PRACTITIONER'S HANDBOOK ON INTERNATIONAL COMMERCIAL ARBITRATION

SECOND EDITION

PRACTITIONER'S HANDBOOK ON INTERNATIONAL COMMERCIAL ARBITRATION

SECOND EDITION

Edited by

Dr Frank-Bernd Weigand

OXFORD
UNIVERSITY PRESS

OXFORD
UNIVERSITY PRESS

Great Clarendon Street, Oxford OX2 6DP

Oxford University Press is a department of the University of Oxford.
It furthers the University's objective of excellence in research, scholarship,
and education by publishing worldwide in

Oxford New York

Auckland Cape Town Dar es Salaam Hong Kong Karachi
Kuala Lumpur Madrid Melbourne Mexico City Nairobi
New Delhi Shanghai Taipei Toronto

With offices in

Argentina Austria Brazil Chile Czech Republic France Greece
Guatemala Hungary Italy Japan Poland Portugal Singapore
South Korea Switzerland Thailand Turkey Ukraine Vietnam

Published in the United States
by Oxford University Press Inc., New York

First published 2009

British Library Cataloguing in Publication Data
Data available

Library of Congress Cataloging-in-Publication Data
Practitioner's handbook on international commercial arbitration / edited by Frank-Bernd Weigand. — 2nd ed.
p. cm.
Rev. ed. of: Practitioner's handbook on international arbitration. 2002.
ISBN 978-0-19-953486-9 (hardback)
1. Arbitration and award, International. 2. Arbitration agreements, Commercial. 3. Conflict of laws—Arbitration and award. I. Weigand, Frank-Bernd, 1960- II. Practitioner's handbook on international arbitration.
K2400.P733 2010
341.5'22—dc22

2009047941

Typeset by Glyph International, Bangalore, India
Printed in Great Britain
on acid-free paper by
CPI Antony Rowe, Chippenham, Wiltshire

ISBN 978-0-19-953486-9

1 3 5 7 9 10 8 6 4 2

PREFACE

This Handbook was first published in 2002. Its concept was to offer 'something different' for the arbitration practitioner: neither another textbook covering arbitration in a particular jurisdiction or international arbitration in general, nor a multi-volume description of the arbitration laws of as many states on earth as possible. Rather, it should offer both in-depth analyses of the major arbitration venues with a strong focus on practical issues and expert commentaries of important *ad hoc* or institutional rules. Today, after several years with numerous new publications on international arbitration, the concept of the first edition of this Handbook has not lost any justification, and its attraction has been confirmed by many practitioners.

Readers of the first edition may have been wondering why the second edition has not been published earlier. The reason for that specific kind of 'delay in arbitration' was mainly the move of the editor to a new publisher and the increase of the contents by several new chapters. In addition, some authors left and some joined the contributors' team. In the second edition, the reader now finds additional country reports (on Belgium and China/ Hong Kong) and further commentaries on institutional arbitration rules (such as the LCIA Rules and the International AAA/ICDR Rules). Furthermore, some countries have enacted new legislation in the meantime (such as eg Austria and Italy), and the UNCITRAL Model Law on International Commercial Arbitration has now been implemented by considerably more states than at the end of the twentieth century. All these recent developments, and, of course, new case law and academic writing, have been taken into account by the existing and new contributors of this Handbook.

As editor of both the first and the second edition, I would like to thank all persons in charge at Oxford University Press who have supported and accompanied this project during the last few years. As well, I do owe thanks to all of my authors who have taken great effort to update their respective chapters or to draft new chapters in accordance with our requirements. Finally, I am very grateful that my family showed remarkable understanding and patience for a husband and dad who, over the last two years, spent a considerable part of his weekend and vacation time with Handbook correspondence and drafts—whether in Germany, other European countries or overseas.

It would be an important reward for me as editor if the new edition were again to become a useful and reliable source of help for the arbitration practitioner, whether he/she is sitting in the office as advocate or arbitrator working on a current proceeding, or is travelling to a foreign country in order to participate in a hearing of an international arbitration case. Of course, both critical remarks or suggestions and positive feedback are welcome and should be addressed either to the publisher or directly to me.

Hamburg (Germany) and Eagle Landing (Newfoundland, Canada), July 2009

Frank-Bernd Weigand

CONTENTS—SUMMARY

CONTENTS

EDITOR

Frank-Bernd Weigand is a partner in his law firm Skorczyk & Weigand, Rechtsanwälte, at which he concentrates on national and international arbitration. In addition, he has taught international arbitration at the renowned Bucerius Law School.

After first practising at a Munich law firm, Dr Weigand joined ESSO Germany's legal department in Hamburg and engaged in the then largest ICC arbitration proceeding, dealing with the exploration and production of natural gas. He then joined Marquard & Bahls, at which he built up its new legal department.

In 2004, he was appointed president of the Hamburg Arbitration Circle, of which he is a founder. He is also a member of various arbitration associations, including the LCIA and the IBA committee on dispute resolution.

Frank-Bernd Weigand holds an LLM in international business law and a Doctor Juris on international procedural law.

CONTRIBUTORS

Jane Ballantyne is an Associate Director in the Commercial Litigation & Arbitration team of Barlow Lyde & Gilbert LLP, London. Jane has extensive experience in international commercial arbitration, particularly under the LCIA and ICC rules, as well as in general commercial litigation. She represents both domestic and foreign clients in a wide range of disputes across a variety of sectors including financial services, IT, and energy. She holds a law degree (BA Hons) from Hertford College, University of Oxford and is a member of the Young International Arbitration Group at the LCIA.

Antje Baumann is a principal associate in the Hamburg office of Freshfields Bruckhaus Deringer LLP and a member of the International Arbitration Group. Dr Baumann has extensive experience in domestic and international litigation as well as arbitration proceedings with a primary focus on corporate disputes, in particular post-transaction and shareholder disputes as well as disputes between companies. Dr Baumann studied law at the Universities of Osnabrueck, Geneva, and London. She holds a master of laws (LLM) degree from the University of California at Berkeley and is admitted to the New York Bar. Dr Baumann is a visiting lecturer at the University of Osnabrueck for mediation and negotiation techniques and regularly publishes on dispute resolution matters.

Michael W. Bühler is co-head of Jones Day's International Litigation and Arbitration Practice. He has represented major corporations and state-owned entities in over 100 arbitration cases throughout the world under, amongst others, the Rules of the ICC and of the arbitration associations of Germany, Belgium, Austria, Switzerland, the USA, and under the UNCITRAL Rules. Michael was a member of the ICC Court of Arbitration (1997–2009) and is co-author of the *Handbook of ICC Arbitration* (2nd Edition, 2008).

He is recommended annually in all the major professional dispute resolution/international arbitration guides such as *PLC Which Lawyer?, Legal 500 EMEA and Best of the Best.* He is a member of Düsseldorf, New York and Paris Bars.

James Castello is a Partner at King & Spalding in Paris, practising international arbitration. Since 2001, James has participated in revising the UNCITRAL Arbitration Rules and Model Law on International Commercial Arbitration as a US delegate to UNCITRAL's Arbitration Working Group. James is also a Court member of the London Court of International Arbitration. He speaks and writes frequently on international arbitration and is recognized in the *International Who's Who of Commercial Arbitration and Chambers Global.* His involvement in arbitration began twenty years ago as legal assistant to Judge Holtzmann on the Iran–US Claims Tribunal, following which he clerked on the US Supreme Court. He received his BA from Yale and an MA and JD from the University of California, Berkeley.

John Choong is a senior associate with the International Arbitration Group of Freshfields Bruckhaus Deringer, based in Hong Kong. John has practised in both Hong Kong and Singapore, and has handled matters in the PRC, Hong Kong, Singapore, Indonesia, Taiwan, Malaysia, Brunei, the Philippines, Guam, Jersey, Europe, the US, and elsewhere. He has experience with a broad range of commercial matters, and has successfully represented clients under the major international arbitration rules, and in court proceedings up to the UK Privy Council. John is listed as a leading individual for dispute resolution in *Chambers Global 2008 and Chambers Asia 2009.* He holds an LLB (Hons) and DipICArb, and is admitted in Hong Kong, England and Wales, and Singapore.

Josephine C.P. Davies is a barrister practising from 20 Essex Street (Chambers of Iain Milligan QC), specializing in commercial law and arbitration. Much of her work is concerned with arbitration almost invariably with an international aspect. She has both acted as counsel (appearing and advising) and as tribunal secretary in arbitrations under a range of systems, including arbitrations under the auspices of the LCIA and the UNCITRAL Rules. She has also been instructed as counsel in arbitration applications to the English Commercial Court.

Emmanuel Gaillard is a Professor of Law at the University of Paris XII and Managing Partner of the Paris office of Shearman & Sterling. Emmanuel Gaillard heads the firm's international arbitration practice. Mr Gaillard has represented major corporations, states, and state-owned entities in over 250 international arbitration cases (with emphasis on investment, energy, construction, and mergers and acquisitions disputes). He has acted as sole arbitrator, party-appointed arbitrator or Chairman in more than fifty international arbitrations. He has also appeared as expert witness on choice of law, arbitration law issues and transnational principles in a number of international arbitration proceedings or enforcement actions before domestic courts. He is the author of numerous publications on international arbitration, among others *La jurisprudrence du CIRDI* (Pedone, 2004), *Aspects philosophiques du droit de l'arbitrage international* (ADI-Poche, Martinus Nijhoff Publishers, 2008); he also co-authored *Fouchard Gaillard Goldman On International Commercial Arbitration* (Kluwer, 1999). In 1984–5, Mr. Gaillard was a Visiting Professor at Harvard Law School.

Martin F. Gusy is a Partner of Gusy Van der Zandt LLP in New York. His practice focuses on international commercial and investment treaty arbitration under all major arbitration rules. Mr Gusy has represented parties in about forty international arbitrations and served as arbitrator in international and US domestic arbitrations. He also practises international and US domestic commercial litigation. A native German, US/German dual licensed Attorney at Law and *Rechtsanwalt*, Mr Gusy holds civil and common law degrees from the Johannes Gutenberg-Universität Mainz and Cornell Law School. The founder and past co-chair of ICDR Y & I, Mr Gusy received the American Arbitration Association's Distinguished Service Award in recognition of his distinguished service and support of international arbitration and mediation in 2007.

Inka Hanefeld is a Partner at the law firm Friedrich Korch Hanefeld, a dispute resolution boutique based in Germany. Inka leads the Hamburg office of the firm and is head of the firm's arbitration group. Formerly, Inka was member of the International Arbitration Group of Freshfields and has worked in the firm's Vienna, New York, Frankfurt, and Hamburg offices. She has acted as counsel and arbitrator in numerous arbitrations under various institutional and ad hoc arbitration rules with a particular focus on industrial plant building, international trade, and post M & A disputes. Inka holds a law degree and a doctorate from Hamburg University and an LLM from New York University. She is admitted to the Bars in Germany and New York.

Christian F. Henel is an associate in Howrey LLP's Global Litigation Group, where he represents a wide array of clients in commercial matters before federal and state courts, and in arbitration, mediation, and other dispute resolution settings. Presently, Mr Henel's practice largely consists of advising and representing clients involved in complex construction and infrastructure disputes. He also has experience representing government contractors in disputes with the US government and related concerns. He received his undergraduate education at the College of William & Mary in Virginia, and his JD from the Catholic University of America, Columbus School of Law (cum laude), where he was a member of the school's Willem C. Vis International Arbitration Moot team.

James M. Hosking is a Partner in New York-based international arbitration and litigation boutique Chaffetz Lindsey LLP and was formerly a Partner in Clifford Chance's Americas International Arbitration group. His practice focuses primarily on international commercial arbitration and investment treaty arbitration. Mr Hosking has handled business disputes under the rules of all the world's leading international arbitration institutions. He regularly writes and lectures on arbitration issues. He previously was the New Zealand delegate to the UNCITRAL Working Group on international commercial arbitration, was co-chair of the ICDR young practitioners group and received the Distinguished Service Award from the AAA in 2007. James holds BA and LLB (with honours) degrees from the University of Auckland and an LLM from Harvard Law School. He is admitted to the New York Bar and previously practised in New Zealand.

Sigvard Jarvin was General Counsel to the ICC Court of Arbitration, Paris (1982–7). He graduated from the University of Stockholm in 1966 and holds an honorary doctorate from that university. He practises as *avocat* in Paris with Jones Day. Mainly engaged in international disputes resolution as counsel and arbitrator he has been involved in approximately 225 arbitrations under the rules of the world's major arbitral institutions. Mr Jarvin was General Editor of *Stockholm International Arbitration Review (1999–2008)*, is co-editor of *Collections of ICC Arbitral Awards*, and publishes regular case notes in various periodicals, including *Journal du Droit International.* He was a member of the ICC International Court of Arbitration (1988–95) and chaired the ICC working party revising the ICC/CMI Maritime Arbitration Rules. He is a member of the Bars of Sweden and Paris and speaks English, French, German, and Swedish.

Miranda Karali is a Partner in the London office of Barlow Lyde & Gilbert LLP. She represents mainly foreign clients in commercial litigation and arbitration. She has particular expertise in international arbitration before the LCIA, the ICC, and the LMAA, handling general commercial, shipping and international trade disputes. She has published numerous articles and is co-author of the Shipping chapter in the American Hellenic Institute's *Doing Business in Greece.* She holds an LLB from the University of Athens, an LLM in International Business Law from King's College London, and is fluent in Greek, French, and Spanish. She is a member of the Athens Bar, the Law Society of England and Wales, and a supporting member of the London Maritime Arbitrators Association.

Pierre A. Karrer has been in private practice for thirty-five years and practises as a full-time arbitrator from his 'boutique' premises. He has been chairman and arbitrator in well over 250 international commercial arbitrations all over the world. He is Honorary President of the Swiss Arbitration Association, former Court Member of ICC, Vice President of the Stockholm Institute, former Vice President of the LCIA, FCIArb, and listed arbitrator everywhere. After studies in Zurich, Göttingen, Padova, and The Hague, he obtained a Dr.iur. from the University of Zurich, and an LLM from Yale. He teaches International Arbitration at the University of Zurich and other universities. He chairs arbitrations in English, French, German, and Italian. He also speaks Dutch and some Spanish.

Rachael D. Kent is a Partner in the international arbitration group of Wilmer Cutler Pickering Hale and Dorr LLP in Washington DC. Ms Kent represents clients in a wide variety of arbitration proceedings under numerous substantive and procedural governing laws. Her experience includes ad hoc and institutional arbitrations, sited in both common law and civil law jurisdictions, including Bermuda, Geneva, Hong Kong, London, New York, Paris, Vienna, and Zurich. Ms Kent teaches International Commercial Arbitration at the Duke University School of Law, and she frequently speaks and writes on topics related to international arbitration. Ms Kent has a JD from the Duke University School of Law.

Christopher Lau, Chartered Arbitrator and Senior Counsel, Singapore, has been in practice for over thirty years with extensive experience in commercial disputes. He was called to the English Bar in 1972. A Partner of Allen & Gledhill Singapore from 1989 to 1995, he served as a Judicial Commissioner of the Supreme Court, Singapore from 1995 to 1998. He is an arbitrator at 3 Verulam Buildings, London, is an independent and non-executive director of Neptune Orient Lines Ltd (NOL), chair of its Audit Committee, and member of its Enterprise Risk Management Committee. He is Chairman of CIArb EAB's Singapore Chapter and a member of ICC Commission on Arbitration.

Vesna Lazić is Associate Professor of International Commercial Arbitration and Private International Law at the Molengraaff Instituut voor privaatrecht, Utrecht University and a staff member of the TMC Asser Institute in The Hague. She lectures and publishes in the field of international commercial arbitration, civil procedure, insolvency, and private international law. She is the author of *Insolvency Proceedings and Commercial Arbitration* (Kluwer Law International, 1999).

Julian D.M. Lew QC is a barrister and international arbitrator practising from 20 Essex Street. Involved in international arbitration for over thirty years as a practitioner and an academic, he has conducted arbitrations as counsel and as an arbitrator under all the major systems. He is a professor and Head of the School of International Arbitration (Centre for Commercial Law Studies, Queen Mary, University of London) and has published extensively on all aspects of international arbitration. He was, for many years, a Director of the LCIA and for six years a member of the LCIA Court. He is currently the UK member of the ICC Court and a member of the Council of the ICC Institute of World Business Law.

Christoph Liebscher is a Partner and head of arbitration at Wolf Theiss in Vienna. Having obtained an MBA at Insead (Fontainebleau), he worked in management positions in Germany, France, former Czechoslovakia, Poland, and other European countries before returning to the legal profession. Amongst others he is a member of the ICC Commission on International Arbitration, of the LCIA, and was a member of the ICC International Court of Arbitration and of the expert group for the reform of the Austrian arbitration law. He is listed as arbitrator with International Arbitral Centers of several Economic Chambers in Central Europe including Austria, Slovenia, and the Czech Republic. He lectures on International Commercial Arbitration at the University of Salzburg.

Gerard J. Meijer is a Partner at NautaDutilh (in both the Rotterdam and Amsterdam office), and leads NautaDutilh's International Arbitration Group. Dr Meijer has extensive experience in international arbitration, representing foreign and multi-national corporations, as well as governmental bodies, in high value arbitration matters in a variety of disputes, including international investment disputes arising out of bilateral investment treaties. In addition, Dr Meijer is involved in high profile arbitration associated court litigation. Dr Meijer also sits as arbitrator. Dr Meijer completed his studies at Erasmus University, Rotterdam (*cum laude*), and also holds a PhD from the same university. Dr Meijer regularly publishes and lectures in the fields of civil procedure law and arbitration, and is one of the leading scholars on arbitration in The Netherlands.

Loukas A. Mistelis is the Clive Schmitthoff Professor of Transnational Commercial Law and Arbitration at the Centre for Commercial Law Studies, Queen Mary, University of London and the Director of the School of International Arbitration. He is also Visiting Professor, NYU in London and was a Visiting Scholar at Columbia University Law School. He teaches International Commercial Arbitration, International Trade and Investment Dispute Settlement, International Commercial Litigation and ADR. Professor Mistelis was educated in Greece, France, Germany, and Japan. His publications include more than fifty referred articles and ten books. His arbitration experience covers ICC, ICISD, LCIA, UNCITRAL, SCC, and Moscow cases. He has been listed as one of the 'leading lights in international arbitration', ('45 under 45'), and is also listed on Who's Who (Commercial Arbitration).

Michael J. Moser is an international attorney and arbitrator who specializes in Chinese matters. He is Chairman of the Hong Kong International Arbitration Centre, Vice President of Asia Pacific Regional Arbitration Group, Court Member of the London Court of International Arbitration and a Board Member of the Arbitration Institute of the Stockholm Chamber of Commerce. He is also a Commission Member of the China International Economic and Trade Arbitration Commission and was the first foreigner to be appointed an arbitrator in China. He is the author of many books and articles and the General Editor of the *Journal of International Arbitration*. He was educated at Harvard Law School and holds a PhD from Columbia University. He practises as an arbitrator with 20 Essex Street Chambers in London and maintains offices in Hong Kong and Beijing.

Robin Oldenstam is a Partner with Mannheimer Swartling and co-chairs the firm's Dispute Resolution Group. He specializes in international arbitration and commercial court proceedings and has acted as counsel in numerous arbitrations, ad hoc as well as institutional, in both Sweden and abroad. In addition, he has gained considerable experience as an arbitrator and is a fellow of the Chartered Institute of Arbitrators. He is chief tutor at the Swedish Bar Association's course in procedural techniques and regularly lectures on civil litigation and arbitration law. He is also a member of the Editorial Board of *Global Arbitration Review*, the Executive Committee of the Swedish Arbitration Association and the Global Advisory Board of the ICDR Y & I.

Marianne Roth is Professor at Salzburg University and practising as an arbitrator under various institutional and ad hoc rules. She is President of the European Court of Arbitration's Austrian Chapter and works as a legal advisor and visiting professor for various institutions and universities around the world (eg Thai Ministry of Justice, Ukraine Cabinet of Ministers, McGeorge School of Law Sacramento, University of Puerto Rico). Professor Roth held chairs at Humboldt University Berlin and Christian Albrechts University Kiel. She completed her doctor's degree (distinction) and habilitation at Kepler University Linz and holds an LLM from Harvard Law School. For her numerous writings Professor Roth received several academic awards, eg the Albert S. Pergam Prize of the New York Bar Association.

Mauro Rubino Sammartano is partner of Bianchi Rubino-Sammartano & Associati in Milan. He chairs the European Court of Arbitration in Strasburg. He has been admitted to the Milan and Paris Bars and is an associate member, as an Italian advocate, of Littleton Chambers in London. He has been a visiting professor at the Milan and Padua Universities. His main fields of practice are contract law, international arbitration and litigation, construction, M & A, and sale of goods. He is the author of various books including *Arbitration Law* (Cedam, 2006); *International Arbitration: Law & Practice* (Kluwer, 2001); *Warranties in Cross-Border Acquisitions* (Graham & Trottman, 1994). He has written extensively on arbitration; such as 'The Fall of Taboo – Review of the Merits of an Award by an Appellate Arbitration Panel and a proposal for an International Appellate Court'; 'Is Arbitration to Be Just a Luxury Clinic?'; and 'Developing Countries vis a vis International Arbitration'.

Peter Bowman Rutledge is an Associate Professor of Law at the University of Georgia Law School. He is the co-author of *International Civil Litigation in United States Courts* (3rd edition with Gary Born). He has published widely in the fields of international arbitration and international civil litigation. Professor Rutledge is also a member of the American Arbitration Association's Delegation to the UNCITRAL Working Group of Arbitration and of the Academic Council of the Institute for Transnational Arbitration.

Franz T. Schwarz is a Partner of Wilmer Cutler Pickering Hale and Dorr LLP in London. A member of the firm's International Arbitration Group, Mr Schwarz has been involved in more than sixty international arbitrations as arbitrator or counsel. Mr Schwarz teaches international arbitration at Zurich University and frequently speaks and publishes on topical issues of international arbitration. He is a Member of the Chartered Institute of Arbitrators; the LCIA; the DIS; the Swiss and Austrian Arbitration Associations; the LCIA Working Committee for the UNCITRAL Working Group II; and the IBA Subcommittee on the New York Convention. From 2003–07, Mr Schwarz served on the Executive Board of the ICDR's Young & International Arbitration program, which he co-founded. Mr Schwarz is a member of the Vienna bar. He graduated from University of Vienna (*Magister Juris*, 1995, top of class) and the London School of Economics (LLM).

Peter A. Straub is the head of the Litigation & Arbitration Team of Walder Wyss & Partners Ltd. He is specialized on complex international commercial disputes and represents parties in both state court litigations and before arbitral panels. His main areas are disputes stemming from telecommunications, pharmaceutical products, construction, joint ventures, commodities trading, and high-end consumer goods. He is also sitting as an arbitrator in international arbitrations (ICC, Swiss Rules, UNICITRAL, etc). He also handles international recognition and enforcement matters. He has published on various subjects in his area of expertise and is a frequent panellist in international conferences. Peter Straub was educated at the University of Zurich (lic. iur. 1984, Dr. iur. 1988) and the London School of Economics (LLM 1991).

Hans van Houtte, LLM Harvard, FCIArb, has over thirty years of arbitration practice. He has arbitrated over 150 cases under the rules of the ICC, LCIA, ICSID, AAA, European Development Fund, CEPANI, Netherlands Arbitration Institute, the Vienna Arbitration Centre, Geneva Chamber of International Commerce, Dubai International Arbitration Centre, and UNCITRAL. The subject matters include i.a. investment , state contracts, turn-key projects, construction, public works, BIT's, NAFTA, joint ventures, IT, share evaluations, sales, agency and distributorship, transfer of technology, oil contracts, antitrust issues, M & A, securities, economic sanctions, export insurance, and rescheduling of public debts. He is considered one of the twenty 'most highly regarded individuals' in arbitration (*Global Arbitration Review – Commercial Arbitration*, 2009, p. 2). He teaches arbitration, conflict of laws, and international business law at the Leuven Law School where he also taught international public law.

Johann von Pachelbel is a Partner with Mannheimer Swartling's Dispute Resolution Group. He co-chairs the firm's German Dispute Resolution Group. Johann specializes in dispute resolution through arbitration and court proceedings in the areas of domestic and international business law. Johann has acted as counsel and as arbitrator in numerous ad hoc as well as institutional arbitrations. He has experience in conducting arbitrations under the auspices of the SCC, ICC, DIS, Swiss Chambers of Commerce, LCIA, and ICSID. In addition, he regularly provides advice in the area of cross border enforcement matters.

TABLE OF CASES

LIST OF ABBREVIATIONS

AAA	American Arbitration Association
AALCC	Asian-African Legal Consultative Committee
ABA	American Bar Association
ABGB	Allgemeines bürgerliches Gesetzbuch
AC	Law Reports Appeal Cases
Act. Dr.	Actualités du droit: revue de la Faculté de droit de Liège
ADRLJ	Arbitration and Dispute Resolution Law Journal
AG	Aktiengesellschaft
AG	Amtsgericht (Local District Court, Germany)
AIA	Association for International Arbitration
AJT	Algemeen Juridisch Tijdschrift
All ER	All England Law Reports
All ER (Comm)	All England Law Reports (Commercial Cases)
Am J Comp L	American Journal of Comparative Law
Am Rev Int'l Arb	The American Review of International Arbitration
Ann Dr. Liège	Annales de droit de Liège
Arb Disp Res LJ	The Arbitration and Dispute Resolution Law Journal
Arb Int'l	Arbitration International
ArbAut	Austrian Arbitration Association ("Österreichische Vereinigung für Schiedsgerichtsbarkeit")
ArbGG	Arbeitsgerichtsgesetz (German Labour Court Law)
Arch. giur. OO. PP.	Archivio giuridico Opere Pubbliche
Arr. Cass.	Arresten van het Hof van Cassatie
AS	Amtliche Sammlung des Bundesrechts (official Swiss legislation collection)
ASA	Swiss Arbitration Association (Association Suisse de l'Arbitrage)
ASGG	Arbeits- und Sozialgerichtsgesetz
Asian Dis Rev	Asian Dispute Review
BAC	Beijing Arbitration Commission
BayObLG	Bayerisches Oberstes Landesgericht (Germany)
BB	Betriebs-Berater (German law journal)
BDG	Beamtendienstrechtsgesetz
BGB	Bürgerliches Gesetzbuch (German Civil Code)
BGBl	Bundesgesetzblatt
BGE	Bundesgericht (Swiss Court of Justice)
BGE	Bundesgerichtsentscheid (Swiss Federal Supreme Court decision)
BGH	Bundesgerichtshof (German Federal Court of Justice)
BGHZ	Entscheidungen des Bundesgerichtshofes in Zivilsachen
BIMCO	Baltic and International Maritime Council
BIT	Bilateral Investment Treaty

BLG	Barlow Lyde & Gilbert
BLR	Building Law Reports
BMLA	British Maritime Law Association
BRH	Belgische rechtspraak in handelszaken
BT	Bundestag (German Parliament)
Bull ASA	Bulletin de l'Association Suisse de l'Arbitrage (ASA Bulletin)
Bull.	Bulletin des arrêts de la Cour de cassation
Bull. Civ.	Bulletin des arrêts de la Cour de cassation (chambres civiles)
Bus LR	Business Law Reports
CA	Court of Appeal (Cour d'Appel)
CACNIQ	Quebec National and International Commercial Arbitration Center
CACV	Hong Kong Civil Appeals
Cah. dr. immo.	Cahiers de droit immobilier
CAS	Court of Arbitration for Sport
Cass	Hof van Cassatie – Cour de cassation
Cass 1–3e Civ	Cour de cassation, Première chambre civile (Nb 2e Civ – Deuxième chambre civile, 3e Civ – Troisième chambre civile)
Cass Civ Mixte	Cour de cassation, Chambre mixte
Cass Com	Cour de cassation, Chambre commerciale
Cass Soc	Cour de cassation, Chambre sociale
CC	Code Civil (Swiss Federal Civil Code)
CCC	Commercial Court Committee
CCIG	Chamber of Commerce and Industry of Geneva
CCP*	Code of Civil Procedure
CEAC	Chinese European Arbitration Centre
CEDR	Centre for Effective Dispute Resolution
CEPANI	Centre belge d'Arbitrage et de Médiation
CEPINA - CEPANI	Belgisch Centrum voor Arbitrage en Mediatie - Centre belge pour l'Arbitrage et la Médiation
CFI	Court of First Instance (Hong Kong)
Ch	Law Reports. Chancery Division since 1980
Ch D	Law Reports. Chancery Division 1875–1980
Chin Journ of Intl Law	Chinese Journal of International Law
CIETAC	China International Economic and Trade Arbitration Commission
CILS	Center of International Legal Studies
Cir	Circuit Court of Appeals
CISG or Vienna Convention	United Nations Convention on Contracts for the International Sale of Goods (1980)
Civ	Civil Division
CJEC	Court of Justice of the European Community (European Court of Justice)
CJQ	Civil Justice Quarterly

CLOUT	Case Law On UNCITRAL Text
CLR	Commonwealth Law Reports (Australia)
Cm	Command Paper
CMAC	China Maritime Arbitration Commission
CMLR	Common Market Law Review
Cmnd	Command Paper (of series published 1956 to 1985)
CO	Code des Obligations (Swiss Federal Code of Obligations)
Cod. Jud.	Code Judiciaire (Judicial Code)
Comm	Commercial
Comm. Ct.	Commercial Court
Concordat	Concordat sur l'arbitrage (Swiss Intercantonal Concordat on Arbitration)
CPC	Code de Procédure Civile (Fra.)
CPR*	Civil Procedure Rules
CPR*	International Institute for Conflict Prevention and Resolution
CRCICA	Cairo Regional Centre for International Commercial Arbitration
CRTPA	Contract (Right of Third Parties) Act 1999
D.P.	Recueil périodique et critique Dalloz
DAB	Dispute Adjudication Board
DAC	Departmental Advisory Committee
Dalloz Aff.	Dalloz Affaires
DCCR	Droit de la consommation
DDC	District Court for the District of Columbia
De Verz.	De Verzekering
DIAC	Dubai International Arbitration Centre
Dir. Fall	Diritto Fallimentare
DIS	German Institution of Arbitration e.V. (Deutsche Institution für Schiedsgerichtsbarkeit)
DOCDEX	Documentary Credit Dispute Resolution Expertise
DRiG	Deutsches Richtergesetz (German Law on Judges)
DRS-CIArb	Chartered Institute of Arbitrators' Dispute Resolution
DSt	Disziplinarstatut
EBITT	ICC Commission on E-Business, IT and Telecoms
EBLR	European Business Law Review
EC Treaty	Treaty establishing the European Community
ECJ	European Court of Justice
ECR	European Court Reports
Ed. jeune Barreau Brussels	Editions du Jeune Barreau de Bruxelles
EDI	Electronic Data Interchange
EEC	European Economic Community
EFTA	European Free Trade Association
EGBGB	Einführungsgesetz zum Bürgerlichen Gesetzbuch (German Private International Law Act)
EGCS	Estates Gazette Case Summaries

EGZPO	Einführungsgesetz zur Zivilprozessordnung
EJ	Echtscheidingsjournaal
EO	Exekutionsordnung
ER	English Reports
EstG	Einkommenssteuergesetz (German Income Tax Law)
Eur. Vervoerr.	Europees vervoerrecht – European Transport Law
EuRAG	Bundesgesetz über den freien Diensteistungsverkehr und die Niederlassung von europäischen Rechtsanwältinnen und Rechtsanwälten sowie die Erbringung von Rechtsdienstleistungen durch international tätige Rechtsanwältinnen und Rechtsanwälten in Österreich
EuZW	Europäische Zeitschrift für Wirtschaftsrecht (European Review for Commercial Law)
EvBl	Evidenzblatt
EWCA	Court of Appeal (England & Wales)
EWHC	High Court (England & Wales)
F	Federal Reporter
F Supp	Federal Supplement Reporter
FAA	Federal Arbitration Act
Fasc.	Fascicule (Juris-Classeur)
Fed R App P	US Federal Rules of Appellate Procedure
Fed R Civ P	US Federal Rules of Civil Procedure
Fed R Evid	US Federal Rules of Evidence
FIDIC	Fédération Internationale des Ingénieurs Conseils
FIE	Foreign-invested enterprise
FINRA	Financial Industry Regulatory Authority
Foro it.	Foro italiano
Foro pad.	Il Foro padano
FOSFA	The Federation of Oils, Seeds and Fats Association Limited
FrG	Fremdengesetz
FTA	Free Trade Agreement
G A Res	General Assembly Resolution
GAFTA	Grain and Feed Trade Association
GAOR	United Nations General Assembly Official Records
Gaz. Pal.	Gazette du Palais
GEN	Gerichtsentlastungsnovelle
GesRZ	Der Gesellschafter – Zeitschrift für Gesellschafts – und Unternehmensrecht
GG	Grundgesetz (German Constitution)
GH	Gerichtshof
Giur. Comm.	Giurisprudenza Commerciale
Giur. it.	Giurisprudenza italiana
Giust. Civ.	Giustizia Civile
Global Arb Rev	Global Arbitration Review

GlUNF	Sammlung von zivilrechtlichen Entscheidungen des k.k. Obersten Gerichtshofes
GMAA	German Maritime Arbitration Association
GmbH	Gesellschaft mit beschränkter Haftung
GmbHG	Gesetz über die Gesellschaften mit beschränkter Haftung
GOP	Government of the Republic of the Philippines
HCA	Civil Action (High Court) (Hong Kong)
HCCT	Construction and Arbitration Proceedings (Hong Kong)
HGB	Handelsgesetzbuch
HK Arbitration Ordinance	Hong Kong Arbitration Ordinance (Cap. 341)
HK Hamburg	Handelskammer Hamburg (Hamburg chamber of commerce)
HKC	Hong Kong Cases
HKCA	Hong Kong Court of Appeal
HKDC	Hong Kong District Court
HKEC	Hong Kong Electronic Cases
HKIAC	Hong Kong International Arbitration Centre
HKIAC Procedures	HKIAC Procedures for the Administration of International Arbitration
HKLR	Hong Kong Law Reports
HKLRD	Hong Kong Law Reports & Digest
HKLY	Hong Kong Law Yearbook
HMSO	Her Majesty's Stationery Office
HR*	House Resolution (proposed legislation)
HR*	Hoge Raad der Nederlanden
I.R.	Informations rapides
IAI	International Arbitration Institute
IBA	International Bar Association
IBA Guidelines	IBA Guidelines on Conflicts of Interest in International Arbitration (2004)
IBA Rules of Evidence	IBA Rules on the Taking of Evidence in International Commercial Arbitration (1999)
IBLJ	International Business Law Journal
ICC	International Chamber of Commerce
ICC Bull	ICC International Court of Arbitration Bulletin
ICC Rules	Arbitration Rules of the International Chamber of Commerce, 1998 edition
ICCA	International Council for Commercial Arbitration
ICDR	International Center for Dispute Resolution
ICLQ	International & Comparative Law Quarterly
ICSID	International Centre for Settlement of Investment Disputes
ICSID Convention	Convention on the Settlement of Investment Disputes between States and Nationals of Other States 1965

IHR	Internationales Handelsrecht (German law journal)
ILM	International Legal Materials
ILR	International Law Reports
Incoterms	International Commercial Terms 2000
Int'l Arb. Rep.	International Arbitration Report
Int. Bus. Lawyer	International Business Lawyer
Int ALR	International Arbitration Law Review
Intl Court of Arb Bull	International Court of Arbitration Bulletin
Int'l Handbook	International Handbook for Commercial Arbitration
Intl Lawyer	International Lawyer
InVo	Insolvenz & Vollstreckung (German law journal)
IPR	Internationales Privatrecht (Private International Law)
IPRax	Praxis des Internationalen Privat- und Verfahrensrechts (German law journal)
IPRG	Bundesgesetz über das Internationale Privatrecht
Iran-US CTR / IUSCTR	Iran-United States Claims Tribunal Reports
ITA	Institute for Transnational Arbitration
J Int'l Arb	Journal of International Arbitration
J.C.P.	Juris-Classeur Périodique (La Semaine Juridique)
J.-Cl. Proc. Civ.	Juris-Classeur (Procédure Civile)
J.O.	Journal Officiel
JAMS	Judicial Arbitration and Mediation Services
JBl	Juristische Blätter
JCAA	Japan Commercial Arbitration Association
JCP	JurisClasseur Périodique
JDI	Journal du Droit International (French law journal)
JDSC	Recueil annuel de jurisprudence en droit des sociétés commerciales
JIA	Journal of International Arbitration
JL	Jurisprudence de Liège
JLMB	Revue de jurisprudence de Liège, Mons et Bruxelles
JN	Jurisdiktionsnorm
Journ of Intl Arb	Journal of International Arbitration
Journ of Intl Banking Law and Regulation	Journal of International Banking Law and Regulation
Journ. not. av.	Journal des notaires et des avocats
JT*	Journal des tribunaux (Belgian law journal)
JT*	Juridisk Tidskrift (Swedish law journal)
Jur.	Jurisprudence (Recueil Dalloz)
Jur. Port Anvers	Jurisprudence du port d'Anvers
KartG	Kartellgesetz
KG	Kammergericht (Higher Regional Court of Berlin, Germany)
KO	Konkursordnung
KSchG	Konsumentenschutzgesetz
KTS	Konkurs-, Treuhand- und Schiedsgerichtswesen (German law journal)

L.G.D.J.	Libraire Générale de Droit et de Jurisprudence
LCIA	London Court of International Arbitration
LICA	Law of International Commercial Arbitration
Limb. Rechsl.	Limburgs rechtsleven
LJ	Lord Justice
LJQB	Law Journal Reports, Queen's Bench New Series
Lloyd's Rep	Lloyd's Law Reports
LLP	Limited Liability Partnership
LMAA	London Maritime Arbitrators Association
LOF	Lloyd's Open Form
LPG	Landpachtgesetz
Lugano Convention	Convention on Jurisdiction and the Enforcement of Judgments on Civil and Commercial Matters, 1988
Mass. Foro it.	Massimario del Foro italiano
Mass. Giust. Civ.	Massimario di Giustizia Civile
MDR	Monatsschrift für Deutsches Recht (German law journal)
Mealey's Intl Arb Rep	Mealey's International Arbitration Report
Model Arb. L. Q. Rep.	Model Arbitration Law Quaterly Report
ModG	UNCITRAL Model Law
MR	Master of the Rolls
MvT	Memorie van Toelichting
NAFTA	North American Free Trade Agreement
NAI	Nederlands Arbitrage Instituut
NASD	National Association of Securities Dealers
NCPC	nouveau Code de procédure civile (the "Code")
New York Convention / NYC	Convention on the Enforcement and Recognition of Foreign Arbitral Awards (New York 1958)
NJ	Nederlandse Jurisprudentie
NJA	Nytt Juridisk Arkiv, Decisions of the Swedish Supreme Court
NJW*	Neue Juristische Wochenschrift (German law journal)
NJW*	Nieuw Juridisch Weekblad
NJW-RR	NJW Rechtsprechungsreport Zivilrecht (German law journal)
NotO	Notariatsordnung
Nov. Dig. It.	Novissimo Digesto Italiano
NW2d	Northwest Reports, 2nd series (state court decision reporter)
O&F	Onderneming & Financiering
OECD	Organisation for Economic Co-operation and Development
OGH	Oberster Gerichtshof
OHADA	Organisation pour l'Harmonisation en Afrique du Droit des Affaires
OJ	Official Journal of the European Union
ÖJZ	österreichische Juristen-Zeitung

OLG*	Oberlandesgericht (German Higher Regional Court)
OLG*	Oberlandesgericht (Higher Regional Court)
OLGR	OLG-Report
P&B	Tijdschrift voor Procesrecht en Bewijsrecht
Pas.	Pasicrisie belge
PCA	Permanent Court of Arbitration
PD	Practice Direction
PIL Statute	Swiss Federal Statute on Private International Law
PILA or PIL Act	Private International Law Act (Switz.)
PRC Arbitration Law	Arbitration Law of the People's Republic of China 1994
PRC Civil Procedure Law	Civil Procedure Law of the People's Republic of China (as amended) 2008
PRC Contract Law	Contract Law of the People's Republic of China 1999
Pres. Rb.	President van de Rechtbank
PUF	Presses Universitaires de France
QB	Queen's Bench
R.R.D.	Revue régionale de droit
RabelsZ	Rabels Zeitschrift für ausländisches und internationales Privatrecht (German law journal)
RAO	Rechtsanwaltsordnung
Rass. Arb.	Rassegna dell'Arbitrato
RATG	Rechstanwaltstarifgesetz
Rb.	Rechtbank
RCP (in Italy C.P.C.)	Codice di Procedura Civile
RdA	Das Recht der Arbeit
RDAI	Revue de Droit des Affaires Internationales
RDC	Revue de droit commercial belge
RDIDC	Revue de droit international et de droit comparé
RDIP	Revue de droit international privé
RdW	Recht der Wirtschaft
Recueil	Recueil des Sentences CEPANI
réf.	référé proceedings
Rep. Foro it.	Repertorio del Foro italiano
Res	Resolution
Res Jur. Imm.	Res et jura immobilia : revue trimestrielle du droit de la construction et des biens
Rev Arb	Review of Arbitration (Revue de l'Arbitrage)
Rev. crit. DIP	Revue critique de droit international privé
Rev. dr. int. Com	Revue de droit international et de droit comparé
Rev. Not. B.	Revue du notariat belge
Rev. Rég. Dr.	Revue régionale de droit
RGAR	Revue générale des assurances et des responsabilités
RGZ	Entscheidungen des Reichsgerichts in Zivilsachen
RH	Rättsfall från hovrätterna (Swedish Court of Appeal Case)
RHA	Rechtspraak van de haven van Antwerpen
Riv. Arb.	Rivista dell'Arbitrato

Riv. cr. Dr. Int. Priv.	Rivista critica del Diritto Internazionale Provato
Riv. Dir. Comm.	Rivista di Diritto Commerciale
Riv. Dir. Int.	Rivista di Diritto Internazionale
Riv. Dir. Int. priv. proc.	Rivista di Diritto Internazionale privato e processuale
Riv. Dir. Proc.	Rivista di Diritto Processuale
Riv. Trim. App.	Rivista Trimestrale degli Appalti
RIW	Recht der Internationalen Wirtschaft (German law journal)
RPDB	Répertoire pratique du droit belge – Encylopedie
RPS	Recht und Praxis der Schiedsgerichtsbarkeit (German law journal)
RRD	Revue régionale de droit
Rsp	Rechtsprechung
RStG	Richter-und Staatsanwaltschaftsdienstgesetz
RTD Com	Revue Trimestrielle de Droit Commercial
RUAA	Revised Uniform Arbitration Act
Rv	Wetboek van Burgerlijke Rechtsvordering
RW	Rechtskundig weekblad
RZ	Österreichische Richterzeitung
S Ct	Supreme Court Reporter
S&S	Schip & Schade
SA	Société Anonyme
SAA	Swedish Arbitration Act
SAC	Shanghai Arbitration Commission
SAR	Stockholm Arbitration Report
Sarl	Société à responsabilité limitée
SCC	Stockholm Chamber of Commerce
SCC Institute	Arbitration Institute of the Stockholm Chamber of Commerce
SCCAM	Swiss Chambers' Court of Arbitration and Mediation
SchiedsRÄG	Schiedsrechtsänderungsgesetz
SchiedsVZ	(deutsche) Zeitschrift für Schiedsverfahren
SCMA	Singapore Chamber of Maritime Arbitration
SDNY	Southern District of New York
SFS	Svensk Författningssamling (The Swedish Code of Statutes)
SIAC	Singapore International Arbitration Centre
SIAR	Stockholm International Arbitration Review (Swedish law journal)
SMA	Society of Maritime Arbitrators
SOU	Statens Offentliga Utredningar (Swedish Government Official Reports)
SpA	Società per Azioni
SPC	PRC Supreme People's Court
SPC Interpretation 2006	SPC Interpretation on Certain Issues Relating to the Application of the PRC Arbitration Law 2006

SPC Provisions 2007	Provisions of the SPC for Several Issues related to the Application of Law to the Trial of Disputes involving Foreign-related Civil or Commercial Contracts 2007
SPC Work Notes 2005	Notice of the SPC on the Issuance of the 'Minutes of the Second National Work Conference on the Trial of Foreign-related Commercial and Maritime Cases' 2005
SPILA	Swiss Private International Law Act = PIL Statute
Stb.	Staatsblad
StGB	Strafgesetzbuch (German Penal Code)
StPO	Strafprozessordnung (German Code of Criminal Procedure)
(Swiss) Penal Code	Swiss Federal Penal Code
Swiss Rules	Swiss Rules of International Arbitration
SZ	Entscheidungen des österreichischen Obersten Gerichtshofes in Zivil- (und Justizverwaltungs-)sachen, veröffentlicht von seinen Mitgliedern
T&C Rv	Tekst en Commentaar Burgerlijke Rechtsvordering
T. App.	Tijdschrift voor appartements- en immorecht
TAS	Tribunal Arbitral du Sport = CAS
TBBR	Tijdschrift voor Belgisch burgerlijk recht
TCC	Technology and Construction Court
Temi lomb.	Temi lombardi
Temi nap.	Temi napoletani
Temi rom.	Temi romani
TGI	Tribunal de Grande Instance
TGR	Tijdschrift voor Gentse rechtspraak
TPR	Tijdschrift voor privaatrecht
TRV	Tijdschrift voor rechtspersoon en vennootschap
TvA	Tijdschrift voor Arbitrage
U.N.T.S.	United Nations Treaty Series
UAA	Uniform Arbitration Act
UGB	Unternehmensgesetzbuch
UKHL	United Kingdom House of Lords
UKPC	United Kingdom Privy Council
UN	United Nations
UNCITRAL	United Nations Commission on International Trade Law
UNCITRAL Model Law	UNCITRAL Model Law on International Commercial Arbitration
UNCTAD	United Nations Conference on Trade and Development
UNGA	United Nations General Assembly
UNIDROIT	International Institute for the Unification of Private Law
UNTS	United Nations Treaty Series
USC	United States Code
UstG	Umsatzsteuergesetz
VBG	Vertragsbedienstetengesetz

VIAC	International Arbitral Centre of the Austrian Federal Economic Chamber
Vienna Rules	Rules of Arbitration and Conciliation of the International Arbitral Centre of the Austrian Federal Economic Chamber (2006)
WAMR	World Arbitration & Mediation Review
WBl	Wirtschaftsblatt
WGII	UNCITRAL Working Group II (International Arbitration and Conciliation)
WIPO	World Intellectual Property Organisation
WLR	Weekly Law Reports
WM	Wertpapier-Mitteilungen (German law journal)
WpHG	Wertpapierhandelsgesetz (German Securities Trading Act)
WTO	World Trade Organization
Y.B. Arb. Inst. Stockholm Chamber Com.	Yearbook of the Arbitration Institute of the Stockholm Chamber of Commerce
YCA	Yearbook Commercial Arbitration
ZBl	Zentralblatt für die juristische Praxis
ZfRV	Zeitschrift für Europarecht, IPR und Rechtsvergleichung
ZInsO	Zeitschrift für das gesamte Insolvenzrecht (German law journal)
ZIP	Zeitschrift für Wirtschaftsrecht (German law journal)
ZPO*	Zivilprozessordnung (code of civil procedure)*
ZRVgl	Zeitschrift für Rechtsvergleichung (Austrian law journal)
Zurich Rules	International Arbitration Rules of the Zurich Chamber of Commerce (1989)
ZVN	Zivilverfahrens-Novelle
ZZP	Zeitschrift für Zivilprozess (German law journal)

(*contextual)

1

INTRODUCTION

Frank-Bernd Weigand and Antje Baumann

I. Origin, globalization and modern practice of arbitration

A. History and nature of arbitration

(1) Historical roots

Arbitration is known as maybe the oldest way of adjudication.[1] It was already well known and used at the time of the Roman empire.[2] The current roots of the arbitration laws in continental Europe and in England reach back to the Middle Ages.[3] In continental Europe, the law on arbitration was usually incorporated in the respective Codes of Civil Procedure, the majority of which has its roots and basis in the nineteenth century. Various reforms since the 70s have resulted in modern arbitration laws in almost every European country.[4] With few exceptions, the reforms did not change the incorporation of the law on arbitration in the respective Codes of Civil Procedure.[5] In England, by contrast, the law on arbitration has historically been contained in the common law based on case law and, in addition, in various Arbitration Acts, the roots of which reach back to the seventeenth 1.01

[1] Schwab, K.H. and Walter, G., *Schiedsgerichtsbarkeit* (6th edn, C.H. Beck Verlag, Munich, 2000) 4 no 7. At this point, no comprehensive historical overview will be given. For more historical information regarding the various jurisdictions, see the various country reports in chs 2 *et seq.*

[2] For details, see Ziegler, K.H., 'Das private Schiedsgericht im antiken römischen Recht' (1971).

[3] Briner, R., 'Domestic Arbitration: Practice in Continental Europe and its Lessons for Arbitration in England' (1997) 13 *Arb Int'l* no 2, 155; Mistelis, L.A., Lew, J.D.M., *Arbitration Insights: Twenty Years of the Annual Lecture of the School of International Arbitration* (Kluwer Law International, 2007) 20–16; Mustill, M.J., 'The History of International Commercial Arbitration', in L.W. Newman, and R.D. Hill (eds), *The Leading Arbitrators' Guide to International Arbitration*, 1 *et seq.*

[4] See the country reports in chs 2–13.

[5] As examples, see the French law (Art 1442, NCPC *et seq*), the German (s 1025, ZPO *et seq*) and the Austrian law (s 577, öZPO *et seq*).

century[6], leading to a 'patchwork'[7] of rules.[8] Since the Arbitration Act 1889, the 'piecemeal process of expansion, amendment and consolidation'[9] has led to several additional Acts which, however, did not necessarily repeal its predecessors. The Arbitration Act 1996 has put an end to this unsatisfactory situation and principally contains the current status of the law.[10] In addition to the respective national laws, the relevant sources of the applicable law may be found in international treaties and the rules of the arbitral institutions[11], like the International Chamber of Commerce (ICC) or the London Court of International Arbitration (LCIA). In the international context, given the various applicable national substantive and procedural laws,[12] the often applicable rules of a particular arbitral institution and one or more treaties, the practitioner faces a difficult task to consider all the relevant legal sources at the different stages of the arbitral process.

(2) Legal nature

1.02 Various practical issues of international arbitration can be better understood and resolved by taking into consideration the legal nature of arbitration. Several doctrines have been developed over the decades in the major European countries[13], upon which it is useful to cast a short glance.

1.03 **(2.1) The jurisdictional theory** When looking at litigation as the 'normal way of adjudication', regulated by particular rules of civil procedure, one may conclude that arbitration also, as the alternative way of settling disputes, has a jurisdictional or procedural nature.[14]

---

[6] See eg Steyn, J., 'England's Response to the UNCITRAL Model Law of Arbitration' (1994) 10 *Arb Int'l* no 1, 7; Poudret, J.F. and Besson, S. *Comparative Law of International Arbitration* (Sweet & Maxwell, 2007) no 45 *et seq*; Böckstiegel, K.H., 'Perspective of Future Development in International Arbitration' in L.W. Newman and R.D. Hill (eds), *The Leading Arbitrators' Guide to International Arbitration* (2nd edn, Juris Publishing, New York, 2008) 495, 496.

[7] Mustill, M. and Boyd, S.C., *The Law and Practice of Commercial Arbitration in England* (Butterworths Legal Publishers, 1989) 33.

[8] Weigand, F.-B., 'Das neue englische Schiedsverfahrensrecht', *Recht der Internationalen Wirtschaft (RIW)* (1997) 904.

[9] Mustill, M. and Boyd, S.C. (n 7) 54.

[10] Weigand, F.-B. 'Das neue englische Schiedsverfahrensrecht', *Recht der Internationalen Wirtschaft (RIW)* (1997) 904, 910.

[11] The most important rules are described in more detail below in chs 15 *et seq*.

[12] Redfern, Hunter, Blackaby and Partasides point out that even in a comparatively simple international arbitration, four different systems or rules of law apply: (i) the law governing the arbitration agreement; (ii) the law which governs the arbitration proceedings; (iii) the law or rules to be applied to the substantive matters in dispute; and (iv) the law governing the recognition and enforcement of the arbitration agreement and the award. (Redfern, A., Hunter, M., Blackaby, N. and Partasides, C., *Law and Practice of International Commercial Arbitration* (4th edn, Thomson Sweet & Maxwell, London, 2004) (Redfern, Hunter, Blackaby and Partasides)).

[13] Schlosser, P., *Das Recht der internationalen privaten Schiedsgerichtsbarkeit* (2nd edn, Mohr Siebeck, Tübingen, 1989) no 40; Yu, Hl., 'Total Separation of International Commercial Arbitration and National Court Regime' (1998) 15 *J Int'l Arb* no 2, 145, 148 distinguishes four contemporary theories; Lew, J.D.M., Mistelis, L.A. and Kröll, S., *Comparative International Commercial Arbitration* (Kluwer Law International, 2003) 5–4; Mistelis, L.A. and Lew, J.D.M, *Arbitration Insights: Twenty Years of the Annual Lecture of the School of International Arbitration* (Kluwer Law International, 2007) 20–31 *et seq*.

[14] In English, the current theories are generally described as contractual and jurisdictional, whereas in German the two opposing views are mostly characterized as 'privatrechtlich' or 'jurisdiktionell—prozeßrechtlich'; see Schlosser, P. (n 13) nos 40 *et seq*. For further details on the jurisdictional theory see Berger, K.P., *Private Dispute Resolution in International Business* (2006) 16–5 *et seq;* Lew, J.D.M., Mistelis, L.A. and Kröll, S.

The most prominent jurisdiction where this theory has been advocated so far is Switzerland. There, the procedural nature of arbitration has constantly been relied on by the Swiss Supreme Court.[15] In Germany too, there are many authors who favour the jurisdictional approach.[16] Probably the most important and strongest advocate of this theory was F.A. Mann with his landmark article named *Lex facit arbitrum.*[17] Starting with the historical origin of law as an act of the state, he points out that also all legal powers of arbitrators as private persons emanate from the respective municipal law.[18] The *lex arbitri*, ie the law of the arbitral tribunal's seat, initially governs the whole of the tribunal's life and work, especially the applicable procedural and private international law.[19] Mann's views, which were laid down more than 30 years ago, have nowadays been revived by Hong-lin Yu.[20]

(2.2) The contractual theory The other, probably older, theory sees the origin and roots of arbitration in a private contract.[21] Therefore, the arbitration agreement establishes the jurisdiction of the arbitral tribunal.[22] Thus, arbitration may be characterized as a consensual method of dispute resolution.[23] As the 'home country' of the contractual theory, one may identify England. Both leading authors and the courts take the unanimous view[24] that due to its basis in private law, arbitration is dominated by the law of contract. In the nineteenth century, the contractual theory appears to have been the generally accepted view in Europe,[25] and it was especially favoured by German[26] and French[27] doctrine. In both countries, however, these views were abandoned or modified in the last decades. **1.04**

(n 13) 5–9 *et seq*; Mistelis, L.A. andLew, J.D.M., *Arbitration Insights: Twenty Years of the Annual Lecture of the School of International Arbitration* (2007) 20–32.

[15] BGE 41 II 534; 96 I 334; 103 II 75. See also the ICC award no 4,504, JDI (Clunet) 1986, 1118 ('procedural agreements which are subject to public law').

[16] See Schlosser, P. (n 13) no 42, with further references.

[17] Mann, F.A. in P. Sanders, 'Liber amicorum for Martin Domke' (1967) 157; reproduced in (1986) 2 *Arb Int'l No* 3, 241.

[18] Mann states that 'every arbitration is necessarily subject to the law of a given State. No private person has the right or power to act on any other level other than that of a municipal law. Every right or power a private person enjoys is inexorably conferred by or derived from a system of municipal law', see Mann, in Sanders, *Liber amicorum for Martin Domke* (1967) p 160.

[19] Mann, F.A. in P. Sanders, *Liber amicorum for Martin Domke* (1967) 160, 164 *et seq.*

[20] Yu, H.L. (n 13) 152.

[21] For further details on the contractual theory see Lew, J.D.M., Mistelis, L.A. and Kröll, S. (n 13) 5–16 *et seq*; Berger, K.P., *Private Dispute Resolution in International Business* (2006) 16–7 *et seq*; Mistelis, L.A., and Lew, J.D.M., *Arbitration Insights: Twenty Years of the Annual Lecture of the School of International Arbitration* (2007) 20–33.

[22] Redfern, Hunter, Blackaby and Partasides (n 12)1–11 and 5–25.

[23] Mustill, M. and Boyd, S.C. (n 7) 43; Redfern, Hunter, Blackaby and Partasides (n 12) 5–25 ('consensual arbitration'); Berger, K.P., *Private Dispute Resolution in International Business* (2006) 16–11 and 16–12.

[24] See eg Mustill, M. and Boyd, S.C. (n 7) 4; Veeder, V.V. in M. Hunter, A. Marriott, V.V. Veeder, *The Internationalisation of International Arbitration,* 13, 14; *Hamlyn & Co v Talisker Distillery* (1894) AC 202; Redfern, Hunter, Blackaby and Partasides (n 12) 1–10 and 1–11.

[25] Mayer, P. in M. Hunter, A. Marriott, V.V. Veeder, *The Internationalisation of International Arbitration,* 37, 39.

[26] See Schlosser, P. (n 13) no 42 with further references.

[27] Schlosser, P. (n 13) no 41; David, R., *L'arbitrage dans le commerce international* (Economica, Paris, 1982) 9; *Cour de Cassation of 27 July 1937,* JCP 1937 II, 449 ('Les sentences qui ont pour base un compromis font corps avec lui et participent de son charactère conventionel.').

1.05 (2.3) **Harmonizing (hybrid) theories** Even advocates of the contractual theory have to admit the existence of jurisdictional elements of arbitration and therefore consider the arbitral process to be of a hybrid nature.[28] The fact that arbitration is characterized by elements of both theories, has led to the theory of the 'Doppelnatur' of arbitration. According to the prevailing view in Germany, arbitration unites the elements of both theories so that the arbitration agreement is of substantive as well as of procedural nature.[29] Similarly in France, according to the now prevailing view, both elements are considered to be essential features of arbitration.[30] Finally, the question on the relevance of the differing theories in practice would probably reveal that the discussion is of little practical importance.[31] The only important situation where the application of either theory is of relevance appears to be the discovery of a gap in the parties' agreement or the applicable national law. In such a case, however, it is suggested that general solutions will scarcely help. According to the question to be determined or regulated, it will have to be decided whether an existing gap should be filled by contractual or procedural law. In Germany, for instance, the law on arbitration (as well as general procedural law) does not contain any regulation of the existence, validity and termination of the arbitration agreement. To determine such issues, therefore, one has to refer to the general law of contract.[32] There may be other situations where a gap should be filled by procedural rules so that there is no necessity generally only to adhere to one of the existing theories.

B. Arbitration agreement

1.06 Irrespective of theoretical or doctrinal differences, the paramount importance of the arbitration agreement is universally recognized. Either by incorporation of an arbitration clause or by the conclusion of a submission agreement,[33] the parties agree on the way the arbitration has to be conducted. Defective agreements may—in the worst case—result in

[28] For further details on the hybrid theories see Redfern, Hunter, Blackaby and Partasides (n 12) 1–16; Lew, J.D.M., Mistelis, L.A. and Kröll, S. (n 13) 5–22 *et seq*; Mistelis, L.A. andLew, J.D.M., *Arbitration Insights: Twenty Years of the Annual Lecture of the School of International Arbitration* (2007) 20–34; Berger, K.P., *Private Dispute Resolution in International Business* (2006) 16–5 and 16–6.

[29] Schütze, R.A., *Schiedsgericht und Schiedsverfahren* (4th edn, C.H. Beck Verlag, Munich, 2007) no 107; Lionnet, K. and Lionnet, A., *Handbuch der internationalen und nationalen Schiedsgerichtsbarkeit* (3rd edn, Boorberg, Stuttgart, 2005) 180; Schwab, K.H. and Walter, G. (n 1) 1, no 1; Bundesgerichtshof, BGHZ 23, 200 and BGHZ 40, 320. For an overview with detailed references, see Schwab, K.H. andWalter, G. (n 1) 76 no 37.

[30] Fouchard, P. Gaillard, E. and Goldman, B., *Traité de l'arbitrage commercial international* (Litec, Paris, 1996) (Fouchard, Gaillard, Goldman)14 no 11.

[31] For that conclusion, see eg Schlosser, P. (n 13) no 50.

[32] See eg Schütze, R.A. (n 29) no 107; Schwab, K.H. and Walter, S. (no 1) 79, nos 9 *et seq*.

[33] For the traditional distinction between arbitration clause (*clause compromissoire*) and submission agreement (*compromis*) see Art 1442 and Art1447, NCPC; Redfern, Hunter, Blackaby and Partasides (n 12) 1–06 to 1–08; Fouchard, Gaillard, Goldman (n 30) 209 *et seq* no 386 ('la distinction entre clause compromissoire et compromis ne présente, dans l'arbitrage international, guère d'intérêt pratique.'); Schlosser, P. (n 13) nos 265 *et seq*. In accordance with the Model Law (Art 7(1), Model Law), the word 'arbitration agreement' is hereinafter used as comprising both the typical arbitration clause (designed for a future dispute) and the submission agreement (concluded after a dispute has arisen). In practice, each adviser will have to make sure that the arbitration clause already contains the essential elements described below.

the frustration of the whole arbitral process.[34] Further, the arbitration agreement has important positive and negative effects according to domestic and international law. Before discussing the form and contents of the arbitration agreement and its legal effects, the different views on the law governing its validity are of relevance.[35]

(1) Law governing the validity of the arbitration agreement

One of the most effective defences of the defendant in an arbitration is the contention that the arbitration agreement (either in the form of an arbitration clause at the end of the main agreement or as a separate arbitration agreement) is invalid so that there is no basis for the arbitration. The defendant may invoke defects of the arbitration agreement, be it at the beginning of or after the termination of the arbitral proceeding,[36] or at the enforcement stage at the place of arbitration[37] or in another jurisdiction where the claimant has applied for enforcement.[38] In all those cases, it is important to determine the law which governs the arbitration agreement itself. **1.07**

(1.1) Law chosen by the parties Both the New York Convention and the Model Law determine that the validity of the arbitration agreement has, in the first place, to be decided according to the substantive law chosen by the parties.[39] The party autonomy which is thereby expressed is generally accepted.[40] However, it is rarely the case that the arbitration clause contains an express choice of law provision for the clause itself.[41] Rather, the parties simply include a clause on the substantive law to be applied to the main contract. In practice, therefore, it will be concluded in most cases that according to the presumed will of the parties, the chosen law also governs the validity of the arbitration clause.[42] This interpretation may be opposed by arguing that in most jurisdictions, the arbitration clause is considered to be a separate agreement independent of the main contract.[43] There are, furthermore, arbitral precedents and decisions which expressly do not apply the law which governs the main contract.[44] **1.08**

[34] On 'pathological' arbitration clauses, much has been written, see eg Bond, S., 'How to Draft an Arbitration Clause' (1989) 6 *J Int'l Arb* 65. The risk that arbitration clauses prove to be defective is relatively high since they are often 'midnight clauses' which are drafted and negotiated at the end of complex commercial negotiations. See Redfern, Hunter, Blackaby and Partasides (n 12) 3–02 and 3–63 *et seq* (on defective arbitration clauses); Robine, E., 'What Companies Expect of International Commercial Arbitration' (1992) 9 *J Int'l Arb* no 2, 31, 32.

[35] For a detailed overview on the applicable law see Lew, J.D.M., Mistelis, L.A. and Kröll, S. (n 13) ch 6.

[36] See eg Art 16, Model Law (challenge of the arbitral tribunal's jurisdiction) and Art 34(2)(a)(i), Model Law (challenge of the award based on the allegation of invalidity of the arbitration agreement).

[37] See eg Art 36(1)(a)(i), Model Law.

[38] See Art V 1.(a), New York Convention.

[39] The wording of Art V 1.(a) of the New York Convention was copied in Art 34(2) and Art 36(1) of the Model Law.

[40] Schlosser, P. (n 13) nos 229 *et seq*; Fouchard, Gaillard, Goldman (n 30) 241 no 426.

[41] Lionnet, K. and Lionnet, A. (n 29) 169.

[42] Redfern, Hunter, Blackaby and Partasides (n 12) 3–36. That is also the view expressed by the Bundesgerichtshof in an older decision, BGHZ 59, 23, 27.

[43] See eg Lionnet, K. and Lionnet, A. (n 29) 169. On separability, see in detail para 1.239 *infra*.

[44] See the award and decision in *Société St. Gobain v Société Dow Chemical France*, Cour d'Appel de Paris of 21 October 1983, *Rev arb* 1994, 1984; Rubino-Sammartano, M., *International Arbitration Law* (Deventer, Boston, 1990) 142 *et seq* with further references.

1.09 **(1.2) Law of the place of arbitration** Both the New York Convention and the Model Law do, as a substitute reference, determine the law of the seat of arbitration to be applied.[45] This is also the solution in those jurisdictions which adhere to the jurisdictional theory[46] as, for instance, Switzerland. Based on the assumption that the arbitration agreement is a 'procedural contract', its validity must necessarily be determined according to the locally applicable procedural law.[47] Summarizing the situation in a comparative analysis, French authors came to the conclusion that in view of the various approaches of different jurisdictions, there is an impression of great uncertainty in this respect.[48]

(2) Form and contents

1.10 The fulfilment of some minimum requirements as to the form and the contents of the arbitration agreement is essential both for the initiation and the carrying on of the arbitral proceeding on the one hand, and for the international recognition and enforcement of the arbitration clause and the ensuing award on the other hand.

1.11 **(2.1) Form of the arbitration agreement** As a general principle, an arbitration agreement shall be in writing.[49] Article II(1) of the New York Convention provides that an arbitral agreement *in writing* shall be recognized by the contracting states and enforceable in a foreign state. However, in recent years a lively discussion has been resumed concerning the question of what, apart from a written and mutually signed contract, may be considered to be a clause 'in writing' or whether or not an oral agreement to arbitrate should be admissible. This discussion *inter alia* led to an amendment of the Model Law. Article 7 of the Model Law now provides for two options.[50]

1.12 According to Option I, an arbitration agreement shall be in writing (Art 7(2), Model Law). There are specific definitions indicating what, apart from a written and mutually signed contract may be considered to be a clause 'in writing'.[51] Article 7(3), Model Law provides that an arbitration agreement is in writing if its content is recorded in any form, whether or not the arbitration agreement or contract has been concluded orally, by conduct, or by other means. The requirement is also met by an electronic communication if the information contained therein is accessible so as to be useable for subsequent reference (Art 7(4), Model Law) or if it is contained in an exchange of statements of claim and defence in which the existence of an agreement is alleged by one party and not denied by the other (Art 7(5), Model Law).

---

[45] 'the law of the country where the award was made' (New York Convention) or 'the law of this state' (Model Law). Art Vii(1) of the European (Geneva) Convention contains a similar rule.

[46] For details, see para 1.03 *supra*.

[47] Bundesgericht BGE 57 I 295; 76 I 338; 96 I 334. See also the decision of the Swiss Bundesgericht, JDI (Clunet) 1976, 729.

[48] 'Une impression de très grande incertitude', see Fouchard, Gaillard, Goldman (n 30) 245 no 434, referring to R David, *L'arbitrage dans le commerce international* (1982) no 242.

[49] Art 7(2), Model Law; § 1031 ZPO para 5. See generally Fouchard, Gaillard, Goldman (n 30) 373 *et seq* nos 590, 591, and 383 *et seq* no 606 according to which in international arbitration no written agreement is required in French law.

[50] See Sorieul, R., 'UNCITRAL's Current Work in the Field of International Commercial Arbitration', (2005) *22 J Int'l Arb* no 6, 543.

[51] According to modern laws, an exchange of letters or other written means of communication is sufficient as long as it provides a record of the agreement, see e g s 1031(1), ZPO; Art 178, SPILA; s 577, öZPO.

Finally, according to Art 7(6), Model Law, the reference to a contract in any document containing an arbitration clause constitutes an arbitration agreement in writing, provided that the reference is such as to make that clause part of the contract. The writing requirement as set out in Option I of Art 7 was specifically drafted with the objective of demonstrating the intent of the parties to arbitrate and to prevent that a party is drawn into arbitral proceedings irrespective of any evidence as to the existence and the content of an alleged arbitration agreement.[52]

Since the situation concerning the oral conclusion of an arbitration agreement was and is amongst the most disputed issues in the area of the form requirements in international arbitration,[53] Art 7, Model Law now provides for an Option II. According to Option II, an arbitration agreement is an agreement by the parties to submit to arbitration all or certain disputes which have arisen or which may arise between them in respect of a defined legal relationship, whether contractual or not. By following this 'Mexican Proposal',[54] the Model Law now offers states alternative texts in drafting arbitration law.[55] 1.13

In some countries, the national legislator has also provided for specific regulations on the inclusion of arbitration clauses in general business conditions and, in the maritime sector, in a bill of lading.[56] 1.14

(2.2) Minimum contents of the arbitration agreement Although the mandatory elements of an arbitration agreement are mostly defined by the respective national laws which sometimes differ considerably,[57] there appear to exist at least two minimum elements.[58] They are to be found in Art II(1) of the New York Convention and in Art 7(1) of the Model Law.[59] Further, they are contained in the model arbitration clauses which are recommended by major arbitration institutions.[60] 1.15

---

[52] Kucherepa, P., 'Reviewing Trends and Proposals to Recognize Oral Agreements to Arbitrate in International Arbitration Law' (2005) *Am Rev Int'l Arb* 16, 409, 414.

[53] Binder, P., 'International Commercial Arbitration and Conciliation in UNCITRAL Model Law Jurisdictions' (2nd edn, Sweet and Maxwell, London, 2005) 76.

[54] Kucherepa, P., 'Reviewing Trends and Proposals to Recognize Oral Agreements to Arbitrate in International Arbitration Law' (2005) *Am Rev Int Arb* 16, 409, 425.

[55] For further details, see ch 14.

[56] See eg s 1031(2) to (4), ZPO.

[57] Schlosser, P. (n 13) no 355. For an overview, see Rubino-Sammartano, M. (n 44) 127 *et seq.*

[58] Redfern, Hunter, Blackaby and Partasides (n 12) 3–44; Derains, Y. andSchwartz,E.A., *A Guide to the New ICC Rules of Arbitration* (Kluwer Law International, The Hague, London, Boston, 1999) 355 *et seq*; Schütze, R.A. (n 29) no 133. A third element, named by C. Schmitthoff, *JBL* 1975, 9, 11, concerning the indication of who shall be the arbitrators, appears mostly to be redundant since either the rules of an institution or the national law provide for the situation that the parties have not agreed on details of the arbitral tribunal.

[59] Art 7(1), Model Law reads: '..an agreement by the parties to submit to arbitration all or certain disputes which have arisen or may arise between them in respect of a defined legal relationship, whether contractual or not. . . .'.

[60] The ICC Model Clause, as amended in accordance with the 1998 Rules of Arbitration, reads: 'All disputes arising out of or in connection with the present contract shall be finally settled under the Rules of Arbitration of the International Chamber of Commerce by one or more arbitrators appointed in accordance with said Rules'. The 1998 LCIA brochure recommends the following clause: 'Any dispute arising out of or in connection with this contract, including any question regarding its existence, validity or termination, shall be referred to and finally resolved by arbitration under the LCIA Rules, which Rules are deemed to be incorporated by reference into this clause.'

1.16 *(2.2.1) Decision of a legal dispute by arbitration* The wording of the agreement must generally provide for mandatory arbitration, ie the decision of a dispute by an arbitral tribunal. That applies similarly, if one of the parties, who has an option to refer a dispute to litigation or arbitration, elects to initiate arbitration proceedings.[61] The wording of the agreement must clearly show that the parties did not want any kind of amicable settlement, be it promoted or assisted by a mediator or conciliator or in any other manner,[62] and that they did not want only a specific factual issue to be resolved or determined by some person who is not an arbitrator.[63] In addition, the arbitration agreement must provide for a final and binding settlement through arbitration without the possibility of any recourse other than those challenge procedures provided for in the respective institutional rules or national laws.

1.17 *(2.2.2) A defined legal relationship to be settled by arbitration* The exact definition of the legal relationship, eg parts or all of the main contract containing the arbitration clause, is of crucial importance since it determines and limits the jurisdiction of the arbitral tribunal. As already suggested by C. Schmitthoff almost 35 years ago,[64] the recommended wording of standard clauses ('all disputes arising out of or in connection with this contract') shall ensure that not only contractual but also other related kinds of legal claims (eg claims based on tort or unjust enrichment) shall be decided by the arbitrators.[65] In view of these two essential elements, one might conclude that arbitration clauses may be drafted in one short sentence, leaving all other related issues to the relevant institution or a state court. However, the inclusion of other additional elements is strongly recommended by leading writers and institutions.

1.18 *(2.2.3) Seat of the arbitration* The fixing of the seat or place of the arbitration is of high importance since, generally, the law of the seat applies to the conduct of the arbitration, in particular the procedure, and regulates how to determine the substantive law to be applied by the arbitrators.[66] The law of the seat will determine, in particular, the degree of possible court intervention during the arbitration proceeding[67] and possible means of recourse after the rendering of the award. Thus, the parties have a chance to choose a location which is 'arbitration friendly' or not.[68]

---

[61] On 'optional arbitration', for further details, see Schlosser, P. (n 13) nos 388 *et seq*. In most cases, mandatory arbitration will be intended without any option for either side, see eg Derains, Y. and Schwartz, E.A. (n 58) 356.

[62] Since arbitration is true adjudication on an equal level with litigation before courts, there must be a clear distinction of arbitration from other forms of alternative dispute resolution; see Redfern, Hunter, Blackaby and Partasides (n 12) 1–51.

[63] Arbitration is mostly distinguished from related forms of third party intervention, be it called valuation, *expertise amiable* or *Schiedsgutachten*. For a comparative analysis, see Schlosser, P. (n 13) nos 19 *et seq*.

[64] Schmitthoff, C., 'Defective Arbitration Clauses' *JBL* 1975, 9, 14.

[65] On US decisions in this respect, see Bond, S., 'How to Draft an Arbitration Clause' (1989) 6 *J Int'l Arb* no 2, 70. In Germany, there is specific case law on the question whether arbitration clauses with a general wording have to be interpreted in a narrow or wide manner, see *BGH Neue Juristische Wochenschrift (NJW)* 1980, 2022, 2024; *BGH Neue Juristische Wochenschrift (NJW)* 94, 136.

[66] The importance of the seat of the arbitration is discussed in detail at III. B. (1) *infra*.

[67] For example, England is more interventionist than Germany which has a more liberal approach, see Weigand, F.-B., 'Das neue englische Schiedsverfahrensrecht' *Recht der Internationalen Wirtschaft* (*RIW*) 1997, 904, 911.

[68] Derains, Y. and Schwartz, E.A. (n 58) 357 *et seq*.

(2.3) **Optional elements of an arbitration agreement** In order to avoid lengthy discussions and potential legal problems at a later stage, the parties should include specific regulations on the following items.[69] **1.19**

(2.3.1) Ad hoc *or institutional arbitration* Nowadays, modern national laws on arbitration provide solutions for many issues and questions arising at any possible stage of the arbitration procedure. Nevertheless, it may well be advisable to include a reference to an experienced arbitration institution, the Rules of which are then incorporated in the arbitration agreement. In most cases, one gets 'value for money',[70] whereas in an *ad hoc* arbitration, the parties themselves have to provide for all the details of the arbitral procedure.[71] Whether institutional rules like the ICC Rules or *ad hoc* rules like the UNCITRAL Arbitration Rules are included in the arbitration clause, it is essential to be as clear and specific as possible.[72] **1.20**

(2.3.2) Number of arbitrators If there is no indication in the arbitration agreement itself, in case of institutional rules, the institution will decide whether the dispute shall be decided by one or three arbitrators.[73] Since, however, the number of the arbitrators has influence on the costs and probably the duration of the arbitration, it is advisable to include a specific regulation of that question.[74] Further, a party may have more influence on the composition of the tribunal if it is able to nominate one arbitrator who then determines the chairman, together with the other party-appointed arbitrator. **1.21**

(2.3.3) Applicable substantive law If the parties do not want this important issue to be decided by the arbitrators, who often enjoy wide discretion in this respect,[75] they have to specifically determine the applicable substantive law. Frequently, the contract contains a choice-of-law clause at another place outside the arbitration clause, which then determines the substantive law to be applied by the arbitrators.[76] In the absence of such choice-of-law, the arbitrators determine the substantive law either by referring to the normal conflict of law rules[77] or, by the so-called *voie directe*, to those national rules of law which have the closest connection to the dispute.[78] **1.22**

---

[69] The following recommendations should also be followed in jurisdictions like England where traditionally the courts give effect to the scarcest clauses conceivable, see Schmitthoff, C., 'Defective Arbitration Clauses' *JBL* 1975, 9, 12 ('arbitration in the city of London'), with further references. For a detailed overview on other relevant issues to be included in an arbitration clause see Lew, J.D.M., Mistelis, L.A. and Kröll, S. (n 13) ch 8.

[70] Bond, S., 'How to Draft an Arbitration Clause' (1989) 6 *J. Int'l Arb* no 2, 68.

[71] For a more detailed discussion of institutional versus *ad hoc* arbitration, see para 1.172 *infra*.

[72] It often happens that the chosen institution or rules are not clearly designated, see eg Bond, S., 'How to Draft an Arbitration Clause' (1989) 6 *J Int'l Arb* no 2, 67 *et seq*; for an ambiguous clause referring to arbitration in Hamburg without a clear determination which institutional rules shall be applied, see BGH Neue Juristische Wochenschrift (NJW) 1983, 1267.

[73] See eg Art 7–12, ICC Rules.

[74] Derains, Y. and Schwartz, E.A. (n 58) 358.

[75] See eg Art 17, ICC Rules 1998. The Rules of the Chinese European Arbitration Centre (CEAC) Hamburg, Art 3(8), expressly provide for the possibility that the parties choose the UNIDROIT Principles of International Commercial Contracts as governing law.

[76] Redfern, Hunter, Blackaby and Partasides (n 12) no 2–26.

[77] That is the solution of the Model Law (see Art 28(2)).

[78] This is the solution chosen by the German legislator (s 1051(2) ZPO); institutional rules often contain similar provisions.

1.23 *(2.3.4) Language of the arbitration* There will be indications (ie the language of the contract, the relevant correspondence etc) as to the presumed will of the parties which language shall be used throughout the arbitral proceedings. Since, however, the language influences the manner of the taking of evidence (translation of documents and witness testimony) and, even more important, the choice of the arbitrators (who have to conduct the hearings etc in the particular language),[79] it is definitely advisable to specify expressly the applicable language in the arbitration agreement itself.

(3) Effects

1.24 **(3.1)'Positive effects' of the arbitration agreement** The so-called positive effects of the arbitration agreement consist in the establishment of the arbitral tribunal's jurisdiction and the definition of the scope of the arbitral proceedings and the ensuing award.

1.25 By inserting an arbitration clause in their main agreement, the parties accept a contractual obligation to refer any future dispute to arbitration.[80] The duty of each party to cooperate for that purpose entails that any failure to do so results in a claim for damages of the other party and/or its right to terminate the agreement because of breach of contract.[81] However, given the difficulty of calculating any damage suffered, a claim for damages is not very helpful.[82] Nor is the wording of international treaties or the Model Law that the court has to 'refer the parties to arbitration',[83] of immediate practical relevance since a court order directly enforcing the arbitration agreement by compelling arbitration is only rarely provided for in national law.[84] Rather, the claimant may, in view of the obstructive behaviour of its opponent, ask the state courts for assistance at the stage of the formation of the tribunal.[85] Further, most rules of arbitral institutions and of national laws on arbitration provide for regulations ordering the continuation of the arbitral proceeding after a failure of a party properly to participate.[86] Therefore, only in very rare cases will an obstructive defendant succeed in totally blocking the arbitration.[87]

1.26 Another important positive effect of the arbitration agreement consists in the definition and limitation of the scope of the proceedings and of any award.[88] On the one hand, this

---

[79] Derains, Y. and Schwartz, E.A. (n 58) 357.

[80] See eg Fouchard, Gaillard, Goldman (n 30) 396 no 627 (*pacta sunt servanda*).

[81] For the majority view in this respect in German law, see eg Schütze, R.A. (n 29) no 143; Lachmann, J.P., *Handbuch für die Schiedsgerichtspraxis* (3rd edn, Dr Otto Schmidt Verlag, Cologne, 2008) nos 295 *et seq*.

[82] Fouchard, Gaillard, Goldman (n 30) 398 no 631.

[83] Art II (3) New York Convention; Art 8(1), Model Law.

[84] Such orders containing explicit steps to be taken by the defendant are eg known in the United States (s 4 US Arbitration Act) and, in a more general way, possible and issued in practice in France by the *Tribunal de Grande Instance de Paris* (Art 1493 and 1457, NCCP); see Schlosser, P. (n 13) no 397. For anti-suit injunctions which sometimes have been issued by English courts, see van Houtte, H., 'May Court Judgments that Disregard Arbitration Clauses and Awards be Enforced under the Brussels and Lugano Conventions?' (1997) 13 *Arb Int'l* no1, 85, 91.

[85] Schlosser, P. (n 13) nos 586 *et seq*; see eg Art 11(4) and (5), Model Law; and Fouchard, Gaillard, Goldman (n 30) 400 no 632.

[86] Art 25(b), Model Law; Art 15(8) LCIA Rules; Art 6(2) ICC Rules.

[87] Fouchard, Gaillard, Goldman (n 30) 401 no 633.

[88] Redfern, Hunter, Blackaby and Partasides (n 12) 3–39 *et seq*; Fouchard, Gaillard, Goldman (n 30) 407 *et seq*, nos 647 *et seq*.

concerns the objective scope of the claims, ie whether according to the wording and interpretation of eg the arbitration clause, claims in tort etc, which are not contractual, may be decided by the arbitrators. In view of a generally wide construction of arbitration clauses and the wording of recommended standard clauses[89], those non-contractual claims will be within the scope of the tribunal's jurisdiction. On the other hand, the arbitration clause also defines the subjective scope of the arbitration: it determines which parties are bound by the arbitration agreement. In this respect, arbitrators and courts have, in recent times, shown a tendency also to include third parties in the arbitral proceedings who were not direct parties of the underlying main contract.[90] In view of general principles of the law on contracts, this is, however, a doubtful practice which lacks a firm legal basis.[91]

(3.2) 'Negative effects' of the arbitration agreement The denial of its own jurisdiction of a court which is seized despite the existence of an arbitration agreement is considered to be one of the main effects of such an arbitration agreement.[92] The solution of early international treaties and its successors, including the Model Law, that the court has to refer the parties to arbitration,[93] is rather general and must be seen in the context of existing national laws. In many jurisdictions, the party opposing the litigation initiated by its opponent must raise the objection timeously in form of an explicit legal objection to the action ('Einrede'). This is the law in eg France, Germany, the Netherlands and Sweden.[94] Other jurisdictions provide for a mandatory declaration of lack of jurisdiction by the court (*ex officio*), as eg in Switzerland.[95] In any case, the party concerned will invoke the arbitration clause out of its own motion before the court in order to stop the litigation proceedings. A further active way of preventing the opponent from initiating litigation proceedings is the use of so-called anti-suit injunctions which have in some cases been issued by English courts.[96] In the international context, this appears, however, to be rather the exception than the rule. **1.27**

C. Dispute resolution in a globalized world

(1) Domestic and international arbitration

Since the early days of arbitration, this private way of adjudication was often used by merchants and companies for disputes arising from contracts with foreign parties. Both during the arbitral proceeding and after the rendering of the award at the stage of challenge or enforcement procedures, the questions arose whether the application of purely domestic **1.28**

---

89 For a wide interpretation of arbitration clauses, see Schlosser, P. (n 13) nos 420 *et seq.*

90 See Fouchard, Gaillard, Goldman (n 30) 317 *et seq* nos 518 *et seq.* For a detailed discussion of the problems of multi-party arbitration, see Massuras, K., *Dogmatische Strukturen der Mehrparteienschiedsgerichtsbarkeit* (Frankfurt, 1998).

91 For inclusion of third parties in arbitration proceedings, see para 1.282 *et seq.*

92 Rubino-Sammartano, M. (n 44) 156; see Schlosser, P. (n 13) no400.

93 See commentary on Art 8, Model Law, ch 14.

94 Art 1458(3), NCCP; s 1032(1), ZPO; Art 1022(1), WBR; s 4 SAA.

95 Art 7, SPILA; Schlosser, P. (n 13) no 400. For more details, see commentary on Art 8, Model Law, ch14.

96 See eg as maritime cases '*The Angelic Grace*' (1995) 1 Lloyd's Rep P 87 and *Continental Bank NA v Aeakos* (1994) 1 Lloyd's Rep 505 (A).

standards (eg for procedural issues) was appropriate in the international context.[97] This question was especially justified in situations where no party was a national or resident of the jurisdiction at the seat of the arbitration. As a consequence, case law and the national legislators started to establish different rules of law for domestic and international arbitration. This development, however, also gave rise to criticism and the legitimate question whether such distinction does have any merits and justification. Also the terms used and the criteria applied are not uniform. 'National' arbitration concerns all arbitral proceedings within a particular jurisdiction, as opposed to 'foreign' arbitration which, from the viewpoint of the particular jurisdiction, is conducted within and governed by a foreign jurisdiction. 'Domestic' as opposed to international arbitration does not have any foreign or international element as for instance arbitration in London between two English companies according to English law. Finally, 'a-national' or de-localized arbitral proceedings or awards do not have any firm link to a particular jurisdiction.[98] A definition of 'international' arbitration will be given below.[99]

1.29 **(1.1) Historical introduction** A description of the situation in three important jurisdictions which are frequently chosen as places for international arbitration shows how differently arbitration with international elements may be regulated.

1.30 England is a jurisdiction which, although often chosen as a place for international arbitral proceedings, for a long time did not develop specific rules for non-domestic arbitration. The majority of the arbitration proceedings in the nineteenth century were not based on the free will of the parties, and the close ties with the courts and their supervisory powers created a regime firmly based in the English judicial system.[100] Apart from a courageous modern draft Arbitration Act of the 1880s,[101] for many decades English law kept the strong supervisory and interventionist powers of the courts which managed to maintain a 'true English' character of (domestic and international) arbitration.[102] Not until the 1970s, as the result of a growing fear that the City of London would lose its leading role as a place for international arbitration, were specific rules for non-domestic arbitration introduced.[103] The Arbitration Act 1979 contained for the first time provisions which enabled the parties to exclude the reference of questions of law to the High Court in London, a choice which was not granted in important specific areas of the law, such as in maritime and commodity

[97] On the reasons why specific rules for international arbitration have been adopted, see Poudret, J.-F. and Besson, S., *Comparative Law of International Arbitration* (n 6) nos 22 *et seq.*

[98] A-national or de-localized arbitration is sometimes also called 'truly international' as opposed to international arbitration which, in many jurisdictions, has the same roots in the national jurisdiction as domestic arbitration. See Fouchard, Gaillard, Goldman (n 30) 48 no 82. Generally on a-national arbitration or delocalization of arbitration, Mayer, P. in M. Hunter, A. Marriott, V.V. Veeder, *The Internationalisation of International Arbitration,* 37 *et seq*; Rensmann (1998) 15 *J Int'l Arb* no 2, 37.

[99] See *infra* para 1.35.

[100] Veeder, V.V. in M. Hunter, A. Marriott, V.V. Veeder, *The Internationalisation of International Arbitration,* 13 *et seq.*

[101] The so-called Bramwell's Code of 1883 was not taken into account when the Arbitration Act 1889 was enacted and fell into oblivion until the beginning of the 1980s; see Veeder, V.V. in M. Hunter, A. Marriott, V.V. Veeder, *The Internationalisation of International Arbitration,* 14.

[102] See eg Weigand, F.-B., *Recht der Internationalen Wirtschaft* (*RIW*) 1997, 904 *et seq.*

[103] See eg Steyn, 'England's Response to the UNCITRAL Model Law of Arbitration' (1994) 10 *Arb Int'l* no 1, 7.

matters.[104] The recent Arbitration Act 1996 does not generally distinguish international from national or domestic arbitration and does not contain specific exclusion agreements or anything similar for international arbitration.[105]

The development in France showed a more liberal approach towards international arbitration. In general, however, since the time of the French Revolution, arbitration was traditionally looked at with distrust, because, in a state where the rule of law governs, it belongs to the courts of the state to decide on questions of law and justice.[106] In contrast to this attitude, international arbitration was already being treated differently by the end of the 19th century. In 1899, the *Cour de Cassation* decided that an award rendered in France by application of English law was to be regarded as 'English', and for that reason was not subject to an appeal in France.[107] In the first half of the twentieth century, various decisions held that French law, which was more stringent at that time than today, did not apply to (and nullify) a 'foreign' arbitration clause if it involved elements of international trade.[108] Immediately before the enactment of the new French law on arbitration (Decree of 1981), the *Cour d'Appel de Paris* confirmed, in the famous *Götaverken* decision, the impossibility of attacking 'international' arbitral awards with a plea for nullity as it is provided for in case of a national or domestic arbitration.[109] Since 1981, there have been two completely different systems for domestic and international arbitration with a much more liberal standard and narrowly defined means of recourse in international arbitral proceedings.[110] **1.31**

Switzerland has, today, a similar situation as France in as much as there are two different regimes for domestic and international arbitration. Such 'internationalism', however, is a rather recent development. Traditionally, according to the jurisdictional approach, arbitration was seen as a procedural phenomenon so that, in principle, the law of the canton where the seat of the arbitration was, applied. Since this state of the law did not favour the development of a modern law on international arbitration, in 1969 the Swiss Concordat was agreed which harmonized the various cantonal provisions on arbitration. However, this law, too, proved to be an obstacle for international commerce since it allowed a judicial review of awards on grounds that included 'arbitrariness'. Under that heading, the losing **1.32**

[104] See s 3(1) Arbitration Act 1979. This exclusion of exclusion agreements was dependent on the application of English substantive law to the arbitration, a requirement showing that the further development of English law in the area of the special category disputes was the decisive motive of the legislator. The criterion for the definition of a non-domestic, international arbitration was the foreign nationality or habitual residence (or the seat in case of a legal person) of one or all the parties at the time when the arbitration agreement was concluded, see s 3(7) Arbitration Act 1979.

[105] The possible exclusion of appeals applies to domestic and international arbitration alike; in addition, there are some specific rules (ss 85 *et seq*) on consumer and small claims arbitration; see Weigand, F.-B., *Recht der Internationalen Wirtschaft (RIW)* (1997) 904, 905.

[106] Delvolvé, J.L. in M. Hunter, A. Marriott, V.V. Veeder, *The Internationalisation of International Arbitration,* 141, 142 *et seq.*

[107] Decision as quoted by Mayer, P. in M. Hunter, A. Marriott, V.V. Veeder, *Internationalisation of International Arbitration,* 37, 44.

[108] Cour de Cassation, 19 February 1930 and similarly of 27 January 1931, quoted in Fouchard, Gaillard, Goldman (n 30) 60 no 108 at fn 174. The wording used at the time ('met en jeu des intérêts du commerce international') is practically identical with the wording of Art 1492, NCCP.

[109] Decision of 21 February 1980, JDI (Clunet) 1980, 660 = *Rev arb* 1980, 524. See also Fouchard, Gaillard, Goldman (n 30) 61, no 110.

[110] See Art 1492, NCCP and, for challenge procedures, Art 1502, NCCP.

party could attack the award bringing forward almost any factual or legal argument,[111] so that awards did not appear to be actually final. According to the new Private International Law Act of 1987 (SPILA),[112] in international arbitration, the parties have a choice between three possibilities, one of which is a total exclusion of all setting-aside proceedings. The prerequisite for such an option is that both parties are foreign nationals or have their residence outside Switzerland.[113]

1.33 The Model Law, as the final example, does distinguish international from domestic arbitration since it is meant to apply only to international arbitration.[114] According to Art 1(3), Model Law, an arbitration may be called international on the basis of various elements, the most important of which is the place of business or permanent residence of the parties in different states. While several countries have maintained this distinction and enacted modern arbitration laws, based on the Model Law, for international arbitration only, there are other countries, as for instance Germany, which have decided to omit such distinction. Therefore, the German law which is based on the Model Law, applies to domestic and international arbitration alike.[115]

1.34 **(1.2) Justification for distinguishing international from domestic arbitration** The notion of international arbitration is so commonly used, be it in textbooks or legal instruments, that it is either not defined at all, assuming that its meaning is obvious anyway, or it is associated with various definitions.[116] To many authors, the need for a definition of 'international' arbitration appears to be obvious,[117] whereas it has rightly been pointed out that one should primarily not simply look at the features of a certain phenomenon but rather consider why it or its notion should be defined at all.[118] The common ground appears to be that a definition (and a distinction by such definition from purely domestic arbitration) is required since more freedom may be allowed in an international arbitration than in a domestic arbitration, thereby giving more weight to party autonomy.[119] As expressed by a well known expert and arbitrator, international arbitration is simply generally recognized

[111] See Art 36(f) of the Concordat which allows the challenge on an award 'based on findings which were manifestly contrary to the facts appearing on the file, or one that constitutes a clear violation of law or equity'.

[112] For details, see Blessing, M., 'The New International Arbitration Law in Switzerland', (1988) 5 *J Int'l Arb* no 1, 1. See also Park, W.W., *International Forum Selection* (Kluwer Law International, Boston, 1995) 89.

[113] Art 192(1), SPILA.

[114] For the reasons for that approach, see commentary on Art 1, Model Law, ch14.

[115] According to the official governmental report on the new law, the reason for that non-distinction was that the Model Law is equally suitable for domestic arbitration and that two different regimes would entail problems of drawing the borderline between each other. See Berger, K.P., *Das neue Recht der Schiedsgerichtsbarkeit—The New German Arbitration Law* (RWS Verlag Kommunikationsforum GmbH, Cologne, 1998) 137.

[116] See eg Redfern, Hunter, Blackaby and Partasides (n 12) 1–17 *et seq.*

[117] See eg Fouchard, Gaillard, Goldman (n 30) 47 no 78: 'La question de savoir ce qu'il faut entendre par arbitrage international est évidemment essentielle.'

[118] Schlosser, P. (n 13) no 36.

[119] Redfern, Hunter, Blackaby and Partasides (n 12) 1–18; Mayer, P. in M. Hunter, A. Marriott, V.V. Veeder, *Internationalisation of International Arbitration,* 37, 40; Park, W.W. (1983) 32 *ICLQ* 21, 30; Yu, Hl (1998) 15 *J Int'l. Arb* no 2, 145, 146; Lalive, P., Poudret, J.E. and Reymond, C., *Le droit de l'arbitrage interne et international en Suisse* (Helbing & Lichtenhahn Editions Payot, Lausanne, 1989) 276 no 25.

to be a 'different animal'.[120] A reason for that may be that states feel a need for firmer control of purely domestic arbitration where it is considered to be an equal alternative to national litigation,[121] whereas internationally active companies and global players appear not to need the same degree of legal protection. Those companies, by preferring a neutral place of arbitration to international litigation and its potential pitfalls, demonstrate their objective to escape state intervention as far as possible. Thus, it is legitimate to establish a 'privileged' framework for a basically private form of dispute resolution among commercial parties. That may be done either by requiring generally a less firm control by the weaker standard of 'international public policy' (as opposed to domestic or national public policy),[122] or by introducing a system of its own for international arbitration. Some experts even suggest to free 'truly international' arbitration proceedings completely from the constraints of national law by introducing the term of a-national or delocalized arbitration.[123] Without going into details, it may be suggested here that both domestic and international arbitration belong to the category of 'national' arbitration in the meaning that they are both governed by the law of the seat of arbitration. Many states provide for different rules on domestic and international arbitration, and therefore the definition of 'international' arbitration plays an important role in practice.

(1.3) Criteria for distinguishing international from domestic arbitration In principle, there are many factors conceivable which may give an arbitration clause or proceeding an international character.[124] For general purposes, it may be sufficient to identify some link with a foreign country, be it the place of the signing or the performance of the main contract or quite a number of other features, in order to consider an arbitration to be international.[125] If, however, the applicability of a certain national law or international treaty is concerned, a clear and exclusive definition is required. There are two groups of criteria which are suitable for a definition.[126] First, the subjective criterion which looks at the parties of the arbitration, and, secondly, the objective criterion which qualifies the subject matter and other objective factors of the arbitration as national or international. **1.35**

The subjective criterion. The European Convention of 1961 refers to the habitual place of residence or the seat of the parties of the arbitration and defines an arbitration as international if the parties have their residence or seat in different contracting states.[127] Also the English Arbitration Act 1979, when defining 'domestic arbitration', considers as international any **1.36**

[120] Lalive, P. in M. Hunter, A. Marriott, V.V. Veeder, *Internationalisation of International Arbitration,* 49, 50. Similar Lalive, Poudret and Reymond (n 119) 276 no 25 ('L'arbitrage interne et l'arbitrage international sont. . . des institutions différents').

[121] Redfern, Hunter, Blackaby and Partasides (n 12) 1–18.

[122] On 'transnational' or 'truly international' public policy, see Lalive, in ICCA Congress Series no 3, 257 and *Rev Arb* 1986, 329.

[123] For a recent comprehensive discussion, see Rensmann, T., (1998) 15 *J Int'l. Arb* no 2, 37. For a more detailed discussion see Lew, J.D.M., Mistelis, L.A. and Kröll, S. (n 13) 68 nos 46 *et seq.*

[124] See eg the long list in Fouchard, Gaillard, Goldman (n 30) no 86 which describes decisive factors. See generally for the definition of international arbitration, Fouchard, P., 'Quand un arbitrage est-il international' *Rev Arb* (1970) 59.

[125] See the listing at Schlosser, P. (n 13) no 36.

[126] Lew, J.D.M., Mistelis, L.A. and Kröll, S. (n 13) 58.

[127] Art I 1(a), European (Geneva) Convention of 1961.

arbitration where none of the parties is a national or resident in the United Kingdom or has its seat there.[128] The Model Law defines an arbitration as international if, at the time of concluding the arbitration agreement, the parties had their places of business in different states.[129]

1.37 The objective criterion. The nature of the dispute is often regarded as the decisive feature for a distinction. For example, the ICC Rules are intended to apply to 'business disputes of an international character' without, however, explaining the meaning of that notion.[130] In practice, any foreign element is considered to be enough for such qualification.[131] The most important legal instrument containing an objective criterion for the definition of 'international' is the French decree of 1981 and the respective rule of Art 1492, NCPC.[132] According to this provision, an arbitration is international 'if it implicates international commercial interests'.[133] This wording which is a summary of the existing French case law at the time[134], has been interpreted as only referring to objective, economic criteria.[135] The nationality of the parties, the applicable substantive law and the place of arbitration are not decisive criteria.[136] Finally, the Model Law contains a lengthy list of factual elements which may, apart from the residence of the parties, serve as an objective factor for the definition as international.[137]

1.38 Whereas for legal instruments there are specific distinctive features which do not have to be commented on here, for general purposes and specifically for this handbook, it is suggested that the subjective approach be followed.[138] If both parties are nationals or residents of the same state where the place of the arbitration is situated, there appears to be no need to grant those parties a lower standard for court supervision etc, only because some interests of international trade may be involved.[139] The difficulties concerning the wide wording of

[128] See s 3(7) for excluding the possibility of so-called exclusion agreements.

[129] See Art 1 (3)(a), Model Law; the place of business is only one of several connecting factors listed in Art 1(3), Model Law.

[130] See Art 1(1), ICC Rules 1998.

[131] Redfern, Hunter, Blackaby and Partasides (n 12) 1–21, referring to the explanatory booklet of the ICC, ICC publication no 301 (1977) 19.

[132] Lew, J.D.M., Mistelis, L.A. and Kröll, S. (n 13) 58.

[133] The wording of Art 1492 ('Est international l'arbitrage qui met en cause des intérêts de commerce international') may also be translated as . . . 'when it involves the interests of international trade', see Redfern, Hunter, Blackaby and Partasides (n 12) 1–22.

[134] For details, see Fouchard, Gaillard, Goldman (n 30) 59 *et seq* nos 108–13.

[135] See Fouchard, Gaillard, Goldman (n 30) 64 no 115. The French courts have taken a liberal approach in order to delimit the purely economic definition of international arbitration: an arbitration is international if it results from a dispute involving the economies of more than one different country, see Lew, J.D.M., Mistelis, L.A. and Kröll, S. (n 13) 58 no 31.

[136] See Fouchard, Gaillard, Goldman (n 30) 66 nos 121 *et seq*, with references to recent case law.

[137] According to Art 1(3)(b), Model Law, these factors are the place of arbitration, place of performance of the commercial relationship or the place with which the subject matter of the dispute is most closely connected.

[138] Lew, J.D.M., Mistelis, L.A. and Kröll, S. (n 13) 60 *et seq*, nos 36 *et seq* for a third approach combining both the subjective and objective criteria.

[139] If two Swiss parties agree on a sale of a machine to be delivered to Germany in a contract that is governed by Swiss law, the 'international' element of the place of delivery (which may be abroad only for the reason that the buyer himself has sold the machine to a German customer) is not strong enough to demand the application of a system of international rules which is primarily designed for totally different cases.

Art 1492, NCPC and the broad and somewhat vague wording of the Model Law show that the subjective approach is more reliable. Objective elements are only rarely strong enough to make an arbitration international although both parties are residents or nationals of the same state. Therefore, an arbitration is international, if at least one party to the arbitration proceedings has its habitual residence or seat outside the jurisdiction where the arbitration has its place or seat. Finally, as already indicated, a simple distinction between national arbitration (and its sub-species of domestic and international arbitration) and foreign arbitration appears to be sufficient. This is also the terminology used by most legal instruments and leading authors,[140] and there is no compelling reason why one should introduce or acknowledge a third category of 'truly international' or a-national arbitration.[141]

(2) Arbitration services

Over the last decades, arbitration, especially in the international context, has changed considerably. Apart from theoretical and often idealistic descriptions of this particular kind of dispute resolution, companies and commercial 'users' are entitled to expect certain arbitral services. **1.39**

(2.1) The creation of an 'international arbitration industry'[142] Especially those practitioners who were early promoters of arbitration as opposed to commonly used litigation regret that arbitration changed from 'a small artisan speciality' to a true arbitration or service industry.[143] Certainly, there was a true explosion of arbitration in the 1970s, 80s and 90s, which did have an influence on the character of international arbitration.[144] In particular, the growth of arbitral institutions competing with each other has shown that those experts involved are parts of a service industry which not only aims at the promotion of justice and fairness but also at the promotion of the arbitration business.[145] One should, however, not deplore that situation for the following reasons: first, even in 'the old glorious days', arbitration was a service rendered by specialists who earned at least part of their living by related activities as counsel and/or arbitrators. Second, companies as the main users have a right to obtain appropriate services whose growth is also an answer to the globalization of **1.40**

---

[140] This territorial approach is the basis for the Model Law (Art 1(2), Model Law) and those jurisdictions which have adopted the Model Law (as eg Germany, see s 1025(1), ZPO), and the national law of other important jurisdictions like the Dutch and Swiss law. See Fouchard, Gaillard, Goldman (n 30)no 92; Redfern, Hunter, Blackaby and Partasides (n 12) 1–18 *et seq.*

[141] Rensmann, T., 'Anational Arbitral Awards—Legal Phenomenon or Academic Phantom?' (1998) 15 *J Int'l. Arb* no 2, 37, concludes that owing to the deregulation of arbitration laws, the concept of a-national arbitration is of vanishing importance. See, however, in favour of delocalized arbitration, eg Rubino-Sammartano, M. (n 44) 21–4 and the French approach, Fouchard, Gaillard, Goldman (n 30) 94.

[142] Frequently, instead of 'arbitration industry' the term 'arbitration culture' is being used: See the topic of the 1996 ICCA Conference, published as 'International Dispute Resolution: Towards an International Arbitration Culture, ICCA Congress Series no 8, 1998'. For general concern see Rubino-Sammartano, M., 'Is arbitration losing ground?' *Am Rev Int'l. Arb* vol 14, 341.

[143] Cremades, B.M., 'Overcoming the Clash of Legal Cultures: The Role of Interactive Arbitration', (1998) 14 *Arb Int'l* no 2, 157; similarly Mustill, M.J., 'Arbitration: History and Background' (1989) 6 *J Int'l Arb* no 2, 43, 55.

[144] Najar, J.C., 'The Inside View: Companies' Needs in Arbitration' (1996) 12 *Arb Int'l* no 3, 359.

[145] *ibid*, 368 *et seq.*

the economy.[146] Therefore, companies should concentrate on the two most important factors of that 'service industry': good arbitrators and a favourable arbitral infrastructure.

1.41 **(2.2) The arbitrator as the private judge of the parties** Many companies have recognized that in international contracts, it is more favourable to provide for an arbitrator as a private judge than for a state court, the members of which are not predictable.[147] How often, however, arbitration is actually chosen in practice, is open to discussion. Estimates that about 90 per cent of international contracts contain arbitration clauses[148] may not be verified by empirical surveys. However, companies who frequently do international business opt for arbitration in two thirds of all international long-term contracts.[149] The freedom to choose the arbitrators is an essential part of the arbitral process,[150] and the choice of arbitration as private adjudication may be called a fundamental right of the parties.[151] It has even been suggested to consider the recognition and enforceability of arbitration agreements as part of the European public policy,[152] especially in England where anti-suit injunctions are issued in order to enforce arbitration agreements, but also in the Unites States, the liberty to resort to arbitration is considered as one of the main pillars of international trade.[153] In practice, a just result depends mainly on the honesty, the skill and the wisdom of the decision makers.[154] Therefore, the personal qualities of the arbitrators are of utmost importance, and especially the chairman will have the difficult task to bridge cultural differences in order to come to a just decision[155].

1.42 **(2.3) The requirement of an adequate 'arbitral infrastructure'** In order to obtain satisfactory services, the parties must be able to rely on an adequate arbitral 'infrastructure'. This comprises skilled lawyers as counsel and arbitrators as well as suitable institutions and a modern legal arbitration regime of the host country of the arbitral tribunal. Within the last 35 years, arbitration has become a special field of the law for quite a few internationally

---

[146] Cremades, B.M. (n 143) 172.

[147] See eg Mustill, M. and Boyd, S.C. (n 7) 5.

[148] Berger, K.P., 'Aufgaben und Grenzen der Parteiautonomie in der internationalen Wirtschaftsschiedsgerichtsbarkeit' *Recht der Internationalen Wirtschaft (RIW)* (1994) 12 *et seq*. Nevertheless, it appears that arbitration is not yet known to all company lawyers, see Najar, J.C., *The Inside View: Companies' Needs in Arbitration* (1996) 12 *Arb Int'l* no 3, 359, 361.

[149] Schmidt-Diemitz, R., 'Internationale Schiedsgerichtsbarkeit - Eine empirische Untersuchung' *DB* (1999) 369.

[150] Rau, A.S., (1998) 14 *Arb Int'l* no 2, 115, 116, considers 'private ordering and self determination' as the essential characteristic of arbitration as compared to litigation.

[151] Devolvé, J.-L., in M. Hunter, A. Marriott, V.V. Veeder, *The Internationalisation of International Arbitration* (1995) 141.

[152] Schlosser, P. CEPANI, 81, 90 *et seq*.

[153] *ibid*, 81, 91.

[154] Saville, M., 'The Origin of the New English Arbitration Act 1996: Reconciling Speed with Justice in the Decision-making Process' (1997) 13 *Arb Int'l* no 3, 237, 251.

[155] Cremades, B.M. (n 143) 161. For a general discussion of personality and qualification of arbitrators, see Weigand, F.-B. 'Der nebenberuflich tätige Schiedsrichter' in B. Bachmann, S. Breidenbach, D. Coester-Waltjen, B. Heß, A. Nelle and C. Wolf (eds), *Grenzüberschreitungen—Festschrift für Peter Schlosser zum 70. Geburtstag* (Mohr Siebeck, Tübingen, 2005). For more details on the need for ethical guidance in international arbitration, see Benson, C., 'Can Professional Ethics Wait? The Need for Transparency in International Arbitration', (2009) 3 *Disp Res Int'l.* no 1, 78. See also the Chartered Institute of Arbitrators Code of Professional and Ethical Conduct for Members (January 2007) published in (2007) 73 *Arbitration* 2, 231 *et seq*.

active lawyers,[156] and the internationalization of the arbitrators[157] is an important feature for the users of arbitration. With eg Paris and London as important and frequently used places for international arbitration, specialized lawyers must be able to represent their clients there in the respective language.[158] Given the importance of the rules of arbitral institutions and the *lex fori* of the arbitration as the two decisive features for the companies,[159] there have been considerable efforts to modernize such rules at the private and public level. This has resulted in a harmonization of the international arbitral process. Therefore, today users have generally a better and more modern arbitral infrastructure than ever before.

D. Types of arbitration

International arbitration proceedings are governed by one and the same legal regime in a particular jurisdiction regardless of the subject matter to be decided by arbitration. However, there are specific areas of international trade, such as commodity trade or maritime matters, which are governed by rules that generally provide particular regulations for deciding disputes by arbitration. Such arbitrations, therefore, 'tend to belong to a world of their own'.[160] The same is true, even more so, for investment arbitrations. As a special type of arbitration the fast-track proceedings will, furthermore, be dealt with in this section. **1.43**

(1) Commodity trade arbitration

Some areas of international trade of important commodities have, for many decades, been subject to specific rules issued by the leading respective trade association. Examples are the Grain and Feed Trade Association (GAFTA) and the Federation of Oils, Seeds and Fats Association Limited (FOSFA), which are both based in London. GAFTA and FOSFA provide for arbitration in their respective contract patterns.[161] Both organizations give general information of their arbitration procedures,[162] however, they do not provide text documents of the current arbitration rules on the respective websites.[163] **1.44**

The GAFTA and FOSFA arbitration rules have some common features. They are highly specialized rules which are tailor-made for the specific trade and accordingly do not form part of the main stream of international arbitration.[164] In practice, the respective arbitration **1.45**

---

[156] Kerr, M., 'Concord and Conflict in International Arbitration' (1997) 13 *Arb Int'l* no 2, 121, 123.

[157] Lalive, P. in M. Hunter, A. Marriott, V.V. Veeder, *The Internationalisation of International Arbitration*, 51, 55.

[158] Briner, R., 'Domestic Arbitration: Practice in Continental Europe and its Lessons for Arbitration in England' (1997) 13 *Arb Int'l* no 2, 155, 159.

[159] See eg Robine, E., 'What Companies Expect from International Commercial Arbitration' (1992) 9 *J Int'l. Arb* non. 2, 31 *et seq.*

[160] Redfern, Hunter, Blackaby and Partasides (n 12) 4–24.

[161] The current GAFTA Arbitration Rules no 125 are effective as of 1 July 2007. Interestingly, these arbitration rules of GAFTA, FOSFA, etc are, generally, only mentioned briefly in books on international arbitration. In addition, there are no or only scarce guidelines available as interpretation of those rules, which are not always very helpful for practical purposes.

[162] See eg the Guide to Arbitrations and Appeals, issued by FOSFA (October 2005).

[163] The Arbitration Rules are only available upon request and/or for members of the organization; see <http://www.gafta.com> and <http://www.fosfa.com>.

[164] Generally, the practitioner will often be surprised when comparing those rules to the generally accepted standards of international arbitration which are not always met.

rules will mostly apply to quality disputes.[165] Therefore, commercial people are not only preferred as arbitrators but their practical experience is often a condition for the parties' choice. Consequently, the neutrality of those arbitrators who have to belong to the very association that has issued the arbitration rules, is not generally guaranteed.[166] Further, the panel often consists only of two arbitrators who, if they cannot agree, have to appoint an umpire who then decides alone.[167] Lawyers are often not admitted to take part in the proceedings be it as arbitrators or party representatives.[168] Finally, both organizations provide for a two-stage arbitration system with an appeal of facts and law to be addressed to a Board of Appeal to be supervised by the association.[169]

(2) Maritime arbitration

1.46 In maritime matters, which may be defined generously,[170] arbitration has for a long time been the generally accepted manner of dispute resolution. It is, therefore, not surprising that specialized centres and/or rules have developed over the decades.

1.47 New York has for many years been one of the leading places for running maritime arbitrations.[171] Since 1925, the basis of those arbitration proceedings is the Federal Arbitration Act. In addition, the Society of Maritime Arbitrators (SMA) has issued particular rules which recently have been modernized.[172] Disputes shall be decided by experienced arbitrators.[173] The SMA Rules aim at preventing delay by a more or less strict timetable,[174] and

---

165 Therefore, those arbitrations are sometimes called 'look-sniff' arbitrations, see Redfern, A. and Hunter M. (1st edn, 1986) 36.

166 Redfern, A. and Hunter, M. (1st edn, 1986) 153, (3rd edn, 1999) 4–24; Fouchard, Gaillard, Goldman (n 30) 573, no 1,004.

167 In such situations, it is only natural that each of the party-appointed arbitrators acts as an advocate of 'his party's' cause within the arbitral tribunal and not as a neutral member of the panel, see Redfern, Hunter, Blackaby and Partasides (n 12) 4–24. This change of role from arbitrator to advocate (in case an umpire is appointed) is even expressly described, see the Guide to Arbitrations and Appeals, issued by FOSFA (October 2005).

168 See Guide to Arbitrations and Appeals, issued by FOSFA (October 2005): 'No person wholly or principally engaged in legal practice shall be eligible to act as an arbitrator or umpire.' . . . 'Either party . . . may not have present or be represented by any member of the legal profession wholly or principally engaged in legal practice.'

169 For details, see eg the Guide to Arbitrations and Appeals, issued by FOSFA (October 2005) on 'Appeals'.

170 Ambrose, C. and Maxwell, K., *London Maritime Arbitration* (1996), 1 define as maritime arbitration such proceedings . . . 'where the dispute involves in some way a ship—for instance, a dispute under a charter party, a bill of lading or a ship sale agreement'. Similary, s 1 of the Federal Arbitration Act 1925 provides: '"Maritime transaction", as herein defined, means charter parties, bills of lading of water carriers, agreements relating to wharfage, supplies furnished vessels or repairs to vessels, collisions, or any other matters in foreign commerce which, if the subject of controversy, would be embraced within admiralty jurisdiction'.

171 For details, see eg the comprehensive survey of Howard McCormack on Maritime Arbitration Practice in New York, presented at the IBA seminar on 'Arbitration and Transport Disputes', 29–31 May 1997, in Hamburg.

172 Bulow, L.C., 'The revised Arbitration Rules of the Society of Maritime Arbitrators', (1995) 12 *J Int'l Arb* no 1, 87 *et seq*.

173 The two party-appointed arbitrators who are either elected from a list provided by the SMA or otherwise have particular experience in maritime matters (as commercial men or lawyers), determine a third person as chairman of the tribunal. The SMA list comprises about 130 arbitrators, see McCormack, H., 3 and 26.

174 The time limit of 120 days for rendering an award starts only from the day when all evidence has been presented to the panel (SMA r 28) and, in addtion, is frequently extended in practice, McCormack, H. 15.

there are also particular rules for a fast procedure in cases of small claims up to US$ 50,000.[175] A particular feature is the habit to publish awards on a regular basis indicating the arbitrators in charge and the dissenting opinions.[176]

Maritime arbitration in London is governed by the Arbitration Act 1996 and the Rules of the London Maritime Arbitrators' Association (LMAA Terms).[177] Although the association plays a central and supportive role in London maritime arbitration, it is not administering or supervising arbitration proceedings like eg the ICC Court.[178] In LMAA arbitration proceedings the arbitrators shall have experience in maritime matters and generally are 'commercial men' and not lawyers.[179] The panel often consists of only two members, and an umpire is only appointed once both arbitrators cannot agree on an award.[180] Whereas before 2006, no reasons had to be given in an award (unless requested), reasoned awards have now become the rule rather than the exception.[181] **1.48**

Also in Germany, maritime arbitration has a considerable tradition, namely in Hamburg and Bremen. In 1983, the German Maritime Arbitration Association with its own arbitration rules (GMAA Rules) was established.[182] The GMAA is an association of experts and practitioners offering a model arbitration clause for contracts related to sea-trade and shipping or maritime matters. The GMAA does not itself administer arbitral proceedings. The GMAA arbitration rules have similar features as the LMAA Terms; eg there are only two arbitrators who have to appoint an umpire in case they cannot agree.[183] The arbitrators shall ensure an expeditious proceeding by sticking to a strict timetable.[184] The GMAA arbitration rules are increasingly used in practice, eg in insurance policies.[185] **1.49**

Of course, there are many other places world-wide, where maritime arbitration is being practised. In France, eg there is the *Chambre Arbitrale Maritime de Paris*.[186] In Stockholm, maritime arbitration also has a considerable tradition.[187] And of course, in Asia, there are **1.50**

---

175 McCormack, H. (n 171) 8.

176 *ibid*, 17.

177 For more details on the LMAA, which was founded in 1960 already, see Mustill, M. and Boyd, S.C. (n 7) 780. The LMAA Terms were first published in 1987 and are now available in the latest 2006 version; see <http://www.lmaa.org>.

178 Ambrose, C. and Maxwell, K. (n 170) 2.

179 *ibid*, (n 170) 2 *et seq*.

180 The LMAA Terms (2006) provide both for a three-person-tribunal and a two-arbitrator-tribunal who have to appoint an umpire in case both arbitrators do not agree on a matter, see ss 8 and 9 of the Terms.

181 See s 22 of the LMAA Terms (2006).

182 The GMAA Rules are in force as of 1 January 2007 and are available in English, French and German, see <http://www.gmaa.de>.

183 See s 3 and s 4 para 1 of the GMAA Rules (2007).

184 Eight weeks after the constitution of the tribunal, there is a first meeting of the arbitrators in which the hearing date will be fixed. In this hearing, having seen and heard the evidence, the panel will already indicate to the parties its preliminary opinion so as to enable the parties to amicably settle the dispute before the award is rendered.

185 For a more detailed description of German maritime arbitration, see Wölper, J., *Maritime Arbitration in Germany*, in K.H. Böckstiegel, S. Kröll and P. Nacimiento, *Arbitration in Germany* (2008) 889.

186 Fouchard, Gaillard, Goldman (n 30) 187 no 340.

187 See Ramberg, J., 'Maritime Arbitration in Sweden', paper presented at the IBA seminar 1997 in Hamburg.

well known arbitration centres handling maritime matters as eg in Hong Kong.[188] Finally, the so-called ICC/CMI Rules should be mentioned which are applied in disputes which are managed by the International Maritime Arbitration Organisation (IMAO).[189]

(3) Investment arbitration

1.51 Investment Arbitration, also referred to as 'Investment Treaty Arbitration' or 'International Investment Arbitration', has become of growing relevance in the last decades. Investment arbitration deals with conflicts between a foreign capital investor and the state of the investment. The number of such conflicts has significantly increased since the mid 1990s.[190] In 2008, more cases than ever were filed with the International Centre for Settlement of Investment Disputes (ICSID). The number of pending cases rose by approximately 12 per cent each year and reached 145 cases in 2008, the highest yearly number ever administered by ICSID.[191]

1.52 Meanwhile, after four consecutive years of growth, global foreign direct investment inflows rose by 30 per cent in 2007 to reach an all-time high of US$ 1,833 billion.[192] Although this might change in the further course of the global financial crisis, it is to be expected that investment arbitration will be of even greater relevance in the years to come, in particular since the current market developments are prone to promote conflicts.

1.53 Compared to other forms of arbitral dispute resolution, investment arbitration is a relatively young phenomenon. It has essentially developed during the 1960s. Investment arbitration is governed by a specific legal framework, sometimes referred to as the 'network of international investment agreements'.[193] Further, the ICSID provides an arbitration forum with its own rules of procedure.[194]

1.54 **(3.1) History and development of investment arbitration** Although being fairly young in its modern form, the network of international investment agreements is part of a long history. The regulatory treatment of foreigners can be traced back into ancient times, when foreigners faced treatment as enemies, barbarians or outcasts and found themselves in a position of complete outlawry.[195] However, already in the middle ages, predecessors of today's network of international investment agreements began to evolve. By the beginning of the twentieth century, a scholar observed that the status of foreigners had turned into

---

188 See Caldwell, P., 'Maritime Arbitration in Hong Kong', paper presented at the IBA seminar 1997 in Hamburg.

189 Those Rules are a modified version of the ICC Arbitration Rules leaving out typical features like the Terms of Reference. See ICC Publication no 324 and Ramberg, J. 4 *et seq*.

190 For more details on the development see McLachlan, C. Shore, L. and Weininger, M., 'International Investment Arbitration' (Oxford *et al*, 2007) 5.

191 ISCID Annual Report 2008, 3. For more detailed figures see Newcombe, C.W., 'Law and Practice of Investment Treaties', (Kluwer Law International, The Hague, London, Boston, 2009) 59.

192 World Investment Report 2008, XV.

193 Newcombe, C.W. (n 191) 1.

194 See Art 1(2) of the Convention on the Settlement of Investment Disputes between States and Nationals of Other States (ICSID Convention/Convention) for the purpose of ICSID; Jagusch, S. and Gearing, M., 'ICSID' in Rowley (ed), *Arbitration World*, (2nd edn, London, 2006) lxv-lxxxviii.

195 Borchard, E.M., 'The Diplomatic Protection of Citizens Abroad or the Law of International Claims' (New York, 1915) 33.

'practical assimilation with nationals'.[196] However, it took until the second half of the twentieth century until the outlines of today's system of international investment agreements became visible.

The genuine challenges of the promotion and protection of foreign investment were realized early. The difficulties linked to foreign investment were not limited to questions of substantive law but equally focused on the issue of dispute resolution. Since an investor's attempt to initiate legal proceedings in the courts of the host state has always been little promising as the investor runs a risk that the court's decision might be affected by bias, corruption and inefficiency, seeking diplomatic protection by his home state was often regarded as the investor's only resort.[197] Despite its disadvantages,[198] diplomatic protection remained the means of choice into the era after the Second World War. 1.55

(3.2) Bilateral investment treaties In order to solve these disadvantages, special treaties designed to protect foreign investment between single states were concluded after the Second World War. Besides provisions concerning substantive law they assigned an important role to arbitration. 1.56

Commonly, the Federal Republic of Germany is considered as the originator of the new generation of investment agreements[199] since it launched a bilateral investment treaties (BITs) program for international agreements focusing on investment as early as 1959.[200] The problem of diplomatic protection was solved by the inclusion of an arbitration clause. It provided for state-to-state dispute settlement before the International Court of Justice (ICJ) if the parties agreed, or, in the case of disagreement, to an arbitration tribunal upon the request of either party.[201] Thereby, it arranged for a cheap, predictable and de-escalating way of dispute resolution between the contracting states. 1.57

The most important development in the post-1968 standard was the emergence of direct investor-state arbitration. Such direct investor-state arbitration enables the investor to 1.58

[196] Newcombe, C.W. (n 191) 2.

[197] *ibid*, (n 191) 24. See also Zeiler, G., 'Investitionsschutz und Schiedsverfahren', in: Toggler, *Praxishandbuch Schiedsgerichtsbarkeit* 301–20; Escher, A., Nacimiento, P. and Weissenborn, C., 'Investment Arbitration and the Participation of State Parties in Germany' in Böckstiegel *et al* (eds), *Arbitration in Germany*, 1,013 *et seq*, 1,020.

[198] Diplomatic protection by the home state of the investors implicates various risks: The inclination of an investor's home state to assist is uncertain and can be diminished by several reasons hard or impossible to influence. It is often costly and prone to cause severe political tensions not excluding military escalation, see Zeiler, G. (n 197) 301 *et seq*; Escher, A., Nacimiento, P. and Weissenborn, C. (n 197) 1020; Schreuer, C. in Hofmann/Tams (eds), *The International Convention on the Settlement of Investment Disputes (ICSID): Taking Stock after 40 Years* (Nomos) 1.

[199] Newcombe, C.W. (n 191) 42.

[200] Escher, A., Nacimiento, P. and Weissenborn, C. (n 197) 1029; Newcombe, C.W. (n 191) 42. The first treaty was concluded between Germany and Pakistan (Germany-Pakistan) in the same year. This treaty between Germany and Pakistan solved the questions of substantive law by including a broad definition of the term investment. Investments were to enjoy protection and security. Provision was made for compensation in the event of an expropriation, see Art 3(1) and (2), Germany-Pakistan.

[201] See Art 11(2), Germany-Pakistan; Newcombe, C.W. (n 191) 42.

initiate arbitration without any interference of his home state.[202] This is achieved by including a term into the BIT in which the contracting states mutually submit an offer to arbitrate disputes with nationals or companies of the other party. It may be accepted by the investor through declaration as well as by simply submitting a claim under one of the sets of rules referred to in the contract.[203]

1.59 In principle, the treaty concluded between Indonesia and the Netherlands in 1968 was the first BIT to allow direct investor-state arbitration.[204] In the aftermath, the concept of unilateral arbitration clauses became the most successful way of coping with the difficulty of resolving disputes between foreign investors and their host states. Suggestively described as 'arbitration without privity',[205] it turned out to be the model solution to the problem.

1.60 The validity of a unilateral arbitration clause was first upheld in a case filed by *Southern Pacific Properties (Middle East) Limited v Egypt* in 1985.[206] Yet, Egypt's consent for arbitration was not found to be included in a BIT but a provision of its foreign investment law. However, only five years later the first award was issued in a case where arbitration was based on an arbitration clause contained in a BIT.[207] This event, sometimes referred to as the beginning of investment arbitration, marks the starting point of a success story. The number of known investment disputes subject to arbitration has constantly been rising reaching a remarkable growth rate from the mid 1990s to the mid 2000s.

1.61 Just like arbitration under BITs was a success story, BIT programmes turned out to be successful as well. By the end of 1979, approximately only 100 BITs had been concluded.[208] Yet a lot of major capital exporting states had become engaged in negotiations.[209] The US concluded their first BIT in 1982, other OECD states followed their example.[210] By the end of the 1980s, 385 BITs had been concluded.[211] This number even nearly quintupled during the 1990s, not only with a lot of OECD states concluding their first BITs, but also

[202] In fact, Germany-Pakistan did not provide for any direct right of investor action at all, see Newcombe, C.W. (n 191) 70.

[203] Zeiler, G. (n 197) 308 *et seq*; Newcombe, C.W. (n 191) 44; Schreuer, C., 'ICSID Commentary 2001' para 257 *et seq*.

[204] Newcombe, C.W. (n 191) 44. It was followed in 1969 by an agreement between Chad and Italy that provided for direct investor-state arbitration with unqualified state consent. Because of this provision Newcombe, C.W. (n 191) 45 regards this as the 'true beginning of modern BIT practice' rather than Germany-Pakistan.

[205] Newcombe, C.W. (n 191) 44; Paulsson, J., 'Arbitration Without Privity' 10 *ICSID Rev* (1995) 232, 256.

[206] Newcombe, C.W. (n 191) 45; McLachlan, C., Shore, L. and Weininger, M. (n 190) 52 *et seq*.

[207] Newcombe, C.W. (n 191) 46 and 58; McLachlan, C., Shore, L. and Weininger, M. (n 190) 5.

[208] *ibid*, (n 191) 46.

[209] *ibid*, (n 191) 42 *et seq*; Vandevelde, K.J., *United States Investment Treaties: Policy and Practice* (Deventer: Kluwer Law and Taxation Publishers, Boston, 1992) 19. In 1962 and 1967 the Organization for Economic Cooperation and Development (OECD) provided Draft Conventions to BITs.

[210] Newcombe, C.W. (n 191) 47 *et seq*. For further discussion of the US development see Vandevelde, K.J. (n 209) 19 *et seq*.

[211] Newcombe, C.W. (n 191) 47.

having new industrializing states entering the stage.[212] Today investment protection is ensured by a network of approximately 2800 of such bilateral investment treaties.[213]

(3.3) Multilateral agreements All attempts to agree on investment issues on a multilateral level failed.[214] The legal framework created with the foundation of the World Trade Organization (WTO) does not provide for rules on investments. The Agreement on Trade-Related Investment Measures (TRIMs) only reaffirms that WTO members may not apply investment measures in ways inconsistent with their obligations under the General Agreement on Tariffs and Trade (GATT 1994).[215] Irrespective of the lack of multilateral agreements, it is unlikely that any agreement reached within the WTO framework could replace today's network of international investment agreements or make it obsolete, as the dispute settlement mechanism within the WTO does merely provide for state-to-state arbitration. **1.62**

Despite all difficulties on the multilateral level, various agreements provide for dispute resolution by way of arbitration: The Energy Charter Treaty, an agreement designed to improve the legal conditions for investment in the energy sector, unilaterally grants the investor the right to initiate arbitral proceedings in its Art 26.[216] The very same possibility is created by Chapter 11 of the North American Free Trade Agreement (NAFTA).[217] **1.63**

(3.4) Convention on the Settlement of Investment Disputes between States and Nationals of other States (ICSID Convention) Only slightly prior to the development of 'arbitration without privity', the establishment of the ICSID marked another milestone in the history of investment arbitration.[218] Today, with over 140 signatory states to the ICSID **1.64**

---

[212] Newcombe, C.W. (n 191) 47 *et seq*. While the BITs' post-1968 standard in dispute settlement has been set with direct and unconditional investor-state arbitration, the substantive provisions of mature BITs do not contain too many provisions different from Germany-Pakistan but rather more and refined guarantees. Germany began to include clauses providing for national and most favoured nation (MFN) treatment in the early 1960s; see Newcombe, C.W. (n 191) 42. Besides these issues, later BITs clarify the scope and meaning of investment obligations, including the minimum standard of treatment, expropriation and MFN treatment. For an in detail discussion of the various typical contents of contemporary BITs with a focus on and reference to their treatment in jurisprudence, see McLachlan, C., Shore, L. and Weininger, M. (n 190) 109 *et seq*; for details of substantive standards in German BITs see Escher, A., Nacimiento, P. and Weissenborn, C. (n 197) 1030 *et seq*.

[213] See Newcombe, C.W. (n 191) 55 *et seq*. Rules on the treatment of investments have never been included in the International Law Commission's work on state responsibility and diplomatic protection.

[214] For a brief outline of the events see Newcombe, C.W. (n 191) 55 *et seq*. Although in 1995 negotiations on a Multilateral Agreement on Investment (MAI) commenced within the OECD, disagreement on numerous issues resulted in the abandonment of the draft in 1998.

[215] In the Doha Round of negotiations, the issue of trade and investment originally put on the agenda by the Doha Declaration was dropped owing to the opposition of the developing member states in 2003.

[216] For more details, see Zeiler, G. (n 197) 310; Escher, A., Nacimiento, P. and Weissenborn, C. (n 197) 1033. For details on arbitral proceedings under the Energy Charter Treaty, see Happ, R., *Schiedsverfahren zwischen Staaten und Investoren unter Artikel 26 Energiechartavertrag. Eine Studie zum Wandel der Streitbeilegung im Investitionsschutzrecht unter den Bedingungen der globalen Weltwirtschaft*, Schriftenreihe der August Maria Berges-Stiftung für Arbitrales Recht, Bd. 7 (Peter Lang, 2000).

[217] For more details, see Zeiler, G. (n 197) 309 *et seq*.

[218] The ICSID was founded on the basis of the Convention on the Settlement of Investment Disputes between States and Nationals of other States (ICSID Convention), which is also known as the Washington Convention. It was opened for signature on 18 March 1965 and entered into force on 14 October 1966. The Centre's purpose was not to serve as a permanent arbitral tribunal, but to provide a legal and organizational framework for

Convention it may well be considered the leading international institution in the field of investment arbitration with which most cases concerning investment arbitration are filed.[219]

1.65 The ICSID's primary purpose is to provide facilities for conciliation and arbitration of international investment disputes.[220] The ICSID Convention, accordingly, provides for a framework of procedural rules that govern the conduct of an arbitration.[221] Proceedings under the Convention are mainly governed by the 'Rules of Procedure for Arbitration Proceedings' (Arbitration Rules).[222] These Rules have been the core element within the ICSID framework since 1966.[223]

1.66 The application of the 'Rules of Procedure for Arbitration Proceedings' requires that one party's offer to arbitration is accepted by the other. A host state's offer may be contained in a rule of domestic legislation, a BIT or a multilateral agreement and simply be accepted by submitting a claim.[224] Both declarations may also be included in a written contractual agreement between the parties. It is irrelevant if such an agreement has been concluded in advance of the occurrence of a conflict (*clause compromissoire*) or afterwards (*compromis*).[225]

1.67 In addition to an agreement to arbitrate under the ICSID's Arbitration Rules, Art 25 (1) of the ICSID Convention provides for two restrictions in regard to the scope of application: (i) the *ratione materiae* limits the scope of application of the ICSID's arbitration rules to disputes which are at least reasonably close-connected to an investment;[226] and (ii) as to *ratione personae,* the Convention requires that conflicting parties are either signatory states to it or nationals of such states.[227]

---

arbitration in the field of investment disputes, see Art 1(2), ICSID Convention. The ICSID was established as an autonomous international organization. It exerts its functions by a permanent Secretariat under the control of an Administrative Council. For further details, see McLachlan, C., Shore, L. and Weininger, M. (n 190) 4; Jagusch, S. and Gearing, M. (n 194) lxv.

219 Zeiler, G. (n 197) 303. For further information, see the ICSID homepage and its annual reports at <http://icsid.worldbank.org>. The most important ICSID periodical is the foreign investment law journal ICSID Review. For more activities of the Centre see Jagusch, S. and Gearing, M. (n 194) lxix *et seq*.

220 Art 1(2), ICSID Convention.

221 Newcombe, C.W. (n 191) 29.

222 Other rules governing the process are the Administrative and Financial Regulations which in part also apply to proceedings under the Additional Facility Rules.

223 Besides the ICSID Arbitration Rules, the Convention also provides for Conciliation Proceedings and the Additional Facility Rules. These rules allow for the conduct of mere fact finding proceedings and apply in cases otherwise falling outside the scope of the ICSID Convention. For further details, see Jagusch, S. and Gearing, M. (n 194) lxvi; Newcombe, C.W. (n 191) 29; Zeiler, G. (n 197) 319 *et seq*.

224 Newcombe, C.W. (n 191) 44.

225 Zeiler, G. (n 197) 307.

226 The question of whether or not an investment is concerned is subject to determination by ICSID tribunals on a case-to-case basis. McLachlan, C., Shore, L. and Weininger, M. (n 190) 164 *et seq* provide an in-depth discussion of the notion of investment under the ICSID Convention comprising arbitral jurisdiction; see also Zeiler, G. (n 197) 304; Schreuer, C., Commentary, Art 26, no 67; Jagusch, S. and Gearing, M. (n 194) lxxi; Escher, A., Nacimiento, P. and Weissenborn, C. (n 197) 1,022 *et seq*; Escher, A, *Recht der Internationalen Wirtschaft* (*RIW*) (2001) 20, 22.

227 The notion of nationals does not only refer to natural persons holding the nationality of a contracting state. It also includes juridical persons situated in a contracting state other than the state party to the dispute or being under foreign control and agreed to be treated as a foreign national. By the latter provision the Convention provides a solution to the problem of possible preclusion of ICSID jurisdiction by the fact

Proceedings under the auspices of ICSID are exclusively governed by an autonomous legal framework. This framework contains rules from the ICSID Convention and subsequent agreements only, but no reference to any state law.[228] Thereby, the ICSID framework constitutes a self-contained regime. Disputing parties are entitled to agreements of their own merely to the extent set out by the mandatory provisions of the ICSID framework.[229] These ensure in case of disagreement between the parties that a dispute once raised under the ICSID's jurisdiction can be resolved without giving any party the opportunity to seriously delay an award. **1.68**

Signatory states to the Convention are obligated to recognize and enforce ICSID awards just as if they were final judgements of a national court.[230] Hence, ICSID awards are not subject to any further control under a national jurisdiction in contrast to customary arbitral awards being enforced under the 1958 New York Convention on the Recognition and Enforcement of Foreign Arbitral Awards (NYC).[231] Yet, these rules govern enforcement with respect to awards issued pursuant to Additional Facility Rules, as they apply in the event that one party to the dispute is not a signatory state to the Convention.[232] The only rules not derogated by the Convention are those of state immunity.[233] **1.69**

(3.5) **Other institutional and *ad hoc* arbitrations** Although the ICSID framework is predominant, investment disputes can be arbitrated outside this framework nonetheless. Among the different opportunities of institutional arbitration provided for in agreements the International Chamber of Commerce (ICC) Rules of Arbitration and the Stockholm Chamber of Commerce (SCC) Rules of Arbitration appear to have considerable importance.[234] Besides, investment treaties usually provide for the possibility of *ad hoc* arbitration outside an administering institution supplementary.[235] Customarily they do so by referring to the 1976 Arbitration Rules of the United Nations Commission on International Trade Law (UNCITRAL).[236] These rules were in part applied by the Iran-US Claims Tribunal. Addressing claims arising out of the 1979 Iranian revolution, it has decided a large number of investment disputes since its establishment in 1981, contributing substantially to international jurisprudence on state responsibility for injuries to foreigners and being **1.70**

that foreign investments are often accomplished through companies incorporated in the host state owing to requirements of its national legislation. Jagusch, S. and Gearing, M. (n 194) lxxi *et seq;* Zeiler, G. (n 197) 305 *et seq*; Schreuer, C., Commentary, Art 25, no 551.

[228] McLachlan, C., Shore, L. and Weininger, M. (n 190) 55; Zeiler, G. (n 197) 311.

[229] Zeiler, G. (n 197) 311.

[230] Art 53(1), 54 (1) ICSID Convention; Zeiler, G. (n 197) 315; Jagusch, S. and Gearing, M. (n 194) lxxxiv *et seq*; with a focus on enforcement in Germany see the detailed outline in Escher, A., Nacimiento, P. and Weissenborn, C. (n 197) 1,039 *et seq*.

[231] Zeiler, G. (n 197) 315.

[232] *ibid.*

[233] Art 55, ICSID Convention; Zeiler, G. (n 197) 316; concerning the German practice of state immunity see Escher, A., Nacimiento, P. and Weissenborn, C. (n 197) 1,044 *et seq*.

[234] Newcombe, C.W. (n 191) 73; McLachlan, C., Shore, L. and Weininger, M. (n 190) 52.

[235] *ibid.*

[236] *ibid.* See also Horn, N., 'Current Use of the UNCITRAL Arbitration Rules in the Context of Investment Arbitration' (2008) 24 *Arb Int'l* no 4, 587.

extensively cited.[237] Despite being frequently mentioned, the ICJ has played only a minor role in the resolution of investment disputes so far.[238] Investment dispute proceedings pursuant to rules other than those of the ICSID bear no specialities compared to proceedings with regard to other matters.

(4) Fast procedures

1.71 In previous times, the length of proceedings before state courts led parties to consider dispute resolution through arbitration as an attractive alternative. Arbitration was, at least in principle, shorter than litigation.[239] The informal procedure of eg a maritime arbitration or some other smaller commodity arbitration in London was a guarantee for a short duration until an award was rendered.[240] Arbitral procedure was, by definition, 'fast-track'.[241]

1.72 In recent years, however, practitioners have been considering the length of arbitral proceedings as a disadvantage of arbitration. According to probably the majority of practitioners, the duration of arbitration is often too long.[242] Undue delay in arbitral proceedings, therefore, has become a frequent feature of this kind of dispute resolution, and the subject of an extensive legal discussion within the last few years.[243] It is a constant issue which leads authors to the conclusion that arbitration is 'slow-track' or 'pathological'.[244] The official time limits contained in some rules of arbitral institutions are generally considered to be totally unrealistic.[245]

1.73 There are several factors which have led to this development: a major reason for delays may be seen in the increasing domination of the procedures by lawyers and, consequently, a more legalistic conduct of arbitral proceedings.[246] Also, the application of the adversarial

---

[237] Newcombe, C.W. (n 191) 39; McLachlan, C., Shore, L. and Weininger, M. (n 190) 135 *et seq*, 286 *et seq*, 323 *et seq* discuss some of its substantive aspects in detail.

[238] For a detailed analysis of the ICJ's contribution to jurisprudence on investment see Newcombe, C.W. (n 191) 35 *et seq*.

[239] In particular, since there is only one level of a judicial decision. See, as an example, Schütze, R.A. (n 29) no 21.

[240] For English examples, see Mustill, M.J. (1989) 10 *Arb Int'l* no 4, 121.

[241] Müller, E. (1998) 15 *J Int'l Arb* No 3, 5, 16.

[242] According to Schmidt-Diemitz, R., 'Internationale Schiedsgerichtsbarkeit - Eine empirische Untersuchung', *Der Betrieb* (1999) 371, 12% of the companies asked think that the duration of arbitration is 'generally too long', and 49% consider it to be 'frequently too long'. See also Lord Bingham, 'The Problem of Delay in Arbitration', in: L.A. Mistelis and J.D.M. Lew (eds), *Arbitration Insights: Twenty Years of the Annual Lecture of the School of International Arbitration* (Kluwer, The Hague, 2007), 4–1 *et seq*.

[243] See eg the ICCA Congresses 1988, 1994 and 1998, Berger, K.P., 'Die Ergänzenden Regeln für Beschleunigte Verfahren der Deutschen Institution für Schiedsgerichtsbarkeit', *SchiedsVZ* (2008) 106; Berger, K.P., 'The Need for Speed in International Arbitration—Supplementary Rules for Expedited Procedures of the German Institution of Arbitration' (*DIS*) (2008) 25 *J Int'l Arb* 595; Redfern, Hunter, Blackaby and Partasides (n 12) no 6–45.

[244] See Mustill, M.J. (n 240) 123: '..it is a ritualistic process dominated by lawyers, with a presumption that the time-scale will be measured in years rather than weeks.'

[245] Najar, J.C. (n 144) 365, pointing especially at the theoretical six-month period laid down in the ICC Rules. For a description of a multi-million dollar ICC arbitration which was brought to conclusion within two months, see Bühring-Uhle, C., *Arbitration and Mediation in International Business* (2006) 86 *et seq*. On a 'Formula 1 arbitration', see Redfern, Hunter, Blackaby and Partasides (n 12) 6–43 *et seq*.

[246] Müller, E. (1998) 15 *J Int'l Arb* no 3, 5, 16; Mustill, M.J. (n 240) 124.

system is certainly responsible for a long-lasting procedure.[247] Another reason for the long duration is often the heavy workload of the arbitrators and counsel involved.[248]

Since it has been recognized that 'justice delayed is justice denied'[249], there have been several attempts to reform national or institutional rules with the aim to expedite arbitration proceedings. **1.74**

(4.1) **Tools for preventing delay** The national legislator may design a new arbitration law with the intention to avoid delay. An example for such a strategy is the English Arbitration Act 1996, one aim of which is speeding up the arbitration procedure.[250] Of course, the legislator will thrive at 'balancing speed with justice'.[251] By including general provisions, imposing respective duties on the arbitrators and the parties,[252] and, in particular, by inclusion of provisions precluding procedural rights if they have not been exercised in due course,[253] a national legislator has a wide range of possibilities to prevent unnecessary delay. **1.75**

The parties may include in the arbitration clause a deadline for the rendering of an award. An illustrative example has been described some years ago; in that case, the parties had provided for a 60-day-deadline for the rendering of the award, running from the beginning of the arbitration.[254] Whereas that is a possibility to speed up the proceedings considerably, such specific time limits can create jurisdictional and enforcement problems if it turns out that the time limit specified is unrealistic or not clearly defined.[255] The parties, therefore, run the risk that they cannot continue with arbitration but have to go to a state court instead.[256] Therefore, in practice, only in very rare cases such time limits are included in arbitration agreements.[257] **1.76**

Another important tool is the effective and prudent case management by the arbitral tribunal. The chairman in particular is able to set short time limits for written briefs and, for **1.77**

---

247 Saville, M. (1997) 13 *Arb Int'l* no 3, 237, 245.

248 Najar, J.C. (n 144) 365.

249 Saville, M. (n 247) 237.

250 Hunter, M. (1997) 13 *Arb Int'l* no 4, 345 *et seq*. See s 1(a) of the Arbitration Act 1996: 'The object of arbitration is to obtain the fair resolution of disputes by an impartial tribunal without unnecessary delay or expense.'

251 Saville, M., 'The Origin of the New English Arbitration Act 1996: Reconciling Speed with Justice in the Decision-making Process'; see also Müller, E. (1998) 15 *J Int'l Arb* no 3, 5, 15.

252 s 33(1)(a) Arbitration Act 1996 requires the arbitral tribunal to 'adopt procedures suitable to the circumstances of the particular case, avoiding unnecessary delay or expense, ..' and establishes a general duty of the parties to comply 'without delay with any determination of the tribunal as to procedural or evidential matters, or with any order or directions of the tribunal' (s 40(2)(a) of the Arbitration Act 1996).

253 See, for instance, s 1027, ZPO, which requires a party to object to any procedural irregularity immediately.

254 See Silvermann, M. (1993) 10 *Arb Int'l* no 4, 113 *et seq*; Davis, B., 'Fast-Track Arbitration and Fast-Tracking Your Arbitration' (1992) 9 *J Int'l Arb* No 4, 43. 43 *et seq*. This case was of a particular nature since it concerned a price determination in a long-term contract for constant gas deliveries which were continuing even during the ongoing arbitration.

255 ICC (Ed), 'Techniques for Controlling Time and Costs in Arbitration', 2007, *ICC Publ* no 843 no 7.

256 Davis, B. (n 254) 43 *et seq*. The success of the arbitration in the example was based on the good cooperation by all participants concerned (ie the parties, the arbitrators and the institution), and can, therefore, not be taken for granted in other cases as well.

257 Davis, B. (n 254) 44.

example, to fix the hearing at the beginning of the arbitration.[258] The tribunal is, however subject to important procedural constraints: according to the overriding principles of due process and, in particular, equal treatment of the parties, the arbitrators must ensure that each party has enough time for the presentation of its case and that no party suffers a disadvantage by not having the same time for a brief as its opponent.[259]

1.78 (4.2) **Fast-track arbitration** The term 'fast-track arbitration' has been created as a response to the problem of delay in arbitration. Using a broad definition,[260] 'fast-track arbitration' includes several attempts to shorten the time until the award is rendered. The parties may choose a particular set of rules which are designed to be more time-efficient and less costly. The Report by the ICC Commission on Arbitration—released at the end of 2007—explicitly advises the parties to consider fast-track rules.[261] At the same time it cautions them about including such provisions in an arbitration agreement as experience shows that in practice it is difficult at the time of the drafting of the arbitration clause to predict the nature of the disputes and the procedures that will be suitable.[262] However, once a dispute has arisen, an agreement on fast-track rules is often difficult to negotiate. This is where the advantage of institutional fast-track rules lies as parties can easily agree upon such rules due to the fact that they have already referred to the appropriate institutional arbitration rules in their arbitration agreement.[263]

1.79 The discussion has already prompted several arbitration organizations to issue specific rules for 'fast-track' arbitration. Among them are *inter alia* the World Intellectual Property Organisation (WIPO), the Swiss Chambers of Commerce, the Geneva Chamber of Commerce and Industry (CCIG), the China International Economic Arbitration Organisation (CIETAC), the American Arbitration Association (AAA), the Stockholm Chamber of Commerce (SCC)[264] and, just recently, the German Institution of Arbitration (DIS) which presented its Supplementary Rules for Expedited Procedures (SREP) on 25 April 2008.[265] The general features of those rules are:[266]

(i) the application of such rules is either based on an agreement in the arbitration clause or based on an agreement after the dispute has arisen. Section 1.1 of the SREP for instance provides that the Supplementary Rules shall be applicable if the parties have referred to them in their arbitration agreement or if the parties have agreed on their application prior to filing a statement of claim. The Swiss Rules on Expedited

---

258 He may propose and insist on agreeing a time schedule for the whole proceedings at the beginning of the arbitration, eg within the drafting of the Terms of Reference.

259 See *supra* para 1.257.

260 In favour of such a broad definition, Müller, E. (1998) 15 *J Int'l Arb* no 3, 5, 6.

261 ICC (ed), no 6.

262 ICC (ed), no 6.

263 Berger, K.P., 'Die Ergänzenden Regeln für Beschleunigte Verfahren der Deutschen Institution für Schiedsgerichtsbarkeit', *SchiedsVZ* (2008) 106; Berger, K.P., 'The Need for Speed in International Arbitration—Supplementary Rules for Expedited Procedures of the German Institution of Arbitration' (*DIS*) (2008) 25 *J Int'l Arb* 595.

264 Müller, E. (1998) 15 *J Int'l Arb* no 3, 5, 8 *et seq*, and 18 (Appendix); see also Bagner, H. (1997) 13 *Arb Int'l* no 2, 193 *et seq*.

265 cf Annex to the DIS-Arbitration Rules 1998—Supplementary Rules for Expedited Proceedings.

266 Müller, E. (1998) 15 *J Int'l Arb* no 3, 5, 9 *et seq*.

Procedures provide for a further alternative: according to Art 42(2) of the Swiss Rules, they shall be applied automatically if the dispute does not exceed a certain threshold, ie arbitrations involving amounts in dispute of less than CHF 1 million (= US$ 0.8 million) are automatically submitted to mandatory accelerated proceedings unless the Chambers decide otherwise;

(ii) appointment of a sole arbitrator either by the parties or the institution concerned.[267] Also, the Swiss Rules (Art 42 (2)) and the SREP (s 3.1) provide for a decision of the dispute by a sole arbitrator, unless the parties have agreed that the dispute shall be decided by three arbitrators either in the arbitration agreement or prior to the filing of the claim;[268]

(iii) fast-track rules generally provide for shorter time limits for the appointment of arbitrators, limited written submissions and/or—if any—a single hearing;[269]

(iv) restricted time frame for rendering the award. The time limits and the flexibility to exceed such limits differ according to the rules concerned: Art 63(a) of the WIPO Rules, for instance, provides that the arbitration 'should, wherever reasonably possible' follow the time frame set out in the rules. Art 42(1)(d) Swiss Rules provides that the award shall be made within six months from the date when the Chambers transmitted the file to the arbitral tribunal, with the possibility of Chambers to extend this time limit. Section 1.2 of the SREP allows for a duration of the arbitral proceeding of six months in the case of a sole arbitrator or of nine months in a case of three arbitrators. Additionally, some rules provide for the possibility that the arbitral tribunal may only state the reasons upon which it relies in a summary form. Whereas under Swiss Rules 42(1)(e), the parties may even agree that no reasons are to be given, s 7, SREP only allows the arbitral tribunal to abstain from stating the facts of the case in its award; and

(v) although not generally provided for by such rules, it is advisable to exclude any challenge of the award—if possible according to the national law of the seat of the arbitration—in order to match the inherent risk of a potential violation of the principle of due process.

The conduct of fast-track arbitration comes into consideration in all cases in which the parties' interest in obtaining a fast and final award outweighs the interest in an exhaustive and thorough factual and legal analysis of the dispute. In particular types of conflicts, the speed of dispute resolution is of prime importance. For instance, in disputes in connection with plant construction projects or concerning the right to rescind a contract regarding the acquisition of a company (share purchase agreement, leveraged buyouts) between signing **1.80**

[267] See for instance Art 14(1) WIPO Expedited Arbitration Rules, see Bagner, H. (1997) 13 *Arb Int'l* no 2, 194.

[268] According to Art 42(2)(c) Swiss Rules, Chambers shall invite the parties to agree to refer the case to a sole arbitrator if the arbitration agreement provides for a three member tribunal and the amount in question does not exceed CHF 1 million.

[269] According to s 4.3, SREP, one oral hearing, including the taking of evidence, shall take place. The parties shall, however, have a right to waive the requirement to an oral hearing, see Berger, K.P., 'Die Ergänzenden Regeln für Beschleunigte Verfahren der Deutschen Institution für Schiedsgerichtsbarkeit' *SchiedsVZ* (2008) (German Arbitral Journal), 105, 109. Art 42(1)(c), Swiss Rules expressly provide for this possibility of a waiver.

and closing due to a 'Material Adverse Change' (MAC),[270] the use of fast-track arbitration may be indispensable.[271]

1.81 If the parties' interest in a thorough analysis of the factual and legal situation is of greater importance, it is not reasonable to limit the admissible submissions or the number of hearings. In such cases, excessive speed may not only clash with the parties' right to be heard but also diminish one of the main advantages of arbitration: freedom and flexibility in the constitution of the arbitral tribunal and the organization of the arbitration.[272] Accordingly, the parties have to carefully consider when agreeing on a fast-track procedure whether or not the conflict in question is feasible for such a dispute resolution mechanism.

(5) Others

1.82 Apart from commodity and maritime arbitration, there are several other types of arbitration. They are conducted either according to generally applied arbitration rules or within a specific framework.

1.83 One important example is the '*Tribunal Arbitral du Sport*' (TAS) in Lausanne (Switzerland) which was established in 1983 by the International Olympic Committee (IOC). Today, this tribunal has jurisdiction for various international sport disputes involving international sport associations.[273]

1.84 For intellectual property disputes, the WIPO Arbitration Rules provide a comprehensive institutional framework once the parties have agreed on arbitration.[274] In addition, the WIPO Arbitration and Mediation Centre also offers mediation or mediation followed by arbitration.[275] Finally, there are specific rules and procedures for domain name disputes the importance of which is increasing steadily.[276]

1.85 As a last example, the FIDIC dispute resolution mechanism should be mentioned. International construction projects are often subject to the FIDIC Standard Terms[277] which provide for a particular 'internal' dispute resolution procedure, which may be followed by ICC arbitration. Once a dispute has arisen, it has to be submitted to a Dispute Adjudication Board (DAB) which may be appointed at the beginning of the project or on an *ad hoc* basis.[278] If the decision of the DAB is not accepted or complied with by one party, an ordinary ICC arbitration procedure may be initiated after a certain period of time.

---

270 Borris, C., 'Streiterledigung bei (MAC-)Klauseln in Unternehmenskaufverträgen: ein Fall für "Fast-Track"-Schiedsverfahren', 2008 *Betriebsberater* (*BB*) 294.

271 Berger, K.P. (n 269) 106.

272 Scherer, M., 'Acceleration of Arbitration Proceedings—The Swiss Way: The Expedited Procedure under the Swiss Rules of International Arbitration' *SchiedsVZ* (2005) 229.

273 For details, see Haas, U., 'Die Sportschiedsgerichtsbarkeit des Tribunal Arbitral du Sport' (TAS), *ZeuP* (1999) 355.

274 For details, see <http://www.arbiter.wipo.int/arbitration/arbitration-guide/index.html>; Smit, H., 'WIPO Arbitration Rules', Commentary and Analysis (New York, 2000).

275 For the mediation rules, see <http://www.arbiter.wipo.int/mediation/mediation-rules/index.html>.

276 For more details, see <http://www.arbiter.wipo.int/domains/guide/index.html>.

277 For the latest standard terms of the Fédération Internationale des Ingénieurs-Conseils (FIDIC), see Wiegand, C., *Recht der Internationalen Wirtschaft* (*RIW*) (2000) 197 and Mallmann, R.A., *Recht der Internationalen Wirtschaft* (*RIW*) (2000) 532.

278 For details, see Mallmann, R.A. (n 277) 539 *et seq.*

II. Relationship of arbitral tribunals and courts

A. Different national approaches

When drafting international commercial contracts, the parties often include an arbitration clause in order to avoid the jurisdiction of state courts, in particular the jurisdiction of those state courts of the other party's home country. The alternative is an arbitration clause providing for a neutral tribunal in a 'neutral jurisdiction'. However, although including an arbitration clause in their contract, the parties cannot completely escape from national courts. Various instances might arise in which the parties or the arbitral tribunal may be dependent on the 'judicial assistance' by state courts. Obviously, under such circumstances it is vital that the state courts pursue a cooperative approach towards arbitration. Although arbitration has traditionally been chosen frequently by commercial parties for the resolution of disputes, a certain resistance of the local judge to his 'competitor' was for a long time the basis of the attitude towards arbitration in several jurisdictions.[279] During the last decades, this relationship turned from confrontation to cooperation, a change which shall be demonstrated in the light of the particular historical development in three major European jurisdictions.[280] **1.86**

(1) England

In the United Kingdom, and especially in England, arbitration has a long history which may be characterized by a very special relationship with the ordinary courts of law.[281] Those ordinary courts have, over the centuries, assumed for themselves the right and duty to ensure that 'inferior tribunals' operate properly, in accordance with broad principles of justice.[282] That may have been founded in a certain jealousy of judges which was described already more than 150 years ago by Francis Russell.[283] Today, however, there are no reasons to assume an existing hostility towards arbitration.[284] **1.87**

(1.1) Relationship of arbitration and courts This particular relationship between private and ordinary public tribunals showed the following three features:[285] **1.88**

(i) the parallel existence of voluntary arbitration and arbitration pursuant to an order of the court (where arbitration sprang from an action in court and always remained part of it) resulted in inherent powers of control and sanctions which were exercised by the courts. This close involvement of the court in the non-voluntary arbitral proceedings had a long-lasting influence on the general attitude of the courts towards arbitration;

---

[279] Cremades, B.M. (n 143) 170.

[280] For a general overview on the relationship of arbitration and state court system see Lew, J.D.M., Mistelis, L.A. and Kröll, S. (n 13)5–34 *et seq*. In regard to the judicial attitude of US courts towards arbitration, see Weisenberger, K., 'From Hostility to Harmony: Buckeye Marks a Milestone in the Acceptance of Arbitration in the American Jurisprudence' (2005) 16 *Am Rev Int'l Arb* 551.

[281] Mustill, M. and Boyd, S.C. (n 7) 30.

[282] *ibid*.

[283] See the letter of 1853 from Francis Russell Esq, reprinted in (1997) 13 *Arb Int'l* no 3, 253, 256.

[284] Mustill, M. and Boyd, S.C. (n 7) 5. In former times, the hostility towards arbitration was a feature of common law jurisdiction, see Kerr, M. (1996) 12 *Arb Int'l* no 2, 171.

[285] See Mustill, M. and Boyd, S.C. (n 7) 32 *et seq*.

(ii) since the beginning of the nineteenth century, again and again doubts were expressed by courts and text-writers as to the wisdom to choose arbitration which often was seen to be an inefficient procedure.[286] That led to a repeated interference by statutory intervention;

(iii) consequently, there was a tendency to restrict the meddling of the courts in order to safeguard the will of the parties who opted for a private and self-determined method of dispute resolution.

1.89 **(1.2) Interference in arbitral proceedings by the legislator and the courts** The tendency to interfere with arbitration is a permanent feature of the Arbitration Acts and English case law of the twentieth century.[287] By the typical 'deeming provisions', many regulations of the arbitral procedure have been introduced as presumed parts of the arbitration agreement.[288] In addition, the so-called 'statement of case' procedure, introduced by the Arbitration Act 1950, enabled a party of the arbitration to apply to the High Court for a decision of a legal question during the course of the arbitral proceeding.[289] Furthermore, procedural defects were the reason for practically unlimited rights of the courts to set aside an award on the ground of misconduct of the arbitrators or the violation of the principle of natural justice.[290] Some of those deficiencies have been removed by the Arbitration Act 1979 which, however, introduced only some improvements mainly for international arbitration.[291]

1.90 The Arbitration Act 1996 has probably set an end to the often criticized 'piecemeal process of expansion, amendment and consolidation' of the law on arbitration which began with the Arbitration Act of 1889.[292] The Arbitration Act 1996 is totally different from all of its predecessors and has established a 'symbiotic relationship between the Commercial Court and London Arbitration'.[293] However, quite a few positive or even euphoric appraisals of the Arbitration Act 1996[294] fail to address the fact that today, still, a party may refer a question of law to the Court.[295] If the judge considers the question to touch important rights of

[286] A significant minority of respondents consider that the Arbitration Act of 1996 has not made any contribution to the effectivity of arbitral proceedings with regard to costs and duration, Harris, B., 'Report on the Arbitration Act 1996', (2007) 23 *Arb Int'l* no 3, 437, 451 no 92.

[287] For a short overview see Park, W.W. (1983) 32 *ICLQ* 21, 33 *et seq.*

[288] That technique of the legislator has disappeared in the Arbitration Act 1996, see Weigand, F.-B., *Recht der Internationalen Wirtschaft* (*RIW*) (1997) 904, 905; Steyn, J. (1994) 60 *Arbitration* no 3, 184, 186.

[289] s 21 Arbitration Act 1950. For the various possibilities to appeal to the court during or after the arbitral proceeding see eg Steyn, J. (1994) 60 *Arbitration* no 3, 184, 190 *et seq*; Zekos, G. (1998) 15 *J Int'l Arb* no 1, 51, 52 *et seq*. For a historical overview of court control, see also Mustill, M. and Boyd, S.C. (n 7) 431 *et seq.*

[290] Mustill, M. and Boyd, S.C. (n 7) 5.

[291] See eg Zekos, G. (1998) 15 *J Int'l Arb* no 1, 51, 56–60.

[292] Mustill, M. and Boyd, S.C. (n 7) 54. That feature of the legislation had already been criticized by Russell; see his letter of 1853 reprinted in (1997) 13 *Arb Int'l*, no 3, 253, 256. Even at that time, Russell was proposing a general arbitration statute. For an overview of the experiences of 10 years of the Arbitration Act 1996, see Harris, B. (2007) 23 *Arb Int'l* no 3, 437 *et seq.*

[293] Editorial notes in (1997) 13 *Arb Int'l* no 3, IV, and 237.

[294] See eg Fraser, D., 'The New Arbitration Act—A Model Law' (1997) *JBL* March issue, 101 *et seq*. The vast majority think that the possibility to appeal on a point of law should be retained on the basis of the Arbitration Act 1996; see Harris, B (2007) 23 *Arb Int'l* no 3, 437, 448.

[295] A committee, chaired by Bruce Harris, prepared a Report for the Commercial Court Users' Committee, the British Maritime Law Association, the London Shipping Law Centre and other bodies on the Arbitration Act 1996. The Committee concluded that 'no amendments are required or desired'. This finding is criticized

that party, he will issue a binding decision in the course of the arbitral proceeding, thereby neglecting the will of the parties to let the arbitrators decide the dispute.[296] A similar issue arises in connection with the admissibility of evidence. Also, the arbitrator's rulings on the admissibility of evidence are reviewable by the court.[297]

The possibility to exclude such interference in international arbitration proceedings is only a weak consolation since, in practice, such agreement will only rarely be included in arbitration clauses. **1.91**

On the other hand, English courts are empowered to issue anti-suit injunctions by which a party is restrained from commencing or continuing proceedings before state courts on the ground that such proceedings are in breach of an arbitration agreement.[298] Section 44 Arbitration Act 1996 expressly clarifies that the English courts may issue injunctions regarding arbitral proceedings as they may do regarding state court proceedings. **1.92**

(2) Civil law jurisdictions (examples)

(2.1) Switzerland Arbitration in Switzerland has a long tradition, in the domestic context as well as in the international ambit. Although a Swiss seat of international arbitral proceedings had been preferred by commercial parties for many decades, the underlying law regulating those procedures was—until the end of the 1960s—contained in 25 cantonal codes of civil procedure.[299] **1.93**

Only in 1969, an Intercantonal Arbitration Convention (commonly referred to as the 'Concordat') was concluded to unify this area of procedural law. The Concordat was a clear progress since it enabled especially foreign parties to recognize the state of the law and, in particular, the scope of possible court intervention during or after arbitral proceedings taking place in Switzerland.[300] However, after some years, practice and especially numerous court decisions on the Concordat showed that the parties of an international arbitration were not protected from purely local procedural concepts and time consuming, far reaching means of recourse after the rendering of the award.[301] That was one of the reasons why the legislator promoted a new law which was designed only for international arbitration. A particular regulation of international arbitration was introduced by the Private International Law Act (SPILA) of 1987 (ch 12), which entered into force in 1989. The scarce **1.94**

by Cohen, M.M., 'A Missed Opportunity to Revise the Arbitration Act 1996', (2007) 23 *Arb Int'l* no 3, 461.

296 For a critical evaluation of this possibility, see Weigand, F.-B. (n 10) 909; Zekos, G. (1998) 15 *J Int'l Arb* no 1, 51, 60 *et seq.*

297 This has been widely criticized, see Cohen, M.M., 'A Missed Opportunity to Revise the Arbitration Act 1996' (2007) 23 *Arb Int'l* no 3, 461, 462 *et seq.*

298 See eg *West Tankers Inc v RAS Riunione Adriatica di Sicurta SpA* (2007) UKHL 4. For further details see Dutta, A. and Heinze, C.A., 'Anti-suit injunctions zum Schutz von Schiedsvereinbarungen' *Recht der Internationalen Wirtschaft* (*RIW*) 2007, 411; Dundas, H.R., 'Court Support of Arbitration Agreements: Anti-Suit Injunctions and the European Court of Justice' (2007) 73 *Arbitration* no 3, 348.

299 In principle, procedural law is the domain of cantonal legislation, see Blessing, M. (n 112) 1, 9 *et seq.*

300 Schlosser, P. (n 13) no 152.

301 Blessing, M. (n 112), *et seq*, points out that the state court intervention was intense at that stage since the action of setting aside had to be brought before the cantonal court with the possibility of further recourse ('Public Law Appeal') to the Federal Supreme Court.

regulation (19 Articles) and the concept of that chapter show that the legislator intended to grant the parties the widest degree of autonomy.[302] One expression of that autonomy is the right of the parties to exclude chapter 12 altogether and apply the rules of the Concordat instead.[303] The main significance of the law, however, is the reduced degree of possible interference and control by the state judiciary.[304] The self-restraint of the legislator results not only in a large degree of party autonomy and freedom of the arbitral process as a whole, but also in a higher degree of responsibility for the parties to regulate the proceedings if they do not want to leave these matters to the arbitrators' discretion.[305] The limitation and clear enumeration of possible means of recourse (Art 190, SPILA) mean higher certainty and less interference by the state. The formerly often used attack of the award on the ground of its 'arbitrariness' has been abolished,[306] and the parties have now the option to exclude any setting-aside procedure if none of them is of Swiss nationality or has its seat in Switzerland.[307] Those exclusion agreements enable the parties to further reduce any possible court interference after the rendering of the award. Thus, today one may conclude that the evolution of the Swiss law on arbitration since the introduction of the Concordat[308] shows that any previous competition or hostility between national courts of law and international arbitration has disappeared and has given way to the idea of assistance and cooperation.[309]

1.95 (2.2) **Germany** The relationship between the courts and arbitral tribunals in Germany is not easy to assess since Germany does not have a strong and important history of arbitration. Therefore, there is no abundant case law or intense experience until the reform of 1997, although arbitration has always been an important part of legal doctrine.

1.96 The law on arbitration was introduced in the Code on Civil Procedure (ZPO) of 1879 where it is still regulated today. Until the reform of 1997, there have been almost no changes in the written law of the ZPO whereas a considerable body of case law has been laid down by the Federal Supreme Court (*Bundesgerichtshof*).[310] Since the regulation of the legislator eg of the arbitral procedure was very scarce, the courts (and consequently the arbitrators) applied mostly those principles that are laid down for litigation in the Code on Civil

[302] Lalive, Poudret and Reymond (n 119) 272 no 20; Blessing, M., 'The New International Arbitration Law in Switzerland' (n 112), *et seq* (giving an overview where this autonomy has been expressly regulated); Gaillard, E. (1988) 4 *Arb Int'l* no1, 25.

[303] Art 176, SPILA; see Lalive, Poudret and Reymond (n 119) 272 no 20.

[304] Blessing, M. (n 112), 1, 16.

[305] Blessing, M. (n 112) 1, 18; Lalive, Poudret and Reymond (n 119) 280 no 28.

[306] This decision by the legislator has been widely welcomed, especially by foreign experts, see eg Gaillard, E. (1988) 4 *Arb Int'l* No1, 25, 30.

[307] Art 190(1), SPILA, see eg Blessing, M. (n 112) 1, 75 *et seq* and Gaillard, E. (1988) 4 *Arb Int'l* No1, 25, 30.

[308] This evolutionary, continuous development has been pointed out by Lalive, Poudret and Reymond (n 119) 258 no 3.

[309] Lalive, Poudret and Reymond (n 119) 274 no 22 ('L'époque de la concurrence, voire de l'hostilité, entre juridiction étatique et arbitrage international est depuis longtemps dépassée et a fait place à l'idée d'assistance et de collaboration'.).

[310] For a historical survey, see eg Lachmann, J.P. (n 81) 27 nos 88 *et seq*.

Procedure.[311] According to the generally favoured jurisdictional approach,[312] there was no room for a *révision au fond*, since the courts were considered to be bound to the fact finding of the arbitral tribunal.[313]

Generally, however, the law before 1998 was looked upon as arbitration-unfriendly for various reasons.[314] One of those reasons was the possibility of the losing party to challenge the award in a lengthy procedure that reached over three court levels up to the *Bundesgerichtshof*.[315] The state of the law until the enactment of the German arbitration law of 1997 was, however, in many respects not showing any features of hostility of the courts towards arbitration. On the contrary, arbitration has, for a long time, been recognized as 'true' or 'substantive' jurisdiction or decision making, which is seen at equal level with the legal decisions of the courts of law.[316] Both the contractual and jurisdictional elements of the arbitration agreement pointed out by the courts and legal writers[317] show the intention to combine the private nature with the judicial function of arbitration. The assimilation of an arbitral award with a state court's sentence means that awards do not have to be recognized by the courts in order to be effective.[318] Awards are only scrutinized eg when the winning party seeks an order of enforcement.[319] However, there has always been some kind of judicial self-restraint at the state of supervising arbitral proceedings and of challenging awards. In particular, the courts did not interpret extensively the notion of *ordre public*,[320] and arbitration agreements have generally been mostly recognized according to the principle of *in favorem validitatis*.[321] Only in exceptional cases, arbitration clauses (eg as parts of general terms and conditions) were held to be null and void for want of a minimum standard of fairness or quasi-denial of justice.[322] **1.97**

The reform which became law in 1998,[323] did follow that liberal tradition in incorporating almost literally the majority of the UNCITRAL Model Law. Thus, the autonomy of the parties is a constant feature which is only in few cases limited by mandatory procedural **1.98**

---

[311] See Schwab, K.H. and Walter, G. (n 1) 145 *et seq*. s 1034(1), ZPO (old version) only provided for the right of the parties to be heard and for the duty of the tribunal to examine the facts of the case. Apart from that, the procedure should be decided by the parties or the arbitrators (s 1034(2), ZPO, old version).

[312] Schlosser, P. (n 13) no 42.

[313] Schwab, K.H. and Walter, G. (n 1) 248 *et seq* no 1; *Reichsgericht (RG) Juristische Wochenschrift (JW)* 1936, 1894; *Bundesgerichtshof (BGH) Neue Juristische Wochenschrift (NJW)* 1986, 1436.

[314] See Berger, K.P., *The New German Arbitration Law* (n 115) 5 *et seq* who names several features of the old law as eg the general provision that tribunals consist of two arbitrators.

[315] Lachmann, J.P. (n 81) 230, no 549; Berger, K.P. (n 115) 30 *et seq*.

[316] *Bundesgerichtshof (BGH) Neue Juristische Wochenschrift (NJW)* 1986, 1436; Lachmann, J.P. (n 81) 2 nos 7–8; Schwab, K.H. and Walter, G. (n 1) 81.

[317] See Schlosser, P. (n 13) nos 50 *et seq*.

[318] The former s 1040, ZPO corresponds to the new s 1055, ZPO.

[319] Schwab, K.H. andWalter, G. (n 1) 4 no 7.

[320] *ibid*, (n 1) 260 *et seq* no 32 *et seq*; BGH Neue Jurischtische Wochenschrift (NJW) 1990, 3,210 (wrong application of the law is not automatically a violation of the *ordre public*).

[321] See eg *OLG Hamburg Recht der Internationalen Wirtschaft (RIW)* 1989, 574, 578.

[322] See eg *BGH Neue Juristische Wochenschrift (NJW)* 1989, 1,477. Generally, arbitration clauses as part of general conditions have been accepted for a long time (BGHZ 7, 187), and only in exceptional cases such clauses have been held to be null and void, see *BGH Neue Juristische Wochenschrift (NJW)* 1989, 1,477.

[323] For an English version, see Berger, K.P. (n 115) 97 *et seq*.

rules.[324] The arbitration agreement now survives attacks that in former times have led to its nullity,[325] and even the successful challenge of an award does no longer render the arbitration agreement terminated but, on the contrary, leads to a revived arbitration agreement which may give rise to a new or continued old arbitral proceeding.[326] Finally, the former lengthy and costly procedures of setting aside have been replaced by limited grounds of recourse which generally may only be brought forward before the Higher Regional Court (*Oberlandesgericht*).[327] In sum, the former liberal case law and the reform have caused an evolution of the German law on arbitration which shows more and more the spirit of cooperation instead of confrontation with the public system of adjudication. The reform of 1998 is commonly regarded as a successful implementation of the international standard of arbitration into German law.[328]

B. Harmonization by international instruments

1.99 The present state of the law on international arbitration is mainly the achievement of inter-state cooperation and resulting multilateral conventions.[329] The modern development started in the 1920s and came to its preliminary end in the 1980s and 90s. The high degree of harmonization[330] and the growing 'internationalization' of the law on arbitration[331] has not been the result of a continuous and gradual development, but rather of some important steps or stages,[332] the most recent of which was the UNCITRAL Model Law of 1985 with the amendments of 2006 which gave rise to a world-wide trend of unification[333] in the area of arbitration.

(1) The roots of international cooperation

1.100 The origins of this cooperation were laid in the late nineteenth century. The Montevideo Convention of 1889 was the first international convention of modern times to provide for the recognition and enforcement of arbitration agreements (between certain Latin

---

324 Those rules concern the equal treatment of the parties and the right to present one's case, see s 1042(1) to (3), ZPO.

325 A predominant influence of one party at the stage of constituting the arbitral tribunal rendered the arbitration clause null and void according to s 1025(2) of the old law, whereas now it only enables the weaker party to apply to the court for intervention, see s 1034(2), ZPO. For the official report on that point, see Berger, K.P. (n 115) 193.

326 s 1059(4) and (5), ZPO. Schütze, R.A. (n 29) 131, no 272; for the old law, see Schwab, K.H. and Walter, G. (n 1) (5th edn 1995) 235.

327 s 1062(1), ZPO; KP Berger (n 115), 30 *et seq.* Only in exceptional cases is there an appeal to the *Bundesgerichtshof*, see s 1065(1), ZPO.

328 Lachmann, J.P. (n 81) 191 *et seq.*

329 For a chronological overview, see Rubino-Sammartano, M. (n 44) 26 *et seq*. The most important treaties are eg to be found in Labes, H.W. and Lörcher, T., *Nationales und internationales Schiedsverfahrensrecht* (C. H. Beck, Munich, 1998).

330 This fact has frequently been pointed out, especially since there are many other areas of the law which are not unified to such a degree, see McAuley, S., 'Achieving the harmonization of transnational civil procedure: Will the ALI/UNIDROIT Project succeed?' (2004) 15 *Am Rev Int'l Arb* 231, 234 *et seq.*

331 Philip, A., *A Century of Internationalisation of International Arbitration: An Overview*, in Hunter, M., Marriott, A. and Veeder, V.V., *The Internationalisation of International Arbitration* (London, 1995) 25 *et seq.*

332 Schlosser, P. (n 13) no 55.

333 Schütze, R.A. (n 29) nos 13 *et seq.*

American states).[334] The first step in the twentieth century aiming at harmonization was the proposal of the International Congress of Chambers of Commerce and Commercial Associations, which convened in 1914, to draft an 'international convention for the unification of laws on arbitration'.[335] The First World War put a sudden end to such plans.

After the war, the Geneva Protocol of 1923 intended to secure international recognition of the validity of arbitration agreements, at a time, when many states did not recognize arbitration clauses, ie agreements to refer future disputes to arbitration.[336] As a consequence, the contracting states agreed to 'refer the parties on the application of either of them to the decision of the arbitrators', thereby indirectly enforcing the arbitration agreement on an international level.[337] Soon afterwards, the Geneva Convention of 1927 required the states to recognize and enforce foreign arbitral awards, but the requirement of a prior declaration of enforceability in the state where the award was made, resulted in a rather cumbersome enforcement procedure for the winning party.[338] **1.101**

After the *Bustamante Code* of 1928[339] the newly-founded International Institute for the Unification of Private Law (UNIDROIT) started its work with a comprehensive report on the contemporary arbitration law and practice with the aim of unifying national law on arbitration.[340] The draft for a proposed Uniform Law, presented in 1936, consisted of 40 Articles and has to be considered as the predecessor of the UNCITRAL Model Law of 1985. **1.102**

(2) The New York Convention of 1958 as 'model treaty'

Before the project of a uniform law in the field of international arbitration was pursued any further, the next and probably most important step was taken by conclusion of the 'UN-Convention on the Recognition and Enforcement of Foreign Arbitral Awards' of 10 June 1958.[341] **1.103**

The proposal for a new convention, which was originally brought forward by the ICC in 1953,[342] resulted from a widely felt disappointment concerning the operation of the **1.104**

[334] Arts 5, 6 and 7 of the Convention of 11 January 1889. See Redfern, Hunter, Blackaby and Partasides (n 12) no 1–117.

[335] Veeder, V.V. in Hunter, M., Marriott, A. and Veeder, V.V., *The Internationalisation of International Arbitration* (n 331), 13, 17.

[336] Redfern, Hunter, Blackaby and Partasides (n 12) no 1–118; Schlosser, P. (n 13) no 55; Lew, J.D.M., Mistelis, L.A. and Kröll, S. (n 13) 2–11 *et seq.*

[337] Redfern, Hunter, Blackaby and Partasides (n 12)no 1–118.

[338] Schlosser, P. (n 13) no 55; Redfern, Hunter, Blackaby and Partasides (n 12) 1–119; Lew, J.D.M., Mistelis, L.A. and Kröll, S. (n 13)) 2–12 (requirement of 'double-*exequatur*').

[339] This convention was a successor of the Montevideo Treaty of 1889, see Rubino-Sammartano, M (n 44) 32. For practical perspectives on recognition and enforcement, see papers from the 11th IBA International Arbitration Day and United Nations New York Convention Day, in (2008) 2 *Disp Res Int'l* no 1, Special Issue, 'The New York Convention: 50 Years'.

[340] The report and the resulting draft uniform law was the result of intensive comparative research by the young Professor René David; for details, see Veeder, V.V. in Hunter, M., Marriott, A. and Veeder, V.V., *The Internationalisation of International Arbitration* (n 331) 18 *et seq.*

[341] United Nations Treaty Series (1959) 330. The Convention is commonly referred to as the New York Convention of 1958. For a comprehensive discussion, see Van den Berg, A.J., *Improving the Efficiency of Arbitration Agreements and Awards: 40 Years of Application of the New York Convention* (The Hague, 1999).

[342] Redfern, Hunter, Blackaby and Partasides (n 12)no 1–119. For details see Schlosser, P. (n 13) no 57.

Geneva Protocol and Convention which had failed to regulate certain important aspects and had, in addition, given rise to several ambiguities.[343] The Convention, which should replace the Geneva Protocol and Convention[344], builds on the rules of those conventions[345] and concentrates on two main objectives:[346] to oblige the contracting states to recognize both arbitration agreements made abroad and arbitral awards rendered in a foreign country. The various regulations[347] proved to be a reliable and commonly accepted foundation for future attempts of unification.

1.105 The importance which the New York Convention enjoys today could not have been immediately foreseen in its early days. Among the signing states of the first hour, important nations as the United Kingdom and the USA were missing, and only in the early 1970s, when Italy and the United States joined, many other states did follow.[348] To date, the Convention has been ratified by more than 140 states,[349] and there is unanimity on its paramount importance for international arbitration.[350] It has been described as 'the most successful international instrument in the field of arbitration' which could perhaps lay claim to be 'the most effective instance of international legislation in the entire history of commercial law'.[351] Indeed, the success rate of the Convention has been very high[352] so that the enforcement of arbitral awards is almost guaranteed in many countries of the world.

1.106 Other conventions which followed after the New York Convention, could not achieve such an enormous success. The European (Geneva) Convention of 1961, which had a more complicated and different history,[353] intended to improve international arbitration in East-West economic transactions, but, mainly owing to its regional limitation and the general acceptance of the New York Convention, it did never play an important role in arbitral practice.[354] The Convention on the Settlement of Disputes between States and Nationals of Other States of 1965, commonly referred to as the Washington Convention, was designed for international investment disputes.[355]

---

343 See eg Schlosser, P. (n 13) no 56. For the reasons for replacing the Geneva Protocol and Convention by a more modern treaty, see Mustill, M. (1989) 6 *J Int'l Arb* no 2, 43, 49; Mistelis, L.A. and Lew, J.D., *Arbitration Insights: Twenty Years of the Annual Lecture of the School of International Arbitration,* 20–44.

344 Art 7(2), New York Convention.

345 Some authors emphasize that many rules of the New York Convention were already contained in the Geneva Protocol and Convention, see eg Philip, A. in Hunter, M., Marriott, A. and Veeder, V.V., *Internationalisation of International Arbitration,* 25, 27.

346 Kerr, M. (1997) 13 *Arb Int'l* no 2, 121, 128; see Art I and Art II of the Convention.

347 See for more details Van den Berg, A.J., *The New York Arbitration Convention of 1958* (1981).

348 Schlosser, P. (n 13) no 57.

349 For a tabular overview see Redfern, Hunter, Blackaby and Partasides (n 12) app M.

350 Redfern, Hunter, Blackaby and Partasides (n 12) nos 1–120 ('most important international treaty relating to international commercial arbitration'), Schlosser, P. (n 13) no 56 ('..ist in der Zwischenzeit zum zentralen multilateralen Regelungsinstrument der internationalen Handelsschiedsgerichtsbarkeit schlechthin geworden.'). See also Nariman, FS (1998) *Int'l Arb L Rev* 163.

351 Mustill, M. (1989) 6 *J Int'l Arb* no 2, 43, 49.

352 Kerr, M. (1997) 13 *Arb Int'l* no 2, 121, 129 points at estimations reported by A. Van den Berg, according to which 98% of awards in international arbitrations are honoured or successfully enforced, whereas national courts deny enforcement only in about 5% of all cases.

353 For a detailed discussion see Schlosser, P. (n 13) nos 85 *et seq.*

354 Redfern, Hunter, Blackaby and Partasides (n 12)no 1–121.

355 *ibid,* 2–40. See in more detail on the Convention I. D. (4) *supra*; nos 1.51 *et seq.*

(3) The UNCITRAL Model Law: a new approach

Although the New York Convention was an international success, it did not automatically result in a harmonization of national laws. Rather, when enacting new laws in the field of arbitration, national legislators mainly resorted to existing traditions which were founded in the respective national history. This diversity of laws was more and more considered to be a disadvantage for international trade and international arbitral proceedings. **1.107**

The United Nations Commission on International Trade Law (UNCITRAL) started its work on the harmonization of the law of international arbitration in the 70s. In 1976, the UNCITRAL Arbitration Rules were created to foster international arbitration, especially in countries of the developing world where there was considerable suspicion towards arbitration.[356] Those rules, which were with some modifications used as the rules of procedure by the US-Iran Claims Tribunal,[357] serve as a basis for *ad hoc* arbitrations and have had a great influence on the practice of arbitration.[358] Following an initiative during 1978 in Paris, UNCITRAL promoted the project of a model law for international arbitral proceedings.[359] In several sessions over some years, a group of experts worked on a draft uniform law, which, after its adoption by UNCITRAL, was finally approved and recommended by the General Assembly of the United Nations on 11 December 1985. Amendments to the UNCITRAL Model Law 1985 were adopted in 2006. **1.108**

It is appropriate to state that UNCITRAL, by promoting the Arbitration Rules and the Model Law, helped to bring to different nations the benefit of arbitration, especially by bridging historical and cultural differences between countries following different legal traditions.[360] **1.109**

The principal decision by UNCITRAL was, not to draft another convention but rather a model law for national legislators. The advantages of this approach are:[361] (i) no requirement of national ratification and specific reservations hindering international unification; (ii) the possibility for the states to keep national particularities whilst generally adopting the pattern of the Model Law; and (iii) the recognizability for the international practitioner and the users of commercial arbitration.[362] **1.110**

---

[356] Schlosser, P. (n 13) no 182.

[357] See eg van Hof, J. *Commentary on the UNCITRAL Arbitration Rules. The Applications by the Iran-US Claims Tribunal* (Deventer, 1991); Schlosser, P. (n 13) nos 187 *et seq.*

[358] Philip, A. in Hunter, M., Marriott, A. and Veeder, V.V., *The Internationalisation of International Arbitration* (n 331) 25, 29.

[359] For details of the drafting history see Schlosser, P. (n 13) no 122; Hußlein-Stich, G., *Das UNCITRAL-Modellgesetz über die internationale Handelsschiedsgerichtsbarkeit,* in Böckstiegel (Carl Heymanns Verlag, Cologne etc, 1990) 2 *et seq.*

[360] Cremades, B.M. (n 143) 171; Sanders, P., 'UNCITRAL's Model Law on International and Commercial Arbitration: Present Situation and Future' (2005) 21 *Arb Int'l* no 4, 443.

[361] Holtzmann, H. and Neuhaus, J., *A Guide to the UNCITRAL Model Law on International Commercial Arbitration: Legislative History and Commentary* (Deventer, 1989) 11; Schlosser, P. (n 13) no 122.

[362] Berger, K.P. (n 115) 7; G. Hermann, often referred to as the 'father' of UNCITRAL and the Model Law, sometimes called this the 'HiFi-factor'—in other words: anybody, who agrees to arbitration in a 'Model Law country', may be confident to find an arbitration-friendly regime that generally meets modern, international standards.

1.111 The contents of the Model Law may, apart from other important points,[363] be characterized by the following three features: (i) a modern, arbitration-friendly regulation of international arbitration; (ii) a high degree of party autonomy with only few mandatory provisions for the proceedings; and (iii) a limited catalogue of reasons for which an award may be challenged and annulled. Finally, as to the interpretation of national laws based on the Model Law, there are reasons to advocate an autonomous approach,[364] given the origin and purpose of the Model Law as a tool of harmonizing international arbitration.

1.112 In the first years after its adoption, the Model Law encountered some scepticism, especially on the part of those countries that have a well established arbitration law which is mostly founded on a long historical development. Thus, in the first decade of its existence, it did not serve as a model for reforms in France, Switzerland or England.[365] However, many other countries, especially those with a common law tradition, did take the Model Law as ground and pattern for recent reforms in the field of arbitration.[366] Today, more than 50 countries may be considered to be 'Model Law states'.[367] Important reforms in this respect are those of England,[368] Germany[369] and Sweden.[370] Recent reforms took place in Spain,[371] Austria[372] and Japan.[373] Germany has adopted the Model Law almost in its entirety, without distinguishing between domestic and international arbitration.[374] It is, therefore, legitimate to praise the Model Law and its world-wide acceptance as a success story.[375] One of the main reasons for this is the fact that it succeeded in combining elements of the civil and

[363] Schlosser, P. (n 13) nos 123 *et seq* lists six main features, whereas Berger, K.P., *The New German Arbitration Law* (n 115) 40, names five characteristic points of the Model Law.

[364] Berger, K.P., 'The New German Arbitration Law' (n 115) 33 *et seq.*

[365] See eg Mustill, M. (1989) 6 *J Int'l Arb* no 2, 43, 54; Craig, W.L. (1988) 4 *Arb Int'l* no 3, 174, 225. The reason for the non-adoption in Switzerland was the fact that the last reform of 1987 already had its roots some years before the creation of the Model Law.

[366] Sanders, P. (1995) 11 *Arb Int'l* no1, 1, 36; Hunter, M. (1997) 13 *Arb Int'l* no 4, 345; Cremades, B.M. (n 143) 171 (with respect to Latin American states). Among the common law jurisdictions, there are eg Australia, Hong Kong, Canada (at federal and state level) and important states of the USA (as California, Florida and Texas).

[367] For a list of all states which have, more or less, adopted the Model Law, see ch 14; generally, on the adoption of the Model Law, see Sanders, P. (1995) 11 *Arb Int'l* no 1, 1.

[368] Although England has not incorporated the Model Law in its entirety, the Arbitration Act 1996 is largely inspired by, and based on, concepts of the Model Law; see eg Hunter, M. (1997) 13 *Arb Int'l* no 4, 345, 346.

[369] For the reasons and extent of the incorporation of the Model Law, see eg Berger, K.P., *The New German Arbitration Law* (n 115) 15 *et seq* and ch 7.

[370] On the reforms in Germany and Sweden, see Weigand, F.-B. (1995) 11 *Arb Int'l* no 4, 397; Strempel, H. and Hobér, K. *RPS*, Beil 4 zu *Betriebsberater (BB)* 11/1999.

[371] Mantilla-Serrano, F., 'The New Spanish Arbitration Act' (2004) 21 *J Int'l Arb* no 4, 367.

[372] See ch 2.

[373] Nishikawa, R., 'Arbitration Law Reform in Japan' (2004) 21 *J Int'l Arb* no 3, 303

[374] The majority of experts in Germany advocated or approved the acceptance of the Model Law as pattern for both international and domestic arbitration, see Berger, K.P., *The New German Arbitration Law* (n 115) 12 (with further references). However, it is doubtful whether the German reform justifies the general statement that there is a growing tendency of legislators to apply the Model Law to both types of arbitration; see for such an opinion, Lionnet, K. and Lionnet, A. (n 29) 45 *et seq.*

[375] See in this respect eg, Cremades, B.M. (n 143) 171; Schütze, R.A. (n 29) 7 ('best seller'); Sanders, P., 'UNCITRAL's Model Law on International and Commercial Arbitration: Present Situation and Future' (2005) 21 *Arb Int'l* no 4, 443.

common law traditions.[376] In order to ensure that success for the future, arbitration practitioners and courts should aim at a uniform or autonomous interpretation of national arbitration rules that are based on the Model Law.[377]

C. Liberal approach to (international) arbitration

In accordance with the general development towards a spirit of cooperation between judges and arbitrators, modern national regulations of arbitration have as a common feature a more or less liberal approach at the various stages of an arbitration procedure. This becomes evident when looking at the matters which may be brought before arbitrators, the limited interference by the courts during the proceedings and after the rendering of the award at the stage of possible attacks of the award. **1.113**

(1) Arbitrability

(1.1) Definition and distinctive features Although arbitration is recognized as an equivalent alternative to litigation, there are subject matters which the states reserve for their courts of law to decide. **1.114**

An arbitration agreement will only be recognized and enforced, if the subject matter covered is 'capable of settlement by arbitration',[378] or arbitrable. Today, this issue is generally referred to as 'arbitrability' or 'arbitrabilité'.[379] The German notion for it is 'Schiedsfähigkeit'.[380] Further, objective arbitrability is distinguished from subjective arbitrability.[381] A dispute may only be submitted to arbitration if the subject matter in question is not an exclusive domain of the courts (objective arbitrability).[382] In addition, the parties to the dispute must be capable and permitted to refer the matter to arbitration (subjective arbitrability).[383] Finally, the question may come up whether the particular remedy sought for by the claimant, may be ordered in an arbitral award ('arbitral remedy').[384] For example, in certain jurisdictions, arbitrators are not allowed to issue orders to refrain or restrictive injunctions,[385] or eg to determine punitive damages to be paid by the defendant.[386] **1.115**

---

[376] This feature is often pointed out, eg by Cremades, B.M. (n 143) 171, who emphasizes that the Model Law has more or less been accepted by an equal number of common law and civil law countries.

[377] Berger, K.P., *The New German Arbitration Law* (n 115), 33 *et seq*; Trappe, J., 'The Arbitration Proceedings, Fundamental Principles and Rights of the Parties' (1998) 15 *Int'l Arb L Rev* no 3, 102.

[378] This is the wording of the Geneva Protocol of 1923 (Art 1) and of the New York Convention (Art II (1)). See Redfern, Hunter, Blackaby and Partasides (n 12) no 3–22. For an example of a recent statute, see s 1, Swedish Arbitration Act 1999.

[379] There was a special issue on arbitrability in international commercial arbitration of Arbitration International (see (1996) 12 *Arb Int'l* no 2). For the French notion of arbitrabilité, see Fouchard, Gaillard, Goldman (n 30) 328 no 532.

[380] Schwab, K.H. and Walter, G. (n 1) 35; Schlosser, P. (n 13) nos 285 *et seq*; Schütze, R.A. (n 29) no 117. Sometimes, 'Schiedsfähigkeit' is replaced by 'Schiedsgerichtsfähigkeit', Lionnet, K. and Lionnet, A. (n 29) 64.

[381] This distinction is sometimes made in textbooks or articles, see Fouchard, Gaillard, Goldman (n 30) 329 *et seq* no 533 Schlosser, P. (n 13) nos 285 *et seq* and 324 *et seq*; Blessing, M., 'Arbitrability of Intellectual Property Disputes' (1996) 12 *Arb Int'l.* no 2, 191.

[382] See eg Lew, J.D.M., Mistelis, L.A. and Kröll, S. (n 13) 9–2.

[383] This question which includes the issue whether states may be parties to commercial arbitration, is not dealt with here; for details, see Schlosser, P. (n 13) nos 324 *et seq* and in particular nos 342 *et seq*.

[384] For details see Rubino-Sammartano, M. (n 44) 109 *et seq*.

[385] As in England, see Mustill, M. and Boyd, S.C. (n 7) 390; Schlosser, P. (n 13)no 316.

[386] For US–American case law in this respect, see Schlosser, P. (n 13) no 317 with further references.

Also the (in-) ability to grant interest or to adapt or modify a contract are issues which may be discussed within a wider concept of arbitrability.[387]

1.116 When distinguishing arbitrable from non-arbitrable disputes, one may define the underlying concept of arbitrability as a public policy limitation upon the scope of arbitration as a method of settling disputes.[388] In principle, a state is free whether it safeguards its interest to have a particular legal issue decided by its courts, by restricting generally the access to arbitration or by applying a public policy control at a later stage after the rendering of the award.[389] When defining arbitrable disputes, the legislator may refer to general groups of disputes or, alternatively, he may exclude certain disputes from arbitration. He may also combine both methods.

1.117 (i) According to the recognition of party autonomy, a state may consider those disputes to be arbitrable which are capable of being resolved by settlement.[390] This is the concept adopted nowadays or in former times eg in German,[391] Austrian[392] and Swiss[393] law. The apparent drawback of this approach is the requirement to look into various laws or legal instruments where such capability for settlement is regulated.

1.118 (ii) The reforms eg in Switzerland and Germany have introduced the concept of 'vermögensrechtliche Ansprüche' (patrimonial claims or claims involving economic interests[394]) which are subject to arbitration. The intention of the respective legislators was to introduce a concept which is wider than the reference to a settlement by the parties and includes any sort of economic or financial interest.[395] It should be noted that within this concept, as generally in many jurisdictions, the application of

[387] Rubino-Sammartano, M. (n 44) 110 *et seq*. In the USA, arbitrability is a broader concept which eg includes also the scope of the particular arbitration clause in question; see Redfern, Hunter, Blackaby and Partasides (n 12)no 3–21 fn. 61; Schlosser, P. (n 13)nos 296 *et seq* and Park, W.W. (1996) 12 *Arb Int'l* no 2, 137, 143. This wide concept of arbitrability is, however, not universally recognized and will, therefore, not be applied here.

[388] Redfern, Hunter, Blackaby and Partasides (n 12) no 3–22; Craig, W.L., Park, W.W. and Paulsson, J., *International Chamber of Commerce Arbitration* (3rd edn, OUP, New York etc, 1999) 91 *et seq*; Park, W.W. (n 387) 145; Hanotiau, B. in Böckstiegel (ed), *Acts of State and Arbitration,* 31, 34; McLaughlin, J. (1996) 12 *Arb Int'l* no 2, 113, 119. See also Art 2060(1) Code Civil (France) which explicity refers to public policy when defining arbitrability.

[389] Schlosser, P. (n 13) no 285.

[390] 'Vergleichsfähigkeit', see eg s 1025, ZPO (as in force until 1997) and Schwab, K.H. and Walter, G. (n 1) 35 nos 2 *et seq*; s 1, Swedish Arbitration Act 1999.

[391] In s 1030(1), ZPO, this concept now applies only for non-patrimonial matters; therefore, eg matrimonial disputes are mostly excluded from arbitration, see Schütze, R.A. (n 29) no 117.

[392] See s 577(1), öZPO.

[393] See Art 5 of the Concordat, whereas the law on international arbitration (SPILA) applies a different definition, see ch 12 *infra*.

[394] There are different translations of 'vermögensrechtliche Ansprüche'. 'Pecuniary claim' is a term which is too narrow for the concepts of Swiss and German law (which is based on Swiss law in this respect) whereas 'claim involving economic interest' is a better translation, expressing the intentions of the legislator to allow also those claims for arbitration that are not looking for payment of money; see Berger, K.P., *The New German Arbitration Law* (n 115) 24 *et seq* and 49 ('disputes that have an economic character'). See also the translation of Art 177(1) SPILA by Blessing, M. (n 112) 1, 25: 'Any dispute involving financial interests can be the subject-matter of an arbitration.'

[395] Blessing, M. (n 112) 1, 25; Berger, K.P. (n 115) 24; Lachmann, J.P. (n 81) 37 no 130. Also the official governmental report on the new arbitration law (reprinted in Berger, K.P. (n 115) 179) applies a wide interpretation.

mandatory law or the exclusive jurisdiction or venue of certain courts does not mean that the underlying dispute is not arbitrable.[396]

(iii) In some jurisdictions, there is either no general definition of arbitrable disputes (as in England),[397] or the concept applied is rather vague and entails difficult problems of definition and interpretation (as in France).[398] **1.119**

(iv) Finally, the legislator may opt for simply listing non-arbitral disputes without including a general definition of arbitrability.[399] In some jurisdictions, those lists (or the reference to other laws containing restrictions of arbitrability) are combined with a general approach as described above under (i) and (ii). This is eg the solution chosen for the new German law.[400] **1.120**

(1.2) The applicable law for determining arbitrability of a dispute The question which law determines the arbitrability of a particular claim or dispute, cannot be answered generally and with certainty.[401] The answer depends on the stage where the issue is raised, ie whether the point of view is that of the arbitrator or judge who has to decide the question when seized during or after the arbitral proceeding.[402] This judge will generally look at 'his law', ie the law of the state where the seat of the arbitration is or was, or, in case of enforcement of the award in another jurisdiction, where enforcement is sought.[403] The arbitrator will have a different approach since he does not know where a future award will possibly be enforced. He will, therefore, concentrate on some significant connecting factors as the law at the seat of the arbitration and the law applicable to the substance of the dispute. Given the multitude of jurisdictions or laws that may be involved,[404] there is no absolute certainty for the arbitrator.[405] **1.121**

[396] Schlosser, P. (n 13) no 290; Berger, K.P. (n 115) 25; sometimes, however, those conclusions are in fact drawn by local courts, see von Hoffmann, B. in Böckstiegel (ed), *Acts of State and Arbitration,* 3, 17.

[397] For a critical description of English law in this respect, see Schlosser, P. (n 13) no 295.

[398] The French law refers to the concept of *ordre public* which is quite vague as numerous court decisions show, see Schlosser, P. (n 13) nos 292 *et seq* (with further references). See also Fouchard, Gaillard, Goldman (n 30) 345 *et seq,* nos 560 *et seq.*

[399] This is eg the Italian solution, see Rubino-Sammartano, M. (n 44) 103 *et seq.*

[400] Whereas s 1030(1), ZPO refers to patrimonial claims, there is, nevertheless, the reservation in s 1030(3) that restrictions of arbitrability contained in other statutory provisions outside the Code of Civil Procedure remain unaffected.

[401] On the law applicable to questions of arbitrability see in general Lew, J.D.M., Mistelis, L.A. and Kröll, S. (n 13) 9–5 *et seq.*

[402] Schlosser, P. (n 13) nos 306 and 315. Hanotiau, B. (1996) 12 *Arb Int'l* no 4, 391, 393. See also Art 32(2)(b)(i), Model Law.

[403] Schlosser, P. (n 13) no 315. Hanotiau, B. (1996) 12 *Arb Int'l* no 4, 391, 402 *et seq.* For the four steps where arbitrability issues may be involved, see Blessing, M., 'Arbitrability of Intellectual Property Disputes' (1996) 12 *Arb Int'l.* no 2, 191, 194 *et seq.*

[404] For a list of eight jurisdictions which are possibly involved, see Blessing, M. (n 112) 1, 26 and Blessing, M., 'Arbitrability of Intellectual Property Disputes' (1996) 12 *Arb Int'l* no 2, 191, 192. See also Redfern, Hunter, Blackaby and Partasides (n 12) no 3–22.

[405] That is pointed out by Schlosser, P. (n 13) nos 306 and 315. In a similar way, see Craig, W.L., Park, W.W. and Paulsson, J. (n 388) 83. This uncertainty is one of the reasons why some authors prefer to rely on substantive rules for determining the arbitrability of a dispute, see eg Kirry, A., 'Arbitrability: Current Trends in Europe' (1996) 12 *Arb Int'l* no 4, 373, 381 *et seq.*

1.122 In the first instance, the arbitrator (and the judge) will refer to the law chosen by the parties as proper law of the arbitration agreement.[406] In most cases, however, there will be no such choice. Rather, the parties will have chosen the substantive law to be applied on the dispute itself. Generally, the law governing the main contract in dispute (*lex causae*), does also apply to the validity of the arbitration agreement.[407] If the dispute before the arbitrator is not arbitrable according to this law, the arbitration agreement is invalid and, consequently, the arbitrators do not have jurisdiction.[408]

1.123 The jurisdiction which in practice should be closely checked by any arbitrator is that of the seat of the arbitration. International conventions and the Model Law both refer to this law as the decisive law for determining the arbitrability of the dispute.[409] If the dispute is not arbitrable according to this law, it is generally open to challenge before the local courts.[410] In addition, the lack of arbitrability at the seat of the arbitration may be a reason for rejecting the enforcement abroad, whether or not this country is member of the New York Convention.[411]

1.124 Finally, the law of the place of performance of the award should be taken into account. Even if it is doubtful whether the arbitrators must follow such a recommendation,[412] the legal advisers of the parties are obliged to examine the jurisdictions where possibly enforcement of an award may be asked for. If it turns out that a possible future dispute is arbitrable at the place of arbitration, but not at the presumed place of enforcement, the lawyer should rather recommend litigation, if possible.

1.125 (1.3) **Arbitrable and non-arbitrable disputes** Before listing areas of the law where arbitrability is often doubtful, it is helpful to look at the reasons why national legislators exclude certain areas of law from arbitration. In a rather general approach, one may distinguish two groups of non-arbitrable matters.[413]

1.126 (i) There are fundamental issues of the society and its organization for which the states claim a monopoly. That applies to all matters of personal status of the citizens and to matters of public or national interest as eg criminal or tax law.[414]

[406] Hanotiau, B., 'L'arbitrage et le droit européen de la concurrence' in Böckstiegel (ed) *Acts of State and Arbitration* (1997) 31, 36; Hanotiau, B. (1996) 12 *Arb Int'l* no 4, 391, 393 *et seq*; Schütze, R.A. (n 29) no 119 (*lex causae*).

[407] That view is questioned eg by Kirry, A. (1996) 12 *Arb Int'l* no 4, 373, 379 *et seq*.

[408] On the *Kompetenz-Kompetenz* of the arbitrators to rule on their jurisdiction after the invoking of lacking arbitrability, see Park, W.W. (n 387) 137 *et seq*.

[409] Art V. (2)(a), New York Convention; Art 36(1)(b)(i), Model Law.

[410] See eg s 1059(2) no 2(a) ZPO. Blessing, M., 'Arbitrability of Intellectual Property Disputes' (1996) 12 *Arb Int'l* no 2, 191, 192, recommends for practical purposes first to check the *lex arbitri* for an answer on the question of arbitrability. According to Hanotiau, B. (1996) 12 *Arb Int'l* no 4, 391, this law should, as a matter of principle, not be decisive.

[411] See eg Blessing, M., 'Arbitrability of Intellectual Property Disputes' (1996) 12 *Arb Int'l* no 2, 191, 195 and Hanotiau, B. (1996) 12 *Arb Int'l* no 4, 391, 397.

[412] Hanotiau, B., 'L'arbitrage et le droit européen de la concurrence' in Böckstiegel (ed) *Acts of State and Arbitration* (1997) 31, 37 *et seq*.

[413] Fouchard, Gaillard, Goldman (n 30) 347 *et seq* no 563; Hanotiau, B., 'L'arbitrage et le droit européen de la concurrence', in Böckstiegel (ed) *Acts of State and Arbitration* (1997) 31, 35.

[414] On a recent decision of the Brazilian Supreme Court differentiating between the primary public interest and the administrative interest (also referred to as secondary public interest) see Filho, C.V., 'TMC

(ii) Other subject matters are reserved for the courts since they affect social groups that are considered to be worthy of particular protection by the legislator: This applies to labour disputes, disputes between landlord and tenant or consumer related disputes.[415] It is obvious, however, that in international trade, these considerations are mostly irrelevant given the fact that the players here are generally companies and not private parties requiring social protection. **1.127**

This is one of the reasons why national courts and legislators tended to apply more liberal standards of arbitrability in the international context than in the purely domestic sphere. This development was especially furthered by two American cases decided in 1974 and 1985,[416] where the Supreme Court explicitly argued that the growth of international arbitration required lower levels of entry for the parties. Further, national legislators who opted for a separate system of international arbitration, included more liberal provisions in those laws than in the law applicable to domestic arbitration.[417] This liberal trend also reached the level of domestic arbitration where the standards gradually were assimilated to the international standard. Germany is a good example for that tendency since it adopted the Swiss approach designed for international arbitration for its new law on arbitration which does not distinguish international from domestic arbitration.[418] **1.128**

(1.4) Particular categories of disputes The following subject matters are generally discussed as (possibly) non-arbitrable disputes:[419] **1.129**

(i) Competition law. For a long time, it has been discussed whether disputes relating to national or European competition law may be decided by arbitrators. Since the US-decision in '*Mitsubishi*', by which (in the international context) any issue involving national or foreign competition law was held to be arbitrable,[420] there was a parallel development in Europe. Whereas in Germany, the arbitrability of antitrust matters was recognized even before the reform of 1997,[421] decisions in Switzerland[422] and Italy[423] also confirmed this liberal trend. In France, disputes involving competition **1.130**

Terminal Multimodal De Coroa Grande Spe S.A. v Ministro da Ciencia e Tecnologia', (2007) 24 *J Int'l Arb* no 4, 431.

415 von Hoffmann, B., 'Internationally Mandatory Rules of Law Before Arbitral Tribunals' in Böckstiegel (ed), *Acts of State and Arbitration* (1997) 3, 16.

416 *Scherk v Alberto Culver*, 417 US 5066 (1976) I YCA, 203; *Mitsubishi Motors Corp v Soler Chrysler-Plymouth Inc* 105 US 3346 (1986) XI YCA, 555. On *Mitsubishi*, see Redfern, Hunter, Blackaby and Partasides (n 12) no 3–25.

417 Art 177, SPILA, as compared to Art 5 of the Concordat, see Blessing, M. (n 112) 1, 25 *et seq*. See also Fouchard, Gaillard, Goldman (n 30) 347 *et seq* nos 563 *et seq* for the development of French jurisprudence in international matters, and 353 no 568, for the general liberal trend in comparative law.

418 Berger, K.P. (fn 16), 23 *et seq*.

419 See in general Lew, J.D.M., Mistelis, L.A. and Kröll, S. (n 13) 9–35 *et seq*.

420 The development afterwards in domestic arbitration did not show a clear pattern, see McLaughlin, J.T. (1996) 12 *Arb Int'l* No 2, 133. Generally, on arbitrability of antitrust issues in Common Law, see Beechey, J. (1996) 12 *Arb Int'l* no 2, 179 *et seq*; Lew, J.D.M., Mistelis, L.A. and Kröll, S. (n 13) 9–36 and 9–42 *et seq*.

421 Schlosser, P. (n 13) no 318; von Hoffman, B. (n 415) 18; Weigand, F.-B., 'Evading EC Competition Law by Resorting to Arbitration?' (1993) 9 *Arb Int'l* no 3, 249, 250 *et seq*.

422 Decision by the *Bundesgericht (BG)* of 28 April 1992, ASA Bull 1992, 368 *Rev arb* 1993, 124. See also Lionnet, K. and Lionnet, A. (n 29) 68, and Blessing, M. (n 112) 1, 25.

423 Court of Appeal of Bologna, 21 December 1991, (1993) YCA, 422.

law were only partly considered to be arbitrable in as much as the antitrust issue was only of an incidental nature.[424] Since 1993, the French courts generally accept the concept of the arbitrability of matters involving competition law.[425] Especially in matters relating to EC competition law, arbitrators have in many ICC awards assumed jurisdiction and taken the view that those disputes are arbitrable.[426] Today, there is no serious doubt that disputes involving EC competition law are subject to arbitral adjudication.[427]

1.131 (ii) Patents and trade marks. Since intellectual property rights are conferred on private parties by the state, there is a tendency to regard related disputes as non-arbitrable if third parties are affected by a possible ruling on the validity of such right. Therefore, claims involving the validity of a patent or trade mark are mostly distinguished from disputes relating to contractual obligations derived from licence agreements.[428]

1.132 As to disputes about the validity of a patent or trade mark, there are liberal jurisdictions like Switzerland[429] or the United States,[430] where arbitrability of such issues has been recognized. In France, however, those claims are generally excluded from arbitration,[431] and also in Germany, claims arising from the alleged nullity of a patent have to be brought to the *Patentgericht* (a court specially created for such matters) which has exclusive jurisdiction.[432]

1.133 As to licence agreements or similar contractual regulations, in most European countries, related disputes are considered to be arbitrable.[433] This does also apply to France where the *Cour d'Appel de Paris*, in a decision of 1994, has confirmed that view.[434]

1.134 (iii) Bribery and corruption. The opinion that claims involving contracts entered into under the influence of bribery are generally not arbitrable, goes back to a famous award of arbitrator *Lagergreen*, rendered in 1963. He held that due to the illegal nature (based on apparent bribery) of the underlying agreement, he did not have jurisdiction

[424] Schlosser, P. (n 13) no 319; Weigand, F.-B. (1993) 9 *Arb Int'l* no 3, 250 with further references.

[425] Cour d'Appel de Paris, 19 May 1993, *Rev arb* 1993, 645 ('Labinal') and 14 October 1993, *Rev arb* 1994, 164.

[426] See eg ICC case no 2811 (1978), JDI (Clunet) 1978, 984; no 4604 (1984), JDI (Clunet) 1985, 973. For more references, see Fouchard, Gaillard, Goldman (n 30) 363 *et seq* no 581; Lew, J.D.M., Mistelis, L.A. and Kröll, S. (n 13) 9–64 *et seq*.

[427] Weigand, F.-B. (1993) 9 *Arb Int'l* no 3, 249 *et seq*; Hanotiau, B. 38 *et seq*.

[428] Redfern, Hunter, Blackaby and Partasides (n 12) no 3–23; Fouchard, Gaillard, Goldman (n 30) 366 no 583 with further references.

[429] Schlosser, P. (n 13) no 31; Blessing, M., (n 112) 1, 25; Blessing, M., 'Arbitrability of Intellectual Property Disputes' (1996) 12 *Arb Int'l* no 2, 191, 199.

[430] The recent liberal tendency was initiated by legislation from 1982 which expressly provided that patent disputes may be arbitrated. Similarly liberal case law for trade marks did follow; see Schlosser, P. (n 13) no 317 and McLaughlin, J. (1996) 12 *Arb Int'l* No 2,135.

[431] Oppetit, *Rev arb* 1979, 83; Fouchard, Gaillard, Goldman (n 30) 358 no 576; Schlosser, P. (n 13) no 317; ICC Case no 6709 (1991), JDI (Clunet) 1992, 998.

[432] Official governmental report, printed in K.P. Berger (n 115) 179; Berger, *The new German arbitration law*, 25; Lachmann, J.P. (n 81) no 141. For the opposite view (in favour of arbitrability), see Schlosser, P. (n 13) no 317 and Schwab, K.H. and Walter, G. (n 1) 36.

[433] See Fouchard, Gaillard, Goldman (n 30) 366 *et seq* no 583 and Schlosser, P. (n 13) no 317, both with further references.

[434] Decision dated 24 March 1994 ('Deko'), *Rev arb* 1994, 515.

to hear the case.[435] This solution is now generally rejected[436] and has for a long time given way to the current practice of arbitrators to accept jurisdiction in cases where corruption was probably involved.[437] Thus, the agreement in question was held to be null and void by the arbitral tribunal in case no 5,622 (1988) in the matter *Hilmarton*,[438] (and in a decision of 1993 *Westinghouse-Philippines*), the Swiss Federal Supreme Court confirmed the arbitrability of matters involving issues of bribery and corruption.[439] That trend is also to be noted in the United States where claims involving the RICO Act are arbitrable according to some case law.[440]

(iv) Insolvency Law. The issue of arbitrability of procedures touching insolvency law has not found uniform answers.[441] In Germany, for instance, certain insolvency disputes were held not to be arbitrable in a rather old decision of the *Bundesgerichtshof*.[442] It is not clear, however, whether this view will prevail.[443] In the United States, following the liberal trend initiated by the *Mitsubishi* decision of 1985, whenever arbitrability issues come up in bankruptcy-related proceedings, courts show a tendency to favour the enforcement of arbitration agreements in the international context.[444] Although matters intimately involved in the bankruptcy process are not arbitrable, other related claims, eg of a trustee, were held to be arbitrable.[445] French decisions show an even more liberal trend, since they shift the issue from the question of arbitrability to the public policy control at the stage of possible attacks on the award: although insolvency related disputes are considered to be arbitrable, ensuing awards will be nullified if fundamental principles of insolvency law have not been observed.[446] The fact that a party is affected by an insolvency procedure before or after the commencement of an arbitration is not generally seen as a ground to prevent or stop an arbitration proceeding, as long as the dispute is related to contractual claims which are not directly based **1.135**

[435] ICC Case no 1110 (15 January 1963), reprinted in (1994) 10 *Arb Int'l* 282 with comments by G. Wetter, 277. See also Craig, W.L., Park, W.W. and Paulsson, J. (n 388) 83; Lew, J.D.M., Mistelis, L.A. and Kröll, S. (n 13) 9–75 *et seq.*

[436] See eg Fouchard, Gaillard, Goldman (n 30) 368 no 586 with further references. See also Oppetit, JDI (Clunet) 1987, 5 *et seq.*

[437] Redfern, Hunter, Blackaby and Partasides (n 12)no 3–27; for the arbitral case law of recent years, see Fouchard, Gaillard, Goldman (n 30) 368 no 586, fns 447 and 448.

[438] *Rev arb* 1993, 327 (1994) YCA, 105.

[439] *Bundesgericht (BG)* decision of 2 September 1993, ASA Bull 1994, 244, 247.

[440] Schlosser, P. (n 13) no 321, referring to the decision of 8 June 1987, 107 S Ct 2332 (1987).

[441] See generally Lew, J.D.M., Mistelis, L.A. and Kröll, S. (n 13) 9–55 *et seq.*

[442] *Neue Juristische Wochenschrift (NJW)* (1956) 1920. For the opposite view, see Schwab, K.H. and Walter, G. (n 1) 34.

[443] The official governmental report on s 1030, ZPO (see KP Berger (n 115), 179) points out that the exclusive jurisdiction of certain courts does not necessarily mean that the respective disputes to be brought before those courts are not arbitrable. Therefore, it may be argued that claims relating to insolvency procedures (for which the insolvency courts have exclusive jurisdiction) are of a patrimonial or economic nature and are therefore arbitrable, if the rights of third parties are not necessarily affected. See for more details Heidbrink, A. and von der Groeben, M.C. 'Insolvenz und Schiedsverfahren' *ZIP* (2006) 265.

[444] McLaughlin, J. (1996) 12 *Arb Int'l* No 2, 134.

[445] *Hayes & Co v Merill Lynch*, 885 F 2d 1149 (3rd Cir 1989); see also 944 F 2d 114 (2nd Cir 1991); McLaughlin (n 444) 134.

[446] See the decisions of the *Cour de Cassation* of 8 March 1988, *Rev arb* 1989, 473, and of 4 February 1992, *Rev arb* 1992, 663. See also Fouchard, Gaillard, Goldman (n 30) 360 no 578.

on or influenced by the insolvency itself.[447] This question, however, and the issue whether an administrator or trustee is bound by an arbitration agreement, are not issues of objective arbitrability *strictu sensu*.[448]

1.136 (v) Embargoes, acts of state. State courts are, in accordance with the 'Act of State Doctrine', prevented from ruling on the lawfulness of a sovereign act of another state. This doctrine, however, does not apply to private arbitral tribunals.[449] Arbitrators are not precluded from determining questions of public international law, and, consequently, arbitrators have often ruled on foreign acts of expropriation and possible compensation claims arising thereof.[450] Likewise, there are no reasons for arbitral tribunals to refrain from deciding disputes that are based on or connected with embargoes.[451] This view was eg taken by the Swiss Federal Court in 1992 in a dispute regarding the UN embargo against Iraq.[452] In another arbitral award rendered in Geneva in 1994, the tribunal rightly pointed out that an embargo did not render the whole dispute non-arbitrable, but, rather had to be taken into account by the tribunal as a consideration of international public policy.[453]

1.137 (vi) Other disputes which often are not arbitrable. There are certain types of disputes which are regulated by special regimes in many jurisdictions. Those areas of the law are mostly influenced by the intention of the legislator to protect the potentially weaker party.[454] That is mostly the case in matters of employment or whenever consumers are concerned and, partly, in family law matters. Disputes that are governed by labour or employment law are sometimes not arbitrable,[455] or they are arbitrable according to special provisions to be applied instead of the general rules governing arbitration.[456] In some jurisdictions as eg the United States, employment disputes are increasingly accepted as matters suitable for arbitration.[457] This trend may also be noted in disputes involving consumers.[458] In some jurisdictions, there are particular provisions within the law on arbitration which apply exclusively for consumer-related

---

[447] See ICC cases no 6697 (1990), *Rev arb* 1992, 135, and no 6632 (1993), quoted by Fouchard, Gaillard, Goldman (n 30) 370 no 587.

[448] For details in this respect, see Schlosser, P. (n 13) no. 428 with further references.

[449] Schlosser, P. (n 13) no 322; Wetter, G. (1985) 2 *J Int'l Arb* no 1, 15 *et seq*.

[450] Schlosser, P. (n 13) no 322.

[451] von Hoffmann, B. (n 415) 17 *et seq*.

[452] The court held that the dispute was arbitrable and that the embargo only had an influence on the substantive claims; *Bundesgericht (BG)* decision of 23 June 1992, ASA Bull 1993, 58 *Rev arb* 1993, 693.

[453] ICC case no 6,719 (1994), JDI (Clunet) 1994, 1,071.

[454] That is the reason why security claims in the United States were considered as non-arbitrable matters; see *Wilko v Swan*, 376 US 427 (1953), and Kerr, J.J. (1996) 12 *Arb Int'l* no 2, 171, 172.

[455] See eg for France, Fouchard, Gaillard, Goldman (n 30) 356 no 573. For other European countries, see Kirry, A. (1996) 12 *Arb Int'l* No 4387 *et seq*.

[456] This is the solution of German law, see Schwab, K.H. and Walter, G. (n 1) 369 *et seq*, on arbitration according to the 'Arbeitsgerichtsgesetz' (law governing employment courts).

[457] For a description of the recent development since the leading case, *Gilmer* (500 US 20 (1991), see McLaughlin, J.T. 119 *et seq*. In France, there is a similar trend, see Fouchard, Gaillard, Goldman (n 30) 356 *et seq* no 573.

[458] Fouchard, Gaillard, Goldman (n 30) 361 *et seq* no 579; Mc Laughlin, J.T. (n 444) 123 *et seq*; Kirry, A. (n 455) 388 *et seq*.

arbitration.[459] The aim of the legislators is often not to preclude arbitration but to protect the potentially weaker party. In family law and the law on personal status, most states exclude the arbitrability of those subject matters that regard the status of a person. Thus, marital status and capacity are mostly regarded as matters within the exclusive jurisdiction of the courts of law.[460] However, there is a modern trend to admit related pecuniary or economic claims for arbitration as eg claims regarding maintenance or property rights.[461]

(2) Limited court interference during the proceedings

One of the objectives of most of the reforms of national arbitration laws in recent years has been to limit the influence of the courts during the arbitral process. The Model Law includes a provision according to which courts of law may only intervene if provided for in the law on arbitration itself.[462] The necessity of such limitation has also been recognized by 'interventionist' states like England in order to keep arbitration attractive.[463] **1.138**

(2.1) Recognition of the arbitration agreement The first and most important self-restraint by the states is to recognize the wish of the parties to submit a dispute to arbitration rather than to litigation. This recognition of the arbitration agreement is now guaranteed in most states of the world. **1.139**

As has already been discussed above,[464] international treaties reaching back into the last century aim at the recognition of arbitration agreements. The logical consequence of this is that whenever litigation is started in spite of a valid arbitration clause, the respective court must stay the proceeding in order to 'refer the parties to arbitration'.[465] Accordingly, also most domestic laws on arbitration provide for a stay of such court proceedings.[466] However, in England, until recently there was no certainty that such stay would be granted in any case, since the 1975 Arbitration Act left room for some discretion of the courts. If convinced that 'there is not in fact any dispute between the parties', the court could decline to terminate the proceedings initiated before it.[467] Since that gave the defendant a sometimes welcome opportunity to stop the arbitration,[468] the Arbitration Act 1996 does no longer **1.140**

---

459 For German law, see eg s 1031(5), ZPO (stricter requirements as to the form of the arbitration agreement). For England, see s 89 *et seq*, Arbitration Act 1996 on arbitration proceedings involving consumers.

460 Fouchard, Gaillard, Goldman (n 30) 355 no 572; McLaughlin, J.T. (n 444) 127 *et seq*; Schütze, R.A. (n 29) no 117.

461 McLaughlin, J.T. (n 444) 128. For German law, see Lachmann, J.P. (n 81) no 131.

462 Art 5, Model Law; Schlosser, P. (n 13) no 124, considers that provision as one of the most critical of the whole Model Law.

463 See the Report on the Arbitration Bill by the English Departmental Advisory Committee on Arbitration Law (The 1996 DAC Report), published in (1997) 13 *Arb Int'l* no 3, 275, 280 nos 21 *et seq.*

464 See 1.99 *supra.*

465 See Art 4, Geneva Protocol 1923, Art II New York Convention; Art 8 Model Law. For the international recognition of arbitration clauses, see also Schlosser, P. (n 13) nos. 76 *et seq*, and Fouchard, Gaillard, Goldman (n 30) 417 *et seq* nos 664 *et seq.*

466 For this so called negative effect of the arbitration agreement, see 1.27 *supra.*

467 s 1, Arbitration Act 1975 read: '..the court, unless satisfied that the arbitration agreement is null and void, inoperative or incapable of being performed, or that there is not in fact any dispute between the parties with regard to the matter agreed to be referred, shall make an order staying the proceedings.'

468 If the defendant demonstrated that he is liable and therefore does not dispute the claim, such allegation had to be checked by the court in a sometimes lengthy proceeding with the only aim to stop the arbitration commenced by the claimant; see Rawlings, J. (1997) 13 *Arb Int'l* no 4, 421.

contain such provision. Now, an application for a stay will be accepted even if the matter cannot be referred to arbitration immediately.[469] Finally, the reasons, accepted by many national legislators, for rejecting such an application are now quite uniform. For example, the English Arbitration Act 1996 names the three reasons as introduced by the New York Convention, ie that 'the arbitration agreement is null and void, inoperative or incapable of being performed'.[470] Only in these cases a state court shall have jurisdiction in spite of an arbitration agreement, in order to grant the parties alternative means of legal protection.

1.141 States may provide that a court may issue an order to stay the proceeding only on application by a party (*ex parte*) or, alternatively, out of its own motion (*ex officio*).[471] According to the French and German legal tradition, which is shared by some other European nations, a stay may be ordered only on application by a party to do so.[472] This concept is also followed by the relevant international treaties and the Model Law.[473] The rationale behind it is the consensual nature of arbitration which allows both parties—claimant by applying to the court, defendant by tacitly accepting this jurisdiction—to deviate from the original agreement to arbitrate.[474] Other states, however, have chosen the other approach according to which the court has to stay the proceeding *ex officio* if it is convinced that a valid and operable arbitration agreement exists. The most important example for that solution is Switzerland.[475]

1.142 **(2.2) The powers of courts during arbitral proceedings** It may generally be presumed that the parties, by electing arbitration for resolving potential disputes, intend to exclude unsolicited interference of the local courts with their private arbitration proceeding. This has recently been formally recognized by the English legislator who, as a consequence, now tries to reduce more than before any potential intervention by a court of law.[476] Thus, the role of the national judge should be supportive rather than interventionist or disruptive.[477]

1.143 The supportive function of the courts starts even before the formal commencement of an arbitral proceeding. Provisional measures may be applied for with the court before or often also after the constitution of the arbitral tribunal in order to safeguard vital interests of the claimant.[478] The inclusion of this exception from the arbitrators' jurisdiction into national

469 s 9(4), Arbitration Act 1996; for the reasoning for the change, see also DAC Report 1996, 286 no 53.

470 s 9(4); see also the same wording eg in s1032(1), ZPO.

471 See 1.27 *supra*.

472 Art 1458(3), NCPC; s 1032(1), ZPO; Art 1022(1), WBR. For other countries, see Schlosser, P. (n 13) no 400; Fouchard, Gaillard, Goldman (n 30) 419 no 669.

473 See eg Art II(3), New York Convention; Art 8(1), Model Law; for details, see Fouchard, Gaillard, Goldman (n 30) 419 no 670.

474 Fouchard, Gaillard, Goldman (n 30) 419 no 669.

475 Art 7, SPILA; however, unconditional appearance of both parties, especially of the defendant, establishes the jurisdiction of the court, see Art 7(a) SPILA. The *ex officio* solution was also chosen by the former socialist countries of Eastern Europe, see Schlosser, P. (n 13) no 400 with further references.

476 For the explicit intention of the English legislator, see the 1996 DAC Report, 280 no 21: '. . .there is no doubt that our law has been subject to international criticism that the Courts intervene more than they should in the arbitral process, thereby tending to frustrate the choice the parties have made to use arbitration rather than litigation as the means for resolving their disputes.'

477 See the 1996 DAC Report, 280 no 22. On the 'partnership' between national courts and arbitral tribunals, see generally Redfern, Hunter, Blackaby and Partasides (n 12) no 7–01 *et seq.*

478 See eg s 1033, ZPO; Art 9 Model Law; s 44 Arbitration Act 1996; Art 183(2), SPILA. In many jurisdictions, there is an alternative power of the arbitral tribunal to issue provisional orders.

laws constitutes an indispensible and effective support for the arbitral process since the claimant mostly depends on an easily enforceable order for the requested interim measure.[479]

Most jurisdictions also provide for support with respect to the constitution of the arbitral tribunal. Either at the initial stage, eg when the two party elected arbitrators fail to agree on the chairman, or at a later stage, eg after the challenge of an arbitrator, help by the state court is useful and often welcome.[480] At the stage of the taking of evidence, a party may also require support in moments where the tribunal's order eg for the appearance of a witness is not followed and thus coercion by the court is indispensable.[481] Whether other, possibly useful supportive measures should be allowed by insertion of a general rule granting jurisdiction to assist the arbitral tribunal, is, however, open to debate. English law has refused to accept such general power already some decades ago,[482] and the legislator of the Arbitration Act 1996 did also reject such a concept in order to avoid undue intervention in a private procedure. There are, however, examples of French decisions showing that the *Tribunal de Grande Instance de Paris* is sometimes prepared to claim jurisdiction for intervening at the commencement of arbitral proceedings to a degree that even replaces the will of the parties.[483] Also in Switzerland, Art 185, SPILA grants the competent court a general power 'for any further judicial assistance' the limits of which are not clearly to be defined. **1.144**

Finally, the supportive powers of the courts are not disturbed or influenced by the Brussels and Lugano Conventions. In a landmark decision of 1991, the European Court of Justice held that the European system regulating jurisdiction and competence of the courts in civil matters, does not apply to court proceedings which are ancillary to arbitration.[484] In the underlying case, the claimant had requested judicial help for initiating an arbitration proceeding in London. Following parallel judicial proceedings in Italy, the defendant's home jurisdiction, the question had to be determined whether the Italian and/or English courts were competent in accordance with the Brussels Convention. The European Court's decision, which exempted supportive judicial orders from the Convention's scope, was commonly welcomed as a clear intention to safeguard the traditional interrelation between arbitral tribunals and locally competent courts.[485] **1.145**

Generally speaking, the state courts have no influence on the substantive decision. The arbitration proceeding is, as a matter of principle, independent from the judicial system of **1.146**

[479] This increased effectiveness of provisional measures ordered by a court is the reason why practitioners often prefer such orders to equally available orders issued by the arbitral tribunal.

[480] See eg Art 11, Model Law; s 1035, ZPO; Art 179, SPILA.

[481] See eg Art 27, Model Law; s 1050, ZPO; Art 184, SPILA.

[482] *South Indian Shipping Corp Ltd v Bremer Vulkan Schiffbau und Maschinenfabrik* (1981) 2 WLR 141; *Paal Wilson & Co v Partenreederei Hannah Blumenthal* (1982) 3 All ER, 394; see also the 1996 DAC Report (fn 83), 309 no 215.

[483] *Rev arb* 1987, 351; for details, see Schlosser, P. (n 13) no 590.

[484] *Marc Rich v Società Italiana Impianti* (1991) ECR 3855 (1991) 7 *Arb Int'l* no 2, 253; Weigand, F.-B., *EuZW* (1992) 529. Regulation No 44/2001 of 22 December 2000 has not changed the law in this respect.

[485] See eg Weigand, F.-B., *EuZW* 1992, 529, 531 *et seq*; Hascher, D.T. (1997) 13 *Arb Int'l* no 1, 33, 61. The court's intention may be concluded from the Advocate General's pleadings, according to which '..the specific legal requirements of international arbitration, a universal method of resolving disputes in international trade', should not be ignored by the European Community; see (1991) 7 *Arb Int'l* no 2, 197.

the state and, therefore, free from any influence on the substantive decision (no *révision au fond*). Thus, the taking of evidence and the application of the relevant substantive law to the facts are matters reserved for the arbitrators.

1.147 It may be questionable, however, whether those duties also extend to the application of European law. According to several decisions of the European Court of Justice, there is no doubt that arbitrators have to apply EC law which forms an integral part of the respective law of each member state.[486] This duty applies also in cases where the arbitrators are entitled to decide as *amiable compositeurs*[487] or where they apply provisions of the so-called *lex mercatoria*.[488] However, an arbitral tribunal is not entitled to refer a preliminary question as to the interpretation of EC law to the European Court of Justice. Since the respective procedure (Art 177 of the EC Treaty) is reserved for national courts, the arbitrators must ask such courts for support in situations where the contents of a provision of EC law is debatable.[489]

1.148 English law constitutes an exception to the principle of non-interference in the substantive decision. In London, there is a tradition of close supervision of arbitration by the courts. Since the introduction of the 'special case' procedure according to which a specific question during an ongoing arbitral proceeding could be decided by the court,[490] the possibility to refer a preliminary question of law to the High Court has survived the Arbitration Act 1979[491] and the reform of 1996. According to s 45 of the Arbitration Act 1996,[492] 'any question of law arising in the course of the proceedings which the court is satisfied substantially affects the rights of one or more of the parties' may be determined by the court, provided both parties, or at least the tribunal, have agreed.[493] Thus, English law still deviates from the commonly accepted principle that it is up to the arbitrators to determine all questions of fact and law without substantive interference by the courts.[494]

---

486 See case *Broekmeulen* 1981 ECR 2311; *Nordsee Deutsche Hochseefischerei v Reederei Mond* 1982 ECR 1095, 1111. For details, see Weigand, F.-B. (1993) 9 *Arb Int'l* no 3, 249, 251 *et seq*.

487 Weigand, F.-B. (1993) 9 *Arb Int'l* no 3, 249, 252, with further references.

488 *ibid*.

489 See the *Nordsee* decision, and, as an early example for the referral of such question by the national court to the European Court of Justice, *Bulk Oil (Zug) v Sun International Ltd* (1983) 1 Lloyd's Rep 655.

490 s 21, Arbitration Act 1950, see eg Triebel, V. and Lange, D.G.F., *Recht der Internationalen Wirtschaft* (*RIW*) 1980, 616, 618 *et seq*.

491 s 2, Arbitration Act 1979; see Triebel, V. and Plaßmeier, H. *RPS* (1997) (Beilage 13 zu *Betriebsberater (BB)*, 11 September 1997) 2, 10.

492 For details, especially the modification of the 1979 rule by the 1996 Act, see Triebel, V. and Plaßmeier (*ibid*) 10.

493 s 45(2). If only the tribunal has agreed (and not the other party), the application to the court is only admissible if the court is satisfied that the determination of the question is likely to produce substantial savings in costs and that the application was made without delay (s 45(2)(b), Arbitration Act 1996).

494 Although some authors have welcomed the new regulation as clear improvement of English law in this respect (see Triebel, V. and Plaßmeier, H. (n 491) 10 and 14), there is no doubt that the new law falls behind the general intention to get into line with other modern laws and especially the Model Law on arbitration; see Weigand, F.-B., *Recht der Internationalen Wirtschaft* (*RIW*) (1997) 904, 911.

(3) Restricted grounds for setting aside awards

The control of the award[495] at the seat of arbitration is the necessary counterpart of a policy of abstention during the course of the proceedings.[496] The more liberal a state's approach is when judging the arbitrability of a dispute, the more important is the potential of control of the award by that state. This control is mostly exercised based on the principle of territoriality, ie the state where the place or seat of arbitration was located, claims such powers as part of its national sovereignty.[497] A former tendency to exercise such control independent of the place of arbitration if the arbitration had been conducted according to the law of the controlling state, was either the exception[498] or expressly abandoned by recent reforms.[499] **1.149**

The losing party of the arbitration has, in principle, two ways of defence before the state courts: either it attacks the award in the proceedings of enforcement, which are initiated by the winning party, or it initiates an action for setting the award aside. Whereas in the first option, the losing party may succeed in rejecting the application of enforcement in the particular state only where enforcement has been sought, in the second alternative, the action of setting aside may render the award null and void and, consequently, unenforceable almost throughout the world.[500] The grounds for setting aside an award, are chosen by the respective states at their discretion, without any obligation or limitation derived from a treaty; the New York Convention does not restrict a nation's liberty in this respect.[501] **1.150**

(3.1) Limited means of recourse against arbitral awards To begin with, one should address the terminology used for describing the possibilities to 'attack' an award.[502] Whereas general terms as 'judicial review' or 'recourse' to a court are quite frequently used in literature, among **1.151**

[495] For an analysis which arbitral awards are subject of challenge, see Poudret, J.-F. and Besson, S., *Comparative Law of International Arbitration* (n 6) 773 *et seq*. The German Federal Supreme Court held in a recent decision of 18 January 2007 (III ZB 35/06) that in regard to a partial award on jurisdiction an application for enforcement is admissible in regard to the costs, see BGH Recht der Internationalen Wirtschaft (RIW) 2007, 466.

[496] Fouchard, Gaillard, Goldman (n 30) 899 no 1,558.

[497] See for a comparative view, Fouchard, Gaillard, Goldman (n 30) 925 no 1,593.

[498] See eg *Hiscox v Outhwaite* (1991) 3 WLR, 297; (1992) YCA, 599.

[499] In France, the procedural approach favoured by the courts since the famous *Götaverken* decision (JDI (Clunet) 1980, 660; *Rev arb* 1980, 524) and the *Norsolor* case (*Rev arb* 1981, 306) has been abandoned by the 1981 decree, see Fouchard, Gaillard, Goldman (n 30) 920 *et seq* no 1,590. Likewise, the German legislator abolished the procedural theory as established by the Bundesgerichtshof (BGHZ 21, 365; 96, 40) by adopting the territorial approach of the Model Law, see eg Berger, K.P., *The New German Arbitration Law* (n 115), 16 *et seq*.

[500] This applies at least to the member states of the New York Convention according to which the enforcement of an award may be refused if it has been set aside in the country where it was made (Art V. (1) (e)). Van Den Berg, A.J. in Lew (ed), *Arbitration Insights: 20 years of the annual lecture of the School of International Arbitration* (2007) 7–18; Smit, H. in L.W. Newman and R.D. Hill (eds), *The Leading Arbitrators' Guide to International Arbitration* 462 *et seq* criticizes as undesirable *inter alia* that the New York Convention provides for the possibility to conduct annulment procedures.

[501] This is emphasized by Park, W.W., 'Uses and Abuses of Appeal from Awards' (1988) 4 *Arb Int'l* no 3, 174. There is, however, a tendency for national legislators to refer to the grounds for attacking awards as expressed in the New York Convention and the Model Law.

[502] For an overview, see Park, W.W. (*ibid*) 176 *et seq*; Redfern, Hunter, Blackaby and Partasides (n 12) no 9–03.

other notions to be discovered,[503] the Model Law and the English Arbitration Act 1996 and a leading textbook both use the terms 'setting aside an award' and/or 'challenging an award'.[504] Therefore, these terms will primarily be used hereinafter and in the remaining parts of the present handbook, whereas other general expressions such as 'judicial review' or 'recourse' are not necessarily excluded. As to the substance of the reasons for challenging an award, it should be noted that, at least in international arbitration, there is a tendency to concentrate the grounds for such a challenge in the relevant provisions of the law on arbitration, thereby eliminating other 'ordinary' means of recourse which are applicable for decisions of a state court.[505]

1.152 From a comparative point of view, there is the almost universally shared conviction that any judicial process which is carried out in the territory of a state, requires the possibility for the parties to refer the ensuing decision to a court of law for some basic control. In England, a country devoted to the constitutional principle of 'no man above the law', this necessity has been expressed as follows: 'no-one below the highest tribunals should have unreviewable legal powers over others'.[506] The counterpart to this starting point is the general observation derived from the contractual nature of arbitration, that any review of a 'binding award' is a deviation from the will of the parties.[507] Therefore, in order to balance the state's interest to guarantee the safeguard of basic principles of justice on the one hand, and the private interest of at least one party to enforce the result of a freely chosen private means of dispute settlement on the other hand, the catalogue of grounds for setting aside an award must be limited.[508] On the level of the enforcement of foreign arbitral awards, this has been recognized by many states who have accepted the limited grounds for refusing an application for enforcement as laid down in the New York Convention. More recently, the Model Law, by almost literally copying those grounds for the purpose of invoking them at the stage of setting aside an award, has confirmed that wish of limited judicial review of arbitral awards.[509]

1.153 The finality of awards and the judicial self-restraint at the stage of a possible challenge of an award require necessarily that there is no *révision au fond* of the award by the state court. This, one may say, 'goes without saying', especially in international arbitration[510], and the

[503] W.W. Park lists also words as 'appeal' from an award or 'nullification', 'annulment' or 'vacation' of an award.

[504] ss 67 and 68, Arbitration Act 1996. Redfern, Hunter, Blackaby and Partasides (n 12) no 9–03.

[505] This is the aim of the Model Law, which expressly provides in Art 5 that 'in matters governed by this Law, no court shall intervene except where so provided in this Law'. See for similar wording, s 1026 of the ZPO and for more details, ch 14, commentary on Arts 5 and 34 of the Model Law. Also in France, other ordinary means of recourse have been abolished for international arbitral proceedings, see Fouchard, Gaillard, Goldman (n 30) 930 no 1,596.

[506] Park, W.W. 185.

[507] *ibid*, 195.

[508] This is almost universally recognized, see eg Redfern, Hunter, Blackaby and Partasides (n 12) no 9–06 and Park, W.W. 183. The limitating character of the respective provision in French law has been pointed out by French case law, see Fouchard, Gaillard, Goldman (n 30) 936 no 1,603 with further references.

[509] For further details, see ch 14.

[510] See eg Fouchard, Gaillard, Goldman (n 30) 930 no 1,597, 936 no 1,603; Cour de Cassation, *Rev arb* 1,994, 683; Van Den Berg, A.J. in Lew (ed), *Arbitration Insights: 20 years of the annual lecture of the School of International Arbitration* (2007) 7–14.

principle is recognized in all major jurisdictions with a considerable tradition as home jurisdiction of international arbitration. There are, however, countries where a factual possibility of a *révision au fond* was abolished only two decades ago (as is the case in Switzerland),[511] or where there is still a risk of the court examining the entire case by itself, even if formally it is only looking at a specific point of law (as is the case in England).[512] Nevertheless, generally, a 'wrong decision', be it by an erroneous application of the law to the facts, or by a wrong appreciation of the evidence, is never a reason to challenge an award.[513] On the other hand, in order to decide the ground on which a challenge has been based, the court is not limited to examining the factual or legal background of such a ground.[514] This does not, of course, amount to a general or complete *révision au fond.*

(3.2) The particularities of judicial review in international arbitration In accordance with the recognition of international arbitration as a phenomenon which is to be distinguished from purely domestic arbitration, there are, in principle, two possibilities for the legislator: Either, a different, more liberal regime for setting-aside procedures is established for awards rendered in an international arbitration, or, the parties are granted an option to exclude the normal grounds for judicial review before or after the rendering of the award. **1.154**

The liberal tendency of limiting the grounds for setting aside in international arbitration is based on the fact that generally, international arbitration proceedings mostly take place in a third or neutral jurisdiction.[515] There are accordingly no connecting factors between the arbitral proceedings and the state where the seat or place of the arbitration is located. This applies all the more if the seat of the arbitration has been fixed by an arbitral institution and not the parties themselves.[516] Based on that minimal or non-existing link, there is mostly no interest of such state to closely control the private adjudication carried out in its territory.[517] Finally, it is not suitable to perceive (international) arbitration as part of the domestic judicial system and to consider the arbitral tribunal as an inferior tribunal which has to be controlled by a higher instance.[518] All those are reasons why certain aspects which **1.155**

---

[511] The 'Willkürbeschwerde' of the Concordat, based on the allegation that the findings of the award were 'arbitrary', has been abandoned in the international context by the SPILA of 1987.

[512] See on the doctrine of manifest disregard of the law in the US, Smit, H., 'The time is ripe for the US Supreme Court to bury the misconceived doctrine of manifest disregard of the law' (2005) *Am Rev Int'l Arb* no 16, 211; Smit, H., 'Another judicial misstep in correcting an arbitral award' (2001), *Am Rev Int. Arb* no 12, 435.

[513] See eg Fouchard, Gaillard, Goldman (n 30) 937 no 1,603. For a German decision, see in this context Hanseatisches Oberlandesgericht Hamburg, 12 March 1998 (unreported), discussed by Trappe, J. (1998) 15 *J Int'l Arb* no 3, 93, 95.

[514] Fouchard, Gaillard, Goldman (n 30) 939 no 1,605; see also Cour de Cassation, *Rev arb* 1987, 469, and the Swiss Federal Tribunal in the matter *Westinghouse*, ASA Bull 1994, 244, 246. See generally, and especially on the Swiss case law, Karrer, P. and Kälin-Nauer, C. (1996) 13 *J Int'l Arb* no 3, 31.

[515] For an assessment of the motives of the legislator to limit the grounds for setting aside an award, see Van Den Berg, A.J. 7–46 *et seq.*

[516] Park, W.W. 190 *et seq.* Generally, on the liberal tendency in international arbitration, see Schlosser, P. (n 13) no 755.

[517] Park, W.W. 191: 'There is no national to protect; there is no national interest to protect; there may be little domestic law that the arbitral panel can be accused of having misunderstood or misapplied. All that is left is the most abstract of sovereign interests—a pure concern of the government for what happens on its sovereign territory.'

[518] *ibid*, 185.

have weight in purely domestic arbitration, such as form requirements, do not play a role in international arbitration.[519]

1.156 These arguments have induced courts and legal experts in the field of arbitration to propose the delocalization of international arbitration. This trend was furthered by the well known French decisions in *Götaverken* and *Norsolor*,[520] and was, subsequently, for a considerable time an important focus of the international arbitration community.[521] Today—to cut a long story short—the majority view of legal writers, courts and national legislators appears to have returned to the conservative approach which was the general opinion of the old days: there are several reasons why an arbitration, even when it is 'international', should be based in a certain jurisdiction, ie the 'home jurisdiction' of the arbitral proceedings. One of those reasons is the simple finding that without such 'residual jurisdiction', the party who wants to oppose the award for certain legal reasons (eg for serious procedural defects), will have to invoke these reasons wherever the winning party chooses to enforce the award.[522] That deficiency has also been recognized by some national legislators who first abolished any recourse to the national courts, and later corrected that law by reintroducing such means of recourse to its courts.[523]

1.157 As to the statutory provisions regulating the judicial review in international arbitration, the different solutions depend mostly on the specific traditions of each country.

1.158 (i) In England, a monistic approach has been preserved and is still the basis of the Arbitration Act 1996, ie for international arbitration, there is no entire particular statutory regime parallel to the provisions on domestic arbitration.[524] Rather, the approach chosen for the first time in the 1979 Act was that the parties could exclude a challenge of an award in international arbitral proceedings as long as certain conditions were fulfilled.[525] The Arbitration Act 1996 distinguishes appeals for procedural reasons[526] from appeals on a question of law: whereas the former means of recourse are mandatory, the parties may exclude any appeal on a question of law without further

[519] See eg Fouchard, Gaillard, Goldman (n 30), 937 no 1,604.

[520] *Götaverken, Rev arb* (1980) 524; *Norsolor, Rev arb* (1981) 306. Both decisions held that the rendering of the award in France was not sufficient for applying French arbitration law in order to challenge the award, see Fouchard, Gaillard, Goldman (n 30) 920 no 1,590.

[521] See eg Paulsson, J., 'Arbitration Unbound: Award Detached from the Law of its Country of Origin' (1981) 30 *ICLQ*, 358; Mayer, P. in M. Hunter, A. Marriott, V.V. Veeder, *The Internationalisation of International Arbitration,* 37 *et seq* with further references.

[522] For such criticism of the delocalization theory, see Mann, F.A., 'Zur Nationalität des Schiedsspruchs' in FS Oppenhoff (Munich, 1985) 215; Böckstiegel, K.H. 1, 10; Mayer, P. (n 521) 45; Schlosser, P. (n 13) no 755.

[523] For the respective legislation in Belgium, see Verbist, H. *RPS*, Beilage 9 zu Betriebsberater (BB) 1998, 4 *et seq*.

[524] In the original bill for the new arbitration act, some separate provisions for domestic arbitration had been introduced but were, 'in the last minute', not brought into force for reasons of European Community law; see the 1997 DAC Supplementary Report on the English Arbitration Act, (1997) 13 *Arb Int'l* no 3, 317, 326 nos 47 *et seq*.

[525] The so-called exclusion agreements were only possible without limitation if they were entered into after the dispute had arisen or if the law to be applied to the substance of the arbitration was not English law; in all the remaining cases, exclusion agreements were not admissible in admiralty, insurance and commodity disputes, see s 4(1), Arbitration Act 1979.

[526] See s 67 (lacking jurisdiction of the arbitral tribunal) and s 68 (serious irregularity) Arbitration Act 1996.

conditions.[527] These exclusion agreements are, however, no particularity of international arbitration since they are also available in purely domestic cases.

(ii) In France, the *Cour de Cassation* introduced a separate regime for judicial review of awards in international arbitration in 1980.[528] Thus, any means of recourse was in fact excluded in arbitral proceedings if the procedural law applied by the arbitral tribunal was foreign or international, ie a law other than French law. This procedural criterion was, of course, open to criticism,[529] and the French legislator by the decree of 1981 (introducing the new Arts 1492 *et seq*, NCPC) showed its intention to apply a different regime for challenging international arbitral awards.[530] In addition, the traditional distinction between *ordre public interne* and *ordre public international* results in a less strict control of international arbitration in France.[531] **1.159**

(iii) In Switzerland, the reform of 1987 introduced a separate legal regime for international arbitration by inserting a respective chapter in the Private International Law Act (SPILA) which entered into force in 1989.[532] For any international arbitration which is governed by the Act, there is now a modern system of law which eg no longer enables a party to attack an award alleging that its findings are 'arbitrary'.[533] In addition, the parties may exclude any appeal against the award by an express agreement to that effect (Art 192, SPILA).[534] The requirements for such an 'express' exclusion agreement are, however, quite strict.[535] **1.160**

(iv) The German approach, as opposed to the Swiss one, is different in as much as it neither provides for a separate regime for international arbitration, nor enables the parties to exclude any challenge of the award. The 10th book of the ZPO incorporates the UNCITRAL Model Law without restricting its application to international arbitration.[536] In addition, no need was seen to deviate from the Model Law by **1.161**

---

[527] s 69(1), Arbitration Act 1996. See Triebel, V. and Plaßmeier, H. *RPS*, Beilage 13 (1997), 2 *et seq*, 12 *et seq*; Weigand, F.-B., *Recht der Internationalen Wirtschaft* (*RIW*) 1997, 904, 909 *et seq*.

[528] For the decisions in *Götaverken* and *Norsolor*, see paras 1.31 and 1.156 and Park, W.W. 199; Van Den Berg, A.J. 7–35 *et seq*.

[529] See eg Fouchard, Gaillard, Goldman (n 30) 919 *et seq* nos. 1589 *et seq*; Mayer, P. (n 521) 44.

[530] The grounds for setting aside international awards as listed in Art 1502 are different from those applicable in domestic arbitration (Art 1484, 1491 NCPC); for details, see Fouchard, Gaillard, Goldman (n 30) 918 nos 1,586 *et seq*.

[531] See Fouchard, Gaillard, Goldman (n 30) 968 no 1,647. For the distinction in the present law, see Art 1484 for domestic and Art 1502 for international arbitration.

[532] See ch 12. For further details on the Swiss Law, see Geisinger, E. and Frossard, V. in Kaufmann-Kohler (ed), *International Arbitration in Switzerland*, (2004) 136 *et seq* (ch 8) and Bernet, M. and Müller, A.K. in Kaufmann-Kohler (ed), *International Arbitration in Switzerland* (2004) 167 *et seq* (ch 9).

[533] On the 'Willkürbeschwerde', see eg Park, W.W. 207; Blessing, M. (n 112) 1, 69.

[534] Blessing, M. (n 112) 1, 75; Fouchard, Gaillard, Goldman (n 30) 927 no 1,594. For details, see Karrer, P., Schütze, R.A. (n 29) (1999), 338, 341 *et seq*; Van Den Berg, A.J. 7–28 *et seq*; Newman 474.

[535] The inclusion of the former ICC Rules in the arbitration clause, thereby incorporating the former Art 24 (which dealt with the finality of the award and exclusion of attacks against it), was considered not to be sufficiently express; see Bundesgericht, *Rev arb* (1991) 709; Blessing, M. (n 112) 1, 75.

[536] The reason for that was firstly the difficulty of defining 'international', and, secondly, the opinion that a parallel system for domestic arbitration would be very similar without major deviations from the Model Law, so that no justification for such similar parallel systems was recognized. See Berger, K.P. *The new German Arbitration Law* (n 115) 19 *et seq*.

introducing exclusion agreements which are not provided for in the Model Law itself.[537]

1.162 (v) The Swedish legislator has, as the German one, opted for the monistic approach by enacting one arbitration act both for domestic and international arbitration.[538] However, it also introduced the possibility to exclude or limit the application of the grounds to set an award aside if the parties do not have any contact with Sweden.[539]

1.163 (vi) Finally, most radical was the solution in Belgium which aimed at attracting international arbitration proceedings by generally excluding any appeal against awards if both parties to the arbitration proceedings are non-Belgian.[540] After some years of experience and also as a consequence of serious criticism by experts,[541] the Belgian legislator overruled its former approach and re-introduced challenge procedures for international arbitral proceedings by the recent reform of 1998.[542]

1.164 (3.3) **Scrutiny and challenge of awards** On the international level, there is no convention governing the extent to which a state may exercise its control over arbitral awards.[543] However, there are two important legal instruments which have considerably influenced the various national laws on that subject: The New York Convention of 1958 practically serves as a guarantee for almost world-wide enforcement of arbitral awards.[544] Generally, this unique treaty with more than 140 member states renders any additional research for the national laws of the respective countries superfluous, thereby giving a very high degree of legal certainty. The same is true in light of the fact that the Model Law is the basis in particular of the most recent reforms of national arbitration laws.

1.165 *(3.3.1) The New York Convention and the UNCITRAL Model Law as guidelines* The grounds—for rejecting the enforcement of or for challenging an award—laid down in both instruments reflect a broad consensus on the principal reasons for setting aside (international) arbitral awards. The convergence of modern national systems of law has primarily been based on the internationally successful New York Convention.[545] When the Model Law was drafted, the New York Convention served as a model for the reasons for challenging an award; the intention to have an international harmonization resulted in almost identical catalogues for resisting enforcement of and for the setting aside of awards.[546]

---

537 There was the common aim within the drafting process to streamline the challenging procedures eg by preventing a party from lengthy appeal procedures over many instances, without, however, generally depriving a party of the limited possibilites to challenge the award, as provided for by the Model Law; see Berger, K.P. 30 *et seq*; Van Den Berg, A.J. 7–31.

538 See s 46, Swedish Arbitration Act 1999 (SAA).

539 s 51(1), SAA, applying if none of the parties is domiciled in Sweden.

540 Van Den Berg, A.J. 7–23 *et seq*; Newman 474.

541 See eg Park, W.W. 200 *et seq*.

542 Verbist, H. *RPS*, Beilage 9, Betriebsberater (BB) 1998, 4, 9: Now, the new law allows exclusion agreements for international arbitration, similarly as in Switzerland and Sweden.

543 For a general overview of the grounds for challenge in different national laws, see Liebscher, C. (n 543) 147 *et seq*.

544 Kerr, M. 129 concludes that, due to a success rate of the Convention of about 98%, it is far easier to enforce arbitration awards than judgments.

545 Redfern, Hunter, Blackaby and Partasides (n 12) no 1–120.

546 Schlosser, P. (n 13) no 129; Redfern, Hunter, Blackaby and Partasides (n 12) nos 1–123 *et seq*; see for further details ch 14. Some authors of books on the Model Law even simply refer to commentaries

Today, the catalogue of the Model Law may be considered as the internationally accepted basis for attacking an award.[547] Both the New York Convention and the Model Law provide that an award which has been set aside in the country of its origin, is not enforceable in the Convention or Model Law state.[548] However, the common structure of the respective provisions is not perfect, and some reasons for attacking an award are overlapping.[549]

(3.3.2) Reasons for challenging an award When trying to build significant categories of the reasons for challenging an award, the bases are recent national statutes which partly follow a different pattern (mostly not as to the substantive reasons) from the New York Convention and the Model Law. Whereas the latter both have listed six groups of reasons, national statutes tend to list five or six different categories.[550] From a comparative perspective, and for practical, not dogmatic purposes, one may distinguish the following categories of reasons relating to (i) the jurisdiction of the arbitral tribunal; (ii) the arbitral tribunal itself; (iii) the procedure applied; (iv) the award; and (v) the public interest concerning the entire arbitral process. **1.166**

(i) Defects related to the jurisdiction of the tribunal **1.167**

The jurisdiction or competence of the arbitral tribunal is dependent on an existing and valid arbitration agreement. Therefore, any award may be set aside if it was based on an invalid or void arbitration agreement.[551] This comprises, of course, circumstances where there was no existing arbitration agreement at all[552] or, although there was one at some point in time, it had expired, thereby depriving the arbitrators of any jurisdiction.[553] Generally, a party must have raised the lack of jurisdiction in time during the proceedings in order not to be prevented to raise it later for setting the award aside.[554] A particular case of invalidity of the arbitration agreement is a situation where there was some incapacity or lack of personal arbitrability which, as well, prevented any arbitral agreement from becoming valid.[555]

---

on the New York Convention when dealing with the reasons for challenging awards, see Hußlein-Stich, G (n 359) 177.

547 Holtzmann, H. and Neuhaus, J. (n 361) 911 *et seq.*

548 See Art V(1)(e) New York Convention and Art 36(1)(a)(v) Model Law.

549 See eg Schütze, R.A. (n 29) nos 306 *et seq.*

550 See eg Switzerland (Art 192, SPILA: five categories), Austria (s 595, öZPO: six categories), France (Art 1502, NCPC: five categories), Germany (s 1059, ZPO: six categories). See also Redfern, Hunter, Blackaby and Partasides (n 12) nos 9–20 to 9–31 (six groups of reasons); Schütze, R.A. (n 29) nos 306 *et seq* (six groups). Generally, for more details on the grounds for challenge, see Van Den Berg, A.J. 7–12; Poudret, J.-F. and Besson, S., *Comparative Law of International Arbitration* (n 6) 785 *et seq*; Liebscher, C. (n 543) 152 *et seq.*

551 Art V(1)(a), New York Convention; Art 34(2)(a)(i), Model Law; Austria: s 595(1) no1, öZPO; England: ss 67(1)(a) and 30(1)(a), Arbitration Act 1996; France: Art 1502 no1, NCPC; Germany: s 1059(2) Nr 1 (a); Italy: Art 829, (1) RCP; Netherlands: Art 1065(1)(a), WBR; Sweden: s 34(1) no 1, SAA; Switzerland: Art 190(2)(b), SPILA. See also Poudret, J.-F. and Besson, S., *Comparative Law of International Arbitration* (n 6) 792 *et seq.*

552 This is expressly mentioned in Art 1502 no1, NCPC, but is, of course, also covered by the wording of the other national laws.

553 For an express wording to this effect, see the French Art 1502 no 1, NCPC and in Sweden s 34(1) No, 2 SAA.

554 See eg Art 16(2), Model Law and the respective commentary in ch 14.

555 The New York Convention and the Model Law mention incapacity expressly, although, strictly speaking, this is only a sub-alternative of a void or invalid arbitration agreement, see Schütze, R.A. (n 29) no 306

1.168 (ii) Defects related to the arbitral tribunal

Most jurisdictions provide for a possibility to challenge the award if the composition or constitution of the arbitral tribunal was not in accordance with the law or the parties' agreement.[556] Sometimes as a particular defect the situation is listed where one or more arbitrators do not fulfil the qualification required by law or party agreement.[557] It is interesting to note that the lack of impartiality or independence of an arbitrator is generally not expressly mentioned as a reason for setting aside an award.[558] There is a common tendency, supported by the Model Law, to urge any party to bring forward reasons for challenging an arbitrator as early as possible during the arbitral proceedings.[559] Thus, the arbitrators are mostly required to reveal any ground which might cause doubt as to their impartiality,[560] and the parties have to come forward with a motion to remove an arbitrator within a certain time limit. If, after an unsuccessful challenge before the tribunal, a party fails to appeal to the competent court within the given time limit, it is afterwards precluded from invoking those grounds against the award itself.[561] Thus, there is only one opportunity to challenge an arbitrator before a state court.[562]

1.169 (iii) Defects related to the procedure

The New York Convention and the Model Law establish as a reason for challenging the award that the losing party was not given proper notice of the institution of arbitral proceedings and, especially of the appointment of an arbitrator, or that the defendant for another reason was not able to present his case.[563] This principle of due process is generally established in the national laws at the stage of describing the duties of the tribunal and as part of the reasons to set an award aside.[564] In most countries, it is more or less generally worded,[565] in others it is acknowledged as part of the *ordre public*. In addition, some countries allow a challenge of an award if the procedure as agreed by

with further references. The Swiss legislator uses a broader wording which covers several alternatives of lack of jurisdiction—see Art 190(2)(b), SPILA: 'if the tribunal wrongfully assumed or declined jurisdiction'.

556 Art V(1)(d), New York Convention; Art 34(2)(a)(iv), Model Law; Austria: s 595(1) no3, öZPO; England: ss 67(1)(a) and s 30(1)(b), Arbitration Act 1996; France: Art 1502 no 2, NCPC; Germany: s 1059(2) no 1 (d), ZPO; Italy: Art 829, RCP; Netherlands: Art 1065(1)(b), WBR; Sweden: s 34(1) no 4, SAA;. Switzerland: Art 190(2)(a), SPILA. See also Poudret, J.-F. and Besson, S., *Comparative Law of International Arbitration* (n 6) 790 *et seq*.

557 See Italy: Art 829(3), 812, RCP.

558 The USA expressly include 'evident partiality or corruption' on the side of an arbitrator in the reasons for attacking an award, see § 10(b), US Arbitration Act. In Sweden, the law is similar, see s 34 (1) no 5, SAA.

559 Schlosser, P. (n 13) nos 532 *et seq*. See Art 12(2) and 13(3), Model Law.

560 See eg Art 12(1), Model Law; s 1036(1), ZPO.

561 Art 13(2) and (3), Model Law; ss 1037(2) and (3), 1065(1), 1062(1), ZPO. See also ch14.

562 The decision of the court is, according to the Model Law and in countries following this pattern, not subject to appeal; see preceding footnote.

563 Art V(1)(b), NY Convention; Art 34(2)(a)(ii), Model Law. See in general Poudret, J.-F. and Besson, S., *Comparative Law of International Arbitration* (n 6) 797 *et seq*; Liebscher, C. (n 543) 243 *et seq*.

564 In England, for example, the Arbitration Act 1996 refers in the section on the challenge of awards (s 68(2)(a)) to the duty of the tribunal of 'giving each party a reasonable opportunity of putting his case and dealing with that of his opponent'; see s 33(1)(a).

565 As in Austria (s 595(1) no 2, öZPO: 'das rechtliche Gehör nicht gewährt wurde'), France (Art 1502 no 4, NCPC: 'principe de la contradiction' not followed) and Switzerland (Art 190(2)(d), SPILA : 'wenn der Grundsatz der Gleichbehandlung der Parteien oder der Grundsatz des rechtlichen Gehörs verletzt wurde.').

the parties or laid down by the law has not been followed by the arbitral tribunal.[566] In modern statutes, however, those grounds are precluded if they have not been brought forward in time during the arbitral proceedings.[567]

(iv) Defects related to the award **1.170**

The contents of the award itself may be the basis for setting-aside procedures. The national legislator may either generally criticize that the arbitrators did not comply with their mandate[568] or more specifically blame the award if it decides issues not submitted to the tribunal *(ultra petita)*[569] or fails to decide matters that have been submitted for determination *(infra petita)*.[570] Some legislators name, as another reason, that formal requirements of the award have not been met[571] or the award is ambiguous or contradictory.[572] A particular reason for a challenge is included in the English Arbitration Act where, in special circumstances, the wrong application of the law may be the basis for setting the award aside.[573]

(v) Defects related to the public interest **1.171**

Both the Convention and the Model Law[574] and practically all jurisdictions[575] provide that an award may be set aside if the *ordre public* has been violated, either by the contents of the award and/or the manner in which it was rendered.[576] According to a modern trend, the standard is the *ordre public international*, ie a body of basic legal principles or requirements the content and scope of which is less strict than the purely domestic *ordre public*.[577] As a sub-category of the *ordre public*, the lack of objective

566 England: s 69(2)(c), Arbitration Act 1996; Italy: Art 829 (7), 816 RCP; Germany: s 1059(2) no 1 (d), ZPO. See also Art V (1)(d) New York Convention and Art 34(2)(a)(iv), Model Law. See also *supra* at h) bb) (1) [lack of jurisdiction].

567 See eg Art 4, Model Law and s 1027, ZPO. Sweden lists 'an irregularity in the course of the proceedings…' as a reason for challenging the award, see s 34(1) no 6, SAA.

568 France: Art 1502 no3, NCPC; Netherlands: Art 1065(1)(c), WBR.

569 Art V(1)(c), New York Convention; Art 34(2)(a)(iii), Model Law; Austria: s 595(1) no 5, öZPO; England: ss 67(1)(a) and 30(1)(c), Arbitration Act 1996; Germany: s 1059(2) no 1(c), ZPO; Netherlands: Art 1065(5), WBR; Sweden: s 34(1) no 2, SAA; Switzerland: Art 190(2)(c), SPILA. See generally, Schlosser, P. (n 13) no 860; Liebscher, C. (n 543) 305 *et seq*.

570 England: s 68(2)(d), Arbitration Act 1996; Sweden: s 36(1), SAA (no challenge, only amendment of award); Switzerland: Art 190(2)(c), SPILA. See in general Poudret, J.-F. and Besson, S., *Comparative Law of International Arbitration* (n 6) 812 *et seq*.

571 England: s 68(2)(h), Arbitration Act 1996; Netherlands: Art 1065(1)(d), WBR; Sweden: s 33 no 3, SAA.

572 England: s 68(2)(f), Arbitration Act 1996; Italy: Art 829(4), RCP.

573 s 69, Arbitration Act 1996 allows an appeal on a point of law if the decision of the tribunal is 'obviously wrong' and if further requirements have been met; for details, see ch 5.

574 Art V(2)(b), New York Convention; Art 34(2)(b)(ii), Model Law. For the contents of the *ordre public*, see ch 14.

575 See eg Liebscher, C. (n 543) 310 *et seq*.

576 Austria: s 595 (1) no 6, öZPO; England: s 68(2)(g), Arbitration Act 1996; France: Art 1502 no 5, NCPC; Germany: s 1059(2) no 2 (b), ZPO; Netherlands: Art 1065(1)(e), WBR; Sweden: s 33 no 2, SAA; Switzerland: Art 190(2)(e), SPILA. See eg Poudret, J.-F. and Besson, S., *Comparative Law of International Arbitration* (n 6) 816 *et seq*; Smit, H., 'Comments on Public Policy in International Arbitration' (2002) *Am Rev Int'l Arb* no 13, 65 stressing that international public policy, not local public policy should provide the applicable standard.

577 See eg explicitly Art 1502 no 5 NCPC; for Switzerland, Blessing, M. (n 112) 1, 70. See generally, Schlosser, P. (n 13) no 868; Smit, H. (2002) *Am Rev Int'l Arb* no 13, 65.

arbitrability of the subject matter of the arbitration is sometimes specifically listed as a ground for challenging the award.[578]

III. Rules governing the arbitral proceedings

A. The procedure according to chosen rules

(1) Party autonomy

1.172 It has been suggested that 'international commercial arbitration is the expression of a free world'.[579] Especially since the promulgation of the UNCITRAL Model Law, there is a world-wide trend towards modernization and liberalization of arbitration laws.[580] Based on the contractual origins of arbitration, party autonomy, therefore, has become the central focus or *Leitmaxime* (guiding principle) of modern legislators and drafters of institutional rules.[581] Party autonomy is universally recognized as a basic feature of arbitration.[582] Consequently, the intention of the parties is paramount,[583] based on their freedom to choose the seat of the arbitration, the *lex arbitri* and the applicable substantive law. This party autonomy has been addressed as the 'prerequisite to the development of harmonized procedures based on the best of a diverse range of approaches'.[584]

1.173 In practice, the parties tend to make at least two choices, ie they determine the applicable procedural and the substantive law of the arbitration.

1.174 As to the procedural rules, the parties may choose: (i) the place of the arbitration and thereby, if no other rules are agreed, the national applicable procedural law or, at least, its mandatory provisions; (ii) a national procedural law other than that of the place of arbitration—a possibility which is not granted by all jurisdictions;[585] (iii) institutional or *ad hoc* arbitration rules; (iv) specific, tailor-made rules as agreed either in the arbitration agreement or at a later stage.

1.175 As to the substantive rules, the parties may determine the application of: (i) a specific national law, either in its entirety—as usually—or only parts of it;[586] (ii) the *lex mercatoria*,

---

[578] Art V(2)(a), NY Convention; Art 34(2)(b)(i), Model Law; Germany: s 1059(2) no 2(a), ZPO; Sweden: s 33 no 1, SAA. For further details on arbitrability, see eg Liebscher, C. (n 543) 168 *et seq.*

[579] Plantey, A. (1994) 5 *ICC Bull* no1, 3, 18.

[580] Derains, Y. and Schwartz, E.A. (n 58) 200. See also Sanders, P., 'Unity and Diversity in the Adoption of the Model Law' (1995) 11 *Arb Int'l* no1, 1.

[581] Redfern, Hunter, Blackaby and Partasides (n 12) 6–01 *et seq*; Lalive, Poudret and Reymond (n 119) 257; DAC Report 1996, no 19, 279 *et seq*; Berger, K.P., *Recht der Internationalen Wirtschaft* (*RIW*) 1994, 12, 14 ('Leitmaxime'); Trappe, J. (1998) 15 *J Int'l Arb* no 3, 93, 98. See also, as to procedural autonomy, ch 14.

[582] According to Trappe, (1998) 15 *J Int'l Arb* no 3, 93, 98, the freedom of the parties to agree on the arbitration procedure (Art 19(1), Model Law) is the most important provision of the Model Law. On party autonomy and its limits in general, see Redfern, Hunter 6–03 *et seq.*

[583] See eg Schlosser, P. (n 13) no 229 *et seq*; Rubino-Sammartano, M. (n 44) 34.

[584] Cremades, B.M. (n 143) 158.

[585] In Germany, for example, the law does not allow the choice of a foreign procedural law in its entirety but only subject to the mandatory norms of German law; see Berger, K.P., *The New German Arbitration Law* (n 115) 17.

[586] The German law, in accordance with the Model Law, gives the possibility to choose the applicable 'rules of law', thereby enabling the parties to determine the application of rules of various jurisdictions; see

a body of internationally recognized and often applied legal principles; although most of the national and institutional arbitration rules today acknowledge the respective choice of the parties, the justification and contents of *lex mercatoria* are still debated;[587] scientific comparative research has enabled the practitioner to refer to a specific set of rules as the UNIDROIT Principles, the Principles of European Contract Law or the CENTRAL List of Principles, Rules and Standards of the *Lex Mercatoria*;[588] (iii) principles of equity (*amiable composition, ex aequo et bono*) which are specifically addressed in many national and institutional rules.[589]

Already by agreeing on the place of the arbitration the parties make—at least to some extent—a choice with regard to the mandatory procedural law to be applied.[590] However, the most important decision of the parties when drafting the arbitration agreement is whether the arbitration shall be institutional or *ad hoc*.[591] **1.176**

(2) Ad hoc arbitration

(2.1) **Institutional or *ad hoc* arbitration** As may easily be acknowledged, a mere reference to pre-fabricated rules is much easier and convenient than to set up those rules explicitly. This applies to arbitration clauses which mostly are discussed at the end of long and difficult commercial negotiations.[592] The opposite of institutional or administrated arbitration is a so-called *ad hoc* arbitration. In its purest form, in this kind of arbitration all procedural rules and details have to be regulated by the parties either in the arbitration clause itself or at a later stage. However, there are also pre-formulated rules as the UNCITRAL Arbitration Rules which may be incorporated by reference, without thereby automatically agreeing on any administrative body. **1.177**

(2.2) ***Ad hoc* arbitration rules** The advantages of this type of arbitration are quite evident: the parties have the opportunity to dress up a tailor-made procedure that fits to the particular contract and business relationship.[593] Furthermore, there are procedural rules like the UNCITRAL Arbitration Rules which help to overcome the difficulty that otherwise, all the different procedural issues have to be specifically regulated by the parties themselves.[594] However, there are several disadvantages to take into account. The full effectiveness **1.178**

Berger, K.P., *The New German Arbitration Law* (n 115) 21; and s 1051(1), ZPO; Art 28(1), Model Law. For this possibility of 'dépecage', which is also to be found in Art 17 (1) ICC Rules 1998, see Derains, Y. and Schwartz, E.A. (n 58) 217 *et seq*.

[587] For critical voices, see Park, W.W. (n 112) 73 *et seq*; Schlosser, P. (n 13) 197 *et seq*. Adamant proponents of *lex mercatoria* are Fouchard, P., *L'arbitrage commercial international* (1965); Gaillard, E. in Fouchard, Gaillard, Goldman (n 30) 814 *et seq*, nos 1,444 *et seq* with extensive further references; Berger, K.P., *The Creeping Codification of the Lex Mercatoria* (Kluwer, 1998).

[588] For details, see CENTRAL (Center for Transnational Law) (ed), *Transnational Law in Commercial Legal Practice, CENTRAL Practice and Study Guide*, vol. 1 (1999), with contributions by Bonell (UNIDROIT Principles), O. Lando (Principles of European Contract Law), and K.P. Berger (CENTRAL Principles).

[589] See eg Art 187(2), SPILA; s 1051(3), ZPO; Art 17(3), ICC Rules; Art 16(2), Vienna Rules; Art 28(3), ICDR Rules.

[590] For the importance of the place of arbitration, see III. B. (1).

[591] See eg Poudret, J.-F. and Besson, S., *Comparative Law of International Arbitration* (n 6) no 93 *et seq*.

[592] This is eg pointed out by Schlosser, P. (n 13) no 162.

[593] Redfern, Hunter, Blackaby and Partasides (n 12) 1–83; Park, W.W. (n 112) 70.

[594] See eg Redfern, Hunter, Blackaby and Partasides (n 12) 1–83.

of *ad hoc* arbitration depends on the cooperation by the parties and their lawyers and an adequate judicial system at the place of arbitration to support the arbitration if necessary.[595] There are plenty of opportunities for a party to use delaying or obstructive tactics, be it at the stage of appointing the arbitral tribunal or at any later stage. Here, the 'lack of institutional oversight'[596] may be seriously regretted by the other side. Finally, the enforcement of an award obtained by default might be more difficult in the case of an *ad hoc* arbitration than in a case of an institutional arbitration since in the latter instance, the competent court will more easily acknowledge that the other party's procedural rights have been safeguarded by the respective institutional rules.[597]

1.179 The UNCITRAL Arbitration Rules are the consequence of an initiative of third world nations which wanted to escape the factual obligation to accept arbitration in Europe or the United States according to well established pro-western procedural rules.[598] Therefore, after extensive preparation by experts, in 1976 UNCITRAL agreed on a new set of rules which were formally adopted by the UN General Assembly and recommended for worldwide use.[599] The Rules had great influence on subsequent national reforms.[600] The comprehensive and detailed rules regulate generally all the major steps of arbitral proceedings from the appointment of arbitrators to the taking of evidence and the correction or interpretation of an award. The Rules were, at the time of its formal approval by the UN the most modern rules for arbitration.[601] The main feature is that an Appointing Authority may, in place of the party or parties, help to constitute the arbitral tribunal since there is no organization or institution available to undertake this task. If the parties have agreed on such an Appointing Authority, it may be approached for completing the appointing procedure or replacing challenged arbitrators.[602] In the absence of such choice by the parties, the Secretary-General of the Permanent Court of Arbitration in The Hague will act as Appointing Authority. The wide acceptance of the UNCITRAL Arbitration Rules is also a result of a balanced mixture of civil and common law elements, especially at the stage of taking evidence.[603] Generally, the Rules are nowadays quite often used because they are apparently quite attractive for parties from different legal cultures.[604]

(3) Institutional arbitration

1.180 Institutional arbitration is nowadays often chosen by commercial parties. The advantages of this kind of arbitration are evident: the automatic incorporation of a comprehensive set of procedural rules is the principal advantage of institutional arbitration. Those rules provide for a regulation of most of the conceivable situations and especially those critical

595 Redfern, Hunter, Blackaby and Partasides (n 12)1–81.

596 Park, W.W. (n 112) 70.

597 *ibid*,(n 112) points at this advantage of an award 'bearing the imprimatur' of an institution like the ICC or the AAA.

598 Schlosser, P. (n 13) no 182.

599 *ibid*, *et seq*; Lionnet, K. and Lionnet, A. (n 29) 534 *et seq*.

600 See Lionnet, K. and Lionnet, A. (n 29) 534 *et seq*.

601 *ibid* (n 29) 534–5; Schlosser, P. (n 13) no 185 *et seq*.

602 Practically all international arbitration institutions have accepted that task; see Lionnet, K. and Lionnet, A. (n 29) 209.

603 Schlosser, P. (n 13) no 184.

604 Lionnet, K. and Lionnet, A. (n 29) 534 *et seq*; Wetter, G. (1995) *Arb Int'l* 117, 122.

instances where either at the outset or at a later stage one party (mostly the defendant) tries to boycott or obstruct the proceedings by not cooperating as required.[605] The respective rules are normally administered by trained staff of the institution concerned which helps to run the proceedings as smoothly as possible, thereby enabling the parties to concentrate on the substantive issues of the case. The existence of standard clauses which are recommended by all of the leading arbitral institutions are an additional factor which makes it convenient to choose institutional arbitration. This aspect and the fact that institutions like the International Chamber of Commerce are well known world-wide, makes it easier to convince the other party or the manager in charge that arbitration is not more uncertain than litigation.[606] This aspect of predictability is of high importance, and it may also be the reason why institutional arbitration appeals in particular to parties of different nationality.[607] It may, therefore, be easily understood why company lawyers tend to favour arbitration before a generally known and respected arbitral institution.[608]

There are, of course, also disadvantages of institutional arbitration. It may be quite expensive since the administrative costs and the arbitrators' fees are calculated on the basis of the amount in dispute so that especially in cases dealing with large sums of compensation etc, the procedural costs are a major discouraging factor.[609] In addition, there may be delays caused by the 'bureaucratic machinery' which is critically noted, in particular, by English practitioners.[610] Further, at least for some authors, the increasing 'processualization' or 'legalization' of arbitration, which is of course mainly due to heavily regulated institutional proceedings, is a matter of concern:[611] for those authors, the flexibility and the conciliatory or the peaceful character of arbitration, are thereby seriously endangered. **1.181**

Some of the most important institutional arbitration rules will be outlined in the following paragraphs. **1.182**

(3.1) The ICC Rules of Arbitration (ICC Rules) The International Chamber of Commerce is probably the best known international institution for the regulation of various areas of international commerce. The International Court of Arbitration, a subdivision of the ICC, has been administering international arbitration proceedings for many decades, and its rules reach back to 1923. The latest version entered into force in 1998.[612] **1.183**

---

605 Redfern, Hunter, Blackaby and Partasides (n 12) 1–80; Park, W.W. (n 112) 69. A Plantey, a former chairman of the International Court of Arbitration of the ICC, summarized this advantage as follows (see (1994) 5 *ICC Bull* no 1, 3, 19): The ICC . . . 'offers the greatest possible freedom to the parties, whilst providing them with fundamental guarantees that they will have a "judge" and that if necessary they will be able to circumvent those obstructive and delaying tactics which are a major risk of non-institutional arbitration'.

606 Najar, J.C. (1996) 12 *Arb Int'l* no 3, 359, 364.

607 Najar, J.C. (1996) 12 *Arb Int'l* no 3, 359 mentions the fact that, at least in former times, eg Russians preferred the Stockholm Chamber of Commerce Rules since they were well known and often used in East-West arbitrations.

608 Robine, E. (1992) 8 *Arb Int'l* 31, 39 *et seq*; Najar, J.C. (1996) 12 *Arb Int'l* Nr 3, 363.

609 See eg Redfern, Hunter, Blackaby and Partasides (n 12)1–81.

610 See as one example, Redfern, Hunter, Blackaby and Partasides (n 12) 1–81.

611 See Lalive, P. in M. Hunter, A. Marriott, V.V. Veeder, *Internationalisation of International Arbitration*, 49, 54.

612 See Derains, Y. and Schwartz, E.A., *A Guide to the New ICC Rules of Arbitration* (1998); Kreindler, R., 'Aktuelle (Streit-)Fragen bei der Anwendung der ICC-Schiedsgerichtsordnung 1998—Praxisüberblick', *Recht der Internationalen Wirtschaft* (*RIW*) (2002) 249; Weigand, F.-B., 'Die neue ICC Schiedsgerichtsordnung

The ICC Rules are probably the most often used institutional arbitration rules in the context of international business transactions.[613] There are at least two significant features of ICC arbitration: the existence of the International Court of Arbitration with its supervisory role and the obligatory setting up of Terms of Reference at the outset of the arbitration proceedings.[614] Both elements have been criticized for many years,[615] but were maintained within the last revision since it was felt that the disadvantages of those features are clearly outweighed by their advantages.[616] The workload of the International Court of Arbitration has steadily increased over the last decades. Whereas in 2002 590 requests for arbitration have been filed with the ICC, the respective number has increased to 599 in 2007 and to 663 in 2008.[617] In some countries like eg Switzerland, ICC cases are on the top of the yearly statistics on international arbitration proceedings.[618]

1.184 (3.2) **The Arbitration Rules of the London Court of International Arbitration (LCIA Rules)** The London Court of International Arbitration is probably the longest-established of all the major international arbitration institutions.[619] Its origins reach back to the last decade of the 19th century,[620] and the institution is today connected with the Chartered Institute of Arbitrators. The LCIA administers arbitrations world-wide under its rules in any venue under any system of law. Now, there are 46 Users Councils for Europe, North America, Latin-America and Caribbean, Arabia, Asia-Pacific and Africa. The main features of the LCIA are the appointment of arbitrators and the administration of arbitral proceedings without any control of the award. Its Rules have been amended and brought into harmony with the UNCITRAL Model Law and, especially the English Arbitration Act 1996.[621] The arbitral tribunal normally consists only of a sole arbitrator, and in case of a three-member tribunal, all arbitrators are selected and appointed by the LCIA Court itself, unless expressly provided otherwise. This unique feature may not easily be discovered,[622] and the parties should provide for party-nominated arbitrators if they want to secure some

---

1998' *Neue Juristische Wochenschrift* (*NJW*) (1998) 2,081. Generally on ICC arbitration, Fouchard, Gaillard, Goldman (n 30) 191 *et seq*, nos 349 *et seq*. For further references, see ch 15.

[613] See eg the survey of R Schmidt-Diemitz (n 149) *DB* (1999) 369, 370, according to which the ICC rules are the first choice among the institutional rules that are frequently used by German companies. On current features including the most recent numbers, see ch 15.

[614] See eg Weigand, F.-B., *Neue Juristische Wocheschrift* (*NJW*) (1998) 2,081, 2,082 with further references and Redfern, Hunter, Blackaby and Partasides (n 12) 1–92.

[615] For a strong criticism, see Habscheid, W. *Recht der Internationalen Wirtschaft* (*RIW*) (1998) 421.

[616] Derains, Y. and Schwartz, E.A. (n 58) 7 *et seq*.

[617] See for more details the Statistical Reports of the International Court of Arbitration of the respective years and ch 15.

[618] In 2006, 95 ICC cases were conducted in Switzerland, whereas there were only 51 international arbitration proceedings (in 2007) under the Swiss Rules; see ch 12, nos 12.25 *et seq*.

[619] See *Arbitration and the LCIA*, a brief introduction, published by the LCIA (1997) [hereinafter LCIA Brochure], 4.

[620] In 1892, the London Chamber of Arbitration was formed, which later, in 1903, became the London Court of Arbitration: In 1981 it was named London Court of International Arbitration. See for further details Lionnet, K. and Lionnet, A. (n 29) 511; Redfern, Hunter, Blackaby and Partasides (n 12) 1–93. For a summary of the institution's history, see ch 18, no 18.22 *et seq*.

[621] The LCIA Brochure, 13, emphasizes that the Rules provide 'a combination of the best features of civil and common law systems'. The current version of the rules came into force in 1998.

[622] See Art 7.1, LCIA Rules 1998. The chairman is in any case appointed by the LCIA Court (Art 5.6 of the Rules), unless expressly provided otherwise by the parties.

kind of influence on the constitution of the tribunal.[623] The case load of the LCIA has increased steadily over the years: in 2008, 221 new cases were filed.[624]

(3.3) The ICDR International Arbitration Rules (ICDR Rules) The American Arbitration Association (AAA) was founded in 1926 and is, today, the most important American arbitral institution with more than 35 regional offices throughout the United States.[625] The AAA Commercial Arbitration Rules have been designed for national arbitration proceedings. In 1986, they have been amended by a Supplement for International Commercial Arbitration, and since 1991, there exist separate International Arbitration Rules (the AAA or ICDR International Arbitration Rules), the current version of which is in force as of 1 July 2003.[626] The International Centre for Dispute Resolution (ICDR) is the international arm of the AAA.[627] The AAA/ICDR holds and updates lists for arbitrators; the 'international list' contains about 2,500 arbitrators world-wide. The main feature of the ICDR Rules is that the AAA/ICDR administration is more liberal and exercises a less strict control than the ICC. A useful tool are optional 'pre-hearing conferences' which, similar to the preparation for the ICC Terms of Reference, provide an opportunity to agree on important practical details which have not been regulated in the arbitration clause itself. As a tool for limiting (electronic) discovery, the 2008 'ICDR Guidelines for Arbitrators Concerning Exchange of Information' deal with the production of documents by the parties, prior to the beginning of the hearing.[628] Since 2001, more than 600 international proceedings are administered each year; in 2008, 703 new cases were filed with the ICDR.[629] 1.185

(3.4) European institutional arbitration rules In Europe, there are plenty of arbitral institutions, be it as part of local chambers of commerce, be it as part of other public or private organizations.[630] Since it is impossible to only give a nearly comprehensive overview, only some examples are mentioned below.[631] 1.186

The Deutsche Institution für Schiedsgerichtsbarkeit, DIS, (German Institution for Arbitration), in its present form was established in 1992 as the result of a merger of several 1.187

[623] See <http://www.lcia-arbitration.com>.

[624] *ibid.* In 2007, 137 new cases were registered, whereas in 2008, 221 new files were registered; see ch 18, no 18.26.

[625] For details, see Lionnet, K. and Lionnet, A. (n 29) 515 *et seq*; Schlosser, P. (n 13) nos 166 *et seq*; ch 19, nos 19.3 *et seq*.

[626] Fouchard, Gaillard, Goldman (n 30) 190 no 344; Redfern, Hunter, Blackaby and Partasides (n 12) 1–94; Lionnet, K. and Lionnet, A. (n 29) 517. For details on the ICDR, see ch 19, nos 19.8 *et seq*. The International Centre for Dispute Resolution is the international arm of the AAA.

[627] For the history and more details of the ICDR, including its offices outside the United States, see ch 19, no 19.8.

[628] See ch 19, no 26.

[629] See ch 19, no 19.16 *et seq*.

[630] eg on the various Swiss-based Arbitral Institutions see Stucki, B. and Geisinger, E., 'Chapter 10—Swiss and Swiss-based Arbitral Institutions' in G. Kaufmann-Kohler and B. Stucki (eds), *International Arbitration in Switzerland, Handbook for Practitioners* (Kluwer Law International, 2004)181.

[631] The omission of an institution does not mean that the institution concerned has only little practical relevance or importance. For some more institutions, see eg Fouchard, Gaillard, Goldman (n 30) 334 *et seq*, no 184 *et seq*.

West and East-German arbitral institutions. Its origins start already in 1920.[632] As the leading German arbitral institution, the DIS administers national and international arbitration proceedings. The latest edition of its arbitration rules is in effect as of July 1998. The replacement of the former rules of 1992 was the logical consequence of the new German law on arbitration which entered into force on 31 January 1998. Originally based on the 'model' of the UNCITRAL Arbitration Rules, the DIS Rules are now 'tailor-made' for (international) arbitrations carried out in Germany. Its quite detailed 42 sections contain usual regulations which, for the first time, also include a provision on multi-party arbitration. The DIS does not publish any official list of arbitrators, nor does it examine the award or any formal requirements of it. The arbitrators' fees listed in the schedule are based on the amount in dispute, and they are, as the administration fee, quite modest as compared to other institutions.[633] The workload of the DIS has considerably increased in the last years: approximately 80 new cases are filed each year.[634]

1.188 The European Court of Arbitration (*Cour Européen d' Arbitrage*) was already formed nearly 50 years ago, but is, so far, only little known.[635] Originally formed by the *Strasbourg* bar as a body for the administration of German-French disputes in the Rhine area, it has had four national delegations since 1995. International arbitrations, however, are only administered by the Strasbourg-based Court of Arbitration.[636] The revised arbitration rules entered into force in 1997 and are supplemented by other related rules.[637] The main aim of the institution is to render effective services for a quick and inexpensive arbitral procedure, and the arbitration rules are focused on small and medium-sized arbitrations.[638] The most distinctive feature is the strict timetable aiming at a first award after nine months. Each procedural step is contained in a detailed timetable which allocates specific time limits for each step.[639] The sole arbitrator shall be elected at a pre-appointment conference. The second distinctive feature consists in the general introduction of appellate arbitral proceedings in order to avoid challenge procedures before state courts. The parties may, however, exclude such second arbitral instance.[640] The appeal is subject to leave by the Court who will grant such leave only once the losing party has deposited the amount in dispute with the Secretariat. After the appellate award, the winning party will be entitled to directly receive such amount.

---

632 For details, see Lionnet, K. and Lionnet, A. (n 29) 506 *et seq*, and the DIS brochure 'Schiedsgerichtsordnung 98' (Vorwort/preface).

633 See for details of the fee schedule in the DIS homepage <http://www.dis-arb.de>. There is also a cost calculator available.

634 Bredow, J. and Mulder, I. in K.H. Böckstiegel, S. Kröll and P. Nacimiento, *Arbitration in Germany* 658.

635 For details, see Rubino-Sammartano, M. (1998) 15 *J Int'l Arb* no 3, 75 *et seq*.

636 There are delegations in Germany, Italy, Turkey and Croatia; Rubino-Sammartano, M. 15 *J Int'l Arb* no 3, 75.

637 These are the Documents-Only Arbitration Rules, the Pre-arbitral Reference Rules and the Mediation Rules.

638 Rubino-Sammartano, M. 15 *J Int'l Arb* no 3, 76.

639 The first preliminary hearing will take place after 29 days from the filing of the claim, the tribunal shall be appointed after 39 days, and—after several intermediary steps—the final hearing shall follow after 230 days.

640 Rubino-Sammartano, M. 15 *J Int'l Arb* no 3, 79.

The Arbitration Institute of the Stockholm Chamber of Commerce (SCC) was founded already in 1917.[641] The institute which administers domestic and international arbitration, is 'very Swedish' concerning its staff and the arbitrators appointed and regards itself as 'one of the leading arbitration centres in the world'.[642] The board and the secretariat supervise arbitrations according to the SCC Rules of 2007 which are suitable both for domestic and international cases.[643] The tribunal will normally consist of three persons, and the chairman is generally determined by the SCC itself. The arbitrators will mostly be Swedish nationals even if one party is Swedish. There is no scrutiny of the award by the SCC for whatever reason. As to the frequency of its use, the east-west trade which has long been the main supplier of arbitration cases under the Rules, has not lost its importance after the dissolution of the USSR, its successor states taking the place of the former USSR. Also for Asia-related disputes, Stockholm has gained importance in recent years.[644] **1.189**

The International Arbitral Centre of the Austrian Federal Economic Chamber of Commerce (*Internationales Schiedsgericht der Wirtschaftskammer Österreich*) has existed since 1975 and received its current name in 1995.[645] Its 'Vienna Rules' are mainly designed for international proceedings (ie cases where at least one party is non-Austrian). The Rules have been revised in 2006 in order to incorporate the recent developments of international arbitration in general and the practical experience of the Vienna Centre since the previous reform of 2001.[646] By the end of 2006, 51 international arbitration cases were pending before the Arbitration Court of the Vienna Economic Chamber.[647] **1.190**

The Zurich Chamber of Commerce has handled (international) arbitrations since 1911. In 2004, the Swiss Chambers of Commerce (of Zurich, Basel, Bern, Geneva, Lausanne, Lugano, Neuchatel) replaced their former individual rules for international arbitration with the Swiss Rules of International Arbitration ('Swiss Rules'). In 2007, they also adopted the Swiss Rules of Commercial Mediation and integrated their services in the 'Swiss Chambers' Court of Arbitration and Mediation' (SCCAM). SCCAM offers international arbitration based on the 'Swiss Rules of International Arbitration' (Swiss Rules). The Swiss Rules of January 2006 provide an extensive and detailed regulation (44 Articles) of practically all aspects of arbitral proceedings.[648] They are based on the UNCITRAL Arbitration **1.191**

---

[641] See Lionnet, K. and Lionnet, A. (n 29) 526 *et seq*; Schlosser, P. (n 13) no 172; Hobér, K., 'Neue Regeln für das Schiedsgerichtsinstitut der Handelskammer Stockholm' in *DIS Mitteilungen* 1/1989, 13; Hobér, K. and McKechnie, W., 'New Rules of the Arbitration of the Stockholm Chamber of Commerce' (2007) 23 *Arb Int'l* no 2, 261. For details, see also the brochure 'Arbitration under the Rules of the Arbitration Institute of the Stockholm Chamber of Commerce—An Introduction (1988)' [hereinafter 'The Brochure'].

[642] See The Brochure, at no 1.

[643] For the history of the rules and its versions, see ch 11, no 11.11.

[644] In 2008, a record number of 176 new cases were filed with the Arbitration Institute of the SCC, see ch 11, no 11.10.

[645] Before 1 January 1995, the name was 'Bundeskammer für Gewerbliche Wirtschaft'; see for details Lionnet, K. and Lionnet, A. (n 29) 523 *et seq*.

[646] On the 2001 reform, see Reiner, A., 'The 2001 Version of the Vienna Rules' (2001) 18 *J Int'l Arb* no 6, 661.

[647] See ch 2, no 2.7; for the frequency of filings, see also Reiner, A., 'The 2001 Version of the Vienna Rules' (2001) 18 *J Int'l Arb* no 6, 661.

[648] For more details on the Swiss Rules, see Zuberbühler, T., Müller, C. and Habegger, P. (eds), *Swiss Rules of International Arbitration* (Kluwer, 2005); Lachmann, J.P. (n 81) no 3,734 *et seq*. See also ch 12.

Rules and the Model Law although changes and additions reflecting modern practice and comparative law in the field of international arbitration have been made.[649] In 2007, 51 arbitration cases were handled by the Swiss Chambers.[650]

1.192 (3.5) **Arbitration Rules in Asia and the Middle East** In 1985, the Hong Kong International Arbitration Centre (HKIAC) was established. Mainly due to the adoption of the UNCITRAL Model Law in Hong Kong in 1990, the HKIAC became one of the leading arbitral centres in Asia.[651] Also after the inclusion of Hong Kong into the Peoples Republic of China in 1997, the importance of Hong Kong as a seat of international arbitration cases has not diminished. The HKIAC acts as Appointing Authority and provides the framework for proceedings under the UNCITRAL Arbitration Rules. In 2008, additionally the HKIAC Administered Arbitration Rules have been published.[652] Acting either in an administrative capacity or as an appointing authority, the HKIAC was involved in 139 new cases in 1993, a number which has substantially increased ever since to 448 in 2007.[653]

1.193 For many years, the China International Economic and Trade Arbitration Commission (CIETAC) has been the most important institution in China for foreign-related disputes.[654] CIETAC has modernized its arbitration rules in 2006.[655] In recent years, CIETAC has handled about 1000 arbitrations per year, approximately half of which were foreign-related.[656] In the past, agreement to a CIETAC arbitration clause appeared to be almost inevitable for foreign parties engaging in trade with or investment in China.

1.194 Looking for alternative venues for China-related disputes, parties have also turned to European arbitration centres and rules as those of Stockholm or Switzerland.[657] In 2008, as a further alternative arbitral institution, the Chinese European Arbitration Centre (CEAC) has been established in Hamburg (Germany).[658] Based on the UNCITRAL Arbitration Rules, the Hamburg-CEAC Arbitration Rules in combination with the UNIDROIT

---

649 A comparative version of the Swiss Rules in which the changes and additions compared to the Model Law are italicized can be found on the homepage of the SCCAM, <http://www.sccam.org>.

650 See ch 12, no 12.26.

651 See ch 4, no 4.6.

652 *ibid*, no 4.43.

653 *ibid*, no 4.45.

654 For other so called arbitration commissions (CMAC, BAC and SAC), see ch 4, no 4.36.

655 See Schroeter, U.G., 'Schiedsverfahren im China-Geschäft: Die neue Schiedsordnung der China International Economic and Trade Arbitration Commission (CIETAC)' *Recht der Internationalen Wirtschaft* (*RIW*) (2006) 296. See also Moser, M.J. and Jianlong, Y., 'CIETAC and its Work', (2007) 24 *J Int'l Arb* no 6, 555; Tao, J., 'Chinese Legal Environment for International Arbitration' (2008) 2 *Disp Res Int'l* no 2, 295.

656 In 2007, of the 1,118 pending cases, 429 were foreign related. However, also a part of the 689 domestic cases had an international element, eg in case of a dispute over a joint venture with a foreign shareholder. See ch 4, no 4.38.

657 In recent years, both the Swiss Chambers and the Stockholm Chamber of Commerce have offered particular seminars and conferences for China-related dispute resolution under their respective arbitration rules. For possible alternatives for arbitration proceedings outside China, see Aglionby, A., 'Arbitration Outside China: The Alternatives' (2007) 24 *J Int'l Arb* No 6, 673. See also Tao, J. and von Wunschheim, C., 'Articles 16 and 18 of the PRC Arbitration Law: The Great Wall of China for Foreign Arbitration Institutions' (2007) 23 *Arb Int'l.* no 2, 309.

658 For details see <http://www.ceac-arbitration.com>. Hamburg, as one of the leading European ports and import gateway for Chinese products, is also a seat of many affiliated companies with Chinese origin.

Principles as applicable substantive law (unless provided otherwise) shall ensure dispute resolution in a neutral manner and in a neutral venue.[659]

Another important venue for international arbitration in Asia is Singapore with the Singapore International Arbitration Centre (SIAC). Established in 1991, the SIAC offers state-of-the-art arbitral rules and services. Its current rules date as of 2007.[660] Since its establishment, the number and value of disputes handled by SIAC have steadily increased, covering a broad range of matters including joint ventures, technology and maritime matters.[661] **1.195**

In the Middle East, until recently, there has been no major international arbitral centre. The Dubai International Arbitration Centre (DIAC), which was established already in 1994, had offered domestic arbitration rules only which were not suitable for international proceedings. Now, with the 2007 DIAC Rules, there is an international framework enabling parties from different regions and cultures to conduct arbitral proceedings according to internationally accepted standards.[662] **1.196**

(4) Supplementary Regulations

Institutional and ad hoc arbitration rules, and often also laws governing arbitral procedure, typically leave the arbitral tribunal broad discretion in the conduct of the proceedings.[663] Given that general rules on 'natural justice' or 'due process' or similar principles are open to specification and interpretation, the parties may wish to avoid any uncertainty resulting thereof by agreeing eg on a set of rules on the taking of evidence.[664] **1.197**

(4.1) IBA Rules of Evidence Cultural differences between parties and jurists from different legal backgrounds become manifest in particular at the stage of taking evidence in international arbitration proceedings.[665] The need for rules of evidence in international arbitration[666] was felt within the International Bar Association already more than 25 years ago: in 1983, the 'Supplementary Rules Governing the Presentation and Reception of Evidence in International Commercial Arbitration' were issued by the IBA.[667] The Rules are a useful guide to arbitration[668] and a workable compromise between the common law **1.198**

---

659 For more details, see also the *Global Arbitration Review Dispute Resolution Compendium 2009.*

660 See <http://www.siac.org> and ch 10.

661 For more details, see ch 10.

662 See for example Kratzsch, 'DIAC-Schiedsverfahren im Mittleren Osten', *Recht der Internationalen Wirtschaft* (*RIW*) (2007) 767.

663 See eg Art 19(2) of the UNCITRAL Rules or Art 20, ICC Rules.

664 Without a predictable and reliable procedure, and without some guiding rules, there may be unpleasant surprises for the parties, see Bagner, H. (1997) 25 *Int'l Bus Lawyer*, no 4, 175, 178.

665 Cremades, B.M. (n 143) 165.

666 See Bagner, H., 'The Need for Rules of Evidence in International Arbitration' (1997) 25 *Int'l Bus Lawyer* no 4, 175.

667 The text is reproduced at Shenton (1985) 1 *Arb Int'l*, 118, and in Labes, H.W. and Lörcher, T. (n 329) 583 *et seq* no 35. The Rules are recommended as a supplement to any other rules applicable to the arbitration, be it institutional or not; see Art 1(1) and Bagner, H., 'The Need for Rules of Evidence in International Arbitration' (1997) 25 *Int'l Bus Lawyer* no 4, 177.

668 Redfern, Hunter, Blackaby and Partasides (n 12) 1–126.

and civil law approach.[669] Although they might not often be formally agreed in practice, they are a remarkable codification of international arbitral practice and a helpful guidance for arbitrators and parties.[670] A revision of the Rules has resulted in a 'second edition'. A first draft had been presented in 1998 in Vancouver,[671] and the new version was formally adopted on 1 June 1999.[672] Now, the Rules are longer (nine Articles) and cover more aspects in more detailed rules.[673] As with the 1983 version, the Rules tend to favour the civil law approach rather than incorporating strictly Anglo-American features.[674]

1.199 **(4.2) UNCITRAL notes on organizing arbitral proceedings** The Notes have been prepared and issued by UNCITRAL (in 1996) and are intended to supplement any kind of arbitration rules. They are, however, not themselves arbitration rules but provide only a list (and annotations) of matters on which the arbitral tribunal and the parties may wish to formulate decisions.[675] While the more than 90 notes address procedural issues which should be regulated eg in a pre-hearing conference,[676] they do not describe particular arbitral practices in detail nor do they express a preference for any of them.[677] Some of the matters addressed may already have been covered by the applicable institutional rules which, in such a situation, will prevail.[678] The matters listed reach from the language and place of arbitration over the way of communications up to details of the evidentiary procedure and the conduct of the hearings. The Notes are only a rough guidance or checklist for the arbitrators who, as suggested, eg may simply inform the parties on how they will proceed.[679]

1.200 **(4.3) IBA Guidelines on Conflicts of Interest in International Arbitration** On 22 May 2004, the long-awaited IBA Guidelines on Conflict of Interest in International Arbitration

[669] Bagner, H., 'The Need for Rules of Evidence in International Arbitration', (1997) 25 *Int'l Bus Lawyer* no 4, 178; Fouchard, Gaillard, Goldman (n 30) 193 no 352.

[670] Bagner, H., 'The Need for Rules of Evidence in International Arbitration' (1997) 25 *Int'l Bus Lawyer* no 4, 178.

[671] After the Vancouver meeting, the IBA working group amended the draft which was then reproduced for discussion in (1998) 3 *Arbitration* and *ADR* no 2, 27 *et seq.* (Newsletter of the IBA Section on Business Law, Committee D, October 1998).

[672] IBA Rules on the Taking of Evidence in International Commercial Arbitration, available on the homepage of the International Bar Association: <http://www.ibanet.org/Publications/publications_IBA_guides_and_free_materials.aspx>. See also Redfern, Hunter, Blackaby and Partasides (n 12) 1–126.

[673] The Rules cover almost all aspects of the taking and production of evidence from documents, witnesses, party- or tribunal-appointed experts to details of the evidentiary hearing.

[674] Bagner, H., 'The Need for Rules of Evidence in International Arbitration' (1997) 25 *Int'l Bus Lawyer* no 4, 177.

[675] For the purposes of the Notes, see nos 1 to 5, and for the list, nos 10 to 13 of the Notes. For more details, see Redfern, Hunter, Blackaby and Partasides (n 12) 6–34 *et seq.*

[676] On the various stages of the proceedings for taking particular decisions, see no 10 of the Notes.

[677] See in particular no 11 of the Notes.

[678] See no 13 of the Notes.

[679] If there is no provision in the applicable arbitration rules or in the specific provisions agreed by the parties eg at the beginning of the proceedings, it is within the discretion of the tribunal how it will eg require a party to produce documents (see note 50). This may be criticized (Bagner, H., 'The Need for Rules of Evidence in International Arbitration', (1997) 25 *Int'l Bus Lawyer* no 4, 178), but timely information to this effect is in any case better than to leave the parties uninformed until the very decision in a particular procedural situation.

were approved by the Council of the International Bar Association.[680] Although those Guidelines are legally not binding, it can be hoped that—similarly to the IBA Rules on the Taking of Evidence in International Commercial Arbitration— the Guidelines on Conflicts of Interest are at least used as a reference for practitioners and will, thereby, foster a more consistent approach to the complex issues of disqualifications and challenge of arbitrators.[681]

The Guidelines are divided into two parts:[682] in Part I, seven general standards regarding impartiality, independence, disclosure and waiver are set. These general standards are accompanied by explanations illustrating further details. Part II consists of a practical application of the general standards. In order to provide the practitioner faced with a conflicts issue a pragmatic solution, the IBA Working Group decided to reflect situations that are likely to occur in today's arbitration world and submit specific guidance. For this purpose, the members of the Working Group analysed the relevant case law and categorized situations. These have found their way into the Guidelines in the form of non-exhaustive lists arranged according to various colours: a Red List, an Orange List and a Green List. The Red List consists of a non-waivable and a waivable Red List, whereby the non-waivable Red List includes situations deriving from the overriding principle that no person can be his or her own judge. The waivable Red List encompasses situations that are serious but not as severe. The Orange List reflects situations which in the eyes of the parties may give rise to justifiable doubts as to the arbitrator's impartiality or independence, resulting accordingly in a duty to disclose. Finally, the Green List contains specific situations where no appearance of and no actual conflict of interest exists from the relevant objective point of view.[683] **1.201**

The Guidelines aim to provide guidance for the various stages in which conflict of interests may arise, ie when accepting an appointment ('disqualification phase'), when deciding as to which facts must be disclosed ('disclosure phase') and finally in the course of the parties' decision on a challenge of the arbitrator ('challenge phase'). **1.202**

---

680 The text of the guidelines can be found on the homepage of the IBA <http://www.int-bar.org>.

681 The need for guidance on the decision whether to nominate or challenge an arbitrator, see Nicholas, G. and Partasides, C., 'LCIA Court Decisions on Challenges to Arbitrators: A Proposal to Publish' (2007) 23 *Arb Int'l* no 1, 1. Guidelines on the Interviewing of Prospective Arbitrators have been published by the Chartered Institute of Arbitrators, see Friedman, M.W., 'Regulating Judgment: A Comment on the Chartered Institute of Arbitrators' Guidelines on the Interviewing of Prospective Arbitrators' (2008) 2 *Disp Res Int'l* no 2, 288. See also Dundas, H.R., 'The Chartered Institute Good Practice Guidelines: Guidelines on the Interviewing of Prospective Arbitrators' (2008) 2 *Disp Res Int'l* no 2, 276.

682 For a comment on the Guidelines, see Shore, L. and Cabrol, E., 'A Comment on the IBA Guidelines on Conflict of Interests: The fragile balance between principles and illustrations, and the mistery of the "subjective test"' (2004) 15 *Am Rev Int'l Arb* 599. See also Gill, J. 'The IBA Conflicts Guidelines—Who's Using Them and How?' (2007) 1 *Disp Res Int'l* no 1, 58.

683 Shore, L. and Cabrol, E. (2004) 15 *Am Rev Int'l Arb* 599 point out that an 'objective test' is used for disqualification and challenge of an arbitrator by the parties and a 'subjective test' based on the parties' point of view in order to determine whether to make a disclosure.

B. Applicable procedural and substantive rules

(1) Significance of the place of arbitration

1.203 There is no doubt that the choice of the place where the arbitration is going to be held is of great importance.[684] Whereas the fixing of the place where hearings shall be held is a geographical choice, the determination of the 'juridical seat'[685] or 'Legaldomizil'[686] is the connection of the arbitration to a particular jurisdiction. Both aspects are often addressed in national laws and arbitration rules, without, however, applying a common terminology. Traditionally, the *situs*, ie the legal basis of the arbitration has been called 'seat' or 'siège'.[687] 'Seat' has been preferred eg in England where this term is to be found in the Arbitration Act 1996 and the revised LCIA Rules.[688] On the contrary, the ICC Rules use the term 'place of the arbitration' (Art 14) and may, in this respect, refer to a similar provision in the UNCITRAL Model Law (Art 20). It appears, therefore, appropriate to use both terms as synonym with the meaning of 'legal place' or 'juridical seat'.

1.204 **(1.1) *Lex arbitri* and *lex loci arbitri*** There is an almost generally shared view that an arbitration cannot be held in a vacuum but must have roots in a particular jurisdiction.[689] The 'law governing the arbitration' or *lex arbitri* is the legal framework within which the arbitral proceedings are conducted.[690] It is mainly of procedural nature, but may also contain substantive aspects.[691] In most proceedings, the *lex arbitri* is identical with the law of the place of arbitration (*lex loci arbitri*).[692]

1.205 In former times, for example in the case of ICC arbitration, the lack of a particular provision in the rules and of a chosen law of procedure, meant that the arbitrators had to look to

---

[684] See eg Berger, K.P., *Private Dispute Resolution in International Business* (Kluwer Law International, 2006) 16–65 *et seq*; Derains, Y. and Schwartz, E.A. (n 58) 200; Redfern, Hunter, Blackaby and Partasides (n 12) 2–08 ('The seat of an arbitration is thus its central point or its centre of gravity so to speak'). Poudret, J.-F. and Besson, S., *Comparative Law of International Arbitration* (n 6) no 956 *et seq* provide an assessment on the similarities and differences of the various national arbitration statutes. See also Kreindler, R., 'Arbitral Forum Shopping: Observations on recent developments in international commercial and investment arbitration' (2005) 16 *Am Rev Int'l Arb* 157.

[685] s 3 of the English Arbitration Act 1996 defines the 'seat of the arbitration' as the 'juridical seat of the arbitration designated by the parties, an arbitral institution or the arbitral tribunal'. See also Berger, K.P., 'Sitz des Schiedsgerichts oder Sitz des Schiedsverfahrens' *Recht der Internationalen Wirtschaft* (*RIW*) (1993) 10 *et seq*.

[686] Lionnet, K. and Lionnet, A. (n 29) 205 *et seq* defines the seat of the arbitral tribunal as the legal domicile, as determined by the parties or the arbitral tribunal, which has the purpose of establishing a conflict of laws connection with the national procedural law on arbitration, which is governing the arbitral proceedings and the arbitral award.

[687] Fouchard, Gaillard, Goldman (n 30) 690 nos 1,239 *et seq*; Redfern, Hunter, Blackaby and Partasides (n 12) 6–13.

[688] s 3, Arbitration Act 1996; Art 16, LCIA Rules which distinguish the seat of arbitration from the place of hearings.

[689] See Redfern, Hunter, Blackaby and Partasides (n 12) 2–04 *et seq*, especially 2–20. English Court of Appeal, *Bank Mellat v Helliniki Techniki SA* [1984] QB 291.

[690] Park, W.W., *Arbitration of International Business Disputes: Studies in Law and Practice* (OUP, 2006). 157 *et seq*; Redfern, Hunter, Blackaby and Partasides (n 12) 6–12 *et seq*.

[691] See Redfern, Hunter, Blackaby and Partasides (n 12) 2–04 *et seq* (with examples of matters governed by the *lex arbitri*), pleading against labelling the *lex arbitri* as merely procedural.

[692] For an instructive overview, see Park, W.W., 'The lex loci arbitri and international arbitration' (1983) 32 *ICLQ* 21, 22 *et seq*; Park, W.W. (n 690) 157.

'the law of the country in which the arbitrator holds the proceedings'.[693] Therefore, arbitral proceedings were often copies of the respective national procedural law which, however, was designed for litigation and not arbitration. Thus, the procedural law of the arbitration, the *lex arbitri*, was often identical with the *lex loci arbitri*. With the 1975 revision of the ICC Rules, the respective provision changed drastically in determining that the arbitrators were authorized to decide procedural issues at their discretion, without reference to any national law or a comprehensive body of procedural rules.[694] According to the modern view, the arbitrators have to take notice of the local procedural law only insofar as the respective mandatory law must be applied.[695]

Furthermore, today it is generally accepted that the arbitrators may hold hearings, meetings and deliberations at places which are different from the formal seat of the arbitration. Modern rules and laws often contain express provisions to this effect.[696] In addition, the fact that the award is signed at another place other than the seat of the arbitration has no influence on the juridical seat as determined by the parties.[697] According to some national laws, the place of the arbitration, ie the legal seat has to be mentioned in the award and is, consequently, deemed to be the place where it has been rendered.[698] **1.206**

(1.2) Importance of the law at the seat of the arbitration Apart from the law chosen by the parties (eg institutional arbitration rules), the law of the 'home jurisdiction' of the arbitral proceedings has considerable importance. **1.207**

The supportive role of the local courts is required in those situations which are not provided for by institutional rules or which require the help of the state courts, for example:[699] appointment or challenge of arbitrators; provisional measures; taking of evidence; decision as to competence or jurisdiction of the arbitral tribunal; determination of preliminary questions of law. **1.208**

The extent and kind of judicial control of the award[700] as well as the interpretation, correction or amendment of the award are dependent on the locally applicable law and the attitude of the local courts (arbitration friendly or hostile atmosphere).[701] The rules in force for challenging awards and the practical application of such rules by the courts are probably the most important factor for the parties when fixing the place of arbitration. **1.209**

693 See Art 16 of the 1955 ICC Arbitration Rules; Derains, Y. and Schwartz, E.A. (n 58) 208 *et seq.*

694 Art 11 of the 1975 ICC Arbitration Rules. This fundamental principle continues to characterize Art 15 of the 1998 ICC Arbitration Rules, Derains, Y. and Schwartz, E.A. (n 58) 208 *et seq.*

695 Redfern, Hunter, Blackaby and Partasides (n 12) 2–06 *et seq.*

696 Art 14, ICC Rules 1998; Art 16.2, LCIA Rules; Art 20(1) and (2), Model Law; Art 176(3), SPILA; s 1043(2), ZPO.

697 This is expressly provided for by s 53 of the English Arbitration Act and Art 16.2 of the LCIA Rules. There are, however, significant cases where the signing of the award at a place other than the juridical seat led to serious problems with respect to the applicable law for challenge or enforcement procedures; see eg *Hiscox v Outhwaite* [1992] 1 AC 562.

698 See Art 31(3), Model Law and, based on it, ss 1054(3) and 1043(1), ZPO.

699 Fouchard, Gaillard, Goldman (n 30) 690, no 1,239; Redfern, Hunter, Blackaby and Partasides (n 12) 2–06 *et seq.*

700 For the importance of the law of the seat for a possible recourse, see Fouchard, Gaillard, Goldman (n 30) 920 *et seq* no 1,590; Park, W.W. (1983) 32 *ICLQ* 21, 29.

701 Najar, J.C. (1996) 12 *Arb Int'l* no 3, 357, 366.

1.210 **(1.3) The nationality of the award** The fact that the arbitral proceedings are in principle subject to the law of the seat of the arbitration may be explained by an analogy to the principle of *lex fori* which is valid for litigation[702] or the so-called principle of territoriality.[703] Arguments for a detachment of international arbitration from the law of the seat of arbitration have initiated intense discussions; finally, however, the delocalization theory appears to have ended in failure.[704] Rather, radical solutions like those chosen by the French courts[705] or the Belgian legislator[706] have been corrected by subsequent legislation.[707] The Model Law and national legislation based on it have reinforced the principle of territoriality which today is generally accepted.[708] Thus, according to general opinion, each (international) arbitration must have a nationality which is generally determined by the place of the arbitral proceedings or where the award was made.[709] Other, formerly applied principles for determining the nationality, as eg the reference to the procedural law applied, have been abandoned in countries like Germany[710] or England.[711] Therefore, potential competence conflicts at the stage of challenging the award have mostly been excluded.[712]

1.211 The importance of the nationality becomes mainly apparent at the stage of enforcement of the award.[713] The New York Convention enables the winning party to enforce the award as a foreign award in any Convention state other than where the arbitration took place.[714] Those provisions according to which enforcement may be resisted, refer to the invalidity of the arbitration agreement, the violation of procedural principles of the place of arbitration

[702] For such analogy to litigation, see eg Mann, F.A. in *Liber Amicorum for Martin Domke* (1967) 167; Gentinetta, J., *Die lex fori internationaler Schiedsgerichte* (1973); Berger, K.P., *The New German Arbitration Law* (n 115) 17. Schlosser, P. (n 13) nos 209 and 726, however, points out that arbitral tribunals do not have a *lex fori*.

[703] Since the creation of the Model Law, this principle has been advocated by legal writers, see eg Berger, K.P., *The New German Arbitration Law* (n 115) 16 *et seq*.

[704] For an overview, see Redfern, Hunter, Blackaby and Partasides (n 12) 2–16 to 2–19.

[705] The French courts rejected any appeals against international arbitrations conducted in France, see the decisions in *Götaverken* and *Norsolor* (*supra* 1.31 and 1.165). See also Park, W.W. (n 690) 165 *et seq*.

[706] The Belgian legislator introduced a new provision in 1985 according to which there was no judicial review whatsoever in international arbitral proceedings conducted in Belgium, see ch 3.

[707] The 1981 decrees regulating domestic and international arbitration in France and the arbitration law reform of 1998 in Belgium; Redfern, Hunter, Blackaby and Partasides (n 12) 2–18.

[708] See Art 1(2), Model Law; s 1025(1), ZPO; Berger, K.P., *The New German Arbitration Law* (n 115) 16 *et seq;* Lionnet, K. and Lionnet, A. (n 29) 207; Fouchard, Gaillard, Goldman (n 30) 51 no 92; Mann, F.A. (1984) 33 *ICLQ* 193; Mann, F.A., 'Zur Nationalität des Schiedsspruchs' in FS Oppenhoff (Munich, 1985) 215 *et seq*. Critical, Schlosser, P. (n 13) no 230.

[709] See eg Redfern, Hunter, Blackaby and Partasides (n 12) 2–08 (with further references). For the most recent regulation by the Swedish legislator, see ss. 46 and 52 Swedish Arbitration Act 1999 ('An award made abroad shall be deemed to be a foreign award').

[710] s 1025(1), ZPO; Berger, K.P., *The New German Arbitration Law* (n 115) 16. For the old law, which determined the nationality according to the 'Verfahrenstheorie', see BGHZ 21, 365 and BGHZ 96, 40, 41.

[711] s 2 para 1, Arbitration Act 1996. For the old law which sometimes looked mainly at the procedural law applied, see Park, W.W. (n 112) 84 with further reference.

[712] For those conflicts, see Schlosser, P. (n 13) no 210 *et seq*.

[713] For more details on procedural intricacies a party seeking enforcement may face in the US, see Strong, S.I., 'Invisible Barriers to the Enforcement of Foreign Arbitral Awards in the United States' (2004) 21 *J Int'l Arb* no 6, 479.

[714] Redfern, Hunter, Blackaby and Partasides (n 12) 10–22 *et seq*. See Najar, J.C. (1996) 12 *Arb Int'l* no 3, 359, 366 ('international currency of the award').

or the setting aside of the award in the country where the award was made.[715] Although the wording used by the draftsmen of the New York Convention was not unequivocal, it has been argued with good reasons that an award is made at the seat of the arbitration.[716] Finally, apart from the enforcement, any judicial intervention depends, as described, on the national seat of the arbitration.[717] Therefore, the juridical seat of the arbitration determines, for all practical purposes, the nationality of the arbitration and, in particular, the award.

(2) Institutional and national arbitration rules

If the parties have agreed to apply institutional arbitration rules, there are sometimes situations where it is doubtful which rule of the national or institutional law prevails. The establishment of a particular hierarchy depends on the drafting pattern of the respective law makers. **1.212**

(2.1) **Drafting techniques of national legislators and institutional law-makers** First, it should be examined whether there is a specific rule regulating the order of precedence of procedural norms. For instance, Art 182, SPILA determines that the parties may regulate the procedure, and, failing such regulation, the applicable procedural law will be determined by the arbitral tribunal which, however, in any case has to respect the principles of due process. Similarly, the English Arbitration Act 1996 grants the parties the freedom to agree on procedural matters, subject to public interest (s 1(b)). There is a list of mandatory provisions which may not be deviated from, and the remaining provisions apply only if there is no agreement to the contrary (s 4). The German law contains a similar provision and leaves an issue to the discretion of the arbitrator if there is neither a party agreement nor a fall-back rule in the law.[718] The ICC Rules follow the same pattern.[719] **1.213**

In addition and especially if there is no such explicit provision naming or indicating mandatory rules, the user should check the wording of the norm concerned. Thus, following the pattern of the Model Law, the German legislator indicated in many provisions whether they are subject to a deviating agreement of the parties.[720] In a similar fashion, the English legislator indicated in many provisions that they apply only if the parties have not agreed otherwise. If, therefore, a rule of a chosen arbitral institution exists, the respective national provision does not apply.[721] **1.214**

[715] Art V. (1)(a), (d) and (e) New York Convention.

[716] Mann, F.A., 'Where is an award 'made'?' (1985) 1 *Arb Int'l* no 1, 107 *et seq.*

[717] Redfern, Hunter, Blackaby and Partasides (n 12) 2–06 *et seq.*

[718] See s 1042, ZPO, which is based on Art 18 and 19, Model Law which, however, is not equally clear.

[719] See Art 15, ICC Rules 1998, according to which an agreement of the parties prevails over the rules which, in addition, leave a decision to the discretion of the arbitral tribunal if there is neither an institutional rule nor a party agreement.

[720] See the official governmental report, in Berger, K.P., *The New German Arbitration Law* (n 115) at 228 commenting on s 1042, ZPO. According to the report, the mandatory character of a norm may only be established, if it is 'neither explicitly nor by implication in accordance with its purpose, subject to party agreement'.

[721] For party autonomy as one of the basic principles of the new English law, see the DAC Report 1996, (1997) 13 *Arb Int'l* no 3, 279 *et seq* no 19.

1.215 **(2.2) General order of precedence** The hierarchy of the norms, ie the order of precedence of the various norms may, therefore, be established as follows: (i) mandatory rules of the *forum*; (ii) mandatory provisions of the institutional rules; (iii) party agreement on subjects left for their discretion by the institutional rules; (iv) failing such an agreement, non-mandatory fall-back rules of the institution; (v) discretion of the arbitrators if so determined by the institutional rules or rules of the *forum*.

(3) Arbitral substantive law

1.216 The *lex arbitri* and the *lex loci arbitri* have to be distinguished from the substantive law applicable to the merits of the case. The applicable substantive law will in the majority of cases be chosen by the parties, be it by an express agreement or an implied choice. In the absence of a choice-of-law by the parties, the arbitrators generally enjoy wide freedom to determine the applicable law. Additionally, also the arbitral case law may be of relevance when deciding questions of substantive law.

1.217 **(3.1) Choice of law or *voie directe*** In most international contracts, the parties explicitly agree on the applicable law in a choice-of-law clause or at least make an implied choice by eg referring to national norms or to standard contract forms which have been adapted to a certain legal system.[722] In such cases, the arbitrators, as a matter of course, have the duty to respect the parties' intentions and choice as to the law applicable on the substance of the dispute.

1.218 In the absence of an explicit or implied choice of law, the arbitrators in principle enjoy a wide freedom in determining the applicable law. In principle, there currently exist three methods for the determination of the applicable substantive law: (i) the application of a choice of law rule identified by the arbitrators; (ii) the application of a specific choice of law rule of the seat; or (iii) the direct choice method.

1.219 The first approach is the one that is followed by the Model Law. According to Art 28(2), Model Law, failing any designation of the applicable law by the parties, the arbitral tribunal shall apply the law determined by the conflict of laws rules which it considers applicable.[723] Similar provisions are contained in the English Arbitration Act of 1996 (s 46 (3)) and the German arbitration law (s 1051(2) Code of Civil Procedure). The arbitrators basically have absolute freedom on the choice of law rules which they will apply.[724]

1.220 Another method is the application of the choice of law rule of the law of the seat of the arbitration which is specifically intended to be applied in international arbitration proceedings. Art 187, SPILA has opted for this approach by providing that in the absence of a

[722] On the law applicable on the limitation regime in international sales contracts, see Schwenzer, I. and Manner, S., 'The Claim is Time-Barred: The Proper Limitation Regime for International Sales Contracts in International Commercial Arbitration', (2007) 23 *Arb Int'l* no 2, 293.

[723] This approach dates back to the 1961 European Convention on International Commercial Arbitration and was also adopted by the UNCITRAL Arbitration Rules of 1976, see Gaillard, E. 'Chapter 10—The role of the arbitrator in determining the applicable law' in: L.W. Newman and R.D. Hill (eds), *The leading arbitrators' guide to international arbitration* 185, 202.

[724] See for the differences between the 'cumulative method' and the method of general principles of private international law, Gaillard, E., 'Chapter 10—The role of the arbitrator in determining the applicable law' in: L.W. Newman and R.D. Hill (eds), *The leading arbitrators' guide to international arbitration*, 185, 203 *et seq.*

choice of law by the parties, the case shall be decided 'according to the rules of law with which the case has the closest connection'.

Finally, the most liberal is the 'direct choice-' method or *voie directe*. According to this approach, the arbitrators may choose directly the rules of law they consider to be appropriate for the resolution of the dispute. This method has in the last decade been adopted by some of the leading arbitration institutions like the AAA, the LCIA, the ICC and the Stockholm Chamber of Commerce[725] and by a number of modern national arbitration statutes.[726] **1.221**

Whereas the foregoing methods—although different in their approaches—aim at determining a national law to apply to the substance of the dispute, there also exists the possibility for the parties to authorize the arbitral tribunal to decide *ex aequo et bono* or as *amiable compositeur*.[727] Hence, the tribunal is not bound to apply specific rules of law, but may decide the case according to what it deems 'fair and equitable'. Owing to the wide freedom associated with this possibility, an express authority by the parties is required. **1.222**

(3.2) Arbitral case law If the parties have not empowered the arbitral tribunal to apply *lex mercatoria* or principles of equity, it must apply a particular national law. Court decisions form a part of the applicable substantive law. For common law jurisdictions, precedents are the main source of the law (doctrine of *stare decisis*), but also in civil law systems, case law plays an important role. The decisions of the highest courts are considered as an authoritative interpretation of the codified law[728] and in some jurisdictions, such decisions have even the formal quality of binding law.[729] Therefore, there is no doubt that in principle, international arbitral tribunals must apply legal precedents of the applicable substantive law.[730] There may be exceptions where a decision does not fit into the international context and is therefore not applied in an international arbitration, but such exception is debatable.[731] **1.223**

Arbitral awards are, as opposed to court decisions, the result of a private adjudicatory process which is based on an agreement of two or more parties. Irrespective of the legal system under which or according to which such awards are made,[732] they do not have the same legal quality as the sentences of state courts. This fundamental difference becomes even more evident if the award takes the form of an 'award by consent' which is, of course, **1.224**

[725] Art 28(1) of the 1997 AAA International Arbitration Rules; Art 22.3 of the 1998 LCIA Rules; Art 17(1) of the 1998 ICC Rules; s 24(1) of the 1999 Rules of the Stockholm Chamber of Commerce.

[726] See eg Art 1496(1) of the French Code of Civil Procedure or Art 1054(2) of the Netherlands Code of Civil Procedure.

[727] See eg Art 28(3), Model Law. For more details, see ch 14.

[728] The theoretical foundation of this phenomenon has been discussed intensively among legal scholars, see Berger, K.P., *The New German Arbitration Law* (n 115) 8–10 with further references.

[729] Examples are the decision of the German Constitutional Court and the Spanish Tribunal Supremo; see Berger, K.P., *The New German Arbitration Law* (n 115) 8.

[730] Berger, K.P., *The New German Arbitration Law* (n 115) 10.

[731] In favour of this approach Berger, K.P., *The New German Arbitration Law* (n 115) 7, 15. There are, however, concerns related to such a wide discretion of arbitrators.

[732] ie which *lex arbitri* or which substantive law applies and whether the applicable law is a common law or civil law system.

no decision in a judicial process.[733] There is, parallel to the growing importance of international arbitration, an increasing number of arbitral awards, of which only a part is published. Nevertheless, the existing *fundus* is large enough to serve as a source of arbitral precedents.

1.225 Similar to judges of state courts, arbitrators tend to build on awards of other arbitrators in related cases. There are several reasons for such a tendency, one of which is the wish to give one's own decision additional weight and hopefully a greater chance for acceptance by the parties. Whereas the upcoming of a 'self-contained judicial system' is praised in this context,[734] the concept of arbitral precedents is at least debatable. Although the question of the legal quality of arbitral case law is of great practical importance, it has, so far, been seldom discussed to a great extent among experts. The importance and necessity of arbitral precedent is rightly pointed out by Gabrielle Kaufmann-Kohler with the words:

> Finally, it is important to remember that the credibility of the entire dispute resolution system depends on consistency, because a dispute settlement process that produces unpredictable results will lose the confidence of the users in the long term and defeat its own purpose. These final points lead to the overall conclusion that 'arbitral precedent' is a necessity for certain types of disputes, if not only for the sake of the rule of law.[735]

1.226 Based on the paramount principle of party autonomy, arbitrators are obliged to respect the will of the parties. Consequently, practically all national or institutional provisions reflect such duty of the arbitral tribunals which, apart from being bound by the parties' choice of the substantive law, may only refer to trade usages in addition.[736] Whereas the application of court cases as a valid source of the applicable national law does not exceed the boundaries set by the parties, the situation is different with arbitral awards which, so far, are no generally accepted source of any national law. It is, therefore, amazing to note that a sound, general doctrinal discussion of this issue is missing to date. A deeper analysis, which cannot be presented here, would have to distinguish between the kind of legal issue decided by a particular award[737] and the 'leading' or ancillary character of such award.

1.227 Finally, there is the potential situation that an arbitral tribunal relies in its award on a particular other arbitral award which is not known to the parties. Here, the tribunal should be very careful: if an arbitral precedent is neither in the public domain, nor has it been introduced by the parties or the tribunal itself, the arbitrators must not take the parties by surprise by relying on such precedent in their award. Otherwise, such behaviour would constitute a breach of the principle of due process.[738] Therefore, there is a case for

---

[733] Whereas in litigation, a settlement normally only results in some kind of protocol which frequently is an enforceable instrument, the agreed award may not necessarily be distinguished or recognized as such.

[734] Berger, K.P., *The New German Arbitration Law* (n 115) 19 with further references; Berger, K.P. (1992) 9 *J Int'l. Arb* no 4, 5.

[735] Kaufmann-Kohler, G., 'Arbitral Precedent: Dream, Necessity or Excuse?' (2007) 23 *Arb Int'l* no 3, 357, 378.

[736] See eg Art 28(4), Model Law and Art 17(2), ICC Rules.

[737] There is, of course, a fundamental difference whether the precedent concerns a procedural or substantive issue and whether it reflects a common practice in accordance with arbitral laws and rules or some minor and remote question which is normally not regulated by any national law.

[738] Berger, K.P., *The New German Arbitration Law* (n 115) 21.

advocating a more generous practice of publishing awards[739] which would not only remove the described concerns, but would also enhance the legitimacy of the entire international arbitral process.[740]

C. Features of institutional and national procedural rules

(1) The limits of party autonomy

As has been outlined above,[741] party autonomy is the central focus or *Leitmaxime* in international arbitration. However, certain rules of procedural and substantive law are considered mandatory and therefore cannot be opted out of by the parties. **1.228**

(1.1) Mandatory procedural law Both in litigation and in arbitration, there are certain mandatory rules of law which the parties cannot contract out of. This applies to certain substantive rules and, in arbitration, also to essential procedural principles.[742] Which essential procedural principles of the seat of the arbitration are considered as mandatory depends, of course, on the particular jurisdiction. In many jurisdictions, the principle of 'due process' including equal treatment of the parties and the right to be heard belong to the obligatory national procedural law.[743] The English legislator, in the course of the recent reform of the arbitration law, has decided to mention expressly which provisions of the Act are mandatory or not.[744] In other jurisdictions, it is more difficult to determine the mandatory character of certain procedural provisions. In Switzerland, the wording of Art 182(3), SPILA shows that this provision regarding due process cannot be deviated from by the parties or arbitrators. In accordance with the paramount importance of party autonomy, there are no other mandatory rules.[745] In Germany, the arbitration law only mentions that, apart from due process and the right to be represented by a lawyer, the parties are free to determine the procedure 'subject to the mandatory provisions of this book' (s 1042(3), ZPO). Since, as in the Model Law, the mandatory character of a particular provision is not always expressly indicated in the text, the user has to refer to the official governmental report in **1.229**

---

[739] Lew, J.D.M., 'The Case for the Publication of Arbitral Awards' in *The Art of Arbitration, Liber Amicorum Pieter Sanders* (1982) 231 *et seq.*

[740] Berger, K.P., *The New German Arbitration Law* (n 115) 21, is right to point out that '. . . a negligent treatment of arbitral case law by the arbitrators themselves might ultimately undermine the legitimacy and attractiveness of the international arbitral process as such'.

[741] See III. A. (1) *supra.*

[742] On the question of whether a request for arbitration must be signed see Wilske, S. and Gack, C., 'Commencement of Arbitral Proceedings and Unsigned Requests for Arbitration' (2007) 24 *J Int'l Arb* no 3, 319. For an analysis of confidentiality and privacy in international arbitration, see eg Hargrove, J., 'Misplaced Confidence? An Analysis of Privacy and Confidentiality in Contemporary International Arbitration' (2009) 3 *Disp Res Int'l* no1, 47.

[743] See eg Art 182, (3), SPILA and s 1042(1), ZPO. For details of due process, see para 1.257 *et seq.*

[744] s 4(1) of the Arbitration Act 1996; DAC Report 1996, no 28, 281. Sch 1 of the Arbitration Act 1996 contains a list of nearly 30 sections relating, amongst others, to the court's power to remove arbitrators, determine preliminary questions of law and to annul awards eg in case of serious irregularities or a lack of substantive jurisdiction of the arbitral tribunal.

[745] See, on the importance of party autonomy and its limitations in the SPILA, Lalive, Poudret and Reymond (n 119) 273 *et seq* and Blessing, M. (n 112) 1, 43 *et seq*: The almost complete detachment of the procedure from local rules was only accepted after a lengthy debate within the discussion of the new law on international arbitration; see Blessing, M. (n 112) 1, 47 *et seq.*

order to recognize the relevant intention of the legislator.[746] Finally, in the case of certain procedural usages or rules that are unknown in the home jurisdiction of the arbitral proceedings, the local textbooks and the particular case law have to be consulted in order to establish whether those principles would be accepted by the local courts. Examples are US-style (pre-trial) discovery and punitive damages which principles are not generally acknowledged in continental Europe.[747]

1.230 (1.2) **Mandatory substantive law** The question which mandatory rules of law have to be applied by arbitrators is discussed under various headings.

1.231 The terminology used does not follow a universally shared pattern. For the purpose of international arbitration, the term of 'international public policy' has been chosen for mandatory norms.[748] In France, the respective issue is mostly discussed under the concept of *lois d'application immédiate* or *lois de police*,[749] and German authors often prefer the term of *Eingriffsnormen.*[750] Since in the area of procedural law, the term of 'mandatory rules of law' is mostly applied, this terminology will hereinafter be used generally, ie also with respect to substantive rules of a public policy nature.

1.232 In order to establish whether arbitrators must apply substantive mandatory rules, the distinction has to be made whether those rules are domestic, ie part of the jurisdiction of the seat of the arbitration, foreign or of an international character.[751] It may be stated that it is highly controversial whether or not an international arbitral tribunal has to apply internationally mandatory rules of a legal system which is not the proper law of the contract.[752] There are important studies on the issue of application by arbitrators of internationally mandatory norms,[753] the result of which shows that there is no consensus on this very

[746] Since the report is often silent in this respect, the mandatory character may not easily be recognized; therefore, the wording of each norm, which often contains reference to an overriding party agreement, is the most important clue for the user; see Berger, K.P., *The New German Arbitration Law* (n 115) 99.

[747] See Schlosser, P. (n 13) nos 638 *et seq*; Weigand, F.-B., 'Discovery in der internationalen Schiedsgerichtsbarkeit', *Recht der Internationalen Wirtschaft* (*RIW*) (1992) 361–5. For a case where damages with punitive character have been rejected for reasons of local public policy, see ICC case no 5,946 (1990), (1991) YCA, 97 *et seq*, 113. For another example in which the arbitrators rejected the plea for treble damages, see ICC case no 6,320 (1991), (1995) YCA, 62.

[748] See eg Domke, M., 'Towards an "international public policy" in commercial arbitration', in FS Bülow (1981), 49 *et seq.*

[749] See Batiffol, H. and Lagarde, P., *Droit International Privé I* (8th edn, 1993) 254; Fouchard, Gaillard, Goldman (n 30) 860, no 1,516.

[750] Drobnig, U., 'Internationale Schiedsgerichtsbarkeit und wirtschaftsrechtliche Eingriffsnormen' in FS Kegel (1987) 95 *et seq*; Juenger, E., 'Lex mercatoria und Eingriffsnormen' in FS Rittner (1991) 233 *et seq*; Soergel, T. and von Hoffmann, B., 'Kommentar zum BGB', *Bd X Einführungsgesetz* (10th edn, 1996) Art 34 no 3.

[751] For this distinction, see the comprehensive study of Blessing, M., 'Impact of Mandatory Rule on International Contracts', paper presented to the Second IBA International Arbitration Day in Düsseldorf (12/13 November 1998) 6 *et seq.*

[752] von Hoffmann, B., 'Internationally Mandatory Rules of Law Before Arbitral Tribunals', in Böckstiegel (ed), *Acts of State and Arbitration* (1997) 3, 8.

[753] Domke, M., 'Towards an "international public policy" in commercial arbitration' in FS Bülow (1981); 49 *et seq*, Lalive, P., 'Transnational (or Truly International) Public Policy and International Arbitration', *ICCA Congress Series* No 3, 1987, 257 *et seq*; Drobnig, U., 'Internationale Schiedsgerichtsbarkeit und wirtschaftsrechtliche Eingriffsnormen', in FS Kegel (1987) 95 *et seq*; Juenger, E., 'Lex mercatoria und Eingriffsnormen' in FS Rittner (1991) 233 *et seq*; Hochstrasser, D., 'Choice of Law and "Foreign" Mandatory Rules in

difficult matter.[754] Therefore, only an overview shall be given addressing the public interests which mandatory norms shall protect and the jurisdictions which the arbitrators possibly have to take into account in this respect.

There are various kinds of interests and motivations of states to enact substantive rules which are intended to be applied irrespective of the parties' or the arbitrators' choice of law. Those rules may belong to the national, international or transnational public policy[755], and may be structured in the following categories: (i) economical and fiscal interests in general; (ii) exchange control regulations or other monetary interests;[756] (iii) political and military interests, as manifested by trade-sanctions, embargoes and boycotts;[757] (iv) maintenance of free and fair trade;[758] (v) social considerations including the protection of the economically weaker party;[759] and (vi) general interests of human mankind, eg protection of the environment, of animals and plants or the cultural heritage.[760] **1.233**

The rules belonging to these categories may be part of the following jurisdictions:[761] **1.234**

(i) the proper law of the contract *(lex causae)*. Although there are several awards applying mandatory norms of the *lex causae*,[762] it is nevertheless suggested that their 'application-worthiness' under a rule of reason has to be carefully checked;[763]

International Arbitration' (1994) 11 *J Int'l Arb* No 1, 57 *et seq*; Lazareff, S., *Mandatory Extraterritorial Application of National Law,* (1995) 11 *Arb Int'l* 137 *et seq*; von Hoffmann, B., 'Internationally Mandatory Rules of Law Before Arbitral Tribunals' in Böckstiegel (ed), *Acts of State and Arbitration* (1997) 3 *et seq*, 8; Blessing, M., *Mandatory Rules of Law vs Party Autonomy in International Arbitration* (1997) 14 *J Int'l Arb* no 4, 23 *et seq*; Blessing, M., 'Impact of Mandatory Rule on International Contracts', paper presented to the Second IBA International Arbitration Day in Düsseldorf (12/13 November 1998) 6 *et seq*.

[754] von Hoffmann, B., 'Internationally Mandatory Rules of Law Before Arbitral Tribunals' in: Böckstiegel (ed), *Acts of State and Arbitration* (1997) 3 *et seq* 12. Blessing, M., 'Impact of Mandatory Rule on International Contracts', paper presented to the Second IBA International Arbitration Day in Düsseldorf (12/13 November 1998) 2 *et seq*, considers the matter as 'one of the most difficult questions with which an arbitrator may be confronted in more than fifty per cent of the cases'. See also Landolt, P., 'Limits on Court Review of International Arbitration Awards Assessed in light of States' Interests and in particular in light of EU Law Requirements' (2007) 23 *Arb Int'l* no 1, 63.

[755] von Hoffmann, B., 'Internationally Mandatory Rules of Law Before Arbitral Tribunals' in: Böckstiegel (ed), *Acts of State and Arbitration* (1997) 22 *et seq*; Fouchard, Gaillard, Goldman (n 30) 874 *et seq*, nos 1,533 *et seq*.

[756] See Berger, K.P., 'Exchange Control Regulations' in Böckstiegel (ed) *Acts of State and Arbitration* (1997) 99 *et seq*.

[757] Blessing, M., 'Impact of Mandatory Rule on International Contracts', paper presented to the Second IBA International Arbitration Day in Düsseldorf (12/13 November 1998) 8 *et seq*.; Matray, L., 'Embargo and Prohibition of Performance; in Böckstiegel (ed), *Acts of State and Arbitration* (1997) 69 *et seq*.

[758] For national and European competition law and its application by arbitrators, see Hermanns, F., in Böckstiegel (ed), *Acts of State and Arbitration* (1997) 61 *et seq*; Weigand, F.-B. (1993) 9 *Arb Int'l* no 3, 249 *et seq*.

[759] This concerns the protection of consumers, workers or exclusive dealers, see eg von Hoffmann, B., 'Internationally Mandatory Rules of Law Before Arbitral Tribunals', in Böckstiegel (ed), *Acts of State and Arbitration* (1997) 3.

[760] Blessing, M., 'Impact of Mandatory Rule on International Contracts', paper presented to the Second IBA International Arbitration Day in Düsseldorf (12/13 November 1998) 6, 8.

[761] See Blessing, M., 'Impact of Mandatory Rule on International Contracts', paper presented to the Second IBA International Arbitration Day in Düsseldorf (12/13 November 1998) 6.

[762] See the examples discussed by Drobnig, U., 'Internationale Schiedsgerichtsbarkeit und wirtschaftsrechtliche Eingriffsnormen' in FS Kegel (1987) 106 *et seq*; von Hoffmann, B., 'Internationally Mandatory Rules of Law Before Arbitral Tribunals', in Böckstiegel (ed), *Acts of State and Arbitration,* (1997) 13 *et seq*.

[763] Blessing, M., 'Impact of Mandatory Rule on International Contracts', paper presented to the Second IBA International Arbitration Day in Düsseldorf (12/13 November 1998) 6 *et seq*.

(ii) the law of the place of arbitration *(lex fori)*; whereas the application of these mandatory rules is partly considered to be of no importance in the practice of arbitral tribunals,[764] there are, nevertheless, differing views on the question whether those rules should be applied by arbitrators in order not to run the risk of a subsequent challenge of the award before the local courts;[765]

(iii) the law of a third country, which eg has enacted trade sanctions that effected the contractual performance; there are several examples of arbitral awards discussing such issues;[766]

(iv) the law of a supranational legal system like the law of the UN or the European Union; here, mainly embargoes and European competition law are concerned;[767] and

(v) the law of the country where potentially enforcement will be sought.[768]

1.235 Finally, whether or not a particular provision or norm must be applied by the arbitral tribunal due to its mandatory nature, has to be determined in a detailed analysis. Various criteria have been developed for such an exercise.[769] The 'application-worthiness' of a rule depends on the jurisdiction it belongs to, which interests it shall protect and whether there is a close enough connection to the dispute and the underlying contract concluded by the parties.[770] Whereas arbitrators will at least have to carefully examine the relevant mandatory rules of the home jurisdiction of the arbitration (which form part of its international public policy),[771] they should also check whether potentially applicable rules of another jurisdiction or of an international character belong to the transnational public policy. It appears to be a commonly shared view that those rules have to be applied in any case by international arbitrators.[772] Arbitrators have not only a responsibility towards the parties

---

764 Drobnig, U., 'Internationale Schiedsgerichtsbarkeit und wirtschaftsrechtliche Eingriffsnormen' in FS Kegel (1987) 106.

765 In favour of the application, von Hoffmann, B., 'Internationally Mandatory Rules of Law Before Arbitral Tribunals' in Böckstiegel (ed), *Acts of State and Arbitration* (1997) 9; against the application, Blessing, M., 'Impact of Mandatory Rule on International Contracts', paper presented to the Second IBA International Arbitration Day in Düsseldorf (12/13 November 1998) 6 *et seq*.

766 See eg Drobnig, U., 'Internationale Schiedsgerichtsbarkeit und wirtschaftsrechtliche Eingriffsnormen', in FS Kegel (1987) 107 *et seq*; von Hoffmann, B., 'Internationally Mandatory Rules of Law Before Arbitral Tribunals', in Böckstiegel (ed), *Acts of State and Arbitration* (1997) 14 *et seq*; Blessing, M., 'Impact of Mandatory Rule on International Contracts', paper presented to the Second IBA International Arbitration Day in Düsseldorf (12/13 November 1998) 7 *et seq*.

767 Hochstrasser, D., 'Choice of Law and "Foreign" Mandatory Rules in International Arbitration' (1994) 11 *J Int'l Arb* no 1, 75 *et seq*.

768 In France, for example, an award violating international public policy will not be enforced, see Arts 1498 and 1502 no 5, NCPC and Fouchard, Gaillard, Goldman (n 30) 967 *et seq*, nos 1,645 *et seq*.

769 See Hochstrasser, D., 'Choice of Law and "Foreign" Mandatory Rules in International Arbitration', (1994) 11 *J Int'l Arb* no 1, 85 *et seq*; Blessing, M., 'Impact of Mandatory Rule on International Contracts', paper presented to the Second IBA International Arbitration Day in Düsseldorf (12/13 November 1998) 30 *et seq*, offers a list of six criteria forming a 'rule of reason' test.

770 Drobnig, U., 'Internationale Schiedsgerichtsbarkeit und wirtschaftsrechtliche Eingriffsnormen', in FS Kegel (1987) 112 *et seq*; Hochstrasser, D., 'Choice of Law and "Foreign" Mandatory Rules in International Arbitration' (1994) 11 *J Int'l Arb* no 1, 86.

771 There is the serious risk that otherwise the award may be challenged and subsequently set aside.

772 See eg von Hoffmann, B., 'Internationally Mandatory Rules of Law Before Arbitral Tribunals' in Böckstiegel (ed), *Acts of State and Arbitration* (1997) 22 *et seq*; Berger, K.P., 'Exchange Control Regulations' in Böckstiegel (ed) *Acts of State and Arbitration* (1997) 124.

but also towards the international business community and, therefore, should assure that under all aspects, sound and carefully reflected justice is done.[773]

(2) Competence-competence *and separability*

For many years, the principles of *competence-competence* of the arbitrators and the separability of the arbitration clauses have been discussed and referred to by scholars and practitioners. Although interconnected, both terms have to be clearly distinguished.[774] The competence of the arbitral tribunal to decide on its own jurisdiction ('*Kompetenz-Kompetenz*' according to its German origin)[775] is a matter of interpretation and scope of the arbitration agreement and of the relationship between arbitrators and courts of law. According to the doctrine of separability, on the other hand, the arbitration clause has to be considered as a contract of its own which is separate from the main contract which it forms part of. Thus, any defect of the main agreement resulting in its nullity, does not automatically lead to the nullity of the arbitration clause.[776] Each of both concepts has its own scope of application. The question who shall decide jurisdictional matters (and with which consequence) may come up in situations where the validity of the arbitration clause (and therefore the problem of separability) is not at stake. Likewise, the validity of the arbitration clause and the jurisdiction of the arbitrators may be debated before a state court of law (eg as an argument within an annulment or enforcement procedure) without any discussion of the *competence-competence* of the arbitral tribunal. Nevertheless, there is a mutual interdependence: for instance, the *competence-competence* may only be relied on if the arbitration clause conferring such power is not null and void due to the nullity of the main contract.[777] **1.236**

(2.1) *Competence-competence* The doctrine of '*Kompetenz-Kompetenz*' means, in its original concept, that the arbitral tribunal may finally determine whether it has jurisdiction, such decision having binding effect for state courts of law.[778] This result, which had mainly been dogmatically supported by *Habscheid*,[779] was also approved by the German Supreme Court *(Bundesgerichtshof)* which held that this kind of final and binding competence of the arbitrators could be derived from a separate and clear 'additional arbitration clause' conferring such jurisdiction expressly on the arbitral tribunal.[780] A similar jurisprudence has been established by the US Supreme Court in the decision *First Options v Kaplan*.[781] There, the Supreme Court established a true *competence-competence*, if the parties had established such jurisdiction of the arbitral tribunal. In view of such power of the **1.237**

[773] Hochstrasser, D., 'Choice of Law and "Foreign" Mandatory Rules in International Arbitration' (1994) 11 *J Int'l Arb* no 1, 84 *et seq*, emphasizes that 'in the long run, only a reasonable application of mandatory law by arbitral tribunals serves the purpose of arbitration as a well-respected and efficient institution of international dispute resolution'.

[774] Schlosser, P. (n 13) nos 392 and 546. The clear distinction has been pointed out by the English legislator, see the DAC Report 1996, no 43, 284.

[775] Schlosser, P. (n 13) no 546.

[776] See eg Schlosser, P. (n 13) no 392 *et seq*.

[777] See Jalili, M. (1996) 13 *J Int'l Arb* no 4, 169.

[778] For details, see Schwab, K.H. and Walter, G. (n 1) 56 *et seq* no 9

[779] KTS (1955) 37 and (1964) 152.

[780] BGH Betriebsberater (BB) (1955) 532; Neue Juristische Wochenschrift (NJW) (1977) 1397.

[781] (1995) 115 S Ct 1920 (US Lexis 3463, 1995). See Jalili, M. (1996) 13 *J Int'l Arb* no 4, 176 *et seq*.

arbitrators, the court would only in exceptional circumstances review the tribunal's decision on its jurisdiction.[782]

1.238 The modern notion of *competence-competence* as used in the current arbitration laws and institutional arbitration rules,[783] has a weaker meaning and establishes the power of the tribunal to rule on its own jurisdiction only subject to later court review.[784] This solution makes sense from a practical point of view since it enables the arbitrators to decide the dispute on the merits once they have ruled positively on their jurisdiction.[785] In addition, in some jurisdictions, the party who does not want to accept such a positive decision of the arbitral tribunal has to challenge it immediately before the state court, since otherwise it will be precluded from it by law.[786] Due to this reservation of the final decision for the state courts, it would be more appropriate to replace the term of *competence-competence* by 'preliminary competence' of the arbitral tribunal to rule on its own jurisdiction. If, as mentioned, the positive decision of the tribunal is not challenged in time, then it becomes the final and binding decision on the arbitrators' jurisdiction.

1.239 **(2.2) Separability of the arbitration clause** In commercial relationships which are subject to an arbitration clause, the dispute to be decided is often closely connected to a termination or alleged nullity of the underlying contract. It would, therefore, in many cases deprive the arbitral tribunal of its jurisdiction if the (alleged) nullity of the main contract would automatically affect the arbitration clause as well. Therefore, the doctrine of separability (or severability) or autonomy of the arbitration clause has been developed.[787] Within the last decades, this doctrine was accepted in many jurisdictions by the respective national courts[788] and in arbitral case law.[789] With the help of this doctrine, the arbitration proceedings may continue and the arbitral tribunal may decide on the validity of the main

[782] Jalili, M. (1996) 13 *J Int'l Arb* no 4, 177 *et seq*, names corruption, fraud and undue influence as set out in § 10 of the Federal Arbitration Act. If no such *competence-competence* has been conferred by the parties to the arbitrators, the courts shall independently decide on the tribunal's jurisdiction.

[783] Art 6 (2) sentence 2, ICC Rules; Art 21(1) UNCITRAL Rules; Art 186(1), SPILA; Art 1466, NCPC; Art 16(1), Model Law; s 1040(1), ZPO.

[784] For a drastic example of an ICC arbitration in Switzerland which came to an end since the Supreme Court annulled the award (more than a year after the rendering of it) on the basis of lack of jurisdiction of the arbitral tribunal (decision of 17 August 1995, unreported), see Karrer, P. and Kählin-Nauer, C. (1996) 13 *J Int'l Arb* no 3, 31.

[785] For such practical considerations in an older English case, see *Christopher Brown Ltd v Genossenschaft Österreichischer Waldbesitzer* [1954] 1 QB 8, 12 *et seq.*

[786] See eg the new German arbitration law, where the motion to the state court has to be brought within a month of the arbitrators' decision (s 1040(3), ZPO).

[787] For the terminology and justification of the doctrine, see Schwebel, S.M., *International Arbitration: Three Salient Problems* (Cambridge University Press, 1987) 2 *et seq*. In France, scholars refer generally to the 'autonomie de la convention d'arbitrage', see Fouchard, Gaillard, Goldman (n 30) 213 *et seq*, no 389. For the discussion on the severability doctrine in the US, see Sheppard, B.H., 'The Moth, the Light and the United States Severability Doctrine' (2006) 23 *J Int'l Arb* 5, 479 and Weisenberger, K., 'From Hostility to Harmony: Buckeye Marks a Milestone in the Acceptance of Arbitration in the American Jurisprudence' (2005) 16 *Am Rev Int'l Arb* 551.

[788] France: Cour de Cassation, *Rev arb* 1963, 60 (*Gosset*); USA: Decision of 12 June 1967, 388 US 395, *Rev arb* 1968, 91 (*Prima Paint*); Germany: Bundesgerichtshof 27 February 1970, BGHZ 53, 315; Switzerland: Bundesgericht, BGE 59 I, 178; England: *Harbour Assurance v Kansa* [1993] QB 701.

[789] See Derains, Y. and Schwartz, E.A. (n 58) 105 with further references.

contract.[790] However, the doctrine does not preclude arguments that the arbitration clause itself is null and void for particular factual and legal reasons. In those cases, it has to be demonstrated why and to which extent those reasons did affect the arbitration clause itself.[791]

Today, the principle of separability has been expressly regulated in statutes and institutional arbitration rules. It may be found, for example, in the Swiss, English and German statutes[792] and in the Model Law (Art 16(1)). Whereas already the 1955 ICC Rules and the 1976 UNCITRAL Arbitration Rules introduced a provision on separability,[793] now almost all of the major institutional arbitration rules contain respective provisions.[794] Nevertheless, there are still examples of decisions of national courts which simply ignore the doctrine of separability of the arbitration clause.[795] **1.240**

(3) Impartiality and independence of arbitrators

The principle of neutrality of the arbitrators is a much discussed general requirement of arbitration. **1.241**

(3.1) Definition and scope According to the expectation of the parties of an international arbitration, none of the arbitrators, including those appointed by the parties, should be predisposed towards any of the parties.[796] Traditionally, the main concern was that of the neutrality of the party appointed arbitrators,[797] although it has correctly been pointed out that in view of the method of dispute resolution chosen, it is unrealistic to expect a complete isolation especially of those unilaterally elected arbitrators.[798] Whereas 'national neutrality' of the sole arbitrator or the chairman is generally accepted and mostly provided for if an institution or appointing authority has to appoint the arbitral tribunal,[799] there are in addition provisions on the 'independence and impartiality' of all arbitrators.[800] In several rules, however, only one of these terms is used.[801] **1.242**

---

790 Schlosser, P. (n 13) no 392.

791 Derains, Y. and Schwartz, E.A. (n 58) 105, referring to ICC case no 6,401 (1992). It appears not justified to distinguish between nullity and non-existence of the main contract, see Fouchard, Gaillard, Goldman (n 30) 226, no 411.

792 Art 178(3), SPILA; s 7, Arbitration Act 1996; s 1040(1), ZPO.

793 See Derains, Y. and Schwartz, E.A. (n 58) 104; Art 21(2), UNCITRAL Arbitration Rules.

794 Art 6(4), ICC Rules 1998; Art 23.1, LCIA Rules; Art 15(2), ICDR International Arbitration Rules.

795 For an Australian decision of 1991 (*IBM Australia Ltd v National Distribution Services Ltd*), see Rogers, A. and Launders, R., 'Separability—The Indestructible Arbitration Clause', (1994) 10 *Arb Int'l* no1, 77 *et seq.*

796 Derains, Y. and Schwartz, E.A. (n 58) 108 with further references. See also Lachmann, J.P. (n 81) no 967 *et seq.*

797 This is clearly demonstrated by the 1975 ICC Rules which only addressed the independence of the party-appointed arbitrators; see Derains, Y. and Schwartz, E.A. (n 58) 109.

798 Rau, A.S. (1998) 14 *Arb Int'l* no 2, 115, 120 *et seq.*

799 Donahey, S. (1992) 9 *J Int'l Arb* no 4, 32. See eg Art 6(4), UNCITRAL Rules.

800 Arts 9, 10, UNCITRAL Arbitration Rules; Art 7, ICDR International Arbitration Rules; Art 5.2, LCIA Rules; Art 12, Model Law; s 1036(2), ZPO.

801 England: s 24(1)(a) (impartiality); Switzerland: Art 180(1)(c), SPILA (independence); USA: s 10(b), Federal Arbitration Act (evident partiality or corruption); ICC: Art 7(1), 1998 Arbitration Rules (independence).

1.243 As to a definition of each of both notions, there appears to be confusion rather than unanimity.[802] It has been suggested that even an 'independent' arbitrator may be biased or partial, and that one should, therefore, consider 'independence' to be the objective term, as opposed to 'impartiality' as a more subjective term which describes a particular state of mind.[803] Indeed, independence or a lack of it is based on previous or present contacts or relationships between arbitrator and party, whereas a lack of impartiality results from the relationship between the arbitrator and the subject matter of the dispute[804] or may be concluded from a particular behaviour in the conduct of the reference.[805]

1.244 In practice, it will be difficult to have 'complete impartiality' or neutrality of the party-appointed arbitrator since he almost invariably will share the same nationality and economical or political background and therefore, shows at least some sympathy for 'his party's' position.[806] The 'candidate' of a party may have expressed an opinion on a certain legal issue, and such a statement may influence the party in its selection process.[807] It is, therefore, not uncommon that such an arbitrator is 'predisposed towards the party who appointed him',[808] and there are even examples of jurisdictions which openly apply a much more liberal standard for the party-appointed arbitrator as opposed to the chairman.[809] Consequently, there is a narrow borderline between 'sympathies' for a party and undue 'partiality'. Depending on personal views and experiences, one may either conclude that nevertheless, generally this apparent paradox (of party appointment and independence) works well in international arbitration,[810] or that true independence and impartiality are only wishful thinking.[811]

1.245 (3.2) **Examples and practice** Before addressing the most important groups of typical situations in practice,[812] it should be pointed out that it is the appearance of bias rather than actual bias which may disqualify an arbitrator.[813]

---

[802] See Craig, W.L., Park, W.W. and Paulsson, J. (n 388) 221.

[803] Derains, Y. and Schwartz, E.A. (n 58) 109 *et seq*; Benson, C., 'Can Professional Ethics Wait? The Need for Transparency in International Arbitration' (2009) 3 *Disp Res Int'l* no 1, 78.

[804] Hunter, M., 'Ethics of the International Arbitrator' *Arbitration* (1987) 219, 222 *et seq*; Benson, C., 'Can Professional Ethics Wait? The Need for Transparency in International Arbitration' (2009) 3 *Disp Res Int'l* no 1, 78.

[805] For 'partiality in the conduct of the reference', see Mustill, M. and Boyd, S.C. (n 7) 253.

[806] Donahey, S. (1992) 9 *J Int'l Arb* no 4, 41.

[807] Derains, Y. and Schwartz, E.A. (n 58) 111.

[808] Redfern, Hunter, Blackaby and Partasides (n 12) no 4–52; Donahey, S. (1992) 9 *J Int'l Arb* no 4, 41.

[809] See for the respective liberal rules of the (domestic) US American AAA Commerical Arbitration Rules, Rau, A.S. (1998) 14 *Arb Int'l* no 2, 123 *et seq*. However, in international arbitration, there is no room for a different treatment of the party-appointed arbitrator, Rau, A.S. (1998) 14 *Arb Int'l* no 2, 129.

[810] See Donahey, S. (1992) 9 *J Int'l Arb* no 4, 39: 'In international arbitrations, the party-appointed arbitrator, who has often been selected because of his perceived predisposition to the party and its legal position, is expected to maintain his independence and impartiality. That this paradox works well in practice is one of the strengths of international commercial arbitration.'

[811] Blessing, M. (n 112) 1, 39 *et seq*.

[812] Derains, Y. and Schwartz, E.A. (n 58) 114 *et seq*, for example, list five groups of 'risky' relationships or behaviour of an arbitrator. For a list of typical situations and an assessment as to possible conflict of interests in these situations, see IBA Guidelines on Conflict of Interests, III. A. (3)(c). See also on the various situations which might give rise to reasons for challenge of an arbitrator, Lachmann, J.P. (n 81) no 981 *et seq*.

[813] See eg Mustill, M. and Boyd, S.C. (n 7) 250 *et seq*.

An arbitrator's personal connection to one party before his appointment as arbitrator may affect his independence. Examples are formal and continuous business relationships between the arbitrator and a party and, not seldom in practice, the previous acting of a member of the arbitrator's law firm for 'his' party.[814] The decision on the question of bias will depend on the facts of each particular case. A possible reason for concern is the relationship between an arbitrator and a party′s counsel, although normal previous business contacts should not be considered as actually detrimental.[815] Similarly, frequent previous appointments as arbitrator by the same party may be critical.[816] However, so far, such facts have not automatically been considered to be a reason for assuming bias.[817] **1.246**

Another area of potential bias is the connection between the arbitrator and the subject matter of the arbitration.[818] Typically, here situations are named where the arbitrator has taken up a position in relation to some or all of the issues of the arbitration which casts doubts on his ability to assess them fairly. However, earlier legal positions advocated by the arbitrator, which may often have caused a party to nominate him as arbitrator, are so general and remote, that it would not be realistic to consider that to be a reason for potential bias.[819] **1.247**

Frequently, examples for bias are taken from an arbitrator's behaviour after the initiation of the arbitration. If, for example, a prospective arbitrator is approached by a party, discusses broadly the merits of the case with it before being nominated or shares his views of the merits with the other party-appointed arbitrator prior to the election of the chairman, this will inevitably raise justified doubts as to such arbitrator's impartiality.[820] On the other hand, early contacts between the party and the proposed party-appointed arbitrator are generally acceptable, if they serve only the purpose of identifying a particular personal qualification or experience or the availability of such future arbitrator.[821] *Ex parte* communications **1.248**

---

[814] These facts and circumstances may be part of the (waivable) Red or the Orange List of the IBA Guidelines on Conflict of Interests in International Arbitration; see Pt II 2 and 3 of the Guidelines. For the details on Red, Orange and Green List, see III A(4)(c).

[815] Derains, Y. and Schwartz, E.A. (n 58) 116, referring eg to an earlier arbitration in which both the arbitrator and the counsel were involved. See also Pt II 2 and 3 of the IBA Guidelines on Conflict of Interests in International Arbitration.

[816] Pt II 3.1.3 of the IBA Guidelines on Conflict of Interests in International Arbitration considers the fact that the arbitrator has within the past three years been appointed as arbitrator on two or more occasions by one of the parties as belonging to the Orange List. See in general also Hunter, M., 'Ethics of the International Arbitrator' *Arbitration* 1987, 222, who points at the possible interest to be appointed again in future arbitrations. See also Rau, A.S. (1998) 14 *Arb Int'l* no 2, 140.

[817] At least the ICC Court of Arbitration has, so far, been reluctant to draw such adverse conclusions; see Derains, Y. and Schwartz, E.A. (n 58) 117.

[818] For instance, the fact that an arbitrator has a significant financial interest in one of the parties or the outcome of the case belongs to the non-waivable Red List, see Pt II, 1.3 of the IBA Guidelines on Conflict of Interests in International Arbitration. The arbitrator's direct or indirect interest in the case is part of the waivable Red List, see Pt II, 2.2 of the IBA Guidelines on Conflict of Interests in International Arbitration.

[819] See in this respect the Green List in Pt II, 4 of the IBA Guidelines on Conflict of Interests in International Arbitration.

[820] See Donahey, S. (1992) 9 *J Int'l Arb* no 4, 41, and Derains, Y. and Schwartz, E.A. (n 58) 120 (both with further references). Art 5.2, LCIA Rules provides that 'No arbitrator, whether before or after appointment, shall advise any party on the merits or outcome of the dispute'.

[821] Derains, Y. and Schwartz, E.A. (n 58) *et seq.* In this respect, see the Guidelines of the Interviewing of Prospective Arbitrators prepared by the Chartered Institute. On the Guidelines, see Dundas, H.R.,

between a party and 'its arbitrator' are almost always not acceptable since secret communications are generally considered to be improper.[822] This applies similarly to social contacts which must not give rise to the impression that the case is being discussed.[823] If that is apparently not the case, for instance at a large public reception, those contacts, which may be purely by chance, should be tolerated.[824] Of course, a sound judgment of the risk of partiality depends on the particular circumstances of each case, and not all situations are as evident as the often quoted example of the claimant's lawyer (female) who, during some days of an arbitral hearing, was observed when leaving the hotel room of the (male) chairman early in the morning.[825]

1.249 **(3.3) Duties of disclosure and challenge of arbitrators** The means for preventing or sanctioning bias, are the following: firstly, each arbitrator must disclose circumstances showing a risk of bias, and, secondly, if there are facts that show a serious potential for bias, the respective arbitrator will be removed from office.[826]

1.250 Nowadays, many arbitration rules aim at an early disclosure of the relevant facts in order to judge the independence of an arbitrator.[827] In addition to the possibility of a challenge, this disclosure at an early stage is desirable as a matter of process efficiency, since it may prevent the disruption of the running arbitration at a later stage.[828]

1.251 Thus, the UNCITRAL Arbitration Rules require that a potential arbitrator 'discloses any circumstances likely to give rise to justifiable doubts as to his impartiality or independence'.[829] The ICC Arbitration Rules require a prospective arbitrator to sign a 'statement of independence' (Art 7(2)) which shall be communicated to the parties who are invited to comment on it within a fixed time limit.[830] Likewise, during the arbitration, each arbitrator shall immediately disclose any fact or circumstance which might endanger his independence (Art 7(3), ICC Rules).

'The Chartered Institute Good Practice Guidelines: Guideline on the Interviewing of Prospective Arbitrators' (2008) 2 *Disp Res Int'l* no 2, 276; Friedman, M.W., 'Regulating Judgment: A Comment on the Chartered Institute of Arbitrators' Guidelines on the Interviewing of Prospective Arbitrators' (2008) 2 *Disp Res Int'l* no 2, 288.

822 Alvarez, G.A. (1990) 6 *Arb Int'l* no 3, 203, 216 *et seq*, Donahey, S. (1992) 9 *J Int'l Arb* no 4, 42.

823 For early English case law in that respect, see Mustill, M. and Boyd, S.C. (n 7) 255; for a more liberal approach, see Derains, Y. and Schwartz, E.A. (n 58) 120.

824 For more details, see Derains, Y. and Schwartz, E.A. (n 58) 120, quoting Art 5(5) of the IBA Rules of Ethics for International Arbitrators, which contains quite a detailed recommendation for an arbitrator's behaviour as far as social or professional contacts are concerned.

825 See Rau, A.S. (1998) 14 *Arb Int'l* no 2, 117 with further references.

826 See on the duty to disclose, Lachmann, J.P. (n 81) no 1,031 *et seq.*

827 Donahey, S. (1992) 9 *J Int'l Arb* no 4, 36. See in this respect the IBA Guidelines on Conflicts of Interest in International Arbitration. Pt 1(3)(a) provides that facts or circumstances which may give rise to impartiality or independence, they shall disclose such facts prior to accepting his or her appointment or as soon as he or she learns about them. For more details on the IBA Guidelines, see III. A. (4) (c) *supra.*

828 Rau, A.S. *supra* (1998) 14 *Arb Int'l* no 2, 118.

829 Art 9, UNCITRAL Rules. The wording has been copied by Art 7, ICDR International Arbitration Rules.

830 For details, see Derains, Y. and Schwartz, E.A. (n 58) 123 *et seq*. See also the LCIA Rules (Art 5.3) which are, in this respect, very similar to the ICC Rules.

National statutes partly require disclosure expressly, or such duty has been established by the courts or by leading scholars. A duty of disclosure exists, for example, in France,[831] possibly in Switzerland[832] and in the United States.[833] Germany, following the Model Law, has also included an express provision to this effect.[834] England, however, has not introduced such a duty as part of the Arbitration Act 1996.[835] Several other states acknowledge a duty of disclosure before or after the commencing of an arbitration.[836] **1.252**

Of course, disclosure is worthless if it is not supplemented by a challenge procedure. In fact, challenge of a partial arbitrator was a commonly shared standard of arbitration rules and statutes even before the formal duty of disclosure was established. **1.253**

(i) The challenge of an arbitrator, either at the appointment stage or later during the arbitration, is generally provided for in the rules of institutional and *ad hoc* arbitration.[837] In an ICC arbitration, for instance, the statement of independence is communicated to the parties who shall then in a given time limit comment on it and, in particular, state whether an arbitrator is accepted or rejected.[838] Respective provisions form part of most national statutes.[839] The remedies provided for by applicable institutional rules, however, have to be first exhausted,[840] or they replace the respective remedy before the state court.[841] As a consequence of a challenge, the arbitrator concerned will either resign, or the other party agrees to the challenge (and the arbitrator will be replaced consequently) or, at least, the institution or the competent state court has to decide whether the arbitrator shall be removed or approved.[842] **1.254**

(ii) If an arbitrator whose impartiality or independence was doubtful participated in the rendering of the award, such award may be challenged before the state courts.[843] Frequently, however, such a motion is dependent on the interested party's prior exhaustion of the applicable remedies.[844] **1.255**

(iii) According to a modern trend, a challenge may be excluded if it is brought forward too late and therefore, is considered to be waived (principle of *estoppel*). Almost all rules **1.256**

---

831 See Art 1452(2), NCPC; Smith, M.L. (1990) 6 *Arb Int'l* no 4, 320, 327 *et seq.*

832 Although there is no express provision in the SPILA, such duty is confirmed by Donahey, S. (1992) 9 *J Int'l Arb* no 4, 36 with further references.

833 *Commonwealth Coatings v Continental Casualty Co*, 393 US 145, 149. See also Donahey, S. (1992) 9 *J Int'l Arb* no 4, 37 with further references.

834 s 1036(1), ZPO. See also Art 12(1), Model Law.

835 The Act includes only a possible challenge before the respective arbitral institution or the High Court, see s 24.

836 For more details, see the Country Reports in the following chapters.

837 Art 7(4) ICC Rules; Art 10.4 LCIA Rules; Art 11(1) and (2) Vienna Rules; Art 7, SCC Rules; s 18.1, DIS Rules; Art 11(3), UNCITRAL Rules.

838 For details, see Derains, Y. and Schwartz, E.A. (n 58) 123 *et seq.*

839 See eg Art 180, SPILA; s 24(1)(a) Arbitration Act 1996; s 1037(2), ZPO.

840 This has been expressly regulated in s 24(2) Arbitration Act 1996, whereas according to most other national rules, the predominance of the respective institutional procedure may be derived from the non-mandatory character of the rules on a challenge of arbitrators.

841 This results from Art 180 (3) SPILA, see Blessing, M. (n 112) 1, 38.

842 Art 7(4), ICC Rules; Art 10.4, LCIA Rules; s 18.3, DIS Rules; Arts 11(3) and 12(1), UNCITRAL Rules.

843 See eg Art 190(1) lit a, SPILA; s 1059(2) Nr. 1(d), ZPO; s 10(b), Federal Arbitration Act.

844 See, for instance, the comment of Blessing, M. (n 112) 1, 68.

provide that a party-appointed arbitrator may not be challenged by the nominating party if the grounds for such challenge are based on circumstances or facts that were known to such party before the appointment.[845] In addition, arbitral rules frequently contain specific or more general requirements to bring forward any challenges without delay or within a certain time limit with the result that later attempts of challenge are excluded.[846] Finally, modern arbitration statutes require an immediate attack of a negative decision of the arbitral tribunal (or the respective institution) before the competent state court, thereby preventing a party from waiting with a potential challenge until the outcome of the award.[847]

(4) Due process

1.257 Although arbitration is different from litigation since the parties may freely determine the procedure to be followed by the arbitrators, there are fundamental procedural rights and principles to be safeguarded in order to establish a system of dispute resolution which is equivalent to the administration of justice by state courts of law.[848] Therefore, there is practically universal acceptance of the principle of 'due process'[849] or, in the English terminology, 'natural justice' as basic and mandatory rule for the parties and arbitrators.[850] The principles of equal treatment of the parties and each party's right to be heard and to present its case were, in the course of the preparation of the Model Law, considered to be the 'Magna Carta of Arbitral Procedure',[851] and today, both are more or less expressly regulated in modern arbitration laws and rules. For instance, the overriding requirement of the arbitrators to act fairly and impartially has been comprehensively regulated by the English legislator.[852]

1.258 **(4.1) Equal treatment of all parties** This principle is basic to all systems of justice,[853] and it is regulated in most national and institutional arbitration rules. There is a particular provision for it in the Model Law (Art 18) and, following it, in the new German arbitration law (s 1041(1), ZPO). It was specifically laid down in the Swiss law of 1987[854] and, for instance, in the UNCITRAL Arbitration Rules (Art 15) and the ICDR International

[845] Art 10(2), UNCITRAL Rules; Art 10.3, LCIA Rules; s 18.1, DIS Rules; Art 180(2), SPILA; s 1036(2), ZPO; Art 12(2), Model Law. The ICC Rules, however, allow later attacks based on facts that were disclosed in the arbitrator's statement of independence; see Derains, Y. and Schwartz, E.A. (n 58) 124 *et seq.*

[846] See eg Art 10.4 LCIA Rules; Art 11(3), Vienna Rules; Art 7(2), SCC Rules.

[847] See, for instance, the German arbitration law, which provides for a two-week deadline for a challenge before the arbitral tribunal and then for a challenge before the state court within a month after the tribunal's decision, s 1059(2) Nr 1(d), § 1027, s 1037(2), ZPO. This solution is based on Art 13(3), Model Law.

[848] This has been emphasized by the German legislator, see the Official Governmental Report on s 1042, ZPO, in Berger, K.P., *The New German Arbitration Law* (n 115) 228.

[849] See eg Derains, Y. and Schwartz, E.A. (n 58) 213.

[850] For English law, see Saville, M. (1997) 13 *Arb Int'l* no 3, 237, 238 *et seq.*

[851] Analytical Commentary, A/CN. 9/264, Art 19 para 1; see for more details ch 14.

[852] ss 1 and 33, Arbitration Act 1996. On the mandatory duty to act fairly, see Hunter, M. (1997) 13 *Arb Int'l* no 4, 345 *et seq.*

[853] Redfern, Hunter, Blackaby and Partasides (n 12) 6–07.

[854] See Art 182(3) SPILA: 'Whatever procedure is chosen, the arbitral tribunal shall assure equal treatment of the parties and of the right of the parties to be heard in an adversarial procedure.'

Arbitration Rules.[855] In England, it forms part of the general duty to act fairly,[856] and in France, the principle of equal treatment is considered to be closely connected to the expressly mentioned *principe du contradictoire* which forms part of the *ordre public international*.[857]

There are, of course, various practical situations where the principle of equal treatment has to be applied. 1.259

(i) The right to nominate one's own arbitrator was intensively discussed after the important French decision in *Dutco*[858] in a multi-party arbitration where two parties on the same side had to agree on a common nomination of 'their' arbitrator. Since that time, there have been several attempts to find a fair and correct solution for such situations, and respective provisions are now contained in the ICC Arbitration Rules and the German DIS Arbitration Rules.[859] Generally, no party must exercise an overriding influence on the composition and constitution of the arbitral tribunal.[860] 1.260

(ii) There are many other situations where equal rights or opportunities must be granted to both parties. Thus, following a particular request of one party, the tribunal has to grant an equivalent extension of a time limit to the other party as well. Another example is the admission of particular means of evidence which must be equally granted to both parties.[861] 1.261

(4.2) Right to be heard or opportunity to present one's case This right is often regulated together with the principle of equality, sometimes even under the same heading.[862] In England, both principles are part of the arbitrators' duty 'to act fairly and impartially as between the parties, giving each party a reasonable opportunity of putting his case and dealing with that of his opponent', (s 33(1)(a) of the Arbitration Act 1996).[863] Similarly, also the ICC Rules establish the duty of the arbitral tribunal to 'ensure that each party has a reasonable opportunity to present its case' (Art 15(2), ICC Rules),[864] whereas the UNCITRAL Rules and the Model Law insist on each party having 'a full opportunity of 1.262

---

855 See Art 16 (1): 'Subject to these rules, the tribunal may conduct the arbitration in whatever manner it considers appropriate, provided that the parties are treated with equality and that each party has the right to be heard and is given a fair opportunity to present its case.'

856 The DAC Report 1996 (no 150, 298 *et seq*) points out that the respective provisions in ss1 and 33 of the Arbitration Act 1996 are based on Art 18, Model Law. See also the respective rule in Art 14.1, LCIA Rules.

857 See Art 1502 no 4 NCPC; Fouchard, Gaillard, Goldman (n 30) 542 no 922, 962 no 1,638, 626 no 1,129.

858 *Sociétés BKMI et Siemens v Société Dutco Construction*, Cour de Cassation, *Rev arb* (1992) 470.

859 Art 10, ICC Rules 1998. For a detailed discussion of the *Dutco* decision and the new provision, see Derains, Y. and Schwartz, E.A. (n 58) 165 *et seq*. See also s 13 of the DIS Arbitration Rules 1998. For more details on multi-party arbitration, see III. C. (6).

860 See eg Blessing, M. (n 112) 1, 48 *et seq*.

861 Lachmann, J.P. (n 81) nos 1,290 *et seq*.

862 See the heading of Art 18, Model Law: 'Equal treatment of the parties'.

863 For more details and the intention of the legislator, see DAC Report 1996, nos 150 *et seq*, 298 *et seq*. An identical rule may be found in Art 14.1, LCIA Rules.

864 The 'reasonable' as opposed to 'full' opportunity to present his case shall not grant less rights but only point out that also this right may not be used without limits but only as far as necessary; see Derains, Y. and Schwartz, E.A. (n 58) 213.

presenting his case'.[865] In Switzerland and Germany,[866] the term of granting *rechtliches Gehör* (right to be heard) is derived from the respective constitution and/or law of civil procedure.[867]

1.263 There are several examples of the application of the principle in various situations of an arbitral proceeding.[868] It includes the opportunity to comment on the arguments and motions of the other party, the right to see the evidence presented by the other party and comment on it, and the duty of the arbitral tribunal to take all arguments and legal opinions into account.[869] The tribunal must hear the witnesses if their testimony is relevant;[870] however, it is not a violation of due process or natural justice to reject an offer for a witness testimony if it is apparently completely unnecessary.[871]

1.264 The arbitral tribunal is also entitled to fix reasonable time limits for briefs and sometimes to formally close the proceedings in order to prevent unnecessary delay. In England, the duty to prevent 'unnecessary delay'[872] is a procedural principle to be observed both by the arbitrators and the parties,[873] the violation of which may justify the challenging of the award.[874] In ICC arbitrations, the arbitrators also have the right and duty to close the proceedings when they are satisfied that the parties have had a reasonable opportunity to present their cases.[875]

(5) Taking of evidence

1.265 The combination of the inquisitorial and adversarial approaches in institutional rules becomes mainly apparent at the stage of taking evidence.[876]

1.266 **(5.1) Witness testimony** Evidence by witness testimony shows elements of both the continental and the common law system.[877] Different approaches, however, still remain: whereas continental arbitrators seem to be more inclined to rely on contemporaneous documents, arbitrators coming from a common law jurisdiction put more weight on oral

---

865 Art 15(1) UNCITRAL Arbitration Rules; Art 18 UNCITRAL Model Law.

866 Art 182(3), SPILA; s 1042(1), ZPO.

867 For Germany, see Official Governmental Report on s 1042, ZPO, in Berger, K.P., *The New German Arbitration Law* (n 115) 228; for the constitutional basis, see Art 103(1), Grundgesetz (GG).

868 See on the '*droit de la defense*' or '*le principe de la contradiction*', Fouchard, Gaillard, Goldman (n 30) 961 *et seq*, nos. 1,638 *et seq*.

869 For more details on the principle of the right to be heard, see eg Lachmann, J.P. (n 81) no 1,295 *et seq*.

870 Lachmann, J.P. (n 81) nos 1,340 *et seq*; Schlosser, P. (n 13) no 835.

871 For case law, see eg Cour d'Appel de Paris, 21 June 1990, *Rev arb* 1991, 96, and *Dalmia Dairy Industries Ltd v National Bank of Pakistan* [1978] 2 Lloyd's Rep 223, 269. For more jurisprudence, see Derains, Y. and Schwartz, E.A. (n 58) 256 *et seq*.

872 s 1(1) and s 33(1)(b), Arbitration Act 1996.

873 cf s 40, Arbitration Act 1996.

874 s 68(2)(a), Arbitration Act 1996.

875 Art 22, ICC Rules 1998. For more details, see ch 15.

876 For an overview, see eg Schlosser, P. (n 13) no 642 with further references; Wirth, M., 'Ihr Zeuge, Herr Rechtsanwalt—Weshalb Civil-Law-Schiedsrichter Common-Law-Verfahrensrecht anwenden' *Zeitschrift für Schiedsverfahren* (*SchiedsVZ*) (2007) 9. On evidence in arbitration proceedings in general, see Redfern, Hunter, Blackaby and Partasides (n 12) 6–61 *et seq*.

877 Cremades, B.M. (n 143) 167. See also Wirth, M., 'Ihr Zeuge, Herr Rechtsanwalt—Weshalb Civil-Law-Schiedsrichter Common-Law-Verfahrensrecht anwenden' *SchiedsVZ* (2007) 9.

testimony of witnesses.[878] They will mostly favour a typical cross-examination which, however, is not a typical feature of civil law jurisdictions where the witnesses are questioned by the judge or arbitrator.[879] It is, therefore, advisable to clarify beforehand with the parties how witnesses should be examined in the hearing.[880] In most cases, there will be limitations as to the scope and time for such questioning.[881]

(5.2) Experts and expert witnesses According to the continental tradition, the expert is elected and appointed by the judge or arbitrator. The common law system, on the contrary, knows the presentation of expert witnesses by each party and the cross-examination of the expert in a manner comparable to the testimony of witnesses. Consequently, it was practically unheard of in England that in international commercial matters, the arbitral tribunal would appoint the expert.[882] In view of the delay and the generally higher costs incurred in a 'battle of expert witnesses',[883] international arbitration rules either provide for the continental, civil law solution[884] or an admission of both approaches.[885] It is interesting to note that the English legislator in the reform of 1996 opted for the tribunal-appointed expert, thereby deviating from the traditional English approach.[886] 1.267

(5.3) Documentary evidence, including discovery of documents As to documents, each party shall or may produce those documents on which it relies at an early stage of the proceeding.[887] In view of this, pre-trial discovery is considerably more limited in international arbitration than in US court practice.[888] Rather, it is up to the arbitrators to request additional documents which shall be specified as clearly as possible.[889] 1.268

---

878 Briner, R., (1997) 13 *Arb Int'l* no 2, 163; Wirth, M., 'Ihr Zeuge, Herr Rechtsanwalt—Weshalb Civil-Law-Schiedsrichter Common-Law-Verfahrensrecht anwenden' *SchiedsVZ* (2007) 9.

879 Institutional rules, therefore, show a liberal approach including elements of both systems, see Art 20.5, LCIA Rules; Art 20(3), ICC Rules (more concentrating on interviews by the tribunal); Art 25(4), UNCITRAL Rules (discretion of the arbitrators).

880 Briner, R. (1997) 13 *Arb Int'l* no 2, 162; Hunter, M. (1997) 13 *Arb Int'l* Nr 4, 353.

881 Although this is not the traditional English approach, limitations are increasingly accepted in international arbitration. As early as 1978, the Court of Appeal upheld the arbitrators' rejection of a request for extensive witness testimony, see *Dalmia Dairy Industries Ltd (India) v National Bank of Pakistan* (1987) 2 Lloyd's Rep 223.

882 Briner, R. (1997) 13 *Arb Int'l* no 2, 164.

883 Of course, two experts are more expensive than one, and costs rise further in cases where the arbitral tribunal decides on its own initiative to hear another, 'neutral' expert.

884 See eg Art 20(4), ICC Rules; s 27.2, DIS Rules.

885 See Art 21.2, LCIA Rules and Art 27.4, UNCITRAL Rules, which both provide for a tribunal-appointed expert who may be questioned by the party-appointed expert witnesses.

886 s 37 Arbitration Act 1996. Hunter, M. (1997) 13 *Arb Int'l* Nr 4, 354; Briner, R. (1997) 13 *Arb Int'l* no 2, 164. Prior to the Arbitration Act 1996, English law would generally assume that in the absence of an explicit choice to the contrary, the parties had intended the arbitral procedure to be adversarial rather than inquisitorial; see *Chilton v Saga Holidays* (1986) All ER 841, at 844.

887 See Art 20(2), ICC Rules; Art 15.6, LCIA Rules; Art18(2) and 19(2), UNCITRAL Arbitration Rules; Art 23(1), Model Law.

888 Frank, J. and Bédard, J., 'Electronic Discovery', *Am Arb Assoc Disp Res J* (November 2007) III. A.; Meier, A., 'The Production of Electronically Stored Information in International Commercial Arbitration' *SchiedsVZ* (2008) 181; Hunter, M. *supra* (1997) 13 *Arb Int'l* no 4, 349 *et seq*; Kerr, M. (1997) 13 *Arb Int'l* no 2, 126.

889 Hunter, M. (1997) 13 *Arb Int'l* no 4, 350. See eg Art 22.1 8 (e), LCIA Rules; Art 20(5), ICC Rules; Art24 (3), UNCITRAL Arbitration Rules.

1.269 However, US courts continue to extend the scope of discovery proceedings to international arbitration. While the courts adopted discovery proceedings in international arbitration rather reluctantly in the past, US-style discovery is today applied not only to state-related arbitration proceedings but also to solely private arbitration proceedings.[890] US courts therewith put arbitration proceedings on a par with external court proceedings, for which a discovery was already previously allowed under the Federal Rules of Civil Procedure (FRCP).[891] Thus, the party who has the burden of explanation and proof is provided the opportunity of a comprehensive US-style discovery, as far as the opponent of the requested discovery—who does not have to be identical to the opponent of the arbitral proceeding—comes across the United States.[892]

1.270 This development is not without controversy, as discovery is usually time-consuming, expensive and burdensome. Furthermore, the question whether a party has the right to refuse to submit evidence on grounds of privilege is still not answered according to an autonomous standard but rather differs according to the applicable national law.[893] Particularly individuals from civil-law countries fear that the extension of the scope of discovery proceedings comprises the inherent danger of undermining the advantages of arbitral proceedings.[894] The dispute has taken on added weight and meaning, as even in arbitral proceedings without US participation an expansion of discoveries has been identified in recent years.[895]

1.271 (5.4) **Electronic discovery in international arbitration** Of increasing relevance in this context is the discovery of electronically stored information ('e-discovery'). Since 1 December 2006, parties to US-court proceedings have also been bound to produce electronically stored information within the scope of a discovery (FRCP, 34(a)).[896] Thereby, the term 'electronically stored information', also referred to as 'ESI', is construed extensively covering all current types of computer-based information.[897] Consequently, the diversity of the information to be considered as electronically stored should not be undervalued.[898] This can easily be verified by means of the following examples of electronically stored data: emails, document drafts, document changes not saved, metadata associated

[890] Kraayvanger, J., Richter, M. and Wendler, J., 'US-Beweishilfe in Schiedsverfahren—ein Anschlag auf die internationale Schiedsgerichtsbarkeit?' *SchiedsVZ* (2008) 161; see *Intel Corp v Advanced Micro Devices Inc* (2004) 542 US 241; *In Re Application of Oxus Gold PLC For Assistance Before A Foreign Tribunal* (2006) US Dist LEXIS 74118 (DNL 10 October 2006); *In Re Application of Roz* (2006) US Dist LEXIS 91461.

[891] 28 USC § 1782(a) (2008).

[892] See Kraayvanger, J., Richter, M. and Wendler, J., 'US-Beweishilfe in Schiedsverfahren—ein Anschlag auf die internationale Schiedsgerichtsbarkeit?', *SchiedsVZ* (2008) 161.

[893] See on privilege in more detail Meyer, O., 'Time to take a Closer Look: Privilege in International Arbitration' (2007) *J Int'l Arb* 24(4), 365 *et seq.*

[894] See Lionnet, K. and Lionnet, A. (n 29) 314; Kraayvanger, J., Richter, M. and Wendler, J., 'US-Beweishilfe in Schiedsverfahren—ein Anschlag auf die internationale Schiedsgerichtsbarkeit?', *SchiedsVZ* (2008) 162 with further references.

[895] Kreindler, R.H., Schaefer, J.K. and Wolff, R., *Schiedsgerichtsbarkeit, Kompendium für die Praxis* (Verlag Recht & Wirtschaft, Frankfurt *et al*, 2006) 241 no 827; see Art 3(2), (3) IBA Rules on Taking of Evidence.

[896] All amendments to the FRCP relating to e-discovery and the respective notes of the Advisory Committee are available at <http://www.uscourts.gov/rules/congress0406.html>.

[897] See Committee Notes on FRCP 26(a); Meier, A., 'The Production of Electronically Stored Information in International Commercial Arbitration' *SchiedsVZ* (2008) 181.

[898] Hilgard, M.C., 'Electronic Discovery im Schiedsverfahren' *SchiedsVZ* (2008) 123.

with specific data files, (deleted) voice mail messages, history of internet searches by search criteria, spreadsheets and deleted data files.[899]

First-hand experience gives rise to the expectation that e-discovery will increase the burden of discovery in significant ways. According to US court decisions, companies are facing heavy responsibilities regarding document management, document storage and document production. Furthermore, courts have already imposed significant sanctions for not properly preserving and producing emails and other electronic data.[900] Although the introduction of e-discovery by the FRCP can be seen as a legitimate development in reaction to the advancement of communication means and technologies, thus reflecting the zeitgeist,[901] parties are rightly concerned as to how e-discovery will affect their potential chances and about the impact it will have on costs.[902] **1.272**

Although the FRCP do not govern arbitration proceedings, e-discovery has already become a commonly occurring component in US arbitration and also continues to gain in significance in today's international commercial arbitration.[903] **1.273**

Miscellaneous sources may make the production of electronic documents available for the parties in international commercial arbitration, such as any subsequent stipulation on procedural issues or the applicable rules of the arbitration institution which govern the proceedings. However, the rules of international arbitration institutions address the taking of evidence in a very general way, as can be seen by means of some of the most common institutional arbitration rules. **1.274**

With regard to arbitral proceedings according to the Commercial Arbitration Rules of the American Arbitration Association, which are designed for domestic use, it is mostly out of the question that the explicitly mentioned discovery also covers electronically stored information.[904] **1.275**

According to the ICC Rules, the arbitrator has wide discretion. Article 20(1) of the ICC Rules provides that 'the arbitral tribunal shall proceed within as short a time as possible to establish the facts of the case by all appropriate means'. The interpretation of 'all appropriate means' as well as, for example, the question in what form electronic data has to be produced largely depends on the personal approach, preferences and experience of the **1.276**

---

[899] For further examples see: Hilgard, M.C., 'Electronic Discovery im Schiedsverfahren' *SchiedsVZ* (2008) 123.

[900] Meier, A., 'The Production of Electronically Stored Information in International Commercial Arbitration' *SchiedsVZ* (2008) 180, referring to *Qualcomm Inc v Broadcom Corp*, 2008 US Dist Lexis 911 (SD Cal 7 January 2008), ordering Qualcomm to pay more than US$ 8.5 million in sanctions for not producing emails.

[901] Meier, A., 'The Production of Electronically Stored Information in International Commercial Arbitration' *SchiedsVZ* (2008) 180.

[902] *ibid.*

[903] Frank, J. and Bédard, J., 'Electronic Discovery', *Am Arb Assoc Disp Res J* (November 2007) III. B; Hilgard, M.C., 'Electronic Discovery im Schiedsverfahren', *SchiedsVZ* (2008) 122.

[904] Hilgard, M.C., 'Electronic Discovery im Schiedsverfahren' *SchiedsVZ* 2008, 122, referring to the amendments to the FRCP of 1 December 2006.

arbitrator.[905] However, in August 2008, an 'ICC Task Force on Production of Electronic Documents in Arbitration' was created. The purpose of the task force is to study and identify the essential features and effects of the disclosure of electronic documents in international arbitration and establish a report, possibly in the form of notes or recommendations for the production of electronic documents in international arbitration.[906]

1.277 The International Dispute Resolution Procedures offered by the International Centre for Dispute Resolution (ICDR) as the international arm of the American Arbitration Association pursue a similar broad approach under 16(1).[907] The ICDR recently issued guidelines for arbitrators concerning the exchange of information including electronically stored data, which became effective in all international cases administered by the ICDR commenced after 31 May 2008.[908]

1.278 More specific but still broad rules on document production are contained in the Arbitration Rules of the LCIA.[909] Article 22 of the LCIA Arbitration Rules provides the tribunal with the power to 'order any party to produce (...) any document or classes of documents in their possession, custody or power which the arbitral tribunal determines to be relevant'. Although the LCIA Rules do not explicitly mention electronic data, the wide discretion of the arbitrator suggests to allow the production of electronic data to the same extent as paper documents, provided that the general principles of the procedure are obeyed.[910]

1.279 Aiming to balance the differences between the Anglo-American and continental European legal systems with regard to the taking of evidence, the International Bar Association in London compiled the IBA Rules on the Taking of Evidence in International Commercial Arbitration as a workable compromise between the different approaches.[911] Article 3 of the IBA Rules establishes a procedure for the exchange of documents: each party shall not only submit to the arbitral tribunal and to the other party the documents available to it on which it relies, but may also submit a 'Request to Produce' with regard to documents under the control of the other side.[912] Thereby, document production under the IBA Rules is not limited to paper documents but explicitly includes electronically stored data.[913] Given further provisions, for example, requiring that the requesting party must describe the requested document or category specifically and provide a description of how the documents

[905] Hilgard, M.C., 'Electronic Discovery im Schiedsverfahren' *SchiedsVZ* (2008) 122; see also Meier, A., 'The Production of Electronically Stored Information in International Commercial Arbitration' *SchiedsVZ* (2008) 184 with further references.

[906] See at <http://www.iccwbo.org/policy/arbitration/index.html?id=23620>.

[907] Art 16(1) of the ICDR International Dispute Resolution Rules: 'Subject to these Rules, the tribunal may conduct the arbitration in whatever manner it considers appropriate, provided that the parties are treated with equality and that each party has the right to be heard and is given a fair opportunity to present its case.'

[908] The ICDR Guidelines for Arbitrators Concerning Exchanges of Information are available at <http://www.adr.org/icdr>.

[909] Meyer, A. 'The Production of Electronically Stored Information in International Commercial Arbitration' *SchiedsVZ* (2008) 184.

[910] *ibid.*

[911] Fouchard, Gaillard, Goldman (n 30) 193 no 352.

[912] Art 3(1) and (2) of the IBA Rules.

[913] Pursuant to Art 1 of the IBA Rules the term 'document' within the scope of a 'document request' is defined as 'a writing of any kind, whether recorded on paper, electronic means, audio or visual recording or any other mechanical or electronic means of storing or recording information'.

are relevant and material to the outcome of the case,[914] overbroad e-document requests may be avoided under the IBA Rules. Hence, the IBA Rules are largely seen as being capable of handling the particularities involved with electronically stored data.[915]

Although the institutional arbitration rules in general do not offer any specific guidance as to what standards apply when the requested party refuses to produce (electronic) documents, it is admitted that there are basically four possibilities for the arbitral tribunal to react. The tribunal may draw an adverse inference: It will infer from the party's failure to comply with the production that the contents of the document would have been harmful to that party.[916] The tribunal may shift the burden of proof to the party with access to the evidence or deliver an interim award or partial award to commit a party to produce certain documents.[917] As far as the opponent of the request for e-discovery is located in the United States, there is also the possibility to have recourse to the national courts. **1.280**

Considering the increasing importance of e-discovery, arbitrators as well as all other participants in international arbitration proceedings should aim at familiarizing themselves with the particularities of electronically stored information.[918] For parties, it is advisable to assess at the very beginning of the arbitration proceedings whether the production of electronic data would be rather beneficial or detrimental to their own case. Accordingly, the parties should, clarify beforehand whether and to what extent the discovery of electronically stored data shall be allowed. **1.281**

(6) Multi-party arbitration

As in litigation, in arbitration too there are not seldom situations where several parties are affected by a legal dispute. The problems involved from a contractual and procedural point of view are commonly discussed under the notion of 'multi-party arbitration' although there is no uniform terminology.[919] **1.282**

(6.1) Problems with more than two parties in arbitration Nowadays, there is a lot of literature[920] on the frequent situation that at any stage of the arbitral process, there are three **1.283**

---

[914] See Art 3 (3) of the IBA Rules.

[915] Frank, J. and Bédard, J., 'Electronic Discovery' *Disp Res J* (November, 2007); Meier, A., 'The Production of Electronically Stored Information in International Commercial Arbitration' *SchiedsVZ* (2008) 188.

[916] Kaufmann-Kohler, G. and Baertsch, P., 'Discovery in International Arbitration: How much is too much?' *SchiedsVZ* (2008) 21.

[917] Hilgard, M.C., 'Electronic Discovery im Schiedsverfahren' *SchiedsVZ* (2008) 123 *et seq.*

[918] *ibid*, 128.

[919] Modern provisions tend to refer to 'multiple party arbitration'; see eg Art 10, ICC Rules 1998. Some authors use a wider notion as eg 'multicontract—multiparty arbitration', see Hanotiau, B. (1998) 14 *Arb Int'l* no 4, 369 *et seq.*

[920] See eg Bartels, M., 'Multi-Party Arbitration Clauses' (1985) 2 *J Int'l Arb* 62; Geimer, R., 'Beteiligung weiterer Parteien im Schiedsgerichtsverfahren, insbesondere die Drittwiderklage' in Böckstiegel, Berger, Bredow (eds), *Die Beteiligung Dritter an Schiedsverfahren* (Carl Heymanns Verlag, Cologne,2005); von Hoffmann, B, 'Schiedsgerichtsbarkeit in mehrstufigen Vertragsbeziehungen, insbesondere in Subunternehmerverträgen in Böckstiegel, Berger, Bredow (eds), *Die Beteiligung Dritter an Schiedsverfahren* (Carl Heymanns Verlag, Cologne, 2005); Markfort, R., 'Mehrparteien-Schiedsgerichtsbarkeit im deutschen und ausländischen Recht' (Cologne, 1994); Massuras, K., *Dogmatische Strukturen der Mehrparteienschiedsgerichtsbarkeit* (Frankfurt etc, 1998); Mustill, M.J., 'Multipartite Arbitrations: An Agenda for Law-Makers' (1991) 7 *Arb Int'l* no 4, 393; Nicklisch, F., 'Mehrparteienschiedsgerichtsbarkeit und Streitbeilegung bei Großprojekten' (FS Glossner 1994) 221; Sandrock, O., 'Wirkungen von Schiedsvereinbarungen im

or more parties involved. Each year, these situations represent about 20 per cent of the new ICC arbitration proceedings.[921]

1.284 The following are examples of typical situations, which generally occur in the construction industry and similar international joint ventures.[922] Either, the employer has contractual relations with several contractors, architects and engineers; if he then initiates arbitration proceedings against several of his partners, this may be called horizontal or multi-party arbitration in a strict sense. Or, the employer arbitrates against the main contractor, with whom he has only contracted and who, in turn, will start proceedings against one or more subcontractors; this situation may be characterized as vertical or multi-party arbitration in a wider sense.[923] In this case, the main contractor (defendant) may also try to include his contractors who he wants to hold liable, by way of *Streitverkündung, intervention forcée* etc.[924]

1.285 There are parallel or rather diverging interests to be taken into account: generally, the advantages of one proceeding as opposed to separate proceedings and the time- and money-saving objective of a uniform process are pointed out.[925] The aim of preventing differing results of various proceedings concerning one economic project and related arguments of *Prozessökonomie* reflect the 'broad interest of justice',[926] which has been generally summarized by Lord Denning in an English case.[927] On the other hand, the basic fact that arbitration is consensual (and thus requires explicit agreements of all parties to be included in one proceeding),[928] is supplemented by the also basic observation of *Nicklisch* that arbitration, as litigation, is designed as a two-party system following the bilateral

Konzern' in Böckstiegel, Berger, Bredow, *Die Beteiligung Dritter an Schiedsverfahren* (Carl Heymanns Verlag, Cologne,2005); von Schlabrendorff, F., 'Parallele Verfahren, Aufnahme von Dritten, Verbindung von Verfahren: Erfahrungen aus der Praxis der ICC' in Böckstiegel, Berger, Bredow (eds), *Die Beteiligung Dritter an Schiedsverfahren* (Carl Heymanns Verlag, Cologne, 2005). On the Guideline on Multi-Party Arbitrations prepared by the Chartered Institute of Arbitrators, see (2006) 72 *Arbitration* 2, 151.

[921] Hanotiau, B (1998) 14 *Arb Int'l* no 4, 372; Massuras, K., *Dogmatische Strukturen der Mehrparteienschiedsgerichtsbarkeit* (Frankfurt etc, 1998) 15 with further references.

[922] For practical examples, see Hanotiau, B. (1998) 14 *Arb Int'l* no 4, 371; Redfern, Hunter, Blackaby and Partasides (n 12) 3–70; Schlosser, P. (n 13) no 559; Lachmann, J.P. (n 81) no 1,237. There are, of course, many more complex contractual situations with more than two interested parties, eg in (international) transport, insurance and finance; for an overview, see Massuras, K., *Dogmatische Strukturen der Mehrparteienschiedsgerichtsbarkeit* (Frankfurt etc, 1998) 5 *et seq* with further references.

[923] For those definitions see Hanotiau, B. (1998) 14 *Arb Int'l* no 4, 371; Lionnet, K. and Lionnet, A. (n 29) 431 *et seq*. See also Redfern, Hunter, Blackaby and Partasides (n 12) 3–72. Horizontal situations are also those where the claimant sues several parties who are jointly and severally liable, as eg a company and its shareholders.

[924] See eg Schlosser, P. (n 13) no 570.

[925] See eg Schiffer, K.J., *Wirtschaftsschiedsgerichtsbarkeit* (Carl Heymanns Verlag, Cologne, etc, 1999) 65; Lachmann, J.P. (n 81) no 624; Massuras, K., *Dogmatische Strukturen der Mehrparteienschiedsgerichtsbarkeit Frankfurt etc* (1998) 22.

[926] Redfern, Hunter, Blackaby and Partasides (n 12) 3–69.

[927] *Abu Dhabi Gas Liquefaction Co Ltd. v Eastern Bechtel Corporation* [1982] 2 Lloyd's Rep 425, 427: '. . . there is a danger of having two separate arbitrations in a case like this. . . . It is most undesirable that there should be inconsistent findings by two separate arbitrators on virtually the self-same question, such as causation. It is very desirable that everything should be done to avoid such a circumstance.'

[928] This is pointed out by all authors, see eg Hanotiau, B. (1998) 14 *Arb Int'l* no 4, 372; Redfern, Hunter, Blackaby and Partasides (n 12) 3–69.

contractual structure.[929] Thus, the particular interest of a party, eg the employer in the above-mentioned examples, may well be contrary to including any other subcontractor who is bound only to the main contractor.[930] As a result, public and private interests may well diverge.

There are two legal principles which having been pointed out by Fouchard in 1980,[931] which form the focus of law-makers and parties when drafting particular provisions on multi-party situations: first, the contractual nature of arbitration requires a binding arbitration agreement or at least the consent of all parties to be included in one arbitral proceeding;[932] and second, especially at the stage of the appointment of arbitrators, equal treatment of all parties involved must be ensured.[933] **1.286**

This requirement of consent is also generally taken into account for the purpose of consolidation of two or more arbitral proceedings;[934] whereas there was, as an exception, in the United States the possibility of court-ordered obligatory consolidation of several arbitration proceedings,[935] this practice has been abandoned,[936] and modern statutes like the English Arbitration Act 1996 require all parties to agree to a consolidation by the court.[937] **1.287**

(6.2) Leading cases and recent legislation (statutes and rules) The best known decision regarding multi-party arbitration was issued by the *Cour de Cassation* in the matter of *Dutco*,[938] which gave rise to an intensive discussion in literature.[939] The company, Dutco, **1.288**

929 Nicklisch, F. (1999) 27 *Int'l Bus Lawyer* no 5, 212, 213 *et seq*; 'In reality, the contracts do form contract networks, legally, however, they remain separate and independent two-party contracts.'

930 Redfern, Hunter, Blackaby and Partasides (n 12) 3–73; Hanotiau, B. (1998) 14 *Arb Int'l* no 4, 372. For the various interests of the parties, see also Massuras, K., *Dogmatische Strukturen der Mehrparteienschiedsgerichtsbarkeit* (Frankfurt etc, 1998) 14 *et seq*.

931 Multi-Party Business Disputes, Institute of International Business Law and Practice, ICC Document no 359 (1980) 59.

932 For a detailed inquiry, see Massuras, K., *Dogmatische Strukturen der Mehrparteienschiedsgerichtsbarkeit* (Frankfurt etc, 1998) 87 *et seq*.

933 For details, see Schlosser, P. (n 13) nos 560 *et seq*; Lachmann, J.P. (n 81) no 1,250; Schütze, R.A. (n 29) no 86; Lionnet, K. and Lionnet, A. (n 29) 436; Massuras, K., *Dogmatische Strukturen der Mehrparteienschiedsgerichtsbarkeit* (Frankfurt etc, 1998) 24 *et seq*.

934 For more details, see eg Barron, W.M., 'Court-ordered Consolidation of Arbitration Proceedings in the United States' (1987) 4 *J Int'l Arb* no 1, 81; Massuras, K., *Dogmatische Strukturen der Mehrparteienschiedsgerichtsbarkeit* (Frankfurt etc, 1998) 25 *et seq*, 278 *et seq*; Wallace, R.E., 'Consolidated Arbitration in the United States—Recent Authority Requires Consent of the Parties' (1993) 10 *J Int'l Arb* no 4, 5. For the omission of a rule on consolidation in the Model Law, see ch 14 on Art 8, Model Law.

935 See Barron, W.M., 'Court-ordered Consolidation of Arbitration Proceedings in the United States' (1987) 4 *J Int'l Arb* no 1, 81; Massuras, K., *Dogmatische Strukturen der Mehrparteienschiedsgerichtsbarkeit* (Frankfurt etc, 1998) 39 *et seq*.

936 *United Kingdom v Boeing* (2nd Cir 1993), (1994) XIX YCA p 240; Wallace, R.E., 'Consolidated Arbitration in the United States—Recent Authority Requires Consent of the Parties' (1993) 10 *J Int'l Arb* no 4, 5; Massuras, K., *Dogmatische Strukturen der Mehrparteienschiedsgerichtsbarkeit* (Frankfurt etc, 1998) 48 *et seq*.

937 s 35(1) and (2): 'Unless the parties agree to confer such power on the tribunal, the tribunal has no power to order consolidation of proceedings or concurrent hearings.' For other jurisdictions, see the country reports in the following chapters.

938 *Sociétés BKMI et Siemens v Société Dutco Construction*, Cour de Cassation (7 January 1992), *Rev arb* (1992) 470.

939 Berger, K.P., 'Schiedsrichterbestellung in Mehrparteienschiedsverfahren: Der Fall "Dutco Construction" vor französischen Gerichten', *Recht der Internationalen Wirtschaft* (*RIW*) (1993) 702; Delvolvé, J.L.,

commenced in Paris a single arbitration proceeding, pursuant to an ICC arbitration clause, against two consortium partners. Both defendants rejected the claimant's request jointly to appoint one arbitrator, arguing that each defendant had the right to designate an arbitrator. In order to avoid the nomination of a single arbitrator for themselves by the ICC, the defendants nominated a joint arbitrator under protest and applied to the tribunal and later the court to stop the claimant's action for violation of the arbitration agreement. The *Cour d'Appel de Paris* argued that there was no violation of the principle of equal treatment since the agreement of all parties to have a three member tribunal involved the anticipation that two parties on one side would be forced to jointly nominate an arbitrator. The *Cour de Cassation*, on the contrary, held that the right of equal treatment at the stage of constituting the arbitral tribunal belonged to the *ordre public* and could not be waived in an arbitration agreement before a dispute had arisen.

1.289 Other case law, at least partly, took another view than the court in the *Dutco* matter. In the *Westland* case, the *Cour de Justice de Genève*, in 1982, held that the then common practice of the ICC to nominate an arbitrator for several defendants if they failed to agree on a joint nomination, was not giving *Westland* (the claimant) a preponderant influence on the constitution of the tribunal.[940] There are, however, numerous other Swiss decisions which kept emphasizing the non-excludable right of equal influence on the constitution of the arbitral tribunal.[941] Similarly, the German *Bundesgerichtshof* rejected the agreed appointment of the tribunal by one party only.[942] In England, the Court of Appeal appointed a single arbitrator for two arbitration proceedings in a construction case where the two arbitration clauses were identical, both referring to London arbitration with a single arbitrator.[943]

1.290 In some arbitration statutes, there are specific regulations on the issue. The Netherlands have included a provision on the participation of a third party in the 1986 Arbitration Act which, as usual, requires consent by all parties involved.[944] There is also a provision on the consolidation of several arbitral proceedings.[945] In England, there is a provision which

---

'Multipartism: The Dutco Decision of the French Cour de Cassation' (1993) 9 *Arb Int'l* 197; Schwartz, E.A., 'Multi-Party Arbitration and the ICC in the Wake of Dutco' (1993) 10 *J Int'l Arb* no 3, 5. See also Derains, Y. and Schwartz, E.A. (n 58) 166 *et seq*; Fouchard, Gaillard, Goldman (n 30) *et seq*, no 792; Massuras, K., *Dogmatische Strukturen der Mehrparteienschiedsgerichtsbarkeit* (Frankfurt etc, 1998) 302 *et seq*.

[940] Républic arabe d'Egypte v Westland Helicopters Ltd, Cour de Justice de Genève (26 November1982), affirmed by the Tribunal Fédéral (16 May 1983), (1986) XI YCA, 127. For a discussion, see Schlosser, P. (n 13) no 564; Derains, Y. and Schwartz, E.A. (n 58) 169; Massuras, K., *Dogmatische Strukturen der Mehrparteienschiedsgerichtsbarkeit* (Frankfurt etc, 1998) 227 *et seq*. The award was later annulled on the ground that not all parties were bound by the arbitration agreement, see Swiss Supreme Court (BG 19 July 1988), *Rev arb* 1989, 525.

[941] Bundesgericht, BGE 57 I 205; 72 I 90; 97 I 489; 107 Ia 155.

[942] BGH Neue Juristische Wochenschrift (NJW) (1989) 1,477. See also the decision of 3 July 1975, BGHZ 65, 59 *et seq*, 64, 66, which emphasized the equal influence of all parties on the constitution of the tribunal.

[943] See Schlosser, P. (n 13) no 582.

[944] Art 1045 of the Dutch Arbitration Act (WBR), which is practically identical to Art 41 of the Rules of the Netherlands Arbitration Institute (NAI), provides that a third party may request to join an arbitration or a party may serve a notice of joinder on a third party which then, with the consent of all parties, becomes a party to the arbitral proceeding.

[945] According to Art 1046, the competent court may order the consolidation of several arbitration proceedings, following which order the parties are required jointly to appoint the arbitrators; failing such appointment, the President of the court appoints the tribunal.

addresses the situation that there are more than two parties and that there occurs a failure of the agreed appointment procedure. The court, then, is entitled to make the necessary appointments itself and to revoke nominations already made.[946] There is also a rule on the consolidation of arbitral proceedings.[947] The German legislator omitted to regulate multi-party situations and delegated all related problems to the courts.[948] The *Bundesgerichtshof*, however, already in 1996, prior to the new arbitration law, felt unable to generally resolve the issue and rejected to take on the role of a quasi-legislator.[949] There are, nevertheless, provisions in the new law on arbitration which might be used for restoring or safeguarding the principle of equality in multi-party situations.[950]

The UNCITRAL Model Law with its amendments of 2006 has not yet addressed the problems of multi-party arbitration. However, taking into consideration the growth of multi-party disputes, the Arbitration Working Group has acknowledged the necessity of specific rules to be included in the Model Law.[951] The Working Group intends to confirm the possibility of multiple claimants or respondents in UNCITRAL arbitrations. It has, therefore, agreed to revise the process for constituting tribunals in multi-party cases to avoid the method of appointment that was condemned as unfair by France's *Cour de Cassation* in the *Dutco* matter. **1.291**

Most major arbitral institutions already revised their rules to provide that, where multiple claimants or respondents do not agree on their preferred appointee to the tribunal and the choice has to be made for them, then the other 'party-appointed' arbitrator must also be appointed by the institution that administers the arbitration. So eg Art 10 of the ICC Arbitration Rules regulates the appointment of the arbitrators in the case of a three-person arbitral tribunal.[952] The general rule, still, is that each side, ie the claimant(s) and defendant(s), shall nominate one arbitrator respectively. If the defendants fail to jointly nominate one arbitrator, the ICC Court will then appoint both the two party-appointed arbitrators and the chairman. The claimant, thus, loses his right to nominate an arbitrator, as well. Similarly, the London Court of International Arbitration, according to the LCIA Arbitration Rules, now enjoys the right to appoint the arbitral tribunal if all parties have **1.292**

---

[946] ss 16(7) and 18, Arbitration Act 1996.

[947] s 35 allows the consolidation of several arbitral proceedings or the holding of common hearings, provided that the parties have agreed so specifically.

[948] See eg Berger, K.P., *The New German Arbitration Law* (n 115) 179 *et seq.* (Official Report on s 1030 ZPO); Schiffer, K.J., *Wirtschaftsschiedsgerichtsbarkeit,* 65.

[949] BGH (29 March 1996), Betriebsberater (BB) (1996) 1074 *et seq.*

[950] s 1034(2), ZPO provides that the court may appoint the arbitrator or arbitrators if the arbitration agreement 'grants preponderant rights' to one party, placing the other party at a disadvantage. This provision might be used for multi-party situations, see Berger, K.P., *DIS-Mat IV* (1998) 11, 19 *et seq.* Further, s 1035(4), ZPO allows a party to seek the assistance of the court if the parties were 'unable to reach an agreement expected of them' under the agreed appointment procedure. K.P. Schlosser refers to s 1032(2), ZPO which might give some help by providing that the court may be seized in order to decide whether an arbitral proceeding in a particular case is admissible or not; see *Recht der Internationalen Wirtschaft* (*RIW*) (1994) 724.

[951] The lack of a specific rule is regretted, see Schlosser, P., *Recht der Internationalen Wirtschaft* (*RIW*) (1994) 723 *et seq*, 724; Massuras, K., *Dogmatische Strukturen der Mehrparteienschiedsgerichtsbarkeit* Frankfurt etc (1998) 32.

[952] On the new rules and the historical background, see Derains, Y. and Schwartz, E.A. (n 58) 165–73, and Grigera Naón, H.A., *DIS-Mat II* (1998) 45, 52 *et seq.*

not agreed in writing to the contrary.[953] In addition, the joinder of a third party is possible if this third party agrees.[954] Finally, the Rules of the German Institution of Arbitration (DIS Rules) contain a similar provision as that of the ICC Rules (s 13, DIS Rules).[955] Only if several defendants fail to jointly nominate one arbitrator, the DIS appointing authority will appoint two arbitrators, who then have to elect the chairman.

IV. Bibliography

General bibliography

Berger, Klaus-Peter, *Das neue Recht der Schiedsgerichtsbarkeit—The New German Arbitration Law* (RWS Verlag Kommunikationsforum GmbH, Cologne, 1998) (Berger, The new German arbitration law).

Berger, Klaus-Peter, *Private Dispute Resolution in International Business* (Kluwer Law International, The Hague, London, Boston, 2006).

Craig, Laurence W., Park, William W. and Paulsson, Jan, *International Chamber of Commerce Arbitration* (3rd edn, OUP, New York, etc, 1999).

Derains, Yves and Schwartz, Eric A., *A Guide to the New ICC Rules of Arbitration* (Kluwer Law International, The Hague, London, Boston, 1999).

Eijsvogel, Peter (ed), *Evidence in International Arbitral Proceedings* (ICC Publishing SA, Paris, 1994).

Fouchard, Philippe, Gaillard, Emmanuel and Goldman, Berthold, *Traité de l'arbitrage commercial international* (Litec, Paris 1996).

Gottwald, Peter (ed), *Internationale Schiedsgerichtsbarkeit: Generalbericht und Nationalberichte* (Gieseking, Bielefeld, 1997).

Hunter, Martin, Mariott, Arthur and Veeder, Van Vechten, *The Internationalisation of International Arbitration* (Graham & Trotman/M. Nijhoff, London, 1995) (The Internationalisation of International Arbitration).

Labes, Hubertus W. and Lörcher, Torsten, *Nationales und internationales Schiedsverfahrensrecht* (C. H. Beck, Munich, 1998).

Lachmann, Jens-Peter, *Handbuch für die Schiedsgerichtspraxis* (3rd edn, Dr Otto Schmidt Verlag, Cologne, 2008).

Lalive, Pierre, Poudret, Jean E. and Reymond, Claude, *Le droit de l'arbitrage interne et international en Suisse* (Helbing & Lichtenhahn, Editions Payot, Lausanne, 1989).

Lew, Julian D. M., Mistelis, Loukas A. and Kröll, Stefan, *Comparative International Commercial Arbitration* (Kluwer Law International, The Hague, London, Boston, 2003).

Lionnet, Klaus and Lionnet, Annette, *Handbuch der internationalen und nationalen Schiedsgerichtsbarkeit* (3rd edn, Boorberg, Stuttgart, 2005) (Lionnet).

Mustill, Michael and Boyd, Stewart C., *The Law and Practice of Commercial Arbitration in England* (Butterworths Legal Publishers, 1989).

Newman, Lawrence W. and Hill, Richard D. (eds), *The Leading Arbitrators' Guide to International Arbitration* (2nd edn, Juris Publishing, New York, 2008).

[953] See Art 8.1 which, in order to exclude such power of the court, requires an agreement in writing that the parties accept to be treated as 'two separate sides for the formation of the Arbitral Tribunal, as Claimant and Respondent respectively'.

[954] Art 22.1(h), LCIA Rules.

[955] See Bredow, J., *DIS-Mat IV* (1998) 111, 115 *et seq*.

Poudret, Jean-Francois and Besson, Sébastien, *Comparative Law of International Arbitration* (Sweet & Maxwell, 2007).

Redfern, Alan, Hunter, Martin, Blackaby, Nigel and Partasides, Constantine, *Law and Practice of International Commercial Arbitration* (4th edn, Thomson Sweet & Maxwell, London, 2004).

Rubino-Sammartano, Mauro, *International Arbitration Law* (Deventer, Boston, 1990).

Schiffer, Jan K., *Wirtschaftsschiedsgerichtsbarkeit* (Carl Heymanns Verlag, Cologne, etc, 1999) (Schiffer).

Schlosser, Peter, *Das Recht der internationalen privaten Schiedsgerichtsbarkeit* (2nd edn, Mohr Siebeck, Tübingen, 1989).

Schütze, Rolf A., *Schiedsgericht und Schiedsverfahren* (4th edn, C.H. Beck Verlag, Munich, 2007).

Schwab, Karl Heinz and Walter, Gerhard, *Schiedsgerichtsbarkeit* (6th edn, C.H. Beck Verlag, Munich, 2000).

History and nature of arbitration

Ambrose, Claire and Maxwell, Karen, *London Maritime Arbitration,* (Informa Law, London, 1996).

Blessing, Marc, 'The New Swiss Law on International Arbitration' (1988) 5 *J Int'l Arb* no1, 1.

Böckstiegel, Karl-Heinz, 'Perspective of Future Development in International Arbitration' in L.W. Newman and R.D. Hill (eds), *The Leading Arbitrators' Guide to International Arbitration* (2nd edn, Juris Publishing, New York, 2008) 495.

Bond, Stephen, 'How to Draft an Arbitration Clause' (1989) 6 *J Int'l Arb* no 2.

Briner, Robert, 'Domestic Arbitration: Practice in Continental Europe and its Lessons for Arbitration in England' (1997) 13 *Arb Int'l* no 2, 155.

Bulow, Lucienne Carasso, 'The revised Arbitration Rules of the Society of Maritime Arbitrators' (1995) 12 *J Int'l Arb* no1, 87.

Caldwell, Peter, 'Maritime Arbitration in Hong Kong', Paper presented at the IBA Seminar on Arbitration and Transport Disputes, 29-31 May 1997, Hamburg.

David, René, *L' arbitrage dans le commerce international* (Economica, Paris, 1982).

Delvolvé, Jean-Luis, 'The Fundamental Right to Arbitration', in: Hunter, Marriott, Veeder, *The Internationalisation of International Arbitration* (Graham & Trotman/M. Nijhoff, London, 1995, 141).

Haas, Ulrich, 'Die Sportschiedsgerichtsbarkeit des Tribunal Arbitral du Sport (TAS)' *ZeuP* (1999) 355.

Holtappels, Peter, 'Maritime Arbitration in Germany', Paper presented at the IBA Seminar on Arbitration and Transport Disputes, 29–31 May 1997, Hamburg.

Houtte, Hans van, 'May Court Judgements that Disregard Arbitration Clauses and Awards be Enforced under the Brussels and Lugano Conventions?' (1997) 13 *Arb Int'l* no1, 85.

Mallmann, Roman A., 'Neue FIDIC - Standardbedingungen für Bau- und Anlageverträge', *Recht der Internationalen Wirtschaft* (*RIW*) 2000, 532.

Mann, Francis A., 'Lex facit arbitrum', in: Sanders (ed), *Liber amicorum for Martin Domke* (1967) 157, reproduced in (1986) 2 *Arb Int'l* no 3, 241.

Mayer, Pierre, 'The Trend of Delocalisation in the Last 100 Years', in Hunter, Marriott, Veeder, *The Internationalisation of International Arbitration* (Graham & Trotman/M. Nijhoff, London, 1995) 37.

McCormack, Howard, 'Maritime Arbitration Practice in New York', Paper presented at the IBA Seminar on Arbitration and Transport Disputes, 29–31 May 1997, Hamburg.

Mistelis, Loukas A. and Lew, Julian D.M., *Arbitration Insights: Twenty Years of the Annual Lecture of the School of International Arbitration* (Kluwer Law International, 2007).

Park, William W., *International Forum Selection* (Kluwer Law International, Boston, 1995).

Ramberg, Jan, 'Maritime Arbitration in Sweden', Paper presented at the IBA Seminar on Arbitration and Transport Disputes, 29-31 May 1997, Hamburg.

Rensmann, Thilo, 'Anational Arbitral Awards (Legal Phenomenon or Academic Phantom?)' (1998) 15 *J Int'l Arb* no 2, 37.

Robine, Eric, 'What Companies Expect from International Commercial Arbitration' (1992) 9 *J Int'l Arb* no 31.

Schmitthoff, Clive, 'Defective Arbitration Clauses', *JBL* (1975) 9.

Smit, Hans (ed), *WIPO Arbitration Rules: Commentary and Analysis* (Juris Publishing, New York, 2000).

Veeder, Van Vechten, 'Two Arbitral Butterflies: Bramwell and David', in: Hunter, Marriott, Veeder, *The Internationalisation of International Arbitration* (Graham & Trotman/M. Nijhoff, London, 1995) 13.

Weigand, Frank-Bernd, 'Das neue englische Schiedsverfahrensrecht', *Recht der Internationalen Wirtschaft* (*RIW*) (1997), 904.

Wiegand, Christian, '"Adjudication"—Beschleunigte außergerichtliche Streiterledigungsverfahren im englischen Baurecht und im internationalen FIDIC—Standardvertragsrecht', *Recht der Internationalen Wirtschaft* (*RIW*) (2000) 197.

Yu, Hong-lin, 'Total Separation of International Commercial Arbitration and National Court Regime' (1998) 15 *J Int'l Arb* no 2, 145.

Ziegler, Karl-Heinz, *Das private Schiedsgericht im antiken römischen Recht* (Munich, 1971).

Arbitration agreement

Binder, Peter, *International Commercial Arbitration and Conciliation in UNCITRAL Model Law Jurisdictions* (2nd edn, Sweet & Maxwell, 2005).

Bond, Stephen, 'How to Draft an Arbitration Clause' (1989) 6 *J Int'l Arb* no 1, 2.

Houtte, Hans van, 'May Court Judgments that Disregard Arbitration Clauses and Awards be Enforced under the Brussels and Lugano Conventions?' (1997) 13 *Arb Int'l* no1, 85.

Kucherepa, Peter, 'Reviewing Trends and Proposals to Recognize Oral Agreements to Arbitrate in International Arbitration Law' (2005) *Am Rev Int'l Arb* 16, 409.

Sorieul, Renaud, 'UNCITRAL's Current Work in the Field of International Commercial Arbitration', (2005) 22 *J Int'l Arb* no 6, 543.

Dispute resolution in a globalized world

Benson, Cyrus, 'Can Professional Ethics Wait? The Need for Transparency in International Arbitration' (2009) 3 *Disp Res Int'l* no 1, 78.

Berger, Klaus-Peter, 'Aufgaben und Grenzen der Privatautonomie in der internationalen Wirtschaftsschiedsgerichtsbarkeit' *Recht der Internationalen Wirtschaft* (*RIW*) (1994) 12.

Blessing, Marc, 'The New Swiss Law on International Arbitration' (1988) 5 *J Int'l Arb* no 1, 1.

Briner, Robert, 'Domestic Arbitration: Practice in Continental Europe and its Lessons for Arbitration in England' (1997) 13 *Arb Int'l* no 2, 155.

Cremades, Bernardo M., 'Overcoming the Clash of Legal Cultures: The Role of Interactive Arbitration' (1998) 14 *Arb Int'l* no 2, 157.

Delvolvé, Jean-Luis, 'The Fundamental Right to Arbitration', in Hunter, Marriott, Veeder, *The Internationalisation of International Arbitration* (Graham & Trotman/M. Nijhoff, London, 1995) 141.

International Council for Commercial Arbitration (ICCA), *International Dispute Resolution: Towards an International Arbitration Culture,* ICCA Congress Series no 8 (The Hague, 1998).

Kerr, Michael, 'Concord and Conflict in International Arbitration' (1997) 13 *Arb Int'l* no 2, 121.

Lalive, Pierre, 'The Internationalisation of International Arbitration: Some Observations', in: Hunter, Marriott, Veeder, *The Internationalisation of International Arbitration* (Graham & Trotman/M. Nijhoff, London, 1995) 53.

Mayer, Pierre, 'The Trend of Delocalisation in the Last 100 Years' in: Hunter, Marriott, Veeder, *The Internationalisation of International Arbitration* (Graham & Trotman/M. Nijhoff, London, 1995) 37.

Mustill, Michael John, 'Arbitration: History and Background' (1989) 6 *J Int'l Arb* no 2, 43.

Najar, Jean-Claude, 'The Inside View: Companies' Needs in Arbitration' (1996) 12 *Arb Int'l* no 3, 359.

Park, William W., *International Forum Selection* (Kluwer Law International, Boston etc, 1995) (Park, Forum Selection).

Rau, Alan Scott, 'On Integrity in Private Judging', (1998) 14 *Arb Int'l* no 2, 115.

Rensmann, Thilo, 'Anational Arbitral Awards (Legal Phenomenon or Academic Phantom?)' (1998) 15 *J Int'l Arb* no 2, 37.

Robine, Eric, 'What Companies Expect from International Commercial Arbitration', (1992) 9 *J Int'l Arb* no 2, 31.

Rubino-Sammartano, Mauro, 'Is Arbitration to be just a Luxury Clinic?' (1990) 7 *J Int'l Arb* no 3, 25.

Rubino-Sammartano, Mauro, 'Is arbitration losing ground?' *Am Rev Int'l Arb* vol 14, 341.

Saville, Mark, 'The Origin of the New English Arbitration Act 1996: Reconciling Speed with Justice in the Decision-making Process' (1997) 13 *Arb Int'l* no 3, 237.

Schlosser, Peter, 'Arbitration and the European Public Policy', in: *L'arbitrage et le droit européen,* Actes du Colloque International du CEPANI du 24 avril 1997 (Bruylant, Bruxelles, 1997) 81 (Schlosser, CEPANI).

Schmidt-Diemitz, Rolf, 'Internationale Schiedsgerichtsbarkeit - Eine empirische Untersuchung', *Der Betrieb (DB)* 1999, 369.

Weigand, Frank-Bernd, 'Der nebenberuflich tätige Schiedsrichter' in Bachmann, B., Breidenbach, S., Coester-Waltjen, D., Heß, B., Nelle, A. and Wolf, C., (eds) *Grenzüberschreitungen—Festschrift für Peter Schlosser zum 70. Geburtstag* (Mohr Siebeck, Tübingen, 2005).

Types of arbitration

Ambrose, Claire and Maxwell, Karen, *London Maritime Arbitration* (2nd edn, Informa Law, London, 2002) (C Ambrose, K Maxwell).

Bagner, Hans, 'Expedited Arbitration Rules: Stockholm and WIPO' (1997) 13 *Arb Int'l* no 2, 193.

Berger, Klaus-Peter, 'Die Ergänzenden Regeln für Beschleunigte Verfahren der Deutschen Institution für Schiedsgerichtsbarkeit' *SchiedsVZ* (2008) 105.

Berger, Klaus-Peter, 'The Need for Speed in International Arbitration—Supplementary Rules for Expedited Procedures of the German Institution of Arbitration (DIS)' (2008) 25 *J Int'l Arb* 595.

Bingham Lord, 'The Problem of Delay in Arbitration', in: L.A. Mistelis, J.D.M. Lew (eds), *Arbitration Insights: Twenty Years of the Annual Lecture of the School of International Arbitration* (Kluwer, The Hague, 2007), 4–1 *et seq.*

Borchard, Edwin Montefiore, *The Diplomatic Protection of Citizens Abroad or the Law of International Claims* (Banks Law Publishing, New York, 1915).

Borris, Christian, 'Streiterledigung bei (MAC-)Klauseln in Unternehmenskaufverträgen: ein Fall für "Fast-Track"—Schiedsverfahren' 2008 *Betriebsberater* (*BB*) 294.

Bühring-Uhle, Christian, *Arbitration and Mediation in International Business* (2006).

Bulow, Lucienne Carasso, 'The revised Arbitration Rules of the Society of Maritime Arbitrators' (1995) 12 *J Int'l Arb* no1, 87.

Caldwell, Peter, 'Maritime Arbitration in Hong Kong', Paper presented at the IBA Seminar on Arbitration and Transport Disputes, 29-31 May 1997, Hamburg.

Davis, Benjamin, 'Fast-Track Arbitration and Fast-Tracking Your Arbitration', (1992) 9 *J Int'l Arb* no 4, 43.

Escher, Alfred, Nacimiento, Patricia and Weissenborn, Christoph, 'Investment Arbitration and the Participation of State Parties in Germany', in Böckstiegel *et al* (eds) *Arbitration in Germany* (Kluwer Law Interantional, Alphen Aan Den Rijn, 2007).

Escher, Alfred, 'Weltbank-Schiedszentrum: Zuständigkeit für die Beilegung von Investitionsstreitigkeiten' *Recht der Internationalen Wirtschaft* (*RIW*) (2001) 20.

Haas, Ulrich, 'Die Sportschiedsgerichtsbarkeit des Tribunal Arbitral du Sport' (TAS) *ZeuP* 1999, 355.

Happ, Richard, 'Schiedsverfahren zwischen Staaten und Investoren unter Artikel 26 Energiechartavertrag. Eine Studie zum Wandel der Streitbeilegung im Investitionsschutzrecht unter den Bedingungen der globalen Weltwirtschaft', *Schriftenreihe der August Maria Berges-Stiftung für Arbitrales Recht, Bd 7* (Peter Lang, 2000).

Holtappels, Peter, 'Maritime Arbitration in Germany', Paper presented at the IBA Seminar on Arbitration and Transport Disputes, 29-31 May 1997, Hamburg.

Horn, Norbert, 'Current Use of the UNCITRAL Arbitration Rules in the Context of Investment Arbitration', (2008) 24 *Arb Int'l* no 4, 587.

ICC (Editor), 'Techniques for Controlling Time and Costs in Arbitration'—Report from the ICC Commission on Arbitration.

Jagusch, Stephen and Gearing, Matthew, 'ICSID' in: Rowley (ed), *Arbitration World,* European Lawyer Reference (2nd edn, London, 2006).

Mallmann, Roman A., 'Neue FIDIC—Standardbedingungen für Bau- und Anlageverträge' *Recht der Internationalen Wirtschaft* (*RIW*) 2000, 532.

McCormack, Howard, 'Maritime Arbitration Practice in New York', paper presented at the IBA Seminar on Arbitration and Transport Disputes, 29-31 May 1997, Hamburg.

McLachlan, Campbell, Shore, Laurence and Weininger, Matthew, *International Investment Arbitration* (OUP, Oxford *et al*, 2007).

Müller, Eva, 'Fast-Track Arbitration: Meeting the Demands of the Next Millenium' (1998) 15 *Int'l Arb* no 3, 5.

Newcombe, Charlotte W., *Law and Practice of Investment Treaties* (Alphen Aan Den Rijn, 2009).

Paulsson, Jan, 'Arbitration Without Privity', 10 *ICSID Rev* (1995) 232.

Ramberg, Jan, 'Maritime Arbitration in Sweden', paper presented at the IBA Seminar on Arbitration and Transport Disputes, 29-31 May 1997, Hamburg.

Saville, Marc, 'The Origin of the New English Arbitration Act 1996: Reconciling Speed with Justice in the Decision-making Process' (1997) 13 *Arb Int'l* no 3, 237.

Scherer, Matthias, 'Acceleration of Arbitration Proceedings—The Swiss Way: The Expedited Procedure under the Swiss Rules of International Arbitration' *SchiedsVZ* (2005) 229.

Schreuer, Christoph, 'Keynote Address: The Dynamic Evolution of the ICSID System' in Hofmann/Tams (eds), *The International Convention on the Settlement of Investment Disputes (ICSID): Taking Stock after 40 Years* (Nomos) 15.

Schreuer, Christoph, 'The ICSID Convention: A Commentary', (Cambridge *et al*, 2001).

Silverman, Moses, 'The Fast-Track Arbitration of the International Chamber of Commerce' (1993) 10 *Arb Int'l* no 4, 113.

Smit, Hans (ed), *WIPO Arbitration Rules: Commentary and Analysis* (Juris Publishing, New York, 2000).

Vandevelde, Kenneth J., *United States Investment Treaties: Policy and Practice* (Deventer: Kluwer Law International, The Hague, London, Boston, 1992).

Wiegand, Christian, '"Adjudication"—Beschleunigte außergerichtliche Streiterledigungsverfahren im englischen Baurecht und im internationalen FIDIC—Standardvertragsrecht' *Recht der Internationalen Wirtschaft* (*RIW*) (2000) 197.

Zeiler, Gerold, 'Investitionsschutz und Schiedsverfahren', in Torggler, *Praxishandbuch Schiedsgerichtsbarkeit* (Schulthess Juristische Medien Verlag Österreich Nomos, Wien *et al*, 2007).

Different national approaches

Blessing, Marc, 'The New International Arbitration Law in Switzerland' (1988) 5 *J Int'l Arb* no 1, 9.

Cohen, Michael Marks, 'A Missed Opportunity to Revise the Arbitration Act 1996' (2007) 23 *Arb Int'l* no 3, 461.

Cremades, Bernardo M., 'Overcoming the Clash of Legal Cultures: The Role of Interactive Arbitration' (1998) 14 *Arb Int'l* no 2, 157.

Dundas, Hew R., 'Court Support of Arbitration Agreements: Anti-Suit Injunctions and the European Court of Justice' (2007) 73 *Arbitration* no 3, 348.

Dutta, Anatol and Heinze, Christian A., 'Anti-suit injunctions zum Schutz von Schiedsvereinbarungen' *Recht der Internationalen Wirtschaft* (*RIW*) 2007, 411.

Fraser, Davidson, 'The New Arbitration Act—A Model Law' (1997) *JBL*, March issue, 101.

Gaillard, Emmanuel, 'A Foreign View on the New Swiss Law on International Arbitration' (1988) 4 *Arb Int'l* no 1, 25.

Harris, Bruce, 'Report on the Arbitration Act 1996' (2007) 23 *Arb Int'l* no 3, 437.

Kerr Jr, John J., 'Arbitrability of Securities Law Claims in Common Law Nations' (1996) 12 *Arb Int'l* no 2, 171.

Russel, Francis, 'A Letter of 1853 from Francis Russel Esq MA to the Rt. Hon Lord Brougham & Vaux on the Improvement and Consolidation of the Law of Arbitration', reproduced in (1997) 13 *Arb Int'l* no 3, 253.

Steyn, Jonathan, '1993 Freshfields Arbitration Lecture: England's Response to the Model Law of Arbitration' (1994) 60 *Arbitration* no 3, 184.

Weigand, Frank-Bernd, 'Das neue englische Schiedsverfahrensrecht' *Recht der Internationalen Wirtschaft* (*RIW*) 1997, 904.

Weisenberger, Kirsten, 'From Hostility to Harmony: Buckeye Marks a Milestone in the Acceptance of Arbitration in the American Jurisprudence' (2005) 16 *Am Rev Int'l Arb* 551.

Zekos, Georgios, 'The Role of Courts in Commercial and Maritime Arbitration Under English Law' (1998) 15 *J Int'l Arb* no 1, 51.

Harmonization by international instruments

Craig, Laurence W., 'Uses and Abuses of Appeal from Awards' (1988) 4 *Arb Int'l* no 3, 174.

Hof, Jacomijn van, *Commentary on the UNCITRAL Arbitration Rules. The Application by the Iran-US Claims Tribunal* (Deventer, 1991).

Holtzmann, Howard and Neuhaus, Joseph, *A Guide to the UNCITRAL Model Law on International Commercial Arbitration: Legislative History and Commentary* (Deventer, 1989).

Hunter, Martin, 'The Procedural Powers of Arbitrators Under the English 1996 Act' (1997) 13 *Arb Int'l* no 4, 345.

Hußlein-Stich, Gabriele, *Das UNCITRAL-Modellgesetz über die internationale Handelsschiedsgerichtsbarkeit,* in Böckstiegel (Carl Heymanns Verlag, Cologne etc, 1990).

Kerr, Michael, 'Concord and Conflict in International Arbitration' (1997) 13 *Arb Int'l* no 2, 121.

Lew, Julian D.M., Mistelis, Loukas A. and Kröll, Stefan, *Comparative International Commercial Arbitration* (Kluwer Law International, 2003).

McAuley, Stephen, 'Achieving the harmonisation of transnational civil procedure: Will the ALI/UNIDROIT Project succeed?' (2004) 15 *Am Rev Int'l Arb* 231.

Mantilla-Serrano, Fernando, 'The New Spanish Arbitration Act' (2004) 21 *JJ Int'l Arb* no 4, 367.

Mistelis, Loukas A. and Lew, Julian D.M., *Arbitration Insights: Twenty Years of the Annual Lecture of the School of International Arbitration* (Kluwer Law International, 2007).

Mustill, Michael John, 'Arbitration: History and Background' (1989) 6 *J Int'l Arb* no 2, 43.

Nariman, Fali S., 'Some Thoughts on the Fortieth Anniversary of the New York Convention 1958' (1998) *Int'l Arb L Rev* 163.

Nishikawa, Rieko, 'Arbitration Law Reform in Japan' (2004) 21 *J Int'l Arb* no 3, 303.

Philip, Allan, 'A Century of Internationalisation of International Arbitration: An Overview' in M. Hunter, A. Marriott, V.V. Veeder, eds, *The Internationalisation of International Arbitration* (Graham & Trotman/M. Nijhoff, London, 1995) 25.

Sanders, Pieter, 'University and Diversity in the Adoption of the Model Law' (1995) 11 *Arb Int'l* no1, 1.

Sanders, Pieter, 'UNCITRAL's Model Law on International and Commercial Arbitration: Present Situation and Future' (2005) 21 *Arb Int'l* no 4, 443.

Strempel, Hans and Hobér, Kaj, 'Das neue schwedische Gesetz über Schiedsverfahren, neue Regeln für das Schiedsinstitut der Handelskammer Stockholm' *RPS, Beilage 4 zu Betriebsberater (BB)* 11/1999, 8.

Van den Berg, Albert Jan, *The New York Arbitration Convention of 1958* (1981) (AJ van den Berg).

Van den Berg, Albert Jan, *Improving the Efficiency of Arbitration Agreements and Awards: 40 Years of Application of the New York Convention*, ICCA Congress Series no 9 (The Hague, 1999).

Veeder, Van Vechten, 'Two Arbitral Butterflies: Bramwell and David' in M Hunter, A Marriott, VV Veeder, eds, *The Internationalisation of International Arbitration* (Graham & Trotham/M. Nijhoff, London, 1995) 13.

Weigand, Frank-Bernd, 'The UNCITRAL Model Law: New Draft Arbitration Acts in Germany and Sweden' (1995) 11 *Arb Int'l* no 4, 397.

Liberal approach to (international) arbitration

Beechey, John, 'Arbitrability of Antitrust / Competition Law Issues—Common Law', (1996) 12 *Arb Int'l* no2, 179.

Bernet, Martin and Müller, Anna K., 'Chapter 9—Recognition and Enforcement of Foreign Arbitral Awards' in Kaufmann-Kohler, *International Arbitration in Switzerland* (Kluwer Law International, 2004) 167.

Blessing, Marc, 'The New International Arbitration Law in Switzerland' (1988) 5 *J Int'l Arb* no 1, 1.

Blessing, Marc, 'Arbitrability of Intellectual Property Disputes' (1996) 12 *Arb Int'l* no 2, 191.

Böckstiegel, Karl-Heinz, 'Zu den Thesen von einer delokalisiserten internationalen Schiedsgerichtsbarkeit' in FS Oppenhoff (Munich, 1985) 1.

Filho, Clávio Valenca, 'TMC Terminal Multimodal De Coroa Grande Spe S.A. v. Ministro da Ciencia e Tecnologia' (2007) 24 *J Int'l Arb* no 4, 431.

Geisinger, Elliott and Frossard, Viviane, 'Chapter 8—Challenge and Revision of the Award' in Gabrielle Kaufmann-Kohler, *International Arbitration in Switzerland* (Kluwer Law International, 2004) 136.

Hanotiau, Bernard, 'L'arbitrage et le droit européen de la concurrence' in Böckstiegel, *Acts of State and Arbitration* (Carl Heymanns Verlag, Cologne, 1997) 31.

Hanotiau, Bernard, 'What Law Governs the Issue of Arbitrability?' (1996) 12 *Arb Int'l* no 4, 391.

Hascher, Dominique T., 'Recognition and Enforcement of Judgements on the Existence and Validity of Arbitration Clauses under the Brussels Convention' (1997) 13 *Arb Int'l.* no 1, 33.

Heidbrink, Alfried and von der Groeben, Marie-Christine, 'Insolvenz und Schiedsverfahren' *ZIP* 2006, 265.

Hoffmann, Bernd von, 'Internationally Mandatory Rules of Law Before Arbitral Tribunals' in Böckstiegel (ed), *Acts of State and Arbitration* (Carl Heymanns Verlag, Cologne etc, 1997) 3.

Karrer, Pierre, 'Judicial Review of International Arbitral Awards, up to a Point' in *Festschrift für Rolf A. Schütze* (Munich, 1999) 338.

Karrer, Pierre and Kälin-Nauer, Claudia, 'Is there a Favor Jurisdictionis Arbitri? Standards of Review of Arbitral Jurisdiction Decisions in Switzerland' (1996) 13 *J Int'l Arb* no 3, 31.

Kaufmann-Kohler, Gabrielle (ed), *International Arbitration in Switzerland* (Kluwer Law International, 2004).

Kerr, John J., 'Arbitrability of Securities Law Claims in Common Law Nations' (1996) 12 *Arb Int'l* no 2, 171.

Kirry, Antoine, 'Arbitrability: Current Trends in Europe' (1996) 12 *Arb Int'l* no 4, 373.

Liebscher, Christoph, *The Healthy Award*, (Kluwer, The Hague, London, Boston, 2003).

Mann, Francis A., 'Zur Nationalität des Schiedsspruchs' in FS Oppenhoff (Munich, 1985) 215.

Mayer, Pierre, 'The Trend Towards Delocalisation in the Last 100 Years' in M. Hunter, A. Marriott, V.V. Veeder, eds, *The Internationalisation of International Arbitration* (Graham & Trotman/ M. Nijhoff, London, 1995) 37.

McLaughlin, Joseph T., 'Arbitrability: Current Trends in the United States' (1996) 12 *Arb Int'l* no 2, 113.

Park, William W., 'Uses and Abuses of Appeal from Awards' (1988) 4 *Arb Int'l* no 3, 174; 'Judicial Controls in the Arbitral Process' (1989) 5 *Arb Int'l* 230; 'The Arbitrability Dicta in First Options v Kaplan: What Sort of Kompetenz-Kompetenz Has Crossed the Atlantic?' (1996) 12 *Arb Int'l* no 2, 137.

Paulsson, Jan, 'Arbitration Unbound: Award Detached from the Law of its Country of Origin' (1981) 30 *ICLQ*, 358.

Rawlings, Jonathan, A., 'Mandatory Stay' (1997) 13 *Arb Int'l* no 4, 421.

Smit, Hans, 'The time is ripe for the US Supreme Court to bury the misconceived doctrine of manifest disregard of the law' (2005) *Am Rev Int'l Arb* no 16, 211.

Smit, Hans, 'Another judicial misstep in correcting an arbitral award' (2001) *Am Rev Int'l Arb* no 12, 435.

Smit, Hans, 'Comments on Public Policy in International Arbitration' (2002) *Am Rev Int'l Arb* no 13, 65.

Trappe, Johannes, 'The Arbitration Proceedings, Fundamental Principles and Rights of the Parties' (1998) 15 *J Int'l Arb* no 3, 93.

Triebel, Volker and Lange, Dieter G.F., 'Reform des englischen Schiedsgerichtsrechts' *Recht der Internationalen Wirtschaft* (*RIW*) 1980, 616.

Triebel, Volker and Plaßmeier, Heiko, 'Das neue englische Schiedsgerichtsgesetz' *RPS* 1997, *Beilage 13 zu Der Betrieb (DB)* 1997, 2.

Van Den Berg, Albert Jan, in Lew (ed), *Arbitration Insights: 20 years of the annual lecture of the School of International Arbitration* (Kluwer Law International, 2007) 7–18.

Verbist, Herman, 'Reform des belgischen Rechts der Schiedsgerichtsbarkeit', *RPS* 1998, *Beilage 9 zu Betriebsberater (BB)* 1998, 4.

Weigand, Frank-Bernd, 'Die internationale Schiedsgerichtsbarkeit und das EuGVÜ' *EuZW* 1992, 529.

Weigand, Frank-Bernd, 'Evading EC Competition Law by Resorting to Arbitration?' (1993) 9 *Arb Int'l* no 3, 249.

Weigand, Frank-Bernd, 'Das neue englische Schiedsverfahrensrecht' *Recht der Internationalen Wirtschaft* (*RIW*) 1997, 904.

Wetter, Gillis (1985) 2 *J Int'l Arb* no 1, 15.

The procedure according to chosen rules

Aglionby, Andrew, 'Arbitration Outside China: The Alternatives' (2007) 24 *J Int'l Arb* No 6, 673.

Bagner, Hans, 'Need for Rules of Evidence in International Arbitration' (1997) 25 *Int'l Bus Lawyer* no 4, 175.

Berger, Klaus-Peter, 'Aufgaben und Grenzen der Parteiautonomie in der internationalen Wirtschaftsschiedsgerichtsbarkeit' *Recht der Internationalen Wirtschaft* (*RIW*) 1994, 12.

Berger, Klaus-Peter, *The Creeping Codification of Lex Mercatoria* (The Hague, London, Boston, 1998).

Böckstiegel, Karl-Heinz, Kröll, Stefan and Nacimiento, Patricia, *Arbitration in Germany* (Kluwer Law International, The Hague, London, Boston, 2007).

Cremades, Bernardo M., 'Overcoming the Clash of Legal Cultures: The Role of Interactive Arbitration' (1998) 14 *Arb Int'l* no 2, 157.

Derains, Yves and Schwartz, Eric A., 'A Guide to the New ICC Rules of Arbitration' (The Hague etc, 1999).

Dundas, Hew R., 'The Chartered Institute Good Practice Guidelines: Guidelines on the Interviewing of Prospective Arbitrators' (2008) 2 *Disp Res Int'l* no 2, 276.

Friedman, Mark W., 'Regulating Judgment: A Comment on the Chartered Institute of Arbitrators' Guidelines on the Interviewing of Prospective Arbitrators' (2008) 2 *Disp Res Int'l* no 2, 288.

Gill, Judith, 'The IBA Conflicts Guidelines—Who's Using Them and How?' (2007) 1 *Disp Res Int'l* no 1, 58.

Habscheid, Walter, 'Die sogenannte Schiedsgerichtsbarkeit der Internationalen Handelskammer' *Recht der Internationalen* (*RIW*) 1998, 421.

Hobér, Kaj and McKechnie, William, 'New Rules of the Arbitration of the Stockholm Chamber of Commerce' (2007) 23 *Arb Int'l* no 2, 261.

Hobér, K., 'Neue Regeln für das Schiedsgerichtsinstitut der Handelskammer Stockholm', in *DIS Mitteilungen* 1/1989, 13.

Hof, Jacomijn van, *Commentary on the UNCITRAL Arbitration Rules, 'The Application by the Iran-US Claims Tribunal'* (Deventer, 1991).

Kratzsch, Susanne, 'DIAC-Schiedsverfahren im Mittleren Osten' *Recht der Internationalen Wirtschaft* (*RIW*) 2007, 767.

Kreindler, Richard, 'Aktuelle (Streit-)-Fragen bei der Anwendung der ICC-Schiedsgerichtsordnung 1998—Praxisüberblick' *Recht der Internationalen Wirtschaft* (*RIW*) 2002, 249.

Moser, Michael J. and Jianlong, Yu, 'CIETAC and its Work' (2007) 24 *J Int'l Arb* no 6, 555.

Najar, Jean-Claude, 'The Inside View: Companies' Needs in Arbitration' (1996) 12 *Arb Int'l* no 3, 359.

Nicholas, Geoff and Partasides, Constantine, 'LCIA Court Decisions on Challenges to Arbitrators: A Proposal to Publish', (2007) 23 *Arb Int'l* no 1, 1.

Plantey, Alain, 'A Major Realisation of the ICC: International Arbitration' (1994) 5 *ICC Bulletin* no 1, 3.

Reiner, Andreas, 'The 2001 Version of the Vienna Rules' (2001) 18 *J Int'l Arb*no 6, 661.

Robine, Eric, 'What Companies Expect from International Commercial Arbitration' (1992) 9 *Arb Int'l* no 2, 31.

Sanders, Pieter, 'Unity and Diversity in the Adoption of the Model Law' (1995) 11 *Arb Int'l* no1, 1.

Schmidt-Diemitz, Rolf, 'Internationale Schiedsgerichtsbarkeit - eine empirische Untersuchung' *Der Betrieb (DB)* (1999) 369.

Schroeter, Ulrich G., 'Schiedsverfahren im China-Geschäft: Die neue Schiedsordnung der China International Economic and Trade Arbitration Commission (CIETAC)' *Recht der Internationalen Wirtschaft* (*RIW*) 2006, 296.

Shore, Laurence and Cabrol, Emmanuelle, 'A Comment on the IBA Guidelines on Conflict of Interests: The fragile balance between principles and illustrations, and the mistery of the "subjective test"' (2004) 15 *Am Rev Int'l Arb* 599.

Stucki, B. and Geisinger, E., 'Chapter 10—Swiss and Swiss-based Arbitral Institutions' in G. Kaufmann-Kohler and B. Stucki (eds), *International Arbitration in Switzerland,* A Handbook for Practitioners (Kluwer Law International, 2004) 181.

Tao, Jingzhou and von Wunschheim, Clarisse, 'Articles 16 and18 of the PRC Arbitration Law: The Great Wall of China for Foreign Arbitration Institutions' (2007) 23 *Arb Int'l.* no 2, 309.

Tao, Jingzhou, 'Chinese Legal Environment for International Arbitration' (2008) 2 *Disp Res Int'l* no 2, 295.

Trappe, Johannes, 'The Arbitration Proceedings, Fundamental Principles and Rights of the Parties' (1998) 15 *J Int'l Arb* no 3, 93.

Weigand, Frank-Bernd, 'Die neue ICC Schiedsgerichtsordnung 1998' *Neue Juristische Wochenschrift* (*NJW*) (1998) 2,081.

Zuberbühler, Tobias, Müller, Christoph and Habegger, Philipp (eds), *Swiss Rules of International Arbitration* (Kluwer, 2005).

Applicable procedural and substantive rules

Berger, Klaus-Peter, 'Sitz des Schiedsgerichts oder Sitz des Schiedsverfahrens' *Recht der Internationalen Wirtschaft* (*RIW*) (1993) 10.

Derains, Yves and Schwartz, Eric A., *A Guide to the New ICC Rules of Arbitration* (The Hague etc, 1999).

Gentinetta, Jörg, 'Die lex fori internationaler Schiedsgerichte' in Schütze, Tscherning, Wais, *Handbuch des Schiedsverfahrens* (2nd edn, Walter de Gruyter Verlag, 1973).

Kaufmann-Kohler, Gabrielle, 'Arbitral Precedent: Dream, Necessity or Excuse?' (2007) 23 *Arb Int'l* no 3, 357.

Kreindler, R., 'Arbitral Forum Shopping: Observations on recent developments in international commercial and investment arbitration' (2005) 16 *Am Rev Int'l Arb* 157.

Mann, Francis A., 'Lex facit arbitrum' in *Liber Amicorum for Martin Domke* (Martinus Nijhoff, The Hague, 1967) 157.

Mann, Francis A., 'Zur Nationalität des Schiedsspruchs' in FS Oppenhoff (Munich, 1985) 215.

Mann, Francis A., 'Where is an award "made"?' (1985) 1 *Arb Int'l* no 1, 107.

Najar, Jean-Claude, 'The Inside View: Companies' Needs in Arbitration' (1996) 12 *Arb Int'l* no 3, 359.

Park, William W., *International Forum Selection* (Kluwer Law International, Boston, 1995).

Park, William W., 'The lex loci arbitri and international commercial arbitration' (1983) 32 *ICLQ* 21.

Park, William W., *Arbitration of International Business Disputes: Studies in Law and Practice* (OUP, 2006).

Schwenzer, Ingeborg and Manner, Simon, 'The Claim is Time-Barred: The Proper Limitation Regime for International Sales Contracts in International Commercial Arbitration' (2007) 23 *Arb Int'l* no 2, 293.

Strong, Stacie I., 'Invisible Barriers to the Enforcement of Foreign Arbitral Awards in the United States' (2004) 21 *J Int'l Arb* no 6, 479.

Features of institutional and national procedural rules

Aguilar Alvarez, Guillermo, 'The Challenge of Arbitrators' (1990) 6 *Arb Int'l* no 3, 203.

Bagner, Hans, 'Need for Rules of Evidence in International Arbitration' (1997) 25 *Int'l Bus Lawyer* no 4, 175.

Bagner, Hans, 'Expedited Arbitration Rules: Stockholm and WIPO' (1997) 13 *Arb Int'l* no 2, 193.

Barron, William M., 'Court-ordered Consolidation of Arbitration Proceedings in the United States' (1987) 4 *J Int'l Arb* no 1, 81.
Bartels, Martin, 'Multi-Party Arbitration Clauses' (1985) 2 *J Int'l Arb* 62.
Batiffol, Henri and Lagarde, Paul, *Droit International Privé I* (8th edn, Dalloz-Sirey, 1993).
Benson, Cyrus, 'Can Professional Ethics Wait? The Need for Transparency in International Arbitration' (2009) 3 *Disp Res Int'l* no 1, 78.
Berger, Klaus-Peter, 'Schiedsrichterbestellung in Mehrparteienschiedsverfahren: Der Fall "Dutco Construction" vor französischen Gerichten', *Recht der Internationalen Wirtschaft* (*RIW*) (1993) 702.
Berger, Klaus-Peter, 'Exchange Control Regulations' in Böckstiegel, (ed), *Acts of State and Arbitration* (1997) 99.
Klaus-Peter Berger, *The New German Arbitration Law* (Carl Heymanns Verlag, Cologne, 1998).
Blessing, Marc, 'The New International Arbitration Law in Switzerland' (1988) 5 *J Int'l Arb* no 9.
Blessing, Marc, 'Globalisation (and Harmonisation) of Arbitration' (1992) 9 *J Int'l Arb* no 1, 79.
Blessing, Marc, 'Mandatory Rules of Law vs. Party Autonomy in International Arbitration' (1997) 14 *J Int'l Arb* no 4, 23.
Bredow, Jens, 'Die DIS-Schiedsgerichtsordnung 1998' in *Neues Deutsches Schiedsverfahrensrecht, DIS-Mat IV* (1998), 111.
Briner, Robert, 'Domestic Arbitration: Practice in Continental Europe and its Lessons for Arbitration in England' (1997) 13 *Arb Int'l* no 2, 155.
Carbonneau, Thomas E. and Jaeggi, Jeanette A., *American Arbitration Association—Handbook on International Arbitration & ADR* (Juris Publishing, New York, 2006) (T.E. Carbonneau, J.A. Jaeggi).
Center For Transnational Law (CENTRAL) ed, *Transnational Law in Commercial Legal Practice, CENTRAL Practice and Study Guides* vol 1, 1999.
Cremades, Bernardo M., 'Overcoming the Clash of Legal Cultures: The Role of Interactive Arbitration' (1998) 14 *Arb Int'l* no 2, 157.
Davis, Benjamin, 'Fast-Track Arbitration and Fast-Tracking Your Arbitration' (1992) 9 *J Int'l Arb* no 4, 43.
Delvolvé, Jean-Louis, 'Multipartism: The Dutco Decision of the French Cour de Cassation', (1993) 9 *Arb Int'l* no 2, 197.
Domke, Martin, 'Towards an "International" Public Policy in Commercial Arbitration', in FS Bülow (Cologne, 1981) 49.
Donahey, Scott, 'The Independence and Neutrality of Arbitrators' (1992) 9 *J Int'l Arb* no 4, 31.
Drobnig, Ulrich, 'Internationale Schiedsgerichtsbarkeit und wirtschaftsrechtliche Eingriffsnormen' in FS Kegel (1987) 95.
Dundas, Hew R., 'The Chartered Institute Good Practice Guidelines: Guideline on the Interviewing of Prospective Arbitrators', (2008) 2 *Disp Res Int'l* no 2, 276.
Frank, Jonathan and Bédard, Julie, 'Electronic Discovery' (2007) 62 *Disp Res J* no 4, 62.
Friedman, Mark W., 'Regulating Judgment: A Comment on the Chartered Institute of Arbitrators Guidelines on the Interviewing of Prospective Arbitrators' (2008) 2 *Disp Res Int'l* no 2, 288.
Frommel, Stefan and Rider, Barry, *Conflicting Legal Cultures in Commercial Arbitration: Old Issues and New Trends* (The Hague, 1999).
Geimer, Reinhold, 'Beteiligung weiterer Parteien im Schiedsgerichtsverfahren, insbesondere die Drittwiderklage' in Böckstiegel, Berger, Bredow (eds), *Die Beteiligung Dritter an Schiedsverfahren* (Carl Heymanns Verlag, Cologne, 2005).
Grigera Naón, Horacio A., 'The 1998 ICC Rules of Arbitration: Certain New Aspects Regarding the Functions of the ICC International Court of Arbitration' in *Die ICC-Schiedsgerichtsordnung 1998, DIS-Mat II* (1998), 45.
Hanotiau, Bernard, 'Complex—Multicontract-Multiparty—Arbitrations', (1998) 14 *Arb Int'l* no 4, 369.

Hargrove, James, 'Misplaced Confidence? An Analysis of Privacy and Confidentiality in Contemporary International Arbitration', (2009) 3 *Disp Res Int'l* no1, 47.

Hermanns, Ferdinand, 'Public Policy and Arbitration: Cartel Law' in Böckstiegel (ed), *Acts of State and Arbitration* (Carl Heymanns Verlag, Cologne etc, 1997) 61.

Hilgard, Mark C., 'Electronic Discovery im Schiedsverfahren' *SchiedsVZ* (2008) 122.

Hochstrasser, Daniel, 'Choice of Law and "Foreign" Mandatory Rules in International Arbitration' (1994) 11 *J Int'l Arb* no 1, 57.

Hoffmann, Bernd von, 'Schiedsgerichtsbarkeit in mehrstufigen Vertragsbeziehungen, insbesondere in Subunternehmerverträgen in Böckstiegel, Berger, Bredow (eds), *Die Beteiligung Dritter an Schiedsverfahren* (Carl Heymanns Verlag, Cologne, 2005).

Hoffmann, Bernd von, 'Internationally Mandatory Rules of Law Before Arbitral Tribunals' in Böckstiegel (ed) *Acts of State and Arbitration* (Carl Heymanns Verlag, Cologne, 1997) 3.

Hunter, Martin, 'Ethics of the International Arbitrator' *Arbitration* (1987) 219.

Hunter, Martin, 'The Procedural Powers of Arbitrators Under the English 1996 Act' (1997) 13 *Arb Int'l* no 4, 345.

Jalili, Mahir, '"Kompetenz-Kompetenz": Recent U.S. and U.K. Developments' (1996) 13 *J Int'l Arb* no 4, 169.

Juenger Ernst, 'Lex mercatoria und Eingriffsnormen', in FS Rittner (1991) 223.

Karrer, Pierre and Kälin-Nauer, Claudia, 'Is there a Favor Jurisdictionis Arbitri? Standards of Review of Arbitral Jurisdiction Decisions in Switzerland' (1996) 13 *J Int'l Arb* no 3, 31.

Kaufmann-Kohler, Gabrielle and Baertsch, Philippe, 'Discovery in International Arbitration: How much is too much?' *Schieds VZ* (2008) 13.

Kerr, Michael, 'Concord and Conflict in International Arbitration' (1997) 13 *Arb Int'l* no 2, 121.

Kraayvanger, Jan, Richter, Malte and Wendler, Jan, 'US-Beweishilfe in Schiedsverfahren—ein Anschlag auf die internationale Schiedsgerichtsbarkeit?', *SchiedsVZ* (2008) 161.

Kreindler, Richard H., Schaefer, Jan K. and Wolff, Reinmar, *Schiedsgerichtsbarkeit, Kompendium für die Praxis* (Verlag Recht & Wirtschaft, Frankfurt *et al*, 2006).

Lalive, Pierre, 'Transnational (or Truly International) Public Policy and International Arbitration' in ICCA Congress Series no 3, 257, (*Rev arb*, 1986) 329.

Lazareff, Sergey, 'Mandatory Extraterritorial Application of National Law' (1995) 11 *Arb Int'l* no 1, 137.

Landolt, Phillip, 'Limits on Court Review of International Arbitration Awards Assessed in light of States' Interests and in particular in light of EU Law Requirements' (2007) 23 *Arb Int'l* no 1, 63.

Markfort, Rainer, *Mehrparteien-Schiedsgerichtsbarkeit im deutschen und ausländischen Recht* (Heymann Verlag, Cologne, 1994).

Marriott, Arthur, 'Evidence in International Arbitration' (1989) 5 *Arb Int'l* no 3, 280.

Massuras, Konstadinos, *Dogmatische Strukturen der Mehrparteienschiedsgerichtsbarkeit* (Europäische Hochschulschriften, Reihe II Bd 2419, Frankfurt, 1998).

Matray, Lambert, 'Embargo and Prohibition of Performance', in: Böckstiegel (ed) *Acts of State and Arbitration* (Carl Heymanns Verlag, Cologne, etc, 1997) 69.

Meier, Anke, 'The Production of Electronically Stored Information in International Commercial Arbitration' *SchiedsVZ* (2008) 179.

Meyer, Olaf, 'Time to take a Closer Look: Privilege in International Arbitration' (2007) 24 *J Int'l Arb* no 4, 365.

Müller, Eva, 'Fast-Track Arbitration: Meeting the Demands of the Next Millenium' (1998) 15 *J Int'l Arb* no 3, 5.

Mustill, Michael John, 'Multipartite Arbitrations: An Agenda for Law-Makers', (1991) 7 *Arb Int'l.* no 4, 393.

Nicklisch, Fritz, 'Mehrparteienschiedsgerichtsbarkeit und Streitbeilegung bei Großprojekten' in FS Glossner, (1994) 221.

Rau, Alan Scott, 'On Integrity in Private Judging' (1998) 14 *Arb Int'l* no. 2, 115.

Reymond, Claude, 'Common Law and Civil Law Procedure: Which is the More Inquisitorial? A Civil Lawyer's Response' (1989) 5 *Arb Int'l* no 3, 357.

Rogers, Andrew and Launders, Rachel, 'Separability—The Indestructible Arbitration Clause' (1994) 10 *Arb Int'l* n 1, 77.

Sandrock, O., 'Wirkungen von Schiedsvereinbarungen im Konzern' in: Böckstiegel, Berger, Bredow (eds), *Die Beteiligung Dritter an Schiedsverfahren* (Carl Heymanns Verlag, Cologne, 2005).

Saville, Marc, 'The Origin of the New English Arbitration Act 1996: Reconciling Speed with Justice in the Decision-making Process', (1997) 13 *Arb Int'l* no 3, 237.

Schlabrendorff, F. von, 'Parallele Verfahren, Aufnahme von Dritten, Verbindung von Verfahren: Erfahrungen aus der Praxis der ICC' in: Böckstiegel, Berger, Bredow (eds), *Die Beteiligung Dritter an Schiedsverfahren* (Carl Heymanns Verlag, Cologne,2005).

Schwarz, Eric A., 'Multi-party Arbitration and the ICC in the Wake of Dutco' (1993) 10 *J Int'l Arb* no 3, 5.

Schwebel, Stephen M., *International Arbitration: Three Salient Problems* (Cambridge University Press, 1987).

Sheppard, Ben H., 'The Moth, the Light and the United States Severability Doctrine' (2006) 23 *J Int'l Arb* 5, 479.

Silverman, Moses, 'The Fast-Track Arbitration of the International Chamber of Commerce' (1993) 10 *Arb Int'l* no 4, 113.

Smith, Murray L., 'Impartiality of the Party—Appointed Arbitrator' (1990) 6 *Arb Int'l* no 4, 320.

Soergel, Theodor and von Hoffmann, Bernd, 'Kommentar zum BGB', *Bd X Einführungsgesetz* (10th edn, Kohlhammer, 1996) Art 34 no 3.

Staughton, Christopher, 'Common Law and Civil Law Procedure: Which is the More Inquisitorial? A Common Lawyer's Response' (1989) 5 *Arb Int'l* no 3, 351.

Wallace, Richard, E., 'Consolidated Arbitration in the United States—Recent Authority Requires Consent of the Parties' (1993) 10 *J Int'l Arb* no4, 5.

Weigand, Frank-Bernd, 'Discovery in der internationalen Schiedsgerichtsbarkeit', *Recht der Internationalen Wirtschaft* (*RIW*) (1992) 361.

Weigand, Frank-Bernd, 'Evading Competition Law by Resorting to Arbitration?' (1993) 9 *Arb Int'l* no 3, 249.

Weisenberger, Kirsten, 'From Hostility to Harmony: Buckeye Marks a Milestone in the Acceptance of Arbitration in the American Jurisprudence' (2005) 16 *Am Rev Int'l Arb* 551.

Wilske, Stephan and Gack, Christine, 'Commencement of Arbitral Proceedings and Unsigned Requests for Arbitration' (2007) 24 *J Int'l Arb* no3, 319.

Wirth, Markus, 'Ihr Zeuge, Herr Rechtsanwalt—Weshalb Civil-Law-Schiedsrichter Common-Law-Verfahrensrecht anwenden' *Zeitschrift für Schiedsverfahren* (*SchiedsVZ*) (2007) 9.

2

AUSTRIA

Christoph Liebscher

I. Introduction

A. Current status of the law on arbitration

(1) Short history

The first version of the Austrian Code of Civil Procedure ('CCP') of 1895 contained rules on arbitration in pt 6, ch 4. The rules were amended in 1929[1] to correct an editorial mistake in s 583(3), and a more comprehensive amendment took place in 1983[2] to adapt the rules to the necessities of modern international trade. **2.01**

(2) Law in force and future projects

On 1 July 2006 a new arbitration law came into force in Austria ('SchiedsRÄG 2006'), based in the large part on the UNCITRAL Model Law ('ModG'), and using the German implementation as a role model. Similar to the previous law, the new law is not separate legislation, but continues to be pt 6, ch 4 of the CCP.[3] The new arbitration law governs all arbitration proceedings that were initiated on or after 1 July 2006. Arbitration proceedings that were initiated before this date continue to be governed by the old law. The only other **2.02**

[1] 6. Gerichtsentlastungsnovelle (GEN) BGBl 222/1929.
[2] Zivilverfahrens-Novelle 1983 (ZVN) BGBl 135/1983.
[3] SchiedsRÄG 2006, BGBl I 2006/7.

legal regime for arbitration applies to certain arbitrations with respect to stock exchange transactions. Owing to their limited importance, these will not be covered in this country report.

2.03 Although there is a wish list for further reform, currently, there are no legislative projects.

(3) Distinction between national and international arbitration

2.04 In order to simplify matters, it was decided not to create different legal foundations for national and international arbitration proceedings. Therefore, the current Austrian arbitration rules are, in principle, valid for all arbitration proceedings if the seat of the arbitral tribunal is in Austria.[4] There are, however, different regimes for the enforcement of Austrian and foreign awards (see sections VII and VIII of this country report).

2.05 (3.1) **If there are different systems and rules for national/international arbitration: what are the criteria for the distinction between both systems?** Not applicable.

B. Practice of arbitration

(1) Frequency of arbitration as opposed to litigation

2.06 There are no statistics available recording the number of disputes referred to domestic arbitration in Austria. However, it appears that most domestic commercial disputes are decided by litigation rather than by arbitration. This is probably due to Austria's specialized commercial courts which seemingly meet the expectations of the population, as only a small number of first instance decisions are appealed.[5]

(2) Leading arbitral institutions and statistics (if available)

2.07 The International Arbitral Centre of the Austrian Federal Economic Chamber has its own rules of arbitration (the Vienna Rules). The modified Vienna Rules became applicable on 1 July 2006, on the same day the new Austrian arbitration law came into force. With regard to domestic arbitrations, it is practically only the Arbitration Court of the Vienna Economic Chamber that has pending cases on a regular basis. With regard to international arbitrations, 51 international arbitration cases with a total amount of approximately one billion Euros were pending before the Arbitration Court of the Vienna Economic Chamber by the end of 2006.[6] In 2007, the Arbitration Court of the Vienna Economic Chamber registered 40 new cases. 35 cases were closed in 2007.[7]

---

[4] Fremuth-Wolf, A., 'Section 577' in Riegler *et al, Arbitration Law of Austria: Practice and Procedure* (Juris Publishing Inc, 2007) s. 577, marg no 5.

[5] Melis, W., 'Arbitration in Austria', s I.2 under <http://wko.at/arbitration> (accessed 25 November 2008).

[6] *ibid.*

[7] The author would like to thank Dr Manfred Heider, Secretary-General of the Arbitration Court of the Vienna Economic Chamber for providing us with this information.

II. Jurisdiction of the arbitral tribunal

A. Arbitration agreement

(1) Arbitration clause and submission agreement

According to s 581[8] an arbitration agreement may apply to all, or certain disputes which have arisen or may arise between the parties in respect of a defined legal relationship. In general, Austrian law does not treat arbitration clauses and submission agreements differently. Therefore, the term 'arbitration agreement' should be understood to include both arbitration clause and submission agreement. In consumer arbitration, only submission agreements are valid (s 617). In labour law arbitration the same limitation applies, except for members of managing boards (ss 9(2), 50(1) of the Labour and Social Court Act). **2.08**

(2) Requirements as to the contents of the arbitration agreement

An arbitration agreement must contain the names of the parties and clearly state that the parties wish to submit the respective dispute, or any dispute, arising out of their defined legal relationship to arbitration. The arbitration agreement must also state the subject matter of the agreement.[9] Generally, if one of the mandatory requirements is not included, the arbitration agreement is invalid. However, it is sufficient if all the mandatory criteria are, at least, determinable from the main contract in which the arbitration agreement is embedded.[10] In addition, the agreement may contain provisions regarding the arbitral procedure, or include a reference to the Rules of a particular arbitral institution such as the VIAC, ICC or LCIA.[11] It is also important to consider that there is a strict distinction between an arbitration agreement and other forms of dispute resolution such as expert determination.[12] **2.09**

(3) Form of the arbitration agreement (eg 'in writing' requirement)

The arbitration agreement must be contained either in a document signed by the parties or in letters, faxes, emails or other forms of communication that prove the existence of the agreement (s 583). For the second alternative (exchange of communication), a signature of the parties is not required.[13] The form of the arbitration agreement is not restricted to **2.10**

---

[8] References to a section without indication of the statute are references to the Austrian Code of Civil Procedure.

[9] Fremuth-Wolf, A., 'Section 581' in S. Riegler *et al*, *Arbitration Law of Austria* (n 4) s 581, marg nos 31 *et seq*.

[10] Zeiler, G., *Schiedsverfahren: ss 577–618 ZPO idF des SchiedsRÄG* 2006 (Neuer Wissenschaftlicher Verlag, 2006) s 581, marg no 21.

[11] Zeiler, G. and Steindl, B., *Arbitration in Austria: A Basic Primer* (2nd edn, Neuer Wissenschaftlicher Verlag, 2007) sec 582, marg no 5.

[12] Hausmaninger, C. '§§ 577 bis 618 ZPO' in H. Fasching and A. Konecny (eds), *Kommentar zu den Zivilprozeßgesetzten* (2nd edn, vol IV/2, Manzsche Verlags- und Universitätsbuchhandlung, 2007, s 581, marg nos 142 *et seq*.

[13] Hausmaninger, C. in H. Fasching and A. Konecny, *Kommentar* (n 12) s. 583, marg nos 61 *et seq;* Zeiler, G., *Schiedsverfahren* (n 10) s 583, marg no 18; Hahnkamper, W., 'Neue Regeln für Schiedsvereinbarung' *SchiedsVZ* 2 (2006) 65, 66; Aburumieh, N., Koller, C. and Pöltner, E., 'Formvorschriften für Schiedsvereinbarung' *ÖJZ 27* (2006) 439, 441.

'paper' but also includes other electronic modes of communication provided that they show a record of the arbitration agreement.[14] It is generally understood that an acceptable record must be visually perceivable and reproducible.[15] Furthermore, the parties must have exchanged the documents. A written record by one party that was not exchanged with the other party is insufficient to prove the existence of an arbitration agreement.[16]

2.11 It was the clear intention of the law maker to apply the same standard as the New York Convention to the form requirement.[17]

2.12 An arbitration agreement which does not comply with the form requirement will have no legal effect. However, under s 583(3) a defect in the form of the arbitration agreement can be cured by entering an appearance in the case. The first entering of an appearance in the case will generally occur in the answer to the claim. Purely procedural acts, for example the appointment of an arbitrator, do not represent an entering of an appearance in the case.[18] There are stricter form requirements for consumer and certain labour arbitration agreements (ss 617, 618).

2.13 **(3.1) Are there special requirements for a power of attorney/authority to enter into an arbitration agreement on behalf of a third party?** Under s 1008 of the Civil Code, a contractually authorized agent, ie a person concluding an arbitration agreement on behalf of another person or entity on the basis of a contractually issued power of attorney, always requires that the special power of attorney be in writing.[19] A suggestion was made by the drafting group that this special written power of attorney be abolished under the new law as being obsolete and not in accordance with other national laws, but this suggestion was not accepted.[20] However, there are two exceptions to this rule: (i) 'Prokurists' (holders of a special statutory power of 'Prokura' under Austrian law); and, (ii) agents authorized by entrepreneurs ('Handlungsvollmacht').

2.14 According to s 49 of the Business Enterprise Code regarding powers of procuration, and s 54(1) of the Business Enterprise Code pertaining to powers of agents of entrepreneurs, no special power of attorney is necessary.

(4) Incorporation of an arbitration clause contained in general terms and conditions

2.15 Section 583(2) states that as long as a reference in a document to another document containing an arbitration clause fulfils the form requirements of s 583(1), then such reference

---

[14] Kloiber, B. and Haller, H., 'Das neue Schiedsverfahrensrecht—eine Einführung' in B. Kloiber *et al*, *Das neue Schiedsrecht: Schiedsrechts-Änderungsgesetz* 2006 (Manzsche Verlags- und Universitätsbuchhandlung, 2006) 20.

[15] Hausmaninger, C. in H. Fasching and A. Konecny, *Kommentar* (n 12) s 583, marg no 67 with further refs.

[16] Fremuth-Wolf, A., 'Section 583' in S. Riegler *et al*, *Arbitration Law of Austria* (n 9) s 583, marg no 27.

[17] '[...] due to the necessary consonance of the form requirements, Austria—also in terms of the enforcement and recognition—risks degenerating into a place of enforcement, rather than strengthing its position as a place of arbitration, if in Austria awards are enforced which would not be enforced internationally according to the New York Convention', 1158 der Beilagen XXII. GP—Regierungsvorlage—Materialien, 9.

[18] Liebscher, C., *The Austrian Arbitration Act 2006: Text and Notes* (Kluwer Law International, 2006) 9, Art 583 (3).

[19] Zeiler, G., *Schiedsverfahren* (n 10) s 583, marg nos 28 and 29.

[20] Oberhammer, P., *Entwurf eines neuen Schiedsverfahrensrechts* (Manzsche Verlags- und Universitätsbuchhandlung, 2002) 158.

constitutes a valid arbitration agreement, if the reference is such that it makes the arbitration agreement part of the contract. This requirement refers to the general rules of contract law on incorporation.

The issue of the incorporation of documents into contracts is governed by ss 864a and 879(3) of the Civil Code.[21] **2.16**

Generally, according to s 864a of the Civil Code an arbitration clause contained in the standard business conditions ('Allgemeine Geschäftsbedingungen') or standard agreements is not considered part of the contract if it is disadvantageous to the other party and the overall circumstances do not justify inclusion into the underlying contract between the parties.[22] Particular consideration should be given to the external appearance of the documents, whether the parties consider the documents when deciding to conclude the contract and whether the document containing the arbitration clause was specifically referred to in the standard business conditions or standard agreements. **2.17**

Furthermore, an arbitration clause contained in standard business conditions or standard agreements may be void, pursuant to s 879(3) of the Civil Code, if it is severely prejudicial to the interests of the other party.[23] **2.18**

(5) Law applicable to the interpretation of arbitration clauses

It was debated whether rules concerning the applicable law should be included in the Act, however it was felt that the national and international discussion regarding this issue was still ongoing; therefore, the question was left open for elaboration by legal literature and case law.[24] **2.19**

Generally, parties have the right to determine the law applicable to the arbitration clause. Theoretically, the applicable law could be different for each aspect of the parties' agreement.[25] Thus far, the Austrian Supreme Court (Oberster Gerichtshof—'OGH') has ruled that failing a disposition by the parties, the validity of the arbitration agreement is to be judged according to the law of the country where the arbitral award was made or is to be rendered.[26] **2.20**

According to Austrian legal scholarship and case precedent an arbitration agreement should be interpreted according to the rules contained in Austrian civil procedural law. Consequently, interpretation of an arbitration clause should not be viewed as a substantive legal agreement that would govern other contractual relationships. To the extent that the provisions of the civil procedure law are sufficient, the general rules of interpretation of contract law are applicable.[27] **2.21**

---

[21] Fremuth-Wolf, A., 'Section 583' in S. Riegler *et al*, *Arbitration Law of Austria* (n 9) s 583, marg no 29.

[22] OGH 25 January 1995 JBl 1995, 596 with annots, Rummel, P.

[23] Deimbacher, O., 'Schiedsverträge und Schiedsklauseln in anderen Verträgen und in ABG' *GesRZ* 1995, 17 *et seq*.

[24] Fremuth-Wolf, A., 'Section 581' in S. Riegler *et al*, *Arbitration Law of Austria* (n 9) s 581, marg no 67; Oberhammer, P., *Entwurf* (n 20) 39.

[25] Hausmaninger, C. in H. Fasching and A. Konecny, *Kommentar* (n 12) s 581, marg no 268.

[26] Fremuth-Wolf, A., 'Section 581' in S. Riegler *et al*, *Arbitration Law of Austria* (n 9) s 581, marg no 68.

[27] Hausmaninger, C. in H. Fasching and A.Konecny, *Kommentar* (n 12) s 581, marg no. 183 *et seq*.

2.22 (5.1) **Do courts accept a wide competence of the arbitral tribunal or do they restrict arbitral competence? Do claims which arise in connection with the agreement submitted to arbitration generally fall within the arbitral jurisdiction even if based on a tortious legal basis? Does there exist case law with respect to the wording in an arbitration clause as 'arising out of/under/in connection with the present contract' and its specific meaning?** The OGH construes an arbitration agreement broadly.[28] Accordingly, the OGH decided that an arbitration agreement providing for an appointment of the arbitral tribunal 'pursuant to the corresponding provisions' is not vague but is to be interpreted as a reference to the provisions of ss 577 *et seq*.[29] Similarly, the OGH construed an arbitration agreement providing for the invocation of the arbitral tribunal 'according to the ÖNORM (Austrian Standard)' as a reference to the ÖNORM 2060 and consequently a reference to the provisions of the CCP.[30]

2.23 Whether an arbitral tribunal may decide upon claims for damages which are not based on the violations of a contract depends upon the scope of the arbitration agreement.

2.24 According to a decision of the OGH, an arbitration clause which provides for the competence of the arbitral tribunal for 'all disputes which concern the affairs of the association' does not cover claims for damages against this credit association for incorrect information about the signing authority for a bank guarantee.[31] An arbitration agreement providing for the competence of the arbitral tribunal for 'all disputes arising out of the business relationship' creates jurisdiction for disputes out of every single legal transaction.[32]

2.25 With regard to an arbitration clause which provides for arbitration for 'all disputes out of the contract', the OGH decided that this wording also covers disputes about the revocation of the contract, its annulment or termination without notice or claims derived from its termination, provided that the main contract was originally valid, even if a party alleges the original nullity of the contract.[33]

2.26 However, the principle that arbitration agreements are to be interpreted broadly is not applied without limits by the OGH. In that sense, the OGH stated that an arbitration clause providing for arbitration for 'all disputes arising out of the contract' does not include—unless otherwise agreed—disputes out of bills of exchange.[34] Another decision dealt with an arbitration agreement contained in a cooperative contract.[35] In this particular case, a dispute had arisen over a loan relationship. The arbitration agreement at the time of the signing of the cooperative contract merely provided for 'disputes arising out of the cooperative relationship'. This was later expanded during an extraordinary general assembly to

[28] OGH 25 January 1995 JBl 1995, 596 with annots, Rummel, P.; 11 July 1990 SZ 63/123; 5 October 1988 WBl 1989, 30; 22 May1986 RdW 1986, 273; Hausmaninger, C. in H. Fasching and A. Konecny, *Kommentar* (n 12) s 581 marg no 193.

[29] OGH 5 May 1998, 3 Ob 2372/96m; 22 May 1986, 7 Ob 544/86 SZ 59/86.

[30] OGH 5 May 1998, 3 Ob 2372/96m.

[31] OGH 25 May 1995 JBl 1995, 598 with annots, Rummel, P.

[32] OGH 22 December 1926, 1 Ob 1062/26 SZ 8/351.

[33] OGH 17 April 1996, 7 Ob 2097/96z, ecolex 1996, 756 RdW 1997, 135; 16 June 1982, 1 Ob 628/82 SZ 55/89; 9 October 1929, 3 Ob 727/29 JBl 1930, 18.

[34] OGH 18 April 1985, 7 Ob 551,552/85; 25 November 1965, 2 Ob 334/65 EvBl 1966/169.

[35] OGH 17 June 2003, 5 Ob 112/03m RdW 2003, 563; 22 December 2002, 6 Ob 62/02i.

include 'all disputes arising out of the cooperative relationship and common bank transactions [. . .] and also disputes between a member of the cooperative and the cooperative'. The OGH found that the declaration of accession to the cooperative did not automatically cover a statutory change to the arbitration agreement and therefore an expansion of the arbitration agreement to include 'common bank transactions' was not operative on the claimant.

(6) Binding effect of an arbitration clause on third parties (eg in case of a guarantee or assignment)

As a general principle, only the parties to an arbitration agreement are bound by the agreement. Austrian courts are reluctant to bind third parties to arbitration agreements.[36] For example, normally shareholders in partnerships or corporations are not bound to arbitration agreements concluded by the partnership. **2.27**

Even though courts will not bind third parties to an arbitration agreement, there are a few limited cases mainly concerning legal successors, beneficiaries of contracts in the favour of the third party and assumption of debt ('Schuldbeitritt'), where the courts have bound third parties to an arbitration agreement.[37] **2.28**

(6.1) What is the law/leading authorities' position on multi-party situations? Especially, (i) with respect to the objection that the arbitration clause does not specifically provide for a plurality of parties in the same procedure; **2.29**

Austrian law does not require a special consent for multi-party arbitration. Section 587(5) shows that the legislator was conscious of multi-party situations but did not provide for any consent requirements in this respect.

(ii) with respect to the constitution of the arbitral tribunal; **2.30**

If several parties who must appoint an arbitrator together fail to do so within four weeks of receipt of a written request to do so, the court will appoint the arbitrator at the request of a party. However, the parties may provide for a different appointment procedure (s 587(5)).

(iii) with respect to the consolidation of two or more running arbitration proceedings? **2.31**

The Austrian Arbitration Act does not contain any provisions dealing with the consolidation of two or more arbitration proceedings. A consolidation will require the consent of all parties and arbitrators.

(6.2) Is there case law/authorities with respect to the admissibility of third party participation in an arbitration without being a claimant or defendant (Nebenintervention/ Streitverkündung; intervention forcée/volontaire; vouching in; amicus curiae etc)? What are the prerequisites and effects of such participation (if permitted)? Austrian arbitration law contains no provision with regard to the admissibility of third party participation in arbitration without being a claimant or defendant. However, according to Austrian doctrine, a person who is not a party to the arbitration agreement may not intervene, if **2.32**

[36] Zeiler, G. and Steindl, B., *Basic Primer* (n 11) s 582, marg no 7.

[37] Zeiler, G., *Schiedsverfahren* (n 10) s 581, marg no 105.

both claimant and defendant object. In case only one party objects, one has to differ: if the third party shall become a party to the arbitration agreement, both parties have to agree. In case the third party shall only obtain the rights to participate at hearings and to pose questions, the arbitral tribunal has discretion to grant the third party's admission without the agreement of both parties, unless institutional arbitration rules or the implicit will of the parties provide for an exclusion of a third party participation.

2.33 If a person who is a party to the arbitration agreement wishes to participate in the arbitration and at least one of the parties objects, the arbitral tribunal has discretion to admit or not to admit this party.[38]

(7) Termination of an arbitration agreement by a party (reasons and case law)

2.34 Unilateral termination of an arbitration agreement is only permissible for important reasons.[39] The OGH has held that the termination by one party may be permissible if due to the unforeseeable deterioration of the economic situation of that party, it can no longer be expected to abide by the arbitration agreement.[40] If one of the parties failed to pay an advance on the costs (for whatever reason), the other party has the right unilaterally to terminate the agreement.[41]

B. Arbitrability

(1) 'Personal arbitrability' (capacity to conclude arbitration agreements)

2.35 Under Austrian law, any natural person who is fully capable of entering into a contract, as well as legal entities and partnerships may conclude an arbitration agreement, with the exception of civil law partnerships and silent partnerships according to the Civil Code.[42]

2.36 A party's capacity validly to conclude an arbitration agreement is determined by its personal status, which is established pursuant to ss 9 and 10 of the Law of the Conflict of Laws. According to these provisions, the status of an individual, as well as a legal entity, is determined by the *lex personalis* (ie in general, the law of the state of which the individual is a citizen or the law of the state where the actual management of the legal entity resides). In Austria, a natural person has the legal capacity validly to enter into an arbitration agreement at the age of 18.[43]

---

[38] Hausmaninger, C. in H. Fasching and A. Konecny, *Kommentar* (n 12) s 594, marg nos 138 *et seq.*

[39] OGH 4 September1936 1 Ob 813/36 SZ 18/151; Respondek, A., 'Die Aufhebungsklage gegen Schiedssprüche nach österreichischem Recht' *RIW* 1993, 378; Rummel, P., 'Schiedsvertrag und ABGB' *RZ* 1986, 148; Backhausen, G., *Schiedsgerichtsbarkeit unter besonderer Berücksichtigung des Schiedsvertragsrechts* (Manz, 1990) 88 *et seq* with further annots; *contra*: Fasching, H., *Schiedsgericht und Schiedsverfahren im österreichischen und im internationalen Recht* (Manz, 1973) 38.

[40] OGH 26 March 1996 1 Ob 641/95 SZ 69/73.

[41] Under the old law: OGH 26 March 1996 1 Ob 641/95 SZ 69/73; Hausmaninger, C. in H. Fasching and A. Konecny, *Kommentar* (n 12) s 581, marg no 132.

[42] Fasching, H., *Lehrbuch des österreichischen Zivilprozeßrechts* (2nd edn, Manz, 1990) marg no 346 *et seq* 2,172.

[43] Backhausen, G., *Schiedsgerichtsbarkeit* (n 39) 22 and 23 with further annots; Fasching, H., *Lehrbuch* (n 42) marg no 334.

(1.1) May a state (or state agency) as party invoke sovereign immunity before the arbitral tribunal or before a state court (eg in a procedure of enforcement)?

Persons with sovereign immunity which conclude an arbitration agreement are deemed to submit to arbitration within the scope of ss 577 *et seq.*[44] Therefore, such persons cannot claim immunity either before the arbitral tribunal or before the courts. **2.37**

(2) 'Objective arbitrability' (eg of patent, trade mark and antitrust matters)

Any claim involving an economic interest that would lie within the jurisdiction of the courts, as opposed, for example, to administrative agencies, is arbitrable (s 582(1)). Consequently, claims that would normally be decided by regulatory or supervisory authorities, as well as all claims which are to be decided by the Patent Office are not arbitrable.[45] Antitrust law knows two systems of antitrust enforcement: public and private. In the private branch of enforcement, nullity and damages are the most likely sanctions. The private remedies are fully arbitrable, the public remedies are not. **2.38**

All other matters are arbitrable if the parties may conclude a settlement on the issue in dispute. **2.39**

However, family law matters and matters concerning contracts subject to the Landlord and Tenant Act or the Limited-Profit Housing Act as well as condominium law are not arbitrable (s 582(2)). **2.40**

Finally, statutory provisions that exclude or limit arbitrability outside the arbitration chapter of the CCP remain unaffected. There are no such restrictions relevant for international arbitration.[46] **2.41**

C. Decision on the arbitral tribunal's jurisdiction ('*competence-competence*')

(1) Separability (independence of the arbitration agreement from the main agreement)

Austrian arbitration law does not explicitly adopt the doctrine of separability of arbitration agreements. An arbitration clause contained in a contract is treated as a separate agreement that is independent from the other terms of the contract. Thus, the validity of an arbitration agreement is generally independent from the validity of the underlying contract.[47] **2.42**

(2) Competence of the tribunal to decide on its own jurisdiction (including form and time of the tribunal's decision)

The competence of an arbitral tribunal to decide on its own jurisdiction is set forth in s 592(1). The arbitral tribunal has the initial say regarding its jurisdiction over a particular dispute. According to s 592(1), the ruling can be made together with the ruling on the case **2.43**

---

44 Zeiler, G., *Schiedsverfahren* (n 10) s 577, marg no 17 with further refs.

45 Reiner, A., *The New Austrian Arbitration Law—Arbitration Act 2006* (LexisNexis, 2006) s 582, fn 33.

46 See Hausmaninger, C. in H. Fasching and A. Konecny, *Kommentar* (n 12) s 582, marg nos 56 *et seq.*

47 Power, J., *The Austrian Arbitration Act: A Practitioner's Guide to Sections 577—618 of the Austrian Code of Civil Procedure* (Manzsche Verlags- und Universitätsbuchhandlung, 2006) s 592, marg no 3; Hausmaninger, C. in H. Fasching and A. Konecny, *Kommentar* (n 12) s 581, marg nos 98 *et seq.*

or it can be made in a separate award.[48] The ruling of the arbitral tribunal as to its own jurisdiction may therefore appear in the form of a final or an interim award. To the (final or interim) award, the formal requirements of s 606 apply.

2.44 Thus, if a party timely objects to the arbitral tribunal's jurisdiction, the arbitral tribunal may either decide the question of jurisdiction only in the final award, may render an affirmative award on jurisdiction, or may render an award denying its own jurisdiction. There are no specific time requirements for rendering the award.

(3) Extent of the 'competence-competence' *and role of the courts (including form and time limits of a challenge of the tribunal's decision)*

2.45 Under the new law there is no true *competence-competence*, because the arbitral tribunal's (interim or final) award, in which the arbitral tribunal—from a party's point of view—wrongly confirms or denies its jurisdiction, continues to remain subject to judicial court review by claim for annulment pursuant to s 611(2) nos 1 and 3.

2.46 The lack of an arbitration agreement is one of the grounds to set aside an award (s 611(2) no 2) as well as the unjustified denial of jurisdiction by the arbitral tribunal.

2.47 However, if the objection concerning the lack of the required form of the arbitration agreement is not made at the latest together with entering the first appearance in the case, the party may not argue that point later.

2.48 On the other hand, a lack of objective arbitrability may be reviewed in the context of a challenge of the award also *ex officio*, even if no objection was raised by a party (ss 611(2) no 7, 611(3)).

2.49 According to s 611(4) an action to set aside an award (either a partial or final award) must be brought within three months from the day the parties received the award. If the parties fail to observe the deadline, then a party can only suggest an official examination by a court or other authority in the context of proceedings pending before such court or agency within the scope of s 613.[49] Pursuant to s 613 any Austrian court and any other Austrian authority can examine an award in terms of its objective arbitrability as well as compatibility with the standards of Austrian public policy and disregard the award if it does not meet one of the two prerequisites. However, the effect is limited to the respective proceeding.[50]

D. Enforcement of an arbitration agreement within or by court proceedings

(1) Effect of invoking an arbitration clause within a court proceeding (and time limits for such a motion)

2.50 The text of s 584 supports the two fundamental ideas about the decision on the jurisdiction of the arbitral tribunal; first, in matters where the parties have included an arbitration clause, a court must dismiss any claim which is subject to that clause unless it finds that the clause is null and void. Hence an arbitration proceeding cannot be impeded by a court

[48] Liebscher, C., *Austrian Arbitration Act 2006* (n 18) 19, Art 592(1).
[49] *ibid* 39, Art 611 (1).
[50] *ibid* 42, Art 613.

proceeding. However the court has the last word on the existence or non-existence of an arbitration clause.[51]

Secondly, once arbitration proceedings have been initiated, no other legal disputes may be brought before a court on the asserted claim. Any such action is to be rejected by the courts; even if the court holds that an arbitration clause is null, it must still dismiss the related action. Thus, this results in a *de facto* precedence of the arbitration procedure before the court procedure. This general principle is invalid if an objection to the jurisdiction of the arbitral tribunal was raised later in the proceedings, for instance together with the first submissions on the merits of the claims, and a decision on the arbitral tribunal's jurisdiction is not to be expected in reasonable time.[52] **2.51**

(1.1) If a party has invoked successfully the arbitration agreement in a court proceeding, is it then entitled to deny within the arbitral proceeding that there is a valid and binding arbitration agreement? Such behaviour by a party might be seen as 'bad faith' and would, therefore, be in violation of the principle of good faith.[53] This principle is also expressed by s 584(5) for the reverse situation. In addition, one could consider the following: if the court holds that it does not have jurisdiction and thereby confirms the validity of the arbitration agreement, then the suit is rejected. Once this decision becomes final, it can be argued that the arbitral tribunal is bound.[54] The finality of the decision excludes identical claims as well as claims directly opposed to the final decision.[55] Therefore, one could take the view that the party who has successfully invoked a valid arbitration agreement before the court may not object to the validity of the arbitration agreement in the arbitral proceedings. **2.52**

(1.2) Vice versa, if a party has successfully objected to an arbitral proceeding by denying that there is a valid arbitration agreement, may it then invoke such agreement in the ensuing court proceeding? According to s 584(5) a party that has invoked the existence of an arbitration agreement at an earlier point in time in any court or arbitration proceedings may not at a later point in time claim that such agreement does not exist, unless the circumstances have changed. This provision represents a clear sanction for violating the basic principle of *non venire contra factum proprium*.[56] **2.53**

(2) Legal remedies and proceedings to enforce an arbitration agreement

Pursuant to s 578 an Austrian court may only become active in matters governed by the arbitration part of the CCP where provided for in this part. **2.54**

According to prevailing Austrian doctrine, s 578 effects that an autonomous statutory application for a declaration of the existence or non-existence and the invalidity of an **2.55**

[51] Liebscher, C., *Austrian Arbitration Act 2006* (n 18) 9, Art 584.
[52] See s 584 (3), second sentence; Hausmaninger, C. in H. Fasching and A. Konecny, *Kommentar* (n 12) s 584, marg no 36.
[53] Fasching, H., *Lehrbuch* (n 42) marg nos 135 *et seq.*
[54] *ibid* marg nos 1,507, 1,512.
[55] *ibid* marg no 1,517.
[56] Liebscher, C., *Austrian Arbitration Act 2006* (n 18) 10, Art 584(5).

arbitration agreement respectively is not allowed under Austrian arbitration law, neither during arbitration proceedings nor before.[57]

2.56 However, a minority view argues that pursuant to s 584—which provides that a court may not reject an application regarding matters which are subject to an arbitration agreement, if it determines that no arbitration agreement exists or that it is inexecutable—prior to the initiation of arbitral proceedings, at least in exceptional cases, a statutory application for a declaration of the incompetence of the arbitral tribunal or the infeasibility of the arbitral proceedings is possible. According to this view, such an application for a declaration is also possible after the initiation of arbitral proceedings.[58]

2.57 **(2.1) Which would be the internationally competent court (i) for obtaining a declaration that an arbitration agreement is valid and binding; or (ii) to compel arbitration? (the defendant's courts? The courts of the place of arbitration? The claimant's courts, cf Article 6(2) in fine, ICC Rules?)** As outlined above, according to prevailing Austrian doctrine, there is no statutory basis for any action to obtain a declaration concerning an arbitration agreement or to compel arbitration.

III. The arbitral tribunal

A. Number and qualification of arbitrators

(1) Sole arbitrator or arbitral tribunal with several arbitrators

2.58 In principle, Austrian law allows the parties free choice regarding the number of arbitrators (s 586(1)). If not determined otherwise by the parties, the number of arbitrators shall be three (s 586(2)). Under the Vienna Rules, the parties are free to choose between a sole arbitrator and an arbitral tribunal consisting of three arbitrators (s 14(1) of the Vienna Rules). If the parties do not agree on the number of arbitrators, the Board of the International Arbitral Centre of the Austrian Federal Economic Chamber shall choose between a sole arbitrator and an arbitral tribunal, taking into account the difficulty of the case, the magnitude of the amount in dispute and the interest of the parties in a rapid and cost-effective decision (s 14(2) of the Vienna Rules).

2.59 **(1.1) Are arbitral tribunals with an even number of arbitrators acceptable?** According to s 586(1) it is mandatory that the arbitral tribunal consists of an uneven number of arbitrators. If the parties have agreed on an even number of arbitrators, then these shall appoint a further person to be the presiding arbitrator.

(2) Qualification of the arbitrators

2.60 The parties can select any person who has full legal capacity to enter into legal transactions.

2.61 **(2.1) Are there mandatory requirements for the qualification of arbitrators (statutory requirements or indirect requirements through eg general conditions of insurance**

[57] See references at Hausmaninger, C. in H. Fasching and A. Konecny, *Kommentar* (n 12) s 578, marg no 19.
[58] Hausmaninger, C. in H. Fasching and A. Konecny, *Kommentar* (n 12) s 578, marg nos 19 *et seq.*

contracts)? There are no additional statutory requirements regarding the qualification of arbitrators, provided the parties have not agreed upon any special additional qualification requirements.

(2.2) Which national arbitration institutions may be contacted for obtaining information about qualified (and specialized) arbitrators? The International Arbitral Centre of the Austrian Federal Economic Chamber maintains a list of arbitrators which contains the contact details and languages spoken. However, this list is only updated every three years.[59] ICC Austria and ArbAut[60] are also sources of information. **2.62**

(2.3) Are judges or civil servants required to obtain permission by their employer to act as arbitrator? Are these permissions given generally or case-by-case? What are the consequences if such permission has not been obtained? According to s 63(5) of the Law on the Employment of the Judiciary, active judges are excluded from being arbitrators. The sanctions for a violation are disciplinary only; the award may not be challenged because of a violation of this provision.[61] **2.63**

Non-judicial civil servants may act as arbitrators. However, the civil servant's employment as an arbitrator of an arbitral tribunal may qualify as an additional occupation ('Nebenbeschäftigung') within the meaning of s 56 of the Civil Servant Act. Under this provision, the civil servant must inform his department and apply for permission if he receives remuneration for acting as an arbitrator. For other employees that work for the state and who are not civil servants, there is an obligation to inform their respective department of all additional paid income if it is likely to exceed a period of four weeks (s 8 of the Public Servant Act). **2.64**

B. Appointment of arbitrators

(1) Extent of party autonomy to establish appointment procedure

The parties are free to agree on a procedure for appointing the arbitrators (s 587(1)). This includes allowing the parties to agree on appointment by an arbitral institution. **2.65**

(2) Procedure in absence of an agreement by the parties

Failing such an agreement on the procedure of appointing the arbitrator(s), the law provides a default procedure for appointing the arbitrator(s) (s 587(2)). In an arbitration with a sole arbitrator, if the parties are unable to agree on the arbitrator within four weeks of receipt of a written request to reach an agreement on a sole arbitrator, the arbitrator shall be appointed, upon request of a party, by the court (s 587(2) no 1). In an arbitration with multiple arbitrators, should the parties fail to reach an agreement, or fail to appoint their **2.66**

---

59 Availiable at <http://portal.wko.at/wk/dok_detail_html.wk?AngID=1&DocID=688948&StID=329164> (accessed 2 June 2008).

60 Austrian Arbitration Association ('Österreichische Vereinigung für Schiedsgerichtsbarkeit'). The Austrian Arbitration Association, which was established in 2000 at the initiative of members of the Board of the International Arbitral Centre of the Austrian Federal Economic Chamber, is neither an arbitration court nor does it administer arbitrations. Its main purpose is the promotion of domestic and international arbitration through public events, professional opinions and publications, as well as training and educational events.

61 Haumaninger, C. in H. Fasching and A. Konecny, *Kommentar* (n 12) s 587, marg no 116.

party-appointed arbitrator(s), or should the notification regarding the presiding arbitrator not be achieved within the time limit, then the appointment shall be made by the court, upon the request by one party. However, the court may only substitute the appointment of arbitrator(s), not other functions, which under the agreed appointment procedure may have been entrusted to a third party entity such as an arbitral institution (s 578).

(3) Effect of the refusal of one party to cooperate in the constitution of the arbitral tribunal

2.67 If a party fails to appoint an arbitrator within four weeks of receipt of a written request to do so from the other party, the appointment shall be made upon the request of either party by the court, if the parties have not provided for another procedure (s 587(2) no 4).

(4) Circumstances and valid reasons for an arbitrator to resign

2.68 In accordance with s 590(1), the mandate of an arbitrator can be terminated at any stage of the proceedings by the parties, or by the resignation of the arbitrator. An arbitrator does not have to show good cause when resigning from his office.[62] If the arbitrator did not have important reasons for the resignation, he may be liable to pay damages for breach of the arbitrator's contract.[63] Important reasons may be illness, refusal of the parties to pay advances on fees or modification of the arbitration agreement that impacts the role of the arbitrator.[64]

C. Challenge and replacement of arbitrators

(1) Grounds, procedure and deadlines for challenging an arbitrator

2.69 The parties are free to agree on a procedure to challenge an arbitrator (s 589(1)). Similar to the appointment procedure, the challenge procedure may be assigned to an arbitral institution (s 589(1)). Failing such agreement, the deadline for challenging an arbitrator is four weeks within becoming aware of the composition of the arbitral tribunal or after becoming aware of any circumstances which give rise to justifiable doubts as to his impartiality or independence (s 589(2)). A challenge of this nature, or any other challenge based on the circumstances referred to in s 588(2), must be made in writing to the arbitral tribunal including the reasons for the challenge (s 589(2)). Unless the challenged arbitrator withdraws, or the other party agrees to the challenge, the arbitral tribunal, including the challenged arbitrator, shall decide on the challenge.[65] If the arbitrator is not challenged within the deadline, the alleged grounds for challenge cannot be used as a reason for challenging an award at a later date.[66]

2.70 **(1.1) Do state courts review challenge procedures which took place in accordance with a specific procedure agreed upon by the parties (eg Art 11, ICC Rules)? If so, at what point in time? May such review be excluded?** If a challenge is unsuccessful, the challenging party may within four weeks of receiving the decision reject the challenge and request

[62] Power, J., *Practitioner's Guide* (n 47) s 590, marg no 2.
[63] Hausmaninger, C. in H. Fasching and A. Konecny, *Kommentar* (n 12) s 590, marg no 44.
[64] For further reasons see Hausmaninger, C. in H. Fasching and A. Konecny, *Kommentar* (n 12) s 587, marg no 253.
[65] Liebscher, C., *Austrian Arbitration Act 2006* (n 18) 16, Art 589(2).
[66] Zeiler, G., *Schiedsverfahren* (n 10) s 589, marg no 12.

the court to decide on the challenge. This decision is not subject to appeal.[67] If the request is denied by the court, or if no such request is made, then the grounds for challenge may not be newly asserted, for example in a proceeding to set aside an award.[68] However, while such a request is pending, the arbitral tribunal, including the challenged arbitrator, may continue the arbitral proceedings and make an award.[69] Section 589(3) constitutes mandatory law which cannot be altered by agreement of the parties.[70]

(1.2) Is there case law with respect to truncated arbitral tribunals? (cf Art 12(5), ICC Rules) Austrian law does not provide for specific rules concerning truncated tribunals. If an arbitral tribunal loses one of its members, a new member will have to be appointed. **2.71**

(2) Procedure for appointing a new arbitrator

In the event the mandate of an arbitrator terminates early, a new arbitrator shall be appointed according to the original rules that were applicable to the appointment of the arbitrator being replaced.[71] Unless otherwise agreed by the parties, the arbitral tribunal may continue the proceedings using the results of the proceedings up to the appointment of the substitute arbitrator, or the tribunal can decide to repeat all or part of the proceedings.[72] **2.72**

IV. The arbitral procedure

A. General principles

(1) Extent of party autonomy to determine the arbitral procedure

Subject to any mandatory provisions of the section pertaining to the general principles and conduct of arbitral proceedings, the parties are free to determine the arbitral procedure.[73] Failing any such agreement between the parties, the arbitral tribunal shall determine the procedure as the tribunal considers appropriate.[74] **2.73**

(1.1) Are the parties free to choose any national or international law governing the procedure before the arbitral tribunal? In principle, the parties to an arbitration agreement are free to determine the procedural rules for the arbitration either by themselves or by reference to procedural rules. Section 594(1), second sentence, expressly provides that arbitral proceedings may also be conducted under entire 'rules of procedure'. 'Rules of procedure' means institutional arbitration rules (eg of the ICC, the VIAC or the LCIA), but also the UNCITRAL Arbitration Rules, as well as the non-arbitration provisions of the CCP and provisions of a foreign arbitration law as a whole.[75] **2.74**

---

[67] Liebscher, C., *Austrian Arbitration Act 2006* (n 18) 17, Art 589(3).
[68] *ibid.*
[69] *ibid.*
[70] Power, J., *Practitioner's Guide* (n 47) s 589, marg no 6.
[71] Liebscher, C., *Austrian Arbitration Act 2006* (n 18) 18, Art 591(1).
[72] *ibid*, Art 591(2).
[73] *ibid*, 25, Art 594 (1).
[74] *ibid.*
[75] Hausmaninger, C. in H. Fasching and A. Konecny, *Kommentar* (n 12) s 594, marg no 85; Platte, M., 'Section 594' in S. Riegler *et al*, *Arbitration Law of Austria* (n 9) s 594, marg no 8.

(2) Basic procedural principles or mandatory rules to be applied by the arbitral tribunal

2.75 The following mandatory procedural rules apply (s 594):

- the parties shall be treated fairly;.
- each party shall be given an opportunity to be heard; and
- each party has the right to be represented by a representative of its choice.

2.76 Therefore, the parties must be given sufficient opportunity to present to the arbitral tribunal all elements,[76] which they consider relevant, and they must have the possibility to participate in the taking of evidence.[77]

2.77 Examples of a violation of the right to be heard were found in the following cases:

- one party was not provided with important documents by the arbitral tribunal and was not even told what the other party claimed in the arbitration;[78]
- an arbitral tribunal failed to inform one party of changes in the facts of the case;[79] and
- a sole arbitrator appointed two persons to hear the parties and consequently rendered an award based on their findings.[80]

2.78 The Supreme Court held that as long as the arbitral tribunal respected the procedure provided for in the arbitration agreement, the right to be heard cannot be violated.[81] A violation of the right to be heard was not found in the following cases:

- the parties had not taken advantage of an opportunity offered by the arbitral tribunal;[82]
- the exclusion of further submissions after the expiry of a deadline did not violate the above principle as long as the opportunity offered by the arbitral tribunal was sufficient for the party to submit its views;[83]
- a party which was not able to present its case because its employees, acting upon the employer's instructions, did not accept a registered letter which contained the details of the hearing;[84]
- a party was not heard by all members of the arbitral tribunal;
- the parties were heard by the co-arbitrators (without the chairman) and the arguments of the parties were all presented by the two arbitrators to the chairman; and
- the parties' submissions were not included in the minutes of the arbitration.

---

[76] In general cf Fasching, H., *Lehrbuch* (n 42) marg nos 692 *et seq*, for arbitration proceedings marg no 2207.

[77] OGH 6 September 1990 [1991] RdW 327; 24 September 1981 [1982] EvBl no 77; 13 January 1955 [1955] 77 JBl 503; 21 November 1951 Neuteufel no 257.

[78] OGH 24 September 1981 [1982] EvBl no 77.

[79] OGH 12 May 1961 [1961] EvBl no 387.

[80] OGH 3 May 1899 no GlUNF 603.

[81] OGH 4 May 1928 (1928) 10 SZ no 123.

[82] OGH 6 September 1990 [1991] RdW 327; 13 January 1955 (1955) 77 JBl 503.

[83] Fasching, H., *Schiedsgericht* (n 39) 103.

[84] OGH 4 May 1928 (1928) 10 SZ no 123.

In fact it seems to be sufficient that the arbitrators have knowledge of the party's position and that the party had the opportunity to express its position at some stage of the proceedings.[85] 2.79

In addition, there are some other mandatory provisions,[86] such as the rule that the arbitral tribunal is authorized to decide on the permissibility of taking of evidence, to carry it out, and to weigh its results freely (s 599 (1)). 2.80

(3) Oral hearing or proceeding on basis of written documents

Unless otherwise agreed by the parties, the arbitral tribunal shall decide whether to hold oral hearings, or whether the proceedings shall be conducted in writing.[87] If a party makes a motion to hold an oral hearing, this does not have the effect that all subsequent steps in the proceedings be conducted orally.[88] There must be only at least one oral hearing on the merits.[89] 2.81

(4) Power of the tribunal (in particular the chairman) to issue procedural orders

It follows from s 594(1) that the arbitral tribunal may issue procedural orders. Questions of procedure may be decided by the chairman alone if so authorized by the parties or all members of the arbitral tribunal (s 604 no 1).[90] 2.82

(5) Distinction of matters of substance and matters of procedure

Section 604 no 1 distinguishes matters of substance and procedural questions without providing a definition of either. The term 'questions of procedure' denotes questions that exclusively affect the course of the arbitration proceedings. This also includes, for example, the determination of the language(s) of the arbitration proceedings (s 596), but not the determination of the seat of the arbitral tribunal. The latter also has effects on the jurisdiction of the courts (s 595(1)). 2.83

(5.1) Are the statutes of limitations a matter of substance or rather of procedure? The statutes of limitation are a matter of substance.[91] 2.84

(6) Persons able to represent a party in an arbitral proceeding

Section 594(3) provides that each party has the right to be represented or advised by a representative of the party's choosing. This is a right that cannot be excluded or restricted.[92] The representative does not have to be a lawyer. 2.85

---

85 OGH 13 January 1955 (1955) 77 JBl 503.

86 See Zeiler, G., *Schiedsverfahren* (n 10) s 594, marg nos 8 *et seq*; Hausmaninger, C. in H. Fasching and A. Konecny, *Kommentar* (n 12) s 594, marg no 80.

87 Liebscher, C., *Austrian Arbitration Act 2006* (n 18) 27, Art 598.

88 *ibid.*

89 *ibid.*

90 Hausmaninger, C. (in H. Fasching and A. Konecny, *Kommentar* (n 12) s 604, marg no 61 states that a chairman may always issue procedural orders alone (in matters such as dates, order of evidence taken) as opposed to a decision on questions of procedure. This view is not convincing.

91 Fasching, H. *Lehrbuch* (n 42) marg no 1,175; Riegler, S., 'Section 603' in S. Riegler *et al*, *Arbitration Law of Austria* (n 9) s 603, marg no 10; Liebscher, C., 'Austria' in C. Liebscher and A. Fremuth-Wolf (eds), *Arbitration Law and Practice in Central and Eastern Europe* (JurisNet LLC, 2006) AUS-44; OGH 23 June 1967, 2 Ob 98/67, 2 Ob 97/67 SZ 40/88.

92 Liebscher, C., *Austrian Arbitration Act 2006* (n 18) 25, Art 594(2).

B. Place of arbitration

(1) Determination of the place of arbitration in absence of an agreement by the parties

2.86 If there is no agreement between the parties on the place of arbitration, then the seat of the arbitral tribunal shall be determined by the arbitral tribunal who shall take into account the circumstances of the case (s 595(1)).

(2) Importance and legal effect of place (seat) of the arbitration

2.87 The choice of the seat of the arbitral tribunal is important for determining legal issues such as the question of whether Austrian law applies to the proceedings ('*lex arbitri*'). According to s 577(1), the application of the Austrian arbitration law (s 577 *et seq*) requires that the arbitral tribunal has its seat in Austria. However, some provisions are applicable even if the seat is outside of Austria or has not yet been determined (s 577(2)).

2.88 The seat of the arbitral tribunal may also determine the law applicable to the arbitration agreement.[93]

2.89 The seat of the arbitral tribunal furthermore determines which domestic courts have jurisdiction over the arbitration procedure (eg regarding the execution of interim measures (see s 593) and the award (eg setting aside an award (see s 615)) and whether the New York Convention ('NYC') is applicable.[94]

2.90 According to s 606(3), the award has to contain the seat of the arbitral tribunal and is deemed to be made at this place.

2.91 As in particular political factors, such as the independence of jurisdiction, the membership of international conventions and the risk of political commotion may have an effect on the enforceability of an award, the choice of an arbitral tribunal's seat may also have a factual importance.

2.92 **(2.1) Are the arbitrators and parties free to convene at other places than the official seat of the arbitration?** The concept of the seat of the arbitration is purely a legal concept. The arbitrators are free to convene at any place they consider appropriate (s 595(2)). Stricter rules apply in an arbitration between an entrepreneur and a consumer (s 617(4)) and in certain labour law arbitrations (s 618).

2.93 **(2.2) Are there visa requirements to enter the country which apply to lawyers and/or arbitrators? Where may current information on that subject be obtained?** Visa requirements to enter Austria vary depending on the individual's nationality. The Austrian law relating to aliens contains the regulations that apply to the requirements of individuals of various nationalities and their respective visa requirements. For current information or to apply for a visa it is necessary to contact the nearest Austrian embassy or consulate.

[93] Hausmaninger, C. in H. Fasching and A. Konecny, *Kommentar* (n 12) s 581, marg nos 283 *et seq*.
[94] Petsche, A., 'Section 595' in S. Riegler *et al*, *Arbitration Law of Austria* (n 9) s 595, marg no 3.

C. Submissions, deadlines and default

(1) Contents and form of submissions (in particular request for arbitration and answer to request)

In *ad hoc* arbitration, the arbitration starts with a request by one party to the other to appoint an arbitrator (s 587(4)). This written request must already state which claim is being asserted and which arbitration agreement the party is invoking.[95] **2.94**

Section 597 deals with the statements of claim and defence. The claimant shall state its claim and the facts supporting this and the defendant shall respond to these. The parties may either submit all documents they consider relevant or may simply refer to these. These requirements suffice to define the subject matter of the arbitration. There is no specific time period for filing these. This can either be agreed by the parties or, if no agreement has been made, set by the arbitral tribunal.[96] **2.95**

(1.1) **From what point in time is a claim considered to be pending with the arbitral tribunal? What are the legal effects of such fact (eg on statutes of limitations)?** As a general rule, the point in time when the defendant receives the claimant's request to appoint an arbitrator is seen as the point when the arbitration commences.[97] This request to appoint an arbitrator is sufficient to interrupt the statute of limitation.[98] It is argued that this rule also applies in institutional arbitration.[99] **2.96**

(1.2) **When is a time limit according to statutes of limitations deemed to be interrupted in case of (i) *ad hoc*; and (ii) institutional arbitration?** It suffices to take the first step in the arbitration according to the arbitration agreement to interrupt the statute of limitation, if the claim is sufficiently substantiated at that time.[100] **2.97**

With regard to *ad hoc* arbitrations, the statute of limitation is deemed to be interrupted on the day the defendant receives the notification of the claimant's intention to initiate arbitration. **2.98**

In institutional arbitrations, the statute of limitation is deemed to be interrupted with receipt of the claim by the arbitral institution.[101] **2.99**

(1.3) **What is the effect of the withdrawal of the request for arbitration?** Section 608 governs the termination of arbitration proceedings. This section is mandatory law.[102] The proceedings will be terminated if the claimant withdraws his claim at any stage of the proceedings. This does not require the claimant to waive his claim or the defendant to **2.100**

---

[95] Zeiler, G., *Schiedsverfahren* (n 10) s 584, marg nos 14 *et seq.*

[96] Power, J., *Practitioner's Guide* (n 47) s 597, marg no 2.

[97] Zeiler, G. and Steindl, B., *Basic Primer* (n 11) s 597, marg no 2.

[98] Liebscher, C., *Austrian Arbitration Act 2006* (n 18) 15, Art 587(4).

[99] Hausmaninger, C. in H. Fasching and A. Konecny, *Kommentar* (n 12) s 584 marg no 35.

[100] *ibid*, marg no 67; Reiner, A., *Handbuch der ICC-Schiedsgerichtsbarkeit* (Manz, 1989) 38 *et seq*; doubtful: Liebscher, C., 'Reform of Austrian Arbitration Law' *JIA*, 2001, 211.

[101] See references in Hausmaninger, C. in H. Fasching and A. Konecny, *Kommentar* (n 12) s 584, marg no 71.

[102] *ibid*, s 594, marg no 80.

agree to the withdrawal. The defendant may however object to the withdrawal. If the arbitral tribunal sees a legitimate interest for the defendant in obtaining a final resolution of the dispute (for example, if it is possible that the claimant files the same claim against the defendant at a later point in time), then the arbitral tribunal may deem the withdrawal ineffective and continue the proceedings.[103]

(2) Legal deadlines (provided by law or set by the tribunal) and effect of non-compliance by a party

2.101 If there are no procedural rules provided by the parties, the arbitrators are free to set deadlines for specific procedural steps.[104] The expiration of these deadlines may result in the exclusion of submissions. If the parties or the arbitrators determine time limits and the consequences of default, it should be noted that such provisions may not violate the parties' right to be heard.

2.102 (2.1) **What are the powers of the tribunal if a party fails to comply with the time limits set up by the tribunal?** If a party fails to perform any procedural act then the arbitral tribunal may continue the proceedings and may make an award based on the basis of the evidence taken. If such failure has been excused to the satisfaction of the arbitral tribunal, then it may still be performed by the party. If the claimant fails to file his statement of claim in accordance with s 597(1) then the arbitral tribunal shall terminate the proceedings. If the defendant fails to respond to the statement of claim within the agreed time period, then the arbitral tribunal shall, unless agreed otherwise by the parties, continue the proceedings without treating such failure in itself as an admission of the claimant's allegations. As this provision is not mandatory, the parties may agree that the arbitral tribunal shall render an award by default if the defendant does not submit a statement of defence.[105]

2.103 (2.2) **Is the tribunal bound by any mandatory time limits for certain procedural steps (eg hearings, making of the award)?** Austrian arbitration law does not provide for time periods within which the arbitrator must perform certain procedural steps. Negligent delay of the proceedings could, however, result in the liability of the arbitrators (s 584(2)).

(3) Statutory requirements as to notifications during an arbitration (with respect to the request for arbitration and other written pleadings; with respect to notifications by the tribunal)

2.104 Section 580 provides rules for the receipt of written communications. There are no other statutory rules concerning notifications.

(4) Effect of the insolvency of a party

2.105 The fact that one of the parties is subject to insolvency proceedings is not in itself sufficient to render a dispute non-arbitrable *per se*.

[103] Power, J., *Practitioner's Guide* (n 47) s 608, marg no 5.
[104] Fasching, H., *Schiedsgericht* (n 39) 104 with additional refs.
[105] Power, J., *Practitioner's Guide* (n 47) s 601, marg no 3.

Insolvency of a party does not entitle the other party to withdraw from the arbitration agreement.[106] The receiver is bound by the arbitration agreement.[107] **2.106**

Only the non-fulfilment of the arbitration agreement, such as a default by the insolvency estate to pay the required advances justifies the extraordinary termination of the arbitration agreement.[108] **2.107**

Pending arbitration proceedings are suspended by the opening of bankruptcy proceedings.[109] **2.108**

D. Facts and evidence: general

(1) Burden of proof (inquisitorial/adversarial procedure)

Under Austrian law, the rules of burden of proof are considered part of the applicable substantive law.[110] **2.109**

Under Austrian law, the general rule is that each party has the burden of proof for the facts supporting its respective legal position.[111] **2.110**

(2) Power of the tribunal to determine the admissibility and weight of the evidence produced by the parties

The arbitral tribunal is authorized to decide on the permissibility of taking of evidence, to carry it out, and to weight its results freely (s 599(1)). This rule is mandatory.[112] **2.111**

The arbitral tribunal may consider any type of evidence in determining the facts of the case. It is not restricted by more closely-regulated means of proof in the CCP.[113] The taking of evidence cannot be carried out by other persons, for example, by an expert alone.[114] If there are no other procedural rules provided by the parties or the arbitrators, the evidence does not have to be presented in the presence of all arbitrators.[115] **2.112**

(2.1) Is the tribunal entitled to take the claimant's factual allegation as proven if the defendant does not participate in the arbitral proceedings? If the defendant fails to appear before the arbitral tribunal, the claimant must, in spite of his absence, stay and prove the facts for which the claimant bears the burden of proof (s 600(1)). This failure is not in itself an admission of the defendant's allegations (s 600(2)). **2.113**

---

[106] Hausmaninger, C. in H. Fasching and A. Konecny, *Kommentar* (n 12) s 581, marg no 132.

[107] *ibid*, marg no 199.

[108] *ibid*, marg no 132.

[109] Schubert, G, '§§ 6–9 KO' in A. Konecny and G. Schubert, (eds), *Kommentar zu den Insolvenzgesetzen* (vol 1, Manzsche Verlags- und Universitätsbuchhandlung, 1997), s 7, marg no 10; Kuhn, G. and Uhlenbruck, W., *Kommentar zu Konkursordnung* (11th edn, Vahlen, 1994) before s 10–12, marg no 5c; different view Petschek, G. *et al*, *Das österreichische Insolvenzrecht—Eine systematische Darstellung* (Manzsche Verlags- und Universitätsbuchhandlung, 1973) 594.

[110] See eg Rechberger, W.H., 'Allgemeine Beweislehre' in H. Fasching and A. Konecny (eds), *Kommentar zu den Zivilprozeß-gesetzen* (2nd edn, vol 3, Manz, 2004) before s 266, marg no 27.

[111] See eg Rechberger, W.H. in H. Fasching and A. Konecny, *Kommentar* (n 110) before s 266, marg no 29.

[112] See Zeiler, G., *Schiedsverfahren* (n 10) s 594, marg nos 8 *et seq*; Hausmaninger, C. in H. Fasching and A. Konecny, *Kommentar* (n 12) s 594, marg no 80.

[113] Fasching, H., *Schiedsgericht* (n 39) 107.

[114] OGH 3 May 1899 GlUNF 603.

[115] OGH 13 January 1955 JBl 1955, 503; Fasching, H., *Lehrbuch* (n 42) marg no 2, 209.

2.114 (2.2) **May the arbitral tribunal consider an allegation of one party as agreed fact if the other party did not (specifically) dispute the allegation?** The same rules apply as set forth under 2.1 (para 2.113), *supra*.

2.115 (2.3) **What is the standard of proof that must be met in order for a fact to be considered to have been established (preponderance of the evidence; beyond reasonable doubt)? Must a stringent requirement be met for certain facts?** According to legal precedent in proceedings before a state court, only a 'high probability' is deemed sufficient.[116] There are no statutory rules that apply in arbitration.[117] Under Austrian law, the standard of proof is a matter of procedural law. According to the general rule of s 594(1), the arbitral tribunal may determine the standard of proof absent any agreement by the parties.

2.116 (2.4) **May the arbitral tribunal rely on its own knowledge to consider certain facts as proven?** Under the old law it was argued that according to s 587 (old) arbitrators may make use of their private knowledge.[118] However, to respect the parties' right to be heard, the arbitrator should disclose such knowledge. Although the rule of s 587 (old) was not included in the text of the new arbitration law, it can be argued that this situation continues.

E. Witnesses

(1) Ability of a person to act as a witness

2.117 The arbitration rules do not contain any regulations on who may appear as a witness before an arbitral tribunal. All persons whose testimony could clarify the dispute may appear as a witness. Any relationships between a witness and a party may be taken into account in the free assessment of evidence.

2.118 (1.1) **Is there a legal difference between a party testifying and a witness? If yes, what are the criteria for such differentiation? Does the testifying of a party have the same weight as a witness testimony?** There are no provisions of Austrian law that differentiate between the testimony of a party and that of a witness. Thus, the testimony of a party can have the same weight as a witness testimony. However, according to its free consideration of evidence (s 599(1)), the tribunal may give different weight to a party testifying as to a witness testifying. Nevertheless, according to the Austrian law, which regulates judicial court proceedings, a party may not be forced to testify (s 373 CCP). This is relevant when the state court is asked to interrogate a witness by way of court assistance under s 602.

(2) Preparation of witnesses and limits thereof

2.119 There are no such rules under Austrian law. In practice, parties and their lawyers are generally allowed to meet with and to prepare a witness. Limits of the preparation of witnesses may derive from s 146 of the Austrian Penal Code ('StGB'), which establishes criminal liability for fraud, if a party encourages a witness to a false witness statement.

---

116 See eg Rechberger, W.H. in H. Fasching and A. Konecny, *Kommentar* (n 110) before s 266, marg no 11.

117 Liebscher, C., 'Beweisaufnahme im Schiedsverfahren' in H. Torggler (ed), *Schiedsgerichtsbarkeit* (Verlag Österreich GmbH, 2007) at 176 *et seq.*

118 Fasching, H., *Schiedsgericht* (n 39) 106, with additional refs, s 587 (1).

Furthermore, preparing a witness in an influencing way is a breach of s 9 of the Austrian Bar Code of Practice ('RAO') and may entail disciplinary consequences for the lawyer.

(2.1) **Do US-style depositions violate any procedural rules or principles?** There are no express procedural rules or principles of Austrian law that would prohibit US-style depositions. However, under s 599(1) the arbitral tribunal has the authoritative say in matters relating to the taking of evidence. 2.120

(2.2) **May a party or its counsel approach a witness whom it has nominated (only before or also after the proceeding has started)? Are interviews permitted?** It is generally permitted that the parties or their lawyers meet with a witness. However, an attorney that gives the appearance of influencing the witness is in breach of s 9 of the RAO and could be subject to disciplinary consequences. 2.121

(3) Admissibility of written witness statements

There are no provisions contained in the Austrian law regarding the method of examining witnesses or the admissibility of written statements by witnesses. It is within the discretion of the arbitral tribunal to permit them if the parties have not agreed otherwise (s 594(1)). 2.122

(3.1) **If the parties agree on written statements, is a party entitled to request an oral hearing for questioning those witnesses (provided such right has not been agreed upon)?** This is a matter within the discretion of the arbitral tribunal (s 594(1)). In general, s 598 (second sentence) provides that upon a party's request, the arbitral tribunal has to hold an oral hearing, if the parties have not excluded the conduction of oral hearings. The agreement to use written witness statements in the proceedings does not exclude the possibility of holding an oral hearing for questioning those witnesses.[119] In practice, written witness statements are usually followed by an oral hearing in which the witnesses are examined. 2.123

(4) Entitlement of a party to have a hearing or cross-examination of witnesses

If there are no rules of procedure provided by the parties the arbitrators may, at their discretion, determine the method of questioning the witnesses. The arbitral tribunal is not obligated to hold a hearing for the questioning of a witness.[120] 2.124

(4.1) **What are the methods used to establish a record of the arbitral proceedings, in particular witness examinations (tape recording, verbatim court reporters, dictated minutes, other methods)?** All methods are used to record the arbitration proceedings. There is no single preferred method. 2.125

(4.2) **May the arbitral tribunal take an oath from a witness?** Arbitrators do not have the authority to question witnesses, parties and experts under oath. If the arbitrators require that the testimony is given under oath they have to apply to the courts for judicial assistance from the competent court.[121] 2.126

---

119 Reverse from Hausmaninger, C. in H. Fasching and A. Konecny, *Kommentar* (n 12) s 598, marg no 30.

120 For the old law (still pertinent under the new law): OGH 13. 1. 1955 JBl 1955, 503; Rechberger, W.H. and Melis, W., 'Schiedsverfahren' in W.H. Rechberger (ed), *Kommentar zur ZPO* (2nd edn, Springer-Verlag, 2000) marg no 3 to s 588 with additional refs.

121 Hausmaninger, C. in H. Fasching and A. Konecny, *Kommentar* (n 12) s 602, marg no 1.

2.127 **(4.3) Does the arbitral tribunal have the power to compel witnesses?** Neither the parties nor the witnesses or the experts are obligated to appear before the arbitral tribunal. The arbitrators cannot impose any sanction upon an individual who does not appear before the tribunal,[122] but the tribunal may seek judicial assistance in accordance with s 602.

F. Documents

(1) Form and kind of documents to be presented to the arbitral tribunal

2.128 If there are no procedural rules provided by the parties the arbitrators may determine in which form documents should be submitted to the arbitral tribunal (eg originals, plain copy or certified copy) and whether documents should be translated (s 594(1)).

2.129 **(1.1) Is the submission of 'agreed documents' permitted? If yes, what is the extent and effect of such an agreement of the parties (authenticity, existence, acknowledgement of such documents' contents)?** 'Agreed documents' are unknown under Austrian law. Given the fact that it is within the mandatory authority of the arbitral tribunal to decide on the taking of evidence and to weigh the evidence (s 599(1)), such an agreement will not be legally binding on the arbitral tribunal.

2.130 **(1.2) How may electronic documents (eg emails) be presented and proven?** There are no statutory rules on electronic documents in arbitration. Also the Vienna Rules do not contain any such rules. In Austrian state court proceedings, electronic documents generally qualify as evidence by inspection ('Augenscheinsbeweis'); they qualify as documents ('Urkunden') if they contain a written record. Emails will therefore be regularly subsumed under the term 'documents' and may be presented and proven either in electronic or printed form. Owing to the principle of material immediacy of taking evidence ('Grundsatz der materiellen Unmittelbarkeit der Beweisaufnahme'), such documents will, however, only be admissible if the immediate evidence (eg the witness) is not available.[123]

2.131 According to arbitral practice, an arbitral tribunal will generally have no legal concerns to allow a party to present electronic documents and to use emails as evidence.

2.132 **(1.3) Does discovery (US- or UK- style), after the procedure has started, violate any procedural rules or public policy considerations?** There are no express procedural rules or principles of Austrian law that would prohibit discovery. However, it will be for the arbitral tribunal to decide whether this is permitted (s 599(1)). Discovery as such will not violate Austrian public policy.

(2) Requirement to produce certain documents (as requested by the tribunal) and consequences of a failure to do so

2.133 The arbitral tribunal may request the disclosure of documents, but the arbitral tribunal cannot enforce this request. With regard to a request for the production of documents directed against the parties, judicial assistance is very limited as there is no comprehensive enforcement mechanism provided for by Austrian law. The non-compliance with the

---

122 Hausmaninger, C. in H. Fasching and A. Konecny, *Kommentar* (n 12) s 602, marg no 1.

123 Rechberger, W.H., 'Verfahren bis zum Urteile' in W.H. Rechberger, *ZPO* (n 120) before s 292, marg no 4.

request for the production of documents by a party is subject to the free assessment of evidence by the arbitrators.[124]

(2.1) Which documents may the tribunal request to be produced (eg also documents which are in the possession of third parties)? The arbitral tribunal could also ask third parties to produce documents or authorize a party to do so. However, a request to produce documents that is directed against third parties is enforceable only by way of court assistance pursuant to ss 308, 309 CCP. **2.134**

(3) Protection of the confidentiality of documents (legal privilege etc)

In principle, arbitration proceedings are held *in camera* and are not open to the public.[125] It is, however, unclear whether there is a general obligation of confidentiality in the absence of an agreement of the parties. There are no court decisions in Austria which deal with the issue of confidentiality. It appears, however, that a comprehensive confidentiality cannot be inferred from an arbitration agreement without a specific provision for confidentiality.[126] Within its general authority to determine the procedure (s 594(1)), the arbitral tribunal may issue rules for the protection of confidentiality. Moreover, almost all institutional arbitration rules contain some rules of confidentiality.[127] **2.135**

G. Experts

(1) Appointment and presentation of experts by the party or the arbitral tribunal

The appointment of experts is governed by s 601. Unless otherwise agreed by the parties, the arbitral tribunal may appoint one or more experts to report to it on specific issues to be determined by the arbitral tribunal. The arbitral tribunal may require a party to give the expert any relevant information or to produce, or to provide access to, any relevant documents or property for the making of a report. Section 601(3) stipulates that the provisions on the challenge of an arbitrator (s 588) and the challenge procedure (s 589(1) and (2)) apply *mutatis mutandis* to an expert appointed by the arbitral tribunal. The parties have a right to question tribunal-appointed experts and be assisted by their own experts. **2.136**

(1.1) By which methods are tribunal-appointed experts selected? What are the rights of the parties during the selection process? There are no statutory rules on the subject. Usually, the arbitral tribunal will give the parties the opportunity to jointly propose an expert. The grounds and the procedure for the challenge of arbitrators apply *mutatis mutandis* to tribunal-appointed experts (s 601(3)). **2.137**

(2) Admissibility and role of expert witnesses

Unless otherwise agreed by the parties, each party has the right to produce reports of its own experts who may also be asked to participate in an oral hearing and be questioned by the other party (s 601(4)). **2.138**

[124] See Liebscher, C. in H.Torggler, *Schiedsgerichtsbarkeit* (n 117) marg no 78 *et seq*.
[125] Hausmaninger, C. in H. Fasching and A. Konecny, *Kommentar* (n 12) s 594, marg no 134.
[126] Fremuth-Wolf, A., 'Confidentiality in Arbitration' in Riegler *et al*, *Arbitration Law of Austria* (n 9) 671.
[127] Hausmaninger, C. in H. Fasching and A. Konecny, *Kommentar* (n 12) s 594, marg no 66.

(3) Influence of the parties upon the selection of questions to be submitted to the expert

2.139 To what extent the parties may be involved in the wording of the questions is determined by the arbitrator's discretion; however, it is frequent that the arbitral tribunal together with the parties determines in advance the questions to be addressed to the expert.

(4) Independence and impartiality of the expert and the right to reject a proposed/appointed expert

2.140 Section 601(3) provides that an expert appointed by the arbitral tribunal—but not one appointed by a party—may be challenged on the same grounds as those applicable to an arbitrator. Experts are thus under a duty to disclose any circumstances relating to their impartiality or independence in the same way as an arbitrator. It is up to the arbitral tribunal to decide whether to uphold a party's challenge or not. This decision cannot be challenged and is not subject to court review. The decision of the arbitral tribunal is thus final and binding on the parties. Any possible bias on the part of the expert only constitutes grounds for challenging an award if thereby the procedural public policy is breached.[128]

2.141 **(4.1) May a party or its counsel approach an expert (or expert witness) whom it has nominated (only before or also after the proceeding has started)? Are interviews admissible?** It is generally permitted that the parties or their lawyers meet with an expert witness. However, an attorney that gives the appearance of influencing the witness is in breach of s 9 of the RAO and could be subject to disciplinary consequences.

2.142 An *ex parte* meeting with a tribunal-appointed expert may create the appearance of bias and, thus, justify a challenge of the expert.

(5) Oral examination of an expert in a hearing

2.143 Unless otherwise agreed by the parties, if a party so requests or if the arbitral tribunal considers it necessary, the expert shall, after delivering his report participate in an oral hearing. In the hearing the parties not only have the opportunity to put questions to him but to present reports from their own expert(s) on the points at issue. The parties' right to examine experts is a reflection of the parties' right to be heard and thus may not be limited by agreement.[129] It is incumbent on the arbitral tribunal to evaluate the relevance of the questions. In complex matters it may indeed be advisable to instruct the parties to submit a list of their own questions within a reasonable time prior to the hearing, so as to ensure compliance with all persons' right to be heard.

H. Interim measures of protection

(1) Kind of interim measures which the tribunal may order

2.144 According to the new arbitration law, arbitrators are not only entitled to render interim measures of protection between the parties to the arbitration agreement, but such interim measures rendered by arbitrators are now enforceable in Austria by the state courts in the same way as interim measures rendered by the courts.

[128] Kloiber, B. and Haller, H. in B. Kloiber *et al*, *Das neue Schiedsrecht* (n 14) 44; Power, J., *Practitioner's Guide* (n 47) s 601, marg no 4.

[129] Power, J., *Practitioner's Guide* (n 47) s 601, marg no 3.

The power of the arbitral tribunal to render interim measures is determined by s 593(1).[130] **2.145**

In accordance with s 17 ModG and s 1041 GCCP,[131] s 593 does not contain a list of interim measures the arbitral tribunal may order. Accordingly, Austrian law does not provide for a *numerus clausus* of such measures. In particular, the arbitral tribunal may also take measures which are unknown to Austrian law.[132] **2.146**

Potential measures are: **2.147**

- measures for securing the enforcement of the award;
- measures for securing the conduct of the proceedings, including the preservation of evidence;
- measures which preliminarily shall govern a legal relationship or which declare an action or omission as preliminarily justified;
- measures which serve the purpose of the preliminary enforcement of an alleged claim;
- preliminary or securing measures with regard to costs.[133]

(1.1) Which are, in general, the procedural and substantive prerequisites for the ordering of interim and conservatory measures (eg reduced degree of evidence; urgency; summary evaluation of the claim)? Section 593 only provides limited guidance. According to s 593(1), the arbitral tribunal may only order such measures it deems necessary with regard to the subject matter in dispute. Nevertheless, Austrian doctrine allows recourse to the broad interpretation and thus even such measures which do not directly concern the subject matter in dispute but the conduct of the proceedings (eg conservation of evidence). **2.148**

Additionally, the ordering of such a measure requires that the enforcement of the claim would be frustrated or considerably impeded or that there is a danger that irreparable damage would occur. **2.149**

Furthermore, an arbitral tribunal may only order an interim or conservatory measure after the parties have been heard. Only a national court may order *ex parte* measures. **2.150**

(1.2) Are the prerequisites for interim measures ordered by the arbitral tribunal more or less the same as if those are requested from the state court? Is there case law/leading authorities on whether those measures are faster and enforced more easily if taken by the arbitral tribunal or the state court? In general, the practice of Austrian courts to grant interim measures is restrictive. The framework for the granting of such measures by arbitral tribunals is more flexible. **2.151**

[130] s 593(1) reads: 'Unless otherwise agreed by the parties, the arbitral tribunal may, at the request of a party, order such provisional or protective measures against another party, after hearing such party, as the arbitral tribunal may consider necessary in respect of the subject matter of the dispute, as otherwise the enforcement of the claim would be frustrated or considerably impeded or there is a danger that irreparable damage will occur. The arbitral tribunal may require any party to provide appropriate security in connection with such measure'.

[131] 'German Code of Civil Procedure'.

[132] Hausmaninger, C. in H. Fasching and A. Konecny, *Kommentar* (n 12) s 593, marg no 53.

[133] See references in Hausmaninger, C. in H. Fasching and A. Konecny, *Kommentar* (n 12) s 593, marg no 56 *et seq*.

2.152 Nevertheless, some arguments may favour the application of state courts: first, arbitral tribunals may order measures only against the parties of the arbitration agreement, ie *inter partes*, whilst state courts may also order measures against third parties (eg third party prohibitions). Second, since prior to its constitution, an arbitral tribunal may not order conservative or interim measures, a party would have to apply for a state court measure in such a case. Finally, the requirement of s 593(1), that the parties need to be heard prior to the ordering of conservative or interim measures by the arbitral tribunal, may be detrimental.[134]

(2) Limits of the tribunal's powers to order interim measures

2.153 The arbitral tribunal may not issue *ex parte* orders (s 593(1)) and may not order interim measures prior to its constitution. The arbitral tribunal may also not issue such orders without having heard the parties.

(3) Orders to provide security for the costs of the proceeding

2.154 There are no specific rules governing an arbitrator's authority to order a party to present security for the costs of the proceedings. However, such an order is possible within the general language of s 593 ('interim or protective measures against the other party as (the arbitral tribunal) deems necessary in respect of the subject-matter in dispute'). Claims for costs form a part of the matter in dispute.[135] Such orders may be applied for, by and granted to both parties.

(4) Attachment of assets by an order of the tribunal

2.155 There are no specific rules governing the attachment of assets. Such an order would be possible within the general framework of s 593.

I. Assistance by the courts

(1) Extent of court assistance in the gathering of evidence

2.156 According to s 602 the courts are obliged to grant judicial assistance to arbitral tribunals. However, under this provision the obligation to grant judicial assistance only covers judicial, sovereign acts, eg summons, examination, administration of oath, appointment of experts, implementation of judicial inspection, of documentary evidence etc. Additionally, the request for assistance may only refer to those judicial acts that are considered necessary by the arbitral tribunal and for which it has no jurisdiction in accordance with s 602. However, the courts are not allowed to review the expedience of the required judicial act. In our experience, judicial assistance is not used very frequently.

2.157 (1.1) **Is it for the arbitral tribunal or for the party to obtain the assistance of state courts with respect to the gathering of evidence?** Either the arbitral tribunal, an arbitrator, or a party with the authorization of the arbitral tribunal may request assistance.

---

[134] Rechberger, W.H. and Melis, W., 'Durchführung des Schiedsverfahrens' in W.H. Rechberger, *ZPO* (n 120) s 594, marg nos 2 *et seq.*

[135] Reiner, A., *The New Austrian Arbitration Law* (n 45) s 593, n 101.

(1.2) According to case law and practical experience, are there considerable delays involved when asking a court to give assistance (eg for the obtaining of evidence)? A request for judicial assistance may take several months. Generally, the length of time depends upon the nature of the request. 2.158

(2) Assistance for enforcing the attachment of assets

Any interim measure ordered by an arbitral tribunal sitting in Austria or abroad may be enforced by the Austrian courts. 2.159

According to s 593(4) the court shall reject the enforcement of the measure if: 2.160

- the seat of the arbitral tribunal lies within the country and the measure suffers from a defect that, for a domestic award, would be a ground for setting aside under s 611(2);
- the seat of the arbitral tribunal does not lie within the country and the measure suffers from a defect that, for a foreign award, would be a ground for the refusal of the recognition or enforcement;
- the enforcement of the measure is inconsistent with a previously applied for, or issued domestic court measure or a previously issued foreign court measure which is to be recognized; or
- the measure provides for a measure that does not exist under domestic law and no appropriate domestic measure was claimed.

The court may grant a hearing to the opposing party according to s 593(5). If the opposing party has not been heard before the decision has been made, that party may make an objection in terms of s 397 of the Enforcement Act to the granting of the enforcement ('Widerspruch'). In either case, the opposing party may only argue that a ground for the refusal of the enforcement as described above according to s 593(4) exists.[136] 2.161

The court shall repeal the enforcement if:[137] 2.162

- the period of validity for the measure determined by the arbitral tribunal has expired;
- the arbitral tribunal has modified or set aside the measure;
- a ground specified in s 399(1) nos 1-4 of the Enforcement Act exists; or,
- security was provided.

(3) Other examples of possible assistance

Other examples of court assistance include the appointment of representatives of absent parties, service of documents and request for assistance to other Austrian authorities or to foreign courts or authorities. 2.163

(4) Dependence of the power of state courts to intervene during the proceedings on the (national) procedural law applied by the arbitral tribunal.

Austrian courts will render assistance under s 602 irrespective of the procedural law to be applied by the arbitral tribunal or its seat (s 577(2)). 2.164

136 Liebscher, C., *Austrian Arbitration Act 2006* (n 18) 22, Art 593 (5).
137 *ibid*, Art 593 (6).

V. The award

A. Types of award

(1) Interim award (eg on interim measures or the jurisdiction of the tribunal)

2.165 The arbitral tribunal may render interim awards. Interim awards are awards, which are neither final awards terminating the arbitration completely nor partial awards, finally resolving at least one claim.

(2) Partial award

2.166 The arbitral tribunal may also render partial awards. A partial award finally deals with at least one claim.

2.167 **(2.1) Are awards, especially partial awards, binding in the same arbitral proceeding? Does it make a difference if after the rendering of such a partial award, one arbitrator is successfully challenged and removed on grounds that prevailed even before the partial award was rendered?** According to s 597 an award has the legal effect of a final and binding court judgment. Therefore, it will also be binding in the same arbitral proceedings.

2.168 If the partial award was not challenged in time, it remains binding even if an arbitrator was successfully challenged subsequently.

(3) Final award

2.169 A final award decides all substantive matters not yet decided by previous partial awards.

2.170 **(3.1) If a party fails to participate in the arbitration, may the tribunal proceed and issue an award on the merits? Is such an award enforceable as any other award? Are there special remedies for the defendant at the enforcement stage?** If a party fails to participate in the arbitration, the arbitral tribunal may proceed and render an award on the merits (s 600(2)). The only exception is a claimant's default to submit a statement of claim. In this case the arbitral tribunal shall just terminate the proceedings (s 600(1)). Such an award is enforceable as any other award and does not give the defendant any special remedies at the enforcement stage.

B. Deliberations and agreement on the award

(1) Time limits (and possible extensions) for making the award

2.171 There exists no time limit in the new law for the making of an award in Austria. This does not exclude that parties may agree upon such time limit or that an arbitral tribunal having its seat in Austria has to apply arbitration rules providing for a time limit for the making of an award. If arbitrators need an extension of the time limit set by the parties or the applicable rules, they have either to ask the parties to agree upon the requested extension of time or to follow the procedure provided for this case in the applicable arbitration rules. Since the arbitration law does not provide for a time limit for the making of an award, Austrian courts would have the authority to extend a time limit agreed by the parties.

(2) Procedure for the decision of the arbitrators (majority vote etc)

2.172 Unless the parties have agreed otherwise, any decision shall be made by a majority of all members of an arbitral tribunal. If so authorized by the parties or by all members of the arbitral tribunal, the presiding arbitrator may decide questions of procedure alone (s 604(1)).

When one or more arbitrators do not participate in a vote without providing a reasonable justification, the remaining arbitrators may decide. In such case, a simple majority of votes has to be calculated on the basis of the total number of arbitrators. If such a situation occurs, the parties must be notified ahead of time of the intention of the participating majority to proceed in this manner (s 604(2)). **2.173**

(2.1) If an arbitrator fails or refuses to take part in oral deliberation meetings, although having been given sufficient notice of such meetings, may an award be rendered on the basis of written deliberations (or deliberations without this arbitrator) only? When one or more arbitrators do not participate in a vote without justified reason, the other arbitrators may decide without them. In this case as well, the necessary majority of votes is to be calculated by the total of all participating and non-participating arbitrators. In the case of a vote on an award, the parties must receive prior information on the intention to proceed in this matter. **2.174**

(3) Admissibility of dissenting opinions

There are no statutory rules on dissenting opinions. Austrian authors are controversial whether dissenting opinions are admissible.[138] A dissenting opinion is in any case not part of an award. If an arbitrator sends the Secretary-General of VIAC a dissenting opinion, he serves it on the parties with the remark that it is not a part of the award. **2.175**

(3.1) Are there any court decisions or positions of leading authorities on the issue of dissenting opinions (admissibility, disclosure to the parties and publication)? There is no available case law on dissenting opinions. Austrian doctrine is controversial whether dissenting opinions are admissible and if so, under what circumstances. According to German law, dissenting opinions are usually accepted, although it is controversial whether they require a respective agreement of the parties. An argument often brought forward against the admissibility of dissenting opinions is that it would infringe the principle of confidential deliberations.[139] **2.176**

(4) Signature by the arbitrators and potential failure of one arbitrator to sign

If there is more than one arbitrator, the new law provides that '[. . .] the signatures of the majority of all members of the arbitral tribunal shall suffice, provided that the reason for any omitted signature is stated on the arbitral award by the presiding or another arbitrator' (s 606(1)). However, an action may be brought against the arbitrator who failed to sign and whose signature is necessary for the effectiveness of the award.[140] **2.177**

[138] See references in Hausmaninger, C. in H. Fasching and A. Konecny, *Kommentar* (n 12) s 606, marg no 76.

[139] *ibid.*

[140] OGH 29. January 1970 JBI 1971, 528.

C. Form of the award and deposition

(1) Form and minimum contents of an award

2.178 According to s 606, the form requirements of an arbitral award are:

- the award has to be made in writing;
- the award must be signed by the arbitrators;
- generally, the award must state the date when, and the place where, it was made; and,
- unless agreed otherwise by the parties, the award shall state the reasons.

2.179 The arbitral award has to be signed by the arbitrators and must state the date when it was made.

2.180 There are some other, obvious, form requirements such as the indication of the parties.

2.181 The Austrian CCP does not contain any other specific provisions regulating the minimum content of an award. An award is a decision of the arbitral tribunal which at least partially decides a claim.[141]

(2) Requirement to give reasons in the award

2.182 According to s 606(2) unless the parties have agreed otherwise '[. . .] the award shall state the reasons upon which it is based'. The parties may also implicitly, at any time, even after the rendering of the award, without any specific form requirements, exclude such an obligation to give reasons.

(3) Necessity to specify place and time where and when the award was made

2.183 According to the OGH, the lack of the date is not a ground for challenge,[142] which clearly establishes that the date is not an essential element. The same applies to the indication of the seat.[143] The specification of the seat in the award has only declaratory effect, since the seat of the arbitration is determined in accordance with s 595.

(4) Other requirements (registration, delivery etc)

2.184 According to s 606(4), after the award is made, a copy signed by the arbitrators shall be delivered to each party. Normally in domestic cases this is achieved by registered mail with return receipt, and in international cases also by international courier services. Section 606(5) states that the award and the documentation of its service are joint documents of the parties and the arbitrators. The arbitral tribunal shall discuss with the parties a possible safekeeping of the award and the documentation of its service (s 606(5)). Therefore, it is the parties' and the arbitrator's responsibility to determine whether and how an original of the award and the documentation of its service shall be registered.

2.185 **(4.1) Does the award have to be laid down or registered with a state court or agency (even if it has been rendered according to a foreign procedural law)?** There are no

[141] Hausmaninger, C. in H. Fasching and A. Konecny, *Kommentar* (n 12) s 606, marg no 45; for the 'non-award' see *ibid*, s 606, marg no. 45 *et seq*; Liebscher, C., *The Healthy Award* (Kluwer Law International, 2003) 116 *et seq*.

[142] OGH 18 September 1991 (1992) 114 JBl 192; Hausmaninger, C. in H. Fasching and A. Konecny, *Kommentar* (n 12) s 606, marg no 92.

[143] Hausmaninger, C. in H. Fasching and A. Konecny, *Kommentar* (n 12) s 606, marg no 91.

statutory registration requirements. According to s 27(5) of the Vienna Rules, one copy of the award and the records of the service shall be deposited with the Secretariat at the Centre.

(4.2) Does a foreign award which has been rendered abroad according to this country's national procedural law, have to be laid down or registered with a state court or agency? Is there a fee or tax for such registration of an award? The new Arbitration Law has a specific provision for the recognition and enforcement of foreign arbitral awards. According to s 614(1) '(t)he recognition and order for enforcement of foreign awards shall be made in accordance with the provisions of the Enforcement Act, unless otherwise provided in international law or in legal instruments of the European Union'. As there are so far no other provisions in international law or legal instruments of the European Union, ss 79–86 of the Enforcement Act apply.[144] **2.186**

No registration is required; for the enforcement procedure as such see under section VIII (paras 2.280–3), *infra*. **2.187**

(4.3) How long after the rendering of the award must the file/award be stored by the lawyers and the arbitral tribunal? There are no statutory rules in this respect. However, it can be argued that the award must be kept for the time period within which it is enforceable. According to Austrian law, the right to enforce an award is time-barred after 30 years following the legal finality of the award (so-called 'Judikatsschuld').[145] **2.188**

D. Applicable substantive law

(1) Party autonomy to choose the applicable substantive law

The parties may choose any legal rules (s 603(1)). This includes as such non-binding legal texts, such as the UNIDROIT Principles or the Principles of European Contract Law. **2.189**

(1.1) Is there a public policy exception to the chosen substantive law? In Austria, the parties' choice of law has its boundaries *inter alia* in the Austrian public policy. The choice of a foreign law does not replace such provisions which are part of Austrian public policy. A choice of law contrary to the basic values of the Austrian legal system will make an award challengeable.[146] **2.190**

(1.2) Does the principle of '*iura novit curia*' apply? Or must the applicable law be proven (by which means)? The principle '*iura novit curia*' applies in Austrian state court proceedings.[147] **2.191**

The content of foreign law is referred to in s 271 CCP, as well as ss 3 and 4 of Austrian Private International Law. According to these provisions the court must ascertain the **2.192**

[144] Melis, W., 'Austria' in P. Sanders and A.J. Van den Berg, *International Handbook on Commercial Arbitration* (Supplement 50, Kluwer Law International, October 2007) 35–6.

[145] Bydlinski, P., 'Judikatsschuld' in P. Rummel (ed), *Kommentar zum Allgemeinen bürgerlichen Gesetzbuch* (3rd edn, vol 1, Manz, 2002) s 1478, marg no 7.

[146] Hausmaninger, C. in H. Fasching and A. Konecny, *Kommentar* (n 12) s 603, marg no 54.

[147] Rechberger, W.H., 'Verfahren bis zum Urteile' in W.H. Rechberger, *ZPO* (n 120) before s 266, marg no 16.

applicable foreign law *ex officio*. The principle '*iura novit curia*' is not part of Austrian public policy. Therefore, its application is optional. If the parties failed to provide for any rules, the arbitral tribunal may in its discretion require the parties to prove the applicable law (ss 594(1), 599(1)).[148]

(2) Decisions according to equity or as amiable compositeur

2.193 Decisions according to equity or as *amiable compositeur* are only permitted if the parties have expressly authorized an arbitral tribunal to do so (s 603(3)).

2.194 However, the question of whether the arbitral tribunal, in determining the amount of loss, may make its decision in accordance with equitable discretion ('billiges Ermessen') or only after having made a detailed examination of the loss, is merely a question of procedure which may not provide a ground for setting aside the award in accordance with s 595 of the old CCP (now s 611).[149] Estimation of a quantum is not a decision according to equity and, therefore, does not require authorization by the parties.

(3) Application of lex mercatoria, *general principles etc*

2.195 Under s 603(1) the parties may provide for the application of such rules.

2.196 Under the old law, the OGH has held, that in absence of a choice-of-law provision, an arbitral tribunal may decide according to the principles of *lex mercatoria* common to the jurisdictions involved.[150] Under the new law, such an approach would require qualification. In the absence of a choice of law, the arbitral tribunal may only select binding legal rules.

2.197 (3.1) **Is the application of *lex mercatoria* considered as the application of law or as a kind of amiable composition?** Apart from statutory law, Austrian substantive law recognizes trade usages and customary law.[151] Only to the extent, the alleged rule of *lex mercatoria* qualifies as one of the two, it is to be applicable. In case, the choice-of-law clause refers to '*lex mercatoria*', the choice will, in principle, be valid (see *supra* under (1) (para 2.189)). It will be for the arbitral tribunal to establish the content. Such a choice-of-law clause would not be an explicit authorization under s 603(3) which allows the arbitral tribunal to decide *ex aequo et bono*.

(4) Applicable substantive law if there is no choice of law by the parties

2.198 In the absence of a choice-of-law clause by the parties in the arbitration agreement or any other additional agreement, the arbitral tribunal shall apply the legal provisions that it considers appropriate (s 603(2)). It may not choose non-binding legal rules such as the UNIDROIT Principles or the Principles of European Contract Law.

---

[148] See Liebscher, C. in H. Torggler, *Schiedsgerichtsbarkeit* (n 117) marg no 34.
[149] OGH 18 November 1982 [1983] GesRZ 102.
[150] *ibid.*
[151] Koziol, H. and Welser, R., *Grundriß des bürgerlichen Rechts* (13th edn, vol I, Manzsche Kurzlehrbuch-Reihe, 2006) 36 *et seq*; Rummel, P., 'Ergänzende Auslegung' in P. Rummel, *Kommentar* (n 145) s 914, marg nos 13 *et seq*; Schauer, M., 'Gebräuche im Geschäftsverkehr' in H. Krejci, *Reform-Kommentar UGB ABGB* (Manz, 2007) s 346, marg nos 1 *et seq*.

(4.1) Is there an autonomous conflict of law rule in the national arbitration law? Is it considered mandatory? No, the parties' choice of a substantive law is to be interpreted as a direct reference to the material law of a state (*voie directe*), and not to its conflict of laws.[152] 2.199

(4.2) What is the law applicable to interest? In principle, interest has to be awarded in accordance with the law applicable to the merits of the dispute.[153] Austrian law provides for legal interest of 4 per cent generally (s 1000(1) of the Civil Code) and—implementing the EC Directive on Late Payment in Commercial Transactions[154]—8 per cent above the base rate on purely commercial transactions if there is no special agreement (s 1333(2) of the Civil Code). 2.200

Compound interest is only available on a statutory basis or by agreement of the parties (s 1000(2) of the Civil Code). However, interest on pre-filing interest can be claimed (s 1000 (2) of the Civil Code). 2.201

(4.3) What is the law and practice with respect to legal interest on foreign currency debts? Interest has to be awarded and calculated in accordance with the substantive law applicable to the dispute. Austrian law does not contain specific rules for interest on foreign currency debt. 2.202

(5) Binding effect of state court decisions

In principle, an arbitral tribunal is bound by a decision of a court. According to the Austrian literature, arbitral tribunals must take into consideration final judgments of the civil courts to the same extent as other courts. A judge cannot rule on the main subject of a previous binding court decision in subsequent court proceedings.[155] The judge must use the previous court decision—without further investigation—as the basis for the judgment.[156] In support of this position, Austrian scholars take the view that the provisions concerning *res judicata* are mandatory law,[157] which is why the parties cannot enter into an agreement about the recognition or non-recognition of *res judicata*.[158] 2.203

(5.1) Is an arbitral tribunal bound by a decision of another arbitral tribunal? The parties and another arbitral tribunal are bound by the finality of an award. Section 607 provides that an award has the effect as a final and binding court judgment between the parties. It can be argued that the principle of legal certainty requires that other arbitral tribunals recognize the *res judicata* effect of an award, if the parties are the same. 2.204

[152] Hausmaninger, C. in H. Fasching and A. Konecny, *Kommentar* (n 12) s 603, marg no 51.

[153] Liebscher, C. in C. Liebscher and A. Fremuth-Wolf, *Arbitration Law and Practice* (n 91) AUS-57.

[154] Directive 2000/35/EC.

[155] Rechberger, W.H. and Simotta, D.-A., *Grundriß des österreichischen Zivilprozessrechts* (6th edn, Manzsche Kurzlehrbuch-Reihe, 2003) marg no 698; Rechberger, W.H., 'Urteile und Beschlüsse' in W.H., Rechberger, *ZPO* (n 120) s 411, marg no 3.

[156] Rechberger, W.H. and Simotta, D.-A., *Grundriß* (n 155) marg no 698; Rechberger, W.H. in W.H. Rechberger, *ZPO* (n 120) s 411, marg no 3.

[157] Hausmaninger, C. in H. Fasching and A. Konecny, *Kommentar* (n 12) s 594, marg no 80; Rechberger/ Simotta, *Grundriß* (n 155) marg no 698; Rechberger, W.H., 'Urteile und Beschlüsse' in W.H. Rechberger, *ZPO* (n 120) ss before 390, marg nos 25 *et seq*, 411, marg no 3.

[158] Hausmaninger, C. in H. Fasching and A. Konecny, *Kommentar* (n 12) s 594, marg nos 80 and 82.

2.205 (5.2) **Does a decision in a criminal case bind an arbitral tribunal?** With its decision dated 17 October 1995, the OGH—with a consolidated senate—stated that decisions in a criminal case are binding on civil courts.[159] A convicted person must accept that the civil court takes the decision in the criminal case as a basis for subsequent civil proceedings.[160] The convicted person cannot argue that the criminal conviction was unlawful. The civil court is bound by all facts included in the decision, whether included in the declarative part of the decision or the reasoning.[161] By contrast, acquitting decisions do not bind the civil court.[162]

2.206 If a state court disregards this binding effect, the judgment is subject to annulment.[163] Grounds for annulment are so severe that they will be considered to pertain to procedural public policy, allowing the challenge of an award.[164]

E. Settlement

(1) Settlement by agreement of the parties with or without support of the arbitral tribunal

2.207 The parties may settle their dispute at any time of the arbitral proceedings with or without support from the arbitral tribunal. If the parties have settled a dispute during the arbitral proceedings, they have three options. First, the parties can request the tribunal to draw up a record of the settlement which is an enforceable title in Austria (s 605 no 1). Second, the parties may request the tribunal to record the settlement in the form of an arbitral award (s 605 no 2). Third, they can just request the termination of the arbitration proceedings (s 608(2) no 3).

2.208 (1.1) **May an arbitrator who has initiated settlement discussions be challenged when agreement on a settlement has failed?** There are no direct grounds for challenging an arbitrator when a settlement agreement that was initiated by the arbitrator fails. However, the arbitrator may be removed pursuant to the general grounds for challenging an arbitrator under s 588, if the arbitrator has demonstrated some pre-disposition towards the settlement discussions which can be construed as a lack of impartiality with regard to his mandate.

(2) 'Private settlement' and its impact on the arbitral procedure

2.209 A private settlement of the parties does not automatically terminate the arbitral proceedings. It only terminates the proceedings if the parties agree on a termination (s 608(2) no 3) and communicate their agreement to the arbitral tribunal. Only an award on agreed terms leads to a termination of the proceedings *ipso iure*.[165]

---

[159] OGH 17 October 1995, 1 Ob 612/95 (verst Senat) = ecolex 1995, 790 (Oberhammer, P.) SZ 68/196 JBl 1996, 117. The Austrian Civil Code included s 268 which stated that civil courts are bound by criminal court decisions. s 268 ABGB was abrogated by the Austrian Constitutional Court in 1990. For further discussion of the effect of criminal decisions on subsequent civil court proceedings see Forgó-Feldner, B., 'Die Bindung des Zivilrichters an strafgerichtliche Verurteilungen' *ÖJZ* (2005) 51.

[160] Rechberger, W.H. and Simotta, D.-A., *Grundriß* (n 155) marg no 715.

[161] Burgstaller, A., 'Grenzender Bindung an Strafurteil' *RdA* (2000) 53.

[162] Rechberger, W.H. and Simotta, D.-A., *Grundriß* (n 155) marg no 715.

[163] See Kodek, G., 'Berufung' in W.H. Rechberger, *ZPO* (n 120) s 477, marg no 1.

[164] See Hausmaninger, C. in H. Fasching and A. Konecny, *Kommentar* (n 12) s 611, marg no 176.

[165] *ibid*, s 605, marg no 62.

(3) Form and effect of a settlement (eg award on agreed terms)

A party may request that the arbitral tribunal record the settlement in the form of an arbitral award on agreed terms provided that the content of the settlement is not in conflict with Austrian public policy. Such award has to meet the form requirements of arbitral awards according to s 606 and has the same status and effects as any other award on the merits of the case (s 605(2)). It shall, therefore, also state the reasons upon which it is based (the content of the settlement between the parties) unless the parties have agreed otherwise. **2.210**

As an alternative, the parties can request the tribunal to draw up a record of the settlement which is an enforceable title in Austria, provided its content is not in conflict with Austrian public policy. **2.211**

F. Costs of the arbitration

(1) General allocation of the costs of the proceedings

After termination of the arbitral proceedings, the arbitral tribunal shall, unless the parties have agreed otherwise, decide on the obligation for the reimbursement of costs. The arbitral tribunal may use its discretion when determining the circumstances of the individual case, in particular the outcome of the proceedings (s 609(1)). Simultaneously with the decision regarding the reimbursement of costs, the arbitral tribunal shall fix the amount of the costs to be reimbursed, provided that this is already possible and that the costs are not offset against each other (s 609(3)). **2.212**

The arbitral tribunal shall, when deciding on the obligation to reimburse costs, consider at its discretion the circumstances of the individual case, in particular the outcome of the proceedings (s 609(1)). Austrian law does not contain any specific provision as to the allocation of costs in the arbitration. If expressly provided for in the arbitration agreement or in a separate order or if the arbitrators have declared s 41 of the CCP is applicable, the arbitrators may award costs to one party to be paid to the other party in the award or in a separate order (ss 41 *et seq*, CCP). Sections 41 *et seq* of the CCP provide that the unsuccessful party has to compensate the other party for the costs of the arbitral procedure, costs of representation as well as certain expenses. **2.213**

(2) Deposits or advances for costs or fees

The CCP itself does not contain any provision as to the advance on costs in arbitral proceedings. Guidance can be found in ss 1170 and 1014 Civil Code. According to these sections and based on the analogous application of the cost determination provisions for state court proceedings, the arbitrators have the right to receive advanced payment of the arbitration fees.[166] In analogy to ss 365 and 332(2) of the CCP, the arbitrators can refrain from commencing their work until the parties provide them with the advance on costs.[167] **2.214**

In institutional arbitration, for example, according to the Vienna Rules, the institution fixes the amount of a deposit against the expected costs of arbitration and asks the parties **2.215**

[166] Fasching, H., *Schiedsgericht* (n 39) 75 *et seq*.
[167] *ibid*, 76.

to pay it in equal shares before the transmission of the file to the arbitrators (s 34(2) of the Vienna Rules). If the defendant refuses to pay, the claimant will be asked to also advance the defendant's share. If the full amount of the requested deposit is not paid, the claim or counterclaim will no longer be considered. The institution also determines the total costs of the arbitration which the arbitrators may distribute between the parties in their award. The practice in *ad hoc* arbitration is the same. The arbitrators have to agree with the parties on their fees, the deposit for the fees and the consequences of non-payment of the full deposit. They will in practice request the parties to pay the agreed deposit for their fees and expected expenses and they will refuse to administer the case if the full deposit has not been paid.

2.216 (2.1) **Is there case law authorizing or prohibiting arbitrators to order a party to pay an advance on the arbitration costs?** There is no case law in Austria authorizing or prohibiting arbitrators to order a party to pay an advance on the arbitration costs.

2.217 (2.2) **May the raising of a set-off claim or counterclaim be made contingent upon payment of the corresponding advance for the relating arbitration costs (cf eg Article 30(5), ICC Rules)? May such a condition be agreed upon when entering into the arbitration agreement?** In general, the parties can be asked to pay advances on the fees and expenses of the arbitrators. The arbitrators may refrain from acting as long as these advances have not been paid.[168] This also applies to set-off or counterclaims.

2.218 (2.3) **What remedies exist against a party which does not pay its part of the advance on the arbitration costs (eg termination of the arbitration agreement)? How may the other party enforce its rights?** It is argued that a party may bring suit against the other party with regard to the payment of the advance before the courts.[169] Where the other party has paid the advance of the defaulting party, a suit can only be filed before the courts if the arbitration proceedings were concluded without making an award.[170]

2.219 Furthermore, a party has the right to terminate an arbitration agreement for an important reason, for example the party's inability to pay the advance.[171]

(3) Costs of the administration by an arbitration institution

2.220 According to the rules on arbitration of the International Arbitral Centre of the Austrian Federal Economic Chamber (Vienna Rules), the administrative costs of the Centre and the arbitrators' fees shall be fixed on the basis of the amount in dispute, according to the schedule of arbitration costs attached in Annex 1 (s 24(1) of the Vienna Rules). If the arbitral proceedings are terminated other than by means of an arbitral award or a settlement, the Secretary shall determine the administrative costs of the Centre and the arbitrators' fees at the appropriate levels (s 24(1) of the Vienna Rules).

---

168 Hausmaninger, C. in H. Fasching and A. Konecny, *Kommentar* (n 12) s 587, marg no 231.

169 Fasching, H., 'Kostenvorschüsse zur Einleitung schiedsgerichtlicher Verfahren' *JBl* 1993, 551 with additional refs.

170 Fasching, H., *JBl* 1993 (n 169) 551.

171 OGH 4 September 1936 SZ 18/151; Rummel, P., *RZ* 1986 (n 39) 48; Hausmaninger, C. in H. Fasching and A. Konecny, *Kommentar* (n 12) s 581, marg no 132.

(4) Arbitrators' fees: law and practice, judicial control

There are no statutory provisions regulating fees and expenses of arbitrators. **2.221**

The claim for compensation derives from ss 1151(1) and 1152 Civil Code. The amount of compensation can be determined in the arbitrators' agreement. Lacking an agreement, the amount has to be adequate. According to legal practice, an adequate remuneration is determined by consideration of all circumstances and everything that happens or has happened under similar circumstances.[172] The tables of fees of arbitral institutions or a general practice in similar cases may give guidance for determining the adequacy of the amount. In practice, the parties frequently agree on the application of the attorney's fees ('Rechtsanwaltstarif'). The enforcement of pecuniary claims of the arbitrators is made in the appropriate forum, ie the competent state court in the absence of an arbitration agreement between the arbitrator and the parties.[173] In practice, the amount of the arbitrators' fees is frequently suggested by the arbitrators themselves. **2.222**

(4.1) May arbitrators fix their own fees in the award? Arbitrators cannot decide on their own fees and expenses, but they can order the parties to reimburse advances made. The arbitrators' fees and expenses are determined by agreement.[174] **2.223**

(4.2) How can the parties change the arbitrators' fees once they are fixed? The parties cannot change the fees once they are fixed. If the fees are fixed, this implies either that the arbitrator and the parties agreed on them or that a third party, such as an arbitral institution, determined them. In these circumstances, a judicial review of the fee level would only be possible if, in the first alternative, the agreement was not valid, or, in the second alternative, the third party violated the applicable rules. **2.224**

(4.3) Are the arbitrator's fees subject to income tax if (i) the place of arbitration; or (ii) the normal residence or place of business of the arbitrator is located in this country? Yes, both are correct. The arbitrator's fees are subject to Austrian income tax; (i) if the arbitrator is either subject to unlimited income tax liability ('unbeschränkte Einkommensteuerpflicht') in Austria by virtue of having a domicile and/or his/her habitual abode here; or (ii) if the arbitrator is merely subject to limited income tax liability ('beschränkte Einkommensteuerpflicht') in Austria by virtue of the arbitrator physically acting in Austria or by virtue of the arbitrator's activities being utilized in Austria. Most of the double taxation treaties concluded by Austria provide that a non-resident arbitrator entitled to the benefits of such a treaty rendering his services in Austria may not be taxed in Austria if the arbitrator does not maintain a permanent establishment ('Betriebsstätte') or a fixed base ('feste Einrichtung') in Austria. **2.225**

(4.4) Are arbitrator's fees submitted to VAT? If yes, is the duty to pay such tax linked to (i) the place of arbitration; or (ii) the arbitrator's general residence? Yes, the latter is correct. The arbitrator's fees are subject to Austrian VAT, if the arbitrator carries out his business from Austria or from a permanent establishment in Austria (cf s 3a(12) of the **2.226**

[172] OGH 7 July 1981 5 Ob 633/81.

[173] Hausmaninger, C. in H. Fasching and A. Konecny, *Kommentar* (n 12) s 587, marg no 226.

[174] *ibid*, marg no 223.

Austrian Value Added Tax Act ('Umsatzsteuergesetz'); Art 9(1) of the Sixth Council Directive 77/388/EEC of 17 May 1977 on the harmonization of the laws of the Member States relating to turnover taxes—Common system of value added tax: uniform basis of assessment; ECJ 16 September 1997, C-145/96 - Bernd von Hoffmann).

(5) Attorneys' fees and the winning party's claim for reimbursement

2.227 As a basic principle it is stated that, where the arbitral proceedings are terminated, the arbitral tribunal shall decide upon the obligation to reimburse the costs of the proceedings provided that the parties have not agreed otherwise (s 609(1)). The arbitral tribunal shall, at its discretion, take into consideration the circumstances of the individual case, in particular the outcome of the proceedings. The obligation to reimburse may include any and all reasonable costs appropriate for bringing the action or defence. If the parties have agreed on the termination of proceedings and have communicated this to the arbitral tribunal, the parties may request a decision on costs together with the notification of the agreement to terminate the proceedings (s 609(1)).

2.228 **(5.1) May in-house lawyers charge fees or may a party request costs of in-house lawyers to be reimbursed?** The reimbursement of the fees of in-house lawyers is not excluded. To grant such reimbursement is within the discretion of the arbitral tribunal. It can be argued that the arbitral tribunal may also take into account the costs of in-house lawyers unless otherwise agreed by the parties.

(6) Time and form of the decision on costs

2.229 The decision on costs shall be rendered when the arbitration is terminated (s 609(1)); the decision shall be rendered in the form of an award (s 609(4)). This may be the award on the merits of the case or a subsequent separate award (s 609(5)). Even the determination of the costs in an award for interpretation or supplementation according to s 610 is possible.[175] Contrary to the old law, a decision in the form of a separate order is not possible.

2.230 **(6.1) May the arbitrators' decision on the costs (allocation and amount of costs to be reimbursed) be challenged separately from the award itself? Are there time limits for such a remedy?** If the decision on costs is part of an award that deals also with other matters, this award may be challenged. If it was rendered in a separate award, then this award may be challenged.[176]

2.231 **(6.2) Are the arbitrators entitled and/or legally obliged to rule on the amount of one or both parties' costs that are recoverable?** Together with the decision on the liability to pay the costs of arbitration, the arbitral tribunal shall determine the amount of costs to be reimbursed (s 609(3)).

G. Publication of the award

(1) Publication with or without the consent of the parties

2.232 In Austria, arbitral awards are considered to be confidential documents. Consequently, whether the award can be published and under what conditions, may be determined by the

[175] Hausmaninger, C. in H. Fasching and A. Konecny, *Kommentar* (n 12) s 609, marg no 80.
[176] *ibid*, marg no 81.

parties. The publication of the award by the arbitral tribunal without the consent of the parties does not provide a ground for setting aside the award. Nevertheless, this is inadmissible.

(2) Practice of publication (eg in specific legal journals)

In general, awards are not published in Austria. However, the Vienna Rules have a provision entitling the Board of VIAC to publish an award in legal journals or in its own publications in anonymous form, unless publication is objected to by at least one party within 30 days after service of the copy of the award. Only two decisions of the International Arbitral Centre of the Austrian Federal Economic Chamber have been published. Both of these decisions involve the UN Convention on Contracts for the International Sale of Goods. **2.233**

VI. Amendment and challenge of the award; liability of arbitrators

A. Amendment, correction or interpretation of the award

(1) Motion to amend or correct an award

According to s 610, within four weeks of receipt of the award, the parties may request the arbitral tribunal to: **2.234**

- correct in the award any errors in computation, any clerical or typographical errors, and any errors of a similar nature (s 610(10)); or
- make an additional award as to claims presented in the arbitral proceedings, but not covered in the award (s 610(3)).

However, the content of the decision may not be changed and errors in the reasoning and justifications of the award may not be corrected.[177] **2.235**

According to s 610(3), the arbitral tribunal shall make the corrections or provide an explanation within four weeks and upon an additional award within eight weeks.[178] **2.236**

(2) Interpretation of the award by the tribunal

Unless the parties have agreed upon another period of time, each party may within four weeks of receipt of the award request the arbitral tribunal to interpret certain parts of the award, if so agreed by the parties (s 610(1) no 2). **2.237**

B. Appeal on the merits

(1) Admissibility and procedure of an appeal on the merits

According to Austrian law, an arbitral award has the status of a final and binding court judgment. It follows that an appeal to a court on the merits of the award is not possible.[179] **2.238**

177 Fasching, H., *Schiedsgericht* (n 39) 130.
178 Liebscher, C., *Austrian Arbitration Act 2006* (n 18) 37, art 610 (3).
179 Melis, W. in P. Sanders and A.J. Van den Berg, *Int'l Handbook* (n 144) 30.

2.239 **(1.1) May the parties agree on an appeal to another arbitral tribunal?** There are no provisions in the new law for an appeal from an arbitral award to a second arbitral panel for review on the merits. This does not exclude the possibility to agree upon such two-tier system, if the parties so wish.[180]

(2) Possibility to exclude an appeal (eg in the arbitration clause)

2.240 Since there are no statutory provisions for an appellate body, there is no need for excluding an appeal.

C. Setting aside of the award

(1) Reasons for setting aside an award

2.241 The grounds for challenge are contained in an exhaustive list in s 611.

2.242 Upon application of a party, an arbitral award shall be set aside if:

- a valid arbitration agreement does not exist, or if the arbitral tribunal denies its jurisdiction despite the existence of a valid arbitration agreement, or if a party was not capable of concluding a valid arbitration agreement under the law which was personally relevant to that party;
- a party was not given proper notice of the appointment of an arbitrator or of the arbitral proceedings or for another reason was unable adequately to defend itself or challenge the claims of the opposing party;
- the award deals with a dispute not falling within the terms of the arbitration agreement, or contains decisions on matters beyond the scope of the arbitration agreement or beyond the claims of the parties; however, if the defect concerns a separable part of the award only, then only that part of the award shall be set aside;
- the formation or composition of the arbitral tribunal is not in accordance with a provision of Austrian arbitration law or with an admissible agreement of the parties;
- the arbitral procedure was not carried out in accordance with the basic values of the Austrian legal system (*ordre public*); or
- the requirements have been met according to which a judgment of a court can be appealed under s 530(1) nos 1-5 via an application for the proceedings to be reopened.

2.243 An arbitral award shall be set aside upon application of a party or by the court *ex officio*:

- when the subject matter of the dispute is not arbitral under Austrian law; or
- if the award is in conflict with the basic values of the Austrian legal system (*ordre public*).

2.244 According to the special provisions for consumers (s 617), which apply also to some labour law cases (s 618), an arbitral award shall also be set aside for the following reasons:

- mandatory provisions of the law have been violated and these provisions of the law could not have been waived by the parties by choice of law even in a case with international relevance (s 617(6) no 1); or

[180] Melis, W. in P. Sanders and A.J.Van den Berg, *Int'l Handbook* (n 144) 30.

- the requirements are fulfilled according to which under s 530(1) nos 6 and 7 (partly concerning new facts and evidence), a procedure before a court could be reopened; or
- the consumer or respectively the employee did not receive written legal advice on the significant differences between arbitration and court proceedings prior to concluding the arbitration agreement.

Violations of rules of public policy always provide a ground for refusal of enforcement of an award and for setting aside an award (s 611(8)). Austrian law does not make a distinction between international public policy and local public policy. Also, in the context of international arbitration only the criterion of Austrian public policy is applicable. It should also be mentioned that the notion of public policy is interpreted very restrictively by the Austrian courts. It is held to encompass the fundamental principles of Austrian law.[181] However, as regards EC law, the notion seems to be stretched by the ECJ, potentially encompassing any rule of EC law.[182] **2.245**

(1.1) May an award made according to international or foreign procedural rules be the object of an application for setting aside before the national courts? Austrian courts are competent to hear the challenge of an award, if the seat of arbitration is in Austria (s 577(1)). The applicable procedural rules are irrelevant for the international jurisdiction of Austrian courts. **2.246**

(2) Procedure and deadlines for challenging an award

The action for setting aside must be brought to the competent court as specified in s 615 within three months, beginning with the day on which the claimant has received the award or the additional award (s 611(4)). An application to correct in the award any errors or to give an interpretation of certain parts of the award shall not extend this time period (s 610(1) nos 1 and 2). **2.247**

In the case of setting aside proceedings on the grounds according to which a judgment of a court of law can be appealed by an action for revision under s 530(1) because of certain criminal offences, the time period for the action for setting aside shall be judged by the respective provisions regarding the action for revision. **2.248**

The filing period for setting aside an award on these grounds ends four weeks after the relevant criminal judgment has become final, but at the latest 10 years after the relevant award has become final and binding. **2.249**

For the additional reopening grounds applicable in consumer and certain labour arbitrations the filing period for setting aside an award ends four weeks from the date on which the applicant party was able to use the final decision or to submit to the court facts or **2.250**

[181] See Liebscher, C., *Healthy Award* (n 141) 310 *et seq.*

[182] See Liebscher, C., 'Case C-168/05, *Elisa Maria Mostaza Claro v Centro Móvil Milenium SL*, judgment of the Court of Justice (First Chamber) of 26 October 2006 ECR I-10421' *CMLR* 45/2008, 545; Liebscher, C., 'EU Member State Court Application of Eco Swiss: Review of the Case Law and Future Prospects' in P. Landolt and G. Blanke, *The Treatment of US Antitrust and EC Competition Law in International Arbitration - A Handbook for Practitioners* (Kluwer Law International, forthcoming 2009).

evidence which it had discovered (s 534(2) no 2 CCP), but at the latest 10 years after the award has become final and binding (s 534(3) CCP).

2.251 (2.1) **Who may (or must) represent a party in a proceeding for setting aside an award?** With a few exceptions, which are without practical importance in international arbitrations, parties have to be represented by an Austrian attorney. EC attorneys can represent parties in consultation with an Austrian lawyer.[183]

2.252 (2.2) **Do specific time limits exist for setting-aside procedures concerning awards on jurisdiction?** There are no specific time limits for setting-aside procedures concerning awards on jurisdiction. The general time limit of three months applies.[184]

(3) Effect of a court decision which sets the award aside

2.253 The decision resets the situation to the stage before the initiation of the arbitration.[185]

2.254 The setting aside of an arbitral award has no effect on the validity of the underlying arbitration agreement. It follows that after the setting aside of an award, new arbitration proceedings can be commenced within the framework of the arbitration agreement. However, when an arbitral award on the same subject matter has already been finally set aside twice and when a further arbitral award on the same subject matter is to be set aside, upon application of a party, the court shall concurrently declare invalid the arbitration agreement with respect to that matter (s 611(5)).

2.255 If an award is set aside for lack of jurisdiction, the statute of limitation remains interrupted if the action is immediately brought before the court or arbitral tribunal (s 584(4)).[186]

2.256 (3.1) **Does the setting-aside action suspend the enforcement? If so, do remedies exist to reinstate enforcement?** An action to set aside an award entitles the debtor to file a claim for suspension of the enforcement procedure, pursuant to s 42(1) no 2 of the Enforcement Act.[187] Where the debtor requests a suspension, he must allege that the commencement of the enforcement procedure involves the risk of pecuniary damage which cannot be recovered, also known as 'suspension interest'.[188] Under certain circumstances, the enforcement procedure is dependent upon the provision of security by the defendant, pursuant to s 44(2) of the Enforcement Act. A suspended enforcement procedure may only be continued by an application to the court (s 44(5) of the Enforcement Act). The court's judgment to set aside the award provides a ground to discontinue the enforcement of the award (s 39(1) no 1 of the Enforcement Act).

---

[183] Bundesgesetz über den freien Diensteistungsverkehr und die Niederlassung von europäischen Rechtsanwältinnen und Rechtsanwälten sowie die Erbringung von Rechtsdienstleistungen durch international tätige Rechtsanwältinnen und Rechtsanwälten in Österreich (EuRAG), s 5 (BGBl I 27/2000).

[184] See Hausmaninger, C. in H. Fasching and A. Konecny, *Kommentar* (n 12) s 611, marg no 235.

[185] *ibid*, marg no 274.

[186] *ibid*, s 584, marg no 67 *et seq*.

[187] OGH 23 May 1990 SZ 63/82.

[188] Rechberger, W.H. and Simotta, D.-A., *Exekutionsverfahren*, (2nd edn, WUV-Universitätsverlag, 1992) marg nos 271 *et seq* with additional refs.

(3.2) After an award has been set aside, does the underlying arbitration agreement revive or remain in force or is it exhausted or deemed terminated? The setting aside of an arbitral award has no effect on the validity of the underlying arbitration agreement. It follows that after the setting aside of an award, new arbitration proceedings can be commenced within the framework of the arbitration agreement. However, when an arbitral award on the same subject matter has already been finally set aside twice and when a further arbitral award on the same subject matter is to be set aside, upon application of a party, the court shall concurrently declare invalid the arbitration agreement with respect to that matter (s 611(5)). **2.257**

(4) Appeal against the court's decision to set aside or not set aside the award

Each party has the right to lodge an appeal against the court's decision to set aside or not set aside the award. The time limit to file the appeal is four weeks and starts with the service of the written copy of the judgment (s 464, CCP). The appeal may be based on the following grounds: nullity (s 464, CCP), error in the court's procedure (s 496(1) no 2 CCP), mistakes in ascertainment of facts that fail to conform to matters in the record and erroneous evaluations of the evidence (ss 488 and 498, CCP), and mistakes in legal judgment.[189] In addition to the general prerequisites, an appeal must fulfil specific procedural requirements such as admissibility, timeliness, identification of the appellant, grievance of the appellant, the lack of a waiver of the right to appeal or of the withdrawal of appeal.[190] Against judgments of the court of appeal the parties may lodge a revision on points of law considered important. **2.258**

(5) Possibility of the parties to exclude actions for setting aside

Any waiver of an action to set aside an award is ineffective.[191] According to the OGH the waiver of an action to set aside an award is effective if it was made after the award was issued, if the ground for setting aside an award was known.[192] **2.259**

D. Liability of arbitrators

(1) Duties and liabilities of arbitrators regarding the conduct of the proceedings

According to s 594(4), an arbitrator who does not fulfil in time or at all the obligations assumed by his acceptance of office is liable to the parties for all the loss caused by his wrongful refusal or delay. Even though this provision does not constitute an ultimate limitation of liability, the Austrian Supreme Court held for the identical provision of the old law that this provision is intended to limit the indefinite contractual liability.[193] In applying what is now s 594(4), the court concluded, that an arbitrator can only be held liable, if the arbitral award was successfully challenged based on the arbitrator's fault.[194] **2.260**

---

189 Kodek, G. 'Berufung' in W.H. Rechberger, *ZPO* (n 120) s 467, marg no 5.

190 Kodek, G. 'Rechtsmittel' in W.H. Rechberger, *ZPO* (n 120) before s 461, marg nos 5 *et seq.*

191 Hausmaninger, C. in H. Fasching and A. Konecny, *Kommentar* (n 12) s 611, marg no 255.

192 GH 25 November 1936 Rsp 1937/17; Hausmaninger, C. in H. Fasching and A. Konecny, *Kommentar* (n 12) s 611, marg no 256.

193 OGH 6 June 2005 9 Ob 126/04a.

194 *ibid.*

2.261 **(1.1) Do the courts and/or authorities rely on a contractual relationship between the parties and the arbitrator(s), irrespective of whether institutional or *ad hoc* arbitration is concerned? What is the legal qualification of such a contract (eg provision of services)?** There is no distinction between *ad hoc* arbitration and institutional arbitration as regards the qualification of the arbitrator's contract.[195] The contract is considered a contract for works.[196]

2.262 **(1.2) Are there court decisions (or authorities) determining which law governs the question of liability of an arbitrator? What is the position of those courts/authorities as to whether and to which extent a legal liability of an arbitrator (or arbitral institution) may be established?** If the law applicable to the arbitrators' agreement is a foreign law, it is not self-evident that s 594(4) applies in this case, since a foreign court which applies foreign law may not directly be bound by the specifications of s 594(4). Nevertheless, according to Austrian authorities, s 594(4) applies to a certain extent (which is determined by jurisprudence),[197] if the parties agree on the application of Austrian law for the proceedings and the arbitrators do not object. However, the parties may expressly agree on a different liability standard.[198]

2.263 An arbitrator may become liable for a damage due to his wrongful refusal or delay in performing his function (s 594(4)). An arbitrator who resigns from his appointment without reasonable grounds is liable for damages.[199] According to the jurisprudence of the OGH, an arbitrator is further liable for culpable mistakes in procedure or in the declaratory part of the award.[200] Such liability becomes effective in case the award was challenged successfully.

2.264 **(1.3) Is an arbitrator subject to criminal prosecution?** Austrian law does not provide any special criminal provisions for arbitrators. However, the general rules of the Criminal Code do apply to an arbitrator's criminal liability.

(2) Possibility to restrict or exclude the arbitrators' liability

2.265 The parties and arbitrators are free to determine the rules for liability in the arbitrators' agreement. It has to be noted that exclusion of liability for intention and severe gross negligence would contradict the principle of *bonos moros*.[201]

---

195 Liebscher, C., 'Wiener Regeln' in R. Schütze (ed), *Institutionelle Schiedsgerichtsbarkeit* (Carl Heymanns, 2006) 268 *et seq*.

196 Liebscher, C. in R. Schütze, *Institutionelle Schiedsgerichtsbarkeit* (n 195) 269.

197 See Hausmaninger, C. in H. Fasching and A. Konecny, *Kommentar* (n 12) s 587, marg nos 202 and 205.

198 *ibid*, s 594, marg no 126.

199 OGH 7 May 1918, ZBl 1919, 222; OGH 12 July1899, GlUNF 676.

200 OGH 6 June 2005, 9 Ob 126/04a, RdW 2005, 610 SZ 2005/85 JBl 2005, 800; see also Hausmaninger, C. in H. Fasching and A. Konecny, *Kommentar* (n 12) s 594, marg no 118.

201 Hausmaninger, C. in H. Fasching and A. Konecny, *Kommentar* (n 12) s 594, marg no 128; Liebscher, C. in R. Schütze, *Institutionelle Schiedsgerichtsbarkeit* (n 195) 271.

VII. Enforcement of national awards

(1) Requirement of a particular procedure to make an award enforceable (leave for enforcement, exequatur*)*

According to s 597 an award has the legal effect of a final and binding court judgment. Therefore, s 1(16) of the Enforcement Act lists an award as one of the enforceable titles. The only formal requirement for enforceability is that the presiding arbitrator, or in the case he is prevented another arbitrator, shall upon request of one of the parties confirm the final and binding nature and the enforceability of the award on a copy of the award (s 606(6)). No *exequatur* by the courts is required. **2.266**

(1.1) Does the national law make any difference between foreign and domestic awards, and if so, what are the criteria? Does there exist an additional notion of award for the purpose of obtaining *exequatur* (France: international awards)? Pursuant to s 577(1), an award is a domestic award when the place of arbitration was in Austria. When the place of arbitration was not in Austria, an award is a foreign award. **2.267**

(1.2) May awards granting conservatory/interim measures be subject to enforcement? Conservatory/interim measures by arbitral tribunals sitting in Austria or abroad are enforced by the Austrian courts (ss 593(3) and 577(2)). **2.268**

According to s 593(4) the court shall reject the enforcement of the measure if: **2.269**

- the seat of the arbitral tribunal lies within the country and the measure suffers from a defect that, for a domestic award, would be a ground for setting aside under s 611(2);
- the seat of the arbitral tribunal does not lie from the country and the measure suffers from a defect that, for a foreign award, would be a ground for the refusal of the recognition or enforcement;
- the enforcement of the measure is inconsistent with a previously applied for, or issued domestic court measure or a previously issued foreign court measure which is to be recognized; or
- the measure provides for a measure that does not exist under domestic law and no appropriate domestic measure was claimed.

The court may grant a hearing to the opposing party according to s 593(5). If the opposing party has not been heard before the decision has been made, that party may make an objection in terms of s 397 of the Enforcement Act to the granting of the enforcement. In either case, the opposing party may only argue that a ground for the refusal of the enforcement as described above according to s 593(4) exists.[202] **2.270**

The court shall repeal the enforcement if:[203] **2.271**

- the period of validity for the measure determined by the arbitral tribunal has expired;
- the arbitral tribunal has modified or set aside the measure;

[202] Liebscher, C., *Austrian Arbitration Act 2006* (n 18) 22, Art 593 (5).
[203] *ibid*, Art 593 (6).

- a ground specified in s 399(1) nos 1–4 of the Enforcement Act exists; or,
- security was provided.

(2) Details of such enforcement procedure (competent court, reasons for rejection of motion etc)

2.272 To enforce an award, a party must make a request to the appropriate state court for an enforcement authorization. Jurisdiction for enforcement requests follows ss 3, 4 and 17–19 of the Enforcement Act. Enforcement requests must generally be addressed to the competent district court. The competent district court grants enforcement as is the case with any other title for enforcement. The state court's review is limited to ss 1 no 16 and 7–9 of the Enforcement Act. Enforcement authorization must be granted in case the domestic award contains the names of the persons of the beneficiary and the obligor, object, nature and amount of the claim and an order to perform, cease or tolerate a particular action. Furthermore, the time period in which these obligations must be performed must have elapsed. Other issues, such as whether a valid arbitration agreement exists will not be reviewed.

(3) Appeal against the decision granting exequatur

2.273 The defendant may appeal against the state court's enforcement authorization (s 65 *et seq* Enforcement Act). The appeal must be filed within 14 days. New submissions may not be introduced. Furthermore, according to s 35 of the Enforcement Act, the defendant may claim fulfilment or a set-off by submitting a counteraction ('Oppositionsklage').[204] With this counteraction, the defendant may only claim on the basis of facts which the party was unable to present in the prior proceedings. Subject to a lack of the confirmation of enforceability the defendant may apply for a discontinuation of the execution (s 39, Enforcement Act). Furthermore the defendant may claim that he has already settled the claim after the title became enforceable (s 40, Enforcement Act).

(4) Appeal (and procedure) if exequatur *has been refused*

2.274 If the court denies enforcement authorization, the applicant may file an appeal within 14 days after receipt of the denying decision (s 65 *et seq*, Enforcement Act). The appeal is subject to the interdiction of new submissions. In general, the court rules on such requests for enforcement authorization without hearing the defendant.[205]

(5) Procedure of enforcement (attachment of bank accounts etc)

2.275 The state court issues an order of execution. Both the enforcement authorization and the order of execution will be delivered to the debtor, which means that neither party will receive a notice of the existence of the enforcement proceedings in Austria prior to receiving the court's order of execution. The enforcement order will be executed by the court itself or by bailiffs acting on behalf of the court.

[204] Riegler, S., 'Enforcement and Recognition of Arbitral Awards' in S. Riegler *et al*, *Arbitration Law of Austria* (n 9) 696.

[205] *ibid.*

The bailiff has to summon the debtor to performance prior to the execution (s 25a(1), Enforcement Act). The bailiff may accept the outstanding payment or any other goods from the debtor (s 25a(2), Enforcement Act). The bailiff may also seize bank accounts, which means that a financial institution must cease all other payments from the account. The free assets of the account (on the date of delivery) are subject to the order of attachment. The financial institution must provide an accounting of the accounts standing, which includes the account balance within four weeks of the date of service of the execution order. 2.276

(5.1) At the stage of enforcement, may the losing party invoke arguments and circumstances which are based on facts which have occurred before (or after) the award was made? In a counteraction the debtor asserts eg fulfilment, set-off, limitation of action, novation or additional time for performance. The debtor may only raise such a counteraction on the basis of facts which he was unable to present in the prior proceedings (s 35(1), Enforcement Act). According to Austrian scholarship, the time that the debtor became aware of these facts is not relevant.[206] The debtor can request the discontinuance of the execution if, for example, the confirmation of the enforceability is missing (s 39(1) no 10, Enforcement Act) or he has settled his debt to the creditor after the enforceable legal title came into existence (s 40, Enforcement Act). 2.277

(5.2) May the losing party invoke a set-off based on claims that are not related to the matter of the arbitral proceeding? Is it material whether such claim came into existence before or after the award was made? A losing party may also invoke a set-off on claims that are not related to the matter of the arbitral proceedings. According to Austrian law, the principal claim and counterclaim do not have to stem from the same legal ground or be in the same amount. The liabilities only have to be of a homogenous nature and quality, which particularly applies for monetary claims. 2.278

Austrian scholarship and case precedent take the view that set-off claims in enforcement proceedings must be made by filing a counteraction in accordance with s 35 of the Enforcement Act. However, such a counteraction is only permissible if the set-off claim could not have been made in the prior proceedings, pursuant to s 35(1) of the Enforcement Act.[207] 2.279

VIII. Foreign awards

A. Recognition and/or enforcement of foreign awards (national law)

(1) Rules according to national law

It is important to differentiate between domestic and foreign awards. Pursuant to s 577(1), an award is a domestic award when the place of arbitration was in Austria. When the place 2.280

[206] Heller, L.V. *et al*, *Kommentar zur Exekutionsordnung* (4th edn, Manz, 1969) 397.

[207] Rechberger, W.H. and Simotta, D.-A., *Exekutionsverfahren* (n 188) marg no 347 with additional annotations.

of arbitration was not in Austria, an award is a foreign award. Sections 79-86a of the Enforcement Act provide the basis for the enforcement of foreign awards in Austria.

2.281 In principle, the requirements to be fulfilled by the creditor to enforce a foreign award are contained in multilateral and bilateral international treaties on the enforcement of foreign awards of which Austria is a signatory state. This follows from s 86 of the Enforcement Act, according to which ss 79-85 of the Enforcement Act are not applicable to the extent that treaties (eg the New York Convention) contain different provisions with respect to the leave for enforcement. In a case where two international treaties are applicable, the OGH held that the enforcement may only be refused if both of these treaties provide grounds for the refusal of enforcement.[208]

2.282 In the absence of multilateral or bilateral conventions, ss 79-85 Enforcement Act are applicable. Pursuant to s 79 of the Enforcement Act, the order granting enforcement of foreign awards presumes, that leave for enforcement has been declared in Austria. The leave for enforcement ('Vollstreckbarerklärung, *Exequatur*') may only be granted, if the foreign award is enforceable according to the provisions of the country of origin and if the reciprocity is guaranteed (s 79(2) of the Enforcement Act). Section 84b of the Enforcement Act makes it clear, that the leave for enforcement ensures the equal treatment of foreign and domestic awards. Sections 80 and 81 of the Enforcement Act provide grounds for refusing the leave for enforcement. However, these grounds are not of particular practical importance, as international treaties contain special provisions which supersede the provisions of the Enforcement Act (s 86, Enforcement Act).[209] The local court is competent to grant enforcement and leave for enforcement for foreign awards (s 82, Enforcement Act). Usually, the territorial jurisdiction is determined by the seat of the debtor. In the absence thereof, the court, in the district, where the award would be enforced, is competent (ss 18 and 19, Enforcement Act). According to s 83 Enforcement Act, the court must rule upon an application for the leave for enforcement without a hearing. Sections 1-78 of the Enforcement Act concerning the enforcement of domestic awards are also applicable (s 83(2), Enforcement Act).

(2) Requirements to be fulfilled by the applicant (procedure, time limits)

2.283 In accordance with s 54(2) Enforcement Act, the application for granting the enforcement on the basis of a foreign award must include an official copy of the enforceable award, the confirmation that the award is finally binding and enforceable and the leave for enforcement. According to s 84a(1) Enforcement Act the request for leave for enforcement ('Antrag auf Vollstreckbarerklärung') may be combined with the request for granting the enforcement ('Antrag auf Bewilligung der Exekution') in a single application.[210] There is no time limit for the application for recognition and enforcement of an arbitral award after this award has become final and binding upon the parties.

---

[208] OGH 20 October1993 EvBl 1994/105.

[209] Mohr, F., 'Vereinfachtes Bewilligungsverfahren und andere am 1.10.1995 in Kraft getretene Bestimmungen der EO-Nov 1995' *ÖJZ* (1995) 895.

[210] OGH 29 May1996 ZfRV 1996/73.

(3) Remedies against decisions granting or declining enforcement

The creditor and the debtor may file an appeal against the decision granting or refusing leave for enforcement. This appeal must be made within four weeks. Only the debtor is entitled to a so-called 'protest' ('Widerspruch') in addition to the appeal (s 84(1), Enforcement Act). The protest can only be made if the court granting the leave for enforcement failed to comply with the requirements of ss 79-81 of the Enforcement Act. The deadline for a protest is generally one month. It is two months, if the debtor has his domicile or his seat abroad. In addition, the provisions concerning the proceedings before the regional courts (s 431 *et seq* CCP) apply to the procedure of protest. **2.284**

B. Recognition and/or enforcement of foreign awards (conventions, treaties)

(1) Specific bilateral or multilateral treaties

Austria has concluded bilateral treaties dealing with the recognition and enforcement of awards with the following states:[211] the former Yugoslavia (BGBl 155/1961), which is now applicable between Austria and Bosnia-Herzegovina, Croatia, Macedonia, the Federal Republic of Yugoslavia; Belgium (BGBl 287/1961); British-Columbia (BGBl 314/1970); Germany (BGBl 105/1960); Russia (BGBl 193/1956); Switzerland (BGBl 125/1962); the Republic of Slovenia (BGBl 115/1961; 714/1993); Liechtenstein (BGBl 114/1975) and Malaysia (BGBl 601/1986). Articles 20 and 21 of the bilateral treaty with Turkey (BGBl 90/1932) concerning the recognition and enforcement of awards were terminated by the Convention of 23 May 1989 (BGBl 571/1992 amended by BGBl 949/1994); however, this is of no practical relevance as Turkey acceded to the New York Convention on 2 July 1992. **2.285**

Austria has concluded the following multilateral treaties dealing with the recognition and enforcement of awards: Protocol on Arbitration Clauses, Geneva, 24 September 1923 (BGBl 57/1928); Convention on the Execution of Foreign Arbitral Awards, Geneva, 26 September 1927, BGBl 343/1930; Convention on German Foreign Debts, London, 27 February 1953 (BGBl 203/1958); Convention on the Recognition and Enforcement of Foreign Arbitral Awards, New York, 10 June 1958 (BGBl 200/1961); Austria withdrew the reciprocity reservation according to Art I para 3 of the New York Convention on 25 February 1988 (BGBl 191/1988); European Convention on International Commercial Arbitration, Geneva, 21 April 1961 (BGBl 107/1964); Convention on the Application of the European Convention on International Commercial Arbitration, 17 December 1962 (BGBl 19/1965); Convention on the Settlement of Investment Disputes between States and Nationals of other States, Washington, 18 March 1965 (BGBl 357/1971); Convention Concerning International Carriage by Rail (COTIF) together with the Protocol on Privileges and Immunities of the International Organisations Concerning International Carriage by Rail (OTIF), Appendix A—Uniform Rules Concerning the Contract for International Carriage of Passengers and Luggage by Rail (CIV) and Appendix B—Uniform Rules Concerning the Contract for International Carriage of Goods by Rail, 19 May 1980 (BGBl 225/1985). **2.286**

[211] Duchek, A., Schütz, W. and Tarko, I., *Zwischenstaatlicher Rechtsverkehr in Zivilrechtssachen* 133 *et seq.*

2.287 Austria is a party to the Convention on the Settlement of Investment Disputes Between States and Nationals of Other States, concluded in Washington, DC, on 18 March 1965; signed on 17 May 1966, ratified on 25 May 1971 and entered into force on 24 June 1971; The Hague Convention Of Civil Procedure, concluded at The Hague, Netherlands on 1 March 1954, signed on 1 March 1954, ratified on 22 February 1956 and entered into force on 12 April 1957 (BGBl 91/1957); the Geneva Convention on the Execution Of Foreign Arbitral Awards, signed on 26 September 1927, ratified on 22 May 1930 and entered into force on 18 October 1930 (BGBl 343/1930); and the United Nations Convention On Contracts for the International Sale of Goods, concluded in Vienna, Austria, signed on 11 April 1980, ratified on 29 December 1987 and entered into force on 1 January 1988 (BGBl 96/1988).

2.288 The enforcement on the basis of a foreign enforceable legal title is regulated by ss 79 to 86 of the Enforcement Act. However, the provisions contained in the multilateral and bilateral treaties on the enforcement of foreign awards prevail.

2.289 As to the extent of the control of the award, the courts will only apply eg the New York Convention, regarding the leave for enforcement, when it is applicable.[212] In this case, enforcement can be denied only on the grounds provided in Art V of the New York Convention. The courts will not consider the merits of the decision of the arbitral tribunal.

(2) Existence of a standard procedure for the enforcement of foreign awards

2.290 See section VIII.A.1 of this report (paras 2.280–3).

(3) Extent of examination and review of the award by the court

2.291 See section VIII.B.1 (para 2.289).

C. Application of the New York Convention

(1) Application of the New York Convention in practice

2.292 Austria has been a signatory to the New York Convention since 2 May 1961. Effective from 25 February 1988, Austria withdrew the reservation it originally made pursuant to Art I(3) of the NYC.[213] Accordingly, Austrian courts recognize and enforce foreign awards made in accordance with this convention.

2.293 The OGH dealt with several issues regarding the interpretation of the NYC. The decisions will be regrouped in the following according to the substance matter, not necessarily following the qualifications given by the court.

2.294 As regards the form requirement, two decisions of the OGH can be stated here:

- when analysing Art II(2) of the NYC, the Austrian Supreme Court held that the signature of one party on a letter submitted by the other party was sufficient as to fulfil the writing requirement. The Austrian Supreme Court was addressed with the enforcement

[212] OGH 29 May 1996 ZfRV 1996/73.
[213] BGBl 191/1988.

of an Italian award in Austria. In this case, the applicant and defendant agreed to the sale of certain goods. Referring to this sale, the applicant sent two order confirmations to the defendant. Both documents included an arbitration clause. Whilst the defendant signed the order confirmations, the applicant's signature was missing. The Austrian Supreme Court considered the order confirmations to be letters from the applicant, which contained an arbitration clause. The Court further held the defendant's reply to be signed copies of these letters. It was not held to be necessary that the defendant had drafted the text. The Italian award was consequently declared enforceable; and[214] in another decision, the Supreme Court held that under Art II(2) NYC an agreement in writing includes an agreement contained in an exchange of telegrams.[215]

The OGH dealt with three cases concerning the invalidity of the arbitration agreement: **2.295**

- in a case where enforcement of a Yugoslav award was sought in Austria, the parties had concluded an arbitration clause providing for arbitration at the arbitration court of the Federal Economic Chamber of Yugoslavia, further providing that the next instance be the competent international law court. Even though the provision concerning the next instance was unclear, this was not a reason to conclude that the arbitration agreement was invalid as a whole. The Supreme Court reasoned that in general, an arbitration clause is not ineffective when only a procedural arrangement is ineffective. Only if the void parts concerned the core of the agreed arbitration, would this also entail the nullity of the entire arbitration agreement. The court concluded that this was not so in the case at issue, as in East-West trade it is not unusual that an arbitration agreement refers only to one instance; and[216]
- the Supreme Court also held that an arbitration agreement was valid which reads

> This agreement, including its conclusion, validity, performance, is subject to exclusive competence of the arbitral tribunals of the Economic Chamber, Budapest, as well as the Federal Economic Chamber, Vienna.

This clause was not held to lack sufficient clarity. It was deemed to grant a choice to the claimant.[217]

- in another case the OGH considered the following arbitration clause:

> Where possible legal questions are concerned the court attached to the Hungarian Chamber of Commerce is competent.

The OGH held that the clause could with certainty be construed as providing for arbitration at the Arbitration Court of the Hungarian Chamber of Commerce.[218]

As regards the incorporation by reference the OGH found an arbitration agreement lacked the required written form because the applicant had failed to prove that the general conditions which contained the arbitration clause had been annexed to the special conditions at **2.296**

---

214 OGH 21 February 1978 (1985) 10 Ybk Comm Arb 418.
215 OGH 17 November 1971 1 Ybk Comm Arb 183.
216 OGH 9 September 1987 (1990) 15 Ybk Comm Arb 367.
217 OGH 11 November 1990 (1990) 3 SZ no 132.
218 OGH 5 October 1988 [1989] WBl 30.

the time the letter was signed. The Supreme Court reasoned that even if at the time of conclusion the general conditions including the arbitration clause were in the possession of the defendant and were known to it, this was insufficient to meet the requirement of written form. In such a situation it cannot be certain that the parties are fully aware of the meaning of the arbitration agreement, which is tantamount to the valid exclusion of the ordinary courts.[219]

2.297 The OGH has dealt with several cases which regarded violation of public policy:

- the Supreme Court refused enforcement of an award rendered in the Netherlands, as the underlying contracts were sale and purchase agreements on a margin basis and thus invalid under Austrian law. According to Austrian law, enforcement of awards has to be refused if they grant claims, which under Austrian law could not be brought before Austrian courts. The Austrian Supreme Court held that the enforcement court is authorized to investigate the legality of the contract if this issue has not been dealt with by the arbitral tribunal as well as in cases where the arbitral tribunal had investigated this question, but had wrongly resolved the issue. It further reasoned that it is irrelevant that the transactions concluded between the parties were subject to Dutch law, because domestic law is applicable to the issue of whether the transaction was valid for determining whether enforcement is to be refused;[220]
- however, the Supreme Court held in a later decision that *exequatur* may only be refused if the recognition or enforcement of an award would be totally incompatible with the Austrian legal order;[221]
- the Supreme Court also rejected any difference between 'domestic' and 'international' public policy;[222]
- transactions that are qualified as gambling or betting violate Austrian public policy.[223] This does not apply to commodity futures transactions[224] nor to other stock exchange transactions;[225]
- the right to set aside is not part of public policy;[226]
- enforcement was sought of an award rendered in Serbia in favour of the Yugoslav seller. The Austrian buyer objected that the award violated public policy because it was based on a false statement by the sole witness, the rate of interest of 73 per cent per annum was excessive and the arbitration agreement was invalid owing to a forged signature. The Supreme Court reasoned that under the combined effect of the 1961 European Convention and the 1958 NYC, which both applied here, the annulment of the award

[219] OGH 2 May 1972 (1985) 10 Ybk Comm Arb 417.
[220] OGH 11 May 1983 (1985) 10 Ybk Comm Arb 421.
[221] OGH 25 April 2001 (2001) 42 ZfRV no 76.
[222] OGH 11 May 1983 (1985) 10 Ybk Comm Arb 421.
[223] OGH 11 May 1983 (1985) 10 Ybk Comm Arb 421; OGH 23 February 1983 (1983); 34 ZfRV no 206.
[224] OGH 11 May 1983 (1985) 10 Ybk Comm Arb 421.
[225] OGH 23 February 1983 (1983) 34 ZfRV no 206.
[226] OGH 25 April 2001 (2001) 42 ZfRV no 76.

on public policy grounds in the country of origin was not a ground for refusing enforcement. The court further held that neither the allegedly false witness statement nor the alleged forgery of the buyer's signature were a basis for refusing enforcement on public policy grounds. The court, however, upheld the buyer's allegation that the rate of interest was excessive and violated Austrian public policy. The court concluded that it was possible to separate the award on the main sum, which was enforceable, from the award on interest, which was not;[227]

- the Supreme Court confirmed enforcement of an award noting that the defendant alleged several procedural defects in the arbitration which allegedly amounted to a violation of due process. The Supreme Court held that the content of Art V(1)b of the NYC implies an infringement of the right to be heard, as does the ground for challenging an award under Austrian law. Therefore the Supreme Court applied its case law to the interpretation of s 595(1) no 2 (after the reform in 2006 s 611(2) no 2) as regards the interpretation of the content of Art V(1)b of the NYC. The Supreme Court concluded that the fact that the arbitral tribunal ignored motions to admit evidence or insufficiently investigated the facts could not be equated to a violation of due process.[228]

The OGH held that the content of Art V(1) lit b NYC implies an infringement of the right to be heard as does the ground for challenging an award under Austrian law. Therefore, the OGH applied its judicature regarding the interpretation of s 595(1) no 2 (after the reform in 2006 s 611(2) no 2) as regards the interpretation of the content of Art V(1) lit b NYC and concluded, that a defect of the arbitral award, caused through the fact that the arbitral tribunal ignored motions for the admission of evidence or insufficiently investigated the facts, cannot be considered to be an infringement of the right to be heard.[229] **2.298**

The OGH has not yet dealt with questions regarding the scope of the arbitration agreement, the issues of representation, waiver, irregular composition of the arbitral tribunal, violation of procedural rules, *ultra petita* and lack of arbitrability. **2.299**

(2) Examples of decisions which do not apply the Convention correctly

As far as we are aware, there are no decisions of the OGH that have incorrectly applied the New York Convention. **2.300**

IX. Appendix

A. National legislation

All national laws and regulations are available on the website of the department of the federal chancellor at <http://ris.bka.gv.at/jus/>.[230]

[227] OGH 26 January 2005 3 Ob 221/04b, [2005] XXX Ybk Comm Arb 421.
[228] OGH 31 March 2005 3 Ob 35/05a, [2006] XXXI Ybk Comm Arb 583.
[229] OGH 31 March 2005 3 Ob 35/05a.
[230] A limited list of Austrian laws in English is available at: <http://www.ris.bka.gv.at/hilfe/erv/law_list.html> (accessed 25 November 2008).

English	German	Amendments
Code of Civil Procedure ('CCP')	Zivilprozeßordnung—ZPO	1.8.1895 in amends, BGBl 140/1997
Introductory Law to the Code of Civil Procedure	Einführungsgesetz zur Zivilprozeßordnung—EGZPO	1.8.1895, RGBl 112
Judicature Act	Jurisdiktionsnorm—JN	1.8.1895 in amends, BGBl 140/1997
Enforcement Act	Exekutionsordnung—EO	27.5.1896 in amends, BGBl 759/1996
Civil Code	Allgemeines bürgerliches Gesetzbuch—ABGB	1.6.1811 in amends, BGBl 30/1997
Federal Statute on Private International Law	Bundesgesetz über das Internationale Privatrecht—IPRG	15.6.1978, BGBl 304/1978
Rome Convention on the Choice of Law for Contracts	Europäisches Schuldvertragsübereinkommen (EVÜ)	1980, 19.6.1980, BGBl 18/1999
Commercial Code	Handelsgesetzbuch—HGB	10.5.1897 in amends, BGBl 114/1997
Limited Liability Company Law	Gesetz über die Gesellschaften mit beschränkter Haftung—GmbHG	6.3.1906 in amends, BGBl 114/1997
Antitrust Law	Kartellgesetz—KartG	19.10.1988 in amends, BGBl 140/1993
Bankruptcy Code	Konkursordnung—KO	10.12.1914 in amends, BGBl 114/1997
Labour and Social Court Law	Arbeits- und Sozialgerichtsgesetz—ASGG	7.3.1985 in amends, BGBl 104/1985
Consumer Protection Act	Konsumentenschutzgesetz—KSchG	8.3.1979 in amends, BGBl 140/1997
Tenure of Land Law	Landpachtgesetz—LPG	26.11.1969 in amends, BGBl 451/1969
Criminal Code	Strafgesetzbuch—StGB	23.1.1974 in amends, BGBl 12/1997
Income Tax Law	Einkommenssteuergesetz—EstG	7.7.1988 in amends, BGBl 49/1998
Value Added Tax Law	Umsatzsteuergesetz—UstG	1994 in amends, BGBl 9/1998
Civil Servant Act	Beamtendienstrechtsgesetz—BDG	27.6.1979 in amends, BGBl 30/1998
Public Servant Act	Vertragsbedienstetengesetz—VBG	1948 in amends, BGBl 30/1998
Notary Code	Notariatsordnung—NotO	31.7.1945 in amends, BGBl 25/1947
Law relating to Aliens	Fremdengesetz—FrG	1.1.1998, BGBl 75/1997
Bar Code of Practice	Rechtsanwaltsordnung—RAO	6.7.1868 in amends, BGBl 140/1997
Attorney Tariff Act	Rechstanwaltstarifgesetz—RATG	22.5.1969 in amends, BGBl 140/1997
Disciplinary Statute	Disziplinarstatut—DSt	28.6.1990 in amends, BGBl 517/1991
Business Enterprise Code	Unternehmensgesetzbuch—UGB	10.5.1897 in amends, BGBl I Nr. 120/2005
Law on the Employment of the Judiciary	Richter- und Staatsanwaltschaftsdienstgesetz—RStG	14.12.1961 in amends, BGBl I Nr. 53/2007
Federal Law on Delivery of Official Documents	Bundesgesetz über die Zustellung behördlicher Schriftstücke—Zustellgesetz	1.4.1982 in amends, BGBl 357/1990

B. Arbitral institutions

The Arbitral Centre of the Federal Economic Chamber was created in 1974. Its rules are specifically designed for international commercial arbitration. It is located at:

Wiedner Hauptstraße 63
Post Office Box 319
A-1045 Vienna
Telephone: +43 (0)5 90 900-4397, 4398, 4399
Fax: +43 (0)5 90 900-216
Email: arb@wko.at
Website: <http://wko.at/arbitration> (English, German, Russian and Czech)

The Court of Arbitration of the Vienna Commodity Exchange is located at:

Wallnerstraße 8
Post Office Box 192
A-1014 Vienna
Telephone: +43 1 531 65 0
Fax: +43 1 532 97 40
Email: info@wienerborse.at
Website: <http://www.wienerborse.at> (English and German)

C. Model arbitration clauses and other patterns

The International Arbitral Centre of the Austrian Federal Economic Chamber recommends the following arbitration clause:

All disputes arising out of this contract or related to its violation, termination or nullity shall be finally settled under the Rules of Arbitration and Conciliation of the International Arbitral Centre of the Austrian Federal Economic Chamber in Vienna (Vienna Rules) by one or more arbitrators appointed in accordance with these Rules.

Appropriate supplementary provisions:

(a) **The number of arbitrators shall be _______ (one or three);**
(b) **The substantive law of _______ shall be applicable;**[231]
(c) **The language to be used in the arbitral proceedings shall be _______.**[232]

[231] In this context, consideration may be given to the possible application of the United Nations Convention on Contracts for the International Sale of Goods 1980.

[232] 'Recommended Arbitration Clause' is availiable at: <http://portal.wko.at/wk/format_detail.wk?angid=1&stid=328039&dstid=8459&opennavid=0>.

Annex 1
VIAC schedule of arbitration costs
Registration fee:
EUR 2,000[233]

Administration charges[234]

Amount in dispute in Euros from	to	Rate in Euros		
0	100,000	3,000		
100,001	200,000	3,000	+ 1.5 % of excess over	100,000
200,001	500,000	4,500	+ 1 % of excess over	200,000
500,001	1,000,000	7,500	+ 0.7 % of excess over	500,000
1,000,001	2,000.000	11,000	+ 0.4 % of excess over	1,000,000
2,000,001	5,000,000	15,000	+ 0.1 % of excess over	2,000,000
5,000,001	10,000,000	18,000	+ 0.05 % of excess over	5,000,000
Over 10,000,000		20,500	+ 0.01% of excess over	10,000,000

Administration charges[235]

Amount in dispute in Euros from	to	Rate in Euros		
0	100,000		6 % minimum fee:	1,000
100,001	200,000	6,000	+ 3 % of excess over	100,000
200,001	500,000	9,000	+ 2.5 % of excess over	200,000
500,001	1,000,000	16,500	+ 2 % of excess over	500,000
1,000,001	2,000.000	26,500	+ 1 % of excess over	1,000,000
2,000,001	5,000,000	36,500	+ 0.6 % of excess over	2,000,000
5,000,001	10,000,000	54,500	+ 0.4 % of excess over	5,000,000
10,000,001	20,000,000	74,500	+ 0.2 % of excess over	10,000,000
20,000,001	100,000,000	94,500	+ 0.1 % of excess over	20,000,000
Over 100,000,000		174,500	+0.01% of excess over	100,000,000

D. Bibliography

Aburumieh, Nora, Koller, Christian and Pöltner, Elisabeth, 'Formvorschriften für Schiedsvereinbarung' *ÖJZ 27* (2006) 439.

Backhausen, Georg, *Schiedsgerichtsbarkeit unter besonderer Berücksichtigung des Schiedsvertragsrechts* (Manz, 1990) (Backhausen, *Schiedsgerichtsbarkeit*).

Burgstaller, Alfred, 'Grenzender Bindung an Strafurteil' *RdA* (2000) 53.

Deimbacher, Otto, 'Schiedsvertäge und Schiedsklauseln in anderen Verträgen und in AGB' *GesRZ* (1995), 12.

[233] See Art 33 para 1.
[234] See Art 36 para 1.
[235] See Art 36 para 6.

Fasching, Hans W., *Schiedsgericht und Schiedsverfahren im österreichischen und im internationalen Recht* (Manz, 1973) (Fasching, *Schiedsgericht*).

Fasching, Hans W., *Lehrbuch des österreichischen Zivilprozeßrechts* (2nd edn, Manz, 1990) (Fasching, *Lehrbuch*).

Fasching, Hans W., 'Kostenvorschüsse zur Einleitung schiedsgerichtlicher Verfahren' *JBl* (1993) 545.

Fasching, Hans W. and Konecny, Andreas (eds), *Kommentar zu den Zivilprozeßgesetzen* (2nd edn, vol 3, Manz, 2004).

Forgó-Feldner, Birgit, 'Die Bindung des Zivilrichters an strafgerichtliche Verurteilungen' *ÖJZ* (2005) 51.

Hahnkamper, Wolfgang, 'Neue Regeln für Schiedsvereinbarung' *SchiedsVZ* 2 (2006) 65.

Hausmaninger, Christian '§§ 577 bis 618 ZPO' in Hans W. Faschingand and Andreas Konecny (eds), *Komentar zu den Zivilprozeßgesetzen* (2nd edn, vol IV/2 Manzsche Verlags- und Universitätsbuchhandlung, 2007).

Heller, Ludwig, Berger, Franz and Stix, Leopold, *Kommentar zur Exekutionsordnung* (4th edn, Manz, 1969).

Kloibel, Barbara, Oberhammer, Paul, Rechberger, Walter H. and Haller, Hartmut, *Das neue Schiedsrecht: Schiedsrrechtsänderungsgestz 2006'* (Manzsche Verlags- und Universitätsbuchhandlung, 2006).

Konecny, Andreas and Schubert, Günter (eds), *Kommentar zu den Insolvenzgesetzen* (vol 1, Manzsche Verlags- und Universitätsbuchhandlung, 1997).

Koziol, Helmut and Welser, Rudolf, *Grundriß des bürgerlichen Rechts* (13th edn, vol I, Manzsche Kurzlehrbuch-Reihe, 2006).

Krejci Heinz, *Reform-Kommentar UGB ABGB* (Manz, 2007).

Kuhn, Georg and Uhlenbruck, Wilhelm, *Kommentar zu Konkursordung* (11th edn, Vahlen, 1994).

Liebscher, Christoph, 'European Public Policy after Eco Swiss' *American Rev of Int'l Arb* [1999] 81.

Liebscher, Christoph, 'Fair Trial and Challenge of Awards in International Arbitration' *Croatian Arb Ybk* (1999) 83.

Liebscher, Christoph, *Schiedsrichtervertrag und anwendbares Recht, Recht und Praxis der Schiedsgerichtsbarkeit* (1999) 2.

Liebscher, Christoph, 'La responsabilité civile de l'arbitre' *Rev arb* [1999] 392.

Liebscher, Christoph, 'European Public Policy—A Black Box?' *JIA* [2000] 73.

Liebscher, Christoph, 'European Public Policy and the Austrian Supreme Court' *AI* [2000] 357.

Liebscher, Christoph, 'Reform of Austrian Arbitration Law' *JIA* [2001], 211.

Liebscher, Christoph, *The Healthy Award* (Kluwer Law International, 2003).

Liebscher, Christoph, 'Der Entwurf des neuen österreichischen Schiedsrechts' *SchiedsVZ*, 2 [2003] 65.

Liebscher, Christoph, *The Challenge of Awards on the Basis of Criminal Acts*, ICCA Congress Series no 11 (2003).

Liebscher, Christoph, 'Arbitration and EC Competition Law—The New Competition Regulation: Back to Square One?' *IALR* [2003] 84.

Liebscher, Christoph, 'Schiedsinstitutionen' in Paul Oberhammer (ed), *Schiedsgerichtsbarkeit in Zentraleuropa* (NWW Neuer Wissenschaftlicher Vertrag, 2005).

Liebscher, Christoph, 'Drafting Awards in ICC Arbitrations' *ICC International Court of Arb Bull*, vol 16 no 2 [2005].

Liebscher, Christoph, *The Austrian Arbitration Act 2006: Text and Notes* (Kluwer Law International, 2006).

Liebscher, Christoph/Fremuth-Wolf Alice (eds), *Arbitration Law and Practice in Central and Eastern Europe* (JurisNet LLC, 2006).

Liebscher, Christoph, 'Looking at the new Austrian Arbitration Law through the spectacles of the English Arbitration Act 1996' vol 9 Issue 4, *IALR* [2006].

Liebscher, Christoph, 'Austria's new Arbitration Law and Federal Arbitration Law in the U.S.—a Comparison', vol 21 Issue 5, *Mealey's Int'l Arb Rep* [2006] 34.

Liebscher, Christoph, 'Autriche: le nouveau droit de l'arbitrage' *Les Cahiers de l'Arbitrage*, 1 [2006] 14.

Liebscher, Christoph, 'Wiener Regeln' in Rolf Schütze (ed), *Institutionelle Schiedsgerichtsbarkeit* (Carl Heymanns, 2006).

Liebscher, Christoph, 'Austria adopts the UNCITRAL Model Law', vol 23 no 4 *AI* [2007] 523.

Liebscher, Christoph, 'Beweisaufnahme im Schiedsverfahren' in Hellwig Torggler (ed), *Schiedsgerichtsbarkeit* (Verlag Österreich GmbH, 2007).

Liebscher, Christoph, 'Case C-168/05, *Elisa Maria Mostaza Claro v Centro Móvil Milenium SL*, judgment of the Court of Justice (First Chamber) of 26 October 2006 ECR I-10421' *CMLR* 45 [2008] 545.

Liebscher, Christoph, 'EU Member State Court Application of Eco Swiss: Review of the Case Law and Future Prospects' in Phillip Landolt and Gordon Blanke (eds), *The Treatment of US Antitrust and EC Competition Law in International Arbitration—A Handbook for Practitioners* (Kluwer Law International, forthcoming 2009).

Melis, Werner, 'Arbitration in Austria', <http://wko.at/arbitration>. Mohr, Franz, Vereinfachtes Bewilligungsverfahren und andere am 1.10.1995 in Kraft getretene Bestimmungen der EO-Nov 1995' *ÖJZ* (1995) 889.

Melis, Werner, 'Country Report Austria' in Pieter Sanders and Albert JanVan den Berg, (eds), *International Handbook on Commercial Arbitration* (Supplement 50 Kluwer Law International, October, 2007).

Oberhammer, Paul, *Entwurf eines neuen Schiedsverfahrensrechts* (Manzsche Verlags- und Universitätsbuchhandlung, 2002).

Petschek, Georg, Reimer, Otto and Schiemer, Karl, *Das österreichische Insolvenzrecht—Eine systematische Darstellung* (Manzsche Verlags- und Universitätsbuchhandlung, 1973).

Power, Jenny, *The Austrian Arbitration Act: A Practitioner's Guide to Sections 577–618 of the Austrian Code of Civil Procedure* (Manzsche Verlags- und Universitätsbuchhandlung, 2006).

Rechberger, Walter H. (ed), *Kommentar zur ZPO* (2nd edn, Springer-Verlag, 2000).

Rechberger, Walter H. and Simotta, Daphne Ariane, *Exekutionsverfahren* (2nd edn, WUV-Universitätsverlag, 1992).

Rechberger, Walter H. and Simotta, Daphne Ariane, *Grundriß des österreichischen Ziviprozessrechts* (6th edn, Manzsche Kurzlehrbuch-Reich, 2003).

Reiner, Andreas, *Handbuch der ICC-Schiedsgerichtsbarkeit* (Manz, 1989).

Reiner, Andreas, *The New Austrian Arbitration Law—Arbitration Act 2006* (LexisNexis, 2006).

Respondek, Andreas, 'Die Aufhebungsklage gegen Schiedssprüche nach österreichischen Recht' *RIW* (1993) 376,

Riegler, Stefan, Petsche, Alexander, Fremuth-Wolf, Alice, Platte, Martin and Liebscher, Christoph, *Arbitration Law of Austria: Practice and Procedure* (Juris Publishing Inc, 2007).

Rummel, Peter, 'Schiedsvertrag und ABGB' *RZ* (1986) 146.

Rummel, Peter (ed), *Kommentar zum Allgemeinen bürgerlichen Gesetzbuch* (3rd edn, vol 1, Manz 2002).

Zeiler, Gerold, *Schiedsverfahren §§ 577–618 ZPO idF des SchiedsRÄG 2006* (Neuer Wissenschaftlicher Verlag, 2006).

Zeiler, Gerold and Steindl, Barbara, *Arbitration in Austria: A Basic Primer* (2nd edn, Neuer Wissenschaftlicher Verlag, 2007).

3

BELGIUM

*Hans van Houtte**

I. Introduction

A. Current status of the law on arbitration

(1) Short history

Initially Belgium assumed the arbitration provisions of the 1806 French Code de procédure civile. In 1876 and 1958 attempts to amend the Belgian arbitration law failed.[1] It was not until 1972 that a more modern arbitration statute was adopted. **3.01**

(2) Law in force and future projects

The present arbitration law is based upon a statute of 4 July 1972.[2] In fact, this statute incorporates the Uniform Law on Arbitration, which was contained in a Council of Europe Convention of 20 January 1966.[3] This Convention, which aimed to introduce a uniform arbitration law in Europe, had, however, failed: it never got the three ratifications to enter into force. In fact it was only signed by Austria and Belgium in 1966. The Convention got its sole—belated—ratification from Belgium in 1972. On that occasion Belgium introduced **3.02**

* The author hereby thanks Iasson Yi, Kristof Cox and Govert Coppens, researchers at the Institute for International Trade Law of the KULeuven, for their help in finalizing the report.

[1] Keutgen, G. and Dal, G.A., L'arbitrage en droit belge et international (2nd edn, Bruylant, 2006) 7.

[2] Moniteur belge, 8 August 1972.

[3] European Convention providing a uniform Law on Arbitration (Convention no 56).

the uniform law into its domestic legal system,[4] with the legislature welcoming the European draft to update its century-old arbitration law, and made the uniform law Book VI of its 1967 Code of Civil Procedure (in French 'Code Judiciaire', in Dutch 'Gerechtelijk Wetboek'; hereinafter abbreviated as: 'Cod Jud'). Articles 1676 to 1723 Book VI of this Code, however, are not an exact copy of the uniform law. The Belgian legislature has added provisions to the uniform law, *inter alia* limiting the capacity of public entities to arbitrate and the possibility to arbitrate employment disputes.[5]

3.03 In 1985, Art 1717, para 4 was added to the arbitration law. This provision excluded annulment proceedings before Belgian courts for arbitrations where none of the parties was a Belgian national or established in Belgium.[6] This automatic exclusion of annulment proved, however, to be counterproductive: instead of attracting international arbitrations to Belgium (except some notorious cases, such as the Eurotunnel arbitration), the new provisions, on the contrary, generally deterred foreign parties from establishing the seat of their arbitration in Belgium. Moreover, the ICC no longer chose Belgium as a seat for arbitrations when the parties had not explicitly chosen Belgium as the place of arbitration: the Belgian exclusion was deemed to have too much impact to warrant selecting Belgium when not expressly provided for by the parties. Article 1717, para 4 was finally amended in 1998. In its new version—and still when none of the parties has a Belgian nationality or establishment—it allows parties to agree beforehand on the exclusion of annulment proceedings.

3.04 The 1998 statute which amended Art 1717, para 4 updated some other provisions and added new features to the arbitration law as well.[7] They were largely inspired by suggestions from the Belgian Centre for Arbitration and Mediation (CEPANI) and in line with some features of the UNCITRAL model law as well as the Swiss, French and Dutch arbitration statutes.

3.05 CEPANI, the Belgian arbitration centre, has established a working group to discuss the introduction of a new arbitration law, which would be largely modelled on the UNCITRAL arbitration Model Law. However, no proposition has been finalised yet.

(3) Distinction between national and international arbitration

3.06 **(3.1) If there are different systems and rules for national/international arbitration: what are the criteria for the distinction between both systems?** Belgian law generally does not differentiate between national and international arbitration. The same procedural rules apply to both.[8]

[4] Several other European countries have been inspired by the Convention when modifying their arbitration law, but did not ratify the Convention as such; see de Bournonville, P., 'Droit judiciaire: l'arbitrage' (Bruylant, 2000), 55.

[5] See Dermine, L., 'L'Arbitrage commercial en Belgique' (Larcier, 1975).

[6] Statute of 27 March 1985, *Moniteur belge* 13 April 1985. See van Houtte, H., 'La loi belge du 27 mars 1985 sur l'arbitrage international' [1986] *Rev arb* 29.

[7] Statute of 19 May 1998, *Moniteur belge* 7 August 1998. See for an analysis of the arbitration law after 1998 : de Bournonville (n 4); Hanotiau, B. and Block, G., 'La loi du 19 mai 1998 modifiant la législation belge relative à l'arbitrage' [1998] *ASA Bull* 528; Horsmans, G., 'La loi belge du 19 mai 1998 sur l'arbitrage' [1999] *Rev arb* 475; Verbist, H., 'Reform of the Belgian Arbitration Law' [1998] *Revue Droit Affaires Internationales*, 842.

[8] de Bournonville, P. (n 4) 216, no 291.

However, Art 1717, para 4 permits the parties to agree in the arbitration agreement or at a later date that the Belgian courts will have no jurisdiction to annul the award. This possibility is only available if none of the parties 'is a physical person of Belgian nationality or a physical person having his normal residence in Belgium or a legal person having its registered office or a branch office in Belgium'.[9]

B. Practice of arbitration

(1) *Frequency of arbitration as opposed to litigation*

There are no statistics available about the use of arbitration compared to litigation. In all events, however, settlement through arbitration seems to be an extreme exception for domestic disputes.[10] Commodity and business–branch arbitrations are very rarely used. Also disputes with parties from other European countries are generally submitted to the courts, *inter alia.* because the EU Regulations and the Lugano Convention facilitate transnational proceedings within Europe. For agreements with non-European partners, where jurisdiction and enforcement of judgments are more problematic, arbitration becomes more popular.[11] **3.07**

(2) *Leading arbitral institutions and statistics (if available)*

In Belgium, for already 40 years, the leading arbitral institution has been the CEPANI (*Centre Belge pour l'Etude et la Pratique de l'Arbitrage National et International*) [in Dutch *Centrum voor de Studie en de Praktijk van de Internationale en Nationale Arbitrage*, in abbreviation: CEPINA]. It operates under the auspices and from the premises of the Federation of Belgian Enterprises (*Fédération des Entreprises de Belgique*—in Dutch, *Verbond van Belgische Ondernemingen*). Besides administering its own arbitrations under the CEPANI rules, it also functions as appointing committee on behalf of the Belgian National Committee of the International Chamber of Commerce and as appointing authority under the UNCITRAL rules. It also organizes workshops and colloquia on arbitration. The reports of its colloquia are published.[12] CEPANI has started the publication of its awards, with commentaries.[13] **3.08**

The CEPANI is directed by of a President, three Vice-Presidents, a Board of Directors (approximately 25 people), a secretariat (some five people) and has approximately 200 members with various backgrounds. The CEPANI rules on arbitration, mediation, mini-trial and technical expertise can be found in the English, French, Dutch and German language on <http://www.cepani.be>. **3.09**

[9] de Bournonville, P. (n 4) 216–17, no 292.

[10] de Meulemeester, D., *Arbitrage: boetiekrecht?* (Maklu, 2007) 56. De Meulemeester notes that the frequency of arbitration as opposed to litigation is limited; hence, he refers to arbitration as 'boutique law'.

[11] The 2005 statistics of CEPANI, Belgium's most important arbitration institution, show that 63.64 % of all CEPANI arbitrations for that year were exclusively between Belgian parties, while 35.36 % involved at least one non-Belgian party. These 'international' parties were primarily Swiss (18.75 %) or Spanish (12.50 %) and—in general—European.

[12] A list and description of these publications can be found on <http://www.cepani.be>.

[13] See *Receuil des Sentences arbitrales du CEPANI (1985–1995)* (Bruylant, 2005).

3.10 CEPANI does not make public the number of cases it handles. This number may be estimated to be between 70 and 80 new cases per year. CEPANI, however, publishes the allocation of its cases over the respective types of disputes. More than half of the CEPANI cases concern commercial sales, agency and distribution or other business transactions. Moreover, a quarter of its caseload concerns mergers and acquisitions, corporate disputes and shareholder litigation; the rest mainly involves patent and trade mark, construction and banking disputes. One third of CEPANI arbitrations involve one or more non-Belgian parties.

3.11 Some specialized arbitration institutions deal with specific disputes such as those involving the diamond exchange, the grain trade, dry cleaning, the sale of furniture, disputes between footballers or other sportsmen and their clubs or sport federations, etc.[14] The Commission for Travel Disputes ('Commission de litiges Voyages'—'Geschillencommissie Reizen') handles disputes between travellers and travel agents or tour operators.[15] Disputes in the diamond trade may be submitted to the Arbitration Council of the Federation of Diamond Exchanges.[16] Disputes over grain may be brought before the Antwerp Arbitration Chamber for Grain and Seeds.[17] Disputes in the potato trade may be submitted to Belgapom, and in appeal to RUCIP arbitration.[18] A detailed inventory of all Belgian arbitration institutions, of which most are dormant, can be found in *Arbitrage et Modes alternatifs de Règlement des Conflits en Belgique*.[19]

II. Jurisdiction of the arbitral tribunal

A. Arbitration agreement

(1) Arbitration clause and submission agreement

3.12 The Belgian arbitration statute does not formally distinguish between, on the one hand, a submission to arbitration after the dispute has arisen ('compromis') and, on the other hand, an arbitral clause in a contract to submit future disputes to arbitration ('clause compromissoire'—'arbitrage beding'). Both are covered by the term 'arbitration agreement' ('convention d'arbitrage'—'arbitrage overeenkomst').[20]

3.13 In fact, however, the possibility of concluding binding arbitration clauses is more restricted than to submit disputes that have actually arisen, to arbitration. For instance, parties cannot agree in an arbitration clause on an arbitration '*ex aequo et bono*' (Art 1700) or submit

[14] An excellent analysis of the operation of these minor arbitration institutions can be found in Piers, P., *Sectorale Arbitrage* (Intersentia, 2007).

[15] Since most 'package deals' in Belgium are governed by the General Conditions of the Commission, including an arbitration clause electing the Commission as the arbitral institution, the Commission handles an important portion of travel dispute litigation. See <http://mineco.fgov.be/PROTECTION_CONSUMER/DISPUTES/voyages/disputes_voyages_fr_001.htm> (last accessed 26 August 2008).

[16] See Piers, M., Sectoriële Arbitrage (Intersentia, 2007) 29 *et seq.*

[17] See *ibid* (n 16), 39 *et seq.*

[18] 'Règles et Usances du Commerce des Pommes de Terre'; See Piers (n 16), 47 *et seq.*

[19] Verbist, H. and De Vuyst, B., *Arbitrage et Modes alternatifs de Règlement des Conflits en Belgique* (La Charte, 2002).

[20] Before the 1972 Statute, a distinction between arbitration clauses and submission agreements was made; see Keutgen, G. and Dal, G.A. (n 1) 55–6, no 42.

employment disputes (Art 1678, para 2) and insurance disputes (Insurance Law, Art 36) to arbitration before the dispute has arisen. Court decisions have also declared ineffective arbitration clauses when the dispute that arose thereafter concerned the termination of a sales concession or of an agency contract—at least when the seat of arbitration would be outside Belgium and Belgian law would not be applicable to the merits; once the dispute had arisen parties would be entitled to submit that dispute to arbitration.[21]

Further, Art 1676 requires that the arbitration clause concerns future disputes that may arise from *a given legal situation*. Therefore, parties cannot agree to submit whatever future dispute to arbitration without any reference to a specific legal situation (eg a specific contract).[22] **3.14**

(2) Requirements as to the contents of the arbitration agreement

Belgian law requires only that the parties' intention to submit a dispute to arbitration be certain and unambiguous (Art 1677).[23] It does not impose further requirements as to its content. The agreement does not have to specify the cause of action or the name of the arbitrators.[24] **3.15**

The only further restriction as to the contents of the arbitration agreement can be found in Art 1678, 1, which states that the arbitration clause shall not be valid if it grants advantages to a party with respect to the appointment of the arbitrator(s). Courts have given a wide interpretation to this restriction. The relevant criteria are the independence and impartiality of the arbitrators and the equality of arms. In particular, arbitration agreements providing for arbitration administered by a (professional) organization to which only one of the parties is a party have come under fire on this basis.[25] **3.16**

CEPANI recommends the following arbitration clause to be included in contracts : **3.17**

> Any dispute arising out of or in relation with this Agreement shall be finally settled under the CEPANI Rules of Arbitration by one or more arbitrators appointed in accordance with those Rules.

There might also be further provisions regarding the composition of the tribunal, the seat of arbitration, the language and the applicable rules of law. **3.18**

(3) Form of the arbitration agreement (eg 'in writing' requirement)

Article 1677, Cod Jud states that 'an arbitration agreement shall be constituted by an instrument in writing signed by the parties or by other documents binding on the parties and showing their intention to have recourse to arbitration'.[26] **3.19**

---

[21] See Cass 28 June 1979, *Pasicrisie* 1979, I, 1260 ; *Journal des Tribunaux* 1979, 625 ; Cass 22 December 1988, Cass 15 October 2004, *Revue de droit commercial belge* 2005, 488 ; Comm Ct Brussels 6 May 1993, Rechtskundig Weekblad 1993, 474 ; Comm Ct Hasselt 24 December 1996, *Revue de droit commercial belge* 1998, 255.

[22] Storme, M., 'Aspects importants du droit arbitral belge' [1976] *RDIP* 119, no 7.

[23] Court of Appeal, Antwerp 9 November 1983, *Limb Rechtsl* 1984, 62.

[24] Keutgen, G. and Dal, G.A. (n 1) 143, no 146; de Bournonville (n 4) 98, no 73.

[25] See *inter alia* Court of Appeal Brussels 23 June 1992, *Res Jur Imm* 1993, 83. For futher reference see Van Houtte, H., Cox, K. and Cools, S., 'Overzicht van Rechtspraak: Arbitrage' [2007] *RDC* 133–5, no 73–6.

[26] In the French version: '*Toute convention d'arbitrage doit faire l'objet d'un écrit signé des parties ou d'autres documents qui engagent les parties et manifestent leur volonté de recourir à l'arbitrage.*' Note the requirement that

3.20 Although the text of Art 1677 requires a document signed by the parties, the 'instrument' referred to in this Article, actually does not require a formal contract by the parties. Also an exchange of letters, telexes[27] or emails may suffice. Even the exchange of letters between the parties' lawyers, in which they appoint their respective arbitrators and describe their claims, has been considered as an agreement to arbitrate.[28]

3.21 The arbitration agreement has to be laid down in writing as a matter of evidence; not as a condition for its validity.[29] Consequently, the agreement to arbitrate can also be proven by the circumstance that the parties appear without reservations before the arbitrators and participate in the arbitration.[30] Likewise, a party is bound by a draft contract, containing an arbitration clause, when it performs this contract even though it did not sign it.[31]

3.22 **(3.1) Are there special requirements for a power of attorney/authority to enter into an arbitration agreement on behalf of a third party?** The arbitration agreement can be concluded by the parties' representatives or proxies.[32] However, such representation requires a specific authority, since submission to arbitration disposes of the party's rights (Art 1988, s 2 Civil Code).[33] Moreover, since the representative's authority has to be interpreted restrictively, it is important to specify the representative's power in detail.[34] Likewise, even though the 'avocat' is not required to prove his power of attorney in as far as he stays within the limits of his mandate *ad litem*, he needs a specific power of attorney to sign an arbitration agreement on behalf of his client.[35]

(4) Incorporation of an arbitration clause contained in general terms and conditions

3.23 An arbitration clause in the general conditions of one of the parties is effective when the other party was aware or should have been aware of this clause and has accepted the general conditions as such.[36] Thus, a contractor is bound by the arbitration clause, contained in the

---

the written document must be signed by the parties. cf The New York Convention, 1958. Convention on the Recognition and Enforcement of Foreign Arbitral Awards 330 UNTS 38 (4738) 1958, art 2.2.

[27] Cass 27 October 1995, Arr Cass 1995, 922; Bull 1995, 952; Pas 1995, I, 952; RW 1995–96 (excerpt), 1097.

[28] Arbitral award 4 December 1979, [1980] *European Transport Law* 46. See also Labour Court of Appeal Mons 15 November 1979, RRD, 1980, 141, in which the arbitration followed was derived from letters of both parties to the arbitration institution.

[29] The writing is only required *ad probationem* and not *ad validitatem*; see Court of Appeal, Brussels, 4 November 1991, JT 1992, 60; Court of Appeal, Ghent, 6 January 2005, P&B 2005, 148.

[30] Storme, M., 'Aspects importants du droit arbitral belge' [1976] *Rev dr int Com* 119, no 2; Linsmeau, J., 'L'arbitrage volontaire en droit privé belge' *RPDB*, compl Vol VII (Bruylant, 1990), no 80.

[31] Court of Appeal, Liège, 3 March 1982, JL 1982, 301; Court of Appeal, Brussels, 4 November 1991, JT 1992, 60; Commercial Court, Hasselt, 14 June 2000, RW 2000–2001, 1283.

[32] Award 4 December 1979, [1980] *European Transport Law* 46.

[33] Commercial Court, Brussels, 31 May 2001, DCCR 2001, 407.

[34] Keutgen, G. and Dal, G.A. (n 1) 72–3, no 61.

[35] Court of First Instance, Liège, 10 November 1976, *Res Jur Imm* 1977, 137. In this case, the court invalidated an arbitration agreement signed by the counsel of the parties, without a specific power of attorney to that respect. Such a specific power was held to be necessary, as it is also for a renunciation of claim (art 824 Cod Jud) or a resignation (art 1045, Cod Jud).

[36] Court of Appeal, Brussels, 4 November 1991, JT 1992, 60; Court of Appeal, Ghent, 6 January 2005, P&B 2005, 148.

general conditions of the procurement to which he tendered.[37] Similarly, a contractor is bound by the arbitration clause in the general conditions to which the draft agreement referred if he has started the works after he received that draft agreement, even if he did not sign this draft.[38] Similarly, an arbitration clause in general conditions on the reverse of the invoice, if sent after the agreement was concluded, is generally considered to be binding when they have not been objected to.[39]

The party's actual knowledge of the arbitration clause is not relevant. Thus, an arbitration clause in the general conditions of an insurance policy applies even if the insured was not aware of them: the insured has the duty to verify these general conditions before signing the policy.[40] The fact that a party may not have paid attention to the general conditions—and the arbitration clause in particular—does not—as a general rule—prevent that party from being bound.[41] **3.24**

However, a mere mention in the contract that the general conditions can be consulted at the registry of a foreign court, is insufficient to make such a clause binding.[42] **3.25**

(5) Law applicable to the interpretation of arbitration clauses

Arbitration clauses, as part of a contract, have to be interpreted under the law which governs that contract. The Belgian Code de Droit International Privé (16 July 2004)[43] Art 98, has extended the applicability of the 1980 Rome Convention on the Law applicable to Contractual Obligations, which itself did exclude arbitration clauses, to the latter.[44] The Code did not yet refer to the Rome I Regulation which now replaces the Rome Convention. **3.26**

(5.1) Do courts accept a wide competence of the arbitral tribunal or do they restrict arbitral competence? Do claims which arise in connection with the agreement submitted to arbitration generally fall within the arbitral jurisdiction even if based on tortious legal basis? Does there exist case law with respect to the wording in an arbitration clause as 'arising out of/under/in connection with the present contract' and its specific meaning? Belgian courts tend to consider the true intention of the parties, rather than the literal meaning of their agreement. Nevertheless, if the intention of the parties is unclear, the courts interpret the arbitration clause restrictively.[45] For instance, a dispute about the termination of an agreement could not be submitted to arbitration but had to be brought **3.27**

[37] Court of Appeal, Liège, 3 March 1982, JL 1982, 301; Court of Appeal, Brussels, 4 November 1991, JT 1992, 60; see also Court of Appeal, Ghent, 31 October 1996 (unpublished).

[38] Commercial Court, Hasselt, 14 June 2000, JDSC 2002, 59 (summary), RW 2000-01, 1283.

[39] See Van Houtte, H. *et al*, 'Overzicht van Rechtspraak: Arbitrage' (n 25) 111, nos 37–9.

[40] *inter alia,* Court of Appeal, Brussels, 4 November 1991, JT 1992, 60; Court of Appeal, Ghent, 6 January 2005, P&B 2005, 148; Commercial Court, Hasselt, 4 December 2002, P&B 2004, 160; President Commercial Court, Hasselt, 15 February 1999, RDC 1999, 872.

[41] Court of First Instance, Bruges, 4 October 1993, TBR 1994, 90.

[42] Court of Appeal, Ghent, 17 December 2002, P&B 2003, 227.

[43] *Moniteur belge* 27 July 2004.

[44] See Van Houtte, H., 'Commentary on Art. 98' in *Le Code de Droit International Privé Commenté* (Intersentia, 1996) 504.

[45] Keutgen, G., 'L'interprétation de la convention d'arbitrage' in *Liber Amicorum CDVA* (Bruylant, 1997) 344 *et seq*.

before the court because the parties only submitted disputes with regard to the 'interpretation' of the agreement to arbitration.[46]

3.28 Further, claims based on a tortious legal basis do not fall under a clause submitting 'all claims arising from this contract or the construction' to arbitration.[47]

3.29 However, some courts have taken a more lenient approach when interpreting the arbitration clause. Thus, it was found that a (former) shareholder's claim objecting to its exclusion from the company fell under the arbitration clause that submitted all disputes 'between the shareholders' to arbitration, even if the claimant was not a shareholder anymore. Deciding otherwise would give the arbitration clause an overly restrictive scope.[48]

(6) Binding effect of an arbitration clause on third parties (eg in case of a guarantee or assignment)

3.30 Principally, the arbitration agreement only binds those who have made the agreement (Art 1165, Civil Code).[49] Third parties cannot be bound by the arbitration agreement, even if their dispute is closely related to a dispute between the parties to the arbitration agreement. Thus, the courts have jurisdiction to decide a claim between the claimant and one of the respondents, even if the claimant and all other respondents are bound by an arbitration agreement.[50]

3.31 Likewise, a third party cannot be forced to intervene in an arbitration between others.[51] Therefore, the guarantor can only be joined in the arbitration if both the guarantor and all original parties to the arbitration (debtor *and* creditor) agree.[52]

3.32 However, when a contract has been assigned, the assignee is bound by the arbitration clause to the same extent as the assignor originally was.[53] Likewise, the insurer, who has paid the insured on a contractual claim and has been subrogated in its rights, can invoke the arbitration clause from the contract between the insured and his contract partner against the latter.[54]

[46] Court of Appeal, Antwerp, 29 September 1992, *European Transport Law* 1994, 309. See also Court of Appeal, Brussels, 27 April 1999, RDC 2000, 619; Justice of the Peace Berchem, 26 November 1996, T Ap1997, 1, 34. *Contra*: Court of Appeal, Liège, 4 September 1987, JL 1988, 309.

[47] Court of Appeal, Liège, 4 September 1987, JLMB 1988, 309.

[48] Court of Appeal, Brussels, 27 April 1999, JDSC 2001, 92, RDC 2000, 619, TRV 1999, 525.

[49] See *inter alia*, Commercial Court, Verviers, 5 March 1966, JL 1966-67, 93; Commercial Court, Brussels, 12 April 1978, *De Verz* 1981, 258; Justice of the Peace, Ostend, 5 November 2003, *Res Jur Imm* 2005, 347; CEPANI award no 1092, *Receuil*, 385. Not only must the parties be the same, they must also act in the same capacity: see Court of First Instance, Nivelles, 4 June 1993, JLMB 1993, 1155.

[50] Court of Appeal, Liège, 25 June 1982, JL 1982, 341. In the opposite situation, the Commercial Court of Brussels found that the participation of one party that is not bound by the arbitration clause is not an obstacle to the application of that clause vis-à-vis the other parties that are bound by the clause: Commercial Court, Brussels, 30 September 1986, RGAR 1989, no 11.493.

[51] Court of Appeal, Brussels, 22 January 1959, Pas 1959, II, 196. See de Bournonville, P. (n 4) 135 *et seq.*

[52] de Bournonville, P. (n 4) 136–7, no 142. Likewise, the guarantor cannot be joined in an action before the courts if he can invoke an arbitration agreement between himself and the debtor: Cass 20 June 1946, Pas 1946, I, 250; Court of Appeal, Ghent, 14 April 1969, RW 1968-69, 165; Commercial Court, Brussels, 9 August 1973, JT 1974, 623; Commercial Court, Liège, 27 June 1985, *Eur Vervoerr* 1985, 572; Court of Appeal, Ghent, 28 October 1980, RHA 1981-82; Cass 9 November 1995, AJT 1996-97, 46, Arr Cass 1995, 986, Bull 1995, 1018, JT 1997, 97, P&B 1996, 118, Pas 1995, I, 1018, Arr Cass 1996, 383.

[53] See de Bournonville, P. (n 4) 242, no 322.

[54] CEPANI Award 1068, *Receuil*, 48.

Further, under the statute of 29 June 1993, all successor companies are bound by the obligations of their predecessor in case of a company split.[55]

The insurer may invoke the arbitration clause in the insurance contract against the victim, who sues him in court.[56] By contrast, the insurer cannot rely on the arbitration clause in the contract between victim and the insured.[57] Similarly, the bank cannot rely on the arbitration clause in the contract (to which the bank itself is not a party) underlying a documentary credit.[58] **3.33**

On the other hand, it is uncertain to what extent the third holder of the goods will be bound by an arbitration clause in a bill of lading, issued by the carrier to the shipper.[59] **3.34**

(6.1) What is the law/leading authorities' position on multi-party situations? Especially, (i) with respect to the objection that the arbitration clause does not specifically provide for a plurality of parties in the same procedure; (ii) with respect to the constitution of the arbitral tribunal; and (iii) with respect to the consolidation of two or more running arbitration proceedings? Belgian courts apply the privity of the arbitration agreement strictly: when a dispute has arisen among several parties, the parties bound by an arbitration agreement have to go to arbitration to have their part of the dispute settled; on the other hand, the (part of the) dispute between parties that are not bound by an arbitration clause has to be decided by the court. Only when it is strictly impossible to split the settlement of the dispute(s), will the court very exceptionally assume jurisdiction, even over the parties who are bound by an arbitration clause. In case of such 'indivisibility', the proceedings are consolidated before the court.[60] **3.35**

The Arbitration Statute does not provide for multi-party arbitrations or consolidation of arbitration proceedings. The CEPANI Arbitration Rules, however, provide that where there are multiple parties, whether as claimant or as respondent, and where the dispute is referred to three arbitrators, the multiple claimants, jointly, and the multiple respondents, jointly, shall nominate one arbitrator. CEPANI will appoint each member of the arbitral tribunal when the multiple parties on the claimant and/or respondent side cannot agree on the appointment of one arbitrator (Art 9, 3 *in fine*). **3.36**

Moreover, when several contracts, containing an arbitration clause entrusting CEPANI with the arbitration, give rise to disputes which are indivisible *or connected*, CEPANI may order the consolidation of the arbitration proceedings and will appoint its arbitral tribunal, **3.37**

[55] For the situation before this statute, see CEPANI award 1068, *Receuil des Sentences CEPANI* (1985-1995) (Bruylant, 2005) 174.

[56] Court of Appeal, Antwerp, 23 September 2002, P&B 2002, 281.

[57] Justice of the Peace, Brussels, 7 October 1999, DCCR 2000, 363.

[58] Commercial Court, Tongeren, 27 February 2002 (unpublished). The court found that this was a consequence of the autonomous character of the documentary credit.

[59] Court of Appeal, Antwerp, 26 May 2003, NJW 2003, 1296 (third party holder is not bound by arbitration clause in bill of lading since it was not a party when the contract was concluded); Commercial Court, Antwerp, 10 May 1995, Jur Anv 1996, 43 (when deciding whether the holder of the bill of lading is a third party, only the wording of the bill of lading is relevant).

[60] Labour Court of Appeal, Mons, 15 November 1979, R.R.D. 1980, 141; Commercial Court, Hasselt, 4 December 2002, P&B 2004, 160; Commercial Court, Kortrijk, 6 September 2004, TGR 2004, 302; Court of First Instance, Nivelles, 17 June 1975, *Res Jur Imm* 1976, 29.

which may—if necessary—be composed of five arbitrators. Such consolidation, though, is no longer possible when a decision has already been taken in one of the proceedings (CEPANI Rules, Art 12). Belgian authors have extensively examined in detail the several aspects of multi-party arbitration.[61]

3.38 (6.2) **Is there case law/authorities with respect to the admissibility of third party participation in an arbitration without being a claimant or defendant (*Nebenintervention/Streitverkündung*; *intervention forcée/volontaire*; vouching in; *amicus curiae* etc)? What are the prerequisites and effects of such participation (if permitted)?** A third party cannot be obliged to participate in the arbitration proceedings against its will. However, it may request or consent to intervene in arbitration proceedings, so that the award is also binding for it. The third party's intervention will only be admitted when all the parties to the arbitration, as well as each of the arbitrators, agrees with this intervention (Art 1696, bis Cod Jud).

3.39 CEPANI rules do not contain a provision on joinder, intervention or any other type of participation of third parties.

3.40 Belgian law does not provide for submissions by an *amicus curiae* and Belgian arbitration practice is unfamiliar with this phenomenon.

3.41 In any event, the participation of third parties in the arbitral hearings would generally be prevented by Art 17.5, which stipulates that the hearings are private and not open to third parties, unless both the arbitral tribunal and the parties agree.

(7) Termination of an arbitration agreement by a party (reasons and case law)

3.42 An arbitration clause survives the termination of the agreement of which it forms part; it only becomes ineffective when no further dispute, covered by that clause, may arise out of the contract.

3.43 As a rule, the arbitration agreement can only be terminated by the common will of the parties to that agreement. The possibility of a unilateral termination (eg on the basis of fraud) depends on the provisions of the law applicable to the arbitration agreement. The Belgian Code of Civil Procedure does not provide specific reasons for such unilateral termination, nor is there any (published) case law on the subject.[62]

3.44 Nevertheless, there are certain circumstances in which a party can argue that its counterparty may not—or no longer—invoke the arbitration agreement.

3.45 Article 1679, s 1, Cod Jud states that the arbitration agreement must be invoked before every other exception or defence (*in limine litis*). This requirement is not fulfilled when a party before the court starts to argue that the period of limitation has passed and invokes the arbitration agreement only in the alternative that this would not be the case.[63] Similarly, a

[61] See Van Compernolle, J., 'L'arbitrage multipartite' in 'L'Arbitrage –Travaux offerts au Professeur A. Fettweis' (Story, 1989) 81 *et seq*; Van Ommeslaghe, P., 'L'arbitrage multipartite' in *L'arbitrage* (Ed jeune Barreau, Brussels, 1983) 110 *et seq*.

[62] See de Bournonville, P. (n 4) 138–9, no 146.

[63] Court of First Instance, Brussels, 26 June 1990, RGAR 1992, 11.968.

party, who had argued in its first *conclusions* that the claim is inadmissible and that it reserves its arguments on the substance until the expert report is filed, can no longer validly invoke the arbitration clause in its later *conclusions*.[64]

In another case, the parties appointed a medical doctor on the basis of their arbitration agreement. The doctor, however, conducted the proceedings as if he were a mere factual expert and did not render an arbitral award determining the rights of the parties. Because the parties had not objected to the doctor's conduct, they were held to be estopped from invoking the arbitration agreement before the court at the later stage of the proceedings.[65] **3.46**

It is important to note, however, that the arbitration clause is not terminated by the fact that a party has waived the application of the arbitration clause in a particular dispute: the clause remains in force for future disputes. **3.47**

Further, if the arbitration clause determines that a party must appoint its arbitrator within a certain period of time and this party fails to do so, this does not imply that it can no longer invoke the arbitration clause.[66] **3.48**

Finally, bankruptcy of one of the parties does not automatically terminate the arbitration agreement, neither is it a basis for termination. The same is true where a company, which has underwritten the arbitration clause, is dissolved.[67] **3.49**

B. Arbitrability

(1) *'Personal arbitrability' (capacity to conclude arbitration agreements)*

Under Belgian law, any person who may conclude a settlement may agree to arbitration (Art 1676(2), Cod Jud). This implies that minors,[68] mentally incapacitated persons and spendthrifts are subject to specific restrictions and formalities. Spouses may also be restricted to engage in arbitration to the peril of the family patrimony.[69] Parties who have been declared insolvent can no longer agree to arbitration; the receiver, who administers the insolvent estate, has this capacity, but subject to the control of the Insolvency Court. **3.50**

Before the statutory amendment of 1998 Belgian public entities had no capacity to agree to arbitration, except when such capacity was expressly granted by treaty or statute.[70] Since 1998 **3.51**

---

[64] Cass 18 March 1983, Arr Cass 1982-83, 883, Bull 1983, 786, Pas 1983, I, 786, RW 1983-84, 80; see also Court of First Instance, Brussels, 17 March 2000, JT 2001, 740.

[65] Court of Appeal, Brussels, 31 March 1987, JL 1987, 740. See also Commercial Court, Antwerp, 13 June 1983, RHA 1985, 71.

[66] Court of Appeal, Brussels, 27 April 1999, RDC 2000, 619.

[67] Keutgen, G. and Dal, G.A. (n 1) 204, no 198. See also 65, no 49 on arbitration agreements concluded by a party in bankruptcy.

[68] A parent may only conclude an arbitration agreement in the name of their children with the specific permission of the court; see President Court of First Instance, Brussels, 25 June 1993, JT 1993, 668.

[69] cf President Court of First Instance, Mechelen, 27 June 1996, EJ 1997, 11; in this case, the President of the court decided that one of the spouses can conclude an arbitration agreement concerning their common patrimony without the other.

[70] For an overview of the case law in this period, see Van Houtte, H. *et al*, (n 25) 121–2, no 31.

they can conclude arbitration agreements to settle disputes regarding the conclusion or the performance of a contract and for matters authorized by law or royal decree.[71]

3.52 Moreover, under the 1961 European Convention on International Commercial Arbitration, the Belgian state can still agree to arbitration for disputes 'arising or which may arise from international trade'.[72] Under the 1965 ICSID Convention[73] and many bilateral investment treaties Belgium can also participate in investment arbitrations.

3.53 Belgian law does not restrict foreign parties from agreeing to arbitration. Their capacity is governed by their national law.

3.54 (1.1) **May a state (or state agency) as party invoke sovereign immunity before the arbitral tribunal or before a state court (eg in a procedure of enforcement)?** A state has waived its immunity of jurisdiction by agreeing to arbitration. Immunity of enforcement normally depends on the nature of the assets against which enforcement is sought. In one instance, however, the court has inferred a waiver of immunity of enforcement from a treaty provision that the award would be binding once it has obtained the *exequatur* from the court.[74]

(2) 'Objective arbitrability' (eg of patent, trade mark and antitrust matters)

3.55 Arbitration aims at the settlement of a legal dispute. Unlike a (non-binding) expert decision, arbitration implies a decision on legal rights and duties, not on mere facts.[75] Moreover, parties can only submit the legal dispute to arbitration when they can also settle themselves the rights and duties involved (Art 1676.1, Cod Jud). Consequently, some issues of domestic and EU competition rules are not arbitrable. For instance, an arbitrator cannot individually exempt an agreement under the Belgian 1999 Competition Statute or the EU competition rules, decide on a complaint of antitrust violation or allow a merger to occur; only the *Conseil de la Concurrence* (and/or the EU Commission) has the authority to do so. However, the arbitrator may determine that an infringement of competition law has been committed and grant compensation.[76]

3.56 Moreover, parties cannot validly include an arbitration clause in employment contracts (save for contracts engaging senior management);[77] employment disputes can, however,

[71] Keutgen, G., 'La nouvelle loi sur l'arbitrage' [1998] *JT* 761 *et seq.*

[72] European Convention on International Commercial Arbitration signed in Geneva on 25 April 1961 (Belgian Law of 19 July 1975).

[73] *Convention on the Settlement of Investment Disputes Between States and Nationals of Other States* (Washington Convention) (adopted 18 March 1965, entered into force 14 October 1966) 575 UNTS 159, 17 UST 1270 (Belgian Law of 17 July 1970).

[74] Court of First Instance, Brussels, 13 March 1992, *Act Dr* 1992, 1377.

[75] Leuven, 22 January 1997, TBBR 1998, 154. See also Arbitral Award 23 August 1984, RGAR 1989, no. 11.534; Criminal Court of First Instance, Nivelles, 9 January 1981, JT 1981, 416; Court of Appeal, Ghent, 27 May 1983, RDC 1987, 209; Criminal Court of First Instance, Marche-en Famenne, 27 February 1992, JLMB 1991, 821; Court of Appeal, Liège, 29 February 2000, JLMB 2000, 1164; Court of Appeal, Mons, 28 October 1999, RRD 2000, 90 and Court of Appeal, Mons, 12 January 1993, JLMB 1993 (excerpt), 1002.

[76] Keutgen, G. and Dal, G.A. (n 1), no 117–18.

[77] Verheyden, T., 'Les contrats de travail' *Rénot,* t. XVI, 1, I, éd 1988, no 100; Labour Court, Hasselt, 24 June 1974, RW 1975-76, 372; Labour Court, Mons, 15 November 1979, *Rev rég dr,* 1980, 141; arbitral award 22 February 1982, TSR 1983, 221; Labour Court of Appeal, Brussels, 8 March 1982, JTT, 1982, 268; Labour Court, Ieper, 24 May 1985, De Verz. 1986, 391; Labour Court of Appeal, Ghent, 28 March 1986, RW 1987-88, 817; Brussels, 13 March 1992, Act dr, 1992, 1377.

always be submitted to arbitration by common agreement of the parties after the dispute has arisen (Art 1678.2, Cod Jud).

Likewise, an arbitration clause in a Belgian distribution contract is invalid for disputes with regard to the termination of that contract when the arbitration would take place outside of Belgium and non-Belgian law would be applicable.[78] Similarly, no arbitration clause with regard to an agency in Belgium would be valid when the arbitration would have its seat outside the EU and a non-EU law would be applicable.[79] **3.57**

Corporate disputes, even over the dissolution of a company, can be arbitrated.[80] However, a company's nullity can only be established by the state courts. **3.58**

Disputes over patents are generally arbitrable (Art 73.6, Patent Law 1984).[81] Also disputes involving trade marks (except for '*licences mandatoires*'), design and copyright are arbitrable. **3.59**

However, for many types of insurance,[82] such as car or fire insurance, future disputes cannot be the subject matter of an arbitration clause;[83] it is only after the dispute has arisen that parties may agree to submit it to arbitration.[84] **3.60**

C. Decision on the arbitral tribunal's jurisdiction ('*competence-competence*')

(1) Separability, (independence of the arbitration agreement from the main agreement)

The invalidity of the contract does not automatically entail the nullity of the arbitration clause it contains (Art 1697.2, Cod Jud).[85] This is *inter alia* also confirmed by CEPANI Rules, Art 5.4: 'unless otherwise agreed, the Arbitral Tribunal shall not cease to have jurisdiction by reason of the nullity or non-existence of the contract, provided that the Arbitral Tribunal upholds the validity of the arbitration agreement.' **3.61**

(2) Competence of the tribunal to decide on its own jurisdiction (including form and time of the tribunal's decision)

The arbitral tribunal has the (exclusive) power to decide on its own jurisdiction and thus on the validity of the arbitration agreement (Art 1697.1, Cod Jud).[86] The arbitral tribunal **3.62**

---

[78] See *inter alia* Cass 15 October 2004, RW 2004-2005, 1063, TBH 2005, 488; Hollander, P., 'L'arbitrabilité des litiges en matière de résiliation de concession de vente soumises à la loi du 27 juillet 1961: fin de la controverse ?' *TBH* 2005, 493 *et seq*; Keutgen, G. and Dal, G.A. (n 1) no. 126- 8.

[79] For an overview and analysis of the caselaw in this field, see Van Houtte, H. (n 25) 116–20, no 16–23.

[80] *Contra* Cass 2 February 1973, Arr Cass 1973, 555 and Pas 1973, I, 529; meanwhile, however, it is generally accepted that disputes touching public policy issues can be subject to arbitration; therefore, the reasoning in this decision would no longer apply; see Van Houtte, H. *et al* (n 25) 120, no 26.

[81] De Gryse, L., 'Quelques propos sur l'arbitrage en matière de brevets d'inventions' in *Mélanges A Braun Jura Vigilantibus* (Larcier, 1987) 89.

[82] This restriction is aimed at protecting the insured's right of acces to the Courts. For an interesting analysis, see arbitral award 30 December 1991, *Act Dr* 1992, 1413.

[83] An arbitration clause in a hospitalization insurance contract, however, is admissible; see Commercial Court, Brussels, 16 June 2003, RDC 2003, 900.

[84] Van Houtte, H., 'Arbitrage en assurances' [2002] *Bulletin des Assurances*, 285– 99.

[85] Confirmed *inter alia* by Cass 22 October 1987, Pas 1988, I, 107; Commercial Court, Tournai 18 October 1984, RDC 1986, 70; Brussels, 5 November 2004, NJW 2005, 671. *Contra (incorrectly)*: Court of Appeal, Brussels, 24 September 1980, *De Verz* 1981, 285.

[86] *Inter alia* Commercial Court, Tournai, 18 October 1984, RDC 1986, 70. *Contra (incorrectly)*: Court of Appeal, Brussels, 24 September 1980, *De Verz* 1981, 285.

may either address the challenge to its jurisdiction together with the merits or render a preliminary, partial award on jurisdiction. The latter can only be challenged with the award on the merits (Art 1697.3, Cod Jud).

3.63 In CEPANI arbitrations, the institution only carries out a prima facie examination of the arbitration agreement to set up the arbitration tribunal; it is this tribunal which will have full jurisdiction to decide on its own competence (Art. 4 and 5.3 CEPANI Rules).

(3) Extent of the 'competence-competence' *and role of the courts (including form and time limits of a challenge of the tribunal's decision)*

3.64 Once the arbitral tribunal (with seat in Belgium) has established its jurisdiction and proceeds to the merits, Belgian courts can no longer hear the merits of the case. They cannot set aside the award on jurisdiction either, but have to wait until an award on the merits has been rendered too. When the tribunal renders a partial award on the merits, the award on jurisdiction has to be challenged together with this partial award on the merits. The time limits to challenge the award on the merits have to be respected for a challenge of the award on jurisdiction. If the court then finds that the tribunal has incorrectly assumed jurisdiction, it will set aside the award on the merits (and also the preliminary award on jurisdiction if a separate award has been rendered) because the arbitral tribunal has exceeded its jurisdiction (Art 1704.2.f, Cod Jud).[87]

3.65 A challenge based on the lack of jurisdiction of the arbitral tribunal, follows the same form as a challenge based on other grounds (see at 3.263, *infra*).

D. Enforcement of an arbitration agreement within or by court proceedings

(1) Effects of invoking an arbitration clause within court proceedings (and time limits for such a motion)

3.66 A Belgian judge will refuse to hear a case on the merits in the face of a valid arbitration agreement (Art 1679.1, Cod Jud)—regardless whether the seat of arbitration will be in Belgium or abroad. Thereto, however, the arbitration clause must be invoked *in limine litis*, ie at the beginning of the procedure and before any other arguments (Art 1679(1), Cod Jud).[88] A party has accepted the court's jurisdiction if it raises the existence of the arbitration agreement for the first time in additional briefs[89] or only on appeal.[90] The court may not invoke the arbitration clause *sua sponte,*[91] since it does not affect public policy.[92]

3.67 There is no *lis pendens* when a party has started an arbitration proceeding and the other party starts court proceedings. Indeed, there can be no *lis pendens* between the state courts

---

[87] See eg Court of First Instance, Tongeren, 15 January 1997, *Limb Rechsl* 1997, 158.

[88] Court of First Instance, Neufchâteau, 21 June 1978, RRD 1979, 743; Commercial Court, Brussels, 16 January 1991, RDC.1992, 137. *Contra* (incorrectly) Commercial Court, Antwerp, 22 June 1992, *Eur Vervoerr* 1994, 74.

[89] Cass 18 March 1983, Arr Cass 1982-83, 883, Bull 1983, Brussels, 17 March 2000, JT, 2001, 740.

[90] Court of Appeal, Mons, 23 September 1992, JLMB, 549.

[91] Commercial Court, Tongeren, 18 March 1976, BRH 1976, 501.

[92] Court of First Instance, Neufchâteau, 21 June 1978, RRD 1979, 743; Mons 23 September 1992, JLMB 1994, 549.

and an arbitral tribunal.[93] It is up to the parties themselves to end the proceedings before the courts by invoking the arbitration clause. The arbitral tribunal does not have to order the parties to do so.[94]

Further, pursuant to Art 1679(2), Cod Jud, parties can still petition the state court for preservation or interim measures. 3.68

(1.1) **If a party has invoked successfully the arbitration agreement in a court proceeding, is it then entitled to deny within the arbitral proceeding that there is a valid and binding arbitration agreement?** The judgment dismissing the case because of a valid arbitration clause would be *res judicata* between the same parties; its recognition could be requested from the arbitrators so that the arbitrators have to accept their jurisdiction. However, it is uncertain what would be the consequences if the arbitrators were not to recognize the court's decision declaring that they have jurisdiction, eg because in their opinion there is no valid and binding arbitration agreement. It is unlikely that the arbitral award, dismissing the claim for lack of jurisdiction, could be challenged on that basis. 3.69

(1.2) ***Vice versa*, if a party has successfully objected to an arbitral proceeding by denying that there is a valid arbitration agreement, may it then invoke such agreement in the ensuing court proceeding?** The arbitral decision that the arbitrators had no jurisdiction because of the invalidity of the arbitration clause has *res judicata* and its recognition could be requested from the court. Moreover, the admission by a party that the arbitration clause was invalid can be considered as an 'aveu judiciaire', which binds this party in other proceedings (Art1356, Civil code). 3.70

(2) Legal remedies and proceedings to enforce an arbitration agreement.

A Belgian court cannot force an unwilling party to participate in arbitration proceedings. It will only refuse to hear itself the merits of the case. Moreover, upon request, it may also appoint an arbitrator instead of that unwilling party, so that the arbitral tribunal can be constituted and the arbitration can proceed—if necessary with the unwilling party defaulting. 3.71

Further, courts have systematically rejected unwilling parties' attempts to challenge the jurisdiction of the arbitral tribunal (directly or indirectly) at stages in the proceedings where such a challenge is not possible (yet). It has been suggested that courts may/should strengthen the principle that the arbitrators' jurisdiction should not be challenged before they have rendered an award on the merits by granting compensation for such frivolous or vexatious proceedings.[95] 3.72

(2.1) Which would be the internationally competent court: (i) for obtaining a declaration that an arbitration agreement is valid and binding; or (ii) to compel arbitration? 3.73

---

[93] Labour Court of Appeal, Mons, 15 November 1979, RRD 1980, 141; Court of Appeal, Liège, 25 June, 1982, JL 1982, 341.

[94] Arbitral award 22 February 1991, *Eur Vervoerr* 1992, 400.

[95] See *inter alia* Court of Appeal, Brussels, 30 November 2004, *Tijdschrift@ipr.be* 2006, no 1, 43 and the note by K. Cox, 'Wie niet horen wil, moet verzet aantekenen tegen de benoeming van een arbiter door de rechter' 99.

(The defendant's courts? The courts of the place of arbitration? The claimant's courts, cf Art 6(2) in fine, ICC Rules?) Any court, where the case on the merits is brought, may address an objection to its jurisdiction and thus rule on the validity of the arbitration clause. In the present state of the law, it seems excluded that Belgian courts, which have not been requested to decide on the merits, would issue a mere declaratory judgment that an arbitration agreement is valid.

III. The arbitral tribunal

A. Number and qualification of arbitrators

(1) Sole arbitrator or arbitral tribunal with several arbitrators

3.74 The arbitrators have to be uneven in number. If the parties have not agreed otherwise, Art 1682, Cod Jud states that a tribunal should be composed of three arbitrators; the CEPANI Rules, by contrast, opt in that event for a sole arbitrator unless CEPANI decides, in view of the importance of the dispute, to appoint three arbitrators at the request of one of the parties or on its own motion (Art 9.5, CEPANI Rules).

3.75 (1.1) **Are arbitral tribunals with an even number of arbitrators acceptable?** An even number of arbitrators is a ground for setting aside the award for the reason that the tribunal has been irregularly composed (Art 1704.2, Cod Jud). However, when the parties had been aware of this irregularity during the proceedings, they have waived this ground for annulment.[96] An exception has been made in a case where the parties were laymen for whom it was not possible to figure out which one of the persons present at the hearing was an arbitrator or merely a case reporter.[97]

3.76 Nevertheless, if the arbitration agreement provides for an even number of arbitrators, the agreement is not invalid; an even number merely entails that an additional arbitrator has to be appointed.[98]

3.77 A (sole) arbitrator is allowed to rely on a legal adviser. This adviser is not deemed to be a (second) member of the 'arbitral tribunal'.[99]

(2) Qualification of the arbitrators

3.78 An arbitrator must in all events have the capacity to conclude contracts and dispose of his political rights (Art 1680, Cod Jud). Apart from that, Belgian law does not impose specific requirements to be an arbitrator. The parties, however, are free to demand from their arbitrators certain characteristics or exclude certain categories of persons (Art 1692.1, Cod Jud).

---

96 Court of First Instance, Mons, 21 March 2000, RRD 2001, 55.

97 Court of First Instance, Mons, 3 November 1998, *Cah dr immo* 1999, 15.

98 Arbitration award 4 December 1979, *Eur Vervoerr* 1980, 46; Court of Appeal, Antwerp, 14 October 1987, Pas 1988, II, 31; see also Brussels, 26 June 1990, RGAR 1992, 11.968 in which the court remarked that according to the arbitration agreement each party had to appoint one arbitrator, without attaching further consequences to this remark.

99 Court of Appeal, Antwerp, 11 February 1991, Pas 1991, II, 108.

(2.1) Are there mandatory requirements for the qualification of arbitrators (statutory requirements or indirect requirements through eg general conditions of insurance contracts)? There are no further statutory or other requirements to act as an arbitrator. 3.79

(2.2) Which national arbitration institutions may be contacted for obtaining information about qualified (and specialized) arbitrators? CEPANI has a members' yearbook which can be consulted at the CEPANI secretariat and which will be soon made available on its website. 3.80

(2.3) Are judges or civil servants required to obtain permission by their employer to act as arbitrator? Are these permissions given generally or case-by-case? What are the consequences if such permission has not been obtained? It seems excluded that a full time judge in function will get the authorization from his superiors to sit in an arbitration. Part-time judges, such as the 'lay-judges' in the Commercial Court may act as arbitrators but will have to ask for permission. In no event, however, may a judge—even after his retirement—be remunerated for his arbitration services (Art 298, Cod Jud).[100] Contrary to the situation in other countries, (former) judges will thus very seldom be arbitrators. 3.81

B. Appointment of arbitrators

(1) Extent of party autonomy to establish appointment procedure

The parties are quite free in the appointment of the arbitrators. They can specify the mechanics of the appointment in the arbitration clause or merely refer therein to the rules of an arbitral institution. However, under the CEPANI Rules (Art 9), the appointment committee of this arbitration institution needs to approve the parties' nominations, taking into account the availability, the qualifications and the ability of the arbitrator to conduct the arbitration in accordance with the Rules. Where the CEPANI Appointments Committee or its chairman refuses to approve the nomination of the arbitrator, that party shall proceed with the replacement within one month of the notification of this refusal. 3.82

(2) Procedure in absence of an agreement by the parties

If the parties have to nominate a sole arbitrator but cannot reach agreement on an appointment within one month after the request for arbitration, the CEPANI Appointment Committee (in case of CEPANI arbitration) will nominate the sole arbitrator. In the case of an *ad hoc* arbitration the appointment will be made by the President of the Civil Court if parties have not reached an agreement on the appointment within one month; his decision is not open for appeal (Art 1684. 2; Art 1686.1, Cod Jud). 3.83

In the event three arbitrators need to be appointed, the claimant should nominate 'his' arbitrator in the request for arbitration and invite the respondent to nominate 'his' arbitrator within 30 days (Art 1684.1). 3.84

In case of CEPANI arbitration, when the respondent does not nominate 'his' arbitrator in due time the CEPANI Appointment Committee will do so instead. The chairman then 3.85

[100] Krings, E., 'Un magistrat de l'ordre judiciaire peut-il être désigné en tant qu'arbitre?' [1976] *RDIDC* 278.

should be appointed by CEPANI, unless the parties have agreed that the appointment would be made by the two arbitrators, already appointed. However, if they fail to make such appointment, CEPANI will make it.

3.86 With *ad hoc* arbitration, on the other hand, the general principle is that the two arbitrators should in common agreement appoint a third arbitrator-chairman. If they are unable to make such appointment within 30 days, the President of the Civil Court, once again, can make the appointment and his decision is not open for appeal (Art 1685; Art 1686.1 Cod Jud).

(3) Effect of the refusal of one party to cooperate in the constitution of the arbitral tribunal

3.87 If the arbitral tribunal consists of three arbitrators, a party has to appoint an arbitrator within one month after the notice of arbitration. If no such appointment has been made within that period, the other side can request the President of the Court of First Instance to make such appointment (Art 1684.1, Cod Jud). In the event of an arbitration by a sole arbitrator and if no agreement on the identity of the sole arbitrator can be reached by the parties within one month after the notice of arbitration, any party can likewise request the President of the Court of First Instance to make such appointment (Art 1684.2, Cod Jud).

3.88 Under the CEPANI Rules, Arts 9, 2 and 3, the parties likewise have to agree on the nomination of a sole arbitrator within one month after the request for arbitration has been submitted to the CEPANI Secretariat or within any other time period granted by the CEPANI Secretariat. In the event of an arbitral tribunal with three arbitrators, the defendant has equally to nominate an arbitrator in principle within one month after the submission of the request for arbitration or within any other period authorized by the CEPANI Secretariat. In the event that no such nomination has been made within the imposed time frame, the CEPANI Appointment Committee will make such nomination instead and appoint the arbitrator.

(4) Circumstances and valid reasons for an arbitrator to resign

3.89 An arbitrator may resign because of illness or legal impediment (Art 1680, Cod Jud). He has to request the authorization of the Court of First Instance to resign (Art 1689, Cod Jud). Whenever an arbitrator has been successfully challenged, his resignation follows from the institution's or court's decision to remove the arbitrator.

C. Challenge and replacement of arbitrators

(1) Grounds, procedure and deadlines for challenging an arbitrator

3.90 Article 1690.1, Cod Jud provides that arbitrators may be challenged 'when circumstances arise which cause legitimate doubts regarding their impartiality or independence'.

3.91 According to Art 1690.1, Cod Jud, arbitrators must be independent and impartial. Being the spouse, parent, business associate, counsel, notary, employee or important shareholder of one of the parties makes one unfit to be arbitrator in a dispute with such party as bias is presumed.

3.92 The arbitrators need to be independent at the moment they are appointed *and* must remain so throughout the whole procedure. Otherwise they can be challenged. However, parties can renounce this independence and impartiality requirement. A 'party-arbitrator', ie an arbitrator appointed by a party, does not represent the latter's interests and must stay as independent and impartial as eg a sole arbitrator or a tribunal's chairman.

CEPANI requests their arbitrators to sign a 'statement of independence' in which they have to disclose 'in writing to the Secretariat any facts or circumstances which might be of such a nature so as to call into question the arbitrator's independence in the eyes of the parties'. Facts or circumstances of a similar nature arising during the arbitration procedure should be disclosed immediately whenever they arise (Art 8 CEPANI Rules). The requirements of independence and impartiality are further specified in the CEPANI's 'Rules of Good Conduct', which state, *inter alia*, that once the tribunal has been appointed, all contacts with the arbitrators will go through the chairman and that the arbitrator will avoid any suspicion of partiality, eg when questioning parties at the hearing. **3.93**

An arbitrator can be challenged for lack of independence until the award is rendered. However, the arbitrator must be notified of the reasons for challenge as soon as the circumstances giving rise to doubts regarding his impartiality or independence are known to the party (Art 1691.1, Cod Jud). Otherwise, it will be assumed that the party did not consider these doubts legitimate or important enough. Indeed, the lack of independence or impartiality of an arbitrator is no ground for setting aside an award (1704.5, Cod Jud) if the relevant facts were known before the award was rendered. **3.94**

Under Art 1690.2, Cod Jud, the arbitrator is given 10 days to decide whether to withdraw because of the challenge. In the meanwhile the arbitral proceedings are suspended. In the event that the arbitrator does not withdraw within 10 days, the arbitral tribunal notifies the challenging party thereof. The latter then has 10 days to summon the challenged arbitrator and the other parties before the Court of First Instance. If this time bar is not respected, the right to challenge is forfeited and the arbitral proceedings resume (Art 1691.2, Cod Jud). **3.95**

Challenges of CEPANI arbitrators have to be brought before a specific Committee on Challenges. A party has, however, 30 days after the discovery of the ground for challenge, to submit his request. The challenged arbitrator, the other arbitrators and all the parties are invited to submit their written comments on the request for challenge. The Committee on Challenges then decides on the challenge.[101] **3.96**

(1.1) Do state courts review challenge procedures which took place in accordance with a specific procedure agreed upon by the parties (eg Art 11 ICC Rules)? If so, at what point in time? May such review be excluded? It is generally accepted that the reference to the arbitration rules which provide for procedures regarding the challenge of an arbitrator (eg Art 10 of the CEPANI Rules), constitutes the parties' waiver of their right of challenge before a state court. Conversely, the Court of Appeal of Brussels has held that a party always has the right to petition the state court to challenge an arbitrator; that right is only suspended as long as the challenge is brought before the arbitration institution, but revives once the institution has denied the challenge.[102] **2.97**

[101] See <http://www.cepani.be> under 'Comité de Récusation'.

[102] Court of Appeal, Brussels, 21 June 2005, R.G. 2004/AR/3106, unpublished.

3.98 (1.2) **Is there case law with respect to truncated arbitral tribunals? (cf Article 12(5) ICC Rules)** Article 1691.3, Cod Jud expressly provides that the arbitrator who has withdrawn from the case, has to be replaced.

(2) Procedure for appointing a new arbitrator

3.99 Under Art 1691.3, Cod Jud, an arbitrator who has withdrawn or has been successfully challenged has to be replaced and a new arbitrator has to be appointed in the way provided for the original appointment. Article 11 of the CEPANI Rules gives the Appointments Committee or the chairman discretion to decide whether or not to follow the original appointment process.

IV. The arbitral procedure

A. General principles

(1) Extent of party autonomy to determine the arbitral procedure

3.100 The parties can establish the arbitral procedure in the arbitration agreement, or at a later stage but within the time limit set by the arbitral tribunal. If they fail to do so, the arbitral tribunal will determine the procedural rules (Art 1693.1, Cod Jud).

3.101 However, the procedural rules, which the arbitrators establish, should be fair and treat the parties equally. If they would favour one side, parties would no longer be bound to the arbitration agreement (Art 1678.1, Cod Jud).

3.102 (1.1) **Are the parties free to choose any national or international law governing the procedure before the arbitral tribunal?** The parties can choose any national or international law to govern the proceedings before the arbitral tribunal on condition that the rules are fair and equitable and comply with the mandatory principles of Belgian arbitration procedure. Indeed, a breach of these principles may entail the setting aside of the award (Art 1704.2g Cod Jud).

(2) Basic procedural principles or mandatory rules to be applied by the arbitral tribunal

3.103 The main limitations to the freedom of the parties or the tribunal regarding the arbitral procedure concern the fundamental procedural guarantees: equality of the parties, contradictory debate, rights of defence, the neutrality of the tribunal and the obligation to motivate the award.[103]

(3) Oral hearing or proceeding on basis of written documents

3.104 The arbitral tribunal generally renders its award after the 'oral presentations' of the parties (Art 1694.2 Cod Jud), except if they have waived this possibility (Art 1694.3, Cod Jud). The tribunal sets the date of the hearings taking into account the convenience and availability of the parties and notifies them thereof.

[103] Keutgen, G. and Dal, G.A.(n 1) 307–11, nos. 374–7.

In case a validly notified party fails to appear at the hearings, the tribunal is allowed to proceed and settle the dispute (Art 1695 Cod Jud), unless the party that is present requires a postponement or unless the absent party has a 'legitimate excuse'. Obviously, if a party is validly notified and cannot present a 'legitimate excuse', it is barred from arguing that it has not been heard. 3.105

(4) Power of the tribunal, especially the chairman, to issue procedural orders

The arbitration statute and the CEPANI Rules do not expressly provide for procedural orders. However, in fact, procedural orders are commonly issued to arrange practical matters or procedural issues. In proceedings with three arbitrators, they very often are only signed by the chairman but after consultation with his co-arbitrators. It is good practice to include in the terms of reference the possibility of procedural orders and of the chairman alone signing them. 3.106

(5) Distinction of matters of substance and matters of procedure

Belgian arbitration law interprets matters of procedure quite restrictively: whenever the merits are affected, substance and not procedure is at stake. 3.107

(5.1) Are the statutes of limitations a matter of substance or rather of procedure? Under Belgian law—as confirmed by its international private law—statutes of limitations are a matter of substance.[104] 3.108

(6) Persons able to represent a party in an arbitral proceeding

The parties do not need to be represented by an 'avocat', although that is often the case. The 'avocat' has not to prove his '*mandatio ad litem*'. He can sign briefs, attend hearings, etc without specific powers of attorney. However, the parties themselves should sign the arbitration agreement, the terms of reference and possible requests to challenge arbitrators. If their 'avocat' signs such documents, the latter should have specific powers of attorney therefor. 3.109

The parties can appear themselves before the arbitrators or be represented by any person admitted by the arbitrators as their representative. However, representation by 'agents d'affaires'—ie persons who operate in the border zone between law and business, such as brokers, accountants, debt collectors—is excluded (Art 1694.4, Cod Jud). 3.110

B. Place of arbitration

The parties are free to choose the place of arbitration. They can do so in the arbitration clause or thereafter. If the arbitral tribunal has been constituted but the parties have still failed to choose the place of arbitration, the arbitrators may impose a deadline to do so. 3.111

(1) Determination of the place of arbitration in absence of an agreement by the parties

If the parties have not agreed on the place of arbitration within the deadline imposed by the arbitral tribunal, the arbitrators may select themselves the place of arbitration. 3.112

[104] Erauw, J., *Handboek Belgisch Internationaal Privaatrecht 2006* (Kluwer, 2006) nos 143, 491 and 500.

3.113 In CEPANI arbitrations, the Appointment Committee will determine the place of arbitration if the parties have not done so (Art 15, CEPANI Rules).

3.114 If no seat of arbitration has been chosen by either the parties or the tribunal, the place of arbitration is presumed to be the place where the award was rendered, as stated in the award.

(2) Importance and legal effect of place (seat) of the arbitration

3.115 The seat of arbitration determines the court that has jurisdiction to intervene during the arbitral procedure and to decide on annulment proceedings after the award has been rendered (Art. 1717.2, Cod Jud). Art 1717.2 thus helps to select the territorially competent court within Belgium. However, the principle underlying Art 1717.2 is also relevant to determine the transnational jurisdiction of Belgian courts as a whole. It grants Belgian courts jurisdiction over each arbitration which has its seat in Belgium so that the arbitration process falls under the scrutiny of Belgian courts which will apply the Belgian arbitration law to it. The law of the seat of arbitration determines the rules regarding the composition of the tribunal, the validity of the arbitration agreement and the effect of the award.

3.116 (2.1) **Are the arbitrators and parties free to convene at places other than the official seat of the arbitration?** Arbitrators are free to set up hearings and meetings in a location other than the place of arbitration, unless the parties have agreed otherwise (Art 1993.2, Cod Jud).

3.117 In CEPANI arbitrations and after consultation with the parties, the arbitral tribunal may decide to hold its hearings and meetings at any other location that it considers appropriate, unless the parties agree otherwise (Art 15.2, CEPANI Rules).

3.118 (2.2) **Are there visa requirements to enter the country which apply to lawyers and/or arbitrators? Where may current information on that subject be obtained?** Information about possible visa requirements can be obtained from the website of the Belgian Ministry of Foreign Affairs: <http://www.diplomatie.be/en/travel/visa/default.asp>.

C. Submissions, deadlines and default

(1) Contents and form of submissions (in particular request for arbitration and answer to request)

3.119 Article 1683 of the Cod Jud requires that the request for arbitration refers to the arbitration agreement and mentions the subject matter of the dispute. When the parties have to select the arbitrators, the request should indicate the arbitrator selected by the claimant and invite the respondent to do the same. If a third body has to appoint the arbitrator, the request should also invite it to do so.

3.120 The request for arbitration can be submitted by ordinary mail, although registered mail is the general practice.

3.121 For CEPANI arbitrations, Art 1 of the CEPANI Rules specifies what the request for arbitration should contain, *inter alia*, the full identity of the parties, a description of the dispute, of the claims and their grounds and, if possible, an estimate of the amounts claimed, all useful information for the appointment of the arbitrator(s) and—whenever proper—a suggested nomination and specifics about the place of arbitration and the applicable rules of law. A copy of the arbitration agreement, of the relevant contracts and correspondence between the parties and of other useful documents should be attached to the request. The request has to be submitted to CEPANI in as many copies as there will be arbitrators plus one extra copy for the CEPANI Secretariat.

The Code of Civil Procedure does not discuss the answer to the request. In CEPANI arbitrations, the answer, which has to address the several elements of the request, should be submitted within a month after CEPANI has received said request (Art 2, CEPANI Rules). 3.122

(1.1) From what point in time is a claim considered to be pending before the arbitral tribunal? What are the legal effects of such fact (eg on statutes of limitations)? The arbitral proceedings start with the submission of the request for arbitration; ie in CEPANI arbitrations when the secretariat receives the request (eg Art 1.3, CEPANI Rules); in *ad hoc* arbitrations, when the request for arbitration has been notified to the respondent (Art 1683, Cod Jud). This submission suspends eg time bars and statute of limitations. In transnational disputes, it is the *lex causae*, ie the law applicable to the merits (generally the proper law of contract), that provides for the relevant time bars and statutes of limitations.[105] 3.123

(1.2) When is a time limit according to statutes of limitations deemed to be interrupted in case of: (i) *ad hoc*; and (ii) institutional arbitration? In CEPANI arbitrations a time limit is deemed to be interrupted as of the submission of the request for arbitration to the CEPANI Secretariat;[106] in *ad hoc* arbitrations as of its notification to the respondent. 3.124

(1.3) What is the effect of the withdrawal of the request for arbitration? By analogy to the rules on 'désistement d'instance' in Belgian courts,[107] a request for arbitration can only be withdrawn without the consent of the respondent as long as the latter has not yet submitted its answer to the request. If the respondent has submitted its answer, the respondent's consent is required. 3.125

(2) Legal deadlines (provided by law or set by the tribunal) and effect of non-compliance by a party

The Belgian arbitration statute does not impose legal deadlines to submit briefs and documents. The arbitral tribunal, however, often establishes a procedural calendar for these submissions. CEPANI Rules, Art 16.3, for instance instructs the arbitral tribunal to establish such a calendar together with the terms of reference or as soon as possible thereafter. When a party considers an imposed deadline too short, eg because of the occurrence of unforeseen difficulties, it has to request the arbitral tribunal for an extension sufficiently ahead of the deadline to be extended. Arbitrators have decided that a small delay in the submission of briefs should not be sanctioned as long as it does not hurt the opposing party. In their opinion, non-respect of these deadlines should not be sanctioned by nullity or exclusion and arbitrators should not engage in strict formalism. However, when a party has received an extension of a deadline or has overrun the deadline, very often the corresponding deadline of the other party will be extended to restore equality. 3.126

105 Erauw, J., *Handboek Belgisch Internationaal Privaatrecht 2006* (Kluwer, 2006) no 143, 491 and 500.
106 See CEPANI Rules, art 1.3.
107 art 820–7, Cod Jud.

3.127 (2.1) **What are the powers of the tribunal if a party fails to comply with the time limits set up by the tribunal?** In principle, arbitrators have the power to discard whatever has not been submitted within the time limits. In fact they will not easily do so and try to find a compromise between the necessity to respect procedural time limits and the preservation of a party's right to present its arguments.

3.128 (2.2) **Is the tribunal bound by any mandatory time limits for certain procedural steps (eg hearings, making of the award)?** Before any arbitrator has accepted his appointment, the parties can agree on a time limit for rendering the award or on a time schedule for the successive procedural steps. Once the first arbitrator has accepted his appointment, they are unable to impose time limits.

3.129 Under the CEPANI Arbitration Rules, the award should be rendered within four months after the tribunal's signature of the terms of reference. However, the CEPANI Secretariat may extend this time limit, either on its own initiative or on the reasoned request of the tribunal (Art 19 of the CEPANI Rules).

3.130 In the event that no time limits have been imposed by the parties or the arbitration rules to which they referred, and when the arbitrators have already been in office for six months but are being slow in rendering their award, each of the parties can request the *Tribunal de Première Instance/Rechtbank van Eerste Aanleg* to impose a time limit upon the arbitral tribunal (Art 1698.2, Cod Jud).

(3) Statutory requirements as to notifications during an arbitration (with respect to the request for arbitration and other written pleadings; with respect to notifications by the tribunal)

3.131 The arbitration statute requests a 'notification/kennisgeving' for the request for arbitration, for a challenge of an arbitrator and for the Award (Arts 1683, 1691 and 1702, Cod Jud). Such notification may be made by ordinary mail (Art 33, Cod Jud). However, the date of these notifications is often crucial to assess whether the notification has occurred within the imposed time frame; sometimes the notification itself may be the starting point of a time period to be respected. Consequently, it is wise to make these notifications with registered mail (with acknowledgement of receipt) or by special courier—so that the exact date of the notification can be easily proven.

3.132 The arbitration statute does not mention specific mechanics for the submission of pleadings. Under Art 7.1 of the CEPANI Rules notifications may be made by registered mail, against acknowledgement of receipt, by special courier, by telecopy or by any other means which gives evidence of notification.

(4) Effect of the insolvency of a party

3.133 Whenever a party becomes insolvent, the *curateur* of the insolvent estate *has* to decide whether he will continue the arbitral proceedings and will have to ask to that effect the approval of the court supervising the bankruptcy.[108]

[108] Loi du 8 août 1997 sur les faillites, art 58. See also T'Kint, F., 'Convention d'arbitrage et faillite' in *L'Arbitrage dans la vie des sociétés* (Bruylant, 1999) 226.

D. Facts and evidence: general

(1) Burden of proof (inquisitorial/adversarial procedure)

Arbitrators do not have the task of gathering evidence. This is the parties' responsibility. Belgian arbitration practice applies an adversarial procedure to gather evidence whereby each party has the burden to submit its own evidence (*actori incumbit probation).* **3.134**

The arbitration statute grants the tribunal the power to order an investigation or examination, to oblige a party to be personally present at the hearing, to order a witness to take an oath and to order a party to produce a document (Art 1696.1, Cod Jud). These powers will only be used when requested by a party and when the tribunal considers these measures essential for the conduct of the proceedings. **3.135**

(2) Power of the tribunal to determine the admissibility and weight of the evidence produced by the parties

According to Art 1696.2, Cod Jud, 'unless otherwise agreed by the parties, the Arbitral Tribunal shall freely assess the admissibility and weight of the evidence'. **3.136**

(2.1) Is the tribunal entitled to take the claimant's factual allegation as proven if the defendant does not participate in the arbitral proceedings? In default proceedings, the arbitral tribunal is supposed to exercise a cursory review of the claimant's allegations and should not rubber-stamp whatever the claimant submits. **3.137**

(2.2) May the arbitral tribunal consider an allegation of one party as agreed fact if the other party did not (specifically) dispute the allegation? When both sides participate in the proceedings, the arbitral tribunal should not question allegations from one party which are not rebutted by the other party—at least when the matter does not concern public policy. **3.138**

(2.3) What is the standard of proof that must be met in order for a fact to be considered to have been established (preponderance of the evidence; beyond reasonable doubt)? Must a stringent requirement be met for certain facts (for which ones)? A fact is considered to be established when it meets the arbitrator's 'intime conviction', ie his internal conviction.[109] **3.139**

(2.4) May the arbitral tribunal rely on its own knowledge to consider certain facts as proven? Arbitrators are often chosen because of the expert knowledge they have. Consequently, they should be able to make use of this knowledge. However, they cannot merely rely on their own expertise without having submitted their views to the parties and having given them the opportunity to comment. **3.140**

E. Witnesses

(1) Ability to act as a witness

Any person can be a witness. The rule of Art 931, Cod Jud, that a party or its representative or employee cannot be a witness, applies in the courts, but not in arbitration. **3.141**

[109] Hanotiau, B., 'Satisfying the Burden of Proof: the Viewpoint of a 'Civil Law' Lawyer' (1994) 10 *Arb Int'l* 341.

3.142 **(1.1) Is there a legal difference between a party testifying and a witness? If yes, what are the criteria for such differentiation? Does the testifying of a party have the same weight as a witness testimony?** In fact there is no legal difference between a party testifying and a witness. For instance, both can be asked to testify under formal oath (Art 1696.1, Cod Jud). As a rule, however, the testimony of a party or its representative or employee will be given much less weight than witness testimony.

(2) Preparation of witnesses and limits thereof

3.143 In Belgian state courts, witnesses are examined directly by the judge and should not have had preliminary contact in respect of their questioning with the parties or the parties' lawyers. That implies that any witness preparation is excluded in state court proceedings. The same rule would be applicable to arbitration proceedings. However, as the parties and the arbitrators are free to frame the procedural rules, they could agree to some witness preparation. However, in that event for the sake of transparency it is suggested that the extent of this preparation is well defined beforehand and known by all parties and the tribunal.

3.144 **(2.1) Do US-style depositions violate any procedural rules or principles?** Although depositions are not common practice in Belgian arbitration practice, parties may agree on US style depositions as they are free to determine themselves the procedural rules to gather evidence in the arbitration (Art 1693.1, Cod Jud).

3.145 **(2.2) May a party or its counsel approach a witness whom it has nominated (only before or also after the proceeding has started)? Are interviews permitted?** Belgian court practice, which is often adopted in arbitration, excludes a party or its counsel from approaching a witness before or during the proceedings. Preliminary witness interviews are likewise excluded. However, the parties can agree to deviate from this practice, but should do so in full transparency towards the other parties and towards the arbitral tribunal.

(3) Admissibility of written witness statements

3.146 Witnesses in Belgian state court proceedings are not allowed to rely on a written statement (Art 935, Cod Jud). The arbitration law or Belgian arbitration rules do not contain provisions on this matter. However, when witnesses are called upon in arbitration, they generally submit a preliminary statement, especially when the arbitration is not purely domestic.

3.147 **(3.1) If the parties agree on written statements, is a party entitled to request an oral hearing for questioning those witnesses (provided such right has not been agreed upon)?** The examination of witness evidence is preliminary at the oral hearing. Only when the parties have agreed thereupon and when the arbitral tribunal does not request the witness to be examined at the hearing (Art 1696.1, Cod Jud), can witness evidence be limited to written statements.

(4) Entitlement of a party to have a hearing or cross-examination of witnesses

3.148 Witnesses in Belgian state court proceedings first make an oral statement and are then questioned solely by the judge who asks his own questions as well as questions suggested by a party (Art 938, Cod Jud). Although this pattern is sometimes followed in arbitration, very often the parties agree—or the arbitral tribunal allows—to cross-examine the witnesses.

(4.1) Which are the methods used to establish a record of the arbitral proceedings, in particular witness examinations (tape recording, verbatim court reporters, dictated minutes, other methods)? There is no general practice to establish a record of the witness examinations. Sometimes—like in the state courts—the arbitral tribunal either dictates or writes down a summary of the witness examination. Sometimes the witness examination is recorded on tape; sometimes it is registered by verbatim court reporters. 3.149

(4.2) May the arbitral tribunal take an oath from a witness? The arbitral tribunal may take an oath from a witness (Art 1696.3, Cod Jud). In practice, however, this appears never to occur. 3.150

(4.3) Does the arbitral tribunal have the power to compel witnesses? If a witness refuses to appear, take the oath or testify, the arbitral tribunal may grant a party leave to request the Court of First Instance to compel a witness to appear before that court and to have a magistrate take the oath and conduct the examination of the witness (Art 1696.4, Cod Jud). However, this possibility never seems to be made use of. 3.151

F. Documents

(1) Form and kind of documents to be presented to the arbitral tribunal

Documents submitted are generally in written form, although sometimes arbitrators also accept documents solely in electronic form. Moreover, and especially in international arbitration, arbitrators ask for a an electronic backup of written documents. These backups very often are submitted on a USB stick or on a CD-Rom. 3.152

Written documents are always submitted in copied form. When the other side challenges the authenticity of the copied document, however, the other side may request that the original document be submitted to the sole arbitrator or to the President of the tribunal. 3.153

(1.1) Is the submission of 'agreed documents' permitted? If yes, what is the extent and effect of such an agreement (authenticity, existence, acknowledgement of such documents' contents)? Formally 'agreed documents' are not a specific part of the arbitration procedure as documents submitted by one party are in principle not contested as to their existence, authenticity and content by the other side when not formally objected to. 3.154

(1.2) How may electronic documents (eg emails) be presented and proven? Emails and other electronic documents can be submitted in printed form. 3.155

(1.3) Does discovery (US- or UK-style), after the procedure has started, violate any procedural rules or public policy considerations? US- or UK-style discoveries are not common in Belgian arbitrations. However, when the parties and the arbitrators agree, proper discovery proceedings can be conducted. 3.156

(2) Requirement to produce certain documents (as requested by the tribunal) and consequences of a failure to do so

Arbitrators seldom have recourse to Art 1696.3, Cod Jud, which allows them to order, at one of the parties' request, the production of a relevant document that is in possession of another party if it is believed that such document may contain evidence regarding a material fact. Whenever such production would be refused, the tribunal may grant the requesting 3.157

party leave to apply within a given time limit to the Court of First Instance for a court order to produce such document (Art 1696.5, Cod Jud). In fact, however, arbitrators generally will draw adverse conclusions from an unjustified refusal to produce documents and no application will be made to the court for an order to produce.

3.158 For issues regarding 'verification of signatures', objection to the production of documents or the forgery of documents, the tribunal can set a time frame during which the parties will be allowed to petition the Civil Court for a decision on such matters (Art 1696.3, Cod Jud).

3.159 **(2.1) Which documents may the tribunal request to be produced (eg also documents which are in the possession of third parties)?** The arbitral tribunal cannot order the production of documents in the possession of a third party. Such production has likewise to be requested by one of the parties to the arbitration with a petition to the Court of First Instance within a time limit set by the tribunal (Art 1696.5, Cod Jud).

(3) Protection of confidentiality of documents

3.160 There are no specific rules to protect the confidentiality of documents. Whenever justified, the production of a confidential document may be refused or the document could be edited or sanitized.

G. Experts

(1) Appointment and presentation of experts by the party or the arbitral tribunal

3.161 Pursuant to Art 1696.3, Cod Jud, arbitrators can appoint an expert, at the request of a party or on their own motion, for a very specific assignment, preferably after having heard the parties' views on the issue. The mechanics of the assignment have to be determined by the tribunal, after consultation with the parties. Articles 962 and 991, Cod Jud, which cover the appointment of court-appointed experts, may be used as guidelines.

3.162 Proceedings before Belgian state courts very rarely formally involve party-appointed experts who are examined in court. The experts engaged by the parties generally interact with the court-appointed expert at the earlier stage when the court expert is preparing his opinion. In arbitrations, however, it is more and more the case that the parties' experts inform the arbitral tribunal directly of their views.

3.163 The expert should not delay the proceedings unnecessarily and the arbitrators should therefore set a deadline for the report to be delivered. If the expert fails to meet the set date, the tribunal shall relieve him of his task.

3.164 **(1.1) By which methods are tribunal-appointed experts selected? What are the rights of the parties during the selection of an expert?** The arbitral tribunal appoints the tribunal's expert autonomously after consultation with the parties about the latter's profile, qualifications and assignment.

3.165 In any event, the challenge of an expert is always possible since it falls within the ambit of public policy. Moreover, the parties should be entitled to comment on the findings of an expert.

(2) Admissibility and role of expert witnesses

As the parties have full liberty to present their arguments and analysis of the facts, they also may have recourse to expert witnesses. Belgian procedural law regulates the admissibility and role of expert witnesses. They are considered as 'technical counsel' of the parties who may assist the parties *inter alia* in dealing with the court-appointed expert. The arbitration law or the arbitration rules do not contain specific rules on expert witnesses. In practice, however, parties sometimes rely on expert witnesses who submit their statements to the other side and the tribunal and who generally will be heard and questioned at the hearing as part of the evidence submitted by the party who presents them. **3.166**

(3) Influence of the parties upon the selection of questions to be submitted to the expert

It is good practice for the arbitral tribunal to consult the parties on the questions to be submitted to the expert. However, the arbitral tribunal has the final word in the selection and phrasing of the questions to be submitted. **3.167**

(4) Independence and impartiality of the expert and the right to reject a proposed/appointed expert

The tribunal-appointed expert should be independent and impartial and is open to challenge by analogy to what Art 966–970, Cod Jud provides for state court appointed experts. The challenge of a tribunal-appointed expert has to be brought before the arbitral tribunal that nominated him.[110] No arbitral decisions on such challenge are known. **3.168**

(4.1) May a party or its counsel approach an expert (or expert witness) whom it has nominated (only before or also after the proceeding has started)? Are interviews admissible? Party-appointed experts are part of a party's defence team and can communicate with that party or its counsel before and during the proceedings. Tribunal-appointed experts cannot be approached by a party or counsel unless with the involvement of the other side. **3.169**

(5) Oral examination of an expert in a hearing

Contrary to state court practice, where court-appointed experts confine their opinion to a written report and are rarely examined at a hearing, experts in arbitration generally also explain their views orally at a hearing. **3.170**

H. Interim measures of protection

(1) Kind of interim measures which the tribunal may order

Arbitrators can order all kinds of interim and conservatory measures, with the exclusion of attachment orders (Art 1696.1, Cod Jud; Art 18.1, CEPANI Rules).[111] **3.171**

[110] Keutgen, G. and Dal, G.A. (n 1) 369, no 455.

[111] The wording of art 1696.1, Cod Jud grants concurrent powers to the arbitrators and the state judge regarding interim relief, thus enabling the parties to turn to the judge even in the presence of an arbitration agreement. The parties can always renounce this possibility, only if the arbitrator is appointed and is able to order interim relief. However, this path should only be chosen if the parties are sure that they will execute without resistance any conservatory or provisional measure ordered. Art 1679.2, Cod Jud provides that an action for interim measures brought before a court does not contradict the existence of an arbitration agreement and cannot be construed as a waiver.

3.172 Thus, arbitrators can grant the same interim measures as state judges can do on the basis of either Art 19.2, Cod Jud (interlocutory measures to introduce the procedure or settle temporarily the situation between the parties) or Art 584, Cod Jud (provisional interim relief in case of urgency).

3.173 **(1.1) Which are, in general, the procedural and substantive prerequisites for the ordering of interim and conservatory measures (eg reduced degree of evidence; urgency; summary evaluation of the claim)?** Interim and conservatory measures can only be ordered by the arbitral tribunal if they have been requested by a party. They do not require a detailed analysis of the factual and legal aspects of the merits. It is sufficient that the request appears justified after a summary analysis and that the advantages of the measures outbalance their disadvantages. Urgency is not a general prerequisite to obtaining interim or conservatory measures. In the event of urgency, however, the evaluation of the claim may be even less stringent but the measure should then be revised if it appears unjustified.[112]

3.174 **(1.2) Are the prerequisites for interim measures ordered by the arbitral tribunal more or less the same as if those are requested from the state court? Is there case law/leading authorities on whether those measures are faster and enforced more easily if taken by the arbitral tribunal or the state court?** The prerequisites for interim measures to be ordered by the arbitral tribunal are largely the same as those requested from the state court. The compliance of interim measures ordered by the arbitral tribunal largely depends on the authority of the arbitrators and the desirability to comply with their instructions in order not to be sanctioned in the coming award. If enforcement is an issue, court measures are easier to enforce than measures ordered by the arbitrators: the enforcement of the latter need a court *exequatur*, while the first are enforceable without further ado.

(2) Limits of the tribunal's powers to order interim measures

3.175 The arbitral tribunal has the same powers as the state court to grant interim measures. As a rule, parties have the alternative to request such measures from either of them (Art 1696.1, Cod Jud). In fact, courts will be rather reluctant to grant interim measures once the arbitral tribunal has been constituted but will refer the parties to the arbitrators.[113] However, the parties may exclude by agreement the possibility of the arbitral tribunal granting interim measures, leaving the courts as the only possibility. In that event, not only the parties, but also the arbitral tribunal can request the state court to order the necessary interim measures.[114]

(3) Orders to provide security for the costs of the proceeding

3.176 Article 18.1 of the CEPANI Rules explicitly mentions security for costs as an example of an interim measure which can be granted by arbitrators. The arbitration statute does not contain such explicit reference but security for the costs would fall under the general powers of arbitrators to grant interim measures.

[112] Keutgen/Dal (n 1) no 421, referring to art 19.2, Cod Jud (general regime) and art 584 Cod Jud (interim measures in case of urgency).

[113] Van Houtte, H., 'Voorlopige maatregelen bij arbitrage' [1989–90] RW 532–6.

[114] Keutgen, G. and Dal, G.A. (n 1) no 420.

(4) Attachment of assets by an order of the tribunal

Article 1696.1 of the Cod Jud explicitly forbids arbitrators to grant attachments of assets. **3.177**

I. Assistance by the courts

(1) Extent of court assistance in the gathering of evidence

Arbitrators may assist the parties in evidence gathering to the same extent a state judge may do. They may order an investigation, an expert examination, the production of a document or they may visit the site to see for themselves whatever is at stake. They also may compel a party to appear in person and they may invite a party to take an oath on the veracity of their statements. In the event a party would not comply with its instructions, the arbitral tribunal may allow the other side to request state court assistance (Art 1696, 3 and 4, Cod Jud). **3.178**

(1.1) Is it for the arbitral tribunal or for the party to obtain the assistance of state courts with respect to the gathering of evidence? It is for the parties to obtain the assistance of state courts to examine a reluctant witness and to order production of a document (Art 1696.4 and 5, Cod Jud). **3.179**

(1.2) According to case law and practical experience, are there considerable delays involved when asking a court to give assistance (eg for the obtaining of evidence)? In fact, parties, however, never seem to request such court assistance as the arbitrators generally draw adverse conclusions from an unjustified refusal to testify or to produce a document. **3.180**

(2) Assistance for enforcing the attachment of assets

As only the state courts may order attachment of assets, no assistance to enforce an arbitrator's order to attach is needed. **3.181**

(3) Other examples of possible assistance

Whenever the arbitral tribunal considers itself unable to properly investigate a matter, it may request a Belgian court or even a foreign judicial authority with a '*commission rogatoire*' to perform that investigation.[115] **3.182**

(4) Dependence of the power of state courts to intervene during the proceedings on the national procedural law applied by the arbitral tribunal

In law, in case of urgency a Belgian '*juge en référé/rechter in kort geding*' may always order interim and conservatory measures after the commencement of the arbitration proceedings (Art 1679.2, Cod Jud). In fact, however, the judge will be rather reluctant to intervene, giving priority to the arbitral tribunal to order the necessary measures. Once the arbitral tribunal has been installed, the parties may exclude the possibility to have recourse to the '*juge en référé/rechter in kort geding*'.[116] **3.183**

[115] Keutgen, G. and Dal, G.A. (n 1) no 471.

[116] Van Houtte, H., 'Arbitrage en Kort geding' [1989] *RW* 532; Keutgen, G. and Dal, G.A. (n 1) no 422.

V. The award

A. Types of award

3.184 An arbitral tribunal can render final, partial and interim awards (Art 1699, Cod Jud).

(1) Interim award (eg on interim measures on the jurisdiction of the tribunal)

3.185 Interim awards, which cover interim measures but do not decide on jurisdiction or the merits of the case, may eg be issued to order an expertise, the personal appearance of the parties or an on-site visit. Its content must meet the same requirements as for a final award. Moreover, it has the force of *res judicata* (Art 1703, Cod Jud) and is immediately enforceable. However, the arbitral tribunal has full discretionary powers to issue either an interim award or a less formal Procedural Order. Article 18 of the CEPANI Rules, for instance, explicitly provides that provisional or conservatory measures shall take the form of an order, setting out the reasons for the decision, or, if the arbitral tribunal considers it appropriate, an award.

(2) Partial award

3.186 Partial awards are definitive awards which deal with jurisdiction or decide on some aspects of the merits. Partial awards are useful when the arbitral tribunal has to deal with several claims that can be addressed separately.

3.187 The content of a partial award must meet the same requirements as for a final award. Moreover, a partial award has the force of *res judicata* (Art 1703, Cod Jud and is immediately enforceable.

3.188 It surely is noteworthy to know that a partial award on jurisdiction cannot be challenged separately but must be attacked together with the subsequent award on the merits (Art 1697.3, Cod Jud).

3.189 The arbitral tribunal can be barred by the parties from issuing partial awards. Arbitrators, who would not abide by the parties' will, commit an excess of power, thus exposing their award to a setting aside procedure.

3.190 (2.1) **Are awards, especially partial awards, binding in the same arbitral proceeding? Does it make a difference if after the rendering of such a partial award, one arbitrator is successfully challenged and removed on grounds that prevailed even before the partial award was rendered?** Partial awards and interim awards, which have not been annulled by the state court, are *res judicata* between the parties (Art 1703, Cod Jud) and are binding in the same proceedings. The circumstance that an arbitrator has been successfully challenged after rendering a partial award, does not *per se* affect the validity of that award.

(3) Final award

3.191 A final award is the award which decides on all the matters before the arbitral tribunal in case the arbitrators have not rendered partial awards or, it is the last award that decides on all issues that are still outstanding, when partial awards have been rendered before.

3.192 (3.1) **If a party fails to participate in the arbitration, may the tribunal proceed and issue an award on the merits? Is such an award enforceable as any other award? Are there special remedies for the Defendant at the enforcement stage?** A defaulting party does not prevent the arbitral tribunal to proceed with the arbitration and render an award on the merits (Art 1695, Cod Jud). However, the arbitrators should verify that the arbitration agreement is valid and that the defaulting party has been duly notified of the proceedings. Otherwise their award will be annulled by the court at the request of the defaulting party (Art 1704, Cod Jud).

B. Deliberations and agreement on the award

(1) Time limits (and possible extensions) for making the award

Pursuant to Art 1698.1, Cod Jud, before the first arbitrator accepted his appointment, the parties may set a time limit within which the tribunal must render its award (Art 1698.1, Cod Jud). However, when the arbitrators have been appointed already for more than six months but failed to act swiftly and the parties did not impose such a time limit, a party can request the Court of First Instance to impose a time limit to render the award (Art 1698.2, Cod Jud). The arbitrators' mission is terminated if they did not issue their award within the time limit set by the parties or by the Civil Court (Art 1698.3, Cod Jud. However, procedural incidents preventing the tribunal from performing its duties automatically suspend the time limit (Art 1696.6, Cod Jud). When an award is rendered after the time limit imposed, it may be set aside because of the arbitrators' loss of jurisdiction. **3.193**

Article 19.1 and 2 CEPANI Rules require that the award be rendered within four months after the signature of the terms of reference. However, the CEPANI Secretariat will extend this time limit upon a motivated request from the tribunal or on its own motion. **3.194**

(2) Procedure for the decision of the arbitrators (majority vote etc)

All arbitrators have to participate in the rendering of an award. Their decision must be taken by an absolute majority of votes, except if the parties agreed otherwise (Art 1701.1, Cod. Jud). The parties can also grant the decisive vote to the chairman of the arbitral tribunal in case no majority can be reached (Art 1701.2, Cod Jud; Art. 20, CEPANI Rules). **3.195**

If the arbitrators cannot agree on the amount to be awarded, the votes for the highest amount will be added to those for the next lower sum, until a majority is formed (Art 1701.2, Cod Jud). **3.196**

(2.1) If an arbitrator fails or refuses to take part in oral deliberation meetings, although having been given sufficient notice of such meetings, may an award be rendered on the basis of written deliberations (or deliberations without this arbitrator) only? It is the arbitrator's duty to participate in the deliberations. Belgian arbitration law has no specific provisions on the arbitrators' participation in deliberations, or on whether these deliberations have to imply a meeting, may be conducted over the telephone or may be limited to an exchange of writings. **3.197**

(3) Admissibility of dissenting opinions

Belgian law does not authorize formal dissenting opinions since it is contrary to the principle of the secrecy of the deliberations.[117] The award can nevertheless mention whether it **3.198**

[117] See eg Keutgen, G. and Dal, G.A. (n1) no 495; Court of First Instance, Charleroi, 1 December 1978, *Revue régionale du droit* 1979, 935; Court of First Instance, Brussels, 6 December 2000, JT 2001, 572.

was rendered by unanimity or by a majority. Moreover, an arbitrator can always express his dissent by refusing to sign the award.

3.199 **(3.1) Are there any court decisions or positions of leading authorities on the issue of dissenting opinions in international arbitration (admissibility, disclosure to the parties and publication)?** Formal dissenting opinions are not admissible in arbitrations with their seat in Belgium. As awards are considered similar to court judgments, the secrecy of the deliberations ('secret du délibéré'), which excludes judges from rendering dissenting opinions, likewise applies to arbitrators.[118]

(4) Signature by the arbitrators and potential failure of one arbitrator to sign

3.200 The award must be signed by at least the majority of arbitrators. Moreover, when one or more of the arbitrator(s) cannot or refuse to sign, this fact must be mentioned in the award without having to give the reasons. An award that does not respect these rules on signature, risks being set aside (Art1704.2.h, Cod Jud).

C. Form of the award and deposition

(1) Award in writing and minimum contents of an award

3.201 According to Art 1701.4, Cod Jud, the award must be rendered in writing; otherwise it may be set aside (Art 1701.4 and 1704.2, Cod Jud).

3.202 Moreover, the award must contain (Art 1701.5, Cod Jud):

- the names and domiciles of the arbitrators (usually their professional domiciles);
- the names and domiciles of the parties;
- the object of the dispute (i.e. the relevant facts and legal issues);
- the date on which the award is issued; and
- the seat of arbitration and place where the award is rendered.

3.203 These requirements are *ad probationem* and can be substituted in other ways. Failure to comply does not necessarily entail the setting aside of the award.[119]

(2) Requirement to give reasons in the award

3.204 The award must be reasoned (Art 1701.5, Cod Jud). Not only the holding ('dispositif') of the award, but also its reasons enjoy *res judicata*.[120]

3.205 The necessity of reasons in an award, rendered in Belgium, is a matter of public policy; a lack of reasons leads to setting aside the award (Art 1704.2.i, Cod Jud). However, if an award is rendered in a country where the motivation is not required, it can still be enforced in Belgium.

[118] See Storme, M., 'Aspects importants du droit arbitral belge' [1976] *RDIDC* 123; Van den Heuvel, J., 'Arbitrage: capita selecta' in *Liber Amicorum L. Simont* (Bruylant, 2002) 341; see also Charleroi, 1 December 1978, *Rev Rég Dr* 1979, 935; Brussels, 6 December 2000, JT 2001, 572.

[119] See reference to discussion of art 1701.5 in Parliament in Keutgen, G. and Dal, G.A. (n 1) 398, no 498.

[120] Keutgen, G. and Dal, G.A., 'Belgium' in J. Paulsson (ed), *International Handbook on Commercial Arbitration*, Suppl 49 (Kluwer, 2007) 27.

(3) Necessity to specify place and time where and when the award was made

Article 1701.5 of the Cod Jud requires the award to state the place and the date it has been rendered. **3.206**

(4) Other requirements (registration, delivery etc)

Article 1702.1 of the Cod Jud demands the chairman of the arbitral tribunal (or the sole arbitrator) to notify a signed copy of the award to each of the parties. However, parties may agree on a different procedure. For instance, by referring to the CEPANI Arbitration Rules, they have delegated the duty to notify to the CEPANI Secretariat (Art 23.2, CEPANI Rules). **3.207**

It is recommended to notify the award to the parties by registered mail with delivery against receipt. As soon as its new provision will enter into force, Art 32.3, Cod Jud will also allow the use of a telecopy or an electronic mail instead of a registered letter 'provided that the receiver delivers a receipt'. **3.208**

The notification of the award entails the following important consequences: **3.209**

- *res judicata* of the award (Art 1703, Cod Jud);
- start of the 30-day time limit to request correction or interpretation of the award (Art 1702 bis, Cod Jud); and
- start of the three-month period to request the setting aside of the award (Art 1707.1, Cod Jud).

(4.1) Does the award have to be laid down or registered with a state court or agency (even if it has been rendered according to a foreign procedural law)? Under Art 1702.2 of the Cod Jud the chairman of the arbitral tribunal (or the sole arbitrator) has to file the original copy of the award rendered in Belgium, with the Registry of the Court of First Instance, territorially competent for the place of arbitration, and informs the parties thereof. The arbitrators become *functus officio* after the filing of the final award. **3.210**

The parties may, however, waive the requirement to file the award at the court registry. In that event arrangements have to be made about who will keep the original of the award. Parties who eg have referred to the CEPANI Arbitration Rules have waived the requirement to file the award at the court registry, except when one of the parties requests the CEPANI Secretariat to do so within one month after the notification of the award (Art 23, CEPANI Rules). In the absence of court filing, CEPANI will keep the original of the award. **3.211**

Although there is no deadline to deposit the award at the court registry, failure to do so without a waiver from the parties could lead to the arbitrators' liability, but would not give a ground for setting aside the award. **3.212**

(4.2) Does a foreign award which has been rendered abroad according to this country's national procedural law, have to be laid down or registered with a state court or agency? Is there a fee or tax for such registration of an award? Domestic and foreign awards have to be registered at the court's registry when their enforcement is sought through an *exequatur* from a Belgian court. **3.213**

3.214 **(4.3) How long after the rendering of the award must the file/award be stored by the lawyers and the arbitral tribunal?** Under Belgian law court and attorney files have to be kept for five years (Civil Code Art 2276 and 2276 bis). By analogy it could be argued that the arbitrators and the lawyers likewise should keep the arbitration file for five years. Arbitrators, however, may request the parties to allow them to return the arbitration documents to the respective party which has submitted the document in its time or to dispose of the arbitration file altogether. When the award has not been filed at the court registry (see *supra* at no 3.210), the chairman of the tribunal, the sole arbitrator or the arbitration institution has to keep the award.

D. Applicable substantive law

(1) Party autonomy to choose the applicable substantive law

3.215 The parties are free to choose the applicable substantive law to a transnational dispute with due respect for mandatory law and public policy. In case the parties did not decide on the applicable law, the arbitral tribunal will have to do so.[121]

3.216 Article 1700.1 of the Cod Jud provides that the tribunal must then decide according to the law, just like a national judge; when arbitrators would not decide in law, their award may be set aside for excess of power (Art 1704.2.d, Cod Jud). When arbitrators are appointed as *amiables compositeurs* (see *infra*), they can apply equity and 'ignore' some rules.

3.217 **(1.1) Is there a public policy exception to the chosen substantive law?** However, when the parties have chosen a legal system with rules, that go against Belgian international public policy, these rules will not apply.[122] The arbitrators furthermore are entitled to apply relevant mandatory rules from a legal system, other than the one chosen by the parties, when there is a close connection between that other legal system and the case.

3.218 **(1.2) Does the principle of '*Iura novit curia*' apply? Or must the applicable law be proven (by which means)?** The principle of *Iura novit curia* applies in the Belgian courts. Likewise arbitrators also can find the applicable rules on their own initiative. However, due process requires that the arbitrators subject their findings to the parties for comments.

(2) Deciding according to equity/as amiable compositeur

3.219 Arbitrators decide in accordance with the rules of law, except when otherwise agreed by the parties that they are allowed to decide as *amiable compositeurs*, ie 'in equity'. (Art 1700.1, Cod Jud). However, whenever one of the parties to the arbitration is a (Belgian) public entity ('personne morale de droit public'), no waiver to apply the rules of law is possible. In fact, arbitrations in equity seem to occur very seldomly.

(3) Application of lex mercatoria, *general principles etc*

3.220 The *Code Judiciaire* does not contain any provision on the law the arbitrators have to apply on the merits. However, arbitrators have to follow the instructions of the parties, whenever they have agreed on the application of *lex mercatoria*, general principles or the like. In such

[121] Commercial Court, Ghent, 12 October 1989, RDCB, 1991, 548.
[122] Keutgen, G., 'La nouvelle loi sur l'arbitrage' [1998] JT 764, no 20 *et seq.*

situations, the arbitrators have to apply these legal rules as long as Belgian public policy or relevant mandatory law is respected.

(3.1) Is the application of *lex mercatoria* considered as the application of law or as a kind of *amiable composition*? *Lex mercatoria* should be considered as a system of law and therefore, does not require an agreement for 'amiable composition' to be applied.[123] **3.221**

(4) Applicable substantive law if there is no choice of law by the parties If the parties did not choose the applicable substantive law, the tribunal is competent to determine the applicable substantive rules. They generally will follow as guidelines the standards of the Rome (1980) Convention on the Law applicable to Contractual Obligations—in the future the Rome I Regulation.[124] **3.222**

(4.1) Is there an autonomous conflict of law rule in the national arbitration law? Is it considered mandatory? There is no autonomous conflict of law rule in the Belgian arbitration law. **3.223**

(4.2) What is the law applicable to interest? Under Belgian conflict of law rules, and following the principles of the Rome (1980) Convention—to be succeeded by the Rome I Regulation—the proper law of the dispute, eg generally the law of the contract—governs matters of interest due on amounts to be paid under the contract. **3.224**

(4.3) What is the law and practice with respect to legal interest on foreign currency debts? As legal interests are governed by the substantive law, applicable to the dispute, interests on foreign currency debts generally are determined by the law applicable to these debts. However, sometimes arbitrators follow UNIDROIT Principle 7.4.9 of International Commercial Contracts and apply the legal interest of the currency of the debt. **3.225**

(5) Binding effect of state court decisions

No statute determines that a state court decision is binding in later arbitration proceedings. Thus, the arbitral tribunal has some discretion to determine the effects it attaches to such decisions. **3.226**

If the tribunal opts to apply Belgian law to those questions, in all events two provisions are relevant. **3.227**

On the one hand, under Art 1350 of the Civil Code the authority which the law attaches to the decisions of the courts ('la chose jugée', 'het rechterlijk gewijsde') is a 'legal presumption' ('presumption légale', 'wettelijk vermoeden'). Pursuant to Art 1352 this legal presumption is sufficient and irrefutable evidence. On the other hand, Art 25 of the Cod Jud provides that the authority of the decisions of the courts ('autorité de chose jugée', 'gezag van het rechterlijk gewijsde') prevents the same claim from being relitigated when the claim, the cause of action and the parties are identical. **3.228**

[123] de Bournonville, P. (n 4), 233, no 313.

[124] van Houtte, H., 'Toepassingsgebied van het EVO, in Europese IPR—Verdragen' (Acco, 1997), 189, 199.

3.229 In other words, if a party brings a claim before the arbitral tribunal that is identical as to its object, its cause of action and the parties, the tribunal may declare such claim inadmissible at the request of the other party; if there is no such complete identity, the findings of a prior court decision may still be relevant as evidence.[125]

3.230 However, if the arbitral tribunal disregards the prior decision of the court, either as a ground for inadmissibility, or as evidence of its findings, this will not be a ground to challenge the tribunal's award since *res judicata* is generally not considered to affect public policy.

3.231 (5.1) **Is an arbitral tribunal bound by a decision of another arbitral tribunal?** No statute regulates specifically the effects an arbitral tribunal should attach to a decision of another arbitral tribunal. If the award from the first arbitral tribunal would have been rendered in Belgium under Art 1703, 1, Cod Jud and unless it is contrary to public policy or unless the dispute is not arbitrable, that first award shall have the authority of a judicial decision, once it has been notified in accordance with Art 1702, para 1—at least on condition that it can no longer be contested before the arbitrators. The first award thus would have the same effects as a Belgian court judgment. Consequently, a party to an arbitration may invoke that the claim is inadmissible if the object of the claim, the cause of action and the parties are identical to the claim, cause of action and parties which were subject matter of a prior Belgian arbitration award (Art 23 *et seq*, Cod Jud). Moreover, in all events, if they wish to do so, the arbitrators may rely on a prior arbitral award as evidence of the findings made in that award (Art 1350 *et seq*, Civil Code).

3.232 However, if the arbitral tribunal disregards the decision of another arbitral tribunal, this will not be a ground to challenge the second tribunal's award since *res judicata* is generally not considered to touch public policy.

3.233 (5.2) **Does a decision in a criminal case bind an arbitral tribunal?** No statute determines the effects which an arbitral tribunal should attach to a decision in a criminal case. Thus, principally the tribunal has the same possibilities as for decisions in civil cases. However, unlike the effects of a civil judgment, the effects of a criminal decision are considered to touch public policy. Therefore, inconsistency between the award and a prior criminal decision, may be a ground to set the award aside for reasons of public policy.

3.234 Moreover, when an arbitral tribunal has requested the criminal court to investigate an allegation of forged documents under Art 1696.5 of the Cod Jud, it will be bound by that court's decision.

E. Settlement

(1) Settlement by agreement of the parties with or without support of the arbitral tribunal

3.235 During the arbitration proceedings, the parties can settle the case. Although the arbitral tribunal generally does engage in detailed settlement discussions with the parties, they may suggest the parties explore possibilities to settle their dispute.

[125] A prior decision may also serve as evidence of its findings, even if the claim, cause of action or the parties to the subsequent proceedings are not identical.

(1.1) May an arbitrator who has initiated settlement discussions be challenged when agreement on a settlement has failed? Arbitrators should not suggest the terms of a possible settlement, but should at most encourage the parties to find a common ground for settlement. An arbitrator who has given his opinion on the terms of settlement may have undermined his impartiality and independence and may be subject to challenge whenever the settlement fails. 3.236

(2) 'Private settlement' and its impact on the arbitral procedure

A private settlement of the dispute makes an arbitration procedure over that dispute moot. The proceedings should then be brought to an end, either by a Procedural Order, stating that the case has been settled, or—if the parties so wish—by a consent award. 3.237

(3) Form and effect of a settlement (eg award on agreed terms)

A settlement reached by the parties can be incorporated in a consent award, which has to be signed by the parties as well as by the arbitrators. As any other award, this consent award may be filed at the court registry. At the request of one of the parties the President of the Court of First Instance can order the enforcement of the consent award. However, enforcement will be denied when the dispute was not arbitrable or the settlement goes against public policy (Art 1715, Cod Jud). 3.238

F. Costs of the arbitration

(1) General allocation of the costs of the proceedings

The costs of the arbitration as well as the respective share of the parties are fixed by the tribunal in the award. The parties may beforehand agree on the allocation of the costs as long as this would not be systematically unfair to one of them or violate their equal access to arbitral justice.[126] 3.239

(2) Deposits or advances for costs or fees

Arbitrators usually request a deposit for their fees and expenses. Arbitral institutions, such as CEPANI, handle the deposits and the advances for costs and fees. In general, claimant and defendant have to contribute to the advances in equal shares. 3.240

The arbitral proceedings may be stayed until full payment of the fees. If necessary, the claimant may advance the part of a reluctant defendant to allow the arbitration to proceed. 3.241

(2.1) Is there case law authorizing or prohibiting arbitrators to order a party to pay an advance on the arbitration costs? The arbitrators are entitled not to proceed as long as the advances have not been paid. However, they cannot actually order a party to advance said costs. 3.242

(2.2) May the raising of a set-off claim or counterclaim be made contingent upon payment of the corresponding advance for the relating arbitration costs (cf eg Article 30(5), ICC Rules)? May such a condition be agreed upon when entering into the arbitration 3.243

[126] Arbitral award, *Actualités du droit*, 1992, 1413.

agreement? In the event of a counterclaim and at the request of a party or on its own initiative, the CEPANI Secretariat may request the claimant and the defendant to cover respectively the advances for the claims and the counterclaims (Art, 26.4 CEPANI Rules).

3.244 (2.3) **What remedies exist against a party which does not pay its part of the advance on the arbitration (eg termination of the arbitration agreement)? How may the other party enforce its rights?** Arbitrators may terminate the proceedings when the deposits and advances have not been paid in full.

3.245 Whenever advances have been fixed separately for claims and counterclaims, the arbitrators shall not decide on the claims, respectively counterclaims as long as the related advances have not been paid. However, even when they cannot decide on the counterclaims because of non-payment of the advance, they have to take all the defendants' arguments against the claim into account.

(3) Costs of the administration by an arbitration institution

3.246 In CEPANI arbitrations the administrative costs of CEPANI are fixed at 10 per cent of the arbitrators' fees and are subject to VAT. Moreover, each request for CEPANI Arbitration must be accompanied by an advance payment of €500 on administrative costs. Such payment is non-refundable, and is credited to the claimant's portion of the advance on costs for arbitration. For arbitrations of limited financial importance the amount is set at €250.

(4) Arbitrators' fees: law and practice, judicial control

3.247 In institutional arbitrations, fees are fixed by the arbitral institution and mentioned in the award. As a matter of principle, courts do not exercise judicial control over the fees parties have to pay in institutional arbitration because the parties have agreed on the fee schedule when choosing the arbitration institution and its rules.

3.248 Fees generally depend to a great extent on the amount in dispute and to a lesser extent on the time spent.

3.249 CEPANI, like other arbitral institutions, has established a scale for arbitrator's fees.

3.250 The fee schedule for CEPANI arbitrations is printed on page 219.

3.251 (4.1) **May Arbitrators may fix their own fees in the award?** In *ad hoc* arbitrations, arbitrators may fix their own fees in the award. They generally have indicated at the start of the proceedings how their fees would be determined (eg by analogy to the CEPANI fee schedule) and they have asked the parties for sufficient retainers to cover the fees.

3.252 In institutional arbitrations the fees are determined by the arbitration institution and their amount, as well as their allocation between the parties and the possible amounts to be reimbursed, are mentioned in the award (eg CEPANI Rules, Art 25 and 27).

3.253 (4.2) **How can the parties change the arbitrators' fees once they are fixed?** Parties, who do not accept the arbitrators' fees, can bring this matter before the Court of First Instance. Such disputes are probably extremely rare and there is no published case law on this matter. Fees for arbitrators in institutional arbitrations are established by the institution on the basis of the fee schedule on which the parties have agreed when choosing the arbitration

Sum in dispute (in euro)				Fees (in euro)					
				Minimum fees			Maximum fees		
from	0,00	to	12.500,00	625,00			1.250,00		
from	12.501,00	to	50.000,00	1.250,00	+	1,00% otae 12.500	1.250,00	+	5,00% otae 12.500
from	50.001,00	to	100.000,00	1.500,00	+	3,00% otae 50.000	3.000,00	+	4,00% otae 50.000
from	100.001,00	to	500.000,00	3.000,00	+	1,50% otae 100.000	6.000,00	+	1,50% otae 100.000
from	500.001,00	to	1.000.000,00	10.000,00	+	0,75% otae 500.000	12.500,00	+	1,50% otae 500.000
from	1.000.001,00	to	5.000.000,00	17.000,00	+	0,70% otae 1.000.000	20.000,00	+	0,75% otae 1.000.000
from	5.000.001,00	to	10.000.000,00	45.000,00	+	0,30% otae 5.000.000	60.000,00	+	0,30% otae 5.000.000
from	10.000.001,00	to	50.000.000,00	70.000,00	+	0,025% otae 10.000.000	80.000,00	+	0,025% otae 10.000.000
Above			50.000.000,00	90.000,00	+	0,012% otae 50.000.000	140.000,00	+	0,012% otae 50.000.000

The administrative costs of CEPANI are fixed at 10% of the fees and are subject to VAT.

(otae: of the amount exceeding)

institution. Because of this preliminary agreement with the schedule, court challenges to fees will be more difficult in institutional arbitration. Likewise, it will be more difficult for a party to challenge the fees determined by *ad hoc* arbitrators when they had agreed on these fees when the arbitration started.

3.254 (4.3) **Are the arbitrator's fees subject to income tax if (i) the place of arbitration or (ii) the normal residence or place of business of the arbitrator is located in this country?** Under Belgian law arbitrators' fees are subject to income tax at the domicile of the arbitrator or at the seat of the legal entity in whose framework (eg law firm, professional company) he acted as an arbitrator.

3.255 (4.4) **Are the arbitrator's fees submitted to VAT? If yes, is the duty to pay such tax linked to (i) the place of arbitration; or (ii) the arbitrator's general residence?** As a general rule arbitrators who are member of the Belgian bar, are not subject to VAT.[127] Arbitrators, however, who are not a member of the Belgian bar but who act regularly as an arbitrator, are subject to VAT.

(5) Attorneys' fees and the winning party's claim for reimbursement

3.256 Since the judgment of the Cour of Cassation of 2 September 2004, the fees of lawyers and technical experts can be reimbursed.[128] As a result, the winning party can claim its fees from the losing one.[129]

3.257 (5.1) **May in-house lawyers change fees or may a party request costs of in-house lawyers to be reimbursed?** Belgian courts have very recently accepted that the winning party has to be reimbursed to some extent for its attorney's fees.[130] In Belgian arbitration practice, the reimbursement of attorney's fees is also slowly being introduced.[131] Reimbursement of costs of in-house lawyers is not yet asked for. Nothing, however, excludes the parties to do so. As the assessment of these costs will be delicate, parties and arbitrators should best agree at the start of the proceedings how these costs will be evaluated.

(6) Time and form of the decision on costs

3.258 The decision on costs is part of the Final Award.

3.259 (6.1) **May the arbitrators' decision on the costs (allocation and amount of costs to be reimbursed) be challenged separately from the award itself? Are there legal provisions, especially time limits for such a remedy?** The arbitrators' decision on costs is incorporated in the final award and can only be challenged as part of the award. However, it will be very

---

[127] See *inter alia* Bigwood, J. and Wasserman, D., 'Fiscalité des honoraires des arbitres' in *Arbitrage et Fiscalité*, Collection CEPANI (Bruylant, 2001) 125 *et seq*.

[128] Cass 2 September 2004, JT, 2004, p 684, and obs De Coninck, B., 'Répétibilité et responsabilité civile: un arrêt de principe'.

[129] For an analysis of how CEPANI arbitrators allocate legal costs of outside counsel and in-house lawyers between the parties, see Van Houtte, H., 'Partijkosten in CEPINA Arbitrage' in *Liber Amicorum Guy Keutgen* (Bruylant, 2008).

[130] See Cass 2 September 2004, *JLMB* 2004, 1320; J.T. 2004, 684; *NJW* 2004, 953, *Rev Not B* 2004, 471; *RGAR* 2005, no 13946; *RW* 2004-05, 535; *TBBR* 2004, 461 and the more detailed provisions of the Statute on the Recuperation of Defence Costs of 21 April 2007.

[131] See eg an analysis of recent CEPANI awards in Van Houtte, H., 'Partijkosten in CEPINA Arbitrage' in *Liber Amicorum Guy Keutgen* (Bruylant, 2008).

exceptional that these costs will offer one of the grounds for annulment of the award under Art 1704, Cod Jud. They will rarely violate public policy. A possible ground could be a contradiction in the reasoning where the costs are allocated inconsistently in view of the reasons and the outcome of the decision. Another ground would be that the arbitrators did not comply with what had been agreed between the parties and the arbitral tribunal. In all events requests for annulment of the award have to be submitted within three months after the notification of the award to the requesting party.

(6.2) Are the arbitrators entitled and/or legally obliged to rule on the amount of one or both parties' costs that are recoverable? The arbitrators are only obliged to rule on a party's legal costs when this has been explicitly requested by that party. On the other hand, whenever a retainer for arbitration costs has been paid in the course of the arbitration proceedings, they have to decide on the allocation of the arbitrators' costs and expenses and on the fate of the advances made thereupon by the parties (CEPANI, Art 27.2). **3.260**

G. Publication of the award

(1) Publication with or without the consent of the parties

Arbitration being a confidential process, awards should not be published unless both parties have permitted to do so. The confidentiality of the awards is confirmed by Art 10 of the CEPANI Rules of Conduct, which imposes upon the arbitrators, the parties and their counsel not to publish awards, unless without the names of those involved and with the express authorization of all parties. Moreover, the CEPANI Secretariat has to be informed in advance of such publication.[132] **3.261**

(2) Practice of publication (which periodicals or legal journals)

Arbitral awards are very rarely published in legal journals. An annotated selection of CEPANI awards can be found in *Receuil des Sentences arbitrales du CEPANI.*[133] **3.262**

VI. Amendment and challenge of the award; liability of arbitrators

A. Amendment, correction or interpretation of the award

(1) Motion to amend or correct an award

In the event of a material or typographical error, or 'any error of a similar nature' the award can be corrected (Art 1702 bis, Cod Jud). A correction can be requested by a party (with notification to the other parties) within 30 days after the notification of the award. The tribunal then has 30 days (with the possibility of extension) to examine the request and decide upon it. **3.263**

Within 30 days after the notification the arbitral tribunal can likewise correct the award on its own motion. The tribunal cannot extend the deadline for corrections on its own motion. **3.264**

---

132 See <http://www.cepani.be>.

133 *Recueil des Sentences arbitrales du CEPANI* (Bruylant, 2005) 441 p.

3.265 The tribunal can issue a new version of the original award or render a specific award on the points corrected.[134] The correction has to comply with all the formalities of an award, eg it must have been subject of deliberation by all the arbitrators and contain the necessary signatures.

3.266 In the event that it is impossible for the tribunal to reconvene to issue a corrected award, the parties can either petition the Court of First Instance for an interpretation or appoint a new arbitral tribunal.[135]

3.267 After the arbitral proceedings are terminated, the arbitral tribunal can issue an additional award at the request of one of the parties when it failed to address some issues, which are disconnected from the issues on which the arbitrators had already decided (Art 1708.1, Cod Jud). In the event, the other party considers the issues, which the arbitral tribunal failed to address, to be connected with the issues on which it had already decided, the President of the Court of First Instance will examine that matter: if he considers the issues not connected, he will refer those issues to the arbitrators for an additional award (Art 1708.2, Cod. Jud.). If, on the other hand, the issues are considered connected, that fact may become a ground for setting aside the award (Art 1704.2, eCod Jud).

(2) Interpretation of the award by the tribunal

3.268 When the parties have agreed thereupon in the arbitration clause or in a subsequent agreement, one party may request the arbitrators to interpret a specific matter or paragraph of the award (Art 1702 bis 1b, Cod Jud). It cannot solicit the interpretation of the whole award, as this could lead to a completely new decision.

3.269 Unless the parties agreed otherwise, a request for interpretation must be submitted within 30 days of the notification of the award. The other party must also be notified of the request.

3.270 The tribunal then has 30 days to examine the request and interpret its award if necessary. This time limit can be extended by the arbitrators.

3.271 Like the original award of which it is an integral part, the interpretation must comply with the formalities of an award.

3.272 In the event that it is impossible for the tribunal to reconvene to decide on an interpretation, the parties can either petition the Court of First Instance for an interpretation or appoint a new arbitral tribunal.

B. Appeal on the merits

(1) Admissibility and procedure of an appeal on the merits

3.273 Under Art 1703 Cod Jud, the parties can agree in the arbitration agreement that an appeal on the merits could be lodged before another arbitral tribunal. If they did not make such an agreement the award cannot be appealed on the merits.

---

134 Keutgen, G. and Dal, G.A. (n 1) 444, no. 550.
135 *ibid*, no. 551.

(1.1) May the parties agree on an appeal to another arbitral tribunal? The parties may provide in the arbitration agreement that the arbitral award shall be subject to appeal before another arbitral tribunal (Art 1703, Cod Jud). **3.274**

An award may be appealed before another arbitral tribunal whenever the parties have agreed to such appeal. Otherwise the award is definite. The parties are free to provide for the practicalities of the appeal procedure, such as for instance whether a partial award can only be appealed with the final one. If the parties did not decide upon a time limit for an appeal, Art 1703.2, Cod Jud states that the latter can be lodged within a month of the notification of the award by a 'huissier' (Art 1703.2, Cod Jud). **3.275**

In fact, the parties rarely provide for an appeal of an award. Furthermore, many arbitration rules (eg CEPANI Rules, Art 24) confirm that the award is definite and do not provide for the possibility of an appeal. **3.276**

(2) Possibility to exclude an appeal (eg in the arbitration clause)

The parties are not required to exclude the possibility of appeal in the arbitration agreement. Unless they explicitly agreed on such appeal—which happens extremely rarely—the appeal is excluded (Art 1703, Cod Jud). **3.277**

C. Setting aside of the award

(1) Reasons for setting aside an award

The grounds for setting aside an award are listed exhaustively in the Code of Civil Procedure (Art 1704, Cod. Jud). The parties cannot waive any of these grounds. **3.278**

There is no time limit to raise the following grounds: **3.279**

- award contrary to public policy (Art 1704.2.a, Cod Jud):

  Public policy encompasses *inter alia* the provisions of the Constitution and of the human rights treaties ratified by Belgium, as well as the Belgian rules on the powers of the arbitrators.[136]

- non-arbitrability of the dispute (Art 1704.2.b, Cod Jud):

  An award on a dispute, which the parties have no legal possibility to settle, is to be set aside.

Some grounds must be raised within three months of the notification of the award. In the event the award has obtained an *exequatur*, this setting aside has to be petitioned within one month after the notification of this *exequatur*: **3.280**

- no valid arbitration agreement (1704.2.c, Cod Jud):

  An award, rendered upon an arbitration clause which favoured one of the parties because the arbitration was organized by the professional organization to which the latter belonged, can eg be set aside.[137] The lack of an arbitration agreement in written form, however, does not lead to setting aside the award as long as it can be established that there

---

[136] Court of Appeal, Brussels, 6 December 2000, JT, 2001, 572.

[137] Van Houtte, H., 'De geldigheid van het arbitragebeding dat arbitrage toevertrouwt aan een beroepsorganisatie', note on Commercial Court, Leuven, 11 September 1989, RDC 1990, 1022.

was an agreement to arbitrate. Likewise, the absence of an invalid arbitration agreement can no longer be invoked as a ground to set aside the award when this invalidity has not been objected to during the arbitration proceedings.

- excess of jurisdiction or power of the arbitral tribunal (Art 1704.2.d, Cod Jud):

  An award can be set aside whenever the tribunal has granted more than what was claimed, has decided on claims not submitted or has decided in equity when the parties had not validly agreed thereupon. Whenever possible, the award will only be partially set aside, ie with regard to the part where the arbitrators decided *ultra petita*.

- absence of a decision on some aspects of the dispute submitted, which cannot be separated from issues already decided by the award (Art 1704.2.e, Cod Jud):

  Whenever these aspects can be separated from the other issues, decided by the award, a party may ask the arbitral tribunal to decide on these aspects in an additional award (Art 1708 Cod. Jud).

- irregular composition of the arbitral tribunal (Art 1704.2.f, Cod Jud):

  An award can, for instance, be set aside when the arbitrator had no capacity to act as an arbitrator (Art 1680, Cod Jud) or when the arbitral tribunal consisted of an even number of arbitrators (Art 1681.1, Cod Jud). However, a party cannot claim the setting aside of the award because of the irregular composition of the tribunal, whenever it was or should have been aware of that matter in the course of the arbitral proceedings and did not raise an objection at that time.

- non-respect of the rights of defence and of mandatory procedural rules (Art 1704.2.g, Cod Jud) :

  Each party has to assert its rights and to bring forward its arguments in an adversarial debate. For the setting aside of the award because of non-respect of the rights of defence, it is only required to prove a violation of the right of defence and not the impact of that violation upon the award. Conversely, the impact of a disregard of the mandatory arbitral procedural rules (cf Arts 1694, 1695, 1696 and 1701.1, Cod Jud) upon the award must be established to result in a setting aside of the award.

- non-respect of the formal requirements for the award (Art 1704.2.h, Cod Jud):

  Art 1701.4, Cod Jud requires that the award be signed by the arbitrators. Whenever one of the arbitrators cannot sign or refuses to sign, this impossibility or refusal has to be mentioned in the award. In all events the award needs to have been signed by the majority of the arbitrators. Failure to respect these requirements is a ground for setting aside the award under Art 1704.2.h, Cod Jud.

- insufficient reasoning of the award (Art 1704.2.i, Cod Jud):

  Under Belgian arbitration law, the award should be as well reasoned as a court decision.[138] The award can be set aside when it did not address all arguments from the parties; the content of these reasons cannot be reviewed.[139]

---

[138] See Linsmeau, J., 'L'arbitrage sectoriel' in *Les modes non judiciaires de règlements des conflits* (Bruylant, 1995) 59, no 31 *et seq.*

[139] Court of First Instance, Anwerp, 15 March 2000, *Algemeen Juridisch Tijdschrift*, 2000–2001, 915.

- contradictions in the award (Art 1704.2.j, Cod Jud) :

  An award can be set aside when the holding ('le dispositif') of the award is incompatible with the reasoning of the award or when there is a contradiction between the reasons of the award.[140]

Finally, the Code of Civil Procedure provide for three grounds for setting aside an award, which have to be raised within three months after their discovery but in all events within five years after the notification of the award: **3.281**

- fraud (Art 1704.3.a, Cod Jud):

  Fraud, however, only can lead to the setting of the award when its impact upon the outcome of the award has been established.

- false evidence (Art 1704.3.b, Cod Jud):

  Again, if an award is based on documents, witnesses, expert reports, exhibits etc, recognized by a judicial decision or by the parties to be false, it can be set aside.

- discovery (Art 1704.3.c, Cod Jud):

  The discovery of 'a document or any other piece of evidence that would have had a decisive influence on the award and that had been retained by the other party' is a ground for setting aside the award.

(1.1) May an award made according to international or foreign procedural rules be the object of an application for setting aside before the national courts? Any award, where the place of arbitration was in Belgium, can be the object of an application for setting aside before the Belgian court of the place of arbitration. The procedural rules, followed in the arbitral proceedings, are irrelevant in this respect. However, whenever an arbitration procedure is governed by international public law (eg between states or other international public law entities), Belgian courts have no jurisdiction and the Belgian arbitration statute is not applicable. **3.282**

(2) Procedure and deadlines for challenging an award

Applications for setting aside the award have to be submitted to the Court of First Instance of the place of arbitration. All the grounds for setting aside the award have to be submitted at the same time (except for the grounds under Art 1704.3, Cod Jud, when not yet found out) (Art 1706.1, Cod Jud). The court must, however, examine *ex officio* the conformity of the award with the provisions of public policy and the arbitrability of the dispute, Art 1707.4, Cod Jud). **3.283**

As indicated above, the invalidity of the arbitration agreement, excess of jurisdiction, the absence of decision on some aspects of the dispute, the irregular composition of the arbitral tribunal, the non-respect of the rights of defence and of mandatory procedural rules, the absence of formal requirements of the award, insufficient reasoning and contradictions in the award are grounds which have to be invoked within three months after notification of **3.284**

[140] Keutgen, G. and Dal, G.A., 'Belgium' in J. Paulsson (ed), *International Handbook on Commercial Arbitration*, Suppl 49 (Kluwer, 2007) 43.

the award. Fraud, false evidence and discovery of decisive evidence have to be invoked within three months after a party has become aware of these grounds for annulment, but cannot be invoked later that five years after the award has been notified.

3.285 (2.1) **Who may (or must) represent a party in a proceeding for setting aside an award?** In proceedings for setting aside an award, parties are usually represented by a Belgian 'avocat', although theoretically they may also appear in person and argue their own case.

3.286 (2.2) **Do specific time limits exist for setting-aside procedures concerning awards on jurisdiction?** The annulment of an award on jurisdiction has to be requested together with the first award on the merits, ie within three months after the notification of the latter (Art 1697.3, Cod Jud).

(3) Effect of a court decision which sets the award aside

3.287 A request for setting aside an award does not suspend the enforcement of the award. However, if the parties provided for the possibility to appeal the award, it would only be enforceable if the tribunal pronounced it provisionally enforceable.

3.288 If the court decides to set aside an award, it becomes null. An award can be partially set aside when the criticized part can be separated from the rest of the award (Art 1705, Cod Jud).

3.289 (3.1) **Does the setting-aside action suspend the enforcement? If so, do remedies exist to reinstate enforcement?** A request to set aside an award does not suspend its enforcement.

3.290 (3.2) **After an award has been set aside, does the underlying arbitration agreement revive or remain in force or is it exhausted or deemed terminated?** Unless an award has been set aside because the dispute was inarbitrable or because there was no valid arbitration agreement, the latter remains in force and a new arbitral tribunal has to be constituted. However, when the specific arbitrators have been designated *nominatim* in the arbitration clause, this clause becomes ineffective once their award has been set aside.

(4) Appeal against the court's decision to set aside or not set aside the award?

3.291 Appeal against a decision of the Court of First Instance, setting aside the award or not, can be lodged before the Court of Appeal.[141]

(5) Possibility of the parties to exclude actions for setting aside

3.292 Whenever none of the parties to an arbitration is a physical person having his normal residence in Belgium or a legal person having its registered office or a branch in Belgium, they may agree in advance (eg in the arbitration clause) to waive the possibility for the setting aside of the arbitral award (Art 1717.4, Cod Jud—amended by Statute of 19 May 1998).

3.293 Moreover, once the award has been rendered, and if public policy has not been violated, they can always waive their entitlement to request the setting aside of an award.

[141] Court of Appeal, Mons, 4 October 1984, 1984 *Rev Reg Dr* 295; Court of Appeal, Brussels, 25 February 1987, 1988 *Ann Dr Liège* 59.

D. Liability of arbitrators

(1) Duties and liabilities of arbitrators regarding the conduct of the proceedings?

By accepting to sit as an arbitrator, the arbitrator has committed himself to be sufficiently available to carry out this task. He cannot delegate this assignment which is personal and *intuitu personae*. Further, he is obliged to respect the confidentiality of the dispute and the arbitration and is bound and protected by the rules of professional secrecy.[142] **3.294**

The arbitrator's contractual liability can be engaged: **3.295**

- if he fails to render the award within the time limit provided;
- if the time limit has expired without the arbitrator having asked for an extension;
- if the arbitrator, after having accepted his mission, withdraws without having been authorized by the Court of First Instance (Art 1689, Cod Jud);
- if the arbitrator has not made in time the necessary disclosures about his impartiality and independence, which, if made, would have led to his removal;
- if the arbitrator unjustifiably refuses to hear a party so that his award has been set aside (Art 1704.2, Cod Jud); or
- if the arbitrator has not notified the award to the parties or has not complied with the request to file the award at the Registry of the Court of First Instance.

The collegial character of the arbitral tribunal and the secrecy of the deliberations entail that the action in liability must be introduced against all the arbitrators.[143] Any division of tasks among the arbitrators during the proceedings is irrelevant. **3.296**

The party, who holds the arbitrators liable, has to prove their tortuous behaviour, the damage it suffered and the causal link between both. **3.297**

Arbitrators cannot be held liable for an error in judgment,[144] except in case of fraud, wilful deception ('dol') or gross negligence equivalent to 'dol'. **3.298**

(1.1) Do the courts and/or authorities rely on a contractual relationship between the parties and the arbitrator(s), irrespective of whether institutional or *ad-hoc* arbitration is concerned? What is the legal qualification of such a contract (eg provision of services)? Although the arbitrator cannot be assimilated to a state judge, he carries out a judicial function. Unlike a state judge he can refuse an appointment to decide a case. The initial source of his authority is the agreement of the parties, with whom he has concluded a contract *sui generis*, irrespective of whether he sits as an *ad hoc* arbitrator or in an institutional arbitration.[145] **3.299**

(1.2) Are there court decisions (or authorities) determining which law governs the question of liability of an arbitrator? What is the position of those courts/authorities as to **3.300**

[142] See Keutgen, G. and Dal, G.A. (n 1) nos 223-31.

[143] Dalcq, R.O. and van Oevelen, A., 'La responsabilité de l'arbitre' in *L'arbitre: pouvoirs et statuts* (Bruylant, 2003) 201, n 14.

[144] Court of Appeal, Brussels, 8 January 2002, JT, 2002 at 792.

[145] de Bournonville, P. (n 4) no 147; Keutgen, G. and Dal, G.A. (n 1) no 205.

whether and to which extent a legal liability of an arbitrator (or arbitral institution) may be established? No decision is known whereby the court discussed the contractual liability of an arbitrator vis-à-vis a party.

3.301 **(1.3) Is an arbitrator subject to criminal prosecution?** An arbitrator can be subject to criminal prosecution whenever he participates in a criminal operation, such as knowingly rendering an award on the basis of a fraud or as part of a tax-dodging or money laundering scheme.

3.302 Moreover, an arbitrator may also possibly be prosecuted for breaches of his professional duty of secrecy.[146]

(2) Possibility to restrict or exclude such liability

3.303 To the extent allowed by Belgian contract law, the arbitrators' liability can be restricted by the arbitrators or by the arbitration rules under which they operate. However, they cannot exclude their liability for fraudulent behaviour and gross negligence.[147]

VII. Enforcement of national awards

(1) Requirement of a particular procedure to make an award enforceable (leave for enforcement, exequatur*)*

3.304 An arbitral award has the authority of *res judicata* when it has been notified to the parties. However, a party to any award may petition the President of the Court of First Instance in order to obtain an *exequatur* to make the award legally enforceable. The parties may have agreed on the court competent to decide on an *exequatur*; otherwise the court of the seat of arbitration will have jurisdiction (Art 1717, Cod Jud).

3.305 **(1.1) Does the national law make any difference between foreign and domestic awards, and if so, what are the criteria? Does there exist an additional notion of award for the purpose of obtaining *exequatur* (France: international awards)?** Under Belgian arbitration law, the conditions and the procedure for the enforcement of domestic awards are regulated by Arts 1710–1714, Cod Jud; those of a foreign award by Arts 1719–1723, Cod Jud.

3.306 **(1.2) May awards granting conservatory/interim measures be subject to enforcement?** Awards granting conservatory or interim measures may receive an *exequatur* as well as other awards do.

(2) Details of such enforcement procedure (competent court, reasons for rejection of motion etc)

3.307 Once the award has obtained the *exequatur* it becomes enforceable.

3.308 However, even without an *exequatur* as long as a domestic award is not set aside, it can be the basis for a conservatory attachment on the assets of the debtor or on assets a third party owes the debtor under Art 1414, Cod Jud. Indeed, under Art 1414, Cod Jud an award can be considered similar to a judgment which may give rise to such a conservatory

[146] See Lambert, P., *Le secret professionel,* RPDB vol XI (Bruylant, 2005) no 334.
[147] van Oevelen, A., 'La résponsabilité de l'arbitre' in *L'arbitre: pouvoirs et statut* (Bruylant, 2003) 198.

attachment.[148] Moreover, under Art 1445, Cod Jud, an award is a written document that certifies that a specific amount is due by the debtor—which again may be the basis for a conservatory attachment.[149]

The petition has to be drafted in the language (Dutch or French) of the court—depending where the court is located. If the award, to be attached to the petition, is in another language, a translation has to be added. The petition has to be submitted in two copies at the court's registry and is examined by the judge *in camera*. The procedure does not involve contradictory debates or the submission of additional files and briefs. **3.309**

If the judge deems such necessary, he can request some additional information from the petitioner (Art 1028, Cod Jud). An *exequatur* request is generally dealt with *ex parte* as the party against whom enforcement is sought is not invited to submit its objections. However, when that party is aware of the petition, it may solicit to be heard (Arts 1028 and 1710.1, Cod Jud). **3.310**

The judge will only perform a cursory examination of the award and will not re-examine the full dispute *ab initio*. Legal or factual errors are no ground to refuse an *exequatur*. **3.311**

The judge can only grant or refuse the *exequatur* of the award. The *exequatur* will be refused if: **3.312**

- the award is not open for appeal before another arbitral tribunal unless the first tribunal has granted provisional enforcement (Art 1710.2, Cod Jud);
- the enforcement of the award would violate public policy (Art 1710.3, Cod Jud); or
- the dispute was not arbitrable (Art 1710.3, Cod Jud).

Within five days after the judge had decided on the *exequatur*, the petitioner is notified thereof. **3.313**

If an *exequatur* has been granted, the successful petitioner has to notify the party against whom enforcement is sought of this decision by 'huissier'. **3.314**

Petitioners generally ask for the *exequatur* decision to remain enforceable in spite of the opposition to the *exequatur* or of a request to set aside the award from the party against whom enforcement is sought. In that event, the *exequatur* decision remains enforceable and can be used as a title for a conservatory attachment. In practice an *exequatur* decision often leads first to a conservatory attachment before it is notified to the other side. To the extent necessary the conservatory attachment may then ultimately be converted in an *exequatur* attachment. **3.315**

(3) Appeal against the decision granting exequatur

Within one month after the notification of the *exequatur* decision, the party against whom enforcement is sought can oppose the *exequatur* decision on the basis of the grounds mentioned above and stated in Art 1710, Cod Jud. At the same time it may also request the judge to order a stay of the enforcement or—at least—to order the enforcing party to post **3.316**

[148] See annotation De Leval, G. under Attachment Court of First Instance Antwerp, 7 December 1979, *Jurisprudence du port d'Anvers*, 1987, 111. See also Keutgen, G. and Dal, G.A. (n 1) no 40.
[149] Van Houtte, H. *et al*, 'Overzicht van Rechtspraak: Arbitrage' (n 25) no 158.

a security (Art 1714.1, Cod Jud. It may also request the setting aside of the award—on the basis of the more ample grounds of Art 1704, Cod Jud (see *supra* nrs 3-279 – 3.293).

(4) Appeal etc if exequatur *has been refused*

3.317 If an *exequatur* would be denied by the President of the Court of First Instance, the petitioner may request the competent Court of Appeal to reconsider this refusal. Within one month after notification the appeal has to be lodged and the party, against whom enforcement was sought, has to be summoned by 'huissier' before the Court of Appeal (Art 1711.1, Cod Jud).

(5) Procedure of enforcement (attachment of bank accounts etc)

3.318 Final awards, which are *res judicata*, are similar to Belgian court judgments and can be a basis for a conservatory attachment of bank accounts or other assets without further specific court proceedings.[150] Whenever the conservatory attachment has to be converted into an executory attachment, the enforcement proceedings, provided for in Arts 1710–1714, Cod Jud, have to be followed and the award has to receive the *exequatur* from the Court of First Instance of the 'arrondissement' where the arbitration had its seat.

3.319 **(5.1) At the stage of enforcement, may the losing party invoke arguments and circumstances which are based on facts which have occurred before (or after) the award was made?** No other facts, other than those submitted to the arbitrators, can be invoked in the *exequatur* proceedings to block enforcement. Only the grounds, referred to in Art 1710, Cod Jud, can lead to a refusal of the *exequatur*. However, whenever a party discovers after the award has been rendered that fraud has been committed or that false written or oral evidence has been submitted to the arbitrators, it may request the setting aside of the award (Art 1707.3, Cod Jud). Whenever the award would already have been enforced before it is set aside, whatever has been paid as a consequence of the court enforcement order, will have to be reimbursed.

3.320 **(5.2) May the losing party invoke a set-off based on claims that are not related to the matter of the arbitral proceeding? Is it material whether such claim came into existence before or after the award was made?** An *exequatur* procedure only focuses on the award and does not take into account matters not related to the arbitration. Consequently the *exequatur* decision stands on its own and is not subject to set-off. The *exequatur* judge does not carry out a judicial set-off between what is due under the award and what may be due to the party against whom enforcement is sought (and who in the first instance was even not given an opportunity to be heard).

VIII. Foreign awards

A. Recognition and/or enforcement of foreign awards (national law)

(1) Rules according to national law

3.321 An *exequatur* of a foreign award has to be solicited from the President of the Court of First Instance of the place where the party against whom enforcement is sought has its

[150] See Art 1414, Cod Jud and Juge Saisies, Antwerp, 7 December 1979, *Jur Port Anvers* 1987, 111 with annotation G. De Leval (which incorrectly applied this principle to a foreign award).

domicile[151] or residence; or in case it has no such domicile or residence in Belgium, from the President of the Court of First Instance where the award is to be enforced (Art 1719.2, Cod Jud). The petitioner has to choose a domicile for the purpose of the enforcement proceedings in the resort of the court. And all notifications to him will be made to this address.

(2) Requirements to be fulfilled by the applicant (procedure, time limits)

The party seeking the enforcement should submit the original or authenticated copy of the award and of the arbitration agreement (Art 1719.2, Cod Jud). **3.322**

When enforcement is not governed by a specific treaty (see hereunder), *exequatur* can be denied on the following four grounds, of which the three first must be verified *ex officio* by the judge (Art 1723, Cod Jud): **3.323**

(i) if the award can still be appealed before the arbitrators and if the arbitrators did not make the award provisionally enforceable notwithstanding an appeal;
(ii) if the award or its enforcement is contrary to public policy. The scope of this 'public policy' is, however, more limited than that of Belgian 'public policy' as referred to in Art 6, Code Civil. The former only concerns the most fundamental principles of the Belgian social, political or economic order, while the latter covers all Belgian mandatory rules;
(iii) if the dispute is not arbitrable according to Belgian law;[152] or
(iv) if a ground for setting aside the award pursuant to Art 1704 is established.[153]

Moreover, there is no need for the award to have already been declared enforceable (double *exequatur*) or to be confirmed by a court in the country where it was rendered in order to be enforced in Belgium.[154] **3.324**

The Belgian judge has no power to set aside a foreign award, but can only deny the *exequatur*. If one of the parties seeks the setting aside of an award rendered abroad, it should petition the court of the country where the award has been rendered and follow the relevant procedural rules of that country. **3.325**

A foreign award, which has received an *exequatur* from the Belgian court, is enforceable in Belgium as an enforceable Belgian court judgment (Art 1494, Cod Jud). **3.326**

---

[151] A 'domicile' under Belgian law is the place where a person is officially registered to have his domicile in the population records.

[152] See eg Cass 28 June 1979, JT 1979, 626, RCJB 1981, 332 and RW 1980-1981, 539, whereby an award, rendered in Switzerland, could not be recognized and enforced in Belgium because the dispute concerned the termination of a concession agreement, covering Belgian territory and subject to the 1961 Statute on the Termination of Exclusive Concession Agreements, which excludes an arbitration clause that envisages the resolution of such disputes in an arbitration outside Belgium and with a non-Belgian law applicable to the merits.

[153] See eg Court of First Instance, Brussels, 29 September 1998 and 14 April 1999, *Jurisprudence du Port d'Anvers* 1999, 271 and 303, where it was argued that a French award would not be enforceable in Belgium because of a lack of a written arbitration agreement (Art 1704.2.c, Cod Jud), but where the Belgian court nevertheless accepted the existence of such agreement because it had been recognized by a French Court.

[154] See Court of First Instance, Brussels, 24 January 1997, JT 1997, 319 and *Rev arb* 1998, 181.

(3) Remedies against decisions granting or declining enforcement

3.327 If an *exequatur* has been granted, the successful petitioner has to notify the party against whom enforcement is sought of this decision by 'huissier'.

3.328 Within one month after this notification, the party against whom enforcement is sought can oppose the *exequatur* decision on the basis of the grounds mentioned above and stated in Art 1723, Cod Jud. At the same time it also may request the judge to order a stay of the enforcement or—at least—to order the enforcing party to post a security (Art 1714.1, Cod Jud).

3.329 If an *exequatur* would be denied by the President of the Court of First Instance, the petitioner may request the competent Court of Appeal to reconsider this refusal. Within one month after notification the appeal has to be lodged and the party against whom enforcement was sought has to be summoned by 'huissier' before the Court of Appeal (by analogy with the appeal against a refused *exequatur* of a domestic award: Art 1711.1, Cod Jud).

B. Recognition and/or enforcement of foreign awards (conventions, treaties)

(1) Specific bilateral or multilateral treaties

3.330 Belgium is a party to various multilateral conventions regarding the enforcement of foreign arbitral awards:

- the Geneva Convention of 26 September 1927, regarding the enforcement of awards in commercial matters (Law of 15 April 1929 (*Moniteur belge*, 11 July 1929));
- the New York Convention of 10 June 1958 (Law of 5 June 1975 (*Moniteur belge*, 5 June 1975));
- the Convention for the Settlement of Investment Disputes between States and Nationals of Other States, concluded in Washington on 18 March 1965 (Law of 17 July 1970, *Moniteur belge*, 24 September 1970); and
- the European Convention on International Commercial Arbitration and appendixes, signed in Geneva on 21 April 1961, and the Arrangement concerning the application of this Convention, signed in Paris on 17 December 1962 (Law of 19 July 1975 , *Moniteur belge*, 17 February 1976).

3.331 Belgium also signed a number of bilateral conventions:

- the Franco-Belgian Convention of 8 July 1899 (Law of 13 March 1900, *Moniteur belge*, 30-31 July 1900);
- the Dutch-Belgian Convention of 28 March 1925 (Law of 16 August 1926, *Moniteur belge*, 27 July 1929);
- the German-Belgian Convention of 30 June 1958 (Law of 10 August 1960, *Moniteur belge*, 18 November 1960);
- the Swiss-Belgian Convention of 29 April 1959 (Law of 21 May 1962, *Moniteur belge*, 11 September 1962); and
- the Austrian-Belgian Convention of 16 June 1959 (Law of 10 August 1960, *Moniteur belge*, 27 October 1961).

(2) Existence of a standard procedure for the enforcement of foreign awards

Article 1723, Cod Jud only covers the grounds for refusal of an *exequatur* of a foreign award. The procedure to be followed is generally the same as the procedure with regard to an *exequatur* of a domestic award. However, for recognition and enforcement under the bilateral treaties with France, the Netherlands and Germany some aspects of the procedure differ from the procedure under the *Code Judiciaire*.[155] The provisions in the bilateral treaties with France and Germany, which require an *exequatur* in the country of the seat before the *exequatur* can be granted by a Belgian court, are in all events overtaken by the exclusion of the 'double *exequatur*' under the Belgian common regime of Art 1723, Cod Jud and by the New York Convention. **3.332**

The petition has to be drafted in the language (Dutch or French) of the court—depending where the court is located. If the award, to be attached to the petition, is in another language, a translation has to be added. The petition has to be submitted in two copies at the court's registry and is examined by the judge *in camera*. The procedure does not involve contradictory debates or the submission of additional files and briefs. **3.333**

If the judge deems such necessary, he can request some additional information from the petitioner (Art 1028, Cod Jud). An *exequatur*-request is generally dealt with *ex parte* as the party against whom enforcement is sought, is not invited to submit its objections. However, when that party is aware of the petition, it may solicit to be heard (Arts 1028 and 1710.1, Cod Jud). **3.334**

The judge will only perform a cursory examination of the award and will not re-examine the full dispute *ab initio*. Legal or factual errors are no ground to refuse an *exequatur*. **3.335**

The judge can only grant or refuse *exequatur* of the award. **3.336**

If an *exequatur* would be denied by the President of the Court of First Instance, the petitioner may request the competent Court of Appeal to reconsider this refusal. Within one month after notification the appeal has to be lodged and the party against whom enforcement was sought has to be summoned by 'huissier' before the Court of Appeal (Art 1711.1, Cod Jud). **3.337**

If an *exequatur* has been granted, the successful petitioner has to notify the party against whom enforcement is sought of this decision by 'huissier'. **3.338**

Within one month after this notification, the party against whom enforcement is sought can oppose the *exequatur*—decision on the basis of the grounds mentioned above and stated in Art 1723, Cod Jud. At the same time it may also request the judge to order a stay of the enforcement or—at least—to order the enforcing party to post a security (Art 1714.1, Cod Jud). **3.339**

(3) Extent of examination and review of the award by the court

When the recognition or enforcement of a foreign award is pursued under a treaty, the court will review the award in light of the review criteria of that treaty. If more than one **3.340**

[155] See Keutgen, G. and Dal, G.A. (n 1) nos 642–6.

treaty applies, the court will only apply the criteria and standards of the treaty which is most favourable towards recognition and enforcement of the award.

C. Application of the New York Convention

(1) Application of the New York Convention in practice

3.341 Belgium has ratified the New York Convention on the Recognition and Enforcement of Foreign Awards (1958) by Statute of Law of 5 June 1975 (*Moniteur belge*, 5 June 1975) which is applicable in Belgium with the 'reciprocity' reservation, ie it applies only when the award is rendered in a country which likewise has adopted the New York Convention.

3.342 Under Art III of the New York Convention enforcement proceedings have to follow the domestic law. Consequently, Belgian courts have applied Art 1719, Cod Jud thereto.[156] A foreign award does not need an *exequatur* in its country of origin to be enforced under the New York Convention.[157] However, when in its country of origin the award is subject of proceedings to set it aside, the Belgian judge may suspend enforcement proceedings under Art VI of the New York Convention;[158] if the Belgian judge considers that the award will probably not be set aside, he may continue enforcement proceedings.[159] A foreign award rendered without any written arbitration agreement cannot be enforced under Art V.1.a of the New York Convention.[160] Similarly a foreign award will not be recognized or enforced in Belgium when the dispute it resolves is not arbitrable under Belgian law; consequently a Swiss award, which stated that no compensation was due for termination of an exclusive Belgian distributorship-agreement was not recognized because such dispute, covered by the 1961-statute on exclusive distributorship-agreements, was not arbitrable under Belgian law (see *supra* 3.013).

(2) Examples of decisions which do not apply the Convention correctly

3.343 There are no instances where the Belgian courts have applied the New York Convention incorrectly.

IX. Appendix

A. National legislation

Code of Civil Procedure, Pt 6, as introduced by the Statute of 4 July 1972 (*Moniteur belge*, 8 August 1972) and amended by the Statutes of 27 March 1985[161] and 19 May 1998.[162]

B. Arbitral institutions

CEPANI-CEPINA
Stuiversstraat 8/Rue des Sols 8

[156] Ct Mechelen, 2 June 1992, *Pasicrisie* 1992, III, 81.
[157] Cass 5 June 1998, *Journal des Tribunaux* 1998, 701.
[158] Appeal, Ghent, 1 April 1994, *Rechtskundig Weekblad* 1994-95, 1057.
[159] Ct Brussels, 25 January 1996, *Journal des Tribunaux* 1997, 234.
[160] Ct Brussels, 29 September 1998, *Jurisprudence du Port d'Anvers* 1999, 271.
[161] *Moniteur belge*, 13 April 1985.
[162] *Moniteur belge*, 7 August 1998.

B-1000 Brussels
Website: <http://www.cepani.be>

Arbitrage van de Nederlandse Orde van Advocaten bij de Balie te Brussel
Gerechtsgebouw
Poelartplein
B-1000 Brussels

Arbitrage de l'Ordre français des avocats du barreau de Bruxelles
Palais de Justice
Place poelaert
B-1000 Brussels

Belgische Arbitragecommissie van de Koninklijke Belgische Voetbalbond/Commission d'arbitrage de l'Unuin Royale Belge de Sociétés de Football
Avenue Houba de Strooperlaan 145
B-1020 Brussels

Belgische Arbitragecommissie voor de Sport/Commission belge d'arbitrage pour le sport
Avenue de Boechoutlaan 9
B-1020 Brussels

Geschillencommissie Meubelen vzw/Commission de Litiges Meubles asbl
B.I. Trade Mart
Atomiumsquare PB 613
B-1020 Brussels

Geschillencommissie Reizen vzw/Commission de Litiges Voyages asbl
Avenue de Koning Albert II-laan 16
B-1000 Brussels

LEGIBEL E.S.V./LEGIBEL G.I.E.
Koningsstraat 55/Rue Royale 55
B-1000 Brussels

Belgapom
Rue de Spastraat 8
B-1000 Brussels

Arbitrage- en Verzoeningskamer voor Granen en Zaden van Antwerpen vzw
Borzestraat 29
B-2000 Antwerpen

Beurs voor Diamanthandel
Pelikaanstraat 78
B-2018 Antwerpen

Geschillencommissie Verbruikers—Textielreinigers (GVT)/Commission d'arbitrage Consommateurs—Entreprises de l'Entretien du Textile (CACET)
Brusselsesteenweg 478
B-1731 Zellik

C. Model arbitration clauses and other patterns

See eg the model CEPANI arbitration clause:

Any disputes arising out of or in relation with this Agreement shall be finally settled under the CEPANI Rules of Arbitration by one or more arbitrators appointed in accordance with those Rules

The following provisions may be added to this clause:

'The Arbitral Tribunal shall be composed of (one) or (three) arbitrators' (1)
'The seat of the arbitration shall be (town or city)'
'The arbitration shall be conducted in the (...) language'
'The applicable rules of law are (...)'

D. Bibliography

Bigwood, J. and Wasserman, D., *Fiscalité des honoraires des arbitres, in Arbitrage et Fiscalité* (coll CEPANI, Bruylant, Brusselss, 2001) 125.

Caprasse, O., 'Interpréter, rectifier ou compléter une sentence arbitrale; incidence sur la procédure du recours en annulations' *Rev Dr Liège* (2006) 61.

Dal, G.A. and Leroy, Ph., 'Existe-t-il une déontologie et une discipline des arbitres', in *L'arbitre: pouvoirs et statut* (coll CEPANI, Bruylant, Brussels, 2003) 165.

Dalcq, R.-O. and Van Oevelen, A., 'La responsabilité de l'arbitre', in *L'arbitre: pouvoirs et statut* (coll CEPANI, Bruylant, Brussels, 2003) 191.

De Bournonville, Ph. and Van Doosselaere, G., 'La nomination de l'arbitre', in *L'arbitre: pouvoirs et statut* (coll CEPANI, Bruylant, Brussels 2003) 37.

De Bournonville, Ph., 'Au sujet des demandes incidentes en matière d'arbitrage', in *L'arbitrage: Travaux offerts au professeur Albert Fettweis* (Story Scientia, Brussels, 1989) 55.

De Gryse, L., 'Quelques propos sur l'arbitrage en matière de brevets d'inventions', in *Jura Vigilantibus* (Antoine Braun, Larcier, Brussels, 1994) 89.

De Leval, G., 'Les mesures provisoires et conservatoires en matière d'arbitrage', in *L'arbitrage: Travaux offerts au professeur Albert Fettweis* (Story Scientia, Brussels, 1989) 111.

De Leval, G., 'Les mesures provisoires et l'arbitrage', in *Arbitrage et modes alternatifs de règlement des litiges* (CUP, Liège, 2002) 168.

Hanotiau, B., 'Le principe du contradictoire devant les tribunaux arbitraux', obs. under Brussels, 25 September 1997, *JT* (1998) p 312.

Hollander, P., 'L'arbitrabilité des litiges en matière de résiliation de concession de vente soumises à la loi du 27 juillet 1961: fui de la controverse?', note under Cass 15 October 2004, *RDC* (2005) 498.

Hollander, P., 'L'arbitrabilité des litiges relatifs aux contrats de distribution commerciale en droit belge', in *L'arbitrage et la distribution commerciale* (coll CEPANI, Bruylant, Brussels, 2005) 25.

Keutgen, G. and Dal, G.A., *L'arbitrage en droit belge et international, Tome I—Le droit belge* (2nd edn, Bruylant 2006).

Keutgen, G., *International Handbook on Commercial Arbitration*, Suppl 49, April 2007.

Linsmeau, J., *L'arbitrage volontaire en droit privé belge* (Bruylant, 1991).

Linsmeau, J. and Van Houtte, V., 'Honoraires et frais des arbitres', in *L'arbitrage: pouvoirs et statut* (coll CEPANI, Bruylant, Brussels, 2003) 233.

Nelissen-Grade, J.-M., 'The annulment of arbitral rewards in Belgium' *International Financial L Rev* (1986) 35.

Storme, M. and Demeuelnaere, B., *International commercial arbitration in Belgium: a handbook* (Kluwer, Deventer, 1989).

Van Houtte, H. and Valgaeren, E., *De exequatur van arbitrage-uitspraken* (RDC, 1997) 275.
Van Houtte, H., 'Aanduiding van arbiters door de rechtbank', note under Cass 7 December 1989, *Pas* (1990) 439.
Van Houtte, H., 'De geldigheid van het arbitragebeding dat arbitrage toevertrouwt aan een beroepsorganisatie', note under Comm, Louvain, 19 September 1989, *RDC* (1990) p 1022.
Verbist, H. and Erauw, J., *Résultats de l'enquête concernant les entreprises et les juristes d'entreprise en Belgique face à l'arbitrage commercial et la conciliation* (RCDP, 2000) 341.
Verbist, H., *Het echte, becijferde beeld van arbitrage in België* (RW, 1998–1999) 345.

Overview of court decisions on arbitration.

Keutgen, G. and Huys, M., 'Chronique de jurisprudence—L'arbitrage (1950 to 1975)' *JT* (1976) 53.
Keutgen, G. and Huys, M., 'Chronique de jurisprudence—L'arbitrage (1975 to 1982)' *JT* (1984) 53.
Keutgen, G., 'Chronique de jurisprudence—L'arbitrage (1982 to 1987)' *JT* (1988) 419.
Keutgen, G., 'Chronique de jurisprudence—L'arbitrage (1987 to 1992)' *JT* (1993) 678.
Keutgen, G., 'Chronique de jurisprudence—L'arbitrage (1993 to 2003)' *JT*, (2004) 429.
Van Houtte, H., Cox, K. and Cools, S., 'Overzicht van Rechtspraak Arbitrage (1972–2006)' *Revue de Droit Commercial belge* (2007) 111.

4

CHINA AND HONG KONG

Michael J. Moser and John Choong

I. Introduction

In recent years, the People's Republic of China ('PRC') has gained increasing recognition as an important player in international arbitration. Hong Kong, which reverted to Chinese sovereignty in 1997 but retains its own separate arbitration regime, has long held one of the premier positions among Asian international arbitration venues. **4.01**

This chapter covers the arbitration regime in both the PRC and Hong Kong. The two systems are discussed separately under each header, using the following notations: **4.02**

(i) '(A)' refers to a section discussing the PRC position; and
(ii) '(B)' refers to a section discussing the Hong Kong position, focusing on international arbitration.

A. Current status of the law on arbitration

(1) Short history

(A) Prior to 1995, the PRC's arbitration law was embodied in a number of different pieces of legislation.[1] In addition, the arbitration regime was set out in various regulations, **4.03**

[1] These included the Economic Contract Law of the People's Republic of China (effective from 1 July 1982, repealed by the Contract Law of the People's Republic of China on 1 October 1999), and the Civil

interpretations, notices and explanations issued by the PRC Supreme People's Court ('SPC'), China's highest judicial body.

4.04 The piecemeal nature of PRC arbitration legislation changed with the coming into force of the Arbitration Law of the People's Republic of China (the 'PRC Arbitration Law') in 1995.[2] The new law represented a 'great leap forward' and fundamentally changed the PRC's arbitration landscape.

4.05 Although the PRC Arbitration Law is based on a number of international norms, PRC arbitral law and practice differs in a number of significant ways from that practised in Hong Kong and in other leading arbitral jurisdictions.

4.06 (B) In contrast to the PRC, Hong Kong has long been one of the leading arbitral seats in Asia. The prominence of Hong Kong is due in part to the establishment of the Hong Kong International Arbitration Centre ('HKIAC') in 1985, as well as Hong Kong's adoption in 1990 of the United Nations Commission on International Trade Law ('UNCITRAL') Model Law,[3] for international arbitrations.

4.07 In 1997, the PRC resumed sovereignty over Hong Kong. Under the principle of 'one country, two systems', Hong Kong's previous legal system continues in place as the foundation of the rule of law, whilst the change of sovereignty is reflected in Hong Kong's new status as a part of the PRC. Importantly, arbitration law and practice in Hong Kong has remained unaffected by the handover.[4] Hong Kong's international arbitration system therefore remains very much based on the UNCITRAL Model Law,[5] as adopted into Hong Kong by the Arbitration Ordinance (c 341) ('HK Arbitration Ordinance').

(2) Law in force and future projects

4.08 (A) The PRC Arbitration Law was adopted at the Ninth Meeting of the Standing Committee of the Eighth National People's Congress, promulgated by Order no 31 of the President of the People's Republic of China on 31 August 1994, and effective as of 1 September 1995.

4.09 It was the result of over three years of drafting, and was based on a number of well recognized norms in international arbitration practice. The PRC Arbitration Law's provisions have also been influenced by the provisions of the UNCITRAL Model Law, although the PRC is not considered a 'model law country' by the UNCITRAL.[6]

Procedure Law of the People's Republic of China (the 'PRC Civil Procedure Law', effective from 9 April 1991, with the revised version effective from 1 April 2008).

[2] Effective from 1 September 1995.

[3] UNGA Res 40/72 (11 December 1985), 40 GAOR Supp No 53, A/40/53, 308.

[4] Save for the recognition and enforcement of Hong Kong awards in the PRC and vice versa, which is discussed at VIII.A.(1) *infra*.

[5] Save for the 2006 amendments to the UNCITRAL Model Law, which have, to date, not been adopted in Hong Kong, although they are set out in the new draft arbitration bill as at the time of writing.

[6] It is not listed as a country which has adopted arbitral legislation based on the UNCITRAL Model Law; cf Hong Kong and Macau, both of which are found on the list: UNCITRAL Model Law on International Commercial Arbitration—status: <http://www.uncitral.org/uncitral/en/uncitral_texts/arbitration/1985Model_arbitration_status.html> (accessed 30 January 2008).

There have been indications that the PRC Arbitration Law is currently being reviewed to bring it more in line with international practice, and to address various shortcomings which have become apparent since its enactment. However, as at the time of writing, it is unclear when the revised law will be promulgated. 4.10

(B) Hong Kong's international arbitration regime is based on the UNCITRAL Model Law, which forms the Fifth Schedule to the HK Arbitration Ordinance. 4.11

The ordinance does not provide a complete code for the conduct of arbitrations, but is intended to provide a framework within which all kinds of *ad hoc* and institutional arbitrations may be carried out in Hong Kong. 4.12

The HK Arbitration Ordinance in its present form (with the complicated numbering of its sections) is the result of many amendments, driven by changes in English law, local legal reform proposals, reactions to developments in the sphere of international arbitration law, and by amendments made necessary by Hong Kong's reversion to PRC sovereignty. 4.13

Some of its key features include judicious court support of arbitration (including the power to suspend court proceedings brought in breach of an arbitration agreement, and the availability of interim relief in aid of arbitration), and the right of all parties to equal treatment and a proper opportunity to present their case. 4.14

Parts I and IA of the HK Arbitration Ordinance apply both to international and domestic arbitration.[7] Part II deals exclusively with domestic arbitration. Part IIA applies the UNCITRAL Model Law to international arbitrations conducted in Hong Kong. The remaining parts deal with enforcement of awards. 4.15

Hong Kong has adopted the UNCITRAL Model Law by reproducing it as the Fifth Schedule to the HK Arbitration Ordinance, with an express provision stating that an international arbitration agreement is governed by chs I to VII of the Model Law.[8] The application of the Model Law is subject to the HK Arbitration Ordinance provisions, which fill a number of perceived gaps in the Model Law and, in a few cases, exclude or limit provisions of the Model Law, either expressly or by implication. 4.16

Throughout this chapter, references have been made to UNCITRAL Model Law provisions. Such a reference means that the relevant Model Law provision is applicable in Hong Kong, as a result of the HK Arbitration Ordinance. Where it is clear that the Model Law provision has to be read in conjunction with a provision in the HK Arbitration Ordinance proper, an additional reference has been included. 4.17

In addition to the HK Arbitration Ordinance, case law (precedent) is still applicable in Hong Kong. This follows from the fact that Hong Kong continues to be a common law jurisdiction by virtue of the Basic Law which governs the transfer of sovereignty to the PRC. 4.18

[7] The terms 'international arbitration' and 'domestic arbitration' are explained in I.A.(3).(B) *infra*.
[8] Section 34C(1), HK Arbitration Ordinance.

4.19 The HK Arbitration Ordinance is currently the subject of an ongoing review, which seeks to abolish the distinction between domestic and international arbitrations. A long-awaited consultation paper and draft of the arbitration bill was published by the Department of Justice in December 2007.[9] As at the time of writing, the Arbitration Bill had received its first reading before the Legislative Council and it is expected that in the near future, Hong Kong will have in place a largely unitary regime for domestic and international arbitrations, both based on the UNCITRAL Model Law.

(3) Distinction between national and international arbitration

4.20 (A) PRC law draws a distinction between foreign-related arbitrations and domestic arbitrations. To some extent, this split corresponds to the 'international' and 'non-international' distinction under the UNCITRAL Model Law.

4.21 The PRC Arbitration Law generally applies to both 'foreign-related' and domestic arbitrations.[10] The exception is ch VII ('Special Provisions for Arbitration involving Foreign Elements'), which sets out provisions applying specifically to economic, trade, transportation and maritime activities involving a foreign element.

4.22 For the reasons explained at IV.B.(1) *infra*, the distinction between 'foreign-related' arbitration and domestic arbitration is a significant one.

4.23 (B) The HK Arbitration Ordinance creates two distinct arbitration regimes in Hong Kong, one dealing with domestic arbitrations and the other with international arbitrations. The HK Arbitration Ordinance permits parties to an international arbitration agreement to opt to treat it as a domestic arbitration agreement instead.[11]

4.24 In contrast to the international regime, the domestic regime confers a number of additional powers on the Hong Kong courts to supervise or assist the arbitration process.[12] However, as a result of the ongoing review of the HK Arbitration Ordinance, it is likely that many of these differences will fall away, as Hong Kong moves towards a unitary regime for domestic and international arbitration.

(3.1) If there are different systems and rules for national/international arbitration, what are the criteria for the distinction between both systems?

4.25 (A) Under PRC law, an arbitration is generally considered 'foreign-related' if it involves:[13]

(i) at least one foreign party; or

---

[9] Available at: <http://www.gov.hk/en/residents/government/consultation/docs/2008/arbitration.pdf> (accessed 3 March 2008).

[10] See Art 65, PRC Arbitration Law.

[11] s 2M, HK Arbitration Ordinance.

[12] These powers include the following:

(i) the court may order that two or more arbitration proceedings be consolidated or may order any of them to be stayed until after the determination of any of them (s 6B(1));

(ii) the court may, in limited circumstances, determine a preliminary point of law (s 23A); and

(iii) the court may order that the arbitrators' fees be taxed (ie subject to a verification process by the courts in Hong Kong) (s21).

[13] Art 304 of the SPC, 'Several Opinions on the Application of PRC Civil Procedure Law' (issued 14 July 1992); and Art 178 of the SPC, 'Several Opinions on the Implementation of PRC General Principles of the Civil Law (Trial Implementation)' (issued 2 April 1988).

(ii) if all the parties are Chinese parties, where:
  a. either the facts establishing the legal relationship between the parties occurred in a foreign country; or
  b. the subject matter in dispute is in a foreign country.

There are three points to note about the above test: **4.26**

(i) First, Chinese entities which are owned by foreign parties (referred to as foreign-invested enterprises ('FIEs')), including wholly foreign-owned enterprises, are generally considered 'Chinese parties'. Importantly, this includes Chinese subsidiaries of foreign companies and Chinese entities which are Sino-foreign joint ventures. Conversely, Hong Kong- (and Macau-) incorporated entities are considered 'foreign parties'.

(ii) Secondly, although a foreign party is sometimes nominally included in a contract, to satisfy the 'foreign party' requirement, it is debatable if such an approach will always be effective under PRC law. In particular, if the foreign party does not appear to have an active role to play in the contract, and does not appear to have a direct interest in any dispute, the contract may not be considered 'foreign-related'. It will then be subject to the limitations of a domestic contract, as explained at IV.B.(1) *infra.*

(iii) Thirdly, whereas the 'foreign party' element in limb (i) is relatively objective, the elements in limb (ii) *supra* are more subjective, and less capable of certain determination. For example, the mere fact that a contract has been executed overseas may not be sufficient to satisfy the requirement that the 'facts establishing the legal relationship have occurred in a foreign country'.

Given the above difficulties with satisfying limb (ii), in practice, the best assurance that a matter is 'foreign-related' is where at least one of the genuine parties to the contract is a foreign party.

(B) The HK Arbitration Ordinance adopts the definition in the UNCITRAL Model Law,[14] that an arbitration is international if: **4.27**

(i) the parties to an arbitration agreement have, at the time of the conclusion of that agreement, their places of business in different states;[15] or

(ii) one of the following places is situated outside the state in which the parties have their places of business:
  a. the place of arbitration if determined in, or pursuant to, the arbitration agreement;
  b. any place where a substantial part of the obligations of the commercial relationship is to be performed or the place with which the subject matter of the dispute is most closely connected;[16] or

[14] Art 1(3), UNCITRAL Model Law.

[15] References to 'state' and 'states' include a reference to Hong Kong: s 2(4) of the HK Arbitration Ordinance.

[16] In practice this is the part of Art 1(3) of the UNCITRAL Model Law which has proven to have the greatest significance in Hong Kong. See *Fung Sang Trading Ltd v Kai Sun Sea Products and Food Co Ltd* [1992] 1 HKLR 40; *Orienmet Minerals Co Ltd v Winner Desire Ltd*, unreported, 7 April 1997 (A 14689/1996).

(iii) the parties have expressly agreed that the subject matter of the arbitration agreement relates to more than one country.

4.28 A 'domestic arbitration agreement' is defined in the HK Arbitration Ordinance as an arbitration agreement that is not an international arbitration agreement. Accordingly, arbitration agreements which would not be international in accordance with the above criteria are domestic arbitration agreements. However, the HK Arbitration Ordinance does provide that parties may, after a dispute has arisen, agree in writing that what would otherwise be a domestic arbitration agreement is to be treated as an international arbitration agreement.[17] In practice, such agreement is rare.

B. Practice of arbitration

(1) Frequency of arbitration as opposed to litigation

4.29 (A) Arbitration plays a significant role in the resolution of commercial disputes in the PRC, both in purely domestic disputes, and in those involving foreign parties.

4.30 There are close to 200 local arbitration commissions in the PRC, and in recent years, the larger commissions have reported handling thousands of cases each year. A number of these arbitration commissions handle significant numbers of 'foreign-related' disputes, with the largest (the China International Economic and Trade Arbitration Commission ('CIETAC')) handling hundreds of foreign-related arbitrations each year.

4.31 By comparison, the PRC courts reportedly handled approximately 8 million civil and commercial disputes in 2006. The judicial caseload is also growing.

4.32 (B) In recent years, the HKIAC has recorded a significant increase in the number of international arbitration cases it handles. In 2004, it reported a total of 280 cases, and this increased to 394 by 2006, and 448 by 2007.

4.33 By comparison, in recent years, the Court of First Instance (a Hong Kong superior court) has had a caseload of about 20,000 civil matters each year. Of these, in 2007, 2,877 were High Court actions.[18]

4.34 In practice, a significant number of cross-border contracts, including many PRC-related contracts, provide for arbitration instead of litigation.

(2) Leading arbitral institutions and statistics

4.35 (A) The PRC Arbitration Law draws a distinction between an 'arbitration commission' (*zhongcai weiyuanhui*) and an 'arbitration institution' (or organization, *zhongcai jigou*). 'Arbitration commission' is generally understood to be a reference to PRC arbitral bodies, whereas 'arbitration institution' is a broader umbrella term which encompasses both 'arbitration commissions' and foreign arbitration bodies such as the International Chamber of Commerce ('ICC').

---

[17] s 2L, HK Arbitration Ordinance.

[18] See <http://www.judiciary.gov.hk/en/publications/annu_rept_2007/eng/caseload02.html> (accessed 26 June 2008).

In the PRC, the leading arbitration commission handling foreign-related disputes is CIETAC. Other significant arbitration commissions include the China Maritime Arbitration Commission ('CMAC') for maritime disputes, and the Beijing Arbitration Commission ('BAC') and Shanghai Arbitration Commission ('SAC'). 4.36

In recent years, CIETAC has handled about 1,000 arbitrations each year (both domestic and 'foreign-related'). This makes it one of the busiest arbitration institutions in the world. 4.37

In 2006, CIETAC accepted 981 cases, 442 of which were foreign-related and 539 were domestic. Of the 539 domestic cases, a majority were cases between FIEs (such as joint ventures or wholly foreign-owned companies) or between an FIE and a purely Chinese business entity.[19] In 2007, CIETAC's caseload had grown to 1,118 arbitrations, of which 429 were foreign-related and 689 were domestic. In 2008, CIETAC established a new record of 1,230 new cases, of which 548 were foreign-related cases and 682 domestic ones. A total of 1,097 cases with a total claim amount of RMB20.9 billion were resolved. 4.38

Other institutions such as the Wuhan Arbitration Commission, Guangzhou Arbitration Commission, Shenzhen Arbitration Commission, the BAC and the SAC also handle thousands of cases each per year. However, the caseload of the BAC, SAC and other PRC arbitral commissions is much more heavily skewed towards domestic cases.[20] 4.39

Given the popularity of CIETAC arbitrations in foreign-related disputes, throughout this chapter, references have been made to the CIETAC Arbitration Rules where appropriate. 4.40

For the reasons explained at II.A.(2) *infra*, there are restrictions on foreign arbitral institutions administering arbitrations seated in the PRC. There are therefore very few such arbitrations in the PRC—for example, in 2006, there was only one ICC arbitration seated in the PRC (outside of Hong Kong).[21] 4.41

(B) The HKIAC is the leading arbitral institution in Hong Kong. It was established in 1985 to promote the use of arbitration and other forms of alternative dispute resolution in the territory. Formed as a non profit-making company limited by guarantee under Hong Kong law, the HKIAC was originally funded by contributions from the business community and the Hong Kong government. Today the HKIAC is completely independent of both business and government and operates with its own budget and funds. The HKIAC has grown to become a major international arbitration institution, and in its current role, it provides the focus for arbitration activity in Hong Kong. 4.42

---

19 Of the 981 cases accepted by CIETAC in 2006, the total amount in dispute was approximately RMB 9.2 billion, or US$1.18 billion. On average, a CIETAC case involved an amount of approximately RMB 9.38 million, or US$1.2 million. See Moser, M., 'CIETAC and its Work—An Interview with Vice Chairman Yu Jianlong' (2007) 24(6) *J Int'l Arb* 555.

20 For example, in 2006, the BAC accepted 2,464 cases, of which only about 56 were foreign-related cases; in 2007, they accepted 1,863 cases of which 162 were foreign-related.

21 ICC '2006 Statistical Report' (2007) 18(1) *ICC International Court of Arbitration Bulletin* 12. In comparison, over the same period, nine arbitrations in Hong Kong and 12 in Singapore were filed with the ICC, even though both jurisdictions have a much smaller overall arbitration caseload than the PRC.

4.43 In the past, the HKIAC adopted the UNCITRAL Arbitration Rules as its rules for international arbitrations. It was also common to agree that the HKIAC Procedures for the Administration of International Arbitration ('HKIAC Procedures') would apply. The HKIAC Procedures clarified the administrative role of the HKIAC within the overall framework of an UNCITRAL arbitration. However, the HKIAC has recently published the HKIAC Administered Arbitration Rules, effective from 1 September 2008, for use in arbitrations administered by the HKIAC. The HKIAC also has a set of Domestic Arbitration Rules.[22]

4.44 Although the publication of the HKIAC Administered Arbitration Rules is an important development, in the immediate future, the use of the UNCITRAL Arbitration Rules is likely to remain widespread in Hong Kong. Accordingly, in this chapter, where examples are taken from arbitration rules, the focus is on the UNCITRAL Arbitration Rules (and the HKIAC Procedures), but with footnote references to key provisions from the HKIAC Administered Arbitration Rules.

4.45 The role of the HKIAC has grown substantially over the last decade. In 1993 the HKIAC (acting either in an administrative capacity or as an appointing authority) had an involvement in 139 new international arbitration cases, rising to 218 in 1997, 257 in 1999, 307 in 2001 and 448 in 2007. In 2007, construction cases constituted about 41 per cent of this caseload, with commercial cases constituting a further 23 per cent.[23] Out of the 448 cases in 2007, 195 involved PRC parties.

4.46 Other significant arbitration organizations in Hong Kong include The East Asia branch of the Chartered Institute of Arbitrators, and the Hong Kong Institute of Arbitrators. There are also a number of industry-specific organizations that are active in arbitration-related areas.

II. Jurisdiction of the arbitral tribunal

A. Arbitration agreement

(1) Arbitration clause and submission agreement

4.47 (A) In general, an arbitration clause is a provision in a contract by which parties agree to arbitrate future disputes. In contrast, a submission agreement is generally an agreement to submit existing disputes to arbitration.

4.48 The PRC Arbitration Law recognizes that arbitration agreements comprise both arbitration clauses stipulated in a contract, as well as agreements to submit disputes to arbitration (whether these are concluded 'before or after disputes arise').[24]

4.49 (B) Hong Kong law also recognizes the distinction between an arbitration clause and a submission agreement. In practice, arbitration clauses are much more common than

[22] The Domestic Arbitration Rules 1993, to be read in conjunction with the HKIAC's revised Guide to Arbitration 1998.

[23] Source: <http://www.hkiac.org/> (accessed 3 October 2008).

[24] Art 16, PRC Arbitration Law.

submission agreements. A submission agreement is sometimes referred to as an '*ad hoc*' arbitration agreement.

(2) Requirements as to the contents of the arbitration agreement

(A) The PRC Arbitration Law provides that a valid arbitration agreement must: **4.50**

(i) be in writing;[25]
(ii) express an intention to refer disputes to arbitration;
(iii) stipulate the matters referable to arbitration; and
(iv) designate an 'arbitration commission' to hear the dispute.[26]

The first three requirements are relatively straightforward. However, requirement (iv) has proven controversial, for two reasons. **4.51**

First, it suggests that an 'arbitration commission' must be expressly designated in the arbitration agreement, failing which the agreement is invalid.[27] There is no such requirement in international arbitral practice, where parties frequently refer to an agreed set of arbitration rules without expressly designating a particular institution. **4.52**

As a result of this peculiarity, in the past, such arbitration agreements have been struck down for being invalid. This rigorous requirement has to some extent been ameliorated by a recent, and significant, SPC Interpretation on Certain Issues Relating to the Application of the PRC Arbitration Law ('SPC Interpretation 2006').[28] **4.53**

The Interpretation sets out various saving provisions: **4.54**

(i) even though the name of the arbitration institution that has been designated is not accurate, if it can nevertheless be determined, that arbitration institution shall be deemed selected; and
(ii) it provides, in effect, that where the arbitration institution is not expressly designated in the arbitration agreement, the arbitration agreement is not invalid if, *inter alia*, the arbitration institution can be ascertained pursuant to the arbitration rules which have been agreed by the parties.

An important corollary of the above requirement for an arbitration commission is that *ad hoc* arbitration does not appear to be recognized under PRC law. **4.55**

[25] The original text of the PRC Arbitration Law in Chinese does not clearly mandate that an arbitration clause must be in writing (in contrast, the reference to 'written form' is clear in the case of a submission agreement). Nonetheless, the written form requirement is generally interpreted as applying to both arbitration clauses and submission agreements.

[26] Art 16, PRC Arbitration Law.

[27] Art 18 of the PRC Arbitration Law sets out a saving provision, stating that if the arbitration agreement contains no or 'unclear provisions' (*yueding bumingque*) regarding, *inter alia*, the designation of an arbitration commission, the parties may attempt to reach a supplementary agreement. In practice, this provision will be of limited use since such agreement will often be difficult after a dispute has arisen.

[28] Effective 23 August 2006. For a more detailed discussion of many of the issues relating to the SPC Interpretation 2006 raised in this chapter, see Yuen, P. and Choong, J., 'Supreme People's Court's Draft Interpretation On Application Of The PRC Arbitration Law' (August 2006) 21(8) *Mealey's Int'l Arb Rep* 52. The article is based on a draft that is substantively identical to the SPC Interpretation 2006, as promulgated.

4.56 The second controversy with requirement (iv) is its reference to 'arbitration commission', and not to 'arbitration institution'. As explained at I.B.(2) *supra*, 'arbitration commission' is a reference to local PRC arbitration commissions, not foreign arbitration institutions. The existence of this requirement has therefore been widely interpreted as meaning that PRC law, implicitly, does not recognize the validity of arbitration agreements designating a foreign arbitration institution (such as the ICC or LCIA) to administer an arbitration held in the PRC. Instead, parties who arbitrate in the PRC have to designate a (Chinese) arbitration commission.

4.57 (B) The HK Arbitration Ordinance provides that the term 'arbitration agreement' has the same meaning as in the UNCITRAL Model Law.[29] The UNCITRAL Model Law states that an 'arbitration agreement' is

> . . . an agreement by the parties to submit to arbitration all or certain disputes which have arisen or which may arise between them in respect of a defined legal relationship, whether contractual or not. An arbitration agreement may be in the form of an arbitration clause in a contract or in the form of a separate agreement.[30]

4.58 There are no explicit formality requirements on content for an arbitration agreement to be valid. Therefore, the parties are free to agree whatever wording they choose, so long as they express a clear intention to submit their disputes to arbitration.

(3) Form of the arbitration agreement (eg 'in writing' requirement)

4.59 (A) As noted above, the PRC Arbitration Law provides that a valid arbitration agreement must be in writing. The SPC Interpretation 2006 clarifies that a 'written' arbitration agreement may be reached by express agreement in writing, exchange of letters and electronically transmitted documents (including telegrams, telefaxes, facsimiles, electronic data interchange and emails).[31]

4.60 (B) The UNCITRAL Model Law contains a provision dealing with the writing requirement.[32] However, in Hong Kong, this provision of the UNCITRAL Model Law has been excluded by the HK Arbitration Ordinance,[33] which significantly alters the meaning of 'agreement in writing'.[34]

4.61 The most obvious effect of the amendment is the removal of the requirement that an arbitration agreement must be 'signed' by the parties. In addition, the amendment also brings arbitration agreements that are partly in writing and partly oral within the scope of the HK Arbitration Ordinance. However, arbitration agreements that are entirely oral continue to fall outside the Ordinance. In the rare event that a party seeks to commence arbitral proceedings based on a wholly oral arbitration agreement, such proceedings would be governed by the common law.[35]

---

[29] Section 2(1), HK Arbitration Ordinance.
[30] Art 7(1), UNCITRAL Model Law.
[31] Art 1, SPC Interpretation 2006.
[32] Art 7(2), UNCITRAL Model Law.
[33] s 2AC, HK Arbitration Ordinance.
[34] The amendments were introduced by the Arbitration (Amendment) Ordinance 1996, which took effect on 27 June 1997.
[35] Unless, of course, s 2AC(2)(f) of the HK Arbitration Ordinance brings such an agreement within the scope of the 'writing' requirement.

Applying the test under the HK Arbitration Ordinance, an 'agreement in writing' will be found to exist if:[36] **4.62**

(i) the agreement is in a document, whether signed by the parties or not;
(ii) the agreement is made by an exchange of written communications;
(iii) although the agreement is not itself in writing, there is evidence in writing of the agreement;
(iv) the parties to the agreement agree otherwise than in writing by referring to terms that are in writing;
(v) the agreement, although made otherwise than in writing, is recorded by one of the parties to the agreement, or by a third party, with the authority of each of the parties to the agreement; or
(vi) there is an exchange of written submissions in arbitral or legal proceedings in which the existence of an agreement otherwise than in writing is alleged by one party against another party and is not denied by the other party in response to the allegation.

(3.1) Are there special requirements for a power of attorney/authority to enter into an arbitration agreement on behalf of a third party (A) The requirements are governed by the general PRC law on agency. **4.63**

In addition, a 1999 opinion[37] issued by the Beijing Higher People's Court deals with the validity of an arbitration agreement executed by an unauthorized agent or an agent whose acts are not subsequently ratified by the principal or an agent acting beyond the scope of its authority. The court's opinion was that an arbitration agreement executed in any of the foregoing situations will not be binding on the unauthorized agent or the principal. If a third party submits an application for arbitration based on such an arbitration agreement, the arbitral institution will have no jurisdiction. **4.64**

(B) There are no special requirements under the HK Arbitration Ordinance, and this issue is governed by the general law of agency. **4.65**

(4) Incorporation of an arbitration clause contained in general terms and conditions

(A) PRC law recognizes the doctrine of incorporation, under which an arbitration clause contained in a separate document (such as general conditions) or agreement can be validly incorporated into a signed contract.[38] The SPC Interpretation 2006 also addresses this issue, by providing that where a contract stipulates that a valid arbitration clause in another contract or document shall be applied to resolve disputes under the contract, the parties shall refer the dispute to arbitration in accordance with such a clause.[39] **4.66**

[36] s 2AC(2), HK Arbitration Ordinance.

[37] Beijing Higher People's Court, 'Opinion on Some Issues regarding the Determination of an Application for Ascertaining the Validity of an Arbitration Agreement and Motions to Revoke an Arbitration Award' (3 December 1999). This opinion will have to be read in conjunction with the PRC Contract Law dealing with the law of agency.

[38] See SPC, 'Reply on Determining Jurisdiction in a Sino-Mongolian Contract that Fails to Provide for Arbitration' (issued 14 December 1996).

[39] Art 11, SPC Interpretation 2006.

4.67 It is not entirely clear whether the contract in question must contain an express reference to the arbitration clause *specifically*, or whether a reference to the general conditions is sufficient. Although debatable, it appears likely from the wording of the SPC Interpretation 2006 that a general reference to the other contract or document is sufficient. Such a reading would also be consistent with previous opinions issued by the SPC and lower PRC courts.

4.68 (B) The HK Arbitration Ordinance provides that a reference in an agreement to:

(i) a written form of arbitration clause; or
(ii) a document containing an arbitration clause,

constitutes an arbitration agreement if the reference is such as to make that clause part of the agreement.[40]

4.69 Such documents might include a party's standard terms and conditions of a contract, or a standard form contract or a prior contract entered into between the parties.

4.70 The agreement making the reference does not itself need to be in writing, although it must be able to be evidenced in writing. The reference made by the parties may be to a specific written arbitration clause found elsewhere or simply to a document containing the clause. There is no requirement that specific words of incorporation be used.[41]

(5) Law applicable to the interpretation of arbitration clauses

4.71 (A) PRC law recognizes that the law governing the *arbitration clause* may be different from the law governing the other provisions in the underlying contract. The SPC Interpretation 2006 states that in determining the validity of an arbitration agreement, the PRC courts shall apply:[42]

(i) the 'law' agreed by the parties; or
(ii) if the parties have not agreed on 'the applicable law' but have agreed on the place of arbitration, the law of the country (or region) in which the arbitration takes place; or
(iii) if the parties have not agreed on the place of arbitration or the agreement on the place of arbitration is unclear, the law of the place 'where the court is located'.

4.72 Therefore, unless the parties have agreed on 'the applicable law', the law of the place of arbitration will determine the validity of the arbitration agreement.[43] If the parties expressly

[40] s 2AC(3), HK Arbitration Ordinance.

[41] *Astel-Peiniger Joint Venture v Argas Engineering & Heavy Industries Co Ltd* [1994] 3 HKC 328.

[42] Art 16, SPC Interpretation 2006.

[43] There is some debate over what constitutes an agreement on 'the applicable law'. Is agreement on the governing law of the contract sufficient? Or do parties have to agree on a law governing the arbitration clause specifically?

There is some support for the view that it is the latter, in a Notice of the SPC on Issuance of the 'Minutes of the Second National Work Conference on the Trial of Foreign-related Commercial and Maritime Cases' ('SPC Work Notes 2005', issued 26 December 2005). On this view, the law of the place of arbitration will, in most cases, govern the validity of the arbitration clause. This is because it is rare for parties to specifically choose a law to govern the arbitration clause (as opposed to a law to govern the contract).

However, even if that question is resolved, there may be a further question over whether under PRC conflict rules, the law governing the validity of the arbitration agreement also governs the scope and interpretation of the arbitration agreement. Some PRC commentators assume this is the case, although there is scope for argument.

stipulate in their contracts a law to govern the arbitration agreement, they would avoid the above uncertainties.

(B) Under traditional English conflict of law rules, an arbitration agreement is a contract, so the choice of law rules that determine which law governs the contract are the same rules for determining which law governs the arbitration agreement. Parties are usually free to select the system of law which will govern their contract, and to expressly select a governing law for the arbitration agreement that differs from this law. However, in practice, the latter choice is rarely made. As a result, the substantive law governing the underlying contract is usually also the law governing the arbitration agreement. This has been the approach taken in previous Hong Kong cases.[44] **4.73**

However, this view is not universally held, and the main competing view is that the law of the place of arbitration should also be the law governing the interpretation of the arbitration agreement. Some recent English authorities have tended to support this competing view.[45] **4.74**

It remains to be seen if the Hong Kong courts will move towards adopting this competing approach. **4.75**

(5.1) Do courts accept a wide competence of the arbitral tribunal or do they restrict arbitral competence? Do claims which arise in connection with the agreement submitted to arbitration generally fall within the arbitral jurisdiction even if based on a tortious legal basis? Does there exist case law with respect to the wording in an arbitration clause as 'arising out of/under/in connection with the present contract' and its specific meaning? (A) Parties to foreign-related contracts in the PRC typically adopt wording providing for disputes 'arising from or in connection with' the contract to be arbitrated, or other similar broad wording.[46] Such wording is sufficient to bring most normal commercial disputes within the tribunal's jurisdiction. There was previously some debate over whether tortious claims were arbitrable. This was because of a provision in the PRC Civil Procedure Law suggesting that tortious claims could only be resolved in court.[47] However, this issue has probably now been resolved,[48] and the better view is that tortious claims are arbitrable. **4.76**

(B) The Hong Kong courts are strongly supportive of international arbitration, and a broad range of matters are considered arbitrable. These include tort claims, and the standard wording of the HKIAC model clause[49] is broad enough to encompass them. **4.77**

---

[44] See eg *Karaha Bodas Company LLC v Perusahaan Pertambangan Minyak Dan Gas Bumi Negara (otherwise known as Pertamina)* (HCCT 28/2002) (CFI) (27 March 2003). The case was also appealed to the Court of Appeal.

[45] See generally, *C v D* [2007] EWHC 1541 (Comm) (CA).

[46] See eg the CIETAC model arbitration clause which provides for 'Any dispute arising from or in connection with this Contract' to be submitted to arbitration.

[47] Art 29, PRC Civil Procedure Law.

[48] Art 7, SPC Work Notes.

[49] 'Any dispute, controversy or claim arising out of or relating to this contract, including the validity, invalidity, breach or termination thereof, shall be settled by arbitration in Hong Kong ...'.

4.78 Recent English authorities have also highlighted the trend of construing arbitration clauses broadly and of moving away from technical constructions based on the precise wording of the clause.[50] This approach has been viewed favourably in Hong Kong.[51]

(6) Binding effect of an arbitration clause on third parties (eg in case of a guarantee or assignment)

4.79 (A) PRC law does not clearly recognize the alter ego or corporate veil-piercing theory.[52] There is also no clear recognition of the US non-signatory/estoppel doctrine and the 'group of companies' concept, both of which have been used in other jurisdictions to bind third party non-signatories.

4.80 Despite this, in PRC-related arbitrations (such as those held in Hong Kong) attempts have occasionally been made to join third parties, by relying on these concepts. However, the traditional view is that PRC law adopts a relatively restrictive approach to such attempts.[53]

4.81 A related concept that PRC law recognizes is that the rights and obligations under a contract are transferable to third parties. The SPC Interpretation 2006 provides that where rights and obligations are transferred in part or in whole, the arbitration agreement shall be binding on the transferee, unless:

(i) the parties agree otherwise;
(ii) the transferee expressly objects; or
(iii) the transferee is not aware of the existence of a separate arbitration agreement at the time of the transfer.

4.82 The exact scope of limb (iii) is uncertain. Accordingly, where a transfer of rights is involved, it would be prudent to ensure that the transferee expressly acknowledges its awareness of the existence of the separate arbitration agreement.

4.83 (B) Under Hong Kong law, an arbitration agreement is binding on parties to it, as well as persons claiming through or under them.[54] Parties claiming 'through or under them' include an assignee, a successor (such as a personal representative) and a trustee in bankruptcy who adopts the contract.[55] Such parties are entitled to, but also bound to arbitrate any claim, and can participate in pending arbitration proceedings.

4.84 Hong Kong law also recognizes the alter ego or corporate veil-piercing theory. However, unlike the case in some jurisdictions, there has to date been no clear recognition of a broader basis for joining in third parties. Thus, concepts such as the 'group of companies' doctrine, which allows non-signatories to be made party to an arbitration agreement, have

50 *Fiona Trust and Holding Corp and Ors v Privalov and Ors* [2007] UKHL 40 (HL).

51 *UDL Contracting Ltd v Apple Daily Printing Limited and Lai Chee Ying Jimmy* HCA 1209/2007.

52 But see eg Arts 76 to 83 of the SPC, 'Regulations of the Supreme People's Court regarding Certain Issues in relation to Enforcement (Effective on Trial Basis)' (effective from 18 July 1998) which appears to envisage some degree of piercing of the corporate veil at the *enforcement* stage.

53 For a discussion, see Yeoh, F. and Fu, Y., 'A Snapshop of Recent Judicial Attitudes on Arbitrability and Enforcement' (2007) 24(6) *J Int'l Arb* 635, 639.

54 See generally, s 18, HK Arbitration Ordinance, which applies to domestic arbitrations. See also *Ryoden Engineering Co Ltd v The New India Assurance Co Ltd* [2008] HKDC 19.

55 See generally, s 5, HK Arbitration Ordinance, which applies to domestic arbitrations.

not yet been widely applied in Hong Kong. Given the relatively conservative approach under English law,[56] it is questionable if such doctrines will be given full effect under Hong Kong law.

(6.1) What is the law/leading authorities' position on multi-party situations? Especially, (i) with respect to the objection that the arbitration clause does not specifically provide for a plurality of parties in the same procedure; (ii) with respect to the constitution of the arbitral tribunal; and (iii) with respect to the consolidation of two or more running arbitration proceedings? (A) The CIETAC Arbitration Rules contain provisions dealing with the constitution of the arbitral tribunal in a multi-party situation.[57] It assumes that there will be two sides to the arbitration, and provides for joint appointment of one arbitrator by each side. **4.85**

In the event either side fails jointly to appoint (or jointly to entrust the chairman of CIETAC to appoint) an arbitrator, the arbitrator shall be appointed by the chairman of CIETAC. The provision therefore appears to envisage a situation where the claimants are able jointly to exercise their right to appoint an arbitrator (because their interests are aligned and they agree on the identity of the arbitrator) whereas the respondents (because their interests are not aligned) may be unable to agree, in which case the chairman of CIETAC steps in to appoint the respondents' arbitrator. **4.86**

This approach is more liberal than that taken under certain rules (eg the ICC Rules),[58] where upon the failure of *either* side to nominate an arbitrator, the arbitration institution may step in to appoint *all* three members of the arbitral tribunal. **4.87**

The PRC Arbitration Law is silent on the consolidation of arbitrations. **4.88**

(B) In Hong Kong, the UNCITRAL Arbitration Rules, read together with the HKIAC Procedures, are frequently chosen for international arbitrations. Neither the Rules[59] nor the Procedures deal expressly with a multi-party situation. In practice, parties desiring to use the UNCITRAL Arbitration Rules for multi-party arbitration will include supplementary provisions in the arbitration clause. The newly adopted HKIAC Administered Arbitration Rules contain provisions dealing with multi-party appointment and can be expected to become increasingly widely used.[60] **4.89**

In addition, the Hong Kong courts are very supportive of international arbitration and can be expected to seek to uphold agreements to arbitrate, even in multi-party situations. For example, in one case,[61] the Hong Kong courts considered a multi-party arbitration **4.90**

---

[56] See eg *Peterson Farms v C & M Farming Ltd* [2004] EWHC 121 (Comm) where the English courts found that the 'group of companies doctrine' did not form part of English law.

[57] Art 24, CIETAC Arbitration Rules.

[58] Art 10, ICC Rules.

[59] In its current version; the UNCITRAL Arbitration Rules are currently being revised.

[60] Art 8.2, Hong Kong Administered Arbitration Rules. In addition, Art 14.6 states that the tribunal shall have the power, upon the application of a party, to allow third parties to be joined in the arbitration as a party, provided that the third party and the applicant consents. On the face of it, consent from the second party to the arbitration is unnecessary. See also Art 22.1(h), LCIA Arbitration Rules.

[61] *Karaha Bodas Company LLC* (*supra*, n 44). The case was appealed to the Court of Appeal on different grounds.

involving two separate contracts with two separate arbitration agreements, in the context of enforcement under the Convention on the Recognition and Enforcement of Foreign Arbitral Awards 1958 (the 'New York Convention'). The respondent argued that there had been wrongful consolidation of the proceedings, and that the arbitrators had not been properly appointed. These arguments were not accepted by the Hong Kong court.

4.91 Quite unusually, the HK Arbitration Ordinance contains a provision expressly dealing with the consolidation of arbitrations. However, this applies only to domestic arbitrations.[62] Consolidation by the court is also generally not available where one contract provides for domestic arbitration while a related contract provides for international arbitration conducted under the UNCITRAL Model Law.[63]

4.92 (6.2) **Is there case law/authorities with respect to the admissibility of third party participation in an arbitration without being a claimant or defendant (Nebenintervention/ Streitverkündung; intervention forcée/volontaire; vouching in; *amicus curiae* etc)? What are the prerequisites and effects of such participation (if permitted)?** (A) Foreign-related arbitrations in China are generally private[64] and, in the absence of consent from all the parties, third parties are generally not permitted to participate. The question of whether *amicus curiae* are entitled to participate, in the context of treaty arbitrations, has not previously come up for consideration.

4.93 (B) Arbitration proceedings in Hong Kong are private and third parties are generally not permitted to participate, absent consent from all the parties to the arbitration. This is acknowledged, for example, by the UNCITRAL Arbitration Rules (which are widely used in Hong Kong), which provide that hearings shall be held *in camera* unless the parties agree otherwise.[65]

(7) Termination of an arbitration agreement by a party (reasons and case law)

4.94 (A) The parties may agree to terminate an arbitration agreement. In the absence of mutual consent, it is generally difficult for the obligations under an arbitration agreement to be terminated. For example, if a party passes away, the arbitration agreement is valid in respect of the party's successors.[66] Furthermore, PRC law recognizes the doctrine of separability, under which an arbitration agreement is independent of the underlying contract. As a result, even if the contract is terminated, this will not automatically result in a termination of the arbitration agreement itself.

---

[62] s 6B, HK Arbitration Ordinance. The relevant provision states that where, in relation to two or more arbitration proceedings it appears to the court:
(i) that some common question of law or fact arises in both or all of them; or
(ii) that the rights to relief claimed therein are in respect of or arise out of the same transaction or series of transactions; or
(iii) that for some other reason it is desirable to make an order under this section,
the court may order those arbitration proceedings to be consolidated on such terms as it thinks just or may order them to be heard at the same time, or one immediately after another, or may order any of them to be stayed until after the determination of any other.

[63] *Ho Kwok Hung (t/a Kim Kwok Co) v Hung Dat Trading Co* [1992] HKCFI 60 (HCA009219/1991).

[64] See eg Art 40, PRC Arbitration Law; Art 33, CIETAC Arbitration Rules.

[65] Art 25(4), UNCITRAL Arbitration Rules.

[66] SPC Interpretation 2006.

Having said that, PRC law does recognize that if a party fails to object to court proceedings brought in breach of an arbitration agreement, he may have waived his rights. In effect, the party loses the benefit of the arbitration agreement. **4.95**

(B) It is open to the parties mutually to agree on the termination of an arbitration agreement. Absent mutual agreement by all the parties, it is difficult for an arbitration agreement to be terminated. Two examples, both in the context of domestic arbitrations, illustrate the point. First, the HK Arbitration Ordinance expressly provides that an arbitration agreement shall not be discharged by the death of any party, but shall in such an event be enforceable by or against the personal representative of the deceased.[67] Secondly, the bankruptcy of a party also does not automatically discharge a party from the arbitration agreement.[68] **4.96**

Hong Kong case law also indicates that it is difficult for a party to revoke its right to arbitrate. In one case, the parties agreed that they would attempt an amicable resolution of an ongoing construction dispute, and that they 'will not bring any arbitration . . . forever'.[69] The Hong Kong courts construed this to mean the parties only agreed to refrain from exercising their right to arbitrate. This did *not* revoke the submission to arbitration altogether. **4.97**

B. Arbitrability

(1) 'Personal arbitrability' (capacity to conclude arbitration agreements)

(A) The PRC Arbitration Law provides, in effect, that PRC nationals, legal persons and other organizations have capacity to conclude arbitration agreements.[70] 'Legal persons' refers to an organization that has capacity for civil rights and capacity for civil conduct, and independently enjoys civil rights and assumes civil obligations in accordance with the law.[71] **4.98**

(B) Under Hong Kong law, in general, any person who has contractual capacity may enter into an arbitration agreement. This is because an arbitration agreement is essentially contractual in nature. However, legal disabilities affecting a person's right to enter into contracts may affect their ability to agree to arbitration. Examples of persons with such disabilities include infants (persons under 18 years of age) and mentally disordered persons. In addition, special rules apply to certain individuals, including bankrupts, agents, partners and personal representatives. **4.99**

(1.1) May a state (or state agency) as party invoke sovereign immunity before the arbitral tribunal or before a state court (eg in a procedure of enforcement)? (A) There is no comprehensive legislation on sovereign immunity, although the PRC has promulgated the Law on Judicial Immunity from Measures of Constraint for the Property of Foreign Central Banks[72] and has also signed the United Nations Convention on Jurisdictional Immunities **4.100**

[67] s 4, HK Arbitration Ordinance.

[68] s 5, *ibid.*

[69] *Hyundai Engineering and Construction Co Ltd v Vigour Ltd* [2004] HKEC 1261; see also the Court of Appeal's decision reported in [2005] 3 HKLRD 723.

[70] PRC Arbitration Law.

[71] Art 36, General Principles of the Civil Law of the People's Republic of China (adopted 12 April 1986).

[72] See Zhu, L., 'State Immunity from Measures of Constraints from the Property of Foreign Central Banks: The Chinese Perspective' (2007) 6(1) *Chin J Int'l Law* 67.

of States and Their Property.[73] In the past, the PRC appeared to subscribe to the theory of absolute immunity and had claimed sovereign immunity in a few cases brought in other countries.[74] However, it is generally believed that today, the PRC differentiates between 'state action'/'state assets' and 'private action'/'private assets'. The PRC's position appears to be that companies which are independent legal entities, even if they are state-owned, are not entitled to protection by claiming sovereign immunity. Conversely, it is likely that the PRC as a state will be entitled to (at a minimum) some degree of sovereign immunity. In such cases, the PRC is likely to adopt a relatively broad view on the scope of protection offered by sovereign immunity.

4.101 (B) It is clear that the Government of the Hong Kong Special Administrative Region is bound by the HK Arbitration Ordinance.[75]

4.102 As for sovereign immunity of foreign states or state agencies, Hong Kong law is currently in a state of transition.[76] The better view is probably that the Hong Kong position on sovereign immunity is still based on the common law, but may also take into account the position under PRC law.

4.103 The Hong Kong common law position (at least shortly before the coming into force of the English State Immunity Act) recognized the theory of restrictive immunity.[77] In contrast, as noted above, the PRC does not appear to formally recognize the theory of restrictive immunity. Accordingly, PRC law, unlike the common law, does not have a well recognized exception to the application of sovereign immunity relating to commercial activities or commercial assets.

4.104 Given the above, it is likely that the Hong Kong courts recognize that where a state or state agency has submitted in writing to refer disputes to arbitration, it will generally be subject to the jurisdiction of the arbitral tribunal. However, it is probably still open to the state to seek to resist enforcement and execution of any resulting award, on the basis of sovereign immunity.

4.105 The above position is consistent with the comments made in a recent Hong Kong case.[78] In addition, in another case involving a foreign award, the Hong Kong courts granted enforcement of the award against a state-owned oil and gas company.[79]

---

[73] GA Res 59/38 (2 December 2004). Signed by the PRC on 14 September 2005 but not yet ratified. See generally, Qi, D., 'State Immunity, China, and its Shifting Position' (2008) 7(2) *Chin J Int'l Law* 307.

[74] See eg *Jackson v People's Republic of China* 550 F Supp 869 (ND Ala 1982), (1986) 25 ILM 1466, involving Chinese railway bonds.

[75] s 47, HK Arbitration Ordinance (except Pt IV of the HK Arbitration Ordinance, which deals with the Enforcement of Convention Awards, does not apply).

[76] Prior to the handover in 1997, the English State Immunity Act applied in Hong Kong. However, following the handover, the Act ceased to apply. In addition, no mainland law currently applies. Nevertheless, Art 19 of the Basic Law provides that the courts of Hong Kong have no jurisdiction over 'acts of state', such as defence and foreign relations.

[77] *Philippine Admiral, The* [1976] 2 WLR 214; [1976] 1 All ER 78 (Privy Council, on appeal from Hong Kong).

[78] See *FG Hemisphere Associates LLC v Democratic Republic of Congo & Ors* [2009] 1 HKC 111.

[79] *Karaha Bodas Company LLC v Perusahaan Pertambangan Minyak Dan Gas Bumi Negara* [2007] HKCA 414 (CACV000121/2003) (CA). However, note that this case involved a commercial arbitration award, and state immunity was apparently not specifically raised as a defence.

(2) 'Objective arbitrability' (eg patent, trade mark and antitrust matters)

(A) The PRC Arbitration Law provides that a wide range of disputes are presumed to be arbitrable, including contractual disputes and disputes involving property rights between citizens, legal persons and other organizations.[80] **4.106**

The SPC Interpretation 2006 further provides that where the scope of the arbitration agreement is unclear, 'arbitrable matters' include (but are not limited to) disputes relating to contractual formation, validity, modification, assignment (*zhuanrang*), performance, liability for breach of contract, interpretation and rescission of contract.[81] **4.107**

Conversely, the PRC Arbitration Law provides that the following disputes are not arbitrable: **4.108**

(i) marital, adoption, guardianship, support and succession disputes; and
(ii) administrative disputes that by law are required to be handled by administrative authorities.[82]

(B) In general, any dispute affecting the civil interests of parties is arbitrable. This includes claims for breach of contract, tort, breach of trust and claims relating to real or personal property. Conversely, certain disputes, such as those relating to family (marriage, divorce, children), intellectual property (where third party rights are affected—in particular, validity of copyrights, patents, registered designs or trade marks) and criminal matters may not be arbitrable. **4.109**

C. Decision on the arbitral tribunal's jurisdiction ('*competence-competence*')

(1) Separability (independence of the arbitration agreement from the main agreement)

(A) The PRC Arbitration Law recognizes the doctrine of separability by providing that an arbitration agreement exists independently, and the amendment, rescission, termination or invalidity of a contract will not affect the validity of the underlying arbitration agreement.[83] The doctrine of separability has been recognized by the PRC courts on many occasions. **4.110**

On the face of it, the CIETAC Arbitration Rules appear to go further than the PRC Arbitration Law, by providing that the validity of an arbitration clause is not affected by the 'non-existence' of the contract.[84] **4.111**

(B) In Hong Kong, it is widely accepted that under the doctrine of separability, an arbitration agreement is considered to be an agreement *separate* from the primary contract between the parties. This is true even when the arbitration agreement is drafted as a single clause within a larger contract. This doctrine is expressly provided for in relation to both domestic and international arbitration agreements in the HK Arbitration Ordinance.[85] **4.112**

---

[80] Art 2, PRC Arbitration Law.
[81] Art 2, SPC Interpretation 2006.
[82] Art 3, PRC Arbitration Law.
[83] Art 19, *ibid.*
[84] Art 5(4), CIETAC Arbitration Rules. See also Art 10, SPC Interpretation 2006 which states (in effect) that where there is an arbitration agreement, the validity of the arbitration agreement shall not be affected if no contract is formed. This provision was intended to deal with certain previous cases in the PRC which had suggested otherwise.
[85] Art 16(1) of the UNCITRAL Model Law and s 13B of the HK Arbitration Ordinance.

(2) Competence of the tribunal to decide on its own jurisdiction (including form and time of the tribunal's decision)

4.113 (A) Under international practice, the validity of an arbitration agreement is primarily determined by the arbitral tribunal. However, under PRC law, questions over both the validity of the arbitration agreement and the tribunal's jurisdiction are reserved for determination by either the arbitration commission or the PRC courts.[86] The tribunal is ordinarily not competent to decide on its own jurisdiction. Notwithstanding this, the current version of the CIETAC Arbitration Rules state that CIETAC may, 'if necessary, delegate such power to the arbitral tribunal'.[87]

4.114 (B) Hong Kong law recognizes and gives effect to the doctrine of *Kompetenz-Kompetenz* (or *competence-competence*), under which the arbitral tribunal is authorized to rule on its own jurisdiction, including on the existence or validity of the arbitration agreement.[88]

(3) Extent of 'competence-competence' *and role of the courts (including form and time limits of a challenge to the tribunal's decision)*

4.115 (A) The above emphasis on 'institutionality' is a cause for concern to some foreign parties, who usually agree to arbitration so that their dispute (including any dispute as to the validity of their arbitration agreement) is decided by their chosen arbitral tribunal, and not by either the arbitration commission or by the local courts.

4.116 Where an application is made to both the arbitration commission and to the PRC courts, the PRC courts will decide the matter.[89] However, as between the two, most parties prefer the arbitration commission to decide the question.[90] It is therefore fortunate that the above rule suggesting that the PRC courts take precedence has been qualified:

(i) if one party applies to the arbitration commission and the other to the PRC courts, the PRC court shall not accept the case where the arbitration commission has already accepted the application and has made a decision.[91] If the arbitration commission has not yet made a decision, the PRC court should accept the case and notify the arbitration commission to suspend the arbitration;[92] and
(ii) the SPC Interpretation 2006 reaffirms this, by providing that after an arbitration institution has made its decision on the validity of an arbitration agreement, the PRC court shall not entertain any application by a party either to determine the validity of

---

86 Art 20, PRC Arbitration Law.

87 Art 6(1), CIETAC Arbitration Rules. The extent to which this provision is strictly consistent with the literal wording of the PRC Arbitration Law may be debatable. See also Art 6(4) of the current BAC Arbitration Rules, which state that the tribunal 'if authorized by the BAC', 'shall have the power to rule on jurisdictional objections and objections to the validity of an arbitration agreement'.

88 Art 16, UNCITRAL Model Law.

89 Art 20, PRC Arbitration Law.

90 In the context of PRC law, having this issue dealt with by an arbitration commission such as CIETAC has two advantages: the arbitration will proceed notwithstanding such a challenge to the validity of the arbitration agreement, and on the face of it, CIETAC may 'if necessary' delegate the power to determine the existence and validity of an arbitration agreement to the arbitral tribunal. See Art 6(4) and 6(1), CIETAC Arbitration Rules.

91 See SPC, 'Reply on Several Questions Regarding the Determination of the Validity of Arbitration Agreements' (issued 26 October 1998).

92 cf Art 6 of the CIETAC Arbitration Rules, which state that CIETAC has the power to determine the existence and the *validity* of an arbitration agreement.

the arbitration agreement or to set aside the decision of the arbitration institution.[93] This provides some certainty once the arbitration institution has ruled on the validity of the arbitration agreement.

As for when the objection has to be raised, the PRC Arbitration Law provides that a challenge to the validity of the arbitration agreement shall be raised prior to the arbitral tribunal's first hearing.[94] The CIETAC Arbitration Rules further provide that where CIETAC is satisfied by prima facie evidence that an arbitration agreement providing for arbitration by CIETAC exists, it may decide that it has jurisdiction over the arbitration case, and the arbitration shall proceed.[95] **4.117**

This helps to avoid unnecessary delay to the arbitration process. However, this decision may subsequently be revised by CIETAC based on facts and/or evidence found by the arbitral tribunal during the arbitration proceedings that are inconsistent with the prima facie evidence.[96] **4.118**

(B) The HK Arbitration Ordinance (read together with the UNCITRAL Model Law) provides that a plea that the arbitral tribunal does not have jurisdiction shall be raised not later than the submission of the statement of defence.[97] However, a party is not precluded from raising such a plea by the fact that he has appointed, or participated in the appointment of, an arbitrator. In the case of a plea that the arbitral tribunal is exceeding the scope of its authority, such a plea shall be made as soon as the matter alleged to be beyond the scope of its authority is raised during the arbitral proceedings. **4.119**

The arbitral tribunal may, in either case, admit a later plea if it considers the delay justified. **4.120**

The arbitral tribunal may rule on the plea either as a preliminary question or in an award on the merits. If the arbitral tribunal rules as a preliminary question that it has jurisdiction, any party may request, within 30 days after having received notice of that ruling, that the Court of First Instance decide the matter, which decision shall be subject to no appeal. While such a request is pending, the arbitral tribunal may continue the arbitral proceedings and make an award.[98] **4.121**

In practice, where the arbitral tribunal rules on the plea as a preliminary question, the decision may take the form of either an award on jurisdiction, or a decision. **4.122**

D. Enforcement of an arbitration agreement within or by court proceedings

(1) Effect of invoking an arbitration clause within a court proceeding (and time limits for such a motion)

(A) The PRC Arbitration Law recognizes that if there is an arbitration agreement and one party commences an action in a PRC court, the PRC court shall not accept the case, unless the arbitration agreement is null and void.[99] **4.123**

93 Art 13, SPC Interpretation 2006.
94 Art 20, PRC Arbitration Law.
95 Art 6(2) and 6(4), CIETAC Arbitration Rules.
96 Art 6(2), CIETAC Arbitration Rules.
97 *ibid.*
98 *ibid.*
99 Art 5, PRC Arbitration Law.

4.124 It also provides that if one party commences an action in a PRC court without declaring the existence of the arbitration agreement and, after the PRC court has accepted the case, the other party submits the arbitration agreement prior to the first hearing, the PRC court shall dismiss the case unless the arbitration agreement is null and void.[100] However, if the other party does not object prior to the 'first hearing', he shall be deemed to have renounced the arbitration agreement and the PRC court shall continue to try the case.[101] The 'first hearing' means the first hearing conducted by the PRC court upon the expiry of the time limit for the submission of the defence, and does not include pre-hearing procedures.[102]

4.125 (B) In Hong Kong, if a party to an arbitration agreement commences court proceedings in respect of a dispute which is subject to an arbitration agreement, the other party (usually the defendant) may apply to the Court of First Instance for an order to stay those proceedings if the dispute is subject to the agreement. The only significant limitation on a defendant's right to obtain a stay of court proceedings is that the stay must be sought not later than submission of his first statement on the substance of the dispute before the court. If a party files a defence (or other pleading) without requesting a stay in favour of arbitration, it will be unable to have the court proceedings stayed at a later stage.[103]

4.126 **(1.1) If a party has invoked successfully the arbitration agreement in a court proceeding, is it then entitled to deny within the arbitral tribunal proceeding that there is a valid and binding arbitration agreement?** (A) In practice, it would be unusual for a party to apply for a stay of court proceedings, relying on an arbitration agreement, while denying the existence of that very agreement before a properly constituted arbitral tribunal. In any event, in the context of the PRC, challenges to both court and arbitral jurisdiction are likely to take place before the PRC court (or, possibly, the arbitration commission), so there is little scope for a party to take inconsistent positions before the same forum.

4.127 (B) This issue is not addressed by the HK Arbitration Ordinance and it does not appear to have directly come up for consideration before the Hong Kong courts. However, it is likely that a party will not be successful in adopting such an inconsistent position, owing to the doctrines of estoppel, waiver or abuse of process. In addition, the Hong Kong courts may well order a stay of court proceedings only upon an undertaking from the applicant that it will forthwith commence arbitration.

4.128 **(1.2) Vice versa, if a party has successfully objected to an arbitral proceeding by denying that there is a valid arbitration agreement, may it then invoke such agreement in the ensuing court proceeding?** (A) See II.D.(1.1) *supra*. Similar reasoning would apply in such a situation.

4.129 (B) See II.D.(1.1) *supra*. Similar reasoning would apply in such a situation.

---

[100] Art 26, PRC Arbitration Law.
[101] *ibid.*
[102] Art 14, SPC Interpretation 2006.
[103] Art 8, UNCITRAL Model Law.

(2) Legal remedies and proceedings to enforce an arbitration agreement

(A) The CIETAC Arbitration Rules provide that an objection to an arbitration agreement and/or the arbitral tribunal's jurisdiction shall be raised in writing 'before the first oral hearing'.[104] Thus, if a party fails to register its objection, but continues to participate in the running of the arbitration proceeding, it will be difficult for the party subsequently to deny in court proceedings that it is not bound by the arbitration proceedings. **4.130**

(B) Once a defendant has made out a prima facie case for the existence of a valid arbitration agreement covering the dispute, the court must order a stay unless it finds that the arbitration agreement is null and void, inoperative or incapable of being performed. **4.131**

The Hong Kong courts have also made it clear that the court's role is not to investigate whether the defendant has an arguable basis for disputing the claim. If a claim is made against him in a matter which is the subject of an arbitration agreement and he does not admit the claim, then there is a dispute within the meaning of the article. And if he seeks a stay of the action, the court must grant a stay unless the plaintiff can show that the arbitration agreement is null and void, inoperative or incapable of being performed.[105] **4.132**

(2.1) Which would be the internationally competent court (i) for obtaining a declaration that an arbitration agreement is valid and binding; or (ii) to compel arbitration? (The Defendant's courts? The courts of the place of arbitration? The claimant's courts, cf Art 6 (2) in fine, ICC Rules?) (A) In general, if the arbitration agreement provides for arbitration in the PRC, the PRC courts would be competent to adjudicate on the validity and effectiveness of the arbitration agreement, and to compel arbitration. **4.133**

(B) In theory, the Hong Kong courts should be the most appropriate court to grant a 'declaration' that a Hong Kong arbitration agreement is valid and binding. Where the respondent is within jurisdiction, the Hong Kong courts would also be a sensible choice for such an application. However, if the respondent is outside jurisdiction, it may be preferable to apply to the court where competing actions have been launched by the respondent, particularly if the foreign courts are perceived as being arbitration friendly. **4.134**

III. The arbitral tribunal

A. Number and qualification of arbitrators

(1) Sole arbitrator or arbitral tribunal with several arbitrators

(A) The PRC Arbitration Law provides that an arbitral tribunal may be composed of either a sole arbitrator or three arbitrators.[106] In practice, an arbitral tribunal comprising three arbitrators would be more common. **4.135**

[104] Art 6(3), CIETAC Arbitration Rules.

[105] *Tai Hing Cotton Mill Ltd v Glencore Grain Rotterdam BV and another* [1995] HKAC 580, (CACV000143a/1995).

[106] Art 30, PRC Arbitration Law.

4.136 (B) The parties may agree upon the number of arbitrators, either in their arbitration agreement, or after a dispute has arisen. In international arbitrations, if the parties fail to agree on the number of arbitrators, the number will be one or three as determined by the HKIAC.[107] In making its decision, the HKIAC will take into consideration:

(i) the amount in dispute;
(ii) the complexity of the claim;
(iii) the nationalities of the parties;
(iv) any relevant customs of the trade, business or profession involved in the dispute;
(v) the availability of appropriate arbitrators; and
(vi) the urgency of the case.[108]

4.137 The HKIAC has also published a guide on the basis upon which it decides on the number of arbitrators.

4.138 (1.1) **Are arbitral tribunals with an even number of arbitrators acceptable?** (A) No. The PRC Arbitration Law states that an arbitral tribunal may be composed of either three arbitrators or one arbitrator.[109] PRC law does not recognize the concept of 'umpires'.

4.139 (B) Yes. The UNCITRAL Model Law gives parties the freedom to choose an even number of arbitrators.[110] The HK Arbitration Ordinance also contains a provision specifically dealing with this, for domestic arbitrations.[111] In practice, international arbitrations overwhelmingly comprise tribunals with either one or three arbitrators.

(2) Qualification of the arbitrators

4.140 (A) The PRC Arbitration Law states that arbitrators shall be appointed from among fair and upright persons, and shall meet one of the following conditions:

(i) to have been engaged in arbitration work for at least eight years;
(ii) to have worked as a lawyer for at least eight years;
(iii) to have served as a judge for at least eight years;
(iv) to have been engaged in legal research or legal education, possessing a senior professional title; or
(v) to have knowledge of law, be engaged professionally in fields such as economic relations and trade, etc or to have a senior title or equivalent professional standard.[112]

4.141 In the case of foreign-related arbitrations, a foreign-related arbitration commission may appoint arbitrators from among foreigners with special knowledge in the fields of law,

---

[107] s 34C(5), HK Arbitration Ordinance. See also Art 6, HKIAC Administered Arbitration Rules, which sets out the procedure and factors the HKIAC Council will apply in deciding on the number of arbitrators, where the parties have not agreed otherwise.

[108] s 9, Arbitration (Appointment of Arbitrators and Umpires) Rules.

[109] Art 30, PRC Arbitration Law.

[110] Art 10(1), UNCITRAL Model Law.

[111] It provides that unless otherwise stated, every arbitration agreement shall, where the reference is to two arbitrators, be deemed to include a provision that the two arbitrators may appoint an umpire at any time after they are themselves appointed and shall do so forthwith if they cannot agree. The purpose of the provision is for the umpire to enter in on the reference in lieu of the arbitrators, where the arbitrators are at a deadlock. See s 10, HK Arbitration Ordinance.

[112] Art 13, PRC Arbitration Law.

economy and trade, science and technology etc.[113] In addition, the arbitration commissions have issued various stipulations on the qualifications of arbitrators.

(B) Consistent with the approach under the UNCITRAL Model Law, the HK Arbitration Ordinance grants parties the freedom to select an arbitrator of their choice.[114] It expressly states that no person shall be precluded by reason of his nationality from acting as an arbitrator, unless otherwise agreed by the parties.[115] **4.142**

In practice, parties sometimes include restrictions on the choice of arbitrators in their arbitration agreement. For example, in Sino-foreign disputes, it is not uncommon for there to be a nationality restriction against appointing arbitrators who are of the same nationality as any of the parties. If an arbitrator does not possess qualifications agreed by the parties, he may be removed.[116] **4.143**

The HKIAC maintains a panel of arbitrators (as well as a separate 'list of arbitrators' who do not possess such experience as to enable them to be on the HKIAC panel). There are currently about 300 arbitrators on the panel, including many leading international and Hong Kong-based arbitrators. The HKIAC applies various criteria for arbitrators who seek appointment on the panel. Parties to HKIAC arbitrations are not obliged to select arbitrators from HKIAC's panel. **4.144**

(2.1) Are there mandatory requirements for the qualification of arbitrators (statutory requirements or indirect requirements through eg general conditions of insurance contracts)? (A) Yes, see III.A.(2) *supra*. **4.145**

(B) No, unless otherwise agreed by the parties. However, arbitrators (including party-appointed arbitrators) have an obligation to be and remain impartial and independent of the parties.[117] **4.146**

(2.2) Which national arbitration institutions may be contacted for obtaining information about qualified (and specialised) arbitrators? (A) The leading body for foreign-related arbitrations in the PRC is CIETAC. Contact details are in IX. **4.147**

(B) The HKIAC. Contact details are in IX. **4.148**

(2.3) Are judges or civil servants required to obtain permission from their employer to act as arbitrator? Are these permissions given generally or on a case-by-case basis? What are the consequences if such permission has not been obtained? (A) The SPC has issued a notice that judges on active duty may not serve as arbitrators.[118] The rationale is to **4.149**

113 Art 67, PRC Arbitration Law.

114 Where the HKIAC Administered Arbitration Rules apply, all designations of arbitrators made by the parties or the arbitrators are subject to confirmation by the HKIAC Council: Art 10.

115 Art 11, UNCITRAL Model Law. If the HKIAC Administered Arbitration Rules apply, Art 11.2 provides that where the parties are of different nationalities, the sole arbitrator and the chairman shall not have the same nationality as any party, unless otherwise agreed.

116 Art 12, UNCITRAL Model Law.

117 *ibid.*

118 SPC, 'The SPC Notice relating to Restrictions on Judges accepting Arbitral Appointments' (13 July 2004). See also Art 13, PRC Arbitration Law which suggests a similar restriction.

allow judges to focus on performing their judicial duties, and to protect the parties' interests.[119]

4.150 (B) Judges may, in domestic arbitrations and in certain circumstances, be permitted to accept appointments as arbitrators. The HK Arbitration Ordinance provides that the judge shall not accept appointment as an arbitrator or umpire unless the Chief Justice has informed him that, having regard to the state of business in the courts, he can be made available to do so.[120]

B. Appointment of arbitrators

(1) Extent of party autonomy to establish appointment procedure

4.151 (A) Under PRC law, the parties are in general free to agree on an appropriate method for constituting the arbitral tribunal. In the past, this was subject to a number of restrictions under the applicable arbitration rules. However, in the case of CIETAC, these restrictions have now been relaxed. Parties may now agree:

(i) on a modification of the Rules, and such an agreement shall prevail except where it is inoperative or in conflict with a mandatory provision of the law of the place of arbitration;[121] and

(ii) may appoint arbitrators outside CIETAC's Panel of Arbitrators, subject to the appointment being confirmed by the chairman of CIETAC in accordance with the law.[122] In recent years, the number of appointments from outside CIETAC's panel has increased significantly, and it is likely that CIETAC takes into account the factors set out in III.A.(2) *supra* in deciding whether to confirm the nomination.

4.152 (B) The HK Arbitration Ordinance provides that parties are, in general, free to agree on a procedure for appointing the arbitrator or arbitrators.[123] In practice, parties often adopt the appointment procedure found in leading international rules, such as the UNCITRAL Arbitration Rules (and the HKIAC Procedures), either by default, or by largely reproducing the salient points from those rules in the arbitration clause proper.

(2) Procedure in absence of an agreement by the parties

4.153 (A) The PRC Arbitration Law sets out a default appointment mechanism, which applies only if the parties fail to agree on a method for constitution of the arbitral tribunal or to appoint the arbitrators within the time limit specified in the rules of arbitration. In such a

[119] A related issue is that in the past, one criticism of CIETAC's appointment process was its tendency in some cases to appoint CIETAC staff members (or other closely associated individuals) as presiding arbitrators. To address these concerns, CIETAC has now stated that a CIETAC staff member may no longer sit as a party-appointed arbitrator, and may only be appointed as arbitrator by the chairman of CIETAC for small claims cases. In addition, CIETAC has indicated that possible future changes include altogether ending the practice of appointing CIETAC staff as arbitrators. See Moser, M., 'CIETAC and its Work—An Interview with Vice Chairman Yu Jianlong' (2007) 24(6) *J Int'l Arb* 555.

[120] s 13A, HK Arbitration Ordinance; see also sch 4, HK Arbitration Ordinance.

[121] Art 4, CIETAC Arbitration Rules.

[122] Art 21, *ibid.*

[123] Art 11(2), UNCITRAL Model Law.

situation, the arbitrators shall be appointed by the chairman of the arbitration commission.[124]

(B) Where the parties have not agreed to any set of rules or other procedural guidelines for the appointment of arbitrators, the provisions contained in the HK Arbitration Ordinance provide a procedural framework which will have effect in domestic and international arbitrations.[125] **4.154**

(3) Effect of the refusal of one party to cooperate in the constitution of the arbitral tribunal

(A) In practice, the default provisions under the PRC Arbitration Law seldom apply and it is more common for the arbitral tribunal to be constituted in accordance with more detailed procedures set out in the arbitration rules. Under the CIETAC Arbitration Rules, the more salient provisions are as follows:[126] **4.155**

(i) the default number of arbitrators is three;
(ii) where three arbitrators are appointed, within 15 days from receipt of the notice of arbitration, the claimant and the respondent shall each appoint one arbitrator or entrust the chairman of CIETAC to make such an appointment. If a party fails to do so, the arbitrator shall be appointed by the chairman of CIETAC;
(iii) within 15 days from the respondent's receipt of the notice of arbitration, the presiding arbitrator shall be jointly appointed by the parties or appointed by the chairman of CIETAC upon the parties joint authorization;
(iv) the appointment of the presiding arbitrator is by way of the 'list' system. Where there is no common candidate in the lists, the presiding arbitrator shall be appointed by the chairman of CIETAC from outside the lists which have been submitted;
(v) where a sole arbitrator is appointed, the arbitrator shall be appointed by agreement or by way of the list system, failing which the chairman of CIETAC makes the appointment.

There is no prohibition on the presiding arbitrator having the same nationality as one of the parties. In practice, this has in the past sometimes resulted in a Chinese national being appointed presiding arbitrator of the arbitral tribunal, even where foreign interests are involved. **4.156**

(B) In Hong Kong, in the case of international arbitrations, where there are three arbitrators and the parties have not pre-determined the selection procedure, each party will appoint one arbitrator and the two appointed arbitrators will, in turn, appoint the third.[127] **4.157**

The HK Arbitration Ordinance provides, in effect, that the two party-appointed arbitrators are given 30 days to agree on the third arbitrator. If they fail to agree within the 30 days, **4.158**

[124] Art 32, PRC Arbitration Law.

[125] If the HKIAC Administered Arbitration Rules apply, section III, dealing with the appointment of arbitrators, will be relevant.

[126] Art 22, CIETAC Arbitration Rules.

[127] Art 11(3)(a), UNCITRAL Model Law. Where the HKIAC Administered Arbitration Rules apply, Art 8.1, dealing with the appointment of a three-member tribunal, will be relevant.

the HKIAC can make the appointment upon request.[128] There is no right of appeal from the decision of the HKIAC.

4.159 In the case of a sole arbitrator, if the parties are unable to agree on his identity, he shall be appointed upon the request of a party, by the HKIAC.[129]

4.160 In making the appointment, the HKIAC will consult at least three members of an independent Appointment Advisory Board.[130] Although the HKIAC is not bound by the advice received, in practice, it is invariably taken into account when reaching a decision.

4.161 The Arbitration (Appointment of Arbitrators and Umpires) Rules set out criteria to be taken into account by the HKIAC in making appointments.[131]

4.162 In practice, the HKIAC will attempt to appoint an arbitrator who is on HKIAC's Panel of Arbitrators. Where the appointment sought requires skills and experience not readily available on the Panel, the HKIAC may appoint non-panelists.

(4) Circumstances and valid reasons for an arbitrator to resign

4.163 (A) The CIETAC Arbitration Rules provide that in the event an arbitrator is prevented *de jure* or *de facto* from fulfilling his/her functions, or he/she fails to fulfil his/her functions in accordance with the requirements of the Rules, or within the time period specified in those Rules, the chairman of CIETAC shall have the power to decide whether the arbitrator shall be replaced. It also provides that the arbitrator may withdraw from his/her office.[132]

4.164 (B) The HK Arbitration Ordinance recognizes that where an arbitrator is challenged, he may withdraw from his office. It expressly provides that a withdrawal in such a situation does not imply acceptance of the validity of the challenge.[133]

4.165 The HK Arbitration Ordinance also provides that in international arbitrations, where an arbitrator becomes *de jure* or *de facto* unable to perform his functions (for example, by reason of insanity or serious illness), or who for any other reason fails to act without undue delay, any party may request the Court of First Instance to decide on the termination of the mandate, which decision shall be subject to no appeal.[134]

4.166 Apart from the above, the relationship between the parties and the arbitrator is generally one of quasi-contract. It would therefore seem that an unwilling arbitrator cannot be forced to perform his functions.[135]

---

[128] Art 11, UNCITRAL Model Law.

[129] *ibid.*

[130] See also Art 9.1 of the HKIAC Administered Arbitration Rules, if the Rules apply.

[131] These are:

(i) the nature of the dispute; (ii) the availability of arbitrators or umpires, as the case may be; (iii) the identity of the parties; (iv) the independence and impartiality of the arbitrator or umpire; (v) any stipulation in the relevant arbitration agreement; and (vi) any suggestions made by the parties themselves.

See s 7, Arbitration (Appointment of Arbitrators and Umpires) Rules.

[132] Art 27, CIETAC Arbitration Rules.

[133] Art 14, UNCITRAL Model Law.

[134] *ibid.*

[135] This view is supported by the *travaux preparatoires* to the UNCITRAL Model Law. See generally, UNCITRAL A/CN.9/246 'Report of the Working Group on International Contract Practices on the Work

C. Challenge and replacement of arbitrators

(1) Grounds, procedure and deadlines for challenging an arbitrator

(A) The PRC Arbitration Law provides that the parties have a right to challenge the arbitrator in various circumstances, including where the arbitrator has a personal interest in the matter or his relationship with one of the parties may affect his impartiality.[136] **4.167**

In addition, ethical rules or codes of conduct issued by the arbitration commissions are also relevant. **4.168**

The PRC Arbitration Law also provides that if a party challenges an arbitrator, he shall submit his challenge, with a statement of the reasons thereof, prior to the 'first hearing'. If the matters giving rise to the challenge only become known after the first hearing, the challenge may be made before the conclusion of the final hearing of the case.[137] **4.169**

The individual arbitration rules set out the grounds for challenge in greater detail. Under the CIETAC Arbitration Rules, arbitrators are to furnish a Declaration stating any facts or circumstances likely to give rise to justifiable doubts as to the impartiality or independence of the arbitrator.[138] A party which intends to challenge the arbitrator on the grounds of facts or circumstances disclosed by the arbitrator shall forward the challenge in writing to CIETAC within 10 days of receipt of the Declaration, failing which it 'shall not' challenge an arbitrator later on the basis of matters disclosed by the arbitrator. **4.170**

The request for the arbitrator's withdrawal shall be in writing, and the facts and reasons on which the request is based shall be stated with supporting evidence. A party may also challenge an arbitrator in writing within 15 days from the date of receipt of the notice of formation of the arbitral tribunal. Where a party becomes aware of the reasons for a challenge after receipt of the notice, the party may challenge the arbitrator in writing within 15 days after such reasons become known, but no later than the conclusion of the last oral hearing.[139] **4.171**

Under the Rules, CIETAC shall promptly communicate the challenge to the other party, the arbitrator being challenged and the other members of the arbitral tribunal. The other party may agree to the challenge, or the arbitrator may withdraw voluntarily, neither of which would imply that the challenge made is sustainable. Otherwise, the chairman of **4.172**

---

of its Seventh Session' (1984). Nonetheless, given the quasi-contractual nature of the relationship, an arbitrator who withdraws without justification may run the risk of being in breach of contract. See also *Jung Science Information Technology Co Ltd v ZTE Corp* [2008] 4 HKLRD 776 (CFI).

[136] The circumstances are as follows:

(i) the arbitrator is a party in the arbitration or a close relative of a party or an agent in the arbitration;
(ii) the arbitrator has a personal interest in the case;
(iii) the arbitrator has another relationship with a party or an agent in the case which may affect the impartiality of the arbitration; or
(iv) the arbitrator has privately met with a party or agent or accepted an invitation to entertainment or gift from a party or agent.

See Art 34, PRC Arbitration Law.

[137] Art 35, *ibid.*

[138] Art 25, CIETAC Arbitration Rules.

[139] Art 26, *ibid.*

CIETAC shall make a final decision on the challenge. The Rules expressly provide that reasons may or may not be stated.[140]

4.173 (B) In the case of Hong Kong, if a party to an international arbitration wishes to challenge an arbitrator, in the absence of an agreed procedure, the party must send a written statement of the reasons for the challenge to the arbitral tribunal within 15 days of becoming aware of the constitution of the tribunal or of becoming aware of the existence of one of the stipulated grounds for challenge.[141] An arbitrator may be challenged where circumstances exist that raise justifiable doubts as to the arbitrator's neutrality or independence or if the arbitrator does not possess the requisite qualifications.[142]

4.174 If the other party does not agree to the challenge, or the arbitrator refuses to step down, the arbitral tribunal will then make its own decision.[143] If the arbitral tribunal rejects the challenge, the challenging party may apply to the Hong Kong courts. The procedure for this is set out in the Rules of the High Court.[144] In order to avoid delay, the arbitral tribunal may continue with the proceedings during the period that the application is pending.[145] However, if the challenge is ultimately successful, any interim award may be set aside by the challenging party. Therefore, in such cases it may be in the parties' interest to wait for the outcome of the challenge before proceeding with the arbitration.

4.175 **(1.1) Do state courts review challenge procedures which took place in accordance with a specific procedure agreed upon by the parties (eg Article 11, ICC Rules)? If so, at what point in time? May such review be excluded?** (A) The PRC Arbitration Law provides that the 'final decision' as to whether or not the arbitrator should withdraw shall be made by the chairman of the arbitration commission. If the chairman of the arbitration commission is one of the arbitrators, the decision shall be made collectively by the arbitration commission.[146] There is no express provision for a further review by the PRC courts of the decision. However, in practice, there is a risk that the PRC courts may set aside an arbitration award if there exist legitimate grounds for challenging the impartiality or independence of the arbitrator.[147] See VI.C.(1) *infra*.

4.176 (B) Under Hong Kong law, the parties are free to agree on a procedure for challenging an arbitrator. Thus, parties who agree to arbitrate under the UNCITRAL Arbitration Rules will have agreed to be subject to the challenge procedure set out in those Rules. Where the HKIAC is involved, the HKIAC's Challenge Rules[148] will also apply.

---

140 Art 26, CIETAC Arbitration Rules.

141 Art 13(2), UNCITRAL Model Law.

142 Art 12(2), *ibid.* See *Jung Science Information Technology Co Ltd v ZTE Corp* [2008] 4 HKLRD 776 (CFI). Where the HKIAC Administered Arbitration Rules apply, Art 11, dealing with the independence, challenge and removal of arbitrators, is also relevant.

143 Art 13(2), UNCITRAL Model Law.

144 c 4 sub leg A.

145 Art 13(3), UNCITRAL Model Law.

146 Art 36, PRC Arbitration Law.

147 For example, one of the grounds for setting aside a domestic award is where the arbitrators have committed malpractice for personal benefit or perverted the law in the course of the arbitration. Thus, if this was the basis for an unsuccessful challenge of the arbitrator, it may be relied upon before the PRC courts as a basis for setting aside the resulting award.

148 Adopted by the Council of the Hong Kong International Arbitration Centre on 7 March 2005.

However, the parties' freedom to agree on a challenge procedure is subject to the court's overriding power to intervene. Thus, if a challenge under the agreed procedure is not successful, the challenging party may within 30 days after notice of the decision rejecting the challenge, request that the Court of First Instance decide the challenge, which decision shall be subject to no appeal.[149] **4.177**

(1.2) **Is there case law with respect to truncated arbitral tribunals? (cf Article12(5), ICC Rules)** (A) The CIETAC Arbitration Rules provide that if, after the last oral hearing, an arbitrator on a three-member tribunal is unable to participate in the deliberation and/or to render the award owing to his/her demise or removal from CIETAC's Panel of Arbitrators, the other two arbitrators may request the chairman of CIETAC to replace the arbitrator. However, it also provides that after consulting with the parties, and upon the approval of the chairman of CIETAC, the remaining two arbitrators may continue the arbitration and make decisions, rulings or the award.[150] **4.178**

(B) The UNCITRAL Arbitration Rules (widely used in HKIAC arbitrations) provides that in the event of the death or resignation of an arbitrator during the course of the arbitral proceedings, a substitute arbitrator shall be appointed or chosen pursuant to the procedure applicable to the appointment or choice of the arbitrator being replaced.[151] The HKIAC Procedures expand on this, by providing that replacement of an arbitrator will be effected by the HKIAC in accordance with the Rules, as necessary.[152] **4.179**

The UNCITRAL Arbitration Rules further provide that if the sole or presiding arbitrator is replaced in this manner, any hearings held previously shall be repeated; if any other arbitrator is replaced, such prior hearings may be repeated at the discretion of the arbitral tribunal.[153] Previous cases conducted under the UNCITRAL Arbitration Rules also provide guidance on how truncated arbitral tribunals should act,[154] and this may be considered persuasive in the context of Hong Kong. **4.180**

(2) Procedure for appointing a new arbitrator

(A) The PRC Arbitration Law provides that if an arbitrator withdraws, a substitute arbitrator shall be selected and appointed in accordance with the Law. After the substitute arbitrator has been selected or appointed, a party may request that the arbitration proceedings already carried out be carried out anew. The decision on whether to approve the request is made by the arbitral tribunal.[155] **4.181**

(B) Where the mandate of an arbitrator terminates due to a challenge or a failure or impossibility to act, or because of a withdrawal from office for any other reason or because of the **4.182**

---

[149] Art 13, UNCITRAL Model Law.

[150] Art 28, CIETAC Arbitration Rules.

[151] Art 13, UNCITRAL Arbitration Rules.

[152] Art 7, HKIAC Procedures. Where the HKIAC Administered Arbitration Rules apply, Art 12, dealing with the replacement of arbitrators, will be relevant.

[153] Art 14, UNCITRAL Arbitration Rules. If the HKIAC Administered Arbitration Rules apply, Art 13, setting out the consequences of the replacement of an arbitrator, will be relevant.

[154] See eg *Himpurna California Energy Ltd and Republic of Indonesia* (2000) XXV YCA 186.

[155] Art 37, PRC Arbitration Law.

revocation of the mandate by agreement of the parties or in any other case of termination of his mandate, a substitute arbitrator may be appointed. Such appointment shall take place according to the rules that applied to the appointment of the arbitrator being replaced.[156]

IV. The arbitral procedure

A. General principles

(1) Extent of party autonomy to determine the arbitral procedure

4.183 (A) In the past, the PRC arbitration regime has generally been more 'institutionalized' and inflexible than the systems in more mature arbitral jurisdictions. However, over the years, parties have been given increasing autonomy to determine their own procedure. This is reflected in revisions to the CIETAC Arbitration Rules.

4.184 In the current 2005 version, the Rules provide that where the parties have agreed on the application of other arbitration rules, or on any modification of the CIETAC Arbitration Rules, the parties' agreement shall prevail, except where such agreement is incapable of being performed or is in conflict with a provision of the mandatory laws of the place of arbitration.[157]

4.185 (B) The HK Arbitration Ordinance provides that subject to the provisions of the UNCITRAL Model Law, the parties are free to agree on the procedure to be followed by the arbitral tribunal in conducting the proceedings.[158] Thus, they may opt for an elaborate, full-blown court-type proceeding with solicitors, barristers, extensive written submissions, and lengthy oral hearings involving the presentation of evidence and the examination and cross-examination of witnesses. Alternatively, they may choose to conduct the proceedings by the simple exchange of written statements without any hearings at all.

4.186 (1.1) **Are the parties free to choose any national or international law governing the procedure before the arbitral tribunal?** (A) Conflict of law rules under PRC law are still in a state of development. The rules recognize a distinction between the procedural law and governing law. However, it is unclear if parties are permitted to choose a foreign procedural law to govern an arbitration seated in the PRC. Even if such a choice is in theory permitted, parties are likely to encounter considerable practical difficulties. It is also likely that they will not be permitted to contract out of mandatory provisions of PRC arbitration law.

4.187 (B) Previous Hong Kong cases have indicated that parties to a Hong Kong arbitration are free to choose a foreign procedural law.[159] In practice, an express choice of a procedural law that is different from the law of the seat would be highly unusual. In addition, it can lead to various legal complications, and arguments may arise over a perceived overlap in the

[156] Art 15, UNCITRAL Model Law.
[157] Art 4, CIETAC Arbitration Rules.
[158] Art 19, UNCITRAL Model Law.
[159] See eg *Karaha Bodas Company LLC* (*supra* n 44).

matters to be dealt with by the law of the seat (eg Hong Kong law) and of the chosen procedural law (or *lex arbitri*).

Most tribunals (and the Hong Kong courts) are likely to seek to construe the arbitration agreement in a way so as to avoid such a result.[160] **4.188**

(2) Basic procedural principles or mandatory rules to be applied by the arbitral tribunal

(A) The PRC Arbitration Law, unlike the case in some other jurisdictions, does not contain an express provision stating that the parties have a 'full opportunity' to present their case.[161] However, it does provide that disputes are to be resolved 'in compliance with the law and in an equitable and reasonable manner'. The arbitration rules tend to elaborate on this requirement.[162] **4.189**

(B) Under Hong Kong law, an arbitral tribunal is required to observe the following duties: **4.190**

(i) in accordance with the objectives spelled out in the HK Arbitration Ordinance, the arbitrators must facilitate the fair and speedy resolution of disputes without unnecessary expense (s 2AA(1));
(ii) the arbitral tribunal must act fairly and impartially as between the parties, giving them a reasonable opportunity to present their cases and to deal with the cases of their opponents (s 2GA(1)(a)); and
(iii) the arbitral tribunal shall employ procedures that are appropriate to the circumstances of the particular case, avoiding unnecessary delay and expense (s 2GA(l)(b)).

In addition, in an international arbitration where the UNCITRAL Model Law applies, the following specific duties are imposed on the arbitral tribunal: **4.191**

(i) to treat the parties with equality and to give each party a full opportunity of presenting his case (Art 18); and
(ii) to be impartial and independent throughout the course of the proceedings (Art 12(1)).

The UNCITRAL Model Law refers to the parties' entitlement to be given a 'full opportunity of presenting his case'.[163] In contrast, the HK Arbitration Ordinance proper refers to **4.192**

---

[160] See generally the approach taken by the English courts, which are likely to be persuasive in Hong Kong: *Naviera Amazonica Peruana SA v Compania Internacional de Seguros del Peru* [1988] 1 Lloyd's Rep 116; the *Channel Tunnel* decision [1993] 1 All ER 664; and *Paul Smith Ltd v H & S International Holding Inc* [1991] 2 Lloyd's Rep 127.

[161] eg Art 18 of the UNCITRAL Model Law, the 'Magna Carta' provision, states that,

> The parties shall be treated with equality and each party shall be given a full opportunity of presenting his case.

[162] eg the CIETAC Arbitration Rules provide that the arbitral tribunal shall act impartially and fairly and shall afford reasonable opportunities to all parties for presentations and debates: see Art 29, CIETAC Arbitration Rules. The BAC Arbitration Rules (effective from 1 April 2008) provide that the arbitral tribunal shall treat the parties fairly and impartially and give each party a reasonable opportunity to present and argue its case: see Art 23, BAC Arbitration Rules. It is pertinent to note that both formulations are couched in terms of a 'reasonable' opportunity to present one's case, instead of the more rigorous 'full' opportunity formulation found in some jurisdictions, and under the UNCITRAL Model Law.

[163] Art 18, UNCITRAL Model Law.

a 'reasonable opportunity to present their cases'.[164] In practice, this distinction has not been material. It is thought by some commentators that the use of 'reasonable opportunity' merely underscores the objective of the HK Arbitration Ordinance to facilitate the fair and speedy resolution of disputes whilst preserving the rules of natural justice.[165]

(3) Oral hearing or proceeding on basis of written documents

4.193 (A) The PRC Arbitration Law provides that the arbitration 'shall' be conducted by means of oral hearings. However, if the parties agree to arbitration without oral hearings, the arbitral tribunal may render an arbitration award on the basis of the written submissions and other material.[166] The provision in the CIETAC Arbitration Rules differs slightly, and states that oral hearings may be dispensed with if the parties so request or agree and the arbitral tribunal deems that oral hearings are unnecessary.[167]

4.194 (B) In a Hong Kong international arbitration, the parties may agree to hold oral hearings for the presentation of evidence and oral argument. Alternatively, they may agree to have the case decided by the arbitrator without a hearing on a 'documents-only' basis. Where the parties cannot agree, the arbitral tribunal will decide whether to hold oral hearings. However, unless the parties have agreed that no hearings shall be held, the arbitral tribunal must hold hearings at an appropriate stage of the proceedings if requested to do so by one of the parties.[168] In practice, it is common for oral hearings to be held in international arbitrations.

(4) Power of the tribunal (in particular the chairman) to issue procedural orders

4.195 (A) The PRC Arbitration Law sets out some general powers and obligations of the arbitral tribunal, including the obligation to notify the parties of the date of hearing; the power to decide whether to postpone a hearing on the request of a party; the power to render a default award in the absence of a party; and the power to render partial awards.[169] However, it does not contain a list of extensive procedural powers as is the case in more mature jurisdictions.

4.196 The arbitration rules often supplement the arbitral tribunal's powers as set out in the PRC Arbitration Law. For example, the CIETAC Arbitration Rules set out the general principle that the arbitral tribunal shall examine the case in any way that it deems appropriate unless otherwise agreed by the parties, and that the arbitral tribunal may hold its deliberations at any place or in any manner it considers appropriate. The CIETAC Arbitration Rules also expressly provide that the arbitral tribunal may, if it considers it necessary, issue procedural

---

[164] s 2GA, HK Arbitration Ordinance.

[165] See Art 14.1 of the HKIAC Administered Arbitration Rules, which also recognizes this balance, by providing that the tribunal shall adopt suitable procedures for the conduct of the arbitration, in order to avoid unnecessary delay or expenses, 'provided that' such procedures ensure equal treatment of the parties and afford them a reasonable opportunity to be heard and to present their case.

[166] Art 39, PRC Arbitration Law.

[167] Art 29, CIETAC Arbitration Rules; see also Art 54 where the summary procedure applies.

[168] Art 24(1), UNCITRAL Model Law. See also Art 14.2 of the HKIAC Administered Arbitration Rules, where the Rules apply.

[169] See generally, ch IV, s 3 of the PRC Arbitration Law.

directions and lists of questions, hold pre-hearing meetings and preliminary hearings, and produce terms of reference 'etc', unless otherwise agreed by the parties.[170]

Significantly, there is no express power in either the PRC Arbitration Law or the CIETAC Arbitration Rules for the arbitral tribunal (or the arbitration commission) to order document disclosure. In practice, such orders are sometimes made by tribunals in foreign-related arbitrations, although the scope of such orders can be unpredictable. **4.197**

(B) The HK Arbitration Ordinance sets out various powers which an arbitrator or arbitral tribunal may exercise.[171] **4.198**

In practice, in Hong Kong arbitrations, it is not uncommon for the chairman or presiding arbitrator to decide procedural matters on his own (although he may sometimes consult the co-arbitrators before reaching a decision). The UNCITRAL Arbitration Rules expressly provide for this, by stating that in questions of procedure, when there is no majority or when the arbitral tribunal so authorizes, the presiding arbitrator may decide on his own, subject to revision, if any, by the arbitral tribunal.[172] **4.199**

(5) Distinction between matters of substance and matters of procedure

(A) Although PRC law recognizes the distinction between substance and procedure, the exact line between the two is not clearly drawn and the technical rules in other jurisdictions **4.200**

---

[170] Art 29, CIETAC Arbitration Rules.

[171] These include the power:

(i) to conduct the proceedings without regard to the strict rules of evidence (s 2GA(2));
(ii) to order security for costs (s 2GB(l)(a));
(iii) to order security for money in dispute (s 2GB(1)(b));
(iv) to order discovery of documents or delivery of interrogatories (s 2GB(l)(c));
(v) to order evidence to be given by affidavit (s 2GB(1)(d));
(vi) to order the inspection, preservation, custody, detention or sale of relevant property (s 2GB(1)(e)(i));
(vii) to grant interim injunctions or other interim measures (s 2GB(1)(f)) although in international cases this power is subject to contrary agreement (Art 17 of the UNCITRAL Model Law);
(viii) to act inquisitorially in the course of the proceedings, unless the parties agree otherwise (ss 2GB(6) and (9));
(ix) to administer oaths and take affirmations, unless the parties agree otherwise (ss 2GB(7)(a) and (9));
(x) to direct the appearance of witnesses, unless the parties agree otherwise (ss 2GB(7)(c) and (9));
(xi) to extend the time for commencing arbitration proceedings (s 2GD);
(xii) to dismiss a claim or counterclaim for want of prosecution (s 2GE);
(xiii) to make interim or partial final awards (s 16 in domestic cases and by practice in international cases);
(xiv) to award simple or compound interests on sums awarded as well as sums claimed in the arbitration and paid late but before the issuance of the award (s 2GH);
(xv) to award costs (s 2GJ);
(xvi) to limit recoverable costs (s 2GL);
(xv) to correct awards (s 19 in domestic cases and Art 33(l)(a) of the UNCITRAL Model Law in international cases);
(xvi) to interpret specific points contained in or parts of an award (in international cases only pursuant to Art 33(1)(b) of the UNCITRAL Model Law); and
(xvii) to make an additional award (UNCITRAL Model Law Art 33(3)—in international cases only).

[172] Art 31, UNCITRAL Arbitration Rules. In the case of the HKIAC Administered Arbitration Rules, Art 29.2 provides that with the prior authorization of the tribunal, the presiding arbitrator may decide questions of procedure on his own.

have not yet found their way into PRC law. In general, it is likely that disputes over the formation, validity or performance of the contract, modification and assignment of a contract, termination and liability for breach would be considered substantive matters, falling within the ambit of the governing law of the contract.[173]

4.201 (B) Hong Kong's conflict of law rules are almost entirely based on the conflict of law principles under common law. The following matters are generally governed by the procedural law:

(i) the constitution of the arbitral tribunal and any grounds for challenge of the arbitral tribunal;
(ii) the arbitral tribunal's entitlement to rule on its own jurisdiction;
(iii) the obligation to treat parties equally;
(iv) the parties' autonomy to agree on the procedure;
(v) the arbitration proceedings and oral hearing;
(vi) default proceedings;
(vii) evidential matters; and
(viii) grounds for setting aside an award.

4.202 Issues governed by the substantive law include, most importantly, the legal effect of a written contract.

4.203 (5.1) **Are statutes of limitation a matter of substance or of procedure?** (A) Under PRC law, the position is not entirely settled. Some PRC law provisions suggest that statutes of limitation merely act as a procedural bar to the right to bring an action, while other provisions appear to extinguish the underlying substantive right. In its judgments, the PRC courts have not always drawn a clear distinction between procedural and substantive rights.

4.204 (B) It appears that Hong Kong continues to adhere to the traditional view that limitation periods are procedural in nature. On this basis, limitation is governed by Hong Kong law and any limitation provision of the substantive governing law is ignored. However, where it is shown that the effect of a foreign limitation statute is to extinguish the underlying legal right (and not just to bar the remedy), the Hong Kong courts will look to the foreign substantive limitation and apply it.[174]

4.205 In the context of PRC-related disputes, it is not uncommon for parties to arbitrate their dispute in Hong Kong, but to agree to PRC law as the governing law. Difficult limitation questions can arise, because of uncertainty over whether the PRC law provisions merely act as a procedural bar, or if they extinguish the underlying substantive right altogether.

---

[173] By analogy to Art 2 of the 'Provisions of the SPC for Several Issues related to the Application of Law to the Trial of Disputes involving Foreign-related Civil or Commercial Contracts' (11 June 2007, the 'SPC Provisions 2007'). On limitation generally, see also the 'Regulations of the Supreme People's Court concerning the Limitation Period System applicable to the Hearing of Civil Cases' (effective from 1 September 2008).

[174] For a discussion of this issue, see Johnston, G., *The Conflict of Laws in Hong Kong* (2005) 26–8.

(6) Persons able to represent a party in an arbitral proceeding

(A) The PRC Arbitration Law provides that a party may appoint a lawyer or other agent to carry out arbitration activities.[175] This therefore suggests that a foreign (or foreign-related) party should be entitled to choose counsel of its choice, whether this is a local PRC lawyer, a foreign lawyer, or even a non-lawyer. Similarly, the CIETAC Arbitration Rules expressly state that either Chinese or foreign citizens may be authorized by a party to act as its representative.[176] However, as a result of certain regulations limiting the scope of legal activities that may be undertaken by foreign law firms, the right of foreign lawyers to act as counsel in arbitrations where the governing law is PRC law is currently unclear.[177] There have been certain incidents, including a memorandum issued by the Shanghai Bar Association, which have called into question the right of foreign lawyers to represent parties in CIETAC arbitrations. **4.206**

In practice, it is not uncommon for foreign parties to be represented in substantial CIETAC arbitrations by both a foreign lawyer agent, as well as by a local PRC counsel. In addition, a power of attorney is usually submitted to the arbitration commission.[178] **4.207**

(B) The HK Arbitration Ordinance enshrines the principle that parties to an arbitration have complete freedom to choose their own representatives, advisers and advocates regardless of their qualifications or nationality.[179] This contrasts with the requirement that only Hong Kong-admitted barristers and solicitors may conduct litigation in the Hong Kong courts. Hong Kong-admitted barristers and solicitors must, however, be retained to present any arbitration-related applications in the courts. **4.208**

B. Place of arbitration

(1) Determination of the place of arbitration in absence of an agreement by the parties

(A) The CIETAC Arbitration Rules provide that where the parties have agreed on the place of arbitration in writing, the parties' agreement shall prevail. Where the parties have not agreed, the place of arbitration shall be the domicile of CIETAC or its sub-commission.[180] **4.209**

It is important to appreciate that PRC law appears to impose a significant limitation on the freedom of PRC parties (including FIEs) to arbitrate outside the PRC, where there are no foreign parties to the contract, and the contract is not otherwise foreign-related.[181] **4.210**

This limitation arises due to a provision in the Contract Law of the People's Republic of China ('PRC Contract Law'),[182] which provides that parties to a foreign-related contract may resolve their disputes before either a Chinese arbitration institution *or* 'another' **4.211**

[175] Art 29, PRC Arbitration Law.

[176] Art 16, CIETAC Arbitration Rules.

[177] See eg Regulations on the Administration of Representative Offices of Foreign Law Firms operating in China (effective from 1 January 2002); Implementation Rules of the Ministry of Justice for the Regulations on the Administration of Representative Offices of Foreign Law Firms operating in China (effective from 1 September 2002, amended 2 September 2004).

[178] Art 29, PRC Arbitration Law.

[179] s 2F, HK Arbitration Ordinance.

[180] Art 31, CIETAC Arbitration Rules.

[181] See I.A.(3.1) on when a contract is considered 'foreign-related'.

[182] Effective from 1 October 1999.

arbitration institution.[183] The latter reference is commonly interpreted as referring to a foreign arbitral institution such as the ICC. Based on this, it appears that where the contract is *not* foreign-related, the dispute must be arbitrated before a Chinese arbitration institution. The argument is often made, by extension, that where a contract only comprises PRC parties (including FIEs), they cannot agree to arbitrate outside the PRC.[184]

4.212 On this basis, if an FIE owned by a US corporation had a dispute with another FIE owned by a UK corporation, in the absence of any foreign element, this would be deemed a 'domestic' dispute, with the consequence that the parties may be prohibited from arbitrating their dispute outside China. A guide issued by the SPC in 2004 supports this view.[185]

4.213 (B) The HK Arbitration Ordinance provides that the parties are free to agree on the place of arbitration. Failing such agreement, the place of arbitration shall be determined by the arbitral tribunal having regard to the circumstances of the case, including the convenience of the parties.[186] In practice, parties usually agree in their arbitration agreement on the place of arbitration.

4.214 The HKIAC Procedures also provide that in light of the administrative services provided by the HKIAC under the HKIAC Procedures, unless otherwise stated, the arbitral tribunal will be presumed to have chosen the offices of the HKIAC in Hong Kong as the place of hearings for all arbitrations under the HKIAC Procedures.[187]

(2) Importance and legal effect of place (seat) of the arbitration

4.215 (A) The place of arbitration is significant for three reasons. First, it determines the arbitration laws which govern the conduct of the arbitration.

4.216 Secondly, the place of arbitration determines which court may exercise supportive and supervisory powers over arbitrations. Therefore, attempts to set aside the award should ordinarily be made at the place of arbitration. The PRC Arbitration Law provides that parties may apply to the Intermediate People's Court to set aside an arbitration award in the place 'where the arbitration commission is located'.[188]

4.217 Thirdly, the place of arbitration fixes the place of the award.[189] This is important in the context of enforcement of the award. Given that the PRC is a signatory to the New York

[183] Art 128.

[184] However, on one reading, the prohibition is simply against domestic disputes being arbitrated before a *non*-Chinese arbitration institution. On this view, there may be an argument that a CIETAC arbitration between PRC parties, whether held within *or outside* the PRC, is permissible. This possibility arises because the current 2005 version of the CIETAC Arbitration Rules envisages that a CIETAC arbitration may take place either inside or outside the PRC.

[185] See SPC, 'Explanations and Answers to Practical Questions on the Trial of Foreign-related Commercial and Maritime Cases' (issued April 2004), para 83.

[186] Art 20, UNCITRAL Model Law. In the case of the HKIAC Administered Arbitration Rules, Art 15.1 provides that the seat of all arbitrations under those Rules shall be the Hong Kong Special Administrative Region, unless the parties have expressly agreed otherwise.

[187] This presumption notwithstanding, the HKIAC is prepared to administer arbitrations in accordance with the Procedures in a location other than Hong Kong and will do so at the request and mutual agreement of the parties. See Art 5, HKIAC Procedures.

[188] Art 58, PRC Arbitration Law.

[189] See eg the CIETAC Arbitration Rules, which expressly recognize that the arbitral award is deemed as being made at the place of arbitration: Art 31.

Convention, an award 'made' in the PRC will be considered an award made in a Convention member state for purposes of enforcement abroad.

(B) As in the case of the PRC, the significance of the place of arbitration under Hong Kong law is threefold. First, it determines which jurisdiction's arbitration laws govern the conduct of the arbitration. Unless the parties agree otherwise, an arbitration which has Hong Kong as its seat will be governed by the HK Arbitration Ordinance. **4.218**

Secondly, the place of the arbitration fixes the place of the award. Where Hong Kong is designated as the *situs* of the arbitration, the award will be considered to have been 'made' in Hong Kong.[190] Because Hong Kong is a part of the PRC, and the PRC is a member of the New York Convention, an award 'made' in Hong Kong will be considered an award made in a Convention member state for purposes of enforcement abroad. **4.219**

Thirdly, the place of arbitration specifies which court may exercise supportive and supervisory powers over arbitrations. Where Hong Kong is the place of arbitration, it is the Hong Kong courts which exercise primary supportive and supervisory jurisdiction over the arbitration. **4.220**

(2.1) Are the arbitrators and parties free to convene at places other than the official seat of the arbitration? (A) The CIETAC Arbitration Rules distinguish between the place or 'seat' of the arbitration, and the place (or venue) for hearings. The rules recognize that parties are free to select the seat of the arbitration;[191] furthermore, where they have agreed on the place for oral hearings, the arbitration shall ordinarily be heard at that agreed place. In the absence of such agreement, a case accepted by CIETAC shall be heard in Beijing, or if the arbitral tribunal considers it necessary, at other places with the approval of the Secretary-General of CIETAC.[192] The Rules also provide that the arbitral tribunal may hold its deliberations at any place or in any manner that it considers appropriate.[193] **4.221**

(B) Yes. The HK Arbitration Ordinance expressly provides that, notwithstanding the place (or seat) of arbitration, the arbitral tribunal may, unless otherwise agreed by the parties, meet at any place it considers appropriate for consultation among its members, for hearing witnesses, experts or the parties, or for inspection of goods, other property or documents.[194] **4.222**

(2.2) Are there visa requirements to enter the country which apply to lawyers and/or arbitrators? Where may current information on that subject be obtained? (A) In general, yes. Information can be obtained from the embassy or consulate general or commissioner offices of the Ministry of Foreign Affairs of the PRC. **4.223**

[190] In the case of the HKIAC Administered Arbitration Rules, Art 15.4 provides that the award shall be deemed to have been made at the seat of the arbitration.

[191] Art 31, CIETAC Arbitration Rules.

[192] Art 32, *ibid.*

[193] Art 29, *ibid.*

[194] Art 20, UNCITRAL Model Law. Where the HKIAC Administered Arbitration Rules apply, Art 14.2 expressly provides that the tribunal may hear witnesses, oral argument and hold meetings for consultation at any place it deems appropriate, having regard to the circumstances.

4.224 (B) In the case of Hong Kong, work visas may be required. In practice, these are usually fairly easy to obtain, once the formalities are complied with. Additional information can be obtained from the Hong Kong International Arbitration Centre and from the Hong Kong SAR Immigration Department Employment and Visit Visas Section or (in the case of mainland residents), from the Mainland Residents Section.

C. Submissions, deadlines and default

(1) Contents and form of submissions (in particular request for arbitration and answer to request)

4.225 (A) The PRC Arbitration Law provides that a party's application for arbitration shall meet the following requirements:[195]

(i) there is an arbitration agreement;
(ii) there is a specific arbitration claim and there are facts and reasons; and
(iii) the application is within the scope of the arbitration commission's jurisdiction.

4.226 In addition, a party shall submit to the arbitration commission the written arbitration agreement and a written application for arbitration, together with copies thereof.[196] The PRC Arbitration Law also sets out specific particulars to be included in the application for arbitration:

(i) the parties' names, sex, ages, occupations, work units and domiciles, and in the case of legal persons or other organizations, their names and domiciles and the names and positions of their legal representatives or principal officers;
(ii) the arbitration claim and the facts and reasons on which the claim is based; and
(iii) the evidence, the source of the evidence and the name and domicile of witnesses.

4.227 The PRC Arbitration Law is largely silent on the content of subsequent submissions. The individual arbitration rules elaborate on some of the above provisions.[197]

4.228 (B) Under Hong Kong law, there are no strict rules or technical requirements on the form of submissions.

4.229 However, certain basic requirements are set out in the HK Arbitration Ordinance. It provides that within the requisite time, the claimant shall state the facts supporting his claim, the points at issue and the relief or remedy sought, and the respondent shall state his defence in respect of these particulars, unless the parties have otherwise agreed on the required elements of such statements. The parties may submit with their statements all documents they consider to be relevant or may add a reference to the documents or other evidence they will submit.[198] Arbitration rules may sometimes contain more detailed provisions on the form and contents of particular documents, such as the request for or notice of arbitration.[199]

---

195 Art 21, PRC Arbitration Law.
196 Art 22, *ibid.*
197 See eg Art 10, CIETAC Arbitration Rules.
198 Art 23, UNCITRAL Model Law.
199 See eg Arts 17 and 18 of the HKIAC Administered Arbitration Rules.

The parties' submissions are important as they set out the background to the substantive matters that will be decided. They also form the basis for the decisions to be made in a number of interlocutory matters, such as discovery applications and decisions on whether to have preliminary issues. 4.230

(1.1) From what point in time is a claim considered to be pending with the arbitral tribunal? What are the legal effects of such a fact (eg on statutes of limitations)? 4.231
(A) Arbitration in the PRC is almost invariably conducted by using the arbitral rules of an institution. These rules often deal with when an arbitration is deemed to commence. The CIETAC Arbitration Rules, for example, provide that the arbitral proceedings shall commence on the date on which CIETAC (or one of its sub-commissions) receives a request for arbitration.[200] Notably, the relevant commencement date is fixed by reference to the date of *receipt* of the request for arbitration, and not the date of *acceptance* of an application for arbitration.[201] Fixing the date of commencement of arbitration by reference to the date of receipt of the request should help provide greater certainty than would be the case if the relevant date is when the application is accepted.

(B) For Hong Kong international arbitrations, unless otherwise agreed, the arbitral proceedings commence on the date on which a request for that dispute to be referred to arbitration is received by the respondent.[202] 4.232

(1.2) When is a time limit according to statutes of limitations deemed to be interrupted in case of (i) *ad hoc*; and (ii) institutional arbitration? (A) PRC law appears to only recognize institutional arbitrations, and not *ad hoc* arbitrations.[203] For institutional arbitrations, the time under the statute of limitation generally stops running once the arbitration proceedings have commenced. When proceedings commence will generally depend on the applicable arbitration rules and any specific provisions in the relevant contract. The situation involving the CIETAC Arbitration Rules has been discussed above. In the case of other arbitration rules, it is possible that an application for arbitration may be rejected and the limitation period may well continue running until a revised application for arbitration is accepted by the arbitration commission.[204] 4.233

(B) In general, under Hong Kong law, the limitation period is interrupted once arbitration proceedings commence. The HK Arbitration Ordinance envisages that the rule on when a dispute commences applies 'unless otherwise agreed by the parties'.[205] Thus, if parties have agreed on a different commencement date, their agreement will prevail. For example, under the ICC Rules, the date on which the request for arbitration is received by the 4.234

[200] Art 9, CIETAC Arbitration Rules.
[201] cf Art 24 of the PRC Arbitration Law which provides that the arbitration commission may accept or reject an application for arbitration.
[202] Art 21, UNCITRAL Model Law. Where the HKIAC Administered Arbitration Rules apply, Art 4.2 provides that arbitral proceedings shall be deemed to commence on the date on which the notice of arbitration is received by the HKIAC Secretariat.
[203] See II.A.(2) *supra*.
[204] See eg Art 8 of the BAC Arbitration Rules which states that arbitral proceedings shall be deemed to commence on the date on which the BAC accepts the Application for Arbitration.
[205] Art 21, UNCITRAL Model Law.

Secretariat is the deemed commencement date (and not the date on which the respondent receives the request).[206] This approach may sometimes be beneficial where there are difficulties locating the Respondent(s).[207]

4.235 **(1.3) What is the effect of the withdrawal of the request for arbitration?** (A) The CIETAC Arbitration Rules provide that a party may file a request with CIETAC to withdraw its claim or counterclaim in its entirety. If the claimant withdraws its claim in its entirety, the arbitral tribunal shall proceed with examining the counterclaim and rendering an arbitral award thereon. If the respondent withdraws its counterclaim in its entirety, the arbitral tribunal shall also proceed with examining the claim and rendering an arbitral award thereon. Where a case is dismissed before the constitution of the arbitral tribunal, the decision shall be made by CIETAC. Where the case is dismissed after the constitution of the arbitral tribunal, the decision shall be made by the arbitral tribunal.[208]

4.236 The CIETAC Arbitration Rules also state that where a party files a request for arbitration for a claim which has been withdrawn, CIETAC has the discretion to decide whether or not to accept the request anew.[209]

4.237 (B) In the case of international arbitrations, the HK Arbitration Ordinance provides that the arbitral tribunal shall issue an order for the termination of the arbitral proceedings when the claimant withdraws his claim, unless the respondent objects and the arbitral tribunal recognizes a legitimate interest on his part in obtaining a final settlement of the dispute.[210] A party may, however, be liable for costs if it seeks to unilaterally withdraw its claim.

(2) Legal deadlines (provided by law or set by the arbitrators) and effect of non-compliance by a party

4.238 (A) The deadline for submissions will be based on the provisions of the PRC Arbitration Law, the applicable arbitration rules and (where silent) as fixed by the arbitral tribunal. In general, submissions in arbitrations in the PRC are relatively shorter and less detailed than in other jurisdictions. Consequently, timelines can be relatively short.

4.239 Arbitration rules commonly used in the PRC set out timelines for submissions, but they also provide for these timelines to be extended.[211] In relation to the production of evidence, the CIETAC Arbitration Rules provide that the arbitral tribunal may specify a time period within which evidence should be produced. The arbitral tribunal may refuse to admit evidence produced out of time, although a party may apply for an extension.[212]

206 Art 4(2), ICC Rules.
207 cf the deemed service provision in s 31, HK Arbitration Ordinance; Art 3, UNCITRAL Model Law.
208 Art 41, CIETAC Arbitration Rules.
209 *ibid.*
210 Art 32, UNCITRAL Model Law.
211 For example, the CIETAC Arbitration Rules expressly provide that the arbitral tribunal may extend the time for filing the Statement of Defence if it believes that there are justifiable reasons. See Art 12, CIETAC Arbitration Rules.
212 Art 36, CIETAC Arbitration Rules.

(B) In Hong Kong international arbitrations, the claimant and the respondent are required to submit a statement of claim and a defence, respectively. If the parties cannot agree, the tribunal shall decide on the time limits for the statements of claim and defence to be exchanged.[213] 4.240

The HK Arbitration Ordinance also provides that, unless otherwise agreed, if, without showing sufficient cause, 4.241

(i) the claimant fails to duly communicate his statement of claim, the arbitral tribunal shall terminate the proceedings;
(ii) the respondent fails to duly communicate his statement of defence, the arbitral tribunal shall continue the proceedings without treating such failure in itself as an admission of the claimant's allegations; or
(iii) any party fails to appear at a hearing or to produce documentary evidence, the arbitral tribunal may continue the proceedings and make the award on the evidence before it.[214]

Apart from the above, the HK Arbitration Ordinance does not clearly provide for the consequences if a party fails to comply with deadlines. However, in practice, the arbitration rules adopted by the parties will frequently provide that the timelines may be extended. For example, in connection with the time for submission of written statements (the statement of claim and defence), the UNCITRAL Arbitration Rules provide that the arbitral tribunal may extend the time limits if it concludes that an extension is justified.[215] 4.242

(2.1) What are the powers of the tribunal if a party fails to comply with the time limits set up by the tribunal? (A) The CIETAC Arbitration Rules provide that a party having justifiable reasons may request a postponement of the oral hearing, provided that any such request is made at least 10 days prior to the oral hearing date.[216] However, the Rules also provide that if the parties fail to appear at an oral hearing without showing sufficient cause or withdraws from an on-going oral hearing without permission, the arbitral tribunal may proceed with the arbitration and make a default award. 4.243

(B) In practice, tribunals in Hong Kong international arbitrations do not ordinarily make peremptory (or 'unless') orders, for a party to comply by a certain date or face certain consequences. Instead, where deadlines cannot be met, it is fairly common for extensions of time to be agreed upon by the parties, or granted by the arbitral tribunal. That said, there has been a greater emphasis in recent years on reducing delays in international arbitration, and for tribunals to adopt a more robust approach, in response to dilatory tactics. Peremptory orders may therefore become a more important tool in the future. 4.244

(2.2) Is the tribunal bound by any mandatory time limits for certain procedural steps (eg hearings, making of the award)? (A) Under the PRC Arbitration Law, there is no mandatory time limit within which the award has to be rendered. Nonetheless, the PRC 4.245

[213] Art 23(1), UNCITRAL Model Law.
[214] Art 25, *ibid.*
[215] Art 23, UNCITRAL Arbitration Rules.
[216] Art 30, CIETAC Arbitration Rules.

Arbitration Law acknowledges the importance of ensuring the impartial and 'prompt' arbitration of economic disputes.[217]

4.246 The CIETAC Arbitration Rules state that the arbitral tribunal shall render an award within six months from the date the arbitral tribunal is formed, and in the case of domestic arbitrations, within four months.[218] In practice, this period may be extended, and the Rules provide that upon the request of the arbitral tribunal, the chairman of CIETAC may extend the time period if it is considered truly necessary and the reasons for the extension are truly justified.

4.247 (B) The HK Arbitration Ordinance does not specify any time limit for the making of an international award. However, if an arbitrator fails to act in a timely manner, he or she can be removed by agreement of both parties or by order of the Hong Kong courts.[219] In this instance, a substitute arbitrator would be appointed in accordance with the rules that applied to the original appointment.

(3) Statutory requirements as to notifications during an arbitration (with respect to the request for arbitration and other written pleadings; with respect to notifications by the tribunal)

4.248 (A) The CIETAC Arbitration Rules provide that all documents, notices and written materials may be sent to the parties and/or their representatives in person, or by registered mail or express mail, facsimile, telex, cable, or by any other means considered proper by CIETAC.[220] Furthermore, any written correspondence shall be deemed to have been properly served if delivered to the addressee or delivered at his place of business, registration, domicile, habitual residence or mailing address, or where, after reasonable inquiries by the other party, none of these addresses can be found, the correspondence is sent by CIETAC to the addressee's last known place of business, registered address, domicile, habitual residence or mailing address by registered mail or other means.

4.249 (B) As a general rule in international arbitrations, the HK Arbitration Ordinance provides that unless otherwise agreed by the parties:

(i) any written communication is deemed to have been received if it is delivered to the addressee personally or if it is delivered at his place of business, habitual residence or mailing address; if none of these can be found after making a reasonable inquiry, a written communication is deemed to have been received if it is sent to the addressee's last-known place of business, habitual residence or mailing address by registered letter or any other means which provides a record of the attempt to deliver it; and

(ii) the communication is deemed to have been received on the day it is so delivered.[221]

4.250 In connection with statements of claim and defence, the HK Arbitration Ordinance provides that the claimant shall state the facts supporting his claim, the points at issue and the

---

[217] Art 1, PRC Arbitration Law.

[218] Arts 42 and 65, CIETAC Arbitration Rules.

[219] Art 14(1), UNCITRAL Model Law.

[220] Art 68, CIETAC Arbitration Rules.

[221] Art 3, UNCITRAL Arbitration Law. In the case of the HKIAC Administered Arbitration Rules, see Art 2, dealing with notices and calculation of periods of time.

relief or remedy sought, and the respondent shall state his defence in respect of these particulars, unless the parties have otherwise agreed as to the required elements of such statements. The parties may submit with their statements all documents they consider to be relevant or may add a reference to the documents or other evidence they will submit.[222]

(4) Effect of the insolvency of a party

(A) The insolvency of one party in and of itself will generally not automatically discharge a party from its obligations under an arbitration agreement. **4.251**

(B) In general, the mere insolvency or bankruptcy of a party does not automatically discharge a party from the arbitration agreement. For domestic arbitrations, the HK Arbitration Ordinance provides that where it is provided in a contract that any disputes shall be referred to arbitration, the term shall, if the trustee in bankruptcy adopts the contract, be enforceable by or against him so far as relates to any such disputes. In addition, in certain circumstances, a party is permitted to apply to court for an order directing that a matter to which an arbitration agreement applies shall be referred to arbitration. The court may, having regard to all the circumstances of the case, make an order accordingly.[223] **4.252**

D. Facts and evidence: general

(1) Burden of proof (inquisitorial/adversarial procedure)

(A) The PRC Arbitration Law does not expressly deal with whether the arbitral tribunal should adopt an inquisitorial or adversarial procedure. However, the CIETAC Arbitration Rules provide that, having regard to the circumstances of the case, the tribunal may adopt an inquisitorial or adversarial approach when examining the case.[224] **4.253**

In practice, many PRC arbitral tribunals, even in foreign-related arbitrations, will adopt an inquisitorial approach that is more interventionist than is the practice in common law jurisdictions. **4.254**

(B) The HK Arbitration Ordinance authorizes an arbitral tribunal, in conducting arbitration proceedings, to decide whether and to what extent it should itself take the initiative in ascertaining the facts and the law relevant to those proceedings.[225] However, this is subject to contrary agreement between the parties.[226] **4.255**

As for the burden of proof, the HKIAC Administered Arbitration Rules provides that each party shall have the burden of proving the facts relied on to support its claim or defence.[227] **4.256**

(2) Power of the tribunal to determine the admissibility, and weight of the evidence produced by the parties

(A) There is no express provision empowering the arbitral tribunal to determine the admissibility and weight of evidence produced by the parties. Strict rules of evidence do not apply **4.257**

222 Art 23, UNCITRAL Model Law.
223 s 5, HK Arbitration Ordinance.
224 Art 29, CIETAC Arbitration Rules.
225 s 2GB(6), HK Arbitration Ordinance.
226 See s 2GB(9), HK Arbitration Ordinance.
227 Art 23.1, HKIAC Administered Arbitration Rules.

in CIETAC arbitrations, and in practice, considerable weight will be given to documentary evidence.

4.258 The PRC Civil Procedure Law also expressly recognizes various categories of evidence.[228]

4.259 (B) In examining the evidence, a Hong Kong arbitral tribunal is not bound by the strict rules applicable to court proceedings, but can receive any evidence (excluding evidence protected by privilege) that it considers relevant to the proceedings.[229]

4.260 It is up to the arbitral tribunal to decide what evidence is relevant and to admit such evidence even though they do not comply with the strict rules of evidence. Having admitted the evidence, it is for the tribunal to decide on the weight of such evidence. Naturally, evidence which is hearsay would carry less weight than direct evidence.

4.261 (2.1) **Is the tribunal entitled to take the claimant's factual allegations as automatically proven if the respondent does not participate in the arbitral proceedings?** (A) No. However, the PRC Arbitration Law does provide that if the respondent fails to appear before the tribunal without justifiable reasons after having been notified in writing, or leaves the hearing prior to its conclusion without the permission of the arbitral tribunal, the arbitral tribunal may (not must) render a default award.[230]

4.262 (B) Under Hong Kong law, if a party fails to appear at the hearing or fails to produce documentary evidence in support of its case, the tribunal has the power to continue the proceedings and make a default award in the absence of the party.[231] The party present (eg the claimant) still has to prove its claim.

4.263 (2.2) **May the arbitral tribunal consider an allegation of one party as agreed fact if the other party did not (specifically) dispute the allegation?** (A) In foreign-related arbitrations in the PRC, in practice, strict rules on admissibility of evidence are often not applied and parties are given reasonable leeway to present their case. It is usually not necessary for a party to specifically dispute each and every allegation.

4.264 (B) In Hong Kong arbitrations, strict rules on evidence do not apply and it is not necessary for a party to specifically dispute every allegation.

4.265 (2.3) **What is the standard of proof that must be met in order for a fact to be considered to have been established (preponderance of the evidence; beyond reasonable doubt)? Must a stringent requirement be met for certain facts?** (A) In general, it is on a preponderance of the evidence.[232] The PRC Arbitration Law states that parties shall provide

[228] Art 63, PRC Civil Procedure Law. These are:
(i) documentary evidence; (ii) material evidence; (iii) audio-visual material; (iv) testimony of witnesses; (v) statements of the parties; (vi) expert conclusions; (vii) records of inspection.

[229] s 2GA(2), HK Arbitration Ordinance. In the case of the HKIAC Administered Arbitration Rules, Art 23.10 provides that the tribunal shall determine the admissibility, relevance, materiality and weight of any matter presented by a party, 'including as to whether or not to apply strict rules of evidence'.

[230] Art 42, PRC Arbitration Law.

[231] Art 25(c), UNCITRAL Model Law.

[232] See generally, SPC, 'Some Provisions of the Supreme People's Court on Evidence in Civil Procedures' (effective from 1 April 2002).

evidence in support of their own arguments.[233] The CIETAC Arbitration Rules state that each party shall have the burden of proving the facts relied on to support its claim, defence or counterclaim, and if a party having the burden of proof fails to produce evidence on time, or the produced evidence is not sufficient, it shall 'bear the consequences thereof'.[234]

(B) This is for the arbitral tribunal to decide and in general, it will be on a balance of probabilities. However, in some situations (eg where allegations of fraud are made), the arbitral tribunal may require more definitive proof. **4.266**

(2.4) May the arbitral tribunal rely on its own knowledge to consider certain facts as proven? (A) Yes, the PRC Arbitration Law expressly provides that the arbitral tribunal may, if it considers it necessary, collect evidence on its own.[235] The CIETAC Arbitration Rules further provide that when investigating and collecting evidence by itself, the arbitral tribunal shall promptly notify the parties to be present at such investigation *if it considers it necessary.* If one or both parties fail to be present, the investigation and collection will proceed regardless.[236] **4.267**

(B) Yes. Under the HK Arbitration Ordinance, a tribunal may take the initiative to ascertain the facts relevant to the proceedings.[237] However, the arbitrator or tribunal should not decide solely on the basis of evidence obtained through their own investigations without sharing such evidence with the parties beforehand. If an award is based in whole or in part on evidence ascertained through the arbitral tribunal's own investigations or specialized knowledge, the tribunal must first put that evidence before the parties for comment. Otherwise the award may be set aside or refused enforcement for not having given the party a reasonable opportunity to present his case.[238] **4.268**

E. Witnesses

(1) Ability of a person to act as a witness

(A) Under PRC law, although various persons are permitted to testify as witnesses, their testimony may be considered less persuasive in particular situations. For example, in PRC court practice, the testimony of a minor or other person suffering from an incapacity and the testimony of any witness who is related to a party or is his agent is, if uncorroborated, generally considered insufficient for establishing the facts.[239] In practice, these court provisions are likely to influence an arbitral tribunal's assessment of evidence taken from such individuals. **4.269**

---

[233] Art 43, PRC Arbitration Law.

[234] Art 36, CIETAC Arbitration Rules.

[235] Art 43, PRC Arbitration Law.

[236] Art 37, CIETAC Arbitration Rules.

[237] Section 2GB(6), HK Arbitration Ordinance.

[238] See *Brunswick Bowling & Billiards Corporation v Shanghai Zhonglu Industrial Co Ltd and Chen Rong* HCCT 66/2007 (10 February 2009).

[239] SPC, 'Certain Provisions of the Supreme People's Court on Evidence in Civil Actions' (effective from 21 December 2001).

4.270 (B) Under Hong Kong law, there are no strict rules on which persons may give evidence as a witness.[240] This is consistent with the general approach in arbitration of disregarding technical rules on admissibility of evidence. Thus, for example, employees of a party to the arbitration are allowed to testify. However, the tribunal has the discretion to give less weight to the testimony of a witness, if this is justified in the circumstances.

4.271 (1.1) **Is there a legal difference between a party testifying and a witness? If yes, what are the criteria for such differentiation? Does the testimony of a party have the same weight as a witness' testimony?** (A) See IV.E.(1) supra. In practice, it is quite common for the evidence of a witness who is an employee of one of the parties to be given less weight than that of an independent party.

4.272 (B) Under Hong Kong law, there is no legal difference and there is no rule preventing a party from testifying in support of his own case, or preventing an employee of a company involved in the proceedings from testifying. Indeed, in practice, it is common for such individuals to testify. However, the relationship between the witness and one of the parties may, of course, influence the weight given to his testimony.

(2) Preparation of witnesses and limits thereof

4.273 (A) There are no formal restrictions in the PRC Arbitration Law on the preparation of witnesses. However, various ethical rules will apply in the case of PRC lawyers. Furthermore, in practice, cross-examination is far more limited in arbitrations held in the PRC than in other jurisdictions. It is not unusual for oral hearings to take no more than a day. Correspondingly, the importance of preparing witnesses is much diminished and among PRC lawyers, witness preparation is not necessarily considered an important task.

4.274 (B) Under Hong Kong law and arbitral practice, there are no specific restrictions against preparing witnesses for the oral hearing.[241] However, ethical and other bar restrictions may apply. For example, 'coaching' of witnesses is not permissible.

4.275 (2.1) **Do US-style depositions violate any procedural rules or principles?** (A) US-style depositions are highly unusual and not used in the PRC.

4.276 (B) US-style depositions do not violate any procedural rules or principles. However, these are unusual and not ordinarily used in international arbitrations in Hong Kong.

4.277 (2.2) **May a party or its counsel approach a witness whom it has nominated (only before or also after the proceeding has started)? Are interviews permitted?** (A) The PRC Arbitration Law is silent on this. Approaching and interviewing a witness in preparation for the proceedings is acceptable.

4.278 (B) In general, a party or its counsel may approach a witness whom it has nominated, both before and after the proceedings have started. However, once a witness has started giving

[240] In the case of the HKIAC Administered Arbitration Rules, Art 23.5 expressly provides that any person may be a witness or an expert witness.

[241] This is also reflected in Art 23.9 of the HKIAC Administered Arbitration Rules, which provides that a party, its officers, employees, legal advisers or counsel may interview witnesses, potential witnesses or expert witnesses.

evidence orally, he should not discuss his evidence with anyone else until he has finished. Ethical and bar rules may also apply to limit the extent to which counsel may communicate with a witness directly.

(3) Admissibility of written witness statements

(A) In the PRC, written witness statements setting out the testimony of a witness are admissible, and they are used quite widely, particularly in foreign-related arbitrations. Used properly, written witness statements can be an effective tool, by reducing the time required for the oral hearing, allowing witnesses to set out their testimony in a more logical and considered manner, and allowing parties to prepare for the oral hearing in an efficient manner. **4.279**

(B) In Hong Kong, written witness statements are admissible and indeed, are frequently used in international arbitrations.[242] They are typically prepared and signed by each witness to be called, and exchanged before the hearing. It is also common for witness statements to refer to and explain supporting documents, which are exhibited either as part of the earlier submissions or document disclosure, or attached to the witness statements. It is also quite common to have more than one round of witness statements, with supplemental or responsive statements submitted in reply to points made in first round witness statements from the other party. **4.280**

(3.1) If the parties agree on written statements, is a party entitled to request an oral hearing for questioning those witnesses (provided such right has not been agreed upon)? **4.281**
(A) Yes. Even though written witness statements may have been adduced, the PRC Arbitration Law expressly provides that the parties have a right to an oral hearing[243] (during which witnesses may be examined).

(B) Yes. Even though the parties have agreed on written statements, a party is ordinarily still entitled to request an oral hearing for questioning those witnesses. Furthermore, the HK Arbitration Ordinance expressly provides that unless the parties have agreed that no hearings shall be held, the arbitral tribunal shall hold hearings at an appropriate stage of the proceedings, if so requested by a party.[244] **4.282**

(4) Entitlement of a party to have a hearing or cross-examination of witnesses

(A) Even though a party is entitled to an oral hearing, in practice, any cross-examination of witnesses during the hearing will be subject to the arbitral tribunal's sanction, and lengthy cross-examination of witnesses would be unusual.[245] **4.283**

In PRC disputes, it is important to be alive to the difficulties caused by language issues. Although the CIETAC Arbitration Rules recognize that parties may agree on the language of the arbitration, in the absence of such agreement, the default language is the **4.284**

---

[242] See eg Art 23.8 of the HKIAC Administered Arbitration Rules which provides that evidence of witnesses or expert witnesses may also be presented in the form of written statements or reports signed by them.
[243] Art 39, PRC Arbitration Law.
[244] Art 24, UNCITRAL Model Law.
[245] The PRC Arbitration Law does, however, recognize that the evidence may be 'examined' by the parties which, in theory, should include a right to cross-examine witnesses. See Art 45, PRC Arbitration Law.

Chinese language.[246] For foreign parties, having the proceedings conducted in Chinese can place them at a tactical disadvantage, and it can also significantly increase the costs of the proceedings, if there are many English language documents (eg disclosed documents) which have to be translated.[247] As a commercial compromise, parties often agree to the proceedings being conducted in both English and Chinese. While this may appear to be an easy compromise, it is not recommended, as it significantly adds to the cost and complexity of the proceedings.

4.285 (B) Even though a party is entitled to an oral hearing, any cross-examination of witnesses during the hearing will be subject to the arbitral tribunal's sanction. In practice, cross-examination of witnesses in Hong Kong international arbitrations would generally be less intensive than in court practice, although much will depend on the composition of the arbitral tribunal and the parties' counsel. In addition, it is increasingly common for tribunals in Hong Kong to adopt a chess-clock type procedure, either by strict time keeping, or by way of an understanding that the available time should be shared equally (or in some other appropriate way) among all parties to the proceedings.

4.286 (4.1) **What are the methods used to establish a record of the arbitral proceedings, in particular witness examinations (tape recording, verbatim court reporters, dictated minutes, other methods)?** (A) Hearings are usually recorded by the secretariat of the arbitration commission in writing. The parties have the right to apply for a correction of the record if it contains omissions or errors.[248] The major arbitration commissions also have facilities for recording the hearing by audio. In the case of foreign-related arbitrations, these rules are less stringent.[249]

4.287 The CIETAC Arbitration Rules recognize that during the oral hearing, the arbitral tribunal may arrange a stenographic and/or audio-visual record. The arbitral tribunal may, when it considers it necessary, take minutes stating the main points of the oral hearing and requesting the parties and/or their representatives, witnesses and/or other persons involved to sign and/or affix their seals to the minutes. The CIETAC Arbitration Rules also provide that the stenographic and/or audio-visual record of the oral hearing shall be available for the use and reference of the arbitral tribunal.[250]

4.288 (B) For most international arbitrations of any significance, it is common for the witness hearing to be recorded and for daily transcripts to be produced.[251] It is also quite common to have a 'live' transcript of the proceedings.

4.289 (4.2) **May the arbitral tribunal take an oath from a witness?** (A) There are no specific provisions in the PRC Arbitration Law on witnesses taking an oath.

---

[246] Art 67, CIETAC Arbitration Rules.

[247] In this regard, Art 67(3) of the CIETAC Arbitration Rules provides that the arbitral tribunal and/or CIETAC may, 'if it considers necessary', request the parties to submit a corresponding version of the documents and evidence by the parties in Chinese or in other languages.

[248] Art 48, PRC Arbitration Law.

[249] Art 69, *ibid.*

[250] Art 35, CIETAC Arbitration Rules.

[251] See also Art 23.6 of the HKIAC Administered Arbitration Rules, which provides that the tribunal may make directions for a record of the hearing if it deems that this is necessary in the circumstances of the case.

(B) Yes. The HK Arbitration Ordinance provides for the possibility of a witness swearing or affirming his statements under oath.[252] **4.290**

(4.3) Does the arbitral tribunal have the power to compel witnesses? (A) The PRC Arbitration Law is silent on this issue. In any event, this would be unusual in practice, particularly in connection with a witness who is not under the control of any of the parties to the arbitration. **4.291**

(B) Yes. Under the HK Arbitration Ordinance, the arbitral tribunal may direct the attendance before the tribunal of witnesses in order to give evidence or to produce documents or other material evidence;[253] this power is, however, subject to contrary agreement by the parties.[254] However, if a witness summons is required to compel the attendance of a witness or the production of evidence, the HK Arbitration Ordinance requires that this must be obtained by a court application.[255] **4.292**

F. Documents

(1) Form and kind of documents to be presented to the arbitral tribunal

(A) In PRC court practice, there are fairly detailed rules on assessing the value and weight of documentary evidence. Although these technical rules are not often applied in foreign-related arbitrations, this emphasis on the value of formal documentary evidence has influenced PRC arbitral practice. It is therefore not unusual for there to be considerable emphasis placed on formal documentary evidence, and parties do expend considerable effort in assessing the authenticity of documents and examining originals. For example, original documents may be considered of greater evidential value than copies of documents, particularly where the copy is not an exact reproduction of the original. **4.293**

The PRC Arbitration Law also provides that the evidence shall be presented during the hearings and may be examined by the parties.[256] However, the full extent of a party's obligation under this provision is the subject of debate. **4.294**

(B) There are no strict rules on the form in which documents are presented. This is a matter for agreement between the parties and the arbitral tribunal. In practice, at the first instance, it is common for copies of documents (not originals) to be provided to the other side (and sometimes, to the arbitral tribunal). Copies of documents produced should ordinarily conform to the original. If there is a serious dispute between the parties as to the authenticity of documents, the originals may then be produced. **4.295**

(1.1) Is the submission of 'agreed documents' permitted? If yes, what is the extent and effect of such an agreement of the parties (authenticity, existence, acknowledgement of such documents' contents)? (A) It is open to the parties to agree on the authenticity, existence or other aspects of documents disclosed in the arbitration. **4.296**

---

252 s 2GB(7)(b) and (9), HK Arbitration Ordinance.
253 s 2GB(7), *ibid.*
254 s 2GB(9), *ibid.*
255 s 2GC(3), *ibid.*
256 Art 45, PRC Arbitration Law.

4.297 (B) Yes. Parties may (and often will) agree on whether there is a dispute as to the authenticity of certain documents. Documents setting out an agreed chronology, or *dramatis personae*, are also frequently used. It is also common to have agreed hearing bundles and core bundles. For PRC-related disputes, agreement on translations may also sometimes be reached prior to the witness hearing.

4.298 (1.2) **How may electronic documents (eg emails) be presented and proven?** (A) For the reasons explained at IV.F.(1) *supra*, in PRC arbitral practice, considerable emphasis is quite often placed on formal documentary evidence, and in assessing the authenticity of documents. However, there are no specific rules on how electronic documents are presented and proven, and similar principles are often applied as with other types of documents.[257]

4.299 (B) There are no specific rules on how electronic documents are presented and proven. In practice, where they are not voluminous, it is common for electronic documents to be presented as hard copy documents. Where there is a dispute over their authenticity, the documents may be produced in their native electronic format, for verification. Where electronic documents are voluminous, other arrangements may be agreed upon. In addition, reference may also be made to the principles and protocols developed in the US and elsewhere.

4.300 (1.3) **Does discovery (US- or UK-style), after the procedure has started, violate any procedural rules or public policy considerations?** (A) No, although as explained above, documentary disclosure is relatively limited in the PRC.

4.301 (B) No, although in practice, documentary discovery in the manner practised in US litigation would be rare.

(2) Requirement to produce certain documents (as requested by the tribunal) and consequences of a failure to do so

4.302 (A) There is no express power in the PRC Arbitration Law or the CIETAC Arbitration Rules for the arbitral tribunal (or the arbitration commission) to order document disclosure (although the arbitral tribunal has the power to request the parties to deliver or produce to an appointed expert or appraiser any relevant documents).[258]

4.303 In practice, orders for the disclosure of documents are sometimes made by tribunals in foreign-related arbitrations. Such orders are typically more limited in ambit than in court practice in common law jurisdictions.

4.304 (B) The parties to an arbitration are generally free to agree the terms and mode of discovery and inspection of documents relating to the dispute. In some arbitrations, no discovery and inspection of documents is necessary as all relevant documents have been appended to the submissions. In others, further discovery and inspection of documents is limited to those which the parties specifically request.

257 cf CIETAC's new Online Arbitration Rules (effective from 1 May 2009).
258 Art 38, CIETAC Arbitration Rules.

Under the HK Arbitration Ordinance, the arbitral tribunal is granted the power to order discovery.[259] However, it is under no obligation to do so.[260] **4.305**

In practice, it is also common to refer to the IBA Rules on the Taking of Evidence in International Commercial Arbitration ('IBA Rules'), either because the parties have agreed that the rules apply, or because it is said that the rules codify accepted practice in international arbitration. **4.306**

(2.1) Which documents may the tribunal request to be produced (eg also documents which are in the possession of third parties)? (A) Orders for the production of documents, if made, would usually cover documents that are relevant and material to the issues in dispute. However, it would be extremely rare for such orders to be directed at third parties. **4.307**

(B) The tribunal would ordinarily order the production of documents which are relevant and material to the outcome of the dispute, applying tests such as those set out in the IBA Rules. A party may also be obliged to take steps to source for documents in the possession of third parties, but which are within that party's control to obtain (eg documents held by a subsidiary). Although unusual, the tribunal may also take steps to assist a party to obtain the production of documents from a third party. **4.308**

(3) Protection of the confidentiality of documents (legal privilege etc)

(A) The PRC Arbitration Law does not contain any express provisions imposing an obligation of confidentiality, although it does recognize that arbitrations are private.[261] **4.309**

The CIETAC Arbitration Rules go further, and recognize that for hearings held *in camera* (ie in private), the parties, their representatives, witnesses, interpreters, arbitrators, experts consulted by the arbitral tribunal and appraisers appointed by the arbitral tribunal and the relevant staff-members of the secretariat of CIETAC shall not disclose to any outsiders any substantive or procedural matters of the case.[262] **4.310**

Although this does not impose an express obligation of confidentiality with respect to documents, in practice, it does offer some degree of protection over the confidentiality of documents. **4.311**

PRC law does not recognize a concept of privilege. However, a similar concept is indirectly recognized in, for example, the CIETAC Arbitration Rules, which provide that where a conciliation fails, communications made in the course of the conciliation process shall not be invoked as grounds for any claim, defence or counterclaim in subsequent proceedings.[263] **4.312**

---

[259] s 2GB(1)(c), HK Arbitration Ordinance.

[260] In the case of the HKIAC Administered Arbitration Rules, Art 23.3 provides that, at any time, the tribunal may require the parties to produce documents, exhibits or other evidence within such a period of time as the tribunal shall determine.

[261] Art 40, PRC Arbitration Law.

[262] Art 33, CIETAC Arbitration Rules.

[263] Art 40, *ibid.*

4.313 In practice, tribunals in foreign-related arbitrations do grant some protection to privileged communications, particularly where the arbitrators are familiar with international judicial practice and foreign parties are involved.

4.314 (B) Under Hong Kong law, an obligation to keep disclosed documents confidential may arise either by express agreement, or (possibly), as an implied obligation.[264]

4.315 The UNCITRAL Arbitration Rules do not impose an express confidentiality obligation on the parties.[265] Similarly, parties often do not include an express confidentiality obligation in their arbitration agreement or the underlying contract. In the absence of such agreement, parties would ordinarily not be under an express obligation to keep the documents confidential, unless the agreed arbitration rules contain such an obligation or they agree on one after the arbitration commences (such as, by adopting the IBA Rules).

4.316 Even if there is no express obligation, there may be an implied duty of confidentiality. Under English law, for example, such a duty is taken to be an implied term of an arbitration agreement.[266] The duty is not absolute, however. To date, the duty of confidentiality attaching to arbitration proceedings has not been directly addressed by the Hong Kong courts; however, it is likely that the Hong Kong courts would be inclined to follow English law.[267]

4.317 The HK Arbitration Ordinance contains separate provisions dealing with the confidentiality of arbitration-related *court* proceedings.[268]

4.318 The HK Arbitration Ordinance expressly recognizes that certain types of documents need not be produced for inspection as they are subject to legal privilege.[269] The three most commonly encountered types of privilege are:

(i) *legal professional privilege*, which covers communications between lawyers and their clients for the purpose of obtaining or giving legal advice;
(ii) *litigation privilege*, which covers documents created for, or in contemplation of, litigation or arbitration proceedings; and
(iii) *without prejudice privilege*, which covers communications made between the parties to a dispute in a *bona fide* attempt to settle the dispute.

---

[264] See also the new draft arbitration bill, which as at the time of writing, contains a confidentiality obligation.

[265] Although a number of other rules do contain confidentiality provisions, for example, Art 39.1 of the HKIAC Administered Arbitration Rules. See also Art 32 of UNCITRAL Arbitration Rules, which provides that the award may be made public only with the consent of both parties.

[266] See generally *Hassneh Insurance Co of Israel v Stuart J Mew* [1993] 2 Lloyd's Rep 243; cf the more liberal Australian position expressed by the High Court of Australia in *Esso Australia Resources Ltd v Plowman* (1995) 183 CLR 10.

[267] See generally *Hong Kong Housing Authority v Sui Chong Construction & Engineering Co Ltd and Anor* [2008] 1 HKLRD 84; *Nam Tai Electronics Inc v PricewaterhouseCoopers* [2008] 1 HKLRD 666 for a discussion of some of the general confidentiality issues.

[268] s 2E, HK Arbitration Ordinance. See also cl 18, Department of Justice, 'Consultation Paper on the Reform of the Law of Arbitration in Hong Kong and the Draft Arbitration Bill' (December 2007) 19 at <http://www.doc.gov.hk/eng/public/pdf/2007/arbitration.pdf> (accessed 14 March 2008), setting out a confidentiality provision in Hong Kong's draft arbitration bill.

[269] s 2GB(8), HK Arbitration Ordinance.

In the context of PRC-related disputes held in Hong Kong, difficult questions can sometimes arise as to what rules of privilege should be applied, given that PRC law does not have a law of privilege as such. 4.319

G. Experts

(1) Appointment and presentation of experts by the party or the arbitral tribunal

(A) If experts are appointed, the usual practice in the PRC is for tribunal-appointed experts, rather than party-appointed experts, to be appointed. The PRC Arbitration Law recognizes that if the arbitral tribunal considers that a special issue requires appraisal, it may refer the issue for appraisal to an 'appraisal department' agreed on by the parties, or to an appraisal department designated by the arbitral tribunal. If requested by a party or required by the arbitral tribunal, the appraisal department shall send its appraisers to attend the hearing.[270] Subject to the permission of the arbitral tribunal, the parties may question the appraiser. 4.320

The CIETAC Arbitration Rules also recognize that experts and appraisers may be consulted or appointed by the arbitral tribunal. The Rules expressly state that copies of the expert's report and the appraiser's report shall be communicated to the parties, who shall be given an opportunity to comment on the report. However, they provide that at the request of either party *and with the approval of the arbitral tribunal*, the expert and appraiser may be heard at an oral hearing where, if considered necessary and appropriate by the arbitral tribunal, they may explain their reports.[271] 4.321

(B) In Hong Kong arbitrations, it is common for expert evidence to be adduced by way of party-appointed experts. However, tribunal-appointed experts are certainly also permitted, as envisaged by the HK Arbitration Ordinance, which provides that unless otherwise agreed by the parties, the arbitral tribunal may appoint one or more experts to report to it on specific issues to be determined by the arbitral tribunal; and may require a party to give the expert any relevant information or to produce, or provide access to, any relevant documents, goods or other property for his inspection.[272] The parties are also entitled to put questions to the expert in a formal hearing, and to present their own rebuttal expert witnesses. 4.322

Usually, the arbitral tribunal will give specific directions on such evidence, after consulting with the parties. Evidence from party-appointed experts may be adduced concurrently, or sequentially. In the case of tribunal-appointed experts, the written expert report would usually be communicated to both parties for comments and the parties may also apply to respond to it prior to the hearing.[273] It is also increasingly common to consider more novel 4.323

[270] Art 44, PRC Arbitration Law.

[271] On the face of it, there may be a slight discrepancy between the provision in the PRC Arbitration Law, and the CIETAC provision. Under the PRC Arbitration Law, the party appears to be entitled as of right to have the appraiser attend the hearing. In comparison, under the CIETAC Arbitration Rules, this right is subject to the sanction of the arbitral tribunal. See Art 38, CIETAC Arbitration Rules. However, in both cases, the parties do not have an automatic right to put questions to the appraiser/expert.

[272] Art 26, UNCITRAL Model Law.

[273] Where the HKIAC Administered Arbitration Rules apply, the procedures set out in Art 25, dealing with tribunal-appointed experts, would be relevant.

methods of dealing with expert evidence, such as expert witness conferencing (on a 'without prejudice' basis or otherwise) or joint agreed statements or reports.

4.324 (1.1) **By which methods are tribunal-appointed experts selected? What are the rights of the parties during the selection process?** (A) There is no express legal requirement in the PRC Arbitration Law for the arbitral tribunal to consult the parties in appointing tribunal-appointed experts. However, in practice, such consultation does take place in foreign-related arbitrations.

4.325 (B) The arbitral tribunal will consult the parties prior to appointing any tribunal-appointed experts, and will usually outline the scope of the proposed advice and seek the parties' views and input. It is also good practice to inform the parties of the expected fee basis for the expert. On occasion, counsel who are more accustomed to an adversarial procedure may resist the appointment of tribunal-appointed experts and seek to persuade the tribunal to permit party-appointed experts instead.

(2) Admissibility and role of expert witnesses

4.326 (A) Although the usual practice in the PRC is to appoint tribunal-appointed experts, rather than party-appointed experts, there is no provision in the PRC Arbitration Law prohibiting evidence from party-appointed experts. In practice, foreign parties to PRC arbitrations do, quite frequently, submit expert evidence from their own party-appointed experts and such evidence may be admitted. Although the expert may be appointed by a party, the expert's role is not to act as a 'hired gun' advocate or mere mouthpiece of his client. Instead, his role is to assist the tribunal in an objective manner, by drawing on his specialist experience.

4.327 (B) In the case of Hong Kong, it is much more common for expert evidence to be adduced by party-appointed experts. As in other jurisdictions, the expert's role is to give his evidence in an objective manner. In practice, party-appointed experts in Hong Kong arbitrations are also frequently held to various ethical standards.

(3) Influence of the parties upon the selection of questions to be submitted to the expert

4.328 (A) The arbitral tribunal is under no obligation to consult with the parties before putting questions to the expert. This stands in contrast to the position in other jurisdictions, where the parties are often involved in this process. However, in practice, foreign arbitrators will usually seek to involve the parties in this process.

4.329 (B) If tribunal-appointed experts are appointed, the arbitral tribunal will usually consult with the parties on the proposed nature and scope of advice to be provided by the expert. This is important because it helps to avoid any subsequent dispute over the expert's role, as well as any allegations that the arbitral tribunal has delegated its duty to decide to the expert. Under the HK Arbitration Ordinance, there is also an obligation that any expert report which the tribunal may rely on in making its decision is communicated to the parties.[274]

[274] Art 24, UNCITRAL Model Law.

(4) Independence and impartiality of the expert and the right to reject a proposed/appointed expert

(A) Under PRC law, there is no express requirement that the tribunal- or party-appointed expert is impartial and independent of the parties. However, in practice, if this is not the case, it may undermine the weight given to the expert's evidence. In extreme cases, it is likely that an expert who is not impartial or independent of one of the parties may also be successfully challenged. **4.330**

(B) The primary duty owed by a party-appointed expert is to the arbitral tribunal, and not to the party who appointed him. An expert witness is therefore obliged to be impartial, and to be and remain independent both in preparing the report and in giving expert evidence before the arbitral tribunal.[275] Experts who fail to be impartial or independent of the parties may be successfully challenged and in extreme cases, may also be subject to sanctions from their relevant regulatory or professional body. **4.331**

(4.1) May a party or its counsel approach an expert (or expert witness) whom it has nominated (only before or also after the proceeding has started)? Are interviews admissible? (A) There is no prohibition under the PRC Arbitration Law against a party or its counsel being in contact with the expert it has appointed. **4.332**

(B) A party or its counsel may approach an expert (or expert witness) whom it has nominated, either before or after the proceedings have commenced.[276] Indeed, it is common for the party or its counsel to be in contact with the expert to assist him in preparing the report to be provided to the arbitral tribunal. **4.333**

(5) Oral examination of an expert in a hearing

(A) While the CIETAC Arbitration Rules expressly state that copies of the expert's report and the appraiser's report shall be communicated to the parties and the parties shall be given an opportunity to comment on the report,[277] there is no automatic right to cross-examine the expert and, based on the CIETAC Arbitration Rules, it is unclear if parties have a right to insist that the expert appear at the oral hearing. **4.334**

(B) Under the HK Arbitration Ordinance, any expert report on which the arbitral tribunal may rely on in making its decision shall be communicated to the parties.[278] In addition, unless otherwise agreed by the parties, if a party requests (or if the arbitral tribunal considers it necessary), the expert shall, after delivery of his written or oral report, participate in a hearing where the parties have the opportunity to put questions to him and to present expert witnesses in order to testify on the points at issue. **4.335**

H. Interim measures of protection

(1) Kind of interim measures which the tribunal may order

(A) In contrast to the position in more developed jurisdictions, an arbitral tribunal in the PRC generally has no power to order interim measures. Instead, applications for preservation **4.336**

---

[275] See generally, *UBC (Construction) Ltd v Sung Foo Kee Ltd* [1993] 2 HKC 458.
[276] In the case of the HKIAC Administered Arbitration Rules, see Art 23.9.
[277] Art 38, CIETAC Arbitration Rules.
[278] Art 24, UNCITRAL Model Law.

of property and preservation of evidence are made to the arbitration commission (eg CIETAC), which then forwards the application to the competent court. In the case of preservation of evidence, this is the court at the place where the evidence is located.[279] In the case of the preservation of property, it is the place where the domicile of the party against whom the order is sought is located or where the property of the party is located.[280]

4.337 Foreign parties seeking to obtain interim relief from the PRC courts are likely to experience significant difficulties. For example, applications are dealt with by the provincial courts and this can be a concern, particularly where the Chinese party is well-connected at the local level. In this regard, there is one significant distinction between applications for interim measures in domestic cases, and in foreign-related cases. In foreign-related cases, applications are submitted to the Intermediate People's Court, whereas for domestic cases, it is an inferior court which handles the application.[281]

4.338 (B) Under the UNCITRAL Model Law, the arbitral tribunal has the power to order a party 'to take such interim measure of protection as the arbitral tribunal may consider necessary in respect of the subject-matter of the dispute'.[282] The qualification that the measures of protection should be 'in respect of the subject matter of the dispute' limits the tribunal's powers.[283]

4.339 The HK Arbitration Ordinance[284] extends the tribunal's general powers, to include the power to:

(i) require money in dispute to be secured;
(ii) direct the inspection, preservation, custody, detention or sale of relevant property; and
(iii) grant interim injunctions.[285]

4.340 (1.1) **Which are, in general, the procedural and substantive prerequisites for the ordering of interim and conservatory measures (eg reduced degree of evidence; urgency; summary evaluation of the claim)?** (A) To succeed in an application for preservation of property, the applicant must generally demonstrate that execution of a judgment may become impossible or difficult because of acts of the other party or for other reasons.[286] If the application is made wrongly, the applicant shall be liable for any resulting loss.

4.341 Alternatively, any interested party whose lawful rights and interests would, due to urgent circumstances, suffer irretrievable damage without immediately applying for property

---

[279] Art 18, CIETAC Arbitration Rules.
[280] Art 17, *ibid.*
[281] SPC, 'Notice on some issues concerning the enforcement of the Arbitration Law' (effective from 26 March 1997); Art 68, PRC Arbitration Law.
[282] Art 17, UNCITRAL Model Law.
[283] For example, while the tribunal may order measures such as the preservation, custody or sale of goods that are the subject matter of the dispute, measures intended solely to protect a party's personal or financial interests (such as a freezing order over the assets of the opponent) may not be granted.
[284] s 2GB.
[285] Where the HKIAC Administered Arbitration Rules apply, see Art 24, dealing with interim measures of protection.
[286] Art 28, PRC Arbitration Law; Art 92, PRC Civil Procedure Law.

preservation may, before filing a lawsuit, apply to the PRC court for property preservation measures.[287]

(B) In general, Hong Kong tribunals will be influenced by the principles applied by the courts, in deciding whether to order an interim measure.[288] In addition, given Hong Kong's position as an UNCITRAL Model Law country, the test laid down in the amendments to the UNCITRAL Model Law may also be persuasive. Under the amended article, to succeed, the party requesting an interim measure shall satisfy the arbitral tribunal that: 4.342

(i) harm not adequately reparable by an award of damages is likely to result if the measure is not ordered, and such harm substantially outweighs the harm that is likely to result to the party against whom the measure is directed if the measure is granted; and
(ii) there is a reasonable possibility that the requesting party will succeed on the merits of the claim.[289]

(1.2) Are the prerequisites for interim measures ordered by the arbitral tribunal more or less the same as if those are requested from the state court? Is there case law/leading authorities on whether those measures are faster and enforced more easily if taken by the arbitral tribunal or the state court? (A) As explained at IV.H.(1) *supra*, an arbitral tribunal in the PRC is not empowered to order interim measures. 4.343

(B) The prerequisites set out above are similar to, but not identical to the test applied in ordinary court proceedings. In practice, an application to the courts will typically be faster than an application to the arbitral tribunal. This is particularly the case where the arbitral tribunal has not yet been constituted. In addition, there are certain procedural advantages with applying to the courts for such relief, for example, where third parties are involved or where it is necessary for the application to be made *ex parte*. 4.344

However, the Hong Kong courts may decline to grant relief if the matter is already the subject of arbitration proceedings and it would be more appropriate for the matter to be dealt with by the arbitral tribunal. In such situations, the courts will likely defer to the tribunal unless there is a particular reason why the court (rather than the tribunal) should grant the order.[290] 4.345

(2) Limits of the tribunal's powers to order interim measures

(A) As explained above, a PRC arbitral tribunal generally has no power to order interim measures. Instead, this power is reserved for the PRC courts. However, even where the PRC courts intervene, there is no clear legislative basis upon which they can grant the full suite of interim relief available in other jurisdictions. For example, orders such as security for costs, interim injunctions and other orders to assist in arbitration are generally not available. 4.346

287 Art 93, PRC Civil Procedure Law.

288 See generally *American Cyanamid Co v Ethicon Ltd* [1975] AC 396, for the applicable principles.

289 Art 17A, UNCITRAL Model Law (as amended in 2006). This provision is also adopted in the new draft arbitration bill, as at the time of writing. It is also recognized that the determination on whether the requesting party will succeed will not affect the discretion of the arbitral tribunal in making any subsequent determination. In the case of the HKIAC Administered Arbitration Rules, Art 24.1 provides that at the request of either party, the tribunal may order any interim measure it deems 'necessary or appropriate'.

290 See generally *Leviathan Shipping Co Ltd v Sky Sailing Overseas Co Ltd* [1998] 4 HKC 347.

4.347 (B) There are a number of limitations on the tribunal's powers to order interim measures: such orders cannot be made *ex parte*, they will generally not be effective against third parties, and the tribunal generally has less coercive powers of enforcement than a court.

(3) Orders to provide security for the costs of the proceeding

4.348 (A) As noted above, a PRC arbitral tribunal generally has no power to order interim measures, and this power is reserved for the PRC courts. Orders for security for costs are generally not available.

4.349 (B) The HK Arbitration Ordinance empowers the arbitral tribunal to make an order requiring a claimant to give security for the costs of the arbitration.[291] However, the arbitral tribunal must not make such an order simply because the claimant:

(i) is a natural person who is ordinarily resident outside Hong Kong; or
(ii) is a body corporate that is incorporated, or an association that is formed, under a law of a place outside Hong Kong, or whose central management and control is exercised outside Hong Kong.

4.350 In making an order for security for costs, an arbitral tribunal:

(i) must specify a period within which the order is to be complied with; and
(ii) may extend that period or an extended period.

4.351 An arbitral tribunal may dismiss or stay a claim if it has made an order requiring the claimant to provide security for costs and the order has not been complied with within the required period. Subject to the above, the arbitral tribunal's discretion to decide whether to order security for costs is generally unfettered. Factors such as the solvency of the claimant and whether the application for security is being used to stifle a genuine claim are examples of factors that may be considered relevant.

(4) Attachment of assets by an order of the tribunal

4.352 (A) As noted above, a PRC arbitral tribunal generally has no power to order interim measures, and this power is reserved for the PRC courts.

4.353 (B) It is highly unusual for an arbitral tribunal to grant an order for attachment of assets, not least because such orders may impact third parties.

I. Assistance by the courts

(1) Extent of court assistance in the gathering of evidence

4.354 (A) The PRC Arbitration Law is silent on the type of relief that may be obtained from the courts to assist in preserving evidence. In general, orders sought may include an order for the delivery up of the evidence or prohibiting its destruction.

4.355 (B) The HK Arbitration Ordinance limits the intervention of the courts to what has been expressly provided in the Ordinance.[292] This is consistent with the general approach of party autonomy, and a recognition that the arbitral tribunal should be the body primarily

[291] s 2GB(1), HK Arbitration Ordinance.
[292] s 2AA(2)(b), *ibid.*

deciding the dispute between the parties. However, the Ordinance does recognize a role for the courts in the taking of evidence.[293]

These include the power to grant:[294] 4.356

(i) an order directing the inspection, photographing, preservation, custody, detention or sale of relevant property by the tribunal, a party or an expert;
(ii) an order directing samples to be taken from, observations to be made of, or experiments to be conducted on the property; and
(iii) an interim injunction or any other interim measure.

(1.1) Is it for the arbitral tribunal or for the party to obtain the assistance of state courts with respect to the gathering of evidence? (A) It is usually the party who applies directly to the state court, when assistance is required. 4.357

(B) In practice, it is usually the party who applies directly to the state court, when assistance is required. Hong Kong arbitral tribunals would usually be hesitant to initiate such applications, because of a desire to be and appear to be neutral before both parties. 4.358

(1.2) According to case law and practical experience, are there considerable delays involved when asking a court to give assistance (eg for the obtaining of evidence)? (A) Although the PRC courts have, in the past, granted orders to assist in preserving evidence, various practical difficulties are often encountered. For example, the court dealing with the application may not be familiar with the procedure, there may be difficulties with effectively policing the orders locally, and there may be considerable delay, thereby defeating the very purpose of obtaining assistance in preserving evidence. 4.359

(B) The Hong Kong courts are experienced with granting interim assistance in aid of an arbitration, and they are prepared and able to grant orders on an urgent and *ex parte* basis, where necessary. In addition, Hong Kong maintains a specialist 'Construction and Arbitration List', and all matters concerning arbitration are set down in this list, and dealt with by a specialist arbitration and construction judge. However, one practical difficulty is with enforcing a Hong Kong court order where (as is often the case in international arbitrations), the respondent is effectively out of jurisdiction. 4.360

(2) Assistance for enforcing the attachment of assets

(A) The PRC Civil Procedure Law states that the property preservation shall be effected by sealing up, distraining, freezing or other methods as prescribed by law.[295] There may be difficulties where the relevant property is overseas. 4.361

(B) The HK Arbitration Ordinance provides that the courts may: 4.362

(i) make an order directing an amount in dispute to be secured;
(ii) in relation to relevant property, make an order directing, *inter alia*, the preservation, custody, detention or sale of the property; or

293 Art 27, UNCITRAL Model Law.
294 s 2GC, HK Arbitration Ordinance.
295 Art 94, PRC Civil Procedure Law.

(iii) grant an interim injunction or direct any other interim measure to be taken.[296]

4.363 Property is considered 'relevant' if,

(i) the property is owned by or is in the possession of a party to the arbitration proceedings concerned; and
(ii) the property is subject to the proceedings, or any question relating to the property has arisen in those proceedings.

(3) Other examples of possible assistance

4.364 (A) Apart from the above, there is no clear legislative basis upon which the PRC courts can grant the full suite of interim measures available in other jurisdictions. For example, orders such as security for costs, interim injunctions and other orders to assist in the arbitration are generally not available.

4.365 (B) The Hong Kong courts have a variety of other powers available to assist in the arbitration process, such as the power to:

(i) order a person to attend proceedings before an arbitral tribunal to give evidence or to produce documents or other material evidence; and
(ii) order a writ of *habeas corpus ad testificandum* to be issued requiring a prisoner to be taken for examination before an arbitral tribunal.

(4) Dependence of the power of state courts to intervene during the proceedings on the (national) procedural law applied by the arbitral tribunal

4.366 (A) In general, the power of the PRC courts to order interim measures only applies where the seat of the arbitration is in the PRC and where PRC procedural law applies. It is questionable if the PRC courts have the power to grant interim relief in aid of a foreign arbitration or where a foreign procedural law applies.

4.367 (B) The Hong Kong courts have the jurisdiction to grant interim measures of protection in aid of foreign arbitral proceedings. The court's jurisdiction derives from the Ordinance, or from the court's inherent jurisdiction.[297] By analogy, it is arguable that the Hong Kong courts may grant interim measures in aid of an arbitration taking place in Hong Kong, even though the parties have agreed on a foreign procedural law. This is supported by the text of the UNCITRAL Model Law.[298]

V. The award

A. Types of award

(1) Interim award (eg on interim measures or the jurisdiction of the tribunal)

4.368 (A) In PRC arbitration practice, both interim awards and partial awards are made.

[296] s 2GC, HK Arbitration Ordinance.
[297] See generally, *The Lady Muriel* [1995] 2 HKC 320.
[298] Art 1, UNCITRAL Model Law which applies the territorial criterion ('place of arbitration') in deciding on the extent to which the law applies.

In international practice, an interim award is used more often where an important procedural issue is being decided. In the PRC, the practice with respect to interim awards may differ from that in other jurisdictions. Thus, for example, an interim award granting interim relief or dealing with jurisdiction would not be common, given the arbitral tribunal's limited powers to grant such orders. 4.369

(B) In Hong Kong, two types of awards are generally recognized: 4.370

(i) a *final award*, which disposes of all the issues currently before the tribunal; and
(ii) an *interim* or *partial award*, in which the tribunal deals with some of the issues, such as jurisdiction, a preliminary point of construction or the law applicable to the merits or liability.[299] If the parties have reached a settlement, the terms can be incorporated into the form of a consent award.[300]

(2) Partial award

(A) In international practice, a partial award is often used where the arbitral tribunal is setting out its decision on one of the substantive issues in dispute between the parties. The award is partial in the sense that it does not finally determine the arbitration; however, it is final with respect to the issues it has addressed. Partial awards may typically be made where liability is dealt with separately from quantum. 4.371

The PRC Arbitration Law recognizes that in arbitration proceedings, if part of the facts involved have already become clear, the arbitral tribunal may first make an award in respect of such part of the facts.[301] It therefore envisages that several awards may be made in the same arbitration. Similarly, the CIETAC Arbitration Rules recognize the concept of 'interlocutory arbitral awards' and 'partial awards'.[302] 4.372

(B) Although the terminology is not universal, a partial award is often made where the arbitral tribunal is setting out its decision on one of the substantive issues in dispute between the parties. The award is partial in the sense that it does not finally determine the arbitration; however, it is final with respect to the issues it has addressed. In international practice, partial awards may typically be made where liability is dealt with separately from quantum. 4.373

(2.1) Are awards, especially partial awards, binding in the same arbitral proceeding? Does it make a difference if after the rendering of such a partial award, one arbitrator is successfully challenged and removed on grounds that prevailed even before the partial award was rendered? (A) Yes, partial awards, once made, are ordinarily binding on the parties. The PRC Arbitration Law is silent on whether the subsequent removal of an arbitrator will affect the validity of a partial award made previously. However, in practice, if an 4.374

[299] See also Art 24.2 of the HKIAC Administered Arbitration Rules which provide that an order for interim measures may be established in the form of an interim award.

[300] See also Art 32.1 of the HKIAC Administered Arbitration Rules which provide that the tribunal shall, if requested by both parties and accepted by the tribunal, record the settlement in the form of an arbitral award on agreed terms.

[301] Art 55, PRC Arbitration Law.

[302] Art 44, CIETAC Arbitration Rules.

arbitrator is successfully removed, this may well provide a valid ground for challenging a partial award which he was a party to.

4.375 (B) Yes, partial awards are binding in the same arbitral proceeding. Such an award is ordinarily final once made; accordingly, the subsequent removal of one of the arbitrators will not automatically impugn the award. However, the removal of the arbitrator may well provide a valid ground for challenging a partial award which he was a party to.

(3) Final award

4.376 (A) Usually, the final award finally disposes of all issues in dispute between the parties.

4.377 (B) Usually, the final award finally disposes of all issues in dispute between the parties.

4.378 **(3.1) If a party fails to participate in the arbitration, may the tribunal proceed and issue an award on the merits? Is such an award enforceable as any other award? Are there special remedies for the defendant at the enforcement stage?** (A) The PRC Arbitration Law states that if the respondent fails to appear before the tribunal without justifiable reasons after having been notified in writing, or leaves the hearing prior to its conclusion without the tribunal's permission, a default award may be made.[303] The CIETAC Arbitration Rules go further and state that where the respondent has filed a counterclaim, the respondent may be deemed to have withdrawn its counterclaim.[304]

4.379 (B) If a party fails to appear at the hearing, the HK Arbitration Ordinance gives the tribunal the power to continue the proceedings and make a default award in the absence of the party.[305] The party present still has to prove its claim.

4.380 A default award is an enforceable award. At the enforcement stage, depending on the applicable jurisdiction, it may be possible for the respondent to seek to resist enforcement on the basis that it did not participate in the arbitration. However, this will be a difficult argument for the respondent to make if it was given due notice of the hearing but elected not to participate.

B. Deliberations and agreement on the award

(1) Time limits (and possible extensions) for making the award

4.381 (A) The CIETAC Arbitration Rules state that the arbitral tribunal shall render an award within six months from the date the arbitral tribunal is formed, and in the case of domestic arbitrations, within four months.[306] In practice, although this period may be extended,[307] it is generally the case that CIETAC arbitrations progress more rapidly than international arbitrations elsewhere.

4.382 (B) The HK Arbitration Ordinance does not specify any time limit for the making of an award in international arbitrations. However, if an arbitrator fails to act in a timely manner,

303 Art 42, PRC Arbitration Law.
304 Art 34, CIETAC Arbitration Rules.
305 Art 25(c), UNCITRAL Model Law.
306 Arts 42 and 65, CIETAC Arbitration Rules
307 Art 65 of the Rules provide that upon the request of the arbitral tribunal, the chairman of CIETAC may extend the time period if it is considered truly necessary and the reasons for the extension are truly justified.

he or she can be removed by the agreement of both parties or by order of the Hong Kong courts.[308]

(2) Procedure for the decision of the arbitrators (majority vote etc)

(A) The PRC Arbitration Law provides that the arbitration award shall be made in accordance with the opinion of the majority of the arbitrators. If the arbitral tribunal is unable to form a majority opinion, the arbitration award shall be made in accordance with the opinion of the presiding arbitrator.[309] **4.383**

(B) The HK Arbitration Ordinance provides that where there is a panel of arbitrators, a majority decision is binding.[310] Article 29.1 of the HKIAC Administered Arbitration Rules further provides that if there is no majority, the award shall be made by the presiding arbitrator alone. **4.384**

(2.1) If an arbitrator fails or refuses to take part in oral deliberation meetings, although having been given sufficient notice of such meetings, may an award be rendered on the basis of written deliberations (or deliberations without this arbitrator) only? (A) The PRC Arbitration Law does not expressly deal with this issue. The CIETAC Arbitration Rules state that the tribunal may hold its deliberations at any place or in any manner that it considers appropriate.[311] **4.385**

However, where an arbitrator refuses outright to participate in the deliberations, the CIETAC Arbitration Rules appear to envisage that the solution is in the first instance, to replace the recalcitrant arbitrator rather than for the arbitral tribunal to continue in truncated form with only two arbitrators. **4.386**

Thus, the CIETAC Arbitration Rules provide that if an arbitrator, *inter alia*, fails to fulfil his or her functions in accordance with the requirements of the Rules or within the time period specified in the Rules, the chairman of CIETAC shall have the power to decide whether the arbitrator shall be replaced.[312] **4.387**

(B) There is no strict requirement that oral deliberations are held although in practice, some form of oral deliberation would be usual. However, if an arbitrator fails to act altogether, this will often be a valid basis for removing the arbitrator. For example, under the UNCITRAL Arbitration Rules, if an arbitrator fails to act, he may be challenged and replaced.[313] In practice, such a challenge would be brought by one of the parties. **4.388**

(3) Admissibility of dissenting opinions

(A) The PRC Arbitration Law provides that the opinion of the minority of the arbitrators may be entered on the record.[314] The CIETAC Arbitration Rules elaborate on this, by **4.389**

[308] Art 14(1), UNCITRAL Model Law. In the case of domestic arbitrations, a time limit for the making of an award may be extended by court order, either before or after the time limit has expired. The court may also remove an arbitrator who fails to issue an award 'with reasonable dispatch'. See s 15(3), HK Arbitration Ordinance.

[309] Art 53, PRC Arbitration Law.

[310] Art 29, UNCITRAL Model Law.

[311] Art 29, CIETAC Arbitration Rules.

[312] Art 27, *ibid.*

[313] Art 13, UNCITRAL Arbitration Rules.

[314] Art 53, PRC Arbitration Law.

clarifying that while a written dissenting opinion shall be docketed into the file and may be attached to the award, it shall not form a part of the award. Similarly, it provides that where the arbitral tribunal cannot reach a majority opinion and the award is rendered in accordance with the presiding arbitrator's opinion, the written opinion of other arbitrators shall be docketed into the file and may be attached to the award, but it shall not form a part of the award.[315]

4.390 (B) In Hong Kong, a dissenting arbitrator cannot insist on his dissenting reasons forming part of the award, unless the arbitration agreement or arbitration rules provide otherwise. In practice, if the dissenting arbitrator requests, his opinion will usually be included with the award.

4.391 (3.1) **Are there any court decisions or positions of leading authorities on the issue of dissenting opinions (admissibility, disclosure to the parties and publication)?** (A) As noted above, both the PRC Arbitration Law and the CIETAC Arbitration Rules recognize that the minority opinion may be entered on the record. The CIETAC Arbitration Rules also expressly note that the dissenting opinion 'may' be attached to the award. Although the dissenting opinion is kept on the file docket, if it has not been attached to the award, it is unlikely that parties will have access to the opinion. In contrast, the BAC Arbitration Rules provide that an arbitrator who chooses not to sign the award shall issue a dissenting opinion, which 'shall' be sent to the parties together with the award but does not form part of the award.[316]

4.392 (B) There is English authority dealing with how dissenting opinions should be treated.[317] In the absence of direct Hong Kong authority on the point, the English authorities will be persuasive.

(4) Signature by the arbitrators and potential failure of one arbitrator to sign

4.393 (A) The PRC Arbitration Law stipulates that an arbitrator with dissenting opinions as to the arbitration award may either sign or not sign the award.[318] The CIETAC Arbitration Rules are to similar effect.[319]

4.394 (B) The HK Arbitration Ordinance states that the award shall be made in writing and shall be signed by the arbitrator or arbitrators. It expressly provides that where there is more than one arbitrator, the signatures of the majority shall suffice, provided that the reason for any omitted signature is stated.[320]

C. Form of the award and deposition

(1) Form and minimum contents of an award

4.395 (A) The PRC Arbitration Law provides that the arbitration award shall specify the arbitration claim, the facts of the dispute, the reasons for the decision, the result of the award, the

[315] Art 43, CIETAC Arbitration Rules.
[316] Art 44(3), BAC Arbitration Rules.
[317] See eg *Cargill International SA v Sociedad Iberica de Molturacion SA* [1998] 1 Lloyd's Rep 489.
[318] Art 54, PRC Arbitration Law.
[319] Art 43, CIETAC Arbitration Rules.
[320] Art 31, UNCITRAL Model Law.

allocation of arbitration costs and the date of the award. If the parties do not wish the facts of the dispute and the reasons for the decision to be specified in the written arbitration award, these may be omitted.[321]

(B) There are no detailed statutory requirements for an arbitral award to be valid and the basic requirements are provided by the common law. These are, essentially, that the award must be final in relation to the issues dealt with, in a manner that is cogent, consistent, clear and unambiguous and capable of enforcement by a court. If it is a final award, it will have to deal with all matters in dispute. The HK Arbitration Ordinance does, however, provide that the award shall be in writing.[322] **4.396**

(2) Requirement to give reasons in the award

(A) Under PRC law, by default, a reasoned award must be issued. However, under PRC practice, the reasoning set out in the award may be somewhat declaratory in nature, with less detailed analysis than would be the case with, for example, awards issued in Hong Kong. **4.397**

(B) The HK Arbitration Ordinance provides that the award shall state the reasons upon which it is based, unless the parties have agreed that no reasons are to be given or the award is an award on agreed terms.[323] **4.398**

(3) Necessity to specify place and time where and when the award was made

(A) The award is legally effective as of the date on which it is made;[324] it is also generally deemed as being made at the place of arbitration.[325] The place of arbitration has taken on added significance because the current version of the CIETAC Arbitration Rules envisages that CIETAC arbitrations may take place outside the PRC. **4.399**

(B) The HK Arbitration Ordinance provides that the award shall state its date and the place of arbitration, and that the award shall be deemed to have been made at that place.[326] The place of arbitration is significant in enforcement proceedings under the New York Convention (which primarily applies the territorial criterion), as well as applications to set aside the award, which can usually only be made at the place (or legal seat) of the arbitration. The date is significant for purposes of various timelines under the HK Arbitration Ordinance, such as when the time for correction of errors expires.[327] **4.400**

(4) Other requirements (registration, delivery etc)

(A) The arbitration award shall be signed by the arbitrators (save that a dissenting arbitrator may choose not to sign the award) and sealed by the arbitration commission.[328] PRC **4.401**

[321] Art 54, PRC Arbitration Law.
[322] Art 31, UNCITRAL Model Law.
[323] *ibid.*
[324] Art 57, PRC Arbitration Law.
[325] See eg Art 31, CIETAC Arbitration Rules.
[326] Art 31, UNCITRAL Model Law.
[327] Art 33, *ibid.*
[328] Art 54, PRC Arbitration Law.

awards will always include the name of the arbitration commission, given the emphasis on 'institutionalized' arbitration.

4.402 Under CIETAC practice, the arbitral tribunal also has to submit its draft award for scrutiny before signing the award. As part of the scrutiny process, CIETAC may remind the arbitral tribunal of issues in the award, but this role is subject to the express proviso that the arbitral tribunal's independence in rendering the award is not to be affected.[329]

4.403 (B) Under Hong Kong law, the award in an international arbitration must be signed by the arbitrator(s), and it shall state the date and place of arbitration. In addition, after the award is made, a copy signed by the arbitrators shall be delivered to each party.[330] There is no requirement for the award to be registered, or deposited in court.

4.404 (4.1) **Does the award have to be laid down or registered with a state court or agency (even if it has been rendered according to a foreign procedural law)?** (A) The arbitration award is to contain the seal of the arbitration commission.[331] The award is legally effective as of the date it is made;[332] on the face of it, this appears to be independent of when the parties receive the award.

4.405 (B) There is no requirement under Hong Kong law for Hong Kong awards to be registered to be effective. However, the HKIAC does provide an authentication service for Hong Kong awards. This can be useful if a party is seeking to enforce a Hong Kong award overseas.

4.406 (4.2) **Does a foreign award which has been rendered abroad according to this country's national procedural law, have to be laid down or registered with a state court or agency? Is there a fee or tax for such registration of an award?** (A) The PRC Arbitration Law is silent on this issue. In any event, it is debatable if the PRC courts will give full effect to a foreign award purportedly made pursuant to PRC procedural law.

4.407 (B) No.

4.408 (4.3) **How long after the rendering of the award must the file/award be stored by the lawyers and the arbitral tribunal?** (A) There are no specific requirements under the PRC Arbitration Law.

4.409 (B) There are no specific requirements under the HK Arbitration Ordinance.

D. Applicable substantive law

(1) Party autonomy to choose the applicable substantive law

4.410 (A) The parties to a contract with a foreign element may choose the law to apply to the resolution of contractual disputes, except as otherwise provided by law.[333]

[329] Art 45, CIETAC Arbitration Rules.
[330] Art 31, UNCITRAL Model Law.
[331] Art 54, PRC Arbitration Law.
[332] Art 57, *ibid.*
[333] Art 126, PRC Contract Law.

However, PRC law imposes a number of significant exceptions to this general principle. In particular, attempts to circumvent mandatory provisions under PRC law or administrative regulations, and to choose a foreign law which contravenes social public interests will not be permitted. **4.411**

In addition, the SPC Provisions 2007[334] has expanded the list of contracts where PRC law is mandatory. As a result of that provision, PRC law applies to various other categories of contracts, where their performance is effected within the PRC.[335] **4.112**

(B) In general, Hong Kong law gives the parties considerable freedom in their choice of governing substantive law. This freedom is subject to certain well known restrictions, such as where the choice made is not *bona fide* and legal;[336] where there is an issue over foreign illegality and violation of foreign public policy; and where the choice violates mandatory principles of Hong Kong law. These restrictions only apply in extreme circumstances. **4.413**

(1.1) Is there a public policy exception to the chosen substantive law? (A) Yes. See V.D.(1) *supra.* **4.414**

(B) Yes. See V.D.(1) *supra.* **4.415**

(1.2) Does the principle of '*iura novit curia*' apply? Or must the applicable law be proven (by which means)? (A) In PRC court practice, the applicable provisions issued by the SPC provides that parties are to provide or substantiate the content of foreign law. Where the PRC court determines that foreign law is applicable, it may generally conduct a review on such foreign law within its terms of reference and may require the parties to provide or substantiate the content of such foreign law. If both the parties and the PRC court cannot ascertain the content of the foreign law via proper channels, the PRC court may apply the laws of the PRC.[337] **4.416**

---

334 n 173 *supra.*

335 These categories are:

(i) Sino-foreign equity joint venture contracts;
(ii) Sino-foreign cooperative joint venture contracts;
(iii) Sino-foreign cooperative exploration and natural resources development contracts;
(iv) contracts for the transfer of shares of Sino-foreign equity joint ventures, Sino-foreign cooperative joint ventures and wholly-owned foreign enterprises;
(v) contracts for contracting-in by a foreign natural person, legal person or other organization in the operation of a Sino-foreign equity joint venture or Sino-foreign cooperative joint venture established in the PRC;
(vi) contracts for acquisition by a foreign natural person, legal person or other organization of the equity interests held by shareholders of a non-FIE in the PRC;
(vii) contracts for subscription by a foreign natural person, legal person or other organization of the increased capital of a non-foreign-invested limited liability company or joint stock limited company in the PRC;
(viii) contracts for acquisition by a foreign natural person, legal person or other organization of assets of a non-FIE in the PRC; and
(ix) other contracts of which the laws of the PRC shall apply under the laws and administrative regulations of the PRC.

See Art 8, SPC Provisions 2007.

336 *Vita Food Products Inc v Unus Shipping Co Ltd* [1939] AC 277.

337 Art 9, SPC Provisions 2007.

4.417 In addition, if following cross-examination, the parties have no objection to the ascertained content of the foreign law, a PRC court shall acknowledge this accordingly. If the parties oppose the application of such foreign law, the PRC court shall make its determination accordingly, after examination.[338] A similar, if somewhat more flexible approach, is usually applied in foreign-related arbitrations in the PRC.

4.418 (B) This principle is not usually applied in Hong Kong arbitrations, particularly where the tribunal members come from a common law background (which is often the case). Instead, the usual practice is for parties to adduce evidence on the applicable law, although tribunal members have been known to draw on their own past experience. This is particularly the case in arbitrations where the governing law is PRC law, which sometimes raises similar issues (for example, on the question of good faith).

4.419 International tribunals do not adopt the strict technical rule that the foreign law is assumed to be identical to Hong Kong law unless it is proven as a question of fact, by expert evidence. Instead, in practice, tribunals adopt a variety of approaches to avoiding this strict technical rule, where appropriate, and usually with the agreement of all parties.

(2) Decisions according to equity or as amiable compositeur

4.420 (A) The PRC Arbitration Law does not expressly refer to the concept of *amiable compositeur* or *ex aequo et bono*. However, it does contain references to non-legal standards as factors to be taken into account in arriving at the arbitral tribunal's decision. For example, the PRC Arbitration Law states that disputes shall be resolved on the basis of facts, in compliance with law and in an equitable and reasonable manner.[339] Although the concept of 'equitable and reasonable manner' may not be equivalent to the concept of *amiable compositeur* and *ex aequo et bono*, it does point to the relatively important role played by notions of 'fairness' under PRC law. This is also borne out by arbitral decisions in the PRC, which usually place some degree of emphasis on such considerations.

4.421 That said, the better view is probably that notions of fairness will generally not override the express provisions of the law, and the parties' agreement as recorded in their contract. The PRC Arbitration Law provision itself suggests this, since the reference to 'equitable and reasonable ' appears to be subordinate to the facts and to 'compliance with law'.

4.422 (B) The HK Arbitration Ordinance expressly envisages that the arbitral tribunal may decide *ex aequo et bono* or as *amiable compositeur*; however, this is the case only if the parties have expressly authorized it to do so.[340] In reality, while the concepts of *ex aequo et bono* and *amiable compositeur* tend to attract academic discussion, they are rarely expressly agreed to in practice.

4.423 Where PRC law is the governing law, Hong Kong international arbitration tribunals have sometimes adopted a less legalistic approach than they would under the common law, in line with the perception that PRC law is more malleable.

---

[338] Art 10, SPC Provisions 2007.
[339] Art 7, PRC Arbitration Law.
[340] Art 28(3), UNCITRAL Model Law.

(3) Application of lex mercatoria, *general principles etc*

(A) The PRC Arbitration Law does not expressly envisage the possibility of parties adopting the *lex mercatoria* as their source of law. However, PRC law does contain tangential references to the role played by international trade practice and usage. For example, the CIETAC Arbitration Rules state that the arbitral tribunal shall make its award on the basis of, *inter alia*, 'international practices'.[341] **4.424**

(B) The question of whether Hong Kong law permits parties to designate the *lex mercatoria* or 'international practice' or 'international rules of law' as their choice of law has not been directly addressed by the Hong Kong courts. In principle, the mere fact that parties have chosen a non-'state' law should not *ipso facto* render the choice invalid.[342] In addition, it is likely that an international arbitration tribunal may be prepared to adopt a less rigid approach in giving effect to the parties' choice. One argument in favour of such an approach is that under the UNCITRAL Model Law, the relevant provision refers to 'rules of law' (and not law), and that parties may agree for the tribunal to decide *ex aequo et bono* or as *amiable compositeur* (neither of which are a strict 'legal system').[343] **4.425**

(3.1) Is the application of *lex mercatoria* considered as the application of law or as a kind of *amiable composition*? (A) This question has not yet been clearly addressed under PRC law. **4.426**

(B) This question has not been directly addressed by the Hong Kong courts. Although there may be some overlap between the two concepts, it is clear that *lex mercatoria* is not identical to, nor is it a subset of *amiable composition*. Some local commentators also clearly treat the two concepts as distinct.[344] See also V.D.(3). **4.427**

(4) Applicable substantive law if there is no choice of law by the parties

(A) The PRC Contract Law sets out the general principle that where the parties to a contract with a foreign element have not chosen an applicable law, the law of the state with the closest connection to the contract shall apply.[345] Thus, the general conflict of law rule applied in the PRC is the 'closest connection' test. **4.428**

The SPC Provisions 2007 elaborate on this test, by clarifying that in applying this test, the court shall take into account the nature of the contract, the obligations of a party that could best reflect the essence and features of the contract and other factors. The provisions also provide specific guidance on determining the applicable law for 17 types of contracts, categorized by reference to the PRC Contract law.[346] **4.429**

---

341 Art 43, CIETAC Arbitration Rules.

342 eg the choice of Taiwanese law is generally assumed to be valid under Hong Kong law.

343 cf however, *Halsbury's Laws of Hong Kong* [2003] 1(2), at [25.146] suggesting that the wording of the UNCITRAL Model Law appears to commit the parties to designating an applicable law which is linked to an identifiable national system of law and makes no allowance for designating transnational principles of law, such as the *lex mercatoria*, as the applicable law.

344 See eg Morgan, R., *The Arbitration Ordinance of Hong Kong: A Commentary* (Butterworths, 1997) 605.

345 Art 126, PRC Contract Law.

346 eg in the case of a sale and purchase contract, the law of the domicile of the vendor at the time of concluding the contract applies as a general rule, unless the negotiation and execution of the contract took place at the place of domicile of the purchaser, or it is specified in the contract that the vendor shall fulfil its delivery

4.430 (B) In the absence of an express (or implied) agreement on the choice of substantive governing law, the law with the closest and most real connection would usually apply.[347] Factors that might be considered relevant include:

(i) location of the subject matter of the contract;
(ii) place of performance;
(iii) place of making or negotiation of the contract;
(iv) place of residence of the parties;
(v) related contracts or past practice; and
(vi) agreed place of arbitration or litigation (if any).

4.431 **(4.1) Is there an autonomous conflict of law rule in the national arbitration law? Is it considered mandatory?** (A) The PRC Arbitration Law does not set out an autonomous conflict of law rule which applies specifically to arbitration.

4.432 (B) The HK Arbitration Law envisages that where parties have not expressly agreed on a choice of foreign governing law, the tribunal will apply the law determined by the conflict of laws rules 'which it considers applicable'.[348] It is therefore clear that the tribunal is not bound to apply the conflict of law rules of the *lex fori* (Hong Kong law), although it appears that it should apply a conflict of law rule which it considers appropriate.

4.433 In practice, Hong Kong tribunals do not always apply a technical conflicts rule as such, but may refer to a range of factors to justify their eventual choice of substantive governing law.[349]

4.434 **(4.2) What is the law applicable to interest?** (A) Interest is payable, and is often awarded.

4.435 (B) Under the HK Arbitration Ordinance, an arbitral tribunal has discretion to award simple or compound interest on the principal sum awarded (or on an amount claimed in the arbitration but paid before the award is made) from such dates, and at such rates as it considers appropriate for any period up to the date of payment.[350] Unless the award provides otherwise, simple interest is payable on the amount of the award from the date of the award at the same rate as for a judgment debt (as specified from time to time by the court).[351]

4.436 **(4.3) What is the law and practice with respect to legal interest on foreign currency debts?** (A) Interest on foreign currency debts appears to be permitted under PRC law. In practice, such interest is awarded.

obligation at the place of domicile of the purchaser, in which case the governing law of the place of domicile of the purchaser shall apply.

[347] See generally *Halsbury's Laws of Hong Kong* [2006] 7(1), at [100.044].

[348] Art 28, UNCITRAL Model Law.

[349] See also Art 31 of the HKIAC Administered Arbitration Rules which provides that the tribunal shall decide the case in accordance with the rules of law agreed by the parties and in the absence of a choice of law, 'by applying the rules of law with which the dispute has the closest connection'.

[350] s 2GH, HK Arbitration Ordinance.

[351] s 2GI, *ibid.*

(B) Interest may be awarded in a foreign currency, provided that the award has been made in that currency. Such interest is commonly awarded, where appropriate. 4.437

(5) Binding effect of state court decisions

(A) PRC law does not recognize a strict doctrine of *stare decisis*. Nonetheless, decisions of higher level PRC courts, especially if on point and if properly reasoned, will be of persuasive value to arbitral tribunals. 4.438

(B) A Hong Kong tribunal will be bound by a decision of a Hong Kong court resolving an issue in dispute between the parties (for example, on the tribunal's jurisdiction). It will not ordinarily be 'bound' by a decision of a state court, in the *stare decisis* sense, since it is not in the same court system as a Hong Kong court. However, insofar as Hong Kong law applies, a Hong Kong tribunal will apply decisions reached by a Hong Kong court. 4.439

(5.1) Is an arbitral tribunal bound by a decision of another arbitral tribunal? (A) The arbitral award is final and binding on the parties to the arbitration.[352] On this basis, the decision of one tribunal should be binding on another tribunal as between the same parties. 4.440

(B) In general, an arbitral award is final and binding on the parties to the arbitration. Therefore, as between the same parties, a party may not seek to relitigate an issue before a second tribunal, where that issue has already been disposed of by the first tribunal. Indeed, in some circumstances, it may also be possible to prevent issues being raised in subsequent proceedings where these could and should have been raised in the first proceedings. 4.441

However, absent special agreement, a decision of one tribunal would usually not be binding on different parties to a second arbitration, even if the same issues are raised. 4.442

(5.2) Does a decision in a criminal case bind an arbitral tribunal? (A) In general, no. 4.443

(B) It would not be strictly 'binding' but it would be applied by a Hong Kong tribunal insofar as the applicable law is Hong Kong law, and it sets out a principle of law that is directly applicable. 4.444

E. Settlement

(1) Settlement by agreement of the parties with or without support of the arbitral tribunal

(A) For historical and cultural reasons, conciliation is an important element of the dispute resolution process in the PRC. The PRC Arbitration Law expressly recognizes that the arbitral tribunal may carry out conciliation prior to making an award, and that the arbitral tribunal shall conduct conciliation if both parties voluntarily seek conciliation.[353] 4.445

The CIETAC Arbitration Rules elaborate on this, by providing that where the parties consent, the arbitral tribunal may conciliate the case during the course of the arbitration proceedings. The arbitral tribunal may conciliate the case in the manner it considers appropriate, and the arbitral tribunal shall terminate the conciliation and continue the 4.446

352 Art 43, CIETAC Arbitration Rules.
353 Art 51, PRC Arbitration Law.

arbitration proceedings if one of the parties requests a termination or if the arbitral tribunal believes that further efforts to conciliate will be futile.[354]

4.447 On the face of it, the CIETAC Arbitration Rules do not appear too exceptional, since it permits conciliation to take place only with the consent of both parties, and the arbitral tribunal is obliged to terminate the conciliation process upon the request of one party.

4.448 In practice, however, it is estimated that in 80 per cent of the cases, at least some efforts to conciliate or mediate the dispute will be made by arbitrators during the oral hearings. In the past, this has led to some concern, particularly on the part of foreign parties, that they may be 'forced' to participate in the conciliation process, or risk incurring the displeasure of the arbitral tribunal. In theory, positions or opinions adopted in conciliation proceedings do not prejudice a party's position in any subsequent arbitration. In reality, there can understandably be concern that such confidence may not be strictly observed, or where members of the arbitral tribunal are involved in the conciliation process, that this may indirectly prejudice the arbitral tribunal's determination in any subsequent arbitral award. This concern is heightened because there is no prohibition against a conciliator who has received potentially prejudicial information in the course of a failed conciliation, from continuing to act as an arbitrator in the proceedings.

4.449 In practice, a number of solutions have been attempted to address this problem. For example, parties may request that an independent conciliator be appointed, or that only one of the arbitrators participate in the conciliation.

4.450 Supporters of the PRC's conciliation-arbitration mechanism often point to the benefits of combining the two. One statistic indicates that in about 30 per cent of CIETAC cases, parties reportedly settled their disputes through conciliation.[355] In the case of the BAC, a reported 45 per cent of all the cases from September 2004 to August 2007 were resolved through mediation.[356]

4.451 In addition, in recent years, with the growing internationalization of PRC arbitral commissions, greater care has been taken in ensuring that the process is perceived by all parties as being fair and neutral.

4.452 (B) The HK Arbitration Ordinance expressly envisages that if all parties to a reference consent in writing, and so long as no party withdraws his consent, an arbitrator may act as a conciliator. An arbitrator acting as a conciliator may communicate with the parties to the reference collectively or separately; and shall treat information obtained by him from a party to the reference as confidential, unless that party otherwise agrees or where the conciliation is terminated and arbitration resumes. Where confidential information is obtained

---

[354] Art 40, CIETAC Arbitration Rules.

[355] Moser, M., 'CIETAC and its Work—An Interview with Vice Chairman Yu Jianlong' (2007) 24(6) *J Int'l Arb* 555, 560. This mirrors statistics previously released by CIETAC for earlier periods.

[356] Harpole, S., 'The Combination of Conciliation with Arbitration in the People's Republic of China' (2007) 24(6) *J Int'l Arb* 623, 632. The discrepancy between the CIETAC and the BAC figures could be due in part to the higher proportion of domestic cases in BAC arbitrations. In comparison, reportedly, one-third of the civil cases dealt with by the PRC courts in 2007 were resolved through non-mandatory judicial mediation: 'Supreme court: More mediation for civil cases' *China Daily* (21 November 2008).

by an arbitrator from a party and those proceedings terminate without the parties settling, the arbitrator shall, before resuming the arbitration proceedings, disclose to all other parties as much of that information as he considers is material to the arbitration proceedings. The HK Arbitration Ordinance also provides that no objection shall be taken to the conduct of arbitration proceedings by an arbitrator solely on the ground that he had acted previously as a conciliator in accordance with the provision.[357]

In practice, this mediation-arbitration provision is not often invoked in international arbitrations. **4.453**

(1.1) May an arbitrator who has initiated settlement discussions be challenged when agreement on a settlement has failed? (A) Ordinarily, no. The CIETAC Arbitration Rules also provide that where conciliation fails, any opinion, view or statement and any proposal or proposition expressing acceptance or opposition by either party or by the arbitral tribunal in the process of conciliation shall not be invoked as grounds for any claim, defence or counterclaim in subsequent arbitration proceedings, judicial proceedings or any other proceedings.[358] **4.454**

(B) Ordinarily, no. See V.E.(1) *supra*. **4.455**

(2) 'Private settlement' and its impact on the arbitral procedure

(A) The CIETAC Arbitration Rules provide that where parties reach a settlement agreement privately through negotiation or conciliation without involving CIETAC, either party may, based on an arbitration agreement, request CIETAC to constitute an arbitral tribunal to render an arbitral award in accordance with the terms of the settlement agreement. In such a situation, unless the parties agree otherwise, the chairman of CIETAC shall appoint a sole arbitrator, who shall examine the case and render an award. The specific procedure and the time limit for rendering the award is not subject to the usual provisions in the CIETAC Arbitration Rules.[359] **4.456**

(B) In the case of Hong Kong, if, during arbitral proceedings, the parties settle the dispute, the arbitral tribunal shall terminate the proceedings. It may also, if requested by the parties and not objected to by the arbitral tribunal, record the settlement in the form of an arbitral award on agreed terms.[360] **4.457**

(3) Form and effect of a settlement (eg award on agreed terms)

(A) The PRC Arbitration Law provides that if conciliation leads to a settlement, the arbitral tribunal shall make a written conciliation statement or render an arbitration award in accordance with the settlement agreement. It states that a written conciliation statement and a written arbitration award shall have equal legal validity and effect. This, in practical terms, appears to elevate the legal status of a written conciliation statement, within the PRC.[361] **4.458**

357 s 2B, HK Arbitration Ordinance.
358 Art 40, CIETAC Arbitration Rules.
359 *ibid.*
360 Art 30, UNCITRAL Model Law.
361 Art 51, PRC Arbitration Law.

4.459 The PRC Arbitration Law also states that the written conciliation statement shall specify the arbitration claim and the result of the settlement reached between the parties. The written conciliation statement shall be signed by the arbitrators, sealed by the arbitration commission, and served on both parties. The written conciliation statement shall become legally effective immediately after both parties have acknowledged receipt. If the written conciliation statement is repudiated by a party before he acknowledges receipt, the arbitration tribunal shall promptly make an arbitration award.[362]

4.460 The CIETAC Arbitration Rules also state that where settlement is reached through conciliation by the arbitral tribunal, the parties 'shall' sign a written settlement agreement, and, unless otherwise agreed, the arbitral tribunal will close the case and render an arbitral award in accordance with the settlement terms.[363]

4.461 In practice, foreign parties will usually ask for an arbitration award instead of a written conciliation statement, whenever this is practicable.

4.462 (B) Under the HK Arbitration Ordinance, where the parties to an arbitration settle their dispute and enter into a settlement agreement, the settlement agreement may be treated as an arbitration award for the purposes of its enforcement and may, with the Hong Kong courts' permission, be enforced in the same manner as an arbitration award.[364] In practice, parties may also ask for the settlement agreement to be recorded as an award.

F. Costs of the arbitration

(1) General allocation of the costs of the proceedings

4.463 (A) In general, under PRC law and practice, the unsuccessful party in foreign-related arbitrations typically bears the costs of the arbitration, and the reasonable legal costs of a party. In the past, these amounts were sometimes artificially constrained,[365] although under the current CIETAC Arbitration Rules, the cap on costs has been abolished.[366] Costs will be assessed by the tribunal according to various factors including the complexity of the case, the expenses actually incurred by the winning party, the disputed amount and the reasonableness of the expenses.

4.464 (B) Under the HK Arbitration Ordinance, the arbitral tribunal may include directions in respect of the costs of the arbitration proceedings in its award. The costs of arbitration proceedings include:

(i) the costs of the reference, that is the parties' own costs, including the costs of their professional advisers and experts; and
(ii) the costs of the award, including the tribunal's fees and expenses and other costs of the hearing.

---

362 Art 52, PRC Arbitration Law.
363 Art 40, CIETAC Arbitration Rules.
364 s 2C, HK Arbitration Ordinance.
365 In particular, under the previous version of the CIETAC Arbitration Rules, the amount of costs or expenses which a party could claim against the losing party was artificially capped at 10 per cent of the total amount awarded to the winning party.
366 Art 69, CIETAC Arbitration Rules.

With regard to both categories, the tribunal may, subject to contrary agreement between the parties: 4.465

(i) direct by whom and in what manner costs are to be paid;
(ii) assess, tax and settle the amount of such costs; and
(iii) direct that costs be paid on any basis that costs can be awarded in Hong Kong court proceedings.[367]

If the tribunal makes no order regarding costs in its award, either party may apply to the tribunal for an order within 30 days after notification of the award.[368] 4.466

The HK Arbitration Ordinance also provides that a prior agreement that the parties or any of the parties must pay their own costs in any event is void. However, such a provision is not void if it is part of a submission agreement made after the dispute has arisen.[369] In addition, unless the parties have agreed otherwise, the ordinance empowers the arbitral tribunal to direct that the recoverable costs are limited to a specified amount. Such a direction can be varied at any stage provided that the variation can be made sufficiently in advance of when the costs are incurred, so that the limit can be taken into account.[370] 4.467

(2) Deposits or advances for costs or fees

(A) Under the CIETAC Arbitration Rules, at the time the request for arbitration is submitted, advance payment of the arbitration fee (based on an *ad valorem* scale) together with a registration fee is due from the claimant. Similarly, if a counterclaim is filed, at the time of filing, the respondent shall pay an arbitration fee in advance according to the *ad valorem* fee schedule. 4.468

(B) Typically, parties will pay a deposit for the costs of the arbitration, prior to the costs being incurred. This is the case, for example, where the HKIAC is providing administrative services.[371] 4.469

(2.1) Is there case law authorizing or prohibiting arbitrators to order a party to pay an advance on the arbitration costs? (A) There is no clear case law addressing this issue. However, unlike, for example, ICC arbitrations, under the CIETAC Arbitration Rules, the arbitration fee for the claim is borne by the claimant, and the arbitration fee for any counterclaim is borne by the respondent. Thus, a party has a clear incentive to pay the necessary deposit in support of its claim or counterclaim (as the case may be). 4.470

(B) There is no clear case law on this issue. Under the HKIAC Procedures, if the required deposits are not paid in full by both parties, the HKIAC administrator shall inform the parties in order for one of them to make the required payment. It provides that if such payment is not made, the arbitral tribunal, after consultation with the HKIAC, may order the 4.471

[367] s 2GJ(l), HK Arbitration Ordinance.
[368] s 2GJ(4), *ibid.*
[369] s 2GJ, *ibid.*
[370] s 2GL,*ibid.*
[371] See also Art 37 of the HKIAC Administered Arbitration Rules, where those Rules apply.

suspension or termination of the arbitral proceedings.[372] There is no express reference to the possibility of arbitrators making an order (or award) for payment of advance on costs.

4.472 In the past, the trend has been for the claimant to pay the respondent's share, where the respondent refuses to pay the necessary deposit and the arbitration is otherwise at risk of being suspended. The claimant would then seek to recover the total advance as part of the costs of arbitration. However, in line with ICC practice, there have in recent years been increasing requests for tribunals to take on a more pro-active role, and to grant appropriate orders to deal with recalcitrant respondents.

4.473 **(2.2) May the raising of a set-off claim or counterclaim be made contingent upon payment of the corresponding advance for the relevant arbitration costs (cf eg Article 30(5), ICC Rules)? May such a condition be agreed upon when entering into the arbitration agreement?** (A) Under the CIETAC scheme, the respondent is responsible for bearing the entire arbitration fee relative to any counterclaim it raises. The CIETAC Arbitration Rules provide that this deposit is payable at the time the counterclaim is filed.[373] Thus, this in itself acts as a strong incentive to persuade the respondent to pay the arbitration fee in advance in support of its counterclaim.

4.474 (B) The HKIAC Procedures provide that the HKIAC administrator shall prepare an estimate of the cost of arbitration and may request each party to deposit an equal amount as an advance for those costs.[374] On the face of it, the provision does not envisage that separate advances will be ordered, but that the advance will be a global sum which will then be initially borne in equal shares by the parties.[375]

4.475 **(2.3) What remedies exist against a party which does not pay its part of the advance on the arbitration costs (eg termination of the arbitration agreement)? How may the other party enforce its rights?** (A) The answer is unclear, although the CIETAC Arbitration Rules do provide that the parties shall proceed with the arbitration 'in *bona fide* cooperation'.[376] In practice, this difficulty tends to arise only where the advance on costs is shared (such as, for example, under ICC practice). This is not the practice under the CIETAC Arbitration Rules.[377]

[372] Art 12, HKIAC Procedures. In the case of the HKIAC Administered Arbitration Rules, Art 37.4 provides that if the required deposits are not paid within 30 days, the HKIAC Secretariat shall so inform the parties in order that one or another of them may make the required payment. If such payment is not made, the tribunal may suspend or terminate the proceedings, or continue on such basis as it sees fit.

[373] Art 13, CIETAC Arbitration Rules.

[374] Art 12, HKIAC Procedures.

[375] cf Art 37.2 of the HKIAC Administered Arbitration Rules which provides that if the Respondent submits a counterclaim or it otherwise appears appropriate in the circumstances, the HKIAC Secretariat may establish separate deposits.

[376] Art 7, CIETAC Arbitration Rules.

[377] However, there are situations where a related difficulty may arise. Under CIETAC practice, as explained at V.F.(4) *infra*, CIETAC may collect from the appointing party an additional deposit to cover the extra cost incurred in appointing a foreign arbitrator. Where the party (usually, a foreign party) fails to pay this deposit in advance, the CIETAC Arbitration Rules state that the party shall be deemed not to have appointed the arbitrator, and the chairman of CIETAC may appoint an arbitrator for the party pursuant to the Rules. See Art 69, CIETAC Arbitration Rules.

4.476 The Rules also provide that where parties fail to advance a deposit to cover the cost of oral hearings at a place other than CIETAC's domicile, the oral hearing shall be held at the domicile of CIETAC.[378]

4.477 (B) This question has not directly come before the Hong Kong courts. If it does, case law from other common law jurisdictions which have considered this issue in the ICC context is likely to be persuasive. It may be possible to obtain an interim award ordering a party to comply with its obligation to pay its part of the advance on costs.

(3) Costs of the administration by an arbitration institution

4.478 (A) The arbitration fee paid by the claimant and/or respondent, is calculated according to the CIETAC fee schedule, and includes both the administrative fee of CIETAC and the arbitrators' fees and expenses.

4.479 Indicative arbitrators' and administration fees for both CIETAC and BAC, for foreign-related arbitrations with three arbitrators, are as follows:

Amount in dispute (USD)	Fees (USD)[379]	
	CIETAC	BAC
1 million	25,300	10,800
10 million	104,300	52,800
20 million	154,300	92,800
50 million	304,300	212,800

4.480 (B) The HKIAC charges various fees depending on the services provided. For administration services conducted pursuant to the HKIAC Procedures, it charges administrative fees according to a tiered structure, by reference to the following fee schedule:

Amount of Claim	Fees
Up to HK$1 million	HK$15,000
Up to HK$5 million	HK$25,000
Up to HK$50 million	HK$50,000
Up to HK$100 million	HK$100,000
Over HK$100 million	As determined by HKIAC Council

(4) Arbitrators' fees: law and practice, judicial control

4.481 (A) The arbitrators' fees are fixed by CIETAC, taking into account the amount in dispute, the workload of the case and its complexity. The arbitrators' fees and expenses are usually included in the lump sum arbitration fee paid by the claimant and/or respondent. These fees are substantially lower than what would be customary by international standards.

4.482 Many foreign arbitrators are more accustomed to being paid on an hourly rate basis, which often results in a higher fee than under the CIETAC domestic scale. To overcome this

378 Art 69, CIETAC Arbitration Rules.

379 Based on three arbitrators, inclusive of administration and registration fees for foreign-related arbitrations, with some rounding of figures. Figures are only for general guidance and specific reference should always be made to the current fee scale and exchange rates. In addition, some of the figures have been simplified, for ease of comparison. Note also that there may be additional expenses for foreign arbitrators; see V.F.(4).

difficulty, CIETAC will in practice, as permitted under its Rules,[380] collect from parties an additional 'actual expense' for appointment of a non-Chinese arbitrator or presiding arbitrator so as to cover his or her remuneration and expenses. In practice, this additional fee is often borne by the party which appointed the foreign arbitrator.

4.483 (B) Arbitrators in Hong Kong international arbitrations typically charge by reference to work done by them in connection with the arbitration, at hourly rates (or daily rates in the case of hearing days). These fees are not included as part of the HKIAC's administrative fees; the HKIAC also does not set arbitrator's fees (except under the new HKIAC Administered Arbitration Rules—*infra*). Where the HKIAC does not fix the fees, it will, at the parties' request, consult with the arbitrators to assist the parties in setting fees for arbitration.

4.484 Where the HKIAC Administered Arbitration Rules apply, the parties may also elect for the fees of the tribunal to be determined based on the HKIAC's published fee schedule. Indicative arbitrators' and administrative fees for three arbitrators, are as follows:

Amount in dispute (USD)	Average Fees (USD)[381]
1 million	89,900
10 million	203,900
20 million	244,400
50 million	365,900

4.485 Where the fee schedule applies, the tribunal's actual fees are fixed by the HKIAC Council, taking into account factors set out in the rules.[382]

4.486 (4.1) **May arbitrators fix their own fees in the award?** (A) No, the arbitrators' fees are fixed by the arbitration commission, such as CIETAC.

4.487 (B) Yes.[383]

4.488 (4.2) **How can the parties change the arbitrators' fees once they are fixed?** (A) The fees are fixed by CIETAC.

4.489 (B) The arbitrators' terms of appointment are usually agreed between the parties and the members of the arbitral tribunal; these terms may therefore be changed by agreement. For domestic arbitrations, there is also provision for fees to be taxed by the courts.[384]

4.490 (4.3) **Are the arbitrators' fees subject to income tax if (i) the place of arbitration; or (ii) the normal residence or place of business of the arbitrator is located in this country?** (A) No special rules apply and this is subject to the usual tests under revenue law. In the PRC, tax is typically deducted at source.

[380] Art 69, CIETAC Arbitration Rules.

[381] Based on three arbitrators (average fees), inclusive of administration and registration fees, with some rounding of figures. Some of the figures have been simplified. Figures are only for general guidance and specific reference should always be made to the current fee scale.

[382] Art 36.3, HKIAC Administered Arbitration Rules.

[383] s 2GJ, HK Arbitration Ordinance. Where the HKIAC Administered Arbitration Rules apply, the fees may be fixed by the HKIAC Council. See V.F.(4).

[384] s 21, HK Arbitration Ordinance.

(B) No special rules apply and this is subject to the usual tests under revenue law. **4.491**

(4.4) Are arbitrators' fees submitted to VAT? If yes, is the duty to pay such tax linked to (i) the place of arbitration; or (ii) the arbitrator's general residence?

(A) Ordinarily, no. **4.492**

(B) Ordinarily, no. There is no value added tax in Hong Kong. **4.493**

(5) Attorneys' fees and the winning party's claim for reimbursement

(A) In general, the unsuccessful party bears the costs of the arbitration, and the reasonable legal costs of a party. The CIETAC Arbitration Rules provide that the arbitral tribunal has the power to decide in the award, according to the circumstances of the case, that the losing party shall compensate the winning party for expenses 'reasonably incurred' by it in pursuing its case. In deciding whether the winning party's expenses incurred in pursuing its case are reasonable, the arbitral tribunal shall consider such factors as the outcome and complexity of the case, the workload of the winning party and/or its representative(s), and the amount in dispute.[385] **4.494**

In practice, the award of costs can vary widely, depending on the arbitral tribunal's composition and whether they are familiar with the amount of work necessary and typical fees incurred in international arbitrations. **4.495**

(B) Although the arbitral tribunal has a wide discretion in awarding costs, it will normally apply principles broadly similar to those in the Hong Kong courts. Therefore, in accordance with the principle of 'costs follow the event', usually the losing party will pay the winning party its 'reasonable' costs.[386] However, there may be situations where this is not the case, for example, where the unsuccessful party has incurred unnecessary costs and expenses by virtue of the successful party's conduct during the proceedings. A successful party may also be denied recovery of some of its costs if it has failed on discrete issues. **4.496**

(5.1) May in-house lawyers charge fees or may a party request costs of in-house lawyers to be reimbursed? (A) Recovery of in-house counsel fees is at the discretion of the arbitral tribunal. **4.497**

(B) Recovery of in-house counsel fees is at the discretion of the arbitral tribunal, and may be awarded in appropriate cases. **4.498**

(6) Time and form of the decision on costs

(A) The decision on costs is often included as part of the arbitral award, and issued at the same time. This is particularly the case in smaller disputes. **4.499**

(B) The decision on costs may either be included as part of the award, or issued as a separate costs award, after parties have made submissions dealing only with costs. Where proceedings are carried out in stages, separate costs awards may also be issued at each stage. **4.500**

[385] Art 46, CIETAC Arbitration Rules.

[386] In the case of the HKIAC Administered Arbitration Rules, Arts 36.4 and 36.5 would be relevant. In respect of the costs of legal representation and assistance, Art 36.5 provides that the tribunal, taking into account the circumstances of the case, shall be free to determine which party shall bear such costs and may apportion it between the parties if it determines that apportionment is reasonable.

4.501 **(6.1) May the arbitrators' decision on the costs (allocation and amount of costs to be reimbursed) be challenged separately from the award itself? Are there time limits for such a remedy?** (A) The arbitrators' decision on who should bear the legal fees and costs is often included as part of the award. Therefore, any challenge to this decision will indirectly be a challenge to the award, and ordinarily be subject to the same limitations as apply to a challenge of the award proper. There is no provision for taxation of costs as such.

4.502 (B) Costs awarded in respect of arbitration proceedings (other than the fees or expenses of the arbitral tribunal) are taxable by the Court of First Instance, unless the award otherwise directs (or the parties otherwise agree).[387] However, taxation only relates to the quantum of recoverable costs, not the applicable principles for recovery. In respect of how costs are allocated, the tribunal has broad discretion to decide. However, the tribunal has to act fairly and impartially as between the parties.[388]

4.503 **(6.2) Are the arbitrators entitled and/or legally obliged to rule on the amount of one or both parties' costs that are recoverable?** (A) The arbitrators are, in theory, obliged to rule on costs as the PRC Arbitration Law states that the arbitration award 'shall' include the allocation of arbitration costs.[389]

4.504 (B) Ordinarily, the tribunal will rule on the allocation of costs. In some cases, they may also specify the amount of costs payable. If the award fails to provide for payment of costs, any party to the proceedings may apply to the arbitral tribunal for an order directing by whom and to whom those costs are to be paid. Such an application must be made within 30 days after the notification of the award or within such further period as the tribunal allows.[390]

G. Publication of the award

(1) Publication with or without the consent of the parties

4.505 (A) The CIETAC Arbitration Rules recognize that for hearings held *in camera* (ie in private), the parties, their representatives, witnesses, interpreters, arbitrators, experts consulted by the arbitral tribunal and appraisers appointed by the arbitral tribunal and the relevant staff members of the secretariat of CIETAC shall not disclose to any outsiders any substantive or procedural matters of the case.[391]

4.506 (B) The UNCITRAL Arbitration Rules are widely used in Hong Kong. They provide that the arbitral award may be made public only with the consent of both parties.[392]

(2) Practice of publication (eg in specific legal journals)

4.507 (A) Selections or extracts of arbitral awards are sometimes published in conjunction with the relevant arbitration commissions. These are often not translated into English. For an English resource, see Cheng, D., Moser, M. and Wang, S.C., *International Arbitration in*

[387] s 2GJ, HK Arbitration Ordinance.
[388] s 2GA, HK Arbitration Ordinance.
[389] Art 54, PRC Arbitration Law.
[390] s 2GJ, HK Arbitration Ordinance.
[391] Art 33, CIETAC Arbitration Rules.
[392] Art 32, UNCITRAL Arbitration Rules. In the case of the HKIAC Administered Arbitration Rules, Art 39.3 sets out guidelines on when an award may be published.

the People's Republic of China: Commentary, Cases and Materials (2nd edn, Butterworths Asia, 2000).

(B) There is no official journal which regularly publishes Hong Kong arbitral awards. Significant decisions are sometimes summarized in *Asian Dispute Review* and the *Asian International Arbitration Journal*. **4.508**

VI. Amendment and challenge of the award; liability of arbitrators

A. Amendment, correction or interpretation of the award

(1) Motion to amend or correct an award

(A) The PRC Arbitration Law provides that if there are literal or calculation errors in the arbitration award, or if matters which have been decided by the arbitral tribunal are omitted in the arbitration award, the arbitral tribunal shall correct or supplement the award.[393] **4.509**

The CIETAC Arbitration Rules elaborate on this, providing that either party may request for a correction of any clerical, typographical, or calculation errors or any errors of a similar nature contained in the award. If such an error does exist in the award, the arbitral tribunal shall make a correction in writing within 30 days from the date of receipt of the written request for the correction. The arbitral tribunal may likewise correct any such errors in writing on its own initiative within a reasonable time after the award is issued.[394] **4.510**

The CIETAC Arbitration Rules expressly provide that such a correction in writing shall form a part of the arbitral award. **4.511**

In addition, the CIETAC Arbitration Rules empower the arbitral tribunal to make an additional award on any claim or counterclaim omitted from the award.[395] **4.512**

(B) The HK Arbitration Ordinance provides that a party may request the arbitral tribunal to correct in the award any errors in computation, any clerical or typographical errors or any errors of a similar nature. The arbitral tribunal may also correct such an error on its own initiative within 30 days of the date of the award.[396] **4.513**

The tribunal is also empowered to make an additional award as to claims presented in the arbitral proceedings but omitted from the award. **4.514**

(2) Interpretation of the award by the tribunal

(A) There is no express provision in the CIETAC Arbitration Rules for the arbitral tribunal to issue an interpretation of the award. **4.515**

(B) If so agreed by the parties, a party may request the arbitral tribunal to give an interpretation of a specific point or part of the award. If the arbitral tribunal considers the request **4.516**

[393] Art 56, PRC Arbitration Law.
[394] Art 47, CIETAC Arbitration Rules.
[395] Art 48, *ibid.*
[396] Art 33, UNCITRAL Model Law.

justified, it shall give the interpretation within 30 days of receipt of the request. The interpretation shall form part of the award.[397]

B. Appeal on the merits

(1) Admissibility and procedure of an appeal on the merits

4.517 (A) Under PRC law, there is no appeal procedure as such which allows a party to substitute the decision reached by the arbitral tribunal with one reached by the PRC courts. The CIETAC Arbitration Rules expressly provide that the arbitral award is final and binding and neither party may bring a suit or make a request to any organiszation for the award to be revised.[398] However, in considering whether to set aside a domestic award, the courts are entitled to look into the merits of the substantive decision reached by the arbitral tribunal. See VI.C.(1) *infra.*

4.518 (B) Under Hong Kong law, there is no provision for an appeal on the merits against an international arbitration award. For domestic arbitration awards, parties may appeal against an award on points of law, subject to leave being obtained.[399]

4.519 (1.1) **May the parties agree on an appeal to another arbitral tribunal?** (A) Yes, subject to agreement by the parties (and possibly, by the arbitration commission). In practice, this is extremely rare.

4.520 (B) Yes. In practice, this is extremely rare.

(2) Possibility to exclude an appeal (eg in the arbitration clause)

4.521 (A) See VI.B.(1) *supra.* Under PRC law, there is no appeal on the merits as such, to the PRC courts.

4.522 (B) See VI.B.(1) *supra.* Under Hong Kong law, there is no appeal on the merits to the Hong Kong courts against an international arbitration award.

C. Setting aside of the award

(1) Reasons for setting aside an award

4.523 (A) Under PRC law, the applicable standard for setting aside awards varies, depending on whether the award is a domestic or a foreign-related award.

4.524 (1.1) **Domestic Awards** For domestic awards (ie one that has no foreign elements), the grounds for setting aside the award are relatively broad, and include both procedural and substantive grounds. These grounds are as follows:[400]

(i) there is no arbitration agreement;
(ii) the matters decided in the award exceed the scope of the arbitration agreement or are beyond the authority of the arbitration commission;

[397] Art 33, UNCITRAL Model Law.
[398] Art 43, CIETAC Arbitration Rules.
[399] s 23, HK Arbitration Ordinance.
[400] Art 58, PRC Arbitration Law.

(iii) the formation of the arbitral tribunal or the arbitration procedure was not in conformity with the statutory procedure;
(iv) the evidence on which the award is based was forged;
(v) the other party has withheld evidence which is sufficient to affect the impartiality of the arbitration;
(vi) the arbitrators have committed embezzlement, accepted bribes or committed malpractice for personal benefit or perverted the law in the course of the arbitration; or
(vii) the award violates social and public interest.

The first three grounds are relatively unexceptional. **4.525**

On paper, grounds (iv) and (vi) also appear unobjectionable. However, there is some uncertainty over what amounts to 'forged' evidence, where the line is drawn between 'forged' and 'misleading' evidence, and how critical the 'forged' evidence must be before it taints the award. The legislative history to this provision suggests that 'forged' should be given a relatively narrow interpretation. As for ground (vi), there is uncertainty over what amounts to 'malpractice' and 'perverting the law'. However, in view of both the context and the severity of the consequences,[401] it is likely that this limb should only apply in the most serious of cases. **4.526**

Grounds (v) and (vii) are potentially more problematic. Ground (v) refers to a party withholding (or concealing) evidence sufficient to affect the impartiality of the arbitration. This ground is complicated by the fact that there is often no extensive document disclosure in PRC arbitrations, so it is not entirely clear when a party is entitled to withhold evidence, and when this amounts to concealment of evidence. **4.527**

Ground (vii) is potentially the most controversial, but it reflects the overriding role played under PRC law by the concept of 'social and public interest'. The concern of many foreign parties is that 'social and public interest', which is an inherently vague concept, may be interpreted broadly and used by courts to re-examine the merits of the award. In particular, in the past, there was case law indicating that this term may be interpreted more broadly than the public policy exception under the New York Convention. However, in more recent cases, the SPC has adopted a relatively narrow reading of the provision, and it is likely that today, it is restricted to violations of fundamental moral standards, sovereignty and the like. **4.528**

If one of the above grounds is made out, the PRC court 'shall' rule to set aside the arbitration award. Therefore, the court does not appear to have any residual discretion to save the award.[402] **4.529**

---

[401] Art 38, PRC Arbitration Law provides for a serious sanction if ground (vi) is established: the relevant arbitrator shall assume legal liability according to law and the arbitration commission shall remove his name from the list of arbitrators.

[402] Art 58, PRC Arbitration Law.

4.530 (1.2) **Foreign-related Awards** In contrast, the grounds for setting aside foreign-related awards are significantly narrower, being generally confined to the following procedural or jurisdictional defects:[403]

(i) there is no arbitration clause in the contract and the parties have not subsequently reached a written arbitration agreement;
(ii) the party against whom the application for enforcement is made was not given notice of the appointment of the arbitrator or of the commencement of the arbitration or was unable to present its case due to reasons for which it is not responsible;
(iii) the composition of the arbitral tribunal or the arbitration procedure was not in conformity with the arbitration rules; or
(iv) the matters dealt with by the award fall outside the scope of the arbitration agreement or outside the jurisdiction of the arbitration commission.

4.531 On the face of it, the standards above appear unobjectionable. In practice, there have been cases where the courts have applied a relatively low standard and set aside an award on the basis, for example, that the arbitration procedure did not conform with the agreed arbitration rules.

4.532 (B) The HK Arbitration Ordinance adopts the narrow setting-aside grounds found in the UNCITRAL Model Law, which are essentially based on the New York Convention grounds[404] for resisting enforcement. In essence, an arbitral award may be set aside only for procedural defects, lack of jurisdiction or public policy grounds:

(i) The arbitral award may be set aside by the court of its own volition if it finds that:
   a. the subject matter of the dispute is not capable of settlement by arbitration under the laws of Hong Kong; or
   b. the award is in conflict with the public policy of Hong Kong.
(ii) An award may also be set aside if the losing party proves that:
   a. a party to the arbitration was under some incapacity or the arbitration agreement is not valid under Hong Kong law—there is therefore no valid agreement or arbitration agreement;
   b. the applicant was not given proper notice of the appointment of an arbitrator or of the arbitral proceedings, or the applicant was otherwise unable to present its case—thereby being in breach of rules of natural justice or due process;
   c. the award deals with a dispute not contemplated by or not falling within the terms of the submission to arbitration, or contains decisions on matters beyond the scope of the submission to arbitration—the arbitrator exceeded the jurisdiction given to him, and if that part of the award can be severed it would be severed so as to preserve the rest of the award which does not exceed jurisdiction;

---

403 Art 70, PRC Arbitration Law; Art 258, PRC Civil Procedure Law. The Chinese text of Art 70 is not entirely clear and two alternative interpretations have been suggested:

(i) the grounds for setting aside a foreign-related award is restricted only to limb (i) of Art 258; limbs (ii) to (iv) do not apply;
(ii) the grounds for setting aside a foreign-related award apply not only to limbs (i) to (iv) of Art 258, but in addition, the 'social and public interest' limb also applies.

404 Art V, New York Convention.

d. the composition of the arbitral tribunal or the arbitral procedure was not in accordance with the agreement of the parties or was not in accordance with the UNCITRAL Model Law—thereby not preserving party autonomy and being in breach of the arbitration agreement/arbitration law.[405]

Instead of setting aside an award, it is open to the Hong Kong courts, where appropriate and if requested by a party, to suspend the setting aside proceedings and to remit the award to the arbitral tribunal. The tribunal is then given an opportunity to resume the arbitral proceedings or to take such other action to eliminate the grounds for setting aside.[406] **4.533**

(1.1) May an award made according to international or foreign procedural rules be the object of an application for setting aside before the national courts? (A) This question has not been clearly considered by the PRC courts. **4.534**

(B) No. Although this question has not directly come up in Hong Kong, the Hong Kong courts have had occasion to consider the legal effect of a foreign court decision purporting to set aside an award not made under that foreign court's procedural law.[407] The court's comments in that case strongly suggest that it would not ordinarily consider itself empowered to set aside an award made under a foreign procedural law.[408] **4.535**

(2) Procedure and deadlines for challenging an award

(A) In the PRC, the application to set aside an award is made to the Intermediate People's Court in the place where the relevant arbitration commission is located.[409] **4.536**

A party that wishes to set aside an arbitration award should submit its application within six months of the date of receipt of the award.[410] The PRC court that has accepted the application shall decide whether to set aside the award or to reject the application within two months from the date of acceptance. **4.537**

However, if the PRC court considers that re-arbitration can be carried out by the arbitration tribunal, it shall notify the tribunal that it should 're-arbitrate' the dispute within a certain time limit and shall stay the setting-aside procedure. If the arbitral tribunal refuses to reconsider the dispute, the PRC court shall resume the setting-aside procedure.[411] **4.538**

(B) An application to set aside an international arbitration award must be made by originating summons to the judge in charge of the Construction and Arbitration List. An application must be made within three months of the date on which the applicant received the award or, if a request has been made to correct or interpret the award (or for an additional **4.539**

[405] Art 34, UNCITRAL Model Law.

[406] *ibid.*

[407] *Karaha Bodas Company LLC, supra* n 44.

[408] However, one possible exception is if the award is made in Hong Kong, but under a foreign procedural law. See generally, 'Report of the United Nations Commission on International Trade Law on the work of its Eighteenth Session' (Vienna, 3-21 June 1985) (A/40/17), paras 72–81 and 272–6.

[409] Art 58, PRC Arbitration Law.

[410] Art 59, *ibid.*

[411] Art 60, *ibid.*

award),[412] from the date on which that request has been disposed of by the arbitral tribunal.[413]

4.540 **(2.1) Who may (or must) represent a party in a proceeding for setting aside an award?** (A) In PRC court proceedings, parties are represented by PRC lawyers. Foreign parties often select PRC lawyers who are well-connected, and also seek the assistance of foreign lawyers, to navigate them through the minefield of local issues.

4.541 (B) The parties to a Hong Kong arbitration are free to choose their own representatives, advisers and advocates. For court proceedings arising out of an arbitration agreement or arising in the course of, or resulting from, arbitration proceedings, it is necessary to use Hong Kong-admitted barristers and solicitors.[414]

4.542 **(2.2) Do specific time limits exist for setting-aside procedures concerning awards on jurisdiction?** (A) As explained at II.C.(2) *supra*, in PRC practice, the validity of an arbitration agreement, and the arbitral tribunal's jurisdiction, is generally determined by either the arbitration commission or the PRC court.[415] Where an application is made to both the arbitration commission and to the PRC court, the PRC court shall decide the matter.

4.543 Neither the PRC Arbitration Law nor the CIETAC Arbitration Rules expressly envisage a further procedure by which the decision of the court or commission (as the case may be) is set aside. On the contrary, the SPC Interpretation 2006 provides that after an arbitration institution has made its decision on the validity of an arbitration agreement, the PRC court shall not entertain any application by a party to either determine the validity of the arbitration agreement or to set aside the decision of the arbitration institution.[416]

4.544 (B) As noted at II.C.(3) *supra*, the HK Arbitration Ordinance (read together with the UNCITRAL Model Law) provides that the arbitral tribunal may rule on a plea that the tribunal does not have jurisdiction or has exceeded the scope of its authority, either as a preliminary question or in an award on the merits:

(i) if the arbitral tribunal rules as a preliminary question that it has jurisdiction, any party may request within 30 days that the Court of First Instance decide the matter, which decision shall be subject to no appeal. Strictly speaking, this is not an application for 'setting aside', and the application is made outside of the normal provisions that govern applications to set aside an award;[417] and

(ii) where the decision is set out in the award on the merits, the usual time lines apply for setting aside an award.[418]

(3) Effect of a court decision which sets aside the award

4.545 (A) An award that has been set aside is usually invalid and of no legal effect, such that it is unenforceable in the place where it has been set aside (in this case, the PRC). In general, it

[412] Art 33, UNCITRAL Model Law.
[413] Art 34(3), *ibid.*
[414] s 2F, HK Arbitration Ordinance.
[415] Art 20, PRC Arbitration Law.
[416] Art 13, SPC Interpretation 2006.
[417] Art 16, UNCITRAL Model Law.
[418] Art 34, *ibid.*

is also unenforceable in foreign jurisdictions.[419] Comments expressed at the time the PRC Arbitration Law was drafted suggest that the preferred view in the PRC is that an award that has been set aside is also not enforceable in other countries.

(B) An award that has been set aside is usually invalid and of no legal effect, such that it is unenforceable in the place where it has been set aside (in this case, Hong Kong). In general, it is also unenforceable in foreign jurisdictions. **4.546**

(3.1) **Does the setting-aside action suspend the enforcement? If so, do remedies exist to reinstate enforcement?** (A) The PRC Arbitration Law provides that if one party applies to enforce an arbitral award and the other party applies to set aside the award, the PRC court shall suspend the enforcement proceedings.[420] The SPC Interpretation 2006 reiterates this.[421] Thus, enforcement proceedings will be delayed where a party applies to set aside an award. In practice, experienced parties will often still commence proceedings to enforce the award, notwithstanding a pending setting-aside application, to avoid any risk of being time-barred. **4.547**

The SPC Work Notes 2005 deals with the effect of foreign proceedings to set aside a non-PRC award. It provides that where an action has been brought outside the PRC to set aside a foreign arbitral award or to suspend its enforcement and that action is pending, the PRC court 'may' (not 'shall') suspend the proceedings for recognition and enforcement in the PRC.[422] That article then continues by providing that if, in similar circumstances, the foreign court is not prepared to suspend its enforcement proceedings, the PRC court may, in effect, reciprocate by similarly not suspending the PRC enforcement proceedings. **4.548**

(B) Under the New York Convention, if an application for setting aside (or suspension) of a foreign award has been made to a competent court, the Hong Kong courts may, if it considers it proper, adjourn its decision on enforcement. It may also, on the application of the party claiming recognition or enforcement of the award, order the other party to provide appropriate security.[423] This provision however, only applies to foreign Convention awards which are sought to be enforced in Hong Kong. **4.549**

In the case of the enforcement of Hong Kong awards, where there is a pending application for setting aside, the courts will likely also adjourn the hearing of any enforcement applications until after disposal of the setting-aside application. **4.550**

(3.2) **After an award has been set aside, does the underlying arbitration agreement revive or remain in force or is it exhausted or deemed terminated?** (A) The PRC Arbitration Law states that if an arbitration award is set aside or its enforcement is refused, a party may **4.551**

---

[419] But compare eg *Hilmarton Ltd v Omnium de Traitement et de Valorisation* (1997) XXII Ybk Comm Arb 696; *Chromalloy Aeroservices v Arab Republic of Egypt* (1997) XXII Ybk Comm Arb 691.

[420] Art 64, PRC Arbitration Law.

[421] Art 25, SPC Interpretation 2006.

[422] Art 83, SPC Work Notes 2005.

[423] Art VI, New York Convention.

apply for arbitration on the basis of a 'new arbitration agreement' reached between the parties, or institute proceedings in the PRC court on the same dispute.[424]

4.552 Thus, it appears that if the arbitral award is set aside or enforcement is refused, the claimant is not permitted to invoke the arbitration agreement again, unless the parties agree on a new arbitration agreement. This reading of the provision is consistent with the views expressed at the time it was drafted.

4.553 In practice, such agreement may be rare, as it is often in the interests of the party challenging the award to derail any attempt at re-arbitrating the dispute. Thus, in such a situation, there is a strong likelihood that the parties may have to resolve their dispute by litigation.

4.554 (B) The effect of setting aside an award on the underlying arbitration agreement depends on the reason why the award has been set aside. For example, if it has been set aside because the arbitration agreement is null and void, then the underlying arbitration agreement will not remain in force. Absent such situations, although arguable, the better view is probably that where an arbitration award is set aside, the arbitration agreement remains in force and the claimant can recommence arbitration (subject to any time bar issues).

(4) Appeal against the court's decision to set aside or not set aside the award

4.555 (A) The PRC courts have in place an important 'reporting system' which applies to foreign-related awards.[425] This system was introduced to give foreign parties greater confidence in the PRC's arbitration regime, and to send a signal that the PRC was supportive of arbitration. It provides that if the people's court decides that there is a basis for setting aside the award, then before setting aside the award or notifying the arbitral tribunal to re-arbitrate the case, a report should be made for examination by the Higher People's court, within 30 days after receipt of the application. If the Higher People's Court shares the view of the first court, its opinion should be reported to the SPC within a further 15 days. It is only after the SPC has replied, that a decision can then be made to set aside the award or to notify the arbitral tribunal to re-arbitrate the case. However, significantly, there is no time limit on when the SPC has to issue its decision. In addition, commentators have criticized the system for not being transparent, as parties are not given the right to participate in the various stages of the 'reporting up' system.[426]

---

424 Art 9, PRC Arbitration Law. cf Arts 213 and 259 of the PRC Civil Procedure Law, which predates the PRC Arbitration Law, and states that if enforcement of the award is disallowed, the parties may, in accordance with a written arbitration agreement reached between them, commence arbitration again, or they may also bring an action before the PRC court; and Art 278 of the SPC, 'Several Opinions on the Application of PRC Civil Procedure Law' (issued 14 July 1992).

425 SPC, 'Notification concerning the Setting aside of Foreign-related arbitral awards by the People's Court' (23 April 1998).

426 However, one of the previous criticisms has, in theory, been addressed by amendments to the PRC Civil Procedure Law, effective from 1 April 2008. Art 203 provides that where a People's Court has failed to act on the enforcement within six months from receipt of the application, the applicant may apply to a higher level People's Court for enforcement. Upon examination, the higher level People's Court may order the original People's Court to take enforcement action or decide on the application itself or designate another People's Court to take action. This helps to address the criticism of some commentators that there can be undue delay in the 'reporting up' system.

Other than this reporting mechanism, the court's decision to set aside an award is final and cannot be appealed.[427] There is a supervisory administrative process which appears to allow for the review of court decisions, but its effectiveness is open to doubt. **4.556**

(B) The Hong Kong High Court Ordinance (c 4) provides that an appeal lies as of right to the Court of Appeal from the Court of First Instance's decision on a setting-aside application.[428] The procedure for appeals is set out in the Rules of the High Court. In general, an appeal to the Court of Appeal shall be by way of rehearing (on the documents) and is brought by way of a notice of appeal. The notice of appeal may be given either in respect of the whole or part of the judgment of the Court of First Instance, and such notice must specify the grounds of the appeal and the precise form of the order which the appellant is seeking. The notice of appeal must be served on all parties to the proceedings in the Court of First Instance within 28 days following the date on which the Court of First Instance judgment was sealed.[429] **4.557**

(5) Possibility of the parties excluding actions for setting aside

(A) The PRC Arbitration Law does not expressly address the possibility of the parties agreeing to exclude actions for setting aside (exclusion agreements). However, it is likely that such agreements will not be effective, or wholly effective. For example, at a minimum, the PRC courts will likely retain the right to set aside a domestic award if it is contrary to social and public interest, regardless of what the parties have purportedly agreed to. This is supported by the fact that under the relevant provision, the PRC courts are empowered to set aside the award on this basis on its own volition, independent of any application by either party. In addition, the SPC has issued an opinion suggesting that it is not open to the parties to agree upon the standard of review in an application to revoke part of an arbitral award.[430] **4.558**

(B) The provision in the HK Arbitration Ordinance dealing with actions for setting-aside of an international award is likely to be a mandatory provision.[431] As such, parties cannot contract out of it. The HK Arbitration Ordinance also contains separate provisions dealing with the validity of exclusion agreements in connection with domestic arbitration agreements, but these deal with leave to appeal and determination of preliminary points of law, and not with excluding the right to set aside an award.[432] **4.559**

D. Liability of arbitrators

(1) Duties and liabilities of arbitrators regarding the conduct of the proceedings

(A) CIETAC has published its Ethical Rules for Arbitrators ('CIETAC Ethical Rules'), and BAC has published its Ethical Standards for Arbitrators.[433] **4.560**

[427] See the SPC, 'Reply concerning Questions over whether to accept an Application to a People's Court for a rehearing by a party dissatisfied with the People's Court's decision to set aside an award' (issued 29 January 1999); Art 9, PRC Arbitration Law.

[428] s 14, High Court Ordinance.

[429] Ord 59, Rules of the High Court.

[430] 'Letter of Reply of the SPC to the request for instructions in the case of application of Hong Kong Qihao Tucano Group Co, Ltd for Revocation of part of the award No 641 (2002) of Shenzhen Arbitration Commission' (effective from 14 September 2004).

[431] Art 34, UNCITRAL Model Law.

[432] s 23B, HK Arbitration Ordinance.

[433] Art 4.1, CIETAC Ethical Rules provide, generally, that an arbitrator:

(i) will hear cases in an independent and impartial manner;

4.561 These rules supplement provisions already contained in the law and arbitration rules. For example, the PRC Arbitration Law provides that disputes are to be resolved 'in compliance with the law and in an equitable and reasonable manner',[434] and the CIETAC Arbitration Rules provide that the arbitral tribunal shall act impartially and fairly and shall afford reasonable opportunities to all parties for presentations and debates.[435]

4.562 Unlike the position under a number of international rules,[436] and in certain jurisdictions, neither the PRC Arbitration Law nor the CIETAC Arbitration Rules contain a provision expressly excluding an arbitrator's liability in connection with the conduct of proceedings. In the absence of contrary agreement, it would therefore appear that the arbitrators may potentially be liable to the parties under general principles of contract law and tort.

4.563 In addition, the PRC Arbitration Law sets out express sanctions in two situations:

(i) where the arbitrator has privately met with a party or agent or has accepted an invitation to entertainment or a gift from a party or agent; and the circumstances are serious; or
(ii) while arbitrating the case, the arbitrators committed embezzlement, accepted bribes, practised graft or made an award that perverted the law.

4.564 In these circumstances, the PRC Arbitration Law provides that the arbitrator shall assume liability according to the law, and the arbitration commission shall remove his name from the list of arbitrators.[437]

4.565 (B) The HK Arbitration Ordinance provides that an arbitral tribunal is liable in law for an act done or omitted to be done by the tribunal, or by its employees or agents, in the exercise or performance (or the purported exercise or performance) of the tribunal's arbitral functions, only if it is proved that the act was done or omitted to be done dishonestly.[438]

4.566 The HK Arbitration Ordinance also addresses the liability of the appointing authority, and of any institution providing administrative services. It provides that a person who appoints an arbitral tribunal or who exercises or performs administrative functions in connection with arbitration proceedings, is liable in law for the consequences of doing or omitting to do an act in the exercise or performance of the function only if it is proved that the act was done or omitted to be done dishonestly. It also contains provisions extending this protection to an employee or agent of the appointing authority or institution.[439]

(ii) comply with the principles of fairness and reasonableness;
(iii) not act as a representative of any party, but treat all parties involved in the arbitration equally;
(iv) strictly comply with the arbitral procedure and provide each party with ample opportunities for making statements;
(v) ensure he or she has sufficient time to deal with the case;
(vi) must carefully and meticulously review all files and materials; and
(vii) must strictly maintain the confidentiality of all information in the arbitration.

[434] Art 7, PRC Arbitration Law.
[435] Art 29, CIETAC Arbitration Rules.
[436] See eg Art 34, ICC Rules (dealing with exclusion of liability).
[437] Art 38, PRC Arbitration Law.
[438] s 2GM, HK Arbitration Ordinance.
[439] s 2GN, *ibid.* In the case of the HKIAC Administered Arbitration Rules, Art 40 sets out provisions excluding the liability of the HKIAC and affiliates.

(1.1) Do the courts and/or authorities rely on a contractual relationship between the parties and the arbitrator(s), irrespective of whether institutional or *ad hoc* arbitration is concerned? What is the legal qualification of such a contract (eg provision of services)? (A) In general, under PRC practice, the relationship between the parties and the arbitrators is less direct than in other jurisdictions. This arises from the more important role played by the arbitration commissions, and the fact that in most cases, parties appoint arbitrators from the panels of the arbitration commissions. As a result, there tends to be a closer relationship between the arbitration commissions and the arbitrators, than as between the parties and the arbitrators. That said, there is probably a quasi-contractual relationship involving the parties, the arbitrators and the arbitration commission, although the exact nature of that relationship has not yet come up for close examination under PRC law. **4.567**

(B) The relationship between the parties and the arbitrator(s) is partly founded on contract, but not entirely so. Instead, it is likely that the relationship is only quasi-contractual in nature, and arbitrators also derive their rights and obligations from their status and from arbitration law. **4.568**

(1.2) Are there court decisions (or authorities) determining which law governs the question of liability of an arbitrator? What is the position of those courts/authorities as to whether and to which extent a legal liability of an arbitrator (or arbitral institution) may be established? (A) This question has not come up for detailed consideration by a PRC court. In practice, it is likely that the PRC courts will, as a starting point, assume that PRC law applies. This is implicit from the provisions set out in VI.D.(1) *supra*. **4.569**

(B) This question has not directly come up for consideration before the Hong Kong courts. The answer is likely to depend in part on whether the relationship between the parties and the arbitrator(s) is considered to be essentially contractual in nature (akin to a contract for services), or one that arises from the status of the arbitrator and the arbitration law. In practice, in determining the liability of an arbitrator, a Hong Kong court is likely to be heavily influenced by the position under Hong Kong law (in particular, the provisions under the HK Arbitration Ordinance—see VI.D.(1) *supra*), and any other relevant terms in the applicable arbitration rules and the arbitrator's terms of appointment. **4.570**

(1.3) Is an arbitrator subject to criminal prosecution? (A) Yes. **4.571**

(B) Yes. **4.572**

(2) Possibility to restrict or exclude the arbitrators' liability

(A) As explained above, neither the PRC Arbitration Law nor the CIETAC Arbitration Rules contain a provision expressly excluding the liability of the arbitrators in connection with the conduct of proceedings. This contrasts with the position in a number of other jurisdictions. In theory, it ought to be possible for the arbitrators, by agreement with the parties, to exclude or limit their liability. However, there will likely be limits. For example, attempts to exclude liability under Art 38 of the PRC Arbitration Law (see VI.D.(1) *supra*) will likely not be allowed. **4.573**

(B) As noted above, the HK Arbitration Ordinance confers some degree of immunity on the arbitrator(s). In addition, the arbitration rules may also include provisions further **4.574** excluding liability.[440] In addition, it is open to arbitrators to seek to include provisions in their terms of appointment expressly limiting their liability. However, there may be limits to the extent of such exclusions, and they may be ineffective for particularly serious violations, such as outright fraud committed by the arbitrator(s).

VII. Enforcement of national awards

4.575 (A) For enforcement of awards, it is useful to distinguish between the following sub-categories:

(i) *national awards,* comprising:
  a. domestic PRC awards (ie awards without a foreign element);
  b. foreign-related PRC awards (ie awards made in the PRC with a foreign element).
  National awards are awards made in the PRC. Domestic awards are awards made in the PRC by PRC arbitration commissions and which do not involve a foreign element. Foreign-related awards are awards made in the PRC by PRC arbitration commissions which involve a foreign element. See I.A.(3.1) *supra* on the test for determining if there is a foreign element. It is important to appreciate that foreign-related awards are made in arbitrations seated *in the PRC.*

(ii) *foreign awards,* comprising:
  a. New York Convention (excluding Hong Kong/Macau) awards;
  b. Hong Kong/Macau awards;
  c. non-New York Convention awards.
  Foreign awards are awards made outside the PRC. They comprise awards made in New York Convention states; in Hong Kong and Macau (which are treated separately from New York Convention states because both of them are special administrative regions of the PRC); and in non-New York Convention states.

4.576 This section VII. deals with the enforcement of national awards (both domestic and foreign-related awards). The next section VIII. deals with the enforcement of foreign awards.

4.577 (B) In the context of enforcement of awards in Hong Kong, it is useful to distinguish between the following:

(i) *Hong Kong awards,* comprising:
  a. awards made in Hong Kong domestic arbitrations; and
  b. awards made in Hong Kong international arbitrations; and

(ii) *non-Hong Kong awards,* comprising:
  a. awards made in New York Convention states other than the PRC;
  b. awards made in the PRC;
  c. awards made in non-New York Convention states, such as Taiwan.

4.578 This section VII. deals with the enforcement of awards made in Hong Kong. The next section VIII. deals with the enforcement of awards made outside Hong Kong.

---

[440] See eg, Art 40 of the HKIAC Administered Arbitration Rules.

(1) Requirement of a particular procedure to make an award enforceable (leave for enforcement, exequatur*)*

(A) The PRC Arbitration Law sets out a general obligation on parties to comply with an arbitration award. If a party fails to comply, the successful party is entitled to apply for enforcement of the award.[441] However, if the party resisting enforcement is able to establish that the arbitration award involves one of the grounds set out in the PRC Civil Procedure Law, the court may refuse to enforce the award. **4.579**

The application is made to the PRC court either in the location where the assets are or the place of domicile of the respondent.[442] In the case of domestic awards, there was previously some uncertainty over which level of the courts (Basic Level People's Court or Intermediate People's Court) had jurisdiction. It now appears clear that the Intermediate People's Court has jurisdiction.[443] **4.580**

For foreign-related awards, it is clear that the application is made to the Intermediate People's Court in the place the losing party has its domicile or where its property is located.[444] **4.581**

(B) Awards made in Hong Kong (whether domestic or international) may be enforced either by summary action or by an action on the award. The summary enforcement procedure provides various procedural advantages and is therefore the mode usually adopted. However, in certain circumstances, such as where there is no written arbitration agreement,[445] it may be necessary to enforce by way of an action on the award, instead of adopting the summary enforcement route. **4.582**

(1.1) Does the national law differentiate between foreign and domestic awards, and if so, which are the criteria? Does there exist an additional notion of award for the purpose of obtaining *exequatur* (France: international awards)? (A) As noted above, PRC law differentiates between national awards (comprising domestic and foreign-related PRC awards), and foreign awards (comprising New York Convention awards, Hong Kong/Macau awards and non-New York Convention awards). **4.583**

The criteria has been set out above. **4.584**

(B) As noted above, for enforcement purposes, a distinction can be drawn between awards made in Hong Kong (both awards made in domestic arbitrations and in international arbitrations) and awards made outside Hong Kong. **4.585**

The criteria for distinguishing between Hong Kong domestic and international arbitrations has been set out at I.A.(3.1) *supra*. The criteria for distinguishing between the various categories of awards made outside Hong Kong is generally based on territoriality.[446] **4.586**

441 Art 62, PRC Arbitration Law.
442 Art 10, 'Regulations of the SPC regarding Certain Issues in relation to Enforcement' (Effective on Trial Basis) (effective from 18 July 1998).
443 Art 29, SPC Interpretation 2006.
444 Art 257, PRC Civil Procedure Law.
445 See s 2GG read with 2AC, HK Arbitration Ordinance.
446 But note the proviso in Art I(1) of the New York Convention, referring to non-domestic awards.

4.587 (1.2) **May awards granting conservatory/interim measures be subject to enforcement?** (A) As explained above, applications for the preservation of evidence and the preservation of property are dealt with by the PRC courts, not the arbitral tribunal. The question of the enforceabilty of arbitral awards granting interim relief has therefore generally not come up.

4.588 (B) Yes. The HK Arbitration Ordinance expressly provides that an award, order or direction made or given in or in relation to arbitration proceedings by an arbitral tribunal is enforceable in the same way as a judgment, order or direction of the court that has the same effect, with the leave of the court or a judge of the court. If that leave is given, the court may enter judgment in terms of the award, order or direction. It is also noteworthy that this provision extends not only to an order granted in the form of an award, but also to orders or directions.[447]

(2) Details of such enforcement procedure (competent court, reasons for rejection of motion etc)

4.589 (A) The PRC Civil Procedure Law sets out the grounds upon which a court may refuse enforcement of an award. These are to some extent similar to the grounds in the case of setting aside of awards and as in the case of setting aside, a distinction is drawn between resisting enforcement of domestic awards, and of foreign-related awards.

4.590 (2.1) **Domestic awards** In the case of domestic awards, if the party against whom enforcement is sought presents evidence which proves that the arbitration award involves one of the following circumstances, the PRC court shall, after examination and verification by a collegiate bench formed by the PRC court, refuse enforcement where:

(i) the parties have neither included an arbitration clause in their contract nor subsequently reached a written arbitration agreement;
(ii) matters decided in the award exceed the scope of the arbitration agreement or are beyond the arbitral authority of the arbitration institution;
(iii) the formation of the arbitration tribunal or the arbitration procedure was not in conformity with statutory procedure;
(iv) the main evidence for ascertaining the facts was insufficient;
(v) the application of law was truly incorrect; or
(vi) the arbitrators committed embezzlement, accepted bribes, practised graft or made an award that perverted the law.

In addition, enforcement shall be refused if the PRC court determines that the execution of the award is against social and public interest.[448]

4.591 The grounds for refusing enforcement of domestic awards are broader than those in the case of foreign-related awards. The PRC court can refuse enforcement for both procedural defects, and on substantive grounds, such as where the 'main evidence for ascertaining the

[447] s 2GG, HK Arbitration Ordinance. See also Art 24.2 of the HKIAC Administered Arbitration Rules, which provides that interim measures ordered by a tribunal may be established in the form of an interim award.

[448] Art 213, PRC Civil Procedure Law.

facts was insufficient' or the application of the law was truly incorrect. These standards are inherently vague and only introduce further uncertainty as to how the courts will exercise their discretion.

(2.2) **Foreign-related awards** In the case of foreign-related awards, the PRC courts shall refuse enforcement of the award if the party resisting enforcement furnishes proof that:[449] **4.592**

(i) there is no valid agreement to arbitrate;
(ii) it was not given notice of the arbitrator's appointment or the commencement of the arbitration proceedings or it was unable to present its case due to causes for which it was not responsible;
(iii) the composition of the arbitral tribunal or the arbitral procedure was improper; or
(iv) the award deals with matters outside the scope of the arbitration agreement or the scope of matters that could be submitted for arbitration.

In addition, if the PRC court determines that the enforcement of the award goes against social and public interest, enforcement shall be refused.

In general, these grounds are similar to those under the New York Convention, and are narrower than the grounds in the case of domestic awards. **4.593**

(B) Under the HK Arbitration Ordinance,[450] the Hong Kong courts may grant leave to enforce both international and domestic awards made (and directions given by tribunals) in Hong Kong summarily (ie without the need to bring fresh proceedings) and to enter judgment in terms of the award. Where such an order is granted, the award may be enforced in the same manner as a Hong Kong judgment. As noted above, this summary enforcement procedure has advantages over commencing an action on the award. **4.594**

The procedure for applying for leave to enforce is governed by the Rules of the High Court.[451] The initial application for leave to enforce should be made to the Court of First Instance without the respondent having notice of the application unless there is good reason for an *inter partes* summons to be issued. Assuming an order granting leave to enforce is obtained *ex parte*, the respondent then has 14 days after service of the order (or such other period if the order is served out of jurisdiction) to apply to set aside the order. During this period, the award shall not be enforced. If the respondent applies within the period to set aside the order, the award shall not be enforced until after the application is finally disposed of. **4.595**

The Hong Kong courts may refuse leave to enforce an international or a domestic arbitral award made in Hong Kong if there are procedural or jurisdictional defects which are similar to the setting-aside grounds in the UNCITRAL Model Law,[452] or the New York Convention grounds for resisting enforcement.[453] If the circumstances justify leave to appeal against a domestic award, the court may (but not must) refuse leave to enforce. The court may (but **4.596**

[449] Art 258, PRC Civil Procedure Law.
[450] s 2GG, HK Arbitration Ordinance.
[451] Ord 73 r 10, Rules of the High Court.
[452] Art 34, UNCITRAL Model Law.
[453] s 44, HK Arbitration Ordinance.

not must) stay the application pending a determination of a challenge against a domestic award.

(3) Appeal against the decision granting exequatur

4.597 (A) The decision to enforce or refuse enforcement of an award cannot be appealed.[454]

4.598 (B) An appeal against a court's grant or refusal to grant leave to enforce an award under s 2GG of the HK Arbitration Ordinance may be made to the Court of Appeal.

4.599 A further appeal may be made to the Court of Final Appeal, if the relevant threshold requirements are met and the court's leave to appeal is obtained.[455]

(4) Appeal (and procedure) if exequatur *has been refused*

4.600 (A) There is a supervisory administrative process that appears to allow for the review of court decisions refusing enforcement, although its effectiveness is open to doubt. In the case of foreign-related awards (but not domestic awards), if the Intermediate People's Court refuses enforcement of the award, the 'reporting system' described above will apply.[456] See VII.(3) *supra.*

4.601 (B) Appeals may be made to the higher courts against a court's refusal to grant leave to enforce an award. See VII.(3) *supra.*

(5) Procedure of enforcement (attachment of bank accounts etc)

4.602 (A) If the respondent fails to comply with an enforcement order of the court, the PRC courts may take various compulsory measures to enforce its orders, including orders to freeze or transfer deposits and to sell off property.[457]

4.603 (B) The Hong Kong courts may make various orders to facilitate the enforcement of an arbitral award where the respondent fails to comply with the enforcement order. These include enforcing a money judgment by seizure and sale of the debtor's goods and chattels; garnishee proceedings; and charging orders over the debtor's land, securities or other interests.

4.604 **(5.1) At the stage of enforcement, may the losing party invoke arguments and circumstances which are based on facts which have occurred before (or after) the award was made?** (A) As noted at VII.(2.1) *supra*, the grounds for resisting enforcement of a domestic award are relatively broad. For example, enforcement may be refused where the main

[454] Art 140, PRC Civil Procedure Law.

[455] See Hong Kong Court of Final Appeal Ordinance (c 484).

[456] See VIII.A.(3).

[457] These include the power to:

(i) make inquiries with financial institutions and to freeze or transfer deposits;

(ii) seal up, distrain, freeze, sell by public auction, or sell off part of the property of the person subjected to execution for the fulfilment of his obligations (but with certain limited exceptions);

(iii) issue a search warrant to search the respondent, his domicile or the place where the property is concealed;

(iv) summon the parties concerned to deliver up property or negotiable instruments; and

(v) compulsorily evict occupants.

See ch XXII, PRC Civil Procedure Law.

evidence for ascertaining the facts was insufficient. There therefore appears to be scope for a losing party to seek to invoke arguments and circumstances arising from subsequent developments. In practice, parties resisting enforcement have also made such arguments.

However, the SPC Interpretation 2006[458] does provide, in effect, that a party waives its right to set aside or resist enforcement of an award on the basis that the arbitration agreement is invalid, if it raises the argument only after the arbitral award is made, and not during the course of the proceedings. This therefore restricts the scope of arguments that a party may make if it fails to make a jurisdictional objection promptly, during the arbitration. **4.605**

(B) In theory, generally yes. However, this is subject to several caveats. First, the grounds for resisting enforcement of an award are very narrow, so the scope of relevant facts would be limited. Secondly, in practice, the courts are likely to view with some scepticism attempts to raise issues that ought to have been, but were not raised before the arbitral tribunal.[459] In addition, a number of arbitration rules contain express waiver provisions, which apply where a party knows that any provision of the rules has not been complied with and yet proceeds without promptly stating his objection.[460] **4.606**

A more topical issue is whether at the enforcement stage, the losing party may invoke arguments which it could have but failed to raise before the courts of the place of arbitration. In one Hong Kong case, the court held that the failure of a party to apply in the PRC to set aside an award did not preclude it from raising the same point before the Hong Kong courts.[461] However, the Hong Kong courts have also recognized that the failure to raise a point may amount to an estoppel or want of *bona fides*, thereby precluding a party from raising the point at the enforcement stage.[462] **4.607**

(5.2) May the losing party invoke a set-off based on claims that are not related to the matter of the arbitral proceeding? Is it material whether such a claim came into existence before or after the award was made? (A) There is some debate as to the proper position under PRC law, and it is currently unsettled. **4.608**

(B) The question of whether a losing party may invoke a set-off at the enforcement stage based on claims that are not related to the arbitral proceeding is a difficult one which has not been directly addressed by the Hong Kong courts. However, in principle, any such attempt is likely to lead to a number of complications. In particular, in order to invoke such a set off, the losing party would have to explain why it did not raise the claim at the arbitration stage, and also, to overcome any objection that its claim has not yet been adjudicated upon.[463] **4.609**

---

458 Art 27, SPC Interpretation 2006.

459 See eg *Medison Co Ltd v Victor (Far East) Ltd* [2000] 2 HKC 502; *Hebei Import and Export Corpn v Polytek Engineering Co Ltd* [1999] 2 HKC 205.

460 See eg Art 30, UNCITRAL Arbitration Rules.

461 *Paklito Investment Ltd v Klockner East Asia Ltd* [1993] 2 HKLR 39.

462 *Hebei Import & Export Corporation v Polytek Engineering Co Ltd.* [1998] HKCA 388; see also *Polytek Engineering Company Ltd v Hebei Import & Export Corp* [1999] 2 HKC 205 (CFA).

463 But cf the situation where an award has already been rendered. In such a scenario, the HK Arbitration Ordinance recognizes that a New York Convention award shall be treated as binding for all purposes on the

VIII. Foreign awards

A. Recognition and/or enforcement of foreign awards (national law)

4.610 (A) This section deals with the recognition and enforcement of the following categories of foreign awards made outside mainland China:

(i) New York Convention awards (excluding Hong Kong/Macau);
(ii) Hong Kong/Macau awards; and
(iii) non-New York Convention awards.

4.611 (B) This section deals with the recognition and enforcement of the following categories of foreign awards, made outside Hong Kong:

(i) New York Convention awards (excluding the PRC);
(ii) PRC awards; and
(iii) non-New York Convention awards.

(1) Rules according to national law

4.612 (A) The PRC acceded to the New York Convention in 1987, subject to two reservations permitted under the Convention.[464]

4.613 (1.1) **New York Convention awards (excluding Hong Kong/Macau)** See VIII.B.(1) *infra.*

4.614 (1.2) **Awards made in Hong Kong/Macau** Following the reversion of Chinese sovereignty over Hong Kong and Macau, the PRC extended its application of the New York Convention to these two territories. However, it was unclear if the Convention allowed for the mutual enforcement of awards between the two territories, and the PRC. As a result, in 2000, the Arrangement Concerning Mutual Enforcement of Arbitral Awards Between the Mainland and the Hong Kong Special Administrative Region (the 'Arrangement')[465] was entered into between the mainland and Hong Kong, providing that where a party fails to comply with an arbitral award, whether made in the mainland or in Hong Kong, the other party may apply to the relevant court in the place where the defendant is domiciled or in the place where the property of the defendant is situated to enforce the award.[466] A similar arrangement was entered into between the mainland and Macau on 30 October 2007.

4.615 The grounds for refusing enforcement of awards generally mirror those found in the New York Convention (although the Arrangement refers to a social and public interest exception applicable in the mainland, whereas under the Convention, the reference is to public policy). The SPC has also recently issued a document confirming that awards made

persons as between whom it was made, and may be relied on by any of those persons by way of, *inter alia*, set-off in any legal proceedings in Hong Kong: see ss 40B and 42, HK Arbitration Ordinance.

[464] Art I(3), New York Convention.
[465] Effective from 1 February 2000.
[466] Art 1, the Arrangement.

in *ad hoc* arbitration proceedings in Hong Kong are enforceable in the PRC. This is of some significance, by removing any doubt over the enforceability of such awards in the PRC.[467]

(1.3) Non-New York Convention Awards The PRC Civil Procedure Law envisages that foreign awards may be enforced in accordance with international treaties (ie most notably, the New York Convention) or 'based on the principle of reciprocity'.[468] Thus, it appears that if the award is issued in a country which recognizes and enforces PRC arbitral awards, then on the basis of reciprocity, that award will similarly be enforceable in the PRC. In practice, this provision does not appear to have been successfully invoked previously, no doubt because most major economies (save for Taiwan)[469] are signatories to the New York Convention, and it is more straightforward to simply rely on the Convention route for such awards. **4.616**

The PRC Civil Procedure Law is silent on the grounds for refusing to enforce a non-Convention award. However, they are likely, at a minimum, to be based on grounds similar to those under the Convention. Otherwise, it would be anomalous if it were easier to enforce a non-Convention award than a Convention award. **4.617**

(B) The section *supra* (VII.(1) to VII.(5)) dealt with the enforcement of awards made in Hong Kong (comprising awards made both in domestic and international arbitrations in Hong Kong). **4.618**

This section deals with foreign awards. **4.619**

(1.4) New York Convention awards (excluding the PRC) See VIII.B.(1) *infra*. **4.620**

(1.5) Awards made in the PRC Prior to the handover, arbitral awards made in Hong Kong were treated as Convention awards for purposes of enforcement in the PRC and vice versa. After 30 June 1997, however, it became unclear how Hong Kong awards would be treated by China's domestic courts when enforcement was sought in the PRC (and vice versa).[470] **4.621**

These concerns were put to rest with the signing on 21 June 1999 of the Arrangement. It was enacted in Hong Kong as Part IIIA of the HK Arbitration Ordinance from 1 February 2000. **4.622**

Part IIIA of the HK Arbitration Ordinance provides for enforcement of 'Mainland awards' in Hong Kong on almost identical terms as for New York Convention awards under Part IV. Accordingly, it is now clear that a Mainland award shall, subject to the defences to enforcement **4.623**

---

[467] See generally, Yuen, P. and Choong, J. 'Enforceability of Ad Hoc Awards' [2007] 2(6) *Global Arb Rev* 25.

[468] Art 267, PRC Civil Procedure Law.

[469] As to which, see the 'SPC Provisions on the People's Court's Recognition of Civil Judgments Made by Courts in the Taiwan Region' (effective from 26 May 1998) and the recent 'Supplementary Rules on the Recognition of Civil Judgments made in Taiwan', promulgated by the Supreme People's Court on 14 May 2009.

[470] The situation became urgent in January 1998, when the Court of First Instance in Hong Kong in *Ng Fung Hong Ltd v ABC* [1998] 1 HKC 213 held that a CIETAC award could not be enforced in Hong Kong under the general provision for enforcement of awards, nor as a Convention award (as it was not made in another contracting state of the New York Convention).

set out below, be enforceable as a judgment of a Hong Kong court in the same manner as an award enforceable under the general enforcement provision.[471]

4.624 One significant effect of the definition of 'Mainland award' is that awards rendered in the Mainland by foreign arbitral institutions or tribunals established pursuant to the rules of a foreign arbitral body (such as the ICC) and awards made in the Mainland pursuant to *ad hoc* proceedings will fall outside the scope of the Arrangement.[472] Such awards may, however, be enforceable in Hong Kong by means of a common law action on the award (ie an action for breach of an implied term in an arbitration agreement to comply with the terms of the award).[473]

4.625 **(1.6) Non-New York Convention Awards** Where enforcement of an award made in non-New York Convention states is sought, an application may be made under the HK Arbitration Ordinance, which provides that an award, order or direction made or given in or in relation to arbitration proceedings by an arbitral tribunal is enforceable in the same way as a judgment, order or direction of the court, with the leave of the court. If that leave is given, the court may enter judgment in terms of the award, order or direction.[474]

4.626 It is clear that this summary procedure for enforcement of awards, orders, and directions under the Ordinance applies to awards, orders, and directions made *outside* Hong Kong, regardless of whether they were made in a contracting state to the New York Convention.[475] This provision therefore ensures the enforceability in Hong Kong of arbitral awards made in Taiwan, Macau and other jurisdictions which are not signatories to the New York Convention.

(2) Requirements to be fulfilled by the applicant (procedure, time limits)

4.627 (A) The procedure for enforcement of foreign-related awards, and foreign (non-New York Convention and Hong Kong/Macau) awards is broadly similar:

(i) the application is made to the Intermediate People's Court in the place where the respondent has its domicile or where its property is located;[476]
(ii) there is a two-year time limit for submission of an application for enforcement;[477]
(iii) Documents to be submitted include the written application setting out the reasons for and description of the matters of the proposed enforcement and the object to be enforced; original or notarised copies of the arbitral award and arbitration agreement; proof of the applicant's identity; and power of attorney.[478]

---

471 s 40B, HK Arbitration Ordinance.

472 In any event, as PRC law does not appear to recognize *ad hoc* arbitrations, an award rendered in the PRC pursuant to an *ad hoc* arbitration may well contravene the requirement that eligible awards be 'made pursuant to the Arbitration Law of the People's Republic of China' anyway.

473 Conversely, as noted above, the SPC has recently clarified that Hong Kong *ad hoc* awards do not face a similar difficulty, and they are enforceable in the PRC. See generally, Yuen, P. and Choong, J., 'Enforceability of Ad Hoc Awards' [2007] 2(6) *Global Arb Rev* 25 and the letter dated 25 October 2007 from the SPC.

474 s 2GG, HK Arbitration Ordinance.

475 s 2GG(2), *ibid.*

476 Art 257, PRC Civil Procedure Law.

477 See Art 215, *ibid*, as a result of amendments effective from 1 April 2008.

478 See generally 'Regulations of the SPC regarding certain issues in relation to Enforcement' (Trial Implementation) (effective from 8 July 1999).

In practice, confusion can arise as to what documents are required. For example, judges have been known to insist that evidential documents relied on in arriving at the award be supplied. Similarly, there can be considerable practical difficulties in obtaining the documents and arranging for official translations, which can also be a time-consuming task; and

(iv) fees and expenses are also payable. These vary according to the monetary value of the award. The respondent is liable for these fees and expenses unless the application for enforcement is denied in whole or in part.[479]

(B) The procedure in Hong Kong for the enforcement of PRC awards and of non-New York Convention awards is similar, and also generally follows the procedure for enforcement of Hong Kong awards. A two-step process is envisaged: **4.628**

(i) at the first stage, the applicant applies *ex parte* to the court for an order granting leave to enforce the award and an order entering judgment in the terms of the award; and

(ii) at the second stage, the respondent may apply to set aside the order, at an *inter partes* hearing. Where the order has been served within jurisdiction, the respondent has 14 days to challenge it. Where it has been served out of jurisdiction, the court will fix a period of time within which the respondent may apply to set aside the order. The award shall not be enforced during this period or, if the respondent applies to set aside the order, until after the application is finally disposed of.[480]

The *ex parte* application to enforce the award is made on affidavit to the judge and on the papers. The relevant supporting documents (such as the arbitration agreement and the award) must be exhibited. In addition, the applicant must make full and frank disclosure of all relevant information in support of the application. The court may decline to grant the order *ex parte* and direct that a summons be issued instead. **4.629**

At the second stage, the Hong Kong courts may only refuse to enforce a foreign award in circumstances broadly reflecting the New York Convention grounds for resisting enforcement of awards. **4.630**

(3) Remedies against decisions granting or declining enforcement

(A) As in the case of applications to set aside an award, PRC law also has a 'reporting system' to deal with cases where enforcement of the award is refused.[481] If the Intermediate People's Court refuses enforcement of a foreign-related arbitral award, or refuses recognition and enforcement of a foreign award, it must report its decision to the Higher People's Court. If the Higher People's Court agrees with the proposal of the Intermediate People's Court to deny enforcement, it must in turn refer the matter to the SPC. It is only if the SPC concurs that the Intermediate People's Court may then issue its order to refuse enforcement. The relevant regulations do not state explicitly that the reporting system applies to **4.631**

[479] 'Measures of the SPC on Litigation Fees' (effective from 1 September 1989).

[480] Ord 73, Rules of the High Court.

[481] See 'Notice of the SPC on several issues regarding the handling by the people's courts of certain issues pertaining to foreign-related arbitration and foreign arbitration' (effective from 28 August 1995).

Hong Kong awards. However, it appears clear that the reporting system also applies, and Hong Kong awards are clearly not domestic awards.

4.632 There have been a number of criticisms of the reporting system:

(i) it is not transparent as parties are not given the right to participate in the various stages of the 'reporting up' system;
(ii) the obligation to report up only applies where the enforcing court refuses to grant enforcement. Cases of 'partial' enforcement may not be caught by the system; and
(iii) there is no time limit on when the SPC has to issue its decision. In practice, in the past, this has reportedly resulted in delays of years in certain cases.

4.633 (B) Under Hong Kong law, an appeal against a court's grant or refusal to grant leave to enforce an award may be made to the Court of Appeal.

B. Recognition and/or enforcement of foreign awards (conventions, treaties)

(1) Specific bilateral or multilateral treaties

4.634 (A) The PRC acceded to the New York Convention in 1987. Pursuant to the New York Convention, an arbitral award made in a foreign territory is recognized as binding in a contracting state (ie the PRC), and is enforceable in accordance with the rules of procedure of that state. The PRC's accession to the New York Convention is subject to two reservations permitted under the Convention.[482] Consequently, awards are enforceable in the PRC only where they are:

(i) awards made in the territory of other contracting states (the reciprocity reservation); and
(ii) awards which result from disputes arising from commercial legal relationships (whether contractual or not) in accordance with PRC law (the commercial reservation).

4.635 The procedure for enforcement of New York Convention awards is broadly similar to that for foreign-related awards, as set out above. Thus:

(i) the application is made to the Intermediate People's Court. Unlike the position with foreign-related awards, under the Convention regime, a hierarchical order applies in determining which Intermediate People's Court should handle the application:
    a. If the respondent is a natural person, the Intermediate People's Court where that person has its registered domicile or where the person is actually located handles the case;
    b. If the respondent is a legal person or organization, the Intermediate People's Court of the place where the principal business office is located;
    c. If the respondent has no domicile or place of residence or principal business office, the Intermediate People's Court at the place where the assets are located.[483]
(ii) there is a two-year time limit for submission of an application for enforcement;[484]

---

482 Art I(3), New York Convention.

483 'Notice of the SPC on the Implementation of China's Accession to the Convention on the Recognition and Enforcement of Foreign Arbitral Awards' (effective from 10 April 1987).

484 See Art 215, PRC Civil Procedure Law, as amended (effective from 1 April 2008).

(iii) documents are submitted, as above;[485] and
(iv) fees and expenses are payable, as above.

Apart from the New York Convention, another important multilateral treaty that the PRC has concluded is the Convention on the Settlement of Investment Disputes between States and Nationals of Other States 1965 ('ICSID Convention'). Pursuant to the ICSID Convention, each contracting state shall recognize an award rendered pursuant to the Convention as binding and enforce the pecuniary obligations imposed by that award within its territories as if it were a final judgment of a court in that State. In general, the ICSID Convention provides for a more favourable enforcement regime than the New York Convention. However, it applies only to investor-state disputes. To date, no ICSID award has been rendered against the PRC. **4.636**

(B) A foreign arbitral award, ie an award made outside Hong Kong and the rest of the PRC, may be enforced in Hong Kong under the New York Convention or under s 2GG(2) of the HK Arbitration Ordinance. **4.637**

Apart from the New York Convention, as noted above, another important multilateral treaty is the ICSID Convention. Prior to the handover, the ICSID Convention applied in Hong Kong, by virtue of the UK Arbitration (International Investment Disputes) Act 1966, which was extended to Hong Kong by Order in Council in 1967. However, following the handover, the Act ceased to apply to Hong Kong. The PRC is a contracting state to the ICSID Convention. It was reportedly agreed by the Sino-British Joint Liaison Group that the Convention would continue to apply to Hong Kong. However, the PRC has not formally declared that the Convention will continue to apply. Notwithstanding this, it is generally assumed that the Convention is intended to be in force and applicable to Hong Kong.[486] **4.638**

(2) Existence of a standard procedure for the enforcement of foreign awards

(A) As can be seen, the general procedure for enforcement of a New York Convention award is broadly similar to that for a foreign-related award. **4.639**

As with foreign-related awards, the 'reporting system' applies to New York Convention awards sought to be enforced in the PRC. However, it is less clear if the reporting system applies to *ad hoc* foreign awards. This is because the relevant notice[487] appears to assume that foreign awards are made by a foreign arbitral institution (by analogy to the PRC system). **4.640**

(B) The HK Arbitration Ordinance[488] provides that a Convention award is enforceable 'in the same manner as the award of an arbitrator by virtue of section 2GG'. Accordingly, the **4.641**

[485] See VIII.A.(2).

[486] For example, the Department of Justice website lists the ICSID Convention under its 'List of Treaties in Force and Applicable to the Hong Kong Special Administrative Region': <http://www.legislation.gov.hk/interlaw.htm> (accessed 7 March 2008). For a discussion of some of the key issues, see Rosa, A. and Choy, J., '"One Country, Two Systems" and Country Risk Protection for Hong Kong Listed Companies', *Hong Kong Lawyer* (June 2008) 32.

[487] See 'Notice of the SPC on several issues regarding the handling by the people's courts of certain issues pertaining to foreign-related arbitration and foreign arbitration' (effective from 28 August 1995).

[488] s 42(1), HK Arbitration Ordinance.

general procedure set out in VIII.A.(2) applies and the Hong Kong courts are empowered to grant leave to enforce Convention awards summarily (ie without the need to bring a common law action on the award).

(3) Extent of examination and review of the award by the court

4.642 (A) At the enforcement stage, the PRC courts' power to examine the arbitral award is strictly circumscribed, and limited only to the grounds set out in the New York Convention. These grounds for refusing enforcement are generally restricted to procedural or jurisdictional defects only. Of the various grounds listed, the 'public policy' ground might be thought to be an issue, given the comparatively broad wording of 'social and public interest' adopted by the PRC as a basis for refusing enforcement of foreign-related awards. In practice, however, there is case law in which the PRC courts have adopted a pro-enforcement approach and construed 'public policy' relatively narrowly.

4.643 (B) As noted above, an application for leave to enforce is usually made *ex parte*. Thereafter, the onus is on the party against whom enforcement is sought to apply to set aside the order granting leave. That party must demonstrate that at least one of the limited grounds on which the enforcement of a Convention award may be refused is applicable.

4.644 The Hong Kong courts have an excellent record in enforcing foreign arbitral awards in accordance with the New York Convention. In particular, the Hong Kong courts recognize that they have a residual *discretion* to permit enforcement of a Convention award. This is reflected in the use of the word 'may' in the relevant provision in connection with the court's power to nevertheless permit enforcement where one or more of the statutory grounds has been made out.[489]

C. Application of the New York Convention

(1) Application of the New York Convention in practice

4.645 (A) Much has been written about the track record of the PRC courts in enforcing awards under the New York Convention, and the material is not always consistent. On the one hand, foreign writers have historically been critical, drawing on anecdotal evidence or surveys suggesting that enforcement rates are relatively low. Conversely, a number of PRC studies, cited by local authors, suggest that success rates are very good. To cite three examples:

(i) a 1997 limited survey carried out by the Arbitration Research Institute of the China Chamber of International Commerce indicated that out of 14 surveyed foreign awards over the period 1990 to 1997, 10 had been recognized and enforced. Three were denied enforcement and one was still pending. Out of the three denied enforcement, only one was a 'genuine' case of a refusal to grant enforcement.[490] On this basis, the ratio of non-enforcement of foreign awards was apparently a very low 7.14 per cent;[491]

[489] s 44(2), HK Arbitration Ordinance.

[490] One involved a mistake in nominating the proper party against whom enforcement should be sought and in the other case, no assets were available for enforcement.

[491] Wang, S.C., 'Enforcement of Foreign Arbitral Awards in the PRC' in C. Drahozal (ed), *Towards a Science of International Arbitration: Collected Empirical Research* (2005) 282–3.

(ii) in contrast, a survey by a foreign scholar of selected awards from 1991 to 1999 totalling about 25 foreign awards indicated a 52 per cent enforcement rate. Even where enforcement was granted, this did not mean that there was 100 per cent recovery of the award amount;[492] and

(iii) based on the information available, a senior CIETAC official recently pointed out that between 2000 and 2006, there were 26 cases of non-enforcement of arbitral awards reported to the SPC for approval. Half of these were CIETAC awards. Out of the 26 cases, there were reportedly only 10 awards which were eventually denied enforcement. This therefore suggests that only 10 out of 'thousands of awards' over that period were refused enforcement.[493]

The authors' own experience suggests that the reality lies at neither extreme. Some of the horror stories that make the rounds simply represent high profile anecdotes (sometimes overstated) at one extreme of the spectrum. Conversely, there is sufficient anecdotal evidence to call into question the accuracy of some of the more optimistic statistics cited by PRC writers. **4.646**

Despite some genuine concerns, there is reason to be optimistic. It is likely that as the legal system in the PRC becomes more sophisticated, and given the pro-enforcement stance in the PRC's arbitral legislation, enforcement rates will improve over time, particularly in the outlying provinces which have historically had a patchy record. **4.647**

(B) The Hong Kong courts are clearly pro-enforcement. For example, in considering the scope of 'public policy', the Court of Final Appeal has definitively stated that Hong Kong courts should take a 'pro-enforcement' approach to Convention awards.[494] In its decision, the court held that the expression 'contrary to public policy' in the Convention and in the HK Arbitration Ordinance[495] meant 'contrary to the fundamental conceptions of morality and justice of the forum in which enforcement was sought' and that the 'public policy' ground for refusing enforcement is to be narrowly construed and applied. **4.648**

(2) Examples of decisions which do not apply the Convention correctly

(A) In the PRC, one of the most well known enforcement cases gone wrong is the *Revpower* case. The case involved a dispute between Revpower (an affiliate of a US company) and a Shanghai company over a joint venture contract involving industrial batteries. The contract contained an arbitration agreement. A price dispute arose, and in July 1991, Revpower proceeded with Stockholm arbitration proceedings against the Shanghai company. **4.649**

---

[492] Peerenboom, R., 'Seek truth from facts: An Empirical Study of Enforcement of Arbitral Awards in the PRC' in Drahozal (ed), *Towards a Science of International Arbitration: Collected Empirical Research* (2005) 292. For a more recent view, cf Peerenboom and He Xin, 'Dispute Resolution in China: Patterns, Causes and Prognosis' (28 January 2008), <http://ssrn.com/abstract=1265116> at 7.

[493] Moser, M., 'CIETAC and its Work—An Interview with Vice Chairman Yu Jianlong' (2007) 24(6) *J Int'l Arb* 555. It is pertinent to note that over the same period, many cases were successfully enforced. Therefore, the figure of 26 cases refers only to cases where enforcement was initially refused. This is because the reporting system does not apply where enforcement is granted. Note that the reporting mechanism does not apply to domestic awards. See also Xin He, 'The Enforcement of Commercial Judgments in China', on file with author.

[494] *Hebei Import & Export Corp v Polytek Engineering Co Ltd* [1999] 1 HKLRD 665.

[495] s 44, HK Arbitration Ordinance.

A challenge by the Shanghai company to the jurisdiction of the arbitral tribunal failed. The Shanghai company then initiated proceedings before the Shanghai Intermediate People's Court, on the basis that the arbitration clause was ambiguous and failed to specify the Stockholm Chamber of Commerce as the arbitral institution. The intermediate courts accepted jurisdiction, and the Shanghai company then withdrew from the Stockholm proceedings. In the arbitration, Revpower obtained an award of US$4.5 million, together with substantial interest. The Shanghai company failed to comply with the award, and Revpower initiated enforcement proceedings before the Shanghai Intermediate People's Court. Despite considerable political pressure, little progress was made. Eventually, after more than two years, the Shanghai Intermediate People's Court granted enforcement of the award, in 1996. However, Revpower was unable to enforce the award because, by then, the Shanghai company had declared bankruptcy. Ultimately, Revpower's application was therefore dismissed on the ground that the Shanghai company had filed for bankruptcy and there were no assets against which the award could be enforced.

4.650 This case is but one of the most notorious ones involving the enforcement of foreign awards in the PRC. That said, it is clear that the legislative framework in the PRC has improved, and there is reason to be cautiously optimistic that the PRC's track record for successfully enforcing awards will continue to improve.

4.651 (B) Examples of cases in which the Hong Kong courts have exercised their discretion to refuse enforcement include where:

(i) one party was denied the opportunity to cross-examine experts appointed by the tribunal and to deal with their evidence;[496]
(ii) the tribunal carried out its own investigations (as permitted under the relevant arbitration rules) but neither notified the results of its enquiries to the parties, nor invited submissions thereon before making its award;[497] and
(iii) an award was procured by unlawful or oppressive conduct by one party.[498]

4.652 However, these decisions are widely regarded as having been correctly decided.

4.653 Examples of cases where the Hong Kong courts have found *in favour of enforcement* of an award notwithstanding a ground set out in the Ordinance having been made out include circumstances where:

(i) the party resisting enforcement waived (by conduct) any objection to an irregularity in the appointment of the tribunal;[499]
(ii) the party resisting enforcement kept silent about a procedural irregularity of which it was aware during the proceedings;[500]

---

496 *Paklito Investment Ltd v Klockner East Asia Ltd* [1993] 2 HKLR 39.
497 *Apex Tech Investment Ltd v Chuang's Development (China) Ltd* [1996] 2 HKC 293.
498 *J J Agro Industries (P) Ltd v Texuna International Ltd* [1992] 2 HKLR 391.
499 *China Nanhai Oil v Gee Tai Holdings* [1995] HKLR 215.
500 *Hebei Import & Export Corp v Polytex Engineering Co Ltd* [1999] 1 HKLRD 665.

(iii) the party resisting enforcement deliberately took no part in the arbitral proceedings;[501] and
(iv) the appointed arbitral body had changed its name and/or its rules had been amended.[502]

IX. Appendix

A. National legislation

PRC Arbitration Law 1994
PRC Civil Procedure Law (as amended) 2008

Arbitration Ordinance (c 341)
Arrangement Concerning Mutual Enforcement of Arbitral Awards between the Mainland and the Hong Kong Special Administrative Region

B. Arbitral institutions and government organizations

China International Economic and Trade Arbitration Commission

6F, CCOIC Building
No 2, Huapichang Lane
Xicheng District
Beijing 100035
People's Republic of China
Telephone: +86 10 6464 6688
Fax: +86 10 6464 3500
Email: cietac@public.bta.net.cn
Website: <http://www.cietac.org.cn/ENGLISH/E_index.htm>
Hong Kong International Arbitration Centre
38/F, Two Exchange Square
8 Connaught Place
Hong Kong SAR
China
Telephone: +852 2525 2381
Fax: +852 2524 2171
Email: adr@hkiac.org
Website: <http://www.hkiac.org>
Gary Soo, Secretary-General
Primrose Law, Deputy Secretary-General

501 *Shejiang Province Garment Import and Export Co v Siemssen & Co (Hong Kong) Trading Ltd* [1996] ADRLJ 183.

502 *Tai Hing (Asia) Commercial Co Ltd v Trinity (China) Supplies Ltd* (unreported, no A6585 of 1987, digested at [1989] HKLY 57); *Shenzhen Nan Da Industrial and Trade United Co v F M International Ltd* [1992] 1 HKC 328.

HKSAR Immigration Department Employment and Visit Visas Section
24/F, Immigration Tower
7 Gloucester Road
Wan Chai
Hong Kong SAR
If the applicant is a PRC national:
Mainland Residents Section
9/F, Immigration Tower
7 Gloucester Road
Wan Chai
Hong Kong SAR

C. Model arbitration clauses and other patterns[503]

The CIETAC model arbitration clause is as follows:

> Any dispute arising from or in connection with this Contract shall be submitted to China International Economic and Trade Arbitration Commission for arbitration which shall be conducted in accordance with the Commission's arbitration rules in effect at the time of applying for arbitration. The arbitral award is final and binding upon both parties.

Note: In practice, practitioners frequently adapt the standard CIETAC model clause, because it may be inadequate in particular situations.[504]

The ICC recommended clause for ICC arbitrations conducted in the PRC is as follows:

> All disputes arising out of or in connection with the present contract shall be submitted to the International Court of Arbitration of the International Chamber of Commerce and shall be finally settled under the Rules of Arbitration of the International Chamber of Commerce by one or more arbitrators appointed in accordance with the said Rules.[505]

The HKIAC recommended clause for international arbitrations administered by the HKIAC is as follows

> Any dispute, controversy or claim arising out of or relating to this contract, or the breach, termination or invalidity thereof, shall be settled by arbitration in Hong Kong under the Hong Kong International Arbitration Centre Administered Arbitration Rules in force when the Notice of Arbitration is submitted in accordance with these Rules.
>
> * The number of arbitrators shall be . . . (one or three).
>
> The arbitration proceedings shall be conducted in . . . . (insert language).
>
> *Optional

[503] These clauses are provided for ease of reference only. For specific transactions, reference should always be made to the latest versions of the model clauses, and specialist advice should be sought.

[504] See generally <http://arbitration.practicallaw.com/9-381-9852> and <http://arbitration.practicallaw.com/7-381-9853> on the PLC website, for drafting notes on the CIETAC clause (subscription required), accessed 18 October 2008, and Yuen, P., 'Arbitration Clauses in a Chinese Context' (2007) 24(6) *J Int'l Arb* 581.

[505] Note that it is by no means certain that an agreement to conduct ICC arbitration in the PRC is valid under PRC law. See II.A.(2) *supra*.

D. Bibliography

Articles

Briner, R., 'Arbitration in China Seen from the Viewpoint of the International Court of Arbitration of the International Chamber of Commerce' in Albert van den Berg (ed), *New Horizons in International Commercial Arbitration and Beyond: ICCA Congress Series no12* (Kluwer Law International, The Hague, 2005).

Choong, John, 'Clarifying the PRC Arbitration Law' (2006) 20(9) *China Law & Practice* 14.

Chua, Eu Jin, 'Arbitration in the People's Republic of China' (2005) 20 *J Int'l Banking L and Regulation* 559.

Harpole, S., 'The Combination of Conciliation with Arbitration in the People's Republic of China' (2007) 24(6) *J Int'l Arb* 623.

Hilmer, Sarah and Wang, Sheng Chang, 'China Arbitration Law v UNCITRAL Model Law' 9 *Int'l Arb L Rev* 1.

Kaplan, N., 'HKIAC's Perspective on Arbitration and Conciliation Concerning China' in Albert van den Berg (ed), *New Horizons in International Commercial Arbitration and Beyond: ICCA Congress Series no 12* (Kluwer Law International, The Hague, 2005).

Lee, James, 'A Review of the Enforcement of Hong Kong Awards in China' [April 2006] *Asian Dis Rev* 52.

Livdahl, David and Qin, Xiao Dan, 'ICC Arbitration Administered in China' [April 2006] *Asian Dis Rev* 49.

Marriot, Arthur and Wang, Sheng Cheng, 'Enforcement of Foreign Arbitral Awards in China' (2002) 68 *J of the Chartered Inst of Arbitrators* 31.

Morgan, Robert and Gu, Weixia, 'Improving Commercial Dispute Resolution in China' [2005] *Asian Dis Rev* 98.

Moser, M., 'CIETAC and its Work—An Interview with Vice Chairman Yu Jianlong' (2007) 24(6) *J Int'l Arb* 555.

Moser, M. and Harwood, J., 'Commentary on Arbitration and Conciliation Concerning China' in Albert van den Berg (ed), *New Horizons in International Commercial Arbitration and Beyond: ICCA Congress Series no 12* (Kluwer Law International, The Hague, 2005).

Moser, Michael and Yeoh, Friven, 'Hong Kong and Mainland China Proposal on Reciprocal Enforcement of Judgments: An Alternative Means of Resolving Sino-Foreign Business Disputes?' (Sept 2006) 21(9) *Mealey's Int'l Arb Rep* 43.

Moser, Michael and Yuen, Peter, 'The New CIETAC Arbitration Rules' (2005) 21(3) *Arb Int'l* 391.

Moser, Michael and Yuen, Peter, 'Chinese Supreme People's Court Provides Clarification—and Confusion—On Arbitration Issues' in Albert van den Berg (ed), *New Horizons in International Commercial Arbitration and Beyond: ICCA Congress Series No 12* (Kluwer Law International, The Hague, 2005).

Rosa, A. and Choy, J., '"One Country, Two Systems" and Country Risk Protection for Hong Kong Listed Companies', *Hong Kong Lawyer* [June 2008] 32.

Wang, S.C.. 'Enforcement of Foreign Arbitral Awards in the PRC' in Drahozal (ed), *Towards a Science of International Arbitration: Collected Empirical Research* (2005).

Yeoh, Friven and Fu, Yu, 'A Snapshot of Recent Judicial Attitudes on Arbitrability and Enforcement' (2007) 24 (6) *J Int'l Arb* 635.

Yuen, Peter and Choong, John, 'Supreme People's Court's Interpretation on Application of the PRC Arbitration Law' (August 2006) 21(8) *Mealey's Int'l Arb Rep* 52.

Yuen, Peter and Choong , John, 'Enforceability of Ad Hoc Awards' (2007) 2(6) *Global Arb Rev* 25.

Yuen, Peter, 'Arbitration Clauses in a Chinese Context' (2007) 24(6) *J Int'l Arb* 581.

Books

Cohen, Jerome, Kaplan, Neil and Malanczuk, Peter (advisory eds) and Fung, Daniel and Wang S.C. (general eds), *Arbitration in China: A Practical Guide—Volumes One and Two* (Sweet & Maxwell, Hong Kong, 2004).

Dejun, Cheng, Moser, Michael and Wang, Sheng Chang, *International Arbitration in the People's Republic of China: Commentary, Cases and Materials* (2nd edn, 2000).

Halsbury's Laws of Hong Kong [2006] 7(1) (LexisNexis).

Ma, Geoffrey and Kaplan, Neil (eds), *Arbitration in Hong Kong: A Practical Guide—Volumes One and Two* (Sweet & Maxwell, Hong Kong, 2003).

Morgan, Robert, *The Arbitration Ordinance of Hong Kong: A Commentary* (Butterworths, 1997).

Moser, Michael (ed), *Managing Business Disputes in Today's China—Duelling with Dragons* (Kluwer Law International, The Hague, 2007).

Moser, Michael and Cheng, Teresa, *Hong Kong Arbitration—A User's Guide* (2nd edn, 2008).

Tao, Jing Zhou, *Arbitration Law and Practice in China* (2nd edn, Kluwer Law International, The Hague, 2008).

5

ENGLAND

Miranda Karali and Jane Ballantyne ***

I. Introduction

A. Current status of the law on arbitration

(1) Short history

This section is concerned only with the laws of England, Wales and Northern Ireland, for the sake of brevity, referred to herein as 'English' law. Scotland has a separate legal system with which this section is not concerned. **5.01**

English arbitration law mirrors that of English law generally, in that it is embodied both in common law (case law) and statute (legislation). The seventeenth century saw the **5.02**

---

* Miranda Karali, Partner, Marine, Energy & Trade team, Barlow Lyde and Gilbert LLP ('BLG') and Jane Ballantyne, Associate Director, Commercial Litigation & Arbitration team, BLG.

** With the generous contribution throughout the England chapter of:

Peter Flint, Partner, Commercial Litigation and Arbitration team, BLG;
Leigh Williams, Partner, Reinsurance and International Risk team, BLG;
Robert Merkin, Professor of Commercial Law at the University of Southampton, and Consultant at BLG;
Judith Pastrana, Professional Support Lawyer, Marine, Energy & Trade team, BLG;
Monique Matosian-Bharucha, Legal Assistant (New York qualified), Commercial Litigation and Arbitration team, BLG;

Contributors to individual sections are acknowledged at the beginning of each section.

introduction of the first recorded English arbitration legislation, in the form of the Arbitration Act 1697.

5.03 The Arbitration Act 1889 that followed repealed much of the Arbitration Act 1697, keeping only one of three forms of arbitration, namely that which allowed parties to retain control of the proceedings but enabled them to make use of the court's regulatory powers. This single system remained the position through the subsequent Acts to the present day, where the Arbitration Act 1996 provides for a system of support for the contractual agreement to arbitrate and a procedure for enforcement of that agreement by the courts.

5.04 The role of the courts was not altogether welcomed, as seen by the introduction of the Arbitration Act 1979, which came about following wide discontent over the extent to which the judiciary could interfere in arbitrations, and which reflected the growing desire for party autonomy as identified by the UK government's Commercial Court Committee on Arbitration 1978 ('the 1978 CCC').[1] The 1978 CCC noted the criticism of the previous Acts, in particular that they provided a low threshold for appeals thereby almost encouraging parties to appeal, and leading to a more uncertain and expensive process.

5.05 The Arbitration Act 1979 did not, however, address the procedural concerns that were identified by the 1978 CCC. The 1989 Departmental Advisory Committee on Arbitration Law (the '1989 DAC'), chaired by (the now) Lord Mustill, recommended the enactment of new arbitration legislation to take into account some but not all of the UNCITRAL Model Law provisions.[2]

5.06 The Report led to widespread debate amongst lawyers and arbitrators, such that a private member's bill was commissioned to address issues raised and propose revised arbitration legislation. The 1996 Departmental Advisory Committee on Arbitration Law (the '1996 DAC') proposed that the new legislation should restate the English principles of arbitration and avoid areas that are 'unsettled', for example, confidentiality which is largely left to the principles established in common law.[3] The 1996 DAC Report swiftly became the Arbitration Act 1996, discussed further below.

(2) Law in force and future projects

5.07 The Arbitration Act 1996 governs arbitration in England and Wales, and Northern Ireland. The Arbitration Act 1996 came into force on 31 January 1997 and applies to all arbitration proceedings commenced on or after that date. The stated object of the Arbitration Act 1996 is the principle that 'the object of arbitration is to obtain fair resolution of disputes by an impartial tribunal without unnecessary delay or expense'.[4]

---

[1] Commercial Court Committee, *Report on Arbitration*, Cmnd 7284, Lord Donaldson (chair) (HMSO, London, 1978).

[2] Departmental Advisory Committee on Arbitration Law, *New Arbitration Act? The response of the Departmental Advisory Committee to the UNCITRAL Model law on International Commercial Arbitration*, Sir Mustill LJ (chair) (HMSO, London, 1989).

[3] Departmental Advisory Committee on Arbitration Law, *Report on the Arbitration Bill*, Sir Saville LJ (chair) (Department of Trade and Industry, London, 1996) 10.

[4] Arbitration Act 1996 s 1(a).

The Arbitration Act 1996 incorporates the Convention on the Recognition and Enforcement of Foreign Arbitral Awards 1958 (the 'New York Convention') and is largely based upon the UNCITRAL Model Law with a number of significant additions and alterations. 5.08

It is now over a decade since the coming into force of the Arbitration Act 1996. In November 2008 the landmark of 1,000 cases decided under the 1996 Act was reached, and a number of reviews have taken place. The most noteworthy is the non-governmental report dated November 2006, prepared under the chairmanship of Bruce Harris for, amongst others, the Commercial Court Users' Committee, the British Maritime Law Association (BMLA), and the London Shipping Law Centre, known as the Harris Report.[5] 5.09

The Harris Report based its findings upon a world-wide survey of English arbitration users and practitioners. The Report concluded that no changes are needed or desirable but its conclusion was controversial. 5.10

(3) Distinction between national and international arbitration

The Arbitration Act 1996 does have the concept of a domestic arbitration agreement.[6] However, the differences in the statutory regime applicable to domestic arbitration agreements (compared to other, ie 'international', arbitration agreements) have not been brought into force and are likely to be repealed. Accordingly, there is no practical significance in the distinction between domestic arbitrations and international arbitrations (or arbitration agreements) as a matter of English law. 5.11

(3.1) If there are different systems and rules for national/international arbitration: What are the criteria for the distinction between both systems? See para 5.11 *supra*. 5.12

B. Practice of arbitration

(1) Frequency of arbitration as opposed to litigation

Owing to the private nature of English arbitration, arbitration statistics are not readily available and there are no statistics that compare the number of arbitration claims against those of litigation. Yet, after gathering information from English arbitration centres, the Harris Report estimated that there are over 5,000, and potentially as many as 10,000, arbitrations each year in England.[7] 5.13

The Ministry of Justice's 2006 Annual Report, by contrast, provides litigation statistics on claims and originating proceedings arising in the Chancery and Queen's Bench Divisions of the court, these being those divisions concerned with civil matters.[8] When the Chancery Division's insolvency and bankruptcy proceedings are deducted from the total, approximately 25,000 litigation proceedings took place before the court in 2006. Applying the 5.14

[5] *Report on the Arbitration Act 1996*, Harris (chair): <http://www.idrc.co.uk/aa96survey/Report_on_Arbitration_Act_1996.pdf> (accessed 3 July 2008).

[6] Arbitration Act 1996 s 85.

[7] Harris Report (n 5) 19.

[8] Ministry of Justice, Judicial and Court Statistics 2006, Cm 7273 (HMSO, November 2007) <http://www.justice.gov.uk/docs/judicial-court-stats-2006-tag.pdf> (accessed 3 July 2008).

Harris Report estimates, it appears that in England arbitration is employed in place of litigation in 20 to 40 per cent of disputes.

(2) Leading arbitral institutions and statistics

- The London Court of International Arbitration (LCIA)

5.15 The LCIA is a leading English international arbitration forum. The majority of these cases have London as their seat of arbitration.

- International Chamber of Commerce Court of Arbitration (ICC)

5.16 The ICC, whilst an international arbitral forum, regularly sees London as the chosen seat of arbitration.

- Chartered Institute of Arbitrators' Dispute Resolution Service (DRS-CIArb)

5.17 Founded in 1915 and now with 11,000 members across more than 100 countries, the DRS-CIArb is a leading centre for the global promotion and facilitation of arbitration. DRS-CIArb offers nominating and appointing services for *ad hoc* arbitrations, adjudications and mediations.

- London Maritime Arbitrators Association (LMAA)

5.18 A leading maritime arbitration forum dealing with international and domestic based arbitrations. In 2006, approximately 2,500 LMAA Members were appointed arbitrators, publishing over 360 awards.[9]

- Lloyd's Salvage Arbitration Branch

5.19 A leading arbitration forum linked with Lloyd's of London that administers salvage arbitrations undertaken under the Lloyd's Open Form of maritime salvage agreement (LOF). Since the coming into force of the Arbitration Act 1996 it has seen some 1,041 arbitrations with a combined value of US$2,082 million.[10]

- Commodity disputes are heard in accordance with the arbitration rules of the relevant trade association, for example the Grain & Feed Trade Association (GAFTA); the Federation of Oils, Seeds & Fats Associations (FOSFA); the Sugar Association of London and the Refined Sugar Association; the London Metal Exchange; and the Coffee Trade Federation.
- English arbitration regularly sees the use of *ad hoc* arbitrations, although due to the nature of these particular arbitrations no statistics are available.

[9] LMAA Introduction.

[10] <http://www.lloyds.com/Lloyds_Worldwide/Lloyds_Agents/Salvage_Arbitration_Branch/LOF_facts_And_figures.htm> (accessed 3 July 2008).

II. Jurisdiction of the arbitral tribunal*

A. Arbitration agreement

(1) Arbitration clause and submission agreement

The Arbitration Act 1996 applies only where the seat of the arbitration is in England, Wales or Northern Ireland.[11] Under English law an arbitration agreement is an agreement between two or more parties to resolve disputes—whether present or future, contractual or not—through arbitration proceedings.[12] Arbitration agreements may be contained in contracts for the resolution of future disputes, or arise through a 'submission agreement', ie a specific agreement, unconnected to another contract, wherein the disputing parties agree to refer their dispute to arbitration. Further, whilst rare, an arbitration agreement may be implied,[13] although such an arbitration agreement may not meet the Arbitration Act's requirement that the agreement be in writing and thus fall outside its scope.[14] **5.20**

(2) Requirements as to the contents of the arbitration agreement

In order for an arbitration agreement to be valid and enforceable under the Arbitration Act 1996, it must (i) properly identify the parties, whether in the main contract or in the arbitration agreement itself;[15] (ii) clearly refer the parties to arbitration for the definitive resolution of the dispute(s);[16] and (iii) have a seat of the arbitration.[17] **5.21**

The parties' agreement to refer disputes to arbitration must be clear and certain,[18] unequivocally reflecting the parties' wishes to make arbitration the means for the final and binding resolution of disputes between them.[19] The type of dispute which may be submitted to arbitration must be specified (and arbitrable),[20] and the procedure envisaged by the clause must be consistent with arbitration.[21] **5.22**

---

* The authors wish to thank Carmel Nye, Associate, Commercial Litigation and Arbitration team, BLG, for her contribution to this section.

[11] Certain provisions apply even where the seat is outside or is not designated, eg stay of legal proceedings, enforcement and certain powers in support of the arbitral process if appropriate: Arbitration Act 1996 s 2(2)-(5).

[12] Arbitration Act 1996 s 6. See also UNCITRAL Model Law Art 7(1). Note, 'dispute' is defined to include 'difference': Arbitration Act 1996 s 82(1).

[13] *Athletic Union of Constantinople v National Basketball Association* [2002] 1 All ER (Comm) 70 (Comm).

[14] Arbitration Act 1996 s 5.

[15] *Internaut Shipping GmbH v Fercometal Sarl ('The Elikon')* [2003] EWCA Civ 812, [2003] 2 Lloyd's Rep 430.

[16] *AIG Europe SA v QBE International Insurance Ltd* [2001] 2 All ER (Comm) 622.

[17] *Naviera Amazónica Peruana v Cía Internacional de Seguros del Perú* [1998] 1 Lloyd's Rep 116 (CA), 119-20 (Kerr LJ); *Dubai Islamic Bank PJSC v Paymentech Merchant Services Inc* [2001] 1 Lloyd's Rep 65 (Comm).

[18] *Lobb Partnership Ltd v Aintree Racecourse Co Ltd* [2000] BLR 65 (Comm).

[19] *Finnegan v Sheffield City Council* (1988) 43 BLR 124 (QB).

[20] *Fiona Trust & Holding Corp and Ors v Privalov and Ors* [2007] UKHL 40, [2007] Bus LR 1719.

[21] *AIG Europe* (n 16); Sutton, D., Gill, J., and Gearing, M., *Russell on Arbitration* (23rd edn, Sweet & Maxwell, London, 2007) 2-065.

5.23 In addition, an arbitration agreement may, and arguably should, contain a number of other provisions setting out the arbitration procedure. Such provisions may concern:

- the seat of the arbitration and the choice of the procedural and/or governing law of the arbitration;
- the selection of an arbitral institution or *ad hoc* rules;
- the number of arbitrators;
- the choice of location for the arbitration;
- the language of the arbitration;
- any additional confidentiality requirements;
- the powers of the tribunal to issue provisional awards;
- the procedures relating to multi-party arbitrations;
- whether costs are to be capped;
- the exclusion of appeals to court; and
- any special requirements regarding an arbitrator's qualifications and/or how the issues should be determined.

In the absence of such provisions, the Arbitration Act 1996 provides a general framework for the resolution of procedural issues.

(3) Form of the arbitration agreement (eg 'in writing' requirement)

5.24 To constitute an arbitration agreement to which the Arbitration Act 1996 applies, the agreement must be 'in writing',[22] but is broadly interpreted to include 'being recorded by any means'.[23] The writing requirement is met even where an unwritten agreement refers to other terms which are in writing,[24] where the arbitration agreement is 'evidenced in writing', whether that of the parties or of a third party acting with the authority of the parties,[25] or where written submissions allege the existence of an unwritten arbitration agreement and the allegation is not denied.[26] Nor is it necessary for the agreement to be signed by the parties, although this may cause problems at the enforcement stage in jurisdictions outside England.[27]

5.25 A wholly oral agreement to refer an existing or future dispute to arbitration is valid at common law but will be outside the scope of the Arbitration Act 1996.[28] Such an agreement is generally regarded as undesirable as, in most cases, the agreement is revocable by either party up to the award and the agreement will lack the default provisions otherwise provided by the Arbitration Act 1996.

---

22 Arbitration Act 1996 s 5; cf s 81(1)(b).
23 *ibid*, s 5(6).
24 *ibid*, s 5(3); *Heifer International Inc v Christiansen* [2007] EWHC 3015 (TCC), [2008] Bus LR D49.
25 Arbitration Act 1996 s 5(4).
26 *ibid*, s 5(5).
27 *ibid*, s 5(2)(a); cf *Russell* (n 21) 2-043. 2006 revisions to the Model Law have introduced the possibility of an unsigned arbitration agreement despite doubts as to enforceability of awards.
28 Arbitration Act 1996 s 81(1)(b).

(3.1) Are there special requirements for a power of attorney/authority to enter into an arbitration agreement on behalf of a third party? No. The only requirement is that the person executing the arbitration agreement on behalf of a principal must satisfy the English law rules relating to the question of authority of agents. That is to say that the agent must have actual, implied or ostensible authority as recognized by English law.[29] 5.26

As a matter of practice, of course, it is always sensible to request that a counterparty's representative produces adequate evidence of corporate authority to bind his principal to the agreement. 5.27

(4) Incorporation of an arbitration clause contained in general terms and conditions

Under s 6(2) of the Arbitration Act 1996, parties need not set out the terms of their arbitration agreement in the contract itself—it is sufficient for the arbitration clause to be incorporated by reference to either a standard form of clause or to a set of trade terms which themselves include provisions requiring disputes to be submitted to arbitration. 5.28

In principle, where parties seek to incorporate a standard form contract or set of terms and conditions, the arbitration clause may be incorporated.[30] This has been the case even where parties have not made express reference to the clause, provided it is clear that the parties intended the arbitration clause to apply.[31] 5.29

However, the position may not be the same if incorporation is attempted by reference to another contract (as opposed to standard contract terms). In *Aughton v M F Kent Services*, the Court of Appeal held that specific and distinct words are necessary to incorporate an arbitration clause.[32] In this case, a reference in a subcontract to another contract's terms and conditions did not suffice to incorporate an arbitration clause into the subcontract. 5.30

Recent judicial decisions seem to follow the approach in *Aughton*; thus, in the absence of special circumstance, s 6 of the Arbitration Act 1996 requires an express reference to the relevant arbitration agreement.[33] In particular, this rule will apply to 'two contract' cases which involve, for example, the incorporation of charterparty arbitration clauses into negotiable bills of lading, as the party to the bill of lading may not have seen the charterparty terms.[34] The English test for incorporation is stricter than that adopted in many Model Law jurisdictions. 5.31

(5) Law applicable to the interpretation of the arbitration agreement

The law of the arbitration agreement regulates substantive matters relating to that agreement, including the interpretation, validity, voidability and discharge of the agreement to arbitrate. 5.32

[29] Reynolds, F.M.B., *Bowstead and Reynolds on Agency* (18th edn Sweet & Maxwell Ltd, London, 2006).

[30] *Modern Building (Wales) Ltd v Limmer and Trinidad Co Ltd* [1975] 1 WLR 1281 (CA); *Extrudakerb (Maltby Engineering) Ltd v Whitemountain Quarries Ltd* [1996] CLC 1747 (QB).

[31] *Pine Top Insurance Co Ltd v Unione Italiana Anglo Saxon Reinsurance Co Ltd* [1987] 1 Lloyd's Rep 476 (Comm); *Heifer International* (n 24).

[32] *Aughton Ltd v M F Kent Services Ltd* (1991) 57 BLR 1 (CA), 31 ff (Sir Megaw).

[33] *AIG Europe (UK) Ltd v Ethniki* [2000] 2 All ER 566 (CA); *Trygg Hansa Insurance Co Ltd v Equitas Ltd* [1998] 2 Lloyds Rep 439 (Comm).

[34] *Trade Maritime Corp v Hellenic Mutual War Risks Association (Bermuda) Ltd ('The Athena')* [2006] EWHC 2530 (Comm), [2007] 1 All ER (Comm) 183.

5.33 The arbitration agreement itself is separable from the main contract between the parties and, although unusual, it may have a different law from that of the law applicable to the substantive contract. The parties may specify the governing law of the arbitration agreement in the agreement itself. If it is not, the essential choice is between the law of the seat of the arbitration and the governing law of the substantive contract.

5.34 Where neither the proper law of the contract nor of the arbitration agreement are stated but the seat of the arbitration is specified, the law of the seat may govern both the substantive contract and the arbitration agreement. On the other hand, where the proper law of the contract is specified but no provision is made in respect of the governing law of the arbitration agreement, there is a presumption that the arbitration agreement is governed by that law which governs the substantive contract.[35]

5.35 **(5.1) Do courts accept a wide competence of the arbitral tribunal or do they restrict arbitral competence? Do claims which arise in connection with the agreement submitted to arbitration generally fall within the arbitral jurisdiction even if based on tortious legal basis? Does there exist case law with respect to the wording in an arbitration clause as 'arising out of/under/in connection with the present contract' and its specific meaning?** Section 1(b) of the Arbitration Act 1996 provides that parties should be free to determine how they wish to resolve their disputes, subject to any safeguards necessary for the public interest. Thus, provided the subject matter of the dispute is arbitrable, the scope of the arbitral tribunal's competence is limited only by the wording of the arbitration agreement.

5.36 In *Fiona Trust*, first the Court of Appeal[36] and then the House of Lords[37] articulated a 'fresh start' for the interpretation of arbitration agreements. The Court of Appeal decided and the House of Lords affirmed that arbitration clauses should be broadly construed so as to give effect to the commercial purpose of the agreement, thereby eliminating any distinction between the phrases 'out of', 'under', 'in relation to' or 'in connection with'.[38] The House of Lords further affirmed that even where one of the parties disputes the validity of the contract, the arbitral tribunal will generally retain competence due to the separability of the arbitration agreement from the underlying contract.[39]

(6) Binding effect of an arbitration agreement on third parties (eg in the case of an assignment or guarantee)

5.37 The effect of arbitration agreements on third parties is subject to two separate regimes in England: (1) that where the Contract (Rights of Third Parties) Act 1999 (the 'CRTPA 1999') applies; and (2) that where the CRTPA 1999 does not apply. Although the Arbitration Act 1996 defines a party as anyone 'claiming under or through a party to an arbitration agreement',[40] in those situations where the CRTPA 1999 does not apply, the

---

35 *Sonatrach Petroleum Corp v Ferrell International Ltd* [2002] 1 All ER (Comm) 627 (Comm).

36 *Fiona Trust & Holding Corp and Ors v Privalov and Ors* [2007] EWCA Civ 20, [2007] 1 All ER (Comm) 891.

37 *Fiona Trust* (n 20 - HL).

38 (n 36 - CA) 17-19 (Longmore LJ); (n 20 - HL) 8, 12-15 (Lord Hoffmann).

39 *Fiona Trust* (n 20 - HL) 16-18 (Lord Hoffmann), applying Arbitration Act 1996 s 7.

40 Arbitration Act 1996 s 82(2).

binding effect of the arbitration agreement differs between assignment, guarantees and novation.

5.38 Under the CRTPA 1999, a third party outside the agreement may initiate arbitration proceedings where it has a substantive right under the contract[41] or if the contract grants the third party such rights.[42] The latter of these rights of enforcement may equally be characterized as a requirement, under which the third party is required to submit disputes to arbitration.[43] Notably, even tortious disputes may fall within the CRTPA 1999's remit.[44]

5.39 Where the third party is a guarantor, surety or indemnifier[45] and the underlying contract (relating to the undertaking) contains an arbitration agreement, the CRTPA 1999 may or may not apply. Where the CRTPA 1999 applies, the guarantor is brought within the remit of the arbitration agreement. Where, however, the CRTPA 1999 does not apply, the arbitration agreement (and therefore award) will only be enforceable against the guarantor where the arbitration agreement makes express provision to that effect.[46] Further, it is worthy of note that the situation of guarantors in arbitration is also problematic with respect to issues of *lis pendens*: most guarantees allow creditors to enforce the guarantee directly against the guarantor without first obtaining an award against the principal debtor, thereby leaving open the possibility for conflicting court and arbitration decisions. Russell thus suggests that guarantees must be well drafted so as to (i) bring the guarantor within the arbitration agreement; and (ii) allow consolidation of proceedings under s35(1) of the Arbitration Act 1996.[47]

5.40 Assignment, by contrast, falls squarely within the definition of a 'party to an arbitration agreement' found in s 82(2) of the Arbitration Act 1996 provided the assignment is valid. Under English law, legal assignment is valid where both the parties and tribunal are notified of the assignment within a reasonable time,[48] and equitable assignment is valid where the parties are notified and the assignee submits to the tribunal's jurisdiction.[49] The arbitration agreement is thus binding on the assignee, who may then commence proceedings, join proceedings and also be bound by proceedings, unless the agreement states otherwise.[50]

5.41 A transferee under novation is not in effect a third party. Rather, when the transferee becomes substituted for the original party, a new contract is formed and new remedies may become available. In practice, however, this will most likely mean that the transferee may take the place of the original party in arbitration proceedings.[51]

---

41 Contract (Rights of Third Parties) Act 1999 s 1.

42 *ibid*, s 8(1).

43 *Nisshin Shipping Co Ltd v Cleaves & Co Ltd* [2003] EWHC 2602 (Comm), [2004] 1 All ER (Comm) 481.

44 Contract (Rights of Third Parties) Act 1999 s 8(2).

45 Hereinafter, the 'guarantor'.

46 *Re Kitchen, ex p Young* (1881) LR 17 Ch D 668; *Sabah Shipyard (Pakistan) Ltd v Government of Pakistan* [2008] 1 Lloyd's Rep 210; *Russell* (n 21) 3-015.

47 *Russell* (n 21) 3-015]

48 *The Republic of Kazakhstan v Istil Group Inc* [2006] EWHC 448 (Comm), [2006] 2 Lloyd's Rep 370.

49 *Baytur SA v Finagro Holding SA* [1992] QB 610 (CA).

50 *Shayler v Woolf* [1946] Ch 320 (CA).

51 *Charles M Willie & Co (Shipping) Ltd v Ocean Laser Shipping Ltd ('The Smaro')* [1999] 1 Lloyd's Rep 225 (Rix J).

5.42 **(6.1) What is the law/leading authorities' position on multi-party situations? Especially (i) with respect to the objection that the arbitration clause does not specifically provide for a plurality of parties in the same procedure; (ii) with respect to the constitution of the arbitral tribunal; and (iii) with respect to the consolidation of two or more running arbitration proceedings?** The Arbitration Act 1996 does not permit either the arbitral tribunal or the court to consolidate arbitration proceedings or order concurrent hearings, unless the parties have expressly so agreed.[52] Third parties not subject to the arbitration agreement may be joined to the proceedings by way of (a) the approval of the parties and, after the initiation of proceedings, the tribunal; or (b) an express provision in the agreement allowing such.[53]

5.43 Yet, a number of problems may arise to frustrate a multi-party arbitration or concurrent hearings; eg where the arbitration agreement fails to provide a mechanism for the appointment of the tribunal, the award may not be enforceable in other jurisdictions. One party may object to the introduction of additional parties (even where such is contemplated by the agreement) owing to concerns over additional costs and time. Further, additional parties may identify tactical advantages in remaining outside the confines of the arbitration. The joining of a third party also introduces potential confidentiality problems.

5.44 The scope of the arbitration agreement will therefore be of great importance, setting out in sufficient detail the procedure for and scope of multi-party disputes. This was illustrated in *City & General (Holborn) v AYH*.[54] There, the court recognized the need to avoid multiplicity of proceedings which carried the risk of excessive costs and inconsistent judgments.

5.45 **(6.2) Is there case law/authorities with respect to the admissibility of third party participation in an arbitration without being a claimant or defendant (Nebenintervention/Streitverkündung; intervention force/volontaire; vouching in; *amicus curiae* etc)? What are the prerequisites and effects of such participation (if permitted)?** Under s 37 of the Arbitration Act 1996, the arbitral tribunal may appoint non-parties to assist with the proceedings, specifically experts, legal advisers or technical assessors. The Arbitration Act does not provide for any other third party participation, subject of course to the express approval of both parties.[55]

(7) Termination of an arbitration agreement by a party (reasons and case law)

5.46 Given that arbitration is based on the consent of the parties, the parties may decide to terminate the arbitration agreement itself.[56] However, the enduring nature of an arbitration clause means that, even if parties decide to adopt a different mechanism for resolving a particular dispute which arises out of the contract, the arbitration agreement will nevertheless continue in force for subsequent disputes.

---

52 Arbitration Act 1996 s 35; *Elektrim SA v Vivendi Universal SA* [2007] EWHC 571 (Comm), [2007] 2 Lloyd's Rep 8; *Russell* (n 21) [3-048]-[3-050].

53 *The Bay Hotel and Resort Ltd v Cavalier Construction Co Ltd* [2001] UKPC 34.

54 *City & General (Holborn) Ltd v AYH Plc* [2005] EWHC 2494, [2006] BLR 55 (TCC).

55 Bellhouse, J. and Lavers, A., 'The Modern Amicus Curiae: a role for arbitration?' (2004) 23 *CJQ* 187.

56 Arbitration Act 1996 s 23(4).

An arbitration agreement may also come to an end where a party, expressly or impliedly, repudiates the agreement (by acting inconsistently with the agreement) and the other accepts the breach.[57] The repudiation must be clear and intentional to be effective.[58] In practice, however, in these circumstances the innocent party may seek a default award from the arbitrators, so that the issues cannot be reopened in another forum. **5.47**

Finally, in rare circumstances, the arbitration agreement may be found to have come to an end through abandonment,[59] in particular where there is a clear intention to abandon the arbitration agreement coupled with the other party's detrimental reliance.[60] **5.48**

B. Arbitrability

(1) 'Personal arbitrability' (capacity to conclude arbitration agreements)

Any natural or legal person who has the capacity to enter into a binding contract has the capacity to be a party to an arbitration. Broadly speaking, that is any adult of sound mind or a properly incorporated or established company or other legal entity. **5.49**

(1.1) May a state (or state agency) as party invoke sovereign immunity before the arbitral tribunal or before a state court (eg in a procedure of enforcement)? There is no general principle of English law that arbitrators are not entitled to deal with issues touching the interests of a state.[61] The English law is contained in the State Immunity Act 1978. Under s 1(1) of the State Immunity Act 1978, a State is generally immune from the jurisdiction of the UK courts, subject to the following exceptions: **5.50**

- (i) under s 2(1), a state is not immune if it has 'submitted' to the jurisdiction of the English courts, which can also be deemed by instituting a claim or intervening or taking another step in proceedings other than raising the immunity defence; and
- (ii) under s 9, which relates specifically to arbitrations, a state that has agreed in writing to submit a dispute to arbitration is deemed to have submitted to the jurisdiction of the UK courts for the purposes of proceedings relating to that arbitration (including enforcement proceedings).[62] This does not apply to arbitration agreements between states. Further, in *Svenska Petroleum v Lithuania (No 2)*[63] the Court of Appeal held that there was no general rule of international law that a state is bound by an arbitration clause only if it has given express consent to be so bound.

(2) 'Objective arbitrability' (eg of patent, trade mark and antitrust matters)

Arbitrability is the question of 'the susceptibility of a particular kind of dispute to a binding objective decision', and should not be confused with the question of what disputes fall **5.51**

---

[57] *Traube v Perelman* (Ch D 25 July 2001).

[58] *BEA Hotels NV v Bellway LLC* [2007] EWHC 1363 (Comm), [2007] 2 Lloyd's Rep 493.

[59] *Wakefield (Tower Hill Trinity Square) Trust v Janson Green Properties Ltd* [1998] EG 95 (CS) (Ch).

[60] *Shell International Petroleum Co Ltd v Coral Oil Co Ltd (No 1)* [1999] 1 Lloyd's Rep 72 (Comm).

[61] Mustill, M. and Boyd, S., *Commercial Arbitration: 2001 Companion Volume to the Second Edition* (Butterworths, London, 2001), 74.

[62] *Tsavliris Salvage (International) Ltd v The Grain Board of Iraq* [2008] EWHC 612 (Comm).

[63] *Svenska Petroleum Exploration AB v Republic of Lithuania (No 2)* [2006] EWCA Civ 1529, [2007] QB 886.

within the terms of an arbitration agreement (scope of agreement).[64] The Arbitration Act 1996 does not define 'a dispute not capable of settlement by arbitration', but it acknowledges the existence of such disputes in English law:

- in s1(b), the Act states the general proposition that parties may decide how to resolve their disputes except where public interest overrides;
- in s 81(1)(a), the Act allows the court to apply any rule of law concerning 'matters which are not capable of settlement by arbitration'; and
- in s103(3), the Act allows the court to refuse recognition and enforcement of a foreign arbitral award on the grounds that it concerns a matter not capable of settlement by arbitration.

5.52 Lord Mustill and Stewart Boyd QC discount the traditional notion that rights *in rem* are not arbitrable, instead defining objective arbitrability having regard to the commercial nature of arbitration. Thus, whilst the registration of (and disputes concerning the grant of) patents and trade marks are monopoly rights of the state and outside the scope of arbitration, disputes between, for example, licensors and licensees of IP rights are frequently referred to arbitration.[65]

5.53 Similarly, although EC competition law issues are a matter of English public policy,[66] they are also capable of resolution by arbitration but only as between the parties to the arbitration agreement and only if the competition law issues in question fall within the scope of the particular arbitration agreement.[67] In the event an arbitral tribunal does not take into account EC competition law where the matter in dispute may impinge thereon, the award may be unenforceable—even where the parties did not raise the issue during proceedings.[68]

C. Decision on the arbitral tribunal's jurisdiction ('*competence-competence*')

(1) Separability (independence of the arbitration agreement from the main agreement)

5.54 The arbitration agreement is both separate and different from the contract in which it is contained, which means that it will survive the termination or invalidity of the underlying contract. This is known as the doctrine of separability and is codified in s 7 of the Arbitration Act 1996.[69] The question for the court in deciding whether a dispute should be referred to arbitration is therefore whether the arbitration agreement itself has been impeached.

5.55 In *Fiona Trust*,[70] both the Court of Appeal and the House of Lords recognized and reaffirmed the principle of separability of an arbitration agreement in the context of invalidity

---

64 *Mustill and Boyd 2001* (n 61), 73.

65 Redfern and Hunter, *Law and Practice of International Commercial Arbitration (*4th edn, Sweet & Maxwell, London 2004), 139, citing Lew, '*Intellectual Property Disputes and Arbitration*', *Final Report of the Commission on International Arbitration* (ICC Publication 1997).

66 Case C-126/97 *Eco Swiss China Time Ltd v Benetton International NV* [1999] ECR I-3055.

67 See *ET Plus SA v Welter* [2005] EWHC 2115, [2006] 1 Lloyd's Rep 251 [51].

68 This problem has not yet been confronted by the English courts.

69 cf UNCITRAL Model Law Art 16(1).

70 See (n 36) and (n 20) respectively.

of the contract. Any allegation of invalidity would not prevent the invalidity issue being determined by an arbitrator.[71]

In *Heifer International v Christiansen*,[72] the court held that in circumstances where the provisions of an agreement have ended upon expiry of the contract, but the relationship between the parties continues thereafter, the separability of the arbitration agreement means that it would continue to take effect beyond that date. **5.56**

It is therefore only in very limited circumstances that an arbitration agreement will be potentially invalid, namely where the arbitration agreement itself is impeached[73] or if the existence of an arbitration agreement is disputed.[74] **5.57**

(2) Competence of the tribunal to decide on its own jurisdiction (including form and time of the tribunal's decision)

The principle of *Kompetenz-Kompetenz* represents the ability of the arbitral tribunal to rule on the question of whether it has jurisdiction. Section 30(1) of the Arbitration Act 1996 provides that an arbitral tribunal possesses the competence to determine 'its own substantive jurisdiction' on matters relating to the validity of the arbitration agreement, the proper constitution of the tribunal and the scope of the arbitration agreement. This power is, however, subject to challenge by any available arbitral process of appeal or review, or by the court in accordance with the relevant sections of the Arbitration Act 1996.[75] **5.58**

Under the Arbitration Act 1996 the arbitral tribunal also has the power 'to decide all procedural and evidential matters'.[76] Moreover, in the event a party defaults, the Arbitration Act 1996 provides that the tribunal may dismiss the claim, continue the proceedings in the absence of the defaulting party,[77] issue a peremptory order which prescribes the time limit within which the defaulting party must comply with the order,[78] and apply the default against the defaulting party. **5.59**

(3) Extent of the principle of 'Kompetenz-Kompetenz' *and role of the courts (including form and time limits of a challenge to the tribunal's decision)*

The Court of Appeal in *Fiona Trust*,[79] recognized that the Arbitration Act 1996 as a whole contemplates that, in general, it will be right for the arbitrators to be the first tribunal to consider whether it has jurisdiction to determine a dispute. The decision demonstrates that arbitrators will have the power to determine their own jurisdiction in almost all circumstances. **5.60**

---

[71] *Fiona Trust* (n 36 - CA) 22-31 (Longmore LJ); (n 20 - HL) 16-19 (Lord Hoffmann).
[72] (n 24).
[73] *Vee Networks Ltd v Econet Wireless International Ltd* [2004] EWHC 2909 (Comm), [2005] 1 All ER (Comm) 303.
[74] *Albon (t/a NA Carriage Co) v Naza Motor Trading Sdn Bhd (No 3)* [2007] EWHC 327 (Ch), [2007] 1 All ER (Comm) 813.
[75] Arbitration Act 1996 s 30(2); cf. UNCITRAL Model Law Art 16.
[76] Arbitration Act 1996 s 34(2)(a)-(h), (3).
[77] *ibid*, s 41(4)(a), (b).
[78] *ibid*, s 41(5).
[79] (n 36).

5.61 However, the Arbitration Act 1996 sets out a framework by which the substantive jurisdiction of the tribunal may be challenged. This makes it clear that an arbitral tribunal's power to decide the issues is still subject to challenge before the court in a number of ways and, as a result, under English law an arbitrator is still unable to determine conclusively his own jurisdiction.

5.62 The procedures for challenging the jurisdiction are as follows:

- by taking an objection to the tribunal that it lacks substantive jurisdiction under s 31 of the Arbitration Act 1996. The tribunal may rule on the objection,[80] though any award may be subsequently challenged by an application to the court under s 67(1) of the Arbitration Act 1996;
- by applying, with the agreement of the other parties or with the permission of the tribunal, for a preliminary ruling by the court as to the substantive jurisdiction of the tribunal in accordance with s 32 of the Arbitration Act 1996;[81]
- by resisting an application to enforce the award pursuant to s 66 of the Arbitration Act 1996, provided that the party's right to resist enforcement on that ground has not been lost or waived by participation in the arbitration itself, further to s 73; and
- by applying to the court for a declaration that the tribunal has no jurisdiction or for an injunction restraining the further conduct of the arbitration under s 72 of the Arbitration Act 1996.

D. Enforcement of an arbitration agreement within or by court proceedings

(1) Effect of invoking an arbitration clause within a court proceeding (and time limits for such a motion)

5.63 Under s9(4) of the Arbitration Act 1996, the English court must grant a stay of court proceedings on the application of a party to the arbitration agreement unless the court is satisfied that the arbitration agreement is 'null and void, inoperative, or incapable of being performed'. The stay is mandatory.[82]

5.64 The timing of the application is prescribed by s9(3). The application may not be made before the applicant has taken the appropriate steps to acknowledge the legal proceedings against him or after the applicant has taken any step in the proceedings to answer the substantive claim. By taking a substantive step in the proceedings, that applicant will be deemed to have submitted to the jurisdiction of the court and to have waived its right to invoke the court's jurisdiction to grant a stay under s 9(4) of the Act.

5.65 (1.1) **If a party has invoked successfully the arbitration agreement in a court proceeding, is it then entitled to deny within the arbitral proceeding that there is a valid and binding arbitration agreement?** No. As a matter of English law, such party would almost certainly be estopped from so doing and the arbitral tribunal would have jurisdiction to strike out a case pleaded on that basis. In addition, if the successful invocation of the arbitration

80 Arbitration Act 1996 s 30(1).
81 *ibid*, s 31(5).
82 *ibid*, s 4(1), sch 1.

agreement is reflected in an order of court terminating (or staying) the court process, such order may constitute *res judicata* as between the parties.

(1.2) Vice versa, if a party has successfully objected to an arbitral proceeding by denying that there is a valid arbitration agreement, may it then invoke such agreement in the ensuing court proceeding? No. The party would be estopped from so doing. See para 5.65 *supra*. 5.66

(2) Legal remedies and proceedings to enforce an arbitration agreement

The English court has jurisdiction to stay legal proceedings commenced in breach of an arbitration agreement,[83] as well as to issue an 'anti-suit injunction',[84] although there is no power to issue an anti-suit injunction where proceedings have been or are about to be brought in another court in the European Union or the European Free Trade Association.[85] 5.67

It is highly unlikely that the English court would make an order effectively compelling parties to arbitrate their dispute. Its only power is to stay its own proceedings, not to order the parties to arbitrate.[86] If both (or all) parties to an arbitration agreement refuse to arbitrate their dispute, such refusal probably constitutes a consensual abandonment of the arbitration reference. If one party to the agreement refuses to arbitrate then, in most circumstances, the appropriate tribunal will be constituted in default and will proceed with the arbitration in the absence of the non-participating party.[87] 5.68

Where the court grants a stay of legal proceedings, the arbitration must proceed. If the court grants an anti-suit injunction, the order will be binding. In the event that the breaching party takes no notice of the anti-suit injunction, the other party may also be able to recover damages.[88] 5.69

(2.1) Which would be the internationally competent court (i) for obtaining a declaration that an arbitration agreement is valid and binding, or (ii) to compel arbitration? (The defendant's courts? The courts of the place of arbitration? The claimant's courts, cf Article 6(2) in fine of the ICC Rules?) Under English law, the court considered most competent to make declarations on the validity of an arbitration agreement is that of the seat of the arbitration.[89] Nonetheless, the English court may also determine the existence and validity of an arbitration agreement governed by the procedural law of another country, particularly where recognition or enforcement of an arbitration award is sought in England under the New York Convention.[90] However, it would seem that declaratory relief is precluded if there is any prospect that judicial proceedings (possibly in breach of the arbitration clause) may be brought elsewhere in the EU or EFTA.[91] 5.70

---

83 Arbitration Act 1996 s 9.

84 Supreme Court Act 1981 s 37.

85 Case C-185/07 *Allianz SpA (formerly Riunione Adriatica di Sicurta SpA) v West Tankers Inc* [2009] 1 All ER (Comm) 435 (ECJ Grand Chamber).

86 cf UNCITRAL Model Law Art 8.1, where the courts may order the dispute to be arbitrated.

87 Arbitration Act 1996 ss 17, 18; LCIA Rules Art 5; ICC Rules Art 9.

88 *A v B (Costs)* [2007] EWHC 54 (Comm), [2007] 1 All ER (Comm) 633 [16].

89 Arbitration Act 1996 ss 31-2, 45, 67, 103(2)(f).

90 *Svenska* (n 63) 104 (Moore-Bick LJ).

91 Case C-185/07 *West Tankers* (n 85).

5.71 In contrast to the ICC Court's limited power to make a prima facie, non-binding assessment of the existence of the arbitration agreement,[92] the English court is empowered to make binding decisions on both the existence and the validity of an arbitration agreement, although, whenever possible, its decision is limited to the existence of the agreement.[93]

III. The arbitral tribunal*

A. Number and qualification of arbitrators

(1) Sole arbitrator or arbitral tribunal with several arbitrators

5.72 The basic principle underlying the statutory provisions is that of party autonomy. Accordingly, any relevant contractual provisions or rules relating to the number and qualification of arbitrators will be given full effect.

5.73 In the absence of any relevant agreement, s 15(3) of the Arbitration Act 1996 provides that the tribunal should consist of a single arbitrator. This 'presumption' in favour of a sole arbitrator reflects the policy of efficient and speedy arbitration, while at the same time recognizing that in some cases the nature of the dispute means that a three-man tribunal is appropriate. Where an arbitration agreement provides for an even number of arbitrators, it is to be read as requiring the appointment of an additional arbitrator as chairman unless otherwise agreed by the parties.[94]

5.74 **(1.1) Are arbitral tribunals with an even number of arbitrators acceptable?** Yes. Despite the presumption in favour of a tribunal with an odd number of arbitrators, the parties may choose to appoint an even number of arbitrators and an umpire, although such appointments are highly exceptional.[95] In arbitrations with two arbitrators and an umpire, the umpire takes over the tribunal's role and acts as a sole arbitrator in the event the arbitrators cannot reach agreement.[96]

(2) Qualification of the arbitrators

5.75 As with the number of arbitrators, the necessary qualifications of the tribunal depend upon the arbitration agreement, and when making any default appointment the court must have regard to any specified qualification.[97]

5.76 **(2.1) Are there mandatory requirements for the qualification of arbitrators (statutory requirements or indirect requirements through eg general conditions of insurance contracts)?** There are no mandatory requirements relating to the qualification of arbitrators,

---

[92] Derains, Y. and Schwarz, E., *A Guide to the ICC Rules of Arbitration* (2nd edn, Kluwer Law International, The Hague, 2005), 76-80.

[93] *Russell* (n 21) [7-025]-[7-036].

* The authors wish to thank Alex Kershaw, Associate, Commercial Risk and Reinsurance team, BLG, for his contribution to this section.

[94] Arbitration Act 1996 s 15(2).

[95] *ibid*, ss 15(1), 21. The parties may choose to appoint two arbitrators with no umpire or chairman and are free to agree how decisions are to be made: s 22.

[96] *ibid*, s 21(4), (5).

[97] *ibid*, s 19.

either as a matter of statute, common law, or practice. However, there are certain contractual formulae (eg 'commercial man' or 'current officer of an insurance or reinsurance company') which provide some guidance as to the particular requirements sought from an arbitrator and which the parties may, therefore, choose to adopt in their contract.

(2.2) Which national arbitration institutions may be contacted for obtaining information about qualified (and specialized) arbitrators? In the context of international arbitration in England, the two main bodies are the ICC and the LCIA. Addresses and contact numbers are given in the Appendix. **5.77**

(2.3) Are judges or civil servants required to obtain permission from their employer to act as arbitrator? Are these permissions given generally or case-by-case? What are the consequences if such permission has not been obtained? Section 93 of the Arbitration Act 1996 provides that a judge of the Commercial Court or of the Technology and Construction Court[98] may accept appointment as a sole arbitrator or as umpire. However, a judge shall not accept such an appointment unless the Lord Chief Justice has informed him that, having regard to the state of business in the courts, he can be made available. **5.78**

B. Appointment of arbitrators

(1) Extent of party autonomy to establish appointment procedure

Again, the procedure for appointment of a tribunal is, in the first instance, within the power of the parties to agree. The Arbitration Act 1996 was drafted with institutional appointments in mind, and arrangements for such appointments are fully recognized. **5.79**

(2) Procedure in absence of an agreement by the parties

In the absence of any agreement governing appointment, s 16 of the Arbitration Act 1996 sets out default provisions which regulate the appointment procedure for various types of tribunals, with time limits. Section 16 regulates tribunals up to three arbitrators or two arbitrators and an umpire. In any other case, s 18 of the Act applies to the appointment procedure.[99] **5.80**

In order to make an appointment, s 16 of the Act requires the service of a notice requesting the recipient to make an appointment. **5.81**

(3) Effect of the refusal of one party to cooperate in the constitution of the arbitral tribunal

If one party, having been notified of the other party's appointed arbitrator, refuses to cooperate in the appointment procedures by not appointing its own arbitrator, then s 17 of the Arbitration Act 1996 permits the other party to notify the defaulting party that it proposes its appointee to act as sole arbitrator. If within seven clear days of that notice being given, the defaulting party does not make the required appointment and fails to notify the other party that it has done so, the other party may appoint its arbitrator as sole arbitrator. This procedure is almost unique to England, and has given rise to concerns that an award **5.82**

---

[98] Technology and Construction Court Guide (2nd edn), s 18 <http://www.hmcourts-service.gov.uk/docs/tccguidefirstrevision.pdf> (accessed 10 March 2009). Judges of the Technology and Construction Court were called Official Referees until 1998, at which point they were given their current title.

[99] Arbitration Act 1996 s 16(7).

made by an arbitrator appointed in this way may not be enforceable in other jurisdictions.

5.83 Section 18 of the Arbitration Act 1996 then confers on the court a wide-ranging discretion to make default appointments in the event of a failure in the appointment procedure.

(4) Circumstances and valid reasons for an arbitrator to resign

5.84 The Arbitration Act 1996 does not specifically address the circumstances in which an arbitrator is entitled to resign. As a matter of English law, the resignation of the arbitrator is, in the absence of some express or implied contractual entitlement to resign, prima facie a breach of contract. Nevertheless, the 1996 DAC recognized that circumstances may well arise in which it would be reasonable for an arbitrator to wish to resign.[100] In such circumstances, the arbitrator may apply to the court under s 25 of the Arbitration Act 1996. The court may relieve the arbitrator if it is of the view that it was reasonable for him to resign.

C. Challenge and replacement of arbitrators

(1) Grounds, procedure and deadlines for challenging an arbitrator

5.85 The Arbitration Act 1996 recognizes that an arbitrator may be challenged and/or removed both by virtue of any relevant institutional rule and also by the court itself. The first avenue of recourse is always under any relevant institutional rules or agreement. Indeed, s 24 of the Arbitration Act 1996 expressly precludes the English court from exercising its own power of removal unless satisfied that the applicant has first exhausted any available recourse to the relevant arbitral institution.

5.86 Assuming there is no relevant contractual provision permitting removal or challenge, the grounds upon which the English court may remove an arbitrator are very limited and are exhaustively listed in s 24 of the Arbitration Act 1996. The grounds set out in s 24 are in some respects narrower than the UNCITRAL Model Law and the LCIA and ICC Rules.

5.87 As far as the procedure for a challenge is concerned, a party seeking the removal of an arbitrator must make an arbitration application to the court by means of an arbitration claim form. The application must be made as soon as the applicant becomes aware of grounds for doing so. A failure by the applicant to act immediately may give rise to a finding of waiver under s 73 of the Arbitration Act 1996.

5.88 **(1.1) Do state courts review challenge procedures which took place in accordance with a specific procedure agreed upon by the parties (eg ICC Rules Article 11)? If so, at what point in time? May such review be excluded?** The English courts do not review specific challenge procedures agreed upon by the parties, save to check that the parties have exhausted such procedures before applying to the court.[101] The application to the court to remove the arbitrator must be made promptly after the specified procedure has concluded.[102] The court's power to remove an arbitrator may not be excluded by the parties as

---

[100] 1996 DAC (n 3) 111-15

[101] Arbitration Act 1996 s 24(2); see para 5.85 *supra*.

[102] See para 5.87 *supra*.

s 24 is a mandatory provision and, thus, applies to all arbitrations with their seat in England.[103]

(1.2) Is there case law with respect to truncated arbitral tribunals? (cf ICC Rules Article 12(5)) Although the provision in Art 12(5) of the ICC Rules for the establishment of a 'truncated tribunal' should in principle be recognized by English law as a valid consensual method of continuing an arbitration speedily and efficiently, there is as yet no case law confirming this. **5.89**

(2) Procedure for appointing a new arbitrator

Section 27 of the Arbitration Act 1996 provides that the parties are free to agree whether (and if so how) any vacancy on the arbitral tribunal should be filled, whether the proceedings should stand and what the effect should be on any appointments which have been made by the arbitrator who has ceased to hold office (for whatever reason). By appointing an arbitration institution, the parties will often have implicitly incorporated a procedure for the appointment of a new arbitrator. If there is no such agreement, s 27 provides that the provisions of ss 16 and 18 of the 1996 Act shall apply to govern the appointment of a replacement tribunal. **5.90**

IV. The arbitral procedure*

A. General principles

(1) Extent of party autonomy to determine the arbitral procedure

The parties' autonomy to determine the arbitral procedure relevant to their dispute is a basic principle of English arbitration law. This principle is stated in s 1(b) of the Arbitration Act 1996. **5.91**

English law, however, recognizes two major limitations to party autonomy over procedural matters in English arbitrations. The first is found in s 34 of the Arbitration Act 1996, which provides that matters of evidence and procedure are to be determined by the arbitrators, subject to the right of the parties to agree on any matter. The second limitation to party autonomy found in the Arbitration Act 1996 is the 'mandatory provisions' listed in Sch 1.[104] **5.92**

Finally, the parties are not free to confer powers upon an arbitral tribunal that would cause the arbitration to be conducted in a manner contrary to the mandatory provisions of the law or the public policy of the state in which the arbitration is held. **5.93**

(1.1) Are the parties free to choose any national or international law governing the procedure before the arbitral tribunal? The Arbitration Act 1996 implicitly permits the **5.94**

---

[103] Arbitration Act 1996 sch 1.

* The authors wish to thank Lyall Hickson, Associate (admitted in Australia), Marine, Energy & Trade team, BLG, and Jennifer Salmon, Associate, Marine, Energy & Trade team, BLG, for their contribution to this section.

[104] Introduced by Arbitration Act 1996 s 4(1).

parties to choose some other national or international law as the curial law[105] by virtue of s 4(5).

(2) Basic procedural principles or mandatory rules to be applied by the arbitral tribunal

5.95 The overriding procedural principle that guides all arbitrations in England is the mandatory provision found at s 33 of the Arbitration Act 1996.[106] It provides that arbitrators must act fairly and impartially, and adopt suitable procedures for the fair and timely resolution of the dispute.[107]

5.96 Of course, the other mandatory provisions listed in Sch 1 of the Act must be respected in all arbitrations with their seat in England, Wales and Northern Ireland.[108]

5.97 Some of the key mandatory provisions are listed below:

- ss 9-11: power of the court to stay legal proceedings;
- s 24: power of the court to remove an arbitrator;
- s 31: objections to the tribunal's substantive jurisdiction;
- ss 33 and 40: general duties of the tribunal and the parties;
- s 66: power of the court to enforce an award; and
- s 73: loss of a party's right to object.

5.98 In addition, under s 40 of the Arbitration Act 1996, the parties are obliged to further the fair and speedy resolution of the dispute.

(3) Oral hearing or proceeding on basis of written documents

5.99 Section 34(2)(h) lists the issue of 'whether and to what extent there should be oral or written evidence or submissions' as an example of the type of matter the tribunal can decide upon. Furthermore, the tribunal must proceed to make its award without a hearing if the parties have expressly so agreed. There are, however, many examples of documents-only arbitrations in the international context, such as charterparty disputes conducted by the London Maritime Arbitrators Association (LMAA). Whilst not usual practice, the arbitrator can order a 'documents-only' hearing if suitable.

(4) Power of the tribunal (in particular the chairman) to issue procedural orders

5.100 The power of a tribunal to issue procedural directions and orders is conferred by s 34 of the Arbitration Act 1996, with a corresponding duty on the parties to comply with directions. It is generally accepted that directions may be given in respect of any matter which the arbitrators have power to determine. The tribunal also has statutory powers under the Arbitration Act 1996 to order security for costs[109] and to obtain evidence.[110]

---

[105] Curial law refers to the law governing the arbitral proceedings and is different from substantive law, which refers to the law governing the contract which is the subject of the dispute.

[106] Arbitration Act 1996 sch 1.

[107] *ibid*, s 33(1)(a), (b).

[108] *ibid*, sch 1.

[109] *ibid*, s 38(3).

[110] *ibid*, s 38(4)–(6).

Like the other arbitrators, subject to the parties' contrary agreement, the chairman may participate in all directions, orders and awards. Where, however, there is neither unanimity nor a majority in the making of a direction, order or award, the Arbitration Act 1996 provides that the chairman's opinion prevails.[111] **5.101**

(5) Distinction of matters of substance and matters of procedure

As far as English law is concerned, matters of procedure are governed by the law of the seat. **5.102** In the rare instance where an arbitration clause provides for the seat in England but a foreign procedural law, the mandatory provisions of the Arbitration Act 1996 still apply.[112] Matters of substance are governed by the law applicable to the substantive dispute as determined by the tribunal. In order to differentiate between the two, one must consider the purpose of the distinction and its consequences.

(5.1) Are the statutes of limitations a matter of substance or procedure? Under English **5.103** common law, issues of limitation are generally procedural rather than substantive and, accordingly, tend to bar a remedy rather than extinguish a right.[113] Where English law governs a contract, the domestic limitation periods will be applied.[114] However, where a contract is governed by a foreign law, the limitation rules of the foreign law generally will be applied, not domestic limitation rules.[115] The foreign law on limitation will not, however, be applied to the extent that it would violate English public policy by causing undue hardship to a (potential) party.[116] In such circumstances, domestic law on limitation would apply.

(6) Persons able to represent a party in an arbitral proceeding

Under s 36 of the Arbitration Act 1996, there are no restrictions upon a party's choice of **5.104** representatives, whether a lawyer or not, unless the parties have agreed otherwise.

B. Place of arbitration

(1) Determination of the seat of the arbitration in absence of an agreement by the parties

Where the seat of the arbitration is not specified, the seat may be determined by reference **5.105** to a provision regarding (i) the procedural law governing the arbitration agreement; (ii) the location where the arbitration is to take place;[117] or (iii) the governing law of the arbitration

---

[111] Arbitration Act 1996 s 20.

[112] *ibid*, s 4(1), (5), sch 1.

[113] Although some limitation provisions of the Limitation Act 1980 may be considered substantive as they extinguish the title of the former owner in certain property matters, eg ss 3(2), 17; Collins, L. *et al* (eds), *Dicey, Morris and Collins on the Conflict of Laws* (14th edn, Sweet & Maxwell, London, 2006) 7-045.

[114] Limitation Act 1980; *Dicey and Morris* (n 113) 7-045–7-046.

[115] Foreign Limitation Periods Act 1984 s 1 and the Rome Convention (Convention on the law applicable to contractual obligations 1980, implemented by the Contracts (Applicable Law) Act 1990 sch 1) Art 10(1)(d), Rome I Regulation (Regulation 593/2008 on the law applicable to contractual obligations, coming into force 17 December 2009) Art 12(1)(d) and Rome II Regulation (Regulation 864/2007 on the law applicable to non-contractual obligations) Art 15(h).

[116] Foreign Limitation Periods Act 1984 s 2. A public policy ('*ordre public*') exception also exists in the Rome Convention (n 115) Art 16, Rome I Regulation (n 115) Art 21 and Rome II Regulation (n 115) Art 26.

[117] *ABB Lummus Global Ltd v Keppel Fels Ltd* [1999] 2 Lloyd's Rep 24 (Comm).

agreement;[118] or, by 'having regard to the parties agreement and all the relevant circumstances'.[119] In determining the seat through 'relevant circumstances', the court will examine any connections with one or more countries identified in relation to (i) the parties; (ii) the dispute which will be the subject of the arbitration; (iii) the proposed procedures in the arbitration; and/or (iv) the issue of the award or awards, which were in existence when the arbitration was commenced.[120]

(2) Importance and legal effect of the seat of the arbitration

5.106 Although an arbitration agreement must have a seat, the seat does not have to be specified explicitly in the contract. Section 3 of the Arbitration Act 1996 defines the seat of the arbitration as the 'juridical seat', ie the legal—rather than the physical—place of the arbitration.[121] If the seat of an arbitration is in England or Wales, the arbitration will be subject to the supervision of the English courts. [122] It has recently been held that where an arbitration agreement is contained in a contract and no curial law is specified for the arbitration agreement, the curial law of the arbitration will be that of the seat of the arbitration.[123]

5.107 Determination of the seat will also have implications for the enforceability of an award. The United Kingdom has been a signatory to the New York Convention since 1975 and therefore awards made in England and Wales can be enforced outside the jurisdiction pursuant to the Convention.[124] The seat is also important for the purpose of determining whether a foreign award may be enforced in England and Wales as a New York Convention award.[125]

5.108 (2.1) **Are the arbitrators and parties free to convene at places other than the official seat of the arbitration?** Section 34(2)(a) of the Arbitration Act 1996 gives the tribunal the freedom to decide where any part of the proceedings is to be held, subject to the right of the parties to agree on the matter. Holding the proceedings elsewhere will not change the seat, which, once determined, can only be altered by the express agreement of the parties.[126]

5.109 (2.2) **Are there visa requirements to enter the country which apply to lawyers and/or arbitrators? Where may current information on that subject be obtained?** Please refer to your local British consular authorities for any specific visa requirements. General information is available online at the UK Border Agency website, accessible at <http://www.ukvisas.gov.uk>.[127]

---

118 *Egon Oldendorff v Libera Corp (No 1)* [1995] 2 Lloyd's Rep 64 (Comm).
119 Arbitration Act 1996 s 3.
120 *Dubai Islamic Bank v Paymentech* (n 17), 73-4.
121 *Braes of Doune Wind Farm (Scotland) Ltd v Alfred McAlpine Business Services Ltd* [2008] EWHC 426 (TCC), [2008] 2 All ER (Comm) 493.
122 Arbitration Act 1996 ss 2, 4(5).
123 *C v D* [2007] EWCA Civ 1282, [2008] 1 All ER (Comm) 1001.
124 Arbitration Act 1996 s 53.
125 *ibid*, Pt III.
126 *Union of India v McDonnell Douglas Corp* [1993] 2 Lloyd's Rep 48 (Comm).
127 (Accessed 3 November 2008).

C. Submissions, deadlines and default

(1) Contents and form of submissions (in particular request for arbitration and answer to request)

The accepted practice in arbitrations held in England is for submissions to be in writing. However, there are no hard and fast rules, and certainly the law does not dictate a specific form that submissions must be in. Section 34(2)(c) gives the tribunal the power to decide 'whether any and if so what form of written statements of claim and defence are to be used, when these should be supplied and the extent to which such statements may be either formal or informal'. However, some institutional rules provide specific guidelines for the content and style of submissions in arbitrations. **5.110**

(1.1) From what point in time is a claim considered to be pending with the arbitral tribunal? What are the legal effects of such fact (eg on statutes of limitations)? The Arbitration Act 1996 deals with the situation when an arbitration is deemed commenced, which has implications for limitation periods. Section 14 of the Arbitration Act 1996 allows the parties to agree when proceedings are regarded as having been commenced for the purposes of all of the provisions of the Act, as well as for the purposes of the Limitation Acts,[128] including the Foreign Limitation Periods Act 1984.[129] However, in the absence of such an agreement, s 14 provides that where the arbitrator is named or designated in the arbitration agreement, arbitral proceedings are commenced when one party serves on the other party a notice in writing requiring him to submit that matter to the person so named or designated.[130] Where the arbitrator(s) needs to be chosen and appointed, arbitral proceedings are commenced when one party serves on the other party notice in writing requiring him to appoint an arbitrator or to agree to the appointment of an arbitrator.[131] Finally, where the arbitrator or arbitrators are to be appointed by a person other than a party to the proceedings, arbitral proceedings are commenced when one party gives notice in writing to that person requesting him to make the appointment.[132] It is also noted that if the arbitration clause refers to institutional rules, the arbitration proceedings must be commenced in accordance with those rules. **5.111**

(1.2) When is a time limit according to statutes of limitations deemed to be interrupted in case of (i) *ad hoc*; and (ii) institutional arbitration? Section 13 of the Arbitration Act makes specific provision for the interruption of time for the purposes of limitation periods, and provides the court with a discretion to exclude the time between the commencement of an arbitration and an award that the court orders to be set aside or declared to have no effect. It follows that time limits can be interrupted in England if an award or part thereof is subsequently overturned. These rules apply generally to both *ad hoc* and institutional arbitrations, and the Arbitration Act 1996 does not envisage any other situation in which the time limits for the statute of limitations may be interrupted. **5.112**

128 Arbitration Act 1996 s 13(4).
129 *ibid*, s 13(4)(a).
130 *ibid*, s 14(3).
131 *ibid*, s 14(4).
132 *ibid*, s 14(5).

5.113 (1.3) **What is the effect of the withdrawal of the request for arbitration?** The Arbitration Act 1996 does not explicitly address the effect of withdrawing the request for arbitration. Tribunals tend to be more lenient on extensions of time than is the court. Given, however, that the arbitration agreement continues in force unless expressly terminated by the parties, the withdrawal of a request for arbitration has no effect on the arbitration agreement itself.[133] Thus, unless the dispute is settled or the statue of limitations has expired, the dispute remains susceptible to arbitration.

(2) Legal deadlines (provided by law or set by the tribunal) and effect of non-compliance by a party

5.114 The Arbitration Act 1996 gives a discretionary power to the tribunal, subject to the parties' contrary agreement, to fix or extend the time within which to comply with any directions it gives.[134] Generally, when a party defaults there are no immediate statutory effects and the tribunal is unlikely to impose sanctions. In practice, the parties agree on an extension of time and inform the tribunal.

5.115 (2.1) **What are the powers of the tribunal if a party fails to comply with the time limits set up by the tribunal?** The Arbitration Act 1996 provides that the parties are free to agree the extent of the tribunal's powers in the event of non-compliance with time limits. Thus, where the parties agree to the rules of an arbitral institution, the institution's provisions for delay and failure to adhere to deadlines will apply against the parties.

5.116 In the absence of such agreement, however, the Arbitration Act 1996 provides a series of default powers to the tribunal. First, the tribunal may extend the time for compliance under s 34(3). Secondly, if the delay is such that the arbitrators conclude that the parties in fact have decided to bring the arbitration agreement itself to an end, or if the claimant has lost its right to proceed, then the arbitrators may decline jurisdiction on the basis of s 30. Third, where the claimant's delay is inordinate and inexcusable and this impedes the fair hearing of the claim, the arbitrators may dismiss the claim altogether.[135] Fourth, the arbitrators may continue with the proceedings and/or issue the award where a party has not complied with the submission of written evidence or submissions.[136] Fifth, the arbitrators may make a peremptory order against the defaulting party, non-compliance with which empowers the tribunal to either seek the court's enforcement of the peremptory order,[137] or to proceed with the arbitration by taking the non-compliance into account, whether by disregarding the subject matter of the order in the proceedings and/or award, drawing adverse inferences from the non-compliance, or reflecting the non-compliance in the costs.[138]

5.117 (2.2) **Is the tribunal bound by any mandatory time limits for certain procedural steps (eg hearings, making of an award)?** The tribunal has a general duty under s 33 of the

---

133 Arbitration Act 1996 ss 6-8.
134 *ibid*, s 34(3).
135 *ibid*, s 41(3).
136 *ibid*, s 41(4).
137 *ibid*, s 42(2)(a).
138 *ibid*, s 41(5), (7).

Arbitration Act 1996 to adopt procedures that are suitable to the dispute and to avoid unnecessary delay and expense. The Arbitration Act 1996 does not, however, impose any specific mandatory time limits on the tribunal.

Nonetheless, many of the institutional rules adhere to specific time limits for hearing dates or awards. However, it is important to note that there is a statutory right to extend time for making an award under the Arbitration Act 1996.[139] **5.118**

(3) Statutory requirements as to the notifications during an arbitration (with respect to the request for arbitration and other written pleadings; with respect to notifications by the tribunal)

The Arbitration Act 1996 provides some default provisions that apply in the absence of the parties agreeing on an effective mode of serving notifications/pleadings. Section 76 details that, in the absence of agreement, documents or notices can be served by any 'effective means'. For institutional arbitrations, the rules will generally provide for the requirements for effective service of notifications. **5.119**

(4) Effect of insolvency of a party

It is widely accepted that insolvency does not affect the ability of a party to proceed with arbitration against the affected party *per se*. However, in the case of a company that is wound up or subject to an Administration Order in England, there will be an automatic moratorium on all legal process, including arbitration.[140] A party wishing to commence or continue arbitration in these circumstances needs to seek leave of the administrator/liquidator or of the court in the absence of consent by the administrator/liquidator. **5.120**

Further, it is also possible for the insolvency of a foreign party to affect an English arbitration. Specifically, Art 4(2)(e) of EC Regulation on Insolvency Proceedings 1346/2000 provides that the law of the state in which proceedings are opened is that which governs 'the effects of insolvency proceedings'. **5.121**

D. Facts and evidence: general

(1) Burden of proof (inquisitorial/adversarial procedure)

A party asserting any fact has the burden of proving it by adducing appropriate evidence before the tribunal. Findings of fact on which an award is based can be challenged as errors of law if they are not based on evidence.[141] **5.122**

Arbitrators have the freedom to determine procedural matters, including whether and to what extent the tribunal should take the initiative itself in ascertaining the facts and the law, subject to any agreement by the parties.[142] This allows the tribunal to decide to adopt an inquisitorial approach if it considers that this is appropriate. However, when adopting an inquisitorial approach, the tribunal should be conscious of its duty to allow each side to put **5.123**

---

[139] Arbitration Act 1996 s 50.

[140] In administration, Insolvency Act 1986 sch B1 [43(6)] as inserted by the Enterprise Act 2002 sch 16; and in liquidation, Insolvency Act 1986 s 130.

[141] Arbitration Act 1996 s 69.

[142] *ibid*, ss 34(1), 34(2)(g).

its case.[143] It should be noted that England and Wales have a strong adversarial tradition in dispute resolution. If the parties wish the inquisitorial procedure to be used, they would be wise to state this expressly in the arbitration agreement.

(2) Power of the tribunal to determine the admissibility and weight of the evidence produced by the parties

5.124 The tribunal is free to decide on procedural rules as to admissibility and weight in the absence of stipulation by the parties, subject only to the arbitrators' general duty set out in s33 of the Arbitration Act 1996.[144] If arbitrators fail to admit admissible evidence, this can be regarded as an error of law but one which is unlikely to be a sufficient ground for an award to be set aside.[145] However, this may be sufficient for an appeal if the evidence is critical to the dispute.[146] If the arbitrators admit evidence which would be inadmissible under the English law of evidence, there is little the parties can do to challenge this as the arbitrators' discretion is subject only to s 33 of the Act. As concerns the question of the weight to attach to evidence, the arbitrators have complete discretion subject again to s 33.[147]

5.125 (2.1) **Is the tribunal entitled to take the claimant's factual allegation as proven if the defendant does not participate in the arbitral proceedings?** The arbitrator's overriding duty to act fairly[148] means that the failure by one side to present evidence does not allow the tribunal to find in favour of the participating party on that basis alone. However, the tribunal is able to carry on with proceedings in the absence of one of the parties if that party fails without sufficient cause to attend or be represented.[149]

5.126 In circumstances where a party is absent from the proceedings, the tribunal may make findings on the basis of the evidence which is before it, which may include evidence submitted by the absent party prior to the hearing. The arbitrator should give the absent party notice that he intends to proceed in their absence before doing so.[150]

5.127 (2.2) **May the arbitral tribunal consider an allegation of one party as agreed fact if the other party did not (specifically) dispute the allegation?** The failure of one party to dispute an allegation cannot be taken as agreement with it. Any evidence adduced in support of such an allegation may well be all that is available to the tribunal and should therefore be scrutinized carefully. Only if it is sufficient to support the facts asserted may the tribunal find in that party's favour.

5.128 (2.3) **What is the standard of proof that must be met in order for a fact to be considered to have been established (preponderance of the evidence; beyond reasonable doubt)? Must a stringent requirement be met for certain facts?** The standard of proof for arbitrations with their seat in England and Wales is not prescribed by law and is usually left to

143 Arbitration Act 1996 s 33(1)(a).
144 *ibid*, s 34(2)(f).
145 *ibid*, s 69.
146 *Fairclough Building Ltd v Vale of Belvoir Superstore Ltd* (1990) 56 BLR 74 (QB).
147 Cross, R. and Tapper, C., *Cross and Tapper on Evidence* (OUP, Oxford, 2007).
148 Arbitration Act 1996 s 33(1)(a).
149 *ibid*, s 41(4).
150 *Owners of the MV Myron v Tradax Export SA ('The Myron')* [1970] 1 QB 527 (Comm).

the tribunal to decide. However, it is not unusual for the English law civil standard of proof to be applied, that is, a party must prove facts on the balance of probabilities. Where there is conflicting and equally convincing evidence presented by both sides in relation to a fact, it is the duty of the tribunal to consider that it has not been proved.[151] In general, the standard of proof, once set, does not vary. However, it has been suggested that a higher standard of proof should be set where allegations of fraud are made.[152]

(2.4) **May the arbitral tribunal rely on its own knowledge to consider certain facts as proven?** The specialist knowledge of the tribunal in relation to the subject matter of the dispute is often considered a powerful factor in persuading parties to choose arbitration as a method of dispute resolution. However, an arbitrator is clearly obliged to base his decision on the evidence before him. English courts have resolved these conflicting factors to conclude that the arbitrator may use information that it could reasonably be expected that a person possessing the qualifications/qualities required of him under the arbitration agreement would have. However, he cannot use his own knowledge to provide evidence not introduced by the parties or to derogate from the evidence of a party's experts without telling the parties and allowing them to respond.[153] **5.129**

E. Witnesses

(1) Ability of a person to act as a witness

The Arbitration Act 1996 makes no specific provision concerning the capacity of an individual to act as a witness in arbitration proceedings. **5.130**

(1.1) **Is there a legal difference between a party testifying and a witness? If yes, what are the criteria for such differentiation? Does the testifying of a party have the same weight as a witness testimony?** There is no legal difference between evidence given by a party and that given by a witness. The LCIA Rules provide that an individual testifying before a tribunal will be treated as a witness notwithstanding that they are a party to the arbitration.[154] However, the testimony of an independent witness is likely to carry more weight than the testimony of a party. **5.131**

(2) Preparation of witnesses and limits thereof

The limits to the preparation of witnesses is not addressed in the Arbitration Act 1996, but rather in the Codes of Conduct for barristers and solicitors.[155] These codes, which are similar in effect, provide that neither barristers nor solicitors may seek to influence a witness. Witnesses may, however, be familiarized with the process of giving evidence, provided the issue in dispute is not addressed, the process is supervised or conducted by someone experienced with the process and without personal knowledge of the events in issue, and records **5.132**

---

[151] *Montedipe SpA v JTP-RO Jugotanker ('The Jordan Nicolov')* [1990] 2 Lloyd's Rep 11 (Comm).
[152] *Redfern and Hunter* (n 65) 6-68.
[153] *Checkpoint Ltd v Strathclyde Pension Fund* [2003] EWCA Civ 84, [2003] L & TR 22.
[154] LCIA Rules Art 20.7.
[155] *The Code of Conduct of the Bar of England and Wales* (8th edn, Bar Council, 2004). *The Solicitors' Code of Conduct 2007* (revised edn, The Law Society, 29 June 2007) <http://www.rules.sra.org.uk> (accessed 10 November 2008).

are maintained.[156] Further, before proceedings witnesses may be provided copies of their witness statement(s) and corresponding supporting documents, but may not review any other witnesses' statements.[157]

5.133 **(2.1) Do US style depositions violate any procedural rules and principles?** US style depositions do not violate any procedural rules or principles, however they are rarely used. A deposition will only be required where it is appropriate under English law and where it is necessary for the purpose of establishing information.[158]

5.134 **(2.2) May a party or its counsel approach a witness whom it has nominated (only before or also after the proceedings have started)? Are interviews permitted?** Before proceedings have commenced, no rule of arbitration law specifically precludes discussions between a party or its counsel and a witness.[159] English barristers and solicitors must not, however, breach the rules of professional conduct which preclude any sort of 'coaching' of witnesses.[160] Once proceedings have started and the witness has begun giving evidence, it is generally accepted that he should not discuss the case with anyone until his evidence is complete.[161]

(3) Admissibility of written witness statements

5.135 In the absence of agreement between the parties, it is again within the domain of the tribunal to decide issues of the admissibility of witness statements.[162] In the case of institutional arbitrations, such as the LCIA, it is contemplated that the testimony of a witness may be presented by a party in written form, either as a signed statement or as a sworn affidavit.[163]

5.136 **(3.1) If the parties agree on written statements, is a party entitled to request an oral hearing for questioning those witnesses (provided such right has not been agreed upon)?** A party can always request an oral hearing even if this has not been expressly agreed between the parties, as the tribunal has the discretion to decide whether an oral hearing is necessary pursuant to s 34 of the Arbitration Act 1996. However, if the parties have agreed on a 'documents only' arbitration, the arbitrators have no power to require them to provide oral evidence.

(4) Entitlement of a party to have a hearing or cross-examination of witnesses

5.137 Again, the tribunal has power to decide, in the absence of party agreement, whether to permit a hearing or cross-examination of a witness. For institutional arbitrations, such as the LCIA, there is a right of the parties to have an oral hearing if they so request, subject to agreed 'documents only' arbitrations.[164] Furthermore, the institutional rules also provide

---

156 *R v Momodou and Limani* [2005] EWCA Crim 177, [2005] 2 All ER 571 [61]-[5].

157 *R v Richardson* [1971] 2 QB 484 (CA), 490–1.

158 *Commerce & Industry Insurance Co (Canada) v Lloyd's Underwriters* [2002] 1 WLR 1323 (Comm).

159 *Bar Code of Conduct* (n 155) s 3 [6.2.1]-[7].

160 *ibid*, (n 155) s 1 [705(a)]; *Solicitors' Code of Conduct* (n 155) [11.01(1)] and Guidance Notes to Rule 11 [12(e)(f), 18].

161 *Bar Code of Conduct* (n 155) s 1, Pt VII [705(c)].

162 Arbitration Act 1996 s 34.

163 LCIA Rules Art 20.3.

164 *ibid*, 19.1.

permission for cross-examination of witnesses and also permit the tribunal to question the witness.[165]

(4.1) Which are the methods used to establish a record of the arbitral proceedings, in particular witness examinations (tape recording, verbatim court reporters, dictated minutes, other methods)? A record of the arbitral proceedings can be established through any of the above methods. In practice, the use of a transcript service is most common. The tribunal and the parties' legal representatives will also usually take detailed notes of the proceedings. **5.138**

(4.2) May the arbitral tribunal take an oath from a witness? Subject to the parties agreeing otherwise, s 38(5) of the Arbitration Act 1996 provides that the arbitral tribunal may direct that a party or witness be examined on oath or affirmation. **5.139**

(4.3) Does the arbitral tribunal have the power to compel witnesses? The arbitral tribunal does not have the power to compel the attendance of witnesses. Rather, a party may use the same court procedures that are available in legal proceedings to compel the attendance of a witness, subject to permission being granted by the tribunal or following the agreement of the parties. However, the court procedures may only be used if the witness is in the United Kingdom and the arbitral proceedings are being conducted in the United Kingdom. **5.140**

F. Documents

(1) Form and kind of documents to be presented to the arbitral tribunal

The tribunal has wide powers to decide whether any, and if so which, documents or classes of documents should be disclosed between and produced by the parties and at what stage.[166] The tribunal's powers, as in all procedural matters, are subject to any contrary agreement made by the parties. **5.141**

(1.1) Is the submission of 'agreed documents' permitted? If yes, what is the extent and effect of such an agreement of the parties (authenticity, existence, acknowledgement of such documents' contents)? Yes. Agreed documents refers to the parties' agreement as to the documents' authenticity (and thus existence), but 'does not involve any agreement as to their admissibility'.[167] **5.142**

(1.2) How may electronic documents (eg emails) be presented and proven? Relevant electronic documents are a major component of any party's disclosure nowadays. The procedure for the submission of these is at the discretion of the tribunal. Usually these documents would be printed out and submitted to the tribunal along with paper documents in the arbitration hearing bundles. **5.143**

(1.3) Does discovery (US or UK style), after the procedure has started, violate any procedural rules or public policy considerations? No. Subject to the parties' contrary **5.144**

---

165 LCIA Rules Art 20.5.
166 Arbitration Act 1996 s 34(2)(d).
167 *Mustill and Boyd 2001* (n 61), 355.

agreement, the tribunal determines all aspects of disclosure, including whether late disclosure is permitted.[168] In so deciding, the tribunal must balance the value of hearing relevant evidence against the prejudice suffered by the other party.

(2) Requirement to produce certain documents (as requested by the tribunal) and consequences of a failure to do so

5.145 As is the case when a party fails to comply with any order made by the tribunal, the arbitrator can make a peremptory order (an order requiring compliance with the tribunal's previous order within a specified time).[169] Remedies are available should the defaulting party fail to comply with the peremptory order.[170] This can be enforced by an application to the court made by the tribunal itself or by one of the parties with the permission of the tribunal.[171]

5.146 Where non-compliance with the tribunal's peremptory order occurs, the tribunal may order that the party may not rely on the documents covered by the order, may draw appropriate adverse inferences, may proceed to make an award without the evidence and/or may oblige the defaulting party to pay any costs incurred as a result of its default.[172]

5.147 (2.1) **Which documents may the tribunal request to be produced (eg also documents which are in the possession of third parties)?** The tribunal has no power to require the production of documents by third parties. However the court is empowered to make such an order and the tribunal may consider it helpful to remind the parties that they may request such an order from the court.[173] A court order is likely only to be made where a legal ground for disclosure can be made out.[174]

(3) Protection of the confidentiality of documents (legal privilege etc)

5.148 Although not expressly stated in the Arbitration Act 1996, there is an implied obligation of confidentiality. No document disclosed in the arbitration may be used by any party for any purpose other than the arbitration without the permission of the other party or pursuant to a court order, with the exception of documents already in the public domain.[175]

5.149 Documents which English law regards as privileged will be protected from inspection by the other side. Privileged documents include those containing legal advice and those brought into existence after litigation is contemplated or commenced and whose sole or dominant purpose is to provide advice in relation to the litigation or to gather evidence for it.[176] Without prejudice communications between the parties will also be exempt from disclosure.

---

168 Arbitration Act 1996 s 34(1), (2)(d).
169 *ibid*, s 41(5), 40(2)(a).
170 *ibid*, s 41(7).
171 *ibid*, s 42.
172 *ibid*, s 41(7).
173 *ibid*, s 43.
174 *Aoot Kalmneft v Denton Wilde Sapte* [2002] 1 Lloyd's Rep 417 (Mercantile).
175 *Hassneh Insurance Co of Israel v Mew* [1993] 2 Lloyd's Rep 243 (Comm).
176 Passmore, C., *Privilege* (2nd edn, XPL Publishing, St Albans, 2006); *Emmott v Michael Wilson and Partners Ltd* [2008] EWCA Civ 184, [2008] 1 Lloyd's Rep 616.

G. Experts

(1) Appointment and presentation of experts by the party or the arbitral tribunal

As with judicial proceedings, the parties are usually allowed to introduce expert evidence/testimony, ie expert witnesses, in an arbitration. Further, the Arbitration Act 1996 empowers the tribunal to appoint experts or legal advisers to report to it and appoint assessors to assist it on technical matters. In addition, the rules of many institutions also confer powers upon arbitrators.[177] **5.150**

The actual presentation of expert evidence—whether from a party-appointed or tribunal-appointed expert—is ultimately in the hands of the tribunal. With respect to party-appointed expert witnesses, the usual method is for exchange of written reports followed by an oral hearing with cross-examination. With respect to tribunal-appointed experts, s37(1)(a)(ii) empowers the tribunal to allow the expert to attend the proceedings and give evidence. The parties must be permitted to comment on the 'information, opinion or advice' provided by the tribunal-appointed expert.[178] **5.151**

(1.1) By which methods are tribunal-appointed experts selected? What are the rights of the parties during the selection process? It is within the power of the tribunal to appoint an expert without consultation, subject to the parties' agreement otherwise.[179] However, in practice the tribunal may wish to consult with the parties prior to appointment, such as envisaged by the International Bar Association ('IBA') Rules on the Taking of Evidence.[180] Some institutions respect the parties' involvement in the selection process by allowing the parties to have a full opportunity to challenge the expert's opinion, whether it be at the terms of reference stage, or at the appointment stage. For instance, if there are concerns with the independence of a proposed expert, the parties may require an oral hearing.[181] **5.152**

(2) Admissibility and role of expert witnesses

The admissibility of expert witness evidence will be guided by Pt 35 of the Civil Procedure Rules 1998 ('the CPR')[182] and the guidelines provided in the judgment of Creswell J in *National Justice Compania Naviera SA v Prudential Assurance SA ('The Ikarian Reefer')*.[183] The general effect of Pt 35 is to ensure that an expert's opinion is disclosed within a reasonable time prior to the trial so that the opposing party has an opportunity to read the expert evidence. Cresswell J emphasized that an expert witness serves foremost as an assistant to the court, a role best achieved by acting independently and objectively. Notwithstanding the above, the overriding principle remains that arbitrators are masters of their own procedure. **5.153**

---

177 ICC Rules Art 20(3)–(4).

178 Arbitration Act 1996 s 37(1)(b).

179 *ibid*, s 37.

180 IBA Rules on the Taking of Evidence Art 6.

181 UNCITRAL Model Law Art 26(2).

182 Civil Procedure Rules 1998, SI 1998/3132; Merkin, R., *Arbitration Law* (1st edn service issue 51 (10 March 2009), Informa Professional, London 1991) 15.368.

183 *National Justice Compania Naviera SA v Prudential Assurance SA ('The Ikarian Reefer')* [1993] 2 Lloyd's Rep 68 (Comm), 81-2.

(3) Influence of the parties upon the selection of questions to be submitted to the expert

5.154 Under the Act and most arbitration rules, the parties may examine a tribunal-appointed expert's evidence at a hearing.[184] By contrast, the IBA Rules expressly contemplate party involvement in drafting an expert's terms of reference,[185] and the ICC Rules go even further in providing that a tribunal may only appoint an expert after first (i) consulting the parties on the expert's terms of reference, identity and cost; and (ii) allowing them to question the expert at an oral hearing.[186]

(4) Independence and impartiality of the expert and the right to reject a proposed/appointed expert

5.155 The independence and impartiality of an expert is of utmost importance. If a party-appointed expert, ie an expert witness, is found not to be independent or impartial, it is open for the tribunal to simply disregard his/her evidence.[187] However, in the case of a tribunal-appointed expert it is assumed that the expert will be independent of the parties and impartial. In the absence of an express agreement governing a challenge to a tribunal-appointed expert, a party could raise its concerns directly with the tribunal. If this failed, a party could attempt to challenge the award pursuant to s 68(2)(a) of the Arbitration Act on the basis of the tribunal's failure to comply with its general duty under s33.[188]

5.156 **(4.1) May a party or its counsel approach an expert (or expert witness) whom it has nominated (only before or also after the proceeding has started)? Are interviews admissible?** Under English law, counsel may approach, communicate with and interview experts at any stage of the arbitral proceedings or before the expert has been engaged.[189] Generally, solicitors provide experts with instructions on the proceedings and the scope of the enquiry, and experts may communicate with both barristers and solicitors where explaining their expertise or another's.[190] Nonetheless, the professional conduct rules for barristers and solicitors preclude any form of coaching of expert witnesses.[191]

(5) Oral examination of an expert in hearing

5.157 Expert evidence usually comes in the form of a written report. In the likely event that the opinions between the opposing party-appointed experts differ, this is usually resolved by an oral hearing where each expert is cross-examined.[192] Ultimately, it will be for the tribunal to decide whether an oral examination of the expert is required.[193]

H. Interim measures of protection

(1) Kind of interim measures which the tribunal may order

5.158 The tribunal's powers to grant interim relief arise out of ss 38 and 39 of the Arbitration Act 1996. Under s 38(1), the parties can empower arbitrators to make any kind of interim

184 LCIA Rules Art 21; UNCITRAL Rules Art 27; ICDR Rules Art 22.
185 IBA Rules on the Taking of Evidence Art 6.
186 See eg ICC Rules Art 20(4).
187 *Russell* (n 21) 5-154.
188 *ibid*, [8-077]–[8-078].
189 CPR PD 35 Annex [8.1], [11.1], [12].
190 CPR 35.8.
191 *Bar Code of Conduct* (n 155), se 1, Pt VII [705(a)].
192 *Russell* (n 21) 5-151.
193 Arbitration Act 1996 ss 34, 37(1).

order they choose, including freezing orders where agreed by the parties. In the absence of the parties' agreement, the Arbitration Act 1996 provides arbitrators with the default power to make orders in relation to property, the examination of witnesses and the preservation of evidence,[194] although such orders may only be made against a party to the proceedings.[195]

In addition, s 39(1) of the Arbitration Act 1996 allows the parties to empower the tribunal to grant on a provisional basis 'any relief which it would have power to grant in a final award'. The parties must expressly agree to confer this power on the tribunal for this section to apply.[196] The tribunal subsequently may amend or overturn such provisional orders.[197] **5.159**

(1.1) Which are, in general, the procedural and substantive prerequisites for the ordering of interim and conservatory measures (eg reduced degree of evidence; urgency; summary evaluation of the claim)? Procedural prerequisites for the ordering of interim and conservatory measures are that (a) the order is made with notice to all parties; and (b) the measures ordered involve only the parties to the arbitration. Further, where the direction or order relates to property, said property must form the subject of the proceedings, or relate to a question arising out of the proceedings. **5.160**

Arbitrators should only make an interim order if they consider it to be fair and just in all the circumstances, having had due regard to commercial common sense. **5.161**

(1.2) Are the prerequisites for interim measures ordered by the arbitral tribunal more or less the same as if those are requested from the state court? Is there case law/leading authorities on whether those measures are faster and enforced more easily if taken by the arbitral tribunal or the state court? Although the substantive considerations exercised by the tribunal are likely to be similar to those of the court, arbitrators are not constrained to following the same guidance as the court and need only exercise their discretion subject to their general duty under s 33 of the Act.[198] The court faces less procedural prerequisites than the tribunal in ordering interim measures: the court may act without notice to the opposing party, the court may make orders against third parties, and the court may order interim injunctions, subject to the restraints on anti-suit injunctions relating to proceedings before EU and EFTA courts. **5.162**

Urgent cases are matters for the court's determination.[199] The court may only act in non-urgent cases following the permission of the tribunal or agreement of the other party.[200] Regardless of whether urgent or not, the court may only act where the tribunal 'has no power or is unable for the time being to act effectively'.[201] **5.163**

[194] Arbitration Act 1996 s 38(4)–(6).
[195] *ibid*, s 38(4).
[196] *ibid*, s 39(4).
[197] *'The Smaro'* (n 51).
[198] Cato, D.M., *Arbitration Practice and Procedure: Interlocutory and Hearing Problems* (3rd edn, Informa Professional, London, 2002) 9.12.5.
[199] Arbitration Act 1996 s 44(3).
[200] *ibid*, s 44(4).
[201] *ibid*, s 44(5).

(2) Limits of the tribunal's powers to order interim measures

5.164 Tribunals are not prohibited from making orders affecting third parties but, as the tribunal has no jurisdiction over third parties, such orders cannot be enforced against those third parties and are therefore ineffective. Further, a tribunal may not make any interim measure without notice, may lack the power to make interim injunctions such as freezing injunctions or search orders, and has no power to enforce its measures directly.[202] In keeping with the scheme of the Act, however, the extent of the tribunal's powers is largely defined by the parties' agreement.[203]

(3) Orders to provide security for the costs of the proceeding

5.165 The Arbitration Act 1996 provides that it is the tribunal and not the court which can make an order for security for costs in arbitration proceedings. A power to order the claimant to provide security for costs is specifically granted in s 38(3). No particular grounds for the granting of such an order are specified in the Act, but there is a prohibition on exercising the power on the sole ground that the claimant is outside the jurisdiction.[204]

5.166 The court has held that such an order cannot be made unless an application is made by the other party.[205]

(4) Attachment of assets by an order of the tribunal

5.167 Pursuant to s 38(1), the tribunal may make an order for the attachment of assets, most often a 'freezing injunction',[206] where such power has been expressly agreed by the parties.[207] In the absence of such express agreement, it appears that the tribunal lacks the power to make a freezing injunction. The Act does not specifically grant the tribunal the power to order the attachment of assets. The court has not clarified if arbitrators may issue freezing orders under s 38 or 39 of the Act.[208] In one case, the court held that such a power may only be conferred through express agreement and operated under s 39;[209] in a case where there was no express power to grant freezing injunctions, the court held that 'the arbitrator tribunal lacks the power...to act effectively in relation to the preservation of assets' under s 38.[210] Notably, any such measures ordered by the tribunal would not bind third parties, but possibly could be enforced by the court.[211] Care should be taken to distinguish between orders made in the arbitration by the tribunal and freezing orders made by the courts to enforce a final arbitration award.

[202] *Russell* (n 21) 5-075.
[203] Arbitration Act 1996 s 38(1), 39(1).
[204] *ibid*, s 38(3).
[205] *Wicketts and Sterndale v Brine Builders and Anor* (TCC, 8 June 2001); *Merkin* (n 182) 14.72.
[206] CPR 25.1(1)(f); Tweeddale, A. and K., *Arbitration of Commercial Disputes: International and English Law and Practice* (OUP, Oxford, 2005) 25.3844.
[207] *Merkin* (n 182) 14.47-8; cf *Kastner v Jason* [2004] EWCA Civ 1599, [2005] 1 Lloyd's Rep 397 [15]-[19] (Rix LJ).
[208] *Kastner v Jason* (n 207 - CA) 15-19 (Rix LJ); *Merkin* (n 182) 14.47.
[209] *Kastner v Jason* [2004] EWHC 592 (Ch), [2004] 2 Lloyd's Rep 233, [25]–[30].
[210] *Pacific Maritime (Asia) Ltd v Holystone Overseas Ltd* [2007] EWHC 2319 (Comm), [2008] 1 Lloyd's Rep 371.
[211] Merkin, R. and Flannery, L., *Arbitration Act 1996* (3rd edn, LLP, London, 2005) 102.

I. Assistance by the courts

(1) Extent of court assistance in the gathering of evidence

The tribunal is the primary body charged with ensuring the gathering and preservation of evidence pursuant to its default powers under s 38(4)-(6). On occasion, however, the tribunal may not be able to act effectively or at all. In such instances, ss 42 and 44 of the Arbitration Act 1996 provide the court with wide default powers to gather and preserve evidence. **5.168**

The court's s 44(2) powers are greater than those of the tribunal under s 38. These powers extend over third parties where necessary. Further, where a party needs to make a without notice urgent application for an injunction to preserve evidence or assets, it may do so under s 44(3) of the Act. **5.169**

Under s 42, the court may also assist in the gathering of evidence by enforcing a party's compliance with the tribunal's peremptory order.[212] Like s 44, the court's power to act is subject to certain limitations and may be altered by the parties' express agreement. **5.170**

(1.1) Is it for the arbitral tribunal or for the party to obtain the assistance of state courts with respect to the gathering of evidence? The court's powers under s44 of the Act are obtained upon application of the party. Except in cases of an urgent application to the court, the applying party must have the permission of the tribunal or agreement of the other party. However, the court's power to enforce peremptory orders of the arbitral tribunal under s 42 may be obtained upon the application of either of the parties or of the tribunal. **5.171**

(1.2) According to case law and practical experience, are there considerable delays involved when asking a court to give assistance (eg for the obtaining of evidence)? Generally, no. One of the overriding objectives of the CPR was to deal with matters 'expeditiously'.[213] An arbitration claim[214] is usually made on notice, one exception being claims made in cases of urgency to preserve evidence or assets under s 44(3). The claim form[215] must be served on the defendant within one month of issue (unless the court orders otherwise).[216] **5.172**

(2) Assistance for enforcing the attachment of assets

Unlike a tribunal, the courts have power under s 44(2)(e) and (3) to order interim freezing orders.[217] The order must be 'just and convenient', under s 37 of the Supreme Court Act 1981.[218] **5.173**

Often the court receives applications for freezing orders in urgent circumstances where no notice has been given to the opposing party. In these instances, the court may only issue a **5.174**

---

[212] Arbitration Act 1996 s 41(5); *Emmott v Michael Wilson and Partners Ltd* [2009] EWHC 1 (Comm), [2009] 1 Lloyd's Rep 233 [71] (Teare J).

[213] CPR 1.1(2)(d).

[214] *ibid*, 62.2(1).

[215] Form N8: CPR PD 62.4 [8.1]; see *Tweeddale* (n 206) 25.43.

[216] CPR 62.4(2).

[217] *ibid*, 25.1(1)(f).

[218] *Mobil Cerro Negro Ltd v Petróleos de Venezuela SA* [2008] EWHC 532 (Comm), [2008] 1 Lloyd's Rep 684 [17]–[19], [35]–[41].

freezing order for the purposes of preserving evidence or assets pursuant to s 44(3).[219] Where the circumstances are not urgent, application to the court for a freezing order proceeds with notice under s 44(2)(e).

(3) Other examples of possible assistance

5.175 Section 43 of the Arbitration Act 1996 empowers the court to give orders to secure the attendance of witnesses where (i) the court has been granted permission by the tribunal or agreement of the parties; (ii) the witness is in the UK; and (iii) the seat of the arbitration is in England or Wales.[220]

5.176 Other powers which may flow from the court's s 44 powers include ordering the sale of assets which are the subject of the proceedings, appointing a receiver, ordering for the sum in dispute to be secured and ordering an injunction to restrain breach of contract.[221]

(4) Dependence of the power of state courts to intervene during the proceedings on the (national) procedural law applied by the arbitral tribunal

5.177 When acting under the default powers in s 42, the court may only act at the request of the arbitral tribunal or at the request of a party (either (i) with the tribunal's permission and upon notice to the opposing party; or (ii) where the arbitration agreement states that the court has these powers and upon notice to the opposing party).[222] Moreover, if the arbitration agreement provides for a different procedure to ensure compliance, that must first be exhausted before s 42 may be used.[223]

5.178 Section 44, although also an optional provision, operates differently. Where the court operates under the default powers listed in s 44, it may only exercise those powers where the tribunal is unable to act or cannot act effectively.[224] Thus, as Merkin states, '[section] 44 is only of significance either where the arbitrators' powers are limited or where the arbitrators have yet to take up their posts'.[225] The court's s 44 powers are also differentiated between urgent and non-urgent cases. Non-urgent applications proceed under s 44(2) and, thus, the court has greater powers at its disposal. Under s44(2), however, the court only acts with the permission of the tribunal or written agreement of the parties and with notice to the opposing party.[226] Although, the court's exercise of its s 44(3) power may proceed without the tribunal's permission and without notice to the opposing party, the power only exists in urgent cases for the preservation of evidence or assets.[227] As in judicial proceedings, the court will only issue a s 44(3) injunction on a without notice basis where 'it would be likely to defeat the purpose of seeking the injunction if forewarning were given'.[228]

---

219 *Cetelem v Roust Holdings Ltd* [2005] EWCA Civ 618, [2005] 1 WLR 3555.

220 Arbitration Act 1996 s 43(1)–(3).

221 *ibid*, s 44(2)(d), (e). But not an anti-suit injunction in respect of judicial proceedings in the EU or EFTA: Case C-185/07 *West Tankers* (n 85).

222 Arbitration Act 1996 s 42(2).

223 *Russell* (n 21) 7-200.

224 Arbitration Act 1996 s 44(5).

225 *Merkin* (n 182) 14.47.

226 Arbitration Act 1996 s 44(4).

227 See *Russell* (n 21) [7-188]–[7-190].

228 *Petroleum Investment Co Ltd v Kantupan Holdings Co Ltd* [2002] 1 All ER (Comm) 124 (Comm) (Toulson J), quoted in *Merkin and Flannery* (n 211), 122.

Section 43, which enables the court to secure the attendance of witnesses, only applies where the tribunal has given its permission or the parties have agreed.[229] It is also noteworthy that s 45 of the Arbitration Act, which provides for the determination of a preliminary point of law, does not include determinations on procedural matters.[230] **5.179**

V. The award*

A. Types of award

(1) Interim awards (eg on interim measures or the jurisdiction of the tribunal)

The term 'interim award' is not used in the Arbitration Act 1996. For the purposes of the Act, however, an 'award' is 'final and binding as between the parties' on all, one or some of the issues that fall to be determined.[231] Thus, temporary or interlocutory procedural directions and orders are not enforceable 'awards'.[232] **5.180**

The Arbitration Act 1996 nonetheless uses the terminology of 'provisional awards' to describe the tribunal's power 'to order on a provisional basis any relief which it would have power to grant in a final award'.[233] The non-binding nature of provisional awards is emphasized in s 39(3), which requires the tribunal to take any provisional awards into account when making its final award. **5.181**

There are two key points to note on provisional awards. First, the tribunal only has power to make them if the parties specifically agree to such a power.[234] Second, a provisional award is effectively a mechanism by which money or property can be distributed between the parties prior to the tribunal's final award.[235] **5.182**

(2) Partial award

Under s 47 of the Arbitration Act 1996, the tribunal is not required to deal with all issues in a single final award, but may (as long as the parties agree) issue a number of final, ie enforceable, awards at different times on different aspects of the matter to be determined. These awards are commonly referred to as 'partial' awards.[236] **5.183**

In addition to the tribunal's power to issue partial awards, ss 30(1) and 31(4)(a) specifically enable the tribunal to 'rule on its own jurisdiction' in a separate award. **5.184**

(2.1) Are awards, especially partial awards, binding in the same arbitral proceeding? Does it make a difference if after the rendering of such a partial award, one arbitrator is successfully challenged and removed on grounds that prevailed even before the partial **5.185**

---

229 Arbitration Act 1996 s 43(1)–(2). See para 5.175 *supra*.
230 *Merkin and Flannery* (n 211) 114.
* The authors wish to thank Simon Jackson, Associate, Commercial Risk and Reinsurance team, BLG, for his contribution to this section.
231 *Russell* (n 21) 6-018; Arbitration Act 1996 s 58(1).
232 Arbitration Act 1996 ss 47, 58(1), 66; *Russell* (n 21) [6-002]–[6-003], [6-009].
233 Arbitration Act 1996 s 39(1).
234 *ibid*, s 39(4).
235 *Mustill and Boyd 2001* (n 61) 108.
236 Arbitration Act 1996 s 47(2)(b); *Merkin and Flannery* (n 211) 129.

award was rendered? A partial award made under ss 31(4)(a) or 47(2)(b) is a final award under the Arbitration Act 1996, ie it is 'final and binding.[237] Partial awards are therefore immediately enforceable and subject to challenge in the same way as any other final award.[238] Thus, the fact that the arbitrator who made the award was later removed would not, without more, affect the enforceability of the award—although it may well mean that there exist grounds for applying to the court to challenge the award under s 68.[239]

(3) Final award

5.186 The tribunal has the power to publish a single final award dealing with all issues.[240] As with partial awards, final awards are 'final and binding' as between the parties, and thus subject to enforcement or challenge.[241] Note that a tribunal may, if it so decides, include its determination on its substantive jurisdiction in the final award addressing all parts of its mandate.[242]

5.187 **(3.1) If a party fails to participate in the arbitration, may the tribunal proceed and issue an award on the merits? Is such an award enforceable as any other award? Are there special remedies for the defendant at the enforcement stage?** If the party has been given notice of the proceedings and a reasonable opportunity to participate, nothing in the Arbitration Act 1996 precludes the tribunal from proceeding to an enforceable award in these circumstances.[243] The non-participating party would be able to question the reference to arbitration and challenge the award on the grounds of the tribunal's lack of substantive jurisdiction or serious irregularity in the proceedings,[244] but would not have the best chances of success given the lack of participation.[245]

B. Deliberations and agreement on the award

(1) Time limits (and possible extensions) for making the award

5.188 Parties are free to set out a time limit within which an award should be made in the arbitration agreement, and the Arbitration Act 1996 does not specify a time limit in default of a choice except in three exceptional circumstances.[246] However, a party may apply to the court for the removal of an arbitrator if that arbitrator has 'refused or failed. . .to use all reasonable despatch in…making an award, and that substantial injustice has been, or will be caused to the applicant'.[247]

5.189 Where the arbitration agreement specifies a time limit within which an award should be made, the tribunal is bound by that time limit unless it is extended by the agreement of the parties or by application to the court under s 50 of the Arbitration Act 1996. Section 50

237 Arbitration Act 1996 s 58(1); *Russell* (n 21) 6-018.
238 Arbitration Act 1996 s 66, cf ss 67-9.
239 *Russell* (n 21) [5-037], [8-072]–[8-114].
240 Arbitration Act 1996 s 47(1), (2)(a); *Russell* (n 21) [6-004]–[6-007].
241 Arbitration Act 1996 ss 58(1), 66.
242 *ibid*, s 31(4)(b).
243 *ibid*, s 41(7)(c).
244 *ibid*, ss 72(1), (2)(a), (b); 67, 68.
245 *Russell* (n 21) 5-067.
246 Arbitration Act 1997 ss 47(1), 71(3), 57(3)(a), 57(6); *Russell* (n 21) 6-062, 7-081.
247 Arbitration Act 1996 s 24(1)(d)(ii).

allows the court to extend a time limit but only if (a) all other routes for extending time (perhaps, for example, under the rules of an arbitral institution) have been exhausted; and (b) substantial injustice would otherwise be done.[248]

(2) Procedure for the decision of the arbitrators (majority vote etc)

An award will be made by the tribunal in accordance with the decision-making procedure laid down in the arbitration agreement. Where the arbitration agreement is silent on these matters or they are not agreed between the parties, and the tribunal consists of two or more arbitrators, the decision-making process is as follows: **5.190**

(i) where the tribunal has a chairman, the award will be the decision of the majority of the arbitrators or failing this will follow the chairman's decision;[249]

(ii) where the tribunal has an umpire, the umpire has no decision-making power unless and until the other arbitrators cannot agree on an issue, at which point the umpire decides the issue as if he were a sole arbitrator;[250]

(iii) where the tribunal has no chairman or umpire, the award will be made by the decision of all or the majority of the arbitrators.[251]

(2.1) If an arbitrator fails or refuses to take part in oral deliberation meetings, although having been given sufficient notice of such meetings, may an award be rendered on the basis of written deliberations (or deliberations without this arbitrator) only? The Arbitration Act 1996 does not specifically address the consequences of a refusal or failure by the arbitrator to participate in the deliberations. There is a body of English common law to the effect that each member of the tribunal is obliged to participate in the decision-making process, and may not absent himself entirely from the tribunal's deliberations (whether in writing or oral).[252] It is suggested that where an arbitrator failed or refused to participate in oral deliberations despite sufficient notice, such an award would be very vulnerable to challenge under s 68 on the grounds of serious irregularity[253] and there would almost certainly be problems in enforcing such an award in other jurisdictions. **5.191**

(3) Admissibility of dissenting opinions

The Arbitration Act 1996 does not specifically address the admissibility of dissenting opinions, although s 52(3) accepts that awards may be made by the majority of arbitrators. In English law, dissenting opinions have no legal status and thus have little practical significance,[254] although the existence of a dissent may at least prompt the losing party to attempt to appeal against the award.[255] **5.192**

---

248 Arbitration Act 1996 s 50(2), (3).

249 *ibid*, s 20.

250 *ibid*, s 21.

251 *ibid*, s 22.

252 *European Grain and Shipping Ltd v Johnston* [1983] QB 520 (CA).

253 *Russell* (n 21) [7-120]–[7-121], [7-123], [8-072] *et seq*.

254 *Stinnes Interoil GmbH v A Halcoussis & Co ('The Yanxilas') (No 1)* [1982] 2 Lloyd's Rep 445 (Comm) (Bingham J), approved in *Cargill International SA Antigua v Sociedad Iberica de Molturacion SA* [1998] 1 Lloyd's Rep 489 (CA), 496 (Waller LJ); *Russell* (n 21) 6-058.

255 *F Ltd v M Ltd* [2009] EWHC 275 (TCC).

5.193 (3.1) **Are there any court decisions or positions of leading authorities on the issue of dissenting opinions (admissibility, disclosure to the parties and publication)?** The Court of Appeal in *Cargill International SA Antigua v Sociedad Ibérica de Molturación* confirmed that dissenting opinions in arbitration awards are a 'courtesy' often extended to the dissenting arbitrator. Nonetheless, unless expressly provided for in the arbitration agreement, 'a dissenting arbitrator has no right to insist on his dissenting reasons forming part of the reasons for an award'.[256]

(4) Signature by the arbitrators and potential failure of one arbitrator to sign

5.194 The parties are free to agree on the form of their award but, in default of agreement, s 52(3) provides that the award shall be 'signed by all the arbitrators or all those assenting to the award'. This means that dissenting arbitrators may, but are not required to, sign the award, and the failure of an arbitrator to sign will not of itself affect the validity of the award.[257]

C. Form of the award and deposition

(1) Form and minimum contents of an award

5.195 The parties are free to decide the form that the award should take.[258] This means that the parties may decide that they wish the award to be given orally and/or in writing, with or without reasons. If the parties do not specify how the award is to be given, s 52(2) to (5) governs the form of the award, providing that it shall (i) be in writing; (ii) be reasoned (unless it is an agreed award or the parties agree to dispense with reasons); (iii) state the seat of the arbitration; (iv) be dated; and (v) be signed by all of the arbitrators (or at least all of those assenting to the award).

(2) Requirement to give reasons in the award

5.196 As noted above, the parties may agree that no reasons should be given for the award, but, in the absence of agreement, s 52(4) provides that reasons must be given. Should the parties decide to dispense with reasons entirely, this will have the effect of removing the English courts' jurisdiction to hear an appeal from the award on a point of law,[259] although it will not affect appeals alleging a serious irregularity in the arbitral process or that the tribunal has no jurisdiction.[260] Once an appeal has been made to the English court, if no reasons or, in the court's opinion, insufficiently detailed reasons have been given for the award, the court may order the tribunal to state its reasons more fully.[261]

(3) Necessity to specify place and time where and when the award was made

5.197 The statutory requirement of specifying the date of the award and the seat of the arbitration has legal and practical consequences. The time limit for challenging the award is 28 days, running from the date on which the award was made, generally being the date stated in the

256 *Cargill International* (n 255), 497 (Waller LJ).
257 *ibid*, 497; *Merkin* (n 182) 18.21, 18.27; *Russell* (n 21) 6-058.
258 Arbitration Act 1996 s 52(1).
259 *ibid*, s 69(1).
260 *ibid*, ss 67-8.
261 *ibid*, s 70(4).

award itself.[262] Sections 67 to 69 of the Arbitration Act 1996, which confer jurisdiction on the court to entertain challenges, apply only where the seat of the arbitration is in England.[263] If the seat was in another New York Convention country, then the English court is prima facie obliged to enforce the award, the seat being regarded as the place where the award is 'made' for the purposes of enforcement.[264]

(4) Other requirements (registration, delivery etc)

In addition to those requirements stated in s 52 of the Arbitration Act 1996, s 55(2) provides that, absent the parties' agreement otherwise, 'notification' of the award is effected where copies of the award are served on the parties 'without delay after the award is made'. Although the Act does not prescribe any specific time period for the notification of the award, the parties have only 28 days in which to appeal or apply to challenge the award whether or not notification has been given.[265] Requirements in the arbitration agreement regarding 'publishing' of an award are met once the tribunal has notified the parties the award is ready.[266] Where the parties agree an award must be delivered, delivery is equal to the s 55(2) notification procedure.[267] **5.198**

The Act also includes a *de facto* requirement for the full payment of the tribunal's fees as delivery of an award may be withheld where the tribunal's fees remain outstanding.[268] **5.199**

(4.1) Does the award have to be laid down or registered with a state court or agency (even if it has been rendered according to a foreign procedural law)? No, an arbitral award rendered for an arbitration with its seat in England is final and binding between the parties and, thus, 'immediately enforceable', even where it was conducted under a foreign procedural law.[269] The only registration requirements relate to the enforcement of certain foreign arbitral awards pursuant to certain statutory provisions. **5.200**

(4.2) Does a foreign award which has been rendered abroad according to this country's national procedural law, have to be laid down or registered with a state court or agency? Is there a fee or tax for such registration of an award? Foreign arbitral awards which are New York Convention or Geneva Convention awards do not need to be registered to be recognized and enforced in England.[270] Certain arbitral awards—in effect, ICSID awards and those issued in states with whom England has reciprocal jurisdiction arrangements—may be recognized and enforced in England by registering the award with the High Court.[271] **5.201**

---

262 Arbitration Act 1996 ss 54(2), 70(3).
263 *ibid*, s 2.
264 *ibid*, s 100(1), (2)(b).
265 *ibid*, s 70(3); *Russell* (n 21) 6-064; cf CPR 62.9(1).
266 *Brooke v Mitchell* (1840) 6 M&W 473, 9 LJ Ex 269; *Russell* (n 21) 6-065.
267 *Russell* (n 21) 6-067.
268 Arbitration Act 1996 s 56(1); cf s 56(2)–(6).
269 *Russell* (n 21) 6-162; Arbitration Act 1996 s 58.
270 Arbitration Act 1996 ss 99-101. Note, however, that a party must obtain the court's permission to enforce an award.
271 Primarily ICSID awards: CPR 62.20(1), 62.21; cf 62.18(1).

5.202 (4.3) **How long after the rendering of the award must the file/award be stored by the lawyers and the arbitral tribunal?** English law lays down no specific requirement in this regard. Typically, solicitors will retain the awards and other documentation for an arbitration for a long period of time. There is no standard period of time for an arbitrator to retain an award.

D. Applicable substantive law

(1) Party autonomy to choose the applicable substantive law

5.203 Section 46 of the Arbitration Act 1996 expressly recognizes the right of the parties to choose the law applicable to the substance of the dispute. The law applicable to the substance of the dispute does not have to be the same as the law that covers the arbitration agreement or the conduct of the arbitration. Thus, it is possible to conduct an arbitration in England under English procedural law (ie the Arbitration Act 1996) while the substance of the dispute is governed by a foreign law.

5.204 (1.1) **Is there a public policy exception to the chosen substantive law?** The Arbitration Act 1996 does not deal explicitly with the role of English public policy in circumstances where a foreign law, which governs the substance of the dispute, violates English public policy. However, the Act makes clear that a violation of English public policy may be grounds for the successful challenge of an award.[272] If arbitrators are applying English conflict of laws rules, there is a public policy exception to choice-of-law,[273] but there is no case in which it has ever operated to strike down an express choice.[274]

5.205 (1.2) **Does the principle of '*iura novit curia*' apply? Or must the applicable law be proven (by which means)?** English law regards foreign law as a question of fact, to be specifically alleged and proved by the party relying upon it. The usual method of proof is by way of expert evidence from a suitably qualified foreign lawyer.[275]

(2) Decisions according to equity or as amiable compositeur

5.206 The parties are free, should they so wish, to have the substance of their dispute resolved by reference to 'other considerations' rather than strict principles of law.[276] Examples of 'other considerations' include arbitrations where the arbitrators are entitled to disregard express contract wording or rules of construction in order to reach an equitable result or act as *amiables compositeurs*.[277] Arbitrations under such 'other considerations' are rarely encountered in England, although so-called 'honourable engagements' clauses are sometimes to be found in arbitration agreements contained in reinsurance contracts.[278] If the parties have

---

272 Arbitration Act 1996 s 68(2)(g) (for English-seated arbitrations); s 103(3) (for recognition and enforcement under the New York Convention).

273 Rome Convention (n 115) Arts 3, 16; Rome I Regulation (n 115) Arts 3, 21.

274 *Merkin* (n 182) 7.28.

275 *Dicey and Morris* (n 113) ch 9.

276 Arbitration Act 1996 s 46(1)(b); Poudret, J.-F., and Besson, S., *Comparative Law of International Arbitration*, translated by Berti and Ponti (2nd edn, Sweet & Maxwell, London, 2007) 720.

277 *West Tankers Inc v Ras Riunione Adriatica di Sicurta SpA ('The Front Comor')* [2007] UKHL 4, [2007] 1 Lloyd's Rep 391 [19] (Lord Hoffmann); 1996 DAC (n 3) 223.

278 *Mustill and Boyd 2001* (n 61) 75, fn 8. See eg *Home Insurance Co and St Paul Fire and Marine Insurance Co v Administratia Asigurarilor de Stat* [1983] 2 Lloyd's Rep 674 (Comm); *Home and Overseas Insurance Co Ltd v Mentor Insurance (UK) Ltd* [1990] 1 WLR 153 (CA).

selected to have their dispute resolved under equitable principles, 'the parties are in effect excluding any right to appeal to the Court' under s 69 or a request for a preliminary decision under s 45.[279]

(3) Application of lex mercatoria, *general principles etc*

The Arbitration Act allows the parties to choose the principles governing the resolution of their dispute,[280] which includes arbitrations conducted under internationally accepted principles of commercial law (known as '*lex mercatoria*').[281] *Lex mercatoria* only applies where the parties have expressly agreed to it.[282] **5.207**

(3.1) Is the application of '*lex mercatoria*' considered as the application of law or as a kind of *amiable composition*? There is no clear answer in English law. In the context of English civil proceedings, a contract must be governed by the law of a country; thus a non-national system of law (such as *lex mercatoria*) or a religious system of law (such as Sharia) is not valid.[283] Further, it is again noted that *lex mercatoria* only applies where expressly chosen by the parties pursuant to s 46(1)(b). From this, it appears that the application of *lex mercatoria* is most likely considered to be a form of *amiable composition*. **5.208**

(4) Applicable substantive law if there is no choice of law by the parties

Where the parties have not determined the law or 'other considerations' that will apply to the substance of their dispute, s 46(3) provides that 'the tribunal shall apply the law determined by the conflict of laws rules which it considers applicable'. Typically, a tribunal seated in England will apply English conflict of law rules, although this is not necessary.[284] **5.209**

English conflict of law rules are governed by the Rome Convention on the Law Applicable to Contractual Obligations 1980, as given effect by the Contracts (Applicable Law) Act 1990. '[T]he Rome Convention provides that, where the parties have not chosen an applicable law, a contract is governed by the law of the country with which it is most closely connected'.[285] Where the parties have designated a seat this often will indicate the governing law of the contract, but first must be taken to demonstrate the parties' choice 'with reasonable certainty'.[286] **5.210**

(4.1) Is there an autonomous conflict of law rule in the national arbitration law? Is it considered mandatory? There is no special conflict of law rule applying to arbitration. **5.211**

---

279 1996 DAC (n 3) [225]; *Mustill and Boyd 2001* (n 61) 328.

280 Arbitration Act 1996 s 46(1)(b).

281 *West Tankers* (n 278 - HL) 19 (Lord Hoffmann); *Merkin* (n 182) 7.57; *Poudret and Besson* (n 276) 703; *Merkin and Flannery* (n 211) 127; Collins *et al* (eds), *Dicey, Morris and Collins: The Conflict of Laws: Second Supplement to the 14th edition* (Sweet & Maxwell, London, 2008) 16-019.

282 *Merkin* (n 182) 7.57.

283 *Shamil Bank of Bahrain EC v Beximco Pharmaceuticals Ltd* [2004] EWCA Civ 19, [2004] 1 WLR 1784; *Merkin* (n 182) 7.28.

284 *CGU International Insurance Plc v Astrazeneca Insurance Co Ltd* [2005] EWHC 2755 (Comm), [2006] 1 CLC 162; *Russell* (n 21) 2-092; *Dicey and Morris* (n 113) 16-010.

285 *Russell* (n 21) 2-092, citing Rome Convention (n 115) Art 4.1. See Rome I Regulation (n 115) Art 4; *Dicey and Morris* (n 113) [16-019]–[16-020].

286 *Russell* (n 21) [2-092]–[2-093]; *Egon Oldendorff v Libera Corp (No 2)* [1996] 1 Lloyd's Rep 380 (Comm) 387.

Often English conflict of law rules apply.[287] Ultimately, under the Arbitration Act 1996, it is for the arbitrators to assess the appropriate conflict of law rules to apply.[288]

5.212 (4.2) **What is the law applicable to interest?** The parties are free to agree on the tribunal's power to award interest and, if so, on what basis. In the absence of agreement, s 49(3), (4) and (5) gives the tribunal the power to award either simple or compound interest as it sees fit. This is the case irrespective of the law applicable to the substantive contract.

5.213 (4.3) **What is the law and practice with respect to legal interest on foreign currency debts?** For arbitrations where the contract is governed by English law, the award may be expressed in foreign currency.[289] Equally, 'the interest on the sum awarded may be. . .varied to represent the value of that currency'.[290] In instances where interest rates are based on foreign currency, 'the courts have been prepared to be guided by the rate at which a person could "reasonably had borrowed" the foreign currency in the foreign country'.[291]

(5) Binding effect of state court decisions

5.214 If the tribunal is obliged to apply English law, then it must give effect to, and apply, any judgment of the English court which is relevant to the issues. Failure to do so may give rise to an appeal against the award under s 69 of the Arbitration Act 1996 on the ground of an error in law.

5.215 (5.1) **Is an arbitral tribunal bound by a decision of another arbitral tribunal?** No, although previous awards may be of persuasive value.

5.216 (5.2) **Does a decision in a criminal case bind an arbitral tribunal?** Yes. Criminal case law forms part of English law as a whole. Thus, insofar as a criminal case is authority for any relevant proposition of law in the arbitration, it can bind an arbitral tribunal; for example, the tribunal's award could not authorize a criminal act.[292]

E. Settlement

(1) Settlement by agreement of the parties with or without support of the arbitral tribunal

5.217 It is often the case that parties to an arbitration settle their dispute by agreement during the course of proceedings, and the Arbitration Act 1996 expressly recognizes and supports the desirability of settlement of disputes by agreement.[293] The tribunal may assist with the settlement if so requested by the parties.

---

287 Being the Rome Convention (n 115).

288 *Russell* (n 21) 2-092.

289 Arbitration Act 1996 ss 48(4), 49; *Lesotho Highlands Development Authority v Impreglio SpA* [2005] UKHL 43, [2006] 1 AC 221 [22] (Lord Steyn); *Miliangos v George Frank (Textiles) Ltd* [1976] AC 443 (HL); *Services Europe Atlantique Sud (SEAS) of Paris v Stockholm Rederiaktiebolag Svea ('The Folias')* [1979] AC 685 (HL), 700–3 (Lord Wilberforce).

290 *Merkin* (n 182) 18.60; *Lesotho Highlands* (n 289) 39 (Lord Steyn), 43 (Lord Phillips MR).

291 McGregor, H., *McGregor on Damages* (17th edn, Sweet & Maxwell, London, 2003) [15-102]–[3], quoting *Miliangos v George Frank (Textiles) Ltd (No 2)* [1977] QB 489 (QB), 497E (Bristow J); *Lesotho Highlands* (n 289) 47 (Lord Phillips MR).

292 *Wood v Griffith* (1818) 1 Swanst 55, 36 ER 291; *Merkin* (n 182) 18.56.

293 Arbitration Act 1996 s 51.

(1.1) May an arbitrator who has initiated settlement discussions be challenged when agreement on a settlement has failed? If it so wishes, the tribunal can use its broad powers to encourage the parties to reach a settlement in the same way that a court is able to. In one instance, the court found that the fact that an arbitrator had facilitated settlement discussions which subsequently failed would not, of itself, be sufficient grounds for challenging that arbitrator or the tribunal.[294] However, the tribunal's role is ultimately quasi-judicial, and so neither the tribunal nor an arbitrator should seek to act as a mediator or negotiator as this may lead a party to challenge an arbitrator on the ground of bias.[295] **5.218**

(2) 'Private settlement' and its impact on the arbitral procedure

The consensual nature of arbitration means that parties are free to implement their agreement to settle themselves and so, in effect, revoke the mandate of the arbitral tribunal to decide their dispute. Section 51(2) of the Arbitration Act 1996 provides that, should the parties settle the dispute, the tribunal is obliged to terminate the substantive proceedings. **5.219**

(3) Form and effect of a settlement (eg award on agreed terms)

Parties will generally wish to record their settlement in some enforceable manner, and the tribunal may, if it does not object, issue an 'agreed award' which 'record[s] the settlement'.[296] The agreed award mechanism set out in s 51 of the Arbitration Act 1996 is final and binding as between the parties.[297] It will qualify as a New York Convention award for the purposes of enforcement outside of England.[298] **5.220**

F. Costs of the arbitration

(1) General allocation of the costs of the proceedings

Unless the parties agree otherwise, the arbitral tribunal has a wide discretion with regard to the allocation of the 'costs of the arbitration'. While the parties are free to allocate these costs amongst themselves, an agreement which has the effect that a party is to pay the whole or part of the costs of the arbitration in any event is only valid if made after the dispute in question has arisen.[299] **5.221**

If the parties do not agree which costs of the arbitration are to be recoverable, s 63 empowers the tribunal to determine which costs are to be recoverable 'on such basis as it thinks fit'. Guidance is given in relation to this broad discretion by s 63(5). **5.222**

As a matter of English practice, costs will in general follow the event (ie the losing party pays the costs of the winning party), and this fundamental principle is given effect in s 61(2) of the Arbitration Act 1996. **5.223**

One particular area of English law which affects the extent to which costs are recoverable is the existence of any offers to settle during the course of the proceedings. If a party rejects a **5.224**

[294] *Weissfisch v Julius* [2006] EWCA Civ 218, [2006] 2 All ER (Comm) 504, although this was a Swiss-seated arbitration; *Merkin* (n 182) 10.35.
[295] Arbitration Act 1996 s 24(1)(a); *Russell* (n 21) [7-117]–[7-119], [7-123]–[7-128].
[296] Arbitration Act 1996 s 51(2).
[297] *ibid*, s 58.
[298] *Russell* (n 21) 6-027.
[299] Arbitration Act 1996 s 60.

sealed offer to settle and is not awarded more than the offer in the tribunal's final award, it is usual for that party to be penalized in costs.[300]

(2) Deposits or advances for costs or fees

5.225 Often arbitrators or arbitral institutions require advance payments to secure their fees, which may be assured by authorizing the arbitrators to make orders to secure their fees, or by providing in the agreement or institutional rules that costs are covered by a deposit.[301] Advance payments to arbitrators generally must be jointly negotiated and agreed upon by the parties.[302]

5.226 Further, the arbitration agreement or rules may provide, expressly or impliedly, that the tribunal is entitled to interim payments.[303]

5.227 (2.1) **Is there case law authorizing or prohibiting arbitrators to order a party to pay an advance on the arbitration costs?** Section 38(2) of the Arbitration Act 1996 empowers the tribunal (unless the parties have agreed otherwise) to order the claimant in an arbitration to provide security for some or all of the costs of the arbitration, which includes the arbitrator's fees and expenses.[304]

5.228 (2.2) **May the raising of a set-off claim or counterclaim be made contingent upon payment of the corresponding advance for the relating arbitration costs (cf eg Article 30(5) of the ICC Rules)? May such a condition be agreed upon when entering into the arbitration agreement?** If the arbitration agreement provides for this, then it would be possible. Otherwise, there is no clear basis in English law for this.

5.229 (2.3) **What remedies exist against a party which does not pay its part of the advance on the arbitration costs (eg termination of the arbitration agreement)? How may the other party enforce its rights?** Assuming the arbitration agreement itself does not provide for a remedy for the non-payment by one party, the tribunal would be able to bring a direct action against the defaulting party for payment.[305] Alternatively, *Wicketts* appears to confirm that the tribunal may also exercise its general power to issue a peremptory order to a party in default under s 41(5).[306] Failure to comply with such a peremptory order may lead to the tribunal dismissing the claim (if it is the claimant that fails to comply) or exercising one of the powers in s 41(7) to make adverse costs orders, draw adverse inferences, exclude evidence etc.

---

[300] See eg *Cadmus Investment Ltd v Amec Building Ltd* (1997) 51 Con LR 105 (QB).

[301] eg ICC Rules Art 30.2; LCIA Rules Art 1.1(f). Advance deposits were approved in *K/S Norjarl A/S v Hyundai Heavy Industries Co Ltd* [1992] QB 863 (CA). See *Russell* (n 21) [4-060]; Mustill and Boyd, *The Law and Practice of Commercial Arbitration in England* (2nd edn, Butterworths, London 1989), 241; *Merkin* (n 182) 10.72.

[302] *Merkin* (n 182) 10.62, citing *K/S Norjarl* (n 302). See *Turner v Stevenage Borough Council* [1998] Ch 28 (CA), 36B (Staughton LJ); *Andrews (t/a BA Contractors) v Bradshaw* [2000] BLR 6 (CA). cf *Mustill and Boyd 2001* (n 61) 296.

[303] *Turner* (n 303); *Russell* (n 21) 4-061.

[304] Arbitration Act 1996 s 59(1); confirmed in *Wicketts* (n 205), 33C-D, 34A-B.

[305] Arbitration Act 1996 s 28(5).

[306] *Wicketts* (n 205).

The non-defaulting party could apply to the tribunal to continue with the proceedings, either seeking an award dismissing the claim or requesting a peremptory order against the defaulting party,[307] and/or requesting the tribunal to initiate a separate action against the defaulting party for its advanced payment.[308] **5.230**

(3) Costs of the administration by an arbitration institution

Section 59(1) provides that the costs of the administration by an arbitration institution form part of the costs of the arbitration, to be allocated in accordance with the arbitration agreement or as the arbitrators see fit. **5.231**

(4) Arbitrators' fees: law and practice, judicial control

Section 28(1) provides that the parties are jointly and severally liable to pay to the arbitrators such fees and expenses (if any) as are appropriate in the circumstances. Arbitrators may agree their fees with the parties, in which case such fee agreements will be upheld as a matter of contract.[309] These provisions make it clear that the arbitrators have the right to a reasonable fee.[310] **5.232**

In the absence of agreement, s 64 limits the recoverable costs of the arbitration in respect of the fees and expenses of the arbitrators to 'such reasonable fees and expenses as are appropriate in the circumstances' and allows a party to refer this question to the court. **5.233**

(4.1) May arbitrators fix their own fees in the award? As noted above, in the absence of a contractual agreement on fees, s 28 provides that the arbitrators are entitled to a reasonable fee, and s 63 empowers the tribunal to determine such in an award. Indeed, arbitrators often fix their fees in the award. These fees, however, are subject to the court's review.[311] **5.234**

(4.2) How can the parties change the arbitrators' fees once they are fixed? Section 28(2) empowers any party to apply to the court to challenge the arbitrators' fees and expenses and the court may adjust the level of those fees and expenses. Equally, s 64(2) provides a party with the right to apply to court 'if there is any question as to what reasonable fees and expenses are appropriate in the circumstances'. However, the right to challenge the arbitrators' fees does not apply where the arbitrators' fees are agreed with the parties.[312] **5.235**

(4.3) Are the arbitrator's fees subject to income tax if (i) the place of arbitration; or (ii) the normal residence or place of business of the arbitrator is located in this country? While ordinarily an individual would be obliged to pay UK income tax on income attributable to the provision of services carried out in the UK, this will depend on a range of factors including whether the arbitrator is engaged as an individual or through a corporate entity and the arbitrator's personal tax residence and position. For further information on the **5.236**

---

307 Arbitration Act 1996 s 41(5)–(7).
308 *ibid*, s 28(5).
309 *ibid*, ss 28(5), 56(3); *Mustill and Boyd 2001* (n 61), 296.
310 Arbitration Act 1996 s 63(7).
311 *ibid*, ss 28(2), 64(2).
312 *ibid*, ss 28(5), 63(6), 64(4).

subject, please consult Her Majesty's Revenue & Customs website on <http://www.hmrc.gov.uk/rates/>.[313]

5.237 **(4.4) Are arbitrator's fees submitted to VAT? If yes, is the duty to pay such tax linked to (i) the place of arbitration; or (ii) the arbitrator's general residence?** Ordinarily fees attributable to the supply of services carried out in the UK would attract UK VAT at various rates. However, this will depend on the nature of the services supplied, the tax status of the entity they are supplied to and a range of other factors. For further information, please consult the VAT page of Her Majesty's Revenue & Customs website on <http://www.hmrc.gov.uk/vat/index.htm>.[314]

(5) Attorneys' fees and the winning party's claim for reimbursement

5.238 The winning party's legal fees are prima facie recoverable costs. Costs are generally ordered on a standard basis, but may also be ordered on an indemnity basis.[315] When assessing costs on a standard basis, arbitrators must have regard to whether they were proportionately and reasonably incurred, or proportionate or reasonable in amount.[316] By contrast, when assessing costs on an indemnity basis, arbitrators must consider whether costs were unreasonably incurred or unreasonable in amount.[317] In addition, there are a number of other factors which the arbitrators must consider relating to the conduct of the parties and the nature of the arbitration.[318]

5.239 **(5.1) May in-house lawyers charge fees or may a party request costs of in-house lawyers to be reimbursed?** There is no specific provision of the Arbitration Act 1996 dealing with the costs of in-house lawyers. Russell, however, states that 'the costs of in-house counsel... are not usually recoverable on the basis that their salaries would be incurred in any event', unless it can be shown that these individuals were recruited specifically to aid with the arbitration.[319]

(6) Time and form of the decision on costs

5.240 A decision on costs is an award for the purposes of the Arbitration Act 1996.[320] Like other awards, there is no time limit for an award on costs unless specified by the parties. 'The award of costs must be in the form of an award' and is intrinsically linked to the final substantive award.[321]

5.241 **(6.1) May the arbitrators' decision on the costs (allocation and amount of costs to be reimbursed) be challenged separately from the award itself? Are there time limits for such a remedy?** Most often the arbitrators' decision on costs is challenged through the award on costs, which may proceed under s 68 (serious irregularity) or s 69 (appeals on a point of

313 (Accessed 30 March 2009).
314 *ibid.*
315 CPR 44.4(1), (4).
316 *ibid*, 44.5(1)(a).
317 *ibid*, 44.5(1)(b).
318 *ibid*, 44.5(3). See also *Merkin* (n 182) 18.110, relating to 'wasted costs' orders.
319 *Russell* (n 21) 6-131, fn 387.
320 Arbitration Act 1996 s 61.
321 *Merkin* (n 182) 18.75.

law) of the Arbitration Act 1996 in the same way that any other award is challengeable.[322] There is no separate process, remedy or time limit in relation to such a challenge and so the general English law governing the challenge of awards will apply.

(6.2) Are the arbitrators entitled and/or legally obliged to rule on the amount of one or both parties' costs that are recoverable? Unless the parties agree on what costs are recoverable, the arbitrators are entitled to determine by award the recoverable costs of the arbitration.[323] While the arbitrators are not obliged to do so, if they do not, any party may apply to the court for an order determining the recoverable costs of the arbitration.[324] **5.242**

G. Publication of the award

(1) Publication with or without the consent of the parties

While not explicitly provided for in the Arbitration Act 1996, privacy and confidentiality have long been assumed to be core principles of English arbitral law.[325] Confidentiality and privacy are important and beneficial features of arbitral proceedings in England. This being so, awards are not published save for a few well-defined exceptions.[326] One obvious circumstance which may lead to an award being published is where one party has to go to court in order to enforce the award. **5.243**

(2) Practice of publication (eg in specific legal journals)

As arbitration awards are confidential, there is no regular journal or publication in which they are published, despite discussion in the arbitration community regarding the value of publication.[327] In the event of subsequent court proceedings, the published decision of the court may refer to some aspects of the award,[328] which can be accessed through the normal English law reports. If the award raises points of general public importance, the court will order publication but subject to the names of the parties not being disclosed[329] and the judgment not setting out any sensitive commercial or private matters. **5.244**

VI. Amendment and challenge of the award; liability of arbitrators*

A. Amendment, correction or interpretation of the award

(1) Motion to amend or correct an award

In the absence of agreement between the parties to confer powers of correction on a tribunal or to permit the making of an additional award, s 57(3) of the Arbitration Act 1996 **5.245**

322 *Fence Gate Ltd v NEL Construction Ltd* (2001) 82 Con LR 41 (TCC) [30].
323 Arbitration Act 1996 s 63(3).
324 *ibid*, s 63(4).
325 *Dolling-Baker v Merrett* [1990] 1 WLR 1205 (CA), 1213 (Parker LJ).
326 *Ali Shipping Corp v Shipyard Trogir* [1999] 1 WLR 314 (CA).
327 Flint, P., 'Arbitration Proceedings: not so private and confidential?', XIX (April 2008) *PLC Magazine*; Nicholas, G. and Partasides, C., 'LCIA Court Decision on Challenges to Arbitrators: A Proposal to Publish' (2007) 23(1) *Arb Int'l* 1.
328 *Department of Economics, Policy and Development of the City of Moscow and Anor v Bankers Trust Co and Anor* [2004] EWCA Civ 314, [2005] QB 207; *Hassneh Insurance* (n 175) 247–8 (Colman J).
329 *F v M* (n 256).
* The authors wish to thank Patric McGonigal, Associate Director, Marine, Energy & Trade team, BLG, for his contribution to this section.

entitles a tribunal either upon application or of its own volition to (i) remove any accidental clerical mistakes or ambiguities in an award; or (ii) make an additional award in respect of any claim which was presented but not dealt with in an award.[330]

5.246 However, the mistake in question must have arisen as a result of an accidental slip only, and errors 'in forming the intention to write down what they did' may not be corrected under this provision.[331]

5.247 As regards the removal of ambiguities, again while this section cannot be used as a way of rewriting an award, it can be used to enable the arbitrators to reconsider any inconsistencies in the award.

(2) Interpretation of the award by the tribunal

5.248 English law generally does not make provision for a tribunal to interpret its own award and therefore, absent the parties' agreement, a tribunal may not do so.[332] However, the rules of many international arbitral bodies do provide for interpretation by the tribunal.[333]

B. Appeal on the merits

(1) Admissibility and procedure of an appeal on the merits

5.249 Reflecting the principle of finality underlying the Arbitration Act 1996, English law recognizes only a very limited right of appeal to the courts on the merits, ie on a point of law.[334] Where an appeal cannot be brought with the parties' agreement and where all arbitral processes of appeal or review have been exhausted,[335] permission to appeal a reasoned award on a point of law may be obtained if:

(i) the decision concerns an issue which affects substantially the rights of one or more parties;
(ii) the question is one which the tribunal was asked to determine;
(iii) the tribunal was obviously wrong or an issue of general public importance is raised on which a tribunal's decision is at least open to serious doubt; and
(iv) it is just and proper for the court to determine the issue.[336]

5.250 It is not possible to appeal against an award on a finding of fact (including a finding of foreign law).[337] The distinction between questions of law and fact was considered by Mustill J in *The Chrysalis*.[338]

330 Also referred to as the 'slip rule'.
331 *Fuga AG v Bunge AG* [1975] 2 Lloyd's Rep 192 (Comm).
332 Arbitration Act 1996 s 68(2)(f).
333 ICC Rules Art 29; UNCITRAL Model Law Art 33(1); ICSID Rules ch VII.
334 Note an award may also be challenged under Arbitration Act 1996 s 68 for a serious irregularity.
335 Arbitration Act 1996 s 70.
336 *ibid*, s 69(3).
337 This includes a situation where, although foreign law applies, English law principles have been adopted in the absence of any evidence of there being any difference: *Reliance Industries Ltd v Enron Oil and Gas India Ltd* [2002] 1 All ER (Comm) 59 (Comm).
338 *Finelvet AG v Vinava Shipping Co Ltd ('The Chrysalis')* [1983] 1 WLR 1469 (QB).

Pursuant to s 70 of the Arbitration Act 1996, an application under this section must be made by way of an arbitration claim form[339] supported by a witness statement within 28 days of the date of an award or arbitral process of appeal or review, and must identify the question of law to be determined and the grounds on which it is said that an appeal should be granted. Such applications will be determined on paper unless the court considers that an oral hearing is required. A decision granting or refusing leave to appeal may only be appealed if the court gives its permission. **5.251**

(1.1) May the parties agree on an appeal to another arbitral tribunal? English law recognizes a very limited right of appeal to avoid parties taking steps to try and delay enforcement by way of unwarranted appeals. Nevertheless, where both of the parties are of the view that an award is flawed, there is no reason why the parties may not agree on it becoming the subject of a review by another tribunal. There is no authority either way on this point, but as a consensual process the parties to an award may choose to ignore an award and may vary those rights as they see fit. **5.252**

(2) Possibility to exclude an appeal (eg in the arbitration clause)

Whereas jurisdictional challenges[340] or challenges on the grounds of serious irregularity[341] cannot be excluded by agreement, it is possible for the parties to agree to exclude the right of appeal on a question of law.[342] Examples of this include Art 26.9 of the LCIA Rules and Art 28(6) of the ICC Rules. Although some jurisdictions do not allow the parties to waive their right to appeal on a point of law, the English courts uphold such provisions.[343]

C. Setting aside of the award

(1) Reasons for setting aside an award

On an appeal, the court may, if it is satisfied that the tribunal has made an error of law, set aside the award. There are two other bases upon which the court may set aside an award. **5.253**

First, the court may set aside the award under s 67 if it is persuaded that the award was made by the tribunal without jurisdiction. However, if the party making the challenge has in fact participated in the arbitral proceedings, then it may well have lost the right to challenge the award on the basis of its participation.[344] Equally, if a party has failed to raise its objections before the tribunal, s 73 generally bars the challenge to the tribunal's jurisdiction.[345] **5.254**

Second, the court may set aside an award on the grounds of 'serious irregularity' under s 68, which at s 68(2) sets out an exhaustive list of grounds upon which the court can either set aside or remit the award, provided that the matter complained of has caused substantial **5.255**

339 Form N8, CPR PD 62 app A.
340 Arbitration Act 1996 s 67.
341 *ibid*, s 68.
342 *ibid*, s 69(1).
343 Eg *Lesotho Highlands* (n 289): upheld waiver under ICC Rules.
344 Arbitration Act 1996 s 73.
345 *Kazakhstan v Istil* (n 48); *Russell* (n 21) 8-061, 8-065.

injustice, such as, for example, failure by the tribunal to conduct the proceedings in accordance with the procedure agreed by the parties.[346]

5.256 A failure by the arbitrators to act as efficiently or expeditiously as they might, or a minor failure to follow the procedure laid down by the parties, is not of itself enough to justify the granting of s 68 relief.[347]

5.257 **(1.1) May an award made according to international or foreign procedural rules be the object of an application for setting aside before the national courts?** Sections 67 and 68 apply where the seat of the arbitration is England. Usually, this will mean that the procedural law governing the arbitration is also English. However, assuming an English seat, these sections would also apply where the procedural law governing the arbitration was foreign or transnational. Such matters would inevitably be taken into account by the court when deciding whether or not it was appropriate to exercise its discretion to intervene, but would not preclude it from so doing.

(2) Procedure and deadlines for challenging an award

5.258 Any jurisdictional challenge under s 67 and any application under s 68 must be made within 28 days from the date of the award.[348] Moreover, if the challenge has not been made in good time, the right to advance the challenge may be lost altogether by virtue of s 73. Finally, any available arbitral process of appeal or review must be exhausted before the court will even consider intervening.[349]

5.259 In either case, the application is made to the Commercial Court[350] by way of an Arbitration claim form,[351] in accordance with CPR Pt 8 procedure, and which satisfies the detailed requirements of CPR 62.4.

5.260 **(2.1) Who may (or must) represent a party in a proceeding for setting aside an award?** Parties are usually represented by solicitors and, at any court hearings, by a barrister.

5.261 **(2.2) Do specific time limits exist for setting-aside procedures concerning awards on jurisdiction?** The application must be made within 28 days of the date of the award.[352]

(3) Effect of a court decision which sets the award aside

5.262 Where the court orders that the award is to be set aside, the award is no longer of any effect. Where the award has been set aside for want of jurisdiction under s 67, then there is no longer any scope or possibility for referring the dispute in question to arbitration.[353]

---

346 It must be shown that there is a serious irregularity and that it has caused substantial injustice: *Elektrim SA v Vivendi Universal SA* [2007] EWHC 11 (Comm), [2007] 2 All ER (Comm) 365.

347 *Lesotho Highlands* (n 289) 26-32 (Lord Steyn); *ABB AG v Hochtief Airport GmbH* [2006] EWHC 388 (Comm), [2006] 1 All ER (Comm) 529 [63]–[7].

348 Arbitration Act 1996 s 70(3).

349 *ibid*, s 70(2).

350 Building and property disputes go to the Technology and Construction Court.

351 Form N8, CPR PD 62 app A.

352 Arbitration Act 1996 s 70(3).

353 *Russell* (n 21) 8-162; cf *Hussmann (Europe) Ltd v Pharaon* [2003] EWCA Civ 266, [2003] 1 All ER (Comm) 879 [80-3] (Rix LJ).

However, where the award is set aside for misconduct or error of law, the court will usually remit the award for further consideration by the tribunal.[354]

(3.1) Does the setting-aside action suspend the enforcement? If so, do remedies exist to reinstate enforcement? In theory, the existence of an application to challenge an award does not affect its enforceability as a matter of English law. However, it is likely that in any enforcement action, the English court would take into account the existence of an application challenging the award, and may, for example, adjourn the enforcement application pending such challenge or, possibly, grant a stay of execution.[355] **5.263**

(3.2) After an award has been set aside, does the underlying arbitration agreement revive or remain in force or is it exhausted or deemed terminated? If the award has been set aside on the basis that there was, in fact, no arbitration agreement between the parties, it necessarily follows that there is no arbitration agreement which can revive.[356] If, on the other hand, an award is set aside because there was a s 68 serious irregularity, the underlying arbitration agreement continues to exist. In those circumstances, the parties must refer any new dispute(s) covered by the arbitration agreement to arbitration in accordance with its terms. **5.264**

(4) Appeal against the court's decision to set aside or not set aside the award

A further appeal to the Court of Appeal is possible, but it is first necessary to obtain permission to appeal from the court which gave the decision.[357] In cases of appeals on points of law, permission to appeal 'shall not be given unless the court considers the question is one of general importance or is one which for some other special reason should be considered by the Court of Appeal'.[358] **5.265**

(5) Possibility of the parties to exclude actions for setting aside

By contrast with appeals on points of law under s 69, ss 67 and 68 are mandatory and therefore cannot be ousted by agreement.[359] **5.266**

D. Liability of arbitrators

(1) Duties and liabilities of arbitrators regarding the conduct of the proceedings

Some duties will be imposed upon the arbitrators by law. If the arbitration is institutional, some duties may be imposed upon the arbitrators by the relevant institutional rules. Other duties may also be imposed upon the arbitrators by the parties. **5.267**

As regards duties imposed by law, s 33 of the Arbitration Act 1996 imposes upon the arbitral tribunal a fundamental general duty of fairness, specifically (i) to act fairly and impartially as between the parties, giving each party a reasonable opportunity of putting his case and dealing with that of his opponent; and (ii) to adopt procedures suitable to the **5.268**

354 Arbitration Act 1996 ss 68(3), 69(7); *Russell* (n 21) 8-163.
355 eg *Far Eastern Shipping Co v AKP Sovcomflot* [1995] 1 Lloyd's Rep 520 (Comm).
356 *Hussmann* (n 353) 80-3 (Rix LJ); *Russell* (n 21) 8-162.
357 Arbitration Act 1996 ss 67(4), 68(4), 69(8).
358 *ibid*, s 69(8).
359 *ibid*, s 4(1), sch 1.

circumstances of the particular case, avoiding unnecessary delay or expense, so as to provide a fair means for the resolution of the matters falling to be determined.

5.269 As regards duties imposed upon the tribunal by the parties themselves, they may, in the arbitration agreement, require the tribunal to produce an award within a specified number of days after the hearing or in a particular form.

5.270 (1.1) **Do the courts and/or authorities rely on a contractual relationship between the parties and the arbitrator(s), irrespective of whether institutional or *ad hoc* arbitration is concerned? What is the legal qualification of such a contract (eg provision of services)?** The exclusive source of the relationship between the parties and the arbitrator(s) is the arbitration agreement, irrespective of whether the arbitration is institutional or *ad hoc*. This is what gives the arbitrator(s) their jurisdiction. In that sense, the relationship between the parties and the arbitrators is contractual. However, once the relationship comes into existence, it is supplemented by the provisions of the Arbitration Act 1996, again irrespective of the form of the arbitration, and becomes quasi-judicial.[360] Consequently, it is not possible to classify the status of arbitrators as simply contractual.

5.271 (1.2) **Are there court decisions (or authorities) determining which law governs the question of liability of an arbitrator? What is the position of those courts/authorities as to whether and to which extent a legal liability of an arbitrator (or arbitral institution) may be established?** There are no English authorities on this point. It has been suggested that this issue should principally be governed by the law of the seat of the arbitration.[361] Arbitrators are, under s 29 of the Arbitration Act, immune from liability unless they have acted in bad faith.

5.272 (1.3) **Is an arbitrator subject to criminal prosecution?** If the arbitrator commits a crime, he will be subject to criminal prosecution.

(2) Possibility to restrict or exclude the arbitrators' liability

5.273 As mentioned above, s 29 of the Arbitration Act 1996 expressly provides for arbitral immunity from suit. Accordingly, although a breach of duty by an arbitrator (eg of s 33) might give rise to a statutory remedy in respect of the arbitration (eg under s 68), it will not give rise to an enforceable claim for damages for breach of contract/duty, unless bad faith on the part of the arbitrator can be shown.

VII. Enforcement of national awards*

(1) Requirement of a particular procedure to make an award enforceable (leave for enforcement, exequatur*)*

5.274 Section 66 of the Arbitration Act 1996 provides for summary enforcement of awards: 'an award made. . .pursuant to an arbitration agreement may, by leave of the court, be enforced

360 *K/S Norjarl* (n 301), 876 (Leggatt LJ), 884 (Sir Browne-Wilkinson VC). See *Mustill and Boyd 2001* (n 61) 166; *Mustill and Boyd* (n 302) 220–3.

361 *Redfern and Hunter* (n 65) 243; *Merkin* (n 182) 10.41.

* The authors wish to thank Dorothy Herman, Associate, Commercial Litigation and Arbitration team, BLG, for her contribution to this section.

in the same manner as a judgment or order of the court to same effect' and 'judgment may be entered in terms of the award'. This procedure is only available where there is an arbitration agreement in writing, although this is defined broadly.[362]

It is also possible to bring what is commonly referred to as 'an action on the award' which involves the commencement of court proceedings founded upon an implied term that an award will be honoured when made.[363] **5.275**

(1.1) Does the law make any difference between foreign and domestic awards, and if so, what are the criteria? Does there exist an additional notion of award for the purposes of obtaining *exequatur* (France: international awards)? Although certain provisions of the Arbitration Act 1996 apply only where the seat of the arbitration is in England, Wales or Northern Ireland, s 66 also applies where the seat is outside England and Wales or where no seat has been specified.[364] It expressly states that it does not affect the recognition or enforcement of awards under other enactments or rule of law[365] and so where specific provision is made for enforcement of foreign awards (that is where the seat is outside England, Wales and Northern Ireland) such provisions will continue to apply. In the case of an award in a state (other than the UK) which is a party to the New York Convention, the provisions at ss 100 to 104 of the Arbitration Act relating to the recognition and enforcement of New York Convention awards will apply in addition to s 66. **5.276**

(1.2) May awards granting conservatory/interim measures be subject to enforcement? Section 66 simply refers to an 'award', which is not defined in the Arbitration Act 1996, but it is considered that it applies only to an award which is final and binding,[366] and would not therefore apply to a provisional, interim or conservatory award. Where an award deals finally with some of the issues or claims referred to arbitration such awards ought to be capable of being enforced pursuant to s 66. Such awards are referred to as partial awards. **5.277**

The court may make an order of the court to enforce peremptory orders of the tribunal and to take other steps in support of the arbitral process pursuant to ss 42, 43 and 44 of the Arbitration Act 1996, and requiring compliance by a certain deadline; it may not redraft the peremptory order and will generally enforce it unless there are good reasons not to do so.[367] Failure to comply with the court's order is then contempt of court with the usual sanctions. The court's order may be appealed with the permission of the first instance court. **5.278**

(2) Details of such enforcement procedure (competent court, reasons for rejection of motion etc)

Section 66 provides for summary enforcement of awards made pursuant to an arbitration agreement[368] so that they may be enforced in the same manner as a judgment or order of **5.279**

362 Arbitration Act 1996 s 5, 81(1).
363 *Agromet Motoimport Ltd v Maulden Engineering Co (Beds) Ltd* [1985] 1 WLR 762 (QB).
364 Arbitration Act 1996 s 2(2).
365 *ibid*, s 66(4).
366 *ibid*, s 58(1).
367 *Emmott v Wilson* (n 212 – Comm).
368 See Arbitration Act 1996 s 5.

the court. This procedure enables awards which grant declaratory relief or specific performance to be enforced as well as money awards and will extend to any interest[369] or costs[370] where awarded by the tribunal.

5.280 An application for permission to enforce an award under s 66 may be made in the High Court[371] or any county court.[372] They are usually made in the Commercial and Admiralty Court. An application may be served outside the jurisdiction with the permission of the court.[373] Proceedings continue as an arbitration claim under the CPR.[374]

5.281 The master or judge may either grant the application on a without notice basis or will direct that the application be served.[375]

5.282 The court has no jurisdiction to consider the correctness of the award sought to be enforced, only its validity, and it must have a real ground to doubt an award's validity to refuse enforcement.[376]

5.283 Where the application is granted on a without notice basis, the claimant must draw up the order giving permission to enforce,[377] and serve this on the defendant, who then has 14 days from service to apply to set the order aside (or longer if the order is served out of the jurisdiction).[378] The burden of proof is on the defendant to show why the award should not be enforced.

5.284 Although the court has a discretion whether to grant permission to enforce an award, the Arbitration Act 1996 expressly states that it must not do so 'where. . .the person against whom it is sought to be enforced shows that the tribunal lacked substantive jurisdiction to make the award'.[379] However, the right to raise such an objection may have been lost.[380] In addition to the statutory ground set out in s 66, there are limited defences to enforcement available at common law, for example, where the award is 'so defective in form or substance that it is incapable of enforcement, or where it would be contrary to public policy'[381] or where it concerns a matter not capable of settlement by arbitration.[382]

---

369 *Continental Grain Co v Bremer Handelsgesellschaft MBH (No 2)* [1984] 2 Lloyd's Rep 121 (Comm).

370 *Holdsworth v Wilson* (1863) 32 LJQB 90, 122 ER 360.

371 CPR PD 62.3 [2.3].

372 The High Court and County Courts (Allocation of Arbitration Proceedings) Order 1996, SI 1996/3215 Art 4.

373 CPR 62.18(4).

374 *ibid*, 62.8.

375 *Curacao Trading Co BV v J Harkisandas* [1992] 2 Lloyd's Rep 186 (Comm).

376 *Middlemiss & Gould v Hartlepool Corp* [1971] 1 WLR 1643 (CA); Arbitration Act 1996 ss 57, 66.

377 The order must refer to the defendant's right to apply to have the order set aside. It is also advisable to refer to the costs claimed by the claimant and incurred in the application for permission and, if relevant, in obtaining judgment as any judgment obtained in the terms of the award cannot include additional costs above those awarded by the tribunal.

378 CPR 62.18(9).

379 Arbitration Act s 66(3).

380 *Middlemiss* (n 377).

381 *G Middleton Ltd v Berry Creek Overseas Development Ltd* [2007] EWHC 318 (TCC), [2007] TCLR 4 [5]. The common law rules are preserved by Arbitration Act 1996 s 81(1).

382 Arbitration Act 1996 s 81(1).

A party also may not be permitted to enforce an award by the expiry of a limitation period[383] or by a relevant foreign judgment on the merits if the criteria for an estoppel are met.[384] 5.285

It is not open to a sovereign state to challenge enforcement proceedings on grounds of state immunity, where it has agreed in writing to submit a dispute to arbitration. This was considered by the Court of Appeal in *Svenska Petroleum v Lithuania (No 2)*.[385] 5.286

Where permission is given, the terms of the award may be entered as a judgment. The courts interpret this strictly. Section 66 cannot be used to cure a deficiency in the award or to award additional interest or costs;[386] the court is only able to enter judgment in the terms of the award. 5.287

If the award is entered as a judgment, the defaulting party may be held to be in contempt of court, as it would in relation to any other judgment of the English court.[387] However, where the award is entered as a judgment, the original award may be taken to have merged with the judgment so that enforcement provisions contained in various arbitration conventions would no longer be available.[388] 5.288

In *Gater Assets v Nak Naftogaz Ukrainiy*,[389] the Court of Appeal considered that a court should not order security for costs against an applicant seeking to enforce an award under the summary procedure of s 66. 5.289

The court has the jurisdiction to grant freezing orders over English assets in aid of the enforcement of arbitration awards where there is a risk that assets will be removed from the jurisdiction, and may in appropriate circumstances make world-wide freezing orders in support of national, and in exceptional circumstances, foreign awards.[390] The court may exercise its powers at the application for permission stage, or once a judgment has been obtained in the terms of the award. Once such judgment has been obtained, the court may also order the defaulting party to disclose details of its assets both inside and outside the jurisdiction. 5.290

The court may consider an application to stay enforcement of an award.[391] 5.291

---

383 *Agromet* (n 364).

384 See *Carl Zeiss Stiftung v Rayner & Keller Ltd* [1967] 1 AC 853 (HL): in essence there must be identity of parties and subject matter, the judgment must be made by a foreign court of competent jurisdiction and the judgment must be a decision on the merits, it must be final and conclusive and clear and unambiguous.

385 (n 63).

386 See *Walker v Rowe* [1999] 2 All ER (Comm) 961 (Comm) in relation to post-award interest on national awards. cf *Gater Assets Ltd v Nak Naftogaz Ukrainiy* [2008] EWHC 1108 (Comm), [2009] Bus LR 396, which is authority that once judgment has been entered in the terms of the award, the English courts may award interest pursuant to the Judgments Act 1838 from the date of the judgment. Other provisions may be available to correct clerical errors or ambiguities, eg Arbitration Act 1996 s 57.

387 *ASM Shipping Ltd of India v TTMI Ltd of England* [2007] EWHC 927 (Comm), [2007] 2 Lloyd's Rep 155.

388 *Russell* (n 21) 8-007.

389 *Gater Assets Ltd v Nak Naftogaz Ukrainiy* [2007] EWCA Civ 988, [2008] Bus LR 388.

390 *Rosseel NV v Oriental Commercial & Shipping (UK) Ltd* [1990] 1 WLR 1387 (CA).

391 A discretion to stay may arise where permission to enforce is sought under s 66, under RSC 1965 ord 47 r 1(1) (which permits the court to stay execution of judgments where there are special circumstances which make it inexpedient to enforce: *Far Eastern* (n 356)) or under its inherent jurisdiction (*Apis AS v Fantazia Kereskedelmi KFT (No 1)* [2001] 1 All ER (Comm) 348 (Comm)).

5.292 Where the court is asked to stay enforcement on the basis of a challenge to the award, the court will assess the strength of the argument that the award is invalid on a 'brief consideration only'.[392] If the award is plainly valid, the court should enforce or order substantial security to be provided at the very least; if the award is plainly not valid, then there should be no enforcement and no security ordered. Between these two positions, it is a matter for the judgment of the court. The court will also look at the impact of a delay on the ease or difficulty of enforcement.[393] Where there is no challenge to an award but a stay is sought on the basis of a cross-claim, this is not normally sufficient to obtain a stay. Special circumstances must be shown which would render it inexpedient to enforce.[394] Where a stay is granted, a cross-undertaking to make good any damage suffered due to the delay may be required.[395]

5.293 Where the summary procedure under s 66 is not available,[396] a party must rely on the common law, which recognizes an implied term that an award will be honoured when made.[397] An action on an award is a fresh cause of action to enforce a contract, and so the limitation period runs for six years from the date of the failure to honour the award (or 12 years where the arbitration agreement was made under seal). Unlike under s66, there is no presumption that the award was validly made and so the enforcing party must prove that the tribunal had jurisdiction.

(3) Appeal against the decision granting exequatur

5.294 The usual rules of English civil procedure apply to appeals from a decision to enforce an arbitral award.[398] Accordingly, permission to appeal will be required, which is granted where an appeal has a real prospect of success or there is some other compelling reason why the appeal should be heard.[399] A party must apply by way of an appellant's notice setting out clearly the grounds of appeal and whether such grounds are questions of law, disputes about factual findings or Human Rights Act 1998 points. The appeal court's consideration is generally limited to a review of the decision of the lower court; it is not a rehearing or an opportunity to introduce new evidence or issues.

(4) Appeal (and procedure) if exequatur *has been refused*

5.295 The appeal procedure when permission to enforce has been refused is the same as that described in para 5.294 *supra*.

---

392 *Apis* (n 392).

393 *Soleh Boneh International v Uganda and National Housing Corp* [1993] 2 Lloyd's Rep 208 (CA). In *Socadec SA v Pan Afric Impex Co Ltd* [2003] EWHC 2086 (QB), a short stay of enforcement was granted to allow the defaulting party to put up security. In *Apis* (n 392), the court ordered a stay of enforcement on condition of a payment into court.

394 The court will consider factors such as the connection between the claims, the strength of the cross-claim, the likely delay and the risk of prejudice to each party if enforcement were granted or refused: *Burnet v Francis Industries Plc* [1987] 1 WLR 802 (CA).

395 *Hillcourt (Docklands) Ltd v Teliasonera AB* [2006] EWHC 508 (Ch).

396 eg where the arbitration agreement is purely oral: Arbitration Act 1996 ss 5(1), 66(1).

397 *Purslow v Bailey* (1704) Ld Raym 1039, 92 ER 190; *Agromet* (n 364). This implied obligation is made express by the rules of several institutional arbitration bodies including the UNCITRAL Rules Art 32.2, ICC Rules Art 28(6) and LCIA Rules Art 26.9.

398 CPR 52.

399 *ibid*, 52.3(6).

(5) Procedure of enforcement (attachment of bank accounts etc)

Once an order granting permission to enforce has been made or a judgment in the terms of the award has been handed down, it is for the successful party to take enforcement steps. He will be in the same position as any other judgment creditor or successful party, in the sense that the same procedural rules and procedures will apply in relation to enforcement of the award as apply in relation to court judgments generally in England and Wales. **5.296**

In relation to a money judgment, an enforcing party may, again on application to the court:[400] **5.297**

(i) apply for a charging order over the assets of the party in default. A charging order may be obtained over a wide variety of assets, including property;
(ii) apply for third party debt orders (eg over the defaulting party's bank accounts);[401]
(iii) appoint a receiver under the court's equitable powers;[402]
(iv) apply for a writ of *fieri facias* to allow seizure of the debtor's goods by the court's bailiffs so these may be sold to satisfy the debt; or
(v) apply for attachment of earnings orders to require sums due to an individual judgment debtor to be paid directly to the enforcing party.

(5.1) At the stage of enforcement, may the losing party invoke arguments and circumstances which are based on facts which have occurred before (or after) the award was made? Parties often seek to rely on facts which occurred before the award was made, at the enforcement stage, to impeach the validity of the award. For example, a party may rely on a procedural irregularity to challenge the award.[403] However, a party will not generally be able to rely on pre-award facts if that would require the court to go behind the facts as found by the arbitrators. **5.298**

Where a party seeks to challenge enforcement in reliance on facts which are said to have occurred after the award was made, the position is likely to be even more difficult because such cases are less likely to impeach the validity of the award itself, and are more likely to give rise to an argument that enforcement is simply unfair. **5.299**

This was emphasized in *Air India v Caribjet*, where the court considered that once a party has 'its enforceable award', it should 'only be deprived of it if there are special circumstances'.[404] **5.300**

(5.2) May the losing party invoke a set-off based on claims that are not related to the matter of the arbitral proceeding? Is it material whether such claim came into existence **5.301**

---

[400] Specific procedural rules apply depending on the order sought.

[401] Note however the court's inability to grant a third party debt order over assets held outside England to avoid conflicts of jurisdiction and the risk of double payment by the third party (*Société Eram Shipping Co Ltd v Cie Internationale de Navigation and Ors* [2003] UKHL 30, [2004] 1 AC 260; *Kuwait Oil Tanker Co SAK v Qabazard* [2003] UKHL 31, [2004] 1 AC 300) or where there is a real chance that the result of such an order would be the losing party paying twice (*Deutsche Schactbau-und-Tiefbohrgesellschaft mbh v Shell International Petroleum Co Ltd* [1990] 1 AC 295 (HL)).

[402] *Soinco SACI & Anor v Novokuznetsk Aluminium Plant & Ors* [1998] QB 406 (Comm).

[403] *Kanoria & Ors v Guinness* [2006] EWCA Civ 222, [2006] 2 All ER (Comm) 413.

[404] *Air India Ltd v Caribjet Inc* [2002] 2 All ER (Comm) 76 (Comm) [65].

before or after the award was made? Claims which are not related to the subject matter of the arbitral proceedings may be set off at the enforcement stage, provided the criteria for common law set-off are met. Although common law set-off does not require any connection between the claims to be set off, the claim to be set off must be due and payable at the time set-off is claimed, and must either be liquidated, or capable of being quantified by reference to ascertainable facts which do not require estimation or valuation.[405] In addition, the set-off claim must be actionable, so if there is a procedural bar to the claim being asserted in the enforcement proceedings, the set-off will not be permitted.[406]

5.302 Provided that the requirements for common law set-off are met when the claim for set-off is made in the enforcement proceedings, the timing of when the claim to be set off arose ought not to matter.

VIII. Foreign awards*

A. Recognition and/or enforcement of foreign awards (national law)

5.303 In practice, it is the New York Convention, as implemented by Pt III of the Arbitration Act 1996, which governs the recognition and enforcement of 'foreign awards' and on which this section will focus. A foreign award may be enforced under the common law rules where the award does not fall within the New York Convention, or another treaty.

(1) Rules according to national law

5.304 A New York Convention award is defined by s 100 of the Arbitration Act 1996 as 'an award made, in pursuance of a [written] arbitration agreement,[407] in the territory of a state (other than the United Kingdom)[408] which is a party to the New York Convention'. Such an award shall be recognized as binding (and therefore relied on by way of set-off or defence in legal proceedings)[409] and permission given for it to be enforced, in the same manner as a judgment or court order.[410] As with domestic awards, where leave has been given, judgment may be entered in the terms of the award.[411]

(2) Requirements to be fulfilled by the applicant (procedure, time limits)

5.305 The procedure (including appeals) and applicable time limits for enforcement of a foreign award under Pt III of the Arbitration Act 1996 are the same as under s 66. An application may be made without notice, by way of an arbitration claim form, and all the relevant sections of the CPR then apply.[412]

---

[405] *Aectra Refining & Marketing Inc v Exmar NV ('The New Vanguard' and 'The Pacifica')* [1995] 1 All ER 641 (CA) 654.

[406] *'The New Vanguard' and 'The Pacifica'* (n 406).

* The authors wish to thank Dorothy Herman, Associate, Commercial Litigation and Arbitration team, BLG, for her contribution to this section.

[407] As defined in the Arbitration Act 1996 s 5; *Mustill and Boyd 2001* (n 61) 381–4; 1996 DAC (n 3) [34], [348].

[408] But not including Scotland.

[409] Arbitration Act 1996 s 101(1).

[410] *ibid*, s 101(2).

[411] *ibid*, s 101(3).

[412] CPR 62, CPR PD 62.

The party wishing to enforce the award must produce an authenticated original award (or duly certified copy) together with the original arbitration agreement (or duly certified copy). If these documents are not originally in English, a certified translation must also be provided.[413] There is no requirement that the respondent has assets in England. If, however, the respondent is out of the country, the applicant must apply for the court's permission to serve the enforcement proceedings outside the jurisdiction.[414] **5.306**

(3) Remedies against decisions granting or declining enforcement

A party may seek permission to appeal against a decision that grants or declines enforcement of a New York Convention award.[415] The Court of Appeal also recently affirmed that, in rare instances, the English court may revisit an earlier decision adjourning enforcement that is no longer appropriate owing to 'significantly different circumstances'.[416] **5.307**

B. Recognition and/or enforcement of foreign awards (conventions, treaties)

Although the primary tool in recognizing and enforcing foreign awards in England, the New York Convention is not the sole convention or treaty upon which a party may rely for the enforcement of a foreign award. **5.308**

Section 99 of the Arbitration Act 1996 governs enforcement of those foreign awards falling within the 1927 Geneva Convention but not the New York Convention. Part II of the Arbitration Act 1950 continues to apply to such awards, which can therefore be enforced summarily in a similar manner to the s 66 procedure described above, or by action on the award. **5.309**

Under CPR 62.20, awards made in UK Overseas Territories[417] may be enforced in the English courts where such awards are enforceable as a judgment in the jurisdiction in which they were made. **5.310**

Awards falling within the 1965 Washington Convention, as implemented by the Arbitration (International Investment Disputes) Act 1966, may be registered in the High Court and thereby become enforceable in the same manner, as if a High Court judgment. The party seeking enforcement must apply for registration under the CPR Pt 8 procedure.[418] **5.311**

(1) Specific bilateral or multilateral treaties

The UK is a signatory to several multilateral treaties regarding the enforcement of foreign arbitration awards: the 1923 Geneva Protocol on Arbitration Clauses, the 1927 Geneva Convention on the Execution of Foreign Arbitral Awards, the New York Convention and the 1965 Washington Convention for the Settlement of Investment Disputes between **5.312**

---

413 Arbitration Act 1996 s 102.

414 See CPR 62.5, 62.18(4).

415 CPR 52.3, CPR PD 52 [2A.1], Table 1.

416 *Nigerian National Petroleum Corp v IPCO (Nigeria) Ltd* [2008] EWCA Civ 1157, [2008] 2 CLC 550 [24] (Tuckey LJ) and *IPCO (Nigeria) Ltd v Nigerian National Petroleum Corp (No 2)* [2008] EWHC 797 (Comm), [2008] 2 Lloyd's Rep 59 [73], [76] (Tomlinson J). The procedural developments, since the earlier decision, were described as 'catastrophic' and an order enforcing part of the arbitral award was made.

417 As defined by the CPR and/or the Foreign Judgments (Reciprocal Enforcement) Act 1933.

418 CPD 62.21.

Contracting States and Nationals of Other States. The UK is not a signatory to the 1961 European Convention on International Arbitration.

(2) Existence of a standard procedure for the enforcement of foreign awards

5.313 The procedure for obtaining permission to enforce New York Convention awards is as outlined at paras 5.305 to 5.306 *supra*.

5.314 In the case of other foreign awards, different procedures apply depending on the applicable convention or act[419] or whether the award is being enforced at common law.[420]

(3) Extent of examination and review of the award by the court

5.315 In the case of New York Convention awards, the court's substantive approach will be governed by ss 103(2) and (3) of the Arbitration Act 1996, which reflect Art V of the New York Convention, specifying the circumstances in which a court may refuse to enforce an award. Except in those circumstances, recognition or enforcement 'shall not be refused'.[421]

5.316 Generally, the court will not go behind an award, and so will not explore the reasoning of the arbitral tribunal, save to the extent that it has to check that the threshold requirements for enforcement have been met, or the exhaustive grounds for refusing enforcement in s103 are made out.[422] Where enforcement is challenged on one of the grounds set out in s 103, the court is likely to allow a rehearing on the matter, unless the issue has already been finally disposed of between the parties.[423]

5.317 On an application for enforcement of a New York Convention award, the court has power to adjourn the decision where an application for the setting aside or suspension of the award has been made.[424] There is debate as to whether a wider power exists to stay the enforcement of New York Convention awards beyond this, but even if such a power did exist, the English courts have indicated that it should and would rarely be exercised.[425]

C. Application of the New York Convention

5.318 Owing to the wide adoption of the New York Convention,[426] arbitration awards can often be easier and quicker to enforce in the UK than foreign court judgments (especially non-EU judgments).

(1) Application of the New York Convention in practice

5.319 The court's approach in considering the recognition or enforcement of New York Convention awards recognizes the important policy interest in ensuring the effective and speedy enforcement of international arbitration awards.[427] Great weight is also given to

419 eg Washington Convention 1965; Foreign Judgments (Reciprocal Enforcement) Act 1933.

420 See CPR 62.20-1.

421 Arbitration Act 1996 s 103(1); cf the general discretion which the court has on applications under s 66.

422 See *Norsk Hydro ASA v The State Property Fund of Ukraine* [2002] EWHC 2120 (Admin) (Gross J).

423 See *Svenska* (n 63), where the English enforcing court could re-examine whether there was a valid arbitration agreement.

424 See Arbitration Act 1996 s 103(5) reflecting the New York Convention Art VI.

425 *Far Eastern* (n 356).

426 It currently has 144 country signatories.

427 *Norsk Hydro* (n 423).

decisions of the relevant supervisory court; issues which have been conclusively determined by that court will only be revisited in exceptional cases, such as corruption.[428]

Where the court considered an attempt to avoid enforcement on the ground that a party had been unable to present its case,[429] the court held a party must show that it has been unable to do so due to matters outside its control.[430] This ground would normally cover the case where the procedure adopted in the arbitration has been operated in a manner contrary to the rules of natural justice. **5.320**

When a party seeks to resist enforcement on grounds of public policy, there are certain rules of public policy, which if infringed, will lead to non-enforcement by the English court, whatever their proper law and wherever they are to be performed; for example, terrorism and drug trafficking.[431] **5.321**

Where an underlying contract is not in that category (such as contracts for the purchase of influence), it is only if the contract is contrary to the public policy of the country where it is to be performed, as well as that of England that enforcement will be refused.[432] There is nothing which offends English public policy if an arbitral tribunal enforces a contract which does not offend the domestic public policy, under either the proper law of the contract or its curial law, even if English domestic public policy might have taken a different view.[433] **5.322**

When illegality is raised but the tribunal has already investigated the illegality, and found there to be none, the court will not generally conduct a full-scale enquiry reopening the issue. It may, however, perform a preliminary enquiry to decide whether it is proper to give full faith and credit to the award, checking that there is no evidence of bad faith or incompetence or lack of jurisdiction on the part of the tribunal.[434] **5.323**

Where a party wishes to rely on new evidence to resist enforcement of an award on grounds of fraud, normally the issue cannot be reopened unless the evidence was not available to the party at the time of the arbitration and, where the allegation is of perjury, the evidence must be so strong that it could reasonably be expected to be decisive at a hearing.[435] **5.324**

Where an award is challenged on the basis that it relates to a matter which is not capable of settlement by arbitration, the court construes this narrowly, considering that decisions affecting the parties' legal status, competition and antitrust matters are arbitrable.[436] **5.325**

---

428 *Minmetals Germany GmbH v Ferco Steel Ltd* [1999] 1 All ER (Comm) 315 (Comm).

429 Arbitration Act 1996 s 103(2)(c).

430 *Minmetals* (n 429).

431 *Lemenda Trading Co Ltd v African Middle East Petroleum Co Ltd* [1988] QB 448 (Comm); cf. *Westacre Investments Inc v Jugoimport SPDR Holding Co Ltd* [2000] QB 288 (CA).

432 *Westacre* (n 432).

433 *ibid*, where a Swiss award enforcing a contract, said to have involved bribery in Kuwait, was upheld, the tribunal having found no illegality.

434 *Soleimany and Soleimany* [1999] QB 785 (CA), but the appropriateness of such a preliminary enquiry has been doubted in *Westacre* (n 432).

435 *Westacre* (n 432).

436 *ET Plus v Welter* (n 67).

5.326 The court has also recognized the policy of speedy enforcement of arbitral awards, by ordering the enforcement of part of a New York Convention award, despite the absence of an express power to do so.[437]

(2) Examples of decisions which do not apply the Convention correctly

5.327 In *Norsk Hydro*,[438] where the court had initially given permission for an award made against a single party to be enforced against two separate and distinct parties, it subsequently set that permission aside as it required the enforcing court to stray into the arena of the substantive reasoning, and intentions of the arbitral tribunal which was not the right approach.[439]

IX. Appendix

A. National legislation

Arbitration Act 1996 <http://www.opsi.gov.uk/acts/acts1996/ukpga_19960023_en_1> (accessed 3 July 2008).

Civil Procedure Rules 1998, SI 1998/3132 <http://www.justice.gov.uk/civil/procrules_fin/menus/rules.htm> (accessed 19 March 2009).

B. Arbitral institutions

Chartered Institute of Arbitrators' Dispute Resolution Service (DRS-CIArb)
IDRS Limited
24 Angel Gate
City Road
London
EC1V 2PT
Telephone: +44(0) 207 520 3800
Fax: +44(0) 207 421 3829
Email: info@idrs.ltd.uk
Website: <http://www.arbitrators.org/institute>

Centre for Effective Dispute Resolution (CEDR)
International Dispute Resolution Centre
70 Fleet Street
London
EC4Y 1EU
Telephone: +44(0) 207 536 6000
Fax: +44(0) 207 536 6001
Email: info@cedr.com
Website: <http://www.cedr.co.uk>

---

437 *NNPC v IPCO* (n 417 - CA).
438 *Norsk Hydro* (n 423).
439 *Norsk Hydro* (n 423).

The Coffee Trade Federation
Blackfriars Foundry
156 Blackfriars Road
London
SE1 8EN
Telephone: +44 (0) 207 328 5222
Fax: +44 (0) 207 328 5444
Email: secretariat@coffeetradefederation.org.uk
Website: <http://www.coffeetradefederation.org.uk>

The Federation of Oils, Seeds & Fats Association (FOSFA)
FOSFA International
20 St Dunstan's Hill
London
EC3R 8NQ
Telephone: +44(0) 207 283 5511
Fax: +44(0) 207 623 1310
Email: membership@FOSFA.org
Website: <http://www.FOSFA.org>

Grain and Feed Trade Association (GAFTA)
GAFTA House
6 Chapel Place
Rivington Place
London
EC2A 3SH
Telephone: +44(0) 207 814 9666
Fax: +44(0) 207 814 8383
Email: post@GAFTA.com
Website: <http://www.GAFTA.com>

Lloyd's Salvage Arbitration Branch
Lloyd's
One Lime Street
London
EC3M 7HA
Telephone: +44(0) 207 327 1000
Email: enquiries@lloyds.com
Website: <http://www.lloyds.com>

London Court of International Arbitration (LCIA)
The LCIA
70 Fleet Street
London
EC4Y 1EU
Telephone: +44 (0)207 936 7007
Fax: +44 (0)207 936 7008
Website: <http://www.LCIA-arbitration.com>

London Maritime Arbitrators (LMAA)
The LMAA
124 Aldersgate Street
London
EC1A 4JQ
Telephone: + 44(0) 207 490 7334
Fax: +44(0) 207 490 4383
Email: LMAA@btconnect.com
Website: <http://www.LMAA.org.uk>

The London Metal Exchange
56 Leadenhall Street
London
EC2A 2DX
Telephone: +44 (0) 207 264 5555
Fax: +44(0) 207 680 0505
Website: <http://www.lme.com>

The Sugar Association and the Refined Sugar Association
The Secretary
The Sugar Association
154 Bishopsgate
London
EC2M 4LN
Telephone: +44(0) 207 377 2113
Fax: +44(0) 207 247 2481
Email: durhamn@sugar-assoc.co.uk
Website: <http://www.sugarassociation.co.uk>

C. Model arbitration clauses and other patterns

The Chartered Institute of Arbitrators' Dispute Resolution Services model arbitration clause:

> Any dispute or difference arising out of or in connection with this contract shall be determined by the appointment of a single arbitrator to be agreed between the parties, or failing agreement within fourteen days, after either party has given to the other a written request to concur in the appointment of an arbitrator, by an arbitrator to be appointed by the President or a Vice President of the Chartered Institute of Arbitrators.

The LCIA model arbitration clause for future disputes:

> Any dispute arising out of or in connection with this contract, including any question regarding its existence, validity or termination, shall be referred to and finally resolved by arbitration under the LCIA Rules, which Rules are deemed to be incorporated by reference into this clause.
>
> The number of arbitrators shall be [one/three].
>
> The seat, or legal place, of arbitration shall be [City and/or Country].
>
> The language to be used in the arbitral proceedings shall be [ ].

The governing law of the contract shall be the substantive law of [ ].

The BIMCO/LMAA model arbitration clause is available at <http://www.LMAA.org.uk/uploads/documents/BIMCO-LMAA-ArbitrationClause2009.pdf> (accessed 23 March 2009).

Although not unique to English arbitration, the UNCITRAL model arbitration clause is available at <http://www.uncitral.org/pdf/english/texts/arbitration/arb-rules/arb-rules.pdf> (accessed 16 January 2008).

D. Bibliography

Books, articles and reports

The Code of Conduct of the Bar of England and Wales (8th edn, Bar Council, 2004).

The Solicitors' Code of Conduct 2007 (revised edn, The Law Society, 29 June 2007) <http://www.rules.sra.org.uk> (accessed 10 November 2008).

Report on the Arbitration Act 1996, Bruce Harris (chair) (Prepared for the Commercial Court Users' Committee, the British Maritime Law Association, the London Shipping Law Centre and other bodies, November 2006) <http://www.idrc.co.uk/aa96survey/Report_on_Arbitration_Act_1996.pdf> (accessed 3 July 2008).

Bellhouse, John and Lavers, Anthony, 'The Modern Amicus Curiae: a role for arbitration?' (2004) 23 *CJQ* 187.

Cato, Mark D., *Arbitration Practice and Procedure: Interlocutory and Hearing Problems* (3rd edn, Informa Professional, London, 2002).

Collins, Sir Lawrence *et al* (eds), *Dicey, Morris & Collins on the Conflict of Laws* (14th edn, Sweet & Maxwell, London, 2006), and Second Supplement to the 14th Edition (Sweet & Maxwell, London, 2008).

Commercial Court Committee, *Report on Arbitration*, Cmnd 7284, Lord Donaldson (chair) (HMSO, London, 1978).

Cross, Rupert and Tapper, Colin, *Cross and Tapper on Evidence* (OUP, Oxford, 2007).

Departmental Advisory Committee on Arbitration Law, *New Arbitration Act? The response of the Departmental Advisory Committee to the UNCITRAL Model law on International Commercial Arbitration*, Sir Michael Mustill LJ (chair) (HMSO, London, 1989).

Departmental Advisory Committee on Arbitration Law, *Report on the Arbitration Bill (February 1996) and Supplementary Report on the Arbitration Act 1996 (January 1997)*, Sir Mark Oliver Saville LJ (chair) (Department of Trade and Industry, London, 1997).

Derains, Yves and Schwartz, Eric, *Guide to the New ICC Rules of Arbitration* (2nd edn, Kluwer Law International, The Hague, 2005).

Flint, Peter, 'Arbitration Proceedings: not so private and confidential?' XIX (April, 2008) *PLC Magazine.*

McGregor, Harvey, *McGregor on Damages* (17th edn, Sweet & Maxwell, London, 2003).

Merkin, Robert, *Arbitration Law* (1st edn service issue 51 (10 March 2009), Informa Professional, London, 1991).

Merkin, Robert and Flannery, Louis, *Arbitration Act 1996* (3rd edn, LLP, London, 2005).

Ministry of Justice, *Judicial and Court Statistics 2006*, Cm 7273 (Presented to Parliament by the Secretary of State for Justice, November 2007) <http://www.justice.gov.uk/docs/judicial-court-stats-2006-tag.pdf> (accessed 3 July 2008).

Mustill, Sir Michael and Boyd, Stewart, *The Law and Practice of Commercial Arbitration in England* (2nd edn, Butterworths, London, 1989).

Mustill, Lord and Boyd, Stewart, *Commercial arbitration: 2001 Companion Volume to the Second Edition* (Butterworths, London, 2001).

Nicholas, Geoff and Partasides, Constantine, 'LCIA Court Decision on Challenges to Arbitrators: A Proposal to Publish' (2007) 23(1) *Arb Int'l* 1.

Passmore, Colin, *Privilege* (2nd edn, XPL Publishing, St Albans, 2006).

Poudret, Jean-François and Besson, Sébastien, *Comparative Law of International Arbitration*, translated by Stephen Berti and Annette Ponti (2nd edn, Sweet & Maxwell, London, 2007).

Redfern, Alan and Hunter, Martin, *Law & Practice of International Commercial Arbitration* (4th edn, Sweet & Maxwell, London, 2004).

Reynolds, F.M.B., *Bowstead and Reynolds on Agency* (18th edn, Sweet & Maxwell, London, 2006).

Sutton, David St John, Gill, Judith and Gearing, Matthew, *Russell on Arbitration* (23rd edn, Sweet & Maxwell, London, 2007).

Tweeddale, Andrew and Keren, *Arbitration of Commercial Disputes: International and English Law and Practice* (OUP, Oxford, 2005).

Cases

ABB AG v Hochtief Airport GmbH [2006] EWHC 388 (Comm), [2006] 1 All ER (Comm) 529.

ABB Lummus Global Ltd v Keppel Fels Ltd [1999] 2 Lloyd's Rep 24 (Comm).

A v B (Costs) [2007] EWHC 54 (Comm), [2007] 1 All ER (Comm) 633.

AIG Europe (UK) Ltd v Ethniki [2000] 2 All ER 566 (CA).

AIG Europe SA v QBE International Insurance Ltd [2001] 2 All ER (Comm) 622 (Comm).

ASM Shipping Ltd of India v TTMI Ltd of England [2007] EWHC 927 (Comm), [2007] 2 Lloyd's Rep 155.

Aectra Refining & Marketing Inc v Exmar NV ('The New Vanguard' and 'The Pacifica') [1995] 1 All ER 641 (CA).

Agromet Motoimport Ltd v Maulden Engineering Co (Beds) Ltd [1985] 1 WLR 762 (QB).

Air India Ltd v Caribjet Inc [2002] 2 All ER (Comm) 76 (Comm).

Albon (t/a NA Carriage Co) v Naza Motor Trading Sdn Bhd (No 3) [2007] EWHC 327 (Ch), [2007] 1 All ER (Comm) 813.

Ali Shipping Corp v Shipyard Trogir [1999] 1 WLR 314 (CA).

Allianz SpA (formerly Riunione Adriatica di Sicurta SpA) v West Tankers Inc (Case C-185/07) [2009] 1 All ER (Comm) 435 (ECJ Grand Chamber)

Andrews (t/a BA Contractors) v Bradshaw [2000] BLR 6 (CA).

Aoot Kalmneft v Denton Wilde Sapte [2002] 1 Lloyd's Rep 417 (Mercantile).

Apis AS v Fantazia Kereskedelmi KFT (No 1) [2001] 1 All ER (Comm) 348 (Comm).

Athletic Union of Constantinople v National Basketball Association [2002] 1 All ER (Comm) 70 (Comm).

Aughton Ltd v M F Kent Services Ltd (1991) 57 BLR 1 (CA).

BEA Hotels NV v Bellway LLC [2007] EWHC 1363 (Comm), [2007] 2 Lloyd's Rep 493.

The Bay Hotel and Resort Ltd v Cavalier Construction Co Ltd [2001] UKPC 34.

Baytur SA v Finagro Holding SA [1991] QB 610 (CA).

Braes of Doune Wind Farm (Scotland) Ltd v Alfred McAlpine Business Services Ltd [2008] EWHC 426 (TCC), [2008] 2 All ER (Comm) 493.

Brooke v Mitchell (1840) 6 M&W 473, 9LG Ex 269.

Burnet v Francis Industries Plc [1987] 1 WLR 802 (CA).

C v D [2007] EWCA Civ 1282, [2008] 1 All ER (Comm) 1001.

CGU International Insurance Plc v Astrazeneca Insurance Co Ltd [2005] EWHC 2755 (Comm), [2006] 1 CLC 162.

Cadmus Investment Ltd v Amec Building Ltd (1997) 51 Con LR 105 (QB).

Cargill International SA Antigua and Anor v Sociedad Ibérica de Molturación SA and Ors [1998] 1 Lloyd's Rep 489 (CA).

Carl Zeiss Stiftung v Rayner & Keller Ltd [1967] 1 AC 853 (HL).

Cetelem v Roust Holdings Ltd [2005] EWCA Civ 618, [2005] 1 WLR 3555.

Charles M Willie & Co (Shipping) Ltd v Ocean Laser Shipping Ltd ('The Smaro') [1999] 1 Lloyd's Rep 225 (Comm).

Checkpoint Ltd v Strathclyde Pension Fund [2003] EWCA Civ 84, [2003] L & TR 22.
City & General (Holborn) Ltd v AYH Plc [2005] EWHC 2494, [2006] BLR 55 (TCC).
Commerce & Industry Insurance Co (Canada) v Lloyd's Underwriters [2002] 1 WLR 1323 (Comm).
Continental Grain Co v Bremer Handelsgesellschaft MBH (No 2) [1984] 2 Lloyd's Rep 121 (Comm).
Curacao Trading Co BV v J Harkisandas [1992] 2 Lloyd's Rep 186 (Comm).
Department of Economics, Policy and Development of the City of Moscow and Anor v Bankers Trust Co and Anor [2004] EWCA Civ 314, [2005] QB 207.
Deutsche Schactbau-und-Tiefbohrgesellschaft mbh v Shell International Petroleum Co Ltd [1990] 1 AC 295 (HL).
Dolling-Baker v Merrett [1990] 1 WLR 1205 (CA).
Dubai Islamic Bank PJSC v Paymentech Merchant Services Inc [2001] Lloyd's Rep 65 (Comm).
ET Plus SA v Welter [2005] EWHC 2115 (Comm), [2006] 1 Lloyd's Rep 251.
Eco Swiss China Time Ltd v Benetton International NV (Case C-126/97) [1999] ECR I-3055.
Egon Oldendorff v Libera Corp (No 1) [1995] 2 Lloyd's Rep 64 (Comm).
Egon Oldendorff v Libera Corp (No 2) [1996] 1 Lloyd's Rep 380 (Comm).
Elektrim SA v Vivendi Universal SA [2007] EWHC 11 (Comm), [2007] 2 All ER (Comm) 365.
Elektrim SA v Vivendi Universal SA [2007] EWHC 571 (Comm), [2007] 2 Lloyd's Rep 8.
Emmott v Michael Wilson and Partners Ltd [2008] EWCA Civ 184, [2008] 1 Lloyd's Rep 616.
Emmott v Michael Wilson and Partners Ltd [2009] EWHC 1 (Comm), [2009] 1 Lloyd's Rep 233.
European Grain and Shipping Ltd v Johnston [1983] QB 520 (CA).
Extrudakerb (Maltby Engineering) Ltd v Whitemountain Quarries Ltd [1996] CLC 1747 (QB).
F Ltd v M Ltd [2009] EWHC 275 (TCC).
Fairclough Building Ltd v Vale of Belvoir Superstore Ltd (1990) 56 BLR 74 (QB).
Far Eastern Shipping Co v AKP Sovcomflot [1995] 1 Lloyd's Rep 520 (Comm).
Fence Gate Ltd v NEL Construction Ltd (2001) 82 Con LR 41 (TCC).
Finelvet AG v Vinava Shipping Co Ltd ('The Chrysalis') [1983] 1 WLR 1469 (QB).
Finnegan v Sheffield City Council (1988) 43 BLR 124 (QB).
Fiona Trust & Holding Corp and Ors v Privalov and Ors [2007] EWCA Civ 20, [2007] 1 All ER (Comm) 891.
Fiona Trust & Holding Corp and Ors v Privalov and Ors [2007] UKHL 40, [2007] 4 All ER 951.
Fuga AG v Bunge AG [1975] 2 Lloyd's Rep 192 (Comm).
Gater Assets Ltd v Nak Naftogaz Ukrainiy [2007] EWCA Civ 988, [2008] Bus LR 388.
Gater Assets Ltd v Nak Naftogaz Ukrainiy [2008] EWHC 1108 (Comm), [2009] Bus LR 396.
Hassneh Insurance Co of Israel v Mew [1993] 2 Lloyd's Rep 243 (Comm).
Heifer International Inc v Christiansen [2007] EWHC 3015 (TCC), [2008] Bus LR D49.
Hillcourt (Docklands) Ltd v Teliasonera AB [2006] EWHC 508 (Ch).
Holdsworth v Wilson (1863) 32 LJQB 90, 122 ER 360.
Home Insurance Co and St Paul Fire and Marine Insurance Co v Administratia Asigurarilor de Stat [1983] 2 Lloyd's Rep 674 (Comm).
Home and Overseas Insurance Co Ltd v Mentor Insurance (UK) Ltd [1990] 1 WLR 153 (CA).
Hussmann (Europe) Ltd v Pharaon [2003] EWCA Civ 266, [2003] 1 All ER (Comm) 879.
IPCO (Nigeria) Ltd v Nigerian National Petroleum Corp (No 2) [2008] EWHC 797 (Comm), [2008] 2 Lloyd's Rep 59.
Internaut Shipping GmbH v Fercometal Sarl (The Elikon) [2003] EWCA Civ 812, [2003] 2 Lloyd's Rep 430.
K/S Norjarl A/S v Hyundai Heavy Industries Co Ltd [1992] QB 863 (CA).
Kanoria & Ors v Guinness [2006] EWCA Civ 222, [2006] 2 All ER (Comm) 413.
Kastner v Jason [2004] EWHC 592 (Ch), [2004] 2 Lloyd's Rep 233.
Kastner v Jason [2004] EWCA Civ 1599, [2005] 1 Lloyd's Rep 397.
Kuwait Oil Tanker Co SAK v Qabazard [2003] UKHL 31, [2004] 1 AC 300.

Lemenda Trading Co Ltd v African Middle East Petroleum Co Ltd [1988] QB 448 (Comm).
Lesotho Highlands Development Authority v Impreglio SpA [2005] UKHL 43, [2006] 1 AC 221.
Lobb Partnership Ltd v Aintree Racecourse Co Ltd [2000] BLR 65 (Comm).
Middlemiss & Gould v Hartlepool Corp [1972] 1 WLR 1643 (CA).
G Middleton Ltd v Berry Creek Overseas Development Ltd [2007] EWHC 318 (TCC), [2007] TCLR 4.
Miliangos v George Frank (Textiles) Ltd [1976] AC 443 (HL).
Miliangos v George Frank (Textiles) Ltd (No 2) [1977] QB 489 (QB).
Minmetals Germany GmbH v Ferco Steel Ltd [1999] 1 All ER (Comm) 315 (Comm).
Mobil Cerro Negro Ltd v Petroleos de Venezuela SA [2008] EWHC 532 (Comm), [2008] 1 Lloyd's Rep 684.
Modern Building (Wales) Ltd v Limmer and Trinidad Co Ltd [1975] 1 WLR 1281 (CA).
Montedipe SpA v JTP-RO Jugotanker ('The Jordan Nicolov') [1990] 2 Lloyd's Rep 11 (Comm).
National Justice Compania Naviera SA v Prudential Assurance SA ('The Ikarian Reefer') [1993] 2 Lloyd's Rep 68 (Comm).
Naviera Amazónica Peruana v Cía Internacional de Seguros del Perú [1998] 1 Lloyd's Rep 116 (CA).
Nigerian National Petroleum Corp v IPCO (Nigeria) Ltd [2008] EWCA Civ 1157, [2008] 2 CLC 550.
Nisshin Shipping Co Ltd v Cleaves & Co Ltd [2003] EWHC 2602 (Comm), [2004] 1 All ER (Comm) 481.
Norsk Hydro ASA v The State Property Fund of Ukraine [2002] EWHC 2120 (Admin).
Owners of the MV Myron v Tradax Export SA (The Myron) [1970] 1 QB 527 (Comm).
Pacific Maritime (Asia) Ltd v Holystone Overseas Ltd [2007] EWHC 2319 (Comm), [2008] 1 Lloyd's Rep 371.
Petroleum Investment Co Ltd v Kantupan Holdings Co Ltd [2002] 1 All ER (Comm) 124 (Comm).
Pine Top Insurance Co Ltd v Unione Italiana Anglo Saxon Reinsurance Co Ltd [1987] 1 Lloyd's Rep 476 (Comm).
Purslow v Bailey (1704) Ld Raym 1039, 92 ER 190.
R v Momodou and Limani [2005] EWCA Crim 177, [2005] 2 All ER 571.
R v Richardson [1971] 2 QB 484 (CA).
Re Kitchen, ex p Young (1881) LR 17 Ch D 668.
Reliance Industries Ltd v Enron Oil and Gas India Ltd [2002] 1 All ER (Comm) 59 (Comm).
The Republic of Kazakhstan v Istil Group Inc [2006] EWHC 448 (Comm), [2006] 2 Lloyd's Rep 370.
Rosseel NV v Oriental Commercial & Shipping (UK) Ltd [1990] 1 WLR 1387 (CA).
Sabah Shipyard (Pakistan) Ltd v Government of Pakistan [2008] 1 Lloyd's Rep 210.
Services Europe Atlantique Sud (SEAS) of Paris v Stockholm Rederiaktiebolag Svea ('The Folias') [1979] AC 685 (HL).
Shamil Bank of Bahrain EC v Beximco Pharmaceuticals Ltd [2004] EWCA Civ 19, [2004] 1 WLR 1784.
Shayler v Woolf [1946] Ch 320 (CA).
Shell International Petroleum Co Ltd v Coral Oil Co Ltd (No 1) [1999] 1 Lloyd's Rep 72 (Comm).
Socadec SA v Pan Afric Impex Co Ltd [2003] EWHC 2086 (QB).
Société Eram Shipping Co Ltd v Cie Internationale de Navigation and Ors [2003] UKHL 30, [2004] 1 AC 260.
Soinco SACI & Anor v Novokuznetsk Aluminium Plant & Ors [1998] QB 406 (Comm).
Soleh Boneh International v Uganda and National Housing Corp [1993] 2 Lloyd's Rep 208 (CA).
Soleimany and Soleimany [1999] QB 785 (CA).
Sonatrach Petroleum Corp v Ferrell International Ltd [2002] 1 All ER (Comm) 627 (Comm).

Stinnes Interoil GmbH v A Halcoussis & Co ('The Yanxila') (No 1) [1982] 2 Lloyd's Rep 445 (Comm).

Svenska Petroleum Exploration AB v Republic of Lithuania (No 2) [2006] EWCA Civ 1529, [2007] QB 886.

Trade Maritime Corp v Hellenic Mutual War Risks Association (Bermuda) Ltd ('The Athena') [2006] EWHC 2530 (Comm), [2007] 1 All ER (Comm) 183.

Traube v Perelman (Ch D 25 July 2001).

Trygg Hansa Insurance Co Ltd v Equitas Ltd [1998] 2 Lloyds Rep 439 (Comm).

Tsavliris Salvage (International) Ltd v The Grain Board of Iraq [2008] EWHC 612 (Comm).

Turner v Stevenage Borough Council [1998] Ch 28 (CA).

Union of India v McDonnell Douglas Corp [1993] 2 Lloyd's Rep 48 (Comm).

Vee Networks Ltd v Econet Wireless International Ltd [2004] EWHC 2909 (Comm), [2005] 1 All ER (Comm) 303.

Wakefield (Tower Hill Trinity Square) Trust v Janson Green Properties Ltd [1998] EG 95 (CS) (Ch).

Walker v Rowe [1999] 2 All ER (Comm) 961 (Comm).

Weissfisch v Julius [2006] EWCA Civ 218, [2006] 2 All ER (Comm) 504.

West Tankers Inc v RAS Riunione Adriatica di Sicurta SpA ('The Front Comor') [2007] UKHL 4, [2007] 1 Lloyd's Rep 391.

Westacre Investments Inc v Jugoimport SPDR Holding Co Ltd [2000] QB 288 (CA).

Wicketts and Sterndale v Brine Builders and Anor (TCC 8 June 2001).

Wood v Griffith (1818) 1 Swanst 55, 36 ER 291.

6

FRANCE

Emmanuel Gaillard

I. Introduction

A. Current status of the law on arbitration

(1) Short history

France is a very popular seat for international arbitration. Undoubtedly, a significant reason for this popularity is the presence of the International Chamber of Commerce ('ICC'), which has been headquartered in Paris since its creation in 1923. Another factor is the large number of international law firms that have a presence in France. Perhaps most importantly, French law has always encouraged international arbitration as a mechanism for resolving international commercial disputes. Although the rules relating to international arbitration were only codified in 1981, the French courts consistently demonstrated a very pronounced pro-arbitration bias long before the codification of the rules.[1] This pro-arbitration bias was reinforced by the 1981 reform, which created one of the first modern international arbitration statutes, and by subsequent case law. Finally, France has, of course, ratified all of the major international conventions on arbitration, in particular the Geneva Protocol and Convention of 1923 and 1927, the New York Convention of 1958, the Geneva Convention of 1961 and the Washington Convention of 1965. **6.01**

[1] See Gaillard, E. and Savage, J. (eds), *Fouchard Gaillard Goldman On International Commercial Arbitration* (Kluwer, 1999) (hereinafter Fouchard Gaillard Goldman) at paras 130 *et seq.*

(2) Law in force and future projects

6.02 A Decree devoted exclusively to international arbitration was promulgated in 1981 and remains in force to date.[2] Pursuant to the 1981 Decree, the new provisions on international arbitration were incorporated into the French *nouveau Code de procédure civile* ('*NCPC*', or the 'Code'). The specific rules pertaining to 'international arbitration' are set forth in Arts 1492 to 1507 of the Code.[3]

6.03 Apart from minor additions and a small number of provisions concerning arbitration that are contained in other statutes, the French law on arbitration has not undergone any changes since the 1981 reform. The application of the legislation on arbitration by French courts has not given rise to any particular difficulties. Indeed, the French courts appear to have fully grasped the liberal spirit of the new provisions—which followed directly in the line of the pre-existing case law—and have implemented them accordingly. The pre-reform case law has also served as a useful resource for courts when confronting issues covered in insufficient detail by the new legislation.

6.04 The French legislation on international arbitration is considered to be particularly progressive in several important respects, and is still in many ways more liberal than the UNCITRAL Model Law of 1985. This is illustrated in particular by the broad statutory definition of 'international arbitration', to be discussed further at para 6.06 *et seq, infra*, and by the rules regarding the applicable law in the absence of a choice by the parties, to be discussed at paras 6.158 *et seq, infra*.

6.05 A further indication of the progressive nature of the French law on international arbitration is found in its recognition of the decline of the importance of the seat in international arbitration. This is evidenced, for example, in the provisions relating to the constitution of the arbitral tribunal (Art 1493; see at paras 6.47 *et seq, infra*) and the arbitral procedure (Art 1494; see at paras 6.60 *et seq, infra*), both of which are governed by the parties' intentions alone. Thus, party autonomy is considered to be the guiding principle of the French law on international arbitration.

(3) Distinction between national and international arbitration

6.06 As noted, French law draws a distinction between domestic and international arbitration. The provisions at Arts 1492–1507 of the Code deal specifically with international arbitration.

6.07 (3.1) **If there are different systems and rules for national/international arbitration, what are the criteria for the distinction between both systems?** A distinct, more liberal regime for international arbitration was adopted with a view to encouraging international commercial players to submit their disputes to arbitration, the forum which the French legislation considered to be most appropriate for the resolution of such disputes.

[2] Decree no 81–500 of 12 May 1981, enacting the provisions of Books III and IV of the Nouveau code de procédure civile and modifying provisions of that Code, Journal Officiel, 14 May 1981, at 1,380; (1981) *Revue de l'arbitrage* [*Rev arb*] 317.

[3] See eg Fouchard, P., *Journal du Droit International* [*JDI*] (1982) 374; Goldman, B., (1981) *Rev arb* 469; Fouchard Gaillard Goldman at paras 131–51.

According to Art 1492 of the Code, an arbitration is international if it implicates the interests of international trade. In contrast with the more traditional approach still often adopted in other legal systems at the time of the enactment of the 1981 legislation, French law looks to the nature of the dispute rather than the parties' domicile or nationality, the applicable law, or the place of arbitration, in order to determine whether or not an arbitration should be considered 'international' in nature. Accordingly, even a contract between two French entities can give rise to an international arbitration if it implicates international commercial interests.[4] **6.08**

B. Practice of arbitration

(1) Frequency of arbitration as opposed to litigation

Arbitration is frequently used in France as an alternative to litigation, particularly in international matters. **6.09**

(2) Leading arbitral institutions and statistics

Given the nature of international arbitration, and in particular the lack of systematic reporting, it is difficult to obtain any meaningful statistics about the number of arbitrations in France in any given year. However, the statistics that are available are indicative of France's popularity as a venue for arbitration. In 2007, for example, of the 599 new arbitrations filed with the ICC, 110 had their seat in France.[5] **6.10**

II. Jurisdiction of the arbitral tribunal

A. Arbitration agreement

(1) Arbitration clause and submission agreement

Unlike the rules pertaining to domestic arbitration, the French law on international arbitration makes no distinction between submission agreements and arbitration clauses.[6] **6.11**

(2) Requirements as to the contents of the arbitration agreement

Under French law, there are no specific requirements as to what should be contained in an agreement to arbitrate in order for it to be valid. The parties may therefore draft the arbitration agreement as they please so long as their intention to arbitrate is expressed unambiguously. Indeed, a clause which simply provides that any dispute concerning the contract shall be submitted to arbitration in France is valid in international arbitration. For example, although Art 1494 of the Code provides, for domestic matters, that 'an arbitration agreement may . . . appoint the arbitrators or provide for the method of their appointment', this is not required for the arbitration agreement to be valid in international matters. **6.12**

---

[4] See eg *Colas routière v Tracet*, CA Paris, 2 October 1992, (1992) *Rev arb* 625; *Murgue Seigle v Coflexip*, CA Paris, 14 March 1989, (1991) *Rev arb* 355.

[5] See 19 ICC Bulletin no 1 (2008), at 5–11.

[6] Compare the provisions on domestic arbitration set forth in Arts 1442 and 1447 of the Code, which distinguish arbitration clauses and submission agreements, with the provisions on international arbitration set forth in Arts 1493 and 1494 of the Code, which make no such distinction.

(3) Form of the arbitration agreement (eg 'in writing' requirement)

6.13 French law is also particularly liberal as far as the form required for a valid arbitration agreement is concerned. For example, although Art 11 of the New York Convention requires that an arbitration agreement must be in writing (but allows national courts the freedom to apply more favourable national rules, in accordance with Art VII), a written agreement is not required under French law. The agreement will be held to be valid if the common intention of the parties to submit the dispute to arbitration can be established, although the written form is of course preferable for evidentiary purposes.

6.14 **(3.1) Are there special requirements for a power of attorney/authority to enter into an arbitration agreement on behalf of a third party?** French law does not impose any specific requirement for the conclusion of an international arbitration agreement on behalf of a third party.

(4) Incorporation of an arbitration clause contained in general terms and conditions

6.15 The French courts have adopted a relatively liberal approach to the issue of the incorporation of an arbitration agreement by reference. In *Bomar Oil v ETAP*,[7] the *Cour de Cassation* held that an agreement to arbitrate that is not contained in a contract may nonetheless bind the parties if it is contained in a document, such as the parties' standard terms and conditions, to which reference had been made in the contract. The court further held, however, that in these cases, the validity of the agreement depended on whether the party against whom the arbitration clause is invoked had knowledge, at the time the contract was concluded, of the documents which contained the arbitration agreement. The intention of the parties is thus the decisive criterion for the determination of validity of the incorporation by reference of an arbitration agreement (see also the theory of the 'group of companies' recognized by French law, discussed at paras 6.21 *et seq, infra*).

(5) Law applicable to the interpretation of arbitration clauses

6.16 There is no specific provision in the Code on how an arbitration agreement should be interpreted. Consequently, one must follow the method generally adopted in international arbitral practice and by the French courts with respect to issues related to the arbitration agreement, which involves determining the scope of the arbitration agreement in the light of generally accepted principles of international law,[8] instead of resorting to the choice of law rules of the seat of the arbitration or, for that matter, any other choice of law rules. This is in keeping with the *Dalico* approach to the assessment of the existence and the validity of the arbitration agreement.[9] Principles which can be applied include (i) the principle of good faith interpretation; (ii) the principle of effective interpretation; (iii) the principle of consistency or global interpretation; and, according to certain authors, (iv) the principle of

[7] See *Bomar Oil NV v Entreprise Tunisienne d'Activités Pétrolières (ETAP)*, Cass 1e Civ, 9 November 1993, (1994) *Rev arb* 108. See also *Société Prodexport v Société FMT Productions et autres*, Cass 1e Civ, 20 December 2000, (2003) *Rev arb* 1341, 1st decision, and commentary by C Legros.

[8] See eg ICC Award no 5721 (1990), *European Company v American and Egyptian Parties* (1990) JDI 1,020, and observations by Y Derains (regarding the interpretation of the arbitration clause *ratione personae*).

[9] See *Municipalité de Khoms El Mergeb v Société Dalico*, Cass 1e Civ, 20 December 1993, (1994) Rev arb 116.

interpretation *contra proferentem*, pursuant to which the agreement is interpreted not to favour the party that drafted it.[10]

(5.1) Do courts accept a wide competence of the arbitral tribunal or do they restrict arbitral competence? Do claims which arise in connection with the agreement submitted to arbitration generally fall within the arbitral jurisdiction even if based on tortious legal basis? Does there exist case law with respect to the wording in an arbitration clause as 'arising out of/under/in connection with the present contract' and its specific meaning? The traditional approach according to which arbitration was the exception to the ordinary rule of the jurisdiction of the courts and, as such, had to be construed narrowly, has been completely abandoned in French law on international arbitration. On the contrary, it is now widely accepted that arbitration is the normal means of resolving international disputes and that, as a result, an arbitration agreement should be construed neither narrowly nor extensively, rather according to the true intent of the parties. 6.17

There is no restriction under French law as to the ability of arbitrators to hear disputes related to tort or quasi-contract claims, other than restrictions which may result from the language of the arbitration agreement itself. 6.18

The language 'arising out of/under/in connection with the present contract' found in arbitration clauses is in general broadly construed as encompassing any kind of dispute. For example, no specific language is required for arbitrators to be empowered to rule on issues such as security for costs or damages arising from a violation of the arbitration agreement itself by a party who chooses to bring the dispute before the courts. 6.19

(6) Binding effect of an arbitration clause on third parties (eg in case of a guarantee or assignment)

Third parties can become party to an arbitration agreement through assignment. In the case of a voluntary assignment, the assignee who is to become a party to the arbitration agreement must agree to do so. Despite the generally recognized autonomy of the arbitration agreement from the main contract, the French courts have consistently held that the acceptance of the assignment of the main contract gives rise to a presumption of acceptance of the assignment of the arbitration agreement. The assignee of a contract who takes the benefit of the rights assigned thereunder cannot avoid the application of the arbitration agreement, unless the parties expressly agree to this avoidance.[11] As far as the other party is concerned, there is a presumption in French law that, in the absence of any indication to the contrary, the obligor has accepted that the agreement may be assigned.[12] However, there is an exception to this presumption for arbitration agreements that were entered into *intuitu personae* (ie in consideration of the identity of the co-contractor).[13] In these cases, 6.20

---

[10] See Fouchard Gaillard Goldman at paras 477–82.

[11] See *SNTM Hyproc v Banque Générale du Commerce*, CA Aix, 9 January 1997, (1997) *Rev arb* 76, and commentary by D. Cohen.

[12] See *Sté Taurus Film et autres v sté Films du Jeudi*, Cass 1e Civ, 8 February 2000, (2000) Bulletin des arrêts de la Cour de cassation (chambres civiles) [Bull Civ] I, no 36; *Peavy Company v Organisme général des fourrages et autres*, Cass 1e Civ, 6 February 2001, (2001) *Rev arb.* 765, and commentary by D. Cohen.

[13] See *Sté Burkinabé des Ciments et Matériaux v Société des Ciments d'Abidjan*, Cass 1e Civ, 28 May 2002, (2003) *Rev arb* 397, and commentary by D. Cohen.

the consent of the obligor must be given expressly. In addition to voluntary assignment, international arbitration agreements can be assigned by operation of law, eg by legal subrogation or succession.

6.21 **(6.1) What is the law/leading authorities' position on multi-party situations? Especially, (i) with respect to the objection that the arbitration clause does not specifically provide for a plurality of parties in the same procedure; (ii) with respect to the constitution of the arbitral tribunal; and (iii) with respect to the consolidation of two or more running arbitration proceedings?** There is no French legislation explicitly governing multi-party arbitration. However, arbitration that involves more than two parties does not necessarily constitute a multi-party arbitration. French law recognizes, for example, the theory of the 'group of companies'. According to this theory, companies in the same group can be held to be bound by an arbitration agreement to which one is a party, provided that such broader application can be inferred from the express or implied intention of the parties. In a 1983 decision,[14] the Paris *Cour d'Appel* refused to set aside an ICC award in which the arbitral tribunal decided that taking into account the 'undivided economic reality' of a group of companies, and 'irrespective of the distinct juridical identity of each of its members, the arbitration clause expressly accepted by certain of the companies of the group should bind the other companies which, by virtue of their role in the conclusion, performance or termination of the contracts containing said clauses, and in accordance with the mutual intention of all parties to the proceedings, appear to have been veritable parties to these contracts or to have been principally concerned by them and the disputes to which they may give rise'.[15]

6.22 Multi-party arbitration, in the strict sense, only occurs when more than two parties' interests are at stake or when various different claims are brought against various different respondents. The *Cour de Cassation* set forth the rules relating to multi-party arbitration in the *Dutco* decision.[16] The case involved three parties, Dutco, Siemens and B.K.M.I. Dutco initiated proceedings against Siemens and B.K.M.I. on the basis of an arbitration agreement contained in a contract among the three parties, but it brought different claims against each of the two respondents. Siemens and B.K.M.I. were required to nominate a single arbitrator. The Paris *Cour d'Appel* denied an action to set aside the tribunal's award in which it held that it had jurisdiction to hear Dutco's claim. The *Cour de Cassation* reversed that decision, holding that 'the principle of the equality of the parties in the appointment of arbitrators is a matter of international public policy; it can only be waived after the dispute has arisen'. The practical impact of the *Dutco* decision should not, however,

[14] See *Isover-Saint-Gobain v Dow Chemical France*, CA Paris, 21 October 1983, (1984) *Rev arb* 98, and commentary by A. Chapelle.

[15] ICC Case no 4131, (1984) IX Yearbook Commercial Arbitration [Ybk Comm Arb] 136. For a more general discussion of this issue, see Fouchard Gaillard Goldman at paras 502–6.

[16] See *BKMI v Dutco*, Cass 1e Civ, 7 January 1992, (1992) *Rev arb* 470, and note by P. Bellet, (1992) *JDI* 707; for an English translation, see (1993) XVIII *Ybk Comm Arb* 140, (1992) *International Arbitration Report* [*Int'l Arb Rep*] B1.

be overestimated. Arbitral institutions are now well equipped to deal with arbitrations involving more than two parties, as can be seen in the new rules of the ICC, the ICDR and the LCIA.[17]

French law does not allow the judicial consolidation of two or more arbitration proceedings. Consolidation is only possible if the parties have so agreed, either expressly or by reference to arbitration rules, and if the equality of the parties regarding the appointment of the arbitral tribunal is respected. 6.23

(6.2) Is there case law/authorities with respect to the admissibility of third party participation in an arbitration without being a claimant or defendant (Nebenintervention/ Streitverkündung; intervention forcée/volontaire; vouching in; *amicus curiae* etc)? What are the prerequisites and effects of such participation (if permitted)? On the related issue of joinder, there is no French case law allowing third parties to intervene voluntarily in an arbitration to which they are not party. The voluntary intervention of third parties is possible only if all parties concerned consent, either directly or by including a reference to arbitration rules providing for such a possibility in the arbitration agreement. 6.24

(7) Termination of an arbitration agreement by a party (reasons and case law)

Under French law, the expiration of the main contract does not lead to the termination of the arbitration agreement. This is an important consequence of the principle of the autonomy of the arbitration agreement. In the event that a contract expires as a result of a novation, settlement, rescission or avoidance, the arbitration agreement survives.[18] French law does, however, recognize causes of termination that are specific to the arbitration agreement. An arbitration agreement will be terminated, for example, if it is waived by the parties or if it is directly affected by a defect rendering it void.[19] Implicit waiver can occur, for example, if one party submits a dispute to the courts and the other party files a defence on the merits without challenging the jurisdiction of the court or reserving its rights to do so. An arbitration agreement may also have no effect because of a defect which is independent of the main contract, such as the non-arbitrability of the dispute. This non-arbitrability would have to be pronounced first by the arbitrators themselves, however, pursuant to the principle of *competence-competence*. In addition, certain events will extinguish a submission agreement, but will not have the same effect on arbitration clauses. These are the making of a final award, the default (or death) of an arbitrator,[20] the expiration of the agreed deadline for making a final award[21] and the setting aside of an award.[22] 6.25

[17] See 1998 ICC Rules of Arbitration, Art 10; 2008 ICDR International Arbitration Rules, Art 6(5); 1998 LCIA Rules, Art 8.

[18] For cases on the survival of the arbitration agreement in the event of novation and settlement, see *Cosiac v Consorts Luchetti*, CA Paris, 4 March 1986, (1987) *Rev arb* 167, and commentary by C. Jarrosson. The appeal against this decision was denied. See Cass 1e Civ, 10 May 1988, (1988) *Rev arb* 639, and commentary by C. Jarrosson. For rescission, see *Société des mines d'Orbagnoux v Fly Tox*, Cass 2e Civ, 25 November 1966, (1967) Dalloz 359, 2nd decision, and commentary by J. Robert.

[19] See Fouchard Gaillard Goldman at paras 525–31.

[20] See *Laiguède v Ahsen Inox*, CA Paris, 7 July 1992, overturned on other grounds, Cass 1e Civ, 10 May 1995, (1995) *Rev arb* 605.

[21] See *SA Les Carrières de la Meilleraie v Mercier*, CA Amiens, 20 October 1959, (1959) *Rev arb* 122.

[22] See *Paroutian v Société de distribution de produits alimentaires et manufacturés Cedipam Cogedis*, Cass 2e Civ, 16 May 1988, (1988) *Rev arb* 645, and commentary by M.C. Rondeau-Rivier. On this issue, generally,

B. Arbitrability

(1) 'Personal arbitrability' (capacity to conclude arbitration agreements)

6.26 The French courts have adopted a very liberal approach to the issue of arbitrability in the context of international arbitration. In domestic arbitration, the issue of subjective arbitrability is governed by Arts 2059–2061 of the French Civil Code.[23] These provisions do not, however, apply to international arbitration. Thus, private persons, companies and public entities may conclude arbitration agreements. In a seminal 1966 decision, the *Cour de Cassation* held that public entities can validly enter into international arbitration agreements notwithstanding the provisions to the contrary for domestic arbitration set forth in Art 2060 of the French Civil Code.[24] This principle has been reaffirmed by the French courts since the 1981 legislative reform, for instance in a 1994 case in which the Paris *Cour d'Appel* held that 'the prohibition excluding governments from referring their disputes to arbitration is confined to domestic contracts. Consequently, the prohibition is not a matter of international public policy. In order for an arbitration agreement in a contract to be valid, it must simply be established that the contract is international and that it was concluded for the purposes of and in accordance with the usages of international commerce'.[25] Similarly, Art 2060 para 2, concerning the non-arbitrability of disputes relating to local authorities and public entities, has been held to be inapplicable to international arbitration, and the *Cour de Cassation* confirmed that Art 2061 (which, before its rewriting in 2001, provided that issues are only arbitrable to the extent provided by law) is not applicable to international arbitration.[26] The Law of 15 May 2001 modified Art 2061 of the Civil Code, which now provides that '[e]xcept were there are particular statutory provisions, an arbitration clause is valid in the contracts concluded by reason of a professional activity'.[27] This liberal approach applies equally to French public entities and foreign public entities.

6.27 **(1.1) May a state (or state agency) as party invoke sovereign immunity before the arbitral tribunal or a state court (eg in a procedure of enforcement)?** The French courts have consistently held that by entering into an international arbitration agreement, a government or public entity waives any jurisdictional immunity towards the arbitral tribunal that it might have.[28] The same rule applies for actions to set up the arbitral tribunal or actions to set aside the award before state courts.[29] On 6 July 2000, the French *Cour de Cassation*

---

see Moreau, B., 'Les effets de la nullité de la sentence arbitrale' in *Etudes offertes à Pierre Bellet* (Litec, 1991) 403.

23 See de Boisséson, M. and Duprey, P., 'L'arbitrabilité subjective en matière de droit des sociétés' in A. Mourre (ed), *Les Cahiers de l'Arbitrage*, vol II (Gazette du Palais 2004) 121.

24 See *Galakis v Trésor public*, Cass 1e Civ, 2 May 1966, (1966) JDI 648, and commentary by P. Level.

25 See *Ministère tunisien de l'équipement v Bec Frères*, CA Paris, 24 February 1994, (1995) *Rev arb* 275, and commentary by Y. Gaudemet; for an English translation, see (1997) XXI *Ybk Comm Arb* 682.

26 *Zanzi v de Coninck, Sautarel et Torelli*, Cass 1e Civ., 5 January 1999, (1999) *Rev arb* 260, and note by P. Fouchard.

27 See Mourre, A., 'L'impact de la réforme de la clause compromissoire sur les litiges relatifs aux sociétés' in A. Mourre (ed), *Les Cahiers de l'Arbitrage*, vol II (Gazette du Palais 2004) 125.

28 See *National Iranian Oil Co v Israel*, TGI Paris, 10 January 1996, (1996) Bulletin de l'Association Suisse d'Arbitrage [ASA Bull] 319; for an English translation, see (1996) 11 *Int'l Arb Rep* B1; *Société Européenne d'Etudes et d'Entreprises (S.E.E.E.) v République socialiste fédérale de Yougoslavie*, TGI Paris, 8 July 1970, (1971) JDI 131, and note by P. Kahn; (1975) *Rev arb* 328, and note by J.-L. Delvolvé.

29 See *UNESCO v Boulois*, CA Paris, 19 June 1998, (1999) *Rev arb* 343, and note by C. Jarrosson.

held that by agreeing to enforce an award promptly as stipulated in the ICC Rules, a state also waived its immunity from enforcement.[30]

(2) 'Objective arbitrability' (eg of patent, trade mark and antitrust matters)

The courts have also posited a variety of rules relating to objective arbitrability, ie the arbitrability of disputes of a specific nature. Thus, for example, Art 2060 para 1 of the Civil Code, which provides that 'issues concerning the status and capacity of persons, issues concerning divorce and separation . . . and, in general, all issues concerning matters of public policy cannot be submitted to arbitration', has been held not to apply to international arbitration. In the *Ganz* case, the Paris *Cour d'Appel* held that 'in international arbitration, an arbitrator . . . is entitled to apply the principles and rules of international public policy . . . except in cases where the non-arbitrability is a consequence of the subject-matter in that it implicates international public policy and absolutely excludes the jurisdiction of the arbitrators because the arbitration agreement is void . . .'.[31] This would appear to exclude the arbitrability of issues such as human rights, paternity disputes, and divorce, ie disputes which would be characterized in other legal systems as issues which cannot be expressed in monetary terms.[32] **6.28**

The French courts have expressly recognized the arbitrability of matters regarding antitrust law.[33] While no arbitration agreement can validly empower arbitrators to decide bankruptcy disputes, arbitrators do have jurisdiction to rule on certain issues relating to bankruptcy law. For example, they have jurisdiction to apply the public policy provisions of French bankruptcy law which provide that shares held by *de jure* or *de facto* directors of a company in receivership are non-transferable as of the date on which the receivership is opened.[34] Other types of dispute which have been held to be arbitrable include boycotts,[35] regulation of foreign investments,[36] securities,[37] EC agricultural subsidies,[38] termination of exclusive sales concessions, subcontracts,[39] and product liability.[40] In contrast, arbitration **6.29**

[30] *Creighton v Ministère des Finances de l'Etat du Qatar*, Cass 1e Civ, 6 July 2000, (2001) *Rev arb* 114, and commentary by P. Leboulanger. See also Gaillard, E. and Edelstein, J., 'Recent Developments In State Immunity From Execution in France: Creighton v Qatar', 15 *Int'l Arb Rep* 1 (October 2000).

[31] See *Ganz v Société Nationale des Chemins de Fer Tunisiens (SNCFT)*, CA Paris, 29 March 1991, (1991) *Rev arb* 478, and commentary by L. Idot.

[32] See eg Art 177 para 1 of the 1987 Swiss Private International Law Statute, or s 1030, ZPO (Law of 22 December 1998).

[33] See *Aplix v Velco*, CA Paris, 14 October 1993, (1994) *Rev arb* 164, and commentary by C. Jarrosson; *Labinal v Mors*, CA Paris, 19 May 1993, (1993) *Rev arb* 645, and commentary by C. Jarrosson; (1993) JDI 957, and commentary by L. Idot; for an English translation, see (1993) 8 *Int'l Arb Rep* E1, E18.

[34] See *Matra Hachette*, CA Paris, 20 September 1995, (1996) *Rev arb* 87, and note by D. Cohen.

[35] See Moitry, J.H., 'L'arbitre international et l'obligation de boycottage imposée par un Etat', (1991) *JDI* 349.

[36] See *Courrèges Design v André Courrèges*, CA Paris, 5 April 1990, (1991) Revue critique de droit international privé [Rev crit DIP] 580, and commentary by C. Kessedjian; (1992) *Rev arb* 110, and commentary by H. Synvet.

[37] See Fouchard Gaillard Goldman at para 579.

[38] See *Grands Moulin de Strasbourg v Compagnie continentale de France*, Cass 1e Civ, 19 November 1991, (1992) *Rev arb* 76, and commentary by L. Idot.

[39] See *Chambon v Thomson CSF*, CA Paris, 10 September 1997, (1997) Dalloz Affaires 1,253.

[40] See Kreindler, R.H., 'The Arbitration Clause: The Validity of an Arbitration Clause in Matters of Product Liability', in *ASA Special Series no 8, The Arbitration Agreement—Its Multifold Critical Aspects* (1994) 123.

clauses embodied in labour law contracts have been held not to be binding on the employee.[41]

C. Decision on the arbitral tribunal's jurisdiction ('*competence-competence*')

(1) Separability (independence of the arbitration agreement from the main agreement)

6.30 One of the fundamental precepts of the French law on international arbitration is that the arbitration agreement is autonomous from the main contract between the parties.[42] In a landmark 1963 decision in the *Gosset* case, the *Cour de Cassation* held that 'in international arbitration, the arbitration agreement, whether concluded separately or included in the contract to which it relates, shall, save in exceptional circumstances . . . have full legal autonomy and shall not be affected by the fact that the aforementioned contract may be invalid'.[43] This should be distinguished, as is now generally recognized, from the principle of *competence-competence*, which is also fully accepted under French law.

(2) Competence of the tribunal to decide on its own jurisdiction (including form and time of the tribunal's decision)

6.31 The principle of *competence-competence* gives arbitral tribunals jurisdiction to rule upon their own jurisdiction.[44] In domestic arbitration, the principle is expressly recognized by Art 1466 of the Code, which provides that 'if a party challenges in the arbitration the existence or scope of the arbitrator's jurisdiction, the arbitrator shall decide on the issue'. While French judges had already recognized this principle prior to 1981,[45] the courts have interpreted the statutory provision to that effect very broadly.[46] Although there is no express provision to this effect for international arbitration, the *Cour de Cassation* has consistently affirmed that the same rule applies.[47] Contrary to certain other countries, French law also

[41] *Picet v Sacinter*, Cass Soc, 4 May 1999, (1999) *Rev arb* 290, and commentary by M.A. Moreau.

[42] On the autonomy of the arbitration agreement, see, eg Dimolitsa, A., 'Separability and "Kompetenz"' in A.J. van den Berg (ed), *ICCA Congress Series no 9, Improving the Efficiency of Arbitration Agreements and Awards: 40 Years of Application of the New York Convention* (Kluwer, 1999) 217; Ancel, J.P., 'L'actualité de l'autonomie de la clause compromissoire' in *Travaux du Comité Français du Droit International Privé 1991–1993* (1994) at 75. See also *Sté Uni-Kod v Sté Ouralkali*, Cass 1e Civ, 30 March 2004, (2005) *Rev arb* 961, and commentary by C. Seraglini.

[43] See *Etablissement Raymond Gosset v Carapelli*, Cass 1e Civ, 7 May 1963, (1963) Juris-Classeur Périodique [J.C.P.], vol 1., Pt 11, no 13,405, and commentary by B. Goldman; (1964) JDI 82, and commentary by J.D. Bredin; (1963) Rev crit DIP 615. See Fouchard Gaillard Goldman at paras 391–2.

[44] See Fouchard Gaillard Goldman at paras 650–60.

[45] See *Caulliez-Tibergien v Caulliez-Hannart*, Cass Com, 22 February 1949, (1949) JCP vol II, no 4,899, and observations by H. Motulsky; *Kohorn v Dimitrov*, Trib civ Seine, 17 October 1956, (1956) JCP vol II, no 4,647, and observations by H. Motulsky; *Impex v P.A.Z.*, CA Colmar, 29 November 1968, (1968) JCP vol II, no 16,246, and observations by P. Level and B. Oppetit.

[46] See *European Country Hotels Ltd v Consorts Legrand*, TGI Paris, 10 April 1990, (1994) *Rev arb* 545, 1st decision, and observations by P. Fouchard; *Ganz v Société Nationale de Chemins de Fer Tunisien (SNCFT)*, CA Paris, 29 March 1991, (1991) *Rev arb* 478, and commentary by L. Idot; *Labinal v Mors*, CA Paris, 19 May 1993, (1993) *Rev arb* 645, and commentary by C. Jarrosson; (1993) JDI 957, and commentary by L. Idot; (1993) Int'l Arb Rep 7; *National Iranian Oil Co v Israel*, TGI Paris, 10 January 1996, (1996) ASA Bull 319; for an English translation, see (1996) *Int'l Arb Rep* B1; *Cie AXA Corporate Solutions et autres v Nemesis Shipping*, Cass1e Civ, 22 November 2005, (2005) Bull Civ I, no 420.

[47] *Zanzi v de Coninck, Sautarel et Torelli*, Cass Civ 1e, 5 January 1999, (1999) *Rev arb* 260, and note by P. Fouchard. See also *Copropriété maritime Jules Verne v Sté American bureau of shipping et autres*, Cass 1e Civ., 7 June 2006, (2006) *Rev arb* 945, and commentary by E. Gaillard.

recognizes the negative effect of the principle of *competence-competence* pursuant to which courts should refuse to rule on any issues regarding the existence and validity of the arbitration agreement until the arbitrators themselves have ruled on their own jurisdiction.[48]

Typically, an arbitral tribunal will render its decision on its own jurisdiction in the form of an award. If the parties so agree, or in the absence of such agreement if the tribunal so decides, this decision can take the form of a partial award on jurisdiction. Such a decision may be challenged immediately before the courts in an action to set aside the award, but the challenge does not prevent the arbitral tribunal from continuing to perform its duties. **6.32**

An arbitral award may be challenged where the arbitral tribunal has wrongly found in favour of its jurisdiction (Art 1502 para 1 of the Code) or wrongly refused its jurisdiction (Art 1502 para 3). The relevant *Cour d'Appel* will examine, from a legal and factual standpoint, the existence, validity and scope of the arbitration agreement in order to rule on the action to set aside the award. The existence of the arbitration agreement must, however, be raised as soon as the party has knowledge of the arbitration agreement, failing which that party may be deemed to have waived his right to invoke the agreement to arbitrate. If the decision on jurisdiction was issued in the form of a partial award, an action to set aside can be brought immediately, but no later than one month following the notification of the enforcement order of the award (Art 1505 of the Code), the deadline being extended by two months for parties outside France (Art 643 of the Code). The arbitration may proceed on the merits pending the outcome of such an action. **6.33**

D. Enforcement of an arbitration agreement within or by court proceedings

(1) Effect of invoking an arbitration clause within a court proceeding (and time limits for such a motion)

National courts are prohibited from hearing disputes that are subject to an arbitration clause from the time that a party invokes the existence, even only prima facie, of an arbitration agreement. This 'negative effect' of the principle of *competence-competence*, discussed at para 6.31 *supra*, is provided for in Art 1458 of the Code for domestic arbitration and the same rule applies in international arbitration. Article 1458 of the Code reads: 'When a dispute submitted to an arbitral tribunal by virtue of an arbitration agreement is brought before a national court, such court shall decline jurisdiction. If the arbitral tribunal has not yet been seized of the matter, the court shall also decline jurisdiction unless the agreement is manifestly void. [. . .]'. The courts are therefore not entitled to review the arbitral tribunal's jurisdiction, other than on a prima facie basis,[49] until such time as there is an action to **6.34**

[48] See Fouchard Gaillard Goldman at paras 671 *et seq*; Banifatemi, Y. and Gaillard, E., 'Negative Effect of Competence-Competence: The Rule of Priority in Favour of the Arbitrators' in E. Gaillard and D. Di Pietro (eds), *Enforcement of Arbitration Agreements and International Arbitral Awards—The New York Convention 1958 in Practice* (Cameron May, 2008) 257. On the same issue, see Gaillard, E., 'L'effet négatif de la compétence-compétence' in *Etudes de procédure et d'arbitrage en l'honneur de Jean-François Poudret* (Payot, 1999) 387, at para 6. See also *Sté Stein Heurtey v sté Nippon Steel corporation*, Cass 1e Civ, 30 March 2004, (2004) Bull Civ I, no 96; *Sté Belmarine et autres v sté Trident Marine Agency INC et autres*, Cass Com, 21 February 2006, (2006) Bull Civ IV, no 41.

[49] See Cachard, O., 'Le contrôle de la nullité ou de l'inapplicabilité manifeste de la clause compromissoire', (2006) *Rev arb* 893. See also *Société UOP NV v Société BP France SA et autres*, Cass 1e Civ, 20 February

enforce or set aside the award. The existence of the arbitration agreement must, however, be raised promptly, ie as soon as the party has knowledge of the arbitration agreement, failing which that party may be deemed to have waived its right to invoke the agreement to arbitrate.[50]

6.35 (1.1) **If a party has invoked successfully the arbitration agreement in a court proceeding, is it then entitled to deny within the arbitral proceeding that there is a valid and binding arbitration agreement?** A party who has successfully invoked the existence of an arbitration agreement in court proceedings is precluded from denying its existence before the arbitral tribunal. This would be contrary to the requirements of the principles of good faith and consistency.

6.36 (1.2) **Vice versa, if a party has successfully objected to an arbitral proceeding by denying that there is a valid arbitration agreement, may it then invoke such agreement in the ensuing court proceeding?** Similarly, a party who has successfully objected to arbitral proceedings by denying the existence of a valid arbitration agreement is precluded from invoking the existence of the agreement before the courts.

(2) Legal remedies and proceedings to enforce an arbitration agreement

6.37 If a party invokes the existence of the arbitration agreement and there is even some uncertainty as to whether such agreement is null and void, the courts must decline jurisdiction until the arbitrators themselves have had a chance to rule on this issue. Pursuant to the negative effect of the *competence-competence* principle,[51] the courts have no discretion in this respect.[52]

6.38 When court proceedings are brought subsequent to the commencement of the arbitral proceedings, the courts must, in the same way, decline jurisdiction.

6.39 (2.1) **Which would be the internationally competent court (i) for obtaining a declaration that an arbitration agreement is valid and binding; or (ii) to compel arbitration? (The defendant's courts? The courts of the place of arbitration? The claimant's courts, cf Article 6(2) in fine, 1998 ICC Rules?)** French law does not provide for a procedure for obtaining a declaratory judgment regarding the validity and binding character of a given arbitration agreement. Due to the negative effect of the *competence-competence* principle, no court has jurisdiction to that effect. However, in the case of difficulty in constituting the arbitral tribunal, either party may bring an action before the President of the *Tribunal de Grande Instance* (TGI) of Paris, in accordance with Art 1493 of the Code.

2007, (2007) *Rev arb* 775, and note by F.-X. Train; *Société Levantina de Hydraulica y Motores (Lehimosa et autres) v Scala et autres*, Cass 1e Civ, 23 January 2007, (2007) *Rev arb* 279, and observations by P. Pic. See also *Prodim v Lafarge*, Cass 1e civ, 12 December 2007; *Ocea v Bouet*, Cass 1e Civ, 9 July 2008, Cass Com, *Les Pains du Sud et autres v Spa Tagliavini et autre*, 25 November 2008; *Nuovo Pignone v Dalkia France et autre*, Paris CA, 25 October 2006, (2008) *Rev arb* 677, and note by O. Cachard.

50 See eg *Sociétés Cofief et Codix v Société Alix*, Cass 1e Civ, 23 January 2007, (2007) *Rev arb* 290, and observations by E. Teynier and P. Pic.

51 Seraglini, C., 'Retour sur la force de l'effet négatif du principe de compétence-compétence en droit français' (2006) *JCP*, vol I at 2,100.

52 *V 2000 v Renault*, CA Paris, 7 December 2000, (1996) *Rev arb* 245.

III. The arbitral tribunal

A. Number and qualification of arbitrators

(1) Sole arbitrator or arbitral tribunal with several arbitrators

Under French law, the parties can provide for a sole arbitrator or for a tribunal of two or more arbitrators. **6.40**

(1.1) Are arbitral tribunals with an even number of arbitrators acceptable? Articles 1453 and 1454 of the Code, which require an odd number of arbitrators, apply only to domestic cases. Nonetheless, even in international arbitration, it would be very unusual to have a tribunal composed of an even number of arbitrators. **6.41**

(2) Qualification of the arbitrators

French law imposes few requirements in terms of the qualifications of the arbitrators. There is no requirement, for instance, that the arbitrators be lawyers. However, the parties are free to agree, directly or by reference to institutional arbitration rules, that the arbitrators should have a particular professional qualification, that they should practice in a particular field, or that they should have experience of a certain type of dispute or fluency in a certain language.[53] **6.42**

(2.1) Are there mandatory requirements for the qualification of arbitrators (statutory requirements or indirect requirements through eg general conditions of insurance contracts)? There are thus no particular statutory or indirect requirements regarding the qualification of arbitrators under French law. Furthermore, French law imposes no conditions regarding the nationality of arbitrators. Thus, for example, the Paris *Tribunal de Grande Instance* has held that the requirement, included in some arbitration rules, that the third arbitrator must not be of the same nationality as the parties 'does not impose a duty on the President of the Tribunal de Grande Instance to exclude the possibility of appointing an arbitrator of the same nationality as one of the parties',[54] except, of course, when such arbitration rules are applicable. **6.43**

Similarly, French law does not impose any conditions as to the capacity of the arbitrators, other than requiring that they have the legal capacity to carry out their mission.[55] In international arbitration, arbitrators can also be legal entities. In practice, however, the entity in question would be represented by a physical person when performing its functions as arbitrator, and the appointment of an entity as arbitrator seldom occurs. **6.44**

---

[53] For an illustration of similar requirements in the arbitration clauses used in the Eurodisney project and their interpretation, see *Campenon Bernard v Eurodisney-land SCA*, TGI Paris, 12 and 20 December 1991, (1996) *Rev arb* 516, and commentary by P. Fouchard.

[54] See *Transportacion Maritima Mexicana SA v Alsthom*, TGI Paris, 22 May 1987 and 23 June 1987, (1988) *Rev arb* 699, 2nd and 3rd decisions, and commentary by P. Fouchard.

[55] See Art 1451 para 1 of the Code for domestic arbitration; the applicability of this principle to international arbitration is uncontested.

6.45 **(2.2) Which national arbitration institutions may be contacted for obtaining information about qualified (and specialized) arbitrators?** A useful resource for information regarding international arbitration specialists who are active in arbitration in France is the International Arbitration Institute (IAI), described further at App (2) *infra*.

6.46 **(2.3) Are judges or other civil servants required to obtain a permission by their employer to act as arbitrator? Are these permissions given generally or case-by-case? What are the consequences if such permission has not been obtained?** As provided in Decree no 94–314 of 20 April 1994, judges are permitted to serve as arbitrators. Active judges need special authorization from their superiors in order to sit as arbitrators. Such permission can only be obtained on a case-by-case basis. In contrast, a retired judge is entirely free to accept his appointment as an arbitrator.

B. Appointment of arbitrators

(1) Extent of party autonomy to establish appointment procedure

6.47 The parties have great freedom as to the procedure to follow for the appointment of arbitrators.[56] Article 1493 of the Code provides that 'the arbitration agreement may, directly or by reference to arbitration rules, appoint the arbitrator or arbitrators or provide for a mechanism for their appointment'.

6.48 The appointment of arbitrators is considered by the French courts to be a contract, rooted in the common intention of the parties, even though the appointment may have been initiated by one party alone. Given the contractual relationship between the parties and the arbitrators, the arbitrators' acceptance is required in order for the appointment of the arbitral tribunal to be valid. This acceptance does not have to be given in any specific form. It is sufficient that the arbitrator indicate his acceptance by a 'personal and irrevocable manifestation of his intention'.[57]

(2) Procedure in absence of an agreement by the parties

6.49 Difficulties can arise in the event that the parties either refuse to appoint an arbitrator or disagree as to which arbitrator to appoint. In these situations, the parties will generally require the assistance of an appointing authority. In the case of institutional arbitration, the appointing authority will in principle be the arbitral institution itself. In the event that the parties do not submit their dispute to the rules of an arbitral institution, Art 1493 para 2 of the Code provides that, at the request of any party, the *Tribunal de Grande Instance* of Paris can intervene in international arbitration proceedings to resolve difficulties concerning the constitution of the arbitral tribunal. One interesting feature of French law is the centralization of all disputes which may arise in this respect before the President of the *Tribunal de Grande Instance* of Paris, who has jurisdiction to rule on these issues irrespective of where in France the arbitration is to take place.

6.50 The same provisions also apply in the event of difficulties in the appointment of a chairman of the arbitral tribunal. The chairman is ordinarily selected by the parties themselves, by the

---

[56] See Fouchard Gaillard Goldman at paras 748–827.

[57] See *Consorts Legrand v European Country Hotels Ltd*, CA Paris, 14 November 1991, (1994) *Rev arb* 545, 2nd decision, and observations by P. Fouchard.

party-appointed arbitrators when entrusted with this task or, in case of difficulty, by the appointing authority, unless the parties have agreed otherwise either directly or by reference to arbitration rules.

(3) Effect of the refusal of one party to cooperate in the constitution of the arbitral tribunal

In the event that one party refuses to cooperate in the constitution of the arbitral tribunal, or if the party-appointed arbitrators cannot agree upon a chairman when they are required to do so, the President of the *Tribunal de Grande Instance* of Paris may, in his role as appointing authority, either appoint the required arbitrator himself, or take the necessary measures to ensure that the arbitrators are appointed. Generally, he will grant a short deadline to the defaulting party to appoint the missing arbitrator, or to the two party-appointed arbitrators to appoint a third one, failing which he will proceed with the appointment. Appeals of a decision of the President of the *Tribunal de Grande Instance* are only possible in exceptional cases.[58] It should be noted, furthermore, that according to Art 1493 para 2 of the Code, the court's jurisdiction is not mandatory. The parties are thus free to choose their own method to resolve difficulties concerning the constitution of the arbitral tribunal. **6.51**

(4) Circumstances and valid reasons for an arbitrator to resign

In principle, an arbitrator is required to carry out his mission until completion, ie until the final award has been rendered (Art 1462 para 1 of the Code). However, an arbitrator may resign for just cause, for instance if it becomes impossible for health or personal reasons to carry out his mission, or if circumstances independent of his will arise which affect his impartiality. There are no particular requirements in terms of form or proof. **6.52**

C. Challenge and replacement of arbitrators

(1) Grounds, procedure and deadlines for challenging an arbitrator

The grounds for challenging an arbitrator can be either the arbitrator's lack of independence or impartiality, or the lack of any other special qualifications imposed by the arbitration agreement. Arbitrators must be independent and impartial to exercise their judicial function. In a 1972 decision concerning a domestic arbitration, the *Cour de Cassation* expressly confirmed this principle, holding that 'an independent mind is indispensable in the exercise of judicial power, whatever the source of that power may be, [and it is] one of the essential qualities of an arbitrator'.[59] Various other decisions also add the requirement of impartiality.[60] For domestic arbitrations, arbitrators are required, pursuant to Art 1452 **6.53**

[58] See eg *Laiguède v Ahsen Inox*, Cass 1e Civ, 10 May 1995, (1995) *Rev arb* 605, 2nd decision, and commentary by A. Hory; *Wasteels v Ampafrance*, CA Paris, 9 November 1983, (1985) *Rev arb* 101; *Alexandre Giuliani v Colas*, CA Paris, 9 July 1986, (1987) *Rev arb* 179, 5th decision, and commentary by P. Fouchard; *Société Industrialexport v GECI and GFI*, CA Paris, 19 December 1995, (1996) *Rev arb* 110, and commentary by A. Hory.

[59] See *Ury v Galeries Lafayette*, Cass 2e Civ, 13 April 1972, (1975) *Rev arb* 235, and commentary by E. Loquin.

[60] See eg *Editions Médicafrique v le concours médical*, Cass 2e Civ, 8 November 1989, unpublished; *Forges et Ateliers de Commentry Oissel v Hydrocarbon Engineering*, Cass 2e Civ, 20 February 1974, (1975) *Rev arb* 238; *KFTCIC v Icori Estero*, CA Paris, 13 June 1996, (1997) *Rev arb* 251, referring to the arbitrator's independence as being '*the essence of his judicial role*', and commentary by E. Gaillard; (1997) *JDI* 151, and commentary by E. Loquin; *Phillip Brothers v Icco*, CA Paris, 6 April 1990, (1990) *Rev arb* 880, referring to the independence as '*an absolute requirement of all arbitral proceedings*', and commentary by M. de Boisséson; Bredin, J.-D,

para 2 of the Code, to inform the parties of all circumstances potentially affecting their independence or impartiality at the time of acceptance of their appointment. In international arbitration, the courts have applied the same principle without reference to Art 1452, referring instead to the arbitrator's duty of disclosure as being a substantive rule directly applicable in international cases.[61]

6.54 For international arbitrations having their seat in France or made subject by the parties to French procedural law, the competent court for the challenge of an arbitrator is the President of the *Tribunal de Grande Instance* of Paris, as the challenge is qualified as a difficulty in the setting up of the arbitral tribunal within the meaning of Art 1493 para 2 of the Code. The intervention of the President of the *Tribunal de Grande Instance* of Paris may be requested either by a party or by the arbitral tribunal. The President rules in summary proceedings (*référé*), for which there is no appeal.[62]

6.55 The right of the parties to challenge an arbitrator is limited in time; the court's jurisdiction expires when the arbitral proceedings come to an end. This has been confirmed by the *Tribunal de Grande Instance* of Paris, which held that 'as the arbitrator has discharged his duties, there can no longer be any difficulty regarding the constitution of the arbitral tribunal such as might warrant the intervention of the President of the Tribunal de Grande Instance of Paris. [The plaintiff] should therefore resort to the forms of recourse available against the arbitral award if it considers that there are grounds on which to set aside the award'.[63]

6.56 The jurisdiction of the *Tribunal de Grande Instance* of Paris is only subsidiary in nature, however. The arbitration agreement can provide for another body, or individual, to resolve such issues. If such provision is made, it is binding on the parties.

6.57 **(1.1) Do state courts review challenge procedures which took place in accordance with a specific procedure agreed upon by the parties (eg Art 11, 1998 ICC Rules)? If so, at what point of time? May such review be excluded?** Because the jurisdiction of the *Tribunal de Grande Instance* is only subsidiary in nature, the court will not intervene if the challenge was or could have been brought before another body under a procedure agreed by the parties.[64]

'La révélation; Remarques sur l'indépendance de l'arbitre en droit interne français' in *Etudes de procédure et d'arbitrage en l'honneur de Jean-François Poudret* (Payot 1999) 349. See also *SIAB et autres v Valmont et autre*, Cass 2e Civ. 25 March 1999, (1999) *Rev arb* 319, and note by C. Jarrosson; Bouche, N. and Fourtoy, F., 'L'indépendance de l'arbitre et les moyens de la garantir' in A. Mourre (ed), *Les Cahiers de l'Arbitrage*, vol I (Gazette du Palais, 2002) 123.

61 See *T.A.I. v. S.I.A.P.E.* and *Germanco v S.I.A.P.E.*, CA Paris, 2 June 1989, 2 decisions, (1991) *Rev arb* 87; *KFTCIC v Icori Estero*, CA Paris, 28 June 1991, (1992) *Rev arb* 568, and commentary by P. Bellet; *Annahold BV v L'Oréal*, CA Paris, 9 April 1992, (1996) *Rev arb* 483, 2nd decision; *Gouvernement de l'Etat du Qatar v Creighton Ltd.*, CA Paris, 12 January 1996, (1996) *Rev arb* 428, 2nd decision, and commentary by P. Fouchard.

62 See, however, *Société GECI et GFE v Société Industrialexport*, CA Paris, 19 December 1995, (1996) *Rev arb* 110, and commentary by A. Hory, where an appeal was deemed possible because of the violation of a fundamental principle of public policy.

63 See *Annahold BV v L'Oréal*, TGI Paris, 2 July 1990, (1996) *Rev arb* 483, 1st decision.

64 See *Raffineries de pétrole d'Homs et de Banias*, CA Paris, 15 May 1985, (1985) *Rev arb* 141; *Opinter France v S.A.R.L. Dacomex*, Cass 2e Civ, 7 October 1987, (1987) *Rev arb* 479, and commentary by E. Mezger.

(1.2) Is there case law with respect to truncated arbitral tribunals? (cf Art 12(5), 1998 ICC Rules) A much debated issue concerns truncated tribunals. The issue relates to whether the parties can agree not to replace an arbitrator who resigns in bad faith. If this were possible, the arbitral tribunal would proceed with the arbitration with only two arbitrators. Some argue that this can be an effective measure to counter disruptive steps taken by arbitrators for the benefit of the party which appointed him or her. It was therefore adopted by the ICC Rules in 1998 (Art 12 (5)). The validity of such a provision has not, however, been tested before the French courts to date.[65] **6.58**

(2) Procedure for appointing a new arbitrator

An arbitrator may need to be replaced subsequent to a successful challenge, default, resignation, removal agreement or death. The replacement procedure is either chosen by the parties, or provided for in the institutional rules that the parties have chosen to apply. In the event that the parties' agreement or the institutional rules they have chosen do not contain adequate provisions to allow for the replacement of an arbitrator, the President of the *Tribunal de Grande Instance* of Paris will assist the parties with the reconstitution of the arbitral tribunal. **6.59**

IV. The arbitral procedure

A. General principles

(1) Extent of party autonomy to determine the arbitral procedure

Under French law, the law governing the arbitral proceedings is distinct from the law governing the merits of the dispute[66] and from the law of the seat of the arbitration.[67] The parties are free to choose the law or the 'rules of law' applicable to the arbitral procedure. This freedom of the parties is expressed in particular in Art 1494 of the Code, which provides that 'an arbitration agreement may, directly or by reference to arbitration rules, determine the arbitral procedure or subject it to any procedural law'. Thus, the parties are also free not to choose any law governing the proceedings, in fact often the preferred course of conduct. **6.60**

In the event that the parties have not agreed upon the applicable procedural rules, or have not done so in sufficient detail, it is up to the arbitral tribunal to do so, either directly or by reference to a law or to arbitration rules, in accordance with Art 1494 para 2 of the Code. In such circumstances, the arbitrators are thus as free as the parties to determine the applicable rules, and are not obliged to refer to a particular national law or to any particular **6.61**

---

[65] For a case in which the Paris *Cour d'Appel* set aside an award rendered by a truncated arbitral tribunal, but in which the parties had not provided for such a possibility, see *ATC-CFCO v Comilog*, CA Paris, 1 July 1997, (1998) *Rev arb* 131.

[66] See *O.C.P.C. v Wilhem Diefenbacher KG and O.C.P.C. v Diefenbacher*, CA Paris, 18 June 1974, (1975) *Rev arb* 179, and commentary by J. Robert; *Wasteels v Ampafrance*, Cass 1e Civ, 10 May 1988, (1989) *Rev arb* 51, and commentary by J.L. Goutal.

[67] See *Chambre arbitrale de Paris v République de Guinée*, CA Paris, 4 May 1988, (1988) *Rev arb* 664, and commentary by P. Fouchard; see also *Industrialexport v K*, TGI Paris, 15 February 1995, (1996) *Rev arb* 503, 2nd decision, and commentary by P. Fouchard; E. Gaillard, (1990) *Rev arb* 759, especially at 761 *et seq.*

arbitration rules. The arbitral tribunal may also choose not to select any law or set of rules and instead decide upon each procedural issue as and when it arises. Should the parties or the arbitral tribunal designate French procedural law, Art 1495 of the Code provides that the rules governing French domestic arbitration only apply in the absence of a specific agreement between the parties determining which procedural rules to apply.[68]

6.62 (1.1) **Are the parties free to choose any national or international law governing the procedure before the arbitral tribunal?** The parties have total freedom under French law to select any national or international law or 'rules of law' to govern the procedure before the arbitral tribunal.

(2) Basic procedural principles or mandatory rules to be applied by the arbitral tribunal

6.63 Despite the considerable party autonomy regarding the determination of the arbitral procedure, there are certain mandatory fundamental principles which must be observed in order to ensure that due process is respected.

6.64 The mandatory fundamental principles which must be observed in all arbitral proceedings are the principles of due process and the equality of the parties. Although not stipulated expressly by the French legislation, there is no doubt that if these principles are not respected, the arbitral award can be declared null and void by the courts of the seat.[69] Furthermore, enforcement of foreign awards can be refused on that basis, provided that the party has appropriately reserved its rights in this respect upon the occurrence of the event which constitutes a breach of these fundamental principles.

(3) Oral hearing or proceeding on basis of written documents

6.65 Even though it will very rarely occur in practice, French international arbitration law allows the arbitrators to dispense with hearings and reach their decision on the basis of the parties' written submissions unless otherwise provided for by the rules chosen by the parties.[70]

(4) Power of the tribunal (in particular the chairman) to issue procedural orders

6.66 Under French law, the arbitral tribunal may, unless the parties have agreed otherwise, resolve procedural issues by way of procedural orders. Procedural orders do not constitute arbitral awards and therefore cannot be the subject of an action to set aside.[71] According to Art 1461 para 1 of the Code, which is applicable on a subsidiary basis whenever French procedural law is to be applied in an arbitration, the procedural orders 'shall be made by all the arbitrators unless the arbitration agreement authorizes them to delegate this task to one of them'. In practice, any such delegation would be to the chairman of the arbitral tribunal.

[68] See also *Raffineries de Pétrole d'Homs et de Banias v Chambre de Commerce Internationale*, CA Paris, 15 May 1985, (1985) *Rev arb* 141.

[69] See Art 1502 paras 4 and 5 of the Code.

[70] See *Compagnie Honeywell Bull SA v Computacion de Venezuela CA*, CA Paris, 21 June 1990, (1991) *Rev arb* 96, and commentary by J.-L. Delvolvé.

[71] See *Pia Inv v Cassia*, CA Paris, 7 July 1987, (1988) *Rev arb* 649, and commentary by E. Mezger; *Sardisud v Technip*, CA Paris, 25 March 1994, (1994) *Rev arb* 391, and commentary by C. Jarrosson.

(5) Distinction of matters of substance and matters of procedure

Matters of substance include all contractual issues pertaining to the merits of the dispute which is the subject of the arbitration (such as contractual interpretation, determination of liability etc), to be distinguished from matters of procedure which concern the judicial element of the arbitration (conduct of the arbitral proceedings, such as the method of examining witnesses or the admissibility of discovery). **6.67**

(5.1) Are the statutes of limitations a matter of substance or rather of procedure? Statutes of limitations are considered to be a matter of substance. For example, a request for arbitration may be declared inadmissible if the law governing a contract for the sale of goods stipulates that an action in respect of a latent defect must be brought within a certain time limit. However, this situation must be distinguished from any time limits laid down by procedural law which may also be applicable in a given case. **6.68**

(6) Persons able to represent a party in an arbitral proceeding

The parties can defend their case themselves or be represented by any person of their choice. There is no requirement that this person be a lawyer or a French national.[72] **6.69**

B. Place of arbitration

(1) Determination of the place of arbitration in the absence of an agreement by the parties

The parties to an international arbitration are generally free to determine the place of arbitration in the arbitration agreement or in a subsequent agreement. If they fail to do so, the designated arbitration institution or, in *ad hoc* arbitration, the arbitrators themselves, will determine the place of arbitration. **6.70**

(2) Importance and legal effect of place (seat) of the arbitration

If France has been designated as the place of arbitration, or if the arbitration is subject to French procedural law, French courts will have jurisdiction to give assistance in the appointment of the arbitral tribunal. If France has been designated as the place of arbitration, the French courts will have jurisdiction to set aside the award in the event that the fundamental principles of due process and equality of the parties have been violated. There are no legal requirements or specific taxes resulting from the choice of France as the place of arbitration. **6.71**

(2.1) Are the arbitrators and parties free to convene at places other than the official seat of the arbitration? There is no French law provision that requires the arbitrators and parties to convene only at the seat of the arbitration. The French courts accept that it is perfectly legitimate to perform some procedural steps in places other than the seat of the arbitration. **6.72**

(2.2) Are there visa requirements to enter the country which apply to lawyers and/or arbitrators? Where may current information on that subject be obtained? The visa requirements to enter France are the same for lawyers and arbitrators as for other business **6.73**

[72] See *SARL Primor v Société d'exploitation industrielle de Bétaigne*, Cass 1e Civ, 19 June 1979, (1979) *Rev arb* 487.

travellers. Current information on French visa requirements may be obtained from any French consulate.

C. Submissions, deadlines and default

(1) Contents and form of submissions (in particular request for arbitration and answer to request)

6.74 An arbitration is initiated by a request for arbitration, followed by an answer, enabling each of the parties to present its initial claims. French international arbitration law does not contain any mandatory requirements as to the form of such a request. The party's intention to initiate arbitral proceedings must, however, be explicit.[73] Of course, any requirements that are set forth in the institutional rules that the parties have chosen, or in the parties' agreement itself, must be respected.

6.75 French law does not require the parties to respect any set deadlines during the arbitral process.[74] In practice, such deadlines are either agreed upon by the parties, expressly or by reference to institutional rules, or set by the arbitral tribunal.

6.76 (1.1) **From what point in time is a claim considered to be pending with the arbitral tribunal? What are the legal effects of such fact (eg on statutes of limitations)?** The arbitral proceedings are deemed to commence by the request for arbitration. From that time, the dispute is pending before the arbitral tribunal with the effect that, for instance, the statute of limitations for the action in question is interrupted; this may also have an important impact on the calculation of interest on amounts subsequently awarded.

6.77 (1.2) **When is a time limit according to statutes of limitations deemed to be interrupted in case of (i) *ad hoc*; and (ii) institutional arbitration?** The point in time at which time limits are interrupted due to the commencement of arbitral proceedings is the date of receipt of the request for arbitration by the opposing party in the case of *ad hoc* arbitration, and by the arbitral institution in the case of institutional arbitration.

6.78 (1.3) **What is the effect of the withdrawal of the request for arbitration?** The withdrawal of a request for arbitration has the result of terminating the arbitral proceedings, although the respondent must consent to the termination in the event that it has brought counterclaims against the claimant.

(2) Legal deadlines (provided by law or set by the tribunal) and effect of non-compliance by a party

6.79 There is no French law provision that governs the effect of a party exceeding a procedural deadline. The effect of such an event will be determined by reference to the parties' agreement. In the absence of any such agreement, the arbitral tribunal typically determines the consequences, with the freedom to draw negative inferences from the party's failure to meet the deadline.

---

[73] See Fouchard Gaillard Goldman at paras 1,209 *et seq.*

[74] See *Sonidep v Sigmoil*, Cass 1e Civ, 15 June 1994, (1995) *Rev arb* 88, 1st decision, and commentary by E. Gaillard; *Communauté urbaine de Casablanca v Degrémont*, Cass 1e Civ, 15 June 1994, (1995) *Rev arb* 88, 2nd decision, and commentary by E. Gaillard.

(2.1) What are the powers of the tribunal if a party fails to comply with the time limits set up by the tribunal? When a party fails to comply with a procedural time limit set by the arbitral tribunal, the arbitral tribunal has the power to sanction this failure, and the French courts will not censor the award at the enforcement stage for having done so.[75] Regarding the case where a party fails to appear at all in the proceedings, it should be noted that French law does not contain any specific provisions applying to default proceedings. However, two general principles govern.[76] First, default does not constitute an admission of liability and does not validate the arguments of the non-defaulting party. Second, arbitral proceedings can go forward despite the absence of the defaulting party. The defaulting party must, however, be informed of the commencement of the arbitral proceedings and of the progress thereof, and must be given the opportunity at every stage of the arbitral process to present its case, in order to observe the requirements of due process.[77] If the defaulting party fails to appear throughout the proceedings, a default award can be rendered against it and, as opposed to a default judgment rendered by a court, such award is not subject to appeal.[78] **6.80**

(2.2) Is the tribunal bound by any mandatory time limits for certain procedural steps (eg hearings, making of the award)? No mandatory procedural time limits are set by French law. **6.81**

(3) Statutory requirements as to notifications during arbitration (with respect to the request for arbitration and other written pleadings; with respect to notifications by the tribunal)

French law imposes no statutory requirements as to the notification of written pleadings and procedural orders during the arbitral proceedings. **6.82**

(4) Effect of the insolvency of a party

The insolvency of a party does not affect the binding force of an arbitration agreement to which it is a party. Thus, in principle, the insolvency of a party will not have the effect of terminating the proceedings, although it may have the effect of causing a stay of the arbitration. **6.83**

---

[75] See eg *Europmarkets v Argogolicos Gulf Shipping Co*, CA Paris, 1e Ch Supp, 16 January 1986 (unpublished).

[76] See Tunik, D., 'Default Proceedings in International Commercial Arbitration', (1998)1 *Int'l Arb L Rev* 86.

[77] See Gaillard, E., 'Laws and Court Decisions in Civil Law Countries' in A.J. van den Berg (ed), *ICCA Congress Series no 5, Preventing Delay and Disruption of Arbitration* (Kluwer, 1991) 104 at 106.

[78] See eg *Dovert et Tabourdeau v Confex*, CA Paris, 7 February 1991, (1992) Rev. arb 634, and observations by J. Pellerin; *Bin Saud Bin Abdel Aziz v Crédit Industriel et Commercial de Paris*, CA Paris, 24 March 1995, (1996) *Rev arb* 259, and commentary by J.-M. Talau. See also Hanotiau, B., 'Le défaut d'une partie dans la procédure d'arbitrage international' in *Mélanges offerts à Raymond Vander Elst* (Nemesis 1986), vol I at 375; Schwebel, S. and Lahne, S., 'Public Policy and Arbitral Procedure' in P. Sanders (ed), *ICCA Congress Series no 3, Comparative Arbitration Practice and Public Policy in Arbitration* (Kluwer, 1987) 205.

D. Facts and evidence: general

(1) Burden of proof (inquisitorial/adversarial procedure)

6.84 The parties are free to agree upon the rules of evidence to be applied in the arbitral procedure. Failing such special agreement, the arbitrators will apply those contained in the applicable institutional rules or national law or the rules selected to govern procedural aspects of the arbitration. For the arbitrators as for the parties, this freedom even goes so far as to allow them to refrain from determining the applicable rules in advance, so as to retain the possibility of resolving each procedural issue as and when it arises. The only limits to this freedom, other than those resulting from the intentions of the parties, are those which derive from the requirements of international public policy, such as the principles of due process and of equality of the parties.

6.85 Where French procedural law is specifically chosen, Art 1460 of the Code provides that the general principles of French procedure should apply. An arbitral tribunal which applies these rules or which is inspired by these rules will typically employ evidentiary techniques such as the hearing of witnesses and experts. Pursuant to Art 9 of the Code, for example, each party bears the burden of proving the facts that are necessary to support its contentions.

6.86 No provision of French law precludes parties from presenting evidence as they see fit. Subject to the procedural rules agreed between the parties, or those set by the tribunal, parties are thus free to adduce documentary evidence, fact witnesses, and expert witnesses.

(2) Power of the tribunal to determine the admissibility and weight of the evidence produced by the parties

6.87 The arbitral tribunal has full discretion to determine the admissibility and weight of the evidence produced by the parties. In addition, Art 11 of the Code provides that the tribunal may draw whatever conclusion it sees fit from the refusal of a party to produce an item of evidence.

6.88 (2.1) **Is the tribunal entitled to take the claimant's factual allegation as proven if the defendant does not participate in the arbitral proceedings?** It is a general principal of French law that default does not constitute an admission of liability, and does not automatically validate the arguments of the claimant. Although there is no obligation on the arbitrators to impose an enhanced burden of proof on the party which is present or represented in compensation for the opposing party's failure to participate, the arbitral tribunal must duly examine the merits of the claimant's factual—and legal—arguments.

6.89 (2.2) **May the tribunal consider an allegation of one party as agreed fact if the other party did not (specifically) dispute the allegation?** No provision of the French law prevents the arbitral tribunal from doing so.

6.90 (2.3) **What is the standard of proof that must be met in order for a fact to be considered to have been established (preponderance of the evidence; beyond reasonable doubt)? Must a stringent requirement be met for certain facts?** The arbitral tribunal is free to determine the standard to be employed for the assessment of evidence, as long as the principle of due process is respected.

(2.4) May the arbitral tribunal rely on its own knowledge to consider certain facts as proven? The arbitral tribunal may assess and determine which facts may be considered as proven based on the knowledge of the arbitrators, and which facts must be evidenced. To meet the requirements of due process, the arbitral tribunal must, however, afford the parties the possibility to discuss all facts. **6.91**

E. Witnesses

(1) Ability of a person to act as a witness

The parties to the arbitration or their representatives, third parties or experts may appear as witnesses. It is up to the parties, and, failing agreement, the arbitral tribunal, to decide whether to hear the testimony of witnesses, and its refusal to do so cannot be a reason to set aside the award in an action before a state court.[79] **6.92**

(1.1) Is there a legal difference between a party testifying and a witness? If yes, what are the criteria for such differentiation? Does the testifying of a party have the same weight as a witness testimony? There is no legal differentiation under French law, but the arbitrators have the power to assess and distinguish the weight to be given to their respective testimony. **6.93**

(2) Preparation of witnesses and limits thereof

It is generally admissible for a party to approach a witness, so long as the same rules and standards apply to both parties and their representatives. **6.94**

(2.1) Do US-style depositions violate any procedural rules or principles? US-style depositions have not been held to violate any procedural rules or principles by the French courts. They are not, however, customary in arbitrations held in France. **6.95**

(2.2) May a party or its counsel approach a witness whom it has nominated (only before or also after the proceeding has started)? Are interviews permitted? It is admissible for a party to communicate with a witness so long as the same rules and standards apply to all parties and their representatives. In the absence of an agreement of the parties, this should be verified by the arbitral tribunal, particularly where the parties belong to different legal traditions.[80] **6.96**

(3) Admissibility of written witness statements

Witness statements will normally be submitted in writing and witnesses allowed to testify orally at a later stage. These written affidavits are often deemed to replace direct examination of the witness, and as such, oral testimony frequently begins directly with cross-examination of witnesses.[81] **6.97**

---

[79] See *Soubaigne v Limmareds Skogar*, CA Paris, 15 March 1984, (1985) *Rev arb* 285; *SGN v PAEC*, CA Paris, 13 July 1987, unpublished.

[80] See Fouchard Gaillard Goldman at para 1,285.

[81] See Goldman, B., 'The Complementary Roles of Judges and Arbitrators in Ensuring that International Commercial Arbitration is Effective' in *International Arbitration—60 Years of ICC Arbitration—A Look at the Future* (ICC Publication no 412, 1984) (ICC Publication no 412) 257, 292; Loquin, E., 'Les pouvoirs des arbitres internationaux à la lumière de l'évolution récente du droit de l'arbitrage international' (1983) *JDI* 293, at 308; in French domestic arbitration, see Art 1461, para 2 of the Code.

6.98 (3.1) **If the parties agree on written witness statements, is a party entitled to request an oral hearing for questioning those witnesses (provided that such right has not been agreed upon)?** Written witness statements are frequently produced in international arbitrations in France and do not violate any procedural rules or principles of French law. The submission of a written witness statement does not automatically create an entitlement to question the witness, even though in most cases the witness is questioned. It is for the parties and, failing agreement, for the arbitral tribunal to assess the preferable course of conduct. There is no mandatory right under French law to examine orally a witness.

(4) Entitlement of a party to have a hearing or cross-examination of witnesses

6.99 In the absence of a specific agreement of the parties, the tribunal will decide upon how to examine witnesses. They can either be examined by the arbitral tribunal or by the parties' representatives or by both. Although there is no specific provision of French law that requires parties to make witnesses available for cross-examination, the parties are free to enter into an agreement to that effect. In the absence of such agreement, the arbitral tribunal will decide whether cross-examination should be allowed. In practice, cross-examination is becoming increasingly prevalent in large international arbitrations having their seat in France.

6.100 (4.1) **Which are the methods used to establish a record of the arbitral proceedings, in particular witness examinations (tape recording, verbatim court reporters, dictated minutes, other methods)?** The method used to establish a record of the arbitral proceedings is left entirely to the discretion of the parties and, subsidiarily, of the arbitrators. In practice, court reporters are frequently used.

6.101 (4.2) **May the arbitral tribunal take an oath from a witness?** In French law, it is generally accepted that an arbitrator is a private individual and, as such, is not empowered to take an oath from a witness.[82] Arbitrators generally remind the witnesses that they are required to tell the truth and that false testimony may lead to criminal sanctions.

6.102 (4.3) **Does the arbitral tribunal have the power to compel witnesses?** The arbitral tribunal does not have subpoena power, under French law, to compel witnesses to attend hearings. The interested party or the arbitrators can seek the assistance of the courts to that effect.

F. Documents

(1) Form and kind of documents to be presented to the arbitral tribunal

6.103 Parties are required to submit identical copies of every document produced to each member of the arbitral tribunal and to the other party simultaneously, in order to safeguard against any violation of due process. There are no specific statutory rules relating to the production of documents in a language other than the language of the arbitration. This issue is typically addressed by the parties and, subsidiarily, by the arbitral tribunal in the terms of reference, when requested, or in a procedural hearing.

[82] See Art 1461 para 2 of the Code, for French domestic arbitration.

(1.1) Is the submission of 'agreed documents' permitted? If yes, what is the extent and effect of such an agreement of the parties (authenticity, existence, acknowledgement of such documents' contents)? The concept of 'agreed documents' does not exist in French law, and due process requires that all evidence be communicated simultaneously and in an identical form to each arbitrator and to the other party. **6.104**

(1.2) How may electronic documents (eg emails) be presented and proven? Before French courts, according to Art 1316–1 of the French Civil Code, '[a] writing in electronic form is admissible as evidence in the same manner as a paper-based writing, provided that the person from whom the document emanates can be duly identified and that it be established and stored in conditions calculated to secure its integrity'. Under French law, an electronic document has the same probative value as a paper document (Art 1316–3 of the French Civil Code). In arbitration, arbitrators are free to deal with the matter in any way they see fit. **6.105**

(1.3) Does discovery (US- or UK-style), after the procedure has started, violate any procedural rules or public policy considerations? Discovery does not violate any procedural rules or public policy considerations of French law. **6.106**

(2) Requirement to produce certain documents (as requested by the tribunal) and consequences of a failure to do so

The parties and the arbitral tribunal are free to determine the modalities and scope of presenting documentary evidence. Although there is no discovery as such under French law, a tribunal does have the power to compel the production of documents from a recalcitrant party. Article 1460 para 3 of the Code—applicable to international arbitration by virtue of Art 1495—provides that 'if a party is in possession of an item of evidence, the arbitrators may also order that party to produce it'. **6.107**

It is not unusual that a party will be unwilling to produce documents to the other party for reasons of confidentiality. Some institutional rules have anticipated this problem, for example Art 20 para 7 of the 1998 ICC Rules which contemplates that '[t]he Arbitral Tribunal may take measures for protecting trade secrets and confidential information'. Pursuant to this provision, a party may ask for documents to be submitted only to the arbitral tribunal or even only the chairman of the tribunal. This is deemed admissible in French law so long as all parties agree, although such limited production may raise issues of due process.[83] Other means of protecting confidentiality such as the conclusion of a confidentiality agreement restricting the circulation of the document to certain specific representatives of the parties, are also used. **6.108**

(3) Protection of the confidentiality of documents (legal privilege etc)

Only correspondence between attorneys, to the extent it is not labelled as 'official', is considered privileged and cannot be produced to the arbitral tribunal. **6.109**

[83] See *SARL Anciens Ets Harognan Comptoir Euro-Turc v Turkish Airlines 'Turk Hava Yollari AO'*, CA Paris, 14 June 1985, (1987) *Rev arb* 395, and observations by J. Pellerin.

G. Experts

(1) Appointment and presentation of experts by the party or the arbitral tribunal

6.110 There are no specific provisions concerning expert evidence in French international arbitration law. Nevertheless, it is recognized that the arbitral tribunal may appoint its own expert,[84] as well as hearing the testimony of any expert witnesses retained by the parties.

6.111 (1.1) **By which methods are tribunal-appointed experts selected? What are the rights of the parties during the selection process?** In the absence of any express agreement between the parties, the arbitral tribunal may select experts according to the method of its choice. The arbitral tribunal has no obligation to consult the parties during the selection process, although in practice they often do, and is never required to grant a party's request for the appointment of an expert.[85]

(2) Admissibility and role of expert witnesses

6.112 The role of the expert witness is to give an impartial and independent opinion on an area that is within his expertise. Parties are free to appoint legal experts to opine on the applicable law or issues such as generally accepted principles of law.

(3) Influence of the parties upon the selection of questions to be submitted to the expert

6.113 The arbitral tribunal will set the scope of the expert's mandate. The tribunal is not required to consult the parties when drafting the expert's terms of reference, although again, in practice, it will normally do so.

(4) Independence and impartiality of the expert and the right to reject a proposed/appointed expert

6.114 Experts appointed by the tribunal must be neutral and therefore independent of the parties and they can be challenged if they lack independence or impartiality. The arbitral tribunal has the power to rule on any such challenge.[86]

6.115 (4.1) **May a party or its counsel approach an expert (or expert witness) whom it has nominated (only before or also after the proceeding has started)? Are interviews admissible?** As for fact witnesses (see at para 6.96 *supra*), it is admissible for a party to interview or communicate with an expert witness it has appointed, so long as the same rules and standards apply to both parties.

(5) Oral examination of an expert in a hearing

6.116 In general, the expert's investigation will culminate in the submission to the arbitral tribunal and to the parties of a written expert report. There is no requirement under French law for an expert witness to make an oral presentation of the expert report or to be examined upon it. The parties are, of course, free to agree upon such a procedure and, in the absence

---

[84] See Arts 10 and 1460 para 2 of the Code.

[85] See *Air Intergulf v SECA*, CA Paris, 1e Ch Supp, 13 May 1980, no G9097 (unpublished); *ITP Interpipe v Hunting Oilfield Services-Hos.*, CA Paris, 1e Ch, Sec C, 3 December 1998, (1999) *Rev arb* 601, and note by C. Jarrosson.

[86] See Gaillard, E., 'Arbitrage commercial international—instance arbitrale—organisation et développement de la procédure arbitrale—intervention du juge étatique', *J-Cl Proc Civ*, Fasc 1068, para 75.

of an agreement, the arbitral tribunal will decide. Any oral hearing of an expert witness must be held in the presence of the parties or their representatives, who will usually be authorized by the arbitral tribunal to question the expert witness directly.

Similarly, there is no requirement that an expert witness attend a hearing, but such attendance can be permitted, either by agreement between the parties or by order of the arbitral tribunal. **6.117**

H. Interim measures of protection

(1) Kind of interim measures, which the tribunal may order

Arbitrators may order provisional or conservatory measures, if the circumstances of the case require it. They normally do so by rendering an interim award. In principle, and unless otherwise provided by the parties, courts and arbitrators have concurrent jurisdiction to take such measures.[87] **6.118**

(1.1) Which are, in general, the procedural and substantive prerequisites for the ordering of interim and conservatory measures (eg reduced degree of evidence; urgency; summary evaluation of the claim)? Interim and conservatory measures may be ordered when it is urgent to take action to prevent irreparable harm. These measures are ordered on an urgent basis by the court or arbitral tribunal on summary examination of the application, without prejudice to a subsequent decision on the merits. **6.119**

(1.2) Are the prerequisites for the interim measures ordered by the arbitral tribunal more or less the same as if those are requested from the state court? Is there case law/ leading authorities on whether those measures are faster and enforced more easily if taken by the arbitral tribunal or the state court? The prerequisites are similar, but it is often considered more effective to turn to the courts where emergency measures are needed, in that the courts can hear an application as a matter of urgency, which may be more problematic for an arbitral tribunal, and because their decisions will be readily enforceable. **6.120**

A particularity of French law is the procedure known as '*référé-provision*', whereby a creditor may use an emergency procedure to have its rights enforced, fully or in part, if these rights are not seriously disputable.[88] The French courts have accepted that, unless expressly excluded by the parties, a *référé-provision* may be granted, even when the application is founded on a substantive issue covered by an arbitration agreement, so long as the arbitral tribunal has not been constituted and there is urgency.[89] **6.121**

[87] See *Atlantic Triton v République populaire révolutionnaire de Guinée*, Cass 1e Civ, 18 November 1986, (1987) Rev crit DIP 760, and commentary by B. Audit.

[88] See Arts 809 para 2 and 873 para 2 of the Code.

[89] See *République islamique d'Iran v Commissariat à l'Energie Atomique*, Cass 1e Civ, 14 March 1984, (1984) Dalloz 629, and commentary by J. Robert; *Horeva v Sitas*, Cass 1e Civ, 6 March 1990, (1990) *Rev arb* 633; *Commisimpex v République du Congo*, TGI Paris, réf, 17 June 1998, Case no 55138/98 (unpublished); *Rantec v SIDT Europe*, Cass 1e Civ, 21 October 1997, (1998) *Rev arb* 673, 2nd decision, and commentary by L. Degos.

(2) Limits of the tribunal's power to order interim measures

6.122 There are certain measures, however, that can only be ordered by the courts.[90] This is the case in particular for attachment orders or more generally of orders designed to facilitate the enforcement of the award to be rendered. Naturally, arbitrators do not have the power to make orders binding on persons who are not party to the arbitration agreement.

(3) Orders to provide security for the costs of the proceeding

6.123 The arbitral tribunal may order a party to provide a security to cover the costs incurred in the course of the arbitration.[91] However, the mere fact that a party is in difficult financial straits does not suffice to justify the making of such an order. The tribunal has to have serious reasons, such as the choice of a corporate entity without any assets to initiate the arbitration, in order to justify an order for the posting of a security.

(4) Attachments of assets by an order of the tribunal

6.124 An international arbitral tribunal sitting in France is not empowered to order the attachment of assets.

I. Assistance by the courts

(1) Extent of court assistance in the gathering of evidence

6.125 When the parties to an arbitration seek assistance in obtaining documentary evidence, the courts have exclusive jurisdiction to compel third parties to produce documents, pursuant to Art 145 of the Code, applicable until the dispute has been submitted to the arbitral tribunal, and thereafter on the basis of the ordinary principles of French law providing for jurisdiction of the courts to take emergency measures.[92] Only the party who considers the production of such documents to be urgent and necessary can make such request. Similarly, only the courts can compel an unwilling witness to attend a hearing.

6.126 Parties are entitled to apply to the French courts to obtain provisional or protective measures if 'a state of urgency has been duly established'.[93] Such application does not constitute a waiver of the applicability of the arbitration agreement to the merits of the dispute.

6.127 (1.1) **Is it for the arbitral tribunal or for the party to obtain the assistance of state courts with respect to gathering evidence?** There is no basis in French law for either the arbitral tribunal or the parties to request the assistance of the courts in the gathering of evidence,[94] other than the urgent protective measures which may be requested by a party to preserve evidence that might otherwise disappear.

[90] See Gaillard, E., 'Arbitrage commercial international—instance arbitrale—organisation et développement de la procédure arbitrale—intervention du juge étatique', *J-Cl Proc Civ*, Fasc. 1068, para 106.

[91] See Fouchard Gaillard Goldman at para 1,256.

[92] See *Société d'exploitation du cinéma REX v Rex*, Cass 3e Civ, 7 June 1979, (1980) *Rev arb* 78, and commentary by P. Courteault; *Ufremine v Société nouvelle de Saint-Elie A Dieu Vat*, Cass 2e Civ, 17 July 1957, (1957) Bull Civ II, no 546; *Akzo Nobel v Elf Atochem*, CA Versailles, 8 October 1998, (1999) *Rev arb* 57, and note by A. Hory.

[93] See *Société d'exploitation du cinéma REX v REX*, Cass 3e Civ, 7 June 1979, (1980) *Rev arb* 78, and commentary by P. Courteault.

[94] See Fouchard Gaillard Goldman at para 1,338.

(1.2) According to case law and practical experience, are there considerable delays involved when asking a court to give assistance (eg for the obtaining of evidence)? French courts deal on an urgent basis with requests for provisional or protective measures, such that there is rarely a significant delay in obtaining an order. 6.128

(2) Assistance for enforcing the attachment of assets

A party can apply to the courts for an order to attach assets located in France, pending the ultimate resolution of the matter, if the claim can be shown to be 'well-founded in principle'.[95] 6.129

(3) Other examples of possible assistance

Another important role played by the French courts in international arbitration proceedings is in the area of court-ordered expertise proceedings, particularly used to obtain findings of fact where the evidence might change or disappear before an arbitral tribunal could order similar proceedings.[96] In France, these measures can usually be ordered in summary proceedings and do not usually delay the arbitration process. Article 145 of the Code reads: 'If there are legitimate grounds for preserving or establishing, prior to any legal proceedings, proofs of facts which may determine the outcome of the dispute, statutory investigative measures may be ordered on the request of any interested person, in ex parte or emergency proceedings'. It is well established under French law that the existence of an arbitration agreement does not prevent the application of this article;[97] but once the arbitral tribunal is constituted, no request can be based on Art 145 of the Code. However, where urgency is established, the courts can take measures to preserve the evidence at stake on the basis of the ordinary provisions of French law regarding urgent measures, even when the merits of the case are before the arbitral tribunal.[98] 6.130

(4) Dependence of the power of state courts to intervene during the proceedings on the (national) procedural law applied by the arbitral tribunal

Although previously the choice of French law to govern the procedure of an international arbitration was deemed to trigger the jurisdiction of French courts,[99] since the 1981 reform the choice of French law as the procedural law governing an international arbitration does not, in itself, create a basis for the jurisdiction of the French courts to intervene during or after the arbitral proceedings. It is a well recognized principle that courts should, to the contrary, refrain from interfering in any way with the arbitral process. 6.131

---

[95] Art 67 of Law no 91–650 of 9 July 1991, Journal Officiel, 9 July 1991, at 9,228.

[96] Loquin, E., 'Conflits entre la compétence arbitrale et la compétence judiciaire', *J-Cl Proc Civ,* Fasc 1034, paras 9 *et seq.*

[97] *Burneister v Alstom Atlantique*, CA Paris, 30 July 1986, (1989) *Rev arb* 113 and *Eurodisney v Torno*, Cass 2e Civ, 11 October 1995, (1996) *Rev arb* 228. See also *société CSF v société Chays frères et autres*, Cass 1e Civ, 25 April 2006, (2007) *Rev arb* 79.

[98] See *Akzo Nobel v Elf Atochem*, CA Versailles, 8 October 1998, (1999) *Rev arb* 57.

[99] See *General National Maritime Transport Co v Götaverken Arendal AB*, CA Paris, 21 February 1980, (1980) JDI 660, and note by P. Fouchard; for an English translation, see (1981) VI *Ybk Comm Arb* 221; *Aksa v Norsolor*, CA Paris, 9 December 1980, (1981) *Rev arb* 306, and note by F.C. Jeantet; for an English translation, see (1981) *ILM* 887.

V. The award

A. Types of award

(1) Interim award (eg on interim measures or the jurisdiction of the tribunal)

6.132 Arbitrators may render several partial or interim awards or decide the entire dispute in a single award. Partial awards can be rendered to address issues such as jurisdiction or the principle of liability, and interim awards on a request for interim measures of protection.

(2) Partial award

6.133 Partial awards are those in which the arbitrators render a final decision on a particular aspect of the dispute.[100] In French law, arbitrators are deemed to be entitled by the arbitration agreement to render partial awards, unless the parties have explicitly agreed otherwise. If the parties have given clear and precise direction in the arbitration agreement or the terms of reference as to what the arbitrators may rule upon in partial awards, the arbitrators' disregard of these directions may give rise to an action to set aside the award.[101]

6.134 (2.1) **Are awards, especially partial awards, binding in the same arbitral proceeding? Does it make a difference if after the rendering of such a partial award, one arbitrator is successfully challenged and removed on grounds that prevailed even before the partial award was rendered?** An arbitral award is a binding decision, against which an action to set aside may be brought, whether the award is partial or final.[102] The removal of an arbitrator on grounds existing prior to the award does not affect the binding character of the award.

(3) Final award

6.135 A final award is a binding decision putting an end to all or part of a dispute. As such, the final award may be a partial award rendering a final decision on one aspect of the dispute, as discussed above, or a global award, which is a decision on all or the last aspects of the dispute and thus terminates the arbitrators' jurisdiction. Arbitrators can also render consent awards, or awards on agreed terms, whereby the parties agree upon the terms of a settlement which is incorporated into an award that is signed and executed by the arbitrators.

6.136 (3.1) **If a party fails to participate in the arbitration, may the tribunal proceed and issue an award on the merits? Is such an award enforceable as any other award? Are there special remedies for the defendant at the enforcement stage?** A default award is no different from any other type of award, provided due process is observed. There is no bar to the enforceability of such awards and an action to set aside an award merely on the basis that it was rendered by default will be dismissed by French courts.[103]

---

[100] See Fouchard Gaillard Goldman at para 1,360; see also *Sardisud v Technip*, CA Paris, 25 March 1994, (1994) *Rev arb* 391, and *Brasoil v GMRA*, CA Paris, 1 July 1999, (1999) *Rev arb* 834.

[101] See *SOFIDIF v O.I.A.E.T.I.*, Cass 1e Civ, 8 March 1988, (1989) *Rev arb* 481, and commentary by C. Jarrosson.

[102] See Fouchard Gaillard Goldman at para 1,356.

[103] See *Bin Saud Bin Abdel v Crédit Industriel et Commercial de Paris*, CA Paris, 24 March 1995, (1996) *Rev arb* 259, and commentary by J.M. Talau.

B. Deliberations and agreement on the award

(1) Time limits (and possible extensions)

The arbitrators must resolve all disputed issues in one or more decisions, formulated in an award. Whether a tribunal is bound by certain time limits for the rendering of its award depends solely upon the parties' agreement or the procedural law or arbitration rules that the parties have adopted. In the absence of any agreement among the parties, French law does not set any time limits for the making of the award.[104] If the parties have chosen French procedural law to govern the dispute, Art 1456 para 1 of the Code applies, which provides that, in the absence of an explicit agreement, the time limit in which the arbitrators must render their award is 'six months from the day on which the last arbitrator accepts his mission'.[105] Paragraph 2 of the same provision provides that this time limit can be extended by the parties or by court order.[106] In the event that the parties have agreed that the arbitral procedure is to be governed by institutional rules, the French courts have held that the time limits set by such rules are binding upon the parties as if they had set them themselves.[107] **6.137**

In the event that the parties agree upon a time limit, such agreement is generally binding upon the arbitral tribunal. If, however, the parties set unrealistic deadlines, the arbitral clause might be deemed to be 'pathological' although this defect could in all likelihood be cured by the tribunal. The parties can, of course, extend the deadline by mutual agreement. For domestic arbitrations, the President of the *Tribunal de Grande Instance* may, pursuant to Art 1456 para 2, grant the arbitrators an extension of time in the absence of an agreement regarding the extension of a deadline.[108] If the parties choose to apply French procedural law, the same rule would be applied to international arbitration. The French courts cannot, however, resurrect proceedings once the time limit has expired.[109] An award rendered after the expiration of the time limit that has been agreed by the parties can be set aside under Art 1502 of the Code. **6.138**

(2) Procedure for the decision of the arbitrators (majority vote etc)

Even though not explicitly provided for in the Code, the necessity for deliberations is a fundamental requirement of French law. Moreover, all of the arbitrators must have been **6.139**

104 See *Sonidep v Sigmoil*, Cass 1e Civ, 15 June 1994, (1995) *Rev arb* 88, 1st decision, and commentary by E. Gaillard.

105 See *Etude Rochechouard Immobilier v Banque Vernes*, CA Paris, 4 July 1991, (1992) *Rev arb* 626, and observations by J. Pellerin.

106 See *Communauté urbaine de Casablanca v Degrémont*, Cass 1e Civ, 15 June 1994, (1995) *Rev arb* 88, 2nd decision, and commentary by E.Gaillard. See also *Busquet v Peyre*, Cass 2e Civ, 7 November 2002, (2003) *Rev arb* 123, and note by E. Loquin; Moreau, B., 'A propos de la prorogation de la durée de l'arbitrage par le tribunal arbitral' in A. Mourre (ed), *Les Cahiers de l'Arbitrage*, vol II (Gazette du Palais, 2004) 92; Masson, A., 'La durée de l'arbitrage au vue de l'arrêt de la Cour de cassation du 7 novembre 2002', *ibid* at 94.

107 See *Appareils Dragon v Construimport*, CA Paris, 22 January 1982, (1982) *Rev arb* 91, and note by E. Mezger; *Krebs v Milton Stern*, Cass 1e Civ, 16 June 1976, (1977) *Rev arb* 269, and observations by E. Mezger.

108 See *Font Laugière Chimie (Manufactures Jacques Dugniolles) v Moaco*, TGI Paris, réf, 9 May and 19 June 1984, (1985) *Rev arb* 161, and commentary by P. Fouchard.

109 See *Application des Gaz ADG v Wonder Corp of America WCA*, TGI Paris, réf, 3 April 1985, (1985) *Rev arb* 170, and commentary by P. Fouchard.

given the opportunity to participate in the deliberations. The tribunal is free to decide on the form of the deliberations.[110] The fact that an arbitrator refuses to participate in the deliberations does not prevent the remaining members from rendering an award. Just as in a default proceeding, the arbitrators need only to be given equal opportunity to participate in the deliberations.[111] In international arbitrations, the arbitral award must be signed by at least a majority of the arbitrators unless provided for by the parties directly or in the rules they have chosen.

6.140 (2.1) **If an arbitrator fails or refuses to take part in oral deliberation meetings, although having been given sufficient notice of such meetings, may an award be rendered on the basis of written deliberations (or deliberations without this arbitrator) only?** An arbitrator cannot obstruct the making of an award by simply refusing to participate in the deliberations. The requirement for deliberations will be satisfied so long as each of the arbitrators is given an equal opportunity to participate either orally or in writing in the discussions among the arbitrators and in the drafting of the award.[112]

(3) Admissibility of dissenting opinions

6.141 French law is silent as to whether, in the case of a majority decision, the remaining arbitrator may render a dissenting opinion.

6.142 (3.1) **Are there any court decisions or positions of leading authorities on the issue of dissenting opinions (admissibility, disclosure to the parties and publication)?** There is no case law on the issue of dissenting opinions. Some authorities are very sceptical about whether this possibility exists.[113] It has been argued that dissenting opinions would constitute a breach of the principle of the secrecy of the deliberations.[114] Others disagree with this position on the grounds that expressing a dissenting opinion does not necessarily entail breaching the secrecy of the deliberations, as the individual views of the majority arbitrators are not revealed. In international arbitrations where the seat is in France, a dissenting opinion is sometimes found. The dissenting opinion is, however, a mere element of fact, and does not form a part of the award.

(4) Signature by the arbitrators and potential failure of one arbitrator to sign

6.143 Article 1473 of the Code provides: 'the award must be signed by all the arbitrators. However, if a minority of them refuses to sign it, the others shall mention the fact and the award shall have the same effect as though it had been signed by all the arbitrators'. Thus, in French international arbitration law, it is sufficient for the award to be signed by the majority of the arbitrators.

[110] See *Industrija Motora Rakovica v Lynx Machinery Ltd,* Cass 2e Civ, 28 January 1981, (1982) *Rev arb* 425, upholding CA Paris, 22 December 1978, (1979) *Rev arb* 266, and commentary by J. Viatte.

[111] See *Industrija Motora Rakovica,* Cass 2e Civ, 28 January 1981.

[112] *ibid.*

[113] See Robert, J., *L'arbitrage* (Dalloz, 1983) 310; Bredin, J.D., 'Le secret du délibéré arbitral' in *Etudes offertes à Pierre Bellet* (Litec, 1991) 79; de Boisséson, M., *Le droit français de l'arbitrage interne et international* (GNL Joly, 1990) 802.

[114] See *Affichage Giraudi v Consorts Judlin,* note following CA Paris, 15 October 1991, by C. Jarrosson, (1991) *Rev arb* 643, 648.

C. Form of the award and deposition

(1) *Form and minimum contents of an award*

Strictly speaking, French law does not require that the award be in writing. However, as a general rule, awards are rendered in writing. In terms of content, in the absence of any agreement among the parties, the arbitrators or the applicable arbitration rules will determine which items must appear in the award. If the parties choose to apply French procedural law, Art 1473 of the Code requires that an award indicate at a minimum: **6.144**

- the names of the arbitrator(s);
- the date of the award;
- the place where it was rendered;
- the names and the addresses of the parties; and
- if applicable, the names of the counsel or other persons who represented or assisted the parties.

(2) *Requirement to give reasons in the award*

Similarly, there is no explicit requirement that the reasons for the award be explained therein. Parties can, of course, agree upon such a requirement. Generally, the fact that an award contains no reasons will not violate French international public policy.[115] However, the lack of reasons in the award may in some cases hide a violation of due process.[116] In practice, most awards do contain reasons.[117] **6.145**

(3) *Necessity to specify place and time where and when the award was made*

The date on which the award is rendered will determine the time at which it becomes *res judicata*. The place where the award is made need only be mentioned in the award if the parties have specified, directly or by reference to arbitration rules, that it should be included. **6.146**

(4) *Other requirements*

The award does not have to be filed with any judicial authority in France; it merely has to be communicated to the parties. **6.147**

(4.1) Does the award have to be laid down or registered with a state court or agency (even if it has been rendered according to a foreign procedural law)? French law does not provide for any registration requirement for awards rendered in France, unless for **6.148**

[115] See *Gerstlé v Merry Hull*, Cass 1e Civ, 22 November 1966, (1967) JDI 631, and commentary by B. Goldman; (1967) Rev crit DIP 372, and commentary by P. Francescakis; *Sheikh Mahfouz Salem Bin Mahfouz v Al Tayar*, CA Paris, 10 May 1994, (1996) *Rev arb* 66, and commentary by C. Jarrosson; *Société nigérienne des produis pétroliers (SONIDEP) v Sigmoil Resources NV*, CA Paris, 26 March 1992, (1992) Dalloz I.R. 161 and 169.

[116] See *Compagnie d'Armement Maritime (CAM) v Compagnie Tunisienne de Navigation (COTUNAV)*, Cass 1e Civ, 18 March 1980, (1980) *Rev arb* 496, and commentary by E. Mezger; (1980) *JDI* 874, and commentary by E. Loquin.

[117] In two decisions dated 11 May 1999 and 26 October 1999, the French courts have abandoned the review of the potential contradiction between reasons in the award (*Rivers v Fabre*, Cass 1e Civ, 11 May 1999 and *Patou Parfumeur v société Edipar*, CA Paris, 26 October 1999, (1999) *Rev arb* 811, and note by E. Gaillard). Prior to these decisions, contradictory reasons could be considered as amounting to giving no reasons at all.

enforcement or challenge purposes (on enforcement procedures, see paras 6.208 *et seq*; see 6.192 *et seq* regarding challenge procedures).

6.149 (4.2) **Does a foreign award which has been rendered abroad according to this country's national procedural law, have to be laid down or registered with a state court or agency? Is there a fee or tax for such registration of an award?** Similarly, there is no requirement for foreign awards to be registered. Given the absence of any registration requirement, there are no fees or taxes to be paid.

6.150 (4.3) **How long after the rendering of the award must a file/award be stored by the lawyers and the arbitral tribunal?** French law contains no specific rule on how long after the rendering of the award the file must be retained, and this matter is thus left to the discretion of the lawyers (or their particular bar rules) and arbitrators. A good practice is to notify the parties that, failing advice to the contrary, the file will be discarded after a specified period of time.

D. Applicable substantive law

(1) Party autonomy to choose the applicable substantive law

6.151 Under French law, the parties to an international arbitration have complete freedom to determine the law or rules of law applicable to the merits. Article 1496 of the Code provides that 'the arbitrator shall decide the dispute in accordance with the rules of the law chosen by the parties; in the absence of such choice, in accordance with the rules of law he or she considers appropriate. In all cases he or she shall take trade usages into account'. The parties' choice of law may be express or tacit. There are no special requirements of form. They are not bound to choose a national law, but can determine any rules of law to be applicable. They can submit the dispute to general principles of law, to rules that are common to several national systems, to international or even transnational law, often referred to as *lex mercatoria*.

6.152 In the absence of a choice by the parties, the arbitrators are free to determine the applicable law. In doing so, French law does not require the arbitrators to apply a rule, or a system of conflict of laws. Instead, the arbitral tribunal is free to directly designate a rule under the *méthode directe*. In the same way as the parties, the arbitrators may choose not only a given legal system, but also transnational rules or any other type of rules they see fit.

6.153 (1.1) **Is there a public policy exception to the chosen substantive law?** The parties' autonomy is not, however, unlimited. The arbitrators must refuse to apply a law chosen by the parties which does not respect international public policy or, according to certain authors, international mandatory rules ('lois de police').[118]

6.154 (1.2) **Does the principle of '*iura novit curia*' apply? Or must the applicable law be proven (by which means)?** The parties must submit, and prove, their legal argument, whether in French or in foreign law. The French courts have consistently held that the principle of due

[118] See Mayer, P., 'La sentence contraire à l'ordre public au fond' (1994) *Rev arb* 615; Mayer, P., 'L'interférence des lois de polices' in *L'apport de la jurisprudence arbitrale* (ICC Publication no 440/1, 1986) 31. For a more reserved position, see Fouchard Gaillard Goldman at paras 1,533 *et seq*.

process requires the arbitral tribunal to submit to the parties for comments any points of law raised by the arbitrators.[119] The arbitrators may only dispense with this requirement when the rule relied on by the arbitrators is so general in nature that it must have been implicitly included in the pleadings, for instance the principle of good faith in the performance of contracts[120] or the principle that contracts should be interpreted in accordance with their spirit.[121]

(2) Deciding according to equity or as amiable compositeur

According to Art 1497 of the Code, an arbitrator may rule as *amiable compositeur* only if authorized to do so by the parties.[122] The courts have held that an *amiable compositeur* must respect the mandatory principles of procedure and due process, and any award rendered must be reasoned. Nonetheless, an arbitral tribunal, ruling as *amiable compositeur*, is free to disregard the strict effect of a rule of law, if deemed appropriate, to the extent that it does not violate international public policy. **6.155**

(3) Application of lex mercatoria, *general principles etc*

As mentioned above, French law does not preclude the parties and, in the absence of any choice of law by the parties, the arbitrators, from applying general principles of law or *lex mercatoria* to the merits of the dispute.[123] **6.156**

(3.1) Is the application of *lex mercatoria* considered as the application of law or as a kind of *amiable composition*? The French courts have always held that general principles of law or *lex mercatoria* are rules of law, and not a type of equity or *amiable composition* which could not be applied absent any specific agreement of the parties.[124] In more recent decisions, the Cour de Cassation has expressly confirmed the legal nature of the *lex mercatoria*, deciding that an arbitrator who applies usages of international commercial law is applying rules of law.[125] **6.157**

---

[119] See *Thyssen Stahlunion v Maaden*, CA Paris, 6 April 1995, (1995) *Rev arb* 448, 5th decision, and the commentary by C. Kessedjian; *VRV v Pharmachim*, CA Paris, 25 November 1997, (1998) *Rev arb* 684, and note by G. Roland.

[120] See *Paco Rabanne Perfumes v Les Maisons Paco Rabanne*, CA Paris, 25 November 1993, (1994) *Rev arb* 730, and commentary by D. Bureau.

[121] See *Romak v Philip Marine*, CA Paris, 28 May 1993, (1995) *Rev arb* 468, 2nd decision, and commentary by C. Kessedjian.

[122] On this issue, generally, see Loquin, E., 'Arbitrage—Instance arbitrale—Arbitrage de droit et amiable composition' *J-Cl Proc Civ*, Fasc 1,038 (1994).

[123] See Fouchard Gaillard Goldman at paras 1,443 *et seq.*

[124] See *Pabalk Ticaret Sirketi v Norsolor*, Cass 1e Civ, 9 October 1984, (1985) *Rev arb* 431, and commentary by B. Goldman; (1985) *JDI* 679, and commentary by P. Kahn; for an English translation, see (1985) *J Int'l Arb* 67, and observations by D. Thompson; see also commentary by B. Goldman, (1983) *Rev arb* 379; *Fougerolle v Banque du Proche-Orient*, Cass 2e Civ, 9 December 1981, (1982) *Rev arb* 183, and commentary by G. Couchez; (1982) *JDI* 93, and observations by B. Oppetit.

[125] See *Compania Valenciana de Cementos Portland v Primary Coal*, Cass 1e Civ, 22 October 1991, (1992) *Rev arb* 457, and commentary by P. Lagarde; (1992) *JDI* 177, and commentary by B. Goldman; for an English translation, see (1991) 6 *Int'l Arb Rep* B1; *Sonidep v Sigmoil*, Cass 1e Civ, 15 June 1994, (1995) *Rev arb* 88, 1st decision, and commentary by E. Gaillard.

(4) Applicable law if there is no choice of law by the parties

6.158 In the absence of an express choice of law by the parties, an arbitral tribunal sitting in France would consider first whether there is any evidence that reveals a tacit choice of such law by the parties, before proceeding to make its own determination of what law applies.

6.159 (4.1) **Is there an autonomous conflict of law rule in the national arbitration law? Is it considered mandatory?** French law does not require an arbitral tribunal to apply the French choice of law rules or, for that matter, any choice of law rules at all in the absence of an express choice by the parties. French law allows the application of the 'direct choice method' ('méthode directe') according to which arbitrators are free to select the applicable rules of law as the parties themselves would do. Nevertheless, in practice arbitrators sitting in France often rely upon generally accepted principles of private international law to guide their choice.

6.160 (4.2) **What is the law applicable to interest?** The French courts have accepted that an arbitral tribunal is not required to apply a law to the question of the calculation of interest, but may rather apply directly the interest rate which is the most commercially reasonable given the circumstances of the case.[126]

6.161 (4.3) **What is the law and practice with respect to legal interest on foreign currency debts?** It is a well accepted principle that the arbitrators have the freedom to select directly the most appropriate interest rate to apply.

(5) Binding effect of state court decisions

6.162 An arbitral tribunal is generally not bound by a decision of a state court, although the decision may have useful precedential value, particularly if it forms part of the applicable law.

6.163 (5.1) **Is an arbitral tribunal bound by a decision of another arbitral tribunal?** An arbitral tribunal is generally not bound by the decision of another arbitral tribunal, although in certain circumstances an arbitral award may constitute a useful precedent.[127] An award may have a *res judicata* effect if rendered between the same parties in the same matter.

6.164 (5.2) **Does a decision in a criminal case bind an arbitral tribunal?** A criminal sentence generally does not bind a civil arbitrator.

E. Settlement

(1) Settlement by agreement of the parties with or without support of the arbitral tribunal

6.165 The parties to an international arbitration are free to negotiate a settlement at any stage during the arbitral process, either with or without the assistance of the arbitral tribunal. In practice, and given the possibility that the settlement negotiations may fail, parties typically conduct such negotiations without the assistance of the tribunal, so as to preserve their respective positions should they fail to agree upon a settlement.

---

[126] See *KFTCIC v Icori Estero*, CA Paris, 13 June 1996, (1997) *Rev arb* 251, and commentary by E. Gaillard; for an English translation, see (1996) 11 *Int'l Arb Rep* D1.

[127] See Fouchard Gaillard Goldman at paras 371 *et seq.*

(1.1) May an arbitrator who has initiated settlement discussions be challenged when agreement on a settlement has failed? Under French law, there is no ground to challenge an arbitrator who has merely initiated settlement discussions. The arbitrator would have to have pre-judged the matter in the course of the process to be successfully challenged. **6.166**

(2) 'Private settlement' and its impact on the arbitral procedure

The effect of the settlement is to terminate the arbitration proceedings. According to Art 2052 para 1 of the Code, a settlement is *res judicata* such that there is no need for the parties to have the tribunal render an award. Nevertheless, only a consent award may allow the parties to benefit from the recognition and enforcement procedures provided in international conventions. Under French law, the arbitrators are required to render a consent award at the request of the parties unless the settlement violates public policy. It should be noted, however, that the courts are free to classify awards on agreed terms as they deem appropriate. As a result, an award on agreed terms may not necessarily benefit from the enforcement mechanisms available to awards and may not be subject to appeal or an action to set aside.[128] **6.167**

(3) Form and effect of a settlement (eg award on agreed terms)

In the event that the parties succeed in reaching a settlement in the course of the proceedings, they can either conclude an agreement and terminate the arbitral proceedings or have their decision recorded by the arbitral tribunal in a consent award, otherwise known as an award on agreed terms. **6.168**

F. Costs of the arbitration

(1) General allocation of the costs of the proceedings

In the absence of any agreement, the arbitral tribunal is free to apportion the costs as it sees fit. Tribunals having their seat in France have increasingly adopted the common law custom of ordering the losing party to pay a large part or even all of the costs of the arbitration.[129] **6.169**

(2) Deposits or advances for costs or fees

In institutional arbitration, the rules of the institution generally provide that the parties have to pay an advance on the costs at the beginning of the proceedings.[130] Similarly, in *ad hoc* arbitration, the tribunal usually asks the parties to pay such advances. **6.170**

(2.1) Is there case law authorizing or prohibiting arbitrators to order a party to pay an advance on the arbitration costs? Although French law is silent on this point, it is well accepted that the arbitrators may direct the parties to pay an advance on costs. **6.171**

(2.2) May the raising of a set-off claim or counterclaim be made contingent upon payment of the corresponding advance for the relating arbitration costs (cf eg Article 30(5), **6.172**

[128] See *Société Guilliet v Consorts Gillet*, Cass 1e Civ, 7 October 1981, (1984) *Rev arb* 361, and commentary by B. Oppetit.

[129] See Fouchard Gaillard Goldman at para 1,255 and also, in domestic arbitration, Rondeau-Rivier, M.-C., (refonte Loquin, E.), 'Arbitrage—La sentence arbitrale', *J-Cl Proc Civ*, Fasc 1034, paras 63 *et seq.*

[130] See, eg Art 30, ICC Rules; Art VIII, Rules of Arbitration of the Chambre Arbitrale Maritime de Paris.

1998 ICC Rules)? May such a condition be agreed upon when entering into the arbitration agreement? The raising of a counterclaim may be made contingent on the payment of the corresponding advance on costs if agreed by the parties, either directly or by reference to arbitration rules, or decided by the arbitrators.

6.173 **(2.3) What remedies exist against a party which does not pay its part of the advance on the arbitration costs (eg termination of the arbitration agreement)? How may the other party enforce its rights?** The failure of a claimant to pay the advances on costs could be construed by the French courts as a withdrawal of the claim.[131] In one case, a party who had filed a request for arbitration and then refused to pay the advance on costs, was ordered to pay damages.[132] French courts have been known to intervene to order the defaulting party to pay its share of the arbitration costs.[133]

(3) Costs of the administration by an arbitration institution

6.174 The costs of the arbitration consist of the arbitrators' fees, all expenses connected with the hearings, the fees and expenses of any experts and, in institutional arbitration, the fees and expenses of the arbitral institution. French law on international arbitration does not contain provisions on the arbitration costs. They are usually determined in accordance with the parties' agreement, or the applicable arbitration rules chosen by the parties.

(4) Arbitrators' fees: law and practice, judicial control

6.175 French law does not expressly provide any rules concerning the arbitrator's fees. In the absence of an agreement of the parties (including a reference to arbitration rules), the arbitrators set—and modify if necessary—their own fees.

6.176 **(4.1) May arbitrators fix their own fees in the award?** The best practice is for the arbitrators to set the amount of their fees separately from the arbitral award. When they nevertheless do set the amount of their fees in the award itself, this does not create a right which becomes irrevocable if the award is not challenged. Whether or not they are set in the award, the arbitrators' fees may be challenged by the parties in an action which is separate from an action to set aside the award.

6.177 **(4.2) How can the parties change the arbitrators' fees once they are fixed?** An arbitrator's right to be remunerated derives from the contract between the arbitrator and the parties. Accordingly, the arbitrators' fees and expenses will be fixed by that contract. French law authorizes the arbitrators to decide upon the final allocation of liability for the fees and expenses between the parties, bearing in mind the contract and the applicable rules of procedure.

---

131 See *Ferruzzi v Union coopérative agricole de céréale d'Eure-et-Loire*, Cass 2e Civ, 26 January 1994, (1995) *Rev arb* 442 (for domestic arbitration).

132 See *Wenko Wenselaar v SA GB Industries*, Commercial Court of Beaune, 8 July 1994, (1995) *Rev arb* 132, and observations by P. Véron.

133 See *Fertalge Euromade Alger v Kaltenbach Thuring SA*, TGI Beauvais, réf, 9 April 1998, (2002) *Rev arb* 993; *SARL Sifamos v SA Grammer AG*, Paris Commercial Court, réf, 18 December 1998, (2002) *Rev arb* 997. See also Rouche, J., 'Le paiement par le défendeur de sa part de provision sur les frais d'arbitrage: simple faculté ou obligation contractuelle ?' (2002) *Rev arb* 841.

In the event that a party wishes to contest the amount of the arbitrators' fees, it cannot do so by bringing an action to set aside the award before the French courts, unless it can show that the arbitrators deviated from their mission when they set the fees. A party wishing to contest the amount of the arbitrators' fees can do so before the courts as it would for other service providers.[134] **6.178**

(4.3) Are the arbitrators' fees subject to income tax if (i) the place of arbitration; or (ii) the normal residence or place of business of the arbitrator is located in this country? An arbitrator whose residence is in France will, in principle, be subject to income tax in France on the fees he is paid, in the same way as other service providers. In principle, an arbitrator whose residence is not in France, but who receives fees in connection with an arbitration the seat of which is in France, will not be subject to French income tax.[135] In such a case, the relevant international tax treaties should be consulted. **6.179**

(4.4) Are arbitrator's fees submitted to VAT? If yes, is the duty to pay such tax linked to (i) the place of arbitration; or (ii) the arbitrator's general residence? Similarly, an arbitrator's fees are in principle subject to VAT in France in the event that his residence is in France, but not simply on the basis of the seat of arbitration being in France.[136] **6.180**

(5) Attorneys' fees and the winning party's claim for reimbursement

There is no rule of French law that requires the losing party to reimburse the legal costs of the prevailing party. This is a decision that is left to the discretion of the arbitral tribunal, taking into account the facts of the case. **6.181**

(5.1) May in-house lawyers charge fees or may a party request costs of in-house lawyers to be reimbursed? There are no mandatory rules of French law regarding the determination of legal fees. Whether the costs and expenses of in-house lawyers are taken into account is left to the discretion of the arbitral tribunal. **6.182**

(6) Time and form of the decision on costs

French law leaves the issue of time and form of the decision on costs for the determination of the arbitral tribunal. The arbitral tribunal will usually deal with the issue relating to the costs together with the last award on the merits, not in a separate award. **6.183**

(6.1) May the arbitrators' decision on the costs (allocation and amount of costs to be reimbursed) be challenged separately from the award itself? Are there time limits for such a remedy? French law does not provide for the possibility to challenge the arbitrators' decision on the allocation of costs among the parties separately from the award itself. The amount of the arbitrators' fees is a separate matter and should not be settled in the award itself. As discussed earlier at para 6.178, these may be challenged before an ordinary court as for any other service provider. **6.184**

---

[134] See *SARL Bureau Qualitas v Viet*, Cass 2e Civ, 28 October 1997, (1998) *Rev arb* 149, and commentary by C. Jarrosson; *SARL Bureau Qualitas v Viet*, Cass 2e Civ, 10 October 1990, (1991) Journal des notaires et des avocats 729, and commentary by P. Laroche.

[135] See Le Gall, J.-P., 'Le statut fiscal de l'arbitre international en Europe' in *L'internationalité dans les institutions et le droit—Convergences et défis—Etudes offertes à Alain Plantey* (Pedone, 1995) 331.

[136] *ibid.*

6.185 (6.2) **Are the arbitrators entitled and/or legally obliged to rule on the amount of one or both parties' costs that are recoverable?** The arbitrators are entitled to rule on the amount of the parties' costs that are recoverable, and have an obligation to do so when requested by one of the parties.

G. Publication of the award

(1) Publication with or without the consent of the parties

6.186 In international arbitration practice, the arbitral proceedings and the award are strictly confidential. A violation of this principle can give rise to damages.[137] An award may therefore only be published with the consent of the parties.

(2) Practice of publication (eg in specific legal journals)

6.187 However, excerpts from awards, with names and other identifying features redacted, may be published. This is the method employed by the *Journal du Droit International*, and the *Revue de l'Arbitrage* which publish extracts from a variety of sources, including ICC, ICSID and *ad hoc* arbitrations.

VI. Amendment and challenge of the award; liability of arbitrators

A. Amendment, correction or interpretation of the award

(1) Motion to amend or correct an award

6.188 In French domestic arbitration, Art 1475 of the Code states that 'the arbitrator has the power to interpret the award, to correct any error and material omission affecting it and to supplement it in case he has omitted to decide on an element of the claim'. It further provides that 'if it is impossible to reconvene the arbitral tribunal, this power shall lie with the court or tribunal that would have been competent in the absence of the arbitration agreement.' There is, however, no comparable provision for international arbitration. Thus, the courts will only have the power to amend, correct or supplement an award in international arbitration if the law or arbitration rules chosen by the parties to govern the procedure so provides.

(2) Interpretation of the award by the tribunal

6.189 Nothing in French law precludes a tribunal from interpreting, correcting or completing its own award upon the request of one or more parties where the parties have consented to this possibility. Certain institutional rules provide for such an eventuality, such as Art 35 of the UNCITRAL Rules; Arts 50 and 51 of the ICSID Rules; and Art 29 of the ICC Rules.

6.190 There is no legal requirement that the parties make such a motion for an interpretative ruling or amendment before a given deadline; however, the parties may expressly agree upon such deadline, or one may be provided in the institutional rules that they have adopted.

---

[137] See *G. Aita v A. Ojjeh*, CA Paris, 18 February 1986, (1986) *Rev arb* 583.

B. Appeal on the merits

(1) Admissibility and procedure of an appeal on the merits

An international arbitral award, whether rendered abroad or in France, is not subject to any appeal on the merits. In numerous decisions since the 1960s, the *Cour de Cassation* has confirmed that an appeal on the merits is not available.[138] **6.191**

C. Setting aside the award

(1) Reasons for setting aside an award

According to Art 1504, para 1 of the Code, 'an arbitral award made in France in an international arbitration may be the subject of an action to set aside in the cases set forth in Art 1502'. The grounds for setting an award aside enumerated in Art 1502 are limited to the following five grounds: (i) absence, nullity, or expiration, of the arbitration agreement; (ii) the irregular constitution of the arbitral tribunal or the irregular appointment of the sole arbitrator; (iii) the incompatibility of decisions made by the arbitrators with the terms of their mission; (iv) the failure to comply with the requirements of due process; and (v) situations where recognition or enforcement of the award would be contrary to international public policy. French courts have repeatedly confirmed that this list is exhaustive.[139] In particular, in an action to set aside an award, the *Cour d'Appel* is not entitled to revisit the merits of the dispute even in the case of a serious error of fact or law.[140] Nor can an award be set aside for errors of judgment, whether of fact or of law,[141] for gross distortion of documents or, for that matter, any grounds other than the five grounds enumerated at Art 1502. **6.192**

(1.1) May an award made according to international or foreign procedural rules be the object of an application for setting aside before the national courts? Any award rendered in France, regardless of the procedural rules governing the arbitration, may give rise to an action to set aside the award before the French courts. However, only awards rendered in France may be the object of such proceedings. **6.193**

(2) Procedure and deadlines for challenging an award

Pursuant to Art 1505 of the Code, 'an action to set aside . . . shall be brought before the Cour d'Appel of the place where the award was made'. The same provision further provides that the time limit for bringing such an action is one month from the service on the party of the award that has been declared executory, within the additional delay of two months for parties residing abroad (Art 644 of the Code). However, pursuant to Art 1500 of the **6.194**

[138] See *Multitrade*, Cass 1e Civ, 23 February 1994, (1994) *Rev arb* 683; *Fougerolle v Butec Engineering*, Cass 1e Civ, 20 December 1993, (1994) *Rev arb* 126, and commentary by P. Bellet; *Fougerolle v Procofrance*, Cass 1e Civ, 25 May 1992, (1993) *Rev arb* 91, and commentary by M. de Boisséson; (1992) JDI 974, and commentary by E. Loquin; (1992) Rev. crit. DIP 699, and commentary by B. Oppetit.

[139] See eg *SPP v République arabe d'Egypte*, Cass 1e Civ, 6 January 1987, (1987) *Rev arb* 469, and note by P. Leboulanger; CA Paris, 22 January 1988, (1989) *Rev arb* 251, and commentary by Y. Derains.

[140] See *Multitrade*, Cass 1e Civ, 23 February 1994, (1994) *Rev arb* 683, and observations by P. Mayer at 615.

[141] See *Société générale pour l'industrie*, Cass 1e Civ, 28 February 1995, (1995) *Rev arb* 597, and commentary by D. Bureau; CA Paris, 20 May 1994, (1994) *Rev arb* 397, and the commentary by J.-P. Le Gall at 253.

Code, the *Cour d'Appel* has the power to order provisional enforcement of an award submitted to it for review.[142]

6.195 In order to be admissible before the French courts, the ground invoked as the basis for the action to set aside the award must have been raised, whenever possible, before the arbitral tribunal itself in order to comply with the requirements of procedural good faith. Of course, a party will not be penalized for having failed to raise an objection before the arbitral tribunal if it only became aware of the grounds for that objection after the award had been made.

6.196 If the *Cour d'Appel* decides to reject the action to set aside, the award or any part of the award which has not been held void becomes immediately enforceable. In exceptional circumstances, the courts may see fit to grant damages to the prevailing party if it finds that the action to set aside is clearly meritless.[143]

6.197 **(2.1) Who may (or must) represent a party in a proceeding for setting aside an award?** The parties must be represented by a specific type of legal counsel known as an *avoué* in proceedings before the *Cour d'Appel.* The parties may also be represented by an ordinary *avocat.*[144] In proceedings before the *Cour de Cassation,* which are limited to the issue of whether or not the *Cour d'Appel* violated the law, the parties must be represented by an *avocat au Conseil d'Etat et à la Cour de Cassation.*

(3) Effect of a court decision, which sets the award aside

6.198 Where the *Cour d'Appel* sets the award aside, its decision completely or partially vacates the award.

6.199 **(3.1) Does the setting-aside action suspend the enforcement? If so, do remedies exist to reinstate enforcement?** The action to set aside has a suspensive effect, such that the award cannot be enforced until the *Cour d'Appel* has reached a decision, unless the arbitrators themselves have declared the award to be provisionally enforceable (a *clause de style* in awards rendered in France). The *Cour d'Appel* also has the power to order the provisional enforcement of the award or to refuse the determination of the arbitrators to that effect.[145]

6.200 **(3.2) After an award has been set aside, does the underlying arbitration agreement revive or remain in force or is it exhausted or deemed terminated?** Even when an award has been set aside, the arbitration agreement on which the award was based remains effective such that the dispute can, under certain circumstances, be resubmitted to arbitration by the parties.[146] This is not the case, however, when the setting aside of the award is based on the lack of a valid and binding arbitration agreement.

---

142 See commentary by P. Bellet to CA Paris, 27 November 1984, (1985) *Rev arb* 289.

143 See eg *Aïta v Ojjeh,* CA Paris, 18 February 1986, (1986) *Rev arb* 583, and commentary by G. Flécheux.

144 See Art 913 of the Code.

145 See Art 1500 of the Code, referring in turn to Art 1479 and Arts 525 and 526. See *Gouvernement de la Fédération de Russie v société Noga,* CA Paris, Ord cons mise en état, 22 September 2005; *Lassus v Falero,* CA Paris, Ord cons mise en état, 13 December 2005; *SA Genoyer (Phocéenne) v SA Sepco,* CA Paris, Ord cons mise en état, 27 June 2006, (2007) *Rev arb* 523, and note by J. Pellerin.

146 See Fouchard, P., 'L'arbitrage international en France après le décret du 12 mai 1981', (1982) *JDI* 374.

(4) Appeal against the court's decision to set aside or not set aside the award

The decision of the *Cour d'Appel* may be the object of a petition to quash before the *Cour de Cassation* in accordance with the ordinary rules of French law. In the case of a decision of the *Cour d'Appel* rejecting an action to set aside the award, the award must be enforced before the decision may be challenged before the *Cour de Cassation*.[147] **6.201**

(5) Possibility of the parties to exclude actions for setting aside

Unlike some countries, French law does not allow the parties to exclude the possibility to bring an action to set aside an award. **6.202**

D. Liability of arbitrators

(1) Duties and liabilities of arbitrators regarding the conduct of the proceedings

Because the arbitrators are in a contractual relationship with the parties, they may incur liability of a contractual nature for acts or omissions in the exercise of their mission. A fault committed in conducting the arbitral proceedings will thus represent a breach of contract and give rise to the arbitrator's contractual liability. However, arbitrators will not be liable for any errors made in reaching their award, unless they are attributable to fraud or gross negligence.[148] **6.203**

(1.1) Do the courts and/or authorities rely on a contractual relationship between the parties and the arbitrator(s), irrespective of whether institutional or *ad-hoc* arbitration is concerned? What is the legal qualification of such a contract (eg provision of services)? The arbitrator and the parties are, irrespective of the type of arbitration concerned, considered to be in a contractual relationship. The contract between the arbitrator and the parties binds the arbitrator from the time of acceptance of the nomination. French courts have refused to characterize this contract as an agency agreement.[149] Rather, it is considered to be a *sui generis* contract for the provision of services.[150] **6.204**

(1.2) Are there court decisions (or authorities) determining which law governs the question of liability of an arbitrator? What is the position of those courts/authorities as to whether and to which extent a legal liability of an arbitrator (or arbitral institution) may be established? In order to determine the law applicable to the arbitrator's contract, French law has regard to the common intent of the parties; the applicable law is thus the one 'chosen' by the parties. In the absence of an express choice, the applicable law will be the one which has the closest links with the contract. This will in all likelihood be the law chosen to govern the procedure. If, as is frequently the case, no national law has been **6.205**

---

[147] See Art 1009–1 of the Code and Lévis, M., L'effectivité du pourvoi en cassation et l'arbitrage (à propos de l'article 1009–1 NCPC)' (1997) *Rev arb* 169.

[148] See *Bompard v Consorts C.*, TGI Paris, 13 June 1990, (1996) *Rev arb* 476, 1st decision, *Bompard v Consorts C.*, CA Paris, 22 May 1991, (1996) *Rev arb* 476, 2nd decision, *Omnium de Travaux v République de Guinée*, TGI Paris, 29 November 1989, (1990) *Rev arb* 525.

[149] See *Pelfanian v Nurit*, CA Paris, 24 March 1992, (1993) *Rev arb* 277, 2nd decision ('the arbitrators, though appointed by the parties, can under no circumstances become their representatives. That would imply, in particular, that they represent the parties and account for their functions. Such a role and the obligation it entails, are alien to the functions of an arbitrator, which are judicial in nature').

[150] For a detailed analysis of the nature of the contract, see the final report on the status of the arbitrator prepared by the ICC Commission on International Arbitration, (1996) *Rev arb* 559, and the observations of the Commission's chairman, P. Fouchard; see also Fouchard Gaillard Goldman at paras 1101–68.

chosen to govern the procedure, then the law of the seat of the arbitration or possibly, in institutional arbitration, the law of the seat of the arbitral institution, will be held to apply to the contract.[151]

6.206 (1.3) **Is an arbitrator subject to criminal prosecution?** Unlike contractual liability, criminal liability cannot be excluded. Pursuant to Art 434–9 of the French Criminal Code, an arbitrator who engages in 'passive' corruption can be liable for up to 10 years in prison and a fine of up to €150,000.00. French law is applicable when a constitutive element of the offence is committed in France.

(2) Possibility to restrict or exclude the arbitrators' liability

6.207 Arbitrators may freely limit or exclude their contractual liability by agreement with the parties. However, such exclusions are not valid in case of gross fault or willful misconduct.

VII. Enforcement of national awards

(1) Requirement of a particular procedure to make an award enforceable (leave for enforcement, exequatur*)*

6.208 The recognition and enforcement of international arbitral awards is governed by Arts 1498 to 1500 of the Code. Article 1500 of the Code incorporates, for international arbitration, the pertinent provisions on domestic arbitration set forth in Arts 1476 to 1479. French courts recognize the distinction between the entry of judgment upon an award rendering the award enforceable (*exequatur*), and the actual enforcement of the award against identified assets.[152]

6.209 (1.1) **Does the national law make any difference between foreign and domestic awards, and if so, which are the criteria? Does there exist an additional notion of award for the purpose of obtaining *exequatur* (France: international awards)?** The French rules on international arbitration apply to both arbitral awards made outside of France and to international arbitral awards made in France. Although only international awards made in France may give rise to an action to set aside the award in accordance with Art 1504 of the Code, any international arbitral award may be the object of a request for *exequatur*. The same grounds for refusing to give effect to an award are applicable in both cases.

6.210 (1.2) **May awards granting conservatory/interim measures be subject to enforcement?** Arbitral awards ordering conservatory or interim measures of protection are provisionally enforceable in the same way as court decisions, in accordance with Arts 1479 and 1500 of the Code. The procedure is the same as for any award.

(2) Details of such enforcement procedure (competent court, reasons for rejection of motion etc)

6.211 An application for the enforcement of an international arbitral award must be submitted to the *Tribunal de Grande Instance*. For international awards rendered in France, Art 1477

[151] See *République de Guinée v MM. R. . .et O. . .*, TGI Paris, réf, 23 June 1988, (1988) *Rev arb* 657, 3rd decision, and note by P. Fouchard. With respect to the liability of the ICC, see *Société SNF v Chambre de commerce internationale*, TGI Paris, 10 October 2007, (2007) *Rev arb* 847, and note by C. Jarrosson.

[152] See *Société ouest-africaine de bétons industriels (SOABI) v Sénégal*, Cass 1e Civ, 11 June 1991, (1991) *Rev arb* 637, and commentary by A. Broches; for an English translation, see (1992) XVII *Ybk Comm Arb* 754.

of the Code provides that the court that has territorial jurisdiction will be the court 'of the place where the award was made'.

Enforcement will normally be obtained by means of an *ex parte* order. According to Art 1499 para 1 of the Code, the party applying for *exequatur* has to submit the original or a certified copy of the award together with an original or a certified copy of the arbitration agreement. Article 1499 para 2 of the Code further states that 'if such documents are not in the French language, the concerned party shall produce a translation certified by a translator registered on the list of experts'. **6.212**

The decision granting *exequatur* does not have to be reasoned. As provided in Art 1478 para 1 of the Code, to which Art 1500 refers, the *exequatur* granting enforcement merely has to be recorded on the arbitral award. In practice, this consists of placing an official stamp at the bottom of the award, accompanied by the date and the judge's signature. Pursuant to Art 1478 para 2 of the Code, however, a decision refusing enforcement must set forth the reasons why enforcement is refused. **6.213**

(3) Appeal against the decision granting exequatur

Whether or not a decision granting recognition or enforcement may be appealed depends on whether the award was made in France. For awards rendered in France, Art 1504 of the Code provides that 'no form of recourse is available against an order granting enforcement of such an award'. However, as Art 1504 further states, an action to set aside the award will be deemed to constitute recourse against the decision granting enforcement. The review performed by the *Cour d'Appel* in an action to set aside the award is the same as it would be in an appeal of a decision granting enforcement of the award. **6.214**

For arbitral awards rendered outside France, the decision granting enforcement of the award is rendered almost automatically after a prima facie review of the existence of the award and its conformity with international public policy. However, the decision granting enforcement can be appealed against pursuant to Art 1502 of the Code and, at this stage, the *Cour d'Appel* will review the award on the basis of the same five grounds applicable in actions to set aside an award rendered in France. As a result, all awards rendered in France or abroad are ultimately subjected to the same conditions for introduction into the French legal order and, in all cases, this review is performed directly by the *Cour d'Appel*. **6.215**

The decision of the *Cour d'Appel* may in turn be reviewed by the *Cour de Cassation*, on points of law only. **6.216**

French courts have consistently taken the view that, where an award has been set aside in the country where it was rendered, it can nonetheless be recognized and enforced in France if it meets the requirements of French law.[153] In a landmark decision of 29 June 2007, *Putrabali v Rena Holding*, the French *Cour de Cassation* confirmed this case law and held **6.217**

[153] See *Pabalk Ticaret Sirketi v Norsolor*, Cass 1e Civ, 9 October 1984, (1985) *Rev arb* 431, and note by B. Goldman; for an English translation, see (1985) *ILM* 360; *Hilmarton v OTV*, Cass 1e Civ, 23 March 1994, (1994) *Rev arb* 327, and note by C. Jarrosson; for an English translation, see (1995) XX *Ybk Comm Arb* 663; *République arabe d'Egypte v Chromalloy Aero Services*, CA Paris, 14 January 1997, (1997) *Rev arb* 395, and note by P. Fouchard; for an English translation, see (1997) XXII *Ybk Comm Arb* 691.

that an international arbitral award 'is not anchored in any national legal system' and 'is an international judicial decision whose validity must be ascertained with regard to the rules applicable in the country where its recognition and enforcement are sought'.[154]

(4) Appeal (and procedure) if exequatur *has been refused*

6.218 Pursuant to Art 1501 of the Code, 'a decision which refuses recognition or enforcement of an award may be appealed'. Pursuant to Art 1503 of the Code, the appeal must be 'brought before the Cour d'Appel for the circuit in which the enforcement court is located, within one month from the notification of its decision'. The *Cour d'Appel*, when hearing such an appeal, may review the award, applying the five grounds for refusing enforcement enumerated at Art 1502 of the Code.

6.219 This decision may in turn be reviewed by the *Cour de Cassation,* on points of law only.

(5) Procedure of enforcement (attachment of bank accounts etc)

6.220 After the judge's decision of *exequatur,* the opposing party has one month to appeal the decision to the Paris *Cour d'Appel.* Until that period has expired, the party that has been granted *exequatur* cannot enforce the decision.

6.221 The enforcement court only carries out a prima facie review of the award. Article 1498 of the Code states that arbitral awards shall be enforced in France 'if their existence is proven by the party relying on the award and if such recognition is not manifestly contrary to international public policy'. The court is not entitled to amend the award under any circumstances.[155] Moreover, the enforcement court does not have jurisdiction to verify that, prima facie, the award decides a dispute falling within the terms of the arbitration agreement. This issue can be addressed at a later stage by the Paris *Cour d'Appel* pursuant to Arts 1502 and 1504 of the Code.

6.222 (5.1) **At the stage of enforcement, may the losing party invoke arguments and circumstances which are based on facts which have occurred before (or after) the award was made?** Although French law restricts the setting aside of or refusal to enforce an award to the exhaustive and highly limited grounds enumerated by Art 1502, the courts are free, in hearing a challenge, to examine all circumstances of the case, legal or factual.[156] However, with respect to international public policy, the Paris Court of Appeal pointed out in a decision of 23 March 2006 that 'the court, which is the judge of the award rather than of the trial, only carries out an extrinsic control'.[157] This decision was confirmed by the French

---

[154] *Société PT Putrabali Adyamulia v société Rena Holding et société Mnogutia Est Epices*, Cass 1e Civ, 29 June 2007, (2007) *Rev arb* 507, and note by E. Gaillard; for an English translation, see (2007) XXXII *Ybk Comm Arb* 299. See also Gaillard, E., 'The Representations of International Arbitration', *NYLJ*, 4 October 2007; Pinsolle, P., 'The Status of Vacated Awards in France: the Cour de Cassation Decision in Putrabali', (2008) *Arb Int'l* 277.

[155] See *Epoux Convert v Droga*, Cass 1e Civ, 14 December 1983, (1984) *Rev arb* 483, and commentary by M.C. Rondeau-Rivier.

[156] See *Southern Pacific Properties*, Cass 1e Civ, 6 January 1987, (1987) 26 ILM 1006.

[157] See *Société SNF SAS v société Cytec Industries BV*, CA Paris, 23 March 2006, (2006) *Rev arb* 100, and note by S. Bollée; for an English translation, see (2007) XXXII *Ybk Comm Arb* 282.

Cour de Cassation which held that the scope of courts' review is limited to verifying that the alleged breach is 'clear, effective and concrete'.[158]

(5.2) May the losing party invoke a set-off based on claims that are not related to the matter of the arbitral proceeding? Is it material whether such claim came into existence before or after the award was made? A set-off cannot be invoked in an action to set aside an arbitral award or to challenge its enforcement. 6.223

VIII. Foreign awards

A. Recognition and/or enforcement of foreign awards (national law)

(1) Rules according to national law

The rules relating to the recognition and enforcement in France of foreign awards are for the most part identical to the rules applicable to international awards rendered in France. Although only international awards made in France may be the object of an action to set aside, any international arbitral award, French or foreign, may be recognized and enforced in France in accordance with Art 1498 of the Code. 6.224

(2) Requirements to be fulfilled by the applicants (procedure, time limits)

The procedure for an application for the enforcement of a foreign arbitral award is the same as that required for international arbitral awards rendered in France; for a detailed description, see at paras 6.208 *et seq, supra.* French law does not, however, specify which French court will have territorial jurisdiction over such an application, leaving the parties with a great deal of flexibility.[159] The parties may request enforcement of the award at the court of the defendant's domicile, the court of the place where attachable property is located, the Paris courts 'on account of their geographically central situation',[160] or at the court of the plaintiff's domicile. 6.225

(3) Remedies against decisions granting or declining enforcement

If the enforcement court declines to enforce an award, this decision can be appealed pursuant to Arts 1501 and 1502 of the Code (see para 6.218 *supra*). 6.226

B. Recognition and/or enforcement of foreign awards (conventions, treaties)

(1) Specific bilateral and multilateral treaties

France has ratified the 1958 New York Convention on the Recognition and Enforcement of Foreign Arbitral Awards and the 1961 European Convention on International Commercial Arbitration (also known as the Geneva Convention). The latter deals with the recognition and enforcement of awards only indirectly when it lists a limited number of grounds on which a decision to set aside an award at the seat of arbitration or in the country 6.227

[158] See *Société SNF SAS v société Cytec Industries BV*, Cass 1e Civ, 4 June 2008, (2008) *Rev arb* 473, and note by I. Fadlallah.

[159] See *GL Outillage v Stankoimport*, CA Paris, 10 July 1992, (1994) *Rev arb* 142, and commentary by P. Level; for an English translation, see (1992) *Int'l Arb Rep* 7.

[160] See *Mora*, 1e Civ, Cass, 13 June 1978, (1978) Rev crit DIP 722, and note by B. Audit; (1979) JDI 414, and observations by P. Kahn.

under the law of which the award was made will be recognized by the countries applying the Geneva Convention. The French courts are familiar with these instruments, which they consider to be complementary instruments which are 'simultaneously' applicable.[161]

(2) Existence of a standard procedure for the enforcement of foreign awards

6.228 In France, the relevant procedures for obtaining the recognition and enforcement of a foreign arbitral award under the New York Convention are those of Arts 1498 *et seq* of the Code, described at paras 6.208 *et seq* and 6.224 *et seq, supra.*

(3) Extent of examination and review of the award by the courts

6.229 In accordance with Art 1498 of the Code, the French court's review of the award is limited to the verification of the existence of the award and its prima facie compliance with international public policy.

C. Application of the New York Convention

(1) Application of the New York Convention in practice

6.230 In France, because the national rules governing enforcement of foreign arbitral awards are more liberal than those of the New York Convention—which merely provides for a minimum level of recognition afforded to awards—the application of the New York Convention by the French courts is of limited relevance.[162]

(2) Examples of decisions which do not apply the New York convention correctly

6.231 There are no particular decisions which are noteworthy for applying the New York Convention incorrectly given that it is generally not necessary for the French courts to resort to the New York Convention for the reasons set out at para 6.230 *supra*.

IX. Appendix

A. National legislation

The principal statute on international arbitration in France is Book IV of the *Code de procédure civile*, incorporating the provisions of the 1981 Decree on International Arbitration (see at para 6.02 *supra*). An English version of this legislation may be found in *Fouchard Gaillard Goldman On International Commercial Arbitration*, which also contains English translations of the other provisions in French legislation which have a bearing on international arbitration, ie Arts 2059–2061 of the French Civil Code, Arts 631 and 631–1 of the French Commercial Code, and Art L. 311–11 of the French Code of Judicial Organization (see Annex 1 of Fouchard Gaillard Goldman at pp 1,005 *et seq*).

B. Arbitral institutions

France has a number of regional or industry-specific arbitration institutions, as well as one general arbitration institution, the *Association française d'arbitrage* (AFA), which is active in

[161] See *Société Européene d'Etudes et d'Entreprise (S.E.E.E.) v République de Yougoslavie*, CA Rouen, 13 November 1984, (1985) *Rev arb* 115 and commentary by J.L. Delvolvé; for an English translation, see (1986) XI *Ybk Comm Arb* 491.

[162] See Clay, T., 'La Convention de New York vue par la Doctrine Française', (2009) *ASA Bull* 50.

case administration. Further information may be obtained from the AFA at the following address:

Association française d'Arbitrage (AFA)
8, Avenue Bertie Albrecht
75008 Paris
Telephone: 33/01 53 77 24 31
Telefax: 33/01 45 63 93 92
Website: <http://www.afa-arbitrage.com>

The *Comité français de l'arbitrage* (CFA) is a major French institution which, while it does not administer arbitrations, is active in the promotion of arbitration, and publishes the important periodical *La Revue de l'arbitrage.* Its address is as follows:

Comité Français de l'Arbitrage
24, Rue de Prony
75017 Paris
Telephone: 33/01 44 29 33 53
Telefax: 33/01 44 29 33 15
Website: <http://www.arbitrage-fr.org>

A further, useful resource for information regarding international arbitration specialists who are active in France is the International Arbitration Institute (IAI). The IAI, which was created in 1974 by Jean Robert, was relaunched in 2000 with a view to creating a new forum for international arbitration specialists with an emphasis on France. The members of the IAI are academics, arbitrators, attorneys or users of international arbitration, residing in France and throughout the world, who are notably either active or interested in international arbitration in France. The members of the IAI are listed in the IAI Directory of Members, a facebook which was published in 2001 and widely distributed around the world in hard copy in addition to being available on the internet site of the Institute, at <http://www.iaiparis.com>. The Directory is a very useful resource for information about qualified arbitration specialists. Further information regarding the IAI is available on request from the author of this report, c/o Shearman & Sterling LLP, 114 avenue des Champs-Elysées, 75008 Paris, France.

Finally, although it is a genuinely international organization rather than a French institution, the International Court of Arbitration of the International Chamber of Commerce (ICC) clearly plays an important role in international arbitration taking place in France. As well as administering cases under its own arbitration rules, the ICC serves as appointing authority for the appointment of *ad hoc* arbitrators under the UNCITRAL Arbitration Rules. Its contact details are as follows:

International Court of Arbitration of the International Chamber of Commerce (ICC)

38, Cours Albert 1er
75008 Paris
Telephone: 33/01 49 53 28 28
Telefax: 33/01 49 53 29 33
Website: <http://www.iccwbo.org>

C. Bibliography

Treatises and monographs

Blanchin, Claude, *L'autonomie de la clause compromissoire: un modèle pour la clause attributive de juridiction?* (LGDJ, Paris, 1995).

Boisséson, Matthieu de, *Le droit français de l'arbitrage interne et international* (2nd edn, GLN Joly, Paris, 1990).

Bollée, Sylvain, *Les méthodes du droit international privé à l'épreuve des sentences arbitrales* (Economica, Paris, 2003).

Bourque, Jean-François, *Le règlement des litiges multiparties dans l'arbitrage commercial international* (Thesis, University of Poitiers (France), 1989).

Clay, Thomas, *L'arbitre* (Dalloz, Paris, 2001).

Coipel-Cordonnier, Nathalie, *Les conventions d'arbitrage et d'élection de for en droit international privé* (LGDJ, Paris, 1999).

Crépin, Sophie, *Les sentences arbitrales devant le juge français—Pratique de l'exécution et du contrôle judiciaire depuis les réformes de 1980–1981* (LGDJ, Paris, 1995).

David, René, *L'arbitrage dans le commerce international* (Economica, Paris, 1981).

David, René, *Arbitration in International Trade* (Kluwer, The Hague, 1985).

Delaume, Georges, *Transnational Contracts—Applicable Law and Settlement of Disputes (A Study on Conflict Avoidance)* (Oceana Publications, New York, 1995).

De Ly, Filip, *International Business Law and Lex Mercatoria* (Amsterdam, North Holland, 1992).

Delvolvé, Jean-Louis, , Rouche, Jean and Pointon, Gerald H., *French Arbitration Law and Practice* (Kluwer, The Hague, 2003).

Fouchard, Philippe, *L'arbitrage commercial international* (Dalloz, Paris, 1965).

Fouchard, Philippe, Gaillard, Emmanuel and Goldman, Berthold, *Traité de l'arbitrage commercial international* (Litec, Paris, 1996).

Gaillard, E. and Savage, J. (eds), *Fouchard Gaillard Goldman On International Commercial Arbitration* (Kluwer, The Hague, 1999).

Goldman, Berthold, *Les conflits de lois dans l'arbitrage international de droit privé.* Collected Courses of The Hague Academy of International Law, vol 109, Year 1963, Pt I. (Martinus Nijhoff, Dordrecht).

Gouiffès, Laurent, Girard, Pascale, Taivalkoski, Petri and Mecarelli, Gabriele, *Recherche sur l'arbitrage en droit international et comparé.* (LGDJ, Paris, 1997).

Hanotiau, Bernard, *Complex Arbitrations - Multiparty, Multicontract, Multi-Issue and Class Actions* (Kluwer, The Hague, 2006).

Henry, Marc, *Le devoir d'indépendance de l'arbitre* (LGDJ, Paris, 2001).

Jarrosson, Charles, *La notion d'arbitrage* (LGDJ, Paris, 1987).

Kassis, Antoine, *L'autonomie de l'arbitrage commercial international. Le droit français en question* (L'Harmattan, Paris, 2005).

Loquin, Eric, *L'amiable composition en droit comparé et international—Contribution à l'étude du non-droit dans l'arbitrage commercial* (Litec, Paris, 1980).

Mayer, Pierre, *L'autonomie de l'arbitre international dans l'appréciation de sa propre compétence.* Collected Courses of The Hague Academy of International Law, vol 217, Year 1989, Pt V (Martinus Nijhoff, Dordrecht, 1989).

Oppetit, Bruno, *Théorie de l'arbitrage* (PUF, Paris, 1998).

Ortscheidt, Jérôme, *La réparation du dommage dans l'arbitrage commercial international* (Dalloz, Paris, 2001).

Osman, Filali, *Les principes généraux de la lex mercatoria—Contribution à l'étude d'un ordre juridique anational* (LGDJ, Paris, 1992).

Poudret, Jean-François and Besson, Sébastien, *Comparative Law of International Arbitration*, S.V. Berti and A. Ponti trans (2nd edn, Zurich, Sweet & Maxwell—Schulthess, 2007).

Racine, Jean-Baptiste, *L'arbitrage commercial international et l'ordre public* (LGDJ, Paris, 1999).

Robert, Jean (with the assistance of Bertrand Moreau), *L'arbitrage—Droit interne—Droit international privé* (6th edn, Dalloz, Paris, 1993).
Robert, Jean and Carbonneau, Thomas E., *The French Law of Arbitration* (Matthew Bender, New York, 1983).
Rubellin-Devichi, Jacqueline, *L'arbitrage—Nature juridique—Droit interne et droit international privé* (LGDJ, Paris, 1965).
Samuel, Adam, *Jurisdictional Problems in International Commercial Arbitration: A Study of Belgian, Dutch, English, French, Swedish, U.S. and West German Law* (Schulthess Polygraphischer Verlag, Zürich, 1989).
Seraglini, Christophe, *Lois de police et justice arbitrale internationale* (Dalloz, Paris, 2001).

Articles

Ancel, Jean-Pierre, 'L'actualité de l'autonomie de la clause compromissoire' in *Travaux du Comité français du Droit International Privé 1991–1993* (1994) 75.
Banifatemi, Yas and Gaillard, Emmanuel, 'Negative Effect of Competence-Competence: The Rule of Priority in Favour of the Arbitrators' in E. Gaillard and D. Di Pietro (eds), *Enforcement of Arbitration Agreements and International Arbitral Awards—The New York Convention 1958 in Practice* (Cameron May, 2008) 257.
Boisséson, Matthieu de and Duprey, Pierre, 'L'arbitrabilité subjective en matière de droit des sociétés' in A. Mourre (ed), *Les Cahiers de l'Arbitrage*, vol II (Gazette du Palais, 2004) 121.
Bouche, Nicolas and Fourtoy, Frédéric, 'L'indépendance de l'arbitre et les moyens de la garantir' in A. Mourre (ed.), *Les Cahiers de l'Arbitrage*, vol I (Gazette du Palais, 2002) 123.
Bredin, Jean-Denis, 'La révélation: Remarques sur l'indépendance de l'arbitre en droit interne français' in *Etudes de procédure et d'arbitrage en l'honneur de Jean-François Poudret* (Payot, 1999) 349.
Bredin, Jean-Denis, 'Le secret du délibéré arbitral' in *Etudes offertes à Pierre Bellet* (Litec, 1991) 79.
Cachard, Olivier, 'Le contrôle de la nullité ou de l'inapplicabilité manifeste de la clause compromissoire' (2006) *Rev arb* 893.
Clay, Thomas, 'La Convention de New York vue par la Doctrine Française' (2009) *ASA Bull* 50.
Dimolitsa, Antonias, 'Separability and "Kompetenz"' in A.J. van den Berg (ed), *ICCA Congress Series no 9, Increasing the Efficiency of Arbitration Agreements and Awards* (Kluwer, 1999) 217.
Fouchard, Philippe, 'L'arbitrage international en France après le décret du 12 mai 1981' (1982) *JDI* 374.
Gaillard, Emmanuel, 'Impecuniosity of Parties and Its Effects on Arbitration: A French View' in *Financial Capacity of the Parties. A Condition for the Validity of Arbitration Agreements?* (Peter Lang Verlag, 2004) 67.
Gaillard, Emmanuel, 'La distinction des principes généraux du droit et des usages du commerce international' in *Etudes offertes à Pierre Bellet* (Litec, 1991) 203.
Gaillard, Emmanuel, 'La jurisprudence de la Cour de Cassation en matière d'arbitrage international' (2007) *Rev arb* 697.
Gaillard, Emmanuel, 'L'effet négatif de la compétence—compétence' in *Etudes de procédure et d'arbitrage en l'honneur de Jean-François Poudret* (Payot, 1999) 387.
Gaillard, Emmanuel, 'Les manoeuvres dilatoires des parties dans l'arbitrage commercial international' (1990) *Rev arb* 759.
Gaillard, Emmanuel, 'The Representations of International Arbitration' *NYLJ*, 4 October 2007.
Gaillard, Emmanuel, 'The Role of the Arbitrator in Determining the Applicable Law' in L.-W. Newman and R.D. Hill (eds), *The Leading Arbitrators' Guide to International Arbitration* (Juris Publishing, 2004) 185.
Gaillard, Emmanuel, 'Thirty Years of Lex Mercatoria: Towards the Selective Application of Transnational Rules', 10 *ICSID Rev-FILJ* 208.
Gaillard, Emmanuel and Pinsolle, Philippe, 'Advocacy in International Commercial Arbitration: France' in R.D. Bishop (ed), *The Art of Advocacy in International Arbitration* (Juris Publishing, 2004) 133.

Goldman, Berthold, 'The Complementary Roles of Judges and Arbitrators in Ensuring that International Commercial Arbitration is Effective' in *International Arbitration—60 years of ICC Arbitration—A Look at the Future* (ICC Publication no 412, 1984) 257.

Goldman, Berthold, 'La réforme de l'arbitrage international en France—La volonté des parties et le rôle de l'arbitre dans l'arbitrage international' (1981) *Rev arb* 469.

Goldman, Berthold, 'Une bataille judiciaire autour de la lex mercatoria: l'affaire Norsolor' (1983) *Rev arb* 379.

Hanotiau, Bernard, 'Le défaut d'une partie dans la procédure d'arbitrage international' in *Mélanges offerts à Raymond Vander Elst* (Nemesis, 1986), vol I at 375.

Hanotiau, Bernard, 'The Conduct of the Hearings' in L.-W. Newman and R.D. Hill (eds), *The Leading Arbitrators' Guide to International Arbitration* (Juris Publishing, 2004) 369.

Kreindler, Richard H., 'The Arbitration Clause: The Validity of an Arbitration Clause in Matters of Product Liability' in *ASA Special Series no 8, The Arbitration Agreement—Its Multifold Critical Aspects* (1994) 123.

Le Gall, Jean-Pierre, 'Le statut fiscal de l'arbitre international en Europe' in *L'internationalité dans les institutions et le droit—Convergences et défis—Etudes offertes à Alain Plantey* (Pedone, 1995) 331.

Lévis, Marc, 'L'effectivité du pourvoi en cassation et l'arbitrage (à propos de l'article 1009–1 NCPC)' (1997) *Rev arb* 169.

Loquin, Eric, 'Arbitrage—Instance Arbitrale—Arbitrage de droit et amiable composition', Juris-Classeur Procédure Civile, Fasc 1038 (1994).

Loquin, Eric, 'Arbitrage—La décision arbitrale—Voies de recours', Juris-Classeur Procédure Civile, Fasc 1046 (2001).

Loquin, Eric, 'Différences et convergences dans le régime de transmission et de l'extension de la clause compromissoire devant les juridictions françaises' in A. Mourre (ed), *Les Cahiers de l'Arbitrage*, vol II (Gazette du Palais, 2004) 49.

Mayer, Pierre, 'La 'circulation' des conventions d'arbitrage', (2005) *JDI* 251.

Mayer, Pierre, 'La sentence contraire à l'ordre public au fond', (1994) *Rev arb* 615.

Mayer, Pierre, 'L'interférence des lois de police' in *L'Apport de la jurisprudence arbitrale* (ICC Publication no 440/1, 1986).

Moitry, J.H., 'L'arbitre international et l'obligation de boycottage imposée par un Etat', (1991) *JDI* 349.

Moreau, Bertrand, 'Les effets de la nullité de la sentence arbitrale' in *Etudes offertes à Pierre Bellet* (Litec, 1991) 403.

Mourre, Alexis, L'impact de la réforme de la clause compromissoire sur les litiges relatifs aux sociétés' in A. Mourre (ed), *Les Cahiers de l'Arbitrage*, vol II (Gazette du Palais, 2004) 125.

Pinsolle, Philippe and Kreindler, Richard, 'Les limites du rôle de la volonté des parties dans la conduite de l'instance arbitrale' (2003) *Rev arb* 41.

Pinsolle, Philippe, 'L'exécution provisoire des sentences rendues en matière internationale en dépit d'une recours en annulation' in A. Mourre (ed), Les Cahiers de l'Arbitrage, vol III (Gazette du Palais, 2006) 108.

Pinsolle, Philippe, 'The Status of Vacated Awards in France: the Cour de Cassation Decision in Putrabali' (2008) *Arb Int'l* 277.

Rouche, Jean, 'Le paiement par le défendeur de sa part de provision sur les frais d'arbitrage: simple faculté ou obligation contractuelle?' (2002) *Rev arb* 841.

Schwebel, Stephen M. and Lahne, Susan G., 'Public Policy and Arbitral Procedure' in P. Sanders (ed), *ICCA Congress Series no 3, Comparative Arbitration Practice and Public Policy in Arbitration* (Kluwer, 1987) 205.

Tunik, Daniel, 'Default Proceedings in International Commercial Arbitration' (1998) *Int'l Arb L Rev* 86.

7

GERMANY

*Inka Hanefeld**

I. Introduction

A. Current status of the law on arbitration

(1) Short history

Germany has a long tradition of arbitration. In Germany, arbitration is widely used in most areas of business and commerce. German arbitration law was codified for the first time in 1877. Effective as from 1 January 1998, German arbitration law underwent a fundamental reform, which completed a long process to shape a new arbitration environment in Germany fit for modern domestic and international dispute resolution. In the course of the 1998 reform, the old German arbitration law was fully replaced by a new arbitration law based on the UNCITRAL Model Law on International Commercial Arbitration of 1985 ('UNCITRAL Model Law'). As was the case with the old German arbitration law, the new arbitration law has been integrated into and forms part of the German Code of Civil Procedure (*Zivilprozessordnung*—'ZPO'). The arbitration law constitutes the 10th Book of the ZPO and is contained in ss 1025–1066 ZPO. 7.01

(2) Law in force and future projects

The UNCITRAL Model Law background makes access for foreign practitioners to German arbitration law comparatively easy: the major characteristics and the legal phraseology of 7.02

* The author would like to thank Mr Simon Manner, associate in the Hamburg office of Friedrich Korch Hanefeld, for his invaluable help and support in the preparation of this report.

German arbitration law are the same as in the UNCITRAL Model Law. There are only a couple of deviations from the UNCITRAL Model Law, in which German arbitration law narrows, alters, or extends the model provisions of the UNCITRAL Model Law. As such, German arbitration law is perceived as an efficient means for international dispute resolution. The adaptation of the UNCITRAL Model Law has undoubtedly improved Germany's image as an attractive venue for arbitration proceedings.[1] There are no plans to substantially revise German arbitration law in the near future.

(3) Distinction between national and international arbitration

7.03 German arbitration law does not distinguish between national and international arbitrations but applies to domestic and international arbitration proceedings alike. German arbitration law follows the principle of territoriality and, hence, applies to all arbitral proceedings, where the place of arbitration is situated in Germany (s 1025(1) ZPO). Only an enumerated set of provisions applies even if the place of arbitration is situated outside Germany or has not yet been determined (s 1025(2) ZPO). Unlike the UNCITRAL Model Law, German arbitration law is not restricted to commercial disputes but applies to all types of arbitration.

B. Practice of arbitration

(1) Frequency of arbitration as opposed to litigation

7.04 Conclusive statistics regarding the frequency, with which parties resort to arbitration as opposed to litigation, are not available in Germany as significant portions of arbitrations are conducted as unreported *ad hoc* arbitrations. However, it is unquestionable that in Germany the importance of arbitration has significantly increased over the recent years. This is certainly true for international cases. In domestic matters as well as in certain fields of business (eg shipping, mergers and acquisitions, and, to a certain degree, construction) arbitration has become the rule rather than the exception.[2] It has been estimated that 80 to 90 per cent of all international commercial contracts contain an arbitration clause,[3] and presumably this also applies to contracts with German parties.

(2) Leading arbitral institutions and statistics

7.05 In Germany, the German Institution of Arbitration e.V. (*Deutsche Institution für Schiedsgerichtsbarkeit*—'DIS') is the most important arbitration institution. The DIS has approximately 950 members, from Germany and abroad. It aims at promoting national and international arbitration for all kinds of arbitrations. The DIS offers an administered arbitral procedure under the DIS Arbitration Rules ('DIS Rules'). The role of the DIS regarding case administration extends, among other things, to the service of the statement of claim and of the award, to the monitoring of and rendering assistance in the establishment

[1] cf Mark, J. Plassmeier, H. and Quinke, D., 'New Developments in German Arbitration Law' in J. Benedictsson *et al* (eds), *The Baker & McKenzie International Arbitration Yearbook 2007* (Wolters Kluwer, 2008) 41.

[2] Kröll, S., Country Report 'Germany' in *ICCA International Handbook on Commercial Arbitration* (Kluwer Law International, 2007) 5.

[3] Schwab, K.H. and Walter, G., *Schiedsgerichtsbarkeit* (7th edn, CH Beck, 2005) ch 41 para 1.

of the arbitral tribunal, and to other administrative matters. Under the DIS Rules, there is no general monitoring of the proceedings or scrutiny of the draft awards.

The DIS Rules are currently in force as from 1 July 1998 with an amended Schedule of Costs effective since 1 January 2005. Recently, the DIS promulgated fast-track arbitration rules,[4] which allow parties and arbitrators to conduct an arbitration within six months (sole arbitrator) or nine months (three-member arbitral tribunal).[5] The DIS Rules are applicable to both national and international arbitrations.[6] They are available in German, English, French, Russian, Spanish, Turkish and Chinese language.[7] Besides the DIS, there exist numerous other arbitration institutions in Germany, most of which specialize in certain industry sectors, such as the *German Maritime Arbitration Association* ('GMAA'). Some of the regional chambers of commerce, such as the *Handelskammer Hamburg* ('HK Hamburg'), also offer arbitration services. **7.06**

The DIS figures show a steady increase in cases. In 2007 and 2008, 199 arbitration proceedings were filed under the DIS Rules. Of the 537 parties to these proceedings, 444 were German and 93 were foreign parties. 32 cases newly filed are/were conducted in English. The amounts in dispute ranged from approximately €3,000 to € 300,000,000.[8] **7.07**

Recent information of the International Court of Arbitration of the International Chamber of Commerce ('ICC') likewise evidences a frequent involvement of German parties in ICC proceedings. In the years 2005 to 2008, 511 German parties participated in ICC proceedings. In 2007 alone, 158 German parties were involved, which equals a percentage of 9.81 per cent of all parties to ICC arbitrations and gave Germany the lead over any other country when comparing the number of parties involved in ICC proceedings.[9] The number of German arbitrators involved in ICC proceedings was also significant. Over the period 2005 to 2007, 267 German arbitrators were appointed. By way of comparison, 266 UK arbitrators, 264 US arbitrators, 246 French arbitrators and 425 Swiss arbitrators were appointed. **7.08**

Not reflected in any statistics are the numerous *ad hoc* arbitrations that take place in Germany and/or involve German parties. *Ad hoc* arbitration is widely used in Germany. According to estimates, the total number of *ad hoc* proceedings conducted per year is up to 1,000.[10] **7.09**

---

[4] Supplementary Rules for Expedited Proceedings ('SREP'), available at <http://www.dis-arb.de.>.

[5] See Berger, K.P., 'The Need for Speed in International Arbitration, Supplementary Rules for Expedited Proceedings of the German Institution of Arbitration (DIS)' (2008) 25(5) *Arb Int'l* 595 ff.

[6] For a commentary on the DIS Rules, see in English : Böckstiegel, K.-H., Kröll, S. and Nacimiento, P. (eds), *Arbitration in Germany: The Model Law in Practice* (Kluwer Law International, 2007) 655 ff; and in German : Theune, U., 'DIS-Schiedsgerichtsordnung' in R Schütze (ed), *Institutionelle Schiedsgerichtsbarkeit* (Carl Heymanns, 2006) 159 ff.

[7] See <http://www.dis-arb.de>.

[8] The DIS figures are published in the *Zeitschrift für Schiedsverfahren/German Arbitration Journal* (*SchiedsVZ*) once per year.

[9] By way of comparison, the percentage of US parties (136) amounted to a percentage of 8,44 % (rank 2), the percentage of Swiss parties (39) to 2,4 % (rank 10) and the percentage of Austrian parties (27) to 1,68 % (rank 16).

[10] Wilske, S., 'Ad hoc Arbitration in Germany' in K.-H. Böckstiegel, S. Kröll, and P. Nacimiento (eds) (n 6) 809, 811 para 2.

II. Jurisdiction of the arbitral tribunal

A. Arbitration agreement

(1) Arbitration clause and submission agreement

7.10 The arbitration agreement may be in the form of a separate arbitration agreement or in the form of an arbitration clause contained in a contract (s 1029(2) ZPO). Both types of agreement are treated the same way. In addition, German arbitration law does not differentiate between an arbitration clause or arbitration agreement agreed upon before the dispute has arisen and a submission agreement relating to an already existing dispute. The arbitration agreement, as an essential prerequisite for all commercial arbitrations, is defined in s 1029(1) ZPO as an agreement by the parties to submit to arbitration all or certain legal disputes, which have arisen or may arise between them in respect of a defined legal relationship.

(2) Requirements as to the contents of the arbitration agreement

7.11 A valid arbitration agreement requires, as a minimum, that certain or all disputes between the parties shall be finally solved by an arbitral tribunal to the exclusion of the courts.[11] It is essential that the parties' definite intention to arbitrate their dispute and to opt out of court proceedings can be clearly inferred from the agreement.[12] A clause that simply excludes access to the courts without providing for arbitration does not constitute an arbitration agreement.[13] On the other hand, it is not necessary that the parties have already agreed on specific procedural aspects of the arbitration.[14] It is not required either that the parties refer to a specific set of institutional arbitration rules.[15] Even very short arbitration agreements like 'Arbitration: Hamburg' or 'place of arbitration: Hamburg' have been considered as sufficient by German courts to establish the jurisdiction of an arbitral tribunal.[16] If, however, the parties decide in their arbitration agreement to conduct the arbitration under the auspices of an arbitral institution, the arbitral institution must be unambiguously defined or identifiable;[17] otherwise, the arbitration agreement can be considered as being null and void.[18]

[11] See BGH, 25 January 2007, [2007] *SchiedsVZ* 273 ff, in which the court held that an arbitration agreement prevails over a choice of court agreement; see also BGH, 12 January 2006, [2006] SchiedsVZ 101 ff.

[12] But see BGH, 1 March 2007, BGHZ 171, 245 ff = [2008] SchiedsVZ 160 ff, in which the BGH held that the parties do not have to agree on a complete exclusion of the state courts but may opt for a conditional submission to arbitration; cf Mark, J., Plassmeier, H. and Quinke, D. (n 1) 48 ff.

[13] Geimer, R. in R. Zöller, *Zivilprozessordnung* (26th edn, Dr Otto Schmidt, 2007) s 1029 para 9.

[14] See OLG Munich, 23 May 2007 and 26 May 2008, both available at <http://www.dis-arb.de>; KG, 21 April 2008, [2008] NJW 2719 f; but see OLG Hamm, 18 July 2007, [2007] MDR 1438 f; cf Kröll, S., 'Die schiedsrechtliche Rechtsprechung 2007' [2008] SchiedsVZ 62, 63 ff; Trittmann, R. and Hanefeld, I. in K.-H. Böckstiegel, S. Kröll, and P. Nacimiento (eds) (n 6) 100 para 17.

[15] Trittmann, R. and Hanefeld, I. in K.-H. Böckstiegel, S. Kröll, and P. Nacimiento (eds) (n 6) 100 para 17.

[16] OLG Hamburg, 24 January 2003, [2003] SchiedsVZ 284 ff; OLG Hamburg, 25 June 2008, available at <http://www.dis-arb.de>.

[17] See eg OLG Karlsruhe, 4 April 2007, available at <http://www.dis-arb.de>; OLG Oldenburg, [2006] SchiedsVZ 223, 224.

[18] BayObLG, 28 February 2000, available at <www.dis-arb.de>; Geimer, R. in R. Zöller (n 13) s 1029 para 53; Schwab, K.H. and Walter, G. (n 3) ch 3 para 1a.

(3) Form of the agreement (eg 'in writing' requirement)

The 'in writing' requirement of German arbitration law is in certain respects more lenient than that of the UNCITRAL Model Law. Section 1031(1) ZPO provides as a general rule that the arbitration agreement shall be contained either in a document signed by the parties or in an exchange of letters, telefaxes, telegrams or other means of telecommunication, which provide a record of the agreement.[19] According to s 1031(2) ZPO, the form requirement of s 1031(1) ZPO shall also be deemed to have been complied with if the arbitration agreement is contained in a document transmitted from one party to the other party or by a third party to both parties and—if no objection was raised in due time—the content of such document is considered to be part of the contract in accordance with common usage. Section 1031(2) ZPO reflects that, according to German substantive law, the failure to object to a commercial letter of confirmation (*kaufmännisches Bestätigungsschreiben*) is, from a legal point of view and under certain conditions, equivalent to accepting the offer of a contract.[20] Section 1031(3) ZPO provides that the reference in a contract complying with the form requirements of s 1031(1) or (2) ZPO to a document containing an arbitration clause constitutes an arbitration agreement provided that the reference is such as to make that clause part of the contract. Section 1031(4) ZPO contains a special provision relating to bills of lading, commonly encountered in maritime transport. It retains in principle the opportunity for carriers of maritime cargo to enter into arbitration agreements with third parties, to whom they have issued bills of lading even if the arbitration agreement is only contained in the charter contract between carrier and charterer.[21] Particular care with respect to form requirements is required in cases in which consumers are involved. In this respect, German arbitration law imposes stricter form requirements than the UNCITRAL Model Law: if one of the parties is a consumer, s 1031(5) ZPO, in general, requires that the arbitration agreement must be contained in a separate and mutually signed document, which does not contain any other agreement than the agreement to arbitrate. Finally, in view of the prohibition of contradictory behaviour, any non-compliance with the form requirements set out in s 1031(1)–(5) ZPO can be cured by entering into an argument on the substance of the dispute in the arbitral proceedings (s 1031(6) ZPO), for example by filing the first submission on the merits, without raising jurisdictional objections.[22] If no arbitration agreement was ever concluded, s 1031(6) ZPO is inapplicable.[23] **7.12**

(3.1) **Are there special requirements for a power of attorney/authority granting the right to enter into an arbitration agreement on behalf of a third party?** German arbitration law does not specify under which conditions an authority to enter into an arbitration agreement can be assumed. It has been suggested that the mere authority to place a commercial **7.13**

[19] cf OLG Munich, 25 April 2007, [2007] OLGR Munich 681, where the court held that the form requirement does not extend to separate agreements on the arbitration procedure, eg the constitution of the arbitral tribunal.

[20] BGH, 2 November 1995, [1996] *NJW* 919 ff: OLG Hamburg, 4 December 2008, 6 Sch 12/08, available at <http://www.dis-arb.de>; OLG Hamburg, 25 January 2008, SchiedsVZ 2009, 71.

[21] Trittmann, R. and Hanefeld, I. in K.-H. Böckstiegel, S. Kröll, and P. Nacimiento (eds) (n 6) 134 para 21.

[22] Lachmann, J.-P. *Handbuch für die Schiedsgerichtspraxis* (3rd edn, Dr Otto Schmidt, 2008) para 368 with further references.

[23] Trittmann, R. and Hanefeld, I. in K.H. Böckstiegel, S. Kröll, and P. Nacimiento (eds) (n 6) 138 para 31.

contract shall include the authority to enter into an arbitration agreement.[24] On the other hand, the general power of attorney granted to an attorney to represent his client in legal proceedings (*Prozessvollmacht*) does not implicitly grant the power to conclude an arbitration agreement.[25] According to a recent decision of the OLG Munich, the commercial power of attorney (*Handlungsvollmacht*) under s 54 of the German Commercial Code (Handelsgesetzbuch—'HGB') does not implicitly grant the power to conclude an arbitration agreement either.[26] In general, there is no special form requirement for an authority to enter into an arbitration agreement on behalf of a third party (s 167(2) of the German Civil Code [*Bürgerliches Gesetzbuch*—'BGB']).[27]

(4) Incorporation of an arbitration clause contained in general terms and conditions

7.14 Section 1031(3) ZPO permits as due form under certain conditions a reference to other written documents containing an arbitration agreement. The reference must be such as to make the arbitration agreement part of the contract. This requires an unambiguous reference, such as an express reference to the arbitration clause.[28] A general reference to general terms and conditions including an arbitration clause may also suffice if the other side has a reasonable chance to take note of the arbitration agreement.[29] This is, for example, assumed if the other side is in the possession of the standard terms and conditions.[30] In any event, if the arbitration clause is included in standard terms of contract (*Allgemeine Geschäftsbedingungen*), the arbitration clause is subject to specific validity control of standard terms pursuant to ss 305 ff BGB), provided that German law applies to the validity of the arbitration agreement. In particular, the courts will examine whether the arbitration clause satisfies the requirement of a just constitution of the arbitral tribunal and the notions of equality and fairness of the arbitral proceedings.[31] Moreover, in consumer cases even stricter validity control standards may apply.[32]

(5) Law applicable to the interpretation of arbitration clauses

7.15 German arbitration law does not contain a specific provision concerning the law applicable to the arbitration clause and its interpretation. Whereas s 1051 ZPO contains a conflict of laws provision for the applicable substantive law that shall govern the dispute, no such

[24] BGH, 25 January 2007, [2007] WM 698 ff; Schlosser, P. in F. Stein and M. Jonas (eds), *Kommentar zur Zivilprozessordnung* (22nd edn, Mohr Siebeck, 2002) s 1029 para 5.

[25] Geimer, R. in R. Zöller (n 13) s 1029 para 20; Lachmann, J.-P. (n 22) para 276 with further references.

[26] OLG Munich, 19 August 2008, [2009] NJW-RR 417, 418 f.

[27] Lachmann, J.-P. (n 22) para 275.

[28] Saenger, I. in I. Saenger (ed), *Zivilprozessordnung* (2nd edn, Nomos, 2007) s 1031 para 7.

[29] Geimer, R. in R. Zöller (n 13) s 1031 para 10.

[30] See Schlosser, P. in F. Stein and M. Jonas (eds) (n 24) s 1031 para 5, who regards the handing over of the standard terms of contract as a mandatory requirement for a valid incorporation; see also OLG Brandenburg, 13 June 2002, [2002] IHR 94 ff, which requires for a valid incorporation a transmission of the standard terms to the other party as well as behaviour that indicates their acceptance.

[31] See for further details Hanefeld, I. and Wittinghofer, M.A., 'Schiedsklauseln in Allgemeinen Geschäftsbedingungen' [2005] *SchiedsVZ* 217 ff.; see also BGH [2007] NJW-RR 1466, which held that an unjust limitation of one party's right to participate in the constitution of the arbitral tribunal does not render an arbitration clause null and void, as the constitution process may be modified by the court on application of the disadvantaged party.

[32] See Trittmann, R. and Hanefeld, I. in K.-H. Böckstiegel, S. Kröll, and P. Nacimiento (eds) (n 6) 100 para 16.

special conflict of laws provision exists for the arbitration clause as such. However, from s 1059(2) no 1(a) ZPO dealing with the grounds for setting aside an arbitral award one can infer a conflict of laws rule with regard to the arbitration clause and its interpretation.[33] Pursuant to this provision, an arbitration clause is, in principle, governed by the law, to which the parties have subjected the arbitration agreement. As in practice, parties rarely provide for a specific choice of law for their arbitration agreement, German courts have ruled that a choice-of-law clause in the main contract does in the ordinary course extend to the arbitration clause.[34] In turn, absent an express or implicit choice of law for the main contract, German law shall apply to the arbitration clause provided that either the place of arbitration is in Germany or else the German courts, in proceedings to enforce foreign arbitral awards (s 1061 ZPO), may examine the arbitration agreement's validity and interpretation under German law, eg if German law including the application of its conflicts of laws provisions is more favourable to the party claiming enforcement (Art VII New York Convention).[35]

(5.1) Do courts accept a wide competence of the arbitral tribunal or do they restrict arbitral competence? Do claims, which arise in connection with the agreement submitted to arbitration, generally fall within the arbitral jurisdiction even if based on tortious legal basis? Does there exist any case law with respect to the wording in an arbitration clause as 'arising out of/under/in connection with the present contract' and its specific meaning? German courts commonly tend to a broad interpretation of the arbitration agreement reasoning that, in case of doubt, the parties wish to submit all questions to arbitration and wish to avoid a split into different proceedings.[36] Therefore, the arbitration agreement regularly extends to statutory claims arising in connection with the contract, such as tort claims and unjust enrichment claims.[37] Furthermore, the arbitral tribunal's competence includes the competence to decide on the question of whether the contract was null and void *ab initio* or whether there was a valid contract termination.[38] For instance, it has been held that an arbitration clause referring to all disputes 'arising out of or in connection with the present contract' entitles the arbitral tribunal to decide on the validity of the contract.[39] Amendments to the contract and extensions of the contract are also **7.16**

[33] Kröll, S. and Kraft, P. in K.-H. Böckstiegel, S. Kröll, and P. Nacimiento (eds) (n 6) 458 para 53, stating that this provision is applicable in every situation, in which the issue of interpreting an arbitration clause arises.

[34] See BGH, 28 November 1963, BGHZ 40, 320, 323; BayObLG, 16 January 2004, [2004] SchiedsVZ 163, 165; OLG Frankfurt, 24 October 2006, available at <http://www.dis-arb.de>; cf Martiny, D. in K. Rebmann, F.J. Säcker and R. Rixecker (eds), *Münchener Kommentar zum Bürgerlichen Gesetzbuch*, vol 10 (4th edn, CH Beck, 2006) Vorbemerkung zu Art 27 EGBGB para 12.

[35] BGH, 21 September 2005, [2005] SchiedsVZ 305 ff.

[36] BGH, 13 January 2009, [2009] SchiedsVZ 122 ff; BGH, 19 July 2004, [2004] ZIP 1616, 1618; OLG Karlsruhe, 15 July 2008, [2008] SchiedsVZ 311 ff and OLG Frankfurt am Main, 30 March 2006, available at <http://www.dis-arb.de> (both stating that the arbitration clause is not 'used up' by a single arbitration procedure but remains valid for further conflicts falling within its scope); OLG Munich, 13 October 2004, [2005] NJW 832, 833; OLG Düsseldorf, 27 February 2004, [2004] SchiedsVZ 161, 162 ff; Schlosser, P. in F. Stein and M. Jonas (eds) (n 24) s 1029 para 18; Schwab, K.H. and Walter, G. (n 3) ch 3 para 19.

[37] Geimer, R. in R. Zöller (n 13) s 1029 para 80 with further references.

[38] OLG Munich, 25 September 2006, available at <http://www.dis-arb.de>.

[39] BGH, 27 February 1970, BGHZ 53, 315, 322 ff.

regularly covered by the arbitration clause.[40] The same applies to ancillary claims, such as claims for interest.[41] Unless the parties agree otherwise, the arbitration agreement will also be construed to imply that the arbitral tribunal shall allocate the costs of the arbitration between the parties in the award (s 1057 ZPO).

7.17 In contrast, particular care is required in multi-contract situations. Only in very exceptional circumstances may an arbitration agreement be interpreted to extend to 'interrelated contracts' between the same parties.[42]

7.18 The German Federal Court of Justice (*Bundesgerichtshof*—'BGH') as well as most legal scholars also opine that the arbitral tribunal is not competent to hear a respondent's set-off defence with a counterclaim that is not subject to the arbitration agreement, unless the other party does not object timeously, or alternatively, the counterclaim is either undisputed or finally confirmed by a state court.[43]

(6) Binding effect of an arbitration clause on third parties (eg in case of a guarantee or assignment)

7.19 According to the German law notion of privity of contract, arbitration agreements, in principle, bind only the parties to the arbitration agreement and their legal successors.[44] Third parties are bound by the arbitration clause only in exceptional circumstances, either on the basis of a special contractual agreement or by operation of law as a party's legal successor. The extension of an arbitration agreement to third parties by virtue of the 'group of companies' doctrine, which would go beyond the normal rules of interpreting agreements, is the subject of controversial discussion in Germany,[45] but denied by the majority of legal scholars.[46]

7.20 A typical example for a special contractual agreement that extends the arbitration agreement's scope to a third party is a contract in favour of a third party (s 328 BGB).[47]

---

[40] Saenger, I. in I. Saenger (ed) (n 28) s 1029 para 15.

[41] OLG Naumburg, 24 February 2005, available at <http://www.dis-arb.de>.

[42] OLG Munich, 13 October 2004, [2005] NJW 832 ff. In this case, the arbitration agreement in a contract of process financing was exceptionally held to also cover a separate loan contract between the same parties, since both contracts were directly and inseparably linked to each other, thus forming an economic unity.

[43] Schlosser, P. in F. Stein and M. Jonas (eds) (n 24) s 1029 paras 31 ff; Geimer, R. in R. Zöller (n 13) s 1029 paras 85 and 86.

[44] Trittmann, R. and Hanefeld, I. in K.-H. Böckstiegel, S. Kröll, and P. Nacimiento (eds) (n 6) 108 para 36 with further references.

[45] For a detailed overview, see Ahrens, J-M., *Die subjektive Reichweite internationaler Schiedsvereinbarungen und ihre Erstreckung in der Unternehmensgruppe* (Peter Lang, 2001); Sandrock, O., 'Wirkungen von Schiedsvereinbarungen im Konzern' in K.-H. Böckstiegel, K.P. Berger and J. Bredow (eds), *Die Beteiligung Dritter an Schiedsverfahren* (Carl Heymanns, 2005) 93 ff; cf Busse, D., 'Die Bindung Dritter an Schiedsvereinbarungen' [2005] *SchiedsVZ* 118 ff.

[46] Sandrock, O., 'Wirkungen von Schiedsvereinbarungen im Konzern' in K.-H. Böckstiegel, K.P. Berger and J. Bredow (eds) (n 45) 107 ff; Müller, W. and Keilmann, A., 'Beteiligung am Schiedsverfahren wider Willen?' [2007] *SchiedsVZ* 113 ff.

[47] Saenger, I. in I. Saenger (ed) (n 28) s 1029 para 20; for a detailed analysis of the binding effect of an arbitration agreement on third parties, see Mohs, F., *Drittwirkung von Schieds- und Gerichtsstandsvereinbarungen* (Quadis and Sellier, 2006).

In contrast, arbitration agreements to a third party's disfavour are not permitted.[48] Classic examples of succession to an arbitration agreement are the assignment of rights under a contract (s 398 BGB), the global succession into the rights of a party (eg by way of inheritance [s 1922 BGB]), or an assumption of debts (ss 414 ff BGB).[49] Third parties typically bound by an arbitration agreement are the administrative receiver (*Zwangsverwalter*), the administrator of a will (*Testamentsvollstrecker*) and the insolvency administrator (*Insolvenzverwalter*).[50]

A warrantor or guarantor is usually not bound by the arbitration agreement, as his debt exists independently from the principal claim.[51] **7.21**

(6.1) What is the law/leading authorities' position on multi-party situations? Especially (i) with respect to the objection that the arbitration clause does not specifically provide for a plurality of parties in the same procedure; (ii) with respect to the constitution of the arbitral tribunal; and (iii) with respect to the consolidation of two or more running arbitration proceedings? Multi-party arbitral proceedings are in principle permissible under German arbitration law, and they are a frequent occurrence in German arbitration practice.[52] German arbitration law nevertheless does not provide for specific provisions dealing with multi-party arbitrations. Rather, the German legislator gave preference to a case-by-case solution considering the many different constellations, in which multi-party problems can arise. **7.22**

Two conditions for multi-party arbitration are generally accepted: Firstly, a multi-party procedure must be based on a contractual agreement.[53] In practice, however, it is often very difficult to determine whether the parties, in a given case, have consented to multi-party proceedings or not. If the contract, in which the arbitration clause is inserted, is a multi-party contract, the arbitration clause may usually be interpreted as contemplating multi-party arbitration. By contrast, a joinder of third parties that have not agreed to the arbitration agreement is not admissible if not all parties involved have agreed to the joinder or consolidation of proceedings.[54] Secondly, all parties involved must be in a position equally to influence the process of nominating the arbitrators.[55] It is not yet conclusively determined in German case law, what, in practice, ensures such equal influence in the nomination process. For example, the DIS Rules provide that all parties on one side must agree to the **7.23**

[48] Geimer, R. in R. Zöller (n 13) s 1029 para 39.

[49] Trittmann, R. and Hanefeld, I. in K.-H. Böckstiegel, S. Kröll, and P. Nacimiento (eds) (n 6) 108 ff para 38 with further references.

[50] Trittmann, R. and Hanefeld, I. in K.-H. Böckstiegel, S. Kröll, and P. Nacimiento (eds) (n 6) 108 ff para 38 with further references.

[51] Schwab, K.H. and Walter, G. (n 3) ch 7 para 34; Geimer, R. in R. Zöller (n 13) s 1029 para 63; Schlosser, P. in F. Stein and M. Jonas (eds) (n 24) s 1029 para 33.

[52] Böckstiegel, K.-H., Kröll, S. and Nacimiento, P., 'Germany as a Place for International and Domestic Arbitrations' in K.-H. Böckstiegel, S. Kröll, and P. Nacimiento (eds) (n 6) 60 para 59.

[53] Lachmann, J.-P. (n 17) para 2806; Schlosser, P. in F. Stein and M. Jonas (eds) (n 19) s 1034 para 20; Geimer, R. in R. Zöller (n 13) s 1029 para 42.

[54] Sachs, K. and Lörcher, T. in K.-H. Böckstiegel, S. Kröll, and P. Nacimiento (eds) (n 6) 293 para 43; Labes, H., 'Arbitration of Insurance Disputes in Germany' in K.-H. Böckstiegel, S. Kröll, and P. Nacimiento (eds) (n 6) 946 para 50.

[55] Lachmann, J.-P. (n 22) paras 2806 and 2818.

choice of the arbitrator; otherwise, the DIS Appointing Committee will choose the arbitrators (but not the chairman) for both sides (s 13(1) and (2) DIS Rules). Whereas some scholars favour the solution of the DIS also in *ad hoc* proceedings,[56] others prefer the solution of the ICC Rules (cf Art 10 ICC Rules) and demand that the state courts should be entitled to appoint the entire arbitral tribunal, including the chairman.[57]

7.24 With respect to the consolidation of two or more pending arbitration proceedings, in which the parties are not identical, German arbitration law, again, does not contain specific provisions. Yet, it is the prevailing opinion that consolidation requires the consent of all parties involved.[58]

7.25 **(6.2) Is there case law/authorities with respect to the admissibility of third party participation in an arbitration without being a claimant or defendant (Nebenintervention/ Streitverkündung; intervention forcée/volontaire; vouching in; *amicus curiae* etc)? What are the prerequisites and effects of such participation (if permitted)?** German arbitration law does not provide for any kind of formal third party intervention (*Nebenintervention*) or third party notice (*Streitverkündung*). The provisions of the ZPO on state court proceedings relating to third party participation must not—not even analogously—be applied in arbitration proceedings.[59] However, the parties are free to enter into agreements on the joinder of a third party in order to achieve the intended effects, either in the arbitration agreement itself or in the course of the proceedings.[60] If the third party unilaterally consents to the joinder, the question remains whether also the opponent party as well as the arbitral tribunal have to agree on this joinder. This question is highly controversial. The consensual and also confidential character of arbitration speaks at least for a necessary consent of all parties involved.[61]

7.26 *Amicus curiae* briefs are usually not encountered in Germany in commercial arbitral practice.

(7) Termination of an arbitration agreement by a party (reasons and case law)

7.27 According to the notion of separability, an arbitration clause, which forms part of a contract, shall be treated as an agreement independent of the other terms of the contract

[56] Schlosser, P. in F. Stein and M. Jonas (eds) (n 24) s 1034 para 17.

[57] BGH, 29 March 1996, [1996] NJW 1996, 1753, 1755; OLG Frankfurt, 24 November 2005, [2006] SchiedsVZ 219, 221 ff; Schwab, K.H. and Walter, G. (n 3) ch 10 para 15; cf Raeschke-Kessler, H., 'Gesellschaftsrechtliche Schiedsverfahren und das Recht der EU' [2003] *SchiedsVZ* 145, 151; Nacimiento, P. and Abt, A. in K.-H. Böckstiegel, S. Kröll, and P. Nacimiento (eds) (n 6) 205 para 41; see also the nomination procedure set forth in Art 8 LCIA Rules, Art 6(5) AAA Rules, and Art 8 Swiss Rules.

[58] Geimer, R. in R. Zöller (n 13) s 1042 para 44; Voit, W. in H-J. Musielak (ed), *Kommentar zur Zivilprozessordnung* (6th edn, Franz Vahlen, 2008) s 1042 para 13; Berger, K.P., *Internationale Wirtschaftsschiedsgerichtsbarkeit* (De Gruyter, 1992) 302 ff.

[59] Elsing, S.H., 'Streitverkündung und Schiedsverfahren' [2004] *SchiedsVZ* 88, 91.

[60] *ibid.*

[61] Geimer, R., 'Beteiligung weiterer Parteien im Schiedsgerichtsverfahren, insbesondere die Drittwiderklage' in K.-H. Böckstiegel, K.P. Berger and J. Bredow (eds) (n 45) 71, 78 with further references; Wagner, G., 'Bindung des Schiedsgerichts an Entscheidungen anderer Gerichte und Schiedsgerichte' in K.-H. Böckstiegel, K.P. Berger and J. Bredow (eds) (n 45) 7, 47; Schlosser, P. in F. Stein and M. Jonas (eds) (n 24) s 1042 para 27.

(s 1040(1) ZPO).[62] Therefore, the termination of the arbitration agreement is, in general, not dependent on the termination of the main contract.[63] Yet, the arbitration agreement and the main contract may well be affected by the same defect. For example, a lack of consent to the main contract, including a revocation of the offer, may also imply a lack of consent with regard to the arbitration agreement included therein.[64]

The arbitration agreement as such may be invalid or end for a variety of reasons. For instance, the arbitration agreement may expire owing to a contractually agreed time limit or by occurrence of a resolving condition or by mutual agreement.[65] Moreover, the arbitration agreement may be null and void *ab initio* or may become inoperative or incapable of being performed. According to a critically discussed decision of the BGH, the arbitration agreement between two parties, one of which was unable to fund the arbitral proceedings, became incapable of being performed and did not even have to be terminated by the impecunious party.[66] In any event, a unilateral right to terminate an arbitration agreement requires an important reason (termination for good cause—*Kündigung aus wichtigem Grund*), eg where the continuation of the proceedings is unbearable for one of the parties[67] or the continuation of the proceedings has become impossible.[68] **7.28**

B. Arbitrability

(1) 'Personal arbitrability' (capacity to conclude arbitration agreements)

The personal arbitrability (*subjektive Schiedsfähigkeit*) is not specifically regulated in German arbitration law. Rather, it is assumed that a party, which is competent to enter into a contract, may also conclude an arbitration agreement.[69] Yet, there are some exceptions to this general rule. For example, s 37h of the German Securities Trading Act (*Wertpapierhandelsgesetz*—'WpHG') only allows merchants (as opposed to non-merchants) to enter in advance into an arbitration agreement with regard to certain financial service transactions. Similar restrictions exist for arbitration agreements with minors and for arbitration agreements with a party that is subject to insolvency proceedings in Germany.[70] **7.29**

(1.1) May a state (or state agency) as party invoke sovereign immunity before the arbitral tribunal or before a state court (eg in a procedure of enforcement)? The concept of sovereign immunity as a general rule of international law is recognized in Art 25 of the German Constitution (*Grundgesetz*—'GG'). While, in general, a state (or state agency) that has agreed to arbitration is deemed to have waived its immunity from both the arbitral **7.30**

---

[62] See eg OLG Frankfurt, 20 July 2007, available at <http://www.dis-arb.de>.
[63] Kröll, S. (n 2) 18.
[64] See BGH, 27 November 2008, III ZB 59/07, available at <http://www.juris.de>; Kröll, S. (n 2) 18.
[65] Trittmann, R. and Hanefeld, I. in K.-H. Böckstiegel, S. Kröll, and P. Nacimiento (eds) (n 6) 111 para 44.
[66] See BGH, 14 September 2000, *BGHZ* 145, 116 ff; but see OLG Oldenburg, 2 April 2004, available at <http://www.dis-arb.de>; for a detailed discussion, see Wagner, G., 'Impecunious Parties and Arbitration Agreements' [2003] *SchiedsVZ* 206 ff.
[67] BGH, 11 July 1985, [1986] *NJW* 2765, 2766; Geimer, R., in R. Zöller (n 13) s 1029 para 99; Schwab, K.H. and Walter, G. (n 3) ch 8 para 11.
[68] Voit, W. in H-J. Musielak (ed) (n 59) s 1056 para 7.
[69] Lachmann, J.-P. (n 22) para 286 with further references.
[70] *ibid*, (n 22) paras 294 and 295.

proceedings and the enforcement proceedings before a state court,[71] problems may arise when it comes to execution proceedings against a state (or state agency), which may directly affect the assets of a state. According to the German majority view, execution proceedings are only permissible against state assets that do not relate to sovereign activities of the state (or state agency) but are used for commercial purposes only.[72]

(2) 'Objective arbitrability' (eg of patent, trade mark and antitrust matters)

7.31 Section 1030 ZPO deals with the arbitrability of the subject matter ('objective arbitrability'— *objektive Schiedsfähigkeit*). In general, any claim involving an economic interest (*vermögensrechtlicher Anspruch*) can be the subject of an arbitration agreement (s 1030(1) sentence 1 ZPO). An arbitration agreement concerning claims not involving an economic interest shall have legal effect to the extent that the parties are entitled to conclude a settlement on the issue in dispute (s 1030(1) sentence 2 ZPO).

7.32 The German definition of arbitrability reflects the intention of the German legislator that, in general, almost all disputes shall be arbitrable except when public interests require an exception.[73] The German legislator intended a broad interpretation of the term 'economic interest',[74] which may comprise not only claims for the payment of a sum of money (*Zahlungsklagen*), but also declaratory claims (*Feststellungsklagen*), actions for the change of a legal relationship (*Gestaltungsklagen*), prohibitory actions (*Unterlassungsklagen*) and actions for revocations (*Widerrufsklagen*).

7.33 In addition, most disputes not involving an economic interest will still be arbitrable under s 1030 ZPO as they can be the object of a settlement.

7.34 Section 1030(2) ZPO denies under certain conditions the arbitrability of lease agreements, but only relates to residential leases and sublease agreements as opposed to commercial leases.

7.35 Typical examples where arbitrability may indeed be an issue have been resolved by the German legislator and/or German case law as follows: Employment disputes are arbitrable under ss 101 ff Labour Courts Act (*Arbeitsgerichtsgesetz*—'ArbGG'). Claims involving antitrust disputes are arbitrable.[75] In general, disputes involving intellectual property rights—eg in the context of copyright, design, patent, and trade mark licensing—are also arbitrable.[76] Yet, the decision of an arbitral tribunal may not involve the revocation of a registered intellectual right (eg patent, design or trade mark) and has effect only *inter partes*,

---

[71] Geimer, R. in R. Zöller (n 13) s 1061 para 57.

[72] Escher, E., Nacimiento, P. and Weissenborn, C., 'Investment Arbitration and the Participation of State Parties in Germany' in K.-H. Böckstiegel, S. Kröll, and P. Nacimiento (eds) (n 6) 1046 paras 66 ff; Lachmann, J.-P. (n 22) para 2748; cf BGH, 4 October 2005, available at <http://www.dis-arb.de> (execution of a BIT award against Russia in Germany).

[73] Schlosser, P. in F. Stein and M. Jonas (eds) (n 24) s 1030 para 6; see also Explanatory Memorandum on the draft Bill of the Arbitration Law Reform Act, BT-Drucksache 13/5274, 34.

[74] Explanatory Memorandum on the draft Bill of the Arbitration Law Reform Act, BT-Drucksache 13/5274, 34; Schlosser, P. in F. Stein and M. Jonas (eds) (n 19) s 1030 paras 1 ff.

[75] See Bundesgesetzblatt (BGBl) I 1997, 3249; Schwab, K.H. and Walter, G. (n 3) ch 4 para 7.

[76] Geimer, R. in R. Zöller (n 13) s 1030 para 15.

ie between the parties to the arbitration.[77] The arbitrability of disputes regarding shareholder resolutions (*Beschlussmängelstreitigkeiten*) has for a long time been the object of controversial discussion.[78] The BGH has recently held that disputes regarding the validity or nullity of shareholders' resolutions are arbitrable under ZPO provided that all shareholders have agreed to arbitration and the arbitration agreement is of such nature as to grant all shareholders equal possibility to participate in the arbitral proceedings.[79] Hence, arbitration clauses with regard to such disputes must take into consideration that shareholder disputes are multi-party disputes and that the scope of the award extends to all shareholders and the company.[80]

C. Decision on the arbitral tribunal's jurisdiction ('*competence-competence*')

(1) Separability (independence of the arbitration agreement from the main agreement)

Under German arbitration law, an arbitration agreement is legally distinct and autonomous from the main contract. This so-called notion of separability as codified in s 1040(1) second sentence ZPO applies regardless of whether the arbitration agreement is contained in a separate agreement or the arbitration clause is included as a 'contract within the contract' in the main contract. **7.36**

(2) Competence of the tribunal to decide on its own jurisdiction (including form and time of the tribunal's decision)

According to s 1040(1) sentence 1 ZPO, the arbitral tribunal may rule on its own jurisdiction and, in this context, on the existence or validity of the arbitration agreement (*competence-competence*). However, it is important to note that, under German arbitration law, the arbitral tribunal's decision is still subject to control by the courts. The term *competence-competence* is, hence, justified only in so far as the arbitral tribunal is empowered to decide on the issue of its own jurisdiction in the first instance. **7.37**

The arbitral tribunal may rule on its jurisdiction by means of a preliminary ruling, if one party has challenged the arbitral tribunal's jurisdiction (s 1040(2) and (3) ZPO). The plea for lack of jurisdiction shall be raised no later than with the submission of the statement of defence (s 1040(2) ZPO). Only under exceptional circumstances may the arbitral tribunal include the decision regarding its jurisdiction within the final award.[81] **7.38**

(3) Extent of the 'competence-competence' *and role of the courts (including form and time limits of a challenge of the tribunal's decision)*

If the arbitral tribunal has issued a confirmative preliminary ruling on its jurisdiction, any party may request, within one month after having received written notice of that ruling, the **7.39**

---

[77] See Blessing, M., 'Arbitrability of Intellectual Property Disputes' (1996) 12(2) *Arb Int'l* 191, 200; Simms, D.P., 'Arbitrability of Intellectual Property Disputes in Germany' (1999) 15(2) *Arb Int'l* 193 ff; some authors are even in favour of an unlimited arbitrability of intellectual property disputes, see Schwab, K.H. and Walter, G. (n 2) ch 4 para 11; Geimer, R. in R. Zöller (n 13) s 1030 paras 14 and 15.

[78] See in detail Lachmann, J.-P. (n 22) paras 303 ff; Duve, C., 'Arbitration in Corporate Law Disputes in Germany' in K.-H. Böckstiegel, S. Kröll, and P. Nacimiento (eds) (n 6) 975, 983 para 19.

[79] BGH, 6 April 2009, [2009] SchiedsVZ 233 ff = [2009] *BB* 1260 ff (with comments by Manner, S.).

[80] Lachmann, J.-P. (n 22) para 309. Of the supplementary rules for disputes regarding shareholder resolutions promulgated by the DIS in September 2009; available (in German) at <http://www.dis-art.de>.

[81] Explanatory Memorandum on the draft Bill of the Arbitration Law Reform Act, BT-Drucksache 13/5274, 44.

court to decide that matter (s 1040(3) sentence 2 ZPO). The Higher Regional Court (*Oberlandesgericht*—'OLG')[82] designated in the arbitration agreement or, absent such designation, the OLG in whose district the place of arbitration is situated, is competent for the decision (s 1062(1) no 2 ZPO). The courts do not limit themselves to a *prima facie* control of the arbitral tribunal's jurisdiction but rather conduct a full review.[83] While the request is pending before the court, the arbitral tribunal may continue the arbitral proceedings and make the award (s 1040(3) sentence 3 ZPO).

D. Enforcement of an arbitration agreement within or by way of court proceedings

(1) Effect of invoking an arbitration clause within a court proceeding (and time limits for such a motion)

7.40 A court, before which an action is brought in a matter being subject of an arbitration agreement, shall, if the respondent raises an objection prior to the beginning of the oral hearing on the substance of the dispute, reject the action as inadmissible unless the court finds that the arbitration agreement is null and void, inoperative or incapable of being performed (s 1032(1) ZPO).[84] The objection must be invoked prior to the beginning of the oral hearing on the substance of the dispute.[85] If the respondent raises the objection in time, the court will have to examine whether one of the three grounds for the arbitration agreement's invalidity (null and void, inoperative, or incapable of being performed) is given in the present case. The burden of proof with regard to the facts that may lead to the finding that the arbitration agreement must be treated as being non-existent lies with the claimant.[86]

7.41 (1.1) **If a party has successfully invoked the arbitration agreement in a court proceeding, is it then entitled to deny within the arbitral proceeding that there is a valid and binding arbitration agreement?** The arbitration agreement's challenge may violate the notion of good faith (s 242 BGB) and, in particular, the prohibition of '*venire contra factum proprium*', if the party challenging the arbitration agreement's validity has argued the opposite way in previous court proceedings resulting in the dismissal of the claim in the court proceedings.[87] If, prior to the commencement of the arbitral proceedings, the party has expressly invoked the arbitration agreement in an exchange of letters and thereby triggered the commencement of arbitration and in the arbitration proceeding suddenly tries to argue that the arbitration agreement is defective, this may also amount to a violation of the notion of good faith.[88]

7.42 (1.2) **Vice versa, if a party has successfully objected to an arbitral proceeding by denying that there is a valid arbitration agreement, may it then invoke such agreement in the ensuing proceeding?** Similarly, a party that has denied the existence of a valid arbitration

[82] In Berlin, the Higher Regional Court is called *Kammergericht* ('KG').
[83] BGH, 13 January 2005, [2005] SchiedsVZ 95, 96.
[84] The arbitration defence is also available in summary proceedings on a document-only basis (*Urkundenprozess*), cf BGH, 31 May 2007, [2007] SchiedsVZ 215 ff.
[85] BGH, 10 May 2001, [2001] NJW 2176.
[86] Huber, P. in K.-H. Böckstiegel, S. Kröll, and P. Nacimiento (eds) (n 6) 144 para 16 with further references.
[87] BGH, 20 May 1968, BGHZ 50, 191, 194; BGH, 2 April 1987, [1987] WM 1084 ff.
[88] BGH, 2 April 1987, [1987] WM 1084 ff.

agreement before the arbitral tribunal is barred from invoking the arbitration agreement in subsequent court proceedings according to the notion of good faith.[89]

(2) Legal remedies and proceedings to enforce an arbitration agreement

(1.1) Which would be the internationally competent court (i) for obtaining a declaration that an arbitration agreement is valid and binding; or (ii) to compel arbitration? (The defendant's courts? The courts of the place of arbitration? The claimant's courts, cf Article 6(2) in fine, ICC Rules?) Section 1032(2) ZPO provides that, prior to the constitution of the arbitral tribunal, an application may be made to the court to determine whether or not arbitration is admissible. Section 1032(2) ZPO is not based on the UNCITRAL Model Law but is rather a unique rule of German arbitration law.[90] The application may be made by both parties, ie the claimant and the respondent. The competent court to decide on the admissibility or inadmissibility of arbitration is the Higher Regional Court (*Oberlandesgericht*—OLG) designated in the arbitration agreement, or absent such designation, the OLG, in whose district the place of arbitration is situated (ss 1032(2), 1062(1) no 2 ZPO). The decision of the OLG covers both a declaratory judgment that the arbitration agreement is valid and binding and a declaratory judgment that arbitration is not admissible.[91] 7.43

III. The arbitral tribunal

A. Number and qualification of arbitrators

(1) Sole arbitrator or arbitral tribunal with several arbitrators

The parties are free to determine the number of arbitrators; failing such determination, German arbitration law designates that the number of arbitrators shall be three (s 1034(1) ZPO). 7.44

(1.1) Are arbitral tribunals with an even number of arbitrators acceptable? Arbitral tribunals with an even number of arbitrators are in principle permitted.[92] However, parties usually agree on an uneven number of arbitrators and specifically on a three-member arbitral tribunal, as, absent an agreement to the contrary, majority decisions are possible when rendering the award (s 1052(1) ZPO). 7.45

(2) Qualification of the arbitrators

German arbitration law does not contain a definition of the general qualifications required for service as an arbitrator.[93] The drafters of the new German arbitration law regarded the 7.46

[89] BGH, 20 May 1968, BGHZ 50, 191, 196; BGH, 2 February 1987, [1987] NJW-RR 1194, 1195; OLG Frankfurt, 1 October 1998, [1999] IPRax 247, 251.

[90] Huber, P. in K.-H. Böckstiegel, S. Kröll, and P. Nacimiento (eds) (n 6) 150 paras 41 and 42, who assumes that s 1032(2) ZPO is a mandatory provision that cannot be derogated from by the parties.

[91] Huber, P. in K.-H. Böckstiegel, S. Kröll, and P. Nacimiento (eds) (n 6) 153 paras 52 ff.

[92] Explanatory Memorandum on the draft Bill of the Arbitration Law Reform Act, BT-Drucksache 13/5274, 39.

[93] Weigand, F.-B., 'Der nebenberuflich tätige Schiedsrichter' in B. Bachmann *et al* (eds), *Grenzüberschreitungen, Festschrift für Peter Schlosser zum 70. Geburtstag* (Mohr Siebeck, 2005) 1081, 1083 ff.

fact that an arbitrator may be of any nationality, sex, religion, origin or race as self-evident and therefore abstained from codifying qualification requirements.[94] As a consequence, the parties are almost entirely free in their choice of arbitrators within the limits of s 1036(1) ZPO, which requires that arbitrators must be impartial and independent. The arbitrator does not need the qualification for judicial office (*Befähigung zum Richteramt*) and does not need to meet any special requirements as to experience or capacity.[95] The parties are, however, free to agree on certain requirements concerning the arbitrator(s)' qualifications in their arbitration agreement. For example, it is permissible and sometimes encountered in arbitration clauses that the parties require a specific education, an in-depth knowledge in a specific field of law, certain technical competence, or language skills.[96]

7.47 (2.1) **Are there mandatory requirements for the qualification of arbitrators (statutory requirements or indirect requirements through eg general conditions of insurance contracts)?** Even though German arbitration law does not regulate specific requirements for the qualification of arbitrators, it is generally accepted under German law that minors and persons suffering from incapacity may not act as arbitrators.[97] Some of the specialized arbitration institutions, particularly in the commodity and sports sector, require that the sole arbitrator or the chairman of an arbitral tribunal is a member of that organization or named on their arbitrators' list.[98]

7.48 (2.2) **Which national arbitration institutions may be contacted for obtaining information about qualified (and specialized) arbitrators?** Upon request, the DIS makes suggestions for the selection of arbitrators (s 2.3 DIS Rules) and provides the parties with information concerning persons who might be considered as arbitrators based on their respective expertise and experience. Furthermore, a list of DIS members is available online at <http://www.dis-arb.de>. In addition, information regarding arbitrators can be obtained at many regional chambers of commerce, eg the HK Hamburg.

7.49 (2.3) **Are judges or civil servants required to obtain permission by their employer to act as arbitrator? Are these permissions given generally or case-by-case? What are the consequences if such permission has not been obtained?** Judges and civil servants need prior permission to act as arbitrators by their employer.[99] Civil servants usually obtain such permission without any difficulties as long as the fulfilment of their duties is not impeded. On the other hand, permission to act as an arbitrator will be granted to active judges only

[94] Explanatory Memorandum on the draft Bill of the Arbitration Law Reform Act, BT-Drucksache 13/5274, 39.

[95] Weigand, F.-B., in B. Bachmann *et al* (eds) (n 93) 1081, 1083; Nacimiento, P. and Abt, A. in K.-H. Böckstiegel, S. Kröll, and P. Nacimiento (eds) (n 6) 195 para 10.

[96] Weigand, F.-B. in B. Bachmann *et al* (eds) (n 93), 1081, 1083 and 1084; Nacimiento, P. and Abt, A. in K.-H. Böckstiegel, S. Kröll, and P. Nacimiento (eds) (n 6) 195 para 11.

[97] BGH, 5 May 1986, [1986] NJW 3079, 3080; Schlosser, P. in F. Stein and M. Jonas (eds) (n 24) s 1036 para 1; Geimer, R. in R. Zöller (n 13) s 1035 para 6.

[98] Hantke, D., 'Die Bildung des Schiedsgerichts' [2003] *SchiedsVZ* 269, 271 and 272; see eg ss 3.3 and 3.4 of the DIS-Sport-Schiedsgerichtsordnung, in force as of 1 January 2008, available at <http://www.dis-arb.de/sport/default.htm>; cf the arbitrators' lists of the 'German Association of Wholesale Traders in Oils, Fats and Oil Raw Materials' (BRDFOR), available (in German) at <http://www.grefor.de/>

[99] Lachmann, J.-P. (n 22) para 832 with further references.

under stricter conditions (s 40(1) of the German Judiciary Act (*Deutsches Richtergesetz*—'DRiG')). Since this discretion can only be exercised based on the individual circumstances, permission is only given and should be verified on a case-by-case basis.[100]

In the case that the permission has not been obtained or turns out to be invalid, German courts have occasionally held that the arbitral proceedings became incapable of being performed.[101] The prevailing view—especially under the new German arbitration law—is, however, that the validity and enforcement of the arbitration agreement and of the award remain unaffected.[102] **7.50**

B. Appointment of arbitrators

(1) Extent of party autonomy to establish appointment procedure

Under s 1035(1) ZPO the parties are entitled autonomously to agree on an appointment procedure for the arbitrators and the chairman. Only if the arbitration agreement grants preponderant rights to one party with regard to the composition of the arbitral tribunal, is party autonomy restricted. In this case, the disadvantaged party may request the Higher Regional Court (*Oberlandesgericht*—OLG) competent in the individual case to appoint the arbitrator(s) in deviation from the agreed nomination procedure (s 1034(2) ZPO). The request must be submitted at the latest within two weeks of the party becoming aware of the constitution of the arbitral tribunal. With respect to the substitute appointment, the courts shall have due regard to any qualifications required of the arbitrator by the parties' agreement and to such considerations as are likely to secure the appointment of an independent and impartial arbitrator. In the case of a sole or third arbitrator, the court shall also take into account the advisability of appointing an arbitrator of a nationality other than those of the parties (s 1035(5) ZPO). It is, however, common practice and understanding that these nationality considerations only apply if the parties themselves are of different nationalities.[103] **7.51**

(2) Procedure in absence of an agreement by the parties

Absent an agreement by the parties regarding the appointment procedure, German arbitration law provides for statutory default rules. If an agreement on a sole arbitrator cannot be reached, one of the parties may request the competent court to appoint the arbitrator (s 1035(3) sentence 1 ZPO). Even though no deadline is stipulated for the parties' agreement, it is a common understanding that the period of one month, which applies to other situations governed by s 1035 ZPO, should be taken as a guideline.[104] In arbitrations with three arbitrators, each party has to nominate one arbitrator within one month after receiving the respective request by the other party (s 1035(3) sentences 2 and 3 ZPO). Otherwise, the court will appoint an arbitrator upon request of one party. The appointment of an **7.52**

---

[100] Weigand, F.-B. in B. Bachmann *et al* (eds) (n 94), 1081, 1088 ff.

[101] KG, 6 May 2002, [2003] SchiedsVZ 185, 186.

[102] OLG Stuttgart, 16 July 2002, [2003] SchiedsVZ 84, 87; Lachmann, J.-P. (n 22) paras 859 ff.

[103] Nacimiento, P. and Abt, A. in K.-H. Böckstiegel, S. Kröll, and P. Nacimiento (eds) (n 6) 202 para 31 with further references.

[104] *ibid* (n 6) 199 para 21 with further references.

arbitrator will become binding as soon as the other party has received notice of the appointment, unless the parties have stipulated otherwise (s 1035(2) ZPO).

7.53 The chairman will usually be elected by the two arbitrators appointed by the parties (s 1035(3) sentence 2 ZPO). If the two arbitrators fail to agree on the third arbitrator within one month of their appointment, the appointment of the chairman shall be made, upon request of a party, by the court. In exercising their power to appoint an arbitrator, courts tend voluntarily to consider suggestions made by the parties.[105]

(3) Effect of the refusal of one party to cooperate in the constitution of the arbitral tribunal

7.54 Where a party fails to act as required under the agreed upon appointment procedure, any party may request the court to take the necessary measure, unless the agreement on the appointment procedure stipulates other means for securing the appointment (s 1035(4) ZPO). As a general rule, it can be said that German courts try to assist in the nomination process by broadly interpreting their competences under s 1035 ZPO in order to respect the parties' intention to submit their dispute to arbitration.[106]

(4) Circumstances and valid reasons for an arbitrator to resign

7.55 An arbitrator may withdraw from his office if he becomes *de jure* or *de facto* unable to perform his functions or for other reasons fails to act without undue delay (s 1038(1) ZPO). A *de jure* inability can be assumed in the case of material legal impediments, such as legal incapacity or lack or later loss of a previously agreed qualification.[107] Typical examples for a *de facto* inability are death, serious illness of the arbitrator, inability to travel, or similar sustained impossibilities of participating in the arbitration.[108] The question of whether an arbitrator fails to act without undue delay cannot be answered generally but has to be decided on a case-by-case basis.[109] If the arbitrator is only temporarily prevented from fulfilling his duties, it will be decisive whether the arbitrator is able to perform his duties within a reasonable time period.[110]

7.56 If one of the reasons for an arbitrator to resign is fulfilled, the legal relationship with the arbitrator will terminate with the result that a substitute arbitrator shall be appointed according to the rules that were applicable to the appointment of the arbitrator being replaced (s 1039(1) ZPO), unless otherwise agreed between the parties (s 1039(2) ZPO).

---

[105] See BayObLG, 16 January 2000, [2002] NJW-RR 933, 934; OLG Munich, 26 April 2006, available at <http://www.dis-arb.de>; cf Brandenburgisches OLG, 24 May 2005, available at <http://www.dis-arb.de>.

[106] See eg OLG Dresden, 20 October 1998, available at <http://www.dis-arb.de>, in which the court held that in cases, where the applicable arbitration rules provide for an unrestricted discretion of the appointing authority in appointing a substitute arbitrator for one of the parties, the appointing authority was not bound by directions of such party as to specific qualifications of the arbitrator (eg the arbitrator's ability to speak German).

[107] Nacimiento, P. and Abt, A. in K.-H. Böckstiegel, S. Kröll and P. Nacimiento (eds) (n 6) 237 para 10 with further references.

[108] Explanatory Memorandum on the draft Bill of the Arbitration Law Reform Act, BT-Drucksache 13/5274, 42; Schlosser, P. in F. Stein and M. Jonas (eds) (n 24) s 1038 para 4; Geimer, R. in R. Zöller (n 13) s 1038 para 2.

[109] cf Lachmann, J.-P. (n 22) para 1128.

[110] Nacimiento, P. and Abt, A. in K.-H. Böckstiegel, S. Kröll and P. Nacimiento (eds) (n 6) 238 para 12 with further references.

C. Challenge and replacement of arbitrators

(1) Grounds, procedure and deadlines for challenging an arbitrator

The challenge of an arbitrator is restricted to grounds that provoke justifiable doubts with regard to his impartiality or independence or to the case that the arbitrator does not possess the qualifications agreed upon by the parties (s 1036(2) sentence 1 ZPO). In addition, a party may only challenge an arbitrator appointed by him, or in whose appointment the party has participated, based on reasons the party was not aware of at the time of the appointment (s 1036(2) sentence 2 ZPO). **7.57**

With regard to the challenge procedure, the parties have wide discretion (s 1037(1) ZPO). According to a recent decision of the OLG Hamburg, the parties may even waive a preliminary challenge procedure (before the arbitral tribunal or an administrative body of an arbitral institution such as the ICC International Court of Arbitration) entirely.[111] If the parties have not agreed on a specific procedure, a written statement of the reasons for the challenge must be sent to the arbitral tribunal, which then decides on the challenge with all its members. The time limit for the challenge amounts to two weeks after the party became aware of the arbitral tribunal's constitution or the circumstances allowing the challenge of the arbitrator (s 1037(2) ZPO). If a challenge before the arbitral tribunal[112] is not successful, the challenging party may then request the court, within one month after having received notice of the decision rejecting the challenge or within a different time limit agreed between the parties, to decide on the challenge (s 1037(3) sentence 1 ZPO). In order to prevent any abuse of challenges, s 1037(3) sentence 2 ZPO stipulates that the arbitral tribunal remains competent to continue the proceedings and make an award, while such court review is pending. **7.58**

Concerning grounds for challenges of arbitrators, the new German arbitration law no longer refers to the grounds for challenges of judges in civil court proceedings (ss 41 ff ZPO).[113] Rather, it must be carefully considered in each individual case whether the connection between an arbitrator and a party actually justifies doubt concerning the arbitrator's impartiality.[114] In international cases, the list of conflicts of interest prepared by the working group of the International Bar Association ('IBA') is a helpful standard for the determination of impartiality and independence.[115] In German domestic cases, one may encounter even stricter standards.[116] For example, private relations to one side—especially if the arbitrator is related to one of the parties or parties' counsel[117]—or private discussions **7.59**

---

[111] OLG Hamburg, 12 July 2005, [2006] SchiedsVZ 55, 56; but see Lachmann, J.-P. (n 22) para 1090 with further references.

[112] See OLG Naumburg, 11 July 2008, available at <http://www.dis-arb.de>, which held that a challenge procedure must be commenced before the award has been issued.

[113] But see OLG Munich, 3 January 2008, [2008] SchiedsVZ 102, 103, in which the court held that, in general, the criteria for a challenge of a judge and an arbitrator are the same.

[114] See eg OLG Munich, 10 January 2007, available at <http://www.dis-arb.de>, in which the court held that tensions between a counsel and an arbitrator, in general, do not justify a challenge of the arbitrator.

[115] Nacimiento, P. and Abt, A. in K.-H. Böckstiegel, S. Kröll, and P. Nacimiento (eds) (n 6) 216 para 33.

[116] *ibid*, para 30.

[117] See eg OLG Frankfurt, 10 January 2008, [2008] SchiedsVZ 199 ff; OLG Frankfurt, 27 April 2006, [2006] SchiedsVZ 329, 330 ff; but see OLG Frankfurt, 4 October 2007, [2008] SchiedsVZ 96 ff, in which the court *inter alia* held that the professional connections between the chairman of the arbitral tribunal and

of the dispute with one side after the appointment[118] have been considered as possible valid grounds for challenging an arbitrator by the German courts.

7.60 **(1.1) Do state courts review challenge procedures, which took place in accordance with a specific procedure agreed upon by the parties (eg Article 11, ICC Rules)? If so, at what point in time? May such review be excluded?** Challenge procedures, which took place in accordance with the chosen institutional arbitration rules and the specific challenge procedure contained therein, may be reviewed by state courts on request of a party within one month after having received notice of the decision rejecting the challenge or within a different time limit agreed between the parties (s 1037(3) sentence 1 ZPO). In particular, such a review by the courts, under German arbitration law, cannot be waived by the parties.[119]

7.61 **(1.2) Is there case law with respect to truncated arbitral tribunals? (cf Article 12(5), ICC Rules)** Since the parties are empowered to modify the procedure for appointing new arbitrators (s 1039(2) ZPO), it appears possible to abolish the substitution of an arbitrator by providing that the arbitrator shall not be replaced. Yet, s 1052 ZPO contradicts this view, as it implicitly requires the award to be made by all members of the arbitral tribunal. Furthermore, German arbitration law requires equality in the composition of the arbitral tribunal and does not subject equality to the disposition of the parties. Hence, it seems to be the current majority view that truncated arbitral tribunals are not permitted; rather a decision by a truncated arbitral tribunal would form a basis for the challenge of the award (s 1059(2) no 1(d) ZPO).[120]

(2) Procedure for appointing a new arbitrator

7.62 Absent an agreement of the parties relating to the appointment of a new arbitrator, a substitute arbitrator shall be appointed according to the rules that applied to the nomination of the original arbitrator (s 1039 ZPO). It is of no relevance how the original arbitrator actually was appointed.[121]

IV. The arbitral procedure

A. General principles

(1) Extent of party autonomy to determine the arbitral procedure

7.63 Under German arbitration law, the parties enjoy extensive freedom for choosing the rules applicable to the arbitration proceedings. Section 1042(3) ZPO enables the parties to

counsel for the respondent arising from activities for the DIS did not constitute a ground for challenge; cf OLG Munich, 5 July 2006, available at <http://www.dis-arb.de>, in which the court held that the fact that one arbitrator was the godparent of an attorney in the law firm representing one of the parties did not constitute a ground for challenge.

118 OLG Munich, 23 February 1971, [1971] BB 886.

119 BayObLG, 24 February 1999, [2000] NJW-RR 360; Lachmann, J.-P. (n 22) para 1049.

120 Nacimiento, P. and Abt, A. in K.-H. Böckstiegel, S. Kröll, and P. Nacimiento (eds) (n 6) 242 ff para 5.

121 Explanatory Memorandum on the draft Bill of the Arbitration Law Reform Act, BT-Drucksache 13/5274, 43.

determine the procedure themselves or by reference to a set of arbitration rules. The principle of party autonomy granted by German arbitration law finds its limits in a limited set of mandatory rules. Section 1042(3) ZPO provides that the parties' autonomy is restricted by the mandatory provisions of the 10th Book of the ZPO if the arbitration is seated in Germany.

(1.1) Are the parties free to choose any national or international law governing the procedure before the arbitral tribunal? Within the limits of the few mandatory provisions of German arbitration law the parties may substitute the German arbitration law with any other national or international law.[122] If the arbitration is situated in Germany and the parties choose a foreign arbitration law, which rarely happens, the chosen foreign arbitration law will not truly be applied as 'law' but rather as procedural rules agreed upon by the parties. Vice versa, German arbitration law may be chosen for arbitrations seated outside of Germany if the arbitration law of the foreign country acknowledges such party autonomy.[123] In international arbitrations, agreements on the application of international procedural standards, such as the IBA Rules on the Taking of Evidence, are occasionally encountered. 7.64

(2) Basic procedural principles or mandatory rules to be applied by the arbitral tribunal

With its limited set of mandatory rules, German arbitration law provides for a liberal procedural framework. The mandatory rules of German arbitration law set out in s 1042(1) and (2) ZPO are: (i) the equal treatment of the parties; (ii) the right to be heard; and (iii) the principle that counsel may not be excluded from representing the parties in the proceedings. The principle of equal treatment requires that the proceedings be conducted in an even-handed and impartial manner.[124] The right to be heard encompasses the right to be duly informed, the opportunity to comment on the relevant facts and points of law, and the arbitral tribunal's obligation to take into account the parties' arguments.[125] Specifically, if the arbitral tribunal intends to base its decision on aspects, which the parties obviously had failed to take into account, the right to be heard demands that the arbitral tribunal raises these issues with the parties according to the German prohibition of surprising decisions (*Überraschungsverbot*).[126] 7.65

In addition, there are only few other rules in German arbitration law, from which the parties cannot derogate. These include a mandatory court review of any unsuccessful challenges of arbitrators (s 1037(3) ZPO) ZPO and the court's decision on the arbitral tribunal's jurisdiction (ss 1032(2) and 1040(3) ZPO).[127] 7.66

[122] Explanatory Memorandum on the draft Bill of the Arbitration Law Reform Act, BT-Drucksache 13/5274, 47.

[123] *ibid*, 31.

[124] Sachs, K. and Lörcher, T. in K.-H. Böckstiegel, S. Kröll, and P. Nacimiento (eds) (n 6) 280 para 4.

[125] *ibid*, 281 ff paras 8 ff with further references.

[126] *ibid*, 284 para 16 with further references.

[127] Nacimiento, P. and Abt, A. in K.-H. Böckstiegel, S. Kröll, and P. Nacimiento (eds) (n 6) 171 para 8 and 225 para 4; Huber, P. in K.-H. Böckstiegel, S. Kröll, and P. Nacimiento (eds) (n 6) 249 para 4.

(3) Oral hearing or proceeding on basis of written documents

7.67 Under German arbitration law, there exists no obligation to conduct an oral hearing as part of the arbitral procedure.[128] Absent an agreement by the parties, the arbitral tribunal is able to decide whether or not oral hearings shall be conducted (s 1047(1) ZPO). Section 1047(1) sentence 2 ZPO specifically acknowledges the possibility that the parties may agree that the arbitral proceedings shall be conducted only on the basis of documents and other materials. On the other hand, the arbitral tribunal has a duty to hold an oral hearing after a respective request by one party, if oral hearings have not been specifically excluded and the requesting party objects to proceedings on a documents-only basis without undue delay.[129] In arbitral practice, it is the rule that an oral hearing will be held.

(4) Power of the tribunal (in particular the chairman) to issue procedural orders

7.68 As a general rule, s 1052(1) ZPO requires any decision of the arbitral tribunal to be made with a majority of all its members, unless the parties agree otherwise. However, the presiding arbitrator may decide individual questions of procedure alone if so authorized by the parties or all members of the arbitral tribunal (s 1052(3) ZPO).

7.69 In arbitral practice, the authorization of the chairman to decide on individual questions of procedure usually means that the chairman may take any minor decisions concerning the formal structuring of the proceedings on his own. For fundamental procedural decisions the chairman needs specific authority to act individually. The parties and the other members of the arbitral tribunal may not defer such power *en bloc* to the chairman but can only grant the authority on a case-by-case basis.[130]

(5) Distinction of matters of substance and matters of procedure

7.70 There exists no conclusive provision in German law how matters of substance and procedure are to be distinguished. For instance, concerning the law of evidence, the admissibility of certain means of evidence is considered to be a question of procedural law.[131] The question of the burden of proof is seen as part of substantive law.[132] The right of set-off is also classified as a matter of substance.[133]

7.71 (5.1) **Are the statutes of limitations a matter of substance or rather of procedure?** Under German law, the statutes of limitations are considered as forming part of substantive law.[134] The general civil law statutes of limitations are codified in the general provisions of the

[128] Lachmann, J.-P. (n 22) para 1586.

[129] See OLG Naumburg, 21 February 2002, [2003] NJW-RR 71, 72.

[130] von Schlabrendorff, F. and Sessler, A. in K.-H. Böckstiegel, S. Kröll, and P. Nacimiento (eds) (n 6) 369 ff para 16 with further references.

[131] Schack, H., *Internationales Zivilverfahrensrecht* (4th edn, CH Beck, 2006) para 679; Leipold, D. in F. Stein and M. Jonas (eds) (n 24) s 286 para 99.

[132] Leipold, D. in F. Stein and M. Jonas (eds) (n 24) s 286 para 78 ff; Wagner, G., *Prozessverträge* (Mohr Siebeck, 1998) 697.

[133] Wagner, G., 'Die Aufrechnung im Europäischen Zivilprozess' [1999] *IPRax* 69 ff.

[134] Schack, S. (n 132) para 521; Grothe, H. in K. Rebmann, F.J. Säcker and R. Rixecker (eds), *Münchener Kommentar zum Bürgerlichen Gesetzbuch*, vol 1/1 (5th edn, CH Beck, 2006) Vorbemerkung s 194 para 34; for a comparative overview, see Schwenzer, I. and Manner, S. '"The Claim is Time-Barred": The Proper Limitation Regime for International Sales Contracts in International Commercial Arbitration' (2007) 23(2) *Arb Int'l* 293, 296 ff.

German Civil Code (ss 194–225 BGB). Yet, specific limitation periods can also be found in other provisions of the BGB (eg ss 438 (1) no 3; 479; 548; 634a; 651g II BGB) as well as in special legislation (eg ss 159; 113(3) HGB; s 12 of the German Product Liability Act [*Produkthaftungsgesetz*—'ProdHaftG']), which all qualify as substantive law provisions.

(6) Persons able to represent a party in an arbitral proceeding

Persons able to represent a party in an arbitral proceeding can be German lawyers and foreign lawyers but do not necessarily need to be lawyers.[135] In arbitral practice, counsel representation is the rule rather than the exception. Parties can agree that such counsel representation is required.[136] **7.72**

B. Place of arbitration

(1) Determination of the place of arbitration in the absence of an agreement by the parties

The place of arbitration shall be determined by the arbitral tribunal if the parties have not agreed on the place of arbitration (s 1043(1) sentence 2 ZPO). Because of the factual and legal importance of the place of arbitration, it is commonly recognized that the decision on the place of arbitration cannot be made by the chairman alone but the determination has to be made by the arbitral tribunal.[137] The factual circumstances for the place of arbitration's determination are convenience of the parties, convenience of the proposed place for the arbitral tribunal and potential witnesses, and practical considerations such as the necessary infrastructure. The legal circumstances to be considered are, in particular, the implications of the place of arbitration on the applicable procedural rules as well as on the recognition and enforcement of the award.[138] **7.73**

(2) Importance and legal effect of place (seat) of the arbitration

The place of arbitration is of paramount legal significance. It determines the *lex arbitri* and thereby defines whether and to what extent German arbitration law is applicable (s 1025(1) ZPO).[139] Furthermore, the place of arbitration determines the origin of the arbitral award as domestic or foreign (ss 1060 and 1061 ZPO). Finally, the place of arbitration is relevant for determining the local jurisdiction of the Higher Regional Courts (*Oberlandesgerichte*—OLG) with regard to the arbitral proceedings (s 1062 ZPO).[140] **7.74**

(2.1) Are the arbitrators and parties free to convene at places other than the official seat of the arbitration? The arbitral tribunal may, unless otherwise agreed by the parties, meet at any other appropriate place for an oral hearing, for hearing witnesses, experts or the parties, for consultation among its members or for inspection of property or documents (s 1043(2) ZPO). As a result it may happen that the place of arbitration in its legal sense becomes a purely fictitious place and that none or only some of the hearings are actually **7.75**

[135] Explanatory Memorandum on the draft Bill of the Arbitration Law Reform Act, BT-Drucksache 13/5274, 46.

[136] Sachs, K. and Lörcher, T. in K.-H. Böckstiegel, S. Kröll, and P. Nacimiento (eds) (n 6) 286 para 21.

[137] Explanatory Memorandum on the draft Bill of the Arbitration Law Reform Act, BT-Drucksache 13/5274, 47.

[138] Sachs, K. and Lörcher, T. in K.-H. Böckstiegel, S. Kröll, and P. Nacimiento (eds) (n 6) 300 para 4.

[139] *ibid*, 298 para 1.

[140] J Lachmann, J.-P. (n 22) para 1393.

held at the place of arbitration.[141] Owing to its legal importance, the place of arbitration must be stipulated in the award (s 1054(3) ZPO).

7.76 (2.2) **Are there visa requirements to enter the country, which apply to lawyers and/or arbitrators? Where may current information on that subject be obtained?** Visa requirements for lawyers and arbitrators to enter Germany differ widely depending on the particular country of origin of the individual lawyer and/or arbitrator. Current information on that subject may be obtained at the German embassies and consulates.

C. Submissions, deadlines and default

(1) Contents and form of submissions (in particular request for arbitration and answer to request)

7.77 Unless otherwise agreed by the parties, s 1044 sentence 2 ZPO stipulates that a request for arbitration shall state the names of the parties, the subject matter of the dispute and contain a reference to the arbitration agreement. The request does not have to fulfil any specific form requirements unless the parties have agreed otherwise.[142] There are also no specific form requirements regarding the delivery of the request.[143] However, in order to ensure that the arbitration was properly initiated, the claimant is well advised to establish a clear evidentiary record on the commencement of the arbitral proceedings.

7.78 With respect to the subsequent statement of claim, s 1046(1) sentence 1 ZPO provides that, within the period of time agreed by the parties or determined by the arbitral tribunal, the claimant shall state his claim and the facts supporting the claim in his statement of claim.

7.79 With respect to the statement of defence, s 1046(1) ZPO provides that the respondent, within the period of time agreed by the parties or determined by the arbitral tribunal, shall state his defence in respect of the particularities contained in the statement of claim.

7.80 The parties may submit with their statements all documents they consider to be relevant or may add a reference to other evidence they will submit (s 1046(1) sentence 2 ZPO).

7.81 The time limits for these submissions will vary from case to case depending on the complexity of the dispute and other relevant circumstances.

7.82 (1.1) **From what point in time is a claim considered to be pending with the arbitral tribunal? What are the legal effects of such fact (eg on statutes of limitations)?** Unless otherwise agreed by the parties, arbitral proceedings commence on the date, on which a request for the particular dispute to be referred to arbitration is received by the respondent (s 1044 sentence 1 ZPO). The commencement of arbitration proceedings has the legal effect of suspending the applicable limitation period (s 204(1) no 11 BGB).

---

[141] Explanatory Memorandum on the draft Bill of the Arbitration Law Reform Act, BT-Drucksache 13/5274, 47.

[142] Sachs, K. and Lörcher, T. in K.-H. Böckstiegel, S. Kröll, and P. Nacimiento (eds) (n 6) s 1044 para 8 with further references.

[143] *ibid*, 303 ff para 8 with further references.

(1.2) When is a time limit according to statutes of limitations deemed to be interrupted in case of (i) *ad hoc*; and (ii) institutional arbitration? In order to suspend the limitation period, s 1044 ZPO only requires the receipt of the request for arbitration by the respondent. German arbitration law does not require the nomination of an arbitrator.[144] Yet, the parties may agree otherwise on a certain point in time, on which the arbitration is deemed to commence (s 1044 ZPO). The parties can reach such an agreement in *ad hoc* proceedings by virtue of an individual agreement. However, more frequently the agreement will result from the parties' agreement on institutional arbitration rules. For example, s 6.1 of the DIS Rules provides that arbitral proceedings commence upon receipt of the statement of claim by the DIS Secretariat. Section 6.2 of the DIS Rules furthermore provides that the statement of claim contain the nomination of the arbitrator, unless the parties have agreed on a decision by a sole arbitrator. **7.83**

(1.3) What is the effect of the withdrawal of the request for arbitration? Section 1056(2) no 1(b) ZPO implicitly acknowledges the claimant's right to withdraw the request for arbitration. The arbitral tribunal shall issue an order for the termination of the arbitral proceedings when the claimant withdraws his claim, unless the respondent objects thereto and the arbitral tribunal recognizes a legitimate interest on his part in obtaining a final settlement of the dispute (s 1056(2) no 1(b) ZPO). In determining whether the respondent has a legitimate interest in the final settlement of the dispute, the arbitral tribunal shall consider, at which stage the arbitration proceedings are and, in particular, if the claimant merely tries to avoid a certain outcome by withdrawing his request for arbitration.[145] Moreover, the arbitral tribunal shall consider the respondent's interest in not again having to defend itself in arbitral proceedings on the same matter.[146] The effect of the withdrawal is that the claimant can raise the claim again in subsequent proceedings unless the claimant waives his claim or enters into a binding undertaking not to raise the claim again. **7.84**

(2) Legal deadlines (provided by law or set by the tribunal) and effect of non-compliance by a party

German arbitration law provides for no specific deadlines regarding the submissions of the parties. Rather, the claimant and the respondent must submit their statement of claim and defence within the period of time agreed by the parties or determined by the arbitral tribunal (s 1046 (1) sentence 1 ZPO). Should the claimant exceptionally fail to communicate his statement of claim in accordance with s 1046(1) ZPO, the arbitral tribunal shall, in general, terminate the proceedings (s 1048(1) ZPO). If the respondent fails to timely communicate his statement of defence, the arbitral tribunal shall continue the proceedings without treating such failure in itself as an admission of the claimant's allegations (s 1048(2) ZPO). **7.85**

With respect to the appointment of arbitrators, German arbitration law provides for default deadlines. For example, if a party fails to appoint the arbitrator within one month of receipt **7.86**

---

[144] Sachs, K. and Lörcher, T. in K.-H. Böckstiegel, S. Kröll, and P. Nacimiento (eds) (n 6) 304 ff para 11 with further references.

[145] cf Lachmann. J.-P. (n 22) paras 1849 ff.

[146] von Schlabrendorff, F. and Sessler, A. in K.-H. Böckstiegel, S. Kröll, and P. Nacimiento (eds) (n 6) 412 ff para 8.

of a request to do so from the other party, or if the two arbitrators fail to agree on the third arbitrator within one month of their appointment, the appointment shall be made, upon request of a party, by the court (s 1035(3) sentence 3 ZPO).

7.87 In addition, there are certain deadlines for the exercise of legal remedies. For example, requests for a substitute appointment by the courts because of an alleged defective composition of the arbitral tribunal must be submitted at the latest within two weeks of the party becoming aware of the constitution of the arbitral tribunal (s 1034(2) sentence 2 ZPO). Unless the parties have agreed otherwise, an application for setting aside an award may not be made after three months have elapsed (s 1059(3) sentence 1 ZPO).

7.88 **(2.1) What are the powers of the tribunal if a party fails to comply with the time limits set up by the tribunal?** Section 1046(2) ZPO empowers the arbitral tribunal to reject any late amendments or supplements of claim and defence during the course of the proceedings if they would delay the proceedings without sufficient justification. If any party fails to appear at an oral hearing or to produce documentary evidence within a set time limit, the arbitral tribunal may continue the proceedings and make the award on the evidence before it (s 1048(3) ZPO). The parties may agree otherwise on the consequences of default (s 1048(4) sentence 2 ZPO).

7.89 **(2.2) Is the tribunal bound by any mandatory time limits for certain procedural steps (eg hearings, making of the award)?** German arbitration law stipulates for the arbitral tribunal almost no mandatory time limits for arbitral proceedings. Rather, s 1042(4) ZPO clarifies that, absent an agreement by the parties, the arbitral tribunal is empowered to conduct the arbitration in such a manner, as it considers appropriate. One exception to this rule is contained in s 1058(3) ZPO dealing with the correction and interpretation of awards. Section 1058(3) ZPO provides that the arbitral tribunal shall make the correction or give the interpretation of the award within one month and make an additional award within two months.

(3) Statutory requirements as to notifications during arbitration (with respect to the request for arbitration and other written pleadings; with respect to notifications by the tribunal)

7.90 In case oral hearings or any other meetings of the arbitral tribunal for the purpose of taking evidence are conducted, the parties must be given sufficient notice in advance (s 1047(2) ZPO). Furthermore, all statements, documents or information supplied by one party to the arbitral tribunal as well as any expert report or evidentiary documents must be communicated to both parties (s 1047(3) ZPO).

(4) Effect of the insolvency of a party

7.91 Under German insolvency law, in case of a party's insolvency the insolvency administrator as trustee will gain control of the debtor's assets and will reorganize or liquidate these assets. The German courts have constantly ruled that an arbitration agreement extends to this trustee and remains unaffected by the insolvency of one party.[147] Only in the exercise of his

[147] BGH, 28 February 1957, BGHZ 24, 15, 18; OLG Cologne, 13 November 2007, [2008] SchiedsVZ 152, 154; cf Schlosser, P. in F. Stein and M. Jonas (eds) (n 24) s 1029 para 35; Eberl, W., 'Das Schiedsverfahren in der Insolvenz' [2002] *InVo* 393 ff.

insolvency contestation rights is the insolvency administrator not bound by the arbitration agreement (*Insolvenzanfechtungsrecht*).[148]

Section 240 ZPO, according to which court proceedings are automatically interrupted if one party becomes insolvent, is not applicable with regard to arbitral proceedings.[149] Nevertheless, the arbitral tribunal, in accordance with the principle of due process, is required to grant the insolvency administrator sufficient time to decide whether and how to continue the proceedings.[150] Moreover, special consideration must be given to the principle of equal treatment of creditors laid down in German insolvency law. This principle demands every creditor to register his insolvency claim with the insolvency administrator and limits individual proceedings to those aiming at a declaratory judgment on the existence of the claim. Registered claims will then be settled in accordance with the applicable insolvency quota. The respective provisions (ss 87, 174, 184 of the German Insolvency Code [*Insolvenzordnung*—'InsO']) are considered part of the German *ordre public*.[151] **7.92**

D. Facts and evidence: general

(1) Burden of proof (inquisitorial/adversarial procedure)

German arbitration law leaves it to the discretion of the parties and the arbitral tribunal to decide whether the arbitration will be conducted in an inquisitorial civil law style or in an adversarial common law style manner. In particular, the arbitral tribunal has the discretion to either play a rather active role in conducting the arbitration, which is self-evident from a German lawyer's perspective, or to conduct the proceedings in a common law style, or to combine elements from different systems of law in the proceedings.[152] In international proceedings, arbitral tribunals can be expected to make use of their wide discretion with regard to the conduct of the proceedings in order to meet the parties' individual expectations and the needs of each particular case. **7.93**

The issue of the burden of proof is considered to be part of the applicable substantive law.[153] **7.94**

The arbitral proceedings are governed by the principle of limited judicial investigation (*beschränkter Untersuchungsgrundsatz*), ie the arbitral tribunal is entitled to establish the facts of the case by all appropriate means.[154] This does, however, not absolve the parties to present the relevant facts and evidence exhaustively to the arbitral tribunal in order to establish their case and to comply with the burden of proof.[155] **7.95**

(2) Power of the tribunal to determine the admissibility and weight of the evidence produced by the parties

As a general rule, absent an agreement by the parties, the arbitral tribunal may determine the admissibility of taking evidence, take evidence and assess freely such evidence (s 1042 **7.96**

[148] See only BGH, 20 November 2003, [2004] ZInsO 88.
[149] OLG Cologne, 13 November 2007, [2008] SchiedsVZ 152, 154 with further references.
[150] Schlosser, P. in F. Stein and M. Jonas (eds) (n 24) s 1042 para 35; Lachmann, J.-P. (n 22) para 1278.
[151] cf BGH, 29 January 2009, BGHZ 179, 304 ff NJW 2009, 1747 ff.
[152] Sachs, K. and Lörcher, T. in K.-H. Böckstiegel, S. Kröll, and P. Nacimiento (eds) (n 6) 290 ff paras 34 ff with further references.
[153] Schack, H. (n 132) para 674; Leipold, D. in F. Stein and M. Jonas (eds) (n 24) s 286 para 79.
[154] Sachs, K. and Lörcher, T. in K.-H. Böckstiegel, S. Kröll, and P. Nacimiento (eds) (n 6) 289 para 31.
[155] Lachmann, J.-P. (n 22) para 1288.

(4) sentence 2 ZPO). In making these determinations the arbitral tribunal is not bound by the restrictions of the ZPO regarding the admissibility and weight of evidence in state court proceedings.[156] On the other hand, s 1042(1) ZPO requires the arbitral tribunal to treat the parties with equality and to give each party full opportunity to present its case. Specifically, the parties must have the right to comment on any evidence considered by the arbitral tribunal.

7.97 There are, however, limits on the powers of the arbitral tribunal. Firstly and foremost, a common agreement of the parties concerning the conduct of the proceedings will prevail (s 1042(3) and (4) ZPO). Secondly, the arbitral tribunal has no compulsory powers (*Zwangsgewalt*), ie the arbitral tribunal cannot force witnesses or experts to appear, it cannot force non-cooperative parties to produce documents, and it does not have the right to administer oaths or affirmations in lieu of an oath.[157]

7.98 (2.1) **Is the tribunal entitled to take the claimant's factual allegation as proven if the defendant does not participate in the arbitral proceedings?** Section 1048(2) ZPO stipulates that in case the respondent does not participate timely in the arbitral proceedings, the arbitral tribunal may not treat such failure in itself as an admission of the claimant's allegations. The expression 'in itself' indicates, though, that the arbitral tribunal may render an award against the respondent if it independently reaches the conclusion that the claimant's claim is justified.[158] The parties may agree otherwise on the consequences of default, which, in practice, however, rarely happens (s 1048(4) sentence 2 ZPO).

7.99 (2.2) **May the arbitral tribunal consider an allegation of one party as agreed fact if the other party did not (specifically) dispute the allegation?** Beyond the rules of default contained in s 1048 ZPO, German arbitration law does not contain specific rules on whether the arbitral tribunal is entitled to take one party's factual allegation as proven if the other party does not specifically dispute the allegation. In view of the fact that the failure to submit a statement of defence may not as such be considered as an admission of the claimant's allegations, it would appear inconsistent if the arbitral tribunal was entitled to consider an allegation of one party automatically as agreed fact if the other party did not specifically dispute the allegation. Rather, the arbitral tribunal may only treat a fact as an agreed fact if the arbitral tribunal is convinced that the other side does not dispute the fact, eg because the correspondence between the parties shows that the party did not contradict or even expressly agreed to the allegation.[159]

7.100 (2.3) **What is the standard of proof that must be met in order for a fact to be considered to have been established (preponderance of the evidence; beyond reasonable doubt)? Must a stringent requirement be met for certain facts (for which ones)?** Under German law, the parties are free to agree on a certain standard of proof in arbitration proceedings.

[156] Schlosser, P. in F. Stein and M. Jonas (eds) (n 24) s 1042 para 1.

[157] Sachs, K. and Lörcher, T. in K.-H. Böckstiegel, S. Kröll, and P. Nacimiento (eds) (n 6) 292 para 39 with further references.

[158] Explanatory Memorandum on the draft Bill of the Arbitration Law Reform Act, BT-Drucksache 13/5274, 50.

[159] Sachs, K. and Lörcher, T. in K.-H. Böckstiegel, S. Kröll, and P. Nacimiento (eds) (n 6) 331 para 5 with further references.

However, since there usually exists no such specific agreement among the parties, it is regularly up to the arbitral tribunal to determine the applicable standard of proof. As the issue of standard of proof, under German law, contains elements of procedural and substantive law,[160] it is questionable whether the arbitral tribunal in an arbitration situated in Germany has to determine the applicable standard of proof as it considers appropriate (s 1042(4) ZPO) or in accordance with the applicable substantive law (s 1051 ZPO). If the arbitral tribunal applied German substantive law, the standard of proof would, in principle, be 'certainty beyond reasonable doubt'; 'preponderance of evidence' would not suffice.[161]

(2.4) May the arbitral tribunal rely on its own knowledge to consider certain facts as proven? German courts have repeatedly ruled that arbitral tribunals are allowed to rely on their own knowledge in order to establish certain facts.[162] This is based on the assumption that arbitrators are generally appointed because of their superior knowledge and experience in the specific field of business to which the dispute relates. In order to secure the parties' right to a fair hearing (s 1042(1) ZPO), the arbitral tribunal is required to give the parties advance notice and opportunity to comment on the facts that the arbitral tribunal wishes to rely on in its own knowledge.[163] **7.101**

E. Witnesses

(1) Ability of a person to act as a witness

In German arbitration law there are no specific rules concerning the ability of a person to act as witness. Whereas for court proceedings specific rules concerning witnesses, for example a right of refusal to testify (*Zeugnisverweigerungsrecht*), exist (ss 373 ff ZPO), no such rules exist for arbitration proceedings. Hence, it is first of all up to the parties to agree on issues relating to the taking of evidence (s 1042(3) ZPO). Absent an agreement of the parties, the arbitral tribunal will determine the appropriate procedure for the examination of the witnesses (s 1042(4) ZPO). In particular, in international arbitrations, the arbitral tribunal may, for example, wish to consider the IBA Rules on the Taking of Evidence.[164] **7.102**

(1.1) Is there a legal difference between a party testifying and a witness? If yes, what are the criteria for such differentiation? Does the testifying of a party have the same weight as a witness testimony? In German arbitration law there is no distinction between a testifying party and a witness. Whereas for court proceedings a clear distinction between parties and witnesses exists, there is no such differentiation in arbitral proceedings. Rather, the arbitral tribunal may hear a party as any other witness and admit the testimony of a party.[165] However, when assessing the probative value of the testimony, the arbitral **7.103**

---

[160] Schütze, R., *Deutsches Internationales Zivilprozessrecht unter Einschluss des Europäischen Zivilprozessrechts* (2nd edn, de Gruyter, 2005) 132 with further references.

[161] Greger, R. in R. Zöller (n 13) s 286 para 18 ff.

[162] BGH, 12 December 1963, [1964] NJW 593, 595; BGH, 11 November 1982, BGHZ 85, 288, 293; BGH, 29 September 1983, [1983] WM 1207, 1208; BGH, 21 December 1989, available at <http://www.juris.de>.

[163] cf BGH, 8 October 1959, BGHZ 31, 45 ff.

[164] Sachs, K. and Lörcher, T. in K.-H. Böckstiegel, S. Kröll, and P. Nacimiento (eds) (n 6) 327 para 24.

[165] Schlosser, P. in F. Stein and M. Jonas (eds) (n 24) s 1042 para 11; Lachmann, J.-P. (n 22) para 1490; Voit, W. in H.-J. Musielak (ed) (n 59) s 1042 para 25.

tribunal has to take into account a personal interest of the witness or party in the outcome of the case, if any.[166]

(2) Preparation of witnesses and limits thereof

7.104 As a general rule, preparation of witnesses is admissible.[167] Yet, witness preparation has its limits, where it amounts to witness manipulation or the fabrication of evidence.[168] Furthermore, witness preparation may lower the witness' credibility.[169]

7.105 (2.1) **Do US-style depositions violate any procedural rules or principles?** US-style depositions seem to be permissible as long as the parties' right to be heard and their right to equal treatment are respected. However, depositions are not customary in German arbitrations and the arbitral tribunal can be expected to examine the witness later itself.

7.106 (2.2) **May a party or its counsel approach a witness whom it has nominated (only before or also after the proceeding has started)? Are interviews permitted?** In general, a party or a counsel may approach its witness before or after the proceedings have commenced because such contact is *per se* not prohibited. Yet, the same rules apply as to the preparation of witnesses, meaning that active influence aimed at obtaining false testimony is forbidden.[170]

7.107 Interviews of the witness by the parties and their counsel are also permitted in arbitrations situated in Germany.[171]

(3) Admissibility of written witness statements

7.108 Pursuant to the general rule of s 1042(4) sentence 2 ZPO and absent an agreement of the parties, it is in the discretion of the arbitral tribunal to determine whether or not written witness statements shall be admitted. In practice, arbitral tribunals decide on this question taking into account the legal background of the parties and the specifics of the case. At least in international arbitrations, witness statements have become widely accepted practice.[172] There are no formal requirements that must be met for written witness statements, but they should be signed by the witness in order to ensure authenticity.[173]

7.109 (3.1) **If the parties agree on written statements, is a party entitled to request an oral hearing for questioning those witnesses (provided such right has not explicitly been agreed upon)?** Since the parties are generally free to regulate the arbitral proceedings themselves, they are competent to exclude oral hearings. In a case where the parties have agreed that no hearings should be held, the arbitral tribunal generally must not allow such hearings and the questioning of witnesses (s 1047(1) sentence 2 ZPO). However, the arbitral tribunal

---

166 Sachs, K. and Lörcher, T. in K.-H. Böckstiegel, S. Kröll, and P. Nacimiento (eds) (n 6) 322 para 11.

167 Lachmann, J.-P. (n 22) para 1513 with reference to Art 4.3 IBA Rules on the Taking of Evidence; Schlosser, P., 'Verfahrensrechtliche und berufsrechtliche Zulässigkeit der Zeugenvorbereitung' [2004] *SchiedsVZ* 225, 228.

168 Lachmann, J.-P. (n 22) para 1515 with further references.

169 Sachs, K. and Lörcher, T. in K.-H. Böckstiegel, S. Kröll, and P. Nacimiento (eds) (n 6) 323 para 14.

170 cf Lachmann, J.-P. (n 22) para 1515.

171 Lachmann, J.-P. (n 22) para 1508.

172 Sachs. K. and Lörcher, T. in K.-H. Böckstiegel, S. Kröll, and P. Nacimiento (eds) (n 6) 323 para 13.

173 Schwab, K.H. and Walter, G. (n 3) ch 15 para 16.

has to take into account its obligation to give each party a full opportunity of presenting his case (s 1042(1) ZPO). In particular, if a party provides sufficient reasons for the request to question a witness, the arbitral tribunal is well advised to allow an oral hearing in order to ensure the party's right to be heard.

(4) Entitlement of a party to have a hearing or cross-examination of witnesses

Similarly, absent the parties' agreement, it lies within the discretion of the arbitral tribunal to allow a cross-examination of witnesses (s 1042(4) ZPO). Even though cross-examinations are alien to German civil procedure, the parties' and the arbitrators' autonomy to determine the arbitral procedure allows provisions for such interrogations.[174] For the purpose of ensuring procedural fairness and allowing preparation for the interrogation, the arbitral tribunal should give prior notice to the witness and the parties if a cross-examination is envisaged. Moreover, the arbitral tribunal should pay particular attention to the parties' equal treatment if one of the parties, owing to its original civil law background, is not in the same command of these techniques as a common law-trained opponent. **7.110**

(4.1) Which are the methods used to establish a record of the arbitral proceedings, in particular witness examinations (tape recording, verbatim court reporters, dictated minutes, other methods)? Absent an agreement by the parties, it lies within the discretion of the arbitral tribunal whether or not and how the arbitral tribunal wishes to establish a record of the arbitral proceedings.[175] In practice, most arbitral tribunals will establish a record of the arbitral proceedings and of the witness examination in order to establish proof for the course of the proceedings. Whether the arbitral tribunal will resort to tape recording, verbatim court reporters, dictated minutes or a short summary protocol will depend on the nature and complexity of the dispute and other particularities of the case. **7.111**

(4.2) May the arbitral tribunal take an oath from a witness? Under German law, arbitral tribunals may not take an oath from a witness.[176] Yet, arbitral tribunals—and a party with the approval of the arbitral tribunal—may request assistance of the state courts with regard to all judicial acts the arbitral tribunal is not empowered to carry out itself (s 1050 sentence 1 ZPO), including the administration of oath or the affirmation in lieu of an oath.[177] **7.112**

(4.3) Does the arbitral tribunal have the power to compel witnesses? The arbitral tribunal has no power to compel witnesses.[178] Also in this respect, the arbitral tribunal must rely on the assistance of the state courts (s 1050 ZPO). **7.113**

F. Documents

(1) Form and kind of documents to be presented to the arbitral tribunal

In general, it lies within the discretion of the arbitral tribunal to decide, what kind of documents and in which form documents are to be presented to the arbitral tribunal **7.114**

---

174 Voit, W. in H.-J. Musielak (ed) (n 59) s 1042 para 23.

175 Schlosser, P. in F. Stein and M. Jonas (eds) (n 24) s 1042 para 29.

176 Explanatory Memorandum on the draft Bill of the Arbitration Law Reform Act, BT-Drucksache 13/5274, 51.

177 Sachs, K. and Lörcher, T. in K.-H. Böckstiegel, S. Kröll, and P. Nacimiento (eds) (n 6) 292 para 39.

178 Lachmann, J.-P. (n 17) para 1583.

(s 1042(4) ZPO). In practice, the parties must usually submit all documents on which they rely to the arbitral tribunal. The production of the document's original is only required if the other party validly contests its existence. With regard to the language of documents, the arbitral tribunal may order that any documentary evidence shall be accompanied by a translation into the language of the arbitral proceedings (s 1045(2) ZPO).

7.115 (1.1) **Is the submission of 'agreed documents' permitted? If yes, what is the extent and effect of such an agreement of the parties (authenticity, existence, acknowledgement of such documents' contents)?** In order to expedite the production of documents, the parties are free to agree on any form of organizing the files, including the submission of 'agreed documents'. This may be particularly recommended when a large number of documents is to be introduced to the proceedings. The parties' agreement on the authenticity or the content of documents usually binds the arbitral tribunal, in particular if the parties have made clear that they do not wish any further taking of evidence.[179]

7.116 (1.2) **How may electronic documents (eg emails) be presented and proven?** Pursuant to s 1042(4) ZPO and absent an agreement of the parties, the arbitral tribunal has discretion to decide on the way electronic documents shall be presented and proven. In regular arbitral practice, a paper record is the rule, and the parties will be asked to produce a copy of emails and other electronic data and present it to the arbitral tribunal. In particularly complex arbitrations, the arbitral tribunal may wish to seek consent with the parties to establish virtual data rooms with electronic access to the documents.

7.117 (1.3) **Does discovery (US- or UK-style), after the procedure has started, violate any procedural rules or public policy considerations?** In general, US- and UK-style discovery are alien to German civil procedure. When the arbitration is seated in Germany, it is most likely that the parties did not intend to allow for extensive discovery such as 'fishing expeditions'.

7.118 It is possible for the parties to agree to a full US- or UK-style discovery procedure.[180] In contrast, it is debatable whether, absent the parties' agreement, the arbitral tribunal may *ex officio* order a US-style discovery.[181] As doubts still seem to prevail, the arbitral tribunal is well advised to ensure the parties' agreement with discovery proceedings in order to prevent the risk of a later challenge of the award.[182]

(2) Requirement to produce certain documents (as requested by the tribunal) and consequences of a failure to do so

7.119 The arbitral tribunal lacks compulsory powers to force a party to produce documents. The arbitral tribunal's possibilities to request a state court to compel a party to produce a

---

[179] Voit, W. in H.-J. Musielak (ed) (n 59) s 1042 para 21 with further references.

[180] Sachs, K. and Lörcher, T. in K.-H. Böckstiegel, S. Kröll, and P. Nacimiento (eds) (n 6) 326 para 23.

[181] Voit, W. in H.-J. Musielak (ed) (n 58) s 1042 para 25; Schütze, R., 'Die Ermessensgrenzen des Schiedsgerichts bei der Bestimmung der Beweisregeln' [2006] *SchiedsVZ* 1 ff; Schütze, R., 'Two Issues of Taking Evidence in International Arbitration Under Civil and Common Law Systems—Production of Documents and Examination of Witnesses' in R. Schütze (ed), *Ausgewählte Probleme des deutschen und internationalen Schiedsverfahrensrechts* (Carl Heymanns, 2006) 71, 77 ff; Wirth, M., 'Ihr Zeuge, Herr Rechtsanwalt!—Weshalb Civil-Law-Schiedsrichter Common-Law-Verfahrensrecht anwenden' [2003] *SchiedsVZ* 9 ff.

[182] Sachs, K. and Lörcher, T. in K.-H. Böckstiegel, S. Kröll, and P. Nacimiento (eds) (n 6) 326 para 23.

document pursuant to s 1050 ZPO are also limited.[183] Yet, the arbitral tribunal may continue the proceedings and make the award on the evidence before it (s 1048(3) ZPO). When making the award, the arbitral tribunal may treat the failure to produce documentary evidence without a valid excuse as an admission of the other party's allegation.[184] Similarly, Art 9(4) of the IBA Rules on the Taking of Evidence provides that the arbitral tribunal may infer that a document is adverse to interests of a party if the party fails to produce the document without satisfactory explanation.

(2.1) Which documents may the tribunal request to be produced (eg also documents, which are in the possession of third parties)? It is questionable, whether the arbitral tribunal, at least by means of an application to the courts based on s 1050, ZPO, has the possibility to compel a third party to produce documents. Owing to the consensual character of arbitration, there are convincing reasons to argue that the arbitral tribunal cannot direct any orders to any third party that is not party to the arbitration agreement. Other authors, however, take the view that the arbitral tribunal can ask the court for all kinds of assistance that are available to the court itself, including orders for the production of documents against third parties in accordance with s 142 ZPO.[185] **7.120**

(3) Protection of the confidentiality of documents (legal privilege etc)

As no general disclosure obligation exists under German law, German law lacks corresponding detailed regulations on confidentiality and privilege. Rather, rules regarding legal privilege may only be deducted from certain substantive law provisions. Most importantly, s 203 of the German Penal Code (*Strafgesetzbuch*—'StGB') stipulates criminal sanctions for certain professionals, including doctors and lawyers, in case they disclose any information without the permission of their client, which they obtained from a client in the context of their profession. Moreover, the arbitral tribunal is empowered to issue certain protective orders or employ a neutral person in the evaluation of evidence for the purpose of protecting the confidentiality of documents and to preserve trade secrets.[186] **7.121**

G. Experts

(1) Appointment and presentation of experts by the party or the arbitral tribunal

Section 1049 ZPO stipulates the principle that, under German arbitration law, experts are appointed by the arbitral tribunal. The arbitral tribunal may appoint one or more experts to report to it on specific issues to be determined by the arbitral tribunal, unless the parties agreed otherwise (s 1049(1) sentence 1 ZPO). The arbitral tribunal may also require a party to give the expert any relevant information or to produce, or to provide access to, any relevant documents or property for his inspection (s 1049(2) sentence 1 ZPO). The arbitral tribunal's power does not prevent the parties from appointing their own experts.[187] **7.122**

[183] Geimer, R. in R. Zöller (n 13) s 427 para 2.
[184] Sachs, K. and Lörcher, T. in K.-H. Böckstiegel, S. Kröll, and P. Nacimiento (eds) (n 6) 323 para 10.
[185] Lachmann, J.-P. (n 22) para 1578.
[186] cf Derains, Y. and Schwartz, E.A., *A Guide to the new ICC Rules of Arbitration* (Kluwer Law International, 1998) 264 ff.
[187] Sachs, K. and Lörcher, T. in K.-H. Böckstiegel, S. Kröll, and P. Nacimiento (eds) (n 6) 336 para 3.

7.123 **(1.1) By which methods are tribunal-appointed experts selected? What are the rights of the parties during the selection process?** The methods, by which tribunal-appointed experts are to be selected, are not regulated by German arbitration law. Nevertheless, the arbitral tribunal will often voluntarily take the equivalent provision for German court proceedings in s 404 ZPO as a guideline, which provides for certain selection criteria, such as making primary use of officially nominated experts.

7.124 No consent of the parties is necessary in order to select a tribunal-appointed expert. However, it is advisable and common practice to involve the parties in the selection process. If both parties agree on one expert or unanimously reject a certain expert, the arbitral tribunal is obliged to appoint or exclude this person because of the party autonomy's prerogative.[188]

(2) Admissibility and role of expert witnesses

7.125 Absent a contrary agreement, the parties may introduce their own expert witnesses in order to challenge the findings of the tribunal-appointed expert or to emphasize the parties' positions (s 1049 (2) sentence 2 ZPO). Some German scholars argue that the testimony of expert witnesses has almost no evidentiary value, as party-appointed experts unlike tribunal-appointed experts are expected to support the party appointing them.[189] However, even if this may be true in a number of cases, in other instances the testimony of a party-appointed expert may indeed be considered as full evidence in case the expert witness renders an impartial and convincing report.

(3) Influence of the parties upon the selection of questions to be submitted to the expert

7.126 In general, the selection of questions to be submitted to the tribunal-appointed expert will be determined by the arbitral tribunal alone (s 1049(1) sentence 1 ZPO). However, absent an opposite agreement by the parties, the parties may request an oral examination of the expert, in the course of which the parties are allowed to ask their own questions (s 1049(2) ZPO). Where the parties agreed to present their own expert witnesses, each party is competent to set up the terms of reference for the respective expert on its own.

(4) Independence and impartiality of the expert and the right to reject a proposed/ appointed expert

7.127 The statutory rules regarding the challenge of arbitrators and the challenge procedure apply *mutatis mutandis* to tribunal-appointed experts (s 1049(3) ZPO). Specifically, tribunal-appointed experts are required to disclose any circumstances likely to give rise to justifiable doubts as to their impartiality or independence. Moreover, they must possess the qualifications agreed upon by the parties.

7.128 The motion to challenge an expert must be raised in a timely manner, ie within two weeks after becoming aware of the expert's appointment or after becoming aware of the circumstance giving rise to the challenge (s 1037(1) ZPO). The only difference between the challenge of arbitrators and experts—based on the fact that s 1037(3) ZPO is not declared

---

188 cf Lachmann, J.-P. (n 22) para 1536.

189 See eg Voit, W. in H.-J. Musielak (ed) (n 58) s 1049 para 11.

applicable by s 1049 ZPO—is that the challenge of an expert cannot be submitted to a state court in case the arbitral tribunal has rejected the challenge. Nonetheless, such rejection might open the possibility to challenge the award afterwards and the arbitral tribunal will therefore usually consider its decision with care.[190]

(4.1) May a party or its counsel approach an expert (or expert witness) whom it has nominated (only before or also after the proceeding has started)? Are interviews admissible? Party-appointed experts may be interviewed and approached by a party or its counsel before and after the proceedings have started, as the expert is deemed to be acting in one party's support anyway. However, the more influence the party exerts on the expert, the less weight the arbitral tribunal will ascribe to the expert's testimony. Hence, in order to ensure the value of the expert report issued by the expert witness, a party is well advised to restrain its communication with the expert. As with regard to the preparation and interviewing of witnesses, expert manipulation and fabrication of evidence is inadmissible. **7.129**

(5) Oral examination of an expert in a hearing

Unless otherwise agreed by the parties, if a party so requests or if the arbitral tribunal considers it necessary, the expert shall, after delivery of his written or oral report, participate in an oral hearing where the parties have the opportunity to put questions to him and to present expert witnesses in order to testify on the points at issue (s 1049(2) ZPO).[191] **7.130**

H. Interim measures of protection

(1) Kind of interim measures which the tribunal may order

At the request of a party, the arbitral tribunal may order such interim measures of protection as it considers necessary in respect of the subject matter of the dispute, unless the parties agreed otherwise (s 1041(1) sentence 1 ZPO). The arbitral tribunal is not limited to interim measures of protection available to German courts, ie attachment (*Arrest*) or preliminary injunction (*einstweilige Verfügung*).[192] Rather, the arbitral tribunal may grant all necessary measures, such as pre-award attachment orders or freezing injunctions. Under very exceptional circumstances, if there is no other way to secure interim relief, the arbitral tribunal is also competent to preliminarily grant the relief sought for in the main proceedings.[193] **7.131**

(1.1) Which are, in general, the procedural and substantive prerequisites for the ordering of interim and conservatory measures (eg reduced degree of evidence; urgency; summary evaluation of the claim)? The procedural prerequisites for the ordering of interim measures under German law are, first of all, (i) a party's application; and (ii) the arbitral tribunal's jurisdiction. Under German arbitration law, the arbitral tribunal can grant an interim measure only on the motion of a party and not *ex officio*.[194] In addition, the arbitral tribunal must satisfy that is has prima facie jurisdiction concerning the subject matter and **7.132**

[190] Explanatory Memorandum on the draft Bill of the Arbitration Law Reform Act, BT-Drucksache 13/5274, 51.

[191] Lachmann, J.-P. (n 22) para 1545.

[192] Schroth, H.-J.,'Einstweiliger Rechtsschutz im deutschen Schiedsverfahren' [2003] *SchiedsVZ* 102, 103.

[193] See eg OLG Frankfurt, 5 April 2001, [2001] NJW-RR 1078.

[194] Lachmann, J.-P. (n 22) para 2900.

the scope of the interim measure. For example, the arbitral tribunal is not entitled to direct an interim measure against a third party not being party to the arbitration agreement.

7.133 The substantive prerequisites for ordering an interim measure are *expressis verbis* limited to the 'necessity' requirement stipulated in s 1041 ZPO. In practice, this requirement is often understood to mean that there is a risk that the applicant's rights might be violated.[195] Moreover, s 1041 ZPO requires that the interim measure relate to the subject matter of the dispute. In addition, the interim measure may, in general, not pre-empt the dispute,[196] unless the applicant would otherwise suffer irreparable harm.[197]

7.134 The standard of proof in interim relief proceedings is that the applicant has to make a prima facie showing (*Glaubhaftmachung*) that his allegations are correct.[198]

7.135 If an interim measure of protection ordered by the arbitral tribunal proves to have been unjustified from the outset, the party, who obtained its enforcement, is obliged to compensate the other party for damages resulting from the enforcement or from his security payment in order to avoid enforcement (s 1041(4) sentence 1 ZPO).

7.136 (1.2) **Are the prerequisites for interim measures ordered by the arbitral tribunal more or less the same as for those requested from the state court? Is there case law/legal authorities on whether those measures are faster and enforced more easily if taken by the arbitral tribunal or the state court?** The prerequisites for interim measures ordered by the court and by an arbitral tribunal differ. Whereas the arbitral tribunal has wide discretion to order any appropriate measure under the necessity requirement stipulated in s 1041 ZPO, the courts are subject to the strict statutory requirements for granting preliminary injunctions or attachments provided for in the ZPO.

7.137 In arbitral practice, the parties will in many cases nevertheless resort to the German courts to seek injunctive relief. Firstly, resort to the courts is the only option in all cases, in which the arbitral tribunal is not yet constituted. Secondly, German courts enjoy a high reputation of granting effective and prompt relief if a motion for injunctive relief is well founded. Finally, as the arbitral tribunal lacks compulsory powers to enforce interim measures, the courts are the right address for motions for interim relief in all cases, in which the opponent will in all likelihood not honour the arbitral tribunal's order voluntarily anyway. In contrast, an application for injunctive relief to the arbitral tribunal should be considered, where the arbitral tribunal is already constituted, the arbitral tribunal enjoys the parties' particular confidence in a competent and fast decision, and the order will be respected by both sides in regular course.

(2) Limits of the tribunal's power to order interim measures

7.138 An important limit of the arbitral tribunal's power to order interim measures can be deducted from s 1041(1) sentence 1 ZPO, according to which the interim measure must

[195] Kreindler, R. and Schäfer, J. in K.-H. Böckstiegel, S. Kröll, and P. Nacimiento (eds) (n 6) 266 para 12 with further references.

[196] Lachmann, J.-P. (n 22) para 2895.

[197] *ibid*, para 2896.

[198] Kreindler, R. and Schäfer, J. in K.-H. Böckstiegel, S. Kröll, and P. Nacimiento (eds) (n 6) 267 para 17 with further references.

relate to the subject matter. This is understood to exclude anti-suit injunctions as these measures serve to protect the arbitral process rather than the subject matter of the dispute.[199]

In addition, some legal scholars argue that the arbitral tribunal cannot grant *ex parte* orders.[200] According to the majority view, however, the arbitral tribunal is empowered to proceed *ex parte* without a prior oral hearing, as s 1063(3) ZPO even allows the presiding judge of the civil court to enforce an interim measure issued by a arbitral tribunal without a prior hearing of the other side.[201] In any event, the arbitral tribunal must give the opposing party *ex post* an effective opportunity to present its case.[202] **7.139**

(3) Orders to provide security for the costs of the proceeding

The arbitral tribunal may require any party to provide appropriate security for costs in connection with any interim measures of protection pursuant to s 1041(1) sentence 2 ZPO. As s 1041(1) sentence 1 ZPO empowers the arbitral tribunal to order any interim measures of protection that it considers necessary, the arbitral tribunal is also authorized to oblige the parties to provide security for the costs of the overall arbitral proceedings.[203] **7.140**

(4) Attachment of assets by an order of the tribunal

The arbitral tribunal may issue an order directed against a party to the arbitration not to dispose of the property in dispute.[204] In very exceptional cases, arbitral tribunals may even be competent to seize the respondent's property by way of an attachment (*Arrest*).[205] Owing to the intrusiveness of an attachment, arbitral tribunals should, however, be very cautious with such an order and not make too abundant use of this form of interim relief.[206] **7.141**

I. Assistance by the courts

(1) Extent of court assistance in the gathering of evidence

The courts assist the arbitral tribunal in the taking of evidence pursuant to the courts' rules on the taking of evidence, unless the courts regard an application for court assistance inadmissible (s 1050 sentence 2 ZPO). In order to determine the admissibility of the measure, courts are not entitled to review whether the requested measure, eg the taking of witness **7.142**

---

199 Kreindler, R. and Schäfer, J. in K.-H. Böckstiegel, S. Kröll, and P. Nacimiento (eds) (n 6) 266 para 13. On after-suit injunctions after the so-called *West Tankers* decision of the ECJ, 10 February 2009, Case C-185/07, *Allianz SpA (formerly Riunione Adriatica di Sicurtà SpA) and Generali Assicurazioni Generali SpA v West Tankers Inc*, see Seelmann-Eggebert, S., and Clifford, P., 'Lost at sea? Anti-suit injunctions after West Tankers' [2009] *SchiedsVZ* 139; Geimer, R. in R. Zöller (n 13) s 1041 para 1.

200 See eg Münch, J. in T. Rauscher, P. Wax and J. Wenzel (eds), *Münchener Kommentar zur Zivilprozessordnung* (3rd edn, CH Beck, 2008), s 1041 para 25.

201 See Lachmann, J.-P. (n 22) para 2906; Geimer, R. in R. Zöller (n 3) s 1041 para 1.

202 Kreindler, R. and Schäfer, J. in K.-H. Böckstiegel, S. Kröll, and P. Nacimiento (eds) (n 6) 268 para 19.

203 Sachs, K. and Lörcher, T. in K.-H. Böckstiegel, S. Kröll, and P. Nacimiento (eds) (n 6) 294 para 47.

204 OLG Frankfurt, 5 April 2001, [2001] NJW-RR 1078; H-J Schroth (n 192) 103.

205 Lachmann, J.-P. (n 22) para 2890; Voit, W. in H.-J. Musielak (ed) (n 58) s 1041 para 4.

206 Explanatory Memorandum on the draft Bill of the Arbitration Law Reform Act, BT-Drucksache 13/5274, 45.

evidence, is necessary for the proper conduct of the arbitral proceedings.[207] Yet, inadmissibility can be assumed, for example, if the arbitral tribunal itself would be able to undertake the requested measure, such as the determination of the amount in dispute.[208]

7.143 (1.1) **Is it for the arbitral tribunal or for the party to obtain the assistance of state courts with respect to the gathering of evidence?** The arbitral tribunal and the parties may request the assistance of the state courts with regard to the gathering of evidence or performance of other judicial acts (s 1050 sentence 1 ZPO). However, a party is only allowed to make such a request with the approval of the arbitral tribunal. This means that the arbitral tribunal has to agree to the request.[209]

7.144 (1.2) **According to case law and practical experience, are there considerable delays involved when asking a court to give assistance (eg for the obtaining of evidence)?** The competent court for rendering assistance in the taking of evidence is the Local Court (*Amtsgericht*—'AG'), in whose district the judicial act is to be carried out (s 1062(4) ZPO).[210]

7.145 So far, no incidents of considerable delays regarding the support granted by the German courts have been reported. The impression is rather that most parties and arbitrators are satisfied with the way German courts render the requested assistance.[211]

(2) Assistance for enforcing the attachment of assets

7.146 While the arbitral tribunal may order interim measures, only state courts may permit enforcement of the interim measures including attachment of assets upon request of a party (s 1041(2) ZPO). The competent court to grant leave for enforcement is the Higher Regional Court (*Oberlandesgericht* - OLG) (s 1062(1) no 3 ZPO). So far, there is no conclusive opinion on the extent of the courts' discretion to grant leave for enforcement[212] and, in particular, on the question of whether the courts are entitled not to permit enforcement if they find that the arbitral measure lacks proportionality.[213] In any event, the courts must refuse enforcement of any interim measures that are incompatible with German public policy.[214]

(3) Other examples of possible assistance

7.147 Section 1050 ZPO extends the possible court assistance to other judicial acts, which the arbitral tribunal is not empowered to carry out. Such other judicial acts include the application to government authorities for permission for a civil servant to testify or the ordering of

---

207 Sachs, K. and Lörcher, T. in K.-H. Böckstiegel, S. Kröll, and P. Nacimiento (eds) (n 6) 342 ff para 4 with further references.

208 *ibid*, 342 para 4 fn 10.

209 *ibid*, 342 para 3 with further references.

210 Explanatory Memorandum on the draft Bill of the Arbitration Law Reform Act, BT-Drucksache 13/5274, 51 and 64.

211 Wirth, M. and Hoffmann-Nowotny, U., 'Rechtshilfe deutscher Gerichte zugunsten ausländischer Schiedsgerichte bei der Beweisaufnahme—ein Erfahrungsbericht' [2005] *SchiedsVZ* 66, 69.

212 Lachmann, J.-P. (n 22) para 2917.

213 *ibid*, para 2920; Kreindler, R. and Schäfer, J. in K.-H. Böckstiegel, S. Kröll, and P. Nacimiento (eds) (n 6) 271 ff paras 31 ff.

214 Lachmann, J.-P. (n 22) para 2917; Kreindler, R. and Schäfer, J. in K.-H. Böckstiegel, S. Kröll, and P. Nacimiento (eds) (n 6) 272 para 33 with further references.

documents to be served by public notice in accordance with ss 185 ff ZPO (*öffentliche Zustellung*).[215]

According to the prevailing opinion among legal scholars,[216] an arbitral tribunal may also request the assistance of the state courts with regard to preliminary references to the European Court of Justice ('ECJ') under Art 234(2) of the Treaty establishing the European Community ('EC Treaty'). Such an 'indirect reference' to the ECJ by way of court assistance would accord to the ECJ's ruling in *Nordsee*, in which the ECJ expressly mentioned that state courts may be called upon in an arbitration to examine questions of Community law in the context of their collaboration with arbitral tribunals.[217] Furthermore, an 'indirect reference' would align with the practical implications of the ECJ's ruling in *Eco Swiss*, pursuant to which arbitral tribunals are to attend to Community law issues as an integral part of public policy in cases in which the award may be executed on Community territory.[218] **7.148**

In addition, German courts have developed the possibility to obtain assistance by state courts in cases where evidence might be lost prior to the constitution of the arbitral tribunal.[219] **7.149**

(4) Dependence of the power of state courts to intervene during the proceedings on the (national) procedural law applied by the arbitral tribunal

The court support provided for by s 1050 ZPO as well as the right to request interim measures of protection from the courts under s 1033 ZPO do not require that the place of arbitration be situated in Germany. Rather, said provisions apply irrespective of the seat of the arbitration (s 1025(2) ZPO).[220] **7.150**

V. The award

A. Types of award

(1) Interim award (eg on interim measures or the jurisdiction of the tribunal)

Interim awards do not contain a final decision but address in advance specific procedural or substantive issues, which are of relevance for the entire arbitration. Unlike partial awards, **7.151**

---

[215] Sachs, K. and Lörcher, T. in K.-H. Böckstiegel, S. Kröll, and P. Nacimiento (eds) (n 6) 341 para 1; Lachmann, J-P. (n 22) para 1621.

[216] See Schwab, K.H. and Walter, G. (n 3) ch 16 para 51; Schlosser, P. in F. Stein and M. Jonas (eds) (n 24) s 1050 para 4; Schütze, R., 'Die Vorlageberechtigung von Schiedsgerichten an den EuGH' [2007] *SchiedsVZ* 121, 124; for a critical view, see Lachmann, J.-P. (n 22) para 1626; Münch, J. in T. Rauscher, P. Wax and J. Wenzel (eds) (n 202) s 1050 para 11.

[217] ECJ, 23 March 1982, Case 102/81, *Nordsee Deutsche Hochseefischerei GmbH Bremerhafen v Reederei Mond Hochseefischerei Nordstern AG & Co KG et al* [1982] ECR 01095 para 14.

[218] ECJ, 1 June 1999, Case C-126/97, *Eco Swiss China Time Ltd v Benetton International NV*, [1999] ECR I-03055 paras 36 and 39; Blanke, G., 'The Role of EC Competition Law in International Arbitration: A *Plaidoyer*' [2005] *EBLR* 169, 175 ff; cf Schütze, R. (n 219) 124.

[219] OLG Koblenz, 15 July 1998, [1999] MDR 502.

[220] Explanatory Memorandum on the draft Bill of the Arbitration Law Reform Act, BT-Drucksache 13/5274, 31 and 51.

interim awards may neither be challenged nor enforced.[221] They are binding for the tribunal as regards its subsequent final decision.[222]

7.152 There is some dispute whether a tribunal's interim decision affirming jurisdiction under s 1040(3) ZPO constitutes an interim award or rather a preliminary ruling.[223] In any event, the decision may only be challenged by way of the specific procedure provided by s 1040(3) ZPO. By contrast, a decision denying jurisdiction is not an interim but a final decision, which may be reviewed in proceedings according to s 1059 ZPO.[224]

(2) Partial award

7.153 The tribunal has discretion to issue a partial award that disposes of certain parts of the dispute, if the legal issues at hand are separable from the remainder of the issues and ready for decision.[225] Partial awards must meet the same formal requirements as final awards, as laid down in s 1054 ZPO.[226] They can be separately challenged by (s 1059 ZPO) or enforced against a party (ss 1060, 1061 ZPO).[227]

7.154 **(2.1) Are awards, especially partial awards, binding in the same arbitral proceeding? Does it make a difference if, after the rendering of such a partial award, one arbitrator is successfully challenged and removed on grounds that prevailed even before the partial award was rendered?** Partial awards are final and binding for an arbitral tribunal. They have a binding effect to the extent that the award finally resolves a claim and fulfils all formal requirements pursuant to s 1054 ZPO.[228] If an arbitrator, after the rendering of the partial award, has been successfully challenged and removed on grounds that prevailed even before the partial award was made, the award will not be rendered void automatically but the aggrieved party may challenge the award in the courts.

(3) Final award

7.155 A final award disposes of all yet undecided issues presented in the arbitral proceedings.[229] The final award terminates the arbitral proceedings (s 1056(1) ZPO). It has the same effect between the parties as a final and binding court judgment (s 1055 ZPO)[230] and may be challenged by a party or enforced against a party in the procedures provided for in ss 1059 ff ZPO. The final award shall contain a decision on the costs of the arbitration (s 1057 ZPO).[231]

---

[221] Schwab, K.H. and Walter, G. (n 3) ch 18 para 10.

[222] Schlosser, P. in F. Stein and M. Jonas (eds) (n 24) s 1054 para 3.

[223] Voit, W. in H.-J. Musielak (ed) (n 58) s 1040 paras 8–9 and s 1054 para 2; Schwab, K.H. and Walter, G. (n 3) ch 18 para 10; S Kröll (n 2) 38.

[224] von Schlabrendorff, F. and Sessler, A. in K.-H. Böckstiegel, S. Kröll, and P. Nacimiento (eds) (n 6) 402 para 14 with further references.

[225] Lachmann, J.-P. (n 22) para 1719.

[226] BGH, 7 October 1953, [1953] NJW 1913, 1914; Geimer, R. in R. Zöller (n 13) s 1054 para 3.

[227] Voit, W. in H.-J. Musielak (ed) (n 58) s 1054 para 2 and s 1055 para 2; Kröll, S. (n 2) 37.

[228] von Schlabrendorff, F. and Sessler, A. in K.-H. Böckstiegel, S. Kröll, and P. Nacimiento (eds) (n 6) 401 para 10.

[229] *ibid*, 400 para 9.

[230] cf OLG Karlsruhe, 15 July 2008, [2008] *SchiedsVZ* 311 ff.

[231] Schwab, K.H. and Walter, G. (n 3) ch 18 para 5.

(3.1) If a party fails to participate in the arbitration, may the tribunal proceed and issue an award on the merits? Is such an award enforceable as any other award? Are there special remedies for the defendant at the enforcement stage? Section 1048(4) sentence 2 ZPO leaves the consequence of non-participation of a party in the arbitration to the discretion of the parties. Absent a party agreement on the issue of non-participation, the tribunal must not treat a failure to participate in itself as an admission of the other party's allegations, but may continue the proceedings and make the award on the evidence before it (s 1048 ZPO). The award will be enforceable as any other award. There are no special remedies for the respondent at the enforcement stage. **7.156**

B. Deliberations and agreement on the award

(1) Time limits (and possible extensions) for making the award

In German arbitration law there are no time limits for making the award. However, according to the principle of party autonomy, the parties may agree upon such time limits. **7.157**

(2) Procedure for the decision of the arbitrators (majority vote etc)

In arbitral proceedings with more than one arbitrator any decision of the tribunal shall be made, unless otherwise agreed by the parties, by a majority of its members (s 1052(1) ZPO). If an arbitrator refuses to take part in the vote, the other arbitrators may take the decision without him, unless otherwise agreed by the parties. The parties shall be given advance notice of the tribunal's intention to make an award without the arbitrator refusing to participate in the vote (s 1052(2) ZPO). **7.158**

A tie-breaking vote of the chairman is not foreseen in German arbitration law. The German legislator took the position that a tie-breaking mechanism could impede efforts to reach an amicable solution and could potentially deprive the other members of the tribunal of adequate influence.[232] **7.159**

(2.1) If an arbitrator fails or refuses to take part in oral deliberation meetings, although having been given sufficient notice of such meetings, may an award be rendered on the basis of written deliberations (or deliberations without this arbitrator) only? If an arbitrator refuses to take part in the deliberation and voting process, the other arbitrators are empowered to take decisions without him, thus effectively barring an arbitrator from delaying without valid reasons or even blocking the making of an award (s 1052(2) sentence 1 ZPO). The tribunal has to inform the parties of its intent to make an award without the defaulting arbitrator before it actually takes the vote (s 1052(2) sentence 2 ZPO). **7.160**

(3) Admissibility of dissenting opinions

German arbitration law does not contain an express provision on dissenting opinions. The majority view among German scholars, which is supported by the legislative materials relating to the new German arbitration law,[233] favours the idea that dissenting opinions are **7.161**

---

232 von Schlabrendorff, F. and Sessler, A. in K.-H. Böckstiegel, S. Kröll, and P. Nacimiento (eds) (n 6) 364 ff para 5.

233 Explanatory Memorandum on the draft Bill of the Arbitration Law Reform Act, BT-Drucksache 13/5274, 56.

generally permitted.[234] Others see a potential conflict with the fundamental principle of the secrecy of deliberations and argue that attaching a dissenting opinion to the award violates the confidentiality of deliberations and should therefore only be permitted if the arbitrators (in case of communication of the dissenting opinion to the parties) and/or the parties specifically agree to this effect.[235]

7.162 (3.1) **Are there any court decisions or positions of leading authorities on the issue of dissenting opinions (admissibility, disclosure to the parties and publication)?** There are no German court decisions conclusively dealing with the issue of dissenting opinions in arbitration proceedings. However, it is common understanding that an international arbitral award including a dissenting opinion is enforceable in Germany.[236]

(4) Signature by the arbitrators and potential failure of one arbitrator to sign

7.163 The award shall be signed by the sole arbitrator or the arbitrators (s 1054(1) sentence 1 ZPO). The signature requirement is mandatory, ie the parties are not free to deviate from it by agreement.[237]

7.164 If the tribunal consists of more than two arbitrators and one of them fails to sign, the signatures of the majority of all arbitrators are sufficient (s 1054(1) sentence 2 ZPO), provided that the reason for any omitted signature is stated in the award.

C. Form of the award and deposition

(1) Form and minimum contents of an award

7.165 The award shall be made in writing (s 1054(1) sentence 1 ZPO). The purpose behind this mandatory requirement is that there shall be certainty about the award's existence and content for both the tribunal and the parties during the decision-making process and after receipt of the award. Furthermore, the award has to be signed by the arbitrators (s 1054(1) sentence 1 ZPO). Moreover, it is recommended to name the award as an 'award'.[238]

(2) Requirement to give reasons in the award

7.166 The award shall state the reasons, upon which it is based (s 1054(2) ZPO), unless the parties have agreed that no reasons are to be given or the award is an award on agreed terms in terms of s 1053 ZPO. At the minimum, the statement of reasons requires that the tribunal comments at least briefly, not necessarily comprehensively, on the substance of the claims

---

[234] Kröll, S. (n 2) 39.

[235] cf Schütze, R., 'Dissenting opinions im Schiedsverfahren' in R. Schütze (ed) (n 181) 189, 197 (parties have to agree on this effect); Lachmann, J.-P. (n 22) para 1695 (arbitrators have to agree on this effect); but see Münch, J. in T. Rauscher, P. Wax and J. Wenzel (eds) (n 200) s 1054 para 22 (neither the parties nor the arbitrators may agree on this effect).

[236] Münch, J. in T. Rauscher, P. Wax and J. Wenzel (eds) (n 200) s 1054 para 22; von Schlabrendorff, F. and Sessler, A. in K.-H. Böckstiegel, S. Kröll, and P. Nacimiento (eds) (n 6) 395 para 19; but see Schütze, R. 'Dissenting opinions im Schiedsverfahren' in R. Schütze (ed) (n 181) 189, 198, who argues that the award can be set aside.

[237] Explanatory Memorandum on the draft Bill of the Arbitration Law Reform Act, BT-Drucksache 13/5274, 56.

[238] cf Lachmann, J.-P. (n 22) para 1741.

and defences.[239] A complete and exhaustive account of all relevant considerations is not required although many awards include an exhaustive and detailed reasoning.[240] A largely incomplete or entirely missing reasoning leaves the award open to challenge under s 1059 ZPO.[241]

(3) Necessity to specify place and time where and when the award was made

As an additional formal requirement for the award, the award shall state the date, on which it was rendered and the place of the arbitration (s 1054(3) ZPO). These data entail a non-rebuttable presumption that the award shall be deemed to have been made on that date and at that place.[242] **7.167**

The specification of the date provides for certainty with regard to the date, on which the award became existent. As far as the entering into effect for the parties and the time limit for challenging the award are concerned, the date of the award's communication rather than the date of the award is decisive.[243] **7.168**

The place of arbitration's specification is of considerable legal importance. For example, the question of whether an award is a foreign or domestic award depends on the place of arbitration. **7.169**

Failure to specify the date and the place of the award does not lead to the invalidity of the award but can be corrected.[244] **7.170**

(4) Other requirements (registration, delivery etc)

Section 1054(4) ZPO provides that a copy of the award signed by the arbitrators shall be delivered to each party. As such delivery does not have to meet the formal standards of service required in court proceedings,[245] postage by simple mail is sufficient. Nonetheless, it is advisable and common practice to send the copy of the award by registered mail or courier service including a return receipt.[246] **7.171**

(4.1) Does the award have to be laid down or registered with a state court or agency (even if it has been rendered according to a foreign procedural law)? German arbitration law does not require a domestic award to be deposited or registered with a state court or agency.[247] **7.172**

---

[239] von Schlabrendorff, F. and Sessler, A. in K.-H. Böckstiegel, S. Kröll, and P. Nacimiento (eds) (n 6) 390 para 9 with further references.

[240] *ibid*, para 9.

[241] Explanatory Memorandum on the draft Bill of the Arbitration Law Reform Act, BT-Drucksache 13/5274, 59 ff; Geimer, R. in R. Zöller (n 13) s 1059 para 45.

[242] Explanatory Memorandum on the draft Bill of the Arbitration Law Reform Act, BT-Drucksache 13/5274, 56; Voit, W. in H.-J. Musielak (ed) (n 58) s 1054 para 8.

[243] Voit, W. in H.-J. Musielak (ed) (n 58) s 1054 para 8.

[244] OLG Stuttgart, 4 June 2002, [2003] NJW-RR 1438, 1439; von Schlabrendorff, F. and Sessler, A. in K.-H. Böckstiegel, S. Kröll, and P. Nacimiento (eds) (n 6) 391 para 12.

[245] Schwab, K.H. and Walter, G. (n 3) ch 20 para 11.

[246] Kreindler, RH., Schäfer, J.K. and Wolff, R., *Schiedsgerichtsbarkeit, Kompendium für die Praxis* (Recht und Wirtschaft, 2006) para 1022.

[247] Explanatory Memorandum on the draft Bill of the Arbitration Law Reform Act, BT-Drucksache 13/5274, 56.

7.173 **(4.2) Does a foreign award, which has been rendered abroad according to this country's national procedural law, have to be laid down or registered with a state court or agency? Is there a fee or tax for such registration of an award?** Foreign awards do not have to be deposited or registered with a state court or agency, either. Therefore, no fee or registration tax is required.

7.174 **(4.3) How long after the rendering of the award must the file/award be stored by the lawyers and the arbitral tribunal?** In German arbitration law there is no requirement for the arbitral tribunal or the parties' lawyers to keep the files for a specific time. However, the participants to the proceedings are well advised to keep their files for a considerable time. The files may, for example, be needed for recognition and enforcement proceedings or for setting aside proceedings. Moreover, potential liability claims against the arbitrators and/or the lawyers may become time-barred long after the rendering of the award.

D. Applicable substantive law

(1) Party autonomy to choose the applicable substantive law

7.175 The arbitral tribunal shall decide the dispute according to the rules of law agreed upon by the parties (s 1051(1) sentence 1 ZPO). Such a choice of law shall be construed, unless otherwise expressed, as directly referring to the substantive law of a state and not to its conflict of law rules (s 1051(1) sentence 2 ZPO).

7.176 The parties are free to choose the entire substantive law of a state but also single rules from different national laws, international conventions such as the Convention on Contracts for the International Sale of Goods (CISG), or international principles such as the UNIDROIT Principles of International Commercial Contracts 2004.[248]

7.177 In the absence of an express choice of law the arbitral tribunal may infer the parties' choice of law from the terms of the contract (s 1051(4) ZPO) and the surrounding circumstances. Such an implied choice is, however, often difficult to prove.[249]

7.178 **(1.1) Is there a public policy exception to the chosen substantive law?** Although not mentioned in s 1051 ZPO, there are certain public policy exceptions, which limit the parties' choice of law and have to be taken into account by arbitral tribunals. These limits are not necessarily the same as the national public policy standards laid down, for example, for German state courts in Art 34 of the German Private International Law Act (*Einführungsgesetz zum Bürgerlichen Gesetzbuch*—'EGBGB').[250] Rather, the applicable standard of public policy is to be found on a transnational level.[251] For example, if a distribution contract or a joint venture agreement violates European competition law, an arbitral award may not be

[248] Explanatory Memorandum on the draft Bill of the Arbitration Law Reform Act, BT-Drucksache 13/5274, 52; Friedrich, B. in K.-H. Böckstiegel, S. Kröll, and P. Nacimiento (eds) (n 6) 352 ff paras 19 ff.

[249] Friedrich, B. in K.-H. Böckstiegel, S. Kröll, and P. Nacimiento (eds) (n 6) 351 para 17.

[250] For a detailed discussion, see Junker, A., 'Deutsche Schiedsgerichte und Internationales Privatrecht (s 1051 ZPO)' in K.P. Berger *et al* (eds), *Festschrift für Otto Sandrock zum 70. Geburtstag* (Recht und Wirtschaft, 2000) 443, 451 ff.

[251] Friedrich, B. in K.-H. Böckstiegel, S. Kröll, and P. Nacimiento (eds) (n 6) 355 para 37.

enforceable in Europe irrespective of whether the said agreement is governed by another system of law.[252]

(1.2) Does the principle of '*iura novit curia*' apply? Or must the applicable law be proven (by which means)? In German court proceedings in civil and commercial matters, it is the court's task to establish the content of the applicable law based on the principle of '*iura novit curia*'. If foreign law applies, s 293 ZPO provides that foreign law is to be proven insofar as it is unknown to the court. **7.179**

In contrast, in arbitration proceedings, since arbitrators cannot be expected to know every possible applicable law, the arbitrators have broad discretion in choosing the means of establishing the law.[253] If necessary, expert advice can be sought. **7.180**

(2) Deciding according to equity or as amiable compositeur

Up to the time of the tribunal's decision, the parties may authorize and require the tribunal to decide the case *ex aequo et bono* or as *amiable compositeur* (s 1051(3) ZPO). The authorization must be given explicitly, meaning doubtlessly and crystal-clear.[254] An authorization cannot simply be inferred from the parties' request to the tribunal to propose a settlement.[255] Furthermore, courts have held that the authorization must be made in writing (s 1031 ZPO).[256] If the tribunal decides *ex aequo et bono* without the express authorization by the parties, the award may be challenged.[257] **7.181**

(3) Application of lex mercatoria, *general principles etc*

The *lex mercatoria* embodies those trade usages and fundamental commercial and legal principles that are thought to be more or less the same throughout the (Western) world, such as for example *pacta sunt servanda* or the principle of equity and good faith. Under German arbitration law, parties may choose the *lex mercatoria* as the rules of law applicable to the substance of the dispute (s 1051(1) ZPO).[258] In all cases, the tribunal shall take into account the usages of the trade applicable to the transaction (s 1051(4) ZPO). **7.182**

(3.1) Is the application of *lex mercatoria* considered as the application of law or as a kind of *amiable composition*? It is subject to controversial debate whether the *lex mercatoria* may be chosen as applicable substantive rules of law under s 1051(1) ZPO[259] or whether **7.183**

---

[252] Friedrich, B. in K.-H. Böckstiegel, S. Kröll, and P. Nacimiento (eds) (n 6) 355 para 37.

[253] Schlosser, P., *Das Recht der internationalen privaten Schiedsgerichtsbarkeit* (2nd edn, Mohr Siebeck, 1989) para 747.

[254] Münch, J. in T. Rauscher, P. Wax and J. Wenzel (eds) (n 200) s 1051 para 44.

[255] OLG Munich, 22 June 2005, [2005] SchiedsVZ 308, 309 ff; Friedrich, B. in K.-H. Böckstiegel, S. Kröll, and P. Nacimiento (eds) (n 6) 360 para 54.

[256] For applicability of the form requirements of s 1031 ZPO, see OLG Munich, 22 June 2005, [2005] SchiedsVZ 308, 309 ff; against the applicability, see Voit, W. in H.-J. Musielak (ed) (n 58) s 1051 para 4; Münch, J. in T. Rauscher, P. Wax and J. Wenzel (eds) (n 200) s 1051 para 45; Kreindler, R.H., Schäfer, J.K. and Wolff, R. (n 246) para 663.

[257] Lachmann, J.-P. (n 22) para 1677.

[258] See on the application of the *lex mercatoria* in German arbitral practice, Ritlewski, K., 'Die Lex Mercatoria in der schiedsgerichtlichen Praxis' [2007] *SchiedsVZ* 130 ff.

[259] Schlosser, P. in F. Stein and M. Jonas (eds) (n 24) s 1051 para 1; Ritlewski, K. (n 258) 130, 134; cf Martiny, D. in K. Rebmann, F.J. Säcker and R. Rixecker (eds) (n 34) Vorbemerkung zu Art 27 EGBGB para 133.

one has to look at the *lex mercatoria* as guidelines for making a decision *ex aequo et bono* under s 1051(3) ZPO.[260] As a compromise, it has been suggested that a decision pursuant to the *lex mercatoria* is a decision pursuant to 'content driven application of equitable principles' taking into account trade practices.[261] To be on the safe side, the parties' agreement should meet the requirements of s 1051(3) ZPO, ie the parties should expressly authorize the tribunal to decide the dispute under the *lex mercatoria*.[262]

(4) Applicable law if there is no choice of law by the parties

7.184 Failing a designation by the parties of the applicable substantive law, the tribunal shall apply the law of the state, with which the subject matter of the proceedings has the closest connection (s 1051(2) ZPO). The 'closest connection' test is an objective test.[263] In the regular course of events, the contract has the closest connection to the law of the country where the party rendering the characteristic performance of the contract has its seat or residence.[264] The tribunal must decide to apply the law of a particular jurisdiction. The tribunal is, in principle, not entitled to apply transnational principles.[265]

7.185 **(4.1) Is there an autonomous conflict of law rule in the national arbitration law? Is it considered mandatory?** Section 1051 ZPO is an autonomous conflict of laws rule. Yet, it is not a mandatory provision and can therefore be derogated from by the parties, eg when choosing institutional arbitration rules containing their own conflict of laws rules. If the parties have failed to designate the applicable law and the tribunal has to apply the 'closest connection' test in accordance with s 1051(2) ZPO, it is questionable whether the arbitrators have to take into account other national conflict of laws rules laid down, for example, for German state courts in Art 28 EGBGB. The prevailing view seems to be that the presumptions of Art 28 EGBGB are not directly applicable[266] but they may still serve as guidelines for determining the 'closest connection' under s 1051(2) ZPO.[267] The same holds true with respect to the Regulation (EC) No 593/2008 of the European Parliament and of the Council of 17 June 2008 on the law applicable to contractual obligations (Rome I-Regulation),[268] which will replace the Rome Convention and the corresponding Art 28 EGBGB by the end of 2009[269] but only apply to international procedures before state courts.[270]

---

[260] Von Hoffmann, B., 'Lex Mercatoria vor internationalen Schiedsgerichten' [1984] *IPRax* 106, 107; Mustill, M.J., 'The New Lex Mercatoria: The First Twenty-five Years' (1988) 4(2) *Arb Int'l* 86, 117.

[261] Friedrich, B. in K.-H. Böckstiegel, S. Kröll, and P. Nacimiento (eds) (n 6) 353 para 26 with further references.

[262] Kreindler, R.H., Schäfer, J.K. and Wolff, R. (n 246) para 682.

[263] Münch, J. in T. Rauscher, P. Wax and J. Wenzel (eds) (n 200) s 1051 para 23.

[264] Friedrich, B. in K.-H. Böckstiegel, S. Kröll, and P. Nacimiento (eds) (n 6) 358 para 44.

[265] Yet in an international commercial setting, at least the International Commercial Terms 2000 ('Incoterms') may already be regarded as a restatement of international trade usages in a given case and, therefore, be taken into account by the arbitrators via s 1051(4) ZPO.

[266] Voit, W. in H.-J. Musielak (ed) (n 58) s 1051 para 6 with further references; but see Explanatory Memorandum on the draft Bill of the Arbitration Law Reform Act, BT-Drucksache 13/5274, 53.

[267] Voit, W. in H.-J. Musielak (ed) (n 58) s 1051 para 6; Geimer, R. in R. Zöller (n 13) s 1051 para 5.

[268] OJ, 4 July 2008, L 177.

[269] Pursuant to its Arts 28 and 29, the Rome I Regulation will apply from 17 December 2009 to contracts concluded after the same date.

[270] cf Mankowski, P., 'Der Vorschlag für die Rom I-Verordnung' [2006] *IPRax* 101 ff.

(4.2) **What is the law applicable to interest?** The law governing the contract between the parties also governs the issue of interest.[271] The law applicable to interest determines among others, which interest rates apply and from which point of time interest has to be paid. **7.186**

(4.3) **What is the law and practice with respect to legal interest on foreign currency debts?** If the laws governing the contract and the currency of the debt are those of the same country, the right to interest and the rate of interest are determined by the law of the contract, regardless of whether the currency and the law in question are foreign. However, if the laws governing the contract and the chosen currency are those of different countries, the situation is more complex. Some commentators hold the opinion that the rate of interest should in this case be determined by the law of the country, in the currency of which the debt has to be paid in.[272] The prevailing view leaves it to the law governing the contract to determine the rate of interest.[273] **7.187**

(5) Binding effect of state court decisions

According to the German law understanding of 'res judicata' (*Rechtskraft*), an arbitral tribunal is only bound by a state court decision that concerned the same parties and the same dispute. In this case, the binding effect is, however, limited to the operative part of the state court decision.[274] **7.188**

(5.1) **Is an arbitral tribunal bound by a decision of another arbitral tribunal?** As an arbitral award has the same effect between the parties as a final and binding court decision (s 1055 ZPO), an arbitral tribunal is similarly bound by a decision of another arbitral tribunal if the decision concerns the same parties and the same dispute.[275] **7.189**

(5.2) **Does a decision in a criminal case bind an arbitral tribunal?** A decision in a criminal case, in general, does neither bind a civil court nor an arbitral tribunal.[276] Yet, as criminal courts under the German Code of Criminal Procedure (*Strafprozessordnung*—'StPO') have to examine the facts *ex officio* (*Amtsermittlungsgrundsatz*), the fact-gathering arising out of criminal proceedings may, in a given case, be very helpful for parties in arbitral proceedings in order to present their case. **7.190**

E. Settlement

(1) Settlement by agreement of the parties with or without support of the arbitral tribunal

It is one of the special characteristics of German arbitration practice that not only the parties but also the tribunal may—and frequently will—suggest settlement negotiations. **7.191**

[271] cf Spellenberg, U. in K. Rebmann, F.J. Säcker and R. Rixecker (eds) (n 34) Art 32 EGBGB para 48 with further references.

[272] Grunsky, W., 'Anwendbares Recht und gesetzlicher Zinssatz' in W. Gerhart *et al* (eds), *Festschrift für Franz Merz zum 65. Geburtstag* (1992) 147, 152 ff; Berger, K.P., 'Der Zinsanspruch im Internationalen Wirtschaftsrecht' (1997) 61 *RabelsZ* 313, 326.

[273] Spellenberg, U. in K. Rebmann, F.J. Säcker and R. Rixecker (eds) (n 34) Art 32 EGBGB paras 48 ff; Heldrich, A. in O. Palandt, *Bürgerliches Gesetzbuch* (67th edn, CH Beck, 2008) Art 32 EGBGB para 5.

[274] On the factual impact of state court and arbitral decisions, see Schütze, R., 'Zur Präzedenzwirkung von Schiedssprüchen' in R. Schütze (ed) (n 181) 93 ff.

[275] cf Schütze, R. (n 279) 93 *et seq.*

[276] Greger, R. in R. Zöller (n 13) s 149 para 1.

Commonly, a German court or tribunal is expected to encourage an amicable settlement of the dispute at every stage of the proceedings. At least for domestic arbitrations in Germany it is estimated that around two thirds of all arbitrations result in such a settlement.[277]

7.192 (1.1) **May an arbitrator who has initiated settlement discussions be challenged when agreement on a settlement has failed?** Against this background, an arbitrator who has initiated non-successful settlement negotiations may not be challenged merely because he tried to encourage an amicable settlement.[278] However, in order to avoid later difficulties, the tribunal should address the issue beforehand, eg ask the parties in advance whether, in what form, and at which point of the proceedings they would like the tribunal to encourage an amicable settlement.[279] To do so is especially advisable if one of the parties is a foreign party, for whom the idea of an arbitral tribunal playing an active role in settlement proceedings may be alien.[280]

(2) 'Private settlement' and its impact on the arbitral procedure

7.193 If, during the arbitral proceedings, the parties settle the dispute, the arbitral tribunal shall terminate the proceedings (s 1053(1) ZPO).

(3) Form and effect of a settlement (eg award on agreed terms)

7.194 If the parties settle their dispute and choose not to apply for an award on agreed terms (*Schiedsspruch mit vereinbartem Wortlaut*), the tribunal shall terminate the proceedings in the form of a termination order under ss 1056(1), 1056(2) no 2 ZPO. Alternatively, the parties may request the tribunal to record the settlement in the form of an award on agreed terms, unless the contents are in violation of public policy (s 1053(1) sentence 2 ZPO). The application has to be filed by both parties but there is no need for a joint application.[281]

7.195 The award on agreed terms must state that it is an award. The award must meet the same form requirements as laid down in s 1054 ZPO, except that there is no reasoning required (s 1053(2) ZPO). Once issued, an award on agreed terms has the same effect as any other award.

7.196 With respect to challenges of an award on agreed terms, it is subject to controversial debate how to deal with situations where—after the award has been issued and became legally binding—it is discovered that the settlement recorded in the award was obtained by fraud, duress or mistake or suffers from illegality. While a large view holds the opinion that the courts should—for example in the case of fraud—set aside the award under s 1059(2) no 1(d) ZPO,[282] others argue that only a claim for damages according to s 826 BGB may lead

[277] Böckstiegel, K.-H., Kröll, S. and Nacimiento, P. in K.-H. Böckstiegel, S. Kröll, and P. Nacimiento (eds) (n 6) 23 para 45.
[278] Münch, J. in T. Rauscher, P. Wax and J. Wenzel (eds) (n 200) s 1053 para 3.
[279] For DIS proceedings, see Theune, U. (n 6) 226 para 3.
[280] Berger, K.P., 'Integration of Mediation Elements into Arbitration' (2003) 19(3) *Arb Int'l* 387, 398.
[281] Mankowski, P., 'Der Schiedsspruch mit vereinbartem Wortlaut' [2001] *ZZP* 37, 70 ff.
[282] Kreindler, R.H., Schäfer, J.K. and Wolff, R. (n 251) para 998 with further references.

to the ignorance of the award.[283] Either way leads to a denial of recognition of the award by the courts, thereby depriving the award on agreed terms of its intended effects.

F. Costs of the arbitration

(1) General allocation of the costs of the proceedings

Unlike the UNCITRAL Model Law, German arbitration law contains an explicit provision on the allocation of the costs between the parties (s 1057 ZPO). Unless the parties agree otherwise, the tribunal shall allocate, by means of an arbitral award, the costs of the arbitration as between the parties, including those costs incurred by the parties necessary for the proper pursuit of their claim or defence. The tribunal shall do so at its discretion and take into consideration the circumstances of the case, in particular the outcome of the proceedings (s 1057(1) ZPO). To the extent that the costs of the arbitral proceedings have been fixed, the arbitral tribunal shall also decide on the amount to be borne by each party. If the costs have not been fixed in the award or if they can only be fixed once the arbitral proceedings have been terminated, the decision shall be taken by means of a separate award (s 1057(2) ZPO). **7.197**

With regard to the criteria, by which the tribunal may allocate the costs, s 1057(1) sentence 2 ZPO makes clear that the arbitrators have full discretion taking into account the particularities of the individual case. Specifically, the arbitrators are not bound by ss 91 ff ZPO, which govern the issue of allocation of costs in state court proceedings. However, at least in domestic arbitration cases, ss 91 ff ZPO will be frequently applied *mutatis mutandis*,[284] thus transferring the principle of 'costs follow the event' into arbitration proceedings. Consequently, in the majority of cases the ratio of success on the merits will determine the allocation of the costs of the proceedings.[285] **7.198**

Only when an award on costs has been rendered are the arbitral proceedings deemed properly terminated under German law.[286] Prior to the decision on costs the arbitral tribunal is under an obligation to gather all necessary information, which in practice will often be done by requesting the parties to hand in statements of costs.[287] The costs may generally comprise costs arising directly from the proceedings, eg the fees of the arbitrators, the expenses of the arbitral tribunal, institutional administrative fees, or potential court fees, but also external fees, such as the incurred expenses of the parties and the parties' attorney fees.[288] **7.199**

(2) Deposits or advances for costs or fees?

The issue of deposits or advances for costs and fees is not explicitly addressed in German arbitration law. However, arbitrators are generally entitled under customary law to claim advance payments. Pursuant to s 273 BGB, the arbitrators may suspend their activities until such payment has been effected.[289] **7.200**

---

[283] Münch, J. in T. Rauscher, P. Wax and J. Wenzel (eds) (n 200) s 1053 para 40; for the admissibility of such a claim, see BGH, 2 November 2000, [2001] NJW 373, 374.

[284] Schwab, K.H. and Walter, G. (n 3) ch 33 para 10; Voit, W. in H.-J. Musielak (ed) (n 58) s 1057 para 3.

[285] Kröll, S. (n 2) 47.

[286] Schwab, K.H. and Walter, G. (n 3) ch 33 para 10.

[287] Kreindler, R.H., Schäfer, J.K. and Wolff, R, (n 246) para 1188.

[288] Schwab, K.H. and Walter, G. (n 3) ch 33 para 1.

[289] von Schlabrendorff, F. and Sessler, A. in K.-H. Böckstiegel, S. Kröll, and P. Nacimiento (eds) (n 6) 421 para 15.

7.201 When fixing the advance, the arbitrators are entitled to request a sum that is high enough to cover the whole amount of the expected costs and fees (including VAT at the current rate of 19 per cent).[290] Usually the tribunal will request each of the parties to pay one half of the advance.[291] After payment of the advance, the money will usually be held in trust by the chairman of the tribunal.[292]

7.202 (2.1) **Is there any case law authorizing or prohibiting arbitrators to order a party to pay an advance on the arbitration costs?** Even though the arbitral tribunal is generally entitled to request the parties to pay advances on costs, case law suggests that an arbitral tribunal cannot compel the parties to actually affect payment.[293] The BGH has ruled that an arbitral tribunal may not decide on its own fees because this would violate the principle that no judge or arbitrator should decide on his own matters (*Verbot des Richtens in eigener Sache*).[294] Instead, the arbitral tribunal may only exercise a right of retention and make fulfilment of its obligation to arbitrate dependent on fulfilment of the parties' obligation to pay advances.[295]

7.203 (2.2) **May the raising of a set-off claim or counterclaim be made contingent upon payment of the corresponding advance for the relating arbitration costs (cf Article 30(5), ICC Rules)? May such a condition be agreed upon when entering into the arbitration agreement?** If the respondent raises a counterclaim the tribunal may request new deposits.[296] By virtue of the tribunal's retention right (s 273 BGB) the tribunal can refuse to decide on the counterclaim until payment of the advance for the counterclaim has been received. By contrast, a set-off, under German law, merely serves as a defence against the claimant's claim and does not constitute a separate legal action. Accordingly, a set-off will, in most cases, not lead to additional arbitration costs justifying any increase of the advance on costs.

7.204 According to the principle of party autonomy, there are no limitations on the parties and the arbitrators to agree in the arbitration agreement on the condition that a counterclaim or set-off can only be raised upon payment of the corresponding advance for the relating arbitration costs.

7.205 (2.3) **What remedies exist against a party, which does not pay its part of the advance on the arbitration costs (eg termination of the arbitration agreement)? How may the other party enforce its rights?** If a party does not pay its part of the advance on costs, the tribunal may, first of all, ask the other party to pay the advance in full, thereby allowing the proceedings to continue. If both parties finally fail to pay the advance, the tribunal can

---

290 Voit, W. in H.-J. Musielak (ed) (n 58) s 1035 para 27.

291 Kröll, S. (n 2) 48.

292 Schlosser, P., 'Der Schiedsgerichtsobmann als Vertragspartner' [2004] *SchiedsVZ* 21, 22.

293 OLG Oldenburg, 31 March 1971, [1971] NJW 1461, 1462; AG Düsseldorf, 17 June 2003, [2003] SchiedsVZ 240; but see von Schlabrendorff, F. and Sessler, A. in K.-H. Böckstiegel, S. Kröll, and P. Nacimiento (eds) (n 6) 421 ff para 16 with further references.

294 BGH, 25 November 1976, WM 1977, 319, 320; BGH, 7 March 1985, [1985] NJW 1903, 1904.

295 BGH, 7 March 1985, [1985] NJW 1903, 1904; OLG Oldenburg, 31 March 1971, [1971] NJW 1461, 1462.

296 Schwab, K.H. and Walter, G. (n 3) ch 16 para 31.

refuse to perform services (s 273 BGB). In addition, the tribunal may declare the arbitral proceedings terminated if it concludes from the non-payment of the advance on costs that the parties fail to pursue the arbitral proceedings (s 1056(2) no 3, first alternative ZPO),[297] or if a party validly terminates the arbitration agreement due to the other party's failure to pay the advance on costs (s 1056(2) no 3, second alternative ZPO).[298]

The opposing party may enforce its right in the continuation of the proceedings firstly by paying the advance in full. Secondly, a party may sue its opponent in court for payment[299] and the tribunal may stay the proceedings.[300] The court may render its decision in summary proceedings on a document-only basis (*Urkundenprozess*).[301] Alternatively, the opposing party may be entitled to terminate the arbitration agreement for cause and claim damages.[302] 7.206

(3) Costs of the administration by an arbitration institution

Similarly to other institutional rules, the arbitration rules of the DIS provide for a fixed fee schedule for the determination of administrative fees (s 40(4) DIS Rules). The administrative fee is determined in relation to the amount in dispute by the amended version of the Appendix to s 40(5) of the DIS Rules, which entered into force on 1 January 2005.[303] The minimum administrative fee is €350.00 and the maximum fee is €25,000.00. 7.207

(4) Arbitrators' fees: law and practice, judicial control

German arbitration law does not contain a provision on arbitrators' fees. The remuneration of arbitrators is primarily governed by the contract between the arbitrator and the parties. If no specific contractual agreement exists, an arbitrator is entitled to fees under s 612(1) BGB, according to which the usual remuneration is deemed to have been agreed if the performance owed is commonly not free of charge.[304] The compensation is at last due with the termination of the proceedings. The parties are jointly and severally liable for the payment.[305] 7.208

The agreement between the parties and the arbitrators concerning the arbitrators' remuneration is generally not subject to judicial control.[306] If the parties have agreed upon the application of institutional arbitration rules, the exact amount of fees of the arbitrators will be determined in accordance with the institutional fee schedule. In *ad hoc* proceedings situated in Germany the parties and arbitrators frequently resort to the provisions of the attorneys remuneration act (*Rechtsanwaltsvergütungsgesetz* - RVG) and adjust these rules to 7.209

297 Lachmann, J.-P. (n 22) para 1861 with further references.
298 von Schlabrendorff, F. and Sessler, A. in K.-H. Böckstiegel, S. Kröll, and P. Nacimiento (eds) (n 6) 414 para 12.
299 Geimer, R. in R. Zöller (n 13) s 1035 para 26.
300 cf BGH, 7 March 1985, [1985] NJW 1903, 1904; AG Düsseldorf, 17 June 2003, [2003] SchiedsVZ 240.
301 Kröll, S. and Kraft, P., 'Ten Years of UNCITRAL Model Law in Germany' (2007) 1(3) *WAMR* 439, 477.
302 Trittmann, R. and Hanefeld, I. in K.-H. Böckstiegel, S. Kröll, and P. Nacimiento (eds) (n 6) 110 para 43.
303 Available at <http://www.dis-arb.de>.
304 Voit, W. in H.-J. Musielak (ed) (n 58) s 1035 para 26.
305 Schwab, K.H. and Walter, G. (n 3) ch 12 para 10.
306 *ibid*, para 11.

the specificities of arbitration proceedings.[307] Less frequent in Germany are agreements that provide for a remuneration per hour of the arbitrators' services at specific hourly rates.

7.210 (4.1) **May arbitrators fix their own fees in the award?** German courts have repeatedly ruled that arbitrators may not fix their own fees by means of an enforceable decision, as this would violate the principle that no judge or arbitrator should decide on his own matters (*Verbot des Richtens in eigener Sache*).[308] Only if an advance on costs including all arbitrators' fees has already been paid to the tribunal, the arbitrators may fix their own fees in the award.[309] Yet, the arbitrators may refuse to perform their service if the advance on costs has not been paid (s 273 BGB).[310]

7.211 (4.2) **How can the parties change the arbitrators' fees once they are fixed?** Once they are fixed, the arbitrators' fees may be changed either by explicit agreement with the parties or by implied consent due to exceptional circumstances (s 612(1) BGB).

7.212 (4.3) **Are the arbitrators' fees subject to income tax if (i) the place of arbitration; or (ii) the normal residence or place of business of the arbitrator is located in this country?** An arbitrator who is a German resident is subject to income tax at his place of residence (s 1 (1) Income Tax Law [*Einkommenssteuergesetz*—'EStG']. Furthermore, foreign arbitrators serving in Germany are, in principle, subject to German income tax and must pay a reduced tax rate, unless a double taxation treaty provides otherwise.[311] Most such treaties provide that a resident of one country rendering services in another country is subject to income tax in that country only if he maintains a 'fixed establishment' there. This means that a foreign arbitrator who simply holds hearings in Germany will usually not be subject to German income tax.[312]

7.213 (4.4) **Are arbitrators' fees submitted to VAT? If yes, is the duty to pay such tax linked to (i) the place of arbitration; or (ii) the arbitrator's general residence?** The fees of an arbitrator with general residence in Germany are subject to VAT, currently in the amount of 19 per cent. In light of an ECJ judgment of 16 September 1997, an arbitrator whose place of business is in Germany must pay VAT in Germany and not in the country where he renders his services.[313] This also means that an arbitrator who renders services in Germany but whose general residence is in a foreign country does not need to pay VAT in Germany and may not charge VAT in addition to the standard fee.[314]

---

[307] cf Bischof, H.H., 'RVG: Erste Gebührenprobleme für Schiedsverfahren und Mediation' [2004] *SchiedsVZ* 252 ff.

[308] BGH, 25 November 1976, [1977] WM 319 ff; see also Kühn, W. and Gantenberg, U., 'Die Kostenentscheidung im Schiedsgerichtsverfahren' in Deutsche Institution für Schiedsgerichtsbarkeit (ed), *Kosten im Schiedsgerichtsverfahren*, (2005) 83 ff.

[309] BGH, 25 November 1976, [1977] WM 319, 320 ff; OLG Dresden, 28 October 2003, [2004] SchiedsVZ 44.

[310] BGH, 7 March 1985, [1985] NJW 1903, 1904.

[311] Wilske, S., 'Ad hoc Arbitration in Germany' in K.-H. Böckstiegel, S. Kröll, and P. Nacimiento (eds) (n 6) 833 para 54 with further references.

[312] *ibid.*

[313] ECJ, 16 September 1997, Case C-145/96, *Bernd von Hoffmann v Finanzamt Trier* [1997] ECR I-4870.

[314] Wilske, S., 'Ad hoc Arbitration in Germany' in K.-H. Böckstiegel, S. Kröll, and P. Nacimiento (eds) (n 6) 833 para 55.

(5) Attorneys' fees and the winning party's claim for reimbursement

The tribunal shall allocate in the award the costs of the proceedings, including all costs incurred by the parties necessary for the proper pursuit of their claim or defence (s 1057(1) ZPO). **7.214**

The costs necessary for the proper pursuit of the proceedings first of all include attorneys' fees, as one can usually expect a party to conduct arbitral proceedings with professional legal assistance. For lawyers' fees to be considered necessary for the proper pursuit of the case the fee amount must appear reasonable and in proportion to the complexity of the case. In this respect the BGH has repeatedly stated that even if the final amount of the fees exceeded the amount of the statutory fees calculated in accordance with the statutory fee schedule for lawyers (*Rechtsanwaltsvergütungsgesetz*—RVG) this alone cannot lead to the inoperativeness of the remuneration agreement provided that the parties agreed on a reasonable hourly rate and the effort spent by the lawyer was necessary.[315] This jurisprudence confirms the general rule under German arbitration law that individual fee agreements are permitted.[316] **7.215**

In addition, the parties can claim reimbursement of their necessary general expenses such as travelling costs and costs for witnesses. In contrast, costs for standard preparations by the party itself, including costs for in-house counsel, are, in general, not reimbursable.[317] **7.216**

(6) Time and form of the decision on costs

It follows from s 1057(1) ZPO that the tribunal shall take the decision on costs in the form of an award.[318] If the final award does not contain a decision on costs, the costs decision must be issued in a subsequent award, which may either take the form of an additional award (s 1058(1) no 3 ZPO) or the form of a separate award (s 1057(2) ZPO).[319] In both cases, the 'final' award is only a partial award, which may be enforceable but does not yet terminate the proceedings according to s 1056(1) ZPO. **7.217**

(6.1) May the arbitrators' decision on the costs (allocation and amount of costs to be reimbursed) be challenged separately from the award itself? Are there time limits for such a remedy? The question whether a decision on costs may be challenged separately from the award is not unanimously answered in German case law and legal commentary. Yet, according to the prevailing view among commentators, a separate award on costs is an award subject to s 1059 ZPO just like any other award and can therefore be challenged separately.[320] Furthermore, the BGH has never overruled a decision by its predecessor, the **7.218**

---

[315] See BGH, 3 April 2003, [2003] NJW 2386, 2387; BGH, 4 July 2002, [2002] NJW 2774, 2775.

[316] In which circumstances the courts would conclude that the hourly fees exceed the appropriate limits cannot be predicted with certainty, as conclusive case law on this point does not yet exist; see von Schlabrendorff, F. and Sessler, A. in K.-H. Böckstiegel, S. Kröll, and P. Nacimiento (eds) (n 6) 426 para 31.

[317] BGH, 18 December 2003, [2004] NJW-RR 856, 856 ff; von Schlabrendorff, F. and Sessler, A. in K.-H. Böckstiegel, S. Kröll, and P. Nacimiento (eds) (n 6) 424 para 24 with further references.

[318] Schwab, K.H. and Walter, G. (n 3) ch 33 para 1.

[319] Münch, J. in T. Rauscher, P. Wax and J. Wenzel (eds) (n 200) s 1057 para 5.

[320] Geimer, R. in R. Zöller (n 13) s 1057 para 2; Schwab, K.H. and Walter, G. (n 3) ch 24 para 26; Lachmann, J.-P. (n 22) para 1917.

Reichsgericht, which held that a decision on costs can be set aside separately.[321] The challenge must be made within three months after receipt of the award (s 1059(3) ZPO).

7.219 (6.2) **Are the arbitrators entitled and/or legally obliged to rule on the amount of one or both parties' costs that are recoverable?** Under German arbitration law, the tribunal's decision on costs necessarily comprises two parts. Firstly, the tribunal must decide to what extent each of the parties has to bear the costs of the proceedings (s 1057(1) ZPO). Secondly, the tribunal must also determine the exact amount of costs the parties have to bear, thereby also deciding on the amount of the parties' costs that are recoverable (s 1057(2) ZPO). In order to ensure equal treatment, the tribunal must consider for its ruling the amount of both parties' costs.

G. Publication of the award

(1) Publication with or without the consent of the parties

7.220 As non-publicity is considered to be one of the essential elements of arbitration, under German arbitration law, the award may not be published without the consent of the parties. If the parties and the arbitrators agree upon publication, the award will be usually published without disclosing the identity of the parties involved.[322]

(2) Practice of publication (eg in specific legal journals)

7.221 There is no specific legal journal solely dealing with the publication of arbitral awards. Rather, arbitral awards may be found at a variety of sources.[323] The DIS publishes from time to time awards in anonymous form and with the consent of the parties in the *Zeitschrift für Schiedsverfahren/German Arbitration Journal* (*SchiedsVZ*) and on its website.[324]

VI. Amendment and challenge of the award; liability of arbitrators

A. Amendment, correction or interpretation of the award

(1) Motion to amend or correct an award

7.222 Section 1058(1) no 1 ZPO allows the parties to request the tribunal to correct any errors in computation, any clerical or typographical errors, or any errors of similar nature. Section 1058(1) no 3 ZPO deals with an application for an additional award as to claims presented in the proceedings but omitted from the award.[325]

---

[321] RG, 29 October 1940, RGZ 165, 142; cf von Schlabrendorff, F. and Sessler, A. in K.-H. Böckstiegel, S. Kröll, and P. Nacimiento (eds) (n 6) 430 para 46.

[322] Kröll, S. (n 2) 52.

[323] See, for example, the following list of sources provided by Kröll, S. (n 2) 52 ff: *Zeitschrift für Schiedsverfahren/German Arbitration Journal* (*SchiedsVZ*, from 2003 onwards); Recht und Praxis der Schiedsgerichtsbarkeit (RPS, semi-annual supplement to the Betriebs-Berater (BB) until 2001); Straatmann, K. and Ulmer, P. (eds), *Handelsrechtliche Schiedsgerichts-Praxis* (Dr Otto Schmidt, 1975 ff), continued online by the HK Hamburg, available at <http://www.hk24.de/produktmarken/recht_und_fair_play/schiedsgerichtemediationschlichtung/schiedsspruchsammlung/index.jsp>); *Recht der Internationalen Wirtschaft (RIW)*; *Ybk Comm Arb*.

[324] See <http://www.dis-arb.de>.

[325] cf OLG Düsseldorf, 14 August 2007, SchiedsVZ 2008, 156 ff.

The time limit for both requests is one month after receipt of the award (s 1058(2) ZPO). In the case of a request by the parties the tribunal shall make the correction within one month (s 1058(3) ZPO) or make an additional award within two months (s 1058(3) ZPO) upon receipt of the request. **7.223**

Any correction or additional award must meet the requirements stipulated by s 1054 ZPO (s 1058(5) ZPO). **7.224**

(2) Interpretation of the award by the tribunal

Any party may request the tribunal to give an interpretation of specific parts of the award (s 1058(1) no 2 ZPO). This requires (i) that there is an express request for interpretation by one party; and (ii) that the request must refer to specific parts of the award but not to the award as a whole. An interpretation request may not be used to challenge or supplement the reasons of the award.[326] **7.225**

B. Appeal on the merits

(1) Admissibility and procedure of an appeal on the merits

Under German arbitration law, the possibility to file an appeal with the courts on the merits against an arbitral award does not exist.[327] Rather, the courts may only control the content of an award by means of the public policy standard provided for in case of a challenge of the award under s 1059 ZPO.[328] **7.226**

In contrast, the parties may stipulate in their arbitration agreement that each party has the right to commence court proceedings within a certain time after receipt of the award.[329] While German courts have not accepted such agreements as valid arbitration agreements under s 1025 ZPO in the past,[330] the BGH recently overruled these decisions and held that the parties may make the arbitration agreement and the binding effect of the award dependant on the condition that no party initiates court proceedings within a specified period of time.[331] **7.227**

(1.1) May the parties agree on an appeal to another arbitral tribunal? German arbitration law is silent on the issue of whether the parties may agree upon a second arbitral instance. As the parties enjoy broad discretion in determining the arbitration proceedings under the principle of party autonomy they seem, however, free to agree on an appeal to another arbitral tribunal.[332] While some arbitral institutions in the commodity sector explicitly provide such a possibility,[333] the parties usually must design the procedural **7.228**

---

326 von Schlabrendorff, F. and Sessler, A. in K.-H. Böckstiegel, S. Kröll, and P. Nacimiento (eds) (n 6) 433 ff para 5.

327 Kreindler, R.H., Schäfer, J.K. and Wolff, R. (n 246) para 111.

328 Kröll, S. (n 2) 53; cf BGH, 30 October 2008, [2009] NJW 1215 ff [2009] SchiedsVZ 66 f.

329 Voit, W. in H.-J. Musielak (ed) (n 58) s 1042 para 29; Geimer, R. in R. Zöller (n 13) s 1042 para 47; Kröll, S. and Kraft, P. (n 301) 448.

330 OLG Frankfurt, 20 December 2005, available at <http://www.dis-arb.de>; see also OLG Naumburg, 20 May 2005, [2006] SchiedsVZ 103, 104.

331 BGH, 1 March 2007, [2008] SchiedsVZ 160, 162.

332 Kröll, S., (n 2) 53; Voit, W. in H.-J. Musielak (ed) (n 58) s 1042 para 29.

333 See eg ss 28 ff of the Arbitration Rules of the Waren-Verein Hamburger Börse, available at <http://www.warenverein.de/pdf/wvb_d_a5_web.pdf#page=69>.

requirements for such appellate proceedings themselves. In the absence of any specifications, the appellate tribunal may constitute itself in accordance with ss 1034 ff ZPO, and conduct the arbitration in such a manner as it considers appropriate (s 1042(4) ZPO).[334] In general, the award of the first arbitral instance only becomes effective in the sense of s 1055 ZPO or terminates the proceedings according to s 1056 ZPO if either no appeal has been made in due time or if the second instance rendered an affirmative decision.[335]

(2) Possibility to exclude an appeal (eg in the arbitration clause)

7.229 The question whether the parties may exclude an appeal to the courts against the award in their arbitration agreement is obsolete under German arbitration law, as there exists no possibility of an appeal under German arbitration law.

C. Setting aside of the award

(1) Reasons for setting aside an award

7.230 With regard to judicial control of the award, German arbitration law rejects the idea of a 'révision au fond' by public courts. Section 1059(1) ZPO rather states that recourse to a court against an award may be made only by a motion to set aside the award for one of the reasons stipulated in s 1059(2) ZPO and in a manner stipulated in s 1059(3) ZPO. These enumerated reasons match those stipulated by Art 34 UNCITRAL Model Law and Art 5 of the New York Convention on the Recognition and Enforcement of Foreign Arbitral Awards of 1958 ('New York Convention') and may be subdivided in two categories.

7.231 The first group of reasons embraced by s 1059(2) no 1 ZPO is mainly concerned with defects as to procedural requirements and must be pleaded by the applicant who needs to show sufficient cause for his allegations. Under subliterae (a)–(d) of s 1059(2) no 1 ZPO, an award may be set aside on account of a defective arbitration agreement (no 1 a), violations of the right to be heard and to fairly present one's case (no 1 b), excess of authority with regard to jurisdiction by the tribunal (no 1 c), or on account of an incorrect constitution of the tribunal or other procedural irregularities (no 1 d).

7.232 The second category of reasons for setting aside an award provided for by s 1059(2) no 2 ZPO deals with severe cases of non-compliance with procedural or substantive law requirements. These reasons must be considered by the court *ex officio*.[336] Specifically, an award may be set aside on account of lack of arbitrability of the subject matter (no 2 a) or because its recognition or enforcement would lead to a result, which would be in conflict with public policy (*ordre public*) (no 2 b).

7.233 In general, German courts construe all reasons for setting aside an award under s 1059 ZPO narrowly.[337] Furthermore, the German courts have recurrently stressed that a party

---

[334] Schwab, K.H. and Walter, G. (n 3) ch 22 para 1.

[335] See Kröll, S. (n 2) 53 and Schwab, K.H. and Walter, G. (n 3) ch 22 para 1.

[336] cf OLG Hamburg, 30 May 2008, [2008] OLGR Hamburg 916, which held that the judicial control of these standards may not be waived by the parties, eg by submitting their disputes to arbitration under the ICC Rules and its Art 28(6), pursuant to which the parties shall be deemed to have waived their right to any form of recourse insofar as such waiver can validly be made.

[337] See Kröll, S. and , Kraft, P. (n 301) 477 ff; Kröll, S. 'Die Entwicklung des Schiedsrechts 2007–2008' [2009] *NJW* 1183, 1187; and Kröll, S., 'Die schiedsrechtliche Rechtsprechung 2008' [2009] *SchiedsVZ* 217, 219 ff with many references to recent court decisions.

must primarily raise its defences during the arbitration proceedings and that not raising them may bar that party from relying on these grounds as a basis for a later challenge of the award (s 1027 ZPO).[338]

(1.1) May an award made according to international or foreign procedural rules be the object of an application for setting aside before the national courts? Most provisions of German arbitration law—including s 1059 ZPO—only apply to awards rendered in proceedings with their place of arbitration in Germany (s 1025 ZPO).[339] Therefore, the decisive criterion, whether setting aside proceedings in Germany are possible, is the place of arbitration. If the place of arbitration was in Germany, an award can be subject to challenge under s 1059 ZPO, regardless of whether it was made according to national, foreign or international procedural rules. In contrast, German courts do not have jurisdiction to set aside foreign awards. Rather, with respect to foreign awards, German courts are limited to declare that the award is not to be recognized in Germany under s 1061(2) ZPO.[340] **7.234**

(2) Procedure and deadlines for challenging an award

The parties have to make an application to set the award aside setting out the reasons and factual allegations, on which the party wishes to base its challenge (s 1059(1) ZPO). The time limit for a motion to set aside the award is three months after receipt of the award, unless the parties have agreed otherwise (s 1059(3) ZPO). **7.235**

An application to set the award aside must be filed with the Higher Regional Court (*Oberlandesgericht*—OLG) that has been designated in the arbitration agreement or, if such designation is missing, the OLG, in whose district the place of arbitration is located (s 1062(1) no 4 ZPO). **7.236**

(2.1) Who may (or must) represent a party in a proceeding for setting aside an award? The application to set aside an award as such may be filed by the parties themselves. As long as no oral hearing has been ordered, the parties do not need any representation by a lawyer, but applications and declarations may be put on record at the court registry (s 1063(4) ZPO). From the moment the court orders an oral hearing, the parties must be represented by counsel (s 78(1), ZPO).[341] **7.237**

(2.2) Do specific time limits exist for setting-aside procedures concerning awards on jurisdiction? Specific time limits for challenging the award exist if the setting-aside procedures concern an award on jurisdiction. If the tribunal has issued a preliminary ruling on jurisdiction, the parties may request the court to decide on the matter within one month after receipt of the tribunals' decision (s 1040(3) ZPO). The BGH has ruled that, after the one-month period has elapsed, the parties are barred from challenging the award in setting-aside or in enforcement proceedings on grounds of defects as to jurisdiction.[342] **7.238**

338 Lachmann, J.-P. (n 22) paras 2434 and 2439 with further references.

339 See BGH, 27 May 2004, [2004] SchiedsVZ 205, 206; Schlosser, P. in F. Stein and M. Jonas (eds) (n 24) s 1059 para 3.

340 Kröll, S. and Kraft, P. in K.-H. Böckstiegel, S. Kröll, and P. Nacimiento (eds) (n 6) 445 ff para 18.

341 *ibid*, 447 para 24.

342 BGH, 27 March 2003, [2003] SchiedsVZ 133, 134.

(3) Effect of a court decision, which sets the award aside

7.239 The setting aside of the award constitutes a retroactive annulment of the award. An award, which has been set aside, is considered to be non-existent *ab initio*.[343]

7.240 The court must decide on the application to set aside the award by means of an order (s 1063(1) ZPO). The court must either set the award aside or uphold it, but may not change the award.[344] If possible, the court may also set aside the award only partially, for example in case of monetary claims.[345]

7.241 **(3.1) Does the setting-aside action suspend the enforcement? If so, do any remedies exist to reinstate enforcement?** Until the award has been set aside, its prejudicial effects must be recognized.[346] Section 1060(2) sentence 2 ZPO stipulates that the grounds for setting aside shall not be considered during enforcement proceedings if a prior challenge of the award under s 1059 ZPO was rejected. Vice versa, an application for a declaration of enforceability under s 1060(1) ZPO must be rendered inadmissible, if a prior challenge of the award was successful.[347]

7.242 **(3.2) After an award has been set aside, does the underlying arbitration agreement revive or remain in force or is it exhausted or deemed terminated?** In the absence of any indication to the contrary, the setting aside of the award shall result in the arbitration agreement becoming operative again in respect of the subject matter of the dispute (s 1059(5) ZPO). The parties can either start arbitration proceedings completely anew or the court may, where appropriate, set aside the award and remit the case to the original arbitral tribunal (s 1059(4) ZPO). In the latter case, the arbitration agreement and the mandate of the arbitrators remain effective,[348] and the tribunal will have to resume the proceedings and render a new decision, eliminating the reason for the challenge.[349]

(4) Appeal against the court's decision to set aside or not set aside the award

7.243 The parties have the right to appeal to the BGH against the court's decision to set aside or not to set aside the award (ss 1065(1), 1062(1) no 4 ZPO). In order for such an appeal to be admissible, no certain amount in dispute must be at stake, but the complaint must be made with regard to a subject matter that is of fundamental importance to the law.[350] The time limit for the appeal is one month after receipt of the court's decision.[351]

(5) Possibility of the parties to exclude actions for setting aside

7.244 It is common opinion among German courts and commentators that the parties may not exclude in advance actions for setting aside an award.[352] However, if the parties have

343 Kröll, S. and Kraft, P. in K.-H. Böckstiegel, S. Kröll, and P. Nacimiento (eds) (n 6) 439 para 3.
344 Schwab, K.H. and Walter, G. (n 3) ch 25 para 14.
345 BGH, 26 September 1985, [1986] NJW 1436, 1438.
346 Kröll, S. and Kraft, P. in K.-H. Böckstiegel, S. Kröll, and P. Nacimiento (eds) (n 6) 476 para 96.
347 Schwab, K.H. and Walter, G. (n 3) ch 25 para 4.
348 cf s 1056(3) ZPO.
349 Lachmann, J.-P. (n 22) para 2393; Kröll, S. and Kraft, P. in K.-H. Böckstiegel, S. Kröll, and P. Nacimiento (eds) (n 6) 475 para 93.
350 Schwab, K.H. and Walter, G. (n 3) ch 31 para 21.
351 Kreindler, R.H., Schäfer, J.K. and Wolff, R. (n 246) para 1122.
352 See only BGH, 26 September 1985, [1986] NJW 1436, 1438; Voit, W. in H.-J. Musielak (ed) (n 58) s 1059 para 39.

received the award, the parties may exclude an action for setting aside the award by mutual agreement at least with respect to certain grounds.[353]

D. Liability of arbitrators

(1) Duties and liabilities of arbitrators regarding the conduct of the proceedings

Arbitrators have the duty to conduct fair and impartial hearings, to take all necessary actions to avoid a delay in the disposition of the proceedings, to maintain order, and to meet the time frame for the rendering of a decision.[354] Furthermore, arbitrators have to conduct their services in person[355] and have to follow the instructions by both parties.[356] In addition, arbitrators have to preserve the confidentiality of the proceedings and have to keep the trade secrets of the parties.[357] If the arbitrator refuses to comply with his duties he may lose his right to remuneration and may be liable for damages.[358] **7.245**

The arbitrator may, however, not be held liable for not having rendered a materially or procedurally accurate decision, since an arbitrator shall not face stricter liability than a state court judge, who is protected by the so-called privilege of judges (*Richterprivileg*).[359] **7.246**

(1.1) Do the courts and/or authorities rely on a contractual relationship between the parties and the arbitrator(s), irrespective of whether institutional or *ad hoc* arbitration is concerned? What is the legal qualification of such a contract (eg provision of services)? Under German law, the relationship between the arbitrator and the parties is considered to be a contractual relationship that comes into existence with the appointment of the arbitrator, regardless of whether a party has signed or refused to sign a contract.[360] The same applies with regard to institutional proceedings, where the arbitrator maintains at the same time a contractual relationship with the institution.[361] The contract between the arbitrator and the parties qualifies as a contract on the provision of services under ss 611 ff BGB.[362] **7.247**

(1.2) Are there court decisions (or authorities) determining which law governs the question of liability of an arbitrator? What is the position of those courts / authorities as to whether and to which extent a legal liability of an arbitrator (or arbitral institution) may be established? Only limited case law on the question of liability of arbitrators exists. For example, there exists one early published court decision, in which an arbitrator was held liable for refusing to sign the award.[363] **7.248**

---

353 See in detail Voit, W. in H.-J. Musielak (ed) (n 58) s 1059 para 39 with further references.

354 BGH, 5 May 1986, [1986] NJW 3077; Kreindler, R.H., Schäfer, J.K. and Wolff, R. (n 246) para 576.

355 Schwab, K.H. and Walter, G. (n 3) ch 12 para 6.

356 Kreindler, R.H., Schäfer, J.K. and Wolff, R. (n 246) paras 578 ff.

357 *ibid*, para 580 with further references.

358 Böckstiegel, K.-H., Kröll, S. and Nacimiento, P., 'Germany as a Place for International and Domestic Arbitrations' in K.-H. Böckstiegel, S. Kröll, and P. Nacimiento (eds) (n 6) 37 para 85.

359 Nacimiento, P. and Abt, A. in K.-H. Böckstiegel, S. Kröll, and P. Nacimiento (eds) (n 6) 176 ff para 30 with further references; on the privilege of judges, see Gal, J., *Die Haftung des Schiedsrichters in der internationalen Handelsschiedsgerichtsbarkeit* (Mohr Siebeck, 2009) 160 ff.

360 OLG Munich, 21 December 2006, 34 SchH 12/06.

361 Kröll, S. (n 2) 25.

362 Schwab, K.H. and Walter, G. (n 3) ch 12 para 1.

363 OLG Hamburg, 8 December 1960, [1961] KTS 174 ff, cited by Lachmann, J.-P. (n 22) para 4308.

7.249 (1.3) **Is an arbitrator subject to criminal prosecution?** Arbitrators abusing their judicial function by accepting an inappropriate advantage may be prosecuted according to s 331(2) and s 332(2) StGB. Furthermore, an arbitrator may, at least in theory, be prosecuted for perversion of justice (*Rechtsbeugung*) according to s 339 StGB.

(2) Possibility to restrict or exclude the arbitrators' liability

7.250 It is possible to restrict the liability of arbitrators in the arbitration agreement.[364] In institutional arbitration, a limitation of liability is often contained in the institutional arbitration rules itself, as is the case in s 44 of the DIS Rules. If German law is applicable, an exclusion of liability for intentional breaches of duties is invalid (s 276(3) BGB).

VII. Enforcement of national awards

(1) Requirement of a particular procedure to make an award enforceable (leave for enforcement, exequatur*)*

7.251 Under German arbitration law, a double regime exists as to the recognition and enforcement of national and foreign awards. For national awards, s 1055 ZPO states that the award has the same effect between the parties as a final and binding court judgment. Hence, by virtue of its very existence a national award has a *res judicata* effect. Only if the award needs to be enforced against a recalcitrant debtor, the award must, in addition, be declared enforceable according to s 1060 ZPO.[365]

7.252 (1.1) **Does the national law make any difference between foreign and domestic awards, and if so, which are the criteria? Does there exist an additional notion of award for the purpose of obtaining *exequatur* (France: international awards)?** The enforcement of foreign arbitral awards by contrast is dealt with by s 1061 ZPO, which states that recognition and enforcement of foreign arbitral awards shall be granted in accordance with the New York Convention. Recognition occurs automatically provided that no grounds to deny enforcement exist.[366] The enforcement of foreign arbitral awards, ie their execution, is only possible after they have been declared enforceable.

7.253 (1.2) **May awards granting conservatory/interim measures be subject to enforcement?** In domestic arbitrations, enforcement of interim measures is possible under the special enforcement procedure provided for under s 1041(2) ZPO, according to which state courts may, at the request of a party, permit enforcement of interim measures, unless an application for a corresponding interim measure has already been made to a court. Section 1042(2) ZPO does, at first glance, not apply to foreign arbitral awards (s 1025(2) ZPO). Yet, German courts may also grant leave for enforcement to foreign interim measures due to the jurisdictional provision contained in s 1062(2) ZPO.[367]

364 Kröll, S. (n 2) 25.

365 See in detail Eberl, W., 'Anerkennung und Vollstreckbarerklärung von Schiedssprüchen' in Wissenschaftlicher Gesprächskreis Schiedsrecht München (ed) *Taktik im Schiedsverfahren* (Dr Otto Schmidt, 2008) 189 ff.

366 Kröll, S. in K.-H. Böckstiegel, S. Kröll, and P. Nacimiento (eds) (n 6) 508 para 2.

367 Kreindler, R. and Schäfer, J. in K.-H. Böckstiegel, S. Kröll, and P. Nacimiento (eds) (n 6) 270 para 27 with further references.

(2) Details of such enforcement procedure (competent court, reasons for rejection of motion etc)

In order to have a national arbitral award enforced, a party must file an application for a declaration of enforceability pursuant to s 1060 ZPO. The competent court for the application is the competent Higher Regional Court (*Oberlandesgericht* – OLG) (s 1062 (1) no 4 ZPO). The application must be made in writing or may be put on record at the court registry (s 1063(4) ZPO). The application has to be accompanied by a certified copy of the award; the certification may also be made by counsel authorized to represent the party in the judicial proceedings (s 1064(1) ZPO). In contrast to foreign arbitral awards,[368] national awards rendered in a foreign language have to be translated.[369] A time limit for the application for a declaration of enforceability does not exist. **7.254**

The court shall only refuse an application for a declaration of enforceability if the court finds that the award suffers from one of the grounds for setting aside enumerated in s 1059(2) ZPO. In case of the reasons stipulated in s 1059(2) no 1 ZPO the party opposing the enforcement must plead these reasons, while the reasons stipulated in s 1059(2) no 2 ZPO have to be considered by the court *ex officio*.[370] If the court finds that there are reasons for setting aside the award, the declaration of enforceability will be denied (s 1060(2) ZPO). In arbitral practice, however, in the vast majority of cases the requested declaration of enforceability will be granted.[371] **7.255**

(3) Appeal against the decision granting exequatur

All decisions rendered in proceedings under s 1060 ZPO may be appealed against on points of law to the BGH (ss 1062(1) no 4, 1065(1) ZPO). The complaint on a point of law requires that the legal matter is of fundamental significance or that the development of the law or the need to secure a uniform case law requires a decision by the BGH (s 574(1) no 1, (2) ZPO). The appeal must be filed by a lawyer specifically admitted to the BGH (ss 575(1), 78(1) sentence 4 ZPO) within one month after service of the decision. **7.256**

(4) Appeal (and procedure) if exequatur *has been refused*

The appeal against a decision refusing enforcement is subject to the same procedural framework as an appeal against a decision granting enforcement (ss 1062(1) no 4, 1065(1) ZPO). **7.257**

(5) Procedure of enforcement (attachment of bank accounts etc)

The procedure of enforcement (eg the attachment of bank accounts) is subject to the national enforcement laws of the country, in which enforcement of the award against the recalcitrant debtor is sought. In Germany, the enforcement law is contained in the 8th book of the ZPO (ss 704–945 ZPO). **7.258**

(5.1) At the stage of enforcement, may the losing party invoke arguments and circumstances, which are based on facts which have occurred before (or after) the award was made? The **7.259**

[368] BGH, 25 September 2003, [2003] SchiedsVZ 281, 282; OLG Cologne, 23 April 2004, [2005] SchiedsVZ 163, 164 ff.

[369] Lachmann, J.-P. (n 22) para 2467.

[370] Schwab, K.H. and Walter, G. (n 3) ch 27 para 8.

[371] Kröll, S. in K.-H. Böckstiegel, S. Kröll, and P. Nacimiento (eds) (n 6) 502 para 40.

basic rule under German law is that once an award has been declared enforceable no arguments based on facts which have occurred before the award was made shall be raised anymore.[372] The only exceptional remedy available to the debtor at the stage of enforcement is a complaint against the enforcement (*Vollstreckungsabwehrklage* or *Vollstreckungsgegenklage*) provided for in s 767 ZPO.

7.260 Under s 767 ZPO, objections with respect to the determined claim shall be permissible in enforcement proceedings to the extent that the grounds, on which they are based, first arose after the end of the hearing, at which the objections could have been raised (s 767(2) ZPO). In this context, German courts have ruled that a party has the choice to invoke such a material defence in proceedings for a declaration of enforceability or, after the award has been declared enforceable, in a complaint against the enforcement.[373]

7.261 (5.2) **May the losing party invoke a set-off based on claims that are not related to the matter of the arbitral proceeding? Is it material whether such claim came into existence before or after the award was made?** A set-off defence with a claim that is *not* related to the matter of the arbitral proceedings, ie for which the arbitral tribunal lacked jurisdiction, may arguably be raised only in a complaint against the enforcement (s 767 ZPO), immaterial of the question of whether such claim came into existence before or after the award was made.[374] In light of the legislative intent behind the German arbitration law to facilitate and streamline the procedure to obtain a declaration of enforceability[375] and with regard to the different allocation of functional jurisdiction for proceedings under s 767 ZPO (jurisdiction of the courts of first instance) and proceedings under s 1060 ZPO (jurisdiction of the Higher Regional Court—*Oberlandesgericht*), respectively,[376] a set-off defence with a claim, for which the arbitral tribunal lacked jurisdiction, would not appear well placed in proceedings to have the award declared enforceable. In any event, there is consensus that a set-off defence with a claim that does not fall under the jurisdiction of the state courts but of another arbitral tribunal may neither be raised in proceedings for the declaration of enforceability nor in a complaint against the enforcement.[377]

---

[372] Kreindler, R.H., Schäfer, J.K. and Wolff, R. (n 246) para 1123.

[373] BGH, 8 November 2007, [2008] SchiedsVZ 40, 43; BGH, 12 July 1990, [1990] NJW 3210, 3211; OLG Hamburg, 22 December 2008–6 Sch 09/08, available at <http:///www.dis-arb.de>; OLG Koblenz, 28 July 2005, [2005] SchiedsVZ 260, 262; OLG Dresden, 20 April 2005, [2005] SchiedsVZ 210, 213 ff; OLG Düsseldorf, 19 January 2005, [2005] SchiedsVZ 214, 215 ff; but see BayObLG, 12 April 2000, [2001] NJW-RR 1363, 1364; for a critical view, see Kröll, S. in K.-H. Böckstiegel, S. Kröll, and P. Nacimiento (eds) (n 6) 563 ff paras 133 ff, arguing that only those material defences should be considered in proceedings for a declaration of enforceability, which are not contested or whose existence has already been determined in a binding court judgment.

[374] Kröll, S. in K.-H. Böckstiegel, S. Kröll, and P. Nacimiento (eds) (n 6) 565 para 136; Hartmann, P in Baumbach, A. *et al. Zivilprozessordnung*, (65th edn, CH Beck, 2007) s 1060 para 10.

[375] Explanatory Memorandum on the draft Bill of the Arbitration Law Reform Act, BT-Drucksache 13/5274, 62 ff; cf Kröll, S. in K.-H. Böckstiegel, S. Kröll, and P. Nacimiento (eds) (n 6) 563 ff para 133.

[376] cf Kröll, S. in K.-H. Böckstiegel, S. Kröll, and P. Nacimiento (eds) (n 6) 564 para 134.

[377] OLG Saarbrücken, 16 September 2005, [2006] OLGR 220; Lachmann, J.-P. (n 22) para 2461; Kröll, S., 'Die Entwicklung des Rechts der Schiedsgerichtsbarkeit 2005/2006' [2007] *NJW* 743, 749.

VIII. Foreign awards

A. Recognition and/or enforcement of foreign awards (national law)

(1) Rules according to national law

German arbitration law provides that recognition and enforcement of foreign arbitral awards shall be granted in accordance with the New York Convention or any other applicable treaty on the recognition and enforcement of foreign arbitral awards (s 1061(1) ZPO).[378] If the declaration of enforceability is to be refused, the court shall rule that the arbitral award is not to be recognized in Germany (s 1061(2) ZPO). If the award is set aside abroad after having been declared enforceable in Germany, an application for setting aside the declaration of enforceability may be made (s 1061(3) ZPO). 7.262

(2) Requirements to be fulfilled by the applicant (procedure, time limits)

The procedural framework governing the recognition and enforcement of foreign arbitral awards under German arbitration law is basically the same as the procedural framework previously explained in cases of domestic awards. Sections 1062 ff ZPO do generally not distinguish between domestic and foreign awards. 7.263

(3) Remedies against decisions granting or declining enforcement

As in the case of domestic awards, the only remedy available against a decision granting or declining enforcement is an appeal to the BGH under s 1065 ZPO. 7.264

B. Recognition and/or enforcement of foreign awards (conventions, treaties)

(1) Specific bilateral or multilateral treaties

Germany has signed a variety of bilateral and multilateral treaties that are relevant in the field of recognition and enforcement of foreign arbitral awards.[379] Bilateral treaties containing provisions on the recognition and enforcement of foreign arbitral awards have been signed with a number of countries, for example with Austria, Italy, Netherlands, Russia, Switzerland and the US. 7.265

Moreover, Germany is a member state of the following multinational treaties: 7.266

- Geneva Protocol on Arbitration Clauses of 1923;
- Geneva Convention on the Execution of Foreign Arbitral Awards of 1927;
- New York Convention on the Recognition and Enforcement of Foreign Arbitral Awards of 1958;
- European Convention on International Commercial Arbitration of 1961; and
- Washington Convention on the Settlement of Investment Disputes between States and Nationals of other States of 1965.

---

[378] On the enforcement of foreign arbitral awards and the so-called 'doctrine of merger', see BGH, 2 July 2009—IX ZR 152/06, available at <http://www.juris.de>.

[379] A complete list is available online at <http://www.dis-arb.de>.

7.267 If an award falls within the scope of a convention or treaty, the latter will supersede s 1061 ZPO by virtue of its international public law character.[380] The most important of these treaties is the New York Convention. The New York Convention is applicable to the recognition and enforcement of almost all foreign arbitral awards in Germany, either directly or on account of the reference to the New York Convention made in s 1061(1) ZPO. The bilateral treaties usually only become important if they contain provisions that are more favourable for the parties than the provisions of the New York Convention (Art VII sentence 1, New York Convention).

(2) Existence of a standard procedure for the enforcement of foreign awards

7.268 The procedure for recognition and enforcement of foreign arbitral awards under multilateral and bilateral treaties is basically determined by the German national enforcement regime.[381] In case of conflicting provisions in the treaty and in national law, the German courts have held that in light of Art VII (1) of the New York Convention, the party applying for recognition and enforcement of an award should benefit from the more favourable requirements.[382]

(3) Extent of examination and review of the award by the court

7.269 In general, the control of arbitral awards by state courts during recognition and enforcement proceedings under the New York Convention is limited to a very minimum. The courts shall only assure the compliance with fundamental procedural and substantive law requirements. Therefore, a court may only refuse recognition and issuance of a declaration of enforceability on account of the reasons enumerated in Art V of the New York Convention. These reasons are almost identical in wording with the ones for refusing a declaration of enforceability and setting aside the award under ss 1060, 1059(2) ZPO for domestic awards.

7.270 In case the court finds that one of the reasons stipulated in Art V of the New York Convention exists, it may refuse to issue a declaration of enforceability and refuse recognition of the award. In contrast to the enforcement of domestic awards, the court may not set aside the award.[383]

7.271 In addition, recognition and enforcement may as well be refused pursuant to Art V(1)(e) of the New York Convention, if the award has not yet become binding on the parties or has been set aside or suspended by a competent authority of the country, in which, or under the law of which, that award was made. Art VI of the New York Convention grants the court the right to stay recognition and enforcement proceedings until the court concerned with the setting-aside proceedings has reached its decision.

[380] Kröll, S. (n 2) 61.

[381] See Art III sentence 1 New York Convention; Schwab, K.H. and Walter, G. (n 3) ch 58 para 1.

[382] BGH, 25 September 2003, [2003] SchiedsVZ 281, 282; OLG Karlsruhe, 14 September 2007, [2008] SchiedsVZ 47, 48; OLG Hamm, 27 September 2005, [2006] SchiedsVZ 106, 108; OLG Koblenz, 28 July 2005, [2005] SchiedsVZ 260, 261.

[383] Kröll. S. (n 2) 63.

C. Application of the New York Convention

(1) Application of the New York Convention in practice

German courts and commentators have taken a very arbitration-friendly approach in interpreting and handling the New York Convention. The courts have granted recognition and enforcement of foreign awards whenever possible and a refusal to recognize or enforce an award has been the very exception.[384] In line with the general principle underlying the New York Convention, German law is based on the assumption that foreign awards should normally be enforced in Germany.[385] **7.272**

For instance, when interpreting the scope of the term 'public policy' stated in Art V(2)(b) of the New York Convention, the BGH uses the concept of 'international public policy',[386] which is narrower than the scope of 'public policy' under s 1059(2) no 2 (b) ZPO.[387] A violation of international public policy can only be assumed where the award would violate the most fundamental principles of procedural or substantive law, eg in case the award was obtained by fraud.[388] **7.273**

Another example of the enforceable-friendly attitude of the German courts is the recent case law of the BGH on the issue of form requirements. The BGH has ruled that in light of Art VII sentence 1 of the New York Convention the arbitration agreement must not meet the requirements of Art II of the New York Conventions but that it is sufficient if the arbitration agreement either meets the form requirements of s 1031 ZPO or those of the law determined by the pertinent provision of the German conflict of law rules (Art 11 EGBGB).[389] **7.274**

(2) Examples of decisions, which do not apply the New York Convention correctly

So far there have been no prominent cases where German courts have shown a significant misinterpretation or misapplication of the New York Convention. **7.275**

IX. Appendix

A. National legislation

German arbitration law forms part of the German Code of Civil Procedure (*Zivilprozessordnung*—'ZPO') and is contained in its ss 1025–1066 (10th Book ZPO). It underwent a fundamental reform effective as of 1 January 1998 (*Schiedsverfahrens-Neuregelungsgesetz*, BGBl 1997 I, 3224) and is now based on the UNCITRAL Model Law. The German Institution of Arbitration e.V. (*Deutsche Institution für Schiedsgerichtsbarkeit*—'DIS') provides for translations of the German arbitration law in English, French, Russian

---

384 See also Kröll, S. (n 2) 63.

385 Kröll, S. in K.-H. Böckstiegel, S. Kröll, and P. Nacimiento (eds) (n 6) 520 para 40.

386 BGH, 18 January 1990, [1990] NJW 2199 ff; BGH, 15 May 1986, [1986] NJW 3027, 3028.

387 cf BGH, 21 April 1998, [1998] NJW 2358; Kreindler, R.H., Schäfer, J.K. and Wolff, R. (n 246) para 1138 with further references.

388 OLG Frankfurt, 16 October 2008–26 Sch 13/08, available at <http://www.juris.de, para 17>; Kröll, S. (n 2) 65.

389 BGH, 21 September 2005, [2005] SchiedsVZ 306, 307; Kröll, S. (n 2) 64.

and Spanish on its website (<http://www.dis-arb.de>). An Explanatory Memorandum on the draft Bill of the Arbitration Law Reform Act (Bundestags-Drucksache 13/5274) is available online (in German) at <http://drucksachen.bundestag.de/drucksachen/index.php>.

B. Arbitral institutions

German Institution of Arbitration e.V. (*Deutsche Institution für Schiedsgerichtsbarkeit*– 'DIS')
Beethovenstr. 5-13
50674 Köln, Germany
Telephone: +49 221 285 520
Fax: +49 221 285 522 22
Email: dis@dis-arb.de
Website: <http://www.dis-arb.de>

German Maritime Arbitration Association ('GMAA')
Kölner Straße 34
28327 Bremen, Germany
Telephone: +49 421 437 90 70
Fax: +49 421 437 90 72
Email: gmaa.germany@t-online.de
Website: <http://www.gmaa.de>

C. Model arbitration clauses and other patterns

DIS Model arbitration clause

> All disputes arising in connection with the contract (. . .description of the contract. . .) or its validity shall be finally settled in accordance with the Arbitration Rules of the German Institution of Arbitration e.V. (DIS) without recourse to the ordinary courts of law.

It is recommended to supplement the arbitration clause by the following provisions:

- The place of arbitration is . . .;
- The arbitral tribunal consists of . . . (number) of arbitrators;
- The substantive law of . . . is applicable to the dispute;
- The language of the arbitral proceedings is . . . .

GMAA Model arbitration clause

> All disputes arising out of or in connection with this contract or concerning its validity shall be finally settled by arbitration in accordance with the Arbitration Rules of the German Maritime Arbitration Association.

D. Bibliography

Ahrens, J.-M., *Die subjektive Reichweite internationaler Schiedsvereinbarungen und ihre Erstreckung in der Unternehmensgruppe* (Peter Lang, 2001).
Baumbach, A. *et al, Zivilprozessordnung*, (65th edn, CH Beck, 2007).
Berger, K.P., 'Der Zinsanspruch im Internationalen Wirtschaftsrecht' (1997) 61 *RabelsZ* 313 ff.
Berger, K.P., 'Integration of Mediation Elements into Arbitration' (2003) 19(3) *Arb Int'l* 387 ff.

Berger, K.P., *Internationale Wirtschaftsschiedsgerichtsbarkeit* (De Gruyter, 1992).

Bischof, H.H., 'RVG: Erste Gebührenprobleme für Schiedsverfahren und Mediation' [2004] SchiedsVZ 252 ff.

Blanke, G. 'The Role of EC Competition Law in International Arbitration: A Plaidoyer' [2005] EBLR 169 ff.

Blessing, M., 'Arbitrability of Intellectual Property Disputes' (1996) 12(2) Arb Int'l 191 ff.

Böckstiegel, K.-H., Kröll, S. and Nacimiento, P. (eds), 'Arbitration in Germany: The Model Law in Practice' (Kluwer Law International, 2007).

Busse, D., 'Die Bindung Dritter an Schiedsvereinbarungen' [2005] SchiedsVZ 118 ff.

Derains, Y. and Schwartz, E.A., A Guide to the new ICC Rules of Arbitration (Kluwer Law International, 1998).

Eberl, W., 'Anerkennung und Vollstreckbarerklärung von Schiedssprüchen' in *Wissenschaftlicher Gesprächskreis Schiedsrecht München (ed) Taktik im Schiedsverfahren* (Dr Otto Schmidt, 2008) 189 ff.

Eberl, W., 'Das Schiedsverfahren in der Insolvenz' [2002] InVo 393 ff.

Elsing, S. H., 'Streitverkündung und Schiedsverfahren' [2004] SchiedsVZ 88 ff.

Gal, J., *Die Haftung des Schiedsrichters in der internationalen Handelsschiedsgerichtsbarkeit* (Mohr Siebeck, 2009).

Grunsky, W., 'Anwendbares Recht und gesetzlicher Zinssatz' in W Gerhart et al (eds), 'Festschrift für Franz Merz zum 65. Geburtstag' (1992) 147 ff.

Hanefeld, I. and Wittinghofer, M., 'Schiedsklauseln in Allgemeinen Geschäftsbedingungen' [2005] SchiedsVZ 217 ff.

Hantke, D., 'Die Bildung des Schiedsgerichts' [2003] SchiedsVZ 269 ff.

von Hoffmann, B., 'Lex Mercatoria vor internationalen Schiedsgerichten' [1984] IPRax 106 ff.

Junker, A., 'Deutsche Schiedsgerichte und Internationales Privatrecht (§ 1051 ZPO)' in K.P. Berger et al (eds), *Festschrift für Otto Sandrock zum 70. Geburtstag* (Recht und Wirtschaft, 2000) 443 ff.

Kreindler, R.H, Schäfer, J.K. and Wolff, R., *Schiedsgerichtsbarkeit, Kompendium für die Praxis* (Recht und Wirtschaft, 2006).

Kröll, S., Country Report 'Germany' in *ICCA International Handbook on Commercial Arbitration* (Kluwer Law International, 2007).

Kröll, S., 'Die Entwicklung des Rechts der Schiedsgerichtsbarkeit 2005/2006' [2007] NJW 743 ff.

Kröll, S., 'Die schiedsrechtliche Rechtsprechung 2007' [2008] SchiedsVZ 62, 63 ff.

Kröll, S., 'Die Entwicklung des Schiedsrechts 2007-2008' [2009] NJW 1183 ff.

Kröll, S., 'Die schiedsrechtliche Rechtsprechung 2008 (Teil 2)' [2009] SchiedsVZ 217 ff.

Kröll, S. and Kraft, P., 'Ten Years of UNCITRAL Model Law in Germany' (2007) 1(3) WAMR 439 ff.

Kühn, W. and Gantenberg, U., 'Die Kostenentscheidung im Schiedsgerichtsverfahren' in 'Deutsche Institution für Schiedsgerichtsbarkeit (ed), Kosten im Schiedsgerichtsverfahren', (2005) 83 ff.

Lachmann, J.-P., *Handbuch für die Schiedsgerichtspraxis* (3rd edn, Dr Otto Schmidt, 2008).

Mankowski, P., 'Der Schiedsspruch mit vereinbartem Wortlaut' [2001] ZZP 37 ff.

Mankowski, P., 'Der Vorschlag für die Rom I-Verordnung' [2006] IPRax 101 ff.

Mark, J., Plassmeier, H. and Quinke, D., 'New Developments in German Arbitration Law' in J Benedictsson et al (eds), *The Baker & McKenzie International Arbitration Yearbook 2007* (Wolters Kluwer, 2008).

Mohs, F., *Drittwirkung von Schieds- und Gerichtsstandsvereinbarungen* (Sellier and Quadis, 2006).

Müller, W. and Keilmann, A., 'Beteiligung am Schiedsverfahren wider Willen?' [2007] SchiedsVZ 113 ff.

Musielak, H.-J., *Kommentar zur Zivilprozessordnung mit Gerichtsverfassungsgesetz* (6th edn, Franz Vahlen, 2008).

Mustill, M. J.. 'The New Lex Mercatoria: The First Twenty-five Years' (1988) 4(2) Arb Int'l 86 ff.

Palandt, O., *Bürgerliches Gesetzbuch* (67th edn, CH Beck. 2008).

Raeschke-Kessler, H., 'Gesellschaftsrechtliche Schiedsverfahren und das Recht der EU' [2003] SchiedsVZ 145 ff.

Rauscher, T., Wax, P. and Wenzel, J., (eds), *Münchener Kommentar zur Zivilprozessordnung* (3rd edn, CH Beck, 2008).

Rebmann, K., Säcker, F.J. and Rixecker, R. (eds), *Münchener Kommentar zum Bürgerlichen Gesetzbuch, Vol 1/1* (5th edn, CH Beck, 2006); vol 10 (4th edn, CH Beck, 2006).

Ritlewski, K., 'Die Lex Mercatoria in der schiedsgerichtlichen Praxis' [2007] SchiedsVZ 130 ff.

Saenger, I., (ed), *Zivilprozessordnung* (2nd edn, Nomos, 2007).

Sandrock, O., 'Wirkungen von Schiedsvereinbarungen im Konzern' in K.-H. Böckstiegel, K.P. Berger and J. Bredow (eds), *Die Beteiligung Dritter an Schiedsverfahren* (Carl Heymanns, 2005) 93 ff.

Schack, H., *Internationales Zivilverfahrensrecht* (4th edn, CH Beck, 2006).

Schlosser, P., *Das Recht der internationalen privaten Schiedsgerichtsbarkeit* (2nd edn, Mohr Siebeck, 1989).

Schlosser, P., 'Der Schiedsgerichtsobmann als Vertragspartner' [2004] SchiedsVZ 21 ff.

Schlosser, P., 'Verfahrensrechtliche und berufsrechtliche Zulässigkeit der Zeugenvorbereitung' [2004] SchiedsVZ 225 ff.

Schroth, H.-J. 'Einstweiliger Rechtsschutz im deutschen Schiedsverfahren' [2003] SchiedsVZ 102 ff.

Schütze, R. (ed), *Ausgewählte Probleme des deutschen und internationalen Schiedsverfahrensrechts* (Carl Heymanns, 2006).

Schütze, R., *Deutsches Internationales Zivilprozessrecht unter Einschluss des Europäischen Zivilprozessrechts* (2nd edn, de Gruyter, 2005).

Schütze, R., 'Die Ermessensgrenzen des Schiedsgerichts bei der Bestimmung der Beweisregeln' [2006] SchiedsVZ 1 ff.

Schütze, R., 'Die Vorlageberechtigung von Schiedsgerichten an den EuGH' [2007] SchiedsVZ 121 ff.

Schütze, R., (ed), *Institutionelle Schiedsgerichtsbarkeit* (Carl Heymanns, 2006).

Schwab, K.H. and Walter, G., *Schiedsgerichtsbarkeit* (7th edn, CH Beck, 2005).

Schwenzer, I. and Manner, S., '"The Claim is Time-Barred": The Proper Limitation Regime for International Sales Contracts in International Commercial Arbitration' (2007) 23(2) Arb Int'l 293 ff.

Seelmann-Eggebert, S., and Clifford, P., 'Lost at sea? Anti-suit injunctions after West Tankers' [2009] SchiedsVZ 139 ff.

Simms, D.P., 'Arbitrability of Intellectual Property Disputes in Germany' (1999) 15(2) Arb Int'l 193 ff.

Stein, F. and Jonas, M. (eds), *Kommentar zur Zivilprozessordnung* (22nd edn, Mohr Siebeck, 2002 ff).

Wagner, G., *Prozessverträge* (Mohr Siebeck, 1998).

Wagner, G., 'Die Aufrechnung im Europäischen Zivilprozess' [1999] IPRax 69 ff.

Wagner, G., 'Impecunious Parties and Arbitration Agreements' [2003] SchiedsVZ 206 ff.

Wirth, M., 'Ihr Zeuge, Herr Rechtsanwalt!—Weshalb Civil-Law-Schiedsrichter Common-Law-Verfahrensrecht anwenden' [2003] SchiedsVZ 9 ff.

Wirth, M. and Hoffmann-Nowotny, U., 'Rechtshilfe deutscher Gerichte zugunsten ausländischer Schiedsgerichte bei der Beweisaufnahme—ein Erfahrungsbericht' [2005] SchiedsVZ 66 ff.

Zöller, R. (ed), *Zivilprozessordnung* (26th edn, Dr Otto Schmidt, 2007).

8

ITALY

Mauro Rubino-Sammartano

I. Introduction

A. Current status of the law on arbitration

(1) Short History

A short history of Italian law on arbitration starts with the previous Civil Procedure Code (1865) which dealt with arbitration at Arts 8 to 34. The new Civil Procedure Code (1940) has replaced those provisions with more modern and liberal ones, which are to be found at Arts 806 to 831 of the Civil Procedure Code. **8.01**

Small but significant amendments were made by Parliament by Act 9 February 9, no 28 (1983). A full Reform was passed by Parliament by Act 5 January no 25 (1994)[1] and subsequently by *Decreto Legislativo* (Executive Order) no 40 of 2 February 2006,[2] both have amended provisions of the Rules of Civil Procedure, and added to them. The consolidated list of such changes is reflected in the updated version of the Civil Procedural Code (hereinafter the Rules of Civil Procedure). **8.02**

[1] The Reform.
[2] The Second Reform.

(2) Law in force and future projects

8.03 As to the law in force, Italian arbitration law is to be found in:

- the Civil Procedure Code 1940;
- Act 9 February no 28 (1983), also referred to as the *Novella* (ie the Amendment);
- Act 5 January no 25 (1994) also referred to as the *Riforma* (or the Reform); and
- *Decreto Legislativo* (Executive Order) no 40 of 2 February 2006 also referred to as the *Second Reform*.

8.04 The provisions of the *Novella* and of the two Reforms are incorporated in the part of the Civil Procedure Code dealing with arbitration. All such statutes will also be referred to as Arbitration Law.

8.05 Apart from said general provisions, specific legislation has been enacted:

- as to contracts entered into between a consumer and a trader or a professional (Act 6 February 6 no 54, 1996), an arbitral clause, unless negotiated directly by the consumer or unless it repeats statutory provisions, is presumed to be burdensome and is of no effect until the opposite is established;
- as to disputes related to public procurement, after the introduction of a series of conflicting legislation regulating the referral of disputes to arbitration,[3] Act 2 June no 216 (1995) has ruled that public procurement disputes be settled through arbitration under the statutory provisions;
- a very recent Bill (Act 24 December 24 2007 no 244) has been approved by Parliament. These new provisions prohibit the Public Administration from entering into arbitration agreements; the subsequent act of Parliament, no 88 of 7 July 2009, has conferred on the government the authority to provide arbitration as the ordinary alternative to court proceedings for public contracts as well.
- as to labour disputes, the rule remains[4] that these are not arbitrable. However, an exception has been made allowing their arbitrability when this is provided for by the law, or by national collective agreements. Nevertheless, in these situations the existence of an arbitration agreement will not prejudice the parties' right to institute court proceedings instead of referring the dispute to arbitration; and
- as to maritime matters, Art 619 *Codice di Navigazione* (Maritime Code) allows the parties to refer the dispute to arbitration.

---

[3] One of which is Legge 10 dicembre 1981, N 741, Ulteriori Norme Per L'accelerazione Delle Procedure Per L'esecuzione Di Opere Pubbliche (Gazzetta Ufficiale 16 dicembre 1981, N. 344)—(Act 10 December 1981, no 741 [Further Rules for the Accelleration of Procedures for the Implementation of Public Works] [Official Gazette, 16 December 1981, no 344]). The Constitutional Court has declared it to be in breach of the Constitution, since it created a compulsory arbitration, in breach of the parties' exclusive right to refer disputes to arbitration.

[4] Legge 11 Agosto 1973, N 533, Disciplina Delle Controversie Individuali Di Lavoro E Delle Controversie In Materia Di Previdenza E Di Assistenza Obbligatorie (Gazzetta Ufficiale, 13 Settembre 1973, no 237) - (Act 11 August 1973, no 533 [Discipline of Individual Labour Dispute and as to Mandatory Social Security and Assistance] [Official Gazette, 13 September 1973, no 237]).

(3) Distinction between national and international arbitration

Italian law on international arbitration was expressly regulated by the Reform in Arts 832–838. However, as will be discussed hereafter, these proceedings are domestic international arbitration. **8.06**

Domestic proceedings which belong to the international subtype were subject to the provisions which govern domestic arbitration, except for derogations related to:[5] **8.07**

- the form of the arbitration clause, which if being part of standard terms or forms, was not subject to the requirement of a second separate and specific acceptance;
- the substantive law, which in the absence of a choice by the parties, was the law with which the relationship has the closest connection;
- the language of the proceedings need not be Italian;
- the challenge of the arbitrators might be regulated differently from the statutory provisions on challenges before state courts;
- the decision of the award might be made through a video conference; and
- attacks against the award, as to which breach of substantive law, *revocazione*, opposition by third parties and review of the merits in the event of setting aside of the award, might be excluded.

The Second Reform has abolished the category of international arbitration, while still providing for different provisions in those arbitrations in which one of the parties resided or operated abroad from those that apply if all the parties, when they entered into the arbitration agreement, resided or operated in Italy.

(3.1) **If there are different legal systems or provisions for national/international arbitration, what are the criteria for the distinction between both systems?** The 1994 Reform Act had introduced special provisions for 'international' arbitration in order to make it easier to conduct arbitral proceedings in Italy which present some element of internationality but which are neither foreign nor procedurally international. The Second Reform has abolished the category of domestic 'international' arbitrations (while providing—as discussed above—in some provisions a derogation from the general rules on arbitration if one of the parties resides or operates abroad). **8.08**

Domestic arbitration between parties having a different residence (or registered offices) and which arise from transactions which belong to international trade remain governed by the Geneva Convention of 21 April 1961, which was followed by the Paris Implementation Agreement of 17 December 1962. **8.09**

The Geneva Convention considers international the domestic arbitration between parties having a different residence (or registered offices) and which arise from transactions that belong to international trade. A different characterization of international arbitration has been suggested by this writer based on the procedural law which governs the proceedings.[6] **8.10**

[5] s 832, Rules of Civil Procedure (hereafter RCP).

[6] Rubino-Sammartano, M., *International Arbitration: Law and Practice* (2nd edn, Kluwer, 2001), 32 *et seq*.

B. Practice of arbitration

(1) Frequency of arbitration as opposed to litigation

8.11 As to frequency of arbitration as opposed to litigation, arbitration is only a very small part of litigation. The majority of domestic arbitrations is *ad hoc*, rather than being administered by arbitral institutions. Trade arbitration is frequent in some areas like the Cotton Industry, the Grain Association, the Hides Association, the Maritime field and commodities.

(2) Leading arbitral institutions and statistics

8.12 The leading arbitral institutions are:

- the *Camera Arbitrale Nazionale e Internazionale di Milano*;
- the *Associazione Italiana per l'Arbitrato*;
- the *Delegazione Italiana of the European Court of Arbitration*;
- the *Curia Mercatorum*; and
- the *Camera Arbitrale della Camera di Commercio di Bologna*.

8.13 As to statistics, in 1996 the backlog of criminal and civil proceedings was in the area of 3.600.000 criminal proceedings and 4.500.000 civil proceedings. The statistics show that civil proceedings pending at the end of 2007 have reached the following level:

Court of Cassation	102,588
Court of Appeal	376,519
Juvenile Court	124,906
High Court	3,208,330
Justices of the Peace	1,371,672
Total:	5,184,015

Administered arbitrations are probably in the area of 300 arbitrations and *ad hoc* arbitrations have probably not exceeded 400 proceedings. This is due to the negative image that has been created of arbitration, as a highly sophisticated and very expensive mechanism reserved for big disputes, ie[7] a luxury clinic.

II. Jurisdiction of the arbitral tribunal

A. Arbitration agreement

(1) Arbitration clause and submission agreement

8.14 Both have been defined[8] as substantive contracts which produce procedural effects. However, as pointed out by precedents,[9] the arbitration clause is different from a submission agreement

[7] See the criticism of this approach made by Mauro Rubino-Sammartano, M., *Is Arbitration Just to be A Luxury Clinic?* (1990) *J Int'l Arb* 3, 25.

[8] *Conti v Com Borgosesia* Court of Cassation (*Corte di Cassazione*) [1967] January 27 no 221, Mass Giust Civ. (1967) 114; in accord *Miserocchi v Soc Agnesi e Figli*, Court of Cassation, [1971] December 13 no 3620, *Mass Giust Civ* (1971) 1952.

[9] *Unione Parmense industriali v Soc SO.AL e altro*, Corte di Cassazione (Court of Cassation) no 2651 (1979), *Rep Foro It* (1981), item Arbitrato c162, 55.

in that the former is entered into prior to the dispute arising while the latter is entered into only after it.

The substance of the arbitration clauses and of submission agreements prevails over their form, which may take a different shape. This is reflected in s 808, Rules of Civil Procedure which provides: 'the parties, in the agreement which they enter into or in a separate document, may provide that disputes arising from it be decided by arbitrators'. **8.15**

(2) Requirements as to the contents of the arbitration agreement

The contents of submission agreements consist of essential and not essential requirements. An essential requirement is the expression of the intention to refer to arbitration a dispute which has already arisen. A further essential element is that the dispute be identified or that the criteria to identify it be set out. **8.16**

The statement of the number of arbitrators and of the way to appoint them was also an essential requirement. However, the Reform has replaced such a requirement with a provision that enables the remedy of the omission by the parties to regulate the number of arbitrators (or their decision to appoint only two arbitrators).[10] **8.17**

Amongst the elements of submission agreements, which are not essential, one should mention: the authority of the arbitrators to mitigate strict law; the determination of the procedure to be followed by the arbitrators; the determination of a time period within which the award must be made, if different from the statutory time period; and the challenge of the award, in the event of the arbitrator not having complied with substantive law. **8.18**

As to the arbitration clauses, they are meant to embrace all the disputes which may arise from the contract which incorporates that clause. The Second Reform has provided at s 808 bis, Rules of Civil Procedure, that the parties may also submit to arbitration their future disputes arising from one or more non-contractual relationships. The related arbitration clause or submission agreement must comply with the same form requirements of the arbitration agreement related to contractual disputes. **8.19**

(3) Form of the agreement (eg in writing requirement)

The agreement is to be in writing.[11] This requirement is not merely *ad probationem*, ie just to prove the existence of the agreement, but according to the prevailing precedents,[12] is a requirement for the validity of the agreement (ie is *ad substantiam*). The notion 'in writing' involves the issue whether the document has also to be signed or not. In this respect, the Arbitration Reforms have clarified that cables, telexes, emails and faxes which comply with the regulations to forward and receive telecommunications are to be treated as documents in writing, even if they are not signed. **8.20**

Under Italian law[13] oppressive clauses have to be accepted specifically by appending a second signature after a reference to each of them. **8.21**

---

10 s 809, RCP.

11 s 807, *ibid.*

12 *Giorgi v Pres reg Sicilia*, Corte di Cassazione (Court of Cassation), no 6847 (2004), *Mass Foro it*, 2004, 620.

13 Civil Code s 1341-2.

8.22 The signing of the arbitration agreement may be replaced by the production, during the proceedings, of the agreement signed by the other party, provided such a production is made in support of the existence of such an agreement.

8.23 It has been submitted[14] that the production of the contract containing the arbitration clause, signed by the other party, amounts to a waiver of the right to challenge the existence of the arbitration agreement on that ground.

8.24 (3.1) **Are there special requirements for a power of attorney/authority to enter into an arbitration agreement on behalf of a third party?** The power of attorney is to be in writing and in order to be validly issued, the issuer must enjoy the capacity to act. If the power of attorney is signed by someone on behalf of a party to it, his/her power to act for that party is required.

(4) Incorporation of an arbitration clause contained in general terms and conditions

8.25 Arbitration agreements are frequently part of a set of standard conditions and are deemed to be incorporated by reference. It has been debated whether a mere general reference to the standard conditions is sufficient. Section 833, Rules of Civil Procedure, which had been introduced by the Reform, required as to domestic 'international' arbitration, that the parties had been aware that the arbitration clause was one of the standard conditions or should have been aware of it by using normal care. This provision has been set aside by the Second Reform. The matter is governed by the law of contract (ss 1341 and 1342, Civil Code). The problem does not arise when there is a specific reference not only to the standard conditions but also to the arbitration clause. This view has been expressed, amongst writers, by *Mirabelli.*[15] The difficulty arises when no specific reference to it is made while incorporating the standard conditions. If so, the reference has been held not to be valid.[16]

(5) Law applicable to the interpretation of arbitration clauses

8.26 The law applicable to the interpretation of arbitral clauses is the law which governs the arbitration clause. The identification of the latter has been the subject of a large debate. The view, according to which one should apply the *lex fori* since the arbitration clause would be a procedural matter, has been excluded by several precedents.[17] The clause being incorporated in a wider contract, the proper law of the latter will then tend to also govern the arbitration clause.

8.27 However, in view of the autonomy of the arbitration clause, it is also conceivable that it be governed by a different law and that the parties have the authority to do so. In the absence of a different choice of law by the parties, it is suggested that the law to be applied to establish whether the arbitration agreement binds the parties is the law which governs the arbitration agreement itself, ie as a rule the *lex contractus*.

---

[14] Rubino-Sammartano, M., *Il Diritto dell'Arbitrato* (5th edn, Cedam, 2006) (hereinafter *Il Diritto dell'Arbitrato*) 359.

[15] Mirabelli, G., 'Clausole compromissorie per relationem ed arbitrato commerciale internazionale' *Rass Arb* (1967) 57.

[16] *Janch v Società Transoceania*, Corte di Cassazione (Court of Cassation), no 6035 (1981), *Rep Foro it* 1981, 53.

[17] *Ditta Hugo Trumpy v Soc Salgoil*, Corte di Cassazione (Court of Cassation), no 269 (1960), *Foro it* 1960, 736.

The question as to which law applies to establish whether a party validly binds itself, should find an answer in the national law of that party. The dilemma does not seem to exist as to a submission, since it is not part of wider contract and is then to be governed by the law applicable to it. 8.28

(5.1) Do courts accept a wide competence of the arbitral tribunal or do they restrict arbitral competence? Do claims which arise in connection with the agreement submitted to arbitration generally fall within the arbitral jurisdiction even if based on tortious legal basis? Does there exist case law with respect to the wording in an arbitration clause as 'arising out of/under/in connection with the present contract' and its specific meaning? As to the construction of arbitration clauses, it is established by precedent that 'arbitration agreements are to be construed restrictively,[18] because they constitute derogation to the jurisdiction of state courts and as such they prevent the parties from being judged by their natural judges'. The Second Reform has amended this trend by providing[19] that arbitration agreements are to be construed as applying to all the disputes arising from that contract or relationship. The wording in an arbitration clause, such as arising out of/under/in connection with the present contract, is then to be construed in a liberal way. 8.29

Except where the tortious dispute is the express object of an arbitration agreement, claims in tort may not fall under the arbitral jurisdiction when the latter arises from an agreement which submits to arbitration disputes arising from a contract. Tortious claims may be included by the parties in the ambit of arbitration clauses. If they are not included in it, either the same fact gives rise to a claim in contract (which is covered by the arbitration clause) and to a claim in tort, and that dispute may be referred to arbitration, or it gives rise only to a claim in tort and then it is excluded from arbitration. For example, an arbitration agreement included in a joint venture contract will normally not refer to arbitration claims for breach of rights on trade marks or for unfair competition, unless it includes commitments as to trade marks or as to competition, or such undertakings are implied in them. The wording used in an arbitration clause, such as 'arising out of/under/in connection with the present contract' is then to be construed in a liberal way. 8.30

(6) Binding effect of an arbitration clause on third parties (eg in case of a guarantee or assignment)

The issue whether a third party may be bound by an arbitration agreement and consequently by the award made under it is separate from the issue whether a third party may intervene in arbitral proceedings. However, the Second Reform has permitted[20] a party which intends to exercise a right or without which the dispute may not be decided, to join its motion, while a third party may not join in other situations or be joined without the consent of all the parties and of the arbitration. In case a third party takes over the rights of a party to the arbitral proceedings, it is entitled to join the proceedings to which the previous holder of a right or obligee was a party. 8.31

18 *Agricola Veneta v Serafino Ferruzzi* (Court of Cassation, 24 October no 5562, [1979], *Mass Giust Civ* 1979, 2444).

19 s 808 quarter, RCP, Second Reform.

20 s 816 quinquies, RCP.

8.32 However, in some situations the obligation of a party to these proceedings may be based on the premise of a fact or duty which is to be established between the other contracting party and a third party. This is the case of the guarantor's duty to pay which depends on the issue whether the principal debtor is in breach of its duty to the creditor and of the rights and duties of the assignee of the credit, which depends on a decision on the existence of the credit if disputed between assignor and debtor. In Italy, the third party, which is affected by the decision of that issue, may not intervene in the proceedings, unless the other parties to the arbitration agreement consent. In order not to leave such a third party without protection, the Reform has granted such parties the right to oppose the award before the Court of Appeal, such proceedings being called *opposizione di terzo* (third party's opposition).[21]

8.33 (6.1) **What is the law/leading authorities' position on multi-party situations? Especially, (i) with respect to the objection that the arbitration clause does not specifically provide for a plurality of parties in the same procedure; (ii) with respect to the constitution of the arbitral tribunal; and (iii) With respect to the consolidation of two or more running arbitration proceedings?** A distinction has to be drawn between several scenarios. In a first scenario several individuals, and or entities, may have entered into an arbitration agreement. The problem here is to ensure that all of them have the same right to appoint the arbitrator/s or that the arbitrator/s be appointed by a neutral party.[22] As held by precedents[23] it is essential that all the parties to a proceeding be placed on an equal footing so far as the appointment of arbitrator/s is concerned. In the absence of a solution to this problem, the arbitral proceedings are split into various proceedings, in each of which one of the other parties will be a defendant. If the dispute cannot be decided without the attendance of all the parties, the proceedings may not take place. If the arbitration agreement does not allow each party to be on an equal footing, the agreement may not give rise to valid proceedings. Appointment of the arbitrator or of all the arbitrators by the arbitral institution is a formula to achieve this object.

8.34 In a second scenario, the arbitration agreement has been entered into only by some of the litigants. Here without the consent of all the parties, it is not possible to add other parties to the proceedings.

8.35 In a third scenario different proceedings, which are somehow interrelated, are pending before the same arbitrator or arbitral tribunal. If so they may proceed in a parallel way, but they must remain separate. In some jurisdictions that may be consolidated. However, consolidation of proceedings is not allowed by Italian arbitration law.

8.36 (6.2) **Is there case law/authorities with respect to the admissibility of third party participation in an arbitration without being a claimant or defendant (Nebenintervention/ Streitverkündung; intervention forcée/volontaire; vouching in, *amicus curiae*; etc)? What are the prerequisites and effects of such participation (if permitted)?** It has been

[21] See *infra*, para 8.265.
[22] See Art 10, 1998 ICC Rules.
[23] *Tino v Soc Coop A.i.a.* Tribunale di Avellino (Tribunal of Avellino) (1961), *Temi nap* 1961, I, 89.

a firm tradition that, while in court proceedings a third party may join the proceedings either in order to assert its own rights on the object of the dispute or to support the arguments of one of the parties (*ad adiuvandum*), the contractual nature of arbitration prevented a third party from joining proceedings unless the parties to them give their consent. This view has been shared by several precedents.[24]

These rules have been changed by the Second Reform (Decreto Legislativo no 40 of 2 February 2006) as discussed under para 8.31 *supra*. **8.37**

(7) Termination of an arbitration agreement by a party (reasons and case law)

In certain circumstances, eg if a time limit for referring a dispute to arbitration has not been complied with, an arbitration agreement may come to an end. In the event of one of the parties to an arbitration agreement being placed in compulsory liquidation, then according to the prevailing precedents,[25] the arbitration agreement loses any effect if the arbitral tribunal has not yet been formed when the order for compulsory liquidation is made. In the opposite case, according to such precedents, the arbitration agreement has effect, provided the claim against the insolvent party is not for payment of money, since all such claims must be made only by filing a proof of debt. According to another view, the arbitration agreement produces effects limited to claims made or to be made by the receiver of the company, or business, which is in compulsory liquidation. **8.38**

It has further been held that even claims which aim to obtain a judgment, which may be the basis for subsequent proceedings, in which the Bankruptcy Court would be unable to challenge the first judgment, are within the exclusive jurisdiction of the Bankruptcy Court.[26] **8.39**

Waiver by the parties, be it express or by conduct, puts an end to the arbitration agreement. If the arbitrator fails to render an award within the term granted to him, provided a party has given a notice to this effect to the arbitrator prior to the arbitrator's decision of the dispute, he will no longer have jurisdiction. It is debatable whether this puts an end to the arbitration agreement too, or whether the parties may start other arbitral proceedings under that arbitration agreement. As held by a precedent, even if in a special situation,[27] the arbitration agreement comes to an end if it becomes impossible to hold arbitral proceedings. **8.40**

Lack of action by the parties during the arbitral proceedings is not seen by the Italian legal system as a withdrawal from them, as long as the parties keep extending the time limit for the award. Lack of response for an unreasonable time period to several orders or directions **8.41**

24 *Valenzi v Cersasismo et al* Corte d'Appello di Roma, (Court of Appeal of Rome) no 1421 (1989), *Rass arb* 1990, 202; in accord *Impresa Giovannini e Micheli v Industrie Pirelli*, Tribunale Arbitrale di Salerno (Arbitral Tribunal of Salerno) (1975), *Arbitrati e appalti*, 1976, 48.

25 *Ditta O.R.M.A. v Tessilmarod* Corte di Cassazione (Court of Cassation) no 30 (1956), *Mass. Giust Civ.* 1956, I, 11; in accord *Chignola v Mueioli* Corte di Cassazione (Court of Cassation) no 2866 (1958), *Foro pad* 1958, I, 969.

26 *Fassi v Fallimento società ALES et al* Corte di Cassazione (Court of Cassation) no 2902 (1992), Dir Fall 1992, II, 673.

27 *Rocco v Agenzia marittima Tomasos*, Corte di Cassazione (Court of Cassation) no 7033 (1992), *Foro it* 1983, I, 1, 2196.

given by the arbitrators may amount to abandonment of those proceedings, although not necessarily also of the arbitration agreement. It has been held[28] that if one of the parties does not respond, the other party may avail itself of all the remedies provided by the law of contract, *inter alia* the right to terminate the arbitration agreement.

8.42 Non-compliance with a former award rendered on the basis of the same arbitration agreement does not entitle the arbitration agreement to be treated as terminated. Violation of the terms of the arbitration agreement may, depending on its relevance, entitle it to be terminated.[29]

B. Arbitrability

(1) 'Personal arbitrability' (the capacity to conclude arbitration agreements)

8.43 The capacity of individuals to submit disputes to arbitration is subject to the general rules and ordinarily does not give rise to difficulties. As to arbitration clauses, the authority to enter into a contract includes the authority to enter into the arbitration agreement, when the latter is one of the terms of that contract. As for submission agreements, in order to enter into them the authority to commit the principal for transactions which go beyond the ordinary day-to-day management of a business (extraordinary management) is required.[30]

8.44 This may give rise to problems in particular as to legal entities. As to state agencies, administrative law shall apply. The main problem here is to ensure that the signatory has due authority to do so. Absence of authority would deprive the arbitration agreement of its effects. It is then advisable to request the government official to proceed to an exchange of 'credentials' as in diplomatic relationships. It has been established by precedent[31] that provided a party has not exercised a lack of care with regard to the authority of the agent of the other contracting party to bind it to the agreement, then the other party may not rely on a lack of authority to defeat the agreement.

8.45 **(1.1) May a state (or state agency) as party invoke sovereign immunity before the arbitral tribunal or before a state court (eg in a procedure of enforcement)?** In general, a foreign state or a state agency may invoke sovereign immunity before state courts when it has acted as a sovereign (*ex jure imperii*) and not when it has acted as a business entity (*ex jure gestionis*). As to arbitral proceedings, a foreign state or a state agency seem not to be entitled to enter into an arbitration agreement and then to argue that—since they are a sovereign—they are not bound by their own earlier free choice. It has been held[32] that the free behaviour of a sovereign on one hand is valid and on the other hand does not detract from his sovereignty.

---

[28] *Soc CIS Milano v Barbera*, Corte di Cassazione (Court of Cassation) no 5499 (1985), *Mediterranean and Middle East Arbitration Quarterly* (1988) 2.

[29] *Soc Rocco v Agenzia Marittima Tomasos Ltd*, Corte di Cassazione (Court of Cassation) no 703 (1982), *Foro it* 1983, I, 2196; Tribunale Arbitrale (Arbitral Tribunal) (1954), *Arch giur oo pp* 1956, I, 35; Punzi, C., *Disegno sistematico dell'arbitrato* (Cedam, 1999) 454 *et seq.*

[30] s 808, last para, RCP.

[31] *Società SAIM v Appio*, Corte di Cassazione (Court of Cassation) no 6246 [1981], *Mass Foro it* 1981, 1, 1276.

[32] *Gouvernment de la Republique populaire du Congo v Agip SpA Societé*, Tribunale Arbitrale (Arbitral Tribunal) (1979), *Rev Cr Dr Int Priv* 1982, 92.

(2) 'Objective arbitrability' (eg of patent, trade mark and antitrust matters)

In general, in order to settle a claim, it must concern a right of which the parties may dispose. Whenever a right may not be disposed of, the dispute is not arbitrable. **8.46**

The Italian legal system—as with many others—has chosen the solution of stating which disputes are non-arbitrable.[33] **8.47**

In principle, labour disputes are not arbitrable,[34] except when this is allowed by national collective agreements, provided a party nevertheless remains free to refer the dispute to the state courts. This matter has been the object of various interventions by Parliament, which have introduced requirements which are not always very clear. **8.48**

Disputes concerning condominiums are in general considered arbitrable.[35] Disputes between two condominium owners over the validity of a condominium resolution are not arbitrable, since the right to have the resolution set aside is not limited to two or several condominium owners, but involves the entire condominium. **8.49**

The distinction highlighted in para 8.49 has to be made also to corporate disputes. In principle, issues involving the right of individual shareholders are arbitrable, while disputes involving collective interests are not.[36] Examples of the latter dealt with by precedents[37] are attacks against corporate resolutions, capital increases or reductions, the winding up of the company, and removal of directors for just cause. Executive Order 17 January 2003 no 5 has widened the scope of corporate disputes which may be referred to arbitration, excluding those to which the *Pubblico Ministero* (Director of Public Prosecution) is mandatorily a party. The Second Reform has allowed third parties to join arbitral proceedings, in specific situations (as explained in no 8.274 *infra*). **8.50**

Arbitrability of the issue of nullity of a contract has to face a difficulty since the requirement for arbitrability is that the parties may dispose of the right in issue and it is generally held that parties may not dispose of the right that a nullity be established or not. However, a distinction has to be made between nullity due to breach of mandatory provisions, which is not arbitrable, and nullity arising from causes which the parties may dispose of, which are arbitrable. Case law[38] confirms this distinction. **8.51**

---

[33] s 806 RCP excludes in fact disputes 'foreseen by ss 429 and 459 as well as those concerning issues of status, of separation between spouses, and those which may not be settled by the parties.

[34] ss 4 and 5 Statute 11 August, no 553, 1973.

[35] *Rossi v Condominio Giardino*, Corte di Cassazione (Court of Cassation) no 3406, *Giust. Civ.* 1985, I, 103; in accord *Caselli v Cond via Lambertenghi 25 Milano*, Corte di Cassazione (Court of Cassation) no 2960 (1968), *Mass Foro it* 1968, 1550.

[36] *Mega c Soc Ital Meeting Executive* Tribunale di Milano (Tribunal of Milan) (2002), *Giurit* 2002, 1014; *Bosè v Vecchiati*, Tribunale di Trieste (Tribunal of Trieste) (1990), *Società* 1991, 818; *Picardi c Soc Picardi,* Tribunale di Napoli (Tribunal of Naples) (1988), *Dir fall* 1989, II, 490; *D'Amico v D'Amico* Corte di Cassazione (Court of Cassation) no 2940, Dir Fall 1988, II, 893.

[37] *Ferrari v Fermi*, Pretura di Sestri Ponente (County Court of Sestri Ponente) (1989), *Foro it* 1989, I, 2356; *Montanari v Nicolini*, Tribunale di Como (Trubunal of Como) (1989), *Società* 1989, 951; *Picaroli v Soc. Piceno*, Tribunale di Napoli, (Tribunal of Naples) (1988), *Dir Fall* 1989, II, 490; *D Mazzetti v Manassei*, Corte di Cassazione (Court of Cassation) no 2731 (1950), *Mass Foro it* 1950, 561.

[38] *Fina v Russi*, Corte di Cassazione (Court of Cassation) no 3003 (1972) *Foro it* 1973, I, 726.

8.52 Even if frequently one believes that tortious liability is not arbitrable; it is nevertheless arbitrable. It is simply that the parties refer such disputes to arbitration less frequently.

8.53 As to intellectual property, a distinction is made between the validity or nullity of the intellectual property right, which is generally held not to be arbitrable, and financial rights arising from it, such as under a licence, which are held to be arbitrable.[39]

8.54 As to bankruptcy, if the proceedings are already pending and the tribunal has been formed, according to the prevailing opinion,[40] the proceedings may continue. Nevertheless, if the matter in dispute is a claim against a company which has been put into compulsory liquidation, it has been held that the matter has to move to the state court before which the bankrupt's debts are to be proved.[41] As discussed above, money claims against a company which is in compulsory liquidation may be exclusively heard by the Bankruptcy Court. The same applies to claims seeking a judgment which would force the Bankruptcy Court to allow a claim based on it.

8.55 The Second Reform has provided at s 817 bis Rules of Civil Procedure that the arbitral tribunal has jurisdiction to hear the defence of setting off within the amount of the claim, even if it is based on a title which is not included in the arbitration agreement. It is submitted that it follows from this that counterclaims which have no basis in the arbitration agreement are outside the jurisdiction of the arbitral tribunal.

C. Decision on the arbitral tribunal's jurisdiction ('*competence-competence*')

(1) Separability (independence of the arbitration agreement from the main agreement)

8.56 **The issue of separability of the arbitration agreement has been debated for a long time.** Precedents[42] and writers[43] have recognized that—with reference to the old Roman rule 'accessorium sequitur principale',[44] the arbitration clause is not an accessory. The contract and the arbitration clause have subsequently been classified as two separate contracts.[45] The autonomy of the arbitration clause from the contract, of which it is physically a part, does not preclude that in some situations, like in the case of the non-existence of the contract, the two agreements be both affected by it.

8.57 The matter has been dealt with by the Arbitration Reforms which provide[46] that 'the validity of the arbitration agreement must be determined autonomously from the contract to which it refers'. According to the Report to the Senate on the Bill which has given birth to the Reform, 'it has been deemed advisable to state in such a way as to avoid any possible

---

[39] *Scherk Enterprises Aktiengesellschaft– Ls Schaft c Soc Des Grandes Marques*, Corte di Cassazione (Court of Cassation), n 3989 (1977), *Mass Giust. Civ.* 1977, 161; *Società Della Pilata v Società Happening*, Corte di Cassazione (Court of Cassation) no 2404 (1989), *Giust. civ.* 1989, 2605.

[40] *Chignola v Muzioli*, Corte di Cassazione (Court of Cassation) no 2866 (1958), *Foro pad* 1958, I, 969.

[41] *CM*, Tribunale di Verona (Tribunal of Verona), no 1100/296 (1989), *Il Fallimento* 1990, 453.

[42] *Soc Purfina It v Soc. Cred Venezia y Rio de la Plata*, Corte di Cassazione (Court of Cassation) no 2161 (1964), *Rep Foro it* 1964, *Arbitrato*, 66, 158.

[43] Carnelutti, F., 'Clausola compromissoria e competenze degli arbitri', *Riv Dir Comm* 1921, II, 63.

[44] The accessory follows the principal.

[45] *Soc tramvie provinciali di Napoli v Manicone*, Corte d'Appello di Napoli (Court of Appeal of Naples) (1950), *Foro it* 1950, I.

[46] s 808, RCP.

misunderstanding on the issue that the arbitration agreement has full_autonomy vis-à-vis the contract to which it refers'.

(2) Competence of the tribunal to decide on its own jurisdiction (including form and time of the tribunal's decision)

The issue has been raised of arbitrators' jurisdiction to rule on their own jurisdiction (*competence-competence*). Under Italian law, arbitrators have jurisdiction to rule on it. However, since their award may be attacked, the final decision belongs to the state courts. Therefore, the Italian legal system deals in this repsect with arbitration as with state courts. When the jurisdiction of the first instance court is challenged before it, it is up to that court to rule on this, subject to review of its decision by the appeal courts. Likewise if the arbitrator's jurisdiction is challenged, it is submitted that it will belong to the arbitrator to decide, subject to review by the state court. The leading precedent has held that[47] 'the arbitrators are themselves judges of their competence' a view which has been confirmed by arbitral awards,[48] and is shared by a leading writer.[49] **8.58**

The time and form of the arbitral tribunal's decision on jurisdiction have also been the object of discussion. The arbitrator may determine his own jurisdiction, or decline it, at the beginning of the arbitral proceedings, or during them, or at the end. There are no statutory provisions regulating this matter. The arbitral tribunal's position on the timing of its decision on such an issue will generally depend on its view on this issue. If the tribunal takes the view that it has no jurisdiction, it will avoid going further through proceedings which would serve no practical purpose. If the tribunal takes the view that it has jurisdiction, it may either render an interim award, in order to decide, or issue an order advising the parties that the decision on this issue will be made together with the merits. Traditionally, such an order is construed as a sign that the tribunal is of the view that the merits must be tried and that it prefers not to take time to render a partial award, also to avoid the proceedings being disturbed by possible attacks. **8.59**

(3) Extent of the 'competence-competence' *and role of the courts (including form and time limits of a challenge of the tribunal's decision)*

The expression '*competence-competence*' (which derives from the German *Kompetenz-Kompetenz*, but which has not kept its original meaning) is construed as meaning that the arbitral tribunal has the authority to decide on its jurisdiction. However, this rule is subject to the authority of the state courts to review that decision. Control by the courts is also a much debated issue. The award which denies jurisdiction and puts an end to the arbitral proceedings must be attacked within 90 days from its service, or in the absence of service within one year from the day the last arbitrator has signed it.[50] **8.60**

---

[47] *Rota v Florè*, Corte d'Appello di Genova (*Court of Appeal* of *Genoa)* (1949), *Foro pad* 1949, 1, 243.

[48] *Soc Speis v Soc CMC*, Tribunale Arbitrale (*Arbitral Tribunal)* (1981), *Rep Foro it* 1983, item *Arbitrato*, 181, 80.

[49] Mortara, L., *Commentario al codice di procedura civile* (Milan, 1923) 88.

[50] *Soc Sic v Soc Cnl*, Corte di Cassazione (Court of Cassation) no 2896 (1993), *Mass Foro it* 1993, 295; Zucconi Galli Fonseca, AAVV *Arbitrato* (Carpi, gen ed, Zanichelli, 2001) 584.

8.61 The award which asserts jurisdiction, and which consequently does not put an end to the arbitral proceedings, may be challenged only together with the award which puts an end to them, within the above time limits.[51] An award which asserts jurisdiction and partly decides the merits may be attacked immediately. The above time limit shall apply. The state court which hears the application for setting aside the award may stay the enforceability of the award. This should not interfere with the continuance of the proceedings, a matter which is left to the arbitrators.[52] The arbitrators might consider staying the proceedings, provided this does not affect the time limit within which they are bound to make the award.

D. Enforcement of an arbitration agreement within or by court proceedings

(1) Effect of invoking an arbitration clause within a court proceeding (and time limits for such a motion)

8.62 There is a need for an *ex parte* plea. The first effect of an arbitration agreement is to deprive the state courts of jurisdiction. Therefore the lack of jurisdiction of the state court, because of the arbitration agreement, is to be submitted by the interested party and may not be raised by the court of its own motion. The Court of Cassation has affirmed this repeatedly.[53] The existence of the arbitration agreement does not have to be raised before the state court in *limine litis*[54] ie before any other defence. However, it must be raised in the statement of defence.[55] The consequence of a failure to challenge timeously the court's jurisdiction by invoking the arbitration agreement amounts to a waiver to it, thereby granting jurisdiction to the state courts.

8.63 The judgment of a state court which asserts or denies its jurisdiction because of an arbitration agreement may be challenged through the *regolamento di competenza* (special proceedings through which the Court of Cassation is seized just in respect of this issue and decides which out of the various state courts has jurisdiction).

8.64 **(1.1) If a party has invoked successfully the arbitration agreement in a court proceeding, is it then entitled to deny within the arbitral proceedings that there is a valid and binding arbitration agreement?** A party may not first oppose court proceedings on the ground of the existence of a valid arbitration agreement and then challenge that agreement during the arbitral proceedings. *Nemo contra factum proprium venire potest.*[56]

8.65 **(1.2) Vice versa, if a party has successfully objected to an arbitral proceeding by denying that there is a valid arbitration agreement, may it then invoke such agreement in the ensuing court proceeding?** Likewise, if a party opposes arbitral proceedings on the ground that the arbitration agreement is not valid, then in subsequent court proceedings it may not argue the existence of that arbitration agreement, since the earlier submission

---

[51] s 827, RCP.

[52] s 830, *ibid.*

[53] *Renzi v Soc Fonderie*, Corte di Cassazione (Court of Cassation) no 278 (1953), *Giur it* 1953, I, 1, 798.

[54] s 38, RCP.

[55] *Mangano v ANPI*, Corte di Cassazione (Court of Cassation) no 751 (1951), *Rep Foro it* 1951, *Arbitramento* n 21.

[56] Nobody can hold the opposite of what he has done.

produces estoppel. This particular situation arose in a case[57] in which a party to a charter-party, Rocco, did not refer the dispute to arbitration according to the arbitration agreement which had been duly entered into, and sued Tomaso before the Court of Naples. Tomaso challenged the court jurisdiction on the ground of the existence of the arbitration agreement. Rocco argued that the time limit to refer the dispute to arbitration had expired and that the arbitration clause was no longer effective. The Court of Cassation ruled that state courts have no jurisdiction if an arbitration agreement has been entered into, even if the time limit for starting arbitration proceedings expired. Rocco then had no right to have the dispute heard, neither by state courts nor by arbitrators.

(2) Legal remedies and proceedings to enforce an arbitration agreement

If a state court is seized by a party and the defendant invokes the arbitration agreement as a defence, the question arises whether the court has any discretion whether to stop the proceedings or not. If the court is convinced that there is a valid arbitration clause, it is under a duty to declare its lack of jurisdiction.[58] **8.66**

Difficulties arise in cases of a simultaneous running of arbitral and court proceedings. Under Italian law prior to the Reform, if arbitral and court proceedings were running simultaneously, this produced the result that the so-called *vis atractiva*[59] of court proceedings absorbed the connected issues pending before the arbitrators.[60] However, it was held[61] that this rule did not apply if it was apparent that the court proceedings had been initiated to cause artificially such an absorption in order to deprive the other party of the right to have such issues determined by arbitrators. A further exclusion to the aforementioned *vis atractiva* was the provision for a foreign award. This has been established by precedents.[62] **8.67**

The Reform has put aside such a *vis atractiva* by providing[63] that 'The arbitrators' jurisdiction is not excluded by a connection between issues submitted to them and proceedings pending before a state court'. The Second Reform has gone further providing (s 819 ter) that the jurisdiction of the arbitral tribunal is not excluded if the same dispute or a connected dispute is pending before a state court. **8.68**

A quite different situation, where arbitral and court proceedings may run simultaneously, arises when a partial award, ie an award which decides some but not all the issues on the merits, is made and attacked. Here, while the arbitrators will decide the remaining issues, the state court will hear the attack against the partial award. **8.69**

[57] *Rocco v Agenzia Tomasos*, Corte di Cassazione (Court of Cassation) no 7033 (1987), *Foro it* 1983, I, 1, 2196.

[58] *Soc Montedison* e *altro v Eni et al*, Corte di Cassazione (Court of Cassation) no 6205 (1996), *Foro it* 1996, I, 2714.

[59] Power to attract.

[60] *Soc Favria v Choa*, Corte di Cassazione (Court of Cassation), no 1108 (1979), Giust Civ Mass 1979, 491; in accord *Lucchi v Livon*, Corte di Cassazione (Court of Cassation) no 5641 (1987) *Rep Foro it*, Arbitrato 183, 96.

[61] *Società Holst italiana v Comune Jesolo*, Corte di Cassazione (Court of Cassation) 29 November, no 5949, *Rep Foro it* 1986, 166, 46.

[62] *Bagnasacco v Mattalia*, Corte d'Appello di Torino (Court of Appeal of Turin) (1984), *Riv Dir Int Priv Proc* (1984) 586.

[63] s 819 bis, RCP.

8.70 **(2.1) Which would be the internationally competent court (i) for obtaining a declaration that a given arbitration agreement is valid and binding; or (ii) to compel arbitration? (The defendant's courts? The courts of the place of arbitration? The claimant's courts, cf Article 6(2) in fine, 1998 ICC Rules?)** The existence of a valid arbitration agreement is normally used as a ground to oppose court proceedings. If this argument succeeds, the court, which has been seized of the claim to which the *exceptio compromissi* is opposed, will declare its lack of jurisdiction. A party may be tempted to block arbitral proceedings by issuing court proceedings seeking a declaratory judgment on the invalidity of the arbitration agreement.[64] It has been debated whether such proceedings may only be initiated before a dispute has been referred to arbitration, or also after the arbitral tribunal has been formed. Some precedents[65] have held that state courts may hear claims concerning the validity or the limits of an arbitration agreement, only if made before the arbitral tribunal is formed. In general, it has been held[66] that a mere claim seeking a declaratory judgment on an arbitration agreement is not admissible, unless it is coupled with a claim to decide a specific dispute, the decision of which involves the issue of the validity of the arbitration agreement. The Second Reform has provided that no court ruling as to the validity of an arbitration agreement may be sought while arbitration proceedings are pending.

8.71 The locally competent court is that of the residence (or place of business) of the defendant or alternatively of the place where the submission, or the arbitration agreement which incorporates the clause, was entered into. Italian courts do not compel arbitration. If they find that the dispute may not be heard by them, because of the existence of a valid arbitration agreement, jurisdiction will be denied.

III. The arbitral tribunal

A. Number and qualification of arbitrators

(1) Sole arbitrator or arbitral tribunal with several arbitrators

8.72 The Reform has removed the nullity which previously[67] affected arbitration agreements which did not state the number of the arbitrators and the way to appoint them, by providing that 'The arbitrators may be one or more, provided their number is always odd'. If an uneven number of arbitrators is appointed, or the number of the arbitrators has not been stated, there shall be three arbitrators and if not appointed by the parties, the President of the *Tribunale*[68] will appoint them. The Second Reform has confirmed this.

8.73 **(1.1) Are arbitral tribunals with an even number of arbitrators acceptable?** According to s 809 Rules of Civil Procedure the arbitrators may be one or more, provided their number

[64] Schizzerotto, G., *Dell'Arbitrato* (2nd edn, Giuffré, Milan, 1982) 651.
[65] *Ferrarini v Odoli*, Corte di Cassazione (Court of Cassation) no 3767 (1955); in Schizzerotto, G., *Arbitrato rituale nella giurisprudenza*, 184.
[66] *Lumi v Soc Edilmark*, Corte di Cassazione (Court of Cassation) no 3361 (1991), *Giur it* 1992, I, 1, 552.
[67] s 809, RCP.
[68] The court which tries cases in the first instance, except for small claims and for some other claims for which the *Pretura* (County Court) has jurisdiction.

is uneven. If the parties have not stated the number of the arbitrators, they shall be three. If the parties have stated that they will be two, a third arbitrator shall be appointed—unless the parties have otherwise agreed—by the President of the *Tribunale* in whose jurisdiction the place of the arbitral proceedings is located.

(2) Qualification of the arbitrators

The qualification of arbitrators includes various aspects: their capacity to act—the absence of other legal obstacles to act in such a capacity; the capacity to decide—the qualification proper. 'The arbitrators may be Italian citizens or not Italian citizens. Minors, persons subject to restrictions to their capacity to act, bankrupts and those who are barred from holding public offices may not be appointed arbitrators'.[69] The Second Reform has amended this provision by providing that a person who is totally or partly deprived of the legal capability to act may not act as arbitrator. Since an arbitrator discharges a quasi-judicial activity, it has been held by precedents[70] and writers[71] that no partnership or corporation may act as an arbitrator. **8.74**

A specific obstacle to act as arbitrator is the lack of independence and/or impartiality. A further requirement which has been mentioned by some writers[72] is the capacity to decide, ie the possession of the knowledge required in order to discharge quasi-judicial tasks. Persons without a legal training are not automatically barred from acting as arbitrators. However, the Court of Cassation has held[73] that an arbitrator who has no legal background may not appoint a lawyer as an expert to advise him on legal issues. **8.75**

In addition to the above-mentioned requirements, an arbitrator must possess the specific qualifications which the parties have stated in the arbitration agreement or in the submission. These qualifications may be positive, such as the possession of a specific training (as being an advocate, or a judge, or a law professor, or an architect, or an engineer, or a quantity surveyor) or may be negative, such as the exclusion of a given profession, eg the choice that the arbitrator shall not be a lawyer or a law professor. **8.76**

(2.1) Are there mandatory requirements for the qualification of arbitrators (statutory requirements or indirect requirements through eg general conditions of insurance contracts)? Legal entities may not be appointed as arbitrators since the decision of a dispute is reserved to individuals.[74] This view was expressed by the Court of Cassation.[75] The requirement for individuals acting as arbitrators, is that they dispose of the capability to act. Consequently, they must not be minors, lunatics or individuals whose capability to **8.77**

[69] s 812, RCP.

[70] *Ditta Di Lieto v Cons Agr Prov Catanzaro*, Corte di Cassazione (Court of Cassation) no 2587 (1962), *Foro it* 1963, I, 58.

[71] Mortara, L., *Commento al Codice di Procedura Civile* (Milan, 1923), 84; Rubino-Sammartano, M., *Il Diritto dell'Arbitrato* (1st edn) 250; in accord but on different grounds Vecchione, R., *L'arbitrato nel sistema del processo civile* (Naples, 1953), 161 and Schizzerotto, G., *Dell'arbitrato* (Milan, 1982), 376.

[72] Rubino-Sammartano, M., *Il Diritto dell'Arbitrato* (2nd edn) 255.

[73] *Silipo c Inadel*, Corte di Cassazione (Court of Cassation), no 2756 (1989), *Foro pad* 1990, I, 4.

[74] Rubino-Sammartano, M., *Il Diritto dell'Arbitrato* (2nd edn) 251.

[75] *Ditta Di Lieto v Cons Agr Prov Catanzaro*, Corte di Cassazione (Court of Cassation), no 2587 (1962), *Foro it*, 1963, I, 58.

act is either excluded (*interdetti*) or restricted (*inabilitati*). Likewise bankrupts are not allowed to act as arbitrators. Arbitrators may be foreign nationals.[76] Judges may act as arbitrators only if they are authorized to do so by the Ministry of Justice. The Court of Cassation[77] has held that the situations which prohibit acting are exhaustive and may not be construed in a liberal way in order to extend them to other situations. Nevertheless, it is suggested that one must add to those specific situations those where the arbitrator is not impartial.

8.78 (2.2) **Which national arbitration institutions may be contacted for obtaining information about qualified (and specialized) arbitrators?** Information as to potential arbitrators may be obtained from:

- the *Camera Arbitrale Nazionale e Internazionale di Milano*;
- the *Associazione Italiana per l'Arbitrato*;
- the *Delegazione Italiana of the European Court of Arbitration*;
- the *Curia Mercatorum*;
- *Camera Arbitrale Italiana*.

Many Chambers of Commerce and other bodies have formed a *Camera Arbitrale* (arbitral institution) and may provide similar information.

8.79 (2.3) **Are judges or other civil servants required to obtain permission by their employer to act as arbitrator? Are these permissions given generally or case-by-case? What are the consequences if such permission has not been obtained?** Judges and public prosecutors may sit as arbitrators if authorized by the Upper Council of the Judiciary.[78] The appointment must concern a dispute involving the public administration or a local authority or a state-controlled corporation. The authorization is not general: it must be sought for each single proceeding. The tendency to grant authorizations is presently restrictive. The consequence of lack of authorization is debated. According to one view,[79] it does not cause nullity but is merely a breach of duty by that person. According to another view,[80] the consequence is the nullity of the appointment. The former view seems preferable.

B. Appointment of arbitrators

(1) Extent of party autonomy to establish appointment procedure

8.80 There is party autonomy to appoint arbitrators. The appointment of an arbitrator is to be made by the party itself or by its special attorney in fact. The appointment of counsel does not by itself include the granting to him of the authority to appoint the arbitrators.[81] The parties are entitled to be on an equal footing as to the appointment of arbitrators. The

[76] s 812, RCP.

[77] *E.D.M.O. v Cons Ricost. Viareggio*, Corte di Cassazione (Court of Cassation) no 835 (1950), *Rep Foro it* 1950, *Arbitramento* 137, 58.

[78] s 14 Statute 2 April 1989, no 97.

[79] Schizzerotto, G., *Dell'Arbitrato* (2nd edn, Giuffré, Milan, 1982), 361; Vecchione, R., *L'arbitrato* (1971) 443.

[80] Satta, S. *cit* at 261.

[81] *Istituto autonomo bustese case popolari v Società CEAAM cooperative* , Corte di Cassazione (Court of Cassation), no 6866 (1992), Riv arb 1992, 713.

Court of Cassation has held[82] that 'an arbitration agreement which entitles one of the parties to appoint the sole arbitrator is null and void', while on another occasion the Court of Appeal (Milan) has held[83] that an arbitration agreement may validly entitle one of the parties to choose the sole arbitrator out of a list of three names submitted by the other party.

If the parties are more than two and the arbitration agreement provides for the appointment of three arbitrators, it has been held that if each party has a position conflicting with that of the other ones,the arbitration agreement shall be unable to produce effects, unless two or more parties spontaneously appoint one arbitrator for all of them. **8.81**

Arbitration law[84] requires that the appointment of the arbitrator be made by notice served by a process server. Since it has been held[85] by a precedent that such a service cannot be carried out by other means and the literal wording of the provision is clear, it is not safe to rely on a more liberal construction. The parties frequently delegate the authority to appoint the arbitrators to an arbitral institution, by accepting its arbitration rules in the arbitration agreement. **8.82**

(2) Procedure in absence of an agreement by the parties

One has to identify the procedure to be followed in the absence of agreement of the parties. The appointment is statutorily regulated[86] and made by the President of the *Tribunale* in whose district the venue of the proceedings is located after hearing—if it deems it fit—also the party which has not applied for it. If the venue has not yet been selected by the parties, the appointment is made by the President of the *Tribunale* of the place where the submission or the contract has been entered into, after hearing—if he deems it fit—also the party which has not applied for it. If that place is outside Italy, the appointment is made by the President of the *Tribunale* of Rome. **8.83**

Also the appointment of the chairman of the arbitral tribunal belongs to the parties. The arbitration agreement will frequently grant such an authority to an arbitral institution or to the party-appointed arbitrators. If the parties have not agreed on how the chairman has to be appointed, or the appointment is not made by those to whom it has been delegated, the appointment will be made by the President of the *Tribunale*, in accordance with the above procedure.[87] **8.84**

(3) Effect of the refusal of one party to cooperate in the constitution of the arbitral tribunal

In the event of refusal by one or more parties to cooperate in the appointment of the arbitral tribunal, the Reform has provided[88] for the intervention of the *Tribunale* in aid of arbitration **8.85**

[82] *Romano c Isotti*, Corte di Cassazione (Court of Cassation) no 419 (1951), *Rep Foro it* 1951, *Arbitramento* 145, 54.

[83] *Ponziano Mazzini Marchesi v Zucchi*, Corte d'Appello di Milano (Court of Appeal of Milan) (1932), *Temi Lomb* 1932, 283.

[84] s 810, para 1, RCP.

[85] *Comune di Porcia v Tomé*, Corte d'Appello di Trieste (Court of Appeal of Trieste) (1991), *Riv Arb* 1992, 488.

[86] s 810, RCP.

[87] ss 809 and 810, RCP.

[88] *ibid.*

in several respects such as: (i) the appointment of an arbitrator, if the party entitled to it does not do so; (ii) the appointment of the chairman of the arbitral tribunal, if the parties cannot agree on it; and (iii) the appointment of the three arbitrators, if the parties have not stated their number and do not agree on it. This procedure shall not apply if the appointment has been delegated by the parties to an arbitral institution or to a third party, and is made by them. The Second Reform has not amended such rules.

(4) Circumstances and valid reasons for an arbitrator to resign

8.86 Because of their acceptance of the appointment, arbitrators are under a duty to make a determination. If they resign without cause, they may be liable for damages[89] if their resignation is challenged.

C. Challenge and replacement of arbitrators

(1) Grounds, procedure and deadlines for challenging an arbitrator

8.87 In the past the grounds for challenge of an arbitrator were the same grounds set forth for the challenge of a judge. The Second Reform has set out new grounds for the challenge of an arbitrator, which are: (i) if the arbitrator does not possess the qualifications agreed upon by the parties; (ii) if he or a body, association or legal entity of which he is a director has an interest in the dispute; (iii) if he, or his spouse, is a relative (up to the fourth degree) of a party or of counsel for a party, or lives with any of them or has regularly meals with them; (iv) if he or his spouse have proceedings pending or are in very bad terms with one of the parties, an officer of it authorized to represent it or any of their counsel; (v) if he is an employee or a permanent adviser or renders paid services to one of the parties, or to a company or persons who control it, or to a company jointly controlled by them, or has other relationships of a financial nature with any of them, or other types of association, which affect his independence; (vi) if he is the guardian or the receiver of one of the parties; or (vii) he has advised, acted for or appeared for one of the parties in a previous stage of the proceedings or has deposed as a witness in them.

8.88 A party may not challenge an arbitrator whom it appointed itself, unless on grounds which have become known to it after his appointment.

8.89 Before the First Reform, it was argued whether an arbitrator who did not attend hearings or meetings or created obstacles to the orderly running of the arbitral proceedings had to be treated as having withdrawn. That view was held by precedents.[90] The First Reform[91] has expressly provided for the replacement of the arbitrator who fails to perform his task or delays performing it. Replacement is to take place by consent of the parties or by resolution of the arbitral institution or other third party appointed to do so in the arbitration agreement or in the submission. In the absence of action by the arbitrator within 15 days after his receipt of a written notice to act, each party may apply to the President of the *Tribunale* for an order to this effect. If the challenge of the arbitrator is manifestly not admissible or

[89] s 813, RCP.

[90] *Polizzi v Ospedale Umberto I Siracusa*, Corte di Cassazione (Court of Cassation) (1949), *Mass Foro it* 1948, 358.

[91] s 813, which was confirmed by the Second Reform, by moving this provision to s 813 bis, RCP .

without any grounds, the challenger may be ordered by the President of the Tribunale to pay to the other party an amount which will be assessed in an equitable way and which in no event will exceed three times the remuneration due to the arbitrator according to the official bar schedule.

The challenge does not stay the arbitral proceedings. The issue has been debated whether—in the event of the parties having already appointed an alternate arbitrator in the arbitration agreement or submission—the latter would step in. This was excluded by precedents[92] on the grounds that one could replace the arbitrator in the event of a temporary impediment only. This solution may not be shared because, in the absence of an express provision to this effect, it does not seem possible that one keeps changing arbitrators. Only when an arbitrator cannot act, and not if he is merely temporarily prevented from doing so, should he be replaced, and that replacement should be for ever. **8.90**

The procedure and deadline for challenging an arbitrator have been debated. The deadline for the challenge of an arbitrator was 10 days after service of the notice of appointment of the arbitrator. It was discussed whether—in the event of absence of service of the notice—time could run from when a party became aware of a ground for challenge. In spite of the strict wording of the statutory provision, several opinions were in favour of this solution. Now, this has been made clear by revised s 815 of the Rules of Civil Procedure, which provides that the time period for the challenge starts to run from service of the notice of appointment or—in the absence of this—from the time that knowledge is acquired.[93] The President of the *Tribunale* decides on challenges by order, after hearing the challenged arbitrator and, if needed, after considering other summary evidence.[94] The order may not be attacked. **8.91**

(1.1) Do state courts review challenge procedures which took place in accordance with a specific procedure agreed upon by the parties (eg Article 11, ICC Rules)? If so, at what point of time? May such review be excluded? The question arises whether if the parties have agreed, either expressly or by incorporating the rules of an arbitral institution, upon a mechanism of 'private' challenge of the arbitrator, state courts have jurisdiction on the challenge of an arbitrator, ie whether the statutory provision which provides for challenge of arbitrators[95] before state courts may or may not be derogated from. The Second Reform provides at s 832 that already existing arbitration rules which are incorporated by reference by the parties into the arbitration agreement may provide for additional grounds to replace challenged (or inactive) arbitrators. It is submitted that it follows from these provisions that the statutory grounds to replace arbitrators may not be derogated from. **8.92**

(1.2) Is there case law with respect to truncated arbitral tribunals? (cf Article 12(5), ICC Rules) Under s 823, Rules of Civil Procedure the determination of the dispute is no longer to be made in personal conference[96] as was provided for before the Reform, but **8.93**

[92] *Perini v Fonzo*, Corte di Cassazione (Court of Cassation) no 4109 (1957), *Mass Giust. Civ.* 1957, 4552.
[93] s 815, RCP.
[94] ie evidence taken by hearing witnesses informally or in an expedited way.
[95] s 815, RCP.
[96] Which in domestic 'international' arbitral proceedings may be replaced by a video conference.

simply with the participation of all the arbitrators, even if unanimity is not required, unless one of the arbitrators requests that it be made in personal conference. In the absence of such request, the decision of the dispute may be made by video or teleconference or by discussion via personal computers. The award is valid even if it is signed only by the majority of the arbitrators, provided it states that the conference has been attended by all the arbitrators, and that the other arbitrators have been unable to sign it or have refused to do so. This view has been confirmed by the Court of Cassation.[97] A different situation arises if for any reason one or all the arbitrators terminate their office.[98] Such arbitrators are then replaced.

(2) Procedure for appointing a new arbitrator

8.94 The procedure for appointment of a new arbitrator is similar to the appointment of the replaced arbitrator. A new arbitrator may be appointed, unless the arbitrator, who has terminated his office, had been appointed *intuitu personae.*[99] This view has been shared by the Court of Cassation.[100] If the arbitrator who has terminated his office was party-appointed, that party will be entitled to appoint another one. In the absence of this, he will be appointed by the President of the *Tribunale.* If that arbitrator is the third arbitrator, the procedure set out by the parties or by the arbitration rules will have to be followed.

IV. The arbitral procedure

A. General principles

(1) Extent of party autonomy to determine the arbitral procedure

8.95 The extent of party autonomy to determine the procedure has to be established. The parties are free to set out the rules which govern the proceedings:[101]

> The parties may state in the arbitration agreement, in the submission, or in a separate written agreement prior to the commencing of the proceedings, the rules to be complied with by the arbitrators during the proceedings. In the absence of that, the arbitrators shall be free to conduct the proceedings in the manner which they consider suitable. In any event they must give to the parties time limits to file documents and pleadings, and to reply to the arguments of the other parties.

8.96 The freedom of the parties finds its limit in the mandatory provisions of the Rules of Civil Procedure and, in general, in the requirements of due process. Any party's directions to the arbitrators contrary to them are then replaced by the latter.

8.97 A further limit to the parties is[102] that, unless consent of the arbitrators to subsequent changes is secured, these rules must be set out before the commencement of the proceedings.

---

97 *Società Lepa v Società Capital*, Corte di Cassazione (Court of Cassation) no 4695 (1988), *Foro it*, 1988, I, 2864.

98 A wide term which encompasses various situations such as death, illness, impossibility to act.

99 ie expressly because of his own specific personality.

100 *Bombaci v Amalfi*, Corte di Cassazione (Court of Cassation) no 1029 (1955), *Rep Foro it* 1955, *Arbitrato rituale* 186.

101 s 816 bis, RCP.

102 *ibid.*

The rationale of this requirement is to allow the arbitrators to be aware of the procedural rules which they will have to apply, before accepting to act in that capacity.

The freedom of the parties to set out the rules governing the proceedings may be exercised by them: (i) by incorporating by reference the rules of an arbitral institution; (ii) by incorporating the Rules of Civil Procedure; (iii) by incorporating rules issued by various arbitral institutions or various Rules of Civil Procedure; or (iv) by setting out themselves rules of their choice. The widespread belief that the arbitrators must apply the Rules of Civil Procedure is therefore not accurate. In fact, if the parties do not impose this on the arbitrators, the latter are free not to apply the Rules of Civil Procedure, except for their mandatory provisions. **8.98**

(1.1) **Are the parties free to choose any national or international law governing the procedure before the arbitral tribunal?** Under s 816 bis Rules of Civil Procedure, the parties are entitled to set out the rules to be complied with by the arbitrators as to the conduct of the proceedings. In the absence of this, the arbitrators are free to conduct the proceedings as they think fit. Even if so, the arbitrators are bound to give time limits to the parties to file documents and briefs and to reply to the other party. In other words in any event, due process of the *lex fori* has to be complied with. In view of this attitude, the parties are free to choose a national or international procedural law, subject to the *lex fori's* mandatory provisions which prevail on it. As held in *Scheepvaarkantor*,[103] the choice of non-Italian arbitration rules may be combined with the choice of Italy as venue of the proceedings. **8.99**

(2) Basic procedural principles or mandatory rules to be applied by the arbitral tribunal.

The arbitrators are bound to respect the basic principles of due process. One of them is the principle of *contraddittorio*[104] which is expressly referred to in the law of arbitration.[105] Strictly speaking, it consists of the right to comment on the position taken by the other party. In practice, *contraddittorio* is given wider contents and other requirements for due process are to be complied with, even if they are not expressly stated. They are: (i) the right to present one's case which is the premise of the other party's right to comment on it (and which frequently is treated as a part of the *contraddittorio*); and (ii) the right to prove it, which is the premise of any submission. While the right to present one's case and to comment on the case of the opposing party are well recognized, the right to prove one's case is not yet well understood. Many arbitrators show a tendency to imitate court proceedings, with the consequence that such right suffers severe limitations.[106] **8.100**

(3) Oral hearing proceeding on basis of written documents?

The question arises whether an oral hearing is compulsory or the arbitrators may decide based on documents only. Oral hearings must be held—in principle—whenever that is needed in order to allow the parties to present their case and/or to comment on the case **8.101**

[103] *Scheepvaarkantor Holwerda v Esperia di Navigazione*, Corte d'Appello di Napoli (Court of Appeal of Naples), 17 March 1979, *Foro pad* 1990, I, 1.

[104] In English: due process, which, as discussed, consists of the right to present one's case and the related evidence, the right to reply to the other party and the right to a fair trial.

[105] s 829, no 9, RCP.

[106] See Rubino-Sammartano, M., *Il Diritto dell'Arbitrato, cit.*

presented by other parties and this cannot be adequately dealt with by the exchange of written pleadings. A hearing must, as a rule, also be held whenever the parties jointly request it. In view of the tradition of a hearing for final address, it will generally be advisable to hold the hearing except if the parties jointly waive it.

8.102 While the Rules of Civil Procedure do not expressly deal with this issue, some arbitration rules, such as those of the Chartered Institute of Arbitrators and of the European Court of Arbitration have a set of rules for documents-only arbitration. The choice of 'documents-only arbitration' implies a waiver by the parties to the right to be heard in person, or by counsel, and to oral evidence. The concern has been authoritatively expressed[107] that such a waiver could affect the right of the arbitrator to decide how to conduct the proceedings. This concern has been addressed by providing that the arbitrator is entitled to check whether the proceedings may take place by 'documents-only arbitration'. The arbitrator is then entitled to refuse the appointment if, in his view, the proceedings may not be decided only by documents.

(4) Power of the tribunal (in particular the chairman) to issue procedural orders

8.103 The tribunal *may* decide procedural issues by an order.[108] The order is to be issued by the arbitral tribunal and not by its chairman alone. However, the parties or the arbitral tribunal may authorize the chairman alone to sign and even to decide issues concerning the conduct of the proceedings. The taking of evidence may be delegated to a member of the tribunal. The tribunal's decision, which puts an end to the proceedings on a procedural ground, should have the form—and in any event the substance—of an award.

(5) Distinction of matters of substance and matters of procedure

8.104 Breach of contract, the doctrine of laches and time bar, are for example substantive matters, while matters such as the standing as a party, representation by counsel, the burden of proof, the taking of evidence and the appointment of an official expert are procedural.

8.105 (5.1) **Are the statutes of limitations a matter of substance or rather of procedure?** The substantive or procedural nature of foreclosures and statutes of limitation has been debated. It has been held by precedents[109] and by writers[110] that foreclosure is a substantive issue, governed by the *lex causae*, a conclusion which seems applicable also to time bar since they both concern the substantive right, and procedural issues concern only the way to enforce that substantive right.

(6) Persons able to represent a party in an arbitral proceeding

8.106 Representation by counsel is not compulsory in Italian proceedings. A party may consequently appear by itself or appoint any other representative. Foreign counsel may consequently represent a party to Italian arbitral proceedings, either jointly with Italian counsel, or alone.[111]

---

107 Ricci, E.F., in the course of an analysis made in a closed scholarly discussion.

108 s 816. para 6, RCP.

109 *W. v W. e G*, Corte d'Appello di Roma (Court of Appeal Rome) (1959), Riv Dir Int 1960, 325.

110 Rubino-Sammartano, M. and Morse, C.G.J., *Public Policy in Transnational Relationship* (Kluwer, Italy, 1991).

111 Rubino-Sammartano, M., *International Arbitration: Law and Practice* (2nd edn, Kluwer, 2001) (hereinafter International Arbitration) 573.

B. Place of arbitration

(1) Determination of the place in absence of an agreement by the parties

The determination of the place of the arbitration is necessary in the absence of a choice by the parties. If the venue of the proceedings has not been fixed, the arbitrators or the arbitral institution if so empowered by the arbitration agreement or by the arbitration rules, may choose the venue which must always be within the territory of the Republic.[112] In the absence of their choice, the venue of the proceedings is in the place where the arbitration agreement has been entered into and if it was entered into abroad, the venue is Rome. **8.107**

The venue of the proceedings is not necessarily the place where all the proceedings take place. However it may not become a mere facade. The decision and the signing of the award do not have to take place in the venue of the proceedings and not even in Italy. The Reform has liberalized all this.[113] **8.108**

(2) Importance and legal effect of place (seat) of the arbitration

The choice of the place of an arbitration produces important effects in various areas such as the involvement of the *lex fori* or at least of its procedural public policy, its enforcement, the setting-aside procedure, the courts competent in aid of arbitration as well as the risk of court interference. The venue of the arbitral proceedings is to be within the territory of the Republic.[114] The award must state the venue of the proceedings;[115] while a failure to mention the venue of the proceedings is no longer a ground for setting the award aside.[116] **8.109**

(2.1) Are the arbitrators and the parties free to convene at places other than the official seat of the arbitration? The arbitrators are free to convene by themselves or with the parties at places other than the official seat of the arbitration, provided that the seat does not become a mere mail box or a façade. **8.110**

(2.2) Are there visa requirements to enter the country which apply to lawyers and/or arbitrators? Where may current information on that subject be obtained? No special visa requirements or special release from them apply to arbitrators or counsel. This consequently depends on their nationality and passport. Some countries are subject to a visa requirement. Information in this respect may be obtained by non-EU residents from the local Italian Consulate. **8.111**

C. Submissions, deadlines and default

(1) Contents and form of submissions (in particular request for arbitration and answer to request)

It is generally held that submissions in arbitral proceedings must be in writing, since this is the common denominator of the proceedings from the arbitration agreement to the award. However, if the parties do not set out the rules which govern the proceedings, it is up to the **8.112**

112 s 816, RCP.
113 s 829 no 2, RCP as amended by the Second Reform.
114 s 816, RCP.
115 s 823, para 2, *ibid.*
116 s 829, *ibid.*

arbitrator to select them. Since in doing so he is not bound—as discussed above—to apply the Rules of Civil Procedure, the arbitrator might request the parties to make their submissions orally. However, if one of the parties insists on written submissions, the arbitrator should be very careful before refusing this, because that might affect that party's right to present its case and give grounds for an attack against the award before the appellate court. The same *caveat* applies if the arbitrator asks the parties to file written submissions only. The practice is that the pleadings be in writing but that the parties argue also orally, if one of them so requests. Instead of dealing in the first pleadings—as in other jurisdictions—with issues of fact only and of admitting or rejecting each specific allegation in the answer, frequently the parties deal from the outset with issues of fact, evidence and issues of law, and reject altogether the opposing party's allegations and submissions.

8.113 **(1.1) From what point in time is a claim considered to be pending with the arbitral tribunal? What are the legal effects of such fact (eg on statutes of limitations)?** A case is considered to be pending from the time it is served on the opposite party—the service of the request for arbitration, containing the claim (and appointing the arbitrator if that party has to appoint one) interrupts the time limit of the claim in issue.[117] Claims may also be made at a hearing. The time limit does not continue to run until the award may no longer be attacked or the judgment made on the award may no longer be attacked.[118]

8.114 If the arbitrators have not yet been appointed at the time of service of the request for arbitration and of the statement of claim, then the claim is pending, conditional upon the arbitral tribunal being duly formed. If arbitration originates from a submission rather than from an arbitration clause and it sets out the claim and counterclaim, the said claim and counterclaim will be pending from then. A statement of claim, or a statement of defence respectively setting out a claim or counterclaim, related to title to real estate may be filed with the Land Registry which gives priority to it, if the claim or counterclaim is successful, over filings[119] made subsequent to the filing of the statement of claim or of defence.

8.115 **(1.2) When is a time limit according to statutes of limitations deemed to be interrupted in the case of (i) *ad hoc*; and (ii) institutional arbitration?** Time limits are interrupted, under s 25, Reform, by service of the written notice of the intention to refer the dispute to arbitration stating one's claims and appointing the arbitrator. The interruption covers the period of time from service of the above notice up to the time the award becomes final or, if the award is challenged, up to the time the judgment made in the challenge proceedings has become final.

8.116 **(1.3) What is the effect of the withdrawal of the request for arbitration?** Withdrawal of the request for arbitration amounts to a withdrawal of the claim. It does not put an end to the proceedings unless the opposing party accepts it, and waives its counterclaim. If not, that issue will have to be determined by the arbitrators, as well as how to deal with the costs of the proceedings.

---

117 Rubino-Sammartano, M., *Il diritto dell'arbitrato* (5th edn, Cedam, Milan, 2006).
118 s 25, Arbitration Reform Act.
119 *ibid.*

(2) Legal deadlines (provided by law or set by the arbitrators) and effect of non-compliance by a party

Deadlines for submissions are statutorily regulated.[120] In any event, the arbitrators must comply with the duty to allow each party to present its case and to respond to the case of the opposing party, by granting to the parties reasonable time and the same opportunities to argue their case. In practice, terms are frequently granted to the parties which are either too short or too long. **8.117**

The issue whether mandatory terms may be imposed by the arbitrators on the parties and whether a term may be mandatory even if it has not been so characterized has been debated. Various views have been held by arbitrators.[121] It is submitted that arbitrators may impose mandatory terms, provided they clearly advise the parties of this in advance. It is generally held[122] that a party may amend its pleadings during the proceedings, provided the new claims fall within the arbitration agreement and the opposing party is not prevented from taking position on them. **8.118**

The effects of non-respect of a deadline are to be considered. Frequently terms are not defined as being mandatory. If a term is mandatory and has not been complied with, then after its expiry, that party will be precluded from carrying it on. Depending on the object of the term, that may affect that party's right to seek leave to call oral evidence or to have that evidence taken, to produce documents or other evidence. If the Rules of Civil Procedure do not apply, a party is free to amend its claims and defences and to make counterclaims within the ambit of the arbitration agreement until, upon the arbitrators' request, the parties have finally to state their claims, counterclaims and defences, before the arbitrators hear final argument and render or reserve judgment. **8.119**

(2.1) What are the powers of the tribunal if a party fails to comply with the time limits set up by the tribunal? The powers of the tribunal in the case of a party's failure to comply with a time limit are as follows: if a term is not mandatory, a late filing will frequently be accepted *de facto* or by issuing an order. If the term is mandatory, the tribunal normally will be unable to extend it, save where there is evidence that a timely filing had been made impossible by reasons outside the control of that party. **8.120**

(2.2) Is the tribunal bound by any mandatory time limits for certain procedural steps (hearings, making of the award etc)? An express time limit is set out for the making of the award.[123] Although no express time limits are set out for the various steps of the proceedings, nevertheless it is suggested that the tribunal must ensure that the parties dispose of the time required in order to present their case and to prove it and that such timing allows **8.121**

[120] s 816 bis, RCP.

[121] See *Soc Impresa L Visconti Costruzioni Sas v IACP di Napoli*, Tribunale Arbitrale (Arbitral Tribunal) (1984), Arch giur oo pp (1991) 247; contra *Soc X v Soc Y*, Tribunale Arbitrale (Arbitral Tribunal) 9 April 1990, Riv Arb 1993, 257.

[122] *Cogepar Costruzioni Generali SpA v IACP di Catania*, Tribunale Arbitrale (Arbitral Tribunal) (1985), Arch giu oo pp (1986) 111.

[123] Unless the parties provide for a time limit to make the award, the statutory time limit applies, which is 240 days from acceptance of the appointment by the arbitral tribunal. s 820, RCP, as amended by the Second Reform, provides for various extentions of this time period.

the arbitrators to decide within the time limit for making the award. No term to produce documents is mandatory unless so defined or unless it is to be clearly implied.

(3) Statutory requirements as to notifications during an arbitration (with respect to the request for arbitration and other written pleadings; with respect to notifications by the tribunal)?

8.122 The appointment of the arbitrators has to be notified by service through an *ufficiale giudiziario*, ('process server') ie a public servant whose task is *inter alia* to serve documents and whose certificate of service is given full faith and credit. The parties will frequently at that time respectively make their claims and state their defences. If the request for arbitration (and statement of claim) and the statement of defence are made in the same document which contains the appointment of the arbitrator by that party, that document will be served through a process server. Subsequent notices during the proceedings may be communicated in writing, without involving a process server, to the parties or to counsel for them. The arbitral tribunal normally sends its notices by registered mail, but other more informal forms of communication are not to be excluded.

(4) Effects of the insolvency of a party

8.123 The effects of compulsory liquidation of a party to an arbitration agreement on that agreement and on the possibility to institute or continue the arbitral proceedings has been debated amongst writers.[124] If the arbitral proceedings are already pending at that time, then according to some,[125] but not to unanimous precedents, the arbitral tribunal keeps jurisdiction, unless the object of the proceedings interferes with the area reserved to the compulsory liquidation procedure, such as the proof of debts.[126]

8.124 As to other forms of insolvency which are less dramatic than compulsory liquidation, such as *concordato preventivo*[127] and *amministrazione controllata*,[128] it is suggested that these 'minor' insolvency proceedings do not detract from the arbitrator's jurisdiction. Their result is to limit the effects of the award as to its enforceability, and as to the right to be paid under it, which may either be delayed or limited to the percentage which has been approved by the general meeting of the creditors.

D. Facts and evidence: general

(1) Burden of proof (inquisitorial/adversarial procedure)

8.125 Evidence turns around the burden of proof. The Italian legal system adheres, as to evidence, to the principle that the claimant must prove the facts on which it bases its claim and the respondent must prove the facts on which it bases its counterclaim or opposition, a rule

---

124 Schizzerotto, G., *Dell'Arbitrato*, 150; Satta, S., *Commentario al codice di procedura civile*, IV, II, 24, Vecchione, R., *L'arbitrato* (1971) 347.

125 *Ditta O.R.M.A. v Tessilmarod*, Corte di Cassazione (Court of Cassation), no 30 (1956), *Mass Giust. Civ.* 1956, I, 11; in accord *Chignola v Muzioli*, Corte di Cassazione (Court of Cassation) no 2866 (1958), *Foro pad* 1958, I, 696.

126 Corte di Cassazione (Court of Cassation) no 2064 (1969) Dir Fall, II, 59.

127 A composition proposal made by the insolvent trader to its creditors, approved by the competent court and accepted by the majority of the creditors, at a specific creditors meeting.

128 Management of a business by the trader who is in temporary difficulty, under the supervision of a court-appointed officer.

which derives from the Roman law principle *'adfirmanti est onus probandi'*.[129] However, the role of the arbitrator is not the one of an umpire who lets the players act and in the end delivers a written notice stating who has won. The arbitrator is requested to establish whether the claimant or the defendant is right. It follows from this that, on the one hand, the arbitrator may not replace counsel of a party and conduct the case for the latter, but on the other hand (provided the parties have not bound him to apply the Rules of Civil Procedure), if he deems it helpful for a better understanding of the facts, he may—clearly avoiding excesses—order that some further witnesses be heard or documents produced.[130]

(2) Power of the tribunal to determine the admissibility and weight of the evidence produced by the parties

The arbitrator's authority as to the admissibility, admission and weight of evidence has been long debated. The first aspect of this matter is whether the admissibility of evidence is a substantive or a procedural issue. According to a leading procedural writer,[131] evidence has two aspects. First a static aspect, for which evidence is a means in order to prove a fact, and second, a procedural aspect, which concerns the way that evidence is taken. According to this view, the admissibility of evidence belongs to the first aspect, with the consequence that it should be governed by substantive law, and that the parties may derogate from statutory provisions, except for the mandatory ones. Admissibility is then to be distinguished from leave to call evidence, which is required under the Rules of Civil Procedure. **8.126**

The limits to the admissibility of evidence belong to the way a party may prove a fact, and therefore are a procedural issue.[132] Unless the arbitrator has been obliged by the parties to apply the Rules of Civil Procedure or has himself chosen to be bound by them, he is not bound to apply statutory limits to admissibility. For example, he will not be bound to exclude evidence of oral agreements contrary and simultaneous to a written agreement. **8.127**

As to the actual admission of evidence, here again, unless the parties have dictated to the arbitrator to apply the Rules of Civil Procedure (or the arbitrator—being free not to do so —has elected to be bound by them), the arbitrator does not have to grant any leave and the parties shall be free to call the evidence which they deem convenient to prove their case. It has been argued[133] that whenever a party that is under a duty to prove a fact is not allowed to prove it, there is a denial of justice, which is the most serious breach of due process and must cause the award, if attacked, to be set aside. **8.128**

As to the weight of evidence, its appreciation is left to the arbitrator with the only exception that the arbitrator must give adequate even if concise reasons for its finding.[134] **8.129**

---

129 The party who states a fact must prove it.

130 *Pizzini v INCIS,* Corte di Cassazione (Court of Cassation) no 916 (1965) in Schizzerotto, G., *L'arbitrato rituale nella giurisprudenza* (Cedam, Padua, 1969).

131 Satta, S., *Diritto processuale civile* (Padua, 1987) 191-2.

132 Carnelutti, F., *La prova civile* (2nd edn, Roma, 1947); Andrioli, *Prova* (Nov Dig II—vol XIV Turin 1967), 260 *et seq*; Ricci, E.F., 'Sul principio dispositivo come problema di diritto vigente' *Riv Dir Proc* 1974, 380.

133 Rubino-Sammartano, M., *Il Diritto dell'Arbitrato* (2nd edn). Art. 403 *et seq; La prova nel processo civile; Foro pad* (1986) 87.

134 *Chiari v Inps,* Corte di Cassazione (Court of Cassation), no 9384 (1995), *Rep Foro it* 1996, item Proc Civile, no 20.

8.130 **(2.1) Is the tribunal entitled to take the claimant's factual allegation as proven if the defendant does not participate in the arbitral proceedings?** If the defendant does not participate in the arbitral proceedings, the tribunal is not entitled to take the claimant's factual allegations as proven and will be satisfied as to them only if the claimant provides adequate evidence of them.

8.131 **(2.2) May the arbitral tribunal consider an allegation of one party as agreed fact if the other party did not (specifically) dispute the allegation?** The arbitral tribunal may not in general consider an allegation of one party as an agreed fact, simply because the other party has not specifically disputed it, unless the defences of such other party show that such circumstance is admitted.

8.132 **(2.3) What is the standard of proof that must be met in order for a fact to be considered to have been established (preponderance of the evidence; beyond reasonable doubt)? Must a stringent requirement be met for certain facts?** The standard of proof is not linked to formulas like 'beyond reasonable doubt' or 'preponderance of evidence'. The tribunal must assess the evidence. A party has met the standard of proof when it has satisfied the arbitral tribunal. Like state courts, the arbitral tribunal may rely on presumptions. Some of them are rebuttable (presumptions *iuris tantum*)[135] other ones are not rebuttable (presumptions *iuris et de jure*).[136]

8.133 **(2.4) May the arbitral tribunal rely on its own knowledge to consider certain facts as proven?** The arbitral tribunal may not use its own knowledge unless it has advised the parties of this specific direct knowledge that it intends to use, giving them the opportunity to comment. In an old decision by the Court of Cassation,[137] the principle was affirmed that the parties must be aware of the factual elements on which the decision will be made.

E. Witnesses

(1) Ability to act as a witness

8.134 One has first to check who may act as a witness. If the arbitrator is bound to apply the Rules of Civil Procedure, or—not being bound by them—has elected to do so, then he is obliged not to hear as witnesses those who have an interest which could make them join or be joined to the proceedings.[138] However even in this situation, if the arbitrator deems it useful, such persons may be heard informally, ie not under oath. When the arbitrator is not bound by such a rule, he may also hear such persons, even if he will be prudent in giving weight to their evidence.

8.135 **(1.1) Is there a legal difference between a party testifying and a witness? If yes, what are the criteria for such differentiation? Does the testifying of a party have the same weight as a witness' testimony?** In court proceedings parties are not treated as witnesses and may

[135] ICC proceedings 1974, no 2216, Clunet 1975 at 916.

[136] Presumptions *juris tantum* correspond to rebuttable presumptions, while presumptions *juris et de jure* correspond to non rebuttable presumptions.

[137] *Soc Comptoir des Broches v Soc Off Mecc Cigardi*, Corte di Cassazione (Court of Cassation) no 331 (1959) *Rep Foro it* 1959, Arbitramento 160, 63–4.

[138] s 246, RCP.

not testify.[139] They may only either be heard informally or be requested to reply to specific questions. Even if so their reply may provide only evidence against that party but not in its favour. Even when the arbitrator is not bound to apply the procedural rules, frequently he tends to behave in the same way and to give no weight to a party's replies in his favour.

(2) Preparation of witnesses and limits thereof

The question arises whether a party may approach a witness. Witnesses must not be influenced. This is why party approach to witnesses is looked at with hostility. If a witness has discussed the matter with a party, this—even if there is no evidence of actual influence—may detract from the witness' creditworthiness. Likewise, counsel for a party should not—as a rule—approach witnesses. He may contact his client's executives, employees and agents to obtain from them information needed for the preparation of the case; they may later be called as witnesses. It may also happen that his client's managers or employees, upon being called as witnesses, request from counsel information as to such hearing. While general information may be provided, preparing a witness and or rehearsing his testimony is not considered acceptable, and would *inter alia* detract from the witness' creditworthiness. On the other hand, a party may by letter inform a witness as to the issues on which he or she will be heard, in order that the witness may concentrate in time on such matters. **8.136**

(2.1) Do US-style depositions violate any procedural rules or principles? Depositions are alien to Italian practice. The maximum which has been reached by the Reform (and the Second Reform has not amended this) is to allow the arbitrators to request witnesses directly to submit statements, a procedure which does not seem to be in breach of public policy. However, the arbitrators shall be free to request to hear such witnesses afresh and to decide what weight to give to their statements and depositions, if conflicting. The arbitrators will meet difficulties in rejecting the application made by one of the parties that they be examined afresh, even if upon the arbitrator's request they have filed a statement. **8.137**

(2.2) May a party or its counsel approach a witness whom it has nominated (only before or also after the proceeding has started)? Are interviews permitted? The fear that counsel may influence a witness has induced the Rules of Conduct of the Bar[140] not to allow counsel, as a rule, to interview witnesses with the aim of inducing them to make statements in favour of his or her client. On the other hand, he or she may contact the managers and employees of their client, in order to elicit from them information in order to present their case and to comment on the case presented by the opposing party. During such contacts, matters which will be later the object of oral evidence, may arise and it is generally felt that counsel may put questions as to them in order to prepare his or her case, without influencing the witness. As to the parties, they enjoy more latitude in this respect. However if they try to influence a witness or to put pressure on him or her, that behaviour is not acceptable; it may affect the weight to be given to that evidence and will make a negative impression on the arbitrator. Apart from this, and subject to the assessment of each situation, in principle interviews with witnesses are not viewed with favour by the disciplinary bodies of the legal **8.138**

139 s 246 and 228, RCP.

140 Art 52, Rules of Conduct for the Italian Bar as of 12 June 2008.

profession and cast a negative light on the testimony, which may be considered as being no longer genuine.

(3) Admissibility of written statements

8.139 The Italian Rules of Civil Procedure[141] do not, as a rule, give relevance to written statements, except in summary proceedings when the judge has no time to hear witnesses. Even here, the written statements' aim is to support an application, rather than to provide absolute evidence of a fact. However, in arbitral proceedings the Reform[142] has entitled the arbitrator to take evidence only by requesting the 'witness' to file a statement which replies to the arbitrator's queries. Even if this is not expressly stated, it is submitted that if a party so requests, the arbitrator must order that witness to appear to be examined. The arbitrator may decide to hear witnesses of his or her own motion, in order to clarify facts or circumstances which he or she considers to be relevant.[143]

8.140 (3.1) **If the parties agree on written statements, is a party entitled to request an oral hearing for questioning those witnesses even if that right has not explicitly been agreed upon?** Until the Reform, witness statements were unknown to Italian practice. Now, the arbitrators are allowed to decide whether to hear a witness by requesting the witness to provide written replies to specific questions within the time limit which they set out. This mechanism is then made available only to the arbitrators, without granting the same powers to the parties. The witness statement mechanism has not yet been much used. The way this provision is structured, there is no express reference to the possibility of a party to seek a hearing of the witness, who has filed a written statement. However, it is suggested that if a party wishes that the witness statement be checked by hearing that witness, the arbitrators should tread very carefully before rejecting such an application. If the parties have waived an oral hearing for questioning the parties, that waiver might appear to be decisive. However, if after the waiver circumstances have arisen which, if known before the waiver, would have affected that decision, it is submitted that the request for an evidentiary hearing should be entertained.

(4) Entitlement of a party to have a hearing or cross-examination of witnesses

8.141 Each party may request a hearing or cross-examination. Under the Italian Rules of Civil Procedure the taking of oral evidence is subject to leave.[144] The witness may be examined only by the judge.[145] When the arbitrator is bound or elects to be bound by the Rules of Civil Procedure, counsel for the parties has no right to call witnesses, to examine and to cross-examine them. The arbitrator may—out of benevolence—allow him from time to time to put to the witness some but not too many questions. The arbitrator is entitled to decide about the relevance of the evidence which he is requested to hear, as to the number

141 s 244, RCP.

142 s 819, ter, *ibid.*

143 *Impresa Costruzioni Graci v ANAS*, Tribunale Arbitrale (Arbitral Tribunal) (1986), *Rep Foro it* 1988, 163, 89; and Rubino-Sammartano, M., *Il Diritto dell'Arbitrato, cit* 420.

144 s 245, RCP.

145 s 253, *ibid.*

of witnesses, and as to their not being barred from testifying because of personal interest.[146] The only protection of a party is that if it calls evidence, which the arbitrator refuses to allow, later rejecting the claim for absence of proof, then a breach of due process has been committed, which is a ground for setting aside the award.[147]

When the arbitrator is not bound by the rules, he may—and it is suggested he should—allow counsel to call witnesses and to cross-examine the witnesses called by the opposing party, subject to the arbitrator intervening only when it is absolutely necessary, such as to questions which are totally outside the ambit of the dispute. **8.142**

(4.1) Which are the methods used to establish a record of the arbitral proceedings in particular witness examinations (tape recording, verbatim court reporters, dictated minutes, other methods)? The practice is to record the arbitral proceedings by minutes generally typed or handwritten as dictated by the chairman. Tape recording or a *verbatim* court reporter may be used if a party so requests and the tribunal agrees, which is less obvious than it might seem since this is not the practice in court proceedings. This may be of special relevance as to oral evidence. The party applying for this will generally be requested to advance the related costs if the application is granted. **8.143**

(4.2) May the arbitral tribunal take an oath from a witness? An extremely old tradition provided that an oath be taken from witnesses. Parliament has abolished that rule in order to avoid creating problems for those who do not believe in God. A lighter even if still solemn formula, stating that the witness is aware of the seriousness of his/her task, has then been replaced for testimony in state courts. It is suggested that when the arbitrators are not bound to apply the Rules of Civil Procedure, they may ask the witness whether he/she agrees that an oath be taken from him/her and, if not, that he requests a solemn affirmation. However, they may not force the witness to make an oath.[148] **8.144**

(4.3) Does the arbitral tribunal have the power to compel witnesses? The arbitrator has no power to compel witnesses to give evidence. The Bill which ended up with the Reform, provided for the state court's intervention to compel witnesses to appear before the arbitrator. However the House of Representatives has voted against it and court intervention in aid of arbitration has then not been introduced. The Second Reform has remedied this situation s 816 ter Rules of Civil Procedure now entitles the arbitral tribunal to obtain from the President of the *Tribunale* (State Court) that he orders witnesses to appear before the arbitral tribunal. **8.145**

F. Documents

(1) Form and kind of documents to be presented to the arbitral tribunal

The original or a photocopy of the document is to be produced. When the original is a tape recording or a film or has a form different from paper, its copy will be such as technology provides for. If the produced copy is challenged by the opposing party, as not being a true **8.146**

[146] s 245–7, RCP.
[147] s 829, no 9, *ibid.*
[148] *Soc Impresa LESI SpA v Agenzia promozione sviluppo del Mezzogiorno*, Tribunale Arbitrale (Arbitral Tribunal) (1989), Arch giur oo pp (1990) 343.

copy of the original, then the original will have to be either produced or exhibited in order that the arbitrator can compare them. If the document is not in Italian, a sworn translation will have to be produced[149] if the Rules of Civil Procedure are to be applied. When the arbitrator is not subject to those Rules of Civil Procedure, he may rule otherwise, such as allowing a mere certification rather than a sworn translation of documents, unless the certification is challenged.

8.147 **(1.1) Is the submission of 'agreed documents' permitted? If yes, what is the extent and effect of such an agreement of the parties (authenticity, existence, acknowledgement of such documents' contents)?** Agreed documents would not conflict with public policy. However this practice would require cooperation between the parties which generally is missing. Documents which are not directly or indirectly challenged by a party are generally treated as admitted by it. This applies to the existence, authenticity and contents of that document.

8.148 **(1.2) How may electronic documents (eg emails) be presented and proven?** Electronic documents such as emails, schedules, websites, or parts of them, and other presentations may be produced by downloading and if authorized by presenting them in power point format. If any of them is challenged, the confirmation of them may be achieved by their being read, or in any event handled, or on their being placed on the website through inspection of the computer system of that party.

8.149 **(1.3) Does discovery (US- or UK-style), after the procedure has started, violate any procedural rules or public policy considerations?** Full discovery is likely to be treated as conflicting with public policy since the Republic of Italy, while ratifying The Hague Convention of 18 March 1970 on Obtaining Evidence Abroad in Civil or Commercial Matters, has refused to accept pre-trial discovery, considering it as oppressive and capable of taking a party by surprise, since a duty to discover is unknown, except in rare situations, to the Italian legal system. However, if the parties agree in writing to proceed to a full discovery, that agreement should be considered valid.

8.150 Partial discovery, ie discovery of specific documents or of a list of documents or of classes of documents may be ordered. However it is very rare in Italian arbitral proceedings that arbitrators issue orders to discover. Breach of an order to discover issued by arbitrators will not be supported by contempt of court or by state courts' intervention in aid of arbitration. However, the arbitral tribunal may infer from such conduct that the party which has not complied with its order has refused to do so, because such documents were not in its favour.

(2) Requirement to produce certain documents (as requested by the tribunal) and consequences of a failure to do so

8.151 Each party is entitled to produce the documents which it deems required or useful in support of its case. The Rules of Civil Procedure do not provide here for leave by the arbitrator. The arbitrator shall be entitled to decide which weight to give to such documents. Documents may be produced as a rule, until the parties have stated in a final way—on the

[149] s 122, RCP.

arbitrator's request—their claims and defences. Earlier mandatory time limits may be set out by the arbitrator for the production of documents, if special reasons make it advisable. A term to file documents shall not be mandatory unless so stated. Too short a term might affect the right of a party to present its case.

(2.1) Which documents may the tribunal request to be produced (eg also documents which are in the possession of third parties? It has been argued whether, like in court proceedings, an arbitrator may order the party to produce a particular document or a class of documents. That right has been denied by an arbitral precedent.[150] However it is submitted that such a right exists provided the existence of the documents and their possession by the opposing party is established. **8.152**

The arbitrator may not issue orders to third parties. However this does not prevent him from requesting documents to third parties. When the arbitrator is not bound to keep to the Rules of Civil Procedure, he will be able to proceed without having to keep to statutory restrictions. An order to a party not to produce further useless documents is conceivable when a party is flooding the proceedings with such type of documents. Privileged documents consist of documents which a party has no duty to produce, such as communications between itself and its lawyers. **8.153**

(3) Protection of the confidentiality of documents (legal privilege etc)

Confidentiality of arbitral proceedings and of its documents is not regulated by Italian procedural law except for hearings that are not open to the public. In fact the privacy which characterizes the arbitration agreement leads to construe all the arbitral hearings as not being open to those who do not have a role to perform in the proceedings.[151] Documents which are produced in the proceedings are consequently not protected by an express duty not to disclose them. Nevertheless, if disclosure causes damages, the liability which may arise from this will have to be taken into account. Apart from this basic protection, it seems difficult always to treat the arbitral proceedings as giving rise to a secret, the disclosure of which amounts to a criminal offence.[152] The parties are free to set out clearly a duty of confidentiality as to the arbitral proceedings, and its ambit. **8.154**

G. Experts

(1) Appointment and presentation of experts by the party or the arbitral tribunal

Experts may be appointed and presented by a party or by the tribunal. Under the Rules of Civil Procedure, the arbitrator may appoint[153] as *consulente tecnico d'ufficio* ('official' expert) one or more persons having a specific technical experience in order to assist him in his accomplishment of a single act or during the entire proceedings. The expert's activity is, therefore, not treated—strictly speaking—as evidence, since the latter has to be provided by the parties to prove their case, but is treated as a support sought and obtained by the arbitrator. **8.155**

[150] *Soc Internacional Forniture Division v Soc Impresa Russotti*, Tribunale Arbitrale (Arbitral Tribunal) (1990), *Rep Foro it* 1992, 182 no 160.

[151] Rubino-Sammartano, M., *Il Diritto dell'Arbitrato* (5th edn) 701.

[152] ss 621-2 Criminal Code.

[153] s 61, RCP.

In court proceedings the official expert takes an oath to perform his task in a proper and impartial way in order to help the tribunal to reach the truth. The tendency is to follow the same procedure in arbitral proceedings.

8.156 It has been held[154] that the tribunal may not appoint an expert to advise on legal issues. However, the above referred to judgment was dealing with a domestic issue and does not necessarily apply to evidence of foreign law.

8.157 Each party may then appoint its '*ex parte*' expert, who may attend meetings with the official expert, discuss such matters with him, and file his report to the latter. Even if the arbitrator does not appoint an official expert, a party may file an *ex parte* expert report, which is treated as a technical submission and does not amount to evidence. Counsel is under a duty arising from its professional Rules of Conduct to contact the court expert only in an official way, ie by writing to him with a copy to the opposing party or during a meeting attended or to be attended by the opposing party. As to the parties' expert, contacts and cooperation with counsel for their client are normal.

8.158 **(1.1) By which methods are tribunal-appointed experts selected? What are the rights of the parties during the selection of an expert?** The arbitral tribunal appoints its expert by basing itself on its own knowledge and previous experience. The parties may propose to the tribunal a list of potential experts. This practice is rather frequent. The arbitrators are not bound to choose any of these persons, but normally go through such lists and occasionally choose one of the experts so proposed.

(2) Admissibility and role of expert witnesses

8.159 As to the admissibility and the role of expert witnesses, under Italian procedural law, witnesses may depose only on facts and may not express technical opinions.[155] The common law practice of each party presenting an expert witness, is therefore unknown to Italian law. This does not prevent the arbitral tribunal, when it is not bound to comply with the Rules of Civil Procedure, from allowing the parties to prove their case by calling expert witnesses.

(3) Influence of the parties upon the selection of questions to be submitted to the expert

8.160 Under the Rules of Civil Procedure, the arbitrator is not bound to involve the parties before deciding which questions to submit to the expert. However, in practice, it is frequent that the arbitrator submits to the parties a draft list of questions to the expert, in order to receive their comments. Occasionally, the arbitrator himself invites the parties to submit draft questions to him.

(4) Independence and impartiality of experts and the right to reject a proposed/appointed expert

8.161 As to the issue of the independence and impartiality of experts as well as the right of a party to reject an expert, in court proceedings the expert takes an oath or makes a solemn affirmation

[154] *Impresa Sacheri v Robotto*, Corte di Cassazione (Court of Cassation), no 2765 (1989), *Foro pad* 1990, I, 278.

[155] ss 244 and 253, RCP.

to perform his task properly and faithfully with the sole purpose of providing the judge with the truth,[156] and consequently, he must be independent and impartial. The tendency in arbitral proceedings is to follow this procedure. The expert may be rejected by a party if he is not independent or based on the other grounds which in court proceedings allow a request to be made that a judge withdraw from the proceedings.[157] These rules also apply to arbitral proceedings when they are subject to the Rules of Civil Procedure.

(4.1) May a party or its counsel approach an expert (or expert witness) whom it has nominated (only before or also after the proceeding has started)? Are interviews admissible? A party or its counsel may approach the expert (or expert witness), whom it has nominated, before or after the proceeding has started, to put or clarify questions, and to understand his responses. However, counsel should not prepare his testimony or draft his report. If it is established that this has occurred and the expert (or expert witness) has been influenced, that will detract from his creditworthiness. **8.162**

(5) Oral examination of the expert in a hearing

The form of presentation of expert's reports and the existence or not of the right of the parties to ask questions to the expert are regulated by the Rules of Civil Procedure. In accordance with such Rules, the official expert must file his written report.[158] The court may, although this is quite rare, invite the expert to appear in order to provide clarifications[159] and if so counsel for the parties may ask for clarification. However, counsel has no right to examine directly the official expert. When the arbitral tribunal is not bound to keep to the Rules of Civil Procedure, he may allow counsel for the parties to examine the expert. **8.163**

A further question is whether the expert is under a duty to appear before the tribunal. Under the Rules of Civil Procedure, the expert has a duty to appear before the state court, since this is a part of the task which he has accepted. Nevertheless while it is expressly provided that a witness who refuses to appear in court proceedings may be forced to appear, this sanction is not expressly repeated as to experts. The same applies to arbitral proceedings. Nevertheless the arbitral tribunal might be tempted to apply to the President of the Court for an order to the expert to appear before the arbitral tribunal. **8.164**

H. Interim measures of protection

(1) Kind of interim measures which the tribunal may order

The Rules of Civil Procedure forbid arbitrators from issuing interim measures,[160] such as sequestrations or other conservatory measures. The parties may apply only to state courts for attachment or interim measure of protection before or during arbitral proceedings. This provision is mandatory, therefore it stands even if the parties exclude the Rules of Civil Procedure. This prohibition does not seem to apply to international arbitral proceedings taking place in Italy but which are not governed by Italian procedural law.[161] **8.165**

---

156 s 193, RCP.
157 s 52, *ibid.*
158 s 195, *ibid.*
159 s 197, *ibid.*
160 s 818, *ibid.*
161 Rubino-Sammartano, M., *Il Diritto dell'Arbitrato* (5th edn) 728.

8.166 **(1.1) Which are, in general, the procedural and substantive prerequisites for the ordering of interim and conservatory measures (eg reduced degree of evidence; urgency; summary evaluation of the claim)?** The prerequisites for the granting by state courts of an interim or conservatory measure is a prima facie good case of the applicant and a risk of irreparable prejudice.[162]

8.167 **(1.2) Are the prerequisites for interim measures ordered by the arbitral tribunal more or less the same as if those are requested from the state court? Is there case law and/or leading authorities on whether those measures are faster and enforced more easily if taken by the arbitral tribunal or the state court?** As discussed above (para 8.158), no interim measures may be ordered by arbitrators.

(2) Limits of the tribunal's powers to order interim measures

8.168 In general the prerequisites for interim measures would be the same as those requested by state courts.

8.169 As earlier discussed, arbitral tribunals have no authority to grant interim or conservatory measures. State courts may order interim measures if prima facie the claim is sound and there is a risk of an irreparable prejudice.

(3) Orders to give security for the costs of the proceeding

8.170 It was argued whether an arbitral tribunal may order a party to give security for the costs of the proceedings. The practice of security for the costs of court proceedings, which is not treated as an interim measure, was well established in Italy.[163] However the Constitutional Court has ruled[164] that this provision was in breach of the Constitution and consequently, the provision lost legal effect. Even if the parties exclude the Rules of Civil Procedure, it is suggested that the arbitrator may not order a security for costs, since this would be in breach of the Constitution.

(4) Attachment of assets by an order of the tribunal

8.171 As discussed above, the arbitral tribunal has no authority to order attachment of assets.

I. Assistance by the courts

(1) Extent of court assistance in the gathering of evidence

8.172 The degree of help from the state courts to obtain evidence which might not be available by order of the arbitral tribunal, has been debated. Under the 1865 Rules of Civil Procedure, it was the practice for arbitrators to apply to state courts in order that they hear witnesses residing in the jurisdiction of that court. Under the 1940 Rules of Civil Procedure that practice has not been followed. This has been based[165] on the ground that the arbitrators' order is not an enforceable instrument. It has been objected to[166] that even a state court's

---

162 s 700, RCP.

163 s 98, *ibid*, no longer in force; Calamandrei, *Introduzione allo studio sistematico dei provvedimenti cautelari* (Padua, 1936).

164 *Carabba v Marcellusi*, Corte Costituzionale (Constitutional Court) no 67 (1960), *Foro it*, 1960, I, 1873.

165 Tarzia, G., 'Istruzione preventiva e arbitrato rituale' *Riv arb* 1991, 719, 222.

166 Rubino-Sammartano, M., *Il Diritto dell'Arbitrato, cit* 536.

order has not that nature and that if there is any reason for a difference between state and arbitral proceedings, it should rather lie in the fact that court intervention is being provided for expressly, while it is not regulated as to arbitral proceedings. The Second Reform has provided at s 816 ter Rules of Civil Procedure that the arbitral tribunal may request the President of the state court of the venue of the arbitral proceedings that he orders a witness, who has not appeared before the arbitral tribunal to do so.

No court intervention is provided for as to witnesses who reside outside the state where the arbitral proceedings take place, except in the event of the court of the venue accepting to apply to the foreign court, in order to support the arbitration (which is extremely unlikely), or if the foreign court entertains applications made to it directly by the arbitrators. **8.173**

(1.1) **Is it for the arbitral tribunal or for the party to obtain the assistance of state courts with respect to the gathering of evidence?** Procedural law does not grant to arbitrators the authority to compel witnesses to appear before themselves nor to produce documents nor to ask, on application from the parties or on their own motion, foreign courts for letters rogatory. The parties are entitled to assistance by state courts in the taking of evidence, limited to what is described herein. **8.174**

As a general rule, as to court proceedings, an application may be made to state courts to hear witnesses who will not be available later.[167] One may try to make use of this remedy even in arbitral proceedings, by calling before state courts a witness who is likely to be unable to appear later. However, except for international conventions for legal assistance, the tendency is that courts intervene only if the merits will be tried by the courts and not when they are to be used in domestic arbitration. **8.175**

In *Attika*,[168] the Court of Cassation has held that applications for *accertamento tecnico preventivo* (ie to hear evidence to be subsequently used in foreign arbitral proceedings) may not be entertained, since the statutory provisions envisage such interventions only as evidence to be heard late by Italian courts. **8.176**

(1.2) **According to case law and practical experience, are there considerable delays involved when asking a court to give assistance (eg for the obtaining of evidence)?** In the event of a state court, being requested to order witnesses to appear before the arbitral tribunal, the matter might be dealt with in about one month from the time the application is filed with the competent court, unless the witnesses are not easily traceable or refuse to appear and have to be brought by the police before the court. The backlog of the great majority of Italian courts may extend such estimate. If a state court is requested from a foreign court to provide assistance to a foreign arbitral tribunal for the taking of oral evidence and agrees to proceed, a large amount of time may be taken by the transmittal of the application to the Italian court and for the return of the file to the foreign court after the evidence has been taken. Subject to that court's backlog, the estimate of the time required for the bureaucratic paperwork to subpoena the witnesses and to hear them should **8.177**

[167] s 692, RCP.

[168] *Attika Shipping Co v Bluemar S.A.*, Corte di Cassazione (Court of Cassation), no 9380, Ybk Comm Arb (1994) 680.

be around three to four months. Assistance of state courts to hear witnesses who have not appeared may be requested by the arbitral tribunal.

(2) Assistance for enforcing the attachment of assets

8.178 Since the arbitral tribunal may not order the attachment of assets, the issue whether it may obtain assistance from state courts for enforcement of its orders to attach assets will not arise. However, a party to arbitral proceedings may apply directly to the state court, even during the arbitral proceedings, in order to obtain an attachment of assets.

(3) Other examples of possible assistance

8.179 The question remains whether there are other situations where court assistance is possible. A party may apply to a state court in order that it appoints an expert in a given field, for example in order to describe a product or a situation. It is argued whether this application may be made if an arbitration agreement exists and even more if the proceedings are already pending. The solution might be positive in the former situation, but negative in the second one, since then the arbitrators themselves may appoint someone to proceed to this.

(4) Dependence of the power of state courts to intervene during the proceedings on the (national) procedural law applied by the arbitral tribunal

8.180 The power of state courts to intervene during the proceedings and after the award is based on the *lex fori*. Under Italian law, state courts may intervene in aid of arbitration at the stage of the appointment and of the challenge of arbitrators. They may also grant conservatory or interlocutory injunctions. After the award, the court grants leave to enforce the award and may, upon application, correct the award after it has been filed with it.[169] State courts may tax the arbitrators' fees and hear disputes between the parties and the arbitrators related to them. State courts may set aside the award and also in special circumstances re-examine the merits or hear oppositions to the award from third parties, and grant leave to enforce foreign or procedurally international awards.

8.181 The power of the state courts to intervene, when the arbitral proceedings are governed by a non-Italian procedural law, has not been the subject of much discussion. It seems that state courts may intervene during the proceedings, if their venue is in Italy, even if the applicable law is not Italian procedural law. However, if the national arbitration rules or the foreign procedural law do exclude courts' intervention, that might induce the Italian courts to refrain from intervening, unless its non-intervention may affect due process.

V. The award

A. Types of award

(1) Interim award (eg on interim measures or the jurisdiction of the tribunal)

8.182 A distinction is made[170] between: (i) awards which partially decide the merits (which are the proper '*partial awards*'); and (ii) those which decide some other issues raised during the

[169] s 826, RCP.
[170] s 827, *ibid.*

proceedings without deciding the dispute (*lodi non definitivi*) which will be referred to as '*interim awards*').

An award which asserts jurisdiction is an interim award, while an award which denies jurisdiction is a final award. Similarly an award which rejects a defence that the claimant has no standing is an interim award, while the award which holds that the claimant has no standing is final. Interim decisions are frequently issued as an order and not by an interim award. Directions of arbitral tribunals as to the conduct of the proceedings are orders, even if defined by the tribunal as awards. **8.183**

(2) Partial award

As provided for by Italian arbitration law[171] a partial award is an award which partially decides the merits, such as an award on liability, or an award on the claimant's claim, while the tribunal continues the proceedings in order to decide on the counterclaim. Even if these awards are partial, nevertheless they definitely decide such issues. Therefore the parties may not ask the arbitrator to revisit them during the rest of the proceedings.[172] However, the award may be challenged before the state courts. **8.184**

(2.1) Are awards, especially partial awards, binding in the same arbitral proceeding? Does it make a difference if after the rendering of such a partial award, one arbitrator is successfully challenged and removed on grounds that prevailed even before the partial award was made? The partial award is then final, in the sense that it may not be reviewed by the arbitrator. Partial awards must be attacked without waiting for the final award. Interim awards may be attacked only together with the final award. Awards may be attacked even if not yet filed with the court. Partial awards may be enforced immediately through their filing with the court. If an arbitrator is challenged and removed after a partial or interim award, this does not affect his earlier decision. No precedents are known as to the different situation where the ground for challenge existed before the partial or interim decision was made. This is probably due to the difficulty of challenging the arbitrator after the partial or interim award, on grounds existing before then, because of the very short time period which must run between the discovery of such a ground and the challenge. Assuming that the time limit is observed, the interested party might try to challenge the partial or interim award for lack of impartiality of the tribunal and/or consequent breach of due process. **8.185**

(3) Final award

The final award decides the entire dispute, be it on an issue of jurisdiction, or of the claimant's or defendant's standing, of estoppel, of time bar or of liability. The final award puts an end to the task of the arbitrator, who subject to the correction of possible material errors,[173] becomes *functus officio*.[174] **8.186**

(3.1) If a party fails to participate in the arbitration, may the tribunal proceed and issue an award? Is such an award enforceable as any other award? Are there special remedies for **8.187**

[171] para 3, s 827, RCP.
[172] *ANAS v Soc Manfredi*, Corte di Cassazione (*Court of Cassation*), no 11209 (1990), *Riv arb* 1991, 790.
[173] s 826, RCP.
[174] Having completed his office.

the Defendant at the enforcement stage? If a party is in default, or from a given time does not participate in the arbitration proceedings, the tribunal may proceed in its default and issue the award, and that award is enforceable as any other award. The party in default has no special remedy against the award, unless it has not been duly notified of the proceedings.[175]

B. Deliberations and agreement on the award

(1) Time limits (and possible extensions) for making the award

8.188 As to time limits and possible extensions, the Reform had fixed the term to make the award at 180 days.[176,177] The parties may by consent extend this term in writing. The Second Reform has introduced new legislation providing at s 820 of the Rules of Civil Procedure that if the parties have not agreed otherwise, the award must be made within 240 days. This term may be extended each time by 180 days, in the event of evidence to be heard, or of the appointment of an official expert, or if a not final or partial award is issued, or if a member of the tribunal is changed. The term starts to run from the date of acceptance of the arbitrators or, if they are more than one, from the acceptance of the last one. Non-compliance with this time limit is not a ground for setting aside the award unless, before the decision is made, that party serves on the arbitrators and on the other parties a notice that it will raise the issue of the expiry of the term.[178]

(2) Procedure for the decision of the arbitrators (majority vote etc)

8.189 Various phases of the arbitral tribunal's decision stage are distinguished by Italian law: (i) the discussion; (ii) the decision; (iii) the drafting; and (iv) signing of the award. The discussion and decision must be made with the participation of all the members of the arbitral tribunal, which may also take place by video or teleconference or by communicating through personal computers.

8.190 It has been held[179] that all the arbitrators must participate in the decision, and the decision may be made by a majority. It follows from this that if one arbitrator does not participate in the discussion, the arbitral tribunal is unable to validly decide, even if, in the event of that absence not being justified, that arbitrator may be liable for breach of his duty. If time is available before the expiry of the term, the arbitrator may be replaced.

8.191 A different situation may arise, where one of the arbitrators attends the discussion but does not share the view of the majority and leaves the meeting before the decision is made and ceases to participate. It is suggested that here, a distinction is to be made between two situations. In a first scenario, when that arbitrator leaves, the discussion was already over and the position of that arbitrator was clearly that he disagreed with the majority. If so, his leaving the meeting merely confirms that he disagrees with the majority. The requirement

---

175 s 829, no 9, RCP.

176 Which does not always correspond to six months.

177 s 820, RCP.

178 s 821, *ibid.*

179 *Impresa edile Lucchetti v Società stalla sociale di Corinaldo*, Corte di Cassazione (Court of Cassation) no 2198 (1989), Rass arb 1989, 308; see also Rubino-Sammartano, M., *Il Diritto dell'arbitrato, cit* at 845 *et seq.*

that he has participated in the discussion has then been complied with.[180] In a second scenario, if an arbitrator leaves before that stage is reached, his departure does not automatically amount to dissent.

(2.1) If an arbitrator fails or refuses to take part in oral deliberation meetings, although having been given sufficient notice of such meetings, may an award be rendered on the basis of written deliberations (or deliberations without this arbitrator) only? The award may be rendered even if one of the arbitrators has participated in the deliberations but leaves or refuses to sign the award. An award may not be rendered if one of the arbitrators does not participate or refuses to attend the deliberations meeting. The deliberation meetings do not require the personal attendance of the arbitrators unless one of them has so requested.[181] **8.192**

If an arbitrator does not participate or refuses to attend within 15 days after a notice to attend, he may be replaced by the President of the Court in the jurisdiction of which is the seat of the arbitration proceeding.[182] A different situation arises if an arbitrator participates in the discussion of the arbitrators, does not share the view of the majority and ceases to participate before a final decision is made. In this case, as discussed earlier, his conduct may amount to disagreement on the decision and not to a failure to participate in the discussion until the end. If so, the other arbitrators may sign the award and state that the decision has been made during the discussion and that such arbitrator has refused to sign it.[183] **8.193**

(3) Admissibility of dissenting opinions

The traditional view in Italy is against dissenting opinions. This position derives from the duty of judges not to disclose what has happened during their discussion of the case. Dissenting opinions are not welcome; in the best case they are tolerated.[184] Dissent is expressed either by a concise statement, or by dealing with the grounds for dissent before signing the award, or by attaching the dissenting opinion to the award or by incorporating it in the award, if the majority agrees. The dissenting opinion is to be provided to the parties by the tribunal or by the dissenting arbitrator. These matters arise from a duty of the arbitrators included in their task, and not from express statutory provisions. **8.194**

(3.1) Are there any court decisions (positions of leading authorities) on the issue of dissenting opinions in international arbitration (admissibility, disclosure to the parties and publication)? Article 26(i) of the Rules of the Italian Arbitration Association provides: 'The dissenting arbitrator is under a duty to sign the award and is only entitled that the award states that the decision is made by majority'. It has been held[185] that the award is not affected by nullity, if it is subscribed by all the arbitrators and decided by a majority, even if **8.195**

[180] Verde, G., 'Collegialità degli arbitri e responsabilità per inadempimento' *Riv dir proc* 1961 at 245.

[181] s 823, RCP.

[182] s 813 bis, *ibid.*

[183] s 823, no 7, *ibid.*

[184] *Ferrenti v Cons Acqued Simbrivio*, Collegio Arbitrale di Roma (Arbitral Tribunal of Rome) (2000), Arch giur oo pp; *Dizzi v Agricola Zootecnica Marchigiana*, Corte d'Appello di Perugio (Court of Appeal of Perugia) (1990), Riv arb 1992, 467; Rubino-Sammartano, M., *cit* (5th edn) 861.

[185] *Pizzi v Agricola Zootecnica Marchigiana*, Corte d'Appello di Perugia (Court of Appeal of Perugia) (1990) *Riv arb* 1992, 467.

it has not been expressed that an arbitrator has dissented. It has been further held[186] that the signature of the award by the arbitrator, stating the items on which he dissented from the majority, is not a ground to set aside the award.

(4) Signature by the arbitrators and potential failure of one arbitrator to sign

8.196 A further question arises whether the award is to be signed by all the arbitrators. Some arbitral tribunals sign the list of their final findings[187] at the end of the discussion. The full award has then to be drafted and signed. All the arbitrators are expected to sign it. However it may happen that an arbitrator is unable to sign it (for example because he is dead or seriously ill) or does not want to sign it, because he disagrees so strongly with it that he does not even accept to sign it stating that it is made by a majority vote. If so, the award is valid even if it is signed only by the majority of the arbitrators, provided they state that it has been discussed by all of them and that those who have not signed it have been unable or have not wished to do so. The Reform has modified the earlier situation, allowing that the award be not only signed but even decided outside Italy, provided the place of the proceedings is in Italy.[188]

C. Form of the award and deposition

(1) Form and minimum contents of an award

8.197 The award must have minimum contents. First it must be in writing. Second it must contain the name of the parties, mention the arbitration clause or the submission agreement and the claims and defences of the parties, state the findings, the concise reasons for them, the place of the proceeding, the way the decision was made and must bear the signature of the arbitrators.[189]

(2) Requirement to give reasons in the award

8.198 The requirement that the award give its concise reasons is mandatory.[190] The reasons must be such as to let the reader understand why the tribunal has decided in that way.

(3) Necessity to specify place and time where and when the award was made

8.199 The place where the award is signed is to be stated, in the opinion of this writer, even if nullity of the award is no more stated in the absence of this requirement as well as of the mention of the venue of the proceedings. The date of the signature of the award too is not considered as a ground for nullity which entitles a party to apply for the setting aside of an award. However, the date of the award is relevant to determine if the award was timely rendered. A non-timely rendered award may be set aside.

(4) Other requirements (registration, delivery etc)

8.200 The existence or not of other requirements must be examined. The tribunal is under a duty to notify each party by dispatching one original, even by registered mail, within ten days

[186] *Impr Mondelli v Prov Bolzano*, Corte d'Appello di Trento (Court of Appeal of Trento) (1956), Mass Giust. Civ. 1956, 24.

[187] *Il dispositivo* ('le dispositif' in French).

[188] s 823, RCP.

[189] *ibid.*

[190] s 823 no 3, *ibid.*

after the signing by the last arbitrator.[191] It is argued[192] whether the award must be delivered or merely dispatched to the parties within this term. Be it as it may, it is safer to see that the award be received by them within this term. Non-compliance with this term is not amongst the grounds for setting aside the award.[193] It is argued whether it may be equated to a late decision. If a party applies for its setting aside on the ground that it is a late decision, the court will have to be satisfied that it was timely made.

(4.1) Does the award have to be laid down or registered with a state court or agency (even if it has been rendered according to a foreign procedural law)? In order that the award can be enforced in Italy, it has to be filed with the court within the territorial jurisdiction in which the venue of the arbitral proceedings is located. The filing may take place at any time. 8.201

(4.2) Does a foreign award that has been rendered abroad according to this country's national procedural law, have to be laid down or registered with a state court or agency? Is there a fee or tax for such registration of an award? An award decided and signed outside Italy may be filed with the court as a domestic award, provided that: (i) the venue of the proceedings was Italy; (ii) that venue has not been a mere façade; (iii) and the arbitral proceedings have been governed by Italian procedural law. No precedents on this issue are known. 8.202

The court order enforcing the award is subject, as with Italian judgments, to registration tax, which is levied by the local Agency of the Ministry of Finance. The rate of the tax varies depending on the contents of the award. If the underlying relationship is not subject to VAT and the award grants to the winning party an amount of money or a right which has an economic value, then, in general the tax rate will be 3 per cent, the tax being different if the contract concerns real estate. 8.203

That rate is due also on interest. In view of the variety of situations and of the different attitude of the local state agencies, also as to the time the tax is levied in case of enforcement of foreign awards, it is advisable to check each time in advance. 8.204

(4.3) How long after the rendering of the award must the file/award be stored by the lawyers and the arbitral tribunal? It is suggested that the file of arbitral proceedings is to be kept by the arbitral tribunal and by counsel at least until the claims under the award have become time-barred. The general rule—which is subject to various exceptions—is that time bar—unless interrupted—expires 10 years after the award. 8.205

D. Applicable substantive law

(1) Party autonomy to choose the applicable substantive law

The parties are free to choose the substantive rules that govern the relationship from which the dispute arises. This provision does not make reference just to *leggi* (statutory provisions) but also to *regole* (rules) (which may also not be statutory provisions). This provision is not 8.206

[191] s 824, RCP.

[192] Schizzerotto, G., *Dell'arbitrato* (2nd edn, Giuffrè 1982) 53.

[193] s 829, RCP.

addressed to domestic arbitration since there the applicable law will generally be Italian substantive law.

8.207 (1.1) **Is there a public policy exception to the chosen substantive law?** Even in this situation the chosen substantive rules may be foreign, provided this is not in *fraude à la loi*.[194]

8.208 The public policy which is to be taken into account in domestic proceedings is Italian domestic public policy. The one to be taken into account in international proceedings is Italian international public policy. The latter is a sort of inner circle within the larger circle made by domestic public policy[195] and puts together the very essential principles of the legal system, which are so important that they cannot be infringed even in non-domestic matters. The duty to comply with public policy has been asserted by several precedents.[196] The controls where there is a conflict with public policy,[197] have to be made based on the public policy existing at the time the control is made, and not before then in case of any difference between the two.

8.209 (1.2) **Does the principle of '*jura novit curia*' apply? Or must the applicable law be proven (by which means)?** The party which argues that a given substantive law applies, should prove its contents. However, under the new Italian Conflict Rules,[198] state courts are under a duty to search of their own motion the contents of the foreign applicable law. Since foreign law is not treated as a fact, the arbitrator too must not be passive, but rather try to achieve appropriate information as to it.

(2) Decisions according to equity or as amiable compositeur

8.210 The parties may also instruct the arbitrators to decide in equity (natural justice), ie to mitigate—when proper—the consequences of statutory provisions, when too strict. This principal goes back to Roman law. Celsius stated that '*jus est ars boni et aequo*'.[199]

8.211 When the Norman Kings were ruling England they were fountains of justice and in that capacity they exercised their judicial power (the prerogative) to decide according to equity. The Roman notion of 'aequitas' and the one at the time of Norman Kings are indeed very close. The authority to decide *ex bono et aequo* is not without limits.

8.212 First, the arbitrator is not entitled to derogate from mandatory provisions. Furthermore the prevailing view is that this discretionary authority concerns only substantive and not also procedural law.

8.213 It has been submitted[200] that to decide *ex bono et aequo* is not a synonym for acting as *amiable compositeur*, which involves settling and which is therefore typical of *arbitrato irrituale*

---

[194] Rubino-Sammartano, M., *Il Diritto dell'Arbitrato* (5th edn) 622.

[195] Rubino-Sammartano, M. and Morse, C.G.J., *Public Policy in Transnational Relationship* (Kluwer, 1991) 105.

[196] *Consorzio autonomo porto Civitavecchia v Società Costamasnaga*, Corte di Cassazione (Court of Cassation) no 5637 (1984), *Mass Foro it* 1984, 1108.

[197] *Anderlan, et al v Reisch*, Corte di Cassazione (Court of Cassation), no 2215 (1984), Riv dir int priv proc 1986, I, 101.

[198] s 14, Statute 31 May 1995, no 218, RCP.

[199] The law is the art of what is fair and equitable.

[200] Rubino-Sammartano, M., *Amiable Compositeur (Joint Mandate to Settle) and Ex aequo et bono (Discretional Authority to Mitigate Strict Law)*, 9 *J Int'l Arb* No 1, 5.

(joint mandate to settle). An *amichevole compositore* (*amiable compositeur*) clause is occasionally inserted by the parties in the arbitration agreement (and not in an *arbitrato irrituale*). This was held[201] to mean that the arbitrators, in applying the law, have the discretionary authority to mitigate it when too strict.

(3) Application of lex mercatoria, *general principles etc*

The latitude granted to the parties to select even non-statutory provisions—as substantive law—makes it possible for them to also choose *lex mercatoria*, even if that will be rare in purely domestic disputes and more frequent in international arbitration. The validity of the choice of *lex mercatoria* has been affirmed by the Court of Cassation in *Töpfer.*[202] **8.214**

Likewise, and perhaps *a fortiori*, the parties are free to select the part of their national law which is common to them, a doctrine called: *le tronc commun*[203] which is reflected in the Channel Tunnel case.[204] **8.215**

Recourse to the principles of international law or to the general legal principles is also possible. It will be extraordinary in purely domestic disputes and infrequent too. **8.216**

(3.1) Is the application of *lex mercatoria* considered as the application of law or as a kind of *amiable composition*? *Lex mercatoria* has been referred to in *Töpfer*[205] as rules of conduct which merchants comply with, in the belief that it is their duty to do so. It is, consequently, to be treated neither as a law nor as *amiable composition*. *Lex mercatoria* has raised large interest amongst writers.[206] **8.217**

(4) Applicable substantive law if there is no choice by the parties

The arbitrators must decide in law, unless the parties have authorized them to decide in *equità* (according to natural justice). However when several legal systems are potentially applicable, a choice amongst them is to be made. If the parties have made no express choice of the applicable law, the arbitrators will first check where an implied choice of that law arises from the contract and conduct of the parties. Only in the absence also of an implied choice, the arbitrators will look for another solution, such as applying the conflicts rules of the various potentially applicable legal systems, if they provide the same result, or apply the doctrine of *depeçage* (ie apply to each performance of the contract the law applicable to the place where it was to take place, or it took place), or apply the *tronc* common doctrine (which applies the part of the potentially applicable substantive laws which is common to them) or apply the doctrine of the *voie directe* (ie to decide the dispute based on the principles arising from the contractual relationships of the parties, without looking for the substantive law). **8.218**

---

201 *Parisi v Parisi*, Corte d'Appello di Messina (Court of Appeal of Messina) (1956), *Rep Foro it* 1957, 174, 24.

202 *Fratelli Damiano snc v August Topfer & Co. GmbH*, Corte di Cassazione (Court of Cassation), no 722 (1982), Riv dir int priv proc (1982) 829.

203 The part of two or more legal system which is common to them. A doctrine submitted by Rubino-Sammartano, M. 'Le "tronc commun" des lois nationales en présence (Réflexions sur le droit applicable par l'arbitre international)' *Rev arb* 1987, 133.

204 *Channel Tunnel Group Ltd et al v Balfour Beatty Construction Ltd et al*, ASA Bull 1993, 1, 97.

205 *Fratelli Damiano snc v August Topfer & Co GmbH*, Corte di Cassazione (Court of Cassation) no 722 (1982), Riv dir int priv proc (1982) 829.

206 Rubino-Sammartano, M., *Il Diritto dell'Arbitrato* (2nd edn) 313 *et seq.*

8.219 **(4.1) Is there an autonomous conflict of law rule in the national arbitration law? Is it considered mandatory?** Contractual obligations are governed, under the law on conflicts,[207] by the Rome Convention 1980,[208] but the Convention does not apply to arbitration.

8.220 **(4.2) What is the law applicable to interest?** If the parties have not otherwise agreed upon, the law applicable to interest is the *lex contractus* (ie the law which governs the contract between the parties from which the dispute has arisen).

8.221 **(4.3) What is the law and practice with respect to legal interest on foreign currency debts?** Unless the parties have otherwise agreed upon, the choice of a foreign currency is in general construed as involving interest to be applied on the principal amount at the legal rate of that currency. This issue is not handled by statutory provisions. Italian courts are not law-makers. They construe the law, but they may change their own construction in subsequent proceedings. Precedents may play a persuasive role.

(5) Binding effect of state court decisions

8.222 State court precedents are not binding on an arbitral tribunal. Exceptions may be envisaged here too such as if a state court has decided a preliminary issue amongst the same parties.

8.223 **(5.1) Is an arbitral tribunal bound by a decision of another arbitral tribunal?** As a rule, court precedents have no binding effects on the decision by the arbitrators. The same applies to awards made by other arbitral tribunals. However, it is submitted that awards made by another arbitral tribunal on a preliminary issue, amongst the same parties, may have a binding or at least a persuasive effect on other arbitral tribunals.

8.224 **(5.2) Does a decision in a criminal case bind an arbitral tribunal?** Final decisions by criminal courts on a preliminary issue or affecting the dispute have to be taken into account by an arbitral tribunal and, subject to the circumstances, may bind it.

E. Settlement

(1) Settlement by agreement of the parties with or without support of the arbitral tribunal

8.225 The parties may settle the dispute during the proceedings. This may be the result of out of court contact between the parties which produces an out of court settlement, as a consequence of which the arbitral proceedings are abandoned, or of an intervention by the arbitrators which induces the parties to put an end to the dispute.[209]

2.226 **(1.1) May an arbitrator who has initiated settlement discussions be challenged when agreement on a settlement has failed?** The lack of success of settlement negotiations entertained by the arbitrator is not a ground to challenge him. The arbitrator may be challenged if he has prejudged or taken sides.

---

[207] Legge 31 maggio 1995, N 218, Riforma del sistema italiano di diritto internazionale private (Gazzetta Ufficiale, 3 giugno, n 128) (Act 31 May 1995, no 218 [Reform of the Italian Law or conflicts of law] [Official Gazette, 3 June, no 128]).

[208] Convenzione di Roma, 19 luglio 1980 sulla Legge applicabile alle obbligazioni contrattuali (Rome Convention, 19 July 1980 on the Law Applicable to Contractual Obligations).

[209] s 185, RCP.

(2) 'Private settlement' and its impact on the arbitral procedure

If the parties settle the dispute outside the proceedings, the most frequent course of action will be their waiver to the proceedings. Upon being so advised, the tribunal will make an order that the proceedings are terminated. 8.227

(3) Form and effect of a settlement (eg award on agreed terms?)

In the event of a settlement being reached in front of the arbitrators, it will be formalized by the parties by entering later into a settlement agreement and waiving the proceedings, or by the tribunal putting the settlement on record and by the minutes of the hearing being signed by the parties and by the arbitrators. The award by consent or on agreed terms is not statutorily regulated and this practice is practically unknown to Italy. The award by consent risks not being enforced because it is not a decision by the arbitrators but a sort of notarial acknowledgement of the settlement reached by the parties. 8.228

F. Costs of the arbitration

(1) General allocation of the costs of the proceedings

The rule as to allocation of costs is that they follow the event.[210] However, the arbitral tribunal may order the winning party to pay the costs of the losing party for the procedural steps of the losing party which have become necessary because of inappropriate conduct of the winning party. The tribunal may order that each party bears its costs when each party loses on one head of claim or where there be other justified grounds. The tribunal may also make the losing party responsible for—if justified reasons exist for it—only a share of the costs of the winning party. A tendency exists to mitigate the loss of a party by ordering that each party bears its legal costs. 8.229

(2) Deposits or advances for costs or fees

As to deposits for costs and fees the view has been expressed that the arbitrators are entitled to advances. Writers generally make reference to an advance on costs. The Second Reform provides at s 816 septies that the arbitrators may make the continuance of the proceedings conditional on the 'advanced payment of the foreseeable expenses'. One has to establish whether expenses include fees. Literally that would not be the case. However, one might construe expenses as costs and costs might include fees. One might turn to the statutory provisions on mandate[211] under which the principal is under a duty to put at the agent's disposal the funds necessary to perform his task.[212] 8.230

(2.1) Is there case law authorizing or prohibiting arbitrators to order a party to pay an advance on the arbitration costs? It has been held[213] by a court of appeal that the arbitrator is entitled to an advance on his costs. The tribunal may make the proceedings conditional on receiving the advance to cover the costs of the proceedings. 8.231

[210] s 91, RCP, see also Andrioli, *Commento al Codice di Procedura Civile*, IV (1974) 817; Vecchione, R., *L'arbitrato* (1971) 459; Schizzerotto, G., *Dell'Arbitrato* (2nd edn, Giuffré, Milan, 1982) 408.

[211] The law of agency (s 1703, Civil Code).

[212] s 1719, Civil Code.

[213] *Ministero dei LL.PP v Imp Gustavo Ungano e Istituto*, Corte d'Appello di Roma (*Court of Appeal of Rome*) 1965, *Arbitrati e Appalti*, 1966.

8.232 **(2.2) May the raising of a set-off claim or counterclaim be made contingent upon payment of the corresponding advance for the relating arbitration costs (cf eg Article 30(5), 1998 ICC Rules)? May such a condition be agreed upon when entering into the arbitration agreement?** No precedents are known on the issue whether the right to make a set-off claim or a counterclaim may be made by the arbitrators conditional upon payment of the related advance by that party. It is submitted that in the absence of limits accepted by the parties, the right to make a set-off claim or counterclaim stands. The question is whether that party is entitled that the proceedings to decide such a claim take place even if it does not pay the requested deposit. Acceptance of arbitration rules which condition the set-off or counterclaim or the continuance of the proceedings upon such a payment has an impact on this.

8.233 **(2.3) Which remedies exist against a party which does not pay its part of the advance on the arbitration costs? Termination of the arbitration agreement? How may the other party enforce its rights?** The arbitral tribunal's order to pay an advance on its fees or costs does not seem to be enforceable. If this order takes the shape of an interim award, which might be argued, then the award might be enforced in the ordinary way. However, collection through enforcement proceedings will take time. Termination of the proceedings for breach by a party of its duties to the arbitrator is conceivable, but has not yet been the object of court decisions.

(3) Costs of the administration by an arbitration institution

8.234 In the case of an administered arbitration, administrative dues will be payable to the arbitral institution. The Rules will generally impose a duty on the parties to pay to that institution the administrative charges provided in the latter's schedule. If not fixed, the arbitral institution will generally be entitled to claim a fair payment for its services. The arbitral institutions which operate in Italy generally deal with this in their rules and schedules. That is the case with the Milan International and National Chamber of Commerce,[214] the *Associazione Italiana per l'Arbitrato*[215] and the Italian Delegation of the European Court of Arbitration.[216]

(4) Arbitrators' fees: law and practice, judicial control

8.235 The arbitrators are entitled to reimbursement of their costs and to a fee for their services, unless they have waived this right. The parties are jointly liable to the arbitrators for the payment of their fees,[217] while, as between themselves, the party which has paid has a claim for reimbursement against the other parties for their respective share. The arbitrators may tax their costs and fees directly. However, the parties are not bound to accept that. If they do not accept it, the taxation is then not binding and upon application by the arbitrators, the President of the *Tribunale* will tax the arbitrators' costs and fees, after hearing the parties. His order[218] is an enforceable instrument. Recourse to the court for taxation of the arbitrators' fees is not infrequent.[219]

[214] Art. 4.1, International Arbitration Rules (1996 edn).

[215] Art. 113, Arbitration Rules (1994 edn).

[216] Art. 8.4, Arbitation Rules (1971 edn).

[217] s 814, RCP.

[218] *ibid*; see *supra* nos Rubino-Sammartano, M., *Arbitrato, Conciliazione e ADR*, (Zanichelli, 2009) 777 *et seq* and 118 *et seq*.

[219] *Infante et al. v Assoc profess Taranto Due et al*, Corte di Cassazione (Court of Cassation) no 2124 (1996), *Riv trim app* 1996, 708.

(4.1) **May arbitrators fix their own fees in the award?** The determination by the arbitrators of their costs and fees is not binding upon the parties.[220] If they do not accept it, then the arbitrator's costs and fees are taxed by the President of the *Tribunale*,[221] on the arbitrator's application after hearing the parties. The arbitrators' taxation of their fees is then just a proposal to the parties. If the latter do not accept it, the arbitrators must apply to the state court for taxation. It has been suggested[222] that from this point of view, the arbitrators' taxation of their fees is not a part of the award even if it is incorporated in it. This view is to be shared. **8.236**

The Court of Cassation has held[223] that arbitrators' fees are to be taxed based on the object of the dispute, the nature and size of the task and its importance. The President of the *Tribunale* taxes the fees by order which is expressly declared not to be capable of attack and which is an enforceable instrument. Nevertheless, it has been held that the order may be the object of a petition to the Court of Cassation provided one of the limited grounds for appeal to such a court exists. However this special procedure is confined to establish the *quantum* of the fees and does not deal also with the separate issue whether the arbitrator is entitled or not to fees. **8.237**

(4.2) **How can the parties change the arbitrators' fees once they are fixed?** In *ad hoc* arbitration, it is rare that fees be fixed in advance. It has been held[224] that the arbitrator is entitled to an advance on his 'costs'. The difficulty for the arbitrator consists in enforcing quickly such a right. The right of the arbitrator to stay his activity in the absence of collection of the advance, on the ground that payment is a condition for performance of his task, requires careful consideration. If so, the issue arises whether the fees may be changed, if the basis for that agreement has changed. If there is a substantial change in the circumstances, each party may apply for its revision. **8.238**

In institutional arbitration the fees are to be determined according to the scale of that arbitral institution, and the arbitrators are generally requested to accept that before being appointed. The scale may provide for adjustment of the fees at the discretion of the arbitral institution. **8.239**

The question whether the parties may influence the arbitrators' remuneration, depends on the specific situation. In *ad hoc* arbitration, the parties may agree upon the arbitrators' fees and make the appointment dependent on the arbitrators' acceptance of those fees, or agree it later with the arbitrators. If not they may refuse the arbitrators' taxation of their fees. In administered arbitration the parties may influence the arbitral institution's determination of the arbitrators' fees, by making comments on how in their view the schedule of that body should be applied. **8.240**

---

[220] s 814, RCP.

[221] In whose jurisdiction the seat of the arbitral proceedings is located.

[222] Satta, S., *Commentario al codice di procedura civile* (1971, vol IV) 200.

[223] *Buizza v Bolognini*, Corte di Cassazione (Court of Cassation) no 21 (1982), *Giur it* 1982, I, 1, 340.

[224] *Ministero dei LL.PP. v Imp. Gustavo Ungaro e Istituto,* Corte d'Appello di Roma (Court of Appeal of Rome) 1965, Arbitrati e appalti 1966, 31.

8.241 A writer has held that one party may not validly commit itself to pay to the arbitrators their entire fees for the proceedings.[225] Nevertheless, without such a commitment, a party becomes liable for the entire fees if the other party does not pay its share. By not allowing one party to make such an unqualified commitment at the beginning, one aims at avoiding to create a direct financial link between the arbitrator and one party. Likewise an agreement between one party and the arbitrator as to the amount of his fees has been held to be invalid.[226]

8.242 (4.3) **Are the arbitrator's fees subject to income tax if (i) the place of arbitration; or (ii) the normal residence or place of business of the arbitrator is located in this country?** The fees collected by arbitrators, if Italian residents, are subject to income tax whether the place of the arbitration is in Italy or abroad.[227] As to non-resident arbitrators, Italian parties to arbitration proceedings taking place in Italy are under a duty to withhold 30 per cent as a final tax and not as an advance, unless an international convention against double taxation exists between Italy and the country of residence of that arbitrator. If a non-resident arbitrator has a permanent establishment or an office in Italy he is subject to full taxation in Italy also on his income from arbitral proceedings.

8.243 (4.4) **Are arbitrator's fees submitted to VAT? If yes, is the duty to pay such tax linked to (i) the place of arbitration; or (ii) the arbitrator's general residence?** VAT is to be applied by Italian arbitrators on the fees due to them by parties which are Italian residents. As to fees due by non-Italian residents, who are residents in an EU member state and hold a VAT position there, no VAT was deemed to apply, as well as if the parties were resident outside the EU.

8.244 This position has been affected by the ruling of the European Court of Justice in *von Hoffmann*[228] which has held that such exclusion from the duty to apply VAT concerns advocates but not arbitrators (even if they are advocates). The consequence of this ruling, until the matter is reviewed or clarified, seems to be that Italian arbitrators, be they advocates or not, have to charge VAT on their fees also to non-Italian residents (be they EU residents or residents in other countries).

(5) Attorneys' fees and the winning party's claim for reimbursement

8.245 Also the fees of the attorneys of the winning party are subject to the rule that costs follow the event. Unless the arbitrators, based on the circumstances, decide otherwise, the losing party will be ordered to pay the fees of the attorneys for the winning party and such fees will be taxed. Italian counsels' maximum fees are determined by an official schedule, which may be derogated by consent only. If a party was represented by its in-house counsel, it may claim, under the heading of reimbursement of costs, for the assistance from its in-house counsel, based on his/her remuneration and on time spent. This claim is quite rare and it is suggested that it would be examined with caution.

8.246 (5.1) **May in-house lawyers charge fees or may a party request costs of in-house lawyers to be reimbursed?** In-house lawyers may not charge fees. It is conceivable, even if not

225 Andrioli, V., *Commento al codice di procedura civile* (Naples, 1947), 817.
226 *Amico v Roxos*, Corte di Cassazione (*Court of Cassation)* no 751 (1936), *Giur it* 1936, I, 1, 294.
227 s 1, Decreto del Presidente della Repubblica (Executive Order), 22 December 1986, no 917.
228 *Von Hoffmann v Finazamt Trier*, European Court of Justice, no 145/96 (1997).

frequent, that the party claiming damages includes in them costs borne as a consequence of its staff, including its in-house lawyers, having wasted time because of the dispute.

(6) Time and form of the decision on costs

The practice is that the decision on costs is made in the final award. **8.247**

(6.1) May the arbitrators' decision on the costs (allocation and amount of costs to be reimbursed) be challenged separately from the award itself? Are there legal provisions, especially time limits for such a remedy? As earlier discussed, as a rule the arbitrator's decision on costs is not a decision, but a mere proposal. This proposal may be rejected by a party separately from the award. If so, the arbitrator will have to apply to the *Tribunale* for the taxation of his or her fees. Contrary to this the decision on who has to bear the costs of the arbitration is a part of the award and if a party wishes to challenge it, it must avail itself of the remedies available against the award. **8.248**

(6.2) Are the arbitrators entitled and/or legally obliged to rule on the amount of one or both parties' costs that are recoverable? The rule being that 'costs follow the event' the loser must pay the costs of the winning party. The arbitrator's decision to grant the principal and interest involves a duty of the arbitrator, if so required, to tax the costs of the winning party to be borne wholly or partly by the loser. **8.249**

G. Publication of the award

(1) Publication with or without the consent of the parties

The possibility to publish awards has long been debated. Awards may be published with the consent of both parties. The confidentiality which is inherent to arbitration, might prevent a party from delivering the award for publication. If in spite of this, the award is received by a third party, there is a tendency to consider that confidentiality binds the parties to the arbitration, but not third parties. Awards are generally published once they are attacked or their enforcement is sought before a state court. **8.250**

(2) Practice of publication (eg in specific legal journals)

Awards, as well as court proceedings related to them, are published in a specialized law report, *Rivista dell'arbitrato*, published by Giuffrè, Milan, under the auspices of the *Associazione Italiana per l'Arbitrato*. Several of them are also published in the law reports *Foro padano*. The main awards and courts proceedings related to them are also published in other main law reports such as *Foro italiano*, *Giurisprudenza italiana*, *Giustizia civile*, and *I Contratti*. **8.251**

VI. Amendment and challenge of the award; liability of arbitrators

A. Amendment, correction or interpretation of the award

(1) Motion to amend or correct an award

Applications to amend or correct the award may be made. The award may be corrected on the application of a party, in the event of it having made omissions or containing clerical mistakes or computation mistakes[229] or of it having omitted to mention the name of the **8.252**

[229] s 826, RCP.

arbitrators or of the parties or the place of arbitration, or the reference to the arbitration agreement or the mention of the requests for relief and respectively for rejection of the relief sought by the other party. It may not be amended in other ways. The application is made to the arbitrator before the award is filed with the court. The arbitral tribunal must decide on the application within 60 days. If the application is made after the award has been filed with the court, the correction is to be sought from the court with which the award has been filed. The correction may also be requested to the court before which the award has been challenged or is asserted.[230]

(2) Interpretation of the award by the tribunal

8.253 The arbitrators have no authority to interpret their award. This power has not been granted to them by any statutory provision. The arbitrators have no authority to reopen and to amend the award, after it is made.

B. Appeal on the merits

(1) Admissibility and procedure of an appeal on the merits

8.254 No appeal on the merits is admissible, in the sense that state courts may not set the award aside on points of fact or because of the appreciation of the evidence by the arbitrator. The issue of reasons, extent and procedure for an appeal on the merits does consequently not arise. The state court may set aside an award for breach of rules of procedure, for nullity of the submission or of the arbitration clause, and for errors as to substantive law[231] if this ground has been expressly provided for by the parties or by a statutory provision. If the award is set aside on such grounds, then the merits will be tried again.[232]

8.255 (1.1) **May the parties agree on an appeal to another arbitral tribunal?** An appeal on the merits to an appellate arbitral tribunal was allowed under the (1865) Rules of Civil Procedure, which made express reference to this.[233] The (1940) Rules of Civil Procedure do not make any more reference to it, and provide[234] that the award is subject only to setting aside and to *revocazione* (re-examination). The general view of courts and writers is that no appeal to a second arbitral instance is allowed.[235] The issue was raised whether the parties may by agreement provide for a second arbitral instance. This has been excluded by the Court of Cassation.[236] This view is not convincing. It has been suggested[237] that the 1940 Code merely aimed at regulating the review by state courts of the product of arbitration, and did not address the issue whether a second arbitral instance could take place. The latter does not consequently seem to be in conflict with Italian procedural public policy. However, the prevailing opinion does not share this view.

---

230 s 826, *ibid.*
231 s 829, *ibid.*
232 s 830, *ibid.*
233 ss 28 and 31.
234 s 827.
235 *Soc Organizz. Tecniche Serv Urbani v Com Firenze*, Corte di Cassazione (Court of Cassation) no 446 (1964), in Schizzerotto, G., *L'arbitrato rituale nella giurisprudenza*, 331.
236 *Soc Organiz. Tecniche Serv Urbani v Com. Firenze* Corte di Cassazione (Court of Cassation) no 446 (1964).
237 Amongst writers see Schizzerotto, G., *L'arbitrato rituale nella giuriusprudenza* (Cedam, 1969) 331; Rubino-Sammartano, M., *Il Diritto dell'Arbitrato, cit* 1173.

(2) Possibility to exclude an appeal (eg in the arbitration clause)

The exclusion of an appeal on the merits is consequently statutorily provided except for the situations referred to at item 8.256 and this provision cannot be derogated from. **8.256**

C. Setting aside of the award

(1) Reasons for setting aside an award

The reasons for setting aside an award[238] may be distinguished in (i) procedural reasons; and (ii) breach of substantive provisions. In turn, procedural reasons may be distinguished in (i) absolute reasons; and (ii) reasons which are subject to conditions or to time limitation. The above two classes of procedural reasons shall be listed separately. **8.257**

The following are absolute procedural reasons[239] (ie grounds for setting aside which do not depend on conditions or time bar): (i) nullity of the arbitration clause or submission; (ii) incapacity of the arbitrator; (iii) lack of decision on an issue raised in the arbitration clause or submission; (iv) conflict between heads of the award; (v) lack of essential requirements of the award; (vi) breach of due process; and (vii) the award not deciding the merits of the dispute when the arbitrators have to decide on the merits. **8.258**

The following are the procedural reasons subject to estoppel or to conditions:[240] (i) irregular appointment of the tribunal; (ii) award deciding beyond the ambit of the arbitration clause or submission; (iii) award made after the expiry of the time limit to make it; (iv) breach of procedural provisions set forth under the sanction of nullity; and (v) conflict with a not attackable award or final judgment. **8.259**

The second class of reasons for setting aside an award consists of breaches of substantive provisions.[241] These grounds for setting aside an award consist in a breach of substantive statutory provisions or of national collective labour agreements and of labour contracts. The nature of the breach one may complain of, is an error in law. In this respect, the ground for setting aside is like the grounds for petition to the Court of Cassation against appellate judgments.[242] This ground for setting aside the award is available only if the parties expressly provided for it or is provided for by a statutory provision. **8.260**

Nevertheless breaches of public policy are always a valid ground for setting aside the award. **8.261**

The above grounds do not include errors in fact. No other grounds for setting aside are available. **8.262**

The application for setting aside the award is excluded in the following circumstances: **8.263**

- the irregular appointment of the tribunal, if this ground has not been raised during the proceedings;[243]

---

[238] s 829, RCP.
[239] s 829, para 1, *ibid.*
[240] s 829, *ibid.*
[241] s 829, para 2, *ibid.*
[242] *Società Digital Angiography v Casa cura Villa Mater Gratiae*, Corte di Cassazione (Court of Cassation), no 11093 (1992), *Foro it* 10 1093, I, 2647.
[243] s 829 no 2, RCP.

- a decision beyond the arbitration agreement, if the party, which attacks it, has had during the proceedings the possibility to raise it (eg because the opposing party had made a claim beyond the arbitration agreement) and has not objected to it; [244]
- the making of the award after the expiry of the time limit if the interested party has not served on the arbitrators and the other party a notice of its intention to attack the award on such a ground;[245] before the dispute has been decided by the arbitrators' signature of the summary of their findings and of the relief which they grant;
- non-compliance with procedural form requirements set forth under the sanction of nullity, when the parties had instructed the arbitrators to comply with such provisions, unless that nullity has been remedied;[246]
- conflict with another previous and no longer attackable award, or with a final judgment, if the previous final judgment or the no longer attackable award has not been produced in the arbitral proceedings; and
- breach of substantive law provisions, if the parties have authorized the arbitrators to decide *ex aequo et bono*.

In addition to setting aside proceedings the attacks that are available against an award, are the following ones.

8.264 First: *Revocazione* (re-examination of the award for fraud or due to false evidence). An application may be made to re-examine the award in the event of the award (i) being the result of fraud of a party or of the arbitrator; (ii) being based on evidence which after the award (or before it but without the interested party having been aware of it) has turned out to be false; or (iii) having been made without the parties having been able to produce decisive documents since they were found only afterwards.[247] The *revocazione* proceedings are governed by the provisions which regulate the *revocazione* of judgments.[248] The application is to be made to the Court of Appeal in the territory of which the venue of the arbitral proceedings was located. If the grounds for *revocazione* arise while setting-aside proceedings are on, the term to file the application for re-examination of the award is stayed until the judgment on the setting-aside proceedings is notified to the parties.[249]

8.265 Second: Third party opposition. The Arbitration Reform Act has introduced[250] a further remedy, in favour of third parties. Under such a remedy, whenever someone, who was not a party to the arbitral proceedings, deems that the award affects his rights, he may oppose the award before the state courts. Assignees and creditors of a party to arbitral proceedings may oppose the award before the state courts when the award is the result of fraud or of conspiracy to their detriment.[251] The opposition is to be made to the Court of Appeal in

[244] s 829 no 4, RCP.
[245] s 829 no 6, *ibid.*
[246] s 829 no 7, *ibid.*
[247] s 831, *ibid.*
[248] s 395 *et seq*, *ibid.*
[249] s 831, *ibid.*
[250] s 831, *ibid.*
[251] s 404, *ibid.*

the territory of the place where the arbitral proceedings was located. The opposition proceedings are governed by the Rules of Civil Procedure for opposition to judgments of state courts.

A joinder of attacks (whenever possible). The Court of Appeal may join applications[252] for setting aside, for *revocazione* and opposition proceedings, unless the stage reached by one of them does not allow to adequately deal with the other ones. **8.266**

(1.1) May an award made according to international or foreign procedural rules be the object of an application for setting aside before the national courts? It has been argued[253] that awards made in Italy according to international or foreign procedural rules may not be the object of an application for setting aside before Italian courts, since the requirement for setting aside is that the judgment or award be made under the procedural rules of the *lex fori*. Neither precedents nor other writers are known on this issue. **8.267**

(2) Procedure and deadlines for challenging an award

As to the procedure and deadlines for setting aside proceedings, it should be noted that those proceedings are not available after the expiry of one year after the signing of the last arbitrator.[254] **8.268**

A shorter time limit exists. In the event of the award being served on a party, that party's application for setting aside has to be served within 90 days after such a date. As to parts of the award which have been corrected through the earlier discussed proceedings, the time limit runs from service of the Correction Order.[255] **8.269**

The writ for setting aside an award may be served and docketed even if the award has not been filed with the court.[256] **8.270**

Awards which decide a part of the merits (partial award), are immediately open to setting aside proceedings. As to awards which decide some of the issues—not concerning the merits—which have been raised (interim awards), without defining the entire dispute, the setting aside procedure may be instituted only simultaneously with the final award.[257] **8.271**

If one of the parties has applied for the setting aside of the award, other parties to the arbitral proceedings may join[258] the application by complying with the provisions for independent joinders and joinders in support and within the time limits for them. **8.272**

Unless all the parties have objected to the review of the merits by it, when the Court of Appeal sets aside the award it re-examines the merits. However if, at the time the arbitration agreement was entered into, one of the parties resided or had its operational centre outside **8.273**

252 s 831, RCP.
253 Rubino-Sammartano, M., *Il Diritto dell'Arbitrato* (2nd edn) 481 *et seq.*
254 s 828, RCP.
255 *ibid.*
256 s 827, RCP.
257 *ibid.*
258 *Società Adriatica navigazione v Società Sperco navigazione*, Corte di Cassazione (Court of Cassation), no 7214 (1990), *Rep Foro it* 1990, 166, no 102.

Italy, the Court of Appeal re-examines the merits only if the parties have so provided in the arbitration agreement or jointly so request.

8.274 As to the setting-aside procedure, the application is to be addressed to the Court of Appeal in the territory of which the seat of the proceedings was located. An application for correction of the award does not stay the term for filing an application to set aside the award.[259] The setting-aside procedure is governed by the procedural provisions which govern proceedings before the Court of Appeal. During the setting-aside procedure, the court may stay the enforcement of the award.[260]

8.275 (2.1) **Who may (or must) represent a party in a proceeding for setting aside an award?** Representation in setting-aside proceedings belongs exclusively to members of the Italian Bar.[261]

8.276 (2.2) **Do specific time limits exist for setting-aside procedures concerning awards on jurisdiction?** If the decision on jurisdiction is made by the arbitrators through an interim award, and it asserts jurisdiction, the interim award may be attacked only together with the final award. If jurisdiction is denied, the award is to be attacked straight away, since it puts an end to the proceedings. Applications for setting aside must be served within 90 days after service of the award. In the absence of service of the award, the application must be served within one year after the signing by the last arbitrator.[262]

(3) Effect of a court decision which sets the award aside

8.277 The effect of the court decision which sets the award aside is that the award is null and void. If only a part of the award is to be set aside, and that part may be severed from is the rest, only that part of the award is declared null and void.[263]

8.278 (3.1) **Does the setting-aside action suspend the enforcement? If so, do remedies exist to reinstate enforcement?** The setting-aside proceedings do not stay by themselves the enforcement of the award. However, the Court of Appeal which hears such proceedings may, upon a party's application, stay the enforcement of the award.[264] If so, the stay will be later replaced by the judgment which either confirms the award, in which case the winning party shall be entitled to enforce it, or which sets it aside, in which case it will not be possible to enforce it.

8.279 (3.2) **After an award has been set aside, does the underlying arbitration agreement revive or remain in force or is it exhausted or deemed terminated?** The setting-aside proceedings consist of two stages: (i) the setting-aside itself; and (ii) after that, the decision of that Court of Appeal on the merits. The Second Reform has provided that the Court of Appeal

---

[259] *Società Cipriani v Tommasi*, Corte di Cassazione (Court of Cassation) no 4364 (1983), *Mass Foro it* 1983, 904.
[260] s 830, RCP.
[261] s 82, para 2, *ibid.*
[262] s 828, *ibid.*
[263] s 830, *ibid.*
[264] *ibid.*

may do so, unless the parties or statutory provisions have expressly excluded this.[265] If the arbitrators complete the proceedings without deciding the merits, the arbitration agreement keeps its effects. This deals with the issue whether the arbitration agreement is extinguished by it being used once (one could say 'consummated') or not. The parties are then free to set forth a new arbitral tribunal or—even if rare—to provide that the previous arbitral tribunal must try the case again.

If one of the parties resides or has its operational centre outside Italy, the Court of Appeal may not re-examine the merits unless the parties have so agreed. **8.280**

(4) Appeal against the court's decision to set aside or not set aside the award

The judgment rendered by the Court of Appeal on attacks against the award may in turn be attacked: **8.281**

- for *revocazione* (re-examination);[266]
- for *regolamento di competenza*[267] which is a ruling on the jurisdiction; on the jurisdiction of that specific state court rather than of another state court of that legal system;
- for errors on points of law (*ricorso per cassazione*);[268] or
- for third party opposition.[269]

The Rules of Civil Procedure which govern attacks against judgments of state courts apply to each of such proceedings.

(5) Possibility of the parties to exclude actions for setting aside

As a rule the parties may not exclude before the award is made attacks against the award.[270] When the parties waive setting aside the award, this waiver produces the limited result that the award may not be set aside because of a breach of substantive law provisions. The same result is produced by the parties having instructed the arbitrators to mitigate strict law.[271] **8.282**

D. Liability of arbitrators

(1) Duties and liabilities of arbitrators regarding the conduct of the proceedings

The issue of arbitrators' legal liability arises in respect of the arbitrators' duty to conduct the proceedings in a fair, expeditious and diligent manner. Not only time, but also quality is relevant in this respect. If unjustified delays occur, the arbitrator may be liable for them. In *Trapani*[272] an arbitrator was held liable for not having decided within the time limit for making the award, due to his not having monitored the time required by his expert to file his report. The Second Reform has provided at s 813 ter Rules of Civil Procedure that arbitrators are liable for damages if they omit or delay action due by them and have been removed for wilful conduct or gross lack of care; if they waive without a good cause the **8.283**

[265] s 830, RCP.
[266] s 395 *et seq*, *ibid.*
[267] s 41 *et seq*, *ibid.*
[268] s 360 *et seq*, *ibid.*
[269] s 404 *et seq*, *ibid.*
[270] ss 829 and 831, *ibid.*
[271] s 829, para 3, *ibid.*
[272] *Trapani v Rapallini*, Corte di Cassazione (Court of Cassation), no 3005 (1987), *Foro pad* 1988, 1, 406.

appointment which they have accepted; or if with a wilful conduct or with gross lack of care, they do not make the award or prevent that it be made within the time limit for it.

8.284 Apart from these breaches, the arbitrators are liable for a wilful breach or for gross lack of care, within the limits set out by Art 2, paras 2 and 3, Statute 13 April 1988, n 1771.

8.285 Court proceedings, based on a claim for damages, may be instituted during the course of the proceedings only on the ground of omission or delay as to action due by the arbitrator.

8.286 If the award has been made, court proceedings may be issued to assert the arbitrator's liability only on the grounds on which the award has been set aside by a final judgment that it has been set aside.

8.287 Except in the event of wilful conduct by the arbitrator, damages may not exceed three times the arbitrator's agreed fees or, in the absence of such agreement, three times the fees provided by the applicable fees schedule.

8.288 If the arbitrator is liable, he is not entitled to fees and to reimbursement of his expenses.

8.289 In case of partial nullity, the amount of his fees and expenses is reduced in proportion.

8.290 Each arbitrator is liable for his own conduct.[273]

8.291 Likewise, if a party has not been given a fair hearing and the requirements of due process have not been complied with, it is possible—depending on the circumstances—that the arbitrator would be liable.

8.292 While slight lack of care might be excluded, liability for wilful conduct or for gross lack of care may not be validly waived by the parties.[274] Breach by the arbitrator of his duties may give rise to his liability for direct damages, as well as for the indirect damages which would be a normal consequence of that breach. It is discussed whether an arbitrator withdrawing without cause is still entitled to be paid his fee. The response to this query will depend on the circumstances. The same issue arises in the event of the award having been set aside. Here too the circumstances and in particular the arbitrator's possible lack of care will play a role.

8.293 **(1.1) Do the courts and/or authorities rely on a contractual relationship between the parties and the arbitrator(s), irrespective of whether institutional *ad hoc* arbitration is concerned? What is the legal qualification of such contract (eg provision of services)?** The nature of the relationship between the arbitrator and the parties is contractual. If the parties accept that the appointment and the proceedings be handled by an arbitral institution, a direct relationship arises between the arbitral institution and the arbitrator, since as a rule the arbitral institution does not act on behalf of the parties, but on its own behalf and for the account of the parties.[275] Some precedents[276] have held that the contract between the arbitrator and the party is a *locatio operis*,[277] and more precisely a contract for professional

273 s 813 ter, RCP.
274 s 1229,Civil Code.
275 Rubino-Sammartano, M., *Il Diritto dell'Arbitrato, cit* 515 *et seq*.
276 *A.T.A.C. v Litardi*, Tribunale di Roma (Tribunal of Rome) (1956), *Temi rom*, 1956, 178.
277 ie a contract for services.

services, whereby the arbitrator undertakes to provide a result, ie to decide the dispute, and not merely to use his best efforts.

(1.2) Are there court decisions (or authorities) determining which law governs the question of liability of an arbitrator? What is the position of those courts/authorities as to whether and to which extent a legal liability of an arbitrator (or arbitral institution) may be established? As to Italian domestic arbitration proceedings the liability of arbitrators has been expressly set forth by s 813 ter of Executive Order, 2 February, no 40 (2006) in case of wilful or grossly negligent acts or omissions. The liability of arbitrators who sit in Italy under a non-Italian procedural law will be subject to that law. However a claim for liability of that arbitrator under Italian law, based on his acts or omissions committed in this jurisdiction, may be justified depending on the circumstance. Italian precedents on arbitrators' liability are extremely rare.[278] **8.294**

(1.3) Is an arbitrator subject to criminal prosecution? No precedents as to the prosecution of arbitrators for crimes committed in their capacity as arbitrators is known. In general, the arbitrator does not benefit from immunity. **8.295**

(2) Possibility to restrict or exclude such liability

The arbitrator's liability may be limited but not totally excluded. In the Italian legal system this area has not been much analysed. It is suggested that, even when liability is excluded, the arbitrator would normally remain liable in the event of wilful conduct or gross negligence. **8.296**

VII. Enforcement of national awards

(3) Requirement of a particular procedure to make an award enforceable (leave for enforcement, exequatur*)*

The procedure to make domestic awards enforceable requires the filing of the award,[279] together with the arbitration clause or submission agreement, with the court in whose jurisdiction the venue of the proceedings is located.[280] As discussed above, the award is binding for the parties even before leave to enforce is granted. It has been discussed whether the award has merely contractual effects or is already a decision. The latter solution has been preferred.[281] From a practical point of view, if leave to enforce the award is not applied for, court proceedings may nevertheless be instituted seeking a judgment which confirms such an award. It is suggested that even an *ex parte* summary judgment may be applied for, based on the award.[282] **8.297**

(1.1) Does the national law make any difference between foreign and domestic awards, and if so, which are the criteria? Does there exist an additional notion of award for the **8.298**

---

[278] *Coniglio v Società SAIM*, Corte di Cassazione (Court of Cassation) no 2800 (1990), *Giust civ* 1990, I, 2365.

[279] Its original or a notarized copy of it.

[280] s 825, RCP.

[281] Ricci, E.F., 'Sull'efficacia del lodo rituale dopo la legge 9 febbraio 1983, n 28' *Riv Dir Proc* 1983, 646; Tarzia, G., 'Efficacia ed impugnabilità del lodo nell'arbitrato rituale' *Riv Arb* (1985) 1.

[282] Rubino-Sammartano, M., *Il Diritto dell'Arbitrato, cit* 891 *et seq.*

purpose of obtaining *exequatur* (France: international awards)? If the award has been rendered in Italy under international or foreign procedural rules, it is submitted[283] that the provision on filing does not apply. However, no precedents are known on this issue. If this view is correct only recognition and enforcement proceedings under the New York Convention, now under s 839 *et seq*, Rules of Civil Procedure, are available as to such award. However, since the criterion to establish the nationality of an award is the place of arbitration, the general opinion of writers is that all awards made in Italy are 'Italian awards'.

8.299 Enforceability of domestic awards is governed by provisions that are different from those which govern foreign awards. As discussed above, enforcement of domestic awards is obtained through an *ex parte* application, and the award becomes enforceable by leave to enforce issued by the Court. The loser in the arbitral proceedings may attack the award by instituting ordinary proceedings before the competent Court of Appeal, aiming to have the award set aside.

8.300 As to foreign (or procedurally international) awards, enforceability is obtained by application to the President of the Court of Appeal, which is competent by territory. The President's control is deeper than the County Court's one, since it involves a control of arbitrability of the dispute under Italian Law and that the award does not conflict with Italian public policy. The opposing party may oppose the President's Order by instituting ordinary proceedings governed by Italian procedural law which, as to grounds for refusing enforceability, is along the same lines of the New York Convention.

8.301 **(1.2) May awards granting conservatory/interim measures be subject to enforcement?** This problem does not arise under Italian law, since the arbitrators may not grant conservatory interim measures.

(2) Details of such enforcement procedure (competent court, reasons for rejection of motion etc)

8.302 The court, after checking whether the award is in order from the point of view of its form requirements, orders that it be enforced. The court's clerk gives to the parties notice of the issue of the order. Only the applicant is involved at this stage. Proceedings are therefore exclusively *ex parte*. Leave to enforce may be refused only if (i) the applicant has not filed the original or a notarized copy of the arbitration clause (or submission) and of the award; or (ii) in the event of the award not being in order from the point of view of form requirements. It has been held[284] that this is the case if the award is not signed, or the venue of the proceedings was outside Italy, or the award is undated, or the name of the parties is not made, or the award contains no decision.

(3) Appeal against the decision granting exequatur

8.303 The Second Reform has introduced a *reclamo* (complaint rather than strictly, technically speaking an appeal) against the granting of the *exequatur*, to be made to the Court of

[283] Rubino-Sammartano, M., *Il Diritto dell'Arbitrato, cit* 1120.
[284] *Court of Cassation*, 9 July no 2601, 1976, *Foro it* 1976, I, 2366.

Appeal within 30 days after the order is communicated.[285] The Court decides in Chambers. In view of the earlier comments, no further appeal should be envisaged against the court order which grants leave to enforce the award. There is a debate as to whether such exclusion also includes appeals to the Court of Cassation against such order. Several precedents[286] have affirmed that they are available.[287]

(4) **Appeal (and procedure) if *exequatur* has been refused** Also the Order which refuses leave to enforce the award may be the object of a request for review by the Court of Appeal, to be made within 30 days after receipt of the Court clerk's notice. The Court of Appeal decides by Order in chambers after hearing the parties.[288] No further appeals are available against the Order made by the Court of Appeal except an appeal to the Court of Cassation. 8.304

(5) Procedure of enforcement (attachment of bank accounts etc)

The award, once declared enforceable by the tribunal, being an enforceable instrument entitles, like an enforceable judgment, to enforce it by serving first an *atto di precetto* (demand for payment served by a process server) and then by asking the court bailiff (*ufficiale giudiziario*) to attach the debtor's real or personal estate or its credits towards third parties (including moneys on its bank account). 8.305

(5.1) **At the stage of enforcement, may the losing party invoke arguments and circumstances which are based on facts which have occurred before (or after) the award was made?** The opposition available against an award based on facts occurred before the award was made, is referred to as *revocazione*[289] (re-examination of the merits due to extraordinary events). Such facts include the wilful conduct of the opposing party, or the award being based on evidence which after the rendering of the award is declared to be false (or which has been so declared before, but without that party being aware of it) or that after the award one or more decisive documents have become available which owing to *force majeure* or to the conduct of the opposing party were not available before the award, being the result of the arbitrator's fraud. 8.306

As to events occurred after the award, one may mention payment of the amount ordered by the award or assignment of the credit under the award to a third party, or transfer of business from the winning party to a third party, or any event such, as time bar, which has extinguished the credit. 8.307

(5.2) **May the losing party invoke a set-off based on claims that are not related to the matter of the arbitral proceeding? Is it material whether such claim came into existence before or after the award was made?** The losing party may,[290] after the leave to enforce is issued, oppose the enforcement of the award on the ground of (i) set-off—based on a 8.308

[285] s 825, RCP.
[286] *Lorenzi v Comunanza*, Corte di Cassazione (Court of Cassation) no 2826 (1995), *Riv Arb* 1995, 445.
[287] Under s 111, Constitution.
[288] s 825, RCP.
[289] *Revocazione* proceedings are to be instituted before the Court of Appeal.
[290] s 615, RCP

credit ascertained and due, even if not yet adjudicated, even if it came into existence after the award was made—or (ii) based on an enforceable judgment.

VIII. Foreign awards

A. Recognition and/or enforcement of foreign awards (national law)

(1) Rules according to national law

8.309 Recognition and enforcement of foreign awards according to the national law has been governed by the Reform,[291] the Second Reform has not modified it. The Reform has basically regulated [292] the grounds for refusal of recognition or enforcement provided for by the New York convention. They belong to two classes.

8.310 First, the following grounds which must be raised by the opposing party:

(i) the parties to the arbitration agreement were, under the law applicable to them, under some incapacity, or the said agreement is not valid under the law to which the parties have subjected it, or failing any indication thereon, under the law of the country where the award was made; or
(ii) the party against whom the award is invoked was not given proper notice of the appointment of the arbitrator or of the arbitration proceedings or was otherwise unable to present its case; or
(iii) the award deals with a difference not contemplated by the submission or arbitration clause or it contains decisions on matters beyond the scope of the submission, provided that, if the decisions on matters submitted to arbitration can be separated from those not submitted, the former may be recognized and enforced; or
(iv) the composition of the arbitral authority or the arbitral procedure was not in accordance with the agreement of the parties, or, failing such agreement, was not in accordance with the law of the country where the arbitration took place; or
(v) the award has not yet become binding on the parties, or has been set aside or suspended by a competent authority of the country in which, or under the law of which, that award was made.

8.311 Second, the grounds which may be raised by the court of its own motion:

(i) the subject matter of the difference was not capable of settlement by arbitration under Italian Law; or
(ii) the award is contrary to the public policy of the country.

(2) Requirements to be fulfilled by the applicant (procedure, time limits)

8.312 Several requirements are to be fulfilled by the applicant. The application for recognition and enforcement of foreign awards is to be made to the Court of Appeal in the territory of which the opposing party resides.[293] If the defendant does not reside in Italy, the application is to be made to the Court of Appeal of Rome.

[291] s 839, RCP.
[292] s 840, *ibid.*
[293] s 839, *ibid.*

The applicant must produce the original[294] or a notarized copy of the award and of the arbitration agreement or of the contract containing the arbitration clause. If such documents are not in Italian, a certified translation of them into Italian is required. The possibility to cure lack of production of the required documents has also been debated. In *Israel Portland*[295] it was held that lack of production of the required documents together with the application for recognition or enforcement may not be cured during the proceedings. The opposite seems now to derive from *Campomarzio*.[296] **8.313**

(3) Remedies against decisions granting or declining enforcement

Remedies are available also against decisions declining enforcement. The applicable statutory provision[297] deals with oppositions both to orders granting recognition and enforcement and to orders rejecting the application. When hearing oppositions made by the applicant against the order which rejects his application, the court has to decide whether grounds for refusal of recognition or enforcement exist. The court order rejecting the application for leave to enforce a foreign award may be opposed by serving, within 30 days after service of said order, a writ of summons before that Court of Appeal. Ordinary proceedings, governed by the provisions before courts of appeal and ending with a judgment will follow. The Court of Appeal's judgment may be appealed to the Court of Cassation.[298] **8.314**

The possibility to apply twice for enforcement has been excluded. In *Israel Portland*,[299] the Italian Court of Cassation has held that if an application for enforcement of a foreign judgment is rejected for lack or inadequacy of the required documents that amounts to a finding on the merits which, upon becoming *res judicata*, prevents applying for enforcement for a second time. This has been shared by the Court of Appeal, Florence.[300] This view has not been fully followed by other precedents[301] which have held that such an application may be filed again. **8.315**

B. Recognition and/or enforcement of foreign awards (conventions and treaties)

(1) Specific bilateral or multilateral treaties

Specific bilateral and multilateral treaties exist dealing with recognition and enforcement of awards. Italy is a party to the following multilateral conventions: **8.316**

- Geneva Protocol on Arbitration Clauses, 24 September 1923;
- Geneva Convention on the Execution of Foreign Arbitral Awards, 26 September 1927;

294 This requirement is different from the New York Convention which provides for production of the duly authenticated original award.

295 *Israel Portland Cement Works Ltd v Moccia Irene SpA*, Corte di Cassazione (Court of Cassation), no 13665 (1991), *Giur it*, 1992, I, 1, 693.

296 *Campomarzio Impianti Srl v Soc Lampart Vegypary Gepgyar*, Corte di Cassazione (Court of Cassation), no 9980 (1995), *Riv Arb* 1996, 78.

297 s 840, RCP.

298 s 360, *ibid.*

299 See *supra*, n 294.

300 *Soc Hackemberg v Soc Sbrolli*, Corte d'Appello di Firenze (Court of Appeal of Florence) (1991), *Riv Arb* 1994, 101.

301 *Lezina Shipping Company v Soc Casillo Grani*, Corte d'Appello di Bari (Court of Appeal of Bari) no 531 (1991), *Riv Arb*, 1993, 4, 639.

- Convention on the Recognition and Enforcement of Foreign Arbitral Awards, New York, 10 June 1958;
- European Convention on International Commercial Arbitration, Geneva, 21 April 1961 (as completed by the Paris Agreement Relating to Application of the European Convention on International Commercial Arbitration);
- Convention on the Settlement of Investment Disputes between States and Nationals of Other States, Washington, 18 March 1965.

Out of those, in particular, the New York and the ICSID Conventions deal with recognition and enforcement of foreign awards.

8.317 Even if they play a less important role, several bilateral conventions concerning recognition and enforcement of foreign arbitral awards have been entered into by the Republic of Italy, such as those with France,[302] Switzerland,[303] Germany[304] and the United States of America.[305]

(2) Existence of a standard procedure for the enforcement of foreign awards?

8.318 If Italy is a party to a multinational or bilateral Convention, which otherwise regulates recognition or enforcement of foreign awards, and the applicant seeks recognition or enforcement under such a Convention, then such a Convention shall apply. In the absence of an applicable international convention, the Rules of Civil Procedure which regulate the enforcement of foreign awards apply.

(3) Extent of examination and control of the award by the court

8.319 As to the extent of examination and control of the award by the court, the President of the Court of Appeal, having checked that the award is in order from the point of view of form requirements, orders that the award produce effects in Italy unless under Italian law: (i) the dispute may not be submitted to arbitration; (ii) the award conflicts with Italian public policy. It has been suggested[306] that state courts may not intervene after the award is rendered if the proceedings were not governed by Italian procedural law, and that this applies both to a filing of non-domestic awards with the court, in order that it be made an enforceable instrument, and to attacks against the award, since their premise is that the arbitral proceedings belong to the Italian legal system. Only enforcement of foreign awards would then be available before the local courts.

C. Application of the New York Convention

(1) Application of the New York Convention in practice

8.320 Italian courts have been applying the 1958 New York Convention, which was implemented in Italy in 1968, for a long time.[307]

[302] The Convention between Italy and France on the Enforcement of Judgments in Civil and Commercial Matters, Rome, 3 June 1930 enacted by Act 7 January no 45 (1932).

[303] The Convention between Italy and Switzerland: on the Recognition and Enforcement of Awards in Commercial and Civil Matters, Rome, 3 January 1933 enacted by Act 15 June no 743 (1933).

[304] Convention, 9 March 1936, enacted by Act 14 January no 106 (1937).

[305] Convention, Washington, 26 September 1951 which has completed the Treaty on Friendship Commerce and Navigation, Rome, 17 February 1988, enacted by Act 4 August no 910, (1960).

[306] Rubino-Sammartano, M., *Il Diritto dell'Arbitrato* (5th edn) 1,110.

[307] Statute 19 January 1968, no 62.

(2) Examples of decisions which do not apply the Convention correctly

In several areas, Italian courts have applied the Convention in a particular way. It is argued whether *arbitrato irrituale*[308] falls within the ambit of the New York Convention.[309] The Court of Cassation[310] has held that *arbitrati irrituali* are to be treated as awards since they are binding on the parties, and therefore comply with the New York Convention's requirement. This view was not shared by some German courts[311] and it is submitted that their criticism is correct. 8.321

When a separate document such as standard terms or a standard form is incorporated in a written contract by a general reference, the question arises whether the fact that this separate document includes the arbitration agreement, without a specific reference being made to it, amounts to consent to arbitration required under the New York Convention.[312] The Italian courts have held[313] that, while a specific reference to the arbitration clause contained in that document amounts to consent, a mere general reference to all the terms of that separate document does not prove consent to the arbitration agreement contained in it. 8.322

IX. Appendix

A. National legislation

General Legislation
Civil Procedure Code 1865 (Royal Order Act June, 1865) (Rubino-Sammartano, M., *cit* at 635).
Civil Procedure Code 1940 (Royal Order Act October 28, 1940 n 1443) (Rubino-Sammartano, M., *cit* at 639).
Act 9 February 1983 no 28 (Rubino-Sammartano, M., *cit* at 645).
Arbitration Reform Act 5 January 1994, no 25 (Rubino-Sammartano, M., *cit* at 646).
Decreto Legislativo (Executive Order 2 February 2006, The Second Reform).

Legislation for Government Contracts
Presidential Order 16 July 1962, no 1063.
Act 20 December 1981 no 741, Official Gazette, 16 December 1981, no 344.
Codice degli Appalti.

Legislation on Labour Disputes
Act 11 August 1973 no 533, Official Gazette, 13 September 1973, no 237.

308 Proceedings conducted by a neutral party entrusted with the task not to decide a dispute but to settle it or to enter, as attorneys for the parties, into a contract which recognizes the existence of a right.

309 See Art I, New York Convention.

310 *Pagnan v Butera*, Corte di Cassazione (Court of Cassation Joint Divisions), no 4167 (1978), Ybk Comm Arb, 1979, Italy no 33.

311 See *Landgericht Hamburg*, 18 January 1979, Ybk Comm Arb, 1981 Germany no 22.

312 Art II.

313 *Min Trasporti v Zonca*, Corte di Cassazione (Court of Cassation, Joint Divisions) no 3620 (1971), Ybk Comm Arb, 1976, Italy, no 5; in accord *Juvakovic v Soc Scagull Shipping*, Corte di Cassazione (Court of Cassation, Joint Divisions) no 1439 (1976), Ybk Comm Arb, 1977, Italy, no 15.

Legislation on maritime transportation
s 619, Maritime Code.

Legislation on industrial property
s 25, Royal Order 29 June 1939, no 1127.
Official Gazette, 14 August 1939, no 189.
Legislation on mediation
Act 29 December 1993, no 580.

Act 5 January 1994, no 25.

Act 14 November 1995, no 481.

Act 31 July 1997, no 249.

Act 18 June 1998, no 192.

Act 29 March 2001, no 135.

Decreto Legislativo (Act) 17 January 2003, no 5.

Decreto Legislativo 9 April 2003, no 70.

Decreto Legislativo 6 February 2004.

Act 6 May 2004, no 129.

Decreto Legislativo 6 September 2005, no 206.

Act 28 December 2005, no 262.

Act 14 February 2006, no 55.

Act 22 February 2006, no 84.

Delibera (Resolution) no 173/07.

Act 24 December 2007, no 244.

Act 28 February 2008, no 31.

Decreto Legislativo, 3 June 2008, no 97.

B. Arbitral institutions

Camera Arbitrale Nazionale e Internazionale di Milano:

Palazzo Mezzanotte, Piazza degli Affari, 6 20123 Milano
Telephone: (0039) (02) 85154536 – 44444515
Fax: (0039) (02) 85154384
Website: <http://www.camera-arbitrale.com>
The *Camera Arbitrale Nazionale e Internazionale* is annexed to the Milan Chamber of Commerce. It organizes seminars with ISDACI Arbitration rules (national arbitration rules and international arbitration rules).

Associazione Italiana per l'Arbitrato:

Rome, Via XX Settembre, 5, 00187.
Telephone: (0039) (06) 4743594
Website: <http://www.arbitratoaia.org>

Arbitration rules: national and international arbitration rules.

The *Associazione Italiana per l'Arbitrato* is closely connected with the Italian Committee of the International Chamber of Commerce, Paris. It organizes seminars.

Italian Delegation of the European Court of Arbitration (Strasbourg)

3, viale Cassiodoro, Milano.
Telephone: (0039) (02) 4889361
Fax: (0039) (02) 48008277
Website: <http://www.cour-europe-arbitrage.org>

The Italian Delegation of the European Court of Arbitration is one of the national delegations of the *Cour Européenne d'Arbitrage* which has its seat in Strasbourg (Europäischer Schiedsgerichtshof, European Court of Arbitration, Corte Arbitrale Europea, Corte Europea de Arbitraje) which is the arbitral institution of the *Centre Européen d'Arbitrage* and has existed for 60 years, and is a legal entity under the laws of Alsace-Moselle, under the patronage of the Council of Europe. It has branches in Milan, Rome, Genoa, the North East, Bologna, Romagna, Tuscany, Puglia and Calabria. The Court's international rules (2004) are available in French, English, German and Spanish; Italian national arbitration rules are also available.

Camera Arbitrale Italiana:

Rome, Via Archimede 116, 00197
Telephone: (0039) (06) 8079359
Website: <www.bo.camcom.it>
The *Camera Arbitrale Italiana* was formed recently.

Curia Mercatorum
Lancenigo di Villorsa (TV) Via Roma 4
Website: <http://www.curiamercatorum.com>

Many Chambers of Commerce have an arbitral institution, but few of them are in full activity.

The following arbitral institutions act also as appointing authorities whenever so requested under the Uncitral Arbitration Rules:

Camera Arbitrale Nazionale e Internazionale di Milano;

Associazione Italiana per l'Arbitrato.

C. Model arbitration clauses

The following are the standard clauses of the above bodies:

Camera Arbitrale Nazionale e Internazionale di Milano

> All disputes arising out of the present contract, including those concerning its validity, interpretation, performance and termination, shall be referred to an arbitral tribunal consisting of three arbitrators, one being the President, according to the International Arbitration Rules of the Chamber of National and International Arbitration of Milan, which the parties declare that they know and accept in their entirety. The arbitrators shall decide according to the norms .... The language of the arbitration shall be ......

Associazione Italiana per l'Arbitrato

Clauses printed in the A.I.A. Arbitration Rules in force as of 1 October 1995 (English version)

Arbitration clause for 'free' or informal arbitration (arbitrato 'irrituale')

> All disputes arising in respect of the present contract, including disputes regarding the validity, performance and termination thereof shall be settled under the arbitration rules of the Associazione Italiana per l'Arbitrato by a sole arbitrator [*] appointed in accordance with the said rules. The parties declare that they are familiar with and accept these rules, also as regards the methods established for the appointment of the arbitrator. The arbitrator shall make his award 'ex aequo et bono' [**] by way of informal arbitration. The parties shall, as of now, recognize his award as the expression of their contractual agreement.

Arbitration clause for formal arbitration (arbitrato 'rituale')

> All disputes arising in respect of the present contract, including disputes regarding the validity, performance, non-performance and termination thereof shall be settled under the arbitration rules of the Associazione Italiana per l'Arbitrato by a sole arbitrator [*] appointed in accordance with the said rules. The parties declare that they are familiar with and accept these rules, also as regards the methods established for the appointment of the arbitrator. The arbitrator shall make his award 'ex aequo et bono' [**] by way of formal arbitration in conformity with the rules of the Italian Code of Civil Procedure from which he cannot derogate.
>
> [*] If the parties wish to submit the dispute to arbitration by three or more arbitrators, always uneven in number, they should specify such number in the clause.
>
> [**] The parties may substitute, if they so wish, 'according to law' for 'ex aequo et bono'.

European Court of Arbitration

Rules for International and National Arbitration (2004 edn)

Standard Mediation and Arbitration Agreements

(Rules applied by the Italian Chapter of the European Court of Arbitration as well as by the other Chapters of the European Court in Europe, in the Mediterranean and Middle East)

> Any dispute between the parties relating to or arising from this contract shall be submitted to a procedure of mediation conducted by a sole mediator, appointed and proceeding in accordance with the Mediation Rules of this body by the local branch—if any—of the

Mediation Centre for Europe, the Mediterranean and the Middle East having its seat in Strasbourg, which Rules are in force at the date of filing of the application for mediation.

In the event of the mediation proceedings not taking place or being unsuccessful, any dispute arising from said relationships between the parties shall be determined in accordance with the Arbitration Rules and the Internal Rules of the European Court of Arbitration—being part of the European Centre of Arbitration having its seat at Strasbourg (in force at the time the application for arbitration is filed), with right to appeal, including—unless forbidden by the applicable procedural law—for wrong choice of the substantive law and or for errors of law, by way of rehearing by an appellate arbitral tribunal (if so allowed by the applicable procedural law), of which adoption of this clause constitutes acceptance.

The arbitration proceedings will be conducted according to the provisions of the said Rules by a sole arbitrator who will be appointed, if the dispute is domestic, by the local Branch—if any—of the European Court of Arbitration and in the absence of a local Branch, as well as to all non domestic disputes, by the Central Registrar competent for that area: Valencia for disputes between parties belonging to Southern Europe, the Mediterranean and the Middle East (as to France, the Department of Provence, Alpes, Côte d'Azur, les Bouches du Rhône, Var, Roussillon and Languedoc) Portugal, the Balkans, Romania, Bulgaria, Ukraine, the Black Sea and in general all the countries of Eastern Europe; Strasbourg for Northern and Central Europe.

The parties undertake to keep, and to cause their Counsel, advisers, managers, employees and agents to keep strictly confidential the dispute, the facts, the documents, the evidence and the award.

The parties agree to conduct and to cause their Counsel to conduct themselves in a manner which limits the duration of the proceedings to six months, and to avoid the production of documents and the calling of witnesses who are unnecessary or irrelevant, restraining motion practices, avoiding delays, vexatious or repetitive conduct and in general any overlawyering and accepting to pay to the other parties all legal costs caused by a breach of such commitment, even in cause of final success in the dispute.

Each party further undertakes to promptly reimburse the other parties which should pay its share of any advance requested by the European Court of Arbitration or by its local competent branch—if any—for the proceedings and to recognise that the other parties shall be entitled to an ex parte summary judgment, or other summary proceedings, against it for such repayment.

The parties request the arbitrator to issue as soon as possible an interim award for the part of a claim or cross claim which is undisputed or manifestly grounded.

Place of Arbitration ____________________

Language of the proceedings ________________

As to the substance of the dispute :

- either the substantive law of ____________

- or ex bono et aequo

D. Bibliography

Books

Alpa (gen ed), *L'arbitrato profili sostanziali* (UTET, Turin, 1999).
Amar, *Dei giudizi arbitrali* (Turin , 1879).
Barbareschi, *Gli arbitrati* (Milan, 1937).
Barbieri-Bella, *Il nuovo diritto dell'arbitrato* (Cedam, Padua, 2007).
Bernardini, P., *L'arbitrato internazionale* (Milan, Giuffrè, 1987).

Bernardini, P. and Giardina, A., *Codice dell'Arbitrato* (Milan, Giuffrè, 1990).
Bernini, A.M., *L'arbitrato* (Clueb, Bologna, 1993).
Buonfrate, A. and Orlandi, C.G., *Codice degli Arbitrati delle Conciliazioni e di altri ADR* (UTET, Turin, 2006).
Carpi (gen ed), *Arbitrato* (2nd edn, Zanichelli, Bologna, 2007).
Deodato, G. and Migliorisi, G., *Codice dell'arbitrato* (Pirola, Milan, 1989).
Fedozzi, P., *L'arbitrato nel diritto processuale civile internazionale* (Palermo, 1908).
Frignani, *L'arbitrato commerciale internazionale* (Cedam, Padua, 2004).
Levoni, A., *L'arbitrato dopo la riforma* (Milan, 1985).
Levoni, A., *Rassegna di giurisprudenza sull'arbitrato e le procedure arbitrali*, (Milan, 1965).
Mirabelli, G. and Giacobbe, D., *Diritto dell'Arbitrato* (Jovene, 1994).
Ricci, E.F., *La prova nell'arbitrato rituale* (Milan, Giuffrè, 1974).
Rubino-Sammartano, M., *L'arbitrato internazionale* (Cedam, 1989).
Rubino-Sammartano, M., *Il diritto dell'arbitrato (interno)* (1st edn (1991) to 5th edn (2006), Cedam, Padua).
Rubino-Sammartano, M. (gen ed), *Arbitrato, Conciliazione e ADR* (Zanichelli, Bologna, 2009).
Rubino-Sammartano, M., *International Arbitration: Law and Practice* (2nd edn, Kluwer, 2001).
Schizzerotto, G., *Dell'arbitrato* (2nd edn, Giuffrè, Milan, 1982).
Schizzerotto, G., *Arbitrato improprio e arbitraggio* (Milan, 1967).
Schizzerotto, G., *L'arbitrato rituale nella giurisprudenza* (Cedam, Padua, 1969).
Sirotti Gaudenzi, A., *Guida al diritto dell'arbitrato* (Il Sole 24 Ore, Milan, 2006).
Vecchione, R., *L'arbitrato nel sistema del processo civile* (1st edn, Morano, Naples, 1953).
Vecchione, R., *L'arbitrato nel sistema del processo civile* (2nd edn, Giuffrè, Milan, 1971).
Verde (gen ed), *Diritto dell'arbitrato* (Giappicchelli, Turin, 2005).

Articles

Andrioli, V., 'La Novella sull'Arbitrato' *Dir e Giur* (1983) 249.
Andrioli, V., 'Sul preliminare di clausola compromissoria' *Riv Dir Proc* 1944-46, II, 88.
Ascarelli, T., 'Arbitri e Arbitratori' *Riv Dir Proc* 1929, I, 308.
Barbareschi, 'Impugnazione per nullità di sentenza arbitrale avanti un giudice competente' *Giur It* 1946, I, 2, 227.
Barbareschi, 'Inammissibilità dei lodi parziali' *Giur It* 1948, I, 493.
Briguglio, 'La riforma dell'arbitrato del 1983: soluzioni giurisprudenziali ed implicazioni sistematiche' *Riv Arb* (1991) 185.
Carnacini, 'Arbitrato rituale' *Nov Dig It* 893, n 24.
Carnacini, Vasetti, 'Arbitri' *Nuovo Dig It* (Turin, 1937) 661.
Carnelutti, 'Arbitri e Arbitratori' *Riv Dir Proc* (1924) I, 121 e ss.
Colesanti, 'Cognizione sulla validità del compromesso in arbitri' *Riv Dir Proc* (1958) 244.
D'Onofrio, 'I lodi liberi' *Riv Dir Proc* (1925) II, 346.
Fazzalari, 'Primo incontro con una…lieta Novella' *Rass Arb* (1983) 1, 2.
Garbagnati, 'Intorno al termine per il deposito del lodo arbitrale' *Foro pad* (1951) II, 74.
Garbagnati, 'Sulla nullità della sentenza arbitrale che abbia pronunciato fuori dei limiti del compromesso' *Foro pad* (1952) I, 337.
Garbagnati, 'In tema di impugnazione per nullità del lodo arbitrale' *Riv Dir Proc* (1947) II, 154.
Giardina, 'Arbitrato transnazionale e lex mercatoria di fronte alla Corte di Cassazione' *Riv Dir Int Priv Proc* (1982) 754.
Giardina, 'La nuova disciplina dell'arbitrato in Italia' *Rass Arb* (1983) 5.
Lessona, 'Arbitramento', in *Enciclopedia Giur Italiana*, (Naples, Milan, 1894)) vol 1, 3, 570.
Liebmann, 'Il principio del contraddittorio nel processo civile italiano' *Mon Trib* (1966) 607.
Lipari, 'Questioni sulla disciplina dell'arbitrato' *Giur It* (1953) IV, 1.
Luzzato, 'Accordi internazionali e diritto interno in materia di arbitrati. La convenzione di New York del 1958' *Riv Dir Int Priv Proc* (1968) 24 e ss.

Micheli, 'Nullità del lodo arbitrale per deposito presso il Pretore incompetente' *Riv Dir Proc* (1937) II, 140.
Mirabelli, 'Clausole compromissorie per relationem ed arbitrato commerciale internazionale' *Rass Arb* (1967) 57.
Mortara, 'Circa l'ammissibilità dell'intervento volontario degli arbitri nel giudizio promosso davanti al tribunale ai sensi dell'art. 32 c.p.c. per la nullità della sentenza da essi emessa' *Giur It* (1900) I, 2, 375.
Ricci, E.F., 'Commentario alla Legge 9 febbraio 1983 n. 28: modificazioni alla disciplina' *Nuove Leggi Civili Commentate* (1983) 744.
Ricci, E.F., 'Contro l'istruzione probatoria segreta nel giudizio arbitrale' *Riv Dir Proc* (1969) 703, (nota a Cass 24 maggio 1968 n 1583).
Ricci, E.F., 'Sull'impugnazione del lodo arbitrale rituale' *Rass Arb* (1985) 243.
Ricci, E.F., 'Sull'impugnazione per errore del lodo arbitrale irrituale' *Riv Dir Proc*, (1977) 443 e 444.
Ricci, E.F., 'Sull'efficacia del lodo arbitrale rituale dopo la Legge 9 febbraio 1983 n. 28' *Riv Dir Proc* 1983, 646.
Rubino-Sammartano, M., '*Amiable Compositeur* (Joint Mandate to Settle) *and Ex Bono et Aequo* (Discretionary Authority to Mitigate Strict Law) Apparent Synonimus Revisited' 9 *J Int'l Arb* 1,5.
Rubino-Sammartano, M., 'Arbitrati Internazionali e Nazionali in Italia' *Foro pad* (1983) I, 39.
Rubino-Sammartano, M., 'Arbitrati italiani, stranieri ed internazionali; Distinzione ed analisi' *Foro pad* (1979) 2, 10 e ss.
Rubino-Sammartano, M., 'Arbitrato semplificato e arbitrato solo su documenti' *Foro pad* (1990) 1, 3.
Rubino-Sammartano, M., 'Arbitrato: l'anti suit injunction e il suo rovescio: l'ordine di proseguire' *Foro pad* (2003) 161.
Rubino-Sammartano, M., 'Arbitrato rituale, mandato a transigere e non ad accertare' *Foro pad* (1988) I, 404 e ss.
Rubino-Sammartano, M., 'Camera Arbitrale per i Lavori Pubblici' *Foro pad* (2001) II, 107.
Rubino-Sammartano, M., 'Developing countries vis-à-vis International Arbitration' 13, *J Int'l Arb* 1, 21.
Rubino-Sammartano, M., 'Diritto Arbitrale: movimento lento' *Foro pad* (1993) II, 23.
Rubino-Sammartano, M., 'Diritto speciale dell'arbitrato societario' *Foro pad* (2003).
Rubino-Sammartano, M., 'Divieto all'arbitro di nominare un consulente tecnico giuridico o incapacità dell'arbitro?' (nota a sentenza) *Foro pad* (1990) I.
Rubino-Sammartano, M., 'Esecutorietà di arbitrati non interni: più formalisti del Re?' (nota a H. & Hackenberg GmbH c Soc Sbrolli, App, Firenze 15 aprile 1992), *Foro pad* (1993) I, 177.
Rubino-Sammartano, M., 'Fulmini sull'arbitrato c.d. obbligatorio' *Foro pad* (1996) n 3-4.
Rubino-Sammartano, M., 'Il contenzioso in tema di lavori pubblici', *Foro pad* (1997) 2.
Rubino-Sammartano, M, 'Il diritto arbitrale in movimento—Progetti di Riforma' *Foro pad* (1989) 121 e ss.
Rubino-Sammartano, M., 'Il nuovo arbitrato internazionale' *Società e dir* (1994) 275. Rubino-Sammartano, M., 'Is Arbitration To Be Just a Luxury Clinic?' *J Int'l Arb* (1990) 3, 25.
Rubino-Sammartano, M., 'La convenzione di New York ad un bivio (tra conservatori e riformisti)' in *Riv Arb* (2002) 807.
Rubino-Sammartano, M., 'La prova nel processo civile' *Foro pad* (1986) 87.
Rubino-Sammartano, M., 'La reciprocità come limite alla capacità dello straniero' *Foro pad* (1991) I, 207.
Rubino-Sammartano, M., 'Le controversie in tema di lavori pubblici' *Foro pad* (1997) n 2.
Rubino-Sammartano, M., 'Le Tronc Commun des Lois Nationales en Présence (Réflexions sur le droit applicable par l'arbitre international)' *Rev arb* (1987) 133.
Rubino-Sammartano, M., 'Ma Dio (o quanto meno la Corte Costituzionale) è veramente con loro?' (nota a Cass, Sez Un, ord.25 giugno 2002, n 9289, Soc Tenolifts servizi c Taglietti), *Foro pad* (2002) I, 454.

Rubino-Sammartano, M., 'Rules of Evidence in International Arbitration' *J Int'l Arb* (1982) 2, 87.

Rubino-Sammartano, M., 'Sede dell'arbitrato in Italia: veramente l'ultimo legame con il territorio nazionale?' (nota a Cass, Sez I, 13 ottobre 2000, n 13648, Soc Il Nuovo Castoro c. Min. esteri) *Foro pad* (2000) I, 312.

Rubino-Sammartano, M., *Sull'arbitro avvocato di una parte* (nota a Trib. Genova 22 marzo 1995, Soc. Sea Searchers c. Società Esercizio Cantieri), *Foro pad* 1996, I, 213.

Rubino-Sammartano, M., 'The Keban Arbitration, Arbitration' *The Journal of the Chartered Institute of Arbitrators* vol 46, n 4, 241.

Rubino-Sammartano, M., 'Third Generation Arbitration –Appeal to a New Panel within arbitration proceedings' *J Int'l Arb* 1987, 76.

Rubino-Sammartano, M., 'Vittoria di tappa, un sogno impossibile' *Foro pad* (2001) 42; *id* nota a Cons Stato 17 ottobre 2003, n 6335, in *Foro pad* (2004).

Rubino-Sammartano, M., 'Il contraddittorio negli arbitrati rituali e irrituali' *Foro pad* (1993) I, 48 (nota a Cass 18 gennaio 1992, n 595).

Rubino-Sammartano, M., 'Ruolo della legge procedurale della sede della procedura arbitrale' *Foro pad* (1992) I, 201.

Rubino-Sammartano, M., 'Arbitrato irrituale come giudizio—ovvero del paradosso perfetto' *Foro pad* (1993 I, 24 (nota a Cass 5 marzo 1992, n 2650).

Rubino-Sammartano, M., 'Arbitrato irrituale: malintesi frutto di una qualificazione e terminologia' *Foro pad* (1990) I, 161 (nota a Trib Venezia ordin 29 novembre 1989).

Rubino-Sammartano, M., 'La fine di un monopolio: arbitrato semplificato e contenzioso ordinario' *Foro pad* (1991) II, 77.

Satta, S., 'Nota sull'arbitrato libero' *Rass Arb* (1974) 1.

Satta, S., 'Questioni in materia di impugnazione del lodo arbitrale' in *Riv Not* (1967) 340.

Scialoja, 'Gli arbitrati liberi' *Riv Dir Comm* (1922) I, 496.

Sraffa, 'Compromessi e lodi stabiliti tra industriali senza le forme dei giudizi' *Riv Dir Comm* (1907) I, 429.

Taruffo, 'Sui vizi di motivazione del lodo arbitrale' *Riv Arb* (1991) 507.

Tarzia, G., 'Efficacia ed impugnabilità del lodo nell'arbitrato rituale' *Rass Arb* (1985) 1.

Tarzia, G., 'Istruzione preventiva e arbitrato rituale' *Riv Arb* (1991) 719.

Tarzia, G., 'Nullità ed annullamento del lodo arbitrale irrituale' *Riv Trim* (1991) 451.

Vasetti, M., 'Arbitraggio' Nov. Dig. It., Torino, 1957.

Vasetti, M., 'Voce Arbitrato irrituale' November Dig, 861.

Vecchione, R., 'Nullità o inesistenza del compromesso in arbitri' *Foro pad* (1953) I, 573.

Vecchione, R., 'Clausola compromissoria apparente, nomina dell'unico arbitro nel dissenso tra le parti' *Giur it* (1954) I, 2, 475.

Vecchione, R., 'Sulla validità della clausola compromissoria unilaterale' *Giur it* (1983) IV, 65.

Verde, G., 'Collegialità degli arbitri e responsabilità per inadempimento' *Riv Dir Proc* (1961) 245.

Vigoriti, V., 'Arbitrato e consulenza tecnica' *Riv Arb* (1993) 185.

Vocino, 'Schema di una teoria della clausola compromissoria' *Foro it* (1932) 1061 ss.

9

NETHERLANDS

Vesna Lazić and Gerard J. Meijer

I. Introduction

A. Current status of the law on arbitration

(1) Short history

From 1 October 1838, statutory arbitration regulation in the Netherlands was contained in Title One of Book Three of the Code on Civil Procedure (*Wetboek van Burgerlijke Rechtsvordering,* hereinafter: Rv), Arts 620–657. Although the Act of 1838 remained virtually unchanged until 1986, case law significantly influenced arbitration law in the Netherlands.[1] Legal writings in this field have also made an important contribution to the development of arbitration law.[2] **9.01**

A new statutory regulation was needed, as the Act of 1838 appeared unable to meet the needs of parties to commercial transactions, particularly those involving international elements. An entirely new Arbitration Act came into effect on 1 December 1986 and is presently in force. The Act of 1838, contained in Title One of the Book Three Rv, was repealed. The 1986 Arbitration Act is contained in a newly introduced Book Four Rv, **9.02**

---

[1] Sanders, P. and Berg, A.J. van den (eds), *The Netherlands Arbitration Act 1986* (Kluwer Law and Taxation Publishers, Deventer, Antwerp, London, Frankfurt, Boston, New York, 1987) 1 (Sanders/Van den Berg).

[2] Snijders, H.J., 'Vierde boek—arbitrage', in *Burgerlijke Rechtsvordering (Civil Procedure)*, a loose-leaf edition (Kluwer, Deventer, 2006), explanatory note 2. (Snijders, Loose-leaf).

consisting of Arts 1020-1076 Rv. It incorporated 'a substantial part' of case law that had been developed by the judiciary.[3] International treaties and arbitration statutes of other countries, in particular those of France and Switzerland, were considered in the process of drafting the 1986 Arbitration Act.[4] Other instruments, such as the 1976 UNCITRAL Arbitration Rules and the 1985 UNCITRAL Model Law on International Commercial Arbitration, were also reviewed.[5]

9.03 Since its enactment, the Act has undergone minor changes on several occasions. In 1991, the only amendment introduced was to correct an editorial mistake in Art 1041, para 1 Rv.[6] The amendments in effect as of 1 January 2002 were mainly adaptations in terminology due to the alterations introduced in Book 1 Rv relating to the procedure in the first instance.[7] The most recent changes came into force on 30 June 2004.[8] In order to implement the Directive on Electronic Commerce of 8 June 2000,[9] the definition or evidence of a 'written form' in Art 1021 Rv was altered (see para 9.19).

(2) Law in force and future projects

9.04 The Arbitration Act is divided into two Titles: Title One (Arts 1020–1073 Rv) which relates to arbitration within the Netherlands; and Title Two (Arts 1074–1076 Rv) which concerns arbitration outside the Netherlands. Article 1074, para 1 relates to a stay of court proceedings in the Netherlands and referral to arbitration abroad. Article 1074, para 2 Rv deals with interim measures of protection, whereas Arts 1075 and 1076 Rv relate to recognition and enforcement of foreign arbitral awards. The division into two Titles provides for a clear criterion with respect to the applicability of the Act (Art 1073, para 1 Rv).[10]

---

[3] Berg, A.J. van den, Delden, R. Van and Snijders, H.J., *Netherlands Arbitration Law* (Kluwer Law and Taxation Publishers, Deventer/Boston, 1993) 1 (Van den Berg/Van Delden/Snijders).

[4] Memorie van toelichting (MvT), (1984) *Tijdschrift voor Arbitrage* (*TvA*), 4A, 19–20 (MvT 1984 *TvA* 1986, 4A).

[5] Korthals Altes, F., Preface to Sanders/Van den Berg. See also Van den Berg/Van Delden/Snijders (n 1). For more particulars on the history of the 1986 Arbitration Act, see Snijders, Loose-leaf, explanatory note 2; Franx, J.P., *Het ontwerp Boek IV van het Wetboek van Burgerlijke Rechtsvordering* (W.E.J. Tjeenk Willink B.V., Zwolle, 1985) 73 *et seq* (Franx).

[6] Law of 31 January 1991, *Stb* 1991, no 50.

[7] Law of 6 December 2001, *Stb* 2001, no 580. The adaptations in terminology include a replacement of the wording 'the President of the District Court' ('*de president van de rechtbank*') with the expression 'the judge competent to decide on provisional relief' ('*voorzieningenrechter*'). The only changes of a substantive nature were those in Arts 1022 and 1068. In Art 1022, para 3 was added. It deals with the requests for the taking of evidence before the tribunal is established. Amendments to Art 1068 relate to the revocation of the award. For more particulars on the amendments to Art 1068, see Meijer, G.J., 'Arbitrage—Boek Vier' in: A.I.M. Van Mierlo, C.J.J.C Van Nispenand M.V. Polak, (eds), *Burgerlijke Rechtsvordering: Tekst & Commentaar* (Kluwer, Deventer, 2008) Art 1068, Nos 108 (Meijer, *T&C Rv*).

[8] Act of 18 June 2004, *Stb* 2004, no 285.

[9] 2002/31/EC, *Stb* 2004, no 210. The text of Art 1021 was amended so as to provide expressly that an arbitration agreement could be evidenced by electronic means. Thereby it is expressly referred to Art 6:227a, para 1 of the Civil Code. See also, Lazić, V., 'Arbitration Law Reforms in the Netherlands: Formal and Substantive Validity of an Arbitration Agreement' in J.H.M. van Erp/L.P.W. van Vliet (eds), *Netherlands Reports to the Seventeenth International Congress of Comparative Law* (Intersentia, Antwerp-Oxford, Utrecht, 2006) 125 (Lazić, Arbitration Law Reforms in the Netherlands).

[10] Berg, A.J. van den, 'The Netherlands' in: Sanders, P./Berg, A.J. van den (eds), *Intl Handbook Comm Arb*, Suppl 7 (Kluwer Law International, The Hague/London/Boston, April 1987, 1 (Van den Berg, *Int Handbook Comm Arb*).

In general, the 1986 Act presents an arbitration-friendly legal framework. Yet reforming statutory law is considered desirable in order to bring it in line with the recent developments in comparative arbitration regulation and modern trends in arbitration practice. With that aim a Working Group led by Prof. A.J. van de Berg drafted 'The Proposals for Changes to Book Four (Arbitration), Articles 1020–1076, Code on Civil Procedure'.[11] 9.05

(3) Distinction between national and international arbitration

There is no dual regime of statutory regulation. The Arbitration Act does not distinguish between 'domestic' and 'international' arbitration. Accordingly, Title One (Arts 1020–1073 Rv) applies to both domestic and international arbitrations taking place in the Netherlands (Art 1073 Rv). The option for a monistic approach in statutory regulation was primarily inspired by a desire to avoid disputes concerning the applicability of the particular regime (ie whether a case is to be defined as domestic or international).[12] It was also considered that a carefully drafted statutory regulation for international arbitration could provide a suitable legislative framework for domestic arbitration.[13] However, the Act does contain provisions in which time limits are extended in cases where at least one party has domicile or actual residence outside the Netherlands. These provisions have particular significance to the appointment of arbitrators (Art 1027, para 2 Rv) and to the challenge of arbitrators (Art 1035, para 4 Rv). The provisions on time extensions apply if at least one party, or the challenged arbitrator, is domiciled or has his actual residence outside the Netherlands. 9.06

(3.1) If there are different legal systems and rules for national/international arbitration, what are the criteria for the distinction between both systems? The Netherlands Arbitration Act applies to national and international arbitration. The same is true for the Netherlands Arbitration Institute's Arbitration Rules, the main Arbitration Institute in the Netherlands. Yet there are certain provisions in the Rules that are adapted to the specific circumstances of international arbitration. These provisions relate, *inter alia*, to certain time limits (time limits may be extended in cases where at least one of the parties, or an arbitrator, has domicile or actual residence outside the Netherlands), the nationality of arbitrators, the language of the proceedings, dissenting opinion and the applicable law to the substance of the dispute. For the purpose of applying these provisions the Rules give a definition of international arbitration. According to Art 1(g) of the Rules, 'international arbitration' is an arbitration in which, at the moment of commencement, at least one party is domiciled or has its seat, or in the absence thereof, has its actual residence outside the Netherlands. 9.07

B. Practice of arbitration

(1) Frequency of arbitration as opposed to litigation

Arbitration, both *ad hoc* and institutional, is a widely used dispute settlement method in the Netherlands. It has significantly expanded in the twentieth century. A frequent insertion of 9.08

---

[11] 'Tekst van de Voorstellen tot wijziging van het Vierde boek (Arbitrage) Artikelen 1020–1076 Rv', (2005) *TvA* 36 (the text is also published on <http://www.arbitragewet.nl>).

[12] MvT, (1984) *TvA*, no 4A, 19. See also Snijder*s*, Loose-leaf, 10, no 2; Hugenholtz, *W.*, *Hoofdlijnen van Nederlands burgerlijk procesrecht* (21st edn, revised by W.H. Heemskerk, Reed Business, The Hague, 2006), no 212 (Hugenholtz/Heemskerk); Van den Berg/Van Delden/Snijders 121; Hugenholtz/Heemskerk, no 212.

[13] Van den Berg, Public Lecture 4.

arbitration clauses in a contract's general conditions and the establishment of different arbitration institutions for various branches of trade, industry and sports have particularly influenced an increased use of arbitration.[14]

(2) Leading arbitral institutions and statistics

9.09 There are more than 30 actively operating arbitration institutions in the Netherlands in the various fields of commerce, industry, consumer matters and sport.[15] Arbitration institutions in the fields of construction, metals, coffee, grain and feed, oils, fats and oilseeds are examples.[16] The arbitral tribunal for the Construction Industry (*Raad van arbitrage voor de Bouw in Nederland*) has been mentioned as an institution with the largest number of arbitrations (more than 700) per year.[17]

9.10 The only general arbitration institution is 'the Netherlands Arbitration Institute' (NAI).[18] It is not specialized for any specific area of industry or trade and, through its Secretariat, administers domestic and international commercial arbitration of practically all kinds. The NAI Arbitration Rules were revised in 1986 in connection with the enactment of the 1986 Arbitration Act, and subsequently amended in 1992, 1997 and 2001. By the changes introduced in 1997, the provisions on interim measures and security were substantially revised. Additionally, a new section '4A' on summary arbitral proceedings was added. The Rules, as amended in 1997, took effect on 1 January 1998 and apply to arbitrations commenced after this date. In 2001 the provisions of Arts 1(d), relating to the definition of an administrator, and 19(8), relating to the challenge of an arbitrator, were adapted. The 2001 amendments took effect on 13 November 2001.

9.11 Statistics are not available for the number of disputes settled by arbitration in the Netherlands. It has been asserted that the number of arbitrations in the Netherlands can be estimated at several thousands per year.[19] It is not clear how many arbitrations relate to 'international arbitration' or arbitration in general.[20]

II. Jurisdiction of the arbitral tribunal

A. Arbitration agreement

(1) Arbitration clause and submission agreement

9.12 With the exception of the procedure for commencing arbitral proceedings (Arts 1024 and 1025 Rv) and the contents of a submission agreement (Art 1024, para 1 Rv), no distinction

[14] Snijders, Loose-leaf, Art 1020, explanatory note 9.

[15] Van den Berg, *In. Handbook on Comm Arb* 3; Snijders, Loose-leaf, Art 1020, explanatory note 2.

[16] A number of arbitration institutions which may be of particular interest in the area of international arbitration are listed in: Van den Berg, *Int Handbook on Comm Arb* 3.

[17] Snijders, Loose-leaf, Art 1020, explanatory note 2.

[18] The address of the NAI Secretariat is: Netherlands Arbitration Institute, Aert van Nesstraat 25 J-K, 3012 CA Rotterdam; P.O. Box 21075, 3001 AB Rotterdam (telephone: +31 10 201 6969; telefax: +31 10 201 6968; email: secretariaat@nai-nl.org; website: <http://www.nai-nl.org>).

[19] Snijders, Loose-leaf, explanatory note 1.

[20] According to ICC statistics for 1992–98, the parties or the ICC Court fixed the Netherlands as the place of arbitration approximately 12 times per year. See Paulsson, J. *et al*, *The Freshfields Guide to Arbitration and ADR: Clauses in International Contracts*, (2nd edn, Kluwer Law International, The Hague/London/Boston, 1999) 30–31 (Paulsson *et al*). The statistics are usually reported in the *ICC International Court of Arbitration Bulletin*.

is made between the arbitration clause and the submission agreement. Article 1020, para 1 Rv provides that 'parties may agree to submit to arbitration disputes which have arisen or may arise between them out of a defined legal relationship, whether contractual or not'. According to Art 1020, para 2 Rv, an arbitration agreement includes a submission, in which the parties agree to submit to arbitration an existing dispute between them, and an arbitration clause, under which the parties bind themselves to submit future disputes between them to arbitration.[21]

The Act provides for their separate treatment only in provisions of Arts 1024 Rv (submission agreement) and 1025 Rv (arbitration clause). In accordance with Art 1024, para 1 Rv, the submission agreement shall describe the matters which the parties wish to submit to arbitration (see para 9.15). Unless the parties have agreed to another method of commencement, the arbitration shall be deemed to have been commenced by the conclusion of the submission agreement (Art 1024, para 2 Rv). In the case of an arbitration clause, the arbitration shall be deemed to have commenced on the day of receipt of a written notice in which a party informs the other that he is commencing arbitration, unless another method of initiating arbitration is agreed upon (Art 1025, paras 1 and 3 Rv). **9.13**

The Act expressly provides that 'the term "arbitration agreement" includes an arbitration clause which is contained in articles of association or rules which bind the parties' (Art 1020, para 5 Rv). Arbitration rules referred to in an arbitration agreement shall be deemed to form part of the arbitration agreement (Art 1020, para 6 Rv). **9.14**

(2) Requirements as to the contents of the arbitration agreement

Besides the requirement provided for in Art 1024, para 1 Rv relating to a submission agreement, there are no specific statutory requirements concerning the contents of the arbitration agreement. The requirement that a submission agreement should include a description of the matters which the parties wish to submit to arbitration under Art1024, para 1 Rv does not mean that all points of difference and arguments of the parties should be indicated. Nor should it be concluded that 'Terms of Reference', as known under Art 18 ICC Rules, are required.[22] Although there are no further statutory requirements with respect to the submission agreement, it is held that a submission agreement should identify the parties and indicate the will of the parties to submit the dispute(s) to arbitration.[23] Inclusion of names of arbitrators or the method of their appointment is not required.[24] **9.15**

(3) Form of the agreement (eg 'in writing' requirement)

Article 1021 Rv provides that an arbitration agreement must be proven by an instrument in writing. Thus, there must be written evidence of the arbitration agreement. Only when a party argues that no arbitration agreement exists, will an agreement have to be proven by an instrument in writing. An arbitration agreement is presumed to exist if the parties to the arbitral proceedings fail to raise the plea of invalidity or non-existence of an arbitration **9.16**

[21] For an extensive study on the arbitration agreement under Dutch law, see Meijer, G.J., *Overeenkomst tot arbitrage* (Kluwer, Deventer, 2008) (Meijer, *Overeenkomst tot arbitrage*).

[22] Snijders, Loose-leaf, Art 1024, explanatory note 2.

[23] Sanders/Van den Berg 14, n 9.

[24] Van den Berg, *Int Handbook on Comm Arb* 6.

agreement before submitting a statement of defence.[25] If a party fails to do so, it is precluded from raising this plea at a later stage in the arbitral proceedings and in the proceedings before the court, unless the objection relates to the non-arbitrability of the dispute (Arts 1052, para 2 Rv and 1065, para 2 Rv).

9.17 If the arbitration agreement must be proven, according to Art 1021 Rv, an instrument in writing which provides for arbitration or which refers to standard conditions providing for arbitration is sufficient, provided that this instrument is expressly or impliedly accepted by or on behalf of the other party. An exchange of documents is not required. Accordingly, the requirement for a written form of agreement is less demanding than the requirement under the New York Convention.[26]

9.18 If a party claims no arbitration agreement exists, an instrument in writing as referred to in Art 1021 Rv is necessary to prove its existence. Witness evidence does not suffice.[27]

9.19 Changes were made to the definition or evidence of a 'written form' in Art 1021 Rv, which came into force on 30 June 2004, to implement the Directive on Electronic Commerce of 8 June 2000.[28] Thereby, it is expressly stated that an arbitration agreement can be evidenced by electronic means and referred to an analogous application of Art 227*a*, para 1 of the Book 6 of the Civil Code (Art 1021 Rv).

9.20 (3.1) **Are there special requirements for a power of attorney/authority granting the right to enter into an arbitration agreement on behalf of a third party?** Article 1021 Rv explicitly provides that an instrument in writing, which provides for arbitration in the meaning of Art 1021 Rv, can be accepted on behalf of a party. No further special requirements exist for a power of attorney to enter into an arbitration agreement.

(4) Incorporation of an arbitration clause contained in general terms and conditions

9.21 Article 1021 Rv expressly deals with standard or general conditions. Accordingly, the following requirements are to be met: (i) reference to general conditions must be proven by a document in writing; (ii) general conditions provide for arbitration as a means of dispute settlement; and (iii) the document in writing must be expressly or impliedly accepted by the other party.[29] Therefore, an instrument in writing which refers to standard conditions providing for arbitration is sufficient. As explained previously, the requirement is simply that such document be accepted expressly or impliedly by the other party (see para 9.16).[30]

9.22 Reference to general conditions in invoices may bring about certain complications. In particular, problems may arise when a reference to general conditions appears only in some of the invoices sent to the other party (eg in invoices sent earlier, but not in invoices sent later). Problems may also arise when no reference to general conditions is made during

---

25 MvT, 4 *TvA* (1986), p 179; Van den Berg, *Int Handbook on Comm Arb* 5.

26 See also, Sanders, P. *Quo vadis arbitration? Sixty years of Arbitration Practice* (Kluwer Law International, The Hague/London/Boston, 1999) 157 (Sanders, *Quo vadis arbitration*).

27 HR 7 May 1993, *NJ* 1993, 655.

28 2002/31/EC, *Stb* 2004, no 210.

29 Snijders, Loose-leaf, Art 1020, explanatory note 2.

30 However, the parties may stipulate that only an express acceptance has binding effect. See HR 17 January 2003 (*ABN AMRO/Teisman*), *NJ* 2004, 280.

negotiations of the agreement, but subsequently reference appears on invoices. The general conditions' binding effect in such situations may be questionable.[31] Consequently, the binding character of an arbitration clause contained in general conditions referred to in an invoice in such manner may also cause problems. The Supreme Court held that a reference to general conditions in an invoice did not comply with the requirement of Art 1021 Rv, because it did not refer to the whole general conditions, but only to the part that related to fees.[32]

When the requirement in Art 1021 Rv, which states that the existence of an arbitration clause has to be 'proven by an instrument in writing', is not met, the arbitration clause contained in general conditions has no binding effect, even if the general conditions are considered applicable as a continuously used stipulation. In exceptional circumstances, an arbitration clause contained in general conditions might be considered unacceptable as being unreasonably onerous, by application of Art 233 of Book 6 of the Civil Code (*Burgerlijk Wetboek*).[33] However, this possibility has very limited practical importance. **9.23**

(5) Law applicable to the interpretation of arbitration clauses

There is no express provision on the law applicable to the arbitration clause and its interpretation. According to Dutch private international law, the applicable law to the arbitration agreement is likely to be the law of the place of arbitration. If the parties have not made a choice concerning the place of arbitration, and this place cannot be determined in another way, it is contended that Dutch law applies. **9.24**

It is also contended that the applicable law to the arbitration agreement is the law applicable to the contract of which the arbitration agreement forms a part.[34] Apart from the applicable law to the arbitration agreement, it should be noted that Dutch courts are well versed in the practice of arbitration and therefore arbitration agreements are likely to be validly interpreted. **9.25**

In general, the same criteria applicable to a contract's interpretation also apply to the interpretation of arbitration agreements.[35] **9.26**

(5.1) Do courts accept a wide competence of the arbitral tribunal or do they restrict arbitral competence? Do claims which arise in connection with the agreement submitted to arbitration generally fall within the arbitral jurisdiction even if based on tortious legal basis? Does there exist case law with respect to the wording in an arbitration clause as 'arising out of/under/in connection with the present contract' and its specific meaning? Claims based on a tortious legal basis may fall within the arbitral tribunal's jurisdiction. In accordance with Art 1020, para 1 Rv, the parties may submit to arbitration existing or future disputes arising out of a defined legal relationship, 'whether contractual or not'. Claims arising in connection with an agreement submitted to arbitration will generally fall within the arbitral **9.27**

[31] See eg HR 5 June 1992, *NJ* 1992, 565; HR 1 June 1993, *NJ* 1993, 688.
[32] HR 7 May 1993, *NJ* 1993, 655.
[33] HR 23 March 1990, *NJ* 1991, 214.
[34] See on the applicable law, Van den Berg/Van Delden/Snijders 146-7.
[35] HR 20 February 2004, *NJ* 2005, 493; HR March 2004, *NJ* 2005, 494; HR 29 June 2007, *NJ* 2007, 576; See also Meijer, *T&C Rv*, Art 1020, note 1g and the literature and case law referred to therein.

jurisdiction even if they are based on a tort (eg claims for damages not based on the violation of the contract).[36]

9.28 In principle, a broad wording of an arbitration clause is recommended 'in order to avoid uncertainties as to whether or not a given dispute falls under the arbitration agreement'.[37] Interpreting an arbitration agreement does not differ from interpreting of agreements in general. According to Dutch contract law, interpretation of a contract is based not only on the wording of the contract. It is based also on the meaning which the parties may reasonably have given to the contract and on the parties' respective expectations.[38] Under specific circumstances, which relate to the nature of the parties and the agreement, the court may also preliminarily conclude that the wording of the contract reflects the meaning thereof. The party that wishes to deny that, on the basis of such presumptive evidence, the wording of the contract reflects its full meaning may proffer to provide rebuttal evidence.[39] When interpreting the arbitration agreement, the right of access to the courts must also be considered.

9.29 An arbitration agreement 'concerning interpretation, performance and termination of the contract' may usually not be interpreted so as to include disputes concerning the existence and nullity of the contract within the scope of the arbitration clause.[40] For subject matter arbitrability, see B.(2).

(6) Binding effect of an arbitration clause on third parties (eg in case of a guarantee or assignment)

9.30 In the case of an assignment of a claim where an arbitration clause is present, the assignee and the debtor are bound by such clause.[41] It follows also from the wording of Art 145 of Book 6 of the Civil Code, according to which the assignment of a claim does not affect the debtor's defences, and from Art 142 of Book 6 of the Civil Code, according to which an assignee acquires the rights which are accessory to the transferred claim. The same is true in case of the transfer of contracts (Art 159 of Book 6 of the Civil Code) [42] and takeover of debts (Art 157, para 1 of Book 6 of the Civil Code).[43]

9.31 A jointly liable co-debtor who has been called upon to contribute to a debt which is discharged at the expense of one of the co-debtors can invoke, against the co-debtor demanding such contribution, the arbitration clause which he could have invoked against the creditor (Art 11, para 1 of Book 6 of the Civil Code). The debtor demanding the aforementioned contribution can also invoke the arbitration clause against a jointly liable debtor.[44]

9.32 The surety who performs an obligation to which the principal debtor is bound can invoke, against the principal debtor, the arbitration clause which the creditor could have invoked

36 Snijders, Loose-leaf, Art 1020, explanatory note 1 (with reference to case law).
37 Van den Berg, *Int Handbook on Comm Arb* 6.
38 HR 13 March 1981, *NJ* 1981, 635.
39 HR 19 January 2007, *NJ* 2007, 575 and HR 29 June 2007, 576.
40 HR 2 November 1990, *NJ* 1991, 123.
41 HR 2 November 1933, *NJ* 1934, p 302; Hof's-Gravenhage 29 December 1988, (1989) *TvA* 102.
42 Rechtbank Groningen, 22 May 1992, (1992) *TvA* 194.
43 Van den Berg/Van Delden/Snijders 36; Sanders, *Het Nederlandse arbitragerecht* 17–18.
44 Snijders, Loose-leaf, Art 1020, explanatory note 7.

against the principal debtor (Art 850, para 3 of Book 7 of the Civil Code in connection with Art 11, para 1 of Book 6 of the Civil Code). However, it is debatable as to whether a surety may invoke, against the creditor, the arbitration clause contained in the contract concluded between the creditor and the principal debtor. According to Art 852, para 1 of Book 7 of the Civil Code, defences which the principal debtor has against the creditor, can also be invoked by the surety if they relate to the existence, content or the time of performance of the obligation of the principal debtor. It is questionable if the obligation to arbitrate can be considered to be the obligation of the principal debtor within the meaning of Art 852 of Book 7 of the Civil Code. This question has not been answered in a consistent manner by the courts.[45] In any case, a suretyship may contain an arbitration clause, whether or not similar to the arbitration clause in the underlying contract between the debtor and the creditor.[46]

It is a controversial issue whether an arbitration clause contained in the charterparty binds a holder of a bill of lading, when there is a reference to it in the bill of lading. A general reference to the charterparty, without explicitly referring to the arbitration clause, has frequently been held as insufficient evidence to consider the holder of the bill of lading bound by the arbitration clause (cf also Art 415, para 1 of Book 8 of the Civil Code).[47] A carrier can invoke an arbitration clause in a charterparty against a receiving agent who acts in his own name on account of the shipper; whereas, the receiving agent can invoke the arbitration clause in the charterparty to the carrier (cf also Arts 410 and 442, para 2 of Book 8 of the Civil Code).[48] In this context it is not relevant that the receiving agent is the holder of a bill of lading. This is because the receiving agent acts on account of the shipper. The conditions of the charterparty apply to his relationship with the carrier as well (cf Art 410 of Book 8 of the Civil Code). 9.33

(6.1) What is the law/leading authorities' position on multi-party situations? Especially, (i) with respect to the objection that the arbitration clause does not specifically provide for a plurality of parties in the same procedure; (ii) with respect to the constitution of the arbitral tribunal; and (iii) with respect to the consolidation of two or more running arbitration proceedings? In principle, arbitral proceedings, may only be commenced by, and against, parties to the arbitration agreement. This means that in case of multiple parties to the arbitration agreement, unless otherwise agreed, a party or multiple parties may commence arbitral proceedings against any other party or against multiple parties to the arbitration agreement, even if the arbitration agreement does not provide for a plurality of parties in the same arbitral proceedings. See also paras 9.37 *et seq* with regard to the consolidation of arbitral proceedings. 9.34

[45] See eg Rechtbank Amsterdam 13 June 1979, *NJ* 1980, 254 (a reliance on the arbitration clause was admitted). Hof Amsterdam, 27 November 1931, *W* 12 485 (a reliance on the arbitration clause was denied). See also Snijders, Loose-leaf, Art 1020, explanatory note 2.

[46] Snijders, Loose-leaf, Art 1020 explanatory note 7.

[47] See also, Sanders, *Het Nederlandse arbitragerecht* 18–19 and the case law indicated therein; Snijders, Loose-leaf, Art 1020 explanatory note 7.

[48] HR 16 January 1998, *NJ* 1999, 284.

9.35 Furthermore, if the arbitration agreement gives one of the parties a privileged position with regard to the appointment of the arbitrator(s), the other party may, despite the method of appointment laid down in that agreement, request the President of the District Court to appoint the arbitrator(s) (Art 1028 Rv). This provision must be broadly interpreted. It applies not only if the method of appointment laid down in the arbitration agreement gives a party a privileged position, but also if the factual circumstances of the specific case give a party a privileged position, for example, when the arbitration agreement does not specifically provide for the plurality of parties.[49]

9.36 As mentioned previously, the arbitrators shall be appointed by any method agreed upon by the parties (Art 1027, para 1 Rv). If the arbitration rules chosen by the parties contain special provisions for the appointment of arbitrators in multi-party situations, the arbitral tribunal will be appointed in accordance with these rules, provided that none of the parties is given a privileged position. For example, Art 10 of the 1998 ICC Rules provides that, in the absence of a joint nomination of an arbitrator by the multiple claimants or the multiple respondents and where all parties are unable to agree to a method for the constitution of the Arbitral Tribunal, the International Court of Arbitration of the ICC may appoint each member of the Arbitral Tribunal. Therefore, Art 10 of the 1998 ICC Rules does not give one of the parties a privileged position with regard to the appointment of the arbitrators within the meaning of Art 1028 Rv.

9.37 If arbitral proceedings have been commenced before an arbitral tribunal in the Netherlands concerning a subject matter which is connected with the subject matter of arbitral proceedings commenced before another arbitral tribunal in the Netherlands, any of the parties may request the President of the District Court in Amsterdam to order a consolidation of these proceedings, provided that such possibility is not excluded by the parties (Art 1046, para 1 Rv). Accordingly, consolidation is possible only between arbitral proceedings pending in the Netherlands and provided that the parties have not excluded it. Reference to arbitration rules which exclude the possibility of consolidation is sufficient.[50] After providing an opportunity for the parties and arbitrators to be heard, the President may wholly or partially grant or refuse the request for consolidation. His decision will be communicated to the parties and the arbitral tribunals involved (Art 1046, para 2 Rv).

9.38 In a full consolidation, the President of the District Court shall appoint the arbitrator(s) and determine the procedural rules which shall apply to the consolidated proceedings if and to the extent that the parties fail to reach agreement on the above within the period of time prescribed by the President of the District Court (Art 1046, para 3 Rv).

9.39 In a partial consolidation, the President of the District Court shall decide which disputes shall be consolidated. The President of the District Court shall, if the parties fail to agree within the period of time prescribed by him, at the request of any party, appoint the arbitrator(s) and determine which rules shall apply to the consolidated proceedings. In this situation the arbitral tribunal, before which arbitral proceedings have already been

[49] President Rechtbank's-Gravenhage, 23 February 1987, (1987) *TvA* 92 and Sanders/van den Berg, Art 1028, explanatory note 3.4.

[50] Sanders/Van den Berg 27, n 52.

commenced, shall suspend those proceedings. The award of the arbitral tribunal appointed for the consolidated arbitration shall be communicated in writing to the other arbitral tribunals involved. Upon receipt of this award, these arbitral tribunals shall continue the arbitral proceedings commenced before them and decide in accordance with the award rendered in the consolidated proceedings.

It has been suggested that offering the parties the option of consolidation would be a more appropriate statutory regulation than the current solution provided by the present Art 1046 Rv.[51] The arbitration clause recommended by the Netherlands Arbitration Institute expressly excludes consolidation under Art 1046 Rv. **9.40**

(6.2) Is there case law/authorities with respect to the admissibility of third party participation in an arbitration without being a claimant or defendant (Nebenintervention/ Streitverkündung; intervention forcée/volontaire; vouching in; *amicus curiae* etc)? What are the prerequisites and effects of such participation (if permitted)? At the written request of a third party, which has an interest in the outcome of the arbitral proceedings, the arbitral tribunal may permit such party to join the proceedings, or to intervene therein. The arbitral tribunal shall send without delay a copy of the request to the parties (Art 1045, para 1 Rv). In addition, a party who claims to be indemnified by a third party may serve a notice of joinder on such a party. A copy of the notice shall be sent without delay to the arbitral tribunal and the other party (Art 1045, para 2 Rv). However, only the arbitral tribunal may permit the joinder and intervention as referred to in Art 1045, para 1 Rv as well as the joinder for the claim of indemnity as referred to in Art 1045, para 2 Rv, if the third party accedes to the arbitration agreement by agreement in writing between him and the parties. The arbitral tribunal must hear the parties before it decides if it will allow the third party to participate in the arbitral proceedings (Art 1045, para 3 Rv). **9.41**

On the grant of a request for joinder, intervention, or joinder for the claim of indemnity, the third party becomes a party to the arbitral proceedings. Unless the parties have agreed thereon, the arbitral tribunal shall determine the further conduct of the proceedings (Art 1045, para 4 Rv). **9.42**

(7) Termination of an arbitration agreement by a party (reasons and case law)

The Arbitration Act contains no express provisions relating to terminating an arbitration agreement. However, the general contract law rule contained in Art 248, para 2 of Book 6 of the Civil Code applies to an arbitration clause as well. It provides that the rule on the binding character of an obligation under the contract will not apply to the extent that, in the given circumstances, this would be unacceptable according to the criteria of reasonableness and fairness. The non-accessibility of the place where arbitration is to be held (owing to war or impossibility of obtaining a visa) can be cited as an example.[52] It is also considered contrary to the criteria of reasonableness and fairness to hold a person of limited means bound by an arbitration clause; if the court was to decline its jurisdiction, such claimant **9.43**

[51] Van den Berg, Public Lecture 14–15.

[52] Van den Berg/Van Delden/Snijders 37.

would be entirely deprived of the right to pursue his claim.[53] Furthermore, the reliance on the arbitration clause is considered contrary to the criteria of reasonableness and fairness owing to the connection between the matters that should be resolved by arbitration and other matters with respect to which no arbitration agreement was entered into.[54]

9.44 An arbitration clause contained in general conditions can be subject to annulment if it is unreasonably onerous to the other party (Art 233 of Book 6 of the Civil Code). An annulment will only occur in very exceptional cases, for example when agreed-upon arbitration rules contain provisions which may be considered unreasonably onerous for one of the parties.[55]

B. Arbitrability

(1) 'Personal arbitrability' (capacity to conclude arbitration agreements)

9.45 In contrast to earlier statutory arbitration law, the present Arbitration Act contains no provision concerning a party's capacity to enter into an arbitration agreement ('personal arbitrability'). Accordingly, the applicable provisions of the general contract law and the applicable provisions on legal capacity, contained in the Civil Code and other statutes shall determine this issue.[56] As in the case when concluding a contract, a party must have legal capacity to enter into an arbitration agreement.

9.46 The state and public entities may also conclude arbitration agreements, provided that certain conditions and formalities are met. Under Dutch private international law restrictions of internal law regarding authority cannot be invoked against the other party who was not familiar—nor was reasonably required to be familiar—with the restrictions. In principle, a party is protected if it relied in good faith on the authority of the other party. This also applies to the formation of arbitration agreements, to which a state or state entity is a party.[57]

9.47 **(1.1) May a state (or state agency) as party invoke sovereign immunity before the arbitral tribunal or before a state court (eg in a procedure of enforcement)?** The distinction between *acta jure imperii* and *acta jure gestionis*, also termed as the doctrine of restricted immunity,[58] was applied by the Supreme Court in a decision of 26 October 1973.[59] The Court rejected Yugoslavia's plea of immunity from jurisdiction, holding there was no immunity from jurisdiction in circumstances when the state had entered into a transaction

---

[53] Kantonrechter Zierikzee, 19 February 1988, (1988) *TvA* 147. The claimant filed the claim before the court after being informed by an arbitration institute that his claim would have been dealt with only after the deposit for costs was made, the amount of which exceeded the amount of his claim.

[54] Rechtbank Haarlem, 11 May 1993, (1993) *TvA* (1993) 238.

[55] HR 23 March 1990, *NJ* 1991, 214. In a transaction concerning flower-bulbs, the rules referred to in general conditions provided that only the members of the association may initiate arbitral proceedings, whereas non-members may rely on an arbitration clause only when raising a counterclaim. Consequently, an arbitration clause referring to such rules was considered as unreasonably onerous. See also, Van den Berg/Van Delden/Snijders 37; Sanders, *Het Nederlandse arbitragerecht* 15–17.

[56] Van den Berg/Van Delden/Snijders 35; Van den Berg, *Int Handbook on Comm Arb* 6.

[57] HR 28 January 2005, *NJ* 2006, 469.

[58] Berg, A.J. van den, *The New York Arbitration Convention of 1958: Towards a Uniform Judical Interpretation*, (Asser/Kluwer, The Hague/Deventer, 1981) 280 (Van den Berg, *New York Convention*).

[59] HR 26 October 1973, *NJ* 1974, 361; (1976) *Yearbook Comm Arb* 196. cf HR 28 January 2005, *NJ* 2006, 469.

with a private party within the sphere of private law. Furthermore, the Netherlands ratified the European Convention on State Immunity of 1972. In Art 12, this Convention deals with a waiver of the right to invoke immunity from jurisdiction when a member state has entered into an arbitration agreement with a private party to settle a dispute arising out of a commercial relationship. Article 12 concerns court proceedings related to arbitration, such as the setting aside of an arbitral award or proceedings concerning the validity or interpretation of the arbitration agreement. Accordingly, the arbitrators are under no obligation to apply the Convention. However, from the provisions of this Convention, it follows that a state may not successfully invoke sovereign immunity before arbitrators in arbitral proceedings taking place in the Netherlands on the same grounds as set out in Art 12 of the aforementioned Convention.

Immunity from jurisdiction does not *eo ipso* imply immunity from execution. With respect to the enforcement of arbitral awards, a state may raise an objection against enforcement, if the assets, with respect to which an attachment is requested, are designated for public service (cf Art 436 Rv). **9.48**

(2) 'Objective arbitrability' (eg of patent, trade mark and antitrust matters)

The Act defines the 'objective' or subject matter arbitrability in Art 1020, para 3 Rv. It provides that 'the arbitration agreement shall not serve to determine legal consequences of which the parties cannot freely dispose'.[60] In practice, considerations of public policy and—in relation to public policy—exclusive jurisdiction of the judiciary determine the actual scope of arbitrability.[61] Thus, public policy matters are not arbitrable.[62] In particular, these are matters with respect to which a decision would have effect *erga omnes* and which are, consequently, not at the parties' free disposal (eg divorce, adoption, appointment of a guardian or a declaration of bankruptcy).[63] **9.49**

The fact that a subject matter is of a public law nature does not necessarily imply that it is not arbitrable; although, arbitration is seldom used in the field of public law. Moreover, the public legal persons' authority to conclude arbitration agreements is limited.[64] **9.50**

When a statute provides for the judiciary's exclusive jurisdiction, arbitration is often considered excluded.[65] Reference to the court in a statute does not necessarily imply non-arbitrability of the subject matter. It is non-arbitrable only when adjudication over a particular subject **9.51**

---

[60] HR 10 November 2006, *NJ* 2007, 561, <http://www.rechtspraak.nl>. The Supreme Court held that the annulment of a decision brought by a legal person is not a legal consequence of which the parties can freely dispose. The reason is that such decisions have legal effects for the legal person itself, as well as for the third parties.

[61] For more particulars, see Lazić, V., *Insolvency Proceedings and Commercial Arbitration* (Kluwer Law International, The Hague/London/Boston, 1998) 143 *et seq* (Lazić, *Insolvency Proceedings and Commercial Arbitration*).

[62] HR 10 June 1955, *NJ* 1955, 570.

[63] Snijders, Loose-leaf, Art 1020, no 5 and HR 10 November 2006, *NJ* 2007, 561. The Supreme Court held that the annulment of a decision taken by a legal person is not a legal consequence of which the parties can freely dispose. The reason is that such decisions *eo ipso* have legal effects for the legal person itself as well as the third parties.

[64] Snijders, Loose-leaf, Article 1020, explanatory note 5a.

[65] Sanders, *Het nieuwe arbitregerecht* 36.

matter is exclusively conferred upon the judiciary and, consequently, is excluded from arbitration.[66] The judiciary's exclusive jurisdiction must clearly follow from the statute's text or legislative history. It is infrequently provided for, so that it does not significantly limit the domain of arbitration.[67]

9.52 The judiciary has exclusive jurisdiction for disputes regarding trade marks under the Uniform Benelux Trademarks Act (Art 14D), drawings and designs under the Benelux Drawings and Designs Act (Art 16) and the validity of patents under the Patents Act (Art 54).

9.53 Although the aforementioned statutes provide for the courts' exclusive jurisdiction, arguably the exclusivity provisions relate only to the courts' jurisdiction in relation to the jurisdiction of other courts and not to arbitration.

9.54 However, disputes arising from licence agreements, and therefore, claims for damages due to patent infringements, are arbitrable anyhow.[68] Disputes relating to the law of succession, matrimonial property, employment contracts and the so-called 'collective employment contracts' are also arbitrable.[69] With respect to disputes arising in bankruptcy, it is clear that claims on behalf of the estate are arbitrable. The same is true for the claims against the estate which are not aimed at payment from the bankruptcy estate. Arbitral proceedings concerning a claim for payment against the estate, which are pending at the moment of the commencement of bankruptcy, may be continued after such claim is contested in the bankruptcy verification proceedings (Art 29 of the Bankruptcy Act). The question of arbitrability of claims for payment contested in verification, when no arbitral proceedings are pending, used to be considered controversial. The prevailing view—which at the same time criticized the relevant provision[70]—was, that Art 122 of the Bankruptcy Act's wording implied non-arbitrability of contested claims (verification disputes).[71] Other interpretations were also maintained.[72] The Supreme Court's decision of 16 April 1999 may be important, although it did not deal with the effect of an arbitration clause.[73] In this situation, effect was given to a forum-selection-clause providing for a foreign court's jurisdiction. Consequently, it may be expected that the same approach will be taken with respect to arbitration agreements.

9.55 The fact that a relationship between parties must be resolved by the application of certain mandatory rules or rules pertaining to public policy does not necessarily imply non-arbitrability of

---

[66] Snijders, Loose-leaf, Art 1020, explanatory note 5a.

[67] Sanders, *Het Nederlandse arbitragerecht* 36.

[68] Van den Berg, *Int Handbook on Comm Arb* 7; Van den Berg/Van Delden/Snijders 33.

[69] Van den Berg/Van Delden/Snijders 33.

[70] Lazić, V., 'Arbitration and Insolvency Proceedings: Claims of Ordinary Bankruptcy Creditors', (1999) 3 *Electronic J of Comparative L* 8 <http://www.ejcl.org/33/art33–2.html> (accessed 10 August 2008) (Lazić, *Electronic J of Comparative L*); Sanders, *TvA* 88/6,169; Ynzonides 394; Snijders, Loose-leaf, Art 1020, explanatory note 6; Lazić, *Insolvency Proceedings and Commercial Arbitration* (n 61) 165.

[71] Sanders, *TvA* 88/6, 169; Sanders, *Het Nederlandse arbitragerecht* 43; Van den Berg/Van Delden/Snijders 33; Van den Berg, *Int Handbook on Comm Arb* 7.

[72] Snijders, H.J. and Buruma, S.L., *Bouwarbitrage en civile rechter*, Publikatie van de Vereniging voor Bouwrecht, no 23 (Kluwer, Deventer, 1995) 50–1 (Snijders/Buruma).

[73] HR 16 April 1999, *NJ* 2001, 1.

the dispute.[74] Thus, issues of competition law (including EC competition law) are arbitrable.[75] Subject to court control, arbitrators may apply mandatory rules. A violation of such rules or the public policy rules may be a reason for refusal of the enforcement or for the annulment of an award. In a similar vein, the fact that a dispute between the parties involves a decision on the issue pertaining to fundamental principles of the EU law does not imply the subject matter's non-arbitrability.[76]

The Arbitration Act enlarged the domain of arbitrability by expressly providing that parties may agree to submit to arbitration 'the determination only of the quality or condition of goods' (Art 1020, para 4(a) Rv), 'the determination only of the quantum of damages or a monetary debt' (Art 1020, para 4(b) Rv), as well as 'the filling of gaps in, or modification of' their legal relationship between the parties (Art 1020, para 4(c) Rv). Arbitrability of these matters was disputable under the previous Act.[77] **9.56**

C. Decision on the arbitral tribunal's jurisdiction ('*competence-competence*')

(1) Separability (independence of the arbitration agreement from the main agreement)

The concept of autonomy or separability of the arbitration clause is incorporated in the Arbitration Act in Art 1053 Rv.[78] According to this provision, an arbitration agreement is considered to be a separate contract from the contract in which it is incorporated or to which it is related. Consequently, arbitrators may decide on the main contract's validity as its invalidity will not affect the arbitrators' jurisdiction resulting from the arbitration clause. A decision on the main contract's validity is not an issue concerning the arbitrators' jurisdiction.[79] **9.57**

However, an arbitration clause's separability in the case of the contract's non-existence, of which it forms part or to which it is related, is a rather controversial issue. Some authors have expressed the view that the separability concept does not apply when the main contract has never been concluded, as non-existence extends also to the arbitration clause.[80] It is stated that in such a case, arbitrators may provisionally rule on this issue, but any decision taken is a decision on jurisdiction and, therefore, is subject to court review.[81] Contrary to this view, other authors express the opinion that the separability of an arbitration clause should be accepted in all cases of the main contract's non-existence.[82] **9.58**

74 Snijders, Loose-leaf, Art 1020, explanatory note 5.

75 Van den Berg, *Int Handbook on Comm Arb* 7.

76 HR 21 March 1997 (*Eco Swiss/Benetton*), *NJ* 1998, 207. See also the decision of the Court of Justice of the European Communities of 1 June 1999 (*Eco Swiss/Benetton*) (C-126/97).

77 It was suggested to exclude arbitration in resolving disputes relating to public procurement, by an express provision to this respect in the Act on Public Procurement. See, Meijer, G.J. and Nieuwendijk, van den, I.P.M., 'Kroniek arbitrage 2004–2006' (2007) 74, *O&R* 21 (Meijer/Nieuwendijk). However, the proposed draft of the statute on public procurement containing such a proposal has not been adopted.

78 The separability of an arbitration clause was assumed already in the decision of the Supreme Court of 27 December 1935 (HR 27 December 1935, *NJ* 1936, 442).

79 Sanders/Van den Berg, Art 1053, 31, fn 65.

80 Van den Berg/Van Delden/Snijders 86; Van den Berg, *Int Handbook on Comm Arb* 8.

81 Van den Berg, *Int Handbook on Comm Arb* 8.

82 Snijders, Loose-leaf, Art 1053, explanatory note 5.

(2) The tribunal's competence to decide on its own jurisdiction (including the tribunal's decision's form and time)

9.59 In accordance with Art 1052, para 1 Rv, the arbitral tribunal shall have the power to decide on its own jurisdiction ('*competence-competence*'). An arbitral tribunal's decision in this respect is, however, subject to subsequent court control. Article 1052, paras 2 and 3 Rv relate to lack of jurisdiction: invalidity of an arbitration agreement (para 2) and the arbitral tribunal's constitution in violation of the applicable rules (para 3). Both cases involving a lack of jurisdiction present grounds for setting aside an award (Art 1065, paras 1(a) and 1(b) Rv).

9.60 From Art 1052, paras 2 and 3 Rv's wording, it may be concluded that a plea that the arbitral tribunal lacks jurisdiction must be raised during the arbitral proceedings. The issue of jurisdiction is first to be decided by the arbitrators, before such plea may be brought before the court, with the exception of the objection of the subject matter's non-arbitrability. A party who appears in arbitral proceedings must ultimately raise the plea that the arbitral tribunal lacks jurisdiction in his statement of defence (Art 1052, paras 2 and 3 Rv).[83] A party who fails to do so is precluded from raising this plea later in the arbitral proceedings and in subsequent proceedings before the court (Art 1052, paras 2 and 3 Rv and Art 1065, paras 2 and 3 Rv). The objection that the arbitral tribunal lacks jurisdiction owing to non-arbitrability of the subject matter is the only plea that may be raised later in arbitral and court proceedings, even if not previously raised (Art 1052, para 2 Rv and Art 1065, para 2 Rv).

9.61 A party who has participated in the arbitral tribunal's constitution may not raise a lack of jurisdiction plea owing to a tribunal's irregular constitution in the arbitral proceedings or in proceedings before the court. A party who has not participated in the tribunal's constitution, but has appeared in the arbitral proceedings, must ultimately raise this objection in his statement of defence (Art 1052, para 3), as already mentioned.

9.62 According to Art 1052, para 4 Rv, any decision of the arbitral tribunal declaring that it has jurisdiction can only be challenged in conjunction with the challenge of a subsequent final or partial final award. This means that, once the arbitral proceeding is running and the arbitral tribunal has declared that it has jurisdiction no court proceedings can successfully be commenced. The arbitral tribunal's decision that it has jurisdiction need not be explicit, but may also be implicitly made, namely in the absence of a timely plea as to the jurisdiction of the arbitral tribunal. If a party then files a claim which is submitted to arbitration, the courts must declare the claim inadmissible. The party must wait for a final (or partial final) arbitral award. Once the arbitral tribunal has rendered a final or partial final award, the party can challenge the arbitral award on the ground that the arbitral tribunal lacks jurisdiction on the ground that there is no valid arbitration agreement (Art 1065, para 1(a) Rv).

(3) Extent of the 'competence-competence' *and role of the courts (including form and time limits of a challenge of the tribunal's decision)*

9.63 The arbitral tribunal's decision that it has jurisdiction may be in the form of an interim award. It can also be made in a subsequent final or subsequent partial final award. It is

[83] See HR 29 April 1994, *NJ* 1994, 488, (1994) *TvA* 187.

questionable whether the arbitral tribunal's decision that it lacks jurisdiction is an arbitral award.[84]

The Act does not provide any time limit for making a decision or award. This includes a decision and an award on jurisdictional issues. According to Art 1048 Rv, '[t]he arbitral tribunal is free to determine the time when the award shall be made'. **9.64**

A tribunal's decision that it has jurisdiction may only be challenged by recourse to the court against a subsequent final or partial final award (Art 1052, para 4 Rv). Time limits for applying to set aside an arbitral award are determined in Arts 1064, para 3 and 1068, para 2 Rv (see paras 9.25–6). These statutory regulations were conceived to prevent a party's delaying tactics in relation to bringing the jurisdiction question before the court during arbitral proceedings.[85] **9.65**

If the arbitral tribunal decides that it lacks jurisdiction, the court shall have jurisdiction to adjudicate the case, unless the parties have agreed otherwise (Art 1052, para 5 Rv). **9.66**

If appeal to a second arbitral tribunal is agreed upon, it will be allowed against both an arbitral tribunal's decision in first instance that it has jurisdiction and an arbitral tribunal's decision in first instance that it lacks jurisdiction (Art 1052, para 6 Rv). In such event the court shall have jurisdiction under Art 1052, paras 4 and 5 Rv only after the decision is made on appeal to the second arbitral tribunal or after the time limit for an appeal has lapsed without an appeal having being lodged or earlier, if the right to appeal is renounced in writing (Art 1052, para 6 Rv). **9.67**

D. Enforcement of an arbitration agreement within or by court proceedings

(1) Effect of invoking an arbitration clause within a court proceeding (and time limits for such a motion)

The Act contains separate provisions on the stay of court proceedings. One relates to an agreement which provides for arbitration in the Netherlands (Art 1022, para 1 Rv) and the other relates to an agreement which provides for arbitration outside the Netherlands (Art 1074, para 1 Rv). Although these provisions are not identical in wording, there is no substantial difference between them. **9.68**

A court seized of a dispute in respect of which an arbitration agreement has been concluded shall declare that it has no jurisdiction if a party invokes the existence of the said agreement before submitting a defence. A court shall only declare that it has jurisdiction if the arbitration agreement is invalid (Art 1022, para 1 Rv) under the law applicable to it (Art 1074, para 1 Rv). The words '*before* submitting a defence' must be *broadly* interpreted, so that a party can invoke the arbitration agreement (somewhere) *in* (the beginning, the middle and the end of) his (statement of) defence.[86] **9.69**

[84] Van den Berg/Van Delden/Snijders 83–5.
[85] Van den Berg, *Int Handbook on Comm Arb* 23.
[86] HR 29 April 1994, *NJ* 1994, 488, (1994) *TvA* 187.

9.70 (1.1) **If a party has invoked successfully the arbitration agreement in a court proceeding, is it then entitled to deny within the arbitral proceeding that there is a valid and binding arbitration agreement?** If a party has successfully invoked the arbitration agreement in court proceedings in the Netherlands, the court will declare that it has no jurisdiction. The court's decision relating to the existence of a valid arbitration agreement has *res judicata* effect (Art 236, para 1 Rv). If the party who successfully invoked the arbitration agreement in court proceedings then denies the existence of a valid arbitration agreement before the arbitral tribunal (when the seat of arbitration is situated in the Netherlands), the other party can invoke the *res judicata* of the court decision before the arbitral tribunal. If a party successfully invoked the existence of the arbitration agreement in court proceedings outside the Netherlands, a party can still deny that a valid arbitration agreement exists before the arbitral tribunal if the place of arbitration is situated in the Netherlands. The final decision on the jurisdiction of the arbitral tribunal lies with the court in the Netherlands (Arts 1064, para 2 Rv and 1065, para 1(a) and (e) Rv).

9.71 (1.2) **Vice versa, if a party has successfully objected to an arbitral proceeding by denying that there is a valid arbitration agreement, may it then invoke such agreement in the ensuing court proceeding?** If a party has successfully objected to an arbitral proceeding by denying that there is a valid arbitration agreement, the arbitral tribunal will have declared that it has no jurisdiction. According to Art 1052, para 5 Rv, the jurisdiction of the court will revive if the tribunal declares that it lacks jurisdiction, unless the parties have agreed otherwise. In practice the parties hardly ever agree otherwise. This means that a party can no longer invoke the arbitration agreement in ensuing court proceedings. The court has jurisdiction to try the case.

(2) Legal remedies and proceedings to enforce an arbitration agreement

9.72 The relevant provisions on stay of court proceedings contained in Arts 1022, para 1, and 1074, para 1 Rv have been addressed separately (see 67 and 68). These are the only provisions that relate to the proceedings to enforce an arbitration agreement. The stay of court proceedings under Arts 1022, para 1, and 1074, para 1 Rv is mandatory. It follows from the words 'shall declare that it has no jurisdiction'. The court has no discretion in this respect and may only examine the validity of the arbitration agreement.[87] It is generally held that, outside the aforementioned provisions, the courts may not compel a party to arbitration.

9.73 (2.1) **Which would be the internationally competent court (i) for obtaining a declaration that an arbitration agreement is valid and binding; or (ii) to compel arbitration? (The defendant's courts? The courts of the place of arbitration? The claimant's courts, cf Article 6 (2) in fine, ICC Rules?)** Apart from Art 1022, para 1 Rv and Art 1074, para 1 Rv, the Dutch Arbitration Act does not contain any provision concerning the possibility of obtaining a declaration that an arbitration agreement is valid and binding. Even the appointment of arbitrators takes place without examining the validity of the arbitration agreement (Art 1027, para 4 Rv).

[87] Van den Berg, *Int Handbook on Comm Arb* 8.

Furthermore, the Act contains no provision on the court's jurisdiction to 'compel' arbitration, which corresponds to ss 4 and 206 of the US Federal Arbitration Act. It is questionable as to whether the parties can obtain a declaration in court proceedings that a given arbitration agreement is valid and binding in court proceedings outside the aforementioned cases. 9.74

III. The arbitral tribunal

A. Number and qualification of arbitrators

(1) Sole arbitrator or arbitral tribunal with several arbitrators

In accordance with Art 1026, para 1 Rv, the arbitral tribunal must be composed of an uneven number of arbitrators (see para 9.73). It may also consist of a sole arbitrator. The parties may agree on the number of arbitrators or on the method of ascertaining the number. If they fail to do so or if the method chosen for determining the number appears inoperable and the parties are unable to agree on this issue, the President of the District Court will determine the number of arbitrators, upon the request of one of the parties (Art 1026, para 2 Rv). No appeal is allowed against the President of the District Court's decision (Art 1070 Rv). 9.75

(1.1) Are arbitral tribunals with an even number of arbitrators acceptable? An even number of arbitrators is not allowed in the Netherlands. Article 1026, para 1 Rv expressly states that 'the arbitral tribunal shall be composed of an uneven number of arbitrators'. However, an arbitration agreement providing for an even number of arbitrators is not regarded as invalid. In such case, the arbitrators shall appoint an additional arbitrator who will act as the chairman of the tribunal (Art 1026, para 3 Rv). If the arbitrators fail to reach agreement on the appointment of the additional arbitrator as provided in Art 1026, para 3 Rv, such arbitrator shall, unless the parties have agreed otherwise, be appointed at the request of either party by the President of the District Court (Art 1026, para 4 Rv).[88] 9.76

An arbitral award rendered in the Netherlands by an even number of arbitrators violates Dutch public policy and can be set aside on the ground that the manner in which the arbitral award was made violates public policy (Art 1065, para 1 (e) Rv). On the same ground, the enforcement of the arbitral award may be refused (Art 1063, para 1 Rv). An arbitral award, rendered abroad by an even number of arbitrators, is enforceable in the Netherlands, if such award is valid under the law of the country where it is rendered.[89] The recognition and enforcement of such award is not considered to be contrary to international public policy (Art V, para 2 (b) New York Convention and Art 1076, Prague 1 Rv). 9.77

(2) Qualification of the arbitrators

There are no particular requirements concerning the qualification of arbitrators under the Act. It provides expressly, in Art 1023 Rv, that any natural person of legal capacity may be appointed as an arbitrator. According to the same provision, no person may be prevented from an appointment for the reasons of his nationality, unless the parties have agreed otherwise. 9.78

[88] Van den Berg, *Int Handbook on Comm Arb* 11.

[89] Hof Den Haag, 3 May 1962, *S&S* 1963, 42, Van den Berg, Public Lecture 7 and Sanders/Van den Berg, Art 1026, 15, note 14.

The Act has abandoned the solution that existed under the previous Act, according to which the judges were precluded from being appointed as arbitrators.[90] According to Art 1023 Rv, only *natural* persons may be appointed as arbitrators.

9.79 **(2.1) Are there mandatory requirements for the qualification of arbitrators (statutory requirements or indirect requirements through eg general conditions of insurance contracts)?** Apart from Art 1023 Rv, no further requirements are imposed on arbitrators. However, according to Art 16, para 2 of the Rules of the Netherlands Arbitration Institute, if a sole arbitrator is to be appointed in arbitration between different nationality parties, the parties may require that the arbitrator be a different nationality from any of the parties. According to Art 16, para 3 of the Rules of the Netherlands Arbitration Institute, the same applies to the arbitral tribunal's chairman if an arbitral tribunal of three arbitrators is to be appointed in arbitration between different nationality parties.

9.80 **(2.2) Which national arbitration institutions may be contacted for obtaining information about qualified (and specialized) arbitrators?** The Netherlands Arbitration Institute's list of arbitrators is not made public. The Netherlands Arbitration Institute will only supply the parties with information about arbitrators if the Arbitration Rules of the Netherlands Arbitration Institute apply. General information about arbitrators can be obtained from the Dutch Chambers of Commerce. Further, information can be obtained from the Dutch National Committee of the ICC.

9.81 **(2.3) Are judges or civil servants required to obtain permission by their employer to act as arbitrator? Are these permissions given generally or case-by-case? What are the consequences if such permission has not been obtained?** As mentioned above, the provision prohibiting Dutch judges from being appointed as arbitrators has been abolished. No specific rules apply in relation to the permission required by Dutch Judges to act as arbitrator. Therefore, internal rules on permissions for additional activities apply. It appears highly unlikely that a failure to obtain the necessary permission would form a ground for setting aside an arbitral award. No case law exists in the context of a failure to gain the necessary permission.

B. Appointment of arbitrators

(1) Extent of party autonomy to establish appointment procedure

9.82 As provided in Art 1027, para 1 Rv, the method of appointment of the arbitrator(s) is to be determined by the agreement of the parties. A third person may be entrusted to appoint the arbitrators. Accordingly, the parties may agree that a third person (eg an arbitration institution, the chamber of commerce, a court or the President of the District Court)[91] appoint all arbitrators, the sole arbitrator or the chairman of a three-member arbitral tribunal.[92]

9.83 The Rules of the Netherlands Arbitration Institute provide for a so-called 'list procedure' for the appointment of arbitrators. Each party may delete from the list (drawn up by the

[90] Sanders/Van den Berg, Art 1023, 13, note 8.
[91] Sanders, *Het Nederlandse arbitragerecht* 98.
[92] Snijders, Loose-leaf, Art 1027, explanatory note 2, 150.

administrator) the names of persons against whom he has overriding objections and number the remaining names in the order of his preference. The administrator shall, taking into account the preferences and objections expressed by the parties, invite one or three persons from the list, as the case may be, to act as arbitrator (Art 14, NAI Rules).

According to Art 1027, para 4 Rv, the third person referred to in Art 1027, para 1 Rv will appoint the arbitrator(s) without examining the arbitration agreement's validity. Party autonomy in determining the method of appointment is limited only by the requirement that the arbitration agreement should not provide a privileged position to one of the parties with respect to the appointment of arbitrators (Art 1028 Rv).[93] An example of a privileged position is when the agreement provides that only one party will have the right to appoint the sole arbitrator or all arbitrators. The stipulation that the arbitrator(s) will be chosen from a list determined by only one party is another example.[94] **9.84**

A party's privileged position does not render the arbitration agreement invalid.[95] The other party may, within one month after the commencement of arbitration, request the President of the District Court to appoint the arbitrator(s) regardless of the method of appointment laid down in the arbitration agreement (Art 1028 Rv). In such a case, the other party shall be given an opportunity to be heard and the provision of Art 1027, para 4 Rv will apply accordingly (see para 9.88). **9.85**

The Act does not provide for the system of 'party-arbitration', whereby each party appoints an arbitrator and the arbitrators so appointed elect a third (as chairman). However, this appointment system is not excluded or forbidden. In accordance with the party autonomy principle as expressed in the Act, the parties may agree on the 'party-arbitration' appointment procedure.[96] Commentators do not recommend this system for use in domestic arbitration, as they consider that a party-appointed arbitrator could lack impartiality.[97] **9.86**

In order to prevent arbitral proceedings from being delayed, the Act provides for a time limit for the appointment of arbitrators. An appointment has to be made within two months from the date of the arbitration's commencement (Art 1027, para 2 Rv). Arbitration is deemed commenced at the moment the submission agreement is concluded, unless the parties have agreed to another method of commencement (Art 1024, para 2 Rv). In the case of an arbitration clause, it is the moment when the respondent receives the notice of arbitration, unless the parties have agreed on a different method of commencement (Art 1025, para 1 Rv). If the parties have not agreed upon the number of arbitrators, the time limit of two months starts to run on the date when the number of arbitrators is determined (Art 1027, para 2 Rv). The Act provides for the possibility to extend the appointment period to three months if at least one of the parties has his domicile or actual residence outside the Netherlands (Art 1027, para 2 Rv). **9.87**

---

93 See also, Van den Berg, Public Lecture 8.
94 Sanders/Van den Berg, Art 1028, 17, note 21.
95 Van den Berg, *Int Handbook on Comm Arb* 13.
96 *ibid*, 11; Snijders, Loose-leaf, Art 1027, explanatory note 2.
97 Van den Berg, *Int Handbook on Comm Arb*.11; Sanders, *Het Nederlandse arbitragerecht* 61; Snijders, Loose-leaf, Art 1027, explanatory note 2.

9.88 In Art 1073, para 2 Rv, the Act provides for the possibility to set the arbitration in motion and appoint the arbitrator(s) when no place of arbitration is determined in the arbitration agreement. Thus, the appointment or challenge of the arbitrator or a secretary may be made in accordance with the relevant provisions of the Netherlands Arbitration Act if one of the parties has domicile or habitual residence in the Netherlands.

(2) Procedure in absence of an agreement by the parties

9.89 According to Art 1027, para 1 Rv, in the absence of an agreement by the parties concerning the method of appointment, the arbitrator(s) shall be appointed by consensus between the parties. This provision means that the parties must agree on the sole arbitrator or on all arbitrators. A participation in the appointment procedure does not entail a waiver of the right to raise the plea of lack of jurisdiction of the arbitral tribunal owing to the absence of a valid arbitration agreement later in arbitral proceedings (Art 1027, para 4 Rv) (see para 9.58).

9.90 In accordance with the principle of party autonomy, the tribunal's chairman will be nominated in the manner agreed by the parties. Thus, the parties may agree on 'party-arbitration', although the Act does not explicitly provide for this system of the appointment procedure. In the absence of an agreement on the appointment method, all arbitrators will be appointed by consensus of the parties (see paras 9.80–9.87). If the appointment is not made within a determined time limit, the President of the District Court will appoint all arbitrators, upon a party's request (see para 9.88).

(3) Effect of one party's refusal to cooperate in the constitution of the arbitral tribunal

9.91 If the arbitrator(s) is not appointed within the period of time provided in Art 1027, para 2 Rv (ie within two months or three months), the arbitrator shall, at the request of either party, be appointed by the President of the District Court. The other party will be given an opportunity to be heard (Art 1027, para 3 Rv). If the parties have not determined the place of arbitration, the appointment of arbitrators may take place in accordance with the provisions of the Netherlands Arbitration Act if at least of one the parties is domiciled or has its actual residence in the Netherlands (Art 1073, para 2 Rv). In this situation a party may request the President of the District Court to appoint the arbitrator(s) as provided in Art 1027, para 3 Rv. A failure to appoint the arbitrator(s) within the time limit includes a failure to appoint the arbitrator(s) according to the method agreed upon by the parties (see para 9.80–9.86) and, in the absence of the agreed-upon method of appointment, a failure of the parties to appoint the arbitrator(s) by consensus.

9.92 If additional arbitrators have to be appointed, the President of the District Court will appoint all arbitrators, even those who have already been nominated.[98] In making the appointment, the President will follow the preferences expressed by the parties in a preceding unsuccessful appointment procedure.[99] The President of the District Court will appoint the arbitrator(s) without examining the validity of the arbitration agreement (Art 1027, para 4, first sentence Rv).

---

98 Sanders/Van den Berg, Art 1027, 16, f 19.
99 *ibid.*

Participation in the appointment of the arbitrator(s) by a party does not entail a waiver of the right to raise the plea that the arbitral tribunal lacks jurisdiction *due to the absence of a valid arbitration agreement* later in arbitral proceedings (Art 1027, para 4, second sentence Rv). A party who has participated in the constitution of the tribunal may not raise a plea of the lack of jurisdiction in the subsequent arbitral or court proceedings *on the ground that the tribunal was established in violation of the applicable rules* (Art 1052, para 3 Rv). A party who has not participated in the establishment of the tribunal, but has made an appearance in the arbitral proceedings, may raise the plea of the lack of jurisdiction *on the ground of improper constitution of the tribunal*, prior to submitting a statement of defence. Thereafter, that party is precluded from raising the plea later in the arbitral proceedings or in proceedings before the court (Art 1052, para 3 Rv). **9.93**

(4) Circumstances and valid reasons for an arbitrator to resign

The arbitrator must accept his mandate in writing (Art 1029, para 1 Rv). The acceptance may be expressed by a letter to the parties or to the arbitration institution or may result from the arbitral award.[100] The ways in which an arbitrator can be released from his accepted mandate are provided for in Art 1029, paras 2–4 Rv. **9.94**

An arbitrator may be released from the mandate at his own request, with the consent of the parties or a third person designated by them, or, in the absence of such person, by the President of the District Court (Art 1029, para 2 Rv). The Act does not require that the reasons for the release be included in the request. Serious illness or an extended stay abroad are examples mentioned in the literature as reasons for the release of a mandate (cf also Art 1029, para 4 Rv).[101] In order to obtain a release, the consent of the parties, a third person or the President is always needed. The President and the third party have discretionary powers when deciding upon a request.[102] **9.95**

An arbitrator may be released from his mandate by mutual agreement of the parties (Art 1029, para 3 Rv). No specific circumstances are mentioned in the Act. Dissatisfaction of the parties with the arbitrator's performance of his duties or inability of the arbitrator to request the release himself, owing to a serious illness, can be cited as examples.[103] **9.96**

An arbitrator may be released from his mandate by a third person designated by the parties, or in the absence of such person, by the President of the District Court, at the request of either party, if he has become *de jure* or *de facto* unable to perform his mandate (Art 1029, para 4 Rv). **9.97**

An arbitrator released from his mandate in accordance Art 1029, paras 2–4 Rv, must be replaced by applying the initial appointment rules. The same applies in the case of an arbitrator's death (Art 1030, para 1) or when there has been a successful challenge (Art 1035, para 3 Rv). **9.98**

---

100 Sanders/Van den Berg, Art 1029, 17, note 22.

101 Snijders, Loose-leaf, Article 1029, explanatory note 3; Sanders/Van den Berg, Art 1029, p 17, fn 23; Van den Berg, *Int Handbook on Comm Arb* 13.

102 Snijders, Loose-leaf, Art 1029, explanatory note 3.

103 Sanders/Van den Berg, Art 1029, 17, fn 24; Snijders, Loose-leaf, Art 1029, explanatory note 4.

9.99 The acceptance and release from the arbitrator's mandate under Art 1029 Rv should be distinguished from the termination of the mandate under Art 1031 Rv. The latter relates to the termination of the arbitral tribunal's mandate either by the parties' agreement[104] or at the request of either party or a third person, if the tribunal carries out its mandate in an unacceptably slow manner. In the case of release made under Art 1029 Rv, a released arbitrator shall be replaced. If an arbitral tribunal's mandate is terminated under Art 1031 Rv, the jurisdiction of the courts will revive, unless the parties have agreed otherwise.

C. Challenge and replacement of arbitrators

(1) Grounds, procedure and deadlines for challenging an arbitrator

9.100 An arbitrator may be challenged 'if circumstances exist that give rise to justifiable doubts as to his impartiality or independence' (Art 1033, para 1 Rv). A resemblance or appearance of partiality may be sufficient to challenge an arbitrator.[105] However, not every type of relationship or connection between an arbitrator and a party or a party's representative will provide a sufficient reason for the challenge.[106] Rather, these are such relationships which may raise justifiable doubts about the arbitrator's impartiality or independence.[107] Thus, an arbitrator may be successfully challenged if he was an attorney for one of the parties in court proceedings relating to the dispute submitted to arbitration.[108] The fact that an arbitrator is a board member of the arbitral institution does not present a reason for his challenge.[109] The same grounds and procedure apply to the challenge of a secretary engaged by the tribunal (Art 1033, para 1 Rv).

9.101 The Act imposes certain limitations with respect to the challenge of an arbitrator. Thus an arbitrator may only be challenged by the party who appointed him on the grounds of which that party becomes aware after the appointment has been made (Art 1033, para 2 Rv). Further limitations concern an arbitrator appointed by a third person or the President of the District Court. A party may not challenge the arbitrator with whose appointment he has consented, unless the grounds for the challenge have become known to this party after the appointment has been made (Art 1033, para 3 Rv).

9.102 The arbitrator's or secretary's duty to disclose the existence of grounds which may form the basis of a challenge are provided in Art 1034 Rv. A prospective arbitrator or a secretary must disclose such grounds in writing to the person who has approached him (Art 1034, para 1 Rv). A person appointed as an arbitrator or secretary shall immediately notify the parties

[104] eg if the parties have reached a settlement. See Sanders/Van den Berg, Art 1031, 18, note 27.

[105] HR 18 February 1994, *NJ* 1995, 765; Pres Rb, Rotterdam, 1 May 1987, (1987) *TvA* 152.

[106] Pres Rb, Amsterdam, 3 June 1988, (1989) *TvA* 105.

[107] On the basis of the requirements of independence and impartiality, arbitrators will, in principle, have to refrain from gathering evidence and from investigating themselves; arbitrators should leave it up to the parties to submit evidence, and confine themselves to an assessment of the evidence presented by the parties (see HR 29 June 2007, *NJ* 2008, 177). Once the arbitral award has been rendered justifiable doubts on the arbitrator's impartiality or independence are not enough to have the arbitral award set aside (see HR 18 February 1994, *NJ* 1995, 765; Pres Rb, Rotterdam, 1 May 1987, (1987) *TvA* 152).

[108] Pres Rb, Rotterdam, 8 January 1993, (1993) *TvA* 104.

[109] Pres Rb Leeuwarden, 4 November 1988, (1989) *TvA* 29.

about the existence of such grounds, if the parties have not already been notified (Art 1034, para 2 Rv).

The procedure for the challenge of an arbitrator is provided in Art 1035. The challenge shall be notified in writing by the challenging party to the challenged arbitrator, the other members of the tribunal, and the other party. The notification should include the grounds for the challenge. A third person shall also be notified, if the challenged arbitrator was appointed by the third person (para 1). Arbitral proceedings may be suspended as of the date of receipt of the notification. The arbitral tribunal has discretionary powers in this respect. Thus, if the challenge is prima facie unjustified, the tribunal may decide to continue the proceedings.[110] **9.103**

If the challenged arbitrator does not withdraw within two weeks' time, running from the day after receipt of notification, the President of the District Court shall decide on the merit of the challenge, at either party's request. If the request is not filed within four weeks, running from the day after receipt of notification, the right to challenge is extinguished. Arbitral proceedings will be continued if previously suspended (para 2). If one or both of the parties or the challenged arbitrator has their domicile or actual residence abroad, the time limits of two and four weeks are extended to six and eight weeks (para 4). Article 1035, para 4 Rv concerns the question of replacement of an arbitrator (see para 9.107). **9.104**

(1.1) **Do state courts review challenge procedures which took place in accordance with a specific procedure agreed upon by the parties (eg Article 11, ICC Rules)? If so, at what point in time? May such review be excluded?** The courts do not, strictly speaking, review challenge procedures which took place in accordance with a specific procedure agreed upon by the parties. However, the fact that the parties have agreed upon a different method of challenging arbitrators does not exclude a decision of the President of the District Court on this issue.[111] It means that if the challenge is unsuccessful in a procedure agreed upon by the parties (eg before an arbitral institution in accordance with its rules), the challenging party may still apply to the President of the District Court to decide on this issue. **9.105**

A decision on a third party's challenge (eg an arbitral institution) should be brought 'in due time as the ultimate decision on the challenge is reserved (without appeal) to the President of the District Court'.[112] Therefore, although the possibility to apply to the President of the District Court may not be excluded by providing for a challenge by a third party, it is rather unlikely that the President of the District Court would bring about a decision deviating from the decision of an arbitral institution on this basis.[113] The decision of the President of the District Court is not subject to appeal (Art 1070 Rv). **9.106**

(1.2) **Is there case law with respect to truncated arbitral tribunals? (cf Article 12(5), ICC Rules)** Article 1057, para 3 Rv provides that, if a minority of the arbitrators refuses **9.107**

[110] Sanders/Van den Berg, Art 1035, 20, note 30.

[111] Van den Berg, *Int Handbook on Comm Arb* 10; cf Rechtbank, Rotterdam, 8 June 2006 (261095/06–1154vr), unpublished, referred to in Meijer/Nieuwendijk 28.

[112] Sanders/Van den Berg, Art 1035, fn 31, 20.

[113] *ibid.*

to sign the arbitral award, the other arbitrators shall mention this beneath the award signed by them. This further statement shall be signed by the dissenting arbitrator(s).[114] A similar statement shall be made if a majority is incapable of signing and if it is unlikely that this impediment will cease to exist within a reasonable time. If an arbitrator has not completely taken part in the process of decision making, the other arbitrators can sign the award on the basis of Art 1057, para 3 Rv. Such an award will not *eo ipso* violate public policy.[115]

(2) Procedure for appointing a new arbitrator

9.108 If a challenged arbitrator withdraws or if the challenge is granted by the President of the District Court, the challenged arbitrator will be replaced in accordance with the procedure of his initial appointment, unless the parties have agreed otherwise (Art 1035, para 3 Rv). Besides the case of a successful challenge, a replacement arbitrator will also be required when an arbitrator dies (Art 1030, para 1 Rv) or if he has been released from his mandate. An arbitrator may be released from his mandate either at his own request (Art 1029, para 2 Rv), or by agreement of the parties (Art 1029, para 3 Rv) or at either party's request if he has become *de jure* or *de facto* unable to perform his mandate (Art 1029, para 4 Rv).

IV. The arbitral procedure

A. General principles

(1) Extent of party autonomy to determine the arbitral procedure

9.109 The Act recognizes a wide freedom of the parties to determine the procedural rules. The arbitral proceedings are to be conducted in a manner agreed upon by the parties. In the absence of such an agreement, the procedure is determined by the arbitral tribunal, subject only to a very limited number of mandatory requirements pertaining mainly to the basic principles of due process (Art 1036 Rv).[116]

9.110 The mandatory provisions express only the basic principles of procedural law and, as such, cannot be considered as a substantial restriction on the parties' freedom.[117] The parties can thus determine the arbitral proceedings freely. The parties' choice of procedural rules, including a reference to Arbitration Rules of an arbitration institution, does not have to be contained in an arbitration agreement. It can be made after a dispute has arisen.[118]

9.111 The equal treatment of the parties requirement and the necessity to give each party an opportunity to present his case and to substantiate his claim are provided in Art 1039, para 1 Rv. A violation of this basic procedural law principle (*audi et alteram partem*) may result

---

[114] HR 5 December 2008, *NJ* 2009, 6; failure to comply with Art 1057, para 3 Rv may lead to the setting aside of the arbitral award; a dissenting opinion that is signed by the third arbitrator cannot replace the lack of his signature in the arbitral award. See para 291.

[115] Hof's-Gravenhage, 17 December 1998, (1999) 3 *TvA* 108–13. It concerns an arbitral award signed by the other arbitrators on the basis of Art 1057, para 3 Rv.

[116] Van den Berg, Public Lecture 12. An exemption to the aforementioned requirements exist in cases of quality arbitration, to the extent that the provisions of s 2 on arbitral proceedings (Arts 1036–48 Rv) do not apply, except Art 1037 Rv relating to the place of arbitration (Art 1047 Rv).

[117] *id.*

[118] Van den Berg, *Int Handbook on Comm Arb* 16.

in setting aside the arbitral award (Art 1065, para 1 (e) Rv). In addition, the right to a hearing may not be denied to the parties (Art 1039, para 2 Rv).

(1.1) Are the parties free to choose any national or international law governing the procedure before the arbitral tribunal? As already mentioned (see para 9.106), parties are free to determine the rules of procedure. In the absence of the parties' agreement in that respect, the arbitrators may determine the rules of procedure, subject only to a few requirements pertaining to due process. **9.112**

Accordingly, parties to an arbitration taking place in the Netherlands are, from a theoretical point of view, free to choose a national procedural law of another country; although to do so would be extremely impractical. Since the Netherlands Arbitration Act accepts the principle of territoriality (Art 1073, para 1 Rv), such choice would not exclude the application of those provisions of the Act which may not be excluded or deviated from by an agreement between the parties. Nor would it exclude jurisdiction of the Dutch courts in exercising their function of support or supervision to arbitration provided by the Act. **9.113**

The provisions which may not be excluded by an agreement of the parties include those relating to the requirements of due process (Art 1039, para 1 Rv), and, for example, those concerning an uneven number of arbitrators, a possibility to request the President of the District Court to decide on the challenge of an arbitrator and the grounds for annulment of the award.[119] **9.114**

(2) Basic procedural principles or mandatory rules to be applied by the arbitral tribunal

The parties's freedom to determine rules of procedure and the tribunal's freedom to determine the procedural rules should the parties fail to do so is subject to the basic procedural principles such as due process. The requirement of equal treatment of the parties and an obligation of the tribunal to give each party an opportunity to present his case are provided in Art 1039, para 1 Rv. An arbitral award rendered in violation of the fundamental principles of due process and fair trial may be set aside (Art 1065, para 1 (e) Rv) and the recognition and enforcement may be refused (Art 1063, para 1 Rv and Art 1076, para 1(B) Rv) on the ground that the manner in which the award was made violates public policy. The recognition and enforcement under the New York Convention may be refused for the reason that the party was unable to present his case (Art V(1)(b) of the Convention) and for the violation of public policy (Art V(2)(b) of the Convention). **9.115**

The requirements mentioned in Art 1039, para 1 Rv, include, *inter alia*, providing an opportunity for a party to react to the other party's claims,[120] or at least to be notified of the claim and any explanatory remarks attached to it.[121] Also included is the requirement that the parties are given an opportunity to express their views on the information on which the award is based.[122] In addition, the arbitral tribunal may not hear a party's submissions in the other party's absence, unless the other party has been given an opportunity to attend **9.116**

119 See Van den Berg/Van Delden/Snijders 6–8.
120 Snijders, Loose-leaf, Art 1039, explanatory note 1.
121 Hof Amsterdam, 16 July 1992, (1993) *TvA* 40.
122 HR 18 June 1993, *NJ* 1994, 449.

such hearing.[123] An arbitrator is also restricted from discussing anything concerning the dispute with a party or its legal counsel outside the arbitral proceedings.[124]

9.117 Whether or not a provision is mandatory follows from the Arbitration Act's text. A provision is supplementary if it uses the formula 'unless the parties have agreed otherwise' or another similar wording. In principle, a provision is mandatory if the aforementioned formula is absent. However, a provision without the formula is only 'in principle' mandatory. In other words, whether a provision is mandatory must be determined on a provision by provision basis. The words 'in principle' leave ample discretion to do so.[125]

9.118 With respect to the conduct of the arbitral proceedings, the requirements concerning due process and fair trial under Art 1039, para 1 Rv mentioned above are mandatory in nature. The provision of Art 1039, para 2 Rv should also be considered as mandatory. It provides that a party's request for an oral presentation cannot be denied, except in the case of quality arbitration. The provisions on the examination of witnesses (Art 1039, para 3 Rv and Art 1041 Rv) and experts (Art 1039, para 3 Rv and Art 1042 Rv) are also mandatory, taking into consideration the general rule with regard to the aforementioned formula.

9.119 Arguably, Art 1038 Rv, which defines the parties' representation in arbitral proceedings, is mandatory. If correct, Art 1038, para 1 Rv would not allow parties' agreements (including Arbitration Rules) which demand legal representation and assistance.[126]

9.120 On the basis of the general rule concerning the use of the criterion 'unless the parties have agreed otherwise', the following provisions would seem to be mandatory: default of a party in the arbitral proceedings (Art 1040 Rv); personal appearance of the parties (Art 1043 Rv); request for information on foreign law (Art 1044 Rv); joinder and intervention of third parties in the arbitral proceedings (Art 1045 Rv); and time limit for making the award (Art 1048 Rv).[127] It should be noted, however, that the provision on consolidation (Art 1046 Rv) is not mandatory, and accordingly, the parties have the discretion to exclude consolidation (Art 1046, para 1 *in fine* Rv).

9.121 There are also mandatory provisions outside the section which relates to the arbitral proceedings (Arts 1036–1048 Rv). Such as, for example, the requirement that there must be an uneven number of arbitrators for arbitral proceedings which take place in the Netherlands (Art 1026, para 1 Rv). In addition, the President of the District Court's jurisdiction in the procedure for challenging arbitrators may not be excluded by an agreement of the parties, as explained above (Art 1035, para 2 Rv) (see para 9.101). In any case, the grounds for setting aside an arbitral award, listed in Art 1065 Rv, are mandatory.[128]

(3) Oral hearing or proceeding on basis of written documents

9.122 Subject to a few mandatory provisions, the parties may agree on the conduct of the proceedings. The same is true for arbitrators in the absence of an agreement between the

123 Snijders, Loose-leaf, Art 1039, explanatory note 1.
124 *id.*
125 See Van den Berg/Van Delden/Snijders 7 with reference to the parliamentary history.
126 *ibid*, 21.
127 *ibid*,19.
128 *id.*

parties. According to Art 1039, para 2 Rv, '[t]he arbitral tribunal shall, at the request of either party or on its own initiative, give the parties an opportunity of making an oral presentation'. The provision's wording implies that a tribunal cannot deny a party's request for a hearing, with the exception of quality arbitration (Art 1047).[129] A tribunal cannot reject a party's request to make an oral presentation even if it considers that an exchange of written pleadings provides sufficient information.[130]

The tribunal is able to hold hearings on its own initiative. The use of the term 'shall' and the absence of the words 'unless the parties have agreed otherwise' or another analogous phrase in Art 1039, para 2 Rv, implies that this provision is mandatory.[131] **9.123**

Moreover, the tribunal can order the parties to appear in person at any stage of the proceedings when it considers it necessary for obtaining information or when attempting to reach a settlement (Art 1043 Rv). **9.124**

(4) Power of the tribunal (in particular the chairman) to issue procedural orders

The Act does not contain provisions relating to the tribunal's power to issue procedural orders. To the extent that the parties have not agreed on the rules of procedure, the conduct of the proceedings will be determined by the arbitrator(s) (Art 1036 Rv), usually in the form of an order. It is common in arbitration, especially in arbitration involving international elements, that an arbitrator, after consulting with the parties, will determine the time limit for the parties' submissions, the date and place for examination of witnesses and other issues of a procedural nature in the form of an order.[132] **9.125**

A procedural order is not considered to be an arbitral award. Rather it is a document in which certain procedural measures are recorded. It is usually in the form of a letter by the tribunal's chairman.[133] **9.126**

(5) Distinction of substantive matters and procedural matters

Substantive matters are those pertaining to the parties' relationship. Procedural matters relate to the conduct and effect of proceedings. The Dutch Arbitration Act contains several provisions relating to substance, eg Art 1020, para 4(c) Rv on the filling of gaps in, or modification of, the legal relationship between the parties and Art 1054, para 3 Rv on the rules applicable to the dispute's substance. **9.127**

(5.1) Are the statutes of limitations substantive or procedural? The periods of limitation are substantive. They are contained in the Dutch Civil Code (Arts 3:306 *et seq*, Dutch Civil Code). **9.128**

(6) Persons able to represent a party in an arbitral proceeding

The Act contains an express provision concerning the representation and assistance of the parties in Art 1038 Rv. According to para 1 of Art 1038 Rv, the parties may appear before **9.129**

129 Sanders/Van den Berg, Art 1039, 22, n 35.
130 Sanders, *Het Nederlandse arbitragerecht* 91.
131 Van den Berg/Van Delden/Snijders 6–8.
132 Sanders, *Het Nederlandse arbitragerecht* 95.
133 *id.*

the tribunal in person, or by an attorney or any person expressly authorized in writing for this purpose may represent them. Attorneys do not require express written authorization. Presumably, a foreign lawyer, who does not require a special written power of attorney to represent his clients under the rules applicable to him, will receive equal treatment in this respect as a practising lawyer in the Netherlands.[134] According to Art 1038, para 2 Rv, any person of their choice may assist the parties. It is arguable that Art 1038 Rv is mandatory (see para 9.118).

B. Place of arbitration

(1) Determination of the place of arbitration in absence of an agreement by the parties

9.130 In the absence of the parties' choice, the arbitral tribunal will determine the place of arbitration. Deciding this also determines the place where the arbitral award shall be made (Art 1037, para 1 Rv and Art 1057, para 4(d) Rv). If no place of arbitration is determined, 'the place of making the award as stated by the arbitral tribunal in the award shall be deemed to be the place of arbitration' (Art 1037, para 2 Rv). The arbitral tribunal may hold hearings, deliberate, and examine witnesses and experts at any other place deemed appropriate, either within or outside the Netherlands (Art 1037, para 3 Rv).

(2) Importance and legal effect of place (seat) of the arbitration

9.131 The fact that the place of arbitration is situated within the Netherlands implies the applicability of Title One of the Netherlands Arbitration Act (Art 1073, para 1 Rv). The place of arbitration determines, *inter alia,* the place where an arbitral award shall be made (Art 1037, para 1 Rv and Art 1057, para 4 (d) Rv). It also determines with which Registry of a District Court a (partial) final arbitral award shall be deposited (Art 1058, para 1 (b) Rv).[135] Through the provision on the deposit of the arbitral award, the place of arbitration determines the District Court to which an application for setting aside an arbitral award must be made (Art 1064, para 2 Rv) and to which President of the District Court a request for a leave for enforcement of an arbitral award must be filed (Art 1062, para 1 Rv).

9.132 (2.1) **Are the arbitrators and parties free to convene at places other than the official seat of the arbitration?** The place of arbitration is a legal concept. It does not imply that the arbitral tribunal must hold hearings, deliberate and examine witnesses and experts at the place of arbitration (Art 1037, para 3 Rv) (para 9.129).

9.133 (2.2) **Are there visa requirements to enter the country which apply to lawyers and/or arbitrators? Where may current information on that subject be obtained?** The general requirements for obtaining a visa to enter the Netherlands also apply to lawyers and/or arbitrators participating in arbitral proceedings in the Netherlands. Normally, visa information can be obtained from any Dutch embassy.

C. Submissions, deadlines and default

(1) Contents and form of submissions (in particular request for arbitration and answer to request)

9.134 There are no specific provisions in the Act concerning the content and form of submissions, with the exception of the notice informing the other party that it has commenced arbitration

134 Sanders/Van den Berg, Art 1038, 22, n 34.
135 *ibid,* Art 1037, 21, n 33.

(see para 9.134). NAI Rules contain an express provision relating to the content and form of the request for arbitration (Art 6, paragraphs 3 and 4) and to a short answer to the request (Art 7).

(1.1) **From which point in time is a claim considered to be pending with the arbitral tribunal? What are the legal effects of such fact (eg on statutes of limitations?)** The Act contains separate provisions concerning the commencement of arbitral proceedings for cases where the parties enter into a submission agreement (Art 1024, para 2 Rv) and for cases where an arbitration clause is concluded (Art 1025 Rv). These provisions determine when arbitral proceedings will be deemed commenced, unless the parties have agreed upon another method of commencement. Therefore, in cases where the parties enter into a submission agreement, the arbitration shall be considered to have been commenced at the moment of the submission agreement's conclusion, unless the parties have agreed otherwise (Art 1024, para 2 Rv). 9.135

If the parties have concluded an arbitration clause, the arbitration is deemed to have been commenced on the date of receipt of the written notice whereby a party informs the other party that he is initiating arbitration. The notice must contain a description of the matters being submitted to arbitration (Art 1025, para 1 Rv). The parties are able to agree on another method of commencement (for example, opting for arbitration rules which provide for commencement by filing a request for arbitration with a particular arbitration institution).[136] The date of an arbitration's commencement is important for *inter alia* determining the period of time in which arbitrators must be appointed in accordance with Art 1027, para 2 Rv. Under NAI Rules, arbitration proceedings are commenced when the request for arbitration is received by the NAI secretariat (Art 6, para 2). 9.136

(1.2) **When is a time limit according to statutes of limitations deemed to be interrupted in case of (i) *ad hoc*; and (ii) institutional arbitration?** If the commencement of legal proceedings interrupts a time limit, the commencement of arbitration—pursuant to the Dutch statute of limitation—also interrupts a time limit (cf Arts 3:316 *et seq* Dutch Civil Code). The question when the arbitration is considered to have been commenced under the Dutch Act has already been addressed (see para 9.86). The relevant provisions of Articles 1024, para 2 Rv (in the case of a submission agreement) and 1025, para 1 Rv (in the case of an arbitration clause) apply only if the parties have not agreed upon another method of commencement. 9.137

Thus, in the case of *ad hoc* arbitration, the relevant provisions of the Act will apply only if the parties have not agreed upon another method of commencement. If the parties have chosen a set of arbitration rules suitable for *ad hoc* arbitration (eg the UNCITRAL Arbitration Rules), the commencement of arbitration will be determined in accordance with these rules. For example, under the UNCITRAL Rules, Art 3(3) of the Rules will apply, irrespective of the question whether the parties concluded an arbitration clause or a submission agreement. 9.138

[136] Sanders/Van den Berg, Art 1025, 14, n 13.

9.139 In the case of institutional arbitration, the parties opt for the rules of a particular institution to be applicable to the arbitral proceedings. In doing so, they also agree to the method governing the commencement of arbitration as provided for in these rules. Accordingly, the rules of the arbitral institution prevail, and as a consequence, Art 4(2) of the 1998 ICC Rules applies (if the parties referred to these Rules).

9.140 (1.3) **What is the effect of the withdrawal of the request for arbitration?** The Arbitration Act does not contain any provision on withdrawing the request for arbitration. Pursuant to Art 35 of the NAI Rules the claimant may withdraw his request for arbitration so long as the respondent has not submitted a statement of defence or, in cases where the arbitration does not take place on the basis of written submissions, so long as a hearing has not been held. Thereafter, withdrawal of the request for arbitration shall be possible only with the express consent of the respondent. By withdrawing the request for arbitration, as far as it is allowed, the arbitral proceedings shall no longer be deemed to have been commenced (cf Art 1025, para 3 Rv) (see para 9.86).

9.141 A withdrawal of the request for arbitration might have effects on the costs incurred by the other party. If a request for arbitration has been withdrawn, the claimant can start proceedings again, unless this is prevented by expiry of limitation periods. A time limit according to statutes of limitations is not deemed to have been interrupted in the case of a withdrawal of a request for arbitration (Art 3:316, para 2 *in fine* Dutch Civil Code) (see para 9.136). If a claimant illegitimately withdraws the request for arbitration and subsequently fails to submit a statement of claim within the meaning of Art 1040, para 1 Rv (see para 9.144) then the arbitral tribunal may terminate the proceedings by means of an arbitral award.

(2) Legal deadlines (provided by law or set by the tribunal) and effect of non-compliance by a party

9.142 The Act does not provide any legal deadlines in connection with the conduct of arbitral proceedings. Thus, the arbitral tribunal may determine the time limits in the absence of the parties' agreement, subject to due process requirements. The only deadline in the Act concerns the pleas as to the arbitral tribunal's jurisdiction. A party who appeared in the arbitral proceedings shall raise a plea that the arbitral tribunal lacks jurisdiction before submitting a defence; thereafter that party will generally be barred from raising this plea in the arbitral proceedings or in proceedings before the court (Arts 1052, paras 2 and 3 Rv) (see para 9.58).

9.143 The Act does not provide a time limit for making an award. According to Art 1048 Rv, the arbitral tribunal is expressly empowered to determine the time when the arbitral award will be made. However, the parties can agree to terminate the arbitral tribunal's mandate if it conducts the proceedings 'in an unacceptably slow manner' (Art 1031, para 2 Rv).

9.144 Besides the provision of Art 1040 Rv, which deals with the default of a party (both of the claimant and of the defendant), there are no specific provisions addressing deadlines and the effects of non-compliance. It is a generally accepted principle that the parties are free to determine the rules of the arbitral proceedings, and, in the absence of such choice, the arbitrators are empowered to do so. It may be concluded that this principle applies also with respect to deadlines and the consequences of non-compliance, providing that the basic principles of due process (such as an equal treatment of the parties and the obligation of providing an opportunity for each party to present his case) are not violated. Accordingly, deadlines can be determined by agreement between the parties and, in the absence of this, by the arbitrators. The same is true for the consequence of non-compliance with the deadlines. For the powers of the tribunal under the Act in case of the claimant's default to submit a statement of claim and the defendant's default to submit a statement of defence, see para 9.144.

(2.1) What are the tribunal's powers if a party fails to comply with the time limits it sets up? Article 1040 Rv relates to the parties' default; whereby, a claimant's default is dealt with in para 1 and a defendant's default in paras 2 and 3. If the claimant, who has been given a reasonable opportunity to communicate his statement of claim or an explanation of it, fails to do so without being able to show a good cause for such failure, 'the arbitral tribunal may terminate the arbitral proceedings by means of an arbitral award' (Art 1040, para 1 Rv). The power of the arbitrator(s) in this respect is discretionary.[137] **9.145**

The defendant's failure to submit the statement of defence, despite being given a reasonable opportunity to do so and without showing good cause for this default, may result in a default award (Art 1040, para 2 Rv). A default award has the same effect as any other award.[138] The arbitrator's power is discretionary. Thus, a defendant's failure to submit the defence will not prevent the arbitrator from rendering an award, provided that the defendant has been duly informed about the arbitral proceedings and has been given a reasonable opportunity to present his defence. The defendant's failure (indicated in Art 1040, para 2 Rv) could, but does not inevitably, result in an award in the claimant's favour. The arbitral tribunal is able to render an award in the claimant's favour, 'unless it considers the claim to be unlawful or unfounded' (Art 1040, para 3). The tribunal can request that the claimant submit evidence supporting his allegation(s). **9.146**

Besides Art 1040 Rv, there are no other provisions concerning the powers of the tribunal in circumstances of non-compliance with time limits. Within their discretion, the arbitrators can either reject or extend the time limits in order to consider the submissions filed outside the given deadline, provided that the requirements of due process are not thereby violated. **9.147**

(2.2) Is the tribunal bound by any mandatory time limits for certain procedural steps (eg hearings, making of the award)? There are no mandatory time limits for any procedural steps governed by the Act. In addition, the tribunal is free to determine the time when an award shall be made (Art 1048 Rv). However, the agreement of the parties may terminate the tribunal's mandate if the proceedings are conducted in an unacceptably slow manner (Art 1031, para 2 Rv). **9.148**

(3) Statutory requirements as to notifications during an arbitration (with respect to the request for arbitration and other written pleadings; with respect to notifications by the tribunal)

In the case of an arbitration clause, the arbitration is deemed to have commenced on the day of receipt of a notice in writing in which a party informs the other that he is commencing **9.149**

137 Sanders/Van den Berg, Art 1040, 23, n 40.

138 *ibid*, n 41.

arbitration (Art 1025, para 1 Rv). If the parties have agreed that a third person shall appoint the arbitrator(s), or any of them, the party who commences the arbitration shall send to this third person a copy of the aforementioned notice (Art 1025, para 2 Rv). In the case of a submission agreement, either party shall send to the third person a copy of the submission agreement (Art 1024, para 3 Rv).

9.150 A person who has been appointed as arbitrator or secretary and who presumes that he could be challenged shall, if the parties have not previously been notified, immediately notify the parties about the existence of the grounds for the challenge (Art 1034, para 2 Rv). In case of a challenge of an arbitrator, the challenge and the corresponding grounds shall be notified in writing by the challenging party to the challenged arbitrator, the other members of the arbitral tribunal, the other party and, if a third person has appointed the challenged arbitrator, such third person (Art 1035, para 1 Rv).

9.151 Regarding the provisions concerning the conduct of proceedings (Arts 1036–1048 Rv), the communication of certain documents is mentioned in Arts 1041, para 3 Rv (communication by the Clerk of the District Court is communication of a copy of the witnesses examination record); 1042, paras 1 and 3 Rv (the tribunal's communication of a copy of the appointment and the terms of reference of the experts and a copy of the expert's report); 1045, para 1 Rv (communication by the tribunal); 1045, para 2 Rv (communication by a party of notification of joinder) and; 1046, para 2 Rv (communication by the President of the District Court in Amsterdam of his decision concerning the consolidation of arbitral proceedings).

(4) Effect of a party's insolvency

9.152 In principle, commencement of an insolvency proceeding entails a limitation of the debtor's right of management and disposal of the property comprising the estate. One of the consequences of commencing bankruptcy liquidation (*faillissement*) is that the right to manage and dispose of the estate passes to the trustee (*curator*) (Art 23 of the Bankruptcy Act, ie the *Faillissementswet*). The debtor's undertakings carried out after the bankruptcy order has been made do not effect the estate, unless and to the extent that it is beneficial for the estate (Art 24 of the Bankruptcy Act). Accordingly, the debtor can neither enter into an arbitration agreement nor can he be a party to arbitral proceedings, either pending ones or those to be initiated, to the extent that such undertakings concern disputes involving the estate. Such legal actions are to be performed by the trustee, who may, however, need to obtain the opinion of the creditors' committee (Arts 78, para 1 and 79 of the Bankruptcy Act) and the authorization of the bankruptcy judge (*rechter-commissaris*) (Art 68, para 2 of the Bankruptcy Act) to institute, defend or continue already instituted legal actions, with the exception of verification disputes.

9.153 The Bankruptcy Act does not specially mention arbitral proceedings. According to the Bankruptcy Act's relevant provisions, pending legal proceedings are suspended after the bankruptcy procedure's commencement. The same Act also contains provisions concerning the continuation of the pending proceedings on the estate's behalf (Art 27) and those against the debtor in respect of the claims other than those for payment from the estate (Art 28).

Pending proceedings involving monetary claims against the estate will be suspended and, if the claim is contested in the verification procedure, will be continued (Art 29).[139] Accordingly, it may be concluded that the pending arbitral proceedings may also be continued. This does not mean that the arbitral tribunal must conduct arbitral proceedings as determined by the relevant provisions of the Bankruptcy Act, but rather, that it would be prudent to consider these provisions when deciding on the conduct of proceedings. In any case, the tribunal should ensure that the requirements of due process are not violated (in particular, providing the opportunity for a party to present his case, bearing in mind the approvals that the trustee may need to obtain) and to avoid a violation of the basic principles of insolvency law (eg the principle *par conduit creditor*).[140] An award rendered in violation of such principles may be subject to challenge for violating public policy (Art 1065, para 1(e) of the Arbitration Act). **9.154**

In the case of the procedure for a suspension of payment (*surséance van betaling*), pending proceedings are not suspended (Art 231, para 1 of the Bankruptcy Act). However, the debtor may not initiate or take part in the proceedings concerning the estate, either on behalf of or against the estate, without the participation of the administrator (*bewindvoerder*) (Art 231, para 3 of the Bankruptcy Act). **9.155**

D. Facts and evidence: general

(1) Burden of proof (inquisitorial/adversarial procedure)

There are no provisions in the Act expressly dealing with the burden of proof. The tribunal has the discretion to decide which evidence rules are to be applied, in the absence of the parties' agreement providing otherwise (Art 1039, para 5 Rv). As indicated previously, the arbitral proceedings are to be conducted in the manner agreed upon by the parties or by the tribunal to the extent the parties have not agreed, subject to the requirements pertaining to due process. From this it can be concluded that these general rules will also apply to the burden of proof and the use of an inquisitorial or adversarial procedure.[141] **9.156**

(2) Power of the tribunal to determine the admissibility and weight of the evidence produced by the parties

The arbitral tribunal may, on its own initiative and in certain circumstances, issue orders during the proceedings, even though a request by a party has not been made. The appointment of one or more experts (Art 1042, para 1 Rv) or an order that the parties appear in person for the purpose of, *inter alia*, providing information (Art 1043 Rv) are both examples **9.157**

139 Ynzonides, M., 'De invloed van faillietverklaring op arbitrage', (1991) 6008 *Weekblad voor privaatrecht, notariaat en registratie* (*WPNR*) 390, 392 (Ynzonides); Sanders, *Het Nederlandse arbitragerecht* (4th edn, Kluwer, Deventer, 2001) 42–3; Rossem, W. Van and Cleveringa, R.P., *Verklaring van het Nederlands Weboek van Burgerlijke Rechtsvordering* (4th edn, R.P. Cleveringa, Zwolle, 1972) Art 620, 1327, note 4. (Van Rossem/Cleveringa).

140 For more particulars on the relationship between insolvency procedure and arbitration, see Lazić, *Insolvency Proceedings and Commercial Arbitration* (n 61) 126, 164–7, 242–3, 284–5 (with references to doctrine and case law).

141 See for a detailed study of the taking of evidence in arbitral proceedings under Dutch arbitration law Fung Fen Chung, C.S.K., *Bewijsmiddelen in het arbitral geding* (SDU Uitgevers, The Hague, 2004) (Fung).

of the tribunals' independent capacity. The tribunal also has the power to call and examine witnesses if a party fails to request so.[142]

9.158 However, some authors have not favoured the tribunal's extensive use of this discretionary power. It is argued that such conduct could be 'in contravention of the passivity, which the arbitrators must also observe'.[143] Also, it is held that the tribunal should take action itself only exceptionally, for example, when a witness' testimony is particularly important for the decision.[144]

9.159 Pursuant to Art 1039, para 5 Rv, the rules of evidence to be applied are at the tribunal's discretion, unless the parties have agreed otherwise. Accordingly, the tribunal has the power to determine the admissibility, weight and relevance of the evidence the parties produce, unless otherwise agreed by them.[145] It is said that the parties' stipulations in the contract, providing that written evidence or authentic deeds are required, must be taken into account.[146] Also, the view has been expressed that the tribunal is bound by the statutory requirements which are considered to be public policy requirements, such as the requirement of written form for certain deeds (eg obligatory written form for the testaments).[147]

9.160 The rules of evidence which courts apply do not bind the arbitral tribunal, unless the parties have made a contrary stipulation. According to the prevailing view, besides the aforementioned agreement between the parties, there is also another restriction to this generally accepted rule. This view maintains that the tribunal should apply the same rules of evidence as a court would apply when deciding on the validity of an arbitration agreement (especially Art 1021 Rv). A decision on this matter is a decision on jurisdiction, which the court may review, by the court. For this reason, the tribunal should apply the same rules as the court uses.[148]

9.161 **(2.1) Is the tribunal entitled to take the claimant's factual allegation as proven if the defendant does not participate in the arbitral proceedings?** As already explained in connection with the defendant's default to submit the statement of defence, the tribunal may, but does not necessarily have to, render a default award. The tribunal may require the claimant to produce evidence in order to support his claims (Art 1040, para 3). Accordingly, the defendant's default 'will not automatically be treated as an admission of the claimant's allegations'.[149] It should be noted that the fact that the defendant does not participate in the proceedings and, as a consequence, does not contest the jurisdiction should not prevent the tribunal from scrutinizing its own jurisdiction.[150]

---

142 See Snijders, Loose-leaf, Art 1039, explanatory note 3.

143 Van den Berg/Van Delden/Snijders 59.

144 *id.*

145 Sanders, *Het Nederlandse arbitragerecht* 106–7.

146 Van den Berg/Van Delden/Snijders 59.

147 Snijders, Loose-leaf, Art 1039, explanatory note 5. In a similar vein, it is said that the arbitrators are bound by statutory provisions concerning evidence and probative value, to the extent that these provisions may not be deviated from (eg marriage contracts, wills and deeds of gifts). Van den Berg/Van Delden/Snijders 60.

148 Snijders, Loose-leaf, Art 1039, explanatory note 5, 316; Van den Berg, *Int Handbook on Comm Arb* 17; Van den Berg/van Delden/Snijders 60.

149 Sanders/Van den Berg, Art 1040, 23, note 42.

150 Sanders, *Het Nederlandse arbitragerecht* 24–5.

There are no express provisions in the Act limiting the parties' freedom to present evidence, except as already indicated in the few basic requirements relating to due process under Art 1039, para 1 Rv. **9.162**

(2.2) May the arbitral tribunal consider an allegation of one party as agreed fact if the other party did not (specifically) dispute the allegation? There are no specific provisions on this issue either in the Act or in the NAI Rules. Presumably the arbitrators will take into consideration all the circumstances of a particular case when deciding whether a certain fact is disputed or not. If from the circumstance of a particular case (eg documents submitted, correspondence between the parties etc) certain facts appear controversial, it would be difficult to consider it an agreed fact merely because a particular allegation is not specifically disputed. **9.163**

(2.3) What is the standard of proof that must be met in order for a fact to be considered to have been established (ie preponderance of the evidence, beyond reasonable doubt)? Must a stringent requirement be met for certain facts? There are no rules concerning the standard of proof in arbitration. See further para 9.158. **9.164**

(2.4) May the arbitral tribunal rely on its own knowledge to consider certain facts as proven? It is argued that the arbitral tribunal may only rely on its own knowledge if it has informed the party and if the parties were given the opportunity to be heard (cf Art 1039, para 1 Rv).[151] An exception to this rule could be made for facts of general knowledge and facts based on general experience. **9.165**

E. Witnesses

(1) Ability of a person to act as a witness

The Act contains no provision pertaining to persons' ability to act as a witness. Presumably, any person who can provide information that may be needed in ascertaining relevant facts in the dispute concerned may appear as a witness. As to the question of who may testify and who is obligated to testify, it is argued that Art 165 Rv, which applies to court proceedings, should be taken into consideration.[152] Article 165 Rv enumerates the reasons for which a person may be exempted from the obligation to testify. This opinion may be based on Art 1041, para 2 Rv. Pursuant to Art 1040, para 2 Rv the court may examine witnesses who do not appear voluntarily or refuse to give evidence. The examination shall take place in the same manner as in ordinary court proceedings. It is arguable that Art 165 Rv forms part of the 'same manner as in ordinary court proceedings'. **9.166**

The application of Art 164 Rv according to which the parties may be examined as witnesses is not recommended for arbitral proceedings. Generally, the parties testifying in arbitral proceedings is not a favoured approach (see para 9.167). Whether or not a party will be allowed to produce witnesses depends on the arbitral tribunal's decision (Art 1039, para 3 **9.167**

151 Snijders/Buruma 80–5.
152 Snijders, Loose-leaf, Art 1039, explanatory note 3.

Rv);[153] although, it is unlikely that the arbitral tribunal will reject evidence which the witnesses or experts submitted.[154]

9.168 (1.1) **Is there a legal difference between a party testifying and a witness? If yes, what are the criteria for such differentiation? Does the testifying of a party have the same weight as a witness testimony?** There is no provision in the Act differentiating between a party testifying and a witness. Generally, it is up to the tribunal to evaluate what weight will to be given to evidence (see para 9.158). Accordingly, the tribunal may consider the value to be attached to a party's statements.[155] The appropriateness, effectiveness and necessity of the parties' testimony in arbitral proceedings are seriously doubted. In particular, party testimony is considered unnecessary, in light of the fact that there is usually an opportunity for the parties to appear in person, and thereby, provide the relevant information. In these circumstances the only difference is that a party may not be examined on oath or affirmation when ordered to appear in person; whereas, a party may give sworn evidence when testifying as a witness. However, the relevance of the difference is questionable.[156]

(2) Preparation of witnesses and corresponding limits

9.169 The Arbitration Act does not contain any provision on the witness preparation and corresponding limits. However, from Art 1041, para 1 *in fine* Rv, it results that a witness shall tell the whole truth and nothing but the truth. It seems that this provision sets the limits of the preparation of witnesses. Preparing a witness which leads to a false testimony may result in setting aside the arbitral award on the ground that the award, or the manner in which the award was made, violates public policy (Art 1065, para 1(e) Rv). On the same ground, an arbitral award's enforcement may be refused (see para 9.326). Further, revocation of the award can take place if the award is wholly or partially based on fraud which is discovered after the award is made and which is committed during the arbitral proceedings by or with the knowledge of the other party (Art 1068, para 1(a) Rv).

9.170 (2.1) **Do US-style depositions violate any procedural rules or principles?** If witness examination takes place, the arbitral tribunal shall determine the time, the place and the manner in which the examination shall proceed (Art 1041, para 1 Rv). US-style depositions (understood as the examination of witnesses by lawyers, in the presence of only a court reporter, who takes the oath from the witnesses and who records their statements), would then be allowed if the arbitral tribunal thus determined the manner of the examination. However, from Art 1039, para 3 Rv it can be concluded that at least one arbitrator must examine the witness(es). Article 1039, para 3 Rv provides that the arbitral tribunal has the power to designate one of its members to examine witnesses or experts.[157]

9.171 (2.2) **May a party or its counsel approach a witness whom it has nominated (only before or also after the proceeding has started)? Are interviews permitted?** The Arbitration

[153] See also, Snijders, H.J. and Meijer, G.J., (eds), 'Arbitrage', *Vademecum Burgerlijk Procesrecht*, (Kluwer, Deventer, 2002) 54 (Snijders/Meijer).

[154] Sanders/Van den Berg, Art 1039, 22, note 36.

[155] Sanders, *Quo vadis arbitration* 260.

[156] Delden, R. Van, *Internationale handelsarbitrage* (Kluwer, Deventer, 1997) 68, n 134 (Van Delden).

[157] Van den Berg/Van Delden/Snijders 59.

Act does not contain any provision on approaching a witness. According to the Dutch Rules of Conduct of Lawyers *(Advocaten)* 1992, persons who have been summoned by the other party to appear in court as witnesses, or who will apparently be so summoned, may not be examined by the lawyer prior to the hearing (Rule 16, para 1). This provision does not apply to a lawyer's own client or to persons employed by or having a special relationship with such client (Rule 16, para 3).

(3) Admissibility of written witness statements

There is no express provision in the Act relating to the admissibility of written statements. Following the general rule provided for in Art 1039, para 1 Rv, the tribunal is free to determine the admissibility, weight and relevance of the evidence submitted, unless the parties have agreed otherwise. The admissibility of written statements is also to be determined by the tribunal, unless the parties' agreement otherwise so provides (cf also Art 4, para 4 IBA Rules on the Taking of Evidence in International Commercial Arbitration). **9.172**

(3.1) If the parties agree on written statements, is a party entitled to request an oral hearing for questioning those witnesses (provided such right has not been agreed upon)? There are no provisions in the Act implying that the written witness statements violate any procedural rules or principles. In principle, the fact that there is a written statement or a sworn affidavit of a witness does not mean that a personal appearance of that witness is unnecessary or redundant (cf also Art 4, paras 7–9 IBA Rules on the Taking of Evidence in International Commercial Arbitration).[158] In particular, a personal appearance provides the opportunity to question the witness on specific issues. From Art 1039, para 3 Rv, it may be concluded that a party can, in principle, request that such witness appear in person for questioning. **9.173**

(4) Entitlement of a party to have a hearing, examination and cross-examination of witnesses

As explained previously (see para 9.108), a party cannot be denied the right to a hearing, ie an opportunity for a party to make an oral presentation (Art 1039, para 2 Rv). With respect to the personal appearance of a witness, this issue falls within the discretion of the tribunal, unless the parties have agreed otherwise according to the general provision of Art 1039, para 5 Rv. The same is true with respect to the question of a party's entitlement to have a cross-examination. In other words, although the tribunal determines the manner in which examination is to proceed (Art 1041, para 1 Rv), the parties may agree on the method of hearing witnesses, and, therefore, the examination and cross-examination of witnesses.[159] In the absence of a parties' agreement as to the method of hearing, it is at the tribunal's discretion to determine and decide on the request for cross-examination. **9.174**

The examination of witnesses is dealt with in Art 1041 Rv. The arbitral tribunal determines the time, place and the manner of examination (Art 1041, para 1 Rv). However, the parties can agree on other methods of hearing witnesses.[160] If the tribunal deems it necessary, the witnesses will be examined on oath or affirmation (see para 9.176). The principle of equal **9.175**

158 Sanders, *Quo vadis arbitration* 259.
159 Sanders/Van den Berg, Art 1041, 24, note 43.
160 *ibid.*

treatment of the parties also applies to the examination of witnesses. This means that, if a person is examined as a witness, the tribunal must, on its own motion, give the other party the opportunity to bring rebuttal witnesses, if necessary at a later stage.[161] In situations where a witness refuses to appear or testify voluntarily, there is the opportunity for a party, with the permission of the arbitral tribunal, to apply for the appointment of a judge before whom the examination of the witness will take place. The particularities of such a case are provided in Art 1041, paras 2–4 Rv, 176.

9.176 (4.1) **Which are the methods used to establish a record of the arbitral proceedings, in particular witness examinations (tape recording, verbatim court reporters, dictated minutes, other methods)?** To our knowledge there is no general method of recording arbitral proceedings. The Arbitration Act does not contain any provision on the record of the proceedings. In international arbitration verbatim court reporters are a frequently used method of establishing a record of the proceedings. If one of the members of the arbitral tribunal examines a witness on the basis of Art 1039, para 3 Rv (see para 9.169), it is advised that the testimony be recorded (in a transcript or minutes).[162]

9.177 (4.2) **May an arbitrator take an oath from a witness?** Article 1041, para 1 Rv expressly provides that, if the arbitral tribunal deems it necessary, it shall examine the witnesses, after they have sworn, in the manner provided by the law, to tell the whole truth and nothing but the truth. This provision also applies to expert witnesses (Art 1042, para 6 Rv).[163]

9.178 (4.3) **Does the arbitral tribunal have the power to compel witnesses?** The arbitral tribunal is not empowered to compel witnesses. However, the Act does provide that the tribunal may allow a party upon request to petition, within the time limit determined by the arbitral tribunal, the President of the District Court to appoint a judge (*rechter-commissaris*) before whom the examination of a witness will be held, if the witness does not appear voluntarily or does appear, but refuses to give evidence before the tribunal. The examination has to take place in accordance with the rules that apply in ordinary court proceedings.

9.179 The Clerk of the District Court will ensure that the arbitrator(s) are given an opportunity to attend the witness examination (Art 1041, para 2 Rv). A copy of the record of the examination will be communicated without delay to the parties and to the arbitral tribunal by the Clerk of the District Court (Art 1041, para 3 Rv). The tribunal may suspend the (arbitral) proceedings until the day of the record of the examination's receipt (Art 1041, para 4 Rv).

F. Documents

(1) Form and kind of documents to be presented to the arbitral tribunal

9.180 The Act expressly provides that the tribunal has the power to order the submission of documents (Art 1039, para 4 Rv). There is no provision concerning the form of documents to be presented. Generally, the parties may agree on the manner for the production of documents.[164]

---

[161] HR 25 May 2007, *NJ* 2007, 294.

[162] Sanders/Van den Berg, Art 1039, 23, note 36.

[163] *ibid*, Art 1041, 24, note 43.

[164] *ibid*, Art 1039, 23, note 37; Van den Berg, *Int Handbook on Comm Arb* 17.

If the parties have not agreed on the form in which documents are to be presented, the tribunal will make the determination.

(1.1) Is the submission of 'agreed documents' permitted? If yes, what is the extent and effect of such an agreement of the parties (authenticity, existence, acknowledgement of such documents' contents)? From Art 1039, para 5 Rv, which provides that the parties are free to set the rules of evidence, it can be concluded that 'agreed documents' will be admissible. Whether this leads to a violation of public policy must be determined in each individual case. **9.181**

(1.2) How may electronic documents (eg emails) be presented and proven? As already explained, the tribunal has the discretion to decide which evidentiary rules will apply, including the admissibility of and the manner in which the evidence will be presented, in the absence of the parties' agreement providing otherwise (Art 1039, para 5 Rv). The same is true with respect to the manner in which emails will be presented and proven. Normally, the parties will be requested to submit a copy of emails and other electronic documents. **9.182**

(1.3) Does discovery (US- or UK-style), after the procedure has started, violate any procedural rules or public policy considerations? Article 1039, para 4 Rv provides that the arbitral tribunal shall have the power to order the production of documents. This provision can be understood to mean—and has so been understood—that the Anglo-American system of the discovery or disclosure of documents will be possible under the Dutch Arbitration Act.[165] An agreement by the parties to submit all documents in their possession to the arbitral tribunal does not violate any procedural rules or public policy considerations. **9.183**

(2) Requirement to produce certain documents (as requested by the tribunal) and consequences of a failure to do so

If a party does not comply with the order to submit documents, the tribunal may draw the conclusions it deems appropriate.[166] In this context it is appropriate to mention Art 1068, para 1 Rv, which lists the grounds for the revocation of the award. One ground for revocation, ground (c), arises when a party after an award is rendered, obtains documents which would have influenced the decision of the arbitral tribunal and which were withheld as a result of the other party's acts. **9.184**

The Act contains no express provision concerning the protection of confidentiality of documents. **9.185**

(2.1) Which documents may the tribunal request to be produced (eg also documents which are in the possession of third parties)? The provision of Art 1039 para 4 states that the tribunal shall have the power to order the production of documents, but does not state which documents may be ordered to be produced. Considering the consensual nature of arbitration, such an order may be directed to the parties to an arbitration agreement, and not to third parties. If the order is not complied with, the arbitral tribunal may draw its own conclusions.[167] **9.186**

---

165 See Van den Berg/Van Delden/Snijders 59 (with a reference to doctrine).

166 Sanders/Van den Berg, Art 1039, 23, note 37; Snijders, Loose-leaf, Art 1039, explanatory note 4, 315; Van den Berg, *Int Handbook on Comm Arb* 17.

167 Sanders/Van den Berg, Art 1039, 23, note 37.

9.187 *(3) Protection of the confidentiality of documents (legal privilege etc)*

It is not clear which rules apply to the attorney-client privilege. Pursuant to Arts 165 Rv and 843*a* para 3 Rv, which apply to ordinary court proceedings, a lawyer/attorney is not obliged to give evidence as a witness nor is he obliged to produce documents. It is arguable that Arts 165 and 843*a* para 3 Rv apply by analogy if the place of arbitration is situated in the Netherlands. Art 165 and 843*a* para 3 Rv apply to legal privilege, but also, *inter alia*, to family privilege, medical and clerical privilege. In addition, parties may refuse to provide documents for serious reasons, for example in the case of trade secrets. It is up to the tribunal's discretion whether the reasons presented by the parties are sufficiently serious.[168]

G. Experts

9.188 Article 1042 Rv governs the arbitral tribunal's appointment of experts. In order to obtain advice, the tribunal may appoint one or more experts. It will communicate a copy of the appointment and the terms of reference to the parties as soon as possible (para 1). Normally, the tribunal will consult the parties about the person to be appointed, as well as about the expert's terms of reference before the actual appointment is made (see also para 187).[169]

(1) Appointment and presentation of experts by the party or the tribunal

9.189 The Act contains separate provisions concerning party-presented experts (expert witnesses) (Art 1039 para 3 Rv) and tribunal-appointed experts (Art 1042 Rv). The parties are able to file with the arbitral tribunal a request to produce witnesses or experts. The tribunal decides whether or not to allow it (Art 1039, para 3 Rv), but it would be unlikely that such a request would be refused.[170] The tribunal may designate one of its members to examine witnesses or experts (Art 1039, para 3 Rv), in order to save costs when witnesses or experts reside abroad. In these situations testimony may be recorded either by transcript or minutes.[171]

9.190 Either party can request for the expert to be examined at the hearing. The party making the request has to inform the tribunal and the other party thereof without delay (para 4). At the hearing, the parties will be given the opportunity to question the tribunal-appointed expert and to provide their own experts (expert witnesses in the meaning of Art 1039, para 3 Rv) (para 5).

9.191 **(1.1) By which methods are tribunal-appointed experts selected? What are the rights of the parties during the selection process?** No method for the selection of tribunal-appointed experts is mentioned in the Act. Presumably, this function is left to the discretion of the tribunal, with the caveat that the requirements of due process or fair trial will not be violated. For example, an appointment of a partial or biased expert may violate the requirement of the equal treatment of the parties expressed in Art 1039, para 1 Rv. The Act provides that the tribunal must inform the parties without delay about the appointment and the terms of reference of the experts (Art 1042, para 1 Rv). In general, however, the tribunal will usually consult the parties before the actual appointment has taken place.[172]

168 *Parl Gesch Herz Rv* 157.
169 Van den Berg, *Int Handbook on Comm Arb* 18.
170 Sanders/Van den Berg, Art 1039, 22, note 36.
171 *id.*
172 Van den Berg, *Int Handbook on Comm Arb* 18.

(2) Admissibility and role of expert witnesses

The parties may request that the tribunal allow them to present expert witnesses (Art 1039, para 3 Rv). It is at the arbitral tribunal's discretion to grant the request. In practice, it is unlikely that the tribunal would refuse a party's application to present expert witnesses (see also para 191).[173] **9.192**

The experts are to be examined at a hearing if either party so requests. The party wishing to make the request must inform the tribunal and the other party without delay (Art 1042, para 4 Rv). The parties will be given an opportunity to examine the tribunal appointed experts and to produce their own experts (so-called expert witnesses in the meaning of Art 1039, para 3 Rv) (Art 1042, para 5 Rv). **9.193**

The time, the place of the examination and the manner in which the examination proceeds shall be determined by the arbitral tribunal. If necessary, the arbitral tribunal shall examine the experts after they have sworn to tell the whole truth and nothing but the truth (para 6). **9.194**

(3) The parties' influence upon the selection of questions to be submitted to the expert

Article 1042 para 1 Rv may give some guidance with respect the involvement of the parties in deciding which questions shall be submitted to the expert. Pursuant to Art 1042, para 1 Rv, the arbitral tribunal shall communicate as soon as possible to the parties a copy of the experts' appointment and the terms of reference. From this provision it may be concluded that the arbitral tribunal decides which questions shall be submitted to the expert. However, the tribunal will usually consult the parties about the person to be appointed as well as the expert's terms of reference before the actual appointment is made (see also paras 187–188). **9.195**

The tribunal may request a party's cooperation in providing to the expert the information he needs (para 2). If the party fails to comply with such request, it is up to the tribunal to draw its own conclusions.[174] A copy of the expert's report will be communicated to the parties without delay (para 3). **9.196**

Either party can request for the expert to be examined at the hearing. The party making the request has to inform the tribunal and the other party thereof without delay (para 4). At the hearing, the parties will be given the opportunity to examine the tribunal-appointed expert and to provide their own experts (expert witnesses in the meaning of Art 1039, para 3 Rv) (para 5). **9.197**

(4) Independence and impartiality of the expert and the right to reject a proposed/appointed expert

The independence and impartiality of experts requirement is not expressly mentioned in the Act. However, the lack of impartiality and independence contravenes the principle of due process and fair trial (including the equality of the parties) (see Art 1039, para 1 Rv according to which provision the parties shall be treated with equality). An arbitral award may be set aside if the award, or the manner in which it was rendered, violates public policy (Art 1065, para 1(e) Rv). An infringement of public policy applies in both the substantive **9.198**

173 Sanders/Van den Berg, Art 1039, 22, note 36.
174 *ibid*, Art 1042, 25, note 45.

and procedural sense, with the latter case including the violation of the basic principles of due process and fair trial.[175] The parties' equality is guaranteed in several ways in Art 1042 Rv itself (see para 9.194). The requirement of independence and impartiality of experts results also from the provision which makes it possible to examine experts after they have sworn to tell the truth and nothing but the truth (Art 1042, para 6 Rv).

9.199 **(4.1) May a party or its counsel approach an expert (or expert witness) whom it has nominated (only before or also after the proceeding has started)? Are interviews admissible?** Nothing in the Act suggests that a party or his counsel are forbidden from approaching an expert witness, either before or after the proceeding has started. However, the influencing of an expert leading to a false testimony, may lead to the setting aside of the arbitral award on the ground that the award, or the manner in which the award was made, violates public policy (Art 1065, para 1(e) Rv). On the same ground enforcement of an arbitral award may be refused (see para 9.327). Further, revocation of the award can take place if the award is wholly or partially based on fraud which is discovered after the award is made and which is committed during the arbitral proceedings by or with the knowledge of the other party (Art 1068, para 1(a) Rv).

(5) Oral examination of an expert in a hearing

9.200 From the provisions on the examination of experts it may be concluded that the Arbitration Act 'expects' the experts to appear in a hearing. Art 1042, para 4 Rv provides that, at the request of either party, the experts shall be examined at a hearing and Art 1042, para 5 Rv provides that the arbitral tribunal shall give the parties an opportunity to examine the experts (cf also Art 6, para 6 IBA Rules on the Taking of Evidence in International Commercial Arbitration). The consequences of the appointed expert refusing to appear in a hearing are not provided. From the aforementioned provisions it might be concluded that a new expert must be appointed who can be examined at a hearing according to Art 1042, paragraphs 4 and 5 Rv, especially if the expert's report is significant and the arbitral tribunal wishes to base its award on this report. Under the circumstances, a violation of Art 1042, paragraphs 4 and 5 Rv in the case of a refusal of the expert to appear, might imply a violation of the right of each party to present its case in the meaning of Art 1039, para 1 Rv.

H. Interim measures of protection

(1) Kind of interim measures which the tribunal may order

9.201 Pursuant to Art 1049 Rv, the arbitral tribunal may render an interim award. There is no provision in the Act specifically stating the type of interim measures that the arbitral tribunal may order. The prevailing view in the literature is that the tribunal has no power to order conservatory attachments of assets, although it may order certain interim measures of protection.[176] An order for an immediate sale of perishable goods, which are the subject of the dispute, and an order for establishing bank guarantees are two examples of provisional

[175] Sanders/Van den Berg, Art 1065, 41, note 99.

[176] Van Delden 71; Snijders, Loose-leaf, Art 1022, explanatory note 4, 86; Van den Berg, *Int Handbook on Comm Arb* 19.

measures which the tribunal may order.[177] Decisions on these type of measures may be brought in the form of an order or an interim award.

9.202 However, orders and interim awards may not be enforced through the courts in the Netherlands. In other words it will be useful to request the tribunal to decide on the interim measure of protection in the form of an order or interim award only when it is expected that a party, against whom a measure is sought, would voluntarily comply with an order or an interim award of the tribunal. Otherwise it is more effective to apply to the President of the District Court to rule on the request in summary proceedings (*kort geding* or *référé*)[178] or to the arbitral tribunal or its chairman if the parties have agreed to empower the arbitral tribunal or its chairman to render an award in summary proceedings.

9.203 In Dutch procedural law, it is possible for a party to obtain an injunction or restraining order in a summary provisional adjudication in *référé* proceedings (*kort geding*) before the President of the District Court (Arts 254 *et seq* Rv). The decision rendered is not a decision on the merits. Instead, the purpose of this procedure is to provide a party with the opportunity to obtain immediate provisional relief in urgent cases, before the competent court has rendered a decision on the merits. It should be noted that the parties are usually not obliged to start the proceedings on the merits (within a certain time limit). Although the President of the District Court's judgment in summary proceedings is provisional, in practice the parties often consider it to be final.[179]

9.204 Article 1051, para 1 Rv provides the possibility for the parties to agree that the arbitral tribunal or its chairman may render an award in summary proceedings 'within the limits imposed by Art 254(1)'. The parties are usually not obliged to start proceedings on the merits (within a certain time limit). The parties' agreement to authorize the arbitral tribunal or its chairman to render an award in summary proceedings can be contained in the Arbitration Rules to which the parties referred to in the arbitration agreement (Art 1020, para 6 Rv). The Arbitration Rules of the Netherlands Arbitration Institute provide for summary arbitral proceedings in Art 37 (summary arbitral proceedings after the appointment of the arbitral tribunal on the merits) and Arts 42a-42o of the NAI Rules (summary arbitral proceedings before the appointment of the arbitral tribunal on the merits).[180]

9.205 An arbitration agreement does not preclude a party from applying to the President of the District Court for a decision in summary proceedings in accordance with Art 289 Rv (Art 1022, para 2 Rv). If one of the parties, notwithstanding the fact that an agreement on summary arbitral proceedings has been concluded, files a request before the President of the District Court, it will be at the discretion of the President to decide whether to refer the case to the agreed summary arbitral proceedings or to decide on the application himself (Art 1051, para 2 Rv). The President's decision referring the matter to summary arbitral proceedings is not subject to appeal (Art 1051, para 4 Rv).

177 Van den Berg, *Int Handbook on Comm Arb* 19.

178 *ibid.*

179 Snijders, *Access to Civil Procedure Abroad* 269.

180 See King, D.B. and Leeuwen, M. Van, 'Summary Arbitral Proceedings, A Powerful New Mechanism in NAI Arbitrations', (2003) 3 *Mealey's Int'l Arbitration Report* 1–8 (King/Van Leeuwen).

9.206 A decision rendered in summary arbitral proceedings is an arbitral award, which can be subjected to enforcement or setting aside by the courts (Art 1051, para 3 Rv). It is argued that an arbitral award in summary arbitral proceedings can be enforced outside of the Netherlands in accordance with the 1958 New York Convention on the Recognition and Enforcement of Foreign Arbitral Awards (see para 9.326).

9.207 (1.1) **Which are, in general, the procedural and substantive prerequisites for the ordering of interim and conservatory measures (eg reduced degree of evidence, urgency, summary evaluation of the claim)?** Article 254, para 1 Rv determines the main conditions of a claim's admissibility in summary proceedings. These conditions are broadly defined. Thus, the claim may be filed with the President of the District Court in all cases where, in the interest of the parties, instant provisional relief is required because of the urgency involved. Owing to urgency, the degree of evidence may be reduced and the claim may be evaluated summarily. Although the President of the District Court in summary proceedings usually makes a decision in which he tries to anticipate the decision in proceedings on the merits (which may be commenced later), it often happens that he allows a provision purely on the basis of a balance of the parties' interests.[181]

9.208 (1.2) **Are the prerequisites for interim measures ordered by the arbitral tribunal more or less the same as if those are requested from the state court? Is there case law/leading authorities on whether those measures are faster and enforced more easily if taken by the arbitral tribunal or the state court?** If the arbitral tribunal or its chairman is, by the parties' agreement, empowered to render an award in summary arbitral proceedings, it will do so within the limits imposed by Art 289, para 1 of the Code of Civil Procedure. It cannot be said with certainty whether an arbitral tribunal's decision (provided that it is a measure that may be ordered by the tribunal) is able to be rendered faster than a court decision when deciding on provisional measures. Usually one is of the opinion that interim measures are faster and easier achieved before the state courts. Mostly arbitrators must still be appointed after a request for interim measures before an arbitral tribunal. However, under the provisions on summary arbitral proceedings of the Arbitration Rules of the Netherlands Arbitration Institute, the administrator can expeditiously appoint an arbitral tribunal.[182]

(2) Limits of the tribunal's powers to order interim measures

9.209 As mentioned previously, there is no express provision in the Act on the types of measures that can be taken by the arbitrators. The prevailing view is that arbitrators are empowered to order interim measures (see Art 1036 Rv).[183] Under the NAI Rules, the arbitral tribunal may order measures which it considers necessary regarding the subject matter of the dispute (Art 38). It should be noted that interim awards are unenforceable through the courts in the Netherlands, as set out above (see para 9.201).

(3) Orders to provide security for the costs of the proceeding

9.210 The Arbitration Act does not contain a provision on the posting of security for the costs of the proceedings. However, it is arguable that a party may request the arbitral tribunal to

[181] Snijders, *Access to Civil Procedure Abroad* 269.
[182] See King/Van Leeuwen 1–8.
[183] Meijer, *T&C Rv*, Art 1051, no 1b.

order the posting of security for costs (in the form of an order or interim award). One should note that an order and an interim award cannot be enforced (see para 9.200). If the parties agree to empower the tribunal to render an award in summary arbitral proceedings, a party may request the posting of security for the costs related to the arbitration on the merits in summary proceedings. An arbitral award in summary proceedings can be enforced (see para 9.200). Article 37, para 1 of the NAI Rules provides that a party may request the arbitral tribunal to order the provision of security on behalf of the party who requests it, in a form to be determined by the arbitral tribunal, regarding costs related to the arbitration on the merits. The order is made in the form of an arbitral award in summary arbitral proceedings (ie an immediate provisional measure) (Art 37, para, 5 NAI Rules). On the basis of the Arbitration Rules of the Netherlands Arbitration Institute it is not possible to request security in arbitral summary proceedings for the arbitration costs related to the summary arbitral proceedings themselves (see Art 42*l*, para 2 Rv). Article 1055 Rv provides that the arbitral tribunal may determine that the enforceability of the arbitral award is subject to the giving of security, in the specific case that it declares that its award is provisionally enforceable on the ground that the parties agreed to arbitral appeal. This provision does not relate to the posting of security for costs as discussed before.

(4) Attachment of assets by an order of the tribunal

In general, arbitrators are empowered to issue orders and protective measures which are **9.211** directed to the parties to an arbitration agreement. As explained above, the prevailing view in Dutch literature is that arbitrators may not order the conservatory attachment of assets (see paras 9.200 *et seq*).

I. Assistance by the courts

(1) Extent of court assistance in the gathering of evidence

With respect to court assistance in the gathering of evidence, the Act provides the possibil- **9.212** ity of petitioning the President of the District Court to appoint a judge before whom a witness will be examined, if a witness does not appear voluntarily or does appear but does not wish to testify (Art 1041, para 2 Rv). If a party so requests, the arbitral tribunal may allow that party to address the President of the District Court within a period of time determined by the arbitral tribunal. The parties and the members of the tribunal (or sole arbitrator) must be given an opportunity to attend the examination of the witness.

A party is entitled to assistance in the examination of a witness who does not appear volun- **9.213** tarily or, having appeared, refuses to give testimony, provided that the party obtains the tribunal's permission to petition the President of the District Court to appoint a judge who will examine the witness. The tribunal will determine the time limit within which such petition is to be made (Art 1041, para 2 Rv).

(1.1) Is it for the arbitral tribunal or for the party to obtain the assistance of state courts **9.214** **with respect to the gathering of evidence?** As already explained (see paras 9.209–10), assistance may be obtained for a witness examination. The party will have to obtain permission from the arbitral tribunal to petition the President of the District Court to obtain the assistance required. It is the party itself, and not the arbitral tribunal, who has to file the petition. The Clerk of the District Court shall give the arbitrator(s) an opportunity of attending the examination of the witness(es) (Art 1041, para 2 Rv).

(2) Assistance for enforcing the attachment of assets

9.215 As mentioned previously, the arbitral tribunal does not have the power to order attachment of assets. In general, orders and interim awards of the arbitral tribunal may not be enforced by the courts (see paras 9.198 *et seq*). However, a party can request the court to grant the attachment of assets (Art 1022, para 2 Rv).

(3) Other examples of possible assistance

9.216 With respect to the arbitral proceedings (s 2, Arts 1036–1048 of the Act), the courts' assistance is provided for in the following provisions: Art 1041, paras 2–3 Rv (assistance in the examination of a witness); Art 1044 Rv (request for information on foreign law); and Art 1046 Rv (consolidation of arbitral proceedings).

9.217 Outside of s 2, which deals with arbitral proceedings, the courts' assistance is provided for in: Art 1022, para 1 Rv (declaration that the court has no jurisdiction if a valid arbitration agreement is invoked); Art 1022, para 2 Rv (request to a court to grant interim measures of protection and application to the President of the District Court for a decision in summary proceedings); Art 1026, para 2 Rv (determination of the number of arbitrators); Art 1026, para 4 Rv (appointment of additional arbitrator); Art 1027, para 3 Rv (appointment of arbitrators); Art 1028 Rv (appointment of arbitrator when an arbitration agreement gives one party a privileged position in the appointment of arbitrators); Art 1029, paragraphs 2 and 4 Rv (arbitrator's release of mandate); Art 1031, para 2 Rv (termination of the arbitral tribunal's mandate); Art 1035 Rv (challenge of arbitrators); Art 1074, para 1 Rv (declaration that the court has no jurisdiction if a valid 'foreign' arbitration agreement is invoked); Art 1074, para 2 Rv (request to a court to grant interim measures of protection and application to the President of the District Court for a decision in summary proceedings in the case of a 'foreign' arbitration agreement). The courts' role in the post-arbitral phase—to the enforcement and the challenge of an arbitral award (Arts 1062–1063 Rv and Arts 1064–1068 Rv)—is not only one of assistance, but also one of a supervisory nature.

(4) Dependence of the power of state courts to intervene during the proceedings on the (national) procedural law applied by the arbitral tribunal

9.218 The Act accepts the principle of territoriality and clearly defines its applicability. If the place of arbitration is situated in the Netherlands, the provisions of Title One of the Dutch Arbitration Act (Arts 1020–1073 Rv) shall apply. As a consequence, the provisions on the court's involvement, which are contained in Title One of the Dutch Arbitration Act, apply when the place of arbitration is situated in the Netherlands (Art 1073, para 1 Rv). However, if the parties have not determined the place of arbitration, the appointment or challenge of the arbitrator(s) or a secretary engaged by an arbitral tribunal may take place in accordance with the provisions contained in s 1 of Title One of the Dutch Arbitration Act if at least one of the parties is domiciled or has his actual residence in the Netherlands (Art 1073, para 2 Rv).

9.219 The role of the Dutch courts, in the case of arbitration which shall take place outside the Netherlands, is limited to the 'indirect enforcement' of an arbitration agreement (Art 1074, para 1 Rv), to interim measures of protection (Art 1074, para 2 Rv) and to the recognition and enforcement of foreign arbitral awards (Arts 1075 and 1076 Rv).

(1.2) According to case law and practical experience, are there considerable delays involved when asking a court to give assistance (eg for the obtaining of evidence)? The Dutch courts are mostly considered to be highly 'arbitration-friendly'. No known considerable delays are involved when asking a court to give assistance. 9.220

V. The award

A. Types of award

(1) Interim award (eg on interim measures or the jurisdiction of the tribunal)

The types of award that an arbitral tribunal may render are indicated in Art 1049 Rv, as follows: a final award, a partial final award and an interim award. An interim award may be rendered on jurisdictional issues, such as the validity of an arbitration agreement and on issues related to the gathering of evidence (such as the examination of witnesses, an expert's report, the appearance in person of parties or a site inspection).[184] Such decisions on evidence are often issued in the form of an order (often as a letter to the parties), without a formal (interim) award being rendered.[185] 9.221

If the arbitral tribunal failed to decide on one or more matters which have been submitted to it, the tribunal may, at the request of either party, render an additional award (Art 1061, para 1 Rv). An additional award shall be regarded as an arbitral award to which Articles 1049–1068 Rv shall be applicable (Art 1061, para 4 Rv). 9.222

(2) Partial award

If the claim, a part of the claim or (at least) one of the claims is decided, the award is called a final award. The arbitral tribunal may decide to separate decisions on the claim(s). For example, it may render a partial final award, for example on a part of the claim or on the first claim. The second part of the claim or the second claim is then left to be decided in a subsequent (last) final award.[186] 9.223

(2.1) Are awards, especially partial awards, binding in the same arbitral proceeding? Does it make a difference if after the rendering of such a partial award, one arbitrator is successfully challenged and removed on grounds that prevailed even before the partial award was rendered? Partial final awards are binding in the same arbitral proceedings, unless a partial final award has been set aside (cf Art 1064, para 4 Rv). It is argued that a so-called 'final decision' on a point of controversy between the parties contained in an interim award (which decision must be distinguished from a 'final award') is binding in the same arbitral proceedings. An interim award can only be set aside in conjunction with a final or partial final award (Art 1064, para 4 Rv).[187] 9.224

---

184 Van den Berg/Van Delden/Snijders 77.
185 Sanders/Van den Berg, Art 1049, 28, note 55 and Van den Berg/Van Delden/Snijders 77.
186 *id.*
187 Snijders, Loose-leaf, Art 1059, explanatory note 2.

9.225 If an arbitrator is successfully challenged, the arbitrator shall, unless the parties have agreed otherwise, be replaced in accordance with the rules governing his initial appointment (Art 1035, para 3 Rv). In case of replacement, the arbitral proceedings shall be suspended by operation of law (Art 1035, para 3 Rv in conjunction with Art 1030, para 3 Rv). The arbitral proceedings shall, after the suspension ceases, continue from the stage they had reached (Art 1035, para 3 Rv in conjunction with Art 1030, para 3 Rv). The parties can agree otherwise. The partial award will certainly remain valid if it was unanimously taken or rendered by a majority vote of the remaining two arbitrators.

(3) Final award

9.226 If the entire claim or all claims are decided, the award is a final award. The same applies to the arbitral tribunal's decision that it lacks jurisdiction (see para 9.220).

9.227 (3.1) **If a party fails to participate in the arbitration, may the tribunal proceed and issue an award on the merits? Is such an award enforceable as any other award? Are there special remedies for the defendant at the enforcement stage?** In the case of the claimant's default, the tribunal may terminate the proceedings by an arbitral award (Art 1040, para 1 Rv). The fact that the defendant has not filed a statement of defence will not prevent the tribunal from rendering an award, when the defendant is unable to show good cause for its failure, and despite being given a reasonable opportunity to do so. Such an award is as enforceable as any other award (cf Art 1062–1063 Rv and Art 1076 Rv). The defendant must have been given a reasonable opportunity to submit his defence. Should this not be the case, the default award may be set aside or refused enforcement, as violating public policy (Articles 1063, para 1 Rv, 1065, para 1(e) and 1076, para 1(e) Rv).

B. Deliberations and agreement on the award

(1) Time limits (and possible extensions) for making the award

9.228 The Act does not provide a time limit within which the arbitral tribunal must render the award. The tribunal has the freedom to determine the time when the award will be rendered (Art 1048 Rv). However, if the tribunal proceeds in an unacceptably slow manner, the arbitral proceedings may be terminated in accordance with Art 1031, para 2 Rv (see paras 9.92–7).

(2) Procedure for the decision of the arbitrators (majority vote, etc)

9.229 The parties may by agreement determine the manner in which the arbitrator(s) are to reach their decision (Art 1057, para 1 Rv). The agreement could mean that the arbitrators will decide by a unanimous vote or that the chairman will decide if no majority can be reached.[188] If the tribunal is composed of more than one arbitrator, and the parties have not agreed on the manner of decision making, it is to decide by a majority of votes (Art 1057, para 1 Rv). As already mentioned, if the tribunal consists of several arbitrators it must always be an uneven number (Art 1026, para 1 Rv).

9.230 (2.1) **If an arbitrator fails or refuses to take part in oral deliberation meetings, although having been given sufficient notice of such meetings, may an award be rendered on the**

[188] Van den Berg, *Int Handbook on Comm Arb* 21.

basis of written deliberations (or deliberations without this arbitrator) only? No provision in the Arbitration Act requires that the deliberations shall take place orally (cf Art 1057, para 1 Rv). It may be argued that Art 1057, para 3 Rv also applies if an arbitrator fails or refuses to take part in oral deliberation meetings (see para 9.229).[189] This means that the other arbitrators shall make a statement of such refusal beneath the award, which they will sign.

(3) Admissibility of dissenting opinions

The Arbitration Act does not contain any provision on dissenting opinions. According to the Arbitration Rules of the Netherlands Arbitration Institute no mention shall be made in the award of the opinion of a minority of the arbitrators. In an international arbitration, however, a minority may express its opinion to other arbitrators and to the parties, in a separate document. This document shall not be deemed to form part of the award (Art 48, para 4 NAI Rules). **9.231**

(3.1) Are there any court decisions or positions of leading authorities on the issue of dissenting opinions (admissibility, disclosure to the parties and publication)? In domestic arbitration dissenting opinions are not favoured. However, in arbitration involving international elements it is possible to attach a dissenting opinion to the award, even though it is not considered part of the award.[190] **9.232**

(4) Signature by the arbitrators and potential failure of one arbitrator to sign

If a minority of arbitrators refuses to sign the award, the other arbitrators will make a statement of the refusal beneath the award that they signed. This statement will be signed by the arbitrators who made the statement. The same will also be done if the minority of arbitrators are not capable of signing, their incapacity being of such nature that it is unlikely to cease to exist within a reasonable time (Art 1057, para 3 Rv). **9.233**

C. Form of the award and deposition

(1) Form and minimum contents of an award

The award must be in writing and signed by the arbitrator(s) (Art 1057, para 2 Rv). Art 1057, para 4(a-e) Rv, states that in addition to the decision itself, the award must contain the following: (i) the names and addresses of the arbitrator(s); and (ii) of the parties; (iii) the date and place of rendering and the reasons for the decision. It is not necessary to indicate reasons if the award merely records settlement or if it relates to the determination of the quality or condition of goods only. If any of these elements, except for the reasons for the decision, is missing or indicated incorrectly, such deficiencies may be corrected as provided in Art 1060, para 2 Rv.[191] **9.234**

(2) Requirement to give reasons in the award

The requirement to give reasons provided in Art 1057, para 4(e) Rv is mandatory. A lack of reasons may result in setting aside the arbitral award rendered in the Netherlands for **9.235**

[189] See also Hof's-Gravenhage, 17 December 1998, (1990) *TvA* 108–13.
[190] Van den Berg, *Int Handbook on Comm Arb* 21.
[191] Sanders/Van den Berg, Art 1057, 33, note 72.

violating public policy (Art 1065, para 1 (e) Rv). Also, the enforcement of the arbitral award may be refused (Art 1063, para 1 Rv). However, if an arbitral award does contain any reasons, but is alleged not to be reasoned adequately, it cannot be set aside and enforcement may not be refused.[192] A non-reasoned foreign arbitral award that is valid under the law of the foreign country may be enforced in the Netherlands, as the doctrine of international public policy is accepted in the Netherlands (see para 9.27).[193]

(3) Necessity to specify place and time and where and when the award was made

9.236 The award's date and the place where it is made must be contained in the award. After the date of the award, the arbitral tribunal shall ensure that without delay a copy of the award is communicated to the parties and the original of the award is deposited with the Registry of the District Court (Art 1058, para 1 Rv). A final or partial final award shall have the force of *res judicata* from the day on which it is made, except for cases in which arbitral appeal is provided (Art 1059 Rv). Leave for enforcement of a final or partial final award can usually be granted from the day on which it is made (Art 1062 Rv). An application for setting aside may be made as soon as the award has acquired the force of *res judicata* (ie on the day on which the award is made) (Art 1064, para 3 Rv).

9.237 The expiration of time limits (such as the time limit for arbitral appeal, the time limit for rectification and correction of the award, the time limit for an additional award and the time limit for setting aside) is usually linked to the deposit of the award with the Registry of the District Court (cf Arts 1050, para 4, 1060, para 1, 1061, para 1 and 1064, para 3 Rv).

9.238 According to Art 1037, para 1 Rv, the parties shall agree to the place of arbitration, or failing such agreement, the arbitral tribunal must decide, which establishes the place where the award shall be made. If, however, the place of arbitration has not been determined either by the parties or the arbitral tribunal, the place of making the award as stated by the arbitral tribunal in the award shall be deemed to be the place of arbitration (Art 1037, para 2 Rv). If the place of making the award as stated by the arbitral tribunal in the award is situated in the Netherlands, the Netherlands Arbitration Act applies (Art 1073, para 1 Rv) (see paragraphs 9.128–129). The place where the award is made (in the meaning of Art 1057 para 4(c) Rv and Art 1037, paragraphs 1 and 2 Rv) is also relevant for the purpose of application of international treaties, such as the New York Convention (see paras 9.327 *et seq*).

(4) Other requirements (registration, delivery etc)

9.239 Article 1058, para 1 Rv provides that a copy of the final award or partial final award, which is signed by the arbitrator or the secretary to the tribunal, must be communicated to the parties without delay (para 1(a)). Furthermore, the tribunal must ensure that the original of the final or partial final award is, without delay, deposited with the Registry of the District Court within whose district the seat of arbitration is located (para 1(b)). With the deposit of the last final award, the mandate of the tribunal will be terminated, unless the award will be corrected or an additional award will be rendered (Art 1058, para 2 Rv).

---

[192] See HR 25 February 2000, *NJ* 2000, 508.

[193] Sanders/Van den Berg, Art 1057, 33, note 74.

(4.1) Does the award have to be laid down or registered with a state court or agency (even if it has been rendered according to a foreign procedural law)? As mentioned, the Act expresses the principle of territoriality in Art 1073, para 1 Rv. Accordingly, the provisions of Title One apply when the place of arbitration is situated in the Netherlands. It implies that the provision of Art 1058, para 1(b) Rv, relating to the requirement to deposit the award, applies always when the place of arbitration is situated within the Netherlands, regardless of whether the parties have agreed on the applicability of another procedural law. **9.240**

(4.2) Does a foreign award which has been rendered abroad according to this country's national procedural law, have to be laid down or registered with a state court or agency? Is there a fee or tax for such registration of an award? The registration under Art 1058, para 1(b) Rv only concerns arbitral awards rendered in the Netherlands. According to Art IV(a) New York Convention, the party applying for the recognition and enforcement shall, at the time of the application, supply the duly authenticated original award or a duly certified copy thereof. A similar requirement exists for the recognition and enforcement without treaty (Art 1076, para 6 Rv in conjunction with Art 986, paras 1 and 2 Rv). **9.241**

The registration fee for the deposit of the arbitral award as mentioned in Art 1058, para 1(b) Rv presently is €102.00. **9.242**

(4.3) How long after the rendering of the award must the file/award be stored by the lawyers and the arbitral tribunal? Under the Netherlands Arbitration Act no direct obligation exists to keep a file of any document related to the arbitral proceedings. However, it should be noted that the documents related to the arbitral proceedings will be of great importance in case of a request for a rectification and correction of an arbitral award, a request for an additional arbitral award, a request for the enforcement of an arbitral award, an application for the setting aside of an arbitral award and an application for revocation of an arbitral award. It is not inconceivable that these proceedings take place a long time after the date of the award (cf also Art 324, para 1 of Book 3 of the Dutch Civil Code). Of course, it should be noted that the arbitrators have to deposit, without delay, a (partial) final arbitral award with the Registry of the District Court of the place of arbitration (Art 1058 para 1(b) Rv). **9.243**

D. Applicable substantive law

(1) Party autonomy to choose the applicable substantive law

According to Art 1054, para 1 Rv, the tribunal must decide and make its award in accordance with the rules of law. It may decide as *amiable compositeur* if the parties by their agreement have authorized it to do so (Art 1054, para 3 Rv). The party autonomy is expressed in Art 1054, para 2. It provides, *inter alia*, that 'if a choice of law is made by the parties, the arbitral tribunal shall make its award in accordance with the rules of law chosen by the parties'. **9.244**

(1.1) Is there a public policy exception to the chosen substantive law? The relevant provision on the applicable law contained in Art 1054 Rv does not mention a public policy exception to the otherwise applicable law in international arbitration. In general, it is not a choice of a particular country's substantive law that may violate public policy. It is rather that the application of a particular provision of the applicable law may lead to a result which **9.245**

is contrary to Dutch public policy. It should be mentioned that public policy exception is usually restrictively applied by the judiciary in the Netherlands, particularly in the context of international arbitration. Should the application of a particular provision result in a decision which would violate public policy according to internationally accepted standards, such an award may be set aside and may be refused the enforcement in the Netherlands.

9.246 Violation of public policy is listed among the reasons for which an arbitral award may be set aside (Art 1065, para 1(e) Rv) and for which it may be refused enforcement (Arts 1063 para 1 Rv and 1076 para 1(B) Rv). Although the Act does not expressly make the distinction between domestic and international public policy, the courts in the Netherlands have accepted the doctrine of international public policy, which is to be generally more narrowly construed than the public policy exception in domestic cases.

9.247 (1.2) **Does the principle of '*iura novit curia*' apply? Or must the applicable law be proven (by which means)?** In court proceedings, the principle of '*iura novit curia*' applies. It is provided in Art 25 Rv that the court shall *ex officio* add to the grounds. It can be argued that it also applies in arbitration, considering that there are no provisions in the Act suggesting that the applicable law must be proven. The International Law Committee has suggested that arbitrators should determine for themselves how to deal with this matter. This might mean that it would be appropriate that a tribunal proposes a text for an agreement between the parties on how the tribunal should determine the applicable law.[194] Art 1044 Rv relates to the request for information on foreign law. It provides, in para 1, as follows: 'The arbitral tribunal may, through the intervention of the President of the District Court at The Hague, ask for information as mentioned in article 3 of the European Convention on Information on Foreign Law, concluded at London, 7 June 1968 (Dutch Treaty Series 1968, 142). The President shall, unless he considers the request to be without merit, send the request without delay to the agency mentioned in Art 2 of said Convention and notify the arbitral tribunal thereof.' It has been argued that this provision, which was also included in the previous statutory law, is virtually never used.[195]

(2) Decisions according to equity or as amiable compositeur

9.248 The parties may authorize the tribunal to decide as *amiable compositeur* (Art 1054, para 3 Rv). If parties have not done so, the tribunal shall decide (only) on the basis of the rules of law (Art 1054, para 1 Rv). One must keep in mind however, that in applying Dutch law, the arbitrators will also need to apply the rules of reasonableness and fairness. If the arbitral tribunal decides as *amiable compositeur* without a party's agreement to do so, the award rendered may be set aside on the ground that the tribunal failed to comply with its mandate. The agreement of the parties in that respect is not subject to any particular formal requirements and may be concluded during the arbitral proceedings.[196]

194 Report of the Committee on International Commercial Arbitration of the International, 'Ascertaining the Contents of the Applicable Law in International Commercial Arbitration' (August 2008) 24.

195 Sanders/Van den Berg, Art 1044, 25, note 48.

196 See also, *ibid*, Art 1075, 31–2, note 68.

(3) Application of lex mercatoria, *general principles etc*

Art 1054, para 2 Rv states that the tribunal shall decide according to the rules of law chosen by the parties. In the absence of their choice of applicable substantive law, the tribunal shall make its award in accordance with the rules of law which it considers appropriate. Accordingly, the parties are not obliged to choose the law of a particular country, but can agree on the application of *lex mercatoria*. The same is true for the arbitral tribunal when determining the applicable law in the absence of the parties' choice. 9.249

(3.1) Is the application of *lex mercatoria* considered as the application of law or as a kind of *amiable composition*? As explained previously, the relevant provision of the Act uses the wording 'rules of law', and not the 'law'. The expression 'rules of law' used in Art 1054, paras 1 and 2 Rv encompasses not only the national rules of law, but also the *lex mercatoria*.[197] In the absence of the parties choice of the applicable substantive law, the arbitral tribunal may determine the applicability of the 'rules of law which it considers appropriate' (Art 1054, para 2 Rv). 9.250

Accordingly, it may decide to apply *lex mercatoria*, without the need to obtain an authorization of the parties in that respect. In contrast, the arbitral tribunal may decide as *amiable compositeur* only if the parties by agreement have authorized it to do so (Art 1054, para 3 Rv). Consequently, it may be said that the application of *lex mercatoria* is considered as the application of the 'rules of law', rather than as a kind of *amiable compositeur*, in the context of the relevant provision of Art 1054 Rv. However, the arbitral tribunal, authorized to decide as *amiable compositeur*, is not precluded from applying *lex mercatoria*. 9.251

(4) Applicable substantive law if there is no choice of law by the parties

When there is no choice of the applicable law by the parties, the tribunal shall make the award in accordance with the rules of law which it deems appropriate (Art 1054, para 2). Accordingly, the relevant provision of the Act allows the so-called 'direct method' (*voie directe*) in determining the applicable law. The arbitral tribunal may make a direct choice of the applicable law, without being required to apply conflict of law rules. 9.252

(4.1) Is there an autonomous conflict of law rule in the national arbitration law? Is it considered mandatory? Pursuant to Art 1054, para 2 Rv, the arbitral tribunal shall make its award in accordance with the rules of law chosen by the parties if the parties have made a choice of law. Failing such choice of law, the arbitral tribunal shall make its award in accordance with the rules of law which it considers to be appropriate. This means that the arbitral tribunal may make a direct choice without being obliged to apply further conflict of law rules. 9.253

(4.2) What is the law applicable to interest? As discussed, the parties are free to determine the law applicable to the substance of the dispute. In the absence of their choice, it will be determined by the arbitral tribunal (Art 1054 para 2 Rv). Thus, if the parties have made an express choice concerning the law applicable to interest, which is different from 9.254

---

197 Van den Berg/Van Delden/Snijders 92. cf Meijer, G.J. and Borelli, S., 'Interview met P. Sanders' (1996) *TvA* 2–12 (Meijer/Borelli).

the otherwise applicable substantive law, it will be the law of their express choice. If no express choice has been made with respect to interest, it will be determined by the arbitral tribunal. In general, it seems appropriate to consider that the law applicable to the substance of the dispute (*lex causae*) will govern the interest as well. Indeed, the arbitral tribunal may determine the applicability of the rules of law which it considers appropriate.

9.255 (4.3) **What is the law and practice with respect to legal interest on foreign currency debts?** As already mentioned, the law applicable to the substance of the dispute will usually govern the question of interest, unless the parties have expressly agreed on the applicability of different law (see para 9.250).

(5) Binding effect of state court decisions

9.256 Court judgments that are *res judicata* are binding in subsequent legal and arbitral proceedings (Art 236 Rv). The same applies to a foreign judgment that is recognized in the Netherlands. A Dutch judgment which acquired *res judiciata* force or a foreign judgment which has been recognized in the Netherlands will prevent any subsequent enforcement of a contradictory arbitral award involving the same parties and the same subject matter of the dispute. Enforcement of such an award would violate public policy (Art 1063, para 1 Rv) and may also be subject to annulment on such ground (Art 1065, para 1(e) Rv).

9.257 (5.1) **Is an arbitral tribunal bound by a decision of another arbitral tribunal?** Article 1059, para 1 Rv provides that a (partial) final award shall have the force of *res judicata* on the day on which it is made. Arbitrators and judges are bound by the arbitral award on the basis of the force of *res judicata* in subsequent arbitral or legal proceedings. The same applies to a foreign arbitral award that is recognized in the Netherlands (see Arts 1075 and 1076 Rv) (see paragraphs 9.325 *et seq*). The existence of a Dutch arbitral award, which has acquired the force of *res judicata* (Art 1059, para 1 Rv), will preclude the enforcement of an award subsequently rendered in arbitral proceedings between the same parties concerning the same subject matter of the dispute. The enforcement of such a subsequently rendered award may be refused as violating public policy (Art 1063, para 1). The same is true when there is a foreign arbitral award which has been recognized in the Netherlands (Arts 1075–1076 Rv). In a similar vein, such a subsequently rendered arbitral award, between the same parties with respect to the same subject matter of the dispute, may be set aside, as contrary to public policy (Art 1065, para 1(e) Rv).

9.258 (5.2) **Does a decision in a criminal case bind an arbitral tribunal?** Pursuant to Art 161 Rv a Dutch criminal court's decision has a binding effect for the Dutch civil court with respect to the facts that the criminal court has held to be proven. Art 161 Rv does not apply to arbitration (Art 1039, para 5 Rv). It seems appropriate, however, that the arbitrators should, if the circumstances of a particular case so require, consider a court decision in a criminal case. It is to be excluded that an arbitral award that disregards such decision violates public policy.

E. Settlement

(1) Settlement by agreement of the parties with or without support of the arbitral tribunal

9.259 In principle, the arbitrators may help the parties to reach a settlement. According to Art 1043 Rv, the tribunal may order the parties at any stage of the proceedings to appear in person in order to provide the necessary information or to attempt to reach a settlement. However, it is said that arbitrators are rather reluctant in taking the initiative to reach a settlement 'in order to avoid the impression of bias'.[198]

It is more likely that the parties will formulate such a proposal. According to Art 1069, para 1 Rv, the arbitral tribunal may, at the joint request of the parties, record the settlement the parties have reached during the arbitral proceedings in the form of an arbitral award. This request may be rejected by the arbitral tribunal without a need to give reasons. **9.260**

(1.1) May an arbitrator who has initiated settlement discussions be challenged when agreement on a settlement has failed? As already explained, the grounds to challenge an arbitrator are dealt with in Art 1033. Thus, an arbitrator may be challenged if circumstances exist that give rise to justifiable doubts as to his impartiality or independence. The fact that an arbitrator has initiated settlement discussions, but the parties have failed to reach a settlement, cannot in itself be considered as ground to challenge an arbitrator. **9.261**

(2) 'Private settlement' and its impact on the arbitral procedure

As mentioned above, the parties may reach a settlement during the arbitral proceedings. At their joint request, the tribunal may, but is not obliged to, record the contents of the settlement in the form of an arbitral award (Art 1069, para 1 Rv). If the tribunal rejects the parties' request to issue an award on agreed terms, it does not have to indicate reasons for such refusal. In general, it will reject a request only in exceptional circumstances. For example, such a request may be refused if the settlement would in the view of the tribunal violate public policy.[199] **9.262**

(3) Form and effect of a settlement (eg award on agreed terms)

If the joint request of the parties is accepted, the tribunal will record the settlement in the form of an arbitral award on agreed terms. The arbitral award on agreed terms has all the characteristics of an arbitral award, with the following differences: it can be set aside only for reasons of public policy; it must be signed not only by the arbitrators but also by the parties; and it does not have to contain reasons (Art 1069, para 2 Rv). **9.263**

F. Costs of the arbitration

(1) General allocation of the costs of the proceedings

The Arbitration Act contains no provision concerning—the allocation of—costs.[200] The issue of costs is only touched upon in Art 1046, para 3 Rv, which relates to the consolidation of arbitral proceedings. It provides, *inter alia*, that the President of the District Court of Amsterdam 'shall determine the remuneration for the work already carried out by the arbitrators whose mandate is terminated by the reasons of the full consolidation'. It has been held that the costs of arbitration will be awarded against the losing party, but that the **9.264**

198 Van den Berg, *Int Handbook on Comm Arb* 24.

199 Sanders/Van den Berg, Art 1069, 44, note 108.

200 See for a general overview on costs in arbitration under Dutch law Van de Hel-Koedoot, M., 'De (kosten)veroordeling in arbitrage. Een overzicht aan de hand van het NAI Arbitrage Reglement' (2009), *TvA* 37–44 (Van de Hel-Koedoot).

arbitral tribunal may divide up the costs among the parties if it considers it justified, for example if each party is successful in a part of his claim.[201]

9.265 The NAI Rules contain the provision on the determination and award of costs in Art 61. The arbitral tribunal shall determine the costs of the arbitration, taking into consideration the provisions on the fees and disbursement of arbitrators contained in Art 58, para 1 (Art 61, para 1 of the Rules). In Art 61, para 2, the Rules provide that the costs will be awarded against the losing party, 'except in special cases at the discretion of the arbitral tribunal'. If both parties have lost in part, the costs may be divided between the parties, wholly or in part (Art 61, para 2 of the Rules). Art 61, para 3 provides as follows, 'In awarding the costs, the arbitral tribunal shall take into account the deposit made in accordance with Art 59. To the extent that a deposit made by a party is used to pay costs that were awarded against the other party in accordance with the provision of the previous paragraph, the latter party shall be condemned to reimburse the former party for these costs'. The costs may be awarded even if they were not expressly claimed by a party (Art 61, para 4 of the Rules). According to Art 56 of the Rules, the costs of arbitration include the administration cost, fees and disbursements of arbitrators, costs of legal assistance, 'as well as other costs which in the opinion of the arbitral tribunal were necessarily incurred in the arbitration'.

(2) Deposits or advances for costs or fees

9.266 The Act contains no provision concerning the deposits for costs or fees. In principle the arbitral tribunal may request both or one of the parties, usually the claimant, to pay a deposit for the fees and costs.[202]

9.267 In NAI arbitrations, the administrator is authorized to require the claimant to pay a deposit. If the respondent has filed a counterclaim, he may also be requested to pay a deposit (Art 59, para 1 of the Rules). The deposit shall serve, *inter alia,* to pay the cost of depositing the award at the registry of the district court, as well as to pay the costs of a secretary, an expert appointed by the tribunal, interpreter and the technical assistance, insofar as the arbitral tribunal incurs such costs (Art 59, para 2 of the Rules). Both the claimant and the respondent may be required by the administrator to pay an additional deposit (Art 59, para 4 of the Rules). (See also para 85.)

9.268 **(2.1) Is there case law authorizing or prohibiting arbitrators to order a party to pay an advance on the arbitration costs?** To our knowledge, no relevant case law in this respect can be found. In any case, orders and interim awards cannot be enforced through the courts in the Netherlands.

9.269 **(2.2) May the raising of a set-off claim or counterclaim be made contingent upon payment of the corresponding advance for the relating arbitration costs (cf eg Article 30(5), ICC Rules)? May such a condition be agreed upon when entering into the arbitration agreement?** The Arbitration Act contains no provisions in that respect. As already mentioned, under the NAI Rules, the respondent may be required to pay a deposit if he has introduced a counterclaim (Art 59, para 1 of the Rules). In accordance with Art 59, para 6

[201] Van den Berg, *Int Handbook on Comm Arb* 26 and Van den Berg/Van Delden/Snijders 100–2.
[202] Van den Berg, *Int Handbook on Comm Arb* 26.

of the Rules, the arbitral tribunal may suspend the proceedings concerning the claim or counterclaim until the party concerned has paid the deposit for costs as required. If the deposit is not paid by a party who has been requested to do so within 14 days (in international cases this time limit is doubled) after the administrator's second reminder in writing, this party shall be deemed to have withdrawn his claim or counterclaim. By choosing the NAI Rules, the parties are considered to have agreed on such a consequence.

(2.3) **What remedies exist against a party which does not pay its part of the advance on the arbitration costs (eg termination of the arbitration agreement)? How may the other party enforce its rights?** The Arbitration Act is silent on this issue. Accordingly, it may be presumed that it is in the discretion of the arbitral tribunal in *ad hoc* arbitral proceedings. However, under the NAI Rules the consequences of the failure of a party to pay the deposit are indicated in Art 59, para 6 of the NAI Rules. As stated above, in accordance with this provision, the arbitral tribunal may suspend the proceedings concerning the claim or counterclaim until the party concerned has paid the deposit for costs as required. If the deposit is not paid by a party who has been requested to do so within 14 days (in international cases this time limit is doubled) after the administrator's second reminder in writing, this party shall be deemed to have withdrawn his claim or counterclaim. **9.270**

(3) Costs of the administration by an arbitration institution

The NAI Rules contain the provision on the costs of the administration in Art 57. Upon commencement of the arbitration, the claimant is to pay a fixed amount for the administration costs. The administrator shall notify the claimant about the amount of the costs as soon as possible after receipt of the request for arbitration (Art 57, para 1 of the Rules). The administration costs are to be determined in accordance with a schedule fixed by the Governing Board. The schedule is contained in the Appendix to the Rules. If the costs cannot be fixed on the basis of the schedule, the administration shall make decision on this issue (Art 57, para 2 of the Rules). The administration costs shall also be due from the respondent if he has filed a counterclaim. The amount of costs will be fixed in the same manner as provided in para 2 (Art 57, para 3 of the Rules). The additional administration costs may be determined if a claim or counterclaim is increased (Art 57, para 4 of the Rules). **9.271**

The collection of the administration costs rests with the administrator. If a party fails to pay the administration costs within 14 days (in an international arbitration this time limit is doubled) after the administrator's second reminder in writing, this party shall be considered to have withdrawn his claim or counterclaim (Art 57, para 5 of the Rules). **9.272**

Half of the administration costs paid by a party shall be reimbursed to him if he withdraws his claim or the counterclaim, as the case may be, before the arbitration file is transmitted to the arbitrators (Art 57, para 6 of the Rules). In case the NAI is required only to appoint the arbitrators, half of the administration costs shall be due from the petitioner (Art 57, para 7 of the Rules). **9.273**

In NAI arbitrations the disbursement of an arbitrator includes reasonable costs for travel and accommodation, secretarial assistance, conference rooms, mailing, telephone, telex and telefax (Art 58, para 2 of the Rules). The administration shall determine the arbitrators' **9.274** fees after consulting the arbitrators. In determining the fees, the following criteria shall be considered: the time spent on the case, the amount in dispute, and the complexity of the case (Art 58, para 1 of the Rules). It is argued that the same criteria usually apply in *ad hoc* arbitrations as well, although sometimes the amount in dispute can be the only criterion. The arbitrators determine the fees themselves, if no arrangement between the parties and the arbitrators in that respect has been made in advance.[203]

9.275 Article 60 of the NAI Rules provides that the arbitral tribunal may order the losing party to pay the costs of legal assistance incurred by the winning party 'if and to the extent that these costs are deemed necessary by the arbitral tribunal'.

(4) Arbitrators' fees: law and practice, judicial control

9.276 The Arbitration Act does not contain any provision on the arbitrators' fees. There are no statutory guidelines or regulations on this issue. According to Art 61, para 1, NAI Rules, the arbitral tribunal shall determine the costs of the arbitration, having regard to the provisions of Art 58, para 1, NAI Rules (see para 9.272) To the extent that sufficient deposits have been made, the legal nature of the award for costs is not an issue in the majority of cases.[204]

9.277 (4.1) **May arbitrators fix their own fees in the award?** The Arbitration Act does not contain any provision on this question. If the provisions on mandate contained in Book 7 of the Dutch Civil Code apply to the agreement between the parties and the arbitrator, the parties owe the arbitrator remuneration as calculated in the habitual manner or, in the absence thereof, a reasonable remuneration, unless the amount of the remuneration has been fixed by the contracting parties (Art 405, para 2 of Book 7 of the Civil Code). To the extent that they are not included in the remuneration, the parties must reimburse the arbitrator for the expenses connected with the performance of the mandate (Art 406 of Book 7 of the Civil Code).

9.278 According to Art 58, para 1 of the NAI Rules, the fees of the arbitrator(s) shall be determined by the administrator after consultation with the arbitrator(s). In determining fees, the time spent on the case by the arbitrator(s), the amount in dispute and the complexity of the case shall be taken into account.

9.279 (4.2) **How can the parties change the arbitrators' fees once they are fixed?** The Arbitration Act does not contain a provision concerning fixing and changing of the arbitrators' fees. As far as institutional arbitration is concerned, parties have little or no influence on the amount of compensation (see para 9.275). As far as *ad hoc* arbitration is concerned, the parties may negotiate with the persons who might be appointed as arbitrators as to the amount of compensation.

9.280 Parties paying the costs of arbitration are not automatically bound to the amounts determined by the arbitrators. If disputed, they become binding after a complete review and determination by the ordinary courts.[205] It is argued, however, that a decision by the

[203] Van den Berg, *Int Handbook on Comm Arb* 25.
[204] Van den Berg/Van Delden/Snijders 101.
[205] *ibid*, 102.

tribunal on the fees in the arbitral award should be considered a *binding advice* (a binding decision based on contract).[206]

(4.3) Are the arbitrator's fees subject to income tax if (i) the place of arbitration; or (ii) the normal residence or place of business of the arbitrator is located in this country? Arbitrators' fees are subject to Dutch income tax if the normal residence of the arbitrator is located in the Netherlands. However, arbitrators' fees may also be subject to income tax in the Netherlands if the place of arbitration is located in the Netherlands. 9.281

(4.4) Are arbitrator's fees submitted to VAT? If yes, is the duty to pay such tax linked to (i) the place of arbitration; or (ii) the arbitrator's general residence? The European Court of Justice held that the remuneration of an arbitrator does not fall within Art 9, para 2(e) of the 6th European VAT Directive on the ground that the services rendered by arbitrators are different from the services rendered by attorneys.[207] However, Resolutions of the Dutch Ministry of Finance make clear that, in principle, arbitrator's fees are submitted to VAT if the arbitrator resides in the Netherlands; if arbitrators do not provide other professional services and hardly ever act as arbitrator, no VAT is due.[208] 9.282

(5) Attorneys' fees and the winning party's claim for reimbursement

As mentioned previously, there are no express provisions relating to the costs of arbitration in the Act. According to the NAI Rules, the winning party may be awarded costs of legal assistance, if these costs are deemed necessary by the arbitral tribunal (Art 60). 9.283

(5.1) May in-house lawyers charge fees or may a party request costs of in-house lawyers to be reimbursed? To our knowledge, there are no mandatory provisions for determining legal fees. Since the Arbitration Act does not contain any (substantial) provision on the costs of arbitration, the costs must be defined on the basis of the applicable arbitration rules. Mostly, arbitration rules do not specifically define the costs of legal assistance. It may be argued that they are not limited to costs of legal representation by an attorney and that costs of in-house lawyers are also included.[209] 9.284

(6) Time and form of the decision on costs

Usually, a decision on costs will be taken in a final award. No decision on costs so far incurred in the proceedings would be contained in an interim award, considering that such decisions cannot be enforced through the courts in the Netherlands. It is likely that the arbitrators would indicate in an interim award the amount of costs incurred so far and what decision on their allocation will be taken in a final award.[210] 9.285

(6.1) May the arbitrators' decision on the costs (allocation and amount of costs to be reimbursed) be challenged separately from the award itself? Are there time limits for such 9.286

---

[206] Sanders, *Het Nederlandse arbitragerecht* 83 and Snijders, Loose-leaf, Art 1057, explanatory note 4.

[207] C-145/96, 16 September 1997 (*Bernd von Hoffmann v Finanzamt Trier*) ECR (1997) I-4857.

[208] Resolution CCP 2006/1796M of the Ministry of Finance of 29 August 2006, *Stcrt* 2006, 174 and Resolution CPP07–285 of the Ministry of Finance of 8 March 2007, *Strct* 2007, 55; see also Pelinck, M.J., 'BTW bij arbitrage' (2007) *TvA* 87–93 (Pelinck).

[209] cf for the developments in this respect Redfern, A. and Hunter, M., *Law and Practice of International Commercial Arbitration* (4th edn, Sweet & Maxwell, London, 2004) paras 8–92 *et seq* (Redfern/Hunter).

[210] Snijders/Meijer 29.

a remedy? The decision on the costs may only be challenged in the setting-aside proceedings against the final or partial final award (Art 1052, para 4 Rv and Art 1064, para 4 Rv) (see paras 9.290 *et seq*).

9.287 **(6.2) Are the arbitrators entitled and/or legally obliged to rule on the amount of one or both parties' costs that are recoverable?** Under the NAI Rules, the arbitrators are entitled to determine the amount of the costs and award these costs even if they were not expressly claimed by a party (Art 61, para 4 of the Rules).

G. Publication of the award

(1) Publication with or without the consent of the parties

9.288 There is no provision in the Act concerning publication of the award. However, the NAI Rules of Arbitration provide for this in Art 55. Thus, the NAI is authorized to have the award published without indicating the names of the parties and other details that might reveal the identity of the parties, unless 'a party communicates in writing to the Administrator his objections thereto within one month after receipt of the award'.

(2) Practice of publication (eg in specific legal journals)

9.289 With respect to the practice of publication, it should be mentioned that the awards in the Netherlands have been published since 1919.[211] In particular, they are published without indicating the names of the parties in the *Tijdschrift voor Arbitrage* (*Journal of Arbitration*).

VI. Amendment and challenge of the award; liability of arbitrators

A. Amendment, correction, or interpretation of the award

(1) Motion to correct or amend an award

9.290 Article 1060 Rv extensively deals with Rectification and correction of the award. A manifest computing or clerical error may be corrected by the tribunal either on its own motion within 30 days after the date of deposit of the award (para 4) or at a party's request made within the same time limit (para 1). An incorrect indication or an omission of some elements concerning the award's content as provided for in Art 1057, para 4 (a)–(d) Rv, including the names of the parties, date and place of rendition of the award, may be corrected by the tribunal either on its own motion or at the request of a party. The 30-day time limit, as indicated above, also applies here. If the arbitral tribunal has failed to decide one or more matters which have been submitted to it, either party may, no later than 30 days after the date of the deposit of the award with the Registry of the District Court, request the arbitral tribunal to render an additional award (Art 1061, para 1 Rv).[212]

9.291 A request for rectification or correction does not suspend enforcement or the setting aside of an award, unless the President of the District Court considers it appropriate to determine otherwise (Art 1060, para 7 Rv).

---

211 Van den Berg, *Int Handbook on Comm Arb* 27.

212 See Nieuwendijk, van den, I.P.M., 'Aanvulling van arbitrale vonnissen' (2002) 1, *TvA* 3–10 (Nieuwendijk).

(2) Interpretation of the award by the tribunal

The Act contains no provisions concerning the interpretation of the award by the tribunal. **9.292** However, there is the opportunity for a party to request the tribunal to render an additional award if one or more matters submitted to arbitration have not been decided upon (see para 9.284).

B. Appeal on the merits

(1) Admissibility and procedure of an appeal on the merits

No appeal on the merits to a court is admissible in the Netherlands. The parties may agree **9.293** on appeal to a second arbitral tribunal, usually by choosing a set of arbitration rules which provides for this possibility (Art 1050 Rv).

(1.1) May the parties agree on an appeal to another arbitral tribunal? If the parties **9.294** agree on appeal to a second arbitral tribunal, the reasons, extent and procedure are usually provided in the arbitration rules chosen by the parties.

(2) Possibility to exclude an appeal (eg in the arbitration clause)

It is not necessary for the parties to exclude appeal to a second arbitral tribunal, as it is pos- **9.295** sible only if the parties have agreed thereto (Art 1050 Rv and Art 1020, para 6 Rv).

C. Setting aside of the award

(1) Reasons for setting aside an award

The following means of recourse against an arbitral award are provided in the Act: an **9.296** application for setting aside (Arts 1064–1067 Rv) and an application for revocation of an award (Art 1068). However, an application for revocation is of little practical importance as the grounds infrequently arise.[213] As revocation of award is rather exceptional, it will not be discussed further.

The grounds for setting aside an arbitral award are provided in Art 1065 Rv. These grounds **9.297** are: (i) no valid arbitration agreement has been entered into (Art 1065, para 1(a) Rv); (ii) the tribunal has been constituted in violation of the applicable rules (Art 1065, para 1(b) Rv); (iii) the tribunal has failed to comply with its mandate (Art 1065, para 1(c) Rv); (iv) the award is not signed (see para 9.106) or does not contain reasons as provided in Art 1057 (Art 1065, para 1(d) Rv);[214] or (v) the award or the manner in which it is made violates public policy or good morals (Art 1065, para 1(e) Rv).

However, the Act limits the parties' possibility to invoke some of the grounds (Art 1065, **9.298** paras 2–4 and 6). In particular, this is the case with respect to the objections concerning

---

213 Van den Berg, *Int Handbook on Comm Arb* 32. Art 1068 was amended by the Act of 6 December 2001, *Stb* 2001, no 580. Thereby, the reasons for revocation listed in Art 1068, para 1 remained unchanged.

214 HR 25 February 2000, *NJ* 2000, 508. According to Art 1057, para 4(e) Rv, an arbitral award shall contain the reasons for the decision, 'unless the award concerns merely the determination only of the quality or condition of goods'. However, when a ground for setting aside under Art 1065 Rv is invoked, the court may not review a decision of the arbitral tribunal on the merits. See eg HR 17 January 2003, *NJ* 2004, 384. Yet, on the basis of Art 1065, para 1(d) Rv, the court may, albeit to a very limited extent, examine whether the arbitral award contains 'solid reasons'. See HR 9 January 2004, *NJ* 2005, 190 and HR 22 December 2006, *NJ* 2008, 4.

invalidity of the arbitration agreement (para 2), irregularity in the constitution of the arbitral tribunal (para 3) and a non-compliance of the tribunal with its mandate (paragraphs 4 and 6). Thus, if a party has participated in arbitral proceedings without raising the plea of invalidity of the arbitration agreement before submitting a defence, that party is precluded from invoking this objection in the annulment procedure. The party will not be estopped from raising this objection only if the validity concerns non-arbitrability of the subject matter (Arts 1065, para 2 and 1052, para 2 Rv). In a similar vein, a party who participated in the establishment of the arbitral tribunal may not invoke the ground mentioned in Art 1065, para 1(b) Rv (irregularity in the constitution of the tribunal). A party who has not participated in the constitution of the tribunal, but did participate in arbitral proceedings is barred from relying on this ground if he failed to raise the objection on the irregularity in the establishment of the tribunal in the arbitral procedure before submitting a statement of defence (Arts 1065, para 3 and 1053, para 3 Rv). Furthermore, the non-compliance of the arbitral tribunal with its mandate shall not be the reason for setting aside the award if the party invoking this ground has participated in the arbitral procedure without raising this objection although he was aware of the arbitral tribunal's non-compliance with its mandate (Art 1065, para 4 Rv). Moreover, if the arbitral tribunal has failed to decide one or more matters submitted to it, the application for setting aside on this ground (non-compliance with the mandate) shall be admissible only if the procedure of requesting an additional award, provided under Art 1061, has taken place (Art 1065, para 6 Rv).

9.299 The award shall be partially set aside 'to the extent that the part of the award which is in excess of or different from the claim can be separated from the remaining part of the claim' (Art 1065, para 5 Rv). An arbitral award can be partially set aside if one of the two parties to arbitral proceedings has not concluded a valid arbitration agreement.[215]

9.300 (1.1) **May an award made according to international or foreign procedural rules be the object of an application for setting aside before the national courts?** Any award rendered in the arbitration having the seat in the Netherlands may be the subject of an application for setting aside before the courts in the Netherlands, regardless of the fact that the parties have chosen foreign procedural rules.

(2) Procedure and deadlines for challenging an award

9.301 The procedure and time limits for an application for setting aside are provided in Art 1064. The application is to be filed with the District Court with whose Registry the award must be deposited (Art 1064, para 2 Rv). An interim award can be challenged only by an application to set aside a final or partial final award (Art 1064, para 4 Rv). The decision brought upon the action for setting aside may be appealed before both the Court of Appeal and the Supreme Court. All grounds for setting aside, on the basis of which a party intends to challenge the award, must be indicated in the writ of summons. All grounds which are not mentioned in the writ cannot subsequently be raised (Art 1064, para 5 Rv). The latter provision may not be applied too strictly.[216]

---

215 HR 20 January 2006, *NJ* 2006, 77; see also Meijer, *T&C Rv*, Art 1065, nos 2d and 9c.

216 HR 5 December 2008, no C07/166HR and HR 27 March 2009, no C07/190HR (see <http://www.rechtspraak.nl>).

The time limits for the application are set forth in Art 1064, para 3 Rv. It provides that the application may be made as soon as the award has *res judicata* effect (ie on the date when it is made, according to Art 1059 Rv). After the expiry of three months from the date of deposit of the award, the right to make an application will be extinguished. When the award is served upon the party together with leave for enforcement, the application for setting aside must be made within three months after the said service. **9.302**

(2.1) Who may (or must) represent a party in a proceeding for setting aside an award General rules and relevant provisions of procedural law, which usually apply with respect to the representation in the proceeding before a competent Dutch court, are applicable with respect to the representation of the party in a proceeding for setting aside as well. Thus, the parties in the procedure for setting aside of the award must be represented by a so-called 'procureur' or by an attorney (*advocaat*). The 'procureur' represents the parties in the court proceeding as far as it concerns the procedural matters and undertaking certain procedural acts, such as the filing of statements and documents to the court. An attorney (*advocaat*) must represent the parties as far as it concerns the content of the case (eg the contents of the writ of summons and the statements, the oral pleadings). **9.303**

(2.2) Do specific time limits exist for setting-aside procedures concerning awards on jurisdiction? If the tribunal decides on the issue of jurisdiction in an interim award, such award can only be challenged by an application for setting aside against the final award. Accordingly, there are no specific time limits for the setting-aside procedure against such awards. **9.304**

(3) Effect of a court decision which sets the award aside

The consequences of a decision setting aside the award are provided in Art 1067 Rv. As soon as such decision becomes final, the jurisdiction of the court shall revive, unless the parties have agreed otherwise. Setting aside of the award shall trigger the annulment of the leave for enforcement by operation of law (Art 1062, para 4 Rv). **9.305**

(3.1) Does the setting-aside action suspend the enforcement? If so, do remedies exist to reinstate enforcement? An application for setting aside does not suspend the enforcement of the award (Art 1066, para 1 Rv). However, the court deciding on the application for setting aside may, upon the request of a party, decide that the enforcement will be suspended if it considers the request to be justified (Art 1066, para 2 Rv). The decision on the request will be brought after the other party has been given an opportunity to be heard (Art 1066, para 4 Rv). When granting or refusing the request the court may order a party to provide security (Art 1066, para 5 Rv). The suspension may be lifted at the request of either party (Art 1066, para 6 Rv). **9.306**

(3.2) After an award has been set aside, does the underlying arbitration agreement revive or remain in force or is it exhausted or deemed terminated? The consequences of the annulment have already been addressed (see para 9.299). In accordance with Art 1067, the jurisdiction of the court shall revive as soon as the judgment setting aside the award becomes final, unless the parties have agreed otherwise. Accordingly, the parties may agree that the arbitration agreement revive or remain in force after an award has been set aside. Indeed, the will of the parties is necessarily limited by the nature or the type of the reason for which the award has been set aside. **9.307**

(4) Appeal against the court's decision to set aside or not set aside the award

9.308 An appeal against the decision granting or refusing the application for setting aside may be brought before the Court of Appeal (Art 1063, para 3 Rv). Furthermore, there is also the possibility of recourse to the Supreme Court against the decision of the Court of Appeal (Art 1063, para 4 Rv).

(5) Possibility of the parties to exclude actions for setting aside

9.309 The possibility to apply for setting aside of an award provided under Art 1065 may not be excluded by an agreement of the parties. There is no possibility for the parties to waive the action for annulment or to exclude one or several grounds for setting aside. However, the parties may agree that only the arbitral tribunal may interpret the arbitration rules that the parties agree to apply to the composition of the arbitral tribunal and to the arbitral proceedings, and they may exclude that the courts, in setting-aside proceedings, may interpret the arbitration rules. Thus, if the parties have agreed to the exclusive interpretation of the arbitration rules by the arbitral tribunal as mentioned above, a decision by the courts in setting-aside proceedings regarding the correct application of the arbitration rules, instigated on the basis of Art 1065, para 1(b) Rv (composition of the arbitral tribunal in violation of the applicable rules) and Art 1065, para 1(c) Rv (violation of the arbitral tribunal's procedural mandate), is practically excluded.[217]

D. Liability of arbitrators

(1) Duties and liabilities of arbitrators regarding the conduct of the proceedings

9.310 With respect to arbitrators' duties and liabilities regarding the conduct of the proceedings, it is generally maintained that arbitrators can only be held liable for damages to the extent that judges may be held liable.[218] Arbitrators can therefore only be held liable for damages if they violate fundamental principles of law, such as impartiality and the right to a fair hearing, and insofar as no recourse can be made or could have been made to the arbitral award.[219]

9.311 **(1.1) Do the courts and/or authorities rely on a contractual relationship between the parties and the arbitrator(s), irrespective of whether institutional or *ad hoc* arbitration is concerned? What is the legal qualification of such a contract (eg provision of services)?** The legal relationship between the parties and the arbitrator(s) is considered to be a mandate (ie services agreement) as referred to in Arts 400–413 of Book 7 of the Civil Code.

9.312 **(1.2) Are there court decisions (or authorities) determining which law governs the question of liability of an arbitrator? What is the position of those courts/authorities as to whether and to which extent a legal liability of an arbitrator (or arbitral institution) may**

[217] HR 9 January 1981, *NJ* 1981, 203, HR 28 September 1999, *NJ* 1991, 230 and HR 17 January 2003, *NJ* 2004, 384; the parties may not exclude that the court decides the question of whether the parties have indeed agreed that only the arbitral tribunal may interpret the arbitration rules.

[218] cf Snijders, Loose-leaf, Art 1029, explanatory note 1; Snijders, H.J., Klaassen, C.J.M. and Meijer, G.J., *Nederlands burgerlijk procesrecht* (4th edn, Kluwer, Deventer, 2007) no 384 (Snijders/Klaassen/Meijer).

[219] Rechtbank Breda, 11 September 1990, (1991) *TvA* 28–31 and Hof's-Hertogenbosch, 28 October 1992, (1992) *TvA* 231.

be established? The law which applies to the agreement between the parties and the arbitrators governs the question of arbitrators' liability. The rules of private international law which were contained in the EC Convention on the Law Applicable to Contractual Obligations, Rome 1980 and in the Rome I Regulation after its entering into force determine the applicable law to this agreement. Thus the law chosen by the parties governs this agreement.

If the parties have chosen the law applicable to the contract, Art 3 EC Convention on the Law Applicable to Contractual Obligations determines that the law of the country with which it is most closely connected is applicable. In arbitrations, this is typically the habitual residence of the arbitrator. **9.313**

Yet it would be more appropriate to consider that the law of the place of arbitration is the law with which the agreement between the parties and the arbitrator(s) is most closely connected, especially since there may be three arbitrators with three different habitual residences (Art 4, para 5, Rome Convention). Thus the law of the Netherlands will be the law governing this agreement, if the place of arbitration is situated in the Netherlands. **9.314**

(1.3) Is an arbitrator subject to criminal prosecution? Dutch law does not contain special provisions which subject arbitrator(s) to criminal prosecution. Therefore the general provisions of the *Wetboek van Strafrecht* (the Dutch Criminal Act) apply. This means that the arbitrators will be subject to the same rules of criminal prosecution as any other person subject to the *Wetboek van Strafrecht.* **9.315**

(2) Possibility to restrict or exclude the arbitrators' liability

According to case law liability can be excluded, with the exception of damages arising from intentional acts and for gross negligence.[220] Article 66 of the NAI Rules excludes the liability of arbitrators. Neither the NAI nor any member of its Governing Board personally, nor the Administrator, nor any arbitrator can be held liable for any act or omission with regard to an arbitration governed by these Rules. **9.316**

VII. Enforcement of national awards

(1) Requirement of a particular procedure to make an award enforceable (leave for enforcement, exequatur*)*

A final or partial final award, which may not be subject to appeal to a second arbitral tribunal, shall have the force of *res judicata* from the date of its rendering. No other type of award is capable of acquiring such force (Art 1059, para 1 Rv). From the date it acquires the force of *res judicata*, the award may be subject to enforcement (Art 1062 Rv) and setting aside (Art 1064, para 3).[221] An award, against which an appeal to a second tribunal is possible, will have *res judicata* effect on the date of expiration of the time limit for appeal or on the date when the second award is rendered (Art 1059, para 2 Rv). **9.317**

---

220 See the case law mentioned in Asser, C. Hartkamp, A.S. and Sieburgh, C.H., *Handleiding tot de beoefening van het Nederlands burgerlijk recht* (Asser serie, 13th edn, Kluwer, Deventer, 2008) 6-I, no 364 *et seq* (Asser/Hartkamp/Sieburgh).

221 Sanders/Van den Berg, Art 1059, 34, note 76.

9.318 According to Art 1062, para 1 Rv, enforcement of a final or partial final award in the Netherlands can take place only after leave for enforcement has been granted by the President of the District Court with whose Registry the original of the award is deposited. The President may grant leave for enforcement of a final or partial final award which is not open to appeal to a second arbitral tribunal or which is rendered on arbitral appeal or with respect to which the tribunal has declared to be provisionally enforceable.

9.319 From the wording of Art 1062, para 2 Rv, it can be concluded that a deposit of the award is not a condition for granting leave for enforcement. Leave for enforcement will be recorded on the original of the award (if deposited) or laid down in the decision, if the award has not been deposited. A certified copy of the award on which leave for enforcement is recorded or of a decision granting leave will be communicated to the parties without delay.

9.320 The provision of Art 1062 Rv relates to the conditions for leave for enforcement of the award with respect to which an appeal may be submitted to a second arbitral tribunal.

9.321 If leave for enforcement is granted, an application for revocation and for setting aside of the award are the only means of recourse available against such decision. Any leave for enforcement will be automatically annulled if an arbitral award is set aside or if revocation of the award has taken place (Art 1062, para 4 Rv).

9.322 (1.1) **Does the national law make any difference between foreign and domestic awards, and if so, which are the criteria? Does an additional motion of award exist for the purpose of obtaining *exequatur* (France: international awards)?** As mentioned, the Act follows the principle of territoriality as expressed in Art 1073, para 1 Rv. The provisions of Title One (Arts 1020–1073 Rv) apply to arbitrations taking place in the Netherlands. Title Two (Arts 1074–1076 Rv) applies to arbitrations held outside the Netherlands. The provision of Art 1075 Rv relates to the recognition and enforcement of foreign arbitral awards under treaties and Art 1076 Rv concerns recognition and enforcement of foreign awards when no treaty is applicable.

9.323 (1.2) **May awards granting conservatory/interim measures be subject to enforcement?** The tribunal may decide on certain types of provisional measures in the form of an order or an interim award. However, neither orders nor interim awards can be enforced through the courts in the Netherlands (see paras 9.198 *et seq*).

(2) Details of such enforcement procedure (competent court, reasons for rejection of motion etc)

9.324 Certain issues concerning the enforcement procedure, in particular the issue of the competent court and the type of awards with respect to which leave for enforcement may be granted, have already been addressed (see paragraphs 9.311 *et seq*). The reasons for refusal of leave for enforcement are provided in Art 1063, para 1 Rv. The President of the District Court may refuse the enforcement of an arbitral award if it or the manner in which it was made violates public policy or good morals. The enforcement can also be refused if the tribunal declares its award provisionally enforceable in violation of Art 1055 Rv or if a penalty for non-compliance determined by the tribunal contravenes Art 1056 Rv. In the latter case refusal shall relate only to the enforcement of the sum of the penalty. The possibility of appeal against the decision granting *exequatur* and further remedies are addressed elsewhere (see paras 9.319 *et seq*).

(3) Appeal against the decision granting exequatur

No appeal against the decision granting leave for enforcement is available. An application for setting aside or for revocation of the award is the only means of recourse available against such decision. Accordingly, the parallel proceedings, upon appeal and upon an application for setting aside, are avoided.[222] Any leave for enforcement is annulled by operation of law if an award is set aside or in the case of revocation of the award (Art 1062, para 4 Rv). **9.325**

The decision rendered on an application for setting aside or revocation of an award may be appealed to the Court of Appeal and to the Supreme Court (Art 1063, para 3 and 4 Rv). **9.326**

(4) Appeal (and procedure) if exequatur *has been refused*

The decision refusing enforcement may be appealed before the Court of Appeal within two months (Art 1063, para 3 Rv). **9.327**

If the decision refusing enforcement is confirmed by the Court of Appeal, then recourse is available to the Supreme Court. The time limit for the recourse is two months from the date the decision is signed (Art 1064, para 4 Rv). If leave for enforcement is granted either on appeal to the Court of Appeal or on the recourse to the Supreme Court, the only remedy against the decision is an application for setting aside or an application for revocation of the award (Art 1064, para 5 Rv). **9.328**

(5) Procedure of enforcement (attachment of bank accounts etc)

If the court has granted the leave for enforcement, the final or partial final award may be enforced on the basis of the provisions that apply to the enforcement of court decisions in general, which include provisions on third party attachments (see also para 311). **9.329**

(5.1) At the stage of enforcement, may the losing party invoke arguments and circumstances which are based on facts which have occurred before (or after) the award was made? It may be argued that if the arbitral award or the manner in which it was made violates public policy or good morals, the enforcement of such award may be refused, regardless of when the facts concerned have actually occurred. **9.330**

(5.2) May the losing party invoke a set-off based on claims that are not related to the matter of the arbitral proceeding? Is it material whether such claim came into existence before or after the award was made? Under Dutch law, a debtor is entitled to a set-off where he has a claim against a party which corresponds to his debt to the same party, and where he has both the right to pay the debt and the right to enforce payment of the claim (Art 127, para 2 of Book 6 of the Dutch Civil Code). However, the question of whether the losing party may actually invoke a set-off based on claims that are not related to the matter of the arbitral proceedings has to be answered on the basis of the applicable rules of substantive law. **9.331**

[222] Van den Berg, *Int Handbook on Comm Arb* 29.

VIII. Foreign awards

A. Recognition and/or enforcement of foreign awards (national law)

(1) Rules according to national law

9.332 The provisions concerning the recognition and enforcement of foreign arbitral awards are contained in Title Two of the Act, 'Arbitration outside the Netherlands' (Arts 1075–1076 Rv). In order for these provisions to apply, the award in question must have been rendered in a country outside the Netherlands.[223] Any other criterion, such as the nationality of the parties or the 'international' character of the relationship, is not relevant for the applicability of the provisions concerned.

9.333 Article 1075 Rv deals with the recognition and enforcement of a foreign arbitral award when a treaty is applicable (for example, the New York Convention). The provision of Art 1076 applies if no treaty concerning the recognition and enforcement can be applied, but also 'if an applicable treaty allows a party to rely upon the law of the country in which recognition and enforcement is sought' (Art 1076, para 1). This provision reflects the possibility provided for in Art VII(1) of the New York Convention. The so-called more-favourable-right provision, expressed in Art VII(1), gives the possibility to the party to rely on the more favourable domestic law of the country where the enforcement and recognition of the award is sought. In practice, the New York Convention is the treaty that will most frequently be applicable, in the light of the number of signatories to the Convention.[224] See also para 9.336 for the question of whether arbitral awards that have been set aside in the country of origin may still be enforced in the Netherlands.

(2) Requirements to be fulfilled by the applicant (procedure, time limits)

9.334 The party seeking enforcement must complete the requirements found either in the provisions of the applicable treaty, or in Art 1076, para 1 Rv. According to Art 1076, para 1, the enforcement may be sought in the Netherlands upon submission of the original or a certified copy of the arbitration agreement and award. These requirements correspond to the conditions that must be satisfied by the party seeking enforcement provided in Art IV of the New York Convention. The enforcement may be refused only if the opposing party asserts and proves one of the grounds for refusal given in Art V New York Convention.

9.335 Under the Act, the party against whom the enforcement is sought may invoke five grounds for disputing enforcement (Art 1076, para 1 (A) Rv). In many respects Art V of the Convention and the provisions of Art 1076, para 1 (A) Rv provide for the same grounds for refusal of the enforcement. These include the lack of a valid arbitration agreement (1076, para 1(A)(a) Rv), improper constitution of the arbitral tribunal (1076, para 1(A)(b) Rv), and non-compliance of the arbitral tribunal with its mandate (1076, para 1(A)(c) Rv). The enforcement and recognition under the Act may also be refused if the 'arbitral award is still

[223] Van den Berg, *New York Convention* 145.

[224] The 1958 New York Convention is viewed in the literature as '[the] most important treaty for the recognition and enforcement of foreign arbitral awards', in: Van den Berg, *New York Convention* 150.

open to an appeal to a second arbitral tribunal, or to a court in the country in which the award is made' (Art 1076, para 1(A)(d) Rv). It is argued that this ground can be understood so as to mean that the award has not yet become 'binding' upon the parties, as expressed in Art V(1)(e) of the New York Convention.[225] Recognition and enforcement may also be refused if the arbitral award has been set aside by a competent authority of the country in which the award was made (Art 1076 para 1 (A)(e) Rv) (see also para 9.336 for the question of whether arbitral awards that have been set aside in the country of origin may still be enforced in the Netherlands). Both the Convention and the Act provide that an award will not be enforced if it would be contrary to public policy (Art 1076, para 1 (B) Rv). This ground is able to be applied by the court *ex officio.* An award could be considered as contrary to public policy if it was found, for example, that the subject matter of the dispute was not capable of settlement by arbitration.

However, the Act limits the possibility to invoke grounds listed in Art 1076, para 1(A) (a)–(c) Rv (the invalidity of the arbitration agreement, irregularity in the constitution of the tribunal and the arbitral tribunal's non-compliance with the mandate). These grounds cannot successfully be invoked in the enforcement procedure by the party who participated in the arbitral proceedings, but failed to raise that objection during the arbitral proceedings (Art 1076, para 2–4 Rv). **9.336**

When drafting Art 1076 of the Act, the provision of Art V of the New York Convention was considered. The main principles expressed in the relevant provision of the Convention have been taken over and incorporated in Art 1076. Thus, any of the grounds listed in Art 1076, para 1(A) Rv must be asserted and proved by the party opposing the enforcement. Moreover, the grounds for refusal under Art 1076, para 1 (A) Rv present an exhaustive list, the number of reasons is limited and the grounds for refusal must be narrowly interpreted. It is important to note that the party bringing a claim for enforcement must use either the New York Convention, (or any other applicable treaty) or Art 1076 Rv of the Act as a basis for enforcement. It is not possible for the party to 'combine elements favourable to him from the two'.[226] **9.337**

(3) Remedies against decisions granting or declining enforcement

Both Arts 1075–1076 Rv provide for Articles 985 to 991 Rv (now Arts 985–990 Rv) of the Code of Civil Procedure to apply to the enforcement proceedings.[227] There is a limitation under Art 1075 Rv that they are only to be applied to the extent that the treaty does not contain provisions deviating therefrom. For Arts 985 to 991 Rv to apply under both Art 1075 Rv and Art 1076, para 6 Rv it is also a requirement that the President of the District Court be appointed as the competent judge for enforcement proceedings brought in the Netherlands. The President of the District Court is interpreted to mean the President of the District Court where the petitioner seeks enforcement or the President of the District Court where the opposing party has his domicile. Importantly, Art 985 Rv states that there **9.338**

225 Sanders/Van den Berg, Art 1076, 50, note 122.
226 Van den Berg, *New York Convention* 161.
227 'Of the procedures required for the enforcement of judgments established in foreign states'.

can be no review on the merits of the award.[228] A decision by the President of the District Court is subject to appeal before the Supreme Court, if recourse is sought by the party within two months from the date of the decision. Legal remedies available against a decision made by the President can be found in Arts 989–990 Rv or the applicable treaty.

9.339 The Act also provides for the possibility of a partial enforcement of an award, if it is found that that the award was in excess of, or different from, what was claimed (Art 1076, para 5 Rv). A court in the Netherlands also has the discretion to suspend its decision on the enforcement if an application to set aside the award is filed by a party in the country where the award was made, but the court has not reached a final decision on this issue (Art 1076, para 7 Rv). In this situation the provisions on the suspension of enforcement contained in Art 1066, paras 2 to 6 Rv shall apply.

B. Recognition and/or enforcement of foreign awards (conventions, treaties)

(1) Specific bilateral or multilateral treaties

9.340 As mentioned previously, Art 1075 Rv relates to the recognition and enforcement of a foreign arbitral award when there is an applicable treaty. The Netherlands has ratified several multilateral treaties concerning the recognition and enforcement of foreign awards. The Netherlands has concluded bilateral treaties that contain provisions concerning the enforcement of arbitral awards: The Belgian–Dutch Convention 1925; The German–Dutch Convention on Enforcement 1962; and The Treaty of Friendship, Commerce and Navigation between the Kingdom of the Netherlands and the United States of America 1956.[229] The latter treaty, which provided for enforcement by recourse to the 1927 Geneva Convention, may be seen as redundant as both signatories are now parties to the New York Convention.

(2) Existence of a standard procedure for the enforcement of foreign awards

9.341 When considering the issue of enforcement, the New York Convention states that its conditions in this area will prevail over possible conditions of national law. However, the manner of enforcement is left to national procedural law.[230] Where there is no applicable treaty governing the enforcement of an award, Dutch law on arbitration applies to enforce a foreign award, as explained above (Art 1076 Rv). The same is true when there is an applicable treaty in force that allows national law to take precedence.[231] As mentioned previously, in the Netherlands, enforcement arises out of the provisions of Arts 985 to 991 Rv, which relate to the enforcement of foreign judgments. These provisions apply to the enforcement of foreign awards under treaties to the extent that the treaty does not contain deviating provisions. It is required that the judge competent to decide on provisional relief (ie the President of the District Court) is substituted for the District Court and the time limit for appeal from this decision is two months (Art 1076 Rv).

[228] Art V of the New York Convention also prohibits a review of the merits of an award.
[229] Van den Berg, *New York Convention* 158.
[230] *ibid*, 152.
[231] *ibid*, 164.

(3) Extent of examination and review of the award by the court

The courts' control is reduced to the examination on the reasons enumerated in Art V of the New York Convention. When the Convention does not apply, the recognition or enforcement may be refused on the grounds listed in Art 1076 of the Act (see para 9.327). It is a generally accepted interpretation of the New York Convention that the court, before which the enforcement of a foreign award is sought, may not review the merits of the award. The grounds for refusal of the enforcement are limited (see Art V, New York Convention). They do not include a mistake in fact or law.[232] The only exception to this rule is when the award violates substantive rules of public policy of the country where the enforcement is sought (see Art V(2)(b), New York Convention).[233] **9.342**

C. Application of the New York Convention

(1) Application of the New York Convention in practice

The Netherlands has been a signatory to the New York Convention since 10 June 1958. Ratification to the Convention took place on 24 April 1964. As already discussed, control of the award by the courts is reduced to the examination on the reasons listed in Art V of the New York Convention. It should be noted that, in special circumstances, a foreign arbitral award that has been set aside may still be enforced in the Netherlands. The Amsterdam Court of Appeal ruled that the New York Convention 1958 pertains to the recognition and enforcement of arbitral awards, but does not provide in the international recognition of decisions by a foreign state courts to set aside arbitral awards. Therefore, the question of whether the decision of a foreign state court to set aside the arbitral awards can be recognized in the Netherlands must be answered on the basis of the rules of general private international law. This means that a Dutch court is at any rate not compelled to refuse the leave to enforce an arbitral award that was set aside if the foreign judgment under which the arbitral award was set aside cannot be recognized in the Netherlands. This particularly applies if the manner in which said judgment was brought about does not satisfy the principles of due process and for that reason recognition of the judgment would lead to a conflict with Dutch public policy, eg if it must be assumed that the foreign judgment was rendered by a judicial instance that was not impartial and independent.[234] **9.343**

(2) Examples of decisions which do not apply the Convention correctly

To our knowledge, there are no decisions of the Dutch Supreme Court in which the New York Convention has been applied incorrectly. **9.344**

IX. Appendix

A. National legislation

Book Four of the Code of Civil Procedure (*Burgerlijke Rechtsvordering—Boek vier*), Articles 1020–1076, came into effect on 1 December 1996, published in English, German, French

232 Van den Berg, *New York Convention* 269 *et seq.*

233 See also, Court of Justice of the EC, 1 June 1999 (C-126/97) *(ECO Swiss/Benetton) NJ* 2000, 339, published also in (1999) XXIV *YCA* 629.

234 Court of Appeal Amsterdam, 28 April 2009, Case no 200.005.269/01 (see <http://www.rechtspraak.nl>).

and Dutch in: Sanders, P. and Berg, A. J. van den (eds), *The Netherlands Arbitration Act 1986*, (Kluwer Law and Taxation Publishers, Deventer, Antwerp, London, Frankfurt, Boston, New York, 1997).

The Netherlands Civil Code (*Burgerlijk Wetboek*) of 1 January 1992, published in English and French in: Haanappel, P.P.C. and Mackaay, E. (eds), *Nieuw Nederlands Burgerlijk Wetboek—het vermogensrecht* (New Netherlands Civil Code—Patrimonial Law), (Kluwer Law and Taxation Publishers, Deventer, Boston, 1990).

The Netherlands Bankruptcy Act (*Faillissementswet*) of 1893, as amended, published in English in Wood, P. and Totty, P.G. (eds.) (Butterworth International Insolvency Laws, Butterworths, 1994).

B. Arbitral institutions

Netherlands Arbitration Institute (NAI),
P.O. Box 21075, 3001 AB Rotterdam.
Visiting address of the NAI Secretariat:
Aert van Nesstraat 25 J-K, 3012 CA Rotterdam.
Telephone (+31)(10)–201 6969
Telefax (+31)(10)–201 6968
Email: secretariaat@nai-nl.org
Website : <http://www.nai-nl.org>

NAI Arbitration Rules in force as of 13 November 2001

A short list of arbitral institutes of particular interest to international trade and industry can be found in Berg, A.J. van den, 'The Netherlands', in J. Paulsson. (ed), *Intl Handbook Comm Arb*, Suppl. 7, April 1987, p 3.

C. Model arbitration clauses

NAI Arbitration clause:

> All disputes arising in connection with the present contract, or further contracts resulting therefrom, shall be finally settled in accordance with the Arbitration Rules of the Netherlands Arbitration Institute (Nederlands Arbitrage Instituut).

Additionally, various matters may be provided for:

- 'The arbitral tribunal shall be composed of one arbitrator/three arbitrators.'
- 'The place of arbitration shall be …….. '(city).
- 'The arbitral procedure shall be conducted in ….'(language).
- 'The arbitral tribunal shall decide as amiable compositeur.'
- 'Consolidation of the arbitral proceedings with other arbitral proceedings pending in the Netherlands, as provided in art 1046 of the Netherlands Code of Civil Procedure, is excluded.'

D. Bibliography

Asser, C., Hartkamp, A.S. and Sieburgh, C.H., *Handleiding tot de beoefening van het Nederlands burgerlijk recht*, 6–1 (Asser serie, 13th edn, Kluwer, Deventer, 2008) (Asser/Hartkamp/Sieburgh).

Berg, A.J. van den, *The New York Arbitration Convention of 1958: Towards a Uniform Judical Interpretation*, (Asser/Kluwer, The Hague/Deventer, 1981) (Van den Berg, *New York Convention*).

Berg, A.J. van den, 'The Netherlands' in P. Sanders and A.J. van den Berg (eds), *Intl Handbook Comm Arb*, Suppl 7 (Kluwer Law International, The Hague, London, Boston, April, 1987) (Van den Berg, *Intl Handbook Comm Arb*).

Berg, A.J. van den, *Hoe gastvrij is Nederland voor de international arbitrage*, Public Lecture held on 11 April 1990 at the Erasmus University Rotterdam (Kluwer, Deventer, 1990) (Van den Berg, Public Lecture).

Berg, A.J. van den, Delden, R. Van and Snijders, H.J., *Netherlands Arbitration Law* (Kluwer Law and Taxation Publishers, Deventer, Boston, 1993) (Van den Berg/Van Delden/Snijders).

Delden, R. Van, *Internationale handelsarbitrage* (Kluwer, Deventer, 1997) (Van Delden).

Franx, J.P., *Het ontwerp Boek IV van het Wetboek van Burgerlijke Rechtsvordering* (W.E.J. Tjeenk Willink BV, Zwolle, 1985) (Franx).

Fung Fen Chung, C.S.K., *Bewijsmiddelen in het arbitraal geding* (SDU Uitgevers, The Hague, 2004) (Fung).

Hel-Koedoot, van de, M., 'De (kosten)veroordeling in arbitrage. Een overzicht aan de hand van het NAI Arbitrage Reglement' (2009), *TvA* 37–44 (Van de Hel-Koedoot).

Hugenholtz, W., *Hoofdlijnen van Nederlands burgerlijk procesrecht* (21 edn revised by W.H. Heemskerk, Reed Business, The Hague, 2006) (Hugenholtz/Hemskerk).

King, D.B. and Leeuwen, M. Van, 'Summary Arbitral Proceedings, A Powerful New Mechanism in NAI Arbitrations' (2003) 3 *Mealey's Int'l Arb Rep* 1–8 (King/Van Leeuwen).

Lazić, V., *Insolvency Proceedings and Commercial Arbitration* (Kluwer Law International, The Hague, London, Boston, 1998) (Lazić).

Lazić, V., 'Arbitration and Insolvency Proceedings: Claims of Ordinary Bankruptcy Creditors' (1999) 3 *Electronic J of Comp L* 1–29 <http://www.ejcl.org/33/art33–2.html> (accessed 10 August 2008) (Lazić, Electronic Journal of Comparative Law).

Lazić, V., 'Arbitration Law Reforms in the Netherlands: Formal and Substantive Validity of an Arbitration Agreement' in J.H.M. van Erp/L.P.W. van Vliet (eds), *Netherlands Reports to the Seventeenth International Congress of Comparative Law* (Intersentia, Antwerpen, Oxford, Utrecht, 2006) 125–47 (Lazić, *Arbitration Law Reforms in the Netherlands*).

Meijer, G.J., 'Arbitrage—Boek Vier' in: A.I.M. Van Mierlo, C.J.J.C.Van Nispen, C.J.J.C. and M.V. Polak (eds), *Burgerlijke Rechtsvordering: Text & Commentaar* (Kluwer, Deventer, 2008) (Meijer, *T&C Rv*).

Meijer, G.J., *Overeenkomst tot arbitrage* (Kluwer, Deventer, 2009) (Meijer, *Overeenkomst tot arbitrage*).

Meijer, G.J. and Borelli, S., 'Interview met P. Sanders', (1996) *TvA* 2–12 (Meijer/Borelli).

Meijer, G.J. and Nieuwendijk, van den, I.P.M, 'Kroniek arbitrage 2004–2006' (2007) 74, *O&R* 21–35 (Meijer/Nieuwendijk).

Memorie van toelichting (MvT), (1984) Tijdschrift voor Arbitrage (*TvA*) 1984, 4A (MvT 1984 *TvA* 4A).

Nieuwendijk, van den, I.P.M., 'Aanvulling van arbitrale vonnissen' (2002) *TvA* 3—10 (Nieuwendijk).

Paulsson, J. *et al*, *The Freshfields Guide to Arbitration and ADR: Clauses in International Contracts*, (2nd edn, Kluwer Law International, The Hague, London, Boston, 1999) (Paulsson *et al*).

Pelinck, M.J., 'BTW bij arbitrage' (2007) *TvA* 87–93 (Pelinck).

Redfern, A. and Hunter, M., *Law and Practice of International Commercial Arbitration* (4th edn, Sweet & Maxwell, London, 2004) (Redfern/Hunter).

Sanders, P., *Het Nederlandse arbitragerecht* (4th edn, Kluwer, Deventer, 2001) (Sanders, *Het Nederlandse arbitragerecht*).

Sanders, P., 'Arbitrage en faillissement' (1988) 6, *TvA* 168 (Sanders, TvA 88/6).

Sanders, P., *Quo vadis arbitration? Sixty years of Arbitration Practice* (Kluwer Law International, The Hague, London, Boston, 1999) (Sanders, Quo vadis arbitration).

Sanders, P. and Berg, A.J. van den (eds), *The Netherlands Arbitration Act 1986*, (Kluwer Law and Taxation Publishers, Deventer, Antwerp, London, Frankfurt, Boston, New York, 1987) (Sanders/Van den Berg).

Snijders, H.J., *Access to Civil Procedure Abroad*, (C.H. Beck Verlag, Munich/Kluwer Law International, The Hague, London, Boston, 1996) (Snijders, *Access to Civil Procedure Abroad*).

Snijders, H.J., 'Vierde boek—arbitrage', in: *Burgerlijke Rechtsvordering (Civil Procedure)*, a loose-leaf edition (Kluwer, Deventer, 2006) (Snijders, Loose-leaf).

Snijders, H.J. and Buruma, S.L., *Bouwarbitrage en civile rechter*, Publikatie van de Vereniging voor Bouwrecht, no 23 (Kluwer, Deventer, 1995) (Snijders/Buruma).

Snijders, H.J., Klaassen, C.J.M. and Meijer, G.J., *Nederlands burgerlijk procesrecht* (4th edn, Kluwer, Deventer, 2007) (Snijders/Klaassen/Meijer).

Snijders, H.J. and Meijer, G.J., (eds), 'Arbitrage', *Vademecum Burgerlijk Procesrecht* (Kluwer, Deventer, 2002) (Snijders/Meijer).

Rossem, W. Van and Cleveringa, R.P., *Verklaring van het Nederlands Weboek van Burgerlijke Rechtsvordering* (4th edn, R.P. Cleveringa, Zwolle, 1972) (Van Rossem/Cleveringa).

Ynzonides, M., 'De invloed van faillietverklaring op arbitrage' (1991) 6008 *Weekblad voor privaatrecht, notariaat en registratie* (*WPNR*) 390 (*Ynzonides*).

10

SINGAPORE

Christopher Lau

I. Introduction

A. Current status of the law on arbitration

(1) Short history

Arbitration has been in use in Singapore since the late 1970s when it gained acceptance primarily in the construction and, to a lesser extent, in the maritime industry as a means of resolving disputes. In the 1980s the country took its first significant step into international arbitration by acceding, on 21 August 1986, to the New York Convention. These early positive developments were, however, marred by a controversial court decision in the mid 1980s barring foreign counsel from appearing in international arbitrations conducted in Singapore. This remained the law in Singapore until the mid-1990s when the ruling was reversed. Until its reversal, notwithstanding the establishing in the early 1990s of an arbitral institution in Singapore—the Singapore International Arbitration Centre ('SIAC')—to administer arbitral disputes, Singapore was not the seat or venue of choice for the arbitration of international disputes. Another 10 years were to pass before Singapore took its next significant step. In 1995, the Model Law came into force as the First Schedule to the International Arbitration Act. Today, with the government's aggressive promotion of Singapore as the seat for international arbitrations in: **10.01**

(i) liberalizing laws permitting foreign counsel to appear in international arbitrations even when the substantive law of the dispute is Singapore law;

(ii) exempting foreign arbitrators from having to pay withholding tax;
(iii) providing for a 50 per cent income tax exemption on 'qualifying incremental income' earned on international arbitration fees by approved law firms;
(iv) the liberalization of immigration laws permitting both foreign counsel and arbitrators to enter and to appear and conduct arbitrations in Singapore; and
(v) the swift enactment of legislation overturning court decisions adverse to the development of Singapore as an international arbitration centre,[1]

and with a very supportive judiciary[2] of party autonomy in arbitration, Singapore is increasingly the seat or venue of choice by parties for the resolution of international disputes.

(2) Law in force and future projects

10.02 There are two statutes governing arbitration in Singapore. First, the Arbitration Act[3] which came into force on 1 March 2002. It is based on the Model Law but it also incorporates provisions from the English Arbitration Act 1996. Second, the International Arbitration Act[4] which was enacted on 31 October 2004 and came into force on 27 January 1995.

10.03 The International Arbitration Act gives the UNCITRAL Model Law on International Commercial Arbitration adopted by the United Nations Commission on International Trade Law on 21 June 1985 ('the Model Law') with the exception of ch VIII of the Model Law, the force of law in Singapore.[5]

10.04 An important future project concerning arbitration in Singapore is an integrated arbitration complex which will contain very modern hearing rooms and facilities. It is expected to be completed in about August 2009. When completed, it will be home to SIAC as well as other international arbitral institutions: see <http://www.maxwell-chambers.com>.

10.05 The International Arbitration Act is also currently under review by the government to 'fine tune' the legislative framework for arbitration. It is expected that there will be amendments to the International Arbitration Act to empower the court to grant interim relief in aid of foreign arbitrations, and to modernize the definition of an 'arbitration agreement' by making it clear that Singapore recognizes that an arbitration agreement can be contained in 'electronic communications'.

---

[1] *Dermajaya Properties v Premium Properties* [2002] 2 SLR 164 and the International Arbitration Act (c 143A, 2002 Rev Ed Sing), s 15A [International Arbitration Act].

The author is deeply indebted to Gemma Kristina Birt MA (Oxon), BCL; to Julia Loh, LLB (NUS) and Ram Kumar Poorna Chandran, BABL (Hons), LLM (NUS) for their invaluable research and assistance without which this Chapter would not have been possible.

[2] See eg *WSG Nimbus Pte Ltd v Board of Control for Cricket in Sri Lanka* [2002] 3 SLR 603, where the Singapore Court took a robust approach and issued an anti-suit injunction restraining a party from proceeding with an action that that party had commenced in the Colombo High Court, Sri Lanka in order that an arbitration in Singapore could proceed.

[3] (c 10, 2002 Rev Ed Sing) [Arbitration Act].

[4] (c 143A, 2002 Rev Ed Sing).

[5] International Arbitration Act s 3(1).

(3) Distinction between national and international arbitration

Arbitration in Singapore may be governed either by the Arbitration Act or the International Arbitration Act. National or domestic arbitration will be governed by the Arbitration Act while international arbitration will be governed by the International Arbitration Act. 10.06

(3.1) If there are different systems and rules for national/international arbitration, what are the criteria for the distinction between both systems? Whilst what is a 'domestic' arbitration is not defined under the Arbitration Act or the International Arbitration Act, what constitutes an 'international' arbitration is. The Arbitration Act therefore acts as the default regime whenever an arbitration falls outside the ambit of the International Arbitration Act. Section 5(2) of the International Arbitration Act states that an arbitration is international if: 10.07

(a) at least one of the parties to an arbitration agreement, at the time of the conclusion of the agreement, has its place of business in any State other than Singapore; or
(b) one of the following places is situated outside the State in which the parties have their places of business:
   (i) the place of arbitration if determined in, or pursuant to, the arbitration agreement;
   (ii) any place where a substantial part of the obligations of the commercial relationship is to be performed or the place with which the subject-matter of the dispute is most closely connected; or
(c) the parties have expressly agreed that the subject-matter of the arbitration agreement relates to more than one country.

Section 5(3) of the International Arbitration Act further provides that: 10.08

(a) if a party has more than one place of business, the place of business shall be that which has the closest relationship to the arbitration agreement;
(b) if a party does not have a place of business, a reference to his place of business shall be construed as a reference to his habitual residence.

A consequence of these provisions is that even where the parties to the arbitration agreement are Singaporean companies having their places of business in Singapore, the arbitration may still be an international arbitration under the International Arbitration Act, if the subject matter of the dispute is closely connected to another place outside Singapore or if the substantial part of the performance of the commercial contract is outside Singapore.[6] 10.09

The International Arbitration Act allows parties to international arbitrations to opt out of the International Arbitration Act. 10.10

Parties must be aware, however, if they choose to opt out of the International Arbitration Act, their arbitration will fall within the domestic arbitration regime[7] which in turn will involve or give opportunity for greater court supervision of the arbitral process. (See further para 10.13 *infra*). 10.11

---

6 *Halsbury's Laws of Singapore, vol 2* para [20.013] 18; and see *Vanol Far East Marketing Pte Ltd v Hin Leong Trading (Pte) Ltd* [1997] 3 SLR 484.

7 International Arbitration Act s 15(1).

10.12 Conversely, parties to a domestic arbitration are able to opt into the International Arbitration Act. This can be done in a number of ways. The parties may agree that even though their arbitration is not an 'international arbitration' under the International Arbitration Act, the Act or the Model Law should apply to the arbitration.[8] They may expressly agree that 'the subject matter of the arbitration agreement relates to more than one country'.[9] In addition, if the parties have chosen Singapore as the seat of their arbitration and if they chose to arbitrate under the Arbitration Rules of the SIAC ('the SIAC Rules'), r 32 of the SIAC Rules provides that: 'Where the seat of arbitration is Singapore, the law of the arbitration under these Rules shall be the International Arbitration Act (Chapter 143A, 2002 Ed, Statutes of the Republic of Singapore) or its modification or re-enactment thereof'. This was affirmed by the Singapore High Court in *Car & Cars Pte Ltd v Volkswagen AG and Another* [2009] SGHC 77 where the court held that parties, in agreeing to adopt the SIAC Rules 2007, elect to have their arbitration treated as an international arbitration, with the International Arbitration Act as the governing regime.

10.13 The bifurcation in the arbitral regime is significant because for arbitrations falling under the Arbitration Act, there is a degree of court supervision in contrast to international arbitrations where there is restricted court intervention. For example, on an application to the court to stay court proceedings by a party to an arbitration agreement, the court, in an arbitration falling under the Arbitration Act, is not compelled to order a stay as it would have to in arbitrations under the International Arbitration Act. It retains a discretion and may order a stay if it is satisfied that:

(i) there is no sufficient reason why the matter should not be referred in accordance with the arbitration agreement; and
(ii) the applicant was, at the time when the proceedings were commenced, and still remains, ready and willing to do all things necessary to the proper conduct of the arbitration.[10] Another example of such supervision arises in the context of an award of costs. The Arbitration Act requires that any costs directed by an award to be paid shall, unless the award otherwise directs, be taxed by the Registrar of the Supreme Court.[11]

A. Practice of arbitration

(1) Frequency of arbitration as opposed to litigation

10.14 There are currently no means available to ascertain the frequency of arbitration as opposed to litigation in Singapore.

(2) Leading arbitral institutions and statistics (if available)

10.15 Although no statistics are available as to the number of disputes being arbitrated in Singapore, such anecdotal evidence as there is indicates that arbitration as a means of resolving disputes is increasingly being employed in preference to litigation and not least

[8] International Arbitration Act s 5(1).
[9] *ibid*, s 5(2)(c).
[10] Arbitration Act s 6(2); International Arbitration Act s 6(2).
[11] Arbitration Act s 39(1).

because of the government's continuing efforts to promote and persuade all sectors of the Singapore economy—financial services, construction and engineering, manufacturing, industrial and maritime—to adopt the arbitral process. For example, SIAC's administration of international disputes continues to grow year on year. In 2008 it administered a total of 99 cases, compared to 58 in 2000.[12]

The principal and premier arbitral institution located in Singapore is the SIAC, an independent and non-profit organization incorporated in March 1990. Since it commenced operations on 1 July 1991, the range, value and international nature of disputes administered by it continue to increase, reflecting initially the types of businesses and investments prevalent to South East Asia[13] and increasingly now, those prevalent to South Asia[14] and East Asia.[15] These disputes include natural resources and energy, building and construction, technology, joint ventures, infrastructure, financial services, mergers and acquisitions, trade, maritime, corporate, insurance and intellectual property. **10.16**

As a reflection of the diverse areas of disputes it is asked to administer, the SIAC in addition to maintaining a panel of arbitrators of different disciplines, skills, expertise and nationality is at liberty to and in practice, has appointed arbitrators from outside its panel when it is or has been necessary for it to do so. **10.17**

The International Centre for Dispute Resolution ('ICDR') has also entered into a joint venture with SIAC to administer regional disputes. **10.18**

There is also an arbitral institution for the maritime industry. The Singapore Chamber of Maritime Arbitration has recently been revamped and relaunched with its own arbitration rules which are modelled loosely on the London Maritime Arbitration Association (LMAA) Rules. The rules are known as the SCMA Arbitration Rules 2nd Edition (2009) and can be found on the SCMA website: <http://www.scma.org.sg>. **10.19**

For the administration of intellectual property disputes there is WIPO's Arbitration and Mediation Centre in Singapore. **10.20**

Finally there is the ICC International Court of Arbitration which, although not located in Singapore, accounts for the largest number of international commercial arbitrations being heard in Asia. **10.21**

II. Jurisdiction of the arbitral tribunal

A. Arbitration agreement

(1) Arbitration clause and submission agreement

A submission agreement is an agreement between parties to submit an existing dispute to arbitration. An arbitration clause is an agreement between parties to refer a dispute **10.22**

[12] Statistics taken from the SIAC website, see <http://www.siac.org.sg/facts-statistics.htm>.
[13] eg Indonesia, Malaysia, Vietnam, Thailand, Philippines.
[14] ie India, Pakistan, Bangladesh, Sri Lanka.
[15] eg China, Korea.

to arbitration. No distinction is drawn in the Arbitration Act or the International Arbitration Act between a submission agreement and an arbitration clause.

(2) Requirements as to the contents of the arbitration agreement

10.23 The test as to what constitutes an arbitration agreement under both the Arbitration Act and the International Arbitration Act essentially is whether the criteria set out in Art 7 of the Model Law has been complied with and it should be noted that in the Arbitration Act, the criteria appears wider in that where an assertion of the existence of an arbitration agreement is made in circumstances in which a reply is called for and the assertion is not denied, the Arbitration Act deems such case to be an effective arbitration agreement as between the parties to the proceedings.[16]

(3) Form of the arbitration agreement (eg 'in writing' requirement)

10.24 What constitutes '*an agreement in writing*' has been widely construed by the Singapore courts. Such an agreement in writing can be contained in a document signed by the parties, or be otherwise in an exchange of letters, fax or other means of communication recording the agreement. No specific form of words is required so long as the intention to arbitrate is clear and unequivocal.[17]

10.25 An instance where the court found there to be no valid agreement to arbitrate is the case of *Teck Guan Sdn Bhd v Beow Guan Enterprise Pte Ltd*.[18] There the court was asked to decide whether there was an arbitration agreement in which the word 'arbitration' was not stated in the following clause:

> Any quality dispute would be settled [SIC] amicably with reference to an independent surveyor. However, any dispute out of this contract to be governed by the rules of the Cocoa Merchants' Association of America Inc . . . . in force on that date.

The court took the view that the reference to the said rules being not sufficiently specific to incorporate the arbitration procedure contained in those rules, there was no arbitration agreement.

10.26 On the other hand, a reference in a bill of lading to a charterparty, or some other document containing an arbitration clause, would constitute an arbitration agreement if the reference were such as to make it clear that that clause is part of the bill of lading.[19] Additionally, on the novel and important legal issue of whether an arbitration agreement may validly provide for one arbitral institution to administer an arbitration under the rules of another arbitral institution, the Singapore Court of Appeal in *Insigma Technology Co Ltd v Alstom Technology Ltd*[20] very recently held that it may do so since such agreement was not inoperative for uncertainty.

---

[16] Arbitration Act s 4(4); see also *L&M Concrete Specialists Pte Ltd v United Eng Contractors Pte Ltd* [2000] 4 SLR 441; [2000] SGHC 166.

[17] There is, however, some suggestion that the agreement needs to be in writing and that the document must be signed by the parties, see *Halsbury's Laws of Singapore*, vol 2, para [20.015], 2003 Reissue.

[18] (2003) 4 SLR 276.

[19] In *Star-Trans Far East Pte Ltd v Norske-Tech Ltd* [1996] 2 SLR 409 it was held that: 'It is well-settled from those cases that the courts will construe words of incorporation used in bills of lading narrowly' (p 416).

[20] [2009] SGCA 24.

(3.1) Are there special requirements for a power of attorney/authority to enter into an arbitration agreement on behalf of a third party? Under Singapore law, there are no specific requirements as to the form or nature of the power of attorney or authority required for an arbitration agreement entered into on behalf of a third party to be binding on such third party. 10.27

Whilst it is open to parties to seek a review of the tribunal's decision that it has jurisdiction whether the arbitration is domestic[21] or international,[22] there is, however, no such recourse or appeal available against a tribunal's decision that it does not have jurisdiction. In *PT Asuransi Jasa Indonesia (Persero) v Dexia Bank SA*,[23] the Singapore Court of Appeal (Singapore's apex court) held that a negative ruling on arbitral jurisdiction is not an 'award' and hence, could not be set aside under Art 34 of the Model Law. 10.28

(4) Incorporation of an arbitration clause contained in general terms and conditions

Arbitration clauses must be expressly brought to the attention of the other contracting party and should not be incorporated in general terms and conditions. See *United Eng Contractors Pte Ltd v L&M Concrete Specialists Pte Ltd*.[24] 10.29

(5) Law applicable to the interpretation of arbitration clauses

Where the seat of arbitration is Singapore, in interpreting whether there is an arbitration agreement, the applicable law is the laws of Singapore. 10.30

(5.1) Do courts accept a wide competence of the arbitral tribunal or do they restrict arbitral competence? Do claims which arise in connection with the agreement submitted to arbitration generally fall within the arbitral jurisdiction even if based on tortious legal basis? Does there exist case law with respect to the wording in an arbitration clause as 'arising out of/under/in connection with the present contract' and its specific meaning? Singapore courts do accept a wide competence of the arbitral tribunal to rule on its own jurisdiction. Article 16 of the Model Law which is in the First Schedule to the International Arbitration Act and s 21(1) Arbitration Act specifically provides that arbitrators have the power to rule on their own jurisdiction. In *PT Tugu Pratama Indonesia v Magma Nusantara Ltd*,[25] the High Court upheld the tribunal's ruling on its own jurisdiction in an international arbitration. In *Sabah Shipyard (Pakistan) Ltd v Government of Islamic Republic of Pakistan*,[26] the High Court held, on the issue as to whether the arbitral tribunal had jurisdiction to determine a dispute on costs arising out of an earlier related arbitration, that the tribunal did have jurisdiction on the basis that the arbitration clause which was in the following terms '. . . any dispute or difference between the parties arising out of or in connection with this Agreement' was sufficiently wide to extend to disputes on costs arising under the first arbitration. 10.31

[21] Arbitration Act s 21(9).
[22] International Arbitration Act s10, Art 16(3), Model Law.
[23] [2006] SGCA 41.
[24] [2000] 2 SLR 196.
[25] [2003] SGHC 204.
[26] [2004] 3 SLR 184.

(6) Binding effect of an arbitration clause on third parties (eg in case of a guarantee or assignment)

10.32 An arbitral tribunal is able to assume jurisdiction over individuals or entities who are not parties to the arbitration agreement where there is an assignment or novation of the agreement and pursuant to the Contracts (Rights of Third Parties) Act[27] in respect of third party beneficiaries.

10.33 In Singapore, a legal assignee of a contract, may upon notice of assignment that is given to the other party,[28] be entitled to rights in the arbitration agreement.[29] The assignment must be an absolute assignment and not by way of charge only.[30] An equitable assignee can only claim the right under the arbitration agreement if notice of assignment has been given and the assignee expressly submits to the jurisdiction of the tribunal.[31] An assignor under an equitable assignment is normally joined in as a party to the arbitration.

10.34 **(6.1) What is the law/leading authorities' position on multi-party situations? Especially, (i) with respect to the objection that the arbitration clause does not specifically provide for a plurality of parties in the same procedure; (ii) respect to the constitution of the arbitral tribunal; and (iii) with respect to the consolidation of two or more running arbitration proceedings?** For there to be a plurality of parties either by way of consolidation or otherwise in one arbitration, the parties' agreement or consent is essential. In the absence of such agreement, Singapore law does not vest jurisdiction in the courts to order consolidation. The same holds true where a party seeks to participate in an arbitration proceeding as an intervener.

10.35 Under s 26 of the Arbitration Act, the arbitral tribunal has the power if parties agree to the consolidation of proceedings and concurrent hearings.

10.36 In practice, where the parties are agreeable, the same arbitrator can be appointed for the separate arbitrations. This, however, does not authorize the arbitrator to order a joint hearing without the consent of the parties. If a joint hearing is ordered, and an award is subsequently made against the objections of one of the parties, that party may be able to challenge its enforcement. The arbitrator cannot order a third party to be joined or consolidate the arbitration without the agreement or consent of all the parties.[32]

10.37 **(6.2) Is there case law/authorities with respect to the admissibility of third party participation in an arbitration without being a claimant or defendant (Nebenintervention/Streitverkündung; intervention forcée/volontaire; vouching in; *amicus curiae* etc)? What are the prerequisites and effects of such participation (if permitted)?** There are no authorities in this regard.

---

[27] (c 53B, 2002 Rev Ed Sing).

[28] *Civil Law Act* (c 43, 1999 Rev Ed Sing).

[29] *Montedipe SpA v JTP-RP Jugotanker, The Jordon Nocolov* [1990] *2* Lloyd's Rep 11.

[30] *L/M International Construction Inc (now Bow International Inc) v The Circle Partnership* (1996) 49 Con LR 12.

[31] *Baytur SA v Finagro Holding SA* [1992] QB 610.

[32] *Halsbury's Laws of Singapore, vol 2, Arbitration, Building & Construction* (2003) Reissue 77.

(7) Termination of an arbitration agreement by a party (reasons and case law)

In general, an arbitration agreement may only be terminated with the consent of the parties to the agreement. **10.38**

B. Arbitrability

(1) 'Personal arbitrability' (capacity to conclude arbitration agreements)

Where an individual person is a party to a commercial transaction, which includes an arbitration agreement, there are no special requirements or formalities which that individual person need to comply with for such arbitration agreement to be valid and enforceable save for the usual requirement that the individual should have capacity to enter into a contract. **10.39**

(1.1) May a state (or state agency) as party invoke sovereign immunity before the arbitral tribunal or before a state court (eg in a procedure of enforcement)? There is legislation in Singapore on parties' entitlement to state immunity: see State Immunity Act.[33] The concept of absolute immunity does not apply. Only qualified immunity does. So if the state does an act related to the state of affairs of the country, it would be entitled to the defence of state immunity: see *West LB AG v Philippine National Bank and Others*.[34] **10.40**

The Singapore government is bound by any contracts so long as it is entered into with proper authority.[35] It is entitled to commence and defend civil proceedings.[36] In international agreements, the International Arbitration Act[37] expressly provides that it is binding on the government. This means that the state is bound in the same manner as any other party to an arbitration agreement to which the International Arbitration Act applies. The government has never raised the issue of immunity in arbitration proceedings. **10.41**

(2) 'Objective arbitrability' (eg of patent, trade mark and antitrust matters)

One way to determine the arbitrability of a dispute is whether the subject matter of the dispute falls within the list of 'commercial' subjects stated in the footnote to Art 1 (1) of the Model Law which provides for the Model Law to apply to commercial arbitrations. Whilst the list is not exhaustive, it does provide guidance in that it states that relationships of a commercial nature include, but are not limited to, any trade transaction for the supply or exchange of goods or services, distribution agreements, commercial representation or agency, factoring, leasing, construction of works, consulting, engineering, licensing, investment, financing, banking, insurance, exploitation agreement or concession, joint ventures and other forms of industrial or business cooperation, carriage of goods or passengers by air, sea, rail or road. Thus, for instance, following the collapse of Lehman Brothers in 2008, some of the disputes between investors of Lehman-linked products and the financial **10.42**

33 (c 313, 1985 Rev Ed Sing).
34 [2007] 1 SLR 967.
35 See Government Contracts Act (c 118, 1985 Rev Ed Sing).
36 See Government Proceedings Act (c 121, 1985 Rev Ed Sing).
37 International Arbitration Act s 34.

institutions in Singapore that sold these products such as Lehman Minibond Notes and Merrill Lynch Jubilee Series 3 Notes, were referred to arbitration.

C. Decision on the arbitral tribunal's jurisdiction (*competence-competence*)

(1) Separability (independence of the arbitration agreement from the main agreement)

10.43 Singapore law clearly recognizes the doctrine of separability. Section 21 of the Arbitration Act states that :

> 21 (2) [For the purpose of subsection (1)], an arbitration clause which forms part of a contract shall be treated as an agreement independent of the other terms of the contract.
> 21 (3) A decision by the arbitral tribunal that the contract is null and void shall not entail ipso jure (as a matter of law) the invalidity of the arbitration clause.

The International Arbitration Act[38] enacts into Singapore law Art 16(1) of the Model Law which provides that an arbitration clause which forms part of a contract shall be treated as an agreement independent of the other terms of the contract. A decision by the arbitral tribunal that the contract is null and void does not, as a matter of law, result in the invalidity of the arbitration clause.

10.44 Institutional rules if adopted by the parties would also provide express recognition of this doctrine.[39] In *Government of the Republic of the Philippines v Philippine International Air Terminals Co Inc*,[40] the High Court of Singapore stated:

> The tribunal's jurisdiction was being challenged, and, at the same time, it was asked to consider the law governing the procedure for the arbitration and the substance of the agreement. It was a prerequisite for the tribunal to consider whether the arbitration agreement could be separated from the main contract and survive, despite the alleged nullity of the main contract. If the principle of severability was not available to the tribunal, then the two questions it was asked to consider were otiose. The issue of severability was a necessary aspect of the tribunal's deliberation. It was within the scope of its jurisdiction. GOP's position was thus untenable. It had been given a fair opportunity to present its case: at [30] to [34].

(2) Competence of the tribunal to decide on its own jurisdiction (including form and time of the tribunal's decision)

10.45 Under Art 16 of the Model Law and s 21(1) of the Arbitration Act, arbitrators have the power to rule on their own jurisdiction and the tribunal may do so by deciding the jurisdictional issue as a preliminary issue before deciding on the merits of the dispute or as part of its final award.

(3) Extent of the 'competence-competence' *and role of the courts (including form and time limits of a challenge of the tribunal's decision*

10.46 Under both the International Arbitration Act and the Arbitration Act,[41] parties seeking a review of the tribunal's decision that it has jurisdiction must apply to the court within 30 days of receipt of the tribunal's decision. Whilst such application is pending, the arbitral

---

38 International Arbitration Act s 3.
39 Singapore International Arbitration Centre (SIAC) Rules 2007, r 25.
40 [2007] 1 SLR 278.
41 International Arbitration Act s10; Arbitration Act s 21(10).

tribunal may still continue the arbitral proceedings and make an award on the merits of the dispute.

A plea that the arbitral tribunal has no jurisdiction must be raised not later than the submission of the statement of defence.[42] A plea that it has exceeded the scope of the reference must be raised as soon as the matter alleged to be beyond the scope of the arbitral authority is raised during the arbitration. The tribunal may rule on the issue of jurisdiction either as a preliminary issue or together with the award on the merits. If a ruling is made as a preliminary issue and the tribunal rules that it has jurisdiction, an appeal lies to the High Court.[43] A further appeal to the Court of Appeal on this issue is permitted with leave from the High Court.[44] If the tribunal rules that it has no arbitral jurisdiction, the matter ends there with no appeal. **10.47**

D. Enforcement of an arbitration agreement within or by court proceedings

(1) Effect of invoking an arbitration clause within a court proceeding (and time limits for such a motion)

The effect of invoking an arbitration within a court proceeding depends on whether the arbitration falls under the Arbitration Act or the International Arbitration Act. In relation to domestic arbitrations, s 6 of the Arbitration Act gives the court discretion in deciding whether or not to grant a stay of proceedings in favour of arbitration pursuant to an arbitration agreement. In its exercise of this discretion, the court must be satisfied that, first, there is no sufficient reason why the matter should not be referred in accordance with the arbitration agreement and secondly, that the applicant for the stay of proceedings was, at the time when the proceedings were commenced, and still remains, ready and willing to do all things necessary for the proper conduct of the arbitration. **10.48**

In contrast, the court in stay applications under the International Arbitration Act has no such discretion. It must order a stay unless it is satisfied that the arbitration agreement is null and void, inoperative or incapable of being performed. Section 6 of the International Arbitration Act provides that: **10.49**

> 6(1) Without prejudice to Article 8 of the Model Law, where any party to an arbitration agreement to which this act applies institutes any legal proceedings in any court in Singapore against any other party to the agreement in respect of any matter which is the subject of the agreement, any party to the agreement may, at any time after appearance and before delivering any pleadings or taking any other steps in the proceedings, apply to that court to stay the proceedings.
> (2) The court to which an application has been made in accordance with subsection (1) shall make an order, upon such terms or conditions as it may think fit, staying the proceedings unless it is satisfied that the arbitration agreement is null and void, inoperative or incapable of being performed.

[42] Arbitration Act s 21(4); Model Law Art 16(2).
[43] Arbitration Act s 21(9); Model Law Art 16(3).
[44] International Arbitration Act s 10.

A positive assertion by the defendant that he is disputing the claim would suffice for the purposes of stay of court proceedings under s 6 of the International Arbitration Act. This would be so even if it could be easily demonstrated that the defendant was wrong: *Tjong Very Sumito and Others v Antig Investments Pte Ltd* [2009] 1 SLR 861.

10.50 In *Yee Hong Pte Ltd v Tan Chye Hee Andrew (Ho Bee Development Pte Ltd, Third Party)*[45] the High Court quoted *Taunton-Collins v Cromie*:[46]

> it was undesirable that there should be two proceedings before two different tribunals (the official referee and an arbitrator) who might eg reach inconsistent findings; accordingly there were special reasons for the exercise of the discretion to refuse a stay of execution.

10.51 In the above case, the High Court of Singapore rejected the contention that it did not have jurisdiction to order the parties to enter into a multi-party arbitration in the absence of an agreement between the contractor and the third party to refer their disputes to arbitration. The court also took the view that, as both disputes arose from the same construction project, it would be unsatisfactory for one dispute to be arbitrated while the other was litigated. There was a possibility of inconsistent findings and decisions and a risk that there would not be a holistic resolution of all the issues between the parties. The court therefore ordered that the contractor's claim against the architect and the architect's claim against the developer be stayed and referred to arbitration with the contractor's claim against the developer.

10.52 In *Car & Cars Pte Ltd v Volkswagen AG and Another*,[47] the Singapore High Court formulated the relevant factors:

> 42 Having discussed the cases across the Commonwealth, I shall attempt to crystallize the relevant factors taken into consideration when a judge exercises his or her discretion in deciding to stay arbitration proceedings on the ground that there will be multiplicity of proceedings. The factors are not exhaustive and in no way conclusive. Based on commonwealth jurisprudence, a stay of proceedings in favour of arbitration will not be granted if:
> (a) the issues for determination in court and arbitration are closely related, such that the resolution of one issue will materially affect the other; in particular, if the evidence adduced in both proceedings is similar (discussed in *Yukon Energy; Bond Corporation; Taunton-Collins; Tasmanian Pulp; Well Hoped Ltd; Prestige Pools*);
> (b) the plaintiff 'induces' the multiplicity (discussed in *Bulk Oil; Morrison; Sunway Damansara; Well Hoped Ltd*);
> (c) the court proceedings have progressed beyond a preliminary stage (discussed in *Yukon Energy; Dawson*);
> (d) it is in the interest of justice that a stay should not be granted (discussed in *Taunton-Collins; Dawson; Prestige Pools; Yee Hong Pte Ltd; W Bruce Ltd*).

10.53 **(1.1) If a party has invoked successfully the arbitration agreement in a court proceeding, is it then entitled to deny within the arbitration proceedings that there is a valid and binding arbitration agreement?** Where a party has successfully invoked the arbitration

[45] [2005] 4 SLR 398; [2005] SGHC 163.
[46] [1964] 2 All ER 332.
[47] [2009] SGHC 77.

agreement in the court proceedings and obtained a stay from the court, it is highly unlikely that it would then be able successfully to deny the validity and enforceability of such an agreement in the arbitral proceedings.

(1.2) Vice versa, if a party has successfully objected to an arbitral proceeding by denying that there is a valid arbitration agreement, may it then invoke such an agreement in the ensuing court proceedings? Where a party has successfully objected to the arbitral proceeding by denying that there is a valid arbitration agreement in the arbitral proceedings, it is highly unlikely that it would then be able to successfully deny the validity and enforceability of such an agreement in the court proceedings.

(2) Legal remedies and proceedings to enforce an arbitration agreement

An arbitration agreement, unless a contrary intention is expressed therein, is binding and will be enforced by the court against the party in breach by referring the defaulting party to arbitrate as agreed.[48] The court has no statutory power to revoke an arbitration agreement. The court may stay proceedings which are commenced or prevent steps which are taken in breach of the agreement to arbitrate.[49] Where the defaulting party fails to appoint or take steps to concur in the appointment of the tribunal, the appointment may be made on its behalf by the appointing authority.[50] **10.54**

(2.1) Which would be the internationally competent court (i) for obtaining a declaration that an arbitration agreement is valid and binding; or (ii) to compel arbitration? (The defendant's courts? The courts of the place of arbitration? The claimant's courts, cf Article 6(2) in fine, ICC Rules? An application for a stay or for a declaration as to the validity or enforceability of an arbitration agreement or to enforce an arbitration agreement is generally made to the court of the seat of the arbitration. In *WSG v Nimbus v Board of Control for Cricket in Sri Lanka*,[51] the Singapore court issued an anti-suit injunction restraining a party from commencing proceedings in another jurisdiction in breach of an arbitration agreement. **10.55**

III. The arbitral tribunal

A. Number and qualification of arbitrators

(1) Sole arbitrator or arbitral tribunal with several arbitrators

Arbitrations in Singapore are usually conducted before either a sole arbitrator or a tribunal of three. The parties are free to determine the number of arbitrators and failing such determination, under the Arbitration Act, a single arbitrator is appointed whereas under the International Arbitration Act, the number is three. **10.56**

48 Model Law Art 8.
49 Arbitration Act s 6.
50 *ibid*, s 13 and Model Law Art 11.
51 [2002] 3 SLR 603.

10.57 In *Bovis Lend Lease Pte Ltd v Jay-Tech Marine & Projects Pte Ltd*,[52] Judith Prakash J held that:

> One of the most important principles in arbitration law is that of party autonomy. This is not only reflected in s 23 of the Act but has also been recognised by this court in *Jurong Engineering Ltd v Black & Veatch Singapore Pte Ltd* [2004] 1 SLR 333. Party autonomy means that the parties are free to decide how their arbitral tribunal is to be constituted and how the arbitration proper is to be conducted. In this case Bovis and Jay-Tech Marine were free to select and agree to the role to be played by the SIAC—whether as appointing authority, account holder, administrator or rule provider. . . .

10.58 (1.1) **Are arbitral tribunals with an even number of arbitrators acceptable?** In principle, an even number of arbitrators is permissible. In reality however, there has been no known arbitration since the advent of the Arbitration Act and the International Arbitration Act where the tribunal has comprised of an even number of arbitrators. Where the parties have agreed to a tribunal consisting of an even number of arbitrators, and as a result there is no majority decision, it is arguable that the award may not be enforceable.[53]

(2) Qualification of the arbitrators

10.59 There is no special qualification required of an arbitrator except those which the parties may contractually agree to. Arbitrators may be of any nationality,[54] and any special qualification may be specified in an arbitration agreement or indirectly incorporated by the rules of arbitration followed.[55] If an arbitrator lacks any qualification as agreed by the parties, that may render the arbitral proceeding void which in turn will affect the enforceability of the award, if subsequently made, as the composition of the tribunal was not in accordance with the arbitration agreement.[56]

10.60 (2.1) **Are there mandatory requirements for the qualification of arbitrators (statutory requirements or indirect requirements through eg general conditions of insurance contracts)?** There are no statutory requirements for the qualification of arbitrators except for the requirement:

(i) both under the Arbitration Act (s 14(1) and (2)) and Art 12(1) of the Model Law that an arbitrator must be impartial and independent; and
(ii) that he must possess the qualifications agreed by the parties.

10.61 (2.2) **Which national arbitration institutions may be contacted for obtaining information about qualified (and specialized) arbitrators?** There are a number of arbitral institutions in Singapore maintaining a panel of arbitrators. The three principal institutions to contact are Singapore International Arbitration Centre (SIAC), Singapore Chamber of Maritime Arbitration (SCMA) and International Centre for Dispute Resolution (ICDR). In addition, the National Committee of the Singapore Business Federation is also able to

52 [2005] SGHC 91 at 18.
53 Arbitration Act s 19(1) and Model Law Art 29 require that the award be made by a majority of the arbitrators.
54 Arbitration Act s 13.
55 *Halsbury's Laws of Singapore, vol 2 Arbitration, Building & Construction* (2003) Reissue, [para 20.055] 62.
56 Arbitration Act s 48(1)(a)(v).

recommend arbitrators and it has in fact, when requested by the Secretariat of the ICC International Court of Arbitration, recommended arbitrators for ICC-administered disputes.

(2.3) Are judges or civil servants required to obtain permission by their employer to act as arbitrator? Are these permissions given generally or case-by-case? What are the consequences if such permission has not been obtained? There are no statutory provisions allowing judges to sit as arbitrators and no sitting judge has sat as an arbitrator. There have, however, been occasions when civil servants (eg civil engineers) have sought the permission of their respective employers to sit as arbitrators. Failure to obtain such permission is unlikely to have an adverse effect on the validity of the arbitral proceedings or the award. 10.62

B. Appointment of arbitrators

(1) Extent of party autonomy to establish appointment procedure

The parties are free to establish the appointment procedure and select the arbitrators of their choice provided the selection complies with any specific requirements that the parties have agreed to, such as qualifications and experience. 10.63

(2) Procedure in absence of an agreement by the parties

Where the parties fail to agree on an appointing procedure or where their chosen method of appointment fails, either party may request the chairman of the SIAC to make the necessary appointment or appointments: s 8 of the International Arbitration Act; s 13 of the Arbitration Act. 10.64

The statutory appointing authority in making the appointment must have regard to the nature of the subject matter in dispute, the availability of the candidate appointed, the identities of the parties to the arbitration, the suggestions from the parties as regards any candidate, the qualifications required of the arbitrator and such other considerations as are likely to secure the appointment of an independent and impartial arbitrator.[57] The decision of the Singapore International Arbitration Centre with regard to the appointment of the arbitrators under these provisions is not subject to any appeal.[58] 10.65

(3) Effect of the refusal of one party to cooperate in the constitution of the arbitral tribunal

If a party fails to appoint the arbitrator within 30 days of the receipt of the first request by either party to do so, or if the parties cannot agree on the third arbitrator, the appointment will be made by the chairman of the SIAC as the statutory appointing authority.[59] 10.66

(4) Circumstances and valid reasons for an arbitrator to resign

There is no legislation providing for when and in what circumstances an arbitrator may resign. Conceivably, however, an arbitrator may resign if for example, circumstances exist that give rise to justifiable doubts as to his impartiality or independence, or even where such 10.67

---

[57] Arbitration Act s 13(6)(a).

[58] *ibid*, s 13(7); Model Law Art 11(5).

[59] Arbitration Act s 13(4); Model Law Art 11(5). The appointment by the SIAC chairman is not a judicial process. Therefore it obviates the need for service of judicial process overseas, which can be a lengthy and complicated procedure.

circumstances do not exist, he considers it necessary to do so in order to preserve the integrity of the arbitral process or if he does not possess the qualifications agreed by the parties. He should also be able to resign for reasons of ill health.

C. Challenge and replacement of arbitrators

(1) Grounds, procedure and deadlines for challenging an arbitrator

10.68 Both arbitrations under the Arbitration Act (ss 14(3), (4) & (5)) and the International Arbitration Act adopt the grounds of challenge and challenge procedure provided in Arts 12(2) and 13 of the Model Law. An arbitrator may be challenged only if:

(i) circumstances give rise to justifiable doubts as to his impartiality or independence; or
(ii) he or she does not possess the qualifications agreed by the parties.

A party may challenge an arbitrator appointed by it only for reasons which it becomes aware of after the appointment is made. If a challenge is to be made, it should be made as soon as the party becomes aware of the grounds for challenge.

10.69 In *Anwar Siraj and another v Ting Kang Chung and another*,[60] Tay Yong Kwang J quoted and followed *Hagop Ardahalian v Unifert International SA ('The Elissar')*[61] in which it was held:

> A subjective lack of confidence in the arbitrator by one party is not a sufficient ground to remove him. The test is an objective one and there must exist real grounds for which a reasonable person would think there is a real likelihood that the arbitrator could not or would not fairly determine the issue on the basis of the evidence and the arguments to be adduced before him.

In the above case, Tay Yong Kwang J held that:

> The fact that an arbitrator seems to be constantly ruling in favour of one party is equally consistent with the merits being on that party's side. The applicants must show that his decision was likely to have been coloured by something which should have no part at all in a fair decision-making process.

10.70 **(1.1) Do state courts review challenge procedures which took place in accordance with a specific procedure agreed upon by the parties (eg Article 11, ICC Rules)? If so, at what point in time? May such review be excluded?** Courts do not generally review challenge procedures agreed upon by the parties and, absent fraud, parties are free to exclude such review.

10.71 **(1.2) Is there case law with respect to truncated arbitral tribunals? (cf Article 12(5), ICC Rules)** There is no reported case law in Singapore on truncated arbitral tribunals. A substitute arbitrator is normally appointed according to the rules applicable to the appointment of the arbitrator being replaced.

(2) Procedure for appointing a new arbitrator

10.72 Parties are free to agree on the procedure for the appointment of a new arbitrator and if rules of arbitration have been agreed, the appointment is made in accordance with the

[60] [2003] 2 SLR 287.
[61] [1984] 2 Lloyd's Rep 84 at 89.

procedure stated in those rules.[62] But where there is no agreement or the agreed procedure fails, any party may apply to the chairman of the SIAC, the statutory appointing authority, to make the appointment.[63]

The parties are free to agree whether and if so to what extent the previous proceedings should stand[64] and what effect the removal or termination of the arbitrator has on any appointment made by him. **10.73**

IV. The arbitral procedure

A. General principles

(1) Extent of party autonomy to determine the arbitral procedure

The parties are at liberty to determine the arbitral procedure.[65] **10.74**

(1.1) Are the parties free to choose any national or international law governing the procedure before the arbitral tribunal? The parties are free to choose any national or international law to govern the proceedings before the tribunal. Under s 15 of the International Arbitration Act: **10.75**

> (1) If the parties to an arbitration agreement (whether made before or after 1st November 2001[66]) have expressly agreed either
> (a) that the Model Law or this Part shall not apply to the arbitration; or
> (b) that the Arbitration Act or the repealed Arbitration Act[67] shall apply to the arbitration, then, both the Model Law and this Part shall not apply to that arbitration but the Arbitration Act or the repealed Arbitration Act (if applicable) shall apply to that arbitration.
> (2) For the avoidance of doubt, a provision in an arbitration agreement referring to or adopting any rules of arbitration shall not of itself be sufficient to execute the application of the Model Law or this Part to the arbitration concerned.

(2) Basic procedural principles or mandatory rules to be applied by the arbitral tribunal

Article 19 of the Model Law and s 23 of the Arbitration Act provide that parties are free to agree on the procedure to be followed by the arbitral tribunal in the conduct of the proceedings. **10.76**

Where the arbitration is seated is Singapore, the tribunal is under a duty to act fairly and impartially and to allow each party a reasonable opportunity to present its case. This is irrespective of whether the arbitration is a domestic or an international arbitration. Section 22 of the Arbitration Act states that: **10.77**

> The arbitral tribunal shall act fairly and impartially and shall give each party a reasonable opportunity of presenting his case.

62 See eg SIAC Rules, r13.
63 Arbitration Act s 13(8); Model Law Art 11(3)(b).
64 Arbitration Act s 18(1)(b).
65 *ibid*, s 23(1).
66 Date of commencement of the International Arbitration (Amendment) Act 2001 (Act 38/2001).
67 (c10, 1985 Rev Ed Sing).

Where the arbitration falls under the ambit of the International Arbitration Act, the Model Law applies and provides:

> Article 18 Equal Treatment of Parties
>
> The parties shall be treated with equality and each party shall be given a full opportunity at presenting his case.

(3) Oral hearing or proceeding on basis of written documents

10.78 The hearing may be oral or it may proceed on the basis of written documents or submissions alone.

10.79 Oral hearing may be held for the presentation of evidence by witnesses or for oral arguments only.[68] Witnesses who attend an oral hearing may be cross-examined by counsel in the usual common law adversarial manner with liberty usually granted for re-examination.[69]

(4) Power of the tribunal (in particular the chairman) to issue procedural orders

10.80 The tribunal may issue procedural orders or in the case of a tribunal consisting of more than one arbitrator with the agreement of the parties, by the tribunal chairman solely.

(5) Distinction of matters of substance and matters of procedure

10.81 (5.1) **Are the statutes of limitations a matter of substance or rather of procedure?** As Singapore is a common law jurisdiction, the determination of what comprises matters of substance and what comprises matters of procedure is based on common law principles. Neither the Arbitration Act nor the International Arbitration Act address the distinction between matters of substance and matters of procedure.

10.82 English common law, which is considered to be persuasive in Singapore, distinguishes two kinds of statutes of limitation: those which merely bar a remedy and those which extinguish a right. Statutes of the former kind are procedural, while statutes of the latter kind are substantive.[70] In Singapore, the position is no different.

10.83 The statutory time limitation applies even where the substantive law applicable to the dispute is not the law of Singapore.[71]

(6) Persons able to represent a party in an arbitral proceeding

10.84 A party is at liberty to decide on who is to represent him in the arbitral proceedings, irrespective of the governing law of the contract. The nationality of the counsel chosen is irrelevant.

10.85 Even though foreign lawyers are permitted to represent parties in arbitration proceedings, including appearing at hearings in the arbitration,[72] in cases where the issues in dispute involve Singapore law, foreign lawyers appearing at the arbitration hearing must do so jointly with a Singapore advocate and solicitor who has in force a practising certificate.[73]

---

68 Arbitration Act s 25; Singapore International Arbitration Rules, r 21.1.

69 *Halsbury's Laws of Singapore, vol 2, Arbitration, Building & Construction* (2003) Reissue, para [20.072].

70 Dicey & Morris, *The Conflict of Laws* (2nd edn, r 17 at 172).

71 *Halsbury's Laws of Singapore, vol 2, Arbitration, Building & Construction* (2003) Reissue, para [20.048] 54.

72 *Turner (East Asia) Pte Ltd v Builders Federal (HK)*[1988] 2 MLJ 280.

73 *Legal Profession Act* (c 161, 2001 Rev Ed Sing), s 35.

B. Place of arbitration

(1) Determination of the place of arbitration in absence of an agreement by the parties

In the absence of agreement by the parties on the place of arbitration, the arbitral tribunal may determine the place of arbitration, depending on the circumstances of the case including the parties' convenience. The Arbitration Act also allows parties to authorize any arbitral tribunal or other institution or third party to decide the place of arbitration. **10.86**

(2) Importance and legal effect of place (seat) of the arbitration

The importance and legal effect of the place (seat) of arbitration is that the seat often determines the nationality of the award and applicable *lex arbitri* and it is also an important factor in determining the governing law of the contract, if none has been agreed. The Arbitration Act and the International Arbitration Act only regulate arbitral proceedings where the *situs* or seat of the arbitration is Singapore.[74] **10.87**

(2.1) Are the arbitrators and parties free to convene at places other than the official seat of the arbitration? The tribunal and the parties are free to convene at places other than the seat of the arbitration. In *PT Garuda v Birgen Air*,[75] the Singapore Court of Appeal distinguished between the 'place of arbitration' and the 'venue of the hearing'. The 'place of arbitration' was a matter to be agreed between the parties, and it does not change even though the tribunal holds its hearings at a different venue or venues—the laws of that state or territory of the seat of arbitration will govern the arbitral process. During the SARS epidemic in Singapore, in a number of arbitrations which had Singapore as its seat, the tribunals and parties agreed to hold their hearings in other venues (eg Melbourne, Australia) with the seat of the arbitration remaining Singapore. **10.88**

(2.2) Are there visa requirements to enter the country which apply to lawyers and/or arbitrators? Where may current information on that subject be obtained? All visitors to Singapore who are neither Singapore citizens nor permanent residents entering Singapore for business or for work purposes must hold a visa in order to enter Singapore. Visas are as a rule, however, liberally issued to visitors entering Singapore to participate in arbitrations. Current information on this and other immigration formalities can be obtained at <http://www.ica.gov.sg>. **10.89**

C. Submissions, deadlines and default

(1) Contents and form of submissions (in particular request for arbitration and answer to request)

Section 9 of the Arbitration Act and Art 21 Model Law provide that, unless the parties otherwise agree, an arbitration to be held in Singapore is commenced on the date the request for the dispute to be referred to arbitration is received by the other party. Where the SIAC Rules apply, r 3 provides that a party wishing to commence arbitration must file with the Registrar a Notice of Arbitration containing various particulars such as names and contact particulars of the parties and their representatives. Rule 3.3 of the SIAC Rules, in **10.90**

[74] *Halsbury's Laws of Singapore, vol 2, Arbitration, Building & Construction* (2003) Reissue, 76.
[75] [2002] 1 SLR 393.

particular, provides that the date of receipt of the Notice of Arbitration by the Registrar of the SIAC is deemed to be the date of commencement of the arbitration.

10.91 (1.1) **From what point in time is a claim considered to be pending with the arbitral tribunal? What are the legal effects of such fact (eg on statutes of limitations)?** When so complied with, time stops to run for limitation purposes.

10.92 (1.2) **When is a time limit according to statutes of limitations deemed to be interrupted in case of (i) *ad hoc*; and (ii) institutional arbitration?** Parties may generally agree when arbitration is deemed to have commenced such that the statutes of limitations is deemed to be interrupted.

(1.3) What is the effect of the withdrawal of the request for arbitration?

10.93 When a party unilaterally withdraws its request for arbitration, it is liable for the costs of the arbitration including the costs incurred by the respondent in responding to the claim and where there is a counterclaim, possibly, an award against it by the respondent in respect of such counterclaim.

(2) Legal deadlines (provided by law or set by the tribunal and effect of non-compliance by a party)

10.94 Neither the Arbitration Act nor the International Arbitration Act provides time-lines within which parties' statements of their respective cases and submissions are to be filed or served. These are left to the tribunals to decide in the absence of the parties' agreement and in accordance with such institutional rules as are applicable. Rule 16 of the SIAC Rules, for instance, provides for the claimant to send its statement of case to the respondent within 30 days of the claimant's being notified by the SIAC Registrar that the tribunal has been constituted and the respondent, its statement of defence within 30 days of its receipt of the claimant's statement of case.

10.95 (2.1) **What are the powers of the tribunal if a party fails to comply with the time limits set by the tribunal?** Both the International Arbitration Act[76] and the Arbitration Act[77] confer power on the tribunal, unless otherwise agreed by the parties, to:

(i) terminate the proceedings where the claimant fails to communicate its statement of claim within the time agreed by the parties or stipulated by the tribunal; and
(ii) continue the proceedings where the respondent fails to communicate its statement of defence within the time stipulated by the tribunal but in doing so, without treating such failure in itself as an admission of the claimant's allegation.

In arbitrations governed by the International Arbitration Act, it is provided, however, that in the exercise of such power the tribunal 'shall' terminate or continue as the case may be. This is in contrast to domestic arbitrations under the Arbitration Act, where the tribunal 'may'. The SIAC Rules mirror the Arbitration Act provisions.[78]

[76] Model Law Art 25.
[77] Arbitration Act s 29(2).
[78] SIAC Rules, r 6.9 & 16.10.

In addition, for arbitration under the Arbitration Act, the tribunal has the additional power to dismiss the claimant's claim if the tribunal decides that there has been an inordinate and inexcusable delay on the part of the claimant in pursuing his claim. The remedy for the respondent in such circumstances is a dismissal of the claim.[79] There is no similar power under the International Arbitration Act. 10.96

(2.2) Is the tribunal bound by any mandatory time limits for certain procedural steps (eg hearings, making of the award)? Neither Act prescribes mandatory time limits for certain procedural steps. That is left to the parties to agree on or, where institutional arbitral rules apply, for the rules to stipulate. Rule 27 of the SIAC Rules, for instance, stipulates that the tribunal shall, unless the parties agree or the Registrar otherwise decides, submit its draft award to the Registrar within 45 days from the date the tribunal decides the proceedings closed. Thus, where the tribunal has agreed to a mandatory time limit or the arbitration is conducted pursuant to institutional rules with such mandatory time limit, the tribunal is, in the absence of agreement by the parties or the relevant arbitral institution to extend time, bound to observe such time limits. 10.97

(3) Statutory requirements as to notifications during an arbitration (with respect to the request for arbitration and other written pleadings; with respect to notifications by the tribunal)

Unless otherwise agreed by the parties, a claimant in an arbitration seated in Singapore is required[80] to state the facts supporting his claim, the points at issue and the relief or remedy sought and the respondent shall state his defence in respect of these particulars. It is also a statutory requirement that these documents as well as any other information or statement supplied to the arbitral tribunal, expert reports and evidentiary documents be communicated to the parties in the arbitration, together with any expert report or evidentiary documents.[81] 10.98

(4) Effect of the insolvency of a party

A party's insolvency does not affect its ability to proceed with arbitration although it may result in an order for security for costs being made by the tribunal as a condition for the continuance of the arbitration and in Singapore.[82] It is necessary to obtain the concurrence of the Official Assignee to proceed where the claimant has been wound up or declared a bankrupt by the Singapore courts. 10.99

D. Facts and evidence: general

(1) Burden of proof (inquisitorial/adversarial procedure)

Section 23 of the Arbitration Act and Art 19 of the Model Law provide that it is for the parties to decide on the procedure to be followed by the arbitral tribunal in the conduct of the proceedings and, failing such agreement, for the tribunal to decide, subject to the overriding requirement under s 22 of the Arbitration Act and Art 18 of the Model Law, that the tribunal must treat the parties with equality and that each party be given a full opportunity 10.100

[79] Arbitration Act s 29(3).
[80] *ibid*, s 24 and Model Law Art 23.
[81] Arbitration Act s 25(5) and Model Law Art 24(3).
[82] Refer to para 10.148.

to present its case. In an international arbitration in addition, s 12(3) of the International Arbitration Act specifically empowers the arbitral tribunal to adopt, if it thinks fit and in the absence of an agreement in writing to the contrary, inquisitorial processes. In practice, whether the procedure adopted is adversarial or inquisitional or both, is usually influenced by the composition of the tribunal as well as the nationalities and legal backgrounds of the lawyers having conduct of the arbitration.

(2) Power of the tribunal to determine the admissibility and weight of the evidence produced by the parties

10.101 The rules of evidence as practised in the courts in Singapore do not apply to arbitrations in Singapore and the application of the Evidence Act[83] is specifically excluded. Section 2(1) of the Evidence Act states that Pts I–III of the Act do not apply to proceedings before an arbitrator (Pt IV of the Act concerns the use of bankers' books as evidence).

10.102 Section 23(2) and 23(3) of the Arbitration Act and Art 19 of the Model Law confer on the arbitral tribunal a power to determine the admissibility, relevance, materiality and weight of any evidence. In this respect, the IBA Rules on the Taking of Evidence in International Commercial Arbitration are increasingly being referred to or agreed on by parties in international arbitrations conducted in Singapore.

10.103 (2.1) **Is the tribunal entitled to take the claimant's factual allegation as proven if defendant does not participate in the arbitral proceedings?** If the respondent does not participate in the arbitral proceedings, the tribunal is not entitled *per se* to take the claimant's factual allegation as proven. It is likely that an enlightened tribunal will still expect the claimant to prove its case. Some assistance on this point is provided by the Arbitration Act and the Model Law. On this point, they both provide that where a respondent fails to provide a statement of defence, the tribunal shall continue the proceedings without treating such failure in itself as an admission of the claimant's case. Further, where any party does not appear at a hearing or produce documentary evidence, the arbitral tribunal may continue the arbitration and resolve the dispute on the evidence before it.[84]

10.104 (2.2) **May the arbitral tribunal consider an allegation of one party as agreed fact if the other party did not (specifically) dispute the allegation?** The tribunal has a wide discretion to determine the weight and admissibility of evidence in an arbitration. Therefore an arbitral tribunal may consider an allegation of one party as agreed fact if the other party did not specifically dispute the allegation.

10.105 (2.3) **What is the standard of proof that must be met in order for a fact to be considered to have been established (preponderance of the evidence; beyond reasonable doubt)? Must a stringent requirement be met for certain facts?** Given the wide discretion that the tribunal has in relation to matters of evidence,[85] the standard of proof that must be met in order for a fact to be considered will be determined by the tribunal taking into account

[83] (c 97, 1997 Ed).
[84] Arbitration Act s 29(2)(b) and (c) and Model Law Art 25 (b) and (c).
[85] See para 10.103.

the nature of the dispute, the nationality of the parties, and the composition of the tribunal.

(2.4) May the arbitral tribunal rely on its own knowledge to consider certain facts as proven? It is clear that the tribunal may not rely on its own knowledge to consider certain facts as proven. If it wishes to do so, it must first put that knowledge to the parties for the parties to have an opportunity to address it. This is not to say that the tribunal is not permitted to use its own knowledge and experience to assess a party's case. After all, this knowledge and experience is a factor considered by parties when choosing the tribunal. **10.106**

E. Witnesses

(1) Ability of a person to act as a witness

Singapore law, as it is based on the common law system, does not impose any restrictions on who may give evidence in an arbitral hearing. **10.107**

(1.1) Is there a legal difference between a party testifying and a witness? If yes, what are the criteria for such differentiation? Does the testifying of a party have the same weight as a witness testimony? In Singapore litigation, there is no difference in principle between the evidence given by the party and by a witness who is not a party to the proceedings. Whilst in theory the evidence of a non-party witness should carry more weight, in practice, each witness' credibility is determined against the entire background and fabric of the case. Therefore, it is likely that where an arbitration in Singapore is before a Singaporean or another arbitrator with a common law background, he or she will probably not assume that the evidence given by a party is any less reliable than that given by a non-party. The author understands that under some civil law legal systems, a distinction is drawn between the evidence given by a party and that given by a non-party. It is therefore conceivable that a tribunal comprised of arbitrators from such differing legal backgrounds, but seated in Singapore, may choose to draw such distinctions. **10.108**

(2) Preparation of witnesses and limits thereof

There are no specific rules in Singapore arbitration laws regarding the preparation of witnesses and the limits of such preparation. Nevertheless it must be appreciated that the evidence of a 'coached witness' runs the risk that it might lose credibility in the eyes of the tribunal. **10.109**

(2.1) Do US-style depositions violate any procedural rules or principles? In theory, US-style depositions do not violate any procedural rules or principles. In practice, however, in the absence of agreement by parties, a tribunal would not generally condone US-style depositions. The parties are free to agree on the procedure to be followed by the arbitral tribunal in conducting the arbitral proceeding.[86] **10.110**

(2.2) May a party or its counsel approach a witness whom it has nominated (only before or also after the proceeding has started)? Are interviews permitted? Although there are no arbitral rules prohibiting a party or counsel approaching a witness whom it has nominated **10.111**

[86] Arbitration Act s 23 and Model Law Art 19.

after the proceeding has started, counsel need to exercise caution when they consider this so as not to breach the professional ethics rules of the Law Society (in the case of Singapore advocates) or compromise the integrity of the witnesses' evidence and their case. In practice, tribunals usually remind witnesses that they should not discuss the case with anyone until their evidence is complete and it may be good practice at the outset of the proceedings to settle any ambiguity about contact with witnesses with the tribunal and the other side.

(3) Admissibility of written witness statements

10.112 As Singapore's legal system is based on the common law system, the use of witness statements is common in litigation and is usually used to stand as a witness' 'evidence in chief'. Consequently, the Arbitration Act and the International Arbitration Act do not prohibit the admissibility of witness statements in arbitrations seated in Singapore. If the arbitration is conducted under the SIAC Rules, r 22.2 provides that:

> The Tribunal may direct the testimony of witnesses to be presented in written form, either as signed statements or sworn affidavits or any other form of recording. Subject to Rule 22.2, any party may request that such a witness should attend for oral examination. If the witness fails to attend, the Tribunal may place such weight on the written testimony as it thinks fit, disregard it or exclude it altogether.

Where the arbitration is not conducted under these rules, the relevant institutional rules should be referred to. The overriding duty of the tribunal is to act fairly and impartially and to give each party a reasonable opportunity to be heard.[87] In addition, the tribunal also has the power, under s 23(2) and 23(3) of the Arbitration Act and Art 19 of the Model Law to determine the admissibility, relevance, materiality and weight of any evidence.

10.113 **(3.1) If the parties agree on written statements, is a party entitled to request an oral hearing for questioning those witnesses (provided such right has not been agreed upon)?** Section 25(2) of the Arbitration Act and Art 24(1) of the Model Law require the arbitral tribunal, unless the parties have agreed that no hearings be held, to hold a hearing at an appropriate stage of the proceedings when so requested by a party. Rule 21.1 of the SIAC Rules imposes a similar obligation on the tribunal to hold a hearing unless the parties have agreed on a documents-only arbitration for the presentation of evidence or for oral submissions.

(4) Entitlement of a party to have a hearing of cross-examination of a witness

10.114 According to r 22.2 of the Arbitration Rules of SIAC, any witness who gives oral evidence may be questioned by each of the parties, their representatives or the tribunal. Also, under s 22 of the Arbitration Act, the tribunal is duty bound to act fairly, impartially and to give each party a reasonable opportunity of presenting its case.

10.115 **(4.1) Which are the methods used to establish a record of arbitral proceedings, in particular witness examination (tape recording, verbatim court reporters, dictated minutes, other methods)?** In Singapore, it is now the practice to have a contemporaneous verbatim recording of the arbitral proceedings as there are live-note service providers established here.

[87] Arbitration Act s 22 and Model Law Art 18.

(4.2) May the tribunal take an oath from a witness The arbitral tribunal in Singapore is empowered to take an oath from a witness: s 28(2)(d) of the Arbitration Act; s 12(2) of the International Arbitration Act. 10.116

(4.3) Does the arbitral tribunal have the power to compel witnesses? The arbitral tribunal does not have the power to compel the attendance of a witness although under s 28(2)(c) of the Arbitration Act and s 12(c) of the International Arbitration Act, the tribunal has the power to compel a party to give evidence by affidavit. However, witnesses may be summoned by a writ of subpoena issued on the application of any party made to the High Court[88] to appear before any arbitral tribunal in Singapore to give oral evidence or to produce documents.[89] 10.117

F. Documents

(1) Form and kind of documents to be presented to the arbitral tribunal

The parties must state what their claim is and also what the other party's defence is. It is common practice in arbitration for this to be submitted in written form. The statement of claim must contain details of the facts supporting the claim, the points in issue and the relief or remedy sought.[90] The respondent must serve a defence in respect of each of the allegations made. Apart from this, there are no other prescriptions on the type of documents to be served. It is usual for parties also to submit any other documents that they consider relevant to the claim or the matters in dispute, and indeed, the Arbitration Act and the Model Law envisage that this will be done.[91] It will be for the tribunal to decide what evidence is admissible and what weight to accord to such evidence.[92] 10.118

Any applicable institutional rules may also dictate what documents are to be supplied. For example, under the SIAC Rules, the parties must submit a written statement of case which sets out in detail the facts and any contentions of law upon which it relies, together with any relief claimed and the amount claimed (insofar as this can be quantified). The respondent must also serve a written statement of defence stating in full detail which of the facts and contentions of law in the statement of case it admits or denies, on what grounds, and on what other facts and contentions of law it relies.[93] The SIAC Rules also state that it will be for the tribunal to decide what other statements should be served by the parties.[94] It also specifies that parties must serve documents to support these statements when serving their written statements.[95] 10.119

(1.1) Is the submission of 'agreed documents' permitted? If yes, what is the extent and effect of such an agreement of the parties (authenticity, existence, acknowledgement of 10.120

[88] Order 38 r 14, The Rules of the Supreme Court of Singapore can be found at <http://app.supreme-court.gov.sg/default.aspx?pgID=97>.
[89] Arbitration Act s 30(1) and (2) and International Arbitration Act s14(1).
[90] Arbitration Act s 24(1) and Model Law Art 23.
[91] Arbitration Act s 24(20) and Model Law Art 23(1).
[92] Arbitration Act s 23(3) and Model Law Art 19(2).
[93] SIAC Rules, r 16.3 and 16.4.
[94] *ibid*, r 16.6.
[95] *ibid*, r 16.8.

such documents' contents)? The submission of 'agreed documents' is permitted and the parties are free to place such conditions as they wish as to the nature and extent of such agreement (for example, as to the truth of what is stated in an agreed document).

10.121 **(1.2) How may electronic documents (eg emails) be presented and proven?** The SIAC Rules do not prescribe a specific procedure for the production of electronic documents and often they are produced in the same manner as other documents are produced. The power to determine the admissibility, relevance, materiality and weight of any evidence lies with the arbitral tribunal.[96] It is common practice for the primary evidence of witnesses to be given in the form of affidavits or sworn statements.[97]

10.122 **(1.3) Does discovery (US- or UK-style), after the procedure has started, violate any procedural rules or public policy considerations?** Discovery (US- or UK-style) after the procedure has started, in principle, does not violate any procedural rules or public policy considerations. However, whether such is permitted by the tribunal is entirely dependent on the tribunal, which, in deciding whether or not to provide such discovery, must be aware that it is under a duty '(a) to properly conduct the proceedings; or (b) to use all reasonable dispatch in conducting the proceedings . . .': s 16(1) of the Arbitration Act.

(2) Requirement to produce certain documents as requested by the tribunal and consequences of a failure to do so.

10.123 Where a tribunal requires that a party produces documents and the party ordered fails to do so, it is open in principle to the tribunal to draw an adverse inference but whether it will in fact do so, depends on the circumstances of each case. For a tribunal to order production of a document, it needs to be satisfied that that document is in the possession, custody or control of the party in respect of whom the production order is being made.[98]

10.124 **(2.1) Which documents may the tribunal request to be produced (eg also documents which are in the possession of third parties)?** Arbitrators have the power to order discovery of documents which are within the possession or control of any of the parties or the persons claiming through them.[99]

(3) Protection of the confidentiality of documents (legal privilege etc)

10.125 Singapore courts' views on confidentiality of the arbitral process mirror the present English position.[100] Hence, a party wishing to preserve confidentiality must either expressly provide for this in the arbitration agreement or adopt institutional rules providing for such confidentiality: see r 34 of the SIAC Rules (3rd edition) in the arbitration.

10.126 Singapore law recognizes that some classes of documents are privileged from disclosure. Without prejudice means 'without prejudice to the maker of the statement'. In most, if not all, common law countries, what this means is that negotiations by parties and letters sent

96 Arbitration Act s 23(3) and Model Law Art 19.
97 Arbitration Act s 28(2)(c) and International Arbitration Act s 12(1)(c).
98 *Halsbury's Laws of Singapore, vol 2, Arbitration, Building & Construction* (2003) Reissue, para [20.086] 85.
99 Arbitration Act s 28(2)(b) and International Arbitration Act s 12(1)(b).
100 *Myanmar Yaung Chi Oo v Win Win Nu* [2003] 2 SLR 547.

to each other labelled 'without prejudice' are privileged, inadmissible as evidence and should not be considered by the judge or arbitrator for deciding the factual issues.

Singapore law recognizes that some classes of documents are privileged from disclosure so it is unlikely that a tribunal would readily order the disclosure of a document to which legal professional privilege applies or the disclosure of 'without prejudice' documents arising out of settlement discussions conducted on a without prejudice basis. **10.127**

It is also interesting to note that in Singapore, the court has the power to grant 'pre-arbitral' discovery, that is, discovery against a party even before the arbitration has commenced.[101] A party to an arbitration agreement may apply for discovery prior to commencing legal proceedings which include that sought by a party to an arbitration agreement. The court has jurisdiction to hear and grant the application for pre-action discovery notwithstanding the fact that the respondent is party to an arbitration agreement to prevent a potential abuse of process (see *Who Up (Pte) Ltd v Lain Tec Construction Pte Ltd*.)[102] **10.128**

In Singapore, documents that are not marked 'without prejudice' are subject to discovery, and in due course considered to be admissible.[103] If the documents in question are ruled to be part of a continuous course of a 'without prejudice' negotiations, all the documents in the series will be treated as being written 'without prejudice', even if some of the documents in the series are not marked 'without prejudice': see *Info-communications Development Authority of Singapore v Singapore Telecommunications*.[104] **10.129**

Order 24 Rule 19 of the Rules of Court in Singapore states: 'Where a party inadvertently allows a privileged document to be inspected, the party who inspected it may use it or its contents only if the leave of the court to do so is first obtained.' In *Dato' Au Ba Chi & Ors v Koh Keng Kheng & Ors*,[105] a privileged document was inadvertently included in a bundle of documents at a trial of an action. There was an application for expungement of the document from the bundle. The court allowed the application, as the document in question was clearly privileged and there was no consent or waiver by the party concerned. **10.130**

G. Experts

(1) Appointment and presentation of experts by the party or the arbitral tribunal

Parties are free to appoint experts and to have their expert evidence admitted as part of their case and where they have so agreed, it is rare for a tribunal—which has the overall responsibility for the fair and expeditious conduct of the arbitration—to refuse to admit such evidence.[106] **10.131**

The parties and tribunal may also agree to engage an expert to assist the tribunal where the dispute is very technical. See *Luzon Hydro Corp v Transfield Philippines Inc*.[107] **10.132**

---

101 Rules of Court (c 322, R5, 2006 Rev Ed), Ord 24 r 6 and Ord 69.
102 [2005] SGCA 26.
103 *Panjacharam Raveentheran v Mookka Pillai Rajagopal* [1998] 1 SLR 28.
104 [2002] 3 SLR 289.
105 [1989] 3 MLJ 445.
106 Rules of Court, Ord 40A r 2, 3.
107 [2004] 4 SLR 705; [2004] SGHC 204.

10.133 **(1.1) By which methods are tribunal-appointed experts selected? What are the rights of the parties during the selection process?** Section 27 of the Arbitration Act and Art 26 of the Model Law confer on the tribunal the power, after consultation with the parties, to appoint experts to report to it on specific issues and to require a party to give to the expert any relevant information or produce or provide access to any relevant document, goods or property for this purpose. It is further provided that when an expert is so appointed, in addition to the requirement that the expert's report be made available to the parties, that he participates in the hearing in order that the parties may question him and for their expert witnesses to testify on the points at issue as well. Rule 23 of the SIAC Rules mirrors these provisions.

10.134 The procedure of 'hot-tubbing' where the parties' experts are all present in the one hearing and permitted to ask questions of each other on specific issues is also gaining considerable popularity in Singapore. It has helped shorten hearing times and brought about meaningful cost savings for the parties. However, for this procedure to succeed, it requires the tribunal both to have a thorough understanding of the issues and to maintain firm control of the proceedings.

(2) Admissibility and role of expert witnesses

10.135 The role and duty of an expert witness is to assist the tribunal in its deliberations on specific issues. He is expected to be independent and impartial and his evidence is intended to be admissible on that basis with the tribunal attaching such weight to it as it considers appropriate. Needless to say, the evidence of an expert witness found to be partial by the tribunal, even though admitted in evidence, will carry very little or no weight before the tribunal. Under s 27 of the Arbitration Act, the arbitral tribunal has the power to appoint experts.

(3) Influence of the parties upon selection of questions to be submitted to the expert

10.136 The tribunal must consult the parties on the questions to be submitted to the witness when it appoints an expert although ultimately it is for the tribunal to decide what these questions should be and the decision as to who to appoint lies ultimately on the tribunal.

(4) Independence and impartiality of the expert and the right to reject a proposed/appointed expert

10.137 Parties may appoint their own experts who are expected to be independent and impartial to assist the resolution of the issues. There is no right stipulated that enables the arbitrator to reject a proposed/appointed expert, but arbitrators may generally determine the admissibility, relevance, materiality and weight of the evidence given by any witness.

10.138 **(4.1) Can a party or its counsel approach an expert (or expert witness) whom it has nominated (only before or after the proceedings has started?) Are interviews admissible?** Nothing in the rules of arbitration law bars discussions between a party or its counsel with an expert. Interviews are permissible.

(5) Oral examination of an expert in a hearing

10.139 Pursuant to s 27(2), unless otherwise agreed by the parties, if a party so requests or if the arbitral tribunal considers it necessary, the expert shall, after delivery of his written or oral report, participate in a hearing where the parties have the opportunity to put questions to him and to present other expert witnesses in order to testify on the points at issue.

H. Interim measures of protection

(1) Kinds of interim measures which the tribunal may order

10.140 The arbitral tribunal has the power to pass the following orders under s 28(2) of the Arbitration Act:

> without prejudice to the powers conferred on the arbitral tribunal by the parties under sub-section (1), the tribunal shall have powers to make orders or give directions to any party for
> (a) security for costs;
> (b) discovery of documents and interrogatories;
> (c) giving of evidence by affidavit;
> (d) a party or witness to be examined on oath or affirmation, and may for that purpose administer any necessary oath or take any necessary affirmation;
> (e) the preservation and interim custody of any evidence for the purposes of the proceedings;
> (f) samples to be taken from, or any observation to be made of or experiment conducted upon, any property which is or forms part of the subject-matter of the dispute; and
> (g) the preservation, interim custody or sale of any property which is or forms part of the subject-matter of the dispute.

10.141 This power is aimed at preserving the status quo as best as possible for the parties in dispute. Such powers are also exercisable by the High Court in support of the arbitration.[108] The High Court has the power to make pre-judgment attachment orders such as Mareva injunctions under its own inherent jurisdiction and to order other interim injunctive reliefs under s 31 of the Arbitration Act. A Mareva injunction restrains a party from removing assets by selling, disposing or otherwise dealing with them or removing them out of the jurisdiction.

10.142 These powers have been used to prevent a party from commencing or maintaining a court action in breach of an arbitration agreement (see *WSG Nimbus Pte Ltd v Board of Control for Cricket in Sri Lanka*).[109]

10.143 In *Econ Corp International Ltd v Ballast-Nedam International BV*,[110] Lai Kew Chai J went a step further by referring to it as a basis for granting leave to serve an originating summons (out of jurisdiction) seeking a grant of an injunction against the calling upon a bond and advance payment guarantees given for a contract which called for arbitration in India.

10.144 **(1.1) Which are, in general, the procedural and substantive prerequisites for the ordering of interim and conservatory measures (eg reduced degree of evidence; urgency; summary evaluation of the claim)?** In both domestic and international arbitrations, the tribunal is given power to order various interim measures of protection such as ordering security for costs, discovery of documents and interrogatories, the preservation, interim custody or sale of any property which is or forms part of the subject matter of the dispute, the taking of samples or the preservation and interim custody of any evidence.[111]

---

108 Arbitration Act s 31.
109 [2002] 3 SLR 603.
110 [2003] 2 SLR 15.
111 Arbitration Act s 28; International Arbitration Act s 12.

10.145 **(1.2) Are the prerequisites for interim measures ordered by the arbitral tribunal more or less the same as if those are requested from the state court? Is there case law/leading authorities on whether those measures are faster and enforced more easily if taken by the arbitral tribunal or the state court?** The prerequisites (procedural and substantive) for the ordering of interim and conservatory measures should be no different from those required by the state courts, viz urgency, full and frank disclosure, a substantial case both on the merits and for the interim relief and an appropriate undertaking to make good any consequent damage.

10.146 The criteria (both procedural and substantive) guiding the tribunal when asked to make an interim order of protection are no different from those that guide the courts. So for example, in an application for an interim injunction where the issue is in essence on the balance of convenience, the status quo needs to be preserved.[112]

(2) Limits of the tribunal's powers to order interim measures

10.147 The tribunal's powers to order interim relief do not extend to third parties or have extra-territorial effect. *Front Carriers Ltd v Atlantic & Orient Shipping Corp*[113] held that the interim measures of protection in s 12(1) of the International Arbitration Act 'are essentially remedies aimed at assisting in the just and proper conduct of arbitration, or in the preservation of property which is the subject matter of the arbitration'. *NCC International AB v Alliance Concrete Singapore Pte Ltd*[114] held that precedence is given to the arbitral tribunal to provide interim relief, with the court's power being incidental to that of the tribunal. The designated functions of the court are purely supportive in nature.

(3) Orders to provide security for the costs of the proceedings

10.148 The arbitral tribunal has power to order security for costs (s 12 International Arbitration Act and ss 28 & 31 of the Arbitration Act). In *Dermajaya Properties Sdn Bhd v Premium Properties Sdn Bhd*,[115] the court held that this power is not compromised even if the applicable rules of arbitration adopted by the parties are silent on the issue.

10.149 The power of the arbitral tribunal to order a claimant to provide security for costs is not to be exercised by reason only of the claimant:

(i) being an individual ordinarily resident outside Singapore; or
(ii) being a corporation or an association incorporated or formed under the law of a country outside Singapore, or whose central management and control is exercised outside Singapore.

(4) Attachment of assets by arbitral tribunal[116]

10.150 In an international arbitration by virtue of s 12(1)(h) of the International Arbitration Act, the tribunal has the power to make an order attaching assets.

---

112 See eg *American Cyanamid Co v Ethican Ltd* (1975) AC 396; *Societe Generale v City Holdings (Pte) Ltd* [1990] SLR 1151.

113 [2006] 3 SLR 854.

114 [2008] 2 SLR 565.

115 [2002] 2 SLR 164.

116 International Arbitration Act s 12(1)(h).

I. Assistance by the courts

(1) Extent of court assistance in the gathering of evidence

Generally, the courts have supportive and limited supervisory functions over arbitrations held in Singapore. These functions are those granted by statute.[117] The court has a wider supervisory role in the arbitrations under the Arbitration Act than those under the international arbitrations. **10.151**

Its supportive function includes the issuing of subpoenas to compel the attendance of witnesses before the arbitral tribunal in Singapore to give oral testimony or to produce documents,[118] to give assistance to the taking of evidence in arbitral proceedings and ordering discovery. **10.152**

(1.1) Is it for the arbitral tribunal or for the party to obtain the assistance of state courts with respect to the gathering of evidence? It is for the party, rather than the arbitral tribunal, to obtain the assistance of state courts with respect to the gathering of evidence. **10.153**

(1.2) According to case law and practical experience, are there considerable delays involved when asking a court to give assistance (eg for the obtaining of evidence)? The Singapore judiciary is efficient and there are seldom delays when a court is asked to give its assistance. **10.154**

(2) Assistance for enforcing the attachment of assets

All orders or directions made or given by an arbitral tribunal in the course of arbitration are, with leave of the court, enforceable in the same manner as if they were orders made by the court and, where leave is so given, judgment may be entered in terms of the order or direction.[119] **10.155**

(3) Other examples of possible assistance

In domestic arbitrations, it is open to a party to apply to court for pre-judgment attachment orders such as Mareva injunctions on the basis of the court's own inherent jurisdiction and for orders in respect of other injunctive reliefs. **10.156**

Further, if a party to an arbitration agreement which comes within the scope of the International Arbitration Act intends to arbitrate his dispute but is unable to do so from the tribunal as it has yet to commence arbitration proceedings, he may apply to the court for such interim relief.[120] **10.157**

In *Swift-Fortune Ltd v Magnifica Marine SA*[121] it was held that s 12(7) of the International Arbitration Act gave the court the power to grant interim measures to assist arbitrations where Singapore was stipulated as the seat of arbitration. It was further held that s 12(7) did not give power to the court to grant interim measures to assist foreign arbitrations. However, the **10.158**

---

117 Arbitration Act s 31.

118 *ibid*, s 30(1); International Arbitration Act s 13 and see generally, *Halsbury's Laws of Singapore, vol 2, Arbitration, Building & Construction* (2003) Reissue, para [20.076 to 20.078] 74–5.

119 Arbitration Act s 28(4); International Arbitration Act s 12(6).

120 *Halsbury's Laws of Singapore, vol 2, Arbitration, Building & Construction* (2003) Reissue, para [20.085] 82.

121 [2007] 1 SLR 629.

court might be able to grant interim injunctions in aid of a foreign arbitration if the court otherwise had personal jurisdiction over the defendants: *Front Carriers Ltd v Atlantic & Orient Shipping Corp* [2006] 3 SLR 854 and *Multi-Code Electronics Industries (M) Bhd v Toh Chun Toh Gordon and Others* [2008] SGHC 193.

10.159 Interim relief such as an interim injunction may be granted by the court. However, it was held in *NCC International AB v Alliance Concrete Singapore Pte Ltd*[122] that the courts would generally play a more interventionist role in granting interim injunctions in domestic arbitration as compared to international arbitration because the Arbitration Act conferred the power to grant interim injunctions solely on the court, whereas the International Arbitration Act conferred the same power on both the court and the arbitral tribunal. However, where the court has concurrent jurisdiction with the arbitral tribunal, it would only intervene to support arbitration, for instance, where third parties over whom the arbitral tribunal had jurisdiction were involved, where matters were very urgent, or where the court's coercive powers of enforcement were required.

10.160 Additionally, where the evidence sought is in the custody or possession of non-parties, parties to arbitrations under s 30 of the Arbitration Act and s 13 of the International Arbitration Act may apply to court for a writ to compel the witness to attend and give evidence or a writ to compel the witness to attend and produce specified documents before the arbitral tribunal in Singapore.

(4) Dependence of the power of state courts to intervene during the proceedings on the (national) procedural law applied by the arbitral tribunal

10.161 The court's power to intervene is not dependent on the national procedural law applied by the arbitral tribunal. But it is to be noted that the national courts do not have jurisdiction under the International Arbitration Act to grant a Mareva injunction in support of arbitration proceedings in which the seat of the arbitration is not Singapore.[123]

V. The award

A. Types of award

10.162 An 'award' is defined in the Arbitration Act[124] and the International Arbitration Act as a decision of the arbitral tribunal on the substance of the dispute and includes any interim, interlocutory or partial award. The test is whether the award, be it final or interim, in any form of words, amounts to a decision on the questions referred for determination by the arbitrator.[125]

(1) Interim award (eg on interim measures of the jurisdiction of the tribunal)

10.163 Unlike 'award', 'interim award' is not defined in the relevant Singapore statutes. In practice, the term 'interim award' is generally used to describe any award that is not the final

[122] [2008] 2 SLR 565; [2008] SGCA 5.

[123] *Swift Fortune Ltd v Magnifica Marine SA* [2006] SGCA 12 where the court declined to grant a Mareva injunction over assets in Singapore in support of a London arbitration.

[124] Arbitration Act s 2(1) and International Arbitration Act s 2(1).

[125] *Halsbury's Laws of Singapore, vol 2, Arbitration, Building & Construction* (2003) Reissue, para [20.094] 91–2.

(last) award in the arbitration. Decisions on issues of the applicable proper law, time-bar defences, joinder of parties and arbitral jurisdiction have been described as interim awards.[126]

Awards that are made on part of the claim, where there has been an admission, or where the award is made after a decision of a part of the decisions which are in dispute are also deemed to be interim awards. When the interim award is made, the arbitrator becomes *functus* in respect of the issues disposed of in the interim award, and not *functus officio* for the matters that are still outstanding and to be determined in the arbitration.[127] **10.164**

(2) Partial award

The term 'partial award' is not defined by the legislation. A partial award is generally known to be an award of only part of the claims or cross claims which are brought, or a determination of only certain issues between the parties. This leaves it open to the parties to either resolve or to continue to arbitrate or litigate the remaining issues. Section 33 of the Arbitration Act and s 19A of International Arbitration Act empower the tribunal 'unless otherwise agreed by the parties' to make more than one award at different points in time during the arbitration on different issues. Rule 27.2 of the SIAC Rules which states that 'the Tribunal may make separate awards on different issues at different times' reflects such power. **10.165**

(2.1) Are awards, especially partial awards, binding in the same arbitral proceeding? Does it make a difference if after the rendering of such a partial awards, one arbitrator is successfully challenged and removed on the grounds that prevailed even before the partial award was rendered? Awards, whether partial or interim, are binding in the same arbitral proceedings. Section 44 of the Arbitration Act and s 19B of the International Arbitration Act does not make any distinction between partial, interim or final awards, and states that 'an award made by the arbitral tribunal pursuant to an arbitration agreement shall be final and binding on the parties and on any person claiming through or under them and may be relied upon by any of the parties by way of defence, set-off or otherwise in any proceedings in any court of competent jurisdiction'. It makes no difference following the rendering of such partial award if one arbitrator is successfully challenged and removed on grounds that prevailed even before the partial award was rendered. **10.166**

(3) Final award

In arbitration, the word 'final' is used with three different meanings. When it is used to describe the effect of an award as final and binding, it is descriptive of all awards made. The term 'final award' is also used to describe the award which is complete, where there are not more issues to be left for determination by another tribunal or any other party. When an award is 'final', that means the award has dealt with all the issues in the arbitration, or that it disposes of all the outstanding issues in the arbitration. An award once made is final and binding. Thenceforth, the arbitrator may not revisit the decision, except to correct clerical mistakes. Once the arbitrator makes the final award, he can make no further awards, nor **10.167**

[126] *Halsbury's Laws of Singapore, vol 2, Arbitration, Building & Construction* (2003) Reissue, para [20.095] 92.
[127] *ibid*, para [20.116] 110.

amend or supplement his award. The concept of a provisional award has not been adopted in Singapore.[128]

10.168 A 'final award' must be the one that decided or completed everything that the arbitral tribunal was expected to decide, including the question of costs. See the case of *Tang Boon Jek Jeffrey v Tan Poh Leng Stanley*[129] where the Court of Appeal held that regardless of the label given to the award by the arbitral tribunal, such label could not be conclusive if there were still matters yet to be adjudicated upon. Until such a final award was given, the arbitral tribunal's mandate still continued and it was not *functus officio*. On the facts of that case, as the arbitrator had not decided on all the issues, his mandate was not terminated and he was entitled to reconsider his decision and, if he thought fit, to reverse himself.

10.169 Once a valid award is made, it is final and binding.[130] It is then enforceable against the party against whom it is made. Section 46 of the Arbitration Act states that an award made by the arbitral tribunal pursuant to an arbitration agreement may, with leave of the court, be enforced in the same manner as a judgment or order of the court to the same effect. Section 19 of the International Arbitration Act states that an award on an arbitration agreement may, by leave of the High Court or a judge thereof, be enforced in the same manner as a judgment or an order to the same effect and, where leave is so given, judgment may be entered in terms of the award. The final award terminates the arbitration and extinguishes the original cause of action. The arbitrator then becomes *functus officio* upon making the final award.[131] The final award must be a valid and binding award. If the final award has been set aside or if it has been declared to be of no effect, this will not cause the tribunal to be rendered *functus*. The jurisdiction is then revived.

10.170 (3.1) **If a party fails to participate in the arbitration, may the tribunal proceed and issue an award on the merits? Is such an award enforceable as any other award? Are there special remedies for the defendant at the enforcement stage?** Both s 29(2)(c) of the Arbitration Act and Art 25 of the Model Law provide that, unless otherwise agreed by the parties, if without showing sufficient cause, any party fails to appear at a hearing or to produce documentary evidence, the arbitral tribunal may continue the proceedings and make the award on the evidence before it. If a party fails to participate in the arbitration, the tribunal may still proceed and issue an award on the merits. This is provided that the party in default has been given every opportunity to participate at each stage of the arbitral proceedings and hearing, and the tribunal is duly satisfied at the hearing of the merits of the successful party's case. Such award when made is enforceable as any other award.

10.171 Section 48 Arbitration Act provides the various bases for the setting aside of such award. They include satisfying the court, for instance, that breach of the rules of natural justice has occurred or that the making of the award was induced or affected by fraud or corruption or that the award deals with an issue not contemplated by or not falling within the terms of

128 *Halsbury's Laws of Singapore, vol 2, Arbitration, Building & Construction* (2003) Reissue, para [20.096] 92.

129 [2001] 3 SLR 237; [2001] SGCA 46.

130 International Arbitration Act s 19B and Arbitration Act s 44.

131 See *Goldenlotus Maritime Ltd v European Chartering and Shipping Inc* [1994] 1 SLR 383; [1993] SGHC 262.

the submission to arbitration. The respondent is further able, in a domestic arbitration, to appeal against the award on a question of law.[132]

It should be noted that parties who wish to appeal against the award must not delay their application. It was held in *Progen Engineering Pte Ltd v Winter Engineering (S) Pte Ltd*[133] that in an appeal against the award, extensions for time to file applications for leave to appeal against an arbitration award should be thoroughly assessed so as not to circumvent the finality of arbitration awards. The longer and more inappropriate the delay, the more reluctant the courts would be in acceding to such applications. **10.172**

A party does not have a similar right of appeal against the award on a question of law in an arbitration governed by the International Arbitration Act. The award may be set aside on the grounds set out in Art 34 of the Model Law and s 24 of the International Arbitration Act. Article 34(2) of the Model Law provides that: **10.173**

> An arbitral award may be set aside by the court specified in Article 6 only if:
> (a) the party making the application furnishes proof that:
> (i) a party to the arbitration agreement referred to in Article 7 was under some incapacity; or the said agreement is not valid under the law to which the parties have subjected it or, failing any indication thereon, under the law of this State; or
> (ii) the party making the application was not given proper notice of the appointment of an arbitrator or of the arbitral proceedings or was otherwise unable to present his case; or
> (iii) the award deals with a dispute not contemplated by or not falling within the terms of the submission to arbitration, or contains decisions on matters beyond the scope of the submission to arbitration, provided that, if the decisions on matters submitted to arbitration can be separated from those not so submitted, only that part of the award which contains decisions on matters not submitted to arbitration may be set aside; or
> (iv) the composition of the arbitral tribunal or the arbitral procedure was not in accordance with the agreement of the parties, unless such agreement was in conflict with a provision of this Law from which the parties cannot derogate, or, failing such agreement, was not in accordance with this Law; or
> (b) the court finds that:
> (i) the subject-matter of the dispute is not capable of settlement by arbitration under the law of this State; or
> (ii) the award is in conflict with the public policy of this State.

Section 24 of the International Arbitration Act states:

> Notwithstanding Article 34 (1) of the Model Law, the High Court may, in addition to the grounds set out in Article 34 (2) of the Model Law, set aside the award of the arbitral tribunal if
> (a) the making of the award was induced or affected by fraud or corruption; or
> (b) a breach of the rules of natural justice occurred in connection with the making of the award by which the rights of any party have been prejudiced.

B. Deliberations and agreement on the award

(1) Time limits (and possible extensions) for making the award

Neither the Arbitration Act nor the International Arbitration Act imposes any time frame for the rendering of the award. An award may be made at different points in time during **10.174**

[132] Arbitration Act s 49.
[133] [2006] SGHC 224.

the proceedings on different aspects of the matters in issue.[134] However, in arbitrations conducted under the rules of arbitral institutions, it is usual for these rules to stipulate the time frame within which the award must be rendered. Rule 27.1 of the SIAC Rules for instance requires that the arbitral tribunal submit a draft of its award to the Registrar of the SIAC within 45 days from the date on which the tribunal declares the closure of the proceedings.[135]

10.175 The absence of statutory time limits, however, does not mean that the rendering of awards can be delayed without reason. Section 16(1)(b)(ii) of the Arbitration Act in relation to arbitrations falling under the Act specifically provides that the court can remove an arbitrator who has refused or failed to use all reasonable dispatch in making an award.

10.176 Whilst the Act does provide that the court may extend time, in the absence of agreement by the parties for the rendering of the award on an application by the party or the tribunal, the exercise of the court's power is conditional on the court being satisfied that substantial injustice would be done if time is not extended.[136]

(2) Procedure for the decision of arbitrators (majority vote etc)

10.177 (2.1) **If an arbitrator fails or refuses to take part in oral deliberation meetings, although having been given sufficient notice of such meetings, may an award be rendered on the basis of written deliberations (or deliberations without this arbitrator) only?** Section 19 Arbitration Act and Art 29 of the Model Law provide, unless the parties agree otherwise, that any decision of the arbitral tribunal shall be made by a majority of its members and that any question of procedure may be decided by a presiding arbitrator if so authorized by the parties or all members of the arbitral tribunal. In practice, on procedural matters, parties frequently agree that the presiding arbitrator decides these unless one or both parties request that the tribunal decides as a whole.

10.178 Where the SIAC Rules apply, r 27.4 provides that where there is more than one arbitrator, the decision of the tribunal is by a majority and that failing such majority decision, the presiding arbitrator is to make the award alone as if he were the sole arbitrator. It further provides that if an arbitrator refuses or fails to sign the award, the signatures of the majority shall be sufficient, provided that the reason for the omitted signature is stated.

10.179 There is no legislation in place providing for the procedure to be followed where an arbitrator fails or refuses to take part in oral deliberation meetings. However, for arbitrations conducted under SIAC Rules, r 27.3 provides that if any arbitrator fails to comply with the mandatory provisions of any applicable law relating to the making of the award, having been given a reasonable opportunity to do so, the remaining arbitrator(s) are to proceed in his absence.

10.180 Where there are differing views which result in the arbitral tribunal being unable to reach a decision, the decision of the presiding arbitrator may form the award. This is subject to the rules adopted during the arbitration.

[134] Arbitration Act s 23; International Arbitration Act s 19A; SIAC Rules, r 27.2 and see *Halsbury's Laws of Singapore, vol 2, Arbitration, Building & Construction* (2003) Reissue, para [20.102] 97.

[135] Art18(1) of the ICC Rules requires an award to be made within six months of the signing of the Terms of Reference.

[136] Arbitration Act s 26.

(3) Admissibility of dissenting opinions

There is no prohibition on the admissibility of dissenting opinions. A dissenting arbitrator is entitled to have his dissenting opinion attached to the majority award, although in practical terms this should have no effect on the validity of the award. **10.181**

(3.1) Are there any court decisions or positions of leading authorities on the issue of dissenting opinions (admissibility, disclosure to the parties and publication)? There are currently no court decisions on the issue of dissenting opinions in Singapore. **10.182**

(4) Signature by the arbitrators and potential failure of one arbitrator to sign

Section 19 of the Arbitration Act and Art 29 of the Model Law provide that, unless the parties agree otherwise, any decision of the arbitral tribunal shall be made by a majority of its members and that any question of procedure may be decided by a presiding arbitrator if it was so authorized by the parties or all members of the arbitral tribunal. In practice, on procedural matters, parties frequently agree that the presiding arbitrator decides these unless one or both parties request that the tribunal decides as a whole. **10.183**

C. Form of the award and deposition

(1) Form and minimum contents of an award

Article 31 of the Model Law and s 38 of the Arbitration Act require that the award is in writing, that it be signed by all the arbitrators (where there is more than one arbitrator) or majority of the arbitrators provided the reason for omission of any arbitrator is stated, that it states the reasons upon which it was based. This is subject to the condition that the parties have agreed that no grounds are to be stated or, that the award is on agreed terms pursuant to a settlement. The date of the award and place of arbitration are also to be stated. A copy of the duly signed award is to be delivered to each party after the award is made. The form of the award is, however, not prescribed. **10.184**

(2) Requirement to give reasons in the award

Section 38 of the Arbitration Act and Art 31 of the Model Law relating to the form and content of the award state that the award shall give the reasons upon which it is based, unless the parties have agreed that no grounds are to be stated, or the award is an award on agreed terms. **10.185**

(3) Necessity to specify the place and time that the award was made

Section 38 of the Arbitration Act and Art 31 of the Model Law relating to the form and content of the award state that the date and place of arbitration must be specified. **10.186**

(4) Other requirements (registration, delivery etc)

A copy of the duly signed award must be delivered to each party. **10.187**

(4.1) Does the award have to be laid down or registered with a state court or agency (even if it has been rendered according to a foreign procedural law)? The award does not have to be laid down or registered with a state court or agency even if it has been rendered according to a foreign procedural law. Under s 44 of the Arbitration Act and s 19B of the International Arbitration Act, the only requirement is that the award be signed and delivered to the parties. **10.188**

10.189 (4.2) **Is there a need for a foreign award which has been rendered abroad according to country's national procedural law, to be laid down or registered with a state court or agency? Is there a fee or tax for such registration of an award?** The position is no different in the case of a foreign award rendered abroad in respect of which the applicable procedural law is Singapore's.

10.190 The fee to be paid is the filing fee payable to the High Court Registry in respect of the application filed in court to register the award as a judgment in order to enforce the award.

10.191 (4.3) **How long after the rendering of the award must the file/award be stored by the lawyers and the arbitral tribunal?** There is no statutory requirement as to the length of time the file or the award is to be stored by the lawyers and the arbitral tribunal following the rendering of the award.

D. Applicable substantive law

(1) Party autonomy to choose the applicable substantive law

10.192 Article 28 of the Model Law and s 32 of the Arbitration Act expressly provide that the tribunal must decide the dispute in accordance with the law chosen by the parties as applicable to the dispute.

10.193 (1.1) **Is there a public policy exception to the chosen substantive law?** Neither the International Arbitration Act nor the Arbitration Act provides for a public policy exception to the chosen substantive law. A court, however, will not enforce or recognize an award if doing so contradicts the public policy of Singapore.

10.194 It was confirmed in the case of *VW and Another v VW*[137] that an award may be set aside, if, *inter alia*, it is in conflict with the public policy of Singapore or a breach of the rules of natural justice occurred in connection with its making.

10.195 (1.2) **Does the principle of '*jura novit curia*' apply? Or must the applicable law be proven (by which means)?** Foreign law has to be proved in the courts as a question of fact with the party adducing such evidence by way of experts. However, for international arbitrations in Singapore, tribunals are increasingly prepared to decide issues of foreign law on the basis of parties' submissions rather than by way of proof in the manner required in the courts.

10.196 Article 28(3) of the Model Law specifically states that the arbitral tribunal 'shall decide *ex aequo et bono* or as *amiable compositeur*' only if the parties have expressly authorized it to do so and Art 28(4) provides that in all cases, the arbitral tribunal is to decide in accordance with the terms of the contract, taking into account the usages of the trade applicable to the transaction.

10.197 Section 32(3) of the Arbitration Act provides that, if the parties so agree, the tribunal may decide the dispute in accordance with such other considerations as are agreed by them or determined by the tribunal.

---

137 [2008] 2 SLR 929; [2008] SGHC 11.

(2) Decisions according to equity or as amiable compositeur

The Sub-Committee Report on Review of Arbitration Law recommended that the concept of '*amiable composition*' in international arbitration should be given the moderate meaning and that in making awards *ex aequo et bono*, the arbitrator should indicate some objective basis for the standards and equity of good sense that he had applied in reaching the decision; and neither concept should be interpreted as a total abandonment of legal principles without regard to mandatory applicable laws and public policy.[138] **10.198**

(3) Application of lex mercatoria, *general principles etc*

There are no known decisions of tribunals in Singapore in which the concepts of *amiable compositeur* or *lex mercatoria per se* have been applied and it is unclear how these principles would apply. **10.199**

(3.1) Is the application of *lex mercatoria* considered as the application of law or as a kind of *amiable composition*? As stated above, there are no known decisions of tribunals in Singapore in which the concepts of *amiable compositeur* or *lex mercatoria per se* have been applied and it is unclear. There has also been no published commentary in Singapore as to whether the application of *lex mercatoria* is considered to be an application of law or as a kind of *amiable composition.* **10.200**

(4) Applicable substantive law if there is no choice of law by the parties

Article 28(2) of the Model Law provides that if there is no choice of law by the parties, the arbitral tribunal is to apply the law determined by the conflict of law rules which it considers applicable. Section 32(3) provides that the tribunal, in such instance, is to apply the law determined by the conflict of law rules. **10.201**

(4.1) Is there an autonomous conflict of law rule in the national arbitration law? Is it considered mandatory? There is no autonomous conflict of law rule in the arbitration laws of Singapore. **10.202**

(4.2) What is the law applicable to interest? The tribunal is given a wide discretion to award interest in international arbitrations, whether simple or compound, at what rate and over what period and where it does not do so, for the sum awarded and directed to be paid to carry interest as from the date of the award and at the same rate as a judgment debt.[139] **10.203**

It was held in *Ahong Construction (S) Pte Ltd v United Boulevard Pte Ltd (No 3)*[140] that the tribunal's power to award interest was derived from the contractual submission of the parties to the tribunal for arbitration. This submission gave the tribunal power to decide 'all matters in difference' according to the existing law of the contract, exercising every right and discretionary remedy of a court except in certain limited examples. Thus, when parties submit to arbitration, they implicitly confer on the tribunal a power to award interest as if the matter were litigated in a court of law. Generally, interest should be awarded on a **10.204**

138 *Halsbury's Laws of Singapore, vol 2, Arbitration, Building & Construction* (2003) Reissue, para [20.115] 107–9.

139 Arbitration Act s 35 and Model Law Art 20.

140 [1995] 1 SLR 548; [1994] SGHC 269.

successful claim. Technically speaking, a tribunal who awarded a sum of money but failed to award interest to compensate the successful claimant accordingly prima facie misconducted itself. The tribunal may decline to award any interest or award interest at a lower rate or for a shorter period but it must have reasonable grounds for doing so and it should set out these reasonable grounds in the award.

10.205 (4.3) **What is the law and practice with respect to legal interest on foreign currency debts?** The tribunal is given a wide discretion to award interest in international arbitrations, whether simple or compound, at what rate and over what period. Where it does not do so, the sum awarded and directed to be paid is to carry interest as from the date of the award and at the same rate as a judgment debt.[141]

(5) Binding effect of state court decisions

10.206 Where the substantive law of the issue in dispute is Singapore law and there is a Singapore court decision on that issue, the arbitral tribunal must apply and give effect to that decision.

10.207 (5.1) **Is an arbitral tribunal bound by a decision of another arbitral tribunal?** The arbitral tribunal is not bound by the decision of another arbitral tribunal.

10.208 (5.2) **Does a decision in a criminal case bind an arbitral tribunal?** If the decision in a criminal case directly and substantially involves a point of law similar to the one in the arbitral proceedings, then the decision on that point of law would bind the arbitral tribunal.

E. Settlement

(1) Settlement by agreement of the parties with or without support of the arbitral tribunal

10.209 Article 30 of the Model Law and s 37 provide for the tribunal to terminate the arbitral proceedings, if during these proceedings, the parties settle the dispute. The tribunal has no discretion in such circumstances: it must terminate the proceedings and, if requested by the parties and it does not object to the settlement, the tribunal is to record the settlement in the form of an award on agreed terms. Such award must be in the same form as an award on the dispute had there not been a settlement and it has the same status and effect as any other award on the merits of the case.

10.210 (1.1) **Can an arbitrator who has initiated settlement discussions be challenged when agreement on a settlement has failed?** There has been no reported case of an arbitrator initiating settlement discussions but not otherwise involved in these discussions or expressing any views on the issues, being challenged when agreement on a settlement has failed. It is to be noted in this context that s 16 of the International Arbitration Act expressly provides that an arbitrator who has, in certain circumstances, acted as a conciliator or mediator in the same dispute may, with the agreement in writing of the parties, serve as an arbitrator in the arbitral proceedings. There does not, however, appear to have been any arbitration proceedings where an arbitrator has also mediated in the proceedings.

[141] *supra,* n 136.

(2) 'Private settlement' and its impact on the arbitral procedure

Section 37 of the Arbitration Act and Art 30 of the Model Law state that if, during arbitration proceedings, the parties settle the dispute, the arbitral tribunal shall terminate the proceedings and, if requested by the parties and not objected to by the arbitral tribunal, record the settlement in the form of an arbitral award on agreed terms. **10.211**

(3) Form and effect of a settlement (eg award on agreed terms)

Section 37 of the Arbitration Act and Art 30 of the Model Law state that the award on agreed terms shall have the same status and effect as any other award on the merits of the case. **10.212**

F. Costs of the arbitration

(1) General allocation of the costs of the proceedings

The award of costs is a matter within the power and discretion of the arbitral award.[142] Whilst it is not the public policy of Singapore to ensure that the costs incurred by parties to the arbitral proceedings, whether domestic or international, are assessed on any particular principle including the proportionality principle, the arbitral tribunal in the exercise of its discretion is expected to follow established legal principles when assessing the costs payable by one party to another.[143] So as a general rule of practice, the costs incurred by a successful party are normally to be borne by the unsuccessful party. **10.213**

In the case of *VW and another v VW*[144] it was disputed that the costs awarded which amounted to $2.8 million was disproportionate to the amount of the dispute which was $927,000. The court granted the successful party the costs of the arbitration, including the costs of its counterclaim. **10.214**

Two sets of costs arise in an arbitration: (i) the costs of the award; and (ii) the costs of the reference.[145] The first includes the joint costs of the parties, eg fees of the tribunal and arbitral institution. The second includes the costs and expenses of the party in bringing or defending the claim. **10.215**

It is to be noted that s 39(2) of the Arbitration Act expressly provides that any provision in an arbitration agreement that each party, in respect of future disputes, is to pay its own costs of the reference or the award or any part thereof is void and shall have no effect. Subsection (3) of the same section expressly provides an exception if such agreement is entered into after the dispute has arisen. There is no such provision in the International Arbitration Act. **10.216**

(2) Deposits or advances for costs or fees

Where the SIAC Rules apply, r 26 of the Rules specifically authorizes the Registrar to request from the parties to the arbitral proceedings advances or deposits towards the costs of the arbitration. **10.217**

142 *Halsbury's Laws of Singapore, vol 2, Arbitration, Building & Construction* (2003) Reissue, para [20.107] 101.
143 *VW and another v VW* [2008] SGHC 11, paras 30 and 31.
144 [2008] SGHC 11.
145 *Halsbury's Laws of Singapore, vol 2, Arbitration, Building & Construction* (2003) Reissue, para [20.107] 101.

10.218 The tribunal's fees and SIAC's fees are ascertained in accordance with the Schedule of Fees in force at the time of commencement of the arbitration.

10.219 The Registrar will fix the advances or deposits on costs of the arbitration to cover the fees and expenses of the tribunal and SIAC. Unless the Registrar directs otherwise, such advances and deposits shall be payable by the parties in equal shares. Where the amount of the claim or the counterclaim is not quantifiable at the time payment is due, the Registrar of SIAC will make a provisional estimate of the costs of the arbitration. This may be adjusted in light of such information as may subsequently become available.

10.220 The Registrar may from time to time direct parties to make further advances or deposits towards costs or expenses of the arbitration incurred or to be incurred on behalf of or for the benefit of the parties.

10.221 (2.1) **Is there case law authorizing or prohibiting arbitrators to order a party to pay an advance on the arbitration costs?** There is no case law prohibiting arbitrators from ordering the payment of advances of costs from the parties.

10.222 (2.2) **Can the raising of a set-off claim or counterclaim be made contingent upon payment of the corresponding advance for the relating arbitration costs (cf eg Article 30.5, ICC Rules)? Can such a condition be agreed upon when entering into the arbitration agreement?** It is uncertain whether the raising of a set-off or counterclaim can be made contingent upon payment of a corresponding advance on costs. Could such a condition be agreed upon when entering into the arbitration agreement? Conceivably, yes.

10.223 (2.3) **What remedies exist against a party which does not pay its part of the advance on the arbitration costs (eg termination of the arbitration agreement)? How may the other party enforce its rights?** Section 41 of the Arbitration Act provides that the tribunal is entitled to refuse to deliver its award until its fees and expenses have been paid in full by the parties with a measure of protection against excessive arbitral fees and also by providing for the national court with some oversight capabilities:

> (1) The arbitral tribunal may refuse to deliver an award to the parties if the parties have not made full payment of the fees and expenses of the arbitrators.
> (2) Where subsection (1) applies, a party to the arbitration proceedings may, upon notice to the other parties and the arbitral tribunal, apply to the court, which may order that
> (a) the arbitral tribunal shall deliver the award upon payment into court by the applicant of the fees and expenses demanded, or such lesser amount as the court may specify;
> (b) the amount of the fees and expenses demanded shall be taxed by the Registrar of the Supreme Court; and
> (c) out of the money paid into court, the arbitral tribunal shall be paid such fees and expenses as may be found to be properly payable and the balance of such money (if any) shall be paid out to the applicant.

10.224 In *Progen Engineering Pte Ltd v Winter Engineering (S) Pte Ltd*,[146] it was held that where a party disputed the fees of the arbitrator, and thereby refused to pay the arbitrator's fees and expenses, the party should have referred the matter to the court for directions or should have sought a

[146] [2006] SGHC 224.

hearing before the arbitrator for a ruling on either the appropriateness of such a condition or the quantum of his professional fees. Such failure to do so was found to be a delay tactic.

Although there is no similar statutory provision that specifically entitles the tribunal to withhold the award until its fees and expenses have been paid, there is no case law prohibiting this and s 21 of the International Arbitration Act provides for a party with access to the Registrar of the SIAC to tax the fees of the arbitral tribunal. **10.225**

Rule 26.5 of the SIAC Rules entitles the tribunal to refuse to hear the claim or counterclaim of a party that has not complied with the Registrar's request for an advance or deposit towards the costs or expenses of the arbitration. Rule 26.7 allows one party to pay the advances and deposits of the non-complying party. It also permits the tribunal to suspend its work should the advances or deposits directed by the Registrar not have been paid. **10.226**

(3) Costs of the administration by an arbitration institution

Where a case is conducted according to SIAC's arbitration rules, or where it has been submitted or referred to SIAC for arbitration, parties pay an administration fee. The administration fee is pegged to the amount of the claim or counterclaim according to a scale. A one-time, non-refundable case filing fee of S$1,000 is payable to SIAC. Administrative claims range from S$2,750.00 for a claim or counterclaim of up to S$50,000, up to S$60,250 for claims above S$50,000,000.00. **10.227**

(4) Arbitrators' fees: law and practice, judicial control

In cases falling outside SIAC's arbitration rules, where SIAC is asked to appoint an arbitrator, an appointment fee is charged. The arbitrator appointment fee, on the other hand, is a flat fee, not dependent on the amount of claim ranging from S$2,000 for a single arbitrator to S$4,000 for three arbitrators. **10.228**

The arbitrator's fee ranges from S$5,000.00 for a disputed amount of less than S$50,000.00 and for disputed amounts of over S$100,000,000.00, the arbitrator's fee is S$273,000 with an additional 0.06 per cent for any excess over S$100,000,000. **10.229**

(4.1) May arbitrators fix their own fees in the award? Arbitrators may fix their own fees in the award, absent agreement by parties,. Although the Court of the Registrar of the SIAC may have some oversight where these have been agreed by parties, it is unlikely that these can be changed, absent fraud. **10.230**

(4.2) How can the parties change the arbitrators' fees once they are fixed? It is unlikely that fees may be changed. **10.231**

(4.3) Are the arbitrator's fees subject to income tax if (i) the place of arbitration; or (ii) the normal residence or place of business of the arbitrator is located in this country? If the arbitrator is resident in Singapore or has his place of business in Singapore, his fees are subject to income tax in Singapore. **10.232**

(4.4) Are the arbitrator's fees submitted to VAT? If yes, is the duty to pay such tax linked to (i) the place of arbitration; or (ii) the arbitrator's general residence? If the income earned by the arbitrator is in excess of S$1 million, GST (a sales tax akin to VAT) currently set at 7 per cent is payable in respect of the arbitrator's fees. **10.233**

(5) Attorney's fees and the winning party's claim for reimbursement

Attorney's fees and the winning party's claim for reimbursement are generally recoverable to the extent that these were incurred reasonably in respect of the arbitration.

10.234 **(5.1) Can in-house lawyers charge fees or can a party request that costs of in-house lawyers be reimbursed?** Common sense dictates that there is no reason why, in principle, in-house lawyers' fees are not claimable provided such fees are clearly shown to have been reasonably incurred in respect of the arbitration.

(6) Time and form of the decision on costs

10.235 Under r 31 of Arbitration Rules of SIAC, the arbitral tribunal has the authority to order in its award that all or part of the legal or other costs of a party (apart from the costs of the arbitration) be paid by another party.

10.236 As a general rule of practice, costs incurred by a successful party in litigation are to be borne by the party that failed. This rule is followed in arbitration too.

10.237 The tribunal must exercise its authority judicially, in accordance with the same principles and be subject to the same limitations as a judge would when exercising a judicial discretion. The award on costs should also be made with reasons and especially so, when the tribunal departs from the general rule.[147]

10.238 **(6.1) May the arbitrators' decision on costs (allocation and amount of costs to be reimbursed) be challenged separately from the award itself? Are there time limits for such a remedy?** It is not possible to challenge the arbitrators' decision on costs separately from the award itself.[148]

10.239 **(6.2) Are the arbitrators entitled and/or legally obliged to rule on the amount of one or both parties' costs that are recoverable?** Section 41 of the Arbitration Act requires the arbitral tribunal to rule on who is to pay and in what amount the costs of the reference on the request of a party, if this has not already been dealt with in the award. Section 21 of the International Arbitration Act provides that costs directed by an award to be paid are to be taxed by the Registrar of the SIAC.

10.240 Where arbitrations are conducted under the SIAC Rules, r 29 requires the tribunal to specify in the award the total amount of the costs of the arbitration and, unless the parties have otherwise agreed, for the tribunal to determine in the award the apportionment of the costs of the arbitration among the parties.

G. Publication of the award

(1) Publication with or without the consent of the parties

10.241 As arbitration is confidential in nature, publication of the arbitration is prohibited without the consent of the parties. In Singapore, although the concept of arbitral confidentiality has been given some limited statutory recognition in s 57 of the Arbitration Act and s 23 of the

---

147 *Halsbury's Laws of Singapore, vol 2, Arbitration, Building & Construction* (2003) Reissue, para [20.110] 103.
148 *VW and another v VW* [2008] SGHC 11.

International Arbitration Act through the imposition of rules restricting publication of arbitration cases which may come before the courts, no judicial pronouncements had come forth until the decision in *Myanma Yaung Chi Oo Co Ltd v Win Win Nu*.[149]

The issue before the judge on appeal was primarily whether parties in arbitration proceedings have a duty to maintain confidentiality of the documents in those proceedings. It was held that because parties in arbitration expected the proceedings to be confidential, disclosures were only to be made in accepted circumstances. One of these circumstances is when the disclosure is reasonably necessary. This exception is grounded on the implied agreement that when it is reasonably necessary to disclose, the duty of confidentiality is lifted. **10.242**

(2) Practice of publication (eg in specific legal journals)

The Singapore Arbitration Centre has published high level commentary in the *Asian International Arbitration Journal* with reporting on cases in Singapore and the rest of Asia. **10.243**

VI. Amendment and challenge of the award; liability of arbitrators

A. Amendment, correction or interpretation of the award

(1) Motion to amend or correct an award

Both the Arbitration Act and International Arbitration Act apply the provisions of Art 33 of the Model Law. Thus arbitrators are allowed to make corrections in the award of any error in computation, any clerical or typographical error or other error of a similar nature.[150] **10.244**

Article 33 provides for a period of no more than 30 days from receipt of the award within which the application for correction, in the absence of agreement to the contrary by the parties, must be made. The tribunal may also on its own initiative within 30 days of the date of the award, correct any clerical or typographical errors or any errors of similar nature. **10.245**

Unless otherwise agreed by the parties, a party, with notice to the other party, may also request, within 30 days of receipt of the award, the arbitral tribunal to make an additional award as to claims presented in the arbitral proceedings but omitted from the award. Provided the arbitral tribunal considers the request to be justified, it must make the additional award within 60 days.[151] **10.246**

(2) Interpretation of the award by the tribunal

Article 33(1)(b) permits the arbitral tribunal, if it considers the request justified, on request by a party made within 30 days of receipt of the award, to give an interpretation of a specific point or part of the award. The interpretation request is not intended to subject the tribunal to answer questions from parties as to the bases or reasoning for the award, nor for a party to seek an additional award to reverse the award already made.[152] **10.247**

---

[149] [2003] 2 SLR 547.

[150] *Halsbury's Laws of Singapore, vol 2, Arbitration, Building & Construction* (2003) Reissue, para [20.112] 105.

[151] Model Law Art 33(3).

[152] *Halsbury's Laws of Singapore, vol 2, Arbitration, Building & Construction* (2003) Reissue, para [20.113] 106, note 2.

B. Appeal on the merits

(1) Admissibility and procedure of an appeal on the merits

10.248 In an international arbitration under the International Arbitration Act, there is no right of appeal against an award. Parties can apply to set aside an award on the limited grounds provided in Art 34 of the Model Law and s 24 of the International Arbitration Act.

Article 34(2) of the Model Law provides that:

> An arbitral award may be set aside by the court specified in Article 6 only if:
> (a) the party making the application furnishes proof that:
> (i) a party to the arbitration agreement referred to in Article 7 was under some incapacity; or the said agreement is not valid under the law to which the parties have subjected it or, failing any indication thereon, under the law of this State; or
> (ii) the party making the application was not given proper notice of the appointment of an arbitrator or of the arbitral proceedings or was otherwise unable to present his case; or
> (iii) the award deals with a dispute not contemplated by or not falling within the terms of the submission to arbitration, or contains decisions on matters beyond the scope of the submission to arbitration, provided that, if the decisions on matters submitted to arbitration can be separated from those not so submitted, only that part of the award which contains decisions on matters not submitted to arbitration may be set aside; or
> (iv) the composition of the arbitral tribunal or the arbitral procedure was not in accordance with the agreement of the parties, unless such agreement was in conflict with a provision of this Law from which the parties cannot derogate, or, failing such agreement, was not in accordance with this Law; or
> (b) the court finds that:
> (i) the subject-matter of the dispute is not capable of settlement by arbitration under the law of this State; or
> (ii) the award is in conflict with the public policy of this State.

Section 24 of the International Arbitration Act states:

> Notwithstanding Article 34(1) of the Model Law, the High Court may, in addition to the grounds set out in Article 34 (2) of the Model Law, set aside the award of the arbitral tribunal if—
> (a) the making of the award was induced or affected by fraud or corruption; or
> (b) a breach of the rules of natural justice occurred in connection with the making of the award by which the rights of any party have been prejudiced.

10.249 Section 48 of the Arbitration Act and Art 34(3) of the Model Law provide that an application for setting aside may not be made after three months have elapsed from the date on which the party making that application had received the award. In *ABC Co v XYZ Co Ltd*[153] it was held that Art 34(3) of the Model Law in force through the International Arbitration Act, did not confer power on the court to extend time beyond the prescribed three months for filing an application to set aside an international arbitration award.

10.250 In a domestic arbitration under the Arbitration Act, parties can appeal against an award on a question of law arising out of a reasoned award made in the proceedings, upon agreement of all parties or by leave of the court under s 49 of the Arbitration Act. However, parties may agree to exclude the jurisdiction of the court to hear the appeal under s 49(2) of the

[153] [2003] 3 SLR 546; [2003] SGHC 107.

Arbitration Act. An agreement to dispense with reasons for the arbitral tribunal's award is treated as an agreement to exclude the jurisdiction of the court under s 49(2) of the Arbitration Act.

Parties must first exhaust any available arbitral process of appeal or review (s 50 of the Arbitration Act). Leave to appeal will be granted by the court only if the court is satisfied that: **10.251**

(i) the determination substantially affects the rights of one or more parties;
(ii) the question is one the arbitral tribunal was asked to determine;
(iii) on the basis of the finding of fact in the award (a) the decision of the tribunal on the question is obviously wrong; or (b) the question is one of general public importance and the decision of the tribunal is open to serious doubt; and
(iv) despite the agreement of parties to resolve the matter by arbitration, it is just and proper in all the circumstances of the case for the court to determine the question.

Leave of the court is required for any appeal from a decision of the court to grant or refuse leave to appeal. On appeal, the court may confirm, vary, remit the award to the arbitral tribunal in whole or part, or set aside the award in whole or in part. Leave to appeal against the decision of the court will only be granted if the question of law is one of general importance, or there is some special reason which should be considered by the Court of Appeal (s 49(11) of the Arbitration Act). **10.252**

The question of law must be a question of Singapore law as an issue of foreign law is always a question of fact and where, therefore, an arbitral award is made under the Arbitration Act, applying substantive law other than that of Singapore, the recourse to appeal may not be available to the parties.[154] **10.253**

Section 50 of the Arbitration Act requires that the application or appeal must be brought within 28 days of the date of the award or if there had been any arbitral process of appeal or review, of the date when the applicant or appellant was notified of the result of the process. **10.254**

Order 69 of the Rules of Court lays down the procedure to be followed. Applications for leave to appeal are heard by a judge in chambers to preserve the confidentiality of the proceedings. The judge has a discretion as to whether an oral hearing is required, determining the application solely on the basis of the papers before him. **10.255**

In practice however, an oral hearing is usually required. **10.256**

(1.1) **Can the parties agree on an appeal to another arbitral tribunal?** The legislature does not appear to prohibit such an agreement. The Arbitration Act recognizes an appeal process from one arbitral tribunal to another. This was also the intention of the drafters of the Model Law. **10.257**

(2) Possibility to exclude an appeal (eg in the arbitration clause)

Parties may agree to exclude the jurisdiction of the court to hear the appeal (s 49(2) of the Arbitration Act). An agreement to dispense with reasons for the arbitral tribunal's award is **10.258**

[154] *Halsbury's Laws of Singapore, vol 2, Arbitration, Building & Construction* (2003) Reissue, para [20.121] 113.

treated as an agreement to exclude the jurisdiction of the court under s 49(2) Arbitration Act.

C. Setting aside of the award

(1) Reasons for setting aside an award

10.259 There are two regimes providing for the setting aside of awards depending on whether the arbitration is domestic (on which event the grounds are set out in s 48 of the Arbitration Act) or international, in which case the reasons for setting aside stipulated in Art 34 of the Model Law would apply. Notwithstanding the two regimes, the grounds are the same. These are subject to the condition that the party proves to the satisfaction of the court that:

(i) a party to the arbitration agreement was under some incapacity;
(ii) the arbitration agreement is not valid under the law to which the parties have subjected it, or failing any indication as to the applicable law, under the laws of Singapore;
(iii) the party making the application was not given proper notice of the appointment of the arbitrator or of the arbitration proceedings or was otherwise unable to present his case;
(iv) the award deals with a dispute not contemplated by or not falling within the terms of the submission to arbitration, except that if the decision on matters submitted to arbitration can be separated from those not so submitted, only that part of the award which contains decisions on matters not submitted to arbitration may be set aside;
(v) the composition of the arbitral tribunal or the arbitral procedure is not in accordance with the agreement of the parties unless such agreement is contrary to any provisions of (in the case of domestic arbitrations)—the Arbitration Act and (in the case of international arbitrations) the Model Law from which the parties cannot derogate or failing such agreement, contrary (in the case of domestic arbitrations) to the provisions of the Arbitration Act or (in the case of international arbitrations) to the provisions of the Model Law;
(vi) the making of the award was induced by fraud or corruption; and
(vii) a breach of the rules of natural justice occurred in connection with the making of the award by which the rights of any party have been prejudiced; or if the court finds that:
   (a) the subject matter of the dispute is not capable of settlement by arbitration in the case of a domestic arbitration, under the provisions of the Arbitration Act, and in the case of an international arbitration, under the laws of Singapore; or
   (b) the award is contrary to the public policy of Singapore.

10.260 **(1.1) Can an award made according to international or foreign procedural rules be the object of an application for setting aside before the national courts?** The setting-aside provisions embodied in the Arbitration Act and the Model Law apply to arbitrations which have their seat in Singapore. In *P.T. Garuda Indonesia v Birgen Air*,[155] the Court of Appeal held that only an award made in Singapore may be set aside. On this basis, conceivably, an

[155] [2002] 1 SLR 393.

arbitration in which the procedural rules of another country are to apply but which has Singapore as its seat, could be set aside.

(2) Procedure and deadlines for challenging an award

The application to set aside is by way of originating summons.[156] The application is heard by a judge. It must be made no later than three months from the date when the party making the application received the award or when its request for correction, interpretation or for an additional award had been disposed of by the tribunal.[157] **10.261**

(2.1) Who may (or must) represent a party in a proceeding for setting aside an award? Parties are usually represented by Singapore counsel as foreign counsel as a rule do not have a right of audience before the Singapore courts. **10.262**

(2.2) Do specific time limits exist for setting-aside procedures concerning awards on jurisdiction? No. Under s 21 of the Arbitration Act, the arbitral tribunal may rule on a plea referred to in the section either as a preliminary question or in an award on the merits. The section provides that if arbitral tribunal rules on a plea as a preliminary question that it has jurisdiction, any party may, within 30 days after having received notice of that ruling, apply to the court to decide the matter. However, the section does not specify any time limits for appeal or setting-aside procedures. **10.263**

(3) Effect of a court decision which sets the award aside

The award is rendered a nullity. **10.264**

(3.1) Does the setting-aside action suspend the enforcement? If so, are there any remedies to reinstate enforcement? In theory, until the setting-aside is decided on and the court sets aside the award, it is enforceable. In practice, however, a court is unlikely to allow enforcement in the face of a setting-aside application and frequently the answer is to have both the application to enforce and the application to set aside heard at the same time and by the same judge. **10.265**

(3.2) After an award has been set aside, does the underlying arbitration agreement revive, remain in force or is it exhausted and deemed terminated? This turns on the basis on which the award has been set aside. Conceivably, if the reason for the setting aside did not turn on the issue of the existence or validity of an arbitration agreement, the underlying agreement should still remain in force. **10.266**

(4) Appeal against the court's decision to set aside or not set aside the award

An appeal against the decision lies to the Court of Appeal.[158] **10.267**

(5) Possibility of the parties to exclude actions for setting aside.

Parties cannot agree to exclude the jurisdiction of the court to hear applications to set aside awards. There are no express provisions in the Arbitration Act or International Arbitration Act regarding this. **10.268**

156 Rules of Court, Ord 69 r 5 and Ord 69A r 2.

157 Arbitration Act s 48(2); Model Law Art 34(3); and see *ABC Co v XYZ Co Ltd* [2003] 3 SLR 546.

158 Rules of Court, Ord 57 r 4.

D. Liability of arbitrators

(1) Duties and liabilities of arbitrators regarding the conduct of the proceedings

10.269 The primary duty of an arbitrator is to act fairly and impartially, to consider all matters in dispute and to make the award.[159]

10.270 The duty to act fairly requires that the tribunal ensures that parties to the proceedings be given reasonable opportunity to present their respective cases and be given equal treatment.[160]

10.271 Breach of this primary duty would result in the arbitrator being removed either by the institution that appointed him or by the court.

10.272 Section 20 of the Arbitration Act and s 25 of the International Arbitration Act provide that an arbitrator is not liable for:

(i) negligence in respect of anything done or omitted to be done in the capacity of an arbitrator; or
(ii) any mistake of law, fact or procedure made in the course of arbitration proceedings or in the making of an arbitral award.

Rule 33.1 of the SIAC Rules mirrors this exemption. It further provides in respect of arbitration that the arbitrator is under no obligation to make any statement to any person concerning the arbitration and that he is not to be made a witness in any legal proceedings arising out of the arbitration whether before, during or after the arbitration.

10.273 Section 16(1)(b)(i) of the Arbitration Act allows an arbitrator who refuses or fails to conduct the proceedings properly to be removed if his failure causes substantial injustice. The case of *Yee Hong Pte Ltd v Powen Electrical Engineering Pte Ltd*[161] held that the power to remove an arbitrator would only be exercised if the failure to conduct the proceedings properly caused substantial injustice, and the court held that the reference to 'substantial' injustice indicated that the use of s 16(1)(b) should be confined to exceptional circumstances only. Each case would depend, *inter alia*, on the surrounding circumstances, the conduct of the arbitrator and terms of reference.

10.274 **(1.1) Do the courts and/or authorities rely on a contractual relationship between the parties and the arbitrator(s), irrespective of whether institutional or *ad-hoc* arbitration is concerned? What is the legal qualification of such a contract (eg provision of services)?** To the extent that the courts will look at the contractual relationship (whether express or implied) between the parties, this presupposes that the relationship does not override or conflict with the primary duties of the arbitrator.

10.275 **(1.2) Are there court decisions (or authorities) determining which law governs the question of liability of an arbitrator? What is the position of those courts/authorities as to**

[159] *Halsbury's Laws of Singapore, vol 2, Arbitration, Building & Construction* (2003) Reissue, para [20.065] 68.
[160] Arbitration Act s 22; Model Law Art 18 and see *Halsbury's Laws of Singapore, vol 2, Arbitration, Building & Construction* (2003) Reissue, para [20.066] 68, also *Turner (East Asia) Pte Ltd v Builders Federal (Hong Kong) Ltd (no 2)* [1988] SLR 532.
[161] [2005] 3 SLR 512; [2005] SGHC 114.

whether and to which extent a legal liability of an arbitrator (or arbitral institution) may be established? There have been no court decisions on this.

(1.3) Is an arbitrator subject to criminal prosecution? Yes, if a criminal offence is established such as, for example, fraud or corruption. Section 16(1)(b)(i) of the Arbitration Act allows an arbitrator who refuses or fails to conduct the proceedings properly to be removed if his failure causes substantial injustice. See *Anwar Siraj and Another v Ting Kang Chung John and Another*[162] where there were allegations of fraud, fraudulent claims and cheating, falsification of bills and/or receipts made against the arbitrator, and criminal negligence owing to loss of documents and evidence resulting from the actions or omissions of the arbitrator. It was held by the court that if any matter were disclosed by the investigations against the arbitrator, the matter would then be referred to the Public Prosecutor to decide whether an offence is made out and if so, whether to prosecute the arbitrator. **10.276**

(2) Possibility of the parties to exclude actions for setting aside.

Parties cannot agree to exclude the jurisdiction of the court to hear applications to set aside awards. There are no express provisions in the Arbitration Act or International Arbitration Act regarding this. **10.277**

VII. Enforcement of national awards

(1) Requirement of a particular procedure to make an award enforceable (leave for enforcement, exequatur*)*

Section 19 of the International Arbitration Act and s 46(1) of the Arbitration Act provide for an award, with leave of the court, to be enforced in the same manner as a judgment or order of the court. **10.278**

Order 69A r 6 of the Rules of Court (which prescribes the procedure for applications to enforce awards made under the International Arbitration Act) and Order 69 r 14 of the Rules of Court (for awards made under the Arbitration Act) provide that an application to enforce an award may be made *ex parte* supported by an affidavit: **10.279**

(i) exhibiting the arbitration agreement and the original award or, in either case, a copy thereof;
(ii) stating the name and the usual or last known place of residence or business of the applicant and the person against whom the award is sought to be enforced; and
(iii) as the case may require, stating either that the award has not been complied with or the extent to which it has not been complied with at the date of the application.

Once leave is obtained, the order granting such leave must be served on the party against whom the order has been obtained and on the expiration of the period prescribed by the court within which such party may apply to set aside the order granting leave and has not done so, the award may be enforced as a judgment of the court. If the party does apply to **10.280**

[162] [2009] SGHC 71.

set aside the leave order, then the enforcement of the award as a judgment of the court is held over until the final disposal of the application to set aside.

10.281 **(1.1) Does the national law make any difference between foreign and domestic awards, and if so, what are the criteria? Is there an additional notion of award for the purpose of obtaining *exequatur* (France: international awards)?** Singapore law does make a distinction between domestic and foreign awards. A foreign award means an arbitral award made in pursuance of an arbitration agreement in the territory of a New York Convention country other than Singapore.[163]

10.282 There is no additional notion of award for the purpose of obtaining *exequatur*.

10.283 **(1.2) May awards granting conservatory/interim measures be subject to enforcement?** Yes.

(2) Details of such enforcement procedure (competent court, reasons for rejection of motion etc)

10.284 Section 28(4) of the Arbitration Act and s 12(6) of the International Arbitration Act provide that all orders or directions made by the arbitral tribunal shall, by leave of the court, be enforceable in the same manner as if they were orders made by the court, and where leave is so given, judgment may be entered in terms of the order of the direction.

10.285 The application for leave is by way of an originating summons to the High Court, which may be made *ex parte* and must be supported by an affidavit setting out fully and fairly the circumstances under which the arbitral tribunal made the interim order or direction and that the interim order or direction has not been complied with.

(3) Appeal against the decision granting exequatur

10.286 Not applicable

(4) Appeal (and procedure) if exequatur *has been refused*

10.287 Not applicable

(5) Procedure of enforcement (attachment of bank accounts etc)

10.288 Once the order granting leave takes effect (ie either on the expiration of the period prescribed by the court for the losing party to apply to set aside the leave order or on the final disposal of any such application) the party obtaining such leave may then apply to the court bailiff for the necessary writs of execution, such as writ of seizure and sale, an attachment order etc.

10.289 **(5.1) At the stage of enforcement, may the losing party invoke arguments and circumstances which are based on facts which have occurred before (or after) the award was made?** No.

10.290 **(5.1) May the losing party invoke a set-off based on claims that are not related to the matter of the arbitral proceeding? Is it material whether such claims came into existence before or after the award was made?** No.

163 International Arbitration Act s 27(1).

VIII. Foreign awards

A. Recognition and/or enforcement of foreign awards (national law)

(1) Rules according to national law

Foreign awards are enforceable in Singapore under the International Arbitration Act only if the awards are made in a country which is party to the New York Convention or under the Reciprocal Enforcement of Commonwealth Judgments Act where the award has been registered as a judgment in that foreign county. In addition, in a recent amendment to the Arbitration Act, s 46(3) of the Arbitration Act provides that an award can be enforced irrespective of whether the place of arbitration was Singapore or elsewhere. **10.291**

Such foreign awards may be enforced by way of a separate action or in the same manner as an award of an arbitrator made in Singapore. Under s 29(2) of the International Arbitration Act, parties may also rely on such an award as a defence, set-off or otherwise in any legal proceedings in Singapore. **10.292**

As a result, in addition to arbitral awards made in New York Convention countries, awards made in any other country can be enforced in Singapore. **10.293**

(2) Requirements to be fulfilled by the applicant (procedure, time limits)

See section VII (1) *supra*. **10.294**

Where the award or agreement is in a foreign language, a translation of it in the English language, duly certified in English as a correct translation by a sworn translator or by an official or by a diplomatic or consular agent of the country in which the award was made, is required to be filed together with the award and arbitration agreement. **10.295**

The application for leave to enforce a foreign award must be made within six years of the making of the award.[164] Where, however, the application is for leave to enforce under the Reciprocal Enforcement of Commonwealth Judgments Act, the application to register must be made within 12 months after the date of the judgment.[165] **10.296**

(2) Remedies against decisions granting or declining enforcement

The possible remedy is, with the leave of the court granting or declining enforcement, by way of an appeal to the Court of Appeal. **10.297**

B. Recognition and/or enforcement of foreign awards (conventions, treaties)

(1) Specific bilateral or multilateral treaties

Singapore acceded to the New York Convention in 1986 with the reservation that it will apply the Convention only to recognition and enforcement of awards made in the territory of another contracting state. The Reciprocal Enforcement of Commonwealth Judgments **10.298**

---

164 Limitation Act (c 163, 1996 Rev Ed Sing) s 6.

165 Reciprocal Enforcement of Commonwealth Judgments Act (c 264, 1985 Rev Ed Sing) s 3.

Act also applies but in practice this Act has limited applicability because at the time of writing this chapter, only judgments in the following countries in the Commonwealth are enforceable pursuant to the provisions of the Act: Australia, Brunei, Darussalam, Sri Lanka, Hong Kong (for judgments obtained on or before 30 June 1997), India (except the State of Jammu and Kashmir), Malaysia, New Zealand, Pakistan, Papua New Guinea, United Kingdom and Northern Ireland and the Windward Islands. Section 46(3) of the Arbitration Act also provides for enforcement of foreign awards not made in the territory of another (New York Convention) contracting state.

10.299 Singapore also ratified the Washington Convention on the Settlement of Investment Disputes in 1968 and a significant number of Bilateral Investment Treaties (BITs) and Free Trade Agreement (FTAs) that allow for recourse to arbitration under the auspices of the International Centre for the Settlement of Investment Disputes (ICSID).

10.300 The BITs presently concluded are with the Republics of Indonesia, Uzbekistan, Peru, Belarus, Mauritius, Latvia and the Kingdom of Cambodia.

10.301 Some of the FTAs which Singapore has concluded allowing for recourse to arbitration under ICSID include FTAs with Australia, India, Japan, the Republic of Korea, New Zealand, the Republic of Panama, the ESFTA States, a free trade area comprising Switzerland, Iceland, Liechtenstein and Norway, and the United States of America. The list of FTAs which Singapore has concluded can be obtained at the website of the International Enterprise Singapore at <http://www.iessingapore.gov.sg>.

(2) Existence of a standard procedure for the enforcement of foreign awards

10.302 The International Arbitration Act, Arbitration Act and the Reciprocal Enforcement of Commonwealth Judgments Act provide for enforcement by the courts. The resulting Awards in BIT and FTA arbitrations are underpinned by the New York Convention or the ICSID Convention which provide for their enforceability as a final judgment of the courts.[166]

(3) Extent of examination and review of the award by the court

10.303 The bases for a Singapore court to examine or review the award are set out in s 31 of the International Arbitration Act which states the grounds on which a court may refuse enforcement; for example incapacity of one party to the arbitration agreement.

C. Application of the New York Convention

(1) Application of the New York Convention in practice

10.304 There is no reported case of a Singapore court refusing enforcement of a New York Convention award.

(2) Examples of decisions which do not apply the Convention correctly

10.305 There is no reported case of a Singapore court refusing enforcement of a New York Convention award.

[166] Savage, J., *Investment Treaty Arbitration Asian Leading Arbitrators' Guide*, 466.

IX. Appendix

A. National legislation

Arbitration Act (c 143A, 2002 Rev Ed Sing).
International Arbitration Act (c 143A, 2002 Rev Ed Sing).
Limitation Act (c 163, 1996 Rev Ed Sing).

B. Arbitral institutions

Singapore International Arbitration Centre (SIAC)
City Hall, 3 St Andrew's Road, Singapore 178958
Telephone: + 65 6334 1277
Fax: + 65 6334 2942
Email: sinarb@siac.org.sg
Website: <http://www.siac.org.sg>

Singapore Chamber of Maritime Arbitration (SCMA)
City Hall, Third Floor, 3 St Andrew's Road, Singapore 178958
Telephone: +65 6334 1277
Fax: +65 6334 2942
Email: info@scma.org.sg
Website: <http://www.scma.org.sg>

International Centre for Dispute Resolution (ICDR)
City Hall, 3 St. Andrew's Road, Singapore 178958
Telephone: (65) 6334 1277
Fax: (65) 6334 2942
Email: BautistaM@adr.org
Website: <http://www.adr.org>

C. Model arbitration clauses and other patterns

SIAC Model Clause

> Any dispute arising out of or in connection with this contract, including any question regarding its existence, validity or termination, shall be referred to and finally resolved by arbitration in Singapore in accordance with the Arbitration Rules of the Singapore International Arbitration Centre ('SIAC Rules') for the time being in force, which rules are deemed to be incorporated by reference in this clause.
>
> The Tribunal shall consist of________ * *[State an odd number. Either state one, or state three]* arbitrator(s) to be appointed by the chairman of the SIAC.
>
> The language of the arbitration shall be __________________.

D. Bibliography

Ambrose, Clare, Maxwell, Karen and Parry, Angharad, *London Maritime Arbitration* (3rd edn, 2009).

Halsbury's Laws of Singapore: Arbitration, Building & Construction, Vol 2, (Butterworths Asia, 2003) Reissue.

Hwang, Michael, Chung, Katie and Cheng, Fong Lee, 'Claims Against Arbitrators for Breach of Ethical Duties' in Arthur Rovine (ed), *Contemporary Issues in International Arbitration and Mediation: The Fordham Papers 2007*, (Martinus Nijhoff Publishers, 2008).
Lau, Christopher and Chandru, Ganesh, 'Singapore' in *The International Comparative Legal Guide to: International Arbitration* (Global Legal Group Ltd, 2007).
Pryles, Michael and Moser, Michael (eds), *Asian Leading Arbitrators' Guide, Volume 1*, (Juris, 2007) Investment Treaty Arbitration, ch 17.

11

SWEDEN

Robin Oldenstam and Johann von Pachelbel

I. Introduction

A. Current status of the law on arbitration

(1) Short history

Sweden has a long history of recognizing arbitration as a means of solving disputes. Commercial disputes are settled in Sweden by arbitration to an extent that surpasses that of many other countries. The first Swedish arbitration statute was enacted over 100 years ago, in 1887, and there are antecedents in fourteenth century provincial codes. In 1929 the Arbitration Act and the related Act on Foreign Arbitration Agreements and Awards were enacted. In order to meet modern requirements, both in the domestic and the international context, the Acts of 1929 were replaced in 1999 by a new Arbitration Act. **11.01**

(2) Law in force and future projects

The present statute on arbitration entered into force 1 April 1999 (*Lag 1999:116 om skiljeförfarande*),[1] hereinafter called 'the Act'. The Act deals with arbitration taking place in **11.02**

[1] cf eg Heuman, L., *Arbitration Law of Sweden* (Juris Publishing, Huntington, 2003); Heuman, L. and Jarvin, S. (eds), *The Swedish Arbitration Act of 1999, Five Years on: A Critical review of strengths and weaknesses* (Juris Publishing, Huntington, 2006); Lindskog, S., *Skiljeförfarande* (Norstedts, Stockholm, 2005); Strempel, H. and Hobér, K., 'Das neue schwedische Gesetz über Schiedsverfahren: neue Regeln für das Schiedsinstitut der Handelskammer Stockholm' [1999] supplement 4 (4) *Recht und Praxis der Schiedsgerichtsbarkeit (RPS)*,

Sweden as well as with arbitration agreements, proceedings and awards having a foreign element. The Act applies equally to domestic and international arbitrations. In form, the Act does not correspond to the UNCITRAL Model Law, but it is very close to it in substance. Notwithstanding that the Swedish legislator did not intend to take the UNCITRAL Model Law as a 'blue-print' there are actually very few material differences between the Act and the Model Law.

(3) Distinction between national and international arbitration

11.03 The rules governing arbitrations in Sweden are the same irrespective of whether it is a national or international arbitration (the Act, s 46). There are, however, some rules paying particular regard to the international character of an arbitration. One important rule refers to the law governing the arbitration agreement (the Act, s 48—see also *infra* at 11.18 *et seq*). Another important rule gives the parties in a commercial relationship, without domicile or place of business in Sweden, the right to exclude or limit the applicability of the grounds for setting aside an award provided for in s 34 of the Act (the Act, s 51, para 1).[2]

11.04 (3.1) **If there are different systems and rules for national/international arbitration, what are the criteria for the distinction between both systems?** There are no different legal systems, but only some provisions in the Act that specifically address arbitration proceedings of an international character.

11.05 To the extent any difference is made between what may be called national arbitration and arbitration having an international connection, such difference is based on whether the parties are, or one of them is, residing outside Sweden at the time of entering into the arbitration agreement, or, even if both parties reside in Sweden, whether the dispute has arisen in connection with a business transaction outside of Sweden.[3]

B. Practice of arbitration

(1) Frequency of arbitration as opposed to litigation

11.06 Although no exact figures are available, a survey in the mid 1990s estimated that some 400 arbitrations took place in Sweden each year. About 20 per cent involve international agreements. In more than 50 per cent of the disputes an award is pronounced after the dispute has been tried on its merits.[4] In view of the development since, the number of arbitrations taking place in Sweden today is likely to be considerably higher.

11.07 In Sweden arbitrations can be conducted either under institutional rules or as *ad hoc* arbitration, where the provisions of the Act will apply. Institutional arbitration, ie arbitration conducted in accordance with the rules of a particular institution, generally offers certain advantages for the parties. The institution may eg assist in the selection of arbitrators and normally continues to keep an eye on the proceedings. Further, the rules of arbitral

---

Deutsche Institution für Schiedsgerichtsbarkeit eV 8–10; Weigand, F.-B. 'The UNCITRAL Model Law: New draft arbitration acts in Germany and Sweden' (1995) 11 (4) *Arb Int'l* 397.

[2] cf also Proposition (Swedish Government Bill, in the following 'Prop') 1998/99:35, 157.

[3] Prop 1998/99:35, 192 and 244.

[4] cf Broomé, B., 'Näringslivets tvistlösning' [1995/1996] *Juridisk Tidskrift*, 457, 458.

institutions are generally designed to avoid or solve those difficulties which occur most frequently in *ad hoc* arbitrations.

(2) Leading arbitral institutions and statistics (if available)

The Arbitration Institute of the Stockholm Chamber of Commerce (the 'SCC Institute') is the leading centre for institutional arbitrations in Sweden. Technically a part of the Stockholm Chamber of Commerce, the SCC Institute is autonomous within the Chamber, having its own Board, and its own Secretariat under the direction of a Secretary-General. **11.08**

For a large number of years, the SCC Institute has maintained its position as one of the major international arbitration institutions and has been in a unique position with respect to trade disputes between, on the one hand, Western businesses and, on the other hand, entities of Eastern Europe and China. For example, under an arrangement, known as the 1992 Optional Clause Agreement, between the American Arbitration Association and the Chamber of Commerce and Industry of the Russian Federation, an arbitration clause designating the SCC Institute as the appointing authority and providing for arbitration in Sweden is proposed for inclusion in contracts between legal or natural persons of the US and Russia. The SCC Institute is further also used in many other international investment and trade disputes and is prepared to act as appointing authority, independent of whether the proceedings are conducted under the SCC Rules or other rules. With regard to proceedings under the UNCITRAL Rules the SCC is acting as appointing authority.[5] Moreover, the SCC Institute is one of the forums designated by the Energy Charter Treaty for the settlement of investment disputes arising under this Treaty (Art 26(4)(c) ECT). Also several bilateral investment treaties provide for the possibility to settle an investment dispute by arbitration under the auspices of the SCC Institute.[6] **11.09**

Arbitrations under the auspices of the SCC Institute cover many areas of international arbitration, such as sales contracts, construction projects, licence agreements, joint ventures and many other categories of commercial issues.[7] Further, a considerable number of disputes involving Chinese parties have traditionally been handled under the auspices of the SCC Institute. Recent statistics show an increasing number of new proceedings filed at the SCC Institute. In 2008 the SCC set a new record with 176 new cases filed.[8] According to the statistics established by the SCC Institute (<http://www.sccinstitute.se>) its international acceptance as a centre for institutional arbitrations is confirmed by the fact that around half of its proceedings during 2008 involved at least one foreign party. **11.10**

The present Rules of the SCC Institute ('SCC Rules') became effective on 1 January 2007 and are applicable to any cases filed after 1 January 2007. These Rules have displaced the former SCC Rules from 1 April 1999, which had been revised in connection with the **11.11**

5 cf Franke, U., 'The Arbitration Institute of the Stockholm Chamber of Commerce' (1983) *Ybk Arb Inst Stockholm Chamber Com* 6, 7.

6 cf, for example, the Agreement for the Promotion and Protection of Investments between the Czech Republic and the United Kingdom of 1990 available at <http://www.unctadxi.org/templates/DocSearch_779.aspx> (accessed 30 September 2008).

7 cf Franke, U., 'International Arbitration in Sweden' (1985) 2 *Int'l Construction L Rev* 159, 160.

8 cf for further statistics <http://www.sccinstitute.se>.

implementation of the Act in 1999. The SCC Rules from 2007 do not substantially differ from the SCC Rules of 1999, but have been further adjusted to adhere to best practices in modern international arbitration. Moreover, they reflect a linguistic revision and a further adoption of generally recognized terminology.[9] Apart from the SCC Rules, the SCC Institute has adopted specific alternative rules including Rules for Expedited Arbitration, Insurance Arbitration Rules, Procedures and Services under the UNCITRAL Arbitration Rules and Mediation Rules.

II. Jurisdiction of the arbitral tribunal

A. Arbitration agreement

(1) Arbitration clause and submission agreement

11.12 An arbitration agreement may concern future disputes as well as an existing dispute (submission). The arbitration agreement may form part of a commercial agreement or may be in the form of a separate agreement. When future disputes are referred to in an arbitration clause, the future dispute should pertain 'to a legal relationship specified in the [arbitration] agreement' (the Act, s 1, para 1). The 'legal relationship' referred to in the arbitration clause should already exist or come into existence at the time of the conclusion of the arbitration clause. A reference to 'any dispute arising under this agreement' is acceptable, but a reference to 'any dispute arising between us' during a specified period, or generally in the future without any limitation to a reasonably specified commercial relationship, is invalid.[10]

(2) Requirements as to the contents of the arbitration agreement

11.13 An arbitration agreement contains the parties' agreement that an existing or a future dispute shall be decided by arbitrators and that the arbitral award shall be final and binding between the parties. This requires that the arbitration agreement is sufficiently distinct in order to be distinguishable from any other kind of dispute resolution.[11] Consequently, an arbitration clause can be very briefly worded according to Swedish law, like, for example: 'All disputes arising out of this contract shall be settled by arbitration'. No further prerequisites for the validity of an arbitration agreement are stipulated in the Act. In the absence of any more detailed agreement it is possible to determine the number of arbitrators, the language of the proceedings or the governing law etc through the application of the statutory rules or the SCC Rules, as the case may be.

11.14 The arbitration agreement must not have been accomplished by duress, fraud, undue influence, or any other such matter that may make the arbitration agreement void according to the ordinary rules of private law.

---

[9] For further information on the revision of the SCC Rules of 1999 cf eg Hobér, K. and McKechnie, W., 'New Rules of the Arbitration Institute of the Stockholm Chamber of Commerce' (2007) 1 (6) *Global Arb Rev* 21; Magnusson, A. and Shaughnessy, P., 'The 2007 Arbitration Rules of the Arbitration Institute of the Stockholm Chamber of Commerce' [2006] (3) *Stockholm Int'l Arb Rev*, 33; Hobér, K. and Foerster, A., 'Die neue Schiedsordnung des Schiedsgerichtsinstituts der Stockholmer Handelskammer' [2007] *SchiedsVZ* 207.

[10] Prop 1998/99:35, 212.

[11] cf Heuman, L., *Arbitration Law of Sweden: Practice and Procedure* (Juris Publishing, Huntington, 2003) 33—with further references.

(3) Form of the arbitration agreement (eg 'in writing' requirement)

The Act does not prescribe any particular form for the arbitration agreement.[12] Nevertheless, in practice most—if not all—arbitration agreements are in writing. It is possible to have an arbitration clause incorporated in an agreement by referring to general conditions. **11.15**

(3.1) **Are there special requirements for a power of attorney/authority to enter into an arbitration agreement on behalf of a third party?** A power of attorney to enter into an arbitration agreement may be given in writing or orally. It is, however, believed that a general power of attorney for legal proceedings according to Swedish law does not authorize a lawyer to enter into an arbitral agreement unless he is specifically authorized to do so.[13] **11.16**

(4) Incorporation of an arbitration clause contained in general terms and conditions

As mentioned above under (11.8), an arbitration clause contained in general conditions is considered incorporated in an agreement if the general conditions have been properly brought to the notice of both parties. For an arbitration clause to be binding in such a situation, it must be proven that the other party actually was informed about the arbitration clause or that such party knew or ought to have known about the clause.[14] If the application of such a clause follows from customs between the parties or from trade usage, a party may be deemed to have known about the arbitration clause.[15] **11.17**

(5) Law applicable to the interpretation of arbitration clauses

An arbitration agreement providing for arbitration in Sweden will be governed by Swedish law, unless the parties have agreed that another law is to be applied.[16] **11.18**

If the arbitration agreement has an international connection, it is governed by the law agreed upon by the parties. A dispute is considered to have an international connection when both parties are, or one of them is, residing outside of Sweden at the time of entering into of the arbitration agreement, or, even if both parties reside in Sweden, when the dispute has arisen in connection with a business transaction outside of Sweden.[17] If the arbitration agreement has an international connection and the parties have not made any such choice of law, the arbitration agreement is governed by the law of the country in which, by virtue of the agreement, the proceedings have taken place or shall take place (the Act, s 48, para 1). However, these principles do not apply with respect to the question whether or not a party was authorized to enter into the arbitration agreement or was duly represented (*ibid*, para 2). Moreover, even if the arbitration agreement is governed by foreign law, Swedish law is applied to determine arbitrability for the purposes of deciding whether an arbitration agreement constitutes a bar to court proceedings, or not (Act, s 49, para 1). **11.19**

---

[12] Prop 1998/99:35, 212.
[13] cf Cars, T., *Skiljeförfarande* 111.
[14] cf eg NJA 1949, 609 (Nytt Juridisk Arkiv, Decisions of the Swedish Supreme Court) and NJA 1980, 46.
[15] cf eg RH 1989:1, RH 1989:51, RH 1989:83 and RH 1990:71.
[16] Prop 1998/99:35, 193, and s 48, para 1 of the Act.
[17] *ibid*, 192 and 244.

11.20 Generally, Swedish law will govern the arbitration agreement if the place of arbitration is located in Sweden (s 48 of the Act), ie questions regarding the interpretation and validity of the agreement will be determined by Swedish contract law.[18]

11.21 (5.1) **Do courts accept a wide competence of the arbitral tribunal or do they restrict arbitral competence? Do claims which arise in connection with the agreement submitted to arbitration generally fall within the arbitral jurisdiction even if based on tortious legal basis? Does there exist case law with respect to the wording in an arbitration clause as 'arising out of/under/in connection with the present contract' and its specific meaning?** When deciding whether a specific dispute is covered by a certain arbitration agreement, the court will construe the arbitration agreement. Such interpretation of an arbitration agreement follows ordinary civil law rules applicable to contract interpretation, considering *inter alia* an evaluation of the parties' intentions when entering into the agreement, the literal meaning of the arbitration agreement and other related circumstances. Arbitration agreements are generally given a wide interpretation. This is based on the assumption that the parties, having agreed to arbitration, will have intended for all of their disputes reasonably connected to the legal relation specified in the arbitration agreement to be settled by the same mechanism.

11.22 There is no case law with respect to the specific above cited wording of an arbitration clause. However, it is generally assumed that the specific wording of an arbitration clause will not affect the wide interpretation generally given to such clauses, unless express limitations or exclusions have been made. In general, a tort claim as opposed to a contractual claim, would not automatically be covered by an arbitration agreement. However, if the tort claim is sufficiently connected to the contractual relationship referred to in the arbitration agreement, the court may construe the arbitration agreement as covering such a claim as well. In a recent decision, the Swedish Supreme Court (*Högsta Domstolen*) thus held that a tort claim could be considered to fall within the scope of an arbitration agreement on the grounds of factual connection if also contractual claims were in dispute.[19] The scope of an arbitration clause will ultimately depend on the intention of the parties, determined against the background of the wording of the arbitration agreement and the factual circumstances of the particular case upon which the claim in question is based.

(6) Binding effect of an arbitration clause on third parties (eg in case of a guarantee or assignment)

11.23 In certain cases it is recognized that an arbitration agreement is not only effective between the contractual parties, but may also become effective in relation to a third party, eg in cases of universal and singular successions, provided that no specific circumstances are opposed. The question whether a guarantor is bound by an arbitration clause which is included in the main contract, eg between creditor and debtor is not addressed in the Act, and the

[18] cf Hobér, K., 'Arbitration Reform in Sweden' (2001) 17 *Arb Int'l* 351, 356; Madsen, F., *Commercial Arbitration in Sweden,* (2nd edn, OUP, Oxford, 2006) 315; see also SCC Arbitral Award 108/1997, [2001] (1) Stockholm Arbitration Report 57 and NJA 2000, 538 (*ATI v Bulbank*).

[19] Swedish Supreme Court (*Högsta Domstolen*) decision of 14 June 2007, Case Ö 2416–04 (*BP v Gatu och Väg AB*).

legislator has referred the issue to be determined by case law.[20] The prevailing opinion is that a guarantor is bound by an arbitration agreement. The issue is probably to be answered by an interpretation of the guarantee agreement in light of all of the circumstances of the case.[21] Further, if a party to a contract transfers all its rights and obligations under a contract including an arbitration clause, the new party is generally considered bound by such arbitration clause. The remaining party is also bound by the arbitration clause in relation to the new party, unless special circumstances exist.[22]

(6.1) **What is the law/leading authorities' position on multi-party situations? Especially, (i) with respect to the objection that the arbitration clause does not specifically provide for a plurality of parties in the same procedure; (ii) with respect to the constitution of the arbitral tribunal; and (iii) with respect to the consolidation of two or more running arbitration proceedings?** There are no provisions under Swedish law dealing with multi-party arbitration, including how the problems which typically arise in such situations are to be remedied. The solutions must be sought in conformity with the basic principle of arbitration, ie the freedom of the parties to agree on how to have their dispute settled. Thus, the initiative rests with the parties. In the absence of an agreement, a party generally cannot be forced into proceedings having more than two parties. The appointment of arbitrators is also up to the parties. However, the parties can agree that the District Court shall appoint an arbitrator, and the District Court is obliged to do so if one party so requests (the Act, s 12, para 3). This rule is *inter alia* meant to facilitate the resolution of multi-party disputes. **11.24**

The application of a typical arbitration clause in a multi-party arbitration involves certain administrative problems. If the parties have so agreed, the District Court at the place of residence of either party, or at the seat of the arbitration proceedings, or the Stockholm District Court, shall appoint an arbitrator (the Act, s 12). Another alternative in case of multi-party arbitration may be, where possible, to separate the parties into two groups in relation to each issue. Then each group appoints one arbitrator and the two arbitrators so appointed select a third. However, the several parties in each respective group must be unanimous in their choice of an arbitrator or arbitrators. If unanimity is not attained, no valid appointment can be made and the rules under which a substitute appointment is to be made become applicable. **11.25**

If the SCC Rules apply, the following procedure is used. In cases where there are two or more parties on either side and in case the dispute is to be resolved by more than one arbitrator, the claimant-side and the respondent-side appoints an equal number of arbitrators each. If the parties on either side cannot jointly agree on an arbitrator or arbitrators, the Board of the SCC Institute will appoint not only the arbitrator(s), but the entire arbitral tribunal, unless the parties have decided otherwise (SCC Rules Art 13, para 4). This procedure comprises a wider possibility for the SCC Institute to appoint arbitrators in **11.26**

20 Prop 1998/99:35, 66.
21 cf Heuman, L., *Arbitration Law of Sweden* (n 1) 97.
22 cf NJA 1997, 866 ('*Emja-case*'; *Braack Schiffahrts KG v Wärtsilä Diesel AB*).

multi-party cases and is in alignment with many other international institutional sets of rules on this point.[23]

11.27 The Act does not address the issue of a potential consolidation of two or more running arbitration proceedings. Thus, this issue is left to be decided by case law. However, if the SCC Rules apply, the Board of the SCC Institute may decide to consolidate several proceedings under certain conditions. According to the rules, the SCC Institute Board may after consulting the parties and the arbitral tribunal, at the request of a party and upon submission of a request for arbitration concerning a legal relationship in respect of which an arbitration between the same parties is already pending, decide to include the claims contained in the request for arbitration in the pending proceedings (SCC Rules, Art 11). This Rule is in alignment with for example Art 4 (6) of the ICC Arbitration Rules.

11.28 (6.2) **Is there case law/authorities with respect to the admissibility of third party participation in an arbitration without being a claimant or defendant (Nebenintervention/ Streitverkündung; intervention forcée/volontaire; vouching in; *amicus curiae* etc)? What are the prerequisites and effects of such participation (if permitted)?** A third party may participate in arbitration proceedings only if such party is bound by the arbitration agreement under which the arbitration proceedings take place and provided that the two other parties consent thereto. In such case, the third party may step into the proceedings as a party.[24] There is no published case law available on this issue.

(7) Termination of an arbitration agreement by a party (reasons and case law)

11.29 A party may terminate an arbitration agreement if the other party is in material breach of the agreement. There are no other possibilities for a party unilaterally to terminate the arbitration agreement, unless the specific arbitration agreement provides otherwise. Thus, a termination may occur by virtue of the provisions in the agreement itself, eg a time limit or other understanding between the parties, or due to the general rules of private law, eg through frustration of the agreement. An arbitration agreement can terminate with respect to an existing dispute only and yet remain in effect with respect to any future disputes.[25] The arbitration agreement probably terminates when the award period, if stipulated by the parties, expires without a valid award having been made.[26] In such a situation, however, the termination is not complete. If the arbitrators render an award after the expiration of the award period, the award is not automatically void, but may be challenged in court proceedings (the Act, s 34 para 2—see also *infra* at 11.258). The arbitral tribunal is thus authorized to render an award, albeit a vulnerable one.

---

[23] cf for example Art 10(2) ICC Rules. According to Art 16 para 3 of the former SCC Rules of 1 April 1999 the SCC was only entitled to appoint the arbitrator(s) which the respective party/parties failed to appoint, however, without encroaching upon the other party's appointment of its arbitrator(s). In contrast thereto, the new ruling is intended to enhance the due process rights of the parties and their equal rights to appoint an arbitrator; cf Magnusson and Shaughnessy, [2006] (3) *Stockholm Int'l Arb Rev* 33, 37; Hobér and McKechnie, (2007) 1 (6) *Global Arb Rev* 21.

[24] cf Westerling, B., 'Rättegångsbalken och skiljeförfarandet' (1981) 11 *Ybk Arb Inst Stockholm Chamber Com* 14.

[25] cf Heuman, L., *Arbitration Law of Sweden* (n 1) 120.

[26] SOU (Statens Offentliga Utredningar (*Swedish Government Official Reports*)) 1994: 81 *Delbetänkande av skiljedomsutredningen*, 110.

B. Arbitrability

(1) 'Personal arbitrability' (capacity to conclude arbitration agreements)

Any legal or physical person may be a party to an arbitration. Such person must, however, have the legal capacity to enter into a binding arbitration agreement. Thus, he may not be a minor or be under a guardianship. **11.30**

A legal entity entering into an arbitration agreement should be properly constituted and validly represented. Parties and their agents must have authority to act. The legal entity must be able to acquire rights and undertake obligations. No restrictions apply with regard to foreign nationals being parties to arbitration in Sweden. **11.31**

The issue of whether a party was authorized to enter into an arbitration agreement, or was duly represented, is typically not to be answered by the law governing the arbitration agreement. Such issue is generally to be answered by the *lex corporationis* or *lex personae* determined pursuant to the principles of applicable private international law. **11.32**

(1.1) May a state (or state agency) as party invoke sovereign immunity before the arbitral tribunal or before a state court (eg in a procedure of enforcement)? The Swedish state has never claimed or enjoyed immunity before its courts or administrative agencies, nor in Swedish arbitral proceedings. Proceedings against a governmental agency of Sweden do not depend on any waiver of immunity by the state. State agencies are, in principle, free to submit to arbitration in their contracts. Each of the central governmental agencies has the power, however, if desirable, to issue instructions to any subordinate local or regional agency that an arbitration agreement would require the approval of the central agency.[27] A sovereign state may, as a matter of principle, claim immunity in Swedish judicial and administrative proceedings, albeit that it is unclear how far such immunity goes.[28] **11.33**

As far as the proper arbitration proceedings are concerned the state immunity defence is not available, since there is nothing to be immune from. Generally speaking, it has been long recognized that there exists a distinction between immunity from jurisdiction and immunity from execution, insofar as lack of immunity from jurisdiction does not necessarily entail lack of immunity from execution.[29] However, there are certain exceptions to the general principle of sovereign immunity. The foreign state may waive its immunity expressly or by conduct. Moreover, a foreign state cannot claim immunity in respect of a counterclaim if it has itself commenced proceedings provided that there is a certain connection between the two claims. It is generally believed that the Supreme Court would recognize the restrictive theory of state immunity, which does not accept state immunity for commercial transactions (*acta gestionis*).[30] Disputes concerning real property may be entertained by the courts notwithstanding a plea of immunity, at least to the extent that the property is not used for the purposes of a diplomatic mission.[31] However, a plea of sovereign **11.34**

---

[27] SOU 1971:88, 113 (Offentlig upphandling : regler och riktlinjer för stat och kommun).

[28] cf Pålsson, P., *Svensk rättspraxis i internationell processrätt* (Norstedts, Stockholm, 1989) 19.

[29] cf Hobér, K., *Enforcing Foreign Arbitral Awards Against Russian Entities* (Transnational Juris, New York, 1994) 85.

[30] cf *Arbitration in Sweden* (SCC, Stockholm, 1984) 12.

[31] cf NJA 1957, 195.

immunity may—at least in connection with truly sovereign acts as opposed to normal commercial acts—be available before the courts and authorities with respect to subsequent enforcement or execution proceedings, unless the foreign state has expressly waived its immunity also as regards execution measures, or it has itself commenced proceedings.

(2) 'Objective arbitrability' (eg of patent, trade mark and antitrust matters)

11.35 Section 1 of the Act defines arbitrability by stating that 'matters in respect of which the parties may reach a settlement' may be the subject of arbitration. A matter which may be comprised by an arbitration agreement is thus one that can be decided in a civil action. Pursuant to Swedish law a wide interpretation of arbitrability applies.[32] Questions regarding punishment, forfeiture and other consequences (except damages) of a criminal case cannot be referred to arbitration. Most questions of family law are also excluded from arbitration.

11.36 As regards patent and trade mark litigation, it is quite clear that cases involving licensing are arbitrable. Arbitration is further believed to be permissible in questions concerning the infringement of industrial property rights.[33] By contrast, other issues in this field, such as the validity of patents are generally not regarded as arbitrable.

11.37 As to arbitration agreements concluded by the debtor prior to bankruptcy proceedings and relating to property which may legally form part of the bankruptcy estate, ie arbitration agreements which may be of importance in disputes between the debtor and third parties (non-creditors), the general rule is that such arbitration agreements are binding on the bankruptcy estate.[34] Nevertheless, the arbitration agreement is binding on the bankruptcy estate only insofar as the debtor and the other party to the agreement could legally have regulated the subject matter by way of agreement. Issues concerning rights *in rem* in relation to the contracting parties may thus not be settled by arbitration if the bankruptcy estate opposes it.[35] Consequently, the validity of a retention of title clause is a matter for the courts. Likewise, if the bankruptcy administrator takes steps to invalidate a transaction which has given a creditor an undue preference, he will not be bound by an arbitration agreement which the debtor has concluded before the bankruptcy with the other party to the transaction. An arbitration agreement entered into by the debtor prior to its bankruptcy is binding on the bankrupt's estate in respect of claims made by a creditor against the debtor.[36]

11.38 Pursuant to s 1, para 3 of the Act the arbitrators may rule on the effects of competition law as between the parties, eg on the validity of contracts. According to the legislator's understanding arbitrators should not, however, decide such issues of their own motion, *ex officio*.[37]

---

32 cf Franke, U., *Swedish Law* (Juristförlaget, Stockholm, 1994) 532, 535.

33 cf Karnell, G., 'Patent och skiljedom, giltighets- och intrångsfrågor' in *Festskrift till Sveriges Advokatsamfund 1887–1987* (Norstedts, Stockholm, 1987) 311.

34 cf NJA 1931, 647.

35 cf Dillén, N., *Bidrag till läran om skiljeavtalet* (Gustaf Larssons, Stockholm, 1933) 254–5; Welamson, L., *Konkursrätt* (Norstedts, Stockholm, 1961) 310; Hassler, A. and Cars, T., *Skiljeförfarande* (2nd edn, Norstedts, Stockhom, 1989) 47; Cars, T., *Skiljeförfarande* 43.

36 cf NJA 1913, 191.

37 Prop 1998/99:35, 58.

Although the legislator reserved to review its position depending on the outcome of the *Eco Swiss v Benetton* case,[38] which was still pending with the European Court of Justice (ECJ) when the Act entered into force in 1999, the Swedish legislator has so far not picked up on the issue again. Neither is there any case law clarifying the arbitrators' duties concerning the principle of party autonomy on the one hand and the implications of mandatory competition law on the other. The ECJ established a national court's obligation to declare an arbitral award invalid where the respective national law requires the court to grant an annulment in case of violation of national rules of public policy, and that the relevant court is obliged to grant such annulment if it is based on a violation of Art 81 of the EC Treaty. Following this ruling it is debated in Swedish legal doctrine whether the arbitral tribunal is obliged to consider the invalidity of an agreement in dispute *ex officio* even if the parties have not presented that argument themselves.[39] Thereby, authors particularly refer to s 33 para 2 of the Act according to which an arbitral award is invalid 'if the award [. . .] is clearly incompatible with the basic principles of the Swedish legal system'. In practice, questions of compatibility with competition law are often hard to determine in advance. Therefore, the issue sometimes may be introduced in the proceedings by the arbitrators through a suitable conduct of the case and thereby inviting the parties to comment on the matter.

Further, it is possible to refer a dispute concerning the alleged nullity of a partnership or a registration of a company to arbitration. A dispute referred to arbitration may also concern the existence of a particular fact (the Act, s 1, para 1). For instance, the arbitrators may rule on whether a defect in sold goods exists or whether a complaint has been made in time. The particular fact must, however, be covered by the arbitration agreement.[40] Arbitrability has also been extended beyond the scope of interpreting agreements to include the supplementing of contracts (the Act, s 1, para 2). This means that arbitrators may fill gaps in contracts if authorized to do so by the parties. The filling of gaps, for example, may take the form of determining the price or other contractual conditions in a long-term agreement.[41] **11.39**

In regard to disputes between business enterprises on the one hand and consumers on the other concerning products or services supplied principally for private use, an arrangement to the effect that future disputes are to be referred to arbitration without a right for the parties to appeal against the award, may not be invoked (the Act, s 6, para 1). This rule does not, however, apply if the dispute concerns an agreement between an insurer and a policyholder concerning insurance based on a collective agreement or group agreement and handled by representatives of the group, nor if an international obligation of Sweden providing to the contrary exists (the Act, s 6, para 2). Moreover, pursuant to s 36 of the Swedish Contracts Act[42] an arbitration agreement may be disregarded if the enforcement **11.40**

[38] cf Case C-126/97 *Eco Swiss China Time Ltd v Benetton International NV* [1999] ECR I-3055.
[39] cf Heuman, L., *Arbitration Law of Sweden* (n 1) 148–52 with further references.
[40] Prop 1998/99:35, 212.
[41] *ibid*, 62.
[42] s 36 of the Swedish Contracts Act reads as follows:

'A contract term or condition may be modified or set aside if such term or condition is unconscionable having regard to the contents of the agreement, the circumstances prevailing at the time the agreement was entered into, subsequent circumstances, and circumstances in general. Where a term is of such significance for the agreement that it would be unreasonable to demand the continued is unreasonable under the particular circumstances, especially in case of consumer contracts. Section 36 of the Contracts Act has also in some specific cases been applied to render an arbitration agreement unenforceable where one party, albeit not a consumer in a strict sense, has an inferior position in relation to the other party and the enforcement of the arbitration agreement would create an unreasonable financial burden on such party.[43] In Swedish legal practice, s 36 of the Contracts Act is applied very restrictively regarding arbitration agreements between commercial parties. Accordingly, an arbitration agreement between two commercial parties has only been declared void pursuant to s 36 of the Contracts Act in very rare cases.

C. Decision on the arbitral tribunal's jurisdiction ('*competence-competence*')

(1) Separability (independence of the arbitration agreement from the main agreement)

11.41 The doctrine of separability, ie that an arbitration clause which is included in the main contract between the parties is, in principle, separable from the rest of the contract, was widely accepted in Swedish case law and literature even before the Act came into force.[44] It is now enshrined in s 3 of the Act without restrictions.

11.42 The arbitration clause may even be subject to a different legal system than the rest of the contract. This means, that in general, the validity of an arbitration clause shall be determined independently and that a party will not be able to obstruct the proceedings simply by maintaining the invalidity of the main contract. However, it may follow from the facts of the relevant case that defects of the main contract also affect the arbitration clause, eg if general requirements for the conclusion of a contract are not met,[45] or where the validity of the arbitration clause depends on the validity of the main contract for some reason.[46] The latter may be the case if the parties agreed on such interdependence between the arbitration clause and the rest of the contract, but according to some authors, it may even follow from the circumstances of the case.[47] However, one should be careful to construe such interdependence without any party agreement to that effect. Otherwise, the idea of the doctrine of separability might too easily be circumvented.

---

enforceability of the remainder of the agreement with its terms unchanged, the agreement may be modified in other respects, or may be set aside in its entirety.

Upon the determination of the applicability of the provisions of the first paragraph, particular attention shall be paid to the need to protect those parties who, in their capacity as consumers or otherwise, hold an inferior bargaining position in the contractual relationship.

The provisions of the first and second paragraphs shall apply mutatis mutandis to questions relating to the terms of legal acts other than contracts.

The provisions of section 11 of the Consumer Contracts Act (SFS 1994:1512) shall also apply to the modifications of contractual terms relating to consumers.'

[43] cf eg NJA 1987, 639. With respect to the application of s 36 of the Contracts Act reference is made to NJA 1976, 706, NJA 1979, 666, NJA 1980, 46, NJA 1981, 711, NJA 1983, 510, NJA 1983, 800, NJA 1983, 853, NJA 1984, 229, NJA 1986, 388.

[44] Prop 1998/99:35, 75 *et seq.*

[45] cf ch 3 of the Contracts Act.

[46] cf Lindskog, *Skiljeförfarande* (n 1) 312.

[47] *ibid.*

(2) Competence of the tribunal to decide on its own jurisdiction (including form and time of the tribunal's decision)

The doctrine of the *compétence de la compétence* is recognized in Swedish law (the Act, s 2, para 1). Thus, the arbitrators may rule on their own jurisdiction to decide the dispute. The arbitrators do not have to rule on their own jurisdiction unless a party has requested them to do so. However, even without such a request by a party, the arbitrators should decide whether the dispute is arbitrable or not and whether an award would be invalid due to *ordre public*.[48] This does not prevent a competent court from ruling on the validity of the arbitration agreement at the request of a party. The arbitrators may, however, continue the arbitral proceedings pending the determination by the court, but the decision of the court once rendered is binding on the arbitrators. **11.43**

An award is challengeable on procedural grounds only and solely in accordance with the provisions of the Act, which, *inter alia*, establishes a three-month period within which the challenge must be filed (the Act, s 34). It is not possible to challenge the award on the merits. **11.44**

A decision by the arbitrators to the effect that the arbitration agreement is invalid is given in the form of an award (the Act, s 27, para 1). **11.45**

A decision by the arbitrators to the effect that the arbitration agreement is valid or that they are competent to try the case is not made in the form of an award, but simply as a decision, making a further trial of the case possible (the Act, s 27, para 3). There is no room for any appeal of the arbitrator's decision during the course of the arbitration proceedings. Thus, there are no remedies against such a decision made by the arbitrators other than a challenge of the final award. **11.46**

(3) Extent of the 'competence-competence' *and role of the courts (including form and time limits of a challenge of the tribunal's decision)*

A decision by the arbitral tribunal to the effect that the arbitration agreement is valid, does not prevent a party from bringing an action before a competent court of law to have the agreement declared invalid (the Act, s 2, para 1). If such action is brought, the arbitral tribunal may continue with the arbitration proceedings or stay the proceedings awaiting the judgment by the court. The decision may also be re-examined when it comes to the enforcement or recognition of the award under the New York Convention.[49] **11.47**

An arbitral award can at a party's request be set aside if there is no valid arbitration agreement (the Act, s 34, para 1). Such challenge of the arbitral award shall be filed in accordance with the provisions of the Act, which, *inter alia*, establishes a three-month period within which the challenge must be filed. However, a party is not entitled to rely on the existence of a circumstance which such party may be considered to have waived by taking part in the proceedings without any objection or otherwise. Nevertheless, a party shall not be treated **11.48**

48 Prop 1998/99:35, 214.

49 cf Hjerner, L., 'On Partial Awards, Orders and Other Decisions in Arbitral Proceedings, in Particular with Respect to Arbitration in Sweden' [1984] *Ybk Arb Inst Stockholm Chamber Com* 31, 37.

as having accepted the arbitrators' jurisdiction to determine the issue referred to arbitration solely by having appointed an arbitrator (the Act, s 34, para 2).

D. Enforcement of an arbitration agreement within or by court proceedings

(1) Effect of invoking an arbitration clause within a court proceeding (and time limits for such a motion)

11.49 A party to a valid arbitration agreement may move for a dismissal on the ground of lack of jurisdiction if the other party commences court proceedings with respect to a matter which is covered by such agreement (the Act, s 4, para 1). Certain prerequisites apply to a court's dismissal on such grounds, viz, the arbitration agreement must cover an issue which is arbitrable, and neither of the parties have forfeited their right to rely on the arbitration agreement as a bar to court proceedings (i) because such a party has opposed a request for arbitration; (ii) because it has failed to appoint an arbitrator in due time; or (iii) because it did not in due time provide its share of the requested deposit or other security for the compensation to the arbitrators (the Act, s 5).

11.50 The objection to the jurisdiction of the court due to an arbitration agreement must be raised on the first occasion when a party pleads its case on the merits before the court. Such a pleading, if made on a later occasion, has no effect unless the party had a valid reason and invoked this as soon as the reason ceased to exist. An arbitration agreement is effective even if the matter has been dealt with earlier in a summary proceeding by another authority (the Act, s 4, para 2). When the existence of a valid arbitration agreement is raised as an objection to jurisdiction, the court must grant a motion for a stay or dismissal. A court may not try an issue that is the subject of concurrent proceedings.[50] Such concurrent proceedings may be arbitration proceedings.[51] Thus, in case of concurrent arbitration proceedings, the court will either declare the court proceedings stayed or dismiss the action.

11.51 (1.1) **If a party has invoked successfully the arbitration agreement in a court proceeding, is it then entitled to deny within the arbitral proceeding that there is a valid and binding arbitration agreement?** A judgment from a court declaring an arbitration agreement valid is binding on the arbitral tribunal in the sense that the tribunal does not have the discretion to rule on the validity of the same arbitration agreement. However, if the court proceedings have been dismissed because of an arbitration agreement, but without reaching the merits of the validity issue, there are no *legal* obstacles for a party having successfully invoked the arbitration agreement to deny before the arbitral tribunal that there is a valid and binding arbitration agreement. However, the arbitrators are likely to consider the fact that the party has invoked the arbitration agreement, when determining whether the arbitration agreement is valid and may also take into account the court's reasons, if any, for its decision on dismissal.

11.52 (1.2) **Vice versa, if a party has successfully objected to an arbitral proceeding by denying that there is a valid arbitration agreement, may it then invoke such agreement in the**

---

50 Code of Judicial Procedure, Ch 13 s 6.

51 cf Fitgers, P. and Mellqvists, M., *Domstolsprocessen—En kommentar till rättegångsbalken* (2nd edn, Norstedts juridik, 2002) 89 *et seq.*

ensuing court proceeding? The short answer is no. A party forfeits its right to rely on the arbitration agreement as a bar to court proceedings where such party has opposed a request for the application of the arbitration agreement (the Act, s 5).

There are certain circumstances, however, in which a motion for a stay or dismissal based on lack of jurisdiction would be denied by the court, despite the existence of a valid arbitration agreement. Examples of such circumstances are, besides the example accounted for above, cases where the respondent has (i) failed to appoint an arbitrator within the required period of time; or (ii) failed, within the required period of time, to provide its share of the deposit or other security for the compensation of the arbitrators (the Act, s 5). **11.53**

The court's powers are not discretionary. When the existence of a valid arbitration agreement is raised as an objection to jurisdiction in a proper case, the courts have to grant such motion. The respondent is required to raise the objection at the earliest possible stage.[52] **11.54**

(2) Legal remedies and proceedings to enforce an arbitration agreement

Swedish law acknowledges the validity and binding effect of arbitration agreements. Unless the dispute falls outside the scope of the arbitration agreement or the agreement is void or ineffective for some other reason (see eg *supra* at 11.14 and 11.40), arbitration agreements should be upheld and enforced by the Swedish courts and by arbitral tribunals sitting in Sweden. In this regard, arbitral tribunals have the ability to assess the validity of an arbitration agreement and determine their own jurisdiction (*supra* at 11.43), although such a determination is subject to legal review by the ordinary courts (*supra* at 11.47). **11.55**

(2.1) Which would be the internationally competent court (i) for obtaining a declaration that an arbitration agreement is valid and binding; or (ii) to compel arbitration? (The defendant's courts? The courts of the place of arbitration? The claimant's courts, cf Art 6(2) in fine, ICC Rules?) Neither the Act nor other Swedish legislation provide for any particular court to be internationally competent to hear an action regarding the validity or applicability of an arbitration agreement. Moreover, the *travaux préparatoires* to the Act do not provide a clear answer to the question. This failure to identify specifically a competent court does not mean that no court is competent. **11.56**

It is generally accepted that Swedish courts will be competent to decide about the validity and applicability of an arbitration agreement also in many cases with the involvement of a foreign element. Such action may be brought both before and after the initiation of arbitral proceedings.[53] The court's competence is determined by analogy to the ordinary Swedish rules as to the jurisdiction of the Swedish courts, thereby considering the subject matter jurisdiction, personal jurisdiction and venue considerations. In practice, and depending on the individual circumstances, such action may, for example, be brought before the court at the place of residence of either party, the court at the place where the disputed contract was executed or before the court at the seat of the arbitral proceedings. It is argued that the Swedish courts may even have jurisdiction over a (negative) declaratory action regarding **11.57**

52 Code of Judicial Procedure, ch 34 s 2.

53 Cars, T., *Lagen om Skiljeförfarande—En kommentar* (fakta Info Direkt Sweden, Stockholm, 1999)53 with reference to the Code of Judicial Procedure ch 13 s 2.

the invalidity or applicability of an arbitration agreement in disputes where the sole connection to Sweden consists of the fact that the place of arbitration is located in Sweden.[54] However, it may also be argued that this is doubtful as this issue has not yet been determined by the Swedish Supreme Court .

III. The arbitral tribunal

A. Number and qualification of arbitrators

(1) Sole arbitrator or arbitral tribunal with several arbitrators

11.58 The parties are given a great deal of freedom with respect to the composition and the appointment of the arbitral tribunal. The statutory framework is non-mandatory and may therefore be modified or replaced by reference to an established set of rules, or otherwise, to conform to the desires of the parties.

11.59 The number of arbitrators is determined by the parties (the Act, s 12, para 1). Sole arbitrators are consequently fully recognized. If the parties have made no agreement as to the number of arbitrators, there shall be three arbitrators (the Act, s 13). In case the SCC Rules are applicable pursuant to the parties' agreement to such effect, there shall be three arbitrators in the absence of any agreement to the contrary (SCC Rules, Art 12). However, in consideration of the complexity of the case, the value of the subject matter or other circumstances, the SCC Institute may decide that the matter shall be decided by a sole arbitrator. If the Rules for Expedited Arbitrations of the SCC Institute are to be applied, Art 1 of the Rules provides for one arbitrator giving no option for the parties to agree differently.

11.60 **(1.1) Are arbitral tribunals with an uneven number of arbitrators acceptable?** Yes. There are no restrictions in such respect. In practice tribunals almost always consist of an uneven number of arbitrators.

(2) Qualification of the arbitrators

11.61 An arbitrator must possess full legal capacity in regard to its actions and its property (the Act, s 7). This means that the arbitrator must be of full age, ie more than 18 years of age, and not have a trustee appointed due to mental disturbance, impaired health or similar circumstances.

11.62 Further, an arbitrator must be impartial (the Act, s 8, para 1). No circumstances which are likely to reduce the confidence in the arbitrator's impartiality may exist (the Act, s 8, para 2). Such circumstances exist, *inter alia*, (i) where the arbitrator or a person closely related to him is a party, or otherwise may expect significant benefit or detriment from the outcome of the dispute; (ii) where the arbitrator or a person closely associated to him is the director of a company or any other association which is a party, or otherwise represents a party or any another person who may expect significant benefit or detriment from the outcome of the dispute; (iii) where the arbitrator has taken a position in the dispute, as an expert or otherwise, or has assisted a party in preparing or conducting its case in the dispute; or

[54] Prop 1998/99:35, 243.

(iv) where the arbitrator has received or demanded remuneration in violation of the provisions of the Act. If an arbitrator owns shares in an investment fund, this fact alone does not mean that he is prevented from serving as arbitrator, in case a company the shares of which are owned by the investment fund is a party.[55] An employee of the Swedish state may also act as an arbitrator in a case where the state is a party, unless he is employed in or by the authority whose activities are directly concerned in such case. There is no general rule which prohibits officials from serving as arbitrators. Thus, Swedish judges may be appointed as arbitrators. A party-appointed arbitrator is under the same duty as an independently appointed arbitrator to be impartial.

A person who is asked to accept appointment as an arbitrator must immediately disclose all circumstances that might prevent him or her from serving as arbitrator. An arbitrator must also inform the parties and the other arbitrators of any such circumstance as soon as all arbitrators have been appointed and thereafter in the course of the proceedings as soon as he or she has learned of any new circumstance (the Act, s 9). Pursuant to the SCC Rules, a person asked to serve as arbitrator must disclose to the person approaching him or her any circumstances which might be deemed to diminish trust in his/her impartiality or independence before being appointed (SCC Rules, Art 14, para 2). Once appointed, the arbitrator shall submit a signed declaration of impartiality and independence to the SCC Institute disclosing any facts and circumstances which may give rise to justifiable doubts in that regard and the SCC Institute Secretariat will provide the parties with copies of the statement (*ibid*). Moreover, an arbitrator, who becomes aware in the course of the arbitral proceedings of any circumstances which may disqualify him or her, is under an obligation immediately to inform the parties and the other arbitrators thereof. 11.63

(2.1) Are there mandatory requirements for the qualification of arbitrators (statutory requirements or indirect requirements through eg general conditions of insurance contracts)? There are no such requirements in addition to the requirement that the arbitrator possesses full legal capacity in regard to its property and that the arbitrator has to be impartial. The parties may provide for additional requirements or grounds for disqualification with respect to the arbitrators. The parties are at liberty to agree in advance on a waiver of specific grounds of disqualification to the extent such agreement is made with full knowledge of all relevant circumstances, and is not so general that it waives all grounds for setting aside an award (the Act, s 34).[56] However, 'foreign' parties have a right to exclude all together their right to challenge the award pursuant to s 34 of the Act (the Act, s 51 para 1). 11.64

(2.2) Which national arbitration institutions may be contacted for obtaining information about qualified (and specialized) arbitrators? Information in this respect may be obtained from the SCC Institute, the address of which is found in the Appendix, s 2. The SCC Institute only gives names of arbitrators. The SCC Institute never gives any recommendation about suitable arbitrators. 11.65

55 Prop 1998/99:35, 84.

56 cf *Arbitration in Sweden* (n 30) 66; Westerling, B., 'Void and Challengeable Awards in Swedish Arbitral Procedure' [1984] *Ybk Arb Inst Stockholm Chamber Com* 45, 47.

11.66 (2.3) **Are judges or civil servants required to obtain permission by their employer to act as arbitrator? Are these permissions given generally or case-by-case? What are the consequences if such permission has not been obtained?** The question whether a judge or a civil servant needs permission to act as an arbitrator ultimately depends on the individual employment contract. However, there is no general rule which prohibits officials from serving as arbitrators, and Swedish judges may thus be appointed. Swedish judges, including the Justices of the Supreme Court, in general only accept appointments as chairmen of arbitral tribunals or as sole arbitrators.[57] In general, a civil servant, including judges, may, however, not undertake an engagement which may affect the confidence in his or in another employee's impartiality in performing his or her duties as a civil servant or otherwise harm the credibility of the agency in question.[58]

B. Appointment of arbitrators

(1) Extent of party autonomy to establish appointment procedure

11.67 The parties enjoy considerable freedom with respect to the appointment of arbitrators (the Act, s 12, para 1). The statutory framework is non-mandatory and may therefore be modified or replaced by a reference to an established set of rules or otherwise in order to conform to the desires of the parties. Thus, the parties may determine in the arbitration agreement the composition of the tribunal, as well as who is to serve as arbitrator. However, the freedom is not unlimited. An arbitration agreement may not provide for the majority of the arbitrators to be appointed by one of the parties.[59] The same principle of party autonomy and respecting appointment procedures agreed upon by the parties apply under the SCC Rules (SCC Rules, Art 12). Hence, the SCC Institute does not maintain any formal list of arbitrators from which the parties would be obliged to choose.

(2) Procedure in absence of an agreement by the parties

11.68 In the absence of any direction from the parties, the tribunal will consist of three arbitrators and each party shall choose one arbitrator and the arbitrators so chosen shall appoint the third (the Act, s 13). The typical tribunal in cases involving large or complex transactions consists of three arbitrators appointed in such manner. If the arbitration agreement refers to the SCC Rules, the tribunal consists of three arbitrators, unless the parties agree otherwise or, due account having been taken of the complexity of the case, the value of the subject matter and other circumstances, the SCC Institute decides that the dispute is to be resolved by one arbitrator (SCC Rules, Art 12). If the dispute is to be resolved by a sole arbitrator, the parties are given 30 days to jointly appoint the arbitrator. In case the parties fail to make the appointment, such arbitrator is appointed by the SCC Institute, unless the parties agree otherwise (SCC Rules, Art 13, para 2). If the arbitral tribunal shall consist of more than one arbitrator, each party shall appoint an equal number of arbitrators and the SCC Institute shall appoint the chairman, unless the parties agree otherwise (*ibid*, para 3). In case of multi-party proceedings and provided that the multiple parties on either side fail jointly to

---

[57] cf Nordenson, U.K., 'The arbitral tribunal' [1990] *Swedish and International Arbitration* 19, 23; Cars, T., *Lagen om Skiljeförfarande* 66; Heuman, L., *Arbitration Law of Sweden* (n 1) 216.

[58] Lag (1994:260) om offentlig anställning (*Public Employment Act*) s 7.

[59] cf NJA 1974, 573; Prop 1998/99:35, 90.

appoint the arbitrator(s), the entire tribunal is appointed by the SCC Institute Board (*ibid*, para 4—and *supra* at 11.26). If the parties have different nationalities, the SCC Institute shall appoint a sole arbitrator or a chairman having another nationality than the parties, unless there exist reasons against it, or the parties otherwise agree (*ibid*, para 5).

In situations where each party is entitled to appoint an arbitrator, the party who acts first shall notify the other party of its choice in writing (the Act, ss 14 and 19). Such notification must be made in that party's request for arbitration. The opposing party must within 30 days of receipt of the notice, notify the first party in writing of its choice of arbitrator (the Act, s 14, para 1). A party who has notified the opposite party of its choice of arbitrator may not revoke the appointment without the consent of the other party (the Act, s 14, para 2). If the opposing party fails to appoint an arbitrator within the stipulated period of time, the District Court at the place of residence of either party, or at the seat of the arbitration proceedings, or the Stockholm District Court, shall appoint an arbitrator within the stipulated period of time at the request of the first party (the Act, ss 14, paras 3 and 44). If the SCC Rules apply, the party that opposes an arbitrator appointed by the other party on grounds of disqualification must file its challenge including the reasons therefore, in writing to the SCC Institute no later than 15 days after the allegedly disqualifying circumstance became known to the party. If no notification is given within the prescribed period of time, the party's right to challenge is precluded (SCC Rules, Art 15, para 2). **11.69**

When the arbitral tribunal is composed of more than one arbitrator, one of them shall be appointed chairman of the tribunal. Unless the parties or the arbitrators have decided otherwise, the chairman shall be the arbitrator appointed by the other arbitrators, or by the District Court (the Act, s 20). If the third arbitrator pursuant to the arbitration agreement is to be appointed by a third party, it follows that such third arbitrator shall be the chairman.[60] If the SCC Rules apply and the arbitral tribunal shall consist of more than one arbitrator, the SCC Institute shall appoint the chairman, unless the parties agree otherwise (SCC Rules, Art 13, para 3). The arbitral tribunal may decide that the chairman may on his or her own make decisions regarding the proceedings. **11.70**

There are no statutory provisions concerning the manner in which the two arbitrators selected by the respective parties are to select the third arbitrator. In practice, the party requesting arbitration will normally notify its appointee of the choice made by the other party, and such appointee will then contact the other appointee and attempt to reach agreement on the third arbitrator. The party-appointed arbitrators should be unanimous in their selection of the final arbitrator, even where there are more than two party-appointed arbitrators.[61] The third arbitrator continues to hold office even if the arbitrators who have chosen him are replaced by someone who would have not agreed to his appointment. **11.71**

If the party-appointed arbitrators fail to agree on the choice of the arbitrator to be appointed by them within 30 days commencing on the date on which the last of them was chosen, either party (but neither of the arbitrators) may apply to a court for it to make the **11.72**

60 Prop 1998/99:35, 225.

61 cf *Arbitration in Sweden* (n 30) 73.

appointment, unless the parties provide otherwise (the Act, s 15, para 1). The competent court is the District Court in the place of domicile of either party or the District Court at the place of arbitration. An application may be entertained also by the District Court of Stockholm. If similar applications have been filed with more than one District Court, the court with which an application was first filed is competent and any decision made by any other court is void. The procedure before the District Court is of a summary character only (the Act, s 44, para 1). No appeal is allowed from the court's decision (the Act, s 44, para 3).

(3) Effect of the refusal of one party to cooperate in the constitution of the arbitral tribunal

11.73 Where the requesting party in its request for arbitration has notified the other party of its own choice of an arbitrator and such other party fails to provide written notice of its choice of an arbitrator within 30 days of receipt, three options are available to the first party:

11.74 (i) The first party may apply to a court for it to make the appointment (the Act, s 14, para 3). Such application will be entertained by the District Court at the place of domicile of either party or by the District Court at the seat of the arbitration proceedings. An application may also be entertained by the District Court of Stockholm. This is the option most frequently used. The procedure before the District Court is of a summary character only. The court shall, if possible, give the other party an opportunity to comment thereon (the Act, s 44, para 1). No appeal is allowed from the decision of the court (the Act, s 44, para 3). If the SCC Rules apply, the SCC Institute makes the appointment (SCC Rules, Art 13, para 3).

11.75 (ii) The party may file a suit in court and request a judgment to the effect that the other party shall select an arbitrator. This option seems to be the most attractive if there is doubt as to the validity or applicability of the arbitration agreement and assuming that the time factor is of no importance.

11.76 (iii) The party may choose to abandon the arbitration agreement and bring the dispute before a court. In such situations the failing party may not invoke the arbitration agreement as a bar to court proceedings (the Act, s 5).

11.77 If any person or entity other than a party or the other arbitrators fails to appoint an arbitrator within 30 days of the date on which it has been requested to do so, the court shall, at the request of a party, appoint the arbitrator. Such application shall be entertained by the District Court at the place of residence of either party or by the District Court at the place of arbitration. An application may also be entertained by the District Court of Stockholm. This is the option most frequently used. If similar applications have been filed with more than one District Court, the court with which an application was first filed is competent and a decision made by any other court is void. The court shall, if possible, give the other party an opportunity to comment on the application (the Act, s 44, para 1). No appeal is allowed from the decision of the court (the Act, s 44, para 3).

(4) Circumstances and valid reasons for an arbitrator to resign

11.78 An arbitrator is considered to have valid reasons for resigning in case of bad health, non-payment of adequate security for compensation etc. In case the parties were to so request, the arbitrator should present some proof in support of such valid reason. An arbitrator may resign, for example, because he finds himself prevented from performing its duties to a sufficient degree.[62] If an arbitrator resigns without valid reason, he may be liable for damages.[63]

C. Challenge and replacement of arbitrators

(1) Grounds, procedure and deadlines for challenging an arbitrator

If an arbitrator is not impartial or has delayed the proceedings (thus not only failed to perform its duties or obstructed), a District Court shall remove him upon the request of a party. There are no deadlines for challenging an arbitrator. The question of impartiality is to be determined solely on objective grounds as confirmed by the Supreme Court in a recent decision.[64] The parties may agree that such a request shall instead be conclusively determined by an arbitration institute (the Act, s 17). The same rules as set out above in respect of the appointment of an arbitrator by a party, the other arbitrators or someone else, apply with respect to the appointment of a new arbitrator. Such application will be considered by the District Court at the place of residence of either party or by the District Court at the place of arbitration. An application may be entertained also by the District Court of Stockholm. If similar applications have been filed with more than one District Court, the court with which an application was first filed is competent and a decision made by any other court is void. The arbitrator whose removal is requested should be heard before the application is granted (the Act, s 44, para 1). No appeal is allowed from the decision of the court (the Act, s 44, para 3). **11.79**

If the SCC Rules apply, the SCC Institute, instead of the court, removes an arbitrator (SCC Rules, Art 16, para 1). The SCC Institute shall release an arbitrator in case it accepts the arbitrator's resignation, or provided the arbitrator has been successfully challenged or if the arbitrator is otherwise prevented from fulfilling its duties or fails to perform its functions in an adequate manner. **11.80**

(1.1) Do state courts review challenge procedures which took place in accordance with a specific procedure agreed upon by the parties (eg Art 11, ICC Rules)? If so, at what point in time? May such review be excluded? The procedure for challenging an arbitrator accounted for above applies only to the extent the parties have not decided otherwise. The parties may agree that this issue shall be conclusively decided by an arbitration institution (the Act, s 11). Thus, if the parties have explicitly provided for certain procedure in respect of challenging an arbitrator and thereby may be deemed to have excluded the **11.81**

---

62 Prop 1998/99:35, 222.

63 cf Schöldström, P., *The Arbitrator's Mandate* (Jure, Stockholm, 1998) 148.

64 Swedish Supreme Court decision of 19 November 2007, Case T 2448–06 (*Jilkén v Ericsson*, unpublished). The Supreme Court had to decide a case where a consultant of a law firm had acted as arbitrator in a dispute which involved a party belonging to a group of companies being client to the law firm where the arbitrator served as a consultant. The Supreme Court annulled the arbitral award and held that a relationship that may diminish confidence must be deemed to exist even if the arbitrator has not had direct client contact with the party, his arbitration practice has been conducted separately from the law practice, or if the arbitral dispute involved questions other than those normally included in the client engagement by the law firm. The court based its objective standpoint and reasoning *inter alia* on international standards by referring to IBA's Guidelines on Conflict of Interest in International Arbitration and case law from the SCC Institute.

possibilities to have a court assist in such respect, a court may not review the challenge procedures unless a party asserts that such challenge procedures have not been in compliance with the parties' agreement.

11.82 (1.2) **Is there case law with respect to truncated arbitral tribunals? (cf Art 12(5), ICC Rules)** No such case law exists.

(2) Procedure for appointing a new arbitrator

11.83 If an arbitrator resigns or is discharged, the court shall at the request of either party appoint a new arbitrator (the Act, s 16, para 1). If the arbitrator cannot perform its duties owing to circumstances arising after the appointment, the person who originally was required to make the appointment shall appoint a new arbitrator (*ibid*). In case an arbitrator is replaced, any hearing at which any oral evidence has been presented should in general be repeated for the benefit of the new arbitrator, unless such evidence was either so well documented and recorded, or was of such minor importance that the failure to repeat may not, in probability, influence the award. [65]

11.84 If the SCC Rules apply, generally the SCC Institute shall appoint a new arbitrator if an arbitrator has been released or if an arbitrator died. However, if the arbitrator being replaced was appointed by one of the parties, such party shall appoint the new arbitrator, unless otherwise deemed by the SCC Institute (SCC Rules, Art. 17, para 1). The arbitrators in their new composition decide to what extent the proceedings must be repeated (SCC Rules, Art 17, para 3).

IV. The arbitral procedure

A. General principles

(1) Extent of party autonomy to determine the arbitral procedure

11.85 According to Swedish law, the parties and the arbitrators are free to determine the procedure appropriate to the circumstances of the case apart from certain restrictions indicated as follows. The arbitrators must deal with the case in an impartial, practical and speedy manner. In doing so, they must act in accordance with the decisions of the parties to the extent that they are not prevented from doing so (the Act, s 21). The arbitrators shall give the parties, to the extent necessary, a full opportunity to present their respective cases in writing or orally. If a party so requests, an oral hearing shall be arranged before a decision is made on an issue referred to the arbitrators (the Act, s 24, para 1). A party shall be given an opportunity to review all documents and all other materials pertaining to the dispute which are supplied to the arbitrators by the other party or any other person (the Act, s 24, para 2). Unless the parties have agreed otherwise, arbitration proceedings are commenced by the party invoking an arbitration agreement by giving a written request for arbitration to its opponent (the Act, s 19). In addition, the arbitrators may decide questions which the parties jointly refer to them in the course of the proceedings. In the absence of any procedural rules agreed by the parties in the arbitration agreement, the arbitrators may look to the

[65] cf *Arbitration in Sweden* (n 30) 75; Heuman, L., *Arbitration Law of Sweden* (n 1) 246 *et seq.*

Code of Judicial Procedure for guidance. It should be noted, however, that the Code of Judicial Procedure is not applicable as a matter of law in arbitration proceedings. If the SCC Rules apply, the chairman may, if so authorized by the other arbitrators, decide questions of procedure on his or her own. No obstruction is possible as the arbitrators may decide the case if a party has failed without valid excuse to present its case (the Act, s 24, para 3). However, the arbitrators must try the case on its merits based on the available materials. A party's failure to appear or to plead may, however, be given evidentiary weight. In case the parties refer to the SCC Rules, the arbitrators have the discretion to decide on how the proceedings are to be conducted. However, the arbitrators must comply with the arbitration agreement and the parties' other wishes (SCC Rules, Art 19, para 1). Some restrictions imposed under the SCC Rules concern the exchange of written pleadings (SCC Rules, Art 24) and each party's right to request that an oral hearing takes place (SCC Rules, Art 27).

(1.1) Are the parties free to choose any national or international law governing the procedure before the arbitral tribunal? Procedural aspects of all arbitrations lawfully carried on in Sweden, by virtue of a 'Swedish' as well as a 'foreign' arbitration agreement, are governed by the Act, ie Swedish law (the Act, s 46). The rules of the Act governing the conduct of proceedings are, however, few in number, and there is consequently ample room for the parties to agree on supplementary rules. Moreover, most of the provisions of the Act are non-mandatory, and to that extent the parties may provide that the procedure is to be governed by alternative rules. **11.86**

(2) Basic procedural principles or mandatory rules to be applied by the arbitral tribunal

The Act contains very few mandatory provisions concerning the procedure. The arbitrators are required to handle the dispute 'in an impartial, practical and speedy manner' (the Act, s 21) and to afford each party an opportunity to present its case (the Act, s 24). In addition, the arbitrators must normally follow the instructions of the parties, including the provisions of any arbitration rules agreed to by them. The parties' ability to deviate from the rules set forth in the Act depends on several circumstances, such as the character of the particular provision, the implication of the deviation and the point of time at which the deviation takes place.[66] **11.87**

(3) Oral hearing or proceeding on basis of written documents

Arbitral proceedings conducted solely on the basis of written documents are admissible according to Swedish law. However, if a party so requests, an oral hearing shall be arranged before a decision is made on an issue referred to the arbitrators (the Act, s 24). Pursuant to the SCC Rules, an oral hearing shall be held if a party so requests or if the arbitral tribunal considers it appropriate. If a hearing is arranged, the arbitral tribunal, taking into account the wishes of the parties, shall determine the date, time and location of the hearing (SCC Rules, Art 27). In practice, oral hearings are usually held. However, there are a few exceptions where proceedings actually are conducted on the basis of written documents only, as for example sometimes under the Expedited Rules of Arbitration of the SCC (Art 27). **11.88**

[66] Prop 1998/99:35, 44.

(4) Power of the tribunal (in particular the chairman) to issue procedural orders

11.89 The powers of the arbitral tribunal, in particular the powers of the chairman, during the proceedings are predominantly administrative in nature, including the organization of the proceedings and the issuance of procedural orders. Nevertheless, the arbitral tribunal may upon request by one party determine that the other party shall take or refrain from taking a certain action in order to secure the claim to be tried. The arbitral tribunal may also decide that the party making such request shall provide security for any loss the other party may suffer (the Act, s 25, para 4). However, such decisions by the arbitral tribunal may not be enforced.

11.90 If the SCC Rules apply the powers of the tribunals, respectively the chairman, are also limited to mostly procedural issues in relation to the administration of the arbitration. Moreover, the arbitral tribunal shall together with the parties promptly after referral of the case to them set up a provisional timetable (SCC Rules Art 23). In case a party fails to comply with such deadlines set by the tribunal the case may be decided without such party having presented its case (the Act, s 24, para 3). The arbitral tribunal is further entitled to decide about interim measures at the request of a party, either in the form of an order or of an award. The tribunal may order the requesting party to provide appropriate security in connection with the interim measure (SCC Rules, Art 32, para 1–3—see *infra* at 11.161 to 11.167).

(5) Distinction of matters of substance and matters of procedure

11.91 In most legal systems the classification of rules and concepts is considered to be part of the conflict of laws. The principles of the *lex fori* are normally applied in connection with such classification, but such principles may be subject to modifications due to the international nature of the matter. Classification is of relevance when determining whether a rule is procedural or substantive in character. When arbitrators in Sweden apply Swedish conflict of laws rules, they will generally apply Swedish rules of classification, since the two sets of rules are interdependent. For example, under Swedish rules of classification, matters concerning the application of the statute of limitation and interest are usually regarded as substantive in character. The application of Swedish principles of classification does not mean that internal Swedish legal concepts are rigidly applied in every detail, since appropriate modifications are made in view of the international aspects of the dispute.[67]

11.92 (5.1) **Are the statutes of limitations a matter of substance or rather of procedure?** The main rule under Swedish law is that the application of statutes of limitations is a matter of substantive law.[68]

(6) Persons able to represent a party in an arbitral proceeding

11.93 A party is entitled to conduct its case through a representative, who need not be a lawyer, or with the aid of an assistant. The representative may also be a foreign lawyer.

---

67 cf *Arbitration in Sweden* (n 30) 55.

68 cf NJA 1930, 692, NJA 1984, 25 and NJA 1984, C 3; cf also Bogdan, M., *Svensk internationell privat- och processrätt* (7th edn, Norstedts, Stockholm, 2008) 266—with further references.

B. Place of arbitration

(1) Determination of the place of arbitration in absence of an agreement by the parties

The choice of country and city where the arbitration is to take place is left to the parties. Alternatively, if they cannot agree, the arbitrators shall determine the place of arbitration (the Act, s 22, para 1). According to the Act and in contrast to the determination of the place (seat) of arbitration, the individual meetings or hearings during the proceeding may be held elsewhere. In case neither the parties nor the arbitrators have determined the place of arbitration it seems unclear whether the chairman's place of business,[69] the place where the award was issued[70] or the place where the award was signed[71] should be regarded as the place of arbitration. From a practitioner's point of view it seems most appropriate to let the respective state court that is first addressed with this question decide on the place of arbitration by taking into account all relevant circumstances of the case.[72] Also, since the *Svea Hovrätt* in Stockholm is always competent to decide on actions for setting aside the award if it does not contain any information on the place of arbitration (s 43, para 1 of the Act), it may not be as important finally to determine the actual location as long as the proceedings took place in Sweden. **11.94**

If the SCC Rules apply, the Board of the SCC Institute shall, after the first exchange of submissions, decide the seat of arbitration, unless otherwise agreed upon by the parties. Notwithstanding this, the tribunal is entitled to deliberate at any place which it considers appropriate and it has the possibility to hold hearings etc at places other than the seat of arbitration (SCC Rules, Art 20, paras 1 and 2). In the latter case, the SCC Rules expressly stipulate that the arbitration—and the award—shall be deemed to have taken place—respectively have been made—at the seat of arbitration (*ibid).* **11.95**

An arbitration may be instituted in Sweden if the arbitration agreement stipulates that the proceedings shall be conducted in Sweden, or if the arbitrators or an arbitral institution in accordance with the agreement have so decided, or if the opposing party otherwise consents thereto (the Act, s 47, para 1). An arbitration may also be instituted in Sweden against a party which is domiciled in Sweden, or that is otherwise subject to the jurisdiction of Swedish courts with regard to the matter in dispute, unless the arbitration agreement provides that the proceedings shall take place abroad (the Act, s 47, para 2). In no other cases may arbitration take place in Sweden under the Act (the Act, s 47, para 3). An award made in disregard of this principle may be set aside at the application of a party (the Act, s 34, para 1, point 3). **11.96**

A non-Swedish party is subject to the jurisdiction of the Swedish courts[73] in disputes concerning money obligations, such as payment of a price, damages or interest if he or she owns real or personal property in Sweden.[74] Furthermore, anyone who has entered into a **11.97**

[69] Cars, T., *Lagen om skiljeförfarande* 105.

[70] Prop 1998/99:35, 114.

[71] cf Lindskog, *Skiljeförfarande* (n 1) 671.

[72] *ibid.*

[73] cf Bogdan, M., 'Some Arbitration - Related Problems of Swedish Private International Law' [1990] *Ybk Arb Inst Stockholm Chamber Com* 70, 75.

[74] Code of Judicial Procedure, ch 10 s 3.

contract or otherwise incurred a debt in Sweden may be sued in Sweden regarding disputes connected to such contract or debt.[75] Of course, the scope of the Swedish provisions on jurisdiction and, accordingly, the ability to institute arbitration proceedings under s 47, para 2 of the Act is limited by the Brussels I Regulation and the Lugano Convention.[76]

(2) Importance and legal effect of place (seat) of the arbitration

11.98 If the chosen place (seat) of arbitration is in Sweden, and thus, taking place in Sweden, the procedural aspects of the arbitration is governed by Swedish law—*lex arbitri* (the Act, s 46). By this, the seat of arbitration is decisive for most questions of a procedural nature arising before, during and after the arbitral proceeding which are to be decided in accordance with the *lex arbitri*.

11.99 (2.1) **Are the arbitrators and parties free to convene at places other than the official seat of the arbitration?** Yes, this is explicitly stipulated both in the Act and the SCC Rules. In case the Act applies in this respect the arbitrators may hold hearings and other meetings elsewhere in Sweden or abroad, unless the parties have agreed otherwise or objected thereto (the Act, s 22, para 2). Provided that the SCC Rules apply, the arbitral tribunal may upon consultation with the parties determine the location of the hearings (SCC Rules, Art 20, para 2 and Art 27, para 2).

11.100 A fairly recent decision of the Svea Court of Appeal in Stockholm in the '*Titan v Alcatel*' case[77] in 2005 cast some doubt on the application of the aforementioned principles in s 22 of the Act. In that case the arbitration agreement and the arbitral award determined Stockholm as the place of arbitration and the award as well as the submissions contained some references to Swedish law. Beyond that, the arbitration had no apparent connection to Sweden, because no hearing or meeting were held in Sweden and neither the arbitrator nor the parties involved were Swedish. The court understood these circumstances to show an insufficient connection to Sweden and the court denied its jurisdiction in the challenge proceedings initiated by one of the parties to the arbitration. This decision has raised some concern about the Swedish courts' understanding of the legal relevance of the seat of arbitration on an international level. However, this decision should not be overstated. The decision of the Svea Court of Appeal has been heavily criticized because of non-compliance with the approved and established principles under Swedish law and Art 22 of the Act.[78] This means, that also in the '*Titan v Alcatel*' case, the requirements for a 'Swedish' arbitration should have been met owing to the fact that the arbitrators determined a place in Sweden to be the seat of arbitration, notwithstanding the decision to hold meetings abroad.

11.101 (2.2) **Are there visa requirements to enter the country which apply to lawyers and/or arbitrators? Where may current information on that subject be obtained?** Unless the

[75] Code of Judicial Procedure, ch 10 s 4.

[76] Council Regulation (EC) 44/2001 of 22 December 2000 on jurisdiction and the recognition and enforcement of judgments in civil and commercial matters [2001] OJ L 12/1, Art 3(2) and Lugano Convention 1988 on jurisdiction and the enforcement of judgments in civil and commercial matters, Art 3, excluding the application of the first sentence of the first paragraph of s 3 of ch 10 of the Swedish Code of Judicial Procedure.

[77] Svea Court of Appeal (Case T 1038–05) [2005] SIAR issue 2, 259.

[78] cf observation by Shaughnessy, P. and Söderlund, C. in [2005] *SIAR* issue 2, 264.

lawyers or arbitrators are citizens of a country within the EU, visa requirements may apply. Information in this respect may be obtained at all Swedish embassies and consulates around the world.

C. Submissions, deadlines and default

(1) Contents and form of submissions (in particular request for arbitration and answer to request)

The law foresees that the parties will exchange written pleadings once or twice prior to the main hearing. The basic rule is, however, that each party shall be given a full opportunity to present its case in writing or orally. The request for arbitration must always be in writing. **11.102**

The request for arbitration shall include (i) an express and unconditional request for arbitration; (ii) details of the issue which is to be resolved by the arbitrators and which is covered by the arbitration agreement; and (iii) details of the party's choice of arbitrator where the party is required to appoint an arbitrator (the Act, s 19). Moreover, unless the parties have agreed otherwise, the claimant shall, within the period of time determined by the arbitrators, state its prayer for relief in respect of the issue stated in the request for arbitration as well as the circumstances invoked by the party in support thereof ('Statement of Claim') (the Act, s 23, para 1). Thereafter, within the period of time determined by the arbitrators, the respondent shall state its position in answer to the claimant's prayer for relief and the circumstances on which the respondent relies in support thereof ('Statement of Defence') (the Act, s 23, para 1). **11.103**

If the SCC Rules apply, the party wishing to initiate arbitration must file a request with the SCC Institute. Such request shall include (i) a statement of the names, addresses, phone and telefax numbers and email addresses of the parties and their counsel; (ii) a summarizing account of the dispute; (iii) a preliminary statement of the relief claimed; (iv) a copy or description of the arbitration agreement or arbitration clause on which the claim is based; (v) any comments on the number of arbitrators; and (vi) where applicable, a statement identifying the arbitrator(s) appointed by the claimant together with relevant addresses, telephone and telefax numbers and email address (SCC Rules, Art 2). The Secretariat of the SCC Institute then forwards the request to the respondent. The respondent is asked to submit an answer to the SCC Institute which shall include (i) objections regarding the existence, validity or applicability of the arbitration agreement (such objections may however also be filed later in the statement of defence); (ii) an admission or denial of the relief sought by claimant; (iii) a preliminary statement of any counterclaim or set-off; (iv) any comments on the number of arbitrators; and (v) a statement identifying the arbitrator(s) appointed by the respondent together with relevant address, telephone and telefax numbers and email address (SCC Rules, Art 5). The respondent's answer is then communicated to the claimant. Following the composition of the arbitral tribunal and fulfillment of further formal requirements the arbitral tribunal then requests the claimant to file its statement of claim followed by the respondent filing its statement of defence (SCC Rules, Art 24). **11.104**

Failure by the respondent to submit a reply does not prevent the proceedings from continuing (SCC Rules, Art 5, para 3). The SCC Institute may further request the parties to submit additional written submissions in case it considers this necessary (SCC Rules, Art 24, para 3). **11.105**

If the claimant fails to comply with such request, the SCC Institute may dismiss the case (SCC Rules, Art 30, para 1). The respondent's failure to comply with such request does not hinder the proceedings from continuing (*ibid*, para 2), unless the request concerns a counterclaim or plea for set-off in which case such claim or plea may be dismissed. If it is obvious that the SCC Institute lacks jurisdiction over the dispute, its Board shall dismiss the case (SCC Rules, Art 10, para 1).

11.106 Unless the parties agree otherwise, the claimant may introduce new prayers for relief and the respondent prayers for relief of its own, provided that the prayers for relief fall within the scope of the arbitration agreement and provided it is not deemed inappropriate to consider them, having regard to the point of time at which they are introduced or to other circumstances (the Act, s 23, para 2). In the course of the proceedings, each party may on the same conditions amend or supplement requests for relief introduced earlier and rely on new circumstances in support of its case. Pursuant to the SCC Rules similar provisions apply to amendments or supplements of a party's claim or counterclaim, defence or set-off (SCC Rules, Art 25).

11.107 (1.1) **From which point in time is a claim considered to be pending with the arbitral tribunal? What are the legal effects of such fact (eg on statutes of limitations)?** In *ad hoc* arbitrations a claim is considered pending when the respondent has received the notice of arbitration. In institutional arbitration the relevant point of time may differ owing to the applicable arbitration rules. In case the SCC Rules are applicable they stipulate that the arbitration shall be deemed to commence on the date on which the request for arbitration is received by the SCC (SCC Rules, Art 4). The point of time at which a claim is considered to be pending has important legal consequences, as, on a substantive level, the filing of the request normally toll the applicable statutory limitation period.

11.108 (1.2) **When is a time limit according to statutes of limitations deemed to be interrupted in case of (i) *ad hoc*; and (ii) institutional arbitration?** In *ad hoc* arbitrations the relevant point of time according to the statute of limitations is generally the receipt of the request for arbitration by the respondent unless otherwise agreed by the parties. Such request shall include an express and unconditional request for arbitration, a statement of the disputed issue which is covered by the arbitration agreement and which is to be resolved by the arbitrators, and a statement of the party's choice of arbitrator where the party is required to appoint an arbitrator (the Act, s 19). In case the request does not comply with these requirements an interruption of the statute of limitation does not become effective before the failure is cured.[79]

11.109 Provided that the SCC Rules apply, an arbitration shall be deemed to commence on the date on which the request for arbitration is received by the SCC. However, in order to achieve the legal effect of eg an interruption of a time limit according to statutes of limitations it is required that the request for arbitration complies with the prerequisites in content stipulated by Art 2 SCC Rules.

---

[79] Prop. 1998/99:35, 103; cf Heuman, *Arbitration Law of Sweden* (n 1) 307; Cars, T., *Skiljeförfarande* (n 35) 95.

(1.3) What is the effect of the withdrawal of the request for arbitration? In case the claimant withdraws its request, the arbitrators shall dismiss the case unless the opposing party requests that the arbitrators rule on the dispute (the Act, s 28). The arbitrators may, upon request of the other party, order the claimant to pay compensation for the respondent's costs during the proceedings (the Act, s 42). 11.110

(2) Legal deadlines (provided by law or set by the tribunal) and effect of non-compliance by a party

In cases where a party must bring an action within a legal deadline, provided either by law or by agreement, and where the action is covered by an arbitration agreement, the claimant must request arbitration in accordance with s 19 of the Act within the deadline in order to avoid a forfeiture of right (the Act, s 45). However, in case the arbitration has been requested in due time but the arbitral proceedings are terminated without a decision of the disputed issue submitted to the arbitrators, and this is not due to the negligence of the party, the action shall be deemed to have been instituted in due time where a party requests arbitration or institutes court proceedings within 30 days of receipt of the award, or where the award has been set aside or declared invalid or an action against the award has been dismissed, from the time that this decision becomes final (*ibid*). 11.111

(2.1) What are the powers of the tribunal if a party fails to comply with the time limits set up by the tribunal? Apart from the award period in the SCC Rules, no deadlines are provided by the statute or the SCC Rules. The arbitrators or, if so authorized by the other arbitrators, the chairman, may, however, set various deadlines in the course of the arbitration proceedings. Provided a party does not adhere to such deadline set by the tribunal, for example regarding the presentation of evidence, the tribunal is entitled to freely assess this fact within its evaluation of evidence. However, the tribunal is not entitled to use compulsory measures towards the disobedient party (the Act, s 25, para 3). 11.112

(2.2) Is the tribunal bound by any mandatory time limits for certain procedural steps (eg hearings, making of the award)? There are no mandatory time limits under Swedish law, unless the parties have agreed on any such time limits. The parties may also stipulate a period within which the arbitral award must be given. If such award period is not observed, the award may be set aside (the Act, s 34, para 1, point 2). 11.113

(3) Statutory requirements as to notifications during an arbitration (with respect to the request for arbitration and other written pleadings; with respect to notifications by the tribunal)

There are no statutory provisions that directly regulate notification in arbitration, but some of the rules in the Service of Documents Act of 1970 may be applicable by analogy.[80] A 'notice' clause regulates the manner in which any notice under an agreement should be given. No unequivocal answer can be given under Swedish law as to whether notices concerning the initiation of arbitration proceedings or other procedural notices in such proceedings given in conformity with the provisions of such a clause will be considered valid and effective in the absence of proof of receipt. 11.114

[80] cf *Arbitration in Sweden* (n 30) 59.

11.115 If the SCC Rules apply, notices shall be delivered to the last known address of the addressee by means of communication that provides a record of the sending thereof. Notices shall be deemed to have been received by the addressee, at the latest on the date they would normally have been received given the chosen means of communication (SCC Rules Art 8).

(4) Effect of the insolvency of a party

11.116 Upon being declared bankrupt, the debtor loses the capacity to deal with property which legally forms part of the bankruptcy estate. The estate, represented by the trustee, is the proper party to all post-bankruptcy proceedings. An application for bankruptcy does not automatically interrupt the arbitral proceedings.

11.117 As to arbitration agreements concluded by the debtor prior to the initiation of bankruptcy proceedings and relating to property which may legally form part of the bankruptcy estate, ie arbitration agreements which may be of importance in disputes between the debtor and third parties (non-creditors), the rule is that such arbitration agreements are binding on the bankruptcy estate.[81] However, this rule is subject to the qualification that the arbitration agreement is binding on the bankruptcy estate only insofar as the debtor and the other party to the agreement could legally have regulated the subject matter by way of agreement, while issues concerning the contracting parties' rights *in rem* may not be settled by arbitration if the bankruptcy estate objects.[82] The same rule applies to actions concerning claims made by a creditor against the debtor. In such a case the creditor is entitled to have its claims considered by an arbitral tribunal notwithstanding the fact that the debtor has been declared bankrupt.[83] Thus, under Swedish law, an arbitration agreement entered into by a debtor prior to bankruptcy is binding on the bankruptcy estate, but only insofar as the debtor and the other party to the agreement could legally have regulated the subject matter by means of agreement.

11.118 The bankruptcy estate will join the proceedings on the same terms as its predecessor. Hence, any admissions or agreements made in the course of the proceedings will continue to bind the party in accordance with general procedural principles, and an award will be binding on the bankruptcy estate.

D. Facts and evidence: general

(1) Burden of proof (inquisitorial/adversarial procedure)

11.119 In Swedish arbitral proceedings the burden of proof generally rests with the party invoking a certain fact (eg the existence of an agreement) as a basis for its claims. This general rule is, however, not without exceptions, and it is ultimately left to the discretion of the arbitrators to decide how the burden of proof should reasonably be allocated for individual circumstances. It is not entirely uncommon that parties will argue for a different allocation of the burden of proof for individual circumstances eg owing to failure by the other party to produce documents as requested.

---

81 cf NJA 1931, 647.

82 cf Åke Hassler and Thorsten Cars, *Skiljeförfarande* (n 35) 47; Cars, T., *Skiljeförfarande* (n 35) 44.

83 cf NJA 1913, 191.

The main principle in arbitration is that it is an adversarial procedure. Arbitrators will very rarely embark upon any fact finding themselves or appoint their own experts. It is up to the parties to present the evidence that they deem necessary (the Act, s 25, para 1). Both written and oral evidence may be submitted. As regards oral testimony, a witness is generally expected to relate its entire story in one flow, without interruption, and without being prompted by direct questions from bench or bar. The arbitrators will base their award upon the facts and evidence presented by the parties. The parties cannot ask the arbitrators to decide which evidence they deem relevant. Nevertheless, unless the parties have otherwise provided, the arbitrators may take certain steps with regard to evidence. The arbitrators may appoint an expert unless the parties oppose such appointment (the Act, s 25, para 1). The arbitrators may also order a party to state which evidence the party will rely on. **11.120**

The principle of an adversarial procedure is also inherent to the SCC Rules. The parties shall on request state the evidence on which they wish to rely and which may be relevant to the outcome of the case, specifying what they wish to prove with each piece of evidence (SCC Rules, Art 26, paras 2 and 3). On request of a party, the tribunal may order a party to produce any document or evidence which may be relevant for deciding the case. The tribunal is thus not entitled to act on its own (*sua sponte*), thereby safeguarding that the parties control the presentation of the case and preventing any unduly inquisitorial administration by the tribunal.[84] Further, the parties shall produce the documentary evidence on which they rely. **11.121**

The arbitrators may, after consultation with the parties, also appoint an expert (SCC Rules, Art 29). However, as a matter of practice, it is relatively uncommon for an arbitral tribunal sitting in Sweden to appoint experts on its on initiative. As a general rule, the arbitrators will leave it to each party to invoke and submit whatever evidence it believes to be appropriate to prove its case including any expert evidence. **11.122**

(2) Power of the tribunal to determine the admissibility and weight of the evidence produced by the parties

There are no restrictions upon the admissibility of evidence. Generally, arbitrators will be guided by the twin principles of freedom to invoke evidence (by each party) and the freedom to assess the weight of the evidence (by the arbitrators). Nevertheless, the arbitrators may refuse to admit evidence which is invoked where such evidence manifestly is not relevant to the case or where such refusal is justified having regard to the time at which the evidence is offered (the Act, s 25, para 2). **11.123**

Also, the SCC Rules stipulate that it is up to the tribunal to determine the admissibility, relevance and weight of evidence provided by the parties (SCC Rules, Art 26, para 1). **11.124**

As a matter of practice it is relatively uncommon for arbitral tribunals to refuse to admit evidence offered by a party, except in extraordinary circumstances. **11.125**

(2.1) Is the tribunal entitled to take the claimant's factual allegation as proven if the defendant does not participate in the arbitral proceedings? The short answer is no. **11.126**

[84] cf Magnusson and Shaughnessy, [2006] *Stockholm Int'l Arb Rev* (3) 18.

However, the arbitrators may give evidentiary weight to the fact that the respondent has not participated in the proceedings. If a party fails without valid excuse to avail itself of the opportunity given to present its case orally or in writing, the arbitrators may also decide the case on the existing materials (the Act, s 24, para 3). Thus, and in such circumstances, the arbitrators are entitled, if they find it appropriate given the burden of proof and the existing material, to base their decision on the claimant's factual allegation.

11.127 (2.2) **May the arbitral tribunal consider an allegation of one party as agreed fact if the other party did not (specifically) dispute the allegation?** Unless a party admits to the truth of any particular allegation, an arbitral tribunal will generally consider such an allegation to be disputed unless the circumstances of the case would lead the tribunal to consider otherwise. In order to avoid any misunderstanding and if a particular, factual circumstance appears material to the outcome of the case, most arbitrators will consider it as part of their duty to clarify to what extent such a circumstance is disputed or accepted as a fact by the parties.

11.128 (2.3) **What is the standard of proof that must be met in order for a fact to be considered to have been established (preponderance of the evidence; beyond reasonable doubt)? Must a stringent requirement be met for certain facts?** There is no general standard of proof applied by arbitrators when they consider whether a certain factual circumstance has been established. However, to the extent the arbitrators choose to be influenced by the Swedish Code of Judicial Procedure, they will generally require disputed facts to be 'shown' (in Swedish '*styrkt*'), which is a standard of proof somewhat above '*the balance of probability*', but below the standard of '*beyond a reasonable doubt*'. The latter standard of proof is generally only used for criminal matters when assessed by a competent court of law.

11.129 (2.4) **May the arbitral tribunal rely on its own knowledge to consider certain facts as proven?** The arbitrators may only base their award on the facts pleaded by the parties. Unless the parties agree otherwise (although this remains an open question as far as arbitration is concerned), it could be argued that the arbitrators would be entitled to rely on their own knowledge, if such knowledge can be deemed as '*notorious*', ie well known to everyone or otherwise publicly accepted as fact.

E. Witnesses

(1) Ability of a person to act as a witness

11.130 Persons testifying before an arbitral tribunal are, technically speaking, not witnesses because they do not testify under oath and do not risk perjury in case of false testimony. Section 25, para 3 of the Act expressly prohibits arbitrators from administering oaths or truth affirmations. There are no particular restrictions on which persons, other than the parties, that may act as witness as long as the ordinary courts are not to be used in connection with hearing a witness.

11.131 If a party wishes to compel a witness or an expert to testify and to do so under oath, or the other party to be examined under truth affirmation, that party may, after obtaining the consent of the arbitrators, submit an application to such effect to the District Court (the Act, s 26, para 1). If the arbitrators consider that the action is justified, they shall approve such a request. The arbitrators may, however, withhold their consent if, eg they believe that sufficient evidence has already been produced on the issue, that the issue is irrelevant[85], that the costs involved would be exorbitant or that the application has been made solely for some extraneous reason, such as a desire to obtain publicity. If consent is given by the tribunal, a party may apply to the District Court designated by the arbitrators or, if no District Court is designated, the District Court of Stockholm (the Act, s 44, para 2). The District Court must grant the application unless the action requested is prohibited by law (the Act, s 26, para 1). Thus, the court's decision shall not be based on whether the action is appropriate or not.[86]

(1.1) Is there a legal difference between a party testifying and a witness? If yes, what are the criteria for such differentiation? Does the testifying of a party have the same weight as a witness testimony? No, there is no such legal difference. However, the sanctions for false testimony given under oath or truth affirmation in a court by a witness and a party, respectively, differ in the sense that a witness' perjury may render a longer period of imprisonment than a party's. In theory this could lead an arbitral tribunal to give less weight to a testimony given by a party, if given under truth affirmation, than to a testimony given by a witness, if given under oath. However, arbitrators are prohibited from administering oaths or truth affirmations in Swedish arbitrations (the Act, s 25, para 3). Furthermore and in practice, whether a person is giving testimony as a party or as a witness is only one of many circumstances that may influence the evidentiary value of such testimony as assessed by an arbitral tribunal. 11.132

(2) Preparation of witnesses and limits thereof

(2.1) Do US-style depositions violate any procedural rules or principles? Depositions are not commonly used in Sweden and are generally not accepted by the Swedish courts. However, to the extent that depositions have been taken in Sweden or another country, in line with the principle of free admissibility of evidence, there are generally no restrictions for a party to rely on testimony given in connection with such deposition before an arbitral tribunal, unless the parties have agreed otherwise. 11.133

(2.2) May a party or its counsel approach a witness whom it has nominated (only before or also after the proceeding has started)? Are interviews permitted? There are no restrictions as regards a party's or counsel's right to approach a witness. It is also common and permitted that witnesses are contacted and interviewed by the parties prior to giving testimony, both before and after proceedings have been started. Furthermore, it is commonly the parties themselves that arrange for the witnesses to be present before the arbitral tribunal. 11.134

(3) Admissibility of written witness statements

There are, as mentioned above (*supra* at 11.123), no restrictions with respect to the admissibility of evidence in an arbitration (including written witness statements). Moreover, the SCC Rules do explicitly allow for (signed) written statements of witnesses and 11.135

[85] Prop 1998/99:35, 229.
[86] *ibid.*

party-appointed experts (SCC Rules, Art 28, para 2). The use of written witness statements is also becoming increasingly common in International arbitrations, ie arbitrations where at least one party is not Swedish. In Swedish, domestic arbitration, which is more influenced by Swedish court procedure, the use of written witness statements remains relatively rare.

11.136 (3.1) **If the parties agree on written statements, is a party entitled to request an oral hearing for questioning those witnesses (provided such right has not been agreed upon)?** The parties may agree that evidence may be submitted in the form of affidavits, ie written witness statements. In international arbitration it is also becoming increasingly common for written witness statements to stand in lieu of the examination in chief. However, in domestic arbitrations affidavits are still considered with some suspicion. The same applies in Swedish court procedure, where they are only accepted under certain circumstances.

11.137 A party who wishes to question a witness that has submitted an affidavit can always ask for such witness to appear in person to be examined at an oral hearing. As a general rule, the arbitrators will require that the opposing party is allowed to cross-examine a witness who has submitted an affidavit. The SCC Rules stipulate in line therewith that any witness or expert, on whose testimony a party seeks to rely, shall attend an oral hearing for examination, unless otherwise agreed between the parties (SCC Rules, Art 28, para 3).

(4) Entitlement of a party to have a hearing or cross-examination of witnesses

11.138 The general expectation is that a witness shall be examined by the parties at an oral hearing by way of examination in chief followed by cross-examination. The arbitrators usually remain and are mostly expected to be passive in connection with the examination of witnesses. Arbitrators do have the right, however, to put questions to witnesses.

11.139 (4.1) **Which are the methods used to establish a record of the arbitral proceedings, in particular witness examinations (tape recording, verbatim court reporters, dictated minutes, other methods)?** There are no statutory provisions with respect to establishing a record of the arbitral proceedings. It is a matter for the parties to agree upon. In practice a tape or digital recording is commonly used. For international arbitration where the language of the proceedings is English, verbatim court reporters are increasingly being used.

11.140 (4.2) **May the arbitral tribunal take an oath from a witness?** No. The arbitrators are not empowered to administer oaths (as regards witnesses) or truth affirmations (as regards parties), and may not order penalties or use other compulsory measures (the Act, s 25, para 3). However and as stated above (*supra* at 11.131), if a party wishes to have a witness or an expert to testify under oath, or the other party to be examined under truth affirmation, that party may, after obtaining the consent of the arbitrators, submit an application to such effect to the District Court (the Act, s 26, para 1).

11.141 (4.3) **Does the arbitral tribunal have the power to compel witnesses?** No. However, and as stated above (*supra* at 11.131), if a party wishes to compel a witness or an expert to testify and to do so under oath, or the other party to be examined under truth affirmation, that party may, after obtaining the consent of the arbitrators, submit an application to such effect to the District Court (the Act, s 26, para 1).

F. Documents

(1) Form and kind of documents to be presented to the arbitral tribunal

There are no legal restrictions on the form of documents or objects that may be produced in arbitration. In practice, documents will be produced by way of copies and accepted as true copies of the original documents unless one party alleges them to be falsified in some way (which very rarely happens). Although the Code of Judicial Procedure provides that documents presented as proof should be produced in the original, the practice in Swedish court procedure is the same as in arbitration. If a document contains information which the possessor is not allowed or not obliged to disclose or which otherwise should not be disclosed, the possessor of such document may be directed to produce, instead of the document, certified relevant excerpts therefrom.[87] The obligation of the possessor may be further limited to permitting a designated person or persons to study the document, eg to determine issues of alleged privilege or confidentiality. However, a document should not only be provided to the arbitrators to study, excluding the other party, as this may potentially amount to a procedural irregularity which could be used as a basis for a subsequent challenge of the award. **11.142**

(1.1) Is the submission of 'agreed documents' permitted? If yes, what is the extent and effect of such an agreement of the parties (authenticity, existence, acknowledgement of such documents' contents)? As mentioned above there are no restrictions as to what kind of documents that may be submitted by the parties. Thus, an 'agreed document', or bundles of 'agreed documents', may be submitted by either party and the arbitrators will generally accept such document as 'agreed' and not make any independent investigation or determination on whether such document in fact is authentic, existing etc. Such determination will only be made by the arbitrators if the other party objects to a document alleging it not to be authentic etc. **11.143**

(1.2) How may electronic documents (eg emails) be presented and proven? There are no restrictions on how to present and prove electronic documents. It is thus open to the parties and the arbitrators to work out an appropriate and efficient method to handle such documents. **11.144**

(1.3) Does discovery (US- or UK-style), after the procedure has started, violate any procedural rules or public policy considerations? Although US- or UK-style discovery is not used in Swedish courts, the parties may agree to use it in arbitration. However, the general expectation in a Swedish arbitration would be that a more limited production of documents, in line with the IBA Rules on the Taking of Evidence in International Commercial Arbitration, would take place between the parties. If the parties have agreed to go further and apply Anglo-American procedural principles including discovery, it is unlikely that such procedure would be deemed to violate any mandatory procedural rules or public policy. **11.145**

[87] Code of Judicial Procedure, ch 38 s 1.

(2) Requirement to produce certain documents (as requested by the tribunal) and consequences of a failure to do so

11.146 Arbitrators cannot impose fines or order other measures to compel production of a document (the Act, s 25, para 3). However, to the extent a tribunal would request certain documents to be produced which are in the possession of a party, such party will generally provide the relevant documents voluntarily in order not to upset the arbitrators. If a party refuses to produce certain evidence, without invoking any valid reason for such refusal, an arbitral tribunal may also potentially draw adverse inferences from such refusal. Although the arbitrators themselves lack coercive powers, ultimately the production of documents may be compelled through the courts (the Act, s 26, para 1). As in respect of compelling witness testimony under oath, if a party wishes to compel the production of certain documents, it may thus, after obtaining the consent of the arbitrators, submit an application to such effect to the District Court (the Act, s 26, para 1). The District Court shall grant the application if the action may be lawfully taken.

11.147 Procedure for production of documents. Before issuing a subpoena, a court of law must give the alleged possessor of a document an opportunity to present objections, eg relating to asserted privilege or disputed importance of the document. If the request for production of a document is granted by the court, an order to such effect may be combined with a penalty of a fine. The court may also specify appropriate conditions concerning the time and manner of production.[88] The concealment or destruction of a subpoenaed document is a criminal offence.

11.148 (2.1) **Which documents may the tribunal request to be produced (eg also documents which are in the possession of third parties)?** An arbitral tribunal draws its mandate from the parties and may only request a party to produce documents. However, if a party wishes to compel the production of certain documents being in the possession of a third party, it may, after obtaining the consent of the arbitrators, submit an application to such effect to the District Court (the Act, s 26, para 1). If the Swedish court approves an application and the document in question can be assumed to be of importance as proof, anyone possessing such a document may be directed to produce it.[89] The obligation to produce documents thus also includes third parties and has in principle the same scope as the duty to give oral testimony. Consequently and to the extent that anyone is obliged to give oral testimony, such a person has a corresponding duty to produce documents which are in its possession, if so ordered by a court of law. The obligation to produce documents does not extend to personal memoranda, or to any other similar notes prepared exclusively for private use, unless compelling reasons exist.[90]

(3) Protection of the confidentiality of documents (legal privilege etc)

11.149 Before a Swedish court of law privilege in respect of a document may be relied on, *inter alia*, with respect to national security,[91] client-lawyer relationship or other relationship of trust

---

88 Code of Judicial Procedure, ch 38 s 1.
89 *ibid*, ch 38 ss 1 and 4.
90 *ibid*, ch 38 s 2.
91 The Official Secrets Act, ch 2 s 1–2, ch 2 s 1.

and for trade secrets.[92] However, when it comes to arbitration, without the involvement of a court to compel production, no such privilege is relevant as the tribunal lacks coercive powers, thus making it up to each party to decide which documents are to be produced and which documents are to be withheld. However, if a party wishes to exclude a particular document from production in an arbitration, it will typically wish to state a valid reason in order not to provoke the arbitral tribunal and potentially have the arbitrators draw adverse inferences from its failure to produce. In international arbitrations conducted in Sweden parties will in such cases often refer to the exceptions to produce provided for in the IBA Rules on the Taking of Evidence in International Commercial Arbitration.

G. Experts

(1) Appointment and presentation of experts by the party or the arbitral tribunal

The parties may rely on experts before the arbitral tribunal. The arbitrators may also appoint an expert at their own initiative, provided, however, that not both parties disapprove of such appointment (the Act, s 25, para 1). The fees of an expert appointed by the tribunal will form part of the costs of the proceedings. In practice, arbitrators will rarely appoint experts at their own initiative, without the prior approval of both parties. **11.150**

If the SCC Rules apply, each party may decide if and to what extent it wishes to appoint an expert of its own. Apart from such party-appointed experts, the arbitral tribunal may appoint an expert to give his or her opinion on a particular matter unless otherwise agreed by the parties (SCC Rules Art 27, para 1). **11.151**

(1.1) **By which methods are tribunal-appointed experts selected? What are the rights of the parties during the selection process?** It is relatively uncommon for arbitral tribunals sitting in Sweden to appoint experts at their own initiative. Most tribunals will leave it to the parties themselves to adduce whatever evidence they see fit to prove their case including expert evidence. However, it is clear that the arbitrators do have the power to summon experts at their own initiative and at the expense of the parties, unless both parties are opposed to such appointment. Arbitrators rarely do so without the prior approval of both parties. The arbitrators would normally also listen to the parties' suggestions with respect to the selection of any experts. **11.152**

If a party wishes an expert to be heard under oath before a court of law, he may seek permission from the arbitrators to apply to the District Court designated by the arbitrators or, if no such designation is made, to the District Court of Stockholm (the Act, s 26, para 1, and s 44, para 2). **11.153**

(2) Admissibility and role of expert witnesses

Expert evidence is freely admissible before an arbitral tribunal. As with any other evidence, the arbitrators may, however, refuse a party to adduce expert testimony if they consider the evidence to be manifestly irrelevant to the case or where such refusal may be justified having regard to the time at which the expert evidence is offered. As with witnesses, an expert is expected to speak the truth even in the absence of his or her testimony being given **11.154**

[92] Code of Judicial Procedure, ch 28 s 8.

under oath. There are no particular procedural rules governing the role of an expert witness and an arbitral tribunal will, as with any other evidence offered by a party, freely assess the evidentiary value of expert testimony.

(3) Influence of the parties upon the selection of questions to be submitted to the expert

11.155 With a party-appointed expert, the party invoking the expert's testimony will generally be in a very good position to influence the selection of questions submitted to the expert. This possibility will be much more limited with an expert appointed by the arbitral tribunal, although most tribunals will consult with the parties and take their suggestions into account when deciding on what questions should be put to an expert.

(4) Independence and impartiality of the expert and the right to reject a proposed/appointed expert

11.156 There are no specific requirements as to an expert's independence and impartiality. However, if the independence and/or impartiality of an expert may be put into question, this may influence the tribunal's assessment of the evidentiary value of the expert's testimony.

11.157 A party cannot reject expert evidence invoked by the other party. As with any other evidence, the arbitrators may, however, refuse a party to adduce expert testimony if they consider the evidence to be manifestly irrelevant to the case or where such refusal may be justified having regard to the time at which the expert evidence is offered. Furthermore, a party has no right to reject an expert proposed by the tribunal. However, most tribunals will consult with the parties and at least consider the views of a party as to the suitability of any particular expert which the tribunal may be considering to appoint.

11.158 (4.1) **May a party or its counsel approach an expert (or expert witness) whom it has nominated (only before or also after the proceeding has started)? Are interviews admissible?** As with witnesses of fact, there are no restrictions as regards a party's right to approach and interview an expert nominated by itself at any time, both before or after the proceedings have started.

(5) Oral examination of an expert in a hearing

11.159 Experts are usually invited to present their views in a written report. The report will then be communicated to the other party which is given the opportunity to comment on the report and, if he or she finds it appropriate, to adduce expert evidence of his/her own. In most cases, experts will also be subjected to oral examination at a main hearing.

11.160 An arbitral tribunal must only base its award on material that has been presented to it by the parties or, if the material has been gathered by the arbitrators themselves (as with a tribunal-appointed expert), that has been communicated with the parties during the proceedings. Although this rule is not spelt out explicitly in the Act, it is a fundamental principle of due process and can *inter alia* be found in the Code of Judicial Procedure. Consequently, an arbitral tribunal may not seek and receive expert advice without employing full transparency as to the content of any such advice vis-à-vis the parties and provide the parties an opportunity to comment thereon.

H. Interim measures of protection

(1) *Kind of interim measures which the tribunal may order*

Interim preservation orders and similar measures are generally granted by the courts. An arbitral tribunal may, however, order certain interim measures. The arbitrators may thus eg order the parties to pay security for the compensation payable to the arbitrators (*supra* at 11.53). The arbitrators cannot, however, order a party to provide security for the other party's costs in connection with the proceedings. The arbitrators may also, unless the parties have agreed otherwise, upon the request of a party, determine that the other party shall take or refrain from taking a certain action in order to secure the claim to be tried by the arbitrators. The arbitrators may also prescribe that the party making such request shall provide reasonable security in respect of the loss that such action may cause the other party (the Act, s 25, para 4). It should be noted that such interim measures decided by the tribunal in an *ad hoc* arbitration may not be enforced, should the party involved refuse to comply with the arbitral tribunal's order in such respect.[93] Here, the only way for a party to achieve an enforceable interim measure is to apply to a competent court of law.[94] 11.161

If the SCC Rules apply the arbitral tribunal is entitled to decide about interim measures at the request of a party either in the form of an order or of an award. The tribunal may order the requesting party to provide appropriate security in connection with the interim measure sought (SCC Rules, Art 32, para 1–3). By empowering the tribunal to issue an award on interim measures the requesting party obtains the possibility, at least in some jurisdictions, to enforce the interim decision. This stipulation has been newly incorporated in the SCC Rules, following various other international arbitration rules providing for the same possibility. Notwithstanding the opportunity of the parties to request interim protection from the arbitral tribunal they are at the same time free to apply for interim measures at the competent judicial authorities. 11.162

(1.1) Which are, in general, the procedural and substantive prerequisites for the ordering of interim and conservatory measures (eg reduced degree of evidence; urgency; summary evaluation of the claim)? To the extent that interim measures are possible to obtain from a Swedish court (*supra* at 11.161), before an attachment or an injunction is granted three conditions must normally be satisfied: (i) the applicant must show probable grounds for its claim, ie the ultimate, substantive claim that the interim measure is supposed to secure; (ii) the property or right in question must be in jeopardy of being removed, destroyed or substantially diminished in value; and (iii) the applicant must furnish security for any damage which the other party may incur in case the applicant's claim is ultimately found to be without sufficient merit. 11.163

(1.2) Are the prerequisites for interim measures ordered by the arbitral tribunal more or less the same as if those are requested from the state court? Is there case law/leading authorities on whether those measures are faster and enforced more easily if taken by the arbitral tribunal or the state court? Decisions by arbitrators with respect to interim 11.164

---

[93] Prop 1998/99:35, 228.
[94] *ibid*, 73.

measures issued in *ad hoc* arbitrations are not enforceable. As explained (*supra* at 11.161 to 11.163), certain conditions must be satisfied before a court of law would grant an interim measure. An arbitral tribunal is likely to apply such, or similar conditions before ordering an interim measure. With respect to security it is explicitly stated that an arbitral tribunal may order security to be posted (the Act, s 25, para 4).

(2) Limits of the tribunal's powers to order interim measures

11.165 The arbitrators may also, unless the parties have agreed otherwise, upon the request of a party, determine that the other party shall take or refrain from taking a certain action in order to secure the claim to be tried by the arbitrators. The arbitrators may also prescribe that the party making such request shall provide reasonable security in respect of the loss that such action may cause the other party (the Act, s 25, para 4). However, such interim measures decided by the tribunal in an *ad hoc* arbitration may not be enforced, should the party involved refuse to comply with the arbitral tribunal's order in such respect. Here, the only way for a party to achieve an enforceable interim measure is to apply to a competent court of law (*supra* at 11.161).

11.166 If the SCC Rules apply the arbitral tribunal is entitled to decide about interim measures at the request of a party either in the form of an order or of an award. The tribunal may order the requesting party to provide appropriate security in connection with the interim measure sought (SCC Rules, Art 32, paras 1–3). By empowering the tribunal to issue an award on interim measures the requesting party obtains the possibility, at least in some jurisdictions, to enforce the interim decision (*supra* at 11.162).

(3) Orders to provide security for the costs of the proceeding

11.167 The arbitrators may order the parties to pay security for the compensation payable to the arbitrators. The arbitrators cannot, however, order a party to provide security for the other party's costs in connection with the proceedings (*supra* at 11.161).

11.168 According to the SCC Rules (Art 45, para 4), if a party fails to pay its half of the advance on costs and such payment is instead provided by the other party, the party having made the payment may request that the arbitral tribunal makes a separate award for reimbursement from the non-paying party.[95] Absent an agreement by the parties to the same effect as the aforementioned SCC Rules, the Act does not provide for the possibility for arbitral tribunals to make separate awards for reimbursement by a party who fails to pay its half of the advance on costs.[96] Consequently, such an opportunity will not be available in an *ad hoc* arbitration under the Act.

(4) Attachment of assets by an order of the tribunal

11.169 As stated above, the arbitrators may, upon the request of a party, determine that the other party shall take or refrain from taking a certain action in order to secure the claim to be tried by the arbitrators. However, such interim measures decided by the tribunal in an *ad hoc* arbitration may not be enforced, should the party involved refuse to comply with the

[95] cf the first separate arbitral award on advance on costs under the new SCC Rules (SCC Arbitration V (113/2007)), published in *Stockholm Int'l Arb Rev* 2008:1, 137.

[96] cf NJA 2000:773 (*3S Swedish Special Supplier AB ('3S') v Sky Park AB*).

arbitral tribunal's order in such respect. Here, the only way for a party to achieve an enforceable interim measure is to apply to a competent court of law (*supra* at 11.161). However, if the SCC Rules apply the arbitral tribunal is entitled to decide about interim measures at the request of a party either in the form of an order or of an award. By empowering the tribunal to issue an award on interim measures the requesting party obtains the possibility, at least in some jurisdictions, to enforce the interim decision (*supra* at 11.162).

I. Assistance by the courts

The courts may assist in the appointment and replacement of arbitrators (*supra* at 11.68 *et seq*, 11.73 *et seq* and 11.79 *et seq*). Similarly, the courts may be of use if a party wishes to disqualify an arbitrator or to challenge the jurisdiction of the arbitrators owing to the absence of a valid arbitration agreement. **11.170**

(1) Extent of court assistance in the gathering of evidence

As explained above in connection with evidence, courts may use their coercive powers to assist in arbitrations with respect to witnesses, production of documents or objects and experts (*supra* at 11.131 and 11.146). **11.171**

(1.1) Is it for the arbitral tribunal or for the party to obtain the assistance of state courts with respect to the gathering of evidence? Only a party may take the initiative to apply for assistance from the courts, but the courts will not act affirmatively with respect to such an application without the consent of the arbitrators (the Act, s 26, para 1). The arbitrators may withhold their consent if, for example, they believe that sufficient evidence has already been produced on the issue, that the issue is irrelevant, that the costs involved would be exorbitant or that the application has been made solely for some extraneous reason, such as a desire to obtain publicity. **11.172**

(1.2) According to case law and practical experience, are there considerable delays involvedwhenaskingacourttogiveassistance(egfortheobtainingofevidence)? Although the time needed to obtain assistance will vary from one court to the next and also depend on the nature of the assistance required, the involvement of a court will generally cause a delay to the arbitral proceedings. A claimant, who may wish for an expeditious arbitration, should therefore carefully consider its options before approaching a court for assistance. Correspondingly, the involvement of a court may sometimes be used by a respondent to try to obstruct and delay the arbitral proceedings. To the extent that the assistance of a court requires the consent of the arbitrators, it will be for them to consider and balance the sometimes conflicting interests of the claimant and respondent in these regards. **11.173**

If the parties have agreed to apply the SCC Rules (or the rules of any other well established institution), many issues that would otherwise fall on the courts to handle will be exclusively handled by the SCC Institute. This includes the appointment and challenge of arbitrators and certain other such matters. **11.174**

(2) Assistance for enforcing the attachment of assets

As stated above, a claimant may—as an interim measure—seek the assistance of the Swedish courts in order to attach the assets of the respondent (*supra* at 11.163 and 11.169). Such assistance may be sought both before or during arbitral proceedings. The Code of Judicial **11.175**

Procedure includes provisions for interim and conservatory measures, which may permit a party to an arbitration agreement to enhance its chances of obtaining a satisfactory, substantial result if he is ultimately successful in the contemplated arbitration. Even before arbitration is requested, an interim measure (injunction, attachment etc) may thus be granted against the future respondent. The most important interim security measure is attachment (in Swedish, *kvarstad*). Whether a Swedish court is competent to hear a request for an interim measure depends on whether such a court, absent the arbitration agreement, would be competent to hear the case on its merits pursuant to the general rules on jurisdiction as provided for by the Code of Judicial Procedure. As an example, attachment is only possible in respect of property which is situated on Swedish territory. The presence of property in Sweden will also provide jurisdiction for a District Court to hear an application for attachment of that property.

(3) Other examples of possible assistance

11.176 In addition to attachment of assets, a claimant may also seek an injunction against the respondent ordering the respondent to take certain actions or abstain from taking certain actions at penalty of a fine.

11.177 The courts may also assist in upholding the arbitration agreement and the procedure itself, eg by appointing and replacing arbitrators (*supra* at 11.73 to 11.77 and 11.79 to 11.80). Similarly, the courts may be of use if a party wishes to disqualify an arbitrator or to challenge the jurisdiction of the arbitrators owing to the absence of a valid arbitration agreement.

11.178 Generally, Swedish courts are very arbitration friendly and will try to uphold and support arbitral proceedings to the extent it falls within their powers to do so.

(4) Dependence of the power of state courts to intervene during the proceedings on the (national) procedural law applied by the arbitral tribunal

11.179 The powers of the Swedish courts do not depend on which procedural law has been applied. As previously stated, arbitration proceedings in Sweden must be conducted in accordance with applicable Swedish legislation of arbitration, ie principally the Act. However, as the Act contains very little in the way of detailed provisions as to the arbitral procedure and as most of the provisions of the Act are anyway permissive in nature, the parties are given great freedom in stipulating the manner in which the arbitral proceedings should be carried on. Thus, foreign procedural rules may in many instances be applied without falling foul of the Act.

11.180 Generally and as a matter of practice, Swedish courts are very arbitration friendly. To the extent that they have any power to do so, the courts will thus rarely intervene with arbitral proceedings.

V. The award

A. Types of award

(1) Interim award (eg on interim measures or the jurisdiction of the tribunal)

11.181 Issues which have been referred to the arbitrators shall be decided by an award. Other determinations, which are not embodied in an award, are designated as 'decisions' (the Act, s 27, para 3). Unless authorized by the parties the arbitrators may not make provisional interim awards for issues concerning interim measures.

As stated above (*supra* at 11.42 to 11.45) the arbitrators may rule on their own jurisdiction. In so doing and if the arbitrators find in favour of jurisdiction, their determination will be given in the form of a decision. If, on the other hand, the arbitrators do not find in favour of jurisdiction, their determination will be given in the form of an award. 11.182

(2) Partial award

It is possible for the arbitrators to render a partial award unless both parties oppose such an award (the Act, s 29, para 1). Correspondingly, if the parties request such an award, the arbitrators must give such an award.[97] However, decisions on the principal claim and a claim operating as a defence by way of set-off must be made in the same award (*ibid*). An interlocutory award may deal with a question of liability, as opposed to the amount of damages, and with allegations or objections pleaded in the alternative.[98] If the SCC Rules apply, the arbitrators may give a separate award in respect of a separate issue or part of the matter in dispute (SCC Rules, Art 38). 11.183

The arbitrators may render a partial award where several distinct claims have been joined, unless both parties are opposed to such partial award. A partial award may also be given if a party has made a (partial) admission (the Act, s 29, para 2). 11.184

(2.1) Are awards, especially partial awards, binding in the same arbitral proceeding? Does it make a difference if after the rendering of such a partial award, one arbitrator is successfully challenged and removed on grounds that prevailed even before the partial award was rendered? Partial awards are binding in the same arbitral proceeding. There is no clear answer today as to whether it would make any difference if one arbitrator is successfully removed on grounds that prevailed even before the partial award was made. In general, however, as long as the award has not been set aside by a competent court of law, it remains binding between the parties. 11.185

(3) Final award

The arbitrators may of course also render a final award, thereby conclusively deciding on the issues which have been referred to them. However, if they terminate the arbitral proceedings without deciding those issues, such a decision is also made in the form of an award. This may eg be the case if the arbitrators find that there is no valid arbitration agreement. If a settlement has been reached between the parties, the parties may request that the arbitral tribunal confirm their settlement in an award. In such case the arbitrators will render an award to that effect (the Act, s 27, para 2). Under the SCC Rules, it is also recognized that the arbitral tribunal may at the request of the parties confirm a settlement in a consent award (SCC Rules, Art 39). 11.186

If a party withdraws a prayer for relief the arbitrators shall dismiss that part of the dispute, unless the opposing party requests the arbitrators to rule on the merits of the claim (the Act, s 28). 11.187

[97] Prop 1998/99:35, 231.
[98] Code of Judicial Procedure, Ch 17 s 5.

If the party does not request such a ruling and the withdrawal implies that there is no remaining dispute, the arbitration proceedings will be terminated by the arbitrators rendering an award to that effect.

11.188 (3.1) **If a party fails to participate in the arbitration, may the tribunal proceed and issue an award on the merits? Is such an award enforceable as any other award? Are there special remedies for the defendant at the enforcement stage?** The arbitrators may not render an award by default, ie they may not base their award solely on the respondent's failure to appear or to plead, but must base their award on the available materials and the applicable law, unless otherwise agreed by the parties. However, if a party fails to participate in the arbitration, the arbitrators may decide the case on the existing materials (the Act, s 24, para 3). Such an award has the same validity as any other award and may also be challenged on the same grounds as any other award. If the SCC Rules apply, the arbitral tribunal is not prevented from proceeding with the case and may render an award if one of the parties, without showing valid cause, fails to appear at a hearing or otherwise to comply with an order of the arbitral tribunal (SCC Rules, Art 30, para 2).

B. Deliberations and agreement on the award

(1) Time limits (and possible extensions) for making the award

11.189 Unless the parties have agreed otherwise, there are no statutory time limits with respect to the rendering of an award. However, if eg the SCC Rules apply, the award must be given no later than six months after the case has been referred to the arbitrators. However, the SCC Institute may grant an extension of this period upon a reasoned request from the arbitral tribunal (SCC Rules, Art 37). In practice, such extensions are commonly sought and granted by the SCC Institute and the average time from referral of the case to the arbitrators until an award is rendered is around 12 months.

(2) Procedure for the decision of the arbitrators (majority vote etc)

11.190 All the arbitrators must take part in the resolution of a dispute. However, if an arbitrator fails, without valid cause, to participate in the deliberations of a particular issue, his or her failure will not prevent the other arbitrators from deciding such issue. With respect to decisions on the merits of a dispute a majority of the arbitrators is necessary and sufficient unless the parties have agreed otherwise. If no majority is attained for any opinion, the opinion of the chairman prevails (the Act, s 30, para 2). It is only the vote itself, not the arbitrator's reasons therefore, which is important in this respect. Consequently, a valid decision may be reached on an issue even if the arbitrators have widely differing opinions on the reasons for their vote.

11.191 If the SCC Rules apply, any award or other decision of the arbitral tribunal 'shall be made by a majority of the arbitrators or, failing a majority, by the Chairperson' (SCC Rules, Art 35, para 1).

11.192 The general practice is for the arbitrators to deliberate and try to decide on the resolution and the contents of the award by unanimity. Only if the chairperson finds that the arbitrators are unable to achieve unanimity will he or she resort to majority and other rules. The chairperson usually drafts the award and then proceeds to invite comments from his or her co-arbitrators.

(2.1) If an arbitrator fails or refuses to take part in oral deliberation meetings, although having been given sufficient notice of such meetings, may an award be rendered on the basis of written deliberations (or deliberations without this arbitrator) only? If an arbitrator fails without valid cause to participate in the deliberations of the arbitral tribunal on any issue, his or her failure does not prevent the other arbitrators from deciding the issue (the Act, s 30, para 1). The same principles apply in case the arbitration is governed by the SCC Rules (Art 36, para 5). 11.193

(3) Admissibility of dissenting opinions

An arbitrator is entitled to express his or her dissenting opinion, with or without a statement of the reasons therefore. A dissenting opinion is usually annexed to the award. 11.194

(3.1) Are there any court decisions or positions of leading authorities on the issue of dissenting opinions (admissibility, disclosure to the parties and publication)? There are no particular authorities on the issue of dissenting opinions nor is there any case law. 11.195

(4) Signature by the arbitrators and potential failure of one arbitrator to sign

The award must be made in writing and must be signed by the arbitrators (the Act, s 31, para 1). It suffices that the award is signed by a majority of the arbitrators provided that the reason why not all of the arbitrators have signed is noted in the award. The parties may also agree that only the chairman shall sign the award (*ibid*). Also the SCC Rules accept that an arbitrator's signature may be missing on such conditions, and failing a majority, the signature of the chairperson is regarded as sufficient (SCC Rules Art 36, para 3). 11.196

C. Form of the award and deposition

(1) Form and minimum contents of an award

The fact that the award has received the arbitrators' final approval does not mean that it has been given. The award is not considered given until it is available to the parties. 11.197

An award must be in writing and the award shall specify the seat of arbitration and the date on which the award is made (the Act, s 31, paras 1 and 2). Further, the award should identify the parties and the dispute and include a clear and definitive decision.[99] The seat at which the award is given is important for two reasons. It determines which court is competent with respect to certain actions (the Act, ss 43 and 44). It also determines whether an award is 'Swedish' or 'foreign'. 11.198

The award shall be delivered to the parties immediately (the Act, s 31, para 3). The winning party may wish to ensure that the award is delivered to the opposite party in a provable manner in order for the three-month period within which the award may be challenged to start running (the Act, s 34, para 3). Similar rules apply under the SCC Rules stipulating that the award shall be delivered to the parties 'without delay' (Art 36, para 4). 11.199

(2) Requirement to give reasons in the award

There is no statutory requirement that reasons for the award must be given.[100] It is, however, considered highly desirable that reasons are included, and the normal practice is that 11.200

[99] cf *Arbitration in Sweden* (n 30) 133; cf also SCC Rules, Art 36, paras 1 and 2.
[100] Prop 1998/99:35, 135.

the award states reasons. If the SCC Rules apply, reasons for the decision shall be included in the award, unless the parties have agreed otherwise (SCC Rules, Art 36, para 1).

(3) Necessity to specify place and time where and when the award was made

11.201 An indication in the award of the place where the arbitration proceedings have taken place is relevant for which court is competent to try challenges of the award (the Act, s 43, para 1). Such indication is also decisive for determining whether the award is Swedish or foreign (the Act, s 52, para 2). The date of the award is in general proof of when the award was rendered. Although it follows directly from the Act (s 31, para. 2) that the place and time shall be specified in the award, there are no sanctions if these requirements are not met. Similar requirements also follow from the SCC Rules (SCC Rules Art 36, para 2).

(4) Other requirements (registration, delivery etc)

11.202 (4.1) **Does the award have to be laid down or registered with a state court or agency (even if it has been rendered according to a foreign procedural law)?** There is no requirement as to filing or registration of an award with any court or other authority. However, under the SCC Rules the arbitral tribunal is under an obligation to submit to the SCC Institute a copy of the award (SCC Rules Art 36, para 4) although failure to abide by this requirement does not affect the validity of the award.

11.203 (4.2) **Does a foreign award which has been rendered abroad according to this country's national procedural law, have to be laid down or registered with a state court or agency? Is there a fee or tax for such registration of an award?** In order to have a foreign award acknowledged and enforced, the award—irrespective of under which procedural law it has been rendered—shall be submitted to the Svea Court of Appeal (the Act, s 56). The original or a certified copy of the award must be attached to the application for acknowledgement and enforcement together with a certified translation into the Swedish language, unless the Court of Appeal decides otherwise (the Act, s 56, para 2). No fee or tax is payable.

11.204 (4.3) **How long after the rendering of the award must the file/award be stored by the lawyers and the arbitral tribunal?** There are no statutory requirements as to how long the lawyers or the arbitrators must keep any file relating to arbitration proceedings. However, if a member of the Swedish Bar Association has been active in the matter either as arbitrator or as counsel, such member is generally obliged to keep his or her files for a period of at least 10 years.

D. Applicable substantive law

(1) Party autonomy to choose the applicable substantive law

11.205 Subject to a few minor exceptions, the parties are entitled to choose the substantive law to be applied to the merits of the case, either through the designation of a particular conflict of laws system or directly through the designation of the applicable substantive law. It should be pointed out that a contractual reference to 'Swedish law' is in general understood to mean Swedish substantive law, thus excluding Swedish conflict of law rules.[101] If the SCC Rules apply and if the parties have not decided on the substantive law to be applied,

[101] cf *Arbitration in Sweden* (n 30) 47.

the arbitrators shall apply the law which they find most appropriate (SCC Rules, Art 22, para 1).

(1.1) Is there a public policy exception to the chosen substantive law? As a matter of principle public policy might prevent the application of a foreign law that would otherwise have been applied. This may occur when such foreign law has been designated by the parties or when such law results from applicable conflict of law rules. A foreign law may thus be set aside if its application would obviously be incompatible with the fundamental principles of the law of Sweden.[102] The scope for applying such public policy exceptions to the law chosen by the parties is relatively narrow. Furthermore, and as regards arbitrations conducted in Sweden in which both parties are non-Swedish, the scope for disregarding the law chosen by the parties owing to Swedish public policy is even more limited.[103] 11.206

(1.2) Does the principle of '*iura novit curia*' apply? Or must the applicable law be proven (by which means)? As regards domestic arbitrations subject to Swedish law, the principle of '*iura novit curia*' certainly applies.[104] However, with respect to international arbitrations, where the applicable law may be more or less familiar to the parties and the arbitrators, it is unclear to what extent this principle does in fact apply.[105] In cases where the arbitrators find that they and/or the parties may be less familiar with the content of the applicable substantive law, the arbitrators will usually require the parties to present some kind of evidence as to the contents of such law. 11.207

(2) Decisions according to equity or as amiable compositeur

The arbitral tribunal may decide *ex aequo et bono* only if the parties have explicitly authorized them to do so.[106] The same principle applies under the SCC Rules (Art 22, para 3). 11.208

(3) Application of lex mercatoria, *general principles etc*

(3.1) Is the application of *lex mercatoria* considered as the application of law or as a kind of *amiable composition*? Under Swedish arbitration law arbitrators are to base their decision on the applicable substantive law, unless otherwise directed by the parties. The generally held opinion is that *lex mercatoria*, Unidroit principles and other such concepts do not constitute 'law' in this sense, nor a system of law. Consequently, the application of *lex mercatoria* or Unidroit principles by arbitrators requires an instruction from the parties to do so. As regards *lex mercatoria*, this further assumes that there is some kind of agreement between the parties on what it can be considered to include. 11.209

(4) Applicable substantive law if there is no choice of law by the parties

If the parties have not agreed on the applicable substantive law, the 1980 EEC Convention On Applicable Law to Contractual Matters would usually govern if Swedish conflict of laws rules are to be applied. Pursuant to this convention the substantive law to be applied 11.210

102 cf *Arbitration in Sweden* (n 30) 78.

103 cf Hobér, K., 'International Commercial Arbitration in Sweden: Two Salient Problem Areas' in *Festskrift till Lars Hjerner, Studies in International Law* (Norstedts, Stockholm, 1990) 257.

104 SOU 1994:81, 150.

105 cf for a critical view Calissendorff, G., 'Jura novit curia i internationella skiljeförfaranden i Sverige' [1995/96] *JT* 141, 147–9.

106 SOU 1994:81, 153 and Prop 1998/99:35, 122.

is the law of the country where the party who is to perform the most characteristic act under the contract in question is domiciled. It should be noted that this presumption does not lead to the place of performance, but rather to the residence or central administration or principal place of business or other place of business, as the case may be, of the party who is to effect the most characteristic performance. The 1964 Act on the Law Applicable to International Sales of Goods[107] will be applied, however, when the dispute concerns an international sales contract. The main principle of the 1964 Act is that, when parties to an 'international' contract of sale have not agreed on a choice of law, the contract will be governed by the law of the jurisdiction where the seller was domiciled at the time he received the order.

11.211 If the SCC Rules apply, the arbitrators do not have to determine the applicable substantive law by way of first applying the applicable conflicts of laws test. Instead the arbitral tribunal may directly apply the substantive law which it considers to be most appropriate (SCC Rules, Art 22, para 1).

11.212 (4.1) **Is there an autonomous conflict of law rule in the national arbitration law? Is it considered mandatory?** There is no conflict of law rule in the Act. Swedish conflict of laws rules are in general not mandatory. The parties may thus agree that other conflict of law rules are to be applied in such respect.[108] The above-mentioned provision in Art 22 of the SCC Rules is an example of how this may work.

11.213 (4.2) **What is the law applicable to interest?** Under Swedish conflict of laws rules, the proper law of the contract also governs a party's obligation to pay interest. The provisions regarding interest forms part of Swedish substantive law.[109]

11.214 (4.3) **What is the law and practice with respect to legal interest on foreign currency debts?** Besides the rules referred to in the previous answer, there is no law on the legal interest on foreign currency debts.

(5) Binding effect of state court decisions

11.215 An arbitral tribunal is generally bound by a decision of a competent court, but only to the extent such decision deals with a specific matter on which the arbitral tribunal also has to decide and the court's decision involves the same parties as in the arbitration proceedings.

11.216 In addition and to the extent Swedish substantive law would apply to the merits of a dispute, an arbitral tribunal would generally and to the extent being aware thereof follow case law dealing with the interpretation of Swedish law. However, to the extent an arbitral tribunal would overlook or even disregard such case law it would not generally be a ground for challenging the award (see *infra* at 11.254).

11.217 (5.1) **Is an arbitral tribunal bound by a decision of another arbitral tribunal?** An arbitral tribunal is not bound by a decision of another arbitral tribunal, unless the parties involved are identical in the two arbitrations and the matter at issue is the same one that has

[107] SFS 1964:528 (Applicable Law (International Sales of Goods) Act).
[108] cf *Arbitration in Sweden* (n 30) 46.
[109] cf Pålsson, L., *Romkonventionen – Tillämplig lag för avtalsförpliktelser* (Norstedts, Stockholm, 1998), 101.

already been the subject of a final decision by the other arbitral tribunal. However, the parties may agree that the previous decision should not be binding or that the matter should again be arbitrated.[110] Other decisions of another arbitral tribunal do not have any binding effect.

(5.2) **Does a decision in a criminal case bind an arbitral tribunal?** Criminal matters are generally non-arbitrable. However, the civil law consequences of a crime may possibly fall to be decided under an arbitration agreement. In such a case, the arbitral tribunal is not necessarily bound by a decision rendered by a criminal court as to whether a particular crime was committed or not, as the burden and standard of proof would be very different in a civil law case as opposed to a criminal case. However, if the criminal court also decided on eg a civil law claim for damages resulting from the crime, such a decision would also bind an arbitral tribunal if it involved the same parties (*supra* at 11.215). **11.218**

E. Settlement

(1) Settlement by agreement of the parties with or without support of the arbitral tribunal

There are no restrictions on arbitrators encouraging the parties to reach a settlement or for arbitrators actively facilitating settlement. **11.219**

(1.1) **May an arbitrator who has initiated settlement discussions be challenged when agreement on a settlement has failed?** An arbitrator, who has merely initiated settlement discussions without expressing any opinion as to the merits of the case, may not be successfully challenged. However, if the arbitrator has expressed an opinion on the merits of all or part of the case, in order to facilitate a settlement, such an arbitrator may potentially be challenged owing to lack of impartiality if no settlement can be achieved. **11.220**

As a matter of practice, most arbitrators will only hint at the possibility of a settlement and will not actively pursue or partake in settlement discussions in order not to create any basis for a party to question subsequently their ability to decide on the merits of the case in an impartial manner. **11.221**

(2) 'Private settlement' and its impact on the arbitral procedure

If the parties have reached a 'private settlement', they may request the arbitrators to terminate the proceedings. The termination will be recorded by way of an award (*supra* at 11.186). **11.222**

(3) Form and effect of a settlement (eg award on agreed terms)

If a dispute is settled, the parties may request that the settlement be confirmed in an award, ie for a consent award to be rendered (the Act, s 27, para 2). The arbitrators may only refuse to render such an award if, for example, the arbitrators find that one of the parties tries to deceive the other party, the award is contrary to public order or the issue in question is not arbitrable.[111] **11.223**

110 cf Hassler, A. and Cars, T., *Skiljeförfarande* (n 35) 31.
111 Prop 1998/99:35, 230.

11.224 Under the SCC Rules, the arbitrators may make an award confirming a settlement ('consent award') if the parties so request (SCC Rules, Art 39, para 1).

11.225 If the parties have reached a settlement, but do not request that it shall be confirmed by way of a consent award, the arbitral tribunal will terminate the proceedings. This will be done by way of an award which will not decide the issues which the parties have referred to the arbitrators (the Act, s 27, para 1). The arbitral tribunal may in such an award determine its own remuneration and impose liability therefore on the parties and decide on the apportionment of liability between the parties for such remuneration and other costs (the Act, s 37).

F. Costs of the arbitration

(1) General allocation of the costs of the proceedings

11.226 Unless the parties have provided otherwise, the arbitrators may, at the request of either party, make an order for the distribution of costs between the parties. The arbitrators' order may include interest, if a party has so requested (the Act, s 42). If a main hearing is held, the party's request for costs must be made no later than at the closing of such hearing, unless otherwise agreed between the parties. A party's claim for costs is usually expressed in a specified amount rather than in a lump sum. An itemized bill specifying the various costs is usually submitted.[112] With respect to the allocation of the costs, the arbitrators will follow any agreement of the parties. If no such agreement exists, by analogy from the Code of Judicial Procedure, the general rule is that the losing party is liable for its own expenses as well as those of the winning party. Such expenses will include a party's share of the compensation payable to the arbitrators, cost of evidence, reasonable fees and expenses of a party's counsel and compensation to a party for its own work and time spent, including loss of salary and other remuneration. Exceptions to this general rule may apply in certain situations, eg when the winning party has negligently brought an unnecessary action or if a party has otherwise negligently caused the other party to incur unnecessary costs or expenses.

11.227 If the SCC Rules apply, the arbitrators shall upon a party's request decide on the apportionment of the costs and determine whether either of the parties, in view of the outcome of the dispute and other circumstances, is to pay the winning party's costs relating to counsel and other expenses, including the compensation to the SCC Institute (SCC Rules, Art 43, para 5 and Art 44).

(2) Deposits or advances for costs or fees

11.228 Most arbitrators will require some form of security or advance from the parties to cover the fees and compensation for costs ultimately due to the arbitrators. This is usually done by the parties being asked to make an advance payment into an account held by the chairperson.

11.229 (2.1) **Is there case law authorizing or prohibiting arbitrators to order a party to pay an advance on the arbitration costs?** The Act expressly provides that the parties may be

112 cf *Arbitration in Sweden* (n 30) 135.

requested to provide security for the compensation ultimately due to the arbitrators (the Act, s 38).

(2.2) **May the raising of a set-off claim or counterclaim be made contingent upon payment of the corresponding advance for the relating arbitration costs (cf eg Article 30(5), ICC Rules)? May such a condition be agreed upon when entering into the arbitration agreement?** The arbitrators may fix separate security amounts for individual prayers for relief. It is thus possible for the arbitrators to make the filing of a set-off claim or counterclaim contingent upon an advance payment (the Act, s 38, para 1). If the SCC Rules apply, the SCC Institute may fix separate sums for the costs for a counterclaim and a plea by way of set-off claim (SCC Rules, Art 45, para 3). In the absence of payment for such separate advances, the counterclaim or set-off claim shall be dismissed (the Act, s 38, para 1 and SCC Rules, Art 45, para 4). **11.230**

(2.3) **What remedies exist against a party which does not pay its part of the advance on the arbitration costs (eg termination of the arbitration agreement)? How may the other party enforce its rights?** If a party fails to provide its share of the security for costs within the period of time stipulated by the arbitrators, the opposing party may provide the whole of the security. In the absence of such security being provided, the arbitrators may terminate the proceedings. A party, who fails to provide his/her share of the requested security, forfeits his/her right to rely on the arbitration agreement as a bar to court proceedings (the Act, s 5, para 3). **11.231**

The Act does not provide a party with the possibility to force the other party to pay its share of the security, neither by requesting a separate award on this issue from the arbitrators, nor by going to a court of law. This has been confirmed in case law.[113] Unless the parties have expressly agreed otherwise, the only remedies available are the ones described above. **11.232**

If the SCC Rules apply and if a party fails to pay his/her share of the advance on costs, the other party will be given the opportunity to pay instead. If such payment is not made, the case will be wholly or partly dismissed or written off (SCC Rules, Art 45, para 4). However, if a party chooses to also pay the advance on costs attributable to the other party, the party having made such a payment may subsequently request that the arbitral tribunal makes a separate award for reimbursement of the payment (*ibid*). **11.233**

(3) Costs of the administration by an arbitration institution

If the SCC Rules apply, a registration fee is payable to the SCC Institute upon filing the request for arbitration and in an amount determined by the SCC Institute's schedule of costs.[114] The SCC Institute shall fix an amount which, together with the accrued interest, shall constitute an advance on the arbitration costs, including the arbitrators' fees and the administrative fee of the SCC Institute. The SCC Institute's decision on the administrative fee is based on the amount in dispute in accordance with a table included in the Regulation for Arbitration Costs issued by the SCC Institute. For the purpose of calculating the **11.234**

113 cf NJA 2000, 773 (*3S Swedish Special Supplier AB ('3S') v Sky Park AB*).

114 cf Art 3 of the SCC Rules with reference to the Schedule of Costs (app II) in force of the date of the Request of Arbitration.

amount in dispute, the value of any counterclaim or set-off claim is to be added to the amount of the claim, with the exemption of claims for interest. Where the amount in dispute is not specified, the SCC Institute will fix the fee on the basis of its assessment of the case. However, if a case has required substantially more or less work than is considered normal, the SCC Institute may deviate from the amounts stated in the table.

(4) Arbitrators' fees: law and practice, judicial control

11.235 If the SCC Rules apply, the SCC Institute will decide on the arbitrators' fees. The decision will be based on the amount in dispute in accordance with a table included in the Regulation for Arbitration Costs issued by the SCC Institute. The principles applicable to such fees correspond to the principles regarding the administrative fee (*supra* at 11.234). The fee due to the co-arbitrator is fixed per person at 60 per cent of the total fee paid to the chairman, unless the SCC Institute decides otherwise in view of any special circumstances of the case. In general the arbitrators are entitled to 'reasonable' compensation for their work and disbursements.

11.236 (4.1) **May arbitrators fix their own fees in the award?** In the absence of an agreement by the parties stipulating otherwise (eg by reference to the SCC Rules), the parties shall be jointly and severally liable to pay reasonable compensation to the arbitrators for work and expenses. Under such circumstances it is for the arbitrators themselves to decide what level of compensation is reasonable and to state such compensation separately for each arbitrator as part of the award (the Act, s 37).

11.237 (4.2) **How can the parties change the arbitrators' fees once they are fixed?** The parties cannot unilaterally change the fees of the arbitrators, once they are fixed. Similarly, the parties cannot bind the arbitrators to an agreement as to the arbitrators' fees, unless the arbitrators were aware of the content of that agreement upon accepting their appointment as arbitrators. If a party is dissatisfied with the fees fixed by the arbitrators or by the SCC Institute (as applicable), it may bring an action in the District Court to have the fees reviewed and, if found to be unreasonable, reduced. If the fees are thus reduced this will apply also with regard to the other party, ie the one who did not bring the action.

11.238 (4.3) **Are the arbitrators' fees subject to income tax if (i) the place of arbitration; or (ii) the normal residence or place of business of the arbitrator is located in this country?** Arbitrators' fees are either regarded as income from employment or as business income if the services are performed in the arbitrator's business.

11.239 If the arbitrator is a Swedish tax resident (as defined), the arbitrator's fees will be subject to income tax in Sweden.[115] If the arbitrator is not a Swedish tax resident, the arbitrator's fees may still be subject to Swedish income tax if they are attributable to a business carried on from a permanent establishment in Sweden. If the foreign arbitrator receives the fee as employment income, he or she may be liable to special income tax for foreigners at a flat

[115] Individuals are tax residents of Sweden if they are domiciled or have their habitual abode in Sweden. In addition, if the individual earlier has been domiciled in Sweden, he or she may be considered tax resident in Sweden if he or she maintains essential ties with Sweden. Companies are tax residents of Sweden if they are incorporated in Sweden.

rate of 25 per cent. However, the fee may be exempt from Swedish income tax if the arbitrator does not stay in Sweden for more than 183 days during a 12-month period and the fee is paid by, or on behalf of, an employer who is not a Swedish resident. Further, the fee may not be borne by a permanent establishment in Sweden.

The above is based on Swedish domestic law. However, Sweden's right to tax a certain income may be reduced under an applicable income tax treaty between Sweden and the country in which the tax payer is tax resident. **11.240**

(4.4) Are arbitrators' fees submitted to VAT? If yes, is the duty to pay such tax linked to (i) the place of arbitration; or (ii) the arbitrator's general residence? If the arbitrator's fee is received as income from employment, it will generally not be subject to VAT. However, if the fee is received as business income, it will in principle be subject to VAT in Sweden if the arbitrator has established his other business or has a fixed establishment from which the service is supplied in Sweden, or, in absence of such a place of business or fixed establishment, the arbitrator has his permanent address or usually resides in Sweden. If none of the foregoing applies, the fees will not be subject to VAT in Sweden. **11.241**

(5) Attorneys' fees and the winning party's claim for reimbursement

Unless otherwise agreed by the parties, the arbitrators may, at the request of a party, order the other party to pay compensation for the party's costs (see the Act, s 42). Such costs will generally include attorney's fees. See further *supra* at 11.226. **11.242**

(5.1) May in-house lawyers charge fees or may a party request costs of in-house lawyers to be reimbursed? There are no mandatory provisions for determining legal fees. However, the costs which may be recovered by the successful party would usually include the following: (i) the party's share of the compensation payable to the arbitrators; (ii) the party's share of fees and charges paid to the arbitration institution under whose auspices the arbitration may have taken place; (iii) costs of evidence produced by the party (such as compensation to witnesses and experts, etc); (iv) fees and expenses for external counsel; and (v) to some extent, compensation to the party itself for work done and time spent on the case, including loss of salary or other remuneration and also cost in respect of in-house lawyers.[116] **11.243**

(6) Time and form of the decision on costs

In Swedish arbitral practice decisions on costs are generally given as a part of the final award on the merits. The decision on cost will thus form a part of the final award. As regards the compensation due to the arbitrators this follows directly from the Act (s 37, para 2). **11.244**

(6.1) May the arbitrators' decision on costs (allocation and amount of costs to be reimbursed) be challenged separately from the award itself? Are there time limits for such a remedy? If a party is dissatisfied with the tribunal's decision in an award relating to compensation due to them, it may bring the matter before a District Court provided that it commences its action no later than three months from the day such party received the award, or in case of a corrected or amended award, no later than three months from the date **11.245**

[116] cf Cars, T., *Lagen om skiljeförfarande*, 188.

such party received the award in its final form (the Act, s 41). Such an action may be brought separately from a challenge of the award itself. An action relating to the allocation as between the parties of the arbitrators' costs is permitted only in the event that the award into which the decision has been incorporated provides that the arbitrators have declined to assume jurisdiction (the Act, s 36, para 2). The award must clearly specify the procedure to be followed by a party wishing to bring an action against the arbitrators' decision as to their own fees (the Act, s 41, para 1). The competent court is the District Court in the place where the arbitral proceedings took place, or if no such place is indicated, the District Court of Stockholm (the Act, s 43, para 3).

11.246 Following a decision by the Swedish Supreme Court,[117] it has been established that a party, who is dissatisfied with the decision of the SCC Institute as to the compensation due to the arbitrators, may also bring the matter before a District Court. This is so notwithstanding that the SCC Rules state that such compensation shall be 'finally determined' by the SCC Institute (SCC Rules, Art 43(2) and (3)), and notwithstanding that the *travaux préparatoires* state that the state court is not competent to decide upon a decision on the compensation of the arbitrators in case the decision is made by a third party like, for example, the ICC International Court of Arbitration in Paris.[118]

11.247 (6.2) **Are the arbitrators entitled and/or legally obliged to rule on the amount of one or both parties' costs that are recoverable?** Unless otherwise agreed between the parties, the arbitrators may, at the request of a party, order the other party to pay compensation for the party's costs and determine the manner in which the compensation to the arbitrators is finally to be allocated as between the parties (the Act, s 42). The arbitrators are thus entitled, but not obliged, to rule on the amount of each party's costs to the extent that they may be recoverable.

G. Publication of the award

(1) Publication with or without the consent of the parties

11.248 An arbitral award may not be published by the arbitrators or by the SCC Institute (if the arbitration has been conducted under the SCC Rules) unless both parties have agreed to publication (SCC Rules, Art 46). However, and as there is no duty of confidentiality covering the parties to an arbitration (unless the parties have agreed otherwise), each party may unilaterally choose to publish the award.[119]

(2) Practice of publication (eg in specific legal journals)

11.249 Publication of an award is unusual. Awards in shipping cases are, however, occasionally published in the Norwegian periodical *Nordiske domme i sjofartsanliggender*. To the extent other awards are published, such publication takes place in various periodicals and legal literature. For instance, awards are now being reported in an anonymous form in the *Stockholm International Arbitration Report* published by the SCC Institute.

[117] Decision of the Swedish Supreme Court of 3 December 2008 (case no Ö 4227–06).

[118] Prop 1998/99:35, 169 and 241.

[119] cf Oldenstam, R. and Pachelbel, J., 'Confidentiality and Arbitration—a few reflections and practical notes' [2006] *SchiedsVZ* 31–5.

VI. Amendment and challenge of the award; liability of arbitrators

A. Amendment, correction or interpretation of the award

(1) Motion to amend or correct an award

At a party's request made no later than 30 days after the party received the award, the arbitral tribunal must rule on a prayer for relief which should have been, but has not been ruled on in the award (the Act, s 27, para 2). Likewise, at a party's request made no later than 30 days after the party received the award, the arbitrators may interpret the award in writing (the Act, s 32, para 1). However, before the arbitrators make any additional ruling or an interpretation, both parties must be given the opportunity to express their views (*ibid*, para 3). **11.250**

(2) Interpretation of the award by the tribunal

If the arbitrators observe that an award contains any obvious error as a consequence of a typographical, computation or other similar mistake committed by the arbitrators or another person, or if the arbitrators by oversight have failed to decide an issue which should have been resolved in the award, they may within 30 days of the delivery of the award decide to correct or supplement the award (the Act, s 32, para 1). If the arbitrators decide to supplement the award, it must be done within 60 days (the Act, s 32, para 2). **11.251**

As mentioned above (*supra* at 11.250) the arbitrators may also correct, supplement or interpret an award if any of the parties should so request within 30 days from receiving the award (the Act, s 32, para 1). If the arbitrators at a party's request decide to correct, supplement or interpret the award, such correction, supplementation or interpretation shall be made within 30 days from the arbitrators' receipt of the party's request (the Act, s 32, para 2). Before any decision to correct, supplement or interpret the award is made, both parties must be afforded an opportunity to express their views on the matter. **11.252**

The SCC Rules contain similar provisions allowing for correction, supplementing and interpretation of an award (SCC Rules, Arts 41 and 42). **11.253**

B. Appeal on the merits

(1) Admissibility and procedure of an appeal on the merits

If the arbitration agreement is silent with regard to the possibility to appeal against the award on the merits, the parties are presumed to have excluded appeal to any court of law.[120] Thus, the main rule is that an award is final and binding when rendered. **11.254**

(1.1) May the parties agree on an appeal to another arbitral tribunal? The parties may stipulate that an appeal on the merits of the case is allowed to a second panel of arbitrators. However, such agreements are very unusual. An arbitration agreement that provides for an appeal to the courts on the merits is valid, but is not covered by the Act. Such an agreement would be equally unusual. **11.255**

[120] Prop 1998/99:35, 139.

(2) Possibility to exclude an appeal (eg in the arbitration clause)

11.256 The parties to an arbitration agreement are—*de iure*—presumed to have excluded the possibility of an appeal against the award on the merits to any court of law, unless otherwise agreed between the parties.

C. Setting aside of the award

(1) Reasons for setting aside an award

11.257 Section 33 of the Act describes the situations in which an award may be void as distinct from challengeable. An award may be void in part only (the Act, s 33, para 2). The circumstances rendering an award void are the following:

(i) the award includes determination of an issue, which under Swedish law, is not arbitrable (*ibid*, para 1, point 1);
(ii) the award or the manner in which the award arose is patently incompatible with the basic principles of the Swedish legal system (*ordre public*) (*ibid*, para 1, point 2); and
(iii) the award does not fulfil the requirements with regard to written form and signing (*ibid*, para 1, point 3).

11.258 An award is challengeable and may be set aside by the court in the following cases (the Act, s 34):

(i) the award is not covered by a valid arbitration agreement between the parties;
(ii) the arbitrators have made the award after the expiration of a period of time stipulated by the parties or have otherwise exceeded their mandate;
(iii) the arbitral proceedings, according to s 47 of the Act, should not have taken place in Sweden;
(iv) an arbitrator has been appointed in a manner contrary to the agreement between the parties or the provisions of the Act;
(v) an arbitrator was unauthorized owing to any circumstance set forth in ss 7 or 8 of the Act; or
(vi) through no fault of the party, any other irregularity has occurred in the course of the proceedings which probably influenced the outcome of the case.

The above does not apply if the award terminates the arbitration proceedings without having determined the matters submitted to the arbitrators (see *infra* at 11.263).

11.259 A party is not entitled to rely on the existence of a circumstance which he may be considered to have waived by taking part in the proceedings without any objection or otherwise. A party is not to be treated as having accepted the arbitrator's jurisdiction to determine the issue referred to arbitration solely by having appointed an arbitrator.

11.260 (1.1) **May an award made according to international or foreign procedural rules be the object of an application for setting aside before the national courts?** As stated above the characterization of an arbitral award as foreign or national does not depend on the procedural rules under which the arbitration proceedings have been conducted. A Swedish award (definition see *infra* at 11.286) can be challenged in Sweden, while a foreign award (definition see *infra* at 11.287)—in accordance with the New York Convention—can only be refused acknowledgement and enforcement in connection with proceedings being brought for such acknowledgement and enforcement (see *infra* at 11293–4).

(2) Procedure and deadlines for challenging an award

If an award is void according to s 33 of the Act it is not necessary to take any steps to have it set aside. A declaratory judgment to such effect by an ordinary court may, however, be desirable for a number of practical reasons. There is no time limit for bringing such an action. **11.261**

A party who wishes to challenge an award must bring an action in a court no later than three months after he or she received the award. The competent court is the relevant Court of Appeal for the place of arbitration. If no place of the arbitration proceedings is indicated, an action is to be tried by the Svea Court of Appeal (the Act, s 43, para 1). If a ground for challenge is substantiated, the court will set aside the award. The court can set aside the award only partially (the Act, s 34), if the part affected by the ground of challenge is severable from the remaining part of the award.[121] **11.262**

If the award merely terminates the arbitration proceedings without the arbitrators having determined the matters which have been submitted to them, ie an award dismissing the proceedings, a party may appeal the award to the relevant Court of Appeal for the place of arbitration or, if no such place is indicated, to the Svea Court of Appeal (the Act, ss 36 and 43). Such an appeal must be made within three months from the date on which the party received the award, or in the case of an amended or interpreted award, from the date on which the party received the award in its final form (the Act, s 36, para 1). **11.263**

In this context it should be noted that the court may stay proceedings concerning the invalidity or setting aside of an award for a certain period of time in order to provide the arbitrators with an opportunity to resume the arbitral proceedings or to take some other measures which will eliminate the invalidity or the ground for challenging the award, provided, however, that the court holds that the claim in the case shall be accepted and either of the parties requests a stay or that both parties request a stay (the Act, s 35, para 1). **11.264**

(2.1) Who may (or must) represent a party in a proceeding for setting aside an award? There are no restrictions as to who may or must represent a party in the proceeding for setting aside an award. Thus, eg a foreign lawyer may represent a party in such an action. However, as the proceedings before the courts in Sweden are conducted in Swedish, language may pose a practical barrier for anyone not Swedish to assume such representation. **11.265**

(2.2) Do specific time limits exist for setting-aside procedures concerning awards on jurisdiction? No, the same time limit of three months apply to such awards (the Act, s 34, para 3). **11.266**

(3) Effect of a court decision which sets the award aside

(3.1) Does the setting-aside action suspend the enforcement? If so, do any remedies exist to reinstate enforcement? A court action does not delay the execution since it constitutes no ground for suspension. Enforcement is impossible, however, if the award is void.[122] When a court has set aside an award, the award is no longer valid and may not form the basis for any execution proceedings. **11.267**

---

[121] cf *Arbitration in Sweden* (n 30) 154–5.

[122] Enforcement Code (181:774), ch 3 s 15, para 1.

11.268 **(3.2) After an award has been set aside, does the underlying arbitration agreement revive or remain in force or is it exhausted or deemed terminated?** The generally held opinion is that an arbitration agreement is still applicable even though the award is void or set aside, unless the award is void because no valid arbitration agreement existed.[123]

(4) Appeal against the court's decision to set aside or not set aside the award

11.269 A decision by the Court of Appeal to set aside or not set aside an award may not be appealed. However, the Court of Appeal may grant leave to appeal the decision if it is of importance, as a matter of precedent, that the appeal be considered by the Supreme Court.

(5) Possibility of the parties to exclude actions for setting aside

11.270 The parties may not exclude the statutory provisions rendering an award void.[124] If neither of the parties in a commercial relationship has its domicile or place of business in Sweden, the parties may, however, by express agreement in writing exclude or limit the applicability of the grounds for setting aside an award (the Act, s 51). A party may lose its right to challenge an award by waiving the irregularity by acquiescence, for example by taking part in the proceedings without objection or otherwise (the Act, s 34, para 2). However, a party shall not be treated as having accepted the arbitrator's jurisdiction merely by having appointed an arbitrator (*ibid*). As regards an allegation that an arbitrator has not been qualified, the party loses its right to challenge the award on such ground if such party has not complied with the period of time stipulated in respect of any objections against the appointment of arbitrators (*ibid*).

D. Liability of arbitrators

(1) Duties and liabilities of arbitrators regarding the conduct of the proceedings

11.271 **(1.1) Do the courts and/or authorities rely on a contractual relationship between the parties and the arbitrator(s), irrespective of whether institutional or *ad-hoc* arbitration is concerned? What is the legal qualification of such a contract (eg provision of services)?** The relationship between an arbitrator and the parties is contractual in nature and concerns the provision of a service. This would apply regardless of whether the proceedings are *ad hoc* or institutional.

11.272 **(1.2) Are there court decisions (or authorities) determining which law governs the question of liability of an arbitrator? What is the position of those courts/authorities as to whether and to which extent a legal liability of an arbitrator (or arbitral institution) may be established?** The liability of an arbitrator follows general principles of contract, ie an arbitrator may be held liable in damages if he or she causes a loss, cost or expense to one or both of the parties through negligence in the performance of his or her duties. There are no particular court decisions or authorities on this subject.

11.273 **(1.3) Is an arbitrator subject to criminal prosecution?** Yes; if an arbitrator has committed a criminal offence in performing his or her duties as an arbitrator, he or she may be subject to criminal prosecution.

123 SOU 1994:81, 109.
124 Prop 1998/99:35, 156.

(2) Possibility to restrict or exclude the arbitrator's liability

It is possible for an arbitrator to restrict his or her liability by way of contract. However, an arbitrator may not exclude his or her liability altogether as it is generally not deemed possible to exclude liability for wilful misconduct or gross negligence. Article 48 of the SCC Rules provides an example of a contractual restriction on liability, as it provides that '[n]either the SCC Institute nor the arbitrator(s) are liable to any party for any act or omission in connection with the arbitration unless such act or omission constitutes wilful misconduct or gross negligence'. **11.274**

VII. Enforcement of national awards

(1) Requirement of a particular procedure to make an award enforceable

An *award* is enforceable without a court order or other *exequatur* when given, unless the award is purely of a declaratory nature. If the losing party does not perform voluntarily, the award may simply be brought to the relevant execution authority (*Kronofogdemyndighet*) if the winning party desires execution of the award in Sweden. It would also be possible to bring an action in court based on the award, but such procedure is not often used. **11.275**

Unlike in respect of a judgment of a court, the execution authority will make a summary check of the award prior to the execution thereof. In making the summary check the execution authority will first ascertain that the arbitration agreement does not contain any provision giving a party the right to appeal against the award (see *infra* under 'Setting aside of the award') or, if such right exists, that the *period* for such appeal has expired. It will also check summarily that the award is not void under the Act (see *infra* under 'Setting aside of the award'). Finally, the execution authority will ascertain that the award is made in writing and is duly signed. If an action has been initiated in court with the purpose of having the award declared void or set aside, execution is possible only if the court decides that execution may take place. **11.276**

If an arbitrator wishes to enforce the order in the award as to its compensation, the rules and procedure accounted for above are subject to the following modifications. The arbitrator must attach to the application evidence that the award has been served on the party against whom enforcement is sought. The period of three months within which a party may challenge in court the amount of compensation must have expired. **11.277**

(1.1) Does the national law make any difference between foreign and domestic awards, and if so, which are the criteria? Does there exist an additional notion of award for the purpose of obtaining *exequatur* (France: international awards)? An arbitral award is 'foreign' if it has been rendered abroad (the Act, s 52). Consequently, all awards rendered in Sweden are considered 'Swedish', even if all parties are non-residents of Sweden, the transaction in dispute has no relation to Sweden and Swedish law does not govern the substance of the case. In classifying an award as foreign or Swedish a territorial test is applied: an award is regarded as having been given in the state in which the arbitration proceedings have taken place (the Act, s 52, para 2). Accordingly, the place where the award has been signed or made available to the parties is not decisive. Furthermore, it is immaterial which arbitration law or which system of arbitration procedure has been used. The procedure for **11.278**

enforcement of a foreign award is different to the enforcement procedure with respect to Swedish awards.

11.279 (1.2) **May awards granting conservatory/interim measures be subject to enforcement?** As mentioned *supra* at 11.162, in *ad hoc* arbitrations under the Act such measures will not be given as awards but as decisions and are not enforceable. However, under the SCC Rules in force since 2007 a party is entitled to apply to the tribunal to render a decision on a conservatory or interim measure by an enforceable award.

(2) Details of such enforcement procedure (competent court, reasons for rejection of motion etc)

11.280 The procedure of enforcement of a Swedish award is as follows: if the execution authority is satisfied, the application will be transmitted to the other party with an invitation to state any objection it may have. Such party may raise any of the matters included in the execution authority's *preliminary* inquiry (eg that the award is void). Nonetheless, if the execution authority finds reasons to believe that the award is void, the authority shall order the applicant to initiate an action in court unless such action is already pending. The execution authority will, however, not assess whether the award may be set aside upon a party's challenge.

(3) Appeal against the decision granting exequatur

11.281 A party being subject to execution proceedings may appeal against the execution decision of the execution authority. Such appeal is made to the applicable District Court not later than three weeks after the decision on the execution has been communicated to the party in question. Further appeals to the Court of Appeal are not possible unless the Court of Appeal grants leave to appeal. An appeal does not delay the execution. Only a special order by the District Court or, if applicable, the Court of Appeal can stop the execution.

(4) Appeal (and procedure) if exequatur *has been refused*

11.282 In case execution is refused, the party seeking enforcement may appeal against such decision. Such appeal is also made to the relevant District Court, and further appeal to the Court of Appeal is possible only if the Court of Appeal grants leave to appeal.

(5) Procedure of enforcement (attachment of bank accounts etc)

11.283 The procedure of enforcement of a national arbitral award regarding a specific attachment of accounts etc follows the same general rules as applicable to a respective enforcement of a judgment of a national court.

11.284 (5.1) **At the stage of enforcement, may the losing party invoke arguments and circumstances which are based on facts which have occurred before (or after) the award was made?** The losing party may raise any objections to the effect that the award is void as to make enforcement impossible. In addition, it may claim that the award is challengeable, but it can only prevent execution if it is able to prove that there is a reasonable chance of success in an action brought to challenge the award. Consequently, if the period for challenging the award has expired by the time execution is applied for, the execution authority will not refuse enforcement on this ground, unless proceedings challenging the award have actually been commenced. It should be noted that the grounds which can be invoked are principally of a procedural nature.

(5.2) May the losing party invoke a set-off based on claims that are not related to the matter of the arbitral proceeding? Is it material whether such claim came into existence before or after the award was made? The losing party may invoke a set-off as an objection to execution provided that the set-off claim is established by a judgment, an award or other decision upon which execution may be based or otherwise is established by a promissory note, and provided that other prerequisites for a set-off are fulfilled, including that the set-off claim is due and that the claim is of such nature that it can be used as a set-off.[125] **11.285**

VIII. Foreign awards

A. Recognition and/or enforcement of foreign awards (national law)

(1) Rules according to national law

As stated above (*supra* at 11.278), under Swedish law an award is 'foreign' if it has been rendered abroad (the Act, s 52, para 1). Consequently, all awards rendered in Sweden are considered 'Swedish', even if all parties are non-residents of Sweden, the transaction in dispute has no relation to Sweden and Swedish law does not govern the substance of the case. **11.286**

As regards 'foreign' awards, ss 52-60 in the Act constitute the incorporation into Swedish law of the provisions of the New York Convention. Consequently, Swedish law corresponds to that convention. Subject to certain reservations, a foreign arbitral award is valid and enforceable in Sweden (the Act, s 53). **11.287**

A foreign arbitral award will not be valid and enforceable in Sweden if the challenging party, ie the party against whom the award is invoked, can prove any of the following circumstances (all of which are exhaustively set forth in the Act, ss 54 and 55): **11.288**

(i) one of the parties to the arbitration agreement under the applicable law did not have authority to enter into it or was not properly represented, or the agreement is invalid under the law to which the parties have subjected it or, failing any indication thereon, under the law of the country where the award was made;
(ii) it was not given proper notice of the appointment of the arbitrator or of the arbitration proceedings or was otherwise unable to present its case;
(iii) the award deals with a difference not contemplated by or not falling within the terms of the submission to arbitration, or it contains decisions on matters beyond the scope of the arbitration agreement, provided that, if the decision on a matter which falls within the mandate can be separated from those which fall outside the mandate, that part of the award which contains decisions on matters falling within the mandate may be recognized and enforced;
(iv) the composition of the arbitral tribunal or the arbitral procedure was not in accordance with the agreement of the parties, or, failing such agreement, was not in accordance with the law of the country where the arbitration took place;

[125] Enforcement Code (1981:774), ch 3 s 21, para 1.

(v) the award has not yet become binding on the parties, or has been set aside or suspended by a competent authority of the country in which, or under the law of which, the award was made;

(vi) the award includes the resolution of an issue which is not arbitrable under Swedish law; or

(vii) the recognition or enforcement of the award would be patently incompatible with the basic principles of the Swedish legal system (*ordre public*).

(2) Requirements to be fulfilled by the applicant (procedure, time limits)

11.289 An application for the enforcement of a foreign arbitral award is submitted to the Svea Court of Appeal in Stockholm (the Act, s 56, para 1). The application must include the original or a certified copy of the award and, unless the court decides otherwise, a certified Swedish translation thereof (the Act, s 56, para 2). If the party against whom enforcement is sought alleges that the parties have not entered into any valid arbitration agreement, the applicant must also submit the original or a certified copy of the arbitration agreement together with a certified translation thereof into the Swedish language or otherwise show that a valid arbitration agreement has been concluded (the Act, s 58, para 1). There are no particular time limits applicable to the enforcement procedure.

(3) Remedies against decisions granting or declining enforcement

11.290 If the Court of Appeal grants the application for enforcement, the arbitral award will become enforceable in the same manner as a final and binding judgment of a competent Swedish court (the Act, s 59). Both parties may appeal to the Supreme Court. A decision to grant execution will not be suspended owing to such appeal. However, if the Supreme Court reverses the decision of the Court of Appeal the decision will be revoked and any property transferred by virtue thereof must be returned.

11.291 In case the Svea Court of Appeal declares a foreign arbitral award unenforceable, such decision may also be appealed to the Supreme Court.

B. Recognition and/or enforcement of foreign awards (conventions, treaties)

(1) Specific bilateral or multilateral treaties

11.292 Sweden has ratified both the Geneva Protocol of 1923, the Geneva Convention of 1927, and the New York Convention of 1958, without availing itself of any of the reservations open to the contracting states. As Sweden did not make any reciprocity reservation when acceding to the New York Convention, the conditions of the Convention, which have been incorporated into the Act, apply to awards irrespective of where they were made. Accordingly, the rule of the New York Convention that no *exequatur* is necessary from the country where the award was made, is applicable to all cases. Sweden has also ratified the Convention on the Settlement of Investment Disputes between States and Nationals of Other States (the Washington Convention) of 1965. A special statute of 1966 declares that awards made in accordance with this Convention are valid in Sweden. They are immediately enforceable in the same manner as ordinary court judgments if they contain an order for payment of money.

(2) Existence of a standard procedure for the enforcement of foreign awards

As stated above (*supra* at 11.289) an application for the enforcement of a foreign arbitral award shall be submitted to the Svea Court of Appeal in Stockholm (the Act, s 56, para 1). The Court of Appeal will notify the party against whom enforcement is sought and give such party an opportunity to raise any objection that it may have (the Act, s 57). A party that opposes enforcement on the ground that it has applied to have the award set aside or suspended in the jurisdiction of origin, may be required by the Court of Appeal to provide security if the applicant so requests. In such case, the Court of Appeal may also postpone its decision (the Act, s 58, para 2). If the Court of Appeal finds it desirable, it may request a further exchange of written statements and may arrange a hearing. **11.293**

(3) Extent of examination and review of the award by the court

The Court of Appeal will determine whether any of the circumstances accounted for *supra* at 11.288 are present and may, if this is found to be the case, render the award unenforceable in whole or part. Unless any such circumstance is manifestly present the Court of Appeal will limit its review to such circumstances (if any) alleged to be present by the party against whom enforcement is sought. The burden will also be on that party to prove the existence of any such circumstance. The list of circumstances set forth *supra* at 11.288, which may render an award unenforceable, is exhaustive and the Court of Appeal will not review any other aspects of the award. **11.294**

C. Application of the New York Convention

(1) Application of the New York Convention in practice

The principles as laid down in the New York Convention have been incorporated in the Act and are applied by Swedish courts as described *supra* at 11.293. **11.295**

(2) Examples of decisions which do not apply the Convention correctly

The Swedish courts apply the New York Convention (*supra* at 11.293) as incorporated in the Act. Legal practice complies with the principles of the New York Convention. **11.296**

IX. Appendix

A. National legislation

Lag om skiljeförfarande 1999:116 = Swedish Arbitration Act, entered into force: 1 April 1999.

B. Arbitral institutions

The Arbitration Institute of the Stockholm Chamber of Commerce (SCC)
POBox 16050
SE-103 22 Stockholm, Sweden
Telephone: + 46 8 555 100 00
Fax: + 46 8 566 316 50
Email: arbitration@chamber.se

The present rules of the SCC Institute became effective from 1 January 2007. They are available in Russian, English, French, German, Chinese, Spanish and Swedish. Since 1995, the SCC Institute furthermore provides optional Rules for Expedited Arbitrations which have been amended as of 1 April 1999. Further, the SCC Institute provides Insurance Arbitration Rules, Procedures and Services under the UNCITRAL Arbitration Rules and Mediation Rules.

The SCC Institute was established in 1917 and has over the past few decades emerged as one of the leading international arbitral institutions in the world. In most cases handled by the SCC Institute both parties are from countries other than Sweden. The SCC Institute can therefore be regarded as a truly international institution. It has for a number of years been in a unique position with respect to trade disputes between Western businesses or nations and the trading activities of Eastern countries. Arbitrations under the auspices of the SCC Institute cover the usual range of subjects of international arbitration, such as sale of goods, construction projects, licence agreements and many other categories of commercial issues as well as investment disputes.

The SCC Institute has in many cases acted as appointed authority under the UNCITRAL Arbitration Rules.

C. Model arbitration clauses and other patterns

The SCC Institute provides several model clauses, each selecting different rules for arbitration. Depending on the subject matter of the case and the parties' intentions, model clauses concerning insurance arbitration or expedited arbitration as well as med-arb clauses are available besides the clause for 'regular' SCC arbitration. The Model Arbitration Clause providing for the Arbitration Rules of the Arbitration Institute of the Stockholm Chamber of Commerce is as follows:

> Any dispute, controversy or claim arising out of or in connection with this contract, or the breach, termination or invalidity thereof, shall be finally settled by arbitration in accordance with the Rules of the Arbitration Institute of the Stockholm Chamber of Commerce.

D. Bibliography

Arbitration in Sweden (2nd edn, Stockholm Chamber of Commerce, Stockholm, 1984).

Bogdan, Michael, *Svensk internationell privat- och processrätt* (7th edn, Norstedts, Stockholm, 2008).

Bogdan, Michael, 'Some Arbitration-Related Problems of Swedish Private International Law' [1990] *Ybk Arb Inst Stockholm Chamber Com* 70–9.

Broomé, Bo, 'Näringslivets tvistlösning' [1995/1996] *JT* 457.

Calissendorff, Gotthard, 'Jura novit curia i internationella skiljeförfaranden i Sverige' [1995/1996] *JT* 141–9.

Cars, Thorsten, *Lagen om skiljeförfarande—En kommentar* (fakta Info Direkt Sweden, Stockholm, 1999).

Dillén, Nils, *Bidrag till läran om skiljeavtalet* (Gustaf Larssons, Stockholm, 1933).

Fitger, Peter and Mikael Mellqvist, *Domstolsprocessen - En kommentar till rättegångsbalken* (2nd edn, Norstedts, Stockholm, 2002).

Franke, Ulf, 'International arbitration in Sweden' (1985) 2 *Int'l Construction L Rev* 159.

Franke, Ulf, 'The Arbitration Institute of the Stockholm Chamber of Commerce' [1983] *Ybk Arb Inst Stockholm Chamber Com* 6–8.

Franke, Ulf, '*Arbitration*' in *Swedish Law* (Juristförlaget, Stockholm, 1994) 532.
Hagberg, Lennart, 'Salient Features of the Swedish Arbitral Procedure' [1990] *Ybk Arb Inst Stockholm Chamber Com* 34–54.
Hassler, Åke and Cars, Thorsten, *Skiljeförfarande* (2nd edn, Norstedts, Stockholm, 1989).
Heuman, Lars, *Arbitration Law of Sweden: Practice and Procedure* (Juris Publishing, Huntington, 2003).
Heuman, Lars and Jarvin, Sigvard (eds), *The Swedish Arbitration Act of 1999, Five Years on: A Critical review of strengths and weaknesses* (Juris Publishing, Huntington, 2006).
Heuman, Lars, 'Rättelse av skiljedom' [1992] *Ybk Arb Inst Stockholm Chamber Com* 19–30.
Heuman, Lars, 'Power of Attorney—In Swedish Arbitration' [1994] *Ybk Arb Inst Stockholm Chamber Com* 45–54.
Hjerner, Lars, 'Recourse to Law Courts in International Arbitration in Sweden' in ICC Publication no 321, *Hommage à Frédéric Eisemann* (Paris, 1978) 61.
Hjerner, Lars, 'On Partial Awards, Orders and Other Decisions in Arbitral Proceedings, in Particular with Respect to Arbitration in Sweden' [1984] *Ybk Arb Inst Stockholm Chamber Com* 31–44.
Hobér, Kaj, 'Svensk domstolspraxis i skiljedomsrätt 1987–1990' [1991] *Ybk Arb Inst Stockholm Chamber Com* 7–34.
Hobér, Kaj, 'International Commercial Arbitration in Sweden: Two Salient Problem Areas' in Ove Bring, Said Mahmoudi and Jan Ramberg (eds), *Festskrift till Lars Hjerner, Studies in International Law* (Norstedts, Stockholm, 1990) 235–97.
Hobér, Kaj, *Enforcing Foreign Arbitral Awards Against Russian Entities* (Transnational Juris, New York, 1994) 85.
Hobér, Kaj, 'Arbitration Reform in Sweden' (2001) 17 *Arb Int'l* 351.
Hobér, Kaj and Foerster, Alexander, 'Die neue Schiedsordnung des Schiedsgerichtsinstituts der Stockholmer Handelskammer' [2007] *SchiedsVZ* 207.
Hobér, Kaj and McKechnie, William,'New Rules of the Arbitration Institute of the Stockholm Chamber of Commerce' (2007) 1 (6) *Global Arb Rev* 21.
Karnell, Gunnar, 'Patent och skiljedom, giltighets- och intrångsfrågor' in *Festskrift till Sveriges Advokatsamfund 1887–1987* (Norstedts, Stockholm, 1987) 285–312.
Lindskog, Stefan, *Skiljeförfarande: En kommentar* (Norstedts, Stockholm, 2005).
Madsen, Finn, *Commercial Arbitration in Sweden* (2nd edn, OUP, Oxford, 2006).
Magnusson, Annette and Shaughnessy, Patricia, 'The 2007 Arbitration Rules of the Arbitration Institute of the Stockholm Chamber of Commerce' [2006] (3) *Stockholm Int'l Arb Rev* 33.
Nordenson, Ulf K., '*The arbitral tribunal*' [1990] in Swedish and *Int'l Arb* 19.
Oldenstam, Robin and v. Pachelbel, Johann, 'Confidentiality and Arbitration—a few reflections and practical notes' [2006] *SchiedsVZ* 31–5.
Pålsson, Lennart, Romkonventionen—Tillämplig lag för avtalsförpliktelser (Norstedts, Stockholm, 1998).
Pålsson, Lennart, *Svensk rättspraxis i internationell processrätt* (Norstedts, Stockholm, 1989).
Schöldström, Patrik, *The Arbitrator's Mandate* (Jure, Stockholm, 1998).
Shaughnessy, Patricia and Söderlund, Christer, 'Observation' [2005] *SIAR* issue 2, 264.
Strempel, Hans and Hobér, Kaj, 'Das neue schwedische Gesetz über Schiedsverfahren: neue Regeln für das Schiedsinstitut der Handelskammer Stockholm' [1999] supplement 4 (4) *Recht und Praxis der Schiedsgerichtsbarkeit (RPS)*, Deutsche Institution für Schiedsgerichtsbarkeit e.V.
Weigand, Frank-Bernd, 'The UNCITRAL Model Law: New draft arbitration acts in Germany and Sweden' (1995) 11 (4) *Arb Int'l* 397.
Welamson, Lars, *Konkursrätt* (Norstedts, Stockholm, 1961).
Westerling, Bengt, 'Rättegångsbalken och skiljeförfarandet' [1981] *Ybk Arb Inst Stockholm Chamber Com* 11–18.
Westerling, Bengt, 'Void and challengeable Awards in Swedish Arbitral Procedure' [1984] *Ybk Arb Inst Stockholm Chamber Com* 45–53.

12

SWITZERLAND

Pierre A. Karrer and Peter A. Straub

I. Introduction

A. Current status of the law on arbitration

(1) Short history

Since medieval times, in Switzerland, arbitration has been used to resolve disputes. In the law of nations, Switzerland has always been a promoter of arbitration. The well known Alabama arbitration was conducted in 1872 in Geneva.[1] **12.01**

Switzerland is a federal state. Under the Swiss Federal Constitution, substantive private law is a federal matter. There is a civil-law style codification in the Swiss Federal Civil Code (CC) and the Swiss Federal Code of Obligations (CO). Switzerland is also a member of the Vienna Convention on the International Sales of Goods. By contrast, procedural law is a still cantonal (state) matter and will remain so until 2011. Accordingly, there are codes of civil procedure in each of the 26 cantons. There is no dual system of cantonal and federal courts. Rather, the judicial system is cantonal at the trial and intermediate appellate levels (District Court; Cantonal Supreme Court, in some cantons also a Commercial Court, and, in some cantons, additionally a Court of Cassation), and there is one Swiss Federal Supreme Court for civil (and other) matters. **12.02**

[1] For a brief account, see Newsletter of East Asia Branch of the Chartered Institute of Arbitrators, July 2008.

12.03 In the twentieth century, Switzerland became one of the leading countries for international commercial arbitration. No particular connection with Switzerland is required for an arbitration to have its seat in Switzerland. For most of the twentieth century, namely until 1989, there was no distinction between domestic and international arbitration. Arbitration was considered a procedural matter, and covered under the various cantonal codes of civil procedure. In 1969, various cantons entered into an inter-cantonal treaty agreeing on a uniform law on arbitration, the Intercantonal Concordat on Arbitration (Concordat), to replace the provisions in the various codes of civil procedure. By now, all cantons have joined the Concordat, and none of the special cantonal provisions survive. The cantons enacted accompanying legislation to go with the Concordat.

(2) Law in force and future projects

12.04 In 1989 international arbitration law was put on a new, federal, basis, while domestic arbitration remained cantonal. Since 1989, except in the very rare opting out cases,[2] all international arbitrations having their seat[3] in Switzerland are exclusively[4] governed by the Swiss Federal Statute on Private International Law (PIL Statute or SPILA, Swiss Private International Law Act), which then came to displace the cantonal law on arbitration (then already the Concordat in most cantons), but only for 'international' arbitration. The PIL Statute is a comprehensive codification of the law of international jurisdiction, conflicts of substantive law, and recognition and enforcement of foreign decisions. Moreover, international bankruptcy and international arbitration are covered. The Convention on Jurisdiction and the Enforcement of Judgments on Civil and Commercial Matters (Lugano Convention) does not apply to arbitration.[5] The cantons enacted accompanying legislation to go with the PIL Statute. Minor amendments were made to the PIL Statute's chapter on international arbitration in 2006 and 2007. After 1989, the Concordat remained the law on domestic arbitration in all of Switzerland.

12.05 However, from 2011 onwards, domestic arbitration will also be on a new, federal, basis, but remain distinct from international arbitration. Legislation on civil procedure will become federal, and so will legislation on domestic arbitration. The Concordat (which is cantonal law) will then be replaced by a chapter of the new Swiss Federal Code of Civil Procedure.[6] This will introduce a provision (in the Swiss Federal Code of Civil Procedure) allowing opting out of the Swiss Federal Code of Civil Procedure and into the PIL Statute. There are no further projects to revise federal international arbitration law in the near future.

[2] Private International Law Statute (PIL Statute) Art 176(2), to be amended in 2011.

[3] Geneva Cour de Justice, (1991) ASA Bull 269, 273-4.

[4] Swiss Federal Supreme Court decision (BGE) 117 II 94, 96; BGE 115 II 288, 290; BGE 115 II 97, 100.

[5] Convention on Jurisdiction and the Enforcement of Judgments in Civil and Commercial Matters (Lugano Convention) Art 1(2) para 4; Kassationsgericht Zurich, 13 June 2002, Kass,-Nr 2002/032 Z (unpublished).

[6] The draft of the Swiss Code of Civil Procedure, as of 21 June 2007, Art 351 *et seq*, is available in English translation in Schöll, M. (ed), *Sourcebook of International Arbitration (Switzerland)* (Schulthess, 2008). The final numbering of articles differs slightly. The final version of 19 December 2008 is at <http://www.admin.ch/ch/d/ff/2009/21.pdf>.

(3) Distinction between national and international arbitration

(3.1) **If there are different systems and rules for national/international arbitration, what are the criteria for the distinction between both systems?** There are different legal systems or provisions for national (domestic) and international arbitration.[7] The reason for the distinction between domestic and international arbitration and the various options offered in the PIL Statute is mostly (but by no means exclusively) historical. In 1989, supporters of cantonal (state) rights had to be mollified. In all cantons, domestic arbitration is to this day governed by the Concordat and accompanying cantonal legislation, even though this is expected to change in 2011. The differentiation between domestic and international arbitration will, however, remain. Presently it is still possible for the parties of an international arbitration to opt in writing into cantonal arbitration law,[8] ie the Concordat and accompanying cantonal legislation. Both the exclusion of the 12th Chapter of the PIL Statute and the reference to cantonal law must be expressed in writing. This 'nostalgic option' is rarely exercised. It will be replaced in 2011 by an option to opt into the Swiss Federal Code of Civil Procedure. What follows is limited to international arbitration under the PIL Statute and will not cover international arbitration under the Concordat of the new Swiss Federal Code of Civil Procedure. **12.06**

The criterion for the distinction between national and international arbitration is (and will remain) an objective test based on the domicile of the parties. The national or international nature of the transaction is irrelevant. An arbitration having its seat in Switzerland is international if at least one of the parties had its registered seat outside Switzerland.[9] Thus, if a French company sells goods to a Swiss company to be shipped from Berne to Lausanne, this will be international for the purposes of PIL Statute Art 176, even though the interests of international trade are not involved. In France, the transaction would be considered domestic. By contrast, if a Swiss corporation sells goods to another Swiss company to be shipped to Kolkata, this will be domestic for the purposes of PIL Statute Art 176. In France, this transaction would be considered international. This may seem odd at times, but the 'international nature' test is not always easy to apply, while the 'seat of the parties' test is. For the purposes of the 'seat of the parties' test of PIL Statute Art 176 one must define which 'parties' are the relevant parties since the original parties to the arbitration agreement may have been replaced (through assignment, legal succession, or assumption of liability, for example) by other parties. According to an unfortunate decision of the Swiss Federal Supreme Court, the parties to the present arbitration are those that are relevant for the test,[10] not the original parties to the arbitration agreement. The opposite would make better sense, since the nature of the dispute resolution regime should not be subject to being altered by a subsequent assignment of contractual rights under the main contract. **12.07**

[7] See PIL Statute Art 176 (1) in conjunction with PIL Statute Art 20 and 21.

[8] See *ibid* Art 176 (2), to be amended in 2011.

[9] See *ibid* Art 176 in conjunction with Arts 20 and 21.

[10] BGE, (2003) ASA Bull 131, 134, justly criticized by Kaufmann-Kohler, G. and Rigozzi, A., 'When is a Swiss arbitration international?' in *Jusletter*, 7 October 2002 <http://www.weblaw.ch/jusletter> (accessed 7 April 2009).

B. Practice of arbitration

(1) Frequency of arbitration as opposed to litigation

12.08 In domestic cases, litigation is predominant; arbitration is not frequent. It is encountered in construction, partnerships, family business and commodities disputes. In international cases, arbitration is the normal way of resolving disputes. Many international arbitrations are conducted in Switzerland that have hardly any connection with Switzerland, or none at all.

(2) Leading arbitral institutions and statistics (if available)

12.09 The leading arbitration institution for international arbitration in Switzerland is the International Chamber of Commerce (ICC). In 2006, the ICC[11] conducted 95, or 16 per cent of all its international commercial arbitrations, in Switzerland, one per cent less than in France, and more than in any other country. Switzerland also had 16 per cent of all ICC arbitrators, more than from any other country, and also more Swiss chairpersons and sole arbitrators than from any other country. Swiss substantive law was applied more often than any other law.

12.10 The leading arbitration institution based in Switzerland is the Swiss Chambers. This is operated by the Zurich Chamber of Commerce, the Geneva Chamber of Commerce and Industry and the Chambers of Commerce of Basel, Berne, Neuchatel, Lugano and Vaud. The Chambers international arbitration rules were designed specifically to work with the arbitration 12th Chapter in the PIL Statute. The Swiss Chambers had 51 international arbitrations in 2007.

12.11 Numerous other institutions that have arbitration rules of their own are based in Switzerland, including the Court of Arbitration for Sport (about 300 arbitrations a year) and WIPO. Occasionally, international arbitrations are conducted in Switzerland under the auspices of foreign local institutions, such as the Stockholm Institute or the Vienna Center. *Ad hoc* international arbitration, with or without the UNCITRAL arbitration rules, is also important, though less frequent than many believe.

12.12 Accordingly, hundreds of international commercial arbitrations are conducted in Switzerland every year. By contrast, maritime arbitrations and international commodity arbitrations having their seat in Switzerland are very rare. Every year, about 14 international arbitration awards rendered in Switzerland are challenged by complaint to set aside before the Swiss Federal Supreme Court; of these, only about one a year are successful (half of these about jurisdiction). Accordingly, of all Swiss international arbitration awards, a fraction of one per cent is successfully challenged, less than anywhere else.[12]

---

[11] See ICC International Court of Arbitration Bulletin (2007) 5 '*2006 Statistical Report*'.

[12] See Dasser, F., 'International Arbitration and Setting Aside Proceedings in Switzerland: A Statistical Analysis' (2007) *ASA Bull* 444 *et seq*, also for further statistical information.

II. Jurisdiction of the arbitral tribunal

A. Arbitration agreement

(1) Arbitration clause and submission agreement

PIL Statute, Art 178(1) and (2) provides as follows: 12.13

> (1) The arbitration agreement must be made in writing, by telegram, telex, telecopier or any other means of communication which permits it to be evidenced by a text.
>
> (2) Furthermore, an arbitration agreement is valid if it conforms either to the law chosen by the parties, or to the law governing the subject matter of the dispute, in particular the main contract, or to Swiss law.

A distinction is made between an arbitration clause and a separate submission agreement (*compromis arbitral*).[13] However, both types of agreements to arbitrate are treated the same way: they are considered separable agreements and are subject to their own form requirements. There is no distinction between agreements to arbitrate made in advance and those made only *in limine litis*. This includes multi-party arbitration clauses which may be agreed to in advance. An arbitration agreement may be included in the bylaws of a partnership or legal entity and will then bind its members, partners or shareholders.

It is conceivable that an arbitration agreement might be tainted by lack of consensus, in which case, if Swiss law applies by virtue of PIL Statute Art 178(2), it may be nullified *ex tunc* within a year of the discovery of the mistake (CO Art 31). By contrast, an arbitration agreement can probably neither be cancelled nor terminated (for cause) *ex nunc*. 12.14

If a party fails to provide the required advances, Art 41(4) of the Swiss Rules of International Arbitration of the Swiss Chambers of Commerce (Swiss Rules) provides the following: 12.15

> 4. If the required deposits are not paid in full within 30 days after the receipt of the request, the arbitral tribunal shall so inform the parties in order that one or another of them may make the required payment. If such payment is not made, the arbitral tribunal may order the suspension or termination of the arbitral proceedings.

The arbitration clause as such remains valid, though. All this is probably good law even in other types of arbitration. If a party fails to advance the arbitration costs, it fails to live up to its commitment to the arbitration clause. It is then estopped (*venire contra factum proprium*) from invoking the arbitration clause as a defence in state court proceedings in the same dispute.

(2) Requirements as to the contents of the arbitration agreement

For an arbitration agreement providing for international arbitration in Switzerland to exist, it must be clear from its content that the parties agree to *arbitration* as distinguished from litigation or conciliation, even though the word 'arbitration' need not be mentioned. 12.16

[13] See PIL Statute Art 178.

Moreover, it is advisable, though not essential,[14] that the arbitration agreement should specify the seat of arbitration in Switzerland. It is sufficient for the parties to refer to arbitration rules pursuant to which the seat of the arbitration may be put in Switzerland, as the ICC Rules. Occasionally, the seat may result from interpretation. If an arbitration clause does not specify the city in Switzerland that should be the seat of the arbitration, the arbitral tribunal, if set up, has the power to determine the seat of the arbitration within Switzerland.[15] However, if the parties provide only for 'arbitration in Switzerland', without providing for a mechanism for setting up the arbitral tribunal, the auxiliary provisions of the PIL Statute providing for the appointment of arbitrators by the courts at the seat of the arbitration[16] cannot be used against the will of the other party in order to set up the arbitral tribunal. This means that an agreement to arbitrate 'in Switzerland' will often be valid, but remain inoperative.[17] Some believe that cantonal law, including Concordat Art 3 letters a and b, may help here, but definitely not the Lugano Convention which is not applicable to arbitration.[18]

(3) Form of the agreement (eg 'in writing' requirement)

12.17 PIL Statute Art 178(1) does not require an arbitration agreement to be in writing and signed,[19] nor to be acknowledged in writing.[20] It is sufficient for the agreement to arbitrate to be ascertainable in its text, eg in the tape recording of a telephone conversation. In the authors' view,[21] the acceptance of that text need not be evidenced in writing or by a text. It may be given orally or by conclusive action, eg by shipping the goods.[22] A specific reference to the text of an arbitration clause is sufficient.[23] A global reference to the arbitration clause may be sufficient.[24] Do any of the three laws mentioned in PIL Statute Art 178(2) apply to validate a reference to a text, or just Swiss substantive law, or some international standard, such as analogous application of Lugano Convention Art 17(1)? In the authors' view, PIL Statute Art 178(2) should apply, in favour of arbitration.[25]

---

14 Vaud Chambre de Recours 11 July 2001, 11 (unpublished), against Zurich Obergericht 31 May 2001 Y/O/PG 0006 Wi (unpublished).

15 See PIL Statute Art 176(3).

16 See *ibid* Art 179(2).

17 BGE 130 III 66, 72; BGE 129 III 675, 680.

18 See Obergericht Zürich, U/O/PG 970003 Wi, 3-5 (unpublished); Kassationsgericht Zürich, (1999) ASA Bull 363.

19 As did Swiss Intercantonal Concordat on Arbitration of 27 August 1969 (Concordat) Art 6.

20 As in the United Nations Convention of 1958 on the Recognition and Enforecement of Foreign Arbitral Awards (New York Convention) Art II (2), see BGE 121 III 38, 43, against BGE 111 1b 253, 255; BGE 110 II 54, 57.

21 Contra Wenger, W. and Müller, C., *'PIL Statute Art 178'* note 16 in: H. Honsell *et al* (eds), *Basler Kommentar Internationales Privatrecht* (2nd edn, Helbing Lichtenhahn, 2007).

22 See the following articles in the PIL Statute for the form requirements concerning:

- opting into Concordat, Art 176(3);
- choice of procedure, Art 182(1);
- choice of law applicable to the merits, Art 187(1);
- choice of a cantonal court for an action to set aside, Art 191(2); and
- waiver of a complaint to set aside, Art 192(2).

23 BGE 110 II 54, 58-9.

24 BGE, (2002) ASA Bull 482, 487; BGE, (2002) ASA Bulletin 299, 305; BGE, (2001) ASA Bull 516, 528.

25 BGE 128 III 50, 62; BGE 119 II 380, 384.

(3.1) Are there special requirements for a power of attorney/authority to enter into an arbitration agreement on behalf of a third party? No. Such form requirements exist only where there are form requirements for the transaction itself, such as founding a company. However, making an arbitration agreement is not subject to particular form requirements designed to protect parties against themselves. The law applicable to the power of a person signing or accepting an arbitration agreement to bind another person to it is governed, in the authors' view, by PIL Statute Art 178(2).[26] 12.18

(4) Incorporation of an arbitration clause contained in general terms and conditions

An arbitration clause may be incorporated, and generally, an arbitration agreement may be made, by referring to an arbitration clause contained in general conditions.[27] There are no specific form requirements for the way a reference should be made to such general conditions, nor on the way such general conditions must be accepted. How one should fill this lacuna is not clear. 12.19

(5) Law applicable to the interpretation of arbitration clauses

It is unclear which law applies to the interpretation of arbitration clauses. Some say, the principles generally applicable to the interpretation of declarations of will *in favorem validitatis*[28] or use similar general expressions.[29] The authors believe that PIL Statute Art 178(2) applies, in favour of arbitration. It provides, *in favorem validitatis*, for the application of three substantive laws and should lead to a wide scope of the arbitration clause.[30] One might also think that principles of Swiss private international law would apply, which would again lead to a broad scope. One might finally think of international standards of interpretation such as Unidroit Principles Art 4.1, leading again to a wide scope. 12.20

(5.1) Do courts accept a wide competence of the arbitral tribunal or do they restrict arbitral competence? Do claims which arise in connection with the agreement submitted to arbitration generally fall within the arbitral jurisdiction even if based on tortious legal basis? Does there exist case law with respect to the wording in an arbitration clause as 'arising out of/under/in connection with the present contract' and its specific meaning? In any event, a wide interpretation is favoured.[31] No distinction is made (as for a long time has been the case in England) according to the wording ('arising out of' or 'in connection with'). 12.21

Pathological clauses should be interpreted by analogy to the general law of contracts[32] and *in favorem validitatis*,[33] particularly as to the designation of an arbitration institution or an appointing authority. Examples: 'ICC Zurich': ICC arbitration in Zurich;[34] 'Swiss Arbitration 12.22

[26] Contra, BGE 96 I 334, 340.
[27] BGE 110 II 54, 59.
[28] BGE 130 III 66, 71.
[29] BGE 116 Ia 56, 58–9.
[30] Contra, BGE 129 III 675, 681.
[31] See eg BGE 117 II 98; BGE 116 II 56 *et seq*; BGE 116 1a 56, 58–9.
[32] BGE 130 III 66, 71.
[33] Obergericht Zürich, U/O/PG970003 Wi, 4–5 (unpublished).
[34] BGE 129 III 675, 681.

Court, Zurich': Swiss Chambers Arbitration in Zurich;[35] 'Tribunal de Commerce de Genève': Cour de Justice.[36]

12.23 Does the arbitration agreement extend to non-connected set-off defences, even if, for the claim that is used for setting-off, there is a separate arbitration clause or a jurisdiction clause? This is specifically accepted in Swiss Rules Art 21(5):

> 5. The arbitral tribunal shall have jurisdiction to hear a set-off defence even when the relationship out of which this defence is said to arise is not within the scope of the arbitration clause or is the object of another arbitration agreement or forum-selection clause.

Concordat Art 29 has the contrary rule, and was much criticized at the time when the PIL Statute was drafted. It was consciously omitted from the PIL Statute. Leading authorities in Switzerland are of the opinion that in international arbitration Swiss Rules Art 21(5) applies generally,[37] unless the parties have expressly agreed to the contrary, eg for claims for damages not based on the violation of a contract, counterfeiting claims etc. This follows from the principle of a wide interpretation of arbitration clauses.

(6) Binding effect of an arbitration clause on third parties (eg in case of a guarantee or assignment)

12.24 Probably the *lex arbitri* applies.[38] Third parties are bound by the arbitration agreement contained in the original contract if the benefit of an agreement subject to the arbitration clause is assigned (which under Swiss substantive law must be done 'in writing', which for that purpose includes the signature of the assignor). A joint debtor ('Schuldbeitritt') is bound by an arbitration clause. The specific formal requirements under Swiss law, if any, for such a transfer must be met. There may be other cases when a non-signatory to an arbitration clause may be bound by it (group of contracts theory, group of companies theory). The Swiss Federal Supreme Court did not set aside an award finding that a non-signatory was bound when the non-signatory had involved himself deeply in the performance of the agreement.[39]

12.25 **(6.1) What is the law/leading authorities' position on multi-party situations? Especially, (i) with respect to the objection that the arbitration clause does not specifically provide for a plurality of parties in the same procedure; (ii) with respect to the constitution of the arbitral tribunal; and (iii) with respect to the consolidation of two or more running arbitration proceedings?** If the contract in which the arbitration clause is inserted is a multi-party contract, the arbitration clause is understood to contemplate multi-party arbitration, no matter whether it specifically says so or not. Such an agreement between the parties is possible from the outset, not only *in limine litis*. It may provide for an unequal treatment of the parties in the appointment of arbitrators (for instance, the arbitration

---

[35] BGE 129 III 675, 681.

[36] Geneva Court of Justice, (1991) ASA Bull 155, 269, 277.

[37] See Reymond, C., in '*PIL Statute Art 186*' note 8 in: P. Lalive, J-F. Poudret and C. Reymond, *Le Droit de l'Arbitrage Interne et Internationale en Suisse* (Payot, 1989).

[38] BGE, (1996) ASA Bull 623.

[39] BGE 129 III 727.

clause may require multiple respondents to agree on one arbitrator, while the claimant may nominate an arbitrator all by itself). Swiss Rules Arts 4 and 8 on the constitution of the arbitral tribunal are based on similar provisions in the Zurich International Rules and the Geneva Rules which, when they were still in force, were not challenged on grounds of unequal treatment. In the still earlier *Westland case*, which was conducted under the old ICC Rules and still under the Concordat, a multi-party arbitral tribunal had been formed by the ICC in accordance with its then practice, a practice then not yet mentioned in the ICC Rules, which was that co-defendants should agree on an arbitrator. The arbitral tribunal was unsuccessfully challenged as improperly constituted.[40] In sum, there was already then no '*Dutco*' problem with the constitution of multi-party arbitral tribunals in Switzerland. There is none now.[41] The appointing authority (which may be a state court) may have to form groups of parties for this purpose.[42] In a multi-party arbitration, the arbitral tribunal may always be constituted as provided in the arbitration agreement between the parties.[43] By now, ICC Rules Art 10, (referring to Art 9), constitutes such an agreement and resolves the issue.

There is no statutory provision for the consolidation of two or more arbitral proceedings running. Swiss Rules Art 4 reads as follows: **12.26**

> 1. Where a Notice of Arbitration is submitted between parties already involved in other arbitral proceedings pending under these Rules, the Chambers may decide, after consulting with the parties to all proceedings and the Special Committee, that the new case shall be referred to the arbitral tribunal already constituted for the existing proceedings. The Chambers may proceed likewise where a Notice of Arbitration is submitted between parties that are not identical to the parties in the existing arbitral proceedings. When rendering their decision, the Chambers shall take into account all circumstances, including the links between the two cases and the progress already made in the existing proceedings. Where the Chambers decide to refer the new case to the existing arbitral tribunal, the parties to the new case shall be deemed to have waived their right to designate an arbitrator.
>
> 2. Where a third party requests to participate in arbitral proceedings already pending under these Rules or where a party to arbitral proceedings under these Rules intends to cause a third party to participate in the arbitration, the arbitral tribunal shall decide on such request, after consulting with all parties, taking into account all circumstances it deems relevant and applicable.

(6.2) Is there case law/authorities with respect to the admissibility of third party participation in an arbitration without being a claimant or defendant (Nebenintervention/ Streitverkündung; intervention forcée/volontaire; vouching in; *amicus curiae* etc)? What are the prerequisites and effects of such participation (if permitted)? Formal third party participation ('*third party practice*', '*Nebenintervention/Streitverkündung*'; '*intervention forcée/intervention volontaire*'; '*vouching in*') in international arbitration is practically unknown in Switzerland, except in sport arbitration. There are no court cases on this, nor **12.27**

40 See BGE 120 II 155 *et seq.*
41 For France, see (1998) *Rev arb* 390, note by Delvolvé, J.-L.
42 See Tribunal Cantonal Neuchâtel, (1995) ASA Bull 51, 54 (a domestic case).
43 See PIL Statute Art 179(1).

is there scholarly writing. It is, however, frequently the case that non-parties (for instance, insiders, parent companies, sellers) participate in an arbitration in an informal manner, particularly in support of a party.

(7) Termination of an arbitration agreement by a party (reasons and case law)

12.28 There is no case law on cancellation or termination of arbitration clauses. Because of the separability principle,[44] an arbitration clause survives the termination of the agreement into which it is inserted. It also survives (and is not 'used up') if an award was rendered based on it, or if that award is set aside.

B. Arbitrability

12.29 Arbitrability is a prerequisite for the validity of the arbitration agreement.[45] Lack of arbitrability leads to declining jurisdiction, but unlike jurisdiction, arbitrability cannot be created (or lack of arbitrability waived) by an unconditional appearance. The consequences of obvious lack of arbitrability are unclear.[46]

(1) 'Personal arbitrability' (capacity to conclude arbitration agreements)

12.30 Anybody may conclude an arbitration agreement, ie individuals, companies, state agencies etc. The question whether a particular individual may act as an officer of a company or state agency or whether a particular individual has a power of attorney to act on behalf of another person is possibly governed by the law governing the status of the person for whom the alleged officer or representative acts,[47] or by the law of the seat of the arbitration which governs the arbitration agreement.

12.31 **(1.1) May a state (or state agency) as party invoke sovereign immunity before the arbitral tribunal or before a state court (eg in a procedure of enforcement)?** Sovereign immunity by a state or state agency may not be invoked before an arbitral tribunal. PIL Statute Art 177(2) provides:

> A state, an enterprise owned by a state, or an organization controlled by a state, which is party to an arbitration, cannot invoke its own law in order to contest its capacity to be a party to arbitration or the arbitrability of a dispute covered by the arbitration agreement.

12.32 With respect to sovereign immunity before a state court (eg in a procedure of enforcement) the law is different: Swiss case law is to the effect that sovereign immunity is a defence, but may be overcome in Switzerland for reasons of Swiss public policy, which presuppose a close link ('Binnenbeziehung') with Switzerland.[48] This does not apply to state court proceedings ancillary to an arbitration foreseen in the PIL Statute. To these, PIL Statute Art 178(3) applies by analogy.[49]

---

[44] PIL Statute Art 178(3).
[45] BGE 118 II, 353, 355.
[46] See para 12.202 *infra*.
[47] See (1990) ASA Bull 270.
[48] See Bucher, A., *Droit international privé suisse, tome I* (Helbing & Lichtenhahn, 1995) 600.
[49] Eg PIL Statute Arts 183, 184, 185, 190.

(2) 'Objective arbitrability' (eg of patent, trade mark, antitrust matters)

The non-arbitrability of particular subject matters is governed exclusively,[50] and regardless of the law applicable to the merits[51] or UN sanctions,[52] by PIL Statute Art 177 which provides for a 'Sachnorm im IPR'.[53] Any dispute of financial interest may be the subject of an arbitration. Accordingly patents, trade marks,[54] antitrust matters,[55] labour matters,[56] marital property, disputes between heirs, and sports law disputes[57] are all arbitrable. Even contracts involving bribery or other illegal or immoral purposes are arbitrable[58] (but then may well be found to be void on their merits). Whether an award will be enforceable elsewhere is irrelevant.[59] Bankruptcy proceedings are not arbitrable.[60] Lack of objective arbitrability may be examined at any time *sua sponte* by the arbitral tribunal.[61] **12.33**

C. Decision on the arbitral tribunal's jurisdiction ('*competence-competence*')

(1) Separability (independence of the arbitration agreement from the main agreement)

The doctrine of separability, under which for certain purposes the arbitration clause is regarded as independent of the agreement on the substantive issues, is accepted in PIL Statute Art 178(3). There may, however, be cases where a lack of consent (PIL Statute Art 178(2)) does not only affect the main contract but also the arbitration clause therein contained. One also occasionally encounters cases where the arbitration agreement is so closely connected with the illegal or immoral purpose of the main contract that it becomes affected by it. **12.34**

If a contract is novated, the arbitration agreement presumably survives.[62] If a contract is terminated, the arbitration agreement presumably survives.[63] If a claim is assigned, the benefit arising from the arbitration agreement is presumably transferred to the assignee.[64] If a dispute is settled, the arbitration agreement in the agreement that gave rise to the dispute presumably survives and applies to the settlement.[65] **12.35**

50 BGE 118 II 193, 196.
51 *ibid*, 356.
52 *ibid*, 356–8.
53 *ibid*, 355.
54 Schweizerisches Patent-, Muster- und Markenblatt 1976 I 9 *et seq.*
55 BGE 118 II 193, 198.
56 BGE 119 II 271.
57 BGE 129 III 445, 463.
58 See Briner, R., '*PIL Statute Art 177*' note 16 *et seq*, especially note 18 in: H Honsell *et al* (eds), *Basler Kommentar Internationales Privatrecht* (2nd edn, Helbing Lichtenhahn, 2007).
59 BGE 118 II 253, 258.
60 Obergericht Thurgau, (2003) ASA Bull 418.
61 Obergericht Zurich, 30 June 2003, PN 030117/U/Wi, 7 (unpublished).
62 BGE, (1997) ASA Bull 291, 300.
63 BGE 116 Ia 56, 59.
64 BGE 103 II 75; BG 128 III 50, 55-6.
65 BGE 121 III 495, 497.

(2) Competence of the tribunal to decide on its own jurisdiction (including form and time of the tribunal's decision)

12.36 The arbitral tribunal shall rule on its own jurisdiction (see PIL Statute, Art 186(1)). This decision is subject to judicial review.[66] Arbitral tribunals have a wide jurisdiction. Arbitration agreements are interpreted in a liberal sense to include all claims in connection with the arbitration agreement, regardless of the specific wording of the clause. PIL Statute Art 186(3) provides, as a rule, that the arbitral tribunal shall decide on its jurisdiction by preliminary award (if it accepts jurisdiction—if it declines jurisdiction, that award is a final award).

(3) Extent of the 'competence-competence' *and role of the courts (including form and time limits of a challenge of the tribunal's decision)*

12.37 In ICC arbitration, a preliminary award on jurisdiction (as any other award) must be scrutinized and approved by the International Court of Arbitration of the ICC. A positive or negative award on jurisdiction may be challenged directly before the Swiss Federal Supreme Court pursuant to PIL Statute Art 190(2)(b) and 191(1) by complaint to set aside, unless this was waived.[67]

12.38 Where the arbitral tribunal has decided on its constitution or jurisdiction in a preliminary award, that preliminary award can be set aside only by a challenge to be filed in 30 days[68] from the notification of the preliminary award. If it is left unchallenged, it will be *res judicata*, and it will not be possible to challenge it with the final award. If jurisdiction is accepted in the final award, the time limit runs from the notification of the final award. In both cases, the challenge goes directly to the Swiss Federal Supreme Court. If jurisdiction was accepted, further arbitral proceedings are not suspended by a challenge of the preliminary award on jurisdiction before the Swiss Federal Supreme Court.[69] The President of the Swiss Federal Supreme Court may however grant suspensive effect to the challenge. Suspensive effect is consistently denied in practice, though. If in due course the award accepting jurisdiction is not set aside, any suspensive effect is lifted, and the arbitration continues. If the arbitral award accepting jurisdiction is set aside, the question of costs may still be remanded to the arbitral tribunal. If the arbitral tribunal has declined jurisdiction and this is set aside by the Swiss Federal Supreme Court, the (same) arbitral tribunal must resume its activities and decide on the merits.[70]

D. Enforcement of an arbitration agreement within or by court proceedings

(1) Effect of invoking an arbitration clause within a court proceeding (and time limits for such a motion)

12.39 As provided in PIL Statute Art 7(1), if, in an arbitrable dispute, the parties have concluded an arbitration agreement, the Swiss courts must decline jurisdiction unless, *inter alia*, the

[66] PIL Statute Art 190(2)(b).
[67] See para 12.210; para 12.215.
[68] See para 12.211.
[69] PIL Statute Art 190(1).
[70] BGE 117 II 94, 96.

defendant has entered in an unconditional appearance. The time limit for such a plea of lack of jurisdiction depends on the applicable cantonal civil procedure.[71] In Zurich, the plea must be raised at the latest together with the answer on the merits.[72] The court's powers in that aspect are not discretionary. It must apply PIL Statute Art 7.

If the arbitration seat is in Switzerland, the Swiss State Court must decide on the basis of the PIL Statute,[73] but only prima facie.[74] If the seat is abroad, the New York Convention, Art II(2) applies,[75] and the Swiss State Court has full powers to decide on this.[76] 12.40

(1.1) If a party has invoked successfully the arbitration agreement in a court proceeding, is it then entitled to deny within the arbitral proceeding that there is a valid and binding arbitration agreement? If a party has invoked successfully the arbitration agreement in a court proceeding, it is no longer entitled to deny before the arbitral tribunal that there is a valid and binding arbitration agreement. In Switzerland, such behaviour would be considered against good faith in the sense of CC Art 2 which is applicable also in procedural matters and in international arbitration.[77] The word 'successfully' is essential here. It is not contrary to good faith to argue inconsistent positions in different fora, but once the point has been finally decided, inconsistency is no longer permitted. 12.41

(1.2) Vice versa, if a party has successfully objected to an arbitral proceeding by denying that there is a valid arbitration agreement, may it then invoke such agreement in the ensuing court proceeding? Vice versa, and for the same reasons as above, if a party has successfully objected to an arbitral proceeding by denying that there is a valid arbitration agreement, it may then not invoke such agreement before the court in the ensuing proceeding. However, there is no case law yet on these questions. 12.42

(2) Legal remedies and proceedings to enforce an arbitration agreement

Once an arbitration is pending, even before an arbitral tribunal, there is *lis pendens* which has the same effect as pending state court proceedings in Switzerland.[78] If the arbitration is pending outside Switzerland, PIL Statute Art 9 applies. Any foreign arbitral award is recognizable in Switzerland pursuant to the New York Convention. Switzerland withdrew the 'reciprocity' reservation to the convention.[79] 12.43

(2.1) Which would be the internationally competent court (i) for obtaining a declaration that a given arbitration agreement is valid and binding; or (ii) to compel arbitration? (The defendant's courts? The courts of the place of arbitration? The claimant's courts, cf Article 6(2) in fine, ICC Rules?) In Switzerland, it is not possible to obtain a declaration 12.44

---

71 BGE 127 III 279, 287; BGE 111 II 62, 66.

72 Para 111 Zürich Zivilprozessordnung (ZPO), Cantonal Code of Civil Procedure; BGE 111 III 62, 65-6.

73 BGE 122 III 139, 141–2.

74 BGE 121 III 139, 141–2.

75 *ibid*, 38, 42.

76 *ibid*, 139, 142; *ibid*, 38, 42.

77 Wenger, W. and Müller, C. *'PIL Statute Art 178'* note 45 in: H. Honsell *et al* (eds), *Basler Kommentar Internationales Privatrecht* (2nd edn, Helbing Lichtenhahn, 2007).

78 PIL Statute Art 181 applies.

79 See Amtliche Sammlung des Bundesrechts (AS) 1993, p 2139, and PIL Statute Art 194.

by a (lower) state court that a given arbitration agreement is valid and binding,[80] or is not binding, nor an order compelling or staying arbitration. If a defendant is sued before a (lower) Swiss court and invokes the arbitration agreement in defence (*exceptio fori alieni*), the Swiss state court must dismiss the case without prejudice.[81] The only competent body to declare with binding effect the validity or invalidity of an arbitration clause is the arbitral tribunal therein designated (but an interest in a mere declaration will normally not be worthy of protection), subject only to a complaint to set aside, in which case the Swiss Federal Supreme Court has jurisdiction.

III. The arbitral tribunal

A. Number and qualification of arbitrators

(1) Sole arbitrator or arbitral tribunal with several arbitrators

12.45 Pursuant to PIL Statute Art 179(1) and (2), the arbitrators shall be appointed in accordance with the private and autonomous agreement of the parties.[82] In the absence of an agreement by the parties, the court where the arbitral tribunal has its seat shall apply, by analogy, the provisions of cantonal law on the appointment of arbitrators, ie in all cantons, Concordat Art 10. Thus, if the parties did not agree otherwise or empower an institution to decide otherwise (as in the ICC Rules or the Swiss Rules) the arbitral tribunal will consist of three arbitrators.

12.46 **(1.1) Are arbitral tribunals with an even number of arbitrators acceptable?** Arbitral tribunals must be formed in accordance with the agreement of the parties.[83] An even number of arbitrators is acceptable,[84] but an uneven number is of course recommended. If the parties fail to agree, PIL Statute Art 176(2) provides that arbitral tribunals are formed in analogy with the cantonal law at the place of arbitration, which is in all Cantons the Concordat. Concordat Art 10(1), provides for a three-member arbitral tribunal as the default solution.

(2) Qualification of the arbitrators

12.47 There are no provisions on the qualification of arbitrators in international arbitration. Sometimes arbitration clauses specify the qualification of arbitrators, but the parties can again waive this.

12.48 **(2.1) Are there mandatory requirements for the qualification of arbitrators (statutory requirements or indirect requirements through eg general conditions of insurance contracts)?** Probably only individuals may be arbitrators.[85] There are no express

[80] See Poudret, J-F., 'Une action en constatation de droit au sujet de l'existence ou la validité d'une clause arbitrale est-elle recevable en droit fédéral ou cantonal?' in Recht und Rechtsdurchsetzung: Festschrift für Hans Ulrich Walder zum 65. Geburtstag, pp 341, 352, against an old BGE in SJIR 1988, 487.

[81] See PIL Statute Art 7.

[82] BGE, (2003) ASA Bull 402, 409.

[83] See PIL Statute Art 179(1).

[84] BGE 121 I 81.

[85] BGE 117 III 57.

mandatory requirements for the qualification of arbitrators. By virtue of general law, an arbitrator should presumably have a capacity to understand and to act ('Urteilsfähigkeit, Handlungsfähigkeit': CC, Art 13) which under Swiss law is not tied to a particular coming of age limit ('Mündigkeit').

(2.2) Which national arbitration institutions may be contacted for obtaining information about qualified (and specialized) arbitrators? The Swiss Arbitration Association (which is not an arbitral institution) publishes profiles of arbitrators, which contain extensive information about qualified and specialized arbitrators in Switzerland. This is accessible on <http://www.arbitration-ch.org>. It also regularly publishes full updated lists of its members in the *ASA Bulletin*. 12.49

(2.3) Are judges or civil servants required to obtain permission by their employer to act as arbitrator? Are these permissions given generally or case-by-case? What are the consequences if such permission has not been obtained? Judges or civil servants may act as arbitrators, but in some courts or administrations this is subject to internal guidelines.[86] A failure to comply with such internal guidelines, regardless of whether they are known to the parties to the arbitration, would not affect the validity of an award. 12.50

B. Appointment of arbitrators

(1) Extent of party autonomy to establish appointment procedure

PIL Statute Arts 179(1) and 180 give the parties full power to regulate the appointment procedure.[87] This can be done by reference to arbitration rules that regulate the appointment of arbitrators.[88] It is possible to name an arbitrator already in an agreement to arbitrate.[89] The agreement to arbitrate could not derogate blatantly from the principle of equal treatment of the parties by providing that one party may appoint more arbitrators than the other, or the arbitrator must be appointed by a federation that is a party to the arbitration while the other party is a member only of an association that is a member of the federation, or chosen from a list on which a party has a preponderant influence.[90] However, in multi-party arbitration, *Dutco* is not good law in Switzerland.[91] 12.51

The decision of an institution making an appointment or an institution's decision on challenge, removal or replacement of an arbitrator may not as such be challenged in Swiss courts. However, an award may be set aside pursuant to PIL Statute, Art 190(2)(a) if the sole arbitrator was not properly appointed or if the arbitral tribunal was not properly constituted. When a judge has been designated as the authority for appointing an arbitrator, the appointment shall be made unless a summary examination[92] shows that no arbitration 12.52

---

86 See Swiss Federal Statute on the Swiss Federal Supreme Court, Art 7. It would stretch the scope of this handbook to go into details.

87 BGE, (2003) ASA Bull 402, 409.

88 BGE 110 Ia 59, 63-4; BGE 102 Ia 493, 501-2.

89 See Bezirksgericht Affoltern am Albis, (1997) ASA Bull 262, 271, also (1998) ICCA Ybk 754, a Swiss New York Convention case concerning a Turkish award.

90 BGE 129 III 445, 456–7.

91 See para 12.25.

92 BGE 108 Ia 308, 310–11.

agreement exists between the parties.[93] For this obligation, no link with Switzerland is required except that the seat of the arbitration must be in Switzerland. Validity and scope of the arbitration agreement are matters for the arbitral tribunal. If these are in doubt the appointment should be made.[94]

(2) Procedure in absence of an agreement by the parties

12.53 In the absence of an agreement by the parties, PIL Statute, Art 179(2) provides that the court where the tribunal has its seat may be seized.[95] Which court is determined by the cantonal law of the seat. The cantonal court then applies, by analogy, the provisions of cantonal law on appointment, removal or replacement of arbitrators, thus the provisions of the Concordat and accompanying cantonal legislation.[96] If no Swiss seat is specified in the agreement to arbitrate, and one of the parties does not cooperate, there are different views on whether an arbitral tribunal may nevertheless be formed, and how.

12.54 In the absence of an agreement by the parties, the appointment of the chairman is made by the co-arbitrators or, if they cannot agree, by a judicial authority.[97] The judicial authority is determined by cantonal law.[98] In most cantons, the judicial authority designated is the Cantonal Supreme Court.[99] By operation of Concordat Art 45(2) (to which Concordat Art 3 refers), in the absence of a determination by the canton[100] or the judicial authority, that judicial authority is the Cantonal Supreme Court. Since several fora have jurisdiction to decide (some only prima facie) whether an agreement to arbitrate exists, one may have to resolve conflicts.[101]

12.55 A judicial remedy against an appointment by a cantonal court may be provided by cantonal law,[102] but neither Zurich nor Geneva do this. The appointment is reviewable by the Swiss Federal Supreme Court on constitutional law grounds only, but the interpretation of cantonal law is reviewable only for arbitrariness.[103] There is no other federal judicial remedy against an appointment by a cantonal court.[104] A refusal to appoint is subject to constitutional review.[105] It amounts to a final decision.[106] However, the interpretation of cantonal law is reviewable only for arbitrariness (which is contrary to the Swiss Federal Constitution).

[93] See PIL Statute Art 179 (3).

[94] BGE 118 Ia 20, 27 is probably not good law.

[95] Kassationsgericht Zürich, Kass-No 90/138 Z, 6-12.

[96] Art 10 *et seq* Concordat: in the absence of an agreement by the parties, the co-arbitrators are appointed by the parties (Art 11 Concordat applied by analogy).

[97] See Art 12 Concordat applied by analogy.

[98] See Art 3 Concordat.

[99] In Zurich, the Obergericht, para 239(2), ZPO.

[100] In Geneva, the Tribunal de première instance.

[101] BGE 127 III 279, 284; BGE 121 III 495, 502.

[102] BGE 119 Ia 421.

[103] *ibid*, 422.

[104] BGE 121 I 81, 83; BGE 115 II 294, 295, 296.

[105] BGE 121 I 81, 83.

[106] BGE 118 Ia 20, 23.

(3) Effect of the refusal of one party to cooperate in the constitution of the arbitral tribunal

If there was no agreement between the parties on the appointment and one party fails to cooperate, the appointment is made as just described by the Swiss court system. When a judge has been designated as the authority for appointing an arbitrator, and the seat of the arbitration is in Switzerland, he or she shall make the appointment unless a summary examination shows that no arbitration agreement exists between the parties.[107] **12.56**

(4) Circumstances and valid reasons for an arbitrator to resign

The legal relationship between an arbitrator and the parties is contractual and contains elements of mandate.[108] Even though under Swiss private law a mandate may be abandoned at will and at any time,[109] except at an inappropriate moment ('zur Unzeit'),[110] an arbitrator may step down only for good cause[111] (including medical reasons). Reasons should be given, but it would be unusual to require proof. **12.57**

C. Challenge and replacement of arbitrators

(1) Grounds, procedure and deadlines for challenging an arbitrator

The grounds for challenge of an arbitrator are primarily governed by the agreement between the parties. This agreement frequently provides that an arbitrator must have or may not have particular citizenship. The parties can agree on the procedure of a challenge and provide that an arbitrator is successfully challenged as soon as the request of challenge will find the approval of the other party. If the parties do not find a consent, they can provide to submit the question to a third person or to an arbitral institution. If the parties give the institution *exclusive* power over challenges, which is presumed,[112] the state courts are excluded.[113] **12.58**

Grounds for challenging an arbitrator must be invoked immediately after they are (or should have been)[114] discovered,[115] or they are forfeited. The 15-day deadline in UNCITRAL Arbitration Rules Art 11(1) is considered too short; the ICC 30-day deadline reasonable.[116] When taking a decision the third person has to consider the peremptory guarantee of PIL Statute Art 180(1)(c). This ground for challenge (lack of independence) is applicable even if there is no specific arbitration agreement or no reference is made to a by-law concerning procedural rules. In practice, the IBA Guidelines are regularly referred to.[117] **12.59**

---

107 See PIL Statute Art179 (3); BGE 118 Ia 20, 24; para 12.52 *supra*.

108 Voser, N. and Gola, P. in G. Kaufmann-Kohler and B. Stucki, *International Arbitration in Switzerland* (Kluwer Law, 2004) 32.

109 Swiss Federal Code of Obligations (CO) Art 396.

110 CO Art 404 (2). BGE 117 Ia 169.

111 BGE 117 Ia 166, 169.

112 BGE 118 II 359, 361.

113 As provided by PIL Statute Art 179(1), but always subject to PIL Statute Art 190(2)(a).

114 BGE 129 III 445, 465. A party should at least 'google' a candidate.

115 *ibid*; BGE 126 III 249, 253-4; BGE 124 I 121, 122–3; BGE 120 II 155.

116 The Swiss Federal Supreme Court said in case BGE 111 Ia 72 that towards the end of an arbitration a challenge should be raised particularly quickly, but this is hard to defend.

117 See Scherer, M.,'New Case Law from Austria, Switzerland and Germany regarding the IBA Guidelines on Conflict of Interest in International Arbitration' (2008) *Transnational Dispute Management* 5 (4).

12.60 In the absence of a determination by the parties an arbitrator may be challenged, *inter alia*, if at any time during the whole proceedings[118] circumstances exist that give rise to justifiable doubts as to his or her independence.[119] The fact that impartiality is not mentioned in the PIL Statue may or may not be relevant.[120] In practice, Swiss courts proceed on a case-by-case basis.[121] The relationship between arbitrator and party representative is relevant[122] only if there is a special relationship. That a decision has been set aside is not *per se* a ground to challenge an arbitrator.[123] If the parties did not agree upon a specific challenge procedure, the judge at the seat of the arbitral tribunal shall make the final decision regarding the challenge.[124] The court is the same court as the court having jurisdiction for the appointment.[125] There is no statutory deadline, but in practice it is advisable to file a challenge promptly, say within 30 days of notice of the grounds for challenge. As a base for the final decision, only the grounds of PIL Statute Art 180, that is (i) not meeting the requirements set by the parties; (ii) ground for challenge in the arbitration rules; and (iii) lack of independence), are applicable, not the rules of challenge of the cantonal law at the seat of the arbitral tribunal. The decision of the judge is final.[126] Some cantons nevertheless permit an appeal on the constitutional ground of denial of justice where the judge refused to address the matter at all. As of today, the Swiss Federal Court has not yet decided on this matter.[127]

12.61 **(1.1) Do state courts review challenge procedures which took place in accordance with a specific procedure agreed upon by the parties (eg ICC Rules Art 11)? If so, at what point in time? May such review be excluded?** State courts may not review challenge procedures that took place in accordance with a specific procedure agreed upon by the parties.[128] PIL Statute Art 197 is specifically designed to exclude a review of challenge procedures before the International Court of Arbitration of the ICC, the Swiss Chambers Special Committee and other similar judiciary or non-judiciary[129] bodies supervising arbitrators pursuant to an agreement by the parties included in the arbitration rules. This appears to be the law also in Sweden and Austria. While a challenge of an arbitrator is pending, the arbitration may proceed.[130] If an arbitral award was rendered by an arbitral tribunal that was improperly constituted, it may be set aside in accordance with PIL Statute Art 190(2)(a).

---

118 BGE, (1992) ASA Bull 381, 390.

119 See PIL Statute Art 180 (1); BGE 129 III 445, 454, 466; BGE, (1998) ASA Bull 634, 648.

120 BGE 129 III 445, 454; BGE, (1997) ASA Bull 99, 104; BGE, (1998) ASA Bull 634, 644-5.

121 BGE 129 III 445, 466; BGE, (1997) ASA Bull 99, 107; BGE 124 I 121, 123; BGE 115 Ia 400, 404.
Challenge unsuccessful: Kantonsgerichtsausschuss Graubünden, (1996) ASA Bull 264, 266–7.
Challenge successful: BGE 124 I 121, 125-6; BGE 116 Ia 485, 488-90; BGE, (2002) ASA Bull 321, 326; BGE 111 Ia 72, 74; BGE 92 I 271, 276-7.

122 BGE, (1998) ASA Bull 634, 646, 648-9 (challenge rejected); BGE, (1997) ASA Bull 99, 105, 107 (challenge rejected).

123 BGE, (2003) ASA Bull 829, 838; BGE 112 Ia 344, 347.

124 See PIL Statute Art 180(3).

125 See paras 12.52 and 12.53 *supra*.

126 BGE 128 III 330, 332; BGE 122 I 370, 372–3.

127 See BGE 118 I 20, 23.

128 BGE 120 II 155.

129 BGE 110 Ia 59, 61.

130 BGE, (2003) ASA Bull 829, 835.

This is not a challenge of arbitrators, but a (different) challenge of the award, which is possible by filing a complaint to set aside within 30 days of the issuance of the award.[131] (But that can be excluded by virtue of PIL Statute Art 192(1), which provides for the possibility of a waiver agreement at any time).[132] Grounds already invoked in the proceedings to challenge an arbitrator may be brought again against the award.[133]

(1.2) Is there case law with respect to truncated arbitral tribunals? (cf Article 12(5), ICC Rules) There was a case still under the Concordat in which a truncated ICC arbitral tribunal was involved. A party-appointed arbitrator abusively purported to resign, but his resignation was not 'accepted' by the ICC. The two other arbitrators continued their deliberations without him and rendered an award (arguably as a truncated tribunal). The award was then challenged successfully under the Concordat before the Zurich Supreme Court as having been rendered by an improperly constituted arbitral tribunal. A constitutional complaint against that court's decision was unsuccessful before the Swiss Federal Supreme Court.[134] The law under the PIL Statute is probably different. PIL Statute Art 179(1) upholds the will of the parties, including the arbitration rules to which they refer which may provide (as the ICC Rules now do expressly) for jurisdiction of a truncated arbitral tribunal. However, there is no case law on truncated arbitral tribunals under the PIL Statute. **12.62**

(3) Procedure for appointing a new arbitrator

If the parties did not agree otherwise, the procedure for the appointment of a new arbitrator will be the same as the procedure used for the original appointment. However, some arbitration rules, which are to be seen as the will of the parties, provide for a different procedure for the replacement of arbitrators, at least if they were removed for reasons other than ill health or death.[135] This is valid even if the parties are, as a result, treated unequally. Unless the parties agree otherwise, the newly constituted arbitral tribunal decides how to continue the arbitration.[136] Normally, the proceedings will continue from where the predecessor arbitrator left it. **12.63**

IV. The arbitral procedure

A. General principles

(1) Extent of party autonomy to determine the arbitral procedure

According to party autonomy, the parties may freely, and not necessarily in writing, determine the arbitral procedure, subject only to the restrictions in PIL Statute Art 182 which reads as follows: **12.64**

> 1 The parties may, directly or by reference to arbitration rules, determine the arbitral procedure; they may also submit the arbitral procedure to a procedural law of their choice.

---

[131] BGE 128 III 330, 332; BGE 120 II 155; BGE 118 II 359, 361.
[132] See paras 12.201 and 12.222 *infra*.
[133] BGE 126 III 249, 253; BGE 118 II 359, 361.
[134] See BGE 117 Ia 166-9.
[135] See International Arbitration Rules of Zurich Chamber of Commerce (Zurich Rules) Art 18(2).
[136] PIL Statute Art 182.

2 If the parties have not determined the procedure, the arbitral tribunal shall determine it to the extent necessary, either directly or by reference to a statute or to arbitration rules.

3 Regardless of the procedure chosen, the arbitral tribunal shall guarantee equal treatment of the parties and the right of both parties to be heard in adversarial proceedings.

The questions on which the procedure may be freely agreed include those conveniently listed in English Arbitration Act 1996 s 34 (which, as such, is of course not applicable in Switzerland). It is possible for an arbitral tribunal to limit the number of hearings,[137] to omit final oral pleadings,[138] or to request *sua sponte* additional information.[139]

12.65 **(1.1) Are the parties free to choose any national or international law governing the procedure before the arbitral tribunal?** In an arbitration having its seat in Switzerland, which is subject to the Swiss *lex arbitri*, the parties are free to choose any national or international law governing the procedure before the arbitral tribunal.[140] If a non-Swiss procedural law was applied in the arbitral proceedings, this has no impact whatsoever on Swiss state courts (assistance;[141] deposition of award;[142] setting aside[143]). The parties may also choose any set of arbitration rules.[144] In case of doubt, the text of the law currently in force applies, not the text at the time of the agreement to arbitrate.[145] The parties may also modify the arbitration rules chosen, or mix and match arbitration rules, neither of which is, however, recommended.

(2) Basic procedural principles or mandatory rules to be applied by the arbitral tribunal

12.66 Regarding mandatory rules of procedure, all that is required is that 'regardless of the procedure chosen, the arbitral tribunal shall guarantee equal treatment of the parties[146] and the right of both parties to be heard[147] in adversarial proceedings. See paras 12.204 and 12.211 *infra*. The principle of good faith is part of the principles of arbitral procedure that bind the parties[148] and the arbitral tribunal.[149] A stay of the arbitration is proper only in exceptional cases.[150] The right to submit evidence is not unlimited. Only relevant evidence must be heard.[151] In particular, the right to an expert opinion must be exercised in the proper form and at the right time, the requested report must be relevant to the outcome of the arbitration, and the arbitral tribunal must itself lack the necessary expertise.[152] The right to be

[137] BGE, (1996) ASA Bull 646, 649–50.

[138] BGE 117 II 346, 348.

[139] BGE, (1998) ASA Bull 653, 658.

[140] See PIL Statute Art 182.

[141] See para 12.125 and para 12.129 *infra*.

[142] See para 12.150.

[143] See para 12.209.

[144] For *ad hoc* arbitration (non-institutional) arbitration rules are available from the United Nations Commission on International Trade Law (UNCITRAL) and from the International Institute for Conflict Prevention and Resolution (CPR).

[145] BGE, (1994) ASA Bull 226, 228.

[146] Swiss Federal Constitution, Art 8; BGE, (2003) ASA Bull 596, 598; BGE 129 III 445.

[147] Swiss Federal Constitution, Art 29 (2); BGE 130 III 35, 38; BGE 129 III 445.

[148] BGE 111 1a 259, 262.

[149] *ibid*, 72, 76.

[150] BGE 119 II 386, 389; BGE 116 I1 154, 158-60; BGE 109 Ia 81, 84–5.

[151] BGE 116 II 639, 644; BGE, (1992) ASA Bull 391, 398.

[152] BGE 121 III 331, consid 2; BGE 119 II 386, 389.

heard on the law has its limits in *iura novit curia.*[153] The arbitral tribunal normally gives reasons, but this may be waived.[154] Even without a waiver, failure to give reasons is not *per se* a ground to set aside an award.[155]

(3) Oral hearing obligatory or proceeding on basis of written documents

An oral hearing is not mandatory,[156] but PIL Statute Art 182 (1) refers to the agreement of the parties, which may provide for the right of any party to require a hearing.[157] **12.67**

(4) Power of the tribunal (in particular the chairman) to issue procedural orders

The arbitral tribunal, in particular the chairman, has the power to issue procedural orders[158] (usually in writing). The rules stated by the arbitral tribunal are subsidiary to the rules provided by the parties. The arbitral tribunal is free to make reference to any kind of regulations, such as a law or any other arbitration rules. It can make a detailed regulation or just give an answer to a single question. State law is not applicable, neither subsidiarily nor *per analogiam*. The arbitral tribunal is not constrained by any time limit to regulate the arbitral procedure. Generally, it will regulate it at the beginning of the proceedings. By regulating the procedure, it shall come in contact with concerned parties. Often, the tribunal develops together with the parties a whole set of written rules. Such discussions (*pre-hearing conferences*), may result in terms of reference or 'acte de mission', or a 'Constitution Order', and also in an 'Order for directions',[159] and in a procedural timetable.[160] None of this is considered an award, but an award that violates PIL Statute Art 190 (2) may in due course be set aside.[161] **12.68**

(5) Distinction of matters of substance and matters of procedure

To distinguish between matters of substance and procedure, there is no hard and fast rule. One author[162] writes the following: **12.69**

> Whether a question is substantive in its nature (Art 187) or procedural (Art 182) (in other words, the 'substance v procedure' issue) must be answered by the Swiss Private International Law functionally or autonomously (that is independently inter alia from 'lex fori' and 'lex causae', in this sense Schlosser, N 742). For this question Art V(1)(d) of the New York Convention is irrelevant.

In doubtful cases one will characterize a question as substantive. From a functional point of view, one should consider to be substantive all questions that have a substantial impact on the outcome of the case apart from the facts of the case. Therefore, the following questions must be characterized as substantive questions of law:

- who must prove what;

[153] BGE 130 III 35, 38–9; see para 12.158 *infra*.
[154] PIL Statute Art 189 (1).
[155] BGE 116 II 373, 375.
[156] BGE 117 II 346, 348.
[157] eg in International Chamber of Commerce (ICC) Rules Art 20 (2).
[158] PIL Statute Art 182.
[159] Subjects often covered: see UNCITRAL Notes.
[160] Required by ICC Rules Art 18(4).
[161] See paras 12.68, 12.204, 12.207 *infra* but do not overlook para 12.215.
[162] Karrer, P.A., '*PIL Statute Art 187*' note 12-14 in: H. Honsell *et al* (eds), *Basler Kommentar Internationales Privatrecht* (2nd edn, Helbing Lichtenhahn, 2007).

- deadlines to observe;
- deadlines of *mise en demeure*;
- statute of limitations;
- interest;
- presumptions and burden of proof;
- the question, whether an interest worthy of protection exists to justify issuing a declaratory judgment;
- *locus standi*;[163]and
- set-off

By contrast, where the equal treatment of the parties and their right to be heard, in short, procedural due process (Art 182), must be guaranteed, one will characterize a question as procedural. One should pay attention to the fact that procedural law is the handmaiden of substantive law. Procedural questions should remain without substantial influence on the outcome of the dispute. Therefore long-term predictability is less important. Accordingly, the following must be characterized as procedural:

- all questions listed in s 34 Arbitration Act 1996;
- duty to particularize allegations within reason;
- singular procedural provisions of the applicable substantive law such as limitations on proof, for instance, exclusion of parol evidence, prohibition to use as evidence information illegally obtained (exclusionary rule);
- taking of evidence;
- questions covered by the IBA Rules of Evidence, including assessment of the evidence and adverse inferences if evidence is withheld;
- advances and recourse of party that made the advance instead of the other against the defaulting party;
- security for party representation costs;
- establishing and allocating costs.

All the measures taken by the tribunal regarding procedure are qualified as a procedural order or resolution, not as an arbitral award. Thus, PIL Statute Arts 188–194 are not applicable, not even in an indirect way. No appeal is available against procedural orders, except if they can be classified as a decision concerning the jurisdiction of the arbitral tribunal.[164] Decisions concerning procedure may be changed by the arbitral tribunal at any time, although it must consider that the procedure has to be foreseeable for the parties.

12.70 (5.1) **Are statutes of limitations a matter of substance or rather of procedure?** Statutes of limitation are seen as a matter of substantive law.

(6) Persons able to represent a party in an arbitral proceeding

12.71 As far as Swiss arbitration law is concerned, anybody may represent a party before an arbitral tribunal. There is no requirement for specific expertise or admission to any bar. There are no restrictions or special requirements for a legal counsel to act on behalf of his party.

[163] BGE of 5 May 2001, (2002) ASA Bull 80.
[164] See para 12.135 *et seq, infra*.

However, general rules on professional behaviour still apply (eg to avoid conflicts of interest etc).

B. Place of arbitration

(1) Determination of the place of arbitration in absence of an agreement by the parties

The determination of the seat of arbitration in the absence of an agreement by the parties is regulated by PIL Statute Art176(3): **12.72**

> The seat of the arbitral tribunal shall be determined by the parties, the arbitral institution designated by them, or, failing both, by the arbitrators.

(2) Importance and legal effect of place (seat) of the arbitration

The seat of arbitration has exclusively the legal effect of providing the *lex arbitri*. In other words, the seat of the arbitration creates a link with the arbitration law at the seat. By choosing the seat, the parties choose the *lex arbitri*. This has nothing to do with the place where the hearings are held; hearings may be conducted elsewhere.[165] Nor does it have any effect on the law applicable to the procedure before the arbitral tribunal which may be freely chosen and in case of default is not the law at the seat,[166] nor on the law applicable to the merits which also may be freely chosen and in case of default is not the law at the seat.[167] **12.73**

(2.1) Are the arbitrators and parties free to convene at other places than the official seat of the arbitration? Yes.[168] This is regularly done by the so-called *ad hoc* panels of the Court of Arbitration for Sport (CAS). **12.74**

(2.2) Are there visa requirements to enter the country which apply to lawyers and/or arbitrators? Where may current information on that subject be obtained? As many Western and Central European countries, Switzerland is a party to the 'Schengen' treaty under which no passport or identity card is required from anybody entering Switzerland from another 'Schengen' country. Otherwise, for citizens of many countries, a valid passport is sufficient. Swiss visa requirements apply only to citizens of a few countries. For lawyers or arbitrators from such countries who wish to travel to Switzerland for an arbitration, entry visas are regularly granted by the Swiss consulate having jurisdiction for the place of the applicant's residence on the basis of a letter from the chairman of the arbitral tribunal. Current information may be obtained from any Swiss consulate, preferably the consulate having jurisdiction as above. **12.75**

C. Submissions, deadlines and default

(1) Contents and form of submissions (in particular request for arbitration and answer to request)

There are no provisions in the PIL Statute on how submissions should be made. Some arbitration rules provide details, though.[169] **12.76**

165 BGE, (1997) ASA Bull 316, 330.
166 PIL Statute Art 182.
167 *ibid*, Art 187. See ICC Rules Art 14.
168 BGE, (1997) ASA Bull 316, 330.
169 See, for instance, Zurich Rules Art 29.

12.77 **(1.1) From what point in time is a claim considered to be pending with the arbitral tribunal? What are the legal effects of such fact (eg on statutes of limitations)?** PIL Statute Art 181 defines the time when a claim is considered to be pending before an arbitral tribunal:

> The arbitral proceedings shall be pending from the time when one of the parties seizes with a claim either the arbitrator or arbitrators designated in the arbitration agreement or, in the absence of such designation in the arbitration agreement, from the time when one of the parties initiates the procedure for the appointment of the arbitral tribunal.

For the purposes of Swiss law, the effect of *lis pendens* means that a statute of limitations is interrupted and that (because of *lis pendens*) the case may not be made pending elsewhere.[170]

12.78 **(1.2) When is a time limit according to statutes of limitations deemed to be interrupted in case of (i) *ad hoc*; and (ii) institutional arbitration?** Under Swiss law, statutes of limitations are deemed interrupted by bringing suit or by raising a defence in court or in arbitration,[171] be it *ad hoc* or institutional arbitration. PIL Statute Art 181 on *lis pendens* (quoted inpara 14.98 *supra*) applies. Accordingly, the relevant time is the time of receipt of claim by the institution or the arbitral tribunal. ICC Rules Art 4(2) has no effect on *lis pendens* in Switzerland.

12.79 **(1.3) What is the effect of the withdrawal of the request for arbitration?** The withdrawal of a request for arbitration is with prejudice, no matter what the withdrawing party says or reserves unilaterally. In other words, the closing order or award based on the withdrawal will have *res judicata* effect, and the withdrawing party will be prevented from asserting its claim elsewhere once again. Switzerland does not have the equivalent of UNCITRAL Model Law Art 32(2)(a).

(2) Legal deadlines (provided by law or set by the tribunal) and effect of non-compliance by a party

12.80 It is customary for arbitral tribunals to set the parties deadlines for their submissions. There is no statutory deadline to render an award, but the parties may set a deadline, which is not recommended.[172] The Statute does not provide for any deadlines, except for the action to set aside an arbitral award pursuant to PIL Statute Art 190/191.[173] If that deadline is missed, the action to set aside is forfeited.

12.81 **(2.1) What are the powers of the tribunal if a party fails to comply with the time limits set up by the tribunal?** The effect of a party exceeding a deadline is determined by the applicable procedural law. Swiss Rules Art 28 provides as follows:

> DEFAULT
>
> 1. If, within the period of time set by the arbitral tribunal, the Claimant has failed to communicate its claim without showing sufficient cause for such failure, the arbitral tribunal

170 See CO Art 135(2) in connection with PIL Statute Art 9.
171 See CO Art 135(2).
172 See ICC Rules Art 32.
173 Art 191 refers to Statute on the Federal Supreme Court Art 77 which refers, with exceptions, to Art 72 *et seq*, including a 30-day deadline.

shall issue an order for the termination of the arbitral proceedings. If, within the period of time set by the arbitral tribunal, the Respondent has failed to communicate its Statement of Defence without showing sufficient cause for such failure, the arbitral tribunal shall order that the proceedings continue.

2. If one of the parties, duly notified under these Rules, fails to appear at a hearing, without showing sufficient cause for such failure, the arbitral tribunal may proceed with the arbitration.

3. If one of the parties, duly invited to produce documentary evidence, fails to do so within the established period of time, without showing sufficient cause for such failure, the arbitral tribunal may make the award on the evidence before it.

The arbitral tribunal has the right attributed to it under the rules applicable to the procedure.[174] There are no strict rules as to when a party is estopped from bringing in late submissions or communications to the arbitral tribunal.

(2.2) **Is the tribunal bound by any mandatory time limits for certain procedural steps (eg hearings, making of the award)?** There are no statutory mandatory time limits for certain procedural steps (hearings, issuing the award etc) to be observed by the tribunal. However, the Arbitration Rules may provide for certain time limits.[175] The parties sometimes provide for time limits, but this should be discouraged. 12.82

(3) Statutory requirements as to notifications during an arbitration (with respect to the request for arbitration and other written pleadings; with respect to notifications by the tribunal)

There are no statutory requirements as to notifications during an arbitration (with respect to the request for arbitration, other written pleadings or notifications by the tribunal) beyond the requirements following from PIL Statute Art 182(3) which reads as follows: 12.83

Regardless of the procedure chosen, the arbitral tribunal shall guarantee equal treatment of the parties and the right of the parties to be heard in adversarial proceedings.

This means that the arbitral tribunal must make every effort to reach the parties, but if a party that entered into an arbitration agreement becomes unreachable, this is the party's problem, not the arbitral tribunal's or the other party's.

(4) Effect of the insolvency of a party

Generally, the arbitral proceeding remains unaffected by the insolvency of one party. However, since the capacity to act on behalf of a party is governed by the law governing that party,[176] the effect of insolvency may be that a trustee in bankruptcy becomes capable to act on behalf of that party. Such a trustee must be given the time to decide whether to continue the proceedings, or whether the proceedings should be let go their course. 12.84

D. Facts and evidence: general

(1) Burden of proof (inquisitorial/adversarial procedure)

The burden of proof decides who is disadvantaged if the evidence concerning a particular fact is in *equipoise*. The question as to who has the burden of proof is a question characterized 12.85

[174] PIL Statute Art 182(3), and para 12.64 *et seq, supra*.
[175] As per ICC Rules Art 32.
[176] See para 12.71 *supra*.

as substantive. It is governed by the law applicable to the substance of the dispute as determined by PIL Statute Art 187. Burden of proof is rarely relevant in international arbitration. A Swiss arbitral tribunal will normally proceed in an adversarial manner, but, it may proceed in an inquisitorial manner, subject to treating the parties equally and the right to be heard.

(2) Power of the tribunal to determine the admissibility and weight of the evidence produced by the parties

12.86 The PIL Statute says nothing on the power and limits of the tribunal to determine the admissibility and weight of the evidence produced by the parties. Swiss Rules Art 25(7) establishes the principle of free assessment of the evidence ('freie Beweiswürdigung'). A party is not limited in its choice as to what to present as evidence. An arbitral tribunal may, however, exclude evidence that serves no useful purpose, particularly under circumstances of anticipated assessment of the weight of evidence ('antizipierte Beweiswürdigung').[177] An arbitral tribunal may, but is not required to, issue an evidentiary order ('Beweisbeschluss').[178]

12.87 **(2.1) Is the tribunal entitled to take the claimant's factual allegation as proven if the defendant does not participate in the arbitral proceedings?** If the defendant does not participate in the arbitral proceedings, the general view is that the tribunal should not take the claimant's factual allegation as proven at face value. It should, to the extent possible, investigate the facts of the case by all appropriate means, as is expressly mandated by the ICC Rules and applies to any international arbitration in Switzerland.

12.88 **(2.2) May the arbitral tribunal consider an allegation of one party as agreed fact if the other party did not (specifically) dispute the allegation?** Yes. This is civil procedure law in many Swiss cantons.

12.89 **(2.3) What is the standard of proof that must be met in order for a fact to be considered to have been established (preponderance of the evidence; beyond reasonable doubt)? Must a stringent requirement be met for certain facts?** The standard of proof that must be met in order for a fact to be considered to be established is not regulated anywhere. 'Preponderance of the evidence' should in general be the test. More stringent requirement must probably be met for facts which, in a criminal court, could lead to a criminal conviction. For this, the test should be 'beyond any reasonable doubt'.

12.90 **(2.4) May the arbitral tribunal rely on its own knowledge to consider certain facts as proven?** The arbitral tribunal may also rely on its own knowledge to consider certain facts as proven. The parties should be heard about the allegations of fact before the arbitral tribunal relies on its own knowledge.

---

177 BGE 106 II 170, 171.
178 BGE 116 II 639, 644.

E. Witnesses

(1) Ability of a person to act as a witness

12.91 There are no rules in the PIL Statute as to who may act as a witness. Swiss Rules Art 25(2) provides as follows:

> Any person may be a witness or an expert witness...

12.92 (1.1) **Is there a legal difference between a party testifying and a witness? If yes, what are the criteria for such differentiation? Does the testifying of a party have the same weight as a witness testimony?** If the Swiss Rules apply, there is no legal difference between a party testifying and a witness.[179] If different procedural rules apply, they may provide for a differentiation according to criteria of their own, which, in the international context, are sometimes difficult to apply. If a party testifies, the weight to be given to that testimony is usually freely assessed.[180]

(2) Preparation of witnesses and limits thereof

12.93 In continental Europe, proof by contemporary documents is considered generally more reliable than proof by testimony of witnesses. In many state courts in continental European countries and in most Swiss cantons, the parties are not allowed to discuss the contents of a statement of the witness before the questioning of the witness starts. This restriction not to contact witnesses before they are questioned is not applicable in international arbitration. On the contrary, the parties are regularly asked to produce written witness statements before the actual hearings of the witnesses take place, which implies approaching the witnesses. The limits are imposed by criminal law, namely that an intentionally wrong witness statement is a criminal offence.[181]

12.94 Each party has responsibility to arrange for the witness to appear at the hearing. The arbitral tribunal may help with obtaining visas. In cases where the parties do not have the power to give instructions to a reluctant witness to appear, they should contact the arbitral tribunal. The arbitral tribunal may then invite the witness. It is possible to obtain a summons from the *juge d'appui*.[182]

12.95 (2.1) **Do US-style depositions violate any procedural rules or principles?** US-style depositions do not violate any procedural rules or principles, but are neither customary in international arbitration, nor feasible in an even-handed way, as mandated by PIL Statute Art 182(3) (in an international context). Depositions (for any purpose) may not be taken within the territory of Switzerland since this is considered a sovereign act that is the prerogative of the Swiss state. There are criminal sanctions against acting for a foreign state in Switzerland without specific authorization: Swiss Federal Penal Code (Penal Code) Art 271.

---

179 See para 12.91 *supra*.
180 See para 12.86 *supra*.
181 Swiss Penal Code Art 307, equally applicable in arbitration.
182 See examples in (1994) ASA Bull 283, 306.

12.96 (2.2) **May a party or its counsel approach a witness whom it has nominated (only before or also after the proceeding has started)? Are interviews permitted?** A party or its counsel may approach and interview a witness whom it has nominated (before or also after the proceedings have started), Swiss Rules Art 25(6). However, they must not induce false testimony or suborn witnesses. The fact that the parties must bring and indemnify their own witnesses is not contrary to due process.[183]

(3) Admissibility of written witness statements

12.97 Written witness statements are permitted and frequently required by international arbitral tribunals having their seat in Switzerland.[184]

12.98 (3.1) **If the parties agree on written statements, is a party entitled to request an oral hearing for questioning those witnesses (provided such right has not been agreed upon)?** Written witness statements do not violate any procedural rules or principles. They are used routinely in Switzerland. Swiss Rules Art 25(5) expressly permit them. The right to be heard[185] probably means that there is a right to cross-question witnesses orally.[186]

(4) Entitlement of a party to have a hearing or cross-examination of witnesses

12.99 All that PIL Statute Art 182(3) provides is that, regardless of the procedure chosen, the arbitral tribunal shall guarantee equal treatment of the parties and the right of both parties to be heard in adversarial proceedings. There is no absolute right to a hearing.[187] In the case of the testimony of witnesses, the right to be heard will normally mean that a party can request a hearing for cross-questioning.

12.100 (4.1) **Which are the methods used to establish a record of the arbitral proceedings, in particular witness examinations (tape recording, verbatim court reporters, dictated minutes, other methods)?** Any of these methods are used. However, the preference lies on the first two, ie on tape recording and on minutes made by verbatim court reporters.

12.101 (4.2) **May the arbitral tribunal take an oath from a witness?** Many say that an arbitrator may not take an oath from a witness, but there is no known basis for this. Consequently, the answer is yes, although oaths are rarely taken. As a matter of Swiss criminal law, witnesses must tell the truth in arbitration regardless of having taken an oath.

12.102 (4.3) **Does the arbitral tribunal have the power to compel witnesses?** The arbitral tribunal has no power to compel anybody or anything. It can, pursuant to PIL Statute Art 183 request the *juge d'appui* to order a witness to appear before it, and such an order may be accompanied by criminal sanctions.[188]

---

[183] BGE 119 II, 271.
[184] See (1993) ASA Bull 302, with numerous practical examples.
[185] PIL Statute Art 182(3).
[186] See para 12.207 *infra*.
[187] BGE 117 II 346, 348, but see ICC Rules Art 20(2).
[188] For an example of how this was done in Switzerland, see (1994) *ASA Bull* 300.

F. Documents and site inspection

(1) Form and kind of documents to be presented to the arbitral tribunal

In international arbitration conducted in Switzerland, photocopies are normally presented, and the arbitral tribunal provides that originals must be submitted when the conformity of a copy is challenged. In international arbitration conducted in Switzerland, translations into the language of the arbitration are not routinely required, except for the convenience of the parties. Most Swiss arbitrators can handle documentation in various languages. Even before the state courts, translations are not provided as a matter of course. Translation into an official language of Switzerland may be required, but documents in English in support of written submissions are frequently accepted even though English is not an official language. Arbitral tribunals frequently require parties to present documents in their entirety where this is reasonable, or in such excerpts as to allow an assessment of the context. **12.103**

(1.1) Is the submission of 'agreed documents' permitted? If yes, what is the extent and effect of such an agreement of the parties (authenticity, existence, acknowledgement of such documents' contents)? Agreed bundles are little known, but admissible. The effect of having an agreed bundle depends on the agreement of the parties which, if unclear, must be clarified by them. If nothing is agreed, the agreed bundle is just a collection of selected documents for convenience only. **12.104**

(1.2) How may electronic documents (eg emails) be presented and proven? Printouts or electronic files may be filed. **12.105**

(1.3) Does discovery (US- or UK-style), after the procedure has started, violate any procedural rules or public policy considerations? Discovery (US- or UK-style) after the start of the procedure does not violate any procedural rules or public policy considerations as such. Some sort of production of documents proceedings is frequent in international arbitration in Switzerland by way of IBA Rules of Evidence Art 3. **12.106**

(2) Requirement to produce certain documents (as requested by the tribunal) and consequences of a failure to do so

See IBA Rules of Evidence Art 3(3) which is often followed in international arbitration in Switzerland. As IBA Rules of Evidence Art 9 provides, failure to produce a document may lead to specific adverse inferences as to its content. However, the party requesting the document to be produced should allege its content, as should be possible—otherwise this is a prohibited 'fishing expedition' (*Ausforschungsbeweis*). **12.107**

(2.1) Which documents may the tribunal request to be produced (eg also documents which are in the possession of third parties)? See IBA Rules of Evidence Art 3(3)(c). Only documents of any kind may be requested, but only those in the custody or control of a party, not third parties. A party can be ordered to provide its best efforts that a document in possession of a subsidiary be provided. **12.108**

(3) Protection of the confidentiality of documents (legal privilege etc)

Regarding the confidentiality of documents, arbitral tribunals having their seat in Switzerland sometimes make special provisions for the protection of business secrets, see Penal Code Art 273. There is a class of privileged documents, but which law applies to **12.109** determine the nature and extent of *various* privileges is unclear. The same is true for the right of witnesses to refuse testimony.[189] Swiss Rules Art 25(7) provides as follows:

> 7. The arbitral tribunal shall determine the admissibility, relevance, materiality and weight of the evidence offered.

The law on confidentiality of documents is unsettled in Switzerland, and certainly in international arbitration in Switzerland.

(4) Site inspection

12.110 Site inspection should follow clear ground rules set in advance by the arbitral tribunal.[190]

G. Experts

(1) Appointment and presentation of experts by the party or the arbitral tribunal

12.111 Most international arbitral tribunals having their seat in Switzerland provide for the possibility of using party-appointed experts or tribunal-appointed experts as the case requires. In practice, tribunal-appointed experts are used only in a minority of cases.[191]

12.112 (1.1) **By which methods are tribunal-appointed experts selected? What are the rights of the parties during the selection process?** The rights of the parties during the selection of an expert are those listed in PIL Statute Art 182(3). Accordingly, the parties should be heard on whether a tribunal-appointed expert should be appointed. The parties should also be heard with respect to the appointment as such, which profile the expert to be appointed by the arbitral tribunal should match, and the parties should be asked to suggest names of possible candidates. The parties should also have an opportunity to suggest questions to be asked. The arbitral tribunal then selects an expert, not necessarily from the names submitted, and instructs the expert by formulating questions, not necessarily the questions suggested by the parties. The whole process must, at some time in the proceedings, be open and transparent for the parties, but not necessarily at the time when it happens. The expert's report should be submitted in writing to the parties, and they must have an opportunity to ask additional questions to the tribunal-appointed expert concerning the instructions received, the method followed, and the preparation of the expert's report. This is normally done at a hearing with the tribunal-appointed expert.[192]

(2) Admissibility and role of expert witnesses

12.113 Expert witnesses are frequently used in international arbitration having its seat in Switzerland. The experts usually provide a written report similar to a witness statement, and are cross-examined on the basis of that report.

(3) Influence of the parties upon the selection of questions to be submitted to the expert

12.114 In practice, the parties are often asked to provide lists of questions which they suggest should be submitted to the expert before the expert is appointed by the arbitral tribunal.[193]

---

189 'To take the fifth', as the Americans say.
190 BGE 104 Ia 69, 71.
191 See (1993) ASA Bull 446, with numerous practical examples.
192 See para 12.117 *infra*.
193 See BGE 116 II 373.

There is no right of the parties to attend the initial meeting between the expert and the arbitral tribunal or to review, at the time when they are issued, the instructions given by the arbitral tribunal to the tribunal-appointed expert. The arbitral tribunal is, however, not limited or bound by these questions, and the questions to be submitted to the expert are frequently worked out between the arbitral tribunal and the expert. The parties need not be present at the instruction of the expert, but the process which led to the appointment of the expert and the instruction of the expert must be documented in such a way that the parties' right to be heard with respect to these matters is safeguarded in accordance with PIL Statute Art 182(3).

(4) Independence and impartiality of the expert and the right to reject a proposed/appointed expert

Swiss case law provides that experts should be as independent and impartial as required of arbitrators or judges.[194] There is no statutory procedure to reject a proposed expert, but an award rendered on the basis of a report by a tribunal-appointed expert who is not suitably independent and impartial in the sense of PIL Statute Art 180 is subject to being set aside by operation of PIL Statute Art 190(2)(d). In practice, the courts proceed on a case-by-case basis.[195] **12.115**

(4.1) May a party or its counsel approach an expert (or expert witness) whom it has nominated (only before or also after the proceeding has started)? Are interviews admissible? A party or its counsel may approach an expert (or an expert witness) whom it has nominated to become a tribunal-appointed expert (before or also after the proceeding has started). Interviews are admissible. The expert may be questioned about the way he or she was interviewed, and must of course answer truthfully. **12.116**

(5) Oral examination of an expert in a hearing

An expert is usually required to appear at a hearing in order to be questioned. This is provided in the instructions to the expert.[196] The obligation of the expert to appear at the hearing may be derived from PIL Statute Art 182(3). There may be an oral presentation of the expert's report in addition to a presentation in writing prior to the hearing. Questions may be asked orally at the hearing. The correspondence and drafts of experts' reports are privileged. The parties also must have an opportunity to comment on the assessment of the expert's report and answers to additional questions, either orally, or by post-hearing brief. **12.117**

H. Interim measures of protection

(1) Kind of interim measures which the tribunal may order

Unless the parties have otherwise agreed, the arbitral tribunal may, on motion of a party, order provisional or conservatory measures.[197] Some say that the arbitral tribunal may not **12.118**

[194] BGE 126 III 249, 253.
[195] See para 12.86 *supra.*
[196] For an example, see Schneider, M., '*Technical Experts in International Arbitration*' (1993) *ASA Bull* 446, 470–1.
[197] PIL Statute Art 183(1).

order such measures *motu proprio*,[198] but there is no good reason why this should be so. The arbitral tribunal is not limited to a particular kind of interim measures of protection, but may not impose *per diem* fines on parties (*astreintes*),[199] nor issue attachment orders against third parties or Mareva injunctions to third parties.

12.119 (1.1) **Which are, in general, the procedural and substantive prerequisites for the ordering of interim and conservatory measures (eg reduced degree of evidence; urgency; summary evaluation of the claim)?** The ordering of interim and conservatory measures is at the full discretion of the arbitral tribunal. PIL Statute Art 183 simply provides:

> 1. Unless the parties have otherwise agreed, the arbitral tribunal may, on motion of one party, order provisional or conservatory measures.
> 2. If the party concerned does not voluntarily comply with these measures, the arbitral tribunal may request the assistance of the competent court; the court shall apply its own law.
> 3. The arbitral tribunal or the state court may make granting the provisional or conservatory measures subject to appropriate sureties.

12.120 (1.2) **Are the prerequisites for interim measures ordered by the arbitral tribunal more or less the same as if those are requested from the state court? Is there case law/leading authorities on whether those measures are faster and enforced more easily if taken by the arbitral tribunal or the state court?** There is no particular reason why the prerequisites for interim measures ordered by an arbitral tribunal should be more or less the same as those requested from 'the' cantonal state court at the seat. In practice, *periculum in mora* and *fumus boni iuris* are required.[200] Prima facie jurisdiction and reasonable chance of success on the merits are sometimes also said to be required, but this is doubtful. Nor need the interim measures be more or less the same as those normally ordered by the cantonal state court at the seat. Experience shows that provisional and conservatory measures issued by an arbitral tribunal are, as a rule, fast and efficient and are normally complied with. This was the reason why the arbitral tribunal was given this power in PIL Statute Art 183. Note that the *juge d'appui* may be asked for assistance, and that he or she in turn may issue a rogatory request to some other courts anywhere in the world.[201]

(2) Limits of the tribunal's powers to order interim measures

12.121 The arbitral tribunal's powers are wider than those of a Swiss cantonal state court,[202] but they are limited to the parties in the arbitration. Against them the arbitral tribunal has no coercive powers, let alone against third parties.[203] Swiss cantonal state courts do not have the power to order penalties for non-compliance (*astreintes*), except in criminal law. It is doubtful that arbitral tribunals have that power.[204] Whether, and if so, to what extent, Swiss arbitral tribunals can issue anti-suit injunctions and anti-arbitration injunctions, is unclear.

---

198 Girsberger, D. and Voser, N., *International Arbitration in Switzerland* (Schulthess, 2008) 244.
199 In favour, Levy, L., '*Les astreintes et l'arbitrage international en Suisse*' (2001) *ASA Bull* 21.
200 Wirth, M., '*Interim or Preventive Measures in Support of International Arbitration in Switzerland*' (2000) *ASA Bull* 37.
201 See PIL Statute Art 184(2).
202 See para 12.118 *et seq, supra*.
203 Geneva Cour de Justice, Semaine Judiciaire 1990, 196, 199.
204 Levy (n 199).

Interim measures may be ordered subject to providing specified security. The arbitral tribunal has jurisdiction to deal with damages claims in connection with interim measures that it ordered in an arbitration. 12.122

(3) Orders to provide security for the costs of the proceeding

Arbitral tribunals do regularly order the parties to pay advances for the costs of the proceeding.[205] Security for party costs may also be ordered by an arbitral tribunal sitting in Switzerland, but only in a proper case. The view to the contrary expressed in a Zurich Chamber of Commerce decision[206] is not followed in practice. 12.123

(4) Attachment of assets by an order of the tribunal

The attachment of assets with third parties cannot be ordered by an arbitral tribunal. It is conceivable that an arbitral tribunal would order the seizure of assets of a party in a party's hands, but it has never been tried. 12.124

I. Assistance by the courts

(1) Extent of court assistance in the gathering of evidence

PIL Statute Art 184(2) provides that the arbitral tribunal, or one party by agreement with the arbitral tribunal, may request the assistance of the state court at the seat of the arbitral tribunal. Which court this is, is determined by the cantonal law of the seat. Normally in Switzerland, but not necessarily,[207] it is the trial court at the Swiss seat. The assistance may be rendered within Switzerland, in which case the state court applies its own procedure. This means that it is limited to the orders that it can issue itself, eg it can order the appearance of a witness before the arbitral tribunal and underline this by the threat of criminal sanctions following Penal Code Art 292.[208] Another possibility is that the state court at the seat of the arbitration issues letters rogatory to courts abroad.[209] Switzerland's world-wide network of judicial assistance treaties is in this way put to the benefit of international arbitration conducted in Switzerland. An arbitral tribunal having its seat in Switzerland is not precluded from seeking direct assistance by state courts outside Switzerland, if the foreign legal system allows this.[210] 12.125

(1.1) Is it for the arbitral tribunal or for the party to obtain the assistance of state courts with respect to the gathering of evidence? The request must be made by or with the consent of the arbitral tribunal. PIL Statute Art 184 provides: 12.126

1. The arbitral tribunal shall itself conduct the taking of evidence.
2. If the assistance of the state judiciary authorities is necessary for the taking of evidence, the arbitral tribunal, or one party by agreement with the arbitral tribunal, may request the assistance of the state court at the seat of the arbitral tribunal; the court shall apply its own law.

205 On recourse, see para 12.176 *et seq, infra*.
206 See (1995) ASA Bull 84-91.
207 Geneva Cour de Justice, (1990) Semaine Judiciaire 196, 199.
208 For an example, see (1993) ASA Bull 307–8.
209 For an example, see (1993) ASA Bull 316–18.
210 For the converse case, see PIL Statute Art 10.

12.127 (1.2) **According to case law and practical experience, are there considerable delays involved when asking a court to give assistance (eg for the obtaining of evidence)?** There is limited practical experience. No considerable delays are experienced at the Swiss end. However, if a Swiss court issues letters rogatory to a foreign court, the non-Swiss court may be slow. Obtaining testimony from the United States took six months.

(2) Assistance for enforcing the attachment of assets

12.128 There is no right of an arbitral tribunal to order the attachment of assets. Accordingly, the state courts at the seat of the arbitration cannot render 'assistance' to that end. However, a Swiss court at the place of assets may, in a proper case, itself order the attachment of assets within its jurisdiction if the prerequisites of the applicable Swiss Statute on Debt Enforcement and Bankruptcy are met. To give an example, the state court at the place of a bank branch may order the attachment of a bank account with that bank branch. Under Swiss law, an attachment must be 'validated' ('prosequiert') within a certain deadline by a court. This includes an arbitral tribunal if it has jurisdiction in the relation between the debtor and the creditor.

(3) Other examples of possible assistance

12.129 The state court at the seat of the arbitration may also provide other types of assistance; for example, the state court maintains a list of interpreters for various languages. This list is not available to the public, but upon request will be communicated to an arbitral tribunal (treated as a fellow court). If an award or a decision of an arbitral tribunal must be notified to a party, this may be done by way of judicial assistance, using the state court system and diplomatic channels. A state court may permit an arbitral tribunal to hold a hearing on its premises, which it would not do for other types of private meetings. Some believe that PIL Statute Art 185 gives the state court at the seat wide powers for further judicial assistance.[211] Experience shows that Swiss courts render assistance promptly. Once letters rogatory are issued, the process may be cumbersome, unless the Swiss courts can communicate directly with foreign courts, as they are allowed with respect to adjacent Germany, Austria or Italy. Obtaining testimony by letters rogatory in the United States took six months. With other countries, the process may be even slower.

(4) Dependence of the power of state courts to intervene during the proceedings on the (national) procedural law applied by the arbitral tribunal

12.130 The power of state courts to intervene during the proceedings and after the rendering of an award does not depend on which procedural law has been applied. The state court's power is unrelated to the issue of the procedural law applied in the arbitration.

V. The award

A. Types of award

(1) Interim award (eg on interim measures or the jurisdiction of the tribunal)

12.131 There is substantial confusion as to the various types of awards.[212] Various words in various languages are used. The authors suggest that, when several awards are issued in an

[211] See list in Girsberger, D. and Voser, N. (n 198) 253.
[212] Definition of award: BGE 129 II 445; BGE 126 III 529, 534; BGE 119 II 271, 275.

arbitration, the following distinctions be made according to various criteria (frequently used expressions in boldface italics):

Interim award (Zwischen-Schiedsspruch, issued pending arbitration)	as opposed to	**Last award** (the last to be issued in this arbitration)
Partial award (Teilschiedsspruch, putting an end to some, but not all, prayers for relief)	as opposed to	**Full award** (on all prayers for relief in this arbitration)
Preliminary award (Vorschiedsspruch or Vorabschieds-spruch, on a preliminary question, without putting an end to a prayer for relief)	as opposed to	***Final award*** (on one of the prayers for relief, not just on a preliminary question, putting an end to that prayer for relief)

Since the criteria are different, an award may be described by all of them (eg interim partial final award).[213]

In PIL Statute Art 186(3), the statement that the arbitral tribunal shall decide on its jurisdiction by preliminary award is correct only if jurisdiction is accepted. If jurisdiction is declined, the award will on the contrary be a final award (and also a full and last award). The award is not preliminary to anything else. **12.132**

Interim measures of protection are not ordered by interim award,[214] but rather by virtue of PIL Statute Art 183 by the arbitral tribunal or, if need be, by the state court, issuing independent orders. **12.133**

(2) Partial award

Unless the parties otherwise agree, the arbitral tribunal may render 'partial awards'.[215] This means all types of awards, such as interim, preliminary and partial awards. A (preliminary or final) award on the constitution of an arbitral tribunal or on its jurisdiction is subject to a separate complaint to set aside, PIL Statute Art 190(2) and (3).[216] **12.134**

Accordingly, if a preliminary award on constitution or jurisdiction, or both, is made by implication in a preliminary award deciding other matters, the award is, in respect of these other matters, not subject to a separate complaint to set aside, but it is subject already to a separate complaint to set aside in respect of the final constitution or jurisdiction decision. Even if the decision on costs is deferred (also) with respect to the respondents against whom jurisdiction is declined, the partial award declining jurisdiction over them is already subject to complaint to set aside because it is already an award on jurisdiction for the purpose of PIL Statute Art 190(3). Failure to timely file a complaint to set aside such an award **12.135**

[213] For a discussion of the terminology, see BGE 130 III 76, 78, 79, putting an end to earlier confusion. Earlier case law should be used only with caution. See, para 12.134 *et seq, infra*.

[214] See para 12.131 *supra*.

[215] See PIL Statute Art 188.

[216] BGE 130 III 66, 75, 76, 86, putting an end to earlier confusion.

separately leads to the complaint being forfeited.[217] By contrast, all other decisions may be set aside only with the final award, unless they are themselves partial final awards.[218] There is already a partial final award on costs with respect to some respondents if an arbitral tribunal declines jurisdiction over them, and deals with costs with respect to them, even though the arbitration continues against the others.[219] A preliminary award on the merits, but already imposing costs to date, is a partial final award on the costs already incurred. This is important because the 30 days deadline of Swiss Federal Statute on the Federal Supreme Court Art 77 must be observed, or the complaint is forfeited.

12.136 (2.1) **Are awards, especially partial awards, binding in the same arbitral proceeding? Does it make a difference if after the rendering of such a partial award, one arbitrator is successfully challenged and removed on grounds that prevailed even before the partial award was rendered?** Awards, especially partial awards, are binding in the same arbitral proceeding. It makes no difference that one arbitrator was subsequently removed. However, the partial award, if it is a final award,[220] may conceivably be set aside on the basis of PIL Statute Art 190(2)(a) as having been rendered by an arbitral tribunal improperly constituted. It may also be possible to revise the partial award.

(3) Final award

12.137 A final award is an award on one of the prayers for relief, as distinguished from a preliminary award which is only a stepping stone on the way to a final award.

12.138 (3.1) **If a party fails to participate in the arbitration, may the tribunal proceed and issue an award on the merits?** If a party fails to participate in the arbitration, the arbitral tribunal may proceed, and its award is enforceable as any other award. There are no special remedies for the respondent at the enforcement stage.

B. Deliberations and agreement on the award

12.139 All arbitrators must have a reasonable opportunity to participate in the deliberations.[221]

(1) Time limits (and possible extensions) for making the award

12.140 There are no statutory time limits for making the award. Some arbitration rules provide for time limits.[222] Some arbitration agreements provide for deadlines as well. The effect of such a deadline is unclear. It is also unclear how such a deadline may be extended, if the parties do not provide for the possibility of an extension.[223] Some authors believe that this belongs to the realm of the '*juge d'appui*' in the sense of PIL Statute Art 185. Others[224] believe that this belongs in the realm of policing of arbitrators, and thus in PIL Statute Art 179.

---

[217] BGE 130 III 66, 75; BGE 127 III 279, 282; BGE 121 III 495, 502; BGE 118 II 353, 355.

[218] See 12.137 *infra*, BGE 130 III 76, 82, 85; BGE 130 III 66, 75; BGE 128 III 50, 53; BGE 118 II 353, 355.

[219] BGE 116 II 80, 83.

[220] Using the terminology of para 12.131 *supra*.

[221] BGE 111 Ia 336, 338-9.

[222] See eg ICC Rules Arts 24 and 32.

[223] As in ICC Rules Art 32.

[224] Karrer, P.A., '*Le Chapitre 12 LDIP: trois ans après*' (1992) *ASA Bull* 45.

(2) Procedure for the decision of the arbitrators (majority vote etc)

There are no specific provisions on the internal procedure for the decision of the arbitrators. The arbitration rules to which the parties usually refer are silent on this point as well. PIL Statute Art 189 provides that the award shall be rendered in conformity with the rules of procedure and in the form agreed upon by the parties. PIL Statute Art 189 expressly provides that in the absence of such an agreement, the arbitral award shall be made by majority, or in default of a majority by the presiding arbitrator alone. Confidentiality of deliberation covers all aspects of the deliberation.[225] 12.141

(2.1) If an arbitrator fails or refuses to take part in oral deliberation meetings, although having been given sufficient notice of such meetings, may an award be rendered on the basis of written deliberations (or deliberations without this arbitrator) only? All that is required is that the arbitrator has an opportunity to take part in the deliberation, whichever form these take, which is for the presiding arbitrator to decide. If an arbitrator had that opportunity, but did not use it, this is that arbitrator's problem. 12.142

(3) Admissibility of dissenting opinions

Confidentiality of deliberation covers all aspects of the deliberation as such. In Swiss Cantonal Civil Procedure, dissenting opinions may be put on record by dissenting judges. This is very rarely done, though. In international arbitration dissenting opinions are possible, but infrequent. Sometimes, the opinion of a dissenting arbitrator is set out 'embedded' in a reasoned award. 12.143

(3.1) Are there any court decisions or positions of leading authorities on the issue of dissenting opinions (admissibility, disclosure to the parties and publication)? No. Since dissenting opinions are possible in state court proceedings and are available to the parties there, and nobody claims that this is contrary to the secrecy of the deliberation, one does not see how the secrecy of deliberation could be violated by a dissenting opinion in an arbitration, let alone how this might affect the validity of the majority award. The dissenting opinion can be enclosed in the award or communicated to the parties together with it only with the agreement of the majority.[226] 12.144

(4) Signature by the arbitrators and potential failure of one arbitrator to sign

The award shall be in writing, supported by reasons dated and signed, but the signature of the chairperson is sufficient.[227] 12.145

C. Form of the award and deposition

(1) Form and minimum contents of an award

The arbitral award shall be rendered in conformity with the rules of procedure and in the form agreed by the parties, PIL Statute Art 189(1). There is no requirement that the award be in writing or contain a certain minimum content. The requirement that the parties be 12.146

[225] BGE 128 III 234, 238, 239. Dissenting opinions, see para 12.143.

[226] BGE, (1992) ASA Bull 381, 386.

[227] See PIL Statute Art 189(2).

identified is implied.[228] In the absence of an agreement, the award shall be in writing, supported by reasons,[229] dated and signed at the very least by the chairperson, see PIL Statute Art 189(2). The parties may waive this (even by conclusive action). Absent of a waiver, failure to give reasons does not lead to the award being set aside. PIL Statute Art 190(2)(d) refers to PIL Statute Art 182, not to PIL Statute Art 189(2) which is *lex imperfecta.*[230]

(2) Requirement to give reasons in the award

12.147 Unless otherwise agreed by the parties, reasons must be given.[231]

(3) Necessity to specify place and time where and when the award was made

12.148 The award must be dated. It is good practice to specify the seat of arbitration in the award itself. There is no requirement that the place of the making of the award be specified. If no place is indicated, the award will be deemed to have been made at the seat of the arbitration in the sense of PIL Statute Art 176(3).

(4) Other requirements (registration, delivery etc)

12.149 As implied in PIL Statute Art 190(1) the award must be notified in the way agreed by the parties, otherwise it must be handed over in writing to the party representatives.[232] If the notification has achieved its aim, a flaw in the notification is irrelevant.[233] No deposit of any kind is required.[234] A certificate equivalent to deposit may be obtained by any party from the arbitral tribunal itself.[235] A certificate of enforceability may be obtained from the Cantonal Court at the seat of the arbitration.[236] However, to be able to certify enforceability, the Cantonal Court must receive information from the Swiss Federal Supreme Court that no complaint to set aside was received to date, and that date must be later than the deadline for a timely complaint to set aside.[237]

12.150 **(4.1) Does the award have to be laid down or registered with a state court or agency (even if it has been rendered according to a foreign procedural law)?** Which procedural law was applied is irrelevant. The award need not, but may, be deposited by any party at the Swiss Court at the seat.[238]

12.151 **(4.2) Does a foreign award which has been rendered abroad according to this country's national procedural law, have to be laid down or registered with a state court or agency? Is there a fee or tax for such registration of an award?** There is no Swiss national procedural

[228] Obergericht Zürich, PG 020009/V/Wi, 2–3 (unpublished).
[229] BGE 130 III 125, 130.
[230] BGE 116 II 373, 375.
[231] See PIL Statute Art 189(2).
[232] BGE, (2001) ASA Bull 481, 485.
[233] BGE 120 II 155.
[234] See PIL Statute Art 193.
[235] PIL Statute Art 193(2).
[236] *ibid,* 193(3); BGE 130 III 129–30; BGE 107 Ia 318, 323–4
[237] This cumbersome procedure is the result of the hasty drafting process of ch 12 of the PIL Statute. The drafters failed to take into account that PIL Statute Art 191(1) had been amended at a late date to provide for an immediate complaint to the Swiss Federal Supreme Court, by-passing the Cantonal Court. As a result, the Cantonal Court must now certify something of which it has no direct knowledge.
[238] PIL Statute Art 193.

law. The 'procedural law according to which the award was rendered' is in any event irrelevant. No registration of a foreign award is required, or even possible. Foreign awards are recognized and enforced as provided in the New York Convention.

(4.3) **How long after the rendering of the award must the file/award be stored by the lawyers and the arbitral tribunal?** There are no specific rules for international arbitration, but Swiss lawyers are required to keep a file for 10 years.[239] In institutional arbitration, arbitral awards are often kept by the institution. It is also possible to deposit arbitral files, free of charge, with the Zurich Supreme Court, but only if the seat was in the canton of Zurich. **12.152**

D. Applicable substantive law

(1) Party autonomy to choose the applicable substantive law

The arbitral tribunal shall decide the merits of the case[240] according to the rules of law agreed upon by the party, PIL Statute Art 187(1) pt 1 French text. The German text is too narrow. The expression, 'rules of law', was deliberately chosen by analogy to UNCITRAL Model Law, Art 28(1) to include UNIDROIT Principles or *lex mercatoria* etc. **12.153**

The law of the country of execution is irrelevant.[241] **12.154**

(1.1) **Is there a public policy exception to the chosen substantive law?** Yes. This is not mentioned in PIL Statute Art 187, but is normal in private international law (PIL). The PIL of international arbitral tribunals is different from the PIL applicable by Swiss state courts. There is no reason to apply the same standard of public policy. Thus, PIL Statute Arts 17–19 are applicable only in Swiss state courts. The standard in international arbitration should be truly transnational.[242] **12.155**

A distinction is made between negative and positive public policy. Negative public policy excludes the application of the otherwise applicable law in cases where such application leads to a result repugnant to fundamental notions.[243] These fundamental notions are different from those mentioned in PIL Statute Arts 17–19 and must be understood to be of a truly transnational nature. Thus, an arbitral tribunal is not prevented from the outset to award punitive damages. **12.156**

Positive public policy means that intervening public law may be applied in certain circumstances. It is perhaps irrelevant whether this law was expressly chosen by the parties.[244] The place of enforcement of a possible award is probably also irrelevant and not predictable anyway.[245] A close connection between the intervening public law and the case is required. **12.157**

---

239 See CO Art 962 (by analogy).

240 But not other, logically earlier questions such as jurisdiction, capacity or power of parties to enter into a contract.

241 BGE 118 II 353.

242 See Karrer, P.A. and Imhoff, A.-C., '*Ordre public in Schiedssachen: Thema mit Variationen und Schlussakkord*' (1996) *IPRax*, 282-7; Karrer, P.A., '*Public policy in Swiss International Arbitration Law: For once, adjectives make a difference*' (2008) *Stockholm Int'l Arb Rev* 135-41.

243 eg BGE, (1993) ASA Bull 253, 254, also (1994) *ICCA Ybk* 220 (Hilmarton).

244 In this sense, however, BGE 118 II 193.

245 BGE 118 II 353.

Moreover, the policies pursued by the intervening public law must be accepted on a truly transnational scale. An arbitral tribunal may not enforce an agreement providing for activity considered illegal and repugnant in most countries. This, however, does not include agreements contrary to antitrust law. If the arbitral tribunal failed to take into account foreign law or positive public policy nature that was not argued, this will not lead to the award being set aside as contrary to public policy in the sense of PIL Statute Art 190(2)(e).[246] By contrast, the Swiss Federal Supreme Court has decided that failure to examine a positive public policy defence that has been argued amounts to wrongful denial of arbitral jurisdiction.[247]

12.158 (1.2) **Does the principle of '*iura novit curia*; apply? Or must the applicable law be proven (by which means)?** The principle *iura novit curia* applies as it does in state court proceedings.[248] The applicable law must not be proven, but the arbitral tribunal often will request the parties to plead it extensively, with supporting documentation. The arbitral tribunal may, but is not required to, conduct its own research into the applicable law. The parties may then comment, if the content of the applicable law on a particular part remains unclear. The arbitral tribunal may apply a closely-related law or transnational law. The right to be heard that must be granted the parties means that the parties should not be surprised by the arbitral tribunal applying a certain legal theory 'out of the blue'. The parties must be given an opportunity to comment on the theory. It is, however, unclear when this opportunity was sufficiently granted, which makes for a tricky decision towards the close of an arbitration.

(2) Decisions according to equity or as amiable compositeur

12.159 The parties may authorize and require the arbitral tribunal to decide the case *ex aequo et bono,* but they must do so unequivocally.[249] Otherwise, the case must be decided according to rules of law.[250] However, a decision *ex aequo et bono* instead of according to the rules of law agreed by the parties will be set aside only if the result is fundamentally (different and) incompatible with public policy.[251] Conversely a decision according to law instead of *ex aequo et bono* may also stand.[252]

(3) Application of lex mercatoria, *general principles etc*

12.160 The parties may choose *lex mercatoria*, general principles etc, or the arbitral tribunal may apply these as the 'rules of law' with which the dispute has the closest connection.[253]

12.161 (3.1) **Is the application of *lex mercatoria* considered as the application of law or as a kind of *amiable composition*?** It is considered as the application of rules of law in the sense of PIL Statute Art 187(1) pt 1.

[246] BGE, (1999) ASA Bull 529, 535, also (2000) *ICCA Ybk* 511.
[247] BGE 118 II 193.
[248] PIL Statute Art 16; BGE 130 III 35, 38-40; BGE 120 II 172; BGE, (2001) ASA Bull 531; BGE, (2002) ASA Bull 493; BGE, (2006) ASA Bull 318; BGE, (2007) ASA Bull 152; BGE, (2007) ASA Bull 582.
[249] PIL Statute Art 187(2).
[250] *ibid,* Art 187(1).
[251] BGE 116 II 634, 637.
[252] BGE 110 Ia 56, 58.
[253] PIL Statute Art 187(2).

(4) Applicable substantive law if there is no choice of law by the parties

In the absence of a choice of law by the parties, the arbitral tribunal shall decide the case according to the rules of law with which the dispute has the closest connection.[254] This is a conflict of laws rule. Note the inclusion of 'rules of law' which allows the arbitral tribunal to apply UNIDROIT Principles, *lex mercatoria* etc. The closest connection should be established on a case-by-case basis, not following the contract-type formula which applies in PIL Statute Art 117.[255] **12.162**

(4.1) Is there an autonomous conflict of law rule in the national arbitration law? Is it considered mandatory? PIL Statute Art 187 is an autonomous conflict of laws rule that any arbitral tribunal sitting in Switzerland pursuant to the PIL Statute must apply. The rule is considered mandatory, but the parties may designate the applicable rules of law pursuant to PIL Statute Art 187(1) pt 1 in an indirect fashion, namely by designating choice-of-law rules which in turn designate the applicable rules of law. This occurs each time the parties designate arbitration rules that contain a choice-of-law rule, as many do. **12.163**

(4.2) What is the law applicable to interest? The law applicable to interest is characterized as a question of substance, not procedure. Accordingly, the law applicable to the merits is often applied. However, the result of applying a statutory interest rate of one law to the currency of another country is unsatisfactory. **12.164**

(4.3) What is the law and practice with respect to legal interest on foreign currency debts? The law is unsettled. Swiss statutory interest is simple interest at 5 per cent per annum. This seems low on some weak currencies, but high on some hard currencies, presently including Swiss francs. It would seem reasonable to gear the interest rate to the particular currency of payment. The only reasonably convenient route to this fair result is UNIDROIT Principles Art 7.4.9.(2), which reads as follows: **12.165**

> The rate of interest shall be the average bank short-term lending rate to prime borrowers prevailing for the currency of payment at the place of payment, or where no such rate exists at that place, then the same rate in the State of the currency of payment. In the absence of such a rate at either place the rate of interest shall be the appropriate rate fixed by the law of the State of the currency of payment.

(5) Binding effect of state court decisions

If the *res judicata* effect of an earlier award by the same arbitral tribunal is disregarded, this is said to violate 'procedural public policy',[256] but may simply be a wrong acceptance of jurisdiction. Apart from public policy considerations, and apart from *stare decisis* (which is not part of Swiss law), only Swiss state court decisions can have a binding effect on Swiss arbitral tribunals. However, which state court decisions? The place of arbitral tribunals within the Swiss legal system is arguably just below the Swiss Federal Supreme Court (which is the only Swiss state court that can set aside awards, and even that only in a very limited way). Accordingly, there is no good reason for Swiss arbitral tribunals to follow lower Swiss **12.166**

---

254 PIL Statute Art 187(1) pt 2.

255 For further details, see Karrer, P.A., '*PIL Statute Art 187*' note 105 *et seq* in H. Honsell *et al* (eds), *Basler Kommentar Internationales Privatrecht* (2nd edn, Helbing Lichtenhahn, 2007).

256 See BGE 128 III 191, 194.

state court precedents, which still lower Swiss state courts may wish to do. However, even Swiss Federal Supreme Court precedents are not binding on the Swiss Federal Supreme Court itself. One may argue that therefore they cannot bind Swiss international arbitral tribunals either. One might therefore even say that for their decisions international arbitral tribunals having their seat in Switzerland are on a par with the Swiss Federal Supreme Court. Still, if an award has been set aside by the Swiss Federal Supreme Court and the case remanded to the arbitral tribunal, the arbitral tribunal is bound by the views of the Swiss Federal Supreme Court, which are then *res judicata*. State court decisions concerning the content of the applicable law may be sources of law, and, as such, may bind a Swiss international arbitral tribunal, but subject to the above considerations about levels.

12.167 A state court decision anywhere in the world may be *res judicata* for the arbitral tribunal, but only if rendered between the same parties and by a court that had jurisdiction based on the agreement of the parties—in other words, in the view of the authors, only where the New York Convention would require recognition had the state court been an arbitral tribunal, see forthwith.

12.168 (5.1) **Is an arbitral tribunal bound by a decision of another arbitral tribunal?** Yes, provided the other arbitration was between the same parties, and the conditions for recognition as provided in the New York Convention are met.

12.169 (5.2) **Does a decision in a criminal case bind an arbitral tribunal?** A decision in a criminal case does not as such bind an arbitral tribunal. The principle, *le pénal tient le civil en l'état* was rejected by the Swiss Federal Supreme Court.[257] It may well be contrary to Swiss Federal Law. If the criminal court decided civil aspects (exercising 'adhesion' jurisdiction), its jurisdiction would have to be specifically acknowledged to bind the arbitral tribunal.

E. Settlement

(1) Settlement by agreement of the parties with or without support of the arbitral tribunal

12.170 It is proper for arbitral tribunals having their seat in Switzerland to seek to induce the parties, at least with their agreement, to reach a settlement.[258] If a settlement is reached, the case must be closed.

12.171 (1.1) **May an arbitrator who has initiated settlement discussions be challenged when agreement on a settlement has failed?** No.

(2) 'Private settlement' and its impact on the arbitral procedure

12.172 Parties are well advised in a private settlement to deal with the following questions:

- should the arbitral tribunal retain jurisdiction until certain payments have been made or certain things are done? Normally not.
- should the arbitral tribunal render an award by consent (stating the content of the settlement and making it enforceable with the New York Convention) or just a closing order (simply closing the case)? Normally, a private settlement will lead to a closing order by the arbitral tribunal, not to an award by consent.

---

[257] See BGE 119 II 386, 389–98.

[258] This may explain why pure mediation is less frequent in Switzerland than in some other countries.

- how should the arbitral tribunal allocate the arbitration costs? What should happen to the advances? Normally, the arbitration costs are split evenly.
- should the arbitral tribunal award party costs, and how? Normally, each party pays its own party costs.

(3) Form and effect of a settlement (eg award on agreed terms?)

Normally, an award by consent is issued only if all the parties request it. See Swiss Rules Art 34(2). In an exceptional case, an arbitral tribunal can refuse to issue an award by consent. **12.173**

F. Costs of the arbitration

(1) General allocation of the costs of the proceedings

Generally, the costs follow the event, ie the losing party pays proportionally the costs of the arbitration to the extent that it lost. **12.174**

(2) Deposits or advances for costs or fees

Normally, there are deposits for costs and fees. **12.175**

(2.1) **Is there case law authorizing or prohibiting arbitrators to order a party to pay an advance on the arbitration costs?** There is no case law prohibiting advances, and few arbitrators would work on a case without being secured. Under the Zurich Law in force until 1987, a party that advanced costs in substitution for the defaulting other party had a statutory right of recourse *pendente lite.* After that, the Concordat and later the PIL Statute applied, which say nothing about this. It is nevertheless possible for an arbitral tribunal to issue an interim award providing for such a recourse. In the ICC system, this type of interim award is by now regularly issued. **12.176**

(2.2) **May the raising of a set-off claim or counterclaim be made contingent upon payment of the corresponding advance for the relating arbitration costs (cf eg ICC Rules Article 30(5))? May such a condition be agreed upon when entering into the arbitration agreement?** A counterclaim may be made contingent upon payment of the corresponding advance (as may the main claim). In Swiss private law a set-off is a defence based on substantive law which may be raised at any time. The parties could exclude by agreement the right to set-off entirely or make it contingent upon the payment of an advance. This is never done, and is in our view neither done in ICC Rules Art 30(5). **12.177**

(2.3) **What remedies exist against a party which does not pay its part of the advance on the arbitration costs? (eg termination of the arbitration agreement)? How may the other party enforce its rights?** If another party pays in its place and stead, this party may be granted a right of recourse.[259] If the arbitration fails because of a failure to pay advances, Swiss Rules Art 41(4) and (5) provides as follows: **12.178**

> 4. If the required deposits are not paid in full within thirty days after the receipt of the request, the arbitral tribunal shall so inform the parties in order that one or another of them may make the required payment. If such payment is not made, the arbitral tribunal may order the suspension or termination of the arbitral proceedings.

[259] See para 12.176 *supra.*

5. In its final award, the arbitral tribunal shall render an accounting to the parties of the deposits received. Any unexpended balance shall be returned to the parties.

This is probably the law generally accepted in Switzerland. This means that the arbitral proceedings are suspended or terminated so that they cannot be resumed, but the agreement to arbitrate remains in force, and another arbitration concerning a different dispute remains possible, based on the same agreement to arbitrate.

(3) Costs of the administration by an arbitration institution

12.179 Under Swiss Rules Art 3(3)(h) and Fee Schedule Art 1, there is an initial fee that covers the registration and the work of the arbitral tribunal up to the making of the constitution order. After that, the arbitral tribunal itself administers deposits. It is required, above a certain threshold, to send a percentage contribution to the general costs of Swiss Chambers arbitration which is payable over and above the arbitration costs.

(4) Arbitrators' fees: law and practice, judicial control

12.180 Arbitrator's fees may be freely agreed between the parties and the arbitrators. Lump sum fees are rare. As any other agreement, an agreement on fees may be changed later. Failing an agreement, fees are set by the arbitral tribunal itself. For *ad hoc* arbitration, the Zurich Bar Association has guidelines. If the parties referred to arbitration rules, the costs are set by them or (more often) by a schedule of costs attached to them. The fees schedule of the Swiss Chambers is *ad valorem,* in conformity with the arbitration costs schedule, with supervision by the institution. In ICC arbitration, the amount of arbitration costs is determined by the International Court of Arbitration of the ICC, but entered in the award by the arbitral tribunal. The arbitral tribunal is free to have its fees secured by advances.[260]

12.181 The costs are normally entered in the last award by the arbitral tribunal. There is normally no separate award on costs.

12.182 There is a decision that no reasons must be given for an order for costs.[261]

12.183 The judicial remedy against an excessive costs award is not different from the judicial remedy against any other decision on the merits. Accordingly, only procedural points may be taken under PIL Statute Art 190(2)(a) to (d), and on substance (principle and *quantum* of costs), only. Thus, PIL Statute Art 90(2)(e) applies.

12.184 (4.1) **May arbitrators fix their own fees in the award?** Yes, arbitrators may fix their own fees in the award. The remuneration is subject to an agreement between the parties and the arbitrators; the parties' influence on the remuneration is limited, though. Sometimes a hide-and-seek game is played between the parties and the arbitrators: The parties try to keep the value in litigation low or undetermined as long as possible, particularly in arbitration systems which have an *ad valorem* fee schedule, such as the ICC.

12.185 (4.2) **How can the parties challenge the arbitrators' fees once they are fixed?** There is no specific provision on judicial control of arbitration costs, but an award of excessive costs might be set aside presumably under PIL Statute Art 190(2)(e), see para 12.208 *infra*.

[260] BGE, (2003) ASA Bull 829, 837; BGE, (2003) ASA Bull 822, 825–6.
[261] BGE, (2001) ASA Bull 102, 111 (doubtful in this generality).

(4.3) Are the arbitrator's fees subject to income tax if (i) the place of arbitration; or (ii) the normal residence or place of business of the arbitrator is located in this country? Foreign arbitrators arbitrating in Switzerland are not subject to Swiss income tax. Arbitrators having their residence or place of business in Switzerland are subject to income tax in Switzerland, and the arbitrators' fees that they earned world-wide are included in their income for this purpose. 12.186

(4.4) Are arbitrator's fees submitted to VAT? If yes, is the duty to pay such tax linked to (i) the place of arbitration; or (ii) the arbitrator's general residence? There is no Swiss VAT on arbitrator's fees, regardless of whether the arbitration is domestic or international, whether the arbitrator has his or her residence or place of business in Switzerland or abroad, and regardless of the parties.[262] This will remain after the current revision of the Federal VAT Statute. 12.187

(5) Attorneys' fees and the winning party's claim for reimbursement

Generally, the winning party (*pro rata* of its success) is compensated for its reasonable party representation fees. This includes regularly its outside lawyers fees, but also the costs of outside experts, interpreters, witnesses, and, in a proper case, may also include internal costs, particularly where a case is handled exclusively in-house.[263] 12.188

(5.1) May in-house lawyers charge fees or may a party request costs of in-house lawyers to be reimbursed? In-house lawyers may not charge fees directly. Fees are an internal matter between them and their employer. There has been a case where a party that had used in-house lawyers had its costs reimbursed on the basis of what outside counsel would have charged in a similar case (and opposing outside counsel did charge in this case). 12.189

(6) Time and form of the decision on costs

The decision on costs is taken in writing, and normally at the end of the entire arbitration, forming part of the last award. Interim decisions on costs are possible, for instance in a preliminary award on jurisdiction, but in institutional arbitration this may be contrary to the arbitration rules applicable. 12.190

(6.1) May the arbitrators' decision on the costs (allocation and amount of costs to be reimbursed) be challenged separately from the award itself? Are there time limits for such a remedy? It is usually part of the final award, and a complaint to set aside is possible in that connection. It is possible to challenge only the costs part of an award. If, English-style, a separate costs award is issued after the main partial award on the merits, that costs award is subject to complaint to set aside separately. Is the main partial award conversely subject to its own complaint to set aside already when issued, or is a complaint to have it set aside available only at the time of the costs award which puts an end to the arbitration? The former, because the main partial award is a final award on its merits. 12.191

The same legal provisions apply as for any challenge of an award, and the deadline is the same, 30 days.[264] 12.192

262 See Karrer, P.A., Roos, C. and Nordin, M., '*Wie verschieden sind Leistungen von Schiedsrichtern und Anwälten für die Zwecke der Mehrwertsteuer?*' (1998) *ASA Bull* 5.

263 See para 12.189.

264 See para 12.211 *infra*.

12.193 (6.2) **Are the arbitrators entitled and/or legally obliged to rule on the amount of one or both parties' costs that are recoverable?** Party representation costs are regularly assessed and allocated by the arbitral tribunal in its last award. These include costs of private experts, translators, court reporters, travel costs, witnesses' costs.

G. Publication of the award

(1) Publication with or without the consent of the parties

12.194 Awards generally may not be published without the consent of the parties. Swiss Rules Art 43(1) provides:

> Unless the parties expressly agree in writing to the contrary, the parties undertake as a general principle to keep confidential all awards and orders as well as all materials submitted by another party in the framework of the arbitral proceedings not otherwise in the public domain, save and to the extent that a disclosure may be required of a party by a legal duty, to protect or pursue a legal right or to enforce or challenge an award in legal proceedings before a judicial authority. This undertaking also applies to the arbitrators, the tribunal-appointed experts, the secretary of the arbitral tribunal and the Chambers.
>
> 2. The deliberations of the arbitral tribunal are confidential.
> 3. An award may be published, whether in its entirety or in the form of excerpts or a summary, only under the following conditions:
>   (a) A request for publication is addressed to the Chambers;
>   (b) All references to the parties' names are deleted; and
>   (c) No party objects to such publication within the time–limit fixed for that purpose by the Chambers.

(2) Practice of publication (eg in specific legal journals)

12.195 Some awards rendered by arbitral tribunals having their seat in Switzerland are published in *the ASA Bulletin* and other international arbitration publications such as *the ICCA Yearbook*, *Mealey's*, *the Journal of International Arbitration*, *Arbitration International* etc. The entire Swiss state court case law on international arbitration has been published in English translation in *Swiss International Arbitration Law Reports*, since 2007.

VI. Amendment and challenge of the award; liability of arbitrators

12.196 Once issued, an award has *res judicata* effect.[265] This applies to the operational part of the award. The reasons may be taken into account to understand the operational part but are not *res judicata*.[266]

A. Amendment, correction or interpretation of the award

(1) Motion to amend or correct an award

12.197 This is an area where there are no statutory provisions. The arbitration rules may cover this, see ICC Rules Art 29; Swiss Rules Arts 36 and 37. Clerical errors may be corrected at any

---

[265] BGE 128 III 191, 194.
[266] *ibid*, 195.

time by the arbitral tribunal, *sua sponte* or upon request by a party. Other corrections of an award are possible if the parties agree to confer jurisdiction for this on the arbitral tribunal. A party may, within 90 days of (sufficient) notice of the mistake,[267] error or need for interpretation of the award, request a revision of the award from the Swiss Federal Supreme Court.[268] Such a revision will be granted if the award was affected by a crime. Whether it may also be granted in other cases is unclear. If the request is granted, the case is remanded to the arbitral tribunal for correction or interpretation,[269] and a new complaint to set aside becomes available within 30 days of the correction or interpretation inasmuch as it relates to the correction or interpretation. All this is based on dicta in case law.

(2) Interpretation of the award by the tribunal

The tribunal may not interpret the award rendered, unless the parties confer jurisdiction upon it for this purpose. In analogy to the action to set aside within a relatively short deadline in international commercial arbitration, the deadline for such request for interpretation (if granted by the parties to the arbitral tribunal) is 30 days.[270] **12.198**

B. Appeal on the merits

(1) Admissibility and procedure of an appeal on the merits

No appeal to Swiss state courts on the merits is possible in the sense of a full review of the facts and the law, and the parties cannot, by agreement, extend the jurisdiction of Swiss state courts in this respect. Any previous decision by an arbitral institution such as the ICC Court is irrelevant for the Swiss Federal Supreme Court deciding on a complaint to set aside and is not as such subject to being set aside.[271] The only judicial remedy available is a 'complaint' (to set aside) to the Swiss Federal Supreme Court.[272] Swiss Federal Statute on the Swiss Federal Supreme Court Art 77 applies. However, the statutory value in dispute threshold of Swiss Federal Statute on the Swiss Federal Supreme Court Art 74(1)—currently CHF 30,000—does most probably not apply even though Art 77 does not exclude it expressly. The legislator simply wished to continue previous law on international arbitration under new terminology, not further limit party rights and leave certain parties without any remedy at all. **12.199**

(1.1) May the parties agree on an appeal to another arbitral tribunal? Yes. **12.200**

(2) Possibility to exclude an appeal (eg, in the arbitration clause)

There is no appeal to Swiss state courts on the merits. The far more limited review by the Swiss Federal Supreme Court in complaint to set aside proceedings may be excluded by non-Swiss parties at any time (waiver agreement).[273] **12.201**

---

[267] For the calculation, see para 12.211 *infra*.

[268] BGE 122 III 492, 493; BGE 119 II 271; BGE 118 II 199, 200–204; PIL Statute Art 191(2) is no longer the law.

[269] BGE 119 II 199, 205.

[270] BGE 130 III 125, 131.

[271] BGE 118 II 359, 361.

[272] PIL Statute Art 191.

[273] See para 12.222 *infra*.

C. Setting aside of the award

12.202 Swiss International Arbitration law does not say anything about the possibility that an award might be absolutely null and void (examples: an award pronouncing a divorce, an award issued by a pseudo-arbitral tribunal) and would not have to be set aside, but could simply be ignored.[274]

(1) Reasons for setting aside an award

12.203 If an award is based on several alternative or subsidiary reasonings, the complaint must request and achieve that all of them be set aside, or the award will stand.[275] A party must *complain* immediately or without delay to the arbitral tribunal of a procedural irregularity, or it will have waived its right to have the award set aside on this ground.[276]

12.204 The only reasons for which the Swiss Federal Supreme Court[277] may set aside an award[278] are set out as follows in PIL Statute Art 190(2):

(a) if the sole arbitrator was not properly appointed or when the arbitral tribunal was not properly constituted;[279]
(b) if the arbitral tribunal wrongly accepted or declined jurisdiction;[280]
(c) if the arbitral tribunal's decision went beyond the prayers for relief submitted to it, or failed to decide one of the items in the claim;[281]
(d if the principle of equality of the parties or the right of the parties to be heard was breached;[282] and
(e) if the award is contrary to public policy.[283]

This list is exhaustive.[284] No ground to set aside an arbitral award may be derived from the European Convention on Human Rights Art 6.[285]

12.205 With respect to the proper constitution and the jurisdiction of the arbitral tribunal,[286] the Swiss Federal Supreme Court is free in its appreciation of the law and its application to the

[274] For a discussion, see BGE 130 III 125, 132; BGE of 21 June 1995, 4 p 267/1994, (unpublished). See para 12.29 *supra*.
[275] BGE 115 II 288, 293.
[276] BGE 127 III 576; BGE 119 II 386, 388; BGE 116 II 639, 644; BGE, (2002) ASA Bull 271.
[277] PIL Statute Art 191(1).
[278] This means, the operative part of the award, not the reasoning, BGE 120 II 155, 167.
[279] Selected case law: BGE 130 III 66, 75; BGE 129 III 445, 449; BGE 119 II 271; BGE 118 II 359, 360; BGE 117 Ia 166, see para 12.58 *et seq, supra*.
[280] Selected case law: BGE 130 III 125, 129; BGE 128 III 50, 54; BGE 121 III 495, 502; BGE 121 III 38, 41; BGE 120 II 155, 164; BGE 118 II 193, 195; BGE 117 II 94, 98; BGE 116 II 639, 641–2.
[281] Selected case law: BGE 128 III 234, 242; BGE 128 III 50, 59; BGE 122 III 492; BGE 120 II 172, 175, 176; BGE 116 II 81, 85; BGE 116 II 639, 641; BGE 115 II 288, 293.
[282] Selected case law: BGE 130 III 125, 130; BGE 130 III 35, 37–8; BGE 129 III 445; BGE 128 III 234, 243; BGE 127 III 576, 579; BGE 120 II 155, 116; BGE 119 II 386, 388–90; BGE 117 II 346, 347, 348; BGE 116 II 639, 642–3; BGE 116 II 373, 375; BGE, (1990) ASA Bull 171, 176–7.
[283] Selected case law: BGE 128 III 191, 198; BGE 128 III 50, 58; BGE 120 II 155, 166; BGE 117 II 604, 606; BGE 116 II 634, 635; BGE 115 II 288, 292. It should be noted that, since the PIL Statute came into force in 1989, not a single arbitral award was ever set aside based on PIL Statute Art 190(2)(e).
[284] BGE 128 III 191; BGE 119 II 380, 382–3; BGE 116 II 721, 723, 728; BGE 115 II 102, 105.
[285] BGE, (1998) ASA Bull 634, 645.
[286] PIL Statute Art 190(2)(a) and (b).

facts as found.[287] A general reasoning by the arbitral tribunal on this point is accordingly sufficient even with respect to foreign law.[288]

The Swiss Federal Supreme Court cannot find new facts.[289] It is bound by the facts as found by the arbitral tribunal, unless the finding of these facts was itself based on a violation of the principle of equality of the parties or the right of the parties to be heard or (doubtful) if the finding of facts is contrary to procedural public policy.[290] By contrast, a finding of fact that is arbitrary, manifestly erroneous, or contrary to the file, is not a ground for setting aside,[291] unless there is procedural denial of justice.[292] If findings of fact were successfully set aside by the Swiss Federal Supreme Court, it may, by exception make its own new findings of fact.[293] **12.206**

With respect to the procedure followed before the arbitral tribunal, only a violation of PIL Statute Art 190(2)(d), which refers back to PIL Statute Art 182,[294] may lead to setting aside an award. If there is such a violation, the award is set aside regardless of why the denial of due process occurred, whether the violation led to the outcome, or its correction would lead to a different outcome.[295] Some decisions by the Swiss Federal Supreme Court[296] make *obiter* reference to 'procedural public policy' apparently found in PIL Statute Art 190(2)(e), but fail to specify how this might differ from the content of PIL Statute Art 190(2)(d), or add to it, or to the principle of *res judicata* (*ne bis in idem*).[297] **12.207**

With respect to the application of the law, PIL Statute Art 190(2)(e) applies. A plain *error in law* or even an arbitrary application of the law[298] is not sufficient to set aside an award.[299] This includes the application of the wrong law or the wrong application of the right law, or the wrong application of the wrong law, or applying *ex aequo et bono*, instead of law,[300] or the other way around,[301] always as long as the outcome does not in itself violate public policy.[302] In this connection, public policy is understood as truly transnational public policy[303] and goes beyond the substantive public policy applicable before a Swiss state court.[304] Somewhat more specific statements about the content of public policy say that this includes **12.208**

---

287 BGE 128 III 50, 54; BGE 121 III 495, 502; BGE 121 III 38, 41; BGE 120 II 155, 164; BGE 117 II 94, 97; BGE, (1996) ASA Bull 496, 501.

288 BGE, (2003) ASA Bull 842, 846.

289 BGE 124 I 208, 212.

290 BGE 120 II 155, 166; BGE 119 II 380, 383; BGE, (1995) ASA Bull 217, 223.

291 BGE 121 III 331, 333; BGE 117 II 604, 606; BGE 116 II 634, 636-7; BGE 115 II 102, 105.

292 BGE 121 III 331, 333–4.

293 BGE, (2003) ASA Bull 842, 844–5.

294 BGE 119 II 386, 388–9.

295 A 'formal' denial of justice suffices: BGE 127 III 576; BGE 121 III 331, 333–4.

296 BGE 120 II 155.

297 BGE 129 III 445, 465; BGE 128 III 191, 194; BGE 127 III 279, 283, since then superseded by PIL Statute Art 186 (1bis); BGE 126 III 249, 252, 253; BGE 117 II 346, 347; BGE 116 II 373, 375.

298 BGE 120 II 155, 166; BGE 119 II 271; BG 115 II 288, 292; BGE 116 II 634, 636–7.

299 BGE 116 II 634, 637.

300 *ibid.*

301 See BGE 110 Ia 56, 58.

302 BGE 127 III 576, 578; BGE 25 November 1993, 4 p 99/1993 (unpublished).

303 BGE 120 II 155, 166–7; BGE 117 II 604, 606–7; BGE 116 II 634, 635, 637.

304 Pursuant to PIL Statute Art 17, Art 135(2) and Art 137(2). See BGE 126 III 534, 538; BGE 125 III 443, 447.

pacta sunt servanda,[305] privity of contractual rights (*pacta tertiis nec prosunt nec nocent*),[306] good faith,[307] the prohibition of discrimination on the basis of gender, race, etc,[308] expropriation without compensation,[309] prohibition to pay bribes,[310] but not statutes of limitation,[311] or interest.[312] Interventionist norms ('Eingriffsnormen') might constitute 'positive' public policy, but they would have to have a universal basis.[313]

12.209 (1.1) **May an award made according to international or foreign procedural rules be the object of an application for setting aside before the national courts?** That foreign procedural rules were followed is irrelevant.[314] As long as the seat of the arbitration was in Switzerland, the Swiss *lex arbitri* applies, and setting-aside proceedings before the Swiss Federal Supreme Court are possible, unless there was a waiver agreement.

(2) Procedure and deadlines for challenging an award

12.210 If a party believes that a ground for complaint to set aside has been set, it must without delay inform the arbitral tribunal and the other party, or the complaint is waived.[315]

12.211 With regard to the procedure and deadlines of a complaint for setting aside an award PIL Statute Art 191(1) refers to the Federal Statute on the Federal Supreme Court regarding complaints which has, in its Art 77, a time limit of 30 days. The 30 days start on the day after notification of the award unless this is a cantonal holiday, presumably at the seat of the arbitration, not anywhere else, but federal court vacations also apply.[316] The complaint to set aside goes straight to the Swiss Federal Supreme Court,[317] but filing it abroad with any Swiss embassy or consulate also keeps the deadline, PIL Statute Art 12. Within the 30 days,[318] the complainant must set out in writing its full complaint to set aside. In theory, the deadline can be extended or reinstated, but this has never happened in practice.[319] The complaint must be based on the record as it was before the arbitral tribunal at the time of the making of the award; no new proof may be adduced. The precise grounds on which the award should be set aside must be stated. Only these will be examined. No reference to earlier submissions is permitted.[320] Mere appellatory criticism of the award is useless.[321]

---

305 BGE 116 II 634, 638; but this is not violated each time a contract is not applied the way a party would wish.

306 BGE 120 II 155, 169; but this is only the counterpart of *pacta sunt servanda.*

307 BGE, (2001) ASA Bull 781, 792.

308 BGE, (2000) ASA Bull 582, 601.

309 BGE 102 Ia 574.

310 BGE 119 II 380.

311 BGE, (1992) ASA Bull 365, 366.

312 BGE, (2002) ASA Bull 660, 675.

313 BGE 128 III 234, 243.

314 See para 12.208, *supra.*

315 See para 12.215 *infra*; BGE 120 II 155. However, if the party discovers the defect only during the time limit for the complaint to set aside, it is sufficient for it to keep the deadline.

316 See n 318 *infra.*

317 PIL Statute Art 191(2) was abolished, effective from 1 January 2007.

318 For details, see Arts 44 to 46 Swiss Federal Supreme Court Statute. Caveat: The European Convention on Time Limits (SR 0.221.122.3) is not (yet) uniformly applied in Switzerland with respect to local holidays.

319 BGE, (1997) ASA Bull 113, 114, also (1998) *ICCA Ybk* 197.

320 BGE, (2003) ASA Bull 570, 574.

321 BGE 129 III 445; BGE 128 III 191; BGE 116 II 634, 637.

A complaint to set aside is often combined with a request for suspensive effect. The respondent is then given two deadlines, a shorter one to respond to the request for suspensive effect, and a longer one to respond on the merits. It is good practice for the respondent to answer both requests simultaneously within the short deadline. Suspensive effect is regularly denied. 12.212

The Swiss Federal Supreme Court may then order a hearing, but usually does not do that[322] and more often than not renders its decision within less than five months. Even where the decision is on the constitution of the arbitral tribunal or its jurisdiction, the proceedings usually do not take longer. 12.213

Where the arbitral tribunal decided on its constitution or jurisdiction in a preliminary award, it can be set aside only if the action to set aside was brought within 30 days from the notification of the preliminary award.[323] If a plea of lack of jurisdiction was not raised prior to any defence on the merits,[324] the party is considered to have entered an unconditional appearance. An unconditional appearance is treated as an agreement to arbitrate. In such a case, the party no longer can challenge the jurisdiction of the arbitral tribunal. 12.214

An action to set aside an arbitral award because of failure to guarantee equal treatment of the parties or the right of both parties to be heard in adversarial proceedings can be brought only if the objection was raised without delay with the arbitral tribunal.[325] Otherwise, the complaint to set aside is waived. 12.215

(2.1) Who may (or must) represent a party in a proceeding for setting aside an award? Anybody may represent a party (in one of Switzerland's official languages) in a complaint before the Swiss Federal Supreme Court to set aside an award.[326] It is wise to retain a Swiss lawyer. The details of the procedure before the Swiss Federal Supreme Court justify this.[327] 12.216

(2.2) Do specific time limits exist for setting-aside procedures concerning awards on jurisdiction? The time limit is 30 days from the rendering of the interim award on jurisdiction, if any is rendered, otherwise, of the final award recognizing (possibly by implication) the jurisdiction of the arbitral tribunal.[328] See para 12.211 *supra*. 12.217

---

[322] BGE, (2003) ASA Bull 842, 845; BGE, (2003) ASA Bull 585, 588.

[323] PIL Statute Art 190 (3); BGE 116 II 721, 731; BGE, (1997) ASA Bull 113, 114.

[324] As provided in PIL Statute Art 186(2).

[325] BGE 116 II 644; BGE 113 Ia 67; BGE 119 II 388; BGE 120 II 155.

[326] For the procedure before the Swiss Federal Supreme Court, PIL Statute Art 191 since 2007 refers to Art 77 of the Swiss Federal Statute on the Swiss Federal Supreme Court in the section on procedure for complaints in civil matters. In Art 40, that statute refers for civil matters to the Swiss Federal Statute on lawyers and limits the right to appear before the Swiss Federal Supreme Court to lawyers. However, the intention was to continue the previous law. In the PIL Statute, Art 191(1) originally referred to the now abolished special recourse procedure in constitutional matters where there was no limitation to lawyers, as confirmed by BGE 116 II 373 consideration 1 (unpublished).

[327] See Geisinger, E. and Frossard, V., 'Challenge and Revision of the Award' in G. Kaufmann-Kohler and B. Stucki (eds), '*International Arbitration in Switzerland*' (Kluwer Law, 2004) 140.

[328] Pursuant to PIL Statute Art 190(3) in conjunction with Art 77 of the Swiss Federal Statute on the Swiss Federal Supreme Court; BGE, (1992) *ASA Bull* 381, 383.

(3) Effect of a court decision which sets the award aside

12.218 If the award is set aside by the Swiss Federal Supreme Court,[329] the case is normally remanded to the same arbitral tribunal for a new decision taking into account the reasons for setting aside.[330] There is no statutory right of the Swiss Federal Supreme Court to issue a new decision of its own. There is no other forum left but the arbitral tribunal. The mere fact that an award was set aside is not sufficient ground to challenge an arbitrator, let alone all members of the arbitral tribunal. Accordingly, if some or even all of its members should be replaced in the wake of the setting-aside proceedings, the arbitral tribunal is legally speaking still the same.

12.219 (3.1) **Does the setting-aside action suspend the enforcement? If so, do remedies exist to reinstate enforcement?** No to both questions,[331] but the complainant for setting-aside may request an order to suspend enforcement from the President of the Swiss Federal Supreme Court, which is regularly denied.[332] If an order to suspend enforcement is issued, the President may reconsider it at any time.

12.220 (3.2) **After an award has been set aside, does the underlying arbitration agreement revive or remain in force or is it exhausted or deemed terminated?** The underlying arbitration agreement remains in force, and the case goes back to the same arbitral tribunal (remission).

(4) Appeal against the court's decision to set aside or not set aside the award

12.221 The decision of the Swiss Federal Supreme Court is final; no appeal is possible against its decision to set aside or not to set aside.

(5) Possibility of the parties to exclude actions for setting aside

12.222 At any time,[333] the parties acting freely may exclude fully the complaint to set aside[334] or limit it to one or several of the grounds listed in PIL Statute Art 190(2)[335] ('Waiver agreement'). Such a waiver agreement *à la Suisse* must be made unequivocally and expressly,[336] for instance in the arbitration agreement which must be ascertainable by a text.[337] It is wise to mention PIL Statute Art 192. There was a decision of the Swiss Federal Supreme Court[338] according to which in sport arbitration a waiver agreement (concerning any

[329] BGE 128 III 50, 53; BGE 127 III 279, 282.

[330] BGE 117 II 94, 96.

[331] See BGE 109 Ia 81, 84–5.

[332] Sometimes on the ground that the complaint has no reasonable chance of success, in which case it is high time to take the hint and cut one's losses.

[333] BGE, (2007) *Swiss Int'l Arb L Rep* no 5.

[334] BGE 118 II 359, consideration 2, unpublished. Unpublished BGE 4A 234/2008 of 14 August 2008 contains a dictum leaving the question open whether a waiver agreement extends to the remedy of revision altogether, or only with respect to the grounds on which the waiver already excluded the primary remedy.

[335] See PIL Statute Art 192 (1).

[336] BGE 131 III 173; BGE 129 III 675, 681; BGE 117 II 94; BGE 116 II 639 (Art 28 ICC Rules insufficient); BGE, (1997) ASA Bull 494, 497; BGE 116 II 721; BGE 115 II 390, 391, 395.

[337] See para 12.17, *supra*.

[338] BGE, 22 March 2007, 4 p 172/2006, unpublished.

appeals decision by the Court of Arbitration for Sport) by an athlete (in a case involving no Swiss party) may be invalid if the athlete had no real choice.[339]

D. Liability of arbitrators

(1) Duties and liabilities of arbitrators regarding the conduct of the proceedings

The duties of arbitrators are not spelled out, but one agrees that arbitrators must act fairly, diligently, and speedily to decide the dispute before them. Their liability is not specifically stated either, but appears limited to wilful misconduct and criminal actions. **12.223**

(1.1) Do the courts and/or authorities rely on a contractual relationship between the parties and the arbitrator(s), irrespective of whether institutional or *ad-hoc* arbitration is concerned? What is the legal qualification of such contract (eg provision of services)? There is a procedural[340] contractual relationship, probably also in case of institutional arbitration (*receptum arbitri*). This is generally seen as a contract *sui generis*.[341] Private law may apply by analogy. In private law terms, the contractual relationship probably is between the parties forming a *société simple* for this purpose on the one hand, and the arbitrators, forming a *société simple* (the arbitral tribunal), on the other hand. There may also be a contract with the individual arbitrators. Mostly the rules of mandate for services in Swiss law would apply by analogy.[342] There are already pre-contractual obligations (*culpa in contrahendo*) such as the duty to disclose facts on which a challenge could be based. The contract may not be terminated at will (as a mandate could be, as a matter of principle), and certainly not at an inappropriate time/'zur Unzeit', but only for good cause. **12.224**

(1.2) Are there court decisions (or authorities) determining which law governs the question of liability of an arbitrator? What is the position of those courts/authorities as to whether and to which extent a legal liability of an arbitrator (or arbitral institution) may be established? The applicable law governing the question of liability of an arbitrator is probably the law at the place where the agent is to exercise its function, which should be the seat of the arbitration. Accordingly, Swiss law would apply. However, there is no case law as to this. This subject is not discussed by legal writers who prefer to let sleeping dogs lie. **12.225**

(1.3) Is an arbitrator subject to criminal prosecution? An arbitrator may also be subject to criminal prosecution. However, again there are no cases known. **12.226**

(2) Possibility to restrict or exclude the arbitrators' liability

The liability of the arbitrators is probably intrinsically limited to best efforts. In Swiss law, liability may be excluded or limited (say, to the amount covered by a lawyer's liability insurance), but not for intentional acts or gross negligence.[343] All this is theoretical. No case has ever arisen in Switzerland. **12.227**

---

339 Nobody argued that a similar reasoning might invalidate the arbitration clause altogether.
340 BGE 111 Ia 72.
341 Girsberger, D. and Voser, N. (n 198) 4.
342 For a discussion, see BGE 111 Ia 72, 76. Voser, N. and Gola, P., 'The Arbitral Tribunal' in G. Kaufmann-Kohler and B. Stucki (eds), *International Arbitration in Switzerland* (Kluwer Law, 2004) 35.
343 See CO Art 100.

VII. Enforcement of national awards

(1) Requirement of a particular procedure to make an award enforceable (leave for enforcement, exequatur*)*

12.228 There is no particular *exequatur* procedure for enforcing a Swiss award[344] in Switzerland. The Swiss award is treated as any court decision under Swiss Federal Constitution Art 122(3), its full faith and credit clause.

12.229 **(1.1) Does the national law make any difference between foreign and domestic awards, and if so, which are the criteria? Does there exist an additional notion of award for the purpose of obtaining *exequatur* (France: international awards)?** The criterion is the seat of the arbitration. If the seat of the arbitration was in Switzerland, the award is final when rendered (unless subsequently set aside with *ex tunc* effect). It is enforceable in Switzerland as any Swiss final court decision.[345]

12.230 An award rendered abroad by an arbitral tribunal having its seat that is final in the country of the foreign seat is (regardless of whether considered there a domestic or an international award) enforceable in Switzerland as any Swiss arbitral award or court judgment pursuant to the New York Convention, with the exceptions there listed.[346]

12.231 What the decision is called is irrelevant. A distinction is made between orders and awards. An award decides in a final manner on a prayer for relief; and order deals with procedural matters, conservatory or interim measures and is subject to change.[347] There is no additional notion of award for *exequatur* purposes.

12.232 **(1.2) May awards granting conservatory/interim measures be subject to enforcement?** Such 'awards' are not considered awards, but orders, and are not enforced. However, a Swiss state court may issue conservatory or interim measures in support of a foreign arbitration and may pattern them after measures already issued by other *fora*.[348]

(2) Details of such enforcement procedure (competent court, reasons for rejection of motion etc)

12.233 The competent authority for the enforcement of money awards or judgments is the Debt Enforcement Office at the domicile of the debtor which is asked to issue a payment order. If the debtor files opposition, opposition may then be removed by the summary judge at the domicile of the debtor on the basis of the award. The procedure before the enforcement of debts office is *ex parte,* but the proceedings before the summary judge involve both parties. Once a Swiss award is final in Switzerland, there are no grounds for refusal of enforcement in Switzerland, except by showing that the award was honoured.

---

344 That is an award rendered by an arbitral tribunal having its seat in Switzerland.
345 Swiss Federal Constitution Art 61.
346 See para 12.240 *et seq.*
347 See paras 12.69, and 12.133.
348 See PIL Statute Art 10.

(3) Appeal against the decision granting exequatur

The decision of the summary judge removing opposition on the basis of a Swiss (or foreign) arbitral award ('definitive Rechtsöffnung'/'mainlevée définitive') may be challenged as such. However, there is no review of the arbitral award as such. The decision of the intermediate appellate court on removal of opposition is still subject to further revision, say on constitutional grounds, by the Swiss Federal Supreme Court. **12.234**

(4) Appeal (and procedure) if exequatur *has been refused*

If opposition was not removed by the summary judge, this is subject to the same remedies as just described,[349] up to the Swiss Federal Supreme Court. **12.235**

(5) Procedure of enforcement (attachment of bank accounts etc)

Assets of the debtor may be attached under the circumstances foreseen by the Swiss Federal Statute on the enforcement of debts and bankruptcy. A summary judge may grant attachment. The attachment must then be 'validated' which is done by debt enforcement procedure (or by filing suit, including in arbitration in Switzerland or abroad, but here the assumption is that there is already a Swiss arbitral award). **12.236**

(5.1) At the stage of enforcement, may the losing party invoke arguments and circumstances which are based on facts which have occurred before (or after) the award was made? The party may claim that the award was paid in the meantime, as is possible with any money judgment. **12.237**

(5.2) May the losing party invoke a set-off based on claims that are not related to the matter of the arbitral proceeding? Is it material whether such claim came into existence before or after the award was made? On set-off *pendente lite,* see para 12.23 *supra.* Set-off against a judgment or award claim is possible only between claims having an equally recognized status in Switzerland, as another court judgment or arbitral award having force of law between the same parties in a different dispute, or an internal set-off between various claims awarded in an arbitral award (say, some on the merits and some for party representation costs). Whether the claim that is set off came into existence before or after the award was made is irrelevant, but both claims must be presently due and payable and recognizable on an equal footing as just explained. **12.238**

Non-monetary awards are enforced under cantonal law. **12.239**

VIII. Foreign awards

A. Recognition and/or enforcement of foreign awards (national law)

While cantonal civil procedure law may allow a special separate cantonal procedure to declare *exequatur* with *res judicata* effect,[350] foreign arbitral awards are normally recognized and enforced the same way as Swiss arbitral awards.[351] This is internally the effect of PIL **12.240**

[349] See para 12.234.
[350] BGE 116 Ia 394. See para 12.241 *infra.*
[351] See para 12.241.

Statute Art 194, in force since 1 January 1989, which made the New York Convention applicable *erga omnes*, but still as an international treaty[352] and externally of the fact that Switzerland withdrew its reciprocity reservation, effective from 23 April 1993.[353] The grounds for non-recognition and non-execution of foreign awards are similar to those for setting aside Swiss awards.[354]

(1) Rules according to national law

12.241 The Swiss national rules on enforcement are the same as for the enforcement of a Swiss court decision. Money awards are enforced as follows:[355] The debt enforcement office is asked *ex parte* to issue an order to pay to the debtor. This is notified to the debtor, if required, through letters rogatory. The debtor then has a deadline of (in Switzerland) 10 or (abroad) 20 days to file 'opposition'. Opposition may then be removed in summary proceedings before a judge at the place of enforcement in Switzerland.[356] One reason to grant final removal of opposition ('definitive Rechtsöffnung') is the existence of an arbitral award, so a copy of the agreement to arbitrate and of the final award must be submitted,[357] possibly a certificate of enforceability.[358] While the New York Convention requires 'due authentication' of the award, in Swiss practice, even a photostat copy of the final award is sufficient if its authenticity is not challenged by the debtor.[359] Translation into a Swiss official language may not be necessary. Missing documents may be filed later. Once opposition is removed with final effect, the debt enforcement office continues the enforcement procedure, which, depending on the debtor, may lead to bankruptcy. The cantons may, but are not required to, provide for a special cantonal *exequatur* procedure. If, according to that procedure, enforceability had already been certified, this binds the (summary) enforcement judge. Otherwise, the decision is made by the enforcement judge.

12.242 Non-monetary awards are enforced under cantonal law.

(2) Requirements to be fulfilled by the applicant (procedure, time limits)

12.243 The applicant must follow the procedures as described in para 12.241 *supra*. It is wise to retain a local lawyer.

(3) Remedies against decisions granting or declining enforcement

12.244 The decision by the summary judge declining enforcement may be attacked, first to an intermediate appellate court (a cantonal court), and ultimately to the Swiss Federal Supreme

---

[352] Patocchi, P.M., '*The New York Convention: the Swiss Practice*' in M. Blessing (ed), *The New York Convention of 1958*, ASA Special Series 9 (ASA 1996) 151.

[353] AS 1993, 2,139.

[354] See para 12.204.

[355] Federal Enforcement of Debt and Bankruptcy Statute Art 38.

[356] *ibid*, Art 81(3); BGE 101 Ia 521, 523.

[357] New York Convention Art IV (1); BGE 130 III 125, 129; Geneva Cour de Justice, (2000) ASA Bull 786, 790.

[358] BGE 130 III 125, 129.

[359] BGE, (2001) ASA Bull 294, 298; Commercial Court of the Canton of Zurich, in (1992) ICCA Ybk 584.

Court for violation of a federal treaty, namely the New York Convention, or constitutional law[360] but not by a complaint to set aside[361] or civil or administrative appeal.[362]

B. Recognition and/or enforcement of foreign awards (conventions, treaties)

(1) Specific bilateral or multilateral treaties

The New York Convention is in practice the only treaty that still plays a role,[363] since the few bilateral treaties that are still in place are superseded *pro tanto*,[364] except in the relationship with Liechtenstein which is not a member of the New York Convention, but with which Switzerland has a treaty on the basis of reciprocity. Taiwan is not a member of the New York Convention, but applies it anyway. Switzerland reciprocally recognizes and enforces awards rendered in Taiwan. Switzerland acceded to the ICSID Convention, effective from 14 June 1996. **12.245**

(2) Existence of a standard procedure for the enforcement of foreign awards?

The *exequatur* procedure is wrapped into the enforcement procedure as already described.[365] **12.246**

(3) Extent of examination and review of the award by the court

The examination and control of the award by the court goes along the lines of the New York Convention. In the wrapped-in procedure, any defences to the enforcement of a foreign arbitral award based on the New York Convention (eg violation of public policy) will be examined. No civil complaint is available, no administrative complaint and no complaint to set aside. The last cantonal court's decision on recognition and enforcement is subject to complaint to the Swiss Federal Supreme Court on ground of violation of an international treaty—the New York Convention.[366] The Federal Supreme Court has unfettered powers of review[367] on the law, which of course includes the New York Convention. **12.247**

C. Application of the New York Convention

(1) Application of the New York Convention in practice

The New York Convention is regularly applied. Switzerland dropped the 'reciprocity' reservation.[368] Swiss awards are recognized and enforced outside Switzerland under the New York Convention, under bilateral treaty (Liechtenstein), or under local law (Taiwan). **12.248**

(2) Examples of decisions which do not apply the Convention correctly

There are no final decisions in Switzerland which do not apply the convention correctly. **12.249**

---

360 BGE 120 II 270, 271–2.
361 BGE 118 Ia 118, 119–20.
362 BGE 120 II 270, 271.
363 See para 12.240 *supra*.
364 BGE 110 II 54, 57; BGE 110 Ib 191, 193–8. Theoretically, if a bilateral treaty is more favourable to recognition or enforcement, it applies.
365 See para 12.233.
366 BGE 128 I 354, 356; BGE 120 II 270, 271; BGE 118 Ia 118, 119–20.
367 BGE 108 Ib 85, 87.
368 See PIL Statute Art 194 and AS 1993, p 2139.

12.250 The following are two cases where Swiss courts probably were not overly formalistic: in a Swiss Federal Supreme Court case[369] the burden to prove that the arbitration agreement in a charter party had been acknowledged in writing was put on the claimant even though the respondent had performed the charterparty. One might argue that the burden of proof should have been shifted to the respondent to prove ignorance of the arbitral agreement. The *translation* of the award must be *certified* by an official or sworn translator. The translation by an employee of a Moscow public notary was considered insufficient by a cantonal court. One might argue that the notary should have been characterized as an official translator.[370]

12.251 There was an extreme case where enforcement of a particular Turkish award was rightly refused by a trial and an intermediate appellate court in Switzerland on public policy grounds. That case did not go before the Swiss Federal Supreme Court.[371]

IX. Appendix

A. National legislation

Federal Statute on Private International Law (PIL Statute) of 18 December 1987, as amended, SR 291.

English translation in Switzerland's Private International Law (Karrer/Arnold/Patocchi, 2nd edn, Boston/Zurich, 1994).

Swiss Federal Statute on the Federal Supreme Court of 17 June 2005.

B. Arbitral institutions

ASA Association Suisse de l'Arbitrage/
Swiss Arbitration Association
Aeschenvorstadt 67
CH–4051 Basel
PO Box CH-4010 Basel
Switzerland
Telephone: +41 61 270 6015
Fax: +41 61 270 6005
Email: info@arbitration-ch.org
Website: <http://www.arbitration-ch.org>

The Swiss Arbitration Association (ASA) is a non-profit association with about 1,200 individual members (a good 300 outside Switzerland) and some 20 corporate members. ASA is not as such an arbitral institution hosting or administering international arbitral proceedings. ASA Membership is open to all those interested in international arbitration,

369 BGE 128 I 354, also (2003) ICCA Ybk 835.
370 Obergericht Zug, (2000) ASA Bull 363.
371 Bezirksgericht Affoltern am Albis, 26 May 1994, affirmed by Zurich Supreme Court, (1998) ICCA Ybk 754.

irrespective of nationality. Many of the most distinguished names in international arbitration are ASA Members.

Swiss Chambers Arbitration

Zurich Chamber of Commerce
Bleicherweg 5
PO Box 3058
CH-8022 Zurich
Switzerland
Telephone: +41 44 217 40 50
Fax: +41 44 217 40 51
Email: direktion@zurichcci.ch
Website: <http://www.zurichcci.ch>

Geneva Chamber of Commerce and Industry
4, Bd. du Théâtre
CH–1204 Geneva
Case postale 5039, 1211 Geneva
Telephone: +41 22 819 91 11,
Fax: +41 22 819 91 00
Email: ccig@cci.ch
Website: <http://www.ccig.ch>

Basle Chamber of Commerce
Aeschenvorstadt 67
4051 Basel
Postfach 4010 Basel
Switzerland
Telephone: +41 61 270 60 60
Fax: +41 61 270 60 65
Email: h.gruen@hkbb.ch
Website: <http://www.hkbb.ch>

Bernese Chamber of Commerce
Gutenbergstr. 1
CH-3011 Berne
PO Box 3001, Berne
Switzerland
Telephone: +41 31 388 87 87
Fax: +41 31 388 87 88
Email: hk@bern-cci.ch
Website: <http://www.bern-cci.ch>

Neuchâtel Chamber of Commerce
Rue de la Serre 4
Case Postale
2001 Neuchâtel

Switzerland
Telephone: +41 32 722 15 15
Fax: +41 32 722 15 20
Email: cnci@cnci.ch
Website: <http:/www.cnci.ch>

Camera di commercio dell'industria e dell'artigianato del cantone Ticino
Corso Elvezia 16
CH-6900 Lugano
Switzerland
Telephone: +41 91 911 51 11
Fax: +41 91 911 51 12
Email: cciati@cci.ch

Chambre vaudoise du commerce et de l'industrie
Av. d'Ouchy 47
Case postale 315,
CH–1001 Lausanne
Switzerland
Telephone: +41 21 613 35 35
Fax: +41 21 613 35 05
Email: cvci@cvci.ch
Website: <http://www.cvci.ch>

Other institutions

German–Swiss Chamber of Commerce
Tödistrasse 60
CH-8002 Zurich
Switzerland
Telephone: +41 1 283 61 61
Fax: +41 1 283 61 00
Email: auskunft@handelskammer-d-ch.ch
Website: <http://www.handelskammer-d-ch.ch>

Bilateral arbitration rules

Swiss-American Chamber of Commerce
Talacker 41
CH-8001 Zürich
Switzerland
Telephone: +41 43 443 72 00
Fax: +41 43 497 22 70
Email: info@amcham.ch
Website: <http://www.amcham.ch>

Bilateral arbitration rules

TAS–Tribunal Arbitral du Sport
av de Beaumont 2
CH-1012 Lausanne
Switzerland
Telehone: +41 21 613 5000
Fax: +41 21 613 5001
Email: info@tas-cas.org
Website: <http://www.tas-cas.org>

Specialized arbitration system for sport arbitration, with special '*ad hoc*' tribunals for Olympic games.

Arbitration and Mediation Centre

World Intellectual Property Organization
34, chemin des Colombettes
PO Box 18
CH–1211 Geneva 20
Telephone: +41 22 338 8247
Fax: +41 22 740 3700
Email: arbiter.mail@wipo.int
Website: <http://www.wipo.int>

Arbitration rules especially for intellectual property disputes.

C. Model arbitration clauses

Clause providing for appointment of all three arbitrators by the Swiss Chambers:

> Any dispute, controversy or claim arising out of or in relation to this contract, including the validity, invalidity, breach or termination thereof, shall be resolved by arbitration in accordance with the Swiss Rules of International Arbitration of the Swiss Chambers of Commerce in force on the date when the Notice of Arbitration is submitted in accordance with these Rules.
>
> The number of arbitrators shall be . . . (one or three);
>
> The seat of the arbitration shall be . . . (city)
>
> The arbitral proceedings shall be conducted in ..... (insert desired language).

D. Bibliography

Periodicals and websites
ASA: <http://www.arbitration-ch.org/>.
ASA Bulletin.
Swiss International Arbitration Law Reports.
Bundesgericht: <http://www.bger.ch>.

General Bibliography:

Berger, Bernhard and Kellerhals, Franz, *Internationale und interne Schiedsgerichtsbarkeit in der Schweiz* (Stämpfli Verlag, 2006).

Bucher, Andreas and Tschanz, Pierre-Yves, *International Arbitration in Switzerland* (Helbing & Lichtenhahn, Basel, 1989).

Corboz, Bernard, 'Le recours au Tribunal fédéral en matière d'arbitrage international' (2002) *Semaine Judiciaire* II, 1 *et seq*.

Dutoit, Bernard, *Commentaire de la Loi féderale du 18 décembre 1987* (Helbing & Lichtenhahn, Basel, 1996) 487 *et seq*.

Girsberger, Daniel and Voser, Nathalie, *International Arbitration in Switzerland* (Schulthess, 2008).

Heini, Anton *et al* (eds), *IPRG Kommentar* (Schulthess, 1993).

Honsell, Heinrich *et al* (eds), *Kommentar zum Schweizerischen Privatrecht, Internationales Privatrecht* (2nd edn, Helbing & Lichtenhahn, Basel, 2007).

Kaufmann-Kohler, Gabrielle and Rigozzi, Antonio, *Arbitrage international* (Schulthess 2006).

Kaufmann-Kohler, Gabrielle and Stucki, Blaise (eds), *International Arbitration in Switzerland* (Kluwer Law, 2004).

Karrer, Pierre A., Arnold, Karl W. and Patocchi, Paolo Michele, *Switzerland's Private International Law* (2nd edn, Kluwer Law, 1994).

Knoepfler, François and Schweizer, Philippe, *Arbitrage international* (Schulthess, 2003).

Kronke, Herbert, Melis, Werner and Schnyder, Anton (eds), *Handbuch Internationales Wirtschaftsrecht* (Otto Schmidt Verlag, 2005).

Lalive, Pierre, Poudret, Jean-François and Reymond, Claude, *Le droit de l'arbitrage interne et international en Suisse* (Payot, 1989).

Müller, Christoph *International Arbitration* (Otto Schmidt Verlag, 2004).

Patocchi, Paolo Michele and Geisinger, Elliott, *Code de Droit International Privé Suisse Annoté* (Payot, 1995).

Poudret, Jean-François and Besson, Sébastien, *Comparative Law of International Arbitration* (2nd edn, Schulthess, 2007).

Reiner, Andreas *Handbuch der ICC-Schiedsgerichtsbarkeit* (Manz Verlag, 1989) 218 *et seq*, 241–7.

Rüede, Thomas and Hadenfeldt, Reimer, *Schweizerisches Schiedsgerichtsrecht* (2nd edn, Schulthess, 1993).

von Thulen Rhoades, Rufus, Kolkey, Daniel M. and Chernick, Richard (eds), *Practitioner's Handbook on International Arbitration and Mediation* (2nd edn, Juris Publishing, 2007).

Torggler, Hellwig (ed), *Praxishandbuch Schiedsgerichtsbarkeit* (Nomos, Verlag, 2007).

Walter, Hans Peter, 'Praktische Probleme der staatsrechtlichen Beschwerde gegen internationale Schiedsentscheide (Art 190 IRPG)' (2001) *ASA Bull* 2.

Zuberbühler, Tobias, Müller, Christoph and Habegger, Philipp (eds), *Swiss Rules of International Arbitration* (Schulthess, 2005).

13

UNITED STATES

Peter Bowman Rutledge, Rachael Kent and Christian Henel

I. Introduction

A. Current status of the law on arbitration

(1) Short history

International commercial arbitration enjoys a long history in the United States, but judicial acceptance of arbitration is of more recent vintage. The historical record contains many instances of arbitration, particularly industry-specific arbitration and post-dispute arbitration.[1] Until the first part of the twentieth century, however, courts in the United States rarely enforced pre-dispute arbitration agreements.[2] Such agreements were void contracts, contrary to public policy because they ousted courts of jurisdiction.[3] **13.01**

This 'judicial hostility' began to break down in the first part of the twentieth century. The watershed moment, however, came in 1925 with the enactment of the Federal Arbitration Act ('FAA'), which continues to serve as the core arbitration law in the United States, for both international and domestic arbitrations.[4] While legislative history on the FAA is **13.02**

---

[1] Bernstein, L., 'Merchant Law in a Merchant Court: Rethinking the Code's Search for Immanent Business Norms' (1996) 144 *University of Pennsylvania L Rev* 1765.

[2] Born, G. and Rutledge, P., *International Civil Litigation in the United States* (Aspen/Kluwer, 2007) 1091.

[3] Born, G., *International Commercial Arbitration in the United States* (Kluwer, 2009) 565.

[4] 9 USC s 1 *et seq.*

sparse, it was modelled on the arbitration law adopted by New York a few years earlier.[5] At its core, the FAA provided (and continues to provide) that arbitration agreements are enforceable (subject only to generally applicable contract defences) and that arbitral awards are judicially enforceable (subject only to a limited number of non-merits defences).[6]

13.03 In the decades following the FAA's enactment, courts displayed a greater solicitude toward arbitration agreements, but their support was not unconditional. Specifically, courts declined to enforce arbitration agreements with respect to claims arising under federal statutes such as the federal securities laws.[7] The theory here was one of statutory interpretation—to permit arbitration of such public law disputes would be contrary to Congress' intent to create a federal forum for such disputes.[8] From 1925 until the 1970s, the non-arbitrability doctrine set an important limit on arbitration in the United States.

13.04 Beginning in the early 1970s, the legal architecture became even more supportive of arbitration. In 1970, the United States ratified the New York Convention.[9] Shortly thereafter, the non-arbitrability doctrine began to wane, initially in international cases. In *Scherck v Alberto-Culver Co*, the Supreme Court held that claims arising under federal antitrust laws were arbitrable in an international arbitration between two companies.[10] *Scherck* ushered in an era of greater toleration for international arbitration of public law claims. In the following decades, that tolerance only grew. In the 1980s, the United States ratified the Panama Convention (a regional convention modelled on the New York Convention supporting the enforcement of agreements and awards in North and South America).[11] Also beginning in the 1980s, courts adapted the logic of *Scherck* to domestic arbitration of antitrust, securities and other public law claims.[12]

13.05 Strong support for arbitration, including international arbitration, continues to reign today. Ironically, however, the statutory architecture has not undergone much change since the FAA's enactment in 1925. Apart from adopting legislation to implement the New York and Panama Conventions, the United States has made relatively few changes to the FAA since 1925. While Congress has tinkered with the law on the edges,[13] most of the law governing arbitration in the United States has unfolded through judicial decision rather than legislation. As discussed in the next section, Congress presently is considering some of the most significant changes to the FAA since its enactment, yet, as of the date of this publication, it has not adopted that legislation.

---

[5] Born, G., *International Commercial Arbitration* (Kluwer, 2001) 35.

[6] 9 USC ss 2, 10.

[7] Born, G., *International Commercial Arbitration* (Kluwer, 2009) 781–5.

[8] eg *Wilko v Swan*, 346 US 427, 74 SCt 182 (1953).

[9] United Nations Convention on the Recognition and Enforcement of Foreign Arbitral Awards (the New York Convention) (New York, 10 June 1958, 330 UNTS 38); Act of 31 July 1970, *Pub L* 91-368, 84 Stat 692, codified at 9 USC ss 201–208 (implementing legislation).

[10] 417 US 506, 94 SCt 2449 (1974).

[11] Inter-American Convention on International Commercial Arbitration (the Panama Convention) (Panama, 13 January 1975, OASTS no 42, 1438 UNTS 245).

[12] See *Shearson/American Exp, Inc v McMahon*, 482 US 220, 232, 107 SCt 2332, 2340 (1987) (collecting cases).

[13] See 9 USC s 15-16; 15 USC s 1226.

(2) Law in force and future projects

The FAA, along with the judicial decisions interpreting it, is the critical source of law governing international commercial arbitration in the United States. The FAA consists of three chapters. Chapter I sets forth general provisions regarding the enforcement of arbitration agreements, the selection of arbitrators and the arbitral forum (in case of party default), and vacatur and enforcement of awards (including in international cases).[14] Chapter II implements the New York Convention and sets forth provisions specific to agreements and awards arising under the Convention.[15] Chapter III contains similar implementing legislation for the Panama Convention.[16] Critically, both ch II and ch III contain 'residual application' clauses which effectively incorporate ch I (the general provisions) to the extent that chapter is not inconsistent with the specific provisions of ch II or ch III.[17] **13.06**

While the FAA is by far the most important piece of international arbitration legislation in the United States, practitioners should be aware of several other bodies of law. The United States is a party to several other treaties, including notably the Washington Convention of 1965.[18] It also is party to several bilateral investment and trade treaties which contain arbitration obligations that may be relevant in a commercial dispute.[19] **13.07**

Additionally, practitioners should be aware of the unique system of shared authority between federal and state governments in the United States. While practitioners will be accustomed to suits arising under the Federal Arbitration Act, the 50 state governments of the United States (plus the District of Columbia) all have their own arbitration laws (many of which are based on a uniform domestic arbitration law called the Revised Uniform Arbitration Act). Some states also have passed laws specifically addressing international arbitration, several of which replicate (or are based upon) the UNCITRAL Model Law.[20] In the practice of international arbitration, these laws rarely matter: the cases typically end up in federal court, and federal law governs the matter. **13.08**

Periodically, though, state practice may matter—because the case is being heard in state court, because state law fills some gap in federal law, or because of a choice-of-law clause in the contract. Given the centrality of federal courts and federal law in most international cases, we focus much of the analysis in this chapter on federal practice and pause to consider state practice only where it is particularly relevant and peculiarly distinct. Nonetheless, the practitioner should always keep this dual system in mind, both because of the potential forum-selection benefits and for the occasional case where state practice becomes relevant. **13.09**

As of the time of this publication, two current developments are of particular importance to practitioners of international arbitration. First, Congress is currently contemplating a **13.10**

---

[14] 9 USC ss 1-16.

[15] *ibid* ss 201-8.

[16] *ibid* ss 301-7.

[17] *ibid* ss 208, 307.

[18] Convention on the Settlement of Investment Disputes Between States and Nationals of Other States ('Washington Convention') (Washington, 18 March 1965, 575 UNTS 160).

[19] eg US-Chile Investment Incentive Agreement, 35 UST 2958 (22 September 1983); North American Free Trade Agreement, 32 ILM 289, 605 (17 December 1992).

[20] See Revised Uniform Arbitration Act (Introductory note).

series of legislative proposals, most notably the Arbitration Fairness Act, which would constitute the most significant alteration of arbitration law in the United States since the FAA's enactment.[21] Although many of the Arbitration Fairness Act's provisions are directed solely at domestic arbitration, some provisions, as currently proposed, could alter the law governing international arbitration on questions such as *competence-competence*.[22] Second, the prestigious American Law Institute is preparing a 'Restatement' of the Law on International Commercial Arbitration. Restatements attempt to synthesize the current jurisprudence in a field and, in some cases, to resolve disagreements among courts on a particular point of law. Courts in the United States often consult and cite restatements as an authoritative expression of the law of the United States, so, once this project is completed, it should have an important impact on future legal developments in this area.[23]

(3) Distinction between national and international arbitration

13.11 Unlike many other countries, the United States does not draw a firm boundary between its law governing international arbitration and its law governing domestic arbitration. As for domestic arbitrations, ch 1 will generally supply the governing law. As for international arbitrations, chs 2 and 3 generally serve as a starting point, so long as the jurisdictional prerequisites for application of the New York Convention or the Panama Convention are satisfied. Even where those prerequisites are satisfied, ch 1 may still apply to the extent its general provisions do not conflict with the specific provisions under ch 2 or 3.[24]

13.12 Owing to the lack of a distinct body of law governing international arbitrations, practitioners should be aware that precedent arising in domestic arbitrations may supply legal principles equally applicable in international arbitrations. For example, both of the seminal Supreme Court decisions articulating principles of separabilty and *competence-competence* involved domestic arbitrations, yet the principles announced by those cases have been extended to the international field.[25]

13.13 (3.1) **If there are different systems and rules for national/international arbitration, what are the criteria for the distinction between both systems?** As noted above, cases arising under the New York and Panama Conventions are the primary area in which different rules govern international commercial arbitrations. Generally, the criteria for distinction are the same ones necessary for application of the conventions generally: an agreement in writing, a commercial relationship, and arbitration in the territory of a signatory country.[26] In cases involving two United States citizens, federal law sets forth an additional prerequisite to

[21] Arbitration Fairness Act of 2009 (HR 1020, S 931) (introduced 12 February 2009 in House; 29 April 2009 in Senate).

[22] Arbitration Fairness Act s 3.

[23] The website of the American Law Institute, the organization overseeing the Restatement, provides status reports on its development. See <http://www.ali.org./>.

[24] In *Vaden v Discover Bank* (no 07-773) (2008), the Supreme Court very recently expanded the scope of a federal court's jurisdiction and held that a Court may 'look through' the arbitration dispute and determine whether the underlying claim presents a basis for federal subject matter jurisdiction (such as the presence of a federal cause of action).

[25] *Prima Paint Corp v Flood & Conklin Manufacturing Co*, 388 US 395, 87 S Ct 1801 (1967) (separability); *First Options of Chicago, Inc v Kaplan*, 514 US 938, 115 S Ct 1920 (1995) (*kompetenz-competence*).

[26] eg *Ledee v Ceramiche Ragno*, 684 F 2d 184 (US Ct of Apps (1st Cir) 1982).

application of both the New York Convention and the Panama Convention—namely that the case involve property abroad, performance abroad or some reasonable relationship with a foreign country.[27] A few cases have construed this 'reasonable relationship' requirement narrowly and declined to apply the Convention.[28]

B. Practice of arbitration

(1) *Frequency of arbitration as opposed to litigation*

The United States is home to a high volume of litigation which dwarfs the frequency of arbitration. Civil cases can be filed in either federal or state court. In 2007, over 250,000 new cases were filed in federal court.[29] In 2005 (the most recent year for which reliable aggregate statistics are available), over 5 million civil cases were filed in state courts of general jurisdiction.[30] By contrast, as detailed in the next section, probably fewer than 200,000 commercial arbitrations were commenced in the United States in 2007. **13.14**

(2) *Leading arbitral institutions and statistics*

The United States has successfully served as the seat for arbitration pursuant to a number of internationally accepted rules such as the ICC Rules and the UNCITRAL Arbitration Rules. Parties wishing to designate a US-based institution have a number of options, including the American Arbitration Association ('AAA') (through its International Centre for Dispute Resolution, 'ICDR'), Judicial Arbitration and Mediation Services Inc ('JAMS'), and the International Institute for Conflict Prevention and Resolution ('CPR'). Each of these institutions maintains detailed websites containing their model clauses, international arbitration rules and, in some cases, arbitrator lists. In addition to maintaining international rules, these institutions often also provide industry-specific rules, such as construction or insurance which, in a particular case, may be better tailored to a party's needs. **13.15**

One aspect of the arbitral institutions in the United States deserves special mention. Many arbitrations in the securities industry—including investor-related and employment-related disputes—occur under the auspices of the Financial Industry Regulatory Authority ('FINRA'). Created in 2007, FINRA, among other things, consolidated the dispute resolution functions of the major American securities exchanges (NYSE, NASD). Unlike most arbitral institutions (such as the AAA or the ICC), FINRA is subject to the express oversight of the Securities and Exchange Commission ('SEC'), the body regulating the securities industry generally. Otherwise, it operates in a manner not unlike any other arbitral institution—with its own set of rules (approved by the SEC), its own list of arbitrators and its own library of awards. **13.16**

A large number of arbitrations take place in the United States each year, but only a fraction of them can be classified as international arbitrations. In terms of sheer caseload, the AAA is the largest, with 128,000 case filings in 2007 of which 622 were international cases.[31] **13.17**

---

27 9 USC ss 202, 302.

28 See Born, *International Commercial Arbitration* 119–26.

29 Administrative Office of the United States Courts (2007) Judicial Business of the United States Courts, 2007 Annual Report of the Director 52, Table S-7.

30 National Center for State Courts (2006) State Court Caseload Statistics 105.

31 Minutes of the AAA Executive Committee (7 February 2008); AAA Annual Report (2007) 5.

FINRA has the next largest overall caseload (3238 new filings in 2007), but virtually all of these undoubtedly were domestic cases (FINRA does not break out its international caseload).[32] JAMS received 2,020 new filings in 2007, of which 21 were international.[33] As CPR arbitrations are generally 'self-administered', the organization does not maintain statistics on the number of disputes taking place under its rules.[34]

II. Jurisdiction of the arbitral tribunal

A. Arbitration agreement

(1) Arbitration clause and submission agreement

13.18 Parties may agree to arbitrate at any time, and generally, the timing of their agreement will dictate the form of that agreement. Parties that agree at the outset of their relationship to arbitrate any dispute arising in the future will often include an arbitration clause as part of the main contract. Parties consenting to arbitrate disputes after the dispute arises may enter into a submission agreement. Either form generally will be enforced under United States law.[35]

(2) Requirements as to the contents of the arbitration agreement

13.19 The Federal Arbitration Act does not provide specific requirements for the content of an arbitration agreement, although the text of section two does state some general limits on the enforceability of the agreement. Generally speaking, under the FAA, agreements will be enforceable, provided (i) a true agreement exists (both parties formed the requisite intent to arbitrate); (ii) the agreement is in writing; (iii) the dispute arises within the scope of the agreement; (iv) the agreement has not been terminated or waived expressly or by conduct; and (v) the agreement is not invalid under 'such grounds as exist at law or in equity for the revocation of any contract'.[36] Courts have interpreted this quoted language to mean that an arbitration clause is still subject to general contract defences and, consequently, have declined to enforce arbitration agreements on grounds such as fraud, duress, unconscionability, lack of definiteness, or lack of mutuality.[37]

13.20 In the international context, an arbitration agreement also enjoys a presumption of enforceability, under the applicable arbitration convention (typically the New York Convention or the Panama Convention).

13.21 If a convention applies to the relationship between the parties, the arbitration agreement will be enforceable subject only to the exceptions from enforcement in that convention.

---

32 FINRA 'dispute resolution' statistics can be found at its website <http://www.finra.org>.

33 Email of Robert Davidson, JAMS, to Peter B. Rutledge (14 October 2008).

34 Email of Russ Bleemer, CPR, to Peter B. Rutledge (21 May 2008). Periodically, CPR will become involved in cases where the parties seek help (often in the selection of neutral arbitrators). In 2006, CPR became involved in 122 such arbitrations. CPR Annual Report (2006) 13.

35 Federal Arbitration Act, 9 USC s 2 (2008).

36 9 USC s 2; Macneil, I., Speidel, R. and Stipanowich, T., *Federal Arbitration Law: Agreements, Awards, and Remedies under the Federal Arbitration Act* (Little Brown, 1999) s 15.1.1.

37 eg *Lea Tai Textile Co Ltd v Manning Fabrics, Inc*, 411 F Supp 1404 (US Dist Ct (SDNY) 1975) (inconsistent arbitration clauses in competing forms canceled arbitration clause).

For example, an agreement which falls within the New York Convention will be enforceable if it meets the requirements for enforceability under Art II(3) of that treaty.[38] Under that provision, arbitration agreements are enforceable unless they are 'null and void, inoperative or incapable of being performed'.

If the relationship between the parties is international in character, but for some reason does not fall within an applicable convention, the FAA will govern enforceability and the agreement will be enforced subject only to generally applicable contract principles. Perhaps the most controversial of those generally applicable contract principles which may render an agreement unenforceable is the doctrine of unconscionability. Under that doctrine, procedural or substantive unfairness in the contract can render it unenforceable. California courts have become somewhat infamous for the use of that state's unconscionability doctrine to invalidate arbitration agreements, particularly in the context of contracts between companies and consumers.[39] **13.22**

The complexity of arbitration clauses in US practice may vary widely, although a typically useful arbitration clause will set forth a choice of arbitral forum, number of arbitrators, language of the arbitration, and choice of arbitral rules.[40] It is also important to note that a few US courts have interpreted s 9 of the FAA to require parties to agree to enforcement of the award in the United States. Although these decisions are a minority and are almost certainly not applicable to international arbitration agreements, it is advisable to include in the arbitration clause an 'entry-of-judgment provision' which ensures that the award may be enforced in the United States.[41] **13.23**

Additionally, because the United States has taken a unique position regarding the extent of an arbitral tribunal's initial *competence-competence*,[42] parties would be well advised to indicate whether threshold jurisdictional questions should be referred initially to the arbitral tribunal or United States courts. Major arbitral institutions offer model arbitration clauses that are ordinarily expected to withstand judicial challenge. Practitioners drafting an arbitration clause might consider beginning with the model clause of the arbitral institution they wish to conduct the proceedings and then, after careful analysis, customizing the model clause according to their needs.[43] **13.24**

(3) Form of the arbitration agreement (eg 'in writing requirement')

Section 2 of the Federal Arbitration Act will only extend presumptive enforceability to arbitration agreements that are in writing. Unlike the UNCITRAL Model Law, the Federal Arbitration Act does not indicate whether the writing must be comprised of a single **13.25**

[38] 9 USC s 202. The statute provides that provisions from the domestic FAA may be used to supplement provisions in the foreign FAA to the extent they are not inconsistent.

[39] For a thorough discussion, see generally, Broome, S., 'An Unconscionable Application of the Unconscionability Doctrine: How the California Courts are Circumventing the Federal Arbitration Act' (2006) 3 *Hastings Bus LJ* 39.

[40] A thorough guide to the drafting of arbitration agreements may be found in Born, G., *International Arbitration and Forum Selection Agreements: Drafting and Enforcing* (Kluwer, 2006).

[41] Born, *International Arbitration and Forum Selection Agreements* (Kluwer, 2006) 86.

[42] See *First Options of Chicago v Kaplan*, 514 US 938, 115 S Ct 1920 (1995), and Section II.C.2–3.

[43] Born, *International Forum Selection Agreements* 44–58.

document bearing the signatures of the consenting parties or evidenced by an exchange of letters or other written correspondence. Currently, federal case law does not address whether the arbitration clause must exist in a single document, but every federal court of appeals that has considered the extent of the writing requirement has held only that the agreement must be written—a party need not have signed the agreement to be bound by its terms, provided that the party manifested assent to the written provision in some other legally recognizable manner.[44] Perhaps surprisingly, some courts have held in the context of computer and internet-based transactions that an online consumer may be bound by an arbitration clause contained in the seller's terms and conditions, provided the arbitration clause is conspicuous to the user and the user proceeds to do business with the seller.[45] In cases implicating the New York Convention, Art II of the Convention provides that an arbitration agreement may be signed by both parties or created through an exchange of documents.

13.26 (3.1) **Are there special requirements for a power of attorney/authority to enter into an arbitration agreement on behalf of a third party?** Authority of an agent to enter into arbitration agreements on behalf of a third party will be governed by state law of agency, in many cases modelled after the American Law Institute's Restatement on Agency (second or third edition).[46] Under general agency principles, a third party will be bound by the signature of another person only if the signatory had authority to enter into an agreement, or the third party later ratifies the action of the third party signatory, expressly or by conduct. Courts have applied these principles in the arbitration context.[47]

(4) Incorporation of an arbitration clause contained in general terms and conditions

13.27 It is not uncommon for an arbitration clause to exist in a separate document that is incorporated into the main contract, such as the general conditions to the contract. Courts generally enforce these arbitration clauses, provided it would be objectively reasonable for the signatory to the main contract to believe it was subject to the arbitration clause. In employment cases, the arbitration clause contained in the collective bargaining agreement may be incorporated by reference when parties initiate an employment relationship.[48] In certain industries, such as the construction industry, a signatory may be bound by an arbitration clause in the general conditions if normal trade usage includes incorporation of

---

[44] See *Seawright v American Gen Fin Svcs.*, 507 F 3d 967, 978 (US Ct of Apps (5th Cir) 2007); *Caley v Gulf Stream Aero Corp*, 428 F 3d 1359, 1369 (US Ct of Apps (11th Cir) 2005); *Tinder v Pinkerton Sec*, 305 F 3d 728, 736 (US Ct of Apps (7th Cir) 2002); *Valero Refining Inc v M/T Lauberhorn*, 813 F 2d 60, 64 (US Ct of Apps (5th Cir) 1987); *Genesco Inc v T. Kakiuchi & Co*, 815 F 2d 840, 846 (US Ct of Apps (2nd Cir) 1987); *Medical Dev Cor. v Industrial Molding Corp*, 479 F 2d 345, 348 (US Ct of Apps (10th Cir) 1973). See also *Ross v American Express Co*, 478 F 3d 96, 99 (US Ct of Apps (2nd Cir) 2007) (finding an arbitration agreement to be in writing on the basis of equitable estoppel).

[45] eg *Hubbert v Dell Inc*, 835 NE 2d 113 (Ill 2005); *Provencher v Dell Inc*, 409 F Supp 2d 1196 (US Dist Ct (CD Cal) 2006). But see *Wigginton v Dell, Inc*, 890 NE 2d 541 (Ill 2008) (arbitration clause must be conspicuous).

[46] American Law Institute, Restatement (Third) of Agency (2006).

[47] eg *Oregon-Pacific Forest Products Corp v Welsh Panel Co*, 248 F Supp 903 (US Dist Ct (Or) 1965); *Hall v Internet Capital Group Inc*, 271 F Supp 2d 332 (US Dist Ct (Me) 2003).

[48] *Roman Associates Inc v Local 94, 94-A, 94-B, Int'l Union of Operating Engineers*, 24 F 3d 447, 449 (US Ct of Apps (2nd Cir) 1994).

general conditions into the main contract.[49] The requisite knowledge for incorporation is somewhat more stringent in shipping cases, where courts have held that a bill of lading may not incorporate an arbitration clause from a charter party unless the bill specifically names the charter party.[50]

(5) Law applicable to the interpretation of arbitration clauses

The question of what law will govern the interpretation of arbitration clauses will depend upon a somewhat complicated interaction between federal law, international treaties (which for most arbitration purposes have the force of federal law), and state law. The application of these three legal frameworks is largely determined by two factors: (i) whether the arbitration falls within an applicable international convention; and (ii) whether the parties have provided a choice of law in their agreement. As a general rule, federal law governs the interpretation of the arbitration agreement unless the parties have chosen state law and the state law promotes arbitration, which is consistent with the federal policy favouring arbitration. **13.28**

In a case where the agreement falls under an applicable convention, s 201 of the FAA states that federal law shall apply. However, if the parties have chosen state law to govern their dispute, state law may apply, to the extent it is not inconsistent with the FAA and federal common law applying the FAA. For example, in *Volt Information Sciences v Stanford* (a domestic case), the Supreme Court refused to strike a California arbitration rule which permitted the state court to continue proceedings rather than stay them in favour of arbitration. The court reasoned in *Volt* that the essence of the FAA policy favouring arbitration was not to promote arbitration at all costs, but to permit the parties to arbitrate according to the terms of their agreement, which includes the parties' choice of law. However, the court left open in *Volt* the possibility that certain state laws would be stricken as violative of the FAA if they sufficiently impaired the policy favouring arbitration.[51] **13.29**

The scope of *Volt*'s rule remains unclear, and subsequent decisions have trimmed back on its potentially broad interpretation. In *Mastrobuono v Sherman Lehman Hutton Inc*, the Supreme Court held that even though the parties specifically chose New York law to govern the arbitration, the parties could not have intended a New York decisional rule limiting the power of arbitrators to award punitive damages to apply in their arbitration proceedings.[52] More recently, in *Preston v Ferrer*, the Supreme Court held that, despite a California choice-of-law clause, the FAA pre-empted a California state law requiring exhaustion of administrative remedies before pursuing arbitration. The Court distinguished *Volt* on the ground that that case involved the rights of third parties who were not signatories to the arbitration agreement.[53] Thus, while the Court has not explicitly overruled *Volt*, its post-*Volt* jurisprudence has consistently sought to trim the scope of its holding that a state choice-of-law **13.30**

[49] See *Aceros Prefabricados SA v TradeArbed Inc*, 282 F 3d 92 (US Ct of Apps (2nd Cir) 2002).

[50] *Keytrade USA Inc v Ain Temouchent M/V*, 404 F 3d 891 (US Ct of Apps (5th Cir) 2005).

[51] *Volt Information Sciences Inc v Board of Trustees of Leland Stanford Junior University*, 489 US 468, 472 (1989) (holding that federal law does not preempt all state law as applied to an arbitration, but allows parties to choose which law will apply, subject to the strong federal policy favouring arbitration).

[52] *Mastrobuono v Sherman Lehman Hutton Inc*, 514 US 52, 62–3 (1995).

[53] *Preston v Ferrer*, 128 S Ct 978 (2008).

clause can permit the enforceability of state arbitration law provisions potentially inconsistent with the FAA.

13.31 **(5.1) Do courts accept a wide competence of the arbitral tribunal or do they restrict arbitral competence? Do claims which arise in connection with the agreement submitted to arbitration generally fall within the arbitral jurisdiction even if based on tortious legal basis? Does there exist case law with respect to the wording in an arbitration clause as 'arising out of/under/in connection with the present contract' and its specific meaning?** The Supreme Court has held that 'as a matter of federal law, any doubts concerning the scope of arbitral issues should be resolved in favour of arbitration'.[54] As such, clauses which refer to all disputes, disputes arising out of, or disputes related to the main contract are generally read very broadly, although some courts have interpreted 'arising under' language more narrowly than 'related to' language.[55] In addition, there exists almost no bar to arbitrability of statutory claims in the United States (a state of affairs that could change if Congress enacted the Arbitration Fairness Act, discussed above).[56] In theory, this broad rule of scope would permit parties to arbitrate even claims based on tort, or quasi-contractual claims such as unjust enrichment or estoppel.[57] As such, unless parties expressly limit the scope of their arbitration agreement, they will most likely find any dispute referred to arbitration.

13.32 Moreover, even parties that carefully draft their arbitration clauses may find federal courts will attempt to broaden the scope of their agreement. For example, in *Mastrobuono v Sherman Lehman Hutton Inc* the Supreme Court affirmed the holding by the Second Circuit Court of Appeals that the parties could not have intended a New York decisional rule limiting the power of arbitrators to award punitive damages to apply in their arbitration proceedings.[58] This rationale seemingly ignored the fact that the parties specifically chose New York law—and presumably, therefore, the punitive damages limitation—to govern the arbitration. Thus, in an attempt to broaden the power of arbitrators, the *Mastruobuono* court essentially revised the nature of the proceeding the parties initially agreed upon. In light thereof, it may be that US courts are willing to prioritize the power and utility of arbitration proceedings over and above the nature of the agreement itself. Parties may hedge this risk of scope-broadening by clearly and precisely defining the scope of their arbitration clause.

---

[54] *Moses H Cone Mem Hosp v Mercury Const Corp*, 460 US 1, 103 S Ct 927 (1983).

[55] *Prima Paint v Flood Conklin Mfg*, 388 US 395, 87 S Ct 1801 (1967); *Cummings v Fedex Ground Package Sys Inc*, 404 F 3d 1258, 1261 (US Ct of Apps (10th Cir) 2005); *Homestead Lead Co v Doe Run Resources Corp*, 282 F Supp 2d 1131(US Dist Ct (ND Cal) 2003) (holding that arbitration clause referring to claims arising out of or relating to a contract are broad and the presumption of arbitrability therefore high). But see Born, G., *International Arbitration and Forum Selection Agreements* (Kluwer, 2006) 39–41 (noting that some courts draw 'fine lines' to distinguish 'arising under' from 'related to' in arbitration agreements).

[56] See s14.

[57] Born, *International Commercial Arbitration* (Kluwer, 2009) 781–5.

[58] *Mastruobuono*, 514 US 52, 115 S Ct 1212 (1995). Although the Supreme Court held in *Volt* that the purpose of the FAA was not to find enforceable arbitration agreements at the expense of forcing parties to arbitrate against their will, it appears in some cases the courts will find creative ways to bolster arbitration. *Accord Preston v Ferrer*, 128 S Ct 978 (2008) (upholding parties choice of California law, but excluding those parts of CA law which would limit the arbitrator's authority).

(6) Binding effect of an arbitration clause on third parties (eg in the case of a guarantee or assignment)

Generally, under US law, the common law rule of privity prevents a party to a contract from seeking to bind a non-signatory party. This rule is generally applicable in the case of arbitration agreements as well. There are, however, exceptions to this rule, and they arise frequently in American arbitration law.[59] **13.33**

The first theory which justifies binding a non-signatory is the doctrine of incorporation by reference. A non-signatory to an arbitration agreement may be compelled to arbitrate if the contract that the non-signatory entered into incorporated an arbitration agreement by reference. For example, a third party to a construction case may not have directly signed the arbitration agreement, but may nonetheless be bound by its terms if the contract signed by the third party incorporates the general conditions of the main contract into its terms.[60] **13.34**

A second situation arises where the non-signatory has essentially assumed the obligation to arbitrate by its conduct. Examples of assumption of the obligation to arbitrate might include proceeding with arbitration, waiving one's right to object to the tribunal's jurisdiction in court, or failing to disavow an obligation to arbitrate during the course of performance of the contract.[61] **13.35**

A third way arises under state law agency principles. For example, a non-signatory may be bound by the signature of its authorized agent, or even an agent who was unauthorized at the time of signing, but whose signature is later ratified by the principal.[62] These principles might apply where one company purchases or otherwise affiliates with another company—absent any agreement to the contrary, the purchasing company would be liable for the arbitration obligations of its subsidiary or affiliate. **13.36**

A fourth theory used to bind non-signatories is the doctrine of veil-piercing, or alter-ego theory. As in most countries, US courts will, on extraordinary occasions, strip a corporation or shareholder of the protection of separateness and limited liability if (i) the two entities are so closely related that there has been a 'virtual abandonment of separateness, or (ii) to prevent fraud or injustice.[63] If the court pierces the veil, non-signatories may be forced to assume the arbitration obligations of its alter-ego. **13.37**

Another theory used to bind non-signatories is the doctrine of assignment. The general rule in the US is that a party who has been assigned rights under a contract will assume the obligation to arbitrate. **13.38**

---

59 See *Ross v American Express*, 478 F 3d 96 (2007). 'Arbitration is strictly a matter of contract . . . . As such, ordinary contract principles apply, and we have recognized a number of common law principles of contract law that may allow non-signatories to enforce an arbitration agreement.' *id* (quoting *Thomson-CSF SA v Amercian Arbitration Ass'n* 64 F 3d 773 (US Ct of Apps (2nd Cir) 1995) (internal quotation marks and citations omitted).

60 *Prefabricados SA v TradeArbed Inc*, 282 F 3d 92, (US Ct of Apps (2nd Cir) 2002).

61 See *Thomson*, 64 F 3d at 777; *Gvosdenovic v United Airlines Inc*, 933 F 2d 1100, 1105 (US Ct of Apps (2nd Cir) 1991).

62 *Thomson*, 64 F 3d at 777.

63 *ibid.*

13.39 Finally, under US law, a non-signatory may be bound by principles of estoppel. Under an estoppel theory, a court may compel arbitration if it determines that it would be unfair for a non-signatory to deny the existence of any obligation to arbitrate.[64] This theory is based in fairness; it can be argued that a party may not enjoy the benefits of a contract while avoiding any obligation thereunder.

13.40 Importantly, even in cases where a party has signed the arbitration agreement, courts may apply equitable estoppel to force the signatory to arbitrate claims that may technically fall outside the scope of the clause. The key to this application of estoppel is whether it may be said that all of the claims are 'inextricably intertwined'. For example, in *Ross v American Express*, plaintiffs brought antitrust claims against two credit card companies, of which one was a signatory to the arbitration agreement and the other was not. The District Court compelled arbitration, because the claims against the non-signatory were 'inextricably intertwined' with those against the signatory.[65]

13.41 Finally, it bears emphasis that arbitration without privity may arise in certain specific fields such as investment disputes. In disputes under a bilateral investment treaty, or BIT, a sovereign non-signatory may be compelled to arbitrate if it has made itself amenable to arbitration in the BIT.[66]

13.42 (6.1) **What is the law/leading authorities' position on multi-party situations? Especially, (i) with respect to the objection that the arbitration clause does not specifically provide for a plurality of parties in the same procedure; (ii) with respect to the constitution of the arbitral tribunal; and (iii) with respect to the consolidation of two or more running arbitration proceedings?** Multi-party litigation is prominent in the US,[67] and it has been gaining momentum in the arbitration context. Two primary ways in which parties arbitrate jointly in the United States are through consolidation of proceedings and class action arbitration. Where there are multiple proceedings involving related factual issues, with at least some common parties, one or more of the parties may seek to consolidate the proceedings with the intention to resolve the issues for a maximum number of parties in the most efficient manner. Class action claims work differently. In a class arbitration, one or more named claimants assert claims on behalf of a 'class' of similarly situated, but unnamed, claimants, who are then bound by the decision of (and entitled to share in any relief granted by) the tribunal.

13.43 Current US law appears to permit consolidation of separate arbitrations where all of the parties have consented to the consolidation.[68] Regarding class action arbitration, the

---

[64] *Thomson*, 63 F 3d 777; see also *American Bankers Group v Long*, 453 F 3d 623, 627 (US Ct of Apps (4th Cir) 2006) (citing *Int'l Paper Co v Schwabedissen Maschinen & Anlagen GMBH*, 206 F 3d 411, 416 (4th Cir 2000).

[65] *In re Currency Conversion Fee Antitrust Litigation*, 2005 WL 2364969 (US Dist Ct (SDNY) 2005).

[66] Born, G., *International Commercial Arbitration* (Kluwer, 2009) 107–8.

[67] US Federal Rule of Civil Procedure 23 (class action filings), and 42 (consolidation).

[68] See *Gov't of United Kingdom v Boeing Co*, 998 F 2d 68 (US Ct of Apps (2nd Cir) 1993) (holding the FAA policy favouring arbitration supersedes interests of judicial efficiency where the parties have not agreed to consolidate proceedings); *Weyerhauser Co v Western Seas Shipping Co*, 743 F 2d 635 (US Ct of Apps (9th Cir) 1984), *cert denied*, 469 US 1061, 105 S Ct 544 (1984); *American Centennial Ins Co v Nat'l Casualty Co*, 951 F 2d 107, 108 (US Ct of Apps (6th Cir) 1991); *Protective Life Ins Corp v Lincoln Nat'l Life Ins Corp*, 873 F 2d 281

Supreme Court has strongly suggested that class action arbitrations do not violate the FAA in at least some circumstances.[69] As a result, some arbitral institutions are making it easier to proceed with multi-party arbitrations. For example, the American Arbitration Association (AAA) has published a set of class action arbitration rules, and its website makes available its class action arbitration docket.[70]

It is of practical importance to note that the current law gives arbitrators the power to decide whether consolidation or class action is permissible, but does not in any way define that discretion. Parties should remain alert to possible consolidation and class action issues which may be subject to arbitrator interpretation when a dispute arises. 13.44

(6.2) Is there case law/authorities with respect to the admissibility of third party participation in an arbitration without being a claimant or defendant (Nebenintervention/ Streitverkündung; intervention force/volontaire; vouching in; *amicus curiae* etc)? What are the prerequisites and effects of such participation (if permitted)? As a general rule, a third party with an interest in the dispute is not permitted to inject his or herself into the proceedings without the consent of the signatory parties. This is because arbitration is regarded as a private and consensual arrangement. In some cases, tribunals may allow *amici curiae* ('friends of the court') to participate in an arbitration proceeding. This is more common in investor-state arbitrations than in arbitrations arising under commercial contracts. 13.45

(7) Termination of an arbitration agreement by a party (reasons and case law)

Parties may mutually agree to terminate an arbitration agreement, but there are relatively few cases in which a party would be justified in unilaterally terminating the arbitration agreement. Under American contract law, generally only a material breach of the arbitration agreement itself would justify unilateral termination by the other party. 13.46

US law recognizes the separability doctrine, which holds that an allegation that the underlying contract is invalid does not defeat the arbitration agreement unless the illegality touches the arbitration agreement itself.[71] Consequently, termination of the underlying agreement does not result in the termination of the arbitration agreement. A party may escape the obligations of an arbitration agreement, however, if the other party has waived its rights under the arbitration agreement. Courts currently use a totality of the circumstances test to determine whether a party has acted in a manner 'inconsistent' with the right to arbitrate.[72] Important considerations in applying such a test in the arbitration context include, but are not limited to: (i) whether the party moving to compel arbitration has 13.47

(US Ct of Apps (11th Cir) 1989); *Del E Webb Construction v Richardson Hospital Authority*, 823 F 2d 145 (US Ct of Apps (5th Cir) 1987). See also Carbonneau, T., *The Law and Practice of Arbitration* (Juris, 2007) 34–5.

[69] See *Gilmer v Interstate/Johnson Lane Corp*, 500 US 20, 111 S Ct 1627 (1991).

[70] AAA Class Action Arbitration Policy and links to rules and docket, available at <http://www.adr.org/Classarbitrationpolicy>.

[71] See *Prima Paint Corp v Flood Conklin Mfg Co*, 388 US 395, 87 S Ct 1801 (1967); *Buckeye Check Cashing Inc v Cardegna*, 546 US 440, 126 S Ct 1204 (2006).

[72] *National Foundation for Cancer Research v A.G. Edwards & Sons Inc*, 821 F 2d 772 (US Ct of Apps (DC Cir) 1987); *Khan v Parssons Global Services Ltd*, 521 F 3d 421 (US Ct of Apps (DC Cir) 2008).

taken a 'substantial step in litigation'; and (ii) whether the party has allowed a 'substantial delay' to lapse prior to invoking the arbitration clause.[73]

B. Arbitrability

(1) 'Personal arbitrability' (capacity to conclude arbitration agreements)

13.48 Currently, any party may agree to arbitration, provided the party possesses the requisite capacity to enter into any contract under state contract and agency principles. Those requirements are generally relaxed; for example capacity is generally satisfied if the signor is of sound mind and not below the legal age to enter into contracts. However, if the pending Arbitration Fairness Act is passed to amend the FAA it may render unenforceable many arbitration agreements negotiated with consumers, employees and franchisees.

13.49 **(1.1) May a state (or state agency) as party invoke sovereign immunity before the arbitral tribunal or before a state court (eg in a procedure of enforcement)?** If the tribunal or state court finds a valid arbitration agreement exists, a sovereign that is a party to that agreement will be held to have waived its sovereign immunity as to arbitration.[74] This is also true in the case of investment arbitrations where a sovereign waives its immunity by consenting to arbitrate against a national of another sovereign under a bilateral treaty.[75] With respect to state and federal court jurisdiction, the sovereign immunity of a foreign state transacting business in the United States will be determined under the Foreign Sovereign Immunities Act (FSIA).[76] As a general rule, under the FSIA a sovereign state that agrees to arbitrate a dispute in the United States waives its immunity from suit in US courts.[77]

(2) 'Objective arbitrability' (eg of patent, trade mark and antitrust matters)

13.50 Application of the non-arbitrability doctrine has significantly declined in importance in American arbitration law, especially in cases arising out of an international relationship.[78] The US courts have held that virtually all commercial claims are arbitrable, including antitrust, securities, intellectual property, employment, and consumer protection claims.

13.51 The preference toward arbitrability in US law extends in many cases to claims created or protected by statute. In *Mitsubishi Motors Corp v Soler*, the Supreme Court held that parties may freely contract to arbitrate federal antitrust claims in international cases, but the court there expressly reserved its opinion on whether antitrust issues were capable of resolution by arbitration in purely domestic cases.[79] Cases since *Mitsubishi* have found as arbitrable

---

[73] *National Foundation for Cancer Research v A.G. Edwards & Sons Inc*, 821 F 2d 772 (US Ct of Apps (DC Cir) 1987); *Khan v Parssons Global Services Ltd*, 521 F 3d 421 (US Ct of Apps (DC Cir) 2008).

[74] But see *B.V. Bureau Wijsmuller v USA*, 1976 A.M.C. 2514 (US Dist Ct (SDNY) 1976).

[75] Born, *International Commercial Arbitration* (Kluwer, 2009) 107–8.

[76] 28 USC ss 1602–11 (Foreign Sovereign Immunities Act).

[77] Carbonneau, T., *The Law and Practice of Arbitration* (Juris, 2007) 132–3.

[78] See *Scherk v Alberto-Culver Co* 417 US 506, 94 S Ct 2449 (1974); *The Bremen v Zapata Off-Shore Co*, 407 US 1, 92 S Ct 1907 (1972); See also Born and Rutledge, *International Civil Litigation in United States Courts* (Aspen/Kluwer, 2007) 1110–11.

[79] *Mitsubishi Motors Corp v Soler Chrysler Plymouth Inc*, 473 US 614, 10 S Ct 3346 (1985).

claims involving securities and employment discrimination disputes, as well as claims under the Racketeer Influenced and Corrupt Organizations Act (RICO).[80]

In a case where arbitration of a statutory claim is at issue and the Supreme Court has not specifically addressed the arbitrability of that claim, the question will likely depend on the Supreme Court's arbitrability analysis in *Shearson/American Express v McMahon*. In *McMahon*, the Court held that statutory issues will be arbitrable provided that arbitration does not inherently conflict with the purpose of the statute (based on the text and legislative history).[81] **13.52**

C. Decision on the arbitral tribunal's jurisdiction ('*competence-competence*')

(1) Separability (independence of the arbitration agreement from the main agreement)

The doctrine of separability, which treats an arbitration agreement as separate from the main contract, is not addressed expressly by the FAA. However, the United States Supreme Court adopted the doctrine of separability in a landmark decision, *Prima Paint Corp v Flood*.[82] The Court recently affirmed its *Prima Paint* holding in *Buckeye Check Cashing Inc v Cardegna*. In both cases, the Court held that an arbitration agreement is separable from the main contract, and in cases where the main contract is illegal or void the defect in the main contract does not necessarily impeach the arbitration agreement.[83] A corollary to that rule, of course, is if the defect to the main contract can be said to infect the arbitration clause, the arbitration clause cannot stand. **13.53**

Importantly, the Court in *Prima Paint* and *Buckeye* did not address the case where one party challenges the arbitration clause on the ground that the underlying contract never came into existence. In fact, the Court in *Buckeye* expressly declined to resolve that question.[84] Until the Court does so, an arbitration clause contained in a main contract is in theory vulnerable to challenge on the ground that the main contract never came into existence. **13.54**

(2) Competence of the tribunal to decide on its own jurisdiction (including form and time of the tribunal's decision)

The FAA does not expressly define the competence of the arbitral tribunal, nor does it provide requirements regarding the form or timing of challenges to the tribunal's jurisdiction. The rules of most major arbitral institutions contain *competence-competence* clauses which establish the competence of an arbitral tribunal to decide whether it has jurisdiction. As the next paragraph will explain, these *competence-competence* provisions can have real significance under current US law. **13.55**

(3) Extent of the 'competence-competence' *and the role of the courts (including form and time limits of a challenge of the tribunal's decision)*

Like its treatment of separability, the FAA does not expressly mention the widely accepted doctrine of *competence-competence*, which imbues arbitral tribunals with power to decide **13.56**

---

80 Born and Rutledge, *International Civil Litigation* (Aspen/Kluwer, 2007) 1112 and note 120, 121.

81 *Shearson/American Express v McMahon*, 482 US 220, 107 S Ct 2332 (1987).

82 *Prima Paint Corp v Flood Conklin Mfg Co*, 388 US 395, 87 S Ct 1801 (1967); *Buckeye Check Cashing Inc v Cardegna*, 546 US 440, 126 S Ct 1204 (2006).

83 *Buckeye Check Cashing Inc v Cardegna*, 546 US 440, 126 S Ct 1204 (2006).

84 *ibid.*

whether they have jurisdiction. In *First Options of Chicago v Kaplan*, the Supreme Court held that questions related to the validity of an arbitration agreement were presumptively for the courts and not the arbitrators, unless there was 'clear and unmistakable evidence' that the parties intended to arbitrate questions related to the arbitrators' jurisdiction.[85] The courts have generally held that incorporating arbitral rules that provide for the tribunal's *competence-competence* satisfies this test. After *First Options*, the Supreme Court held in *Howsam v Dean Witter Reynolds* that certain 'gateway questions' (ie procedural matters, such as whether a party has filed within a time limit, or whether a party satisfied prerequisites for filing arbitration under the contract) must be resolved by the arbitrators. The Court maintained, however, that the core question of whether the parties agreed to arbitrate a dispute is presumptively a question for the courts.[86]

D. Enforcement of an arbitration agreement within or by court proceedings

(1) Effect of invoking an arbitration clause within a court proceeding (and time limits for such a motion)

13.57 A party seeking to invoke an arbitration clause may make a motion to compel arbitration under the FAA. For domestic arbitrations, s 4 of the FAA provides that any party aggrieved by another party's refusal to submit to a written arbitration agreement may petition the US District Court which would have jurisdiction absent an arbitration agreement.[87] In an arbitration falling under the New York Convention or Panama Convention, ss 206 and 303 provide that the courts 'may direct that arbitration be held in accordance with the agreement at any place therein provided for, whether that place is within or without the United States'.

13.58 In addition to seeking a court order to compel, s 3 of the FAA provides that the party seeking to compel arbitration may also request the court to stay the court proceedings while arbitration proceeds. Importantly, however, the s 3 stay application is not limited to cases where the court grants an order compelling arbitration. A stay may be granted even if the court denies the motion to compel, if sufficient grounds exist for granting the stay.[88]

13.59 The FAA does not impose a time limit on a party's ability to bring a motion to compel. But courts have found waiver in cases where a party proceeds to litigate in court without seeking to compel arbitration. In considering waiver, courts most often look at factors such as (i) whether the party moving to compel arbitration has taken a 'substantial step in litigation'; and (ii) whether the party has allowed a 'substantial delay' to lapse prior to invoking the arbitration clause.[89] The issue of waiver is decided on a circumstantial basis, and no one factor will be decisive. Recently, the US Court of Appeals for the District of Columbia Circuit held in *Khan v Parssons Global* that filing a motion to dismiss in the trial court waived that party's ability to invoke arbitration.[90]

---

[85] *First Options of Chicago Inc v Kaplan*, 514 US 938, 115 S Ct 1920 (1995).

[86] *Howsam v Dean Witter Reynolds*, 537 US 79, 123 S Ct 588 (2002).

[87] 9 USC s 4.

[88] 28 USC s 2283 (federal anti-injunction act).

[89] *National Foundation for Cancer Research v A.G. Edwards & Sons Inc*, 821 F 2d 772 (US Ct of Apps (DC Cir) 1987); *Khan v Parssons Global Services Ltd.*, 521 F 3d 421 (US Ct of Apps (DC Cir) 2008).

[90] *ibid.*

(1.1) If a party has invoked successfully the arbitration agreement in a court proceeding, is it then entitled to deny within the arbitral proceeding that there is a valid and binding arbitration agreement? Unless the parties expressly agree otherwise, a tribunal may permissibly apply equitable principles to estop a party in the arbitration from denying an agreement exists, where the party first raised the agreement in a motion to compel. 13.60

(1.2) Vice versa, if a party has successfully objected to an arbitral proceeding by denying that there is a valid arbitration agreement, may it then invoke such agreement in the ensuing court proceeding? Both federal and state courts in the United States will similarly estop a party from invoking an arbitration agreement if it denied the existence of the agreement before a tribunal. 13.61

(2) Legal remedies and proceedings to enforce an arbitration agreement

If a party seeks to enforce an arbitration agreement, it may make a motion to compel in federal court. Section 4 of the FAA provides that the court can review the arbitration agreement and order the parties to arbitrate if it finds a valid agreement to arbitrate exists. The act also provides 'if the making of the arbitration agreement or the failure, neglect, or refusal to perform the same be in issue, the court shall proceed summarily to the trial thereof'. 13.62

Any trial on the issue of formation of the agreement must follow the analysis set forth by the Supreme Court in *First Options* and its successor cases, meaning that the doctrine of separability will apply to save the arbitration agreement from deficiencies which would render the underlying contract void, but it is for the courts to decide the issue of whether the tribunal has jurisdiction unless there is 'clear and unmistakable evidence' that the parties intended for the arbitrators to decide.[91] The FAA provides that the party alleged to be in default under the arbitration agreement may demand trial by jury. 13.63

(2.1) Which would be the internationally competent court (i) for obtaining a declaration that an arbitration agreement is valid and binding; or (ii) to compel arbitration? (The defendant's courts? The courts of the place of arbitration? The claimant's courts, cf Article 6(2) in fine, 1998 ICC Rules?) As discussed previously, an international arbitration agreement is generally governed by federal law, and s 203 confers subject matter jurisdiction over any agreement falling under the convention.[92] Section 206 grants federal courts the authority to compel arbitration. As in the case of domestic arbitration agreements, a party seeking to compel arbitration must do so early on, and avoid acting in a manner 'inconsistent' with the arbitration right.[93] 13.64

One problem which arises with some frequency involves establishing that a United States court has personal jurisdiction over the litigants in the case. Generally, personal jurisdiction will be satisfied over a defendant if (i) the defendant is incorporated or has its principal place of business in the United States; (ii) the defendant is personally served with process 13.65

[91] *First Options*, 514 US 938, 115 S Ct 1920 (1995); *Howsam*, 537 US 79, 123 S Ct 588 (2002).

[92] 9 USC s 203

[93] *National Foundation for Cancer Research v A.G. Edwards & Sons Inc*, 821 F 2d 772 (US Ct of Apps (DC Cir) 1987); *Khan v Parssons Global Services Ltd*, 521 F 3d 421 (US Ct of Apps (DC Cir) 2008).

in the United States; (iii) the defendant consents to jurisdiction in the United States; or (iv) the defendant has contacts with the United States which arise out of the transaction in dispute. This last category is known as the 'minimum contacts' requirement for personal jurisdiction. In *International Shoe v Washington*, the Supreme Court held that a court will have jurisdiction over a defendant if the defendant has 'certain minimum contacts with [the forum state] such that the maintenance of the suit does not offend 'traditional notions of fair play and substantial justice'.[94]

13.66 In a case where parties have agreed to arbitrate in the United States, personal jurisdiction presents no hurdle because both parties consent to the jurisdiction of US courts by virtue of their agreement. Similarly, in cases where US law applies because it is the seat of arbitration, it will often be the case that by agreeing to arbitrate in a particular state, the parties have made sufficient minimum contacts with the state to make jurisdiction constitutional. In cases where neither party has consented to arbitration under US law or in US territory, however, personal jurisdiction may be lacking, creating an obstacle to access to the US courts.

III. The arbitral tribunal

A. Number and qualification of arbitrators

(1) Sole arbitrator or arbitral tribunal with several arbitrators

13.67 There are no requirements imposed by US law regarding the number of arbitrators in US-sited arbitrations. The parties have broad discretion to agree on the number of arbitrators, either directly or by reference to a set of procedural rules. Tribunals comprised of a sole arbitrator or a panel of several arbitrators are equally acceptable. Section 5 of the FAA (which governs domestic arbitrations and may have residual effect in international arbitrations) provides that, where the courts are called on to appoint arbitrators for the parties, 'unless otherwise provided in the agreement the arbitration shall be by a single arbitrator'.[95]

13.68 **(1.1) Are arbitral tribunals with an even number of arbitrators acceptable?** Tribunals with an even number of arbitrators are acceptable, but uncommon. All of the leading institutional and non-institutional arbitral rules provide for either a sole arbitrator or a panel of three arbitrators.[96]

(2) Qualification of the arbitrators

13.69 Aside from the impartiality standards discussed below, US law imposes no requirements for the qualifications of arbitrators. The parties are free to include specific qualifications

[94] *International Shoe Co v Washington*, 326 US 310, 66 S Ct 154 (1945); *Asahi Metal Industry Co v Superior Court*, 480 US 102, 107 S Ct 1026 (1987).

[95] 9 USC s 5.

[96] AAA (ICDR) International Rules, Art 5; AAA Commercial Rules, R-15; AAA Procedures for Large, Complex Commercial Disputes, r L-2; CPR International Rules, r 5.

required of the arbitrators, such as particular language skills, industry experience, or technical expertise, in their arbitration agreement or by adoption of a set of arbitration rules. If they do so, those requirements will be respected.

(2.1) Are there mandatory requirements for the qualification of arbitrators (statutory requirements or indirect requirements through eg general conditions of insurance contracts)? There are no mandatory requirements imposed by US law for the qualification of arbitrators in international arbitrations or domestic commercial arbitrations. The parties are free to choose as arbitrators whomever they view as best suited to resolving their dispute. Some institutional rules impose specific qualification requirements for the arbitrators.[97] **13.70**

(2.2) Which national arbitration institutions may be contacted for obtaining information about qualified (and specialized) arbitrators? The International Institute for Conflict Prevention and Resolution provides a publicly accessible database of arbitrators (available at <http://www.cpradr.com>). The Judicial Arbitration and Mediation Services also provides a publicly accessible database (available at <http://www.jamsadr.com>). There are also numerous publications listing and ranking arbitration specialists and arbitrators, including Chambers USA,[98] Expert Guides: Experts in Commercial Arbitration,[99] *Dispute Resolution Directory*,[100] and *A Roster of International Arbitrators*.[101] **13.71**

(2.3) Are judges or civil servants required to obtain permission by their employer to act as arbitrator? Are these permissions given generally or case-by-case? What are the consequences if such permission has not been obtained? Although it is common for retired judges to sit as arbitrators in private commercial disputes, sitting US judges generally do not accept appointments as arbitrators. The Code of Conduct for United States Judges provides that a sitting federal judge may not act as an arbitrator (or mediator) or provide other private judicial services, unless authorized by law.[102] Most states have similar restrictions.[103] Civil servants are not explicitly precluded from acting as arbitrators, but they may be limited in the situations and circumstances in which they may do so. **13.72**

---

[97] eg NASD Code of Arbitration Procedure for Customer Disputes, Arts 12400, 13400 (requiring that the chairman of a panel of arbitrators in a securities arbitration under the NASD Rules must have completed the NASD's training for chairpersons of NASD tribunals and must have previously served as an arbitrator in a certain number of arbitrations administered by a self-regulatory organization in which hearings were held); AAA Employment Arbitration Rules, Art 12 (requiring that neutral arbitrators 'shall be experienced in the field of employment law.').

[98] Published by Chambers and Partners and available at <http://www.chambersandpartners.co.uk/usa/>.

[99] Published by Legal Media Group and available at <http://www.expertguides.com/>.

[100] Martindale-Hubbell, *Dispute Resolution Directory*, available at <http://www.dispute.martindale.com/index.php>.

[101] Smit, H. and Pechota, V., *A Roster of International Arbitrators* (Smit's Guides to International Arbitration, updated quarterly).

[102] Code of Conduct for United States Judges Canon 5E (Judicial Conference 2000).

[103] eg California Code of Judicial Ethics Canon 4F (2007); Massachussetts Code of Judicial Conduct Canon 5E (1998).

B. Appointment of arbitrators

(1) Extent of party autonomy to establish appointment procedure

13.73 The parties have broad discretion to establish the procedure for appointing arbitrators, and the FAA expressly gives effect to any agreement by the parties.[104] It is important to note that the parties may agree on a mechanism for appointing the arbitrator(s) either directly in the arbitration agreement itself, or by selecting a set of procedural rules that contains a mechanism for appointing the tribunal.

13.74 Under the AAA (ICDR) International Arbitration Rules, if the parties have not agreed on an appointment procedure, the AAA (ICDR) will appoint the arbitrators directly.[105] Some other institutional rules widely used in the US, including the AAA Commercial Rules, use a list mechanism, under which the institution sends both parties an identical list of potential arbitrators. Each party strikes the names of the individuals that are not acceptable to it, ranks the remaining names in order of preference, and returns the list to the institution. The institution then appoints the highest-ranked name that is common to both lists. If there is no common name remaining on the lists, the institution generally appoints the arbitrator directly (without reference to the lists).[106]

(2) Procedure in absence of an agreement by the parties

13.75 The FAA is somewhat ambiguous as to the power of the courts to appoint arbitrators in international cases in the absence of an agreement by the parties. Most courts that have considered the issue have concluded that ss 5 and 206, taken together, allow the courts to appoint arbitrators in international arbitrations even if the parties have not agreed on an appointment mechanism.

13.76 Section 206, which governs arbitrations falling under the New York Convention, provides that the courts may appoint arbitrators in international arbitrations 'in accordance with the provisions of the [parties' arbitration] agreement'. However, if the parties have not agreed on a particular appointment mechanism, either directly or through reference to a set of procedural rules, the courts have generally held that they can appoint arbitrators under s 5 of the FAA, which governs domestic arbitrations but can have residual effect in international cases. Section 5 provides that '[i]f no such [appointment] method be provided therein . . . then upon the application of either party to the controversy the court shall designate and appoint an arbitrator or arbitrators or umpire, as the case may require, who shall act under the said agreement with the same force and effect as if he or they had been specifically named therein'.[107] This provision expressly allows courts to act in the absence

---

[104] 9 USC s 5 ('If in the agreement provision be made for a method of naming or appointing an arbitrator or arbitrators or an umpire, such method shall be followed'.); s 206 (providing that where the courts are called on to enforce the parties' arbitration agreement by appointing arbitrators for the parties, the courts must do so 'in accordance with the provisions of the [parties' arbitration] agreement'). See also Revised Uniform Arbitration Act (2003) ('RUAA'), s 11(a).

[105] AAA (ICDR) International Rules, Art 6.

[106] eg AAA Commercial Rules, R-11; JAMS International Rules, Art 7; NASD Code of Arbitration Procedure for Customer Disputes, r 12400-6; NASD Code of Arbitration Procedure for Industry Disputes, r 3400-6.

[107] 9 USC s 5.

of an agreement by the parties on an appointment mechanism. Most courts have interpreted s 5, in combination with s 206, as allowing them to make appointments in international, as well as domestic, arbitrations, even in the absence of an agreed appointment mechanism.[108]

(3) Effect of the refusal of one party to cooperate in the constitution of the arbitral tribunal

Where the parties have agreed to an appointment mechanism but that mechanism has failed (for example, because one party refuses to cooperate in the constitution of the tribunal), the courts may appoint arbitrators directly. As discussed above, s 206 of the FAA allows the courts to appoint arbitrators in international arbitrations in accordance with the parties' arbitration agreement, and s 5 of the FAA expressly allows courts to appoint arbitrators where the parties' agreed appointment mechanism has failed. Courts regularly appoint arbitrators in international arbitrations under these provisions. **13.77**

(4) Circumstances and valid reasons for an arbitrator to resign

Once the arbitrators have accepted their appointment, they have a contractual obligation to the parties to hear the case and decide the dispute. If an arbitrator becomes incapacitated or unable to carry out his or her mandate, he or she may resign.[109] **13.78**

An arbitrator's resignation can have serious implications for the resolution of the parties' dispute. Thus, if an arbitrator has resigned without good cause, that arbitrator may (at least theoretically) be held liable for any damages caused by his or her breach of contract.[110] **13.79**

C. Challenge and replacement of arbitrators

Historically, in domestic arbitrations, party-appointed arbitrators were not required or presumed to be neutral, and US arbitral institutions and US courts drew clear distinctions between party-appointed arbitrators and 'neutrals'. In the past decade, this presumption has been reversed, and it is now generally presumed that, unless the parties have specifically provided otherwise, all of the arbitrators are independent and impartial. This is now specifically provided in the AAA/ABA Code of Ethics for Arbitrators,[111] the AAA Commercial Rules,[112] and other institutional arbitration rules.[113] **13.80**

[108] eg *Jain v de Mere*, 51 F 3d 686 (US Ct Apps (7th Cir) 1995); *CAE Indus Ltd v Aerospace Holdings Co*, 741 F Supp 388 (US Dist Ct (SDNY) 1989); *Astra Footwear Indus v Harwyn Int'l*, 442 F Supp 907, 910 (US Dist Ct (SDNY) 1978).

[109] eg Domke on Commercial Arbitration vol 1, s 24:1 (2003) ('Arbitrators have an unqualified right to resign and cannot be forced by the courts to continue to serve if they are unwilling to do so.'); *Florasynth v Pickholz*, 750 F 2d 171, 174 (US Ct Apps (2nd Cir) 1984) (arbitrators have an 'unqualified right' to resign if they believe it is in the best interests of the parties).

[110] See paras 13.264–13.75 *infra*.

[111] AAA/ABA Code of Ethics, Note on Neutrality (effective 1 March 2004) ('it is preferable for all arbitrators including any party-appointed arbitrators to be neutral, that is independent and impartial, and to comply with the same ethical standards. This expectation generally is essential in arbitrations where the parties, the nature of the dispute, or the enforcement of any resulting award may have international aspects. . . . This Code establishes a presumption of neutrality for all arbitrators, including party-appointed arbitrators, which applies unless the parties' agreement, the arbitration rules agreed to by the parties or applicable laws provide otherwise').

[112] AAA Commercial Rules, R-12(b), R-17 (effective 1 July 2003).

[113] eg CPR International Rules, r 7.1; JAMS International Rules, Art 8.1.

13.81 The FAA allows the courts to overturn an arbitral award '[w]here there was evident partiality or corruption in the arbitrators or either of them'.[114] This is the only procedural avenue by which the courts may consider a challenge to an arbitrator. As a consequence, parties may raise challenges to an arbitrator's independence and impartiality with an arbitral institution or with the arbitrators themselves during the arbitral proceeding, but they can seek judicial review of such issues only after the award has been rendered, in an action to vacate (or in defence of an action to enforce) the award.[115]

(1) Grounds, procedure and deadlines for challenging an arbitrator

13.82 Most procedural rules contain provisions allowing parties to challenge an arbitrator at the appointment stage. Under these rules, the parties generally submit their challenge to the relevant arbitral institution or appointing authority, or, less commonly, to the arbitrators themselves, for a decision.[116]

13.83 The FAA allows US courts to consider objections regarding an arbitrator's independence only after the award has been rendered. Section 10 provides that an arbitral award may be vacated '[w]here there was evident partiality or corruption in the arbitrators, or either of them'.[117]

13.84 'Evident partiality' is generally evaluated under an objective standard, and arbitrators should therefore 'disclose to the parties any dealings that might create an impression of possible bias'.[118] The courts are divided regarding the consequences of a failure to disclose such matters where there is no evidence of actual bias. Some courts have held that any failure to disclose facts that might objectively create an impression of bias is grounds for vacating the tribunal's ultimate award.[119] Other courts have held that failure to disclose a fact that would not be grounds for seeking to disqualify the arbitrator cannot be grounds for seeking to vacate the tribunal's award.[120] Although US practice has moved decidedly away from the historical presumption that party-appointed arbitrators are not neutral,

[114] 9 USC s 10.

[115] eg *Aviall Inc v Ryder System Inc*, 110 F 3d 892, 895 (US Ct Apps (2nd Cir) 1997) ('it is well established that a district court cannot entertain an attack upon the qualifications or partiality of arbitrators until after the conclusion of the arbitration and the rendition of the award') (quotation omitted); *Gulf Guaranty Life Ins Co v Connecticut General Life Ins Co*, 304 F 3d 476, 489–91 (US Ct Apps (5th Cir) 2002); *Florasynth*, 750 F 2d 174 ('The Arbitration Act does not provide for judicial scrutiny of an arbitrator's qualifications to serve, other than in a proceeding to confirm or vacate an award.'). But see *Metropolitan Property and Casualty Ins Co v JC Penney Casualty Ins Co* 780 F Supp 885, 894 (US Dist Ct (D Conn) 1991) ('In light of this reality, it simply does not follow that the policy objective of an expeditious and just arbitration with minimal judicial interference is furthered by categorically prohibiting a court from disqualifying an arbitrator prior to arbitration.').

[116] eg AAA (ICDR) International Rules, Arts 8–9; AAA Commercial Rules, r R-17; CPR International Rules, Art 7.6–7.8.

[117] 9 USC s 10.

[118] *Commonwealth Coatings Corp v Continental Casualty Co*, 393 US 145, 89 S Ct 337 (1968).

[119] eg *Olson v Merrill Lynch, Pierce, Fenner & Smith Inc*, 51 F 3d 157, 159 (US Ct of Apps (8th Cir) 1995); *Schmitz v Zilvetti*, 20 F 3d 1043, 1046–48 (US Ct of Apps (9th Cir) 1994); *Middlesex Mutual Ins Co v Levine*, 675 F 2d 1197, 1200 (US Ct of Apps (11th Cir) 1982). See also RUAA s 12(d) ('If the arbitrator did not disclose a fact as required . . . the court . . . may vacate an award.').

[120] eg *Positive Software Solutions Inc v New Century Mortgage Corporation*, 476 F 3d 278, 281 (US Ct of Apps (5th Cir) 2007); *Nationwide Mutual Ins Co v Home Ins Co*, 429 F 3d 640, 644–45 (US Ct of Apps (6th Cir) 2005); *Sphere Drake Ins Ltd v All Amercian Life Ins Co.*, 307 F 3d 617, 621 (US Ct of Apps (7th Cir) 2002).

some judicial decisions continue to apply different standards of independence to party-appointed and 'neutral' arbitrators.[121]

In considering issues related to arbitrator disclosure, some courts and arbitral institutions have looked to the AAA/ABA Code of Ethics for Arbitrators in Commercial Disputes[122] for guidance. The AAA/ABA Code of Ethics, which is published jointly by the AAA and the American Bar Association, provides: 13.85

A. Persons who are requested to serve as arbitrators should, before accepting, disclose:
   (1) any known direct or indirect financial or personal interest in the outcome of the arbitration;
   (2) any known existing or past financial, business, professional or personal relationships which might reasonably affect impartiality or lack of independence in the eyes of any of the parties. For example, prospective arbitrators should disclose any such relationships which they personally have with any party or its lawyer, with any co-arbitrator, or with any individual whom they have been told will be a witness. They should also disclose any such relationships involving their families or household members or their current employers, partners, or professional or business associates that can be ascertained by reasonable efforts;
   (3) the nature and extent of any prior knowledge they may have of the dispute; and
   (4) any other matters, relationships, or interests which they are obligated to disclose by the agreement of the parties, the rules or practices of an institution, or applicable law regulating arbitrator disclosure.[123]

The AAA/ABA Code of Ethics also provides that '[a]ny doubt as to whether or not disclosure is to be made should be resolved in favor of disclosure'.[124] Consistent with these principles, the AAA Rules (and most other commonly used procedural rules) provide for broad disclosure by the potential arbitrators at the time of their appointment.[125] 13.86

(1.1) Do state courts review challenge procedures which took place in accordance with a specific procedure agreed upon by the parties (eg Article 11, ICC Rules)? If so, at what 13.87

[121] See Born, G., *International Commercial Arbitration* (Kluwer, 2009) 1496–9.

[122] The Code of Ethics for Arbitrators in Commercial Disputes is not binding, but it aims to 'set[] forth generally accepted standards of ethical conduct for the guidance of arbitrators and parties in commercial disputes, in the hope of contributing to the maintenance of high standards and continued confidence in the process of arbitration'.

[123] Code of Ethics for Arbitrators in Commercial Disputes, effective 1 March 2004, Canon II. See also RUAA s 12 (requiring potential arbitrator to disclose 'any known facts that a reasonable person would consider likely to affect the impartiality of the arbitrator in the arbitration proceeding, including: (1) a financial or personal interest in the outcome of the arbitration proceeding; and (2) an existing or past relationship with any of the parties to the agreement to arbitrate or the arbitration proceeding, their counsel or representatives, a witness, or other arbitrators.').

[124] Code of Ethics for Arbitrators in Commercial Disputes, effective 1 March 2004, Canon II.

[125] AAA (ICDR) International Rules, Art 7 ('Arbitrators acting under these rules shall be impartial and independent. Prior to accepting appointment, a prospective arbitrator shall disclose to the administrator any circumstance likely to give rise to justifiable doubts as to the arbitrator's impartiality or independence.'); AAA Commercial Rules, R-16 ('Any person appointed or to be appointed as an arbitrator shall disclose to the AAA any circumstance likely to give rise to justifiable doubt as to the arbitrator's impartiality or independence, including any bias or any financial or personal interest in the result of the arbitration or any past or present relationship with the parties or their representatives. Such obligation shall remain in effect throughout the arbitration.').

point in time? May such review be excluded? As discussed above, US courts will review challenges to the independence or impartiality of the arbitrators only after the award has been made, in connection with an action to vacate or enforce the award.

13.88 (1.2) **Is there case law with respect to truncated arbitral tribunals? (cf Art 12(5), ICC Rules.)** If the parties have selected a set of procedural rules to govern their arbitration, those rules may contain provisions regarding whether, in the event of the death, resignation, or non-participation of one of the arbitrators, the remaining arbitrators may proceed to make an award.[126]

13.89 Where the parties have not agreed on the consequences of a truncated tribunal, either directly or by reference to a set of procedural rules, the courts have generally held that upon the death or resignation of one member of an arbitral tribunal, the panel loses its authority to render a final award and a new tribunal should be constituted to hear the proceedings anew.[127] Some courts have found exceptions to this rule where the evidentiary proceedings were already closed and where the two remaining arbitrators were in agreement on the award.[128]

(2) Procedure for appointing a new arbitrator

13.90 If the parties have selected a set of procedural rules to govern their arbitration, those rules will typically contain provisions regarding how a vacancy on the tribunal should be filled and whether any or all of the prior proceedings should be repeated.[129]

13.91 In the absence of provisions in the parties' arbitration agreement or any applicable procedural rules, US courts have generally held that, upon the death or resignation of an arbitrator, the entire panel loses its jurisdiction to render an award and should be disbanded.[130] In special circumstances—such as where the proceedings are at a very early stage or where the remaining issues to be determined are relatively discrete from those already decided by the original tribunal—some courts have allowed the appointment of a substitute arbitrator and the continuation of the arbitration proceedings.[131]

---

[126] eg AAA (ICDR) International Rules, Arts 10–11; AAA Commercial Rules, R-19; CPR International Rules, rules 7.9–12.

[127] eg *Marine Products Export Corp v M.T. Globe Galaxy*, 977 F 2d 66, 68 (US Ct of Apps (2nd Cir) 1992); *Backus-Brooks Co v Northern Pacific Railway Co*, 21 F 2d 4, 13 (US Ct of Apps (8th Cir) 1927); see also 1 Domke on Commercial Arbitration s 26:4. The RUAA, however, provides that if an arbitrator is unable to act, 'a replacement arbitrator must be appointed . . . to continue the proceeding and to resolve the controversy'. RUAA s 15(e).

[128] eg *Zeiler v Deitsch*, 500 F 3d 157, 166–8 (US Ct of Apps (2nd Cir) 2007); *Trade and Transport Inc v Natural Petroleum Charters Inc*, 738 F Supp 789, 791–2 (US Dist Ct (SDNY) 1990); *Republic of Colombia v Cauca Co*, 190 US 524, 528, 23 S Ct 704, 706 (1903).

[129] eg AAA (ICDR) International Rules, Arts 10–11; AAA Commercial Rules, R-19; CPR International Rules, rules 7.9–12.

[130] eg *Marine Products*, 977 F 2d at 68; *Jones v St Louis-San Francisco Railway Co*, 728 F 2d 257, 263–4 (US Ct of Apps (6th Cir) 1984); *Association of Flight Attendants, AFL-CIO v Aloha Airlines Inc*, 158 F Supp 2d 1200, 1207–8 (US Dist Ct (D Hawaii) 2001); *In re CIA De Navegacion Omsil SA*, 359 F Supp 898, 899 (US Dist Ct (SDNY) 1973).

[131] eg *Dow Corning Corp v Safety National Casualty Co*, 335 F 3d 742, 749 (US Ct of Apps (8th Cir) 2003); *Wellpoint Health Networks Inc and UniCare Life & Health Co v John Hancock Life Ins Co*, 547 F Supp 2d 899, 914–15 (US Dist Ct (N D Ill) 2008).

IV. The arbitral procedure

A. General principles

(1) Extent of party autonomy to determine the arbitral procedure

There is relatively little US legal authority regarding the procedures to be followed in an arbitration. Most issues are left to the agreement of the parties (including their agreement as to any particular procedural rules) and to the discretion of the arbitral tribunal. **13.92**

(1.1) Are the parties free to choose any national or international law governing the procedure before the arbitral tribunal? There are no statutory provisions regarding the choice of a foreign procedural law. US courts recognize the significant difficulties raised by choosing a foreign procedural law and generally will not interpret an arbitration agreement as providing for a foreign procedural law unless there is clear and unequivocal evidence that this is what the parties intended.[132] There is no express prohibition on choosing a foreign procedural law, however, and the few cases that address the issue suggest that the courts would respect a clear and unambiguous choice of a foreign procedural law.[133] **13.93**

(2) Basic procedural principles or mandatory rules to be applied by the arbitral tribunal

US law grants the arbitrators broad discretion to determine the procedures to be used in the arbitration.[134] The only mandatory rules regarding arbitral procedure concern basic due process protections. The FAA allows the courts to set aside an arbitral award where there has been corruption, fraud, or evident partiality on the part of the arbitrators, or where 'the arbitrators were guilty of misconduct in refusing to postpone the hearing, upon sufficient cause shown, or in refusing to hear evidence pertinent and material to the controversy; or of any other misbehaviour by which the rights of any party have been prejudiced'.[135] **13.94**

---

[132] eg *Karaha Bodas Co v Perusahaan Pertambangan Minyak Dan Gas Bumi Negara,* 364 F 3d 274, 291 (US Ct of Apps (5th Cir) 2004) ('An agreement providing that one country will be the site of the arbitration but the proceedings will be held under the arbitration law of another country [is] "exceptional"; "almost unknown"; a "purely academic invention"; "almost never used in practice"; a possibility "more theoretical than real"; and a "once-in-a-blue-moon" set of circumstances').

[133] eg *Karaha Bodas Co,* 364 F 3d at 292–94; *Int'l Standard Elec Corp v Bridas Sociedad Anonima Petrolera,* 745 F Supp 172, 177 (US Dist Ct (SDNY) 1990) ('Parties to an international arbitration might prefer to equalize travel distance and costs to witnesses by selecting as a *situs* forum A, midpoint between two cities or two continents, and submit themselves to a different procedural law by selecting the arbitration procedure of forum B').

[134] *D.E.I., Inc v Ohio and Vicinity Regional Council of Carpenters,* 155 Fed Appx 164, 170 (US Ct of Apps (6th Cir) 2005) ('Arbitrators are not bound by formal rules of procedure and evidence, and the standard for judicial review of arbitration procedures is merely whether a party to arbitration has been denied a fundamentally fair hearing.') (quoting *Nat'l Post Office Mailhandlers v US Postal Service,* 751 F 2d 834, 841 (US Ct of Apps (6th Cir) 1985)); *Int'l Union, United Mine Workers of America v Marrowbone Development Co,* 232 F 3d 383, 389 (US Ct of Apps (4th Cir) 2000) ('An arbitrator typically retains broad discretion over procedural matters . . ..'); *Local 12934 of Int'l Union etc v Dow Corning,* 459 F 2d 221, 223 (6th Cir 1972) ('[I]t has long been settled that where the substantive issues of a dispute are a proper subject for arbitration, procedural matters arising out of that dispute are for the arbitrator, not the courts, to determine.').See also Born, G., *International Commercial Arbitration* (Kluwer, 2009) 1761–2.

[135] 9 USC s 10(a)(3). *See also* RUAA s 15(d) ('At a hearing under subsection (c), a party to the arbitration proceeding has a right to be heard, to present evidence material to the controversy, and to cross-examine witnesses appearing at the hearing.').

These provisions reflect the tribunal's obligation to ensure that the parties are treated fairly and that each has a full opportunity to present its case. Other than this, there are no mandatory procedural rules imposed by US law.

(3) Oral hearing or proceeding on basis of written documents

13.95 A tribunal can proceed solely on the basis of written documents without an oral hearing if the parties agree,[136] but if either party requests an oral hearing, the tribunal will generally accommodate that request. There is no due process requirement for an oral hearing, however, and refusal to hold an oral hearing will not be grounds for vacating an arbitral award so long as each party was given a full and fair opportunity to present its case.[137]

(4) Power of the tribunal (in particular the chairman) to issue procedural orders

13.96 As a matter of practice, it is well accepted that the tribunal can issue procedural orders. It is also widely accepted that the chairman of the tribunal acting alone can issue procedural orders in appropriate circumstances, such as for routine administrative matters.[138]

(5) Distinction of matters of substance and matters of procedure

13.97 As a general rule, the tribunal will decide the dispute in accordance with the substantive law chosen by the parties or selected by the tribunal, while matters of procedure will be determined by the procedural law, which is generally the law of the arbitral seat (or, uncommonly, a foreign procedural law selected by the parties). In application, however, this rule can be quite complex, because there is not always a clear distinction between matters of substance and matters of procedure.

13.98 (5.1) **Are the statutes of limitations a matter of substance or rather of procedure?** Under US law, statutes of limitation are often considered to have both substantive and procedural aspects, depending on the context and issues involved. With respect to the appropriate choice of law, statutes of limitation are generally held to be governed by the procedural law of the forum.[139] US courts have generally held that arbitrators have jurisdiction to determine issues regarding the statute of limitations.

(6) Persons able to represent a party in an arbitral proceeding

13.99 Parties may generally be represented by a lawyer or non-lawyer representative of their choice.[140] In the past, there have been efforts by individual states to restrict the rights of foreign lawyers (ie lawyers not licensed to practice in that state) to appear in international

[136] eg AAA Commercial Rules, R-30(c); CPR International Rules, r 12.2; JAMS International Rules, Art 23.1.

[137] eg *Griffin Industries Inc v Petrojam Ltd*, 58 F Supp 2d 212, 219–0 (US Dist Ct (SDNY)1999) ('While hearings are advisable in most arbitration proceedings, arbitrators are not compelled to conduct oral hearings in every case.'); *Federal Deposit Ins Corp v Air Florida System Inc*, 822 F 2d 833, 842 (US Ct of Apps (9th Cir) 1987); *British Ins Co of Cayman v Water Street Ins Co Ltd*, 93 F Supp 2d 506, 517 (US Dist Ct (SDNY) 2000).

[138] eg AAA (ICDR) International Rules, Arts 16.1, 26.2; CPR International Rules, r 9.1; JAMS International Rules, Art 20.5.

[139] Restatement (Second) of Conflict of Laws s 142.

[140] eg AAA (ICDR) International Rules, Art 12; AAA Commercial Rules, R-24; CPR International Rules, r 4; JAMS International Rules, Art 19.1.

arbitrations sited in that state.[141] These efforts were severely criticized and were withdrawn.[142]

B. Place of arbitration

The parties generally have broad autonomy to agree on the place (seat) of arbitration. Most parties select the place of arbitration in their arbitration agreement. **13.100**

(1) Determination of the place of arbitration in absence of an agreement by the parties

In a domestic US arbitration, if the parties have not agreed on the place of the arbitration, s 4 of the FAA allows the US federal court that would have had jurisdiction in the absence of the parties' arbitration agreement to compel arbitration within its own judicial district. **13.101**

In an international arbitration, s 206 allows the US courts to 'direct that arbitration be held in accordance with the agreement at any place therein provided for, whether that place is within or without the United States'.[143] Where the parties to an international arbitration have not selected the *situs* in their arbitration agreement or by reference to a set of procedural rules, most courts will not compel arbitration under s 206. However, the courts may still act under s 4 to compel arbitration in their own judicial district.[144] **13.102**

(2) Importance and legal effect of place (seat) of the arbitration

As in other jurisdictions, the legal seat of the arbitration has particular significance in US law. Many provisions of the FAA apply only where the place of the arbitration is within the US, and the US courts will offer substantially more assistance in aid of an arbitration that is seated within the US than one that is seated elsewhere. **13.103**

In addition, the place of the arbitration is particularly important for the enforcement of arbitral awards. The US is a signatory to the New York Convention, which establishes a separate legal regime that governs the enforcement of foreign arbitration awards. Thus, under US law, arbitral awards rendered within the US are subject to judicial review under the grounds listed in s 10 of the FAA and established by common law, while arbitral awards rendered elsewhere are subject to review only in accordance with the narrower grounds set out in the New York Convention. **13.104**

---

[141] eg *Birbrower, Montalbano, Condon & Frank, PC v ESQ Business Services Inc*, 17 Cal 4th 119, 949 P 2d 1 (Cal S Ct 1998) (holding that a lawyer representing a party in a non-international arbitration sited in California must be a member of the California State Bar); *Florida Bar v Rappaport*, 845 So 2d 874 (Fla S Ct 2003) (holding that an out-of-state lawyer representing a party in a non-international arbitration sited in Florida was engaged in the unauthorized practice of law). See also Nayar, R., 'Unauthorized Practice of Law in Private Arbitral Proceedings: A Jurisdictional Survey' (2007) 6 *J of American Arbitration* 1.

[142] The California legislature adopted new legislation in response to *Birbrower* providing that an out-of-state lawyer may represent a party in a California-sited arbitration if the lawyer associated with California counsel and agreed to be subject to local jurisdiction for disciplinary purposes. Cal Civ Proc Code s 1282.4. Similarly, the Florida bar regulations were amended to allow out-of-state lawyers to represent parties in arbitrations sited in Florida. Fla Bar Reg R 4-5.5 (2006).

[143] 9 USC s 206.

[144] eg *Jain v de Mere*, 51 F 3d 686, 690 (US Ct of Apps (7th Cir) 1995); *Bauhinia Corp v China National Machinery & Equipment Import & Export Corp*, 819 F 2d 247, 250 (US Ct of Apps (9th Cir) 1987); *Oil Basins Ltd v Broken Hill Proprietary Co*, 613 F Supp 483, 487–8 (US Dist Ct (SDNY) 1985).

13.105 **(2.1) Are the arbitrators and parties free to convene at other places than the official seat of the arbitration?** It is generally accepted that hearings or other proceedings can take place outside of the *situs* without affecting the legal seat of the arbitration.[145]

13.106 **(2.2) Are there visa requirements to enter the country which apply to lawyers and/or arbitrators? Where may current information on that subject be obtained?** Individuals entering the US are subject to immigration and visa requirements, which vary according to their nationality. Current information may be obtained from the United States Citizen and Immigration Services at <http://www.uscis.gov>.

C. Submissions, deadlines and default

(1) Contents and form of submissions (in particular request for arbitration and answer to request)

13.107 There are no legal requirements for the contents or form of the parties' submissions. These are left entirely to the procedural rules chosen by the parties or to the discretion of the tribunal.

13.108 **(1.1) From what point in time is a claim considered to be pending with the arbitral tribunal? What are the legal effects of such fact (eg on statutes of limitations)?** There are no statutory or case law requirements regarding the initiation of a claim. The procedural rules adopted by the parties, if any, may contain provisions regarding the initiation of the arbitration.[146]

13.109 **(1.2) When is a time limit according to statutes of limitations deemed to be interrupted in case of (i) *ad hoc*; and (ii) institutional arbitration?** There are no statutory provisions regarding the initiation of an arbitration and the interruption of the statute of limitations. If the parties have adopted a set of procedural rules that provides when the arbitration shall be deemed to have commenced, that will be the point at which the statute of limitations is interrupted. In the absence of relevant procedural rules, the arbitration will generally be considered to have commenced with the filing of a demand for arbitration.[147]

13.110 **(1.3) What is the effect of the withdrawal of the request for arbitration?** It is generally within the discretion of the tribunal to consider whether, in light of the stage of the proceedings and the potential prejudice to the respondent, the claimant should be allowed to withdraw its claims with or without prejudice to its ability to refile the arbitration at a later time.[148] It is also within the tribunal's discretion to award costs in connection with the claimant's withdrawal of the action.[149]

---

145 eg AAA (ICDR) International Rules, Art 13; CPR International Rules, r 9.5; JAMS International Rules, Art 14.2.

146 eg AAA (ICDR) International Rules, Art 2(2); CPR International Rules, r 3.2.

147 1 Domke on Commercial Arbitration s 17.6, s 18.5.

148 eg *Howard, Weil, Labouisse, Friedrichs Inc v Tower Hill Trading Co Ltd*, no 94 Civ 4709, 1995 WL 548846 (SDNY 1995).

149 *ibid.*

(2) Legal deadlines (provided by law or set by the tribunal) and effect of non-compliance by a party

There are no deadlines imposed by US law for the arbitration procedure. Tribunals are generally granted broad discretion to set procedural deadlines and to determine the consequences of non-compliance with those deadlines. Although tribunals have discretion to enforce their deadlines, they must also ensure that each party is given a full opportunity to present its case. Indeed, the FAA expressly provides that 'refusing to postpone the hearing, upon sufficient cause shown' is 'misconduct' and may justify vacating the tribunal's award. For this reason, tribunals are generally willing to grant reasonable extensions of time when requested by the parties. **13.111**

(2.1) What are the powers of the tribunal if a party fails to comply with the time limits set up by the tribunal? The tribunal may refuse to consider evidence or submissions that are not made within the time limits established by the tribunal. Tribunals are generally reluctant to exercise this power, however, because there is a risk that this could give rise to objections that one of the parties was not given a full opportunity to present its case. When one party fails to comply with the tribunal's deadlines, the tribunal can also extend the time limits of the other party so that the parties have equal amounts of time to prepare their cases. **13.112**

(2.2) Is the tribunal bound by any mandatory time limits for certain procedural steps (eg hearings, making of the award)? There are no mandatory time limits imposed by US law, but most sets of procedural rules do contain time limits. For example, many sets of procedural rules contain time limits for appointing the tribunal and submitting an answer or statement of defence. Some procedural rules also contain deadlines for oral hearings or rendering the award.[150] **13.113**

(3) Statutory requirements as to notifications during an arbitration (with respect to the request for arbitration and other written pleadings; with respect to notifications by the tribunal)

There are no legal requirements regarding notifications. Most procedural rules contain provisions regarding the submission of correspondence and written submissions. **13.114**

(4) Effect of the insolvency of a party

Under the US bankruptcy laws, upon the filing of a petition for bankruptcy or reorganization, there is an automatic stay of all ongoing legal proceedings, including arbitrations.[151] The bankruptcy courts may lift the stay in appropriate cases.[152] Some courts have exercised **13.115**

[150] eg AAA Commercial Rules, R-41; CPR International Rules, r 15.7; JAMS International Rules, Art 31.1.

[151] 11 USC s 362.

[152] Biesterfeld, L., 'Parties to International Commercial Arbitration Agreements Beware: Bankruptcy Trumps Supreme Court Precedent Favoring Arbitration of International Disputes' (2006) *J Dispute Resolution* 273; Rosell, J., 'International Arbitration and Bankruptcy: United States, France and the ICC' (2001) 18 *J Int'l Arb* 417.

this power to allow international arbitration proceedings to continue.[153] Other courts have held that if the claims in the arbitration are significant (ie so-called 'core' proceedings), the policy favouring centralizing all claims in the bankruptcy process should take precedence over the policy favouring the enforcement of international arbitration agreements.[154]

D. Facts and evidence: general

13.116 Under US law, tribunals have broad discretion to control the disclosure, admissibility, and evaluation of evidence.[155] The FAA also grants tribunals broad powers to compel the disclosure of information, including from third parties.

(1) Burden of proof (inquisitorial/adversarial procedure)

13.117 Although US civil procedure is based on the adversarial system, there is no requirement that arbitrations sited in the US follow this approach. Most US-sited arbitrations are adversarial, however, and it is generally accepted that the claimant bears the burden of proof in establishing the elements of its claim. (The respondent may have the burden of proving specific points that are relevant to its defence.)

(2) Power of the tribunal to determine the admissibility and weight of the evidence produced by the parties

13.118 The tribunal generally has the authority to determine the admissibility and weight of the evidence submitted by the parties.[156] The tribunal is not required to apply any particular rules of evidence, including the US Federal Rules of Evidence.[157]

13.119 **(2.1) Is the tribunal entitled to take the claimant's factual allegation as proven if the defendant does not participate in the arbitral proceedings?** Generally, where the respondent does not participate in the proceedings, the tribunal may not take the claimant's factual allegations as proven. Rather, the claimant still has the burden of establishing the elements of its claim, and the tribunal must evaluate the evidence and make a determination on the merits.[158]

---

[153] eg *In re Matter of Dollar Corp*, 139 BR 192, 196 (US Bankrcy Ct (E D Mich) 1992); *Societe Nationale Algerienne Pour la Recherche, la Production, le Transport, la Transformation et la Commercialisation des Hydrocarbures v Distrigas Corp*, 80 BR 606, 610–14 (US Dist Ct (D Mass) 1987); *Quinn v CGR*, 48 BR 367, 369–70 (US Dist Ct (D Colo) 1985).

[154] eg *In re White Mountain Mining Co*, 403 F 3d 164, 169–70 (US Ct of Apps (4th Cir) 2005); *In re United States Lines Inc*, 197 F 3d 631, 640–1 (US Ct of Apps (2nd Cir) 1999).

[155] eg 9 USC s 7; RUAA ss 15, 17; *Supreme Oil Co v Abondolo*, 568 F Supp 2d 401, 408 (US Dist Ct (SDNY) 2008) ('Arbitrators possess great latitude to determine the procedures governing their proceedings and to restrict or control evidentiary submissions, without the need to follow "all the niceties observed by the federal courts."') (quoting *Tempo Shain Corp v Bertek Inc*, 120 F 3d 16, 20 (US Ct of Apps (2nd Cir) 1997); *Rosensweig v Morgan Stanley & Co Inc*, 494 F 3d 1328, 1333 (US Ct of Apps (11th Cir) 2007); *Eljer Manufacturing v Kowin Dev Corp*, 14 F 3d 1250, 1255 (US Ct of Apps (7th Cir) 1994).

[156] eg AAA (ICDR) International Rules, Arts 16.3, 19.2, 20.6; AAA Commercial Rules, R-31; CPR International Rules, r 12; RUAA ss 15, 17; *Rosensweig*, 494 F 3d at 1333.

[157] eg AAA Commercial Rules, R-31; CPR International Rules, r 12; *Rosensweig*, 494 F 3d at 1333; *Nationwide Mutual Ins Co. v Home Ins Co*, 278 F 3d 621, 625 (US Ct of Apps (6th Cir) 2002); *Coppinger v Metro-North Commuter Railroad*, 861 F 2d 33, 39 (US Ct of Apps (2nd Cir) 1988).

[158] eg AAA (ICDR) International Rules, Art 23; AAA Commercial Rules, R-29; CPR International Rules, r 16; RUAA s 15(c) ('The arbitrator may hear and decide the controversy upon the evidence produced although a party who was duly notified of the arbitration proceeding did not appear.').

(2.2) May the arbitral tribunal consider an allegation of one party as agreed fact if the other party did not (specifically) dispute the allegation? If a particular factual allegation is undisputed, a tribunal will often accept that fact as proven. There is no requirement that the tribunal do so, however, and even if a factual allegation is undisputed, the tribunal may reach a contrary factual determination. 13.120

(2.3) What is the standard of proof that must be met in order for a fact to be considered to have been established (preponderance of the evidence; beyond reasonable doubt)? Must a stringent requirement be met for certain facts? In US courts, civil claims must generally be proven by a preponderance of the evidence. US civil procedure establishes higher thresholds for proof of certain allegations, such as fraud. These standards of US civil procedure do not necessarily apply to an arbitration sited in the US. 13.121

(2.4) May the arbitral tribunal rely on its own knowledge to consider certain facts as proven? In US courts, judges are empowered to take 'judicial notice' of certain facts that are within common knowledge or in the public domain.[159] It is reasonable to assume that arbitrators, who are given wide discretion in admitting and evaluating evidence, would also be empowered to consider their own knowledge and experience. This is particularly true where parties have selected the arbitrators for their specific expertise in a particular industry or area of law. 13.122

E. Witnesses

(1) Ability of a person to act as a witness

Any person can be a witness in an arbitration seated in the US. 13.123

(1.1) Is there a legal difference between a party testifying and a witness? If yes, what are the criteria for such differentiation? Does the testifying of a party have the same weight as a witness testimony? There is no limitation on a party or its representatives testifying as a witness in an arbitration, and a party witness is generally treated in the same way as a third party witness. The tribunal is free to give whatever weight it considers appropriate to the testimony of any witness, including a party witness. 13.124

(2) Preparation of witnesses and limits thereof

It is common for counsel for each party to 'prepare' witnesses for their testimony by talking about the case, the way the witness' testimony fits into the overall factual and legal theories, and possible questions the witness may be asked on cross-examination. It is also common for counsel to demonstrate typical cross-examination styles and questions in order to familiarize witnesses with the cross-examination process. Of course, counsel may not tell a witness what to say or ask a witness to change the substance of his or her testimony. 13.125

(2.1) Do US-style depositions violate any procedural rules or principles? US-style depositions do not violate any procedural rules or principles, and it is within the tribunal's broad discovery powers to allow or not allow them. US-style depositions are not uncommon in US domestic arbitrations, but they are less common in international arbitrations sited in the US. 13.126

159 US Federal Rules of Evidence, r 201.

13.127 The AAA (ICDR) has recently issued *Guidelines for Arbitrators Concerning Exchanges of Information* in international arbitrations, in which it cautions that:

> Depositions, interrogatories, and requests to admit, as developed in American court procedures, are generally not appropriate procedures for obtaining information in international arbitration.[160]

13.128 In its *Guide for Commercial Arbitrators* in domestic cases, the AAA also cautions that:

> Although this rule vests in the arbitrators the discretion to direct documentary exchanges, it does not contemplate full-blown, litigation-like discovery. . . . Some arbitrators, albeit rarely, interpret . . . [the rules] to provide for depositions.[161]

13.129 **(2.2) May a party or its counsel approach a witness whom it has nominated (only before or also after the proceeding has started)? Are interviews permitted?** Witness interviews are permitted at any point in the arbitral process, including before and after the arbitration has begun. There may be ethical limitations on approaching potential witnesses if they are represented by counsel or are employed by the opposing party (in which case the proper approach is through that person's or his employer's counsel).[162]

(3) Admissibility of written witness statements

13.130 Written witness statements are admissible and are commonly used in international arbitrations. They are less common in domestic arbitration and are generally not used in litigation proceedings.

13.131 **(3.1) If the parties agree on written statements, is a party entitled to request an oral hearing for questioning those witnesses (provided such right has not been agreed upon)?** There are US cases that hold that parties do not have an absolute right to cross-examine witnesses, and that refusing to allow cross-examination is not a violation of a party's due process rights.[163] Nevertheless, if a party has submitted written witness statements, tribunals will almost always schedule an oral hearing for cross-examination of the witnesses.

(4) Entitlement of a party to have a hearing or cross-examination of witnesses

13.132 Parties do not have an absolute right to an oral hearing or to cross-examination of witnesses. Where a party has requested an oral hearing, or the right to cross-examine witnesses, however, tribunals will almost always grant that request.

---

160 AAA (ICDR) Guidelines for Arbitrators Concerning Exchanges of Information, available at <http://www.adr.org>.

161 AAA *Guide for Commercial Arbitrators*, available at <http://www.adr.org>.

162 eg ABA Model Rules of Professional Conduct, rules 4.2, 4.3.

163 eg *Alexander v Gardner-Denver Co*, 415 US 36, 57, 94 S Ct 1011, 1024 (1974) (noting that in arbitration, the 'rights and procedures common to civil trials, such as discovery, compulsory process, cross-examination and testimony under oath, are often severely limited or unavailable'); *Mitsubishi Motors Corp v Soler Chrysler-Plymouth Inc*, 473 US 614, 649, 105 S Ct 3346, 3365 (1985); *Generica Ltd v Pharmaceutical Basics, Inc*, 125 F 3d 1123, 1130 (US Ct of Apps (7th Cir) 1997); *Papapetropoulous v Milwaukee Transport Services Inc*, 795 F 2d 591, 598–601 (US Ct of Apps (7th Cir) 1986). The RUAA, however, provides that 'a party to the arbitration proceeding has a right to be heard, to present evidence material to the controversy, and to cross-examine witnesses appearing at the hearing'. RUAA, s 15(d).

(4.1) Which are the methods used to establish a record of the arbitral proceedings, in particular witness examinations (tape recording, verbatim court reporters, dictated minutes, other methods)? In international arbitration proceedings seated in the US, oral hearings are often recorded in a verbatim written transcript by private court reporters. In domestic arbitration proceedings, oral hearings are sometimes recorded in a verbatim transcript, but are often not recorded by any means. **13.133**

(4.2) May the arbitral tribunal take an oath from a witness? Yes. Witnesses are generally heard under oath, and the tribunal generally administers the oath. **13.134**

(4.3) Does the arbitral tribunal have the power to compel witnesses? Under s 7 of the FAA, tribunals have the power to compel the attendance of any person, including non-parties, at an arbitration hearing.[164] Under this section, tribunals also have the power to compel any person to produce documents 'which may be deemed material as evidence in the case'.[165] Individuals served with such a subpoena may resist it—either by moving to quash the subpoena or by refusing to comply and forcing the requesting party to move to compel. The US courts are expressly authorized to enforce subpoenas issued by arbitral tribunals to secure the attendance of witnesses or the production of documents.[166] **13.135**

F. Documents

(1) Form and kind of documents to be presented to the arbitral tribunal

Arbitral tribunals enjoy broad discretion in connection with the disclosure of documents and presentation of documentary evidence. **13.136**

(1.1) Is the submission of 'agreed documents' permitted? If yes, what is the extent and effect of such an agreement of the parties (authenticity, existence, acknowledgement of such documents' contents)? The use of 'agreed documents' is not common in US arbitration practice. **13.137**

(1.2) How may electronic documents (eg emails) be presented and proven? The production and presentation of emails falls within the broad discretion of the arbitral tribunal. The US Federal Rules of Civil Procedure contain provisions regarding the production of electronic evidence.[167] While these rules are not binding in arbitration proceedings, tribunals may refer to them in crafting procedural orders regarding the disclosure of documents stored electronically. **13.138**

(1.3) Does discovery (US- or UK- style), after the procedure has started, violate any procedural rules or public policy considerations? No. **13.139**

---

[164] 9 USC s 7. This power is obviously limited to persons residing in the US and subject to the jurisdiction of the US courts.

[165] *ibid.*

[166] *ibid.* There are geographic limitations on the power of the federal courts to enforce subpoenas, including those issued by arbitral tribunals. US Federal Rules of Civil Procedure, r 45.

[167] See eg Federal Rules of Civil Procedure, rules 26, 34.

(2) Requirement to produce certain documents (as requested by the tribunal) and consequences of a failure to do so

13.140 Tribunals have the power to order the parties to produce documents.[168] They also have the power to enforce their document production orders, including by drawing adverse inferences from the failure of a party to comply with a disclosure order. The threat of adverse inferences is often a sufficient incentive to convince the parties to comply with the tribunal's orders.

13.141 In addition, the US courts are authorized to enforce subpoenas issued by arbitral tribunals under s 7 of the FAA.

13.142 **(2.1) Which documents may the tribunal request to be produced (eg also documents which are in the possession of third parties)?** Tribunals have broad authority to order the disclosure of documents, including from third parties (at least those who are located in the US and subject to the tribunal's subpoena power under s 7 of the FAA). Courts have reached different conclusions as to whether the subpoena power in s 7 extends to pre-trial discovery, or only to the production of documents at an oral hearing.[169]

(3) Protection of the confidentiality of documents (legal privilege etc)

13.143 Tribunals have broad authority to determine issues of privilege and confidentiality, and the courts generally defer to these decisions.[170]

G. Experts

(1) Appointment and presentation of experts by the party or the arbitral tribunal

13.144 There are no legal requirements or restrictions regarding the use of expert witnesses. Although some sets of procedural rules allow for the appointment of independent experts by the tribunal,[171] it is far more common for the parties to submit expert evidence from experts retained by the parties.[172]

13.145 **(1.1) By which methods are tribunal-appointed experts selected? What are the rights of the parties during the selection process?** Where tribunal-appointed experts are used, tribunals often seek the agreement of the parties and their views on potential experts.

---

[168] eg 9 USC s 7; RUAA, ss 15, 17; AAA (ICDR) International Rules, Arts 19; AAA Commercial Rules, R-21, R-31; CPR International Rules, r 12; *National Broadcasting Co v Bear Stearns & Co*, 165 F 3d 184, 187 (US Ct of Apps (2nd Cir) 1999).

[169] Compare *In re Security Life Ins Co*, 228 F 3d 865, 870–1 (US Ct of Apps (8th Cir) 2000) (allowing pre-trial production of documents from third parties), with *Hay Group Inc v E.B.S. Acquisition Corp*, 360 F 3d 404, 406–10 (US Ct of Apps (3rd Cir) 2004) (holding that arbitrators do not have power to order pre-trial production of documents from third parties) and *COMSAT Corp v NSF*, 190 F 3d 269, 276 (US Ct of Apps (4th Cir) 1999) (same).

[170] eg *Howard University v Metropolitan Campus Police Officers Union*, 512 F 3d 716, 721–2 (US Ct of Apps (DC Cir) 2008); *Picco v General Electric Co*, 114 Fed. Appx 227, 2004 WL 2486631 (US Ct of Apps (7th Cir) 2004).

[171] eg AAA (ICRD) International Rules, Art 22.

[172] eg Fenton, R, 'A Civil Matter for a Common Expert: How Should Parties and Tribunals Use Experts in International Commercial Arbitration?' (2006) 6 *Pepperdine Disp Res* J 279, 288.

(2) Admissibility and role of expert witnesses

Tribunals have broad discretion to determine the scope of expert testimony and to assess expert evidence. 13.146

(3) Influence of the parties upon the selection of questions to be submitted to the expert

If tribunal-appointed experts are used, tribunals will generally consult with the parties regarding the questions to be submitted to the expert. 13.147

(4) Independence and impartiality of the expert and the right to reject a proposed/appointed expert

Where party-appointed experts are used, they are not generally regarded as or expected to be neutral. Nor are they expected to be advocates. Rather, they can consult with the party that appointed them, and they can help to formulate that party's positions on legal or technical issues, so long as they do not compromise their own views in the process.[173] 13.148

By contrast, tribunal-appointed experts are generally required to be independent and impartial. The parties are usually given an opportunity to object to a proposed expert on the grounds of lack of independence or lack of required expertise. 13.149

(4.1) May a party or its counsel approach an expert (or expert witness) whom it has nominated (only before or also after the proceeding has started)? Are interviews admissible? Parties are permitted to meet with a party-appointed expert and to participate in the preparation of the expert report. Parties and their counsel are also permitted to meet with a party-appointed expert prior to an oral hearing to prepare for cross-examination. 13.150

(5) Oral examination of an expert in a hearing

Party-appointed experts are generally subject to cross-examination by the opposing counsel and questioning by the tribunal. Tribunal-appointed experts are often subject to questioning by both parties' counsel. The tribunal also has broad discretion to employ other techniques of hearing expert evidence, including 'witness conferencing'. 13.151

H. Interim measures of protection

(1) Kind of interim measures which the tribunal may order

Tribunals have broad authority to issue interim measures of protection.[174] Although some early cases held that tribunals could issue interim measures of protection only where expressly authorized by the parties, more recent authorities hold that tribunals have inherent power to issue interim measures of protection. In addition, virtually all procedural rules 13.152

[173] eg Ruttinger, G. and Meadows, J., 'Using Experts in Arbitration,' [2007] *Disp Res J* 1; Wilske, S. and Gack, C., 'Expert Evidence in International Commercial Arbitration,' (2007) 29 *Comp L Ybk of Int'l Bus.*

[174] eg *Banco de Seguros del Estado v Mutual Marine Office Inc*, 344 F 3d 255, 262–3 (US Ct of Apps (2nd Cir) 2003); *Yasuda Fire & Marine Ins Co Ltd. v Continental Cas Co*, 37 F 3d 345, 351 (US Ct of Aps (7th Cir) 1994); *Pacific Reinsurance Management Corp v Ohio Reinsurance Corp*, 935 F 2d 1019, 1022–3 (US Ct of Apps (9th Cir) 1991); *Island Creek Coal Sales Co v City of Gainesville*, 729 F 2d 1046, 1049 (US Ct of Apps (6th Cir) 1984); *Certain Underwriters at Lloyds, London v Argonaut Ins Co*, 264 F Supp 2d 926, 937–8 (US Dist Ct (N D Cal) 2003); *Sperry International Trade Inc v Government of Israel*, 532 F Supp 901, 904–6 (US Dist Ct (SDNY) 1982).

grant tribunals (and sometimes specially-appointed interim panels prior to the constitution of the tribunal) broad authority to issue interim measures of protection.[175]

13.153 Common forms of interim relief include orders to preserve the status quo, orders to prevent a party from disposing of assets, orders to preserve evidence, preliminary injunctions requiring or preventing certain acts, and anti-suit or anti-arbitration injunctions.[176]

13.154 **(1.1) Which are, in general, the procedural and substantive prerequisites for the ordering of interim and conservatory measures (eg reduced degree of evidence; urgency; summary evaluation of the claim)?** Although the precise requirements for issuing interim or conservatory relief vary by jurisdiction, US courts generally require a showing (i) of irreparable harm; (ii) that the threatened harm outweighs the potential prejudice to the party against whom the relief is awarded; (iii) that the party requesting the relief has a likelihood of success on the merits of the claim; and (iv) that the relief is not adverse to the public interest.

13.155 **(1.2) Are the prerequisites for interim measures ordered by the arbitral tribunal more or less the same as if those are requested from the state court? Is there case law/leading authorities on whether those measures are faster and enforced more easily if taken by the arbitral tribunal or the state court?** Arbitral tribunals often apply broadly similar legal standards to requests for interim relief. However, it is sometimes faster to obtain interim measures from the courts. Under US civil procedure rules, it is possible to obtain emergency, temporary interim relief, including in *ex parte* proceedings, sometimes in a matter of days, in the appropriate circumstances. (These emergency measures remain in effect until the court can more fully consider the merits of the request for interim relief.) This kind of emergency relief is generally not available in arbitration.

13.156 Moreover, interim relief granted by a court may be more effective. The courts can make orders directed to third parties and can issue orders attaching assets. In addition, a court order is immediately enforceable, while an award from an arbitral tribunal granting interim relief is subject to challenge or enforcement proceedings in the courts (and a procedural order—as opposed to an award—granting interim relief may not be enforceable through the courts at all).

(2) Limits of the tribunal's powers to order interim measures

13.157 There are no specific limits on the power of tribunals to award interim measures. A tribunal's jurisdiction is, of course, limited to the parties to the arbitration, and tribunals therefore do not have jurisdiction over third parties with respect to interim measures of relief.

(3) Orders to provide security for the costs of the proceeding

13.158 There is no specific limitation on the tribunal's power to order security for costs. Tribunals, like courts, often require a party requesting interim measures of protection to provide security for any potential harm to the other party in connection with such interim measures.

---

[175] eg AAA (ICDR) International Rules, Art 21; AAA Commercial Rules, R-34 and Optional Rules O1–O7; CPR International Rules, rules 13–14.

[176] Rau, A., 'Provisionsal Relief in Arbitration: How Things Stand in the United States' (2005) 22 *J Int'l Arb* 1.

It is relatively uncommon in US-sited arbitrations, however, to order security for the costs of the underlying proceedings. This is in part because there is no tradition of fee-shifting in US civil litigation and therefore no tradition of ordering security for costs in that forum.

(4) Attachment of assets by an order of the tribunal

Although an arbitral tribunal can order one of the parties to the arbitration to refrain from disposing of particular assets, the tribunal cannot make enforceable orders that bind third parties. Therefore, parties seeking the attachment of assets generally do so through the courts. **13.159**

I. Assistance by the courts

(1) Extent of court assistance in the gathering of evidence

US courts will provide judicial assistance to enforce subpoenas issued by a US-sited arbitral tribunal.[177] The courts generally will not otherwise interfere with a tribunal's authority to control the disclosure and presentation of evidence. **13.160**

It is unclear to what extent US courts will provide judicial assistance in connection with gathering evidence for use in a foreign-sited arbitration. US courts have authority under 28 USC s 1782 to order the production of documents and witness testimony 'for use in a proceeding in a foreign or international tribunal'.[178] Although early decisions held that arbitral tribunals were not 'foreign or international tribunal[s]' for purposes of s 1782,[179] in recent years, several federal courts have reached the opposite conclusion and have issued orders for the disclosure of evidence for use in international arbitrations sited outside of the US.[180] Under s 1782, the parties to the foreign proceeding are entitled to petition US courts for disclosure orders without first obtaining the consent of the foreign tribunal. **13.161**

(1.1) **Is it for the arbitral tribunal or for the party to obtain the assistance of state courts with respect to the gathering of evidence?** Requests for judicial assistance with respect to gathering evidence are typically made by the parties to the proceeding rather than the tribunal. **13.162**

(1.2) **According to case law and practical experience, are there considerable delays involved when asking a court to give assistance (eg for the obtaining of evidence)?** As a general matter, the courts will act reasonably quickly with respect to requests for judicial assistance, although there are sometimes delays. **13.163**

[177] 9 USC s 7.

[178] 28 USC s 1782.

[179] eg *Bear Stearns*, 165 F 3d at 187–91; *Republic of Kazakhstan v Biedermann Int'l*, 168 F 3d 880, 881–3 (US Ct of Apps (5th Cir) 1999).

[180] *In re Application of Oxus Gold PLC*, no Misc 06-82, 2006 WL 2927615 (US Dist Ct (D NJ) 2006); *In re Application of Roz Trading Ltd*, 469 F Supp 2d 1221, 1223–28 (US Dist Ct (N D Ga) 2006). These courts relied on dicta in the US Supreme Court's decision in *Intel Corp v Advanced Micro Devices Inc*, 542 US 241, 124 S Ct 2466 (2004). In *Intel*, the Supreme Court wrote that 'foreign and international tribunals' include 'investigating magistrates, administrative and arbitral tribunals, and quasi-judicial agencies, as well as conventional civil, commercial, criminal, and administrative courts'.

(2) Assistance for enforcing the attachment of assets

13.164 US courts will generally enforce arbitral awards granting interim relief subject to the same standards of review as any other arbitral award.

13.165 US courts also have the power to issue interim measures of protection to parties in arbitration proceedings.[181] Although a few courts have refused to grant interim measures of protection where there is a pending international arbitration, reasoning that the policies underlying the New York Convention require minimal interference by the courts,[182] the better view, adopted by the vast majority of courts, is that the courts should provide judicial assistance to the parties in international arbitration proceedings, including by issuing interim measures of protection where appropriate, to ensure that the arbitral process functions smoothly and that the resulting award provides effective relief.[183]

(3) Other examples of possible assistance

13.166 Among other things, US courts provide judicial assistance to parties in arbitration proceedings by enforcing subpoenas issued by arbitral tribunals, granting orders to preserve assets, granting preliminary injunctions or orders to preserve the status quo, granting anti-suit injunctions where appropriate to give effect to the parties' arbitration agreement, and appointing arbitrators where the parties are unable to do so.

(4) Dependence of the power of state courts to intervene during the proceedings on the (national) procedural law applied by the arbitral tribunal

13.167 Although there is no authority specifically addressing the issue, it seems likely that US courts would provide appropriate judicial assistance for any US-sited arbitration, regardless of the procedural law chosen by the parties, unless the parties had specifically excluded the possibility of seeking relief from the US courts.

V. The award

A. Types of award

13.168 Most commonly used procedural rules expressly grant the arbitrators authority to grant interim and partial, as well as final, awards.[184] Even in the absence of an express authorization

---

[181] eg RUAA, s 8 (authorizing courts to award interim measures of relief (i) before the tribunal is appointed; or (ii) after the tribunal is appointed if the matter is urgent and the arbitrator is unable to provide timely and effective relief); *Ortho Pharmaceutical Corp v Amgen Inc.*, 882 F 2d 806, 812–13 (US Ct of Apps (3rd Cir) 1989); *PMS Distributing Co v Huber & Suhner AG*, 863 F 2d 639, 642 (US Ct of Apps (9th Cir) 1988); *Teradyne Inc v Mostek Corp*, 797 F 2d 43, 57 (US Ct of Apps (1st Cir) 1986); *Roso-Lino Beverage Distrib Inc v Coca-Cola Bottling Co*, 749 F 2d 124, 125 (US Ct of Apps (2nd Cir) 1984).

[182] eg *Merrill, Lynch, Pierce, Fenner & Smith v Hovey*, 726 F 2d 1286, 1292 (US Ct of Apps (8th Cir) 1984); *McCreary Tire & Rubber Co v CEAT SpA*, 501 F 2d 1032 (US Ct of Apps (3rd Cir) 1974); *Cooper v Ateliers de la Motobecane SA*, 442 NE 2d 1239 (NY Ct of Apps 1982).

[183] eg *Borden Inc v Meiji Milk Products Co*, 919 F 2d 822, 826 (US Ct of Apps (2nd Cir) 1990) ('We hold that entertaining an application for a preliminary injunction in aid of arbitration is consistent with the court's powers pursuant to s 206.'); *Sauer-Getriebe KG v White Hydraulics Inc*, 715 F 2d 348, 351–2 (US Ct of Apps (7th Cir) 1983); *Carolina Power & Light Co v Uranex*, 451 F Supp 1044, 1051–5 ((N D Cal) 1977).

[184] AAA (ICDR) International Rules, Art 27.7; AAA Commercial Rules, R-43(b); CPR International Rules, r 15.1. See also RUAA, s 18.

in the relevant procedural rules, US courts have generally upheld a tribunal's power to issue interim or partial awards,[185] although the courts have not always been consistent in defining or distinguishing between 'interim', 'partial', and 'final' awards. The determination of whether an award is subject to immediate review by the courts depends primarily on whether the award is intended to finally dispose of the issues in dispute, rather than on the particular label attached to it.[186]

(1) Interim award (eg on interim measures or the jurisdiction of the tribunal)

Some courts have refused to allow immediate enforcement of interim or partial awards, reasoning that a 'final' award must dispose of all issues that have been submitted to the arbitrator.[187] Most courts, however, have held that where an award is intended to fully dispose of a particular issue (eg the need for conservatory measures), that award may be immediately enforceable by the courts, even though it does not fully dispose of the parties' claims and counterclaims.[188] **13.169**

If the award is intended to be subject to immediate review and enforcement by the courts, the tribunal should consider designating the award a 'final' award on interim measures, or otherwise indicating that it is binding on the parties and not subject to further consideration by the tribunal. If an 'interim' award is intended to be merely provisional, and is subject to further review or consideration by the tribunal, the courts should decline to review and enforce the award until after it has become 'final'. **13.170**

(2) Partial award

US courts have also generally held that arbitrators have the authority to issue partial awards, which dispose completely of one or more issues while reserving the tribunal's decision on other issues in dispute. For example, a tribunal may issue a partial award on jurisdiction, while reserving a decision on the merits, or it may issue a partial award on liability, while reserving its award on damages. Most commonly used procedural rules specifically grant this power to the tribunal.[189] **13.171**

---

[185] eg *Metallgesellschaft AG v M/V Capitan Constante*, 790 F 2d 280 (US Ct of Apps (2nd Cir) 1986); *Island Creek Coal Sales Co v City of Gainesville*, 729 F 2d 1046 (US Ct of Apps (6th Cir) 1984); *Southern Seas Navigation Ltd v Petroleos Mexicanos of Mexico City*, 606 F Supp 692 (US Dist Ct (SDNY) 1985); *Sperry International Trade Inc v Government of Israel*, 532 F. Supp 901 (US Dist Ct (SDNY) 1982). The FAA also implicitly acknowledges that tribunals have this authority. 9 USC s 16(a)(1)(D).

[186] eg *Publicis Communication v True North Communications, Inc*, 206 F 3d 725 (US Ct of Apps (7th Cir) 2000).

[187] eg *International Shipping Agency, Inc v Union Empleados de Muelles de Puerto Rico*, 547 F Supp 2d 116 (US Dist Ct (D P R) 2008); *Orion Pictures Corp v Writers Guild of America West, Inc*, 946 F 2d 722 (US Ct of Apps (9th Cir) 1991).

[188] eg *Arrowhead Global Solutions, Inc v Datapath Inc*, 166 Fed Appx 39 (US Ct of Apps (4th Cir) 2006); *Publicis Communication v True North Communications Inc*, 206 F 3d 725 (US Ct of Apps (7th Cir) 2000); *Yasuda Fire & Marine Ins Co of Europe v Continental Cas Co*, 37 F 3d 345 (US Ct of Apps (7th Cir) 1994); *Metallgesellschaft AG v M/V Capitan Constante*, 790 F 2d 280 (US Ct of Apps (2nd Cir) 1986); *Island Creek Coal Sales Co v Gainesville*, 729 F 2d 1046 (US Ct of Apps (6th Cir) 1984); *Sperry International Trade Inc v Government of Israel*, 532 F Supp 901 (US Dist Ct (SDNY) 1982).

[189] AAA (ICDR) International Rules, Art 27.7; AAA Commercial Rules, R-43(b); CPR International Rules, r 15.1.

13.172 As long as an award is intended to be 'final' in that it fully decides an issue before the tribunal, the award is subject to immediate review and enforcement by the courts. US courts have reviewed and enforced (or annulled) partial awards, including partial awards on jurisdiction and partial awards on one or more substantive claims or issues in dispute.[190] In a few cases, however, even where a partial award is 'final', courts have elected to reserve their review and consideration of any requests to annul or enforce the award until the tribunal has issued an award fully disposing of all remaining issues in dispute.[191]

13.173 (2.1) **Are awards, especially partial awards, binding in the same arbitral proceeding? Does it make a difference if after the rendering of such a partial award, one arbitrator is successfully challenged and removed on grounds that prevailed even before the partial award was rendered?** US courts recognize that once an arbitral tribunal has issued a final award, the tribunal has fulfilled its mandate, and it is *functus officio.*[192] Once a tribunal has issued a partial award that fully disposes of an issue in dispute, the tribunal has fulfilled its mandate with respect to that issue and the award should be binding on the tribunal throughout the remainder of the arbitration. If a tribunal wants to retain jurisdiction to revise or reconsider its decision after further proceedings in the arbitration, the tribunal should issue an order (as opposed to an award) or otherwise expressly state that its decision is not final and is subject to further reconsideration.

(3) Final award

13.174 The term 'final' award is sometimes understood as the tribunal's last award, finally disposing of all remaining issues before it, but a 'final' award is better understood as any award that finally disposes of a particular issue in dispute. Final awards are subject to immediate review and enforcement by the courts.

13.175 (3.1) **If a party fails to participate in the arbitration, may the tribunal proceed and issue an award on the merits? Is such an award enforceable as any other award? Are there special remedies for the defendant at the enforcement stage?** If a party fails to participate in the arbitration, the tribunal may proceed to issue an award on the merits. Most commonly used procedural rules expressly grant the arbitrators authority to issue default awards,[193] and US courts have held that default awards are generally enforceable.[194] Unlike in US litigation, where a court may issue a default judgment against a party who fails to appear

[190] eg *McGregor Van De Moere Inc v Paychex Inc*, 927 F Supp at 618; *The Home Insurance Company v RHA/Pennsylvania Nursing Homes*, 127 F Supp 2d 482 (US Dist Ct (SDNY) 2001); *Trade & Transport Inc v Natural Petroleum Charterers Inc*, 931 F 2d 191 (US Ct of Apps (2nd Cir) 1991).

[191] eg *Texaco Panama Inc v Duke Petroleum Transport Corp*, 1996 WL 502437, no 95 CIV 3761 (US Dist Ct (SDNY) 1996).

[192] eg *Local 2322, Int'l Brotherhood of Electrical Workers v Verizon New England, Inc*, 464 F 3d 93 (US Ct of Apps (1st Cir) 2006); *RGA Reinsurance Co v Ulico Cas Co*, 355 F 3d 1136 (US Ct of Apps (8th Cir) 2004); *Glass Molders, Pottery, Plastics & Allied Workers Int'l Union v Excelsior Foundry Co*, 56 F 3d 844, 845 (US Ct of Apps (7th Cir) 1995); 1 Domke *Commercial Arbitration* (2009) s 26.1.

[193] AAA (ICDR) International Rules, Art 23; AAA Commercial Rules, R-29; CPR International Rules, r 16.

[194] *Comprehensive Accounting Corp v Rudell*, 760 F 2d 138 (US Ct of Apps (7th Cir) 1985); *Kentucky River Mills v Jackson*, 206 F 2d 111 (US Ct of Apps (6th Cir) 1953); *Energoinvest DD v Democratic Republic of Congo*, 355 F Supp 2d 9, 11–12 (US Dist Ct (D DC) 2004); *Real Color Displays Inc v Universal Applied Tech Corp*, 950 F Supp 714, 716–717 (US Dist Ct (E D NC) 1997).

without considering the merits of the case, an arbitral tribunal may only issue a default award if it considers the evidence submitted by the non-defaulting party and determines on the merits that the non-defaulting party has adequately discharged its burden of proof.[195] A default award is subject to review by the courts under the same standards as any other award.[196]

B. Deliberations and agreement on the award

(1) Time limits (and possible extensions) for making the award

US law imposes no requirements regarding the time within which an arbitral award should be issued. If the parties have specified a time limit in their arbitration agreement or by reference to a set of procedural rules,[197] that time limit will form part of the parties' agreement, and the arbitrators have an obligation to respect it. **13.176**

Parties—and institutional rules—are sometimes overly ambitious in setting short deadlines for a tribunal's award. Particularly where the issues are complex or where one or both parties seek to delay the proceedings or extend the timetable for their submissions, it can be virtually impossible for a tribunal to meet the time limit imposed by the parties or the applicable procedural rules. In these cases, the parties and/or the relevant institution generally grant extensions of time for the tribunal's award. Even where the parties have not agreed to extend the deadline, courts are reluctant to set aside arbitral awards solely on the ground that they were issued after the time limit specified in the parties' agreement.[198] **13.177**

(2) Procedure for the decision of the arbitrators (majority vote etc)

An arbitral award is valid if it is made by a majority of the arbitrators; there is no requirement for a unanimous award (unless the parties have agreed otherwise).[199] Most commonly used sets of procedural rules expressly allow majority awards.[200] **13.178**

(2.1) If an arbitrator fails or refuses to take part in oral deliberation meetings, although having been given sufficient notice of such meetings, may an award be rendered on the **13.179**

[195] eg AAA (ICDR) International Rules, Art 23; AAA Commercial Rules, R-29; CPR International Rules, r 16; RUAA, s 15(c).

[196] eg *National Development Co, v Triad Holding Corporation*, 930 F 2d 253, 258 (US Ct of Apps (2nd Cir) 1991); *Energoinvest*, 355 F Supp 2d at 11–12; *Frontier Construction Inc v Tri-State Management Company*, 262 F Supp 2d 893, 895 (US Dist Ct (N D Ill) 2003); *Bevona v 820 Second Avenue Associates*, no 93 Civ 2039 (JSM), 1993 WL 541657, at *1–*2 (US Dist Ct (SDNY) 1993) (default arbitral award vacated where defendant was clearly under no contractual obligation to arbitrate termination of employees of subcontractor).

[197] For example, the AAA Commercial Arbitration Rules provide that the tribunal's award should be issued within 30 days of the closure of the hearings. AAA Commercial Rules, R-41. See also CPR International Rules, r 15.7 (providing that the arbitral award 'should in most circumstances' be made within one year of the initial pre-hearing conference).

[198] eg *West Rock Lodge no 2120 v Geometric Tool Co*, 406 F 2d 284 (US Ct of Apps (2nd Cir) 1968) (time limits imposed on rendering an arbitral award are directory, not mandatory, and late award should be enforced absent showing of harm caused by delay). Other cases have reached the opposite conclusion and have invalidated awards that were rendered after the proscribed period of time. eg *Jones v St Louis-San Fransisco Railway Co*, 728 F 2d 257 (US Ct of Apps (6th Cir) 1984); *Hunting Alloys Inc v United Steelworkers of America*, 623 F 2d 335 (US Ct of Apps (4th Cir) 1980).

[199] eg RUAA, s 13.

[200] AAA (ICDR) International Rules, Art 26.1; AAA Commercial Rule, R-40; CPR International Rules, r 15.2; JAMS International Arbitration Rules, Art 31.2.

basis of written deliberations (or deliberations without this arbitrator) only? Given that the courts have upheld majority awards, it follows that if one member of a three-person tribunal refuses to participate in deliberations, or otherwise seeks to obstruct the functions of the tribunal, the two remaining members can proceed to issue an award without the concurrence or participation of the third member. Most commonly used procedural rules expressly authorize the majority of the arbitrators to continue even if one arbitrator refuses to participate in deliberations or in signing the award.[201]

(3) Admissibility of dissenting opinions

13.180 **(3.1) Are there any court decisions or positions of leading authorities on the issue of dissenting opinions (admissibility, disclosure to the parties and publication)?** There is a strong tradition in US courts of issuing dissenting opinions, and there is no prohibition against doing so in arbitration proceedings. Many commonly used sets of procedural rules expressly allow dissenting opinions.[202]

(4) Signature by the arbitrators and potential failure of one arbitrator to sign

13.181 There is no specific requirement under US law that the arbitrators sign the award, but it is common practice to do so (and most sets of procedural rules do expressly require this).[203] If one arbitrator fails to sign the award, this is generally not viewed as an obstacle to the validity and enforcement of the award.[204]

C. Form of the award and deposition

(1) Form and minimum contents of an award

13.182 There are no specific requirements regarding the form or contents of an arbitral award.

(2) Requirement to give reasons in the award

13.183 There is no general requirement for a reasoned award, unless the parties have agreed otherwise.[205] In domestic arbitrations, many arbitrators choose not to provide reasons with their award in order to limit the ability of the reviewing court to consider the merits of the award. Indeed, the AAA specifically instructs arbitrators appointed under its rules that:

> Commercial arbitrators are not required to explain the reasons for their decisions. As a general rule, the award consists of a brief direction to the parties on a single sheet of paper. One reason for brevity is that written opinions might open avenues for attack on the award by the losing party.

---

201 AAA (ICDR) International Rules, Arts 11, 26.1; CPR International Rules, rules 7, 15.2.

202 eg CPR International Rules, r 15.3; JAMS International Rules, Art 31.4.

203 AAA (ICDR) International Rules, Art 26; AAA Commercial Rules, R-42; CPR International Rules, r 15.2; JAMS International Rules, Art 32.4.

204 eg AAA (ICDR) International Rules, Art 26.1; CPR International Rules, r 15.2.

205 eg *United Steelworkers of America v Enter. Wheel & Car Corp*, 363 US 593, 80 S Ct 1358 (US S Ct 1960); *D.H. Blair & Co v Gottdiener*, 462 F 3d 95 (US Ct of Apps (2nd Cir) 2006); *Stark v Sandberg, Phoenix & von Gontard, PC*, 381 F 3d 793 (US Ct of Apps (8th Cir) 2004); *Wallace v Buttar*, 378 F 3d 182 (US Ct of Apps (2nd Cir) 2004); *El Dorado School District v Continental Cas. Co.*, 247 F 3d 843 (US CT of Apps (8th Cir) 2001); *Eljer Manufacturing Inc v Kowin Development Corp*, 14 F 3d 1250, 1254–55 (US Ct of Apps (7th Cir) 1994).

> Courts will not review arbitrators' decisions on the merits of the case, even where the conclusions are different from those that a court might reach. But a carelessly expressed thought in a written opinion could afford an opportunity to delay enforcement of the award. The obligations to the parties are better fulfilled when the award leaves no room for attack. In situations where you feel it necessary to write such an opinion, it should be contained in a separate document.[206]

In international arbitrations, the usual practice is to provide a reasoned award (unless the parties agree otherwise), and most of the commonly used sets of procedural rules for international arbitration require a reasoned award. For example, the AAA (ICDR) International Arbitration Rules provide that '[t]he tribunal shall state the reasons upon which the award is based, unless the parties have agreed that no reasons need be given'.[207] **13.184**

(3) Necessity to specify place and time where and when the award was made

There is no general requirement imposed by US law that the award state the time and place where it was made, but it is common practice to do so. Many sets of procedural rules expressly require this,[208] and when such rules apply, US courts will give them effect. If the award does not state the time and place that it was made, the parties may need to offer other evidence establishing these facts in an annulment or enforcement action, because they can be relevant to whether the award is characterized as a domestic or foreign award and can determine whether the award has been submitted to the court within the time periods established for enforcement under ss 9 and 207 of the FAA. **13.185**

(4) Other requirements (registration, delivery etc)

(4.1) Does the award have to be laid down or registered with a state court or agency (even if it has been rendered according to a foreign procedural law)? There is no requirement that an arbitral award be registered in order to be valid in the US. However, the FAA does provide a mechanism under which a party to the arbitration can seek to have a US court issue an order confirming the award. For domestic arbitration awards governed by ch I of the FAA, the parties can seek confirmation under s 9 within one year of the award being made. For international awards subject to ch II of the FAA, parties can seek confirmation under s 207 within three years of the award being made. **13.186**

(4.2) Does a foreign award which has been rendered abroad according to this country's national procedural law, have to be laid down or registered with a state court or agency? Is there a fee or tax for such registration of an award? As discussed above, there is no requirement that arbitral awards be registered in order to be valid in the US, but there is a three-year statute of limitations for enforcement of a foreign award under s 207 of the FAA. There are no special fees associated with confirming or enforcing arbitral awards, but there **13.187**

[206] AAA *Guide for Commercial Arbitrators*, available at <http://www.adr.org>. See also AAA Commercial Rules, R-42 ('The arbitrator need not render a reasoned award unless the parties request such an award in writing prior to appointment of the arbitrator or unless the arbitrator determines that a reasoned award is appropriate').

[207] AAA (ICDR) International Rules, Art 27.2. See also CPR International Rules, r 15.2.

[208] eg AAA (ICDR) International Rules, Art 27.3; CPR International Rules, r 15.2; JAMS International Rules, Art 32.4.

may be generally applicable court filing fees. Parties should check the applicable court rules for details.

13.188 **(4.3) How long after the rendering of the award must the file/award be stored by the lawyers and the arbitral tribunal?** There are no requirements imposed by US law regarding the retention of arbitration files and awards. Ethical rules of some state bars may, however, impose document preservation requirements on counsel for a party.

D. Applicable substantive law

(1) Party autonomy to choose the applicable substantive law

13.189 Under US law, parties have broad autonomy to select the applicable substantive law to govern their dispute. The parties can select any system of national law, or even a non-national system of law, such as the Convention on the Sale of Goods or the UNIDROIT Principles of International Commercial Contracts. The parties' broad autonomy in this regard is also reflected in all leading sets of procedural rules.[209]

13.190 **(1.1) Is there a public policy exception to the chosen substantive law?** Parties are generally free to choose the substantive governing law. However, the New York Convention allows enforcing courts to refuse to enforce an arbitral award if enforcement of the award would be contrary to public policy.[210] Thus, US courts (and the courts in any other signatory state) can refuse to enforce an award if the law chosen by the parties would violate US public policy (for example, because a foreign law was applied to claims arising under a US statute, such as the securities or antitrust laws).[211]

13.191 **(1.2) Does the principle of '*iura novit curia*' apply? Or must the applicable law be proven (by which means)?** Consistent with its common law tradition, the general expectation and practice in US arbitration is for the parties to provide the tribunal with the applicable legal authorities and written argument applying those authorities to the specific facts of the case. This is particularly important where one or more of the arbitrators is from a legal system other than that which provides the substantive law to be applied to the dispute.

(2) Decisions according to equity or as amiable compositeur

13.192 Parties are free to grant the arbitrators the power to decide their dispute in accordance with general principles of equity (ie *ex aequo et bono*).[212] In the absence of such agreement by the parties, and particularly where the parties have agreed to a particular substantive governing law, the arbitrators are generally obligated to apply a specific system of law.[213]

---

[209] eg AAA (ICDR) International Rules, Art 28; CPR International Rules, r 10.1.

[210] New York Convention, Art V(2)(b).

[211] eg *Rodriguez de Quijas v Shearson/American Express Inc*, 490 US 477, 109 S Ct 1917 (US S Ct 1989); *Shearson/American Express Inc v McMahon*, 482 US 220, 107 S Ct 2332 (US S Ct 1987); *Mitsubishi Motors Corp v Soler Chrysler-Plymouth Inc*, 473 US 614, 105 S Ct 3346 (US S Ct 1985); *PPG Indus, Inc v Pilkington plc*, 825 F Supp 1465 (US Dist Ct (D Ariz) 1993).

[212] eg *Island Territory of Curacao v Solitron Devices Inc*, 489 F 2d 1313 (US Ct of Apps (2nd Cir) 1973).

[213] eg AAA (ICDR) International Rules, Art 28.3 ('The tribunal shall not decide as *amiable compositeur* or *ex aequo et bono* unless the parties have expressly authorized it to do so.'); CPR International Rules, Art 10.3.

(3) Application of lex mercatoria, *general principles etc*

Although the parties are free to agree that the arbitrators should apply principles of *lex mercatoria* instead of a particular national law, this is uncommon as a matter of practice. **13.193**

(3.1) Is the application of *lex mercatoria* considered as the application of law or as a kind of *amiable composition*? There is no legal authority discussing the application of *lex mercatoria* by the arbitrators. If the arbitrators are given the mandate to apply *lex mercatoria* to the parties' dispute, they should strive to apply specific legal principles to the facts of the particular dispute rather than rely on general principles of equity.[214] **13.194**

(4) Applicable substantive law if there is no choice of law by the parties

(4.1) Is there an autonomous conflict of law rule in the national arbitration law? Is it considered mandatory? There is no autonomous choice-of-law principle for the substantive law to be applied in US-sited arbitrations. If the parties have not selected an applicable substantive law to govern their dispute, the arbitrators have broad discretion to select the substantive law.[215] **13.195**

While some sets of procedural rules contain choice-of-law principles that would apply in the absence of an express choice by the parties, most leave the choice of law entirely to the tribunal's discretion.[216] **13.196**

(4.2) What is the law applicable to interest? US courts have generally held that arbitrators have the authority to award interest on arbitral awards. The decision to award interest and the applicable rate of interest are within the discretion of the tribunal, unless the parties have provided otherwise.[217] Courts usually uphold an arbitrator's award of pre-award interest (interest from the time of the breach or wrongful action up to the final arbitration award) and will not disturb the rate applied by the tribunal.[218] **13.197**

---

214 Born, *International Commercial Arbitration*, 2232–7 (Kluwer, 2009).

215 eg *ATSA of California Inc v Continental Ins Co*, 754 F 2d 1394, 1396 (US Ct of Apps (9th Cir) 1985) (reversing trial court's holding that Egyptian law should apply, on grounds that arbitrator had authority to determine applicable law); *Chloe Z Fishing Co v Odyssey Re (London) Ltd*, 109 F Supp 2d 1236, 1253 (US Dist Ct (S D Cal) 2000); *Zurich Ins Co v Ennia Gen Ins Co*, 882 F Supp 1438, 1440 (US Dist Ct (SDNY) 1995) ('The issue of the law to be applied in the arbitration proceeding—including the question whether the choice of law clause in the Management Agreement applies—is for the arbitration panel'); *American Construction Machinery & Equipment Corp v Mechanized Construction of Pakistan Ltd*, 659 F Supp 426 (US Dist Ct (SDNY) 1987), *affirmed*, 828 F 2d 117 (US Ct of Apps (2nd Cir) 1987).

216 AAA (ICDR) International Rules, Art 28.1 ('The tribunal shall apply the substantive law(s) or rules of law designated by the parties as applicable to the dispute. Failing such a designation by the parties, the tribunal shall apply such law(s) or rules of law as it determines to be appropriate.'); CPR International Rules, r 10.1 ('The Tribunal shall apply the substantive law(s) or rules of law designated by the parties as applicable to the dispute. Failing such a designation by the parties, the Tribunal shall apply such law(s) or rules of law as it determines to be appropriate.').

217 eg AAA (ICDR) International Rules, Art 28.4 ('The tribunal may award such pre-award and post-award interest, simple or compound, as it considers appropriate, taking into consideration the contract and applicable law'); CPR International Rules, r 10.6.

218 eg *Horton Inc v NSK Corp*, 544 F Supp 2d 817, 822, 827 (US Dist Ct (D Minn) 2008) (upholding arbitrator's award and pre-award interest); *T-Mobile USA Inc v Qwest Comm. Corp*, no C07-0976 MJP, 2008 WL 217730, at *2 (US Dist Ct (W D Wash) 2008); *Hendrik Delivery Svc Inc v St. Louis Post-Dispatch, LLC*, no 4:07CV1516 JCH, 2007 WL 3071827, at *2, *9 (US Dist Ct (E D Mo) 2007); *Bryant Motors Inc v Blue Bird Body Co*, no 5:06-CV-353(CAR), 2007 WL 2422133, at *2 (US Dist Ct (M D Ga) 2007). Courts

13.198 In connection with an enforcement action, courts will sometimes award additional interest for the time between the issuance of the arbitral award and payment. The granting of post-award interest is generally within the discretion of the courts.[219] Courts awarding post-award interest will often apply the applicable rate of post-judgment interest for federal civil actions.[220] They may also look to the substantive law governing the contract[221] or to state law.[222]

13.199 **(4.3) What is the law and practice with respect to legal interest on foreign currency debts?** If a foreign arbitral award provides for interest according to a foreign interest rate, US courts generally will not disturb the award of interest,[223] unless the rate is 'penal' under the law of the foreign forum.[224] If a foreign arbitral award does not include interest, a US court in an action to enforce the foreign award has broad discretion to determine whether to award interest and, if so, what interest rate to apply.[225]

(5) Binding effect of state court decisions

13.200 An arbitral tribunal can be bound by prior judgments of the courts under the general principles of *res judicata*. The extent to which a tribunal is bound by prior court judgments will depend, in part, on the applicable substantive and procedural law, and on whether the general requirements for the application of *res judicata* (ie, final judgment issued on the merits of the same claim between the same parties)[226] or collateral estoppel (ie final determination of a particular issue that was actually litigated and was necessary to the court's judgment on a different claim)[227] are met.

---

may decline to enforce an award of interest where it serves penal, rather than compensatory, purposes. See *Laminoirs-Trefileries-Cableries de Lens, SA v Southwire Co*, 484 F Supp 1063 (US Dist Ct (N D Ga) 1980).

[219] eg *Industrial Risk Insurers v MAN Gutehoffnungshutte GmbH*, 141 F 3d 1434, 1446–47 (US Ct of Apps (11th Cir) 1998); *Pend Oreille Public Utility District no 1*, 28 F 3d 1544, 1553 (US Ct of Apps (9th Cir) 1994). Federal courts are required to apply the FAA even to cases involving diversity jurisdiction; however, application of the FAA itself does not independently provide a basis for federal question jurisdiction.

[220] The applicable rate of interest in federal civil actions is provided at 28 USC s 1961. See *United States v Gordon*, 393 F 3d 1044, 1058 n 12 (US Ct of Apps (9th Cir) 2004); *Gutehoffnungshutte*, 141 F 3d at 1446–7; *T-Mobile*, 2008 WL 217730, at *2.

[221] *Zachary Construction Corp v Natkin Contracting LLC*, Civil Action no SA-04-CA-0405 FB (NN), 2006 WL 1169545 (US Dist Ct (W D Tex) 2006) (because arbitration agreement provides for Oklahoma law to be applied to the state contract dispute, interest is awarded pursuant to Oklahoma law).

[222] *Estate of Riddle v Southern Farm Bureau Life Ins*, 421 F 3d 400, 409 (US Ct of Apps (6th Cir) 2005); *Fidelity Federal Bank, FSB v Durga Ma Corp*, 387 F 3d 1021, 1024 (US Ct of Apps (9th Cir) 2004); *Executone Info Sys Inc v Davis*, 26 F 3d 1314, 1329 (US Ct of Apps (5th Cir) 1994); *Bryant Motors Inc*, 2007 WL 2422133, at *2; *General Electric Co v Anson Stamping Co Inc*, 426 F Supp 2d 579, 597 (US Dist Ct (W D Ky) 2006); *Lewis*, 304 F Supp 2d at 1351–2.

[223] eg *Proton Shipping Inc v Sovarex SA*, no 05 Civ 10295(PAC), 2006 WL 177005 (US Dist Ct (SDNY) 2006); *American Construction Machinery Equipment Corp v Mechanized Construction of Pakistan Ltd.*, 659 F Supp 426, 428–30 (US Dist Ct (SDNY) 1987).

[224] eg *Oh Young Indus Co v E & J Textile Group*, no B179884, 2005 WL 2470824, at *6 (Ca Ct App 2005); *Aasma v American S.S. Owners Mut. Protection and Indemnity*, 238 F Supp 2d 918, 922 (US Dist Ct (N D Ohio) 2003); Laminoirs-Trefileries-Cableries de Lens SA v Southwire Co, 1980 US Dist. LEXIS 9898, at *14 (US Dist Ct (N D Ga) 1980) (holding that a 14.5% and 15.5% interest rate were penal rather than compensatory, bearing no reasonable relation to any damage resulting from delay in recovery of the sums awarded).

[225] eg *Sarhank Group v Oracle Corp*, no 01 Civ 1285(DAB), 2004 WL 324881, at *4 (US Dist Ct (SDNY) 2004).

[226] Restatement (Second) of Judgments s 19 (1982).

[227] *ibid* s 27 (1982).

(5.1) Is an arbitral tribunal bound by a decision of another arbitral tribunal? US courts have generally recognized that arbitral awards can have *res judicata* and collateral estoppel effect, both in subsequent arbitrations and in court actions, in the same manner as court judgments.[228] Courts sometimes require a showing that the prior arbitration included adequate adjudicatory procedures before according it full preclusive effect.[229] 13.201

(5.2) Does a decision in a criminal case bind an arbitral tribunal? It is difficult to see how an arbitral tribunal could ignore the outcome of a prior criminal proceeding, but there is no specific requirement that the tribunal reach the same decisions on the predicate factual issues as that reached by a jury or judge in a related criminal proceeding. It is important to note that the standards of proof differ in criminal and civil proceedings, and although a criminal proceeding may involve similar factual issues as a parallel civil proceeding, these differences mean that it is not at all implausible that a criminal proceeding and a parallel civil claim could be decided in different ways. 13.202

E. Settlement

(1) Settlement by agreement of the parties with or without support of the arbitral tribunal

There is no requirement in US law that arbitrators encourage or facilitate settlements between the parties. There also is no prohibition on arbitrators doing so, although active encouragement of or participation in the parties' settlement efforts may conflict with the arbitrator's adjudicatory mandate. Parties are, of course, always free to settle their disputes without the participation of the tribunal. 13.203

(1.1) May an arbitrator who has initiated settlement discussions be challenged when agreement on a settlement has failed? Some commentators have suggested that arbitrators who encourage or participate in settlement discussions run the risk of undermining their neutrality and violating their mandate as arbitrators.[230] The AAA/ABA Canon of Ethics does not bar arbitrators from participating in settlement discussions, but it does caution arbitrators about the potential tension between their role as arbitrator and the role of mediator: 13.204

> Although it is not improper for an arbitrator to suggest to the parties that they discuss the possibility of settlement or the use of mediation, or other dispute resolution processes, an arbitrator should not exert pressure on any party to settle or to utilize other dispute resolution processes. An arbitrator should not be present or otherwise participate in settlement discussions or act as a mediator unless requested to do so by all parties.[231]

---

[228] eg *IDS Life Ins Co v Royal Alliance Ass'n*, 266 F 3d 645 (US Ct of Apps (7th Cir) 2001); *Stulberg v Intermedics Orthopedics Inc*, 997 F Supp 1060 (US Dist Ct (N D Ill) 1998); *City of Gainesville v Island Creek Coal Sales Co*, 618 F Supp 513 (US Dist Ct (M D Fla) 1984), *affirmed*, 771 F 2d 1495 (US Ct of Apps (11th Cir) 1985); *Matter of American Insurance Co*, 371 NE 2d 798 (NY Ct of Apps 1977). For commentary, see Gordon, R., 'Only One Kick at the Cat: A Contextual Rubric for Evaluating Res Judicata and Collateral Estoppel in International Commercial Arbitration' (2006) 18 *Florida J Int'l L* 549.

[229] eg *Jacobs v CBS Broad Inc*, 291 F 3d 1173 (US Ct of Apps (9th Cir) 2002); *Pritchard v Dent Wizard Int'l Corp*, 275 F Supp 2d 903 (US Dist Ct (S D Ohio) 2003).

[230] Plant, D.W., 'Mediation in International Commercial Arbitration: Some Practical Aspects' (1998) 4 *J Int'l & Comp L* 329, 335-6; Abramson, H.I., 'Protocols for International Arbitrators Who Dare to Settle Cases: Some Practical Aspects' (1999) 10 *Am Rev Int'l Arb* 1.

[231] American Arbitration Association, Code of Ethics for Arbitrators in Commercial Disputes.

13.205 The AAA Commercial Arbitration Rules also reflect this concern. Rule 8 provides:

> At any stage of the proceedings, the parties may agree to conduct a mediation conference under the Commercial Mediation Procedures in order to facilitate settlement. The mediator shall not be an arbitrator appointed to the case.[232]

Other rules contain similar provisions.[233]

(2) 'Private settlement' and its impact on the arbitral procedure

13.206 When parties reach a settlement during the course of an arbitration, they generally agree to terminate the arbitration proceedings 'with prejudice', which means that both parties are precluded from asserting the same claims or counterclaims in a subsequent proceeding. The parties will still be responsible for paying the fees of the arbitrators and any applicable institutional fees. If the parties have selected a set of procedural rules, those rules may contain provisions that expressly govern the payment of fees and the return of any deposits in the event of a settlement.

(3) Form and effect of a settlement (eg award on agreed terms)

13.207 Most procedural rules provide that the arbitrators have authority to issue awards memorializing the terms of any agreed settlement by the parties.[234] These so-called 'consent awards' can provide significant advantages for the parties by giving their contractual settlement the force and effect of a binding and enforceable arbitral award. Some commentators have raised concerns that such awards could be used by unscrupulous parties to launder money or evade their legal obligations, and arbitrators are therefore advised to investigate the details of the parties' dispute and their agreed settlement to satisfy themselves that there is no evidence of collusion before incorporating the terms in an arbitral award.[235]

F. Costs of the arbitration

(1) General allocation of the costs of the proceedings

13.208 There are no statutory provisions governing the allocation of the costs of the arbitration. Most procedural rules, both institutional and *ad hoc*, contain detailed provisions regarding the assessment and allocation of arbitration costs, including administrative costs, arbitrators' fees, and the parties' legal and other costs.[236] Arbitrators are generally granted broad discretion to allocate the administrative costs of the arbitration, including arbitrators' fees, unless the parties have agreed otherwise. Courts are split on whether arbitrators have the

---

[232] AAA Commercial Rules, R-8.

[233] eg CPR International Rules, r 19 ('The Tribunal may suggest that the parties explore settlement at such times as the Tribunal may deem appropriate. With the consent of the parties, the Tribunal at any stage of the proceeding may arrange for mediation of the claims asserted in the arbitration by a mediator acceptable to the parties. The mediator shall be a person other than a member of the Tribunal. . . The Tribunal will not be informed of any settlement offers or other statements made during settlement negotiations or a mediation between the parties, unless both parties consent.').

[234] AAA (ICDR) International Rules, Art 29; CPR International Rules, r 19.4; AAA Commercial Rules, R-44.

[235] Redfern, A., Hunter, M.,Blackaby, N. and Partasides, C., *Law and Practice of International Commercial Arbitration* (2004) s 5-29; Derains, Y. and Schwarz, E., *A Guide to the ICC Rules of Arbitration* (2005) 311–12.

[236] AAA (ICDR) International Rules, Art 31; AAA Commercial Rules, Rule 43(c); CPR International Rules, rules 17.2, 17.3.

authority to award the payment of the parties' legal fees in the absence of express agreement by the parties.

(2) Deposits or advances for costs or fees

There are no statutory provisions regarding the costs of the arbitration. Most procedural rules (both institutional and *ad hoc*) allow the relevant arbitral institution or the arbitrators directly to require the parties to pay deposits or advances on the costs of the arbitration, including the arbitrators' fees.[237] **13.209**

(2.1) Is there case law authorizing or prohibiting arbitrators to order a party to pay an advance on the arbitration costs? There are no prohibitions on the arbitrators' authority to order the parties to pay deposits or advances on the arbitration costs, including the arbitrators' fees. **13.210**

(2.2) May the raising of a set-off claim or counterclaim be made contingent upon payment of the corresponding advance for the relating arbitration costs (cf eg Article 30(5), ICC Rules)? May such a condition be agreed upon when entering into the arbitration agreement? The arbitrators or the relevant arbitral institution can require that the respondent pay its share of an advance on costs before accepting a counterclaim or a set-off claim. The parties can specifically agree on such a rule in their arbitration agreement directly or by referring to a set of procedural rules that include this rule. **13.211**

(2.3) What remedies exist against a party which does not pay its part of the advance on the arbitration costs (eg termination of the arbitration agreement)? How may the other party enforce its rights? If the claimant (or counterclaimant) does not pay its share of the advance on costs, the arbitral institution or the arbitrators can terminate the arbitration or refuse to accept the counterclaim. If the respondent (or counterclaim respondent) does not pay its share of the advance, all of the commonly used procedural rules allow the claimant (or counterclaimant) to pay the full advance on costs related to the claim (or counterclaim) in order for the arbitration to proceed.[238] **13.212**

The claimant can seek compensation for having to pay the respondent's share in a final cost award by the tribunal. Alternatively, the claimant may seek an immediate partial award from the tribunal directing the respondent to pay its share of the cost deposit on the ground that the respondent's refusal to do so is a breach of its contractual obligation to arbitrate in good faith. **13.213**

(3) Costs of the administration by an arbitration institution

All arbitration institutions charge a fee for administering the arbitration. The amount of the administrative fee and the authority of the arbitrators and the institution to allocate that fee among the parties are determined by the institution's procedural rules.[239] **13.214**

---

237 AAA (ICDR) International Rules, at Art 33; AAA Commercial Rules, R-52; CPR International Rules, r 17.4.

238 AAA (ICDR) International Rules, at Art 33.3; AAA Commercial Rules, R-54; CPR International Rules, r 17.5.

239 AAA (ICDR) International Rules, at 'Administrative Fees' (providing a sliding scale of administrative fees based on the amount in dispute; for a $10 million claim, the administrative fee is $14,000); AAA

(4) Arbitrators' fees: law and practice, judicial control

13.215 Generally, there are no statutory provisions regarding the costs of the arbitration.[240] Arbitrators (and/or arbitral institutions) generally have broad discretion regarding issues related to the costs of the arbitration, including with respect to the arbitrators' fees.[241]

13.216 (4.1) **May arbitrators fix their own fees in the award?** If the parties have selected a set of procedural rules to govern the arbitration, those rules will generally contain detailed provisions regarding the arbitrators' fees and the scope of the arbitrators' discretion in setting those fees.[242]

13.217 (4.2) **How can the parties change the arbitrators' fees once they are fixed?** The parties are contractually obligated to pay the fees that are assessed by the arbitral institution or contractually agreed with the arbitrators. The only way to change those fees is to seek agreement from the arbitrators or the institution to provide for a different fee arrangement. For a variety of reasons, this is generally not recommended.

13.218 (4.3) **Are the arbitrator's fees subject to income tax if (i) the place of arbitration; or (ii) the normal residence or place of business of the arbitrator is located in this country?** The US Internal Revenue Service has not published specific guidance on the tax implications of fees earned for service as an arbitrator in an arbitration sited in the US. The tax treatment of such fees is potentially complex and may depend on the arbitrator's citizenship and residence, the amount of the fees earned, where the fees are paid, and a number of other factors. Arbitrators are advised to seek the advice of an experienced tax specialist for guidance.

13.219 (4.4) **Are arbitrator's fees submitted to VAT? If yes, is the duty to pay such tax linked to (i) the place of arbitration; or (ii) the arbitrator's general residence?** The US tax laws do not include imposition of VAT, but an arbitrator's fees may be subject to income tax, as discussed above.

(5) Attorneys' fees and the winning party's claim for reimbursement

13.220 In US civil litigation, there is no rule providing for fee-shifting (except in very limited circumstances), and each party generally bears its own legal costs regardless of the outcome of the case. In light of this rule, some US courts have held (primarily in connection with domestic arbitrations) that arbitrators lack the power to award legal fees unless the parties have expressly conferred this authority on the tribunal.[243] This approach is misguided,

Commercial Rules, at 'Administrative Fees' (providing a sliding scale of administrative fees based on the amount in dispute; for a $10 million claim, the administrative fee is $14,000); JAMS Schedule of Fees and Costs (providing for administrative fees of $1,000 plus 10% of the fees charged by the arbitrators).

[240] US case law does suggest, however, that in arbitration involving consumers, an arbitration agreement may be unenforceable if the costs of the arbitration would be 'prohibitively expensive' for the consumer. See *Green Tree v Randolph*, 521 US 79, 121 S Ct 513 (US Sup Ct 2000).

[241] AAA (ICDR) International Rules, Art 31; AAA Commercial Rules, r 43(c); CPR International Rules, r 17.2.

[242] *ibid.*

[243] eg RUAA, s 21(b); *McNabb v Riley*, 29 F 3d 1303, 1306–07 (US Ct of Apps (8th Cir) 1994); *Bacardi Corp v Congreso de Uniones Industriales de Puerto Rico*, 692 F 2d 210 (US Ct of Apps (1st Cir) 1982); *Prudential-Bache Sec Inc v Depew*, 814 F Supp 1081, 1082 (US Dist Ct (M D Fla) 1993) (in context of arbitration, observing that '[l]itigants in the United States must follow the so-called "American rule" for attorneys' fees',

particularly in the context of international arbitration proceedings, where it is undisputed that tribunals and courts are not bound by rules of US civil procedure. The better view—which has been adopted by a number of US courts—[244] is that arbitrators have inherent authority to award attorneys' fees in international arbitration proceedings unless the parties have agreed otherwise.[245]

US parties often expressly agree in their contracts that each side will bear its own legal costs in arbitration proceedings. Where parties have excluded the power of the arbitrators to award costs to the winning party, that agreement will be upheld, and failure to respect the parties' agreement can be grounds for refusing to enforce the tribunal's award.[246] **13.221**

(5.1) May in-house lawyers charge fees or may a party request costs of in-house lawyers to be reimbursed? Reimbursement for the costs of in-house lawyers is at the discretion of the arbitrators and/or the arbitral institution. In practice many parties do not seek reimbursement for the costs of in-house lawyers or executives for their time in connection with the arbitration. **13.222**

(6) Time and form of the decision on costs

Most procedural rules contain provisions regarding the arbitrators' award on costs. Most tribunals include their award on costs in their final award on the merits, but some tribunals issue a separate final award on costs. **13.223**

(6.1) May the arbitrators' decision on the costs (allocation and amount of costs to be reimbursed) be challenged separately from the award itself? Are there time limits for such a remedy? If the arbitrators issue their award on costs in a separate award, then that award can (at least theoretically) be subject to review by the courts in a proceeding separate from the award on the merits. If the cost award is part of the tribunal's final award on the merits, the extent to which it can be challenged or enforced separately from the award on the merits will depend on the law of the enforcing forum. **13.224**

(6.2) Are the arbitrators entitled and/or legally obliged to rule on the amount of one or both parties' costs that are recoverable? Unless otherwise agreed by the parties, the arbitrators are generally entitled (but not obliged) to issue an award directing one party to pay all or part of the costs of the other party. Some US statutes contain specific mandatory provisions regarding the recovery of attorneys' fees in connection with certain statutory claims. **13.225**

G. Publication of the award

(1) Publication with or without the consent of the parties

The scope of confidentiality of arbitral awards is, at least to some extent, within the control of the parties. The parties can agree in their arbitration agreement, either directly or by **13.226**

---

and that '[a] litigant cannot collect attorneys' fees from the losing party unless a statute or contract provides for the award, or the losing party willfully disobeyed a court order or brought suit in bad faith').

244 eg *MCT Shipping Corp v Sabet*, 497 F Supp 1078 (US Dist Ct (SDNY) 1980); *J.R. Snyder Co v Soble*, 226 NW 2d 276 (Mich Ct of App 1975); *Comm. Metals Co v Int'l Union Marine Corp.*, 1973 A.M.C. 515 (US Dist Ct (SDNY) 1972).

245 Born, *International Commercial Arbitration*, 2491–4 (Kluwer, 2009).

246 eg *Kristian v Comcast Corp*, 446 F 3d 25 (US Ct of Apps (1st Cir) 2006); *Ergobilt Inc v Neutral Posture Ergonomics Inc*, 2002 WL 1489521 (US Dist Ct (N D Tex) 2002).

reference to a set of procedural rules, that any award will be confidential and will not be subject to publication. They can also consent to publication of their award, either by adopting a set of procedural rules that provide for publication of the award or by agreeing to publication after the award is issued. The parties' agreement regarding confidentiality will generally be upheld.[247]

13.227 Arbitrators are generally required to maintain the confidentiality of the arbitral proceedings and any awards. Canon VI(B) of the AAA/ABA Code of Ethics states: 'Unless otherwise agreed by the parties, or required by applicable rules or law, an arbitrator should keep confidential all matters relating to the arbitration proceedings and decisions.'[248]

13.228 If an award is subject to confirmation or annulment proceedings, the award must be submitted to the enforcing court and may be publicly available in the court records.

(2) Practice of publication (eg in specific legal journals)

13.229 Some arbitral institutions do publish arbitral awards,[249] but most do not. Institutions sometimes publish awards in a redacted form, without any party names or identifying information. Awards under the AAA Commercial Rules and the AAA (ICDR) International Rules are not published and are kept entirely confidential by the AAA.[250]

VI. Amendment and challenge of the award; liability of arbitrators

A. Amendment, correction or interpretation of the award

(1) Motion to amend or correct an award

13.230 Section 11 of the Federal Arbitration Act expressly authorizes a party to request the courts to modify or amend an arbitral award.[251] The motion should be brought in the court of the district wherein the award was made.[252] Section 11 sets forth limited grounds under which a court, in its discretion, may modify or correct an award.[253] These include where the award contains an evident calculation or descriptive error, where the arbitrators have issued an award upon a matter not submitted to them, or where the form of the award is imperfect in some respect.[254]

---

[247] eg *Guyden v Aetna Inc*,—F 3d—, 2008 WL 4426478 (US Ct of Apps (2nd Cir) 2008); *Iberia Credit Bureau Inc v Cingular Wireless LLC*, 379 F 3d 159, 175 (US Ct of Apps (5th Cir) 2004).

[248] AAA/ABA Code of Ethics, Canon VI(B).

[249] eg NASD Code of Arbitration Procedure for Customer Disputes, Art 12904(g); NASD Code of Arbitration Procedure for Industry Disputes, Art 13904(g).

[250] AAA (ICDR) International Rules, Art 27.4 and Art 27.8. The AAA rules provide exceptions: for instance, the presumption of privacy and confidentiality does not apply to class arbitrations, and all class arbitration hearings and filings may be made public, subject to the authority of the arbitrator to provide otherwise in special circumstances. American Arbitration Association, Supplementary Rules for Class Arbitrations. Additionally, all employment dispute awards are also published and made available to the public, with the names of the parties and identifying factors redacted.

[251] 9 USC s 11.

[252] *ibid.*

[253] *Sociedad Armadora Aristomenis Panama, S A v Tri-Coast S. S. Co.*, 184 F Supp 738 (US Dist Ct (SD N Y) 1960).

[254] 9 USC s 11(a)–(c).

Periodically, litigation arises over whether a request to modify an award falls outside the scope of a court's authority and, in fact, represents a back-door attempt to obtain judicial review of the merits. Thus, on the one hand, a court may not rely on its s 11 power to correct erroneous factual findings in the award.[255] On the other hand, courts disagree over whether this section allows them to correct material calculation errors even though the arbitrators were not responsible for the errors.[256] Particularly when it comes to damages calculations, litigation can arise over whether a damages award (particularly one not explained very well) results from a miscalculation by the arbitrator (which can be corrected) or, instead, reflects a careful determination about the merits of the case and the prevailing party's entitlement to relief (which cannot).[257] **13.231**

Other provisions of the FAA set forth detailed procedural requirements for motions to modify or correct an award. The motion must be served upon the adverse party within three months of entry or delivery of the award.[258] Motions filed beyond this deadline are generally dismissed as time-barred, though courts have implied that late motions might be excused by reference to tolling principles or the diligence of the moving party.[259] **13.232**

(2) Interpretation of the award by the tribunal

The FAA does not contain any specific provision authorizing the tribunal to interpret the award after it has been rendered. Some courts have recognized the *functus officio* doctrine under which arbitrators are divested of jurisdiction (and thus further opportunity for interpretation or review) after they render an award.[260] However, recent decisions have developed broad exceptions to the *functus officio* doctrine that may allow the arbitrator some scope to interpret or amplify his award after rendering it.[261] For example, these exceptions allow the arbitrator to clarify, complete or interpret his award so long as he does not **13.233**

---

[255] *San Martine Compania De Navegacion, S A v Saguenay Terminals Limited*, 293 F 2d 796 (US Ct of Apps (9th Cir) 1961); *Amicizia Societa Navegazione v Chilean Nitrate & Iodine Sales Corp*, 274 F 2d 805 (US Ct of Apps (2nd Cir) 1960).

[256] Compare *Transnitro Inc v M/V Wave*, 943 F 2d 471 (US Ct of Apps (4th Cir) 1991), with *U S for Use and Benefit of Chicago Bridge & Iron Co v Ets-Hokin Corp*, 284 F Supp 471 (US Dist Ct (ND Cal) 1966).

[257] eg *ARW Exploration Corp v Aguirre*, 45 F 3d 1455 (US Ct of Apps (10th Cir) 1995); *Atlantic Aviation Inc v EBM Group Inc*, 11 F 3d 1276 (US Ct of Apps (5th Cir) 1994); *Hesfibel Fiber Optik & Elektronik San Ve Tic AS v Four S Group Inc*, 315 F Supp 2d 1365 (US Dist Ct (SD Fla) 2004); *Data-Stream AS/RS Technologies, LLC v China Int'l Marine Containers Ltd*, 2003 WL 22519456 (US Dist Ct (SD NY) 2003); *Fried, Krupp, GmbH, Krupp Reederei Und Brennstoff-Handel-Seeschiffarht v Solidarity Carriers Inc*, 674 F Supp 1022 (US Dist Ct (SD N Y) 1987).

[258] *Webster v A. T. Kearney Inc*, CA7 (Ill.) 2007, 507 F 3d 568; *Tokura Const Co Ltd v Corporacion Raymond*, SA, SDTex1982, 533 F Supp 1274.

[259] 9 USC s 12. See *Choice Hotels Int'l Inc v Shiv Hospitality, LLC*, 491 F 3d 171 (US Ct of Apps (4th Cir) 2007); *Taylor v Nelson*, 788 F 2d 220 (US Ct of Apps (4th Cir) 1986); *Florasynth Inc v Pickholz*, 750 F 2d 171 (US Ct of Apps (2nd Cir) 1984); *Piccolo v Dain, Kalman & Quail Inc*, 641 F 2d 598, 601 (US Ct of Apps (8th Cir) 1981). Depending on the claim and the basis for subject matter jurisdiction, issues will arise about whether federal or state law supplies the relevant limitations period. Compare *eg Rodriguez v Prudential-Bache Securities Inc*, 882 F Supp 1202 (US Dist Ct (D P R) 1985), with *Brown v Hyatt Corp*, 128 F Supp 2d 697 (US Dist Ct (D Hawaii) 2000). In the specific context of international arbitration (at least those where the awards fall under the New York Convention), federal law will almost always govern.

[260] See eg *Office & Professional Employees Int'l Union, Local no 471 v Brownsville General Hospital*, 186 F3d 326 (US Ct of Apps (3rd Cir) 1999) (discussing the doctrine's evolution in the United States).

[261] eg *Local 2322, Int'l Brotherhood of Electrical Workers v Verizon New England Inc*, 464 F3d 93 (US Ct of Apps (1st Cir) (2006).

'alter' it.[262] Many sets of institutional rules contain provisions allowing tribunals to modify or correct an award after it has been issued.

B. Appeal on the merits

(1) Admissibility and procedure of an appeal on the merits

13.234 Judicial review of an arbitration award rendered in the US is governed by s 10 of the FAA. That section provides that the US court 'in and for the district wherein the award was made may make an order vacating the award upon the application of any party to the arbitration' if any of the specific enumerated grounds is met. As discussed below, the grounds for vacatur of an arbitral award under s 10 of the FAA are directed to procedural issues and do not allow a substantive review of the arbitrator's decision on the merits.

13.235 The US courts have also historically applied additional common-law grounds in reviewing arbitral awards and have occasionally vacated arbitral awards on the basis that they are 'contrary to public policy', 'irrational', in 'manifest disregard of the law', or do not 'draw their essence from the agreement'.[263] Relying on these common-law grounds, US courts have, not infrequently, looked beyond the procedural aspects of the arbitration and, at least partly, considered the substantive merits of the award. As discussed below, when applying these doctrines, US courts have consistently held that they cannot be invoked to challenge mere errors of fact or law, but rather should be limited to extreme circumstances, such as where the arbitrator knew of a binding rule of law but consciously chose to disregard it.

13.236 As also discussed below, recent Supreme Court jurisprudence has cast doubt on these common-law doctrines by suggesting that the statutory grounds for vacatur set forth in s 10 of the FAA may be exclusive and may not allow judicial review of arbitral awards for manifest disregard of the law.[264] There is now considerable uncertainty surrounding the doctrine. Recent decisions of the circuit courts of appeals regarding whether the courts may continue to review arbitral awards for manifest disregard of the law are divided,[265] and it is likely that the Supreme Court will be asked to return to this question in the near future.

13.237 (1.1) **May the parties agree on an appeal to another arbitral tribunal?** In general, the parties can agree on an appeal to another arbitral tribunal (a possibility expressly contemplated by some institutional rules and implicitly by others).[266] Though the issue has arisen infrequently, courts have not questioned the enforceability of arrangements under which a

[262] Macneil, Speidel & Stipanowich, *Federal Arbitration Law* (1994) s 37.6.6.

[263] 4 Am Jur 2d, *Alternative Disp Res* s 207.

[264] See *Hall Street Assocs LLC v Mattel Inc*, 128 S Ct 1396 (2008).

[265] See *Citigroup Global Markets Inc v Bacon*, 2009 WL 542780 (US Ct of Apps (5th Cir) 2009); *Comedy Club Inc v Improv West Assocs*, 2009 WL 205046 (US Ct of Apps (9th Cir) 2009); *Coffee Beanery Ltd v WW. LLC*, 2008 WL 4899478 (US Ct of Apps (6th Cir) 2008); *Stolt-Nielsen SA v AnimalFeeds Int'l Corp*, 548 F3d 85 (US Ct of Apps (2d Cir) 2008).

[266] See generally Marrow, P.B., 'A Practical Approach to Affording Review of Commercial Arbitration Awards: Using an Appellate Arbitrator' [August 2005] *Disp Res J* 10 (August–October 2005).

second arbitral panel can review an award.[267] This position flows from the principle of party autonomy that underpins much arbitration law in the United States.[268]

Courts have sometimes held appellate arbitral review provisions unconscionable where they systematically favour one party. This may arise in the consumer or employment setting where, for example, a company requires arbitration of disputes and is likely to be the respondent in any arbitration, and where the clause sets a monetary threshold on appellate review.[269] It may also arise in cases of arbitration agreements that grant only one party the right to appellate arbitral review.[270] Such clauses effectively provide a one-sided opportunity for the company to get a 'second bite at the apple' in cases where they do not prevail initially. **13.238**

Although issues of unconscionability and one-sided arbitration clauses are unlikely to arise in international commercial relationships between sophisticated businesses, practitioners should be aware that such doctrines exist. **13.239**

(2) Possibility to exclude an appeal (eg in the arbitration clause)

The Supreme Court's recent decision in *Hall Street v Mattel*, while not directly addressing the question, strongly suggests that parties may not contractually limit the scope of judicial review of the award. While *Hall Street* concerned a party's attempt to *expand* the grounds for judicial review, the Supreme Court's rejection of that effort, and the underlying scepticism over party autonomy in this area, supports the view of appellate courts that have rejected contractual attempts to exclude an appeal.[271] **13.240**

C. Setting aside of the award

(1) Reasons for setting aside an award

Section 10 of the FAA sets forth the main grounds for setting aside an award. Generally speaking, these grounds focus on serious procedural irregularities in the arbitration rather than substantive error or defects in the agreement itself. Section 10 provides that a court may vacate the award where: **13.241**

- the award was procured by corruption, fraud or undue means;
- there was evident partiality or corruption in the arbitrators;
- the arbitrators were guilty of misconduct in refusing to postpone the hearing upon sufficient cause shown; or in refusing to hear evidence pertinent and material to the controversy, or of any other misbehaviour by which the rights of any party have been prejudiced; or

267 *Kyocera v Prudential-Bache Trade Services Inc*, 341 F 3d 987, 1000 (US Ct of Apps (9th Cir) 2003) (*en banc*); *Bowen v Amoco Pipeline Co*, 254 F 3d 925, 936–37 (US Ct of Apps (10th Cir) 2001); *UHC Management Co Inc v Computer Services Corp*, 148 F 3d 992, 998 (US Ct of Apps (8th Cir) 1998); *Chicago Typographical Union no 16 v Chicago Sun-Times Inc*, 935 F 2d 1501, 1505 (US Ct of Apps (7th Cir) 1991); *Marshall v Pontiac*, 287 F Supp 2d 1229 (US Dist Ct (S D Cal) 2003).

268 See *Hall Street Assocs, LLC v Mattel Inc*, 128 S Ct 1396 (2008); Revised Uniform Arbitration Act s 23, Comment B.6.

269 See *Little v Auto Stiegler Inc*, 29 Cal 4th 1064, 63 P 3d 979 (Cal 2003).

270 See *Beynon v Garden Grove Medical Group*, 100 Cal App 3d 698, 161 Cal Rptr 146 (Cal 1980).

271 See *Hall Street Assocs LLC v Mattel Inc*, 128 S Ct 1396 (2008).

- the arbitrators exceeded their powers, or so imperfectly executed them that a mutual, final and definite award upon the subject matter submitted was not made.[272]

13.242 Courts have created additional common-law grounds for vacatur that have the potential to broaden the scope of judicial review beyond the grounds enumerated in s 10. These court-made doctrines take a variety of forms—courts have vacated arbitral awards on the basis that they are 'contrary to public policy', 'irrational', in 'manifest disregard of the law', or do not 'draw their essence from the agreement'.[273] Whether these judge-made doctrines form distinct grounds or merely represent different verbal formulations of the same concept is unclear. What is clear, however, is that these doctrines permit a reviewing court to look beyond the procedural aspects of the arbitration and, at least partly, to peer behind the substantive merits of the award.

13.243 The most frequently cited, and thus most controversial, of these doctrines is manifest disregard of the law. While lower courts consistently have maintained that this doctrine does not permit a reviewing court to set aside an award on the basis of mere disagreement with the arbitrator's legal conclusions, they have been less clear on what else is required.[274] A consistent formulation has not emerged in the case law, but the dominant one appears to be that the arbitrator was aware of the applicable law and proceeded to disregard it.[275] So formulated, the doctrine would appear to have an objective and a subjective component. The objective component requires proof that a particular legal rule governed a case. The subjective component requires proof that the arbitrator was both aware of and disregarded this rule.

13.244 Applied broadly, the manifest disregard of the law doctrine would have the potential to undermine one of the primary advantages of arbitration—to limit (if not exclude entirely) judicial review of the merits of the dispute. In practice, while the doctrine is often raised in vacatur proceedings, it rarely succeeds. Courts have overturned arbitral awards on this ground where an arbitrator utterly ignored the applicable law brought to his attention despite overwhelming evidence, where a party urged the arbitrator to disregard the law in a case built on weak evidence, and where the arbitrators erroneously read a limitations period into the contract.[276]

13.245 Despite its frequent invocation in the lower courts, the manifest disregard of the law doctrine has never formally been approved by the Supreme Court. The Court has referred to the doctrine in only three opinions. In the first two (one of which it has overruled), the Court suggested, albeit in dicta, that courts could overturn arbitral awards for manifest

---

[272] 9 USC s 10.

[273] 4 Am Jur 2d, Alternative Dispute Resolution s 207.

[274] eg *Yusuf Ahmed Alghanim & Sons, WLL v Toys 'R' Us Inc*, 126 F 3d 15 (US Ct Aps (2nd Cir) 1997); *Northrop Corp v Triad Int'l Marketing*, 811 F 2d 1265 (US Ct of Apps (9th Cir) 1987).

[275] *Compare San Martine Compagnia de Navegaciano v Saguenay Terminals*, 293 F 2d 796, 801 (US Ct of Apps (9th Cir) 1961), *with DiRussa v Dean Witter Reynolds*, 121 F 3d 818, 821 (US Ct of Apps (2nd Cir) 1997).

[276] *Patten v Signator Insurance Agency Inc*, 441 F 3d 230 (US Ct of Apps (4th Cir) 2006); *Halligan v Piper Jaffray Inc*, 148 F 3d 197 (US Ct of Apps (2nd Cir) 1997); *Montes v Shearson Lehman Brothers Inc*, 128 F3d 1456 (US Ct of Apps (11th Cir) 1997).

disregard of the law.[277] More recently, however, in *Hall Street v Mattel*, the Supreme Court expressed a more sceptical view.[278] While not formally disapproving of the manifest disregard doctrine, the Court strongly hinted that the vacatur grounds set forth in s 10 were exclusive and that the manifest disregard of the law doctrine did not fall under any of those grounds. There is now considerable uncertainty surrounding the doctrine. While the lower courts grapple with the meaning of the *Hall Street* decision, practitioners can expect that the manifest disregard of the law doctrine (and similar court-made merits-based grounds for judicial review) will continue to be regularly invoked, though rarely successful.

(1.1) May an award made according to international or foreign procedural rules be the object of an application for setting aside before the national courts? The FAA does not explicitly address the situation of an award rendered in the United States in an arbitration subject to another country's procedural law, and case law does not appear to have addressed this precise issue.[279] The FAA and US judicial decisions would not limit the power of the US courts to consider a setting-aside application simply because the arbitration was subject to a foreign procedural law, and precedent suggests that the US courts would not decline to exercise their power on that basis.[280] **13.246**

(2) Procedure and deadlines for challenging an award

The deadlines for vacatur actions are identical to those governing actions to modify the award, discussed above. The motion must be filed within three months of the date when the award is delivered or filed.[281] Late motions are dismissed as time-barred. By contrast, the FAA sets forth a longer deadline for motions to confirm the award (three years in case of awards falling under the New York Convention; one year in case of non-Convention awards).[282] The combination of these different deadlines for vacatur and confirmation actions effectively forces the party seeking vacatur to move first. Some authority holds that if a party fails to make a timely vacatur motion, it waives any vacatur defences in a subsequent confirmation action (the Supreme Court has never embraced this view, and as authors we are sceptical whether it is correct. Nonetheless, prudent practitioners must be aware of this line of authority).[283] **13.247**

277 *First Options of Chicago Inc v Kaplan*, 514 US 938 (1995) 115 S Ct 1920; *Wilko v Swan*, 346 US 427 (1953)74 S Ct 182, overruled by *Rodriguez de Quijas v Shearson/American Express Inc*, 490 US 477 (1989), (109 S Ct 1917).

278 *Hall Street v Mattell*, 128 SCt 1396 (2008).

279 Born, G., *International Commercial Arbitration* (Kluwer, 2001) 428.

280 eg *Gas Natural Aprovisionamientos SDG SA v Atlantic LNG Co. of Trinidad and Tobago*, 2208 WL 4344252 (US Dist Ct (SDNY) 2008); *Telenor Mobile Communications AS v Storm* LLC, 524 FSupp2d 332 (US Dist Ct (SDNY) 2007); *International Thunderbird Gaming Corp v United Mexican States*, 473 FSupp2d 80 (US Dist Ct (DDC) 2007); *Loewen v United States*, 2005 WL 3200885 (US Dist Ct (DDC) 2005); *Liberia Eastern Timber Corp v Liberia*, 650 FSupp 73 (US Dist Ct (SDNY) 1986).

281 9 USC s 12.

282 *ibid*, ss 9, 207.

283 Compare eg *Cullen v Paine, Webber, Jackson & Curtis Inc*, 863 F 2d 851 (US Ct of Apps (11th Cir 1989) and *Florasynth Inc v Pickholz*, 750 F 2d 171 (US Ct of Apps (2nd Cir) 1983) with *Chauffeurs, Teamsters, Warehousemen and Helpers Local Union no 364 v Ruan Transport Corp*, 473 F Supp 298 (US Dist Ct (N D Ind) 1979) and *Paul Allison, Inc v Minikin Storage of Omaha Inc*, 452 F Supp 573 (US Dist Ct (D Neb) 1978).

13.248 In addition to giving parties the right to appeal an order confirming or vacating an arbitral award, s 16 of the FAA also allows parties to appeal certain interlocutory orders. Parties may appeal an interlocutory order that enjoins an arbitration, and any order (i) denying a motion to stay an action pending arbitration under s 3 of the FAA; or (ii) denying a motion to compel arbitration under ss 4 or 206 of the FAA.[284] However, parties may not appeal an order (i) granting a motion to stay under s 3; or (ii) granting a motion to compel under ss 4 or 206.[285]

13.249 A motion to vacate should be brought in the court of the district in which the award was made.[286] The party moving to vacate the award must append a number of documents to the motion, including a copy of the arbitration agreement, a copy of the award, any arbitral orders relating to extension of the deadline for rendering the award and any judicial orders pertaining to the proceeding.[287]

13.250 Finally, the moving party must establish that the court has subject matter and personal jurisdiction. To the extent an award falls within the ambit of the New York Convention, then a federal court will have subject matter jurisdiction under ch II of the FAA.[288] However, in cases of awards falling outside the Convention, the moving party must establish an independent basis for subject matter jurisdiction.[289] Likewise, personal jurisdiction must exist over the defendant in the setting-aside action, typically based on the defendant's 'contacts' with the state in which the suit is filed or with the state where property is located (*in rem* jurisdiction).[290]

13.251 (2.1) **Who may (or must) represent a party in a proceeding for setting aside an award?** In most respects, federal law does not set forth specific requirements for the identity of the parties' legal representative in a vacatur proceeding (or any other proceeding for that matter). Instead, the matter is regulated by a combination of state law, state bar rules, and the rules of the particular court. In general, at least one of the party's counsel must be admitted to appear in the court of the district where the proceeding is brought. So long as that condition is satisfied, other counsel may appear through an application to the court for admission *pro hac vice*. Generally speaking, such applications (which are routinely granted) enable a counsel, provided that he is a member in good standing of at least one state bar, to appear for purposes of the case. He may perform most acts in the proceeding but generally must appear with the actual member of the local court and may not be able to sign pleadings that are filed in the court. Foreign counsel, who are not members of any state bar, generally may not be admitted *pro hac vice*.

---

284 9 USC s 16(a) (1) (A–C).
285 *ibid,* s 16(b).
286 *ibid,* s 12.
287 *ibid.*
288 *ibid,* s 203.
289 *Moses H Cohn Memorial Hospital v Mercury Construction Corp*, 460 US 1, 103 S Ct 927 (1983).
290 See Fed R Civ P 4(k); *Glencore Grain Rotterdam BV v Shivnath Rai Harnarain Co*, 284 F 3d 1114 (US Ct of Apps 9th Cir) 2002); *Base Metal Trading Ltd v OJSC 'Novokuznetsky Aluminum Factory'*, 283 F 3d 208 (US Ct of Apps (4th Cir) 2002).

(2.2) Do specific time limits exist for setting-aside procedures concerning awards on jurisdiction? Unlike the UNCITRAL Model Law, the FAA does not expressly authorize immediate review of jurisdictional awards. Consequently, little case law has addressed this question.[291] 13.252

Jurisdictional awards in which the arbitrators fully decline jurisdiction are likely subject to the three-month time limit for vacatur actions. These awards are unquestionably 'final' for purposes of the s 12 deadline and, thereby, trigger the three-month deadline for vacatur actions. 13.253

It is more difficult to say whether the time limits apply to awards in which the arbitrators uphold their jurisdiction. Rather surprisingly, the federal courts do not appear to have confronted this question directly. As discussed above, if a jurisdictional award finally determines the tribunal's jurisdiction, it should be considered a 'final' award for purposes of judicial review. 13.254

As noted above, under the Supreme Court's decision in *First Options of Chicago Inc v Kaplan*,[292] courts in the United States have jurisdiction to resolve challenges to the validity of the arbitration agreement, absent 'clear and unmistakable' evidence that the parties intended for the arbitrators to decide. Consequently, in many cases, the party objecting to the arbitrator's jurisdiction can obtain a judicial ruling on the matter even prior to the tribunal's issuance of an award on jurisdiction. 13.255

(3) Effect of a court decision which sets the award aside?

In the event that a court vacates an arbitral award, that award will cease to have legal effect in the United States. The losing party in the vacatur action may seek to appeal the adverse decision to an appellate court. The vacatur of the arbitral award does not necessarily deprive the arbitration agreement of continuing effect, and the parties' dispute may be referred to new arbitral proceedings. 13.256

(3.1) Does the setting-aside action suspend the enforcement? If so, do any remedies exist to reinstate enforcement? While the FAA does not explicitly address this scenario, case law and practice in the United States supports the idea that a setting-aside action does not suspend enforcement proceedings. Rather, the two proceedings occur in parallel, and the reviewing court renders a single opinion simultaneously addressing the vacatur motion and the enforcement (or confirmation) petition.[293] 13.257

(3.2) After an award has been set aside, does the underlying arbitration agreement revive or remain in force or is it exhausted or deemed terminated? The vacatur of an arbitral award should not, by itself, render the arbitration agreement unenforceable. Section 10 of 13.258

291 *Storm LLC v Telenor Mobil Communications AS*, 2006 WL 3735657 at *3 (US Dist Ct (SD NY) 2006); *Poponin v Virtual Pro, Inc.*, 2006 WL 2691418 (US Dist Ct (N D Cal) 2006); *Transportacion Maritima Mexicana SA v Companhia de Navegacao Lloyd Brasiliero*, 636 F Supp 474, 475 (US Dist Ct (SDNY) 1983). For a thorough treatment of the subject, see J Gaitis, *The Federal Arbitration Act: Risks and Incongruities Relating to the Issuance of Interim and Partial Awards in Domestic and International Arbitrations* (2005) 16 *Am Rev Int'l Arb* 1.

292 514 US 938, 115 S Ct 1920 (1995).

293 eg *Yusuf Ahmed Alghanim & Sons, W.L.L. v Toys 'R' Us*, 126 F3d 15 (US Ct of Apps (2nd Cir) 1997).

the FAA implies this result by providing that the vacating court has discretionary authority to remand the case to the arbitral tribunal if its deadline for entering an award has not lapsed.[294] Moreover, several courts vacating awards have remanded cases with instructions that the parties can proceed with another arbitration if they so desire.[295] Of course, if the court sets aside the award based on a defect in the arbitration clause itself, such a finding could extinguish the agreement.

(4) Appeal against the court's decision to set aside or not set aside the award

13.259 A party can appeal a district court's decision vacating (or refusing to vacate) an arbitral award. The appeal would be governed by the ordinary rules governing appeals from final judgments of the district courts.[296] The losing party normally must file a notice of appeal within 30 days of the entry of the judgment.[297] The notice would be filed, and the appeal subsequently briefed, in the relevant appellate court with jurisdiction over decisions from the district court which rendered the judgment.

(5) Possibility of the parties to exclude actions for setting aside

13.260 While the Supreme Court has not definitively addressed this precise issue, it is almost certain that the US courts will not enforce a contractual provision attempting to exclude set-aside actions. A few lower courts have confronted this precise issue, and they have uniformly refused to enforce such clauses on the ground that control over the vacatur grounds is a congressional prerogative.[298] In *Hall Street*, the Supreme Court employed similar reasoning to refuse to enforce a contractual provision that expanded the grounds for judicial review of an award. Contractual provisions that seek to reduce (or eliminate) judicial review would represent an even more significant intrusion into congressional prerogative. Thus, in light of the Supreme Court's decision in *Hall Street*, US courts almost certainly will not enforce a contractual provision that excludes judicial review.

D. Liability of arbitrators

(1) Duties and liabilities of arbitrators regarding the conduct of the proceedings

13.261 As a general matter, arbitrators and arbitral institutions have long enjoyed absolute immunity from civil liability for arbitral acts taken within the scope of their jurisdiction. This rule is premised on the idea that arbitrators perform a function similar to judges (who likewise enjoy absolute immunity from civil liability) and, thus, need the immunity in order to ensure their independence and the integrity of the arbitral process. Like judicial immunity, arbitral immunity in many jurisdictions does not derive from statute but, instead, is fashioned by court-made common-law principles.[299] (Some states have codified the immunity

---

[294] 9 USC s 10.

[295] *Champion Int'l Corp v United Paperworks Intern. Union, AFL-CIO*, 168 F 3d 725 (US Ct of Apps (4th Cir) 1999); *Texas Eastern Transmission Corp v Barnard*, 285 F 2d 536 (US Ct of Apps (2nd Cir) 1960); *Los Angeles Newspaper Guild, Local 69, American Newspaper Guild, AFL-CIO, CLC v Hearst Corp*, 352 F Supp 1383 (US Dist Ct (C D Cal) 1973).

[296] 28 USC s 1291.

[297] Fed R App P 4 (a)(1)(A).

[298] *Bowen v Amoco Pipeline Co*, 254 F 3d 925 (US Ct of Apps (10th Cir) 2001).

[299] *Kalina v Fletcher*, 522 US 118, 133, 118 S Ct 502, 511 (1997).

rule, and the Revised Uniform Arbitration Act, available for adoption by the states, does so as well). While this approach has been the subject of academic criticism,[300] courts have continued to adhere to it and only created a few narrow exceptions.

The absolute immunity of arbitrators and arbitral institutions encompasses an array of acts.[301] The arbitrator is immune in case of a factually or legally erroneous award or failure to disclose a conflict.[302] Some courts even have extended this principle to situations where the aggrieved party has alleged bad faith, malice or deliberate misconduct. As an indication of the immunity's breadth, courts even have extended it to suits filed by parties alleging either that they were not signatories to the arbitral agreement or that the arbitrator lacked authority to resolve the dispute.[303] **13.262**

The immunity is equally broad with respect to arbitral institutions.[304] The underlying rationale for the extension is that it is necessary to give effect to the arbitrator's own immunity (otherwise institutions might be unwilling to administer arbitrations).[305] Courts have extended the immunity to circumstances where the institution appointed an allegedly incompetent arbitrator, spoiled evidence, engaged in procedural irregularities, mistakenly released the arbitral award, provided defective notice or even acted contrary to its own rules (including prior to the commencement of the arbitration).[306] Even where the claim alleges that the arbitration association lacked jurisdiction, courts will extend immunity to the association unless there is a clear absence of jurisdiction.[307] **13.263**

While the immunity of both arbitrators and arbitral institutions is broad, there are limits, both as to specific acts and as to the type of relief. As to the acts falling outside the immunity, some courts make an exception from immunity in the case of arbitrators who act in bad faith.[308] An additional exception is where the arbitrator engaged in some act unrelated **13.264**

---

300 See Rutledge, P., 'Toward a Contractual Approach for Arbitral Immunity' (2004) 39 *Ga L Rev* 151.

301 eg *Waysl Inc v First Boston Corp*, 813 F 2d 1579 (US Ct of Apps (9th Cir) (1987).

302 *Blue Cross Blue Shield of Texas v Juneau*, 114 SW 3d 126 (Tex App 2003).

303 eg *International Medical Group v American Arbitration Ass'n*, 312 F 3d 833, 843 (US Ct of Apps (7th Cir) 2003); *Tamari v Conrad*, 552 F 2d 778, 780–81 (US Ct of Apps (7th Cir) 1977).

304 eg *Pfannenstiel v Merrill Lynch, Pierce, Fenner & Smith*, 447 F 3d 1155, 1159 (US Ct of Apps (10th Cir) 2007); *New England Cleaning Services Inc v American Arbitration Ass'n*, 199 F 3d 542 (US Ct of Apps (1st Cir) 1999); *Hawkins v NASD, Inc*, 149 F 3d 330, 332 (US Ct of Apps (5th Cir) 1998); *Barbara v New York Stock Exchange Inc*, 99 F 3d 49 (US Ct of Apps (2nd Cir) 1996). For a rare case denying immunity on an unusual set of facts (arbitration mandated by a city that appointed the arbitrator), see *United States v City of Hayward*, 36 F 3d 382 (US Ct of Apps (9th Cir) 1994).

305 *Ozark Air Lines Inc v National Mediation Bd*, 797 F 2d 557, 564 (US Ct of Apps (8th Cir) 1986).

306 eg *International Medical Group v American Arbitration Ass'n*, 312 F 3d 833, 843 (US Ct of Apps (7th Cir) 2003); *Honn v National Ass'n of Securities Dealers, Inc*, 182 F 3d 1014 (US Ct of Apps (8th Cir) 1999);. *Olson v NASD*, 85 F 3d 381, 382 (US Ct of Apps (8th Cir) 1996); *Boraks v American Arbitration Ass'n*, 517 NW 2d 771, 773 (Mich Ct of Apps 1994); *Theile v RML Realty Partners*, 18 Cal Rptr 2d 416, 417 (Cal Ct App 1993); *Cort v American Arbitration Ass'n*, 795 F Supp 2d 970, 972 (US DCt (N D Cal) 1992); *Austern v Chicago Bd. Options Exchange*, 898 F 2d 882, 886 (US Ct of Apps (2nd Cir) 1990); *Corey v New York Stock Exchange*, 691 F 2d 1205, 1211 (US Ct of Apps (6th Cir) 1982); *Cort v American Arbitration Ass'n*, 795 F Supp 970 (US Dist Ct (N D Cal) 1992); *Thiele v RMI Realty Partners*, 14 Cal App 4th 1526, 18 Cal Rptr 2d 416 (Cal Ct App 1993).

307 *New England Cleaning Services Inc v American Arbitration Ass'n*, 199 F 3d 542 (US Ct of Apps (1st Cir) 1999).

308 eg *Postma v First Federal Sav & Loan of Sioux City*, 74 F 3d 160 (US Ct of Apps (8th Cir) 1996); *I & F Corp Int'l Ass'n of Heat and Frost Insulators and Asbestos Workers*, 493 F Supp 147 (US Dist Ct (S D Ohio)

to his jurisdiction. In some cases, this may be a purely private act (like harassment); in others it might be an official act (like an architect or accountant who both resolves disputes but is also involved in other aspects of a project such as the design work).[309] A final exception is for non-feasance. Recall that the immunity protects arbitral 'acts'. Consequently, the arbitrator's failure to act may not fall within the immunity's protection. This was the logic employed by the California Court of Appeal in *Baar v Tigerman*.[310] In that case, the arbitrator failed to render a timely award, violating both the arbitral rules and an extension granted him by the administering institution. While the California legislature eventually overruled *Baar* by statute, the case exemplifies another important, if narrow, limit on arbitral immunity.[311]

13.265 As to relief, the arbitrator is not immune from criminal prosecution. Additionally, some authority holds that the doctrine does not protect the arbitrator from depositions, particularly where there is some prima facie showing of fraud or misconduct.[312] (In that case, the scope of the deposition will often be limited to the alleged fraud or misconduct in order to avoid re-examination of any award that the arbitrator has rendered).[313] Finally, there is a disagreement among lower courts over whether the immunity protects the arbitrator and arbitral institutions against requests for injunctive relief or contempt orders.[314]

13.266 Owing to the broad scope of arbitral immunity, the case law on liability does not contain an extensive exposition on an arbitrator's duties. A few of the exceptional cases finding the arbitrator liable for acts of fraud, corruption or non-feasance do talk in terms of the arbitrator's breaching a duty of 'fair dealing' or talk in terms of his duty to render a reasonable, timely decision, The implications of these conceptions of the arbitrator's duties have not, however, been developed in other contexts.

13.267 Beyond the context of liability, cases in other contexts (particularly vacatur and enforcement actions) have expounded generally on an arbitrator's duties. For example, an arbitrator has a duty to investigate and to disclose potential conflicts of interest.[315] Likewise, while

---

1980); *Grane v Grane*, 143 Ill App 3d 979, 493 NE 2d 1112 (Ill Ct App 1986); *Beaver v Brown*, 56 Iowa 565, 9 NW 911 (Iowa, 1881).

[309] eg *Cahn v International Ladies' Garment Union*, 203 F Supp 191 (US Dist Ct (ED Pa) 1962); *Lundgren v Freeman*, 307 F 2d 104 (US Ct of Apps (9th Cir) 1962); *Peterka v Dennis*, 744 N W 2d 28 (Minn App 2008); *Craviolini v Scholer & Fuller Associated Architects*, 89 Ariz. 24, 357 P 2d 611, 614 (1960).

[310] 140 Cal App 3d 979 (Cal Ct App 1983).

[311] eg *E.C. Ernst Inc v Manhattan Construction Co*, 551 F 2d 1026, 1033 (US Ct of Apps (5th Cir) 1977); *Morgan Phillips Inc v JAMS/Endispute, LLC*, 140 Cal App 4th 795, 44 Cal Rptr 3rd 782 (Cal Ct App 2006) (unexplained withdrawal from arbitration not entitled to immunity).

[312] eg *MCI Construction v Hazen and Sawyer*, no 199CV00002, 2003 WL 22061226 (M.D.N.C. Aug. 29, 2003); *Carolina-Virginia Fashion Exhibitors Inc v Gunter*, 291 N C 208, 230 SE 2d 380 (1976).

[313] eg *Container Tech Corp v Gadsden Pty Ltd.*, 781 P 2d 119, 121 (Colo Ct App 1989). But see eg *Garzella v Borough of Dunmore*, 237 FRD 271 (US Dist Ct (M D Pa) 2006) (relying on immunity to bar deposition of arbitrator).

[314] *Compare Tamari v Conrad*, 552 F 2d 778 (US Ct of Apps (*7th* Cir) 1977) *and Global Gold Mining, LLC v Robinson*, 533 F Supp 2d 442 (US Dist Ct (SDNY) 2008), *with Kemmner v District Council of Painting and Allied Trades no 36*, 768 F 2d 1115 (US Ct of Apps (9th Cir) 1985); *Real Estate One Inc v American Arbitration Ass'n Inc*, 2005 WL 233554 (Mich App 1 February 2005).

[315] eg *Commonwealth Coatings Corp v Continental Casualty Co*, 393 US 145, 89 SCt 337 (1968); *Applied Industraial Materials Corp v Ovalar Makine Ticaret Ve Sanayi, AS*, 492 F 3d 132, 138 (US Ct of Apps

arbitrators do not have a duty independently to investigate the law, the manifest disregard of the law doctrine (to the extent it remains valid) implies a duty not to ignore the applicable law presented by the parties and not to ignore the contract giving rise to their jurisdiction.[316] These various conceptions of the arbitrator's duties (largely uncontroversial vis-à-vis most international arbitral rules) have not been extended into the liability context to support claims for money damages based on misconduct by the arbitrator. Rather, the proper remedy for such 'breaches' of duty is to seek vacatur (or oppose enforcement) of the award.

(1.1) Do the courts and/or authorities rely on a contractual relationship between the parties and the arbitrator(s), irrespective of whether institutional or *ad hoc* arbitration is concerned? What is the legal qualification of such a contract (eg provision of services)? Owing to the 'functional analysis' that guides the absolute immunity of arbitrators in the United States, courts typically have not had occasion to consider the precise nature of the relationship between the arbitrators and the parties (contractual or otherwise). The few cases finding arbitrators liable in case of non-feasance do couch their analysis in terms of a breach of contract by the arbitrator of the agreement between himself and the parties to resolve their dispute.[317] This conception of the relationship has not been more fully developed, nor has it distinguished between institutional and *ad hoc* arbitration. **13.268**

(1.2) Are there court decisions (or authorities) determining which law governs the question of liability of an arbitrator? What is the position of those courts/authorities as to whether and to which extent a legal liability of an arbitrator (or arbitral institution) may be established? Owing to the widespread acceptance of absolute immunity for arbitrators and arbitral institutions, few cases have meaningfully addressed the applicable law governing liability of these entities. Generally, courts in the United States apply their own law (eg federal courts applying federal law), though they occasionally cite precedent from other jurisdictions as persuasive authority.[318] **13.269**

The little authority addressing the matter, mostly arising in the context of whether a particular form of dispute resolution qualified as 'arbitration' (and thus entitled the decision maker to immunity) is mixed. Some cases hold that state law controls the definition of arbitration and, thus, indirectly at least the availability of immunity.[319] Other cases, stressing the need for uniformity in this field of law (an especially compelling consideration in the context of international arbitration), conclude that federal law defines the meaning of arbitration and, thus, the scope of immunity.[320] **13.270**

(2nd Cir) 2007); *Al-Harbi v Citibank, N.A.*, 85 F 3d 680 (US Ct of Apps (DC Cir) 1996); *Schmitz v Zilveti*, 20 F 3d 143 (US Ct of Apps (9th Cir) 1994).

[316] eg *Wallace v Butler*, 378 F 3d 182, 191 n 3 (US Ct of Apps (2nd Cir) 2004); *Champion Int'l Corp v United Paperworks Int'l Union, AFL-CIO*, 168 F 3d 725 (US Ct of Apps (4th Cir) 1999).

[317] See *supra* note 311.

[318] See Lew, J.M., *The Immunity of Arbitrators* (Lloyd's of London,1990) 85–6.

[319] eg *Waysl Inc v First Boston Corp*, 813 F 2d 1579 (US Ct of Apps (9th Cir) (1987).

[320] eg *Salt Lake Tribunal Publishing Co LLC v Management Planning, Inc*, 390 F 3d 684 (US Ct of Apps (10th Cir) 2004).

13.271 The correct answer probably should depend on several factors—(i) the forum (federal versus state); (ii) the basis for subject matter jurisdiction (as it affects the applicable law); and (iii) the choice-of-law clause in the contract (under the logic of the *Volt* decision, it may justify application of a state rule to the extent that rule is most supportive of the arbitral process). As a practical matter, in international arbitration, cases tend to end up in federal court, fall within the court's federal question jurisdiction (arising under ch II of the Federal Arbitration Act) and do not include a choice-of-law clause specifying application of a particular state law. Consequently, in international cases at least, federal law should govern the issue.

13.272 (1.3) **Is an arbitrator subject to criminal prosecution?** Yes. While the case law is sparse, it does hold that an arbitrator is subject to criminal prosecution.[321] This principle follows from the analogy to judicial immunity. Judges are subject to criminal prosecution, for criminal acts *ipso facto* are not 'official acts' within the scope of their jurisdiction.

(2) Possibility to restrict or exclude the arbitrators' liability

13.273 Given the broad immunity accorded to arbitrators as a matter of law, courts in the United States have had little reason to opine on the enforceability of contractual restrictions or exclusions on an arbitrator's liability. If the issue were to arise (eg where a state changed its immunity rule or where the legal immunity did not attach), case law from analogous settings suggests that, under some circumstances, a court would enforce a contractual provision that sought to limit the arbitrator's liability (though probably not a provision that sought to exclude liability altogether).[322] Within limits, courts generally will enforce liability limits in other professional services contracts. Depending on the jurisdiction, the extent of enforceability may turn on factors such as the procedural protections underpinning the decision to waive, the scope of the waiver and the type of claim at issue (with courts generally less willing to enforce waivers in cases of intentional torts).[323]

VII. Enforcement of national awards

(1) Requirement of a particular procedure to make an award enforceable (leave for enforcement, exequatur*)*

13.274 A domestic arbitration award is not automatically enforceable at the time it is rendered in the sense that the prevailing party may not judicially attach the unsuccessful party's assets. In order to enforce a domestic arbitral award, the prevailing party must have the award confirmed under s 9 of the FAA in the court for the district where the award was made.

13.275 (1.1) **Does the national law make any difference between foreign and domestic awards, and if so, which are the criteria? Does there exist an additional notion of award for the purpose of obtaining *exequatur* (France: international awards)?** The question of whether an award may be considered domestic or international under the FAA is answered

321 eg *L & H Airco Inc v Rapistan Corp*, 446 NW 2d 372 (Minn 1989); *Earle v Johnson*, h, 334 (Minn, 1900).

322 See Lee, B., *Modern Tort Law: Liability and Litigation* (Thomson West) s 22:7.

323 See Restatement (Second) of Torts s 496B, comment d.

by FAA s 202. Section 202 provides that an award does not fall under the New York Convention if it is between two US citizens, 'unless that relationship involves property located abroad, envisages performance or enforcement abroad, or has some other reasonable relation with one or more foreign states'.[324]

In the case of a domestic award, ch I of the FAA provides a framework for confirmation and vacatur of the award. In the case of an international award, ss II and III of the FAA enable the standards of the New York or Panama Conventions to govern recognition and enforcement. As mentioned above, the grounds for declining enforcement under the Conventions are narrower than the grounds for vacatur set forth in the text of s 10 of the FAA and the accompanying common law grounds. **13.276**

Generally, US courts honour the distinction between domestic and international awards, applying the enforcement standards of the applicable Conventions to international awards, and reserving the FAA standards for vacatur for domestic awards. As explained more fully below, some US courts have held that in cases where an arbitration that falls under the New York Convention is conducted in the US, review of the award is not limited to Art V grounds, but may be reviewed and vacated on FAA s 10 grounds, including common law grounds such as manifest disregard of the law.[325] **13.277**

(1.2) May awards granting conservatory/interim measures be subject to enforcement? **13.278**
The language of the FAA contemplates that federal courts may confirm partial awards,[326] and US courts have upheld orders enforcing partial arbitral awards, provided the award finally decided an issue before the tribunal.[327] As discussed above, however, courts sometimes refuse to enforce such awards on the basis that they are not 'final.'

(2) Details of such enforcement procedure (competent court, reasons for rejection of motion etc)

In the case of a domestic award, s 9 of the FAA sets forth the requirements for confirmation. The party seeking confirmation must apply to a federal district court within one year of the date when the award was made. If the parties have agreed in their arbitration agreement on a specific court for the entry of judgment, they must bring the motion to confirm in that court. In the absence of such specification, venue is proper in the district where the award was made. The court must confirm the award, unless the award has been modified, vacated, or corrected under the FAA.[328] **13.279**

The unsuccessful party to an arbitral award may resist confirmation by bringing a motion to vacate or modify pursuant to FAA ss 10 and 11. As discussed above, such a motion must **13.280**

---

[324] 9 USC s 202.

[325] eg *Yusuf Ahmed Alghanim & Sons, WLL v Toys R Us Inc*, 126 F 3d 15, 20 (US Ct of Apps (2nd Cir) 1997). Further discussion and examples are provided in section VIII of this Report, which focuses on how US courts enforce non-domestic awards.

[326] 9 USC s 16(a)(1)(d) (confirming 'an award or partial award').

[327] eg *Metallgesellschaft AG v M/V Capitan Constante*, 790 F 2d 280 (US Ct of Apps (2d Cir) 1986); *Sperry International Trade Inc v Government of Israel*, 532 F Supp 901 (US Dist Ct (SDNY) 1982); *Employers Surplus Lines Ins Co*, 2008 WL 337317 (US Dist Ct (SDNY) 2008).

[328] See 9 USC ss 10–11 (modification, vacatur and correction procedures).

be brought in the court for the district where the award was made, within three months of the rendition of the award.

(3) Appeal against the decision granting exequatur

13.281 A party may appeal from an order confirming an award under s 16 of the FAA.[329] The party seeking to appeal will follow the normal steps for appealing against a final order in US courts.[330]

(4) Appeal (and procedure) if exequatur *has been refused*

13.282 Just as a party may appeal against an order confirming an award, s 16 allows a party to appeal against a court's decision to vacate or modify an award.[331]

(5) Procedure of enforcement (attachment of bank accounts etc)

13.283 After an arbitral award has been confirmed, it has the force of a legal judgment, and the creditor party may attach the debtor's assets to satisfy the award. Generally, the law governing the attachment will be the law of the US state where the assets are located. Most states have adopted Art 9 of the Uniform Commercial Code, which gives judgment lien creditors priority on a 'first in time' basis.[332] Federal bankruptcy law may also apply; if the losing party has filed for bankruptcy in federal court, the party holding a judgment will be precluded from executing the judgment, and the bankruptcy court will allocate the debtor's assets among all creditors.[333] Practitioners should consult state and federal law for further information on these collection matters.

13.284 **(5.1) At the stage of enforcement, may the losing party invoke arguments and circumstances which are based on facts which have occurred before (or after) the award was made?** A party whose assets are subject to attachment may not introduce new facts to alter the judgment, after final judgment has been rendered.

13.285 **(5.2) May the losing party invoke a set-off based on claims that are not related to the matter of the arbitral proceeding? Is it material whether such claim came into existence before or after the award was made?** If a party seeks to invoke a set-off during the arbitration proceeding itself, it may do so if the arbitrators so permit. Under the *First Options* and *Howsam* line of cases, the scope of the arbitration agreement is generally a matter that is decided by arbitrators. Once the tribunal has rendered its award and that award has been merged into a final judgment, no set-off claims may be raised.

VIII. Foreign awards

A. Recognition and/or enforcement of foreign awards (national law)

(1) Rules according to national law

13.286 The law governing the recognition and enforcement of arbitral awards in the United States depends on whether the award satisfies the requirements for application of one or more of

329 9 USC s 16(a) (1) (D).
330 28 USC s 1291-4 (federal appeals statute); 28a USC (Federal Rules of Appellate Procedure).
331 9 USC s 16(a) (1) (E).
332 UCC s 9–317, 322.
333 11 USC s 362 (2008) (federal bankruptcy law; automatic stay provision).

the enforcement treaties to which the United States is a party. The question whether a treaty applies to recognition and enforcement of an award generally boils down to satisfying four requirements:

- Was there an agreement in writing within the meaning of the relevant convention?
- Did the arbitration take place in a country that is a signatory to the relevant convention?
- Does the agreement arise out of a legal relationship that would be considered commercial?
- Does the agreement have the necessary foreign connection (either by virtue of at least one party not being an American citizen or the transaction having a 'reasonable relationship' with a foreign country)?[334]

If all these requirements are satisfied, a treaty generally will govern enforcement of the award in the United States; the next two subsections of this chapter explore that regime. If any of these requirements is not satisfied, then domestic law will govern enforcement of the award in the United States; the balance of this subsection focuses on that regime. **13.287**

As noted above, s 10 sets forth most of the grounds upon which an award can be vacated—matters such as bias, fraud, and lack of notice. Additionally, as detailed elsewhere in this chapter, federal courts have created a number of common law (ie non-statutory) doctrines under which courts can decline to give effect to an award, such as public policy and irrationality. The most significant—and frequently litigated—of these doctrines is manifest disregard of the law. Under that doctrine, a court may refuse to enforce an award if the arbitrator was aware of the applicable law and consciously ignored it. This makes the United States one of the few important arbitral jurisdictions in the world where courts retain some opportunity to scrutinize the merits of the decision. As noted above, the Supreme Court's recent decision in *Hall Street* has cast new doubt on the continued validity of that doctrine as an independent ground for vacating (or refusing enforcement of) an award. **13.288**

(2) Requirements to be fulfilled by the applicant (procedure, time limits)

The Federal Arbitration Act provides various rules governing the procedures for award enforcement, including the venue of the enforcement action, the items that must be included in an enforcement action and a filing deadline. As to venue, the FAA expressly provides that the confirmation petition may be brought in the district wherein the award was rendered,[335] but the Supreme Court has made clear that this is a permissive—not mandatory provision.[336] Consequently, the action may be brought in any jurisdiction that would be proper under the general venue statute.[337] As noted above, some courts also have required an 'entry of judgment' in the arbitration clause as well. As to necessary items, the party moving for confirmation shall attach the agreement, the award, orders of the arbitrators' **13.289**

[334] *Bergesen v Joseph Muller Corp*, 710 F 2d 928 (US Ct of Apps (2nd Cir) 1983); *Ledee v Ceramiche Ragno*, 684 F 2d 184 (US Ct of Apps (1st Cir) 1982). See also New York Convention Arts I, II & V; 9 USC s 202.

[335] 9 USC s 10.

[336] *Cortez Byrd Chips Inc v Bill Harbert Construction Co*, 529 US 193 (2000).

[337] 28 USC s 1391.

appointment, orders extending the deadline for the award, and any other papers used in a prior action to confirm, modify or correct the award.[338]

(3) Remedies against decisions granting or declining enforcement

13.290 The primary remedy against a decision granting or declining enforcement is to file an appeal with the federal circuit court of appeal with jurisdiction over the district court that enforced the award. Parties do not need to petition for the appellate court to exercise jurisdiction but, instead, have an appeal as of right provided that they comply with the general rules governing appeals (the most important of which is to file a notice of appeal, typically within 30 days of the entry of the district court's judgment enforcing the award).[339]

13.291 A second potential remedy, of particular importance to parties appealing against a decision that grants enforcement, is an application to stay the district court's mandate. The mandate—essentially the court's order that the losing party comply with its judgment—typically issues 7–10 days following entry of the judgment. Following its issuance, the prevailing party in an enforcement action could then conceivably begin attachment proceedings against the losing party's assets. An application to stay the mandate—which may be filed either with the district judge who issued the decision or with the appellate court that would review the decision—is one device that the losing party might consider in order to forestall attachment proceedings. Counsel should be aware, however, that an application to stay the mandate, particularly in a money judgment action, may require the applicant to post a bond or other security in order to ensure that assets are available to satisfy any judgment.

B. Recognition and/or enforcement of foreign awards (conventions, treaties)

(1) Specific bilateral or multilateral treaties

13.292 The United States is party to several multilateral treaties governing the recognition and enforcement of foreign arbitral awards. Treaties familiar to the international arbitration practitioner will include the New York Convention of 1958 and the Washington Convention of 1965 (governing investment disputes). Less well known but periodically important is the Interamerican Convention on International Commercial Arbitration of 1975 ('Panama Convention'), a regional convention between the United States and various countries in Central and South America. As to enforcement issues, its provisions mimic those of the New York Convention.

13.293 The United States also is party to several bilateral treaties, mostly concerning investment disputes. The United States has ratified BITs with approximately 40 nations.[340] Additionally, a number of trade treaties (such as the North American Free Trade Agreement) contain arbitration provisions. Of course, these treaties would not cover purely commercial disputes between private parties and, consequently, are not further discussed here.

13.294 This robust treaty regime governing the enforcement of arbitral awards in the United States stands in stark contrast to the non-existent regime governing the enforcement of foreign

[338] 9 USC s 13.

[339] Fed R App P 4(a)(1).

[340] <http://tcc.export.gov/Trade_Agreements/Bilateral_Investment_Treaties/index.asp>.

judgments. In fact, the United States is not a party to any multilateral or bilateral treaty governing judgment enforcement. It has signed (but not yet ratified) the Hague Choice of Courts Convention. Consequently, this contrast between enforcement regimes makes forum selection decisions (arbitration versus litigation) particularly important when considering a commercial relationship that might eventually entail enforcement proceedings in the United States.

(2) Existence of a standard procedure for the enforcement of foreign awards

The Federal Arbitration Act sets forth a standard procedure for the enforcement of foreign awards. Section 203 of the Act grants federal courts subject matter jurisdiction over such cases.[341] However, a party seeking enforcement of a foreign award must consider both what courts will have personal jurisdiction over the losing party in the arbitration and what courts will be the proper venue for an enforcement action.[342] **13.295**

In general, the exercise of personal jurisdiction requires a court to be sitting in a state with which the losing party in the arbitration has 'minimum contacts'.[343] Even where the minimum contacts exist, the exercise of personal jurisdiction must be reasonable, according to a series of factors set forth in decisions of the US Supreme Court.[344] Enforcement actions arising under the Convention will be dismissed if they fail to meet these twin requirements.[345] **13.296**

Proper venue will depend on where the arbitration took place. If the arbitration took place within the United States, venue lies in the court of the district of the arbitral seat.[346] If the arbitration took place outside the United States, venue lies in the court of any district that, but for the arbitration clause, would have jurisdiction.[347] Even where venue is proper, however, an enforcement action may be subject to dismissal on the ground of *forum non conveniens*, a doctrine under which a court in the United States will dismiss a case over which it properly has jurisdiction in favour of an adequate alternative forum where a complex balancing test of public and private interest factors favours dismissal.[348] **13.297**

Once personal jurisdiction and venue are established, the New York Convention and Federal Arbitration Act set forth the requirements for what must accompany an enforcement petition: the award (original or certified copy) and the written arbitration agreement[349] (original or certified copy); where relevant, the documents must be officially translated (by an **13.298**

[341] 9 USC s 203. See *Glencore Grain Rotterdam BV v Shivnath Rai Hamarain Co*, 284 F 3d 1114 (US Ct of Apps (9th Cir) 2002).

[342] *Telcordia Tech Inc v Telkon SA Ltd*, 458 F 3d 172 (US Ct of Apps (3rd Cir) 2006); *Glencore Grain Rotterdam BV v Shivnath Rai Hamarain Co*, 284 F 3d 1114 (US Ct of Apps (9th Cir) 2002). Different rules may apply to foreign-government defendants. See *TMR Energy Ltd v State Property Fund of Ukraine*, 411 F 3d 296 (US Ct of Apps (DC Cir) 2005).

[343] *International Shoe Co v State of Washington*, 326 US 310, 66 S Ct 154 (1945).

[344] *Asahi Metal Industry v Superior Court*, 480 US 102, 107 S Ct 1026 (1987).

[345] eg *Transatlantic Bulk Shipping Ltd v Saudi Chartering SA*, 622 F. Supp. 25, 1985 A.M.C. 2432 (SD NY 1985).

[346] 9 USC s 204.

[347] *id.*

[348] *In re Arbitration between Monegasque de Reasssurances S.A.M. v NAK Naftogaz of Ukraine*, 311 F 3d 488 (US Ct of Apps (2nd Cir) 2002).

[349] *Czarina LCC v WF Poe Syndicate*, 358 F 3d 1286 (US Ct of Apps (11th Cir) 2004).

official translator, diplomat or consular agent) into the official language of the country where enforcement is sought.[350] Under the FAA, an enforcement action must be brought within three years after the award is made (a longer deadline compared to the one-year deadline governing confirmation actions for arbitrations not covered by the treaty).[351]

(3) Extent of examination and review of the award by the court

13.299 Section 207 of the FAA (part of the legislation implementing the New York Convention) provides that a court '*shall* confirm the award *unless* it finds one of the grounds for refusal or deferral of recognition or enforcement of the award specified in the [New York] Convention'.[352] United States courts display a 'pro-enforcement' bias to the review of foreign arbitral awards under a multilateral treaty.[353] They apply this principle in a number of ways. First, a number of decisions have stressed that the grounds for refusing enforcement, such as those set forth in Art V of the New York Convention, should be construed narrowly so as not to undermine the treaty regime and its commerce-promoting goals.[354] Second, courts have repeatedly stressed that the grounds set forth in the treaty for refusing enforcement are exclusive and, thereby, have refused to apply the potentially stricter domestic standards, such as manifest disregard of the law.[355] Courts uniformly have held that the party resisting enforcement bears the burden of proving that one of the defences set forth in Art V applies to the arbitration.[356] Finally, a few US courts have held (or suggested) that application of the Art V grounds is not mandatory, but rather leaves a court the discretion whether to enforce an award even when the party resisting arbitration has met its burden of proof.[357]

C. Application of the New York Convention

(1) Application of the New York Convention in practice

13.300 Beyond the application of the general principles noted in the preceding section, United States courts have interpreted and applied each of the major grounds for refusing

[350] New York Convention Art IV. See *Matter of Arbitration between Continental Grain Company and Foremost Farms Inc,* 1998 WL 132805 (US Dist Ct (SDNY) 1998).

[351] 9 USC s 207. See *Seetransport Wiking Trader Schiffarhtsgesellschaft MBH & Co, Kommanditgesellschaft v Navimpex Centrala Navala,* 989 F 2d 572, 1993 A.M.C. 2693 (2d Cir 1993).

[352] 9 USC s 207.

[353] eg *Scherck v Alberto-Culver Co,* 417 US 506, 94 SCt 2449.

[354] eg *Karaha Bodas Co LLC v Perusahaan Petrambangan Minyak Dan Gas Bumi Negara,* 364 F 3d 274, 288 (US Ct of Apps (5th Cir) 2004); *Parsons & Whittemore Overseas Co v Societe Generale de L'Industrie du Papier,* 508 F 2d 969 (US Ct of Apps (2nd Cir) 1974).

[355] eg *Admart AG v Stephen and Mary Birch Foundation Inc,* 457 F 3d 302, 308 (US Ct of Apps (3d Cir) 2006); *China Nationall Metal Products Import/Export Co v Apex Digital Inc,* 379 F 3d 796, 798–800 (US Ct of Apps (9th Cir) 2004); *Baxter Int'l Inc v Abbott Laboratories,* 315 F 3d 829 (US Ct of Apps (7th Cir) 2003); *Industrial Risk Insurers v M.A.N. Gutenhoffnungshutte GmbH,* 141 F 3d 1434, 1445 (US Ct of Apps (11th Cir) 1998); *Yusuf Ahmed Alghanim & Sons, WLL v Toys R Us Inc,* 126 F 3d 15, 20 (US Ct of Apps (2nd Cir) 1997); *M & C Corp v Erwin Behr GmbH & Co,* 87 F 3d 844, 851 (US Ct of Apps (6th Cir) 1996).

[356] eg *Karaha Bodas Co LLC v Perusahaan Petrambangan Minyak Dan Gas Bumi Negara,* 364 F 3d 274, 288 (US Ct of Apps (5th Cir) 2004); *Imperial Ethiopian Gov't v Baruch-Foster Corp,* 535 F 2d 334, 336 (US Ct of Apps (2nd Cir) 1976).

[357] For other cases holding (or suggesting) that a refusal to enforce is discretionary even if an Art V ground applies, see *Four Seasons Hotels and Resorts, BV v Consorcio Barr SA,* 377 F 3d 1164, 1171 (US Ct of Apps (11th Cir) 2004).

enforcement under Art V of the New York Convention. In doing so, they have addressed a number of unresolved choice-of-law questions embedded within that Article. Close examination of these choice-of-law determinations helps to shed light on how courts will apply these grounds in a given case.[358]

In practice, application of the New York Convention has reflected the pro-enforcement bias described above. United States courts reject most enforcement challenges based on the grounds set forth in Art V.[359] They have been especially sceptical of arguments based on the Art V.2 exceptions of non-arbitrability and public policy[360] (except in occasional cases involving arbitration against non-signatories).[361] **13.301**

Nonetheless, courts occasionally have refused enforcement of awards under each of the major headings of Art V. Some of the red flags that can call an award's enforceability into doubt include where the underlying agreement did not satisfy the New York Convention's writing requirement[362] and where a party only had notice of the arbitration after completion of the proceedings.[363] While generally unwilling to entertain objections as to the conduct of the arbitral proceedings, they have occasionally refused to enforce awards where, for example, a tribunal changed evidentiary rules in the middle of the proceeding and punished a party which had relied on an earlier ruling[364] and where irregularities arise over the manner of the tribunal's appointment.[365] **13.302**

One area of New York Convention practice that has generated much controversy in the international arbitration community—the question of 'local standards' annulments under Art V.1.e—deserves special mention. United States courts have offered conflicting views on whether the New York Convention allows them to enforce an award that has been set aside in the arbitral forum (or, if different, the country supplying the procedural law).[366] The majority view holds that enforcement is unavailable and treats the Art V grounds as mandatory.[367] Nonetheless, a minority view continues to endure (albeit barely). The most famous example of the minority view is *Chromalloy v Arab Republic of Egypt*, which enforced **13.303**

---

358 For a regularly updated collection of US judicial decisions regarding enforcement under the New York Convention, see Rosenhouse, M.A., 'Confirmation of Foreign Arbitral Award Under Convention on Recognition and Enforcement of Foreign Arbitral Awards' *194 ALR Fed 291* (rev ed 2008).

359 For a regularly updated collection of US judicial decisions regarding enforcement under the New York Convention, see Rosenhouse, M.A., 'Confirmation of Foreign Arbitral Award Under Convention on Recognition and Enforcement of Foreign Arbitral Awards' (rev'd 2008) 194 *ALR Fed* 291.

360 See generally Campbell, A., 'Refusal to Enforce Foreign Arbitration Awards on Public Policy Grounds' 144 *ALR Fed* 481.

361 See *Sarhank Group Oracle Corp*, 404 F 3d 657 (US Ct of Apps (2nd Cir) 2005).

362 *Czarina LLC ex rel Halvanon Ins Co Ltd. v W.F. Poe Syndicate*, 254 F Supp 2d 1229 (US Dist Ct (MD Fla) 2002).

363 *Sesostris SAE v Transportes Navales SA*, 727 F Supp 737 (US Dist Ct (D Mass) 1989).

364 *Iran Aircraft Industries Inc v Avco Corp*, 980 F2d 141, 146 (US Ct of Apps (2nd Cir) 1992).

365 *Encyclopedia Universalis SA v Encyclopedia Brtiannica Inc*, 403 F 3d 85 (US Ct of Apps (2nd Cir) 2005); *Cargill Rice Inc v Empresa Nicaraguesne Delimentos Basicos*, 25 F 3d 223 (US Ct of Apps (4th Cir) 1994).

366 Courts have interpreted the phrase 'the country . . . under the laws of which that award was made' to refer to a country (other than the arbitral forum) supplying the procedural law of the arbitration. eg *Karaha Bodas Co LLC v Perusahaan Pertambangan Minyak Dan Gas Bumi Negara*, 364 F 3d 274, 308–9 (US Ct of Apps (5th Cir) 2004); *Yusuf; International Standard Electric Corp v Bridas*, 754 F Supp 172, 178 (US Dist Ct (SDNY) 1990).

367 *Baker Marine (Nig.) Ltd v Chevron (Nig) Ltd*, 191 F 3d 194 (US Ct of Apps (2d Cir) 1999).

an award that had been set aside in the arbitral forum (Egypt).[368] *Chromalloy* involved an unusual set of facts—the arbitral clause could be interpreted to foreclose a vacatur action in the forum and the losing party was a sovereign (Egypt) that had obtained vacatur in its own courts. While *Chromalloy* remains a valid precedent, recent case law has called the continued validity of the decision into doubt (without quite overruling it).[369]

(2) Examples of decisions which do not apply the Convention correctly

13.304 As the foregoing discussion should demonstrate, United States Courts largely have a fine track record when it comes to interpreting and applying the New York Convention. They do not display the parochial interests that the New York Convention was designed to avoid and have erred in favour of enforcement. Thus, we have little to criticize. Nonetheless, we acknowledge that some decisions have sparked controversy and flag four for special consideration here.

13.305 First, the *Chromalloy* decision, enforcing an award notwithstanding its vacatur in the arbitral forum, reached at least a debatable result.[370] Both defenders and opponents of the decision can invoke colourable arguments. On the one hand, the notion of a 'floating award' does seem to do violence to the underlying principles of the New York Convention, as embodied in its structure and the *travaux préparatoires*, all of which indicate that the drafters intended to give great weight to the views of the arbitral forum's courts, not only as to enforceability within the forum itself but also as to its enforceability in other countries. On the other hand, a strictly textualist interpretation of Art V does support the decision, insofar as Art V is drafted in permissive terms ('may refuse enforcement' rather than mandatory ones).

13.306 Second, we are sceptical of decisions that allow enforcement actions to be dismissed on grounds of *forum non conveniens*.[371] As with *Chromalloy*, these decisions are not entirely without foundation—the New York Convention does not preclude application of the enforcement forum's procedural law, and *forum non conveniens* is unquestionably embedded in federal law. Nonetheless, the idea that an enforcement proceeding should be dismissed in favour of another, more convenient forum appears to undercut two goals of the Convention. First, it undercuts the Convention's aspiration to shield arbitral awards from parochial domestic doctrines that hinder their enforcement. Second, it runs contrary to the Convention's idea that, subject to a few exceptions (such as arbitrability and public policy), the law governing enforcement should not vary wildly across different fora. The suggestion that another country is somehow more convenient to an enforcement action when the substantive standard should not vary (and the enforcement action is not especially factually intensive) strikes us as at least debatable.

13.307 Third, while we laud the United States' generally pro-enforcement bias toward international awards, some decisions arguably overstretch this point in cases where the arbitrators

[368] 939 F Supp 907 (US Dist Ct (DDC) 1996).

[369] *TermoRio SA, E.S.P. v Electranta SP*, 487 F 3d 928 (US Ct of Apps (DC Cir) 2007).

[370] *Chromalloy v Arab Republic of Egypt*, 939 F Supp 907 (US Dist Ct (DDC) 1996).

[371] eg *In re Arbitration between Monegasque de Reasssurances S.A.M. v Nak Naftogaz of Ukraine*, 311 F 3d 488 (US Ct of Apps (2nd Cir) 2002).

award remedies apparently precluded by the agreement itself.[372] This issue typically arises in the context of clauses that either limit damages or prohibit awards of certain types of damages (such as lost profits or exemplary damages). Where arbitrators award such damages, despite the prohibitory clause, courts have still upheld the award, reasoning that the arbitrator is simply interpreting the contract, and the court should not second-guess the arbitrator's interpretation. While this principle of judicial second-guessing is an especially important one in arbitration, Art V.1.c of the New York Convention would appear to countenance a degree of just such oversight when it comes to the scope of the agreement and the submission. Accordingly, decisions upholding award of damages despite clauses prohibiting such remedies deserve closer examination.

Finally, we believe there is reason to be sceptical of decisions that compel arbitration in a **13.308** *situs* other than the one chosen by the parties. This issue arose in the 1980s following the Iranian revolution where federal courts declined to compel parties to arbitrate in Iran. Rather than concluding that the arbitration agreement was unenforceable, however, the court took the unusual step of compelling arbitration in the United States, even though the parties had not consented to such a forum. Again, we recognize good arguments on both sides. In defence of this line of cases, one can argue that the parties did consent to arbitration, so the rule attempts to effectuate that intent as closely as possible. On the other hand, the decision flies in the face of the consensual underpinnings of arbitration by compelling a party to arbitrate in a country to which it never agreed, an action that has important implications both for arbitral procedure and the judicial review of the award.

IX. Appendix

A. National legislation

Federal Arbitration Act, 9 U.S.C. ch. 1 (2006).
Federal Arbitration Act, 9 U.S.C. ch. 2 (2006).
Federal Arbitration Act, 9 U.S.C. ch. 3 (2006).
Uniform Arbitration Act, U.A.A. s 1 (1956).
Revised Uniform Arbitration Act, U.A.A. s 1 (2000).

B. Arbitratal institutions

American Arbitration Association
1633 Broadway
10th Floor
New York, NY 10019
Telephone: 1-800-778-7879
Email: websitemail@adr.org
Website: <http://www.adr.org>

[372] *Jacada (Europe) Ltd v International Marketing Strategies Inc*, 404 F 3d 1701 (US Ct of Apps (6th Cir) 2005).

International Institute for Conflict Prevention & Resolution
575 Lexington Avenue
21st Floor
New York, NY 10022
Telephone: 212.949.6490
Email: info@cpradr.org
Website: <http://www.cpradr.org>

JAMS
1920 Main Street
Suite 300
Irvine, CA 92614
Telephone: 212-751-2700
Email: smandava@jamsadr.com
Website: <http://www.jamsadr.com>

Society of Maritime Arbitrators, Inc
30 Broad Street
7th Floor
New York, NY 10004
Telephone: 212-344-2400
Email: info@smany.org
Website: <http://www.smany.org>

C. Model arbitration clauses and other patterns

American Arbitration Association model international arbitration clauses:

> Any controversy or claim arising out of or relating to this contract, or the breach thereof, shall be determined by arbitration administered by the International Centre for Dispute Resolution in accordance with its International Arbitration Rules.

or

> Any controversy or claim arising out of or relating to this contract, or the breach thereof, shall be determined by arbitration administered by the American Arbitration Association in accordance with its International Arbitration Rules.

The parties may wish to consider adding:

(a) 'The number of arbitrators shall be (one or three)';

(b) 'The place of arbitration shall be (city and/or country)'; or

(c) 'The language(s) of the arbitration shall be ________.'

International Institute for Conflict Prevention & Resolution model international arbitration clause:

> Any dispute arising out of or relating to, this contract, including the breach, termination or validity thereof, shall be finally resolved by arbitration in accordance with the International Institute for Conflict Prevention and Resolution Rules for Non-Administered Arbitration of International Disputes, by (sole arbitrator) (three arbitrators, of whom each party shall appoint one) (three arbitrators, none of whom shall be appointed by either party). Judgment upon the award rendered

by the arbitrator(s) may be entered by any court having jurisdiction thereof. The seat of the arbitration shall be (city, country). The arbitration shall be conducted in (language). The Neutral Organization designated to perform the functions specified in Rules 5, 6, and 7 shall be (name of CPR or other organization).

JAMS model international arbitration clause:

Any dispute, controversy or claim arising out of or relating to this contract, including the formation, interpretation, breach or termination thereof, including whether the claims asserted are arbitrable, will be referred to and finally determined by arbitration in accordance with the JAMS International Arbitration Rules. The tribunal will consist of [three arbitrators] [a sole arbitrator]. The place of arbitration will be [location]. The language to be used in the arbitral proceedings will be [language]. Judgment upon the award rendered by the arbitrator(s) may be entered by any court having jurisdiction thereof.

D. Bibliography

Born, G., *International Commercial Arbitration* (Kluwer, 2009).

Born, G., *International Commercial Arbitration* (2nd edn, Kluwer, 2001).

Carbonneau, T., *International Litigation and Arbitration* (Juris, 2007).

Coe, J., *International Commercial Arbitration: American Practices and Principles in Global Context* (Transnational, 1997).

Coulson, R., *Business Arbitration—What You Need to Know* (American Arbitration Association, 1992).

Drahozal, C., *Commercial Arbitration: Cases and Problems* (2nd edn, LEXIS, 2006).

Drahozal, C., *New Experiences of International Arbitration in the United States*, 54 *Am J Comp L* 233 (2006).

Goldsmith, J. (ed), *International Dispute Resolution: The Regulation of Forum Selection* (Transnational, 1997).

Hellman, R., 'Arbitration Agreements and the Conflicts of Law' (1928) 43 *Yale LJ* 617.

Hoellering, M., 'How the AAA International Arbitration Program Works', in *Handbook on International Arbitration and ADR* (JURIS, 2006).

Jones, S., 'Historical Development of Commercial Arbitration in the United States' (1927) 12 *Minn L Rev* 240 (1927).

Jones, S., 'Three Centuries of Commercial Arbitration in New York: A Brief Survey' [1956] *Wash U L Q* 193.

Kellor, F., *American Arbitration: Its History, Functions and Achievements* (Beard, 2000).

Lew, J., *Applicable Law in International Commercial Arbitration* (Kluwer, 1978).

Lowenfeld, A., *International Litigation and Arbitration* (3rd edn, West, 2006).

Lowenfeld, A., 'The Party-Appointed Arbitrator in International Controversies: Some Reflections' (1995) 30 *Tex Int'l LJ* 59.

Macneil, I. *et al, Federal Arbitration Law* (Little Brown, 2006).

McConnaughay, P., 'The Risks and Virtues of Lawlessness: A "Second Look" at International Commercial Arbitration' (1999) 93 *NW U L Rev* 453.

O'Hara, E. *et al, The Law Market* (Oxford, 2009).

Park, W., 'Determining Arbitral Jurisdiction: Allocation of Tasks Between Courts and Arbitrators' (1997) 8 *Am Rev Int'l Arb* 133.

Park, W., 'Determining Arbitral Jurisdiction: Allocation of Tasks between Courts and Arbitrators' 9 *Arb & Disp Res L J* (2000).

Park, W., 'Private Adjudicators and the Public Interest: The Expanding Scope of International Arbitration' (1986) 12 *Brooklyn J Int'l L* 629.

Quigley, L., 'Accession by the United States to the United Nations Convention on the Recognition and Enforcement of Foreign Arbitral Awards' (1961) 70 *Yale LJ* 1049.

Rau, A., 'Everything You Needed to Know About Separability in Seventeen Simple Propositions' (2003) 14 *Am Rev Int'l Arb* 1.
Reisman, M. *et al*, *International Commercial Arbitration* (Foundation, 1997).
Silberman, L., 'International Arbitration: Comments from a Critic' 13 *Am Rev Int'l Arb* 9 (2002).
Smit, H., 'Substance and Procedure in International Arbitration: The Development of a New Legal Order' (1991) 65 *Tulane L Rev* 1309.
Stipanowich, T., 'Arbitration and the Multiparty Dispute: The Search for Workable Solutions' (1987) 72 *Iowa L Rev* 473.
Ware, S., 'Default Rules Through Mandatory Rules: Privatizing Law through Arbitration' (1999) 83 *Minn L Rev* 703.

14

UNCITRAL MODEL LAW ON INTERNATIONAL COMMERCIAL ARBITRATION

Marianne Roth

I. Introduction

On 11 December 1985 the United Nations General Assembly (UNGA) adopted a resolution[1] recommending all states to give due consideration to the Model Law on International Commercial Arbitration. This law was prepared by the United Nations Commission on International Trade Law (UNCITRAL) in only six years' time and has been partially amended in 2006. The rationale behind the Model Law was that trading nations would benefit from having an international text as a basis for harmonizing national legislation in the field of international commercial arbitration. Business people who consider entering into foreign trade transactions look for reliable and known procedures to resolve disputes which may arise in connection with the transaction. Thus, in view of national laws on arbitral proceedings which differed widely in different jurisdictions, the need for uniform standards of arbitral procedure had been felt for decades. **14.01**

The first draft for a uniform law was adopted by the International Chamber of Commerce (ICC) back in 1937. In 1966 the Council of Europe adopted the Strasbourg Uniform Law. However, only Belgium ratified the *loi uniforme*. Based on this experience, UNCITRAL did not consider the vehicle of a uniform law; instead, it debated whether a model law or a convention would be the best tool to achieve its goal of unifying international commercial arbitration law. UNCITRAL chose the way of a model law that simply sets an example for countries looking for a proper basis for their arbitration legislation. Owing to its flexibility, such a law is more likely to fit into a state's existing procedural law than would an inherently inflexible convention. **14.02**

[1] UNGA Res 40/72 (11 December 1985) UN Doc A/40/53.

14.03 The output of the drafting process was a great success. After 23 years of the recommendations made by the UNGA, the Model Law has been enacted in more than 50 states, often with only minor modifications. Furthermore, it has also inspired numerous countries and several arbitral institutions to revise their national laws or their arbitration rules. It has thus emerged as one of the most important texts in international commercial arbitration and the basis for further developments in this field, which is now recognized as a specific sector that should not be governed by national particularities.

A. The process of drafting the Model Law

(1) UNCITRAL

14.04 A brief look at the organization of the United Nations Commission on International Trade Law (UNCITRAL) may be helpful in understanding the drafting process. UNCITRAL is a specialized Commission of the UN, established by the UNGA in 1966 with the aim of promoting the unification and harmonization of international trade law.[2] Its membership is limited to 36 states chosen to represent all regions of the world, but its annual sessions may be attended by representatives of other UN member states or by international organizations.

14.05 When UNCITRAL undertakes a specific project, such as the preparation of the Model Law, it usually sets up a Working Group composed of a restricted number of experts, who then work continually and intensively on the project. Working Groups report on their progress at the annual sessions of the Commission. Their completed work is reviewed by the Commission. If the Commission approves the work, it is submitted to the UNGA for adoption.

14.06 The Commission and the Working Groups are supported by the International Trade Law Branch of the UN Office of Legal Affairs, which serves as the Secretariat to UNCITRAL. The Chief of the Branch is the Secretary-General of the Commission. The Secretariat provides major assistance in researching, analysing and drafting.

(2) Background

14.07 The history of the drafting of the Model Law goes back to a recommendation addressed to the Commission by the Asian-African Legal Consultative Committee (AALCC) in 1976. This recommendation was to draft a protocol to the 1958 Convention on the Recognition and Enforcement of Foreign Arbitral Awards (the New York Convention). The objective was to ensure that national laws would not hinder parties from conducting arbitration proceedings in accordance with rules they had freely chosen, for example the UNCITRAL Arbitration Rules, which were completed in the same year.[3] At the time, differences undoubtedly existed between frequently used arbitration rules and national laws which had often been drafted only in view of national arbitration. This recommendation led to a consultative meeting in Paris in 1978 with representatives of the UNCITRAL Secretariat and the AALCC as well as members of the International Council for Commercial Arbitration (ICCA) and the Arbitration Commission of the ICC.[4]

[2] UNGA Res 2205 (XXI) (17 December 1966).

[3] See Secretariat Note reporting AALCC Decision, UN Doc A/CN.9/127, Annex, para 3.

[4] See Secretariat Note on Further Work, UN Doc A/CN.9/169, para 3.

The conclusion of this meeting was that UNCITRAL should initiate steps resulting in uniform standards of arbitral procedure by preparing a model law.[5] The concept of a protocol to the New York Convention was not supported, as representatives felt that this widely accepted and successful document should not be altered.[6] At the 1979 Commission session, where the Secretariat also submitted an extensive report on the interpretation and application of the New York Convention,[7] the Commission decided that the Secretariat should be requested to prepare a preliminary draft of a model law on arbitral procedure in consultation with interested international organizations, particularly AALCC and ICCA.[8] The draft was to be based on the provisions of the New York Convention and the UNCITRAL Arbitration Rules. Its scope of application was to be restricted to international commercial arbitration in view of the specific features inherent in the settlement of international disputes.[9] **14.08**

(3) The drafting process

After a careful study of national arbitration laws, the Secretariat submitted a report on possible features of a model law on international commercial arbitration at the 1981 Commission session.[10] After considering this report, the Commission decided to entrust work on the draft to its Working Group on International Contractual Practices and to request the Secretariat to assist the Working Group.[11] **14.09**

In February 1982 the Working Group considered the Model Law for the first time.[12] Four two-week sessions followed.[13] After each session, the Secretariat prepared draft texts of articles of the Model Law that reflected the Working Group's discussions.[14] These drafts were reviewed at subsequent sessions of the Working Group. Initially, the Working Group consisted of 15 member states of the Commission.[15] Observers from 27 states and six international organizations attended the first Working Group session on the Model Law.[16] Owing to increased interest, the Commission decided to expand the membership of the Working Group to include all 36 member states of the Commission at its 1983 session.[17] After the Working Group had adopted the Fifth Draft and thus completed its work in **14.10**

---

[5] *ibid* paras 6–9.

[6] *ibid* paras 4–5.

[7] Secretariat Study on the New York Convention, UN Doc A/CN.9/168.

[8] See 1979 Commission Report, UN Doc A/34/17, para 81.

[9] *ibid.*

[10] First Secretariat Note, UN Doc A/CN.9/207 (14 May 1981).

[11] 1981 Commission Report, UN Doc A/36/17, para 70.

[12] See First Working Group Report, UN Doc A/CN.9/216 (23 March 1982). This commentary follows the approach of Holtzmann and Neuhaus to cite the Working Group's first report concerning its work on the Model Law as the 'First Working Group Report', although it is a report of its third session.

[13] Second Working Group Report, UN Doc A/CN.9/232 (10 November 1982); Third Working Group Report, UN Doc A/CN.9/233 (28 March 1983); Fourth Working Group Report, UN Doc A/CN.9/245 (22 September 1983); Fifth Working Group Report, UN Doc A/CN.9/246 (6 March 1984).

[14] First Draft, UN Doc A/CN.9/WG.II/WP.37 (15 July 1982); Second Draft, UN Doc A/CN.9/WG.II/WP.40 (14 December 1982); Third Draft, UN Doc A/CN.9/WG.II/WP.45 (13 June 1983); Fourth Draft, UN Doc A/CN.9/WG.II/WP.48 (29 November 1983); Fifth Draft, UN Doc A/CN.9/246 (Annex) (6 March 1984).

[15] See 1981 Commission Report, UN Doc A/36/17, para 67 note 23.

[16] First Working Group Report, UN Doc A/CN.9/216, paras 5–6.

[17] 1983 Commission Report, UN Doc A/38/17, para 143.

March 1984, in its June-July 1984 session the Commission requested the Secretary-General to transmit the draft text to all governments and interested international organizations for their comments.[18]

14.11 The Secretariat conducted a detailed analysis of the comments received[19] and also prepared an analytical commentary on the draft.[20] Before the 1985 Commission session the ICCA held a meeting in Lausanne to discuss the draft, in which approximately 550 experts from 39 nations participated. The Commission adopted the Model Law on 21 June 1985 after carefully reviewing the proposed provisions. Members and observers of 62 states and 18 international organizations participated in the extensive review of the Fifth Draft. The Commission's work at this session is documented in the Summary Records[21] and in its Report.[22]

14.12 The legislative history shows that the Model Law was drafted by arbitration experts—scholars and practitioners—from around the world in order to meet the expectations of all kinds of legal systems and to provide a truly international approach in this specific field.

(4) Amendment in 2006

14.13 On 7 July 2006 the Model Law was amended by the Commission at its 39th session.[23] In its Resolution of 4 December 2006 the UNGA recommended 'that all States give favourable consideration to the enactment of the revised articles of the UNCITRAL Model Law on International Commercial Arbitration, or the revised UNCITRAL Model Law on International Commercial Arbitration, when they enact or revise their laws'.[24]

14.14 The revision of the Model Law contains a new Art 2A, which refers to internationally accepted principles to make it easier to interpret the provisions of the Model Law and to develop a uniform understanding of the Model Law.[25] Furthermore, the original language of Art 7, which was based on the wording of Art II(2) of the New York Convention, was adopted to address modern trade practices and new technological developments.[26] Owing to the growing importance of interim measures of protection in international arbitration, Art 17 was modified and a new ch IV A (Art 17-17 J) was introduced.[27] This new chapter includes a set of preliminary orders and an enforcement regime. Article 35(2) was amended to liberalize formal requirements concerning the recognition and enforcement of arbitral awards and to reflect the amendment on the form of the arbitration agreement in enforcement proceedings.[28]

---

[18] 1984 Commission Report, UN Doc A/39/17, para 101.
[19] Analytical Compilation of Government Comments, UN Doc A/CN.9/263.
[20] Analytical Commentary, UN Doc A/CN.9/264.
[21] UN Docs A/CN.9/SR.305–33.
[22] Commission Report, UN Doc A/40/17.
[23] See Commission Report, UN Doc A/61/17.
[24] See UNGA Res 61/32 (18 December 2006), UN Doc A/RES/61/33, para 1.
[25] See Commission Report, A/61/17, para 174.
[26] See *ibid*, paras 146 *et seq*.
[27] See *ibid*, para 88.
[28] See *ibid*, para 171.

Legislation based on the amendments as adopted in 2006 has so far only been enacted in Ireland (2008), Mauritius (2008), New Zealand (2007), Peru (2008) and Slovenia (2008). 14.15

(5) Travaux préparatoires *as interpretive guide*

The *travaux préparatoires* consist of all documents that emerged from the drafting process described above. As legislative history, this material represents an important guide for legislators, practitioners and courts when interpreting the Model Law. The drafters of the Model Law also recognized the *travaux préparatoires* as an essential means for clarifying the text.[29] This is all the more important because the Model Law frequently employs general language in order to meet the expectations of the various legal systems and uses wording that has the same meaning in all its official languages: English, French, Spanish, Russian, Chinese and Arabic. 14.16

Consultation of the *travaux préparatoires* also increases the likelihood of a uniform international interpretation of the Model Law.[30] Correspondingly, many states expressly refer to them as interpretive guidelines.[31] Canada, however, restricts the recourse to the Commission Report and the Analytical Commentary.[32] Nevertheless, as many provisions can only be properly understood by considering the complete history of the drafting process, this commentary is based on the complete set of the *travaux préparatoires*. 14.17

In this context it should be noted that the 2006 amendments of the Model Law introduced a separate provision on the issue of interpretation (Art 2A).[33] 14.18

B. Objectives and principles

The explicit aim of the Model Law is to harmonize and unify national arbitration laws in order to meet the demands of international arbitral practice. It is intended to provide certainty and clear legal principles in international trade, thus promoting international commercial arbitration and international business. Given that the Model Law is tailored for use in all legal systems, covering both *ad hoc* and institutional arbitration for all kinds of disputes, it codifies internationally acceptable standards of arbitral procedure. 14.19

However, its carefully prepared text not only represents the lowest common denominator of arbitral practice and doctrine in the various legal systems but also establishes an elaborate framework for international commercial arbitration. This framework is characterized by 14.20

[29] eg Commission Report, UN Doc A/40/17, para 60; Summary Record, UN Doc A/CN.9/SR.306, para 19. See also Davidson, F.P., *International Commercial Arbitration: Scotland and the UNCITRAL Model Law* (Green/Sweet & Maxwell, 1991) para 1.10.

[30] Brunel, A.J., 'A Proposal to Adopt UNCITRAL's Model Law on International Commercial Arbitration as Federal Law' (1990) 25 *Texas Int'l L J* 64.

[31] eg *Australia*: s 17(1) of the International Arbitration Act 1974; *British Columbia*: s 6 of the British Columbia International Commercial Arbitration Act 1986; *Bermuda*: s 24 of the Bermuda International Conciliation and Arbitration Act 1993; *Hong Kong*: s 2(3) and Sixth sch of the Arbitration Ordinance 1996; *New Zealand*: s 3 of the Arbitration Act 1996; *Scotland*: s 66(3) of the Law Reform (Miscellaneous Provisions) (Scotland) Act 1990; *Singapore*: s 4(1) of the International Arbitration Act 1994; *Zimbabwe*: s 2(3) of the Arbitration Act 1996.

[32] See s 4(2) of the Federal Commercial Arbitration Act 1986.

[33] See commentary on Art 2A at para 14.72 *et seq*.

broad party autonomy in fashioning the arbitral process, the functioning of the proceedings even where the parties have not made respective provisions, the guarantee of fairness and equal treatment of the parties and minimal court intervention restricted to the necessary assistance and correction.

(1) Procedural autonomy of parties and arbitrators

14.21 Arbitration is by definition a consensual process. Parties may therefore design the rules of procedure in accordance with the needs of their particular case, whether by individual agreement or by reference to proven standard arbitration rules. Hence, it is up to them to decide on matters such as the place of arbitration, the rules for appointing arbitrators and the substantive law.

14.22 If, however, the parties do not make use of their freedom to tailor the arbitral process, the Model Law, in line with the UNCITRAL Arbitration Rules, confers pertinent powers to the arbitral tribunal in order to ensure the functioning of the proceedings. Thus, the Model Law has established a special dispute resolution regime that is freed from national procedural law.

(2) Mandatory law

14.23 There are some mandatory provisions restricting the autonomy of the parties and arbitrators in order to ensure fair and efficient proceedings. The paramount principle in this context is laid down in Art 18, which provides that the parties shall be treated with equality and each party shall be given full opportunity to present its case.

(3) Minimal judicial intervention

14.24 The Model Law reflects the trend towards less court control in international commercial arbitration. Article 5 sets out that no court shall intervene in matters governed by the Model Law except where so provided in this Law. Consequently, the Model Law completely enumerates the courts' intervention powers in the enacting state, so that parties do not have to fear unexpected judicial intervention based on some unknown principle derived from national procedural law. Nevertheless, it must be noted that some judicial assistance and supervision is inevitable, particularly at the post-award stage.

(4) Lex specialis

14.25 The Model Law represents a special legal regime prevailing over any domestic law that deals with the same subject. This standing is explicitly stated in Art 2 of *Bahrain's* 1994 Decree Law no 9 on the Issue of the International Business Arbitration Law. Outside the scope of the Model Law,[34] domestic laws remain applicable, for example laws regulating arbitrability, the fixing of fees, or requests for deposits. In contrast to its priority over domestic law, the Model Law by virtue of Art 1(1) yields to international treaties in force between the enacting state and any other state or states.

[34] For matters not governed by the Model Law see paras 14.102 and 14.371.

C. Structure

The Model Law consists of nine chapters and 36 Articles. Chapter I (Arts 1–6) contains basic definitions and general provisions. Chapters II–VI follow the progress of an arbitration in chronological order: ch II (Arts 7–9) deals with the arbitration agreement; ch III (Arts 10–15) with the composition of the arbitral tribunal; ch IV (Arts 16–17) with the jurisdiction of the arbitral tribunal,; ch IV A with interim measures of protection and preliminary orders (Arts 17–17 J); ch V (Arts 18–27) with the conduct of arbitral proceedings and ch VI (Arts 28–33) with the making of the award and termination of the proceedings. Chapters VII and VIII cover the post-award stage: ch VII allows recourse against the award and ch VIII ensures recognition and enforcement of foreign awards. **14.26**

D. Adoption of the Model Law

Since the recommendation of the UNGA in 1985 an amazing number of states have adopted the Model Law, either verbatim or with some modifications. UNCITRAL lists the following jurisdictions as Model Law states:[35] **14.27**

Armenia (2006), *Australia* (1991), *Austria* (2005), *Azerbaijan* (1999), *Bahrain* (1994), *Bangladesh* (2001), *Belarus* (1999), *Bulgaria* (2002), *Cambodia* (2006), *Canada* (1986), *Chile* (2004), in *China*: Hong Kong Special Administrative Region (1996), Macau Special Administrative Region (1998); *Croatia* (2001), *Cyprus* (1987), *Denmark* (2005), *Dominican Republic* (2008), *Egypt* (1996), *Estonia* (2006), *Germany* (1998), *Greece* (1999), *Guatemala* (1995), *Hungary* (1994), *India* (1996), *Iran* (Islamic Republic of) (1997), *Ireland* (1998), *Japan* (2003), *Jordan* (2001), *Kenya* (1995), *Lithuania* (1996), the former Yugoslav *Republic of Macedonia* (2006), *Madagascar* (1998), *Malta* (1995), *Mexico* (2005), *New Zealand* (1996), *Nicaragua* (2005), *Nigeria* (1990), *Norway* (2004), *Oman* (1997), *Paraguay* (2002), *Peru* (1996), the *Philippines* (2004), *Poland* (2005), *Republic of Korea* (1995), *Russian Federation* (1993), *Serbia* (2006), *Singapore* (2001), *Slovenia* (2008), *Spain* (2003), *Sri Lanka* (1995), *Thailand* (2002), *Tunisia* (1993), *Turkey* (2001), *Ukraine* (1994), within the United Kingdom of Great Britain and Northern Ireland: *Scotland* (1990); in *Bermuda*, overseas territory of the United Kingdom of Great Britain and Northern Ireland; within the *United States of America*: California (1996), Connecticut (2000), Illinois (1998), Louisiana, Oregon and Texas; *Uganda* (2000), *Venezuela* (Bolivarian Republic of) (1998), *Zambia* (2000) and *Zimbabwe* (1996).

Legislation based on the Model Law, with amendments as adopted in 2006, has been enacted in *Ireland* (2008), *New Zealand* (2007), *Mauritius* (2008), *Peru* (2008) and *Slovenia* (2008).

Other countries were inspired by the Model Law to a greater or lesser extent. In fact, every country that has enacted a new law concerning international commercial arbitration after 1985 has at least examined the Model Law in the drafting process.

---

[35] UNCITRAL website at <http://www.uncitral.org/uncitral/en/uncitral_texts/arbitration/1985Model_arbitration_status.html>.

(1) Form of implementing legislation

14.28 Most states incorporated the Model Law by enacting a separate new law for arbitration in general or one specifically for international commercial arbitration.[36] Only a few states incorporated the Model Law in an existing Act.[37] Besides, incorporation is possible either by mere reference to the Model Law (which is then annexed in a schedule) or by direct insertion of the Model Law provisions into the respective national law.

(2) Alterations

14.29 For the sake of harmonization and uniformity as well as in the interest of the users of international arbitration—primarily foreign parties and their lawyers—the Secretariat advised the states to follow the Model Law as closely as possible in preparing new arbitration laws.[38] However, certain drafting changes are unavoidable in order to fit the Model Law into the legal structure of the adopting state, which often has a different form, language and style. The above-mentioned direct insertion encourages such alterations. In the case of adoption by reference as well, additions and alterations are almost always attached to the reference. Some states list the changes in the incorporating act;[39] others modify the Model Law text itself.[40] Only the *Bahrain* Decree on International Commercial Arbitration incorporates the Model Law without any alterations.

(3) Additions

14.30 Certain matters are beyond the purview of the Model Law. These matters include conciliation and mediation, consolidation in multi-party disputes, fees and costs, interest, liability of arbitrators and representation. Various states, however, implemented some of these matters into their arbitration laws when adopting the Model Law.

(4) The Model Law and domestic arbitration

14.31 *Austria, Bulgaria, Canada, Egypt, Germany, Hungary, India, Japan, Kenya, Quebec, Mexico, New Zealand, Spain* and *Sri Lanka* also adopted the Model Law provisions for domestic arbitrations.[41] The laws of *Hong Kong, Malta, Nigeria, Scotland* and *Singapore* allow the parties to a domestic arbitration to opt into the Model Law.[42] *Hong Kong* and *Singapore* require this agreement to be in writing and contained in the arbitration agreement or in any

---

[36] *Bahrain, Bulgaria, Cyprus, Connecticut, Egypt, Hungary, India, Iran, Kenya, Malta, Nigeria, Peru, Russian Federation, Sri Lanka, Tunisia, Ukraine, Zimbabwe.*

[37] *Germany, Quebec, Mexico.*

[38] Explanatory Note by the UNCITRAL Secretariat, para 3.

[39] *Australia, Bermuda, Canada* and Canadian common law provinces and territories, *Hong Kong, Singapore.*

[40] *New Zealand, Scotland, Zimbabwe.*

[41] *Austria*: s 577(1) of the Austrian Code of Civil Procedure; *Bulgaria*: s 3(1) of the Transitory and Final Provisions LICA; *Canada*: Art 1(1) of the Federal Commercial Arbitration Act 1986; *Egypt*: Art 1 of the Law Concerning Arbitration in Civil and Commercial Matters; *Germany*: s 1025 of the ZPO; *Hungary*: s 1 of Act LXXI of 1994 on Arbitration; *India*: s 2(2) of the Arbitration and Conciliation Ordinance 1996; *Japan*: Art 3 of the Arbitration Act 2003; *Kenya*: s 2 of the Arbitration Act 1995; *Quebec*: Title I of Book VII CCP; *Mexico*: Art 1415 of the Commercial Code; *New Zealand*: s 6 of the Arbitration Act 1996; *Spain*: Art 1 of the Spanish Arbitration Act 2003; *Sri Lanka*: s 2(1) of the Arbitration Act 1995.

[42] *Hong Kong*: ss 2L, 34B of the Arbitration Ordinance 1996; *Malta*: s 14(2) of the Arbitration Act 1996; *Nigeria*: s 57(2)(d) of the Arbitration and Conciliation Decree 1988; *Scotland*: s 66(4) of the Law Reform (Miscellaneous Provisions) (Scotland) Act 1990; *Singapore*: s 5(1) of the International Arbitration Act 1994.

other document. On the other hand, a number of states, namely *Australia, Bahrain, Bermuda, Hong Kong, Malta, Nigeria* and *Singapore* provide opt-out provisions,[43] that is the parties to an international arbitration may agree not to apply the Model Law but to apply the domestic law or other rules instead. Except for *Bahrain,* all these states require the opt-out arrangement to be in writing and included in the arbitration agreement or in any other document.

II. Commentary on the UNCITRAL Model Law

Chapter I. general provisions

Special literature:

Beraudo, Jean-Paul, 'Case Law on Articles 5, 8, and 16 of the UNCITRAL Model Arbitration Law' (2006) 23 *J Int'l Arb* 101.
Bianca, C.M. and Bonell, M.J., *Commentary on the International Sales Law* (Giuffrè, 1987).
Felemegas, John, *An International Approach to the Interpretation of the United Nations Convention on Contracts for the International Sale of Goods (1980) as Uniform Sales Law* (Cambridge University Press, 2007).
Herrmann, Gerold, 'The UNCITRAL Model Law on International Commercial Arbitration: Introduction and General Provisions' in Petar Sarcevic (ed), *Essays on International Commercial Arbitration* (Graham & Trotman/Martinus Nijhoff, 1989).

Article 1. Scope of application*

(1) This Law applies to international commercial arbitration, subject to any agreement in force between this State and any other State or States.**

(2) The provisions of this Law, except articles 8, 9, 17 H, 17 I, 17 J, 35 and 36, apply only if the place of arbitration is in the territory of this State.

(Article 1(2) has been amended by the Commission at its 39th session, in 2006)

(3) An arbitration is international if:
(a) the parties to an arbitration agreement have, at the time of the conclusion of that agreement, their places of business in different States; or
(b) one of the following places is situated outside the State in which the parties have their places of business:
(i) the place of arbitration if determined in, or pursuant to, the arbitration agreement;
(ii) any place where a substantial part of the obligations of the commercial relationship is to be performed or the place with which the subject-matter of the dispute is most closely connected; or
(c) the parties have expressly agreed that the subject-matter of the arbitration agreement relates to more than one country.

(4) For the purposes of paragraph (3) of this article:
(a) if a party has more than one place of business, the place of business is that which has the closest relationship to the arbitration agreement;

[43] *Australia*: s 22 of the International Arbitration Act 1974; *Bahrain*: Art 1 of Decree Law no 9 of 1994; *Bermuda*: s 29 of the Bermuda International Conciliation and Arbitration Act 1993; *Hong Kong*: ss 2 M, 34 A(2) of the Arbitration Ordinance 1996, Chapter 341; *Malta*: s 60(1) of the Arbitration Act 1996; *Nigeria*: s 53 of the Arbitration and Conciliation Decree 1988; *Singapore*: s 15 of the International Arbitration Act 1994.

(b) if a party does not have a place of business, reference is to be made to his habitual residence.

(5) This Law shall not affect any other law of this State by virtue of which certain disputes may not be submitted to arbitration or may be submitted to arbitration only according to provisions other than those of this Law.

*** Article headings are for reference purposes only and are not to be used for purposes of interpretation.**

**** The term 'commercial' should be given a wide interpretation so as to cover matters arising from all relationships of a commercial nature, whether contractual or not. Relationships of a commercial nature include, but are not limited to, the following transactions: any trade transaction for the supply or exchange of goods or services; distribution agreement; commercial representation or agency; factoring; leasing; construction of works; consulting; engineering; licensing; investment; financing; banking; insurance; exploitation agreement or concession; joint venture and other forms of industrial or business co-operation; carriage of goods or passengers by air, sea, rail or road.**

A. Meaning and purpose

14.32 Art 1 shapes the scope of application of the Model Law, both in the substantive and the territorial respect. In substantive terms, it sets forth that the Model Law applies to international commercial arbitration and provides guidelines for the interpretation of these terms. With regard to the territorial scope of application it clarifies that the provisions of the Model Law only apply to international arbitrations held in the enacting state, with some exceptions. The scope of application was the subject of extensive deliberations during the drafting process.

B. Substantive scope of arbitration

14.33 The primary goal of the Model Law is to establish a special regime for international commercial arbitration in order to overcome local constraints and peculiarities which create difficulties and adversely affect the functioning of the arbitral process.[44] Accordingly, at the outset the Commission decided that the substantive scope of arbitration should be limited to international commercial arbitration.[45] The reason for this self-restraint may be seen in UNCITRAL's aim to provide a model law that meets the expectations of a variety of legal systems and can therefore be adopted by many countries.

14.34 However, the drafters did not intend to hinder national legislatures from giving the Model Law a wider application, for example by also adopting the model provisions for domestic commercial arbitration.[46] Many Model Law states chose this approach.[47] Although in principle the scope of application was clear from the beginning, the definition of the term 'international commercial arbitration' was the subject of considerable discussion.

(1) Arbitration, paragraph (1)

14.35 The term 'arbitration' has been left undefined in the Model Law, as in most national laws and international conventions. Article 2(a) simply clarifies that this term means both *ad hoc*

---

[44] See Analytical Commentary, UN Doc A/CN.9/264, Art 1 para 22.

[45] 1979 Commission Report, UN Doc A/34/17, paras 79, 81.

[46] See Analytical Commentary, UN Doc A/CN.9/264, Art 1 para 22.

[47] See the Introduction to this commentary.

and institutional arbitration. The drafters intended the Model Law to cover consensual arbitration, that is, arbitration based on the voluntary agreement of the parties. Thus, the Model Law does not comprise compulsory or 'free' arbitration such as the Dutch *bindend advies*, the German *Schiedsgutachten* or the Italian *arbitrato irrituale*.[48]

(2) International, paragraphs (1), (3), (4)

Recognizing that many countries have different laws applicable to international and domestic arbitrations it was necessary to define the word 'international', because parties and arbitrators must know under which system the proceedings are taking place from the outset of the arbitration. This is of particular interest, for example, where a party can apply for leave to appeal in domestic arbitration.[49] The definition was among the most controversial issues that arose during the drafting process. In its final version, Art 1(3) provides four criteria for determining when a commercial arbitration is governed by the Model Law rather than a state's domestic law of arbitration. This approach was preferred to a general formula such as that adopted in the French Code of Civil Procedure of 1981, which considers an arbitration to be international if it involves international commercial interests.[50] **14.36**

(2.1) Place-of-business test, paragraphs (3)(a) and (4) The most important criterion for the vast majority of cases provides that an arbitration is international if the parties have their places of business in different states.[51] Paragraph (4) clarifies two practical situations: first, if a party has various places of business, the place with the closest relationship to the arbitration agreement prevails; second, if a party has no place of business, its habitual residence is relevant. The place-of-business criterion corresponds with the test employed in Arts 1(1) and 10 of the 1980 UN Convention on Contracts for the International Sale of Goods (CISG), also known as the Vienna Convention.[52] *India*, however, did not adopt this approach.[53] **14.37**

(2.2) Further tests In order to encompass disputes not involving business places in different states but showing another international element, the Working Group decided to expand the scope of application and provide for further tests. Hence sub-para (3)(b) qualifies an arbitration as international if one of the following places is situated outside the state in which the parties have their places of business: **14.38**

(2.2.1) Place of arbitration, sub-paragraph (3)(b)(i) A foreign *situs* renders the arbitration international if it is determined in or pursuant to the arbitration agreement. **14.39**

(2.2.2) Place of contract performance or place of subject matter of the dispute, sub-paragraph (3)(b)(ii) Any place where a substantial part of the obligations of the commercial **14.40**

[48] See Analytical Commentary, UN Doc A/CN.9/264, Art 1 para 15; for the arbitration agreement see Art 7.

[49] eg *Hong Kong*: ss 23–23B of the Arbitration Ordinance 1996, c 341.

[50] Art 1492 of the 1981 Code of Civil Procedure.

[51] eg *Vibroflotation A G v Express Builders Co Ltd*, High Court of Hong Kong (Kaplan), 15 August 1994, CLOUT Case 77.

[52] Vienna, 11 April 1980, UN Doc A/Conf. 97/18. CISG is currently in force in more than 70 countries.

[53] See s 2(f) of the Arbitration and Conciliation Ordinance 1996.

relationship is to be performed or the place with which the subject matter of the dispute is most closely connected qualifies an arbitration as international.

14.41 The High Court of Hong Kong clarified the far-reaching consequences of this provision in *Fung Sang Trading Ltd v Kai Sun Sea Products & Food Co Ltd*. The High Court was faced with two Hong Kong companies with their places of business in *Hong Kong*. The sale of goods contract they had entered into contained an arbitration clause which provided that the place of arbitration was *Hong Kong* and that the arbitration was to be governed by Hong Kong law. Payment and nomination of the vessel were to be made in *Hong Kong* as well. The fact that the delivery of goods was to be made in *China*, however, rendered the arbitration international by virtue of Art 1(3)(b)(ii).[54] The High Court of Hong Kong relied upon this decision in subsequent cases.[55]

14.42 In *Vanol Far East Marketing Pte Ltd v Hin Leong Trading Pte Ltd* the High Court of Singapore took a similar view. Both parties had their place of business in *Singapore*, payment and nomination of vessel were performed in *Singapore* and Singapore law governed the contract. On the other hand, the providing of the cargo, the tendering of notice of readiness, the transfer of risks and the loading operations were all performed in *Korea*. In addition, the demurrage claimed was purportedly incurred at the loading port in *Korea*. Thus, the High Court held that the place of substantial performance of the contract as well as the place with which the subject matter of the dispute was most closely connected was *Korea*. Accordingly, the arbitration was deemed international.[56]

14.43 *(2.2.3) Opt-in provision, sub-paragraph (c)* An arbitration will be deemed international if the parties have expressly agreed that the subject matter of the arbitration agreement relates to more than one country. Some Model Law states omitted this provision.[57]

14.44 *(2.2.4) Additional provisions* *Tunisia* provides for an additional general test supplementing the Model Law criteria with the French definition of 'international'.[58] Thus, under Tunisian law an arbitration is also considered to be international if it involves international commercial interests.[59]

---

[54] *Fung Sang Trading Ltd v Kai Sun Sea Products & Food Co Ltd*, High Court of Hong Kong (Kaplan), 29 October 1991, CLOUT Case 20, excerpts published in (1992) XVII YCA, 289 and (1992) 1 Hong Kong Law Reports 40, summarized and commented on by Kaplan, Spruce and Moser 173.

[55] *Katran Shipping Co Ltd v Kenven Transportation Ltd*, High Court of Hong Kong (Kaplan), 29 June 1992, CLOUT Case 39, published in (1992) Hong Kong Law Digest, G 9, (1992) ADRLJ, 235 and (1993) XVIII YCA 175 (excerpts), commented on by Kaplan, Spruce and Moser 186; *Ananda Non-Ferrous Metals Ltd v China Resources Metals and Minerals Co Ltd.*, High Court of Hong Kong (Kaplan), 22 June and 12 July 1993, CLOUT Case 58, excerpts published in (1993) 2 Hong Kong Law Reports 331; *D. Heung & Associates, Architects & Engineers v Pacific Enterprises (Holdings) Company*, High Court of Hong Kong (Leonard), 4 May 1995, CLOUT Case 108.

[56] *Vanol Far East Marketing Pte. Ltd v Hin Leong Trading Pte Ltd*, High Court of Singapore (Lau, Judicial Commissioner), 27 May 1996, CLOUT Case 209, published in (1997) 3 Singapore Law Reports 484.

[57] eg *Ontario*: s 2(3) of the International Commercial Arbitration Act 1990; *Hungary*: s 47 of Act LXXI of 1994 on Arbitration; *Mexico*: Art 1416(III) of the Commercial Code; *Russian Federation*: Art 1 of the Law on International Commercial Arbitration; *Ukraine*: Art 1 of the Law on Commercial Arbitration 1994.

[58] Art 1492 of the 1981 Code of Civil Procedure.

[59] Art 48(1)(b)(2)(d) of the 1993 Arbitration Code.

(3) *Commercial, paragraph (1)*

The term 'commercial' is deliberately left undefined as no satisfactory definition could be found.[60] Article 1, however, contains a footnote which calls for a wide interpretation so as to cover matters arising from all relationships of a commercial nature, whether contractual or not. It then provides an illustrative and non-exhaustive list of relationships that are considered commercial under the Model Law. Though such a list was regarded as a useful guidance in interpreting the Model Law,[61] it was not included in the Model Law text primarily because the enumeration of examples is contrary to the legislative techniques in a number of states. Moreover, some of the examples mentioned do not qualify as commercial in all legal systems.[62] Yet, some Model Law states embraced the text of the footnote in the body of their arbitration laws.[63] **14.45**

The list clarifies that the qualification as 'commercial' under the Model Law depends on the objective nature of the relationship or transaction and not on the subjective status of the parties as merchants, as provided in some civil law countries. The *travaux préparatoires* emphasize that, unlike Art I(3) of the New York Convention, the term 'commercial' should be interpreted autonomously in order to achieve the aim of wide interpretation.[64] Such an interpretation, however, was rightly understood not to touch on state immunity. **14.46**

The examples illustrate the wide variety of cases encountered in international arbitral practice. Thus, several relationships not included in the list should nevertheless be considered commercial matters, such as arrangements to supply electrical energy or to transport liquefied gas via pipeline; the same is true for 'non-transactions' such as claims for damages arising in a commercial context.[65] *Ukraine* expressly added scientific-technical supervision.[66] Other disputes, however, should not be covered despite their relation to business, for example labour and employment disputes[67] as well as consumer claims.[68] **14.47**

---

[60] See Commission Report, UN Doc A/40/17, para 20; for an extensive debate see eg First Working Group Report, UN Doc A/CN.9/216, para 19; Second Working Group Report, UN Doc A/CN.9/232, para 32; Fifth Working Group Report, UN Doc A/CN.9/246, para 158; Analytical Compilation of Government Comments, UN Doc A/CN.9/263, paras 13–17; Summary Record, UN Doc A/CN.9/SR.306, Art 1 paras 7–39; SR.319, paras 23–40; Commission Report, UN Doc A/40/17, paras 19–26.

[61] Fifth Working Group Report, UN Doc A/CN.9/246, para 159; Analytical Commentary, UN Doc A/CN.9/264, Art 1 paras 16–17, 19; Commission Report, UN Doc A/40/17, para 20.

[62] See Third Working Group Report, UN Doc A/CN.9/233, para 53; for a general discussion about the footnote technique see Analytical Commentary, UN Doc A/CN.9/264, Art 1 paras 16–17; Commission Report, UN Doc A/40/17, paras 19–20.

[63] eg *British Columbia*: s 1(6) of the British Columbia International Commercial Arbitration Act 1986; *Cyprus*: s 2(5) of the International Commercial Arbitration Law 1987; *Nigeria*: s 57(1) of the Arbitration and Conciliation Decree 1988; *Scotland*: Art 2(g) of the Law Reform (Miscellaneous Provisions) Act 1990; *Ukraine*: Art 2 of the Law on Commercial Arbitration 1994.

[64] eg Analytical Commentary, UN Doc A/CN.9/264, Art 1 paras 19–20; Commission Report, UN Doc A/40/17, paras 22, 26; Fifth Working Group Report, UN Doc A/CN.9/246, para 158.

[65] Analytical Commentary, UN Doc A/CN.9/264, Art 1 para 18.

[66] Art 2 of the Law on Commercial Arbitration 1994.

[67] Confirmed by the Alberta Court of Queen's Bench (Murray) in *Borowski v Heinrich Fiedler Perforiertechnik GmbH*, 12 August 1994, CLOUT Case 111, published in (1994) 10 Western Weekly Reports 623. But see *Ross v Christian and Timbers, Inc*, Ontario Superior Court of Justice (Swinton), 30 April 2002, published in (2002) Ontario Judgments no 1609 (Lexis), CLOUT Case 505.

[68] *ibid* Second Working Group Report, UN Doc A/CN.9/232, para 32.

14.48 A number of Model Law states omitted the list of examples.[69] *India* expressly provides that the term 'commercial' shall be interpreted under the law in force in *India*.[70] Many other states deleted not only the list, but also the reference to 'commercial' in general.[71] The scope of application of their arbitration laws is therefore much wider than that of the Model Law.

(4) Non-arbitrability, paragraph (5)

14.49 Although the drafters regarded it as desirable to limit the amount of non-arbitrable subject matter, they considered it impossible to provide an exhaustive list of such matters, which could be an easy reference for foreign lawyers and businessmen.[72] The Commission finally adopted Art 1(5) deferring to the enacting state's domestic law provisions on arbitrability. Hence, subject matters not arbitrable under national law may not be submitted to Model Law arbitration, ie they are excluded from its scope of application. Common examples for matters exempt from the domain of arbitration are bankruptcy, antitrust, security, patent, trade mark, copyright and customs issues.[73] As the question of arbitrability is also important in the context of Arts 7, 8 and 34(2)(b)(i), when choosing the place of arbitration, the parties should carefully examine whether the matter in dispute is arbitrable under the laws of this state.

14.50 Some Model Law states expressly stipulate that an enactment confers jurisdiction on a court or other tribunal with respect to any matter, but failure to refer to determination by arbitration does not, by itself, indicate that a dispute regarding that matter is non-arbitrable.[74] In *Automatic Systems Inc v Bracknell Corp* the Ontario Court of Appeal was faced with the question of whether the Ontario Construction Lien Act, providing only for domestic arbitration, rendered the international dispute non-arbitrable. The Court held that only very clear language in a statute could preclude international arbitration. Thus, any doubt as to the intention of a statute should be resolved in favour of the Model Law.[75]

(5) Overriding treaties, paragraph (1)

14.51 Another limitation of the scope of application of the Model Law emerges from Art 1(1), which provides that the Model Law yields to any contrary treaty obligation binding the enacting state.[76] This proviso was introduced to clarify the legislative intent, not to affect the validity and operation of multilateral and bilateral treaties in force in the enacting state. The Model

[69] eg *Canada*: Art 1(1) of the First sch of the Federal Commercial Arbitration Act 1986; *India*: s 2(1)(f) of the Arbitration and Conciliation Ordinance 1996; *Mexico*: Art 1416 of the Commercial Code; *Russian Federation*: Art 1(2) of the Law on International Commercial Arbitration 1993.

[70] s 2(1)(f) of the Arbitration and Conciliation Ordinance 1996.

[71] eg *Germany*: s 1025 of the ZPO; *Hong Kong*: s 34C(2) of the Arbitration Ordinance 1996, Chapter 341; *Kenya*: s 2 of the Arbitration Act 1995; *New Zealand*: Art 1 of the First sch of the Arbitration Act 1996; *Peru*: Art 1 of Decree Law no 25935; *Sri Lanka*: s 2(1) of the Arbitration Act 1995; *Tunisia*: Art 47 of the Arbitration Code 1993; *Zimbabwe*: Preamble of the Arbitration Act 1996.

[72] See First Secretariat Note, UN Doc A/CN.9/207, para 56; First Working Group Report, UN Doc A/CN.9/216, para 40.

[73] First Secretariat Note, UN Doc A/CN.9/207, paras 55–6.

[74] eg *New Zealand*: s 10(2) of the First sch of the Arbitration Act 1996; *Zimbabwe*: s 4(3) of the Arbitration Act 1996.

[75] *Automatic Systems Inc v Bracknell Corp*, Ontario Court of Appeal (Morden, Blair and Austin), 25 April 1994, CLOUT Case 73, published in (1994) 18 Ontario Reports (3d), 257.

[76] Analytical Commentary, UN Doc A/CN.9/264, Art 1 paras 9–11.

Law thus recognizes that arbitration is not only governed by national law but also by international agreements, such as the 1958 New York Convention, the 1961 European Convention, the 1965 Washington Convention or the 1975 Panama Convention. The proviso also covers agreements which, though not primarily concerned with arbitration, contain pertinent provisions, for example Art 22 of the 1978 Hamburg Convention on Carriage of Goods by Sea.

C. Territorial scope of application, paragraph (2)

(1) Strict territorial criterion

As a rule, the place of arbitration determines the applicability of the Model Law.[77] Thus, the Model Law governs the procedure of all those arbitrations that take place in the enacting state. After long and intensive debates, the Commission decided to adopt this strict territorial criterion, though there was also support for the alternative approach, the so-called autonomy criterion. **14.52**

According to the autonomy concept the place of arbitration is not the exclusive determining factor for the application of the Model Law. Rather, it was suggested that the Model Law should also apply if the parties so specify in their arbitration agreement, regardless of whether the place of arbitration is in the adopting state. Hence, this concept, envisioned by the New York Convention, would allow the parties to choose the arbitration law of a state other than that of the place of arbitration. Such autonomy, however, may lead to difficulties if a court of the place of arbitration considers itself competent to intervene in the arbitral proceedings and if the remedies prescribed in the chosen procedural law are essentially different from the remedies in the law of the place of arbitration.[78] Nevertheless, among the adopting states *Tunisia* and *Egypt* enacted the autonomy principle as an addition.[79] **14.53**

The Commission, however, preferred the above-stated strict territorial criterion on the basis that it was used by the great majority of national laws. It further pointed out that the Model Law itself granted the parties wide freedom in tailoring the rules of the arbitral proceedings, including the possibility of agreeing on the procedural provisions of another country, so long as they did not conflict with the mandatory provisions of the Model Law.[80] **14.54**

(2) Exceptions

Articles 8, 9, 17 H, 17 I, 17 J, 35 and 36—provisions dealing with court assistance—apply to any international commercial arbitration regardless of the place of arbitration.[81] Germany added Art 27, which provides for court assistance in taking evidence, to these exceptions.[82] **14.55**

---

[77] eg *Deco Automotive Inc v G. P. A. Gesellschaft für Presseautomation GmbH*, Ontario District Court, York Judicial District (Mandel), 27 October 1989, CLOUT Case 13, as to the applicability of Arts 5 and 16.

[78] Fifth Working Group Report, UN Doc A/CN.9/246, para 167.

[79] *Tunisia*: Art 47(2) of the Arbitration Code 1993; *Egypt*: Art 1 of the Law Concerning Arbitration in Civil and Commercial Matters 1994.

[80] Commission Report, UN Doc A/40/17, paras 73, 80.

[81] See Fifth Secretariat Note, UN Doc A/CN.9/WG.II/WP.49, paras 18–27.

[82] See s 1025(2) of the Code of Civil Procedure with reference to s 1050 of the Code of Civil Procedure, which corresponds to Art 27.

In this respect, Germany considered the proposal to embrace taking evidence abroad discussed in the drafting process but finally dropped it.[83]

14.56 Under Art 8(1) any court before which an action is brought in a matter that is the subject of a valid arbitration agreement must refer the parties to arbitration on request of a party, irrespective of the place of arbitration or the law governing the arbitration agreement. The reason for such universal recognition of arbitration agreements is that an arbitration agreement can only be effective if it prevents the parties from bringing a court action in any state.[84]

14.57 Similarly, Art 9, which provides that a request to a court for interim measures should be compatible with an arbitration agreement, allows a party to make such a request not only to a court in the state where the arbitration takes place, but also to a court in any country.

14.58 Articles 17 H and 17 I allow that recognition and enforcement of interim measures ordered by arbitral tribunals can be sought in any state, irrespective of the place of arbitration.

14.59 Article 17 J expressly empowers state courts to grant interim measures in support of arbitral proceedings, regardless of where the arbitration takes place.

14.60 Under Arts 35 and 36 recognition and enforcement of both domestic and foreign awards can be sought. The scope of application of these articles is therefore wider than the general scope of application of the Model Law.

(3) Floating arbitrations

14.61 A consequence of adopting the strict territorial criterion is that the Model Law does not govern situations in which the place of arbitration is not yet fixed. If a party needs court assistance at this stage—for example, in the process of appointing an arbitrator under Art 11, in a challenging procedure under Art 13 or in connection with the arbitrator's failure to act under Art 14—it must obtain the assistance under laws other than the Model Law.[85]

14.62 Lengthy deliberations were made to extend the applicability of Arts 11, 13 and 14 to the time before the place of arbitration was determined, but the issue was finally left outside the scope of the Model Law because no entirely satisfactory connecting factor could be provided. Five possible connecting factors to the state were proposed: (i) place of business of the defendant; (ii) place of business of the claimant; (iii) place of business of either the claimant or defendant; (iv) conclusion of the arbitration agreement; and (v) in certain circumstances, the residence of an arbitrator.[86] It was also suggested that the Secretary-General of the Permanent Court of Arbitration at The Hague, which is the authority specified in the UNCITRAL Arbitration Rules, might make the necessary decisions.[87]

14.63 *Germany* explicitly provides that in case the place of arbitration has not yet been determined, the German courts will be competent to perform the court functions specified

---

[83] See commentary on Art 27 at paras 14.439–44.
[84] Fifth Secretariat Note, UN Doc A/CN.9/WG II/WP.49, para 19.
[85] See Commission Report, UN Doc A/40/17, para 80.
[86] *ibid*, paras 76, 109.
[87] Summary Record, UN Doc A/CN.9/SR.312, Art 1 para 69; SR.314, Art 1 paras 37–9.

under ss 1034, 1035, 1037 and 1038 of the Code of Civil Procedure, which correspond to Arts 10, 11, 13 and 14 of the Model Law, if the respondent or claimant has its place of business or habitual residence in *Germany*.[88]

(4) Conflict of procedural laws issues

14.64 The drafters did not include a rule to deal with the conflict of procedural laws. Such conflicts may arise if the criterion for the delimitation of the application scope in a state which has not adopted the Model Law differs from the strict territorial criterion of a Model Law state in that it allows parties to select a foreign procedural law. In this case, the courts of both states might consider themselves competent to provide judicial assistance, or both might decline to assist.[89] After consideration, the Working Group came to the conclusion that as conflict rules were generally contained in other laws of the enacting state, it was inappropriate to deal with this question in the Model Law.[90] Thus, the conflict of procedural laws is an issue regulated by domestic law.[91]

D. Transitional scope of application

14.65 Some Model Law states provide that the Model Law shall apply to every arbitration agreement and every arbitral award, regardless of whether they have been made before or after the date of commencement of the enactment.[92] Other states, however, only apply the Model Law provisions to arbitration agreements that were concluded before the commencement of the enactment, if the parties so agree.[93]

Article 2. Definitions and rules of interpretation

For the purposes of this Law:

(a) 'arbitration' means any arbitration administered by a permanent arbitral institution or not;

(b) 'arbitral tribunal' means a sole arbitrator or a panel of arbitrators;

(c) 'court' means a body or organ of the judicial system of a State;

(d) where a provision of this Law, except article 28, leaves the parties free to determine a certain issue, such freedom includes the right of the parties to authorize a third party, including an institution, to make that determination;

(e) where a provision of this Law refers to the fact that the parties have agreed or that they may agree or in any other way refers to an agreement of the parties, such agreement includes any arbitration rules referred to in that agreement;

(f) where a provision of this Law, other than articles 25(a) and 32(2)(a), refers to a claim, it also applies to a counter-claim, and where it refers to a defence, it also applies to a defence to such counter-claim.

---

88 s 1025(3) of the ZPO.

89 Fifth Secretariat Note, UN Doc A/CN.9/WG.II/WP.49, paras 28–30.

90 See Fifth Working Group Report, UN Doc A/CN.9/246, paras 198–201.

91 See Holtzmann and Neuhaus 37 *et seq.*

92 eg *Bermuda*: s 38 of the Bermuda International Conciliation and Arbitration Act 1993; *New Zealand*: s 19 of the First sch of the Arbitration Act 1996; *Ontario*: s 2(2) of the Ontario International Commercial Arbitration Act 1990; *Sri Lanka*: s 2(1) of the Arbitration Act 1995; *Zimbabwe*: s 6(2) and (4) of the Arbitration Act 1996.

93 *Australia*: s 30 of the International Arbitration Act 1974; *Malta*: s 68 of the Arbitration Act 1996; *Singapore*: s 26(1) of the International Arbitration Act 1994.

A. Definitions

(1) Arbitration, paragraph (a)

14.66 Article 2(a) avoids giving a specific definition to the term 'arbitration'. It simply clarifies that the Model Law applies to both *ad hoc* arbitration and to any type of administered or institutional arbitration.[94]

(2) Arbitral tribunal and court, paragraphs (b) and (c)

14.67 Article 2(b) states that an arbitral tribunal can be composed of a sole arbitrator or a panel of arbitrators. Thus, it permits the parties to select the number of arbitrators they wish, which is an expression of the basic principle of party autonomy. Paragraph (c) refers to the national judicial system and clarifies that all competent authorities[95] of a country are included in the definition of the term 'court', not only those organs actually called a 'court'. The primary purpose of these definitions was to draw a precise line between judicial and arbitral dispute settlement organs in order to avoid confusion in terminology.[96] This seemed necessary because some arbitral organizations bear the name 'court', for example the ICC International Court of Arbitration or the London Court of International Arbitration. The definition should also prevent misunderstanding in languages such as French or Spanish where the term 'tribunal'—the word for 'court'—is an abbreviated form of the term 'arbitral tribunal'.[97]

B. Rules of interpretation

(1) Parties' freedom, paragraph (d)

14.68 The freedom of the parties to determine a certain issue includes the right to authorize a third person, including an institution, to make that determination. This is of essential relevance for the determination of the number of arbitrators under Art 10(1) or the place of arbitration under Art 20(1). The Commission added the important restriction that the parties cannot authorize a third party to determine the rules of law applicable to the substance of the dispute under Art 28. This choice can only be made by the parties themselves or by the arbitral tribunal.

(2) Agreement, paragraph (e)

14.69 Article 2(e) clarifies that the agreement of the parties on any matter under the Model Law includes any arbitration rules referred to in their agreement, for example the UNCITRAL Arbitration Rules, the ICC Rules, the LCIA Rules, the American Arbitration Association (AAA) Rules etc.

(3) Counterclaim, paragraph (f)

14.70 Article 2(f) explicitly states that a reference to a claim also applies to a counterclaim, and a reference to a defence includes a defence to a counterclaim. Originally, this provision was modelled on Art 21(3) of the UNCITRAL Arbitration Rules and only concerned the

[94] See also Art 1(1).
[95] This is the expression used in the New York Convention.
[96] Analytical Commentary, UN Doc A/CN.9/264, Art 2 para 1.
[97] *ibid*, para 2.

timing of pleas that the arbitral tribunal does not have jurisdiction over.[98] During the drafting process, a broader understanding was responsible for the result that any provision of the Model Law referring to the claim would apply *mutatis mutandis* to a counterclaim.[99] The Commission added Art 2(f) in order to stress this immanent feature.[100] Art 25(a) and 32(2)(a) are excluded from the general rule regarding counterclaims, as it would not be appropriate to terminate proceedings in cases where the counterclaimant fails to communicate his statement of counterclaim or where he withdraws his counterclaim.

C. No definition of the term 'award'

Both the Working Group and the Commission engaged in considerable debate as to a definition of the term 'award'. A definition appeared to be desirable, especially with respect to Art 34, determining which types of decisions would be subject to recourse. The Working Group considered the following proposal: '"Award" means a final award which disposes of all issues submitted to the arbitral tribunal which finally determine[s] any question of substance or the question of its competence or any other question of procedure but, in the latter case, only if the arbitral tribunal terms its decision an award.'[101] While the first part of the proposed definition—up to the word 'substance'—was widely supported, serious concerns were expressed with regard to the latter part, particularly the reference to decisions on questions of procedure.[102] As there was insufficient time for in-depth consideration of the important implications to a number of provisions of the Model Law, for example Arts 31, 33, 34, 35 and 36, the Working Group left this question open.[103] In view of the difficulty in finding an acceptable general definition, the Commission decided to regulate only the types of decisions where it is important, such as in setting-aside procedures under Art 34.[104] Following the example of the New York Convention, which does not define the term 'arbitral award', no definition was provided.[105] Some Model Law states explicitly state that 'award' means a decision of the arbitral tribunal on the substance of the dispute.[106] **14.71**

Article 2 A. International origin and general principles
(As adopted by the Commission at its thirty-ninth session, in 2006)

(1) In the interpretation of this Law, regard is to be had to its international origin and to the need to promote uniformity in its application and the observance of good faith.
(2) Questions concerning matters governed by this Law which are not expressly settled in it are to be settled in conformity with the general principles on which this Law is based.

---

[98] First Draft, UN Doc A/CN.9/WG.II/WP.37, Art 28 and note 13.
[99] Fifth Working Group Report, UN Doc A/CN.9/246, para 196.
[100] See Commission Report, UN Doc A/40/17, para 327; Summary Record, UN Doc A/CN.9/SR.331, Art 2 paras 10–14; SR332, Art 2 para 2.
[101] Fifth Working Group Report, UN Doc A/CN.9/246, para 192.
[102] *ibid* para 193.
[103] *ibid* para 194.
[104] Commission Report, UN Doc A/40/17, para 49.
[105] See Art 32 for the different types of awards.
[106] eg *British Columbia*: s 2(1) of the British Columbia International Commercial Arbitration Act 1986; *New Zealand*: s 2(1) of the Arbitration Act 1996; *Singapore*: s 2(1) of the International Arbitration Act 1994.

A. Meaning and purpose

14.72 The 1985 draft text of the Model Law did not comprise a provision on interpretation.[107] The current revised Art 2A provides guidance for a uniform interpretation of the Model Law by demanding that due regard be given to the Model Law's international origin, the need of uniformity and the principle of good faith when interpreting it. Where a question is governed by the Model Law but is not expressly settled in it, reference may be made to the general principles upon which it is based. The Commission agreed that the inclusion of such a provision would be useful and desirable because it would promote a more uniform understanding of the Model Law.[108]

14.73 Art 2A was modelled along the lines of Art 2 of the UNCITRAL Model Law on International Commercial Conciliation, Art 3 of the UNCITRAL Model Law on Electronic Commerce, Art 8 of the UNCITRAL Model Law on Cross-Border Insolvency and Art 4 of the UNCITRAL Model Law on Electronic Signatures.[109] The origin of and inspiration for these provisions is to be found in Art 7 of the UN Convention on CISG (the Vienna Convention). Despite the fact that the CISG is a multilateral convention and Art 2A deviates from it on some minor points, the substance of the provision essentially remains the same. As the *travaux préparatoires* of the 2006 amendment of the Model Law only provide very little information on Art 2A, the comprehensive case law and extensive scholarly writings on Art 7 CISG should be taken into consideration when construing the revised provision of Art 2A.[110]

B. Internationality, uniformity and good faith, paragraph (1)

(1) International origin and uniform interpretation

14.74 The first limb of Art 2A(1) provides that when interpreting the Model Law, consideration is to be given 'to its international origin' and 'to the need to promote uniformity in its application'. A closer examination shows the second criterion is only apparently separated and turns out to be a consequence of the first.[111]

14.75 To have regard to the Model Law's international origin means to be aware of the fact that the provisions of the Model Law, while enacted as part of domestic legislation and therefore becoming domestic in character, should not be interpreted by reference to the concepts of local law. This is particularly relevant in common law countries, where national and domestic statutes are traditionally interpreted narrowly to limit their interference with the law developed through jurisprudence. In this context, reference can be made to Bianca and Bonell's commentary on the CISG regarding Art 7(1): 'Instead of sticking to its literal and

---

[107] However, in its Res A/40/72 the UNGA requested that the text of the Model Law together with the *travaux préparatoires* should be submitted to governments, arbitral institutions and other interested bodies. Thus, the UNGA indirectly introduced the *travaux préparatoires* as a means of interpretation.

[108] See UN Doc A/61/17, para 175.

[109] See UN Doc A/CN.9/506, para 49; UN Doc A/61/17, para 174.

[110] cf Binder, P., *International Commercial Arbitration in UNCITRAL Model Law Jurisdictions* (Sweet & Maxwell, 2005) para 10–027, who suggests this method of interpretation for construing Art 2 of the UNCITRAL Model Law on International Commercial Conciliation.

[111] See Bonell, M.J. in C. M. Bianca and M. J. Bonell (eds), *Commentary on the International Sales Law* (Giuffrè, 1987), Art 7, para 2.2.1.

grammatical meaning, courts are expected to take a much more liberal and flexible attitude and to look, wherever appropriate, to the underlying purposes and policies of individual provisions as well as of the Convention as a whole.'[112]

Owing to the international character of the Model Law, reference to its international origin should ensure uniformity in the interpretation of the Model Law in various countries.[113] This implies interpreting its provisions autonomously in the context of the Model Law itself, without referring to traditional principles and concepts of domestic law. In fact, a nationalistic approach to the interpretation of the Model Law would be contrary to its uniform application and to its international nature. To achieve uniformity, the world-wide application of the 'Case Law on UNCITRAL Texts' Database by courts and arbitral tribunals in particular would be a major step. **14.76**

(2) Observance of good faith

Neither the Model Law nor the *travaux préparatoires* provide a definition of the term 'observance of good faith'. Thus, reference is to be made to literature on Art 7 of the CISG. Scholarly opinions on the scope and function of this principle in the context of the CISG are divided. Under the first opinion, good faith 'is merely a tool of interpretation at the disposal of the judges to neutralize the danger of reaching inequitable results'.[114] Under the second opinion, the principle of good faith 'is also necessarily directed to the parties to each individual contract of sale'.[115] It seems sensible to follow the second approach for the Model Law, as good faith should be observed by the parties and arbitrators in all stages of arbitral proceedings and not only in terms of interpretation. Moreover, Arts 4, 8(1), 12(2) and 13(2) of the Model Law refer to that principle by directing the parties to act in conformity with good faith. **14.77**

C. Settlement in conformity with general principles (2)

Article 2A(2) provides assistance in relation to issues that are deemed to be dealt with within the Model Law but not expressly regulated in its text. Thus, the provision has a quasi gap-filling function. Neither the Model Law nor the *travaux préparatoires* provide a definition or a clarification of 'general principles'.[116] However, procedural autonomy of parties and arbitrators, the assurance of fair and efficient proceedings and minimal intervention of state courts may be regarded as general principles within the Model Law.[117] **14.78**

[112] *ibid* para 2.2.1; cf Felemegas, J., *An International Approach to the Interpretation of the United Nations Convention on Contracts for the International Sale of Goods (1980) as Uniform Sales Law* (Cambridge University Press, 2007) (Felemegas) 11 who points out that the paradox 'that internationalism might be better served by a narrow interpretation (. . .) is merely an aberration, or rather an illusion'.

[113] cf Guide to Enactment of the UNCITRAL Model Law on International Commercial Conciliation, para 44.

[114] Felemegas, 12.

[115] Bonell in Bianca, C.M. and Bonell, M.J., *Commentary on the International Sales Law* (Giuffrè, 1987) Art 7, para 2.4.1.

[116] Only the Guide to Enactment of the UNCITRAL Model Law on International Commercial Conciliation (in its para 41) provides a non-exhaustive list of principles that should be considered as 'general principles'.

[117] See ch A. II. of this commentary.

Article 3. Receipt of written communications

(1) Unless otherwise agreed by the parties:

(a) any written communication is deemed to have been received if it is delivered to the addressee personally or if it is delivered at his place of business, habitual residence or mailing address; if none of these can be found after making a reasonable inquiry, a written communication is deemed to have been received if it is sent to the addressee's last-known place of business, habitual residence or mailing address by registered letter or any other means which provides a record of the attempt to deliver it;

(b) the communication is deemed to have been received on the day it is so delivered.

(2) The provisions of this article do not apply to communications in court proceedings.

A. Meaning and purpose

14.79 Art 3 regulates the method of delivering written communications in arbitral proceedings and determines their receipt. The drafters found this issue too important to leave to national laws. Article 3 is modelled on Art 2(1) of the UNCITRAL Arbitration Rules, but differs from it in several details. Yet, none of the changes are substantive.[118]

14.80 Art 3 is a non-mandatory rule of procedure.[119] The parties may agree otherwise, for example, by agreeing on arbitration rules such as the ICC Rules or the UNCITRAL Arbitration Rules which will then prevail pursuant to Art 2(e). However, if the parties wish Art 3 to apply in such a situation, they must exclude any conflicting provisions from the applicability of the arbitration rules.[120]

B. Methods of delivering communications and receipt, paragraph (1)

14.81 Paragraph (1)(a) lists three methods of delivering written communications: (i) delivery to the addressee personally (actual receipt); (ii) delivery to the addressee's place of business, habitual residence or mailing address (constructive receipt); (iii) if none of these can be found after making a reasonable inquiry, sending the written communication to the addressee's last-known place of business, habitual residence or mailing address by registered letter or other means which provide a record of the attempt to deliver it (constructive receipt). The expression 'last-known' refers to the knowledge of the sender.[121] If the communication is delivered by means of one of these methods, it will be treated as received on the day of delivery pursuant to para (1)(b). Thus, the methods of delivery listed in para (1)(a) are not only conclusive of the fact of receipt, but also of the date of receipt.[122]

14.82 After considering further details, the Commission decided that the provision should not set forth excessively detailed procedural requirements, as doing so might hinder adoption

[118] See Holtzmann, H.M. and Neuhaus, J.E., *A Guide To The UNCITRAL Model Law On International Commercial Arbitration: Legislative History and Commentary* (Kluwer Law and Taxation Publishers, 1989) (Holtzmann and Neuhaus), 186 *et seq.*

[119] See Commission Report, UN Doc A/40/17, Art 3 para 45; the Commission placed this provision, which was originally drafted as Art 2(e), in a separate article because it was neither a definition nor a rule of interpretation but a rule of procedure.

[120] Broches, A., *Commentary on the UNCITRAL Model Law on International Commercial Arbitration* (Kluwer Law and Taxation Publishers, 1990) (Broches) 26.

[121] Commission Report, UN Doc A/40/17, para 41.

[122] Dore, I.I., *The UNCITRAL Framework for Arbitration in Contemporary Perspective* (Graham & Trotman/Martinus Nijhoff, 1993) 104.

by national legislatures.[123] Many Model Law states brought this provision in line with their national procedural requirements.[124]

C. Scope of application, paragraph (2)

Article 3 only applies to written communications, either from a party or from the arbitral tribunal, and only in arbitral proceedings. This includes any steps by a party, an arbitrator or an appointing authority in the appointment process.[125] Paragraph (2) clarifies that this provision does not apply to documents sent in court proceedings, including measures.[126] When a state designates an authority other than a court to exercise the functions set forth in Art 6, eg a Chamber of Commerce acting as appointing authority pursuant to Art 11(4), Art 3 is applicable, as only proceedings of courts as defined in Art 2(c) are exempted.[127] **14.83**

Article 3 applies to written communications by a party, an arbitrator, or an appointing authority in the process of appointing arbitrators prior to any court involvement (Art 11), the request that a dispute be referred to arbitration (Art 21), statements of claim and defence (Art 23) and delivery of the arbitral award (Art 31(4)). **14.84**

Article 3 does not apply to documents filed in courts under the challenge procedures (Art 13(3)), requests to courts to decide on the jurisdiction of the arbitral tribunal (Art 16(3)), proceedings to seek court assistance in taking evidence (Art 27) and proceedings to set aside or enforce the arbitral award (Arts 34–36). **14.85**

Article 4. Waiver of right to object

A party who knows that any provision of this Law from which the parties may derogate or that any requirement under the arbitration agreement has not been complied with and yet proceeds with the arbitration without stating his objection to such non-compliance without undue delay or, if a time-limit is provided therefore, within such period of time, shall be deemed to have waived his right to object.

A. Meaning and purpose

As a general rule, a party has the right to object to any failure to comply with a procedural requirement, whether laid down in a provision of the Model Law or in the arbitration agreement. Article 4 contains an implied waiver of this right under certain conditions, based on a general principle known in various legal systems as 'waiver', 'estoppel' or '*venire contra factum proprium*'. There was extensive discussion on the appropriateness of such a provision. However, the Commission was of the opinion that a general waiver rule would help the arbitral process function efficiently and in good faith and would help achieve greater uniformity on the matter.[128] Article 4 is modelled on Art 30 of the UNCITRAL Arbitration Rules, but in view of its rigorous effect the prerequisites were softened. A party **14.86**

123 Commission Report, UN Doc A/40/17, paras 42–3.
124 eg *Bulgaria* Art 32 of the LICA .
125 Commission Report, UN Doc A/40/17, Art 2 para 106.
126 See *ibid.*
127 *ibid*; Holtzmann and Neuhaus, 185.
128 Commission Report, UN Doc A/40/17, para 53.

shall only be deemed to have waived his right to object if a number of expressed conditions are fulfilled.

B. Conditions for the operation of the waiver rule

(1) Non-compliance with a non-mandatory provision or the arbitration agreement

14.87 The procedural requirement that has not been complied with must have been contained either in a non-mandatory provision of the Model Law or in the arbitration agreement.

14.88 **(1.1) Non-mandatory and mandatory provisions** The scope of Art 4 is limited to provisions from which the parties may derogate, ie non-mandatory provisions. This implies that a party cannot waive his right to object to failure to comply with a mandatory provision of the Model Law. In its original form Art 4 provided for a waiver from both mandatory and non-mandatory provisions, but the effect of waiver resulting from a non-compliance with a mandatory provision was felt to be too rigid.[129] Mandatory provisions that cannot be waived under Art 4 are the requirements that the arbitration agreement be in writing (Art 7(2)), that the parties be treated with equality and that each party be given a full opportunity to present his case (Art 18), that a party be given notice of any hearing and be sent any materials supplied to the arbitral tribunal by the other party (Art 24(2), (3)), that an award—including an award on agreed terms pursuant to Art 30(2)—be in writing (Art 31(1)), that it state its date and the place of arbitration (Art 31(3)) and that it be delivered to each party (Art 31(4)).

14.89 However, some mandatory provisions contain a waiver of sorts. Article 7(2) sets out that an arbitration agreement is in writing if it is contained in an exchange of statements of claim and defence in which the existence of an agreement is alleged by one party and not denied by another. Under Art 12(2) a party would not be permitted to challenge an arbitrator on a ground that he was aware of at the time of his participation in the appointment or if he had the option to veto the appointment but failed to do so. Under Art 16(2) a plea that the arbitral tribunal does not have jurisdiction must be raised at a certain time, unless the delay is justified.

14.90 **(1.2) Arbitration agreement** The procedural requirement that has not been complied with must be contained in an arbitration agreement, must be valid and not in conflict with a mandatory provision of the Model Law.[130] It is doubtful whether the definition of the term 'arbitration agreement' in Art 7—that is, an agreement to submit disputes to arbitration—is appropriate in this context. At one time the Secretariat rightly noted that parties commonly agree on procedural issues long after the arbitration clause has been included, which means whenever a dispute arises or even during the arbitral proceedings.[131] The Working Group did not address this issue even though it is of importance. The solution provided by Holtzmann and Neuhaus[132] seems to be a sound one: if the separate procedural agreement is in writing, it shall be considered part of the arbitration agreement as

[129] See Fourth Working Group Report, UN Doc A/CN.9/245, para 178; Fifth Working Group Report, UN Doc A/CN.9/246, paras 180, 182; Analytical Commentary, UN Doc A/CN.9/264, Art 4 para 2.

[130] Analytical Commentary, UN Doc A/CN.9/264, Art 4 para 2.

[131] Fourth Secretariat Note, UN Doc A/CN.9/WG.II/WP.50, paras 12–14.

[132] Holtzmann and Neuhaus, 197.

defined in Art 7. If the separate procedural stipulation is made orally, the arbitral tribunal, in view of its general power under Art 19(2), shall recognize such an oral agreement only to the extent that the agreement is invoked in a timely manner.

(2) Knowledge

The second condition for a waiver is that the respective party was aware of the non-compliance. The first drafts embraced the case that a party 'ought to have known' of the non-compliance, but the Commission decided to delete those words from the corresponding provision in the UNCITRAL Arbitration Rules, as they might create more problems than they solve.[133] Thus, positive knowledge of the waiving party is required. **14.91**

(3) Time limit

The third condition is that the party does not state his objection within the time limit provided for in the Model Law or in the arbitration agreement. The Model Law, in Art 13, provides a time limit for challenging an arbitrator. Arbitration agreements referring to a set of arbitration rules incorporate the time limits of those rules. If there is no explicit time period imposed, the objection must be raised without undue delay. Originally, the Model Law used the term 'promptly', as provided in Art 30 of the UNCITRAL Arbitration Rules. In order to soften the provision, the Working Group changed the wording to 'without delay'[134] and later to 'without undue delay'[135], a term used in Art 19(2) of the Vienna Convention of 1980. Thus, only a delay that cannot be properly justified is not encompassed in the party's right to object. **14.92**

(4) Proceeding with the arbitration

A party who does not state his objection loses his right to object only if he proceeds with the arbitration. This means an appearance at a hearing, communication to the arbitral tribunal or to the other party or other acts relating to the arbitral proceedings. The Secretariat commented that a party would not be deemed to have waived his right to object if a postal strike or similar impediment prevented him from sending any communication at all for an extended period of time.[136] It may be noted that in case a party does not proceed with the arbitration but instead refuses to continue with the proceedings, Art 25(c) regulates that the arbitral tribunal may continue the proceedings and make the award on the evidence before it. **14.93**

C. Effect of waiver

A party who is deemed to have waived his right to object is precluded from raising the objection during the subsequent stages of the arbitral proceedings and after the rendering of the award. In particular, the party may not invoke the non-compliance as a ground for setting aside the award or as a reason for refusing its recognition or enforcement.[137] The Commission confirmed the view that the effect of a waiver under Art 4 is not limited to the **14.94**

---

[133] Commission Report, UN Doc A/40/17, para 54.
[134] Fourth Working Group Report, UN Doc A/CN.9/245, para 178.
[135] Commission Report, UN Doc A/40/17, para 56.
[136] Analytical Commentary, UN Doc A/CN.9/264, Art 4 para 5.
[137] *ibid*, para 6.

arbitral proceedings alone, but extends to subsequent court proceedings in the context of Arts 34 and 36.[138] It has to be noted, however, that the court in the setting aside or enforcement proceedings is not bound by the decision of the arbitral tribunal, so that it might come to a different conclusion as to whether a party has waived his right to object.[139] Yet, the court may be expected to have a healthy respect for the judgment of the arbitrator who knew the particular circumstances of the case.[140]

Article 5. Extent of court intervention

In matters governed by this Law, no court shall intervene except where so provided in this Law.

Special literature:

Herrmann, Gerold, 'The role of the courts under the UNCITRAL Model Law script' in Julian D.M. Lew (ed), *Contemporary Problems in International Arbitration* (Martinus Nijhoff Publishers, 1987) 164.

Hunter, J. and Martin, H., 'Judicial assistance for the arbitrator' in Julian D.M. Lew (ed), *Contemporary Problems in International Arbitration* (Martinus Nijhoff Publishers, 1987) 195.

Melis, Werner, 'Arbitration and the Courts', in P. Sanders (ed), *UNCITRAL's Project for a Model Law on International Commercial Arbitration*, Interim meeting Lausanne, 9–12 May 1984 (ICCA Congress Series no 2, 1984) 83.

A. Meaning and purpose

14.95 One of the objectives of the Model Law is to limit the involvement of national courts in international commercial arbitration. This brief provision is of utmost importance for this objective. The purpose of Art 5 is to compel the drafters of the Model Law and national legislators to state all instances of court control in the law on international commercial arbitration, in order to achieve certainty as to the maximum extent of court involvement to parties and arbitrators alike.[141] Parties and arbitrators shall not be confronted with unexpected general or residual powers of a court granted under the respective domestic system.[142]

14.96 Art 5 was the subject of considerable debate regarding its restrictive scope of court control and its categorical wording. It should be noted that the drafters of a law on international commercial arbitration will not be hindered from extending the scope of court involvement if this is felt to be necessary.[143] However, the drafters should exercise restraint in this important issue in view of the desirability of promoting uniformity in Model Law jurisdictions and being mindful that extensive court control is regarded as an obstacle in practice.

138 Commission Report, UN Doc A/40/17, Art 4 para 57; Seventh Secretariat Note, UN Doc A/CN.9/264, Art 4 para 6; Fifth Working Group Report, UN Doc A/CN.9/264, Art 4 para 181.

139 Commission Report, UN Doc A/40/17, Art 4 para 57; Summary Record, UN Doc A/CN.9/SR.308, Art 4 para 61.

140 Holtzmann and Neuhaus, 200.

141 Commission Report, UN Doc A/40/17, para 63.

142 Analytical Commentary, UN Doc A/CN.9/264, Art 4 para 2.

143 Commission Report, UN Doc A/40/17, para 63.

B. Court involvement under the Model Law

During the drafting process it was widely agreed that the term 'intervene' covers both assistance from the courts and judicial intervention.[144] Therefore, Art 5 deals with the whole scope of court involvement under the Model Law. 14.97

(1) Provisions

The Model Law provides for court involvement in the following instances: 14.98

- (i) under Art 8(1) where, if a party so requests, the court before which an action is brought in a matter that is the subject of a valid arbitration agreement must refer the parties to arbitration;
- (ii) under Art 9 where the court may grant interim measures of protection;
- (iii) under Art 11(3) and (4) where the court appoints an arbitrator when the appointment procedure fails;
- (iv) under Art 13(3) where the court decides on the challenge of an arbitrator when the challenge under priority procedures is not successful;
- (v) under Art 14(1)(2) where, at a party's request, the court decides on the termination of an arbitrator's mandate;
- (vi) under Art 16(3) where, if a party so requests, the court reviews an arbitral tribunal's decision on its own jurisdiction;
- (vii) under Art 27 where a party requests the court's assistance in taking evidence;
- (viii) under Art 34 where the court decides upon an application for setting aside an arbitral award; and
- (ix) under Arts 35 and 36 where the court recognizes and enforces an arbitral award, or refuses recognition and enforcement.

(2) Matters governed by this Law

Article 5 is limited to 'matters governed by this Law'. Therefore, courts can assist or intervene in an area not governed by the Model Law. There was serious debate about the distinction between these two areas, as the silence of the Model Law on an issue does not necessarily mean that this issue is a matter not governed by the Model Law. It could rather mean that the drafters had considered the situation and decided that it was a matter governed by the Model Law, but had determined to exclude court involvement; alternatively, it could mean that the drafters had not considered the situation at all.[145] The Commission rightly pointed out that in the great majority of cases the normal rules of statutory interpretation, taking into account the principles underlying the text of the Model Law, lead to an answer.[146] 14.99

(2.1) Guidelines for interpretation Not every issue relating to 'international commercial arbitration' is governed by the Model Law. The scope of Art 5 is narrower than the substantive scope of arbitration provided in Art 1. Article 5 was intended to refer only to 14.100

---

[144] See Summary Record, UN Doc A/CN.9/SR.309, Art 4 para 40.

[145] See Analytical Compilation of Government Comments, UN Doc A/CN.9/263/ADD.2 (UK Comments), Art 5 paras 20–6.

[146] Commission Report, UN Doc A/40/17, para 61.

those matters that were, in fact, governed by or regulated in the Model Law, whether expressly or implicitly.[147]

14.101 The Secretariat submitted that deciding whether a matter is implicitly governed by the Model Law is not always an easy task. It suggested, for example, that Art 11(2), which grants the parties freedom to agree on a procedure for appointing arbitrators, implied the exclusion of any court intervention in this regard, such as court confirmation as required under some laws. On the other hand, Art 17, which governs the arbitral tribunal's power to order interim measures of protection, does not regulate the possible enforcement of these measures. The question of enforcement is therefore a matter not governed by the Model Law but by domestic law.[148]

14.102 (2.2) **Matters not governed by the Model Law** The Working Group and the Secretariat provided non-exhaustive lists of matters not governed by the Model Law.[149] Examples of such matters are: the capacity of the parties to conclude the arbitration agreement; the contractual relations between the parties and the arbitrators or the arbitral institution; the question of arbitrability; representation and assistance; the impact of state immunity; the competence of the arbitral tribunal to adapt and supplement contracts; the burden of proof; fees and other costs, including security thereof; the liability of the arbitrators; the role of the courts prior to the selection of the place of arbitration; the period of time for the enforcement of the arbitral award; the consolidation of the arbitral proceedings.

(3) No opting-out provision

14.103 The Commission rejected a proposal to allow parties to agree on a wider scope of court intervention, primarily because it did not believe that the parties could deal properly with this complex issue.[150] Thus, the issue of court involvement remains a matter regulated by legislature.

Article 6. Court or other authority for certain functions of arbitration assistance and supervision

The functions referred to in Articles 11(3), 11(4), 13(3), 14, 16(3) and 34(2) shall be performed by . . . [Each State enacting this model law specifies the court, courts or, where referred to therein, other authority competent to perform these functions.]

A. Meaning and purpose

14.104 Article 6 calls upon each state enacting the Model Law to designate a court or other authority which is to perform certain functions of assistance and intervention under the Model Law. Its intention is to concentrate the listed arbitration-related functions in a single body that would help foreign parties to locate the competent court or authority and obtain information on its practices and previous decisions. Furthermore, the experience of one competent court would be beneficial to the functioning of international commercial arbitration.[151]

---

[147] See Analytical Commentary, UN Doc A/CN.9/264, Art 4 para 5.

[148] See *ibid*, para 6.

[149] Fifth Working Group Report, UN Doc A/CN.9/246, para 188; Analytical Commentary, UN Doc A/CN.9/264, Art 4 para 5; see also Introduction of this commentary.

[150] Commission Report, UN Doc A/40/17, para 64.

[151] Analytical Commentary, UN Doc A/CN.9/264, Art 6 para 2.

However, the wording makes clear that the enacting state may designate more than one court or authority.

Especially large states or federal states may wish to designate a type of court, for example any commercial courts or commercial chambers of district courts. It was understood that the state may designate any court, type of court or authority which is deemed appropriate in its system. 14.105

B. Court functions

Article 6 does not refer to all court functions under the Model Law. It lists the appointment of arbitrators under Art 11, the decision to challenge an arbitrator under Art 13, the decision on the termination of an arbitrator's mandate under Art 14, the ruling on the jurisdiction of the arbitral tribunal under Art 16 and the decision upon an application for setting aside under Art 34. Article 6 makes no reference to the obligation of the court to refer matters subject to a valid arbitration agreement to arbitration under Art 8, to the power of the court to grant interim measures of protection under Art 9, to court assistance in taking evidence under Art 27 or the decision on an application for recognition and enforcement under Arts 35 and 36 because these provisions apply to all courts of a Model Law state. 14.106

In departing from the Model Law, the arbitration law of *Japan* gives the Japanese courts certain powers of jurisdiction, such as to appoint arbitrators if there is a possibility that the place of arbitration will be in Japan and one of the parties has its principal place of business in Japan.[152]

Chapter II. Arbitration agreement

Special literature:

Bachand, Frederic, 'Does article 8 of the Model Law call for full or prima facie review of the arbitral tribunal's jurisdiction?' (2006) 22 *Arb Int'l* 463.

Beraudo, Jean-Paul, 'Case Law on Articles 5, 8, and 16 of the UNCITRAL Model Arbitration Law' (2006) 23 *J Int'l Arb* 101.

Bösch, Axel and Farnsworth, Joanna (eds), *Provisional Remedies in International Commercial Arbitration—A Practitioner Handbook* (Walter de Gruyter, 1994).

Castellani, Luca, 'UNCITRAL Developments on Arbitration Agreements in Electronic Form' (2005) 24 *The Arbitrator & Mediator* 19.

Herrmann, Gerold, *The Arbitration Agreement as the Foundation of Arbitration and Its Recognition by the Courts, in International Arbitration Congress, International Arbitration in a Changing World: Conference, Bahrain, 14–16 February 1993* (ICCA Congress Series no 6, Kluwer Law and Taxation Publishers, 1994).

Horn, Norbert, 'The Arbitration Agreement in Light of Case Law of the UNCITRAL Model Law (Arts 7 and 8)' (2005) 8 *Int'l Arb L Rev* 146.

Jacobs, Marcus, S., 'Requirement of writing and of signature under the UNCITRAL Model Law and the New York Convention' (2006) 21 *Mealey's Int'l Arb Rep* 46.

Kaplan, Neil, 'Is the need for writing as expressed in the New York Convention and the Model Law out of step with commercial practice?' (1996) 5 *Asia Pacific L Rev* 1.

[152] Art 8 of the Japanese Arbitration Act 2003.

Kröll, Stefan, '20 Year UNCITRAL Model Law: Selected problems of the arbitration agreement in light of the jurisprudence' (2006) 21 *Mealey's Int'l Arb Rep* 33.
Kucherepa, Peter, 'Reviewing trends and proposals to recognize oral agreements to arbitrate in international arbitration law' (2005) 16 *Am Rev Int'l Arb* 409.
Lew, Julian D.M., 'Arbitration Agreements: Form and Character' in Petar Sarcevic (ed), *Essays on International Commercial Arbitration* (Graham & Trotman/Martinus Nijhoff, 1989).
Liebscher, Christoph, 'Interpretation of the Written Form Requirement Art 7(2) UNCITRAL Model Law' (2005) 8 *Int'l Arb L Rev* 164.
Senni, Tommaso, 'Electronic signatures: the UNCITRAL Model Law' (2005) *Revue de droit des affaires internationales* 55.
Szurski, Tadeusz, 'Arbitration Agreement and Competence of the Arbitral Tribunal' in Pieter Sanders (ed), *UNCITRAL's Project for a Model Law on International Commercial Arbitration, Interim meeting, Lausanne, 9–12 May 1984* (ICCA Congress Series no 2 1984).

Option I

Article 7. Definition and form of arbitration agreement

(As adopted by the Commission at its 39th session, in 2006)

(1) 'Arbitration agreement' is an agreement by the parties to submit to arbitration all or certain disputes which have arisen or which may arise between them in respect of a defined legal relationship, whether contractual or not. An arbitration agreement may be in the form of an arbitration clause in a contract or in the form of a separate agreement.

(2) The arbitration agreement shall be in writing.

(3) An arbitration agreement is in writing if its content is recorded in any form, whether or not the arbitration agreement or contract has been concluded orally, by conduct, or by other means.

(4) The requirement that an arbitration agreement be in writing is met by an electronic communication if the information contained therein is accessible so as to be useable for subsequent reference; 'electronic communication' means any communication that the parties make by means of data messages; 'data message' means information generated, sent, received or stored by electronic, magnetic, optical or similar means, including, but not limited to, electronic data interchange (EDI), electronic mail, telegram, telex or telecopy.

(5) Furthermore, an arbitration agreement is in writing if it is contained in an exchange of statements of claim and defence in which the existence of an agreement is alleged by one party and not denied by the other.

(6) The reference in a contract to any document containing an arbitration clause constitutes an arbitration agreement in writing, provided that the reference is such as to make that clause part of the contract.

Option II

Article 7. Definition of arbitration agreement

(As adopted by the Commission at its thirty-ninth session, in 2006)

'Arbitration agreement' is an agreement by the parties to submit to arbitration all or certain disputes which have arisen or which may arise between them in respect of a defined legal relationship, whether contractual or not.

A. Meaning and Purpose

14.107 Article 7 defines the term and thereby the scope of the arbitration agreement, which establishes the foundation of an arbitration. The arbitration agreement is one of the most important elements of arbitration, representing the first step towards a binding and enforceable arbitral award. Bearing this in mind, the parties to an arbitration agreement should make every effort to draw up an agreement within the scope set forth in Art 7.

Article 7 was revised by the Commission at its 39th session.[153] The original 1985 text of Art 7 closely followed Art II(2) of the New York Convention, which requires an arbitration agreement to be in writing. If an arbitration agreement does not meet the form requirements, any party may object to the jurisdiction of the arbitral tribunal. The Commission considered that in cases where the willingness of the parties to arbitrate is not in question, the validity of the arbitration agreement may as well be recognized. Therefore, Art 7 was amended to meet modern trade practices and new technological developments in communication.

The Commission adopted two options, which provide two different approaches regarding the definition and form of an arbitration agreement. The first approach follows the detailed structure of the 1985 text of the provision. The second approach defines the arbitration agreement without any form requirement. The Commission did not express any preference in favour of the first or the second option. Instead, the Commission considered offering both options to enacting states. Thus, enacting states may adopt either the first or the second option depending on the particular circumstances under which the Model Law is enacted in their domestic laws. In the view of the Commission, both options are adequate to ensure enforceability of arbitration agreements under the New York Convention.

B. The arbitration agreement, Option I, paragraph (1)

Article 7(1), which is taken from Art II(1) of the New York Convention,[154] provides a broad definition of the term 'arbitration agreement'. Article 7(1) was not subject to the Commission's revision of Art 7 in 2006. It comprises an agreement to submit to arbitration existing disputes (*compromis*, submission agreement) as well as an agreement to arbitrate future disputes (*clause compromissoire*, arbitration clause). The dispute must arise from a 'defined legal relationship' between the parties, but the relationship need not be contractual. The agreement may be in the form of a clause in a contract or in the form of a separate agreement. Unlike some legal systems, no further formalities such as a public deed or recording in court are required. **14.108**

(1) No distinction between a submission agreement and an arbitration clause regarding their legal consequences

Pursuant to the Protocol on Arbitration Clauses (Geneva Protocol) of 1923, the New York Convention of 1958 and the European Convention on Arbitration of 1961, the Model Law permits an arbitration agreement to relate to existing and future disputes. It intends to unify national arbitration laws in this regard because arbitration clauses are not given full effect under some national laws. As arbitration clauses are frequently used in international trade nowadays, there is a vital need to recognize them in international commercial arbitration. **14.109**

153 See Commission Report, UN Doc A/61/17, para 146 *et seq.*

154 See First Draft, UN Doc A/CN.9/WG.II/WP.37, Art 2 note 9.

Mexico,[155] *Egypt*[156] and *Iran*,[157] for example, changed their approach to arbitration clauses and now recognize them as valid arbitration agreements. All Model Law states adopted this provision. The Model Law as *lex specialis* then supersedes any provisions of domestic law denying the validity of arbitration clauses in international arbitration.

(2) Defined legal relationship

14.110 The Analytical Commentary of the Secretariat states that the term 'defined legal relationship' should be given a wide interpretation so as to cover all non-contractual commercial cases occurring in practice, such as third party interference with contractual relations, infringement of trademark or other unfair competition.[158] Thus, disputes arising out of contract, quasi-contract and tort can be encompassed, as long as they fall within the substantive scope of application of the Model Law as stated in Art 1. It depends on the wording of the concrete arbitration agreement whether disputes based on a non-contractual legal basis are encompassed. If the parties wish to refer such disputes to arbitration, they should choose broad and unambiguous wording in the arbitration agreement to make this point clear.

(3) Form

14.111 Pursuant to the last sentence of Art 7(1), the term 'arbitration agreement' comprises of arbitration clauses in a contract as well as separate arbitration agreements. If a country adopts this provision, it must recognize both forms in international commercial arbitration, regardless of any conflicting domestic law. This results from the nature of the Model Law as *lex specialis*. It should be noted that for certain purposes an arbitration clause is treated as an agreement independent of the other terms of the contract as a whole. This principle is known as the 'separability/autonomy of the arbitration agreement'.[159]

(4) Matters not dealt with

14.112 Some matters were discussed in connection with this provision during the drafting process but were finally not dealt with in this provision or elsewhere. First, there is no concrete definition of the term 'arbitration'.[160] Second, although Art 7(1) is modelled on Art II(1) of the New York Convention, it omits the Convention's limitation to differences 'concerning a subject matter of settlement by arbitration'.

14.113 The Working Group recognized the importance of the requirement of arbitrability but saw no need for an express provision because, *inter alia*, a non-arbitrable subject matter would normally be regarded as null and void and the issue of non-arbitrability was adequately addressed in Arts 34 and 36.[161]

14.114 Art 1(5) was introduced to clearly state that the Model Law only gives full effect to arbitration agreements covering an arbitrable subject matter but does not touch upon the

155 Art 1416(I) of the Commercial Code.
156 Art 10(1) of the Law Concerning Arbitration in Civil and Commercial Matters.
157 Art 1(C) of the International Commercial Arbitration Act.
158 UN Doc A/CN.9/264, Art 7 para 4.
159 See commentary on Art 16(1)(2) and (1)(3) at paras 14.258–60.
160 See commentary on Arts 1 and 2 at paras 14.33–5 and 14.66 respectively.
161 Analytical Commentary, UN Doc A/CN.9/264, Art 7 para 5.

question of what disputes are arbitrable. This question will be governed by the applicable law.[162]

Third, the question of the legal capacity of parties to conclude an arbitration agreement is not governed by the Model Law but by the applicable domestic law.[163] **14.115**

Fourth, the Model Law does not deal with questions of sovereign immunity.[164] It is up to the domestic law to determine whether a state that enters into a valid arbitration agreement in a commercial transaction waives immunity. Yet, most of the adopting states declare that the state is bound by the Model Law. **14.116**

Finally, the validity of the arbitration agreement is a matter left to the applicable law, as the formulation of an exhaustive list of clearly defined grounds for the invalidity of the agreement was regarded as impossible.[165] As to the applicable law, Arts 34(2)(a)(i) and 36(1)(a)(i) provide that for purposes of setting aside, recognition and enforcement of an award, the law of the place of arbitration governs the validity of the arbitration agreement unless the parties have chosen another law. The drafting history suggests expanding this specific choice-of-law rule into a general rule on the law governing the arbitration agreement.[166] **14.117**

C. In writing, Option I, paragraphs (2)–(5)

The revised Art 7(2) follows Art II(1) of the New York Convention in requiring an arbitration agreement to be in writing.[167] However, the revised Art 7(3)–(5) recognizes a record of the contents of the agreement in any form as equivalent to 'writing'. While the 1985 text of the Model Law required the signatures of the parties to enter into a valid arbitration agreement, the new rule no longer requires signatures or an exchange of messages. The arbitration agreement may also be concluded orally, by conduct or by any other means, as long as the content of the agreement is recorded. **14.118**

Prior to the revision of Art 7 the arbitration agreement itself had to be in writing; an oral agreement evidenced in writing did not suffice.[168] Oral agreements, whether evidenced in writing or not, were generally null and void. However, the parties could have resolved the formal defect under Art 16(2) if a plea that the arbitral tribunal lacked jurisdiction because the arbitration agreement was not in writing—and therefore deemed null and void—was not raised until the submission of the statement of defence, by which the respondent would have waived his right to object. The arbitration agreement would then be regarded as valid for the arbitration proceedings. **14.119**

[162] See commentary on Art 1(5) at paras 14.49–50.

[163] See First Working Group Report, UN Doc A/CN.9/216, para 28; Second Working Group Report, UN Doc A/CN.9/232, para 39.

[164] See First Working Group Report, UN Doc A/CN.9/216, para 29.

[165] See *ibid,* para 25.

[166] Fifth Secretariat Note, UN Doc A/CN.9/WG.II/WP.49, Art 34 para 37. See also commentary on Art 8 II 3.

[167] It should be noted, however, that the Convention, by virtue of its Art VII(1), also recognizes a more favourable position, eg as to the writing requirement, a party may have under the law of a country where the award is sought to be relied upon.

[168] See Second Working Group Report, UN Doc A/CN.9/232, para 42.

(1) Extent of the writing requirement

14.120 In requiring a written form for any agreement to submit a dispute to arbitration it is to be assumed that Art 7(2) extends to modifications of the original arbitration agreement by which further issues are submitted to arbitration, even if this is done during the arbitral proceedings.[169]

(2) Methods of satisfying the writing requirement

14.121 The Secretariat conducted a study of the application and interpretation of the New York Convention by courts in a variety of countries and noted a number of varying court decisions in the interpretation of the writing requirement under the Convention.[170] The Working Group decided to modify the wording of Art II (2) of the New York Convention in order to provide a more precise and refined definition of what is meant by 'the arbitration agreement shall be in writing'.[171] The Commission was of the opinion that these modifications to the wording were merely elaborations and should also be applied in the interpretation of the New York Convention.[172]

14.122 In that context, at its 39th session the Commission adopted a recommendation regarding the interpretation of Art II(2) and Art VII(1) of the New York Convention.[173] In its resolution of 4 December 2006 the UNGA declared that a promotion of a uniform interpretation of the New York Convention in connection with the modernization of the Model Law 'is particularly timely'.[174]

14.123 The recommendation encourages states to recognize that the circumstances described in Art II(2) of the New York Convention are not exhaustive. Thus, the more favourable regime of both options of Art 7 shall be applied instead of the restrictive form requirements under Art II(2) of the New York Convention. This is possible by virtue of the provision contained in Art VII(1) of the New York Convention.[175] In this context, the Working Group considered that existing interpretations of the notion of writing contained in case law should be preserved and not endangered by Art 7(2).[176] There are several ways to fulfil the writing requirement under Art 7(2), as explained below.

14.124 (2.1) **Signed document** The classic contractual form in writing is an agreement contained in a document signed by the parties. In this case, a person who signs the contract on behalf of one party must have the necessary powers to do so.[177]

---

[169] See Fourth Working Group Report, UN Doc A/CN.9/245, para 182; Holtzmann and Neuhaus, 261.

[170] Secretariat Study on the New York Convention, UN Doc A/CN.9/168, paras 19–26.

[171] See First Working Group Report, UN Doc A/CN.9/216, para 23.

[172] See Commission Report, UN Doc A/40/17, para 87.

[173] Commission Report, UN Doc A/61/17, Annex 2.

[174] UNGA Res 61/33 (4 December 2006) UN Doc A/Res/61/33.

[175] See Explanatory Note by the UNCITRAL Secretariat, 2006, para 40. In its Res 61/33 of 4 December 2006 the UNGA clarifies that by virtue of this 'more favourable provision', 'any interested party' should be allowed 'to avail itself of rights it may have, under the laws or treaties of the country where an arbitration agreement is sought to be relied upon, to seek recognition of the validity of such an arbitration agreement'.

[176] See Working Group Report, UN Doc A/CN.9/487, para 25.

[177] Moscow City Court, 13 December 1994, CLOUT Case 147.

(2.2) **Recorded in any form, paragraph (3)** According to Art 7(3) an arbitration agreement is considered to be in writing if it is concluded orally, by conduct or by any other means, as long as its content is recorded in any form. In this context, 'recorded' means that information should be 'accessible so as to be usable for subsequent reference'.[178] The provision was drafted along the lines of Art 7(2) of the UN Convention on Independent Guarantees and Standby Letters of Credit, which provides that '[a]n undertaking may be issued in any form which preserves a complete record of the text of the undertaking [. . .]'; and Art 6(1) of the UNCITRAL Model Law on Electronic Commerce, which provides that '[w]here the law requires information to be in writing, that requirement is met by a data message if the information contained therein is accessible so as to be usable for subsequent reference'.[179] During the drafting process of the provision, the Working Group considered that the notion 'recorded' in connection with 'data message' in para 4 should make it unambiguously clear that records other than traditional paper documents are included among the acceptable forms of recording an arbitration agreement.[180] **14.125**

(2.3) **Electronic communication, paragraph (4)** In deviating from the wording of the New York Convention, which merely refers to an exchange of letters or telegrams, the drafters of the original text of the Model Law intended to clarify that the Model Law encompasses modern and future means of communication,[181] such as fax, data transmission via satellite or email. However, in its 39th session the Commission considered that any form of electronic communication should fulfil the writing requirement as long as the agreement is recorded.[182] Article 7(4) defines 'electronic communication' as communication by means of 'data messages'.[183] 'Data message' is in turn defined as information generated, sent, received or stored by electronic, magnetic, optical or similar means. **14.126**

Furthermore, Art 7(4) provides a non-exhaustive list of means of communication that can be defined as 'data message'. The terms email, telegram, telex and telecopy are self explanatory. However, the term 'electronic data interchange (EDI)' is not explained in Art 7(4) and requires further examination. A definition of 'electronic data interchange' is provided by Art 2(b) of the UNCITRAL Model Law on Electronic Commerce 1996, but the definition was unfortunately not included in the revised Art 7(4). According to this provision, 'electronic data interchange (EDI)' means the 'electronic transfer from computer to computer of information using an agreed standard to structure the information'.[184] It is advisable for adopting states to include this provision in their domestic law so as to clarify this term.[185] **14.127**

[178] Working Group Report, UN Doc A/CN.9/508, para 23.

[179] *ibid*, para 22.

[180] *ibid*, para 23.

[181] See First Working Group Report, UN Doc A/CN.9/216, para 23; Second Working Group Report, UN Doc A/CN.9/232, para 43; Third Working Group Report, UN Doc A/CN.9/233, para 67; Analytical Commentary, UN Doc A/CN.9/264, Art 7 para 7; Note by the Secretariat UN Doc A/CN.9/WG.II/WP.118, para 14.

[182] For the definition of 'recorded' see the commentary on Art 7(3) at para 14.125.

[183] This provision was inspired by Art 2(a) of the UNCITRAL Model Law on Electronic Commerce 1996, UN Doc A/Res/51/162; see UNGA A/51/628. See Note by the Secretariat UN Doc A/CN.9/WG.II/WP.118, para 14.

[184] Art 2(b) of the UNCITRAL Model Law on Electronic Commerce 1996.

[185] See Binder, para 2-059.

14.128 (2.4) **Exchange of statements of claim and defence in which the existence of an agreement is alleged by one party and not denied by another, paragraph (5)** An exchange of statements of claim and defence would probably constitute an exchange of letters in most jurisdictions.[186] However, with Art 7(5) the Commission wanted to make clear that in this situation the agreement can be concluded tacitly. This provision has the same purpose as Art 16(2). As to the interpretation of the phrase 'statements of claim and defence', in *Gay Constructions PTY Ltd and Spaceframe Buildings (North Asia) Ltd v Caledonian Techmore (Building) Limited and Hanison Construction Co Ltd.* the High Court of Hong Kong noted that the phrase was not defined and was interpreted as not only referring 'to pleadings in the formal sense once an arbitration has commenced', but also to other letters exchanged between the parties.[187] Later, *Hong Kong* amended the term 'statements of claim and defence' in 'written submissions'.[188] At any rate, an exchange of such documents constitutes an exchange of letters that provide a record of the agreement.[189]

14.129 *Bulgaria* added that a declaration of the respondent recorded in the minutes of the arbitration hearing will also be deemed as an arbitration agreement, even if it is not signed by the parties.[190]

14.130 (2.5) **Reference in a contract to a document containing an arbitration clause, if the reference makes the clause part of the contract, paragraph (6)** By adding Art 7(6), the drafters clarified that the writing requirement is met by references in contracts to general conditions in separate documents or to another contract. The reference must be such as to make the arbitration clause part of the contract and the reference need only be to the document containing the arbitration clause, not explicitly to the arbitration clause itself.[191] The wording clarifies that the general conditions or the other contract must have been intended to be a part of the contract. However, an explicit reference is not necessary.[192]

14.131 In this context, the Explanatory Note by the UNCITRAL Secretariat states that the applicable contract law remains available to determine the level of consent necessary for a party to become bound by an arbitration agreement made by reference.[193]

---

[186] Summary Record, UN Doc A/CN.9/SR.311, Art 7 para 11; but see Aboul-Enein (1995) 11 *Arb Int'l* 78, who denies this interpretation for *Egypt*, as the Law concerning Arbitration in Commercial and Civil Matters omits the reference to an exchange of statements of claim and defence.

[187] *Gay Constructions PTY Ltd and Spaceframe Buildings (North Asia) Ltd v Caledonian Techmore (Building) Limited and Hanison Construction Co Ltd*, 17 November (1994), CLOUT Case 87.

[188] See s 2AC(1)(e) of the Arbitration Ordinance 1996.

[189] *Oonc Lines Limited v Sino-American Trade Advancement Co Ltd, High Court of Hong Kong* (Kaplan), 2 February 1994, CLOUT Case 62, published in (1994) ADRLJ, 291 (292) as to telexes and faxes; see also the decision of the Presidium of the Supreme Court of the Russian Federation, 24 November 1999, published in (2004) Mezhdunarodnyy kommercheskiy arbitrazh [International Commercial Arbitration] no 11, CLOUT Case 637.

[190] See Art 7(3) of the Law in International Commercial Arbitration.

[191] Fifth Working Group Report, UN Doc A/CN.9/246, para 19; Analytical Commentary, UN Doc A/CN.9/264, Art 7 para 8.

[192] *Gay Constructions PTY Ltd and Spaceframe Buildings (North Asia) Ltd v Caledonian Techmore (Building) Limited and Hanison Construction Co Ltd*, High Court of Hong Kong (Kaplan), 17 November 1994, CLOUT Case 87; *Skandia International Insurance Company and Mercantile & General Reinsurance Company and various others* (Meerabux), Supreme Court of Bermuda, 21 January 1994, CLOUT Case 127.

[193] Explanatory Note by the UNCITRAL Secretariat, para 19.

In *Skandia International Insurance Company and Mercantile & General Reinsurance Company and various others* the Supreme Court of Bermuda held that under reference to the *travaux préparatoires* of the Model Law, general words of incorporation suffice. Thus, a reference to insurance coverage 'as per wording attached' incorporates the arbitration clause contained therein into the reinsurance agreement.[194] The document containing the arbitration clause does not have to be between the same parties as the contract into which the arbitration clause was incorporated by reference.[195] **14.132**

Bulgaria[196] and *Sri Lanka*[197] omitted the provision for incorporation by reference. In *Bulgaria*, however, it is the standing practice of the Court of Arbitration at the Bulgarian Chamber of Commerce and Industry to recognize such references as valid.[198] **14.133**

D. Arbitration Agreement, Option II

Article 7, Option II provides an alternative approach for national legislators in defining an arbitration agreement. The wording of the provision is similar to Art 7(1), Option I; however, any form requirement is omitted. During the drafting process, the view was expressed that this alternative proposal might depart too radically from traditional legislation, including the New York Convention, to be readily acceptable in many countries.[199] After comparing several jurisdictions the Commission noted, however, that there was a trend towards relaxing the form requirement for the arbitration agreement and that the Model Law should therefore offer national legislators the choice to opt for the alternative proposal.[200] **14.134**

Article 8. Arbitration agreement and substantive claim before court

(1) A court before which an action is brought in a matter which is the subject of an arbitration agreement shall, if a party so requests no later than when submitting his first statement on the substance of the dispute, refer the parties to arbitration unless it finds that the agreement is null and void, inoperative or incapable of being performed.

(2) Where an action referred to in paragraph (1) of this article has been brought, arbitral proceedings may nevertheless be commenced or continued, and an award may be made, while the issue is pending before the court.

A. Meaning and purpose

Article 8 represents a protective barrier between the institution of international commercial arbitration and national court systems. Paragraph (1), which is modelled on Art II(3) of the New York Convention,[201] obliges any court to refer a matter to arbitration when it is the subject of a valid arbitration agreement and when a party requests the court to do so within a certain time limit. **14.135**

---

194 *Skandia International Insurance Company and Mercantile & General Reinsurance Company and various others* (Meerabux), 21 January 1994, CLOUT Case 127.

195 *Astel-Peiniger Joint Venture v Argos Engineering & Heavy Industries Co Ltd*, High Court of Hong Kong (Kaplan), 18 August 1994, CLOUT Case 78.

196 See Art 7(2), LICA.

197 See s 3(2) of the Arbitration Act 1995.

198 Stalev, 'Bulgaria' in *Int'l Handbook on Comm Arb* Suppl 19, (August 1995) 5.

199 See Commission Report, UN Doc A/61/17, para 164.

200 See *ibid*, para 165.

201 Analytical Commentary, UN Doc A/CN.9/264, Art 8 para 2.

14.136 Article 8 pertains to the non-territorial provisions listed in Art 1(2). This means that a party can even rely on Art 8 when the place of arbitration is in a different state and perhaps the only connection to the adopting state is that the court action was brought there.

B. Reference of a matter subject to an arbitration agreement to arbitration, paragraph (1)

14.137 A court seized of a dispute which is the subject of an arbitration agreement is obliged to refer the parties to arbitration unless it finds that the agreement is null and void, inoperative or incapable of being performed. The reference depends on a request of a party made no later than the submission of its first statement on the substance of the dispute. Article 8(1) is addressed to all courts of the Model Law states.[202]

(1) Dispute within the scope of the arbitration agreement

14.138 Article 8(1) demands a dispute to be referred to arbitration. When the defendant unequivocally admits liability, there is no dispute to be arbitrated and hence the court cannot refer the parties to arbitration.[203]

14.139 If there is a dispute, it must be within the scope of the arbitration agreement in order to be referred to arbitration. This is because the arbitral tribunal derives its jurisdiction from the arbitration agreement. The power of the tribunal to decide regarding the subject matter in question depends on the wording of the arbitration agreement. In *Crystal Rose Home Ltd v Alberta New Home Warranty Programme* the Alberta Court of Queen's Bench held that an arbitration clause that provided for arbitration of any dispute 'with respect to any matter in relation to this agreement' was not limited to claims for breach of contract but would extend, for example, to a claim in tort for which the existence of the contract was a relevant fact.[204]

14.140 In *Onex Corp v Ball Corp* the Ontario Court of Justice held that the expression arising 'under' or 'in relation to the construction' of the agreement is broad enough to cover rectification of the agreement. The court noted that in case of doubt the arbitration clause should be interpreted in a manner that would be conducive to arbitration.[205] This interpretation perfectly fits the aim of the Model Law: to promote international commercial arbitration.

---

[202] Analytical Commentary, UN Doc A/CN.9/264, Art 8 para 2.

[203] *Guangdong Agriculture Company Limited v Conagra International (Far East) Limited*, High Court of Hong Kong (Barnett), 24 September 1992, CLOUT Case 41, published in (1992) Hong Kong Law Digest 11; (1993) XVIII YCA 187 (191); *Zhan Jiang E & T Dev Area Service Head Co. v An Hau Company Limited*, High Court of Hong Kong (Kaplan), 21 January 1994, CLOUT Case 61, published in (1994) ADRLJ 307; *Joong and Shipping Co. Limited v Choi Chong-sick (alias Choi Chong-sik) and Chu Ghin Ho trading as Chang Ho Company*, High Court of Hong Kong (Kaplan), 31 March 1994, CLOUT Case 63; *Tai Hing Cotton Mill Limited v Glencore Grain Rotterdam B V and another*, Court of Appeal of Hong Kong (V P Nazareth, Bokhary and Liu), 24 November 1995, CLOUT Case 128, published in (1996) 1 Hong Kong Cases 363; *Nassetti Ettore S p a v Lawton Development Limited*, High Court of Hong Kong (Leonard), 19 April 1996, CLOUT Case 129.

[204] *Crystal Rose Home Ltd v Alberta New Home Warranty Programme*, Alberta Court of Queen's Bench (Mater Funduk), 23 November 1994, CLOUT Case 115.

[205] *Onex Corp v Ball Corp*, Ontario Court of Justice, General Division (Blair), 24 January 1994, CLOUT Case 69; See also *Bitumat Ltd v Multicom Ltd*, High Court of Zimbabwe (Smith), 31 May 2000, CLOUT Case 370.

In *T1T2 Limited Partnership v Canada* the same court held that an arbitration clause which provided that differences between the parties should be resolved through arbitration, with the exception of differences 'involving a question of law', did not cover the application of legal principles to a set of facts that would have been necessary to resolve the plaintiff's claim. It thus rejected the application for a stay of proceedings.[206] 14.141

Another example where a dispute was not encompassed by the words of the arbitration agreement was decided by the Canadian Federal Court of Appeal in *Nanisivik Mines Ltd and Zinc Corporation of America v Canarctic Shipping Co Ltd and Others*. One of the defendants was a party to a bill of lading, but not to the charterparty out of which the dispute arose. The Court held that the arbitration clause of the charterparty incorporated in the bill of lading by general reference to the terms and conditions of the charterparty did not bind the parties to the bill of lading, because it only referred to disputes under the charterparty. It noted that the result of making the arbitration clause of a charterparty applicable to disputes arising under a bill of lading could only be achieved in two ways: either the bill of lading should specifically refer to the charterparty's arbitration clause or, in case of general reference to the terms of the charterparty, the arbitration clause in the charterparty should expressly provide that it also applied to disputes under bills of lading issued pursuant to it.[207] 14.142

How carefully arbitration clauses should be drafted was also illustrated in a case before the High Court of Hong Kong. The parties had entered into a sales contract providing for arbitration in Beijing. As payment, a bill of exchange was drawn on a Hong Kong party and accepted by the defendant. The court held that, under both Chinese law applicable to the sales contract as well as under Hong Kong law applicable to the bill of exchange, the bill was to be treated as a separate contract that was not covered by the arbitration clause contained in the sales contract. Therefore, the application for a stay of the court proceedings was dismissed and the claim on the bill referred to the appropriate court. 14.143

(2) *Request of a party*

The reference to arbitration operates only if one of the parties requests the court to refer the matter to arbitration. Thus, the court is not empowered to refer the matter on its own motion, ie *ex officio*.[208] The principle of party autonomy calls for the condition that a party must invoke the arbitration agreement. If the claimant brings an action before a court and the defendant remains silent, he will be deemed to have waived his right to go to arbitration.[209] The defendant therefore cannot simply rely on the arbitration agreement, but has to react to a claim before the court when he wants to have the matter arbitrated. 14.144

[206] *T1T2 Limited Partnership v Canada*, Ontario Court of Justice—General Division (Borins), 10 November 1994, CLOUT Case 113.

[207] *Nanisivik Mines Ltd and Zinc Corp of America v Canarctic Shipping Co Ltd and Others*, Canada: Federal Court of Canada, Appeal Division (Mahoney, MacGuigan and Linden), 10 February 1994, CLOUT Case 70, published in (1996) ADRLJ 117 (123 *et seq*).

[208] Fifth Working Group Report, UN Doc A/CN.9/246, para 22; Analytical Commentary, UN Doc A/CN.9/264, Art 8 para 3. See also High Commercial Court of Croatia, Pž-7481/03, 27 April 2004, published (abstract) at <http://www.vtsrh.hr>, with comments in Lovrić, 'Ugovor o arbitraži u praksi trgovačkih sudova' [Arbitration agreement in the case law of the commercial courts] Pravo u gospodarstvu (2005) 41, CLOUT Case 657.

[209] cf Broches, 43.

Case law is divided as to whom the request has to be made. While the Canadian Federal Court of Appeal rightly demands a request to the court,[210] the Ontario Court of Justice found a request to the other party sufficient.[211]

14.145 Unlike the New York Convention, but in line with Art VI(1) of the 1961 European Convention, the Model Law requires the party to file the request within a certain time limit, which is no later than the submission of his first statement on the substance of the dispute. Failure to make a timely request precludes the party from invoking the arbitration agreement at all further stages of the court proceedings.[212] During the drafting process there was wide support of the view that a party should also be precluded from relying on the arbitration agreement in other contexts or proceedings. However, the Working Group decided not to incorporate a provision on such a general effect, because it would be impossible to devise a simple rule covering all aspects of this complex issue.[213]

14.146 Various court decisions discuss the timeliness of the request. It was held that the defendant's numerous procedural steps, including discovery, undertaken in judicial proceedings before invoking the arbitration clause did not amount to renunciation of the arbitral procedure.[214] Likewise, the fact that the defendant responded to the plaintiff's motion to enjoin him from continuing with the arbitration was not considered to constitute the taking of a step in the court proceedings so as to justify refusal of the requested stay of court proceedings.[215]

14.147 Interestingly, the Ontario Court of Justice in *Bab Systems Inc v McLurg* held that the word 'statement' in Art 8(1) meant the first statement in the arbitral process, in contrast to the court proceedings. Within only hours, the plaintiff's application to the court seeking judicial relief was followed by a notice advising the defendant of the plaintiff's intention to submit the dispute to arbitration pursuant to an arbitration clause in their agreement. Even assuming that the plaintiff had (unilaterally) waived arbitration by having initiated litigation, the Court concluded that such a waiver had been effectively retracted by a reasonable notice of the intention to arbitrate. The court further reasoned that as the plaintiff had not submitted its first statement in the arbitral proceedings, its request for submission to arbitration was timely.[216] Though contrary to the wording of Art 8, this interpretation, under the particular circumstances of the case, led to a fair result. However, the decision would

[210] *Ruhrkohle Handel Inter GmbH and National Steel Corp et al v Fednav Ltd. and Federal Pacific (Liberia) Ltd. and Federal Calumet (The)*, Federal Court of Canada, Appeal Division (Marceau, Desjardings and Décary), 29 May 1992, CLOUT Case 33, published in (1992) 3 Federal Court Reports 98, commented on by Tetley in (1993) *Lloyd's Maritime and Commercial L Q* 238.

[211] *Bab Systems Inc v McLurg*, Ontario Court of Justice, General Division (Borins), 21 December 1994, CLOUT Case 118.

[212] See Fifth Working Group Report, UN Doc A/CN.9/246, para 22.

[213] See *ibid*; Analytical Commentary, UN Doc A/CN.9/264, Art 8 para 4.

[214] *A. Bianchi S R L v Bilumen Lighting Ltd*, Superior Court of Québec (Ryan), 18 May 1990, CLOUT Case 186, published in (1990) Recueil de jurisprudence du Québec 1681.

[215] *Globe Union Industrial Corp v G. A. P. Marketing Corp*, British Columbia Supreme Court (Lysyk), 18 November 1994, CLOUT Case 114, published in (1995) 2 Western Weekly Reports 696.

[216] *Bab Systems Inc v McLurg*, Ontario Court of Justice, General Division (Borins), 21 December 1994, CLOUT Case 118. But see *Ruhrkohle Handel Inter GmbH and National Steel Corp et al v Fednav Ltd and Federal Pacific (Liberia) Ltd and Federal Calumet (The)*, Federal Court of Canada, Appeal Division (Marceau, Desjardins and Décary), 29 May 1992, CLOUT Case 33.

have been in perfect harmony with Art 8 if it had considered the plaintiff's court action as withdrawn and therefore not constituting a first statement on the substance of the dispute under Art 8(1).

In *ABN Amro Bank Canada v Krupp Mak Maschinenbau GmbH* the Ontario Court of Justice again took a position contrary to the wording of Art 8(1); this time, however, refusing reference to arbitration. The court held that a request for a stay filed together with the statement of defence and counterclaim in the court proceedings was untimely, because it implied acceptance of the court's jurisdiction.[217] **14.148**

Correspondingly, the British Columbia Court of Appeal ruled that the defendants were not entitled to a stay, as they had filed statements of defence after their applications to stay the proceedings.[218] This excessively strict practice requires that a party to an arbitration agreement who has received a statement of claim in court proceedings must apply for stay without submitting a statement of defence, not together with or after his application for a stay. **14.149**

Mexico and *Scotland* did not adopt the time limit stipulated by the Model Law. The Scottish Law Reform Act 1990 allows a party to request the reference to arbitration '. . . at any time before the pleadings in the [court] action are finalized'.[219] The Mexican Code of Commerce, which completely dropped the time limit provision, took an even more far-reaching approach.[220] Nevertheless, the recommended practice is to raise the request of reference at a similar point of time as provided in the Model Law in order to avoid inconsistencies with Mexican procedural law.[221] **14.150**

There is one restriction to the party's right to request that the dispute be referred to arbitration. If a party has raised the plea that the arbitral tribunal has no jurisdiction according to Art 16(2), it is not allowed to request a reference to arbitration. Such a request would contradict the principle of good faith[222] and possibly lead to the unsatisfactory result that the case cannot be settled either in court or in arbitration. **14.151**

(3) Scope of the court's inquiry into the validity of the arbitration agreement

The court may refuse to refer the parties to arbitration if it finds the arbitration agreement 'null and void, inoperative or incapable of being performed'. These terms have been taken over, without any comment, from Art II(3) of the New York Convention.[223] On the basis **14.152**

[217] *ABN Amro Bank Canada v Krupp Mak Maschinenbau GmbH,* Ontario Court of Justice (Haley), 23 December 1994, CLOUT Case 119, published in (1994) 21 Ontario Reports (3rd), 511, excerpts published in (1995) *Int'l Arb Rep* 11.

[218] *Stancroft Trust Limited, Berry and Klausner v Can-Asia Capital Company, Limited, Mandarin Capital Corporation and Asiamerica Capital Limited,* British Columbia Court of Appeal (Carrothers, Southin and Wood), 26 February 1990, CLOUT Case 17, published in (1990) 3 *Western Weekly Reports* 665.

[219] Art 8(1), sch 7 of the Law Reform Act 1990.

[220] Art 1424 of the Code of Commerce 1993.

[221] See in particular Arts 1090, 1092 and 1094 of the Commercial Code 1993; Trevino, J.C., 'The New Mexican Legislation on Commercial Arbitration' (1994) 11 *J Int'l Arb* 20.

[222] Hußlein-Stich, G., *Das UNCITRAL-Modellgesetz über die internationale Handelsschiedsgerichtsbarkeit* (C. Heymanns Verlag, 1990) (Hußlein-Stich) 45.

[223] Holtzmann and Neuhaus, 302 *et seq*; Broches, 45 *et seq.* For the interpretation of these terms concerning the New York Convention see van den Berg, A.J., *The New York Arbitration Convention of 1958: Towards a*

of the separability doctrine, it is merely the arbitration agreement itself and not the contract as a whole which must be valid for the matter to be referred to arbitration.[224]

14.153 A number of judicial decisions reveal the interpretation of the last part of Art 8(1) in the adopting states. Concerning a dispute resolution clause that provided for either arbitration or litigation in *China*, the High Court of Hong Kong held that such a clause was not void for uncertainty, but gave the parties a choice within the range of options agreed upon. As the plaintiff opted for a method of dispute resolution not foreseen in the contract, namely litigation in *Hong Kong*, it was open for the defendants to exercise that choice. By applying for a stay of proceedings under Art 8, they opted for arbitration.[225]

14.154 In the famous 'Hamburg Coffee Case', the *Hanseatische Oberlandesgericht* (Hanseatic higher regional court) Hamburg held an arbitration clause, despite its minimal content ('Arbitration: Hamburg') as valid because, when read in conjunction with the contract, it referred to the arbitration rules of the German Coffee Association.[226] The Higher Regional Court of Bavaria declared an ambiguous arbitration agreement, which provided for two different chambers of handicrafts, as void for uncertainty, because it was impossible to determine the competent arbitral tribunal from it.[227]

14.155 In another case, the High Court of Hong Kong concluded that the reference to an unspecified third country, to a non-existent organization and to non-existent rules did not render the arbitration agreement inoperative or incapable of being performed, as arbitration could be held in any country other than the countries where the parties had their places of business and under the law of the place of arbitration, which could be chosen by the plaintiff.[228]

In *Jean Charbonneau v Les Industries A. C. Davie Inc et al* the Superior Court of Quebec held an arbitration agreement under which a party to the contract was to arbitrate the dispute inoperative. The reason was obvious: a party cannot act as an impartial arbitrator, even if it is the Minister of Agriculture.[229]

14.156 The reference to arbitration cannot be declined on the ground that the award would be unenforceable in the forum state, ie the state in which the court is located. The Working Group pointed out that such a criterion for refusing reference to arbitration would be

---

Uniform Judicial Interpretation (Asser/Kluwer, 1981) (van den Berg) 123 *et seq*, 158; Born, G.B., *International Commercial Arbitration in the United States: Commentary and Materials* (Deventer, 1994) 203 *et seq*.

[224] See commentary on Art 16(1)(2) and (1)(3) at paras 14.258–60.

[225] *William Company v Chu Kong Agency Co Ltd and Guangzhou Ocean Shipping Company*, High Court of Hong Kong (Kaplan), 17 February 1993, CLOUT Case 44, published in (1993) Hong Kong Law Digest, B 7.

[226] Hanseatisches Oberlandesgericht (Hamburg), 24 January 2003, 11 Sch 6/0, published in German DIS-Online Database on Arbitration Law <http://www.dis-arb.de>, CLOUT Case 571.

[227] Higher Regional Court of Bavaria, 4Z SchH 13/99, 28 February 2000, published in German: BetriebsBerater, Beilage 8 zu Heft 37/2000 (RPS), 15, DIS-Online Database on Arbitration Law <http://www.dis-arb.de>, Comment by Kröll and Heidkamp in (2002) *Int'l Arb L Rev*, N-41, CLOUT Case 557.

[228] *Lucky-GoldstarInternational (H. K.) Limited v Ng Moo Kee Engineering Limited*, High Court of Hong Kong (Kaplan), 5 May 1993, CLOUT Case 57, published in (1993) 2 Hong Kong Law Reports 73.

[229] *Jean Charbonneau v Les Industries A. C. Davie Inc et al*, Superior Court of Quebec (Moisan), 14 March 1989, CLOUT Case 66, published in (1989) Recueil de jurisprudence du Québec 1255.

contrary to the objective of the Model Law, which is to promote international commercial arbitration, on two grounds: first, the award might well be enforceable in other states; second, until the award has been made it might not be clear whether it would, in fact, be unenforceable.[230]

In taking this position, the Working Group revealed its assumption that the law governing the validity of the arbitration agreement for the purposes of Art 8 is not the law of the forum. Though the Model Law does not specify which law governs the validity of the arbitration agreement at the stage of reference to arbitration, the *travaux préparatoires* suggests applying the same solution as provided in Arts 34(2)(a)(i) and 36(1)(a)(i) for purposes of setting aside, recognition and enforcement.[231] Accordingly, the predominant view refers to the law chosen by the parties and, failing such, to the law of the place of arbitration.[232] There are two reasons why the Model Law does not explicitly extend this conflict of laws rule to the arbitration agreement in general. First, the territorial application of the Model Law, which is a prerequisite of that rule, was not included until the last stage of the drafting process. Second, the drafters wanted to wait for the results of the expected Hague Convention on the law applicable to arbitration agreements; such a convention, however, never came into existence.[233] **14.157**

Yet, in the absence of a specific stipulation by the parties as to a national law governing the arbitration agreement, an increasing number of arbitrators, particularly under the ICC Rules, determine the validity and effects of an arbitration agreement without reference to any national law. Instead, they refer to the common intent of the parties,[234] as revealed by the circumstances of the negotiation and performance of the contract, and the usages of international trade.[235] Nevertheless, prudent arbitrators should take account of the law of the seat of arbitration as provided in Arts 34(2)(a)(i) and 36(1)(a)(i) of the Model Law as well as in Art V(1)(a) of the New York Convention, as they are obliged to make every effort to render an enforceable award.[236] **14.158**

---

[230] Second Working Group Report, UN Doc A/CN.9/232, para 51.

[231] Fifth Secretariat Note UN Doc A/CN.9/WG.II/WP.49, Art 34 para 37.

[232] Holtzmann and Neuhaus, 303; Hußlein-Stich, 48 *et seq*; Granzow, J.H., *Das UNCITRAL-Modellgesetz über die internationale Handelsschiedsgerichtsbarkeit von 1985* (Verlag V Florentz 1988) 95; Berger, K.P., *International Economic Arbitration* (Kluwer Law and Taxation Publishers, 1993) 157; van den Berg, A.J., *The New York Arbitration Convention of 1958: Towards a Uniform Judicial Interpretation* (Asser/Kluwer, 1981) 126 *et seq* as to the analogous provisions of the New York Convention. But see *BWV Investments Ltd. v Saskferco Products Inc UHDE-GmbH et al*, Saskatchewan Court of Queen's Bench (MacPherson C J QB), 19 March 1993, CLOUT Case 28, in which the Court considering the question of inconsistency between an arbitration agreement and the Builders' Lien Act did not apply the law of the place of arbitration (Swiss Law) but its own domestic law. See discussion on arbitrability, *infra*.

[233] Fifth Working Group Report, UN Doc A/CN.9/246, Art 1 para 200.

[234] Kammergericht Berlin, 28 Sch 17/99, 15 October 1999, CLOUT Case 373.

[235] *Isover St. Gobain v Dow Chemical France et al*, ICC Case 4131/1982, I ICC Awards 146, 465 upheld by the Paris Court of Appeal, decision of 21 October 1983, *Rev arb* 1984, 98, extracts in English in (1984) IX *YCA* 132 JDI (Clunet) 1983, 899 with note *Derains*; ICC Case 4381/1986, II ICC Awards 264.

[236] cf Art 35 ICC Rules; Craig, Park and Paulsson 54; Lew, J.D.M., 'The Law Applicable to the Form and Substance of the Arbitration Clause' (1998) *ICCA Congress Series no* 14, paras 130 *et seq*; Redfern, A and Hunter, M., *Law and Practice of International Commercial Arbitration* (4th edn, Sweet & Maxwell, 2004) paras 3–51; Berger, 159.

14.159 The Working Group declined to add an express term that a non-arbitrable subject matter was a ground for refusing reference to arbitration, primarily because it was noted that an arbitration agreement concerning a non-arbitrable subject matter would normally be regarded as null and void.[237] Moreover, as in the question of the law governing the arbitration agreement in general, the Model Law is silent as to which law should apply to considerations of arbitrability at the stage of referral to arbitration. Looking to the provisions on setting aside, recognition and enforcement of an award, there are two sets of potentially applicable rules.[238] Articles 34(2)(a)(i) and 36(1)(a)(i) of the Model Law subject the validity of an arbitration agreement, as noted above, to the law chosen by the parties and, failing such, to the law of the place of arbitration, while Arts 34(2)(b)(i) and 36(1)(b)(i) of the Model Law authorize judges to determine the arbitrability of a dispute on the basis of their own law. Hence, with respect to arbitrability, courts generally tend to look at the *lex fori*, not only at the post-award stage but also when asked to refer the matter to arbitration.[239] Nevertheless, opinion on this issue is divided: some writers favour the law of the place of arbitration as opposed to the law of the forum, while others argue for a cumulative application of the mentioned laws.[240]

14.160 Moreover, the proposal to add the term 'manifestly' before 'null and void', which would have limited the court to a prima facie finding that the arbitration agreement was valid, was rejected during the drafting process. It was felt that the issue should be settled by the court without first referring it to an arbitral tribunal which allegedly lacked jurisdiction.[241] Notwithstanding this clear statement in the *travaux préparatoires* and despite the fact that the opposing party explicitly challenged the existence of an arbitration clause, in *Skandia International Insurance Company* the Supreme Court of Bermuda contented itself with such a prima facie finding as to the validity of the arbitration clause. The Court pointed out that in any event a challenge to the existence, validity or scope of the arbitration agreement was a matter to be first determined by the arbitral tribunal under Art 16(3) of the Model Law. It thus granted the requested injunction restraining the opposing party from continuing with court proceedings in Kuwait.[242]

(4) Reference to arbitration

14.161 The term 'refer to arbitration' stems from the 1923 Geneva Protocol on Arbitration Clauses,[243] from which it was taken over in the New York Convention. Primarily for the

[237] Fifth Working Group Report, UN Doc A/CN.9/246, para 23; accord Fourth Working Group Report, UN Doc A/CN.9/245, para 187; see also *BWV Investments Ltd. v Saskferco Products Inc et al and UHDE GmbH*, Saskatchewan Court of Appeal, 25 November 1994, CLOUT Case 116, published in (1995) 2 Western Weekly Reports 1, which considered the question of inconsistency between an arbitration agreement and the Builder's Lien Act under the headline 'null and void, inoperative or incapable of being performed'.

[238] Holtzmann and Neuhaus, 304.

[239] See eg *BWV Investments Ltd. v Saskferco Products Inc UHDE-GmbH, et al* Saskatchewan Court of Queen's Bench (MacPherson C J QB), 19 March 1993, CLOUT Case 28. As to court practice under the parallel provisions of the New York Convention see van den Berg, 152 *et seq.*

[240] For further references see van den Berg, 154.

[241] Third Working Group Report, UN Doc A/CN.9/233, para 77.

[242] *Skandia International Insurance Company and Mercantile & General Reinsurance Company and various others*, Supreme Court of Bermuda (Meerabux), 21 January 1994, CLOUT Case 127.

[243] League of Nations Treaty Series, vol XXVII, 158, no 678, Art 4.

sake of consistency with the New York Convention, the Working Group decided not to stipulate what type of decision the court should render when the arbitration agreement was invoked. This matter was left to the respective court to determine according to its procedural law.[244]

In some legal systems such as that of *Canada*, the courts, by referring a matter to arbitration, do not deprive themselves of jurisdiction but only refrain from exercising it: they order a stay of proceedings. Such a stay is not unconstitutional, in that it precludes access to the courts because any denial of access results from a consensual surrender of the right to litigate.[245] In other legal systems a party's request to refer the matter to arbitration leads to a definite end of the court proceedings. Here, the action is dismissed. **14.162**

When the conditions of Art 8(1) are fulfilled, the court has no discretion, but must refer the parties to arbitration. 'Shall' in this article means 'must', not 'may'.[246] Correspondingly, the British Columbia Court of Appeal held that the court may exercise its residual jurisdiction to refuse a stay of proceedings only when a party clearly established that it was not a party to the arbitration clause, the alleged dispute did not come within the terms of the arbitration agreement or the application was out of time. The Court further rightly noted that if these points were arguable, the stay of the legal proceedings should be granted and the issues left to be resolved in the arbitration.[247] **14.163**

Besides, the court's involvement under Art 8(1) is restricted to a determination of whether the arbitration agreement is null and void, inoperative or incapable of being performed.[248] In any event, the court is not concerned with investigating whether the defendant has an arguable basis for disputing the claim. This is the primary task of the arbitral tribunal.[249] **14.164**

---

[244] See First Working Group Report, UN Doc A/CN.9/216, para 56; Third Working Group Report, UN Doc A/CN.9/233, para 76; Fourth Working Group Report, UN Doc A/CN.9/245, para 186.

[245] *Stancroft Trust Limited, Berry and Klausner v Can-Asia Capital Company Limited, Mandarin Capital Corporation and Asiamerica Capital Ltd*, British Columbia Court of Appeal (Carrothers, Southin and Wood,), 26 February 1990, CLOUT Case 17, published in (1990) 3 Western Weekly Reports 665 (666, 670).

[246] eg *Coopers and Lybrand Ltd. (Trustee) for BC Navigation S A v Canpotex Shipping Services Ltd*, Federal Court of Canada, Trial Division (Denault), 2 November 1987, CLOUT Case 9, published in (1987) 16 Federal Trial Reporter 79; *Nanisivik Mines Ltd and Zinc Corporation of America v Canarctic Shipping Co Ltd and Others*, Federal Court of Canada, Trial Division (Walsh), 19 January 1993, CLOUT Case 36; Federal Court of Canada, Appeal Division (Mahoney, MacGuigan and Linden), 10 February 1994, CLOUT Case 70, published in (1996) ADRLJ 117; *A. Bianchi S. R. L. v Bilumen Lighting Ltd*, Superior Court of Québec (Ryan), 18 May 1990, CLOUT Case 186, published in (1990) Recueil de jurisprudence du Québec 1681; cf *Krutov v Vancouver Hockey Club Limited*, British Columbia Supreme Court (Chambers) (Harvey), 22 November 1991, CLOUT Case 19.

[247] *The City of Prince George v A. L. Sims & Sons Ltd.*, British Columbia Court of Appeal, 4 July 1995, CLOUT Case 179, published in (1995) 9 Western Weekly Reports 503; *Gulf Canada Resources Ltd v Arochem International Ltd*, British Columbia Court of Appeal (Hinkson, Southin and Cumming), 10 March 1992, CLOUT Case 31, published in 66 British Columbia Law Reports (2 d), 113 (119 *et seq*).

[248] *Rio Algom Limited v Sammi Steel Co*, Ontario Court of Justice—General Division (Henry), 1 March 1991, CLOUT Case 18, excerpts published in (1993) XVIII *YCA* 166.

[249] See *Guangdong Agriculture Company Limited v Conagra International (Far East) Limited*, High Court of Hong Kong (Barnett), 24 September 1992, CLOUT Case 41, published in (1992) Hong Kong Law Digest, H 11; (1993) XVIII *YCA* 187 (191); *Zhan Jiang E & T Dev Area Service Head Co v An Hau Company Limited*, High Court of Hong Kong (Kaplan), 21 January 1994, CLOUT Case 61, published in (1994) ADRLJ 307; *Tai Hing Cotton Mill Limited v Glencore Grain Rotterdam B V and another*, Court of Appeal of Hong Kong (Nazareth V. P., Bokhary and Liu), 24 November 1995, CLOUT Case 128, published in (1996) 1 Hong

14.165 With regard to third parties not privy to the arbitration agreement, in *Nanisivik Mines Ltd. and Zinc Corporation of America v Canarctic Shipping Co Ltd and Others* the Canadian Federal Court of Appeal distinguished between reference to arbitration on the one hand and stay of court proceedings on the other. Under Art 8, while the court must not refer a third party's claim to arbitration, it nevertheless has discretion under s 50(1)(b) of the Federal Court Act to stay the litigation of said claim pending arbitration of the co-plaintiff's claim.[250]

(5) Matters not addressed

14.166 The Working Group discussed two other issues, but ultimately decided not to deal with them in the Model Law. First, it was agreed that the effectiveness of a stipulated time period for submission of a dispute to arbitration was independent of any prescription period concerning the underlying transactions. Thus, even if the period in an arbitration agreement is shorter than the mandatory prescription period regarding a court action, it will be effective. Yet, the Working Group declined to include a provision on this point, or on related issues such as the right of a party to resort to a court after expiry of that time limit, because it was felt that the solution would vary with each case.[251]

14.167 Second, the Working Group decided not to deal with the problem of consolidation in multi-party disputes. While it was agreed that parties had the freedom to conclude consolidation agreements if they so wished, the Working Group was of the opinion that there was no real need to include a rule on this subject.[252] Some Model Law states such as *Australia*, *British Columbia*, *California*, *New Zealand* and *Ontario*, however, inserted respective consolidation provisions.

C. Commencement or continuation of the arbitral proceedings, paragraph (2)

14.168 Article 8(2) allows the arbitral tribunal to commence or continue the arbitral proceedings while the issue of its jurisdiction is pending with a court; an arbitral award may also be made. Thus, it permits simultaneous proceedings, either in the situation that the matter is brought before a court after the commencement of the arbitral proceedings or in the case that the arbitral proceedings are initiated after the court action. This provision was the subject of considerable debate within the Commission.[253] It was adopted for the sake

Kong Cases, 363; *Nassetti Ettore S p a v Lawton Development Limited*, High Court of Hong Kong (Leonard), 19 April 1996, CLOUT Case 129.

[250] *Nanisivik Mines Ltd and Zinc Corporation of America v Canarctic Shipping Co Ltd and Others*, Federal Court of Canada, Appeal Division (Mahoney, MacGuigan and Linden), 10 February 1994, CLOUT Case 70, published in (1996) *ADRLJ* 117 (120 *et seq*). But see *Nanisivik Mines Ltd and Zinc Corporation of America v Canarctic Shipping Co Ltd and Others*, Federal Court of Canada, Trial Division (Walsh), 19 January 1993, CLOUT Case 36 and *Continental Resources Inc v East Asiatic Co (Canada) et al*, Federal Court of Canada, Trial Division (Strayer), 22 March 1994, CLOUT Case 72, unpublished. cf *Navionics Inc v Flota Maritima Mexicana S A et al*, Federal Court of Canada, Trial Division (Joyal), 17 January 1989, CLOUT Case 15, published in (1989) 26 Federal Trial Reporter 148.

[251] First Working Group Report, UN Doc A/CN.9/216, para 38; Second Secretariat Note, UN Doc A/CN.9/WG.II/WP.35, para 23.

[252] First Working Group Report, UN Doc A/CN.9/216, para 37; Second Secretariat Note, UN Doc A/CN.9/WG.II/WP.35, para 22.

[253] eg Summary Record, UN Doc A/CN.9/SR.312, Art 8 paras 4–41; Commission Report, UN Doc A/40/17, paras 91–3.

of a prompt resolution of the arbitration, thus reducing the effect of a party's dilatory tactics.[254]

The risk of simultaneous proceedings is that two varying decisions may be rendered by the arbitral tribunal and the court. This risk is minimized by the fact that the party that brings an action before a court normally also raises the plea provided in Art 16(2) that the arbitral tribunal has no jurisdiction. When an arbitral tribunal has serious doubts as to its jurisdiction, it should rule on that plea as a preliminary question or stay the proceedings until the decision of the court, taking into account the expenses of the parties.[255] **14.169**

It must be emphasized that the decision to stay the arbitral proceedings is for the arbitral tribunal; the court has no power to order a stay. As the Working Group ultimately deleted the wording 'unless the court orders a stay of the arbitral proceedings',[256] Art 5, which provides that in matters governed by the Model Law no court shall intervene except where so provided in the Model Law, is applicable. **14.170**

Article 9. Arbitration agreement and interim measures by the court
It is not incompatible with an arbitration agreement for a party to request, before or during arbitral proceedings, from a court an interim measure of protection and for a court to grant such measure.

A. Meaning and purpose

Article 9 deals with another effect of the arbitration agreement. It clearly expresses that the arbitration agreement does not prevent parties to an arbitration from requesting interim protective measures from a court, nor does it prevent the court from granting such measures. Thus, the principle of compatibility addresses not only the parties, but also the national courts. Aiming to make the arbitration proceedings efficient and to secure its expected results, this rule reflects the expectations of the parties.[257] **14.171**

As to the relation to Art 17 J, see the commentary on Art 17 J at para 14.359. **14.172**

B. Scope of application

(1) Request for interim protective measures

The first part of Art 9 provides that either party to an arbitration agreement has the right to request provisional orders from a national court. Such a request is not incompatible with the arbitration agreement, ie it is neither prohibited nor to be regarded as a waiver of the agreement.[258] The request can be made either prior to or during the arbitral proceedings. It should be noted that court access is not restricted, for example the requesting party need not seek permission from the arbitral tribunal. **14.173**

---

254 See Commission Report, UN Doc A/40/17, para 92.
255 *ibid.*
256 Fifth Working Group Report, UN Doc A/CN.9/246, para 21.
257 Analytical Commentary, UN Doc A/CN.9/264, Art 9 para 1.
258 *ibid,* para 2; Fifth Secretariat Note, UN Doc A/CN.9/WG.II/WP.49, para 22.

14.174 This part of the provision applies regardless of whether the request is made to a court of a Model Law state or to a court of another state.[259] Therefore, a party's request for an interim measure, either from a court of a country which has adopted the Model Law or from a court of any other country, will not have the effect of waiver of the arbitration agreement.

(2) Granting of interim protective measures

14.175 The second part of the provision, which stipulates that a national court is not prevented from granting interim protective measures by the existence of an arbitration agreement, only addresses the courts of the Model Law state.[260] The interpretation of this rule is that the national court shall not refuse to grant an interim measure of protection permitted by its domestic procedural law on the ground that an arbitration agreement exists between the parties.[261] It seems consistent with the language of Art 9 and the intention of the drafters that the court of the Model Law state shall assist a party to an international arbitration agreement in this respect, regardless of the place of arbitration laid down in the agreement.[262]

14.176 Art 9, which is inspired by Art 26(3) of the UNCITRAL Arbitration Rules, was implemented to establish uniform interpretation on the important issue of court access regarding interim measures of protection, as the Secretariat's study of judicial decisions under the 1958 New York Convention noted divergent approaches by the courts.[263]

14.177 It should be stressed that the court is not allowed to grant interim measures of protection *sua sponte*. Instead, such court assistance depends on the request of a party. This requirement is an expression of the Model Law's intention to minimize judicial intervention.

14.178 Some Model Law states even provide further conditions in this regard, at the same time clarifying the relationship between Arts 9 and 17. In *Zimbabwe*, for example, the court shall not grant an interim order unless the arbitral tribunal has not yet been appointed and the matter is urgent, or the arbitral tribunal is not competent to grant the order, or the urgency of the matter makes it impracticable to seek such an order from the arbitral tribunal. In addition, the court shall not grant any such order where the competent arbitral tribunal has determined an application therefore.[264] In *Hong Kong* the court has discretion to decline making an order when it considers it more appropriate for the matter to be dealt with by the arbitral tribunal.[265] Other Model Law states provide that the court requested for an interim protective measure shall treat the arbitral tribunal's ruling on any matter relevant to the application, as well as any finding of fact made in the course of such

---

[259] See Art 1(2), which excludes Art 9 from the territorial principle.

[260] Analytical Commentary, UN Doc A/CN.9/264, Art 9 paras 2–3; Fifth Secretariat Note, UN Doc A/CN.9/WG.II/WP.49, para 21.

[261] See Fifth Secretariat Note, UN Doc A/CN.9/WG.II/WP.49, para 21.

[262] cf *Interbulk (Hong Kong) Ltd v Safe Rich Industries Ltd*, High Court of Hong Kong (Barmett), 2 March 1992, CLOUT Case 42, published in (1992) 2 Hong Kong Law Reports 185 and (1992) Hong Kong Law Digest, C 7.

[263] See Secretariat Study on the New York Convention, UN Doc A/CN.9/168, para 29; First Secretariat Note, UN Doc A/CN.9/207, para 61.

[264] Art 9(3) of the Arbitration Act 1996.

[265] s 2GC(6) of the Arbitration Ordinance, ch 341.

ruling, as conclusive for the purposes of the application.[266] *Sri Lanka* does not provide for any court assistance with regard to interim protective measures.

(3) Kinds of interim measures

Art 9 applies to any interim measure which can be granted under a given legal system, as Art 9 only expresses the principle of compatibility and does not itself regulate which interim measures of protection are available.[267] Both the Working Group and the Commission took the view that the provision embraced a wide variety of measures, such as measures to conserve the subject matter of the dispute, measures to secure evidence, measures to protect trade secrets and proprietary information, pre-award attachments and similar seizures of assets, measures required from third parties and enforcement of any interim measures ordered.[268] **14.179**

Some Model Law states specifically set out the kinds of interim measures that a court may grant.[269] In *Trade Fortune Inc v Amagalmated Mill Supplies Ltd* the British Columbia Supreme Court held that the concept of 'protection' includes the right of an arbitrating party to obtain a garnishee order before judgment in order to secure funds for payment of the eventual arbitration award.[270] In *Vibroflotation A G v Express Builders Co. Ltd* the High Court of Hong Kong held that subpoenas cannot be characterized as interim measures of protection, but may be granted under Art 27.[271] **14.180**

There is a noticeable trend that courts have become reluctant to intervene in arbitral proceedings. In *Relais Nordik v Secunda Marine Services Limited* the Federal Court of Canada held that a mandatory interim injunction to force the respondent to comply with the terms of a charterparty was not an interim measure covered by Art 9. The applicant was seen as attempting to have the court rather than the arbitrators resolve the substance of the dispute, notwithstanding the respondent's objection pursuant to Art 8.[272] **14.181**

It has to be noted that the range of interim measures which are available from a court under Art 9 is broader than the interim measures that the arbitral tribunal may grant under Art 17. An arbitral tribunal may only grant interim measures 'in respect of the subject-matter of the dispute'. Unlike the court, the tribunal cannot enforce such a measure.[273] **14.182**

---

[266] eg *New Zealand*: Art 9(3) of the First sch of the Arbitration Act 1996; *Kenya*: s 7(2) of the Arbitration Act 1995; *California*: s 1297.94, CCP.

[267] See Commission Report, A/40/17, para 96.

[268] See Fourth Working Group Report, UN Doc A/CN.9/245, para 188; Fifth Working Group Report, UN Doc A/CN.9/246, para 26; Analytical Commentary, UN Doc A/CN.9/264, Art 9 para 4; Commission Report, UN Doc A/40/17, para 96.

[269] eg *Bermuda*: s 35(5) of the Bermuda International Conciliation and Arbitration Act 1993; *California*: s 1297.93, CCP; *Hong Kong*: s 2GC(1) of the Arbitration Ordinance, Chapter 341; *New Zealand*: Art 9(2) of the First sch of the Arbitration Act 1996; *Zimbabwe*: Art 9(2) of the Arbitration Act 1996.

[270] *Trade Fortune Inc v Amagalmated Mill Supplies Ltd*, British Columbia Supreme Court (Bouck), 25 February 1994, CLOUT Case 71, published in (1996) ADRLJ 132.

[271] *Vibroflotation A G v Express Builders Co Ltd*, High Court of Hong Kong, 15 August 1994, CLOUT Case 77.

[272] *Relais Nordik v Secunda Marine Services Limited*, Federal Court of Canada, Trial Division (Pinard), 19 February 1988, CLOUT Case 11, published in 24 Federal Trial Reporter 256.

[273] See also commentary on Art 17 at paras 14.277–87.

(4) Exclusion

14.183 The Commission clarified that the wording of Art 9 does not preclude the parties from excluding all or certain interim measures by agreement. Consequently, Art 9 refers to 'an arbitration agreement' and not to 'the arbitration agreement'.[274]

Chapter III: Composition of arbitral tribunal

Special Literature:

Nakamura, Tatsuya, 'Appointment of Arbitrators According to the UNCITRAL Model Law on International Commercial Arbitration' (2005) 8 *Int'l Arb L Rev* 179.

Okekeifere, Andrew I., 'Appointment and challenge of arbitrators under the UNCITRAL Model Law I' (1999) 2 *Int'l Arb L Rev* 167.

Okekeifere, Andrew I., 'Appointment and challenge of arbitrators under the UNCITRAL Model Law II' (2000) 3 *Int'l Arb L Rev* 13.

Strohbach, Heinz, 'Composition of the Arbitral Tribunal and Making of the Award' in Pieter Sanders (ed), *UNCITRAL's Project for a Model Law on International Commercial Arbitration, Interim meeting, Lausanne, 9–12 May* (ICCA Congress Series no 2 1984).

Voskuil, C.C.A. and Freedberg-Swartzburg, Judith Ann, 'Composition of the Arbitral Tribunal' in Petar Sarcevic (ed), *Essays on International Commercial Arbitration* (Graham & Trotman/ Martinus Nijhoff, 1989).

Article 10. Number of arbitrators

(1) The parties are free to determine the number of arbitrators.
(2) Failing such determination, the number of arbitrators shall be three.

A. Meaning and purpose

14.184 Article 10 constitutes a special expression of the principle of party autonomy. The provision is the first within the Model Law that was structured according to the 'two-level system'.[275] While Art 10(1) leaves it to the parties to determine the number of arbitrators without being bound to any national law, Art 10(2) deals with the case of the parties' inability to reach an agreement.

B. Party autonomy, paragraph (1)

14.185 Art 10(1) includes the free designation of the method for appointing the arbitrators and the free choice of any number of arbitrators. The parties are not bound by any national law provision on this issue.[276] They are free to fix a specific number of arbitrators or just to decide whether the number of arbitrators should be even or odd. It is important to note that some Model Law states restrict the parties' freedom to determine an odd number of arbitrators.[277] However, even if the parties do not comply with this restriction in their arbitration agreement, the agreement will remain valid. In *MMTC v Sterlite Industries*

[274] Commission Report, UN Doc A/40/17, para 97.

[275] See Analytical Commentary, UN Doc A/CN.9/264, Art 10 para 1.

[276] *ibid.*

[277] eg *Hungary*: s 13(1) of Act LXXI of 1994 on Arbitration; *India*: s 10(1) of the Arbitration and Conciliation Ordinance 1996; *Tunisia*: Art 55(1) of the Arbitration Code 1993; *Egypt*: Art 15(2) of the Law Concerning Arbitration in Civil and Commercial Matters.

(India) Ltd the Supreme Court of India held that the relevant provision to determine the (formal) validity of an arbitration agreement is Art 7. As there is no reference to the number of arbitrators within this provision, the number of arbitrators specified in the arbitration agreement does not affect its validity.[278]

In case the parties choose an even number of arbitrators, they should be aware of the increased risk of deadlock. The laws of *Sri Lanka* and *Austria* demand an additional arbitrator who shall act as Chairman if the parties appoint an even number of arbitrators.[279] According to the general rule stated in Art 2(d), third parties or institutions may be authorized to make the necessary determinations. Pursuant to Art 2(e), the parties to the dispute are free to let the process of determination be governed by any arbitration rules[280] to which their agreement refers. **14.186**

C. Supplementary regulation, paragraph (2)

In case the parties fail to determine the number of arbitrators themselves or to agree on the authorization of a third party to make that determination, Art 10(2) provides for a tribunal composed of three arbitrators. The Working Group briefly considered several alternatives for this provision,[281] but adopted the number of three, which is the most common number in international arbitration, following Art 5 of the UNCITRAL Arbitration Rules. The prevailing view was that a panel of three arbitrators is more likely to guarantee equal treatment of both parties.[282] Some Model Law states such as *Alberta*, *India*, *Kenya*, *Mexico*, *Scotland*, *Singapore* and *Spain* changed this supplementary rule and provide for a sole arbitrator in case of the parties' failure to determine the number of arbitrators.[283] The advantage of this provision is that the conduct of the arbitral proceedings by a sole arbitrator is normally less expensive and time-consuming. If the parties want more arbitrators, for example in complex cases, they will be free to agree thereon under Art 10(1). **14.187**

Article 11. Appointment of arbitrators

(1) No person shall be precluded by reason of his nationality from acting as an arbitrator, unless otherwise agreed by the parties.

(2) The parties are free to agree on a procedure of appointing the arbitrator or arbitrators, subject to the provisions of paragraphs (4) and (5) of this article.

(3) Failing such agreement,

(a) in an arbitration with three arbitrators, each party shall appoint one arbitrator, and the two arbitrators thus appointed shall appoint the third arbitrator; if a party fails to appoint the arbitrator within thirty days of receipt of a request to do so from the other party, or if the two arbitrators fail to agree on the third arbitrator within thirty days of

[278] *MMTC v Sterlite Industries (India) Ltd*, Supreme Court of India, 18 November 1996, CLOUT Case 177.

[279] *Sri Lanka*: s 6 of the Arbitration Act 1995; *Austria*: s 586(1) of the Code of Civil Procedure.

[280] eg the UNCITRAL Arbitration Rules, the ICC Rules, the AAA Rules, the LCIA Rules.

[281] Reported by Holtzmann and Neuhaus, 348 *et seq*.

[282] Second Working Group Report, UN Doc A/CN.9/232, para 81.

[283] *India*: s 10(2) of the Arbitration and Conciliation Ordinance 1996; *Kenya*: s 11(2) of the Arbitration Act 1995; *Mexico*: Art 1426 of the Commercial Code; *Scotland*: Art 10(2) of the Law Reform (Miscellaneous Provisions) (Scotland) Act 1990; *Singapore*: s 9 of the International Arbitration Act 1994.

their appointment, the appointment shall be made, upon request of a party, by the court or other authority specified in article 6;

(b) in an arbitration with a sole arbitrator, if the parties are unable to agree on the arbitrator, he shall be appointed, upon request of a party, by the court or other authority specified in article 6.

(4) Where, under an appointment procedure agreed upon by the parties,

(a) a party fails to act as required under such procedure, or

(b) the parties, or two arbitrators, are unable to reach an agreement expected of them under such procedure, or

(c) a third party, including an institution, fails to perform any function entrusted to it under such procedure, any party may request the court or other authority specified in article 6 to take the necessary measure, unless the agreement on the appointment procedure provides other means for securing the appointment.

(5) A decision on a matter entrusted by paragraph (3) or (4) of this article to the court or other authority specified in article 6 shall be subject to no appeal. The court or other authority, in appointing the arbitrator, shall have due regard to any qualifications required of the arbitrator by the agreement of the parties and to such considerations as are likely to secure the appointment of an independent and impartial arbitrator and, in the case of a sole or third arbitrator, shall take into account as well the advisability of appointing an arbitrator of a nationality other than those of the parties.

A. Meaning and purpose

14.188 In general, Art 11 regulates the procedures for the appointment of arbitrators. However, para (1) does not deal with these procedures, but with an important point concerning the qualifications of an arbitrator. The other paragraphs provide different appointment mechanisms. Similar to the structure implemented by Art 10, para (2) establishes the basic principle of party autonomy in this context. Furthermore, para (3) provides a mechanism for appointing a tribunal consisting of three arbitrators or a sole arbitrator when the parties fail to reach an agreement. In cases where neither a procedure agreed on by the parties nor the procedure subsidiarily offered by the Model Law leads to the appointment of a tribunal, para (4) directs the court, or any other authority specified by Art 6 of the Model Law, to take the necessary measure for an appointment. Paragraph (5) establishes certain criteria that must be observed by the court or other authority in appointing the arbitrator.

B. Nationality of arbitrators, paragraph (1)

14.189 Article 11(1) stipulates that no person in a Model Law state shall be excluded from appointment as an arbitrator by reason of his nationality. This refers to foreigners as well as to residents[284] and is an important issue in establishing truly international arbitration.[285] The provision is inspired by Art 2 of the Strasbourg Uniform Law on Arbitration of 1966.[286] It corresponds to regulations incorporated in many national laws and some international texts such as the European Convention on International Commercial Arbitration of 1961

[284] Calavros, C., *Das UNCITRAL-Modellgesetz über die internationale Handelsschiedsgerichtsbarkeit* (Verlag Ernst und Werner Gieseking, 1988) (Calavros) 63.

[285] Holtzmann and Neuhaus, 359.

[286] First Secretariat Note, UN Doc A/CN.9/207, para 64 note 26.

and the Concluding Document of the Madrid Conference on Security and Cooperation in Europe of 1983. The Working Group agreed that the term 'nationality' should embrace the term 'citizenship', which is used in some legal systems.[287]

(1) The parties' freedom to diverge from Article 11(1)

Following the overriding principle of party autonomy, the parties have the freedom to specify, either directly or by incorporating the rules of trade associations or arbitral institutions, that arbitrators may or may not be appointed because of their nationality.[288] **14.190**

(2) The precedence of the Model Law over national legislation

Article 11(1) overrides any restriction grounded in nationality that may be contained in national arbitration laws.[289] It has a legally binding effect on the appointing court or authority specified in Art 6. Yet though the drafters of the Model Law aimed at preventing discrimination against persons in international commercial arbitration because of their nationality, Art 11(1) cannot prevent states from altering the Model Law on this point to reflect their particular policies in national legislation.[290] Apparently, no Model Law state changed the Law in this respect. **14.191**

In this context, problems may arise if the recognition and enforcement of an arbitral award which was rendered beyond the Model Law's territorial scope of application[291] by an arbitral tribunal whose composition was governed by a national law discriminating against arbitrators of a foreign nationality contradicts the public policy of a state that has adopted Art 11(1) and therefore has to be set aside pursuant to Art 34(2)(b)(ii). In view of the aim and object of international commercial arbitration, which is to offer a means of dispute resolution independent from national peculiarities, in a situation where the parties to the dispute did not agree on the question of the arbitrator's nationality it seems sensible to deny recognition and enforcement. The acceptance of precluding foreigners from serving as arbitrators beyond the scope of party autonomy hinders further development of international commercial arbitration and contradicts the Model Law's non-discrimination tendency.[292] **14.192**

C. Appointment pursuant to party agreement, paragraph (2)

Pursuant to Art 11(2) the parties are basically free to agree on a procedure for appointing the arbitrator or arbitrators. The parties' freedom includes the right to authorize a third person or an institution pursuant to Art 2(d) and to refer to arbitration rules pursuant to Art 2(e).[293] However, the agreement of the parties and the possibly chosen arbitration rules are subject to para (4), providing for recourse to the court or authority specified in Art 6 under certain circumstances, and to para (5), which provides criteria to be observed by that court or authority in appointing an arbitrator. **14.193**

287 Fifth Working Group Report, UN Doc A/CN.9/246, para 31.
288 Analytical Commentary, UN Doc A/CN.9/264, Art 11 para 1.
289 *ibid.*
290 Fourth Working Group Report, UN Doc A/CN.9/245, para 193.
291 See Arts 1(2), 35(1).
292 See also Calavros, 63 *et seq.*
293 UN Doc A/CN.9/264, Art 11 para 2.

14.194 However, in *Microtec Sécuri-T Inc v Quebec National and International Commercial Arbitration Centre (CACNIQ)* the Quebec Superior Court refused to intervene on the question of appointment of arbitrators, as the parties had excluded recourse to court supervision by acceding to the CACNIQ arbitration rules, which provide for an appointment procedure in the event of a lack of agreement between the parties.[294]

D. Appointment pursuant to the Model Law mechanism, paragraph (3)

14.195 Article 11(3) provides supplementary rules in the event that the parties have failed to agree on a procedure for the appointment of arbitrators. Mechanisms are provided for appointing either three arbitrators or one arbitrator, recognizing that these are the most common numbers of arbitrators in international commercial arbitration.[295]

(1) Tribunals composed of three arbitrators, sub-paragraph (a)

14.196 If there are to be three arbitrators, regardless of whether this number was determined by the parties under Art 10(1) or whether it follows from Art 10(2) in the absence of such a determination, the mechanism for appointing a three-person tribunal applies. Pursuant to Art 11(3)(a) each of the parties to the dispute shall appoint one arbitrator and the two arbitrators so appointed shall decide on the third. If the two arbitrators fail to agree on an additional arbitrator within 30 days after their own appointment, ie after the date of the appointment of the last appointed arbitrator,[296] any party may request the court or other authority specified in Art 6 to make the necessary appointment. The same provision shall apply if one party entirely fails to nominate any arbitrator within 30 days after receiving a request to do so from the other party.

14.197 Despite the ambiguous wording of para (3)(a)[297] the 30-day period,[298] which derives from Art 7 of the UNCITRAL Arbitration Rules, does not constitute a deadline for the arbitrators' or the party's power to appoint an arbitrator. The primary aim of the provision is to prevent deadlock in the appointment process, allowing the parties to petition the court or other authority to appoint the arbitrator after a certain period of time has elapsed.[299] If no party applies to the court or other authority, this can be interpreted as an implicit agreement to extend the time limit.[300]

14.198 As a result, an appointment made by the two arbitrators or the other party after the 30-day period has expired would be valid.[301] This interpretation is in accordance with the

[294] *Microtec Sécuri-T Inc v Quebec National and International Commercial Arbitration Centre (CACNIQ)*, Quebec Superior Court (Godin), confirmed by the Quebec Court of Appeal, 2 June 2003, published in French: (2003) Quebec Judgments no 2918 (Lexis); confirmed (2003) Quebec Judgments no 6868 (Lexis), CLOUT Case 516.

[295] See First Draft, UN Doc A/CN.9/WG.II/WP.37, Art 16 note 28; Analytical Commentary, UN Doc A/CN.9/264, Art 11 para 5.

[296] Broches, 57.

[297] The ambiguity was pointed out by the Canadian Government; see Analytical Compilation of Government Comments, UN Doc A/CN.9/263/ADD.1, Art 11 para 2.

[298] *Sri Lanka* provides for a 60-day period: s 7(2)(b) of the Arbitration Act 1995.

[299] See Analytical Commentary, UN Doc A/CN.9/264, Art 11 para 6.

[300] See Holtzmann and Neuhaus, 361 *et seq*.

[301] See Davidson *(Scotland)* para 4.8. But see Bayrisches Oberstes Landesgericht, 4ZScH 9/11, 16 January 2002, published in German: (2002) Neue Juristische Wochenschrift-Rechtsprechungsreport 933,

basic principles of the Model Law: to ensure efficient and expedient proceedings, to recognize party autonomy to the utmost degree and to minimize judicial intervention. Similarly, it should still be possible for the two arbitrators or the other party to appoint an arbitrator after the expiration of the time limit when a party has already requested the court or other authority to do so. A sensible solution would be that the requesting party may either withdraw the request, or the court, when informed of the appointment, may confirm the appointment made by the other party or the arbitrators.[302] When requesting judicial assistance, the claimant has to present an arguable case that there is a dispute arising out of a valid arbitration agreement.[303]

(2) Tribunals consisting of a sole arbitrator, sub-paragraph (b)

Where the parties have agreed to nominate a sole arbitrator pursuant to Art 10(1) but are unable to agree on a concrete person, para (3)(b) provides that the arbitrator shall, at either party's request, be appointed by the court or other authority specified in Art 6. The Model Law does not fix a time limit within which the parties must attempt to reach agreement on appointing a single arbitrator before the supplementary mechanism for appointment applies. Sub-paragraph (b) merely refers to the parties' failure to agree, but gives no indication as to when this prerequisite can be assumed. The application of a time limit was suggested in sub-para (b),[304] but was rejected mainly because the situation in this sub-para is different from the situation prescribed in sub-para (a). In this sub-para the persons expected to agree are the parties who initially wanted to submit their dispute to arbitration, and the best evidence of their failure to agree on an arbitrator is the request of one of them to the court or other authority.[305] **14.199**

In case the parties reach no agreement, they should not hesitate to seek court assistance to avoid frustration or any undue delay of procedures. If a party chooses to apply to the court, the court will be obliged to decide upon the request in order to avoid a deadlock.[306] *Nigeria* provides for a time limit of 30 days as well as a special list-procedure.[307] **14.200**

(3) Tribunals composed of a number of arbitrators other than one or three

The Model Law does not deal with the rather rare situation where the number of arbitrators that the parties have agreed upon are other than one or three, for example two arbitrators. The Working Group considered it undesirable to include provisions for any possible number that **14.201**

CLOUT Case 563. See also *Austria*: s 587(7) of the Code of Civil Procedure allowing the appointment of an arbitrator after a request is made to the court by the other party.

[302] Voskuil and Freedberg-Swartzburg, 'Composition of the Arbitral Tribunal' in P. Sarcevic (ed), *Essays on International Commercial Arbitration* (Graham & Trotman /Martinus Nijhoff, 1989) (Voskuil and Freedberg-Swartzburg) 76.

[303] Chairman, Singapore International Arbitration Centre (SIAC), 4 October 1995, SIAC Arb no 21 of 1995, CLOUT Case 110.

[304] See Summary Record, UN Doc A/CN.9/SR.312, Art 11 para 59; see also the time limit provided in Art 6 of the UNCITRAL Arbitration Rules.

[305] See Summary Record, UN Doc A/CN.9/SR.312, Art 11 para 60; Analytical Commentary, UN Doc A/CN.9/264, Art 11 para 6; Commission Report, UN Doc A/40/17, para 103.

[306] But see Voskuil and Freedberg-Swartzburg, 76 who state that it is at the discretion of the court to decide whether such a request may be admitted.

[307] See s 44 of the Arbitration and Conciliation Decree 1988.

parties may select.[308] Hence, there is an intentional gap in the Model Law.[309] It can be assumed that the appointment of arbitrators in such situations is a matter not governed by the Model Law, but by another national law.[310] *New Zealand* and *Hungary* expressly regulate this issue.[311]

E. Appointment by Article 6 authority, paragraph (4)

14.202 Article 11(4) applies where the parties have agreed on a procedure for appointing an arbitral tribunal or a sole arbitrator, either under para (2) or (3), and the agreed procedure fails. Three typical defects are comprised: (i) a party fails to act as expected under the agreed procedure; (ii) an agreement is not reached under the procedure; (iii) an appointing authority fails to act in accordance with the procedure.

14.203 In such an event, any party to the dispute is allowed to request the court or other authority specified in Art 6 'to take the necessary measure' to secure the appointment. The *travaux préparatoires* state that the authority is obliged not merely to order the recalcitrant party or appointing authority to act, but to also make the appointment of the arbitrator or the arbitrators itself.[312] The High Court of Hong Kong modified this approach and allowed the defendant seven days from the date of delivery of the judgment to appoint the arbitrator, who would otherwise be appointed by the Court.[313]

14.204 Article 11(4) ensures the availability of the court or other authority as a remedy of last resort in order to avoid any deadlock or undue delay in the appointment process.[314] However, the assistance of the court or other authority is not needed when the agreement on the appointment procedure provides other means for securing the appointment, and when the means actually do secure the appointment.[315]

14.205 As to the costs of the court proceedings, the High Court of Hong Kong found that under certain circumstances it was proper that the plaintiff should be placed in the same position it would have been in if the defendant had honoured its obligation under the arbitration agreement and appointed an arbitrator. Therefore, the court ordered the defendant to pay the plaintiff's costs, occasioned by the application for the appointment of an arbitrator by the court on behalf of the defendant.[316]

---

[308] See First Draft, A/CN.9/WG.II/WP.37, Art 16 note 28; Second Working Group Report, A/CN.9/232, para 87.

[309] Holtzmann and Neuhaus, 361.

[310] See *ibid*; Davidson *(Scotland)* para 4.7 points out that under this assumption s 3 of the Arbitration (Scotland) Act 1894 would still have effect in the context of international commercial arbitration; but see Voskuil and Freedberg-Swartzburg, 73 and Hußlein-Stich, 61 who consider applying the same systems that are prescribed in the Model Law.

[311] *New Zealand*: Art 11(6) of the First sch of the Arbitration Act 1996; *Hungary*: s 14(3) of Act LXXI of 1994 on Arbitration.

[312] See Fifth Working Group Report, UN Doc A/CN.9/246, para 32; Analytical Commentary, UN Doc A/CN.9/264, Art 11 para 4.

[313] *Pacific International Lines (PTE) Ltd & Another v Tsinlien Metals and Minerals Co Ltd*, High Court of Hong Kong (Kaplan), 30 July 1992, CLOUT Case 40, published in (1993) XVIII *YCA* 180 (186), excerpts published in (1993) 2 Hong Kong Law Reports 249.

[314] See Analytical Commentary, UN Doc A/CN.9/264, Art 11 para 4.

[315] Broches, 57.

[316] *China Ocean Shipping Company v Mitrans Maritime Panama S A*, High Court of Hong Kong (Leonard), 28 September 1993, CLOUT Case 59.

F. Guiding principles for appointments by the Article 6 authority, paragraph (5)

Article 11(5) indicates the guidelines for the court's or other authority's decision in appointing an arbitrator. First, it demands due regard to any qualifications an arbitrator should have pursuant to an agreement by the parties. All qualifications determined by the parties, such as special skills, a certain profession or long-standing experience, impose a duty of consideration on the court or other authority. A failure to observe any requirement stipulated in an agreement between the parties constitutes a reason for setting aside the award pursuant to Art 34(2)(a)(iv) or for refusing its recognition and enforcement under Art 36(1)(a)(iv).[317] 14.206

The second criterion that the court or other authority must duly regard involves such considerations as are likely to secure the appointment of an independent and impartial arbitrator. The prerequisite of an independent and impartial arbitrator is the very essence of arbitration. Any lack of independence or impartiality constitutes a ground for challenging the arbitrator under Art 12(2) and a reason for setting aside the award pursuant to Art 34(2)(a)(iv) or for refusing its recognition and enforcement under Art 36(1)(a)(iv). 14.207

It can be concluded that these two criteria are mandatory and therefore cannot be contracted out by party agreement.[318] 14.208

In the case of the appointment of a sole or a third arbitrator, the appointing authority shall also take into account the advisability of selecting an arbitrator of a nationality other than those of the parties for the sake of neutrality.[319] This criterion can be derived from the principle of party autonomy as expressed by Art 11(1), from the chosen wording 'shall', 'as well' and 'advisability'. It can also be derived from a comparison with Art 6(4) of the UNCITRAL Arbitration Rules, on which Art 11(5) was modelled,[320] that the parties, however, may free the court or other authority from observing this criterion.[321] Some states omitted this guideline.[322] In *British Columbia* and *Iran* the sole or the third arbitrator has to be of a nationality other than that of the parties.[323] 14.209

As the freedom of the parties to agree on an appointment procedure under Art 11(2) is subject to para (5), the parties are obliged to observe the above-mentioned criteria as well. In this context, it should be noted that no provision of the Model Law imposes any duty on the court or the parties to consider professional qualifications, race, religion or other specific characteristics when appointing a person as an arbitrator. *Tunisia* added an article that 14.210

[317] Calavros, 65; Hußlein-Stich, 60 note 293.

[318] Analytical Commentary, UN Doc A/CN.9/264, Art 11 para 8; Broches, 58.

[319] But see Strohbach, ICCA Lausanne 108, who warns against overrating the role of a foreign arbitrator; *Sri Lanka* omitted this guideline: s 7(4) of the Arbitration Act 1995; In *Iran* the law demands that the sole or the third arbitrator must be of a nationality other than that of the parties.

[320] See First Draft, UN Doc A/CN.9/WG.II/WP.37, Art 17 note 30.

[321] Analytical Commentary, UN Doc A/CN.9/264, Art 11 para 8; Broches, 58.

[322] eg *Sri Lanka*: s 7(4) of the Arbitration Act 1995; *Hungary*: s 16 of Act LXXI of 1994 on Arbitration.

[323] *British Columbia*: s 11(9) of the British Columbia International Commercial Arbitration Act 1986; *Iran*: Art 11(4) of the International Commercial Arbitration Act.

prescribes the qualifications of an arbitrator, such as to be of age, legally competent and in full enjoyment of his civil rights.[324] *Hungary* and *Egypt* added similar provisions.[325]

14.211 The High Court of Hong Kong noted that 'when the court is appointing on behalf of the defaulting appointing party, it should go out of its way to ensure that no sense of grievance is felt, however unreasonable that attitude might appear to others'.[326]

14.212 The decision of the court or other authority specified in Art 6 under para (3) or (4) shall be subject to no appeal. The Secretariat noted that finality seemed appropriate in view of the administrative nature of the function, and essential in view of the need to constitute the arbitral tribunal as soon as possible.[327]

G. Acceptance

14.213 The Model Law does not deal with the way an arbitrator is to accept his mandate. Some Model Law states require the acceptance to be in writing.[328]

Article 12. Grounds for challenge

(1) When a person is approached in connection with his possible appointment as an arbitrator, he shall disclose any circumstances likely to give rise to justifiable doubts as to his impartiality or independence. An arbitrator, from the time of his appointment and throughout the arbitral proceedings, shall without delay disclose any such circumstances to the parties unless they have already been informed of them by him.

(2) An arbitrator may be challenged only if circumstances exist that give rise to justifiable doubts as to his impartiality or independence, or if he does not possess qualifications agreed to by the parties. A party may challenge an arbitrator appointed by him, or in whose appointment he has participated, only for reasons of which he becomes aware after the appointment has been made.

A. Meaning and purpose

14.214 Article 12 primarily ensures the arbitrator's compliance with the principle of impartiality and independence,[329] which is the main substance of the legality of arbitration. It does so in two ways: first, a prospective or appointed arbitrator is required to disclose without delay any circumstances likely to give rise to justifiable doubts as to his impartiality and independence; second, those circumstances form grounds for challenging the arbitrator.

[324] Art 10 of the Arbitration Code 1993.

[325] *Hungary*: s 12 of Act LXXI of 1994 on Arbitration; *Egypt*: Art 16(1) of the Law Concerning Arbitration in Civil and Commercial Matters.

[326] *Fung Sang Trading Limited v Kai Sun Sea Products and Food Company Limited*, High Court of Hong Kong (Kaplan), 29 October 1991, CLOUT Case 20, published in (1992) 1 Hong Kong Law Reports, 40 (54); (1992) XVII YCA 289 (303).

[327] Analytical Commentary, UN Doc A/CN.9/264, Art 11 para 7.

[328] eg *Hungary*: Art 17 of Act LXXI of 1994 on Arbitration; *Egypt*: Art 16(3) of the Law Concerning Arbitration in Civil and Commercial Matters; *Spain* (omitting the writing requirement): Art 16 of the Arbitration Act 2003; *Tunisia*: Art 11 of the Arbitration Code 1993.

[329] Strohbach, 109.

B. Duty of disclosure

Article 12(1) imposes a duty upon any prospective or appointed arbitrator to promptly disclose any circumstances likely to give rise to justifiable doubts regarding his impartiality or independence. Paragraph (1) does not specify the recipient for the disclosure of a person who is approached in connection with a possible appointment as an arbitrator. It can be assumed that the disclosure is to be made to the person that has made the approach, whether that person is a party, a third party such as an arbitral institution, or the court or other authority specified in Art 6.[330] The disclosure must be made to the parties from the time of the arbitrator's appointment. In *India* the disclosure must be made in writing.[331] **14.215**

Article 12(1) was modelled on Art 9 of the UNCITRAL Arbitration Rules, but the drafters of the Model Law clarified and emphasized the obligation of the arbitrator by stipulating that the duty of disclosure is a continuing one at all stages of the arbitral proceedings[332] and must be carried out without delay. As Art 12(1) constitutes a mandatory provision,[333] it prevails over Art 9 of the UNCITRAL Arbitration Rules in arbitral proceedings pursuant to the UNCITRAL Arbitration Rules taking place in a Model Law state. From the mandatory character of this provision, it follows that the parties may not exclude their right to challenge an arbitrator. **14.216**

C. Grounds for challenge, paragraph (2)

Article 12(2)(1), a mandatory provision,[334] sets forth the grounds for challenging an arbitrator. The drafters of the Model Law agreed that they would not attempt to list in detail all possible circumstances that would justify a challenge.[335] It was preferred to provide two general formulae to define situations giving rise to taking action against an arbitrator by focusing on the person's impartiality and independence as well as on his compliance with qualifications agreed on by the parties. In using general tests rather than detailed criteria, the drafters expected wide acceptance of this provision. Almost all Model Law states have adopted this provision. **14.217**

(1) Impartiality and independence

Pursuant to the first part of Art 12(2)(1) an arbitrator may be challenged if circumstances exist that give rise to justifiable doubts as to his impartiality or independence. This provision was modelled on Art 10 of the UNCITRAL Arbitration Rules.[336] Owing to their contractual nature, the regulation in the UNCITRAL Arbitration Rules cannot affect the application of any other grounds for challenge provided in mandatory rules of the applicable law. In contrast, the Model Law lists the grounds for challenge exhaustively, as **14.218**

---

330 Voskuil and Freedberg-Swartzburg, 80; Davidson *(Scotland)* para 4.12.
331 s 12(1) of the Arbitration and Conciliation Ordinance 1996.
332 Second Working Group Report, UN Doc A/CN.9/232, para 58; Third Working Group Report, UN Doc A/CN.9/233, para 106.
333 Strohbach, 109.
334 See Analytical Commentary, UN Doc A/CN.9/264, Art 13 para 1.
335 First Working Group Report, UN Doc A/CN.9/216, para 43.
336 See First Secretariat Note, A/CN.9/207, para 66; Broches, 60.

clarified by the use of the word 'only'.[337] However, most of the grounds for challenge set forth in national laws may be comprised in the general rule of the Model Law.[338]

14.219 The Model Law neither contains a definition of the terms 'impartiality' and 'independence', nor does it set out any circumstances giving rise to justifiable doubts as to this criterion. As a guideline for interpretation, the Secretariat suggested that this proviso should cover instances of biased behaviour or misconduct.[339] These may arise out of a previous involvement in the subject matter in dispute, a financial interest in the case or a close personal or business relationship with one of the parties.[340] Some Model Law states explicitly state that the arbitrators are not the representatives of the parties and may not receive any instruction in the course of their action.[341]

(2) Qualifications agreed on by the parties

14.220 An arbitrator may be challenged if he does not possess qualifications agreed on by the parties, for example the requirement of a certain profession or long-standing experience. In conformity with the regulation in Art 11(1) the parties may agree that the arbitrator must or must not be of a particular nationality.[342] Some Model Law states omitted the ground of lack of qualifications.[343]

(3) Deferred cognition, sentence (2)

14.221 Pursuant to Art 12(2)(2) a party may challenge an arbitrator appointed by him, or in whose appointment he has participated, only for reasons which he becomes aware of after the appointment has been made. Therefore, a party would not be permitted to challenge an arbitrator on a ground which he already knew of at the time of his participation in the appointment procedure or if he could have forestalled the appointment at that time but failed to do so.[344] Such behaviour would contradict the overriding principle of good faith. Thus, Art 12(2)(2) contains a special form of waiver, which is generally dealt with in Art 4. If a party is deemed to have waived a particular ground for challenge, he is precluded from invoking the said ground not only in arbitration, but also in setting-aside and enforcement proceedings. However, the court in these proceedings is not bound by the arbitral tribunal's decision on the challenge.

14.222 Article 12(2)(2) covers direct appointments by one or both parties[345] as well as indirect appointments under list procedures, such as those provided in Art 6(3) of the UNCITRAL

---

337 Commission Report, UN Doc A/40/17, para 119.

338 Analytical Commentary, UN Doc A/CN.9/264, Art 12 para 4; Calavros, 67; Hußlein-Stich, 64; see also Commission Report, UN Doc A/40/17, paras 116–19.

339 Analytical Commentary, UN Doc A/CN.9/264, Art 12 para 5.

340 See First Secretariat Note, UN Doc A/CN.9/207, para 65; see also eg Oberlandesgericht Naumburg, 10 SchH 3/01, 19 December 2000, published in German: (2003) Neue Zeitschrift für Schiedsverfahren (German Arbitration Journal) 135, commented on by Kröll, 17 *Mealey's Int'l Arb Rep* no 6, CLOUT Case 665.

341 eg *Hungary*: s 11 of Act LXXI of 1994 on Arbitration.

342 See Commission Report, UN Doc A/40/17, para 116.

343 eg *Nigeria*: s 45 of the Arbitration and Conciliation Decree 1988; *Sri Lanka*: s 10(2) of the Arbitration Act 1995.

344 Broches, 61.

345 Fifth Working Group Report, UN Doc A/CN.9/264, para 34.

Arbitration Rules.[346] Among the Model Law states, only *Nigeria* did not adopt this provision on deferred cognition.

Article 13. Challenge procedure

(1) The parties are free to agree on a procedure for challenging an arbitrator, subject to the provisions of paragraph (3) of this article.

(2) Failing such agreement, a party who intends to challenge an arbitrator shall, within fifteen days after becoming aware of the constitution of the arbitral tribunal or after becoming aware of any circumstances referred to in article 12(2), send a written statement of the reasons for the challenge to the arbitral tribunal. Unless the challenged arbitrator withdraws from his office or the other party agrees to the challenge, the arbitral tribunal shall decide on the challenge.

(3) If a challenge under any procedure agreed upon by the parties or under the procedure of paragraph (2) of this article is not successful, the challenging party may request, within thirty days after having received notice of the decision rejecting the challenge, the court or other authority specified in article 6 to decide on the challenge, which decision shall be subject to no appeal; while such a request is pending, the arbitral tribunal, including the challenged arbitrator, may continue the arbitral proceedings and make an award.

A. Meaning and purpose

Article 13 deals with the procedure to be applied when an arbitrator is challenged on the grounds set forth in Art 12. Following the principle of party autonomy, Art 13(1) stipulates that the parties are basically free to model the challenge procedure. In case the parties fail to agree on such a procedure according to the 'two-level system' inherent in Art 13, para (2) provides that the party who intends to challenge an arbitrator may request the arbitral tribunal to decide on the challenge. Should neither a procedure agreed upon by the parties nor the tribunal's efforts be successful under any circumstances, recourse may be made to the court or other authority specified in Art 6 for a final decision pursuant to Art 13(3). **14.223**

It should be noted that challenge procedures only take place when the arbitrator or the other party does not accept the challenge. In practice, it is more likely that either the arbitrator who recognizes a ground for challenge will withdraw from his office or the parties will agree on the termination of the arbitrator's mandate.[347] **14.224**

B. Challenge procedure pursuant to party agreement, paragraph (1)

Article 13(1) acknowledges the parties' freedom to determine the challenge procedure. Pursuant to Art 2(d) and (e) this includes the right to authorize a third party, including an institution, to make that determination and to agree on a set of arbitration rules. However, party autonomy as to the challenge of an arbitrator is not unrestricted. First, Art 18 requires equal treatment of the parties in all procedural contexts[348] and second, Art 13(3) demands a last resort to the court in any challenge procedure.[349] Hence, a decision on the challenge **14.225**

[346] Analytical Commentary, UN Doc A/CN.9/264, Art 12 para 6.
[347] See Strohbach, 121.
[348] Analytical Commentary, UN Doc A/CN.9/264, Art 19 para 7.
[349] *ibid*, Art 13 para 2.

by the arbitral tribunal or an authorized arbitral institution is in any case subject to court review.

It has to be noted that contrary to the stipulations contained in Art 13(2) and (3), parties are not bound to certain time limits when tailoring the challenge procedure. However, if parties choose a set of arbitration rules providing time limits, they have to comply with those rules. A number of Model Law states do not grant the parties any freedom to agree on a challenge procedure.[350]

C. **Default challenge procedure, paragraph (2)**

14.226 When the parties have not agreed on a procedure for an arbitrator's challenge, pursuant to Art 13(2) the arbitral tribunal shall decide on the challenge, unless the challenged arbitrator withdraws from his office or the other party agrees to the challenge. This decision is subject to ultimate court review as provided for in Art 13(3). In *Tunisia* the arbitral tribunal cannot decide on the challenge.[351]

(1) Prerequisites

14.227 The challenging party must submit a written statement of reasons for the challenge within 15 days.

14.228 (1.1) **Written statement of reasons** The party who intends to challenge an arbitrator pursuant to Art 13(2) must send a written statement of reasons for the challenge to the arbitral tribunal. The document must specify the grounds for challenge. In addition, its content must raise justifiable doubts as to the impartiality or independence of the arbitrator or his compliance with the qualifications demanded by the parties. The word 'challenge' does not have to be mentioned expressly. It suffices when the party makes it unambiguously clear that he will not accept a certain arbitrator for the stated reasons.

14.229 (1.2) **Time limit** The challenging party must send the arbitral tribunal the written statement of reasons for the challenge within a time limit of 15 days[352] after becoming aware of the constitution of the arbitral tribunal or of any circumstance referred to in Art 12(2). Although the Model Law is not perfectly clear on this point, it may be assumed that an arbitral tribunal is constituted when all the arbitrators have been designated and have accepted their mandate. Article 13(2) also covers the situation in which a party, at the time of the tribunal's constitution, believes in the impartiality and independence of an arbitrator as well as in his compliance with any qualifications agreed on by the parties but later discovers a ground for challenge.

14.230 The question as to what effect a failure to raise a timely challenge should have was left unresolved by the drafters of the Model Law. It is clear from the conditions set out in Arts 12(2) and 13(2) that a party who fails to raise a challenge in a timely manner is precluded

[350] eg *Nigeria*: s 45(9) of the Arbitration and Conciliation Decree 1988; *Sri Lanka*: s 10(3) of the Arbitration Act 1995. The arbitration laws of *Egypt* and *Oman* also do not have provisions conforming to Art 13(1).

[351] See Art 58 of the Arbitration Code 1993.

[352] In *Peru* within three days following the notice of the appointment; see Art 23 of Decree Law no 25935.

from raising this issue later in the arbitral proceedings. Moreover, it seems reasonable that a party who knows of a ground for challenge and does not raise its objection in time should be barred from relying on it in setting-aside or enforcement proceedings under Art 34(2)(a)(iv) and Art 36(1)(a)(iv).[353] Such behaviour would be contrary to the principle of good faith.

(2) Applicability of Article 13(2)

The clear wording of Art 13(2) states that the arbitral tribunal shall decide on the challenge. The Commission rejected a proposal that the mandate of a sole arbitrator who was challenged but did not withdraw from his office terminated on account of the challenge. It noted that the refusal of a sole arbitrator to resign would constitute a rejection of the challenge, making available resort to the court under para (3).[354] This seems sound, and should also apply to the rare situation when all arbitrators of a tribunal are challenged and refuse to withdraw from their office. **14.231**

However, in the case of a multi-arbitrator tribunal the Commission decided not to adopt a suggestion to exclude the challenged arbitrator from the deliberations and the decision of the tribunal on the challenge.[355] As the tribunal's decision on a challenge is not a question of procedure within the meaning of Art 29 sentence (2) and is therefore entrusted to all members of the tribunal pursuant to Art 29 sentence (1),[356] the challenged arbitrator would have to decide on his own challenge. This contradicts the basic principle that no person shall be allowed to judge a case he himself is involved in.[357] It seems reasonable that in such a situation the arbitral tribunal shall decide the challenge without the vote of the challenged arbitrator. **14.232**

D. Resort to Article 6 authority, paragraph (3)

In cases where a challenge procedure agreed upon by the parties or decided by the arbitral tribunal turns out to be unsuccessful, Art 13(3) allows the challenging party to request the court or other authority specified in Art 6 to decide on the challenge as a final instance. There was considerable debate in both the Working Group and the Commission as to the scope of court intervention in deciding challenges.[358] Ultimately, the drafters opted for an immediate court review of unsuccessful challenges. Article 13(3) is mandatory.[359] **14.233**

In order to reduce the risk of delay and dilatory tactics, the following features were included. First, a time limit of 30 days[360] must be imposed, which starts to run when notice of the **14.234**

[353] See Analytical Compilation of Government Comments, UN Doc A/CN.9/263, Art 13 para 4 (Norway); Strohbach, 111; Hußlein-Stich, 72; but see Holtzmann and Neuhaus, 409 *et seq* with reference to Art 4.

[354] Commission Report, UN Doc A/40/17, paras 127–9.

[355] *ibid*, paras 128–9.

[356] Fifth Working Group Report, UN Doc A/CN.9/246, para 38; Analytical Commentary, UN Doc A/CN.9/264, Art 13 para 2.

[357] See Hußlein-Stich, 75; Calavros, 72.

[358] eg Fourth Working Group Report, UN Doc A/CN.9/245, paras 209–12; Analytical Compilation of Government Comments, UN Doc A/CN.9/263, Art 13 para 10; ADD.1, Art 13 para 1; Summary Record, UN Doc A/CN.9/SR.310, paras 34–8; SR.313, paras 44–5; SR.314, para 1; Commission Report, UN Doc A/40/17, paras 122–5.

[359] Analytical Commentary, UN Doc A/CN.9/264, Art 13 para 2.

[360] In *Tunisia*: 45 days; see Art 58 of the Arbitration Code 1993.

decision rejecting the challenge is received. Second, the decision made by the Art 6 authority shall be subject to no appeal. Third, the arbitral tribunal may continue the arbitral proceedings and even make an award while the request for challenge is pending. It may be assumed that when the award is issued and the arbitral proceedings are thus terminated pursuant to Art 32(1), the court is no longer allowed to decide on the challenge.[361] The challenging party who is unwilling to accept this award then has the possibility to initiate setting-aside or enforcement proceedings under Art 34(2)(a)(iv) or Art 36(1)(a)(iv).

14.235 Distinguished arbitrators will consider suspending the arbitration during the court proceedings. However, if they find the challenge totally unfounded, they should continue the arbitration in order to prevent postponement of the proceedings. Some Model Law states, such as *Tunisia* and *Bulgaria*, changed para (3), stating that the arbitral proceedings shall be suspended while the request is pending.[362] In *British Columbia* and *Oregon* the court may refuse to decide on the challenge if it is satisfied that, under the procedure agreed upon by the parties, the party making the request had the opportunity to have the challenge decided by an authority other than the arbitral tribunal, for example by an arbitral institution.[363] *India* does not allow any court intervention in the challenge procedure.[364]

Article 14. Failure or impossibility to act

(1) If an arbitrator becomes *de jure* or *de facto* unable to perform his functions or for other reasons fails to act without undue delay, his mandate terminates if he withdraws from his office or if the parties agree on the termination. Otherwise, if a controversy remains concerning any of these grounds, any party may request the court or other authority specified in article 6 to decide on the termination of the mandate, which decision shall be subject to no appeal.

(2) If, under this article or article 13(2), an arbitrator withdraws from his office or a party agrees to the termination of the mandate of an arbitrator, this does not imply acceptance of the validity of any ground referred to in this article or article 12(2).

A. Meaning and purpose

14.236 Article 14(1) sets out grounds and methods for the termination of an arbitrator's mandate. In order to facilitate an arbitrator's voluntary withdrawal or a party's consent to the termination, Art 14(2) stipulates that a termination of mandate does not imply acceptance of the grounds asserted.

B. Grounds for termination, paragraph (1)

14.237 Article 14(1)(1) specifies three grounds for terminating the mandate of an arbitrator: (i) *de jure* inability to perform his functions; (ii) *de facto* inability to perform his functions; (ii) any other failure to act without undue delay. In addition, the death of an arbitrator automatically leads to the termination of his mandate. This consequence was regarded as

[361] See Hußlein-Stich, 77; but see Voskuil and Freedberg-Swartzburg, 87 and Calavros, 72 *et seq* who consider concurrent challenge and setting-aside procedures.

[362] See *Tunisia*: Art 58(3) of the Arbitration Code 1993; *Bulgaria*: Art 16(2) LICA.

[363] *British Columbia*: s 13(5) of the British Columbia International Commercial Arbitration Act 1986; *Oregon*: s 36.478 of the International Commercial Arbitration and Conciliation Act 1991.

[364] s 13 of the Arbitration and Conciliation Ordinance 1996.

so self-evident that no such stipulation was expressly adopted.[365] The grounds were taken from Art 13(2) of the UNCITRAL Arbitration Rules.[366] *De jure* inability to perform the arbitrator's function refers to the law of the place of arbitration; d*e facto* inability refers to instances such as illness, change of profession and the like.

As to the interpretation of the rather vague term 'failure to', the Analytical Commentary provides some guidelines. First, this term is meant to cover the wide range of situations in which retention of a 'non-performing' arbitrator becomes intolerable.[367] Second, the following considerations should be taken into account: what action was expected or required of him in light of the arbitration agreement and the specific procedural situation? If he has not done anything in this regard, has the delay been so inordinate as to be unacceptable in light of the circumstances, including technical difficulties and the complexity of the case? If he has done something and acted in a certain way, did his conduct clearly fall below the standard of what may reasonably be expected from an arbitrator? Amongst the factors influencing the level of expectations are the ability to function efficiently and expeditiously, and any special competence or other qualifications required of the arbitrator by agreement of the parties.[368] **14.238**

In order to put the time element inherent in this provision into concrete terms, the words 'without undue delay' were added. The Commission Report expressly notes that the additional words were merely elucidatory and did not imply a change in meaning.[369] Other phrases such as 'with due dispatch and with efficiency' or 'with reasonable speed' were rejected, because the criteria of speed and efficiency should not be the primary conditions in this regard. Especially the criterion of efficiency was not adopted, as it would imply the unintended effect of court review.[370] In *Tunisia* the mandate of an arbitrator terminates when he does not fulfil his duty within 30 days.[371] **14.239**

C. Procedure for termination, paragraph (1)

If one of the above-mentioned grounds is present, there are three ways of terminating an arbitrator's mandate: (i) the withdrawal of the arbitrator; (ii) an agreement of the parties on the termination, including the authorization of a third party such as an arbitral institution to decide on the termination pursuant to the general rule laid down in Art 2(d);[372] or (iii) a decision by the court or authority specified in Art 6 if a controversy remains concerning any of these grounds.[373] This decision is not appealable. **14.240**

365 See Analytical Commentary, UN Doc A/CN.9/264, Art 14 para 1.
366 See *ibid,* para 3; Commission Report, UN Doc A/40/17, para 137.
367 Analytical Commentary, UN Doc A/CN.9/264, Art 14 para 3.
368 *ibid,* para 4.
369 Commission Report, UN Doc A/40/17, para 139.
370 *ibid,* para 138.
371 See Art 59(1) of the Arbitration Code 1993.
372 See Commission Report, UN Doc A/40/17, para 15.
373 *Bermuda* provides for another concept: If an arbitrator on a three-person or five-person arbitral tribunal fails to participate in the arbitration, unless the parties otherwise agree, the other arbitrators have the power and the sole discretion to continue the arbitration and to make any decision, ruling or award notwithstanding the non-participation of an arbitrator; see s 30 of the Bermuda International Conciliation and Arbitration Act 1993.

14.241 The final text does not provide any particular procedure for a party to follow when he wishes that the mandate of an arbitrator be terminated. The first draft set out that the party should send a written statement of the reasons to the other party and to all arbitrators and if, within 20 days after notification, the other party does not agree to the termination and the arbitrator does not withdraw from his office, the party may request the Art 6 authority to make a final decision.[374] This procedure was not adopted because it was deemed to be too detailed.[375]

14.242 However, the sending of a written statement of reasons to the other party and all arbitrators so that they can decide on their conduct seems reasonable.[376] If the arbitrator neither withdraws from his office nor does the other party agree to the termination, the party who wishes that the mandate of an arbitrator be terminated can apply to the Art 6 authority. The court or other authority can then rely on the existence of a controversy concerning the grounds for termination.

14.243 If the parties have entrusted an arbitral institution or an appointing authority with the decision regarding the termination, this decision will be final and not subject to court review. As clearly stated in Art 14(1)(2), the court or other authority specified in Art 6 may only decide on the termination of the mandate if there is a controversy concerning the grounds of termination. When the parties have jointly authorized a third party to decide, this decision is included in the parties' freedom to agree on the termination. There is no controversy between the parties and the condition for court review is therefore not fulfilled.[377]

D. Exoneration, paragraph (2)

14.244 This provision applies both to this article and to the challenge procedure under Art 13(2). It emphasizes that neither an arbitrator's withdrawal nor a party's agreement to the termination of an arbitrator's mandate implies acceptance of the validity of any ground referred to in this article or in Art 13(2). There is a similar provision in Art 11(3)(3) of the UNCITRAL Arbitration Rules. It was included to help facilitate withdrawal or consent.[378] Many arbitrators may prefer to withdraw from their office when reproached with prejudice that indicates a lack of confidence in them, even if the charge is false.[379] Such a withdrawal should not be deemed an admission of the charge.

Article 15. Appointment of substitute arbitrator

Where the mandate of an arbitrator terminates under article 13 or 14 or because of his withdrawal from office for any other reason or because of the revocation of his mandate, a substitute arbitrator shall be appointed according to the rules that were applicable to the appointment of the arbitrator being replaced.

---

374 First Draft, UN Doc A/CN.9/WG.II/WP.37, Art 11.

375 See Second Working Group Report, UN Doc A/CN.9/232, para 67.

376 See Holtzmann and Neuhaus, 438.

377 *ibid,* 440 *et seq.*

378 See Analytical Commentary, UN Doc A/CN.9/264, Art 14 *bis* para 1.

379 Strohbach, 111.

A. Meaning and purpose

Article 15 not only provides a mechanism for appointing substitute arbitrators, but also widens the scope of grounds for the termination of an arbitrator's mandate. **14.245**

B. Reasons for termination of an arbitrator's mandate

Article 15 sets out four different categories of reasons giving rise to the termination of an arbitrator's mandate. First, termination of mandate under Arts 13 or 14, including withdrawal and the parties' agreement to terminate; second, withdrawal from office for any other reason; third, revocation of the arbitrator's mandate by agreement of the parties; and fourth, termination for any other reason. This provision reflects the unlimited freedom of the parties to terminate an arbitrator's mandate as well as the unlimited possibility of an arbitrator to resign.[380] **14.246**

The Working Group rejected requiring just cause for the resignation because it was felt that an unwilling arbitrator should not be forced to perform his functions.[381] The recognition of an unlimited possibility of an arbitrator to resign led to the concern that a party-appointed arbitrator could abuse the mechanism for resignation and replacement, particularly by using it repeatedly. The Working Group decided not to deal with this question.[382] However, this problem can be resolved with reference to Art 19 and Art 29. It seems appropriate that in such a situation the remaining arbitrators are entitled to continue the arbitral proceedings and to make an award.[383] In *Bulgaria* the mandate of an arbitrator only terminates when he becomes unable to perform his functions or fails to act without justifiable reasons.[384] In *Bermuda* any resignation by an arbitrator shall not be effective unless the arbitral tribunal determines that there are sufficient reasons to accept the resignation.[385] **14.247**

C. Procedure for appointing a substitute arbitrator

When an arbitrator's mandate terminates, a substitute arbitrator shall be appointed according to the rules that were applicable to the appointment of the arbitrator being replaced. This does not mean that the new appointment has to be made in exactly the same way as the original one. It means that the same set of rules under Art 11 will apply, either as laid down in the arbitration agreement or based on the supplementary rules provided in the Model Law.[386] **14.248**

The principle of party autonomy recognized in Art 11 for the original appointment of an arbitrator applies with equal force to the procedure of appointing a substitute arbitrator.[387] **14.249**

---

[380] See Fifth Working Group Report, UN Doc A/CN.9/246, para 44; Analytical Commentary, UN Doc A/CN.9/264, Art 15 paras 2–3.

[381] Fifth Working Group Report, UN Doc A/CN.9/246, para 44; Analytical Commentary, UN Doc A/CN.9/264, Art 15 para 3.

[382] See Fourth Working Group Report, UN Doc A/CN.9/245, para 219.

[383] See Holtzmann and Neuhaus, 466; see generally Schwebel, S.M., *International Arbitration: Three Salient Problems* (Grotius, 1987) 296.

[384] See Art 17(1) LICA.

[385] See s 30(1) of the Bermuda International Conciliation and Arbitration Act 1993.

[386] See Analytical Commentary, UN Doc A/CN.9/264, Art 15 para 4; Holtzmann and Neuhaus, 465.

[387] Commission Report, UN Doc A/40/17, para 147.

This includes the freedom not to appoint a substitute arbitrator at all, but to terminate the arbitral proceedings if the parties do not want to continue without a particular arbitrator.[388] The parties' freedom includes, of course, the right to entrust an appointing authority or an arbitral institution with the decision on the appointment of a substitute arbitrator pursuant to Art 2(d).

14.250 Unlike Art 14 of the UNCITRAL Arbitration Rules, the Model Law does not demand the repetition of previously held hearings when an arbitrator is replaced. However, under Art 19 the parties and the arbitral tribunal are free to do so when they find it appropriate. *India* emphasizes this by stipulating that, unless otherwise agreed by the parties, any hearings previously held may be repeated at the discretion of the arbitral tribunal. It added that an order or ruling of the arbitral tribunal made prior to the replacement of an arbitrator shall not be invalid solely because there has been a change in the composition of the tribunal.[389] The latter provision derives from the *British Columbia* International Commercial Arbitration Act and is also recognized in *New Zealand* and *Zimbabwe*. In addition, *British Columbia* and *New Zealand* adopted Art 14 of the UNCITRAL Arbitration Rules of 1976.[390] *Sri Lanka* explicitly states that *de novo* proceedings shall not be initiated unless the parties otherwise agree.[391] In *Egypt* all previously held hearings, including any possible award, are considered to be null and void.[392] In *Ontario* any hearing held prior to the replacement or removal of an arbitrator shall start afresh, subject to the contrary agreement of the parties.[393] The law of *Spain* provides that the parties shall decide if it is appropriate to repeat any prior proceedings before the appointment of the substitute arbitrator.[394]

Chapter IV. Jurisdiction of arbitral tribunal

Special literature:

Beraudo, Jean-Paul, 'Case Law on Articles 5, 8, and 16 of the UNCITRAL Model Arbitration Law' (2006) 23 *J Int'l Arb* 101.

Bösch, Axel and Farnsworth, Joanna (eds), *Provisional Remedies in International Commercial Arbitration—A Practitioner Handbook* (Walter de Gruyter, 1994).

Cobb, Matthew B., 'Article 16 (1) of the UNCITRAL Model Law: The Related Doctrines of Kompetenz-Kompetenz and Separability' (2001) 16 *Mealey's Int'l Arb Rep* 32.

Mádl, Ferenc, 'Competence of Arbitral Tribunals in International Commercial Arbitration' in Petar Sarcevic (ed), *Essays on International Commercial Arbitration* (Graham & Trotman/Martinus Nijhoff, 1989).

Szurski, Tadeusz, 'Arbitration Agreement and Competence of the Arbitral Tribunal' in Pieter Sanders (ed), *UNCITRAL's Project for a Model Law on International Commercial Arbitration, Interim meeting, Lausanne, May 9–12, 1984* (ICCA Congress Series no 2, 1984).

---

[388] Analytical Commentary, UN Doc A/CN.9/264, Art 15 para 5.

[389] s 15(3) and (4) of the Arbitration and Conciliation Ordinance 1996.

[390] *British Columbia*: Art 15(3) and (4) of the British Columbia International Commercial Arbitration Act 1986; *New Zealand*: s 15(2) of the First sch of the Arbitration Act 1996; *Zimbabwe*: Art 15(2) and (3) of the Arbitration Act 1996.

[391] s 8(3) of the Arbitration Act 1995.

[392] Art 19(4) of the Law Concerning Arbitration in Civil and Commercial Matters.

[393] s 4(1) of the International Commercial Arbitration Act 1990.

[394] Art 20(2) of the Arbitration Act 2003.

Article 16. Competence of arbitral tribunal to rule on its jurisdiction

(1) The arbitral tribunal may rule on its own jurisdiction, including any objections with respect to the existence or validity of the arbitration agreement. For that purpose, an arbitration clause which forms part of a contract shall be treated as an agreement independent of the other terms of the contract. A decision by the arbitral tribunal that the contract is null and void shall not entail *ipso iure* the invalidity of the arbitration clause.

(2) A plea that the arbitral tribunal does not have jurisdiction shall be raised no later than the submission of the statement of defence. A party is not precluded from raising such a plea by the fact that he has appointed, or participated in the appointment of, an arbitrator. A plea that the arbitral tribunal is exceeding the scope of its authority shall be raised as soon as the matter alleged to be beyond the scope of its authority is raised during the arbitral proceedings. The arbitral tribunal may, in either case, admit a later plea if it considers the delay justified.

(3) The arbitral tribunal may rule on a plea referred to in paragraph (2) of this article either as a preliminary question or in an award on the merits. If the arbitral tribunal rules as a preliminary question that it has jurisdiction, any party may request, within thirty days after having received notice of that ruling, the court specified in article 6 to decide the matter, which decision shall be subject to no appeal; while such a request is pending, the arbitral tribunal may continue the arbitral proceedings and make an award.

A. Meaning and Purpose

Article 16 regulates the competences of the arbitral tribunal and the national court when proceedings have been initiated before the arbitral tribunal.[395] It provides that the arbitral tribunal may rule on its own jurisdiction in the first instance. Thus, the Model Law adopts the concept of *competence-competence*. In this context, the doctrine of separability of the arbitration clause is recognized. In addition to stating these principles, Art 16 contains rules governing the tribunal's decision of its competence and specifies the extent of court review regarding that decision. It should be noted that Art 16 only applies by virtue of Art 1(2) when the place of arbitration is in the enacting state.[396] **14.251**

B. Concept of *competence-competence*, paragraph (1)(1)

Article 16(1)(1) lays down the concept of *competence-competence* (*Kompetenz-Kompetenz, compétence de la compétence*) in providing that the arbitral tribunal may rule on its own jurisdiction. This sentence was patterned after Art 21(1) of the UNCITRAL Arbitration Rules,[397] with two differences. **14.252**

The first difference is that, while the UNCITRAL Arbitration Rules give the arbitral tribunal the power to rule '*on objections* that it has no jurisdiction', the Model Law deletes the reference to objections, thus allowing the tribunal to raise and decide jurisdictional issues on its own initiative.[398] The phrase that the arbitral tribunal's power includes 'any objections with respect to the existence or validity of the arbitration agreement' merely gives a non-exhaustive example of the most important question regarding the tribunal's **14.253**

[395] For the opposite situation, when an action is brought before a court in a matter which is the subject of an arbitration agreement, see Art 8.

[396] *Deco Automotive Inc v G. P. A. Gesellschaft für Pressenautomation mbH*, Ontario District Court, York Judicial District (Mandel), 27 October 1989, CLOUT Case 13.

[397] See First Draft, UN Doc A/CN.9/WG.II/WP.38, Art 29 note 17.

[398] See Commission Report, UN Doc A/40/17, para 150.

jurisdiction, and does not limit the tribunal's competence-competence to those cases where a party has raised an objection.[399] However, the difference between the Model Law and the UNCITRAL Arbitration Rules in this regard is not intended to be as significant as the wording suggests. The Working Group was of the opinion that, except for certain jurisdictional issues concerning arbitrability or public policy, the failure to raise a jurisdictional plea should be deemed as a waiver of the point.[400] The principle of party autonomy does not allow that the tribunal can then raise this issue on its own motion.

14.254 The second difference between the UNCITRAL Arbitration Rules and the Model Law is that the words 'has the power to rule' were substituted by the less vigorous term 'may rule'. In doing so, the Commission merely intended to align the English text with the French, and not to deviate in substance from the wording in the Rules.[401]

14.255 The arbitral tribunal derives its competence to rule on its own jurisdiction from the arbitration agreement. If the agreement is sufficiently broadly drawn, it might encompass not only contractual but also non-contractual claims, for example on a tortuous legal basis, which then fall within the jurisdiction of the tribunal. The competence of the tribunal to rule on its own jurisdiction includes the finding that no arbitration agreement existed between the parties.[402]

14.256 Article 16(1)(1) does not provide for an exclusive and final power of the arbitral tribunal to rule on its own jurisdiction after the commencement of arbitral proceedings. The tribunal merely has the initial and primary competence to decide on its own jurisdiction. This decision is subject to court review, immediate under Art 16(3), later in a setting-aside procedure under Art 34 or in an action for recognition and enforcement under Art 36. The competence-competence of the arbitral tribunal supports the goal of the Model Law to facilitate international commercial arbitration and to ensure its proper functioning. It prevents delays that would occur if an arbitral tribunal had to suspend or terminate its proceedings each time a party raised jurisdictional objections. The court review ensures that the arbitral tribunal does not exceed its jurisdiction.

14.257 As the procedural law principle of competence-competence is mandatory, the parties cannot agree to limit the power of the arbitral tribunal to decide on its jurisdiction. The Commission rejected a proposal to give the parties such freedom, but noted that a state which adopted the Model Law could exclude or limit the tribunal's power in this respect.[403] Apparently, no Model Law state touched on the arbitral tribunal's power.

C. Doctrine of separability, paragraphs (1)(2), (1)(3)

14.258 Article 16(1)(2) and (1)(3) explicitly recognize the doctrine of separability (severability, autonomy) of the arbitration clause. This provision, which was modelled on Art 21(2)(2)

---

[399] See Commission Report, UN Doc A/40/17, para 150; Holtzmann and Neuhaus, 479 note 6; see also Szurski, 75.

[400] See Fifth Working Group Report, UN Doc A/CN.9/246, para 51; see also *infra*.

[401] Commission Report, UN Doc A/40/17, para 152.

[402] Moscow City Court, 13 December 1994, CLOUT Case 147.

[403] Commission Report, UN Doc A/40/17, para 151.

and (2)(3) of the UNCITRAL Arbitration Rules,[404] lays down a principle recognized in most countries.[405] It states that for the purpose of the arbitral tribunal's competence to rule on its own jurisdiction with respect to the existence or validity of the arbitration agreement, the arbitration clause is regarded as independent of the other terms of the contract. Therefore, a decision by the arbitral tribunal that the underlying contract is null and void does not automatically invalidate the arbitration clause.[406] It should be emphasized that, unlike in some national laws, an initial defect is not automatically a ground for the nullity of the arbitration clause.[407]

Article 16 does not explicitly state which law the arbitral tribunal has to apply in determining the validity of the arbitration agreement and the various issues relating to its jurisdiction. However, the Secretariat suggested that the applicable law should be the same law as the one the court specified in Art 6 would apply in setting-aside proceedings under Art 34.[408] Article 34 sets out in para (2)(a)(i) that the validity of the agreement will be governed by the law to which the parties have subjected it or, in the absence of such an indication, the law of the Model Law state. The capacity of the parties will be decided according to the law determined by the conflict of laws rules of the place of arbitration. As provided in Art 34(2)(b), arbitrability and other issues of public policy will be governed by the law of the Model Law state. **14.259**

The practical importance of the doctrine of separability lies in the fact that the arbitral proceedings may generally be continued even though the contract is found to be null and void, which helps to make the arbitral proceedings more effective.[409] **14.260**

D. Raising of jurisdictional pleas, paragraph (2)

(1) Timing

Article 16(2) primarily regulates the timing of pleas concerning whether an arbitral tribunal is without jurisdiction or is exceeding the scope of its authority. Its purpose is to make the parties raise jurisdictional pleas promptly. A plea that an arbitral tribunal does not have jurisdiction, for example because the arbitration agreement is invalid, must be raised no later than at the submission of the statement of defence. Thereafter, as a rule, the parties have waived their right to raise such a plea. However, sentence (4) allows the arbitral tribunal to admit a later plea if it considers the plea justified. **14.261**

404 See First Draft, UN Doc A/CN.9/WG.II/WP.37, Art 4 note 13.

405 See also *Enrique C. Wellbers S. A. I.C. AG v Extraktionstechnik Gesellschaft für Anlagenbau M. B. M.: S/Ordinario*, Argentina: Cámara Nacional de Apelaciones en lo Commercial—Sala, 26 September 1988, CLOUT Case 27, which applies the principle of separability laid down in Art 16(1), although the Model Law has not been adopted in *Argentina* because it reflects a generally-accepted principle.

406 See also *Globe Union Industrial Corp v G. A. P. Marketing Corp.*, British Columbia Supreme Court (Lysyk), 18 November 1994, CLOUT Case 114, published in (1995) 2 Western Weekly Reports 696; *NetSys Technology Group AB v Open Text Corp*, Ontario Court of Justice, 29 July 1999, CLOUT Case 367.

407 See Analytical Commentary, UN Doc A/CN.9/264, Art 16 para 2; see also *Fung Sang Trading Ltd v Kai Sun Sea Products & Food Co Ltd*, High Court of Hong Kong (Kaplan), 29 October 1991, CLOUT Case 20, excerpts published in (1992) Hong Kong Law Reports, 40 (50 *et seq*, 54); (1992) XVII *YCA* 289 (298, 302).

408 Analytical Commentary, UN Doc A/CN.9/264, Art 16 para 3.

409 Mádl, 106.

14.262 Sentence (2) clearly states that a party is not precluded from raising such a plea by having appointed or participated in the appointment of an arbitrator. Thus, a party who intends to invoke lack of jurisdiction of the arbitral tribunal may take part in the constitution of the tribunal without making a reservation, which is necessary under some national laws for excluding the effect of waiver or submission.[410] This provision is patterned after Art 18(4) of the Strasbourg Uniform Law on Arbitration of 1966.[411]

14.263 As to the content of the plea, it is important to note that the respective party has to refer to the lack of jurisdiction of the arbitral tribunal. The Moscow City Court held that a mere submission of the defendant in his statement of defence that he is not the legal successor of the party to the arbitration agreement, and therefore not a party to the contract, is not sufficient.[412] The *Hanseatisches Oberlandesgericht* Hamburg stated that the deadline in Art 16(2) would not apply if the party challenging the tribunal's jurisdiction had not been properly informed about the commencement of the arbitral proceedings.[413]

14.264 A plea that the arbitral tribunal is exceeding the scope of its authority must be raised as soon as the matter alleged to be beyond the scope of the arbitral tribunal's authority comes up during the arbitration proceedings. This provision is modelled on Art V(1) of the European Convention on International Commercial Arbitration of 1961.[414] It has to be stressed that not only can the arbitral tribunal raise a matter beyond the scope of the tribunal's authority, for example when requesting or examining evidence on an issue not submitted to it for decision, but so too can a party in his written or oral statement. The other party would then have to object promptly.

14.265 The Commission recognized that parties who were not sophisticated in international commercial arbitration might not realize that a matter exceeding the tribunal's jurisdiction had been raised and that they need to react immediately. Moreover, in some cases it might not be possible to raise such a plea until the time of award, because the governing law—and therefore limitations on arbitrability—may not be determined until that time.[415] In such situations the delay would presumably be considered justified and the plea allowed by the arbitral tribunal under Art 16(2)(4). Furthermore, the Commission suggested that in such cases the court could allow the plea in setting-aside, recognition or enforcement proceedings.[416]

(2) Effect of failure to raise a plea

14.266 A party who fails to raise a timely plea under Art 16(2) has waived his right to object. Thus, during the later stages of the arbitral proceedings, the party is precluded from raising a plea

---

410 Analytical Commentary, UN Doc A/CN.9/264, Art 16 para 6.

411 See First Draft, UN Doc A/CN.9/WG.II/WP.38, Art 28(2) note 15.

412 Moscow City Court, 10 February 1995, CLOUT Case 148. As to the question of whether an arbitration agreement is binding on a legal successor see Bundesgerichtshof Germany, XII ZR 42/98, 3 May 2000, published in German: (2000) *Neue Juristische Wochenschrift* 2346; (2000) BetriebsBerater 1544, DIS-Online Database on Arbitration Law <http://www.dis-arb.de>, CLOUT Case 561.

413 Hanseatisches Oberlandesgericht Hamburg, 6 Sch 4/01, 8 November 2001, published in German: DIS—Online Database on Arbitration Law, –<http://www.disarb.de>, CLOUT Case 562.

414 First Draft, UN Doc A/CN.9/WG.II/WP.38, Art 28(2) note 14.

415 Commission Report, UN Doc A/40/17, Art 16 para 155.

416 *ibid.*

referring to the existence, validity or scope of the arbitration agreement. As a rule, this is also true for the post-award stages.[417] The Working Group and the Secretariat took the view that failure to object in a timely manner would also preclude the party from relying on the objection in setting-aside or enforcement proceedings.[418] Although the Commission did not explicitly take a position, the *travaux préparatoires* clearly indicate this rule.

However, there are exceptions to the rule of preclusive effect.[419] Matters concerning public policy and arbitrability may be decided upon by a court irrespective of when they are raised.[420] Moreover, pleas concerning violations of any mandatory rules, for example the violation of Art 7(2), can be raised at a later point in time during both the arbitral and the court proceedings.[421] **14.267**

E. Court review of arbitral tribunal's jurisdictional rulings, paragraph (3)

Article 16(3) makes it clear that a challenge to the jurisdiction of the arbitral tribunal is a matter first determined by the arbitral tribunal itself.[422] Yet, the drafters agreed that the arbitral tribunal's rulings on its own jurisdiction should be subject to some sort of court review.[423] However, the views widely diverged on the time and the conditions of that review.[424] Article 16(3) in its final form provides for a flexible solution that enables the arbitral tribunal to assess in each particular case whether the risk of dilatory tactics is greater than the danger of wasting money and time.[425] Some Model Law states such as *Egypt*, *India* and *Oman* omitted Art 16(3). **14.268**

The provision empowers the arbitral tribunal to rule on its own jurisdiction either as a preliminary question or in the final award. If the tribunal chooses to decide this question in the final award, review will be available in setting-aside or in enforcement proceedings under Arts 34 and 36. If the tribunal chooses to rule on a plea as a preliminary question, this decision will be subject to immediate review by a court. The preliminary question can suffer from the same type of irregularities as an award on the merits (see Art 34 and 36) and **14.269**

---

[417] See Moscow City Court, 10 February 1995, CLOUT Case 148.

[418] See Fifth Working Group Report, UN Doc A/CN.9/246, para 51; Analytical Commentary, UN Doc A/CN.9/264, Art 16 paras 8–9.

[419] Broches, 81; Holtzmann and Neuhaus, 483; but see Calavros, 91 who denies any exception to the rules of Arts 16(2) and 4 of the Model Law.

[420] See Analytical Commentary, UN Doc A/CN.9/264, Art 16 para 10.

[421] Holtzmann and Neuhaus, 483 *et seq*; Broches, 86 *et seq*.

[422] See also *Fung Sang Trading Ltd v Kai Sun Sea Products & Food Co Ltd.*, High Court of Hong Kong (Kaplan), 29 October 1991, CLOUT Case 20, excerpts published in (1992) Hong Kong Law Reports, 40 (52); (1992) XVII YCA 289 (300).

[423] First Working Group Report, UN Doc A/CN.9/216, para 82; Commission Report, UN Doc A/40/17, para 157.

[424] eg First Draft, UN Doc A/CN.9/WG.II/WP.38, Arts 28(3), 30; Second Working Group Report, UN Doc A/CN.9/232, paras 155–6; Second Draft, UN Doc A/CN.9/WG.II/WP.40, Arts IV(3), XIII(3); Fourth Working Group Report, UN Doc A/CN.9/245, paras 62–5; Fourth Draft, UN Doc A/CN.9/WG.II/WP.48, Arts 16, 17; Fifth Draft, UN Doc A/CN.9/246 (Annex), Arts 8, 16(3); Analytical Compilation of Government Comments, UN Doc A/CN.9/263, Art 16 paras 7–10; ADD.1, Art 16 paras 1–2; Commission Report, UN Doc A/40/17, paras 157–60.

[425] Commission Report, UN Doc A/40/17, para 159.

thus, may affect the parties' rights in the same way.[426] The party's request for review must be made to the court specified in Art 6 within 30 days after having received notice of the tribunal's ruling. The court's decision is subject to no further appeal.[427] While the request is pending, the arbitral tribunal has discretion to continue the proceedings; the arbitrators may even reach a binding decision.

Chapter IV A. Interim measures and preliminary orders

Special literature:

Bachand, Frederic, 'The UNCITRAL model law's take on anti-suit injunctions' in Emmanuel Gaillard (ed), *Anti-suit injunctions in international arbitration* (Juris Publishing, 2005) 87–112.

Bahmaei, Mohammed-Ali, *L'intervention du juge étatique des mesures provisoires et conservatrices en présence d'une convention d'arbitrage. Droits français, anglais et suisse* (LDGJ, 2002).

Baykitch, Alex and Truong, Jacqueline, 'Innovations in international commercial arbitration - interim measures a way forward or back to the future' (2005) 24 *The Arbitrator & Mediator* no 2, 95.

Berger, Bernhard 'Prozesskostensicherheit (cautio judicatum solvi) im Schiedsverfahren' (2004) 22 *ASA Bull* no 1, 4.

Branson, Cecil, *The Enforcement of Interim Measures of Protection 'Awards'*, ICCA Congress Series no 11, (Kluwer, 2003) 163.

Branson, Cecil, 'Interim measures of protection in a changing international commercial arbitration world' (2002) 9 *Croatian Arb Ybk* 9.

Castello, James, 'Arbitral Ex Parte Interim Relief: The View in Favor' (2003) 58 *Disp Res J* no 3, 60, 65 *et seq*.

Chao, Elaine and Menon, Sundaresh, 'Reforming the Model Law Provisions on Interim Measures of Protection' (2006) *2 Asian Int'l Arb* no 1, 1.

Derains Yves, 'The view against arbitral ex-parte interim relief' (2003) 58 *Disp Res J* no 3, 61.

Donovan, Donald F., '*The Scope and Enforceability of Provisional Measures in International Commercial Arbitration: A Survey of Jurisdiction, the Work of UNCITRAL and Proposals for Moving Forward*' ICCA Congress Series no 11 (Kluwer, 2003) 82.

Fraraccio, Victoria 'Ex-parte preliminary orders in the UNCITRAL Model Law on International Commercial Arbitration' (2006) 10 *Vindobona J of Int'l Commercial L and Arb* no 2, 263.

Hacking, David, 'Ex parte interim relief and the UNCITRAL model law' (2003) 58 *Disp Res J* no 3, 63.

Hamilton, Calvin A. and Vázquez, Eva M., 'Interim measures and the new Spanish Arbitration Act' (2005) 20 *Mealey's Int'l Arb Rep* no 6, 22.

Horning, Richard Allan, 'Interim Measures of Protection; Security for Claims and Costs; and Commentary on the WIPO Emergency Relief Rules (in Toto): Article 46' (1998) 9 *Am Rev Int'l Arb* 155.

Howell, David, 'Interim measures of protection in international arbitration proceedings: towards a new paradigm?' (2006) *Asian Dis Rev* 18.

Huntley, Christopher, 'The Scope of Article 17: Interim Measures under the UNCITRAL Model Law' (2005) 9 *Vindobona J of Int'l Commercial L and Arb* no 1, 69.

[426] Hanseatisches Oberlandesgericht Hamburg, 30 August 2002, 11 Sch 2/00, published in German DIS-Online Database on Arbitration Law <http://www.dis-arb.de>, CLOUT Case 570.

[427] But see *Singapore*: appeal to the Court of Appeal with the leave of the High Court, s 10 of the International Arbitration Act 1994.

Karrer, Pierre A. and Desax, Marcus, 'Security for Cost in International Arbitration, why, when, and what if...' in Robert Briner (ed), *Liber Amicorum Karl-Heinz Böckstiegel: Law of International Business and Dispute Settlement in the 21st Century* (Heymann, 2001) 330.

Marchac, Gregoire, 'Note & Comment: Interim Measures in International Commercial Arbitration under the ICC, AAA, LCIA and UNCITRAL Rules' (1999) 10 *Am Rev Int'l Arb* 123.

Montineri, Corinne and Musolino, Franca 'UNCITRAL's current work on interim measures of protection granted by arbitral tribunals and their enforcement' (2004) 23 *The Arbitrator and Mediator* no 3, 1.

Naimark, Richard W. and Keer, Stephanie E, 'Analysis of UNCITRAL questionnaires on interim relief' (2001) 16 *Mealey's Int'l Arb Rep* no 3, 23.

Poudret, Jean-François, 'Les mesures provisionnelles et l'arbitrage: aperçu comparatif des pouvoirs respectifs de l'arbitre et du juge' in François Bohnet (ed), *Mélanges en l'honneur de François Knoepfler* [Anthology in honour of Francious Knoepfler] (Basel, 2005) 235.

Roth, Marianne, 'Arbitration Costs—Advance Payments and Reimbursement' *CILS Comparative Law Yearbook of International Business*, (Kluwer, 2007) 99.

Roth, Marianne, 'Arbitration Costs—Austrian and International Perspectives' in: Roger Jones and Gabriel Moens (eds), *Int'l Trade and Business L Rev Vol XII* (Routledge Cavendish, 2008) 1.

Schaefer, Jan K., *New Solutions for Interim Measures of Protection in International Commercial Arbitration: English, German and Hong Kong Law Compared*, <http://www.ejcl.org/22/abs22-2.html>.

Schroth, Hans-Jürgen, 'Einstweiliger Rechtsschutz im deutschen Schiedsverfahren' (2003) *SchiedsVZ* no 3, 102.

Thomas, J. C., 'Interim measures in international arbitration: finding the best answer' (2005) 12 *Croatian Arb Ybk* 213.

'UNCITRAL achieves consensus on interim measures in arbitration' (2005) 16 *World Arbitration and Mediation Report* no 3, 83.

Uzelac, Alan, 'Jurisdiction of the Arbitral Tribunal: Current Jurisprudence and Problem Areas Under the UNCITRAL Model Law' (2005) 8 *Int'l Arb L Rev* no 5, 153.

Van Haersolte-Van Hof, Jacomijn J, 'Interim Measures of Protection—A European and Continental Perspective' ICCA Congress Series no 11 (Kluwer, 2003), 150.

Van Houtte, Hans, 'Ten reasons against a proposal for ex parte interim measures of protection in arbitration' (2004) 20 *Arb Int'l* no 1, 85.

Wang, William, 'International arbitration: the need for uniform interim measures of relief' (2003) 28 *Brooklyn J of Int'l L*, 1059.

Winstanley, Adrian, 'UNCITRAL heralds the age of ex parte measures' (2005) 5 *Model Law Materials* no 1, 5.

Wong, Jarrod, 'The issuance of interim measures in international disputes: a proposal requiring a reasonable possibility of success on the underlying merits' (2005) 33 *Georgia J of Int'l and Comp L* 605.

Yesilirmak, Ali, *Provisional Measures in International Commercial Arbitration* (Kluwer, 2005).

Section 1. Interim measures

Chapter IV A, s 1, replaces the existing Art 17 with entirely new provisions regarding the power of the arbitral tribunal to order interim measures. However, so far only five Model Law states, namely *Ireland*, *Mauritius*, *New Zealand*, *Peru* and *Slovenia*, have enacted legislation based on the amendments on interim measures as adopted in 2006. Therefore, before providing commentary on the amended text of Art 17, it seems sensible to first have a look at the old version of Art 17 regulating the power of the arbitral tribunal to order interim measures. **14.270**

Original version of Article 17. Power of arbitral tribunal to order interim measures

(Before the amendments adopted by the Commission at its 39th session, in 2006)

Unless otherwise agreed by the parties, the arbitral tribunal may, at the request of a party, order any party to take such an interim measure of protection as the arbitral tribunal may consider necessary with respect to the subject matter of the dispute. The arbitral tribunal may require any party to provide appropriate security in connection with such a measure.

A. Meaning and Purpose

14.271 In its original version Art 17 empowers the arbitral tribunal to order interim measures of protection with respect to the subject matter of the dispute at the request of a party. The parties can exclude or modify this power by agreement.[428] In addition, the arbitral tribunal has the discretion to order appropriate security in connection with such measures. Thus, a party has the choice to request interim protective measures either from the arbitral tribunal under this provision or from a court under Art 9. Article 17 is modelled on Art 26(1) and (2) of the UNCITRAL Arbitration Rules, with a number of changes.

B. The order of interim measures, sentence (1)

(1) Implied power to order interim measures

14.272 The term 'unless otherwise agreed by the parties' makes it clear that the power of the arbitral tribunal to order certain interim measures of protection is implied in an arbitration agreement. Hence, there is no need for the parties to confer this power on the arbitral tribunal explicitly.[429]

(2) Scope of the implied power

14.273 Regarding the scope of the arbitral tribunal's power to order interim protective measures, Art 17 provides for a general formula permitting any interim measures of protection with respect to the subject matter of the dispute. There was some support for limiting the measures to the ones explicitly provided in the non-exclusive list of examples in Art 26(1) of the UNCITRAL Arbitration Rules,[430] but ultimately it was decided that the tribunal's power should not be so limited.[431] During the drafting process, the following measures were assumed to be within the power of the arbitral tribunal under Art 17: measures to conserve goods (such as by depositing them with a third person or selling perishable goods),[432] the opening of bank letters of credit,[433] using or maintaining machines or completing phases

---

[428] In *Egypt* the arbitral tribunal may make orders for interim measures only if this power is expressly conferred upon it by the parties: see Art 24(1) of the Law Concerning Arbitration in Civil and Commercial Matters; in *Quebec* the arbitral tribunal has no such power.

[429] Fourth Working Group Report, A/CN.9/245, para 71; Broches, 91.

[430] See Second Working Group Report, UN-Doc. A/CN.9/232, para 121; Second Draft, UN Doc A/CN.9/WG.II/WP.40, Art XIV.

[431] Fourth Working Group Report, UN Doc A/CN.9/245, para 71.

[432] See eg First Working Group Report, UN Doc A/CN.9/216, para 66; First Draft, UN Doc. A/CN.9/WG.II/WP.37, Art 23.

[433] Analytical Compilation of Government Comments, UN Doc A/CN.9/263/ADD.1, Art 18 para 1 (*Sudan*).

of construction where necessary to prevent irreparable harm,[434] measures to secure evidence,[435] and measures to protect trade secrets and proprietary information.[436] This listing is merely indicative of the measures that may be granted by an arbitral tribunal. The power of an arbitral tribunal is limited to orders directed to the parties of the arbitration agreement because the arbitral tribunal derives its jurisdiction from this agreement. Therefore, the scope of Art 17 is not as wide as the scope of Art 9, which also includes interim measures relating to third parties. Some Model Law states list the interim measures that an arbitral tribunal may grant.[437] In *Kenya and Zimbabwe* the arbitral tribunal, or a party with the approval of the arbitral tribunal, may seek assistance from the High Court in exercising any power conferred upon the arbitral tribunal in this regard.[438]

(3) The enforcement of interim measures ordered by an arbitral tribunal

Article 17 only deals with the question of whether an arbitral tribunal may order interim measures of protection. The question of enforcement of such interim measures is not addressed by the Model Law. The Working Group decided to leave this question unresolved, as it touched on national procedural laws and court competence and was unlikely to be accepted by many states.[439] Therefore, the enforcement of interim measures ordered by an arbitral tribunal is governed by the procedural law of the enacting state. However, the Secretariat noted that it is most likely that a party will comply with the tribunal's order in view of the probability that in deciding the case, particularly in any assessment of damages, the arbitral tribunal would take into account the party's failure to comply.[440] **14.274**

A large number of Model Law states included provisions concerning the enforcement of such interim measures. In some states orders under Art 17 are treated like arbitral awards for the purpose of enforcement.[441] In Scotland the order takes the form of an award.[442] Other states allow a party to request enforcement from a court.[443] In still other states a party may request authorization from the arbitral tribunal to proceed with the execution of the order itself.[444] **14.275**

---

434 Analytical Commentary, UN Doc A/CN.9/264, Art 18 para 2.

435 Analytical Commentary, UN Doc A/CN.9/264, Art 18 para 2.

436 Commission Report, UN Doc A/40/17, para 167.

437 See eg *Hong Kong*: s 2GB(1) of the Arbitration Ordinance; *Singapore*: s 12(1) of the International Arbitration Act 1994; *Zimbabwe*: Art 17(2) of the Arbitration Act 1996.

438 *Kenya*: s 18(2) of the Arbitration Act 1995; *Zimbabwe*: Art 17(3) of the Arbitration Act 1996.

439 Fourth Working Group Report, UN Doc A/CN.9/245, para 72.

440 Analytical Commentary, UN Doc A/CN.9/264, Art 17 para 5.

441 See eg *Bermuda*: s 26 of the Bermuda International Conciliation and Arbitration Act 1993; *British Columbia*: s 2 of the British Columbia International Commercial Arbitration Act 1986; *California*: s 1297.92 CCP; *New Zealand*: Art 17(2) of First sch of the Arbitration Act 1996; *Malta*: s 62 of the Arbitration Act 1996; *Ontario*: s 9 of the Ontario International Commercial Arbitration Act 1990; see also *Australia*: s 23 of the International Arbitration Act 1974.

442 Art 17(2) of sch 7 of the Law Reform (Miscellaneous Provisions) (Scotland) Act 1990.

443 *Germany*: s 1041, ZPO; *Sri Lanka*: s 13(2) of the Arbitration Act 1995; *Hong Kong*: s 2GG of the Arbitration Ordinance, Chapter 341; *Singapore*: s 12(5) of the International Arbitration Act 1994; see also *Tunisia*: Art 62 of the Arbitration Code: the arbitral tribunal can request such assistance.

444 *Egypt*: Art 24(2) of the Law Concerning Arbitration in Civil and Commercial Matters; *Oman*: Art 24(2) of the Law of Arbitration in Civil and Commercial Disputes.

C. Securities in connection with interim measures, sentence (2)

14.276 The arbitral tribunal may require any party to provide appropriate security in connection with the measure ordered by the tribunal. The Model Law uses a more general wording than Art 26(2) of the UNCITRAL Arbitration Rules, which provides for 'security for the costs of such measure'. The Commission changed the language to clarify that the security required could cover not only the costs of such interim measure, but also any possible or foreseeable damage to a party.[445]

Article 17. Power of arbitral tribunal to order interim measures

(As adopted by the Commission at its thirty-ninth session, in 2006)

(1) Unless otherwise agreed by the parties, the arbitral tribunal may, at the request of a party, grant interim measures.

(2) An interim measure is any temporary measure, whether in the form of an award or in another form, by which, at any time prior to the issuance of the award by which the dispute is finally decided, the arbitral tribunal orders a party to:

(a) Maintain or restore the status quo pending determination of the dispute;

(b) Take action that would prevent, or refrain from taking action that is likely to cause, current or imminent harm or prejudice to the arbitral process itself;

(c) Provide a means of preserving assets out of which a subsequent award may be satisfied; or

(d) Preserve evidence that may be relevant and material to the resolution of the dispute.

A. Meaning and purpose

14.277 Article 17(1) entitles the arbitral tribunal to order interim measures as long as the parties have not agreed otherwise. Article 17(2) provides a generic definition of interim measures and provides an illustrative list of possible measures that the arbitral tribunal may grant.

B. Power to order interim measures, paragraph (1)

14.278 Article 17(1) provides that the arbitral tribunal may, at the request of a party, grant interim measures of protection, unless the parties have agreed otherwise. Thus, it is possible that the parties opt out of the regime by agreeing that Art 17 shall not apply. The Commission considered this as a more workable solution than an opt-in scheme. as the parties may not realistically agree on such matters by the time disputes have arisen.[446]

14.279 The limitation of interim measures in respect to the subject matter of the dispute within the original text of Art 17 was omitted. The Commission considered that the shortened new wording should clarify that the arbitral tribunal also may order interim measures that are not directly related to the assets under dispute.[447] It should be noted that Art 26 of the UNCITRAL Arbitration Rules, however, excludes measures that are not related to the goods in dispute.

---

[445] Commission Report, UN Doc A/40/17, paras 165–6.

[446] Chao, E. and Menon, S., 'Reforming the Model Law Provisions on Interim Measures of Protection' (2006) 2 *Asian Int'l Arb* 5.

[447] Working Group Report, UN Doc A/CN.9/508, para 52.

C. Definition of interim measures, paragraph (2)

(1) Form

Article 17(2) describes an interim measure as any temporary measure issued prior to the rendering of the final award 'whether in the form of an award or in another form'. The tribunal may issue the measure in the form of an award, but it is not obliged to do so.[448] Thus, there is no prescribed form for the order of an interim measure.[449] However, by its very nature an interim measure is unlikely to be of the substance of a final award. This is particularly important with regard to the question of enforcement. In this context, the Commission made clear that the wording 'would not be misinterpreted as taking a stand in respect of the controversial issue as to whether or not an interim measure issued in the form of an award would qualify for enforcement under the New York Convention'.[450] Thus, regardless of the form of the measure, only the regime of ch IV A, s 4 is applicable for the enforcement of the measure. **14.280**

(2) Timing

Interim measures may be ordered at any time prior to the issuance of the award by which the dispute is finally decided. Thus, interim measures might be requested at any stage of the arbitral proceeding.[451] **14.281**

(3) Categories of interim measures

Article 17(2)(a)–(d) provides a list of functions characteristic to interim measures. The Working Group agreed that the list should be non-exhaustive[452] in providing 'generic broadly-cast categories describing the functions or purposes of various interim measures without focusing on specific measures'.[453] In preparing these categories, the Working Group compared several jurisdictions to distil the common essence of an interim measure.[454] **14.282**

(3.1) Maintenance of status quo, paragraph (2)(a) Article 17(2)(a) provides that an interim measure should maintain the status quo until a final decision on the merits of the case is rendered. This purpose of interim measures is widely accepted in many legal systems.[455] **14.283**

(3.2) Anti-suit injunctions, paragraph (2)(b) Article 17(2)(b) empowers the arbitral tribunal to prevent a party from employing actions that may cause obstruction or delay in the arbitral process.[456] This includes the tribunal's power to prevent a party from bringing a claim before a court or another arbitral tribunal by issuing anti-suit injunctions,[457] which are defined as an 'interim measure by which an arbitral tribunal would order a party not to pursue court proceedings or separate legal proceedings'.[458] The fundamental idea behind **14.284**

---

448 Chao and Menon, 7.

449 Working Group Report, UN Doc A/CN.9/508, para 65 *et seq.*

450 Note by the Secretariat, UN Doc A/CN.9/WG.II/WP.131, para 10; Working Group Report, UN Doc A/CN.9/547, para 72.

451 Working Group Report, UN Doc A/CN.9/508, para 69.

452 Binder para 4-051; Chao and Menon 7; Montineri Musolino 4.

453 Working Group Report, UN Doc A/CN.9/545, para 21.

454 For a summary of the information obtained from the compared jurisdictions see Note by the Secretariat, UN Doc A/CN.9/Wg.II/WP.119.

455 Working Group Report, UN Doc A/CN.9/545, para 23.

456 *ibid.*

457 Chao and Menon, 6.

458 Working Group Report, UN Doc A/CN.9/547, para 75.

this provision is that it is legitimate for arbitral tribunals to protect their own arbitral process.[459] Although some delegates were in opposition against this provision,[460] within the Working Group the view prevailed that such measures were becoming common and that they served an important purpose in international trade by ensuring protection for arbitral proceedings.[461]

14.285 (3.3) **Preservation of assets, paragraph (2)(c)** Article 17(2)(c) is aimed at avoiding a dissipation of assets from which the final award could be satisfied[462] and therefore empowers the arbitral tribunal to issue interim measures to preserve assets to secure the enforcement of the award.[463] This includes measures 'to avoid loss or damage and measures aimed at preserving a certain state of affairs until the dispute is resolved, such as orders to continue performing a contract during the arbitral proceedings (eg an order to a contractor to continue construction works despite its claim that it is entitled to suspend the works); orders to refrain from taking an action until the award is made; orders to safeguard goods (eg to take specific safety measures, to sell perishable goods or to appoint an administrator of assets); orders to take the appropriate action to avoid the loss of a right (eg to pay the fees needed to extend the validity of an intellectual property right); orders relating to the clean-up of a polluted site'.[464]

14.286 The Working Group agreed that the provision should not deal with the topic of security of costs, as it would not be appropriate to put the defendant under an obligation equal to that of the claimant to provide a guarantee simply to defend itself.[465]

14.287 (3.4) **Preservation of evidence, paragraph (2)(d)** Article 17(2)(d) entitles the arbitral tribunal to preserve evidence that may be relevant or material for the resolution of the dispute on an interim basis. The purpose of this preservation is to facilitate the proper conduct of the arbitral process.[466] The Working Group included this provision because the domestic rules of civil procedure do not sufficiently deal with the topic of preservation of evidence.[467]

Article 17 A. Conditions for granting interim measures

(As adopted by the Commission at its thirty-ninth session, in 2006)

(1) The party requesting an interim measure under article 17(2)(a), (b) and (c) shall satisfy the arbitral tribunal that:

(a) Harm not adequately reparable by an award of damages is likely to result if the measure is not ordered, and such harm substantially outweighs the harm that is likely to result to the party against whom the measure is directed if the measure is granted; and

---

459 Working Group Report, UN Doc A/CN.9/547, para 77.

460 *ibid*, para 76.

461 *ibid*, para 77; Working Group Report, UN Doc A/CN.9/589, para 20 *et seq*.

462 Yesilirmak, para 1–14.

463 Working Group Report, A/CN.9/523, para 77.

464 Report of the Secretary General, UN Doc A/CN.9/WG.II/WP.108, para 63.

465 Working Group Report, A/CN.9/523, paras 37, 77; But with regard to s 593 Austrian Code of Civil Procedure see Reiner, A., Das *neue österreichische Schiedsrecht: The New Austrian Arbitration Law* (LexisNexis ARD Orac, 2006) 27, 89; Roth, 'Arbitration Costs: Advance Payments and Reimbursement' 104 *et seq*; Roth, 'Arbitration Costs—Austrian and International Perspectives' in: Roger Jones and Gabriel Moens (eds), *Int'l Trade and Business L Rev. Vol XII* (Routledge Cavendish 2009) 7 *et seq*.

466 Yesilirmak, paras 5–72.

467 Working Group Report, UN Doc A/CN.9/545, para 27.

(b) There is a reasonable possibility that the requesting party will succeed on the merits of the claim. The determination on this possibility shall not affect the discretion of the arbitral tribunal in making any subsequent determination.

(2) With regard to a request for an interim measure under article 17(2)(d), the requirements in paragraphs (1)(a) and (b) of this article shall apply only to the extent the arbitral tribunal considers appropriate.

A. Meaning and purpose

Article 17A sets out two conditions which must be fulfilled by a party requesting an interim measure. The requesting party has to satisfy the tribunal that there is on the one hand the necessity of irreparable harm and on the other hand a reasonable possibility of the applicant's success on the merits of the case. In addition, the provision addresses the question of the burden of proof to be discharged by the applicant. As interim measures are often used as a dilatory tactic, the provision's main purpose consists of providing an effective means against frivolous and unfounded applications for interim measures. **14.288**

B. Conditions to be satisfied for granting interim measures, paragraph (1)

A party requesting an interim measure has to satisfy the arbitral tribunal that the conditions set forth in sub-paras (a) and (b) are fulfilled: the possibility of not adequately reparable harm and a reasonable possibility of winning on the merits of the case. Both conditions have to be satisfied equally.[468] As to the question of the burden of proof, the Working Group clarified that the applicant has to meet the burden of convincing the arbitral tribunal that both conditions are satisfied.[469] In respect of the standard of the burden of proof, the Working Group chose a neutral formulation and left the question of how the tribunal is to be satisfied open.[470] **14.289**

(1) Risk of harm, paragraph (1)(a)

Under Art 17 A(1)(a) interim measures can only be issued to avoid harm that cannot adequately be compensated in monetary terms.[471] Examples are the loss of a priceless or unique work of art, a business becoming insolvent, an essential business opportunity being lost or harm being caused to the reputation of a business as a result of a trademark infringement.[472] The discussed wording 'irreparable harm', although well known in many legal systems, was deleted and substituted with the wording 'harm not adequately reparable by an award of damages'. The Working Group considered that 'irreparable harm might present too high a threshold',[473] and that the new wording should make clear that the arbitral tribunal has discretion in deciding whether an interim measure should be issued.[474] **14.290**

In addition, Art 17 A(1)(a) requires that the harm should substantially outweigh the harm caused by the interim measure against the other party. Thus, the arbitral tribunal should **14.291**

468 Binder para 4-057.
469 Working Group Report, UN Doc A/CN.9/545, para 28.
470 *ibid*, para 28.
471 *ibid*, para 88.
472 *ibid*, para 86.
473 Report of the Secretary General, UN Doc A/CN.9/WG.II/Wp.131, para 15.
474 *ibid*.

take the effect of an interim measure on the arbitrating parties' rights into account, to ensure that the harm caused by the measure is not out of proportion with the advantage for the applicant. The conditions set out in Art 17 A(1)(a) are comparable to the balance of convenience test, which is commonly applied by courts in common law jurisdictions.[475]

(2) Reasonable possibility to succeed on the merits, paragraph (1)(b)

14.292 Article 17 A(1)(b) sets forth the second condition for granting an interim measure and provides that the arbitral tribunal must believe that there are reasonable chances that the requesting party may win the case. This initial evaluation of the case is limited to a determination of the seriousness of the case.[476] The arbitral tribunal should be satisfied that the requesting party has a case and that the claim is not frivolous or vexatious.[477] It is explicitly stated that the later findings of the arbitral tribunal should not be prejudiced at this stage of the proceeding.[478]

C. Preservation of evidence, paragraph (2)

14.293 Where a request is made for an interim measure for the preservation of evidence, the arbitral tribunal may apply less onerous conditions than set forth in Art 17 A(1) if it considers that appropriate. This seems a sensible solution, as the preservation of evidence is a matter of direct interest to the entire arbitral process and should not be hindered by strict conditions.

Section 2. Preliminary orders

Article 17 B. Applications for preliminary orders and conditions for granting preliminary orders

(As adopted by the Commission at its thirty-ninth session, in 2006)

(1) Unless otherwise agreed by the parties, a party may, without notice to any other party, make a request for an interim measure together with an application for a preliminary order directing a party not to frustrate the purpose of the interim measure requested.

(2) The arbitral tribunal may grant a preliminary order provided it considers that prior disclosure of the request for the interim measure to the party against whom it is directed risks frustrating the purpose of the measure.

(3) The conditions defined under article 17A apply to any preliminary order, provided that the harm to be assessed under article 17A(1)(a), is the harm likely to result from the order being granted or not.

A. Meaning and Purpose

14.294 Article 17 B deals with the application and conditions for the granting of preliminary orders, which provide a means of preserving the status quo until the arbitral tribunal issues an interim measure adopting or modifying the preliminary order.

[475] Chao and Menon 8.

[476] Working Group Report, UN Doc A/CN.9/523, para 43.

[477] Yesilirmak, para 5-28.

[478] Working Group Report, UN Doc A/CN.9/523, para 43; Working Group Report, UN Doc A/CN.9/545, para 32.

By far the most controversial issue in the reforms of the Model Law was whether the Model Law should permit the ordering of interim measures on an *ex parte* basis without hearing the party against whom the measure is directed. There was a wide divergence of views amongst the member states: in support of *ex parte* measures, it was said that there is a general necessity for these kinds of orders in situations where an element of surprise was called for, such as where it was possible that the affected party might try to pre-empt the measure by taking actions to make the measure moot or unenforceable.[479] **14.295**

In opposition against *ex-parte* measures, it was argued that these types of measures could run 'counter to the principles of trust and consensus underlying international arbitration and contradicted the principle that parties to arbitral proceedings should be treated on the basis of fairness and equality'.[480] Although there are strong grounds both for and against *ex parte* measures, the view prevailed that it is more important to develop a regime in which such measures can be monitored than to allow these measures without such a regime.[481] Thus, the Working Group decided to adopt a regime permitting the arbitral tribunal to grant some kind of interim relief on an *ex parte* basis. **14.296**

Parties may opt out of the regime of *ex parte* interim relief by agreeing that Art 17 B would not apply. Thus, it is the default situation under Art 17 B that *ex parte* measures are permitted.[482] **14.297**

B. Application for preliminary orders, paragraph (1)

Article 17 B(1) empowers the arbitral tribunal to issue preliminary orders directed to the party against whom an interim measure is requested. **14.298**

A preliminary order might be regarded as a subset for an interim measure, but has to be distinguished from interim measures in its narrower purpose: preliminary orders are designed to forbid the party against whom an interim measure is requested to take action to frustrate the requested measure until the arbitral tribunal has heard this party and ruled on the application of the measure. **14.299**

According to the Working Group, preliminary orders provide 'a bridging device until an *inter partes* hearing could take place in respect of a requested measure'.[483] Preliminary orders are subject to strict time limits[484] and designed to prevent the frustration of an interim measure by ordering the party to preserve the status quo until further notice.[485] **14.300**

[479] Working Group Report, UN Doc A/CN.9/569, para 15; For the discussion see Castello, J., 'Arbitral Ex Parte Interim Relief: The View in Favor' (2003) 58 *Disp Res J* no 3, 68.

[480] Working Group Report, UN Doc A/CN.9/569, para 16; For the detailed discussion see Van Houtte, H., 'Ten reasons against a proposal for ex parte interim measures of protection in arbitration' (2004) 20 *Arb Int'l* 85; Fraraccio, V., 'Ex-parte preliminary orders in the UNCITRAL Model Law on International Commercial Arbitration' (2006) 10 *Vindobona J of Int'l Commercial L and Arb* (Vienna) 263.

[481] Montineri and Musolino, 7.

[482] Working Group Report, UN Doc A/CN.9/573, para 27.

[483] Working Group Report, UN Doc A/CN.9/569, para 26.

[484] See the commentary on Art 17 C(4) at paras 14.307 and 14.308.

[485] Binder, para 4-074.

Furthermore, the Working Group explained that preliminary orders shall not only require a party to refrain from an action, but also encompass an order for an affirmative action.[486]

C. Conditions for granting preliminary orders

(1) Risk of frustrating the purpose of an interim measure, paragraph (2)

14.301 Article 17 B(2) supports and strengthens what Art 17 B(1) sets forth and thus provides further guidance as to the considerations to be taken into account by an arbitral tribunal when granting a preliminary order. While sub-para (1) deals with the procedure to be followed by a party when applying for a preliminary order, this provision deals with the issue from the perspective of the arbitral tribunal's power.[487]

(2) Conditions of Article 17 A, paragraph (3)

14.302 Article 17 B(3) provides that the conditions of Art 17 A also apply to preliminary orders. The Working Group considered that Art 17 A is to be applied in the context of preliminary orders in a way that the harm to be assessed by the arbitral tribunal in that context is the harm resulting if the preliminary order is not granted, and not the harm resulting if the interim measure is not granted.[488]

Article 17 C. Specific regime for preliminary orders

(As adopted by the Commission at its thirty-ninth session, in 2006)

(1) Immediately after the arbitral tribunal has made a determination in respect of an application for a preliminary order, the arbitral tribunal shall give notice to all parties of the request for the interim measure, the application for the preliminary order, the preliminary order, if any, and all other communications, including by indicating the content of any oral communication, between any party and the arbitral tribunal in relation thereto.

(2) At the same time, the arbitral tribunal shall give an opportunity to any party against whom a preliminary order is directed to present its case at the earliest practicable time.

(3) The arbitral tribunal shall decide promptly on any objection to the preliminary order.

(4) A preliminary order shall expire after twenty days from the date on which it was issued by the arbitral tribunal. However, the arbitral tribunal may issue an interim measure adopting or modifying the preliminary order, after the party against whom the preliminary order is directed has been given notice and an opportunity to present its case.

(5) A preliminary order shall be binding on the parties but shall not be subject to enforcement by a court. Such a preliminary order does not constitute an award.

A. Meaning and Purpose

14.303 Article 17 C employs a special regime for preliminary orders. The provision ensures that the tribunal enables a party against whom a preliminary order is directed to present its case at the earliest time possible. Additionally, an automatic expiry of the order after a limited number of days is established.

---

486 Working Group Report, UN Doc A/CN.9/569, para 31.

487 *ibid*, para 40.

488 Note by the Secretariat, UN Doc A/CN.9/WG.II/WP.141, para 9.

B. Right of the responding party to be heard

(1) Obligation to give notice, paragraph (1)

Article 17 C(1) states that the arbitral tribunal is obliged to provide all documents and information regarding the application of an interim measure or preliminary order to the party against whom the preliminary order was sought. This notice has to be given by the arbitral tribunal immediately after it has ruled on the application of a preliminary order. The provision's purpose, therefore, is to transform an *ex-parte* situation into an *inter-partes* one as quickly as possible.[489] The Working Group clarified that this obligation shall apply regardless of whether the arbitral tribunal issued or refused to issue the order.[490] **14.304**

(2) Opportunity to present the case, paragraph (2)

Article 17 C(2) obliges the arbitral tribunal to give the responding party an opportunity to present its case after it has received notice from the arbitral tribunal pursuant to Art 17 C(1). This opportunity to object to the issuance of a preliminary order and to be heard by the arbitral tribunal has to be given at the earliest possible time.[491] The original draft text of the provision established a time period of 48 hours after notice was given to the corresponding party.[492] The time limit was later removed because the Working Group wanted to avoid the risk that the provision could be misinterpreted, creating an obligation for the responding party to react within a specific time.[493] **14.305**

(3) Prompt decision on the objection, paragraph (3)

After an objection by the responding party against a preliminary order, the arbitral tribunal has to decide on the objection as quickly as possible. In its decision the arbitral tribunal can modify, suspend or terminate the preliminary order.[494] **14.306**

C. Expiry of preliminary orders, paragraph (4)

Article 17 C (4) provides that the preliminary order cannot extend beyond a time limit of 20 days. The Working Group clarified that this time limit was meant to be a 'drop dead date' designed to 'strengthen the principle that an arbitral tribunal could not extend the *ex parte* phase of the proceeding beyond the twenty days'.[495] **14.307**

The arbitral tribunal may only grant preliminary orders beyond the twenty-day limit if the preliminary order is converted into an *inter-partes* interim measure after the party against whom the measure is granted has been heard.[496] Thus, it is necessary to hear the party against whom the measure is granted no later than 20 days after the preliminary order was issued, otherwise the measure would automatically expire. **14.308**

489 Binder, para 4-077.
490 Note by the Secretariat, UN Doc A/CN.9/605, para 14.
491 Working Group Report, UN Doc A/CN.9/569, para 52.
492 *ibid.*
493 *ibid* para 55.
494 See commentary on Art 17 D.
495 Working Group Report, UN Doc A/CN.9/569, para 64.
496 *ibid* para 63; Working Group Report, UN Doc A/CN.9/573, para 56.

D. No court enforcement of preliminary orders, paragraph (5)

14.309 Article 17 C(5) clarifies that no enforcement procedure for preliminary orders is provided by the Model Law, even though preliminary orders are binding on the parties. In addition, this provision states that a preliminary order does not constitute an award.

14.310 The non-enforcement of preliminary orders was the central compromise in order to keep a consensus within the Working Group in the course of the discussion on *ex parte* preliminary orders.[497] The exclusion of court enforcement results from the very temporary nature of a preliminary order[498] and from the system of enforcement of interim measures (Art 17 H), which is expressly limited to interim measures.[499] The Working Group considered that enforcement of preliminary orders 'could raise practical difficulties, such as whether notification to the other party of the preliminary order should be deferred until after the order had been enforced by a court'.[500] It was argued that the parties would comply in the vast majority of cases with preliminary orders, and that it would be vital that parties retain confidence in the tribunal's impartiality, which could be narrowed by the enforcement of *ex-parte* preliminary orders.[501]

Section 3. Provisions applicable to interim measures and preliminary orders

Article 17 D. Modification, suspension, termination

(As adopted by the Commission at its thirty-ninth session, in 2006)

The arbitral tribunal may modify, suspend or terminate an interim measure or a preliminary order it has granted, upon application of any party or, in exceptional circumstances and upon prior notice to the parties, on the arbitral tribunal's own initiative.

A. Meaning and Purpose

14.311 Article 17 D provides strict rules for the modification, suspension and termination of both interim measures and preliminary orders. The arbitral tribunal is not free to alter an interim measure or a preliminary order, but rather can only act *ex officio* under exceptional circumstances and after having notified the parties.

B. Only measures granted by the tribunal

14.312 Article 17 D states that the arbitral tribunal may modify, suspend or terminate an interim measure and a preliminary order that 'it has granted'. According to the Secretariat this wording clarifies that an arbitral tribunal can only alter a measure issued by that tribunal.[502]

---

[497] Note by the Secretariat, UN Doc A/CN.9/605, para 15.

[498] *ibid*; Working Group Report, UN Doc A/CN.9/547, para 66.

[499] Chao and Menon, 16.

[500] Note by the Secretariat, UN Doc A/CN.9/605, para 15; Working Group Report, UN Doc A/CN.9/569, para 46 *et seq*.

[501] Chao and Menon, 15.

[502] Note by the Secretariat, UN Doc A/CN.9/WG.II/WP. 131, para 23.

As interim measures are often sought before the constitution of an arbitral tribunal, there was some discussion on whether an arbitral tribunal should have the power to alter interim measures issued by state courts or other arbitral tribunals.[503] The consensus was that the issue of allowing an arbitral tribunal to review a court-ordered measure raised sensitive issues as to balancing the role of private arbitral bodies against that of courts, which have sovereign powers and an appellate regime.[504] Finally, the view prevailed that the application of the provision should be restricted to measures that had been issued by the same tribunal. 14.313

C. Alteration of a measure upon application of a party

Article 17 D empowers the arbitral tribunal to modify, suspend or terminate an interim measure and a preliminary order upon application of a party. In contrast to the alteration of a measure on the tribunal's own initiative, there are no further conditions required for the modification of a measure upon an application of a party. 14.314

D. Alteration of a measure on the tribunal's own initiative

Article 17 D demands two conditions, namely exceptional circumstances and a prior notification to the parties before the arbitral tribunal may modify, suspend or terminate a measure *ex officio* without an application of a party. The issue whether the arbitral tribunal may alter a measure on its own initiative was hotly debated within the Working Group. According to one view, a measure should only be terminable at the request of the party that had applied for the measure.[505] It was argued that the arbitral tribunal may be seen as unduly protecting the interests of the other party by terminating an interim measure and thus deviating from the principle of impartiality.[506] 14.315

However, the view prevailed within the Working Group that a certain degree of discretion was necessary to make it possible for the arbitral tribunal to correct the—often serious—consequences of interim measures and preliminary orders.[507] 14.316

(1) Exceptional circumstances

The first condition for altering an interim measure or preliminary order *ex officio* without an application of a party is that 'exceptional circumstances' exist. The *travaux préparatoires* offers no explanation of this term provided. The Working Group merely stated that 'while under normal circumstances an interim measure could only be terminated or modified at the request of a party, specific circumstances might justify modification or termination of an interim measure by the arbitral tribunal on its own initiative'.[508] For example, it seems sensible to allow the alteration of a measure without an application of a party on the 14.317

[503] Working Group Report, UN Doc A/CN.9/545, para 41; Working Group Report, UN Doc A/CN.9/547, para 102.
[504] Working Group Report, UN Doc A/CN.9/547, para 104.
[505] Working Group Report, UN Doc A/CN.9/545, para 37.
[506] *ibid.*
[507] *ibid,* para 38.
[508] *ibid,* para 40.

tribunal's initiative where the measure appeared to have been granted on an erroneous or fraudulent basis.[509]

(2) Notification of the parties

14.318 Article 17 D demands prior notice to all parties as the second condition for an alteration of a measure on the tribunal's own initiative.

Article 17 E. Provision of security

(As adopted by the Commission at its thirty-ninth session, in 2006)

(1) **The arbitral tribunal may require the party requesting an interim measure to provide appropriate security in connection with the measure.**

(2) **The arbitral tribunal shall require the party applying for a preliminary order to provide security in connection with the order unless the arbitral tribunal considers it inappropriate or unnecessary to do so.**

A. Meaning and purpose

14.319 Article 17 E empowers the arbitral tribunal to order appropriate security in connection with an interim measure or a preliminary order.

B. Security in connection with interim measure, paragraph (1)

14.320 The arbitral tribunal may require the requesting party to provide appropriate security in connection with the measure ordered by the tribunal. Whether or not security is to be provided is left to the tribunal's discretion.[510] The Model Law uses a more general wording than Art 26(2) of the UNCITRAL Arbitration Rules, which provide for 'security for the costs of such measure'. The Commission changed the language to clarify that the security required could cover not only the costs of such interim measure, but also any possible or foreseeable damage to a party.[511]

14.321 The Working Group maintained the non-mandatory character of the provision, as it was felt that the security in connection with a measure should not be considered a condition precedent to the granting of an interim measure.[512]

C. Security in connection with preliminary order, paragraph (2)

14.322 In contrast to interim measures, where the order for security is left to the tribunal's discretion, in relation to preliminary orders, Art 17 E(2) states as a principle that the tribunal shall require the requesting party to provide security in connection with the order.[513] The arbitral tribunal may refrain from requiring security from the party applying for a preliminary order only if it considers it inappropriate or unnecessary.

---

[509] Working Group Report, UN Doc A/CN.9/545, para 38.

[510] Menon and Chao, 14.

[511] Commission Report, UN Doc A/40/17, paras 165–6.

[512] Working Group Report, UN Doc A/CN.9/547, para 92; Note of the Secretariat, UN Doc A/CN.9/WG.II/WP.131, para 18.

[513] Menon and Chao, 14.

Article 17 F. Disclosure

(As adopted by the Commission at its thirty-ninth session, in 2006)

(1) The arbitral tribunal may require any party promptly to disclose any material change in the circumstances on the basis of which the measure was requested or granted.

(2) The party applying for a preliminary order shall disclose to the arbitral tribunal all circumstances that are likely to be relevant to the arbitral tribunal's determination whether to grant or maintain the order, and such obligation shall continue until the party against whom the order has been requested has had an opportunity to present its case. Thereafter, paragraph (1) of this article shall apply.

A. Meaning and purpose

Article 17 F introduces the parties' obligation to disclose a material change of circumstances on the basis of which an interim measure or a preliminary order was requested or granted. The provision reflects two distinct disclosure obligations for interim measures and preliminary orders that operate in distinct circumstances. Given that the interim measure or preliminary order might be granted at an early stage of the arbitral proceedings, an arbitral tribunal might often be faced with an imperfect record of the facts and would wish to be informed of any changes concerning the facts on the basis of which the measure was granted. Thus, the purpose of this provision is to ensure that a decision to grant a measure would be made on the basis of the most complete record of the facts.[514] **14.323**

B. Disclosure regarding measures, paragraph (1)

Article 17 F(1) empowers the arbitral tribunal to require any party to promptly disclose changed circumstances related to interim measures and preliminary orders.[515] The disclosure has to be made to the arbitral tribunal, which may then proceed according to Art 17 D and suspend, terminate or modify the measure. The Working Group noted that according to Art 24(3) the disclosure also has to be communicated to the other party, which may apply for an alteration of the measure according to Art 17 D.[516] **14.324**

The duty of disclosure is limited to material changes 'in the circumstances on the basis of which the measure was requested or granted'. Thus, there is no duty to disclose all circumstances that the arbitral tribunal is likely to find relevant.[517] **14.325**

The provision does not include a sanction for non-compliance with the obligation to disclose. The Working Group considered that the express inclusion of a sanction was not necessary, as in any case the usual sanction for violation of the duty to disclose would be either the suspension or termination of the measure, or the award of damages. It was noted, however, that an award of damages might not be a solution in all cases, particularly where the other party was not capable of paying damages.[518] **14.326**

---

[514] Commission Report, UN Doc A/61/17, para 123.

[515] See commentary on Art 17 F(2).

[516] Working Group Report, UN Doc A/CN.9/547, para 97.

[517] Working Group Report, UN Doc A/CN.9/569, para 68.

[518] Working Group Report, UN Doc A/CN.9/547, para 100.

C. Disclosure regarding preliminary orders, paragraph (2)

14.327 Article 17 F(2) provides a continuing obligation[519] of the party applying for a preliminary order to disclose all circumstances that are likely to be relevant to the arbitral tribunal's determination to grant or maintain the order. The obligation starts with the application for a preliminary order and continues until the party against whom the order has been requested has had an opportunity to present its case. In contrast to para (1), which limits the duty to disclose to 'material changes', this provision expresses a broader obligation[520] and covers all 'circumstances that are likely to be relevant to the arbitral tribunal's determination whether to grant or maintain the order'.

14.328 The provision was inspired by the rule existing in some jurisdictions that parties had a special obligation to inform the court of all matters, including those that spoke against their position. This rule was considered a fundamental safeguard and an essential condition to the acceptability of preliminary orders. Similarly, in many other legal systems, a comparable obligation arose from the recognized requirement that parties act in good faith.[521]

Article 17 G. Costs and damages

(As adopted by the Commission at its thirty-ninth session, in 2006)

The party requesting an interim measure or applying for a preliminary order shall be liable for any costs and damages caused by the measure or the order to any party if the arbitral tribunal later determines that, in the circumstances, the measure or the order should not have been granted. The arbitral tribunal may award such costs and damages at any point during the proceedings.

A. Meaning and purpose

14.329 Article 17 G addresses the requesting party's liability for any costs or damages caused if an interim measure or preliminary order should later be proved unwarranted.

B. Scope of application

14.330 Where an interim measure or preliminary order ultimately proves to be unjustified, the damages and costs arising from such measure may be awarded by the arbitral tribunal.[522] Such damages should be granted upon request and substantiated by the requesting party.[523] A decision on damages should be rendered in the form of an award at any point during the proceedings, in order to permit a challenge of the decision of the arbitral tribunal regarding costs and damages.[524]

14.331 As to the question of whether Art 17 G should distinguish between *inter partes* and *ex parte* interim measures, the Working Group compared several national laws.[525] It came to the

[519] Working Group Report, UN Doc A/CN.9/569, para 67.

[520] *ibid,* para 68.

[521] Commission Report, UN Doc A/61/17, para 122.

[522] Working Group Report, UN Doc A/CN.9/545, para 65.

[523] Yesilirmak, paras 5–104.

[524] Working Group Report, UN Doc A/CN.9/589, para 48.

[525] These states were Austria, Canada (Province of Quebec), the Czech Republic, Finland, France, Germany, Singapore, Spain, Switzerland and the United States of America. See Note by the Secretariat, UN Doc A/CN.9/WG.II/WP.127.

conclusion that there should not be such a distinction regarding the question of liability within the Model Law.[526]

The term 'cost' is to be interpreted in accordance with Art 38 of the UNCITRAL Arbitration Rules, where a detailed definition is provided.[527] Accordingly, the arbitral tribunal may also award, apart from damages caused by the measure, the fees of the arbitral tribunal, travel expenses and other expenses of arbitrators and witnesses, costs for expert advice, costs of legal representation and expenses of the appointing authority. **14.332**

Section 4. Recognition and enforcement of interim measures

Article 17 H. Recognition and enforcement

(As adopted by the Commission at its thirty-ninth session, in 2006)

(1) An interim measure issued by an arbitral tribunal shall be recognized as binding and, unless otherwise provided by the arbitral tribunal, enforced upon application to the competent court, irrespective of the country in which it was issued, subject to the provisions of article 17 I.

(2) The party who is seeking or has obtained recognition or enforcement of an interim measure shall promptly inform the court of any termination, suspension or modification of that interim measure.

(3) The court of the State where recognition or enforcement is sought may, if it considers it proper, order the requesting party to provide appropriate security if the arbitral tribunal has not already made a determination with respect to security or where such a decision is necessary to protect the rights of third parties.

A. Meaning and purpose

Article 17 H, together with Art 17 I, establishes a regime for recognition and enforcement of arbitral interim measures by state courts. As arbitral tribunals do not have coercive powers to ensure compliance, the provision's purpose consists of providing support for the enforceability of interim measures. The provision's framework is established in a manner similar to that set forth for arbitral awards in Art 35, albeit with such alterations as are necessary due to the very nature of interim measures.[528] **14.333**

B. Interim measures binding and enforceable by courts, paragraph (1)

Under Art 17 H(1) interim measures of protection issued by arbitral tribunals have to be recognized as binding and, unless otherwise provided by the arbitral tribunal, are enforceable upon application to the competent court, irrespective of the country in which they were issued. **14.334**

Article 17 H(1) confirms what is already stated in Art 1(2), that the provisions concerning recognition and enforcement of interim measures apply to all interim measures, irrespective of the country in which they were issued, ie to domestic and foreign interim measures of international commercial arbitration. **14.335**

---

[526] Working Group Report, UN Doc A/CN.9/547, para 105.

[527] Working Group Report, UN Doc A/CN.9/545, para 63; Binder (n 110) para 4-071.

[528] Working Group Report, UN Doc A/CN.9/524, para 20.

14.336 During the Working Group's discussions, the need for enforceability[529] of interim measures was widely supported by the argument that a final award may be of little value to the successful party if, in the meantime, action or inaction by a recalcitrant party has rendered the outcome of the proceedings largely useless, for example by dissipating assets or removing them from the jurisdiction.[530] In the argument against the enforcement of interim measures, it was noted that, as a practical matter, parties tend to comply with such measures anyway, for example to avoid responsibility for costs caused by the failure to implement the measure, or because they are reluctant to displease the arbitral tribunal.[531]

14.337 Article 17 H(1) clarifies that court enforcement of interim measures ordered in arbitral proceedings taking place in the state of the enforcing court or in another state is possible, irrespective of the seat of the arbitral tribunal. This is particularly relevant in cases where arbitrations are held in 'neutral' places where the parties do not have assets.[532]

14.338 The Working Group considered that the right to seek recognition and enforcement of an interim measure should not be conditional upon the approval of the arbitral tribunal.[533] It was argued that an approval was implicit anyway from the fact that the arbitral tribunal had granted the measure and therefore an express approval of enforceability was not necessary.[534] On the other hand, it was brought forward that the arbitral tribunal would be restricted in its discretion to award interim measures without approval of the enforcement.[535] In the end, consensus was reached by inserting the term 'unless otherwise provided by the arbitral tribunal' as a substitution for the approval of the arbitral tribunal to the enforcement.

14.339 The Working Group considered that where an application for enforcement was made before several state courts, these courts should be free to evaluate the best way to proceed. It stated that the mere fact that a party had sought enforcement in two different state courts should not by itself be a ground for non-enforcement, as there could be legitimate grounds as to why the application has been made in different state courts. For example, the applicant may have assets in more than one jurisdiction or it may be unclear which court was the proper court in which to make that application.[536]

14.340 In addition, the Working Group considered that the arbitral tribunal's power to decide on its own jurisdiction according to Art 16 should be preserved and that a court should not rule on an arbitral tribunal's jurisdiction in enforcement proceedings regarding interim measures.[537]

529 For detailed discussions on the need of enforceability see Chao and Menon, 17 *et seq*, *Yesilirmak*, paras 6–12 *et seq*.
530 Note by the Secretariat, UN Doc A/CN.9/460, para 117.
531 *ibid*, para 118.
532 *ibid*, paras 115 *et seq*.
533 Working Group Report, UN Doc A/CN.9/524, para 21.
534 *ibid*, para 25.
535 *ibid*, para 26.
536 *ibid*, para 21.
537 *ibid*, para 22.

A great number of Model Law states included provisions concerning the enforcement of interim measures. In some states interim measures are treated like arbitral awards for the purpose of enforcement.[538] In *Scotland* the order takes the form of an award.[539] Other states allow a party to request enforcement from a court.[540] In still other states a party may request authorization from the arbitral tribunal to proceed with the execution of the order itself.[541] **14.341**

C. Safeguards

(1) Obligation to inform the court, paragraph (2)

Article 17 H(2) imposes an obligation on the party who is seeking enforcement or who has obtained recognition and enforcement of the interim measure to inform the court of any termination, suspension or modification of that measure. It was pointed out that enforcement of an interim measure required that the measure should still be in force as originally issued and that Art 17 H(2) was designed to address the issue of how certainty as to persistence of the interim measure could be achieved by the enforcing court.[542] In enforcement proceedings the provision may become relevant in connection with Art 17 I(1)(a)(iii) where the suspension of an interim measure is recognized as a possible ground for refusing recognition and enforcement. **14.342**

(2) Security, paragraph (3)

Article 17 H(3) addresses the question of whether a court, when faced with an application to enforce an interim measure, should be able to order the applicant to provide security.[543] The provision limits the power of the court to order security to cases where the tribunal has not made a decision in this respect or where it is necessary to protect third party rights. **14.343**

The Working Group considered that, as a general principle, a court should not have the power to review the merits of a decision taken by an arbitral tribunal as to the order to provide security. However, it was considered necessary that if the tribunal had not considered it appropriate to issue an order for security, the court could still review that decision.[544] In addition, the Working Group considered that interim measures ordered by an arbitral tribunal were only binding on the parties to the arbitral proceedings, whereas a court decision could have wider application and thus apply to third parties.[545] **14.344**

---

538 eg *Bermuda*: s 26 of the Bermuda International Conciliation and Arbitration Act 1993; *British Columbia*: s 2 of the British Columbia International Commercial Arbitration Act; *California*: s 1297.92, CCP; *New Zealand*: Art 17(2) of First sch of the Arbitration Act 1996; *Malta*: s 62 of the Arbitration Act 1996; *Ontario*: s 9 of the Ontario International Commercial Arbitration Act 1990; see also *Australia*: s 23 of the International Arbitration Act 1974.

539 Art 17(2) of sch 7 of the Law Reform (Miscellaneous Provisions) (Scotland) Act 1990.

540 *Germany*: s 1041, ZPO; *Sri Lanka*: s 13(2) of the Arbitration Act 1995; *Hong Kong*: s 2GG of the Arbitration Ordinance, ch 341; *Singapore*: s 12(5) of the International Arbitration Act 1994; see also *Tunisia*: Art 62 of the Arbitration Code: the arbitral tribunal can request such assistance.

541 *Egypt*: Art 24(2) of the Law Concerning Arbitration in Civil and Commercial Matters; *Oman*: Art 24(2) of the Law of Arbitration in Civil and Commercial Disputes.

542 Working Group Report, UN Doc A/CN.9/485, para 95.

543 Note by the Secretariat, UN Doc A/CN.9/WG.II/WP.125, para 35.

544 Working Group Report, UN Doc A/CN.9/547, para 56.

545 *ibid*, para 61.

Article 17 I. Grounds for refusing recognition or enforcement***

(As adopted by the Commission at its thirty-ninth session, in 2006)

(1) Recognition or enforcement of an interim measure may be refused only:

(a) At the request of the party against whom it is invoked if the court is satisfied that:

(i) Such refusal is warranted on the grounds set forth in article 36(1)(a)(i), (ii), (iii) or (iv); or

(ii) The arbitral tribunal's decision with respect to the provision of security in connection with the interim measure issued by the arbitral tribunal has not been complied with; or

(iii) The interim measure has been terminated or suspended by the arbitral tribunal or, where so empowered, by the court of the State in which the arbitration takes place or under the law of which that interim measure was granted; or

(b) If the court finds that:

(i) The interim measure is incompatible with the powers conferred upon the court unless the court decides to reformulate the interim measure to the extent necessary to adapt it to its own powers and procedures for the purposes of enforcing that interim measure and without modifying its substance; or

(ii) Any of the grounds set forth in article 36(1)(b)(i) or (ii), apply to the recognition and enforcement of the interim measure.

(2) Any determination made by the court on any ground in paragraph (1) of this article shall be effective only for the purposes of the application to recognize and enforce the interim measure. The court where recognition or enforcement is sought shall not, in making that determination, undertake a review of the substance of the interim measure.

***** The conditions set forth in article 17 I are intended to limit the number of circumstances in which the court may refuse to enforce an interim measure. It would not be contrary to the level of harmonization sought to be achieved by these model provisions if a State were to adopt fewer circumstances in which enforcement may be refused.**

A. Meaning and purpose

14.345 Article 17 I is designed to limit the circumstances in which a court may refuse the enforcement of an interim measure of protection. The provision follows the structure of Art 36 with some alterations that are required due to the nature of interim measures.

B. Interplay with Article 36

14.346 The Working Group pointed out that the recognition and enforcement regime of interim measures set out in Art 17 I was autonomous and that the application of Art 36 is excluded regarding the enforcement of interim measures.[546]

14.347 Following the structure of Art 36, the distinction between sub-paras (a) and (b) refers to the burden of proof. The grounds listed in sub-para (a) have to be proven by the party against whom the enforcement is sought, whereas the defences mentioned in sub-para (b) do not require such a proof. The party resisting recognition or enforcement is not even required to raise these defences himself (though he would be well advised to draw the court's attention to them), because the court can do so on its own motion.[547]

[546] Working Group Report, UN Doc A/CN.9/589, para 78.

[547] Huleatt-James, M. and Gould, N., *International Commercial Arbitration* (2nd edn, LLP, 1999) 116; van den Berg, A.J., *The New York Arbitration Convention of 1958: Towards a Uniform Judicial Interpretation* (Asser/Kluwer, 1981) 389, 391 as to Art V of the New York Convention.

C. No review of the measure's substance, paragraph (2)

Article 17 I is based on the assumption that the court should not repeat the decision-making process of the arbitral tribunal that led to the issuance of the measure and that enforcement proceedings should not be delayed. The court should not review the conclusions of the arbitral tribunal or the substance of an interim measure. Thus, the court's jurisdiction is limited to expressly enumerated grounds under which recognition and enforcement of the interim measure may be refused. **14.348**

D. Grounds for refusing recognition or enforcement, paragraph (1)

(1) Grounds of Article 36 (1)(a)(i)—(iv), paragraph (1)(a)(i)

See commentary on Art 36 (1)(a)(i), (ii), (iii) and (iv) at paras 14.572 to 14.576. **14.349**

(2) Non-compliance with security provisions, paragraph (1)(a)(ii)

At the request of a party, recognition and enforcement of an arbitral interim measure may be refused if a decision of the arbitral tribunal for providing security in connection with the interim measure according to Art 17 E has not been complied with. **14.350**

(3) Measure terminated or suspended, paragraph (1)(a)(iii)

Article 17 I(1)(a)(iii), which is to be read in conjunction with Art 17 D, sets out three authorities under which an interim measure could have been terminated or suspended as a prerequisite for refusing recognition and enforcement: the arbitral tribunal which has issued the measure, the competent court of the state in which the arbitration takes place, or the competent court of the state under the law of which that interim measure was granted. **14.351**

The wording 'where so empowered' limits the possibility of court intervention to situations where state courts are specifically empowered to revise an interim measure issued by the arbitral tribunal.[548] **14.352**

The provision does not refer to the modification of an interim measure. Within the Working Group it was discussed whether the word 'modified' after the word 'suspended' should be added for the sake of consistency with the language used under Art 17 D. That proposal did not receive support for the reason that once an arbitral tribunal had modified an interim measure, the original measure was terminated expressly or implicitly and could no longer be recognized and enforced. However, the Working Group clarified that the enforcement regime set out in Art 17 I applied in respect of any interim measure, whether or not it was modified by the arbitral tribunal.[549] **14.353**

(4) Measure incompatible with court's powers, paragraph (1)(b)(i)

The court may, without a request of a party, refuse recognition and enforcement *ex officio* if the interim measure is incompatible with the powers conferred upon that court. However, the court may decide to reformulate the interim measure to the extent necessary to adapt it to its own powers and procedures, without modifying its substance. **14.354**

---

548 Working Group Report, UN Doc A/CN.9/589, para 83.
549 *ibid*, para 85.

(5) Subject matter of the dispute not arbitrable or measure conflicts with public policy, paragraph (1)(b)(ii)

14.355 See commentary on Art 36(1)(b)(i) and (ii) at para 14.578.

Section 5. Court-ordered interim measures

Article 17 J. Court-ordered interim measures
(As adopted by the Commission at its thirty-ninth session, in 2006)

A court shall have the same power of issuing an interim measure in relation to arbitration proceedings, irrespective of whether their place is in the territory of this State, as it has in relation to proceedings in courts. The court shall exercise such power in accordance with its own procedures in consideration of the specific features of international arbitration.

A. Meaning and Purpose

14.356 Article 17 J completes the set of provisions on interim measures by addressing the issue of court-ordered interim measures in support of arbitration.

B. Scope of application

14.357 Article 17 J expressly empowers state courts to grant interim measures in support of arbitral proceedings. The provision applies regardless of where the arbitration takes place and thus confers upon a state court the power to issue interim measures even if the arbitration takes place outside the country in which the court is constituted.[550] This is also confirmed by the words 'in courts' at the end of the first sentence, which is intended to clarify that there is no intention to refer to specific court proceedings, either domestic or foreign.[551]

14.358 The Commission clarified that the purpose of Art 17 J was to preserve the power of courts to issue interim measures in support of arbitration, but should not be understood as expanding the powers of the courts for interfering in the arbitral process.[552] Art 17 J does not relate to the function of assistance and supervision of arbitration proceedings as referred to in Art 6; consequently, it should not be construed as expanding the powers of courts in relation to those functions.[553]

C. Relationship between Article 9 and Article 17 J

14.359 On the question of the relationship between Art 9 and Art 17 J, the Working Group pointed out that the scope of Art 9 and Art 17 J were different, as Art 9 dealt with the right of parties to request an interim measure of protection from a court, whereas Art 17 J expressly empowered courts to grant such measures in support of an arbitration.[554]

[550] See Art 1(2); Note by the Secretariat, A/CN.9/WG.II/WP.125, para 41.
[551] Commission Report, UN Doc A/61/17, para 141.
[552] *ibid*, para 139.
[553] *ibid*, para 131.
[554] Working Group Report, UN Doc A/CN.9/573, para 93; Note by the Secretariat, A/CN.9/WG.II/WP.119, para 8.

Chapter V. Conduct of arbitral proceedings

Special literature:

Bredow, Jens and Mulder, Isabel, 'Court Assistance in Arbitral Proceedings from the Perspective of Art 27 of the UNCITRAL Model Law' in Gerald Aksen *et al* (eds), *Liber Amicorum Robert Briner: Global Reflections on International Law, Commerce and Dispute Resolution* (ICC Publication no 693, 2005).

Herrmann, Gerold, 'Power of Arbitrators to Determine Procedures under the UNCITRAL Model Law' in Albert Jan van den Berg (ed), *Planning Efficient Arbitration Proceedings – The Law Applicable in International Arbitration, XIIth International Arbitration Congress, Vienna, 3–6 November 1994* (ICCA Congress Series no 7, Kluwer Law International, 1996).

Holtzmann, Howard M., 'The Conduct of Arbitral Proceedings' in Pieter Sanders (ed), *UNCITRAL's Project for a Model Law on International Commercial Arbitration, Interim meeting, Lausanne, 9–12 May 1984* (1984).

van Houtte, Hans, 'Conduct of Arbitral Proceedings' in Petar Sarcevic (ed), *Essays on International Commercial Arbitration* (Graham & Trotman/Martinus Nijhoff, 1989).

Article 18. Equal treatment of parties

The parties shall be treated with equality and each party shall be given a full opportunity to present his case.

A. Meaning and purpose

Article 18, which is based on Art 15(1) of the UNCITRAL Arbitration Rules,[555] states fundamental principles of fairness in requiring that the parties be treated with equality and each party be given full opportunity to present its case. These principles are a substantial part of what the Secretariat called the 'Magna Carta of Arbitral Procedure'.[556] Given that 'due process' is the indispensable foundation of any system of justice,[557] Art 18 is mandatory. A failure to comply with the principles laid down in Art 18 would constitute a ground for setting aside the award under Art 34(2)(a)(ii), (iv) or (b). **14.360**

B. Scope of application

This provision was initially included as a third paragraph in Art 19, restricting the discretion of the arbitral tribunal to conduct the proceedings. It was later recognized that the basic notions of fairness are of central importance for the entire arbitral proceedings, addressing both the arbitrators and the parties. Therefore, it was decided to make it a separate article placed at the beginning of ch V.[558] **14.361**

The wording of the UNCITRAL Arbitration Rules, that each party has the right to be heard 'at any stage of the proceedings', was deleted because it was feared that it might be relied upon to make unnecessary submissions and hence prolong the proceedings.[559] Irrespective of this deletion, however, the principles of fairness are to be followed in all **14.362**

[555] See First Draft, UN Doc A/CN.9/WG.II/WP.37, Art 19 note 34.

[556] Analytical Commentary, UN Doc A/CN.9/264, Art 19 para 1.

[557] Holtzmann and Neuhaus, 550.

[558] Commission Report, UN Doc A/40/17, para 176.

[559] Second Working Group Report, UN Doc A/CN.9/232, para 104.

procedural contexts.[560] In particular, they govern all provisions regarding the conduct of arbitral proceedings established in ch V. Some of these rules, such as those set out in Arts 24(2), (3) and 26(2), even put them in a more concrete form. Yet, the principles of Art 18 also apply to the procedures referred to in Arts 13 and 14, though not directly expressed therein.[561] It must be noted, however, that court proceedings, for example those under Art 34, are governed not by Art 18 but by other provisions of national law.[562]

14.363 In order to ensure efficient and expedient proceedings, a number of provisions covering specific procedural situations, namely Arts 16(2), 23(2), 24(1) and 25(c), place certain restrictions on the right to present one's case. Thus, it is generally admitted that the rights granted in Art 18 do not at any time entitle a party to obstruct the proceedings by dilatory tactics, such as by offering objections, amendments or evidence only on the eve of the award.[563]

The Higher Regional Court Celle emphasized that the right to be heard was not violated because arbitration proceedings were held in the Russian language, as it was the defendant's obligation to obtain assistance from an interpreter in order to fully participate in the proceedings.[564]

Article 19. Determination of rules of procedure

(1) Subject to provisions of this Law, the parties are free to agree on the procedure to be followed by the arbitral tribunal in conducting the proceedings.

(2) Failing such agreement, the arbitral tribunal may, subject to the provisions of this Law, conduct the arbitration in such a manner as it considers appropriate. The power conferred upon the arbitral tribunal includes the power to determine the admissibility, relevance, materiality and weight of any evidence.

A. Meaning and purpose

14.364 In the Analytical Commentary the Secretariat called Art 19, which at that time included a third paragraph that is now Art 18, the 'Magna Carta of Arbitral Procedure' and described the provision as 'the most important provision of the model law'.[565] Article 19 establishes the principle of procedural autonomy by recognizing the parties' freedom to lay down the rules of procedure and by granting the arbitral tribunal, failing agreement of the parties, wide discretion as to the conduct of the arbitral proceedings. The principle of procedural autonomy is the crucial point in establishing truly international commercial arbitration. In international cases there is a special need to be unimpeded by local peculiarities and

[560] Analytical Commentary, UN Doc A/CN.9/264, Art 19 para 7; see Commission Report, UN Doc A/40/17, para 176.

[561] See Summary Record, UN Doc A/CN.9/SR.322, Art 22 para 28; Analytical Commentary, UN Doc A/CN.9/264, Art 19 para 8; see also Analytical Commentary, UN Doc A/CN.9/264, Art 13 para 2 note 45.

[562] Holtzmann and Neuhaus, 552 *et seq*.

[563] Analytical Commentary, UN Doc A/CN.9/264, Art 19 para 8; Holtzmann and Neuhaus, 560; See also *Re Corporacion Transnacional de Inversiones SA de CV et al and STET International SpA et al*, Canada: Superior Court of Justice (Lax), 22 September 1999, CLOUT Case 391.

[564] Higher Regional Court Celle, 8 Sch 3/01, 2 October 2001, affirmed by the Bundesgerichtshof, III ZB 6/02, 30 January 2003, published in German: DIS-Online Database on Arbitration Law <http://www.dis-arb.de>, CLOUT Case 559.

[565] UN Doc A/CN.9/264, Art 19 para 1.

traditional standards that may be found in the existing domestic law of the place of arbitration, as the application of the domestic law would present a major disadvantage to any party not familiar with that system.[566]

B. Parties' freedom to lay down procedural rules, paragraph (1)

(1) Party autonomy

Article 19(1) guarantees the freedom of the parties to determine the procedure to be followed by the arbitral tribunal in conducting the proceedings. The parties are allowed to devise their own set of procedural rules according to their specific needs and wishes. They may also refer to any standard arbitration rules for institutional or *ad hoc* arbitration, as is made clear by Art 2(e). Their freedom indeed allows them to take full advantage of the services of permanent arbitral institutions or established arbitration practices of trade associations.[567] The parties can even apply the civil procedure of a particular legal system, so long as its provisions do not conflict with the mandatory provisions of the Model Law.[568] It must be emphasized that the rules of the chosen civil procedure only govern the proceedings and are not the rules applicable to the substance of the dispute, which is a matter regulated in Art 28. **14.365**

The freedom of the parties is a continuing one throughout the arbitral proceedings and not limited to the time before the first arbitrator is appointed.[569] The time limit was suggested on the grounds that the rules of procedure should be clear from the beginning, so that any arbitrator should know under what rules he is expected to perform his function.[570] However, this suggestion was not adopted, although it was discussed controversially several times during the drafting. It should be noted that under the adopted provision arbitrators cannot be forced to accept procedures which they object to, as they can always resign.[571] Moreover, the time frame for any agreement on procedural matters can be settled between the parties and the arbitrators.[572] **14.366**

(2) Restriction by mandatory provisions of the Model Law

The procedural freedom of the parties is not an unrestricted one. It is limited by the provisions of the Model Law, ie by the mandatory provisions.[573] Above all, it is subject to the fundamental principles of fairness laid down in Art 18. Other mandatory provisions are contained in Arts 23(1), 24(2)–(4), 27, 30(2), 31(1), (3), (4), 32 and 33(1), (2), (4), (5). **14.367**

---

566 Analytical Commentary, UN Doc A/CN.9/264, Art 25 para 1.

567 *ibid,* Art 19 para 2.

568 Commission Report, UN Doc A/40/17, para 276.

569 Fifth Working Group Report, UN Doc A/CN.9/246, para 63; Analytical Commentary, UN Doc A/CN.9/264, Art 19 para 4 note 63; Commission Report, UN Doc A/40/17, para 171–2; Holtzmann, ICCA Lausanne, 132; Hußlein-Stich, 107 *et seq*; Granzow, 143; but see Calavros, 105 *et seq*; see also the similar discussion under Art 26(1).

570 Fourth Secretariat Note, UN Doc A/CN.9/WG.II/WP.50, para 14.

571 Commission Report, UN Doc A/40/17, para 172.

572 Summary Record, UN Doc A/CN.9/SR.316, para 52; Commission Report, UN Doc A/40/17, para 172.

573 Analytical Commentary, UN Doc A/CN.9/264, Art 19 para 3.

C. Procedural discretion of the arbitral tribunal, paragraph (2)

(1) Procedural autonomy, sentence (1)

14.368 When the parties have not agreed on any procedural matter before or during the arbitral proceedings, the arbitral tribunal may conduct the arbitration in such manner as it considers appropriate. The arbitral tribunal's power is subject to provisions of the Model Law that specify and limit the tribunal's power, such as Arts 18, 23(2), 24(1), (2), (3), 25, 26(2). Thus, Art 19(2) gives the arbitral tribunal wide discretionary powers to decide on procedural matters. The Analytical Commentary on Art 19 notes that these powers enable the arbitral tribunal to meet the needs of a particular case and to select the most suitable procedure when organizing the arbitration, conducting individual hearings or other meetings and determining the important specifics of taking and evaluating evidence.[574] Furthermore, the Secretariat gave examples of the exercise of the arbitrators' discretion. The tribunal may adopt a common law procedure using affidavits and pre-hearing discovery if both parties are from that system; otherwise, if the parties are from a civil law tradition, the mode of proceedings may be more inquisitorial than adversary. When the parties are from different legal systems, the tribunal may use a liberal 'mixed' procedure, adopting suitable features from different legal systems and relying on techniques proven in international practice and, for instance, let parties present their case as they themselves judge best.[575] In any event, the arbitral tribunal must be guided by the fundamental principle of fairness as established in Art 18.

(2) Evidence, sentence (2)

14.369 The arbitral tribunal's powers include the determination of the admissibility, relevance, materiality and weight of any evidence. This provision is modelled on Art 25(6) of the UNCITRAL Arbitration Rules[576] and is non-mandatory. The phrase 'the power conferred upon the arbitral tribunal' relates to the power conferred directly by the Model Law in the first sentence of para (2), and not the power conferred by the agreement of the parties under para (1).[577] This means that if the parties agree to exclude certain kinds of evidence, the arbitral tribunal will be bound to respect that decision. Similarly, if the parties have agreed on procedural rules containing rules of evidence,[578] the arbitral tribunal will also be obliged to respect that agreement.[579] In the absence of contrary agreement by the parties, the arbitral tribunal is empowered to adopt a comprehensive set of evidentiary rules.[580]

14.370 **(2.1) Relationship between Article 19(2)(2) and Article 28** During the drafting process, the question arose as to the relationship between Art 19(2)(2) and Art 28, which allows the parties to choose the substantive law that will be applicable to the dispute, as under some legal systems a question of admissibility, relevance, materiality and weight of

574 UN Doc A/CN.9/264, Art 19 para 5.
575 *ibid,* para 6.
576 See First Working Group Report, UN Doc A/CN.9/216, para 60.
577 Holtzmann and Neuhaus, 566; see also First Working Group Report, UN Doc A/CN.9/216, para 59.
578 eg UNCITRAL Arbitration Rules, LCIA Rules.
579 Holtzmann, ICCA Lausanne, 133.
580 Fourth Working Group Report, UN Doc A/CN.9/245, para 75.

evidence is considered to be a matter of substantive law.[581] The Commission determined that the discretion conferred on the arbitral tribunal by Art 19(2) should not be affected by the choice of law applicable to the substance of the dispute under Art 28.[582] This is a prudent solution, as the aim of arbitration is to free the parties of the requirement to follow rigid technical rules of evidence.[583]

(2.2) Evidentiary matters not dealt with in the Model Law First, a proposition that the Model Law should provide that the evidence of witnesses may be presented in the form of signed written statements[584] was not adopted. The Commission preferred to leave this point of detail to the agreement of the parties or to the discretion of the arbitrators.[585] 14.371

Second, it was proposed that the Model Law should clarify that each party has the burden of proving the facts relied on to support his claim or defence,[586] a provision borrowed from Art 24(1) of the UNCITRAL Arbitration Rules. The suggestion was rejected on the basis that it was a generally recognized principle that reliance by a party on a fact required that party to prove the fact. However, it was felt that certain aspects of this question might be regarded to be issues of substantive law and hence subject to Art 28 and, moreover, that such a provision might interfere with the freedom of the parties and the arbitrators in conducting the arbitration proceedings as stated in Art 19.[587] Therefore, this matter is not dealt with in the Model Law. 14.372

Article 20. Place of arbitration

(1) The parties are free to agree on the place of arbitration. Failing such agreement, the place of arbitration shall be determined by the arbitral tribunal having regard to the circumstances of the case, including the convenience of the parties.

(2) Notwithstanding the provision of paragraph (1) of this article, the arbitral tribunal may, unless otherwise agreed by the parties, meet at any place it considers appropriate for consultation among its members, for hearing witnesses, experts or the parties, or for inspection of goods, other property or documents.

A. Meaning and purpose

Representing an emanation of the principle of party autonomy, Art 20(1) recognizes the parties' freedom to choose the place of arbitration (*situs*). In the absence of an agreement by the parties, the arbitral tribunal is called upon to determine this place in the light of the particular circumstances of the case. 14.373

The factual significance of the place of arbitration is that, in principle, the arbitral proceedings would be expected to be held at that place. However, for purposes of convenience and savings on costs, there may be good reasons for meeting elsewhere. Thus, Art 20(2) provides 14.374

581 See Summary Record, UN Doc A/CN.9/SR.316, Art 19(2) para 69 *(Italy)*.

582 Commission Report, UN Doc A/40/17, para 174.

583 Summary Record, UN Doc A/CN.9/SR.330, Art 19(2) para 58.

584 See Art 25(5) of the UNCITRAL Arbitration Rules.

585 Commission Report, UN Doc A/40/17, para 329.

586 See First Secretariat Note, UN Doc A/CN.9/207, para 75; Analytical Compilation of Government Comments, UN Doc A/CN.9/263, paras 9–10 *(Soviet Union* and *United States)*.

587 Commission Report, UN Doc A/40/17, para 328.

for a number of 'exceptions' empowering the arbitral tribunal, unless otherwise agreed by the parties, to meet at any place it considers appropriate for the particular stages of the proceedings. As these actual meetings are completely independent of the 'official' place of arbitration, the factual relevance of the *situs* is somewhat reduced. Yet, the place of arbitration is of great legal relevance, as a number of Model Law provisions expressly or implicitly refer to it, for example the place of arbitration determines which courts or other authorities will perform the functions of assistance and supervision set out in Arts 6 and 27.

14.375 Article 20 was adopted almost uniformly in the Model Law states. Only the arbitration laws of the *Republic of Bulgaria* and *Peru* fail to include the tribunal's discretion to determine meeting places as provided in Art 20(2).

B. Importance of the place of arbitration

14.376 The place of arbitration is of particular importance in three respects. First, it is essential for the Model Law's territorial scope of application: Art 1(2) states that the provisions of the Model Law, except Arts 8(1), 9, 35 and 36, only apply if the place of arbitration is in the territory of the enacting state. Thus, strictly speaking, Art 20(1) would only apply when the place of arbitration had already been determined.[588] This provision, however, primarily intends a restatement of the principle of party autonomy as regards the place of arbitration and hence must be seen as complementing Art 1(2).[589] Yet, due to the territorial approach of the Model Law, the parties' as well as the tribunal's freedom to choose the place of arbitration, as granted in Art 20(1), is restricted to the territory of a Model Law state.

14.377 Second, the place of arbitration is one of the criteria establishing the international character of arbitration. Under Art 1(3)(b)(i), an arbitration is international when the place of arbitration, if determined in or pursuant to the arbitration agreement, is situated outside the state in which the parties have their places of business.

14.378 Third, pursuant to Art 31(3) the award is deemed to have been made at the place of arbitration as determined in accordance with Art 20(1). The place of origin of the award is relevant in recognition and enforcement proceedings, not only in terms of the Model Law under Art 36(1)(a)(i) and (v), but also in terms of the Geneva Convention of 1927 and the New York Convention. Both conventions allow contracting states to take advantage of a 'reciprocity' reservation by restricting recognition and enforcement of non-domestic awards to such awards as have been made in the territory of another contracting state.[590]

C. Determination by the parties, paragraph (1)(1)

14.379 There was general agreement from the outset that the Model Law should recognize the parties' freedom to determine the place of arbitration and that it should contain a supplementary rule empowering the arbitral tribunal to determine the place of arbitration when

[588] Davidson *(Scotland)* para 6.16.
[589] Binder, para 5-037.
[590] For a list of states having made the reciprocity reservation see van den Berg, A.J., *The New York Arbitration Convention of 1958: Towards a Uniform Judicial Interpretation* (Asser/Kluwer, 1981) Annex B.

the parties had not agreed upon that place.[591] As clarified by Art 2(d), the parties' freedom allows them to authorize a third party, including an institution, to make that determination for them,[592] a construction often found in arbitration clauses. Pursuant to Art 2(e) the same freedom permits them to invoke a particular set of arbitration rules.[593] It should be noted that by virtue of Art 1(5) this freedom might be restricted by a mandatory provision of treaties or conventions in force in the enacting state, such as Art 22 of the 1978 Hamburg Convention on Carriage of Goods by Sea.[594]

The Model Law does not stipulate a time limit within which the parties must agree on the place of arbitration. In accordance with the principle of party autonomy, which is to be followed throughout the arbitral proceedings,[595] the parties should be allowed to agree on the place of arbitration at any time during the arbitral proceedings, even when the arbitral tribunal has already determined this place. Because of the above-mentioned important implications of this determination for the arbitral and the enforcement proceedings, the freedom of the parties should be given full effect.[596] Nevertheless, some authors acknowledge this freedom only until the commencement of the arbitral proceedings: at that time, the parties' right to choose the place of arbitration elapses and the arbitrators are called upon to determine the *situs*. According to this view, the parties are not allowed to change the arbitrators' determination.[597] **14.380**

D. Determination by the arbitral tribunal, paragraph (1)(2)

Where the parties do not agree on the place of arbitration, it is to be determined by the arbitral tribunal. In doing so, the tribunal shall show regard to the circumstances of the case. This phrase is lifted almost verbatim from Art 16 of the UNCITRAL Arbitration Rules. It refers not only to practical considerations in connection with the arbitral proceedings—such as the least possible displacement of parties, witnesses and arbitrators, and the necessary infrastructure—but also to the legal consequences of the choice, such as the suitability of the applicable procedural law and the availability of procedures for recognition and enforcement of the award under the New York Convention or other multilateral or bilateral treaties.[598] Because of these important implications of the *situs*, the choice of this place is not a question of procedure that might be decided by the presiding arbitrator under Art 29.[599] In a case where the arbitral award merely stated the arbitrator's address, the *Oberlandesgericht* Düsseldorf defined the place of arbitration to be the actual, effective **14.381**

591 First Working Group Report, UN Doc A/CN.9/216, paras 53–4.

592 eg the ICC Court under Art 14(1) of the ICC Arbitration Rules.

593 eg the LCIA Arbitration Rules, the UNCITRAL Arbitration Rules.

594 First Secretariat Note, UN Doc A/CN.2/207, para 71.

595 See commentary on Art 19.

596 See Hußlein-Stich, 111.

597 Calavros, 107; Sanders, P., 'Commentary on UNCITRAL Arbitration Rules' (1977) II *YCA* 194 as to Art 16(1) UNCITRAL Arbitration Rules; cf Rauh, K., *Die Schieds- und Schlichtungsordnungen der UNCITRAL* (1983) 78 who at least grants the parties the right to request the arbitrators to change their determination.

598 Commission Report, UN Doc A/40/17, para 179; Holtzmann, ICCA Lausanne, 135 *et seq.*

599 Calavros, 108; Hußlein-Stich, 112.

place of arbitration. Only if no particular place could be determined could the place of the last hearing be considered as the place of arbitration.[600]

14.382 The formula 'including the convenience of the parties' was added to the wording taken from the UNCITRAL Arbitration Rules. The highlighting of this issue caused some debate as to whether this phrase limits the considerations of the arbitral tribunal to the displacement of the parties and thus represents a substantive change in comparison with the relevant provision in the UNCITRAL Arbitration Rules.[601] The prevailing view was that the wording should be incorporated in order to emphasize the great importance of this issue and to meet the concerns of some delegates that the arbitral tribunal might impose an inconvenient location on the parties to the arbitration. It was understood that the convenience of the parties should be interpreted to include the above-mentioned considerations regarding the applicable procedural law and the recognition and enforcement of awards.[602] Thus, there is no discrepancy in the interpretation of the provisions of the Model Law and the UNCITRAL Arbitral Rules in this respect.

E. Location of actual meetings, paragraph (2)

14.383 Article 20(2) permits the arbitral tribunal to meet at any place it considers appropriate for consultation among its members, for hearing witnesses, experts or the parties, or for inspection of goods, other property or documents. Yet, the holding of such meetings has no effect on the 'official' place of arbitration. The provision is modelled on Art 16(2) and (3) of the UNCITRAL Arbitration Rules, but was broadened as it was recognized that many good reasons for meeting at locations other than the place of arbitration exist. When looking for an appropriate location, the tribunal will usually consider such matters as convenience and costs.[603]

14.384 Though Art 20(2) does not expressly mention the making of the award, the wording of Art 31(3), '. . . deemed to have been made at the place of arbitration', clearly suggests that this task also may be carried out at any location the tribunal considers appropriate.[604] Hence, it is possible that all proceedings, including the making of the award, take place in another state than that of the *situs*. In any event, the award must be signed as being made at the 'official' place of arbitration.

14.385 Paragraph (2) only applies in the absence of any contrary agreement of the parties. In particular, the parties are free to restrict the tribunal's discretion to determine meeting places, for example by agreeing on standard arbitration rules that contain narrower provisions. Besides, a few Model Law states, namely the *Republic of Bulgaria* and *Peru*, did not adopt the option to hold meetings outside the place of arbitration, as granted in para (2).

---

600 Oberlandesgericht Düsseldorf, 6 Sch 2/99, 23 March 2000, CLOUT Case 374.

601 See Commission Report, UN Doc A/40/17, para 179; Summary Record, UN Doc A/CN.9/SR.321, Art 20 paras 1–26.

602 Commission Report, UN Doc A/40/17, paras 178, 180.

603 See Analytical Commentary, UN Doc A/CN.9/264, Art 20 para 3.

604 See also Analytical Compilation of Government Comments, UN Doc A/9./263, Art 20 para 2; Holtzmann, ICCA Lausanne, 137.

Article 21. Commencement of arbitral proceedings

Unless otherwise agreed by the parties, the arbitral proceedings with respect to a particular dispute commence on the date on which a request for that dispute to be referred to arbitration is received by the respondent.

A. Meaning and Purpose

Article 21 determines the time that the arbitral proceedings commence as the date on which a request for a particular dispute to be referred to arbitration is received by the respondent. It provides a supplementary rule for parties who have not agreed on different rules, especially by reference to rules of arbitral institutions that may state a different point of time, for example the date the request for arbitration is received by the arbitral institution. **14.386**

B. Request for arbitration

(1) Content

The request for arbitration must identify the dispute in question with enough specificity. It must make it clear that arbitration is being resorted to thereby. The name makes no difference, as long as the purpose is clear. Thus, it may be called 'request', 'notice', 'application' or some other name. The request for arbitration may also contain a statement of claim, which will expedite the proceedings. A mere expression of the intention of later initiating arbitral proceedings is not sufficient.[605] **14.387**

Unlike Art 3(3) of the UNCITRAL Arbitration Rules, the Model Law does not provide a detailed list of requirements that the request for arbitration must include. In order to fulfil its function of commencing the arbitral proceedings—which, above all, means to start the process of appointing the arbitrators—and in order to enable the respondent to decide on his reaction, the particulars listed in Art 3(3) of the UNCITRAL Arbitration Rules seem appropriate. These are: (i) a demand that the dispute be referred to arbitration; (ii) the names and addresses of the parties; (iii) a reference to the arbitration clause or the separate arbitration agreement that is invoked; (iv) a reference to the contract out of or in relation to which the dispute arises; (v) the general nature of the claim and an indication of the amount involved, if any; (vi) the relief or remedy sought; (vii) a proposal as to the number of arbitrators, if the parties have not previously agreed thereon. *Germany* explicitly states that the request shall state the names of the parties, state the subject matter of the dispute and contain a reference to the arbitration agreement.[606] As the request does not fix the matter of dispute—this is an effect of the statement of claim—a statement of the facts supporting the claim is not necessary. Of course, if the request for arbitration contains a statement of claim, the statement of claim must include a statement of facts supporting the claim. **14.388**

Article 21 does not explicitly provide that the request for arbitration must be in writing. Yet, with regard to the wording 'received', which refers to Art 3,[607] and keeping in mind the legal consequences of the request for arbitration, a written request is required.[608] **14.389**

605 Analytical Commentary, UN Doc A/CN.9/264, Art 21 para 2; Holtzmann and Neuhaus, 612.
606 s 1044, ZPO.
607 See Analytical Commentary, UN Doc A/CN.9/264, Art 21 para 2 note 67.
608 Hußlein-Stich, 115.

(2) Receipt

14.390 The point of time the request for arbitration is received or deemed to be received is regulated in Art 3.

C. **Legal consequences**

14.391 Article 21 determines when the arbitration proceedings commence. This point of time is not only important for the next steps of the arbitral proceedings—above all, the appointment of the arbitrators—but also for the interpretation of other provisions, eg Art 8(2) ('Where [a court action] has been brought, arbitral proceedings may nevertheless be commenced or continued . . .') or Art 30 (1) ('If, during arbitral proceedings, the parties settle the dispute . . .').[609]

14.392 Under the Model Law the commencement of arbitral proceedings does not have the same legal effect on the running of periods of limitation as the commencement of judicial proceedings.[610] Both the Working Group and the Commission carefully considered this issue of considerable practical importance. It was recognized that a provision which gives a claimant in arbitration a degree of protection against the running of the period of limitation equivalent to that enjoyed by the plaintiff in a court proceeding would enhance the effectiveness of international commercial arbitration,[611] especially because, in many international transactions, arbitration is a substitute for judicial proceedings as the means of settling disputes.[612] Uniformity in that respect seemed desirable, as a number of legal systems accepted the concept that the running of the limitation period ceases when arbitral proceedings commence, while many legal systems did not.[613] A provision was proposed based on Art 14(1) of the Convention on the Limitation Period in the International Sale of Goods of 1974, which had been drafted under the auspices of UNCITRAL.[614] However, neither the Working Group nor the Commission adopted the provision, as it would touch upon questions which were regarded by many legal systems as matters of substantive law and therefore outside the scope of the Model Law.[615] Yet, the Commission invited all states to consider enacting provisions which, in harmony with the principles and norms of the given legal system, would place arbitral proceedings on equal footing with court proceedings in this respect.[616] In *Cyprus* the commencement of the arbitral proceedings results in the suspension of the period of limitation, subject to certain provisions specified in ss 21(3)–(5).[617]

[609] See Holtzmann and Neuhaus, 610.
[610] But see *Fustar Chemicals Ltd v Sinochem Liaoning Hong Kong Ltd*, Supreme Court of Hong Kong, 5 June 1996, CLOUT Case 706, where the Court noted that Art 21 was drafted to define the point in time when the limitation period for bringing a legal action is considered to have been interrupted.
[611] Commission Report, UN Doc A/40/17, Art 21 para 184.
[612] Third Secretariat Note, UN Doc A/CN.9/WG.II/WP.41, Art 21 para 12.
[613] Commission Report, UN Doc A/40/17, Art 21 para 184.
[614] Third Secretariat Note, UN Doc A/CN.9/WG.II/WP.41, Art 21 para 14.
[615] Third Working Group Report, UN Doc A/CN.9/233, Art 21 para 22; Commission Report, UN Doc A/40/17, Art 21 para 185.
[616] Commission Report, UN Doc A/40/17, Art 21 para 186.
[617] s 21(2) of the International Commercial Arbitration Law 1987.

Article 22. Language

(1) The parties are free to agree on the language or languages to be used in the arbitral proceedings. Failing such agreement, the arbitral tribunal shall determine the language or languages to be used in the proceedings. This agreement or determination, unless otherwise specified therein, shall apply to any written statement by a party, any hearing and any award, decision or other communication by the arbitral tribunal.

(2) The arbitral tribunal may order that any documentary evidence shall be accompanied by a translation into the language or languages agreed upon by the parties or determined by the arbitral tribunal.

A. Meaning and purpose

In international arbitration the determination of the language or languages to be used during the proceedings is of considerable practical importance because the parties, their representatives, the arbitrators and witnesses normally speak different languages. The drafters of the Model Law recognized that most national laws did not address this issue. In order to avoid the interpretation that the language for court proceedings at the place of arbitration should be decisive for the arbitral proceedings, it was considered necessary to clearly state that the determination of the language(s) primarily lies within the competence of the parties and, in the absence of an agreement by the parties, within the competence of the arbitral tribunal.[618] Article 22 is closely modelled on Art 17 of the UNCITRAL Arbitration Rules. **14.393**

B. Determination of language(s) of proceedings

(1) Party autonomy, paragraph (1)(1)

Following the general policy referring to proceedings within the Model Law, the parties are free to select the language or languages to be used in the arbitral proceedings. They can judge best whether a single language would be acceptable for them or whether more than one language needs to be used. The freedom of the parties includes a reference to a set of arbitration rules pursuant to Art 2(e). When determining the language, the parties should keep in mind the concept of fairness laid down in Art 18 and the practical fact that the use of more than one language is time- and cost-consuming because of the necessary translations. The costs for translation form part of the overall costs of the arbitration and as such shall be borne, in principle, by the losing party.[619] **14.394**

Article 22 does not expressly state at what point of time the parties must agree on the language. As the proceedings will be carried out in this language, the parties should determine this question before they start to prepare their written statements.[620] However, it seems sensible that the primary right of the parties to determine the language will be a continuing one and as such enables them to override the supplementary determination of the tribunal **14.395**

[618] See Third Working Group Report, UN Doc A/CN.9/233, para 28; Analytical Commentary, UN Doc A/CN.9/264, Art 22 para 1.

[619] Analytical Commentary, UN Doc A/CN.9/264, Art 22 para 4.

[620] Holtzmann, ICCA Lausanne, 141; cf Holtzmann and Neuhaus, 629; but see Calavros, 110 who states that this should be until the commencement of the proceedings.

by agreeing to a different language or languages when they disapprove of the tribunal's decision.[621]

(2) Supplementary rule, paragraph (1)(2)

14.396 The arbitral tribunal will decide on the issue of the language to be used in the proceedings only if there is no party agreement on this issue. In doing so, the arbitral tribunal should consider the language capacities of the parties as well as of the arbitrators, the effects on the parties in terms of time and money and, above all, its duty expressed in Art 18 to treat the parties with equality and permit each party a full opportunity of presenting his case.[622] As the decision on language is a procedural question, the presiding arbitrator may determine this issue alone pursuant to Art 29.[623]

14.397 The Commission was of the opinion that it was inherent in the fundamental principle of fairness that a party had a right to express himself in his own language, provided he arranges for interpretation into the language of the proceedings at his own expense.[624] Proposals that the arbitral tribunal be obliged to use the language of both parties under certain circumstances, or that a party always had the right to present his case in his language—with the costs of interpretation and translation into the language of the arbitral tribunal included in the costs of arbitration—were rejected since they were considered too rigid.[625] Where parties have used only one language in their business dealings, particularly in their contract and their correspondence, a decision by the arbitral tribunal to choose this language as the language of the proceedings would not *per se* conflict with the fairness principle.[626] Unlike Art 17(1) of the UNCITRAL Arbitration Rules, which instructs the arbitral tribunal to decide on the language 'promptly after its appointment', the Model Law does not specify the time when the tribunal has to make the determination. The exigencies of arbitral procedure, however, suggest that any decision on language should be made early on in the arbitration procedure.[627]

C. Scope of the determination of the language(s), paragraphs (1)(2) and (2)

14.398 Pursuant to Art 22(1)(2) the parties' agreement or the tribunal's decision regarding the language of the proceedings applies to any written statement by a party, any hearing and any award, decision or other communication by the arbitral tribunal, unless the parties or the tribunal have determined the scope differently. Documentary evidence, however, does not have to be translated into the procedural language. As para (2) stipulates, it lies within the discretion of the arbitral tribunal to order that documentary evidence be accompanied by a translation. Given that such documents—invoices, computer printouts, financial records, technical specifications or shipping documents, among others—are often voluminous and only partly relevant to the dispute, the tribunal may decide whether and to what

[621] Davidson *(Scotland)* para 6.35; but see Calavros, 110 who precludes the parties from choosing the language after the commencement of the proceedings.
[622] See Analytical Commentary, UN Doc A/CN.9/264, Art 22 para 3.
[623] Calavros, 110; Hußlein-Stich, 117.
[624] Commission Report, UN Doc A/40/17, para 190.
[625] *ibid* para 191.
[626] Analytical Commentary, UN Doc A/CN.9/264, Art 22 para 4.
[627] Holtzmann and Neuhaus, 629.

extent translation is required.[628] Again, in deciding this issue the arbitral tribunal has to consider, on the one hand, the practical effects regarding time and costs and, on the other hand, the fundamental principles of fairness. In multilingual proceedings it might be sufficient in some circumstances to order the translation into only one of the procedural languages in order to reduce costs.[629] For cost-saving reasons the Commission rejected demanding certifications of translations. It should be mentioned that in enforcement proceedings under Art 35(2) such certifications are required.

Article 22(2) does not explicitly state that this provision is subject to contrary party agreement. However, under Art 22(1)(2) the parties have the unlimited power to specify the scope of the determination of the language(s). In light of the Working Group's understanding that the provisions of the Model Law that did not express their non-mandatory character were necessarily of mandatory nature,[630] it can be concluded that Art 22(2) is non-mandatory. If the parties agree that particular documents should or should not be translated, the tribunal cannot refuse to give effect to this agreement.[631] **14.399**

Article 23. Statements of claim and defence

(1) Within the period of time agreed by the parties or determined by the arbitral tribunal, the claimant shall state the facts supporting his claim, the points at issue and the relief or remedy sought, and the respondent shall state his defence with respect to these particulars, unless the parties have otherwise agreed as to the required elements of such statements. The parties may submit with their statements all documents they consider to be relevant or may add a reference to the documents or other evidence they will submit.

(2) Unless otherwise agreed by the parties, either party may amend or supplement his claim or defence during the course of the arbitral proceedings, unless the arbitral tribunal considers it inappropriate to allow such amendment with regard to the delay in making it.

A. Meaning and purpose

Article 23(1) lays down the basic elements of the statements of claim and defence from which the parties cannot deviate. However, the provision is non-mandatory in detail in order to allow the parties to agree on particular arbitration rules. It also provides that the parties may annex to their statements all documents—or a reference to the documents or other evidence—that they consider to be relevant. Under Art 23(2) the parties may amend or supplement their statements, subject to the discretion of the arbitral tribunal. As para (2) is non-mandatory, the parties may agree otherwise. According to Art 2(f), the reference to claims and defences also applies to counterclaims and defences to counterclaims. **14.400**

B. Form and contents of statement of claim or defence, paragraph (1)

Paragraph (1)(1) establishes the essential contents of the statement of claim, which defines the dispute on which the arbitral tribunal is to decide: the relief or remedy sought and the **14.401**

628 See Analytical Commentary, UN Doc A/CN.9/264, Art 22 para 5.
629 Commission Report, UN Doc A/40/17, para 193.
630 Fifth Working Group Report, UN Doc A/CN.9/246, para 177.
631 See Holtzmann and Neuhaus, 628 *et seq.*

facts supporting the claim. It also mentions the points at issue, although these normally cannot be stated until the respondent submits his statement of defence.

14.402 The requirement of some statement from each party expresses a basic principle of arbitral procedure that is mandatory, because by virtue of Art 18 each party must have the opportunity of presenting his case; furthermore, the arbitrators have to be informed of all the facts of the dispute submitted to them.[632] In *Germany* the new arbitration law provides explicitly that the parties cannot derogate from the essential contents of the remedy sought and the facts supporting the claim.[633]

14.403 However, the parties are free to vary the contents of the statements. Hence Art 23(1) is a non-mandatory rule.[634] The right of the parties in this regard was included in order to avoid a conflict between the Model Law and the institutional arbitration rules that require different essential contents in the initial statements, such as Art 4(2) and Art 5(1) of the ICC Rules.[635] Thus, if the parties agree to such arbitration rules, these will override Art 23(1).

14.404 The statements of claim and defence are not required to be in writing.[636] During the Commission's deliberations, it was noted that written pleadings seemed inappropriate, especially in arbitrations relating to claims of damage to goods, where the arbitrators simply inspect the goods on the spot, or claims which are set out in written communications between the parties.[637] Facing these facts the Model Law also covers purely oral proceedings.

14.405 The periods of time within which the claimant must state his claim and the respondent must state his defence are primarily determined by the parties, and otherwise by the arbitral tribunal. This provision is an expression of the party autonomy in procedural matters recognized by Art 19(1), and the general discretion granted to the arbitral tribunal with regard to the conduct of proceedings under Art 19(2) if the parties have not agreed on the issue.

14.406 As Art 23(1)(2) leaves it to each party and his procedural strategy to decide whether to submit documents with his statement or at least refer to documents or other evidence, these issues are not part of the essential contents of the statements.[638] As to the point of time when the parties have to reveal or submit the documents or evidence, it was the drafter's understanding that the parties are not completely free in this regard. Unless otherwise specified in the arbitration agreement, the arbitral tribunal has the power, under the general discretion granted to it under Art 19(2), to require a party to submit a summary of the documents and other evidence which that party intends to present in support of his claim

[632] See Commission Report, UN Doc A/40/17, para 196; Summary Record, UN Doc A/CN.9/SR.322, Art 23 paras 34, 29, 42.

[633] s 1046 (1)(1), ZPO.

[634] Analytical Commentary, UN Doc A/CN.9/264, Art 23 para 2; Commission Report, UN Doc A/40/17, para 196.

[635] See Summary Record, UN Doc A/CN.9/SR.322, Art 23 para 50 (*Russia*); Analytical Commentary, UN Doc A/CN.9/264, Art 23 para 2; Holtzmann, ICCA Lausanne, 143.

[636] Commission Report, UN Doc A/40/17, para 197.

[637] See Summary Record, UN Doc A/CN.9/SR.332, Art 23 paras 31 (*United Kingdom*), 46 (*Australia*).

[638] Analytical Commentary, UN Doc A/CN.9/264, Art 23 para 3.

or defence and, as is clear from Art 25(c), requires a party to produce documentary or other evidence within a certain period of time.[639]

If the claimant fails to communicate his statement of claim in accordance with Art 23(1), the arbitral tribunal will terminate the proceedings pursuant to Art 25(a). If the respondent fails to communicate his statement of defence, Art 25(b) provides for continuation of the proceedings. **14.407**

C. Amending or supplementing the claim or defence, paragraph (2)

Paragraph (2) is non-mandatory. Thus, the parties may agree, for example, that they have the unlimited right to amend or supplement their claim or defence or, conversely, that amendments or supplements are generally prohibited or that they are subject to specified limits, for example time limits.[640] **14.408**

If there is no specific party agreement, either party may amend or supplement his claim or defence during the arbitral proceedings as he sees fit, unless the arbitral tribunal considers it inappropriate to allow such amendment with regard to the delay in making it. Although the text does not explicitly refer to supplements, it is clear from the Analytical Commentary that the reference to amendments is intended to embrace supplements.[641] Art 23(2) expressly states the criterion of delay in submitting an amendment or supplement as a ground for refusing amendments or supplements. Originally, para (2) mirrored the wording of Art 20 of the UNCITRAL Arbitration Rules, which also states the criteria of prejudice to the other party or any other circumstances.[642] After discussing these criteria during the drafting process, the Commission decided not to adopt them.[643] The proponent of this change suggested that the reference to 'any other circumstances' was far too broad. He also proposed the deletion of the reference to prejudice to the other party, as this was already covered by Art 18, which requires that the parties be treated with equality and that each be given a full opportunity of presenting its case.[644] It has to be noted that there was a strong view in favour of deleting all limitations on the parties' right to submit amendments or supplements, as any limitation in that respect would be contrary to Art 18.[645] Other delegations expressed the view that the provision should follow the wording of the UNCITRAL Arbitration Rules,[646] because otherwise the arbitral tribunal **14.409**

---

[639] *ibid* para 3. But see Calavros, 112 fn 475 and Hußlein-Stich, 120 *et seq* who assert that Art 19(2) is not applicable in this case, because it is subject to the provisions of the Model Law and in particular to Art 23(1)(2) which grants the parties the freedom to choose the point of time for revealing and submitting evidence.

[640] Analytical Commentary, UN Doc A/CN.9/264, Art 23. para 6.

[641] *ibid* para 4.

[642] See Third Draft, UN Doc A/CN.9/WG.II/WP.44, Art C(3).

[643] See Summary Record, UN Doc A/CN.9/SR.323, Art 23 paras 29–30; Commission Report, UN Doc A/40/17, Art 23 para 200.

[644] See Summary Record, UN Doc A/CN.9/SR.323, Art 23 para 9 (*France*). This proposal attracted wide support: see paras 15, 16, 18, 19, 20, 22, 23, 25, 27; see also Commission Report, UN Doc A/40/17, Art 23 para 199.

[645] See Summary Record, UN Doc A/CN.9/SR.323, Art 23 paras 2, 4, 5, 6, 13.

[646] *ibid* paras 8, 10, 11, 17, 21.

would not have the power to prevent abuses of an unlimited right.[647] Under the adopted wording, delay in submitting an amendment or supplement and non-observance of the equality of the parties are grounds for disallowing an amendment or supplement.[648] In line with the provision in Art 16(2)(4), it seems appropriate not to refuse an amendment or supplement when the arbitral tribunal considers the delay justified.

14.410 There is one absolute limit on amendments and supplements with respect to which the arbitral tribunal has no discretion at all: an amendment or supplement cannot exceed the scope of the arbitration agreement. This is not expressly stated in Art 23(2), but follows from the fact that the jurisdiction of the arbitral tribunal is based on and limited by the arbitration agreement.[649] However, if a claimant amends its statement of claim to include a new claim that is otherwise outside the scope of the existing arbitration agreement and the respondent fails to raise a timely objection to the lack of an arbitration agreement, under Art 7(2)(2) a new arbitration agreement covering the expanded dispute is created.[650]

D. Analogous application to counterclaim and set-off

14.411 Article 2(f) provides that any provision referring to the claim also applies to a counterclaim and that any reference to a defence also applies to a defence to the counterclaim. Thus, the provisions of Art 23 encompass counterclaims[651] and defences to counterclaims. Unlike 19(3) of the UNCITRAL Arbitration Rules, the Model Law does not explicitly deal with a claim relied on by the respondent for the purpose of a set-off. As the Analytical Commentary treats the set-off like a counterclaim,[652] it may be concluded that the claim of the respondent for the purpose of a set-off must arise out of the same arbitration agreement as the claim.[653]

Article 24. Hearings and written proceedings

(1) Subject to any contrary agreement by the parties, the arbitral tribunal shall decide whether to hold oral hearings for the presentation of evidence or for oral argument, or whether the proceedings shall be conducted on the basis of documents and other materials. However, unless the parties have agreed that no hearings shall be held, the arbitral tribunal shall hold such hearings at an appropriate stage of the proceedings, if so requested by a party.

(2) The parties shall be given sufficient advance notice of any hearing and of any meeting of the arbitral tribunal for the purposes of inspection of goods, other property or documents.

(3) All statements, documents or other information supplied to the arbitral tribunal by one party shall be communicated to the other party. Also any expert report or evidentiary document on which the arbitral tribunal may rely in making its decision shall be communicated to the parties.

---

[647] *ibid*, para 8 (*United States*).

[648] Broches, 121.

[649] Analytical Commentary, UN Doc A/CN.9/264, Art 23 para 5.

[650] Holtzmann and Neuhaus, 649.

[651] See Analytical Commentary, UN Doc A/CN.9/264, Art 23 paras 7–8.

[652] See *ibid*, para 7.

[653] Hußlein-Stich, 123.

A. Meaning and purpose

Article 24 is a specific form of the basic principles laid down in Art 18 that the parties shall be treated with equality and each party should be given a full opportunity of presenting his case. It primarily sets out the mode of the arbitral proceedings. 14.412

B. Mode of the proceedings, paragraph (1)

(1) Oral hearing or written proceedings

Article 24(1) deals with the important procedural question of whether oral hearings will be held before the arbitral tribunal or whether the arbitral proceedings will be conducted solely in writing. Written proceedings are not very common, as the party's right to fully present his case generally calls for oral hearings. It may be emphasized that Art 24(1) only concerns the basic decision on whether there should be oral hearings at all or whether the proceedings should be conducted exclusively on the basis of written documents. The questions of the length of oral hearings, the stage at which they occur or the relationship between oral hearings and documents fall within the general discretionary powers of the arbitral tribunal granted by Art 19(2) and limited by Art 18.[654] 14.413

Article 24(1) is inspired by Art 15(2) of the UNCITRAL Arbitration Rules.[655] As the Arbitration Rules do not regulate the effect of an agreement by the parties to have or not to have hearings—a situation a Model Law must provide for—the provision had to be amended. Divergent views were expressed as to the basic policy in this connection, which caused considerable drafting problems and several amendments of the provision.[656] In the end the following three propositions regarding the availability of an oral hearing were agreed upon: 14.414

(1.1) Party agreement to have a hearing, sentence (1) If there is an agreement by the parties to have a hearing, the arbitral tribunal must hold such a hearing. The tribunal has no discretion.[657] 14.415

(1.2) Party agreement to have written proceedings, sentence (2) If the parties agree not to have a hearing, the tribunal must respect the parties' will.[658] It is not entitled to arrange a hearing. The agreement binds the parties as well, regardless of whether or not it was made before or after the dispute arose, on the basis of the general principle of *pacta sunt servanda*. However, parties can jointly modify their agreement.[659] 14.416

---

654 Commission Report, UN Doc A/40/17, para 203.

655 See First Working Group Report, UN Doc A/CN.9/216, para 57; First Draft, UN Doc A/CN.9/WG.II/WP.37, Art 20 note 35.

656 eg First Working Group Report, UN Doc A/CN.9/216, para 57; Second Working Group Report, UN Doc A/CN.9/232, para 108; Second Draft, UN Doc A/CN.9/WG.II/WP.40, Art XVII(1); Fourth Draft, UN Doc A/CN.9/WG.II/WP.48, Art 24(1); Fifth Working Group Report, UN Doc A/CN.9/246, paras 77–8; Analytical Compilation of Government Comments, UN Doc A/CN.9/263, paras 1–6; ADD.1, para 1; ADD.2 (UK Comments), para 18; Summary Record, UN Doc A/CN.9/SR.323, Art 24 paras 49, 54, 60; Commission Report, UN Doc A/40/17, para 205.

657 See Analytical Commentary, UN Doc A/CN.9/264, Art 24 para 2; cf Commission Report, UN Doc A/40/17, para 205.

658 See Analytical Commentary, UN Doc A/CN.9/264, Art 25 para 3; Commission Report, UN Doc A/40/17, para 205.

659 Commission Report, UN Doc A/40/17, para 205.

14.417 (1.3) **No party agreement, sentences (1) and (2)** In the absence of a party agreement on this issue, which is the most common case, either party may request a hearing. The arbitral tribunal then must hold such hearings at an appropriate stage of the proceedings. The change in wording from 'any stage of the proceedings' as provided for in Art 15(2) of the UNCITRAL Arbitration Rules into 'at an appropriate stage of the proceedings' was made in order to avoid an interpretation that would allow disruption of expeditious proceedings.[660] It may be assumed that a request for an oral hearing at the eve of the award would be at an inappropriate stage and therefore would not be successful.

14.418 If there is no agreement and no request for a hearing, it is left to the discretion of the arbitral tribunal to decide whether or not to hold a hearing.[661] In exercising this discretion the arbitral tribunal has to observe the standards laid down in Art 18.

(2) Scope of oral hearings

14.419 A second change from the language of the UNCITRAL Arbitration Rules concerns the scope of the oral hearings. Article 24(1)(1) deletes the reference to witnesses, including expert witnesses, and simply states that the oral hearings shall be held for the presentation of evidence or for oral argument. The general formula will ensure the interpretation **that all possible types of evidence** recognized in various legal systems are covered, such as evidence by witnesses, expert witnesses, cross-examination of any such witnesses, testimony and cross-examination of a party.[662] The term 'oral argument' is intended to cover arguments not only on the substance of the dispute, but also on procedural or jurisdictional issues.[663]

C. Sufficient advance notice, paragraph (2)

14.420 Article 24(2), which requires that the parties be given sufficient advance notice of any hearing and of any meeting of the arbitral tribunal for the purposes of inspection of goods, other property or documents, is a procedural necessity and therefore mandatory. This means that a party agreement to dispense with notice or to provide for a shorter than 'sufficient' period of notice would not be effective.[664]

14.421 The Model Law refrains from specifying details concerning the notice. A proposal that the notice be given at least 40 days in advance was rejected, because a fixed time period was considered inappropriate in view of the great variety of cases that would be covered by the Model Law.[665]

14.422 The principle laid down in this paragraph is not only fundamental in this context in that it enables the parties to participate effectively in the proceedings, but also in the context of

[660] See Second Working Group Report, UN Doc A/CN.9/232, para 111.
[661] *ibid*, para 207.
[662] See Fifth Working Group Report, UN Doc A/CN.9/246, para 79; Analytical Commentary, UN Doc A/CN.9/264, Art 24 para 5.
[663] See Fourth Working Group Report, UN Doc A/CN.9/245, para 81; Analytical Commentary, UN Doc A/CN.9/264, Art 24 para 5.
[664] Analytical Commentary, UN Doc A/CN.9/264, Art 24 para 7.
[665] Fourth Working Group Report, UN Doc A/CN.9/245, para 82; Analytical Commentary, UN Doc A/CN.9/264, Art 24 para 7.

Art 25(c) in that it is a condition for continuing the proceedings in case a party fails to appear at a hearing.[666]

D. Communication of documents and other information, paragraph (3)

Article 24(3) stipulates the principle that all statements, documents and other information supplied to the arbitral tribunal by one party shall be communicated to the other party, and any expert report or evidentiary document which the arbitral tribunal may rely on in making its decision shall be communicated to the parties. Again, as a specific form of Art 18, this provision is mandatory. Like para (2), this provision does not regulate details such as who is to communicate the information. **14.423**

Article 24(3) is largely based on Art 15(3) of the UNCITRAL Arbitration Rules, but does not demand that the documents supplied to the arbitral tribunal by one party be communicated to the other party at the same time. This change is based on the intent to harmonize the Model Law with arbitration rules such as the ICC Rules, under which documents are first sent to the arbitral institution or the tribunal, which then transmits them to the arbitrators and the other party.[667] **14.424**

The reference in the second sentence of Art 24(3) to any 'evidentiary document' is intended to clarify that research material prepared or collected by the arbitral tribunal does not have to be communicated to the parties.[668] **14.425**

Article 25. Default of a party

Unless otherwise agreed by the parties, if, without showing sufficient cause,

(a) the claimant fails to communicate his statement of claim in accordance with article 23(1), the arbitral tribunal shall terminate the proceedings;

(b) the respondent fails to communicate his statement of defence in accordance with article 23(1), the arbitral tribunal shall continue the proceedings without treating such failure in itself as an admission of the claimant's allegations;

(c) any party fails to appear at the hearing or to produce documentary evidence, the arbitral tribunal may continue the proceedings and make the award on the evidence before it.

A. Meaning and purpose

Article 25 sets out the consequences of a party's default. It was generally agreed that an arbitral law must provide arbitration with its necessary 'teeth'[669] in order for it to function efficiently. It should be emphasized that Art 25 is non-mandatory and the parties may therefore agree on alternative consequences. **14.426**

The provision specifies the three default situations: (i) failure to communicate a statement of claim; (ii) failure to communicate a statement of defence; and (iii) failure to appear at a hearing or to produce documentary evidence. With respect to the different situations, the **14.427**

---

666 *ibid*, para 6.

667 See First Draft, UN Doc A/CN.9/WG.II/WP.37, Art 20 note 36; Second Working Group Report, UN Doc A/CN.9/232, para 109.

668 See Commission Report, UN Doc A/40/17, para 211; see also Analytical Commentary, UN Doc A/CN.9/264, Art 24 para 8.

669 First Secretariat Note, UN Doc A/CN.9/207, para 80.

Model Law provides for different consequences: the arbitral tribunal may either terminate the proceedings or continue them. Some safeguards were included to ensure the fair exercise of the power conferred upon the arbitral tribunal.

B. Consequences of default of a party

(1) Sufficient cause for default

14.428 The first safeguard to ensure fair exercise of the arbitral tribunal's power implemented in the supplementary regulation of Art 25 is that the provisions of this article will not apply if a party shows sufficient cause for his default. This formula was taken from Art 28 of the UNCITRAL Arbitration Rules.[670] The arbitral tribunal is entitled to decide whether or not sufficient cause has been shown. It was suggested that a court would decide, depending on the circumstances of each case, whether *ex parte* proceedings by the arbitral tribunal were permissible.[671] The suggestion was not adopted, as it introduced an element of court supervision of international commercial arbitration, which was felt to be neither necessary nor desirable.[672]

14.429 The sufficient cause for the delay has to exist before the time the action is due. The drafters intentionally gave no exact definition of the point of time when sufficient cause was to be shown to the arbitral tribunal in order not to interfere with the discretion of the tribunal to assess the cause for delay and to extend the period of time for the party to communicate a statement or to produce evidence.[673]

(2) Failure to communicate the statement of claim, sub-paragraph (a)

14.430 If a claimant fails to communicate his statement of claim within the period of time agreed by the parties or determined by the arbitral tribunal,[674] the arbitral tribunal shall terminate the proceedings.[675] The reference to the time period incorporated in Art 23(1) implies that the defaulting claimant should have been duly notified in advance of what he was expected to do. This requirement of advance notice forms another safeguard to ensure fair proceedings.[676]

(3) Failure to communicate the statement of defence, sub-paragraph (b)

14.431 If the respondent fails to communicate his statement of defence within the period of time agreed on by the parties or determined by the arbitral tribunal,[677] the tribunal shall continue the proceedings. As to the legal assessment of such failure, the Model Law provides the safeguard that the defendant's default is not to be considered in itself an admission of

---

[670] See First Draft, UN Doc A/CN.9/WG.II/WP.37, Art 24(A) note 43.

[671] First Working Group Report, UN Doc A/CN.9/216, para 71.

[672] Second Working Group Report, UN Doc A/CN.9/232, para 126.

[673] Commission Report, UN Doc A/40/17, para 123.

[674] See Art 23(1).

[675] As to the form of termination see Art 32. But see Hußlein-Stich, 129 with reference to Holtzmann, ICCA Lausanne, 150 *et seq* (commenting on the Fifth Draft), who points out that the termination occurs automatically without need for an order. However, at the last stage of the drafting there was a change in the wording that aligns Art 25(a) with Art 32.

[676] First Secretariat Note, UN Doc A/CN.9/207, para 81; First Working Group Report, UN Doc A/CN.9/216, para 71; Analytical Commentary, UN Doc A/CN. 9/264, Art 25 paras 2 *et seq*.

[677] See Art 23(1).

the claimant's allegations. This safeguard is particularly important because, under many national laws on civil procedure, default of the defendant is treated as such an admission.[678] The alternative approach that the default is to be considered as a full denial of the claim and all supporting facts was not adopted in order to provide the tribunal with certain discretion.[679] In particular, the wording 'in itself' clarifies that the arbitral tribunal has discretion as to how it assesses the cause of failure and is free to draw those inferences that appear most probable from the silence of the respondent.[680] Another safeguard lies in the reference to the time limit in Art 23(1), which ensures that the defaulting defendant be duly notified in advance.[681]

(4) Failure to appear at hearing or to produce evidence, sub-paragraph (c)

If any party fails to appear at a hearing or to produce documentary evidence, the tribunal may continue the proceedings and make the award on the evidence before it. By intentionally using the term 'may' the drafters stressed the discretion of the arbitral tribunal in this respect.[682] As a result, the tribunal has the power to decide not to continue the proceedings even where the party in default does not show sufficient cause for his default.[683] **14.432**

Article 25 does not stipulate what inferences the arbitral tribunal may draw from a party's failure to appear at a hearing or to produce documentary evidence. However, the *travaux préparatoires* make clear that it was the drafters' understanding that the tribunal is empowered to infer that the evidence would have been to that party's disadvantage.[684] **14.433**

Although this provision does not explicitly state a time limit, the Secretariat points out that the term 'failure to appear at a hearing' presupposes that the party was given sufficient advance notice under Art 24(2), and the term 'failure to produce documentary evidence' presupposes that the party was requested to do so within a specified period of time that was reasonable in accordance with the fundamental principles of fairness of Art 18.[685] **14.434**

Article 26. Expert appointed by arbitral tribunal

(1) Unless otherwise agreed by the parties, the arbitral tribunal
  (a) may appoint one or more experts to report to it on specific issues to be determined by the arbitral tribunal;
  (b) may require a party to give the expert any relevant information or to produce, or to provide access to, any relevant documents, goods or other property for his inspection.

(2) Unless otherwise agreed by the parties, if a party so requests or if the arbitral tribunal considers it necessary, the expert shall, after delivery of his written or oral report, participate in

678 Fifth Working Group Report, UN Doc A/CN.9/264, para 83; Analytical Commentary, UN Doc A/CN.9/264, Art 25 para 4.

679 *ibid*; Holtzmann and Neuhaus, 700.

680 Analytical Compilation of the Government Comments, UN Doc A/CN.9/263, Art 32 para 1 *(Federal Republic of Germany)*; Commission Report, UN Doc A/CN 40/17, para 214.

681 Analytical Commentary, UN Doc A/CN.9/264, Art 25 paras 2 *et seq.*

682 See Commission Report, UN Doc A/40/17, para 215.

683 Davidson *(Scotland)* para 6.61.

684 See Analytical Commentary, UN Doc A/CN.9/264, Art 25 para 5; Summary Record, UN Doc A/CN.9/SR.325, Art 27 paras 84–6; Commission Report, UN Doc A/40/17, para 229.

685 Analytical Commentary, UN Doc A/CN.9/264, Art 25 para 5.

a hearing where the parties have the opportunity to put questions to him and to present expert witnesses in order to testify on the points at issue.

A. Meaning and purpose

14.435 In many commercial arbitrations, such as in business, financial, construction or technical matters, the arbitrators feel the need to seek expert advice. Article 26 only concerns experts appointed by the arbitral tribunal; it does not deal with party-appointed experts. The right of a party to appoint experts is implied in his right to fully present his case under Art 18. Article 26 represents a compromise between the common law system of adjudication in which appointment of experts by the court or tribunal is not usual and the civil law system in which such appointments are common.[686] Art 26 was inspired by Art 27 of the UNCITRAL Arbitration Rules,[687] but is less detailed on the grounds of the general agreement that the Model Law should express only statements of principle and not detailed procedural elements.[688]

B. Power to appoint expert, paragraph (1)

(1) Appointment of expert, sub-paragraph (a)

14.436 Article 26(1)(a) empowers the arbitral tribunal to appoint one or more experts *ex officio* to report to it on any issue it may determine, even if the parties have not specifically authorized it to do so. Because of the non-mandatory character of the provision the parties may exclude this power at any stage of the proceedings. It was considered that the parties should only conclude a contrary agreement before the appointment of the first arbitrator,[689] as an arbitrator might not want to act without having the opportunity to obtain advice from an expert. If the agreement of the parties was reached before the arbitrator's appointment, he would know the terms of his appointment.[690] However, the principle of party autonomy was recognized as being paramount for a number of reasons: first, it was felt that the parties know best by what means their dispute should be settled; second, the parties will be the ones to pay for any expert; third, the parties might not have confidence in an expert proposed for appointment by the arbitral tribunal; fourth, the appointment of experts might increase the costs beyond the amount the parties are willing to spend; finally, if an arbitrator resigns because of the parties' late decision not to allow an expert, and he is free to do so, they would have to bear the cost of wasted time and money.[691] Because of the last reason, the parties should be careful in making a contrary agreement after the appointment of the first arbitrator. It is prudent to agree on the power of the arbitral tribunal to appoint an expert at the outset of the arbitral proceedings.[692] Such an agreement will be implied if the

686 Commission Report, UN Doc A/40/17, para 219.

687 See First Draft, UN Doc A/CN.9/WG.II/WP.37, Art 22 note 38.

688 See Second Working Group Report, UN Doc A/CN.9/232, para 117.

689 See Fourth Working Group Report, UN Doc A/CN.9/245, para 84; Fourth Draft, UN Doc A/CN.9/WG.II/WP.48, Art 26(1); Summary Record, UN Doc A/CN.9/SR.325, Art 26 para 39; Commission Report, UN Doc A/40/17, para 218.

690 See Commission Report, UN Doc A/40/17, para 218.

691 See Analytical Commentary, UN Doc A/CN.9/264, Art 26 para 2; Commission Report, UN Doc A/40/17, para 219.

692 Van Houtte, 124.

parties refer to particular arbitration rules such as the UNCITRAL Arbitration Rules or the ICC Rules.[693]

(2) Duty of the parties to cooperate with the expert, sub-paragraph (b)

Subject to the contrary agreement of the parties, the arbitral tribunal has the power to require a party to give the expert any relevant information or to produce or to provide access to any relevant documents, goods or other property for his inspection. The parties may alter this provision by referring to arbitration rules such as the UNCITRAL Arbitration Rules, which, *inter alia*, set out in Art 27(2) that the expert shall directly request the parties to supply information or materials. Originally, the Model Law provision was exactly in this form.[694] It was amended because it seemed more appropriate that the arbitral tribunal itself, and not the expert, should require any relevant information and materials.[695] Of course the expert can request the parties directly under the Model Law provision as well, which makes the proceedings faster. Yet only the arbitral tribunal can actually order production and sanction non-compliance with this order under Art 25(c).[696] It should be noted in this context that by virtue of Art 27 the arbitral tribunal or a party with the approval of the arbitral tribunal may request assistance in taking evidence from a competent court. **14.437**

C. Expert appearing at hearing, paragraph (2)

Paragraph (2), which is again subject to the contrary agreement of the parties, is a concrete implementation of the fundamental right of the parties to have a full opportunity to present their case under Art 18.[697] It deals with the conduct of the arbitral proceedings after the delivery of the expert's report, which may be in written or oral form.[698] Oral reports may be adequate when the case requires an urgent decision or when the parties are cost-conscious.[699] After the delivery of the report, Art 24(3) requires that it be communicated to the parties, who must then have sufficient opportunity to examine the expert opinion.[700] If either a party then so requests or the arbitral tribunal considers it necessary, the expert shall participate in a hearing. The flexible formulation makes clear that a hearing with an expert does not have to be held in each and every case.[701] In the hearing the parties have the opportunity to question the expert and to present counter-experts in order to testify on the points at issue. In this connection it should be stressed that regardless of whether the arbitral tribunal calls an expert or not, each party is free to choose and present expert witnesses.[702] **14.438**

---

693 See Art 27 of the UNCITRAL Arbitration Rules; Art 20(4) of the ICC Rules.
694 See First Draft, UN Doc A/CN.9/WG.II/WP.37, Art 22(2)(b).
695 Fifth Working Group Report, UN Doc A/CN.9/264, para 88.
696 Holtzmann and Neuhaus, 720.
697 See Analytical Commentary, UN Doc A/CN.9/264, Art 26 para 3.
698 The First Draft contained a more rigid version following Art 27 of the UNCITRAL Arbitration Rules in providing for a report 'in writing'; see UN Doc A/CN.9/WG.II/WP.37, Art 22(1).
699 Holtzmann, ICCA Lausanne, 153; Van Houtte, 124.
700 Van Houtte, 124.
701 Fifth Working Group Report, UN Doc A/CN.9/246, para 89.
702 Holtzmann and Neuhaus, 720.

The Working Group agreed that the arbitral tribunal should hear such expert witnesses as provided for in Art 15(2) of the UNCITRAL Arbitration Rules.[703]

Article 27. Court assistance in taking evidence

The arbitral tribunal or a party with the approval of the arbitral tribunal may request from a competent court of this state assistance in taking evidence. The court may execute the request within its competence and according to its rules on taking evidence.

A. Meaning and purpose

14.439 Article 27 concerns another instance of court intervention in arbitral proceedings. This provision was the subject of considerable disagreement with respect to both its underlying policy and its details and was therefore redrafted several times. One view favoured the deletion of the whole provision as it might be abused for dilatory tactics by the parties and would also be contrary to the private nature of arbitration.[704] The prevailing view, however, was to include a provision dealing with assistance by courts in enforcing procedural decisions of the arbitral tribunal. It was pointed out that such a provision could contribute to the proper and efficient functioning of international commercial arbitration and that there was a practical need for court assistance in obtaining evidence in view of the fact that the arbitral tribunal is not empowered to enforce its procedural decisions for example to inspect property or to compel a person to testify or to produce a document.[705] Under the Model Law it merely has the power to interpret the refusal of a party to comply with an order to produce evidence to that party's disadvantage under Art 25(c).[706]

14.440 Among those who proposed the inclusion of a provision on court assistance in securing evidence, there was some discussion as to the details of this provision. The discussion focused on three concerns: the integration with existing court procedures, the question of international court assistance and the possibility of abuse.[707] In the end, the Commission adopted a version that merely expresses a policy statement that the parties and the arbitral tribunal have a right to such assistance[708] and does not provide for concrete details regarding the procedure for obtaining court assistance in taking evidence, for example the contents of the request or the form of the assistance. Some Model Law states included specifications.[709]

---

[703] First Working Group Report, UN Doc A/CN.9/216, para 63; see also Sanders (1977) II *YCA* 204. The reference to the UNCITRAL Arbitration Rules appears to have been by way of example in order to clarify the underlying principle; see Holtzmann and Neuhaus, 721 note 16.

[704] See First Working Group Report, UN Doc A/CN.9/216, para 61; Fourth Working Group Report, UN Doc A/CN.9/245, para 38; Fifth Working Group Report, UN Doc A/CN.9/246, para 95.

[705] *ibid*; Third Secretariat Note, UN Doc A/CN.9/WG.II/WP.41, para 27; Analytical Commentary, UN Doc A/CN.9/264, Art 27 para 1; but see Melis, 95 who points out that court assistance in taking evidence plays merely a marginal role in international arbitrations.

[706] See Analytical Commentary, UN Doc A/CN.9/264, Art 27 para 1 note 77; Commission Report, UN Doc A/40/17, para 229.

[707] See First Working Group Report, UN Doc A/CN.9/216, para 61.

[708] See Fifth Working Group Report, UN Doc A/CN.9/246, para 94.

[709] eg *Bermuda*: s 35 of the Bermuda International Conciliation and Arbitration Act 1993; *New Zealand*: Art 27(2) of the First sch of the Arbitration Act 1996; *Singapore*: ss 13–14 of the International Arbitration Act 1994; *Zimbabwe*: Art 27 of the Arbitration Act 1996.

B. Request for assistance and its effect

In order to avoid requests for irrelevant or unnecessary evidence which would delay the arbitral proceedings, Art 27 requires that either the arbitral tribunal or a party with the approval of the arbitral tribunal may request assistance from a competent court.[710] Thus, the procedural party autonomy is restricted. In any case, the request by a party depends on the consent of the tribunal. This proviso represents a compromise between the 'investigative' and the 'adversarial' approaches of arbitration.[711] The final version of the Model Law does not specify the contents of the request. The Commission decided to delete a respective proviso because it was felt to be too detailed for a model law.[712] Thus, this is a matter governed by national procedural law.[713] 14.441

The 'competent court' is not necessarily the one specified in Art 6. The drafters recognized from the outset that court assistance formed an integral part of the procedural law of the legal system concerned and that the Model Law should not interfere with existing national laws concerning court assistance in taking evidence.[714] Thus, the competence of the courts is a matter regulated by the procedural law of the respective state. Under general provisions, the court's competence may be based, for example, on the residence of the witness to be heard or the location of the property to be inspected.[715] The Model Law as *lex specialis* would prevail over the general provisions of the procedural law only when the state has entrusted the Art 6 authority with the taking of evidence in international commercial arbitrations. 14.442

The competent court may execute the request according to its rules on taking evidence. The drafters of the Model Law did not draft uniform procedural rules on court assistance or indicate the form in which the court should execute the request, again recognizing state autonomy in this regard and faced with the practical difficulties of drafting rules that would be compatible with many different legal systems. A provision that the court could either take the evidence itself or order the evidence to be provided directly to the arbitral tribunal was deleted in the final text on this ground.[716] Therefore, the court may decide as provided in the applicable procedural law. 14.443

C. Territorial scope of application

During the drafting process, the inclusion of provisions for taking of evidence abroad and assistance to be given by a court in the Model Law state to foreign arbitrations was considered.[717] The Working Group deleted these provisions as a compromise between 14.444

---

[710] See Analytical Commentary, UN Doc A/CN.9/264, Art 27 para 5.

[711] See Commission Report, UN Doc A/40/17, para 226.

[712] Commission Report, UN Doc A/40/17, para 228.

[713] See also *Vibroflotation A G v Express Builders Co Ltd*, High Court of Hong Kong (Kaplan), 15 August 1994, CLOUT Case 77.

[714] First Working Group Report, UN Doc A/CN.9/216, para 61(a); see also Commission Report, UN Doc A/40/17, para 225.

[715] See Analytical Commentary, UN Doc A/CN.9/264, Art 27 para 5.

[716] Commission Report, UN Doc A/40/17, para 230.

[717] See Third Working Group Report, UN Doc A/CN.9/233, paras 27–36; Third Draft, UN Doc A/CN.9/WG.II/WP.44, Art E(2); Fourth Working Group Report, UN Doc A/CN.9/245, paras 42–6; Fourth Draft, UN Doc A/CN.9/WG.II/WP.48, Art 27(2), (3).

those in favour of international court assistance and those opposed to any provision on court assistance.[718] It was further pointed out that while court assistance as such seemed useful, its extension to foreign arbitral tribunals could not be appropriately dealt with by a model law.[719] An acceptable system of international court assistance could not be established unilaterally through a model law but rather by international instruments such as conventions or bilateral treaties, as the principle of reciprocity and bilaterally or multilaterally accepted procedural rules were essential conditions for the functioning of such a system.[720] The Commission agreed with this view.[721] Thus, the territorial scope of application of Art 27 is limited to arbitrations in the Model Law state. *Germany*, however, provides for international court assistance in taking evidence.[722]

Chapter VI. Making of award and termination of proceedings

Special literature:

Blessing, Marc, 'Regulations in Arbitration Rules on Choice of Law' in Albert Jan van den Berg (ed), *Planning Efficient Arbitration-Proceedings: The Law Applicable in International Arbitration, XIIth International Arbitration Congress, Vienna, 3–6 November 1994* (ICCA Congress Series no 7, Kluwer Law International, 1996).

Blessing, Marc, 'Choice of Substantive Law in International Arbitration' (1997) 14 *J Int'l Arb* 39.

Chukkwumerije, Okezie, *Choice of Law in International Commercial Arbitration* (Quorum Books, 1994).

Derains, Yves, 'Possible Conflict of Laws Rules and the Rules Applicable to the Substance of the Dispute' in Pieter Sanders (ed), *UNCITRAL's Project for a Model Law on International Commercial Arbitration, Interim meeting, Lausanne, 9–12 May 1984* (1984).

Drahozal, Christopher R., 'The Making of the Award: Comments on Case Law Developments Under the UNCITRAL Model Law' (2005) 8 *Int'l Arb L Rev* 183.

Grigera Naon, Horacio, 'Choice-of-law Problems in International Commercial Arbitration' (2001) 289 *Recueil des cours de l'Acadmie de droit international de La Haye* 9.

Knoepfler, Francois and Schweizer, Philippe, 'Making of Awards and Termination of Proceedings' in Petar Sarcevic (ed), *Essays on International Commercial Arbitration* (Graham & Trotman/Martinus Nijhoff, 1989).

Kühn, Wolfgang, 'Express and Implied Choice of the Substantive Law in the Practice of International Arbitration' in Albert Jan van den Berg (ed), *Planning Efficient Arbitration Proceedings: The Law Applicable in International Arbitration, XIIth International Arbitration Congress, Vienna, 3–6 November 1994* (ICCA Congress Series no 7, Kluwer Law International, 1996).

Lando, Ole, 'The Law Applicable to the Merits of the Dispute' in Petar Sarcevic (ed), *Essays on International Commercial Arbitration* (Graham & Trotman/Martinus Nijhoff, 1989).

Lew, Julian, D.M., 'Relevance of Conflict of Laws Rules in the Practice of Arbitration' in Albert Jan van den Berg (ed), *Planning Efficient Arbitration Proceedings: The Law Applicable in International Arbitration, XIIth International Arbitration Congress, Vienna, 3–6 November 1994* (ICCA Congress Series no 7, Kluwer Law International, 1996).

[718] See Fifth Working Group Report, UN Doc A/CN.9/246, paras 95–6; Analytical Commentary, UN Doc A/CN.9/264, Art 27 para 4.

[719] *ibid.*

[720] Fourth Working Group Report, UN Doc A/CN.9/245, para 43.

[721] Commission Report, UN Doc A/40/17, para 225.

[722] See s 1025(2), ZPO with reference to s 1050, ZPO, which is the equivalent of Art 27.

Lew, Julian D.M., *Applicable Law in International Commercial Arbitration* (1978).
MacGuinness, Declan, 'Applicable Law Chosen by Arbitrators: A Critical View on the Arbitrator's Use of the Method of voie directe' (2003) *Stockholm Arb Rep* 61.
Nakamura Tatsuya, 'Parallel proceedings before an arbitral tribunal and a national court from the perspective of the UNCITRAL model law' (2004) 19 *Mealey's Int'l Arb Rep* 23.
Schmid, Hans-Rudolf, *Choice of Law by the Arbitrator* (LL M Thesis, Harvard Law School, 1986).
Strohbach, Heinz,'Composition of the Arbitral Tribunal and Making of the Award' in Pieter Sanders (ed), *UNCITRAL's Project for a Model Law on International Commercial Arbitration, Interim meeting, Lausanne, 9–12 May 1984* (ICCA Congress Series no 2, 1984).
Williams, David and Buchanan, Amy, 'Correction and Interpretation of Awards under Article 33 of the Model Law' (2001) 2 *Int'l Arb L Rev* 119.

Article 28. Rules applicable to substance of dispute

(1) The arbitral tribunal shall decide the dispute in accordance with such rules of law as are chosen by the parties as applicable to the substance of the dispute. Any designation of the law or legal system of a given State shall be construed, unless otherwise expressed, as directly referring to the substantive law of that State and not to its conflict of laws rules.

(2) Failing any designation by the parties, the arbitral tribunal shall apply the law determined by the conflict of laws rules which it considers applicable.

(3) The arbitral tribunal shall decide *ex aequo et bono* or as *amiable compositeur* only if the parties have expressly authorized it to do so.

(4) In all cases, the arbitral tribunal shall decide in accordance with the terms of the contract and shall take into account the usages of the trade applicable to the transaction.

A. Meaning and purpose

Article 28 provides for the determination of the rules that the tribunal applies to the substance of the dispute. Hence, Art 28 solely concerns substantive law, whereas Art 19 determines the procedural law of the actual arbitration. **14.445**

One of the great advantages international arbitration has to offer is the flexibility in choosing the appropriate law for the settlement of material disputes. Accordingly, Art 28 grants the parties full autonomy in their choice of the substantive law in para (1). They may even authorize the tribunal to decide *ex aequo et bono*, according to para (3). In the absence of a mutual designation by the parties, para (2) empowers the tribunal to determine the applicable law, albeit under some stricter requirements. In all cases, regardless of whether the parties or the arbitrators are given the choice of law, the decision as to the substance of the dispute must be in line with the terms of the contract and the relevant usages of trade, according to para (4). **14.446**

B. Choice of law by the parties, paragraph (1)

(1) Party autonomy

Paragraph (1) confers the primary choice of the substantive law on the parties, granting them full autonomy. All adopting states embraced this autonomy. As a general principle of law, it forms part of the *lex mercatoria* and the transnational *ordre public*.[723] The parties may also alter their choice of law during the proceedings, provided that rights of third parties are **14.447**

[723] Redfern and Hunter, paras 2–34 *et seq*,.; Berger, 490, 535 with further references; Lew, J.D.M., 'Applicable Law in International Commercial Arbitration' (Kluwer Law International, 1978) 81 *et seq*.

not prejudiced.[724] The freedom of the parties to choose the law applicable to their dispute is only restricted on the grounds of international public policy and mandatory norms of third countries (*lois d'application immédiate*).[725] In particular, the chosen law need not have a special connection to the case at hand.[726]

14.448 The second sentence of Art 28(1) clearly excludes *renvoi* by stating that any choice of law shall be construed, unless otherwise expressed, as referring to substantive law and not to conflict of laws rules.

(2) Rules of law

14.449 In certain cases parties may wish to agree on rules different from those of a particular national system of law, such as when dealing with a state which does not accept foreign law, or when national laws do not adequately reflect the needs of commerce. Article 28(1) meets this desire by employing the term 'rules of law' as opposed to 'law' used in para (2). Hence the parties may 'choose the rules embodied in a convention or similar legal text elaborated on the international level, even if not yet in force', select single rules from different national laws (*dépecage*)[727] or agree to 'stabilize' the law, ie to select a national law at a given moment of time.[728] According to almost unanimous contemporary view, 'rules of law' in para (1) also include general principles of law and the *lex mercatoria* as well as case law developed in arbitral awards and private restatements of international contract law, such as the UNIDROIT Principles.[729] During the drafting process of the Model Law, however, opinion on the proper meaning of the term 'rules of law' was divided. On the one hand, the Fourth Working Group Report rejected a wide interpretation including general legal principles and arbitral case law;[730] on the other hand, the Secretariat, in giving reasons for the terminology in para (1), referred to the identical wording in Art 42 of the 1965 Washington Convention and the arbitration laws of *France* and *Djibouti*.[731] These norms, however, undisputedly hold a broad meaning granting parties the greatest possible freedom.[732]

---

[724] Berger, 493 *et seq* with further references; Redfern and Hunter, paras 2–36 *et seq*.

[725] Berger, 491, 538 with further references; cf Redfern and Hunter, paras 2–37 *et seq*; Rubino-Sammartano, M., *International Arbitration Law* (2nd edn, Kluwer, 2001).

[726] Berger, 491 *et seq*. The sometimes stated 'reasonable interest' does not really limit party autonomy, since parties only lack such interest under extraordinary circumstances where the choice of law is 'evidently arbitrary and the result of child's play'; BGE 91 II 44, 51; Triebel, V. and Petzold, E., 'Grenzen der *lex mercatoria* in der internationalen Schiedsgerichtsbarkeit' (1988) 34 *RIW* 345 *et seq*; cf Schnyder, A.K., *Das neue IPR-Gesetz* (Schulthess Polygraphischer Verlag, 1990) 27 *et seq*; Rubino-Sammartano, 219 *et seq*. But see Art 3(3) of the Rome Convention on the Law Applicable to Contractual Obligations of 19 June 1980 for the restriction on entirely internal cases.

[727] Commission Report, UN Doc A/40/17, para 232.

[728] Summary Record, UN Doc. A/CN.9/SR.326, para 26; Hußlein-Stich, 142.

[729] UNIDROIT, Principles of International Commercial Contracts (1994). See Berger, 556 *et seq* with further references; Redfern and Hunter, 94 n 82 and paras 2–46; Granzow, 168; Calavros, 123; Blessing, *Choice of Substantive Law*, 56. But see Schlosser, P., *Das Recht der internationalen privaten Schiedsgerichtsbarkeit* (2nd edn, 1989) marg no 201.

[730] Fourth Working Group Report, UN Doc A/CN.9/245, para 94.

[731] Seventh Secretariat Note, UN Doc A/CN.9/264, para 4. See Art 42 of the Washington Convention on the Settlement of Investment Disputes between States and Nationals of Other States (ICSID), 575 UNTS 159; *France*: Art 1496 of the Nouveau Code de Procédure Civil; *Djibouti*: Art 12 of the Code on International Arbitration.

[732] Berger, 557 n 396; Gaillard, E., 'The UNCITRAL Model Law and Recent Statutes on International Arbitration in Europe and North America' (1987) 2 *ICSID Review—Foreign Investment L J* 433 *et seq*;

Moreover, in the final discussion on para (1) several representatives still favoured the wide understanding of 'rules of law'.[733] Holtzmann and Neuhaus rightly argue that as, pursuant to para (3), parties may even authorize the tribunal to act as *amiable compositeur*, they should likewise be able to choose any set of rules they wish, as long as these rules are ascertainable.[734]

(3) Express or implied choice

In the absence of an express agreement, the tribunal may still infer a parties' choice of law from the terms of the contract and the relevant surrounding circumstances.[735] Possible indications for such an implied choice are standard contract forms or general conditions which have been adapted to a certain legal system, or other references to national norms.[736] However, the choice of the seat of arbitration is not *per se* an implied choice of the law in force in that country.[737] The parties may have selected the place of arbitration for reasons other than the substantive law, such as geographic distance and neutrality, the seat then having no connection to the case. Hence, only in particular situations may the seat of arbitration be an indication of an implied choice of law, which at any rate must be supported by additional factors.[738] **14.450**

C. Determination by the tribunal, paragraph (2)

In the absence of an express or implied designation by the parties, it is up to the tribunal to determine the law applicable to the merits of the dispute. In contrast to para (1), however, the tribunal's choice is restricted in two ways: first, the tribunal may only apply a national system of law ('law' as opposed to 'rules of law') and second, this law has to be determined by a conflict of laws rule (classical or indirect method). **14.451**

The arbitral tribunal is not bound to apply the conflict of laws rules of the seat of arbitration.[739] However, arbitrators should take care to base their finding on a choice of law which **14.452**

Derains, Y., 'International Commercial Arbitration in Civil Law Countries' in P. Sanders (ed), *Arbitration in settlement of international commercial disputes involving the Far East and arbitration in combined transportation* (1989) 4 *ICCA Congress Series*, 240; Derains, Y., 'Possible Conflict of Law Rules Applicable to the Dispute' in P. Sanders (ed), *2 ICCA Congress Series* 191 *et seq*; von Breitenstein, D., 'Die Arbitrage im französischen Recht' in K.-H., Böckstiegel (ed), *Schiedsgerichtsbarkeit in Frankreich* (1986) 15, 39 *et seq*; Reiner, A., 'Die internationale Schiedsgerichtsbarkeit nach österreichischem und französischem Recht' (1986) *ZRVgl* 210.

[733] See the statements in the Summary Record, UN Doc A/CN.9/SR.326, para 1 *(Italy)*, 7 *(Argentina)*, 9 *(France)*, 23 (The Hague Conference on Private International Law), 28 *(France)*, 29; see also para 8 *(Germany)*, 20 *(Japan)*.

[734] Holtzmann and Neuhaus, 768; cf Summary Record, UN Doc A/CN.9/SR.326, para 8 *(Germany)*, 20 *(Japan)*.

[735] Redfern and Hunter, para 2-76; Blessing, *Choice of Substantive Law* 43 *et seq* with further references; Kühn, '*Express and Implied Choice*' 380 *et seq*.

[736] Rubino-Sammartano, 423 *et seq*; Berger, 494.

[737] However, for *Germany* see Albers, J. in Baumbach *et al*, *Zivilprozessordnung* (58th edn, 2000) s 1051 marg no 2 with further references; cf also US Supreme Court, *Scherk v Alberto Culver*, (1974) 417 US 506, 519 n 13; Lew, J.D.M., *Applicable Law in International Commercial Arbitration* (1978) 190.

[738] Berger, 495 *et seq* with further references; Rubino-Sammartano, 426 *et seq*. Redfern and Hunter, paras 2–78 *et seq* with further references.

[739] Granzow, 171; Berger, 495 *et seq*, 498, 506, 508 *et seq* with further references; Bucher, A., 'Transnationales Recht im IPR' in Schwind (ed), *Aktuelle Fragen zum Europarecht aus der Sicht in- und ausländischer Gelehrter* (1986) 11 *et seq*, 29; Redfern and Hunter, paras 2–79 *et seq* with further references; 16;

convinces the losing party,[740] though the decision on the conflict of laws rules and consequently on the applicable substantive law is not subject to court review. In contemporary practice, arbitral tribunals tend to compare the different conflict of laws rules having a sufficient connection with the case and consequently apply coinciding rules.[741] Frequently, arbitrators cumulatively apply the conflict of laws rules of both parties' home country and as it may also be that of the seat of the arbitration.[742] The recent trend in international arbitration is to widen this comparative approach by applying those conflict of laws rules that are common to the leading legal systems in the world and reflected in international conventions[743] or those conflict rules which are generally followed in international arbitrations of the kind under consideration.[744]

14.453 The traditional approach of Art 28(2) limiting the tribunal's choice to a domestic legal system determined by conflict of laws rules is in harmony with Art VII of the 1961 European Convention[745] and Art 33(1) of the UNCITRAL Rules.[746] Nonetheless, Art 28(2) was criticized during the course of drafting, as the complicated conflict of laws approach is contrary to arbitral practice.[747] It was pointed out that the conflictual approach, in fact, does not provide a higher degree of certainty than a direct determination of the governing law (*voie directe*) considering that the conflict of laws rules differ from one legal system to another and that the reasons which lead the arbitrator to select an appropriate applicable law under the direct method are similar to the connecting factors in conflict rules.[748] Thus, more than half the adopting states rejected the conflicts approach of the Model Law,[749] either by embracing the *voie directe*[750] or by referring the arbitrators to the law with which the case has the closest connection.[751] A number of states, namely *Oregon* and the *Canadian*

---

cf *Sapphire International Petroleums Ltd v National Iranian Oil Company* (1964) 13 ICLQ, 1011 *et seq.* But see *Calavros*, 128.

[740] Commission Report, UN Doc A/40/17, para 236; Berger, 498, 500 *et seq*; Bucher, A., 'Transnationales Recht im IPR' in Schwind (ed), *Aktuelle Fragen zum Europarecht aus der Sicht in- und ausländischer Gelehrter* (1986) 35; Aden, M., 'Die Anwendung materiellen Rechts durch den Schiedsrichter' (1984) *RIW* 934 *et seq.*

[741] ICC Award no 5118 (1986), in Jarvin, S. *et al* (ed), *Collection of ICC Arbitral Awards 1986–1990* (Kluwer, 1994) 249 *et seq*, (1987) JDI (Clunet) 1027 with note Jarvin, 1028; ICC Award no 4996, (1986) JDI (Clunet) 1132; Berger, 497 *et seq.*

[742] eg ICC Award no 6281, (1990) XV YCA 96 *et seq.*

[743] ICC Award no 5713, YCA XV (1990) 70 *et seq* ('general trend in conflict of laws'); ICC Award no 6281, (1991) JDI (Clunet) 1054 with note Hascher, 1056.

[744] ICC Award no 4237, (1985) X YCA 52, 55; van Hof, J., *Commentary on the UNCITRAL Arbitration Rules* (1991) 238 ('general principles of private international law'); Berger, 498 with further references.

[745] European Convention on International Commercial Arbitration, concluded in Geneva on 4 April 1961, 484 UNTS 349.

[746] Analytical Commentary, UN Doc A/CN.9/264, para 6. The additionally mentioned ICC Rules have meanwhile adopted the *voie directe* and changed the terminology to 'rules of law', see Art 17(1), ICC Rules of 1998.

[747] See the statements in the Summary Record, UN Doc A/CN.9/SR.326, para 38 *(Japan)*, 40 *(United States)*, 43 *(Argentina)*, 44 *(France)*, 46 *(Sweden)*, 48 *(Australia)*, 49 *(Italy)*, 54 *(Canada)*; UN Doc A/CN.9/SR.327, para 1 *(Korea)*, 6 *(Switzerland)*, 11 *(Finland)*.

[748] Commission Report, A/40/17, para 237.

[749] All *Canadian Provinces* except for *Quebec*; *Egypt*; *Germany*; *Hungary*; *India*; *Kenya*; *Mexico*; *Oman*; *Spain*; *Tunisia*; within the *USA*: *California, Oregon.*

[750] eg *Canadian Provinces* except for *Quebec*; *Tunisia*; *Oregon.*

[751] eg s 1051(2), ZPO. cf the similar provisions Art 187 s 1 of the Swiss International Private Law and Art 834 of the Italian Law on International Arbitration. The closest connection test is known in almost all

Provinces except for *Quebec*, also replaced the rigid term 'law" by the phrase 'rules of law', thereby harmonizing the parties' and the tribunal's choice-of-law provisions.

Article 28(2), however, is not a mandatory rule. The parties may agree to widen the scope of the arbitrators' determination of the applicable law and authorize them to apply a-national rules of law. Conversely, the parties may also agree on the applicability of a limited number of national legal systems, thereby restricting the tribunal's power to determine the applicable law.[752] **14.454**

Occasionally, arbitral tribunals regard the absence of an express choice-of-law clause as an implied 'negative choice', by which parties exclude the application of domestic laws and thus implicitly choose transnational legal principles to govern their dispute.[753] This negative-choice doctrine could be employed to avoid the restrictive choice-of-law rule in Art 28(2). Before assuming an implied choice of a-national rules, however, the will and true interests of the parties must be carefully investigated. Quite often parties leave the choice of law to the arbitral tribunal, because they do not want to jeopardize their deal by lengthy discussions and an eventual disagreement on the applicable law. Yet, they do not necessarily expect the tribunal to apply a-national rules of law. On the other hand, there may indeed be situations where both parties have concurring intentions to denationalize their contractual relationship. In such a case, however, the omission of a choice-of-law clause is but a mere indication of the parties' will to exclude domestic laws, which requires confirmation by other indicative factors.[754] **14.455**

D. Decision *ex aequo et bono* or as *amiable compositeur*, paragraph (3)

The authority to decide *ex aequo et bono* or as *amiable compositeur* indicates that the tribunal is not bound to apply specific rules of law, but may adjudicate the case according to what it deems fair and equitable under the given circumstances.[755] To protect the inexperienced party, the Model Law, in line with the UNCITRAL, AAA and WIPO Arbitration Rules, requires an express authorization of the tribunal to exercise such freedom.[756] As this **14.456**

legal systems and consequently also applied in international commercial arbitrations: ICC Award no 5717, ICC Bulletin no 2, 1990, 22; ICC Award no 4237, (1985) X YCA 52, 55; Iran-US Claims Tribunal Award *Harnischfeger Corp v Ministry of Roads and Transportation*, (1984) 7 Iran–US CTR 90, 99.

[752] Analytical Commentary, UN Doc A/CN.9/264, para 6; Granzow, 172; Berger, 563.

[753] eg ICC Award no 7375, (1996) *Int'l Arb Rep*; ICC Award no 5065, (1987) JDI (Clunet) 1039; *TEXACO Overseas Petroleum Company (TOPCO)/California Asiatic Oil Company (CAL-ASIATIC) and the Government of Libyian Arab Republic*, (1978) 17 ILM 16; *Sapphire International Petroleums Ltd v National Iranian Oil Company*, (1964) ICLQ 1011 *et seq*; ICC Award no 3572 *Deutsche Schachtbau- und Tiefbohrgesellschaft mbH et al v The Government of the State of R'as Al Khaimah and The R'as Al Khaimah Oil Company (Rakoil)* (1989) YCA 111 *et seq*; ICC Award no 5953 *Primary Coal Inc v Compania Valenciana de Cementos Portland*, Partial Award, (1990) *Rev arb* 701; Berger, 559 *et seq* with further references; Blessing, '*Choice of Substantive Law* 45 *et seq*; Blessing, *Regulations in Arbitration Rules* 396 *et seq.*; Kühn, '*Express and Implied Choice*' 380 *et seq.*

[754] Berger, 559 *et seq.*

[755] cf Analytical Commentary, UN Doc. A/CN.9/264, para 9; Broches, 149 *et seq*; Redfern and Hunter paras 2-73 *et seq.*; Berger, 566.

[756] Analytical Commentary, UN Doc. A/CN.9/264, para 8. But see Art 17(3) ICC Arbitration Rules 1998, Art 42(3) ICSID Arbitration Rules 1984 and Art 10.3 CPR Arbitration Rules 1992, which do not require that the authorization be given expressly.

type of arbitration is not labelled uniformly in the various legal systems, para (3) states both the Latin and the French terms, which have a similar meaning.[757]

14.457 In their authorization the parties may provide additional explications as to the definite form of the tribunal's mandate, either by drawing up specific guidelines or by simply referring to the kind of *amiable composition* developed in a particular legal system.[758] Apart from such directives, arbitrators acting as *amiable compositeurs* need not determine and apply a particular system of law.[759] Yet, they frequently do so,[760] without being required to first employ conflict of laws rules.[761] Certainly, they may also base their decision on the *lex mercatoria*.[762] Even having chosen applicable rules, *amiable compositeurs* may deviate from them, eg by shifting the burden of proof or reducing the damages to be paid, if their strict application would lead to inequitable results.[763] Under such (albeit rare) circumstances arbitrators may also disregard trade usages that, as a general rule according to para (4), have also to be taken into account by *amiable compositeurs*.[764]

14.458 Decisions *ex aequo et bono* are essential in cases where an adequate settlement can only be reached by a flexible approach detached from the constraints of national law, taking account of all circumstances of the dispute. In practice, *amiable compositions* are particularly appropriate for international commodity arbitrations and disputes in the course of complex long-term relationships.[765] Within this context the question arises whether arbitrators are allowed to deviate from contractual stipulations and adapt them to changed circumstances. According to parts of legal doctrine, the principle of *pacta sunt servanda* expressed in para (4) must yield when the nature of the contract reveals that, at the time of its conclusion, the parties were not able to foresee all instances which might occur during the course of their relationship. In such a situation, arbitrators may interfere in the contractual equilibrium and re-evaluate the mutual obligations of the parties. An exception is only made when the contract has been of speculative interest to the parties.[766] In contrast, another

[757] Second Working Group Report, UN Doc A/CN.9/232, para 169; Summary Record, UN Doc. A/CN.9/SR.327, para 26, 27. See also Art 39(4) of the Egyptian Law on Arbitration which in contrast to the Model Law attempts to define these terms.

[758] Analytical Commentary, UN Doc A/CN.9/264, para 9.

[759] But see Rüede, T. and Hadenfeldt, R., *Schweizerisches Schiedsgerichtsrecht* (1980) 278 *et seq*.

[760] eg ICC Award no 5118 in Jarvin *et al* (eds) 318; David, R., *Arbitration in International Trade* (1985) 335.

[761] ICC Award no 3742 (1983) in Jarvin, S. and Derains, Y. (eds), *Collection of ICC Arbitral Awards 1974–1985* (Kluwer, 1990) 486, 487.

[762] ICC Award no 3540 (1980) in Jarvin and Derains (eds) 105, 110; Rubino-Sammartano, 470; Berger, 566 *et seq*.

[763] ICC Award no 5118, in Jarvin, Derains and Arnaldez (eds) 318 *et seq*; Berger, 570 *et seq* with further references; Jarvin, S. in Lew (ed), *Contemporary Problems in International Arbitration* 72.

[764] Nöcker, T., *Das Recht der Schiedsgerichtsbarkeit in Kanada* (1988) 147; Berger, 577.

[765] Horn, N., 'Changes in Circumstances and the Revision of Contracts in Some European Laws and in International Law' in Horn (ed), *Adaptation and Renegotiation of Contracts in International Trade and Finance* (1985) 3 *et seq*; Aden, M., *Internationale Handelsschiedsgerichtsbarkeit* (1988) 108 *et seq*; David, R., *Arbitration in International Trade* (1985) 336; Berger, 566 with further references.

[766] Berger, 573 *et seq*; Sandrock, O., '"Ex aequo et bono" und "amiable composition"-Vereinbarungen: ihre Qualifikation, Anknüpfung und Wirkungen' in Glossner (ed), *Jahrbuch für die Praxis der Schiedsgerichtsbarkeit* (1988) 131 *et seq*; Schlosser, P., *Das Recht der internationalen privaten Schiedsgerichtsbarkeit* (2nd edn, 1989) marg no 751; Mezger, E., (1992) Note, *Rev arb* 220 *et seq*; Funck-Brentano, R., 'Die "Amiable Composition"',

view requires, at any rate, a further explicit authorization if the tribunal is to modify the terms of the contract.[767]

Like other awards, *ex aequo et bono* decisions should be enforceable and therefore may not violate the international *ordre public* of the *lex arbitri* and possible enforcement states[768] nor infringe fundamental principles of arbitral procedure, namely party equality and the possibility to present one's case, as granted in Art 18.[769] **14.459**

Among the adopting states, the Republic of *Bulgaria* and the *Russian Federation* do not provide a rule for *amiable composition*. This omission may be rooted in the scepticism of former communist states as regards the liberalization from the constraints of domestic law.[770] Yet, *Lithuania* and *Ukraine* fully embraced Art 28 including its acknowledgement of *amiable composition*. **14.460**

E. Terms of contract and usages of trade, paragraph (4)

Regardless of whether the parties or the arbitral tribunal choose the applicable substantive law, the last para of Art 28 requires the tribunal to decide in accordance with the terms of the contract and to take the trade usages applicable to the transaction into account. This is generally also valid for decisions *ex aequo et bono*.[771] Being in line with Art VII(1) of the 1961 European Convention and a number of arbitration rules,[772] para (4) declares what many parties in international arbitration expect. Correspondingly, the Sixth Secretariat Note points out that '. . . the law applicable to the contract is, in international business relations, a delicate subject on which, at the end of lengthy negotiations, it may be difficult to reach agreement. Each party will prefer to have its own law be declared applicable, afraid of surprises the law of the other party may present. The question remains therefore often outstanding. It may even be a stimulant for insertion of an arbitration clause into the contract as the parties, not without good reasons, expect from the arbitrators that they will above all base their decisions on the wording and history of the contract and the usages of trade'.[773] **14.461**

in Böckstiegel (ed), *Schiedsgerichtsbarkeit in Frankreich* (1983) 89, 96; Lew, Applicable Law 510 *et seq*. See also *Award SEEE v The Popular Federative Republic of Jugoslavia* (1959) JDI (Clunet) 1075.

[767] See 'Rules for Adaptation of Contracts', ICC Publication no 326, 1978; for a general discussion see Redfern/Hunter paras 8–20 *et seq*; Bernini, G., 'Arbitration during the process of long term contracts' (1977) 43 *Arbitration* 51; Bernini, G., 'Adaptation of Contracts' in P. Sanders (ed), *New Trends in the Developement of International Commercial Arbitration and the Role of Arbitral and Other Institutions* (ICCA Congress Series no 1, 1982) 193.

[768] First Secretariat Note, UN Doc A/CN.9/207, para 90; First Working Group Report, UN Doc A/CN.9/216, para 86; Hußlein-Stich, 150; Berger, 574 *et seq* with further references.

[769] Loquin, E., *L'Amiable Composition en Droit Comparé et International* (1980) 194 *et seq*; Delaume, G., *Law and Practice of Transnational Contracts* (1988) § 9.11; Berger, 572.

[770] See Leloczky, K., 'East-West Arbitration, A Practitioner's Viewpoint from Hungary' (1988) 4 *AI* 266 *et seq*.

[771] Hußlein-Stich, 152; Calavros, 133; cf Sanders, 'Commentary on UNCITRAL Arbitration Rules' (1977) II *YCA* 211 as to Art 33(3) UNCITRAL Arbitration Rules. But see ch IV, *supra*.

[772] eg Art 33(3) of the UNCITRAL Arbitration Rules, Art 10.2. of the CPR Arbitration Rules, Art 17(2) of the ICC Arbitration Rules, Art 59(a) of the WIPO Arbitration Rules and Art 23.4 of the DIS Arbitration Rules as well as Art 28(2) of the AAA International Arbitration Rules.

[773] Analytical Compilation of Government Comments, UN Doc. A/CN.9/263, Art 28 para 12.

14.462 Article 28 remains silent on the relationship of contract terms and trade usages to the applicable substantive law. The major question in this context is whether trade usages are to be employed only if the law applicable to the substance of the dispute acknowledges their existence. This narrow 'conflictualist' approach,[774] however, is increasingly rejected by the view that participants in international trade are subject to an enhanced responsibility and therefore 'considered, unless otherwise agreed, to have impliedly made applicable to their contract and its formation a usage of which the parties knew or ought to have known and which in international trade is widely known to, and regularly observed by, parties to contracts of the type involved in the particular trade concerned' (Art 9(2) CISG, Art 1.6. UNIDROIT Principles for International Commercial Contracts).[775] Hence, irrespective of their standing within the applicable substantive law, an arbitrator should always take account of the relevant trade usages in line with the legitimate interests of the parties. As a general rule, however, mandatory rules of the applicable law are paramount and cannot be deviated from. The same is true for explicit contractual stipulations.[776] Furthermore, trade usages should be disregarded if their application endangers the enforceability of the award, namely by violating the *ordre public* of the *lex loci arbitri* or the laws of possible enforcement states.[777]

Article 29. Decision-making by panel of arbitrators

In arbitral proceedings with more than one arbitrator, any decision of the arbitral tribunal shall be made, unless otherwise agreed by the parties, by a majority of all its members. However, questions of procedure may be decided by a presiding arbitrator, if so authorized by the parties or all members of the arbitral tribunal.

A. Meaning and purpose

14.463 Article 29 concerns arbitral awards and other decisions of the arbitral tribunal. In principle, decisions in arbitral proceedings with more than one arbitrator are to be arrived at by the majority of all its members, unless the parties agree otherwise. However, a presiding arbitrator may decide about matters of procedure if the parties or all members of the arbitral tribunal authorize him to do so. Article 29 is based on Art 31 of the UNCITRAL Arbitration Rules.[778]

---

[774] As to Art VII(1) of the 1961 European Convention Schlosser, P., *Das Recht der internationalen privaten Schiedsgerichtsbarkeit* (1975) marg no 614; for a detailed discussion see von Hoffmann, B., *Internationale Handelsschiedsgerichtsbarkeit* (1970) 123. For Dutch law see Kokkini-Iatridou in Kokkini-Iatridou and Grosheide (eds), *Eenvormig en Vergelijkend Privaatrecht* 329.

[775] Berger, 576 *et seq*; von Hoffmann 123 *et seq* with further references. For an intermediate view see Calavros 134 *et seq*. An earlier draft version of para (4) was largely based on Art 9 of the CISG, but later completely deleted, as it was thought not to be applicable to all contracts covered by the Model Law, eg investment contracts. Moreover it was argued that the legal effect and qualification of trade usages is not uniform in all legal systems. See Second Working Group Report, UN Doc. A/CN.9/232, para 164 et *seq*; Fourth Working Group Report, UN Doc A/CN.9/245, para 98 et *seq*; Analytical Commentary, UN Doc. A/CN.9/264, para 11. The Commission, however, restored Art 28(4) by pointing to the similar provisions of Art 33(3) of the UNCITRAL Rules and Art VII(1) of the European Convention. See Summary Record, UN Doc. A/CN.9/SR.326, para 41.

[776] Hußlein-Stich, 154; Berger, 577.

[777] Lew, Julian, D.M., *Applicable Law in International Commercial Arbitration* (1978) 440; cf Berger, 577.

[778] First Draft, UN Doc A/CN.9/WG.II/WP.38, Art 29 note 5.

B. Majority principle, sentence (1)

Where there is more than one arbitrator, decisions of the arbitral tribunal are to be made by a majority. This is not a mandatory requirement; the parties may agree otherwise. The majority principle applies to all decisions of the arbitral tribunal, whether substantive or procedural. In the latter case, however, sentence (2) permits a different solution. Not insisting on unanimity supports expedient proceedings and reduces the risk that parties may waste time and expense in unsuccessful arbitral proceedings.[779] **14.464**

(1) No actual participation required

Article 29 does not demand actual participation of all arbitrators in the deliberations. The award or other decision is valid provided that all arbitrators had the opportunity to take part in the deliberations.[780] This condition was not expressly mentioned in the Model Law, to avoid the wrong interpretation that an arbitrator had a right to refuse to take part in the deliberations.[781] *Germany* addresses this problem by expressly stating that, subject to contrary party agreement, in case an arbitrator refuses to take part in the vote on a decision, the other arbitrators may decide without him.[782] Under the Model Law a refusal to participate or to vote would be a ground for terminating the arbitrator's mandate under Art 14 and to substitute this arbitrator pursuant to Art 15.[783] An award made by a majority of the arbitrators without giving all arbitrators the opportunity to participate in the deliberations may be set aside under Art 34(2)(a)(iv) on the grounds that the procedure was not in accordance with the Model Law.[784] **14.465**

(2) Ways of voting

The Model Law does not require the physical presence of the arbitrators at the same place when making a decision.[785] They can vote by telephone, fax, telex, mail, email or other means of communication. **14.466**

(3) Deadlock

The wording of sentence (1) leaves no doubt that 'majority' means 'more than half of all appointed arbitrators' and does not mean 'more than half of those who made the award'.[786] This leads to the possibility that a majority decision cannot be reached because the arbitrators have fundamentally different opinions. It was proposed that in such a case the presiding arbitrator should cast the decisive vote, a solution found in the ICC Arbitration Rules and the LCIA Arbitration Rules. The Commission did not adopt this suggestion as doing so might, under certain circumstances, lend itself to precluding the other members of the arbitral tribunal from having an appropriate influence on the decision-making.[787] It was argued **14.467**

---

[779] See Analytical Commentary, UN Doc A/CN.9/264, Art 29 para 2.
[780] See Second Working Group Report, UN Doc A/CN.9/232, para 138.
[781] *ibid.*
[782] See s 1052(2), ZPO; see also Saarländisches Oberlandesgericht, 4 Sch 2/02, 29 October 2002, published in German DIS-Online Database on Arbitration Law <http://www.dis-arb.de>, CLOUT Case 662.
[783] See Hußlein-Stich, 157.
[784] See Davidson *(Scotland)* para 7.18.
[785] See Commission Report, UN Doc A/40/17, para 821.
[786] See Second Working Group Report, UN Doc A/CN.9/232, Art 29 para 139, Hußlein-Stich, 156.
[787] Commission Report, UN Doc A/40/17, Art 29 para 244.

that where a presiding arbitrator was empowered to decide in absence of a majority, he was in effect a sole arbitrator. If the parties wished to appoint a sole arbitrator, they would do so. In addition, requiring a majority decision made it more likely that all issues would be fully considered, as a need to reach agreement existed.[788] Some Model Law states, however, abandon the requirement of a majority decision. Under the laws of *Bulgaria*, *Hungary*, *Peru* and *Tunisia* the presiding arbitrator shall decide alone, if a majority cannot be reached.[789] Yet, Art 39 of the Bulgarian Law on International Commercial Arbitration explicitly requires an arbitrator who disagrees with the award to give his dissenting opinion in writing.

14.468 Article 29 is non-mandatory. Thus, parties are free to authorize a presiding arbitrator to decide alone if the tribunal is unable to reach an agreement. With regard to the award, this result will also be achieved pursuant to Art 2(e) if the parties agree to arbitration under the ICC or the LCIA Arbitration Rules[790] or other rules which contain a corresponding provision. For *quantum* decisions, the parties may agree on a formula for the calculation of the decisive amount.[791] Yet, the parties do not have to settle the issue of voting before the commencement of the arbitral proceedings, but may wait until the decision-making has reached a deadlock.[792] In such a situation the parties may also ask the arbitral tribunal to issue an order for the termination of the proceedings because their continuation has become impossible.[793]

14.469 The Model Law does not touch on the well-established commercial practice to let an umpire decide when an arbitral tribunal consisting of two arbitrators fails to agree. The drafters accepted that the provisions on decision-making in the Model Law should not exclude these practices.[794]

C. Questions of procedure, sentence (2)

14.470 For the sake of expediency and efficiency,[795] a presiding arbitrator may decide questions of procedure alone if the parties or the arbitral tribunal has authorized him to do so. Although the second sentence does not contain the wording 'unless otherwise agreed by the parties', this part of the provision should also be regarded as non-mandatory, as it is closely linked to the first sentence by the word 'however'.[796] The Working Group did not mean that all those provisions of the Model Law which did not express their non-mandatory character were necessarily of mandatory nature.[797] The *travaux préparatoires* also indicate that the article as a whole is intended to be non-mandatory.[798]

---

[788] Summary Record, UN Doc A/CN.9/SR.327, Art 29 para 48.

[789] *Bulgaria*: Art 39 LICA; *Hungary*: s 38(1) of Act LXXI of 1994 on Arbitration; *Peru*: Art 41 of Decree Law no 25935; *Tunisia*: Art 74 of the Arbitration Code 1993.

[790] See Art 25(1) of the ICC Rules and Art 26.3 of the LCIA Rules.

[791] Analytical Commentary, UN Doc A/CN.9/264, Art 29 para 3.

[792] See Summary Record, UN Doc A/CN.9/SR.327, Art 29 para 50.

[793] Berger, 600; see also commentary on Art 32(2)(c).

[794] See First Working Group Report, UN Doc A/CN.9/216, para 77.

[795] See Fourth Working Group Report, UN Doc A/CN.9/245, para 104; Fifth Working Group Report, UN Doc A/CN.9/246, para 108; Analytical Commentary, UN Doc A/CN.9/264, Art 29 para 1.

[796] Holtzmann and Neuhaus, 810 n 8.

[797] Fifth Working Group Report, UN Doc A/CN.9/246, para 177.

[798] See Second Working Group Report, UN Doc A/CN.9/232, para 137; Analytical Commentary, UN Doc A/CN.9/264, Art 29 para 3.

This provision deviates in three respects from Art 31(2) of the UNCITRAL Arbitration Rules. First, a presiding arbitrator is not permitted to decide alone 'when there is no majority'. He must be authorized by the parties or by all members of the tribunal. This leads to the second change: mere majority of the tribunal cannot grant this power. Third, the decision of the presiding arbitrator is not 'subject to revision, if any, by the arbitral tribunal'. The Working Group agreed that once the authorization for the presiding arbitrator to decide alone had been given, his decision should not be subject to the arbitral tribunal.[799] **14.471**

The Model Law neither defines the term 'presiding arbitrator' nor the manner of his appointment. It can be assumed that the parties, by either expressly or implicitly agreeing on a set of arbitration rules which deal with this issue, or the arbitral tribunal may appoint a presiding arbitrator.[800] However, from the carefully chosen wording 'a presiding arbitrator', it follows that the Model Law does not require that a presiding arbitrator be appointed.[801] If no presiding arbitrator has been appointed, the second sentence will not be applicable.[802] **14.472**

As to the impact of the term 'questions of procedure', the *travaux préparatoires* provide some guidelines. During the Commission's deliberations it was noted that, at least in common law countries, the distinction between procedural and substantive matters was not always clear.[803] The response to this was that the power of the arbitral tribunal to decide on matters of both procedure and substance should also imply the power to decide on the distinction between them.[804] Questions of procedure include the determination of oral hearings, the setting of time limits, the decision about the procedural language(s) and the appointment of experts. It may be assumed that decisions regarding the competence-competence of the arbitral tribunal under Art 16, the order of interim measures under Art 17 and the determination of the place of arbitration under Art 20 do not belong to the questions of procedure.[805] **14.473**

Some Model Law states omitted Art 29 sentence (2).[806] In *Bulgaria* and *Peru* a presiding arbitrator may decide on procedural questions as well as substantive issues if a majority cannot be reached. *Egypt*, however, apparently does not empower a presiding arbitrator to decide questions of procedure.[807] **14.474**

Article 30. Settlement

(1) If, during arbitral proceedings, the parties settle the dispute, the arbitral tribunal shall terminate the proceedings and, if requested by the parties and not objected to by the arbitral tribunal, record the settlement in the form of an arbitral award on agreed terms.

[799] Fourth Working Group Report, UN Doc A/CN.9/245, para 104.

[800] See Davidson *(Scotland)* para 7.21; but see Hußlein-Stich, 158: only the arbitral tribunal analogous to Art 7(1) of the UNCITRAL Arbitration Rules.

[801] See Summary Record, UN Doc A/CN.9/SR.327, Art 29 para 44.

[802] Broches, 157.

[803] Summary Record, UN Doc A/CN.9/SR.327, Art 29 para 41 *(Australia)*.

[804] *ibid* para 44.

[805] See Calavros, 138; see also Hußlein-Stich, 157.

[806] eg *Bulgaria*: Art 40 of the Law Concerning Arbitration in Civil and Commercial Matters; *Egypt*: Art 40 of the Law Concerning Arbitration in Civil and Commercial Matters; *Peru*: Art 40 of Decree Law no 25935.

[807] See Aboul-Enein (1995) 11 *Arb Int'l* 82.

(2) **An award on agreed terms shall be made in accordance with the provisions of article 31 and shall state that it is an award. Such an award has the same status and effect as any other award on the merits of the case.**

A. Meaning and purpose

14.475 Article 30 concerns an issue of great practical importance. It allows the parties to settle their dispute during the course of the arbitral proceedings. With regard to the often long-standing business relationships of the parties, a settlement is a method of dispute resolution with many advantages, as it promotes cooperation between the parties. In the case of a settlement, the arbitral tribunal must terminate the proceedings, thereby saving the parties the time and expenses of a complete arbitration. The use of the word 'shall' clearly means 'must' in this context. The important feature of this provision is the permission for effective enforcement of a settlement agreement by recording it in the form of an arbitral award.

B. Arbitral award on agreed terms

(1) Request by both parties, paragraph (1)

14.476 If the parties reach a settlement, they may request the arbitral tribunal to record the settlement in the form of an arbitral award on agreed terms. Although the language is ambiguous, it was the clear intent of the drafters that both parties must agree to have the settlement recorded in the form of an award on agreed terms.[808] However, it is sufficient that only one party makes the formal request, provided that the other party agrees to it.[809] As the arbitral tribunal has to be satisfied as to the dual will of the parties, a joint request is recommended in order to save time.[810] The requirement of a request by both parties, a concept taken from Art 34(1) of the UNCITRAL Arbitration Rules, reduces the risk of one party being treated unfairly where the settlement was ambiguous or subject to conditions that might not be apparent to the arbitral tribunal.[811]

(2) No objection by the arbitral tribunal, paragraph (1)

14.477 Article 30(1) requires the consent of the arbitral tribunal to render an award. Thus, under certain circumstances, the tribunal has the discretion to refuse to record a settlement.[812] In the Commission it was proposed that this prerequisite be deleted, as the arbitral tribunal should not have powers to overrule the will of the parties.[813] Yet, a distinction must be drawn between the right of the parties to have the arbitral proceedings terminated and their right to have their settlement recorded as an award. The arbitrators are not obliged to subscribe to a settlement agreed to by the parties which is unlawful in their view or which violates the public policy of the place of arbitration, including fundamental notions of

---

[808] See Commission Report, UN Doc A/40/17, para 250.

[809] *ibid.*

[810] Broches, 160.

[811] Second Working Group Report, UN Doc A/CN.9/232, paras 174–5; Analytical Commentary, UN Doc A/CN.9/264, Art 30 para 2.

[812] It should be noted that the ICC Rules 1998 and LCIA Rules 1998 changed their approach and now also recognize the discretion of the arbitral tribunal, see Art 26 of the ICC Rules and Art 26.8 of the LCIA Rules.

[813] See Summary Record, UN Doc A/CN.9/SR.328, Art 30 para 4 (*Australia*), 8 (*Iraq*), 10 (*Cuba*), 11 (*France*), 12 (*Mexico*); Commission Report, UN Doc A/40/17, para 248.

fairness and justice.[814] With regard to the principle of party autonomy, this right of refusal should be restricted to such exceptional circumstances.[815] *Germany* put the right of refusal in a concrete form by stating that the arbitral tribunal shall record the settlement unless the contents are in violation of public policy (*ordre public*).[816] *Hungary* stipulates that the arbitral tribunal may refuse to record the settlement only in case the arbitral tribunal considers the settlement as not being in accordance with the law.[817] *Bulgaria* omitted this prerequisite in its arbitration law, but it is assumed that the arbitral tribunal may refuse to record the settlement if the settlement violates mandatory rules of law.[818] Under *Egyptian* law it is assumed that if the parties request the record of the settlement, the arbitral tribunal is obliged to do so.[819]

(3) Award on the merits, paragraph (2)

Once an award of agreed terms is made under the provisions of Art 31 and states that it is an award it has the same status and effect as any other award on the merits. Article 30(2)(2) clarifies this consequence which is already implicit in Art 30(2)(1). The settlement is then enforceable under Art 36 of the New York Convention and nearly all legal systems. Keeping in mind that the award is based on the agreement of the parties, it would be consistent not to allow a party to such an award to invoke the grounds for setting aside under Art 34(2)(a) or to refuse recognition and enforcement under Art 36(1)(a). The grounds provided in Art 34(2)(b) and Art 36(1)(b) are not touched on by this limitation.[820] **14.478**

C. Conciliation and mediation

In some Model Law states the arbitral tribunal is entitled to encourage settlement by using mediation, conciliation or other procedures any time during the arbitral proceedings if the parties so agree.[821] In *Hong Kong*, *Singapore* and *Australia* written consent of all parties is necessary in order to employ conciliation.[822] Other Model Law states regulate conciliation in detail.[823] In *California*, *Oregon* and *Texas* a person who has served as a conciliator is not **14.479**

[814] See Analytical Commentary, UN Doc A/CN.9/264, Art 30 para 2; Commission Report, UN Doc A/40/17, para 249.

[815] See Calavros, 142.

[816] s 1053(1), ZPO.

[817] s 39(2) of Act LXXI of 1994 on Arbitration.

[818] See Art 40, LICA; Stalev, 16.

[819] See Art 41 of the Law Concerning Arbitration in Civil and Commercial Matters; Aboul-Enein (1995) 11 *Arb Int'l* 82.

[820] See Broches, 160 *et seq.*

[821] eg *British Columbia*: s 30 of the British Columbia International Commercial Arbitration Act 1986; *India*: s 30(1) of the Arbitration and Conciliation Ordinance 1996; *Ontario*: s 3 of the Ontario International Commercial Arbitration Act 1990.

[822] *Hong Kong*: s 2B of the Arbitration Ordinance 1996, ch 341; *Singapore*: s 17 of the International Arbitration Act 1994; *Australia*: s 24 of the International Arbitration Act 1974.

[823] eg *Bermuda*: Pt II (ss 3–21) of the Bermuda International Conciliation and Arbitration Act 1993; *California*: Chapter 7 of Title 9.3 of the CCP; *Hong Kong*: ss 2A and 2B of the Arbitration Ordinance 1996, ch 341; *Nigeria*: s 55 and sch 3 of the Arbitration and Conciliation Decree 1988; *Oregon*: ss 36.528-58 of the International Commercial Arbitration and Conciliation Act; *Texas*: Arts 249-34 to 249-43 of the Arbitration and Conciliation of International Disputes Act.

allowed to be appointed as an arbitrator but—except for the law in *Texas*—parties may agree otherwise.[824]

Article 31. Form and contents of award

(1) The award shall be made in writing and shall be signed by the arbitrator or arbitrators. In arbitral proceedings with more than one arbitrator, the signatures of the majority of all members of the arbitral tribunal shall suffice, provided that the reason for any omitted signature is stated.

(2) The award shall state the reasons upon which it is based, unless the parties have agreed that no reasons are to be given or the award is an award on agreed terms under article 30.

(3) The award shall state its date and the place of arbitration as determined in accordance with article 20(1). The award shall be deemed to have been made at that place.

(4) After the award is made, a copy signed by the arbitrators in accordance with paragraph (1) of this article shall be delivered to each party.

A. Meaning and purpose

14.480 Article 31 sets forth minimum formal and substantive requirements of awards issued under the Model Law aiming at establishing uniform standards of arbitral procedure.[825]

B. Award in writing and signed, paragraph (1)

14.481 Article 31(1) requires the award to be in writing and signed, which are common standards in national laws for the sake of certainty. Like Art 29, this provision contains a majority rule. In arbitral proceedings with more than one arbitrator the signatures of the majority of all members of the arbitral tribunal shall suffice, provided that the reason for any omitted signature is stated. It was recognized that some legal systems require all arbitrators to sign the award in order for it to be valid. This was felt to be an unsatisfactory solution, as it would frustrate an arbitration if any of the arbitrators refused to sign the award or was unable to do so, for example because he had died, or had become physically unable to sign or could not be reached anymore.[826] It should be noted that the Model Law does not restrict the reasons for not signing the award.

14.482 At one point the Secretariat suggested fully aligning the signature requirement with Art 29, ie with any agreed decisional system other than decision by majority.[827] The Commission did not act on this suggestion. It may therefore be assumed that Art 31(1) is mandatory regarding the basic requirement that the award has to be signed, but that the issue of who has to sign the award is governed by Art 19, which regulates the conduct of the proceedings. Thus, under the Model Law the parties may agree that the signature of the presiding arbitrator is sufficient.[828]

---

[824] *California*: s 1297.393 of the CCP; *Oregon*: s 542 of the International Commercial Arbitration and Conciliation Act; *Texas*: Art 39(3), Arbitration and Conciliation of International Disputes.

[825] See Secretariat Note on Further Work, UN Doc A/CN.9/169, para 6.

[826] cf Analytical Commentary, UN Doc A/CN.9/264, Art 31 para 2.

[827] *ibid* para 1 note 83.

[828] See Berger, 603; see also Broches, 163 *et seq* who proposes that enacting states might amend the provision to clarify that the majority rule only applies 'in arbitral proceedings with more than one arbitrator, where the award of the arbitral tribunal is to be made by a majority of all its members'; but see Davidson *(Scotland)* para 7.27 who refers to the mandatory character of this provision pointing out that even if the parties have

There was also a proposal that the award should state whether any arbitrator has dissented,[829] on which the Commission did not act. It was understood that if the Model Law did not deal explicitly with this issue, it would be governed by Art 19 as a matter of the conduct of proceedings.[830] Thus, a dissenting opinion may be stated in the award if the parties so agree or if the arbitral tribunal so allows. It has to be noted, however, that the requirement of permission only refers to the way the dissenting opinion is communicated to the parties and not to the admissibility of dissenting opinions in general. Thus, a minority may still render its dissenting opinion separately, if the majority does not agree to issue it in or together with the award.[831] **14.483**

C. Statement of reasons, paragraph (2)

Under para (2) the award must state the reasons upon which it is based, unless the parties have agreed otherwise or the award is an award on agreed terms under Art 30. This solution closely follows Art 32(3) of the UNCITRAL Arbitration Rules. The requirement of stating reasons meets the interests of the parties, particularly of the losing party, to learn why the tribunal made the decision just the way it did. In light of the fundamental principle of party autonomy, it is consistent that the parties are permitted to waive this requirement. This may be appropriate for certain types of arbitration, such as quality arbitrations, or simply in order to accelerate the rendering of the award.[832] A contrary party agreement can either be made expressly, including reference to arbitration rules containing such waiver, or implicitly, for example by submitting the dispute to an established arbitration system which does not require a reasoned award.[833] **14.484**

D. Date and place of award, paragraph (3)

Article 31(3) sets out that the award shall state its date and the place of arbitration as determined in accordance with Art 20(1), which shall be deemed to be the place of the award. The irrebuttable presumption that the award is made at the place of arbitration was included, recognizing the fact that the award is, in practice, often decided by deliberations at various places, by telephone conversation or correspondence, for the sake of convenience.[834] Given that the place at which the award is made determines the law under which the award can be set aside and is also important in the context of recognition and enforcement of the award under Art 36 of this Law and the New York Convention, there is a need for clarity and certainty in this respect. The actual place at which the award was signed can thus differ from the place stated in the award. **14.485**

The date of making the award is not subject to the same presumption. It was felt that the date must be rebuttable, because the arbitrator as well as the parties might have reasons for **14.486**

agreed that the award shall be decided upon by the presiding arbitrator, Art 31(1) still demands that the award should, at the very least, be signed by a majority of the members of the tribunal.

829 Analytical Compilation of Government Comments, UN Doc A/CN.9/263, Art 31 para 2 *(Norway)*.
830 See Analytical Commentary, UN Doc A/CN.9/264, Art 31 para 2; see also Hußlein-Stich, 162.
831 cf Berger 610 *et seq*; Holtzmann and Neuhaus, 837, note 8.
832 See First Working Group Report, UN Doc A/CN.9/216, para 80.
833 Analytical Commentary, UN Doc A/CN.9/264, Art 31 para 3.
834 See Fourth Working Group Report, UN Doc A/CN.9/245, para 114.

stating the date of the award to be earlier or later than the date it was actually rendered.[835] This could be the case when the parties have agreed that the award must be rendered within a particular period of time,[836] the arbitrators failed to do so, and the parties nevertheless want the award to be valid.

E. Delivery of award, paragraph (4)

14.487 After the award is made, a copy signed by the arbitrators, or at least the majority of the arbitrators, must be delivered to each party. This provision, which is mandatory, is based on Art 32(6) of the UNCITRAL Arbitration Rules. Receipt of a copy of the award is a necessary condition for the request to correct or interpret the award under Art 33(1), the request to make an additional award under Art 33(3), the application for setting aside the award under Art 34(3) and for obtaining recognition or enforcement under Art 35(2).

F. Matters not addressed in paragraph (4)

(1) Registration and deposit

14.488 The Model Law does not require any administrative act such as registration or deposit of the award.[837] For the sake of ensuring continued availability of the original award or an authenticated copy thereof, requiring a deposit or registration with a certain court or office was considered.[838] However, in the end the approach of the New York Convention prevailed, which does not require registration or deposit for international awards. As the Convention does not demand any deposit requirements in the country of origin, it was deemed desirable to fully align the requirements for recognition and enforcement of an international award with the result that in practice it would not matter whether recognition and enforcement were sought in the country of origin or somewhere else.[839] At one point there was a proposal to expressly state that registration or deposit of an award is not necessary.[840] Obviously, this proposal was not adopted. However, the silence of the Model Law in this regard should not be interpreted as leaving regulation to domestic laws.[841] On the contrary, it was decided intentionally that no such administrative act is required.[842]

(2) Publication of the award

14.489 There was brief consideration as to whether or not the Model Law should deal with this controversial question. As it was not addressed, the degree of publicity of the award and the arbitral proceedings is left to the agreement of the parties and the arbitration rules they select.

---

835 Commission Report, UN Doc A/40/17, para 254.

836 eg by referring to a set of arbitration rules such as the ICC Rules, which provide for a time limit of six months in Art 24.

837 Analytical Commentary, UN Doc A/CN.9/264, Art 31 para 6.

838 See First Working Group Report, UN Doc A/CN.9/216, para 102.

839 First Secretariat Note, UN Doc A/CN.9/207, paras 97–100.

840 Fourth Secretariat Note, UN Doc A/CN.9/WG.II/WP.50, para 29.

841 See Commission Report, UN Doc A/40/17, paras 316–7, which seems to prefer this interpretation.

842 See Summary Record, UN Doc A/CN.9/SR.320, Art 35 paras 81–4.

(3) Date on which the award becomes binding

The question of when an award becomes binding is particularly important for the recognition and enforcement procedure. Under Art 36(1)(a)(v) of the Model Law and Art V(1)(e) of the New York Convention recognition or enforcement of an award can be refused if the award has not yet become binding on the parties. Article 35(1), which states that an arbitral award shall be recognized as binding, does not specify the point in time when an award becomes binding. The term 'binding' under the New York Convention, and therefore under the Model Law, means that the award is no longer open to ordinary means of recourse, such as appeals to a court or a second arbitration instance.[843] During the drafting process three possible dates were considered at some length: (i) the date the award was made; (ii) the date on which the award was delivered to the parties; (iii) the date on which the three-month period for making an application for setting aside the award mentioned in Art 34(3) expired.[844] The date the award was made was favoured because of its certainty and, moreover, because it was an option adopted by certain national laws.[845] There was also considerable support for the date of delivery, because it seemed strange if the award were to become binding without the parties knowing of it or having a chance to study it.[846] To others it seemed strange that the award could become binding on the parties on different days simply because it was delivered on different days.[847] The date of receipt would also require proof, thus causing many practical difficulties.[848] There was little support for the three-month setting-aside period, but it was suggested that a period of time must elapse before the award became binding.[849] However, in the end no provision on when the award becomes binding was included. Therefore, the question is open to interpretation of the arbitral tribunals and courts. For the sake of certainty, the date of the award seems to be a sensible solution. **14.490**

(4) Res judicata

It was proposed to include a provision to the effect that an arbitral award made in accordance with Art 31 had the force of *res judicata*. The proposal was not adopted because it was considered that the term *res judicata* was a complex one which could have different applications in various legal systems.[850] **14.491**

Article 32. Termination of proceedings

(1) The arbitral proceedings are terminated by the final award or by an order of the arbitral tribunal in accordance with paragraph (2) of this article.

---

[843] See eg Tribunale di Napoli, decision of 30 June 1976, (1979) IV YCA, 277; Landgericht Bremen, decision of 8 June 1967, (1977) II YCA, 234; Secretariat Study on the New York Convention, UN Doc A/CN.9/168, para 41.

[844] See Commission Report, UN Doc A/40/17, para 256; Summary Record, UN Doc A/CN.9/SR328, Art 31 paras 52–8; SR. 329, paras 1–25.

[845] See Summary Record, UN Doc A/CN.9/SR.329, Art 31 paras 4, 11–15, 18, 19, 21, 23; SR328, Art 31 paras 53, 58.

[846] See Summary Record, UN Doc A/CN.9/SR.329, Art 31 para 5; SR 328 Art 31 para 54.

[847] See Summary Record, UN Doc A/CN.9/SR.328, Art 31 para 55; Commission Report, UN Doc A/40/17, para 257.

[848] See Summary Record, UN Doc A/CN.9/SR.329, Art 31 paras 2, 12.

[849] *ibid*, para 6.

[850] Commission Report, UN Doc A/40/17, para 259.

(2) The arbitral tribunal shall issue an order for the termination of the arbitral proceedings when:

(a) the claimant withdraws his claim, unless the respondent objects thereto and the arbitral tribunal recognizes a legitimate interest on his part in obtaining a final settlement of the dispute;

(b) the parties agree on the termination of the proceedings;

(c) the arbitral tribunal finds that the continuation of the proceedings has for any other reason become unnecessary or impossible.

(3) The mandate of the arbitral tribunal terminates with the termination of the arbitral proceedings, subject to the provisions of articles 33 and 34(4).

A. Meaning and purpose

14.492 Article 32 sets out that arbitral proceedings are terminated by a final award or by an order of the arbitral tribunal. As pointed out in the Analytical Commentary,[851] this provision serves three purposes. First, it provides guidance in the last phase of the arbitral proceedings. Second, it regulates the termination of the mandate of the arbitral tribunal. Third, it provides certainty as to the point of time of the termination of the proceedings, which may be of relevance for matters unrelated to the arbitration itself, for example the continuation of the running of a limitation period or the possibility of instituting court proceedings.

B. Termination by final award

14.493 The Model Law neither provides a definition of the term 'award'[852] nor of the term 'final award'. During the drafting process a separate article was proposed to address the different types of awards that a tribunal might issue, such as final, interim, interlocutory or partial awards. The proposal, however, was not adopted for two reasons: first, simply listing these types of awards without specifying the nature and consequence of each type did not seem useful; second, it was recognized that the various types were not clearly defined.[853] The drafters then focused on the effect of the different awards with regard to the termination of the proceedings and to the mandate of the arbitral tribunal. Article 32(1) and (3) clearly states that only a final award—and not interim, interlocutory or partial awards, which were regarded as non-final awards[854]—terminates the proceedings and the mandate of the arbitral tribunal. Although non-final awards do not appear in the final text, it may be assumed that the arbitral tribunal, nevertheless, has the power to render such awards under the Model Law.[855] This was the clear intention of the drafters,[856] and there are no indications as to a change of meaning in changing the wording. The employment of the term

[851] UN Doc A/CN.9/264, Art 32 paras 1–2.

[852] See commentary on Art 2.

[853] See Fifth Working Group Report, UN Doc A/CN.9/246, para 73.

[854] See Second Draft, UN Doc A/CN.9/WG.II/WP.40, Art XXIII, alternative B; Fourth Working Group Report, UN Doc A/CN.9/245, para 118.

[855] Holtzmann and Neuhaus, 868 *et seq*; but see Davidson *(Scotland)* para 7.56: governed by other domestic law.

[856] See Fourth Working Group Report, UN Doc A/CN.9/245, para 118.

'final award' indicates the underlying meaning. Some Model Law states clarified this in their general provisions.[857]

In the first drafts the term 'final award' was defined as the award 'intended to settle the dispute in full',[858] the 'final disposition of the substance of the dispute'[859] or the award 'which constitutes or completes the disposition of all claims submitted to arbitration'.[860] However, in the end the Working Group decided to leave the term undefined 'for the sake of simplicity'.[861] Yet it is clear from the legislative history that only an arbitral decision that decides about the subject matter of the dispute as a whole, thus settling the dispute in full, leads to the termination of the arbitrators' mandate. **14.494**

The Model Law does not set a time limit within which the arbitral tribunal is to make the award. *Egypt* departed from this approach and provides for a time limit of 12 months from the date of the commencement of the arbitral proceedings, unless the parties have agreed otherwise. In all cases, the arbitral tribunal may extend such a time limit by up to six months. The parties may agree on a longer period. If the award is not made within the deadline, each party may request the president of the court, referred to in Art 9 of the Egyptian Law, to order the extension of the time limit or the termination of the arbitral proceedings. In case of termination, each party may refer the dispute to the court which originally had jurisdiction.[862] The law of Spain provides for a six-months time limit for the issuance of the arbitral award.[863] The *Kammergericht* Berlin held that the time limit provision contained in the arbitration agreement, which required the award to be rendered within six months after the appointment of the tribunal's chairman, was not mandatory and purely hortatory. However, the parties should have made every effort to enable the tribunal to render the award within six months after the appointment of the chairman.[864] **14.495**

C. Termination by order of the arbitral tribunal, paragraph (2)

Article 32(2) enumerates situations in which the arbitral proceedings can or will be terminated by an order of the arbitral tribunal. The termination order does not have the effect of *res judicata*. It merely serves to record the discontinuance of the proceedings and the reasons therefore, without closing the door for future proceedings in the same case.[865] Thus, if the tribunal misjudges the status of the arbitration and erroneously issues a termination order, parties are not prevented from instituting new proceedings before another or even **14.496**

[857] eg *British Columbia*: s 2(1) of the British Columbia International Commercial Arbitration Act 1986; *India*: s 2(1) of the Arbitration and Conciliation Ordinance 1996; *Kenya*: s 3(1) of the Arbitration Act 1995; *New Zealand*: s 2(1) of the Arbitration Act 1996; *Singapore*: s 2(1) of the International Arbitration Act 1994.

[858] First Draft, UN Doc A/CN.9/WG.II/WP.38, Art 25.

[859] Second Draft, UN Doc A/CN.9/WG.II/WP.40, Art XXIII, alternative B.

[860] *ibid*, alternative A.

[861] Fifth Working Group Report, UN Doc A/CN.9/246, para 115.

[862] Art 45 of the Law Concerning Arbitration in Civil and Commercial Matters.

[863] Art 37(2) of the Spanish Arbitration Act 2003.

[864] Kammergericht Berlin, 23/29 Sch 21/01, 6 May 2002, published in German DIS-Online Database on Arbitration Law <http://www.dis-arb.de>, CLOUT Case 668.

[865] Berger, 636.

the same arbitral tribunal. The order for termination always refers to the proceedings and not to the claim.[866]

(1) Withdrawal of claim, sub-paragraph (a)

14.497 If the claimant withdraws his claim, the proceedings will not terminate automatically. The drafters recognized that the withdrawal of the claim could either be a renouncement or a means to pursue the claim before another arbitral tribunal. The respondent might have a certain interest in the current proceedings being pursued in order to reduce the risk of harassment by a claimant repeatedly bringing a claim and then withdrawing it[867] or withdrawing his claim at a late stage of the proceedings and then compelling the respondent to participate in other proceedings.[868] Accordingly, the arbitral tribunal was granted discretion to continue the proceedings where the respondent objects to termination and in the objective judgment of the tribunal the respondent has a legitimate interest in obtaining a final settlement of the dispute. A legitimate interest of the respondent may be recognized at any stage of the proceedings.[869]

(2) Party agreement on termination, sub-paragraph (b)

14.498 Pursuant to Art 33(2)(b) the arbitral tribunal must order the termination of the proceedings when the parties agree on it. The provision clearly states that the termination results from the tribunal's order, not directly from the party agreement. Rather, such agreement by the parties serves as a ground for a termination order.[870]

14.499 The primary question in relation to this provision is whether it covers only specific agreements to terminate the proceedings at a particular moment of time or also covers advance agreements setting a deadline for making an award, for example by referring to a set of arbitration rules which demands the award be made within a certain time limit.[871] At one point, the Working Group found it desirable to make clear that the provision includes both types of agreement.[872] However, the Working Group later decided to merely refer to termination by agreement of the parties 'for the sake of simplicity'.[873] Unfortunately, the present language, 'when the parties agree on the termination of the proceedings', does not clearly express the underlying intention of the drafters. In this context, it is important to note that the drafters also discussed the setting of a period of time for the making of an award in relation to Art 14(1) and Art 15. It may be assumed that the appropriate remedy in a situation where the arbitral tribunal fails to render an award in time is not the termination of the proceedings but the termination of the arbitrator's mandate and the appointment of a substitute arbitrator.[874]

[866] Knoepfler, F. and Schweizer, P., 'Making of Awards and Termination of Proceedings' in Petar Sarcevic (ed), *Essays on International Commercial Arbitration* (Graham & Trotman/Martinus Nijhoff, 1989) 173.

[867] Summary Record, UN Doc A/CN.9/SR.329, Art 32 para 30.

[868] Commission Report, UN Doc A/40/17, para 262.

[869] cf Hußlein/Stich, 167 *et seq*; but see Calavros, 143.

[870] Analytical Compilation of the Government Comments, UN Doc A/CN.9/263, Art 32 para 1 (*Soviet Union*).

[871] eg Art 24 of the ICC Rules.

[872] Fourth Working Group Report, UN Doc A/CN.9/245, Art 32 para 50.

[873] Fifth Working Group Report, UN Doc A/CN.9/246, Art 32 paras 114, 115.

[874] cf Holtzmann and Neuhaus, 870 note 27; Davidson *(Scotland)* para 7.63.

(3) Continuation of the proceedings unnecessary or impossible, sub-paragraph (c)

Under Art 32(2)(c), which is modelled on Art 34(2) of the UNCITRAL Arbitration Rules, the arbitral tribunal must issue an order for the termination of the proceedings when it finds that the continuation of the proceedings has become unnecessary or impossible for any reason other than that stated above. In the Third Draft the word 'impossible' was changed to 'inappropriate'. However, as a number of delegations found that this term gave the tribunal too much discretion, the original language was retained.[875] **14.500**

Instances in which the continuation of the proceedings becomes unnecessary or impossible are failure to communicate the statement of claim pursuant to Art 25(a), as explicitly recognized in the Hungarian law,[876] settlement under Art 30(1), agreement of the parties to cancel the arbitration agreement and all other instances in which the arbitration agreement as the basis of arbitration turns out to be null and void or non-existent. In these situations the termination of the proceedings is a more or less self-evident consequence. Nevertheless, the Secretariat recommended the instant rule mainly to exclude termination in circumstances that merely impede the normal course of proceedings without making them impossible. The drafters were thinking of difficulties or delays in appointing the presiding arbitrator, unreasonable delay in rendering the award or other failure of action on part of the arbitrators or the parties.[877] The Arbitration Act of *New Zealand* clarifies that the death of a party does not terminate the arbitral proceedings or the authority of the arbitral tribunal, unless the parties so agree.[878] **14.501**

The drafting history is silent as to the situation where the arbitral tribunal has reached a deadlock in the voting on the merits. One might argue that in such a case the continuation of the proceedings has become impossible and therefore the tribunal must issue an order for termination.[879] However, as it is principally up to the parties to determine the course of the proceedings and to decide on the fate of the arbitration, the deadlocked tribunal should take account of the parties' will and render a termination order only if the parties agree.[880] **14.502**

D. Termination of the arbitral tribunal's mandate

As a rule, the mandate of the arbitral tribunal terminates with the termination of the arbitral proceedings. However, there are two exceptions to this rule. First, the mandate's termination is subject to Art 33. After the award has been made, each party may request the arbitral tribunal to correct any clerical or other errors of similar nature in the award, or to interpret the award or to make an additional award. In the cases of correction and interpretation, the mandate of the tribunal, which has terminated with the rendering of the final award, revives for the purpose of issuing the corrective or interpretive decision. In the case **14.503**

[875] See Analytical Compilation of Government Comments, UN Doc A/CN.9/263, Art 32 para 3 (*Soviet Union*); ADD.1, Art 32 para 1 (*Canada*) and para 2 (*Yugoslavia*); Summary Record, UN Doc A/CN.9/SR.329, Art 32 para 33.

[876] s 42(2)(a) of Act LXXI of 1994 on Arbitration.

[877] See Third Secretariat Note, UN Doc A/CN.9/WG.II/WP.41, Art 32 para 40; Knoepfler and Schweizer, 172.

[878] Art 32 of the First sch of the Arbitration Act 1996.

[879] Granzow, 176, 188.

[880] Berger, 600, 635 *et seq*. See also commentary on Art 29 sentence (1).

of making an additional award as to claims omitted from the award, the arbitrators have not completed their mission, ie their mandate was not terminated by the rendering of the incomplete award.[881]

14.504 The second exception to this provision is stated in Art 34(4). Under this provision a court may suspend the setting-aside proceedings in order to give the arbitral tribunal an opportunity to resume the arbitral proceedings or to take other action, which in the tribunal's opinion will eliminate the grounds for setting aside.

Article 33. Correction and interpretation of award; additional award

(1) Within 30 days of receipt of the award, unless another period of time has been agreed upon by the parties:

(a) a party, with notice to the other party, may request the arbitral tribunal to correct in the award any errors in computation, any clerical or typographical errors or any errors of a similar nature;

(b) if so agreed by the parties, a party, with notice to the other party, may request the arbitral tribunal to give an interpretation of a specific point or part of the award.

If the arbitral tribunal considers the request to be justified, it shall make the correction or give the interpretation within 30 days of receipt of the request. The interpretation shall form part of the award.

(2) The arbitral tribunal may correct any error of the type referred to in paragraph (1)(a) of this article on its own initiative within 30 days of the date of the award.

(3) Unless otherwise agreed by the parties, a party, with notice to the other party, may request, within 30 days of receipt of the award, the arbitral tribunal to make an additional award as to claims presented in the arbitral proceedings but omitted from the award. If the arbitral tribunal considers the request to be justified, it shall make the additional award within 60 days.

(4) The arbitral tribunal may extend, if necessary, the period of time within which it shall make a correction, interpretation or an additional award under paragraph (1) or (3) of this article.

(5) The provisions of article 31 shall apply to a correction or interpretation of the award or to an additional award.

A. Meaning and purpose

14.505 Article 33, which is modelled on Arts 35, 36 and 37 of the UNCITRAL Arbitration Rules, allows the arbitral tribunal to make corrections, interpretations and additional awards within specific time limits and under certain conditions. These three measures of clarification and rectification of minor mistakes are exceptions to the principle of finality of the award. They are based on the fact that the arbitrators who made the award are best able to remove these mistakes. In doing so, the arbitrators help to relieve the workload of the courts in that they avoid actions for setting aside the award.[882]

14.506 In this context it should be noted that another possibility to alter an award after it has been issued is provided by Art 34(4), under which a court, when asked to set aside an award, can suspend the setting-aside proceedings in order to give the arbitral tribunal an opportunity to eliminate the grounds for setting aside.

---

[881] See Berger, 637.
[882] *ibid*, 636 *et seq*.

B. Matters relevant to Article 33 as a whole

(1) Time limits

Article 33 sets out specific time limits both for a request by a party and for the response to that request by the arbitral tribunal. The fixed time limits are safeguards to limit the duration of uncertainty about the definitive contents of the award. They are also necessary to align this provision with Art 34(3), which sets a time limit for an application for setting aside an award.[883] **14.507**

The period for requesting any of the provided measures is 30 days,[884] starting with the receipt of the award. However, due to the overriding principle of party autonomy, the parties can vary this period of time. **14.508**

The arbitral tribunal is permitted 30 days[885] from the receipt of the request to correct or interpret the award and 60 days[886] from the date of the award 'for the usually more difficult and time-consuming task of making an additional award'.[887] It is also allowed to correct the award on its own motion within 30 days[888] of the date of the award. Paragraph (4) empowers the tribunal to extend these time limits where it deems it necessary. This could be the case when the preparation of an interpretation requires consultations between the arbitrators, when the making of an additional award requires hearings or taking of evidence or when sufficient time must be given to the other party for replying to the request.[889] **14.509**

(2) Notice to the other party

A party requesting any modification has to give notice to the other party so that the other party has the opportunity to respond to that request.[890] Art 33 states this prerequisite explicitly for the sake of clarification; however, it already follows from the fundamental principle of procedural fairness laid down in Art 18. **14.510**

(3) Effect of request

The Model Law does not explicitly deal with the effect of a request for modification. It must be assumed that the award remains enforceable while the arbitral tribunal is considering such a request.[891] **14.511**

(4) Form and contents, paragraph (5)

The requirements as regards the form and contents of an award stated in Art 31 apply with equal force to any correction, interpretation or additional award. **14.512**

---

[883] Fifth Working Group Report, UN Doc A/CN.9/246, para 120.

[884] In *Bulgaria*: 60 days as to the request for correction or interpretation, see Art 43(3) LICA; in *Germany*: one month, see s 1058(2) ZPO; in *Sri Lanka*: 14 days, see s 27(1) of the Arbitration Act 1995.

[885] In *Germany*: one month, see s 1058(3) ZPO; in *Sri Lanka*: 14 days, see s 27(2) of the Arbitration Act 1995.

[886] In *Germany*: two months, see s 1058(3), ZPO; in *Sri Lanka*: 30 days, see s 27(4) of the Arbitration Act 1995.

[887] Analytical Commentary, UN Doc A/CN.9/264, Art 33 para 2.

[888] In *Bulgaria*: 60 days, see Art 43(3), LICA.

[889] Analytical Commentary, UN Doc A/CN.9/264, Art 33 para 2.

[890] Fifth Working Group Report, UN Doc A/CN.9/246, para 124.

[891] Davidson *(Scotland)* para 7.75.

C. Correction, paragraphs (1)(a) and (2)

14.513 Under Art 33(1)(a) a party may, within 30 days of receipt of the award, request the arbitral tribunal to correct in the award any errors in computation, any clerical or typographical errors or any errors of a similar nature. The parties may extend the rather short time limit. Hence the provision is non-mandatory in this respect. The general power of the arbitral tribunal to correct the award, however, is not subject to any contrary party agreement. If the tribunal considers the correction justified, it will make the correction. Furthermore, pursuant to para (2) a correction may be made not only at the request of a party, but also on the tribunal's own initiative, within 30 days of the date of the award. In both cases, under Bulgarian law the parties have to be heard regarding the correction either in an oral hearing or through written statements.[892]

D. Interpretation, paragraph (1)(b)

14.514 Under Art 33(1)(b) each party may request the arbitral tribunal to give an interpretation of a specific point or part of the award, if the parties have so agreed. The wording of this provision differs in some aspects from the language of Art 35 of the UNCITRAL Arbitration Rules on which it was modelled, but there seems to be no substantive change. The time limit was shortened in order to align it with the period of time provided for the correction of the award. The specification of the scope of application should be regarded as a mere clarification.[893] The express formula that the interpretation of the award can only be sought if the parties agree to empower the arbitral tribunal to do so fully corresponds with Art 35 of the UNCITRAL Arbitration Rules, as the latter provision itself serves as an express agreement of the parties. The party agreement can be made either in advance or at the time of the request for interpretation.[894] In *Bulgaria* and *Egypt* an agreement of the parties is not a prerequisite for the request for an interpretation of the award.[895]

14.515 This provision was the subject of considerable discussion during the drafting process. A strong view favoured the deletion of this provision, fearing that it would undermine the principle of the finality of the arbitral award and might be abused to open new proceedings in the guise of an interpretation or harass the arbitral tribunal.[896] Others felt that some procedure of interpretation of the award by the arbitral tribunal should be provided in light of the fact that the award in international commercial cases is normally not written in the mother-tongue of the arbitrators, which increases the possibility of ambiguity.[897] The arbitrators who have decided the case would be best able to clarify their intention. Therefore, by general consensus, it was decided that they should be entitled to do so. In order to meet

---

[892] Art 43(4), LICA.

[893] See Holtzmann and Neuhaus 890.

[894] Berger, 641, who rightly points out that an agreement subsequent to the rendering of the award will frequently be hard to obtain for the party interested in the interpretation unless the ambiguity concerns the interests of both parties.

[895] *Bulgaria*: Art 43, LICA; *Egypt*: Art 49 of the Law Concerning Arbitration in Civil and Commercial Matters.

[896] eg Summary Record, UN Doc A/CN.9/SR.325, Art 33 paras 38, 40–1, 44–5, 49–51; Commission Report, UN Doc A/40/17, para 266.

[897] Commission Report, UN Doc A/40/17, para 267.

the above-mentioned concerns, the safeguard that a request for interpretation might be made only if so agreed by the parties was introduced.[898] Another safeguard is that the arbitral tribunal, unlike its power with respect to the correction of the award granted in para (2), cannot interpret the award on its own initiative. *Bulgaria* added a further safeguard; both parties must be heard either in an oral hearing or through written statements.[899]

Although the Commission did not adopt the proposal to change the word 'interpretation' to 'clarification',[900] the provision should be read in this way, only permitting requests for interpretation when the wording of a specific point or part of the award is ambiguous.[901] The fundamental principle of finality of the award calls for this restrictive approach. **14.516**

If the tribunal considers the request justified, it will give the interpretation, which forms part of the award. It should be noted that the parties, irrespective of this provision, are free to request the arbitral tribunal to give an informal oral interpretation of the award, which of course is not binding for courts in a setting-aside or enforcement procedure.[902] **14.517**

E. Additional award, paragraph (3)

Article 33(3) permits either party to request the arbitral tribunal to make an additional award as to claims presented in the arbitral proceedings but omitted from the award, for example where claimed interest was erroneously not awarded. Unlike Art 37 of the UNCITRAL Arbitration Rules on which this provision was modelled, para (3) is subject to contrary party agreement and is thus non-mandatory. Another significant change is that it does not require the omission to be rectified without any further hearings or evidence. It was decided that the arbitral tribunal should also be permitted to resolve claims as to which further hearings or evidence are required, because otherwise such omission would constitute a ground for setting aside the award as a whole.[903] *Hungary* states this explicitly.[904] **14.518**

If the arbitral tribunal considers the request to be justified, it shall make the additional award within 60 days. Pursuant to para (4), the tribunal is entitled to extend the time limit. Examples of unjustified requests would be failure to cite reasons for an issue decided by the tribunal or a late submission that has not yet been submitted to the tribunal for a decision.[905] The additional award is a separate award, which may be set aside or enforced. **14.519**

---

[898] See Commission Report, UN Doc A/40/17, para 270.

[899] Art 43(4) LICA.

[900] See Summary Record, UN Doc A/CN.9/SR.325, Art 33 para 48; Commission Report, UN Doc A/40/17, paras 268–9.

[901] Holtzmann and Neuhaus, 891; see Commission Report, UN Doc A/40/17, para 267; this is the understanding of the corresponding provision of the UNCITRAL Arbitratrion Rules by the Iran-US Claims Tribunal, cf eg *Paul Domin De Rosiere, Panacaviar SA v The Islamic Republic of Iran et al*, 26 CTR 256, 258 *et seq.*

[902] Berger, 644.

[903] See Fourth Secretariat Note, UN Doc A/CN.9/WG.II/WP.50, Art 33 paras 21–3; Fifth Working Group Report, UN Doc A/CN.9/246, para 125; see also commentary on Art 34 para 3 at 14.544 and 14.545.

[904] s 44 of Act LXXI of 1994 on Arbitration.

[905] Knoepfler and Schweizer, 175, fn 381.

Chapter VII. Recourse against award

Special literature:

Broches, Aron, 'Recourse against the Award, Recognition and Enforcement of the Award' in Pieter Sanders (ed), *UNCITRAL's Project for a Model Law on International Commercial Arbitration, Interim meeting, Lausanne, 9–12 May 1984* (ICCA Congress Series no 2, 1984).

Gharavi, Hamid, G., *The International Effectiveness of the Annulment of an Arbitral Award* (Kluwer Law International, 2002).

Ghikas, Gerald, W., 'A Principled Approach to Adjourning the Decision to Enforce Under the Model Law and the New York Convention' (2006) 22 *Arb Int'l* 53.

Kröll, Stefan, 'Setting Aside Proceedings in Model Law Jurisdictions – Selected Procedural and Substantive Questions from the Case Law' (2005) 8 *Int'l Arb L Rev* 170.

Ungar, Kenneth, T., 'The Enforcement of Arbitral Awards Under UNCITRAL's Model Law on International Commercial Arbitration' (1987) 25 *Columbia J of Transnational L* 717.

Viscasillas, Pilar P., 'Case Law On the Recognition and Enforcement of Arbitral Awards Under the UNCITRAL Model Law on International Commercial Arbitration' (2005) 8 *Int'l Arb L Rev* 191.

Article 34. Application for setting aside as exclusive recourse against arbitral award

(1) Recourse to a court against an arbitral award may be made only by an application for setting aside in accordance with paragraphs (2) and (3) of this article.

(2) An arbitral award may be set aside by the court specified in article 6 only if:

(a) the party making the application furnishes proof that:

(i) a party to the arbitration agreement referred to in article 7 was under some incapacity; or the said agreement is not valid under the law to which the parties have subjected it or, failing any indication thereon, under the law of this State; or

(ii) the party making the application was not given proper notice of the appointment of an arbitrator or of the arbitral proceedings or was otherwise unable to present his case; or

(iii) the award deals with a dispute not contemplated by or not falling within the terms of the submission to arbitration, or contains decisions on matters beyond the scope of the submission to arbitration, provided that, if the decisions on matters submitted to arbitration can be separated from those not so submitted, only that part of the award which contains decisions on matters not submitted to arbitration may be set aside; or

(iv) the composition of the arbitral tribunal or the arbitral procedure was not in accordance with the agreement of the parties, unless such agreement was in conflict with a provision of this Law from which the parties cannot derogate, or, failing such agreement, was not in accordance with this Law; or

(b) the court finds that:

(i) the subject-matter of the dispute is not capable of settlement by arbitration under the law of this State; or

(ii) the award is in conflict with the public policy of this State.

(3) An application for setting aside may not be made after three months have elapsed from the date on which the party making the application had received the award or, if a request had been made under article 33, from the date on which that request had been disposed of by the arbitral tribunal.

(4) The court, when asked to set aside an award, may, where appropriate and so requested by a party, suspend the setting aside proceedings for a period of time determined by it in order to give the arbitral tribunal an opportunity to resume the arbitral proceedings or to take such other action as in the arbitral tribunal's opinion will eliminate the grounds for setting aside.

A. Meaning and purpose

Article 34 establishes that an application for setting aside to the court specified in Art 6 is the exclusive recourse against an arbitral award. Furthermore, it lays down the specific grounds upon which an award may be set aside. Developing these standards presented some of the greatest difficulties in the drafting process, as the reasons for challenging an award are of central importance to the balance between the interests of the parties to freely determine the arbitration procedure and the interests of the legal system expected to give effect thereto.[906] It was recognized that national laws provide a number of ways to attack an award with different time limits and varied lists of grounds. For the sake of uniformity and certainty, the drafters decided to provide for only one type of recourse available during a fairly short period of time and to allow recourse for rather limited reasons. Other forms of recourse that might be available under national laws are thus excluded. The limitation ensures that foreign parties contemplating arbitration in a Model Law state are able to determine the conditions under which an award may be set aside. This facilitates practice in international commercial arbitration. The limited opportunity for recourse against the award represents a well-balanced compromise between the party's demand for speedy proceedings that end with a final award and the principle of justice. **14.520**

B. Action for setting aside as only recourse against an award, paragraph (1)

The Model Law provides for only one exclusive method of initiating proceedings for judicial review against the arbitral award.[907] Of course, this decision does not affect the party's right to defend himself against the award by requesting refusal of recognition or enforcement in proceedings initiated by the other party under Arts 35 and 36. Furthermore, it is important to note that the arbitral tribunal has the power to resume the arbitral proceedings, which is made clear by Art 34(4), and that Art 34(1) does not exclude recourse to a second arbitral tribunal where such appeal within the arbitration system is envisaged.[908] **14.521**

The Model Law does not define the term 'arbitral award'[909] nor does Art 34(1) specify which kinds of decision would be subject to the setting aside recourse. However, in the light of Art 34(2), which states the grounds for setting aside, it may be assumed that only final arbitral awards can be the subject of an action for setting aside an arbitral award. **14.522**

Clarified by Art 1(2), territoriality is the basic criterion for the applicability of the Model Law and thus for Art 34. That means that the application for setting aside must be made to the court specified in Art 6,[910] located in the state in which the place of arbitration was located.[911] **14.523**

---

[906] See First Secretariat Note, UN Doc A/CN.9/207, para 107.

[907] In *Tunisia* parties from other countries are allowed to waive their right to institute setting-aside proceedings, see Art 78(6) of the Arbitration Code 1993. *Egypt* and *Oman* prohibit an exclusion of setting aside prior to the making of an arbitral award, see Art 54(2) of the Egyptian Law Concerning Arbitration in Civil and Commercial Matters and Art 54 of the Omani Law of Arbitration in Civil and Commercial Disputes.

[908] Analytical Commentary, UN Doc A/CN.9/264, Art 34 para 2.

[909] See commentary on Art 2 at para 14.66.

[910] See commentary on Art 6 at paras 14.104 to 14.106.

[911] See commentary on Art 20 at paras 14.373 to 14.385.

14.524 The Model Law does not regulate the conduct of the setting-aside proceedings. This issue is governed by the domestic law of civil procedure of the Model Law state. Domestic law also applies on appeals against decisions by courts specified in Art 6, including setting-aside decisions.

C. Grounds for setting aside the award, paragraph (2)

14.525 Article 34(2) lists the grounds on which an award may be set aside. This listing is exhaustive, as expressed by the word 'only' and reinforced by the character of the Model Law as *lex specialis*.[912] The grounds are essentially identical with the grounds on which recognition and enforcement may be refused under the New York Convention and under Art 36 of the Model Law, which is closely modelled on Art V of the New York Convention. Thus, the Working Group and the Commission finally followed the proposal of the Secretariat that urged from the outset that there should be full alignment of the reasons for setting aside and for refusing recognition and enforcement in order to prevent an international award from falling victim to local particularities of law even where the case at hand bears no substantive connection with that respective state.[913] The alignment also has the salutary effect of avoiding 'split' or 'relative' validity of international awards, ie awards which are void in the country of origin but valid and enforceable abroad.[914]

14.526 It was the Commission's understanding that the award might be set aside on any of the grounds listed in Art 34(2), irrespective of whether such a ground had materially affected the award.[915] Thus, even minor procedural errors can give rise to grounds for setting aside the award. However, as indicated by the word 'may' in the opening sentence of para (2), the court has discretion not to set aside the award when such grounds are present.[916]

14.527 As to the interpretation of these grounds, the goal of the Model Law to limit court control should be kept in mind. In *Quintette Coal Limited v Nippon Steel Corporation et al* the British Columbia Court of Appeal held that the appropriate standard of review for arbitral awards is one that preserves the autonomy of the forum chosen by the parties and minimizes judicial intervention.[917]

(1) Concern about restrictive list of grounds

14.528 Some delegates felt that the restrictive approach was too narrow to cover all cases of procedural injustice where annulment was justified. Thus, there was considerable discussion of a number of additional possible grounds, which derived from various national law

[912] Analytical Commentary, UN Doc A/CN.9/264, Art 34 para 5.

[913] First Secretariat Note, UN Doc A/CN.9/207, para 110.

[914] Analytical Commentary, UN Doc A/CN.9/264, Art 34 para 9; as to the potential risk of 'double control' of domestic awards see commentary on Art 36.

[915] Commission Report, UN Doc A/40/17, para 303.

[916] See Summary Record, UN Doc A/CN.9/SR.318, Art 34 para 65; Holtzmann and Neuhaus, 922; see also commentary on Art 36 and *Nanjing Cereals, Oils and Foodstuffs Import & Export Corporation v Luckmate Commodities Trading Ltd.*, High Court of Hong Kong (Kaplan), 16 December 1994, CLOUT Case 88, as to the similar wording in Art 36(1).

[917] *Quintette Coal Limited v Nippon Steel Corporation et al*, British Columbia Court of Appeal (Hutcheon, Proudfoot and Giggs), 24 October 1990, published in (1991) 1 Western Weekly Reports 219. CLOUT Case 16.

provisions, *inter alia* (i) that the arbitral tribunal has omitted to make an award with respect to one or more points of the dispute (decision *infra petita*);[918] (ii) that the award contains conflicting decisions; (iii) that new facts or evidence are discovered or become known only after the award has been made; and (iv) that the award was improperly procured by the other party (eg by fraud, bribery, forgery or other criminal act).[919] An alternative suggestion was to replace all the specific grounds with a general formula, such as 'in cases of procedural injustice', and to rely on the common sense of the judge.[920] None of these proposals was adopted for a number of reasons. One was the view that not all of the proposed additional grounds justified setting aside an award.[921] Another was the feeling that some of the proposed grounds were already embraced by para (2), especially by the public policy ground under Art 34(2)(b)(ii). Above all, the aim of aligning the grounds for setting aside with the grounds for refusing recognition and enforcement and thus diminishing the impact of the place of award was emphasized. It was argued that this would facilitate international commercial arbitration by enhancing predictability and expeditiousness and would go a long way towards establishing a harmonious system of limited recourse against awards and their enforcement.[922] Some Model Law states, however, added other grounds for setting aside or varied the list.[923]

(2) Selected grounds for setting aside

As to content, the grounds listed in Art 34(2) can be divided into three groups:[924] lack of contractual basis (Art 34(2)(a)(i),(iii) and (b)(i)), significant irregularities of the arbitral proceedings (Art 34(2)(a)(ii) and (iv)) and violation of the public policy of a state (Art 34(2)(b)(ii)). In a formal respect, the Model Law distinguishes between sub-para (a), which is to be invoked only if the party seeking to have the arbitral award set aside furnishes proof in relation to one of the grounds specified thereunder, and sub-para (b), where this is not necessary; ie the distinction refers to the burden of proof.[925] In any case, the court specified in Art 6 is not entitled to act unless a party has made an application for setting aside.[926] **14.529**

[918] eg Art 190 s 2c of the Swiss Act on Private International Law and Art 1065 s 1c in connection with ss 4 and 6 of the Netherlands Arbitration Act, ie Book Four of the Dutch Code of Civil Procedure, recognizing such omissions as grounds for setting aside. Berger 663, 664 n 96 points out that notwithstanding the limited list of grounds in Art 34 of the Model Law, the drafters acknowledged that awards *infra petita* also might be set aside. The cited Fourth Secretariat Note, UN Doc A/CN.9/WG.II/WP.50, para 23, however, gives this interpretation only for omissions which, according to Art 33(2), Fourth Draft, could not be rectified by an additional award, because a further hearing or further evidence was required. Yet, in order to avoid the consequence of having the award set aside in such a situation, the Working Group extended the admissibility of additional awards: Art 33(3) of the Model Law empowers the arbitral tribunal to render an additional award in all cases where claims have been omitted from the original award irrespective of whether further hearings or evidence are needed; see Fifth Working Group Report, A/CN.9/246, para 125; Holtzmann and Neuhaus, 891.

[919] See Second Draft, UN Doc A/CN.9/WG.II/WP.42, Art 42(2), n 29.

[920] Third Working Group Report, UN Doc A/CN.9/233, para 186.

[921] Commission Report, UN Doc A/40/17, para 279.

[922] Third Working Group Report, UN Doc A/CN.9/233, para 187.

[923] eg *Egypt*: Art 53(1)(d) and (g) of the Law Concerning Arbitration in Civil and Commercial Matters; *Oman*: Art 53(1)(d) and (g) of the Law of Arbitration in Civil and Commercial Disputes; *Iran*: Art 33 of the International Commercial Arbitration Act.

[924] Calavros, 148 *et seq.*

[925] Summary Record, UN Doc A/CN.9/SR.318, para 7.

[926] *ibid*, Art 34 para 8.

14.530 As the grounds for setting aside essentially conform with those for refusing recognition and enforcement as laid down in Art V of the New York Convention, the following commentary merely highlights the modifications that mainly result from using the grounds for purposes of setting aside.

14.531 (2.1) **Incapacity of party and invalidity of the arbitration agreement, sub-paragraph (a)(i)** This provision states two quite separate grounds for setting aside: that the party to the arbitration agreement was under some incapacity and that the arbitration agreement itself is not valid. The provision is modelled on Art V(1)(a) of the New York Convention.

14.532 *(2.1.1) Incapacity of a party* The wording with respect to subjective arbitrability differs from the New York Convention provision in two respects. First, the New York Convention refers to the incapacity of the parties. As it was felt that the Model Law should clarify that the incapacity of either party was a ground upon which the award could be set aside, the provision was formulated in the singular.[927] Second, the choice-of-law rule of the New York Convention ('under the law applicable to them') was deleted. This phrase was regarded as either incomplete or misleading, as it was not clear whether it refers to the law of nationality, of domicile or of residence of the parties.[928] The phrase was therefore only removed because of its vagueness. No substantive change is attributed to this alteration.[929] It is still necessary to determine the applicable law, which should be done by reference to the conflict of laws rules of the place of arbitration.[930]

14.533 *(2.1.2) Invalidity of the arbitration agreement* With respect to the invalidity of the arbitration agreement, the Model Law contains a choice-of-law rule. Thus, the award may be set aside if the arbitration agreement is not valid under the law to which the parties have subjected it or, failing any indication thereon, under the law of the enacting state. An arbitration clause which submits a future dispute to arbitration normally does not specify the governing law, unless by referring to a set of arbitration rules which incorporate a choice-of-law clause. Consequently, in the most common cases the arbitration agreement is governed by the applicable law of the main contract, unless there are clear indications to the contrary.[931] In the latter case, the law of the place of arbitration (*lex fori*) according to Art 1(2) will be applied.

14.534 In this context, the effect of the waiver rule pursuant to Art 4 has to be considered. A party who is of the opinion that the arbitration agreement is invalid should raise a plea that the arbitral tribunal has no jurisdiction as required by Art 16(2). If he fails to do so, he will, as a rule, be precluded from raising objections with respect to the existence or validity of the arbitration agreement not only during the further stages of the arbitral proceedings, but also in the post-award stage.[932] It was recognized that the failure to raise such a plea might

---

[927] Summary Record, UN Doc A/CN.9/SR.317, paras 18–21.

[928] Commission Report, UN Doc A/40/17, para 280.

[929] Holtzmann and Neuhaus, 916; see also Commission Report, UN Doc A/40/17, para 321 as to the parallel change in Art 36.

[930] See van den Berg, A.J., *The New York Arbitration Convention of 1958: Towards a Uniform Judicial Interpretation* (Asser/Kluwer, 1981) 276.

[931] Davidson *(Scotland)* para 8.15.

[932] Fourth Secretariat Note, UN Doc A/CN.9/WG.II/WP.50, Art 34 para 11; see also Analytical Commentary, UN Doc A/CN.9/264, Art 34 para 10.

not have the effect of a waiver in all circumstances. The Commission decided to leave the question to the interpretation and regulation by the states adopting the Model Law.[933]

(2.2) **Party unable to present his case, sub-paragraph (a)(ii)** An arbitral award may be set aside if a party proves that he was unable to present his case, for example when he was not given proper notice of the appointment of an arbitrator or of the arbitral proceedings. This provision is based on Art V(i)(b) of the New York Convention and is clearly connected with Art 18, which establishes the principle of due process. It is important to note that any violation of Art 18 would constitute a ground for setting aside the award under this provision or under paras (a)(iv) or (b).[934] **14.535**

(2.3) **Infringement of jurisdiction of the arbitral tribunal, sub-paragraph (a)(iii)** This provision is lifted almost verbatim from Art V(1)(c) of the New York Convention. It provides that the award may be set aside if it deals with matters beyond the scope of the jurisdiction of the arbitral tribunal. The waiver rule, which is expressed in Art 4, has the same effect on this setting-aside ground as on the ground of invalidity of the arbitration agreement provided for in sub-para (a)(i). **14.536**

(2.4) **Composition of the arbitral tribunal or arbitral procedure not in accordance with the agreement of the parties or the Model Law, sub-paragraph (a)(iv)** Article V(1)(d) of the New York Convention, on which this provision was modelled, and Art 36(1)(a)(iv) of the Model Law state that recognition or enforcement may be refused if the composition of the arbitral tribunal or the arbitral procedure was not in accordance with the agreement of the parties or, failing such agreement, was not in accordance with the law of the country where the arbitration took place. As Art 34 only deals with domestic awards, the applicable law will be the Model Law if there is no agreement of the parties. Accordingly, the last words were altered. Furthermore, a new phrase was included: 'unless such agreement was in conflict with a provision of this Law from which the parties cannot derogate'. In doing so, the drafters wanted to clearly express that this provision does not give absolute priority to the agreement of the parties, which is the usual interpretation of the New York Convention provision. On the contrary, their intention was to express that the agreement was subject to the mandatory provisions of the Model Law.[935] It was rightly pointed out that the phrase does not clearly reflect this intention.[936] It solely says that if an agreement is in conflict with mandatory provisions of the Model Law, non-observance of such an agreement will not be a ground for setting aside the award. The wording does not comprise the effect of observance of an agreement that violates mandatory provisions. It was clearly intended that this would be a ground for setting aside. The Commission Report states that where the agreement was found to be in conflict with a mandatory provision of this Law, or where the parties had not made an agreement on the procedural point at issue, the provisions of this Law, whether mandatory or not, **14.537**

---

[933] Commission Report, UN Doc A/40/17, paras 288–9.

[934] Analytical Commentary, UN Doc A/CN.9/264, Art 34 para 302.

[935] Third Working Group Report, UN Doc A/CN.9/233, para 149; Analytical Commentary, UN Doc A/CN.9/264, Art 34 para 11.

[936] Summary Record, UN Doc A/CN.9/SR.317, Art 34 para 52; Analytical Compilation of Government Comments, UN Doc A/CN.9/263/ADD.1, Art 34 para 4 (*Canada*); Broches, 196.

provide the standards against which the composition of the arbitral tribunal and the arbitral procedure are to be measured.[937]

14.538 It should be noted that an agreement on the composition of the arbitral tribunal or the arbitral procedure which conflicts with mandatory provisions of the Model Law would also be a setting-aside ground, either on the basis of sub-paras (a)(ii) or (b)(ii). Therefore, the express reference to the mandatory provisions was not absolutely necessary in order to cover these situations, but serves to stress that party autonomy does not prevail in all circumstances.[938]

14.539 (2.5) **Subject matter of the dispute not arbitrable, sub-paragraph (b)(i)** Pursuant to this sub-paragraph an arbitral award may be set aside by the court specified in Art 6 only if the court finds that the subject matter of the dispute is not capable of settlement by arbitration under the law of the enacting state. This provision is based on Art V(2)(a) of the New York Convention and addresses the important question of arbitrability.[939]

14.540 During the drafting process, divergent views were expressed as to the implementation of this provision in its current form. Under one view, it was not appropriate to determine the question of arbitrability by the law of the place of arbitration in view of the fact that the place of arbitration might not be connected in any way with the subject matter of the dispute.[940] Moreover, it was pointed out that the finding of non-arbitrability was not limited to the state of the forum, but extended to all other states by virtue of Art 36(1)(a)(v), thus having a global effect. In light of this global effect, the law applicable to the substance of the dispute should be decisive.[941] This view refers to the approach of certain law systems regarding arbitrability as a matter concerning the validity of the arbitration agreement. Others felt that a different view was justified when the issue of non-arbitrability was part of the public policy of the forum state.[942] Ultimately, the provision was retained for reasons of 'predictability and certainty in this important issue'. It was noted that the parties could, in fact, achieve that goal by selecting a suitable place of arbitration and thus the governing law.[943] Therefore, for purposes of setting aside, the intent of the drafters was that the issue of arbitrability are to be governed by the substantive law of the place of arbitration.

14.541 (2.6) **Award conflicts with public policy, sub-paragraph (b)(ii)** The court specified in Art 6 may set aside an arbitral award if it finds the award to be in conflict with the public policy of the enacting state. Like Art V(2)(b) of the New York Convention, this provision refers to the domestic public policy of the respective state. A proposal to qualify the public policy as international public policy—a concept which is applied by certain states either by statute or judicially—was rejected. Although it was recognized that there was a trend to

[937] UN Doc A/40/17, para 290.
[938] As to the impact of this provision see also the commentary on Art 36(1)(a)(iv).
[939] See also commentary on Art 1(5).
[940] Commission Report, UN Doc A/40/17, para 291.
[941] Fifth Working Group Report, UN Doc A/CN.9/264, para 136.
[942] cf *ibid,* para 136; Commission Report, UN Doc A/40/17, para 292.
[943] Commission Report, UN Doc A/40/17, paras 293–4.

distinguish between the less strict standards of international public order of a state and the standards of that state's domestic public order,[944] there was considerable doubt as to the general acceptance and, above all, accuracy of this concept.[945] *Tunisia* understands the term 'public policy' as in private international law, which seems to refer to the concept of international public policy.[946]

As regards the impact of the term 'public policy', it was the understanding of the Commission that it covered fundamental principles of law and justice in substantive as well as procedural respects, a concept taken from the civil law tradition,[947] and it embraced not only the award itself, but also the manner in which it was arrived at. Thus, instances such as corruption, bribery or fraud and similar serious cases would constitute grounds for setting aside.[948] Some Model Law states explicitly state 'for the avoidance of any doubt', without limiting the generality of this provision, that an award is in conflict with the public policy if the award was induced or effected by fraud or corruption, or if a breach of the rules of natural justice occurred in connection with the making of the award.[949] **14.542**

The Moscow City Court held that the tribunal's dismissal of a claim despite the fact that the defendant had acknowledged the claim brought against him did not constitute grounds for setting aside the award. As the arbitrators were not bound by an acknowledgement of the claim, there was no violation of Art 18 and no conflict with public policy. The Court also noted that a procedural infringement in the arbitral proceedings had no relevance to the notion of 'public policy'.[950] In another case, the same court held that an award ordering the Russian plaintiff to make a payment in foreign currency whereas the plaintiff did not have a foreign currency account was not in conflict with the public policy of the Russian Federation. In this connection, the Court noted that in the enforcement of the award the competent court had the option of modifying the arrangements and procedures for enforcement.[951] As to the interpretation of the term 'public policy', see also the commentary on Art 36(1)(b)(ii) at paras 14.578 to 14.580. **14.543**

---

944 See Secretariat Study on the New York Convention, UN Doc A/CN.9/168, paras 46–7; First Secretariat Note, UN Doc A/CN.9/207, para 21; Second Working Group Report, UN Doc A/CN.9/232, para 16.

945 Third Working Group Report, UN Doc A/CN.9/233, para 154.

946 See Art 78(2) of the Arbitration Code 1993.

947 See also *Navigation Sonomar Inc v Algoma Steamships Ltd.*, Superior Court of Quebec (Gonthier), 16 April 1987, published in (1987) Requeils de Jurisprudence du Quebec 1346, commented on by Tetley (1993) *Lloyd's Maritime and Commercial L Q* 239; See for the common law: *Zimbabwe Electricity Supply Authority v Genius Joel Maposa*, Supreme Court of Zimbabwe (Chief Justice Gubbay and Judges of Appeal Ebrahim and Sandura), 21 December 1999, CLOUT Case 323; *Conforce (Pvt) Ltd v The City of Harare*, Harare High Court (Chinhengo), 5 April 2000, CLOUT Case 342.

948 Commission Report, UN Doc A/40/17, paras 296–7.

949 *Australia*: s 19 of the International Arbitration Act 1974; *New Zealand*: Art 34(6) of the First sch of the Arbitration Act 1996; *Malta*: s 58 of the Arbitration Act 1996; *Zimbabwe*: Art 34(5) of the Arbitration Act 1996; see also *Bermuda*: s 27 of the Bermuda International Conciliation and Arbitration Act 1993; *India*: s 34 of the Arbitration and Conciliation Ordinance 1996; *Scotland*: Art 34(2)(a)(v) of the Law Reform (Miscellaneous Provisions) (Scotland) Act 1990; *Singapore*: s 24 of the International Arbitration Act 1994.

950 Moscow City Court, 10 November 1994, CLOUT Case 146.

951 Moscow City Court, 18 September 1995, CLOUT Case 149.

D. Time limit for application to set aside the award, paragraph (3)

14.544 An application for setting aside may be made within three months[952] of the date on which the party making that application received the award. If a party requests a correction or interpretation of the award or an additional award under Art 33, the three-month period begins to run on the date on which the arbitral tribunal disposes of this request. In the interest of certainty and quick settlement of the dispute, the provision ensures that the exclusive means of recourse against the award are available only during a fairly short period of time.[953] The parties are not allowed to vary the period by agreement.[954] The High Court of Singapore stated that it did not have the power to extend the time limit, as the Court derived its jurisdiction to hear such an application from the Model Law, which does not provide for any extensions of the time period for an application for setting aside the award.[955] In *New Zealand* this paragraph does not apply to an application for setting aside on the ground that the award was induced or effected by fraud or corruption.[956] *Bulgaria* excluded the time limit for the setting-aside grounds stated in sub-para (b).[957]

14.545 There was some lengthy discussion on whether to include a provision to govern the running of the setting-aside period for arbitral awards that are subject to an appeal to a second arbitral tribunal, a concept common in certain commodity arbitrations.[958] Both the Secretariat and the Working Group pointed out that the Model Law should not exclude such arbitral appeals.[959] The Third Draft provided for a setting-aside period beginning on the date of receipt of the decision of that arbitral tribunal.[960] The Working Group later decided to delete this provision because it was thought to be unnecessary.[961]

E. Suspension of setting-aside proceedings for remedial measures, paragraph (4)

14.546 Article 34(4) provides for a concept inspired by the 'remission' known in most common law jurisdictions but unfamiliar to the civilian systems. Consequently, there was considerable discussion on whether or not to provide for this concept. In the end, the view prevailed that it could be a useful mechanism for curing procedural defects without having to set aside the award.[962] The divergent approaches clearly influenced the impact of the provision. In its final form, Art 34(4) states that the court may, upon request of a party and where appropriate, suspend the setting-aside proceedings for a period of time in order to give the

[952] *Egypt*: 90 days, see Art 54 of the Law Concerning Arbitration in Civil and Commercial Matters; *Hungary*: 60 days, see s 55(1) of Act LXXI of 1994 on Arbitration; *Sri Lanka*: 60 days, see s 32(1) of the Arbitration Act 1995.

[953] cf Analytical Commentary, UN Doc A/CN.9/264, Art 34 para 1.

[954] Commission Report, UN Doc A/40/17, para 304.

[955] High Court of Singapore, 8 May 2003, OM no 600027 of 2001, *ABC CO v XYZ CO LTD*, published: (2003) 3 SLR 546, CLOUT Case 566.

[956] Art 34(3) of the First sch of the Arbitration Act 1996.

[957] See Art 48(3), LICA.

[958] See First Secretariat Note, UN Doc A/CN.9/216, para 102.

[959] *ibid*; First Working Group Report, UN Doc A/CN.9/216, para 106; Analytical Commentary, UN Doc A/CN.9/264, Art 34 para 2.

[960] UN Doc A/CN.9/WG.II/WP.46, Art XXX(2).

[961] Fourth Working Group Report, UN Doc A/CN.9/245, para 153.

[962] See Fifth Working Group Report, UN Doc A/CN.9/264, para 139; Analytical Commentary, UN Doc A/CN.9/264, Art 34 para 13.

arbitral tribunal an opportunity to resume the arbitration or to take such other action as will, in the tribunal's opinion, eliminate the grounds for setting aside.

Remission under the Model Law has three basic elements. First, it is formed as an alternative to immediately setting aside the award where appropriate. The drafters could not find a more detailed formula than 'appropriate', which would cover the great variety of cases where remission would either be appropriate or inappropriate.[963] It is thus an issue within the discretion of the court. However, it is certainly inappropriate for a court to ask the arbitral tribunal to correct a defect based on the invalidity of the arbitration agreement or the incapacity of a party.[964] Second, the remission procedure must be requested by a party. Third, the purpose of the remission procedure is to give the arbitral tribunal the opportunity to remove a certain defect that constitutes a ground for setting aside under para (2). Thus, the court cannot invite the arbitral tribunal to correct an error or to deal with a point omitted from the award, as the award may not be set aside on such grounds.[965] By permitting remission the Model Law confirms the continuing mandate of the arbitral tribunal in this regard.[966] During the period of time determined by the court, the arbitral tribunal has the exclusive competence to correct the defect as it finds appropriate.[967] The court will continue with the setting-aside proceedings only if the arbitral tribunal does not take the opportunity to eliminate the grounds for setting aside, or if the court finds that it did not take the appropriate measures.[968] Some Model Law states do not provide for remission.[969] **14.547**

F. Effect of setting aside the award

The final text of the Model Law does not directly address the effect on the arbitration agreement of having an award set aside. The initial draft of what became the remission procedure provided for a re-institution of the arbitral proceedings after the court had set aside the award.[970] The Working Group supported this provision because 'it made clear that the arbitration agreement had not necessarily lapsed'.[971] Later, the remission procedure was altered to a procedure which would take place during a suspension in the setting-aside proceeding. Although the Secretariat later raised the question of the effect of setting aside on the arbitration agreement,[972] neither the Working Group nor the Commission dealt with this issue. *Germany* explicitly states that setting aside the award shall, in the absence of any indication to the contrary, result in the arbitration agreement becoming operative again with respect to the subject matter of the dispute.[973] This represents a reasonable **14.548**

[963] Third Draft, UN Doc A/CN.9/WG.II/WP.46, Art XXX(3), note 17.

[964] Summary Record, UN Doc A/CN.9/SR.319, Art 34 para 2; see also Second Draft, UN Doc A/CN.9/WG.II/WP.42, Art 41(4), note 32.

[965] Davidson *(Scotland)* para 8.36.

[966] Analytical Commentary, UN Doc A/CN.9/264, Art 34 para 14.

[967] But see Sanders (1995) 11 *Arb Int'l* 22: accompanied by the court's opinion as to how the award could be amended or supplemented in order to avoid setting aside.

[968] cf Analytical Commentary, UN Doc A/CN.9/264, Art 34 para 14.

[969] eg *Bulgaria*: Arts 47–8 LICA; *Egypt*: Arts 52–4 of the Law Concerning Arbitration in Civil and Commercial Matters.

[970] Second Draft, UN Doc A/CN.9/WG.II/WP.42, Art 41(4).

[971] Third Working Group Report, UN Doc A/CN.9/233, para 191.

[972] See Fourth Secretariat Note, UN Doc A/CN.9/WG.II/WP.50, paras 24–6.

[973] s 1059(5), ZPO.

solution. *Tunisia* empowers the court which sets aside the award to decide on the merits, if necessary and upon the application of all parties.[974]

Chapter VIII. **Recognition and enforcement of awards**

Special literature: See ch VII.

14.549 Like ch VII, the eighth and final chapter of the Model Law also concerns the post-arbitral phase. While Art 34 addresses the losing party and provides a way for actively attacking the award, Arts 35 and 36 contain rules for recognition and enforcement of the award, which will be requested by the successful party in the arbitration proceedings if the losing party does not comply with his obligations voluntarily. In such a situation—which is fortunately rather rare—there is a need for court assistance. Articles 35 and 36 are lifted, almost verbatim, from the New York Convention, because the drafters wanted to reach as much consistency as possible with the liberal enforcement procedure of this widely accepted convention.

A. Inclusion of provisions on recognition and enforcement

14.550 As there is a convention dealing with recognition and enforcement, the question of whether the Model Law should regulate this matter at all and, if so, whether it should deal with both domestic and foreign awards was raised several times during the drafting process. Obviously, the view prevailed that the regulation of recognition and enforcement for domestic and foreign awards in the Model Law was beneficial. It was felt that the Model Law would be incomplete without provisions on this important issue. As to states which had not acceded to the New York Convention, the hope was expressed that these states might find it easier to adopt the provisions as part of the Model Law rather than to ratify or accede to that convention.[975]

14.551 For states that had acceded to the New York Convention, these provisions would provide a regime for non-convention, eg domestic awards. The concept of uniform treatment of all awards in international commercial arbitration irrespective of the country of origin would reduce the importance of the place of arbitration in international commercial arbitration and therefore promote this kind of dispute settlement.[976]

14.552 It has to be emphasized that the Model Law does not distinguish between foreign and domestic awards, as does the New York Convention. This is a radical approach and a

---

[974] Art 78(5) of the Arbitration Code 1993.

[975] In fact, *Bahrain*, *Canada* and its *Provinces* and *Territories*, *Kenya*, *Lithuania*, *Peru*, *Singapore* and *Zimbabwe* acceded to the New York Convention after the Model Law was recommended by the United Nations. *Iran* and *Oman* enacted the Model Law but are not parties to the New York Convention. It should be noted that approximately 50 countries acceded to the New York Convention after 1985, which is remarkable in view of the total number of parties, now 120 countries.

[976] For details see eg First Working Group Report, UN Doc A/CN.9/216, para 103; Third Working Group Report, UN Doc A/CN.9/233, para 129; Fourth Working Group Report, UN Doc A/CN.9/245, paras 125–33; Fifth Working Group Report, UN Doc A/CN.9/246, paras 142–3; Analytical Compilation of Government Comments, UN Doc A/CN.9/263, paras 1–8; Analytical Commentary, UN Doc A/CN.9/264, Art 34 paras 1–3; Summary Record, UN Doc A/CN.9/SR.320, Art 34 paras 30–57; Commission Report, UN Doc A/40/17, paras 308–10.

great step in international commercial arbitration in view of the fact that this distinction was common ground in bilateral and multilateral agreements as well as in national arbitration laws at the time of drafting the Model Law. However, a number of Model Law states did not adopt this approach. *Bulgaria, California, Connecticut, Hong Kong, India, Iran, Singapore* and *Texas* did not enact ch VIII. In these states the different treatment of domestic and foreign awards remains.

B. Scope of application

In principle, pursuant to Art 35(1) the provisions concerning recognition and enforcement in the Model Law apply to all arbitral awards, irrespective of the country in which they were made, ie to domestic and foreign awards in international commercial arbitration. As the Model Law yields to any treaty in force between the enacting state and any other state or states by virtue of Art 1(1), it does not affect the operation of the New York Convention or other multilateral conventions or bilateral treaties dealing with the enforcement of awards in Model Law states that have acceded to these conventions or ratified these treaties. In this context, it must be stressed that the scope of application of the Model Law is not identical to that of the New York Convention. While the Model Law deals with domestic and foreign awards in international commercial arbitration, the New York Convention concerns foreign awards, whether in international commercial arbitration or in other arbitrations. **14.553**

When a Model Law state accedes to the New York Convention, recognition and enforcement of foreign awards are governed by this convention. If it makes use of the reciprocity reservation provided for in Art I(3) of the New York Convention, ie if it makes the reservation that it will apply the convention only to awards made in the territory of another contracting state, recognition and enforcement of only those foreign awards are governed by the New York Convention. Foreign awards made in the territory of a state which is not party to the New York Convention, however, may be governed by other conventions or treaties when both this state and the Model Law state are parties thereof, such as the Geneva Convention on the Execution of Foreign Arbital Awards of 1927 or the Inter-American Convention on International Commercial Arbitration (Panama Convention) of 1975. Otherwise, these awards are governed by the Model Law. Domestic awards, ie those made within the Model Law state, are governed by Arts 35 and 36 within the scope of application of the Model Law. This concept, which already derives from Art 1(1), is highlighted in s 28 of the *Bermuda* International Conciliation and Arbitration Act 1993, s 59 of the *Malta* Arbitration Act 1996 and s 20 of the *Australia* International Arbitration Act 1974. These provisions are in full alignment with the Model Law.[977] **14.554**

C. Reciprocity

As a substantial number of states have made use of the reciprocity reservation to the New York Convention, it was proposed to include a provision in the Model Law that would allow recognition or enforcement of foreign arbitral awards only on the basis **14.555**

[977] But see Sanders (1995) 11 *Arb Int'l* 24, who erroneously concludes that *Australia* and *Bermuda* omitted ch VIII.

of reciprocity.[978] Both the Working Group and the Commission were of the opinion that the use of territorial links in international commercial arbitration should not be promoted. Furthermore, it was regarded as technically impossible to provide a workable mechanism of reciprocity in a model law that would fit in all legislatures. However, it was noted that each state that wanted to subject the application of the provisions on recognition and enforcement of foreign awards to a requirement of reciprocity could do so, specifying the basis or connecting factor and the technique that it used.[979]

Article 35. Recognition and enforcement

(1) An arbitral award, irrespective of the country in which it was made, shall be recognized as binding and, upon application in writing to the competent court, shall be enforced subject to the provisions of this article and of article 36.

(2) The party relying on an award or applying for its enforcement shall supply the original award or a copy thereof. If the award is not made in an official language of this State, the court may request the party to supply a translation thereof into such language.****

(Article 35(2) has been amended by the Commission at its 39th session, in 2006)

****** The conditions set forth in this paragraph are intended to set maximum standards. Therefore, it would not be contrary to the harmonization able to be achieved by the model law if a State retained even less onerous conditions.**

A. Meaning and purpose

14.556 Article 35 lays down the conditions for recognizing and enforcing awards issued in international commercial arbitration, which tell the party seeking recognition or enforcement how to make out a prima facie case. What type of decision the competent court may render in which procedure is an issue regulated by the domestic law of the enacting state.

14.557 The drafters consciously drew a clear distinction between recognition and enforcement in view of the fact that recognition is not only a step in the enforcement process but may also stand alone.[980] Mere recognition will occur when a successful party invokes the *res judicata* effect of an award in other proceedings. This legal effect obtains automatically without the request of the party.[981]

B. Conditions for recognition or enforcement

(1) Supply of the award, paragraph (2)

14.558 If a party wishes the award to be recognized or enforced, it shall supply the original award or a copy thereof. In addition, if the award is not made in an official language of the enacting state, the court may request the party to supply a translation of it into such language. Article 35(2) sets maximum standards, as is explicitly stated in the footnote. Thus, Model

[978] Analytical Compilation of Government Comments, UN Doc A/CN.9/263, ch VIII paras 9–12 (*Czechoslovakia, Norway, Poland, Soviet Union*).

[979] See Fifth Working Group Report, UN Doc A/CN.9/246, para 144; Commission Report, UN Doc A/40/17, para 330.

[980] Fifth Working Group Report, UN Doc A/CN.9/246, para 146; Analytical Commentary, UN Doc A/CN.9/264, Art 34 para 4.

[981] Fifth Working Group Report, UN Doc A/CN.9/246, para 146.

Law states are free to retain less onerous conditions, which is of particular importance for domestic awards that are treated like domestic court decisions in some states.

The old version of Art 35(2), which was modelled on Art IV of the New York Convention, provided that the party relying on an award or applying for its enforcement should supply the duly authenticated original award or a duly certified copy thereof, as well as the original arbitration agreement or a duly certified copy thereof.[982] The Working Group considered it necessary to ensure that a modified understanding of the writing requirement[983] would be reflected in Art 35(2) through an amendment to that article by deleting the requirement of 'supply of the arbitration agreement or a duly certified copy thereof'.[984] **14.559**

Additionally, the word 'certified' in the first and second sentences of the old version of Art 35(2) was deleted, because inclusion of such a requirement had created, in some cases, uncertainty as to who could undertake the certification and what the certification would consist of.[985] In that respect, the Commission noted that the question of need for certification or similar evidence regarding the authenticity of a text or its translation was a matter that was better left to the general law of evidence or court rules, and to judicial discretion rather than dealt with by way of imposed requirements that could be overly cumbersome and open to differing interpretations.[986] **14.560**

However, the Commission noted that the deletion of the certification requirement should not be read as ruling out the possibility that certification might be required by judges, where appropriate, and in accordance with local law.[987] **14.561**

In relation to the stricter rule of Art IV of the New York Convention, Art 35(2) constitutes the more favourable domestic law. Thus, the application for a declaration of enforceability of an arbitral award is not precluded by the New York Convention, but admissible under Art 35(2).[988] **14.562**

(2) Application in writing

The enforcement procedure is effected only upon application in writing to the competent court. While the setting-aside procedure is conducted before the court specified in Art 6, applications for enforcement have to be addressed to the court designated by the law of the forum state. In *Egypt* and *Oman* enforcement of an arbitral award is not admissible until the period for bringing an action for setting aside expires.[989] **14.563**

---

[982] Commission Report, UN Doc A/61/17, para 171.

[983] See commentary on Art 7 at paras 14.107 *et seq*.

[984] Commission Report, UN Doc A/61/17, para 171; Working Group Report, UN Doc A/CN.9/606, para 22.

[985] Commission Report, UN Doc A/61/17, para 172.

[986] *ibid*.

[987] *ibid*, para 173.

[988] See Highest Regional Court of Bavaria, 4Z Sch 5/00, 11 August 2000, CLOUT Case 401 and Bundesgerichtshof, III ZB 68/02, 25 September 2003, published in German (2003) SchiedsVZ 281 (note by Kröll), published in English: 24 *Ybk Int'l Comm Arb* 767, CLOUT Case 666.

[989] *Egypt*: Art 58(1) of the Law Concerning Arbitration in Civil and Commercial Matters; *Oman*: Art 58(1) of the Law of Arbitration in Civil and Commercial Matters.

(3) No ground for refusal, paragraph (1)

14.564 Recognition and enforcement are subject to Art 36. Therefore, if the court finds that there is a ground for refusing recognition or enforcement it will not recognize or enforce the award.

C. Filing, registration or deposit of awards

14.565 In the Fifth Draft there was a provision that explicitly stipulated that filing, registration or deposit of an award with a court of the country where the award was made was not a pre-condition for its recognition or enforcement in the enacting state.[990] The Commission deleted this provision. It was suggested that this question should be left to each state.[991] As Art 35 in its final form sets out the conditions for recognition and enforcement and does not mention filing, registration or deposit, it should be assumed that under the Model Law these procedures are not required. This assumption is in line with the basic approach of the drafters to align the Model Law with the New York Convention as much as possible. Thus, filing, registration or deposit requirements in the domestic law of the Model Law state does not apply to awards within the scope of the Model Law.[992] *Egypt* and *Oman*, however, require the deposit of the award.[993]

D. Period for enforcement of award

14.566 The Model Law does not state a certain period of time within which an action to enforce an award must be brought. Although the Working Group initially favoured the idea of stating a fixed period of time, it later decided not to include any provision on this point because it was felt that harmonizing the rules already in existence on this subject in the various legal systems would be difficult in view of the differing national policies closely linked to procedural law aspects of states.[994]

E. Recognition as binding

14.567 The Working Group did not adopt a suggestion to clarify that the arbitral award only binds the parties to the respective arbitration; nor did it adopt a proposal to state the exact point of time when an award shall be recognized as binding, which was suggested to be the date of the award.[995] The Secretariat understood that these issues were implicit in the current text.[996] The Commission later discussed the question of the date on which an award becomes binding. As to foreign awards, it was rightly pointed out that it is only consistent with Art 36(1)(a)(v), which refers to the law of the state in which or under the law of which the award was made, that the date on which the award becomes binding is governed by the

[990] Fifth Draft, UN Doc A/CN.9/246 (Annex), Art 35(3).

[991] Summary Record, UN Doc A/CN.9/SR.320, Art 34 para 81 (*India*); Commission Report, UN Doc A/40/17, para 316.

[992] Holtzmann and Neuhaus, 1009 *et seq.*

[993] *Egypt*: Art 47 of the Law Concerning Arbitration in Civil and Commercial Matters; *Oman*: Art 47 of the Law of Arbitration in Civil and Commercial Disputes.

[994] Fourth Working Group Report, UN Doc A/CN.9/245, para 56.

[995] Fifth Working Group Report, UN Doc A/CN.9/246, para 148.

[996] Analytical Commentary, UN Doc A/CN.9/264, Art 35 para 4.

law under which the award was made.[997] As regards awards made in the Model Law state where recognition or enforcement is sought, unfortunately no consensus could be achieved for a concept on when an award becomes binding.[998]

Article 36. Grounds for refusing recognition or enforcement

(1) Recognition or enforcement of an arbitral award, irrespective of the country in which it was made, may be refused only:

(a) at the request of the party against whom it is invoked, if that party furnishes to the competent court where recognition and enforcement is sought proof that:

(i) a party to the arbitration agreement referred to in article 7 was under some incapacity; or the said agreement is not valid under the law to which the parties have subjected it or, failing any indication thereon, under the law of the country where the award was made; or

(ii) the party against whom the award is invoked was not given proper notice of the appointment of an arbitrator or of the arbitral proceedings or was otherwise unable to present his case; or

(iii) the award deals with a dispute not contemplated by or not falling within the terms of the submission to arbitration, or it contains decisions on matters beyond the scope of the submission to arbitration, provided that, if the decisions on matters submitted to arbitration can be separated from those not so submitted, that part of the award which contains decisions on matters submitted to arbitration may be recognized and enforced; or

(iv) the composition of the arbitral tribunal or the arbitral procedure was not in accordance with the agreement of the parties or, failing such agreement, was not in accordance with the law of the country where the arbitration took place; or

(v) the award has not yet become binding on the parties or has been set aside or suspended by a court of the country in which, or under the law of which, that award was made; or

(b) if the court finds that:

(i) the subject-matter of the dispute is not capable of settlement by arbitration under the law of this State; or

(ii) the recognition or enforcement of the award would be contrary to the public policy of this State.

(2) If an application for setting aside or suspension of an award has been made to a court referred to in paragraph (1)(a)(v) of this article, the court where recognition or enforcement is sought may, if it considers it proper, adjourn its decision and may also, on the application of the party claiming recognition or enforcement of the award, order the other party to provide appropriate security.

A. Meaning and purpose

Article 36 contains an exhaustive list of grounds that permit a court to refuse to recognize or enforce an arbitral award in international commercial arbitration. It has to be read in close connection with Art 35, which regulates the conditions for recognition and enforcement. **14.568**

997 Analytical Compilation of Government Comments, UN Doc A/CN.9/263, Art 35 para 2 (*Soviet Union*); Summary Record, UN Doc A/CN.9/SR.320, Art 61 (*Soviet Union*); Commission Report, UN Doc A/40/17, para 313.

998 See commentary on Art 31 at para 14.490.

In its opening sentence Art 36(1) reinforces the basic policy of enforcement under the Model Law, namely that foreign and domestic arbitral awards are treated alike.

14.569 This provision is nearly identical to Arts V and VI of the New York Convention, on which it is closely modelled. The grounds for refusal also found their way into the Model Law as grounds for setting aside under Art 34. As in these corresponding provisions, the distinction between sub-paras (a) and (b) refers to the burden of proof.[999] The grounds listed in sub-para (a) have to be proven by the party against whom the enforcement is sought, whereas the defences mentioned in sub-para (b) do not require such a proof. The party resisting recognition or enforcement is not even required to raise these defences himself (though he would be well advised to draw the court's attention to them), because the court can do so on its own motion.[1000] The selection of the grounds in both sub-paragraphs avoids court review 'on the merits'.[1001]

14.570 The Working Group noted that the opening language 'may be refused' in para (1) was ambiguous in that it might be construed as giving discretion to the court. The prevailing view, however, was that, for the sake of certainty and predictability, the court should not be given such discretion and that that interpretation could be made clear by using the wording 'shall be refused'.[1002] At its next meeting, however, the Working Group rejected this change. Although the Working Group Report offers no explanation, it may be inferred that, in addition to the general desire to align Art 36 with the New York Convention, it was thought preferable to provide some 'flexibility' as regards individual reasons for refusal, such as exclusion of minor, non-material defects of arbitral procedure.[1003] Notwithstanding this legislative history, the High Court of Hong Kong interpreted the term 'may' as discretionary authority of the court. Yet, the Court stated this reasoning only in the alternative: first, it held that there was no ground for refusing enforcement as the defendant had ample opportunity to present its evidence but failed to do so; then the Court added that even if there were such a ground, it was at the Court's discretion to grant enforcement. [1004]

14.571 As the grounds for setting aside, which are nearly similar, are commented on in detail, only differences to Art 34 and to the New York Convention shall be pointed out in the following commentary. When interpreting the grounds it should be kept in mind that the New York

[999] See eg Presidium of the Higher Arbitration Court of the Russian Federation, 22 February 2005, case no 14548/04, published in (2005) *Mezhdunarodnyy kommercheskiy arbitrazh* [*International Commercial Arbitration*] no 3, CLOUT Case 643.

[1000] Huleatt-James, M. and Gould, N., *International Commercial Arbitration* (2nd edn, LLP, 1999) 116; Jan van den Berg, A., *The New York Arbitration Convention of 1958: Towards a Uniform Judicial Interpretation* (Asser/Kluwer, 1981) 389, 391 as to Art V, New York Convention.

[1001] *Société Nationale d'Opérations Pétrolières de la Côte d'Ivoire Holding v Keen Lloyd Resources Ltd*, High Court of the Hong Kong Special Administrative Region, Court of First Instance (Burrell), 20 December 2001, CLOUT Case 530.

[1002] Third Working Group Report, UN Doc A/CN.9/233, Art 36 para 140.

[1003] *ibid*; Summary Record, UN Doc A/CN.9/SR.318, Art 34 para 65; Holtzmann and Neuhaus, 1057 *et seq*.

[1004] *Nanjing Cereals, Oils and Foodstuffs Import & Export Corp v Luckmate Commodities Trading Ltd*, High Court of Hong Kong (Kaplan), 16 December 1994, CLOUT Case 88; see also *Europcar Italia SpA v Alba Tours International Inc*, Ontario Court of Justice, 21 January 1997, CLOUT Case 366, where the Court, in exercising its discretion, considered the balance of convenience to the parties.

Convention only concerns foreign awards, Art 34 only domestic awards and Art 36 both types of awards. Thus, the conflict of laws rules in Art 36 can either refer to the law of a foreign country, which may or may not be a Model Law state, or to the Model Law of 'this state'.[1005]

B. Grounds for refusing recognition or enforcement, paragraph (1)

(1) Incapacity of a party and invalidity of the arbitration agreement, sub-paragraph (a)(i)

As in Art 34, the choice-of-law rule of the New York Convention regarding the incapacity of the party was deleted. The applicable law will be determined by reference to the conflict of laws rules of the place of arbitration.[1006] As regards the invalidity of the arbitration agreement, this provision repeats the choice-of-law rule of the New York Convention. **14.572**

(2) Party unable to present his case, sub-paragraph (a)(ii)

See commentary on Art 34 at para 14.535. **14.573**

(3) Arbitral tribunal exceeding its jurisdiction, sub-paragraph (a)(iii)

For clarity, the Secretariat suggested that the question as to whether the arbitrators had exceeded their authority should be answered by using two standards: the arbitration agreement and the often narrower mandate given to the arbitrators by way of reference, submission or statement of claim.[1007] In order to fully align Art 36 with the New York Convention, the drafters retained the language of this sub-para. However, this proposal gives a useful guideline as to the interpretation of this provision. An example of when a matter does not fall within the arbitration agreement was decided by the Saskatchewan Court of Appeal in *AAMCO Transmissions Inc v Kunz*.[1008] **14.574**

(4) Composition of the arbitral tribunal or arbitral procedure not in accordance with the agreement of the parties or the Model Law, sub-paragraph (a)(iv)

While this sub-para mirrors Art V(1)(d) of the New York Convention, there is a substantial difference to Art 34(2)(a)(iv). An application for setting aside the award shall be refused if the agreement is in conflict with mandatory provisions of the Model Law. There is no such limitation of the party autonomy in enforcement proceedings, either in the New York Convention or in this sub-para. **14.575**

In *China Nanhai Oil Joint Service Corp, Shenzhen Branch v Gee Tai Holdings Co Ltd* the High Court of Hong Kong held that although the composition of the arbitral tribunal was not in accordance with the agreement of the parties, the defendant had waived his right to raise jurisdictional objection. While the arbitration agreement provided for arbitration by the China International Economic and Trade Arbitration Commission (CIETAC), Beijing, the defendant participated in an arbitration by CIETAC, Shenzhen, without clearly reserving his right to later object to the award on the grounds that the arbitral tribunal lacked **14.576**

1005 See Analytical Commentary, UN Doc A/CN.9/264, Art 36 para 4.

1006 See commentary on Art 34 at para 14.532.

1007 Second Draft, UN Doc A/CN.9/WG.II/WP.42, Art 36 note 4.

1008 *AAMCO Transmissions Inc v Kunz*, Saskatchewan Court of Appeal (Vancise, Wakeling and Gerwing), 17 September 1991, published in 97 Saskatchewan Reports 5, CLOUT Case 67.

jurisdiction. The Court further stated that even if the defendant had not waived his right to object, it would still declare the award enforceable because it was satisfied that the defendant basically obtained what he had agreed to: arbitration conducted by three CIETAC arbitrators under CIETAC rules.[1009]

(5) Award not yet binding, set aside or suspended, sub-paragraph (a)(v)

14.577 This sub-para is lifted from Art V(1)(e) of the New York Convention. For obvious reasons, it has no counterpart in Art 34. The term 'binding' has been extensively discussed under the commentaries on Arts 31 and 35 at paras 14.490 and 14.567 respectively.

(6) Subject matter of the dispute not arbitrable or award conflicts with public policy, sub-paragraph (b)

14.578 See commentary on Art 34 at paras 14.539 to 14.543. In *Robert E. Schreter v Gasmac Inc* the Ontario Court of Justice rightly pointed out that the public policy ground should be narrowly defined and should not be used as a means of reopening the merits of the award.[1010] The Court held that a foreign arbitral award is enforceable under the Model Law regardless of its confirmation by court judgment because, first, such a confirmation is not a ground for refusal to enforce the award, and second, that it would be anomalous if the court were precluded from enforcing a confirmed award while retaining the discretion under Art 36(1)(a)(v) to enforce an award that has been set aside in its 'home jurisdiction'. The respondent's argument in this case was that an award which had been confirmed by a court judgment merged into the judgment and therefore only the judgment, and not the arbitral award, could be enforced under the rules for the enforcement of court judgments. In *Murmansk Trawl Fleet v Bimman Realty Inc* the Ontario Court of Justice ordered enforcement in Ontario of a final arbitral award issued in New York, which had not been confirmed under New York law. The court held that it was not necessary to obtain confirmation of a foreign award in the country where it was rendered in order for it to be enforceable in Ontario. The court based this conclusion on a public policy favouring arbitration and disfavouring delays of enforcement.[1011] In another case the same court found that the term 'public policy' refers to the essential morality of the enforcing state; the mere violation of the Canadian Interest Act did not fulfil this requirement.[1012] In *Transport de cargaison (Cargo Carriers) v Industrial Bulk Carriers* the Quebec Court of Appeal held that a ransom may not contradict Canadian public policy. While a bribe is by definition immoral for both the offeror and the receiver and therefore violates public policy, a ransom involves immorality only on the part of the blackmailer. Thus, the other party may successfully seek enforcement of an award that

[1009] *China Nanhai Oil Joint Service Corp Shenzhen Branch v Gee Tai Holdings Co Ltd*, High Court of Hong Kong (Kaplan), 13 July 1994, CLOUT Case 76.

[1010] *Robert E. Schreter v Gasmac Inc*, Ontario Court, General Division (Feldman), 13 February 1992, published in 7 *Ontario Reports* (3 d) 608, commented on by Chukwumerije (1993) 22 *Canadian Business L J* 296, CLOUT Case 30.

[1011] *Murmansk Trawl Fleet v Bimman Realty Inc*, Ontario Court of Justice, General Division (Somers), 19 December 1994, CLOUT Case 117.

[1012] *Arcata Graphics Buffalo Ltd v Movie (Magazine) Corp*, Ontario Court, General Division (Eberle), 12 March 1993, CLOUT Case 37.

provides for reimbursement of the sum paid.[1013] The Russian Federal Arbitration Court found that the failure to apply applicable substantive or procedural legal norms cannot be recognized as a violation of the fundamental principles of Russian law.[1014]

Lack of reasons in a foreign award should not constitute a ground for refusal to enforce the award on grounds of public policy.[1015] An unreasoned domestic award should, however, be unenforceable in view of Art 31(2). In *Navigation Sonomar Inc v Algoma Steamships Ltd.* the Superior Court of Quebec held, with regard to the similar setting-aside ground, that an arbitral award will not be set aside for insufficiency of reasons.[1016] **14.579**

(7) Changes in Model Law states

Hungary only allows refusal to enforce the arbitral award on the grounds of non-arbitrability and conflict with public policy.[1017] *Egypt* and *Oman* also limited the grounds for refusal. Under their respective laws enforcement may only be refused if the award is in conflict with a judgment previously rendered by the Egyptian courts on the subject matter in dispute, if it violates Egyptian public policy or if it was not properly notified to the party against whom it was rendered.[1018] **14.580**

C. Relationship between Articles 34 and 36, paragraph (2)

Article 36(2) is based on Art VI of the New York Convention. It provides for adjournment of the recognition or enforcement proceedings where the defendant has applied for setting aside or suspension of the award to a court in which, or under the law of which, the award was made. The decision about the adjournment lies at the discretion of the enforcement court. If the court adjourns its decision, it may, on the application of the plaintiff, order the defendant to provide appropriate security. **14.581**

Although there are only minor changes in wording, the scope of this provision is wider than that of Art VI of the New York Convention, as it not only covers foreign awards, but also domestic awards. Therefore, the question that arises is about the relationship between Arts 34 and 36. This question is closely connected with the question of 'double control'. If the arbitral proceedings took place in a Model Law state, the losing party can actively attack the award by applying for setting aside the award under Art 34. At the same time, he can rely on the same grounds in recognition and enforcement proceedings initiated by the other party in the same country or elsewhere. Thus, different courts might simultaneously review **14.582**

1013 *Transport de cargaison (Cargo Carriers) v Industrial Bulk Carriers*, Quebec Court of Appeal (Vallerand, Brossard and Dussault), 15 June 1990, published in (1990) *Revue de droit judiciaire* 418, CLOUT Case 185.

1014 Federal Arbitration Court, Northwest District, 20 March 2003, case no A56-34456/02, published in the journal *Mezhdunarodnyy kommercheskiy arbitrazh* [*International Commercial Arbitration*] 2004, no 3, CLOUT Case 639.

1015 See Chukwumerije (1993) 22 *Canadian Business L J* 304.

1016 *Navigation Sonomar Inc v Algoma Steamships Ltd*, Superior Court of Quebec (Gonthier), 16 April 1987, published in Requeils de Jurisprudence du Quebec 1987, 1346, commented on by Tetley (1993) *Lloyd's Maritime and Commercial L Q* 239, CLOUT Case 10.

1017 s 58 of Act LXXI of 1994 on Arbitration.

1018 *Egypt*: Art 58 of the Law Concerning Arbitration in Civil and Commercial Matters; *Oman*: Art 58 of the Law of Arbitration in Civil and Commercial Disputes.

an award on the same grounds. The Working Group agreed that such double control should be avoided not only for the sake of economy and efficiency, but also in order to prevent conflicting decisions.[1019] Two proposals to resolve this problem were discussed, but ultimately not adopted.[1020] The Secretariat was of the opinion that Art 36(2) provided sufficient safeguard against simultaneous proceedings.[1021] As a rule, it seems sensible for a court to postpone the decision on recognition or enforcement until the outcome of the setting-aside or suspension proceedings is known. *Sri Lanka* added that where applications filed in court to enforce an award and to set aside an award are pending, the court shall consolidate the applications.[1022]

III. Appendix

A. Bibliography: General

Alavrez, Henri and Rivkin, David, *Model Law Decisions: Cases applying the UNCITRAL Model Law on International Commercial Arbitration: 1985–2001* (Kluwer, 2003).

Alexander, Nadja, 'The UNCITRAL Model Law on International Commercial Arbitration' (2004) 15 *World Arbitration and Mediation Report* 105.

Aksen, Gerald *et al* (eds), *Liber Amicorum Robert Briner: Global Reflections on International Law, Commerce and Dispute Resolution* (ICC Publishing, 2005).

Béguin, Jacques (ed), *Droit du commerce international* (LexisNexis, Litec, 2005).

van den Berg, Albert J. (ed), *International Council for Commercial Arbitration: International commercial arbitration, important contemporary questions, International Arbitration Conference, London, 12 - 15 May 2002* (Kluwer Law International, 2003).

van den Berg, Albert Jan, 'UNCITRAL Model Law on International Commercial Arbitration: Introductory Note' (1986) XI *YCA* 379.

Berger, Klaus Peter, *International Economic Arbitration* (Kluwer Law and Taxation Publishers, 1993).

Bergsten, Eric E., 'Implementation of the UNCITRAL model law on international commercial arbitration into national legislation' (2003) 10 *Croatian Arb Ybk* 101.

Bianca, C.M. and Bonell, M.J., *Commentary on the International Sales* Law (Giuffrè, 1987).

Binder, Peter, *International Commercial Arbitration in UNCITRAL Model Law Jurisdictions* (Sweet & Maxwell, 2005).

Born, Gary B., *International arbitration and forum selection agreements* (2nd edn, Kluwer Law International, 2006).

Born, Gary B., *International commercial arbitration: commentary and materials* (2nd edn, Transnational Publishers, 2001).

Briner, Robert (ed), *Liber Amicorum Karl-Heinz Böckstiegel: Law of International Business and Dispute Settlement in the 21st Century* (Heymann, 2001).

Broches, Aron, *Commentary on the UNCITRAL Model Law on International Commercial Arbitration* (Kluwer Law and Taxation Publishers, 1990).

[1019] Fourth Working Group Report, UN Doc A/CN.9/245, para 156.

[1020] *ibid* paras 157–8.

[1021] Analytical Commentary, UN Doc A/CN.9/264, Art 36 para 5; see also Analytical Compilation of Government Comments, UN Doc A/CN.9/263 para 1 (*United States*).

[1022] s 35(1) of the Arbitration Act 1995.

Broches, Aron, *The 1985 UNCITRAL Model Law on International Commercial Arbitration: An Exercise in International Legislation, Netherlands Yearbook of International Law*, Volume XVIII (Martin Nijhoff Publishers, 1987) 3.

Calavros, Constantin, *Das UNCITRAL-Modellgesetz über die internationale Handelsschiedsgerichtsbarkeit* (Verlag Ernst und Werner Gieseking, 1988).

Dore, Isaak I., *The UNCITRAL Framework for Arbitration in Contemporary Perspective* (Graham & Trotman Martinus Nijhoff, 1993).

Granzow, Joachim H., *Das UNCITRAL-Modellgesetz über die internationale Handelsschiedsgerichtsbarkeit von 1985* (Verlag V Florentz, 1988).

Griffith, Gavan, 'Insider: UNCITRAL and its model law' (2004) *IAMA national newsletter (Melbourne)* 7.

Hascher, Dominique, 'Arbitrage du commerce international' (2005) *Rép Internat Dalloz.*

Herrmann, Gerold, '13 years experience with the UNCITRAL Model Law on International Commercial Arbitration' in Ana Piaggi and Luis Alejandro Estoup (eds), *Derecho mercantil contemporaneo* (La Ley, 2001).

Herrmann, Gerold, 'The UNCITRAL Arbitration Law: A Good Model of a Model Law' (1998) *Uniform L Rev* 483.

Herrmann, Gerold, 'The UNCITRAL Model Law—its background, salient features and purposes' (1985) *Arb Int'l* 6.

Herrmann, Gerold, 'UNCITRAL adopts Model Law on International Commercial Arbitration' (1986) *Arb Int'l* 2.

Hobér, Kaj, *Essays on international arbitration* (JurisNet LLC, 2006).

Holtzmann, Howard M. and Neuhaus, Joseph E., *A Guide To The UNCITRAL Model Law On International Commercial Arbitration: Legislative History and Commentary* (Kluwer Law and Taxation Publishers, 1989).

Hunter, Martin, 'The UNCITRAL Model Law' (1985) 13 *Int'l Bus Lawyer* 399.

Hußlein-Stich, Gabriele, *Das UNCITRAL-Modellgesetz über die internationale Handelsschiedsgerichtsbarkeit* (C. Heymanns Verlag, 1990).

Jarvin, Sigvard, 'La loi-type de C N U D CI. sur l'arbitrage commercial international' (1986) *Rev arb* 509.

Kavass, Igor and Liivak, Arno (eds), *UNCITRAL Model Law of International Commercial Arbitration: A Documentary History*, vols I–II (William S Hein Company, 1985).

Kerr, Michael, 'Arbitration and the Courts: The UNCITRAL Model Law' (1985) 34 *ICQL* 1.

Lew, Julian *et al*, *Comparative International Commercial Arbitration* (Kluwer, 2003).

Lowenfeld, Andreas F. (ed), *Lowenfeld on international arbitration: collected essays over three decades* (Juris Publishing, 2005).

Merkin, Robert M., *Arbitration Law* (LLP, 2004).

Mistelis, Loukas A (ed), *Pervasive problems in international arbitration* (Kluwer Law International, 2006).

Mourre, Alexis (ed), *Les Cahiers de l'Arbitrage*, vol II (Gazette du Palais, 2002).

Mustill, Lord Justice, 'Contemporary Problems in International Commercial Arbitration: A Response' (1989) 14 *Int'l Bus Lawyer* 161.

Nabil, Antaki and Prujinger, Alain (eds), *Proceedings to the 1st International Commercial Arbitration Conference* (Wilson & Lafleur Itée, 1986) with commentaries by Gerold Herrmann, Jean Thieffry, Laurie Slade, Stephen M. Boyd and Manon Pomerleau.

Newman, Lawrence W. (ed), *The leading arbitrators' guide to international arbitration* (Juris Publishing, 2004).

Okekeifere, Andrew I., 'Public policy and arbitrability under the UNCITRAL model law' (1999) 2 *Int'l Arb L Rev* 70.

Okefeifere, Andrew I., 'The UNCITRAL Model Law and the Problem of Delay in International Commercial Arbitration' (1997) 14 *J Int'l Arb* 127.

Park, William, *Arbitration of International Business Disputes: Studies in Law and Practice* (OUP, 2006).

Paulsson, Jan, 'Report on the UNCITRAL Model Law on International Commercial Arbitration as adopted in Vienna on 21 June 1985' (1986) 52 *Arbitration* 98.

Poudret, Jean-François and Besson, Sébastien, *Comparative law of international arbitration* (2nd edn, Sweet & Maxwell, 2007).

Redfern, Alan and Hunter, Martin, *Law and Practice of International Commercial Arbitration* (4th edn, Sweet & Maxwell, 2004).

Reid, Alan S., 'The UNCITRAL Model Law on International Commercial Arbitration and the English Arbitration Act: Are the Two Systems Poles Apart?' (2004) 21 *J Int'l Arb* 227.

Rubino-Sammartano, Mauro, *International Arbitration Law* (2nd edn, Kluwer, 2001).

Sanders, Pieter, 'Unity and Diversity in the Adoption of the Model Law' (1995) 11 *Arb Int'l* 1.

Sanders, Pieter, *The Work on UNCITRAL on Arbitration and Conciliation*, (Kluwer Law International, 2004).

Sanders, Pieter, 'UNCITRAL's Model Law on International and Commercial Arbitration: Present Situation and Future' (2005) 21 *Arb Int'l* 443.

Sanders, Pieter and van den Berg, Albert Jan (eds), *International Handbook on Commercial Arbitration*, vols I–IV, suppl 27 (Kluwer, 1998).

Sarcevic, Petar (ed), *Essays on International Commercial Arbitration* (Graham & Trotman/Martinus Nijhoff, 1989).

Schwartz, Eric A., 'The ICC Arbitration Rules and the UNCITRAL Model Law' (1993) 9 *Arb Int'l* 231.

Schwebel, Stephen M., *International Arbitration: Three Salient Problems* (Grotius, 1987).

Segesser, Georg von, 'Extract from the "Report of the United Nations Commission on International Trade Law on the work of its thirty-ninth session, 19 June—7 July 2006"—Annex I' (2007) 25 *ASA Bull* no 3.

Shifman, Bette E., 'Developments in the Adoption of the 1985 UNCITRAL Model Law on International Commercial Arbitration' (1990) 1 *Am Rev Int'l Arb* 281.

Smith, Gordon *et al*, 'The UNCITRAL Model Law and the Parties' Chosen Arbitration Rules: Complementary or Mutually Exclusive?' (2002) 6 *Vindobona J of Int'l Commercial L and Arb* 194.

Sorieul, Renaud, 'UNCITRAL's Current Work in the Field of International Commercial Arbitration' (2005) 22 *J Int'l Arb* 543.

Sorieul, Renaud, 'Update on Recent Developments and Future Work by UNCITRAL in the Field of International Commercial Arbitration' (2000) 17 *J Int'l Arb* 163.

Sornarajah, Muthucumaraswamy, 'The UNCITRAL Model Law: A Third World Viewpoint' (1989) 6 *J Int'l Arb* no 4, 7.

Sutton, David St. John *et al*, *Russell on Arbitration* (23rd reviewed edn, Sweet & Maxwell, 2007).

Szász, Iván, 'Introduction to the Model Law of UNCITRAL on International Commercial Arbitration', in Pieter Sanders (ed), *UNCITRAL's Project for a Model Law on International Commercial Arbitration, Interim meeting, Lausanne, 9–12 May 1984* (ICCA Congress Series no 2, 1984, 31).

UNCITRAL Working Group on arbitration proposes reforms to model law (2006) 17 World Arbitration and Mediation Report 178.

UNCITRAL Secretariat, *Explanatory Note by the UNCITRAL Secretariat on the Model Law on International Commercial Arbitration.*

Wetter, Gilles J., 'The Internationalization of International Arbitration: Looking Ahead to the Next Ten Years' in Albert Jan van den Berg (ed), *Planning Efficient Arbitration Proceedings: The Law Applicable in International Arbitration* (XIIth International Arbitration Congress, Vienna, 3–6 November 1994, ICCA Congress Series no 7, Kluwer Law International, 1996).

B. Bibliography: Model Law states

Australia:

Andrew, Romauld, 'The Ill-Favoured Child of Litigation: International Commercial Arbitration and the Australian Trade Practices Act 1974' (2004) 21 *J Int'l Arb* 239.

Baron, Adrian, 'The Australian International Arbitration Act, the Fiction of Severability and Claims for Restitution' (2000) 16 *Arb Int'l* 159.

Barrett-White, Stephen and Kee, Christopher, 'Enforcement of Arbitral Awards where the Seat of the Arbitration is Australia: How the Eisenwerk Decision Might Still be a Sleeping Assassin' (2007) 24 *J Int'l Arb* 515.

Bonnell, Max, 'The Trade Practices Act: Australia's International Arbitration Headache' (2007) 10 *Int'l Arb L Rev* no 5.

Morrison, James, 'Defining the Scope of Arbitrable Disputes in Australia: Towards a "Liberal" Approach?' (2005) 22 *J Int'l Arb* 569.

Morrison, James, 'Drawing a Line in the Sand: Defining the Scope of Arbitrable Disputes in Australia' (2005) 22 *J Int'l Arb* 395.

Pryles, Michael, 'Overview of international arbitration in Australia' (2006) 25 *The Arbitrator and Mediator* 51.

Secomb, Matthew, 'Shades of Delocalisation, Diversity in the Adoption of the UNCITRAL Model Law in Australia, Hong Kong and Singapore' (2000) 17 *J Int'l Arb* 123.

Austria: see country report.

Bangladesh:

Maniruzzaman, Abdul F., 'Bangladesh Embraces the UNCITRAL Model Law on Arbitration: But Not Quite!' (2004) 19 *Mealey's Int'l Arb Rep* 61.

Maniruzzaman, Abdul F., 'International Commercial Arbitration in Bangladesh: The New Law' (2004) 70 *Arbitration* 131.

Maniruzzaman, Abdul F., 'The New Law of International Commercial Arbitration in Bangladesh: A Comparative Perspective' (2003) 14 *Am Rev Int'l Arb* 139.

Maniruzzaman, Abdul F., 'The Bangladesh Arbitration Act 2001: Some reflections' (2005) *Asian Dis Rev* 73.

Belarus:

Shelkoplyas, Natalya, 'The Belarusian Law on International Arbitration Court: The Spirit or the Letter of the Model Law?' (2000) 17 *J Int'l Arb* 155.

Bermuda:

Bermuda, (1994) XIX *YCA* 447.

Narinder, K. *et al*, 'Bermuda', in *Int'l Handbook on Comm Arb* Suppl 18 September 1994.

Rawding, Nigel, 'ADR: Bermuda's International Conciliation and Arbitration Act 1993' (1994) 10 *Arb Int'l* 99.

Bulgaria:

Gueorguiev, Emile, 'La loi bulgare sur l'arbitrage commercial international' (1996) *Rev arb* 39.

Pechota, Vratislav, 'A New Law on International Commercial Arbitration in Bulgaria' (1990) 1 *Am Rev Int'l Arb* 310.

Staikov, Sevdalin, 'International Commercial Arbitration in Bulgaria' in *International Commercial Arbitration in Europe*: *Special Supplement*, (1994) *ICC ICArb Bull* 76.

Stalev, Zhivko, 'Bulgaria', in *Int'l Handbook on Comm Arb* Suppl 19 August 1995.

Stalev, Zhivko, 'Bulgaria' (1994) XIX *YCA* 449.

Stalev, Zhivko, 'Das neue bulgarische Gesetz über die internationale Handelsschiedsgerichtsbarkeit' (1988) 2 *JPS* 208.

Canada: Federal State, Provinces and Territories:

Barin, Babak *et al*, *The Osler guide to commercial arbitration in Canada* (Kluwer Law International, 2006).

Boivin, Richard, 'International Arbitration in Canada' (2003) 20 *J Int'l Arb* 507.

Casey, Brian J., *Arbitration law of Canada: practice and procedure* (Juris Publishing, 2005).

Chibueze, Remigius O., 'The Adoption and Application of the Model Law in Canada Post-Arbitration Challenge' (2001) 18 *J Int'l Arb* 191.

Finn, Annie and Thomson, Claude, 'International Commercial Arbitration: A Canadian Perspective' (2002) 18 *LCIA Arb Int'l* 205 (<http://www.fasken.com/publications/ detail.aspx?publication=2012>).

Kyle, Rodney C., 'Some Analytical Jurisprudence on Canadian Arbitration Law' (2000) 55 *Disp Res J* 24.

Chile:

Biggs, Gonzalo, 'Breakthrough for International Commercial Arbitration in Chile' (2004) 59 *Disp Res J* 65 (<http://findarticles.com/p/articles/mi_qa3923/is_200402/ ai_n9392190>).

Conejero Roos, Christián, 'The New Chilean Arbitration Law and the Influence of the Model Law' (2005) 22 *J Int'l Arb* 149.

Jiménez, Figueres *et al*, 'Notes on the new Chilean law on international arbitration' (2005) 20 *Mealey's Int'l Arb Rep* 21.

Källman, Eva, 'Internationale Handelsschiedsgerichtsbarkeit in Chile' (2006) 6 *Internationales Handelsrecht* 137.

Croatia:

Kresimir, Sajko, *Das kroatische Recht der Internationalen Schiedsgerichtsbarkeit* (Miscelanea, 2005).

Kresimir Sajko, 'New Croation 2001 Arbitration Law: General Analysis and Some Open Issues' in H P Mansel (ed), *Festschrift für Erik Jayne* (vol 1, 2004).

Triva, Siniša, 'Croatian Law on Arbitration' (2002) 9 *Croatian Arb Ybk* 107.

Uzelac, Alan, 'Current Developments in the Field of Arbitration in Croatia' (2002) 19 *J Int'l Arb* 73.

Uzelac, Alan, 'Written form of the arbitration agreement towards a revision of the UNCITRAL Model Law' (2005) 12 *Croatian Arb Ybk* 111.

Cyprus:

Triantafyllides, Antis, 'Cypriot judgment Ioannou and Paraskevaides of Nicosia, Cyprus v Biwetes Europe Ltd. of Nicosia "is in line" with intent of UNCITRAL Model Law draftsmen' (2002) 17 *Mealey's Int'l Arb Rep* 14.

Denmark:

Jorgensen, Jacob C and Terkildsen, Dan, 'The New Danish Arbitration Act' (2005) 8 *Int'l Arb L Rev* 203.

Lookofsky, Joseph and Kristoffersen, Karsten, 'The new Danish Arbitration Act' (2006) *Stockholm Int'l Arb Rev* 43.

López-Rodríguez, Ana M., 'New Arbitration Acts in Denmark and Spain. The Application of Transnational Rules to the Merits of the Dispute' (2006) 23 *J Int'l Arb* 125.

Meurs-Gerken, P.R., 'Distinctive features of the new Danish arbitration act' (2005) 16 *ICC ICArb Bull* 47.

Egypt:

Aboul-Enein, M.I.M., 'Reflections on the New Egyptian Law on Arbitration' (1995) 11 *Arb Int'l* no 1, 75.

El-Ahdab, Abdul Hamid, 'The New Egyptian Arbitration Act in Civil and Commercial Matters' (1995) 12 *J Int'l Arb* no 2, 65.

El-Ahdab, Abdul Hamid, 'Arab North Africa (Algeria, Egypt, Libya, Morocco and Tunisia)' in Eugene Cotran and Austin N.E. Amissah (eds), *Arbitration in Africa* (Kluwer Law International, 1996).

Riad, Tarek F., 'Arbitration and the Legal Business Environment in Egypt' (2000) 17 *J Int'l Arb* 169.

Estonia:

Lezheiko, Kirill, 'Comparative analysis of the new Estonian arbitration law provisions on the choice of law applicable to the international commercial arbitration dispute' (2005) *Stockholm Int'l Arb Rev* 15.

Põldvere, Pirkka-Marja, 'Estonia has taken a new step in (international) commercial arbitration' (2005) *Stockholm Int'l Arb Rev* 1.

Germany: See country report.

Greece:

Kerameus, Konstantinos D., 'The new Greek law on international commercial arbitration' (1999) 52 *Revue hellénique de droit international* 583.

Koussoulis, Stelios, 'Greek arbitration law: Introduction' (2005) 5 *Model Law Materials* 85.

Guatemala:

Ibargüen, Marcos S., 'Arbitration in Guatemala' in *International Commercial Arbitration in Latin America: Special Supplement* (1997) *ICC ICArb Bull.*

'Recent Developments in Arbitration Law and Practice: Introduction' (1997) XXII *YCA* 569.

Hong Kong:

Fitzgerald, Darren, 'Arbitration in Hong Kong after the handover' (2000) 3 *Int'l Arb L Rev* 122.

Fitzgerald, Darren and Polkinghorne, Michael, 'Notes and Current Developments: Arbitration in Southeast Asia: Hong Kong, Singapore and Thailand Compared' (2001) 18 *J Int'l Arb* 101.

O'Hare, Judith, 'Arbitration and Alternative Dispute Resolution: A Hong Kong Perspective' (1996) 7 *Am Rev Int'l Arb* 1.

Kaplan, Neil, 'An update on Hong Kong's arbitration law' in *International Commercial Arbitration in Asia: Special Supplement* (1998) *ICC ICArb Bull* 11.

Ma, Geoffrey and Kaplan, Neil (eds), *Arbitration in Hong Kong: A Practical Guide* (Sweet and Maxwell, Asia, 2003).

Morgan, Robert, 'International Arbitration in Hong Kong' in Peter Gottwald (ed), *Internationale Schiedsgerichtsbarkeit: Generalbericht und Nationalberichte: Arbitrage International: International Arbitration* (Gieseking-Verlag, 1997).

Moser, Michael J. and Cheng, Teresa Y., *Hong Kong Arbitration: A User's Guide* (Kluwer Law International, 2004).

Neoh, Anthony, 'The relationship between Hong Kong and the PRC in arbitration-related matters: The Hong Kong perspective' in *International Commercial Arbitration in Asia: Special Supplement* (1998) *ICC ICArb Bull* 18.

Niu, Jill *et al*, 'Arbitration in Greater China: Hong Kong, Macau and Taiwan' (2007) 24 *J Int'l Arb* 651.

Wang, Sheng Chang, 'Practical differences in arbitration procedures in China and Hong Kong: An overview' in *International Commercial Arbitration in Asia: Special Supplement* (1998) *ICC ICC ICArb Bull* 76.

Yang, Philip, 'Practical differences in arbitration procedures in China and Hong Kong: costs and interest' in *International Commercial Arbitration in Asia: Special Supplement* (1998) *ICC ICArb Bull* 83.

Hungary:

Engelhardt, Hanns, 'New Regulations Concerning Arbitration in Hungary' (1995) 6 *Am Rev Int'l Arb* 375.

Horváth, Eva, 'The Practical Application of the Hungarian Arbitration Act' (2001) 18 *J Int'l Arb* 371.

Pikó, Rita, *Schiedsgerichtsbarkeit in Ungarn* (Verlag Recht und Wirtschaft. 1998).

India:

Bansal, A.K., 'International Arbitration in India' (1995) 6 *Am Rev Int'l Arb* 191.

Bokka, S.R., 'Comments on Indian arbitration law' (2006) 17 *World Arbitration and Mediation Report* 301.

Dewan, Nakul, 'Arbitration in India: An Unenjoyable Litigating Jamboree!' (2007) 3 *Asian Int'l Arb J* 99.

Hilmer, Sarah E., 'Has arbitration failed India or has India failed arbitration?' (2007) 10 *Int'l Arb L Rev* 33.

Jambholkar, Lakshmi, 'International Commercial Arbitration. Recent Developments in Indian Law' (2002) 19 *J Int'l Arb* 601.

Kachwaha, Sumeet, 'The Arbitration Law of India: A Critical Analysis' (2005) 1 *Asian Int'l Arb J* 105.

Kachwaha, Sumeet, 'The Indian Arbitration Law: Towards a New Jurisprudence' (2007) 10 *Int'l Arb L Rev* 13.

Kawatra, G.K. and Khurana, S.L., 'Indian Arbitration Law—Existing and Proposed' (1995) 12 *J Int'l Arb* no 3, 5.

Krishan, Devashish and Singh, Pratibha, 'The Indian 1996 Arbitration Act: Solutions for a Current Dilemma' (2001) 18 *J Int'l Arb* 41.

Nair, Promod, 'Surveying a Decade of the "New" Law of Arbitration In India' (2007) 23 *Arb Int'l* 699.

Raghavan, Vikram, 'New Horizons for Alternative Dispute Resolution in India, The New Arbitration Law of 1996' (1996) 13 *J Int'l Arb* no 4, 5.

Ramaswamy, P., 'Enforcement of Annulled Awards An Indian Perspective' (2002) 19 *J Int'l Arb* 461.

Iran:

Entezari, Shirin, 'Iran Adopts International Commercial Arbitration Law' (1998) 13 *Int'l Arb Rep* 15.

Entezari, Shirin O., 'Iranian Arbitration Proceedings' (1997) 14 *J Int'l Arb* no 4, 53.

Gharavi, Hamid G., 'Le nouveau droit iranien de l'arbitrage commercial international' (1999) *Rev arb* 35.

Gharavi, Hamid G., 'The 1997 Iranian International Commercial Arbitration Law: The UNCITRAL Model Law à L'iranienne' (1999) 15 *Arb Int'l* 85.

Jafarian, Mansour and Rezaeian, Mehrdad, 'The New Law on International Commercial Arbitration in Iran' (1998) 15 *J Int'l Arb* no 3, 31.

Khalilian, Sayyed K., 'A survey of the Iranian legislation on international commercial arbitration' (2001) 16 *Mealey's Int'l Arb Rep* 46.

Khatib-Shahidi, Sassan D., 'Neue Entwicklungen im iranischen Recht der Handelsschiedsgerichtsbarkeit und der Firmenniederlassung' (1998) *RIW* 265.

Krishan, Ranbir, 'Appointment of an arbitrator in arbitration proceedings under the Indian arbitration and conciliation act 1996' (2001) *Int'l Arb L Rev* 90.

Mashkour, Moshkan, 'Building a Friendly Environment for International Arbitration in Iran' (2000) 17 *J Int'l Arb* 79.

Monney, Pierre R., 'Iranian Legislation and International arbitration' (2001) *Int'l Bus Lawyer* 448.

Seifi, Jamal, 'The New International Commercial Arbitration Act of Iran—Towards Harmony with the UNCITRAL Model Law' (1998) 15 *J Int'l Arb* No 2, 5.

Ireland:

Anglade, Leila, 'Ireland as a place for international arbitration' (2001) 12 *Am Rev Int'l Arb* 263.

Bunni, Neal G., 'Ireland's Arbitration (International Commercial) Act' (1999) *Int'l Business L J* 482.

Gaffne, John P. and Fry, William, 'Ireland's International Commercial Arbitration Act' (2000) 15 *Mealey's Int'l Arb Rep*.

'Ireland: The Arbitration (International Commercial) Act 1998' (2000) 4 *Model Arbitration L Q Rep* 149.

Koch, Christopher, 'The New Irish Arbitration Act of 1998' (1999) 17 *ASA Bull* 51.

Reichert, Klaus, 'Current Development: Ireland's New International Commercial Arbitration Law' (2000) 11 *Am Rev Int'l Arb* 379.

Reichert, Klaus, 'Ireland's new international commercial arbitration law' (2001) 4 *Int'l Arb L Rev* 202.

Reichhart, Klaus, 'What You Need To Know About International Arbitration Law And Ireland' (2006) 21 *Mealey's Int'l Arb Rep* 15.

Japan:

Eastman, Richard A., 'New Law, New Changes: An Update On the Japanese Arbitration And ADR Scene' <http://www.metrocorpcounsel.com/pdf/2004/August/04.pdf>.

Iwasaki, Kazuo, 'Key Features of New Japanese Arbitration Law' (2006) 2 *Asian Int'l Arb J* 76.

Livdahl, David A., 'Cultural and Structural Aspects of International Commercial Arbitration in Japan' (2003) 20 *J Int'l Arb* 375.

Masaaki, Kondo *et al*, *Arbitration law of Japan* (Shojihomu, 2004).

Matsumoto, Toshio, 'Recent developments in arbitration in Japan' (2004) 48 *JSE* Bull 1.

Nakamura, Tatsuya, 'Continuing Misconceptions of International Commercial Arbitration in Japan' (2001) 18 *J Int'l Arb* 641.

Nakamura, Tatsuya, 'Japan's new arbitration law and the JCAA new arbitration rules from the perspective of international commercial arbitration: Can Japan become an arbitration center in Asia?' (2006) 21 *Mealey's Int'l Arb Rep* 25.

Nakamura, Tatsuya, 'Salient features of the new Japanese arbitration law based upon the UNCITRAL model law on international commercial arbitration' (2004) 17 *JCAA* newsletter 1.

Nishikawa, Rieko, 'Arbitration Law Reform in Japan' (2004) 21 *J Int'l Arb* 303.

Oda, Hiroshi, 'Arbitration reform in Japan' (2003) 15 *ICC ICArb Bull* 23.

Roughton, Dominic, 'A Brief Review of the Japanese Arbitration Law' (2005) 1 *Asian Int'l Arb J* 127.

Sato, Yasunobu, 'The New Arbitration Law in Japan: Will It Cause Changes in Japanese Conciliatory Arbitration Practices?' (2005) 22 *J Int'l Arb* 141.

Tateishi, Takao, 'Recent Japanese Case Law in Relation to International Arbitration' (2000) 17 *J Int'l Arb* 63.

Thirgood, Russell, 'A Critique of Foreign Arbitration in Japan' (2001) 18 *J Int'l Arb* 177.

Kenya:

Couldrey, J., 'Kenya' in Eugene Cotran and Amissah Austin (eds), *Arbitration in Africa* (Kluwer Law International, 1996).

Lithuania:

Mikelenas, Valentinas, 'Unification and harmonisation of law at the turn of the millennium: The Lithuanian experience' (2000) 5 *Uniform L Rev* 243.

Ryssdal, Anders, 'Interim and Conservatory Measures: Theory, Strategies and a Practical Experience in Lithuania' (2001) *Stockholm Arb Rep* 25.

Macau:

Fockenrath, Holger, 'Das internationale Schiedsverfahren in Handelssachen in Macau und der Volksrepublik China' in Erik Jayme and Christian Schindler (eds), *Rechtsentwicklungen in Portugal, Brasilien und Macau* (Nomos, 2002).

Niu, Jill *et al*, 'Arbitration in Greater China: Hong Kong, Macau and Taiwan' (2007) 24 *J Int'l* Arb 651.

Madagascar:

Ranjeva, Hery, 'Le régime de l'arbitrage international à Madagascar' (2000) *Journal du droit international* 709.

Malaysia:

Davidson, William S. and Rajoo, Sundra, 'The Malaysian Arbitration Act 2005 and the UNCITRAL Model Law' (2006) *Asian Dis Rev* 80.

Davidson, William S. and Rajoo, Sundra, 'The new Malaysian Arbitration Act 2005' (2006) 72 *Arbitration* 257.

Malta:

Carlevaris, Andrea, 'Arbitration in Malta: Current Developments' (2002) 19 *J Int'l Arb* 27.

'Recent Developments in Arbitration Law and Practice: Introduction' (1997) XVII *YCA* 569.

Mexico:

Cook, Jeanne M., 'International Arbitration in the Latin American Context: A Comparative Look At Arbitration in Mexico and the United States' (1999) 3 *The Vindobona J of Int'l Commercial L and Arb* 41.

González de Cossío, Francisco, 'Chauvinism Rejected: Mexican Supreme Court Upholds the Constitutionality of the Mexican Arbitration Statute' (2005) 22 *J Int'l Arb* 163.

New Zealand:

Burnard, Robert, 'The New Zealand Law Commission's Report on the UNCITRAL Model Law' (1992) 8 *Arb Int'l* no 3, 281.

Holt, Saul, 'The Arbitration Act 1996' (1997) 8 *Auckland Univ L Rev* 611.

Keene, Brian, 'The Arbitration Act 1996' (1997) *New Zealand L J* 17.

Kennedy-Grant, Tómas, 'New Zealand', *Int'l Handbook on Comm Arb* Suppl 25 January 1998.

Kennedy-Grant, Tómas, 'New Zealand' (1997) XXII *YCA* 575.

Richardson, Megan, 'Arbitration Law Reform: The New Zealand Experience' (1996) 12 *Arb Int'l* no 1, 57.

Williams, David and Lindsay, Lauren, 'Recent Developments in Arbitration in New Zealand' (2006) 9 *Int'l Arb L Rev* 134.

Williams, David, 'New Zealand: The New Arbitration Act: Adoption of the Model Law with additions' (1998) 1 *Int'l Arb L Rev* 214.

Nigeria, Federal Republic of:

Adaralegbe, Adebayo, 'Limitation Period for the Enforcement of Arbitral Awards in Nigeria' (2006) 22 *Arb Int'l* no 4, 613.

Ajibola, Bola, 'Nigeria' in Eugene Cotran and Austin Amissah (eds), *Arbitration in Africa* (Kluwer Law International, 1996) 91.

Asouzu, Amazu A., 'Arbitration and Judicial Powers in Nigeria' (2001) 18 *J Int'l Arb* 617.

Asouzu, Amazu A., 'The UN, the UNCITRAL Model Arbitration Law and the Lex Arbitri of Nigeria' (2000) 17 *J Int'l Arb* 85.

Atanda, Edward, 'The Nigerian Arbitration and Conciliation Decree of 1988' (1991) 1 *Am Rev Int'l Arb* 452.

Chukwuemerie, Andrew, 'Salient issues in the law and practice of arbitration in Nigeria' (2006) 14 *African journal of international and comparative law/Revue africaine de droit international et compare* 1.

Idornigie, Paul Obo, 'The 1988 Nigerian Arbitration and Conciliation Act; need for review?' (2003) 6 *Int'l Arb L Rev* 49.

Idornigie, Paul, 'The Principle of Arbitrability in Nigeria Revisited' (2004) 21 *J Int'l Arb* 279.

Idornigie, Paul Obo, 'The Relationship Between Arbitral and Court Proceedings in Nigeria' (2002) 19 *J Int'l Arb* 443.

Ikeyi, Nduka, 'When can a Nigerian Court Grant an Injunction in Aid of (International) Arbitration?' (2005) 8 *Int'l Arb L Rev* 78.

Okekeifere, Andrew I., 'International Commercial Arbitration and the UNCITRAL Model Law Under Written Federal Constitutions: Necessity Versus Constitutionality in the Nigerian Legal Framework' (1999) 16 *J Int'l Arb* 49.

Peru:

López, Carlos A.M., 'The Arbitration Agreement in Peruvian Law' (2004) 7 *Int'l Arb L Rev* 196.

Montoya Alberti, Ulises, 'Arbitration in Peru' in *International Commercial Arbitration in Latin America: Special Supplement* (1997) *ICC ICArb Bull* 74.

Simon, Adrian and Rooney, J.H., 'The Law and Practice of International Arbitration in Peru' (1999) 10 *World Arbitration and Mediation Report* 48.

The Philippines:

Foster, David, 'Umbrella Clauses: A Retreat from the Philippines?' (2006) 9 *Int'l Arb L Rev* 100.

Lizares, Eduardo P., 'Arbitration in the Philippines and the Alternative Dispute Resolution Act of 2004' (2005) 1 *Asian Int'l Arb J* 102.

Lizares, Eduardo P., *Arbitration in the Philippines and the Alternative Dispute Resolution Act of 2004* (EPL Publications, 2004).

Poland:

Brockhuis, Jörn and Wildenauer, Eva-Maria, 'Schiedsgerichtsbarkeit in Polen' (2006) 4 *Eastlex* 70.

Kakolecki, Andrzej and Nowaczyk, Piotr, 'Poland's new arbitration legislation' (2005) 16 *ICC ICArb Bull* 41.

Rajski, Lerzy, 'The New Polish Arbitration Law of 2005' (2006) *Int'l Bus L J* 351.

Szurski, Tadeusz, 'Introducing the UNCITRAL Model Law to Poland: Some Remarks on the Polish Law on International Commercial Arbitration' (2001) 18 *J Int'l Arb* 227.

Russian Federation:

Karabelnikov, Boris, 'The Supreme Arbitrazh Court of the Russian Federation does not trust international arbitration' (2006) 72 *Arbitration* 130.

Komarov, Alexander S., 'Russian Federation legislation on international commercial arbitration' in *International Commercial Arbitration in Europe—Special Supplement* (1994) *ICC ICArb Bull* 117.

Märkl, Petra, *Schiedsgerichtsbarkeit in Rußland: Internationale und nationale Schiedsgerichtsbarkeit in der Russischen Föderation und Fragen des anwendbaren Rechts)* (Verlag Recht und Wirtschaft, 1998).

Spiegelberger, William R., 'The Enforcement of Foreign Arbitral Awards in Russia: An Analysis of the Relevant Treaties, Laws, and Cases' 16 *Am Rev Int'l Arb* 261.

Tapola, Diana, 'Enforcement of Foreign Arbitral Awards: Application of the Public Policy Rule in Russia' (2006) 22 *Arb Int'l* 151.

Verschinin, Alexander, 'Internationale Handelsschiedsgerichtsbarkeit in Rußland' in Peter Gottwald (ed), *Internationale Schiedsgerichtsbarkeit: Generalbericht und Nationalberichte—Arbitrage International—International Arbitration* (Gieseking-Verlag, 1997) 759.

Yakovlev, Andrei, 'International Commercial Arbitration Proceedings and Russian Courts' (1996) 13 *J Int'l Arb* 37.

Yoshida, Ikko, 'Intepretation of Separability of an Arbitration Agreement and its Practical Effects on Rules of Conflict of Laws in Arbitration in Russia' (2003) 19 *Arb Int'l* 95.

Scotland:

Davidson, Fraser P., *International Commercial Arbitration—Scotland and the UNCITRAL Model Law* (Sweet & Maxwell, 1991).

Lord Dervaird, 'Scotland and the UNCITRAL Model Law: The Report to the Lord Advocate of the Scottish Advisory Committee on Arbitration Law' (1990) 6 *Arb Int'l* 63.

Lord Dervaird *et al*, 'Arbitration in Scotland: A New Era Dawns' (2004) 70 *Arbitration* 115.

Goodman, Ronald E.M., 'UNCITRAL Model Law on International Commercial Arbitration: Divergent Approaches in England and Scotland: A Question of Appeal?' (1990) *International Business Lawyer* 251.

Singapore:

Boo, Lawrence, 'Singapore' in *Int'l Handbook on Comm Arb Suppl* 21 August 1996.

Dang, Minh and Murugaiyan, Siva, 'Singapore court confuses over arbitration' (2001) *Int'l Financial L Rev* 87.

Duthie, Leigh *et al*, 'International Arbitration in Singapore Opting out of the UNCITRAL Model Law' (2002) 19 *J Int'l Arb* 39.

Fitzgerald, Darren and Polkinghorne, Michael, 'Notes and Current Developments, Arbitration in Southeast Asia: Hong Kong, Singapore and Thailand Compared' (2001) 18 *J Int'l Arb* 101.

Hsu, Locknie, 'Orders for security for costs and international arbitrations in Singapore' (2000) *Int'l Arb L Rev* 108.

Hwang, Michael, 'The state of international commercial arbitration in Singapore' in *International Commercial Arbitration in Asia—Special Supplement* (1998) *ICC ICArb Bull* 41.

Lee Suet Lin, Joyce, 'Much Ado about Errors: The Singapore Perspective' (1998) 15 *J Int'l Arb* 95.

Pillay, Mohan R., 'The Singapore Arbitration Regime and the UNCITRAL Model Law' (2004) 20 *Arb Int'l* 355.

Pillay, Mohan R., 'The Singapore arbitration regime 2002: then, now and why' (2003) *Int'l Construction L Rev* 91.

Secomb, Matthew, 'Shades of Delocalisation, Diversity in the Adoption of the UNCITRAL Model Law in Australia, Hong Kong and Singapore' (2000) 17 *J Int'l Arb* 123.

Tabalujan, Benny S., 'Singapore's Adoption of the UNCITRAL Model Law on International Commercial Arbitration' (1995) 12 *J Int'l Arb* 51.

Spain:

Cairns, David and Stampa, Gonzalo, 'Arbitration law in Spain: taking-off... at last?' (2001) 3 *Int'l Arb L Rev* 84.

Cairns, David and Ortiz, Alejandro López, 'Spain's New Arbitration Act' (2004) 22 *ASA Bull* 695.

Cairns, David, 'The Spanish Application of the UNCITRAL Model Law on International Commercial Arbitration' (2006) 22 *Arb Int'l* 573.

Fröhlingsdorf, Josef, 'Neue Entwicklungen im spanischen Schiedsverfahrensrecht' (2001) *Betriebsberater, Beilage* 6, 2.

Fröhlingsdorf, Josef, 'Spaniens Reform der Schiedsgerichtsbarkeit' (2004) 50 *RIW* 352.

Hamilton, Calvin and Vázquez, Eva M., 'Spain: An Emerging Seat For International Arbitration' (2004) 19 *Mealey's Int'l Arb Rep* no 10.

Hamilton, Calvin A. and Vázquez, Eva M., 'Interim measures and the new Spanish arbitration act' (2005) 20 *Mealey's Int'l Arb Rep* 22.

Herrera, Christian Petrus, 'Spanish Perspectives on the Doctrines of Kompetenz-Kompetenz and Separability: A Comparative Analysis of Spain's 1988 Arbitration Act' (2000) 11 *Am Rev Int'l Arb* 397.

Krasselt-Priemer, Thomas, 'Neuregelung des spanischen Schiedsverfahrensrechts' (2005) *IPRax* 164.

Krishan, Ranbir, 'An Overview of the Arbitration and Conciliation Act 1996' (2004) 21 *J Int'l Arb* 263.

López-Rodríguez, Ana M., 'New Arbitration Acts in Denmark and Spain: The Application of Transnational Rules to the Merits of the Dispute' (2006) 23 *J Int'l Arb* 125.

Mantilla-Serrano, Fernando, 'La nouvelle loi espagnole du 23 decembre 2003 sur l'arbitrage' (2004) *Revarb* 225.

Mantilla-Serrano, Fernando, 'The New Spanish Arbitration Act' (2004) 21 *J Int'l Arb* 367.

Mendez, Francisco R., 'International Arbitration in the new Spanish Arbitration Act' (2004) 7 *Int'l Arb L Rev* 165.

Nadal, Elisabeth de, 'The New Spanish Arbitration Act: An Overview' (2004) 19 *Mealey's Int'l Arb Rep* 42.
Nadal, Elisabeth de, 'The New Spanish Arbitration Act: An Overview (Arbitration Act 60/2003 of December 23, 2003)' (2004) 19 *Mealey's Int'l Arb Rep* no 4.
Obe, Ramon Mullerat, 'Spain Joins the Model Law' (2004) 20 *Arb Int'l* 139.
Stampa, Gonzalo and Cairns, David J.A., 'New Trends in Spanish Arbitration' (2004) 59 *Disp Res J* 62.
Stampa, Gonzalo, 'The 2003 Spanish Arbitration Act' (2004) 22 *ASA Bull* 671.
Tévar, Nicolás Zambrana, 'Das neue spanische Schlichtungsgesetz' (2005) *Zeitschrift für Rechtsvergleichung, Internationales Privatrecht und Europarecht* 225.

Sri Lanka:
Asouzu, Amazu and Raghavan, Vikram, 'The Legal Framework for Arbitration in Sri Lanka Past and Present' (2000) 17 *J Int'l Arb* 111.
Recent Developments in Arbitration Law and Practice, Introduction, (1997) XXII *YCA* 569.

Sweden:
Ek, Ralf, 'Das neue schwedische Schiedsverfahrensrecht' (2000) *RIW/AWD* 31.
Soderlung, Christer, 'A Comparative Overview of Arbitration Laws: Swedish Arbitration Act 1999, English Arbitration Act 1996 and Russian Federal Law on International Commercial Arbitration 1993' (2004) 20 *Arb Int'l* 73.

Thailand:
Fitzgerald, Darren and Polkinghorne, Michael, 'Notes and Current Developments, Arbitration in Southeast Asia: Hong Kong, Singapore and Thailand Compared' (2001) 18 *J Int'l Arb* 101.
Polkinghorne, Michael and Inthasuwan, Chatchai, 'Arbitration in Thailand' (2000) 15 *Mealey's Int'l Arb Rep* 14.
Winckless, Michael L., 'The history and current status of arbitration in Thailand' (2004) *Asian Dis Res* 12.

Tunisia:
Bühler, Michael, 'Tunis als Austragungsort internationaler Schiedsverfahren im "Nord-Süd" -Wirtschaftsverkehr?—Zum neuen tunesischen Schiedsgesetz' in *Betriebs Berater Beilage* 14 vom 14 September 1995, 9.
El-Ahdab, Abdul Hamid, 'Arab North Africa (Algeria, Egypt, Libya, Morocco and Tunisia)' in Eugene Cotran and Austin Amissah (eds), *Arbitration in Africa* (Kluwer Law International, 1996) 261.
Kallel, Sami, 'The Tunisian Law on International Arbitration' (1993) 4 *Am Rev Int'l Arb* 233.
Malouche, Habib, 'Tunisia' in *Int'l Handbook on Comm Arb Suppl* 21 August 1996.
Kalthoum, Meziou and Mezghan, Alii, 'Le Code tunisien de l'arbitrage' (1993) *Rev arb* 521.
Salah, Kamal ben, 'An Overview of the Tunisian Arbitration Regulations' (2000) 17 *J Int'l Arb* 141.

Turkey:
Bezen, Serdar, 'Recent Developments in International Commercial Arbitration in Turkey' (2001) 16 *Mealey's Int'l Arb Rep* 32.
Bezen, Serdar, 'Turkey adopts UNCITRAL Model Law' (2001) 16 *Mealey's Int'l Arb Rep* 42.
Eksi, Nuray, 'General Evaluation of the Turkish International Arbitration Act' (2005) 8 *Int'l Arb L Rev* 87.
Elver, Nazan Candaner, 'Turkish International Arbitration Law and Restrictions on Its Application' (2004) 21 *J Int'l Arb* 453.
Kocasakal, Özdemir H., 'The New Turkish Law on International Arbitration' (2007) *Int'l Bus L J* 211.
Rumpf, Christian, 'Internationale Schiedsgerichtsbarkeit in der Türkei' (2002) *RIW* 843.
Tugrul, Ansay, 'International Arbitration in Turkey' (2003) 14 *Am Rev Int'l Arb* 333.

Yesilirmak, Ali, 'Development Of Effective Arbitration And Alternative Dispute Resolution Regime In Turkey' (2005) 20 *Mealey's Int'l Arb Rep* 18.

Yesilirmak, Ali, 'The Turkish International Arbitration Law of 2001' (2002) 19 *J Int'l Arb* 171.

Ukraine:

Alyoshin, Oleg Y. and Slipachuk, Tatyana, 'Enforcement of Foreign Arbitral Awards in the Ukraine: To Be or Not to Be' (2005) 22 *J Int'l Arb* 65.

Kiszczuk, Laurenti, 'Ukrainisches Gesetz über internationale Handelsarbitrage' (1995) *RIW* 641.

Pobirchenko, Igor G, 'Ukraine' *Int'l Handbook on Comm Arb Suppl* 20 October 1995.

Slipachuk, Tatyana V. and Runeland, Per, 'Kiev: From Zero to 800 Cases Per Year in Less than 10 Years' (2000) 11 *Am Rev Int'l Arb* 585.

Slipachuk, Tatyana, 'International Commercial Arbitration in the Ukraine: Legislation and Practice' (2003) 20*J Int'l Arb* 515.

Sourjikova-Giebner, Valentina, *Schiedsgerichtsbarkeit in der Ukraine: Internationale und nationale Schiedsgerichte*, (Verlag Recht und Wirtschaft, 1998).

Within the United States of America:

Carbonneau, Thomas E., 'International Arbitration: The United States' in Peter Gottwald (ed), *Internationale Schiedsgerichtsbarkeit: Arbitrage International: International Arbitration* (Gieseking-Verlag 1997).

Donahey, Scott M., 'California and Arbitrator Failure to Disclose' (2007) 24 *J Int'l Arb* 389.

Dore, Isaak I., *The UNCITRAL Framework for Arbitration in Contemporary Perspective* (Graham & Trotman/Martinus Nijhoff,1993).

Fry, James D., 'The Federal Arbitration Act, UNCITRAL Model Law and New York' (2004) 7 *Int'l Arb L Rev* 97.

Golbert, Albert S. and Kolkey, Daniel M., 'California's new International Arbitration and Conciliation Code: California is a more attractive venue for resolving international commercial disputes' (1988) 11 *Los Angeles Lawyer* 46.

Golbert, Albert S. and Kolkey, Daniel M., 'California's Adoption of a Code For International Commercial Arbitration and Conciliation' (1988) 10 *Loyola of Los Angeles Int'l and Comparative L Rev* 583.

Kuner, Ch., 'Die neuen internationalen Handelsschiedsgesetze der US-amerikanischen Einzelstaaten' (1994) *RIW* 368.

Rau, Alan Scott, 'The UNCITRAL Model Law in State and Federal Courts: The Case of "Waiver"' (1995) 6 *Am Rev Int'l Arb* 223.

Romeu-Matta, Xavier E., 'New Developments in International Commercial Arbitration: A Comparative Survey of New State Statutes and the UNCITRAL Model Law' (1990) 1 *Am Rev Int'l Arb* 140.

Wright, Kenneth B., 'California's International Commercial Arbitration Act: New Procedures for the Arbitration and Conciliation of International Commercial Disputes' (1989) 17 *Int'l Business Lawyer* 45.

Zambia:

Chapman, Michael, 'Arbitral Law Reform in Africa: Recent Events in Zambia' (2004) 4 *Model Arb LQ Rep* 633.

Zimbabwe:

Asouzu, Amazu A., 'The Arbitration Laws of Kenya, Zimbabwe and Uganda: Some remarks on Remarkable Developments' (2000) 4 *Model Arb L Q Rep* 83.

Donavan, Ian A., 'Zimbabwe', in Eugene Cotran and Austin Amissah (eds), *Arbitration in Africa* (Kluwer Law International, 1996).

McMillan, A.R., 'Zimbabwe Arbitration Act 1996' (2000) 15 *Mealey's Int'l Arb Rep* 42.

Reid-Rowland, John, 'Arbitration in Zimbabwe: the UNCITRAL Model Law in practice in a developing country' (2007) 73 *Arbitration* 216.

15

THE ARBITRATION RULES OF THE INTERNATIONAL CHAMBER OF COMMERCE (ICC)

Michael W. Bühler and Sigvard Jarvin

I. Introduction to the 1998 ICC Rules of Arbitration

A. The International Chamber of Commerce and its organization

With the considerable expansion of international commercial arbitration throughout the world, 'ICC arbitration' has become the world-wide brand name for international commercial arbitration. Businessmen signing contracts with foreign partners and their lawyers recognize the reference to 'ICC arbitration' as meaning the referral of a dispute to arbitration under the Rules of Arbitration of the International Chamber of Commerce. By agreeing to 'ICC arbitration', parties to a contract agree to an arbitration that will be conducted under the auspices of the International Chamber of Commerce (the 'ICC'). As an institution, the ICC will only provide administrative services, but will not itself decide the dispute submitted to arbitration. It is rather the Arbitral Tribunal constituted specifically for each dispute under the ICC Rules of Arbitration of 1998 (the 'Rules' or 'ICC Rules') that will alone have the power and the responsibility of deciding the parties' dispute.[1] **15.01**

The ICC, founded in 1919 by US and European businessmen at a conference in Atlantic City, USA, originally aiming to restore trade and prosperity after World War I, is today an international business organization that groups thousands of member companies and associates from over 130 countries. Since the inception of the ICC, Paris has been its seat. Its purpose is 'to promote an open international trade and investment system and the **15.02**

[1] See *infra* para 15.22.

market economy'. Among a number of rules that govern the conduct of international business,[2] the ICC provides probably the most well known, the ICC Rules of Arbitration.

15.03 The ICC's supreme governing body is the ICC World Council (the 'Council'). Its delegates are mainly senior business executives from around the world and notwithstanding its private nature, the Council is comparable to a general assembly of a major intergovernmental organization.[3] The delegates are named to the Council by the National Committee of each member country. The Council meets once a year, normally in June, and 10 direct members from countries where there is no National Committee may be invited to participate in the Council's work.

15.04 The National Committees represent the ICC in their respective countries. In 2008, there were 92 National Committees[4] bringing in their national business concerns and recommendations to the International Secretariat of the ICC, and making sure that their contributions were reported by the ICC to governments and international organizations.

15.05 The Council elects the President and Vice-President of the ICC for two-year terms. It also elects the Executive Board, responsible for implementing ICC policy on the President's recommendation. The Executive Board has actually 20 members serving for three years, and a rotating system with one third of the members retiring at the end of each year. The ICC Council does not include governmental representatives.

15.06 The International Secretariat of the ICC is presided by the Secretary-General.[5] Together with the National Committees it carries out the ICC's work programme. The Secretary-General is recommended by the Executive Board and appointed by the Council at the initiative of the President.

15.07 ICC conferences and congresses represent important means to communicate ICC business expertise to a broad public. While the conferences always treat a specific topic and often elaborate business policies, the congresses are major business events. The ICC holds its World Congress every two years upon the invitation of a National Committee and always at a different venue. The last ICC World Congress was held at the invitation of ICC Morocco in Marrakech on 6–9 June 2004. No other World Congress has been held since.

15.08 ICC commissions and task forces and special groups, created by the ICC and composed of over 500 members from 90 countries, play an important role in developing, scrutinizing and drawing up international commerce policies, statements, perspectives, national government initiatives, business comments and recommendations.[6] The commissions are set

---

[2] eg the Incoterms for trade and transport of goods, its latest version being the Incoterms 2000, and the UPC 600 Rules for international documentary credits as in effect from 1 July 2007.

[3] See <http://www.iccwbo.org>, link 'ICC Constitution' for further information in the respective fields.

[4] 34 from Europe, 17 from Asia Pacific, 18 from the Americas, 13 from Africa and 10 from the Middle East, for the complete list see <http://www.iccwbo.org>, link 'National Committees'.

[5] It is to be noted that the Secretary-General of the ICC is a different person from the Secretary-General of the ICC Court, see *infra* paras 15.71; 15.137.

[6] eg the Commission on E-business, IT and Telecoms (EBITT) with its factsheets 11 from April 2007, or the Commission on Trade and Investment Policy on ICC recommendations to safeguard freedom of investment from February 2008.

up by the President and Secretary-General in consultation with National Committees. Further, working parties are occasionally created by representatives of more than one commission to support the work of the commissions.[7] The members of ICC commissions and task forces and special groups often consist of experts assigned by ICC member companies and business associations to participate in the work fulfilled by these bodies. The policy statements established by the commissions are submitted, after approval of the Executive Board and the Council, to national governments and international organizations through the ICC National Committees and the ICC's Secretariat.

B. The ICC International Court of Arbitration and its Secretariat

The ICC International Court of Arbitration (the 'ICC Court'), established in 1923 and located at the ICC headquarters in Paris, is composed nowadays of members from some 88 countries. As an internal department of the ICC with no legal personality, the ICC Court ensures the application of the ICC Rules. **15.09**

As provided for in Art 1(2) of the Rules, Art 1(1) of App I to the ICC Rules, (Statutes of the International Court of Arbitration) or in Arts 1(1) and 2(2) of App II to the Rules (Internal Rules of the International Court of Arbitration), the ICC Court does not decide cases, and parties to ICC arbitration and their counsel never appear before the ICC Court. The ICC Court simply administers and supervises the ICC arbitration process from the initial Request for Arbitration to the final award by fulfilling various tasks, such as the appointment and confirmation of arbitrators, the decision upon challenges of arbitrators, the filing and calling of advances on cost, the scrutiny and approval of the awards, and the fixing of the arbitrators' fees. **15.10**

Although the ICC Court exercises important administrative functions, and thereby assists both the parties and the arbitrators in the smooth conduct of the arbitral proceedings, the ICC Court's work is not designed to affect the arbitrators' liberty of decision. It is solely for the arbitrators to decide upon the merits of the dispute, and to take whatever procedural decision that is required to bring the arbitration to an end, normally through the issuance of a final award. The arbitrator's liberty of decision is expressly recognized in Art 27 of the Rules, which gives the ICC Court the right to scrutinize and approve any award. **15.11**

In carrying out its functions the ICC Court acts independently from the ICC and its organs as well as from the National Committees, that is, it receives no instructions as to how to handle individual matters submitted to it by the parties. The work of the ICC Court and its sessions, whether plenary or those of a committee of the ICC Court, are of a confidential nature.[8] **15.12**

The official working languages of the ICC Court are English and French, but Arbitral Tribunals are not limited to using these languages. Pursuant to Art 16 of the Rules, the parties may determine any language of their choice as the language of arbitration, ie the **15.13**

---

[7] eg the Commissions' projects for 2008 provide for a study of the Arbitral Tribunal's role as *amiable compositeur*, explanatory notes for the use of experts in the conduct of expertise proceedings, or specific issues related to trusts and arbitration, see ICC Annual Report 2007.

[8] See *infra* para 15.91.

language used by the parties for communicating with the Arbitral Tribunal, and in the absence of such choice by the parties, the Arbitral Tribunal will determine the language(s).[9]

15.14 The ICC Court is assisted by the Secretariat of the ICC Court (the 'Secretariat'), based at the ICC headquarters in Paris, Art 1(5) of the Rules. Unlike the ICC Court members, the Secretariat officials are employees of the ICC. The Secretariat currently employs an impressive number of 30 lawyers from 19 different countries.[10] Since late 2008, in response to the growing demand from the business and legal communities, the Secretariat has opened a dedicated facility for arbitration hearings and other forms of commercial dispute resolution in Paris and a branch office in Hong Kong. The Hong Kong office provides a neutral forum for conducting China-related arbitration and dispute resolution between Chinese and non-Chinese parties, and enables closer contacts with important economies in the region such as India, Korea and Japan, as well as emerging economies such as Vietnam. The Secretariat of the ICC Court functions above all as the notification body in receiving communications from, and sending communications to, the parties, including the Request for Arbitration and the Answer thereto.

15.15 As regards new technology and communication from and to the parties, the ICC NetCase system was started in 2005.[11] The NetCase system provides an online database for the parties and the members of the tribunal. This database covers administrative aspects of the case (deposits, costs and extensions), correspondence between the parties and provides an online source of all filings of the parties. Use of NetCase is an option, and is one that is being adopted by a few tribunals.

15.16 The Secretariat is run by a Secretary-General of the ICC Court (the 'Secretary-General').[12] In the last 25 years, three Secretaries General were from the United States, one from Argentina and the current one is from New Zealand. The Secretary-General is assisted by a Deputy Secretary-General, currently an Australian, and a General Counsel, a French lawyer, Professor in law. The Secretary-General's powers were expanded with the 1998 Rules to include functions such as the confirmation of arbitrators (Art 9(8)) of the Rules, the fixing of the provisional advance, or the suspension of the Arbitral Tribunals work, where the advance on costs has not been paid.[13]

C. Figures on ICC arbitration

15.17 An ICC arbitration 'commences' with the filing of a Request for Arbitration to the Secretariat of the ICC Court, Art 4(1) of the Rules. In 2008, 663 Requests for Arbitration

---

[9] See *infra* Art l6.

[10] See <http://www.iccwbo.org>, link 'contact us'.

[11] See Philippe, M., 'New IT facility for ICC arbitration users' (2005) 16 *ICC ICArb Bull* no 2, 5; Philippe, M. 'NetCase: A New ICC Arbitration Facility' (2004) *ICC ICArb Bull*, Special Supp, 53; ICC NetCase, 'At The Forefront of IT In Arbitration'.

[12] The current Secretary-General, Mr Jason Fry has a dual nationality, British and New Zealand and was previously a practising lawyer based in Paris.

[13] See para 15.127.

were registered by the ICC Court, the highest number ever since its conception (599 cases were registered in 2007).[14]

(1) Parties to ICC arbitration

The cases registered in 2008 involved 1,758 parties from 120 different countries, and thus virtually from all over the world. **15.18**

In 2008, in 10.7 per cent of the cases at least one party was a state or parastatal entity. **15.19**

The continent from which most parties originated in ICC arbitrations was in 2007, Europe (in particular Western Europe (55.3 per cent), followed by the Americas (22.1 per cent), Asia (17.9 per cent), Africa (3.5 per cent) and Australasia (12 per cent). France (104 parties), Germany (158 parties), Italy (70 parties) and the United Kingdom (69 parties) were the most frequently represented countries followed by Switzerland (39 parties), Spain (47 parties), the Netherlands (46 parties), Turkey (31 parties), Poland (29 parties) and Austria (27 parties). This can be explained by the long established arbitration practice in these countries (both domestic and international), and their highly export-oriented economies, which increases their readiness to accept international commercial arbitration. **15.20**

In 2007, one third of the parties from the Americas came from Canada and the USA (9.7 per cent of the total of parties). In fact, although ICC arbitration is sometimes said to be not that popular in the United States, parties from the USA represent in recent years the largest group of parties in ICC arbitrations. Of all Asian parties, India and China were most often represented with about approximately one quarter of all Asian parties (69 parties out of 288). A significant increase took place with respect to Lebanon and Israel, who were parties in 18 cases out of 98 from Central and West Asia. As regards the African continent, Cameroon and South Africa were the most commonly seen states with 9 out of 33 parties. **15.21**

(2) The Arbitral Tribunal

The selection of a qualified arbitrator is an important condition for the successful conduct of arbitral proceedings. Under the ICC Rules, an Arbitral Tribunal is normally composed of one or three arbitrators. In the latter case one arbitrator is normally nominated by each of the parties and the third is appointed either with the agreement of the parties and/or co-arbitrators, or by the ICC Court. When one arbitrator is foreseen, he or she will be appointed by the ICC Court, if not jointly selected by the parties and/or co-arbitrators. **15.22**

If the parties fail to agree upon the number of arbitrators or, in an arbitration with a sole arbitrator, who that arbitrator should be, the ICC Rules provide that the ICC Court shall appoint a sole arbitrator unless the dispute is such as to warrant the appointment of three arbitrators.[15] **15.23**

With regard to the selection of arbitrators the National Committees play a vital role in identifying potential arbitrators with appropriate qualifications. Unlike some other institutional arbitration rules, the arbitrators acting in an ICC arbitration do not have to be, and are not chosen from a pre-established list of arbitrators, thus enabling the parties **15.24**

[14] ICC website: <http://www.iccwbo.org/court/arbitration/index.html?id=26612>.

[15] See *infra* Art 8(2), para 15.390.

and/or the ICC Court or the co-arbitrators to have unlimited flexibility in the choice of appropriate arbitrators.

15.25 In 2007 a total of 1,039 arbitrators were appointed from 66 different countries with a significant increase of arbitrators from Central and Eastern Europe and Latin America. The most significant increases in Central and Eastern Europe were Polish and Czech arbitrators, whereas in Latin America such increases occurred in Brazil (43 arbitrators). In South East Asia it is Singapore (20 arbitrators) which had the most marked increase.

15.26 In 2007 Switzerland was the country of origin of most of the arbitrators (140), followed by the United Kingdom (98), USA (89), Germany (85) and France (79).

15.27 Parties nominated arbitrators in 596 cases; in 279 cases the arbitrators were proposed by one of the ICC's National Committees; 133 arbitrators were appointed upon the proposal by the co-arbitrators and 31 directly by the ICC Court.

15.28 In 2007, the ICC Court refused to confirm an arbitrator proposed by the parties in 17 instances. In 2007, challenges of arbitrators were made in 22 cases, of which only one was upheld by the ICC Court. Resignations were submitted by 28 arbitrators; all were accepted. Further, the ICC Court replaced arbitrators on its own initiative in three cases, in accordance with Art 12(2) of the Rules.

(3) Place of arbitration

15.29 In 2007, places of arbitration were established in 42 different countries on all five continents. In 2008, the place of arbitration was located in 50 countries. The parties used their right to choose their place of arbitration in most of the cases (85.2 per cent), which has been a constant pattern for over ten years.[16]

15.30 As in past years, most of the ICC arbitrations were held in Europe (74.7 per cent) followed by Asia. In Europe, France was the most favoured place of arbitration (110 cases), followed by Switzerland (97 cases), and the United Kingdom (58 cases). The USA attracted 37 cases. The predominance of Western European cities has been decreasing over the last 10 years in favour of other regions. It is also worth highlighting that for the first time since the ICC Bulletin has been publishing court statistics, arbitrations were based in Chile, Cuba and Malta, while Poland emerged as an increasingly frequent choice.[17]

(4) Applicable law

15.31 In 79.8 per cent of the cases filed in 2007, the parties had determined in their contracts the applicable law to the merits, mostly agreeing on a national law (in all but three contracts) rather than on a supranational law (the three exceptions including the choice of the UNIDROIT Principles of International Commercial Contracts, the Vienna Convention for International Sales, known as CISG and the law of the OHADA). This would seem to

[16] See (2008) 19 *ICC ICArb Bull* no 1, 11. In 2006, in 86.6% of the cases the parties agreed the place of arbitration. In 2002, the ICC Court fixed the place of arbitration in less than 14% of the cases, (2006) 14 *ICC ICArb Bull* no 1, p 13.

[17] (2008) 19 *ICArb Bull* no 1, 11.

infer that as for the place of arbitration, parties agreeing to ICC arbitration know how to make use of their right to select the applicable rules of law.

Among national laws, English and Swiss Law were most commonly chosen, followed by German law, US laws and French law. In only one case the parties had explicitly agreed to give the arbitrators the power to act as *amiable compositeur* (see Art 17(3).) **15.32**

(5) Sector of trades and amounts in dispute

The amounts in disputes varied from less than 50,000 US dollars to over 100 million US dollars, while the majority may be allocated in the middle range. In 2007, the amounts in dispute were in excess of 1 million US dollars in more than half of the cases (57.5 per cent). **15.33**

The new cases registered with the ICC Court in 2007 again covered, as in the past, a wide range of economic sectors, with notable increases in the fields of construction and engineering (14.3 per cent of cases), energy (10.8 per cent of cases), and information technology (10.2 per cent of cases). There were also increases in the number of cases from other sectors, such as finance and insurance, general trade and distribution, and health and food industries.[18] **15.34**

The disputes referred to in ICC arbitration comprised 23.9 per cent sale agreements, 13.3 per cent construction, 9.4 per cent distribution, 8.3 per cent shareholders' agreements and 5.5 per cent intellectual property agreements. **15.35**

(6) Awards

In 2008 a total of 407 awards were rendered by Arbitral Tribunals, as opposed to 349 awards in 2007; 223 were final, and 96 were partial awards; 30 awards were by consent.[19] In 2007, English was the most frequently used language of the awards, approximately 70 per cent. Other languages, in decreasing order of frequency, were: French, Spanish, German, Italian and Portuguese, followed by Chinese, Greek, Polish, Arabic, Russian and Japanese. Three awards were drafted in more than one language, respectively English and Mandarin, English and Portuguese, and English and Spanish. **15.36**

Before the awards are signed by the arbitrator(s) and notified to the parties, the awards are subject to scrutiny by the ICC Court (Art 27). In 2007, the ICC Court approved 32 awards without suggestion of any changes to be made to the award, and 317 awards with such suggestions. 35 awards were not approved when scrutinized for the first time, and were returned by the ICC Court to the arbitrator(s) and therefore needed to be resubmitted to the ICC Court for approval. Most awards were unanimous decisions, but in 27 awards the decision was made by two of the three arbitrators and in one award the decision was made by the chairman alone; 22 of the approved awards represented majority decisions.[20] **15.37**

[18] The 'classic' ICC arbitration economic sectors comprise trade, joint venture and construction, licensing and finance.

[19] (2008) 19 *ICC Court Bull* no 1, 13.

[20] *ibid.*

15.38 In 2007, 28 applications were made for the correction and interpretation of awards (Art 29).[21] In 18 cases the arbitral tribunal acceded fully or partially to the request by issuing a so-called Addendum, and in 15 cases the requests were rejected by so called Decisions (Art 29).

(7) Conciliation requests/ICC ADR Rules

15.39 The ICC offers also as a framework for the amicable settlement of business disputes that is to be distinguished from ICC arbitration, the newly launched ICC ADR Rules ('Amicable Dispute Resolution').[22] These Rules replace the 1988 ICC Rules of Optional Conciliation and are effective as of 1 July 2001. The scope of the ICC ADR Rules corresponds to that of the former Rules of Conciliation, which were in force in their current version as from 1 January 1988, and envisaged the settlement of international business disputes by a conciliator (now called 'neutral') upon a request for conciliation (now called 'mediation') by both parties. The ICC ADR Rules offer, however, different settlement techniques. The parties can freely choose the technique they consider most conducive to a settlement. Four alternative ICC ADR clauses are suggested by the ICC.[23] In 2007, the ICC received 12 ADR requests involving a total of 29 parties from 19 countries and independent territories.

(8) Ad hoc *appointments of arbitrators*

15.40 The ICC received in 2007 a total of 10 requests to serve as appointing authority in *ad hoc* arbitrations. Five requests were made under the UNCITRAL arbitration rules and five in *ad hoc* proceedings. The ICC offers to act as appointing authority in cases where parties choose to use the UNCITRAL arbitration rules to govern their procedure, but also wish to draw on the ICC's long experience in appointing qualified arbitrators. The ICC will not only draw up lists with names of qualified arbitrators and submit the lists to the parties, but it will also, as the case may be, nominate arbitrators if one party has failed to do so, or decide challenges to arbitrators as well as replacements. Parties may ask the ICC to provide a statement on a consultative basis as to the fees charged by the arbitrators and deposits required by them. Upon the request of a party or an arbitral tribunal, the ICC may hold deposits until the fees and costs for arbitration have been settled.

15.41 Each request made to the ICC as appointing authority will entail a charge of currently 2,500 US dollars, payable by the party making the request. Given the fall of the US dollar against major foreign currencies, and the Euro in particular, this makes the use of ICC's services particularly inexpensive.

(9) Expertise requests

15.42 The ICC International Centre for Expertise, created in 1976 at the ICC headquarters in Paris and operating under the 2003 ICC Rules for Expertise, deals with technical, financial, contractual or other questions requiring specialized knowledge.[24] The parties may agree to

[21] See *infra* Art 29.

[22] The ICC ADR Rules can be downloaded together with the Guide to ICC ADR from <http://www.iccwbo.org/court/ADR>.

[23] They are available on the site <http://www.iccwbo.org/court/ADR>.

[24] The rules are available on the site <http://www.iccwbo.org/court/expertise>. See also Wolrich, P.M., 'ICC Expertise–The New, Revised ICC Rules for Expertise: A Presentation and Commentary' (2002) 13 *ICC ICArb Bull* no 2, 11.

use the services of the Centre for the proposal and/or appointment of an expert and the administration of expertise proceedings in connection with international business matters pursuant to the ICC Rules for Expertise.

In 2007, the ICC received 14 requests for the proposal of an expert,[25] covering the heavy industry and the services sector and dealing with expertise in connection with the price of coal, the conformity of equipment with contract specifications, the design, construction, operation and deterioration of industrial facilities, mine clearance procedures, information technology application and financial service.[26] **15.43**

The experts proposed or appointed came from five different countries: France, the Netherlands, Switzerland, the United Kingdom and the USA The parties in these cases came from Western Europe, Latin America, the USA, the Middle East and North Africa. **15.44**

(10) DOCDEX requests

The services of the International Centre for Expertise also include the ICC Rules for Documentary Credit Dispute Resolution Expertise (DOCDEX), revised and in effect as from 15 March 2002.[27] Established in 1997 by the ICC Banking Commission the DOCDEX Rules shall facilitate the rapid settlement of disputes arising under the Uniform Customs and Practice for Documentary Credits (UCP) and the Uniform Rules for Bank-to-Bank-Reimbursement under Documentary Credits (URR). The document-based expert decision is made by three experts, who are appointed from a list kept by the ICC Banking Commission. The decision is not binding upon the parties unless the parties have agreed otherwise. Mostly the parties can expect the final opinion six to twelve weeks following the receipt of the request by the ICC.[28] **15.45**

In 2007 the ICC received seven requests for a DOCDEX decision. The experts appointed came from Austria, Belgium, China, the Czech Republic, Denmark, France, Germany, Greece, Italy, Jordan, Luxembourg, Malaysia, the Netherlands, Switzerland, Turkey and the United Kingdom, whilst the parties involved came from Bulgaria, China, Greece, Japan, Libya, Malaysia, South Korea, Switzerland, Tunisia and the United Kingdom. **15.46**

D. Selected points of interest under the 1998 Rules

In order to reduce delays the Secretary-General has certain powers which the ICC Court exercised before. The Secretary-General may establish provisional advances on costs, thus enabling the transmission of the file at an earlier stage,[29] and may confirm party-nominated arbitrators, if the arbitrators' statement of independence does not raise objections to such confirmation. Also fast-track arbitrations are facilitated by allowing the parties to shorten procedural time limits.[30] **15.47**

---

[25] In comparison to 21 requests for expertise in 1999, see (1999) 11 *ICC ICArb Bull* no 1, 10.

[26] (2008) 19 *ICC ICArb Bull* no 1, 15.

[27] See <http://www.iccwbo.org/court/docdex/id4493/index.html>.

[28] Decisions are given in 30 days following the receipt of all necessary correspondence from the parties. See Collyer, G., 'Documentary Credit Dispute Resolution under the DOCDEX Rules Three Years On' (2000) *ICC Bull*, Special Supp, Finance and Insurance, 67.

[29] Under the 1975/1988 Rules it was the ICC Court that fixed the global advance on costs.

[30] See *infra* Art 32.

15.48 Minimizing unpredictability or improving transparency is enhanced for instance by vesting the Arbitral Tribunal with the power (i) not to list in the Terms of Reference issues to be determined if such listing is deemed to be inappropriate;[31] (ii) to admit new claims and counterclaims not included in the Terms of Reference even if objected by a party,[32] or (iii) to establish the obligation to communicate to all parties the challenge or replacement of an arbitrator and the comments relating thereto.[33]

15.49 The 1998 Rules are available in a total of thirteen languages on the ICC's homepage.[34] Notwithstanding the official languages of the ICC being English and French, and the availability of the Rules in numerous languages, it is important to bear in mind when seeking to interpret legal terms or expressions used in the ICC Rules that they are neither of English, American nor French origin.

15.50 The 1998 Rules apply to all ICC arbitrations that started after 1 January 1998, unless the parties have expressly provided for, and requested that earlier editions of the Rules apply.[35]

15.51 The 1998 Rules meet the requirements for flexibility and expedition in the arbitral process. The main features continue to be:

- the requirement of, and the time limit for, signing Terms of Reference;[36]
- the time limit for making the award;[37]
- the decision by the chairman of the Arbitral Tribunal majority;[38]
- the possibility to render an award by consent;[39]
- the scrutiny and approval of the draft award by the ICC Court;[40] and
- notification and enforceability of an award.[41]

15.52 The 1998 Rules explicitly allow for disputes of both a national and an international character to be handled under the auspices of the ICC.[42]

15.53 The Rules provide in Art 4(6) for an explicit consolidation of requests for arbitration to pending proceedings when these are related to legal relationships that already form the basis of an ICC arbitration between the same parties, and provided the Terms of Reference have not been signed or approved by the ICC Court.

15.54 Conservatory and interim measures: The 1998 Rules contain a notable provision relating to conservatory and interim measures decided by Arbitral Tribunals. The 1998 Rules expressly empower the arbitrators to do so in Art 23, and even if the parties apply to judicial

[31] See *infra* Art 18, para 15.707.
[32] See *infra* Art 19, para 15.772.
[33] See *infra* Art 11 and Art 12.
[34] On the site <http://www.iccwbo.org>: English, French, German, Arabic, Spanish, Russian, Chinese, Portuguese, Dutch, Czech, Polish, Thai and Turkish.
[35] See *infra* Art 6, para 15.317 *et seq.*
[36] ICC 1975/1988 Art 13 corresponds to ICC 1998 Art 18.
[37] ICC 1975/1988 Art 18 corresponds to ICC 1998 Art 24.
[38] ICC 1975/1988 Art 19 corresponds to ICC 1998 Art 25(1).
[39] ICC 1975/1988 Art 17 corresponds to ICC 1998 Art 26.
[40] ICC 1975/1988 Art 21 corresponds to ICC 1998 Art 27.
[41] ICC 1975/1988 Art 23 corresponds to ICC 1998 Art 28.
[42] See ICC 1998 Art 1 in comparison to ICC 1975/1988 Art 1(1).

authorities for such measures, they do not violate or waive the arbitration agreement or the Arbitral Tribunal's power by doing so. In addition, the Arbitral Tribunal may impose a security on the party requesting provisional measures, Art 23(1) of the Rules.

The 'equal treatment' of parties requirement: The 1998 ICC Rules have expressly introduced the principle of equal treatment of the parties, Art 15(2). This axiomatic principle was not reflected in the 1975/1988 Rules, while most of the modern arbitration rules contain a provision to this effect.[43] **15.55**

New claims and counterclaims: Art 19 authorizes the Arbitral Tribunal to allow new claims and counterclaims even after the signing of the Terms of Reference, if the nature of such claim, the stage of the proceedings and/or other relevant circumstances justify it.[44] **15.56**

Truncated tribunals: Earlier versions of the Rules offered no solution to deal with the situation where one of the arbitrators died or had been removed by the ICC Court after the proceedings had been closed. Article 12(5) of the current version gives a the ICC Court express authority to determine after the closing of the proceedings, whether or not to replace the member of the Arbitral Tribunal that had died or was removed. In fact, this provision was incorporated to deal with the situation where one of the arbitrators was seeking to obstruct the decision in order to avoid, through its resignation, the rendering of an award. **15.57**

Applicable rules of law: The issue of the applicable rules of law is dealt with in Art 17(1) Article 17(1) incorporates what may be seen as a significant departure from the approach employed in the 1975/1988 Rules, as it now speaks of the 'rules of law' to be applied, instead of 'the law', 'the applicable law', and 'the law designated as the proper law' as stated in Art 13(3) of the former Rules. This revision expressly authorizes the parties to choose, and the Tribunal to apply, not merely the law of one or perhaps more municipal jurisdictions, but also so-called 'rules of law' taken from other sources, such as generally accepted principles of law or *lex mercatoria*. Article 17(1) thereby expressly authorizes the Arbitral Tribunal to determine the applicable substantive rules of law without taking the preliminary step of selecting an appropriate rule of conflict as was the case since the 1961 European Convention.[45] **15.58**

Correction and interpretation of the award: Art 29, in line with a predominant trend in national arbitration laws and international arbitration rules, provides for the correction and interpretation of awards primarily in order to facilitate the recognition and enforcement of an award. **15.59**

Waiver rule: According to Art 33, a party may not raise untimely objections to the conduct of the proceedings. This rule is not only important for maintaining the integrity of the arbitral proceedings, but even more important for any subsequent proceedings before state courts, eg regarding challenges against the award or enforcement proceedings. **15.60**

---

[43] See Art 16(1) AAA/ICDR, Art 15 UNCITRAL Rules, Art 38 WIPO.

[44] Compare Art 4 AAA/ICDR, Art 44 WIPO, Art 20 UNCITRAL Rules, Art 23 UNCITRAL Model Law.

[45] Blessing M., 'Regulations in Arbitration Rules on Choice of Law' (1996) *ICCA Congress Series no 7*, 391.

15.61 Exclusion of liability: Art 34 provides for the protection of the arbitrators, the ICC Court, the National Committees and any other ICC employees by excluding in broad language any liability. However, after a recent Paris Court of Appeal decision, the validity and effects of this provision remain to be determined.[46]

15.62 Multiple parties: Art 10 requires the joint nomination by all parties of one side, (claimant and/or respondent) and helps to expedite the proceedings and thwart dilatory intentions of recalcitrant parties.

E. International Conventions relevant in ICC arbitration

15.63 The ICC Rules of Arbitration are not stand-alone provisions, unconnected to the arbitration law applicable at the place of arbitration, or to the laws of recognition and enforcement of awards in the countries of origin of the parties, or any other third country where a party might seek to enforce an ICC award. The Rules expressly recognize their connection to a general legal framework, in particular (i) in Art 15, where the existence of 'the rules of procedure of a national law to be applied to the arbitration' is acknowledged;[47] (ii) Art 23(2) where it is accepted that parties 'may apply to any competent judicial authority for interim or conservatory measures', before and even after the file was transmitted to the Arbitral Tribunal;[48] (iii) in Art 28(6), pursuant to which the parties 'shall be deemed to have waived their right to any form of recourse insofar as such waiver can validly be made';[49] and (iv) in Art 35 pursuant to which the ICC Court and the Arbitral Tribunal 'shall make every effort to make sure that the Award is enforceable at law'.[50]

15.64 In countries that have adopted the UNCITRAL Model Law as part of their legislation on international (and possibly even domestic) arbitration, the validity of provisions contained in the ICC Rules will not be questioned. The Model Law was amended in 2006, in order to promote a higher degree of uniformity of arbitral procedures and better address the specific needs of international commercial arbitration practice. The recent amendments include: Art 1(2) (*Scope of application*), Art 2A (*International origin and general principles*), Art 7 (Option I, *Definition and form of arbitration agreement* and Option II, *Definition of arbitration agreement*), ch IV A (*Interim Measures and Preliminary Orders*) and Art 35(2) (*Recognition and enforcement*).[51]

---

[46] Paris TGI, 10 October 2007, *Société SNF v Chambre de Commerce Internationale*, (2007) *Rev arb* no 4, 847, note Jarrosson, ans (2007) Dallorz no 41, 2916, note Clay. In another recent case, the Paris *Cour d'Appel* held that, absent a party agreement on the time limits for making an award, the fact that the arbitrators set their own procedural timelines without considering French domestic law did not engage the tribunal's liability. Looking at the complexity and particular circumstances of the case (ie the challenge of the preliminary award before the *Cour d'Appel*, the resignation of the president of the tribunal followed by the appointment of a new president by the Paris Tribunal de Grande Instance, and a three-month suspension of the deliberations), the Court also noted the arbitrators used all diligence in making the final award, a fact which, again, should not trigger their liability. CA Paris (1ère Ch, Sec C), 6 November 2008, *Jacques Charrasse et Société CNCA-CEC v M Rossi, et al* (2009) Dallorz no 8, 538; Note by Daniel Mainguy, (2009), Recueil Dallorz no 8, 539.

[47] See *infra* Art 15, para 15.612 *et seq*.

[48] See *infra* Art 23, para 15.895.

[49] See *infra* Art 28, para 15.994.

[50] See *infra* Art 35.

[51] For more information, see <http://www.uncitral.org>; see also Bühler, M.W. and Webster, T., *Handbook of ICC Arbitration: Commentary, Precedents, Materials* (2nd edn, Thomson, Sweet & Maxwell, 2008) 333, para 23-1.

15.65 Any jurisdiction that possesses modern arbitration rules, either as part of its Code of Civil Procedure, or as a separate legislative Act or Decree, will find the ICC Rules to be a perfectly acceptable exercise of the parties' autonomy to contract, and of their choice to have their dispute decided pursuant to a private dispute settlement mechanism. This does not mean that any and each provision of the ICC Rules and its application in practice by the ICC Court will be upheld by the national courts in such jurisdictions.[52] In particular, the broad exclusion of liability as provided in Art 34 of the new Rules may find its limits in a particular jurisdiction.[53]

15.66 When a party does not accept to voluntarily honour an ICC award, the winning party may wish to seek its enforcement in the country of origin or elsewhere. The enforcement of foreign awards is greatly enhanced by the New York Convention on the Recognition and Enforcement of Foreign Arbitral Awards of 10 June 1958 which has been adopted by 144 countries (as of 12 January 2009)[54] (the 'New York Convention'). National courts faced with a request not to recognize and to refuse *exequatur* of an ICC award will often be reluctant to follow such request, since, by and large, ICC awards enjoy the respect that stems from the fact that they have been rendered through a fair and transparent process, the supervision by the ICC Court being an additional guarantor thereof.[55]

II. Commentary on Articles 1–35

A. Article 1. International Court of Arbitration

(1) The International Court of Arbitration (the 'Court') of the International Chamber of Commerce (the 'ICC') is the arbitration body attached to the ICC. The Statutes of the Court are set forth in App I. Members of the Court are appointed by the Council of the ICC. The function of the Court is to provide for the settlement by arbitration of business disputes of an international character in accordance with the Rules of Arbitration of the International Chamber of Commerce (the 'Rules'). If so empowered by an arbitration agreement, the Court shall also provide for the settlement by arbitration in accordance with these Rules of business disputes not of an international character.

(2) The Court does not itself settle disputes. It has the function of ensuring the application of these Rules. It draws up its own Internal Rules (App II).

(3) The Chairman of the Court, or, in the Chairman's absence or otherwise at his request, one of its Vice-Chairmen shall have the power to take urgent decisions on behalf of the Court, provided that any such decision is reported to the Court at its next session.

(4) As provided for in its Internal Rules, the Court may delegate to one or more committees composed of its members the power to take certain decisions, provided that any such decision is reported to the Court at its next session.

(5) The Secretariat of the Court (the 'Secretariat') under the direction of its Secretary-General (the 'Secretary-General') shall have its seat at the headquarters of the ICC.

---

[52] Several provisions of the ICC Rules have been challenged in the past before national courts, eg Art 18 of the 1975/1988 Rules (now Art 24) regarding the extension of the six-month time limit to render an award. See para 7 *et seq* (Art 24).

[53] See *infra* Art 34, para 15.1243.

[54] The latest standing of contracting states can be downloaded from <http://www.uncitral.org>.

[55] See the ICC Court's general and broad mandate in Art 35 of the Rules.

(1) Institutional Character

15.67 (1.1) **The institutional character of ICC arbitration** The International Chamber of Commerce ('ICC') is the world's leading business organization, and not exclusively, or even primarily, an arbitral institution. Founded in 1919, its purpose is to promote world-wide an open international trade and investment System and the market economy. Its members are National Committees set up in 2008 in 90 countries, national trade federations, industrial companies and associations from altogether over 130 countries, all of which support free trade.

15.68 One of the essential services offered by the ICC is its System for the resolution of disputes by the International Court of Arbitration, which can be used by any entity doing business, including sovereign states. There is no qualification requirement of membership with the ICC or its National Committees in order to use the arbitration services of the ICC.

15.69 The ICC is a private institution, and is in fact a not-for-profit association created under the laws of France. Although France is the host country of the ICC, the ICC's vocation is entirely international.

15.70 (1.2) **The ICC and its bodies (organization)** The members of the ICC are federated in the ICC's Council, which is the ICC's supreme governing body, composed of chief executives of leading companies around the world. The President and Vice-President of the ICC are elected by the Council for two-year terms. The Council also elects the Executive Board, responsible for implementing ICC policy, on the President's recommendation. The Executive Board is composed of between 15 and 30 members, who serve for three years, with one third of the members retiring at the end of each year.

15.71 The ICC has a Secretary-General who heads its International Secretariat and works closely with the ICC's National Committees. The Secretary-General is appointed by the Council at the initiative of the President and on the recommendation of the Executive Board.

15.72 The ICC has some 15 commissions and one advisory group, the Economists Advisory Group, in areas such as Banking, Competition, and International Commercial Practice, to name but a few. For the user of ICC arbitration, the most important commission is the ICC's Commission on International Arbitration, which meets twice a year, and which was responsible for preparing the 1998 Arbitration Rules.[56] The Chairman, the Vice-Chairmen, the members and alternate members of the ICC Court are all *ex officio* members of the Commission. It is for each National Committee to appoint delegates of its choice to the Commission.

15.73 The Commission has several 'task forces', in 2009, for instance, on '*Amiable Composition* and *ex aequo et bono*', on 'National Rules of Procedure for Recognition and Enforcement of Foreign Arbitral Awards pursuant to the New York Convention of 1958', on 'Guidelines for ICC Expertise Proceedings', on 'Trusts and Arbitration', on 'Production of Electronic Documents in Arbitration', and on the 'Revision of the 1998 ICC Rules of arbitration'. A department called ICC Events organizes arbitration seminars and workshops for practitioners from around the world, as well as colloquia for arbitrators.

[56] See *supra* Introduction para 15.8.

15.74 Another body of the ICC is the International Centre for Expertise which organizes expertise proceedings under its Rules currently in force since 1 January 2003.[57] A special kind of dispute resolution in the field of documentary credit issues is offered by the International Centre for Expertise under Documentary Credit Dispute Resolution Expertise Rules (DOCDEX).[58] DOCDEX decisions may also be found on DC-PRO Focus, ICC's online subscription service for documentary credits. Users from over 25 countries have already taken advantage of the service, which offers fraud alerts, legal background, news stories and opinions. More information is also available on the ICC's Commission on Banking Technique and Practice.[59]

15.75 The ICC has also issued ICC ADR Rules, which came in force on 1 July 2001 to facilitate the amicable settlement of business disputes under the aegis of the ICC. They were launched to replace the 1988 Rules of Optional Conciliation. Over the years, the Conciliation Rules had limited success judging from the declining number of conciliation requests that were filed with the ICC in the 1990s.[60] The ICC ADR Rules are published in the booklet Dispute resolution Services, ICC publication no 847. They can be downloaded from the ICC's homepage on the internet.[61] The ICC's ADR services are distinct from its arbitration services, and are handled by staff other than that of the ICC Court.

15.76 The ICC acts also as appointing authority in *ad hoc* arbitration cases, in particular under the UNCITRAL Rules of Arbitration 1985 and their recent amendments.[62]

15.77 In 2004, the ICC launched a new set of rules for establishing and operating Dispute Boards.[63] These are intended to accompany the performance of a contract and help resolve disagreements and decide disputes as and when they arise. Under these Rules, the ICC's role is limited to appointing Dispute Board members, deciding on challenges made against Dispute Board members and reviewing decisions made by Dispute Boards.[64] In 2006 and 2007 the ICC was required to intervene four times.

---

57 The Rules can be downloaded at <http://www.iccwbo.org>. In 2006 and 2007, respectively, 10 and 14 new requests for expertise were filed with the ICC, see (2007) 18 *ICC ICArb Bull* no 1, 15; (2008) 19 *ICC ICArb Bull* no 1, 15 and *supra* Introduction para 15.42.

58 The revised DOCDEX System came into effect on 15 March 2002. The DOCDEX Rules can be downloaded from www.iccwbo.org. In 2006 and 2007, respectively, 5 and 7 requests were submitted to the ICC, see *ibid*, and *supra* Introduction para 15.45.

59 See <http://www.iccwbo.org/court/docdex/id4493/index.html>, and see *supra* Introduction para 15.45.

60 In 2007, 12 requests for ADR were filed with the ICC (see *supra* Introduction n 42, the same number as in 2006), see also Mackie K., 'The Future of ADR Clauses after *Cable & Wireless v IBM*' (2003) 19 *Arb Int'l* no 3, 345 and Jimenez-Figueres D., 'Amicable Means to Resolve Disputes: How the ICC ADR Rules work' (2004) 21 *J Int'l Arb* no 1, 9.

61 See *supra* Introduction, para 15.39.

62 Amendments to Arts 1(2), 7, 35(2), a new ch IV bis to replace Art 17 and a new Art 2A were adopted on 7 July 2006. In 2006 the ICC acted in 18 *ad hoc* arbitration cases. Eight of these appointments were made under UNCITRAL Rules, see *op cit.* In 2007, 10 *ad hoc* appointments were made, five pursuant to the UNCITRAL Rules, see *supra* Introduction paras 40–1, also as to the ICC Rules on the 'ICC as appointing authority under the UNCITRAL Arbitration Rules'.

63 ICC publication no 847.

64 See ICC, 'ICC Dispute Board Rules: Practitioner's View' (2007) 18 *ICC ICArb Bull* no 1, 43; Jolivet, E., 'Chronique de jurisprudence arbitrale de la Chambre de commerce internationale: Arbitrage CCI et procédure ADR' in *Les Cahiers de l'Arbitrage Volume I* (Gazette du Palais, Paris, 2002) 261; Lazareff, S.,

15.78 **(1.3) Financing the ICC's services** The ICC has three major sources of revenue: (i) the membership fees; (ii) the sale of publications and the organization of seminars; and (iii) the administrative costs paid by parties having recourse to ICC arbitration together with the interest yielded by the advances deposited by these parties.

15.79 The ICC is sometimes criticized on the grounds that a substantial portion of the revenue which stems from the arbitration services is not deployed for the ICC Court and its Secretariat, but for other operations of the ICC. This is not quite correct. The revenue of the ICC derived from the payment of administrative costs covers by and large the direct costs of the Court and its Secretariat, which are significant.

(2) Article 1(1): Organization of the ICC Court

15.80 **(2.1) The International Court of Arbitration** The word 'international' in the Court's name stresses the truly international character of this arbitration institution, given the multinational composition of both its Court and its Secretariat, and the multinational background of its users.[65]

15.81 The ICC Court is not a separate legal entity and has no legal capacity. It is simply the 'arbitration body attached to the ICC', that is to say an internal department within the ICC. Negligence, or errors, if any, committed by the ICC Court are therefore the responsibility of the ICC, against which any legal disputes would have to be directed.[66] In some cases, the French courts and even courts in other countries have been seized of actions brought against the ICC relating to the Court's activities. The French Supreme Court has held several times that there is a contractual relationship between the parties and the ICC with respect to the organization of arbitration.[67]

15.82 Under Art 1(1), the ICC Council is responsible for appointing, and does in fact appoint, the members of the ICC Court.

15.83 Each National Committee of the ICC is empowered to nominate up to two members for appointment to the ICC Court by the ICC Council, which also appoints the Chairman and the Vice-Chairmen, in each case for a term of three years.[68] The members of the Court are not employed by the ICC; they act on a *pro bono* basis. Except for the Chairman and the Vice-Chairmen, not even the travel expenses of the members are reimbursed, but each member receives a *per diem* fee per meeting attended (currently less than 100 US dollars). At the end of the year 2007, the members of the Court came from 90 different countries.

'Aux frontières de l'arbitrage et de l'ADR: La Sentence d'Accord Parties' in *Les Cahiers de l'Arbitrage Volume I* (Gazette du Palais, Paris, 2002) 8.

[65] In 2007 and 2008, a total of 3,369 parties in ICC arbitration originated from a record 126 (120) different countries and independent territories, above Introduction, para 15.18 *et seq.*

[66] See *infra* Art 34.

[67] See Cour de Cassation, Civ 1e, 20 February 2001, *Société Cubic Defense Systems Inc v Chambre de commerce internationale*, (2001) *Rev arb* no 3, , 511, note *Clay*; Paris, 15 September 1998, *Société Cubic Defense Systems Inc v Chambre de commerce internationale*, (1999) *Rev arb* no 1, 103, note *Lalive*; TGI Paris, 21 May 1997, *Société Cubic Defense v Chambre de commerce internationale*, (1997) *Rev arb* no3, 417. More recently, see Paris TGI, 10 October 2007, *Société SNF v Chambre de Commerce Internationale*, (2007) *Rev arb* no 4, 847, note *Jarrosson*; TGI Paris, 16 December 2004, *M Marcel Taffin v Cour internationale d'arbitrage de la Chambre de Commerce Internationale & Société Goather Versicherungsbank VVag*, unreported.

[68] The current term will end on 31 December 2011.

From March 2006 to June 2008, the Chairman of the ICC Court was Professor Pierre Tercier from Switzerland who succeeded Dr Robert Briner, another Swiss lawyer,[69] who had been Chairman since January 1997.[70] From 1 July to 31 December 2008, Carl Salans, a US national served as Chairman of the ICC Court, and was replaced on 1 January 2009 by John Beechey, a UK national. Thus, the predecessor and two successors of Professor Tercier were all former practising attorneys who, prior to becoming the ICC Court's Chairman, all had substantial international arbitration experience. Currently, there are Vice-Chairmen, who are chosen by the Chairman at his own discretion, and like the Chairman, appointed for a term of three years by the ICC World Council. The Vice-Chairmen are not employees of the ICC, nor is the Chairman himself. 15.84

(2.2) The Statutes of the ICC Court (App I to the ICC Rules) As stated in Art 1(1), the Statutes of the ICC Court are set forth in App I.[71] It is for the Council of the ICC Court to issue and to amend these Statutes. The Statutes should be read together with the ICC Rules and the Internal Rules of the ICC Court in App II. 15.85

In the first place, the Statutes describe the functions and powers of the ICC Court. The Court is entrusted with ensuring the application of the Rules and has all the 'necessary powers' to do so. There are two additional clauses, which do not change the position but simply confirm that the ICC Court is an 'autonomous body' which carries out its functions independently from the ICC and its organs as well as from the members of the ICC National Committees (App I, Art 1(2) and (3)). 15.86

The ICC Court is composed of the following persons: a Chairman, Vice-Chairmen, members and alternate members (together referred to as 'members') (App I, Art 2, first sentence). The ICC Court is assisted by the ICC Secretariat. (App I, Art 2, second sentence). 15.87

The Chairman is elected by the ICC World Council upon recommendation of the Executive Board of the ICC (App I, Art 3(1)). The Statutes contain no requirements as to the Chairman's qualifications or experience with ICC arbitration, and the Chairman can be chosen, and in the past has been chosen, from outside the ICC Court.[72] The Vice-Chairmen are appointed from among the members of the Court 'or otherwise' by the ICC Council upon proposal of the Chairman of the Court (App I, Art 3(2)).[73] 15.88

The members of the ICC Court are appointed upon the proposal of the ICC National Committees, that is to say one member for each National Committee (App I, Art 3(3)). Alternate members may be appointed by the Council upon proposal of the Chairman of the Court (App I, Art 3(4)). In the past, an alternate member was appointed in particular where the ordinary member of the ICC Court was based outside of France, and unable to 15.89

69 The two prior Chairmen, Mr Michel Gaudet and Mr Alain Plantey, were from France.

70 Upon completion of Dr Briner's term, see *Liber Amicorum in honour of Robert Briner, Global Reflections on International Law, Commerce and Dispute Resolution* (ICC Publishing, Paris, 2005).

71 Art 1: Function; Art 2: Composition of the ICC Court; Art 3: Appointment; Art 4: Plenary Session of the ICC Court; Art 5: Committees; Art 6: Confidentiality; Art 7: Modification of the Rules of Arbitration.

72 See *supra* Introduction, n 12 and para 15.16.

73 Some of the current Vice-Chairmen were previously members of the Court, which has the advantage of having persons truly knowledgeable about the ICC Court's practice and policy.

attend the ICC Court's sessions regularly. The term of office of such persons is three years. If a member is no longer in a position to exercise his functions, he may be replaced by the ICC Council and such successor will be in office for the remainder of the predecessor's term (App I, Art 3(5)).

15.90 A list of the members and alternate members of the ICC Court can be found on the ICC's website.[74] At the end of 2008, there were 126 members on the ICC Court, 98 regular and 28 alternate members representing 90 different nationalities.

15.91 The decisions of the ICC Court are taken at the monthly plenary sessions presided over by the Chairman, or in his absence by one of the Vice-Chairmen designated by him (App I, Art 4, first sentence). The provisions for voting and quorum at the plenary sessions are as follows: a quorum is attained if six members or alternate members are present, and decisions are taken upon majority vote, the Chairman having the casting vote in the event of a tie (App I, Art 4 second and third sentence). The members and alternate members may attend any plenary session of the Court as they wish. Alternate members have the same standing as the ordinary members of the Court. It therefore happens frequently that a member and alternate member from the same country attend the plenary session of the Court, although this was probably not the original intention. The Court also takes decisions through committees. They are composed of three members including the Chairman of the Court, or one of the Vice-Chairs (App I, Art 5).

15.92 The confidential nature of the work of the ICC Court is set down in the Statutes (App I, Art 6, first sentence). Article 6 refers only to confidentiality in relation to the ICC Court proceedings and not to confidentiality in ICC arbitrations generally.[75] It establishes that the ICC Court has the power to make rules to determine who may attend meetings of the Court and its committees and who may be allowed access to the materials submitted to the ICC Court and its Secretariat. This provision reflects the rules on presence at the Court's sessions contained in the Internal Rules (App II, Art 1).

15.93 Finally, the Statutes lay down the procedure for modification of the Rules: accordingly, the Court is to place proposals before the Commission on International Arbitration, which are then submitted to the Executive Board and the ICC Council for approval (App I, Art 7).

15.94 (2.3) **The functioning of the ICC Court** The function of the ICC Court is described in the Rules, Art 1(1), fourth sentence as follows: '(. . .) to provide for the settlement by arbitration of business disputes of an international character'.

15.95 The Rules and Apps II and III set forth the powers of the ICC Court so that it can fulfil its function. The Court's structure, and the resources at its disposal to fulfil this function, have been described above.

15.96 In principle, the scope of application of the ICC Rules is limited to 'business disputes', provided they are of an 'international character'. This wording is a self-imposed limitation on and safeguard for the kinds of disputes for which the ICC wishes to offer its arbitration

---

[74] <http://www.iccwbo.org>.
[75] See *infra* Art 20(7).

services. ICC arbitration is not only 'international', but also 'universal'[76] in nature as all types of international business disputes may be resolved by the ICC regardless of the particular sectors of trade, industry or services, of the nationality of the parties or of the private or public character of the contracts involved.

In practice, the scope of application of ICC arbitration has rarely posed a problem for the following reason: the vast majority of matters submitted to the ICC Court qualify under the above definition, in particular since the ICC Court has traditionally taken a broad view of what constitutes a 'business dispute of an international character'.[77] Therefore even parties from the same country, ie with the same nationality, may have a dispute of 'international character', if it arises out of a transaction which involves or affects international commerce.[78] **15.97**

Article 1(1) expressly empowers the ICC Court to accept business disputes 'not of an international character'. Strictly speaking, the ICC Court thus 'shall' accept such disputes, 'if so empowered by an arbitration agreement'. The addition of the latter words is superfluous, since the ICC Court will in any event act only if the parties have provided in their arbitration agreement for 'ICC arbitration' as reflected in Art 6 (1). **15.98**

Business disputes: The term 'business' is to be understood in a broad sense, that is to say any dispute involving commercial interests, in whatever field, in the private or public sector. The disputes referred to ICC arbitration cover all kinds of contracts, namely sales and purchase contracts (23.9 per cent), services agreements, intellectual property (5.5 per cent) and cooperation arrangements.[79] While the American Arbitration Association (the 'AAA') offers to entertain large-scale labour (employment) disputes, sport disputes, automobile accident or insurance claims as well as mass claims, the ICC Court considers them to be outside its general vocation.[80] This does not prevent the ICC in a particular case from accepting disputes in these fields. The amount of the parties' dispute is not relevant in defining what is a 'business' dispute, although it is recognized that the current ICC arbitration system is not well suited for 'small claims' disputes. The ICC Rules are not designed to cover consumer disputes, in particular under the aspect that the ICC arbitration costs may be dissuasive in the consumer area.[81] **15.99**

---

[76] Craig, L.W., Park, W.W. and Paulsson, J., *International Chamber of Commerce Arbitration* (3rd edn, Oceana/ICC Publishing, New York, 2000) 1.

[77] Craig/Park/Paulsson, *op cit*, 138 *et seq*.

[78] Craig/Park/Paulsson, *op cit*, 138 *et seq*; Derains, Y. and Schwartz, E., *A Guide to the ICC Rules of Arbitration* (2nd edn, Kluwer, The Hague, 2005) 16 *et seq*; Redfern, A. and Hunter, M. with Blackaby, N. and Partasides, C., *Law and Practice of International Commercial Arbitration* (4th edn, Thompson/Sweet & Maxwell, London, 2004) 14.

[79] In 2007, the following principal economic sectors were: construction and engineering: 14%; energy: 12.5%; information technology: 10.4%; industrial equipment and services: 8.3%; metals and raw materials: 7.1%; finance and insurance: 6.7%; and transports: 5.2%, see (2006) 18 *ICC ICArb Bull* no 1, 11.

[80] The AAA, the most important domestic arbitration institution in the USA, provides a wide range of specific arbitration rates for matters such as labour, sport or accident, insurance or mass claims. These rates may be downloaded from <http://www.adr.org>.

[81] See *Brower et al v Gateway 2000, Inc et al*, (1998) New York Supreme Court, Appellate Division, First Department 676 N.Y.S.2d 569, (1999) YBCA vol XXIVa 343 (ICC arbitration clause in a consumer sales contract for a Gateway computer; the court rejected the enforceability on the grounds of unconscionability considering that the ICC fee structure exceeded the amount at issue).

15.100 Investment disputes under bilateral investment treaties (or 'BITs') may also be submitted to ICC arbitration. BITs often foresee an arbitration clause for certain types of disputes relating to the investment, either under local arbitration, the arbitration rules of the International Center for the Settlement of Investment Disputes ('ICSID'), or under rules of other arbitration institutions, like the UNCITRAL Arbitration Rules or the ICC Rules.

15.101 Article 1(1) states as part of the Court's function that arbitration shall be provided 'in accordance with the Rules'. This proviso applies to both the ICC Court and to the parties. The ICC Court cannot intervene in matters that go beyond its function defined in Art 1. For instance, the ICC Court could not act as an adjudicator or a mediator in a given dispute. At the same time, this provision restricts the freedom of parties to depart unilaterally from the arbitral system contained in the ICC Rules of Arbitration. It is on the basis of these words that the ICC Court may decline to administer a given case where parties seek to deviate significantly from the Rules. This issue is often referred to under the somewhat misleading jargon of 'mandatory' and 'non-mandatory' provisions in the ICC Rules of Arbitration.

15.102 By issuing the ICC Rules, the ICC makes an offer to parties to agree upon the use of its arbitration services, as embodied in its Rules.[82] To the extent that the ICC Rules specifically give the power to the parties to agree on certain matters that may arise in the course of an ICC arbitration, such as the number of arbitrators, the method of their selection, the place of arbitration or the language of the arbitration, the ICC Court is obviously bound by such agreement.

15.103 In all other cases, it would seem that parties cannot unilaterally impose any deviation from the ICC Rules without the agreement of the ICC Court. It then becomes a policy question for the ICC Court whether or not to accept such change. The ICC has to protect its reputation regarding both how satisfactorily the arbitration procedure is conducted, and the enforceability of awards rendered under its auspices.

15.104 It has been the ICC Court's policy not to accept modifications to its Rules on certain points, including:

- the establishment of the Terms of Reference;
- the fixing of arbitrators' fees by the Court; and
- the scrutiny and approval of awards by the Court.[83]

These issues are often referred to as being of 'mandatory' nature.[84]

15.105 In practice, the ICC Court has regularly accepted a modification of its Rules upon a case-by-case decision, so long as they were considered compatible with the ICC arbitral system

[82] See also Art 6(1).

[83] It is worth noting that during the 1998 revision of the Rules, not a single National Committee proposed the deletion of the Terms of Reference from the Rules. Although a few had suggested that they become optional, that suggestion was not pursued.

[84] See also Smit, R.H., 'Mandatory ICC Arbitration Rules' in *Liber Amicorum Robert Briner* (ICC Publishing, Paris, 2005) 845.

as such. However, the drafters of ICC arbitration clauses and agreements must be aware that they depart from the ICC Rules at their own risk, and that the ICC Court is not obliged to agree.

The ICC Court has accepted, for example, arbitration clauses which empowered the arbitrators, rather than the ICC Court itself, to determine the place of arbitration, although this latter function is the responsibility of the Court, where the parties have not agreed upon the place (Art 14). **15.106**

Where parties have stipulated in their arbitration clause a short time limit for the arbitrators to render the final award, the ICC Court would normally explain to the parties the difficulty of implementing such a time limit, and seek to ensure that the parties agree on the possibility for the ICC Court to extend this time limit (see Art 24).[85] **15.107**

(3) Article 1(2): The powers of the ICC Court

(3.1) The role of the ICC Court Notwithstanding its imposing name, the ICC Court does not itself settle the disputes which are submitted to it by parties (Art 1(2)). Since the inception of the ICC Court, this has always been the case.[86] The ICC Court's role is to provide the framework for arbitration under its Rules in a consistent and foreseeable manner. Each dispute submitted to ICC arbitration will be decided by an Arbitral Tribunal, which the ICC Court will supervise from a merely administrative perspective. The ICC Court will not guarantee a uniform application of the ICC Rules and generally leaves it to the Arbitral Tribunal to interpret them. **15.108**

The powers of the ICC Court are those defined in the ICC Rules, ie ensuring the application of the Rules (Art 1(2)). The decisions which the ICC Court has to take under the Rules are to a large extent expressly stated therein (eg determining prima facie the existence of an ICC arbitration agreement, constituting the Arbitral Tribunal, deciding on challenges against arbitrators, and on their replacement, fixing the place of arbitration, approving the Terms of Reference, scrutinizing and approving awards etc). The ICC Court takes these decisions with a view to administering the arbitration case submitted to it by the parties. In this respect, the functions of the ICC Court need to be distinguished from those of the arbitrators, who are principally called upon to decide the substantive issues of a dispute put before them. **15.109**

Article 1(1) of the ICC Court's Statutes (App I) emphasizes that the court 'has all necessary powers for that purpose', that is to say for ensuring the application of the Rules. Such powers **15.110**

[85] To the possibilities and limits to modify time limits set out in the ICC Rules, see *infra* Art 32.

[86] Since the ICC Court is not a court as such, a different name might have been more appropriate. However, 75 years after the inauguration of the ICC arbitration system, it might do more harm than good to rename the ICC Court at this late date. The first set of the ICC Rules provided for the appointment of an 'International Committee on Arbitration', to be known as the 'Court of Arbitration of the International Chamber of Commerce'. The ICC Court has nothing in common with the Permanent Court of Arbitration ('PCA') in The Hague (Netherlands), which was established on the basis of the Hague Conventions of 1899 and 1907 for international disputes arising between states.

are to be exercised with a view to meeting the objectives set forth in Art 35, pursuant to which the Court 'shall make every effort to make sure that the Award is enforceable at law'.

15.111 Based upon such powers, the ICC Court will interpret the ICC Rules as it deems fit. It is to be noted, however, that the ICC Court's interpretation of the Rules is not necessarily binding upon the arbitrators that have been asked to decide a particular dispute. Likewise, national courts are not bound by the ICC Court's view of how the ICC Rules should be applied to a particular case.

15.112 When the ICC Court decides upon the number of arbitrators, appoints a sole arbitrator, replaces a Chairman on the basis of a challenge, fixes the place of arbitration or the costs of arbitration, extends time limits for establishing the Terms of Reference or to render the award, or scrutinizes draft awards under Art 27, it exercises the authority entrusted to it by the parties to take, in a given situation, a decision pursuant to its Rules, on behalf of those parties. The situation is not different when the Court decides that prima facie there is a binding arbitration agreement, under which it is authorized to act, ie to set the arbitration in motion. These decisions are all administrative in nature, as has been confirmed by the French Supreme Court in the *Cubic* case,[87] and the ICC Court is not required to provide reasons for its decisions.

15.113 This does not mean that the ICC Court, in the exercise of the discretion which it is afforded by the parties under its Rules, can render arbitrary decisions. Nor does it mean that certain standards of 'due process' (fairness) do not have to be satisfied. Since the ICC Court's decisions are administrative in nature, national courts may review issues relating to jurisdiction, challenges to arbitrators and the validity of the award. Thus, it has become the common practice of the ICC Court and its Secretariat to seek the views of both parties prior to taking any administrative decision, such as an extension of time requested by a party, even in cases where the ICC Rules do not expressly provide for such a possibility. This fosters the parties' confidence in ICC arbitration, and adds to the transparency of the entire arbitral process.

15.114 If a party should consider that the ICC Court has violated the ICC Rules in taking a specific decision, the party is at liberty to submit the matter to the competent national courts, most likely those in France, since the ICC has its seat in Paris, France.[88] In such cases, the ICC Court's decision on jurisdiction pursuant to Art 6(2) of the ICC Rules is only provisional. The jurisdictional decision will then be made by the Arbitral Tribunal that has been put in place pursuant to the ICC Rules.[89] From a French law perspective, the ICC's obligation is to ensure the organization of the arbitration. French courts will leave it to the arbitrators to decide on the merits and to the courts at the place of arbitration to reach any judicial decisions required (such as the validity of a challenge). They will not interfere with the ICC Court's decisions, provided that these are taken by the ICC Court under its discretion to apply the ICC Rules.

---

[87] See n 67 under para 15.81 *supra*.

[88] As the cases cited in n 67 show, challenges of the ICC Court's decisions before the national courts have rarely, if ever, succeeded.

[89] See *infra* Art 6, paras 15.340 *et seq*.

(3.2) The Internal Rules of the ICC Court Article 1(2) states that the ICC Court draws up its own Internal Rules which, since 1980, appear as App II to the ICC Rules of Arbitration. **15.115**

They comprise six rules, as follows: on the confidential nature of the work of the ICC Court (Art 1); on the participation of members of the ICC Court in ICC arbitration (Art 2); on the relations between members of the Court and the ICC National Committees (Art 3); on the Committee of the ICC Court (Art 4); on the ICC Court Secretariat (Art 5); and, finally on scrutiny of awards by the ICC Court (Art 6). **15.116**

Both the plenary sessions and the committee sessions of the Court are restricted to the members and its Secretariat (App II, Art 1(1)), although exceptionally other persons may be invited by the Chairman provided they agree to respect the confidential nature of the work (App II, Art 1(2)). This applies in particular to interns that spend a few months at the Court's Secretariat as part of their legal training.[90] Therefore the parties and their legal representatives have no access to the Court's sessions and therefore no opportunity to make oral statements, instead they may make written submissions. They may also speak directly with the Secretariat if they feel that an oral explanation may assist the Secretariat in better understanding a party's position. Nevertheless, the Secretariat should ensure that any substantive point raised is presented to the other party as well.[91] The Secretariat sets out the positions of both parties and the Tribunal if necessary.[92] **15.117**

The Internal Rules ensure the confidentiality of documents submitted to the ICC Court and those created by the Court in the course of its proceedings, by restricting communication thereof to the members of the ICC Court, its Secretariat and such persons as are authorized to attend sessions by the Chairman (App II, Art 1(3)).[93] The only other persons who may have limited access to documents, ie awards and other documents of general interest, are researchers undertaking work of a scientific nature on international trade law, such persons being authorized by the Chairman or the Secretary-General of the Court (App II, Art 1(4)). The Rules expressly exclude the possibility of communicating to such persons 'memoranda, notes, statements and documents remitted by the parties within the framework of arbitration proceedings' (App II, Art 1(4)).[94] **15.118**

---

[90] This has been an established practice for many years.

[91] If a party raises a substantive point with the Secretariat, the Secretariat usually invites the party to set out the comment in a letter copied to the other side. The parties' correspondence with the Secretariat usually forms part of the file submitted to the ICC Court.

[92] For a comprehensive description of the valuing system of the ICC Court's Plenary and Committee Services, see Bühler/Webster, Handbook of ICC Arbitration, *op cit*, 496–509.

[93] See para 15.12. See also Rosher, P., 'Legal privilege et confidentialité des communications avocat-client en matière d'arbitrage international—Vers une possible harmonisation?' (2007) *Les Cahiers de l'Arbitrage* no 3, 21.

[94] Jolivet, E., 'Access to information and Awards' (2006) 22 *Arb Int'l* no 2, 265, 273–4. 'A distinction should be drawn between the information that is aimed at being communicated without specific control, such as promotional brochures and controlled information. Control can be exercised on the communication itself or the use of the information. The latter situation is, for example, encountered when arbitral institutions give access to arbitral decisions for research of an academic nature. Once the information has been processed by the researcher in a doctoral thesis, a book or an article, the institution will check that the information chosen and the reference thereto do not contravene its confidentiality policy and are not likely to be detrimental to its image.'

15.119 As regards persons who may be authorized, such authorization is subject to the condition that they give an undertaking to respect the confidentiality of the documents and to refrain from publication of any text without the prior approval of the Secretary-General of the Court (App II, Art 1(5)).

15.120 As to the functioning, statistics and proceedings of ICC arbitration, the ICC and the members of the Secretariat regularly publish articles regarding types of decisions and trends, but without identifying the name of the parties involved,[95] and provide relevant extracts of awards and procedural orders that do not identify either the parties or (the arbitrators).[96]

15.121 In any arbitration proceedings, the ICC Secretariat may receive a large number of submissions, documents and correspondence and it is not practicable for it to keep these in their entirety once the arbitration proceedings have come to an end. The ICC Secretariat notifies the parties prior to destroying documents, communications or correspondence from the parties or arbitrators in any given arbitration. Normally, when the final award is communicated to the parties, or when the file is being closed for other reasons, the Secretariat will invite the parties to indicate within a fixed time limit whether they wish any documents that they have submitted to the ICC in the course of the arbitration to be returned to them. The return of such documents will be at the expense of the party asking for it (App II, Art 1(7)). In the absence of such a request, the ICC will not send the often voluminous briefs and exhibit volumes to its external archives, but rather will simply have them destroyed.

15.122 In any event, the following essential documents are kept in the archives of the ICC Secretariat: originals of all awards, the Terms of Reference, decisions of the ICC Court as recorded in the minutes of the Court's sessions, and pertinent correspondence (App II, Art 1(6)).

15.123 The Chairman and members of the Secretariat are excluded from acting as arbitrators or counsel in ICC arbitrations (App II, Art 2(1)). Only upon nomination by one or both parties, or any other procedure determined by the parties, may the Vice-Chairmen or members of the ICC Court act as arbitrators, although this is also subject to the confirmation of the Court (App II, Art 2(2)). The Vice-Chairmen and Court members may always act as counsel to a party in an ICC arbitration. The Chairman, Vice-Chairmen and members of the Court or Secretariat have a duty to inform the Secretary-General of any involvement in any capacity whatsoever in proceedings pending before the Court, as soon as such persons become aware of this involvement (App II, Art 2(3)). Furthermore, the Internal Rules provide that any such person should not participate in discussions or decisions concerning such proceedings, and should retire from the session of the Court when the matter is considered (App II, Art 2(4)). It follows that material information or documents are not

---

[95] See Jolivet, E., 'Chronique de jurisprudence arbitrale de la Chambre de commerce internationale (CCI): l'incompétence de l'arbitre' (2006) *Les Cahiers de l'Arbitrage* 2006/1, 38.

[96] See eg Arnaldez, J.J., Derains, Y. and Hascher, D., *Collection of ICC Arbitral Awards 1996–2000*, vol IV (ICC Publishing/Kluwer, 2003); Arnaldez, J.J., Derains, Y. and Hascher, D., *Collection of ICC Arbitral Awards 1991–1995*, vol III (ICC Publishing/Kluwer, 1997); Jarvin, S., Derains, Y. and Arnaldez, J.J., *Collection of ICC Arbitral Awards 1986–1990*, vol II (ICC Publishing, Paris, 1994); and Jarvin, S. and Derains, Y., *Collection of ICC Arbitral Awards 1974–1985*, vol I (ICC Publishing, Paris, 1990).

communicated to such persons (App II, Art 2(5)). In practice, and to the best of the authors' knowledge, scrupulous attention is always given in respecting these rules.

The members of the ICC Court are independent of the National Committees by which they were proposed (App II, Art 3(1)) and, apart from specific information which the Chairman may ask them to pass on, they are to treat as confidential in their relations with the ICC National Committees information concerning individual cases with which they become acquainted (App II, Art 3(2)). **15.124**

As stated above, in order to carry out its work, the Court may establish committees and is responsible for establishing the functions and organization of such committees (App I, Art 5).[97] At each plenary session, the members of the committee sessions of the forthcoming month are designated; they will always be formed by members from three different countries (the Chairman or a Vice-Chair of the Court and two members or alternate members (App II, Art 4(2)). Therefore the members of the committee will generally change from month to month. The Chairman convenes the committee, and a quorum is attained if two members are present (App II, Art 4(4)). The plenary session of Court determines the matters to be decided by the committee, and decisions are to be taken unanimously, failing which (or if the committee abstains), the case will normally be transferred to the next plenary session with any suggestions the committee deems appropriate. Otherwise the decision of the committee is brought to the notice of the ICC Court at the next plenary session (App II, Art 4(5)). In general there are four committee meetings a month, usually on Thursday morning, and one plenary session, which is normally held in the afternoon of the last Thursday of each month. **15.125**

It is fair to say that with one monthly plenary session, and four committee sessions per month, the ICC Court works nowadays on a permanent basis throughout the year.[98] **15.126**

The Secretary-General of the ICC Court has the power, in case of absence, to delegate to the General Counsel and/or the Deputy Secretary-General authority under the ICC Rules in respect of confirmation of arbitrators, certification of true copies of Terms of Reference or awards, and request for payment of provisional advances, (App II, Art 5(1)). The Secretariat is empowered with the ICC Court's approval, to issue notes and other documents to the parties and arbitrators, when necessary for the proper conduct of the arbitration proceedings (App II, Art 5(2)).[99] **15.127**

Finally, regarding the duty of the Court to scrutinize awards under Art 27, the Internal Rules provide that the Court consider 'to the extent practicable', the requirements of mandatory law at the place of arbitration (App II, Art 6). The specific references to mandatory rules on giving reasons for the awards, signature of awards and admissibility of dissenting **15.128**

[97] See *supra* para 15.91.

[98] It is a myth that as a Paris-based organization, the ICC Court would not meet during the month of August. Over the last 25 years, there was always a plenary session in August.

[99] See eg 'Note from the Secretariat on the appointment of administrative secretaries to assist the Arbitral Tribunal with its administrative tasks' (1995) 6 *ICC ICArb Bull*, no 2, 77.

opinions which were in the Internal Rules of 1980 are no longer included, the general reference to requirements of the mandatory law being sufficient.[100]

(4) Article 1(3): The Chairman

15.129 (4.1) **Role of the Chairman of the ICC Court and of its Vice-Chairmen** The role of the Chairman is to ensure the effective functioning of the ICC Court, and the ultimate responsibility lies with him. The Statutes provide that the Chairman is to preside over plenary sessions of the Court, and the Chairman has the casting vote (App I, Art 4). Also, alternate members may be appointed by the Council upon the Chairman's proposal (App I, Art 3).[101] The Internal Rules also specifically require that it is only upon the Chairman's invitation that outside persons may attend sessions of the Court and upon the Chairman's authorization (and also the Secretary-General's) that certain persons can have limited access to Court documentation and awards.[102] The Chairman normally also chairs the plenary and committee sessions of the Court.[103] In these tasks, the Chairman, may designate one of the Vice-Chairmen to act on his behalf in his absence.[104]

15.130 The Chairman of the ICC Court has to assume many other more informal, albeit important, functions. The Chairman regularly attends outside arbitration events, and travels frequently to foreign countries to meet the respective National Committees, members of the judiciary, members of government, in particular the Minister of Justice, and representatives of the business community. Explaining on the ground the advantages of international commercial arbitration, and in particular of ICC arbitration, the role of the ICC Court and its Secretariat, and discussing concerns about certain developments in the fields of arbitration that may negatively affect the confidence of the international business community, is of paramount importance. The Chairman of the Court will often be accompanied by the Court's Secretary-General or other members of the Secretariat.

15.131 (4.2) **The taking of 'urgent decisions' by the Chairman of the ICC Court** Pursuant to the Rules, Art 1(3), the Court's Chairman or a Vice-Chairman has the power to take urgent decisions. There are no express restrictions in the ICC Rules upon the ability of the Chairman of the ICC Court (or in his absence, a Vice-Chairman) to render on behalf of the Court an urgent decision. Matters as to which the Chairman may take urgent decisions include approval of awards (eg interim, final and revised final awards, including the fixing of the costs of arbitration etc). There must be a good reason for the urgency that justifies that exceptionally the matter not be submitted for consideration by the entire ICC Court, or one of its (three-member) committees, but simply be decided by the Chairman of the Court.

15.132 In one case where the Chairman of the ICC Court was to approve an interim award, the urgency resulted from the fact that the award had to be notified to the parties immediately so as to allow them to prepare for an upcoming hearing that had been scheduled for quite

[100] See Art 27 for further details.
[101] See *supra* paras 15.83 *et seq.*
[102] See *supra* paras 15–117.
[103] See *supra* para 15.91.
[104] Or exceptionally a member of the Court, see *supra* para 15.91.

some time by the Tribunal. In another case, the parties had agreed on a 'fast-track' arbitration procedure, according to which the award was to be notified within six weeks after the hearing.[105] The existence of urgency was also accepted where a Respondent had filed for bankruptcy, and where the Claimant was required to declare its claims before a certain date by producing the award. In another case, an award had to be made before a certain date; otherwise the assets held in custody by a third party would have been released.

The decision of the Chairman is to be reported to the Court 'at its next session', ie at the next monthly plenary session of the Court. This report is only for purposes of information, not for ratification. 15.133

It may, however, be assumed that the Chairman will make use of its prerogative only in truly urgent cases such as fast-track arbitrations, in order not to reduce the breadth of the decision-making power normally reserved to, and to be exercised by the Court alone. Further, in truly complex and sensitive matters, however urgent they may be, the Chairman would always be well advised to seek informally the views of other members of the Court, in particular the Vice-Chairmen, prior to rendering his decision, and that is what he normally does. 15.134

(5) Article 1(4): The committees

With the impressive increase of workload resulting from the ever increasing number of new cases being filed every year[106], the ICC Court can only function properly if some of the matters which require its attention are delegated to Committees. Article 1(4) gives the basis for such delegation by referring to the ICC Court's Internal Rules, which more fully set out the organization of the ICC Court's committees (App II, Art 4). The Internal Rules do not limit the subject matters of the committees, which can take the same type of decisions as the plenary session of the Court. Pursuant to Art 4(5)(a) of the Internal Rules, it is for the Court to decide which types of decisions it wishes to reserve to the plenary session alone.[107] Thus, committees of the Court can also approve awards. In practice, awards raising particular issues, or being of particular importance because of the identities of the parties (eg a sovereign state), or the amounts involved, continue to be submitted to the plenary session. This is also the case where a dissenting opinion has been submitted by an arbitrator. The plenary session of the Court decides challenges and replacements of arbitrators. In any event, decisions of a committee are deemed to be decisions of the entire Court. The plenary session of the Court will not review a decision taken by one of the committees, merely take note of it. 15.135

Some parties feel in certain cases that a matter should be examined at the plenary session, not just by a committee, or once a committee has taken a decision, that the matter should be reviewed at a plenary session. A committee has entire discretion whether or not a matter should be submitted for decision by the plenary session. In general, once the ICC Court 15.136

[105] See *infra* Art 32 on fast-track arbitration.

[106] See *supra* Introduction para 15.17.

[107] See also Art 4(5)(b) and (c) of the Internal Rules, App II, as to the decisions taken by the committee or transferred to the Court's plenary sessions.

has taken a decision at a plenary or committee session it will not revisit it absent the showing by a party that new elements have emerged, which might alter the Court's decision.

(6) Article 1(5): The Secretariat

15.137 (6.1) **The organization of the ICC Court's Secretariat** The Secretary-General of the ICC Court (who is often confused with, but is different from, the Secretary-General of the ICC)[108] is the head of the Secretariat of the ICC Court. The Secretary-General is assisted by a Deputy Secretary-General and a General Counsel.

15.138 In 2007, the Secretariat of the ICC Court had over 60 full-time employees. The Secretariat's employees included 30 lawyers from 19 different countries of whom six are counsel. The staff speaks 18 languages, including English, French, German, Italian, Spanish, Russian, Mandarin, Polish, Arabic, Latvian, and Romanian. The Secretariat handles day-to-day administration of approximately 1,300 cases pending with the ICC Court. Each counsel heads a team composed of three Deputy-counsel who administer, under the counsel's supervision, the pending cases, and two secretaries. The counsel are of different nationalities and are fluent in at least two languages. They report directly to the Secretary-General. The counsel prepare the documents for submission to the ICC Court and attend sessions of the ICC Court where they report on the status of the cases, and answer questions that members of the ICC Court may have prior to taking a decision in a particular cases.

15.139 (6.2) **The seat of the ICC Court's Secretariat** The ICC Court's Secretariat has its seat at the headquarters of the ICC, in Paris. Since late 2008, the Secretariat has had a branch office in Hong Kong, which enables parties from the Asian-Pacific Rim easier contacts with the ICC in their time zone.[109] In 2003, a liaison position was created in Santiago, Chile, now relocated in Panama for the Latin American market, and in 2005 in Tunisia for the Middle East and Northern Africa. The ICC Court also has marketing consultants in New York for North America and in the United Kingdom. Irrespective of the ICC Court's Secretariat seat and regional offices, parties to an ICC arbitration can conduct their arbitration in any other place on the globe.[110]

15.140 (6.3) **The role of the ICC Court's Secretariat** The ICC Court is assisted by the Secretariat (Art 2 of the Statutes, App I). The Secretariat is the executive body of the ICC Court. It operates under the direction of the Court's Secretary-General. Its function consists of ensuring the effective day-to-day administration of the arbitration cases submitted to the ICC. It is the Secretariat that receives the Request, the Answer and any Reply to the counterclaim and that generally corresponds with the parties with respect to the ICC Rules.

15.141 The Secretariat prepares the decisions to be taken by the ICC Court and its Secretary-General, and it communicates those decisions to the parties.[111] All documentation required by the ICC Court is generally prepared and organized by the Secretariat. The documents

[108] See para 15.71.

[109] See *supra* Introduction, para 15.14.

[110] See *infra* Art 14, paras 15.565 *et seq.*

[111] The Secretariat will set out in an agenda a proposal for the decision to be taken by the ICC Court. If the ICC Court agrees with the Secretariat's proposal, it will endorse it; if not, it will modify or change it as it deems fit.

to be submitted will depend on the issue before the ICC Court and include the correspondence from the parties relevant to the issue together with its extracts or other relevant material.[112] The Secretariat also provides advice to parties and arbitrators concerning the practices of the Court and the Secretariat in applying the ICC Rules. The Secretariat has issued a number of general notes relating to various issues such as expenses and the appointment of administrative secretaries.[113]

Article 2. Definitions

In these Rules:

(1) 'Arbitral Tribunal' includes one or more arbitrators.

(2) 'Claimant' includes one or more claimants and 'Respondent' includes one or more respondents.

(3) 'Award' includes, *inter alia*, an interim, partial or final award.

(1) Introduction

It is convenient for the user of the Rules to find at the beginning three defined terms, which frequently appear in the Rules. It is now clear that a sole arbitrator may be referred to as the arbitral tribunal, that a Claimant or Respondent may comprise several entities and that several types of awards can be rendered.[114] **15.142**

(2) 'Arbitral Tribunal'

The definition of 'Arbitral Tribunal' in Art 2(i) of the Rules reflects the text of the standard ICC arbitration clause. This article, read with Art 7(6) of the Rules, makes it plain that in an ICC arbitration an Arbitral Tribunal can be constituted with more than three arbitrators when the parties have so agreed.[115] However, in practice this is unusual for the reasons that are discussed in Art 8. **15.143**

The ICC Rules confer identical powers and duties on the arbitrators, that is the members of the Arbitral Tribunal, except as to the chairman's position pursuant to Art 21(3) and 25(1).[116] **15.144**

(3) 'Claimant and Respondent'

In conformity with most other international arbitration rules, the 1998 ICC Rules have substituted the term 'Respondent' for that of 'Defendant', and thus ended an inconsistency, since the word 'Respondent' goes with 'Claimant', and the word 'Defendant' is used with 'Plaintiff'. The latter terms are reserved for court proceedings; owing to the consensual nature of arbitration, the reference to 'Claimant'/'Respondent' is normally preferred. **15.145**

---

[112] See Art 5 of the Internal Rules, App I.

[113] See, eg ICC, 'Note from the Secretariat on the appointment of administrative secretaries to assist the Arbitral Tribunal with its administrative tasks', *op cit;* ICC, 'Note on correction and interpretation of arbitral award' (1999) 10 *ICC ICArb Bull*, no 2, 4; and the Secretariat's 'Statement on VAT and other taxes applicable to arbitrator's fees' (2006) *ICC ICArb Bull*, no 2, 4.

[114] Comparable arbitration rules: Art 1 SIAC; Art 1 WIPO; comparable rule in the UNCITRAL Model Law: Art 2.

[115] See para 15.417.

[116] See as to the duties: Art 7, 15(2), 18(1) and 20(1), (2), (6); and as to the powers: Art 14(2), 15(1), 17(1), 20, 23(1), 29 (1) of the ICC Rules.

15.146 Of far greater importance is the definition of 'Claimant' as "including one or more claimants and 'Respondent' as including 'one or more respondents'.[117]

15.147 A significant number of the arbitrations the ICC administers involve more than two parties on either side of the arbitration or on both sides.[118] Article 2(ii) indicates from the outset that the ICC Rules may accommodate multi-party arbitration.[119]

(4) 'Award'

15.148 The 1975/1988 Rules did not recognize the existence of or any distinction between different types of awards, except by referring to a 'partial or definite' award. The 1995 Working Group of the ICC Commission on International Arbitration made an attempt to define the terms 'interim', 'interlocutory', 'partial', and 'final' awards.[120] The 1998 Rules now provide a definition which establishes that the term 'award' does not refer only to a 'final' (in the sense of 'last') award. However, the Rules do not provide an exhaustive list of the types of awards encompassed by the terms, and without defining the meaning of an 'interim' and 'partial' award. It is normally the Tribunal that gives its award the title it considers appropriate. As a matter of practice, an interim award would normally settle the issue of jurisdiction, whereas a partial award would decide some element(s) of the merits of the dispute, for example the liability of a party.[121] As there is no internationally accepted definition of these terms, 'partial' award in one jurisdiction may correspond to 'interim' award in another.[122] In the practice of ICC arbitrations, those terms are used interchangedly for anything that is but a final award. The award deciding upon the quantum of damage would be the 'final' award, provided it contains also a decision on costs. Any award ending the arbitral proceedings, and deciding upon the costs of arbitration, is a final award within the meaning of the ICC Rules.[123]

15.149 There are other, more difficult issues that arise in the context of an award. What decisions of the Arbitral Tribunal should be deemed to be 'awards', which must, under the Rules, be scrutinized by the ICC Court before being signed by the arbitrators? May an Arbitral Tribunal fix and allocate between the parties the costs so far incurred in an award which does not finally dispose of the entirety of the issues before it (ie a 'partial' award)? More generally, under what circumstances, may a 'partial' award be issued?

[117] See discussion under Art 10.

[118] See Webster/Bühler, *op cit*.

[119] See Whitesell, A.-M. and Silva-Romero, E., 'Multiparty and Multicontract Arbitration: Recent ICC Experience' (2003) ICC *ICArb Bull*, Special Supp, 7.

[120] See ICC Working Group on Interim and Partial Awards, Final Report (1990) 1 *ICC ICArb Bull* no 1, 26.

[121] See Redfern/Hunter, *op cit*, 354; Delvolvé, J.-L., Rouche, J. and Pointon, G.H., *French Arbitration Law and Practice* (Kluwer, New York, 2003) 167, n 302; Poudret, J.F. and Besson, S., *Comparative Law of International Arbitration* (Thomson/Sweet & Maxwell, London, 2007) Art 1, 631; Fouchard, Ph., Gaillard, E. and Goldman, B., *On International Arbitration* (Kluwer, 1999) 734, Art 1, n 1348–66; Craig/Park/Paulsson, *op cit*, p 358.

[122] See Wirth, M., 'Interim or Preventive Measures in Support of International Arbitration in Switzerland' (2000) 18 *ASA Bull* no 1, 31; Derains/Schwartz, A Guide, *op cit*, 29 for further details.

[123] See also the discussion in Arts 24 and 27.

Article 2(iii) does not answer the question of when a decision by the Arbitral Tribunal constitutes an award. Awards, but not procedural orders, must be scrutinized and approved by the ICC Court, and will be notified to the parties by the Secretariat, unlike procedural orders. It is therefore, as a matter of practice, of utmost importance to know whether the decision of an Arbitral Tribunal constitutes an award or not. The ICC Rules provide no specific guidelines to arbitrators or to the ICC Court that allow a proper qualification in each instance.[124] **15.150**

Under the New York Convention, arbitral decisions are enforceable when they constitute awards. In a well-publicized decision, the US Court of Appeals for the Seventh Circuit held that the order of an Arbitral Tribunal (acting in the particular case under the LCIA Rules) directing a party to release certain tax information was 'final', and could therefore be confirmed pursuant to the New York Convention.[125] The Court of Appeals agreed that substance (content) rather than form (title) should control the determination of whether a particular decision of an Arbitral Tribunal constitutes an 'award' under the New York Convention or not. **15.151**

Likewise, the Paris Court of Appeal qualified a decision of an ICC Arbitral Tribunal entitled 'procedural order' as an arbitrator's award, irrespective of its title.[126] **15.152**

Article 3. Written notifications or communications; Time limits

(1) **All pleadings and other written communications submitted by any party, as well as all documents annexed thereto, shall be supplied in a number of copies sufficient to provide one copy for each party, plus one for each arbitrator, and one for the Secretariat. A copy of any communication from the Arbitral Tribunal to the parties shall be sent to the Secretariat.**

(2) **All notifications or communications from the Secretariat and the Arbitral Tribunal shall be made to the last address of the party or its representative for whom the same are intended, as notified either by the party in question or by the other party. Such notification or communication may be made by delivery against receipt, registered post, courier, facsimile transmission, telex, telegram or any other means of telecommunication that provides a record of the sending thereof.**

(3) **A notification or communication shall be deemed to have been made on the day it was received by the party itself or by its representative, or would have been received if made in accordance with the preceding paragraph.**

(4) **Periods of time specified in, or fixed under the present Rules, shall start to run on the day following the date a notification or communication is deemed to have been made in accordance with the preceding paragraph. When the day next following such date is an official holiday or a non-business day in the country where the notification or communication is deemed to have been made, the period of time shall commence on the first following**

---

[124] For a general discussion of this issue, see Art 27, paras 15.947 *et seq.*

[125] *Publicis Communication v Fine North Communications Inc* [2000] 7th Cir 203 (F 3rd 725); see also *Bull ASA* (2000), 427. See commentary by Lamm, C. and Hellbeck, E.R., 'Report on Publicis S.A. v. True North Communications Inc.' (2000) 3 *Int'l Arb L R*; Goldstein, M., 'Note—Publicis Communications and Publicis S.A. v. True North Communications, Court of Appeals for the Seventh Circuit—14 March 2000' (2000) 18 *ASA Bull* no 4, 830; Smit, R.H. and Turner, A., 'Enforcement by US Court of International Arbitration Interim Orders and Awards under the New York Convention, *Publicis Communication v True North Communications Inc*' (2001) *SAR* 2001:1, 47.

[126] *See Braspetro OU Services v Management and Implementation of the Great-Man Made River Project (GMRP)* (2000) Bull ASA 376 *et seq.* See Bühler/Webster, *op cit*, paras 28–21 *et seq* for further examples.

business day. Official holidays and non-business days are included in the calculation of the period of time. If the last day of the relevant period of time granted is an official holiday or a non-business day in the country where the notification or communication is deemed to have been made, the period of time shall expire at the end of the first following business day.

(1) Introduction

15.153 Article 3 deals with written communications and notifications and the manner of their valid transmission (Art 3(1–3)), as well as with time limits and their calculation under the Rules (Art 3(4)). The rules contained in Art 3 are often completed or modified by rules set out in the Terms of Reference or in procedural orders, to the extent that they concern the relations between the Arbitral Tribunal and the parties.

15.154 Article 3(1) distinguishes between pleadings and other written communications submitted by a party and communications forwarded by the Arbitral Tribunal to the parties. Article 3(2) introduces the notion of 'notification' in addition to communications made by the Secretariat and the Arbitral Tribunal to the parties, but also specifies rules with respect to the addressee. It further details the valid means of transmission under the Rules. Finally, Art 3(3) contains provisions for those cases where a specific addressee cannot be found or has disappeared in the course of the arbitration.

15.155 No provision is made in Art 3 or elsewhere in the Rules for communications between the Arbitral Tribunal and the Secretariat.

(2) Article 3(1): Communications from the parties

15.156 (2.1) **Submissions made by the parties** The parties are obliged to supply all written submissions, except communications between themselves or between their counsel, in a number of copies sufficient to provide one for each party[127] and arbitrator in addition to the ICC Court's Secretariat. The basic rule is explicitly reaffirmed in Art 4(4) for the Claimant's Request for Arbitration and in Art 5(3) for the Respondent's Answer. Although this is not expressly stated, Art 3(1) contemplates hard copies (as opposed to soft copies sent electronically).

15.157 Article 3(1) uses the expression 'pleadings and other written communications'. The term 'communications' was introduced in order to include any type of written submission by the parties (pleadings, briefs, memoranda, applications, motions, letters).[128]

15.158 The purpose of this provision leaves unaffected any rules of privilege that may be binding upon a party or its counsel.[129]

15.159 The question may arise whether, in the context of discovery procedures, all documents exchanged by the parties must be provided in copy for the arbitrators and the Secretariat. Given that the purpose of discovery is principally to allow the parties to correctly and fully

[127] For the term party see *infra* Art 10, paras 15.460 *et seq.*

[128] It follows from this objective that communications between the parties, regarding settlement negotiations or an attempt to agree on procedural issues, need not be communicated to the Arbitral Tribunal or the Secretariat.

[129] See eg *Code of Conduct for Lawyers in the European Union* of 28 October 1988 in its amended version of 28 November 1998 and 6 December 2002, available on <http://www.ccbe.org>.

prepare their cases, documents exchanged in the context of discovery would not seem to fall within the scope of Art 3(1). Moreover, Art 3(1) refers to 'pleadings and written communications' that are 'submitted' by a party. This text indicates that the document in question is intended for the ICC Court's Secretariat and/or the Arbitral Tribunal, in addition to the other party.[130] However, where an Arbitral Tribunal, by virtue of its prerogatives under Art 20(5), requires the submission of all or categories of documents exchanged between the parties, such documents must be provided in accordance with Art 3(1).

If communications between the parties or their lawyers relate to their agreement on procedural matters, the questions may arise whether one party may inform the Arbitral Tribunal thereon and more generally, who controls the arbitration proceedings.[131] The provisions of national laws may differ substantially upon the first question dealing with the confidentiality of such communications.[132] In the practice of ICC arbitrations, the parties should presume that any document exchanged between them and/or between their lawyers is not confidential, unless it states otherwise.[133] **15.160**

Likewise, submissions made in the context of ancillary court proceedings, such as applications for interim measures, letters rogatory etc., would not seem to fall under the scope of Art 3(1). However an *ex parte* application for interim measures should be notified to the Secretariat pursuant to Art 23(2).[134] **15.161**

Article 3(1) also applies to submissions made in the course of an expertise ordered by the Arbitral Tribunal (Art 20(4)).[135] **15.162**

Documents annexed: The obligation to provide copies in a sufficient number extends likewise to all documents of any kind annexed to the submissions concerned, such as contracts, letters, drawings, plans, photographs, pictures, maps and the like, irrespective of their volume. It also applies if such documents are handed in without any accompanying submissions, eg in fulfilment of a specific request of the Arbitral Tribunal or during an oral presentation at a hearing. In the latter case, the Secretariat is not always provided with a copy. An Arbitral Tribunal should make sure that all documents handed out during the oral hearings are dispatched to the Secretariat after the hearing, in order to enable the ICC Court and its Secretariat to perform their respective supervising roles. **15.163**

No express provisions exist with respect to exhibits which are not documents, such as samples or electronic storing devices (floppy disks, CD-ROMs/DVDs, CDs, tapes). **15.164**

---

130 Derains/Schwartz, A Guide, *op cit*, 33.

131 See Kaufmann-Kohler, G., 'Qui controle l'arbitrage? Autonomie des parties, pouvoirs des arbitres et principes d'efficacité' in *Liber Amicorum Claude Reymond* (Litec, Paris, 2004) 153; and Webster, T., 'Party Control in International Arbitration' (2003) 19 *J Int'l Arb* no 2, 119, concerning the control of arbitration proceedings.

132 For example, in France communications between attorneys are regarded as confidential; in Commonwealth legal systems documents need to be sent as 'without prejudice' if they are not to be disclosed.

133 See in this context Art 5.3.1 of the Code of Conduct for Lawyers in the European Union: 'If a lawyer sending a communication to a lawyer in another Member State wishes it to remain confidential or without prejudice he should clearly express his intention when communicating the document', see *supra* n 129.

134 See *infra* Art 23, para 15.904.

135 See *infra* Art 20, para 15.799.

If such devices contain electronically stored documents, which are capable of being printed, they would have to be submitted in the required number of 'copies'.

15.165 Article 3(1) does not expressly specify to whom the submissions must be made. It is, however, implicitly clear from the text of Art 3(1) that copies are to be provided to 'each party, . . . each arbitrator, and . . . the Secretariat'. It is common practice that the parties are required to copy directly to the other party, and, if it has already been provided with the file, also to the Arbitral Tribunal, all other submissions they make in the arbitration.

15.166 Where documents annexed are normally in the form of simple photocopies, in case of a dispute as to their authenticity, the Arbitral Tribunal may require the production of the original.

15.167 (2.2) **Communications made by the Arbitral Tribunal** Article 3(1), second sentence, confirms the commonly accepted practice that arbitrators copy in the Secretariat in their communications with the parties. This allows the ICC Court actively to supervise the arbitral procedure and to take decisions as necessary (eg time extensions under Arts 18 and 24; increases of advance on costs under Art 30(2)).

15.168 The word 'communication' is to be understood broadly, and comprises any written information, order, requests and the like that the Arbitral Tribunal may issue to the parties during the arbitration.

15.169 Only communications of the Arbitral Tribunal to the parties must be copied to the Secretariat under the specific obligation of Art 3(1). Thus, the provision does not provide for communications among the arbitrators or between the Arbitral Tribunal and an expert, a court reporter, or judicial authorities in the context of court assistance to be copied to the parties and/or the Secretariat. This does not prevent the Arbitral Tribunal from copying such correspondence to the parties and/or the Secretariat, if it considers this to be appropriate. The duty towards a good administration of justice may require that it copy such correspondence to the parties and Secretariat. Since the Secretariat is neutral with respect to all participants in the arbitration, and to ensure the good administration of the arbitral procedure on a day-to-day basis, an Arbitral Tribunal may sometimes find it useful to provide the Secretariat with copies of the aforementioned correspondence. However, parties must not gain insight into the decision-making process of the Arbitral Tribunal (*secret du délibéré*). The limited exception hereto by way of a dissenting opinion will be dealt with below.[136]

15.170 The Arbitral Tribunal must always copy in the Secretariat with its communications with the parties.

(3) Article 3(2): Communications from the Secretariat and the Arbitral Tribunal

15.171 (3.1) **Notifications/communications made by the Secretariat of the ICC Court and/or the Arbitral Tribunal** Article 3(2) introduces the notion of notifications in addition to communications. The term 'notification' is intended to designate the official communication by the Secretariat to the parties of the various decisions made by the ICC Court,

[136] See *infra* Art 25, paras 15.927 *et seq.*

including the award rendered by the Arbitral Tribunal (see Art 28(1)). It would have been appropriate to use the word notification also for the communication of the Request for Arbitration to the Respondent, and the communication of Answer to the Claimant, although the Rules use a different terminology (see Art 4(5) using the term 'send' and Art 5 (4) using the term 'communicate'). Article 3 should be read in conjunction with the relevant national law, in particular the law of the place of arbitration. Some national laws have more precise provisions regarding notice.

The essential part of Art 3(2), first sentence, deals with the question which address the Secretariat and the Arbitral Tribunal must use for communications to the parties. However, the provision must be construed also to apply to any communication sent by one party to the other in the arbitral proceedings.[137] In practice, the parties and arbitrators usually agree and set forth in the Terms of Reference[138] the addresses to which notifications are to be made. **15.172**

Last address 'as notified either by the party in question or by the other party': The intended meaning is already contained in the word 'last' address, which is obviously not necessarily the same as 'actual' address. The purpose of this provision is to protect the party incapable of tracing the actual whereabouts of its contractual partner by allowing communications to be made to the last 'known' address. **15.173**

Under the wording 'as notified either by the part in question or by the other party', two situations can be envisioned: either the addressee itself has notified its address, which is regularly the case for the Claimant, or the addressee has not (yet) communicated its address, which normally is the case for a Respondent at the beginning of the arbitration. In the latter case, delivery is attempted at the address notified by the other party. In those cases where delivery does not succeed, delivery may nonetheless be deemed to have been made if the address notified by the other party is the address last known to it. Given the far-reaching consequences of an ineffective notification of a Request for Arbitration,[139] a party must make sufficient efforts to trace the other party's address, and to provide the Secretariat of the ICC Court and the Arbitral Tribunal therewith. The advent of electronic directories and white and yellow pages in telephone directories of almost any place on the globe being available via the internet, makes a Claimant's task much easier nowadays than it was in the past. It is the responsibility of the parties, and not of the Secretariat or the Arbitral Tribunal, to locate the proper address of a Respondent. **15.174**

The words 'or its representative' make it clear that notifications are valid even if delivered to a person other than the party itself, provided that such person represents the party. **15.175**

When providing addresses to the Secretariat for the purposes of notification to corporate entities, or state authorities, parties should make sure that the necessary persons authorized to receive documents are named or at least described by their functions in the address, as **15.176**

[137] See *supra* paras 15.153 *et seq*.

[138] As to name and addresses recorded in the Terms of Reference, see *infra* Art 18, paras 15.710 *et seq*.

[139] Under Art V.l(b) of the New York Convention, an Award will only be recognized and enforced where the Respondent was given 'proper notice of the arbitration proceedings'.

otherwise there is no requirement that notice be made to any particular person of the corporate entity or state authority. In fact, quite a number of state authorities (ministries, regional directorates etc), in particular in Middle East countries, are known to refuse to accept delivery of documents on the grounds that no specific person is named in the address. If physical persons are parties to the arbitration, first names should be given in the address in order to avoid delivery to relatives who might not necessarily be considered as representatives for the receipt of documents.

15.177 (3.2) **Means of transmission** Whereas the first sentence of Art 3(2) contains rules with respect to the recipient's address, the second sentence lists the means by which the notifications and communications mentioned in the first sentence shall be made. The means are listed by way of exclusive enumeration, which, however, allows almost any imaginable means of transmission. Significantly, unregistered mail is excluded, whereas all kind of electronic communications are now included.

15.178 The different means of transmission contained in the list may be divided into three categories: (i) those which provide, factually or potentially, a record of physical receipt of the communication by the addressee or its representative; (ii) those which provide a record of correct transmission; and (iii) those which provide only a record of sending. If all of these categories suffice to effect communication of documents 'validly' under the Rules, requirements of national laws and/or the New York Convention to prove that proper notification was given of the commencement of the arbitration and of the award in the enforcement procedures must not be overlooked, and in fact be satisfied within the arbitration procedure. In any event, parties may validly agree to use only certain forms of communications for their arbitration.

15.179 *(3.2.1) Means which provide a record of physical receipt* Delivery against receipt: Any means of transmission is acceptable if the addressee signs a receipt for the delivery. Therefore, delivery 'by hand' through an international courier service or local messenger whereby the documents are handed over by the carrier to the addressee is a valid means of notification, if the latter confirms with its signature, on a copy of the document delivered or on a delivery slip, that it has received the document. It can be regarded as the classic form of communication for arbitration where delivery is made in countries with reliable postal services. In most cases, it may appropriately complement facsimile transmission, as this combines rapid transmission and signed proof of delivery.

15.180 Courier services: These services are listed separately as a valid means of transmission, without requiring a receipt for delivery. In practice, it is always prudent for the sender to use courier services that obtain signed delivery slips from the recipient.

15.181 *(3.2.2) Means of transmission which provide a record of correct transmission* Registered post: Although it is listed as a means of transmission, the registered letter as such, ie not combined with a return receipt slip, is certainly not a satisfactory means of transmission. Therefore, for all practical reasons, a registered letter only proves that documents were handed over to the post office by the sender, thus leaving the sender in the same situation as ordinary mail. Registered post should therefore be used only with a return receipt requested.

Facsimile transmission: Facsimile transmission is capable of providing not only a record of sending, but also instantaneously alerts the sender of any deficiencies in the transmission process. However, this is not a record of delivery in the meaning of the provision under consideration, as it is not signed by the addressee. Therefore, facsimile transmissions should normally be used only as a complementary means of notification or once a regular communication process has been established whereby actual receipt of a facsimile is demonstrated by the simple fact that the addressee answers to it in the normal course of business. **15.182**

(3.2.3) Means of transmission, which provide record of sending Telegram and telex are today outdated means of transmission in an arbitration, and for years the Secretariat of the ICC Court has not used the ICC's telex machine. **15.183**

(3.2.4) Other means of telecommunication that provide a record of the sending thereof Although formulated in a way to comprise a number of different means of communication, the real impact of that provision is the use of email transmission of documents via the internet as a valid means of communication under the Rules. **15.184**

In order to comply with the requirements of this provision, a record of sending must be provided by the system. This is undoubtedly more than the mere print-out of the message or of the documents transmitted. One must therefore make sure that the internet provider (server) is capable of providing specific sender-reports showing the fact that the communication in question has in fact been sent. In most cases, such reports also comprise information concerning the transmission process (routing) and delivery to the electronic box of the addressee. In such cases, they equal for all practical purposes facsimile transmissions to a computer platform. **15.185**

Email communication is first of all a practical means of instantaneous communication for small messages, such as organizational questions or clarification of minor points outside the sequence of written submissions. Email transmission may also play a role for the transmission of more voluminous submissions and, as the technical performance of scanners increase, exhibits to written submissions. **15.186**

Correspondence and documents can also be posted on ICC's NetCase system rather than be sent by the traditional methods of courier, post or fax. NetCase is a service allowing arbitrations to be conducted in a secure online environment (including password and virus protection as well as sophisticated encryption), and is available at no additional charge. **15.187**

NetCase may, however, only be used if all parties and all arbitrators agree to use it and sign a Statement of Acceptance of the Conditions of Access and Use of NetCase. If so, all participants are able to communicate through a secure website hosted by the ICC having round the clock access from any computer in the world to their case, as to (i) a summary of the case; (ii) the correspondence relating to the arbitration; (iii) procedural documents (including the Terms of Reference and procedural orders); (iv) the various memorials; and (v) exhibits to the memorials. The parties may download all of these documents in pdf format. If used as the primary means of communication, the parties and the Arbitral Tribunal should take into account any mandatory provisions of applicable law regarding the notification of documents. **15.188**

15.189 Particularly in large arbitrations, the amount of documents moved around can become burdensome. Storage, transport and retrieval of documents cost the parties both time and money. NetCase provides one centralized point for the storage of all documents submitted in an arbitration with a standardized system for the retrieval of documents by date, author or title. In addition NetCase sets out a broad range of information, such as details of parties and arbitrators, procedural calendar, and statements of the current financial situation.[140]

(4) Article 3(3): Date on which communications are effective

15.190 As set out above, para (3) looks at the addressee's end of the transmission process and stipulates under which conditions and on what date the communication/notification is effected ('made'). The wording of the provision under consideration envisages, in addition to the actual receipt of the communication by the addressee, the hypothetical receipt ('deemed'), which covers both the situation where the addressee cannot be reached and therefore actual receipt is known not to have occurred, and the lack of sufficient proof for actual receipt.

15.191 Where the addressee or its representative actually receives the communication transmitted, the effects of the notification/communication are achieved by that event on that day. This may be shown by the record of delivery or by an acknowledgement of receipt issued in due course by the addressee. Whether the addressee or its representative only 'receives' a given notification/communication when they physically take possession of the communication, or whether it is sufficient that they have the possibility to take physical possession of the communication by the fact of exercising power, custody or control over the communication, may vary according to the circumstances.

15.192 The provision then determines the hypothetical 'delivery' in order to determine when receipt would have occurred ('would have been received'). This determination is important in connection with the question of when deadlines linked to such notification/communication start to run. However, save the obligation to have made the notification or communication in accordance with Art 3(2), no further indication is given in the Rules how such hypothetical assessment should be carried through or which standards should be applied. An Arbitral Tribunal will take a prudent approach and consider relevant aspects having regard to local customs and circumstances, including prevailing holiday habits in the addressee's country.

(5) Article 3(4): Time limits

15.193 Article 3(4) contains stipulations with respect to when time limits start to run, as well as their precise ending. For the calculation of any specific time period, the provision under consideration tries to respect most different legal and cultural systems. This has to be taken into account when interpreting the provision under consideration, especially when determining what 'official holiday' or 'non-business day' implies.

[140] For a description of NetCase, see Philippe, M., 'NetCase: A New ICC Arbitration Facility', *op cit*; and Philippe, M., 'New Upgrades to the ICC NetCase', *op cit*; more generally, see <http://www.iccnetcase.org>.

The calculation of time periods 'in' the Rules and 'under' the Rules pursuant to Art 3(4) deals with time limits set by the Arbitral Tribunal as well as with time limits applicable to the Arbitral Tribunal. Article 3(4) does not apply generally to time periods under the underlying contract, which must be determined in accordance with the law applicable to the underlying contract or that part of the underlying contract. 15.194

Article 3(4) does not contain any provisions with respect to the calculation of time periods other than those expressed in days. The Rules themselves calculate in months only with respect to the time periods for the establishment of the Terms of Reference (Art 18) and the making of the award (Art 24). In these instances, the Court has always followed the general rule that the ending date of the time period is the day of the relevant month of the expiry period, which bears the same date as the day on which the time period is deemed to have started to run. This rule should apply in general terms if the time period is expressed other than in days. However, rather than to fix time limits by weeks or months, it is preferable to indicate a fixed ending date in order to exclude any ambiguity in this respect. 15.195

(5.1) Time limits specified in the ICC Rules Article 3(4) applies to all time periods specified in the Rules, in particular under Art 5(1) and (6), Art 8(2) and (3), Art 11(2), Art 18(2), Art 24(1), Art 29(1) and (2) and Art 30(4).[141] 15.196

(5.2) Time limits fixed under the ICC Rules Article 3(4) also applies to the various time limits which are fixed in application of the Rules, whether by the Secretariat, the ICC Court or the Arbitral Tribunal. This is true also for the time to be fixed by the Secretariat under Art 1(7) of the Internal Rules (app H) since they form part of the ICC Rules in general. 15.197

(5.2.1) Time limits fixed by the Secretariat There are only a few provisions under the Rules which expressly grant the Secretariat the power to fix at its own volition time limits vis-à-vis a party: Art 4(4) with respect to the administrative closing of the file upon non-compliance with the formal requirements in connection with the filing of the Request for Arbitration; Art 7(2) with respect to collecting parties' comments upon a qualified statement of independence filed by a prospective arbitrator; Art 1(7) of the Internal Rules for the fixing of a time limit to the parties and the arbitrators for any claim of restitution of documents before destroying the file; and Art 30(4) with respect to the final time limit for payment of advances on arbitration costs before administrative withdrawal of the respective claims.[142] Various provisions expressly foresee the possibility for the Secretariat to extend the limits specified in the Rules, such as Art 5(2) and (6) for the Answer to the Request for Arbitration and the Reply respectively, and Art 8(3) for the parties' joint nomination of a sole arbitrator. 15.198

Other provisions grant the Secretariat the power to set time limits vis-à-vis both the parties and the arbitrators. Such is the case for collecting the various comments of the parties and arbitrators under Art 11(3) in the context of a challenge submitted by a party, and Art 12(5) with respect to the question of the replacement of an arbitrator. Likewise, the financial 15.199

[141] With respect to the parties' power to modify these time limits, see *infra* Art 32.

[142] With the express proviso that this time limit is to be fixed by the Secretary-General of the ICC Court, not its Secretariat.

administration of the arbitration by the Secretariat requires fixing time limits under Art 30(1) and (3).

15.200 On a more general level, the Secretariat has the possibility to set time limits for the good administration of the arbitration. In this context, the Secretariat may invite comments from the parties or the arbitrators on various issues to be considered by the Court for determination. Absent a reply within such time limits, or a request for an extension thereof, the Court may proceed under its Rules. Such is the case with the invitation extended to an arbitrator to fill in a statement of independence (Art 7), comments invited from the parties with regard to the number of arbitrators (Art 8), with regard to a qualified statement of independence filed by a prospective arbitrator (Art 9), in regard to the method of constitution of the Arbitral Tribunal in a multiple party context (Art 10), or in the context of the financial administration of the file, such as inviting comments prior to any separation of the advance on costs under Art 30(2).

15.201 *(5.2.2) Time limits fixed by the Court* Under the Rules, it is for the ICC Court to fix time limits, particularly in the context of the constitution of the Arbitral Tribunal. Such is the case for any time limit to complete the procedure of nomination of a chairman of the Arbitral Tribunal agreed upon by the parties if the parties cannot agree upon such time limit (Art 8), or for the various deadlines under Art 9.

15.202 The Court also has the power to extend time limits fixed by the Rules under Art 18(2) for the signature of the Terms of Reference and under Art 24 for the rendering of the award. As a general matter the Court always has the power to extend time limits fixed by the Secretariat, if necessary. This is expressly stated in Art 30(4), because of the drastic consequences linked to that specific time limit. The Secretariat has, however, no power to extend time limits set by the Court.

15.203 *(5.2.3) Time limits fixed by the Arbitral Tribunal* Article 3(4) also applies to the various time limits fixed by the Arbitral Tribunal even in the absence of any specific agreements contained in the Terms of Reference. However, the parties and the Arbitral Tribunal may agree upon different rules for the calculation of time limits.[143] In practice, this may happen with respect to provisions for the timeliness of submissions when the date of dispatching the submission is retained as the relevant event rather than its receipt by the addressee.

15.204 Unless or until otherwise agreed, all deadlines fixed by the Arbitral Tribunal are calculated in accordance with Art 3(4).

15.205 (5.3) **Start and end date of time limits** Article 3(4) states the general principle that the day on which the notification/communication initiating the time period occurs is not taken into account for the calculation of the time period. The first day to be counted for time periods expressed in days is thus the day following the day of the initiating event, unless it is an official holiday or a non-business day at the place of receipt.

[143] See *supra* Art 1, para 15.101 regarding the possibilities to derogate from the provisions of the ICC Rules.

The Rules also state time periods for which the initiating event is not a notification/communication and Art 3(4) will apply. For example, Art 11 requires a party to make a challenge against an arbitrator within 30 days from the date of acquiring knowledge of the facts on which the challenge is based. Such knowledge is not necessarily acquired by receipt of a document.[144] **15.206**

However, the calculation method under Art 3(4) will not apply in those cases where time periods are calculated other than by days. The time period under Art 24 for the making of the award is fixed at six months from the date of the last signature of the Terms of Reference. Article 24(1) defines thereby as the starting date the date of the last signature in the Terms of Reference, and not the next following day. **15.207**

Official holidays in the country where notification or communication is made. The official holidays are determined in the country of the addressee of the notification. **15.208**

Non-business day. Non-business days are the weekly recess days which vary from country to country according to religious influences, ie the Sunday for countries with a Christian cultural background, the Saturday for Jewish communities, and the Friday for most Islamic countries. Given the differing usages in the different countries, the present version of the Rules avoids taking a clear decision on whether the relevant preceding day (very often a non-working day in the producing sector) must be considered a non-business day. Nevertheless, the Secretariat has usually dealt with Saturdays as if they were non-business days. Likewise, where Islamic countries are concerned, the Thursday should be dealt with as if it were a non-business day, given that many business activities, shops and offices close at midday (if not before, in the case of public administration). **15.209**

First following business day. The first day to count for the relevant time period is the first following business day. Thus, if the initiating event for the relevant time period occurs on a Saturday, the first day to count will be the following Monday, unless this would be an official holiday. In some countries, business only restarts the second day after the weekly recess day (eg Jordan on the Sunday). In the same way as the day directly preceding the weekly recess day will not be counted by the Secretariat for the calculation of the time period, such days should also be left aside for calculating the time period. **15.210**

Ending date. For the calculation of the time periods expressed in days, all holidays, non-business or assimilated days are included in the counting. In so far as the time period is expressed in days, the time period expires with the date corresponding to the last day counted in accordance with the time period. As for the starting date, if the last day of the time period happens to be an official holiday or a non-business day, the time period only expires the first following business day. That part of the provision, from its mere wording, also applies to time periods expressed other than in days, when the relevant ending date happens to be an official holiday or a non-business day. **15.211**

[144] See *infra* Art 11, para 15.500. The wording 'from the date when' is also found in Art 5(6) with respect to the 30-day time period for the submission of a 'Reply' by the Claimant.

15.212 The time period regularly expires at the end of the relevant day, ie at 24:00 hours. However, a precise hour may be specified, in particular in fast-track procedures,[145] or in connection with conservatory or interim measures.[146] While specifications like 'before close of business' may not be sufficiently precise for drawing any negative conclusion from an action allegedly out of time, the relevant time limit expires in any case at the end of the day indicated.

Article 4. Request for Arbitration

(1) A party wishing to have recourse to arbitration under these Rules shall submit its Request for Arbitration (the 'Request') to the Secretariat, which shall notify the Claimant and Respondent of the receipt of the Request and the date of such receipt.

(2) The date on which the Request is received by the Secretariat shall, for all purposes, be deemed to be the date of the commencement of the arbitral proceedings.

(3) The Request shall, *inter alia*, contain the following information:

a) the name in full, description and address of each of the parties;

b) a description of the nature and circumstances of the dispute giving rise to the claim(s);

c) a statement of the relief sought, including, to the extent possible, an indication of any amount(s) claimed;

d) the relevant agreements and, in particular, the arbitration agreement;

e) all relevant particulars concerning the number of arbitrators and their choice in accordance with the provisions of Articles 8, 9 and 10, and any nomination of an arbitrator required thereby; and

f) any comments as to the place of arbitration, the applicable rules of law and the language of the arbitration.

(4) Together with the Request, the Claimant shall submit the number of copies thereof required by Article 3(1) and shall make the advance payment on administrative expenses required by Appendix III ('Arbitration Costs and Fees') in force on the date the Request is submitted. In the event that the Claimant fails to comply with either of these requirements, the Secretariat may fix a time limit within which the Claimant must comply, failing which the file shall be closed without prejudice to the right of the Claimant to submit the same claims at a later date in another Request.

(5) The Secretariat shall send a copy of the Request and the documents annexed thereto to the Respondent for its Answer to the Request once the Secretariat has sufficient copies of the Request and the required advance payment.

(6) When a party submits a Request in connection with a legal relationship in respect of which arbitration proceedings between the same parties are already pending under these Rules, the Court may, at the request of a party, decide to include the claims contained in the request in the pending proceedings provided that the Terms of Reference have not yet been signed or approved by the Court. Once the Terms of Reference have been signed or approved by the Court, claims may only be included in the pending proceedings subject to the provisions of Article 19.

(1) Introduction

15.213 Whatever the arbitration rules, an arbitration is started by the party requesting the dispute to be submitted to arbitration. That party will therefore give the other party a 'notice of arbitration', or, as in the case of ICC arbitration, submit a document called the 'Request for

[145] See *infra* Art 32, paras 15.1183 *et seq.*

[146] See *infra* Art 23, paras 15.876 *et seq.*

Arbitration'. The receipt of a Request for Arbitration by the ICC is, for all purposes, the starting point of the arbitral proceedings; it is the moment when an ICC arbitration 'commences'.

The Request may serve as a notification to the Respondent that an arbitration has been commenced, without providing significant detail about the case. It may also constitute a fairly elaborate or even complete presentation of the Claimant's case, both factual and legal.[147] **15.214**

Given the universality of ICC arbitration in terms of nationality of the parties and their counsel, the governing law and applicable procedures, it would be impossible to establish any meaningful requirements as to form without detracting from the universal vocation of the ICC Rules. It would be difficult to impose uniformity as to how a Request for Arbitration is to be drafted and presented. **15.215**

At the same time, it will be recognized that the lack of precision which is the counterpart of flexibility of the ICC Rules, may result in the submission of Requests which may make it more difficult for the ICC Court to set the arbitration in motion, and to take the decisions required therefore, such as deciding upon the number of arbitrators and on their appointment, fixing the place of arbitration, or a proper amount of the provisional advance on costs. **15.216**

Without switching ICC arbitration to a system of 'notice pleading', it was considered by the ICC Working Group that the Rules could be drafted so as to make clear that a *complete* statement of the Claimant's case could, but need not, be included in the Request. It was hoped that more concise Requests would lead to more concise Answers, thereby reducing requests by Respondents for lengthy extensions of time to file the Answer. **15.217**

The Request for Arbitration, contrary to a 'simple notice', has to include information as to the nature of the dispute, a statement of the relief sought, the relevant agreements, the composition of the Arbitral Tribunal and place of arbitration. **15.218**

Before commencing the arbitration itself, often the question arises whether the parties have agreed on pre-arbitral requirements, eg to negotiate or mediate (so-called multi-tiered arbitration clauses). Even if the ICC standard arbitration clause contains no such obligation, the parties are free to adapt the standard clause thereto, and often do so. The terms of such agreement, the law governing it and the law of the place of arbitration will generally decide upon the effect of such agreement.[148] The ICC Dispute Board Rules (September 2004) **15.219**

---

[147] Historically, the Request for Arbitration in ICC Arbitration (which was so denominated even in the 1923 ICC Rules) was not a 'notice pleading'. If the 1923 ICC Rules called for a 'brief statement of claims of the applicant for arbitration', by 1927 the ICC Rules required that the Request contain a 'Statement of the plaintiff's case', which requirement was maintained through the 1975/1988 ICC Rules. Exactly what constituted a 'statement of the Claimant's case' was never the subject of specific requirements within the ICC Rules or of a recommended 'form' by the ICC itself. There have been Requests which comprised nothing more than a few telefaxed pages, and there have been Requests in major construction cases which comprised a dozen boxes of pleadings and exhibits setting out the case legally and factually.

[148] On multi-tiered dispute resolution clauses and their enforcement, see Jolles, A., 'Consequences of Multi-tier Arbitration Clauses: Issues of Enforcement' (2006) 72 *Arbitration* no 4, 329; Jimenez-Figueres, D., 'Multi-Tiered Dispute Resolution Clauses in ICC Arbitration' (2003) 4 *ICC IC Arb Bull* no 1, 71;

state that if the parties have agreed to submit their dispute to a Dispute Review Board (or Dispute Adjudication Board), they will normally have to do so before commencing an ICC arbitration. Even if a party may consider certain procedural requirements as harmful, eg disclosure of information[149] or as causing delay[150], once a dispute has arisen, it will be bound to it. A party may reject requirements of such multi-tiered arbitration clause stating that the condition for its application was no longer at hand because the other party had rejected it or for some other recognized ground.

15.220 The Arbitral Tribunal may state in the Terms of Reference whether and to which extent pre-arbitral conditions are met. If the issue is not resolved with the Terms of Reference, the party who alleges that there is, as a result, a procedural defect is required to raise the issue promptly, both under Art 33 of the Rules and possibly under the applicable law. In a recent case, the Swiss Supreme Court noted eg that the obligation to mediate was an ongoing one that the parties could have invoked during the course of the proceedings. The court held that it was an abuse of right for the party to raise the failure to meet this requirement after the hearings had been terminated.[151]

(2) Article 4(1): Filing with the ICC Court's Secretariat

15.221 Under the ICC Rules, any Request for Arbitration must be filed with the Secretariat of the ICC[152] at the following address: 38 Cours Albert 1er, 75008 Paris, telephone: +33.1.49.53.29.05, telefax: +33.1.49.53.29.33[153], or with the newly-created ICC Asia Office, at the following addresses: Suite 2, 12/F, Fairmont House, 8 Cotton Tree Drive Central, Hong Kong, telephone +852.3607.560, telefax: +852.2523.1619. Its regular business hours are Monday to Friday from 8.30 am to 7 pm. A party may file the Request

Jiminez-Figures, D., 'Amicable Means to Resolve Disputes', *op cit*; Sutton, D., Gill, J. and Gearing, M., *Russell on Arbitration* (23rd edn, Thomson/Sweet & Maxwell, London, 2007), 188; in *England*, see *Cable/Wireless Plc v IBM United Kingdom Ltd* (2002) EWHC 2059, (2002) 2 All ER (Comm) 1041 (11 October 2002); Mackie K., *op cit*; in *France*, see *Cass civ mixte*, 14 February 2003, *Poiré v Tripier*; Jarrosson, Ch., 'Note on Cass. Civ Mixte, 14 Febr. 2003' (2003) 19 *Arb Int'l* no 3, 263 and (2003) *Rev Arb* no 2, 403. See also *Nihon Plast Co v Takata-Petri Aktiengesellschaft*, CA, 4 March 2004, (2005) *Rev arb* no 1, 151, note *Train* (a pre-arbitration clause is a contractual clause which binds not only the parties but also the tribunal). French jurisdictions have opted for the same position in judicial proceedings. See *Cass civ 2e*, 21 April 2005, *Sté Maison girondine v Lonne et al* (2005) JCP ed G II 10153 p 2063, note *Croze* (conciliation is a condition precedent to court action); in *Switzerland*, see Swiss Supreme Court, 6 June 2007, *X. Ltd v Y*, 4A_18/2007, referred to at para 4–4; Swiss Supreme Court, 17 August 1995, *Vekoma v Maran Coal Company*, (1996) 14 ASA Bull no 4, 673, note *Schweizer*; Friedland, P.D., 'The Swiss Supreme Court Sets Aside an ICC Award' (1996) 13 *J Int'l Arb* no 1, 111; in *Sweden*, see *SCC Case 21/1999*, SAR 2002:2, p 59.

[149] The mediation or alternative procedure usually provides for the confidentiality of documents communicated during the procedure. However, by entering into a mediation, it is virtually inevitable that a party will disclose its approach to the case.

[150] Some clauses provide a specific cooling-off period of sometimes several weeks or even months before recourse to arbitration is authorized.

[151] von Segesser, G., 'Note on Swiss Supreme Court, June 6, 2007, X. Ltd v Y, 4A_18/2007' (September 2007) *ITA Monthly Report*, vol V Issue 9.

[152] See *supra* Art 1, paras 15.138 *et seq.*

[153] Trying to get someone from the Court's Secretariat on the phone, by dialing the ICC's general telephone number, is almost impossible, and only the most patient callers will succeed. Direct calling numbers of members of the Secretariat can be found in the ICC's yearly-published Handbook or via the ICC's website <http://www.iccwbo.org>.

by any of the means contemplated by Art 3(2), second sentence.[154] Currently, the ICC's NetCase facility is not available for the Request of Arbitration, even if later on in the arbitration proceedings the Arbitral Tribunal may dispense wholly or partially the delivery of hard copies on the basis of NetCase as agreed with the parties.

The Secretariat notifies the Claimant and Respondent of the receipt of the Request and the date of such receipt by the ICC. Article 4(1) does not stipulate when the parties are to be informed of the receipt of the Request, or that they have to be notified simultaneously. In the Secretariat's practice, the notification under Art 4(1) will be made to the Claimant by a letter signed by the Secretary-General, acknowledging the date of receipt of the Request for Arbitration, assigning a case number, and indicating the contact details of the ICC counsel in charge of the file, and of the members of the counsel's team. The notification to the Respondent pursuant to Art 4(1) will only take place at the time the Secretariat sends the Request for Arbitration to the Respondent as required by Art 4(5).[155] As will be discussed below, a significant lapse of time between the ICC's receipt of the Request, and its notification to the Respondent may occur in certain cases.[156] **15.222**

There is no need for a Claimant to notify the Request directly to the Respondent. Nothing, however, prevents a Claimant from giving advance notice of the Request by sending it simultaneously to the ICC and the other party. Article 5(1) makes clear that the Respondent is to file an Answer only within 30 days of the Respondent's receipt of the Request from the Secretariat. Thus, prior receipt from the Claimant does not matter under the Rules. **15.223**

As long as either the filing fee or the adequate number of copies has not been received by the ICC, the Request is not notified by the Secretariat to the Respondent. This failure does not hinder the commencement of the arbitration proceedings, but will delay the notification of the request to the Respondent.[157] **15.224**

(3) Article 4(2): Commencement of ICC arbitration

Article 4(2) identifies the date of receipt of the Request by the Secretariat as the date of commencement of ICC arbitration proceedings. If the Request is sent to the ICC by advance telefax communication, it is the day of receipt of the telefax which the Secretariat will consider as the receipt date. This applies even where the exhibits to the Request and/or the hard copies of the Request and the advance payment on administrative expenses have not been received by the ICC on that same day.[158] If a party tries to hand deliver the Request to the ICC on a Saturday, Sunday or on a day which is a public holiday in France, when the ICC's Paris offices are closed, the date of receipt will normally be only on the following business day. However, if outside the ICC's regular business hours the delivery of Request is accepted by someone present on the ICC's premises such as a security guard or **15.225**

[154] See *supra* Art 3, paras 15.176 *et seq.*
[155] See *infra* para 15.266.
[156] See *infra* paras 15.230 *et seq.*
[157] See Derains/Schwartz, A Guide, *op cit*, 42.
[158] The receipt stamp will be put on the hard copies of the Request only with the date at which they were actually received by the ICC.

janitor, the latter are instructed to mark the date of receipt of the Request which will then be acknowledged by the Secretariat.

15.226 For all practical purposes, if a party is keen to make a hand delivery, it is preferable to do so on a business day, and to arrange by telephone an appointment with the Secretariat prior thereto. The party will then obtain an ICC receipt stamp with the date of receipt on a copy of its notification letter to the ICC.[159]

15.227 Article 4(2) may be compared favourably with the equivalent provision in Art 3(2) of the UNCITRAL Arbitration Rules, which provides that the arbitral proceedings are deemed to commence when the notice of arbitration is received by the Respondent. Given the number of instances in which the ICC receives a Request just before the expiration of a statute of limitations period, the certainty of knowing that it is the receipt of the Request by the ICC in Paris or, more recently, in Hong Kong that tolls the running of prescription periods has been a source of comfort to numerous Claimants who have been unable to effectuate service of a document on the proper Respondent when, for example, it is an 'authority' of an 'agency' of a governmental entity of a country with a tangled bureaucratic organization and shifting designations for its governmental entities. In ICC arbitration, the sometimes difficult task of notifying the Request to the Respondent is shifted from the Claimant to the arbitral institution.

15.228 In civil law systems, the law applicable to limitation periods is normally the law governing the underlying contract, whereas in common law systems the law applicable to the procedure (if any) is relevant, as may the law of the place of arbitration.[160]

15.229 The US Supreme Court held in the *Howsam v Dean Witter Reynolds case*,[161] that it is for the Arbitral Tribunal to decide whether the limitation is contained in the contract itself. The issue was whether the Claimant had filed a claim within the six-year period provided by the National Association of Securities Dealers (NASD) Code of Arbitration Procedure. Even if the *Howsam* case deals with a contractual limitation period under the NASD Rules and not statutory limitation periods, the justification for having such periods decided by the Arbitral Tribunal and not by national courts would be similar.[162]

---

[159] For that purpose, it is advisable to take to the ICC an extra copy of the notification letter and/or of the Request.

[160] English law was applied with respect to limitations periods based on the place of arbitration prior to the Foreign Limitations Period Act of 1984 to which reference is made in Art 13 of the English Arbitration Act 1996 as amended. See also Russell on Arbitration, *op cit*, 189, 528. For Switzerland, see Vogt, N.P., 'Article 181' in S. Berti, H. Honsell, N.P. Vogt and A.K. Schnyder (eds), *International Arbitration in Switzerland—An Introduction to and a Commentary on Articles 176–194 of the Swiss Private International Law Statute* (Helbing & Lichtenhahn/Kluwer, Basel, 2000) 182.

[161] *Howsam v Dean Witter Reynolds*, 537 United States Reports 79; 2002 US Lexis 9235 (US Supreme Court 2002); (2004) YBCA vol XXIX p 232 (excerpt).

[162] The basic point is that the responsibility for making decisions as to arbitrability under US law depends on the language of the clause and applicable rules. Owing to the wording of the Rules there may be less of a carve-out under an ICC arbitration than otherwise. See *Stone & Webster Asia Inc v Triplefine International Corporation* (2nd Cir 2003), *Apollo Computer, Inc v Berg*, 886 F.2d 469 (1st Cir 1989) and *Daiei v United States Shoe Corp*, 755 F Supp 299 (D Haw 1991).

Under French law, not only is the issue of limitations (*prescription*) a matter for the arbitrator, but, if the arbitrator is authorized to decide *ex aequo et bono* (a possibility under Art 18), the arbitrator may even set aside the limitation period.[163] **15.230**

It has sometimes happened that the Secretariat, in attempting to notify the Request, has required several weeks or even longer to do so. Pursuant to Art 4(2), this is meant to be, and will normally be, without consequence, provided that under the applicable rules of law the receipt of the Request by the ICC is sufficient to interrupt the statute of limitations. The use of the words 'for all purposes' in Art 4(2) reflects such intent. **15.231**

Theoretically, the issue can arise as to whether the receipt by the Secretariat of a Request which is not in compliance with the Rules will constitute the commencement of the arbitration proceedings as from the date of receipt, or only as from the date on which the requirements of the Rules were met. **15.232**

To the authors' knowledge, virtually no serious problems have arisen in practice, since in the past the Secretariat has followed the procedure now codified in Art 4(4) of the Rules. There seem to be no instances in which a national court or an Arbitral Tribunal considered that a limitation period (contractual or statutory) had expired notwithstanding the prior submission of an 'incomplete' Request. **15.233**

Article 4(2) and the certainty of knowing the commencement date of an ICC arbitration are also important when bankruptcy proceedings are opened against one of the parties of the arbitration. If at the time of filing the Request for Arbitration, bankruptcy proceedings were already pending against the Respondent, the Claimant may, pursuant to the relevant rules of bankruptcy, have to file the Request for Arbitration against the court-appointed administrator. **15.234**

(4) Article 4(3): Contents of the Request

Article 4(3) deals with the contents of the Request and has been considerably modified compared to its earlier versions in an attempt to accelerate the initial stages of ICC arbitration. Rather than requiring a 'statement of claim', the ICC Rules simply refer to a 'description of the nature and the circumstances of the dispute' (*lit* b), but expressly seek the Claimant's comments as to the place of arbitration, the applicable law, and the language of the arbitration (*lit* f). However, the Secretariat does not review the Request to determine whether the Claimant has met each requirement of the Rules. That will be a matter for the Arbitral Tribunal, and compliance with the form requirements of Art 4(3) is rarely a serious problem in practice. **15.235**

'(a) the name in full, description and address of each of the parties.' The purpose of this requirement is to properly identify the party (or parties) that a Claimant wishes to call into the arbitral proceedings, and against which it wishes to obtain an award that it may then **15.236**

[163] Cass Civ 2e, May 31, 2001, *Huon v Consorts Huon*, where the French Supreme Court set aside a lower court decision deciding not to appoint an arbitrator based on the expiration of a limitation period, (2002) *Rev arb* no 3 691. See also Paris CA, 28 November 2002, *Panalpina World Transports Holding AG v Transco*, (2003) *Rev Arb* no 4,1359, note Betto.

enforce against that party.[164] Any errors in the Request may be perpetuated in the Terms of Reference and, if not corrected prior to the rendering of the final award, may jeopardize its enforcement.

15.237 The Rules place the Claimant in the favourable position of being able to determine the parties to the arbitration, subject to Art 6(2), but they do not confer expressly any similar right to the Respondent.[165]

15.238 In case of a physical person, it is essential for identification purposes to provide also the person's first name, and where known, date of birth. In case of a legal person, the legal nature of that party should be added (ie a 'SA' or 'Sarl' in France, a 'AG' or 'GmbH' in Germany, an 'Inc' in the USA, etc). If the company is registered with a Commercial Register or Company Register, the name and registration number may also be added.

15.239 It has happened that the Secretariat has notified a Request to the address of the Respondent indicated in the Request only to have the Request returned, with a notice that the party no longer resides at the address indicated. In such cases, as already discussed, Art 3(2) and (3) establish that a Request so returned is 'deemed to have been made' on the date it 'would have been received' by the party at the address indicated. Nonetheless, non-delivery creates an unsatisfactory situation, in particular for the Claimant that may be faced in such circumstances with a Respondent trying to oppose enforcement of an award on the ground that no proper notice of the Request was given to it.

15.240 Accordingly, the Secretariat, if so requested, will notify the Request to multiple, alternative addresses and use its experience to try to find a means of delivery to cities abroad not on the usual routes of international courier services.

15.241 Of course, it is the Claimant which bears the ultimate responsibility for providing a proper address and, if actual delivery of the Request cannot be effected, for proceeding with the arbitration while assuming the risk that an award might be set aside or denied enforcement.

---

[164] See *ICC case no 13645* (2006) Final Award, presently unreported: The Respondent was the holding company of several companies that were the results of mergers and acquisitions with various name changes. After the Respondent challenged the Arbitral Tribunal's jurisdiction, the Claimant argued that the Respondent had a duty to alert it in advance that it had incorrectly named the parent company in its draft Request for Arbitration, which it had provided a month prior to filing the Request for Arbitration. The sole arbitrator, a French lawyer, found: 'While Claimant might have appreciated receiving notice from the Respondent prior to the filing of this arbitration that the latter could not be subject to jurisdiction, the Respondent had no duty to do so. The Respondent was only required to raise lack of jurisdiction as a defence in accordance with the rules of the arbitral proceeding and did so at the first opportunity provided under the Rules, ie in its Answer.' The Tribunal declined jurisdiction over the Respondent, the parent company of the group which 'had no involvement whatsoever in the conclusion, performance or termination of the . . . contract'. The Arbitral Tribunal added that the mere participation of the various group entities in their negotiations with Claimant regarding its claims arising out of the termination of the contract 'cannot form a basis for an express or implied consent to arbitral jurisdiction . . . it would be contrary to common sense and singularly inappropriate to hold that the mere willingness of a party to participate in settlement negotiations results in an admission of liability, waiver of defenses, or other forfeiture of its rights.' The Respondent was represented by one of the co-authors.

[165] See Derains/Schwartz, A Guide, *op cit*, 45–6.

The description of a party may provide for its registered capital, if any, and otherwise be very brief and general (eg 'the largest manufacturer of roller bearings in country x', or 'active in the distribution and sale of liquors and spirits'). But it may also be more detailed if a Claimant feels it is important in the arbitration. Arbitrators coming from a country other than that of the Claimant or Respondent may not necessarily have heard of the party, and thus be unfamiliar with its standing and reputation. There is nothing wrong in trying to favourably impress the Arbitral Tribunal by submitting, for instance, a corporate brochure, or a party's website. **15.242**

Neither Art 4(3) nor the Rules elsewhere deal with the question whether a party may amend its Request for Arbitration. Generally, until Terms of Reference under Art 18 have been drawn up, a Claimant is free to amend its Request, in particular by adding new claims or modifying its prayer for relief.[166] **15.243**

If a Claimant wishes to add a new party to the arbitration by amending a Request, the initial issue is whether arbitrators have already been appointed. If a Claimant wishes to add further Claimants and there is agreement between them on the co-arbitrator, then there should be no due process issue with respect to the appointment of that co-arbitrator. However, if the Claimant is seeking to add another Respondent and the initial Respondent has already appointed a co-arbitrator, then there may well be a due process issue. In a recent case, the Claimant brought proceedings against one party to a shareholders' agreement but then sought to file an amended Request to add a joint venture company that had also signed the shareholders' agreement but which was partly owned by a third party in order to make any award enforceable against the joint venture company. The initial Respondent objected and the proposed additional Respondent did not agree. As a result, the Claimant abandoned the attempt.[167] **15.244**

'(b) a description of the nature and circumstances of the dispute giving rise to the claim(s).' The Request does not need to be a presentation of all legal and factual elements of the Claimant's case, but must not be limited to merely setting out the relief sought. **15.245**

The Claimant is free to make a Request containing a full statement of its case, but is not required to do so. As a practical rule, a Claimant will wish to set out in any Request the contractual situation that in most cases will underlie the dispute, and describe the factual background (eg by providing a historical account of the events leading up to the dispute). The Claimant may also explain the legal basis for its positions and claims, and may attach supporting evidence to the Request. In practice, the contractual documents containing the arbitration agreement will be exhibited, as well as any relevant exchange or correspondence that helps to understand the factual allegations set out in the Request. **15.246**

'(c) a statement of the relief sought, including, to the extent possible, an indication of any amount(s) claimed.' A clear statement in the Request of the relief sought is obviously desirable in terms of encouraging the Claimant to think clearly about its objectives (money, specific performance, permanent injunction, contract interpretation etc), allowing the **15.247**

166 See Derains/Schwartz, A Guide, *op cit*, 53.

167 In such a case, the Claimant could have brought a new arbitration.

Respondent to understand what is at stake and providing information to the ICC which can assist it in deciding, as necessary, upon the number of arbitrators and the expertise of any appointments it must make.[168] The request for relief may be modified up to the Terms of Reference and even thereafter subject to the provisions of Art 19. It is a basic principle that an Arbitral Tribunal cannot award relief that has not been sought.

15.248 This article also encourages the Claimant to quantify any monetary damages being sought. The amount of the claim plays an important, sometimes decisive, role when the ICC Court decides the number of arbitrators.[169] It also enables the Secretary-General to fix more precisely the advance on costs (provisional or otherwise).[170] Although the ICC's advance of costs is fixed in US dollars, a party is free to quantify the monetary relief it seeks in any other currency.[171] Knowledge of the amount in dispute may also influence a decision by a prospective arbitrator whether or not to accept the case.

15.249 Notwithstanding the advantages of quantifying the claim(s) in the Request, this is not always done. Sometimes this is because it is difficult and costly to go through the exercise of quantification, and the Claimant may therefore prefer to await a later stage in the arbitration (for this reason, Claimants sometimes seek a partial award on liability before turning to quantification.) Sometimes the Claimant may not wish to quantify its claims in the Request because the amount in dispute is significant, and the Claimant wishes to avoid the payment of a substantial advance on costs at an early stage. It may thus prefer that the ICC apply its procedures for fixing an initial lump sum advance on costs.[172]

15.250 As is clear from the wording of this article, the failure to quantify a monetary claim does not mean that the Request is not in conformity with the ICC Rules. The ICC will therefore move the arbitration forward in the absence of any quantification. Each Claimant must determine on the basis of the circumstances of its case whether or not to quantify its claims in the Request.

15.251 (d) the relevant agreements and, in particular, the arbitration agreement.' From a purely grammatical point of view it might be understood that only 'information' about the 'relevant agreements and . . . the arbitration clause' is called for, rather than the actual documents themselves. In practice, while the arbitration clause is virtually always quoted *verbatim* in the Request, there is almost always annexed to the Request a complete copy of the contract(s) and/or documents in which the relevant arbitration agreement is to be found. These are almost always the 'agreements' in connection with which the dispute has arisen.

15.252 It is generally advantageous for the Claimant to enclose complete copies of such agreements as they serve to inform the ICC Court about the subject matter and the complexity of the case (important information if the Court is to determine the number of arbitrators

[168] See *infra* Art 8, paras 15.392 *et seq.* and Art 9, paras 15.425 *et seq.*

[169] See *infra* Art 8, para 15.394.

[170] See *infra* Art 30, para 15.1055.

[171] The Secretariat will convert that currency into US dollars at the rate prevailing when the claims are submitted, see *infra* Art 30, para 15.1049.

[172] See *infra* Art 30, para 15.1047 *et seq*, and App III of the Rules, Art 1.

and their expertise). This also avoids any uncertainty as to which contracts are at issue, a point that does not always come through clearly in every Request where there are multiple agreements between the parties. Lastly, most arbitrators are likely to request a copy of these documents anyway.

In any event, a Claimant may produce any other document it wishes to rely on in support of its claims together with the Request. In a construction dispute, the Request may already comprise several volumes of exhibits, if the Claimants considers this to be necessary or advantageous. **15.253**

'(e) all relevant particulars concerning the number of arbitrators and their choice in accordance with the provisions of Arts 8, 9 and 10, and any nomination of an arbitrator required thereby.' The objective of this requirement is to avoid any loss of time in the constitution of the Arbitral Tribunal occasioned by the failure of the Claimant to nominate an arbitrator in those cases where it should do so. In the event the Request fails to include such nomination, the Request will nonetheless be notified to the Respondent, but the Respondent has the right to insist that before it nominates an arbitrator pursuant to Art 5, the Claimant must do so.[173] **15.254**

Particulars concerning the choice of the arbitrators: This provision invites the Claimant to set forth its view on criteria such as the nationality, the residence, the profession, the legal training, the language proficiencies or any other qualification an arbitrator should possess. As provided in Art 9(1), the ICC Court has to consider some of these criteria when appointing or confirming an arbitrator, and the Claimant's early comments in that respect should help the Court to focus on the requirements that a party to the arbitration considers important. Pursuant to Art 5(1)(d), the Respondent is to make the same comments, so that the Court will normally have the views of both parties when taking its decision.[174] **15.255**

'(f) any comments as to the place of arbitration, the applicable rules of law and the language of the arbitration.' While the majority of Requests contain the information called for by this provision, many do not, or at least do not deal with all three of these issues as clearly as would be desirable. **15.256**

Given the significance of the place of arbitration to the conduct of the arbitration,[175] and the obviously crucial importance of the governing law,[176] the Request should be as explicit on these points as possible. Where the arbitration clause fixes the place of arbitration, it will be sufficient for the Claimant to refer thereto. Where no place was agreed, the Claimant may set out its preferences in the hope that the Respondent would accept one or the other place suggested, and/or may indicate the place it would consider unacceptable under the assumption that the ICC Court would fix the place somewhere else.[177] Where the contract contains no governing law clause, the Claimant's indication of its position may be helpful **15.257**

---

[173] See *infra* Art 8, para 15.407 *et seq*.
[174] See *infra* Art 9. When the Court is simply to confirm an arbitrator, it has limited discretion in considering these factors, see *infra* Art 9.
[175] See *infra* Art 14, para 15.565.
[176] See *infra* Art 17, para 15.659 *et seq*.
[177] See *infra* Art 14, para 15.569 *et seq*.

for the Court when it comes to the appointment of an arbitrator. Early agreement on these points may facilitate the constitution of the Arbitral Tribunal, and expedite the arbitration.

15.258 Regarding the language of the arbitration (Art 16), the major issue for the purpose of drafting the Request is in what language it should be done. The ICC Rules provide no clear guidance on this point, unlike, for example, the International Arbitration Rules of the AAA, which stipulate in Art 14 that the language(s) of the arbitration shall be that of the documents containing the arbitration agreement.

15.259 The vast majority of Requests are, indeed, drawn up in the language of the contract in connection with which the dispute has arisen, but a Request in another language will not be deemed inappropriate by the Secretariat, which will treat it as any other Request. The correspondence of the Secretariat concerning the Request, however, will always be in one of the four or five languages in which it is most competent (in particular English, French, German, and Spanish).[178]

15.260 If a party submits a Request in a language unfamiliar to the Secretariat, the latter has two options: one, it may request the Claimant to provide an English or French translation of the Request,[179] or two, it may arrange itself for a translation of the Request, which reflects the current practice. However, the Secretariat will notify the Request to the Respondent only in the original version without providing the translation. The Secretariat considers that the translation is made for internal purposes and does not wish to be held responsible by the Respondent for any errors or inaccuracies contained therein.

(5) Article 4(4): Failure to comply with the requirements

15.261 Articles 4(4) and (5) codify the Secretariat's practice regarding the treatment of Requests that do not meet the requirements of the Rules.[180]

15.262 Where a Request is not accompanied by the required registration fee, it results in a loss of time, sometimes considerable, before the Request can be notified. The explicit mention in Art 4(4) of the advance payment, viz the non-refundable filing fee (2,500 US dollars in the present edition of the 1998 Rules) and a cross-reference to the place in App III to the Rules where details on the payment are to be found, should eliminate such loss of time.

15.263 Article 4(4) also codifies the Secretariat's practice of requiring a 'complete' Request, in terms of the number of copies of the Request to be submitted according to the Rules and the accompanying payment of the 2,500 US dollars filing fee. Although this provision requires the Claimant to submit the advance payment together with the Request, Arts 4(1)

[178] The Secretariat is free to use the language it considers appropriate in its correspondence with the parties and to request that the parties correspond with the staff in a language that it understands for a good administration of the case.

[179] English and French are the official languages of the ICC Court, and of the ICC Rules of Arbitration, see *supra* Introduction, para 15.13.

[180] See *supra* para 15.223.

and (2) appear to indicate that the arbitration is commenced on the date on which the Request itself is received.[181]

It is worth stressing that Art 4 nowhere requires that the person filing a Request for Arbitration on behalf of the Claimant, most often its counsel, ie an attorney-at-law, provide the Secretariat with a power of attorney. It is left to the Arbitral Tribunal to request from either party the submission of a power of attorney.[182] 15.264

The time limit fixed by the Secretariat for the Claimant to 'complete' the Request in order to avoid having the file closed is not necessarily identical for each and every Request. The situation described above where the submission of a Request has tolled the running of any applicable contractual or statutory time periods, without the Respondent being aware thereof, is to remain the exception. 15.265

Although Art 4(4) provides that the 'unperfected' file is closed 'without prejudice' to the Claimant's right to submit the same claim at a later date, the ICC Rules almost certainly do not override any contractual or statutory provisions to the contrary, and the Claimant would have to look to such provisions to determine whether any limitation period continues to run even during the time the 'unperfected' Request had been filed with the ICC and the date on which the Secretariat advises that the file has been closed. 15.266

(6) Article 4(5): Notification of the Request by the Secretariat

This provision constitutes the explanation of what the Secretariat does once a Claimant has 'completed' the Request in a timely manner so that the file is not closed pursuant to Art 4(4). The Secretariat transmits the Request to the address of the Respondent indicated in the Request after receipt of the Claimant's advance payment. This constitutes a notification within the meaning of Art 3(2) of the Rules. The notification letter will indicate: the name and address of the Claimant, its counsel, the date of receipt of the Request for Arbitration by the ICC; a request to submit an Answer to the Request within 30 days from the day following the date of receipt of the notification letter, with the required number of copies of the Answer; information regarding the constitution of the Arbitral Tribunal (eg the name of the arbitrator appointed by the Claimant, if any), and an invitation to copy all correspondence addressed to the Secretariat and to the Claimant. 15.267

(7) Article 4(6): Joinder of two ICC arbitration cases

Article 4(6) deals with the consolidation of several disputes between the same parties in a single arbitral proceeding. The provision provides for claims 'in connection with a legal relationship between such parties' to be joined with a Request for Arbitration already in action. Such joinder of arbitration proceedings is subject to the decision of the ICC Court upon request of a party. Thus, the arbitrators are not given any power by the ICC Rules to join two or more arbitral proceedings in the same proceeding, contrary to state courts, and notwithstanding their competence to admit new claims or counterclaims.[183] 15.268

---

181 See *supra* para 15.224.
182 See *infra* Art 18, para 15.736.
183 See *infra* Art 19, paras 15.755 *et seq.*

15.269 The ICC Court may 'decide to include the claims contained in the Request in the pending proceedings' under the conditions that (i) the existing ICC arbitration and the new Request for Arbitration have the same parties; (ii) the joinder be requested by at least one party; (iii) a legal relationship exists between the proceedings; and (iv) the Terms of Reference have not yet been signed or approved by the ICC Court, or if they have, the claims to be joined to a Request for Arbitration would be admissible as new claims under Art 19. In addition, the pending proceedings must be ICC arbitration proceedings with identical or at least compatible arbitration clauses. There is no provision for consolidation of an ICC arbitration with an *ad hoc* arbitration for example.

15.270 Whenever the new arbitration involves a new third party, the ICC Court is prevented from joining the two arbitrations, unless all parties agree thereto.

15.271 Article 4(6) serves the purpose of efficiency and economy in ICC arbitral proceedings. It happens from time to time that parties to a contract file a Request for Arbitration against each other more or less at the same time. In the case of joinder, the second arbitration would be merged into the first arbitration, so that the Claimant in the second arbitration would become a Respondent and Counter-Claimant in the first arbitration. The Claimant in the first arbitration would become the Counter-Respondent. In the case of such joinder, the ICC Court's Secretariat will normally close the file in the second arbitration, which will become part of the first arbitration.

15.272 Contrary thereto a party may wish to have the disputes decided in separate arbitration proceedings not only for tactical reasons, but for example because it does not want the same arbitrators to decide the cases. Thus, the ICC Court has not only to consider the interest of economy and efficiency, but also the right of a party to nominate a different arbitrator under aspects of 'equality of parties'.

15.273 National legal systems vary in their treatment of consolidation of arbitral proceedings. The UNCITRAL Model Law makes no provision for consolidation. Article 35 of the English Arbitration Act of 1996 permits consolidation basically by agreement of the parties.[184] Article 7 of the Ontario International Commercial Arbitration Act of 1990 permits the court to consolidate arbitrations on motion of a party. Article 24 of the Australian International Arbitration Act of 1974 (as amended) and Art 1046 of the Netherlands Code of Civil Procedure permit Tribunals to order consolidation.

Article 5. Answer to the Request; Counterclaims

(1) Within 30 days from the receipt of the Request from the Secretariat, the Respondent shall file an Answer (the 'Answer') which shall, *inter alia*, contain the following information:

a) its name in full, description and address;

b) its comments as to the nature and circumstances of the dispute giving rise to the claim(s);

c) its response to the relief sought;

[184] Russell on Arbitration, *op cit*, 107, 110. More generally, see Redfern/Hunter, *op cit*, 173–6; Derains/Schwartz, A Guide, *op cit*, 58–62.

d) any comments concerning the number of arbitrators and their choice in light of the Claimant's proposals and in accordance with the provisions of Articles 8, 9 and 10, and any nomination of an arbitrator required thereby; and

e) any comments as to the place of arbitration, the applicable rules of law and the language of the arbitration.

(2) The Secretariat may grant the Respondent an extension of the time for filing the Answer, provided the application for such an extension contains the Respondent's comments concerning the number of arbitrators and their choice, and, where required by Articles 8, 9 and 10, the nomination of an arbitrator. If the Respondent fails to do so, the Court shall proceed in accordance with these Rules.

(3) The Answer shall be supplied to the Secretariat in the number of copies specified by Article 3(1).

(4) A copy of the Answer and the documents annexed thereto shall be communicated by the Secretariat to the Claimant.

(5) Any counterclaim(s) made by the Respondent shall be filed with its Answer and shall provide:

a) a description of the nature and circumstances of the dispute giving rise to the counterclaim(s); and

b) a statement of the relief sought including, to the extent possible, an indication of any amount(s) counterclaimed.

(6) The Claimant shall file a Reply to any counterclaim within 30 days from the date of receipt of the counterclaim(s) communicated by the Secretariat. The Secretariat may grant the Claimant an extension of time for filing the Reply.

(1) Introduction

While Art 4 deals with the Request for Arbitration, Art 5 concerns the Answer thereto. Art 5 is in large part the mirror image of Art 4. It thus requires the Respondent to provide the same type of information as the Claimant, or comments on the information provided by the Claimant in the Request. If the Respondent wishes to pursue a counterclaim against the Claimant, it has, not surprisingly, to submit the same type of information concerning the counterclaim as the Claimant is required to submit in the Request. **15.274**

A Respondent who objects to the arbitral jurisdiction will normally raise such objection in its Answer, [185] since otherwise the Respondent risks waiving its rights to object to jurisdiction under the applicable law.[186] **15.275**

If the Respondent decides not to submit an Answer at all, it is noteworthy that the ICC Court may nevertheless decide, pursuant to Art 6(2), whether it is prima facie satisfied that there may be an arbitral jurisdiction under the ICC Rules. By not submitting an Answer, the Respondent deprives itself not only of the possibility of supplying reasons (eg jurisdiction, pre-arbitral requirements) against the arbitration proceedings themselves but also of the possibility of submitting its comments on the place of arbitration or numbers of arbi- **15.276**

[185] See also *infra* under Art 6, para 15.324.

[186] See for example Art 186(2) of the Swiss PILA which provides that any objection to the jurisdiction must be raised prior to any defence on the merits. Art 16(2) of the UNCITRAL Model Law provides that: 'A plea that the arbitral tribunal does not have jurisdiction shall be raised not later than the submission of the statement of defence.'

trators if the Court, pursuant to the prima facie criteria, puts the arbitration proceedings in motion.[187]

15.277 In case that the Respondent before a state court objects to arbitral jurisdiction the Claimant will certainly invoke Art 2 of the New York Convention[188] (if applicable under national law),[189] whereas concurrent court proceedings do not generally require or result in a stay of the arbitral proceedings.[190]

15.278 A Respondent sometimes refuses to pay its share of the advance on costs while objecting to jurisdiction. In such situation, the Claimant is forced to pay the entire amount of the advance on costs for the claim, at least until the decision on jurisdiction has been taken by the Tribunal.[191]

15.279 The Respondent should also state in its Answer any failures to comply with any applicable pre-arbitral procedure, otherwise the Respondent may risk finding that the right to raise such an objection has been waived. In the *Poiré v Tripier* case, the French Supreme Court held that a contractual clause that provides for the settlement of disputes by conciliation precludes any recourse to judicial redress before the completion of the conciliation process.[192]

15.280 The failure to meet pre-arbitral requirements may be important if there is a statute of limitations issue in which case the Respondent may wish to argue that the arbitration has not been validly commenced in accordance with the Rules.

15.281 In a recent ICC case,[193] an Arbitral Tribunal decided it had no jurisdiction to hear the case, as the Request was filed prematurely, that is prior to the start and completion of the pre-arbitral procedure as foreseen in the arbitration agreement. The Arbitral Tribunal refused

[187] Respondents who do not file an Answer often default with respect to the proceedings as a whole. If the arbitration clause provides for three arbitrators or if the ICC Court decides that the Arbitral Tribunal should consist of three arbitrators, the Claimant will generally nominate one arbitrator and the ICC will generally have the National Committee of the defaulting Respondent propose an arbitrator, who may not be known to the Respondent.

[188] Art 2 states that: 'The court of a Contracting State, when seized of an action in a matter in respect of which the parties have made an agreement within the meaning of this article, at the request of one of the parties, refer the parties to arbitration, unless it finds that the said agreement is null and void, inoperative or incapable of being performed.'

[189] Art 5 of the UNCITRAL Model Law provides, for example, that '(1) A court before which an action is brought in a matter which is the subject of an arbitration agreement shall, if a party so requests not later than when submitting his first statement on the substance of the dispute, refer the parties to arbitration unless it finds that the agreement is null and void, inoperative or incapable of being performed.'

[190] The UNCITRAL Model Law permits the arbitration to continue as does Art 32(4) of the English Arbitration Act of 1996.

[191] If the parties have signed an agreement with an ICC arbitration clause, then the Arbitral Tribunal in first instance is to decide on its jurisdiction in accordance with Art 6(4). By agreeing to the Rules, the parties have agreed to pay the advance on costs in accordance with Art 30(3). Therefore, failure by the Respondent to pay its share of the advance on costs would appear to be a breach of its obligations under the Rules. However, where the claim is that the Respondent is not even a party to the arbitration clause, then it is difficult to see the basis for the claim that the Respondent should pay its share of the advance on fees.

[192] See Cass Civ Mixte, 14 February 2003, (2003) 19 Arb Int'l no 3, 263 and (2003) *Rev arb* no 2, 403, note Jarrosson.

[193] ICC case no 12739 (2004), unreported: place of arbitration was Switzerland and applicable law Tunisian law.

to suspend the arbitration procedure pending the completion of the pre-arbitral phase, considering that such suspension had not been provided for by the parties in the arbitration agreement. While one may question the wisdom of that conclusion, it shows that non-compliance with pre-arbitral procedure requirements puts Claimants at risk.

(2) Article 5(1): Contents of the Answer

Whereas Art 4(3) contains a list of six items which every Claimant should address in the Request for arbitration, Art 5(1) limits this list for the Respondent's Answer to five items. Since these items are essentially identical, the comments under Art 3 apply *mutatis mutandis*. The following additional comments are worth making. **15.282**

(i) The Respondent is asked in *lit* (a) to provide its name in full, a description of itself and its address. If the Claimant has given an improper spelling of the Respondent's name or incomplete address, the Respondent is expected to correct such errors. **15.283**

(ii) The Respondent is not required to submit a full statement of reply, but may do so if it wishes. In practice, the scope and volume of the Respondent's Answer will depend on the nature of the Request for Arbitration. In any event, pursuant to *lit* (b) a Respondent is required only to provide 'its comments as to the nature and circumstances of the dispute giving rise to the claim(s)'. Like the Claimant, the Respondent may wish to, and mostly does, exhibit at least key documents (if not already included in the Request for Arbitration) to its Answer in support of its counter-allegations and counter-arguments. It is not necessary or usual to provide a reference to the evidence that will be submitted to support each allegation of fact. Most Arbitral Tribunals will assume that the evidence will be provided in the course of the proceedings.[194] **15.284**

(iii) Pursuant to *lit* (c), the Respondent is also to give its response to the relief sought by the Claimant. In the vast majority of cases, the Respondent will request that the claims be dismissed, and that the Claimant be ordered to bear the cost of arbitration, including the Respondent's legal cost. **15.285**

In some cases, the Respondent may have a counterclaim against the Claimant. Rather than pursuing it as a separate counterclaim, the Respondent may, as part of its defence against the relief sought, declare a set-off in the Answer to the Request for arbitration. As now follows clearly from Art 30(5), the amount of the claimed set-off may be taken into account by the Court when fixing the advance on costs.[195] **15.286**

(iv) The Respondent is required to comment upon the number of arbitrators and their choice in light of the Claimant's proposal *lit* (d). Whenever the Answer is filed after the 30-day time limit, the Respondent is required to provide such comments together with its applications for an extension of the 30-day time limit. This is stipulated in Art 5(2). In practice, it is relatively rare that an Answer will be submitted within the initial time limit. (A Respondent may nevertheless reiterate in the Answer the comments it may already have given to the Secretariat when submitting its application for time-extension.) **15.287**

[194] See *supra* Art 4, para 15.242.

[195] See *infra* Art 30, paras 15.1092 *et seq.*

15.288 When the arbitration agreement specifies the number or arbitrators and the Claimant does not seek to alter such agreement, the Respondent is bound by such agreement, and will usually not have to comment upon the number.

15.289 Where the arbitration agreement leaves the number of arbitrators open, the Claimant is free to request a sole arbitrator or a three-member panel. If the Respondent agrees with the request, it becomes binding for the ICC Court, as if it had been contained in the initial arbitration agreement. If the Respondent disagrees with the Claimant's proposal, the Claimant may either reconsider its position and change its mind, or leave it to the ICC Court to take a decision upon the number of arbitrators pursuant to Art 8(2). In order to facilitate the ICC Court's decision-making, the Respondent should state the reasons why it considers that a sole arbitrator, or, as the case may be, a three-member panel would be appropriate.[196]

15.290 (v) To the extent that the arbitration agreement or other contractual provision does not specify the place of arbitration, the applicable rules of law, and the language of the arbitration, *lit* (e), the parties are best off agreeing upon such issues once the arbitration has started. The Claimant will have made its position known in this respect in the Request for Arbitration in accordance with Art 4(3)(f).[197] The Respondent may now agree with the Claimant's suggestion, or make different suggestions. If the Respondent provides persuasive reasons for its alternative suggestions, the Claimant may well be willing to accept the Respondent's counter-proposal. Both parties know that either the ICC Court or the Arbitral Tribunal will ultimately have to decide upon these issues as provided in Art 14 (place of arbitration), Art 17 (applicable law) or Art 16 (language of the arbitration), if the parties have not reached an agreement. To the extent that the parties may or may not anticipate the outcome of the decision the Court will make, they will often be inclined to accept the proposal made by one or other side.

15.291 Even if any comments on these issues are preliminary in nature and may be subject to substantial briefing later, they may be relevant in choosing a chairman of the Arbitral Tribunal and in any event will be useful in preparation of the Terms of Reference provided for in Art 18.

(3) Article 5(2): Extension of the time to file an Answer

15.292 Whereas a Claimant has a virtually unlimited amount of time within which to prepare its Request, the Respondent may be caught by surprise when it receives the Request and, indeed, may even have been unaware that the Claimant considered that a dispute had arisen in connection with the relevant contract. By the time the Request has reached the necessary level of decision makers in the Respondent's organization and outside counsel has been selected and consulted by the Respondent, a considerable amount of time may elapse. The problem may be aggravated if the Request is drafted in a language in which the Respondent's key personnel are not fluent, or if the Respondent's usual outside counsel, if it has one, is unfamiliar with the language, the applicable law and/or international

[196] See *infra* Art 8, paras 15.386 *et seq.*
[197] See *supra* Art 4, para 15.255.

commercial arbitration. The Respondent's files on the subject matter of the dispute may have been warehoused or scattered around, requiring time to retrieve and organize them. Even if none of these factors is present, the complexity of many of the cases submitted to ICC arbitration,[198] and the sheer bulk of many Requests and the annexed exhibits, may lead the Respondent to spend a considerable time analysing and understanding the Request.

To require the Respondent to provide within a short period of time an Answer to the claims set out in a Request can constitute a denial of equal treatment of the parties which may be prejudicial to the Respondent. The Secretariat has therefore the right to extend the time for the Respondent's reply. **15.293**

Article 5(2) does not specify how long an extension the Secretariat may grant, and what the Respondent has to do to obtain such extension. Typically, as the 30-day period for filing the Answer is drawing to a close, the Respondent will write to the Secretariat, with a copy to the Claimant, requesting an extension which may run from 15 days to several weeks. The Secretariat will grant extensions of up to 30 days as a matter of routine without specifically seeking the Claimant's views, and without the need for the Respondent to come up with an elaborate set of reasons for its request. If the extension sought is for a period much longer than 30 days (ie the original 30 days plus 30 more days), the Secretariat will normally first seek the Claimant's views and limit any extension to no more and perhaps less than 60 days if the Claimant objects to an extension going beyond this time. **15.294**

The Secretariat seeks often the Claimant's views rather mechanically without trying first to assess the circumstances. If an ill-advised or uninformed Claimant flatly rejects an extension of time beyond the 'standard' 30 days, the Secretariat unnecessarily puts itself in a delicate situation, since it has now to decide in favour of one or other party. In the authors' opinion, there will rarely be good grounds for a Respondent to seek an extension of more than two months, which, if granted, would give it a total of three months to submit an Answer. Likewise, an extension of four to six weeks will rarely result in a delay of the arbitral proceedings, since this is the time it will take in most instances to constitute the Arbitral Tribunal. In a case where it is clear from the outset that the constitution of the Arbitral Tribunal will require more time than that, the Secretariat should take this factor into account when deciding upon a request for extension. **15.295**

The Secretariat may only grant an extension if the Respondent has, within the initial 30-day period after receipt of the Request, submitted its comments concerning the number of arbitrators and their choice, and where required by Arts 8, 9 and 10, the nomination of an arbitrator. In other words, under the Rules and practice of the ICC Court's Secretariat, the constitution of the Arbitral Tribunal should not be delayed by any extension of time granted to the Respondent to file an Answer containing the information required under Art 5(1). **15.296**

[198] Craig/Park/Paulsson, *op cit*, 4, note that 'the ICC has become the forum for the settlement of some of the more difficult and delicate contemporary international commercial conflicts'.

15.297 For example, if the arbitration clause does not specify the number of arbitrators,[199] the Respondent's application for an extension of time to file the Answer must comment on the particulars concerning the number of arbitrators and their choice contained in the Request. If the arbitration clause provides for three arbitrators, the Claimant should have named one in the Request and the Respondent, in its application for an extension, should raise any comments it may have in regard to the arbitrator nominated by the Claimant and must nominate an arbitrator on its own behalf.

15.298 If the chairman is to be appointed by the ICC, the application for an extension is also the occasion for the Respondent to raise any points it may have regarding the expertise, professional experience, nationality or other characteristics it believes the chairman of the Arbitral Tribunal should possess, as well as any proposals regarding alternative procedures for the appointment of the chairman (such as having the co-arbitrators agree upon him) which are not contained in the arbitration clause.[200]

15.299 The last sentence of Art 5(2) may create the impression that, if the Respondent fails to provide its comments on the number of arbitrators and their choice in its application for an extension, or if it does not nominate an arbitrator although required to do so by the Rules, it is thereafter precluded from making such comments or from nominating an arbitrator. In general, however, the Secretariat has applied this language loosely. The ICC Court will normally take into consideration comments made by a Respondent, even if they are made out of time, provided the ICC Court has not yet taken a decision. For example, if a Respondent's nomination is submitted to the Secretariat prior to the time the ICC Court appoints an arbitrator on behalf of the Respondent, the tendency is to accept such nomination. Flexibility is the key word in this context, ie the meeting of the time limit in Art 5 is not viewed by the ICC Court as an objective in itself. One could also say that the ICC Court operates on a 'no harm, no loss' basis, when it comes to accepting nominations of arbitrators made out of time.

(4) Article 5(3): Filing the Answer

15.300 Article 5(3) makes plain that the Answer is to be submitted only to the Secretariat, not to the Claimant and not to the arbitrators, should they have been nominated. It is typically the Secretariat's task to send the Answer to the Claimant, pursuant to Art 5(4), and to the Arbitral Tribunal pursuant to Art 13.

15.301 The required number of copies of the Answer may not be known at this stage, eg if the number of arbitrators was not agreed by the parties and has not yet been fixed by the Court, which may first want to see the Respondent's Answer. In such a case, it will normally suffice that the Respondent submits three copies of the Answer (one each for the ICC, the Claimant and the prospective sole arbitrator), the ICC NetCase Service being currently not available at that stage of the arbitration proceedings.[201] If the Respondent seeks the appointment of three arbitrators, it would seem consistent, and therefore advisable, that the Respondent

---

[199] As in the ICC standard arbitration clause.
[200] See *infra* Art 9, para 15.425 *et seq.*
[201] See *supra* Art 4, para 15.220.

submits five copies of the Answer from the outset, ie as above, with a copy of the Answer for each of the three arbitrators.

(5) Article 5(4): Notification of the Answer to the Claimant

Article 5(4) makes it clear that the Secretariat will communicate the Answer to the Claimant. However, it happens in practice that the Respondent, or its counsel, provides a courtesy copy to the Claimant in advance.[202] **15.302**

(6) Article 5(5): Counterclaim

Any counterclaim is to be filed by the Respondent along with its Answer to the Request. This requirement can constitute another legitimate reason why a Respondent who wishes to file a counterclaim, may need an extension of time for filing its Answer. **15.303**

The requirements as regards the contents of a counterclaim reflect those of a Request. The fact that Art 5(5) does not include provisions which parallel Arts 4(3)(a), (d), (e) and (f) should not be taken as meaning that the information called for in these Articles need not be included. It is clear that when the requirements for filing an Answer and those for filing a counterclaim are taken together, all of the information required under Art 4(3) should be provided by the Respondent. **15.304**

Article 5(5) may be understood as meaning that if a Respondent does not file a counterclaim with its Answer, it is thereafter precluded from filing a counterclaim. This, however, is normally not the case, as can be seen from Arts 18 and 19 of the Rules.[203] **15.305**

In some cases, the Respondent will file a claim for set-off. Some practitioners maintain that this is different from a counterclaim based on the characterization of the set-off claims under the applicable law. However, the distinction is difficult to see. Under most legal systems, to establish a set-off, a party must demonstrate that it has a claim in a certain amount and that the claim arose in a context where the party is entitled to set it off against a corresponding claim of the other party. **15.306**

Article 5(5) refers to a 'counterclaim' which is literally a claim against the Claimant or one of the Claimants. The term does not and has not been interpreted as covering claims against third parties. The term does also not cover so-called cross-claims. As stated under Art 4, the Respondent has generally no possibility to designate the parties of arbitration.[204] If a Respondent has a claim against a third party it has no choice other than seeking to obtain the Claimant's consent to add the third party or bring a new arbitral proceeding. If the Claimant and the third party are part of the same group, they may accept the addition of the related third party. Otherwise, the possibility for the Respondent of adding a third party to an ICC arbitration is limited, but may happen under the following conditions. **15.307**

If the third party is a party to the same arbitration agreement as the parties to the arbitration, the ICC Court has accepted in a number of recent instances that the Respondent join the third party. Pursuant to learned commentators, three conditions must be met (i) the **15.308**

202 See *supra* Art 4, para 15.222 (Claimant's Request sent to Respondent).

203 See *infra* Art 19, para 15.762 *et seq.*

204 See *supra* Art 4, para 15.243.

third party must have signed the arbitration agreement on the basis of which the Request was filed;[205] (ii) the Respondent must have introduced claims against the new party; and (iii) the request for joinder has been made before the Tribunal is constituted.[206]

15.309 Cross-claims are claims litigated between parties on the same side of the arbitration; for instance, by the first Respondent against the second Respondent in an arbitration brought by a Claimant against two Respondents. The 1998 ICC Rules, like those of other arbitral institutions, are premised on a bilateral situation: a Claimant brings claims against a Respondent, with the Respondent being allowed to raise a counterclaim against the Claimant.[207] The current wisdom is that in the absence of an arbitration agreement drafted specifically to cover also cross-claims it is not possible to pursue such claims under the ICC Rules.[208]

(7) Article 5(6): Reply to a counterclaim

15.310 The Claimant has 30 days to reply to the Respondent's counterclaim. Article 5(6) provides that 'the Secretariat may grant the Claimant an extension of time for filing a Reply'. It is intended that any such extension, where requested by the Claimant, will be dealt with along the same lines as an extension for the filing of an Answer.

15.311 In the event Claimant has received a courtesy copy of the Answer and the counterclaim from the Respondent in advance,[209] the time limit to submit a Reply to the counterclaim will only start to run once the counterclaim has been received by the Claimant from the Secretariat. This rule does not prevent the Respondent from sending a courtesy copy directly to the Claimant, when counsel of both parties are well intentioned, and wish the matter to proceed expeditiously.

15.312 The Claimant's Reply to the counterclaim is to be communicated to the Secretariat in the required number of copies.

Article 6. Effect of the arbitration agreement

(1) Where the parties have agreed to submit to arbitration under the Rules, they shall be deemed to have submitted ipso facto to the Rules in effect on the date of commencement of the arbitration proceedings, unless they have agreed to submit to the Rules in effect on the date of their arbitration agreement.

(2) If the Respondent does not file an Answer, as provided by Article 5, or if any party raises one or more pleas concerning the existence, validity or scope of the arbitration agreement, the Court may decide, without prejudice to the admissibility or merits of the plea or pleas, that

---

205 The fact that the third party must have signed the arbitration agreement appears to exclude situations where the third party is allegedly subject to the arbitration clause due to its relationship with the parties for example. In some jurisdictions, this restriction may seem appropriate, but in France, the French Supreme Court has recently reinforced the rule that arbitration clauses can be extended to non-signatories, and therefore this requirement appears restrictive. See *infra* Art 6, para 18.

206 Whitesell/Silva-Romero, *op cit*, 7.

207 See Bühler, M.W., 'Cross-claims in international arbitrations: a common law perspective', paper delivered at the 22nd Symposium of Arbitrators in Paris, 26 March 2007.

208 Delvolvé, J.-L., 'Final Report on Multi-party Arbitrations' (1995) 6 *ICC ICArb Bull* no 1, 32, 34. See also *infra* Art 6, para 15.329, regarding a cross-claim against a third party that was effectively on the Respondent's side.

209 See *supra* Art 4, para 15.222 (re: courtesy copy of the Request).

the arbitration shall proceed if it is prima facie satisfied that an arbitration agreement under the Rules may exist. In such a case, any decision as to the jurisdiction of the Arbitral Tribunal shall be taken by the Arbitral Tribunal itself. If the Court is not so satisfied, the parties shall be notified that the arbitration cannot proceed. In such a case, any party retains the right to ask any court having jurisdiction whether or not there is a binding arbitration agreement.

(3) If any of the parties refuses or fails to take part in the arbitration or any stage thereof, the arbitration shall proceed notwithstanding such refusal or failure.

(4) Unless otherwise agreed, the Arbitral Tribunal shall not cease to have jurisdiction by reason of any claim that the contract is null and void or allegation that it is nonexistent, provided that the Arbitral Tribunal upholds the validity of the arbitration agreement. The Arbitral Tribunal shall continue to have jurisdiction to determine the respective rights of the parties and to adjudicate their claims and pleas even though the contract itself may be nonexistent or null and void.

(1) Introduction

Article 6 of the ICC Rules incorporates two fundamental principles of international arbitration: **15.313**

- *Kompetenz-Kompetenz*, Art 6(2); and
- separability (or autonomy) of the arbitration agreement, Art 6(4).

These two principles are interrelated and can operate in tandem. Article 16(1) of the UNCITRAL Model Law includes both principles and links them. However, these are discrete principles; one could exist without the other.[210] Therefore, it is logical to stipulate *Kompetenz-Kompetenz* and separability in separate provisions, as in Arts 6(2) and 6(4) of the ICC Rules.[211] **15.314**

Article 6(2) also stipulates an important role for the ICC Court. If the Respondent fails to file an Answer, or if any party contests the existence, validity or scope of the arbitration agreement, the ICC Court may decide that the arbitration shall proceed if the Court is prima facie satisfied that an arbitration agreement under the ICC Rules exists. If the Court does so decide, the decision as to jurisdiction shall be taken by the Arbitral Tribunal itself, pursuant to the *Kompetenz-Kompetenz* principle. **15.315**

Article 6(3) contains the important general rule regarding default by a party: Notwithstanding such default, the arbitration shall proceed. **15.316**

Finally, Article 6(1) clarifies which version of the ICC Rules governs the arbitration, a point that was left open in previous versions of the Rules. **15.317**

(2) Article 6(1): The applicable rules

What version of the ICC Rules is applicable? The ICC Rules have been modified on several occasions since they were first published in 1922.[212] Until the publication of the 1998 **15.318**

---

[210] See Craig/Park/Paulsson, *op cit*, 49, noting that: 'Unlike *competence-competence,* which in most situations is a matter of procedure, the autonomy of the arbitration clause is a substantive principle.'

[211] See also AAA International Arbitration Rules, Arts 15(1) and 15(2); English Arbitration Act 1996, s 7 (separability) and s 30 *(competence-competence);* cf LCIA Rules, Art 23.1 (combining *Kompetenz-Kompetenz* and separability). The Swedish Arbitration Act 1999, ss 2 *(Kompetenz-Kompetenz)* and 3 (separability).

[212] See Derains/Schwartz, A Guide, *op cit*, 2.

Rules, the Rules did not stipulate which version of the Rules would apply to a given arbitration. In practice, parties to a standard ICC agreement rarely expressly stipulate that the ICC Rules as currently in force at the time of the agreement shall apply to the arbitration. This could lead to uncertainty and dispute when one version of the Rules was in effect at the time when the parties concluded their arbitration agreement and another version was in effect when the arbitration was commenced. When the ICC Rules were amended in 1988, the Court followed the policy of applying the amended Rules to all arbitrations commenced after the effective date of the new Rules. However, this policy was challenged by some parties, on the basis that, when agreeing to arbitration under the ICC Rules, they agreed to the ICC Rules then in force.[213]

15.319 When the parties have stipulated in their arbitration agreement that a specific version of the Rules shall apply, the ICC Court follows that agreement. In practice, the Secretariat of the Court may, however, invite the parties to consider submitting the arbitration to the current Rules in force. If this is to no avail, the arbitrators may make the same suggestion when drafting the Terms of Reference. The current Rules being an improvement to the previous Rules, one would reasonably expect parties to submit their dispute to the improved set of Rules.

15.320 Article 6(1) clarifies this point.[214] Unless the parties have agreed otherwise, the parties are deemed to have submitted to the Rules in effect on the date of commencement of the arbitration proceedings. This is in accordance with the practice the ICC Court has followed since 1975.

15.321 Caveat: The introduction of Art 6(1) in the 1998 Rules does not, however, fully settle this issue. Parties to a contract concluded before the effective date of the 1998 Rules (1 January 1998) cannot be deemed to have incorporated Art 6(1) in their arbitration agreement. Thus, if the parties to an agreement entered into prior to 1998 disagree upon which version of the Rules applies to an arbitration commenced after 1 January 1998, the ICC Court—and ultimately the Arbitral Tribunal—will have to decide the issue.[215]

(3) Article 6(2): Prima facie decision regarding existence of the arbitration agreement and Kompetenz-Kompetenz

15.322 *Kompetenz-Kompetenz*: The principle of *Kompetenz-Kompetenz* provides that arbitrators have jurisdiction (or competence) to determine whether they have jurisdiction over the matter that is pending before them. The effect of this well known principle is that national courts will normally wait with a decision regarding the existence of arbitral jurisdiction until the arbitrators have ruled on their own jurisdiction. The arbitrators' decision regarding their jurisdiction is subject to review by any court with jurisdiction over the matter (eg, in an annulment action against the award at the place of arbitration or in enforcement

---

213 See eg ICC Final Award in Case no 5622 (1992), extract published in (1997) 8 ICC ICArb Bull no 1, 52. See also cases cited by Craig/Park/Paulsson, *op cit,*145, n 20.

214 See generally Derains/Schwartz, A Guide, *op cit,* 76–8; Craig/Park/Paulsson, *op cit,* 142–5, para 10.03.

215 The policy adopted by the ICC Court for proceeding in this situation is summarized in Derains/ Schwartz, A Guide, *op cit,* 78, n 128.

proceedings wherever they may be brought). Article 6(2) states this principle succinctly: '. . . any decision as to the jurisdiction of the Arbitral Tribunal shall be taken by the Arbitral Tribunal itself.'

While the power of an Arbitral Tribunal to determine its own jurisdiction may be considered an inherent power of the Arbitral Tribunal,[216] treaties, national laws and rules of international arbitration expressly stipulate the principle of *Kompetenz-Kompetenz*.[217] **15.323**

The Court's prima facie decision regarding the existence of the arbitration agreement: Art 6(2) thus stipulates a rule that is generally accepted in international arbitration. However, Art 6(2) also provides for a preliminary, administrative decision on jurisdiction by the ICC Court that is less common. If the Respondent fails to submit an Answer, or if any party raises a plea concerning the existence, validity or scope of the arbitration agreement, the Court will examine the matter and determine whether it is prima facie satisfied as to the existence of the arbitration agreement under the ICC Rules. If it is so satisfied, the ICC Court 'may' decide - and, in practice, *will* decide - that the arbitration shall proceed.[218] **15.324**

The most common situation where the ICC Court must make a determination under Art 6(2) arises when the Respondent either fails to submit an Answer or raises a jurisdictional plea in its Answer. However, Art 6(2) may come into play in other situations. For example, a Respondent may accept jurisdiction and seek, in fact, to expand the arbitral proceedings by filing a claim against a third party that has not been named by the Claimant. If the third party—or, indeed, the Claimant, as Art 6(2) refers to 'any party'—then raises a plea concerning the existence, validity or scope of the arbitration agreement in relation to the Respondent's claim against the third party, the ICC Court will be called upon to consider *the* prima facie existence of such arbitration agreement, pursuant to Art 6(2). **15.325**

It is important to stress that the ICC Court's decision under Art 6(2) is not final or binding; the decision is an administrative, rather than a juridical, act.[219] If the Court decides against the prima facie existence of the arbitration agreement, Art 6(2) expressly stipulates that any party retains the right to seek a decision from a court having jurisdiction that there is a binding arbitration agreement. If the ICC Court is prima facie satisfied that an arbitration agreement under the Rules exists, and accordingly decides that the arbitration shall proceed, its decision in no way binds the Arbitral Tribunal; the ICC Court's decision is 'without prejudice to the admissibility or merits of the pleas or pleas [concerning the existence, validity or scope of the arbitration agreement]'. Indeed, this is the very nature of a prima **15.326**

[216] See Redfern/Hunter, *op cit*, 252.

[217] eg Geneva Convention of 1961 on International Commercial Arbitration, Art 5(3); Art 41(1) Washington Convention of 1965 on the Settlement of Investment Disputes Between States and Nationals of Other States; Art 16, UNCITRAL Model Law; Art 1458, French Code of Civil Procedure; Art 186, Swiss Private International Law Act; s 30, English Arbitration Act 1996; s 2, Swedish Arbitration Act 1999; Art 21, UNCITRAL Arbitration Rules; Art 15, AAA International Arbitration Rules; Art 23, LCIA Rules.

[218] For a description by the Chairman of the ICC Court of the procedure followed by the Court when applying Art 6(2), see Briner, R., 'The Implementation of the 1998 ICC Rules of Arbitration' (1997) 8 *ICC ICArb Bull* no 2, 7.

[219] See *supra* Art 1, paras 15.108 *et seq*.

facie determination: it is subject to revision, in light of a complete development of the relevant facts and law.

15.327 In practice, the ICC Court rarely decides under Art 6(2) that an arbitration shall not proceed. It is, after all, very unusual for a Claimant to submit a Request for Arbitration without some evidence that would at least prima facie establish the existence of an ICC arbitration agreement. Pleas regarding the existence, validity or scope of an arbitration agreement often raise complex issues of fact and/or law that are best decided by the Arbitral Tribunal, rather than by the ICC Court, which has no jurisdictional power.[220]

15.328 Issues that may arise in connection with the ICC Court's application of Art 6(2) include the following:[221]

15.329 *Is there an arbitration agreement?* There is no requirement under the ICC Rules that an arbitration agreement be in writing, although other applicable legal rules—notably, Art II of the New York Convention—may so require.[222] The ICC Court will nonetheless require some probative evidence of the arbitration agreement if its existence is called into question. The ICC Court decided in the *Cekobanka* case (1985) that an exchange of telexes, alleged by the Claimant to constitute an ICC arbitration agreement, was not a prima facie agreement between the parties to arbitrate. Accordingly, the Court declined to allow the arbitration to proceed. The disappointed Claimant then sued the ICC before the Paris Court of First Instance *(Tribunal de Grande Instance)*, seeking an order compelling the ICC Court to set the arbitration in motion. The Paris Court rejected the suit, holding that the ICC Court had properly exercised its discretion under the ICC Rules.[223] The ICC Court's decision in *Cekobanka* was relatively restrictive, and in other analogous cases the Court has allowed the arbitration to proceed, leaving it to the Arbitral Tribunal to decide whether an arbitration agreement existed. In light of the trend in ICC Court decisions since 1985 and the modification of the relevant provision under the 1998 Rules, it is likely that a case presenting the facts of the *Cekobanka* case would be decided differently today.[224]

15.330 *Which parties are bound by the arbitration agreement?* A more common problem than the alleged non-existence of an arbitration agreement concerns the legal effect of an arbitration agreement vis-à-vis a party that has not signed the relevant agreement. It is not unusual for a party to rely upon legal grounds such as assignment, agency, *alter ego*, estoppel or for a group of companies to argue either (i) that it should be allowed to claim on the basis of an arbitration clause that it has not signed; or (ii) that another party should be bound by an arbitration clause that the latter has not signed.[225] The ICC Court will not attempt to

[220] Gélinas, F., 'The Application of the ICC Rules by the Court: 1998 Overview' (1999) 10 *ICC ICArb Bull* no 1, 11.

[221] Derains/Schwartz, A Guide, *op cit*, 87, n 92.

[222] eg Art 583 of the Austrian Code of Civil Procedure. Reiner, A., *The New Austrian Arbitration Law: Arbitration Act 2006* (LexisNexis, ADR ORAC, 2006) 10.

[223] *Ceskilovenska Obchodni Banka AS (Cekobanka) v Chambre de commerce internationale*, Tribunal de Premiere Instance de Paris (8 October 1986), (1987) Rev. arb 367. See also *supra* Art 1.

[224] Derains/Schwartz, A Guide, *op cit*, 85–6.

[225] See eg *International Paper Co v Schwabendissen Maschinen & Anlagen GmbH*, no 98–2482, (14 March 2000), F 3rd (4* Cir 2000) reviewing well-established common law principles under which a non-signatory can enforce, or be bound by, an arbitration provision within a contract executed by other parties and holding

resolve the factual and legal issues that may arise in this context, but it will require at least a plausible theory showing why the non-signatory could enforce or be bound by the relevant arbitration agreement,[226] and some factual support for such theory, preferably evidenced by some documents. The mere allegation of facts is likely to be insufficient to convince the ICC Court of the prima facie existence of an arbitration agreement, or its binding character regarding a party that has not signed it.

Does the agreement effectively provide for arbitration under the ICC Rules? Another situation where the ICC Court can be required to make a decision under Art 6(2) arises from a contractual clause that makes an inaccurate reference to the ICC Rules. Examples include references to 'the International Chamber of Commerce of Geneva', and 'the Arbitration Court of the French Chamber of Commerce, Paris'. The ICC's practice regarding such 'pathological' clauses is relatively liberal.[227] Among the criteria taken into consideration by the ICC Court in determining whether the parties intended to agree upon arbitration under the ICC Rules, are the nationalities of the parties and their lack of connection with the place of arbitration specified in the clause. In particular, the ICC Court will consider whether there is any other institution administering international arbitrations at the place mentioned in the clause.[228] These factors may prima facie satisfy the ICC Court that the parties have agreed to arbitration under the ICC Rules, so that the arbitration may proceed and the issue may be decided by the Arbitral Tribunal. **15.331**

A different but related problem arises where the parties refer unambiguously to ICC arbitration but include some provision in their arbitration agreement that is incompatible with the ICC Rules (eg, the exclusion of scrutiny of the draft award by the ICC Court).[229] Even in the absence of a plea by one of the parties concerning the existence, validity or scope of the arbitration agreement, the ICC Court would be unwilling to allow the arbitration to proceed with such a provision, as this would violate Art 1(1) of the Rules.[230] **15.332**

that the appellant was estopped refusing to comply with the arbitration clause of a contract upon which the appellant sought to rely.

[226] See Craig/Park/Paulsson, *op cit*, 171 *et seq*. The Court may, however, be more reluctant to allow arbitral proceedings to proceed against a physical person who did not sign the relevant agreement, as compared to a non-signatory corporate entity. See Derains/Schwartz, A Guide, *op cit*, 91–2 (discussing the R.E.D.E.C. case).

[227] The term 'pathological' was used by the former Secretary-General of the ICC Court, see Eisenmann, F., 'La clause d'arbitrage pathologique' in *Arbitrage commercial—Essais in memoriam Eugenio Minoli, Colloria di Studi sull'Arbitrator* (AIA 1974) 129. The Paris Cour d'Appel decided on 28 October 1997 that an arbitration clause referring to 'the ICC in Geneva' had to be construed or designated as to the ICC Paris as the organizer of the arbitration, and Geneva, as the place of arbitration, *(Société Procédés de fabrication pour le béton v La grande Jamahira arabe lybienne populaire et socialiste)*, (1998) *Rev arb* 399; see also ICC Award no 2626 (1977), *Collection of ICC awards (1974–1985)* 316; ICC Award no 4472 (1984), *Collection of ICC awards (1974–1985)* 528; ICC Award no 5294 (1988), *Collection of ICC awards (1986–1990)* 182.

[228] A sole arbitrator appointed pursuant to the arbitration rules of the Chamber of Commerce and Industry of Geneva ('CCIG') decided as follows in an interlocutory award on jurisdiction of 29 November 1996: 'The correct designation of an arbitration institution is not a requirement for the validity of an arbitration agreement. An arbitration agreement submitting all disputes to the Arbitration Court at the Swiss Chamber for Foreign Trade in Geneva refers according to the Arbitral Tribunal to the Chamber of Commerce and Industry of Geneva', Chamber of Commerce and Industry of Geneva, Arbitration Matter no 117 (1997) *ASA Bull*, 534.

[229] See *supra* Art 1, paras 15.101 *et seq*.

[230] See *supra* Art 1, paras 15.103 and 15.104.

15.333 A party determined that it should not become part of an ICC arbitration, will sometimes seize the state courts and seek an order that the arbitration cannot take place. As long as the ICC has not become a party to such proceedings (outside Paris, courts would normally have no jurisdiction over the ICC),[231] the ICC Court will not be bound by such decision. If the Claimant decides that it wishes to proceed with the arbitration despite parallel state court proceedings going on, or even by ignoring an order from a state court not to proceed, the ICC Court will normally constitute the Arbitral Tribunal, which will then have to take a decision.[232]

15.334 Is the dispute submitted to arbitration arbitrable? A Respondent may challenge the ICC Court's jurisdiction on the ground that the dispute is not arbitrable, eg because the claim is prohibited, as a matter of domestic mandatory law, from being arbitrated, or otherwise. As long as the ICC Court is satisfied prima facie of the existence of an ICC arbitration agreement, it will leave the issue of arbitrability to be decided by the Arbitral Tribunal.

15.335 This review of the ICC Court's application of Art 6(2) shows that complex issues of fact and/or law often arise in connection with pleas concerning the existence, validity or scope of an arbitration agreement. Under such circumstances, the ICC Court will usually be prima facie satisfied that the arbitration agreement exists, and decide that the arbitration shall proceed. The decision enables the parties to present their evidence and arguments in full and it permits the Arbitral Tribunal to address and decide the issue. The most important element of Art 6(2) thus remains the principle of *Kompetenz-Kompetenz*.

(4) Article 6(3): Consequences of default by a party

15.336 Default by a party. Article 6(3) confirms the ICC Court's and the Arbitral Tribunal's power to proceed with the arbitration in case of any party's refusal or failure to take part in the arbitration or any stage thereof. This is an essential rule for the efficacy of international arbitration. Clearly, if a recalcitrant party could obstruct or block an arbitration by failing to take part in it, international arbitration could not continue as a viable means of resolving disputes. It is an implicit requirement of the rule stated by Art 6(3) that the defaulting party has received proper notice of the arbitration and its various stages. See *supra*, Art 3.

15.337 The ICC Rules also contain provisions regarding specific defaults in the course of the arbitral procedure. See *infra*, Arts 8, 10, 18(3), 21(2) and 30(3)-(4).

15.338 It is noteworthy that Art 6(3) refers to a default by 'any of the parties'. Generally, if a party refuses or fails to take part in an arbitration, it is the Respondent. However, under certain circumstances, it may be the Claimant that ceases to participate and the Respondent may have an interest in pursuing the arbitration and obtaining a final award. For example, the Respondent may have a counterclaim against the Claimant, or it may wish to obtain a final and binding decision on some issue, such as cost. Pursuant to Art 6(3), there is no doubt that the arbitration can proceed even if the Claimant ceases at some stage to participate.

[231] See *supra* Art 1, para 15.113.

[232] See the US Court's *Deutz* case in that context.

If a party refuses or fails to take part in the arbitration, it is likely that that party will also default upon its obligation to pay its share of the advance on costs. In order for the arbitration to proceed, it then becomes necessary for the non-defaulting party to pay the defaulting party's unpaid share of the advance on costs. See *infra*, Art 30(3); see also Art 1(6) of App III of the Rules. **15.339**

No 'default award'. In contrast to the procedure followed before a municipal court, the Arbitral Tribunal does not—and cannot—render a 'default award' in case one party refuses or fails to participate in the arbitration. While the default is likely to affect the non-defaulting party's burden of proof, the Arbitral Tribunal must still examine its jurisdiction, pursuant to Art 6(2), and establish the facts of the case by all appropriate means, Art 20(1). **15.340**

(5) Article 6(4): Separability of the arbitration agreement

Separability of the arbitration agreement. The separability (or autonomy) of the arbitration agreement is, with *Kompetenz-Kompetenz*, one of the fundamental principles of international arbitration contained in Art 6. Under the separability principle, the agreement to arbitrate is deemed to be separate from and independent of the contract in which it is contained. Therefore, the nullity or non-existence of the contract does not necessarily entail the nullity or non-existence of the agreement to arbitrate.[233] Art 6(4) states this principle in broad terms. **15.341**

There may be theoretical difficulties inherent in deeming the arbitration agreement to be a separate and autonomous contract within the main contract. However, this principle enables the Arbitral Tribunal to act effectively to address and resolve the parties' disputes; it is a 'convenient and pragmatic fiction'.[234] Accordingly, the separability principle is widely accepted in national laws and international arbitration rules.[235] **15.342**

The arbitration agreement may be valid even if the contract containing it is invalid. In this context, it is important to recall that the law governing the arbitration agreement may not be the same as the law governing the contract that contains that agreement.[236] On the other hand, certain reasons rendering the contract invalid would also invalidate the arbitration agreement contained within it, eg where the person entering into the contract was not major, or lacked authority to represent the party. **15.343**

The power of the Arbitral Tribunal to determine its own jurisdiction—*Kompetenz-Kompetenz*—gives effect to the separability principle.[237] If the Arbitral Tribunal is to decide upon its own jurisdiction, it must first assume that jurisdiction—even if, or especially when, a party alleges that the contract is null and void or non-existent. Thus, the two **15.344**

---

[233] For discussions on the separability principle, see Derains/Schwartz, A Guide, *op cit*, 111 *et seq;* Craig/Park/Paulsson, *op cit*, 48, 515; Redfern/Hunter, *op cit*, 251, 263 *et seq*.

[234] Redfern/Hunter, *op cit*, 251.

[235] eg Art 16(1), UNCITRAL Model Law; s 7, English Arbitration Act 1996; Swedish Arbitration Act 1999, s 3; Swiss Private International Law Act, s 178(3); Netherlands Arbitration Act, Art 1053; *Prima Paint Co v Flood & Conklin Manufacturing Corp*, 388 US 395, 402 (1967) (United States); UNCITRAL Arbitration Rules, Art 21.2; AAA International Arbitration Rules, Art 15(2); LCIA Rules, 23.1. But cf Craig/Park/Paulsson, *op cit*, 51, n 16 (suggesting that, in some countries where the separability principle is considered to be accepted, the national courts have not yet addressed the issue).

[236] See Craig/Park/Paulsson, *op cit*, 52–4, n 18.

[237] For an illustration of how these two principles may work together in practice, see Craig/Park/Paulsson, *op cit*, 48 *et seq*.

discrete elements of Art 6, Arts 6(2) and 6(4), may operate in tandem in a situation where the Arbitral Tribunal makes decisions that are among the most important that it is called upon to make.

Article 7. General provisions

(1) Every arbitrator must be and remain independent of the parties involved in the arbitration.

(2) Before appointment or confirmation, a prospective arbitrator shall sign a statement of independence and disclose in writing to the Secretariat any facts or circumstances which might be of such nature as to call into question the arbitrator's independence in the eyes of the parties. The Secretariat shall provide such information to the parties in writing and fix a time limit for any comments from them.

(3) An arbitrator shall immediately disclose in writing to the Secretariat and to the parties any facts or circumstances of a similar nature which may arise during the arbitration.

(4) The decisions of the Court as to the appointment, confirmation, challenge or replacement of an arbitrator shall be final and the reasons for such decisions shall not be communicated.

(5) By accepting to serve, every arbitrator undertakes to carry out his responsibilities in accordance with these Rules.

(6) Insofar as the parties have not provided otherwise, the Arbitral Tribunal shall be constituted in accordance with the provisions of Arts 8, 9 and 10.

(1) Introduction

15.345 The constitution of the Arbitral Tribunal and the basic principles and duties relating thereto are covered by six Articles (Arts 7 to 12). The first of these, Art 7, deals with, as its title indicates, general provisions, the main focus of which is the requirement of independence of the Arbitrator (Art 7(1) to (3) and (5)).

15.346 The general provisions enumerate, as a fundamental principle of international commercial arbitration, the independence of the members of the Arbitral Tribunal, imposing an obligation of disclosure on the prospective arbitrator in respect to his independence prior to the appointment (Art 7(2)), and once appointed, a continuing obligation of disclosure during the arbitration (Art 7(3)). Similar provisions are expressed in other international arbitration rules, and may also be found in national laws.[238]

15.347 While paras (1) to (3) and para (5) of Art 7 refer to the status of the arbitrator, paras (4) and (6) make plain the important role of the ICC Court in constituting the Arbitral Tribunal by rendering final and confidential decisions relating thereto.

15.348 Article 7(5) offers the contractual base for the arbitrator's responsibility under the Rules. When the arbitrator accepts to serve, he signs a written acceptance. Thus, the Rules are a principal source of the obligations imposed upon the arbitrator.

15.349 In 2004, the International Bar Association published the IBA Guidelines on Conflict of Interest in International Arbitration (the 'IBA Guidelines').[239] The IBA Guidelines are

---

[238] eg Art 1452 French CPC, Art 58 of the Swiss federal Constitution providing for impartiality of judges including also international arbitration, see decision of the Federal Tribunal of 9 February 1998, (1998) ASA Bull, 634; Swedish Arbitration Act 1999, ss 7, 8 and 9, or German Code of Civil Procedure s 1036(1).

[239] They replace the 1987 IBA's Rules of Ethics for International Arbitrators if the matters are covered by the new IBA Rules, otherwise the 1987 Rules remain valid. See Càrdenas, E. and Rivkin, D.W., 'A Growing Challenge for Ethics in International Arbitration' in *Liber Amicorum in honour of Robert Briner* (ICC Publishing, Paris, 2005) 191.

accompanied by an explanatory comment on each principle (the 'General Standard') and provide concrete examples in application lists (a waivable and non-waivable 'Red list' as well as an 'Orange' and a 'Green' list) that cover various practical situations related to the arbitrator's impartiality, independence and obligation to disclose.[240]

In providing general principles and concrete examples, the IBA Guidelines may be a useful reference for the parties and the arbitrators.[241] However, the IBA Guidelines have no binding effect as such upon the ICC Court, the arbitrators acting under the ICC Rules or the parties, unless adopted by the parties in their arbitration agreement. They are in many respects too general to allow the ICC Court to determine whether or not to accept a challenge in the given circumstances of a case.[242] **15.350**

(2) Article 7(1): The requirement and notion of the arbitrator's independence

The notion of independence is neither defined in the ICC Rules nor in any other comparable international arbitration rules.[243] While the general concept is easily understood in terms of avoiding a close relation between a (prospective) arbitrator and a party, its contours may be more difficult to learn. The ICC Court deals with this issue on a case-by-case basis giving due regard to the specific circumstances of each matter, the applicable law and the nationality of the parties and the arbitrator(s). Therefore the expression 'independence' is to be construed very broadly. **15.351**

Based on the wording 'every arbitrator must be and remain independent of the parties involved . . ' the arbitrator is required to be (directly) independent from all parties, ie, not only from the nominating party.[244] The most frequent case of direct dependence may be assumed where the arbitrator has a direct professional, financial or similar relationship with a party and/or a financial interest in the outcome of the arbitration.[245] The ICC Court's practice in previous cases was to not confirm arbitrators who had important professional links with one of the parties,[246] that created a financial dependence between the (prospective) arbitrator and one party. **15.352**

The independence of an arbitrator may be also violated in cases of indirect relationships between an arbitrator and a third person. These relationships may comprise for instance **15.353**

---

[240] General Standard 1 of the IBA Rules states: '(1) General Principles - Every arbitrator shall be impartial and independent of the parties at the time of accepting an appointment to serve and shall remain so during the entire arbitration proceeding until the final award has been rendered or the proceeding has otherwise finally terminated'. The IBA Rules can be downloaded from <http://www.ibanet.org>.

[241] See the citations of the IBA Rules for example by the court of first instance in *Applied Industrial Materials Corp v Ovalar Makine Ticaret Ve Sanayi A S*, US Dist LEXIS 44789, (2007) *Mealey's Int'l Arb Rev* vol 21 #7, 9 as upheld in *Applied Industrial Materials Corp v Ovalar Makine Ticaret Ve Sanayi AS*, 492 F.3d 132, CA2 (NY), 9 July 2007. The principles were also cited in England but the court did not treat them as helpful. See *ASM Shipping Ltd of India v TTMI Ltd of England* [2005] EWHC 2238 (Comm) (19 October 2005)].

[242] For further comments see Bühler/Webster, ICC Handbook, *op cit*, paras 7.7–7.12.

[243] See the Comparable Arbitration Rules mentioned *supra*. See also General Standard 1 of the IBA Guidelines in n 4 and El Kosheri, A.S. and Youssef, K.Y., 'The Independence of International Arbitrators: An Arbitrator's Perspective' (2007) *ICC ICArb Bull*, Special Supp on Independence of Arbitrators, 43, 44.

[244] Craig/Park/Paulsson, *op cit*, 207, n 15.

[245] *ibid*, 67; Redfern/Hunter, *op cit*, 201.

[246] However, a simple occasional or *ad-hoc* cooperation between an arbitrator and a party related to their professional activities but not to the arbitral case should not, in the authors' opinion, suffice to create a disqualification based on dependence.

the arbitrator's connection to the party's representative or counsel, or the party's connection to the arbitrator's law firm.[247] Whether these relationships affect the independence of the arbitrator in terms of a close relationship differs from case to case. The ICC Court has for instance assumed the existence of an arbitrator's dependence in situations where several partners of the arbitrator's law firm had advised companies within the group of one of the parties, even though the prospective arbitrator had not himself given any legal opinion to any subsidiary of that group. Contrary hereto, where the arbitrator's law firm mandated another law firm to give legal advice for a party's parent company, the relationship was regarded as not sufficiently close as to call upon a non confirmation of the nominated arbitrator. These examples demonstrate that it is advisable to thoroughly check possible conflicts in respect of new clients and to monitor this situation also throughout the arbitration.

15.354 The requirement of independence often comes along with the requirement of impartiality.[248] The ICC Rules refer only to the 'independence' of the arbitrator as a condition for his confirmation or appointment by the ICC Court and provide the obligation of impartiality in terms of fairness in the conduct of the proceedings under Art 15(2).[249] The terms 'independent' and 'impartial' are not identical. It may occur that the arbitrator is financially and otherwise independent, but nevertheless not impartial. The concept of 'independence' can be decided with the help of objective criteria, such as the existence of a relation between the arbitrator and the parties, while 'impartiality' is more of a subjective nature (eg bias of an arbitrator). It is a state of mind, and may not be easily detected before the arbitral proceedings. However, the non-confirmation of an arbitrator on the grounds of dependence will in most cases comprise the suspicion that the arbitrator will not be able to discharge his duties without impartiality.

15.355 Another term used in connection with the independence of the arbitrator is his neutrality. A valid distinction between 'impartiality' and 'neutrality' is on the first sight difficult to achieve. As with the 'impartiality' of the arbitrator this requirement is not necessarily bound to his independence. The neutrality of the arbitrator will frequently be dealt in connection with the arbitrator's nationality as reflected in Art 9(5),[250] which requires the sole arbitrator or chairman to be of another nationality than the parties. Therefore the question of neutrality will arise more often in cases where the arbitrator is party-appointed. A party may be inclined to select one of its own nationals as arbitrator, not only for purposes of a better understanding of its position, which is perfectly legitimate and comprehensible, but also in order to obtain the understanding by a member of the Arbitral Tribunal of a behaviour that obstructs or delays the proceedings, which is not an acceptable attitude.[251] The IBA Guidelines specify in this context that a 'non-neutral' arbitrator is excluded from their scope, thus implicitly only the independent and impartial arbitrator is a neutral one.[252]

---

[247] Derains/Schwartz, A Guide, *op cit*, 123 *et seq.*

[248] Except Art 10 CCIG and Art 16 Zurich, all the comparable rules mentioned *supra* require both independence and impartiality of the arbitrator.

[249] See *infra* Art 15 paras 15.615 *et seq*; Redfern/Hunter, *op cit*, 201.

[250] See *infra* Art 9 paras 15.444 *et seq.*

[251] Craig/Park/Paulsson, *op cit*, 92.

[252] General Standard 5 of the IBA Rules states: '(5) Scope - These Guidelines apply equally to tribunal chairs, sole arbitrators and party-appointed arbitrators. These Guidelines do not apply to non neutral arbitra-

However, there is no need for a dogmatic distinction between the above-described requirements. For instance, in cases of a 'repeat' arbitrator, ie when a particular arbitrator accepts repeated nominations by the same party, and the other party fears that the arbitrator previously has taken the positions of the nominating party[253], the arbitrator could be dependent as well as partial or not neutral even before the commencement of the arbitral proceedings. **15.356**

It is not the arbitrator's own opinion that is determining but how the parties conceive it. This is stated in Art 7(2).[254] The IBA Guidelines refer to the point of view of a 'reasonable and informed third party'.[255] **15.357**

When discussing the arbitrator's independence the question arises what an arbitrator can do and cannot do without calling into question his impartiality. The arbitrator must be vigilant regarding his declarations as they might cause a party to call into question his independence. The arbitrator is obliged to reveal information on his background, qualifications, independence and availability when approached by a party as a prospective arbitrator. In such context, and as long as the arbitrator was not confirmed by the ICC Court, *ex parte* communication as well as preliminary communications between a party and a prospective arbitrator are generally accepted. Further, any information regarding the suitability of other arbitrators for nomination as chairman, where the parties or party-nominated arbitrators are to participate in that nomination, or any information concerning the general nature of the dispute and/or the anticipated proceedings may be regarded as acceptable.[256] Contrary hereto, a discussion of the merits of the dispute with the parties or the parties' counsel may jeopardize the arbitrator's independence and impartiality.[257] More generally, throughout the arbitration procedure the arbitrator should always treat the parties equally in order to ensure his impartiality. **15.358**

The requirement of independence prevails from the beginning to the end of an arbitration. An arbitrator must be independent at the time of his (i) nomination by a party or by the co-arbitrator and subsequent confirmation by the Secretary-General, or, as the case may be, by the Court; or of his (ii) appointment by the ICC Court. Once the arbitrator has been confirmed or appointed, the arbitrator must remain independent of the parties during the arbitration. Most challenges are made in respect of an arbitrator's lack of independence or impartiality.[258] It is worth noting that the New York Convention provides in Art V(1)d as grounds for refusal of recognition and enforcement of an award, *inter alia*, the arbitrator's lack of independence.[259] **15.359**

tors, who do not have an obligation to be independent and impartial, as may be permitted by some arbitration rules or national laws'.

[253] Derains/Schwartz, A Guide, *op cit* 128.

[254] See French Supreme Court, Cass, Civ 1e, 20 June 2006, *Société Prodim v Pierre Nigioni*, (2007) *Rev Arb*, 463, 466. The President of the Commercial Tribunal ordered one party to communicate the number of cases in which it appointed the same arbitrator , the Supreme Court judged the demand of the president of the Commercial Tribunal as justified. See also El-Kosheri/Youssef, *op cit*, 50.

[255] See Bühler/Webster, ICC Handbook, *op cit*, paras 7–16.

[256] eg Art 7 (2) AAA, 21 WIPO.

[257] Derains/Schwartz, A Guide, *op cit*, 131 *et seq.*

[258] See *supra* para 15.353 and *infra* Art 11.

[259] Craig/Park/Paulsson, *op cit*, 68: Art V (1)d of the New York Convention provides for refusal when '. . . the arbitral procedure was not in accordance with the agreement of the parties. . .', ie where agreed rules as for instance ICC Rules are violated.

15.360 As already mentioned above, the IBA Guidelines give practical examples of issues as to whether an arbitrator is impartial and independent. The duty of impartiality and independence shall cover the entire duration of the arbitration proceedings until the final award but not the annulment or enforcement proceedings. The Red List, divided into a waivable and non-waivable part, reflects (non-exhaustive) situations that give rise to justifiable doubts as to the arbitrator's impartiality and independence. In the situations enumerated in the Non-Waivable Red List[260], the arbitrator shall be excluded from his function as such, while within the circumstances included in the Waivable Red List[261] the parties may waive a possible objection.[262]

---

[260] The Non-Waivable Red List is as follows:
1.1. There is an identity between a party and the arbitrator, or the arbitrator is a legal representative of an entity that is a party in the arbitration.
1.2. The arbitrator is a manager, director or member of the supervisory board, or has a similar controlling influence in one of the parties.
1.3. The arbitrator has a significant financial interest in one of the parties or the outcome of the case.
1.4. The arbitrator regularly advises the appointing party or an affiliate of the appointing party, and the arbitrator or his or her firm derives a significant financial income therefrom.
For the complete waivable list, see <http://www.ibanet.org>.

[261] The Waivable Red List reads as follows:
2.1. Relationship of the arbitrator to the dispute
2.1.1 The arbitrator has given legal advice or provided an expert opinion on the dispute to a party or an affiliate of one of the parties.
2.1.2 The arbitrator has previous involvement in the case.
2.2. Arbitrator's direct or indirect interest in the dispute.
2.2.1 The arbitrator holds shares, either directly or indirectly, in one of the parties or an affiliate of one of the parties that is privately held.
2.2.2 A close family member of the arbitrator has a significant financial interest in the outcome of the dispute.
2.2.3 The arbitrator or a close family member of the arbitrator has a close relationship with a third party who may be liable to recourse on the part of the unsuccessful party in the dispute.
2.3. Arbitrator's relationship with the parties or counsel.
2.3.1 The arbitrator currently represents or advises one of the parties or an affiliate of one of the parties.
2.3.2 The arbitrator currently represents the lawyer or law firm acting as counsel for one of the parties.
2.3.3 The arbitrator is a lawyer in the same law firm as the counsel to one of the parties.
2.3.4 The arbitrator is a manager, director or member of the supervisory board, or has a similar controlling influence, in an affiliate of one of the parties if the affiliate is directly involved in the matters in dispute in the arbitration.
2.3.5 The arbitrator's law firm had a previous but terminated involvement in the case without the arbitrator involved himself or herself.
2.3.6 The arbitrator's law firm currently has a significant commercial relationship with one of the parties or an affiliate of one of the parties.
2.3.7 The arbitrator regularly advises the appointing party or an affiliate of the appointing party, but neither the arbitrator not his or her firm derives a significant financial income therefrom.
2.3.8 The arbitrator has a close family relationship with one of the parties or with a manager, director or member of the supervisory board or any person having a similar controlling influence in one of the parties or an affiliate of one of the parties or with a counsel representing a party.
2.3.9 A close family member of the arbitrator has a significant financial interest in one of the parties or an affiliate of one of the parties.

[262] See also Epstein, L., 'Arbitrator Independence and Bias: The View of a Corporate In-house Counsel' (2007) *ICC ICArb Bull*, Special Supp on Independence of Arbitrators, 55.

Contrary thereto, the Orange List is a non-exhaustive enumeration of situations that in the eyes of the parties may give rise to justifiable doubts as to the arbitrator's independence and impartiality. A successful challenge of its matters before a national court based on these situations is uncertain. 15.361

As mentioned, the IBA Guidelines are not binding on the ICC and the ICC Court's decisions are rendered on a case-by-case basis, but the Secretariat may consider the IBA Guidelines and be inspired by them when analysing a potential or actual challenge against an arbitrator, and in practice often does so. 15.362

(3) Article 7(2): The prospective arbitrator's statement of independence

The arbitrator's independence is to be established at the outset when the Arbitral Tribunal is constituted. The prospective arbitrator is therefore required to submit to the ICC Secretariat a statement of independence, before his appointment or confirmation, on an independence/disclosure form supplied by the ICC Secretariat (the 'Arbitrator's Declaration of Acceptance and Statement of Independence') in which he or she must give details of any matters which might influence his or her independence in the eyes of the parties (in the jargon of the Court referred to as 'clean' or 'qualified' statements of independence). 15.363

The Secretary-General may confirm as an arbitrator a person that has been nominated by a party only if the candidate has filed a statement of independence without qualification or a qualified statement of independence that has not given rise to a party's objections (Art 9(2)).[263] A confirmation is much more likely to occur with qualified statements than with non-specified statements of independence. From 1998 to 2006, 76.6 per cent of non-confirmations were based on qualified statements and only 23.1 per cent on non-qualified statements.[264] 15.364

The 'Arbitrator's Declaration of Acceptance and Statement of Independence' form is provided by the ICC Secretariat to each prospective arbitrator, irrespective whether the arbitrator was nominated by one party or all the parties, selected by the co-arbitrator, proposed by a National Committee, or appointed directly by the ICC Court. It is the only document that an arbitrator is required to sign before his appointment and it contains not only the arbitrator's declaration of being 'independent of each of the parties' and intending 'to remain so', but also the arbitrator's consent 'to accept to serve as arbitrator' under Art 7(5). 15.365

The question for an arbitrator is what to disclose. Article 7(2) speaks of 'facts or circumstances which might be of such nature as to call into question an arbitrator's independence in the eyes of the parties'. But how shall the arbitrator know what is included under the expression 'in the eyes of the parties'? In the absence of rules and guidelines of the ICC in this respect, prospective arbitrators should adopt a prudent approach and disclose rather more than less, if there is a doubt as to whether certain facts or circumstances could call into question their independence. The facts and circumstances to be disclosed may comprise 15.366

263 See *infra* Art 9, para 15.439 *et seq.*

264 See Whitesell, A.-M, 'Independence in ICC Arbitration: ICC Court Practice concerning the Appointment, Confirmation Challenge and Replacement of Arbitrators' (2007) *ICC ICArb Bull*, Special Supp on Independence of Arbitrators, 7, 14.

those that are likely to give rise to justifiable doubts as to the arbitrator's independence,[265] or are likely to create an impression of bias or prevent a prompt resolution of the case,[266] further, past and present professional positions,[267] or the extent of any prior knowledge of the case or any commitments which may affect his or her performance as an arbitrator.[268] Effectively, all information that may reasonably affect the arbitrator's independence shall be disclosed.[269]

15.367 Equally, the IBA Guidelines refer in their General Standard 3 to facts and circumstances that in the eyes of the parties give rise to doubts to the arbitrator's impartiality and independence.[270]

15.368 Notwithstanding that the parties may choose how to react when an event puts in question the arbitrator's independence, the arbitrator runs the risk of being challenged if information is not disclosed, even if the non-disclosed information itself does not justify a replacement of the arbitrator based on a lack of independence.[271] Contrary to ICC principles, pursuant to the IBA Guidelines the failure of disclosure does not automatically give grounds for challenges; nor will the stage of the arbitration proceedings be taken into account when a challenge is discussed as is the case under ICC arbitration.[272] However, a failure to disclose information has to be seen in the light of information provided by the parties about themselves in their Request and Answer. Where the information the parties have provided about themselves is scarce, it may be difficult for an arbitrator to know whether there exist circumstances that should be disclosed. Otherwise neither the prospective arbitrator nor the ICC Court may be expected to consider whether the arbitrator was and will be able to realize that the non-disclosed information could have created and could create an appearance of dependence or partiality.

15.369 It is safe to recommend that any matter in the IBA Guidelines' Red List must be disclosed, while the disclosure of matters under the Orange List depends on the circumstances. The matters in the Green List need not, in our view, be disclosed.

---

[265] eg in Art 17(2), SCC; Art 11.3, SIAC; Art 9, UNCITRAL; or Art 22, WIPO.

[266] See eg Arts 12(2) and 20(1).

[267] See Art 5.3, LCIA.

[268] See Art 4.2 of the IBA Rules.

[269] Derains/Schwartz, A Guide, *op cit*, 135.

[270] General Standard 3 of the IBA Guidelines provides as follows:

(a) If facts or circumstances exist that may, in the eyes of the parties, give rise to doubts as to the arbitrator's impartiality or independence, the arbitrator shall disclose such facts or circumstances to the parties, the arbitration institution or other appointing authority (if any, and if so required by the applicable institutional rules) and to the co-arbitrators, if any, prior to accepting his or her appointment or, if thereafter, as soon as he or she learns about them.

(b) It follows from General Standards 1 and 2(a) that an arbitrator who has made a disclosure considers himself or herself to be impartial and independent of the parties despite the disclosed facts and therefore capable of performing his or her duties as arbitrator. Otherwise, he or she would have declined the nomination or appointment at the outset or resigned.

(c) Any doubt as to w]hether an arbitrator should disclose certain facts or circumstances should be resolved in favour of disclosure.

[271] See *supra* n 243; this is actually the reason for resolving doubts in favour of disclosure; it may for instance be found in Art 4 of the IBA Rules, which provides that failure of disclosure creates an appearance of bias and may lead to disqualification. See also Craig/Park/Paulsson, *op cit*, 215.

[272] See explanation of IBA Guideline General Standard 3, *op cit*, *supra*.

Is there a risk of unnecessary or excessive disclosure ('over-disclosure')? The IBA Guidelines General Standard 3(c) provides that 'Any doubt as to whether an arbitrator should disclose certain facts or circumstances should be resolved in favour of disclosure'. This approach corresponds to the approach the ICC Court takes in its standard disclosure form for arbitrators[273] and has support elsewhere, including in the United States.[274] **15.370**

Article 7(2) does not mention explicitly the independence of counsel or other arbitrators; nor does Art 7(2) refer to the relationship between arbitrators. But in certain cases the relationship between an arbitrator and a counsel or another arbitrator may be linked to an indirect relationship with the party. Notwithstanding the lack of such provision, the ICC form for the arbitrator's statement of independence refers to the arbitrator's relation with counsel as well. **15.371**

Where the party-nominated arbitrator gives a qualified statement of independence by disclosing information, the Secretariat will forward such statement to the parties in writing and fix a time limit for any comments from them.[275] Generally the time limit granted to the parties to raise their objections will be short: it will vary from one to two weeks. If a party does not provide comments within the time limit granted, it shall be considered that, as regards the disclosed facts or circumstances, the respective party does not object to the confirmation of the nominated arbitrator. Upon expiry of the time limit or after receipt of the parties' comments, the Court, or pursuant to Art 9(2), the Secretary-General, will decide on the appointment/confirmation of the arbitrator in question on the basis of the information received. It is not the Court's practice independently to check or verify information disclosed by the arbitrator or by the parties. **15.372**

However, a party's failure to object to an arbitrator's appointment will not affect the party's right to challenge the arbitrator pursuant to Art 11, if the challenge is submitted to the Secretariat within the time limit foreseen in para (2) of Art 11.[276] **15.373**

(4) Article 7(3): The arbitrator's continuing obligation to disclose

The arbitrator must disclose all information relevant to his independence not only before his appointment/confirmation but also during the arbitration. 'During the arbitration' comprises the time from the arbitrator's appointment/confirmation by the ICC Court or from his confirmation by the Secretary-General, until expiry of the time limit for the correction or interpretation of notified final awards under Art 29 (30 days), or, as the case may be, until receipt of the corrected or interpreted award by the parties.[277] **15.374**

---

[273] See *supra*, para 15.357.

[274] See *Commonwealth Coatings Corp v Continental Casualty Co,* 393 US 145 (1968) case cited: 'If arbitrators err on the side of disclosure, as they should, it will not be difficult for courts to identify those undisclosed relationships which are too insubstantial to warrant vacating an award.'

[275] In the event that the arbitrator was proposed by a National Committee (Art 9(3)) see *infra* Art 9, paras 15.444 *et seq.*

[276] Derains/Schwartz, A Guide, *op cit*, 136–8.

[277] See the *Applied Industrial Materials Corp* case, (2007) 21 *Mealey's Int'l Arb Rev* no 7, 9 (annulment of an *ad hoc* Award for failure by the chairman of the Tribunal to disclose the commercial relationship between a company controlled by the arbitrator with one of the parties. The ongoing obligation of disclosure is even stronger when the parties had expressly stated in the submission agreement their expectations regarding disclosure of the arbitrators). *Positive Software Solutions Inc v New Century Mortgage et al*, no 01–11432, 436

15.375 Article 7(3) stipulates an immediate obligation to disclose any facts or circumstances that may arise during the arbitration. The arbitrator must therefore disclose without undue delay any facts or circumstances that may reasonably affect his independence after becoming aware thereof. Disclosure shall be made not only to the Secretariat but also to the parties. A failure to disclose such information timely may provide a ground for challenge.

15.376 Among the facts that may arise during an arbitration is a new arbitration that affects an arbitrator's independence. This frequently occurs and causes problems in larger law firms where, eg one office in one city and country may accept to act for a client belonging to a group of companies a member of which is involved as a party in an arbitration taking place in another city and country where a member of the law firm acts as arbitrator.[278]

15.377 Any information revealed by a party regarding the independence of the arbitrator after expiry of the time limit pursuant to Art 29 or after receipt of the 'corrected' or 'interpreted' award may only be revised by national judicial authorities.[279]

(5) Article 7(4): The decision of the ICC Court regarding the appointment, confirmation, challenge or replacement of an arbitrator

15.378 It is the ICC Court that determines whether the arbitrator's appointment can be confirmed in view of the statement of independence, and decides upon the merits of a challenge. In this respect, the ICC Court has wide discretion. Although it decides on a case-by-case basis, the ICC Court's decisions follow a rather consistent path. At the time of the appointment of an arbitrator, the ICC Court will look more strictly into the facts disclosed by an arbitrator to evaluate whether a party may legitimately fear a certain lack of independence of a prospective arbitrator. Once the arbitral proceedings have started, and the more they have advanced, the more critical the ICC Court's analysis will be of the facts and circumstances that are advanced by a party to justify a challenge.

15.379 The ICC Court's decisions are final, which means that its decisions are not subject to any further recourse before the ICC Court or any other body within the ICC. They are regularly made in a Court's plenary session, not in the restricted committee session. A Court member always submits a report on the matter, and these matters are treated first on the Court's agenda. However, the parties are free to seek judicial remedies, for instance apply

F.3d 495, 504 (5th Cir. 2006) (Award vacated for failure of an arbitrator to disclose that seven years before the arbitration he worked with a firm that had an extensive litigation relationship with a firm that represented a party). In contrast, see *HSN Capital LLC et al v Productora Y Comercializador de Television, SA de CV*, 5 July 2006, 2006 WL 1876941 (MDFla) (petition to vacate an ICC Award denied by the court under Art V of the New York Convention. Membership and professional relationship between the chairman of the Tribunal and one of the co-arbitrators during the arbitration proceedings are, alone, casual relationships that do not affect their independence. Failure by the challenging party to provide relevant evidence in this respect); see also *Merrill Lynch, Pierce, Fenner & Smith Inc v Lambros*, 1 FSupp 2d 1337 (M.D.Fla. 1998) (petition to vacate the Award based on the fact that one of the arbitrators was a fraternity brother of one of Merrill Lynch's attorneys. The court found that the relationship between the arbitrator and the counsel was too remote to constitute a conflict of interest and create the appearance of partiality).

[278] Clay, Th., 'La disparition de l'obligation d'indépendance de l'arbitre au profit de l'obligation de révélation', note sous Paris 1re Ch C, 12 February 2009 (2009) *Rev arb* no 1, 186.

[279] Craig/Park/Paulsson, *op cit*, 216 *et seq.*

to a national court for recourse,[280] in particular the courts at the place of arbitration in the context of an action to set aside the award, or the courts at the place of enforcement.[281]

The ICC Court will not communicate the reasons for its decision to the parties, which in that sense are 'confidential'. The main purpose of the final and confidential character of its decisions is to ensure the efficiency of the arbitral proceedings as the parties are prevented from obstructing or delaying the proceedings. It will also save the ICC Court from an overload of work of such nature. In addition, the award will be less 'vulnerable' and therefore more difficult to attack. And, it will avoid an offence or embarrassment of the arbitrators involved as the ICC Court will not only have to consider the arbitrator's independence,[282] but also other matters such as the competence of the arbitrator raised by a party upon a challenge. The parties have to put their confidence in the ICC Court. The parties should be able to do so since the premier consideration of the ICC Court is the position of the parties and the integrity of the arbitral process.[283] **15.380**

(6) Article 7(5): The arbitrator's obligation to carry out his responsibilities in accordance with the Rules

By filling out and signing the 'Declaration of Acceptance and Statement of Independence' form provided by the Secretariat, the arbitrator accepts to serve as arbitrator under the Rules in terms of fulfilling his duties in accordance with the Rules and of being familiarized with the requirements of the Rules. Such acceptance is the precondition for the statement of independence and the disclosure of related facts. **15.381**

The provision also explicitly states that the arbitrator must have time available and be able to proceed with diligence to enable the arbitration to be conducted and completed efficiently and expeditiously.[284] Pursuant to Art 24 of the ICC Rules, the arbitration shall be completed within six months after the signing of the Terms of Reference. Most ICC arbitrations are not completed within this period, simply because the exchange of briefs and hearing up to the closing of the proceedings takes at least as long. This nevertheless raises the interesting question whether, when signing the form, an arbitrator effectively undertakes to ensure that he has the time available to handle the arbitration within the six months time limit. **15.382**

In addition, this express duty comprises an undertaking by the arbitrator to carry out his responsibilities throughout the arbitration; he may not resign during the arbitration without a valid reason, as reflected in Art 12.[285] However, the arbitrator's express duty to act in **15.383**

[280] eg, Art 13 UNCITRAL Model Law providing expressly for application to courts etc.

[281] See with respect to 'indirect challenges', the Swiss Supreme Court, 14 December 2004, *A Ltd v B Ltd* (2005) 23 ASA Bull no 2, 337 at 344: 'Decisions by bodies such as the Court of Arbitration of the International Chamber of Commerce cannot, as such, be contested under Art 190 para 3 PIL Act in the form of proceedings to set aside. However, such decisions are indirectly subject to investigation within the scope of the proceedings to set aside the arbitrators' ruling. An objection on the grounds of irregular composition of the arbitral tribunal as defined by Art 190 para 2 lit. a PIL Act is therefore admissible'.

[282] Derains/Schwartz, A Guide, *op cit*, 139 *et seq.*

[283] See further more detailed provisions in respect to the appointment and confirmation of arbitrators (Art 9), challenge of arbitrators (Art 11) and replacement of arbitrators (Art 12).

[284] Craig/Park/Paulsson, *op cit*, 71.

[285] See *infra* Art 12, paras 15.522 *et seq.*; Derains/Schwartz, A Guide, *op cit*, 141.

accordance with the ICC Rules may be expanded to any other rules or agreements to which the parties may adhere, where the ICC Rules are silent (Art 15(1)),[286] or where they are derogated from by the parties (Art 7(6)). The arbitrator has therefore to give effect to any reasonable agreement of the parties.

(7) Article 7(6): Constitution of the Arbitral Tribunal

15.384 Article 7(6) gives priority to the autonomy of the parties by making the constitution of the Arbitral Tribunal subject to the agreement of the parties. The majority of ICC arbitration clauses do not contain any specific requirements in this respect, be it regarding the number of arbitrators, their nationality, their qualifications, or how they are to be appointed. Indeed, pursuant to the standard ICC arbitration clause proposed and published by the ICC, all that the parties need to provide in respect of the constitution of the Arbitral Tribunal is that the disputes shall be finally settled 'by one or more arbitrators appointed in accordance with the said Rules'.

15.385 The parties' autonomy in constituting the Arbitral Tribunal includes also the possibility to mandate a third institution or third person from outside the ICC to appoint, for instance, the sole arbitrator or chairman of the Arbitral Tribunal, although this is part of the prerogatives of the ICC Court pursuant to Art 8(2).[287] Although the wisdom of such provisions seems questionable, the ICC Court normally accepts the appointment made by a third body. Unlike in the case of a National Committee of the ICC, which can only make a proposal, the ICC Court will be bound by the appointment made by the third body. It will, however, be incumbent upon the ICC Court to confirm the arbitrator, which it will only do if he or she submits a statement of independence as described above.[288]

Article 8. Number of arbitrators

(1) The dispute shall be decided by a sole arbitrator or by three arbitrators.

(2) Where the parties have not agreed upon the number of arbitrators, the Court shall appoint a sole arbitrator, save where it appears to the Court that the dispute is such as to warrant the appointment of three arbitrators. In such a case, the Claimant shall nominate an arbitrator within a period of 15 days from the receipt of the notification of the decision of the Court, and the Respondent shall nominate an arbitrator within a period of 15 days from the receipt of the notification of the nomination made by the Claimant.

(3) Where the parties have agreed that the dispute shall be settled by a sole arbitrator, they may, by agreement, nominate the sole arbitrator for confirmation. If the parties fail to nominate a sole arbitrator within 30 days from the date when the Claimant's Request for Arbitration has been received by the other party, or within such additional time as may be allowed by the Secretariat, the sole arbitrator shall be appointed by the Court.

(4) Where the dispute is to be referred to three arbitrators, each party shall nominate in the Request and the Answer, respectively, one arbitrator for confirmation. If a party fails to nominate an arbitrator, the appointment shall be made by the Court. The third arbitrator, who will act as chairman of the Arbitral Tribunal, shall be appointed by the Court, unless the parties have agreed upon another procedure for such appointment, in which case the

[286] See *infra* Art 15 paras 15.605 *et seq.*

[287] The authors have seen clauses referring to the Chamber of Commerce of Geneva, the *Handelsgericht* of Zurich or the Vice President of the Law Society of England and Wales.

[288] See *supra* para 15.362.

nomination will be subject to confirmation pursuant to Art 9. Should such procedure not result in a nomination within the time limit fixed by the parties or the Court, the third arbitrator shall be appointed by the Court.

(1) Introduction

Once a dispute has been referred to arbitration, one of the first tasks is the constitution of the arbitral tribunal, and implicit in that is the question how many arbitrators are required. 'Disputes' include all issues submitted by the parties to the Arbitral Tribunal for a decision. The number of arbitrators and the manner of their appointment is the subject matter of Art 8 of the ICC Rules. **15.386**

The statistics of the ICC Court for the year 2007 show that 20.1 per cent of Arbitral Tribunals were composed of a sole arbitrator and 79.9 per cent of a three-member panel.[289] **15.387**

(2) The number of arbitrators

In ICC arbitration there will, as a rule, be either a sole arbitrator or a panel of three arbitrators, which reflects a general practice in international arbitration as a similar provision is found in many other arbitration rules (see eg *supra* the comparable arbitration rules of international and national arbitration institutions). This may seem somewhat surprising in light of the wording of the ICC standard arbitration clause which refers to 'one *or more* arbitrators'. This apparent contradiction is, however, resolved through Art 7(6), which authorizes the parties to agree upon the number of arbitrators. It is only in the absence of such agreement that, where there is to be more than one arbitrator, there shall be three arbitrators.[290] **15.388**

In the first place, it is the parties that will settle this question. They may already have done so in their arbitral clause, or may do so once the dispute arises, when they respectively submit the Request for Arbitration and the Answer thereto.[291] The ICC model arbitration clause leaves this matter open, so if parties refer to ICC arbitration using this clause, they will need to make the appropriate adjustment to indicate their choice of either a sole arbitrator or three arbitrators. It may, however, be difficult for parties to reach an agreement on such issue once they are the protagonists in a dispute. Also, it happens sometimes that, for purely tactical reasons, one party is not cooperative in this respect (ie, it does not want the other party to go to arbitration). **15.389**

Failing the parties' decision in this matter, it is the ICC Court which decides whether there is to be a sole or three arbitrators. **15.390**

(3) Making the choice: A sole arbitrator or three arbitrators

In the choice between a sole or three arbitrators the parties have complete freedom. The Rules themselves are silent and provide no guidelines. As the Rules contain in any event criteria to ensure the selection of suitable arbitrators, it may seem less important to the **15.391**

[289] See *supra* Introduction, paras 15.22 *et seq*.
[290] See *infra* para 15.401.
[291] See the statistical data given *supra* in the Introduction, paras 15.22 *et seq*.

parties to choose the number of arbitrators. In practice, this choice depends on the nature, complexity and importance of the dispute, and the likely amount in dispute.

15.392 The advantages of speed and economy speak in favour of having one arbitrator. Dealing with one arbitrator's agenda rather than that of three persons may make scheduling much easier; the fees of one arbitrator will be less than that for three arbitrators; less time may be spent on the arbitration as a sole arbitrator will not have to spend time in consultation as do three arbitrators.

15.393 On the other hand, it may be that with a panel of three arbitrators, there is a better chance that the resulting award will be well balanced and thought-out than with one arbitrator. Three arbitrators can often better analyse complex factual and legal situations, and come to grips with difficult procedural issues. That should not really be a concern if the parties have been able to agree upon a sole arbitrator in whom they have confidence; it may, however, be difficult for them to reach common ground in making such a selection. In the event that parties have already provided in their arbitral clause for three arbitrators and find that the dispute when it arises does not warrant this, they might consider modifying their agreement in order to have a sole arbitrator.

15.394 In the event that the parties have not reached agreement on the number of arbitrators, then the matter falls to the ICC Court to determine, and there is in the Rules a presumption that the ICC Court will decide upon a sole arbitrator unless 'the dispute is such as to warrant the appointment of three arbitrators' (Art 8(2)). While many other international arbitration rules also give preference to a sole arbitrator failing the decision of the parties (ie Art 5 AAA, Art 5.4 LCIA, Art 14 WIPO), this is not always the case (ie, Art 16(1) SCC, Art 5 UNCITRAL, Art 10 UNCITRAL Model Law).

15.395 One of the Court's main considerations is the amount in dispute, whether that amount warrants the additional fees and expenses that necessarily follow from having three arbitrators involved. Generally speaking, if the amount in dispute is small it makes sense to have a sole arbitrator. The ICC Court's 'rule of thumb' was for many years an amount of 1 million US dollars as the watershed between small and big cases. Nowadays the ICC Court's practice is more flexible. In 2007, 9.5 per cent of ICC's arbitrations involved claims less than 1 million US dollars.[292] These were generally decided by a sole arbitrator except where the parties had agreed otherwise.

15.396 Where the amount in dispute is over 10 million US dollars, one may generally expect a panel of three arbitrators. Between 1 million US dollars and 10 million US dollars, the choice of one or three arbitrators depends in particular on the complexity of the dispute.

15.397 Other international arbitration rules have express provisions to this effect.[293] However, although the amount in dispute may not justify a three member panel, there may be good

292 See (2008) 19 ICC *ICArb Bull* no 1 13.

293 Such as the Zurich Rules, Art 10, which provides that a dispute should be decided by three arbitrators, unless the parties have elected to have a sole arbitrator, in the event that the amount in dispute is in excess of SFr 1,000,000.

reasons for the ICC Court to favour the appointment of three arbitrators in a particular case, eg when one of the parties is a state or a state-owned corporation.

The fact that a sole arbitrator may not be fully conversant with the applicable law of the dispute or the law of the country of one of the parties does not normally by itself lead the ICC Court to constitute a three-member panel. In one case, where the law of an Asian country was applicable, the Respondent objected to the appointment of a sole arbitrator who was not a member of the Bar of that country since, pursuant to the contract, the law of that country was applicable to the dispute. Since foreign nationals were not admitted to the Bar of that country, and since the sole arbitrator must have a different nationality than that of the parties, it was clear that the sole arbitrator to be appointed by the ICC Court could have no specialist knowledge of the applicable law. The absence of such specialist knowledge is, however, a frequent feature in international commercial arbitration and in the case of experienced arbitrators it cannot be said that this absence is detrimental to the arbitral process, the quality of awards, and justice. The content of foreign law is then a matter of evidence that the parties must plead before the arbitrator. **15.398**

An important reason for having a panel of three arbitrators is that it gives the parties more control over the selection of the persons that will decide their dispute. If the parties cannot decide on the selection of a sole arbitrator then the matter will be dealt with by the institution, whereas, if they have decided upon three arbitrators, then each party will nominate an arbitrator (the party-appointed arbitrators). Having three arbitrators, thus, gives each party the chance to propose an arbitrator who, though independent, has that party's trust. It is often the case that the party-appointed arbitrator will be well placed to highlight the position of the party who nominated him or her, since the arbitrator may have a certain familiarity with that party's legal, economic and cultural background. **15.399**

(4) Procedures for the nomination or appointment of arbitrators and their confirmation

Parties nominate persons they wish to act as arbitrators, either jointly in the case of a sole arbitrator, or individually in the case of the party-appointed arbitrator who becomes part of the three-member panel. The parties' nomination has to be confirmed by the ICC Court or by the Secretary-General of the Court (see Art 9(2)).[294] In the event that the parties do not make a nomination the ICC Court appoints the arbitrator, provided the parties have not foreseen another method for appointment under the Rules. Whereas Art 8 deals solely with the number of arbitrators, Art 9 details the confirmation and appointment of the arbitrators. **15.400**

Priority is given to the agreement of the parties, and it is one of arbitration's main attractions that the parties can have their dispute referred to the arbitrator(s) of their choice, rather than have an arbitrator imposed on them. The ICC Rules provide a ready mechanism to ensure the appointment of the arbitrators where the parties have failed to exercise their choice. **15.401**

[294] See *infra* Art 9, paras 15.439 *et seq.*

15.402 Where the parties have not agreed on the number of arbitrators, the Secretariat will make a recommendation to the ICC Court as to whether to appoint a sole arbitrator or a panel of three arbitrators. The Secretariat transmits the ICC Court's decision to the parties. The ICC Court does not communicate the reasons for its decision and there is no recourse against it. The ICC Court's decisions as to the appointment of an arbitrator are final (Art 7(4)), which seems to include the fixing of the number of arbitrators.

15.403 If a party fails to appoint an arbitrator within the required time limit, the ICC Court may, despite its right to appoint an arbitrator on behalf of the party, tacitly extend the time limit for the party to appoint its own arbitrator as such time limits are of a purely administrative nature.

(5) The sole arbitrator

15.404 In the event that the parties have decided to refer their dispute to a sole arbitrator, then they are to make a joint nomination of the sole arbitrator for confirmation by the ICC Court pursuant to Art 8(3). The ICC Rules provide a fall-back in the event that parties are unable to agree on a joint nomination; the ICC Court appoints the sole arbitrator. The Court will do so if 30 days have elapsed from the Respondent's receipt of the Request for Arbitration, including any extension of time granted by the Secretariat, without the parties having made such a joint nomination. This effectively disposes of the problem of a party that is seeking to obstruct the process by blocking the nomination, and of course of any deadlock situation between the parties. The provision that the Secretariat may extend the 30-day time limit is new, and reflects a practice of the Secretariat to do so.

15.405 As mentioned, the ICC Court will also appoint a sole arbitrator in the event that the parties have not decided upon the number of arbitrators, and the Court does not consider that the case warrants three arbitrators.

15.406 Upon the parties' joint request the Secretariat may provide a list of suitable arbitrators, from which the parties can select one within a given time period. By choosing an arbitrator from a neutral list, the parties will not have to consider the name of a sole arbitrator proposed by one party to the other, which method often raises questions as to the independence or bias of the party-proposed arbitrator.[295]

(6) Three arbitrators

15.407 Article 8(4) provides for the appointment procedure to be followed whenever there are to be three arbitrators, whether upon the parties' joint request or, failing such request, upon the ICC Court's decision in accordance with Art 8(2). Each of the parties is to nominate an arbitrator. When the arbitration clause provides for three arbitrators the Claimant must nominate an arbitrator in the Request for arbitration, and the Respondent must do so in the Answer to the Request for Arbitration (or if an extension has been requested to file the Answer, in the letter to the ICC making such request).[296] The arbitrators are then to be confirmed by the Secretary-General or the ICC Court. Again, if one of the parties fails to

[295] See Seppälä, C., 'Obtaining The Right International Arbitral Tribunal: A Practitioner's View' (2007) 22 *Mealey's Int'l Arb Rev* no 10, 36.

[296] See *supra* Art 5, paras 15.286 *et seq.*

make such nomination, the ICC Court will step in and make the appointment on behalf of the party in default.

It is an accepted part of this process that the Respondent, therefore, will know the choice of arbitrator made by the Claimant, and can make its own choice in light of this knowledge. **15.408**

The situation is more complicated where the arbitration clause is silent as to the number of arbitrators, and where the ICC Court needs first to determine the number. Let us assume that the Claimant wishes to have a three-member panel, that the Respondent disagrees, and that the ICC Court decides in favour of three arbitrators. The Court will then fix a time limit for the Claimant to appoint an arbitrator. A separate time limit will be fixed for the Respondent. It will start to run, however, only once the Claimant has made its nomination. If a Claimant has already nominated an arbitrator in the Request for arbitration, as it is entitled to do, then the ICC Court will fix only a time limit for the Respondent to nominate an arbitrator. **15.409**

Where the Claimant wishes a sole arbitrator, but the Respondent requests a three-member panel, the Respondent may appoint an arbitrator in the Answer to the Request for arbitration (or in the letter seeking an extension), but may also wait until the ICC Court has decided upon the number. In that case, the ICC Court will invite the Claimant to first appoint an arbitrator (again within a time limit of normally 15 days), and it will thereafter be for the Respondent to appoint an arbitrator within an equivalent time limit. Thus, the slight procedural advantage of the Respondent in the appointment process is preserved, since he will make the appointment only once the Claimant's nominee is known to him. **15.410**

The parties may determine a procedure for the nomination of the third arbitrator. Most commonly he is to be nominated by the two party-appointed arbitrators and confirmed by the ICC Court, failing which the ICC Court will itself make the appointment. The ICC Court will do so with regard to any time limit fixed by the parties or by the ICC Court itself. Unless the parties have agreed a different procedure, the Rules provide that the third arbitrator will be appointed by the ICC Court. **15.411**

Arbitrators are often appointed by the parties upon recommendation of the parties' lawyers, eg because they have acted as arbitrators in prior arbitrations or are otherwise known to the lawyers based on their publications or otherwise. Alternatively, the parties may seek the assistance of the ICC National Committee of their country to obtain a list of names of potential arbitrators, without involving the Secretariat or the ICC Court. Parties (or their lawyers) sometimes wish to interview potential arbitrators either in person, by telephone or by videoconference.[297] In principle, nothing is wrong with such interviews. **15.412**

[297] See Aksen, G., 'The Tribunal's Appointment' in L.W. Newman R.D. and Hill (eds), *The Leading Arbitrators' Guide to International Arbitration* (Juris Publishing/Staempfli Publishers, 2004) 31; Lowenfeld A.F., 'The Party appointed Arbitrator' in L.W. Newman L.W. and R.D. Hill (eds), *The Leading Arbitrators' Guide to International Arbitration* (Juris Publishing/Staempfli Publishers, 2004) 41; Bishop D. and Reed L., 'Practical Guidelines for Interviewing, Selecting and Challenging Party-Appointed Arbitrators in International Commercial Arbitration' (1998) *Arb Int'l* vol 14 no 4, 395, 423; 'Selection of Arbitrators in a Nutshell' (2002) 19 *J Int'l Arb* no. 3, 261, 262.

15.413 If the ICC Court decides that the dispute is such as to warrant a three-member panel, then the Secretariat will notify this decision to the parties and the Claimant will have 15 days to nominate an arbitrator. Within 15 days from the notification by the Claimant of its nomination, the Respondent is to make its nomination. The Secretariat will generally extend these time limits, upon request and good cause, for a limited period of time, for example for 8 to 15 days. If a party fails to nominate a co-arbitrator then the ICC Court will appoint the co-arbitrator for the party. Prior to making such appointment, the ICC Court must first consult with the National Committee that it considers appropriate in accordance with Art 8(4). The ICC Court selects the appropriate National Committee particularly with regard to the place of arbitration, nationality of the parties, the language of the arbitration and complexity of the dispute.[298] The Respondent's failure to nominate an arbitrator will therefore not prevent the Arbitral Tribunal from being constituted.[299]

15.414 Article 8(4) also expressly provides that, where there are three arbitrators, the third arbitrator is to act as the chairman of the Arbitral Tribunal. The chairman will be appointed by the ICC Court unless the parties have agreed otherwise.[300] For example, some ICC arbitration clauses expressly authorize the co-arbitrators to select the chairman of the Arbitral Tribunal, and thereby modify the ICC standard arbitration clause. Or the parties will agree at the beginning of the arbitration to defer the selection process first to the co-arbitrators and only if they cannot reach agreement on a chairman will the ICC Court make the choice. While a chairman chosen by co-arbitrators will have their full support and trust, or may even be

---

[298] See Bühler/Webster, ICC Handbook, *op cit*, 140. In one example, the Secretariat stated as follows in its submission to the ICC Court: 'In the light of the nationality of the parties (Czech and Bulgarian), the language of the arbitration (English), the applicable substantive law (Bulgarian law), the Secretariat suggests that the Court invite the Austrian National Committee to propose the Chairman in this matter.' In another example, the Secretariat stated as follows: 'If the two co-arbitrators do not agree on a joint nomination for the Chairman of the Arbitral Tribunal, in light of the nationality of the parties (German and Algerian), of their legal advisors (Germany, France and Switzerland) and of the co-arbitrators (French and Swiss), of the place of arbitration (Geneva, Switzerland) of the language of the arbitration (French), the Secretariat suggests that the Court invite the Spanish National Committee to propose the Chairman of the Arbitral Tribunal.' These examples are only indicative as to how the ICC Court is being put in a position to exercise its discretion.

[299] For an example of the problems that can arise in *ad hoc* arbitration, see Cass civ 1re, *State of Israel v National Iranian Oil Company* (NIOC), 1 February 2005, case no 404. In that *ad hoc* case, the arbitration clause did not indicate the place of arbitration. Nor did it provide a default mechanism for appointment of a co-arbitrator, although it did provide that the chairman would be chosen by the Chairman of the ICC Court. The State of Israel refused to appoint a co-arbitrator and, after an initial refusal, the French courts appointed an arbitrator in its stead on the basis that France was the least inappropriate jurisdiction to do so and that it would be a denial of justice not to do so. For a discussion of the case, see Tattevin, G., 'NIOC v. Israel: "The End" . . . Or Is It?' (2005) *SIAR* 2005:2, 221 and Train, F.-X., 'Denial of Justice in International Arbitration: How the French "Juge d'appui" Extends Its Jurisdiction' (2005) *SIAR* 2005:2, 230; Lazareff, S., 'De l'amour du juge' (2005) *Les Cahiers de l'arbitrage* 2005/1, 3, and Gazette du Palais, Special Arbitrage, 21–2 October 2005, 3.

[300] For the importance of an agreement see also *Encyclopaedia Universalis SA v Encyclopaedia Britannica*, 2005 US App LEXIS 5157 (2d Cir, 2005); Appellationsgericht Kanton Baselstadt, 6 September 1968, (1976) YBCA 200; 64 Schweizerische Juristenzeitung (1967), 378; Corte di Appello di Firenze, 13 April 1978, *Rederi Aktiebolaget Sally v Srl Termarea*, (1979) YBCA 294. More generally, see Jarvin, S., 'Irregularity in the composition of the Arbitral Tribunal and the Procedure', in E. Gaillard and D. Di Pietro (eds), *Enforcement of Arbitration Agreements and International Arbitral Awards: The New York Convention 1958 in Practice* (Cameron May, London, 2008) 729.

known by the co-arbitrators, the appointment of the chairman by the ICC Court involves an element of surprise for both the parties and the arbitrators.[301]

If the parties or the arbitrators have not complied with the appointment procedure agreed in their arbitration agreement and such compliance has not been waived, an award may be set aside or refused enforcement based on the argument that the Arbitral Tribunal was improperly constituted. **15.415**

The chairman must have a nationality different from those of the parties (this is provided under Art 9(5)). However, the parties are free to derogate from this rule. **15.416**

The chairman has the important role also of ensuring the organization and smooth conduct of the proceedings in consultation with the co-arbitrators. In the making of the award, in the event that no majority decision can be reached, the chairman has the power to make the award on his own (see Art 25(1)). **15.417**

(7) More than three arbitrators

It follows from Art 7(6) of the ICC Rules, that an Arbitral Tribunal constituted under the Rules may be composed of more than three arbitrators, eg four or five or more.[302] This situation may occur in a multi-party arbitration dispute, but is in practice very unusual. **15.418**

More than three arbitrators do not only increase the costs of the arbitration but also the risk that the arbitral proceedings may be slower. In addition, not every jurisdiction allows the constitution of an arbitral tribunal of an even number.[303] **15.419**

(8) Two arbitrators

Some ICC arbitration clauses provide for an arbitral tribunal composed of two arbitrators only. Although the ICC Rules do not expressly prohibit such panel, their compatibility with ICC arbitration may be questionable where the parties did not agree to a so-called 'deadlock' provision. It is not unusual to find for instance in insurance and re-insurance contracts influenced by English law, a provision to the effect that there shall be two arbitrators. If the two arbitrators do not arrive at a joint conclusion, the dispute shall be referred to an umpire who decides alone. The umpire is not bound to adopt the position of the one or the other of the two co-arbitrators, but can form his own opinion. The umpire is not appointed at the beginning of the case, unlike the usual practice in ICC arbitrations where all three arbitrators are appointed at the outset. Thus, the umpire has to rehear the case after the two other arbitrators have been unable to find a common opinion. **15.420**

Clauses of this kind are not compatible with the ICC arbitration system for several reasons. Since there are only two arbitrators appointed at the outset there can be no majority opinion. Since the umpire is appointed only when the other two arbitrators have failed to agree, if the two arbitrators cannot agree and an umpire is appointed, the proceedings will be much longer than if all three arbitrators had been appointed from the outset. There is no **15.421**

[301] See Bühler/Webster, ICC Handbook, *op cit*, paras 4–23, 5–29, 8–35.
[302] See *supra* Art 7, para 15.384.
[303] eg Arts 1453–1454 of the French New Code of Civil Procedure, that apply to domestic arbitration, see also Derains/Schwartz, A Guide, *op cit*, 145.

chairman of the Arbitral Tribunal to manage the arbitration. However, in the past, the ICC Court has accepted that two-member panels be constituted under its Rules, since Art 7(6) grants the parties the possibility to derogate from the provisions of Arts 8, 9 and 10, and thus to submit their dispute to an even number of arbitrators.

15.422 The ICC Court is unlikely to accept an even number of arbitrators where the law applicable at the place of arbitration does not provide such possibility. For instance, Art 1026 of the Dutch Arbitration Act states that the Arbitral Tribunal shall be composed of an uneven number of arbitrators, and where they have agreed on an even number of arbitrators, the arbitrators shall appoint an additional arbitrator who shall act as the chairman of the Arbitral Tribunal. In such case, the ICC Court will, on the basis of Art 6(2), set in motion the arbitration only on condition that a three-member panel will be constituted. Otherwise, it would not act in compliance with its obligation to 'make every effort to make sure that the Award is enforceable at law'.

Article 9. Appointment and confirmation of the arbitrators

(1) In confirming or appointing arbitrators, the Court shall consider the prospective arbitrator's nationality, residence and other relationships with the countries of which the parties or the other arbitrators are nationals and the prospective arbitrator's availability and ability to conduct the arbitration in accordance with these Rules. The same shall apply where the Secretary-General confirms arbitrators, pursuant to Article 9(2).

(2) The Secretary-General may confirm as co-arbitrators, sole arbitrators and chairmen of Arbitral Tribunals persons nominated by the parties or pursuant to their particular agreements, provided they have filed a statement of independence without qualification or a qualified statement of independence has not given rise to objections. Such confirmation shall be reported to the Court at its next session. If the Secretary-General considers that a co-arbitrator, sole arbitrator or chairman of an Arbitral Tribunal should not be confirmed, the matter shall be submitted to the Court.

(3) Where the Court is to appoint a sole arbitrator or the chairman of an Arbitral Tribunal, it shall make the appointment upon a proposal of a National Committee of the ICC that it considers to be appropriate. If the Court does not accept the proposal made, or if the National Committee fails to make the proposal requested within the time limit fixed by the Court, the Court may repeat its request or may request a proposal from another National Committee that it considers to be appropriate.

(4) Where the Court considers that the circumstances so demand, it may choose the sole arbitrator or the chairman of the Arbitral Tribunal from a country where there is no National Committee, provided that neither of the parties objects within the time limit fixed by the Court.

(5) The sole arbitrator or the chairman of the Arbitral Tribunal shall be of a nationality other than those of the parties. However, in suitable circumstances and provided that neither of the parties objects within the time limit fixed by the Court, the sole arbitrator or the chairman of the Arbitral Tribunal may be chosen from a country of which any of the parties is a national.

(6) Where the Court is to appoint an arbitrator on behalf of a party which has failed to nominate one, it shall make the appointment upon a proposal of the National Committee of the country of which that party is a national. If the Court does not accept the proposal made, or if the National Committee fails to make the proposal requested within the time limit fixed by the Court, or if the country of which the said party is a national has no National Committee, the Court shall be at liberty to choose any person whom it regards as suitable. The Secretariat shall inform the National Committee, if one exists, of the country of which such person is a national.

(1) Introduction

Article 9 establishes a complex system of constituting the Arbitral Tribunal, where every arbitrator not appointed by the ICC Court needs to be confirmed either by the Court or its Secretary-General. While most arbitration rules provide simply for an appointment mechanism, the ICC Rules foresee that the arbitrators, once nominated by a party or by the co-arbitrators, must be confirmed by the ICC Court, Art 9(1), otherwise an arbitrator may not act under the ICC Rules.[304] Unlike the situation under other institutional rules, the ICC Court will ensure that the arbitrators are qualified and independent. However the ICC Court excludes liability for the Arbitral Tribunal's actions.[305] **15.423**

Another important principle of the ICC appointment mechanism is that default by a party to appoint an arbitrator, or failure of the parties to reach an agreement on the arbitrator to be appointed, will not as such frustrate the arbitral process. The Court will thus always intervene to appoint an arbitrator a sole arbitrator or chairman when the parties or the party-appointed arbitrators have failed to agree on the sole arbitrator or chairman pursuant to Arts 8(3) and 8(4) of the Rules. **15.424**

The control by the ICC Court is aimed at assuming the enforceability of the award (Art 35) since, pursuant to Art V(1)(d) of the New York Convention, a national court can refuse to enforce an award if 'The composition of the arbitral authority or the arbitral procedure was not in accordance with the agreement of the parties, or, failing such agreement, was not in accordance with the law of the country where the arbitration took place'.[306] **15.425**

(2) Article 9(1): Criteria to be taken into consideration by the ICC Court when appointing or confirming an arbitrator

Article 9 sets forth the different criteria that the ICC Court shall take into consideration when confirming or appointing the arbitrators. Those criteria are: **15.426**

- the prospective arbitrator's nationality;
- the prospective arbitrator's residence and other relationships with the countries of which the parties or the other arbitrators are nationals;
- the prospective arbitrator's availability; and
- the prospective arbitrator's ability to conduct the arbitration in accordance with the Rules.

This list is not exhaustive, but describes reasonably well the factors that play a role at the time of constituting an Arbitral Tribunal. Depending on its role, the ICC Court attitude will be different: when intervening as the confirming authority, the Court will be reluctant to interfere with a party's choice and will generally trust the parties' judgment, although it will systematically verify that the appointed arbitrator is independent. Statistically, the vast **15.427**

304 See also the *Cubic* case *supra* Art 1, n 67.

305 See *infra* Art 34.

306 With respect to the parties' agreement as to the selection of the arbitrators, see the *Encyclopaedia Universalis* case and Jarvin, S., 'Irregularity in the composition of the Arbitral Tribunal and the Procedure', *op cit*, mentioned *supra* in Art 8, para 15.413 and n 300.

majority of the arbitrators proposed by the parties are confirmed by the Court.[307] When acting as the appointing authority, the Court will be more cautious as it will be appointing the arbitrator on behalf of the parties when it appoints either a sole arbitrator or the chairman, or on behalf of one party alone when the latter defaults. Although the independence of the arbitrator is not mentioned in Art 9(1), the ICC Court will not appoint or confirm an arbitrator as long as the prospective arbitrator has not submitted a written statement of independence pursuant to Art 7(2).

15.428 When considering the factors listed in Art 9(1), the ICC Court enjoys wide discretion depending on the circumstances of each particular case. In doing so, it will have the efficacy and fairness of the arbitral process in mind, as well as the parties' presumed expectations.

15.429 (2.1) **Nationality, residence and other relationships with the countries of which the parties or other arbitrators are nationals** The rationale of these criteria is to ensure the neutrality of the arbitrator which would be questioned in case the chairman or the sole arbitrator is of the same nationality or has the same place of residence as one of the parties.

15.430 The nationality of the arbitrator is only important when the ICC Court makes the appointment, although Art 9(5) stipulates as a general rule that the sole arbitrator or the chairman of the Arbitral Tribunal shall be of a nationality other than those of the parties. While, as a general rule, this is binding upon the ICC Court,[308] the parties are free in their choice of an arbitrator's nationality. This applies in the first place when they will themselves appoint an arbitrator,[309] but also when they have the opportunity to select, by way of mutual agreement, the sole arbitrator, or the chairman of the Arbitral Tribunal. The ICC Court, when asked to confirm the prospective arbitrator, can no more than acknowledge his nationality. The ICC Court will also have to consider the nationality of a prospective arbitrator when the latter is to be appointed on behalf of a party pursuant to Art 9(6).

15.431 The residence and other relationships are generally qualified as being a complement to the nationality requirement. The idea is that a potential arbitrator might be influenced when he has been a resident in a country for a long time and has fully integrated in the local community. However, in most cases, the place of residence is unlikely to affect the arbitrator's neutrality.

15.432 (2.2) **The arbitrator's availability** All arbitrators should devote the time necessary to enable the arbitration to proceed as fast as possible according to the circumstances. At the time of the appointment it is, however, difficult to assess whether the prospective arbitrator will be available to conduct the arbitration as this depends to a large extent on the wishes and the conduct of the parties, the complexity of the dispute and other factors, which are all uncertain at the time of the appointment. It is generally not possible for an arbitrator to commit himself to be fully available for the conduct of the arbitration since he cannot at that point in time foresee the extent of his commitment and the development of his or her

[307] In 2007, out of a total of 1,039 arbitrators appointed or confirmed by the Court, 729 were confirmed following their nomination. From a total of 279 proposed arbitrators only 26 were refused by the ICC Court, see *supra* Introduction para 15.25.

[308] For the exceptions see Art 9(5) and *infra* para 15.446.

[309] Parties are not constrained to select a national of their own country.

other professional obligations. There are, however, instances where an arbitrator reasonably foresees to be 'overly busy' for a prolonged period of time, which he should then at least disclose. In the past, the ICC Court has generally not attempted to independently assess an arbitrator's availability. It has, however, the power to replace arbitrators who are not fulfilling their duties (Art 12(2)). In addition, while the ICC Court cannot interfere with a party's choice, it is likely to hesitate to reappoint, upon the proposal of a National Committee, a person that in the past has not been sufficiently available in a specific matter.

(2.3) **Ability to conduct the arbitration in accordance with the Rules** The language of Art 9(1) appears to prompt the Court to refuse to appoint a potential arbitrator in cases where his ability to conduct the arbitration is doubtful. The elements the Court may take into consideration to assess the potential arbitrator's ability are the following. **15.433**

Legal qualifications: The Rules do not require an arbitrator to have any legal training or experience but the parties almost always appoint representatives of the legal profession (mostly practising lawyers). The ICC Court ordinarily assumes that the parties expect to have someone with a legal degree to act as sole arbitrator or chairman. The Court will try to ensure that the person appointed has been trained in or is otherwise familiar with the law to be applied in the arbitration (if a choice of applicable law has been made in the agreement) or a similar legal system. It is not as easy as it sounds. In many instances, the applicable law is the law of one of the parties, and the Court is not allowed, unless both parties agree, to appoint a chairman or a sole arbitrator having the same nationality as a party. The Court will thus often seek to appoint a person who has been trained in the law to be applied in the arbitration without being a national of that country. However, in arbitration the contents of the applicable law are considered to be a matter of evidence. There is no requirement under the Rules that the arbitrator must be qualified in the applicable law. A challenge of the arbitrator on the ground that he is not sufficiently qualified is very unlikely to be successful, in particular when the ICC Court has made the initial appointment. Such challenge would in fact question the suitability of the Court's initial choice of the arbitrator, and absent any new elements that were not known to the ICC Court at the time of the appointment, the ICC Court will in all likelihood reject a challenge brought on such basis. **15.434**

Expertise in the commercial or technical field that is the subject of the arbitration: The ICC Court generally endeavours to identify a person knowledgeable in the relevant area and all prospective arbitrators are required to indicate their areas of expertise on a standard form resume that they are asked to complete prior to their appointment. However, since an arbitrator may be assisted by an expert (Art 20 (4)), the lack of sufficient commercial or technical expertise will rarely be a ground for not appointing, let alone for not confirming, an arbitrator. **15.435**

Experience in arbitration matters: This is specially important for the chairman of an Arbitral Tribunal and for the sole arbitrator. The ICC Court thus generally seeks to identify persons with international arbitration experience, although not necessarily acquired under the ICC Rules. **15.436**

Language: The arbitrator must have a sufficient working knowledge of the language in which the arbitration is to take place. The reason for this requirement is to avoid the delays **15.437** and expenses that would result from the use of an interpreter by an arbitrator. If the arbitration proceedings shall be conducted in two languages, the ICC Court does not necessarily require the arbitrator to be fluent in both languages. The ICC Court has been reluctant to establish any rigid practice in this respect, but there is at least one case under the 1975/1988 Rules when the Court refused to confirm an arbitrator, nominated by a party in replacement of an arbitrator who had resigned, because the nominee did not understand the language stated to be the language of arbitration in the Terms of Reference and the other party objected to the nomination.[310]

15.438 The arbitrator's physical resources: The arbitrator's age and physical resources are generally not taken into account by the Court, although in a case where the mobility of the arbitrator is essential, it might be reluctant to appoint or confirm an arbitrator that who is not able to travel.

15.439 The prospective arbitrator must also have the right to act as an arbitrator. In certain countries national judges may not act as arbitrators, or may need a special authorization from their administrative hierarchy.[311]

(3) Article 9(2): Confirmation of the arbitrator(s)

15.440 Article 9(2) confers limited authority to the Secretary-General of the ICC Court to confirm arbitrators nominated by the parties. Such confirmation allows the time for the constitution of the Arbitral Tribunal to accelerate. The Secretariat is not required to await a session of the ICC Court for the confirmation of an arbitrator, but can seek immediately the confirmation by the Secretary-General. It will do so upon receipt of all information required to decide whether the arbitrator should be confirmed.

15.441 The limited authority conferred to the Secretary-General: The Secretary-General is only authorized to confirm the appointment when it does not give rise to any difficulty: (i) when the arbitrator has filed a statement of independence without qualification; or (ii) when a qualified statement of independence has not given rise to any objection on the part of any of the parties. However, Art 9(2) does not take account of the situations where a prospective arbitrator's appointment may be contested for reasons unrelated to the question of the arbitrator's independence. It should be expected that the Secretary-General would not ordinarily confirm an arbitrator who is subject of an objection, but rather refer the matter to the Court (unless the objection is clearly frivolous). Where the Secretary-General considers that an arbitrator should not be confirmed, he must submit the matter to the Court for a decision. The Secretary-General cannot refuse to confirm an arbitrator, only the Court can.

15.442 The confirmation procedure: Before the arbitrators can be confirmed, they must submit to the Secretariat a completed statement of independence form (Art 7(2)) and their *curriculum vitae* on a form provided by the Secretariat.[312]

---

[310] See Derains/Schwartz, A Guide, *op cit*, 159; Bühler/Webster, ICC Handbook, *op cit*, paras 9–18.

[311] Aboukrat, G., 'A propos du statut de l'arbitre et de celui de la magistrature: quelle place pour le droit français?' in *Les Cahiers de l'Arbitrage Volume I* (Gazette du Palais, Paris, 2002) 121. See also Bühler/Webster, ICC Handbook, *op cit*, paras 9–17.

[312] See *supra* Art 7, paras 15.362 *et seq.*

These documents are sent by the Secretariat to the parties. In case of a qualified statement of independence which gives rise to an objection by a party, the Secretariat will automatically refer the matter to the next session of the ICC Court. **15.443**

Consequences of non-confirmation: If the ICC Court refuses to confirm an arbitrator, it normally invites the party who made the nomination to make a new proposal within a fixed period of time (typically 15 to 30 days), although the ICC Court is not obligated to do so. It might also take the position that the party failed to nominate an 'independent' arbitrator and appoint an arbitrator on its behalf, pursuant to Arts 9(3), 9(4) and 9(5). The ICC Court is, however, very reluctant to deprive a party of its right to make a new nomination at this early stage of an arbitration. **15.444**

D. Articles 9(3), 9(4) and 9(5): Appointment of the sole arbitrator or the chairman by the ICC Court

One of the most important roles that the Court fulfils is ensuring that the chairman or sole arbitrator is qualified to preside over the arbitration. The process of appointing the sole arbitrator has been described in Art 8(3). It is based on the parties' agreement, and it is only in case the parties fail to agree that the Court will intervene as the appointing authority. When the dispute is to be referred to three arbitrators, the rule set forth in Art 8(4) is that each party appoints an arbitrator, while the ICC Court will appoint the chairman. **15.445**

This general rule might be modified by the parties who can, in the arbitration agreement, provide that the chairman will be appointed by the party-appointed arbitrators. Again, as the ICC Court encourages proceedings that have been voluntarily adopted by the parties, it will not intervene as appointing authority unless the party-appointed arbitrators have failed to agree. **15.446**

The parties may also agree that the sole arbitrator or the chairman have the same nationality as the parties, subject to the discretionary power of the ICC Court pursuant to Art 9(1) with respect to confirmation of the sole arbitrator or chairman, or they may even agree to waive this requirement indirectly where they have agreed that the co-arbitrators shall nominate the chairman and the co-arbitrators have chosen a chairman having the nationality of one of the parties. **15.447**

Articles 9(3), 9(4) and 9(5), set forth the principles applicable to the appointment by the Court of the sole arbitrator or of the chairman. As under the previous rules, they require the ICC Court to solicit proposals from ICC National Committees, and leave it to the ICC Court to select a National Committee that is appropriate.[313] **15.448**

[313] National Committees are autonomous organizations created by ICC members to serve as an interface between the members and the ICC headquarters in Paris, see *supra* Introduction, n 4, and Art 1, n 64. They play a central role in the appointment of arbitrators by the ICC Court. Due to their autonomous status, they are not all staffed and organized in the same manner for the purpose of proposing arbitrators to the Court. As a general rule, the National Committees have a formal structure in place for the proposal of arbitrators. Some have permanent staff members while others do not. Some, such as the French and US National Committees have established arbitration committees or commissions composed of independent local practitioners who assist the National Committee in performing their tasks. Others (such as Belgium and Germany) have arrangements with local arbitration institutions.

15.449 Choosing the appropriate National Committee: In selecting a National Committee, the Court will consider the following factors.

15.450 Nationality of the parties: Pursuant to Art 9(5), the chairman or the sole arbitrator must ordinarily be of different nationality than the parties, except 'in suitable circumstances', and only if no party objects. As a consequence, in any given case, certain National Committees will be barred by the nationality requirement of Art 9(5).[314] Then, in case of a three-member panel, the ICC Court will often avoid to appoint a chairman of the same nationality as a co-arbitrator, in order to ensure a balance of nationalities within the tribunal. There will be no such restriction where both parties have appointed arbitrators having the same nationality.

15.451 Language, law applicable to the arbitration: See *supra* our comments at para 15.436.

15.452 Place of the arbitration: The ICC Court does not necessarily look for an arbitrator residing in the country of the seat of the arbitration, except for small cases in order to achieve maximum cost efficiency. The ICC Court is, however, more likely to take into consideration the seat of the arbitration when there exists an agreement of the parties on this issue, as there are fewer chances that a party might raise an objection to the appointment of an arbitrator residing in the place that the parties have agreed to be the place of the arbitration. Another advantage of choosing an arbitrator from the National Committee of the country being the seat of the arbitration is that the arbitrator will be aware of particularities of local law and procedures which might affect the arbitration.

15.453 The geopolitical context: The ICC Court takes into account political problems when making its choice of a National Committee. For instance, the ICC Court is unlikely to ask the National Committee of the country that maintains no diplomatic ties with the country of one of the parties. Countries that are viewed as being politically neutral, such as Switzerland, have therefore better chances to be asked for appointments than others.

15.454 Statistically, the most frequently solicited National Committees so far have been Switzerland, France, England, Belgium, Austria and Lebanon.[315]

15.455 The appointment procedure: When appointing a sole arbitrator or a chairman, the Court must make two decisions: (i) choose an appropriate National Committee; (ii) decide whether to appoint the arbitrator proposed by the National Committee. Those decisions are normally made separately. Upon receipt of a proposal from the Secretariat, the Court decides at a first committee meeting which National Committee to select. The Secretariat then requests from the National Committee one or more proposals, which, when received, are submitted to the ICC Court for consideration at a subsequent Court committee meeting. At the end, the process could take several weeks. In order to accelerate the process, Art 9(3) allows the Secretariat to submit to the ICC Court at the same time the two matters

[314] The Court will thus have to determine the nationality of the parties, which is not as easy as it sounds, as the arbitration might be directed toward an individual having two nationalities or toward a group of companies having different nationalities.

[315] For the arbitration to be conducted in the Middle East.

together.[316] The Secretariat is now allowed, if the Court so wishes, to submit both proposals to the Court during the same session.

Once the ICC Court has selected a National Committee, the National Committee is contacted by the Secretariat, but the parties are not informed of the Court decision until an appointment has been made. The Secretariat provides the National Committee with a written description of the dispute, including the identities of the parties, their counsel and co-arbitrators if applicable. The language, applicable law and place of the arbitration are also specified, together with the amount of the dispute and any other special requirement. The National Committee is then requested to make a proposal within a time limit fixed by the Court. Although the time limit is rarely specified by the Court, the Secretariat usually requests a proposal within 15 days. In truly sensitive cases, it happens that the ICC Court urges the Secretariat to find one or more proposals. Depending on the National Committee, the proposal might be preceded by substantial informal consultation with the Secretariat. When the National Committee finally makes its proposal, it provides the Secretariat with a copy of the prospective arbitrator's *curriculum vitae* and a completed statement of independence. **15.456**

Any appointees proposed by a National Committee have to file an unqualified statement of independence. The reasoning is that parties are not informed of the name or the arbitrator's possible qualifications prior to his appointment. As a result, where a party sees an arbitrator's qualified statement of independence, the qualifications could give rise to challenges under Art 11. Besides, there would rarely be a good reason for the ICC Court to appoint an arbitrator who cannot provide an unqualified statement, as there are normally many equally qualified candidates available who are free of any conflicts, whether actual or potential.[317] **15.457**

Upon receipt of the proposal, the Court has the discretion to either appoint the arbitrator proposed by the National Committee or refuse the proposal, and then either request the National Committee to make a new proposal or request a proposal from another National Committee. In addition, Art 9(4) makes it clear that the ICC Court can choose a sole arbitrator from a country where there is no National Committee, provided no party objects within the time limit fixed by the ICC Court. In practice it is rare that the ICC Court appoints a chairman or a sole arbitrator from a country where there is no National Committee.[318] **15.458**

(5) Article 9(6): Appointment of an arbitrator on behalf of a defaulting party

An important principle of ICC arbitration is that a party's default, at any stage of the proceedings, shall not frustrate the arbitral process. Generally, a party that is not willing to cooperate in the arbitral process (for example by objecting to jurisdiction), will also refuse to appoint an arbitrator. In such a case, and pursuant to Art 8(4) of the Rules, the arbitrator **15.459**

[316] Art 9(3) now provides that the Court's appointment shall be made 'upon proposal' of a National Committee rather than, as under the former Rules, 'after having requested' such proposal.

[317] See Bühler/Webster, ICC Handbook, *op cit*, paras 9–22.

[318] According to Derains/Schwarz, A Guide, *op cit*, 159, only 16 out of 400 appointments made in 1995–1996 were made under this provision.

will be appointed by the ICC Court in order to ensure equal treatment of the parties.[319] Article 9(6) describes the applicable procedure.

15.460 Article 9(6) requires the ICC Court to seek a proposal from a party's National Committee. If the party is from a country that does not have a National Committee, the Court may appoint 'any person whom it regards as suitable'. Then, in soliciting proposals from National Committees, the procedure is almost identical to the one set forth in Art 9(3) except that a decision of the Court is not requested in order to choose the National Committee as the choice is mandated by the rule itself. If there is no National Committee in the country where the defaulting party is a national, the Court will seek a suitable arbitrator who is a national of that country. If it is unable to do so, it may appoint an arbitrator from another country, but will be required to inform the National Committee of that country if it exists.

Article 10. Multiple parties

(1) Where there are multiple parties, whether as Claimant or as Respondent, and where the dispute is to be referred to three arbitrators, the multiple Claimants, jointly, and the multiple Respondents, jointly, shall nominate an arbitrator for confirmation pursuant to Article 9.

(2) In the absence of such a joint nomination and where all parties are unable to agree on a method for the constitution of the Arbitral Tribunal, the Court may appoint each member of the Arbitral Tribunal and shall designate one of them to act as chairman. In such a case, the Court shall be at liberty to choose any person it regards as suitable to act as arbitrator, applying Article 9 when it considers this appropriate.

(1) Introduction

15.461 While Art 10 is headed 'Multiple Parties', its scope is limited to the question of how arbitrators are appointed in a case where (i) there are two or more Claimants or two or more Respondents, or both (that is, 'multiple parties'); and (ii) the dispute is to be referred to three arbitrators. Although this Article does not expressly refer to the situation of multiplicity of parties on both the Claimant's and the Respondent's side, it should, as a matter of common sense, be interpreted as though the words 'or both' were incorporated.

15.462 Approximately one third of the arbitrations administered each year by the ICC Court involve two or more Claimants or two or more Respondents.[320] For example, joint ventures or consortia of contractors for international projects are often constituted among two or more parties. If the members of a joint venture or a consortium become involved as Claimants or Respondents in an international arbitration with a third party or parties, this will give rise to a multi-party arbitration. Similarly, several companies within the same corporate group of companies may jointly enter into a contract with a third party, or they

[319] It is however rare that the ICC Court makes default appointments. In 2007 the ICC Court made 31 direct appointments (ie without nominations of arbitrators by parties) out of 310 appointments, see (2008) 19 *ICC Court Bull*, no 1, 9.

[320] 31% of the new cases in 2007 involved more than two parties, see (2008) 19 *ICC ICArb Bull* no 1, 8. Of the 186 cases concerned, 161 involved between 2 and 5 parties, 21 between 6 and 10 parties, and 4 more than 10 parties. Multi-respondents cases were more frequent than multi-claimant cases or cases involving both several claimants and respondents.

may all be party to a shareholders' agreement. If they have a dispute with such third party or parties, this too will give rise to a multi-party arbitration.

Another multi-party situation which is not unusual is where a dispute arises between the owner and the main contractor in a construction project and where the main contractor wants to involve one or more of the subcontractors that performed the part of the construction work in dispute. **15.463**

Typical multi-party situations also arise in disputes between insurers, ie when an insurance company, respondent in the arbitration, wishes to involve a reinsurance company that will ultimately have to bear the losses.[321] **15.464**

The number of arbitrators in an ICC arbitration is usually one or three.[322] Where the dispute is to be settled by a sole arbitrator, all the parties will either have to agree on a single nominee or the arbitrator will be appointed by the ICC Court, Arts 8(1), 8(2), and 8(3). Thus, where there is to be a sole arbitrator, the multi-party nature of the arbitration should not give rise to any additional difficulty in constituting the Arbitral Tribunal, and Art 10 has no bearing on such situation. However, where a dispute is to be settled by three arbitrators, each of the Claimant and the Respondent must nominate an arbitrator, which may give rise to the difficulty where there are two or more Claimants or Respondents and they are unable to agree on a joint nominee. For example, if there is a single Claimant who nominates an arbitrator but there are two Respondents who cannot agree on a joint nominee, making it necessary for an arbitrator to be appointed on the Respondents' behalf by a third party such as the ICC Court, an issue may arise as to whether each Respondent has, in the appointment of arbitrators, been treated equally with the Claimant. Arguably, each Respondent has not been treated equally since the Claimant has been able to nominate an arbitrator of his choice whereas each Respondent has not been afforded this right. This is the issue which Art 10 is designed to address. **15.465**

(2) The Dutco *case*

Two or more Claimants, having decided to bring an arbitration jointly, are usually able to agree on a jointly-nominated arbitrator but sometimes two or more Respondents are unable to agree, especially if they are unrelated or have different interests in the outcome of the dispute. The ICC Court's previous practice in such cases was to require the two or more Respondents to agree on a joint nomination, failing which the ICC Court would appoint an arbitrator on their behalf. The ICC Court observed this practice until the decision of the French Supreme Court in *Siemens AG and B.K.M.I. Industrieanlagen GmbH v Dutco Construction Co Ltd* in 1992.[323] In that case, three companies were parties to a consortium agreement regarding the construction of a cement plant, each party having assumed a specific scope of the works for the plant. The agreement contained an arbitration clause providing for the final settlement of all disputes among the members by three arbitrators **15.466**

---

[321] With respect to typical multi-party situations (ie, several companies in the same group, multiple signatories, additional parties, class actions, etc). See also Bühler/Webster, ICC Handbook, paras 10–7 *et seq* and 10–33.

[322] Art 8(1) and *supra* Art 8, paras 15.387 *et seq.*

[323] French *Cour de Cassation*, 7 January 1992, (1992) *Rev arb* 520; *YBCA* (1993) XVIII, 140.

appointed in accordance with the ICC Rules. One party commenced an ICC Arbitration against the other two parties and nominated an arbitrator. However, the other two parties claimed that they had different interests in the arbitration, that they could not agree on a jointly-nominated arbitrator and, when the ICC Court appointed one on their behalf, objected to the appointment. The Arbitral Tribunal nevertheless considered that it had been validly constituted, but the two Respondents challenged the award before the Paris Court of Appeal. The Respondents argued, among other things, that they had not agreed to a multi-party arbitration (as distinct from two separate proceedings, one against each Respondent) and that, contrary to the principle that parties should be treated equally, each Respondent had been deprived of the right to appoint his own arbitrator. The Paris Court of Appeal rejected their arguments, stating that inasmuch as the arbitral clause provided for the submission of all disputes among the three parties to arbitration by three arbitrators, it was necessarily implicit from the clause that, in the event of a dispute, two parties would have to agree jointly on the nomination of an arbitrator, whereas one party would nominate an arbitrator. Thus, according to the Court of Appeal, the parties' intention had been respected.

15.467 The French Supreme Court disagreed and quashed the decision, holding that the principle that the parties should be treated equally in the appointment of arbitrators is a matter of public policy and that the parties cannot waive this right until after the dispute has arisen. This meant that a party could not validly waive this right in an arbitration clause signed before a dispute arose.

15.468 The principle that parties should be treated equally in the appointment of arbitrators, which the French Supreme Court referred to, does not necessarily mean that each party should have the right to nominate an arbitrator. Each party does not have that right. Rather, it means that each party should have equal rights in the process of constituting the Arbitral Tribunal.

15.469 The effect of the *Dutco* decision was to call into question not only ongoing multi-party arbitrations in France, where numerous ICC arbitration proceedings take place, but also the enforcement of foreign arbitral awards in France. Moreover, while the Swiss courts appeared to have come to the opposite conclusion on the same issue in the case of an ICC Arbitration taking place in Switzerland,[324] there was a risk that other jurisdictions might align themselves with the position taken by the French Supreme Court in *Dutco*. For these reasons, it was decided to include in the 1998 ICC Rules a new Art 10 to deal with the appointment of arbitrators in multi-party cases.

15.470 Article 10 ensures that, where there are multiple Claimants or Respondents, they can be treated equally in the appointment of arbitrators (unless they waive this right after a dispute arises) since it provides that in such cases:

- the multiple Claimants or the multiple Respondents must jointly nominate an arbitrator; or

[324] *Cour de Justice*, Geneva, 26 November 1982, *Arab Republic of Egypt v Westland Helicopters Ltd* (1989) *Rev arb* 514; *La Semaine Judiciaire*, (1984), Geneva, 509, affirmed by the *Tribunal Fédéral Suisse*, 15 May 1983.

- after the dispute arises and failing such joint nomination, either all parties must agree on 'the method for the constitution of the Arbitral Tribunal' or each member of the Arbitral Tribunal may be appointed by the ICC Court.

Consequently, where an Arbitral Tribunal has been constituted in compliance with Art 10, the validity of its constitution should not be subject to attack on the grounds of *Dutco*. **15.471**

(3) Article 10(1): Multi-party Claimants or Respondents

Article 10(1) deals with the situation where the Claimant or the Respondent consists of two or more parties[325] and where the dispute is to be referred to three arbitrators either because that is what the parties have agreed (eg in the arbitration clause) or, in the absence of such agreement, because the ICC Court has appointed three arbitrators pursuant to Art 8(2). **15.472**

In any such situation, Art 10(1) provides that in accordance with Art 9 the multiple Claimants must jointly nominate an arbitrator and the multiple Respondents must do the same. This means that multiple Claimants should, jointly, make such nomination in the Request for Arbitration, pursuant to Arts 4(1)(e) and 8(4), and multiple Respondents should, jointly, make such nomination in the Answer, pursuant to Arts 5(1)(d) and 8(4). **15.473**

Where the parties have not agreed upon the number of arbitrators but the Court has decided upon three arbitrators, pursuant to Art 8(2), then the multiple claimants must jointly nominate an arbitrator within 15 days from the notification of the Court's decision fixing the number of arbitrators at three and multiple Respondents must jointly nominate an arbitrator within 15 days from receipt of the notification of the Claimant's nomination. **15.474**

As a practical matter, 15 days is a rather short limit for unrelated multiple parties in an international case to select potential arbitrators, ascertain their ability, availability and willingness to act, and to agree upon a suitable candidate. This will be the case in particular where the multiple Respondents are represented by different counsel. Accordingly, they would be well advised to start this process in advance of the 15 days provided for in the Rules. **15.475**

Joint nominations by multiple Claimants or multiple Respondents are, like the nomination of a sole arbitrator, subject to confirmation by the ICC Court pursuant to Art 9.[326] **15.476**

Pursuant to Art 8(4), the chairman of the Arbitral Tribunal will be appointed by the Court, unless the parties have agreed upon another procedure. Pursuant to Art 9(5), the chairman could not ordinarily be of a nationality of any of the multiple Claimants or Respondents, as each is a party to the arbitration. Pursuant to Art 9(1) and in accordance with the practice of the ICC Court, the chairman would also not ordinarily be of the same nationality as either of the arbitrators appointed on behalf of either of the parties. **15.477**

[325] See Art 2 (ii).

[326] See *supra* Art 9, paras 15.439 *et seq.*

15.478 Illustration: Where an arbitration agreement among A, B and C provides for three arbitrators and A and B bring an arbitration against C (or C brings an arbitration against A and B), then A and B must jointly nominate an arbitrator in the Request for Arbitration and C must nominate an arbitrator in the Answer (or C must nominate an arbitrator in the Request for Arbitration and A and B must jointly nominate one in the Answer). The chairman of the Arbitral Tribunal would normally be appointed by the ICC Court from candidates having the nationality of none of the Claimants or Respondents or of the party-nominated arbitrators.

(4) Article 10(2): Appointment by the ICC Court

15.479 Article 10(2) then provides for what is to happen 'in the absence of such a joint nomination and where all parties are unable to agree to a method for the constitution of the Arbitral Tribunal'. Unfortunately, this language could give rise to some differences of interpretation. The reference to 'such a joint nomination' clearly refers to a joint nomination by multiple Claimants or multiple Respondents but does it cover the situation where there are both multiple Claimants and multiple Respondents? The use of 'joint nomination' in the singular suggests that it does not, whereas logic and common sense suggest that it should. This is also suggested by the language in Art 10(1) providing that 'the multiple Claimants, jointly, and the multiple Respondents, jointly, shall nominate . . .'. While not free from doubt, the better interpretation seems to be that it was intended to cover the situation where there are both multiple Claimants and multiple Respondents.

15.480 A possibly more difficult issue is what is meant by 'a method for the constitution of the Arbitral Tribunal'. Supposing the parties agree on a method for the constitution of the Arbitral Tribunal but are, nevertheless, unable to constitute a tribunal using that method? For example, supposing all parties agree that to constitute the Arbitral Tribunal the parties will select three names from a list furnished by the ICC Court, the ICC Court furnishes such a list but then the parties find that they are unable to agree on the three names selected. The parties will have agreed on 'a method' for the constitution of the Arbitral Tribunal but will, nevertheless, have been unable to constitute one. Will the ICC Court be entitled to act under Art 10(2) and appoint each member of the Arbitral Tribunal?

15.481 It should be entitled to do so because Art 10 was designed to overcome the problem raised by the decision of the French Supreme Court in the *Dutco* case,[327] and it is necessary to interpret Art 10(2) to achieve this purpose. Accordingly, the words 'a method for the constitution of the Arbitral Tribunal' need to be read as meaning 'a method for the constitution of the Arbitral Tribunal which allows the constitution of the entire Arbitral Tribunal to be achieved'.

15.482 In summary, Art 10(2) refers to the following four situations:

- where there are multiple Claimants, and they have not jointly nominated an arbitrator either in the Request for Arbitration or within 15 days from the notification of the ICC Court's decision fixing the number of arbitrators as three, pursuant to Art 8(2); or

[327] See *supra* para 15.465.

- where there are multiple Respondents, and they have not jointly nominated an arbitrator either in the Answer or within 15 days from the notification of the Claimant's (or Claimants) nomination, pursuant to Art 8(2); or
- both (a) and (b) above have occurred; or
- the parties have been unable to agree upon a procedure which will enable the entire Arbitral Tribunal to be constituted.

In any of these four situations, the ICC Court 'may' appoint each member of the Arbitral Tribunal and designate one of them as the chairman of the Tribunal even if the Claimant in the case has already nominated its arbitrator. When will the ICC Court do so? In light of the *Dutco* decision, the ICC Court will certainly do so in the case of any arbitration taking place in France or where the award might have to be enforced in France. The ICC Court will also do so in other cases where it believes there is a risk that the courts of any relevant jurisdiction may adopt a similar position to that adopted by the French Supreme Court in *Dutco*. Article 10(2) provides the Court with the flexibility to do whatever is appropriate in light of the facts in each case. Interestingly, since the coming into force of the 1998 Rules, the ICC Court has had to apply Art 10 only in very few cases.[328] **15.483**

Article 10(2) provides that in appointing each member of the Arbitral Tribunal, the Court must apply Art 9 (which sets out general rules with respect to the appointment and confirmation of arbitrators) when it considers it appropriate. Pursuant to Art 9(6), where the multiple Claimants or the multiple Respondents are of the same nationality, then the Court must ordinarily make the appointment upon a proposal of the National Committee of the country of which the Claimants or Respondents, respectively, are nationals. On the other hand, where the multiple Claimants or multiple Respondents are of different nationalities, the Rules do not expressly state how the Court shall make the appointment. The Court will normally not make the appointment upon a proposal of a National Committee of a country of which any of the Claimants or Respondents, respectively, is a national. **15.484**

When the Court designates an arbitrator to act as chairman, it will do so in the same manner as described above in relation to Art 10(1), where the Court appoints the chairman. **15.485**

Illustration: Where an arbitration agreement among A, B and C provides for three arbitrators and A brings an arbitration against B and C (or B and C bring an arbitration against A), and B and C cannot agree on a joint nomination for arbitrator, the ICC Court may refuse to appoint A's nominated arbitrator, and appoint a different arbitrator for A and appoint, jointly, an arbitrator for B and C, as well as appoint the chairman of the Arbitral Tribunal. **15.486**

If there is a sole Respondent who seeks to add another party for purposes of a counterclaim, then there will be a 'cross-respondent' to be added to the proceedings. Until recently it was considered difficult if not impossible for a Respondent to add parties without the agreement of the Claimant. If the ICC Court accepts that a Respondent add parties, the issue arises as to the joint nomination of arbitrators or the application of Art 10(2) to appoint the entire Arbitral Tribunal. **15.487**

[328] It did so for the first time in October 1999.

Article 11. Challenge of arbitrators

(1) A challenge of an arbitrator, whether for an alleged lack of independence or otherwise, shall be made by the submission to the Secretariat of a written statement specifying the facts and circumstances on which the challenge is based.

(2) For a challenge to be admissible, it must be sent by a party either within 30 days from receipt by that party of the notification of the appointment or confirmation of the arbitrator, or within 30 days from the date when the party making the challenge was informed of the facts of and circumstances on which the challenge is based if such date is subsequent to the receipt of such notification.

(3) The Court shall decide on the admissibility, and, at the same time, if necessary, on the merits of a challenge after the Secretariat has afforded an opportunity for the arbitrator concerned, the other party or parties and any other members of the Arbitral Tribunal to comment in writing within a suitable period of time. Such comments shall be communicated to the parties and to the arbitrators.

(1) Introduction

15.488 The challenge of arbitrators is an important mechanism for ensuring the integrity of the arbitral process, which depends on the quality and independence of the persons to whom the parties have referred their dispute. The ICC Rules, like other arbitration rules, therefore allow for the possibility of a party to challenge an arbitrator and, if such challenge is successful, for the removal and replacement of the arbitrator under Art 12(2).

15.489 A challenge will inevitably mean some delay and disruption to the conduct of the arbitration while the challenge is considered, especially if this occurs late in the proceedings, although such consideration is clearly outweighed in the event of a successful challenge and the importance of ensuring that the parties' confidence in the process is maintained.[329]

15.490 The challenge procedure is, however, open to some abuse, ie where a challenge is raised by a party in order to avoid or at least delay the commencement of the arbitral process or, later on, to delay or disrupt the arbitration, or to intimidate the challenged arbitrator about future decisions.[330] Depending on the circumstances, challenges raised late in the proceedings are bound to be judged differently than a challenge at the outset of the arbitration because of the greater disruption this causes, ie where a challenge is made after the exchanges of all briefs, the examination of witnesses or after the close of the hearing. This will very much depend on the ground invoked for the challenge. Some grounds (ie the lack of disclosure of an element, which the arbitrator knew was most relevant for the parties) but which he failed to disclose at the time of his or her appointment, may remain relevant whatever the stage of the proceedings are.[331]

15.491 Besides, the challenge of an arbitrator has to be examined not only during the conduct of the proceedings themselves subject to Art 11, but also during the annulment proceedings pursuant to the law of the place of arbitration and enforcement proceedings in jurisdictions

[329] Derains/Schwartz, A Guide, *op cit*, 185; Redfern/Hunter, *op cit*, 207 *et seq*.

[330] Böckstiegel, K.-H., 'Practices of Various Arbitral Tribunals' in 'Preventing Delay and Disruption of Arbitration: I Conduct by a Party to Disrupt Establishing the Tribunal and Starting the Arbitral Proceedings. Topic 3: Use by a party of challenges to delay or disrupt the arbitration' (1991) *ICCA Congress Series no 5*, 131, 132.

[331] See *supra* Art 7(2), paras 15.362 *et seq*.

in which the successful party seeks to enforce the award.[332] The national case law, particularly at the place of arbitration and at the place of probable enforcement, may serve as a reference for challenges. Under French law for example, the failure to raise a challenge in a timely manner constitutes a waiver.[333]

In any event, the requirements defined in Art 11, ie the submission of a written statement within a fixed time limit by the party intending to challenge an arbitrator, and the ultimate control by the ICC Court, may avoid such delay and disruption in the event that a challenge is raised by a party purely to serve its own agenda. Also, the attention given at the outset of the appointment process to the arbitrator's statement of independence, and the continued duty on the arbitrator in this regard throughout the arbitration is intended and in practice does remove areas of potential challenges. To avoid the parties raising frivolous challenges, there is also a strict time frame within which challenges are to be made in order to be admissible (Art 11(2), and there is a requirement for reasons to be given by a party for any challenge (Art 11(1)). **15.492**

Although in the past it was observed that challenges appeared to be increasing,[334] statistically there are relatively few challenges compared with the number of arbitrators serving on tribunals, and only a minor number of challenges were upheld by the ICC Court in the past.[335] **15.493**

(2) Article 11(1): Bringing a challenge against an arbitrator

The grounds for a party to solicit a challenge under Art 11(1) may be 'for an alleged lack of independence or otherwise', while the grounds for the challenge must have arisen either since the appointment or the confirmation of the arbitrator (Art 11(2)). Independence of the arbitrator is a cornerstone of ICC arbitration, and it thus follows that where a party considers that this standard has not been met this should be a reason for a challenge. The notion of independence is dealt with under Art 7.[336] **15.494**

Article 11(1) is drafted broadly, since the words 'or otherwise' indicate that a challenge may be made on grounds other than an alleged lack of independence. What is meant by 'otherwise' is not defined by the Rules.[337] Thus, the Court has wide discretion to consider any **15.495**

---

[332] For further details see Bühler/Webster, ICC Handbook, paras 11–3, 11–7 *et seq*; see also Clay, Th., *L'arbitre* (Dallorz, Paris, 2001) 231; Bagner, H., 'Arbitrator Impartiality: Appearance is Everything' (2006) 21 *Mealey's Int'l Arb Rev* no 6, 26.

[333] See *BVD Laboratoires et al v BLC Talgo Cosmetic*, Paris, 25 September 2003, *Les Cahiers de l'Arbitrage Volume II, op cit*, 327; *Voith Turbo GmbH v Société Nationale des Chemins de Fer Tunisiens*, Paris, 28 November 2002, *Les Cahiers de l'Arbitrage Volume II, op cit*, 324 (failure to object to arbitrator participating in prior proceedings not raised in timely fashion).

[334] See Càrdenas, E. and Rivkin, D.W., *op cit*, 191.

[335] Hascher, D., 'ICC Practice in Relation to the Appointment, Confirmation, Challenge and Replacement of Arbitrators' (1995) 6 ICC *ICArb Bull* no 2, 4, 11. Out of 1,285 cases pending at year-end 2007, 22 challenges were made pursuant to Art 11, of which 21 were accepted by the Court. The Court's refusal to confirm an arbitrator is often due to an arbitrator's disclosure statement regarding his independence, but is not tantamount to a challenge (2008) 19 ICC *ICArb Bull*, no 1, 9; see *supra* Art 9, para 15.440.

[336] Other arbitration rules allow for challenges in respect of independence or impartiality, such as Art 8(1), AAA; Art 10.3, LCIA; Art 11(1) Vienna; Art 24(a), WIPO; Art 10, UNCITRAL.

[337] The words 'or otherwise' were introduced for the first time in the 1988 Rules; see Derains/Schwartz, A Guide, *op cit*, 187, n 171.

circumstances that a party may bring before it. In this respect, it is worth recalling certain obligations that the arbitrators have under the Rules, such as the duty to act impartially and fairly and ensure that each party has a reasonable opportunity to present its case (Art 15(2)), to proceed within as short a time as possible to establish the facts of the case by all appropriate means (Art 20(1)), and the general mandate under Art 35 to act in the spirit of the Rules and make every effort to ensure that the award is enforceable at law. However, where a party is dissatisfied by the way the Arbitral Tribunal conducts the proceedings, eg because several of that party's procedural requests were rejected, this alone will rarely allow a challenge to be successful. A significant number of challenges brought against ICC arbitrators are in fact a criticism of the way the arbitration is conducted, from which it is then implied by a party that the arbitrator is or appears to be biased. A party's allegation that the arbitrator's conduct of the arbitration constitutes a denial of its right to a fair trial can be interpreted as a challenge for (alleged) lack of impartiality.

15.496 A challenge might be made if an arbitrator has failed to disclose any facts or circumstances likely to give rise to doubts with respect to the arbitrator's independence, or for alleged partiality or bias in the eyes of the parties. A challenge may also be made in case the arbitrator fails to carry out his functions competently and properly, eg if the arbitrator is not conducting the arbitration diligently, or is giving insufficient time and attention to the arbitration, giving rise to an inordinate delay in the conduct of the arbitration, or where the party questions the fair conduct of the arbitration.[338]

15.497 Unless there is manifest misconduct, a challenge based on alleged partiality or failure to fulfil the duties properly may have less chances of success. From the arbitrator's point of view, in order to avoid that a party raises a frivolous challenge in the course of the arbitration, the arbitrator should ensure that the parties are in agreement with the conduct of the arbitration. Experienced arbitrators usually include in the Terms of Reference a statement to the effect that the parties agree that there are no circumstances known to them at the time they sign the Terms of Reference that would give rise to a challenge of the arbitrators. They will do so likewise at the end of hearings, and, where, for instance, (summary) minutes are prepared by the Arbitral Tribunal, it may also include a statement to this effect, and have the minutes signed by both parties.

15.498 A party is unlikely to raise a challenge against its party-appointed arbitrator,[339] and most challenges are with respect to the chairman or sole arbitrator, or the chairman together with the arbitrator appointed by the other party, ie the 'majority' of the Arbitral Tribunal. On a few occasions, a party has directed the challenge against the entire Arbitral Tribunal.

15.499 The party making a challenge against an arbitrator is required to submit a written statement to the ICC Secretariat, which sets out the facts and circumstances on which the challenge is based. Such written statement, pursuant to Art 3(1), is to be sent at the same time to the other party and to the arbitrators and shall provide in as full detail as possible the reasons for the challenge together with any supporting documents. The ICC Court will

[338] Craig/Park/Paulsson, *op cit*, 223 *et seq*.; Derains/Schwartz, A Guide, *op cit*, 187–8; Hascher, D., *op cit*, 13 *et seq*.

[339] Although this has happened in the practice of the ICC Court.

decide on the basis of that written submission, ie there will be no oral argument, and the Rules do not foresee any other subsequent written submission.[340] In practice, however, as long as the ICC Court has not taken its decision, the challenging party may supplement its submission.

In conflicts of interest matters, the IBA Guidelines may be a reference point for the ICC Court notwithstanding that the factual situations are almost invariably more complex than those set out in the IBA Guidelines.[341] **15.500**

(3) Article 11(2): Admissibility of the challenge

In order for a challenge of an arbitrator to be admissible, the party must submit its statement within a 30-day time limit. The time limit seeks to reduce the number of challenges that are made to delay the arbitration, for instance where a party makes a challenge on the basis of facts and circumstances that it already knew about, because it is not pleased with the way a procedural matter has been decided or fears an unfavourable outcome of the arbitration.[342] **15.501**

As regards an arbitrator appointed or confirmed by the ICC Court, a party wishing to raise a challenge, must do so within 30 days from the date that it received notification of the arbitrator's appointment or confirmation in respect of matters raised in the arbitrator's statement of independence or indicated in his *curriculum vitae*.[343] The time period prior to the notification of the appointment or confirmation, during which the party has been able to review the arbitrator's curriculum vitae and statement of independence, is not included in the 30-day time limit. This means that a party may have more than 30 days to make a challenge. In practice the dates on which the time limit starts and expires will be easy to establish, and thus are rarely controversial, and where they are it seems that the Court takes an *in dubio pro re* approach. It is indeed always preferable to be able to look at the merits of a challenge rather than to dismiss it simply because it was out of time. There are, of course, clear-cut cases where a party has simply failed to take action for too long a time, and where this can easily be verified. In such cases the cut-off of the 30-day time limit fully serves its purpose. **15.502**

The IBA Guidelines provide in General Standard 7 that the parties have a duty to carry out the appropriate steps to check on conflicts especially as to publicly available information.[344] In a recent case, a French court deemed that the fact that an arbitrator was a member of an **15.503**

[340] As noted *supra* in Art 1, para 15.10, parties or their counsel never appear before the ICC Court to hear oral argument (see Art 1(2), Art 21, and App I). The communication of the parties and of arbitrators with the ICC Court is exclusively in writing, via the Court's Secretariat. The latter serves an important filter-function, ie, the Secretariat will only submit such correspondence to the ICC Court that it considers relevant.

[341] See also *supra* Art 7, para 15.361.

[342] Derains/Schwartz, A Guide, *op cit*, 188 *et seq*.

[343] See *supra* Art 7, para 15.362.

[344] General Standard 7 states: '(a) A party shall inform an arbitrator, the Arbitral Tribunal, the other parties and the arbitration institution or other appointing authority (if any) about any direct or indirect relationship between it (or another company of the same group of companies) and the arbitrator. The party shall do so on its own initiative before the beginning of the proceeding or as soon as it becomes aware of such relationship. (b) In order to comply with General Standard 7(a), a party shall provide any information already available to it and shall perform a reasonable search of publicly available information.'

association of lawyers was sufficient notice of that relationship, as was information that was available on the internet.[345]

15.504 The 30-day time limit applies likewise to circumstances that arise in the course of an arbitration and cause a party to bring a challenge against an arbitrator. In that case, the 30-day time limit will start to run from the time when the party becomes aware of the facts and circumstances in question. In practice, in particular when the challenge is based on procedural events, the 'circumstances' of a challenge may form a series of events that form a 'single transaction'. In such case, the ICC Court may have to look at the 'end' rather than the start date of such events.

15.505 A party will rarely bring a challenge lightly and where certain procedural events occur that may, in its view, give rise to a challenge, it may be proper for that party to await the end of these events, before lodging the challenge. The criticized events may have given rise to an exchange of correspondence between the parties and the Arbitral Tribunal. As long as that exchange is not completed, a party should not be obliged to bring a challenge simply out of fear that it may otherwise miss the 30-day time limit. Thus, in case of doubt as to when the 30-day time limit starts to run, it seems appropriate for the ICC Court to take a rather liberal view.

(4) Article 11(3): The ICC Court's decision on the challenge

15.506 Pursuant to Art 11(3), the first matter for the ICC Court to consider is the timeliness, and thus the admissibility of the challenge. It is not necessarily a straightforward task to verify the date upon which a party claims to have discovered the facts or circumstances on which it bases its challenge, and in such case it seems that the practice of the ICC Court is to admit the challenge.

15.507 If the ICC Court finds the challenge admissible, it will decide on the merits of such challenge. Article 11(3) provides that the Secretariat shall give the opportunity for the arbitrator concerned, the other party or parties, and any other member of the Arbitral Tribunal to comment on the challenge. A suitable time period will be fixed by the Secretariat, usually 15 days, or less if the Secretariat considers that under the circumstances a shorter time limit is required and appropriate. The Secretariat grants persons only the opportunity for comments; the addressees have no obligation to comment and the ICC Court will proceed even if no comments are received. Usually though, the ICC Court will receive the comments of the challenged arbitrator, the other party or parties not making the challenge, and, if there is a three-member panel, the other members of the Arbitral Tribunal as well. The attitude of the latter will very much depend on the nature of the challenge. If it concerns a purported lack of disclosure, they may refrain from any comments. If it concerns the proceedings and thus events they have personally evidenced, they may feel the need to comment.

15.508 Comments are to be provided in writing. This allows the ICC Court to verify whether and to what extent the allegations made by the challenging party can be corroborated. It does not serve any useful purpose for the other party or the arbitrators to express their view on

[345] See the *Voith Turbo* case, and *BVD Laboratoires case, op cit, supra.*

whether the facts qualify for a challenge, but rather whether the facts are true and accurate and whether or not they were properly understood by the challenging party. Regrettably, the exchange of correspondence sometimes becomes rather emotional and even hostile, and diffuse the distinct impression of partisanship. This is, however, not the purpose of the comments that the Secretariat solicits.

As mentioned, pursuant to Art 11(3), the comments are to be communicated by the Secretariat to all the parties and arbitrators. This provision is new; under the 1975/1988 Rules, the arbitrators' comments were not to be communicated to the parties, and were in fact treated as confidential by the ICC Court.[346] While the communication of the comments ensures transparency and fairness of the process, it may also unnecessarily poison the atmosphere between the parties and the Arbitral Tribunal. **15.509**

Although the Rules do not foresee an opportunity for the challenging party to submit a further statement or a further input by the parties or the arbitrators in respect of the comments of others, the Secretariat may, if considered helpful, include in the comments by the concerned persons the circulating process, if the circumstances permit this. **15.510**

The ICC Court will appreciate at its discretion whether the facts described by the challenging party will qualify for a challenge under Art 11 of the Rules. In doing so, it will take into consideration the comments received from the other party, and from the arbitrators. The Court is however always free to form its opinion on a case-by-case basis; it is not bound by previous decisions. **15.511**

The ICC Court always decides upon challenges at its plenary sessions.[347] As stipulated in Art 7(4) the ICC Court does not communicate reasons for its decision on challenges, whether confirming or rejecting the same.[348] The decision under Art 7(4) is also final insofar as the Court is concerned, which means that it is not subject to further recourse before the ICC Court.[349] The absence of communication of the ICC Court's reasoning means that it remains unknown to the parties and the arbitrators whether a challenge was rejected because it was inadmissible (ie made out of time), or whether it failed on the merits, or for both reasons.[350] Further, even where the ICC Court may find the Arbitral Tribunal's conduct of the proceedings somewhat questionable, the ICC Court will generally not express any views or opinions in that respect. In other words, the ICC Court will either uphold or reject the challenge, and even where it rejects the challenge will refrain from any critical comments regarding an arbitrator's position or conduct. **15.512**

The ICC Court's reasons are, however, noted in its minutes or at least in the ICC Court's own files and can be produced upon request to one of the parties and where the ICC Court **15.513**

---

346 See Craig/Park/Paulsson, *op cit*, 206; Derains/Schwarz, A Guide, *op cit*, 190–1.

347 See *supra* Art 1, para 15.91.

348 See *supra* Art 7, paras 15.379 *et seq.*

349 Unlike Art 13(3) of the UNCITRAL Model Law which provides judicial recourse if a challenge is rejected by the arbitral court, see eg Derains/Schwartz, A Guide, *op cit*, 139.

350 See *supra* Art 7, para 15.378 regarding the final and confidential character of the ICC Court decisions. However, we doubt whether this is a good policy: it might assist the parties if the ICC Court indicated that a challenge was filed too late, and therefore inadmissible. The ICC Court should have no difficulty in communicating to the parties whether the challenge was rejected based on form or on the merits.

finds this to be appropriate. For instance, in one case, the ICC Court supplied the reasons for its decision to a Swiss court, which had to decide upon a recourse against the arbitrator (who had not been removed by the ICC Court following a challenge).

15.514 Under the ICC Rules, no provision exists that would require the Arbitral Tribunal to suspend the arbitral proceedings pending the decision of the ICC Court on a challenge. It is rather a matter left to the discretion of the Arbitral Tribunal, absent the parties' agreement or rules of laws requiring otherwise.[351]

15.515 If the challenge succeeds the challenged arbitrator will be removed and replaced by a new arbitrator as described under Art 12. This clearly has an impact on the schedule of the arbitration while the new arbitrator is put in place, but, as noted, this is outweighed by the importance of ensuring the integrity of the procedure.[352]

15.516 The question arises as to how an arbitrator should deal with a challenge against him that he considers to be unfounded and without merits. The arbitrator may feel that his position is compromised and that it would be in the best interest of the arbitration that he withdraws as he does not have the confidence of the party having made the challenge. It is not the general view that an arbitrator should tender his own resignation because of the challenging party's possible lack of confidence.[353] After all, the challenge may be frivolous and made solely in the interest of delaying the arbitration. In practice, arbitrators faced with a challenge do rarely tender their resignation. Challenges are a matter for the ICC Court, and an arbitrator should let the decision-making process of the Court determine the matter. However, the ICC Court is likely to respect an arbitrator's decision to withdraw in such circumstances (which is dealt with under Art 12).

15.517 In examining a challenge, the ICC Court does not charge an extra fee against the party bringing a challenge, let alone against the unsuccessful challenger. Its work in reviewing a challenge is part of its general case administration and supervision under the ICC Rules, and as such covered by the administrative costs fixed in accordance with Art 31(1) of the Rules.[354] In some cases, parties have sent in multiple challenges (in one arbitration over 16 times), which all needed to be investigated by the Secretariat and addressed by the Court at its plenary sessions, at the expense of a lot of time and costs. Nothing would seem wrong, from a policy perspective, with charging an additional administrative fee in such situations.

15.518 The arbitrator that is removed following a successful challenge remains entitled to fees for the work accomplished by him up to that time. While the fixing of the fees remains a matter of discretion for the ICC Court based on the fee schedule,[355] the Court will rarely if ever sanction an arbitrator by overly reducing his fees.

---

[351] Derains/Schwartz, A Guide, *op cit*, 191.

[352] See *supra* Art 11, para 15.488.

[353] Bond, S., ICC Report in 'Preventing Delay and Disruption of Arbitration: I Conduct by a Party to Disrupt Establishing the Tribunal and Starting the Arbitral Proceedings. Topic 3: Use by a party of challenges to delay or disrupt the arbitration' (1991) *ICCA Congress Series no 5*, 150, 152.

[354] See also *infra* Art 31, paras 15.1109 *et seq*.

[355] See *infra* Art 31, paras 15.1108 *et seq*.

(5) The ICC Court's decision on challenges pursuant to the UNCITRAL Arbitration Rules

Arbitration agreements incorporating the UNCITRAL Arbitration Rules may refer to the ICC as the 'appointing authority'.[356] In such cases, it may be for the ICC to select an arbitrator in accordance with the Rules adopted by the ICC to that effect. Pursuant to Art 12(1) of the UNCITRAL Rules, the appointing authority is also competent to decide upon a challenge, where the other party does not agree to the challenge, and where the challenged arbitrator does not withdraw. Such challenges will be examined by the ICC Court at one of its plenary sessions. In examining the challenges, the ICC Court will look at the admissibility of the challenge (in particular whether the challenge was made in a timely fashion pursuant to Art 11 of the UNCITRAL Arbitration Rules), and based on the facts submitted by the parties, and in accordance with the standards of Art 10 of the UNCITRAL Arbitration Rules, the merits of the challenge.[357] **15.519**

Article 12. Replacements of arbitrators

(1) An arbitrator shall be replaced upon his death, upon the acceptance by the Court of the arbitrator's resignation, upon acceptance by the Court of a challenge, or upon the request of all the parties.

(2) An arbitrator shall also be replaced on the Court's own initiative when it decides that he is prevented de jure or de facto from fulfilling his functions, or that he is not fulfilling his functions in accordance with the Rules or within the prescribed time limits.

(3) When, on the basis of information that has come to its attention, the Court considers applying Article 12(2), it shall decide on the matter after the arbitrator concerned, the parties and any other members of the Arbitral Tribunal have had an opportunity to comment in writing within a suitable period of time. Such comments shall be communicated to the parties and to the arbitrators.

(4) When an arbitrator is to be replaced, the Court has discretion to decide whether or not to follow the original nominating process. Once reconstituted, and after having invited the parties to comment, the Arbitral Tribunal shall determine if and to what extent prior proceedings shall be repeated before the reconstituted Arbitral Tribunal.

(5) Subsequent to the closing of the proceedings, instead of replacing an arbitrator who has died or been removed by the Court pursuant to Articles 12(1) and 12(2), the Court may decide, when it considers it appropriate, that the remaining arbitrators shall continue the arbitration. In making such determination, the Court shall take into account the views of the remaining arbitrators and of the parties and such other matters that it considers appropriate in the circumstances.

(1) Introduction

The rules concerning the replacement of an arbitrator follow from the other provisions contained in Arts 7 and 11. **15.520**

(2) Article 12(1): Replacement of an arbitrator in case of death, resignation, challenge, or upon request of the parties

An arbitrator may need to be replaced in the following circumstances: **15.521**

(i) Death of an arbitrator. As soon as the ICC Court is informed thereof it will normally have to start replacing him. Some or all of the oral hearings may have to be carried out anew **15.522**

[356] See *supra* Introduction para 15.40.

[357] Pursuant to Art 10(1) UNCITRAL Arbitration Rules, 'any arbitrator may be challenged if circumstances exist that give rise to justifiable doubts as to the arbitrator's impartiality or independence'.

as is foreseen under Art 12(4). Having a verbatim transcript of witness testimony will often help in making the decision.

15.523 (ii) Resignation of an arbitrator. The tender of resignation by an arbitrator is not sufficient to trigger his replacement. The resignation becomes effective only if it is accepted by the ICC Court.

15.524 The ICC Court will carefully consider whether to accept a resignation and its discretion is wide; the Rules offer no indications in this respect. The ICC Court might for example consider as valid reasons for the tender of resignation an arbitrator's health conditions, his appointment to a professional position (eg in government or the judiciary) incompatible with the role of an arbitrator, a conflict of interest arising for instance out of the merger of the law firm to which the arbitrator belongs with another law firm (eg one party to the arbitration is a client of that other law firm).

15.525 An arbitrator may consider resignation even where, under the ICC Rules and the applicable law, there is no basis for a challenge, but where the arbitrator considers it appropriate under ethical criteria.[358] The ICC Court is an important control mechanism to prevent frivolous resignations, for instance provoked by pressure brought to bear on an arbitrator by a party as a way of delaying the arbitration. Persons accepting to act as arbitrator take on a serious role, and the ICC Court will not want to see and will not accept frivolous resignations. But the ICC Court does not require an arbitrator to continue where he has good reasons to resign.

15.526 (iii) Challenge of an arbitrator. If a party's challenge is successful, then the arbitrator ceases to act as from the time the Court accepts the challenge, and the decision has been notified to the arbitrator. He thus needs to be replaced.

15.527 (iv) Request of the parties: Circumstances may arise where all the parties are in agreement that an arbitrator is to be replaced; this is different from the challenge procedure under Art 11. Parties appoint arbitrators in whom they have confidence. When parties no longer have such confidence, they can seek the reconstitution of the Arbitral Tribunal.[359] While Art 12(1) does not refer to, and does not require a joint request of the parties to have the arbitrator replaced, in practice, it will normally be on the basis of such joint request. In one case, however, a party brought a challenge against the chairman of the Arbitral Tribunal. The other party objected to the challenge, but felt, because of the particular circumstances of the case, that even if the challenge would be unsuccessful, there was a risk that the chairman would be biased, and that in order to show that he was not, he might take actions actually favouring the challenging party.[360] The party therefore felt that the chairman could no longer maintain his position. The ICC Court, after having rejected the challenge, nevertheless concluded that both parties lacked confidence in the chairman and that they

[358] See Glossner, O., 'Sociological aspects of international commercial arbitration, The art of arbitration' in *Liber Amicorum Pieter Sanders* (Kluwer, 1982) 143, 145, see also *Bühler/Webster, ICC Handbook*, para 12-9.

[359] Craig/Park/Paulsson, *op cit*, 93.

[360] While this type of reasoning may apply in other cases, the opposite may also be true.

were in agreement, although for differing reasons, that he ought to be replaced. The chairman was thus replaced.

(3) Article 12(2): Replacement of an arbitrator on the initiative of the ICC Court

The ICC Court also has the power to replace an arbitrator upon its own initiative when an arbitrator is not fulfilling his functions under the Rules or according to the prescribed time limits. The ICC Court has wide discretion in this respect.[361] **15.528**

One reason is a serious and persistent delay in the conduct of the arbitration in respect to the prescribed time limits. There are other reasons for the replacement of an arbitration such as when an arbitrator is not cooperating with the other members of the tribunal or, in the case of a chairman or sole arbitrator, not ensuring that the arbitration proceeds in accordance with the Rules or in accordance with the time limits. Likewise where the arbitrator is no longer in a position to fulfil his functions, eg because he was appointed as Minister of Justice, he can be replaced. The ICC Court may further take the initiative to replace an arbitrator where, following an order by a municipal court restraining the Arbitral Tribunal from proceeding with the arbitration, an arbitrator declares his unwillingness to participate in any further steps of the arbitration until such order is vacated. In a situation where an arbitrator is detained by local authorities without any indication on the possible length of his incarceration, the ICC Court may wish to replace him having due regard to the uncertainty when he may be able again to act as arbitrator.[362] **15.529**

As regards *de jure* problems, the Secretariat is familiar with the practices and rules in various countries. Therefore, the Secretariat may become aware of a legal issue that the arbitrator and the parties have overlooked.[363] For example, in some countries, judges are not permitted to act as arbitrators. Since the Secretariat is familiar with these requirements, the Secretariat rather than the parties may raise the issue with the arbitrator. **15.530**

The ICC Court's powers under this provision enable it to resolve any difficulties of functioning of an Arbitral Tribunal in respect of one or all of the arbitrators. It is to be recalled that under Art 7(5) an arbitrator has accepted to carry out his responsibilities in accordance with the Rules. If he does not do so, replacement remains the only sanction the Court has against the arbitrator.[364] **15.531**

In both 2006 and 2007, the ICC Court took the initiative to replace an arbitrator in three cases due to the arbitrator's inability or failure to fulfil his functions.[365] **15.532**

---

[361] More generally, see Griffith, G. and Pintos Lopez, R., 'Renegotiating Arbitrators' Terms of Remuneration' (2002) 19 *J Int'l Arb* no 6, 581. Misconduct due to arbitrator's intention to enter into special fee arrangements directly with the parties.

[362] See Ming, W., 'The Strange Case of Wang Shengchang' (2007) 24 *J Int'l Arb* no 1, 63 (detention of an arbitrator, former Vice chairman and Secretary-General of CIETAC by the Chinese authorities on the basis of allegations that he was involved with 'illegal distribution of state assets').

[363] However, it is up to each member of the Arbitral Tribunal to verify that there are no legal incompatibilities.

[364] For the arbitrator's entitlement to receive his fees, see *infra* Art 31, paras 15.1110 *et seq.*

[365] (2008) 19 *ICC ICArb Bull* no 1, 9; (2007) 18 *ICC ICArb Bull* no 1, 9.

(4) Article 12(3): The replacement process

15.533 As the wording of this provision indicates, the ICC Court may consider replacing an arbitrator on the basis of information that has come to its attention, eg if a party has made a complaint, but has not raised a challenge (because the party is reluctant to do so). The Secretariat may be informed by the chairman of the Arbitral Tribunal that one member of the panel does not respond to any correspondence or refuses to attend a hearing. Or the Secretariat may learn through the media that a sole arbitrator has been appointed to a position incompatible with serving as arbitrator. In practice, the most common situation, albeit rare, is the complaint made by a party that does not qualify as a challenge or a request which has become inadmissible because of the time that has passed since the initial event occurred. Article 12(2) is not intended to provide the parties with an additional means to replace arbitrators after the time limit for a challenge has expired.[366]

15.534 In the same way as under the challenge procedure, where the ICC Court considers replacement of an arbitrator for non-fulfilment of his functions or failure to observe a time limit, before making its decision the Court will give an opportunity to the arbitrator concerned, the parties, and the other members of the Tribunal to give their comments. Such comments are to be submitted in writing within a time limit fixed by the ICC Court, usually 15 days.

15.535 In the interest of transparency the comments of each of these persons will be communicated to the others. There is no further exchange of comments foreseen, although the ICC Court may request further comments if considered necessary in the circumstances. In practice, the Court rarely uses this discretion.

15.536 Under Art 7(4), the Court's decision in respect of the replacement of an arbitrator is final, and the reasons for such decision will not be communicated. Of course, in the event of a challenge or the Court initiating the replacement of the arbitrator, the various positions of the challenged arbitrator, the parties and the other members of the Arbitral Tribunal will have been circulated, so that there is transparency regarding such decision reached by the Court, even if the ICC Court's internal decision-making process is not revealed.[367]

15.537 In the event of death, resignation and at the request of all the parties, the reasons for the ICC Court to replace an arbitrator will always be plain.

(5) Article 12(4): Reconstitution of the Arbitral Tribunal

15.538 When the ICC Court proceeds to replace an arbitrator it has the discretion to decide whether or not to follow the original nominating process provided for in Art 8. For instance, if the arbitrator was a sole arbitrator, then the ICC Court may give the parties a time limit to agree upon a sole arbitrator. If they do not, then the ICC Court will appoint him. Where the arbitrator to be replaced was a party-nominated arbitrator, the ICC Court may give the party who had nominated him a time limit within which to nominate a new arbitrator, failing which the ICC Court will step in and make such nomination. Where the third arbitrator was nominated according to a procedure agreed upon by the parties, eg by the

[366] Bond, S., ICC Report, *op cit*, 25.
[367] See *supra* Art 7, para 15.379.

two party-appointed arbitrators, then the ICC Court may invite the party-appointed arbitrators to make a new appointment within a given time limit.

The ICC Court, however, may decide to dispense with the original nomination procedure and make the appointment of the replacement arbitrator directly in accordance with the provisions of Art 9, in the same way as if the party had defaulted.[368] This will rather be the exception. **15.539**

After replacement, one important issue is the extent to which the reconstituted Arbitral Tribunal can continue the proceedings from that point, or whether they need to repeat the earlier proceedings to some extent. This is a matter for decision of the newly composed Arbitral Tribunal. The Arbitral Tribunal has to seek the parties' comments on this issue before taking a decision, as expressly required by Art 12(4). However, if the parties do not agree it is up to the Arbitral Tribunal to decide subject to any mandatory limitations of the *lex arbitri*, which it will have to consider. **15.540**

The issue becomes more difficult the more the arbitral proceedings are advanced. As the written record can easily be assimilated by the replacement arbitrator the need for starting the hearing again is more likely to arise, if at all, in relation to oral witness testimony. Re-staging a week of hearings is a tall order, and may, in many circumstances, not be feasible. If a *verbatim* transcript of the witness testimony was made, it should hardly be necessary to hear the witnesses again, since the transcript will record the position taken by the witness. The Tribunal has a wide discretion in deciding upon the further conduct of the proceedings as far as the ICC Rules are concerned. The arbitration law at the place of arbitration may be more stringent in that respect and may have to be taken into account.[369] **15.541**

Articles 12(1), (2) and (4) are silent regarding the remuneration, if any, of the replaced arbitrator. Such remuneration is indeed subject solely to Art 31(1). **15.542**

(6) Article 12(5): 'Truncated' Tribunal

The death of a member of the Arbitral Tribunal or his removal by the ICC Court after the proceedings have been closed but before the arbitrators have deliberated and reached a decision raises different considerations than if the death or resignation had happened earlier in the proceedings, where it would be appropriate to replace an arbitrator. The ICC Court may decide, if it considers it appropriate, that the remaining arbitrators continue the arbitration alone, ie as a 'truncated' tribunal.[370] **15.543**

Article 12(5) intends to deal with the situation where one of the arbitrators is seeking to obstruct the arbitration through his resignation in order to avoid the rendering of **15.544**

[368] See Derains/Schwartz, A Guide, *op cit*, 200, and the similar, although broader, rule in Art 11(1), LCIA.

[369] See *infra* Art 15, ns 419 *et seq*, as to the role the municipal law at the place of arbitration may play, see also Bühler/Webster, ICC Handbook, *op cit*, para 12–33.

[370] See also Schwebel, S.M., 'The validity of an arbitral award rendered by a truncated tribunal' (1995) 6 *ICC Bull* no 2, 19 and Philippe, M., 'Difficultés procédurales causées par les clauses compromissoires paritaires et les tribunaux arbitraux tronqués' (2005) *Gazette du Palais*, 21, 24.

an award.[371] It is a sound provision made in the interest of the efficiency of the arbitral process. Where the hearing has been closed (Art 22) and the arbitrators are left only to deliberate and render the award, to appoint a new arbitrator would undeniably delay the rendering of the award and often seriously disrupt the arbitral process altogether.

15.545 Before making a decision, the ICC Court must solicit the views of the remaining arbitrators and the parties as well as take account of other matters that it considers appropriate. In this, as in other respects, the decision of the ICC Court will be final and the Court will not give reasons for its decision (Art 7(4)). The ICC Court obviously has a wide discretion to take into account any such factors that it considers appropriate as these are not defined by the Rules. Other arbitration rules offer a wider list of factors than the ICC Rules which allows for the possibility of a 'truncated' tribunal only (i) after the close of the proceedings; or (ii) in the event of death or removal of an arbitrator, not just failure of an arbitrator to participate in the arbitration.[372] Also, under the WIPO Rules, it is for the remaining arbitrators to decide whether or not they ought to continue as a 'truncated' tribunal. It is consistent with the Court's role in ICC arbitration that this decision is part of it', the Court's, sole prerogative.

15.546 In the ICC Court's practice, since its introduction in the Rules in 1998, this provision has so far very rarely been applied.

Article 13. Transmission of the file to the Arbitral Tribunal

The Secretariat shall transmit the file to the Arbitral Tribunal as soon as it bas been constituted, provided the advance on costs requested by the Secretariat at this stage has been paid.

(1) Introduction

15.547 The arbitral proceedings can only start once the arbitrators have received the file from the ICC Court's Secretariat. From this moment the Arbitral Tribunal becomes responsible for the conduct of the arbitration. The purpose of Art 13 is to determine when the arbitrators shall receive the file so that the arbitration proceedings before the arbitrators can start. There are two conditions for the transmission of the file: (i) the Arbitral Tribunal must have been constituted; and (ii) the advance on cost fixed by the Secretary-General must have been paid by one or more of the parties. Thus, the moment when the activities of the Arbitral Tribunal start in an ICC arbitration can easily be identified.

15.548 From the time the arbitrators receive the file the parties shall communicate directly with the arbitrators and must send copies of all correspondence and other documents to the other party(ies) and to the Secretariat for information (Art 3(1)). Likewise, the arbitrators, in case

---

[371] See also Swiss Supreme Court, 1 February 2002, *X Ltd v Y BV*, 4P.226/2001 commented by Tschanz, P.-Y., 'Uncooperative Arbitrators Need Not Delay Award' (2002) <http://www.internationallaw office.com/newsletters/detail.aspx?g=5530550a-086c-4d12-b3c9-838386f5c59c > (accessed 25 May 2009) (the failure of an arbitrator to attend the deliberation of the Tribunal due to the pending challenge of the chairman of the Tribunal before the ICC Court, is not a sufficient ground to set aside the Award).

[372] See Arts 10, 11, AAA, Art, 12 LCIA and Art 35, WIPO.

of a three-member panel normally the chairman, will communicate directly with the parties and send copy to the Secretariat.[373]

(2) Two conditions for transmission of the file

The Arbitral Tribunal may be constituted in one of the many ways provided for in Arts 8, 9 and 10. The constitution of an Arbitral Tribunal may take place quickly in cases where each of the parties promptly nominates an arbitrator, and where the chairman of the Arbitral Tribunal can be designated as promptly. The constitution of the Arbitral Tribunal will only be considered accomplished once all three arbitrators have signed a declaration of acceptance, and once they have been appointed by the ICC Court, or, as the case may be, confirmed either by the ICC Court or the Secretary-General. In practice, the time when the Arbitral Tribunal is fully constituted varies from case to case. Unless the parties have expressly agreed for a specific time limit,[374] the Arbitral Tribunal will rarely, even in the case of a sole arbitrator, be constituted in less than two months from the ICC's receipt of the Request for Arbitration. The Arbitral Tribunal will be operative as soon as the second condition has been fulfilled: payment of the (provisional) advance on costs. **15.549**

Where the Secretariat transmits the file, or a portion of the file (ie at least the Request) to the two co-arbitrators prior to the appointment of the chairman in order to inform them about the nature of the arbitration and with a view to assist them in the selection of a chairman, this will be for information only and remain subject to Art 13. **15.550**

The provisional advance on costs which is payable by the Claimant upon request of the Secretary-General pursuant to Art 30(1) must have been paid, though a 'provisional' advance on costs is not explicitly mentioned in Art 13. No Arbitral Tribunal will be allowed to start working on the file until the ICC has received the provisional advance on costs which is intended to cover the costs of the arbitration until the Terms of Reference have been drawn up (Art 30 (1)). Since the transmission of the file is conditional on the payment of the provisional advance by the Claimant, the latter in reality controls the speed of the transmission of the file, even if it is bound to respect the time limit that the Secretary-General regularly fixes for the payment of the provisional advance.[375] At the Claimant's request, the time limit can be extended by the Secretariat.[376] In some cases, the Respondent may also substitute for the Claimant if the Claimant fails to pay its share of the advance of costs. **15.551**

In a case where the Respondent is in fact the 'true' Claimant in the arbitration and the Claimant has no particular interest in moving quickly, the Respondent might be delayed **15.552**

[373] This contrasts sharply with the practice of some other arbitral institutions, such as the Court of Arbitration attached to the Polish Chamber of Commerce in Warsaw, where the parties and arbitrators are required to communicate through the Secretariat of the Court of Arbitration. Another arbitration institution, the Arbitration Institute of the Stockholm Chamber of Commerce, advises parties not to copy the Institute with the documents that the parties submit to the Arbitral Tribunal.

[374] In their arbitration agreement, for instance for fast-track arbitrations, see *infra* Art 32, paras 15.1185 *et seq.*

[375] See *infra* Art 30, paras 15.1053 *et seq.*

[376] See *infra* Art 30, para 15.1053.

from pursuing its 'claims'. If for such or any other reason the Respondent wishes to and substitutes for the Claimant by paying the provisional advance on costs, the ICC will not raise any objections. It will also accept joint payment or the provisional advance of both parties, although neither practice is expressly foreseen in the Rules.

(3) Transmission and contents of the file

15.553 Upon receipt of the provisional advance on costs the Secretariat will immediately transmit the file to the Arbitral Tribunal, who will only then be able to proceed with the drawing up of the Terms of Reference, establish a procedural timetable (Art 18), and decide other questions that may need to be decided at the beginning of the procedural phase of the arbitration, see Art 14(2), and Arts 15, 16 and 17.

15.554 As the expression 'transmission of the file' indicates, the file is sent to Arbitral Tribunal. The size of the arbitration file will vary according to the length of time and extent of the correspondence which has occurred between the parties and the ICC on preliminary matters, ie if a party questions a prima facie existence of an agreement to arbitrate or if the constitution of the Arbitral Tribunal has taken time.[377] Generally speaking, the file will include the Request for Arbitration, the Answer to the Request for Arbitration and counterclaim, if applicable, and any Reply to the counterclaim. It will further include the written communications submitted by the parties to the ICC, as well as any documents annexed thereto, and the communications of the ICC to the parties.[378]

15.555 The Secretariat draws up a list of the pleadings and written communications which make up the file, commonly referred to as the 'List of Documents', and sends it to the Arbitral Tribunal with a copy to the parties. This practice ensures that no important communications are missed. Parties should verify the list to ensure that the Arbitral Tribunal is appraised of all key correspondence that they consider should be brought before the Arbitral Tribunal regarding the early stages of the arbitral process.

15.556 Parties may wish for certain communications, relating for instance to the constitution of the Arbitral Tribunal, not to be transmitted to the latter. They may have expressed certain preferences as to the characteristics and qualities of the arbitrators, especially arguments against an arbitrator of a certain background or nationality, which need not be known to the Arbitral Tribunal after it has been constituted. Such disclosure may put a party in an uncomfortable position if an arbitrator is chosen of precisely the nationality or training against which a party has objected, although it may later have accepted these. In case of doubt, parties may wish to indicate to the Secretariat that any such communications should not be sent to the Arbitral Tribunal as part of the file.

15.557 At the time of transmission of the file, the Secretariat will generally confirm to the Arbitral Tribunal a number of key elements relating both to their appointment and the arbitration. For example, the Secretariat will indicate the place of arbitration and provide details of the constitution of the Arbitral Tribunal, such as the date of confirmation of its members. It will also notify the Arbitral Tribunal of the full names and addresses of the parties to the

[377] See *supra* Art 6(2).
[378] See *supra* Art 3, paras 15.156 *et seq.*

proceedings and those of their representatives. It will indicate the financial status of the file, by giving the amount in dispute, including the amount of the provisional advance on costs fixed by the Secretary-General, and of the total advance on costs that will often already have been fixed by the ICC Court.[379] The Secretariat will offer some advice to the Arbitral Tribunal as to which arbitrator-related expenses are covered by the provisional advance as well as explain the relevant procedures for reimbursement of arbitrator's expenses and payment of fees,[380] and the use of an administrative secretary by the Arbitral Tribunal.[381] More importantly, the arbitrator will be invited to prepare the Terms of Reference in an expeditious manner in order to ensure that they can be submitted to the ICC Court within two months upon the arbitrator's receipt of the file.[382]

Following the transmission of the file, the Secretariat takes a step back from the proceedings as it is now for the Arbitral Tribunal to take the conduct of the arbitration into its hands and to correspond directly with the parties. The Secretariat will therefore instruct the Arbitral Tribunal that the correspondence shall henceforth take place directly between the parties and the Arbitral Tribunal. The sender of the correspondence, whether the Arbitral Tribunal or the respective party, shall send copies of all correspondence to the Secretariat, which maintains its own records during the ongoing arbitration proceedings.[383] As mentioned under Art 3, the parties and the Arbitral Tribunal may also use the ICC NetCase facility which relieves the Secretariat of the sending of copies. **15.558**

Correspondence among the members of the Arbitral Tribunal need not be copied to the Secretariat,[384] although in practice some chairmen of Arbitral Tribunals do so, a way of showing to the Secretariat that they are working on the file. Sometimes the chairman may also expect some feedback from the Secretariat, such as when he copies to the Secretariat the first draft of the Terms of Reference when that is circulated to the co-arbitrators for their comments. The Secretariat will normally look at it and where appropriate provide the chairman with its comments.[385] **15.559**

(4) Provisional relief by the Arbitral Tribunal

One of the consequences of the transmission of the file is that from this point on, unless the parties have agreed otherwise, the Arbitral Tribunal may order provisional relief at the request of a party, as expressly recognized by Art 23(1). **15.560**

Prior to the transmission of the file parties will have no other option than to apply to the competent state courts for provisional relief.[386] As discussed above,[387] a Claimant may delay the transmission of the file by non-payment of the provisional advance, in which case **15.561**

[379] See *infra* Art 30, paras 15.1059 *et seq.* At this stage the parties will be invited by the Secretariat to pay the total advance on costs within 30 days.

[380] See *infra* Art 31, paras 15.1125 *et seq*, 15.1132 *et seq.*

[381] See *infra* Art 31, para 15.1129.

[382] See *infra* Art 18, para 15.739.

[383] *See supra* Art 3, paras 15.156 *et seq.*

[384] See *supra* Art 3, paras 15.156 *et seq.*

[385] See *infra* Art 18, para 15.693.

[386] See *infra* Art 23, para 15.895.

[387] See *supra* Art 13, para 15.550.

a Respondent seeking provisional relief might be prevented from applying to the Arbitral Tribunal unless the Secretariat is willing to waive the condition or to allow the Respondent to make payment for the Claimant in substitution.[388]

Article 14. Place of the arbitration

(1) The place of the arbitration shall be fixed by the Court unless agreed upon by the parties.
(2) The Arbitral Tribunal may, after consultation with the parties, conduct hearings and meetings at any location it considers appropriate unless otherwise agreed by the parties.
(3) The Arbitral Tribunal may deliberate at any location it considers appropriate.

(1) Introduction

15.562 International arbitration offers the advantage—amongst others—over court of law proceedings of allowing parties a greater choice of forum. The parties are not limited to the other party's place of residence, or the place where that party has assets, as they normally are in litigation, but are free to agree to hold the arbitration in practically any place that suits them. The parties' scope of choice is much wider than it is in litigation thanks to the existence of a number of conventions which make enforcement of arbitration awards easier to obtain abroad than court judgments.

15.563 This freedom of choice has not always existed. For instance, as far as the ICC is concerned, Arts IX and XXIX of the first ICC Arbitration Rules of 1922 provided that 'the arbitration shall take place in the country and town determined by the Court of Arbitration, after examination of the Request for arbitration and before the appointment of arbitrators'. It was thus the ICC Court, not the parties, which fixed the place of arbitration.

15.564 The ICC Rules uphold the principle of the parties' freedom of choice. Only when the parties have not agreed shall the ICC Court fix the place of arbitration.

15.565 The parties may choose the place of arbitration in their contract, when a dispute has arisen, or they may leave it to be made on their behalf by an arbitral institution or by the Arbitral Tribunal itself. At some stage, a choice must be made.

15.566 Where should an international arbitration be held? Should it be in Amsterdam, Buenos Aires, Cairo, Dubai, Geneva, Kuala Lumpur, London, Moscow, New York, Paris, Stockholm or Vancouver (to name a few possibilities)? There are practical considerations to be made, such as availability of suitable hearing rooms, accommodation and other infrastructure. Just as important to know is that a rapid development has taken place in many countries in recent years; the legislation and the practice have been changed to respond to the demands of international arbitration. However, this is not true everywhere. In some places the international movement towards accepting arbitration is still seen with suspicion. As a result, there exist great variations with respect to what matters are arbitrable, what form must be given to an arbitration agreement, the degree of judicial intervention in the arbitration process, the means of challenging an arbitrator, the freedom of choice of the law applicable to the merits, whether several arbitrations may be joined together into one single proceeding, whether discovery of documents is possible, what conservatory measures are available, etc.

[388] See *infra* Art 30, para 15.1086.

Public policy rules of law of *lex fori* must be respected by the arbitrator, not the least since he shall make every effort that the award is enforceable at law (Art 35).[389]

The law of the place of arbitration may indirectly affect the procedural approach chosen by the arbitrator, even if the choice of the place of arbitration is not identical with a choice of procedural law in the terms of Art 15.[390] The different concepts of procedural and substantive law in different countries may cause some surprise to the unwary when choosing the place of arbitration. This is what the parties learnt in one ICC case regarding the question of the statute of limitation.[391] The Claimant asserted that Finnish substantive law applied, but that there is no statute of limitation in Finnish law. The arbitrator applied the rules of *lex fori*, which stipulated that limitation is a matter of procedure, not of substance. Since the arbitrator was sitting in England, the application of *lex fori* on the issue was mandatory and the arbitrator came to the conclusion that the claim was time-barred under English law and dismissed the case.[392] Thus, the choice of place of arbitration may decide the outcome of the case.[393] **15.567**

(2) Article 14(1): Selection of the place of arbitration

(2.1) The choice of the parties It is the experience of the ICC Court that the parties themselves agree on the place of arbitration to an increasing extent, thus leaving limited room for the ICC Court to decide the issue. In 2007, the choice of the place was made by the parties in 85.2 per cent of the cases and by the ICC Court in the remaining 14.8 per cent.[394] France confirmed its lead as the most popular country chosen for ICC Arbitration followed by Switzerland. In fact, for many years now the parties themselves have selected the place of arbitration in well over 80 per cent of ICC arbitrations. This confirms the default character of Art 14(1), when it states that the Court shall fix the place of arbitration, unless agreed upon by the parties. **15.568**

The parties' first concern in selecting a place of arbitration should certainly be that the award be enforceable and the parties' choice will be dictated by the desire to find a place of arbitration to secure this objective. By making the choice themselves, the parties are well **15.569**

[389] See also Crook, J., 'Leading Arbitration Seats in Conflicting Legal Cultures in the Far East: A Comparative View' in S.N. Frommel and B.A.K. Rider (eds), Conflicting Legal Cultures in Commercial Arbitration: Old Issues and New Trends (Kluwer, Boston, 1999) 63; Kaufmann-Kohler, G., 'Identifying and Applying the Law Governing the Arbitration Procedure—The Role of the Law of the Place of Arbitration' (1999) *ICCA Congress Series no 9*, 336; Kaufmann-Kohler, G., 'Le lieu de l'arbitrage à l'aune de la mondialisation—Réflexions à propos de deux formes récentes d'arbitrage' (1998) *Rev arb* no 3, 517.

[390] See ICC Case no 1512 (1971) in *Collection of ICC Arbitral Awards 1974–1985*, vol 1, *op cit*, 3; see also ICC Case no 5485 (1987), 18 August 1987, (1989) YBCA vol XIV, 156; ICC case no 4589 (1984) (Interim Award), (1986) YBCA vol XI, 148; ICC Case no 5080 (1985), (1987) YBCA vol XII, 124; ICC Case no 5073 (1986) (Partial Award), (1988) YBCA vol XIII, 53; ICC Case no 5460 (1987), (1988) YBCA vol XIII, 10.

[391] Extracts of the Award have been published and commented by Jarvin, S., 'Arbitrability of Anti-Trust Disputes: The Mitsubishi v. Soler Case' (1985) 2 *J Int'l Arb* no 3, 69, 75.

[392] English law has since changed. Under the Foreign Limitation Periods Act (1984), where a foreign law applies, the rules of that foreign law relating to limitation should apply.

[393] See also Webster, Th., 'Review of Substantive Reasoning of International Arbitral Awards by National Courts: Ensuring One-Step Adjudication' (2006) 22 *Arb Int'l* no 3, 431.

[394] In 1995 the choice was made by the ICC Court in less than 10% of the cases (see (1996) 7 *ICC ICArb Bull* no 1, 8). In 1990 the parties chose the place of arbitration in 86% of the cases registered with the ICC Court (see (1991) 2 *ICC ICArb Bull* no 1, 4).

positioned to take into account various other parameters that are important for the smooth and efficient running of the arbitration. One such factor is the cost of arbitration, the availability of foreign exchange and the freedom to transfer it. Another factor is the time and the costs of travelling to the place of arbitration. By choosing a place of arbitration in a third country, both parties will have the inconvenience of travelling and staying abroad; neither of the parties is therefore favoured at the expense of the other. A third factor for the parties to consider is *lex causae* and where it had been chosen in the parties' contract, they can fix the place of arbitration in the appropriate country. But where there is no agreement, and since the place of arbitration must be fixed before the arbitrators have decided the choice of *lex causae*, it is convenient to fix the place of arbitration in a neutral country where international arbitration is accepted and developed; the chances of obtaining access to the necessary material and expert legal advice is thereby enhanced.

15.570 (2.2) **Criteria applied by the ICC Court** Where, in the absence of the parties' choice, the ICC Court is called upon to fix the place of arbitration, it will be guided by the effectiveness that could be expected to be given to an award rendered at the place of arbitration, the neutrality of the place, as well as the convenience of the parties. What criteria do the ICC Rules stipulate and what happens in practice, when the ICC Court fixes the place of arbitration? Article 14 gives no indication as to how the choice should be made. A useful list of criteria may in fact be found under the UNCITRAL Notes dealing with arbitration under UNCITRAL Rules and the criteria to be considered by an Arbitral Tribunal in fixing the place of arbitration.

15.571 Where neither a chairman nor a sole arbitrator has been appointed by the parties—and this is the most frequent situation—the ICC Court would consider what nationality the arbitrator is likely to have, and the choice of a place of arbitration and of the presiding arbitrator is then made simultaneously. The Court then proceeds by eliminating various possible places of arbitration.

15.572 (i) Ostensible neutrality being one of the guiding principles in ICC arbitration, the place of arbitration will not, as a rule, be fixed in the country of one of the parties. Ostensible neutrality requires that no party shall have an advantage over the other because of the choice of place of arbitration.[395]

15.573 (ii) The effectiveness of the award must be ascertained (see Art 35) and possible places of arbitration are screened with respect to their adherence to bilateral, multilateral or international conventions recognizing commercial arbitration and enforcement of arbitral awards. Whenever possible, the Court will fix the place in a country that has adhered to the New York Convention.[396]

15.574 (iii) The ICC Court's choice of place will be influenced by the attitude of local courts. Where such courts tend to intervene unnecessarily in the arbitration process and offer a party acting in bad faith an opportunity to obstruct the arbitration, the ICC Court is likely

[395] See also Verbist, H., 'The Practice of the ICC International Court of Arbitration with Regard to Fixing of the Place of Arbitration' (1996) 12 *Arb Int'l* no 3, 347.

[396] See *supra* Introduction, para 15.66.

to go elsewhere when fixing the place of arbitration.[397] On the other hand, where the local courts do not offer assistance in case of need, the parties' interest will not be served either.[398]

(iv) The availability of adequate support services (conference rooms, hotels, secretaries, interpreters, libraries etc) are taken into account. **15.575**

(v) The parties' choice of applicable law, where such a choice has been made, may also be taken into account by the ICC Court, and guide its choice of place of arbitration; there is, however, no imperative rule. **15.576**

(vi) The ICC Court will consider the convenience for the parties of the place; as far as possible, it should be equally convenient (or inconvenient) to both parties. **15.577**

One example may illustrate the practical application of the above principles. In a case between Austrian and Yugoslav parties, the arbitration clause provided that 'Swiss material law' be applied. The ICC Court fixed the place of arbitration in Zurich. By doing so, the ICC Court opted for (i) a neutral place; (ii) adhering to international conventions; (iii) where local courts are mindful of the autonomy of arbitration; (iv) where adequate support services are available; (v) which was in the country of the applicable law chosen by the parties; and (vi) located half-way between the disputing parties. The ICC Court's choice is not always that easy to make. **15.578**

When determining its choice the ICC Court will opt for a 'neutral' site unless strong, specific reasons favour the fixing of the place of arbitration in the country of one of the parties. Unfortunately, the Court's experience with confirming a choice made by the parties to fix the place of arbitration in the Respondent's country is discouraging. In contracts between powerful organizations, mostly state-owned, often in developing countries, which have had a strong bargaining position in their contract negotiations with a private company, it is not unusual to find the place of arbitration fixed by contract in the country of the state organization. In many such cases where the local party has been a Respondent, it has used all kinds of procedures and devices to stop the arbitration from going forward. These may include efforts to exercise influence on local and national authorities in order to obtain refusal by competent authorities to issue visas to the arbitrators or the opposing party's counsel, court litigation against the other party, including sometimes the ICC and injunctions against the arbitrator. The ICC Court's task—to assure enforceable awards, delivered speedily and at reasonable costs—is not enhanced by such behaviour of the parties. It is not surprising, therefore, that the ICC Court pursues the policy of not fixing the place of arbitration in a party's country. **15.579**

[397] See Paulsson, J., 'Arbitration-Friendliness: Promises of Principles and Realities of Practice' (2007) 23 *Arb Int'l* no 3, 477.

[398] In *Titan v Alcatel*, the Svea Court of Appeal, Stockholm, Sweden, found that the arbitral proceedings, which had taken place outside of Stockholm, the contractually agreed place of arbitration, did not have sufficient connection to Stockholm to give Swedish courts jurisdiction to examine an application to set aside the award. See Jarvin, S. and Dorgan, C., 'Are Foreign Parties Still Welcome in Stockholm?—The Svea Decision in Titan v. Alcatel CIT S.A. Raises Doubts' (2005) 20 *Mealey's Int'l Arb Rep* no 7, 42.

15.580 (2.3) **The so-called 'ICC—Paris Clause'** Numerous are the arbitration clauses which refer to 'International Chamber of Commerce Paris', 'la Chambre de Commerce Internationale de Paris', or simply 'ICC Paris', 'la CCI Paris', 'the ICC of Paris', or 'the Chamber of Commerce of Paris' (not to mention the ICC), and the like. The question arises whether the reference to 'Paris' is intended to indicate a reference to the ICC (as it is based in Paris) or whether it is intended to refer to the place of arbitration (as the ICC does not contain a reference to Paris in its name).

15.581 In one case, the arbitration clause in the agreement between Italian and Spanish parties stipulated arbitration 'at *the* International Chamber of Commerce in Paris'. The arbitrators were to decide 'according to International Chamber of Paris regulations'. This clause was not interpreted as an unambiguous agreement between the parties to have the arbitration in Paris. In another recent case, the arbitration clause referred to the 'International Chamber of Commerce, Paris'. The Claimant proposed that Paris, France be the place of arbitration. The Respondent requested that it be in Switzerland as the reference to Paris was only meant as an indication of the arbitral institution. In addition, the parties could not decide at the time of signature of the agreement on the place of arbitration in Paris. In the absence of a clear choice, it is the ICC Court's practice to fix the place of arbitration in Paris. While the wording in the first case could mean that the parties intended the place to be Paris (unless they merely added 'in Paris' to avoid any doubts as to the institution that would administer the arbitration, which is not necessary), the Secretariat in the second case referred to the ICC's usual practice and fixed Paris as place of arbitration as it was at least one party's intention.

15.582 A variation of the 'ICC Paris' clause is a clause referring to 'ICC Geneva', or 'ICC Zurich', or indicating another place where the ICC is thought to exist. Such clauses are usually interpreted as meaning that the parties have agreed to arbitration under the ICC Rules and that they have agreed—or would not disagree—to the fixing of the place of arbitration at the *situs* indicated, ie Geneva, Zurich etc.[399]

15.583 (2.4) **Request to change the place** One or even both parties sometimes request that the place of the arbitration be changed, once the arbitration has started. The reasons for this vary as the following examples from the Court's practice show.

15.584 (i) Owing to difficulties of enforcement. One principle applied by the ICC Court is to reconsider a decision only when new facts, as opposed to new arguments, are presented by a party.[400] In one case, the ICC Court had initially fixed Bangkok as the place of arbitration in a dispute between parties from a Far Eastern country. Following advice as to the impossibility of enforcing an award rendered in Thailand in the Far Eastern country (lack of

[399] See *supra* Art 6, para 15.330. Further examples as to the interpretation of the arbitration agreement at Bühler/Webster, ICC Handbook, paras 14–19 to 14–21; and see also ICC Case no 14190 (2006), unreported; the parties settled their dispute without ever having had a meeting at the place of arbitration.

[400] See *infra* Art 22, paras 15.855 *et seq*.

legislation enabling application of the New York Convention), the ICC Court changed the place of arbitration to Kuala Lumpur.[401]

(ii) Political unrest and insecurity. In another case, the chairman of the Arbitral Tribunal considered the place of arbitration—which had been fixed in the contract—too dangerous (political unrest and insecurity) and requested it to be changed. The parties refused to agree to a change and the chairman's resignation was accepted by the ICC Court under the circumstances.[402] **15.585**

In yet another case before the ICC Court, a Respondent requested that the place of arbitration provided for in the arbitration agreement and located in the Claimant's country should be changed by the ICC pursuant to its implied powers under Art 35. The Respondent relied, *inter alia*, on the doctrine of 'changed circumstances', arguing that unforeseeable changes in that country meant that it was in an unfair and unequal position if it had to arbitrate the dispute in the Claimant's country. It further argued that since the new regime was in place in the Claimant's country the state courts of that country were under the complete control of that regime, and were certain to annul any award rendered in the Respondent's favour. At a plenary session, the ICC Court rejected the Respondent's request. **15.586**

The drafters of the 1998 ICC Rules had in fact considered to give the ICC Court the power to change the place of arbitration agreed by the parties, but it was finally decided not to grant the ICC Court any (express) authority in that respect.[403] Under Art 14(1), the power of the ICC Court to fix the place of arbitration is clearly limited to the case where the parties have not agreed on the place. **15.587**

As an administrative body,[404] the ICC Court has no power to modify the parties' agreement for any reason and, to the authors' knowledge, has never relied on Art 35 (or its predecessor Art 26 of the 1975/1988 Rules) to change a place of arbitration previously agreed to by the parties.[405] **15.588**

It is an entirely different question whether an Arbitral Tribunal can do so, with reference to Art 35 and/or the law applicable to the arbitration agreements. The mere fact that the ICC Court will not interfere, does not mean that an Arbitral Tribunal has no power to deal with such issue. For reasons of neutrality, the ICC Court is also unlikely to interfere with the parties' original choice of the place of arbitration. From a policy standpoint, it does not seem advisable either that the ICC be seen as not respecting the parties' prior agreement. **15.589**

(iii) Once agreed by the parties, the place can only be modified by new agreement. **15.590**

401 See also Jarvin, S., 'The place of arbitration–A review of the ICC Court's guiding principles and practice when fixing the place of arbitration' (1996) 7 *ICC ICArb Bull* no 2, 58.

402 See *supra* Art 12, paras 15.526 *et seq*.

403 The proposed text was drafted as follows: 'In the event that exceptional circumstances make arbitration impossible at the place so fixed or agreed, the Court may fix another place after consulting the parties (. . .)'.

404 See *supra* Art 1, paras 15.107 *et seq*.

405 See Bühler/Webster, ICC Handbook, paras 14–32 *et seq*.

15.591 After the ICC Court had fixed the place of arbitration in Zurich, it rejected a subsequent request by one of the parties to move it to the United States as there was no agreement of the parties to change venue of the arbitration.

15.592 In another case, the parties had agreed to Paris, a choice the ICC Court had confirmed. The Respondent thereafter requested the ICC Court to change the place of arbitration to Tunis. The Claimant would consent only on two conditions: (i) the agreement of all arbitrators; and (ii) the firm undertaking by the Respondent to waive any further challenge or obstruction. The Respondent stated that the acceptance by the Claimant of the place of arbitration cannot be made conditional on the defendant's waiver to challenge an arbitrator. The ICC Court did not modify the place of arbitration.

(3) Article 14(2): Hearings and meetings outside the place of the arbitration

15.593 Article 14(2) allows the Arbitral Tribunal to conduct hearings and meetings at any other location it considers appropriate. Article 14(2) implies that the concept of the place of arbitration is a legal notion. The place of arbitration determines where the award is made, and establishes the jurisdiction of the state courts having jurisdiction competent to set aside an award.[406] Although the legal domicile of an Arbitral Tribunal is at the place of arbitration, it can validly act outside such place, ie hear the parties, or witnesses, deliberate, and sign the award without physically being present at the place of arbitration.[407]

15.594 In many cases it is convenient to hold hearings and meetings at a place other than the place of the arbitration. For instance, where witnesses are to be heard and they all, or most of them, live in another country, sometimes on another continent than the place of the arbitration, it makes economical sense for the arbitrators and counsel to go to that place rather than having the witnesses travel to the place of arbitration.

15.595 In many international arbitrations goods supplied by one of the parties to the other must be inspected, or a construction site, a shipyard, a mine, a road, or a building that is the object of the dispute between the parties, and which by definition cannot be displaced to the place of arbitration, must be examined by an expert and/or the arbitrators. The location of the disputed object is most often elsewhere than the place of the arbitration, since the latter will have been chosen to be a neutral place, halfway between the business addresses of the parties or by applying similar criteria. In situations like these, the Arbitral Tribunal and the parties may find it more appropriate to conduct the hearings all together outside the place of arbitration. The following example from an ICC arbitration may serve as an illustration.

---

[406] See Paris Cour d'Appel, décision of 28 October 1997, *Société Procédés de préfabrication pour le béton v Libye*, (1998) *Rev arb* 399: '*Le siège de l'arbitrage est une notion juridique dont dépend la compétence du juge pour annulation.*' See also *supra* Art 6, n 228. Note however the different approach by the Svea Court of Appeal, Stockholm, Sweden, *supra* para 15.573 and n 398.

[407] Recently, an arbitrator provided as follows in the Terms of Reference: 'The award shall be deemed to be rendered in [x-city], but may be signed by the Arbitrator elsewhere than [x-city]. The parties shall not seek to rely on any argument to the effect that any award or procedural decisions shall be invalid or of limited validity by reason of their having in fact been signed elsewhere than in [x-city].' The need of such provision seems questionable.

The Danish supplier of a cement plant had a dispute with the Canadian buyer of the plant. The place of the arbitration was Copenhagen, the plant was installed outside Montreal and the majority of the witnesses were resident near Montreal. Since an inspection of the plant had been requested by the parties, it was agreed not only to inspect the plant on site, but also to hear the witnesses and the parties' arguments in the office of a law firm in Montreal. 15.596

In another case, where the parties were from India and New Zealand, the place of arbitration New Delhi, the parties' counsel based in New Delhi, and the arbitrators resident in New Delhi, Paris and London respectively, a hearing for the settling of the procedure of the arbitration took place through a video conference. The two European arbitrators sat in London and the third arbitrator and the two counsel sat in front of a video screen in New Delhi. 15.597

Article 14(2) requires the Arbitral Tribunal to consult with the parties before it decides to conduct the hearings and the meetings at another location than the place of the arbitration. This rule will protect against abuses since the Arbitral Tribunal must listen to the parties' arguments for and against holding a hearing outside the place of arbitration, before it decides to do so. The agreement on the place of the arbitration may have been the result of protracted and difficult negotiations between the parties, and based on reasons that are not immediately visible for the Arbitral Tribunal; the Arbitral Tribunal should, in such a situation, not change the venue of a hearing without having consulted the parties. Where a party does not participate in the arbitration, the arbitrator is still required to consult both parties before he decides to hold the hearing in a place other than the place of arbitration. 15.598

The parties have the power to stop the arbitrators from choosing a venue for a hearing outside the place of the arbitration, as the last words of Art 14(2) indicate ('. . . unless otherwise agreed by the parties'). Thus, only agreement among the parties can effectively and definitely stop the arbitrators. 15.599

Related to the issue of the place of hearings is the issue whether alternative means of communication can be made available to substitute, in full or in part, physical meetings of the arbitral tribunal and the parties, such as through the use of video conferencing and telephone conferences. The use of telephone conferences with respect to fact-finding is discussed under Art 20.[408] 15.600

(4) Article 14(3): Place of deliberations among the arbitrators

The arbitrators need not ask the parties' permission to meet between themselves at a place other than the place of arbitration. Article 14(3) authorizes the arbitrators to deliberate at any location they consider appropriate. It derives from Art 25 that each member of the Tribunal should have a full opportunity to participate in the deliberations.[409] In practice, when the arbitrators live in the same city they prefer to meet there, even if it is not the place of the arbitration. This is cost and time effective. 15.601

408 See Art 20, para 15.782.

409 See CA Paris, 16 January 2003, (2004) *Rev arb* no 2, 382, note *Jaeger*; Cass civ 2e, 28 April 1980, *Société Inex Film et autre v Société Universel Pictures*, (1982) *Rev arb* no 4, 424, note *Fouchard*.

15.602 When the arbitrators live in different countries, or even on different continents, the place of the arbitration may be the obvious choice to meet and deliberate, but not in all circumstances. Meeting at the office of the chairman is often the preferred choice, particularly if the chairman, which is usually the case, is the drafter of the award. Meeting at his office will allow the arbitrators to review and modify and finalize the draft award with a minimum loss of time.

15.603 In the authors' experience, a first deliberation often takes place immediately after the end of the hearing, at the place of the arbitration. Thereupon, the chairman produces a first draft of the award and emails or faxes it to the co-arbitrators. If the issues are not too controversial between the arbitrators, they may arrive at a draft award without meeting again after the hearing. The deliberations then take place through an exchange of correspondence rather than through a meeting in person. Article 14(3) does not prevent such a way to proceed. In other cases, one further meeting or more may be necessary.

Article 15. Rules governing the proceedings

(1) The proceedings before the Arbitral Tribunal shall be governed by these Rules and, where these Rules are silent, by any rules which the parties or, failing them, the Arbitral Tribunal may settle on, whether or not reference is thereby made to the rules of procedure of a national law to be applied to the arbitration.

(2) In all cases, the Arbitral Tribunal shall act fairly and impartially and ensure that each party has a reasonable opportunity to present its case.

(1) Introduction

15.604 A fundamental principle in ICC arbitration is that the proceedings are not automatically governed by the local rules of procedure at the place of the arbitration, the so-called *lex arbitri* (with the exception for rules that are mandatory under the law at the place of the arbitration). The ICC Rules do not require that the arbitration be submitted to any municipal procedural law, save for mandatory provisions of such law which should be respected in order to safeguard the validity of the award.

15.605 The parties are free to choose rules of procedure for the arbitration in addition to those already laid down by the ICC Rules of Arbitration. This will usually be done in the Terms of Reference, and/or in the Tribunal's Procedural orders. If the parties fail to agree, the arbitrators will decide on all outstanding procedural issues. Although the ICC Rules do not expressly provide how the arbitrators should decide procedural issues, contrary to decisions on the merits (see Art 25) the latter rules will apply *mutatis mutandis* to procedural decisions. Thus the arbitrators will decide by a majority decision if they cannot agree, or the chairman will decide alone. This is, however, in our experience most unusual, since the arbitrators normally agree on the procedure without much difficulty. The UNCITRAL Notes on Organising Arbitral Proceedings of 1996, as well as the IBA Rules on the Taking of Evidence in International Commercial Arbitration of 1999, may be consulted even by arbitrators acting under the ICC Rules at least as a reference point that may assist and guide them in the conduct of the arbitral proceedings.

(2) Article 15(1): Hierarchy of procedural rules

15.606 (2.1) **Procedural rules agreed by the parties** The basic rules relating to the proceedings before the Arbitral Tribunal are contained in the ICC Rules. It was never the intention of the Rules to be as comprehensive as a Code of Civil Procedure. Besides, the ICC Rules have been designed to be adaptable to all varieties of arbitral proceedings, given the universality of ICC arbitration and the diversity of origins of the parties, their counsel and the arbitration. For instance, the ICC Rules contain no provision on how a witness should testify, and what weight should be given to testimonial evidence.[410] Many other procedural issues are not expressly governed by the ICC Rules. This is the reason why Art 15(1) states that where the Rules are silent regarding the proceedings before the Arbitral Tribunal,[411] it is for the parties, and alternatively the arbitrators to settle them.

There are further limitations, however, since one cannot expect the Arbitral Tribunal to accept any rules made up by the parties; there are limits to what parties can validly agree upon with a binding effect for the arbitrators.[412] Thus, whereas generally speaking the Arbitral Tribunal is bound to comply with the wishes and agreements of the parties, it is not bound to apply procedural rules agreed by the parties if such procedure is illegal or if it turns out to be very burdensome or impractical to carry through.[413] For instance, where a party files an appeal against an interim or a partial award before a state court, the Arbitral Tribunal may upon request of that party, or, in some cases upon its own initiative, suspend the arbitral proceedings for the time the appeal is pending before the state court. In such cases, the ICC Court will normally prolong accordingly the six-month time limit to render an award under Art 24.[414] **15.607**

Also, the arbitrators must consider, before accepting a set of rules agreed upon by the parties, whether the implementation of the rules would make the enforcement of the award impossible or improbable in another country. The arbitrators have a general duty, according to Art 35, to make every effort to make sure that the award is enforceable. **15.608**

An arbitrator who does not approve the procedural rules agreed by the parties has one of two choices: accept the parties' agreement or resign. Resignation is dealt with in Art 12, which provides in para (1) that the ICC Court has a discretion to accept or refuse an arbitrator's resignation. However, the resignation on the ground that the parties have agreed on a procedure that is unacceptable to the arbitrator is unusual in practice.[415] **15.609**

(2.2) Procedural rules settled by the arbitrators The most common situation in ICC practice is, in our experience, that the Arbitral Tribunal settles the procedure, not the parties. Often the Arbitral Tribunal is more experienced in international arbitration than the parties. Where the parties are represented by experienced counsel, they will in practice easily agree with the arbitrators' suggestions, and accept their directions. **15.610**

---

[410] Art 20(3) expressly refers to the possibility of hearing witnesses.

[411] For example, the Rules are considered as silent where the Arbitral Tribunal acts in accordance with Arts 20 or 21; see also Derains/Schwartz, A Guide, *op cit*, 224.

[412] See Jarvin, S, 'To What Extent Are Procedural Decisions of Arbitrators Subject to Court Review?' (1999) *ICCA Congress Series no 9*, 366.

[413] See Kaufmann-Kohler, G.,'Qui controle l'arbitrage?', *op cit*, 153; Karrer P.A., 'Freedom of an arbitral tribunal to conduct proceedings' (1999) 10 *ICC Bull* no 1, 14; Böckstiegel, K.-H., 'Major Criteria for International Arbitration in Shaping Efficient Procedure' (1999) *ICC ICArb Bull*, Special Supp, 49.

[414] See *infra* Art 24, para 15.914.

[415] See *supra* Art 12, para 15.523.

15.611 There is no standardized ICC arbitral procedure and therefore no model to refer to. With the time however, as arbitrators from different countries and continents brought up in various legal environments sit together on ICC Arbitral Tribunals, a certain *rapprochement* has taken place and continues to take place.[416] The IBA Rules of Evidence are a good example hereof; they represent a compromise between the practices found in civil law and common law traditions, adapted to international arbitration. Therefore, it is unusual to find that the arbitrators agree to adopt a purely national procedure, since there will almost always be an international element in an ICC arbitration. Where, in the absence of the parties' choice, the arbitrator determines a point of procedure, he 'is no longer in any way expected to refer to an underlying municipal procedural law, but may determine the rules of procedure freely'.[417] Such freedom is in turn limited by the ICC Rules itself, in particular the requirement of equal treatment of the parties, the parties' right to be heard, and the general requirement for any arbitrator to act in good faith.[418] It is likewise unusual that the arbitrators draft a complete set of rules regulating every single aspect of the procedure. Rather the arbitrators will lay down—in the Terms of Reference or in a procedural ruling—some basic points in order to spare the parties from surprises.

15.612 These basic points may include: the manner in which service of documents will take place; whether written witness statements are permitted, how many briefs the parties should exchange before the hearing; whether post-hearing briefs are allowed; whether certified copies or only original documents may be served as evidence; whether discovery of documents can be ordered; whether the witnesses shall be heard by the arbitrators or whether they may be cross-examined by the parties' counsel, and the like.

15.613 (2.3) **Rules of procedure of a national law, including mandatory legal provision** It is unusual in ICC proceedings to find that the parties or the arbitrators agree to apply purely local or national rules of procedure. It is also unusual to have an ICC arbitrator refer to the municipal or national code of civil procedure at the place or arbitration whenever he is free to fix the arbitral proceedings. Local procedural rules are normally not known to parties or their counsel, and the latter should not be forced to seek the assistance of local counsel at the place of arbitration whenever a procedural issue arises.[419] Where an arbitrator wishes to apply a particular provision of the municipal code of procedure, he should first consult with the parties in order to avoid surprises.[420] Particular aspects of local rules practices and customs may, however, be adopted, and are likely to influence the conduct even of an ICC arbitration, in particular when they prevail at the place of arbitration.

[416] Redfern/Hunter, *op cit*, 264 *et seq*; Craig/Park/Paulsson, *op cit*, 107–8; Derains/Schwarz, A Guide, *op cit*, 223 *et seq*; Craig/Park/Paulsson, *op cit*, 295 *et seq*.

[417] Blessing, 'The Arbitral Process—Part III: The Procedure before the Arbitral Tribunal' (1992) 3 *ICC ICArb Bull* no 2, 18, 19; see also Craig/Park/Paulsson, *op cit*, 296.

[418] Blessing, 'The Arbitral Process', *op cit*, 20.

[419] *ibid*, *op cit*, 23.

[420] Reiner, A., The New Austrian Arbitration Law: Arbitration Act 2006 (LexisNexis, ADR ORAC, 2006) 194, n 451, gives a vivid example of this point when he explains that for an English, a Saudi or Korean party it is probably easier to understand the Austrian rules on warranties than the conduct of an Austrian civil court case.

Article 15(1) should be read in conjunction with App II, Art 6, of the ICC Rules which provides, that when scrutinizing an award, the ICC Court considers the requirements of mandatory law at the place of arbitration. Thus, even if there is no express provision in the ICC Rules that the mandatory rules of a national legal system must be taken into account, this is understood to be the case. Otherwise the risk exists that the award can be set aside at the place of arbitration, by virtue of mandatory national law, or at the place where recognition or enforcement is sought, by virtue of the New York Convention. The said Convention stipulates in its Art V that recognition and enforcement of the award may be refused, 'if a party . . . . furnishes proof that the arbitral procedure (failing an agreement of the parties) was not in accordance with the law of the country where the arbitration took place'. **15.614**

In practice, the Secretariat of the ICC Court, when receiving a draft award from an Arbitral Tribunal, checks the relevant local legislation in order to make sure that no mandatory law has been violated. It reports its findings to the ICC Court and/or the member of the Court who acts as rapporteur of the case.[421] This control of the award before it is approved as to its form, is an essential element of the ICC procedure. **15.615**

(3) Article 15(2): The Arbitral Tribunal's duty to act fairly and impartially

It may seem obvious to require that the Arbitral Tribunal shall act 'fairly and impartially'. It was not an express provision in previous editions of the ICC Rules, but certainly inspired by similar provisions in the rules of other arbitral institutions. The principle is, however, not new in ICC arbitration; it governed ICC arbitration before it was included in the 1998 edition of the Rules.[422] **15.616**

The Arbitral Tribunal shall also ensure that each party has a reasonable opportunity to present its case. The Arbitral Tribunal has a certain amount of discretion in this respect; it is in its power to decide how long time to afford each party to prepare and present its case, how many memorials it can submit, and when the number of witnesses called by a party is sufficient or when the length of hearing witnesses becomes unreasonable. **15.617**

The *Bombardier Transportation* case, which came before the French courts in 2005, provides a good illustration of the power granted to the Tribunal by Art 15(2).[423] The Respondent in the ICC proceedings, attempted to challenge the award on the basis of Art 1502(4) of the French NCPC for violation of the principle of due process. It was argued that the Claimant's failure to comply with the Rules and the procedural orders of the Tribunal including time limits for the submissions did not enable the Respondent to fully prepare its case before the hearing. The Paris Court of Appeal rejected the arguments in the following terms: **15.618**

> . . . time limits fixed by the arbitrators are not an end by itself . . . but are purported to ensure the equality between the parties, the loyalty of the debates and the efficient organization of

[421] See *infra* Art 27, para 15.953.

[422] See Craig/Park/Paulsson, *op cit,* 108, pointing out that the requirement to act fairly and impartially is also an arbitrator's ethical obligation.

[423] Paris, 23 June 2005, *La société Bombardier Transportation Switzerland v La société Siemens AG,* JurisData: 2005-287132. See also Paris, 9 September 1997, *Heilmann v société Graziano Trasmissioni,* (1998) *Rev arb* no 4, 712, note Derains. See also Bühler/Webster, ICC Handbook, *op cit*, para 33–27.

the procedure, the procedural equality between the parties does not require, as alleged by the Respondent, that the decision taken for one party be extended to the other one, the proof that the time imbalance in favour of the Claimant has violated the Respondent's procedural rights remains to be given . . . .[424]

15.619 Interestingly, Art 15(2) does not stipulate that the arbitrators shall handle the dispute in a speedy manner. This requirement is however present. Article 20(1) stipulates that the Arbitral Tribunal shall 'proceed within as short a time as possible to establish the facts of the case', which of course, is a requirement of speed, but which is not so general as one would have expected; it is limited to the establishment of the facts, not the conduct of the arbitration procedure in general.

15.620 The requirement of ensuring 'reasonable opportunity' includes also a requirement and an obligation on the Arbitral Tribunal to handle the dispute in a practical manner. The Rules do not stipulate this and could not stipulate any details in this regard since what is practical in a given case will depend on the circumstances of the particular case and the scope of the dispute, the extent of the evidence, and so forth. Handling the dispute in a practical manner includes the right for the arbitrators to modify the procedure as the case develops and, where necessary, make new procedural rulings amending previous rulings.

Article 16. Language of the arbitration

In the absence of an agreement by the parties, the Arbitral Tribunal shall determine the language or languages of the arbitration, due regard being given to all relevant circumstances, including the language of the contract.

(1) Introduction

15.621 In international arbitration, as in international business transactions, the language of the parties involved is not necessarily one and the same. Whereas the language of the contract may be agreed upon quite easily and the parties show great willingness to find a common denominator at the stage when they enter into a contract, the situation is sometimes radically different when they shall arbitrate their dispute; to reach an agreement at this stage may prove to be a difficult and time-consuming exercise. The ICC recommends that it may be desirable for the parties to stipulate in the arbitration clause itself the language of the arbitration.[425] This is a good recommendation which parties are well advised to follow, simply because it helps in organizing the arbitration.

15.622 The Rules do not define what is meant by 'the language or languages of the arbitration'. It is generally accepted that the term includes the language(s) used by the Arbitral Tribunal and the parties for communicating orally and/or in writing.[426] Thus, the language of arbitration refers to the language of the proceedings, comprising both its written and oral parts. The Request for Arbitration and the Answer thereto, including the documents annexed thereto, need to conform to the language of arbitration. The same applies to oral statements made at hearing or meetings of the Arbitral Tribunal with the parties.

[424] The translation is taken from Bühler/Webster, ICC Handbook, *op cit*, para 15-11.
[425] See ICC Publication no 839, 9.
[426] Lazareff, S., 'The Language of Institutional Arbitration' (1997) 8 *ICC ICArb Bull* no 1, 18 *et seq*.

However, the Arbitral Tribunal is not obliged to extend the language of arbitration to any document submitted. Multi-linguistic arbitrators, who nowadays continue to be found more often outside Anglo-Saxon countries,[427] will find it relatively easy to accept documents in a language other than the arbitration language. In practice, the arbitrators will seek to limit translations because of their often exorbitant costs. As far as legal documents are concerned, an Arbitral Tribunal may accept that only relevant extracts of a court case are translated. However, it will then often be necessary to have the translation cover the entire structure of the document, and the context of the excerpt. The Arbitral Tribunal remains, however, free to request translation of documents in their entirety and of any documents annexed to a party's brief or to a witness statement. **15.623**

There is no official or 'natural' language in ICC arbitration. The ICC is neutral with respect to the language the parties will choose for the arbitration; any language can be used in an ICC arbitration. It does not matter that the English and French versions are the only official texts of the ICC Rules; it is also irrelevant whether the ICC Rules have been translated in the language of the arbitration.[428] In practice, only a few languages are commonly used as the arbitral language in the ICC arbitration. Not surprisingly, English has became the *lingua franca* of international arbitration,[429] but Arabic, French, German, Italian, Japanese, Portuguese and Spanish are used as well. An arbitration is likely to be in one of these languages where the litigants have the same domestic[430] or regional[431] origin. There may be other reasons; for instance, in one dispute concerning the supply and construction of an industrial kiln, the Spanish Claimant appointed counsel based in Germany in a dispute against a German Respondent. The contract provided for the application of German law, and Paris as place of arbitration. Since the Request for arbitration was filed in German, the Respondent accepted this to be the language of the arbitration, although the contract was in English. **15.624**

If parties understand this principle, that there is no predetermined language in ICC arbitration, they are likely to approach the difficulties that the choice of language may give rise to with a more open mind. It is not automatically so that the language of the contract will be the language of the arbitration, although this is frequently the case, in particular where the parties' correspondence has also been exchanged in that language. **15.625**

In the 1975/1988 Rules the language of the contract was emphasized by the words 'in particular'. The wording in the current Rules refers to 'all relevant circumstances including the language of the contract'.[432] This suggests that a more neutral approach is to be made by the Arbitral Tribunal when determining the language of arbitration, notwithstanding its **15.626**

---

427 See Reed, L. and Sutcliffe, J., 'The "Americanisation" of International Arbitration' (2001) 16 *Int'l Arb Rep* 37.

428 See *supra* Introduction, paras 15.49 *et seq.*

429 See <http://www.iccwbo.org/court/arbitration/>.

430 eg to Japanese parties.

431 eg an Egyptian and a U.A.E. party, or a Colombian and a Mexican party.

432 According to Reiner, the language of the contract has diminished in importance for the determination of the language of the arbitration. See Reiner, A., 'Le Règlement d'Arbitrage de la CCI, Version 1998' (1998) *Rev arb* 18.

unchanged authority to decide upon the language of arbitration where there is no agreement of the parties.

15.627 It is very useful for all involved, the parties, their counsel, the ICC Secretariat and the arbitrators to know in advance what the language of the arbitration will be. The parties' choice of counsel, and of arbitrators and sometimes even of expert witnesses, will be influenced by the choice. The language of the arbitration may in some cases also have an impact on the choice of the place of arbitration considering that secretaries and stenographers are more easily found in a country where the language of the arbitration is spoken.

15.628 The language may be used as a 'weapon' by a recalcitrant or an uncooperative party to delay the arbitration and/or to make it more costly. By appointing an arbitrator who does not speak the language of the contract the party can cause extra costs to be incurred and often delay the proceedings.

15.629 One aspect to consider when choosing the language of arbitration is the ability of the parties to present their cases. Article 15(2) provides that the parties shall have a 'reasonable opportunity' to present their case. Likewise, the UNCITRAL commentary on Art 22 of the UNCITRAL Model Law provides that the language of the arbitration must be determined by reference to Art 19(3) of the UNCITRAL Model Law. This provision states that 'the parties shall be treated with equality and each party shall be given a full opportunity of presenting his case'.

15.630 When choosing the language of the arbitration the parties may also have the future enforcement of the award in mind.[433] If the award is drafted in the language used in the country in which the award will be enforced, the enforcement may be quicker.[434] It will be less costly at any rate if the winning party does not have to have the award translated by an official translator. At the time of signing the arbitration agreement, this consideration will rarely be of great help. A Swedish contractor and South Korean owner are likely to prefer English as language of the arbitration, although an award will eventually have to be translated into Swedish or Korean.

(2) Agreement by the parties

15.631 The parties may agree upon 'the language or languages of the arbitration'.[435] The parties do not necessarily have to agree on the language in the arbitration clause as is often the case. The agreement may be also made at a later stage, after a dispute has arisen, in particular when the Terms of Reference are signed. Besides, where an agreement upon the language of arbitration already exists, the parties may add further particulars, eg who bears the translation costs, who selects an interpreter, limit translation to documents other than legal material, etc. Here again, the Terms of Reference are an appropriate moment to reach such agreement, which can also occur during the further conduct of the arbitration.[436]

[433] See Art IV(2) of the New York Convention; see also CA Paris, 18 March 2004, *Sarl Synergie v Société SC Conect SA*, (2004) *Rev arb* no 4, 917, note *Garaud* and *Ziadé* (absence of the translation of the Award by a sworn translator is not a ground for annulment of the *exequatur* decision granted by the French Court).

[434] In particular, when a party wishes to obtain conservatory measures on the basis of the Award.

[435] See *infra*, paras 15.644 *et seq*, the choice of more than one language.

[436] Craig/Park/Paulsson, *op cit*, 97, 281.

An interpreter should be a neutral person. A person chosen by one party to interpret the oral testimony of a witness may be refused by the Arbitral Tribunal on ground of lack of impartiality if the interpreter is an employee of the party. **15.632**

(3) Absence of an agreement

In the absence of an agreement upon the language of arbitration or upon certain details in connection with the chosen language it is the responsibility of the Arbitral Tribunal to decide on the respective matters. As mentioned above the Arbitral Tribunal has to give due regard 'to all relevant circumstances including the language of the contract'. **15.633**

In addition to the language of the contract, there are several other circumstances which may play an important role; probably most important is the language of the parties' correspondence. Further; the language of correspondence between party and counsel, the nationality of parties, counsel and/or the Arbitral Tribunal, the place of arbitration, the applicable law. In determining the language of arbitration the cost factor or the chances to find qualified translators and interpreters should not be underestimated either. **15.634**

Notwithstanding that no general rule exists to determine which circumstance shall prevail, the language of communication between the parties during the time of contract performance is a reliable factor in determining the language of arbitration. **15.635**

The language of arbitration agreed to between the parties or fixed by the Arbitral Tribunal does not bind the Secretariat in its written communications to the parties and the arbitrators. Since many members of the Secretariat are fluent other than in English and French, the two official working languages of the ICC Court, they will, whenever possible, write in the actual language of arbitration, such as German, Italian and Spanish in particular. **15.636**

An arbitrator addressing solely the Secretariat may use the language he deems fit, although most arbitrators would use the language of arbitration also in their written communications with the Secretariat. Arbitrators can have their deliberations in the language of their choice, which does not need to be the language of the arbitration. Where an arbitrator is only familiar with the language of the arbitration, he would be entitled to the deliberations taking place in that language. **15.637**

No matter which circumstances will decide the language of arbitration, at least one arbitrator must master the 'original' language of the witnesses or the parties when poor or incorrect translations of their statements are submitted.[437] When the other party submits a 'counter-translation' the Arbitral Tribunal may only decide the 'battle of translations' if at least one of its members is proficient in the original language. **15.638**

In the *Bombardier Transportation* case,[438] the challenging party attempted to have an ICC award set aside, alleging violation by the arbitral tribunal of the Terms of Reference, which provided for English as the language of the arbitration. It was argued that, by allowing **15.639**

[437] Castineira, E. and Petsche, M., 'The Language of the Arbitration: Reflections on the Selection of Arbitrators and Procedural Efficiency' (2006) 1 *ICC ICArb Bull* no 1, 33, 35 *et seq*.

[438] See CA, Paris 25 June 2005, La Société Bombardier Transportation Switzerland v La société Siemens AG, JurisData: 2005-287132.

communications of exhibits in a language other than English, the arbitral tribunal had exceeded its powers and mission (Art 1502-3 of the French CPC). The Paris Court of Appeal rejected that argument on the grounds that it appeared unreasonable that a party who, during the contract, had accepted to work from French or German documents would now object to the use of such documents, and concluded that the arbitrators had not exceeded their powers.

(4) Correspondence with the ICC Court

15.640 The question of the language arises immediately at the beginning of any ICC arbitration: in which language may the Claimant validly submit its Request and in which language may the Respondent file its Answer?

15.641 This question is to be distinguished from the one in which language the parties may address themselves to the ICC Court, viz. its Secretariat. Since the ICC Court has two official working languages, English and French, correspondence with the ICC will always be accepted by the ICC in any of these two languages. In addition, the staff at the Secretariat are masters of several other languages, such as Arabic, German, Italian, Dutch, Mandarin, Latvian, Polish, Portuguese, Russian, Romanian, Spanish. A party is in no way limited by the official languages of the ICC Court, although, as a practical matter, it is recommended that parties address themselves to the ICC Court in languages which the Secretariat is likely to understand without the need of outside help.

15.642 Another matter is whether the other party in the arbitration accepts the correspondence in a language chosen by the first party, even if the Secretariat accepts it. If for instance, the contract is in English and the German Claimant files a Request for arbitration in German, the Respondent, coming for instance from Latin America, may object and state that it does not understand the Request in German and that therefore, the time limit to answer the Request (Art 5(1)) does not begin to run until the Request has been submitted in, or translated to, a language that the Respondent understands. No provisions in the ICC Rules deal with such situations; it will be for the Secretariat to find a solution in agreement with the parties, or otherwise refer the question to the arbitrators. An early appointment of the arbitrators becomes particularly critical in these situations.

15.643 Where a language of the arbitration has been agreed between the parties or fixed by the Arbitral Tribunal, the Secretariat will systematically correspond with the parties and the arbitrators in the chosen language, provided it is a language that the Secretariat is able to correspond in.

15.644 The internal documents prepared for the sessions of the ICC Court are always in English or French and the documents submitted by the parties in other languages than English or French will be translated for the ICC Court into one of the two languages.

(5) One or two languages of the arbitration?

15.645 Article 16 refers to the language or languages of the arbitration, thus recognizing expressly that in an ICC arbitration more than one language can be used. The authors have been involved in cases where three languages were invariably used by the arbitrators although the award was drafted in the language that was agreed to be the determining language of the arbitration.

The use of more than one language will put parties whose mother tongues are different on an equal footing since each of them can draft its briefs and present its arguments at the hearing in a language with which the party feels absolutely comfortable. If the arbitrators are likewise bilingual and the opposite party also understands the language of the opponent, the situation is an ideal one. Two languages can then be used throughout the arbitration and none of the parties will be at a disadvantage. **15.646**

In practice the situation is often more complicated. Where one party wants to use its own language, the other party may not accept such proposal because it does not sufficiently master the language of the opposing party. In such situations one language is agreed upon or decided by the arbitrators, sometimes coupled with an arrangement for translation of documents and interpretation of the counsel's argument at the hearing.[439] **15.647**

The costs of translation and interpretation will often have to be advanced by the party requesting translation and interpretation, and will become part of the costs of the arbitration and eventually be borne by the losing party in the arbitration. There are, however, no hard and fast rules in this area and the parties and the arbitrators are free to make such arrangements as they see fit.[440] **15.648**

In cases where only one language is agreed or used, the language in which witnesses will testify may pose a special problem. Should a witness be unable or not feel comfortable to speak the language of the arbitration, interpretation must be arranged by the Arbitral Tribunal or by the party calling the witnesses. The costs of interpreters in this situation, where one language has been agreed or decided to be the language of the arbitration, need not necessarily be treated as costs of the arbitration. More often, in our experience, the interpretation costs are the charge of the party whose witness requires interpretation, although the Arbitral Tribunal may in its discretion decide otherwise. **15.649**

Should two (or more) languages be used in the arbitration, it is recommended that the parties agree, or that the arbitrators decide, which of the languages shall be the governing language in case of conflict between them. Where two (or more) languages are the official languages of the arbitration, both the Terms of Reference and the award must be drafted in those languages. Sometimes it is agreed that the award is to be rendered in one language alone. This is, of course, a complication, which speaks against the use of more than one official language, but in certain situations it is simply not possible to do otherwise. **15.650**

In our experience, it is in particular where state enterprises or governments are involved in ICC arbitrations that the language question can become a difficult problem to resolve in a practical manner. Based on what is felt to be national prestige and pride, bureaucratic traditions put an important pressure on a government not to agree using any other language than its own. But in all fairness, the problem is not limited to states, it arises also in arbitrations in which both parties are privately owned companies, and in either case there seems to rest on a fundamental misunderstanding of what international commercial arbitration is all about. **15.651**

---

[439] See also Castineira/Petsche, *op cit*, 36; Bühler/Webster, ICC Handbook, *op cit*, paras 16–28 *et seq*.

[440] See *infra* Art 31, paras 15.1145 *et seq*.

15.652 Flexibility should also in this area be the guiding principle in ICC arbitration. In one recent arbitration in which one of the authors was involved, both parties accepted to arbitrate in English, a foreign language to both of them. Since one party appointed an arbitrator who was not fully comfortable with English, the Arbitral Tribunal appointed an interpreter to be present to assist the arbitrator. The interpreter sat next to the arbitrator and spoke simultaneously in a low voice into the ear of the arbitrator. This arrangement did not disturb the rhythm of the oral hearings.

15.653 Consecutive interpretation is not ideal for the efficiency of witness examination. Where the Arbitral Tribunal's or counsel's questions must first be translated, the witness, who often understands the question as originally put, has more time to think about his answer than a witness who must answer immediately in the same language. We have seen many arbitrations in which efficient cross-examination of a witness is jeopardized because of this process. Simultaneous interpretation, when considered, requires the use of additional facilities, such as a separate interpreter's cabin, microphones, and headphones. It adds seriously to the costs. As a more general point, it is also not always easy to find qualified interpreters at the place of hearing for specialized fields, and it is always advisable to provide the interpreter in advance with relevant documents.

Article 17. Applicable rules of law

(1) The parties shall be free to agree upon the rules of law to be applied by the Arbitral Tribunal to the merits of the dispute. In the absence of any such agreement, the Arbitral Tribunal shall apply the rules of law which it determines to be appropriate.

(2) In all cases the Arbitral Tribunal shall take account of the provisions of the contract and the relevant trade usages.

(3) The Arbitral Tribunal shall assume the powers of an *amiable compositeur* or decide *ex aequo et bono* only if the parties have agreed to give it such powers.

(1) Introduction

15.654 Under the 1998 Rules, there is no requirement that the parties need to select a law applicable to the merits. If the parties wish to agree on an applicable norm for the resolution of their dispute, they may do so, but their choice is not limited to a national law. They can agree to 'rules of law', which is a wider concept than 'law'.[441] If the parties do not agree on rules of law, and the arbitrators step in to decide which norms shall apply, the arbitrators are not restricted to a set of rules applicable at the place of arbitration; they are not even forced to apply the conflict of laws rules of the law applicable at the place of arbitration. This place may have been fixed by the ICC Court of Arbitration, not the parties, and should therefore not be considered a criteria for the choice of the applicable law. The arbitrators can apply those rules of law on the merits which they determine are appropriate without operating the choice through a system of conflict of laws rules.

15.655 Thus, the parties' freedom in the choice of applicable law is almost total. There is one minor restriction on the arbitrators' choice: the rules of law chosen by the arbitrators must, in its view, be 'appropriate'. This freedom will in many cases reduce predictability and will make

[441] An early example from ICC practice is the case 1641 decided in 1969, published and commented in *Collection of ICC Arbitral Awards, Volume I*, 1974–1985, 189.

it more important for parties who desire predictability to specify the law to be applied to the merits in their business agreement. The arbitrators' choice of applicable law on the merits may otherwise come as a surprise to a party.

The parties have, since the beginning of the 1990s, drawn the conclusion that it is in their interest to choose the applicable law: in recent years more than 80 per cent of the disputes submitted to ICC Arbitration provided expressly for the choice of an applicable law.[442] **15.656**

The Request of the Claimant and the Answer of the Respondent should contain the parties' respective comments as to the applicable rules of law under Art 4(3)(f) and Art 5(1)(e). A potential dispute between the parties thereto will therefore become evident prior to the constitution of the Arbitral Tribunal. In such case, the Arbitral Tribunal will decide on the rules of law applicable under Art 18 of the Rules. **15.657**

Where in the absence of a party agreement the arbitrators must make the choice, the arbitral procedure is delayed. Often the parties are invited to submit pleadings with respect to the choice of the applicable law, and the arbitrators then proceed with the rendering of a separate decision on this issue; sometimes in the form of a partial award. The award on applicable law, just like any other award, must be scrutinized and approved by the ICC before it can be notified to the parties.[443] **15.658**

In summary thus, the place of the arbitration exercises—at least in theory—has no influence on the choice of applicable law to the merits and the choice of the law is made without recourse to a conflict of laws rule.[444] **15.659**

(2) Article 17(1): Freedom to chose rules of law

'Rules of law' is a concept that has developed in international commercial, and particularly, ICC Arbitration, over recent decades. The concept is nowhere defined. It is considered to encompass not only rules laid down in national legal systems, national acts of law, but also general principles of law, as for instance reflected in the UNIDROIT Principles of International Commercial Contracts of 2004 as a prominent example of *lex mercatoria.*[445] The rules of law applicable to a dispute can be taken from several national legal systems, the so-called *depeçage* is accepted in ICC Arbitration. The rules of law may be found in principles expressed in draft conventions, not yet adopted through legislative acts. Or they may be reflected in other principles of *lex mercatoria*, principles of general application to international contracts, over which there is an abundant literature with different definitions of the term '*lex mercatoria*'.[446] The use of *lex mercatoria* is, however, limited in ICC practice. **15.660**

---

[442] See *supra* Introduction, paras 15.31 and 15.32.

[443] See *infra* Art 27.

[444] For a more detailed discussion, see also Bühler/Webster, ICC Handbook, *op cit*, in Art 1, paras 17–10 *et seq*.

[445] More generally, see *ICC ICArb Bull*, Special Supp (2005), (2003) *ICC ICArb Bull*, Special Supp *UNIDROIT Principles: New Developments and Applications.* A new edition of the UNIDROIT Principles is in preparation.

[446] Fortier, Y., 'The New Lex Mercatoria, or Back to the Future' (2001) 17 *Arb Int'l* no 2, 121; Jolivet, E., 'La jurisprudence arbitrale de la CCI et la lex mercatoria' (2001) *Gazette du Palais*, 563. See also ICC case no 10422 (2001), (2003), JDI, p 1142, note *Jolivet*, or ICC case no 9797 (2000), *Andersen Consulting Business Unit Member Firms v Arthur Andersen Business Unit Member Firms et al* (2000) 18 ASA Bull no 3, 514; (2001) 12 ICC ICArb Bull no 2, 88.

15.661 The right for the parties and the arbitrators to apply rules of law must however not overshadow the fact that a single national law is the most frequent choice when parties agree on the applicable law in their business contract.

15.662 The Vienna Convention ('CISG') is frequently invoked as applicable rules of law under Art 17. As of 2008, 70 countries had adopted the Vienna Convention, and it has become part of the national law of those countries displacing certain provisions of the national law otherwise applicable. Therefore, the issue of an appropriate application of the Vienna Convention is often raised by the Arbitral Tribunal whether or not invoked by the parties.[447] The rules of the CISG do not cover all contractual issues that may arise in a sales contract, and it is therefore advisable to refer also to a national law in order to be able to fill such 'gaps'. The CISG may be part of that national law, but does not necessarily have to, as long as the parties agree that the CISG should apply to their sales contract.

15.663 (2.1) **No rule of conflict needs to be determined** Where the arbitrators have to determine the applicable law they need not first determine the applicable rule of conflict. This solution is the result of a process over the past years by which it has become more and more accepted that the arbitrators could use the so-called *voie directe* to find the appropriate law to the merits contrary to national courts that are bound to apply national conflicts of law rules.[448]

15.664 Another principle used by ICC arbitrators to choose the applicable substantive law is the cumulative application of several national rules of conflict;[449] if the result is that they all point to the application of, eg the seller's law in a sale of goods contract or the buyer's law in a construction contract, there is no conflict of law that need to be resolved. The arbitrator will arrive at a material choice of law which is identical (the seller's or the buyer's law), whichever law he refers to in order to decide the appropriate rule of conflict.

15.665 (2.2) **Mandatory law** The parties' freedom to agree on the applicable law to the merits is not without limits. The New York Convention, Article V 1(a) stipulates that the recognition or enforcement of an award may be refused if the parties to the arbitration agreement were, under the law applicable to them, under some incapacity. The award may also be refused recognition or enforcement if the arbitration agreement—in the absence of an agreement on the law applicable to it—is invalid under the law of the country where the award was made. Thus, the Arbitral Tribunal, given its duties under Art 35, is subjected to apply the mandatory law of the place of arbitration and enforcement irrespective of the parties' choice of applicable law.[450]

15.666 Consequently, by choosing a 'foreign' applicable law to their contract, the parties cannot avoid the effects of the law of their residence (in the case of a company) or their nationality

---

[447] On this issue, see van Houtte, H., 'The Vienna Sales Convention in ICC Arbitral Practice' (2000) *11 ICC Bull* no 2, 22 and 34.

[448] The *voie directe* is the choice of the appropriate applicable law without reference to any specific choice of law rule.

[449] Derains/Schwarz, A Guide, *op cit*, pp 241–2; Bühler/Webster, ICC Handbook, *op cit*, paras 17–24 *et seq.*

[450] See also Bühler/Webster, ICC Handbook, *op cit*, para 17–49.

(in the case of a physical person) when it comes to deciding whether they are capable of entering into a contract at all. Also, by not agreeing on a law applicable to the arbitration agreement, the parties will be subjected to the law of the country where the award is made when deciding the issue whether the agreement to arbitrate is valid. In the latter case the failure to choose an applicable law has the effect that a law at the place of the arbitration will exercise its full effect; it becomes a mandatory law.

The New York Convention further states in its Art V 2(a) that recognition and enforcement may be refused where the dispute is not arbitrable in the country where enforcement or recognition is sought and, in Art V 2(b) if it would be contrary to the public policy of that country to recognize or enforce the award. **15.667**

The arbitrability of a dispute may, by the parties, be subjected to the provisions of a law that is generous with respect to the kinds of issues that may be arbitrable. But the choice will be of limited effect since, at the recognition and enforcement stage, another norm will be applied: that of the country in which the winning party seeks to enforce the award. That norm will thus have a mandatory effect. **15.668**

It would lead to unfair and unjust results if a party willingly and knowingly enters into an arbitration agreement only to invoke later that the agreement is invalid or inoperable under the laws of its home country or that the enforcement would violate the law in its home country. It is particularly shocking when it is a state, a government or a national enterprise that invokes such grounds as a defence against the enforcement of an award made against it. But such arguments are raised quite frequently in ICC arbitrations, as can be seen in many ICC arbitral awards that have been published. **15.669**

Competition law is a domain in which the issue of the application of national, mandatory law has been much discussed and continues to be much discussed.[451] In a well known case decided by the US Supreme Court in 1985, the *Mitsubishi v Soler Chrysler* case,[452] the Supreme Court held that arbitrators can decide issues involving matters regulated by US antitrust law—which have a mandatory character—and that US courts would exercise a control *a posteriori* over the arbitrator's application of the US antitrust law if the award were presented for enforcement or recognition in the US The applicable law according to the parties' agreement in the business contract was the laws of Switzerland, not US law. But the anti-competitive effect of the agreement took place in the US. Thus, the field of **15.670**

[451] See for example, Dolmans, M. and Grierson, J., 'Arbitration and the Modernization of EC Antitrust Law: New ICC Opportunities and New Responsibilities' (2003) 14 *ICC ICArb Bull* no 2, pp 37, 53; Jolivet, E., 'Chronique de jurisprudence arbitrale de la Chambre de commerce internationale (CCI): Quelques exemples du traitement du droit communautaire dans l'arbitrage CCI' (2003) *Cahiers de l'Arbitrage* 2e partie, 3; von Mehren A T., 'The Eco Swiss and International Arbitration' (2003) 19 *Arb Int'l* no 4, 465; Bensaude, D., 'Thalès Air Defence BV v. GIE Euromissile: Defining the Limits of Scrutiny of Awards Based on Alleged Violations of European Competition Law' (2005) 22 *J Int'l Arb* no 3, 239; Blanke, G., 'Defining the Limits of Scrutiny of Awards Based on Alleged Violations of European Competition Law—A Réplique to Denis Bensaude's "Thalès Air Defence BV v GIE Euromissile"' (2006) 23 *J Int'l Arb* no 3, 249. See also Heitzmann, P. and Grierson, J., 'SNF v Cytec Industrie: National Courts within the EC Apply Different Standards to Review International Awards Allegedly Contrary to Art 81 EC' (2007) *SIAR* 2007:2, 39.

[452] US Supreme Court, decision of 2 July 1985, *Mitsubishi Motors Corp (Japan) v Soler Chrysler-Plymouth, Inc (U.S.)*, YCA XI (1986), 555 *et seq.*

arbitrability was expanded through the decision in *Mitsubishi* but not the public policy criteria under which mandatory law will continue to be applied to control and counter a choice of applicable law made by the parties in their agreement.

(3) Article 17(2): Trade usages

15.671 Reference to the 'relevant trade usages' in Art 17(2), may be understood as a reference to such formalized rules that are widely accepted in international business and trade without having a legally binding character. Examples are rules sprung from the ICC itself, such as INCOTERMS, the Uniform Rules and Practice for Documentary Credits, Rules relating to Letters of Credit etc.[453]

15.672 Other trade usages or practices need to be identified as being generally used by the people in the trade in question before they can be recognized as trade usages for the purpose of this Article.

15.673 Although Arbitral Tribunals tend to rely on provisions of a contract rather than trade usages, *relevant* trade usages must be taken into account pursuant to Art 17(2) of the Rules since they have become part of the parties' contract.

(4) Article 17(3): Amiable compositeur

15.674 In ICC practice, the parties do not often agree to give the arbitrators the powers to act as *amiable compositeur* or to decide *ex aequo et bono*.[454] The practical importance of the rule laid down in Art 17(3) is thus limited in our opinion.

15.675 The *amiable composition* concept has French origins. It remains a feature of today's law in France, where the notion can be found in the *Code de Procédure Civile*, Art 1474: 'The arbitrator shall decide the case in conformity with rules of law, unless the parties have given him the power to decide as *amiable compositeur*.'

15.676 The exact meaning of *amiable compositeur* is disputed.[455] It is generally admitted that an arbitrator who has the powers of *amiable compositeur* can disregard any law from which the party would be free to derogate, ie laws other than mandatory rules of law.[456] The *amiable compositeur* cannot have greater freedom than that of the parties at the time they established his mission. And the parties cannot derogate from mandatory rules of law.

---

[453] See *supra* Introduction para 15.02.

[454] See ICC Case 4761, commented in *Collection of ICC Arbitral Awards, Vol II*, 1986–1990, 298, 299, and *supra* Introduction.

[455] For a further discussion, Kiffer, L., 'Amiable Composition and ICC Arbitration' (2007) 18 *ICC ICArb Bull* no 1, 51; Derains/Schwartz, A Guide, *op cit*, 244 *et seq*; Craig/ Park/ Paulsson, *op cit*, 112; Bühler/ Webster, ICC Handbook, para 17–68; Poudret/Besson, *op cit*, 616, para 7.5. See also Bühler, M.W. and Jarvin, S., 'L'amiable compositeur peut-il laisser la question du droit applicable au fond indéterminée?' in *Mélanges dédié à François Knoepfler, Droit international privé, droit de l'arbitrage et droit comparé* (Helbing & Lichtenhan, Basel, 2005); More generally, see ICC Task Force on *Amiable Composition* and *ex aequo et bono*, which was created in September 2005 and was mandated to identify the essential features of *amiable composition* and *ex aequo et bono* and also to study the role of the arbitrators in this respect. A guideline is expected to be published by the ICC Task Force.

[456] See ICC Case no 2096, *Collection of ICC Arbitral Awards, 1974–1985, op cit*, 186; ICC Case no 2879, *Collection of ICC Arbitral Awards, op cit*, 346; ICC Case no 4434 (*Collection of ICC Arbitral Awards, 1974–1985, op cit*, 458; ICC Case no 4996, *Collection of ICC Arbitral Awards, 1986–1990, op cit*, 293.

If there exists general agreement that the *amiable compositeur* can depart from the strict application of a legal rule in order to reach a 'fair' resolution of a dispute, it is not certain that he may also derogate from the terms of the contract. An arbitrator acting with the powers of *amiable compositeur* in France may depart from the strict application of the contract without being able to modify the basic terms of the parties' bargain. But he may not have the same freedom—to depart from the contract—in other jurisdictions. It has been suggested that the *amiable compositeur* arbitrator would have such freedom when the parties agree to give him *amiable compositeur status* in long-term contracts or in contracts when the risks and the financial consequences for the parties are difficult to predict. In an ordinary contract, such as for the sale of goods or the construction of a building or a road, it would not be justified to let the parties derogate from the terms of the contract. **15.677**

At any rate, the application of the powers of the *amiable compositeur* is limited in ICC arbitration, and the cases where parties give the arbitral tribunal such powers are getting more and more rare. Under Art 17(2), the arbitrator shall in all cases take account of the provisions of the contract. It may be presumed that this rule applies also in those cases mentioned in para 3 of Art 17, in which the arbitrator has assumed the powers of *amiable compositeur*. **15.678**

Article 18. Terms of Reference; Procedural timetable

(1) As soon as it has received the file from the Secretariat, the Arbitral Tribunal shall draw up, on the basis of documents or in the presence of the parties and in the light of their most recent submissions, a document defining its Terms of Reference. This document shall include the following particulars:

a) the full names and descriptions of the parties;

b) the addresses of the parties to which notifications and communications arising in the course of the arbitration may be made;

c) a summary of the parties' respective claims and of the relief sought by each party with an indication to the extent possible of the amounts claimed or counterclaimed;

d) unless the Arbitral Tribunal considers it inappropriate, a list of issues to be determined;

e) the full names, descriptions and addresses of the arbitrators;

f) the place of the arbitration; and

g) particulars of the applicable procedural rules and, if such is the case, reference to the power conferred upon the Arbitral Tribunal to act as *amiable compositeur* or to decide *ex aequo et bono*.

(2) The Terms of Reference shall be signed by the parties and the Arbitral Tribunal. Within two months of the date on which the file has been transmitted to it, the Arbitral Tribunal shall transmit to the Court the Terms of Reference signed by it and by the parties. The Court may extend this time limit, pursuant to a reasoned request from the Arbitral Tribunal or on its own initiative if it decides it necessary to do so.

(3) If any of the parties refuses to take part in the drawing up of the Terms of Reference or to sign the same, they shall be submitted to the Court for approval. When the Terms of Reference are signed in accordance with Art 18(2) or approved by the Court, the arbitration shall proceed.

(4) When drawing up the Terms of Reference, or as soon as possible thereafter, the Arbitral Tribunal, after having consulted the parties, shall establish in a separate document a provisional timetable that it intends to follow for the conduct of the arbitration and communicate it to the Court and the parties. Any subsequent modifications of the provisional timetable shall be communicated to the Court and the parties.

(1) Introduction

15.679 The Terms of Reference are a distinctive feature of ICC Arbitration. No document of this type is required to be drawn up under the rules of any of the other major international arbitration institutions.[457] The Terms of Reference have for many years been the subject of considerable criticism, the principal one being that they are a source of undue delay without any countervailing benefits.

15.680 Terms of Reference are meant to provide, at an early stage of the arbitration, a general procedural framework, which is of use for the parties, the arbitrators, and the ICC Court, and subsidiarily to the national courts that are seized with a request for the annulment, or recognition and enforcement of an ICC award. Usually, the Terms of Reference do not deal with the details of the procedure to be followed, but serve as a 'road-map' from the beginning to the end of an ICC arbitration for all participants in the arbitration, in particular the parties and the Arbitrators. They allow all kinds of pre-hearing organizational activities to be addressed and offer a structure for the subsequent proceedings to be determined in a rational matter, in particular in shaping the procedural rules that are best suited to a particular dispute.[458]

15.681 More or less detailed rules of arbitration procedure will generally be issued by the arbitral tribunal in the form of procedural orders, which will be signed by the Arbitral Tribunal or by its chairman alone.

15.682 In our experience, an increasing number of practitioners have come to appreciate the Terms of Reference as a useful device in the context of international arbitration proceedings since they contribute, in large measure, to the order that they are capable of bringing at an early stage of the arbitral process. Not surprisingly, in many *ad hoc* arbitrations Terms of Reference are drawn up along the model of the ICC Terms of Reference.

15.683 The Terms of Reference have the following advantages, *inter alia*:[459]

- affording the parties and arbitrators the further possibility of identifying the substantive issues that will be required to be addressed in the arbitration;
- delimiting the precise scope of the Arbitral Tribunal's mandate in order to help ensure that the award ultimately rendered is neither *ultra* nor *infra petita*;
- providing the parties and the arbitrators with an opportunity to identify and possibly agree on procedural and other matters, such as the applicable law, the language of the arbitration and the timetable; and

---

[457] Compare between Arts 18 and 15 of the Arbitration Rules of the Cairo Regional Centre for International Commercial Arbitration (CRCICA) pursuant to which the Centre prepares a draft terms of reference. The Rules can be downloaded from <http//www.crcica.org.eg/>.

[458] See Webster, 'Party Control in International Arbitration', *op cit*, 133; Lazareff, S., 'Terms of Reference' (2006) 17 *ICC ICArb Bull* no 1, 21; Lazareff, S. and Schäfer, E., 'The 1992 Practical Guide on Terms of Reference Revisited' (1999) 10 *ICC ICArb Bull* no 2, 14; Sanders, P., 'The Terms of Reference in ICC Arbitration' in *Liber Amicorum in honour of Robert Briner* (ICC Publishing, Paris, 2005) 693.

[459] ICC, 'Practical Guide' prepared by ICC Commission Working Group (S. Lazaroff, Chairman) (1992) 3 *ICC ICArb Bull* no 1, p 24.

- obliging the parties to ensure that all of their claims and counterclaims have been raised (subject, however, to the provisions of Art 19, as discussed *infra).*

Indeed, in relation to the last of the foregoing matters, the Terms of Reference have long served as a useful aid to the ICC Court in checking whether all of the parties' claims and counterclaims (but no others) have been decided, when it scrutinizes the arbitrators' draft award pursuant to Art 27. **15.684**

In ICC arbitrations Terms of Reference are mandatory. In other words, the parties may not opt out of the Terms of Reference since the ICC will not accept an arbitration under its auspices where this particular feature of its Arbitration Rules is absent.[460] **15.685**

Where the Terms of Reference contain detailed procedural rules, there is an issue as to how they can be changed. There is no provision for amending the Terms of Reference and generally they are subject to the consent of the parties (except for adding new claims under Art 19). Procedural orders issued by the Arbitral Tribunal do not require the consent of the parties to be amended.[461] **15.686**

(2) Article 18(1): Preparation of the Terms of Reference

(2.1) The drawing up of Terms of Reference by the Arbitral Tribunal The arbitrators shall proceed expeditiously with the case and the first thing they have to do when they receive the file from the ICC Court is to draw up the Terms of Reference. As has been explained above under Art 13, the Arbitral Tribunal receives the file as soon as the Claimant has paid the provisional advance on costs. **15.687**

The Terms of Reference are to be drawn up on the basis of documents or in the presence of the parties and in the light of their most recent submissions. The words 'their most recent submissions' are important for the understanding of the Rules. It is generally considered that the parties are free to make new claims up until the Terms of Reference have been drafted, even as late as at the meeting being held for the purpose of signing the Terms of Reference. **15.688**

(i) Most recent submissions: The Rules do not define what is meant by the 'most recent submissions'. Normally the submissions include the Request for Arbitration and the Respondent's Answer thereto as well as possible counterclaims and the answer thereto. However, any other submission made by either party prior to the establishment of the Terms of Reference, eg an amendment to the Request for Arbitration, submission of new claims or counterclaims, are admissible and shall be taken into consideration. It may also occur that, even on the eve of a Terms of Reference meeting, a party, usually the Respondent, makes a submission, eg presents its defence or submits counterclaims, and, as a rule, the Arbitral Tribunal then has to consider such submission in the Terms of Reference.[462] A party's letter to the Arbitral Tribunal commenting upon the draft Terms of Reference is **15.689**

---

460 See *supra* Art 1, paras 15.103–15.106.

461 For a fuller discussion about the parties' freedom to change, amend or opt out provisions of the ICC Rules of Arbitration see Webster Th., 'Party Control in International Arbitration', *op cit*, 133.

462 ICC, 'Practical Guide', *op cit*, ns 62–6 on how to cope with the situation of repeated late submissions, with the ensuing risk of delay in signing the Terms of Reference.

also to be considered as a 'submission', and in such letter a party might, for instance, increase the amount of its claims, amend the factual and/or legal basis of its claims and the like.

15.690 If the Arbitral Tribunal considers that the parties' submissions are insufficient to draw up meaningful Terms of Reference, it may request further submissions from one or both parties.[463] In practice, this is the exception rather than the rule, and is more likely to occur where a Respondent has not yet made any submission of substance. The Arbitral Tribunal will consider the most recent submissions and/or address any preliminary matters, eg requests for conservatory and interim measures.

15.691 (ii) In the presence of the parties: The arbitrators have the right to convene a meeting with the parties upon receipt of the file.[464] Before doing so, the Arbitral Tribunal takes into consideration a variety of factors in assessing whether it would be appropriate to convene a meeting with the parties for the sole purpose of signing the Terms of Reference, eg cost effectiveness, whether agreements on subsidiary issues or points may be reached (such as the language of the proceedings, or even the issues of applicable law), and, although more rarely, whether the entire case may be brought to a settlement.

15.692 A Terms of Reference meeting may also have another important functions, eg to make the parties aware of the Arbitral Tribunal's authority and knowledge of the file and more generally to foster the parties' confidence in the Arbitral Tribunal's ability and willingness to act fairly, swiftly and professionally. Therefore, a meeting between the Arbitral Tribunal and the parties may help in obtaining the parties' agreement on contested points, in clarifying any ambiguities, and more generally in getting a better understanding of the nature of the parties' dispute.

15.693 The Terms of Reference meeting may be held not only at the place of arbitration, but at any other place suggested by the Arbitral Tribunal to which the parties have agreed.

15.694 In our experience, the usual way in which the arbitrators proceed to draft the Terms of Reference is the following. A draft is prepared by the sole arbitrator or chairman of the Arbitral Tribunal[465] in the light of the documents submitted by the parties and is circulated to them by the Arbitral Tribunal for comments. This draft may or may not include procedural stipulations. It is then revised by the arbitrators to take into account the comments received and a meeting is organized during which the Terms of Reference are signed. At this meeting procedural details may be further discussed as well as the provisional timetable contemplated in Art 18(4).

15.695 It is most often desirable to hold a meeting for the purpose of finalizing the Terms of Reference. This gives the parties the opportunity to meet the arbitrators and opposing counsel; sometimes for the first time.

---

[463] ICC, 'Practical Guide', *op cit*, ns 24, 28.

[464] For the advantages of such meeting: Böckstiegel K.-H., 'Case Management by Arbitrators: Experiences and Suggestions', in *Liber Amicorum in honour of Robert Briner* (ICC Publishing, Paris, 2005) 115. See also ICC, *Techniques for Controlling Time and Costs in Arbitration* (ICC Publication no 843, 2007).

[465] In that case, it is good practice for the chairman to first submit his draft to his fellow arbitrators for their comments, prior to circulating the draft Terms of Reference to the parties.

Such meeting may also speed up the process of finalizing the Terms of Reference. When the Terms of Reference are drawn up and signed by correspondence exclusively, the process of completing them, particularly if there are disagreements between the parties, may be considerably prolonged. 15.696

But there are situations when proceeding by correspondence is the better alternative: when it is difficult for the arbitrators and parties to find a mutually convenient date for a meeting to sign the Terms of Reference, when the dispute seems to be relatively simple, and where agreeing on the Terms of Reference and on procedural issues, including the timetable appear to be rather uncontroversial, or when owing to geographical diversity, travel cost and travel time are considerable factors. It may be quicker and therefore quite acceptable to proceed by correspondence. 15.697

(2.2) **Summary of the parties' claims** The Terms of Reference must include a summary of the parties' claims. Such summary provides all parties involved in the arbitration with a clear view of the nature and extent of the dispute, especially where the initial submissions are ambiguous. Together with the identification of the issues to be determined such summary will allow them to identify the central contentious points as they exist at the beginning of the proceedings. 15.698

Further, the summary permits the arbitrators to obtain a preliminary view of the likely issues at stake and thus allows them to direct the proceedings in the most efficient manner. 15.699

A useful way to proceed was set out in the Practical Guide on Terms of Reference:[466] 'It may be useful to describe briefly any uncontested factual and legal background out of which the dispute has arisen.' 15.700

The parties' respective prayers for relief *(petita)* should be fully and clearly set out. This should include ancillary *petita* such as interest claimed and the request for costs. The factual allegations which support these prayers for relief should be sufficiently identified.[467] 15.701

The uncontested factual and legal background should be set forth in a separate section of the Terms of Reference while the prayers for relief and the factual allegations that support them may be set forth in another section. Many Terms of Reference also have separate sections for these points. While the parties' claims must be clearly identified, it is necessary to avoid narrow wording that would unnecessarily restrict the Arbitral Tribunal. The appropriate level of detail depends on the nature of the dispute. The Terms of Reference should be a self-contained document; therefore, a mere reference to the parties' submissions is not acceptable.[468] 15.702

The purpose of the Terms of Reference is to describe the parties' claims, but not in any way to replace or supersede the pleadings made by the parties in the Request for Arbitration and 15.703

466 ICC, 'Practical Guide', *op cit*, 34.

467 The term 'claim' is in certain situations difficult to define; for a detailed discussion see comments under Art 19.

468 For a discussion, Webster Th., 'Terms of Reference and French Annulment Proceedings' (2003) 20 *J Int'l Arb* no 6, 561.

the Answer thereto. The signature by a party of the Terms of Reference does not, in any way, constitute an acceptance of any of the claims or defences being asserted by the other party in the arbitration. Rather, it is no more than an acknowledgement that the parties' respective claims have been properly described. If there are difficulties at the stage of the drafting of the Terms of Reference they are often the consequence of a misunderstanding of the effect of the Terms of Reference. If the arbitrators explain to a party that by signing, it does not accept the position taken by the other party with respect to arbitral jurisdiction, or the merits of the case, it is our experience that the party will be more cooperative and willing to sign the Terms of Reference.

15.704 (2.3) **List of issues** Because the summary of the parties' respective claims consists of an outline of the parties' allegations and the remedies sought, the issues to be determined are distinct from the parties' respective prayers for relief.

15.705 The list of issues to be determined identifies the questions of fact and law which at the time of drafting appear to be relevant to the adjudication of the parties' claims. Since in most arbitrations further submissions will be made after the signature of the Terms of Reference some issues may disappear while new issues will arise.

15.706 The determination of the issues to be decided has a practical function. It will shape the subsequent proceedings by focusing the attention of the parties and the Arbitral Tribunal on the essential points for decision; thus enhancing the efficiency of the proceedings and the cogency of pleadings. For example, issues which relate to jurisdiction, the *locus standi* of a party, the applicable law, or the admissibility of claims may be clearly and separately identified. This is especially helpful where such issues may have to be decided by a partial award.

15.707 The variety of substantive issues to be found in Terms of Reference is countless. Normally they are organized by heads of claim and identify the points which are relevant for the adjudication.

15.708 Not all cases, however, will allow a list of issues to be established and agreed without tough dispute over certain points. In such circumstances, the Arbitral Tribunal may simply wish to decide that such list be omitted. To allow the Tribunal to handle such situations with the required flexibility, the general clause suggested in the Practical Guide may be included in the first draft of the Terms of Reference:[469] 'The issues to be determined shall be those resulting from the parties' submissions and which are relevant to adjudication of the parties' respective claims and defences; in particular the Arbitration Tribunal may have to consider the following issues (but not necessarily all of these and only these, and not in the following order)'.

15.709 If the Arbitral Tribunal decides to drop the list of issues it should bear in mind that the wording of Art 18(l)(d) calls for it to explicitly state that it finds it inappropriate to enumerate the issues to be determined. The following clause fulfils this purpose:[470] 'The issues to

[469] ICC, 'Practical Guide', *op cit*, 35, n 121.
[470] Lazareff/Schäfer, *op cit*, 16.

be determined by the Arbitral Tribunal shall be those resulting from the parties' submissions, including forthcoming submissions, and which are relevant to adjudication of the parties' respective claims and defences, without prejudice to the provisions of Article 19 of the 1998 ICC Rules. Therefore, pursuant to Art 18(l)(d) of the Rules, the Tribunal considers it inappropriate to include a specific list of the issues to be determined'.

Finally, one should have in mind that during the course of the arbitration certain issues might disappear while other ones may appear. The possibility to update the list of issues should therefore be foreseen in the Terms of Reference.[471] **15.710**

(2.4) **Names and addresses** The Terms of Reference are a good place to record what address is to be used for notification and communication purposes throughout the arbitration.[472] The contact details for notification and communications in practice includes the telephone, telefax and, in some cases, the telex number of the person concerned, as well as an email address. It is therefore convenient for these numbers and addresses to be included in the Terms of Reference, ie in a single document. **15.711**

The indication of the parties' names and addresses serves to properly identify the parties to the arbitration and later to facilitate the enforcement of the award. The Arbitral Tribunal will normally take the names as they appear in the pleadings submitted by the parties, ie the Request for Arbitration and the Answer thereto, subject to any request for notification of names. A Respondent that has changed its name may wish to add its new name with the reference 'formerly known as', etc. As international transactions often lead to a change in the company's name, it is useful to clarify in the Terms of Reference whether the parties that signed the arbitration agreement are identical to the parties to the arbitration.[473] **15.712**

Although not expressly provided for in Art 18(l)(a), arbitrators regularly include the business address of the parties on the basis of what the parties have indicated in their pleadings.[474] For enforcement purposes, it is advisable to have more than just a PO Box for the address. In light of the general rule contained in Art 35, it is not improper for an Arbitral Tribunal to request the parties to give the proper address of their seat, including any proof thereof such as an extract from the Commercial Registrar at the company's seat or any equivalent thereto. **15.713**

Counsel is regularly authorized to receive communications and notifications on behalf of the party it is representing, whether a party is represented by one or several counsel. While the representation by one counsel is the rule, even in cases where the party(ies) is (are) represented by more than one counsel, all names and addresses of the counsel are to be included in the Terms of Reference as communications and notifications are to be made to all counsel. **15.714**

The Terms of Reference may expressly stipulate that the parties or counsel must immediately notify all signatories of the Terms of Reference and the Secretariat of the ICC Court **15.715**

---

471 For a discussion, see Webster, 'Terms of Reference and French Annulment Proceedings', *op cit*, 564.

472 *Lazareff/Schäfer op Cit*, 11.

473 Arnaldez, J.J., 'L'acte determinant la mission de l'arbitre' in *Etudes offertes à Pierre Bellet* (Litec, Paris, 1991) 5; Schäfer, *op cit*, 11.

474 See *supra* Arts 4, paras 15.235 *et seq*, and 5, paras 15.273 *et seq*.

of any change of names, descriptions, address, telephone or facsimile number. It may be worth adding that failing such notification, communications made to a party in accordance with the provisions contained in the Terms of Reference shall be valid for all purposes.[475]

15.716 The indication of the arbitrators' names and addresses calls for no particular comments. As for the parties, the office telephone and telefax numbers and email addresses of the members of the Arbitral Tribunal must be mentioned. It is left entirely to the arbitrators' own decision whether or not they also wish to provide the parties with their private address and numbers.[476]

15.717 At this stage, it is also appropriate for the parties to state in the Terms of Reference that they consider the appointment of the arbitrator(s) validly made in accordance with the ICC Rules, and to confirm that they have no grounds for challenging the arbitrators.[477] A formula often used in Terms of Reference is: 'By the execution of these Terms of Reference the parties confirm that they have no grounds for objection against any of the arbitrators'. In light of the challenge provisions contained in Art 11, and in particular the time limit to do so, the need for such statements is, however, limited.

15.718 (2.5) **The place of the arbitration** In almost every case, the place of the arbitration will have been determined at the time the Terms of Reference are drafted. The parties may, however, decide to change the place of arbitration, subject to the arbitrators' agreement. In either case, the Terms of Reference will mention the place of the arbitration as per clause (f).

15.719 Although not required, the Terms of Reference often mention the liberty to hold hearings and meetings outside the place of the arbitration which is contemplated in Art 14(2).[478]

15.720 (2.6) **Procedural rules** Pursuant to clause (g), particulars of the applicable procedural rules shall also be included in the Terms of Reference. The practice of ICC arbitrators varies extensively in this respect. Some will include very limited procedural rules; others will try to fix them in an extensive manner. While the latter approach has the advantage of avoiding surprises during the further conduct of the arbitration, it limits the flexibility that is required in almost any arbitration to adapt to the particular circumstances of the case. It may therefore be preferable to simply fix the general principles, but to leave the specifics to subsequent procedural directions.

15.721 However, these procedural rules will set out the 'blueprint' for the proceedings and thus add to their predictability. Pursuant to Art 15(1), where the ICC Rules are silent, procedural rules can be agreed by the parties, or where there is no such agreement, settled by the Arbitral Tribunal.

15.722 The establishment of Terms of Reference is indeed an appropriate moment to seek, and obtain, the parties' agreement on procedural rules not expressly addressed by the ICC

[475] ICC, 'Practical Guide', *op cit*, ns 94–5.
[476] See *supra* Art 7.
[477] Arnaldez, J.J., *op. cit.*, 7.
[478] See *supra* Art 14, paras 15.592 *et seq.*

Rules. Parties may, however, leave it with Art 15(1), viz. with the Arbitral Tribunal to fix the procedural rules not expressly covered by the ICC Rules as the need arises.

Procedural rules established in the Terms of Reference often include the language of arbitration and how it is to be applied to documents in another language (if not agreed upon at an earlier stage), how written communications shall be routed among the parties and the Arbitral Tribunal, questions on witness evidence (eg whether written testimonies shall be used, the procedure for examining witnesses and for recording the oral testimony). It is not unusual to refer to the IBA Rules on the Taking of Evidence in International Commercial Arbitration.[479] **15.723**

It may also be stated, if considered appropriate, that all documents are presumed to be authentic and complete even though furnished in photocopies, unless their authenticity is challenged by the other party.[480] **15.724**

The Terms of Reference may further provide that reasonable particulars of all allegations and denials in the pleadings shall be given. This is more a concern of due process, since it avoids new allegations of facts being made by a party only at the time of the hearing. The Arbitral Tribunal may even provide in the Terms of Reference that at the end of the exchange of pleadings, no new allegations or denials may be made by the parties, except upon showing of good cause and with the express authorization of the Arbitral Tribunal.[481] **15.725**

Parties may include a provision granting the Arbitral Tribunal the power expressly, upon the request of either party or on its own initiative, to order a party to produce any relevant document that is in the possession, custody or control of said party, its servants or agents. This is often referred to as discovery, and the extent and practice varies widely throughout the world. The power to order the production of documents may be limited to documents which the arbitrators may consider to be (actually or potentially) relevant to the determination of any issue or matter in the proceedings. Likewise, parties may also wish to exclude the possibility of being required to produce any privileged documents. **15.726**

It is not uncommon to indicate in Terms of Reference that where a party fails to comply with an order of the Arbitral Tribunal to produce any relevant document, the Arbitral Tribunal shall draw its own conclusions from such failure in making its award. **15.727**

In disputes involving technical issues, the need to appoint an expert may arise. The Arbitral Tribunal may, at the parties' request or on its own initiative, appoint an expert. The Terms of Reference may stipulate the method and details for the appointment of an expert pursuant to Art 20,[482] eg how his mission is to be defined, how the cost for such an expert shall be advanced by the parties, or one of them, whether the parties shall have the right to question the expert prior to his written report, and the like. **15.728**

[479] Adopted on 1 June 1999.

[480] In order for such challenge to be made timely, it may be recommendable to fix in the Terms of Reference a time limit for the making of such challenge, failing which the right to challenge shall be deemed to have been waived. In any event, the Arbitral Tribunal should, at its discretion, be authorized to require the production of any originals.

[481] See *infra* Art 22, paras 15.854 and 15.857 *et seq*, on the closing of the proceedings.

[482] See *infra* Art 20, para 15.801 *et seq*.

15.729 Construction disputes amount on average to some 15 per cent of ICC arbitration cases.[483] It is therefore not surprising that the issue of site inspections by the Arbitral Tribunal comes up with some regular frequency in these cases. The Terms of Reference may be a good place to include a provision regarding the Arbitral Tribunal's and expert's right to visit the site. It may, eg, be stated that such a visit may take place at any time, by giving to the parties reasonable notice, and that the parties may be present at such visits.

15.730 It is not unusual for the chairman of an Arbitral Tribunal to assume certain procedural prerogatives and to set them out in the Terms of Reference.[484] For instance, the chairman will have the right to call meetings and to set and extend time limits on behalf of the Arbitral Tribunal, or the chairman may issue procedural orders with his signature alone, after such consultation with the co-arbitrators and counsel as he considers appropriate in light of the nature and urgency of the matters dealt with in such orders. In cases of urgency, the chairman may even be expressly authorized to act without a prior attempt to consult with his fellow arbitrators.

15.731 The inclusion of many other procedural points may or may not be appropriate in Terms of Reference. Some further examples shall be given, although this is not meant to suggest that parties and ICC arbitrators should always consider such points while establishing Terms of Reference. It depends entirely on the circumstances of each case, including the procedural rules applicable at the place of arbitration.

15.732 Examples: (i) *Waiver*: procedural complaints shall be made within a reasonable time, otherwise they shall be deemed waived;[485] (ii) *Secrecy of deliberations*: no obligation of the Arbitral Tribunal to submit its internal files to a court of any jurisdiction; (iii) *Interlocutory/Procedural matters*: It may be agreed that applications on such matters shall be decided by the Arbitral Tribunal on the basis of written submissions alone; (iv) *Archiving*: In large construction cases and the like, the question constantly arises where to archive the arbitration files that may fill one or more filing cabinets, by whom (the chairman alone or all three arbitrators), and for how long; (v) *Non-appearance*: The ICC Rules contain no general provisions dealing with the situation of default. If signed by both parties, the Terms of Reference may stipulate, eg, that if either party fails within the prescribed time to appear or present its case, or comply with the directions of the Arbitral Tribunal at any stage of the proceedings, the Arbitral Tribunal may, after giving reasonable notice to each party, proceed with the arbitration and make an award; (vi) *Exclusion of the right to seek the annulment of awards*: some arbitration laws leave the parties free to exclude beforehand the right to challenge awards.[486] Such exclusion agreement may be included into Terms of Reference; (vii) *Dissenting opinions*: As the ICC Rules do not contain any express provisions as to whether dissenting opinions may be communicated to the parties, the parties may wish to authorize the arbitrators expressly to do so, or on the contrary, refuse such authority;[487]

[483] In the year 2007, 14.3 % of the cases represented concerned construction, (2008) 19 *ICC ICArb Bull* no 1, 12.
[484] ICC, 'Practical Guide', *op cit*, paras 162–3.
[485] See *infra* Art 33.
[486] See *infra* Art 28, paras 15.994 *et seq.*
[487] See *infra* Art 25, paras 15.927 *et seq.*

(viii) *Confidentiality*: It is generally understood that ICC arbitrators have an obligation inherent in their status to respect the confidential nature of the arbitral proceedings.[488] If in a given case, there are particular concerns or requirements of confidentiality, this may be included in the Terms of Reference; (ix) *Amount in dispute*: The ICC costs are fixed on the basis of the amount in dispute. At the time of signing the Terms of Reference, the parties' respective claims may be known, and have been quantified. It assists the ICC Court in its task of fixing the advance on costs to have the total amount in dispute indicated in the Terms of Reference.[489] Where the claims of a party are not quantified, eg claims for declaratory relief, it might nevertheless be appropriate to include a provisional assessment of the monetary value of such claims; (x) *Deposit of award*: If under the mandatory rules of the place of arbitration, an award needs to be deposited with the courts, the Terms of Reference may say so, and authorize, eg the chairman to proceed with the deposit of the award on behalf of the Arbitral Tribunal. If the parties may, and wish to, waive such deposit requirement, they may expressly say so in addition to the stipulation contained in Art 28(3).

(2.7) **Changes in the Terms of Reference** As mentioned above, nothing is said in the Rules about the possibility of amending the Terms of Reference. During the arbitration, a party's name or address may change as a result of a merger or a party may change counsel. **15.733**

In practice, the ICC Court has never insisted upon such amendments being made. Nor do the Rules require the Terms of Reference to be changed to reflect the replacement of an arbitrator or their signature by the new arbitrator. The Terms of Reference have never been required to reflect faithfully the evolution of the arbitration. **15.734**

In one case, one of the authors, acting as arbitrator, drew up an addendum to the Terms of Reference after the original Terms of Reference had been signed by the parties and submitted to the ICC Court for information. This addendum reflected the most recent prayers for relief submitted by one of the parties, and as a result thereof, a new issue to be determined. Although no 'addendum' is provided for in the 1998 Rules, the Court took note of the document and the Arbitral Tribunal rendered an award deciding the issues enumerated both in the Terms of Reference and the addendum. **15.735**

(3) Article 18(2): Signature of the Terms of Reference and extension of time –limit

The Rules do not specify anything concerning the persons who are to sign the Terms of Reference, nor do they prescribe a particular form for Terms of Reference. ICC arbitrators regularly establish them on plain stationary and number each page, with the option of adding a cover page that mentions the ICC case number, the words 'Terms of Reference', and even the date of signature. In practice, they are signed by a legal representative of each party or by its counsel. **15.736**

Practice varies with respect to the requirement for a party representative or counsel who signs the Terms of Reference to submit a power-of-attorney. Some arbitrators, notably those coming from a jurisdiction where the production of an authority is the norm, request the counsel to produce a power-of-attorney, whereas other arbitrators, used to the norms **15.737**

[488] See *infra* Art 20, para 15.781.
[489] ICC, 'Practical Guide', *op cit*, paras 178–9.

prevailing in, for instance, Great Britain and France, where a *solicitor* or an *avocat* is not required to produce a power-of-attorney before the courts, do not ask for it.

15.738 It should be borne in mind that in many jurisdictions special authority is required to enable an attorney to enter validly into an arbitration agreement on a client's behalf. Thus, insofar as the Terms of Reference may in any way alter the original agreement to arbitrate or otherwise confer jurisdiction on the Arbitral Tribunal, a special power of attorney may be required by any attorney signing that document.[490]

15.739 A prudent arbitrator should thus normally request the production of powers of attorney by the parties' counsel if it is intended that counsel signs the Terms of Reference. If such power is not provided when the Terms of Reference are signed, it may be submitted afterwards.

15.740 When the Secretariat transmits the file to the arbitrators, it advises them that the Terms of Reference must be transmitted to the ICC Court. In its letter to the arbitrators, which is always copied to the parties, the Secretariat stresses that the ICC Court attaches particular importance to the rapid resolution of arbitrations conducted under the ICC Rules, and invites the arbitrators to make every effort to finalize the Terms of Reference within the period provided for in the Rules. Arbitrators are also put on notice that when fixing the arbitrators' fees the ICC Court may take into account 'avoidable delay' in the completion of the Terms of Reference. The attention of the arbitrators is also drawn specifically to Art 12(2), which provides that an arbitrator shall be replaced when the ICC Court decides that he is not fulfilling his functions within the prescribed time limits.[491]

15.741 Pursuant to Art 18(2), the ICC Court may extend the time limit pursuant to a reasoned request from the Arbitral Tribunal, or on its own initiative if it decides it is necessary to do so. Provided there was some action during the first two months upon receipt of the file, the ICC Court will extend the time limit as a matter of routine for further two months, mostly upon the request of the sole arbitrator or the chairman. The reasons why an extension may be required are multiple. When the Arbitral Tribunal wishes to finalize the Terms of Reference at a meeting with the parties, finding a mutually convenient date may become a factor of delay. It may also happen that the Claimant has not yet submitted its Answer to the Respondent's counterclaim, and that the Arbitral Tribunal wishes to see the Answer before finalizing the Terms of Reference.

15.742 In the author's experience, Terms of Reference are most often signed within two months.

(4) Article 18(3): Refusal to sign or draw up Terms of Reference

15.743 If a party refuses to sign the Terms of Reference, or fails to participate in their drawing up, Art 18(3) provides that the Terms of Reference shall be submitted to the ICC Court for approval.

15.744 It is not usual, but it sometimes happens, that a party refuses to sign the Terms of Reference. In cases where a party stays out of the procedure altogether, does not come to the meeting

[490] See, for an example of a case where difficulties were encountered in this regard, *Boisson et autres v Société Totem Holding et autres,* Cour d'Appel de Paris (19 October 1995), (1996) *Rev arb* 82, cited by Derains/Schwartz, A Guide, *op cit*, 260, n 178.

[491] See *supra* Art 12, paras 15.525 *et seq*.

for the drawing up of the Terms of Reference or remains completely passive, its behaviour will be deemed a refusal to sign the document.

The approval by the ICC Court of the Terms of Reference which have not been signed by a party ensures that the rights of that party are protected.[492] The Court will not approve Terms of Reference that include issues for which the agreement of all parties is required. If an Arbitral Tribunal has reason to believe that one of the parties will not sign the Terms of Reference, it is wise, from the outset, not to include any provisions that require the consent of both sides.[493] **15.745**

Upon approving the Terms of Reference, the Court has to grant the defaulting party a time limit for signature. In the ICC Court's practice, it will normally grant 15 days. It has been noted that a party that originally refused to sign Terms of Reference, will almost always maintain its refusal, and the granting of an additional time limit by the ICC Court is therefore considered meaningless.[494] Although the prospects of obtaining such party's signature subsequent to the ICC Court's approval are indeed mostly dim, the granting of an extra time limit is part of the due process mechanism inherent to ICC arbitration. **15.746**

Usually it is the Respondent who refuses to sign the Terms of Reference, but the opposite can happen. Particularly, it has happened in our experience, where the Respondent has presented a surprising and important counterclaim that is many times larger than the Claimant's claim. **15.747**

Nothing in the Rules prevents the ICC Court from approving Terms of Reference that the Claimant refuses to sign as long as the Respondent has signed them. **15.748**

No case can proceed without the signature by the Arbitral Tribunal and either of the Claimant and the Respondent. The ICC Court cannot approve a document that is not signed by all the arbitrators. Article 18(3) does not provide for the case where an arbitrator refuses to sign the Terms of Reference, and the ICC Court may not substitute an arbitrator's signature by approving Terms of Reference. **15.749**

Whatever the reasons may be for an Arbitrator not to sign the Terms of Reference, his refusal would most likely amount to a non-fulfilment of his duties, and be grounds for his removal by the ICC Court pursuant to Art 12(2). **15.750**

(5) Article 18(4): Provisional timetable

Article 18(4) requires all Arbitral Tribunals to establish a provisional timetable after having consulted the parties, and to communicate it to the ICC Court and the parties. This should be done when drawing up the Terms of Reference, or as soon as possible thereafter. The timetable shall be separate from the Terms of Reference. There is no need for the parties to sign or otherwise accept the timetable. Indeed some commentators consider that it would be unwise to have the timetable signed as this could be regarded as an agreement on procedural rules as referred to in Art 15(1), making it difficult for the Arbitral Tribunal to modify **15.751**

492 Craig/Park/Paulsson, *op cit*, 284 *et seq.*
493 ICC, 'Practical Guide', *op cit*, n 68.
494 Reiner, A., *op cit*, 63.

the timetable if the parties do not agree thereto. On the other hand, as pointed out by Lazareff and Schäfer, it is likely that a timetable to which all parties have given their consent will elicit a stronger moral commitment from them, which may make it easier to insist on compliance with time limits and dates for hearings and thereby guard against unnecessary delay.

15.752 The duty imposed on the Arbitral Tribunal to inform the ICC Court and the parties of any subsequent modifications to the provisional timetable is intended to enable the ICC Court to extend the period allowed for making the final award by the time required (Art 24(1)).

15.753 The Rules do not prescribe any particular form that the timetable must take. The only requirement is that the timetable should be laid down in a document that is separate from the Terms of Reference. In practice it can be a letter, or a separate sheet, dated and signed by the sole arbitrator or chairman. The important things are clarity and flexibility, that the timetable is easily identified and that it can be modified when the need arises as the arbitration proceeds.

15.754 The Tribunal shall prepare the timetable in consultation with the parties, ie seek their views. The Arbitral Tribunal may invite the parties to make suggestions in view of the establishment of a timetable, or, more frequently (and generally more efficiently) submit a proposal to the parties for their comments.

15.755 The timetable to be fixed at this stage, as already mentioned, is provisional, ie not invariably binding towards the end of the proceedings. Article 18(4) makes it plain that the timetable is required to show only the conduct of the arbitration that the Arbitral Tribunal 'intends to follow'. It may need to be adapted to the progress made during the proceedings. It may only cover certain 'tranches' of the proceedings, eg only the further round or rounds of exchange of pleadings. Once completed, the Arbitral Tribunal may then amend the timetable by adding new actions and dates of procedure.

Article 19. New claims

After the Terms of Reference have been signed or approved by the Court, no party shall make new claims or counterclaims which fall outside the limits of the Terms of Reference unless it has been authorized to do so by the Arbitral Tribunal, which shall consider the nature of such new claims or counterclaims, the stage of the arbitration and other relevant circumstances.

(1) Introduction

15.756 This Article deals with the right of a party to introduce new claims into the arbitration after the establishment of the Terms of Reference. As long as the new claims remain within the limits of the Terms of Reference, the latter will not constitute a bar for the admission of new claims. But where the new claims fall outside the limits of the Terms of Reference, an authorization by the arbitral tribunal is required for the new claims to be admitted in the proceedings.

15.757 In every arbitration, as in every case before a court of law, there must be a point in time when the parties cannot present new claims any longer. Otherwise the proceedings could be delayed and extended over long periods of time which would cause disorder and disruption and ultimately lead to undesired effects such as denial, in practical terms, for a party to get to justice.[495] Justice rendered too late is no justice.

On the other hand, it is often just and reasonable that further claims relating to the same contract and the same circumstances as those that gave rise to the original claim be dealt with in one and the same arbitration. The arbitrators know the contract and the facts, the parties' counsel are already familiar with the case, the witnesses may be the same to give evidence relating to both the original and the new claim. Economical reasons then speak in favour of permitting a party to introduce a new claim when the arbitration is under way. **15.758**

Article 19 strikes a balance between these conflicting interests. The signing of the Terms of Reference does not put an end to the period during which a party may introduce a new claim, but the introduction of a new claim thereafter is not automatically permitted; its admission will depend on the arbitrator's decision as to whether the new claim falls within the scope of the Terms of Reference,[496] not upon the consent of the other party. Thus, after the signature of the Terms of Reference no party can be certain that a claim it seeks to introduce will be dealt with. Thus, careful consideration before signing the Terms Reference is necessary. **15.759**

A new claim that is not admitted may nevertheless be tried in arbitration. The party is always free to institute a new proceeding by submitting a Request for Arbitration to the ICC. **15.760**

In many such cases the party will appoint the same arbitrator as in the first case. Should the other party do the same, and should the same chairman be appointed in the second case, the possibility of joining the two cases could be envisaged. However, in most situations of this kind, a joinder will not be possible since the proceedings in the first case will be too far advanced and it would be contrary to the interest of celerity to delay it further. **15.761**

The arbitrators who are nominated by the parties to decide a dispute are selected for their knowledge of the business or industry in which the dispute arises and/or the rules of law applicable to the dispute. A new claim can pose a problem if its resolution requires knowledge that goes beyond the arbitrators' expertise. This should be one consideration to take into account before introducing a new claim. **15.762**

(2) The limits of the Terms of Reference

There is some 'jurisprudence',[497] but little clear and authoritative guidance regarding what falls outside the limits of the Terms of Reference, and what remains within its boundary. There is also no definition what constitutes a 'new' claim or counterclaim. Some arbitrators accept any new claim based on the same set of facts. Others include new claims for the same **15.763**

---

[495] See Schwartz, E.A., '"New Claims" in ICC Arbitration: Navigating Art 19 of the ICC Rules' (2006) 17 *ICC ICArb Bull* no 2, 55, 57; Derains, Y., 'Amendments to the claims and new claims: where to draw the line?' in *Arbitral Procedure at the Dawn of the Millennium* (Bruylant, Brussels, 2005) 65.

[496] Derains/Schwartz, A Guide, *op cit*, 269; Webster Th., 'Terms of Reference and French Annulment Proceedings', *op cit*, 563, 583.

[497] See eg ICC cases 4462, 5514, 6309, 6618, in the three Collections of ICC Arbitral Awards (1971–85), (1986–90) and (1991–95), or ICC case 6197 (1995) in (1998) YBCA vol XXIII, 13 at 27 and its discussion at Bühler/Webster, ICC Handbook, para 19–7.

relief although not based on the same facts. Yet other arbitrators reject new claims based on different legal grounds although evolving from the same facts.

15.764 Under the previous Rules, Art 13(l)(c) referred to 'a summary of the parties' respective claims'. This provision has been amended in Art 18(l)(c) of the 1998 Rules to cover also 'the relief sought by each party'. The wording of the former Rules was considered confusing, as it did not distinguish between 'an overview of the *de facto* and/or *de jure* arguments, on the one hand, and the parties' respective claims, on the other'.[498] The Rules now make this distinction, by referring to the actual and/or legal arguments as the 'claims', and to the *petita* arising out of such arguments as the 'relief sought'. The latter is the narrower concept, as specific relief can be based on different factual and/or legal arguments.

15.765 It is our view that the words '*claims or counterclaims*' used in Art 19 are to be understood as the relief sought by a party. It therefore has been more appropriate to change the words '*claims or counterclaims*' in Art 19 by the words '*the relief sought*', rather than *keeping* the old wording of Art 16. In any event, a claim or counterclaim is not tantamount to a new factual statement or to new legal arguments or theories, which the parties may advance after the signing of the Terms of Reference in support of their existing claims, ie in support of the relief they are seeking.

15.766 Based on the view that Art 19 is concerned with a change of relief, the question of when such relief falls *outside* the Terms of Reference can normally be answered without too much difficulty.

15.767 A claimant who, pursuant to the Terms of Reference, is seeking the payment of the purchase price and after the signing of the Terms of Reference adds a claim for royalties based upon the unlawful use of his trade name by the Respondent, pursues a new claim that falls outside the scope of the Terms of Reference.

15.768 An increase of the amount claimed by a party normally also falls outside the scope of the Terms of Reference, as the latter will be concerned with the question of whether the Party A is owed the payment of X (ie the original amount), not of Y (ie the increased amount).

15.769 It is an entirely different question whether such increase should be allowed under the Rules. Under the past Rules, arbitrators have, in fact, used the considerations related thereto to appreciate whether the increase did or did not remain within the limits of the Terms of Reference.[499]

15.770 The parties may expressly provide in the Terms of Reference for the possibility of an increase of the claims, in particular where an increase will automatically flow from the time elapsed since the signing of the Terms of Reference. In such case it should be possible to say that a claim for the payment of a certain sum of money, which is specifically identified and which

---

[498] Reiner, A., *op cit*, 60.

[499] See the example of the ICC Award 6266 (1991), given by Reiner, *op cit*, 67, where the arbitrators approved an increase on the grounds that it did not change the purpose of the proceedings, did not delay the proceedings, and seemed even intended to save additional proceedings.

because of the time lapse, may be subject to increase in the course of the arbitration, remains within the limits of the Terms of Reference.

Where the Respondent by way of defence raises a set-off claim after the signature of the Terms of Reference, the restrictions of Art 19 apply in the same way as any other new claim or counterclaim, if the purpose of Art 19 is to be achieved. 15.771

(3) The Arbitral Tribunal's discretion to accept new claims

A new claim or counterclaim introduced after the signature of the Terms of Reference should only be allowed when it is justified to do so. A new claim that could have been raised before the signature of the Terms of Reference, but was not raised, should normally not be considered as justified, unless the party can show good cause or unless its late introduction has no significant impact on the arbitral proceedings. As a general proposition it would seem that the more the arbitral proceedings are advanced, the less an Arbitral Tribunal will be inclined to admit new claims. 15.772

Since the purpose of the Terms of Reference is to bring order into the arbitration, a party should not be allowed to conceal its claims or counterclaims during the drafting of the Terms of Reference in order to present them at a later time, particularly not if a late presentation would disrupt the planning of the arbitration or the agreed timetable. To avoid being barred by Art 19 in an ongoing arbitration, the party that anticipates the possibility of raising new claims or counterclaims after the signing of the Terms of Reference, should advise the Arbitral Tribunal and the other party as soon as practical. It may, sometimes, be appropriate to include an express reservation in the Terms of Reference regarding the introduction of specific new claims. 15.773

Often, a new claim consists simply of an increase in the amount of a claim. According to our experience, such new claims are generally accepted by the arbitrators. They will be reported to the ICC Court, which may increase the advance on costs as a consequence of the higher total amount in dispute. As soon as the parties, or one of them, have (has) paid the additional advance on costs to the ICC Court, the arbitrators can proceed with the arbitration. 15.774

When taking the decision to allow or disallow a new claim, the Arbitral Tribunal will wish to take the views of the other party into account. The latter may be opposed to the introduction of such claims, but may accept it; in the latter case, an Arbitral Tribunal will rarely go against the will of the parties, but rather allow the new claims or counterclaims. 15.775

Article 19 remains silent as to the form in which the Arbitral Tribunal should authorize a new claim. It would seem appropriate for the Arbitral Tribunal to proceed by procedural order, but a letter may do as well. The Arbitral Tribunal will then deal with the merits of the new claim in the award provided that it is satisfied that the new claim has been properly notified and parties had a reasonable opportunity to be heard with respect to it, in accordance with Art 15 and applicable law. 15.776

Article 20. Establishing the facts of the case

(1) The Arbitral Tribunal shall proceed within as short a time as possible to establish the facts of the case by all appropriate means.

(2) **After studying the written submissions of the parties and all documents relied upon, the Arbitral Tribunal shall hear the parties together in person if any of them so requests or, failing such a request, it may of its own motion decide to hear them.**

(3) **The Arbitral Tribunal may decide to hear witnesses, experts appointed by the parties or any other person, in the presence of the parties, or in their absence provided they have been duly summoned.**

(4) **The Arbitral Tribunal, after having consulted the parties, may appoint one or more experts, define their terms of reference and receive their reports. At the request of a party, the parties shall be given the opportunity to question at a hearing any such expert appointed by the Tribunal.**

(5) **At any time during the proceedings, the Arbitral Tribunal may summon any party to provide additional evidence.**

(6) **The Arbitral Tribunal may decide the case solely on the documents submitted by the parties unless any of the parties requests a hearing.**

(7) **The Arbitral Tribunal may take measures for protecting trade secrets and confidential information.**

(1) Introduction

15.777 The ICC arbitral procedure is in most cases detached from the local law at the place of arbitration, except insofar as it is mandatory. Article 20 of the Rules fits into all legal and procedural systems. The ICC arbitrator has the duty to ascertain facts immediately, a burden that is not, strictly speaking, that of a common law judge. In common law adversary proceedings, the judge has the passive role of evaluating such evidence as the parties may see fit to present.[500] In contrast, the ICC Rules follow the continental civil law approach under which judges have a duty actively to investigate the facts.[501]

15.778 In ICC arbitrations foreign law is not necessarily considered as an issue of fact. Nor is it required that specific rules of law must be proven by expert evidence.[502] However, in many cases the parties will submit expert reports on the material content of the governing law, particularly with respect to the law applicable to a part of the dispute.[503]

(2) Article 20(1): Establishing the facts of the case

15.779 Article 20 thus reflects the inquisitorial element of the civil law tradition. It is the arbitrator's—not the parties'—responsibility to establish the facts, and the arbitrator is given powers to do so 'by all appropriate means'. In that respect the 1998 Rules are more

---

[500] For a more detailed discussion on common law/civil law approaches see Paulsson, J., 'The Timely Arbitrator: Reflections on the Böckstiegel Method' (2006) 22 *Arb Int'l* no 1, 19; Lazareff, S., 'L'arbitre singe ou comment assassiner l'arbitrage', in *Liber Amicorum in honour of Robert Briner* (ICC Publishing, Paris, 2005) 477, 485; Pietrowski, R., 'Evidence in International Arbitration' (2006) 22 *Arb Int'l* no 3, 373; Cordero Moss, G., 'Is the Arbitral Tribunal Bound by the Parties' Factual and Legal Pleadings?' (2006) *SIAR* 2006: 3, 1. See also Blessing, M., 'The ICC Arbitral Procedure Under the 1998 ICC Rules–What Has Changed?' (1997) 8 *ICC ICArb Bull* no 2, 16, 28 and Blessing, M., 'The ICC Arbitral Process - Part III', *op cit.*

[501] Craig/Park/Paulsson, *op cit,* 415 *et seq* and Reed/Sutcliffe, *op cit,* 38.

[502] On the subject of *iura novit curia,* see Kaufmann-Kohler, G., 'Iura Novit Arbiter - Est-ce bien raisonable? Réflexions sur le statut du droit de fond devant l'arbitre international' in A. Héritier Lachat. and L. Hirsch (eds), *De Lege Ferenda, Réflexions sur le droit désirable, en l'honneur du Professeur Alain Hirsch* (Slatkine, Geneva, 2004) 71.

[503] For example, if Swiss law is the substantive governing law but one of the issues relates to corporate formalities under Cayman Islands law, parties may submit expert evidence on Cayman Islands law, while dealing with Swiss law as the law to be argued.

explicit than the previous versions; a leading idea is that the arbitrator shall manage the case, take initiatives, be active.

Establishing the facts of the case depends basically on evidence provided by the parties and their counsel. An Arbitral Tribunal will rarely take the initiative to collect and review evidence from sources other than the parties, unless at the request of a party or through a Tribunal-appointed expert. In that context the IBA Rules on Evidence of 1 June 1999 are often referred to in ICC arbitration.[504] **15.780**

The arbitrator may decide to hear: **15.781**

- a party;
- a witness;
- an expert appointed by a party; or
- any other person.

Further the arbitrator may: **15.782**

- appoint his own expert;
- summon a party to provide additional evidence; or
- take measures for protecting trade secrets and confidential information.

But the Rules are silent with respect to many procedural issues. The arbitrator may issue procedural rulings although this power is not expressly mentioned in Art 20. It is indeed inherent in the arbitrator's function and therefore no specific reference is required. The arbitrator may bifurcate proceedings in order to hold separate, initial hearings on threshold matters that may make further evidence unnecessary. He may order site visits, or the showing of the functioning of machinery and equipment in dispute. He can encourage the parties to use video recordings or other means of modern technology as evidence. **15.783**

The arbitrator must also combat delaying tactics of either party.[505] This reflects an underlying philosophy of the Rules, which aims at making ICC arbitration faster and more efficient. Article 20(1) gives broad powers to the arbitrator which he may use also in order to prevent delays. The ICC 'Task Force' report on *Techniques for Controlling Time and Costs in Arbitration*[506] provides comments on procedural aspects of arbitration, particularly with a view to reducing costs and time involved in the proceedings. **15.784**

There are still limits to what an arbitrator can do and decide. The previous '*memento mori*' rule, contained in Art 26 of the 1975/1988 Rules still prevails: Art 35 provides that '. . . the arbitrator. . .shall make every effort to make sure that the award if enforceable at law'. Although the Rules give the arbitrator wide powers, he must not disregard mandatory procedural rules at the place of arbitration and comply with such rules in order to ensure **15.785**

---

504 Admittedly, many parties and their counsel hear about the IBA Rules on Evidence for the first time when they are being referred to in an arbitration.

505 See generally on this subject ICCA Working Group I, 'Preventing Delay and Disruption of Arbitration' (1991) *ICCA Congress Series no 5*, 197.

506 See ICC Publication no 843.

that the award will not be set aside on the basis of a breach by the arbitrator of a mandatory procedural rule.

15.786 If the authority of the Arbitral Tribunal is far-reaching when it comes to establishing the facts of the case 'by all appropriate means', one may wonder what powers it has to establish the law. Does the Arbitral Tribunal have power, for instance, to raise questions of law and ask the parties to develop legal arguments relating to issues not previously raised by a party? Here again, the answer seems to be affirmative, since such power forms part of the inherent function of the arbitrator under the ICC Rules.

15.787 In addition, certain guidelines as for example the UNCITRAL Notes on Organising Arbitral Proceedings[507] and their comments in the context of *ad hoc* arbitration may also be used in ICC arbitration.

15.788 May the Arbitral Tribunal ask questions as to facts or law that it considers relevant? Is the Tribunal allowed to submit such questions to the parties and order a further hearing, as the case may be, allowing enough time for the parties to respond? There could be good reason to allow such a practice. In many countries, courts and other judicial bodies are increasingly stringent (notably with respect to arbitrators) regarding the requirements of a due hearing of the parties. In cases which are often complex, where parties have no right of appeal nor access to judicial review before the Supreme Court or elsewhere, the maxim *Da mihi factum, dabo tibi ius* is out of place. The debate over the arbitrator's power to raise questions of law applicable to the facts before him is an ongoing one. We conclude that in order to avoid surprises for the parties, where an arbitrator wishes to raise legal arguments that the parties have not debated at all, it is appropriate for the arbitrator to raise them with the parties prior to rendering the award. Like so often in international commercial arbitration, the right answer may lie in some middle ground depending very much on the circumstances of the case.

(3) Article 20(2): Hearing the parties

15.789 Article 20 of the Rules makes a distinction between hearing a party and hearing other persons.[508] The arbitrator must hear a party, and may hear others (witnesses, experts). The arbitrator may limit the evidence to be heard to the evidence he considers necessary in order to reach a decision. The ruling of Professor Lalive in ICC case no 1512 (*Dalmia Dairy Industries*) is still, in our view, good law.[509]

(4) Article 20(3): Hearing witnesses

15.790 The term 'witness' is not defined under the ICC Rules. More generally, anyone capable of describing facts based on his own perception may be a witness, irrespective of his status as a party, director, manager, employee, agent and the like. Such practice is also reflected in Art 4(2) of the IBA Rules on Evidence which provides that '(a)ny person may present evidence as a witness, including a Party or a Party's officer, employee or representative'.[510]

---

507 <http://www.uncitral.org/uncitral/en/uncitral texts/arbitration/1996Notesproceedings>.

508 For a more general discussion, see also Bühler/Webster, ICC Handbook, *op cit*, paras 20 *et seq.*

509 Jarvin/Derains, *op cit*, 3, 33, 206.

510 See Oetiker, C., 'Witnesses before the International Arbitral Tribunal' (2007) *ASA Bull* vol 25, 253; Derains, Y., 'Le témoin en matière d'arbitrage international' in *Mélanges en l'Honneur de François Knoepfler*

The existing practice in ICC arbitration is largely inspired by the practice known in common law systems: the calling and examination of witnesses and the order in which they testify are up to the parties. Each party introduces and questions its own witness, whereafter the other side cross-examines. The party who called the witness is then entitled to a redirect examination of its witness. The arbitrators also ask questions, of course, but they are not normally expected to conduct an extensive examination of their own motion. 15.791

Article 20(3) is permissive. The Tribunal may decide whether or not to hear witnesses, experts or more generally any other person. However, it is not usual in ICC practice that the Arbitral Tribunal decides, on its own motion, to hear witnesses, experts or more generally any other person. 15.792

Continental European arbitrators often prefer taking control of the witnesses themselves, by questioning them first, before the parties' counsel conduct their examination.[511] In our experience, this practice is quickly changing in favour of the common law practice, described above. 15.793

Parties should consider in advance the position they wish to take with respect to the presentation of witness testimony and the hearing of an expert. These matters may be discussed and agreed at the time of signing the Terms of Reference, but also thereafter. In the absence of any agreement, the Arbitral Tribunal is likely to issue a procedural order setting forth the ways witness testimony is to be presented and examined. 15.794

(i) Examination by the Arbitral Tribunal (the less frequent method): Will the examination of the witnesses be conducted by the presiding arbitrator? If so, do the parties have the right to question the witness freely after examination by the Arbitral Tribunal, and if so, directly, or only through the Arbitral Tribunal? 15.795

(ii) Examination by counsel (the more frequent method): If witnesses are to be presented and examined by a party and cross-examined by the adversary, are any specific limitations on the method of examination envisaged? It is current in ICC practice to permit a witness on direct examination to deliver an essentially narrative statement, punctuated by questions by the counsel who has presented the witness. 15.796

(iii) Extent of cross-examination and redirect: Where examination of a witness is conducted principally by the Arbitral Tribunal or by counsel to the party presenting the witness, the adverse party should be entitled to cross-examine the witness. The party calling the witness, is he entitled to a redirect examination? 15.797

(iv) Depositions: A deposition is a written record of oral testimony given prior to hearing and without the presence of the Arbitral Tribunal. Both parties are represented at the taking 15.798

(Helbing & Lichtenhahn, Basel, 2005) 227; Gélinas, P.A., 'Evidence through witnesses' in *Arbitration and Oral Evidence*, ICC Dossier 2004, ICC Publication no 689, 29, 31. More generally: IBA Working Party, 'Commentary on the New IBA Rules of Evidence in International Commerical Arbitration' (January 2000) *IBA Int'l Bus Lawyer,* 14; Bühler, M.W. and Dorgan, C., 'Witness Testimony Pursuant to the 1999 IBA Rules of Evidence in International Commercial Arbitration—Novel or Tested Standards?' (2000) 17 *J Int'l Arb* no 1, 3, 18.

[511] Bühler/Dorgan, *op cit*, 3.

of the deposition of the witness. The written record may be filed in the litigation or arbitration. Pre-trial depositions are an important element in American court litigation but not frequently used in ICC arbitration. While the parties in an ICC arbitration may agree on pre-trial depositions, ICC arbitrators are unlikely to order any such depositions or to intervene in that process. The arbitrators will in any event be reluctant to order a deposition outside the place of arbitration and in their absence, but may authorize it at the request of a party also outside the place of arbitration.

15.799 (v) Expert witnesses: In cases involving technical issues parties frequently wish to present evidence and testimony by experts whom they have consulted, whether the Arbitral Tribunal desires to be aided by a neutral expert or not. The calling of expert witnesses occurs irrespective whether the parties come from civil law or common law jurisdictions. The Rules explicitly state that a party can appoint its own expert witness.[512]

15.800 The testimony of the expert witness will normally be provided in the form of a report submitted in advance of the hearing. The written report is the foundation upon which the oral examination of the expert witness is built. The latter will be allowed to defend his views in response to questions from both the tribunal and the parties' counsel.[513]

15.801 The evidence submitted to an Arbitral Tribunal is generally not subject to any specific rules of evidence. As noted for example in the IBA Rules of Evidence, it is up to the Arbitral Tribunal to decide the weight to be given to particular items of evidence.[514] The procedure presented in the IBA Rules of Evidence is adopted in many international arbitrations, as it provides the lawyers of the parties with the flexibility of testing the evidence while allowing for questioning by the Tribunal.[515]

(5) Article 20(4): appointing an expert

15.802 Not only the parties, but also the Arbitral Tribunal may appoint an expert to give a view on disputed issues. The power given in Art 20(4) is an emanation of the arbitrator's general power 'to establish the facts of the case by all appropriate means', Art 20(1). In practice, the expert will be asked to look into technical issues, typically where the arbitrators lack the expertise and have no means to assess themselves the veracity of a contention.

15.803 The Arbitral Tribunal will rarely appoint an expert upon its own motion, but rather at the request of one or both parties. It will only do so if the parties, or one of them, is willing to advance the costs thereof.[516] Should the Arbitral Tribunal refuse such request, it has to justify its decision in a procedural order or in the award to avoid due process issues.

---

[512] Art 20(3). See also Arts 5 and 6 of the IBA Rules of Evidence that distinguish between party-appointed and tribunal-appointed experts. Schlosser, P. *op cit*, 775.

[513] 'Witness Statements' in A. Héritier Lachat and L. Hirsch (eds), *De Lege Ferenda—Réflexions sur le droit désirable en l'honneur du Professeur Alain Hirsch* (Slatkine, Geneva, 2004) 95.

[514] See Art 8 of the IBA Rules on the Taking of Evidence in International Commercial Arbitration that gives a point of reference to witness procedure in hearings. The text of the IBA Rules can be downloaded from <http://www.ibanet.org>.

[515] See Bühler/Dorgan, *op cit*, 17. See also ICC, *Arbitration and Oral Evidence* (ICC Publishing, Paris, 2005); Peter, W., 'Witness "Conferencing"' (2002) 18 *Arb Int'l* no 1, 47.

[516] Sec *infra* Art 31, para 15.1134; Voser, N. and Mueller, A., 'Appointment of Experts by the Arbitral Tribunal: the Civil Law Perspective' (2006) 7 *Business L Int'l* no 1, 73. For examples of a Tribunal-appointed

Where the Arbitral Tribunal decides to appoint an expert it is free to select him or her at its discretion. The Arbitral Tribunal may find it useful to make an enquiry at the ICC International Centre for Expertise, another service offered by the ICC. The Centre is located in Paris at the same address as the Court Secretariat. It establishes, upon demand, a proposal of one or more names of experts for any particular dispute. Its services are available both to ICC arbitrators and parties, at any time.[517] **15.804**

Defining the expert's Terms of Reference is incumbent on the Arbitral Tribunal in consultation with the parties.[518] **15.805**

The costs of an expert are not included in the general advance on costs paid by the parties to the ICC, but regulated by a separate provision in App III, Art. 1(11). Therefore, unless one or both parties advance the fees for the expert, the arbitrator will not appoint him, or if he was already appointed, not authorize him to start with his mission. **15.806**

Article 20(4) remains silent as to how the Arbitral Tribunal should assess the expert's activities and conclusions.[519] In ICC Case no 12131, an Arbitral Tribunal sitting in Switzerland pointed out as to the expert's statements: **15.807**

> 207. Given the Arbitral Tribunal did not have the specialized knowledge with respect to the technical issues raised....
>
> (...)
>
> 209. In terms of weighing the evidence, one should bear in mind that the Tribunal is not bound by the Expert's finding. However, should the arbitrators decide to have differing opinions from those of the Expert, they ought to provide grounds for their solution in order to preclude any oversight or violation of the right to be heard (see Poudret/Besson, *Droit comparé de l'arbitrage international*, edn 2002, p 595). In other words, there are no reasons for the Arbitral Tribunal to divert from the Expert's findings, unless there is an objectively justified material and different solution (...).[520]

(6) Article 20(5): Production of documents

The authority of an Arbitral Tribunal to order the production of documents is explicit since Art 20(5) authorizes the Arbitral Tribunal to summon a party to provide 'additional evidence'. The conditions under which the production of documents may be requested by the Arbitral Tribunal is an area where there exist marked differences between common law and civil law practices, and these issues are controversial and lively discussed.[521] Article 3(3) of **15.808**

expert, see ICC Case no 6057 (1990), (1993) J Int'l Arb no 4, 1067, and ICC Case no 6673 (1992), (1992) J Int'l Arb no 4, 992, note Hascher. Regarding the consequences of failure of one party to cooperate with the Tribunal-appointed expert, see ICC case no 6497 (1994), (1999) YBCA Vol. XXIV, 71. For an example of a Tribunal-appointed expert and a discussion of his procedure and report in the context of the Iran-US Claims Tribunal, see *Ebrahimi v Iran* Award in cases nos. 44 46 47 (560–44/46/47–3) of 12 October 1994, 30 Iran–USCTR 170.

[517] See *supra* Introduction, para 15.42.

[518] Bühler, M.W., 'Technical Expertise', *op cit*, 138 *et seq.*

[519] See Art 6, IBA Rules of Evidence thereto.

[520] ICC Case no 12131 (2006) (Partial Award), unreported.

[521] Lionnet, K., 'Once Again: Is Discovery of Documents Appropriate in International Arbitration?' in *Liber Amicorum in honour of Robert Briner* (ICC Publishing, Paris, 2005) 491, 492; Kaufman-Kohler, G.,

the IBA Rules of Evidence gives helpful suggestions that may be adopted in situations where different legal traditions meet.

15.809 The issue has been a matter of much debate, and is a matter of great concern to many parties.[522] The origin of the debate is the difference in practice between common law countries and civil law countries with respect to providing evidence. For American litigators, documentary discovery, interrogatories and deposition discovery are an integral part of the judicial fact-finding process.[523] In addition, in American procedure, third parties can be required to provide evidence with respect to court proceedings. English court procedure provides for documentary disclosure by one party to the other party if the documents relate to the matters in issue in the case and, in exceptional cases, for disclosure by third parties. These common law approaches have been contrasted with the civil law approach, where it is basically up to each party to obtain and submit the evidence on which it relies.[524] However, in considering these approaches, it should be noted that American courts and English law both favour limited discovery in arbitration,[525] although the difficulty lies in the practical application of this rule to concrete requests for document production.

15.810 In our view, there is no serious doubt that ICC arbitrators have the power to order the production of documents by a party, since this is part of the authority inherent to their function, and falls within their general power to 'establish the facts of the case by all appropriate means', Art 20(1). The discussions in a particular case turn upon the extent of the production.

15.811 ICC arbitrators typically decline to order broad discovery of documents that would open the doors to 'fishing expeditions' in which parties seek to obtain documents favourable to

'Discovery in International Arbitration: How Much is Too Much?' *SchiedsVZ* (January/February 2004) 13; King D.B. and Bosman L., 'Rethinking Discovery in International Arbitration: Beyond the Common Law/Civil Law Divide' (2001) 12 *ICC ICArb Bull* no 1, 24; Cremades, B., 'Powers of the arbitrators to decide on the admissibility of evidence and to organise the production of evidence' (1999) 10 *ICC ICArb Bull* no 1, 49.

[522] Lionnet, K., *op cit* 492; Kaufman-Kohler, G., 'Discovery in International Arbitration', *op cit*, 13; Bernini, 'The civil law approach to discovery: a comparative overview of the taking of evidence in the anglo-american and continental arbitration systems' in L.W. Newman and R.D. Hill. (eds), *The Leading Arbitrators' Guide to International Arbitration* (Juris Publishing/Staempfli Publishers, 2004) 269; Brower, C. N. and Sharpe, J. K., 'Determining the extent of discovery and dealing with request for discovery: perspectives from the common law' in L.W. Newman and R.D. Hill (eds), *The Leading Arbitrators' Guide to International Arbitration* (Juris Publishing/Staempfli Publishers, 2004) 307; King/Bosman, *op cit*, 24; Cremades, B., *op cit*, 49; Goldman, B., 'Instance judiciaire et instance arbitrale internationale' in *Etudes offertes à Pierre Bellet* (Litec, Paris, 1991) 219; Briner, R., 'The Evaluation of Evidence: Some Observations Based on the Practice of the Iran-United States Claims Tribunal' in *Liber Amicorum Thomas Bär and Robert Karrer* (Helbing & Lichtenhahn, Basel, 2004) 41.

[523] Deposition discovery involves questioning of a witness by the opposing lawyer, under oath and almost invariably not in the presence of the judge or arbitrator.

[524] This is not to say that judges in civil law countries cannot provide a party significant assistance in obtaining documents, although not as a matter of routine and in specific circumstances only.

[525] See eg *COMSAT Corp v NSF*, 190 F3d 269 (4th Cir, 1999): 'Parties to a private arbitration agreement forego certain procedural rights attendant to formal litigation in return for a more efficient and cost-effective resolution of their disputes' cited by Webster, 'Party Control in International Arbitration', *op cit*, 125, n 15; see also s 33 of the English Arbitration Act 1996.

establish their case. Discovery entails costs, and big companies can 'crush' smaller ones with massive discovery demands. This reluctance to order broad discovery is also explained by the fact that ICC arbitrators have no power to compel production or to sanction a party for failure to comply.

In the authors' experience, which we share with other practitioners, there is a growing acceptance of limited discovery of documents in international arbitration.[526] **15.812**

Finally, legal privilege may be an issue in document production since a party may be prevented, under the law applicable to him, from producing a document ordered by the Tribunal. Privilege is related to national law and the place where a lawyer (or other professional) practices. The parties have to be treated equally and the Arbitral Tribunal is frequently confronted with due process issues when dealing with questions of privilege.[527] **15.813**

(7) Article 20(6): Documents arbitration only

Under Art 20(6) the arbitrator can proceed on the sole basis of the documents, unless a party requests a hearing. This rule may be seen as a detail without great practical importance; the number of cases that are decided without a hearing is very small. **15.814**

The Arbitral Tribunal must inform the parties in advance of its intention to proceed without a hearing so as to give the parties an opportunity to object and to request a hearing. In the authors' opinion, there are only a few instances where it would be advisable for a party not to have a hearing. While the virtues of hearings may sometimes be overestimated, they should certainly not be underestimated either: oral argument by skilled counsel often forcefully highlight the truly dispositive issues and underlying facts to the Arbitral Tribunal. A hearing may also allow the Arbitral Tribunal to engage with the parties in a dialogue, which in turn may help in clarifying 'grey' areas, and limiting the issues in contention. **15.815**

A documents only arbitration may be appropriate when solely legal questions are at stake, which the parties have extensively covered in their written pleadings. But for the reasons set out above, even then the authors would generally favour a hearing on the legal issues. Again, it has to be stressed that an award is not subject to appeal, so that the parties have only one opportunity to plead the merits of their case. **15.816**

A hearing may not be required when the claims are not seriously disputed, and in particular when the Respondent does not participate in the arbitration. It might then be a futile and unnecessarily costly exercise to hold a hearing. The classic example is goods sold, but unpaid. When the non-payment seems to be based on no other reason than the buyer's unwillingness to pay the purchase price and when neither party requests a hearing, a decision on the basis of documents may prove to be appropriate. **15.817**

---

[526] See for a general discussion Bühler/Webster, ICC Handbook, *op cit*, paras 20–56 *et seq* and paras 20–70 *et seq*.

[527] See eg European Court of First Instance, 17 September 2007, *Akzo Nobel Chemicals Ltd and Akcros Chemicals Ltd v Commission of the European Communities*, joined case 62003A0253 (T-122/03 and T-253/03) (Commission's powers of investigation—documents seized in the course of an investigation—legal professional privilege protecting communications between lawyers and their clients—admissibility). See also Rosher, P., 'Legal privilege et confidentialité des communications avocat-client en matière d'arbitrage international', *op cit*, 21.

(8) Article 20(7): Protecting trade secrets

15.818 Article 20(7) gives the Arbitral Tribunal the authority to take measures for the protection of trade secrets and confidential information. The general issue of confidentiality is whether the details of the arbitration, the documents produced and the evidence adduced in the arbitration and the final award must be kept confidential between the parties, their counsel and/or the arbitrators. This general problem has led to much debate in the international arbitration community following notably the decisions of the High Court of Australia in the *Esso* case[528] and of the Supreme Court of Sweden in the *Bulbank* case.[529]

15.819 Confidentiality is of particular significance in intellectual property matters because in most licence and franchise agreements the information being licensed and transferred is of a secret, and thus confidential nature: it is common to find provisions written into licence and know-how agreements providing an obligation to keep the information confidential. Such confidentiality clauses rarely extend expressly to arbitration procedures. [530]

15.820 Article 20(7) deals with the power of the arbitrator to regulate the problem of confidentiality in the course of the arbitration. It is inspired by recent case law and the WIPO Arbitration Rules. But unlike the WIPO Rules, which are very detailed, the ICC Rules provide merely a general statement giving the arbitrators the power to take appropriate measures according to the circumstances of each individual case.

15.821 The measures for protection could:

- identify the specific areas of confidentiality, eg witness statements, transcripts, documents produced by a party in the arbitration, and the award; and
- confirm that contractual obligations of confidentiality and secrecy contained, eg, in licence, know-how or other agreements must be upheld, and determine what their effect will be on the arbitration and the parties.

15.822 If the arbitrators take measures, they must consider the sanctions for non-compliance with such measures. Measures should be limited in time and not persist in perpetuity. Exceptions must be made for a party's obligation under law or otherwise to disclose information, eg the party may be forced to disclose, under a stock listing agreement, to its bankers, shareholders, insurers etc. In many instances an Arbitral Tribunal's protective order will only have effect during the course of the arbitration. A party wishing to ensure confidentiality after the end of the arbitration could seek an extended or permanent order before a court of law, or, as part of the award, if the Terms of Reference provide for such claim,[531] and if there is a legal basis for such claim.

---

[528] *Esso Australia Resources Ltd v The Honourable Sidney James Plowman* (1995), 183 CLR 10; also in (1995), 11 *Arb Int'l*, 235.

[529] *A.I. Trade Finance Inc (AIT) USA*, in Bulgarian Foreign Trade Bank (Bulbank), Bulgaria, case N. NT 1881–99, judgment rendered on 27 October 2000, published and commented in Stockholm Arb Rep 2000: 2, 137.

[530] See Bühler, M.W, 'Les clauses de confidentialité dans le commerce international' (2002) 3 *RDAI*, 359.

[531] See *supra* Art 18, para 15.731.

Article 20(7) is a consequence of the interest that parties generally have in preserving the confidentiality of arbitral proceedings. In the authors' view, such interest is normally best served if the arbitral process is covered by confidentiality. Confidentiality should remain the norm in all ICC arbitrations, whether or not the arbitrators have taken particular measures of protection.[532] **15.823**

Article 21. Hearings

(1) When a hearing is to be held, the Arbitral Tribunal, giving reasonable notice, shall summon the parties to appear before it on the day and at the place fixed by it.

(2) If any of the parties, although duly summoned, fails to appear without valid excuse, the Arbitral Tribunal shall have the power to proceed with the hearing.

(3) The Arbitral Tribunal shall be in full charge of the hearings, at which all the parties shall be entitled to be present. Save with the approval of the Arbitral Tribunal and the parties, persons not involved in the proceedings shall not be admitted.

(4) The parties may appear in person or through duly authorized representatives. In addition, they may be assisted by advisers.

(1) Introduction

Article 21 deals with hearings, without giving a definition thereof. Whenever the Arbitral Tribunal meets with the parties, be it to sign the Terms of Reference, discuss procedural issues, listen to testimonial evidence or to the parties' argument, a hearing takes place within the meaning of Art 21. **15.824**

Such hearing will normally bring the parties physically together, but may also take place by means of visioconference.[533] Although a telephone conference between the parties and the Arbitral Tribunal will, in the absence of visual presence, not qualify as a hearing, the Rules contained in Art 21 will apply *mutatis mutandis*. **15.825**

The stipulation in Art 21 must be read together with Art 20(2). There is no absolute requirement under the Rules to convene a hearing at all, but it is done in nearly every case. The arbitrators, if not the parties, usually want to meet the parties and counsel in order to get a better understanding of the case and in order to have an opportunity to put questions to and have an exchange with the parties and their counsel.[534] **15.826**

(2) Article 21(1): Calling a hearing

A hearing should be prepared as early as possible. The experienced arbitrator discusses tentative dates with the parties' counsel in the early stages of the case. A good opportunity **15.827**

[532] For a more detailed discussion see Bühler/Webster, ICC Handbook, *op cit*, paras 20–86 *et seq*, paras 20–92 and 20–97; see Paris, 22 January 2004, *Société National for Fishing and Marketing Nafimco v Société Foster Wheeler Trading Company AG*, (2004) *Rev arb* no 3, 657. See also Loquin, E., 'Les obligations de confidentialité dans l'arbitrage' (2006) *Rev arb* no 2, 324; Müller, Ch, 'La confidentialité en arbitrage commercial international: un trompe-l'oeil? On est souvent satisfait d'être trompé par soi-même' (2005) *ASA Bull* no 2, 216; Dimolitsa, A., 'Quid encore de la confidentialité?' in *Mélanges dédiés à François Knoepfler* (Helbing & Lichtenhahn, Basel, 2005) 249; Cavalieros, Ph., 'La confidentialité de l'arbitrage' (2005) *Les Cahiers de l'Arbitrage* no 3, Gazette du Palais 14–15 December 2005, 6.

[533] See Schäfer, E., 'Videoconferencing in Arbitration' (2003) 14 *ICC ICArb Bull* no1, 35, describes in much detail the many aspects a Tribunal needs to consider prior to authorizing and proceeding with videoconferencing as an aspect of visioconference.

[534] See *supra* Art 20, para 15.788.

to do so is when the Arbitral Tribunal and the parties meet to agree upon and sign the Terms of Reference. At that stage of the case, the parties and the arbitrators have an overview of the case and have a good idea of the issues and the evidence required so that they can plan the length of a hearing. Pursuant to Art 18(4), the Arbitral Tribunal is required at such stage to establish a provisional calendar.

15.828 Since arbitrators and counsel acting in ICC arbitrations are often busy people whose calendars fill up quickly, it is safe to block dates for a hearing and to provide for reserve dates in case the hearing cannot take place on the first dates. To stay on top of events, the arbitrator thus gives procedural directions by fixing tentative hearing dates in the provisional timetable (Art 18(4)), which the arbitrator then confirms when the time is ripe for the hearing by a formal letter or procedural order summoning the parties to attend the hearing. The requirement of giving 'reasonable notice' under Art 21(1) is thereby fulfilled.

15.829 The place of the hearing is normally the place of the arbitration, see Art 14(1). As discussed above, the Arbitral Tribunal may, after consultation with the parties, conduct the hearings at another place that it deems appropriate, Art 14(2).[535]

15.830 The convocation to the hearing should not only indicate the time and the place but also inform the parties of the procedure to be followed at the hearing, if not already done in the Terms of Reference or in a procedural direction given by the Arbitral Tribunal. Particularly in cases where counsel, parties and arbitrators come from countries with different legal traditions it is necessary to be explicit in the convocation to the hearing with respect to issues that are likely to raise questions and pose problems, first among which is the hearing of witnesses.

15.831 Many ICC arbitrations take place in the conference rooms of a major hotel. Such a choice has the advantage of being neutral and easily accessible for all people concerned although it is rather costly. Hotels are also able to provide conference aid material, make suitable arrangements for food and drink, and offer travel services. To preserve confidentiality, the Arbitral Tribunal will instruct the hotel management to make neutral references to the arbitration on the welcome board displayed in the entrance hall, for instance with the mere reference to 'ICC arbitration', or 'ICC Case No' (ie without the name of the parties); or with the name of the chairman only, without a case number.

15.832 In some cases, hearings take place at the offices of one of the arbitrators, often, but not exclusively, at those of the chairman, or even in the offices of counsel of one of the parties. A local Chamber of Commerce or congress centre may also be used.

15.833 The ICC has concluded a number of agreements with other institutions around the world regarding the use of their facilities as hearing rooms. The counsel in charge of the file at the ICC Court Secretariat will inform the arbitrators hereof upon demand. In Paris, at the ICC headquarters, conference rooms and conference services for the conduct of arbitrations are now available. Because of high demand, early booking is essential.[536] More recently, in 2008,

---

[535] See *supra* para 15.592.

[536] The booking conditions can be obtained by calling the ICC at +33 1 49 53 29 05.

in order to respond to a growing demand from the business and legal communities, the ICC opened a hearing facility for arbitration and other forms of commercial dispute resolution. The hearing centre is located in Paris and can be contacted either via internet at: <http://www.icchearingcentre.org> or by telephone at: +33 1 49 53 33 00.

Another issue is the number or periods of hearings to be decided, if more than one hearing **15.834**
is envisaged. The UNCITRAL Notes on Organising Arbitral Proceedings reflect thereto:

> 76. Attitudes vary as to whether hearings should be held in a single period of hearings or in separate periods, especially when more than a few days are needed to complete the hearings. According to some arbitrators, the entire hearings should normally be held in a single period, even if the hearings are to last for more than a week. Other arbitrators in such cases tend to schedule separate periods of hearings. In some cases issues to be decided are separated, and separate hearings set for those issues, with the aim that oral presentation on those issues will be completed within the allotted time. Among the advantages of one period of hearings are that it involves less travel costs, memory will not fade, and it is unlikely that people representing a party will change. On the other hand, the longer the hearings, the more difficult it may be to find early dates acceptable to all participants. Furthermore, separate periods of hearings may be easier to schedule, the subsequent hearings may be tailored to the development of the case, and the period between the hearings leaves time for analysing the records and negotiations between the parties aimed at narrowing the points at issue by agreement.[537]

(3) Article 21(2): Failure by a party to appear

If a party fails to appear at a hearing it must have a valid excuse; otherwise the Arbitral **15.835**
Tribunal will proceed with the hearing. What constitutes a valid excuse is not defined in the Rules and it is left to the arbitrators to decide in each case in light of the circumstances whether a valid excuse exists or not. For example, if a party has created or contributed to the legal impediment that prevents it from attending at a hearing, the Arbitral Tribunal may decide that the excuse is not valid. Similarly, financial reasons rarely give rise to a 'valid excuse', unless the issue is such as to virtually render the arbitration agreement unconscionable.

If the Arbitral Tribunal proceeds and makes an award in spite of a party's failure to appear **15.836**
the Arbitral Tribunal should mention in the award the circumstances and the reasons for its decision to proceed, thereby anticipating possible difficulties at the future enforcement of the award (see Art 35).

Insolvency proceedings may constitute another reason for a party's absence at a hearing. **15.837**
Under the law of the place of incorporation of the insolvent party, proceedings may have to be stayed pending completion of certain formalities due to the insolvency. The trend nowadays is, however, to continue arbitration proceedings where arbitration may take place under the applicable law.[538] This is an area in which much development presently takes place.

[537] The UNCITRAL Notes may be downloaded from <http://www.uncitral.org/pdf/english/texts/arbitration/arb-notes/arb-notes-e.pdf>; see also ICC Publication no 843, *op cit*, paras 36 (Need for a hearing) and 72 (minimizing the length and number of hearings).

[538] For a discussion under American and French law see for example Rosell, J. and Prager, H., 'International Arbitration and Bankruptcy: United States, France and the ICC' (2001) 18 *J Int'l Arb* no 4, 417; see also

15.838 If the Arbitral Tribunal proceeds with the hearing in one party's absence, the absent party has no right under the Rules to be heard at a later time, unless, of course, it had a valid excuse for not being present. The proceedings are considered validly held and the Arbitral Tribunal should proceed to making an award.

15.839 A party's failure to appear at a hearing is not to be considered as an admission of the other party's claim. Thus the Arbitral Tribunal is not entitled to issue a default award. The Claimant must still prove its case and the Arbitral Tribunal is required to examine all the evidence. In practice, in cases where a party fails to appear the Arbitral Tribunal often bends over backwards in its efforts to convince itself that the Claimant's claim should be accepted. How far the Arbitral Tribunal should go will very much depend on the type of claims and the evidence submitted. If the Arbitral Tribunal suddenly becomes the 'devil's advocate' for the Respondent, this would not be compatible with its duty to remain impartial and is generally not desirable.

(4) Article 21(3): The Arbitral Tribunal's power to conduct the hearing

15.840 Careful planning by the Arbitral Tribunal and information to the parties of its plans are essential elements for an efficient hearing. Several questions arise before or during a hearing that need to be considered and answered in a timely manner. The UNCITRAL's Notes on Organising Arbitral Proceedings mentioned above may be a useful help in the planning. Some arbitrators consider it useful to limit the aggregate amount of time each party has for any of the following: (i) making oral statements; (ii) questioning its own witnesses and those of the other party.[539] In general, the same aggregate amount of time is considered appropriate for each party, unless the Arbitral Tribunal considers that a different allocation is justified. A different allocation is generally justified where the number of witnesses for each party is not the same. Before deciding, the Arbitral Tribunal may wish to consult the parties as to how much time they think they will need.

15.841 Practices differ as to whether the parties should make opening and/or closing statements and their level of detail; the sequence in which the Claimant and the Respondent present their opening statements, arguments, witnesses and other evidence; and whether the Respondent or the Claimant has the last word. In view of such differences it may foster efficiency of the proceedings if the Arbitral Tribunal clarifies to the parties, in advance of the hearings, the manner in which it will conduct the hearings. The arbitrator's role in explaining the procedure, the advantages and disadvantages of the various options under

---

Fouchard Ph., 'Arbitrage et faillite' (1998) *Rev arb* no 3, 471. For Swizerland, see Lévy, L., 'Insolvency in Arbitration (Swiss Law)' (2005) *Int'l Arb L Rev* Issue no 1, 23; Brown-Berset, D. and Lévy, L., 'Faillite et arbitrage' (1998) 16 *ASA Bull* no 4, 664; Mantilla-Serrano, F., 'International Arbitration and Insolvency Proceedings' (1995) 11 *Arb Int'l* no 1, 51; Croze, H. and Reinhard, Y., 'Procédures collectives et arbitrage: Conseils pratiques aux parties et aux arbitres' (2005) *JCP Entreprises et Affaires* no 14, 614; see also Cass Com, 14 2004, *Prodim v Logidis*, (2004) *Rev arb* no 3, 591, note Ancel; Cass Com, 2 June 2004, *Gaussin v Société Alstom Power Turbomachines and Industry v Société Alstom Power Turbomachines*, (2004) *Rev arb* no 3, 596, note Ancel.

[539] See UNCITRAL Notes on Organising Arbitral Proceedings, *op cit*, paras 78–9.

consideration will be an important element in allowing the parties to understand and accept the conduct of the hearing.[540]

As regards a record of the hearings the Arbitral Tribunal should decide, preferably after consulting the parties, on the method of recording oral statements and testimony. The most useful, though costly, method is for a professional stenographer to prepare verbatim transcripts for each hearing day, often available the same evening or the next day. In many common law jurisdictions professional court reporters are part of the court systems and therefore easy to find. In Europe court-reporters with experience in international arbitration proceedings are readily available in London, Dublin and Paris. It is usually not too difficult to have them fly to even distant places of arbitration. A verbatim hearing transcript is a very reliable record of oral testimonial evidence and easy to use when preparing post-hearing briefs. A written record may be combined with tape-recording, so as to enable reference to the tape in case of disagreement over the written record. **15.842**

In the Nordic countries it is customary to tape-record the hearing of witnesses or the parties. A tape-recording that has not been transcribed is rarely of particular help to the parties. It is cumbersome and time-consuming to find the relevant passage on a tape, and thereafter to transcribe it. Likewise, the cost of transcribing a tape is rarely a cost-saving factor compared to a verbatim transcript. Whenever the terms at stake in the arbitration are important it seems preferable to choose verbatim transcripts. **15.843**

When it comes to closing arguments some legal counsel are accustomed to giving notes summarizing their oral arguments to the Arbitral Tribunal and to the other party or parties. If such notes are presented, this is usually done during the hearings or shortly thereafter; in some cases, the notes are sent before the hearing. In order to avoid surprise, treat the parties equally and facilitate preparations for the hearings, advance clarification is advisable as to whether submitting such notes is acceptable and the time for doing so. Rather than having closing argument the parties may settle for post-hearing briefs. **15.844**

The arbitrator's decision settling procedural issues can take various forms. It can be an award (interim or partial) although in practice this is rarely done, or a decision, often in the form of a procedural order. **15.845**

Arbitrators may have express or inherent powers to make interlocutory orders relevant to the arbitration. Such orders are generally without binding force,[541] have no *res judicata* effect and cannot be challenged as awards, but there exist exceptions in national law and **15.846**

[540] On the power of the Arbitral Tribunal to conduct the proceedings, see Karrer P. A., 'Freedom of an arbitral tribunal to conduct proceedings', *op cit*; Vicuña, O., 'The binding nature of procedural orders in international arbitration' (1999) 10 *ICC ICArb Bull* no 1, 38; Donovan, D.F., 'Powers of the arbitrators to issue procedural orders, including interim measures of protection, and the obligations of parties to abide by such orders' (1999) 10 *ICC ICArb Bull* no 1, 57; Böckstiegel, K.-H., 'Major Criteria for International Arbitration in Shaping Efficient Procedure', *op cit*, 49.

[541] Jarvin, S., 'Les décisions de procédure des arbitres peuvent-elles faire l'objet d'un recours juridictionnel?' (1998) *Rev arb* nono 4, 611.

various arbitration rules. Compliance by the parties with the arbitrator's orders is voluntary in the absence of a particular provision of national law.[542]

15.847 The state courts at the seat of arbitration are generally not empowered to sanction non-compliance with arbitrators' interlocutory orders, but exceptions exist such as Art 183(2) of the Swiss Private International Law[543] and Art 1041 of the 1997 German Arbitration Act incorporated in the German Code of Civil Procedure, which provide that Arbitral Tribunals have the power to order provisional or conservatory measures and request assistance of the courts if a party does not comply. In any event, national courts normally retain jurisdiction to order interlocutory measures.

(5) Article 21(4): Right of attendance at the hearing

15.848 Only the persons involved in the proceedings can be admitted to the hearing, see Art 21(3). The parties are in the majority of cases represented by counsel. The term 'authorized representative' in Art 21(4) does not designate the party's counsel, but a person who, under the law applicable to the party—in the case of a company the law at the place of its incorporation—is entitled to represent the party, ie a chairman of the board, a manager, a general director, a chief executive officer, or the like.

15.849 There is no requirement under the Rules that a party must be represented by a lawyer. If a lawyer appears on behalf of a party there is no requirement under the Rules that he must submit a power of attorney; it is up to the Arbitral Tribunal to require such power. A prudent Arbitral Tribunal is likely to require from the attorneys that they submit an original power of attorney. This is not to be viewed as a sign of mistrust, but rather as a measure of 'orderly housekeeping'. It avoids any questioning and surprise in the future, and ultimately is in accordance with the arbitrator's duty to 'make every effort to make sure that the award is enforceable at law', Art 35.[544]

15.850 In some countries there are restrictions with respect to foreign legal counsel's right to appear in international arbitrations in the country. In the past, this was a problem in Singapore and China,[545] but this anomaly seems now to have been resolved in these two countries. California remains the possible exception.[546]

[542] Thus, eg, an Arbitral Tribunal proceeding under the ICSID Rules found while it could recommend provisional measures, this would not prohibit the parties from any recourse to a national court, see French *Cour de Cassation,* 18 November 1986 *(Atlantic Triton v Revolutionary People's Republic of Guinea and Soguipêche), YBCA* (1987) XII, 183, n 1.

[543] See Lalive, P., Poudret, J.-F. and Reymond, C., *Le droit de l'arbitrage interne et international en Suisse* (Payot, Lausanne, 1989) 365.

[544] See Art 35.

[545] As regards Singapore, see Rivkin, *YBCA* (1991) XVI, 402, and China, see (1995) *ASA Bull,* 32, 50.

[546] See *Birbower, Montabano, Condon & Frank PC v The Superior Court of Santa Clara,* 949 P 2d 1 (Cal 1998); see also Holtzmann, H. and Donovan, D.F., 'United States Country Report' in Paulsson, J. (ed) *ICCA Handbook,* Supp 28 (Kluwer, 1999). The California Rules of Court were modified in 2004 in order to permit any US-qualified lawyer to represent a party in an arbitration (r 966). However, it remains unclear whether lawyers admitted to foreign bars can represent parties in national or international arbitration.

Article 22. Closing of the proceedings

(1) When it is satisfied that the parties have had a reasonable opportunity to present their cases, the Arbitral Tribunal shall declare the proceedings closed. Thereafter, no further submission or argument may be made, or evidence produced, unless requested or authorized by the Arbitral Tribunal.

(2) When the Arbitral Tribunal has declared the proceedings closed, it shall indicate to the Secretariat an approximate date by which the draft award will be submitted to the Court for approval pursuant to Article 27. Any postponement of that date shall be communicated to the Secretariat by the Arbitral Tribunal.

(1) Article 22(1): Declaring the proceedings closed

After the parties have had an opportunity to present their cases the arbitration enters into its final phase: the deliberation among the arbitrators, followed by their decision. While in the past some arbitrators, as a matter of routine, declared the proceedings closed as of a given time, others did not, thus leaving it up to the parties to make further submissions of briefs and documents whenever they saw fit. Whenever one party made late submissions, the Arbitral Tribunal usually accepted it, the other party requested to respond to it, and was normally allowed to do so. This prolonged the duration of the arbitration. The Rules now make it clear that all arbitrators must apply the same routine. **15.851**

The rule that, at an appropriate stage in a judicial or arbitral proceeding, the judge or arbitrator declares proceedings closed is familiar to civil law lawyers. Thus, s 296a of the German Code of Civil Procedure provides that after closing the oral proceedings (*nach Schluss der mündlichen Verhandlung*) the parties may not make any further statements. Likewise, under French law it is for the presiding judge to order the *clôture des débats*[547] after which neither party may present new arguments or evidence. French law applicable to domestic arbitrations contains a similar provision.[548] **15.852**

The arbitrator must be careful not to close the proceedings before it is convinced that each party has had a reasonable opportunity to present its case. When exercising its discretion to apply Art 22(1), the Arbitral Tribunal must be aware of its duty to 'ensure that each party has a reasonable opportunity to present its case', Art 15(2). In practice, an Arbitral Tribunal will regularly be well advised to consult the parties in respect of their intention to offer any further evidence, hear new witnesses or to make new submissions.[549] **15.853**

As was remarked above under Art 21, if a party fails to appear at a hearing without a valid excuse, the proceedings are nonetheless valid, and the Arbitral Tribunal can declare the proceedings closed under Art 22(1).[550] **15.854**

---

547 While this may be translated literally as the closing of the 'argument' (*débats*), in fact, no evidence may be produced either, after this date, in French court proceedings.

548 Art 1468 of the French Code of Civil Procedure, which reads as follows: 'The arbitrator shall fix the date on which the matter shall be submitted for deliberation (*mise en délibéré*). After that date, no claim can be made nor ground for a claim raised. No observation can be presented nor any document produced, unless it has been requested by the arbitrator.'

549 See Art 29 of the UNCITRAL Rules: 'The arbitral tribunal may inquire of the parties of they have any further proof to offer or witness to be heard, and, if there are none, it may declare the proceedings closed.'

550 See *supra* paras 15.838 *et seq.*

15.855 The result of the closing of the proceedings is that the parties may no longer make any further submission or argument nor produce any further evidence in the case. If any party should do so, then the Arbitral Tribunal may disregard it. A similar rule is contained in other arbitration rules.[551]

15.856 However, a further submission or argument may be made or further evidence may be produced after the closing of the proceedings when 'requested or authorized' by the Arbitral Tribunal. The Arbitral Tribunal may decide that it needs additional information about some aspect of the case. In this event, the Arbitral Tribunal may, on its own initiative, 'request' that the parties provide additional evidence or argument on that particular issue, see Art 20(5). Alternatively, one or more of the parties may request permission from the Arbitral Tribunal to submit additional arguments or provide further evidence, in which event the Arbitral Tribunal has discretion whether to 'authorize' such a request or not.[552]

15.857 It is suggested that where fresh evidence comes to light which could not reasonably have been produced before the closing of the proceedings or where all of the parties join in making the request, the request should ordinarily be granted. But where, for example, a party maintains that the time allocated to it was insufficient, the Arbitral Tribunal will need to decide the issue in light of all of the circumstances, including its obligation to provide the parties with a reasonably expeditious proceeding.[553] It is suggested that the Arbitral Tribunal only grant such requests in exceptional circumstances.[554] An incentive for an Arbitral Tribunal to grant such a request is that if it later proves to have been unjustified or unreasonable, the requesting party can usually be sanctioned sufficiently by being made to bear the additional costs incurred, or by an award of interest (if appropriate) against it, or both.[555]

15.858 The wording of Art 22(1) would seem to indicate that the closing of the entire proceedings in a case is meant, and not merely the closing of proceedings in relation to a specific issue or issues. The better view seems to be, however, that the proceedings can be closed whenever the Arbitral Tribunal intends to issue an award on a particular issue, whether on 'preliminary' issues dealing with jurisdiction, arbitrability of a claim, determination of the applicable rules of law or other matters. The same may apply when the Arbitral Tribunal

---

[551] Art 24 of the AAA Rules; Rule 38 of the ICSID Rules; Art 21.6 of the SIAC Rules; Art 29 of the UNCITRAL Rules; and Art 57 of the WIPO Rules, are similar, except that the AAA, SIAC and UNCITRAL rules refer to the closing of '(h)earing(s)', rather than to the broader expression, closing of 'proceedings'.

[552] See also Taylor, T. and Baruti, R., 'Reopening The Case After The Hearing—To What Extent And Under What Circumstances Should It Be Allowed?' *ASA Special Series* no 29, September 2007, 8 with references to cases of the Iran–USCTR.

[553] Sec Art 20(1) of the Rules which requires the Arbitral Tribunal to proceed within as short a time as possible to establish the facts of the case by all appropriate means and Art 24 of the Rules which requires that the Arbitral Tribunal render its final Award within six months although this time limit may be extended pursuant to a reasoned request from the Arbitral Tribunal or by the Court on its own initiative.

[554] In this connection, see r 38(2) of the ICSID Rules: 'Exceptionally, the Tribunal may, before the award has been rendered, reopen the proceedings of the ground that new evidence is forthcoming of such nature as to constitute a decision factor or that there is a vital need for clarification on certain points.' The UNCITRAL (Art 29) and WIPO (Art 57(b)) Rules also require exceptional circumstances to be shown to justify the reopening of hearings or proceedings.

[555] See Redfern/Hunter, *op cit*, 326. While they discuss this issue in relation to the closing of the hearing, their discussion is also relevant to the closing of proceedings.

wishes to decide on the merits of a party's liability, prior to deciding upon quantum. Each time an award is rendered, the Arbitral Tribunal will reopen the proceedings until it has rendered the final award. In proceeding in this manner, the Arbitral Tribunal will normally best be in a position to achieve the purpose of Art 22(1).

Article 22(1) does not specify in what form or to whom the declaration that the proceedings are closed should be made. While the declaration may initially be made orally, it is highly advisable that it be confirmed by a written order of the Tribunal. The declaration should be addressed to the parties and copied to the Secretariat.[556] The closing of proceedings is, and should be seen by the parties, to be an important step towards the conclusion of the arbitration. **15.859**

Should the Arbitral Tribunal realize during its deliberations and after having closed the proceedings, that it is not fully informed on all points necessary for the resolution of the dispute, it can order the parties to submit complementary documents or evidence, or provide additional explanations, and thereby expressly or implicitly declare the proceedings reopened. In practice, Arbitral Tribunals rarely make use of that facility, often out of fear that the type of question would indicate to the parties the outcome of the dispute. For instance, if an Arbitral Tribunal suddenly becomes concerned by the interest calculations made by the Claimant on its principle claims, and seeks a clarification from the Claimant, it would not be difficult to infer from such request for clarification that the Arbitral Tribunal will in principle uphold the Claimant's claims. **15.860**

(2) Article 22(2): Date of Submission of the draft award to the ICC

The Arbitral Tribunal must inform the ICC Court's Secretariat about the approximate date on which it will submit the draft award to the Court for scrutiny. **15.861**

The time the Arbitral Tribunal will require to prepare a draft award will depend upon the circumstances in each case. Nevertheless, the Arbitral Tribunal must commit itself to finish its work by a certain date. The members of the Arbitral Tribunal are obliged to give their work as arbitrators at least the same importance and urgency as their other pressing professional obligations. **15.862**

If the effect of requiring arbitrators to indicate a date to the Secretariat is to induce arbitrators to study the pleadings and evidence more closely earlier in the case so that, at the closing of the proceedings, they are better prepared to indicate when they should have completed the work, then so much the better. **15.863**

In any event, the Arbitral Tribunal is not bound by the date it has indicated to the Secretariat. The date is only an approximate one and Art 22(2) expressly envisages that the Arbitral Tribunal may communicate a postponement of that date to the Secretariat. While there is no requirement for the Arbitral Tribunal to supply the Secretariat with the reason for the **15.864**

[556] Art 3(1) of the Rules requires that a copy of any communication from the Arbitral Tribunal to the parties be sent to the Secretariat. In any event, the Secretariat will ordinarily know that the proceedings have been declared closed when it receives an indication of the approximate date that a draft Award will be submitted to the Court pursuant to Art 22(2).

postponement, the Arbitral Tribunal is, of course, not precluded from doing so. Ordinarily, the Arbitral Tribunal will not wish itself to appear as the body responsible for delay.

15.865 Delay in meeting the initial date or any later date will normally remain without sanction.[557] Arbitrators' fees are fixed by the Court. When fixing them, the Court is expressly authorized to take into account, among other things, 'the diligence of the arbitrator', 'the time spent', and 'the rapidity of the proceedings'.[558] Thus, if arbitrators fail, without explanation, to submit a draft award to the Court within a reasonable time, the Court may take this into account when fixing their remuneration.[559]

15.866 The Arbitral Tribunal may also provide the parties an approximate date for submitting their draft award to the Court. In doing so, a party's late tactical filings could be prevented, unless a request for reopening the proceedings by seeking to introduce a new document is based on good cause.[560]

15.867 Article 22(2) does not stipulate the form in which the Arbitral Tribunal shall indicate its estimated time for the drafting of the award. We conclude that it need not be made in writing. A simple telephone conversation between the chairman of the Arbitral Tribunal and the counsel in charge of the file at the ICC Court Secretariat would be sufficient. As a matter of good order, some record in writing would seem to be the better practice. While Art 22(2) does not require that the anticipated date of rendering the award be communicated to the parties, nothing prevents an Arbitral Tribunal from doing so. In some instance, by the end of the hearing the Arbitral Tribunal will give the parties some indication of when it expects to deliver its draft award to the ICC.

Article 23. Conservatory and interim measures

(1) Unless the parties have otherwise agreed, as soon as the file has been transmitted to it, the Arbitral Tribunal may, at the request of a party, order any interim or conservatory measure it deems appropriate. The Arbitral Tribunal may make the granting of any such measure subject to appropriate security being furnished by the requesting party. Any such measure shall take the form of an order, giving reasons, or of an award, as the Arbitral Tribunal considers appropriate.

(2) Before the file is transmitted to the Arbitral Tribunal, and in appropriate circumstances even thereafter, the parties may apply to any competent judicial authority for interim or conservatory measures. The application of a party to a judicial authority for such measures or for the implementation of any such measures ordered by an Arbitral Tribunal shall not be deemed to be an infringement or a waiver of the arbitration agreement and shall not affect the relevant powers reserved to the Arbitral Tribunal. Any such application and any measures taken by the judicial authority must be notified without delay to the Secretariat. The Secretariat shall inform the Arbitral Tribunal thereof.

557 Bühler/Jarvin, *op cit,* 251; Bühler, M.W., 'Costs in Arbitration: Some further considerations' in *Liber Amicorum in honour of Robert Briner* (ICC Publishing, Paris, 2005) 179. See Art 12, paras 8 *et seq*, for the possibility to remove an arbitrator that does not fulfil his functions on accordance with the Rules.

558 Art 2 of the App III to the ICC Rules of Arbitration entitled 'Arbitration Costs and Fees', see *infra* paras 15.1110 *et seq.*

559 See *infra* Art 31, para 15.1114.

560 Swiss Federal Tribunal, 16 October 2003, *X S.A.L., Y S.A.L et A v Z Sàrl*, 4P.115/2003, (2004) 22 ASA Bull no 2, 364, at 380–1. See also Derains/Schwartz, A Guide, *op cit*, 294.

(1) Introduction

There is frequently a compelling need to seek interim relief, also called conservatory and provisional measures, in connection with an international arbitration. Interim measures address the requirements of a party for immediate and temporary protection of rights or property pending a decision on the merits by the Arbitral Tribunal. **15.868**

Perhaps the two most common forms of interim relief are attachments and injunctions. For example, an attachment is sought to prevent the dissipation of the assets that are the subject of the arbitration. An injunction is normally requested to protect property rights at issue in the arbitration. Interim relief can also involve the safeguarding and preservation of perishable property. Interim measures can include orders which require corrective measures in environmental disputes or direct advance payment of part of a claim to alleviate hardship. Other interim measures involve security, ie the posting of security for costs and security for the award itself.[561] **15.869**

When agreeing to ICC arbitration, parties accept to submit the merits of their disputes to resolution exclusively under the ICC Arbitration Rules.[562] At the same time, the ICC Rules have long recognized that submission to arbitration under the ICC Rules does not prevent parties from having recourse to national courts to obtain urgent interlocutory measures, before the Arbitral Tribunal is constituted and even thereafter. This is necessary because some measures must be taken urgently if they are to be effective (eg the conservatory attachment of assets) and it may take several months after the submission of a Request for Arbitration for an Arbitral Tribunal to be constituted, to be in possession of the file and, therefore, in a position to order such measures itself. This is also appropriate because even when the Arbitral Tribunal is in a position to act it may and often does not have the coercive sanctions that are available to national courts in order to enforce its orders".[563] Therefore conservatory and interim measures often provide for the interaction between the Arbitral Tribunal and national courts.[564] **15.870**

The arbitrators' power under the ICC Rules to grant interim relief has been the subject of some debate. ICC Arbitral Tribunals have found that they have the power to order interim or conservatory measures 'as directions to the parties', even though the pre-1998 versions **15.871**

---

561 See for example Voser, N., 'Interim Relief in International Arbitration: The Tendency Towards More Business-Oriented Approach' (2007) 1 *Disp Res Int'l* no 2, 171, 179.

562 See Art 6(1) regarding the effect of the parties' arbitration agreement.

563 See Lévy, 'Insolvency in Arbitration (Swiss Law)' *op cit*, as to the possibility for arbitrators sitting in Switzerland to order fines.

564 Poudret, J.-F., 'Les mesures provisionnelles et l'arbitrage. Aperçu comparatif des pouvoirs respectifs de l'arbitre et du juge' in *Mélanges en l'honneur de François Knoepfler* (Helbing & Lichtenhahn, Basel, 2005) 235, 239. The importance of the interaction was also noted by the Federal Court of the Southern District of New York in *Discount Trophy & Co v Plastic Dress-Up Co*, no Civ. 3:03cv2167, 2004 US Dist LEXIS 2659, at 29 (D Conn, 2004): 'Even though this case will be stayed pending the parties' arbitration, the Second Circuit has made it clear in a series of decisions that the Court has both the power and duty to entertain a motion for a preliminary injunction pending the results in the arbitration. And this is true even though, as is the case here, the parties are entitled under the rules of the arbitral tribunal they have chosen to seek pendente lite relief directly from the arbitrator.' More generally on the role of the courts and problems related to the execution of conservatory and provisional measures, see (1993) *ICC ICArb Bull*, Special Supp, *Conservatory and Provisional Measures in International Arbitration*.

of the ICC Rules do not contain any express provision to this effect. For instance, in Egyptian law measures such as putting some assets under judicial sequestration or the attachment of the debtor's assets is permissible. In addition, the arbitral tribunal may also order such measures, and may request the provision of security to cover the cost of expenses required for this purpose.[565]

15.872 Not only is an ICC Arbitral Tribunal now expressly authorized to order interim measures at the request of a party but it is explicitly recognized as being the principal source for such measures. Requests to the Arbitral Tribunal are dealt with in Art 23(1) whereas applications to a judicial authority, which are permitted in more restricted circumstances ('before the file is transmitted to the Arbitral Tribunal, and in appropriate circumstances . . . thereafter'), are dealt with in Art 23(2).

15.873 Article 23(1) aligns the ICC Rules with the most modem international arbitration practice on this subject. Thus, the UNCITRAL Model Law of 1985 in its amended version in 2006 (Art 17),[566] recent national arbitration laws like those of England (Arbitration Act 1996, ss 38 and 39) and Switzerland (Swiss PILS of 1989, Art 183) and modern arbitration rules,[567] all expressly provide that arbitrators may order interim or conservatory measures.

15.874 The concepts and issues in the new provisions of Art 17 of the UNCITRAL Model Law give a useful checklist of what parties and Arbitral Tribunals may consider with respect to such measures.[568] The new amendments distinguish between 'interim measures' that are issued upon notice to the other party (Arts 17 and 17A) and 'preliminary orders' that are made *ex parte* (Art 17B and 17C). An important aspect of the revision to the UNCITRAL Model Law was to legally ensure the enforcement of interim measures irrespective of the country where it was issued.[569]

15.875 As discussed under Art 14,[570] in general the link between the Tribunal and the national courts is through the courts of the place of arbitration. However, with respect to enforcement of conservatory or interim measures this is not necessarily the case. The relevant national court for conservatory and interim measures will usually be the court where the

---

565 El-Sharkawi, M.S., 'New Trends in Egyptian Arbitration Law' (1999) 16 *J Int'l Arb* no 1, 5, 15.

566 Amendments to Arts 1(2), 7, and 35(2), a new ch IV A to replace Art 17 and a new Art 2A were adopted by UNCITRAL on 7 July 2006, see <http://www.uncitral.org>.

567 UNCITRAL Arts 24(3) and 26, LCIA Art 25.

568 As to further details on conservatory or interim measures provided for in the UNCITRAL Model Law, see also Bühler/Webster, ICC Handbook, *op cit*, Art 23; Malinvaud, C., 'Modification de la loi modèle CNUDCI sur les mesures intérimaires: un texte de compromis sur les mesures ex parte' (2007) *Les Cahiers de l'Arbitrage* no 1, 12.

569 Art 17 H provides for enforcement and Art 17 I provides grounds for refusal of enforcement. As regards enforcement, Art 17 H provides:

> (1) An interim measure issued by an arbitral tribunal shall be recognized as binding and, unless otherwise provided by the arbitral tribunal, enforced upon application to the competent court, irrespective of the country in which it was issued, subject to the provisions of article 17 I.
> (2) The party who is seeking or has obtained recognition or enforcement of an interim measure shall promptly inform the court of any termination, suspension or modification of that interim measure.
> (3) The court of the State where recognition or enforcement is sought may, if it considers it proper, order the requesting party to provide appropriate security if the arbitral tribunal has not already made a determination with respect to security or where such a decision is necessary to protect the rights of third parties.

570 See *supra* para 15.565.

conservatory or interim measure is to be carried out. This is frequently not the country of the place of arbitration, although it may well be the country of enforcement. Therefore, one of the key aspects of the revision to the UNCITRAL Model Law was to seek to provide a legal mechanism for the enforcement of interim measures.

To take some examples of the application of Art 23, ICC arbitrators have found that there was a valid application for interim or conservatory measures where a party: **15.876**

- applied to a court for the appointment of an expert in advance of arbitration to record certain facts;[571]
- obtained the attachment of the other party's bank accounts;[572]
- commenced garnishment proceedings to preserve goods that were the subject of the dispute between the parties (unpublished award);
- sought to obtain an order enjoining the payment of a bank guarantee (unpublished award);
- obtained an order authorizing it to contract with a new subcontractor in place of its original subcontractor, who was ordered to leave the site, without prejudice to the party's possible liability for damages in the event that it were found to have wrongfully terminated the subcontract;[573]
- obtained an order for immediate provisional payment of an undisputed debt;[574] or
- obtained an order from an Italian Court temporarily blocking payments under the contract at issue (unpublished award).

(2) Article 23(1): Measures ordered by an Arbitral Tribunal

The Rules now expressly recognize the power of the Arbitral Tribunal to grant interim relief, Art 23(1). The arbitrator may make the granting of such a measure conditional upon appropriate security being provided by the requesting party. **15.877**

Article 23(1) provides that the conservatory and interim measures shall take the form of a reasoned procedural order or an award, at the Arbitral Tribunal's discretion. It is to be noted that in an ICC arbitration, final measures are set out in an award (whether interim, partial or final) and that an award is subject to the scrutiny of the ICC Court under Art 27. **15.878**

Thus, if upon the request of the Claimant the Arbitral Tribunal were to order the Respondent to make a provisional payment (referred to in French as a *provision*) to the Claimant, the Arbitral Tribunal could make such order subject to the supply by the Claimant of a bank guarantee for an equivalent amount. **15.879**

The reference to 'appropriate' security is very broad and could cover not only the direct costs of imposing a measure but also consequential damages to a winning party resulting from the imposition of the measure against that party. **15.880**

[571] Case no 2444, (1997) JDI, 932, case no 4156, (1984) JDI, 937 and case no 5650, YBCA XVI (1991), 85.
[572] Case no 4415, (1984) JDI, 530; see also case no 4998, (1986) JDI, 1139, where this was implicitly admitted.
[573] Case no 4126, (1987) JDI, 934.
[574] Case no 5103, (1988) JDI, 1206.

15.881 The arbitrator is competent to decide an interim or conservatory measure as soon as he has received the file.[575] Thus, he need not wait until the Terms of Reference have been signed or otherwise come into force.

15.882 This gives rise to two questions, namely: (i) as the Arbitral Tribunal may 'at the request of a party order such measures', may it do it *ex parte*? and (ii) what is an 'interim or conservatory measure'?

15.883 The need to act urgently and the element of surprise, which are undoubtedly important in the case of some such measures (eg where the Respondent is apparently defrauding his creditors), normally entitles an arbitrator to order interim or conservatory measures, *ex parte*.[576]

15.884 However, in the authors opinion it is uncertain whether an Arbitral Tribunal may make *ex parte* orders under the ICC Rules. The terms of Art 23(1) need to be reconciled with: (i) Art 15(2) of the ICC Rules providing that 'in all cases, the Arbitral Tribunal shall act fairly and impartially and ensure that each party has a reasonable opportunity to present its case'; and (ii), assuming a hearing were appropriate, Art 21(3) of the ICC Rules which provides that 'all the parties shall be entitled to be present at hearings'.

15.885 Unlike certain other arbitration rules,[577] the measures the Arbitral Tribunal may order are not limited to the subject matter of the dispute. The Arbitral Tribunal may grant 'any' interim or conservatory measure 'it deems appropriate'.

15.886 The ICC Rules contain no definition of 'interim or conservatory measures' and this expression has no generally accepted meaning in common law systems.[578] The French language version of the Rules refers to 'mesures provisoires ou conservatoires', a familiar legal expression under French civil law. Accordingly, as the ICC Rules have always been drafted simultaneously in the English and French languages, it is not inappropriate to refer, in the first instance, to the meaning of this expression in French law.

15.887 An Arbitral Tribunal may not order interim or conservatory measures *sua sponte* (that is on its own initiative), as Art 23(1) expressly provides that the Arbitral Tribunal may only act 'at the request of a party'.

15.888 An interim or conservatory measure ordered by the Arbitral Tribunal may take the form of an order or an award. Since such measure can be issued prior to the signing of the Terms of Reference, it will be possible to render an interim award before the Terms of Reference were signed (Art 18), and before the six-month time limit to render an award has started to run

[575] See Lew, J., 'Commentary on Interim and Conservatory Measures in ICC Arbitration Cases' (2000) 11 *ICC ICArb Bull* no 1, 23; Besson, S., *Arbitrage international et mesures provisoires—Etude de droit comparé* (Schulthess, Zurich, 1998), 31 *et seq*.

[576] Lalive/Poudret/Reymond, *op cit*, 362.

[577] Compare Art 26.1 of the UNCITRAL Arbitration Rules where this is the case.

[578] In *Bank Mellat v Helleniki*, Lord Justice Kerr said that the expression 'stem[s] from the context of other systems of law', at 792, Art 23, n 12. On the other hand, this expression is contained, as he acknowledged, in Art 24 of the European Convention of 27 September 1968 on Jurisdiction and the Enforcement of Judgments in Civil and Commercial Matters.

(Art 24).[579] While the term 'order' is not defined in the Rules, an 'award' is defined in Art 2(iii) of the Rules to include, *inter alia*, an interim award, and according to Art 25(2), an award must state the reasons upon which it is based. It is also subject to scrutiny and approval by the ICC Court under Art 27. The choice of form is in the hands of the arbitrator who, in either case, must give reasons for his decisions.[580] The arbitrator will have to decide which form is the most effective in the circumstances, taking into consideration that an order, contrary to an award, need not be submitted to the ICC Court for approval before it is issued, whereas an award needs to be approved, which involves some additional time before it can become effective. By its nature, the interim or conservatory measure is of provisional nature, even when it is issued in the form of an award.

The effectiveness of an arbitrator's decision will depend on the legal environment of the case. A conservatory or interim measure cannot be enforceable against a recalcitrant party without the assistance of a local court. Ordinarily, in many countries, local courts will be prepared to confirm an interim direction by the Arbitral Tribunal making that direction enforceable by contempt citation. It is, though, far from certain that courts are prepared to cooperate in all parts of the world.[581] The arbitrator and the local court of law may both be competent to grant interim measures; there is a potential risk for jurisdictional conflicts. Also, there will be a risk of conflicting decisions, so that a court of law may take a decision that runs contrary to a measure decided by the arbitrator. **15.889**

Security for costs: ICC arbitrators have awarded security for costs in several reported cases,[582] but have also refused such requests.[583] In two recent ICC cases, the Arbitral Tribunal rejected the Respondent's request to order security for costs given the absence of any special circumstances justifying such a decision, emphasizing in one case the necessity to use such a power in a restrictive manner,[584] and, in the other case, the need for any exceptional circumstances to be proven.[585] **15.890**

In a recent ICC case no 13646, a Swiss Respondent requested that a Tribunal sitting in Geneva order security for costs, covering *inter alia* the Claimant's share of the ICC arbitration and its own legal costs, against a Nigerian Claimant. The Respondent based its request on the alleged fact that the Claimant would encounter difficulties to effect a payment abroad in favour of the Respondent, and that enforcing an award in Nigeria would require lengthy and costly procedures. The Tribunal rejected the Respondent's request given the absence of any special circumstances justifying such a decision. In so doing, the Tribunal **15.891**

[579] See *supra* para 15.880.

[580] See *supra* Art 2, paras 15.147 *et seq*, and *infra* Art 27, para 15.957.

[581] Thereto, see Kojovic, T., 'Court Enforcement of Arbitral Decisions on Provisional Relief—How Final is Provisional?' (2001) 18 J *Int'l Arb*, no 5, 511; Smit/Turner, *op cit*, n 46; Pryles, M., 'Interlocutory Orders and Convention Awards: The Case of *Resort Condominiums v Bolwell*', (1994) 10 *Arb Int'l*, no 4, 385.

[582] eg Case no 6697 (1992) *Rev arb*, 135 and Case no 6632 referred to by Fouchard/Gaillard/Goldman, *op cit*, 701 *et seq*, and Case no 1256; see also the procedure order rendered in 1998 by a sole arbitrator, (1999) *ASA Bull*, 59.

[583] See eg Case no 7047 (1997) 8 *ICC Court Bull* no 1, 61.

[584] ICC Case no13646, Procedural Order no 3 (2005), unreported.

[585] ICC Case no13070 (2006) (Interim Award), unreported.

emphasized in its procedural order the necessity for it to use such a power in a restrictive manner:

> [___]. It is generally admitted, however, that such power must be used in a restrictive manner. In Switzerland, this is, in particular, the opinion of Jean-François Poudret and Sebastien Besson: 'Un security for costs n'est à notre avis justifié que dans des cas très particuliers' (*Droit comparé de l'arbitrage international*, Bruylant L.G.D.J. Schulthess, 2002, s 610). The abovementioned procedural order issued by a tribunal sitting in Zurich expresses the same view: 'Arbitral precedents [. . .] show that security for costs should only be granted in exceptional circumstances and with the greatest reluctance' (*ASA Bull* 2005, at 112). As far as ICC Arbitration is concerned, Y. Derains and E. Schwartz confirm that 'those drafting the 1998 Rules were reluctant to mention security for costs expressly because they did not wish to encourage the proliferation of such applications, which, apart from being rare, are generally disfavoured in ICC arbitration' (*op cit* 297).
>
> [__]. This Arbitral Tribunal shares the view that the mere existence of doubt as to the possibility of enforcing a future award against the other party is not a sufficient ground for granting a request for security for costs. To impose such burden on a party requires more than the ordinary risk that the party ordered to pay may not be willing and may not be easily forced to do so; it requires the existence of special circumstances. Such necessity might be lightened if a very serious likelihood, if not near certainty that the alleged debt exists or will exist could be established (. . .)[586]

15.892 In ICC Case no 13070,[587] a Tribunal sitting in Paris, rejected the Respondent's request for security for costs against the Claimant based on the lack of any exceptional circumstances. The Tribunal, however, appeared to consider deterioration of the financial situation of a Claimant as constituting exceptional circumstances, case considered that the Respondent had failed to provide specific proof thereof in the case:

> [___]. Security for costs should only be granted in exceptional circumstances and with the greatest reticence (Karrer/Desax, Security for Costs in International Arbitration, in: Briner/Fortier/Berger/Bredow (eds), *Liber Amicorum Karl-Heinz Böckstiegel*, Köln *et al* 2001, Weigand (ed), *Practitioner's Handbook on International Arbitration*, Copenhagen 2002, 253). Insolvency must be considered as one of these exceptional circumstances (*ASA Bull* 1997, 377), as well as the situation, where a claimant did no longer conduct its commercial activity (*ASA Bull* 1999, 59).
>
> [___]. As a general rule, security for costs may only be ordered if, *inter alia*, the following conditions are fulfilled: there must be a situation of urgency and a risk of substantial damage for the requesting party. It is usually required to be in presence of a 'fundamental change of the situation since the basic agreement between the parties was entered into' (Karrer/Desax, *op cit* 345). In other words, the financial situation of the counterparty must have deteriorated since the time when the parties concluded their agreement.

---

586 ICC case no13646, Procedural Order no 3 (2005), unreported. See also *Puerto Rico Hospital Supply Inc v Boston Scientific Corp*, 21 October 2005, First Circuit US Court of Appeals, 20 Mealey's Int'l Arb Rev no 10, 16 (denial of injunctive relief pending ICC arbitration by US court in absence of any irreparable harm for the requesting party); *Plama Consortium Ltd v Republic of Bulgaria*, ICSID case no ARB/03/24 of 6 September 2005, 20 Mealey's Int'l Arb Rev no 10, 8 (denial of a request for urgent provisional measures to protect a party's right to non aggravation of a pending arbitration claim in absence of a change of circumstances that threatens the ability of the Tribunal to grant the relief sought by a party and the capability of giving effect to the relief).

587 ICC Case no 13070 (2006) (Interim Award), unreported.

[___]. Respondent does nowhere provide for specific proof for any such deterioration of Claimant's financial situation. Neither has it established that Claimant's financial situation has changed, either since the validity of the agreement or since the beginning of the arbitral proceedings. On the other hand, Claimant rightly observes that 1/ so far, it has assumed the entirety of the arbitration costs, 2/ it is a public institution under the Government monitoring. This last element, indeed, precludes by principle any serious risk of insolvency or bankruptcy.

Given that under Art 31 of the Rules, ICC arbitrators are required to decide on the allocation of the parties' legal costs, and that the largest component of these tends to be a party's legal fees and expenses, and given ICC arbitrators' tendency to apply the principle that 'costs follow the event',[588] it seems entirely reasonable for ICC arbitrators to be prepared to order security for the legal costs of a Respondent (or of a Claimant facing a counterclaim) in appropriate circumstances, eg where there is reason to believe the claiming party lacks the necessary resources[589] and/or is from a country which has not ratified the New York Convention favouring the enforcement of international arbitral awards.[590] **15.893**

(3) Article 23(2): Measures ordered by a judicial authority

Interim or conservatory measures ordered by an Arbitral Tribunal are subject to four limitations or shortcomings: **15.894**

- they will be unavailable before the Arbitral Tribunal bas been constituted and has received the file;
- arbitrators normally lack coercive powers;
- they might not be granted *ex parte*, a serious obstacle whenever the element of surprise is important; and
- the powers of an Arbitral Tribunal cannot be exercised against persons who are not parties to the arbitration.

Article 23(2) stipulates that the parties may apply to any competent judicial authority for interim measures under the conditions described in that paragraph. The Rules do not preclude a party from going to a state court where the urgency of the matter so requires or where the party considers this to be more effective. **15.895**

There is thus an unlimited right for the parties to apply to the state courts for interim or conservatory measures before the file is transmitted to the Arbitral Tribunal. This is necessary as the efficacy of certain relief requires that it be granted urgently (eg an order for the sale of perishable goods or an attachment on the assets of a debtor who is expected to seek to conceal them) and before the file is transmitted (which, as indicated above,[591] may take **15.896**

[588] See *infra* paras 15.1167 *et seq.*

[589] eg a 'shell' company, or a company that filed for bankruptcy proceedings.

[590] Veit, M. D., 'Note–Procedural Order No. 14 of 27 November 2002–Security for Costs in International Arbitration–Some Comments to Procedural Order No 14 of 27 November 2002' (2005) 23 *ASA Bull* no 1, 116; Besson, S., *op cit*, 38, para 37, and 220, para 358; Sandrock, O., 'The Cautio Judicatum Solvi in Arbitration Proceedings or The Duty of an Alien Claimant to Provide Security for the Costs of the Defendant', (1997) 4 *J Int'l Arb* no 2, 17 at 2 3; Karrer, P.A. and Desax, M., 'Security for Costs in International Arbitration; Why, When and What if . . .' in *Liber Amicorum Karl-Heinz Böckstiegel* (Carl Heymanns Verlag, Cologne, 2001) 339.

[591] See *supra* para 15.869.

several months after the filing of the Request for Arbitration). During this phase, only the courts are available to grant such relief. In these circumstances, a request for interim or conservatory measures cannot be permitted to await the constitution of the Arbitral Tribunal.[592]

15.897 However, after the file has been transmitted to the Arbitral Tribunal,[593] Art 23(2) provides that the parties' right to apply to the courts for interim or conservatory measures is more limited as the Arbitral Tribunal, who will be deciding the merits and, therefore, hearing the whole case, is now in a position to receive requests for such measures 'in appropriate circumstances'.

15.898 Article 9 of the UNCITRAL Model Law states that '[i]t is not incompatible with an arbitration agreement for a party to request, before or during arbitral proceedings, from a court an interim measure of protection and for a court to grant such measure'.[594] This has now been confirmed and broadened in Art 17 J of the UNCITRAL Model Law that provides that: '[a] court shall have the same power of issuing an interim measure in relation to arbitration proceedings, irrespective of whether their place is in the territory of this State, as it has in relation to proceedings in courts. The court shall exercise such power in accordance with its own procedures in consideration of the specific features of international arbitration.'

15.899 While, for many years, the ICC Rules have provided that the parties may apply to the courts for interim or conservatory measures in certain circumstances, this provision has not always been recognized by national courts.

---

592 For example, in France, see Versailles, 8 October 1998, *Société Akzo Nobel et autres v SA Elf Atochem* (1999) *Rev arb* no 1, 57, note Houry: '[w]hereas it is a principle of positive French law that the parties to an agreement with an arbitration clause giving jurisdiction to an arbitral tribunal of the ICC may have recourse to the state courts to obtain conservatory measures having in particular as their objective to preserve the situation, the rights or the evidence and in particular the existence of an arbitration clause does not preclude action by the judge for urgent matters.' (Authors' translation); see also Art 185 of the Swiss PILA, s 38 of the English Arbitration Act 1996. See also Cass civ 1re, 18 November 1986, *Atlantic Triton Company v (1) Republic of Guinea and (2) Soguipêche* (1987) YBCA vol XII, 183, note Gaillard (Art 26 of the ICSID Convention does bar one of the parties from resorting to national courts to attach assets until an Award is rendered by the Tribunal).

593 See *supra* paras 15.552 *et seq.*

594 Discussed for example in Federal Court of Canada, *Frontier International Shipping Corp v Tavros* [2000] 2 FC 427; 1999 CanLII 9389 (FC). See also *Brunswick Corp, Mercury Marine Division v Yamaha Motor Co Ltd*, US District Court Eastern District of Wisconsin, case no 04-C-0584 (1 October 2004) (preliminary injunction ordering the Respondent to continue the performance of the contract pending the final resolution of the dispute based on the wording of the contract, the court declining to rule on the substance which is left to the arbitrators); *Peabody Coalsales Co v Tampa Elec* Co, 36 F.3d46 (8th Cir 1994) (preliminary injunction ordered by the court based on the contractual provision stating 'Unless otherwise agreed in writing by the parties during the dispute resolution process'. According to the court, an order compelling arbitration 'in accordance with the terms of the agreement' must necessarily include an order requiring continued performance); *RGI Inc v Tucker & Assocs Inc*, 858F.2d 227 (5th Cir 1988) (a preliminary injunction is appropriate in light of the contract language providing '[i]n the event that a dispute is submitted for arbitration pursuant to this paragraph, this Subcontract shall continue in full force and effect until such decision is rendered . . . in such a circumstance, the court needs not involve itself in balancing the various factors to determine whether a preliminary injunction should be issued').

Thus, in the United States, the courts are divided on whether a party who is bound by an arbitration clause may apply to a court for a conservatory attachment. In *McCreary Tire & Rubber v CEAT SpA*,[595] the US Court of Appeals for the Third Circuit held that a pre-award attachment was contrary to Art II. 3 of the New York Convention which provides that, when a court of a contracting state is seized of an action in respect of which the parties have made an arbitration agreement, the court shall, at the request of one of the parties, 'refer the parties to arbitration'. According to the Court of Appeals, this language precluded the Court from acting in any capacity except to order arbitration and, therefore an order of attachment could not be issued. In *Cooper v Ateliers de la Motobecane*,[596] the Court of Appeals of New York (the highest court in the State of New York) in a 4–3 decision followed the ruling laid down in the *McCreary Tire* case, as have certain other US courts. However, other US courts have held that pre-award attachment is not incompatible with the New York Convention.[597] **15.900**

Where interim or conservatory measures have been sought from the courts prior to arbitration, national procedural laws often require that proceedings on the merits must be commenced within a limited time thereafter. The commencement of an ICC arbitration in the country of the court issuing the interim or conservatory order, or elsewhere, will ordinarily satisfy this requirement. However, if an ICC arbitration is not promptly commenced, a court may, of course, decide to vacate an order earlier granted. **15.901**

As interim or conservatory measures are, by their nature, temporary, they will normally endure only for so long as the merits of the related claim have not been finally decided. Once the Arbitral Tribunal is seized of the file, it might direct a party to renounce or otherwise to take steps to have interim or conservatory measures obtained prior to the commencement of arbitration proceedings removed. Alternatively, the Arbitral Tribunal may require that they be replaced by others under the control of the Arbitral Tribunal. As the Arbitral Tribunal has sole responsibility for deciding the merits of the case, it should be the ultimate judge of any such measures ordered by state courts. **15.902**

In one ICC case the Arbitral Tribunal adopted the following reasoning regarding interim relief sought from a national court in the presence of an arbitration agreement: **15.903**

> If the state court orders or declines to order a measure, the parties cannot subsequently resort to the arbitral tribunal to obtain a more favourable ruling, and *vice versa*. Even if the state court was first approached solely for the reason that the arbitral tribunal was not yet properly constituted, the tribunal cannot later on, after its constitution, reverse or modify the measure ordered by the state judge. What if a subsequent request for reversal or modification of an order is based on changed circumstances? Arguably, such a request should be dealt with by the arbitral tribunal once it is constituted.[598]

---

[595] See 501 F2d 1032 (3d Cir. 1974).

[596] See 57 NY2d 408, 456 NY2d 728 (1982).

[597] See *Carolina Power & Light Company v URANEX*, 451 F Supp 1044 (1977) which referred to an earlier decision of Judge Learned Hand in *Murray Oil Products Co v Mitsui & Co*, 146 F 2d 381 (2nd Cir 1944) holding that pre-judgment attachment was not incompatible with the United States Arbitration Act.

[598] ICC Order no 5 of 2 April 2002, regarding Claimant's Request for Interim Relief, (2003) 21 ASA Bull no 4, 810, 816.

15.904 A party requesting interim or conservatory measures before national courts should take care that its action will not be considered as a waiver or violation of the arbitration agreement despite Art 23(2) that provides that application to a state court 'shall not be deemed to be an infringement or a waiver of the arbitration agreement' as it is a matter for national law.[599] It should also be aware that such an action may affect the willingness of the Arbitral Tribunal to grant the relief.[600] However, Art II(3) of the New York Convention requires a party to apply to dismiss the national court proceedings and thus to compel arbitration if national proceedings are brought.[601]

15.905 A party who applies to a judicial authority for interim measures must report this to the ICC Secretariat. This is expressly provided for in Art 23(2), last sentence. The Secretariat will inform the Arbitral Tribunal of such applications and measures decided by a local judicial authority. In the authors' experience parties inform both the Arbitral Tribunal and the Court Secretariat at the same time, which is more efficient and appropriate.

15.906 The Secretariat of the ICC Court needs to be kept currently informed since it oversees the progress of each case and must inform the ICC Court regarding any delay and the ensuring need for the ICC Court to extend the time limit for the drawing up of the Terms of Reference (Art 18) or the making of the award (Art 24).

15.907 Parties often neglect to notify the Secretariat until the Request for Arbitration or Answer is filed. Thus, the question sometimes arises whether any adverse consequences might follow from any failure to notify the Secretariat 'without delay'. Arbitral Tribunals have been called upon to construe this requirement in at least three cases.[602]

Article 24. Time limit for the award

(1) The time limit within which the Arbitral Tribunal must render its final award is six months. Such time limit shall start to run from the date of the last signature by the Arbitral Tribunal or of the parties of the Terms of Reference or, in the case of application of Article 18(3), the date of the notification to the Arbitral Tribunal by the Secretariat of the approval of the Terms of Reference by the Court.

(2) The Court may extend this time limit pursuant to a reasoned request from the Arbitral Tribunal or on its own initiative if it decides it is necessary to do so.

---

599 Supreme Court of Philippines, 19 May 2006, *Transfield Philippines Inc v Luzon Hydro Corporation, Australia and New Zealand Banking Group Limited and Security Bank Corporation* (ICC case no 11264 with Singapore as place of arbitration): 'As a fundamental point, the pendency of arbitral proceedings does not foreclose resort to the courts for provisional relief. The Rules of the ICC, which govern the parties' arbitral dispute, allow the application of a party to a judicial authority for interim or conservatory measures. Likewise, section 14 of the Republic Act no 876 recognizes the rights of any party to petition the court to take measures to safeguard and/or conserve any matter which is the subject of the dispute in arbitration', <http://elibrary.supremecourt.gov.ph>.

600 For a discussion on anti-arbitration or anti-suit injunctions, see para 24–17. More generally, on the waiver of the arbitration agreement, see Jarvin, S., 'La renonciation à la convention d'arbitrage' in *Liber Amicorum Dobrosav Mitrovic* (Belgrade, 2007).

601 Bühler/Webster, ICC Handbook, *op cit*, para 23–53.

602 Case no 2444, (1977) JDI, 932; Case no 4415, (1984) JDI, 530; and Case no 5103 (1988) JDI, 1206. The two first cases are also published in *Collection of ICC Arbitral Awards 1974–1985, op cit,* and *Collection of ICC Arbitral Awards 1986–1990, op cit.*

(1) Introduction

The time limit for rendering the award in ICC arbitration is six months. This seems to be a very long time in some cases and to be absolutely insufficient in other cases. The variety of the complexity of ICC cases is such that one can wonder if it is useful at all to have any time limits fixed by the Rules. The timetable that the arbitrators must establish pursuant to Art 18(4) should be geared towards a procedure that will permit the arbitrators to render their award within six months from the time of signing the Terms of Reference. The parties themselves are often unable to present their case within such a short time so as to allow an award to be drafted by the arbitrators, scrutinized by the ICC Court (which may take up to one month) and then signed by the arbitrators (which may take one or two weeks when they live in different places) before the end of the six month period.[603] **15.908**

Article 24(1) stipulates that the final award shall be rendered within six months. A final award is an award bringing the arbitration to its end.[604] **15.909**

It is current practice that ICC arbitrators render several awards, called interim, partial, interlocutory or intermediate awards.[605] Such 'non-final' awards typically deal with the Arbitral Tribunal's jurisdiction in cases where it is contested. The arbitrators, in complex cases, eg where much evidence is required to prove damages, often prefer to bifurcate the proceedings and make a first award dealing with a party's *responsibility* for an alleged breach of contract and then a final award deciding the amount of *damages* suffered. There is, in the Rules, no specific time limit imposed for such non-final awards. What matters is that the final award be rendered within six months. **15.910**

(2) Article 24(1) Six-month time limit to render the final award

The six months in question begin to run immediately upon the signature of the Terms of Reference. The time runs from the date of the last signature by the arbitrators or the parties of the Terms of Reference. It does not matter whether the Terms of Reference have already been transmitted to the ICC Court. As soon as the Secretariat has received the signed Terms of Reference it will advise the Arbitral Tribunal in writing, with a copy to the parties, of the date at which the six months have started to run, and that this time limit may be extended pursuant to Art 24(2). In a recent case the question arose whether the making of an addendum to the Terms of Reference extends the starting point for the calculation of the six months so that it would run from the signature of the addendum. The Court's Secretariat denied that. **15.911**

The final award is not considered to have been rendered until it has been approved by the ICC Court pursuant to Art 27, and signed by the Arbitral Tribunal. **15.912**

The arbitrators, in order to create the best possible condition for complying with the six month limit, should keep contact with the ICC Court's Secretariat so as to be informed when they should deliver their draft award in order for it to be examined by the Court at its next session. **15.913**

603 See *infra* Art 32 as to modifying time limits.
604 See *supra* Art 2, paras 15.148 *et seq.*
605 *ibid.*

15.914 Actually, mid-size arbitrations may take longer than 12 months from the date on which the Arbitral Tribunal is constituted. The extending of the originally-foreseen period may be due to external factors, a matter of agreement between the parties or caused by the parties or even by an arbitrator. Therefore, to the extent that the Arbitral Tribunal is able to obtain the parties' agreement on the procedure at an early stage, it will provide a baseline for future reference if there are attempts to delay the proceedings.

15.915 Other issues relevant to the time limit for the award are suspensions due to other proceedings, parallel pending proceedings or anti-arbitration injunctions.[606]

(3) Article 24(2): Extension of the time limit

15.916 The ICC Court has the power to extend the time limit for the award, either on its own initiative or pursuant to a reasoned request from the Arbitral Tribunal. Such extensions are routinely granted by the ICC Court in the same manner as for the Terms of Reference.[607] The Secretariat reports to the first committee meeting of the ICC Court each month on every case in which the deadline will expire in the following month, and the ICC Court extends the deadline in question by an additional three months for as many times as necessary. Where the parties and the Arbitral Tribunal have agreed on a timetable that envisages a duration of the arbitration of more than six months, the ICC Court will grant extensions of more than three months, so as to take the timetable into account.[608]

15.917 Thus, the ICC Court's practice is to routinely grant three-month extensions. However, the ICC Court will refuse to routinely extend the time limit where the Arbitral Tribunal has remained inactive during the past quarter. In such cases, the ICC Court will extend the time limit for a shorter period, since it wishes to promptly receive an update of the status of the arbitration. This is the best way for the ICC Court to assume its role under Art 12(2), pursuant to which it may replace an arbitrator who is not fulfilling his functions 'within the prescribed time limits'.[609]

15.918 It is desirable that the Court closely supervises the time limits and establishes, through the Secretariat, the necessary contacts with the arbitrators in order to encourage them to treat the arbitration as a matter of priority. It is doubtful whether the resources at the Secretariat level are always sufficient to meet this demand, and if they were, whether they would significantly reduce delays.

15.919 Parties should be aware that the ICC Court is not required to give reasons for its decision to extend a time limit. Nor is the Court required to contact the parties—even less ask their view—before it decides to extend a time limit.[610] Only the Arbitral Tribunal is informed of the extension and solicited by the ICC Court's Secretariat to inform the parties at the

---

[606] More generally Bühler/Webster, ICC Handbook, *op. cit*, paras 24–10 to 24–32.

[607] See *supra* Art 18, para 15.740.

[608] Schäfer, E., Verbist, H. and Míos, C., *ICC Arbitration In Practice Schäfer* (Kluwer Law International, 2004) 62.

[609] See *supra* Art 12, para 15.527 *et seq*.

[610] See German Supreme Court, 14 April 1988, (1989) IPRAX 228; Belgian Supreme Court, 8 December 1988, (1989) Journal des Tribunaux (Belgium) 275. Paris Court of Appeal, 25 November 1997 in ICC case no 864 *Sociétée V.R.V. Spa v Sociéte Pharma Chim Ltd Co* (1998) *Rev arb*, 684.

appropriate moment. Upon request by a party, the Secretariat does, however, advise the parties directly of the further time extension that the ICC Court may have granted.

Under Art 24(2), the ICC Court is thus not required to consult with or notify the extension of the period to render the award to the parties. In a recent case the Paris Court of Appeals held that this did not cause the period for the arbitration to expire. The court noted that the party challenging the award participated in the proceedings after the expiration of the period in question.[611] **15.920**

That the institution extends time limits on its own initiative is characteristic for an institutional arbitration, such as the ICC. This is an advantage compared to *ad hoc* arbitration where arbitrators have to take care that such extensions are granted. In the *Consorts Juliet* case, the award was set aside by the French Supreme Court because it was rendered after the time limit set by French law and the Arbitral Tribunal failed to obtain an extension from the French courts in accordance with Art 1456 of the French CPC.[612] **15.921**

Article 25. Making of the award

(1) When the Arbitral Tribunal is composed of more than one arbitrator, an Award is given by a majority decision. If there be no majority, the Award shall be made by the Chairman of the Arbitral Tribunal alone.
(2) The Award shall state the reasons upon which it is based.
(3) The Award shall be deemed to be made at the place of the arbitration and on the date stated therein.

(1) Article 25(1): Decision-making where the Arbitral Tribunal is not unanimous

Article 25(1) applies to all Arbitral Tribunals composed of more than one arbitrator and to all awards, whether final, interim or partial. In the overwhelming majority of cases, tribunals of more than one arbitrator will be composed of three arbitrators.[613] Article 25 applies to awards whether final, interim or partial.[614] To arrive at an award, the Tribunal will have to deliberate. The deliberations of the Tribunal are confidential[615] and require trust among **15.922**

[611] Cass civ 1re, 6 July 2005, *Société AIC v Société Skanska*, <http://www.legifrance.gouv.fr>, case no 15223: (2006) *Rev arb* no 2, 429, note Pic; (2005) Dalloz, 3061, note Clay; Paris, 6 March 2003, Société *AIC-El Amiouny International Contracting et Trading v Société Skanska*, (2004) *Rev arb*3, 886, note Bensaude; see also Paris, 12 June 2003, *SA Citel v Mungovan*, (2004) *Rev arb* no 1, 135.

[612] Cass civ 1re, 6 December 2005, *Consorts Juliet v Castagnet et al*, SIAR 2006:1, 149, note Degos; (2006) *Rev arb* no 1, 126, note Jarrosson; (2006) JCP G II 10066 852, note Clay; Paillusseau, J., 'L'arbitre responsable du délai d'arbitrage' (2006) *JCP* I 129, 666; see also Fouchard, Gaillard & Goldman, *op cit*, 500, paras 868 and 621, para 1149.

[613] See Art 8.

[614] See *supra* paras 15.148 *et seq.*

[615] *Certain Underwriters at Lloyd's, London et al v Argonaut Insurance Company* (United States District Court, Northern District of California, para 11–56 n 30. (Footnote 11: 'Certain Underwriters cite other procedural irregularities. It contends Interim Order No.2 was issued before Certain Underwriters' arbitrator ever learned of . . . it. But this claim gets into the internal deliberation of the panel, which the Court concludes is not warranted in this case.') *In the Matter of the Petition of Fertilizantes Fosfatados Mexicanos SA*, 751 FSupp 467, 468 n 1 (SDNY 1990), 2003 US Dist. LEXIS 8796. ('This case should not be viewed as a precedent in any way for inquiry into the deliberations of an arbitration panel. Such matters should remain confidential and inviolate'). (2003) YBCA vol XXVIII, 1248; 2003 US Dist LEXIS 8796.

the members of the Tribunal.[616] While the arbitrators' deliberations often constitute an ongoing process, they usually begin at the latest during the evidentiary hearings with respect to the credibility of various witnesses. Oral testimony frequently has a significant impact on Tribunals, as it often serves to bring the evidence to life and to highlight discrepancies. The natural tendency of the arbitrators—like counsel—is to review the impact of each day's testimony as the hearings progress. This immediate impact of oral testimony is reduced (or perhaps complemented) if there is a transcript of the proceedings, particularly if that transcript is available on a same-day basis. The Tribunal's deliberations may continue immediately after the evidentiary hearings or after the legal argument and, in many cases, the Tribunal will wish to set aside dates to review the material in detail.

15.923 The most common situation is unanimity. It cannot always be achieved; two of the arbitrators may agree, but the third arbitrator may have a differing opinion.[617] The award will then be made by the two arbitrators, usually the chairman and one of the co-arbitrators. More unusual, but noteworthy, is the situation, which has happened, where the two co-arbitrators agree on the award and the chairman disagrees.

15.924 The power of the chairman of the Arbitral Tribunal to decide alone when there is no majority, stipulated in the second phrase of Art 25(1), is an important characteristic of ICC arbitration, which was for a long time unique for the ICC Rules.[618] Most other arbitration rules used to require that there always be at least a majority vote. The latter approach, as pointed out by two distinguished commentators, has the disadvantage of requiring the chairman to obtain the agreement of at least one of the co-arbitrators, which can force compromises that may be neither legitimate nor reasonable.[619] Thus, for example, in a case of contractual liability, the arbitrator appointed by the Claimant may consider that the Claimant is entitled to damages amounting to US $2,000,000, while the arbitrator appointed by the Respondent believes that the latter has no liability. If the chairman concludes that the Claimant is entitled to US $1,000,000, he can impose his views under Art 25(1). If a majority decision were required, however, he would need to work out a compromise with one of the co-arbitrators.

[616] Madsen, F. and Eriksson, P., 'Deliberations of the Arbitral Tribunal–Analysis of Reasoned Awards from a Swedish Perspective' (2006) *SIAR* 2006: 2, 1; Derains Y., 'La pratique du délibéré arbitral' in *Liber Amicorum in honour of Robert Briner* (ICC Publishing, Paris, 2005) 221; Leboulanger, Ph., 'Principe de collégialité et délibéré arbitral' in *Mélanges en l'honneur de François Knoepfler* (Helbing & Lichtenhahn, Basel, 2005) 259; Fortier, Y., 'The Tribunal's deliberation' in L.W. Newman. and R.D. Hill (eds), *The Leading Arbitrators' Guide to International Arbitration* (Juris Publishing/Staempfli Publishers, 2004) 391; Bredin, J.-D, 'Le secret du délibéré arbitral' in P. Bellet P., *Etudes offertes à Pierre Bellet* (Litec, Paris, 1991) 71 and Bredin, J.-D., 'Retour au délibéré arbitral' in *Liber Amicorum Claude Reymond* (Litec, Paris, 2004) 43.

[617] More generally Bühler/Webster, ICC Handbook, *op cit*, paras 25–4 to 25–11. See also Madsen/Eriksson, *op cit*, 1; Derains, Y., 'La pratique du délibéré arbitral', *op cit*, 16; Leboulanger, Ph., *op cit*, 259; Fortier, Y., 'The Tribunal's deliberation', *op cit*, 391; Bredin, J.-D., 'Le secret du délibéré arbitral', *op cit*, 71; and Bredin, J.-D. 'Retour au délibéré arbitral', *op cit*, 43.

[618] Reymond, C., 'Le Président du Tribunal Arbitral' in *Etudes offertes à Pierre Bellet* (Litec, Paris, 1991) 467.

[619] Derains/Schwartz, A Guide, *op cit*, 306.

In contrast, the ICC approach permits the chairman to maintain a completely independent position and discourages partisan conduct on the part of the co-arbitrators, who know that the chairman is not required to agree with either of them in order to issue an award. 15.925

The rules are silent with respect to the voting process within the Arbitral Tribunal. For instance, in the example above it is conceivable to think that the arbitrators could first vote on the liability, whereby a majority in favour of liability would be obtained. Thereafter, they could proceed to vote with respect to the amount of damages. In such a situation the arbitrator who had found that there was no liability would nonetheless have the opportunity to vote with respect to the amount of damages that should be awarded, now that the majority had found that the Respondent was liable. He might find that the amount should be US $2,000,000 like the other co-arbitrator, and not US$1,000,000, like the chairman thought. It is not inconceivable that the outcome of the award would have been different had the arbitrators agreed on voting rules beforehand. The ICC Rules do not offer any guidance on this important issue, which is left essentially to the discretion and skills of the chairman. 15.926

Likewise, in a construction case before the ICC there were 18 different claims relating to various parts of the construction of a building. The arbitrators were not unanimous on a single claim and ruled by majority, but the majority votes changed for each claim. For instance, on claim no 1 arbitrators A and B formed a majority, on claim no 2 arbitrators B and C formed a majority, on claim no 3 arbitrators A and C, and so on. The total amount awarded was therefore not covered by one majority but decided by a different majority on each individual claim. 15.927

The Rules do not stipulate anything with respect to dissenting opinion. From time to time ICC arbitrators write dissenting opinions.[620] 15.928

Dissenting opinions are not scrutinized and approved by the ICC Court, although the Court studies them in order to check that the issues they raise are addressed in the award. The dissenting opinions are communicated to the parties only with the consent of the non-dissenting majority. In many cases the majority arbitrators agree to the communication of the dissenting opinion to the parties. In some cases, the award expressly identifies the arbitrator who dissented, eg when an arbitrator declines to sign an award because of his dissent. It is then proper for the majority to state so in the award. The majority may also add that the arbitrator has written a dissenting opinion, which the majority has seen, but that it differs with such opinion for the reasons set out in the award. 15.929

The reasons behind a dissenting opinion are not always evident, and vary from case to case. Some arbitrators are sometimes exposed to pressure from the party who appoints them—political pressure where a government or a state enterprise is a party—or economic pressure. But that is certainly not the main, let alone the only, reason for an arbitrator wishing to write a separate opinion. It is to be noted that dissents are not part of the award. For 15.930

[620] See also Smit, R. H., 'Dissenting Opinions in Arbitration' (2004) 15 *ICC ICArb Bull* no 1, 37; Hunter, M., 'Final Report on Dissenting and Separate Opinions' (1990) 1 ICC ICArb Bull no 1, 32.

example, the French courts consider dissents in annulment proceedings as 'elements of fact', and they have no legal value as such.[621]

15.931 Ironically, it has been suggested to the authors in discussions with arbitrators whose most vital interests may be at stake when they are appointed as arbitrators by a powerful (state-owned or private) party, that the ICC ought to prohibit dissenting opinions since that would relieve them from the pressure of having to express a dissenting opinion in situations where they in fact are in agreement with the two other arbitrators. Other arbitrators, however, feel it is important to be able to express a differing view, in particular when it relates to issues of law.

(2) Article 25(2): Reasoned award

15.932 The Court has always required awards to be reasoned, and this was widely assumed to be inherent in the provision for the scrutiny and approval of awards by the Court. The Rules are now, since 1998, explicit in this regard.[622] The Court will not approve an award that does not set out the reasons for the arbitrator's decision; it will be considered a formal flaw regarding which the ICC Court is entitled to refuse approval under Art 27.[623] This control mechanism is important; it constitutes a 'quality control' of ICC awards that does not exist in most other institutional arbitrations, eg the LCIA, DIS or SCC.

(3) Article 25(3): Place where award is deemed to be made

15.933 The presumption that the award is made at the place of the arbitration is a legal fiction of great legal and practical importance.[624] In many cases the arbitrators do not meet at the place of arbitration to deliberate, and to come to their decision, let alone in order to sign the award. Indeed, arbitrators rarely meet solely for the purpose of signing an award. The original copies of the award are regularly circulated among them for signature.

15.934 The place of arbitration provides the link with the place of the proceedings relating to the conduct of the arbitration and any annulment proceedings, as has been recognized by courts of many countries. The new wording in Art 25(3) was inspired by a UK court case, in which it was questioned whether the former practice—unsupported by the 1975/1988 version of the Rules—to approve awards signed outside the place of the arbitration, resulted in a legally binding award. Such doubts have now been dispelled; the Rules reflect the reality of the practice of international commercial arbitration and the award can be validly

---

[621] See Paris, 16 January 2003, *Société des télécommunications internationales du Cameroun (Intelcam) v SA France Télécom*, (2004) *Rev arb* no 2, 369, where the Paris Court of Appeal held that the dissenting opinion reflected the fact that there had been collegial deliberations.

[622] See Lloyd, H., Darmon, M., Ancel, J.-P., Lord Dervaird, Liebscher, Ch. and Verbiest, H., 'Drafting Awards in ICC Arbitration' (2005) 16 *ICC ICArb Bull* no 2, 19. More generally, see Cremades, B., 'The Arbitral Award' in L.W. Newman and R.D. Hill (eds), *The Leading Arbitrators' Guide to International Arbitration* (Juris Publishing/Staempfli Publishers, Huntington, New York, 2004) 397; Tschanz, P.-Y., 'The Award—How To Structure it, How Detailed? Orders And Reasons, Adding Insult To Injury' (September 2007) *ASA Special Series* no 29, 25. See also Wolrich P. M., 'Techniques for Controlling Time and Costs in Arbitration' (2007) 18 *ICC ICArb Bull* no 1, 23. See also discussions under Art 24.

[623] For a detailed discussion on the reasoning, see Bühler/Webster, ICC Handbook, *op cit*, paras 25–15 *et seq*.

[624] See *supra* Art 14, paras 15.565 *et seq*.

signed at any place, as long as it will indicate the place of arbitration as Art 25(3) is referring to where the award is 'deemed to be made', and not where it was signed.[625]

However, a recent Swedish court case casts doubt on the efficiency of this legal fiction. In *Titan Corporation v Alcatel CIT SA*,[626] an ICC case, the parties' contract defined Stockholm as the place of arbitration. When it came to an arbitration, however, the arbitrator conducted the hearings in Paris and London, not in Stockholm. The Svea Court of Appeal found that the case had no 'Swedish judicial interest' and no connection with Sweden and declared that the place of arbitration was not Stockholm and the award was not considered rendered there. **15.935**

Article 26. Award by consent

If the parties reach a settlement after the file has been transmitted to the Arbitral Tribunal in accordance with Article 13, the settlement shall be recorded in the form of an award made by consent of the parties if so requested by the parties and if the Arbitral Tribunal agrees to do so.

Many disputes that are submitted to ICC arbitration are in fact settled during the proceedings, with or without the assistance of the Arbitral Tribunal.[627] When the parties settle their dispute in this way they can simply withdraw the case and request the ICC Court to fix the costs of arbitration. Thereafter the file will be closed by the ICC Court's Secretariat. Article 26 deals only with the consent award as a result of the settlement but not with how the parties have reached their settlement.[628] **15.936**

It is not unusual that the parties wish to keep the contents of their settlement agreement secret from the Arbitral Tribunal. Such practice may reflect a legitimate interest of the parties which arbitrators will respect. For this reason, parties will require no award recording their agreement. Where the undertakings made by one or both parties in the settlement agreement need yet to be performed, one party may have doubts regarding the ability or willingness of the other party to voluntarily implement the settlement agreement once the case will have been withdrawn from the ICC. In that situation, a party may seek the suspension of the arbitral proceedings for a given period of time (eg six or twelve months or more). If the settlement agreement is fully executed, the arbitration may be terminated upon the joint request of the parties.[629] **15.937**

---

[625] See also Art 14, para 15.592.

[626] Svea Court of Appeal, 28 February 2005, comments by Jarvin, S. and Dorgan, C., *op cit*, 42.

[627] In 2007, 30 Awards by consent were rendered out of the 349 Awards that were approved by the ICC Court, see (2008) 19 *ICC Court Bull* no 1, 5.

[628] See ICC, *Techniques for Controlling Time and Costs in Arbitration*, *op cit*, 28, para 43 (the Tribunal's role in promoting settlement); Schneider, M.E., 'Combining Arbitration with Conciliation' (1996) *ICCA Congress Series* no 8, 57: 'The admissibility and appropriateness for an arbitrator to act as conciliator is among the most controversial issues among international arbitration practitioners. The views and practices in this respect differ widely.'

[629] A settlement agreement could also stipulate that it will be for the Claimant to send a letter to the ICC requesting the termination of the arbitration, and for the Respondent to confirm such request within, eg seven days. It could further stipulate that the absence of such confirming letter by the Respondent should be construed as the letter's tacit agreement to the termination of the agreement.

15.938 An alternative solution to a suspension of the arbitration might be the issuance of an award by consent, since it will give one party an instrument for enforcement.[630] An award by consent may be recorded only after the constitution of the Arbitral Tribunal. The arbitration proceedings must at least have advanced to the receipt of the file by the Arbitral Tribunal under Art 13 of the Rules. It is not necessary for Terms of Reference to have been signed before an award by consent can be issued. However, Art 26 does not appear to contemplate the parties waiving these provisions in order to obtain a consent award prior to the constitution of the Arbitral Tribunal.[631]

15.939 An award by consent is an award, and as such it can be enforced against the will of a party, if necessary; the New York Convention and bilateral conventions[632] may then be used in order to obtain satisfaction for the party whose claim was recognized in the award by consent. An award by consent will record the terms of the parties' settlement agreement, and will normally not have to make an independent finding or decision. It is common practice for settlement agreements to contain an agreement on costs, which the arbitrator will record in the award. Many times, parties agree to share the ICC costs for arbitration, each party bearing its own costs, in particular legal fees and expenses.[633]

15.940 Since the award by consent is an award, the ICC Court's scrutiny procedure laid down in Art 27 of the Rules applies. In other words a consent Award is also subject to the same provisions of the Rules as any form of award, including correction and interpretation, as well as annulment and enforcement.[634] An award made by consent will normally be sent to a committee meeting rather than a plenary session of the Court;[635] the time it will take to get the award by consent approved will therefore be rather limited. As with any final award, the Court will fix the costs of arbitration, see Art 31. The rules of Arts 27 through to 29 apply to the award of consent *mutatis mutandis*.

15.941 An award by consent is usually final as it brings the arbitration to an end with prejudice. However, there exist in the annals of the ICC examples of cases where an award by consent was partial (settling only a part of the dispute), which is very unusual.[636]

15.942 The Arbitral Tribunal will record the settlement agreement of the parties in the form of an award by consent, only if the parties have requested so. The settlement agreement will often already contain a joint request to that effect. ICC arbitrators will normally have no reason

---

[630] Bühring-Uhle, C., *Arbitration and Mediation in International Business* (Kluwer Law International, The Hague, London, Boston, 1996) 361.

[631] See Newmark, C. and Hill, R., 'Can a Mediated Settlement Become an Enforceable Arbitration Award?' (2000) 16 *Arb Int'l* no 1, 81; Lazareff, S., 'Aux frontières de l'arbitrage et de l'ADR: La Sentence d'Accord Parties' in *Les Cahiers de l'Arbitrage Volume I* (Gazette du Palais, Paris, 2002) 8; Tchakoua J.-M., 'The Status of the Arbitral Award by Consent: The limits of the Useful' (2002) *RDAI/IBLJ* no 7, 775; Kreindler, R., 'Settlement Agreements and Arbitration in the Context of the ICC Rules' (1998) 9 *ICC ICArb Bull* no 2, 22.

[632] See *supra* Introduction, paras 15.63 *et seq*.

[633] See *infra* Art 31, paras 15.1150 *et seq*.

[634] For an illustration of enforcement of an Award by consent, see Indian Supreme Court, 13 May 1999, *Harendra H. Mehta et al v Mukesh H. Mehta*, (2000) YBCA vol XXV, 641.

[635] See *infra* Art 27, paras 15.947 and 15.954.

[636] ICC case 4761 in *Collection of ICC Arbitral Awards 1986–1991*, vol I, 298, with comments by Sigvard Jarvin.

to refuse to render an award, unless they consider that the settlement agreement violates, for instance public policy at the place of arbitration or under the law applicable to the contract. There is no time limit for rendering an award by consent. As long as no final award has been notified to the parties, the latter can bring an end to the arbitration by way of settlement and have the same recorded in an award by consent.[637]

Article 27. Scrutiny of the award by the Court

Before signing any Award, the Arbitral Tribunal shall submit it in draft form to the Court. The Court may lay down modifications as to the form of the Award and, without affecting the Arbitral Tribunal's liberty of decision, may also draw its attention to points of substance. No Award shall be rendered by the Arbitral Tribunal until it bas been approved by the Court as to its form.

(1) Introduction

Article 27 is probably one of the provisions of the ICC Rules which is the most misunderstood by parties and arbitrators but also the most useful for both of them. The scrutiny of awards by the ICC Court is a typical feature of ICC arbitration which distinguishes it from other arbitration institutions.[638] It is a special service rendered by the ICC Court and the relatively high administrative costs charged by the ICC for administering arbitration cases find their justification, *inter alia*, in that process and the value thereof, which should not be underestimated by the users of ICC arbitration.[639] **15.943**

In ICC arbitrations, like in any other international commercial arbitration, parties choose persons as arbitrators because they have confidence in their intellect, competence, experience, integrity and diligence.[640] When the ICC Court is to appoint an arbitrator it will seek to ensure that its candidate will meet these expectations.[641] In light of the significant amounts often at stake in ICC arbitration, and the complexities of cases, it is not surprising that some of the finest lawyers in the world have the privilege to act as arbitrators in ICC arbitration. It is also hardly surprising that the work product of such arbitrators is impeccable and that the scrutiny of the draft award by the ICC Court will not add much. However, it is submitted that even in these cases, the drafting of top quality awards could hardly be a reason not to have the awards first scrutinized by the Court. **15.944**

It should also not come as a surprise that quite a few awards do not match the expectations one is entitled to have in view of the important responsibility arbitrators assume, and the high standing they often enjoy. Indeed, awards may contain patent errors, be difficult to **15.945**

[637] It has happened that a settlement agreement was reached by the parties after the ICC Court had scrutinized and approved the final award, but prior to its signature and notification. As a consequence the Secretariat was advised by the parties that the final Award should not be communicated to them.

[638] See *supra* Introduction, para 15.51.

[639] In 2007, 349 Awards were approved by the ICC Court. No figure was published as to how many awards were approved with modifications or without. We do not know how many awards were actually scrutinized, either. Their number may have exceeded the number of approved awards.

[640] Craig/Park/Paulsson, *op cit*, 196.

[641] See *supra* Art 8, paras 15.390 *et seq.*, and *supra* Art 9, para 15.425, as to the ICC Court's criteria when appointing an arbitrator.

understand, incomplete inasmuch as not all claims have been fully dealt with and generally poorly composed, both as far as legal reasoning and/or the drafting is concerned.[642]

15.946 The reasons for poorly drafted awards do not matter that much, that is to say whether it is lack of experience and skills, including the arbitrator's linguistic skills,[643] the difficulty of the subject matter coupled with poor pleadings by the parties, or simply the lack of care of the arbitrator. What matters, however, is the ultimate work product that will be given to the parties, once the draft award was approved by the ICC Court. As follows from the very wording of Art 27, and as will be discussed below, the ICC Court is limited in its efforts to improve an arbitrator's work product. It can only require modifications of form; and where issues of substance are concerned, it may only draw the arbitrator's attention thereto. As will also be discussed below, it is not always easy to distinguish between 'form' and 'substance', and there are no hard and fast rules as to what constitutes one or the other.

15.947 In the authors' experience, the members of the ICC Court always seek to respect the arbitrators' autonomy in reaching their decision, and will not impose changes that would be incompatible with the ICC Court's duty of neutrality and the 'judicial' authority which rests exclusively with the arbitrators.

(2) The ICC Court's scrutiny process

15.948 Article 27 requires that 'any Award' be submitted in draft form to the ICC Court. This includes that is to say an interim award on jurisdiction, a partial Award on liability, an Award by consent (Art 26) as much as a final award that deals solely with the issue of costs.

15.949 The distinction between an award and a procedural order has recently been decided in the American and French courts which seem to privilege the substance over form or description when determining whether the decision is an award or a procedural order.[644] In the *Publicis* case,[645] the US Court of Appeals for the Seventh Circuit decided that an order for production of documents rendered by an arbitral tribunal in England could be enforced in

[642] In a different context, *Kurt Heller,* a well-respected Austrian jurist and well known arbitrator stated: 'Anyone who is familiar with arbitration can tell of careless arbitrators (. . .). Arbitrators (. . .) not subject to any controls would most likely tend to be less prudent about the proper establishment of the facts and the law of a case'. Heller, K., 'Constitutional Limits of Arbitration' (2000) *Stockholm Arb Rep* 2000:1, 7.

[643] While the majority of Awards are written in English, the native language of many arbitrators is a language other than English; see *supra* Art 16, paras 15.622 *et seq.*

[644] Paris, 25 March 1994, *Société Sardisud et autre v société Technip et autre,* (1994) *Rev arb* no 2, 391 (an Award is 'the decision of an arbitral tribunal which finally settles, in whole or in part, the underlying dispute either on the merits, on jurisdiction or on any procedural issue which terminates the arbitral proceedings'); see also Paris, 1 July 1999, *Société Braspetro Oil Services (Brasoil) v The Management and Implementation Authority of the Great Man-Made River Project (GMRA),* (2000) ASA Bull vol 18 no 2, 376; (1999) YBCA Vol.XXIVa, 296; (1999) *Rev arb* no 4, 834; Paris, 11 April 2002, *Société ABC International v Société Diverseylever Ltd* (2003) *Rev arb* no 1, 778 and 160, note Bensaude (2003) YBCA vol XXVIII, 209; SAR 2002:1 185, note Kaplan and Cuniberti; see also Jarvin, S., 'To What Extent Are Procedural Decisions of Arbitrators Subject to Court Review?' (1999) *ICCA Congress Series no 9,* 366; Carlevaris, 'La qualification des décisions des tribunaux arbitraux dans le Règlement d'arbitrage CCI et dans la jurisprudence française' in *Les Cahiers de l'Arbitrage, Volume I, op cit,* 153.

[645] See Smit/Turner, *op cit,* 47.

the United States. In the *Braspetro* case, the Paris Court of Appeal annulled an order which it viewed as an award.[646]

In the *Publicis* case,[647] the US Court of Appeals for the Seventh Circuit decided that an order for production of documents rendered by a Tribunal in England could be enforced in the United States. In doing so, the Court dealt with the difference between procedural orders and awards in the following terms: **15.950**

> [4] Publicis says the tribunal's decision was an interim order and, under the convention, only arbitral 'awards' are final and subject to confirmation (. . .)
>
> [5] Publicis' position is that an arbitral ruling can be final in every respect, but unless the document bears the word 'award' it is not final and is unenforceable. This is extreme and untenable formalism. The New York Convention, the United Nations arbitration rules, and the commentators' consistent use of the label 'award' when discussing final arbitral decisions does not bestow transcendental significance on the term. Their treatment of 'award' as interchangeable with final does not necessarily mean that synonyms such as decision, opinion, order, or ruling could not also be final. The content of a decision–not its nomenclature–determines finality. (. . .)
>
> [6] . . . Discovery involves compiling information needed to reach a resolution; it is an early step in moving toward the end result. In the situation at hand, whether or not Publicis had to turn over the tax records is the whole ball of wax. The tribunal's order resolved the dispute, or was supposed to, at any rate. Producing the documents wasn't just some procedural matter–it was the very issue True North wanted arbitrated. The finality of the tribunal's ruling is demonstrated by the deadline. (. . .) A ruling on a discrete, time-sensitive issue may be final and ripe for confirmation even though other claims remain to be addressed by arbitrators. (citations omitted)
>
> [8, 9] . . . Despite some possible superficial technical flaws, and despite its designation as an 'order' instead of an 'award', the arbitral tribunal's decision–as to this chunk of the case–was final.[648]

In the *Braspetro* case, a Tribunal in an ICC arbitration had issued a document that it entitled an order. The Tribunal did not submit the order to the ICC Court for scrutiny and an application was made to annul it for failure to meet the procedural requirements of the Rules regarding scrutiny. The Paris Court of Appeal annulled the order, which it viewed as an award.[649] The Paris Court of Appeal stated as follows: **15.951**

> [1] The qualification of [a decision as an] award does not depend on the terms used by the arbitrators or by the parties. On 15 October 1997, Brasoil requested the arbitrators to review the partial award of 5 March 1995, alleging that GMRA had fraudulently withheld essential documents which it already had in its possession at the beginning of the arbitration and which could have affected the decision on who was responsible for the malfunctioning [of the wells], and that in any case these documents revealed an essential fact of which Brasoil was unaware through no fault of its own. GMRA maintained that the request was inadmissible

[646] See the *Braspetro* case, referred to in n 647, *infra* para 15.950.

[647] See Smit/Turner, *op cit*, 47.

[648] 206 F.3d 725 US Court of Appeals, 7th Circ, 14 March 2000, (2000) YBCA Vol.XXV at 1153–5.

[649] See the *Braspetro* case, referenced in n 646, *supra*.

and unfounded. The parties exchanged statements on this issue and were heard at the hearing of 19 December 1997 together with their 'respective experts'.

[2] In the light of all these elements and after a five-month deliberation, the arbitral tribunal rendered the 'order' of 14 May 1998, by which, after a lengthy examination of the parties' positions, it declared that the request could not be granted because Brasoil had not proven that there had been fraud as alleged. This reasoned decision–by which the arbitrators considered the contradictory theories of the parties and examined in detail whether they were founded, and solved, in a final manner, the dispute between the parties concerning the admissibility of Brasoil's request for a review, by denying it and thereby ending the dispute submitted to them–appears to be an exercise of its jurisdictional power by the arbitral tribunal.

[3] GMRA's objection that the 'order' at issue refuses to open an appellate instance and thus amounts to 'decisions on the administration of the proceedings' made by arbitral institutions to refuse commencement of an arbitration or joinder of a third party, is unfounded. Even if the similarity were perfect, the main reason for which the decisions of the ICC, whatever the nature of the problems they solve and the procedure followed, are not awards, is that they are not rendered by an arbitral tribunal, which clearly is not the case here.

[4] Contrary to GMRA's opinion and notwithstanding its qualification as an 'order', the decision of 14 May 1998, which did not concern the evidence-taking in the arbitration, is thus indeed an award. Hence, Brasoil's request [to the Court of Appeal] is admissible.[650]

15.952 In some cases, the chairman and his co-arbitrators or the chairman alone will sign the draft award before submitting it to the ICC Court. The signature of the draft award is neither required by the Rules, not otherwise necessary and will not change the nature of the award as a draft submitted for approval by the ICC Court.[651] The signature, and/or sometimes the initialling of each page, of the draft award by the Arbitral Tribunal may sometimes be useful as it clearly indicates that the draft is the work product of the entire panel and reflects its position at that time, be it by unanimity or majority.[652] When submitting the final draft of an award to the Secretariat, a chairman should obviously always copy in his co-arbitrators, and provide them with a copy of the final text. It may happen that the chairman makes 'last minute' changes to an award, that may be the result of the final deliberations of the arbitrators, be it at a meeting, over the telephone, or by way of correspondence, or simply the result of the chairman's last careful review of the draft award.

15.953 The Rules do not say in what format the draft award is to be submitted. For reasons of speed, and absent an overly lengthy award, many Arbitral Tribunals will send the draft to the Secretariat by email or telefax. The use of electronic mail with the draft award as an attachment is becoming more and more frequent.

15.954 Once the Secretariat has received the draft award it will read it and examine it against the Terms of Reference to ensure that the claims and issues identified therein have been dealt with by the Arbitral Tribunal. If the counsel in charge of the file has questions he will get in

[650] (1999) YBCA vol XXIVa at 297–8.

[651] (1992) Bull ASA, 381(384–385) No nullity of draft Award that was signed prior to ICC Court's approval.

[652] See *supra* Art 25, paras 15.925 *et seq*, with regard to votes.

contact with the sole arbitrator or chairman of the Arbitral Tribunal, either in writing, or, more frequently, over the telephone. At the same time the Secretariat will prepare an agenda for the Court setting out its views and recommendations for approval or non-approval.

Whenever the award is of particular importance, either because of the amounts at stake, and/or because a government is involved,[653] the Secretariat will submit the draft award to the Court's plenary session. It will ask a member of the ICC Court to draft a written report which the member will then present orally to his fellow members. Thereafter, the Chairman of the ICC Court will seek the views of the other members of the Court, and solicit any additional comments from the Secretariat. **15.955**

At the end of its deliberations the ICC Court will either approve the draft award, with or without the request for modifications, or it will defer the approval to one of its next sessions. **15.956**

(3) Modifications of form and points of substance

Modifications as to form: Whenever an issue of form of the award is at stake, the ICC Court may lay down modifications, that is to say invite the Arbitral Tribunal to correct or amend the award. Clerical errors, such as typographical and computational errors, are probably the most frequent examples in the ICC Court's practice where modifications as to form are requested. Where the final award omits a decision on costs, or the latter is incomplete, or when the Award does not indicate the name of the parties or the place of arbitration, the Arbitral Tribunal will be requested to amend the draft award accordingly. **15.957**

ICC awards need to contain reasons. When an award contains no reason on a given issue or when such reasons remain unclear or are contradictory, the ICC Court will request the Arbitral Tribunal to provide additional reasoning or to improve its reasoning so as to make the point in contention understandable. It is evidently debatable whether more or better reasoning is required to make an award fully intelligible. **15.958**

Unlike the Arbitral Tribunal and the parties, the ICC Court is not familiar with the pleadings and the evidence submitted during the arbitration. Therefore, an issue that may be easily understandable to the Arbitral Tribunal and the parties, may not be understood by the ICC Court. In some cases, it will be sufficient for the Arbitral Tribunal to explain the background in a letter or telephone conversation with, the Secretariat. In other cases the Arbitral Tribunal may have to redraft one or more paragraphs of its award so as to allow a third person, such as the Court, to immediately understand its reasoning. **15.959**

Points of substance: They concern the merit of the Arbitral Tribunal's decision for example its upholding of arbitral jurisdiction, its decision to consider the law of one party as being applicable rather than the law of the other, its decision to consider the termination of a contract to be wrongful or not, to award simple rather than compound interest etc. Any decision that may either change the outcome of the case or that may have an impact on the outcome relates to the substance of the award. Such decisions fall within the entire discretion of the Arbitral Tribunal which alone has studied the parties' pleadings and evidence, **15.960**

[653] See *supra* Art 1, para 15.91.

heard testimony, and examined the relevant law, and which alone has the authority to decide upon the claims as a result thereof.

15.961 When the Arbitral Tribunal's decision on a point of substance appears to be manifestly wrong, or simply questionable, the ICC Court may draw the Arbitral Tribunal's attention thereto. The Court will normally use careful wording in doing so, in order not to give the impression it is trying to infringe upon the Arbitral Tribunal's freedom of decision. In doing so the ICC Court has Art 35 of the Rules in mind, in so far as the latter requires the ICC Court and the Arbitral Tribunal to make every effort to ensure that the award is enforceable at law.[654]

15.962 In the French case *Cubic Defense System v Chambre de Commerce Internationale*, the arbitrators made a procedural decision which they qualified as provisional and subject to later confirmation through a formal, reasoned award.[655] The procedural decision related to certain claims which were distinguishable from others which were time-barred; it was a majority decision, with one arbitrator dissenting. Cubic challenged the majority arbitrators but the ICC Court refused to replace them and Cubic then attacked the ICC in the French courts, asserting that the ICC should have examined and immediately revised the arbitrators' procedural decision since it was nothing else than a disguised award according to Art 21 of the 1975/1988 Rules. Cubic maintained that this practice would lead to a complete freedom for arbitrators to qualify their decisions as provisional or procedural in order to prevent the ICC Court from controlling them. The Paris court of first instance rejected this argument and decided that the ICC Court has no power to substitute its own qualifications to those made by the arbitrators as to the proper character of their decisions; that qualification is the prerogative of the arbitrators. The Court of Appeal confirmed this decision.[656]

(4) The ICC Court's approval of the award

15.963 The draft award can be approved by the ICC Court at any of its sessions, ie not only at its monthly plenary session, but at any of the committee sessions that take place almost every week.[657] Once a draft award has been approved, the Secretariat will inform the Arbitral Tribunal, and will request that it be provided with the required number of duly executed originals of the award. The Arbitral Tribunal can now 'render' its award, ie sign and date it for notification to the parties. If follows from Art 28(1) that the notification of the award is done by the Court's Secretariat not by the Arbitral Tribunal.[658]

15.964 Once the draft award has been approved the Arbitral Tribunal must not make any further changes, other than of a clerical nature, unless it resubmits the award or the amended section thereof to the ICC Court for renewed scrutiny.

[654] This is not to say that an Award that is manifestly wrong on a point of substance must necessarily be set aside and would not be enforced.

[655] See decision of the *Tribunal de Grande Instance* Paris, 8 October 1986, *Rev arb* (1987) 367; Paris, decision of 21 May 1997, *Rev arb* (1997) 417; *Cass. Civ. 1re*, 20 February 2001 *op cit* Bull I, n 39.

[656] See *supra* para 15.950, and *infra* Art 29, fn 699, regarding *Braspetro Oil* Case.

[657] See *supra* Art 1, paras 15.91 and 15.117.

[658] See *infra* Art 28, para 15.966.

Article 28. Notification, deposit and enforceability of the award

(1) Once an Award has been made, the Secretariat shall notify to the parties the text signed by the Arbitral Tribunal, provided always that the costs of the arbitration have been fully paid to the ICC by the parties or by one of them.

(2) Additional copies certified true by the Secretary-General shall be made available on request and at any lime to the parties, but to no one else.

(3) By the virtue of the notification made in accordance with Paragraph 1 of this Article, the parties waive any other form of notification or deposit on the part of the Arbitral Tribunal.

(4) An original of each Award made in accordance with the present Rules shall be deposited with the Secretariat.

(5) The Arbitral Tribunal and the Secretariat shall assist the parties in complying with whatever further formalities may be necessary.

(6) Every Award shall be binding on the parties. By submitting the dispute to arbitration under these Rules, the parties undertake to carry out any Award without delay and shall be deemed to have waived their right to any form of recourse insofar as such waiver can validly be made.

(1) Introduction

The scope of Art 28, as its title indicates, covers the formalities of notification and deposit of the award once the arbitrators have signed it and provides for the finality and enforcement of the award. **15.965**

The award may, as defined in Art 2, be an interim, partial or final award, or an award by consent pursuant to Art 26. **15.966**

(2) Article 28(1): Notification of the award

Once an award has been made it is the Secretariat of the ICC Court, not the Arbitral Tribunal, that will notify the award to the parties. The burden of notifying an award does not fall upon the sole arbitrator, or chairman of an Arbitral Tribunal, as it does in an *ad hoc* arbitration, but upon the administrative body of the arbitral institution. The ICC Court's Secretariat has the exclusive role of notifying awards. Pursuant to Art 28(1), two conditions must be met before the award will be notified to the parties. **15.967**

Article 28(1) operates only 'once an Award has been made', ie signed by the arbitrators. The 'Making of the Award' is the subject of Art 25, and an 'Award by Consent' is dealt with under Art 26. Before an award is signed by the arbitrators, the ICC Court will have to scrutinize and approve it in accordance with Art 27. **15.968**

In case of the final award, or as the case may be, the award by consent, the arbitrators' mission comes to an end upon signature of the award and the arbitrators become *functus officio*. Nevertheless, there is one important, although limited, exception to this general principle: the arbitrators' right to correct or to interpret the award, Art 29.[659] Outside this exception, any request by a party for reopening the proceedings, for reconsideration of an issue or for deciding upon an issue or a claim that was left out of the award would normally have to be rejected by the Arbitral Tribunal as not being admissible.[660] **15.969**

---

659 See *infra* Art 29, para 15.1005.

660 Craig/Park/Paulsson, *op cit*, 406.

15.970 The Secretariat's notification of the award further requires that the costs of arbitration have been paid in full to the ICC, whether by one or both of the parties. The purpose of this provision is obviously identifiable as a 'security device' to ensure that the ICC is not left out of funds to pay the arbitrators once the award is in the hands of the parties.[661] The rule is simple to understand: no payment of the costs in full, no award for the parties. In practice, the arbitration costs have already been paid earlier in the proceedings, by means of the advances on costs, by either both parties or one of the parties if the other defaults.

15.971 The Secretariat will notify one original copy to each of the parties, which may be by registered mail, for example if the parties are in Western Europe, by courier or by hand if the parties come to the ICC to pick up the award. Whatever method is used, the Secretariat maintains a proper record of receipt, ie a signed return receipt from the parties, since it may be called upon for proof if the receipt is ever questioned. Awards are normally not transmitted by telefax or email, although this would be the best way of ensuring that both parties get to learn the findings and holdings of the Arbitral Tribunal at the same time. It is frustrating for a party to learn from its opponent that it has lost the case when it has not yet received the award, whereas the other party has. If both parties, or their representatives, are in Paris, they may agree that the award be simultaneously remitted to both of them at the ICC headquarters. In one case, counsel based in Colombo (Sri Lanka) received the award by courier before the Paris-based counsel for the other party received it by registered mail. Simultaneous transmittal by email or by access to a website is not practised by the Secretariat. An electronic copy of the signed award is posted on the ICC Netcase Services but only after the originals have been notified by the Secretariat and received by the parties.[662]

15.972 Where parties know that the notification is imminent they may agree with the Secretariat personal pick-up of the award at a given date and hour at the ICC headquarters. A special power-of-attorney of the person collecting the award will have to be provided to the Secretariat in advance.

15.973 The general rule is that notification will be made to the parties in accordance with the stipulations in the Terms of Reference regarding 'the addresses of the parties to which notifications and communications arising in the course of the arbitration may be made', Art 18(l)(b).[663] In the event that parties have included more than one addressee, ie where a party is represented by more than one counsel, and since normally only one original copy of the award per party will be notified, the Terms of Reference should preferably state which addressee is to receive the award. For instance, a party may wish to receive 'notification' directly rather than through its counsel.

15.974 It is generally possible for a party to get an indication from the Secretariat as to the status of the issuance of the award and when the Secretariat anticipates that notification will take place.

---

661 Craig/Park/Paulsson, *op cit*, 400.

662 See ICC, 'Conditions of Access and Use of Netcase' (ICC Note of 18 April 2007), <http://www.iccnetcase.org>; see also *supra* Introduction, para 15.15.

663 See *supra* Art 18, para 15.711.

In its notification letter the Secretariat will inform the parties of the date of the session when the award was approved by Court and of the amount of the costs of arbitration, and make a statement that such amount has been fully covered by the payments effectuated by the parties. The Secretariat routinely draws the parties' attention to the binding effect of the award and to their undertaking to carry out the award in accordance with Art 28(6). **15.975**

It is also at this stage that the Secretariat will inform the parties that it will close its file on the arbitration, and archive certain key documents, ie the Terms of Reference and all awards, as well as copies of all pertinent correspondence of the Secretariat and records of the Court's decisions. Parties and arbitrators will be invited to give their instructions to the Secretariat concerning documents submitted to the Secretariat in the course of the arbitration, which will be returned at the request of parties and the arbitrators at their own cost. Failing instructions within a time limit to be fixed by the Secretariat, such documents may be destroyed.[664] **15.976**

(3) Article 28(2): Certified copies of the award

As mentioned above, only one original set of the award is notified to each party. Since the parties may be in need for additional copies for enforcement or annulment proceedings or other purposes,[665] Art 28(2) confirms that parties may obtain, upon request, at any time additional copies of the award, which will be true copies certified by the Secretary-General of the ICC Court, and, if needed, affixed with the apostille.[666] **15.977**

Such certified copies will be provided to the parties at no extra charge and can often be obtained from the Secretariat within a very short time (normally two to three days). Pursuant to Art 5 of the Court's Internal Rules, the Secretary-General may delegate certification powers to the General Counsel and Deputy Secretary-General of the ICC Court. **15.978**

Only parties to the arbitration may be provided with additional copies. **15.979**

(4) Article 28(3): No notification or deposit of the award by the Arbitral Tribunal

By virtue of the notification of the award by the Secretariat, as set out under Art 28(1), the parties are deemed to waive any other form of notification or deposit on the part of the Arbitral Tribunal. **15.980**

Thus, by virtue of agreement of the parties, an Arbitral Tribunal is freed of any requirements of local procedural laws prevailing at the place of arbitration for notifying and/or depositing the award unless such requirements are of a mandatory nature. In some jurisdictions arbitrators may have a duty to register the award with the local court, in particular in domestic arbitrations,[667] or before any recourse against it can be exercised in the courts.[668] The waiver contained in Art 28(3) will only be effective where the laws applicable at the **15.981**

---

[664] See App II, Art 1(6) and (7).

[665] Where the Claimant is a consortium composed of four different companies, they may each wish to have a certified copy of the Award.

[666] See *infra* para 15.985.

[667] See Spanish *Tribunal Supremo*, decision of 28 March 1994, *ABC v Espanola SA*, (1994) *Rev arb*, 749.

[668] See *Cour d'Appel de Paris* decision of 22 March 1996, *N.V. Lernout et Hauspie Speechproducts v Société Compumedia SL*, (1997) *Rev arb*, 83.

place of arbitration uphold the parties' freedom to dispense the arbitrators from carrying out such formalities. This provision follows from the fact that after signature of the award, the arbitrators are *functus officio* and, therefore, play no part in the enforcement process.[669]

15.982 The ICC arbitral process is not dependent upon such requirements of local procedural laws for its conclusion. However, if parties need to or wish to deposit an award with local courts at the place of arbitration, the Secretariat will assist them.[670]

(5) Article 28(4): Deposit of the award at the ICC

15.983 An original set of the award will always be kept by the Secretariat of the ICC Court. Thus, the ICC acts as depository of all awards rendered under its auspices.[671] Obviously, it is important to preserve a copy of the award, as well as to have an original set available in the future in case it is necessary to verify the authenticity of the award or provide additional certified copies to parties for enforcement purposes.

15.984 The Secretariat thus takes over such responsibility from the Arbitral Tribunal, which is not required to play a role in the deposit of the award under national laws. This makes sense since the same procedures for deposit will be applied in all ICC arbitrations and such procedures are kept in the hands of an institution which is permanent and adapted to the preservation of such records.

15.985 As far as the ICC arbitral process is concerned, it is completed upon notification and deposit of the award in accordance with this Article.

(6) Article 28(5): Assistance of the Arbitral Tribunal and the Secretariat

15.986 The ICC as an institution has an obvious interest in the process of enforcement of awards rendered under its aegis, and the Secretariat provides assistance to parties where this is sought in order to execute an award, ie where a party is required or wishes to deposit its award with a local court. When foreign courts (eg, in Spain) request that the certified true copy of the original award be affixed with the apostille, the Secretariat may also assist a party in obtaining the apostille under the Hague Convention of 5 October 1961 from the competent authorities and will normally do so at no extra cost to that party.[672]

(7) Article 28(6): The effects of the award

15.987 Ensuring the finality and enforceability of an award is pivotal to the whole ICC arbitral process and to the extent possible, in view of requirements under national laws, this is embodied in the ICC Rules.

15.988 (7.1) **Binding character of awards** The ICC Rules themselves expressly provide for the finality of the arbitral procedure in that every award, once signed by the arbitrators and

[669] On the different modalities of delivery of Awards, see also van Houtte, H., 'The delivery of the Award, Ten Pitfalls' in *ASA Special Series* no 29 (September 2007) 76; van Houtte, H., 'The delivery of Awards to the Parties' (2005) 21 *Arb Int'l* no 2, 177; see also Bühler/Webster, ICC Handbook, *op cit*, 28–12 *et seq* with respect to delivery of Awards in different legal systems.

[670] See *infra* para 15.985.

[671] They are kept in a safe box at the ICC. It would make sense for the ICC to store copies of the most recent original awards on electronic format.

[672] See *supra* para 15.977.

notified by the Secretariat to the parties, has a legally binding effect upon the parties and enforcement proceedings may be based thereon immediately.

The award disposes of the dispute submitted to arbitration and therefore such matters become *res judicata*, ie they will not be examined before another forum (except in the event that the award is set aside). **15.989**

The award has binding effect only as between the parties to the arbitration. It does not extend to third parties. The findings of an award in one arbitration are not binding in another arbitration where the same parties or facts are involved, although the Tribunal in the subsequent arbitration may refer to such findings. **15.990**

The time at which an award becomes binding on the parties is significant with regards to international conventions concerning the recognition by states of foreign arbitral awards. The most important of such treaties is the New York Convention.[673] Thereunder, signatory states are not required to recognize and enforce an award until the latter has become binding on the parties (Art V(l)(e)).[674] The immediate binding effect of ICC awards is embodied in Art 28(6).[675] **15.991**

(7.2) Parties' obligation to perform an award promptly and waiver of a right to recourse Pursuant to Art 28(b), the parties have undertaken to carry out an award without delay. Accordingly, it is an implied term of the arbitration agreement that the parties will honour the award. This obligation follows from the immediate binding effect of the award in the first part of Art 28(6). At the inception of the ICC Rules, parties were under a moral obligation, which subsequently evolved into a legal obligation, in line with developments in international treaties and conventions allowing for the enforceability of foreign arbitral awards, ie the Geneva Conventions and later the New York Convention. **15.992**

The status of an award may, however, be qualified under national laws and the recognition and enforcement mechanisms available under international treaties and conventions may not exist where a party comes from a country that is not a signatory thereto.[676] **15.993**

Therefore, the undertaking by parties to carry out awards and to respect the final and binding effect thereof is significant and in practice it seems especially so, since a high percentage of the ICC awards are satisfied by the parties voluntarily.[677] Voluntary execution of the awards is indeed one of the cornerstones of international arbitration. Parties that frequently insert ICC or other international arbitration clauses in their contracts know that the arbitral system will only be truly viable if both parties accept to 'play the rules of the game' until the end, that is to say until the award is rendered and satisfied by the losing party. These parties will normally not hesitate to comply voluntarily with the award even **15.994**

[673] See *supra* Introduction, para 15.66.

[674] Craig/Park/Paulsson, *op cit*, 401; Derains/Schwartz, A Guide, *op cit*, 320.

[675] The final and binding effect of Awards is a feature of both institutional and *ad hoc* arbitration rules, see eg UNCITRAL Rules, Art 32(2).

[676] The number of signatories to the New York Convention stands at 144 (as of January 2009), see Introduction, para 15.66.

[677] No statistics are available in that respect, and the figure of 90% of voluntary compliance with ICC Awards, which is often advanced in ICC arbitration circles, may be somewhat on the high side.

where they believe that the arbitrators 'got it wrong' on the merits, or were 'not entirely right' in their decision. It is and should remain the exception that a party not content with the outcome of an arbitration starts an entirely new battle before the national courts of one or several countries.

15.995 A further aspect of finality and enforceability of ICC awards lies in the waiver by the parties to have recourse against the award. Such waiver extends 'insofar as such waiver can validly be made', that is to say appeals to state courts will not be permitted unless under the national laws in question such waiver is invalid. Generally speaking to waive a right to appeal the award is allowed pursuant to the legislation of many countries.

15.996 However, national laws providing for the right to seek the annulment (setting aside) of awards are not waived by this provision. This is due to their mandatory nature, which prevents parties from waiving their rights to challenge an award before the competent state courts in advance.[678]

15.997 The French courts have confirmed this view in several Court of Appeal decisions.[679] Article 28(6) was not intended to and does not amount to a waiver of the basic rights of the parties, including the right to have the award set aside under applicable law or to object to its enforcement under the grounds set out in the New York Convention discussed below. Nor does it permit a party to execute on the award without judicial formality on the award. As the French courts have held:

> Whatever its obligatory effect the undertaking [in Article 28(6)] does not have the effect of conferring on the arbitral award the status of an automatically executory judgment as claimed by the defendants; that it cannot deprive the parties not only of the possibility of seeking to have the award annulled, which is a matter of public policy, but also of that to invoke the generally applicable provisions of the [New Code of Civil Procedure] to seek to block the temporary execution if, as in the present case, it has been ordered; Article 28(6) of the above rules and the obligation of good faith in the carrying out of the award which follows from it imply solely a strict interpretation of the cases in which one can derogate even temporarily from the enforcement of the award and therefore the objection as to admissibility of the defendants must be rejected.[680] (Authors' translation)

15.998 The position of the Paris Court of Appeal was confirmed in the *République du Congo* case where the French Supreme Court took the view that the reference to Art 28 is not to be construed as a waiver of the suspensive nature of the annulment action ('recours en

[678] Under the Swiss PILA (Art 192), the parties can waive their right to bring proceedings to have the award set aside (by the Swiss Supreme Court), provided certain conditions are met Art 28(6) of the ICC Rules does not qualify as an exclusion agreement under Swiss arbitration law; see eg Berti, S.V., Honsell, H., Vogt, N.P. and Schnyder, A.K., *International Arbitration in Switzerland* (Helbing & Lichtenhahn, Basel, 2000), Art 92 n 14. The same applies for exclusion agreements under the English Arbitration Act 1996 s 69, and the Belgian arbitration law (Art 1717 of the *Code Judiciaire*). See the critical appraisal in that respect by Heller, K., *op cit*, 17.

[679] Paris, 5 February 2003, *Société Thalès Air Defence v GIE Euromissile et Eads*, (2004) *Rev arb* no 1, 94; Paris, 22 February 1996, *Société Karl Schlüter GmbH & Co KG v Société Industrielle et Minière (SNIM)*, (1997) *Rev arb* 83 (extracts only); see also Paris, 18 February 1989, *Société Almira Films v Pierrel ès qual* (1989) *Rev arb* 711.

[680] Paris, 5 February 2003, *Société Thalès Air Defence v GIE Euromissile et Eads*, (2004) *Rev arb* no 1, 94.

annulation').[681] Under French law, the *recours en annulation* of the award is suspensive in accordance with Art 1506 of the French CPC, unless the parties have expressly agreed to waive its suspensive effect or when the Tribunal has granted a provisional enforcement of the award in accordance with Art 514 of the French CPC.[682] In other words, in the context of international arbitration, if provisional enforcement has been ordered in the award, it can only be terminated by the judge on appeal on specific grounds, ie if it is prohibited by law or would have patently excessive consequences. The purpose of such declaration is to neutralize a stay of the enforcement of the award pending the challenging procedure of the award before French courts. In the Case of *Groupe Antoine Tabet v République du Congo* the French Supreme Court stated:

> Article 28 of the rules of arbitration of the International Chamber of Commerce which provides that every Award has an obligatory effect for the parties which undertake to carry it out and are presumed to have waived their rights to any possible recourse, does not provide that the award is executory by provision or by law. This undertaking does not confer to the arbitral award the status of an executory decision. It cannot be also inferred from the acceptance of the obligatory character of the award that a party has waived its right to challenge the arbitral award. This right, by virtue of articles 1506, 1500 and 1476 to 1479 NCPC, is suspensive, except when the judgment is granted provisional enforcement or is automatically enforced by law. (Authors' translation)

In most jurisdictions such recourse is nonetheless limited to a few grounds of annulment, ie where the Arbitral Tribunal lacks jurisdiction, fraud and public policy reasons.[683] **15.999**

The position on the recognition and enforcement of awards varies from country to country and parties are well advised to look to the provisions of the law of the place where it may seek to enforce an award in respect of relevant time limits, and whether or not it is required to register or deposit the award before local courts.[684] **15.1000**

Under some arbitration laws the provisional enforcement of an award can be ordered by the Arbitral Tribunal so that an annulment action at the place of arbitration will have no suspensive effect.[685] It is a matter of discretion of the Arbitral Tribunal whether or not to order, upon the Request of a party, the provisional enforcement of the award. It seems doubtful **15.1001**

[681] Paris, 10 March 2005, *République du Congo v SA Total E&P Congo*, (2005) *Rev arb* no 3, 788. See also Cass Civ 1re, 4 July 2007, *Groupe Antoine Tabet v République du Congo et Société Totale E&P Congo*, no 05-16.586; see also (2007) *Rev arb* no 3, 648; see, however, the contrary decision of the Paris TGI, December 2002, *Banque Centrale de Syrie et République arabe de Syrie v Société Papillon Group Corporation (PGC)*, (2003) *Rev arb* no 1, 245; Farhad, *op cit*, 115; Fouchard/Gaillard/Goldman, *op cit*, 1011.

[682] Paris, 2 June 2005, *Bacque et autres v Société Carlyle Luxembourg Holding*, (2005) *Rev arb* no 4, 1015, note Callé.

[683] The limited scope of Art 28(6) is also confirmed under Swiss law as it does not construe a waiver of recourse under Art 192(2) of the Swiss PILA. See Poudret/Besson, *op cit*, 780, para 839; Müller Ch., *International Arbitration, A Guide to the Complete Swiss Case Law* (Unreported and Reported) (Thomson/Schulthess, London/Zurich, 2004) 208, para 1.4. See also Baizeau, D., 'Waiving the Right to Challenge an Award Rendered in Switzerland: Caveats and Drafting Considerations for Foreign Parties' (2005) *Int'l Arb L Rev* no 3, 69.

[684] See *supra* para 15.985; An overview of the decisions of primary and secondary jurisdictions with reference of annulment and enforcement can be found at Bühler/Webster, ICC Handbook, *op cit*, paras 28–30 *et seq*.

[685] In France, see Arts 1500, 1479 (1) of the *Code de Procedure Civile*.

that the undertaking of the parties pursuant to Art 28(6) is, by itself, a sufficient reason to reject a party's request for provisional enforcement.

15.1002 (7.3) **Enforcement of awards that have been set aside** Another issue related to Art 28(6) is the enforcement of annulled awards. It was originally held that an award set aside at its place of arbitration could not be enforced under the 1958 New York Convention. Certain jurisdictions, however, now permit the enforcement of the annulled award in a New York Convention state other than the state of the place of arbitration.

15.1003 Thus, the French Courts permitted enforcement of the awards in the *Norsolor*, *Hilmarton*, *Chromalloy* and *Bechtel* cases irrespective of their annulment in the states of origin.[686] The French Supreme Court has sustained its position in the recent *Putrabali* case.[687] In its opinion, an international arbitral award is a decision of international justice. As such the award is governed by national public policy provisions. It is only necessary to verify whether the rules of recognition and enforcement in the state of enforcement have been respected.

15.1004 A further aspect concerns the questions whether the courts of the place of enforcement should grant a stay until the final decision of the courts at the place of arbitration has been rendered. Thus, Art VI of the New York Convention provides such possibility if considered appropriate by the enforcing court. However, in most New York Convention countries, one would expect that the local courts would be reluctant to suspend enforcement proceedings based on annulment proceedings at the place of arbitration unless the annulment proceedings have a reasonable prospect of success.

Article 29. Correction and interpretation of the award

(1) On its own initiative, the Arbitral Tribunal may correct a clerical, computational or typographical error, or any errors of similar nature contained in an Award, provided such correction is submitted for approval to the Court within 30 days of the date of such Award.

(2) Any application of a party for the correction of an error of the kind referred to in Article 29(1), or for the interpretation of an Award, must be made to the Secretariat within 30 days of the receipt of the Award by such party in a number of copies as stated in Article 3(1). After transmittal of the application to the Arbitral Tribunal, it shall grant the other party a short time limit, normally not exceeding 30 days, from the receipt of the application by that party to submit any comments thereon. If the Arbitral Tribunal decides to correct or interpret the Award, it shall submit its decision in draft form to the Court not later than 30 days following the expiration of the time limit for the receipt of any comments from the other party or within such other period as the Court may decide.

---

[686] Cass Civ 1e 9 October 1984, *Pabalk Ticaret Sirketi v Norsolor SA* (1985), Rev. arb 431, note Goldman; Cass Civ1e 23 March 1994, *Hilmarton Ltd v Omnium de traitement et e valorisation—OTV,* (1995) YBCA Vol. XX, 663 ; Paris CA 14 January 1997 *République arabe d'Egypte v Société Chromalloy Aero Services,* (1997) *Rev arb* 395, note Fouchard; Paris CA 29 September 2005, *Direction générale de l'aviation civile de l'émirat de Dubai v Société Bechtel,* (2006) *Rev arb* 2006, 695, note Muir-Watt; IAR (2005), vol 3, 151, note Pinsolle, 159, and Mourre, 172.

[687] Cass Civ 1e 29 June 2007, *PT Putrabali Adyamulia v Rena Holding et Société Mnogutia Est Epices,* underling the independent legal nature of international arbitration awards. For a discussion see Gaillard, E., 'Enforcement of Awards Set Aside in the Country of Origin: the French Experience' (1999) *ICCA Congress Series no 9,* 505; CA (1re Ch C) 31 March 2005, Note by Gaillard, (2006) 3 *Rev arb,* 665.

(3) **The decision to correct or to interpret the Award shall take the form of an addendum and shall constitute part of the Award. The provisions of Articles 25, 27 and 28 shall apply mutatis mutandis.**

(1) Introduction

Article 29 expressly allows the correction and interpretation of awards. Indeed, many developed systems of national arbitration laws as well as international arbitration rules permit the correction of errors by arbitrators in their award. Some also foresee the possibility of interpretation of an award. **15.1005**

Once an arbitrator has signed his award he is considered to be *functus officio*. Awards finally dispose of the issues they address and arbitrators can normally not reopen decided issues of fact and law. Pursuant to Art 29, ICC arbitrators retain, however, for a limited period of time, narrow jurisdiction confined to the correction of errors and the interpretation of the award. **15.1006**

In theory, as opposed to other institutional systems, a provision relating to the correction and interpretation of an ICC award might seem to be superfluous since every ICC award is scrutinized and approved by the ICC Court prior to being signed by the Arbitral Tribunal and notified to the parties. Errors of clerical, computational, typographical or similar nature, therefore, should be detected by the ICC Court during its scrutiny of the award and corrected prior to the signing of the award by the Arbitral Tribunal. **15.1007**

What is foreseen by the ICC Rules is exactly what happens in practice: out of over 300 awards approved each year by the Court,[688] and despite ICC arbitrators using their best efforts in drafting awards, only a handful pass such scrutiny without the Secretariat and/or the Court finding at least one typographical error.[689] In some cases, the Court also seeks clarification of the reasoning given by the arbitrators, as it is empowered to do under the ICC Rules.[690] This holds true in particular when the award contains ambiguous or unclear language which compels clarification. **15.1008**

(2) General scope of Article 29

Article 29 refers in its paras 1 and 2 to 'an Award', and thus applies to any award, not just to the final award. This is in line with the power of scrutiny of the ICC Court which applies to 'any Award' (Art 27). Pursuant to the definition given in Art 2, an award may be an interim, partial or final award. An award may also be by consent of the parties (Art 26). Although not expressly stated in Art 29, the award in question will always be an award that has already been approved by the ICC Court, and signed by the Arbitral Tribunal. In practice, the award will also have been notified by the Secretariat to the parties, although this is not a prerequisite for an *ex officio* correction by the arbitrator. **15.1009**

[688] In 2007, the ICC Court approved 223 final awards, 96 partial awards and 30 awards by consent. There were 18 corrections/interpretations of Awards made pursuant to Art 29, (2008) 19 *ICC ICArb Bull* no 1, 13–14.

[689] See *supra* Art 27, para 15.956.

[690] *ibid* para 15.958.

15.1010 For the correction of an award to be made, there must be an error contained in the award, which may be of clerical, computational, typographical or of similar nature. The wording covers a wide range of errors, all of which should be non-material and should normally be visible on their face. The reference to errors of a 'similar nature' appears to be intended to cover mechanical errors as well. In interpreting an analogous provision, the English court noted that '[t]he authorities draw distinctions between errors affecting the expression of the tribunal's thought (which can be corrected) and errors in the tribunal's thought process (which cannot) and to not permitting corrections to reflect "second thoughts"'.[691]

15.1011 The word 'error' implies that something is wrong in the award that needs to be rectified. The more difficult question may be how to decide whether the error is of substance (ie material) or simply of form (ie non-material).

15.1012 Article 29 does not provide for a definition of an interpretation of an award. Article 29(2) refers simply to the 'application (. . .) for the interpretation of an Award'.

(3) The correction of an award

15.1013 Under the ICC Rules, the correction of an error in an award can arise in two circumstances: *ex officio* by the Arbitral Tribunal (Art 29(1)) or at the request of a party (Art 29(2)).

15.1014 (3.1) **Article 29(1): Upon the initiative of the Arbitral Tribunal** The first situation is where the Arbitral Tribunal itself detects that it has made an error. It does not matter whether the award has already been notified to the parties as long as the Arbitral Tribunal submits its request to the ICC Court within 30 days of the date of the award, that is to say the date of signature, not the date of notification to the parties.

15.1015 (3.2) **Article 29(2): At the request of a party** The second situation is where one party, upon receipt of the award, detects an error. The party then has 30 days to submit an application for correction to the Secretariat of the ICC Court.[692] It is consistent with ICC arbitration being an administrative and supervised arbitration system to have the party submit its application to the Secretariat of the ICC Court, and not directly to the Arbitral Tribunal. The Secretariat is also best placed to verify whether the Arbitral Tribunal is still in a position to function properly or not. In the event that an arbitrator has either become ill (and incapable to exercise his functions) or died, then the Secretariat would first have to ensure that the Arbitral Tribunal can be reconstituted.

15.1016 The application for the correction of the award shall be addressed to the Secretariat with the number of copies as provided in Art 3(1). The Secretariat will send a copy to the Arbitral Tribunal and to the other party. However, it is not unusual for the applicant to send courtesy copies of his request to the Arbitral Tribunal and the other party simultaneously with his request to the Secretariat. Thus, the Arbitral Tribunal will already have been 'forewarned'. Its duty to act will, however, only start once the Secretariat has notified the Arbitral Tribunal of the request.

---

[691] *Gannet Shipping Ltd v Eastrade Commodities Inc* [2001] EWHC Commercial 483 (6 December 2001).

[692] For the possibility of extending such time limit, see *infra* para 15.1032.

Upon receipt of the request, the Arbitral Tribunal may fix a time limit in which the other party is to submit its comments. The fact that an award was scrutinized and approved by the ICC Court will be no defence to the opponent of the request. Rather, in cases of errors, the ICC Court would have to admit, same as the arbitrators, that such error was overlooked. This will be the assumption anyway, but there is no way for the parties to know whether the point of error was at all considered by the ICC Court during the scrutiny of the award. **15.1017**

The Arbitral Tribunal may reject a request for correction and/or interpretation made by the parties in accordance with Art 29(2) third sentence. In 2007, 18 addenda correcting and/or interpreting arbitral awards were issued by ICC tribunals. **15.1018**

Requests for interpretation of awards run a greater risk of being rejected than requests for correction. As the 'interpretation' of the award is not defined under the Rules, a party could be more tempted to demand an interpretation in terms of an inappropriate supplement or modification of the award. In a recent ICC case the Arbitral tribunal stated: **15.1019**

> Interpretation thus consists of eliminating any ambiguities or uncertainties, if any, and clarifying the genuine meaning of the decision without modifying it. In other words, interpretation consists of restoring the true meaning of the decision where it has been improperly expressed in the operative part, where the latter is at odds with the findings or contains uncertainties or ambiguities. Interpretation does not entail a modification or an addition to the initial decision and thus cannot jeopardize *res judicata*.[693]

Another related question is whether the Arbitral Tribunal, when seized of an application by a party to correct and interpret an award under Art 29(2), may correct another aspect of the award after the 30-day period in Art 29(1) has expired. If such correction does not relate to a correction issue that has been requested by a party under Art 29(2), the Arbitral Tribunal will generally not be entitled to do so.[694] **15.1020**

(3.3) Article 29(3): Addendum to the award or decision Once the Arbitral Tribunal has received the comments, it will decide whether to reject or to accept the application. If the Arbitral Tribunal decides to correct the award *ex officio*, or to accept a party's application to this effect, it will have to submit its decision to the ICC Court in the form of a so-called 'addendum' to the award.[695] If the Arbitral Tribunal arrives at the conclusion that the award does not need to be corrected or interpreted or that the application goes beyond a correction and/or interpretation of the award (so that the Arbitral Tribunal would be *functus officio*), its decision shall be set out in a document entitled 'Decision' giving the reasons upon which it is based (Art 25(2)), and the finding that the application is rejected.[696] **15.1021**

---

[693] ICC case 12131 (Decision of the Tribunal dismissing a request for interpretation) (2006), unreported.

[694] For a discussion, see de Fróes, C.H., 'Correction and Interpretation of Arbitral Awards' in *Liber Amicorum in honour of Robert Briner* (ICC Publishing, Paris, 2005) 285, 289.

[695] Bühler/Jarvin, *op cit*, 299, Art 29. The Swiss Supreme Court took the same view in its decision of 12 January 2005, case no 4 P.219/2004, (2005) 13 ASA Bull. no 2, p 352.

[696] See Note of the Secretariat regarding correction and interpretation of Arbitral Awards, (1999) 10 ICC Court Bull no 2, 5.

15.1022 The ICC Court will then review, scrutinize and approve the addendum or the decision to the award of the Arbitral Tribunal.

15.1023 After signature of the addendum or the decision by the Arbitral Tribunal, the Secretariat will notify it to the parties.

15.1024 The addendum or decision is not a new award nor a replacement of the old award but simply, as the word says, an 'addendum' which will be deemed to be incorporated in the award. It is difficult to see the practical need for a separate award, and even less the justification for allowing a separate action for annulment against such award.[697]

15.1025 If under the *lex arbitri* a separate award would be required, Art 29(3) should not be a hindrance for such a separate award. The addendum is subject to the same form requirement as an award, inasmuch as it will have to be scrutinized and approved by the ICC Court, then signed and dated by the arbitrators, and thereafter notified to the parties by the Secretariat of the ICC Court in the same way as any other award.

15.1026 (3.4) **Costs** At least two questions will regularly arise in connection with the cost aspects of a request for correction: Is an advance for costs payable to meet the costs that will be incurred by the Arbitral Tribunal and/or the ICC Court for rectifying an error or interpreting an award? And if so, which party shall pay the costs?

15.1027 As for any additional costs incurred by the Arbitral Tribunal in the event of correction/interpretation, Art 2(7) of App III to the ICC Rules gives the Court the discretion to fix an advance to cover additional fees and expenses of the Arbitral Tribunal in dealing with applications made under Art 29(2).

15.1028 But the ICC Court may exercise its discretion only if the Secretariat considers that, in view of the particular circumstances of the case, an advance to cover additional fees and expenses of the Arbitral Tribunal is warranted. The Secretariat will then submit the matter to the ICC Court. Otherwise the application is to be transmitted directly to the Arbitral Tribunal. If the ICC Court did not ask for an advance on costs at the time when the application was submitted to the Secretariat, it can, in exceptional circumstances, take a decision on costs at the time of the scrutiny and make the notification of the Decision contingent upon the payment by one or both parties of the costs fixed by the ICC Court.[698]

15.1029 However, the scrutiny and approval of the Addendum by the ICC Court will in no event lead to further administrative expenses on the part of the ICC. At this stage of the arbitration, the services of the ICC Court are free of charge.

---

[697] The title 'Decision' is not to be understood technically as a decision not representing an award, and even generally speaking the question whether an act of the Arbitral Tribunal represents a decision or an award will not depend upon the title, see Note of the Secretariat regarding correction and interpretation of Arbitral Awards, (1999) 10 *ICC Court Bull* no 2, 5. See also Paris Court of Appeal, 1 July 1999 *Braspetro Oil Services Company v The Management and Implementation Authority of the Great Man-Made River Project (Libya)*, YCA (1999) XXIV, 297, and also (2000) Bull ASA, 830.

[698] See ICC, 'Note of the Secretariat of the International Court of Arbitration of the International Chamber of Commerce Regarding the Correction and Interpretation of Arbitral Awards' (1999) 10 *ICC ICArb Bull* no 2, 4.

(4) The interpretation of an award

Unlike the correction of an award, its interpretation can only be made at the request of a party. Even if an arbitrator would find certain parts of his award not to be sufficiently clear, he has no authority under the ICC Rules to modify his award once it was notified to the parties, absent a request from a party for an interpretation. Likewise, when a request for interpretation is made by a party, it cannot question the ICC Court whether, during the scrutiny process, the ICC Court might have considered a given point in the award as not being sufficiently clear, or more generally, what its understanding of such point was. 15.1030

(4.1) **Article 29(2): At the request of a party** The same procedure as described above for the correction of an award applies *mutatis mutandis* to the interpretation of an award.[699] 15.1031

The 30-day time limit to submit a request for interpretation is relatively short. It supposes that the parties have fully analysed the impact of the award on their rights and obligations thereunder. While in many cases this will hardly be difficult, in other cases this may only become fully evident when enforcement measures are initiated. In the authors' experience, the winning party will often first start discussing with the losing party how the award is to be implemented, and it is during such discussion that ambiguities in the award may come to light. The winning party will therefore have to keep a close eye on the 30-day time limit. This is probably the only time limit in the Rules where, if missed, it will operate like a *guillotine*, that is to say make the application inadmissible because it was not timely. 15.1032

The parties remain free to extend the time limit in their arbitration agreement or in the Terms of Reference, even after the award was rendered, upon notification of the award, before the 30-day time limit has expired, and even thereafter. In practice, such extensions are unlikely to happen often. The arbitrators would have to consent to act for the purpose of interpreting an award after the time limit fixed by the Rules. Although not obliged to accept such a request, it can be assumed that arbitrators will normally honour the parties' agreement. 15.1033

(4.2) **Article 29(3): Addendum to the award or decision** As it was rightly noted, the interpretative decision of the Arbitral Tribunal shall only clarify, not modify, the initial award and will therefore not infringe upon the principle of '*res judicata*'.[700] 15.1034

The ICC Rules do not expressly provide for the possibility of remanding a matter back to the Arbitral Tribunal. Under some national laws, it is possible that the courts will refer a matter back to the Tribunal, in a sense instructing the Tribunal to complete the task. The effect is to reopen issues for which the Tribunal was *functus officio* prior to the remand. 15.1035

[699] See *supra* para 15.1012 *et seq*.

[700] More generally, see de Fróes, *op cit*, at 289 and 291; Daly, B., 'Correction and Interpretation of Arbitral Awards under the ICC Rules of Arbitration' including Extracts from ICC Addenda and Decisions on the Correction and Interpretation of Arbitral Awards, (2002) 13 *ICC ICArb Bull* no 1, 61, 72; ICC, 'Note of the Secretariat of the International Court of Arbitration of the International Chamber of Commerce Regarding the Correction and Interpretation of Arbitral Awards', *op cit*, 4; Bühler, M.W., 'Correction and Interpretation of Awards and Advance on Costs' (1997) *ICC ICArb Bull*, Special Supp, 53; Kühn, W., 'Rectification and Interpretation of Arbitral Awards' (1996) 7 *ICC ICArb Bull* no 2, 78.

The ICC Rules do not provide expressly for the possibility of remanding a matter back to the Tribunal, once an award has been set aside in full or in part.

15.1036 As to whether an addendum or a decision is required, see above the comments at para 15.1020.

15.1037 (42.3) **Costs** The need for a special advance might occur in particular if the arbitrators have to meet amongst themselves or even with the parties, in order to decide upon the request for interpretation of the award. A request for interpretation could be used by a losing party as a weapon to gain time, to delay the crucial moment when he has to face the financial consequences of the award. In order to discourage such behaviour, it is fair that the party has to pay a new advance on costs. One may also argue that if there exists a genuine need for clarification of the award through an interpretation, the fault lies with the arbitrators who should have drafted the award in a clearer fashion. The arbitrators should then bear the costs and not be entitled to another fee for this additional work.

15.1038 Under normal circumstances, the interpretation of an award will be a much more time-consuming exercise than the rectification of an award. While it seems difficult to imagine the need for a hearing prior to rectifying an error, such need may well occur in the case when an interpretation is requested. Even then, this should, however, be the exception.[701]

Article 30. Advance to cover costs of the arbitration

(1) After receipt of the Request, the Secretary-General may request the Claimant to pay a provisional advance in an amount intended to cover the costs of arbitration until the Terms of Reference have been drawn up.

(2) As soon as practicable, the Court shall fix the advance on costs in an amount likely to cover the fees and expenses of the arbitrators and the ICC administrative costs for the claims and counterclaims which have been referred to it by the parties. This amount may be subject to readjustment at any time during the arbitration. Where, apart from the claims, counterclaims are submitted, the Court may fix separate advances on costs for the claims and the counterclaims.

(3) The advance on costs fixed by the Court shall be payable in equal shares by the Claimant and the Respondent. Any provisional advance paid on the basis of Article 30(1) will be considered as a partial payment thereof. However, any party shall be free to pay the whole of the advance on costs in respect of the principal claim or the counterclaim, should the other party fail to pay its share. When the Court has set separate advances on costs in accordance with Article 30(2), each of the parties shall pay the advance on costs corresponding to its claims.

(4) When a request for an advance on costs has not been complied with, and after consultation with the Arbitral Tribunal, the Secretary-General may direct the Arbitral Tribunal to suspend its work and set a time limit, which must be not less than 15 days, on the expiry of which the relevant claims, or counterclaims, shall be considered as withdrawn. Should the party in question wish to object to this measure it must make a request within the aforementioned period for the matter to be decided by the Court. Such party shall not be prevented on the ground of such withdrawal from reintroducing the same claims or counterclaims at a later date in another proceeding.

[701] The same cost procedure applies as described *supra* under paras 15.1025 *et seq.* for the correction of an Award.

(5) **If one of the parties claims a right to a set-off with regard to either claims or counterclaims, such set-off shall be taken into account in determining the advance to cover the costs of arbitration in the same way as a separate claim, insofar as it may require the Arbitral Tribunal to consider additional matters.**

(1) Introduction

The advances on costs are intended to secure the payment of the arbitrations costs at the end of the arbitration. In the ICC arbitration system the advances on costs cover the ICC's administrative expenses, the arbitrators' fees and the arbitration-related expenses, eg the arbitrators' out-of-pocket expenses, Art 1(4) of App III to the Rules.[702] Advances on costs are a common feature of both institutional and *ad hoc* arbitration, the legitimate purpose thereof being to 'secure in advance the financial resources necessary for carrying out the arbitration' in respect of both the ICC and the arbitrators. **15.1039**

The ICC advance on costs system gives the parties a reasonable indication of their financial exposure in the arbitration proceedings from the beginning of these proceedings. Such indication is important since the issue of costs, ie the amount of costs, time of payment, and whether, and to what extent, a party can recover such costs, is very important for any party involved in arbitration proceedings. Arbitration being a private method of dispute resolution, it is for the parties to bear the costs of those they have chosen to be their judges, and in the event of administered arbitration, they will have to also pay the costs of the institution for its administration activities in respect of a given arbitration. **15.1040**

It is essential for a party to know the advance on cost mechanisms under the ICC Rules well, since it will assist a party in deciding whether it should file a counterclaim or set-off claim, whether it should advance the arbitration costs in lieu of the other party, or simply discontinue the proceedings. **15.1041**

To appreciate the cost system under the Rules, in addition to Art 30 a party must also refer to Art 31. Article 31 defines the different types of costs of arbitration. The ICC Court has exclusive authority to fix the arbitrators' fees and its own administrative costs. The decision whether the parties' legal costs are allowable and the allocation thereof among the parties is to be made by the Arbitral Tribunal in the final award. **15.1042**

The ICC Rules also deal with costs in App III to the Rules (Arbitration Costs and Fees) which provides additional rules in respect of advances on costs (Art 1), costs and fees (Art 2), appointment of Arbitrators (in an arbitration not conducted under the ICC Rules—Art 3) and scales of administrative expenses and arbitrators fees (Art 4). Articles 1 and 4 particularly concern the issue of costs under Art 30 and will be dealt with under the commentary here. **15.1043**

Under the ICC cost system, three advances will generally have to be paid: a non-refundable filing fee payable by the Claimant at the moment of filing its Request for Arbitration; a provisional advance payable by the Claimant following receipt of the Request for Arbitration, and the 'global' advance on costs payable by both parties. **15.1044**

[702] See *infra* para 15.1042.

15.1045 It is for the Secretary-General to fix the amount of the provisional advance, and for the ICC Court to determine the global advance. The time and manner of payment and the consequences of default in payment of these two advances is normally for the Secretariat to decide. The arbitration will not go forward if the filing fee is not paid, it will not progress as long as the provisional advance is not paid, and if the global advance on costs is not paid, the arbitration proceeding may not go ahead in respect to the claims or counterclaims to which it relates.

15.1046 As of 1 January 2008 new cost scales apply for administrative expenses and arbitrators fees. They replace the cost schedule in place since 1 July 2003. The new cost scales apply to all Requests for arbitration received by the Secretariat on or after 1 January 2008. The minimum amount of the administrative fee charged by the ICC Court for the administration of an arbitration case remains at US$ 2,500 for a dispute worth US$ 50,000 US dollars or less and remains capped at the maximum of US$ 88,800 for disputes worth US$ 80 million or more. The scales for the ICC's administrative fees set out in App III, Art 4(A) remain unchanged. The scales regarding the arbitrators' fees (App III, Art 4(B)) have been increased from those under the previous table.

15.1047 The cost scales are based on a digressive percentage applied to successive tranches of the amount in dispute.[703] The basis of the assessment of the advance on costs is the amount of the sum in dispute between the parties,[704] which is equivalent to the amount of the main claim or the 'aggregate' of all claims, counterclaims and/or set-offs, Art 30(2) and (5). Ancillary claims such as for costs or interest fall outside this computation and are normally irrelevant to the assessment.[705] A set-off, which a party presents as a defence to a principal claim or a counterclaim, will be included in the computation of the amount in dispute 'insofar as it may require the arbitrators to consider additional matters', Art 30(5).

15.1048 Where the amount in dispute is not stated, the ICC Court fixes the amount of the advance of the administrative costs and the arbitrators' fees at its discretion, see App III, Art 2, (1) and (5).[706] In exercising its discretion, the ICC Court may also make its own estimate of the amount in dispute. While an estimation by the ICC Court may be a difficult task without full knowledge and understanding of the file, it has, however, the expertise to make a fair assessment in view of the great number of cases handled every year. At any rate, particularly in small disputes, it is clearly in the parties' own interest to inform the ICC Court of the financial value of their claims on instituting the arbitration.

15.1049 Where a claim is not for damages, parties may indicate the approximate value of the claim they are pursuing. This will allow the ICC Court to apply the cost scale, rather than to take a lump-sum approach. Examples are: a claim for interlocutory relief aimed at prohibiting a party from drawing a performance bond; a claim for the restitution of certain assets, eg service stations leased on the basis of an arguably invalid contract and declaratory

703 Craig/Park/Paulsson, *op cit*, 386.
704 *ibid.*
705 There may be exceptions: eg, if a party only claims interest on a loan.
706 Pursuant to the ICC statistics, in 12% of new cases set in motion in 2000, the amounts in dispute were not quantified, (2001) 12 *ICC Court Bull*, no 1, 11.

relief aimed at having the Arbitral Tribunal find that a contract is null an void, or has not become effective.[707] In these instances, the claims obviously have a financial value, since the Claimant pursues a monetary interest (eg protection against a potential loss or against a potential claim from the other party).

The advances on costs are calculated in US dollars. Therefore, when claims are stated in **15.1050** another currency, the ICC Court converts the sum in dispute into US dollars. The relevant exchange rate is the one prevailing on the date of filing of the claim or counterclaim.

Prior to instituting arbitration proceedings, parties may contact either the ICC directly or **15.1051** one of its National Committees in order to obtain information regarding the foreseeable costs of the arbitration. They may also consult the ICC's website, which contains a very helpful arbitration cost calculator to assess the amount of the advance on costs, ie the arbitrators' fees and administrative expenses, but which does not include the arbitrator's expenses.[708]

The first step in the payment of the advance on costs is the Claimant's duty to pay a non- **15.1052** refundable filing fee (see Art 1(1) App III). The amount of this fee is US$2,500. While non-refundable, the filing fee is effectively an advance on the Claimant's portion of the eventual costs of the arbitration. It is intended to cover the ICC's initial administrative expenses for the commencement of the arbitration, ie opening a file and to notifications of the Request for Arbitration to the Respondent. Article 30(4) expressly states that as long as the filing fee has not been paid, the Request for Arbitration will not be notified to the Respondent.[709]

The filing fee is only payable once, irrespective of the number of parties on the Claimant's **15.1053** or Respondent's side, or of the number of arbitrators. No additional registration fee is due upon Respondent's filing of the Answer or a counterclaim.

(2) Article 30(1): Provisional advance on costs

Fixing of the provisional advance on costs. After receipt of the Request for Arbitration, the **15.1054** Secretary-General 'may' fix a provisional advance on costs. Therefore, in any given arbitration, it is for the Secretary-General to decide whether or not to fix a provisional advance. In practice, the Secretary-General always does so. His decision will be notified to the Claimant together with the letter confirming that the Request for Arbitration has been notified to the Respondent.[710] The Claimant will be given 30 days to make such payment, but upon request, the Secretariat will extend the time limit.

This provisional advance is intended to cover only the costs of the arbitration up to the **15.1055** signature of the Terms of Reference. Therefore the provisional advance will normally not

[707] See eg ICC Award no 5285 (1992) for a case of uncertain quantum of damages, published in (1992) 3 ICC ICArb Bull no 2, 48; Craig/Park/Paulsson, *op cit*, 256.

[708] The cost calculator may be downloaded from <http//www.iccwbo.org/court/>, link 'International Court of Arbitration/Costs'. It enables parties to apply the scales of App III for ICC administrative expenses and arbitrators' fees.

[709] See *supra* Art 4, para 15.261.

[710] See *supra* Art 4, paras 15.266 *et seq*.

exceed the amount obtained by adding together the ICC administrative costs, the foreseeable expenses of the Arbitral Tribunal that the latter may incur while establishing the Terms of Reference, and the minimum fees of the arbitrators provided for in the ICC's scale based on the amount of the claim. In practice the provisional advance normally covers 25 to 35 per cent of the costs as calculated for the entire arbitration.[711]

15.1056 However, if the amount of the claim has not been quantified, the Secretary-General will fix the provisional advance at his discretion. Currently, the amount of the provisional advance will be fixed as a matter of routine at US$18,000 if a sole arbitrator is to be appointed, or at US$30,000 if a three-member panel is to be constituted. The Secretary-General may ask for smaller or higher amounts, if this appears to be more appropriate in a given case.

15.1057 The Arbitral Tribunal's foreseeable expenses will be covered by a lump sum amount. This amount is intended to allow the reimbursement of the arbitrator's out-of-pocket expenses incurred up to the signing of the Terms of Reference.[712] If no meeting takes place between the Arbitral Tribunal and the parties to finalize and sign the Terms of Reference, the arbitrators' out-of-pocket expenses will normally not be significant. Since the work carried out by the Arbitral Tribunal up to the signature of the Terms of Reference is not and should not be too time-consuming, it is justifiable to take into account only the minimum fee to which the arbitrator may be entitled under the cost scale when calculating the amount of the provisional advance on costs.

15.1058 This provisional advance on costs is payable by the Claimant alone. No provisional advance is payable in respect of any counterclaims the Respondent might submit together with its Answer. The payment of the provisional advance is a pre-condition of the transmission of the file to the Arbitral Tribunal.[713]

15.1059 The provisional advance is to be credited to the Claimant's share of the total advance on costs fixed by the ICC Court, App III, Art 1(2).

(3) Article 30(2): Global advance on costs

15.1060 Article 30(2) indicates the moment when the ICC Court becomes actively involved, ie when the ICC Court fixes the global advance on costs. This is the third step in the procedure in respect of advances on costs.

15.1061 Article 30(2) provides that the advance is to be fixed 'as soon as practicable'. The wording leaves wide discretion to the ICC Court to determine the timing of the global advance.

15.1062 The ICC Court's current practice is as follows: First the Secretariat submits the matter before the ICC Court so that the total advance can be fixed. The ICC Court will then have to decide whether it considers the timing to be 'as soon as practicable'. Once the Respondent has submitted an Answer to the Request for Arbitration, and a counterclaim, if any, the ICC Court will have all the elements it needs to determine the proper amount of the total advance on costs. By that time, it will already know the number of arbitrators, the residence

---

[711] See <http://www.iccwbo.org/court/>, link 'International Court of Arbitration—Costs'.
[712] App III, Art 1(2) and (3).
[713] See *supra* Art 13.

of the party-appointed arbitrators, and sometimes even of the chairman,[714] as well as the place of arbitration. If the number of arbitrators and/or the place of arbitration are to be fixed by the ICC Court, it may well take these decisions, at the same time it determines the total advance on costs. While in most cases the ICC fixes the total advance on costs before the file is transmitted to the Arbitral Tribunal, the Secretariat will seek the payment of that the unpaid part of the global advance by the parties only once the file transmission has occurred.[715]

The latest moment at which the global advance will normally be fixed is once the Terms of Reference have been signed, since the amounts at stake will then be known with much more certainty.[716] **15.1063**

The ICC Court will determine the total advance by taking into account the amounts of the claim and of the counterclaim. Article 30(2) specifically says that the advance is to be 'an amount likely to cover . . . costs for the claims and counterclaims'. If the amount of the claims remains unquantified at the time the ICC Court fixes the global advance on costs, it will as a matter of routine set it at US$ 65,000 for a sole arbitrator, and US$ 135,000 for a three-member panel. Prior to 2008, the ICC Court usually fixed the advance on costs for unquantified claims at US$60,000 and US$ 120,000 respectively.[717] The ICC Court may also set the advance at a higher or lower amount, depending on the circumstances of the case. **15.1064**

If the amount of claims is partially quantified, the ICC Court will fix the advance on costs by using the arbitrators' fees at a higher range than the average, ie increasing up to 50 per cent between the average and the maximum depending on the circumstances of the case. **15.1065**

The advance on costs is to comprise the fees of the arbitrators, any foreseeable arbitration-related expenses of the arbitrator(s) and the administrative expenses of the ICC Court, App III, Art 1(4). It may also relate to the costs of a Secretary in the event that an Arbitral Tribunal wishes to have the assistance of such person. The practice in respect of the cost of secretaries is set out in the ICC's Note Concerning the Appointment of Administrative Secretaries by Arbitral Tribunals dated 1 October 1995, as follows: 'The Arbitral Tribunal should inform the ICC Secretariat and the parties as early as possible of the estimated cost of the administrative secretary so that this may be taken into account when the Court fixes the advance on costs for the arbitration'. The fees of the administrative secretary are normally to be paid out of the fees awarded to the arbitrator(s) by the ICC Court and are not to be treated as expenses of the Arbitral Tribunal; reasonable expenses of the administrative secretary may, however, be reimbursed, ie travel expenses. The Note expressly states that the Court will be concerned to ensure that the engagement of such a person does not increase **15.1066**

[714] The residence of the arbitrators is relevant in regard of the place of arbitration and the travel expenses that may have to be incurred.

[715] At this stage, the provisional advance (Art 30(1)) must have been paid; otherwise the file will not be transmitted to the arbitrators (Art 13).

[716] When transmitting the files to the arbitrator, the Secretariat always 'encourages' the latter to state the amount in dispute in the Terms of Reference 'as precisely as possible'.

[717] This corresponds to an amount of dispute of approximately 1.2 million US dollars in the case of a sole arbitrator and of 1 million US dollars in the case of three arbitrators.

the cost of the arbitration to the parties. Parties remain, however, free to agree that the fees of an administrative secretary be treated as expenses of the Arbitral Tribunal. This may be appropriate where the sole arbitrator or chairman appoints a paralegal (legal assistant) to deal with purely administrative matters (such as arranging the services of court reporters and providing them with the necessary documents to prepare for the hearing, or liaising with counsel to find mutually acceptable hearing dates, etc.).

15.1067 The advance does not cover any value-added taxes (VAT), which the arbitrator may have to pay on his fees and expenses, see App III, Art 2(9). The Secretariat invariably takes the position that the recovery of any such taxes that the arbitrator may have to pay is a 'matter solely between the arbitrator and the parties'.[718]

15.1068 In cases with small amounts in dispute, the average fees provided by the scale may be too low in relation to the time necessarily required for the arbitrator to render the award.[719] In the ICC Court's practice, whenever the amount in dispute is under 100,000 US dollars it will look to the upper part of the cost scale with regard to arbitrators' fees when fixing the advance on costs, so as to be in a position to pay adequate fees at the end of the proceedings.

15.1069 Pursuant to the ICC Court's practice, an arbitrator's right to a fee only arises once the arbitrator has received the file. When the co-arbitrators are asked to select the chairman of the Arbitral Tribunal, it is often the case that the Secretariat will have provided them with the Request for Arbitration and, if already available, the Answer thereto. Although this is not considered to be part of the formal file transmission pursuant to Art 13, it is only fair that arbitrators can expect in such case a reading fee, even if the case does not go otherwise forward. Likewise, the time the co-arbitrators spend in selecting the chairman will have to be remunerated even if the parties decide to settle their dispute before the chairman of the Arbitral Tribunal was confirmed by the ICC Court. It is therefore imperative that the provisional advance has been paid, so that the ICC has the funds to pay the arbitrators for these preliminary activities.

15.1070 While there is no provision in the Rules entitling the arbitrator to receive an advance on the fees, it has become the practice for many arbitrators to request the payment of a first account on fees as soon as they have submitted the Terms of Reference to the ICC Court. Such payment is called somewhat misleadingly an 'advance on fees', even though the arbitrators have already performed services which undoubtedly entitle them to a fee.

15.1071 If the dispute is settled following delivery of the file to the Arbitral Tribunal, its members, where they directly contributed to the realization of this settlement, will often claim a 'bonus'. Reference to an hourly fee is alien to the ICC cost system which in no way intends to guarantee fees to arbitrators, particularly to practising lawyers acting as arbitrators, at rates equivalent to their normal working fee rate as counsel.[720] Clearly, in a large arbitration there is a greater degree of responsibility placed on the arbitrator and it is appropriate to

---

[718] See for a further discussion *infra* Art 31, para 15.1120.
[719] Schwartz, *op cit*, 14–15.
[720] See *infra* Art 31, para 15.1114.

appoint an arbitrator who is equal to such responsibility. Doubtless the parties will also want the best arbitrator available on the market. The ICC fee scale is designed to reflect this. As emphasized by Craig/Park/Paulsson, there must of course be a 'garde-fou' to counteract what in a given case might, despite these considerations, be excessive.[721] A safeguard mechanism exists in Art 2(2) of App III and the ICC Court may of course always apply Art 2(2) to fix a lower amount.

Readjustment at any time during the arbitration. The amount of the total advance on costs is a provisional figure that may or may not correspond to the final costs of the arbitration. It remains provisional throughout the arbitration proceedings. The provisional nature is clear from the fact that it is only at the time of the final award that the ICC Court fixes the costs of the arbitration definitively, Art 31. **15.1072**

Thus, Art 30(2) expressly provides that the amount of the total advance on costs may be subject to readjustment at any time in the arbitration, ie it may be either increased or decreased. It is only the ICC Court that may make such adjustment. The advance is likely to be adjusted if the amount in dispute fluctuates significantly for whatever reason, if the estimated expenses of the arbitrators exceed the ceiling initially envisaged, or if the arbitration proceedings become more difficult and time-consuming than anticipated.[722] However, fluctuations in the exchange rate of the currency in which the claims are made, or the effect of accrual of interest on the amount in dispute do normally not give rise to adjustments. **15.1073**

In the course of the arbitration, several adjustments of the advance may occur, in particular after the signing of the Terms of Reference that provide for more precise details as of nature, amount and procedure of the arbitration. However, this possibility does not change the fact that at the outset the advance is fixed with a view to cover the arbitrators' fees and expenses as well as the administrative expenses for the whole procedure. **15.1074**

It is the practice of the ICC Court to inform the parties beforehand of its intent to readjust, viz increase the advance on costs, so as to give them the opportunity to comment. **15.1075**

Separate advances on costs. Upon application of a party, the Court may fix separate advances on costs for principal claims and counterclaims. Where separate advances have been fixed, the ICC Secretariat will invite each party to pay the amount of the advance which corresponds to its respective claim.[723] In practice separate advances on costs often concern complex arbitration cases involving, for example, multi-party cases and cross claims.[724] **15.1076**

Parties have the possibility of posting a bank guarantee if the separate advance fixed for either party's claim exceeds one-half of the global advance, calculated as previously described.[725] If the separate advance is subsequently increased, at least half of the increase is to be paid in cash.[726] **15.1077**

[721] Craig/Park/Paulsson, *op cit*, 272.
[722] App III, Art 1(10).
[723] *ibid*, Art 1(7).
[724] Bühler/Webster, ICC Handbook, *op cit*, paras 30–27 *et seq*.
[725] App III, Art 1(8). The ICC Secretariat establishes the terms governing all bank guarantees which the parties may post in respect of the advance on costs, App III, Art 1(9).
[726] *ibid*, Art 1(8).

(4) Article 30(3): Payment of the advance of costs

15.1078 Payable by the parties in equal shares. Once the global advance is fixed by the ICC Court, 50 per cent is to be paid by the Claimant, less the US $2,500 filing fee and less the provisional advance under Art 30(1) already paid, and 50 per cent is to be paid by the Respondent. The advance on cost will thus be payable by both parties in equal shares.[727] One may question whether the principle to pay the advance on costs in equal shares represents not only a contractual obligation in relation to the ICC but also in relation to the other party. Several ICC awards approve this principle[728], while certain commentators[729] and one ICC award disagree.[730]

15.1079 Another issue concerns the power of the Arbitral Tribunal to order one party to pay half payment of the advance on costs to where the jurisdiction of the Arbitral Tribunal is challenged.[731] In such case, the Arbitral Tribunal, irrespective of the view that it takes in relation to the nature of the obligation under Art 30(3), may refuse to order a non-paying party to pay its share before it has decided on its jurisdiction.[732]

15.1080 In fact, in a recent case the Claimant submitted a request for an injunction asking that the Respondent—which had challenged the Tribunal's jurisdiction—be ordered to pay half of the advance on costs fixed by the ICC Court pursuant to Art 30.[733] According to the Respondent, the Tribunal could not issue such an injunction before it has decided whether

---

[727] Art 9(2), 1975/1988 Rules.

[728] See for example ICC case no 13853 (Partial Award on costs—reimbursement of the Respondents' share of the advance on costs to Claimants; award on costs), unreported ('13. The Tribunal considers that payment should be made direct to the Claimants rather than to the ICC. The Claimants' submission that this is a contract debt is accepted. That debt is owed to the Claimants and if it is they, not the ICC, who should receive payment.'); see also ICC Partial Award of March 27, 2001, *X Company, Panama, v Y SA, Suisse*, (2001) 19 ASA Bull no 2, p. 285.

[729] See on the subject generally, Secomb, M., 'Awards and Orders Dealing with the Advance on Costs in ICC Arbitration: Theoretical Questions and Practical Problems' (2003) 14 *ICC ICArb Bull* no 1, 59; Fadlallah, I., 'Payment of the Advance on Costs in ICC Arbitration: The Parties' Reciprocal Obligations' (2003) 14 *ICC ICArb Bull* no 1, 53; Scherer, M., 'Jurisprudence–Introduction to Case Law Section–Advance on the costs of the arbitration' (2003) 21 *ASA Bull* no 4, 749; Rouche, J., 'Le paiement par le défendeur de sa part de provision sur les frais d'arbitrage: simple faculté ou obligation contractuelle?' (2002) *Rev arb.*no4 at 841; Favre-Bull, X., 'Les conséquences du non-paiement de la provisions pour frais de l'arbitrage par une partie—Un tribunal arbitral peut-il condamner un défendeur au paiement de sa part de l'avance de frais?' (2001) 19 *ASA Bull* no 2 at 227; Reymond, C., 'Note sur l'avance des frais de l'arbitrage et sa répartition', in *Etudes de procédure et d'arbitrage en l'honneur de Jean-François Poudret* (U of Lausanne, 1999) 495.

[730] See ICC Interim Award of 26 March 2002, (2003) 21 ASA Bull no 4, 802 ('[17] The Arbitrator considers that this power of the ICC Court of Arbitration to discharge the parties from the obligation to pay each half of the global advance on costs, by fixing separate advances, implies that the parties are not contractually bound (each towards the other) to pay half of the advance on costs when a counterclaim is raised. This aspect seems not having been considered by the legal literature and the arbitral awards mentioned hereabove (no 14 and 15), but it had been raised by the Arbitrator (letter of July 26, 2001) and has been discussed with the parties at the October 29–30, 2001 hearing').

[731] ICC case no 13645 (2006), unreported.

[732] In ICC case no 12895, Procedural Order no 10 (2005), unreported, a three-member Tribunal recently refused to order a Respondent to pay its share of the advance on costs, see Bühler/Webster, *op cit* para 30-30-36 on further details. See also ICC case no 10439 (2002) (Partial Award) dismissing the non-defaulting party's request '[s]ince the issue of jurisdiction over [the Respondent] is still pending, the relief sought by the [Claimant] cannot be granted' cited by Secomb, M., *op cit*, 63.

[733] ICC Case no 13645 (2006), unreported.

or not it had jurisdiction over the Respondent. In other words, a challenge of the jurisdiction of the Tribunal is a challenge of its power to entertain interim measures as well. Although such a situation is not provided by the ICC costs system, it is, however, a case in which a Tribunal (irrespective of the view that it takes of the nature of the obligation set forth in Art 30(3)) may be reluctant to render a decision ordering a non-paying party to pay before it has decided on its jurisdiction.

It is for the ICC Secretariat to request the parties to pay their share of the advance. The ICC Secretariat normally grants the parties 30 days from the time the file is transmitted to the Arbitral Tribunal. Both parties are free to ask the Secretariat for an extension of this time limit, to which the Secretariat will usually agree with no difficulty, in particular when the request is made for the first time. **15.1081**

The parties are to pay their shares in cash. However, the party has the possibility of posting a bank guarantee for any amount in excess of a ceiling which the ICC Court fixes from time to time.[734] If the total advance exceeds this ceiling, each party can post a bank guarantee for 50 per cent of the excess amount provided it has paid its basic share in cash. Parties rarely use this facility. The ICC Secretariat establishes, in cooperation with the private banking house Sarasin in Basel, Switzerland, terms governing bank guarantees posted by parties in respect of the advance on costs. **15.1082**

Article 30(3) also provides for the eventuality of default in payment of the total advance on costs by one of the parties. As in the past, ICC Rules foresee the possibility of substitution by the other party, where such party has already paid its share in full.[735] Normally, it is the Claimant paying in substitution for the Respondent in default. Whether Claimant decides to do so is to be considered in the light of Art 30(4). **15.1083**

In the event that a party has to pay in lieu of a defaulting party, it has a free choice between payment in cash or by posting a bank guarantee (provided it has already paid its part of the advance on costs fully in cash).[736] **15.1084**

As mentioned above,[737] the payment of the advance on costs has no impact on the Terms of Reference becoming operative, contrary to the system under the 1975/1988 Rules.[738] The coming into force of the Terms of Reference is now unconnected to the payment in full of the advance on cost. **15.1085**

Article 30(4): Non-compliance with a request for an advance on costs

Article 30(4) expressly provides for a mechanism allowing the arbitrators to proceed only with those claims and those counterclaims for which the advance has been paid. **15.1086**

The ICC Secretariat is in general responsible for collecting the advance on costs and will invite the parties to pay the advance on costs, once this has been fixed by the ICC Court. **15.1087**

734 App III, Art 1(5).
735 1975/1988 Rules, Art 9(2); App III, Art 1(6) of the 1998 Rules.
736 App III, Art 1(6).
737 See *supra* para 15.1054.
738 1975/1988 Rules, Art 9(4), second para.

In the event of default in payment, once the file has been transmitted to the arbitrators, the ICC Secretariat and the arbitrators are to consult each other prior to taking further action.

15.1088 The Secretariat has the express right to direct the arbitrators to suspend their work and to fix a time limit in which the party in default is to pay. Such time limit is to be 15 days at a minimum. Often this period will be longer, indeed it may be months, before the ICC Secretariat fixes a final time limit.[739]

15.1089 If, within this time limit the amount has not been paid, or if the time limit is not extended, then the claim will be considered as withdrawn unless the party in default objects.

15.1090 If the party in default does object to the withdrawal of its claim, then it will as a second step have to make the appropriate payment within the new time limit fixed by the Secretariat. If at the end of the time limit there is no payment, the claim will be considered withdrawn, and the file closed by the ICC.

15.1091 Withdrawal of a claim under this Art 30(4) only affects the claim within the scope of the arbitration proceedings at hand. This Article expressly provides that the party is not thereby prevented from reintroducing the same claim or counterclaim in some other proceeding at a later date. Therefore, one cannot infer from the withdrawal of the claim any position of the party as to the merits of such claim. Clearly, a party may at a given time not be in a financial position to pursue a claim or counterclaim, or may have other valid reasons for not doing so, and it should therefore not be automatically deprived of the right to do so at a later time, albeit in new arbitral proceedings.

15.1092 This stipulation may be seen as misleading, since its content is only true with respect to the relations of the parties to the ICC. In other words, the ICC cannot refuse a new Request for Arbitration subsequently filed by the same Claimant. However, Art 30(4) does not affect the question of the validity of the arbitration agreement, and in particular a possible renunciation thereof in the first arbitration,[740] and does not safeguard against the running of the statute of limitations under the applicable rules of law.

(6) Article 30(5): Set-off claims

15.1093 Article 30(5) expressly provides that the value of a set-off, which may have been made by one of the parties in respect of either the principal claim or a counterclaim, may be taken into account in determining the amount of the advance on costs.

15.1094 The effect of this rule is that the amount in dispute will include any set-off, as this Article states, 'in the same way as a separate claim' provided, however, that it leads the Arbitral Tribunal to consider 'additional matters'.

[739] This will mean a lull in the arbitration, and that the arbitrators already seized of the file will not be paid their fees in the interim, but may receive an advance on fees.

[740] The French *Cour de Cassation* held in a judgment of 19 November 1991 that a Respondent in an ICC arbitration that had refrained from paying its advance on costs, leading the ICC Secretariat to fix a final time limit for payment under its Internal Rules, could not in subsequent proceedings before national courts invoke the latter's lack of competence on the basis of the arbitration clause, (1992) *Rev arb* 462 with commentary by Hascher. A clear sanction in case of non-payment of the deposit is contained in the Zurich Rules, Art 55.

This Article is consistent with the aim of discouraging unreasonable claims and counterclaims through the ICC costs system. Even if disguised as a set-off, whenever additional matters are raised, the result in terms of the determination of the advance on costs will be the same as if parties had raised claims or counterclaims. **15.1095**

Additional matters are not defined in the Article. Such definition would seem unnecessary, since it is likely to be clear whether there are new elements, ie the set-off is not closely connected with a claim or counterclaim, or even arises out of a different contract between the parties. The Arbitral Tribunal has to determine whether additional matters are raised. Its answer is likely to be in the affirmative whenever it needs to address new factual or legal issues with regard to the set-off. **15.1096**

Suspension of the proceedings at the request of the parties. In some cases, parties to an ICC arbitration request the ICC Court and/or the Arbitral Tribunal to hold the matter in abeyance for a given period of time. Requests for suspension of the proceedings are normally granted. One consequence of this is that the payment of the total advance on costs, which may still be outstanding at that moment, will also be suspended. Indeed, it is not uncommon that after notification of the Request for Arbitration to the Respondent and prior to the file being transmitted to the arbitrators, but also at any other stage of the proceedings,[741] the parties start discussions in an attempt to settle their dispute. **15.1097**

Security for costs of a party. The ICC Rules make no provision for security for costs and do not grant arbitrators express authority to order such security in favour of one of the parties. They also do not exclude such authority. If it is so provided under the law of the place of arbitration or under the law of the place where the party, from whom security is sought, has its seat, provisional security may be granted by the local courts,[742] or by the Arbitral Tribunal. **15.1098**

Article 31. Decision as to the costs of the arbitration

(1) The costs of the arbitration shall include the fees and expenses of the arbitrators and the ICC administrative expenses fixed by the Court, in accordance with the scale in force at the time of the commencement of the arbitral proceedings, as well as the fees and expenses of any experts appointed by the Arbitral Tribunal and the reasonable legal and other costs incurred by the parties for the arbitration.

(2) The Court may fix the fees of the arbitrators at a figure higher or lower than that which would result from the application of the relevant scale should this be deemed necessary due to the exceptional circumstances of the case. Decisions on costs other than those fixed by the Court may be taken by the Arbitral Tribunal at any time during the proceedings.

(3) The final Award shall fix the costs of the arbitration and decide which of the parties shall bear them or in what proportions they shall be borne by the parties.

[741] Eg after the Terms of Reference have been signed or after an interim or a partial Award has been rendered by the Arbitral Tribunal.

[742] See *supra* Art 23, paras 15.878 *et seq.*

(1) Introduction

15.1099 The issue of costs is a crucial one for all users of international arbitration; it is also an extremely sensitive one since all participants of the ICC arbitral process are concerned thereby—the ICC, the parties, the arbitrators.

15.1100 A key question for parties will be the level of financial commitment the arbitration involves, as well as the likely financial risk, ie to what extent a party can recover costs incurred in the arbitration.

15.1101 Since arbitration is a private means of dispute resolution parties will have to bear, in addition to the usual costs of bringing and defending a claim, the costs and expenses of the Arbitral Tribunal, as well as that of hearing rooms, transcription services and interpreters. The parties also have to bear the institution's administrative costs.

15.1102 The ICC, similar to other international arbitration institutions, has built into its Rules a costs system, which is particularly developed and provides schedules in respect of the ICC's administrative expenses and the costs and fees of the Arbitral Tribunal relating to the amount in dispute.

15.1103 In ICC arbitration there is an element of certainty and uniformity through the cost system. The ICC's practice of requesting an advance on costs (Art 30) also gives some reasonable indication of the parties' financial exposure. Moreover, parties have the certainty that the final award will comprise a decision on costs, not, however, how such costs will be apportioned among them.[743]

15.1104 However, the rules on costs are not always easy to apply and there are many factors which can determine their application in practice, in particular regarding the questions whether certain costs are allowable and their allocation. Moreover, the Rules deal with costs in several places: apart from Arts 30 and 31, parties need to look to App III—Arbitration Costs and Fees, which comprises provisions on advances on costs, costs and fees and the scales of administrative expenses and arbitrator's fees.

15.1105 A further consideration is that the ICC's monetary reference for arbitration expenses and arbitrators' fees is the US dollar. An increase in the US dollar exchange rate is immediately felt by parties which come from outside the US dollar zone. Since all amounts in dispute are first converted by the ICC Court into US dollars the increase of the US dollar will, at the same time, decrease the (US dollar) amount in contention, and thereby lead to a lower assessment of costs pursuant to the scale.

(2) Article 31(1): The scope of ICC costs of arbitration

15.1106 The costs of arbitration under Art 31(1) can be grouped under two categories: procedural costs and parties' costs.

15.1107 Procedural costs comprise (i) the fees and expenses of the arbitrators; (ii) the ICC administrative costs, both of which are fixed by the ICC Court; as well as (iii) the fees and expenses of any experts appointed by the Tribunal. They do not comprise the parties' costs, ie the

---

[743] See *infra* paras 15.1167 *et seq.*

costs expended by the parties for bringing or defending claims in the arbitral proceedings. The administrative costs of the ICC and the fees of the arbitrators are assessed in accordance with the ICC cost scale in force at the time the arbitration proceedings commence, App III, Art 4(1).[744]

Recently, the ICC Commission on Arbitration prepared a report entitled 'Techniques for Controlling Time and Costs in Arbitration'. The report sets out a large number of techniques for organizing arbitral proceedings and controlling their duration and costs. The report is not part of or interpretative of the ICC Rules or in any way binding upon the ICC Court. However, the techniques are designed to assist arbitral tribunals, parties and their counsel and intend to contribute to the ICC's cost effectiveness.[745] **15.1108**

(2.1) **Procedural costs** The ICC administrative costs. The ICC administrative costs are charged at a flat rate depending upon the sum in dispute. There is, however, a cap on the ICC's administrative expenses: where the sum in dispute is over US$ 80 million, a flat amount of US$ 88,800 is to constitute the entirety of the ICC's administrative expenses.[746] The administrative fee includes a non-refundable filing fee, which the Claimant must pay on filing a Request for Arbitration, irrespective of the sum in dispute.[747] Since 1 January 1998 the filing fee has been US$ 2,500. This filing fee constitutes an advance on the Claimant's portion of the advance on costs.[748] **15.1109**

The ICC administrative costs are a flat amount irrespective of the actual expenditure in the individual case. They cover a wide range of services inherent to the ICC arbitration system, and the high degree of intervention of the administering body. These include: notification of the Request for Arbitration and of the Answer thereto; determination of the existence of a prima facie agreement to arbitrate; appointment or confirmation of arbitrators; deciding challenges against arbitrators or removal of arbitrators; determination of the place of arbitration where this has not been chosen by the parties; determination of advance on costs and fixing the costs of the arbitration; approval of the Terms of Reference; extension of time limits; and scrutiny and approval of awards. Moreover, for each case the ICC Secretariat appoints a counsel to advise the parties on the day-to-day running of the case. The number of hours spent by the staff of the ICC Secretariat and by the members of the ICC Court on an arbitration file is not accounted for separately. Furthermore, this flat amount is unaffected by the number of arbitrators involved, the number of parties on each side, the number of counsel representing one party, the distance from the place where the parties reside or where the Tribunal has its seat.[749] **15.1110**

[744] The current ICC cost scale is effective as of 1 January 2008. *See supra* App III, Art 4(1) and Art 30 para 15.1047.

[745] ICC Publication 843, *op cit.*

[746] App III, Art 4(2).

[747] *ibid*, Art 1(1). Prior thereto, and since 1986 the filing fee payable by the Claimant amounted to US $ 2000. Before 1986, each side was asked to pay US $500 dollars, a system which did not work very well.

[748] See *supra* Art 30, para 15.1051.

[749] Telephone communications with, and courier services to, a party residing eg in Bogota and Lagos will obviously increase the actual expenses of the ICC Court which acts from its Paris headquarters. The newly established office in Hong Kong will service parties in Asia and the Eastern hemisphere so that communications

15.1111 The arbitrators' fees. The arbitrators' fees are fixed exclusively by the ICC Court in accordance with the cost scale, App III, Art 2(1). There exists no cap for the arbitrators' fees under the cost scale.

15.1112 The ICC Rules do not allow the parties and the arbitrators to enter into any separate fee agreement, App III, Art 2(4). Under the ICC system, arbitrators, however distinguished they may be, and irrespective of the practices prevailing in their countries of origin, cannot exert any direct influence on the decision determining the amount of their fees. Such protective provisions are clearly to the advantage of the parties,[750] and perhaps to a lesser extent of the arbitrators themselves.

15.1113 The power to fix the arbitrators' fees is one of the key features of ICC arbitration. Allowing exceptions thereto, eg by allowing arbitrators to agree with the parties to a different remuneration, would defeat the objectives of the system, which has to be universally applied in order to be credible.

15.1114 Unlike the ICC administrative expenses, the cost scale provides a range of maximum and minimum arbitrators' fees calculated according to the amount in dispute. This allows large discretion to the ICC Court. Moreover, it is difficult to overcome the fact that the ICC Court can only allocate the parties' advances on costs to the arbitrators' fees to the extent that it has received sufficient funds from the parties, which in turn is dependent on the amount of the total advance on costs fixed by the ICC Court. While the drafting of the final award by definition occurs at the end of the proceedings, and while it is only at this stage that ICC arbitrators can indicate to the Court the time they have spent in order to accomplish their task, there is a certain reluctance on the part of the ICC Court to ask the parties for additional payments at this late stage.

15.1115 Commonly, where a case proceeds to a final award, the fees will fall within the middle of the range established by the ICC cost scale for the applicable sum in dispute. In setting the fees, the ICC Court shall take into account factors such as the diligence of the arbitrators, time spent by the arbitrators, the rapidity of the proceedings as well as the complexity of the dispute, App III, Art 2(2). The usual hourly rates or the usual system of remuneration an arbitrator applies when exercising in his regular profession, are not taken into consideration by the ICC Court in determining the arbitrator's fees. The Secretariat will always inform prospective arbitrators accordingly prior to their appointment or confirmation as arbitrators. At the same time, the hourly rates for which an arbitrator normally works do not constitute a cap, and in a given case an arbitrator may receive a significantly higher hourly fee than he would otherwise. The opposite is also true.

15.1116 The Secretariat will normally invite the arbitrators during the course of the arbitration and at the time the draft final award is submitted for the ICC Court's scrutiny, to indicate the

---

and courier services to parties in eg Jakarta, Sydney and Tokyo will be at less cost compared to when the Secretariat acted from Paris.

[750] Craig/Park/Paulsson, *op cit*, 385 *et seq*; Karrer P.A., 'Freedom of an arbitral tribunal to conduct proceedings', *op cit*, 41; Schwartz, E., 'The ICC Arbitral Process, Part IV: The Costs of ICC Arbitration' (1993) 4 *ICC ICArb Bull* no 1, 8 at 9.

time spent, that is to say how many hours they devoted to a case. Rather than just providing a number of hours, it would seem more appropriate to indicate to the ICC Court the 'visible' part thereof, by listing eg the days spent in hearings, on site visits, at meetings with the members of the Tribunal, travelling and drafting the award, etc.

While the ICC Court rightly seeks to encourage arbitrators to handle the case as swiftly as possible, there seem to be only a few arbitrators who have seen their fees increase because of the rapidity with which they acted. Although a financial incentive for 'fast-track' arbitration makes sense, it is difficult to measure such performance in practice, and no real guarantee is given to the 'dynamic' as opposed to the 'plodding' arbitrator.[751] 15.1117

The time spent is normally a sign of the complexity and difficulty of a case. Further, a complex case will be all the easier for the arbitrator to understand and to resolve, the better and the more professionally it is presented by counsel for the parties. What the ICC Court could, and should compensate under this heading, is also the quality of the award (in terms of its formal presentation, statement of reasons, research and/or discussion of relevant doctrine and jurisprudence, etc). 15.1118

The application of such factors will explain why in a given case fees may be fixed below or above the average allowed under the fee scale. In exceptional circumstances, the ICC Court has the power to depart from the fee scale in fixing the arbitrators' fees, Art 31(2). 15.1119

The cost scale is based on the appointment of a single arbitrator. Where three arbitrators are appointed, the ICC Court has the discretion to increase the amount, App III, Art 2(3). The maximum shall not exceed three times the fee of one arbitrator. Of the total fee, the chairman normally receives 40 per cent and the remaining arbitrators 30 per cent each, unless the arbitrators have come to some other arrangements, and have so notified the ICC.[752] In exceptional cases, the ICC Court may, however, on its own initiative allocate the fees on a different basis than the 40/30/30 rule.[753] 15.1120

Finally, the fees and expenses paid to the arbitrators do not include any value-added taxes (VAT) or other taxes or charges applicable to arbitrator's fees and expenses. Parties are expected to acquit such taxes or charges although recovery is solely a matter between arbitrators and the parties, App III, Art 2(9). Given the variety of cases and the diverse tax treatment of arbitrators according to requirements of their own national tax regime, VAT liability on arbitrators' fees and expenses is a complex issue and on a practical level gives rise to many delicate problems.[754] 15.1121

751 Craig/Park/Paulsson, *op cit*, 388–9.

752 *ibid*, *op cit*, 389.

753 Arbitrators are advised by the Secretariat prior to their appointment/confirmation of this fee allocation.

754 Before the so-called *Hoffmann* case the situation was unclear. The German professor Bernd von Hoffmann had not paid VAT to the German tax authorities on the fees received as an arbitrator in an ICC arbitration having its seat in France. His dispute with the German tax authorities went up to the European Court of Justice, which rendered a very controversial judgment pursuant to which fees of arbitrators resident in Europe (unlike those of attorneys) are subject to VAT even on export transactions, ECJ, 6th Chamber, 16 September 1997, *Bernd von Hoffman and Finanzamt Trier*, (1998) YBCA vol XXIII, 175, also (1997) 12 Mealey's Int'l Arb Rep no 10, H-1; see also Lazareff, S. and Le Gall, J.-P., 'L'assujetissement des arbitres

15.1122 Since the European Union has 27 members, a large number of arbitrators residing in Europe are concerned by the VAT issue.[755] As of November 2006, the ICC offers arbitrators subject to VAT and other taxes a service to have the funds of the VAT and other taxes due on their fees administered by the ICC. As indicated in the ICC Note on VAT, '[w]hen arbitrators take advantage of this service, ICC acts as the "depositary" of the fund. ICC receives funds from the parties who have been instructed to this effect by an arbitrator (chairman of arbitral tribunal on behalf of the other members of the arbitral tribunal, member of an arbitral tribunal subject to VAT or sole arbitrator subject to VAT), and makes the payments corresponding to the VAT at the request of the arbitrators when the latter bill the parties for their fees'.[756]

15.1123 However, since the ICC does not call on parties to make payment of any amount in respect to an arbitrator's VAT liability, there are no guarantees for the arbitrator that the parties will honour any such additional request. Further, since the arbitrators' fees are only fixed at the time of the final award, the exact amount of any VAT liability can only be determined at that stage, and it is only then that the arbitrators can send a (pro forma) invoice to the parties setting out VAT in addition to the fees and expenses. To be on the safe side, arbitrators subject to VAT would have to ask for an advance payment directly from the parties, calculated at the rate of their domestic VAT regime and on the foreseeable amount of fees and expenses.[757] Such advance payment may then be paid into a separate account opened by the chairman of the Arbitral Tribunal (rather than by each arbitrator).

15.1124 For parties outside the European Union that are unable or may have difficulties recovering the VAT paid to the arbitrators, the payment of VAT represents a significant additional charge. Parties may wish to ask an arbitrator at the time of his appointment whether or not he is likely to be liable to account for VAT on his fees and expenses.

15.1125 The arbitrators' expenses. The arbitrators' expenses are distinct from their fees. Not only do such expenses fall outside the cost scale, but the manner in which the expenses are calculated is different. The expenses of ICC arbitrators can be grouped under two categories: (i) personal expenses; and (ii) administrative expenses.

15.1126 (i) The arbitrators' personal expenses. They are reimbursed on a cash basis, limited to what the ICC Court's Secretariat considers to be reasonable.[758] According to the revised Notice

---

à la TVA sous l'empire de l'article 259 du code général des impôts' (2006) *Rev arb* no 2, 543; Le Gall, J.-P., 'The fiscal status of the arbitrator' (1995) *ICC ICArb Bull*, Special Supp, 100; ICC case no 12711 (2004) (Procedural Order), JDI 2006 no 4, 1454, note Jolivet.

[755] See Patocchi, P.M., 'Deciding on the costs of the arbitration - Selected Topics' (2007) *ASA Special Series* no 29, 49, at 60.

[756] See Bühler/Webster, ICC Handbook, Pt II, Document 12.3, ICC Note on VAT, Taxes, Charges and Imposts Applicable to Arbitrators' Fees.

[757] In its Note dated 1 January 1996, the Secretariat advises as follows: 'In the event that an arbitrator is required to pay such taxes, the arbitrator may seek to recover the same from the parties by invoicing them directly for the amount of tax due. In such case, the parties shall pay such amount directly to the arbitrator, in addition to the advance on costs paid to the ICC.'

[758] See also ICSID, Schedule of Fees, para 2; Vienna, Art 29, Note to Schedule of Administrative Charges.

to Arbitrators: Personal and Arbitral Tribunal Expenses, 1 January 2005,[759] (hereinafter 'ICC Notice on Arbitrators' Expenses'), for such expenses incurred on or after 1 January 2005, a flat *per diem* allowance, of US$ 500, applies for each day and night spent on ICC arbitration business out of the arbitrator's town of residence, where hotel accommodation is utilized. A higher allowance of up to a maximum of US$ 800 is authorized if supported by invoices and receipts. If no hotel accommodation is utilized the flat *per diem* allowance is US$ 250. As a general rule, the ICC Court's Secretariat will accept all expenses that are both necessary and reasonable, but will refuse what seem to be unjustifiable 'extras'.

To clarify what is an 'extra' and what is 'unjustifiable expense, the ICC Notice on Arbitrators' Expenses, determines what expenses are covered by the *per diem* allowance as follows: hotel accommodation (where necessary); meals/snacks; laundry/pressing; inner-city transport (including taxis); telephone call, faxes or other communications; tips. It expressly excludes entertainment expenses such as theatre/opera tickets or luxury restaurants or accompanying guests as a reimbursable item. Also, charges for telephone calls, faxes and other communications are limited to what is reasonable. The Notice on Arbitrators' Expenses is automatically sent by the Secretariat to arbitrators once the arbitration file is transmitted to them. **15.1127**

The arbitrators' expenses relate to out-of-pocket personal living disbursements, incurred for travel and accommodation in connection with his attendance at hearings and meetings. All expenses related to activities of the Arbitral Tribunal, such as the hire of a conference room for the hearing, the appointment of court reporters, interpreters or typists, the cost of typewriters, outside messenger and courier services, telephones and faxes, postage, photocopying and similar disbursements are treated as 'Tribunal arbitration expenses', and as such are reimbursable to the arbitrators upon production of the appropriate supporting documents. **15.1128**

The ICC Court's Secretariat will normally not accept separate charges for word processing, secretarial overtime, books, subscriptions to specialized journals, conferences or seminars, office supplies, or storage charges, unless there are specific reasons to burden the parties with such expenses, and special arrangements are made with the Secretariat in time. **15.1129**

The latter also applies, in particular, where a sole arbitrator or the chairman of the Tribunal intends to appoint an administrative secretary (the 'Secretary').[760] Where such appointment is made, the issue of costs is set out in the ICC Secretariat's Note Concerning the Appointment of Administrative Secretaries by Arbitral Tribunals of 1 October 1995. The Arbitral Tribunal is to inform the ICC Secretariat and the parties as early as possible of the estimated fees of the Secretary. The ICC Court will take account of such estimation in fixing the advance on costs. The responsibility for paying the Secretary, however, lies upon the Arbitral Tribunal, which will do so out of the amount of the arbitrators' fees. **15.1130**

The arbitrators are to submit to the Secretariat requests for reimbursement of expenses with the necessary justification, preferably on a continuous basis and at the latest by the date of **15.1131**

[759] See reprinted in Derains/Schwartz, A Guide, 413.

[760] Craig/Park/Paulsson, *op cit*, 337. See *supra* Art 13, para 15.556.

the submission of the draft award. The Secretariat will check the accuracy of the expenses and may ask for receipts to prove such expenses. Such control has the practical advantage of guaranteeing that the calculation of the *per diem* allowance, and the reimbursement of other expenses is carried out in a uniform and proper manner. However, the ICC Court does not normally inform the parties what expenses were incurred by and reimbursed to the individual arbitrator. In its letter notifying the final award, the ICC Court's Secretariat simply indicates the total amount of expenses, without an itemized breakdown thereof.[761] In the final award itself, the arbitrators will often only indicate the total amount of the procedural costs, as fixed by the ICC Court, and which include the expenses.

15.1132 The amount of expenses incurred by the members of the Arbitral Tribunal may be significant. It may be possible for both the parties and the arbitrators to reduce such expenses; for example where the place of arbitration is fixed in the arbitration clause, and therefore known to the parties from the outset, it would cause less expenses to take arbitrators residing at the place of arbitration; the examination of witnesses often takes longer than originally envisaged, and it is therefore always advisable to allow one or two extra days for this at the outset, thus avoiding the need to go to a second hearing and the extra time and cost this would involve.

15.1133 (ii) The arbitrators' administrative expenses. The arbitrators' administrative expenses comprise expenses in respect of hiring conference rooms, audio-visual equipment, appointment of a court-reporter, interpreters and the like.

15.1134 In some cases, where substantial expenses are at stake, the Arbitral Tribunal will, as a matter of caution, obtain a cost estimate and submit same to the parties. The administrative expenses are normally paid out of the advance on costs held by the Secretariat. In some cases, direct arrangements are made between the Secretariat and the services provider, so that the Arbitral Tribunal does not have to make a cash advance for such expenses.[762]

15.1135 The costs of experts. If the Arbitral Tribunal requests an expert, the parties or one of them, will have to bear the fees and expenses of the expert. The experts' fees are to be secured in advance through a cash deposit fixed by the arbitrator at an amount sufficient to cover such fees and expenses, App III, Art 1(11).

15.1136 The advance on costs for the experts' fees and expenses is fixed by the Arbitral Tribunal, not by the ICC Court or its Secretariat. The Arbitral Tribunal may open a separate bank account in its own name for the payment of the advance on the experts' costs or, if desired, may use the bank account held at the ICC's bank in Switzerland. In most cases, Arbitral Tribunals will request that the advance on the experts' costs be paid by both parties in equal shares or by one party alone, for instance where the latter bears the burden of proof.

---

[761] This is criticized by Karrer, P.A., 'Freedom of an arbitral tribunal to conduct proceedings', *op cit*, 35.

[762] In other cases, arbitrators will ask the parties to make direct arrangements with the services providers, and thus to pay them directly. Such expenses do then become part of the 'parties' costs'. Since parties' costs are often treated differently from the procedural costs, as will be discussed below, it may prove to be to the disadvantage of the successful party that these expenses were not part of the procedural costs, as they would have, if their payment would have been made out of the advance on cost paid to the ICC.

The ICC Rules are silent regarding the amount of the experts' costs. Generally, experts will be remunerated for their services on a similar basis as their usual professional fees to be agreed with the Arbitral Tribunal. The Tribunal should endeavour to outline clearly the scope of services to be rendered by the expert, and on that basis obtain an estimate of the experts' costs (including disbursements) which it will submit to the parties for their information and comments. **15.1137**

The Arbitral Tribunal should always make sure that the experts' costs do not exceed the initial estimate, in order to avoid any risk of liability. **15.1138**

(3) The parties' costs

The elements of parties' costs. Parties' costs represent the costs incurred by a party in making or defending an arbitral claim. The ICC Rules are silent as to the various individual items that may constitute parties' costs; the Rules refer to 'legal' costs and to 'other costs'. Article 31(1) offers only the general guidance that parties' costs are 'the reasonable legal and other costs incurred by the parties for the arbitration'. In general such 'costs' vary greatly, and include *inter alia*: (i) fees of legal counsel; (ii) travel expenses and any miscellaneous expenses; (iii) expenses of witnesses; (iv) costs of carrying out discovery; (v) interpreters' and translators' costs; (vi) the costs of obtaining private expert opinion; and (vii) fees of accountants or quantity surveyors or other third parties involved in the preparation of the case. **15.1139**

Attorney fees. Parties have unlimited discretion in choosing and appointing their counsel. Their choice may be made irrespective of the place of arbitration; equally it may be motivated by the complex and special nature of many international arbitrations so that a party may wish to appoint specialist lawyers. Thus, it happens that two or three law firms represent jointly one party in an ICC arbitration. The role of in-house counsel may vary greatly also.[763] The ICC Rules expressly maintain the freedom of the parties to decide who are to be their (legal) advisers, Art 22(4). **15.1140**

In essence, attorney fees are reimbursable costs in ICC arbitration provided they can be said to be 'reasonable'. A method for Arbitral Tribunals to define 'reasonable costs' is to compare the amounts claimed by the two parties for their legal fees, taking into account the legal backgrounds of the parties. If one party's claim of legal fees is significantly less than that of the other party, the Arbitral Tribunal will rather tend to consider these fees as reasonable instead of the higher fees claimed by the other party.[764] **15.1141**

There is no reason to exclude the costs of in-house counsel, if the latter solely or predominantly presented the case to the Arbitral Tribunal.[765] Even where this is not the case, the **15.1142**

[763] Karrer, P.A., 'Freedom of an arbitral tribunal to conduct proceedings', *op cit*, 37.

[764] In some cases, the lawyers for one party will submit a claim which is significantly less than the amount that they have actually billed the client. This reduces the risk of the effect of a comparison and may reflect the fact that the expenditure in legal fees was viewed as necessary to defend a principle going beyond the amounts at issue in the case. See also Swiss Supreme Court, 9 January 2006, 4P.280/2005, *X v Y*, (2006) 24 ASA Bull no 2, 347, note Scherer, at 266.

[765] Schwartz, E., 'The ICC Arbitral Process, Part IV: The Costs of ICC Arbitration', *op cit*, 21. The Arbitral Tribunal accepted a significant amount for in-house legal costs in ICC case no 8786 (1997), (2002) 20 ASA Bull no 1,67; (2000) 11 ICC ICArb Bull no 2, 71.

central role of the in-house counsel as the coordinator between counsel and the party's management and staff should not be underestimated. However, since in-house counsel are often salaried employees of a party, it is often difficult to justify separate costs for them.[766]

15.1143 In the United States, where in principle each party to an arbitration bears the costs of its own counsel, the right to be reimbursed for these costs in ICC arbitration is accepted.[767] In 1987, an ICC Tribunal with its seat in Paris decided that in a dispute between American and French parties, New York law governed the contractual relationship. The American Claimant lost and had to bear the procedural costs. Furthermore, it had to pay attorneys' and witnesses' expenses as well as compensate the Respondent for its expenses for a total sum of almost 1 million US dollars.[768] Another ICC Tribunal in Paris, where the matter was governed by French law, granted the claimant, who was successful in all points of his claim, compensation with regard to his legal expenses 'reasonably' amounting to 300,000 French francs.[769] Neither of the above cases gave more precise details of the amount of compensation, which in each instance came to about 2 per cent of the amount of the claim.

15.1144 Witnesses' expenses. The ICC Rules do not address the question of compensation of witnesses which is to be settled between the parties and their witnesses alone. This is by no means a *lacunae* of the ICC Rules but simply a fact which has its origin in the diversity of rules that may apply to a given ICC arbitration, and the impossibility of subjecting witnesses to a 'code of expenses'. Travel expenses and a daily fee are generally paid to the witness, or his employer, by the party who called the witness.

15.1145 Calling witnesses in international arbitrations can be very costly. It is of considerable importance for the parties to have the possibility to be reimbursed for the cost of witnesses' testimony in case they are successful.[770] A precise breakdown of the individual witnesses' expenses is rare, since in practice parties often do not mention such expenses as a separate heading of their costs. In contrast, the UNCITRAL Rules expressly refer to such expenses, and provide for reimbursement only so far as these are approved by the Arbitral Tribunal (Art 38(d)). It seems appropriate that the Arbitral Tribunal should exert control over the agreement reached between the parties and their witnesses regarding reimbursement.

15.1146 Miscellaneous costs. The services of interpreters or translators are often required in ICC proceedings and can be expensive. Reimbursement of such costs depends on a variety of factors, for instance whether the parties themselves agreed on the official language of the

[766] Likewise, the costs of in-house staff (accountants, engineers, etc) arising in the preparation and supervision of the case are normally not awarded to a party.

[767] Incidentally, it might be noted that the Florida International Arbitration Act 1986, Art. 684, 19 para 4 expressly provides for the reimbursement of attorneys' fees.

[768] ICC Case no 5558 (1987). Both sides were represented by New York attorneys.

[769] ICC Case no 5277 (1987), published in extract, *Collection of ICC Awards 1986–1990, op cit*, 112, (1988) YBCA XIII, 80. This passage is, however, not printed; see also ICC Case no 5418 (1987), (1988) YBCA XIII, 91.

[770] For costs of an expert witness, see ICC Case no 5649 (1987), *Collection of ICC Awards 1986–1990, op cit*, 217, and (1989) YBCA XIV 174, 179. The Moroccan party was awarded damages on its counterclaim. The Tribunal stated expressly that... '[t]he Moroccan party does not have grounds to request payment of the costs of the expert report, which was anyway at his expense'.

arbitration or the Tribunal made an order in this respect. Precise details of the relevant criteria in ICC arbitrations are unavailable.

In a recent case, the French Claimants requested the payment of the equivalent of over 2 million US dollars in internal costs incurred by its employees in relation to a very large arbitration. The New York based Arbitral Tribunal simply reduced them with a broad brush approach for lack of detailed description and justification: **15.1147**

> [837]. The Claimants' bill of costs also includes internal costs in the amount of [___] in respect of the time and expense incurred by their employees in relation to this arbitration. The Tribunal sees no reason in principle not to award internal costs since, if not organized and performed internally, the matters usually encompassed within these types of costs would likely be incurred at a higher cost from outside providers. As the Claimants have not provided a detailed description and justification of these internal costs, the Tribunal believes it appropriate to reduce the internal costs claimed in respect of this arbitration by 50 percent.[771].

Submission of parties' costs. It is normally at the time of the closing of the hearings that the Arbitral Tribunal will invite the parties to submit their application regarding costs.[772] There is no standard for such submissions and the practice of submitting costs varies in form and extent from the mere indication of a flat amount with no breakdown to a submission of a costs brief with invoices and other justifications as exhibits. **15.1148**

In the absence of any instructions from the Arbitral Tribunal, it seems appropriate for a party to submit at least a general breakdown of the costs it has incurred. Parties should also be asked to submit a statement from their Financial Director confirming that the amount of costs claimed has actually been incurred and paid by that party. **15.1149**

The concept of 'reasonable legal and other costs' limits the extent to which an award for parties' costs may be granted. Article 31(1) does not, however, specify what is to be understood by '*reasonable*' costs. In this respect, the arbitrators enjoy wide discretion. **15.1150**

ICC arbitration clauses rarely deal with costs and if they do, this will only relate to their allocation, eg by stating that the winning party shall be entitled to costs or that each party shall bear half of the costs of arbitration.[773] Sometimes, ICC arbitration clauses also refer to criteria such as 'reasonableness' or 'fairness' to establish what costs may be reimbursed. The Terms of Reference will normally not contain any rule on costs either. **15.1151**

Under these circumstances, the arbitrators are free to look at the rules prevailing in this respect at the place of arbitration, or at the place where counsel selected by the parties have their place of residence. The last seems more appropriate, since counsel selected by the **15.1152**

---

[771] ICC case no 12124 (2006) (Final Award), unreported.

[772] See *supra* Art 22, para 15.857 regarding the closing of the proceedings even where only an interim or partial Award is to be rendered.

[773] The standard arbitration clause proposed by the ICC makes no reference to costs. The costs issue is not even considered to be a point 'desirable for the parties' to specify in the arbitration agreement, see the ICC standard arbitration clause that can be downloaded from <http://www.iccwbo.org> link 'International Court of Arbitration'. See also Bond, S., 'How to draft an Arbitration Clause (Revisited)' (1990) 1 *ICC Court Bull* no 2, 21; Craig/Park/Paulsson, *op cit*, 118–19.

parties will calculate their fees in accordance with their own national practices, which will not necessarily be those of the place of arbitration.

15.1153 Admittedly, national practices themselves are not necessarily appropriate in the international arena. Such practices are as diverse as they are conflicting.[774] Some do not even allow a general rule of recovery of parties' costs, as in France or in the United States. Others allow recovery, but limit this by reference to different bases of assessment so that they may be limited to scales of recoverable costs, as in Canada, or fixed according to the amount in dispute, as in Germany,[775] or even on an hourly basis.[776]

15.1154 Thus, in the absence of more explicit guidance, arbitrators will exercise their discretion in the context of setting parties' costs by reference to international practices. The question of costs between parties from the same jurisdiction may well be straightforward. This in itself does not guarantee that the Arbitral Tribunal will deem to be 'reasonable' those costs calculated according to a particular national practice, or arrangements made by counsel with its client.

(4) Article 31(2): The ICC cost scale, and arbitrators' early decision on costs

15.1155 Article 31(2) deals two entirely different subjects:

15.1156 The ICC Court's right to deviate from the ICC cost scale is regulated in the first sentence. The second sentence recognizes the arbitrators' right to fix costs during the arbitration.

15.1157 The Court's right to deviate from the ICC cost scale. The ICC Court is allowed to depart from the cost scale, where 'in the exceptional circumstances of the case', it deems this to be necessary. The ICC Court will do so, for example, where due to the complexity of the dispute and the volume of the parties' submissions, the cost scale would be unlikely to provide adequate remuneration to the arbitrator. Accordingly the ICC Court can fix the amount of the arbitrators' fees at a level higher or lower than the costs and fee scale. There is no limitation in respect of arbitrators' fees, App III, Art 2(2). But it is expressly stated that the administrative expenses 'shall normally not exceed the maximum amount of the scale', App III, Art 2(5).

15.1158 The arbitrators' right to fix costs prior to the final award. The costs referred to in Art 31(1) and to be fixed by the ICC Court are the so-called procedural costs. They are fixed at the end of the proceedings, ie normally once the final award or an award by consent is rendered. Article 31(2) allows the Arbitral Tribunal to decide on parties' costs *at any time* in the course of the arbitration.[777] Generally the arbitrators' decision on costs, both procedural and parties' costs, is made at the time of rendering the final award, but may also be made beforehand. This may be the case where the Arbitral Tribunal determines that it has no jurisdiction

[774] Craig/Park/Paulsson, *op cit*, 394–6; see Wetter, G. and Priem, C., 'Costs and their Allocation in International Commercial Arbitration' (1991) *Am Rev Int'l Arb* vol 2, 249, at 296 with reference to Switzerland.

[775] In Germany, attorneys' fees are regulated by the RVG (*Rechtsanwaltsvergütungsgesetz*) which sets out the fees based on the value of the dispute.

[776] Wetter/Priem, 'Costs and their Allocation in International Commercial Arbitration', *op cit* 264.

[777] See Bühler, M.W., 'Costs of Arbitration: Some further considerations', *op cit*, para 20–34, n 156.

over one of the Respondents to the arbitration, and therefore the second party is no longer party to the continued proceedings. Or, where a party is unsuccessful in a jurisdictional argument, the Arbitral Tribunal may require such party to pay the other party's costs with respect to that application. Article 31(2) does not stipulate the form in which such decision is to be made which could be by interim or partial award or by procedural order of the Arbitral Tribunal.[778] Where a final award follows much later, it is preferable to deal with the issue of costs for such party in the award rejecting jurisdiction over that party.

With jurisdictional applications, it is commonplace that the party who is unsuccessful in a jurisdictional argument is required to pay the other party's costs with respect to that application. The basic justification for that approach is that the unsuccessful application should not have been made. However, there are exceptions to this principle. **15.1159**

(5) Article 31(3): Arbitrators' decision on costs

(5.1) **The fixing of costs in the final award** It is only at the time that the award is submitted to the ICC Court for scrutiny and approval that the latter will make a final determination of the costs of the arbitration, which shall be stated in the award. At this stage, the issue of the allocation of costs between the parties arises. The duty to apportion the costs rests with the Arbitral Tribunal, not with the ICC Court. Even though parties to an ICC arbitration are expected to advance the costs in equal shares, this principle does not apply to the allocation of the costs of the arbitration. **15.1160**

ICC arbitrators enjoy wide discretion in allocating both procedural and parties' costs, since Art 31 does not indicate what factors are to be considered in making such allocation. Since a reasoned award on allocation is scarce, it is difficult to establish a standard practice or to define all the factors which may influence the arbitrators' decision. **15.1161**

Article 31(3) permits the arbitrators to decide both upon the recovery of procedural costs of the arbitration as well as recovery of parties' costs.[779] Parties' costs are calculated on a different basis from procedural costs, the latter being exclusively a matter for the ICC Court, as explained above Art 31(1). **15.1162**

Determination of parties' costs. Where both parties have set forth their costs to the Arbitral Tribunal before the award is made, the Arbitral Tribunal must verify whether these costs have been properly incurred and at the same time determine if, and to what extent, the Claimant and/or the Respondent are entitled to an award for costs. **15.1163**

No hard and fast rules govern how the amount is to be calculated. Article 31(3) does not refer to the rules of law that are applicable to the arbitration. Therefore, the question arises whether and to what extent an Arbitral Tribunal in an ICC arbitration should refer to any rules of law and respectively to its legal system when deciding upon the costs.[780] **15.1164**

---

[778] This may create, however, an enforcement problem.

[779] Craig/Park/Paulsson, *op cit*, 393 *et seq.*

[780] For more details of the law applicable when deciding upon the costs, see Bühler/Webster, *op cit*, paras 31–71 *et seq.*

15.1165 The simplest method is to award a global sum. Generally, this will be a flat rate sum, a breakdown of which is not provided by the arbitrators. Under the standard of 'reasonable legal and other costs', this sum will not necessarily cover the actual costs incurred by the parties.[781] The fact that a party has paid the fees and expenses of its counsel can be viewed as a first indication of their reasonableness. However, since each party is free to manage its litigation resources as it sees fit, the time issue is whether it is reasonable to place the financial burden of that party's decision onto the other side. The use of several counsel and experts by a party may be perfectly legitimate, but may be seen by the Arbitral Tribunal as not essential for defending the case, and may thus not be allowed for lack of reasonableness.

15.1166 Different criteria may be taken into account as follows: the total sum in dispute, the amount of separate claims and counterclaims, the significance and complexity of the matters in dispute and/or the time spent, the need to mobilize independent resources, eg experts on claim assessment and/or on accounting, experts on foreign law, and even the parties' conduct during the proceedings. By comparing the costs of one party with the costs of the other party, the Arbitral Tribunal may also get some sense of the reasonableness. However, a party having the burden of proof with respect to evidence that may be largely located out of its hands, possibly in a distant country, is likely to incur higher costs than its opponent. There may be other reasons why the costs of one side are much higher than those of the other and nevertheless reasonable.[782]

15.1167 It is not unknown for an arbitrator to accept outright a lawyer's fee note which has been submitted to him and which is calculated on the basis of the lawyer's own national practices or of an agreement between the lawyer and his client.[783] In so doing, the arbitrator implicitly agrees that these legal costs have been reasonably expended in preparing and conducting the party's case. In an ICC arbitration, having its place of arbitration in London between Austrian and South African parties, the Claimant was awarded his normal legal costs. The arbitrator, from the UK, allowed 'Mr Y's bill—drawn up in accordance with the principles, and at the normal rates, applicable to Austrian patent agents—amounts (after deduction of the deposits for costs paid to the ICC Court of Arbitration of the ICC, which are included in it) to (. . .)'.[784]

15.1168 Allocation of costs. The allocation of costs is made once the final determination of costs has been settled; it becomes part of the final award. There is a variety of ways in which costs may be allocated and of factors which are likely to influence on this allocation. One may here again distinguish between the procedural costs and the parties' costs. This distinction is a practical one, not a formal one. The terms of Art 31(3) do not make such a distinction with

---

[781] Craig/Park/Paulsson, *op cit*, 393 *et seq.*

[782] See discussion in Kreindler R., 'Final Rulings on Costs: Loser Pays All?' in *Best Practices in International Arbitration* (2006) *ASA Special Series* no 24, 4; Bühler, M.W., 'Awarding Costs in International Commercial Arbitration: An Overview' (2004) 2 *ASA Bull* no 2, 249. See also ICC Study of the final Awards of 1991 cited in Derains & Schwartz, A Guide, *op cit*, 371.

[783] This is more likely where both parties are represented by lawyers of the same nationality and the arbitrator himself understands the basis of the calculation if, for example, he is also a lawyer practicing in the same jurisdiction.

[784] ICC Case no 5460 (1987), published in extract in *Collection of ICC Awards 1974–1985, Vol I, op cit*, 136, and (1988) YBCA XIII, 104.

regard to the exercise of the arbitrators' discretion to allocate costs. The discretion relates to 'arbitration costs', which includes both types of costs.[785]

Allocation of procedural costs. The ICC Rules are silent on cost allocation inasmuch as they do not indicate which party should bear the costs of arbitration nor to what extent, and merely stipulate that the arbitrator shall 'decide which of the parties shall bear them or in which proportions they shall be borne by the parties'. This permits the arbitrators absolute discretion, which to a greater or lesser extent is found in the rules of other arbitral institutions.[786] **15.1169**

Unless otherwise agreed, the arbitrators do not have to follow the judicial rules or practices on cost allocation applicable at the place of arbitration. As discussed under Art 14, the law of the place of arbitration seems not appropriate to be applied for a detailed procedure but rather sets out the minimum procedural standards for international arbitration.[787] However, it seems that many arbitrators yield to such practices.[788] **15.1170**

The merits of this approach are difficult to evaluate—certainly for the parties this represents some practical disadvantages. The lack of a yardstick governing the exercise of this discretion in ICC Rules is combined with the fact that the allocation of costs between the parties in ICC awards is rarely expressed in great detail. This means that it is not only difficult to predict how the costs may be allocated in a particular case, but also to explain the allocation thereafter. **15.1171**

One of the most significant factors in relation to the allocation of procedural costs is the outcome of the dispute and many legal systems of the world provide somehow for the award of costs to the successful party. Depending on the outcome, costs may be dealt with in three ways: one party pays the full costs; a 50/50 split between both parties, or a proportional allocation. In ICC case 11670 the Arbitral Tribunal stated: **15.1172**

> The Rules do not contain any rules or criteria for the decision that the Tribunal must take [regarding costs]. The decision is left to the discretion of the arbitrator. Nevertheless, the results of the arbitration play a predominant role in the exercise of this discretion by the arbitrator. A party who loses his case is, in principle ordered to pay the costs of arbitration. However, other criteria can be taken into account, and notably the manner in which the case was conducted and the costs caused by reckless or abusive request or by delaying tactics.[789]

---

[785] UNCITRAL Rules, Art 40.2, expressly grants the arbitrators greater discretion in relation to parties' costs; Redfern/Hunter, *op cit* 408; Wetter/Priem, *op cit,* 316.

[786] Wide discretion is found in the following rules Art 28.2 LCIA, Art 31 AAA, and Art 28(1) ICSID, which do not specify how the discretion is to be exercised. Art 43(5) SCC, and Art 56 Zurich, both provide a basis of apportionment.

[787] See Art 14, paras 15.573 *et seq.* See also ICC case no 8786 (1997) (Final Award): 'The Arbitrator has to decide within his own discretion to what extent attorney's fees may be determined to be "normal". Thereby, the Arbitrator is not bound by "any local procedural law or practice" [. . .] Therefore, it is not relevant what attorney's fees would be customary or provided for, eg by Turkish law. It is within the free discretion of the Arbitrator to decide to what extent attorney's fees are "normal" and how the attorney's fees are allocated between the parties.' (2002) ASA Bull vol 20 no 1, 67; (2000) ICC ICArb Bull vol 11 no 2, 83.

[788] Craig/Park/Paulsson, *op cit,* 393 *et seq*; Karrer P.A., *op cit,* 38; Redfern/Hunter, *op cit,* 399–400.

[789] ICC case no 11670 (2003) (Final Award), (2004) 22 ASA Bull no 2, 333.

15.1173 Thus, a Claimant prevailing in all of its claims can normally expect the unsuccessful Respondent to be ordered to pay the procedural costs of the arbitration.[790] Where the claim is dismissed or the Arbitral Tribunal considers that it is not competent, a Respondent can expect the Claimant to bear the procedural costs in full.[791] Where neither party is successful outright, it is common practice to allocate the costs in the same proportion as the outcome of the substantive issues. When looking at the outcome, it may be insufficient to take a mathematical view by comparing the amount claimed and the amount awarded. For a Claimant to succeed on the issue of liability may be a major achievement, and may have required significant resources to obtain. Likewise, the scope of work of an Arbitral Tribunal would not necessarily have been reduced if the Claimant had only pursued the strict minimum of its entitlement in the award.[792] On the other hand, the gross exaggeration of a claim may have led to additional work for the Arbitral Tribunal. The failure to obtain a successful outcome on an issue on which a large amount of time and effort were spent may also be taken into account.

15.1174 Factors such as national practices, the principle of equity and the extravagance of a party in the proceedings may also influence the allocation. Thus, the allocation may sanction a party whose conduct prior to or during the arbitration has added unnecessary cost and delay to the proceedings, or take into account the amicable and professional cooperation of parties in the resolution of the dispute.

15.1175 Apportionment of parties' costs. Parties' costs may be apportioned in the same ways as the procedural costs. This may follow the outcome of the case entailing that a party pays the other party's costs in full or an appropriate percentage thereof,[793] and here again, ie for procedural costs, this seems to be a general trend world-wide. Witnesses' expenses may require different treatment, so that such costs are borne by the party calling the witness or by the party in whose favour the witness gives evidence. Similar considerations apply to interpreters' and translation costs.

15.1176 The allocation may be made irrespective of the outcome of the case, particularly where both claims and counterclaims make it impracticable to analyse how much of the costs

---

790 ICC Case nos 3099, 3100 (1979) in *Collection of ICC Awards 1974–1985, op cit*, 67, 365, (1982) YBCA VII, 87, 95; ICC Case no 3316 (1979) in *Collection of ICC Awards 1974–1985, op cit*, 385, (1982) YBCA VII, 106; ICC Case no 5460 (1987), (1988) YBCA XIII, 104, see ICC case no 8445 (1996), (2001) YBCA vol XXVI, 167; ICC case no 10188 (1999), (2003) YBCA vol XXVIII, 68; ICC case no 9466 (1999), (2002) YBCA vol XXVII, 170.

791 See, eg ICC Case no 3383 (1979) in *Collection of ICC Awards 1974–1985, op cit*, 394 and (1982) YBCA VII, 119; Wetter/Priem, *op cit*, 292 quoting ICC Case no 6401, (1991) Int'l Arb Rep, 125.

792 See, eg ICC Case no 2930 (1982) in *Collection of ICC Awards 1974–1985, op cit*, 118, (1984) YBCA IX, 105; ICC Case no 4237 (1984) in *Collection of ICC Awards 1974–1985, op cit*, 167 and (1985) YBCA X, 52–60; see also ICC Case no 3267 (1984) in *Collection of ICC Awards 1974–1985, op cit*, 376, (1987) YBCA XII, 87, 96, where the Arbitral Tribunal held: 'In view of the final result of this arbitration for each party, it is an equitable solution to decide that the costs of the arbitration proper are to be borne by the parties in the same proportion as their advances therefor, which were made approximately one-third by Claimant and two-thirds by defendant. . .'. ICC Case nos 2977, 2978 and 3033 (1978), (1981) YBCA VI, 133 awarded a 50/50 allocation of the costs of the arbitration.

793 See eg (1972) ICC Case no 1803 in *Collection of ICC Awards 1974–1985, op cit*, 40 and (1980) 5 YBCA, 177; (1964) ICC Case no 1250 in *Collection of ICC Awards 1974–1985, op cit*, 30 and (1980) 5 YBCA, 168.

incurred relate to the claims and counterclaims. In such a case, an English arbitrator took what he termed a 'broad brush approach'.

The simplest and an often-used approach in international arbitration is that each party pays its own legal costs. It is striking that this may even be the basis of allocation where a Claimant's claims are rejected as unfounded.[794] The rationale for such approach may be that in an international arbitration it should be the sole responsibility of each party how it presents and defends its case. While there is no universally recognized principle that the losing party has to bear the legal costs of its opponent,[795] the principle that each party bear its own costs is not universally recognized either. Proportional allocation is required by the procedural rules in countries such as Germany, Austria, Sweden, and Switzerland whereas in France, for example, parties to state court proceedings normally have to bear their own legal expenses irrespective of the outcome of the case, and where judges may grant an indemnity on an exceptional basis (Art 700 of the Code of Civil Procedure). Of course, since Arbitral Tribunals generally comprise arbitrators from different legal backgrounds, the allocation is likely to reflect a compromise between the practices of each one's national procedural laws. **15.1177**

In a recent case, an Arbitral Tribunal sitting in France ordered the Respondent to bear its own legal costs in addition to 50 per cent of the Claimant's costs, while the ICC Arbitration Costs were to be borne equally by the parties. It stated: **15.1178**

> Most of the efforts made by the parties concentrated on the question whether the early termination of the [] Agreement was justified. Indeed, both the disputed part of the principal claims and the decisions on the counterclaims largely hinged on the resolution of this central question. It was finally resolved against Respondent and, as mentioned above, Claimant was then successful at the rate of 25 per cent on the disputed part of the principle claims and fully victorious in respect of the counterclaims.[796]

(5.2) **Decision on costs** Pursuant to Art 31(3), the parties are entitled to a decision on costs, even if they do not assert this right at the hearing. Claims for costs are normally made in the Terms of Reference (Art 18). Otherwise, arbitrators will not determine and allocate the normal legal costs, thus forcing each party to bear its own. Thus, if parties neglect to claim their parties' costs, the arbitrators cannot award them. **15.1179**

The arbitrators' decision being limited to an allocation of the procedural costs, whenever arbitrators forward their final award in draft to the ICC Court for scrutiny and approval, they will leave a blank for the amount of the costs of arbitration. When the ICC Court approves the award, it will also fix the procedural costs, and indicate the same to the **15.1180**

---

[794] Craig/Park/Paulsson, *op cit*, 395; Redfern/Hunter, *op cit*, 397.

[795] In arbitration agreements contained in bilateral agreements of states, it is often provided that each side bear its own legal costs. See eg the Treaty between the Federal Republic of Germany and the former USSR on Promotion and the Reciprocal Protection of Investments of 13 June 1989, Art 5, 29 *ILM* 351 (1990). See also cooperation between Belgium, Luxembourg and the former USSR, Art 9(9), *ibid* at 299 and between the United Kingdom and the former USSR, Art 9(5), *ibid* at 366. See also the Agreement between Canada and France establishing a Court of Arbitration for the purpose of carrying out the delimitation of maritime areas of 30 March 1989, Art 8(1), *ibid* at 11 and the Convention on Establishing the Multilateral Investment Guarantee Agency (MIGA Convention), Art 57, Annex 11, Art 4(k), 24 *ILM* 1598 (1985).

[796] ICC Case no 13686 (2007), unreported.

arbitrators so that they can insert the amount in the award prior to its notification to the parties.[797] At this stage, the ICC Court is entitled to charge the full costs according to the cost scale. The cost scale makes no provision for a preliminary decision on procedural costs and it is therefore not possible to include and allocate in a preliminary award the amount of procedural costs to be borne by a party. As for parties' legal and other costs, a decision of the Arbitral Tribunal may be made at any time during the proceedings, Art 31(2).

15.1181 Since Art 31(3) clearly states that the final award shall deal with costs, if an arbitrator decides that a case is outside his competence, he nonetheless remains competent to decide the costs. The 1998 Rules have clarified the position. Under the 1975/1988 Rules it was not clear whether, if an arbitrator found he lacked competence, he was nevertheless competent to determine the costs or whether the decision on costs would be for the national court.[798] In practice, ICC arbitrators who have declined jurisdiction over a dispute have nevertheless proceeded to make a decision on costs and the 1998 Rules confirms this practice.

15.1182 If parties settle their dispute before the final award, then the amount of administrative costs charged by the ICC at its discretion depends on the progress of the arbitration. The Court is to take account of the 'stage attained by the arbitral proceedings and any other relevant circumstances' in doing so, App III, Art 2(6). If the parties cannot reach an agreement on the question of their costs, this may be dealt with in the award. Commonly, if a Claimant wants to withdraw its claim, a Respondent will only agree if either the Claimant assumes the costs or the Arbitral Tribunal decides thereon.

15.1183 The decision on costs should be included in the dispositive part of the final award in a manner that makes it readily enforceable, ie the party entitled to costs should be given the right in the holding of the award to claim from the other side a sum of money.[799] Account will be made for the payment of the advance on costs paid to the ICC by the party entitled to costs. The right to reclaim costs will normally be expressed in the same currency as the costs incurred or already paid, ie in case of the procedural cost, in US dollars, which is the currency in which the advance on costs was paid to the ICC.

Article 32. Modified time limits

(1) The parties may agree to shorten the various time limits set out in these Rules. Any such agreement entered into subsequent to the constitution of an Arbitral Tribunal shall become effective only upon the approval of the Arbitral Tribunal.

---

[797] Craig/Park/Paulsson, *op cit*, 392.

[798] If the Respondent takes no part in the proceedings, that is, he does not appoint an arbitrator, does not pay any advance on costs and does not sign the Terms of Reference, and does therefore not incur any costs, the question of a decision on costs will become academic, since the Claimant will have to bear the costs anyway.

[799] Examples: 'We award that the Claimants pay the costs of this arbitration, fixed by the International Court of the International Chamber of Commerce in the total amount of 400,000 US dollars, and that the Claimants refund to the Respondents the sum of 200,000 US dollars which they had paid to the International Chamber of Commerce by way of an advance on costs. We further order that the Claimants pay the Respondents a contribution to the Respondents' legal costs and expenses, which contribution we assess at FF 1,250,000', or more simply: 'The Respondent shall pay to the Claimant the sum of 150,000 US dollars and the sum of FF 950,000 as costs of arbitration', the first figure being the procedural costs advanced by the Claimant, the second the legal costs incurred by the same.

(2) **The Court may, on its own initiative, extend any time limit which has been modified pursuant to Article 32(1) if it decides that it is necessary to do so in order that the Arbitral Tribunal or the Court may fulfill their responsibilities in accordance with these Rules.**

(1) Introduction

The article regarding the possibility for the parties to modify the time limits was introduced with the 1998 modification of the Rules. The ICC Court had by that time gained some experience from so-called fast-track arbitration proceedings, the first of which was handled by the Court already in the late 1980s. One of these early fast-track cases has been much publicized and commented, since the award was rendered within a period of only 80 (days of the submission of the Request for Arbitration and much of the critical work done by the arbitrators and the Court's scrutiny and approval of the award, took place over Christmas and New Year. **15.1184**

Although the need for faster arbitration proceedings is voiced in many articles and at many seminars, parties and their counsel must not be blind to the difficulties that are inherent in fast-track arbitrations.[800] **15.1185**

There is a limit to how short time periods can be, beyond which it becomes doubtful whether each party has had an appropriate opportunity to present its case and submit its defence. Arbitrators too need time to reflect on difficult questions and the issues that arise in a fast-track arbitration are by no means less complicated or less contentious than those arising in a 'normal' arbitration. Due process requires that an appropriate time is allotted to each party.[801] Against this background no special procedure for fast-track arbitration has been implemented in the 1998 ICC Rules. Article 32 offers simply the possibility for parties to agree to shorten the various time limits set out in the Rules where they deem this to be appropriate. **15.1186**

Article 32 does not cover procedural remedies as motions for summary judgment or dispositive motions that also could shorten arbitral proceedings, like recently invoked at the IAI Seminar on Dispositive Motions in International Arbitration.[802] **15.1187**

In September 2000, the ICC Commission on International Arbitration issued a 'Note on Expedited ICC Arbitration Procedure'. It is addressed to parties wishing to organize an expedited ICC arbitration procedure, and highlights the dos and don'ts, and the pros and cons thereof.[803] Unlike other arbitral institutions, the ICC has no set of rules for fast-track **15.1188**

[800] See Bühler, M.W., 'Die ICC-Schiedsgerichtsordnung 1998 aus Sicht der Parteien' (1998) *DIS-MAT* II, p 34; Reiner, A., 'Le Règlement d'Arbitrage de la CCI', *op cit*, 47.

[801] Kreindler, R., 'Speedier arbitration as a response to changes in world trade: a necessary goal or a threat to the expectations of the parties?' in *Liber Amicorum Michel Gaudet* (ICC Publishing, Paris, 1999) 180.

[802] See IAI Seminar on the 'Dispositive Motions in International Arbitration', 9 November 2006, Paris, reported in (2007) 25 *ASA Bull* no 1, 197, note Knoll and (2006) *Rev arb* no 4, 1129, note Train.

[803] Doc 420/20–005. It can be obtained from the ICC Court's Secretariat, 38, Cours Albert 1er, 75008 Paris, France, Tel: 00-33-1-49-53-28-28, Fax: 00-33-1-49-53-29-33. See also (2002) 13 *ICC Bull* no 1, 29.

arbitrations,[804] and it was decided not to include specific fast-track provisions in the ICC Rules during the revision of the 1975/1988 ICC Rules.[805]

(2) Article 32(1): Agreement to modify the time –limits

15.1189 The following time limits under the Rules can be shortened. The 30 days granted to the Respondent for the filing of an answer (see Art 5(1)); the appointment of an arbitrator (see Art 9); the two month period to sign the Terms of Reference (see Art 18(2)); and the six months period for rendering the award (see Art 24 (1)).

15.1190 The parties cannot agree with a binding effect for the ICC Court that the Court shall be bound by certain deadlines to which the parties may have agreed. The ICC Court maintains in all situations its independence to use the time it considers necessary for the administration of arbitrations taking place under its Rules.

15.1191 If the parties have agreed in their contract that shorter time limits shall apply to an arbitration, the arbitrators will be informed of this before accepting to be appointed as arbitrators. If, on the other hand, the parties agree to modify the time limits after the arbitration has started, one cannot expect the arbitrators who often have a busy schedule to be bound to such an agreement unless they have approved the modified time limits. This is provided for in the second sentence of Art 32(1).

(3) Article 32(2): Power of the ICC Court to extend modified time limits

15.1192 The ICC Court has the last word with respect to fast-track arbitration time limits since the Court overlooks each arbitration and is responsible, to the extent possible, that each award is enforceable at law (Art 35). By choosing the ICC Rules, the parties accept the right of the ICC Court to modify the agreed time limits.[806] Therefore, the ICC Court may on its own initiative extend the time limits, when it becomes clear that the shortened time limits agreed by the parties will be impossible to comply with if the parties are to be given 'a reasonable opportunity to present their case', see Art 15(2).

15.1193 One of the authors had an experience of this situation in a case where the parties had agreed in the arbitration agreement that the award should be rendered within 90 days from the Request for Arbitration. When the arbitration started it soon became manifest to the arbitrators that the complexity of the case was such that the parties were not able to submit extensive briefs in time as to allow the arbitrators to organize the hearing, hear the witnesses and draft an award within the stipulated 90-day period. The ICC Court then on its own initiative, but after having consulted with the Arbitral Tribunal, decided that it was necessary to extend the 90-day time limit and so informed the parties and the arbitrators before the expiry of said time limit.[807]

---

[804] eg the SCC Institute, the WIPO Institute, the AAA Institute, the CCIG Institute provide for institutional rules for fast-track arbitrations.

[805] See *supra* Art 1, para 15.107.

[806] See French Supreme Court decision, Cass. Civ 1re, 15 June 1994, *Communauté urbaine de Casablanca v société Degrémont,* (1995) *Rev arb* no1, 88, note Gaillard.

[807] See ICC Case no 11183 (2001), unreported. The arbitration agreement provided that the Award shall be rendered within four months from the appointment of the arbitrator. The four-month time limit has been

The time limit agreed by the parties in the contract had, however, a positive effect since both the parties and the arbitrators worked with the objective of finishing the case within 90 days. Had no time limit existed in the arbitration agreement it is likely that the award had not been rendered within the 120 days within which it was in fact rendered, but rather within the normal six-month period provided for in the Rules. **15.1194**

However, often when parties agree on short time limits for the issuance of a final award, they assume that there will be only one award dealing with all issues. When, for instance, questions of jurisdiction arise, the arbitrators may feel obliged to render two awards, one on jurisdiction, the other on the merits, making it more difficult, if not impossible to respect the shortened time limit. **15.1195**

Since any award, including a first award on jurisdiction must be scrutinized and approved by the ICC Court before its notification to the parties, the time needed for the Court's scrutiny and approval of the draft award should be anticipated when agreeing to shortened time limits. **15.1196**

Article 33. Waiver

A party which proceeds with the arbitration without raising its objection to a failure to comply with any provision of these Rules, or of any other rules applicable to the proceedings, any direction given by the Arbitral Tribunal, or any requirement under the arbitration agreement relating to the constitution of the Arbitral Tribunal, or to the conduct of the proceedings, shall be deemed to have waived its right to object.

(1) Introduction

Article 33 deals with the principle that a party may not complain about failures to comply with the Rules or with any other procedural rules applicable to the proceedings long after the arbitral proceedings. The provision is in line with many other provisions in international arbitration rules that objections that are not raised in a timely manner will be rejected. A waiver rule as *estoppel* or *venire contra factum proprium* is an important tool for maintaining the integrity of arbitral proceedings and also for any subsequent proceedings before state courts, eg in connection with the enforcement of the award or a challenge against an arbitrator. **15.1197**

In the *Golshani v Gouvernement de la République d'Iran* case the French Supreme Court rejected the Claimant's demand to dismiss the enforcement of the arbitral award in France on the grounds of *estoppel*.[808] The Court stated: **15.1198**

> The decision [of the Court of Appeal] . . . validly decided that Mr. Golshani who himself presented the request for arbitration before the American Iranian Claims Tribunal and who had participated for nine years without reservation in the arbitral proceedings is not permitted by reason of *estoppel* to maintain that that jurisdiction had decided without having an agreement to arbitrate or an invalid one not applicable to him.

---

extended by the ICC Court in accordance with Art 32(2) in order to enable the Arbitral Tribunal to fulfil its task. The Award was finally rendered within six months.

[808] Cass Civ 1re, 6 July 2005, *Golshani v Gouvernement de la République d'Iran*, (2005) *Rev Arb* no 4, 993, note Pinsolle.

15.1199 It is to be welcomed that the ICC Rules contain an express warning signal for the increasing number of parties and counsel who participate in ICC arbitrations with no prior arbitration experience whatsoever, be it international or domestic. Such warning signal will also work as a good reminder for experienced parties seeking to gain advantages by tactical manoeuvres, that a party cannot wait before raising an objection to an arbitrator's or the other party's failure to comply with the ICC Rules, or other rules or directions that are applicable.

15.1200 Irregularities or perceived irregularities should be pointed out by the parties to the Arbitral Tribunal. A party must raise an objection as soon as it becomes aware of the reason justifying that an objection is made, or as soon as possible thereafter, allowing the party a reasonable, but limited, time for reflection before it must take action. Thereafter, it should be deemed to have waived its right to object, unless it can show good cause why it has not raised its objection earlier. The Arbitral Tribunal has discretion to appreciate the timeliness of the objection, and in exercising such discretion will have to be fair to both parties and take into account the relevant circumstances underlying the objection.

(2) Irregularities that can be waived

15.1201 Under Art 33, irregularities concern 'any provisions of these Rules'. This could be, eg that instance, if a party considers that it was not given a reasonable opportunity to present its case in accordance with Art 15(2).

15.1202 Although, in practical terms, the most common cases for a complaint are irregularities committed by the Arbitral Tribunal in the proceedings, the text of Art 33 is not limited thereto. The ICC Court or its Secretariat or a party can commit acts falling under the definition of this provision, and the party who feels that a rule has not been complied with must then react.

15.1203 Unlike many of the rules that contain a provision on waiver, Art 33 is wide in scope: it includes also any failures and irregularities with respect to 'any other rules applicable to the proceedings': Such rules are normally to be found in the Terms of Reference and/or in procedural orders of the Arbitral Tribunal, such as the language to be used, the way witnesses are to be heard, or the time limit for the submission of pleadings. If, for instance, the Terms of Reference provide that submissions that are made late will not be taken into consideration, a party must object to a late filing by the other party in order to avoid the operation of the waiver effect under this Article.

15.1204 'Any direction given by the Arbitral Tribunal'. Such directions may include requests to submit documents, the setting of hearing dates, or the requisites for a site visit.

15.1205 Further irregularities may result from a failure to respect any requirement under the arbitration agreement relating to the constitution of the Arbitral Tribunal. For instance, if a specific language or other skill of knowledge is required from the arbitrator pursuant to the arbitration agreement but is lacking, or if an arbitrator has a nationality that was excluded by agreement, a party must object in order to escape the waiver.

15.1206 There may also be irregularities where the arbitration agreement contained a requirement regarding the conduct of the proceedings. For instance, if it was agreed that 'officers and directors' of a party cannot be heard as witnesses, that the hearing should take place in a specific language, or that witnesses should not be cross-examined and these stipulations are not respected, a party must object.

(3) The failure to comply with rules of law

Rules of law and law are not included in the categories of various provisions enumerated in the Article. Thus, an arbitrator's or a party's failure to comply with a provision of law cannot be deemed to have been waived even if no objection is raised by the party. This would certainly apply to mandatory rules of law, which the parties may not even have pleaded before the Arbitral Tribunal. **15.1207**

An illustrative example of the application of this principle can be found in the *Eco Swiss China Time Ltd v Benetton International BV* case of the European Court of Justice.[809] In that case, the validity of a licence agreement which one of the parties had terminated, became an issue in the annulment proceedings before the Dutch courts. The Arbitral Tribunal found the termination to have been in violation of the parties' agreement and awarded damages. The losing party brought proceedings in the Netherlands to have the award set aside since, in that party's view, the award was invalid as contrary to public policy by virtue of the alleged nullity of the licence agreement under Art 81 EC Treaty (formerly Art 85), contrary to European Community competition law. None of the parties had, however, raised the point during the arbitration proceedings. **15.1208**

The European Court of Justice ruled that provisions of Art 81 EC (ex. Art 85) may be regarded as a matter of public policy within the meaning of the New York Convention. It went on to state that Community Law requires that questions concerning the interpretation of the prohibition laid down in Art 81(1) EC Treaty should be open to examination by national courts when asked to determine the validity of an arbitration award and that it should be possible for those questions to be referred, if necessary, to the European Court of Justice for a preliminary ruling. **15.1209**

The European Community regulations are thus 'rules of law' or 'law" which are not included in the categories enumerated in Art 33 that can be deemed to be waived. The *Eco Swiss* case concerned rules having a public policy character. However, Art 33 does not operate any distinction between public policy and rules of law and law in general, not necessarily of a public policy nature. **15.1210**

French courts seem to be more flexible, as reflected recently by the *Thalès* case and followed by the French Supreme Court in the *SNF v Cytec* decision.[810] In the *Thalès* case, the French **15.1211**

[809] Judgment of 1 June 1999, Case C-126/97, (2001) Stockholm Arb Rep, pp 23–52; (1999) YBCA vol XXIVa, 629; *Rev arb* (1999) no 3, 631, note/dot; CJEC 1 June 1999.

[810] Paris, 5 February 2003, *Société Thalès Air Defence v GIE Euromissile et Eads*, (2004) *Rev arb* no 1, 94; Webster, Th. 'Review of Substantive Reasoning of International Arbitral Awards by National Courts: Ensuring One-Step Adjudication', *op cit*; Mourre, A. and Radicati di Brozolo, L., 'Towards Finality of Arbitral Awards: Two Steps Forward and One Step Back' (2006) 23 *J Int'l Arb* no 2, 171; Senkovic, P. and Lastenouse, P., 'International Arbitration And Antitrust Law: Eco Swiss Judgment Revisited By the Paris Court of Appeal' (2005) 20 *Mealey's Int'l Arb Rev* no 2, 1; (2005) RTD Com 263, note Loquin; Radicati di Brozolo, L.G., 'L'illicéité qui crève les yeux: critère de contrôle des sentences au regard de l'ordre public international (à propos de l'arrêt Thalès de la Cour d'Appel de Paris)' (2005) *Rev arb* no 3, 529; French Supreme Court,

court acknowledged the applicability of EC competition law, but also noted that the review of the merits, including the treatment of competition law issues, is limited to situations where there is a 'manifest violation' of competition law. Therefore a demand of annulment based on a violation of the EU competition law was rejected by the Paris Court of Appeal. In the *SNF v Cytec* decision the Court recalled the principle not to review the merits of a case when international public policy issues are concerned.[811]

15.1212 In the *Thalès* case,[812] Thalès sought to have the award annulled based on a violation of the EU competition law. None of the parties had, however, raised this issue during the arbitral proceedings, nor did the Tribunal. The Paris Court of Appeal rejected the annulment action and noted that the review of awards is limited under French law. Therefore, review of the merits, including the treatment of competition law issues, is limited to situations where there is a 'manifest violation' of competition law.

15.1213 A similar, even less limited approach than the French one is to be found in Switzerland.[813] In the *Tensacciai* case, the Swiss Federal Tribunal rejected a party's demand for annulment stating that: 'the provisions of competition law, whatever they may be, do not belong to the essential and widely recognized values which, according to the prevailing concepts in Switzerland, should constitute the foundation of any legal system. Consequently, the violation of such a provision does not fall within the scope of Art 190(2)(e) PILA. . . .'.

15.1214 Article 33 is helpful in two respects. It reinforces the authority of the Arbitral Tribunal, as it makes it possible to remedy any procedural irregularities prior to the issuance of the award, provided an objection was made in a timely manner. It also limits grounds for annulment or non-recognition of awards before the national courts. There is abundant jurisprudence where the courts have refused to sanction a procedural irregularity on the ground that the party had not objected during the arbitration, and had thus effectively waived its right to raise an objection.

Cass Civ 1e, 4 June 2008, *Société SNF SAS v Société Cytec Industries BV*; may be downloaded from <http://www.courdecassation.fr>, link 'jurisprudence', 'arrêts', 'première chambre civile'.

[811] Paris, 23 March 2006, *Société SNF SAS v Société Cytec Industries BV*, (2006) *Rev arb* no 2, 483; for a comparison, see Tribunal de Première Instance de Bruxelles, 8 March 2007, *Société SNF SAS v Société Cytec Industries*, (2007) *Rev arb* no 2, 303, note Mourre and Radicati di Brozolo; (2007) 25 *ASA Bull* no 3, 630, note de Meulemeester and Piers. See also the discussion in para 17–53; French Supreme Court, Cass Civ 1e, 4 June 2008, *Société SNF SAS v Société Cytec Industries BV*; *op cit*.

[812] See discussion in para 17–55; see the *Thalès* case cited at para 28–23; Webster, 'Review of Substantive Reasoning of International Arbitral Awards by National Courts: Ensuring One-Stop Adjudication', *op cit*, para 14–3 n 4; Mourre and Radicati di Brozolo, 'Towards Finality of Arbitral Awards: Two Steps Forward and One Step Back' (2006) *J Int'l Arb* vol 23 no 2, 171; Senkovic and Lastenouse, 'International Arbitration And Antitrust Law; Eco Swiss Judgment Revisited By the Paris Court of Appeal' (2005) *Mealey's Int'l Arb Rep* vol 20 no 2, 1; (2005) *RTD Com* 263, note Loquin; Radicati di Brozolo, 'L'illicéité qui crève les yeux: critère de contrôle des sentences au regard de l'ordre public international (à propos de l'arrêt Thalès de la Cour d'appel de Paris)' (2005) *Rev arb* no 3, 529; Racine, 'Réflexions sur l'autonomie de l'arbitrage commercial international (II.–L'arbitrage, Deuxième Séance)' (2005) *Rev arb* no 2, 305, at 324. See also Kurkela, Levin, Liebscher and Sommer, 'Certain Procedural Issues in Arbitrating Competition Cases'" (2007) *J Int"l Arb* vol 24 no 2, 189.

[813] Swiss Federal Tribunal, 8 March 2006, *Tensacciai v Terra Armata*, 4P.278/2005 (ICC arbitration—Italian law—place of arbitration: Lausanne), <http://www.bger.ch>; Radicati di Brozolo, L.G., 'Note—Tribunal Fédéral Suisse, 8 mars 2006' *Rev arb* no 3, 769. More generally, see Arfazadeh, H., *Ordre public et arbitrage international à l'épreuve de la mondialisation* (Bruylant, LGDJ, 2nd edn, Schulthess, Zurich, 2006).

Another issue is to define the limits or requirements of a waiver. For example Art 27 of the Rules that deals with the scrutiny of awards cannot be waived under the ICC Rules.[814] In contrast thereto, the failure by a party to object to the fact that some local rules were not applied may constitute a waiver, for example if the parties agree to IBA Rules of Evidence.[815] **15.1215**

What form does an objection take in order to be a valid objection? Article 33 does not give any hints to the form. It will finally be the national courts of the place of arbitration and of any place of enforcement that will decide what constitutes an objection. As to the requirements of a waiver, the Paris Court of Appeal stated in the *Bombardier Case*: **15.1216**

> Considering that in order to be heard in annulment proceedings, the grievance needs to have been invoked in front of the arbitral tribunal each time it was possible to do so; that this rule, which protects procedural loyalty and arbitral awards, would be rendered useless if it was enough to utter menaces and critics in front of the arbitrator, as shown by Bombardier, in order to keep its options open when the time has come, to isolate an element of the procedure and present it as a violation of the adversarial principle.[816]

Article 33 does not provide for any time limit during which to raise an objection and imposes no requirement of 'promptness' or the like. Nor does it state that objections must be made in a 'prompt' manner, in contrast with the LCIA, WIPO and UNCITRAL Rules. However, it is usually limited in those circumstances to challenges to the arbitrators. Article 33 does nevertheless provide an indication as to when the objection should be made when it states that the waiver occurs 'when the party proceeds with the arbitration without raising its objection'. The basic principle is that the party should object prior to further steps being taken in the arbitration. If the party fails to do so, then the waiver may arise. In the normal course of arbitral proceedings, the parties will be called upon to proceed with the arbitration promptly, and therefore objections will have to be made generally in rather prompt fashion to effectively prevent a waiver of rights under Art 33. **15.1217**

Article 34. Exclusion of liability

Neither the arbitrators, nor the Court and its members, nor the ICC and its employees, nor the ICC National Committees shall be liable to any person for any act or omission in connection with the arbitration.

(1) Introduction

Article 34 is a provision which was introduced in 1998. It provides an exclusion of liability of the arbitrators, the ICC Court and its members, the ICC and its employees and the ICC National Committees. This exclusion is very broad as it applies to 'any act or omission in **15.1218**

[814] See Paris Court of Appeal, 1 July 1999, *Braspetro Oil Services v Management and Implementation of the Great-Man Made River Project (GMRP)*, Bull ASA (2000) 376; Smit, R., 'Mandatory ICC Arbitration Rules', *op* cit, 845.

[815] For a further discussion, see Bühler/Webster, ICC Handbook, paras 33–18 *et seq.*

[816] Paris, 23 June 2005, *Société Bombardier Transportation Switzerland v Société Siemens AG*, JurisData: 2005-287132.

connection with the arbitration' by any such person or body.[817] It has been recently tested by French courts who dismissed it as not valid in the particular case.

15.1219 As international arbitration has grown in importance, as there are more cases involving significant amounts of money, and as parties have become more litigious, arbitrators and arbitral institutions are being sued or threatened with suit (with or without justification) more frequently. While there have been few reported cases against ICC arbitrators, there have been several well known cases against the ICC itself in Swiss and Egyptian courts in connection with the *Westland*[818] case where the ICC was sued for a large amount and in France in connection with the *REDEC* case,[819] the *Cubic* case,[820] or the *SNF* case.[821]

15.1220 In the recent *SNF* case, the Paris court stated that the limitation of liability provision in Art 34 is effective in a contractual context in the absence of 'wilful breach, inexcusable or gross negligence approaching fraud'.

15.1221 In light of these developments, when time came to revise the 1975/1988 Rules, the working party of the ICC Commission[822] considered inserting in the Rules an explicit provision dealing with the immunity of arbitrators and of the ICC.[823] It had noted that immunity of arbitrators and of arbitral institutions was increasingly provided for in various international arbitration rules, where immunity was granted in respect of 'conscious and deliberate wrongdoing', in cases of 'fraud and dishonesty' and 'deliberate wrongdoing'.[824]

15.1222 National laws differ widely on the subject of immunity of arbitrators. However, just as most national laws appear to provide judges with some degree of immunity from liability for negligence in performing their judicial duties, so they seem to provide arbitrators with some measure of immunity when performing the same role.

15.1223 The reason for providing immunity is that arbitration is regarded as an important adjunct to the courts in resolving disputes and that without such immunity arbitrators could, as private citizens, fear that they could be subject to suit by disappointed litigants. As stated

---

[817] It is of interest to recall that the ICC Pre-arbitral Reference Procedure of 1990 provided in Art 6.8 that neither the ICC nor any of its employees or persons, acting as Chairman or Vice-Chairman, nor any person acting as Referee shall 'be liable to any person for any loss or damage arising out of any act or omission in connection with the Rules except that the Reference may be liable for the consequences of conscious and deliberate wrongdoing'.

[818] See *Cour de Justice de Genève*, decision of 26 November 1982, *République arabe d'Egypte, A.O.I., A.B.H. v Westland Helicopters Ltd.*, (1989) *Rev arb* 514.

[819] See Tribunal de Grande Instance de Paris, decision of 13 July 1988, *Société R.E.D.E.C. et pharaon v Société Uzinexport Import et Chambre de Commerce Internationale* (1989) *Rev arb* 97. In this case, REDEC sought a suspension of the arbitration as, REDEC claimed, the ICC had wrongly decided under the ICC Rules that there was a prima facie arbitration agreement with R.E.D.E.C. The French court held that the ICC Court's decision was an 'administrative' rather than a 'judicial' act and, as such, could not be challenged before the French courts. See further *infra*, para 15.1243.

[820] See *supra* Art 1, para 15.81 and n 67.

[821] *Tribunal de Grande Instance de Paris*, decision of 10 October 2007, *Société SNF v Chambre de Commerce Internationale* (2007) *Rev arb* no 4, 847, note Jarrosson.

[822] See *supra* Introduction, para 15.61.

[823] See *infra* paras 15.1224 *et seq.*

[824] See *supra* comparable arbitration rules. Other international arbitration rules do not provide for immunity of arbitrators, notably UNCITRAL as well as Zurich, CCIG and Vienna.

recently by the US District Court of the Southern District of New York in the *Global Gold Mining* case:

> The rationale of arbitral immunity is that such immunity is essential to protect the decision maker from undue influence and protect the decision-making process from reprisals by dissatisfied litigants [825]

If a party is dissatisfied with an arbitral award then his recourse, if any, should normally be against the arbitration award and not against the arbitrator or his insurer.[826] **15.1224**

(2) The scope of the exclusion of liability

While the absolute immunity accorded by the text of this article may appear extreme, it is anticipated that in practice, this provision will be subject to qualification under the applicable national law. Indeed, it remains to be seen how this clause will be enforced in those legal systems which have not embraced, or have only partially done so, the concept of immunity of arbitrators and arbitral institutions, and whether therefore it provides sufficient protection of the arbitrators and the ICC. Certainly, any user of ICC arbitration would be well advised to look to the applicable law to fully appreciate what his liability might be. **15.1225**

To the extent that parties are to choose the arbitrators themselves, the immunity of arbitrators provides yet another reason why parties should not underestimate the importance of choosing competent and experienced arbitrators who understand and are able to conduct the proceedings in a proper way and to render an effective award. **15.1226**

The scope of the exclusion of liability is wide. It is not limited to claims of parties but relates to claims of *any person*. Therefore, all users of ICC Arbitration are concerned by this provision. The exclusion relates to *any act or omission* on the part of the arbitrator or the ICC *in connection with* an arbitration. Therefore, it would seem that immunity exists in relation to any act or omission in carrying out relevant functions as well as a failure to act at all. **15.1227**

The immunity of the arbitrators must be viewed in terms of the safeguards against the lack of independence, non-fulfilment of functions, misconduct and delay on the part of arbitrators, provided within the ICC Rules in particular in Arts 7, 11, and 12 as to the duties and rights of arbitrators, or in Arts 7(5), 15(2), 18, 20(1), 23, 24 and 27 regarding the conduct of the proceedings. **15.1228**

The safeguards and recourse under the ICC Rules may nevertheless be insufficient. A party which suffers loss as a result of an act or omission of an arbitrator in the discharge of his duties or his failure to do so, will be without recourse in terms of financial compensation for the consequences thereof and the removal of the arbitrator will offer little consolation. **15.1229**

825 *Global Gold Mining, LLC v Peter Robinson & the ICC*, 2008 WL 336821 SDNY See also *Babylon Milk Cream Co v Horvitz*, 151 NYS. 2d 221 (September, 1956) aff'd 4AD2d 777, 165 NYS 2d 717 (1957).

826 Some countries, like the United States, afford arbitrators close to absolute immunity whereas in certain civil law countries, like France, the immunity provided for by law is much more qualified, see for example *Tamain v Conrad*, 552 F2d 778, 780. Under English law, the immunity of arbitrators is substantially more limited than in the US. s 29(1) of the English Arbitration Act 1996 provides: 'An arbitrator is not liable for anything done or omitted in the discharge of his function as arbitrator unless the act or omission is shown to have been in bad faith.'

15.1230 This provision is mandatory and it will not be possible for *any person* in an ICC arbitration to contract out of it by agreement and thereby deprive either the arbitrators or the institution of its protection. All parties and any person will be deemed to have agreed to such exclusion by the fact there is an arbitration under the ICC Rules.

15.1231 Previously such immunity would have been achieved by agreement of an exclusion clause. The absolute exclusion of liability removes the onus on the arbitrator to seek such protection directly from the parties, which is undoubtedly preferable since liability is a sensitive issue for an arbitrator to discuss with parties, especially at the outset of an arbitration.[827] Moreover, if parties did not agree to such exclusion, then the arbitrator would have to consider whether to act without such protection from immunity or simply not to accept the appointment. Such decision would be particularly important in view of certain national laws which envisage the possibility of actions for damages against an arbitrator.[828]

(3) Immunity of the Arbitrators

15.1232 **(3.1) Nature of the arbitrators' function and rights and duties of arbitrators** The nature of the arbitrators' function can explain the immunity vested in arbitrators in fulfilling their functions: arbitrators exercise a judicial or quasi-judicial function. The arbitrators' immunity may understandably be said to result from the principle of judicial immunity. There are, however, significant differences between judicial and arbitral immunity, the former arising out of public appointment while the latter arises as a matter of private appointment on the basis of the parties' agreement.

15.1233 Contrary to judges, the arbitrators' mission is limited to the particular arbitration for which they have been appointed: it is a personal mission which an arbitrator cannot on his or her own accord assign to a third person. Also, under the ICC Rules, the arbitrator's appointment may be terminated. An arbitrator may be replaced by the ICC Court in the event of death, resignation, upon request of the parties, upon acceptance of a challenge by one of the parties as to the arbitrator's 'alleged lack of independence or otherwise' or upon the ICC Court's own initiative if the arbitrator is prevented from fulfilling or fails to fulfil his functions (see Arts 11 and 12).

15.1234 Indeed, it is the consensual nature of the arbitral process which has led the relationship between arbitrators and parties to be defined in terms of a contract with the rights and duties that go with it and, therefore, arbitrators should not be vested with immunity.[829]

15.1235 Moreover, an arbitrator's functions are not limited to the rendering of a substantive decision on the dispute since the arbitrator also has the role of 'manager' of the arbitration, the responsibility for the proper conduct of the arbitration. Finally, it is also part of the arbitrator's duty to render an enforceable award.

15.1236 In some respects though, the relationship between the arbitrators and the parties is difficult to define in terms of a contractual relationship. Parties normally have the expectation that

---

[827] However, the authors are not aware of extension clauses having been inserted by arbitrators into Terms of Reference.

[828] Redfern/Hunter, *op cit*, 241.

[829] *ibid*, 240 *et seq.*

the arbitrators will act fairly, but it is difficult to characterize fairness as a contractual obligation. It is also difficult to define in contractual terms the relationship between the co-arbitrator, appointed by one party, and the other party, since in any event the arbitrator owes duties to both parties equally.

Taking a closer look at the question of arbitrators' remuneration, it is accepted practice in international arbitration that arbitrators receive remuneration for the exercise of their functions, whether this remuneration is agreed with the parties or one of them or arises out of the agreement of the parties to submit their dispute to institutional arbitration, such as the ICC, which provides for remuneration of arbitrators within its rules (see Arts 30 and 31). On the one hand, the fact that the arbitrators receive remuneration is not inconsistent with the contractual theory, as in principle judges are also remunerated. However, on the other hand judges clearly do not derive their remuneration from the parties. **15.1237**

One rationale for the immunity of arbitrators is where the arbitrators have been selected by the parties: parties should assume responsibility for their choice of arbitrator in the event of failures or omissions by the arbitrator in the conduct of the arbitration.[830] In ICC Arbitration, priority is given to the parties' choice of arbitrator. While the ICC Court confirms the appointment before it becomes effective, this is purely administrative, and the parties should therefore exercise all due care and attention in the selection process to ensure the appointment of a suitably qualified, experienced and independent person as arbitrator. The consequences of not doing so may cause the damage notably with respect to the substantive outcome of the case,[831] for which the parties will have no recourse against the arbitrator. **15.1238**

The parties' choice of arbitrator as a rationale for the immunity of arbitrators may sit uneasily where, in the absence of the parties' choice, the ICC Court selects the arbitrator. However, the position is the same with respect to arbitrators selected by the ICC Court as those chosen by the parties, since the immunity defined in Art 34 is conferred on all arbitrators in ICC Arbitration. **15.1239**

(3.2) **Purpose of protecting the arbitrators from liability** The rule of the arbitrators' immunity has several purposes: to preserve the independence of the arbitrators, especially to avoid dissatisfied parties threatening action for damages against the arbitrators which might unduly influence the decision-making process; to preserve the finality of the award so that dissatisfied parties do not seek to have it opened up on some vexatious or frivolous grounds; and to ensure that there are suitable arbitrators who are ready and willing to act, since in all likelihood suitable arbitrators would be difficult to find if they faced the risk of personal liability in connection with an arbitration.[832] **15.1240**

Also, the general provision of immunity for arbitrators avoids the possibility of parties seeking to establish the exact nature of any act or omission, ie to characterize it as a contractual or administrative function rather than a judicial one. However, it would seem questionable **15.1241**

830 Redfern/Hunter, *op cit*, 241.
831 See *supra* Art 8.
832 Redfern/Hunter, *op cit*, 241 *et seq*.

to extend such rationale to protecting arbitrators against fraud or other misconduct, which as noted above, are not exempted from the scope of the arbitrators' immunity under the ICC Rules.

(4) Immunity of the ICC Court and its members, the ICC and its employees, and ICC National Committees

15.1242 Article 34 extends the same immunity as that vested in ICC arbitrators to the ICC itself. In so doing it has followed the example of other arbitral institutions in recognizing that not only the arbitrators but the arbitral institution which administer the arbitration and may have appointed the arbitrators, should be protected from liability claims. The immunity under the provisions of Art 34 is wider than that of comparable provisions in the other arbitral rules which are qualified by reference to deliberate wrongdoing, fraud and dishonesty.[833] Such immunity, despite the administrative role of the ICC, is a necessary safeguard of the integrity of the arbitral process as a whole.[834]

15.1243 The ICC will therefore be immune in respect of all its functions exercised under the ICC Rules, that is to say for any failings in carrying out of its functions. For instance denial by the ICC Court of the existence of a prima facie arbitration agreement, which prevents an arbitration from proceeding, or a wrongful acceptance of a prima facie arbitration agreement, whereby the Respondent will have to take the matter before the Arbitral Tribunal, or late notification of a Request for Arbitration to the Respondent by the ICC Court's Secretariat, or failure to appoint suitably qualified arbitrators, or negligence in deciding a challenge of an arbitrator, and so forth. The manner in which the ICC carries out its functions will not necessarily be transparent since, in many instances it does not provide reasons for its decision.

15.1244 In *Redec v Société Uzinexport Import*,[835] the *Tribunal de Grande Instance* of Paris was seized with respect to the challenge of the ICC Court's decision that a prima facie agreement to arbitrate existed and that the arbitration could proceed against four named defendants. One of these defendants, an individual, who had signed the arbitration agreement, challenged the ICC Court's decision contending that he had signed the arbitration clause in his capacity of the officer of the relevant company but not, however, in any personal capacity. Another defendant, Redec, challenged the ICC Court's decision as to the existence of a

---

833 Art 31.1 of the LCIA Rules, Art 35 of the AAA Rules and Art 33 of the SIAC Rules provide a wider exclusion in respect of the institution than of the arbitrators, since the latter may be held liable for 'conscious and deliberate wrongdoing'. Art 21 HKIAC does not protect the institution in the event of 'fraud and dishonesty' and Art 77 of the WIPO Rules does not protect the Centre in the event of 'deliberate wrongdoing'. The ICC considered qualifying the exclusion from liability also in respect both of the arbitrators and the ICC so that they would not be immune in the event of 'deliberate wrongdoing or gross negligence'. This qualification was not adopted since some members of the ICC Commission's working party considered it might be used as a 'floodgate' which would be open to exploitation by counsel for a losing party to seek to characterize what went wrong as 'deliberate wrongdoing' or 'gross negligence' and thereby to collect from the ICC what it did not recover or had to pay to the other party under an award.

834 Without such protection, arbitral institutions would have to take out expensive insurance cover to pay such claims (since the institutions themselves would not have the necessary funds). Ultimately, the costs of such insurance would be borne by parties, ie in ICC Arbitration the administrative costs of the ICC would necessarily have to be increased to cover such insurance costs.

835 See *supra* n 821.

prima facie arbitration clause as it was the third party guarantor of one of the defendant companies, and not a party to the arbitration clause. The ICC Court subsequently re-examined its decision and found that the individual was not prima facie bound by the arbitration clause, thus this matter was not decided by the French Court. The ICC Court confirmed its position as to Redec. The Paris district court examined the challenge by Redec—on the basis of Art 809 of the New French Code of Civil Procedure—confirming the ICC Court's decision to be neither 'un trouble manifestement illicite' (a manifestly illicit trouble) nor that it was necessary for it to prevent 'un dommage imminent' (imminent damage) since the arbitrator would anyway decide on the scope of his jurisdiction and Redec would, if necessary, be able to challenge the award. The *Tribunal de Grande Instance* expressly recognized the administrative nature of the ICC Court's decision in this regard.

Vesting the institution with immunity is also intended to protect the integrity of the ICC system. It is understandably necessary that the immunity of the institution be extended to the ICC's members and employees and its National Committee to avoid actions being directed against them in an attempt to circumvent the immunity of the arbitral institution itself. **15.1245**

Article 35. General rule

In all matters not expressly provided for in these Rules, the Court and the Arbitral Tribunal shall act in the spirit of these Rules and shall make every effort to make sure that the award is enforceable at law.

(1) Matters not provided in the Rules

The ICC Rules of Arbitration are far from being a comprehensive code of conduct of an arbitration.[836] The Rules were never intended to be a code covering every aspect of the arbitral procedure. Given the variety of backgrounds of the participants in ICC arbitrations and the diversity of disputes, the Rules only provide the necessary framework, leaving many aspects to the parties and the arbitrators to resolve. This is explained by the fact that the manner in which arbitration is conducted varies widely from one jurisdiction to another. **15.1246**

Consequently, the *arbitrability* of disputes is not treated in the Rules, the *capacity* of parties to be party to an ICC arbitration is also not covered, the death, dissolution, merger, succession and *substitution of parties* is not dealt with by the Rules nor is *bankruptcy* of a party. Many aspects of the agreement to arbitrate are not covered in the Rules, such as *defects and invalidity of the arbitration agreement*. The Rules provide nothing in respect of the manner in which *evidence* shall be taken.[837] **15.1247**

Nor do the rules regulate the weight to be attached to different evidence, whether cross-examination of witnesses is permitted or desirable and similar matters. The possibility of making a dissenting and separate opinion is not mentioned in the Rules.[838] The relationship **15.1248**

[836] See *supra* Art 15, para 15.605.

[837] See, however, Art 20(3) and (4) regarding the possibility to hear witnesses and to appoint experts.

[838] While Art 25(1) stipulates that the Award may be by majority only, it neither authorizes nor excludes the issuing of a dissenting opinion, see *supra* Art 25, paras 15.927 *et seq.*

between the Arbitral Tribunal and the national courts at the place of arbitration is not generally dealt with in the Rules (see, however, Art 23(2)). Finally, the recognition and enforcement of the arbitral award is not treated in any great detail in the Rules (see, however, Art 28(6)).

(2) The spirit of the Rules

15.1249 Article 35 has existed in its present form in the ICC Rules, with only slight alterations, since 1955 and is generally intended to guide both the ICC Court and the arbitrators when a question or issue may arise during the conduct of the arbitration that is 'not expressly provided for' in the Rules. Article 35 serves the useful purpose of providing the ICC Court and arbitrators with both general guidance and authority to act, as appropriate, in respect of matters with which the Rules do not deal explicitly. In the authors' opinion, however, Art 35 does not provide more than very general guidance in addressing many of the questions mentioned above that are not covered by the Rules.

15.1250 When referring to the spirit of the ICC Rules, at least five guiding principles come immediately to mind: (i) party autonomy.[839] Where there is mutual agreement by the parties on issues not expressly covered by the Rules, such agreement will normally prevail over other consideration; (ii) fair and equal treatment of the parties;[840] (iii) impartiality of the arbitral process;[841] (iv) efficiency of the arbitral process;[842] and (v) limited state court intervention.[843]

15.1251 The limits of the powers of the ICC Court under Art 35 are not entirely clear. It has been suggested that the ICC Court might in exceptional circumstances find that it possesses the inherent authority under Art 35 to change the place of arbitration agreed by the parties in order to prevent the arbitration process from grinding to a halt.[844] While an Arbitral Tribunal may have the authority to adopt an agreement by the parties to changed circumstances, the ICC Court is not vested with such powers.[845]

15.1252 Article 35 could be invoked by an arbitrator facing an unreasonable request by the parties with respect to the procedure to be followed, for instance with respect to a party's right to present its case, but also with respect to the arbitrator's right to keep the arbitration procedure within reasonable limits, authorizing the arbitrator to refuse the hearing of witnesses who in the arbitrator's opinion have nothing of pertinence to contribute. It can also be relied on when applying a rule of law that the parties have not pleaded but which the Arbitral Tribunal may consider applicable as a matter of public policy, since the state courts at the place for arbitration will be applying such law because of its public policy character.[846]

---

839 See in particular Arts 7(6), 10(2), 14(2), 15(1), 16, 17, 23(1) and 32(1).
840 See in particular Art 15(2).
841 See in particular Arts 7(1)–(3) and 11.
842 See in particular Arts 18(4), 20(1), 22(1) and 24(1).
843 See in particular Arts 6(2), 11, 12 and 23.
844 See *supra* Art 14, paras 15.582 *et seq.*
845 See the discussion *supra* Art 14, paras 15.586 *et seq.*
846 See *supra* Art 15, paras 15.607 *et seq.*

Under this Article the ICC Court earlier justified its practices in relation to the constitution of the Arbitral Tribunal in multi-party cases, a subject that the Rules did not previously expressly cover (now Art 10). Similarly, in the absence of a provision in the former Rules on truncated tribunals (now Art 12(5)), the ICC Court approved an award, and allowed the signing of the award by the two remaining members on the basis of Art 26, which was the predecessor to Art 35. Likewise, the ICC Court relied upon that provision in authorizing an Arbitral Tribunal to consider an application for the interpretation of an award, which is now expressly provided for in Art 29. In each of these cases, the ICC Court came to the conclusion that in the absence of an express provision in the Rules, the positions adopted by it were those that were most in keeping with the general scheme of the Rules (their 'spirit') and the ultimate enforceability of the award. **15.1253**

Based on a broad construction of that provision, Arbitral Tribunals have sometimes felt obliged when rendering their award to consider the enforceability of their decisions not only at the place of the arbitration but at other possible places of execution. In our view this is going too far; the Article does not require the Arbitral Tribunal to ensure that the award will be subject to execution in any particular country provided that it has been rendered in accordance with the formal requirements of the place where it was made. In any event, an international arbitrator will not necessarily be in a position to know where the winning party will seek to enforce the award.[847] **15.1254**

Where a party challenges the Arbitral Tribunal's jurisdiction, the question arises whether the Arbitral Tribunal would breach its obligation to render an enforceable award if it concluded that it has jurisdiction over the parties contrary to a public court position. In ICC case no 10623 the Arbitral Tribunal denied such position in stating that if the Arbitral Tribunal finds that it has jurisdiction, it cannot fail to exercise it, otherwise it 'would entail a denial of justice and fairness to the parties and conflict with the legitimate expectations they created by entering into an arbitration agreement'.[848] **15.1255**

The ICC Case no 10623 dealt with an arbitration between state 'X' and a private party. The place of arbitration was in state 'X'. The tribunal commented as follows on the requirements of Art 35: **15.1256**

> [140.] A generally accepted principle of international arbitration, reflected in Article 35 of the ICC Rules, compels the Arbitral Tribunal to make every effort to ensure that any award it renders is enforceable at law. In this contact, complying with the law and the judicial decisions of the seat is clearly an important objective, in light of the fact that the courts have the power to set aside an award rendered in their country (. . .).
>
> [142.] This does not mean, however, that the arbitral tribunal should simply abdicate to the courts of the seat the tribunal's own judgment about what is fair and right in the arbitral proceedings. In the event that the arbitral tribunal considers that to follow a decision of a court would conflict fundamentally with the tribunal's understanding of its duty to the parties, derived from the parties' arbitration agreement, the tribunal must follow its own judgment, even if that requires non-compliance with a court order.

---

847 See Derains/Schwartz, A Guide, *op cit*, 385.

848 ICC Case no 10623 (2003) ASA Bull, 59. For more details, see Bühler/Webster, ICC Handbook, *op cit*, paras 35–8 *et seq.*

[143.] To conclude otherwise would entail a denial of justice and fairness to the parties and conflict with the legitimate expectations they created by entering into an arbitration agreement. It would allow the courts of the seat to convert an international arbitration agreement into a dead letter, with intolerable consequences for the practice of international arbitration more generally.

[144.] This conclusion is consistent with principles that are already well established in international arbitration. In particular, it is clear from arbitral case law that the obligation to make every effort to render an enforceable award does not oblige an arbitral tribunal to render awards that are fundamentally unfair or otherwise improper. An arbitral tribunal should not go so far as to frustrate the arbitration agreement itself in the interests of ensuring enforceability. Such an outcome would be, to say the least, a paradox.[849]

15.1257 A key factor for the Tribunal in the above case was that the arbitration involved the state and the courts of a state are an emanation of that state. Therefore, in this exceptional case, the Tribunal decided to ignore the anti-arbitration injunction of the courts of the place of arbitration. The reference in the award to cases where annulled awards have been enforced is the litmus test. If a Tribunal does not believe that any award it renders will be enforced either at the place of arbitration or elsewhere, then it will hardly ignore the courts of the place of arbitration.

15.1258 However, the duty of an Arbitral Tribunal is to consider mandatory principles of law that may affect the enforcement. In the *Eco Swiss* case, for example,[850] neither the parties nor the Arbitral Tribunal raised EU competition law matters during the arbitration proceedings. The award was annulled on public policy grounds based on EU competition law.

III. Appendix

A. Model clauses

Arbitration:

All disputes arising out of or in connection with the present contract shall be finally settled under the Rules of Arbitration of the International Chamber of Commerce by one or more arbitrators appointed in accordance with the said Rules.

Pre-Arbitral referee procedure:

Any party to this contract shall have the right to have recourse to and shall be bound by the pre-arbitral referee procedure of the International Chamber of Commerce in accordance with its Rules for a Pre-Arbitral Referee Procedure.

Pre-arbitral referee procedure and arbitration:

Any party to this contract shall have the right to have recourse to and shall be bound by the pre-arbitral referee procedure of the International Chamber of Commerce in accordance with its Rules for a Pre-Arbitral Referee Procedure.

[849] ICC Case no10623, *op cit*, paras 0–31, n 29, 14–34, fn 28, and 24–6, n 22.

[850] CJEC, 1 June 1999, C-126/97, *Eco Swiss China Time Ltd v Benetton International*, (1999) YBCA vol XXIVa, 629; (1999) *Rev arb* no 3, 631, note Idot.

All disputes arising out of or in connection with the present contract shall be finally settled under the Rules of Arbitration of the International Chamber of Commerce by one or more arbitrators appointed in accordance with the said Rules of Arbitration.

B. Contact details

ICC Headquarters:
The ICC International Court of Arbitration
38, cours Albert 1er
75008 Paris
Telephone: + 33 1 49 53 29 05
Telefax: + 33 1 49 53 29 33
Email: arb@iccwbo.org
Website: <http://www.iccwbo.org>, link 'contact us'

ICC Court's Asian office:
The ICC International Court of Arbitration
Suite 2
12/F Fairmont House
8 Cotton Tree Drive
Central
Hong Kong
Telephone: + 852 3607 560
Telefax: + 852 2523 1619

ICC Hearing Centre in Paris:
112 Avenue Kléber
75016 Paris
Telephone: + 33 1 49 53 33 00
Email: infohearingcentre@iccwbo.org
Website: <http://www.icchearingcentre.org>

C. Bibliography

Aboukrat, G., 'A propos du statut de l'arbitre et de celui de la magistrature: quelle place pour le droit français ?' in *Les Cahiers de l'Arbitrage Volume I* (Gazette du Palais, Paris, 2002) 121.

Aksen, G., 'The Tribunal's Appointment' in L.W. Newman and R.D. Hill (eds), *The Leading Arbitrators' Guide to International Arbitration* (Juris Publishing/Staempfli Publishers, 2004) 31.

Arfazadeh, H., *Ordre public et arbitrage international à l'épreuve de la mondialisation* (2nd edn, Bruylant, LGDJ, Schulthess, Zurich, 2006).

Arnaldez, J.J., 'L'acte determinant la mission de l'arbitre' in *Etudes offertes à Pierre Bellet* (Litec, Paris, 1991) (cited as: Arnaldez J.J.).

Arnaldez, J.J., Derains, Y. and Hascher. D., *Collection of ICC Arbitral Awards 1991–1995*, vol III (ICC Publishing/Kluwer, 1997).

Arnaldez, J.J., Derains, Y. and Hascher. D., *Collection of ICC Arbitral Awards 1996–2000*, vol IV (ICC Publishing/Kluwer, 2003).

Bagner, H., 'Arbitrator Impartiality: Appearance is Everything' (2006) 21 *Mealey's Int'l Arb Rev* no 6, 26.

Baizeau, D., 'Waiving the Right to Challenge an Award Rendered in Switzerland: Caveats and Drafting Considerations for Foreign Parties' (2005) *Int'l Arb L Rev* No 3, 69.

Bensaude, D., 'Thalès Air Defence BV v GIE Euromissile: Defining the Limits of Scrutiny of Awards Based on Alleged Violations of European Competition Law' (2005) 22 *J Int'l Arb* no 3, 239.

Bernini, G., 'The civil law approach to discovery: a comparative overview of the taking of evidence in the anglo-american and continental arbitration systems' in L.W. Newman and R.D. Hill (eds), *The Leading Arbitrators' Guide to International Arbitration* (Juris Publishing/Staempfli Publishers, 2004) 269.

Berti, S.V., Honsell, H., Vogt N.P. and Schnyder A.K., *International Arbitration in Switzerland* (Helbing & Lichtenhahn, Basel, 2000).

Besson, S., *Arbitrage international et mesures provisoires—Etude de droit comparé* (Schulthess, Zurich, 1998) (cited as: Besson, S.).

Bishop, D. and Reed L., 'Practical Guidelines for Interviewing, Selecting and Challenging Party-Appointed Arbitrators in International Commercial Arbitration' (1998) *Arb Int'l* vol 14 no 4, 395.

Blanke, G., 'Defining the Limits of Scrutiny of Awards Based on Alleged Violations of European Competition Law—A Réplique to Denis Bensaude's "Thalès Air Defence BV v GIE Euromissile"' (2006) 23 *J Int'l Arb* no 3, 249.

Blessing, M., 'The Arbitral Process—Part III: The Procedure before the Arbitral Tribunal' (1992) 3 *ICC ICArb Bull* no 2, 18 (cited as: Blessing, The arbitral process).

Blessing, M., 'The ICC Arbitral Procedure Under the 1998 ICC Rules–What Has Changed?' (1997) 8 *ICC ICArb Bull* no 2, 16.

Blessing, M., 'Regulations in Arbitration Rules on Choice of Law' (1996) *ICCA Congress Series no 7*, 391.

Böckstiegel, K.-H., 'Case Management by Arbitrators: Experiences and Suggestions' in *Liber Amicorum in honour of Robert Briner* (ICC Publishing, Paris, 2005) 115.

Böckstiegel, K.-H., 'Major Criteria for International Arbitration in Shaping Efficient Procedure' (1999) *ICC ICArb Bull*, Special Supp, 49 (cited as: Böckstiegel K.-H., Major Criteria).

Böckstiegel, K.-H., 'Practices of Various Arbitral Tribunals' in 'Preventing Delay and Disruption of Arbitration: I Conduct by a Party to Disrupt Establishing the Tribunal and Starting the Arbitral Proceedings. Topic 3: Use by a party of challenges to delay or disrupt the arbitration' (1991) *ICCA Congress Series no 5*, 131.

Bond, S., 'How to draft an Arbitration Clause (Revisited)', (1990) 1 *ICC Court Bull* no 2, 21.

Bond, S., ICC Report in 'Preventing Delay and Disruption of Arbitration: I Conduct by a Party to Disrupt Establishing the Tribunal and Starting the Arbitral Proceedings. Topic 3: Use by a party of challenges to delay or disrupt the arbitration' (1991) *ICCA Congress Series no 5*, 150 (cited as: Bond S., ICC Report).

Bond, S., 'The experience of the ICC in the Confirmation/Appointment Stage of an Arbitration', paper presented at the ICC/ICSID/AAA Colloquium of International Arbitration in Paris, 27 October 1988.

Bredin, J.-D., 'Le secret du délibéré arbitral' in Bellet P., *Etudes offertes à Pierre Bellet* (Litec, Paris, 1991) 71 (cited as: Bredin, J.-D., Le secret).

Bredin, J.-D., 'Retour au délibéré arbitral' in *Liber Amicorum Claude Reymond* (Litec, Paris, 2004) 43 (cited as: Bredin, J.-D., Retour au délibéré).

Briner, R., 'The Evaluation of Evidence: Some Observations Based on the Practice of the Iran-United States Claims Tribunal' in *Liber Amicorum Thomas Bär and Robert Karrer* (Helbing & Lichtenhahn, Basel, 2004) 41.

Briner, R., 'The Implementation of the 1998 ICC Rules of Arbitration' (1997) 8 *ICC ICArb Bull* no 2, 7.

Brower, C.N. and Sharpe, J.K., 'Determining the extent of discovery and dealing with request for discovery: perspectives from the common law' in L.W. Newman. and R.D. Hill (eds), *The Leading Arbitrators' Guide to International Arbitration* (Juris Publishing/Staempfli Publishers, 2004) 307.

Brown-Berset, D. and Lévy, L., 'Faillite et arbitrage' (1998) 16 *ASA Bull* no 4, 664.
Bruna 'Control of time limits by the International Court of Arbitration' (1996) 7 ICC *ICArb Bull* no 2, 72.
Bühler, M.W., 'Awarding Costs in International Commercial Arbitration: An Overview' (2004) 2 *ASA Bull* no 2, 249.
Bühler, M.W., 'Costs in Arbitration: Some further considerations' in *Liber Amicorum in honour of Robert Briner* (ICC Publishing, Paris, 2005), 179 (cited as: Bühler, M., Costs in arbitration).
Bühler, M.W., 'Cross-claims in international arbitrations: a common law perspective', paper delivered at the 22nd Symposium of Arbitrators in Paris, 26 March 2007.
Bühler, M.W., 'Correction and Interpretation of Awards and Advance on Costs' (1997) *ICC ICArb Bull*, Special Supp, 53.
Bühler, M.W., 'Die ICC-Schiedsgerichtsordnung 1998 aus Sicht der Parteien' (1998) *DIS-MAT* II, 34.
Bühler, M.W., 'Les clauses de confidentialité dans le commerce international' (2002) 3 *RDAI*, 359.
Bühler, M.W., 'Technical Expertise: An additional Means for Preventing or Settling Commercial Disputes' (1989) 6 *J Int'l Arb* no 1, 135 (cited as: Bühler, Technical Expertise).
Bühler, M.W. and Dorgan. C., 'Witness Testimony Pursuant to the 1999 IBA Rules of Evidence in International Commercial Arbitration—Novel or Tested Standards?' (2000) 17 *J Int'l Arb* no 1, 3 (cited as: Bühler/Dorgan).
Bühler, M.W. and Jarvin, S., 'L'amiable compositeur peut-il laisser la question du droit applicable au fond indéterminée?' in *Mélanges dédié à François Knoepfler, Droit international privé, droit de l'arbitrage et droit comparé* (Helbing & Lichtenhan, Basel, 2005) (cited as: Bühler/Jarvin).
Bühler, M.W. and Webster, T., *Handbook of ICC Arbitration: Commentary, Precedents, Materials* (2nd edn, Thomson, Sweet & Maxwell, London, 2008) (cited as: Bühler/Webster, ICC Handbook).
Bühring-Uhle, C., *Arbitration and Mediation in International Business* (Kluwer Law International, The Hague, London, Boston, 1996).
Calvo, M.A., 'The Challenge of the ICC Arbitrators: Theory and Practice' (1998) *J Int'l Arb* vol 15 no 4, 63.
Càrdenas, E. and Rivkin, D.W., 'A Growing Challenge for Ethics in International Arbitration' in *Liber Amicorum in honour of Robert Briner* (ICC Publishing, Paris, 2005) 191 (cited as: Càrdenas and Rivkin).
Carlevaris, A., 'La qualification des décisions des tribunaux arbitraux dans le Règlement d'arbitrage CCI et dans la jurisprudence française' in *Les Cahiers de l'Arbitrage Volume I* (Gazette du Palais, Paris, 2002) 153.
Castineira, E. and Petsche, M., 'The Language of the Arbitration: Reflections on the Selection of Arbitrators and Procedural Efficiency' (2006) 1 *ICC ICArb Bull* no 1, 33 (cited as: Castineira/Petsche).
Cavalieros, Ph., 'La confidentialité de l'arbitrage' (2005) *Les Cahiers de l'Arbitrage* no 3, *Gazette du Palais* 14–15 December 2005, 6,
Clay, Thomas, 'La disparition de l'obligation d'indépendance de l'arbitre au profit de l'obligation de révélation', note sous Paris 1re Ch. C., 12 February 2009 (2009) *Rev arb* no 1, 186.
Clay, Thomas, *L'arbitre* (Dalloz, Paris, 2001) p 231 (cited as Clay Th., L'arbitre).
Clay, Thomas, 'Note on *Société Cubic Defense Systems Inc v Chambre de commerce internationale*' (1999) *Rev arb* no 1, 103.
Collyer, G., 'Documentary Credit Dispute Resolution under the DOCDEX Rules Three Years On' (2000) *ICC Bull*, Special Supp, Finance and Insurance, 67.
Cordero Moss, G., 'Is the Arbitral Tribunal Bound by the Parties' Factual and Legal Pleadings?' (2006) *SIAR* 2006:3, 1.
Craig, L.W., Park, W.W. and Paulsson, J., *International Chamber of Commerce Arbitration* (3rd edn, Oceana/ICC Publishing, New York, 2000) (cited as: Craig/Park/Paulsson).

Croze, H. and Reinhard, Y., "Procédures collectives et arbitrage: Conseils pratiques aux parties et aux arbitres" (2005) *JCP Entreprises et Affaires* no14, 614.

Cremades, B., 'Powers of the arbitrators to decide on the admissibility of evidence and to organise the production of evidence' (1999) 10 *ICC ICArb Bull* no 1, 49 (cited as: Cremades, B.).

Cremades, B., 'The Arbitral Award' in L.W. Newman and R.D. Hill (eds), *The Leading Arbitrators' Guide to International Arbitration* (Juris Publishins/Staempfli Publishers, Huntington, New York, 2004) 397.

Crook J., 'Leading Arbitration Seats in Conflicting Legal Cultures in the Far East: A Comparative View' in S.N. Frommel and B.A.K. Rider (eds), *Conflicting Legal Cultures in Commercial Arbitration: Old Issues and New Trends* (Kluwer, Boston, 1999) 63.

Daly B., 'Correction and Interpretation of Arbitral Awards under the ICC Rules of Arbitration' including Extracts from ICC Addenda and Decisions on the Correction and Interpretation of Arbitral Awards, (2002) 13 *ICC ICArb Bull* no 1, 61.

de Fróes C.H., 'Correction and Interpretation of Arbitral Awards' in *Liber Amicorum in honour of Robert Briner* (ICC Publishing, Paris, 2005) 285 (cited as: Fróes).

Delvolvé, J.-L., 'Final Report on Multi-party Arbitrations' (1995) 6 *ICC ICArb Bull* no 1, 32.

Delvolvé, J.-L., Rouche, J. and Pointon, G.H., *French Arbitration Law and Practice* (Kluwer, New York, 2003).

Derains, Y., 'Amendments to the claims and new claims: where to draw the line?' in *Arbitral Procedure at the Dawn of the Millennium* (Bruylant, Brussels, 2005) 65.

Derains, Y., 'La pratique du délibéré arbitral' in *Liber Amicorum in honour of Robert Briner* (ICC Publishing, Paris, 2005) 221 (cited as: Derains, La pratique).

Derains, Y., 'Le témoin en matière d'arbitrage international' in *Mélanges en l'Honneur de François Knoepfler* (Helbing & Lichtenhahn, Basel, 2005) 227.

Derains, Y. and Schwartz, E., *A Guide to the ICC Rules of Arbitration* (2nd edn, Kluwer, The Hague, 2005) (cited as: Derains/Schwartz, A Guide).

Dimolitsa, A., '*Quid* encore de la confidentialité?' in *Mélanges dédiés à François Knoepfler* (Helbing & Lichtenhahn, Basel, 2005) 249.

Dolmans, M. and Grierson, J., 'Arbitration and the Modernization of EC Antitrust Law: New ICC Opportunities and New Responsibilities' (2003) 14 *ICC ICArb Bull* no 2, 37.

Donovan, D.F., 'Powers of the arbitrators to issue procedural orders, including interim measures of protection, and the obligations of parties to abide by such orders' (1999) 10 *ICC ICArb Bull* no 1, 57.

Eisemann F., 'La clause d'arbitrage pathologique' in *Arbitrage commercial—Essais in memoriam Eugenio Minoli*, Colloria di Studi sull'Arbitrator (AIA 1974) 129.

El Kosheri, A.S. and Youssef, K.Y., 'The Independence of International Arbitrators: An Arbitrator's Perspective' (2007) *ICC ICArb Bull*, Special Supp on Independence of Arbitrators, 43 (cited as: El Kosheri/Youssef).

El-Sharkawi, M.S., 'New Trends in Egyptian Arbitration Law' (1999) 16 *J Int'l Arb* no 1, 5.

Epstein L., 'Arbitrator Independence and Bias: The View of a Corporate In-house Counsel' (2007) *ICC Arb Bull*, Special Supp on Independence of Arbitrators, 55.

Estreicher, S. and Bennett, S.C., 'Disqualification of Arbitrators: Before or After the Award?' (2007) 237 *NYLJ* no 86.

Etudes de procédure et d'arbitrage en l'honneur de Jean-François Poudret (U of Lausanne, 1999).

Etudes offertes à Pierre Bellet (Litec, Paris, 1991).

Fadlallah, I., 'Payment of the Advance on Costs in ICC Arbitration: The Parties' Reciprocal Obligations'(2003) 14 *ICC ICArb Bull* no 1, 53.

Farhad, A., 'Provisional Enforcement of International Arbitral Awards Made in France—The Dilatory Effect of the French Set Aside Application' (2006) 23 *J Int'l Arb* no 2, 115.

Favre-Bull, X., 'Les conséquences du non-paiement de la provisions pour frais de l'arbitrage par une partie—Un tribunal arbitral peut-il condamner un défendeur au paiement de sa part de l'avance de frais?' (2001) 19 *ASA Bull*, 227.

Fortier, Y., 'The New Lex Mercatoria, or Back to the Future' (2001) 17 *Arb Int'l* no 2, 121.
Fortier, Y., 'The Tribunal's deliberation' in L.W. Newman and R.D. Hill (eds), *The Leading Arbitrators' Guide to International Arbitration* (Juris Publishing/Staempfli Publishers, 2004) 391.
Fouchard, Ph., Gaillard, E. and Goldman, B., *On International Arbitration* (Kluwer, 1999).
Fouchard, Ph., 'Arbitrage et faillite' (1998) *Rev arb* no 3, 471.
Friedland P.D., 'The Swiss Supreme Court Sets Aside an ICC Award' (1996) 13 *J Int'l Arb* no 1, 111.
Gaillard, E., 'Enforcement of Awards Set Aside in the Country of Origin: the French Experience' (1999) *ICCA Congress Series* no 9, 505.
Gaillard, E. and Di Pietro, D. (eds), *Enforcement of Arbitration Agreements and International Arbitral Awards: The New York Convention 1958 in Practice* (Cameron May, London, 2008).
Gélinas, F., 'The Application of the ICC Rules by the Court: 1998 Overview' (1999) 10 *ICC ICArb Bull* no l, 11.
Gélinas, P.A., 'Evidence through witnesses' in *Arbitration and Oral Evidence*, ICC Dossier 2004, ICC Publication no 689, 29.
Glossner, O., 'Sociological aspects of international commercial arbitration, The art of arbitration' in *Liber Amicorum Pieter Sanders* (Kluwer, 1982) 143.
Goldman, B., 'Instance judiciaire et instance arbitrale internationale' in *Etudes offertes à Pierre Bellet* (Litec, Paris, 1991) 219.
Goldstein, M., 'Note - Publicis Communications and Publicis S.A. v. True North Communications, Court of Appeals for the Seventh Circuit - 14 March 2000' (2000) 18 *ASA Bull* no 4, 830.
Griffith, G. and Pintos Lopez, R., 'Renegotiating Arbitrators' Terms of Remuneration' (2002) 19 *J Int'l Arb* no 6, 581.
Hascher, D., 'ICC Practice in Relation to the Appointment, Confirmation, Challenge and Replacement of Arbitrators' (1995) 6 *ICC ICArb Bull* no 2, 4 (cited as: Hascher, D.).
Heitzmann, P. and Grierson, J., 'SNF v Cytec Industrie: National Courts within the EC Apply Different Standards to Review International Awards Allegedly Contrary to Article 81 EC' (2007) *SIAR* 2007: 2, 39.
Heller, K., 'Constitutional Limits of Arbitration' (2000) *Stockholm Arb Rep* 2000:1, 7 (cited as: Heller, K.).
Héritier Lachat, A. et Hirsch, L. (eds), *De Lege Ferenda, Réflexions sur le droit désirable, en l'honneur du Professeur Alain Hirsch* (Slatkine, Geneva, 2004).
Holtzmann, H. and Donovan, D F., 'United States Country Report' in Paulsson, J. (ed), *ICCA Handbook*, Supp 28 (Kluwer, 1999).
Hunter, M., 'Final Report on Dissenting and Separate Opinions' (1990) 1 *ICC ICArb Bull* no 1, 32.
IAI Seminar on 'Dispositive Motions in International Arbitration' (9 November 2006, Paris) reported in (2007) 25 *ASA Bull* no 1, 197.
IBA Working Party, 'Commentary on the New IBA Rules of Evidence in International Commerical Arbitration' (January 2000) *IBA Int'l Bus Lawyer*, 14.
ICC Working Group on Interim and Partial Awards, Final Report (1990) 1 *ICC ICArb Bull* no 1, 26.
ICCA Working Group I, 'Preventing Delay and Disruption of Arbitration' (1991) *ICCA Congress Series no 5*, 197.
International Chamber of Commerce (ICC), *Arbitration and Oral Evidence* (ICC Publishing, Paris, 2005).
International Chamber of Commerce (ICC), 'Conditions of Access and Use of Netcase' (ICC Note of 18 April 2007).
International Chamber of Commerce (ICC), ICC Dispute Board Rules: Practitioner's View (2007) 18 *ICC ICArb Bull* no 1, 43.

International Chamber of Commerce (ICC), 'Note from the Secretariat on the appointment of administrative secretaries to assist the Arbitral Tribunal with its administrative tasks' (1995) 6 *ICC ICArb Bull*, no 2, 77.

International Chamber of Commerce (ICC), 'Note of the Secretariat of the International Court of Arbitration of the International Chamber of Commerce Regarding the Correction and Interpretation of Arbitral Awards' (1999) 10 *ICC ICArb Bull* no 2, 4.

International Chamber of Commerce (ICC), 'Note on correction and interpretation of arbitral awards' (1999) 10 *ICC ICArb Bull*, no 2, 4.

International Chamber of Commerce (ICC), 'Practical Guide' prepared by ICC Commission Working Group (S. Lazaroff, Chairman) (1992) 3 *ICC ICArb Bull* no 1, 24 (cited as: ICC, Practical Guide).

International Chamber of Commerce (ICC), 'Statement on VAT and other taxes applicable to arbitrator's fees' (2006) *ICC ICArb Bull*, no 2, 4.

International Chamber of Commerce (ICC), *Techniques for Controlling Time and Costs in Arbitration* (ICC Publication no 843, 2007).

Jarrosson, Ch., 'Note on Cass Civ Mixte, 14 Febr. 2003' (2003) 19 *Arb Int'l* no 3, 263 and (2003) *Rev Arb* no 2, 403.

Jarvin, S., 'Arbitrability of Anti-Trust Disputes: The Mitsubishi v. Soler Case' (1985) 2 *J Int'l Arb* no 3, 69.

Jarvin, S., 'Irregularity in the composition of the Arbitral Tribunal and the Procedure', in E. Gaillard and D. Di Pietro (eds), *Enforcement of Arbitration Agreements and International Arbitral Awards: The New York Convention 1958 in Practice* (Cameron May, London, 2008) 729.

Jarvin, S., 'La renonciation à la convention d'arbitrage' in *Liber Amicorum Dobrosav Mitrovic* (Belgrade, 2007).

Jarvin, S., 'Les décisions de procédure des arbitres peuvent-elles faire l'objet d'un recours juridictionnel?' (1998) *Rev arb* no 4, 611.

Jarvin, S., 'The place of arbitration–A review of the ICC Court's guiding principles and practice when fixing the place of arbitration' (1996) 7 *ICC ICArb Bull* no 2, 58.

Jarvin, S., 'To What Extent Are Procedural Decisions of Arbitrators Subject to Court Review?' (1999) *ICCA Congress Series no 9*, 366.

Jarvin, S., Derains, Y. and Arnaldez, J.-J., *Collection of ICC Arbitral Awards 1986–1990*, Vol II (ICC Publishing, Paris, 1994).

Jarvin, S. and Derains, Y., *Collection of ICC Arbitral Awards 1974–1985*, Vol I (ICC Publishing, Paris, 1990) (cited as: Jarvin/Derains).

Jarvin, S. and Dorgan, C., 'Are Foreign Parties Still Welcome in Stockholm?—The Svea Decision in Titan v. Alcatel CIT S.A. Raises Doubts' (2005) 20 *Mealey's Int'l Arb Rep* no 7, 42 (cited as: Jarvin, S. and Dorgan, C.).

Jimenez-Figueres, D., 'Amicable Means to Resolve Disputes: How the ICC ADR Rules work' (2004) 21 *J Int'l Arb* no 1, 9 (cited as: Jimenez-Figueres D., Amicable Means to Resolve Disputes.

Jimenez-Figueres, D., 'Multi-Tiered Dispute Resolution Clauses in ICC Arbitration' (2003) 4 *ICC ICArb Bull* no 1, 71.Jolivet, E.

Jimenez-Figueres, D., 'Access to information and Awards' (2006) 22 *Arb Int'l* no 2, 265.

Jimenez-Figueres, D., 'Chronique de jurisprudence arbitrale de la Chambre de commerce internationale: Arbitrage CCI et procédure ADR' in *Les Cahiers de l'Arbitrage Volume I* (Gazette du Palais, Paris, 2002), 261.

Jimenez-Figueres, D., 'Chronique de jurisprudence arbitrale de la Chambre de commerce internationale (CCI): l'incompétence de l'arbitre' (2006) Les Cahiers de l'Arbitrage 2006/1, 38.

Jimenez-Figueres, D., 'Chronique de jurisprudence arbitrale de la Chambre de commerce internationale (CCI): Quelques exemples du traitement du droit communautaire dans l'arbitrage CCI' (2003) *Cahiers de l'Arbitrage* 2e partie, 3.

Jimenez-Figueres, D., 'La jurisprudence arbitrale de la CCI et la *lex mercatoria*' (2001) *Gazette du Palais* 563.

Jolles, A., 'Consequences of Multi-tier Arbitration Clauses: Issues of Enforcement' (2006) 72 *Arbitration* no 4, 329.

Karrer, P.A., 'Freedom of an arbitral tribunal to conduct proceedings' (1999) 10 *ICC Bull* no 1, 14 (cited as: Karrer P.A., Freedom of an arbitral tribunal).

Karrer, P.A. and Desax, M., 'Security for Costs in International Arbitration; Why, When and What if...' in *Liber Amicorum Karl-Heinz Böckstiegel* (Carl Heymanns Verlag, Cologne, 2001) 339.

Kaufmann-Kohler, G., 'Discovery in International Arbitration: How Much is Too Much?' (*SchiedvsVZ* January/February 2004) 13 (cited as: Kaufmann-Kohler, G., Discovery in International Arbitration).

Kaufmann-Kohler, G., 'Identifying and Applying the Law Governing the Arbitration Procedure—The Role of the Law of the Place of Arbitration' (1999) *ICCA Congress Series no 9*, 336.

Kaufmann-Kohler, G., 'Iura Novit Arbiter - Est-ce bien raisonable? Réflexions sur le statut du droit de fond devant l'arbitre international' in Héritier Lachat, A. et Hirsch, L. (eds), *De Lege Ferenda, Réflexions sur le droit désirable, en l'honneur du Professeur Alain Hirsch* (Slatkine, Geneva, 2004) 71.

Kaufmann-Kohler, G., 'Le lieu de l'arbitrage à l'aune de la mondialisation—Réflexions à propos de deux formes récentes d'arbitrage' (1998) *Rev arb* no 3, 517.

Kaufmann-Kohler, G., 'Qui controle l'arbitrage? Autonomie des parties, pouvoirs des arbitres et principes d'efficacité' in *Liber Amicorum Claude Reymond* (Litec, Paris, 2004) 153 (cited as: Kaufmann-Kohler, G., Qui contrôle l'arbitrage ?).

Kiffer, L., '*Amiable Composition* and ICC Arbitration' (2007) 18 *ICC ICArb Bull* no 1, 51.

King, D.B. and Bosman, L., 'Rethinking Discovery in International Arbitration: Beyond the Common Law/Civil Law Divide' (2001) 12 *ICC ICArb Bull* no 1, 24 (cited as: King/Bosman).

Kojovic, T., 'Court Enforcement of Arbitral Decisions on Provisional Relief—How Final is Provisional?' (2001) 18 *J Int'l Arb*, no 5, 511.

Kreindler, R., 'Final Rulings on Costs: Loser Pays All?' in *Best Practices in International Arbitration* (2006) *ASA Special Series* no 24, 4.

Kreindler, R., 'Settlement Agreements and Arbitration in the Context of the ICC Rules' (1998) 9 *ICC ICArb Bull* no 2, 22.

Kreindler, R., 'Speedier arbitration as a response to changes in world trade: a necessary goal or a threat to the expectations of the parties?' in *Liber Amicorum Michel Gaudet* (ICC Publishing, Paris, 1999) 180.

Kurkela, M.S., Levin, R.C., Liebscher, C.L. and Sommer, P., 'Certain Procedural Issues in Arbitrating Competition Cases' (2007) 24 *J Int'l Arb* no 2, 189.

Kühn W., 'Rectification and Interpretation of Arbitral Awards' (1996) 7 *ICC ICArb Bull* no 2, 78.

Lalive P., 'Note on TGI Paris, May 21, 1997, *Société Cubic Defense v Chambre de commerce internationale*' (1997) *Rev arb* no 3, 417.

Lalive, P., Poudret, J.-F. and Reymond, C., *Le droit de l'arbitrage interne et international en Suisse* (Payot, Lausanne, 1989) 365 (cited as Lalive/Poudret/Reymond).

Lamm, C. and Hellbeck, E.R., 'Report on Publicis S.A. v. True North Communications Inc.' (2000) 3 *Int'l Arb. L. R.*

Lazareff, S., 'Aux frontières de l'arbitrage et de l'ADR: La Sentence d'Accord Parties', in *Les Cahiers de l'Arbitrage Volume I* (Gazette du Palais, Paris 2002) 8.

Lazareff, S., 'De l'amour du juge' (2005) *Les Cahiers de l'arbitrage* 2005/1, 3, and *Gazette du Palais*, Special Arbitrage, 21–22 October 2005, 3.

Lazareff, S., 'L'arbitre singe ou comment assassiner l'arbitrage', in *Liber Amicorum in honour of Robert Briner* (ICC Publishing, Paris, 2005) 477.

Lazareff, S., 'Terms of Reference' (2006) 17 *ICC ICArb Bull* no 1, 21.
Lazareff, S., 'The Language of Institutional Arbitration' (1997) 8 *ICC ICArb Bull* no 1, 18.
Lazareff, S. and Le Gall, J.-P., 'L'assujetissement des arbitres à la TVA sous l'empire de l'article 259 du code général des impôts' (2006) *Rev arb* no 2, 543.
Lazareff, S. and Schäfer, E., 'The 1992 Practical Guide on Terms of Reference Revisited' (1999) 10 *ICC ICArb Bull* no 2, 14 (cited as: Lazareff/Schäfer).
Leboulanger, Ph., 'Principe de collégialité et délibéré arbitral' in *Mélanges en l'honneur de François Knoepfler* (Helbing & Lichtenhahn, Basel, 2005) 259 (cited as: Leboulanger Ph.).
Le Gall, J.-P., 'The fiscal status of the arbitrator' (1995) *ICC ICArb Bull*, Special Supp, 100.
Lévy, L., 'Insolvency in Arbitration (Swiss Law)' (2005) *Int'l Arb L Rev* Issue no 1, 23.
Lévy, L., 'Witness Statements' in Héritier Lachat, A. and Hirsch, L. (eds), *De Lege Ferenda—Réflexions sur le droit désirable en l'honneur du Professeur Alain Hirsch* (Slatkine, Geneva, 2004) 95.
Lew, J., 'Commentary on Interim and Conservatory Measures in ICC Arbitration Cases' (2000) 11 *ICC ICArb Bull* no 1, 23.
Liber Amicorum Dobrosav Mitrovic (Belgrade, 2007).
Liber Amicorum in honour of Robert Briner, Global Reflections on International Law, Commerce and Dispute Resolution (ICC Publishing, Paris, 2005) (cited as: Liber amicorum Robert Briner).
Liber Amicorum Claude Reymond, Autour de l'arbitrage (Litec, Paris, 2004) (cited as: Liber amicorum Claude Reymond).
Liber Amicorum Karl-Heinz Böckstiegel, Law of International Business and Dispute Settlement in the 21st Century (Carl Heymanns Verlag, Cologne, 2001).
Liber Amicorum Michel Gaudet (ICC Publishing, Paris, 1999).
Liber Amicorum Thomas Bär and Robert Karrer (Helbing & Lichtenhahn, Basel, 1997).
Lionnet, K., 'Once Again: Is Discovery of Documents Appropriate in International Arbitration?' in *Liber Amicorum in honour of Robert Briner* (ICC Publishing, Paris, 2005), 491 (cited as: Lionnet, K.).
Lloyd, H., Darmon, M., Ancel, J.-P., Lord Dervaird, Liebscher, Ch. and Verbiest, H., 'Drafting Awards in ICC Arbitration' (2005) 16 *ICC ICArb Bull* no 2, 19.
Loquin, E., 'Les obligations de confidentialité dans l'arbitrage' (2006) *Rev arb* no 2, 324.
Lowenfeld, A.F., 'The Party appointed Arbitrator' in L.W. Newman and R.D. Hill (eds), *The Leading Arbitrators' Guide to International Arbitration* (Juris Publishing/Staempfli Publishers, 2004) 41.
Mackie, K., 'The Future of ADR Clauses after *Cable & Wireless v IBM*' (2003) 19 *Arb Int'l* no 3, 345.
Madsen, F. and Eriksson, P., 'Deliberations of the Arbitral Tribunal–Analysis of Reasoned Awards from a Swedish Perspective' (2006) *SIAR* 2006: 2, 1 (cited as: Madsen/Eriksson).
Malinvaud, C., 'Modification de la loi modèle CNUDCI sur les mesures intérimaires: un texte de compromis sur les mesures ex parte' (2007) *Les Cahiers de l'Arbitrage* no 1, 12.
Mantilla-Serrano, F., 'International Arbitration and Insolvency Proceedings' (1995) 11 *Arb Int'l* no 1, 51.
Mélanges en l'honneur de François Knoepfler (Helbing & Lichtenhahn, Basel, 2005).
Ming, W., 'The Strange Case of Wang Shengchang' (2007) 24 *J Int'l Arb* no 1, 63.
Mourre, A. and Radicati di Brozolo, L., 'Towards Finality of Arbitral Awards: Two Steps Forward and One Step Back' (2006) 23 *J Int'l Arb* no, 2, 171.
Müller, Ch., *International Arbitration, A Guide to the Complete Swiss Case Law (Unreported and Reported)* (Thomson/Schulthess, London/Zurich, 2004).
Müller, Ch., 'La confidentialité en arbitrage commercial international: un trompe-l'oeil? On est souvent satisfait d'être trompé par soi-même' (2005) *ASA Bull* no 2, 216.
Newmark, C. and Hill, R., 'Can a Mediated Settlement Become an Enforceable Arbitration Award?' (2000) 16 *Arb Int'l* no 1, 81.

Newmark, C. and Hill, R., The Leading Arbitrators' Guide to International Arbitration (Juris Publishing/Staempfli Publishers, 2004).

Oetiker, C., 'Witnesses before the International Arbitral Tribunal' (2007) *ASA Bull* vol 25, 253.

Paillusseau, J., 'L'arbitre responsable du délai d'arbitrage' (2006) *JCP* I 129, 666.

Patocchi, P.M., 'Deciding on the costs of the arbitration - Selected Topics' (2007) *ASA Special Series* no 29, 49.

Patocchi, P.M. and Frey-Brentano, H., 'The Provisional Timetable in International Arbitration' in *Liber Amicorum in honour of Robert Briner* (ICC Publishing, Paris, 2005) 575.

Paulsson, J., 'Arbitration-Friendliness: Promises of Principles and Realities of Practice' (2007) 23 *Arb Int'l* no 3, 477.

Paulsson, J., 'The Timely Arbitrator: Reflections on the Böckstiegel Method' (2006) 22 *Arb Int'l* no 1, 19.

Peter W., 'Witness "Conferencing"' (2002) 18 *Arb Int'l* no 1, 47.

Philipp, M., 'Difficultés procédurales causées par les clauses compromissoires paritaires et les tribunaux arbitraux tronqués' (2005) *Gazette du Palais* 21.

Philipp, M., 'NetCase: A New ICC Arbitration Facility' (2004) *ICC ICArb Bull*, Special Supp 53.

Philipp, M., 'New IT facility for ICC arbitration users' (2005) 16 *ICC ICArb Bull* no 2, 5.

Pietrowski R., 'Evidence in International Arbitration' (2006) 22 *Arb Int'l* no 3, 373.

Poudret, J.-F., 'Les mesures provisionnelles et l'arbitrage. Aperçu comparatif des pouvoirs respectifs de l'arbitre et du juge' in *Mélanges en l'honneur de François Knoepfler* (Helbing & Lichtenhahn, Basel, 2005) 235.

Poudret, J.-F. and Besso, S., *Comparative Law of International Arbitration* (Thompson/Sweet & Maxwell, London, 2007).

Pryles, M., ' Interlocutory Orders and Convention Awards: The Case of Resort Condominiums v. Bolwell' (1994) 10 *Arb Int'l* no 4, 385.

Racine, J.-B., 'Réflexions sur l'autonomie de l'arbitrage commercial international (II.—L'arbitrage, Deuxième Séance)' (2005) *Rev arb* no 2, 305.

Radicati di Brozolo, L.G., 'L'illicéité qui crève les yeux: critère de contrôle des sentences au regard de l'ordre public international (à propos de l'arrêt Thalès de la Cour d'appel de Paris)' (2005) *Rev arb* no 3, 529.

Redfern, A. and Hunter, M. with Blackaby, N. and Partasides, C., *Law and Practice of International Commercial Arbitration* (4th edn, Thomson/Sweet & Maxwell, London, 2004) (cited as: Redfern/Hunter).

Reed, L. and Sutcliffe, J., 'The "Americanisation" of International Arbitration' (2001) 16 *Int'l Arb Rep* 37.

Reiner, A., 'Le Règlement d'Arbitrage de la CCI, Version 1998' (1998) *Rev arb* no 3, 47 (cited as: Reiner, A.).

Reiner, A., *The New Austrian Arbitration Law: Arbitration Act 2006* (LexisNexis, ADR ORAC, 2006).

Reymond, C., 'Le Président du Tribunal Arbitral' in *Etudes offertes à Pierre Bellet* (Litec, Paris, 1991) 467.

Reymond, C., 'Note sur l'avance des frais de l'arbitrage et sa répartition' in *Etudes de procédure et d'arbitrage en l'honneur de Jean-François Poudret* (Lausanne, 1999) 495.

Rosell, J. and Prager, H., 'International Arbitration and Bankruptcy: United States, France and the ICC' (2001) 18 *J Int'l Arb* no 4, 417.

Rosher, P., 'Legal privilege et confidentialité des communications avocat-client en matière d'arbitrage international—Vers une possible harmonisation ?' (2007) *Les Cahiers de l'Arbitrage* no 3, 21 (cited as Rosher, Legal privilege).

Rosher, P., 'The Application and Scope of Attorney-Client Privilege in International Arbitration' (2007) *SIAR* 2007: 2, 1.

Rouche, J., 'Le paiement par le défendeur de sa part de provision sur les frais d'arbitrage: simple faculté ou obligation contractuelle?' (2002) *Rev arb* no 4, 841.

Sanders, P., 'The Terms of Reference in ICC Arbitration' in *Liber Amicorum in honour of Robert Briner* (ICC Publishing, Paris, 2005) 693.

Sandrock, O., 'The Cautio Judicatum Solvi in Arbitration Proceedings or The Duty of an Alien Claimant to Provide Security for the Costs of the Defendant' (1997) 4 *J Int'l Arb* no 2, 17.

Schäfer, E., 'Videoconferencing in Arbitration' (2003) 14 *ICC ICArb Bull* no 1, 35.

Schäfer, E., Verbist H. and Míos C., *ICC Arbitration In Practice* (Kluwer Law International, 2004).

Schlosser, P., 'Generalizable Approaches to Agreements with Experts and Witness Acting in Arbitration and International Litigation' in *Liber Amicorum in honour of Robert Briner* (ICC Publishing, Paris, 2005) 775 (cited as: Schlosser, P.).

Schneider, M. E., 'Combining Arbitration with Conciliation' (1996) *ICCA Congress Series no 8*, 57.

Scherer, M., 'Jurisprudence–Introduction to Case Law Section–Advance on the costs of the arbitration' (2003) 21 *ASA Bull* no 4, 749.

Schwartz, E.A., '"New Claims" in ICC Arbitration: Navigating Article 19 of the ICC Rules' (2006) 17 *ICC ICArb Bull* no 2, 55.

Schwartz, E.A., 'The ICC Arbitral Process, Part IV: The Costs of ICC Arbitration (1993) 4 *ICC ICArb Bull* no 1, 8 (cited as: Schwartz).

Schwebel, S.M., 'The validity of an arbitral award rendered by a truncated tribunal' (1995) 6 *ICC Bull* no 2, 19.

Secomb, M., 'Awards and Orders Dealing with the Advance on Costs in ICC Arbitration: Theoretical Questions and Practical Problems' (2003) 14 *ICC ICArb Bull* no 1, 59 (cited as: Secomb, M.).

Senkovic, P. and Lastenouse, P., 'International Arbitration And Antitrust Law: Eco Swiss Judgment Revisited By the Paris Court of Appeal' (2005) 20 *Mealey's Int'l Arb Rep* no 2, 1.

Seppälä, C., 'Obtaining The Right International Arbitral Tribunal: A Practitioner's View' (2007) 22 *Mealey's Int'l Arb Rep* no 10, 36.

Smit, R.H., 'Dissenting Opinions in Arbitration' (2004) 15 *ICC ICArb Bull* no 1, 37.

Smit, R.H., 'Mandatory ICC Arbitration Rules', in *Liber Amicorum Robert Briner* (ICC Publishing, Paris, 2005) 845 (cited as: Smit, R.H., Mandatory ICC Arbitration Rules).

Smit, R.H. and Turner, A., 'Enforcement by US Court of International Arbitration Interim Orders and Awards under the New York Convention, *Publicis Communication v True North Communications Inc*' (2001) *SAR* 2001:1, 47 (cited as: Smit/Turner).

Sutton, D., Gill, J. and Gearing, M., *Russell on Arbitration* (23rd edn, Thomson/Sweet & Maxwell, London, 2007) (cited as: Russell on Arbitration).

Tattevin, G., 'NIOC v. Israel: "The End" . . . Or Is It?' (2005) *SIAR* 2005:2, 221.

Taylor, T. and Baruti, R., 'Reopening The Case After The Hearing—To What Extent And Under What Circumstances Should It Be Allowed?' *ASA Special Series no* 29, September 2007, 8.

Tchakoua J.-M., 'The Status of the Arbitral Award by Consent: The limits of the Useful' (2002) *RDAI/IBLJ* no 7, 775.

Tercier, P., 'Dissenting Opinions and Majority Decision', in *ASA Special Series no 29*, September 2007.

Train, F.-X., 'Denial of Justice in International Arbitration: How the French "Juge d'appui" Extends Its Jurisdiction' (2005) *SIAR* 2005: 2, 230.

Tschanz, P.-Y., 'The Award—How To Structure it, How Detailed? Orders And Reasons, Adding Insult To Injury' (Sept. 2007) *ASA Special Series* no 29, 25.

Tschanz, P.-Y., 'Uncooperative Arbitrators Need Not Delay Award' (2002) <http://www.internationallawoffice.com/newsletters/detail.aspx?g=5530550a-086c-4d12-b3c9-838386f5c59c > (accessed 25 May 2009).

van Houtte, H., 'The delivery of Awards to the Parties' (2005) 21 *Arb Int'l* no 2, 177.

van Houtte, H., 'The delivery of the Award, Ten Pitfalls' in ASA Special Series no 29 (September 2007) 76.

van Houtte, H., 'The Vienna Sales Convention in ICC Arbitral Practice' (2000) 11 *ICC Bull* no 2, 22.

Verbist, H., 'The Practice of the ICC International Court of Arbitration with Regard to Fixing of the Place of Arbitration' (1996) 12 *Arb Int'l* no 3, 347.

Veit, M.D., 'Note–Procedural Order No.14 of 27 November 2002–Security for Costs in International Arbitration–Some Comments to Procedural Order No 14 of 27 November 2002' (2005) 23 *ASA Bull* no 1, 116.

Vicuña O., 'The binding nature of procedural orders in international arbitration' (1999) 10 *ICC ICArb Bull* no 1, 38.

Vogt, N.P., 'Article 181' in S. Berti, H. Honsell, N.P. Vogt and A.K. Schnyder (eds), *International Arbitration in Switzerland—An Introduction to and a Commentary on Articles 176–194 of the Swiss Private International Law Statute* (Helbing & Lichtenhahn/Kluwer, Basel, 2000).

von Mehren, A.T., 'The Eco Swiss and International Arbitration' (2003) 19 *Arb Int'l* no 4, 465.

von Segesser, G., 'Note on Swiss Supreme Court, June 6, 2007, *X. Ltd v Y*, 4A_18/2007' (September 2007) *ITA Monthly Report*, vol V Iss 9.

Voser N., 'Interim Relief in International Arbitration: The Tendency Towards More Business-Oriented Approach' (2007) 1 *Disp Res Int'l* no 2, 171.

Voser, N. and Mueller, A., 'Appointment of Experts by the Arbitral Tribunal: the Civil Law Perspective' (2006) 7 *Business L Int'l* no 1, 73.

Webster, Th., 'Party Control in International Arbitration' (2003) 19 *J Int'l Arb* no 2, 119 (cited as: Webster, Party Control in International Arbitration).

Webster, Th., 'Review of Substantive Reasoning of International Arbitral Awards by National Courts: Ensuring One-Step Adjudication' (2006) 22 *Arb Int'l* no 3, 431 (cited as: Webster, Review of Substantive Reasoning).

Webster, Th., 'Selection of Arbitrators in a Nutshell' (2002) 19 *J Int'l Arb* no 3, 261.

Webster, Th., 'Terms of Reference and French Annulment Proceedings' (2003) 20 *J Int'l Arb* no 6, 561 (cited as: Webster, Terms of Reference).

Wetter G. and Priem C., 'Costs and their Allocation in International Commercial Arbitration' (1991) *Am Rev Int'l Arb* vol 2, 249 (cited as: Wetter/Priem).

Whitesell, A.-M. and Silva-Romero, E., 'Multiparty and Multicontract Arbitration: Recent ICC Experience' (2003) *ICC ICArb Bull*, Special Supp, Complex Arbitration, 7 (cited as: Whitesell/Silva-Romero).

Whitesell, A.-M., 'Independence in ICC Arbitration: ICC Court Practice concerning the Appointment, Confirmation Challenge and Replacement of Arbitrators' (2007) *ICC ICArb Bull*, Special Supp on Independence of Arbitrators, 7.

Wirth, M., 'Interim or Preventive Measures in Support of International Arbitration in Switzerland' (2000) 18 *ASA Bull* no 1, 31.

Wolrich, P.M., 'ICC Expertise–The New, Revised ICC Rules for Expertise: A Presentation and Commentary' (2002) 13 *ICC ICArb Bull* no 2, 11.

Wolrich, P.M., 'Techniques for Controlling Time and Costs in Arbitration' (2007) 18 *ICC ICArb Bull* no 1, 23.

16

UNCITRAL RULES

*James Castello**

I. Introduction

The United Nations Commission on International Trade Law (UNCITRAL or 'the Commission') differs from nearly every other institution in the world that promulgates rules to govern arbitration proceedings in that it plays no role in the proceedings themselves. It never administers arbitrations, nor does it even appoint arbitrators. Rather, the UNCITRAL Secretariat, based in Vienna, Austria, and comprising a small professional staff of lawyers who possess expertise in aspects of commercial law, serves only to support the work of the Commission. And the Commission's work has nothing to do with individual arbitrations; rather, its objective is to harmonize national laws and international commercial legal practices on a wide range of trade-related issues. Those issues include 'dispute resolution, international contract practices, transport, insolvency, electronic commerce, international payments, secured transactions, procurement and sale of goods.'[1] The Commission's formation came about more than 40 years ago in the following circumstances. **16.01**

A. The origins of UNCITRAL

In 1965, a report prepared for the Sixth (ie Legal) Committee of the United Nations General Assembly highlighted 'the difficulties faced by parties engaging in international **16.02**

* This chapter is dedicated to Judge Howard Holtzmann, whose belief in UNCITRAL's importance and whose unflagging commitment to ensuring the excellence of UNCITRAL's work in the field of arbitration over the past 35 years have inspired many. I wish to thank Jernej Sekolec, former Secretary of UNCITRAL, for his very helpful comments and corrections on the 'Introduction' to this chapter; all remaining faults are of course my own. I also express my gratitude to Lorraine de Germiny, an associate in the Paris office of King & Spalding, for her excellent research assistance as well as to Patricia Rosario, a former *stagiaire* at Dewey & LeBoeuf, for her additional research.

[1] See UNCITRAL, 'The UNCITRAL Guide: Basic facts about the United Nations Commission on International Trade Law' ('The UNCITRAL Guide') 1 (United Nations, Vienna, 2007).

commercial transactions as a result of the multiplicity of and divergencies in national laws'.[2] This led the General Assembly to seek a 'comprehensive report' from the UN Secretariat, examining, *inter alia,* 'the United Nations organs and other agencies which might be given responsibilities with a view to furthering cooperation in the development of the law of international trade and to promoting its progressive unification and harmonization'.[3] The Secretariat's subsequent report found, *inter alia,* that the 'progress made in the unification and harmonization of international trade law has been rather slow,' in part because 'none of the formulating agencies commands world-wide acceptance'.[4] Rather,

> In some cases, those agencies have a membership confined either to countries of centrally planned econom[ies] (e.g. CMEA) or to countries of free enterprise economies (e.g. the ICC); in other instances, members must belong to a specific region (e.g. the ECE). In the case of UNIDROIT, although there is no geographical limitation on membership, the present membership is predominantly European.[5]

16.03 The report concluded that the United Nations had an advantage in promoting unification and harmonization because it 'comprises practically all the countries of the world, representing the various legal, economic and social systems as well as all stages of economic development.'[6] It therefore recommended formation of a UN Commission on this subject which, in view of its technical nature, should have a rotating membership of a limited number of member states, whose representatives to the Commission 'should be persons of eminence in the field'.[7] It was further suggested that the Secretariat for this new Commission be located within the UN's Office of Legal Affairs.[8]

16.04 The proposed Commission's goals included, 'Preparing, and promoting the adoption of, new international conventions, model laws and uniform laws, and the codification and wider acceptance of international trade terms, provisions, customs and practices'.[9] Once formed, the Commission ultimately found that some of these legal instruments were better suited than others for harmonizing particular areas of commercial law. For example, as UNCITRAL has since noted, 'conventions afford little flexibility to adopting States,' and therefore, '[i]f a high degree of harmonization cannot be achieved or a greater degree of flexibility is desired and is appropriate to the subject matter under consideration, a different technique of harmonization, such as a model law or legislative guide, might be used'.[10]

---

[2] UNCITRAL, 'The United Nations Commission on International Trade Law' 3 (United Nations, New York, 1986).

[3] GA Res 2102 (XX) (20 December 1965).

[4] Report of the Secretary-General (23 September 1966), paras 210(a) and (c), UN Doc A/6396.

[5] *ibid,* para 210(c).

[6] *ibid,* para 220.

[7] *ibid,* para 226.

[8] *ibid,* para 232.

[9] *ibid,* para 227(c).

[10] The UNCITRAL Guide (n 1) paras 32, 31. The law of procedure is one such field in which strict harmonization is difficult to achieve because countries are often reluctant to depart from their traditional national solutions. Thus, it is not surprising that in the field of dispute resolution, the Commission has promulgated more flexible instruments such as the Model Law of International Commercial Arbitration and the Model Law of International Commercial Conciliation, which can be adopted by national legislatures that generally wish to follow modern, international practice but that may need to make certain adaptations in

At its session in late 1966, the General Assembly adopted a resolution establishing UNCITRAL[11] with a membership of 29 states serving terms of six years and a required distribution of members among the world's geographic regions.[12] In 1973, the General Assembly increased UNCITRAL's membership to 36 and, in 2002, to 60 states.[13] **16.05**

B. Adoption of the UNCITRAL Arbitration Rules

At its second session, the Commission directed a Special Rapporteur to report on problems in the application and interpretation of existing conventions on international commercial arbitration.[14] That report, ultimately presented at UNCITRAL's fifth session, recommended *inter alia* that the Commission consider the desirability of drafting a model set of arbitration rules to unify and simplify national rules on arbitration.[15] At its sixth session in 1973, the Commission considered states' comments on that proposal. Some expressed apprehension as to the difficulty of the task, particularly insofar as 'the procedure in the common law countries was totally different from that in force in the civil law countries'.[16] But a majority believed that development of model arbitration rules particularly for *ad hoc* arbitration would be useful and directed the Secretariat to draw up an initial draft.[17] The Secretariat did so, after seeking the advice and drafting assistance of Professor Pieter Sanders of the Netherlands. The draft presented for the Commission's consideration, which was published in November 1974,[18] benefited from other input as well. As the then Secretary of UNCITRAL later explained, **16.06**

> promptly upon the Commission's decision [requesting preparation of draft arbitration rules], . . . I wrote to every member of [the] International Council for Commercial Arbitration, suggesting concrete programmes for collaboration and more specifically for their designation of a representative consultative group . . . which has worked long and hard with the Secretariat and with our special expert consultant, Dr. Sanders, in the evolution of the draft rules . . . . This consultative group, for instance, commented on two earlier drafts . . . including one session in London at which the second draft was subjected to exhaustive analysis. Comments after that meeting on the second draft led to the third draft in the U.N document of November 1974. . . . [This] draft set of rules . . . will be submitted to the Commission at its forthcoming annual session in April 1975.[19]

---

these instruments. The UNCITRAL Arbitration Rules similarly permit parties to make changes in particular provisions without compromising the basic tenets of a universally negotiated text.

[11] G A Res 2205 (XXI) (17 December 1966).

[12] *ibid*, para 1. Half of the initial members served for only three years in order to facilitate staggered terms.

[13] See G A Res 3108 (XXVIII), para 8 and G A Res 57/20, para 2, respectively. The latter expansion did not take effect until 2004.

[14] *Report of UNCITRAL on the work of its 2nd session* (3–31 March 1969) para 112, UN Doc A/7618.

[15] See Report by Ian Nestor (Romania), Special Rapporteur, 'Problems concerning the application and interpretation of existing multilateral conventions on international commercial arbitration and related matters' (1 March 1972) para 180, UN Doc A/CN.9/64; see also *Report of UNCITRAL on the work of its 6th session* (2–13 April 1973) para 66, UN Doc A/9017.

[16] *ibid*, para 71.

[17] *ibid*, paras 77–8.

[18] 'Report of the Secretary General: preliminary draft set of arbitration rules for optional use in *ad hoc* arbitration relating to international trade' (4 November 1974) fns 2 and 3, UN Doc A/CN.9/97 (hereafter 'Preliminary draft Rules'), *reprinted in* (1975) VI UNCITRAL Ybk 163.

[19] International Council for Commercial Arbitration, 'Proceedings of the Vth International Arbitration Congress, 7–10 January 1975' (Indian Council of Commercial Arbitration, New Delhi, 1975) D-7 (remarks of John Honnold, former UNCITRAL Secretary).

This account confirms the special role in the development of the Rules played by the International Council for Commercial Arbitration ('ICCA'), a non-governmental, international membership organization dedicated to promoting the use and improving the processes of arbitration.

16.07 ICCA's influential role continued after publication of the November 1974 draft of the Rules, when ICCA devoted part of its next Congress, held in January 1975 in New Delhi, to a detailed consideration of the draft. One of the four 'working parties' at the ICCA Congress discussed the draft for several hours during the Congress and reported its findings to the closing plenary session. Professor Sanders served as rapporteur for that working party, and the published proceedings included both a lengthy summary of its discussion as well as the text of its report to the plenary session.[20] It is sometimes said that, because of the prominence of the arbitration practitioners who attended the ICCA conference, the range of their nationalities, and their generally favourable conclusions concerning the draft Rules, state members of UNCITRAL acquired added confidence in the proposed Rules, which contributed to the Commission's willingness thereafter to adopt them within two years.

16.08 By the time the Commission took up the draft Rules in April 1975, it had grown to 36 member states, and its annual session was attended as well by representatives of certain intergovernmental and non-governmental 'observer' organizations. However, almost none of these were primarily concerned with international arbitration.[21]

16.09 The *travaux préparatoires* reflecting the Commission's two years of discussion and revision of the draft arbitration rules are substantial and useful. The UN Secretariat prepared its customary summary of the Commission's proceedings, which describe individual delegates' interventions as well as the determinations reached regarding each provision.[22] These summary records, as well as reports of the session and other working materials, have all been made accessible through a single page of UNCITRAL's website.[23]

16.10 In their 1975 session, the delegations 'concentrated on the basic concepts underlying the draft and on the major issues dealt with in the individual articles thereof'.[24] Based on these comments and discussions, the UNCITRAL Secretariat—again, with the assistance of

---

[20] *ibid*, D1-112 and E 33-49. It was recognized by UNCITRAL that 'the discussions at the [ICCA] Congress . . . [gave] general approval to the preliminary draft' while 'also provid[ing] valuable suggestions as to points in regard to which the draft should be modified or clarified in the light of experience and practice with international commercial arbitration.' See 'Report of the Secretary General suggested modification to the preliminary draft set of arbitration rules for optional use in *ad hoc* arbitration relating to international trade' para 4 (hereafter 'Preliminary draft Rules (Addendum)', UN Doc A/CN.9/97/Add.2, *reprinted in* (1975) VI *UNCITRAL Ybk* 182.

[21] *Report of UNCITRAL on the work of its 8th session* (1–17 April 1975) para 6, UN Doc A/10017, *reprinted in* (1975) VI *UNCITRAL Ybk* 9,10.

[22] In evaluating the significance of these *travaux préparatoires*, it is useful to know that they were prepared by editors within the UN Secretariat who are usually not lawyers but who take notes during the debates and consult audio recordings of proceedings. However, these summaries are not reviewed or approved by the Commission and typically also not by the delegates whose interventions are summarized.

[23] See <http://www.uncitral.org/uncitral/en/uncitral_texts/arbitration/1976Arbitration_rules_travaux.html> (last accessed 3 October 2009).

[24] *Report of UNCITRAL on the work of its 9th session* (12 April–7 May 1976) para 48, UN Doc A/31/17, *reprinted in* (1976) VII *UNCITRAL Ybk* 9, 21.

Professor Sanders—prepared a revised draft for discussion at the following year's meeting, including a commentary on the new proposed text.

At its ninth annual session in 1976, the Commission formed a 'Committee of the Whole II' to review and further revise the draft Rules in detail[25] during 19 half-day meetings.[26] Once again, the UN Secretariat provided a summary of the Committee's proceedings, describing the determinations reached regarding each Article as well as individual delegates' comments. The Committee ultimately reported its proposed revised draft to the Commission, with an accompanying commentary, and after some further debate and modifications, the Commission adopted the Arbitration Rules on 28 April 1976.[27] The *travaux préparatoires* just outlined are helpful in discerning the drafters' intent in certain Articles of the Arbitration Rules, and they are thus referred to repeatedly in the Commentary on the Rules in section II of this chapter. That section examines the meaning and principal applications of each Article. Given the special role that Professor Sanders played as consultant to the Secretariat during this process, his Commentary on the Arbitration Rules (published after UNCITRAL's adoption of them)[28] also carries special weight and is cited in the section II Commentary. **16.11**

C. The jurisprudence of the Iran-United States Claims Tribunal

Another resource concerning the Rules' meaning or scope is the record of how arbitral tribunals have applied them. However, although the UNCITRAL Rules have by now been used in a very large number of arbitrations, little is known about most tribunals' application of the Rules, since UNCITRAL arbitrations are typically protected by confidentiality imposed by the parties and supported by the Rules themselves. Art 32(5), for example, provides that an award may only be made public 'with the consent of both parties,' which is not often given. Although some arbitrators' application of the Rules have become public, particularly in certain investor-state arbitrations whose records tend to find their way into the public domain, the number of tribunal rulings applying the UNCITRAL Arbitration Rules that have become public remains quite limited, with one very substantial exception. **16.12**

In 1981, the governments of the United States and of the Islamic Republic of Iran agreed to the terms of what became known as the Algiers Accords, which established an international arbitral tribunal, seated at The Hague, to resolve certain claims between citizens of either country and the government of the other, as well as certain claims between the two governments. The claims to be adjudicated by this Iran-US Claims Tribunal grew out of the overthrow of the Shah of Iran's government and the upheaval accompanying the seizure of American hostages in Tehran in 1979.[29] In part of the Algiers Accords known as the **16.13**

[25] See *ibid*, para 9; simultaneously, a Committee of the Whole I met to consider a draft of the Convention on the Carriage of Goods by Sea.

[26] *ibid*, para 50.

[27] *ibid*, para 56.

[28] Sanders, P., 'Commentary on UNCITRAL Arbitration Rules' in (1977) II *Ybk Comm Arb* 172.

[29] See Art II of the Declaration of the Government of the Democratic and Popular Republic of Algeria concerning the Settlement of Claims by the Government of the United States of America and the Government of the Islamic Republic of Iran (hereafter, 'The Claims Settlement Declaration'), dated 19 January 1981; *reprinted in* Aldrich, G., *The Jurisprudence of the Iran-United States Claims Tribunal* (Clarendon Press, Oxford,

Claims Settlement Declaration, the two governments agreed that the newly established Tribunal 'shall conduct its business in accordance with the arbitration rules of the United Nations Commission on International Trade Law (UNCITRAL) except to the extent modified by the Parties or by the Tribunal to ensure that this Agreement can be carried out'.[30]

16.14 One of the most important modifications to those Rules that the Tribunal adopted replaced Art 32(5) with new language providing that, 'All awards and other decisions shall be made available to the public', with certain exceptions (to be applied upon party request) permitting deletion of the identity of the parties and 'other identifying facts and trade or military secrets'. One of the original members of the Iran-US Claims Tribunal has explained why—faced with the task of adjudicating hundreds of claims in three different chambers of the Tribunal—the Tribunal decided to revise the Rules in this important way:

> [W]ithout publication[,] parties and the arbitrators themselves would have to keep re-inventing the wheel, whereas the availability of published awards would provide information on Tribunal practice that would greatly assist in the effective presentation and decision of cases. Moreover, publication was needed to assure equality of treatment of parties before the Tribunal because Iranian parties, all of whose cases were handled by a governmental law office, would have access to all awards while U.S. nationals were represented by a variety of different law firms and would not have a similar source of information. Also, transparency was appropriate because awards could affect national interest and result in payment from public funds in the Security Account.[31]

16.15 Quite apart from the benefits that Judge Holtzmann describes for the parties and arbitrators involved in the Tribunal's work, the decision to make 'all . . . decisions' by that Tribunal public has paid rich benefits to parties and arbitrators in other UNCITRAL arbitrations around the globe by providing a sustained record of how the Rules are interpreted and used in practice. All of the awards and many of the orders issued by the Iran-US Claims Tribunal have been published, *inter alia*, in what are thus far 37 volumes of the 'Iran-United States Claims Tribunal Reports,'[32] and these are cited extensively in the Commentary on the Rules in section II of this chapter.

D. UNCITRAL embarks on a revision of its Arbitration Rules

16.16 In 1998, UNCITRAL commemorated the 40th anniversary of the Convention on the Recognition and Enforcement of Foreign Arbitral Awards (1958), better known as the New York Convention, with festivities held at the United Nations in New York. That program included presentations by arbitration experts who highlighted issues in this field that would benefit from further legal regulation. As an outgrowth of those presentations, the Commission requested its Secretariat to prepare a note on future work that the Commission

1996) 546. However, The United States' claims against Iran specifically arising from the seizure and detention of the hostages and related damage to the embassy were expressly excluded from this jurisdiction. *ibid.*

30 See *ibid*, Art III(2).

31 Holtzmann, H., 'Drafting the Rules of the Tribunal' in D. Caron and J. Crook (eds), *The Iran-United States Claims Tribunal and the Process of International Claims Resolution* 75, 83 (Transnational Publishers, Ardsley NY, 2000).

32 (Grotius Publications, Cambridge UK, 1981–).

might undertake to enhance international arbitration.[33] In considering that report the following year, the Commission discussed a number of possible topics for further legal treatment, ranging from the issue of consolidation of cases before arbitral tribunals to the question of decisions by 'truncated' tribunals to the problem of liability of arbitrators.[34] The Commission determined to keep 'an open mind as to the ultimate form that [its] future work . . . might take' on such issues, but the possibility of addressing them in existing texts was implicit in the Commission's further observation that 'the time had arrived to assess the extensive and favourable experience with national enactments of the UNCITRAL Model Law on International Commercial Arbitration (1985) as well as the use of the UNCITRAL Arbitration Rules and the UNCITRAL Conciliation Rules. . .'.[35]

The Commission ultimately assigned the task of developing possible legal texts on these issues to an inter-governmental Working Group on arbitration and conciliation, known as 'Working Group II' ('WGII'), which since 2000 has convened twice each year. Pursuant to the Commission's determination as to priorities, Working Group II turned its attention first to conciliation (drafting a new Model Law on International Commercial Conciliation) and then to drafting revisions in the Model Law on International Commercial Arbitration, before taking up possible modifications in the Arbitration Rules, in the autumn of 2006. **16.17**

The Working Group comprises delegations from each of the states that are members of the Commission. By the time the Working Group turned to the Arbitration Rules, the Commission's (and hence the Working Group's) membership stood at 60 states, but its sessions are typically attended as well by 15 or more delegations from 'observer' states, ie other states that are members of the United Nations and that wish to participate. Moreover, the sessions are also attended by a growing number of representatives of a variety of organizations that have been accorded 'observer' status—ie organizations whose work relates to, or is implicated by, international arbitration. These organizations are both intergovernmental[36] and non-governmental, ranging from arbitral institutions[37] to organizations whose members include arbitration practitioners.[38] Although, in some UN bodies, observers may have no or a limited role in deliberations, it is characteristic of UNCITRAL's Working Groups that observers are allowed to participate actively in the debates and thus influence their outcome. **16.18**

E. The revision work method

The starting point for Working Group II's reconsideration of the Arbitration Rules was a paper prepared by the Secretariat identifying possible areas for revision, based in part on an **16.19**

[33] See *Report of UNCITRAL on the work of its 32nd Session* (17 May–4 June 1999) para 335, UN Doc A/54/17.

[34] *ibid*, paras 340–79.

[35] *ibid*, paras 338, 337.

[36] eg the Permanent Court of Arbitration in The Hague.

[37] eg the American Arbitration Association, International Chamber of Commerce International Court of Arbitration, London Court of International Arbitration, Vienna International Arbitral Centre, and Cairo Regional Centre for International Commercial Arbitration.

[38] eg the International Bar Association, Swiss Arbitration Association, Bar Association of the City of New York, International Council for Commercial Arbitration, Chartered Institute of Arbitrators, Milan Club of Arbitrators and International Arbitration Institute.

'informal and unpublished report' that the Secretariat commissioned from two private arbitration practitioners.[39] That report considered a wide array of potential changes in the Rules but distinguished those that might simply be desirable from those the authors believed to be essential.

16.20 As the Working Group picked its way through these options, it repeatedly adverted to crucial guidance laid down by the Commission at the outset of the revision project:

> any revision of the UNCITRAL Arbitration Rules should not alter the structure of the text, its spirit, its drafting style, and should respect the flexibility of the text rather than make it more complex. It was suggested that the Working Group should undertake to carefully define the list of topics which might need to be addressed in a revised version of the UNCITRAL Arbitration Rules.[40]

Thus, the primary aim of the revision has been to modernize the Rules where this seemed advisable (in light of changes since 1976 in the nature of arbitration or in practitioners' understanding of its requirements). But the Working Group otherwise has sought to avoid changing provisions in these Rules that are widely accepted as successful and effective. Accordingly, the Working Group has decided that a number of provisions (including many in which changes had been proposed by the initial report commissioned by the Secretariat) needed either no revision or only minor wording changes.

16.21 After determining which revisions to consider, the delegations embarked on two full readings through the 41 Articles of the Rules, working out the precise text of any revisions as they progressed. Revisions made in the first reading could if necessary be modified in the second, and some revisions required two discussions before yielding any agreement on a revised text. This process has taken up several working sessions thus far and has again generated significant *travaux préparatoires* that are accessible on a single page of the UNCITRAL website.[41] Because this revision work has been conducted in a Working Group, there are no records summarizing individual delegates' remarks, such as are prepared by the UN Secretariat following the Commission's sessions and which provide a particularly detailed record of the drafting of the 1976 Rules. However, the UNCITRAL Secretariat has prepared reports on each working session that carefully summarize the discussions and set forth the Working Group's decisions regarding the wording of each Article. The Commentary on possible revisions to the Rules in section II of this chapter cites these *travaux préparatoires* extensively.[42]

---

[39] See *Note by the Secretariat, Settlement of commercial disputes: Revisions of the UNCITRAL Arbitration Rules* (20 July 2006) para 3 and fn 4, UN Doc A/CN.9/WG.II/WP.143 (citing its commissioned report: Paulsson, J. and Petrochilos, G., *Revision of the UNCITRAL Arbitration Rules* (2006), available at <http://www.uncitral.org/pdf/english/news/arbrules_report.pdf> (last accessed 4 September 2009)).

[40] *Report of UNCITRAL on the work of its 39th session* (19 June–7 July 2006), para 184, UN Doc A/61/17. See also, eg *Report of WGII on the work of its 45th session* (11–15 September 2006) para 3, UN Doc A/CN.9/614.

[41] See <http://www.uncitral.org/uncitral/en/commission/working_groups/2Arbitration.html> (last accessed 4 October 2009).

[42] In evaluating the significance of the working session Reports as *travaux préparatoires,* it is useful to know that the Secretariat staff preparing these reports are lawyers who have participated in the working sessions and that the Reports themselves are carefully reviewed, corrected and then adopted by the Working Group before the close of each session.

16.22 The Working Group has proceeded by what is essentially a process of consensus, and thus votes are never taken on particular proposals. This approach means that, in revising the Arbitration Rules, the Working Group typically will not recommend a change unless a broadly prevailing view among member delegations supports the change, such that it is believed (including, usually, by any delegation(s) that may not favour the change) that the revision should be recommended. Once the Working Group agrees upon a revised text of for the entire Rules, it will forward this to the Commission, which will review the document and adopt it at one of its annual sessions, with or without modifications. The deliberative process at the Commission level will not necessarily duplicate what has occurred in the Working Group. One reason is that, whereas states' delegations to the Working Group sometimes consist only of private practitioners who serve as consultants to the particular government on arbitration issues, delegations to the Commission's meetings are always led by officials from each state's government. (For that reason, a Working Group may sometimes leave certain more political issues undecided so that they can be resolved at the Commission level.) It is anticipated that the Working Group will complete its work on proposed revisions in the UNCITRAL Arbitration Rules in time for the text to be forwarded to and considered for adoption by the Commission at its annual meeting in June 2010.

F. The possibility of separate rules for investor-state arbitrations

16.23 One overarching question that the Working Group has faced is whether the Arbitration Rules should be maintained in a generic version intended to apply in multiple settings. This question was framed by discussion in the first working session:

> [I]n practice, there [a]re at least four types of arbitration where the UNCITRAL Arbitration Rules [a]re used, namely; disputes between private commercial parties where no arbitral institution was involved (a type sometimes referred to as 'ad hoc'arbitration), investor-State disputes, State-to-State disputes and commercial disputes administered by arbitral institutions. The question was raised whether in revising the UNCITRAL Arbitration Rules, the Working Group should maintain that generic approach or should include provisions, possibly contained in parallel versions or annexes to the UNCITRAL Arbitration Rules, dealing specifically with the different types of arbitration or disputes to which the Rules applied.[43]

In general, the Working Group has decided against developing separate versions of, or annexes to, the Rules to adapt them for specific contexts. Delegates felt that the Rules had already proved themselves adaptable to a wide range of circumstances, that adding specialized provisions could compromise the Rules' flexibility and simplicity and thus make them less attractive, and that any provisions designed to accommodate particular types of arbitrations might more quickly become obsolete.[44]

16.24 However, the Working Group did recognize that its discussion of revisions could yield some 'useful conclusions relating to specific situations, such as investor-State disputes or institutional arbitration'.[45] That expectation was borne out with respect to at least one issue. During the first reading through the Rules, the Working Group was made aware of a

[43] *Report of WGII on the work of its 45th session* (11–15 September 2006) para 17, UN Doc A/CN.9/614.
[44] *ibid*, paras 18–19.
[45] *ibid*, para 19.

proposal to augment transparency in investor-state arbitration, including by (i) making the pleadings filed in such arbitrations public (subject to certain possibilities for redaction); (ii) expressly allowing the submission of amicus briefs from third parties (subject to control by the tribunal); (iii) allowing third parties to attend hearings in such arbitrations; and (iv) providing that all awards, orders and decisions by the tribunal be made public in such cases. This package of revisions was formulated by two of the non-governmental observers.[46] Although the Working Group did not discuss the specifics of that proposal, it did engage in an initial discussion whether the Rules should address suggestions for greater transparency in 'investor-state arbitration'.

16.25 During that debate, it was broadly recognized that there was often a justification for transparency in the arbitration of investment claims against national governments that did not apply to the arbitration of commercial disputes between private parties.[47] It was also recognized that the 1976 Rules made no provision for transparency since they were expected to apply to private commercial disputes, yet since that time the UNCITRAL Rules have become the second most frequently used in investor-state arbitrations, surpassed only by the rules of the International Center for the Settlement of Investment Disputes (ICSID).[48] On the other hand, doubts were expressed as to the wisdom of applying, via the Rules, a blanket transparency provision to all arbitrations deemed to involve 'investment,' and it was also suggested that the more appropriate approach might be to insert such requirements into the treaties under which investment claims arose.[49] Moreover, if this issue were to be addressed via the Rules, it was debated whether this should be by means of an Annex (possibly to be opted into or out of), a model clause, or perhaps guidelines.[50] Above all, there was a widespread concern that if the Working Group undertook to resolve all of these questions at that juncture, completion of the Rules revision would be considerably delayed.

16.26 Ultimately, the Working Group resolved not to risk such delay but rather to take up consideration of transparency after the Rules revision was complete, subject to any contrary directive from the Commission. In fact, the Commission at its next meeting supported this approach, affirming that 'it would not be desirable to include specific provisions on treaty-based arbitration in the UNCITRAL Arbitration Rules themselves' and agreeing that work on investor-state disputes 'should not delay the completion of the revision of the UNCITRAL Arbitration Rules in their generic form'.[51] On the other hand, the Commission 'agreed by consensus on the importance of ensuring transparency in investor-State dispute resolution' and directed that this topic 'was worthy of future consideration and should be dealt with as a matter of priority immediately after completion of the current revision of the . . . Rules'.[52] It is thus expected that the Working Group will turn to this issue in 2010.

[46] *See Report of WGII on the work of its 48th session* (4–8 February 2008)para 65 & Annex III, UN Doc A/CN.9/646.
[47] *ibid*, para 57.
[48] *ibid*, para 58.
[49] *ibid*, para 60.
[50] *ibid*, para 61.
[51] *Report of UNCITRAL on the Work of its 41st session* (16 June–3 July 2008) para 314, UN Doc A/63/17.
[52] *ibid.*

G. The structure of this chapter's Commentary on the Rules

The Commentary on the Rules in section II of this chapter is divided into 41 segments—one for each Article. In turn, each segment has two parts. Part 1 ('Commentary on current text') discusses the Article as it appears in the Rules, including (where appropriate) the record of its application by tribunals or its treatment by commentators. Part 1 usually begins with a summary paragraph enumerating each substantive provision in the Article, and the rest of Part 1 is then divided by sub-headings corresponding to these substantive provisions. In a few cases, an Article is so straightforward that no subheadings are needed. Part 2 ('Contemplated revisions') discusses changes in the Article that Working Group II is considering. For those Articles in which significant revisions are contemplated, Part 2 usually begins with a summary paragraph enumerating the different substantive revisions, and the remainder of Part 2 is again divided into corresponding sub-headings. **16.27**

The discussion of revisions in each Part 2 of the Commentary reflects the progress achieved by Working Group II as of the end of the last working session in 2009. As of that juncture, the Working Group had nearly completed its second reading of the Rules (having reached Art 40), although a few issues were identified in the second reading that will have to be revisited.[53] Where the Working Group appears to have firmly decided to recommend a revision, the text in Part 2 so indicates; where the Working Group has not yet decided whether to recommend a change or is contemplating alternative wordings for a revision, the text in Part 2 describes the inclination of the Working Group as of late 2009. The scope of the revisions contemplated will result in a revised numbering of the Articles in the next version of the Rules. However, the Commentary that follows generally ignores any relocation or renumbering of particular provisions, since final renumbering has not yet been agreed upon and speculation as to such reorganization would add unnecessary complexity. **16.28**

II. Commentary on the UNCITRAL Arbitration Rules

Section I. Introductory rules

SCOPE OF APPLICATION

Article 1

1 **Where the parties to a contract have agreed in writing* that disputes in relation to that contract shall be referred to arbitration under the UNCITRAL Arbitration Rules, then such disputes shall be settled in accordance with these Rules subject to such modification as the parties may agree in writing.**

2 **These Rules shall govern the arbitration except that where any of these Rules is in conflict with a provision of the law applicable to the arbitration from which the parties cannot derogate, that provision shall prevail.**

**MODEL ARBITRATION CLAUSE*

Any dispute, controversy or claim arising out of or relating to this contract, or the breach, termination or invalidity thereof, shall be settled by arbitration in accordance with the UNCITRAL Arbitration Rules as at present in force.

---

[53] See, *eg*, *Report of WGII on the work of its 50th session* (9–13 February 2009) *passim*, UN Doc A/CN.9/669.

Note - Parties may wish to consider adding:

(a) The appointing authority shall be . . . (name of institution or person);

(b) The number of arbitrators shall be . . . (one or three);

(c) The place of arbitration shall be . . . (town or country);

(d) The language(s) to be used in the arbitral proceedings shall be . . .

(1) Commentary on current text

16.29 Article 1 of the Rules contains four significant provisions: (i) requiring that agreements to arbitrate under the Rules be 'in writing'; (ii) identifying which disputes are arbitrable under the Rules; (iii) confirming the parties' ability to modify the Rules; and (iv) clarifying the Rules' relationship to applicable law. A footnote to Art1(1) accomplishes a further purpose: (v) setting forth a Model Arbitration Clause for parties' use. That clause identifies important aspects of an arbitration that are subject to the parties' control in their arbitration agreement and that, if not addressed by the parties, are treated substantively elsewhere in the Rules.

16.30 (1.1) **Written form of arbitration agreement** Article 1(1) requires that the parties' agreement to submit their disputes to arbitration under the Rules be 'in writing.' Since a similar requirement exists under most national laws and since Art II of the New York Convention conditions the obligation of signatory states to enforce a foreign arbitration agreement upon its being 'in writing',[54] the inclusion of this requirement in Art 1 was viewed as enhancing the enforceability of awards issued under the Rules[55] and also avoiding 'uncertainty as to whether the parties had agreed to the applicability of the Rules'.[56] Unlike the New York Convention or the UNCITRAL Model Law, the Rules do not attempt to define what is meant by 'in writing', which the Commission left to the applicable law.[57]

16.31 (1.2) **Arbitrability under the Rules** An unusual feature of Art 1(1) is its provision limiting the Rules' scope of application to 'disputes in relation to that contract,' meaning the contract entered into by 'the parties'. Most arbitration rules leave questions of arbitrability to the applicable law. When the Rules were adopted in 1976, it was assumed they would generally be used in commercial contexts, and thus the provision confining the Rules' application to 'disputes in relation to' the parties' contract did not appear to be a significant limitation and could in any event be modified by the parties.[58] However, when not modi-

[54] Sanders (n 28) 172, 177.

[55] *Report of UNCITRAL on the work of its 8th session*—(1–17 April 1975), Annex I ('Preliminary Draft Set of Arbitration Rules for optional use in *ad hoc* arbitration relating to international trade: Summary of Discussion by UNCITRAL') para 18, UN Doc A/10017, *reprinted in* (1975) VI *UNCITRAL ybk* 26 (hereafter, 'Summary of 8th Session Discussion'); *Report of UNCITRAL on the work of its 9th session* (12 April–7 May 1976) Annex II ('Report of the Committee of the Whole II relating to the UNCITRAL Arbitration Rules' para 9, UN Doc A/61/17, *reprinted in* (1976) VII *UNCITRAL Ybk*, 66, 67 (hereafter, 'Report of the Committee of the Whole II')). See also van Hof, J., *Commentary on the UNCITRAL Arbitration Rules: The Application by the Iran-US Claims Tribunal* (Kluwer, Deventer, 1991) 15.

[56] Sanders (n 28) 177.

[57] *Report of the Committee of the Whole II* (n 55) para 10, *reprinted in* (1976) VII *UNCITRAL Ybk* at 67. UNCITRAL, *Summary Record of the 161st Meeting* (9 April 1975) 120, UN Doc A/CN.9/SR.161.

[58] Sanders (n 28) 174 (noting that 'there is no doubt that the UNCITRAL Arbitration Rules were designed to facilitate the arbitration of disputes arising out of international trade transactions'). The parties' ability to adapt the Rules to resolve non-contractual claims was confirmed, *inter alia*, when Iran and the

fied by the parties, there may be a question whether this provision hinders application of the Rules to non-contractual disputes. For example, there are now about 2,000 bilateral investment treaties (BITs) in force in the world, a significant number of which permit resolution of disputes arising under the treaty by arbitration pursuant to the UNCITRAL Rules. Indeed, by the end of 2005, about 30 per cent of investment arbitrations brought pursuant to treaty had been initiated under the UNCITRAL Rules.[59]

An investor that brings a claim against a state for violation (for example) of 'fair and equitable treatment'[60] often will not have any contractual relationship with the host state, raising the question whether such claims can be said to be 'in relation to that contract' between 'the parties,' within the meaning of Art 1(1). Notwithstanding this language in Art 1, claims in BIT cases have generally been regarded as arbitrable under the Rules, probably because the State that offers (in a treaty) to submit such non-contractual claims to arbitration and the investor that accepts that offer (in filing its notice of arbitration under the Rules) are deemed to have jointly modified the Rules to the extent necessary to accommodate the claims.[61] **16.32**

(1.3) Parties' ability to modify rules Article 1(1) permits the parties to alter the Rules in any way that they 'may agree', although they must do so 'in writing', apparently for reasons of consistency with the like requirement for arbitration agreements.[62] This preservation of complete party autonomy regarding Rules revisions contrasts with the practice of certain arbitral institutions that treat some articles of their rules as non-derogable.[63] Parties that have agreed to arbitrate under the UNCITRAL Rules, as administered by an institution that offers this service, may confront a similar question whether that institution's supervision is conditioned on non-derogation from certain Articles of the Rules.[64] **16.33**

United States conferred jurisdiction in 1981 upon the Iran-United State Claims Tribunal to adjudicate claims under the UNCITRAL Arbitration Rules (as modified) that arose not only 'out of debts, contracts', but also out of 'expropriations or other measures affecting property rights'. See Art II(1) of the Claims Settlement Declaration (n 29), *reprinted in* Aldrich (n 29) 546.

59 UNCTAD, *Investor-State Disputes Arising From Investment Treaties: A Review* (United Nations, New York, 2005) 4–5.

60 See, eg 2004 United States Model Bilateral Investment Treaty, Arts 3 to 6, available at <http://www.state.gov/documents/organization/38710.pdf> (last accessed 4 October 2009).

61 See *Lance Paul Larsen v The Hawaiian Kingdom*, Award (Permanent Court of Arbitration Tribunal, 5 Feb 2001), *reprinted in* 119 ILR 566, 585–6; see also Caron, D., Caplan, L. and Pellonpää, M., *The UNCITRAL Arbitration Rules: A Commentary* (OUP, Oxford, 2006) 21 & fn 14. At the very least, a state that has offered to arbitrate treaty claims under the Rules would likely be estopped from thereafter challenging a tribunal's jurisdiction over such claims by arguing that they were not arbitrable because of this clause in the Rules.

62 Baker, S. and Davis, M., *The UNCITRAL Arbitration Rules in Practice: The Experience of the Iran-United States Claims Tribunal* (Kluwer, Deventer, 1992) 8.

63 See, eg Derains, Y. and Schwartz, E., *A Guide to the New ICC Rules of Arbitration* (2nd edn, Kluwer, Deventer, 2005) 19 n 21 (noting that the ICC Court of Arbitration 'has refused to administer cases where the parties provided in their arbitration clauses for' procedures deemed 'incompatible with the [ICC] Rules').

64 The Swiss Rules of International Arbitration ('the Swiss Rules') are closely modeled on the UNCITRAL Rules and, thus, similarly omit any limitation on the parties' power to revise them. Nevertheless, it is recognized that some of the Swiss Rules are 'mandatory' insofar as they 'concer[n] such a fundamental feature . . . that the Chambers [ie the Arbitration Committee of the six Swiss Chambers of Commerce] would refuse to administer an arbitration without this provision.' Besson, S., 'Introduction' in T. Zuberbühler, C. Müller & P. Habegger (eds), *Swiss Rules of International Arbitration: Commentary* (Kluwer/Schulthess, Zurich, 2005) 9. Mr Besson believes the mandatory provisions include Art 9's requirement of impartiality

16.34 (1.4) **Relationship of rules to national law** Article 1(2) stipulates that the Rules will govern the arbitration except insofar as they 'conflict with a provision of the law applicable to the arbitration from which the parties cannot derogate,' in which case the latter provision would prevail. Professor Sanders cites as a possibly non-derogable national law a provision conferring upon national courts an exclusive jurisdiction over challenges to arbitrators.[65] The drafters chose to refer to non-derogable rather than 'mandatory' provisions of law after noting that the understanding of what were 'mandatory' provisions differed considerably among legal systems.[66] Of course, the scope of any national law preemption will not be affected by the wording of this provision in the Rules, but delegates added the provision because 'the absence of a statement of this fact might mislead businessmen into thinking that the provisions of the Rules were definitive and not subject to review by judicial tribunals'.[67] Nevertheless, Professor Sanders has noted approvingly that 'in cases involving international commercial arbitration, many national courts have become more and more inclined to apply the more restrictive standard of international public policy rather than the wider standard of national public policy' in deciding which laws conflict with the Rules.[68]

16.35 (1.5) **The Model Arbitration Clause** The Model Clause in the footnote to Art 1(1) is intended to be inserted in a contract between the parties. Like the text of Art 1(1), the Model Clause limits the scope of claims that are arbitrable to those 'arising out of or relating to this contract, or the breach, termination or invalidity thereof'. Under the Model Clause, the parties also agree to arbitrate 'in accordance with the UNCITRAL Arbitration Rules as at present in force'. Finally, the Clause suggests that the parties 'may wish to consider adding' language to their agreement addressing four other aspects of an arbitration: (i) the identity of an appointing authority; (ii) the number of arbitrators; (iii) the place of arbitration; and (iv) the language(s) of the arbitration. Each of these choices can be significant, as explained more fully in the commentary accompanying Arts 5–8 and 16–17, which cover these issues substantively.

(2) Contemplated revisions

16.36 The Working Group intends to recommend four changes in this Article: (i) deleting the requirements as to written form; (ii) modifying the limitation on arbitrability; (iii) clarifying when the new version of the Rules will be deemed to apply; and (iv) making certain wording changes in the Model Arbitration Clause.

16.37 (2.1) **Requirement of written form** The Working Group seeks to delete the requirements that an agreement to arbitrate under the Rules and any modification of those Rules

---

and independence for arbitrators and Art 15(1)'s requirement that parties be treated equally and be given an opportunity to be heard. *ibid.*

65 Sanders (n 28) 178. cf Art 12 of the Rules (appointing authority resolves challenges to arbitrators).

66 van Hof (n 55) 15; UNCITRAL, *Summary Record of the 177th Meeting* (28 April 1976) para 1 (remarks of Ghanaian delegate, reporting recommendations of a working group on this issue), UN Doc A/CN.9/SR.177.

67 *Summary of 8th Session Discussion* (n 55) para 4.

68 Sanders (n 28) 178 (citing Strohbach, H., 'General Introduction' (1976) I *Ybk Comm Arb* 4–17).

must be 'in writing'.[69] Although some delegates believe such writing requirements usefully alert parties to the potential risks of seeking to enforce unwritten arbitration agreements, particularly where the applicable law requires a written form,[70] a strong majority feels that retaining these writing requirements (i) conflicts with the more 'liberal understanding of the form requirement' recently adopted in the Model Law on International Commercial Arbitration;[71] (ii) conflicts with those national laws that no longer impose form requirements for arbitration agreements; (iii) regulates an issue that should be left to applicable law; and (iv) would continue to give rise to litigation.[72]

(2.2) **Modified limitation on arbitrability** The Working Group would delete the words describing the parties as 'parties to a contract' and also the words limiting arbitrability to 'disputes in relation to that contract'. The latter phrase would be replaced by broader language taken directly from Art 7 of the UNCITRAL Model Law on International Commercial Arbitration, which authorizes arbitration of all 'disputes . . . in respect of a defined legal relationship, whether contractual or not'.[73] In this way, the Working Group seeks to 'put beyond doubt that a broad range of disputes, whether or not arising out of a contract, could be submitted to arbitration under the Rules'.[74] **16.38**

(2.3) **When would the revised rules apply?** The Working Group has addressed a question prompted by the revision project itself: When will the new version of the Rules apply? Given that arbitration is based on contract, the Working Group believes it should avoid 'retroactive application of the revised version of the Rules to arbitration agreements and treaties concluded before its adoption'.[75] Thus, the Working Group favours adding a paragraph to Art 1 establishing a 'presumption' that parties who conclude an arbitration agreement *after* UNCITRAL adopts the new version of the Rules (which is likely to be in 2010) (i) want the most recent version of the Rules to apply to any arbitration that arises under that agreement, unless (ii) the parties themselves have specified which version of the **16.39**

---

[69] *Report of WGII on the work of its 48th session* (4–8 February 2008), para 71, UN Doc A/CN.9/646, approving revised draft of Art 1(1) set forth in UN Doc A/CN.9/WG.II/WP.147 para 7.

[70] *Report of WGII on the work of its 46th session* (5–9 February 2007) para 30, UN Doc A/CN.9/619.

[71] In revising the Model Law in 2006, the Working Group offered two alternative approaches for national legislatures to adopt concerning the written form of arbitration agreements. Model Law Art 7, Option I still requires that an enforceable arbitration agreement be 'in writing' but substitutes a new, expansive definition of that term: 'An arbitration agreement is in writing if its content is recorded in any form, whether or not the arbitration agreement or contract has been concluded orally, by conduct, or by other means.' Mindful that some national legislatures have eliminated any formal requirement for arbitration agreements, the Working Group also approved Art 7, Option II, which defines 'arbitration agreement' without any reference to written form. The UNCITRAL Commission approved both alternatives when it adopted the revised version of the Model Law. The 2006 amended Model Law is available at <http://www.uncitral.org/pdf/english/texts/arbitration/ml-arb/07-86998_Ebook.pdf>, where it is accompanied by an 'Explanatory Note by the UNCITRAL Secretariat on the 1985 Model Law on International Commercial Arbitration as amended in 2006' (hereafter, 'Explanatory Note'). Paras 19 and 20 of the Explanatory Note provide useful background regarding the Working Group's objectives in proposing (and the practical effect of adopting) Option I.

[72] *Report of WGII on the work of its 46th session* (5–9 February 2007) paras 28–9 and 31, UN Doc A/CN.9/619.

[73] *Report of WGII on the work of its 48th session* (4–8 February 2008) para 71, UN Doc A/CN.9/646, approving draft revision of Art 1(1) set forth in UN Doc A/CN.9/WG.II/WP.147, para 7.

[74] *Report of WGII on the work of its 46th session* (5–9 February 2007) para 23, UN Doc A/CN.9/619.

[75] *Report of WGII on the work of its 48th session* (4–8 February 2008) para 75, UN Doc A/CN.9/646.

Rules will apply.[76] (The Working Group recognizes, however, that this 'presumption' should be drafted carefully so as to take account of the special problem posed by arbitration agreements that may be 'concluded' after the revised Rules are adopted by parties that accept offers to arbitrate made before the revised Rules were adopted.[77]) Similar provisions, presuming that parties (unless they expressly agree otherwise) wish to have any future arbitration governed by the rules in effect at the time their arbitration commences, are included in major institutional rules,[78] but the revision as proposed by the Working Group diverges from the approach recommended in the Rules' Model Arbitration Clause, which the Working Group would delete.[79]

16.40 If the 'presumption' recommended by the Working Group is ultimately included in the Rules, parties thereafter agreeing to arbitrate under the Rules would be on notice that the latest version of those Rules—including, revisions that may be adopted years from now and hence years after the agreement to arbitrate is entered into—will apply when any new arbitration is initiated, unless the parties agree otherwise.

16.41 (2.4) **Rewording the Model Arbitration Clause** In addition to deleting the Model Clause's language stating that parties adopt the Rules 'as at present in force', the Working Group would change the Clause so that it invites parties to specify a 'town *and* country' for the place of arbitration (rather than one or the other) and to choose a single 'language', since inviting a choice of 'language(s)' may unduly encourage dual-language arbitration even though its burdens normally outweigh its advantages. In the unusual case where dual-language arbitration is necessary, the parties of course remain free to agree to such a procedure.

[76] *ibid*, para 73, UN Doc A/CN.9/646 (recording 'considerable support for the wording of the 'Option 1' default provision, set forth in the *Note by the Secretariat*, UN Doc A/CN.9/WG.II/WP.147, para 7); *Report of WGII on the work of its 49th session* (15–19 September 2008) para 19, UN Doc A/CN.9/665 (recording that the Working Group 'considered' a redrafted version of Option 1, as set forth in the *Note by the Secretariat*, UN Doc A/CN.9/WG.II/WP.151, para 2). It should be noted that many parties do not incorporate in their arbitration agreement either the language in Art 1's Model Clause or any other words addressing which version of the Rules to apply.

[77] Particularly under bilateral investment treaties (BITs), there are likely to be arbitration agreements based on longstanding offers to arbitrate that will be concluded after adoption of the revised Rules but will nonetheless have had their *content* fixed *before* that adoption date. For example, a claimant may 'conclude' an arbitration agreement by filing a notice of arbitration in 2011 (after UNCITRAL is expected to have adopted the new Rules) that accepts an offer by a State—as set forth in a BIT that may have entered into force in 2007—to arbitrate claimed violations of 'fair and equitable treatment' of investments under the Rules. It would be inappropriate to 'presume' that the state party in such circumstances submitted to arbitration under a new version of the Rules when the treaty that contains the state's offer to arbitrate entered into force before UNCITRAL had adopted either the new Rules or the presumption as to their future applicability. (Of course, the State could phrase its offer to arbitrate in the treaty so that it expressly submits to future versions of the Rules). The Working Group thus is inclined to exclude from the operation of the 'presumption' any arbitration agreement that is 'concluded' after UNCITRAL adopts the new Rules but that is formed by acceptance of an offer to arbitrate made *before* UNICTRAL adopts the new Rules. *Report of WGII on the work of its 49th session* (15–19 September 2008) para 19, UN Doc A/CN.9/665 (recording that the Working Group 'considered' new language to this effect, contained in the *Note by the Secretariat*, UN Doc A/CN.9/WG.II/WP.151, para 2).

[78] See eg ICC Rules Art 6(1) (1998); AAA ICDR Rules Art 1(1) (2008).

[79] As previously noted, the Model Arbitration Clause appended to Art 1 provides that the Rules to be applied will be those 'at present in effect,' ie in effect at the time that the arbitration agreement is concluded.

NOTICE, CALCULATION OF PERIODS OF TIME

Article 2

1. **For the purposes of these Rules, any notice, including a notification, communication or proposal, is deemed to have been received if it is physically delivered to the addressee or if it is delivered at his habitual residence, place of business or mailing address, or, if none of these can be found after making reasonable inquiry, then at the addressee's last-known residence or place of business. Notice shall be deemed to have been received on the day it is so delivered.**
2. **For the purposes of calculating a period of time under these Rules, such period shall begin to run on the day following the day when a notice, notification, communication or proposal is received. If the last day of such period is an official holiday or a non-business day at the residence or place of business of the addressee, the period is extended until the first business day which follows. Official holidays or non-business days occurring during the running of the period of time are included in calculating the period.**

(1) Commentary on current text

Article 2 deals with two related subjects in two paragraphs: (i) when and how notices are deemed to be 'received' by an addressee; and (ii) how time periods under the Rules are calculated. **16.42**

(1.1) 'Receipt' of notices Article 2(1) requires that a notice or other communication be actually delivered, either to the addressee or to certain of its addresses, as a condition for deeming that the communication has been 'received.' The date of receipt is crucial in calculating time periods pursuant to Art 2(2). The drafters chose to rely on actual delivery in preference to establishing a rebuttable presumption (as repeatedly proposed during the Rules' drafting) that delivery has occurred within a given time if certain conditions of transmittal have been fulfilled (eg if the communication is sent by telegram or registered mail).[80] In requiring actual delivery and in specifying certain acceptable addresses for such delivery, the Commission followed Art 14(2) of the Convention on the Limitation Period in the International Sale of Goods.[81] As leading commentators have noted, 'On the one hand, the drafters were trying to ensure that a party did not face arbitral proceedings without having been first made aware of it . . . [o]n the other hand, the Committee did not want to place an undue burden on the sender by requiring that he know the rules of law on notice and presumption of receipt of the State in which the notice was to be delivered'.[82] As other commentators have noted, there appears to be an interaction between Art 2(1) and Art 4 (duty to communicate details as to party representative) since, 'Once a party has informed the . . . arbitral tribunal about the name and address of its representative, there is an assumption that any communication can validly be notified to the latter; . . . it should be up to the party to clearly state the fact that all communications still have to be made to it directly in spite of this designation.'[83] **16.43**

[80] See Caron, Caplan and Pellonpää (n 61) 378–9; van Hof (n 55) 9.

[81] (adopted 14 June 1974, entered into force 1 August 1988) 1511 UNTS I-26119. Art 14(2) of the Convention contains a default rule as to when arbitration begins for purposes of tolling a limitation period.

[82] Caron, Caplan and Pellonpää (n 61) 379.

[83] Gilliéron, P. and Pittet, L., 'Introductory Rules' in Zuberbühler, Müller and Habegger (eds) (n 64) 23 (discussing identical provisions, borrowed from the UNCITRAL Rules, in the Swiss Rules of International Arbitration).

16.44 (1.2) **Calculation of time periods under the Rules** Article 2(2) provides that time limits 'under the Rules' are calculated as beginning on the day following the receipt of a notice or communication and that, if the last day of the period of time then falls on a non-business day 'at the residence or place of business of the addressee', the period is extended to the next business day. As these terms make clear, the time periods are presumed to relate to the due dates for parties' submissions during the arbitration.

(2) Contemplated revisions

16.45 The Working Group intends to modify Art 2 to refer expressly to the possibility of electronic communication.

16.46 The Working Group intends to insert a new paragraph, prior to the existing ones, stating that notices and other communications may be transmitted not only by traditional modalities such as registered post and telegram but also by more recently developed technologies such as 'facsimile transmission' and other forms of 'electronic communication' that provide some form of record.[84] The initial motive for endorsing 'electronic communication' was both 'to reflect contemporary practice'[85] and to maintain consistency with other UNCITRAL instruments on this subject,[86] such as the 2005 United Nations Convention on the Use of Electronic Communications in International Contracts.[87] The Working Group appears to have resolved that the required 'record' of the electronic communication must evidence its transmission but not necessarily its receipt.[88]

NOTICE OF ARBITRATION

Article 3

1. **The party initiating recourse to arbitration (hereinafter called the 'claimant') shall give to the other party (hereinafter called the 'respondent') a notice of arbitration.**
2. **Arbitral proceedings shall be deemed to commence on the date on which the notice of arbitration is received by the respondent.**
3. **The notice of arbitration shall include the following:**
   (*a*) **A demand that the dispute be referred to arbitration;**
   (*b*) **The names and addresses of the parties;**
   (*c*) **A reference to the arbitration clause or the separate arbitration agreement that is invoked;**
   (*d*) **A reference to the contract out of or in relation to which the dispute arises;**

---

84 *Report of WGII on the work of its 48th session* (4–8 February 2008) para 83, UN Doc A/CN.9/646, discussing possible revisions in the draft version of Art 2 (1bis) set forth in *Note by the Secratariat*, UN Doc A/CN.9/WG.II/WP.147, para 15; *Report of WGII on the work of its 49th session* (15–19 September 2008) paras 23–9, UN Doc A/CN.9/665.

85 *Note by the Secretariat* (6 December 2006) para 25, UN Doc A/CN.9/WG.II/WP.145.

86 *Report of WGII on the work of its 46th session* (5–9 February 2007) para 50, UN Doc A/CN.9/619. The Working Group previously recommended, and the Commission adopted, insertion of a similar paragraph in the 2006 revisions to the Model Law on International Commercial Arbitration, providing that the requirement of written form for arbitration agreements (under Option I of Art 7) 'is met by electronic communication if the information contained therein is accessible so as to be useable for subsequent reference'. See also Explanatory Note (n 71) para 20.

87 GA Res 60/21, UN Doc A/RES/60/21 (9 December 2005).

88 *Report of WGII on the work of its 49th session* (15–19 September 2008) paras 27, 29, UN Doc A/CN.9/665.

(*e*) **The general nature of the claim and an indication of the amount involved, if any;**

(*f*) **The relief or remedy sought;**

(*g*) **A proposal as to the number of arbitrators (i.e. one or three), if the parties have not previously agreed thereon.**

4. **The notice of arbitration may also include:**

(*a*) **The proposals for the appointments of a sole arbitrator and an appointing authority referred to in article 6, paragraph 1;**

(*b*) **The notification of the appointment of an arbitrator referred to in article 7;**

(*c*) **The statement of claim referred to in article 18.**

(1) Commentary on current text

Article 3 achieves three purposes: it (i) specifies how an arbitration is commenced; (ii) establishes a rule for determining the arbitration's date of commencement; and (iii) outlines the information that the notice of arbitration 'shall include' while suggesting other items that it 'may include'. **16.47**

(1.1) Commencement of arbitration Article 3(1) provides that, in order to commence an arbitration, a claimant 'shall give to the other party . . . a notice of arbitration'. Notwithstanding the use of the verb 'give,' there is no requirement that the claimant personally deliver the notice to any other party; rather, the claimant may use any of the modes of delivery described in Art 2. **16.48**

(1.2) Date of commencement Article 3(2) stipulates that 'arbitral proceedings shall be deemed to commence' on the day when the notice of arbitration is received by the respondent. This provision must be read together with Art 2(1), which describes when 'any notice . . . is deemed to have been received'. The drafters debated whether to leave the issue of commencement to be resolved by the applicable law (including the Convention on the Limitation Period)[89] but decided that local prescription of rights might depend on the date of commencement and so included this provision.[90] **16.49**

(1.3) Contents of notice of arbitration Article 3(3) states that the notice of arbitration 'shall include' seven items: a demand that a dispute be referred to arbitration; names and addresses of the parties; a reference to the arbitration clause or agreement relied upon, a reference to the contract in relation to which the dispute arises; a statement as to the general nature of the claim and its amount; the relief sought; and (if not already agreed) a proposal as to the number of arbitrators. Article 3(4) provides that the notice 'may also include' a proposal for appointment of a sole arbitrator[91] or the designation of a party-appointed arbitrator, a proposal for an appointing authority, and the statement of claim. **16.50**

[89] See (n 81) and accompanying text.

[90] van Hof (n 55) 28; *Summary of 8th Session Discussion* (n 55) para 24; 'Report of the Secretary General: revised draft set of arbitration rules for optional use in *ad hoc* arbitration relating to international trade (addendum): commentary on the draft UNCITRAL Rules' (commentary on draft Art 4(2)), UN Doc A/CN.9/112/Add.1, *reprinted in* (1976) VII *UNCITRAL Ybk* 166, 168 (hereafter 'Commentary on Revised draft Rules').

[91] Such a proposal would be governed by the requirements of Art 8(2).

16.51 The reasons for making the latter items optional vary. The decision whether to propose a sole arbitrator or to designate the claimant's party-appointed arbitrator in the notice of arbitration is optional because the Rules do not impose any time limit on the taking of either action. What the Rules regulate is the time for *resolving* selection of a sole arbitrator, once one party has made a proposal, or for *completing* appointment of a three-person tribunal, once one party has appointed one member of a tribunal.[92]

16.52 However, the combined effect of Art 3(3)(g) and Art 3(4) is that the notice of arbitration can *both* propose the number of arbitrators to be agreed *and* simultaneously set the clock ticking for appointing a sole arbitrator or constituting a three-member tribunal. Under Art 5, the respondent has 15 days after receipt of the notice to agree or disagree on the number of arbitrators. Thus, for example, if when the 15 days expire the parties have agreed there should be a sole arbitrator, then if the notice already proposed one or more candidates for that position, the parties will have only 15 more days (under Art 6) to agree on a sole arbitrator. Failing such agreement, the sole arbitrator will be appointed by the appointing authority.

16.53 Similarly, if after 15 days from the respondent's receipt of the notice the parties have either agreed there should be a three-member tribunal or have failed to agree on the number of arbitrators, then there will be three arbitrators (as a result of the default provision in Art 5, requiring three if no number is agreed). In that case, under Art 7, the respondent will have only 15 more days to name its party-appointed arbitrator if the notice of arbitration named the claimant's party-appointed arbitrator.[93]

16.54 As for the option to include the statement of claim in the notice of arbitration, the Commission declined to make this mandatory because, depending on the circumstances, a claimant may wish either to accelerate the commencement of the arbitration (by filing only the notice) or to accelerate adjudication of its claim (by filing a combined notice and statement of claim). Thus, the drafters rejected proposals that the Rules merge the two documents because this might force the claimant to needless expense and effort in the midst of possible settlement discussions or preclude the filing of a notice before the claimant had gathered all the documents required to be included with its statement of claim.[94]

(2) Contemplated revisions

16.55 The Working Group intends to recommend (i) wording changes in Art 3(3) to enhance the contents of a notice of arbitration; (ii) the addition of a significant new provision requiring the respondent to file a response to the notice of arbitration; and (iii) inclusion of a further new provision that would address the possible consequences for the constitution of a tribunal of an incomplete notice of arbitration or the failure to file a response.

---

92 See Arts 6 and 7 of the Rules.

93 Only if application of Art 5 results in a three-member tribunal but the notice of arbitration has not named a party-appointed arbitrator will it be left to one of the parties to set the clock running on constituting the tribunal by designating the first party-appointed arbitrator.

94 van Hof (n 55) 29; Caron, Caplan and Pellonpää (n 61) 344-5; *Summary of 8th Session Discussion* (n 55) para 27; *Report of the Committee of the Whole II* (n 55) paras 22–3.

(2.1) Enhanced contents of the notice of arbitration The Working Group would change sub-para 3(b) to require that the notice contain the parties' 'contact details' (which could include facsimile and email contacts) rather than merely their 'addresses.'[95] Consistent with the proposed relaxation of Art 1's arbitrability requirement, sub-para 3(d) would no longer require 'reference to the contract' from which the dispute arises but rather would seek 'identification of any contract or other legal instrument' from which the dispute may arise.[96] Sub-paragraph 3(e) would also be amended to require a 'brief description' of the claim rather than merely an indication of its 'general nature', while sub-para 3(g) would require a proposal not merely as to the number of arbitrators but also as to the language and place of arbitration if the parties have not already agreed on these matters.[97] Generally, these changes seek to 'include more detailed or additional information in the interests of improving efficiency of the arbitral procedure'.[98] Finally, the Working Group recommends relocating the provision that permits the claimant to include its statement of claim in the notice of arbitration. This option is currently set forth in Art 3(4), but the Working Group proposes to move the provision to Art 18 (Statement of Claim), where it will be rephrased as a statement that the claimant may decide, after the respondent has had an opportunity to file its response (see discussion in the paragraphs immediately below), that it wishes to treat its notice of arbitration as also including its statement of claim.[99] 16.56

(2.2) Response to the notice of arbitration The Working Group intends to recommend that a respondent be required to file a response within 30 days after receiving the notice of arbitration. This requirement would be set forth in two paragraphs that would generally correspond to the provisions governing the notice of arbitration in Art 3(3) and (4): ie, one new paragraph would mandate that the response comment on most of the items that the notice 'shall include' while the other would invite the response to comment on items that the notice 'may . . . include'. However, with respect to Art 3(3)(a)'s requirement that the notice of arbitration include 'a demand that the dispute be referred to arbitration,' the corresponding item to be covered by the response would appear to be a plea that the arbitral tribunal lacks jurisdiction, and the Working Group has decided that this belongs in the list of items whose inclusion in the response will be optional rather than the list of required items. This will have the effect of preserving the provision in Art 21(3) stating that a plea as to the tribunal's lack of jurisdiction 'shall be raised not later than the statement of defence.' The response also 'may' include a brief description of any counterclaim.[100] 16.57

---

95 *Report of WGII on the work of its 46th session* (5–9 February 2007) para 52, UN Doc A/CN.9/617.

96 *ibid*, para 54; see *Report of WGII on the work of its 49th session* (15–19 September 2008) para 35, UN Doc A/CN.9/665, recording the Working Group's adoption of revised text of Art 3 as set forth in *Note by the Secretariat*, UN Doc A/CN.9/WG.II/WP.151 para 11.

97 *Note by the Secretariat* (6 December 2006) paras 34–5, UN Doc A/CN.9/WG.II/WP.145; see also *Report of WGII on the work of its 49th session* (15–19 September 2008) para 35, UN Doc A/CN.9/665, recording the Working Group's adoption of revised text of Art 3 as set forth in *Note by the Secretariat*, UN Doc A/CN.9/WG.II/WP.151 para 11.

98 *Note by the Secretariat* (6 December 2006) para 31, UN Doc A/CN.9/WG.II/WP.145.

99 *Report of WGII on the work of its 49th session* (15–19 September 2008) para 36, UN Doc A/CN.9/665; see also *Report of WGII on the work of its 50th session* (5–9 February 2009) paras 19–22, UN Doc A/CN.9/669.

100 *Report of WGII on the work of its 49th session* (15–19 September 2008) paras 38–41, UN Doc A/CN.9/665, adopting with revisions the drafts of Art 3(5) and (6) set forth in *Note by the Secretariat*, UN Doc A/CN.9/WG.II/WP.151 paras 9, 13.

16.58 Requiring a response to the notice of arbitration is one of the 'main lines of revision' in the Rules that was recommended by two prominent practitioners, in an unofficial report commissioned by the UNCITRAL Secretariat at the outset of the revision project.[101] In support of this change in the Rules, it was noted that (i) the current Rules defer the respondent's first submission until after the statement of claim has been filed, leaving the respondent's position unknown 'perhaps for six months' and thus preventing 'efficient preparation for both litigation and amicable settlement'; (ii) it is 'not good practice to constitute an arbitral tribunal without having any indication of the kind of case that will be mounted in defence, as this may bear on the required attributes of arbitrators, especially if any appointment is to be made by an Appointing Authority'; and, (iii) submission of an early response would enhance the tribunal's ability to issue procedural directions for the case.[102] Based on the Secretariat's presentation of this proposal to the Working Group's first Rules revision session,[103] the Working Group agreed that it offered advantages in constituting the tribunal.[104]

16.59 **(2.3) Consequences of incomplete notice or failure to file response** The Working Group intends to add language that, as so far agreed, would provide that 'the constitution of the arbitral tribunal shall not be hindered' either by an objection to the sufficiency of the notice of arbitration or by the respondent's failure to submit a response to the notice of arbitration.[105] The envisioned new language would also reaffirm the tribunal's authority to 'proceed as it considers appropriate' in the case of either deficiency in the pleadings, and would reaffirm that the tribunal will 'finally resolve[]' any controversy about the notice of arbitration's sufficiency.[106]

REPRESENTATION AND ASSISTANCE

Article 4

The parties may be represented or assisted by persons of their choice. The names and addresses of such persons must be communicated in writing to the other party; such communication must specify whether the appointment is being made for purposes of representation or assistance.

---

[101] Paulsson and Petrochilos (n 39) 5–6. This revision parallels a similar change already incorporated into the Swiss Rules of International Arbitration (see Art 3(7)–(8) thereof, providing for an 'Answer to the Notice of Arbitration'). The Swiss Rules are generally modeled on the UNCITRAL Rules.

[102] *ibid* at 6.

[103] *Note by the Secretariat* (20 July 2006) paras 40–1, UN Doc A/CN.9/WG.II/WP.143.

[104] *Report of WGII on the work of its 45th session* (11–15 September 2006) para 57, UN Doc A/CN.9/614. A similar provision has already been included in the revised Swiss Rules, which are expressly based upon the UNCITRAL Rules. See Swiss Rules of International Arbitration (2004) Art 3(7), 3(8) and 3(9).

[105] *Report of WGII on the work of its 49th session* (15–19 September 2008) para 42, UN Doc A/CN.9/665, recording the Working Group's adoption (with minor edit) of the draft Art 3(7) set forth in *Note by the Secretariat*, UN Doc A/CN.9/WG.II/WP.151 paras 9, 14. See also proposed elaboration of the provision by the Secretariat to cover as well the tardy or incomplete submission of a response: *Note by the Secretariat, 'Settlement of Commercial Disputes: Revision of the UNCITRAL Arbitration Rules'* (8 December 2008) para 19, UN Doc A/CN.9/WG.II/WP.154.

[106] *Report of WGII on the work of its 49th session* (15–19 September 2008) para 42, UN Doc A/CN.9/665, recording the Working Group's adoption (with minor edit) of the draft Art 3(7) set forth in *Note by the Secretariat*, UN Doc A/CN.9/WG.II/WP.151 paras 9, 14.

(1) Commentary on current text

Article 4 serves two functions, set forth in its two sentences. It (i) allows a party to choose those persons who will either represent or assist the party in presenting its case; and (ii) requires a party to identify these persons, including their function as representative or assistant, to the other party. **16.60**

(1.1) Choosing representatives or assistants Article 4's first sentence, which guarantees that parties can have their case presented by—or with the help of—persons of their choice, refers to the right to be 'represented *or* assisted' because the drafters worried that referring only to 'representation' could exclude parties' being aided by non-lawyers.[107] **16.61**

(1.2) Communicating the name and address of a party representative or assistant Article 4's second sentence, requiring communication of the name and address of any person representing or assisting a party, is very broad and, if read literally, might imply that each party must identify to the other(s) all persons lending it any sort of assistance. The possibility of such a misreading results from the drafters' attempt to broaden the Article to include non-lawyers by referring to persons who 'assist' a party. The risk of such an overly expansive reading was noted during the final drafting of the Rules, and a solution was approved by a drafting committee[108] but not ultimately incorporated in the text, perhaps because the solution resurrected concerns that representation was being limited to lawyers.[109] However, the *travaux préparatoires* elsewhere indicate that the persons whose names and addresses must be communicated are those who help to present a party's case in written or oral interactions with the arbitrators.[110] The drafters rejected a suggestion that the Rules require a power of attorney for party representatives,[111] noting that the law in 'most Western countries' did not require such a document.[112] However, the Rules' omission of such a requirement does not preclude a tribunal from ordering a party to produce a power of attorney in a given case, as has been demonstrated by the Iran-US Claims Tribunal.[113] **16.62**

[107] The revised draft of the Rules that was presented at the Commission's 9th session stated that a party may be 'represented by a counsel or agent'. *Report of the Secretary General: Revised draft set of arbitration rules for optional use in* ad hoc *arbitration relating to international trade* (text of draft Art 5), UN Doc A/CN.9/112, *reprinted in* (1976) VII *UNCITRAL Ybk 161* (hereafter 'Revised draft Rules'). The subsequent reformulation of what became Art 4 resulted from delegates' concern that the earlier phrasing (especially when translated into other UN working languages) might exclude assistance by non-lawyers. Report of Committee of the Whole II (n 55) para 25. See also Baker and Davis (n 62) 12; van Hof (n 55) 31–2.

[108] UNCITRAL Committee of the Whole II, *Summary Record of the 15th Meeting* (27 April 1976) paras 23–4, UN Doc A/CN.9/9/C.2/SR.15.

[109] See Baker and Davis (n 62) 12–13.

[110] For example, the initial draft of this Article 'deemed' that the identity of a party's 'counsel or agent' had already been communicated to the other party 'where the notice of arbitration, the statement of claim, the statement of defence, or a counterclaim is submitted on behalf of a party by a counsel or agent.' Revised draft Rules (n 107) (draft of Art 5), *reprinted in* (1976) VII *UNCITRAL Ybk* at 161. Similarly, the commentary to this initial draft explained that 'representation may take place at any stage of the arbitral proceedings, including any hearing . . . or any meeting for the inspection of goods'. Commentary on Revised draft Rules (n 90) (commentary on draft Art 5), *reprinted in* (1976) VII *UNCITRAL Ybk* at 168.

[111] Report of Committee of the Whole II (n 55) para 26.

[112] UNCITRAL Committee of the Whole II, *Summary Record of 2nd Meeting* (15 April 1976) paras 46–50, UN Doc A/CN.9/9/C.2/SR.2.

[113] See *Flexi-Van Leasing Inc v Iran* (Order 36-1) 1 Iran-USCTR 166, 167 (1982) (ordering the claimant, at the respondent's request, to produce a power of attorney); see also *id* (dissenting opinion by Judge Howard

16.63 Article 4's requirement that a party also communicate whether each person it designates is 'for purposes of representation or assistance' seems to have been motivated by a concern that a person merely 'assisting' a party may not have authority to act for the party (although this might also be true of a person said to be a 'representative').[114] This motive may be inferred from the fact that, when the draft Article had focused only on the party's choice of representation by 'counsel or agent', requiring communication of the representative's name and address was intended 'to assure the other party that such counsel or agent possesses the requisite authority to act on behalf of the party whom he claims to represent'.[115]

16.64 The Iran-US Claims Tribunal has addressed the potential difficulties regarding the role of persons who lend 'assistance' to parties in two Notes that it adopted to clarify application of Art 4. Note 2 provides that 'an appointed representative shall be deemed to be authorized to act before the arbitral tribunal on behalf of the appointing party for all purposes' and that its 'acts . . . shall be binding upon the appointing party' even though 'a representative is not required to be licensed to practice law'.[116] By contrast, Note 3 states that 'persons chosen to assist [a party] who are not also appointed as representatives' are deemed unauthorized either to act on behalf of the appointing party, to bind that party, or 'to receive notices, communications or documents on behalf of the appointing party'.[117]

(2) Contemplated revisions

16.65 The Working Group intends to recommend changes in Art 4 that will (i) limit a party's ability to disrupt proceedings by its choice of counsel; (ii) confirm the tribunal's authority to clarify the scope of a representative's authority; and (iii) bring this Article's wording into conformity with other provisions of the Rules.

16.66 **(2.1) Limiting choice of counsel** The Working Group expressed concern that allowing parties to designate 'persons of their choice' to represent them could be read as conferring an absolute right to choose any counsel at any point in the proceedings and thus to impose, for example, 'a busy practitioner that would be unable to meet reasonable time schedules set by the arbitral tribunal'.[118] To preclude such disruption, the Working Group will recommend that 'persons chosen by them' be replaced by 'persons of their choice' in the first sentence of Art 4.[119]

Holtzmann, objecting *inter alia* on the ground that 'no requirement for such a power of attorney is contained in the [Rules]' and further noting that the claimant had already identified its counsel in its statement of claim, in compliance with Arts 4 and 18(1) of the Rules). However, the 'general trend', at the Iran-US Claims Tribunal has been to refrain from ordering the production of a power of attorney. van Hof (n 55) 34.

114 cf *Cherafat v Iran* (Decision no. 106–277-2, 25 June 1992) (claimants assert that attorney who obtained the tribunal's dismissal of their claim was not their representative and therefore could not bind them) *reprinted in* 28 Iran USCTR 216, 219–20 (1992).

115 *Commentary on Revised draft Rules* (n 90) 168 (commentary on draft Art 5).

116 *Reprinted in* Aldrich (n 29) 556.

117 *ibid.*

118 *Report of WGII on the work of its 46th session* (5–9 February 2007) para 63, UN Doc A/CN.9/619.

119 *ibid.* See also *Report of WGII on the work of its 49th session* (15–19 September 2008) paras 44–5, UN Doc A/CN.9/665, recording the Working Group's adoption of final edits in the draft language of Art 4, as set out in *Note by the Secretariat*, UN Doc A/CN.9/WG.II/WP.151 para 15.

(2.2) Clarifying a party representative's authority The Working Group grappled with the issue of how to confirm a party representative's authority or the scope thereof. It declined to require that a party notify other parties of its representative's scope of authority, fearing that this might force disclosure of confidential matters, such as the extent of counsel's settlement authority.[120] Instead, the Working Group intends to recommend language confirming the tribunal's power to seek (including at the request of a party) 'proof of authority granted to the representative . . . in such form as the arbitral tribunal may determine'.[121] **16.67**

(2.3) Conforming changes The Working Group intends to recommend deletion of the words 'in writing', from the second sentence of Art 4, since Art 2(1) already sets forth authorized modes of communication, and the Working Group will also recommend that the words 'the other party' be changed to 'all parties',[122] in accordance with changes being recommended throughout the Rules to reflect the possibility of multi-party proceedings. **16.68**

Section II. Composition of the arbitral tribunal

NUMBER OF ARBITRATORS

Article 5

If the parties have not previously agreed on the number of arbitrators (i.e. one or three), and if within fifteen days after the receipt by the respondent of the notice of arbitration the parties have not agreed that there shall be only one arbitrator, three arbitrators shall be appointed.

(1) Commentary on current text

Article 5 establishes a default rule that the arbitration will be adjudicated by three arbitrators if the parties have not previously agreed on the number of arbitrators and if they do not reach agreement within 15 days after the Respondent receives the notice of arbitration. **16.69**

It is useful for the UNCITRAL Rules to contain a default provision on the number of arbitrators because the Rules are designed to be—and often are—used in *ad hoc* arbitrations, where there is no administering institution that might resolve this issue when the parties do not.[123] **16.70**

The UNCITRAL drafters debated whether to choose a default rule of one or three arbitrators. It was recognized, for example, that considerations as to cost as well as speed in resolving the dispute argued in favour of a default requirement for a sole arbitrator.[124] On the **16.71**

[120] *Report of WGII on the work of its 46th session* (5–9 February 2007) paras 64–7, UN Doc A/CN.9/619.

[121] *Report of WGII on the work of its 49th session* (15–19 September 2008) para 43, UN Doc A/CN.9/665 (recording the Working Group's approval of new language in Art 4 on this point set forth in *Note by the Secretariat*, UN Doc A/CN.9/WG.II/WP.151 para 15).

[122] *ibid*, para 44 (WGII's approval of new wording of Art 4, set forth in UN Doc A/CN.9/WG.II/WP.151 para 15).

[123] cf Art 5 of the American Arbitration Association's International Rules (hereafter 'ICDR Rules') (providing that where parties have not agreed on the number of arbitrators, 'one arbitrator shall be appointed unless the administrator determines in its discretion that three arbitrators are appropriate because of the large size, complexity or other circumstances of the case'); similar provisions can be found in Art 8(2) of the Rules of Arbitration of the International Court of Arbitration of the International Chamber of Commerce (hereafter 'ICC Rules'), in Art 5.4 of the London Court of International Arbitration Rules (hereafter 'LCIA Rules'), and in Art 6(1) of the Swiss Rules.

[124] *Summary of 8th Session Discussion* (n 55) para 39; *Report of the Committee of the Whole II* (n 55) para 27 (discussion of draft Art 6); see also Caron, Caplan and Pellonpää (n 61) 170.

other hand, establishing a three-member tribunal as the default position accommodates each party's desire to select at least one arbitrator who has the knowledge, background and experience that the selecting party deems essential for resolving the case. Having three arbitrators also often assures broader competence within the tribunal for handling large or complex cases. It was further observed that three-member tribunals were the norm in international commercial arbitration.[125] In the end, the latter arguments proved decisive in favour of a default rule requiring three arbitrators.[126]

16.72 Since Art 3 requires that a notice of arbitration contain a proposal for the number of arbitrators if the parties have not previously agreed on this, Art 5's deadline effectively means that the respondent has 15 days after receiving the notice of arbitration either to express agreement with the number that the notice proposes, persuade the claimant to change its mind on the number it proposes, or accept a three-member tribunal by default. As has already been discussed in the context of Art 3,[127] the relatively short period of 15 days also makes it easier for the claimant to use the notice of arbitration to start the clock running on the 30-day deadlines under Arts 6 and 7, respectively, for agreeing on a sole arbitrator or appointing three members of a tribunal. In other words, the effect of the short time limit under Art 5 is that once the number of arbitrators is definitively resolved (no more than 15 days following service of the notice of arbitration), there will then be only 15 more days before the parties' deadline for agreeing upon a candidate for sole arbitrator (assuming the claimant proposed someone in its notice of arbitration) or before the respondent's deadline for appointing its party-appointed arbitrator (assuming, again, that the claimant named its party-appointed arbitrator in the notice of arbitration).

(2) Contemplated revisions

16.73 The Working Group has debated whether the default rule should, in fact, require one arbitrator rather than three arbitrators but, like the drafters more than 30 years ago, has thus far favoured (i) retaining a default rule of three arbitrators, with a possible exception where one party simply fails to express any preference. Meanwhile, the Working Group intends (ii) to amend the Rule to clarify that parties may agree on a number of arbitrators other than one or three.

16.74 **(2.1) Retaining the default rule for three arbitrators** The Working Group considered modifying the default rule slightly, so that it would continue to require three arbitrators if either party requested three but would call for a single arbitrator if one party favoured that solution and the other party was entirely silent.[128] At the end of this debate, there was no

---

[125] *Summary of 8th Session Discussion* (n 55) paras 39–40; see also Caron, Caplan and Pellonpää (n 61) 170.

[126] Although it would not have been anticipated at the time, the choice has proved particularly apt for the subsequent application of the UNCITRAL Rules in resolving disputes under bilateral and multilateral agreements. As one group of commentators has noted, 'A three-member panel has been preferable for the [Iran-US Claims] Tribunal for exactly the reasons stated by the members of the UNCITRAL Drafting Committee: Iranian and American arbitrators often found themselves, for example, explaining aspects of their national laws'. Caron, Caplan and Pellonpää (n 61) 171-2 (also noting the same effect in NAFTA ch 11 arbitrations).

[127] See *supra* paras 16.52–3.

[128] *Report of WGII on the work of its 49th session* (15–19 September 2008) paras 57–60, UN Doc A/CN.9/665.

consensus favouring the change, and thus the Working Group provisionally decided to retain the current rule.[129] However, it was decided that the parties should have 30 days following service of the notice of arbitration (rather than the 15 days that Art5 currently provides) in which to seek to agree on the number of arbitrators. The reason for the change is that the respondent will now have 30 days to file a response to the notice of arbitration and the respondent's preference for the number of arbitrators is one of the matters that the response must set forth.[130]

The Working Group has left open the possibility of amending Art 5 to provide that, where one party favours a single arbitrator and the other party does not agree but also does not appoint its own arbitrator, the party favouring a single arbitrator could ask the appointing authority to resolve whether a sole arbitrator was 'appropriate' in the case and, if so, to appoint that arbitrator.[131] **16.75**

(2.2) Facilitating the parties' choice of a different number of arbitrators Because of the parenthetical phrase ('one or three')in its current text, Art 5 strongly implies that the tribunal may only have one or three arbitrators. Strictly speaking, the parties are not so limited since they are free (pursuant to Art 1(1)) to modify the Rules as they deem necessary. However, the Working Group decided to delete Art 5's parenthetical phrase, noting that (for example) 'a two-member arbitral tribunal, which was allowed by the UNCITRAL Arbitration Model Law . . . was customary in some trades'.[132] A corresponding change has also been adopted at a later point in the Rules to resolve the method of appointing a tribunal that has a number of arbitrators other than one or three. This is further described among the contemplated revisions to Art 7. **16.76**

APPOINTMENT OF ARBITRATORS (Articles 6 to 8)

Article 6

1 If a sole arbitrator is to be appointed, either party may propose to the other:

(a) The names of one or more persons, one of whom would serve as the sole arbitrator; and

(b) If no appointing authority has been agreed upon by the parties, the name or names of one or more institutions or persons, one of whom would serve as appointing authority.

2 If within thirty days after receipt by a party of a proposal made in accordance with paragraph 1 the parties have not reached agreement on the choice of a sole arbitrator, the sole arbitrator shall be appointed by the appointing authority agreed upon by the parties. If no appointing authority has been agreed upon by the parties, or if the appointing authority agreed upon refuses to act or fails to appoint the arbitrator within sixty days of the receipt of a party's request therefor, either party may request the Secretary-General of the Permanent Court of Arbitration at The Hague to designate an appointing authority.

3 The appointing authority shall, at the request of one of the parties, appoint the sole arbitrator as promptly as possible. In making the appointment the appointing authority shall use the following list-procedure, unless both parties agree that the list-procedure should not be

---

[129] *ibid* at para 61.

[130] *ibid* at paras 65–7; see also discussion of new provision for filing of response at paras 16.57–8 *supra*.

[131] *Report of WGII on the work of its 49th session* (15–19 September 2008) paras 62–4, UN Doc A/CN.9/665.

[132] *Report of WGII on the work of its 46th session* (5–9 February 2007) para 83, UN Doc A/CN.9/619.

used or unless the appointing authority determines in its discretion that the use of the list-procedure is not appropriate for the case:

(a) At the request of one of the parties the appointing authority shall communicate to both parties an identical list containing at least three names;

(b) Within fifteen days after the receipt of this list, each party may return the list to the appointing authority after having deleted the name or names to which he objects and numbered the remaining names on the list in the order of his preference;

(c) After the expiration of the above period of time the appointing authority shall appoint the sole arbitrator from among the names approved on the lists returned to it and in accordance with the order of preference indicated by the parties;

(d) If for any reason the appointment cannot be made according to this procedure, the appointing authority may exercise its discretion in appointing the sole arbitrator.

4 In making the appointment, the appointing authority shall have regard to such considerations as are likely to secure the appointment of an independent and impartial arbitrator and shall take into account as well the advisability of appointing an arbitrator of a nationality other than the nationalities of the parties.

(1) Commentary on text

16.77 Article 6 proceeds from the premise that the parties have agreed there will be only one arbitrator. It establishes the process for appointing that arbitrator, according to the possible circumstances: either (i) the parties appoint the arbitrator; or (ii) the parties designate an appointing authority (or call upon the Secretary-General of the Permanent Court of Arbitration to make that designation) ; and (iii) the appointing authority then appoints the sole arbitrator. As Professor Pieter Sanders has noted, the cumulative requirements of this Article are 'perhaps rather complicated,' but they were 'the only acceptable solution UNCITRAL could find without making its arbitration a fully administered, institutional arbitration'.[133]

16.78 **(1.1) The parties' appointment of a sole arbitrator** If the parties have agreed that there will be only one arbitrator, either party may at any time propose one or more persons, one of whom would serve as the arbitrator. As previously noted, Art 3(4) invites but does not require the claimant to include such a proposal in the notice of arbitration, but the proposal may be made later, including by the respondent. There is no limitation as to the background qualification or nationality of candidates the parties may propose for sole arbitrator, but all arbitrators must meet the standards of independence and impartiality implicitly set forth in Arts 9 (arbitrators' disclosure duty) and 10 (challenge of arbitrators). Once one party has received the other party's proposal of candidates for sole arbitrator, Art 6(2) gives the parties 30 days to agree on the sole arbitrator. If no agreement is reached within that time, either party may request that the appointing authority appoint the sole arbitrator.

16.79 Under Art 6(1), the party that first proposes one or more persons who might serve as the sole arbitrator may also propose one or more institutions or persons, one of whom might serve as appointing authority, 'if no appointing authority has been agreed'. Article 6(2)'s 30-day time limit for the parties to reach an agreement applies to 'a proposal made in

[133] Sanders (n 28) 184.

accordance with paragraph 1'. Professor Pieter Sanders has expressed the view that, because para 1 of Art 6 envisions a combined proposal of candidates for sole arbitrator and for appointing authority (when no appointing authority has yet been agreed), 'it is only upon the receipt of a combined proposal, covering both matters, that the period of 30 days mentioned in Art 6, para 2 begins to run'.[134] However, this conclusion seems inconsistent with the permissive wording of Art 6(1) (a party 'may propose' candidates for sole arbitrator 'and' for appointing authority) and with the drafting history of this provision.[135]

Nonetheless, given the language and structure of Art 6(1), what Professor Sanders believes the Rules require is, at the very least, desirable as a matter of practice: if an appointing authority has not already been agreed, a party's initial proposal of candidates for sole arbitrator 'should be a *combined proposal* and contain also the names of one or more institutions or persons, one of whom would serve as appointing authority'.[136] **16.80**

(1.2) Selecting an appointing authority If the parties have not previously agreed on an appointing authority, either party may propose one or more names of institutions or persons, one of whom would serve as the appointing authority. Article 3(4) invites the claimant to include such a proposal in its notice of arbitration, but the proposal may be made later, including by the respondent. Indeed, even Professor Sanders acknowledges that if a party's initial proposal pursuant to Art 6(1) only contains candidates for sole arbitrator, 'either party . . . may still make' the second proposal of candidates for appointing authority if no appointing authority has been agreed.[137] Moreover, although the language of Art 6(1) may be ambiguous on this point, the drafters' apparent intent was that parties may by-pass any attempt to agree on the sole arbitrator and proceed directly to a party's proposal of candidates for appointing authority.[138] If only this second type of proposal is made, pursuant to Art 6(1)(b), presumably the 30-day limit for agreement imposed by Art 6(2) still applies. **16.81**

If the parties haven't designated an appointing authority, if the first proposal for a sole arbitrator is not accompanied by a proposal for an appointing authority, and if the parties then do not agree on a sole arbitrator within 30 days of a party's proposal of one or more candidates, the Rules do not give the parties another 30 days to agree on an appointing authority. Rather, in the circumstances just described, either party can apply immediately to the Secretary-General of the Permanent Court of Arbitration ('PCA') at The Hague to designate an appointing authority. This conclusion follows directly from the wording of Art 6(2)'s two sentences as well as from the drafting history.[139] The practical result is that, **16.82**

---

[134] Sanders (n 28) 182.

[135] See Baker and Davis (n 62) 22–3.

[136] Sanders (n 28) 183 (emphasis in original).

[137] *ibid*, 184.

[138] Baker and Davis (n 62) 23 and fn 73.

[139] See *ibid*, 22. These commentators also point out that, because Art 6(2) allows any party to request the Secretary-General's designation of an appointing authority whenever there is no authority that 'has been agreed upon', the clause might be read as permitting parties to seek successive designations of different appointing authorities in a single arbitration. If (for example) the Secretary-General designates an appointing authority that appoints a sole arbitrator who subsequently dies or resigns, Art 13 provides that his or her replacement shall be 'appointed or chosen pursuant to the procedure provided for in articles 6 to 9 that was

in the case where the parties have not agreed to an appointing authority, if the party that first proposes candidates for sole arbitrator does not combine that with a proposal as to an appointing authority, the parties will need to discuss possible choices for the appointing authority concurrently with their discussion as to the sole arbitrator. If they fail to do so and also fail to agree on an arbitrator within 30 days following the first proposal of one, either party can then immediately seek the PCA's designation of the appointing authority without any discussion on candidates for that position.

16.83 According to Art 6(2)'s final sentence, a party may also ask the PCA Secretary-General to designate an appointing authority if an existing appointing authority 'refuses to act'[140] after a party asks it to act, or if it fails to appoint an arbitrator within 60 days of a party's request that it do so. By its terms, this 60-day deadline only applies to appointing authorities that have been 'agreed upon' by the parties. However, as has already been suggested in the previous paragraph,[141] the words 'agreed upon' in this context should be construed as including appointing authorities designated by the Secretary-General.

16.84 There are several subsequent provisions in the Rules that incorporate by reference the procedure for designating an appointing authority set forth in Art 6. For example, when a challenge to an arbitrator must be decided upon and no appointing authority has yet been named, Art 12(1)(c) provides that an appointing authority shall be 'designated in accordance with the procedure . . . provided for in article 6'. This raises the question whether, in such circumstances, a party may ask the PCA Secretary-General to designate an appointing authority as soon as the challenge arises or whether the parties must first propose candidates to each other and seek to agree upon an appointing authority, as provided under Art 6(1). The Rules do not appear to require this. In a case arising from the Iranian government's challenge to Judge Mangård of the Iran-US Claims Tribunal, the designated appointing authority decided that Art 12's cross-reference to 'the procedure for designating an appointing authority as provided for in Article 6' was 'intended to make it possible . . . to decide on the challenge as quickly and as simply as possible' and therefore that the mechanism in Art 6 'has to be interpreted as meaning that . . . the Secretary-General of the [PCA] is empowered to designate an Appointing Authority to decide on a challenge if he receives a request to that effect from one of the Parties'.[142]

---

applicable to the appointment or choice of the arbitrator being replaced'. In such circumstances, a literal reading of Art 6(2) might allow a party to request the Secretary-General to designate a new appointing authority to appoint the replacement arbitrator because the existing appointing authority was not 'agreed upon'. As Baker and Davis point out, the more plausible construction of Art 6(2)'s second sentence is that its use of the term 'agreed upon' rather than 'designated' was inadvertent and that, in the circumstances just described, no designation of a new appointing authority is required. *ibid*, 30–1.

140 One possible reason for a refusal to act is if the person or institution designated as appointing authority recuses itself from the particular decision. This is less likely in the appointment of an arbitrator than in other contexts, such as the resolution of a challenge, but it should in any event be rare. See Baker and Davis (n 62) 31–3.

141 See n 139.

142 Decision of the Appointing Authority on Iran's Objection to Judge Mangård, 5 March 1982, *reprinted in* 1 Iran–IUSCTR 509, 514 (1981–82); see also Caron, Caplan and Pellonpää (n 61) 176–8.

Once an appointing authority is designated for one purpose, the Rules seem to contemplate that this person or entity should remain the appointing authority for other purposes in the arbitration, including for the possible appointment of a replacement arbitrator under Arts 12 and 13 or for the setting forth of a basis for arbitrators' fees under Art 39. It is true that, according to Arts 12 and 13, the tasks described therein shall be performed by an appointing authority designated 'as provided for in article 6'[143] and, as noted, Art 6(2) provides that an appointing authority should be designated whenever 'no appointing authority has been *agreed upon by the parties*'. Thus, a party might argue that an appointing authority designated for one purpose by the Secretary-General of the PCA does not continue to serve for other purposes because he or she was not 'agreed upon by the parties'. As has already been noted, however, it is doubtful that the UNCITRAL drafters intended Art 6(2) to curtail the service of appointing authorities designated by the Secretary-General of the PCA.[144] 16.85

(1.3) The appointing authority's appointment of a sole arbitrator Once an appointing authority has been chosen (either by party agreement or by the PCA Secretary-General's designation), any party may request that the authority appoint a sole arbitrator (if none has yet been designated), observing the further requirements set forth in Art 8. However, the fact that a party has made such a request does not preclude the parties from subsequently agreeing on a sole arbitrator.[145] Pursuant to Art 6(3), the appointing authority should appoint the arbitrator not only within the 60-day deadline imposed by Art 6(2) but also 'as promptly as possible', and it should do so by means of the 'list-procedure' described in Art 6(3), unless it determines that this is not appropriate to the case or unless the parties have agreed otherwise. Under the list procedure, the appointing authority submits to each party a list of possible candidates for the position of sole arbitrator, each party has 15 days to return the list (after deleting any names to which that party objects and indicating the 16.86

[143] Art 12(1)(c) (the cross-reference in Art 13 is similar but not identical).

[144] See Baker and Davis (n 62) 29–31 and see note 139, *supra*. The likely reason why Art 6(2) refers only to an appointing authority 'agreed upon by the parties' is that appointment of a sole arbitrator occurs at such an early stage of the proceeding that no other circumstance could already have occasioned designation of an appointing authority by the PCA Secretary-General. However, when Art 6(2) is applied to a later arbitral appointment, an appointing authority may by then have been designated by the Secretary-General. As Baker and Davis recount, the question did arise whether the appointing authority who had been designated by the PCA Secretary-General in 1982 (Judge Charles Moons of the Netherlands Supreme Court) to rule upon the government of Iran's challenge to Judge Mangård as a member of the Iran-US Claims Tribunal was eligible in 1983 to appoint a replacement for Judge Bellet, another member of the same Tribunal. Art 13 (which governs replacement of arbitrators upon resignation) invokes 'the procedure ... in articles 6 to 9 that was applicable to the appointment ... of the arbitrator being replaced', which in the case of Judge Bellet meant Art 7(3), since Judge Bellet was a presiding arbitrator in a three-member chamber of the Iran-US Claims Tribunal. Thus, the method for appointing Judge Bellet's successor was that the two party-appointed arbitrators should agree on a successor, but when they failed to agree within 30 days, the successor was to be chosen by an appointing authority. It was arguable that either party could then seek designation of a new appointing authority for this purpose (not least because, pursuant to Art 7(3)'s cross-reference to Art 6, it could be said under Art 6(2) that the existing appointing authority, Judge Moons, had not 'been agreed upon by the parties'). As a precaution against such arguments, the Secretary-General redesignated Judge Moons as appointing authority. Judge Moons' redesignation put to rest any thought of designating a second, competing appointing authority.

[145] This has happened, for example, at the Iran-US Claims Tribunal; see Baker and Davis (n 62) 19 (noting that in 1988 Iranian and US arbitrators finally agreed on presiding arbitrators for Chambers One and Three of the Tribunal just before the appointing authority was to announce his selections).

party's order of preference among the remaining names),[146] and the appointing authority then appoints the sole arbitrator from among the remaining names 'and in accordance with the [parties'] order of preference'. However, Art 6(3)(d) contains an escape clause, allowing the appointing authority to appoint the sole arbitrator simply according to its discretion, 'if for any reason the appointment cannot be made according to this procedure'.[147]

16.87 Article 6(4) requires that the appointing authority take into account 'such considerations as are likely to secure the appointment of an independent and impartial arbitrator' (reflecting Art 10's language) and also directs the authority to 'take into account . . . the advisability of appointing an arbitrator of a nationality other than the nationalities of the parties'.

16.88 At present, the Rules contain no provision regarding the potential legal liability or immunity of an arbitrator, the appointing authority, or the institution designating the appointing authority in the performance of their respective duties. The UNCITRAL Working Group has proposed addition of an Article addressing this issue, which is discussed in para 16.397, *infra.*

(2) Contemplated revisions

16.89 The primary change that the Working Group intends to recommend in Art 6 is (i) to relocate the provisions relating to the designation of the appointing authority in Arts 6, 7 and 8 to a new Article (to be placed between the current Arts 4 and 5 and provisionally denominated 'Art 4bis'), in order to encourage parties to make such designations at an early stage. One result of this reorganization will be (ii) a reduced text in the revised Art 6, which will also be reworded to clarify its operation in multi-party proceedings.

16.90 (2.1) **Creation of a new Article relating to the appointing authority** One of the 'main lines of revision' recommended to the UNCITRAL Secretariat in advance of the Rules revision project was that provisions relating to designation of the appointing authority that are set forth separately in Art 6 (appointment of sole arbitrators) and Art 7 (appointment of arbitrators in three-member tribunals) be consolidated in one Article 'for simplicity and consistency'.[148] A new 'Art 4bis' that the Working Group recommends inserting into the Rules after the current Art 4 implements this recommendation.[149] The new Article would provide that, if the appointing authority has not already been agreed upon, any party 'may at any time propose' to all other parties names of institutions or persons, one of whom would serve as appointing authority and, if all parties do not agree on an appointing

---

[146] See Baker and Davis (n 62) 28 ('it may be supposed that a party who does not return his list on time accepts all the names on the list').

[147] See *id* 28–9 (noting one instance in which Iran and the United States managed to delete all the names on the list and that in subsequent appointments the same appointing authority either abandoned the list procedure or severely curtailed it).

[148] Paulsson and Petrochilos (n 39) 7.

[149] See *Report of WGII's 49th session* (15–19 September 2008) paras 46, 51–6, UN Doc A/CN.9/665, recording the Working Group's adoption, with minor revisions, of the draft Art 4bis set forth in the *Note by the Secretariat* (6 August 2008) para 16, UN Doc A/CN.9/WG.II/WP.151. See also *Note by the Secretariat* (3 August 2007) paras 29–33, UN Doc A/CN.9/WG.II/WP.147, and *Report of WGII on the work of its 46th session* (5–9 February 2007) paras 69–78, UN Doc A/CN.9/619 (summarizing earlier discussion of purposes of proposed Art 4bis).

authority within 30 days of receiving such a proposal, any party may request the Secretary-General of the PCA to designate the appointing authority.[150] A principal purpose of this restructuring is to encourage parties to put an appointing authority in place as soon as possible. Moreover, by consolidating provisions relating to the appointing authority in a separate Article, the revised Rules would, for example, eliminate the uncertainty as to whether the Rules require a party to propose candidates for appointing authority and candidates for sole arbitrator together.

The new Art 4bis will also clarify that the PCA Secretary-General's assigned role as designating authority under the Rules does not preclude parties from agreeing upon the Secretary-General to serve as their appointing authority.[151] The Working Group has also debated whether to go further and to provide in Art 4bis that, where the parties have not agreed on an appointing authority, the Secretary-General of the PCA should act as the appointing authority by default.[152] Ultimately, '[t]he view was . . . expressed [in Working Group II] that . . . the matter was of [a] political nature and could only be settled by the Commission'.[153] When the Commission then took up this issue it voiced several concerns and concluded that, '[i]n light of those policy principles, . . . the UNCITRAL Arbitration Rules should not contain a default rule, to the effect that one institution would be singled out as the default appointing authority'.[154] **16.91**

The proposed new Article would also incorporate the provision in Art 6(2) and its counterpart in Art 7(2)(b) that authorize a party to seek the Secretary-General's designation of a new appointing authority when the existing authority refuses to act or fails to appoint an arbitrator within a fixed period after a party has asked it to do so.[155] The wording of these existing provisions would be modified in three ways. First, the new provision will refer simply to the refusal or failure by 'the appointing authority' to act, thus removing the uncertainty arising, eg from Art 6(2)'s reference to an appointing authority 'agreed upon by the parties.' Secondly, a reference will be added to the possible refusal or failure by the appointing to exercise the new power that is proposed to be given to it (under Art 39) to determine arbitrators' fees.[156] In case of such refusal or failure, the PCA Secretary-General, upon a party's request, will simply make the fee determination itself, rather than designating a new appointing authority. Finally, whereas under current Art 6(2) the appointing authority is given 60 days in which to appoint a sole arbitrator (which, by cross-reference, also governs appointment of a tribunal's presiding arbitrator under Art 7(3)), the revised **16.92**

[150] *Report of WGII on the work of its 49th session* (15–19 September 2008) paras 51–2, UN Doc A/CN.9/665 (approving draft of paras (1) and (2) of new Art '4bis', as set forth in UN Doc A/CN.9/WG.II/WP.151, para 16).

[151] *ibid.*

[152] See *Report of WGII on the work of its 46th session* (5–9 February 2007) paras 71–4, UN Doc A/CN.9/619.

[153] *Report of WGII on the work of its 49th session* (15–19 September 2008) para 50, UN Doc A/CN.9/665. For further discussion of this role of the Commission in the Rules revision process, see para 16.22, *supra*.

[154] *Report of UNCITRAL on the work of its 42nd session* (29 June–17 July 2009) para 297, UN Doc A/64/17.

[155] *Report of WGII on the work of its 49th session* (15–19 September 2008) para 53, UN Doc A/CN.9/665 (approving draft of para (3) of new Art '4bis,' as set forth in UN Doc A/CN.9/WG.II/WP.151, para 16).

[156] *ibid*; see discussion of the Working Group's proposed revisions in Art 39, at paras 16.377 *et seq infra*.

language in proposed Art 4bis would reduce this to 30 days.[157] Article 6(4) would also be transferred to the new Art '4bis'.[158]

16.93 (2.2) **Revised scope of Article 6** The creation of the new Art '4bis' will reduce the text of Art 6 to only two paragraphs.[159] The first paragraph will combine elements of the current Art 6(1) and (2), providing simply that if all parties have agreed that there will be a sole arbitrator but have not agreed on his or her identity within 30 days after one party notifies the others of its proposed candidate(s), then the arbitrator will be appointed, upon a party's request, by the appointing authority. This streamlined version of Art 6(1) and (2) again removes any suggestion that a party's candidates for sole arbitrator must or should be combined with a proposal of candidates for appointing authority. Another effect of this rewording may be that Art 6 would no longer authorize a party immediately to request the PCA Secretary-General to designate an appointing authority once the parties fail to agree on an arbitrator within 30 days. Rather, it appears that the designation of an appointing authority will always follow its own procedure under the new Art 4bis, beginning with one party's proposal of one or more candidates for appointing authority, as described three paragraphs above.

16.94 The second paragraph of revised Art 6 will essentially follow the current text of Art 6(3), with one significant wording change.[160] Whereas the current wording of Art 6(1), (2) and (3)(a) reflects an assumption that each arbitration contains only two parties, the UNCITRAL Working Group proposes new wording that applies equally to two-party or multi-party arbitration.[161]

Article 7

1. **If three arbitrators are to be appointed, each party shall appoint one arbitrator. The two arbitrators thus appointed shall choose the third arbitrator who will act as the presiding arbitrator of the tribunal.**
2. **If within thirty days after the receipt of a party's notification of the appointment of an arbitrator the other party has not notified the first party of the arbitrator he has appointed:**
   (*a*) **The first party may request the appointing authority previously designated by the parties to appoint the second arbitrator; or**
   (*b*) **If no such authority has been previously designated by the parties, or if the appointing authority previously designated refuses to act or fails to appoint the arbitrator within thirty days after receipt of a party's request therefor, the first party may request the Secretary-General of the Permanent Court of Arbitration at The Hague to designate the appointing authority. The first party may then request the appointing authority so**

157 See *Report by WGII's 49th Session* (15–19 September 2008) para 53, UN Doc A/CN.9/665 (approving draft of para (3) of new Art '4bis,' set forth in *Note by the Secretariat*, UN Doc A/CN.9/WG.II/WP.151, para 16).

158 *ibid* at para 56.

159 *Report of WGII on the work of its 49th session* (15–19 September 2008) para 68, UN Doc A/CN.9/665 (recording the Working Group's adoption with minor edits of the draft revised text of Art 6 set forth in *Note by the Secretariat*, UN Doc A/CN.9/WG.II/WP.151 para 18).

160 *ibid.*

161 *ibid.*, recording the Working Group's approval of the revised draft of Art 6 set forth in *Note by the Secretariat*, UN Doc A/CN.9/WG.II/WP.151 para 17 (modifying, for example, Art 6(1)'s provision that 'either party may propose to the other' names of possible sole arbitrators to refer instead to the 'receipt by all parties of a proposal for the appointment of a sole arbitrator').

designated to appoint the second arbitrator. In either case, the appointing authority may exercise its discretion in appointing the arbitrator.

3. **If within thirty days after the appointment of the second arbitrator the two arbitrators have not agreed on the choice of the presiding arbitrator, the presiding arbitrator shall be appointed by an appointing authority in the same way as a sole arbitrator would be appointed under article 6.**

(1) Commentary on current text

Article 7 proceeds from the premise that the arbitration will have a three-member tribunal, pursuant either to the parties' agreement or to the operation of Art 5, which provides for a three-member tribunal when the parties have not agreed within the time limit upon the number of arbitrators. Article 7 describes how such a tribunal will be constituted and, like Art 6, addresses several aspects of this process: (i) the parties' own power to appoint two of the arbitrators; (ii) selection of the third, presiding arbitrator by joint agreement of the first two arbitrators; and (iii) the appointment by an appointing authority of any arbitrator who is not appointed according to the procedures just outlined. **16.95**

(1.1) Each party's power to appoint one arbitrator Article 7(1) establishes a rule for constituting three-member tribunals that the UNCITRAL drafters regarded as 'customary'[162] in international arbitration, namely, that each party appoints one of the arbitrators and these two arbitrators jointly select a third, presiding arbitrator. Pursuant to Art 7(2), this procedure for constituting a three-member tribunal is set in motion by one party's notification to 'the other party' that it has appointed an arbitrator. Article 3(4) invites the claimant to include such a notification in its notice of arbitration but does not require that it do so. Thus, there is no time limit within which the first arbitral appointment must occur, and the first appointment can (though it would not normally) be made by the respondent rather than the claimant. **16.96**

Pursuant to Art 7(2), once a party receives notice that the other party has appointed an arbitrator, the party so notified has 30 days in which to notify the first party that it has also appointed an arbitrator. If the second party does not give such a notice within 30 days, then the first party may request an appointing authority to appoint the second arbitrator. **16.97**

Article 7 does not impose any limitation on the qualifications or characteristics of party-appointed arbitrators, except that such arbitrators must meet the standards of independence and impartiality implicitly set forth in Arts 9 (arbitrators' duty to disclose) and 10 (challenge of arbitrators). **16.98**

(1.2) Appointment of the presiding arbitrator Once the second arbitrator has been appointed—either by the second party or by an appointing authority at the request of the first party—the two arbitrators that have been appointed are to agree on a third, presiding arbitrator. Article 7(3) provides that the two arbitrators must reach this agreement within 30 days after the second arbitrator's appointment and that, if no agreement is reached by that deadline, the presiding arbitrator 'shall be appointed by an appointing authority'. Once again, no restriction is placed upon the first two arbitrators' choice of a presiding **16.99**

[162] Sanders (n 28) 186.

arbitrator, other than that he or she must meet the requirements of independence and impartiality implicitly set forth in Arts 9 and 10.

16.100 It is normal practice for party-appointed arbitrators to keep the parties informed of their progress toward agreeing on selection of a presiding arbitrator.[163] Moreover, quite apart from any procedural considerations, it has been stated that 'it is generally accepted that a party-appointed arbitrator consults with the lawyers of the designating party about the acceptability of potential candidates for the third arbitrator (cf Sect. 5(2) of the IBA Rules of Ethics for International Arbitrators of 1986)'.[164]

16.101 **(1.3) The appointing authority's appointment of arbitrators not appointed by the foregoing procedures** If the second party fails to notify the first party of its appointment of a second arbitrator within 30 days after having been notified of the first arbitrator's appointment, and if no appointing authority 'has been previously designated by the parties', Art 7(2)(b) provides that the party seeking appointment may ask the PCA Secretary-General to designate an appointing authority. (The requesting party does not have to delay this request by seeking first to agree with the second party on an appointing authority.[165]) The same party may also request the Secretary-General to designate an appointing authority if an authority 'previously designated' either refuses to appoint the second arbitrator or fails to do so within 30 days of a request that it do so. The fact that this party may seek designation of an appointing authority if there is none 'previously designated *by the parties*' could be read as authorizing designation of a new appointing authority even if one has already been designated by the PCA Secretary-General. However, as has already been noted with respect to similar language in Art 6, it is unlikely that the drafters intended such a result.[166]

16.102 If the 30-day deadline for the first two arbitrators' appointment of a presiding arbitrator expires without their having agreed on such an appointment and if no appointing authority has yet been designated in the case, then either party may immediately request the PCA Secretary-General to appoint one. Once again, it appears that the requesting party need not delay the request to seek possible agreement with the other party on an appointing authority.[167] If that is so, any discussion by the parties of possible candidates for appointing

---

[163] Baker and Davis (n 62) 24.

[164] Bühler, M., 'Appointment of Arbitrators in Bi-Party or Multi-Party Proceedings,' in Zuberbühler, Müller & Habegger (eds) (n 64) 78.

[165] Sanders (n 28) 186–7; see also para 16.82, *supra*, regarding the similar construction of the appointment mechanism under Art 6.

[166] See Baker and Davis (n 62) 29–31. As has been explained with respect to the similar language in Art 6(2), the likely reason why Art 7(2)(b) refers to an appointing authority 'previously designated by the parties' is that appointment of a second arbitrator occurs at such an early stage of the proceeding that no circumstance could yet have occasioned designation of an appointing authority by the PCA Secretary-General. However, questions can arise when the appointment procedure set forth in Art 7(2)(b) is applied at a later stage of the proceedings (see eg Art 13, cross-referencing the procedure, *inter alia*, in Art 7(2) for replacement of arbitrators who have died or resigned). See n 144 and accompanying text.

[167] Baker and Davis (n 62) 24; Sanders (n 28) 187. Art 7(3) provides that 'the presiding arbitrator shall be appointed by an appointing authority in the same way as a sole arbitrator would be appointed under Article 6'. It will be recalled that, under Art 6, a party may ask the Secretary-General of the PCA to designate an appointing authority if 'no appointing authority has been agreed upon by the parties'. As discussed, *supra*, in nn 139 and 144 and accompanying text, it is unlikely that the drafters intended the phrase just quoted to permit

authority will have to occur while the 30-day period for the first two arbitrators' selection of the presiding arbitrator is running. This is one reason why, as just noted, each of the arbitrators usually keeps the party that appointed them apprised of the progress of discussions concerning appointment of a presiding arbitrator.[168]

Once a party has requested an appointing authority to appoint either the second party-appointed arbitrator or the presiding arbitrator, the appointing authority has 30 days or 60 days, respectively, to make the appointment. If the appointing authority fails to appoint within the relevant deadline, a party may ask the PCA Secretary-General to designate a new appointing authority. The reason that the appointing authority is given 60 days, rather than 30 days, to appoint a presiding arbitrator is that Art 7(3) obliges the arbitrator to apply the list procedure set forth in Art 6 in appointing a presiding arbitrator (subject to Art 6(3)'s authorization for an appointing authority to disregard the list method 'in its discretion'), and the list procedure is assumed to take longer.[169] **16.103**

Article 7 again places no restriction on the characteristics of an arbitrator chosen by an appointing authority, except that the requirements of independence and impartiality implicit in Arts 9 and 10 must be met and, pursuant to Art 6 as cross-referenced in Art 7(3), an appointing authority shall consider 'the advisability of appointing' a presiding arbitrator 'of a nationality other than the nationalities of the parties'.[170] Moreover, if the presiding arbitrator is selected according to the list procedure, the appointing authority may not appoint someone whose name was deleted from the list by one of the parties. It has been observed that party-appointed arbitrators are often reluctant to put forward candidates for presiding arbitrator who are preferred by the party that appointed them for fear that, if the arbitrators fail to reach agreement and the selection then devolves upon an appointing authority that uses the list procedure, each party will then strike off the list any person previously proposed by the opposing party's appointed arbitrator.[171] **16.104**

(2) Contemplated revisions

The Working Group intends to propose two sorts of revisions for Art 7. As already noted in discussing Art 6, the Working Group (i) intends to move those provisions in Art 7(2) pertaining to designation of and actions by an appointing authority to a new Art '4bis', where they would be consolidated with similar provisions in current Arts 6 and 8. The Working Group also intends (ii) to add another article, immediately following current Art 7, addressing special problems that arise in selecting tribunals when there are multiple **16.105**

---

designation of a second appointing authority where one has already been designated by the Secretary-General but not 'agreed upon by the parties'. Similarly, the 60-day deadline that Art 6(2) imposes for the appointing authority's appointment of a sole arbitrator (and that Art 7(3) incorporates as a deadline for such appointment of a presiding arbitrator) literally only applies to appointing authorities 'agreed upon' rather than designated by the Secretary-General, but again it is extremely unlikely that this distinction was intended by the drafters and it has been suggested the distinction should be ignored. See Baker and Davis (n 62) 26–7.

[168] Baker and Davis (n 62) 24.

[169] Sanders (n 28) 187. The Working Group intends nonetheless to reduce this period to 30 days, so that there would be a uniform period for an appointing authority's appointment of any arbitrator. See discussion regarding revision of Art 6, para 16.92 *supra*.

[170] Art 6(4).

[171] See eg Caron, Caplan and Pellonpää (n 61) 181.

claimants or respondents or when the parties have agreed to a number of arbitrators other than one or three.

16.106 **(2.1) Creation of a new Article relating to the appointing authority** The Working Group intends to consolidate provisions relating to the appointing authority that are presently spread over Arts 6, 7 and 8 in a new Article provisionally identified as 4bis. Thus, sub-para (b) of Art 7(2) would be deleted and its substance would be incorporated into the new Art 4 bis.[172] This contemplated rewording of Art 7(2) may change its meaning in at least one respect. As noted, Art 7(2) has been construed as permitting the party that first appoints an arbitrator to request the PCA Secretary-General to designate an appointing authority, as soon as the second party fails to give notice of the second arbitrator's appointment within 30 days of the first arbitrator's appointment. By contrast, it appears that under the new Art 4bis, the procedure for designating an appointing authority will always follow the steps set forth in that Article, according to which the designation process always begins with the parties having 30 days to agree on an appointing authority after one party's proposal of one or more candidates for that position.[173]

16.107 **(2.2) New Article addressing appointment of tribunals in arbitrations with multiple parties or an unusual number of arbitrators** As has been noted, one general revision that the Working Group intends to make throughout the Rules is to replace language that assumes there are only two parties in an arbitration with language that is consistent with the possibility of multiple parties. Multi-party arbitration has substantially increased in recent years; the ICC, for example, has reported that nearly a third of the cases filed with its International Court of Arbitration now have more than two parties.[174] However, the presence of multiple parties can create special difficulties in the selection of a three-member tribunal. Since Art 7(1) provides that 'each party shall appoint one arbitrator' and further provides that this process should yield only two arbitrators who will then jointly select the third arbitrator, this process must obviously be adapted where there are more than two parties (ie two or more claimants or respondents). The Working Group recommends adopting two provisions that will form part of a new Article provisionally designated 'Art 7bis'.

16.108 The first new provision would establish the principle that, where there are multiple parties, unless all parties agree otherwise, the multiple claimants jointly or the multiple respondents jointly shall appoint one arbitrator.[175] This proposal follows the approach of other major arbitration rules in adapting to multi-party arbitral appointments.[176]

16.109 A further provision to be incorporated in Art 7bis would address the problem that can arise if multiple claimants or respondents fail to agree on one arbitrator. In that case, the provision

[172] See *Report of WGII on the work of its 49th session* (15–19 September 2008) paras 17, 69, UN Doc A/CN.9/665, recording the Working Group's adoption of the revised text set forth in *Note by the Secretariat*, UN Doc A/CN.9/WG.II/WP.151 para 18.

[173] See para 16.90, *supra*.

[174] *ICC Arb Bull* vol 19/no 1 (2008) 8 (stating that in 2007, 31% of ICC cases involved more than two parties).

[175] See *Report of WGII on the work of its 49th session* (15–19 September 2008) paras 17, 71, UN Doc A/CN.9/665, recording the Working Group's adoption of the text of Art 7bis as set forth in *Note by the Secretariat*, UN Doc A/CN.9/WG.II/WP.151 para 19.

[176] See eg ICC Rules Art 10(1) (1998); Swiss Rules Art 8(4) (2004).

would allow the appointing authority, at the request of any party, to constitute the entire tribunal, which would include the power to revoke any appointment already made and to 'appoint or reappoint each of the arbitrators'. This proposed provision, which again resembles clauses in other major arbitration rules,[177] has been deemed necessary to respond to a decision more than 15 years ago by France's highest court, in the so-called *Dutco* case.[178] The *Cour de cassation* in *Dutco* sustained the respondents' attack on the method by which an ICC arbitral tribunal had been constituted where the claimant had named one arbitrator but the two respondents initially declined to agree on the second arbitrator and ultimately made a joint appointment only 'under protest,' after the ICC stated it would otherwise appoint the arbitrator for them.[179] The French high court held that a tribunal so constituted violated the parties' right of equality.[180] It is now generally believed that an appropriate way to uphold the principle of equality in circumstances like those that arose in *Dutco* is for the administering institution or appointing authority to appoint all members of the tribunal.[181]

The need to adapt tribunals' appointment procedure to multi-party arbitrations while avoiding the *Dutco* problem was one of the 'main lines of revision' in the UNCITRAL Rules identified to the UNCITRAL Secretariat at the outset of the revision project.[182] The solution proposed in Art 7bis contains one feature not always specified in other rules, allowing the appointing authority to 'reappoint' an arbitrator. The Working Group believed that 'the appointing authority should have the discretion to appoint an arbitrator already appointed by a party that was subsequently deprived of its right to appoint'.[183] **16.110**

A final provision that the Working Group intends to add to the new Art 7bis would address the appointment procedure if parties choose a number of arbitrators other than one or three. Parties usually prefer one or three arbitrators, but the Working Group recognizes that the Rules should accommodate parties who agree on a different number. In such cases, proposed Art 7bis provides that the arbitrators would be chosen 'according to the method agreed upon by the parties', but if that method is not followed the entire tribunal would be appointed by the appointing authority, under the same default provision intended to cover the *Dutco* circumstances.[184] **16.111**

Article 8

1 **When an appointing authority is requested to appoint an arbitrator pursuant to article 6 or article 7, the party which makes the request shall send to the appointing authority a copy of the notice of arbitration, a copy of the contract out of or in relation to which the dispute has arisen and a copy of the arbitration agreement if it is not contained in the contract.**

---

177 See eg ICC Rules Art 10(2) (1998); Swiss Rules Art 8(5) (2004); AAA ICDR Rules Art 6(5) (2008).

178 *Sociétés BKMI et Siemens c/ société Dutco*, Cour de cassation (7 January 1992) *Rev arb* (1992) 470.

179 The background to, and consequences of, the *Dutco* case are described in Derains and Schwartz (n 63) 177–84.

180 *Sociétés BKMI et Siemens c/ société Dutco*, Cour de cassation (7 January 1992) *Rev arb* (1992) 470, 472.

181 See Paulsson and Petrochilos (n 39) 7; Derains and Schwartz (n 63) 183.

182 Paulsson and Petrochilos (n 39) 7.

183 *Report of WGII on the work of its 45th session* (11–15 September 2006) para 63, UN Doc A/CN.9/614; see also *Report of WGII on the work of its 46th session* (5–9 February 2007) para 91, UN Doc A/CN.9/619.

184 See *Report of WGII on the work of its 49th session* (15–19 September 2008) paras 17, 71, UN Doc A/CN.9/665, recording the Working Group's adoption of the text of Art 7bis as set forth in *Note by the Secretariat*, UN Doc A/CN.9/WG.II/WP.151 para 19.

The appointing authority may require from either party such information as it deems necessary to fulfil its function.

2 Where the names of one or more persons are proposed for appointment as arbitrators, their full names, addresses and nationalities shall be indicated, together with a description of their qualifications.

(1) Commentary on current text

16.112 Article 8 seeks to facilitate the appointing authority's appointment of qualified arbitrators by requiring (i) that the appointing authority be supplied with information concerning the nature of the claims and any related information it deems necessary; and (ii) that information about proposed arbitrators' identity and qualifications be disclosed at the time their appointment is proposed.

16.113 **(1.1) Providing relevant information to the appointing authority** Article 8(1) provides that any party seeking appointment of an arbitrator pursuant to Arts 6 or 7 must give the appointing authority copies of the notice of arbitration, of the contract to which the dispute relates and (if not contained in the contract) of the arbitration agreement. The provision further specifies that the appointing authority can 'require from either party' any other information it 'deems necessary to fulfill its function'. It was believed that this would assist the appointing authority in appointing an arbitrator 'who was well qualified to hear the particular dispute'.[185]

16.114 **(1.2) Providing information about proposed arbitrators** Article 8(2) requires that, whenever 'the names of one or more persons are proposed for appointment,' information concerning each prospective arbitrator's qualifications, nationality and contact details shall be provided. The obligation to provide such information when proposing an arbitrator candidate can fall on parties, on arbitrators, or on the appointing authority. A party may propose to other parties 'one or more persons' to serve as arbitrator when seeking agreement on a sole arbitrator under Art 6(1) and arbitrators similarly propose names under Art 7(3). Or, an appointing authority may propose candidates in using the list procedure or in otherwise selecting a sole or presiding arbitrator under Arts 6(3) and 7(3).

(2) Contemplated revisions

16.115 The Working Group intends (i) to transfer a revised Art 8(1) to the new Art 4bis that, as previously described,[186] will consolidate provisions from current Arts 6 to 8 that deal with the selection of and actions by the appointing authority. The Working Group (ii) also intends to delete Art 8(2) from the Rules.

16.116 **(2.1) Creation of a new Article relating to the appointing authority** As noted in discussing revisions in Arts 6 and 7, the Working Group intends to add a new 'Art 4bis' that will consolidate a number of general provisions concerning the appointing authority. A revised version of Art 8(1) is slated for inclusion in new Art 4bis; it would require a party requesting appointment of an arbitrator under Arts 6, 7, 7bis and 13 to provide the appointing authority with not only the notice of arbitration but also, 'if it exists, any response to

[185] *Report of the Committee of the Whole II* (n 55) para 43.
[186] See paras 16.89 to 16.92 and 16.106.

the notice of arbitration'.[187] This provision will no longer require the party to furnish any relevant contract or (if separate) the arbitration agreement. This reflects, in part, the expected effect of a proposed revision in Art 3(3), which would require a notice of arbitration to contain an 'identification of' (and not just 'a reference to,' as Art 3(3) currently provides) the arbitration agreement and 'any contract or other legal instrument out of or in relation to which the dispute arises'. If a claimant 'identifies' the arbitration agreement and any relevant contract without actually submitting these documents with the notice of arbitration, the appointing authority may of course require their submission pursuant to that part of (relocated) Art 8(1) that will continue to authorize an appointing authority to obtain from the parties any other information it deems necessary.[188] Article 8(1), as relocated, will also be revised to require that whenever an appointing authority exercises 'its functions under these Rules . . . it shall give the parties an opportunity to present their views in any manner it considers appropriate'.[189] (This would apply to all appointing authority functions—including (for example) to any determination by such an authority as to arbitrators' fees, pursuant to the proposed revision of Art 39.[190]) A further new sentence will also require that any communications between a party and the appointing authority or the PCA Secretary-General be sent as well to all other parties.[191] At present, Art 15(3) only requires that each party send to the other party copies of all communications with the arbitral tribunal.

(2.2) Deletion of Article 8(2) Although Art 8(2) was also initially proposed for inclusion in the new Art 4bis, the Working Group initially revised this provision to require that the information about proposed arbitrators be supplied by the candidates themselves,[192] rather than by the appointing authority, and then deleted the provision altogether.[193] **16.117**

CHALLENGE OF ARBITRATORS (Articles 9 to 12)

Article 9

A prospective arbitrator shall disclose to those who approach him in connexion with his possible appointment any circumstances likely to give rise to justifiable doubts as to his impartiality or independence. An arbitrator, once appointed or chosen, shall disclose such circumstances to the parties unless they have already been informed by him of these circumstances.

---

[187] See *Report of WGII on the work of its 49th session* (15–19 September 2008) paras 17, 55, UN Doc A/CN.9/665, recording the Working Group's approval of Art 4 bis(5) as set forth in *Note by the Secretariat*, UN Doc A/CN.9/WG.II/WP.151 para 15.

[188] See *ibid*, paras 17, 54, UN Doc A/CN.9/665, recording the Working Group's decision to make only one unrelated change in the draft of Art 4 bis(4) set forth in *Note by the Secretariat*, UN Doc A/CN.9/WG.II/WP.151 para 15.

[189] *ibid.*

[190] See commentary on Art 39, *infra.*

[191] *ibid.*

[192] *Report of WGII on the work of its 46th session* (5–9 February 2007) para 78, UN Doc A/CN.9/619; this decision was implemented in the *Note by the Secretariat*, UN Doc A/CN.9/WG.II/WP.147 para 33.

[193] See draft set forth in August 2008 *Note by the Secretariat*, UN Doc A/CN.9/WG.II/WP.151 para 15 (proposing new text of Art 4 bis(5), deleting the last sentence that appeared in WP.147). The August 2008 draft reflected the Working Group discussions but also 'comments received by the Secretariat at the occasion of conferences and meetings organized to discuss the revision of the Rules'.' *ibid*, para 3. The revised Art 4 bis(5) was adopted without change. See *Report of WGII on the work of its 49th session* (15–19 September 2008) paras 17, 55, UN Doc A/CN.9/665.

(1) Commentary on current text

16.118 Article 9 accomplishes two objectives: it (i) requires disclosure by a potential or appointed arbitrator of facts 'likely to give rise to justifiable doubts as to his impartiality or independence'; and (ii) specifies when and to whom such disclosure must be made.

16.119 (1.1) **Disclosure of circumstances implicating impartiality or independence** The purpose of requiring disclosure is not only to ensure selection of arbitrators who can resolve—and who will appear to resolve—a dispute objectively but also to force parties to bring challenges at the outset of an arbitration, to avoid subsequent disruption and delay.[194] Parties that do not bring a challenge based on facts disclosed under Art 9 will be estopped from raising a challenge on those grounds later, either pursuant to Art 10(2)'s prohibition on challenges by parties to arbitrators they appoint based on facts known before appointment, or pursuant to Art 11(1)'s requirement that any other party bring a challenge based on such facts within 15 days of an arbitrator's appointment or of the date when the circumstances 'became known to that party'. This also prevents a party from strategically deploying a challenge only after the outcome of an arbitration becomes clear.[195]

16.120 The composite standard for disclosure—'*likely* to give rise to *justifiable* doubts'—combines both subjective and objective elements. The requirement that doubts be *justifiable* is objective, as has been made clear in the context of challenges adjudicated under this standard, pursuant to Art 10. Thus, an arbitrator need not reveal all circumstances that could be alleged to reflect bias but only those facts provoking *justifiable* doubts as to bias. On the other hand, the determination whether certain circumstances are *likely* to raise such doubts will necessarily involve a subjective element, since it is the arbitrator who must evaluate the 'likely' impact of certain circumstances.[196] This is not surprising since Art 9 was drafted from the premise that, 'No one knows better than the arbitrator himself whether such circumstances exist'.[197]

16.121 Article 9 is silent as to any consequence of an arbitrator's failure to disclose circumstances that meet the standard for disclosure. However, as is discussed below in the context of Art 10(1), it may be argued that a failure to disclose, in itself, evidences justifiable doubts as to impartiality or independence and thus supports a challenge.

16.122 (1.2) **When and to whom disclosure must be made** Article 9 expressly requires disclosure in two circumstances. First, a person who is approached about possibly serving as an arbitrator 'shall disclose to those who approach him'. The recipient of such disclosure would thus be either one or more parties or arbitrators or an appointing authority. In addition to disclosure by 'a prospective arbitrator', Art 9 requires disclosure by an arbitrator 'once appointed or chosen' unless 'the parties . . . have already been informed by him'. At a

194 *Commentary on Revised draft Rules* (n 90) 170 (commentary to draft Art 9(3)); see also Caron, Caplan and Pellonpää (n 61) 201.

195 UNCITRAL Committee of the Whole II, *Summary Record of 3rd Meeting* (13 April 1976) para 25, UN Doc A/CN.9/IX/C.2/SR.3.

196 See eg Baker and Davis (n 62) 50 ('whether to disclose is left to the arbitrator's good faith discretion').

197 See *Preliminary draft Rules* (n 18) para 3 of 'Commentary' on draft Art 8, *reprinted in* (1975) VI *UNCITRAL Ybk* 163, 171.

minimum, then, a person who has disclosed certain circumstances after being approached by a party about possible appointment must disclose the same circumstances to any other party if he or she is subsequently appointed as an arbitrator.

Article 9 does not specify whether its two disclosure duties are continuous. The phrasing of the first obligation is consistent with the existence of an ongoing duty, since it describes the obligation in terms of a particular relationship—the one between 'a prospective arbitrator' and 'those who approach him'. Arguably, such a duty persists as long as the relationship persists. Some commentators have expressed the firm view that this duty is continuous until the decision as to appointment is made.[198] **16.123**

The wording of the second obligation is more ambiguous. On the one hand, the duty is framed as arising at a particular moment: 'once appointed or chosen' the arbitrator 'shall disclose such circumstances'. When read in context, this appears to refer to a disclosure to additional persons of what has already been disclosed prior to the arbitrator's appointment. The *travaux préparatoires* are also ambiguous, and commentators have construed them divergently.[199] However, several commentators have concluded unequivocally that the duty to disclose is continuous, based either on this same drafting history[200] or on that history combined with the underlying policy of the rule.[201] This view was also espoused by at least one arbitrator on the Iran-US Claims Tribunal.[202] **16.124**

(2) Contemplated revisions

The Working Group intends (i) to modify the language of Art 9 to clarify the continuous nature of the disclosure obligation; and (ii) to add two sample disclosure statements that a prospective or appointed arbitrator can use in responding to his or her disclosure obligations under Rule 9. **16.125**

(2.1) The ongoing duty to disclose The Working Group will recommend a rewording of Art 9 to clarify that the disclosure obligation continues for the duration of an arbitrator's service in an arbitral case.[203] The revised second sentence of this Article would state that an arbitrator has a duty to disclose 'from the time of his or her appointment and throughout the arbitral proceedings' and that such disclosure should be made both to the parties and to any other arbitrators.[204] **16.126**

(2.2) Model statements of disclosure The Working Group will recommend that Art 9 be supplemented by two model statements that an arbitrator could use in responding to his **16.127**

---

[198] Caron, Caplan and Pellonpää (n 61) 201–2.

[199] *Compare* van Hof (n 55) 58 n 97 ('the *travaux* do not explicitly support this view' that the arbitrator has a continuous obligation of disclosure) *with* Caron, Caplan and Pellonpää (n 61) 201 ('such a continuing duty is indicated in the drafting history of the Rules').

[200] Baker and Davis (n 62) 46.

[201] Caron, Caplan and Pellonpää (n 61) 201.

[202] See *Frederica Lincoln Riahi v Islamic Republic of Iran* (DEC 133-485-1, 17 November 2004; Dissenting Opinion of Judge Charles N. Brower) 6, *reprinted in Mealey's Int'l Arb Rep*, vol 19, issue 12, section C.

[203] See *Report of WGII on the work of its 49th session* (15–19 September 2008) paras 17, 74, UN Doc A/CN.9/665, recording the Working Group's adoption with further amendment of the draft new text of Art 9 set forth in *Note by the Secretariat*, UN Doc A/CN.9/WG.II/WP.151 para 22.

[204] *ibid.*

or her disclosure obligations. Each statement will begin by affirming the arbitrator's impartiality and independence and the fact that he or she 'intend[s] to remain so'. Thereafter, the first model statement will affirm that the arbitrator has no circumstances to disclose that would likely give rise to justifiable doubts as to impartiality or independence, while the second model statement would contain a disclosure of any past relationships with the parties or any other circumstances 'that might cause a party to question my impartiality or independence' as well as a statement by the arbitrator that he or she does not believe such circumstances are likely to give rise to justifiable doubts regarding such impartiality or independence. Both statements would conclude with a sentence reaffirming the arbitrator's continuous duty to make disclosure during the arbitration.[205]

Article 10

1 **Any arbitrator may be challenged if circumstances exist that give rise to justifiable doubts as to the arbitrator's impartiality or independence.**

2 **A party may challenge the arbitrator appointed by him only for reasons of which he becomes aware after the appointment has been made.**

(1) Commentary on current text

16.128 Article 10 achieves two purposes: It (i) sets forth the substantive basis for challenging an arbitrator; and (ii) limits the ability of a party that has appointed an arbitrator to challenge that arbitrator.

16.129 (1.1) **The method and substantive basis for challenge** Article 10 establishes the same standard for challenging an arbitrator that already guides the arbitrator's duty to disclose: the existence of circumstances giving rise to 'justifiable doubts' as to impartiality or independence. The disclosure requirement is nonetheless broader since Art 9 requires disclosure of all circumstances '*likely*' to give rise to justifiable doubts, whereas a challenge will be upheld under Art 10 only if an appointing authority finds that circumstances *do* give rise to such doubts.

16.130 The contours of Art 10 and of its substantive standard have been elaborated in several publicly disclosed challenges under the Rules, primarily at the Iran-US Claims Tribunal.[206] The results of those challenges have underscored several points: (i) that a challenge is the only mechanism under the Rules by which a party may seek to remove an arbitrator for bias; (ii) that 'justifiable doubts' is an objective standard and is likely the sole basis for challenge under the Rules; and (iii) that this standard is intended to apply uniformly to all arbitrators, regardless of how appointed, although the achievement of such uniformity may be doubted. The challenges brought at the Iran-US Claims Tribunal have also highlighted, without resolving, questions as to (iv) whether particular circumstances may give rise to 'justifiable doubts'; and (v) whether an arbitrator's failure to disclose under Art 9 may serve as the ground for a challenge.

---

[205] *Report of WGII on the work of its 49th session* (15–19 September 2008) paras 17, 76–80, UN Doc A/CN.9/665, recording the Working Group's adoption, with amendments, of the draft Model Statements set forth in *Note by the Secretariat*, UN Doc A/CN.9/WG.II/WP.151 para 24.

[206] See eg Caron, Caplan and Pellonpää (n 61) 216–40; Baker and Davis (n 62) 37–60; see also Brower, C. and Brueschke, J., *The Iran-United States Claims Tribunal* (Brill, The Hague, 1998) 163 *et seq*.

(1.1.1) Exclusive method for removing arbitrators In an early case at the Iran-US Claims Tribunal, the government of Iran purported to exercise an authority quite apart from a challenge to remove an arbitrator, declaring unilaterally that Judge Nils Mangård, a presiding arbitrator, was 'disqualified' from further service because of his alleged partiality. The appointing authority rejected Iran's action, finding that nothing in the Rules or in the Claims Settlement Declaration (which established the Tribunal) conferred such a power. The appointing authority further noted that, 'the independence of the arbitrators . . . is also scarcely reconcilable with the notion that the arbitrators can be disqualified by a unilateral statement by one of the High Contracting Parties that it no longer has confidence in them'.[207] **16.131**

(1.1.2) 'Justifiable doubts' is an objective standard and is likely the sole basis for a challenge under the Rules Appointing authorities have equated a 'justifiable doubt' with a doubt that would be harboured by a reasonable person informed of the relevant facts. In one of its challenges to Judge Robert Briner, then a presiding arbitrator in a chamber of the Iran-US Claims Tribunal, Iran accepted that 'justifiable doubts' were those that were generated 'in a reasonable man's mind' but argued that a doubt is 'naturally formed on the basis of appearances, not as a result of the careful analysis of the evidence' and that 'the word 'justifiable' does not create a stricter standard of doubt'.[208] The appointing authority appeared to disagree, noting that 'an Arbitrator can be challenged not on the ground of circumstances which have given rise to serious doubts . . . but solely on the ground of circumstances which give rise to justifiable doubts'.[209] Similarly, in another UNCITRAL Rules arbitration, the appointing authority explained: **16.132**

> If the doubt had merely to arise in the mind of a party contesting the impartiality of an arbitrator, 'justifiable' would have been almost redundant. The word must import some other standard—a doubt that is justifiable in an objective sense. . . . In sum, would a reasonably well informed person believe that the perceived apprehension—the doubt—is justifiable? Is it ascertainable by that person and so serious as to warrant the removal of the arbitrator?[210]

The objective standard for 'justifiable doubts' is fairly stringent, and indeed none of the challenges brought against members of the Iran-US Claims Tribunal has been upheld, although some have been resolved before the challenge was ruled upon.[211]

The question has arisen whether the standard of 'justifiable doubts' as to impartiality or independence is the sole basis for a challenge under the Rules. For example, in the case arising from two Iranian arbitrators' physical attack on a presiding arbitrator at the Iran-US Claims Tribunal, the United States challenged the Iranian arbitrators not only under the **16.133**

[207] Decision of the Appointing Authority Ch M J A Moons on the Objections by Iran to Judge Mangård, 5 March 1982, *reprinted in* 1 Iran–USCTR 509, 516 (1981–82).

[208] Caron, Caplan and Pellonpää (n 61) 216 (quoting Reply Memorandum of Iran regarding challenge of Judge Briner in Case no 55, 28 November 1988, *reprinted in* 20 Iran–USCTR 260–73).

[209] Decision of the Appointing Authority on the Second Challenge by Iran of Judge Briner, 19 September 1989, *reprinted in* 21 Iran–USCTR 384, 387 (1989).

[210] Challenge Decision of 11 January 1995, para 23, *reprinted in* XXII *Ybk Comm Arb* 227, 234 (1997).

[211] In particular, the challenge brought by the United States against the two Iranian-appointed arbitrators who physically attacked a presiding arbitrator, Judge Mangård, was resolved when Iran agreed to the challenge and appointed two new arbitrators.

Rules but also based on 'fundamental legal principles governing international arbitration,' which allegedly included a duty to 'adhere to proper judicial decorum'.[212] Although this challenge was never ruled upon by the appointing authority, the United States' contention that a challenge can be based on legal principles outside the Rules has been doubted.[213] Indeed, the appointing authority subsequently rejected the United States' attempt to challenge Judge Broms on a provision of the Rules other than Art 10. The US had argued, *inter alia*, that Judge Broms' disclosure of confidential deliberations demonstrated his inability to perform his functions within the meaning of Art 13(2). The appointing authority found that even the supplemental paragraphs that the Iran-US Claims Tribunal had added in Art 13 addressed 'actual failure to act, or "the impossibility of his performing his functions", rather than a metaphorical failure or impossibility inferred from his views expressed when acting'. The appointing authority thus concluded that Art 13(2) 'was not intended to be used as a supplement or to qualify the meanings of "independence" and "impartiality" in Arts 9 to 12'.[214] Although some commentators characterize Art 13(2) as a basis for challenge,[215] it may be more accurate to state—consistent with Art 13's placement under a caption ('Replacement of an Arbitrator') that is separate from the one that covers Arts 9–12 ('Challenge of Arbitrators')—that Art 13(2) provides a distinct procedure for removing an arbitrator based on his or her *inaction* rather than on his or her *attributes* or *service* as an arbitrator.[216]

16.134 *(1.1.3) The same standard should apply to all arbitrators, regardless of how appointed* During the original drafting of the Rules, there was considerable debate whether party-appointed arbitrators should be subject to the same standards of impartiality and independence as sole or presiding arbitrators.[217] Ultimately, the drafters concluded that, consistent with the domestic laws of many countries, it was best to subject all arbitrators to the same obligations.[218] It has been suggested, however, given the nature of the challenges brought at the Iran-US Claims Tribunal and their results, that the expectations as to impartiality may be somewhat different for party-appointed arbitrators.[219] Nevertheless, as Sir Robert

212 See Caron, Caplan and Pellonpää (n 61) 229 (quoting from the US agent's memorandum to the appointing authority, supporting the challenge against Judges Kashani and Shafeiei).

213 *id*, 230; see also van Hof (n 55) 78 (Art 10 'must be considered as exhaustive and exclusive').

214 Decision of the Appointing Authority of the Iran-US Claims Tribunal, Sir Robert Jennings, on the Challenge of Judge Bengt Broms ('Decision on Judge Broms Challenge') 7 May 2001 at 4; *cited in Mealey's Int'l Arb Rep*, vol 16, issue 5 (May 2001) 2.

215 See eg Baker and Davis (n 62) 57.

216 See van Hof (n 55) 78 ('it seems inappropriate to construct Art 13.2 [of the Tribunal Rules] as an additional ground for challenge'). Art 13(2) states that, where an arbitrator, eg 'fails to act . . ., the procedure in respect of the challenge . . . of an arbitrator . . . shall apply', which is not the same as stating that a request for removal pursuant to Art 13(2) constitutes a challenge.

217 *Summary of 8th Session Discussion* (n 55) para 68.

218 *Commentary on Revised draft Rules* (n 90) 170 (commentary on draft Art 9(1)).

219 See eg Caron, Caplan and Pellonpää (n 61) 212 (noting that relatively few challenges to party-appointed arbitrators have been initiated at the Iran-US Claims Tribunal and that, 'Over time, less and less impartiality and independence was expected of the Iranian arbitrators.' See also Baker and Davis (n 62) 55–7 ('in closely nuanced cases, it is not irrational to suggest that the kind of relationship that might give rise to doubts as to a chairman's impartiality does not cross that line in the case of a party-appointed arbitrator,' *id* at 57).

Jennings wrote when, as the appointing authority, he reviewed the challenge to Judge Broms at the Iran-US Claims Tribunal:

> One ought to resist an assumption that the independence and the impartiality of the Members of the Tribunal who are nominated by a Party are different in their juridical nature from the requirements for one of the 'neutral' judges. No such distinction is made in the rules governing challenges.[220]

(1.1.4) Whether certain circumstances give rise to 'justifiable doubts' The original drafters considered incorporating into the Rules examples of facts that would reflect partiality or dependence or, alternatively, categories of circumstances giving rise to justifiable doubts.[221] Ultimately, that approach was deemed unworkable, both because of the risk of under-inclusiveness and the difficulty of stating an invariable result for circumstances whose significance could depend on small factual details.[222] Thus, the consequence under Art 10 of particular circumstances has been left to appointing authorities to determine. Several fact patterns have given rise to challenges at the Iran-US Claims Tribunal, including prior relationships to a party or witness. **16.135**

Judge Briner was first challenged by Iran for having previously had a relationship with the Swiss subsidiary of the company that had furnished expert testimony on valuation in Case no 55. Both parties agreed that close relationships between an arbitrator and a witness *could* give rise to justifiable doubts, although neither party could cite a case where a challenge had been sustained on this ground.[223] In the end, Judge Briner resigned from the case, under protest, before the appointing authority had ruled on the case.[224] In another case, Judge Noori, an arbitrator appointed by Iran, was challenged by the claimant in *Carlson v Melli Industrial Group* for failing to disclose that he had formerly served as legal counsel and as a director of the National Industries Organization of Iran (NIOI), a government agency that owned the respondent. The appointing authority rejected the challenge on the ground, *inter alia*, that Judge Noori had not worked on the particular case when he was briefly employed at NIOI and that the respondent was one of many companies that NIOI owned.[225] Several commentators have cautioned against extrapolating a general rule from this result, believing that it is very much the product of its particular facts.[226] **16.136**

In a second challenge to Judge Briner, the government of Iran alleged several improprieties in his conduct of Case no 39, including that he 'slanted' evidence in the case and threatened **16.137**

---

220 Decision on Judge Broms Challenge (n 214) 11.

221 *Commentary on Revised draft Rules* (n 90) 170 (commentary on draft Art 9(2)).

222 *Summary of 8th Session Discussion* (n 55) paras 70–4 and *Report of the Committee of the Whole II* (n 55) para 59; see also Caron, Caplan and Pellonpää (n 61) 213.

223 Caron, Caplan and Pellonpää (n 61) 217.

224 *ibid.*

225 Decision of the Appointing Authority on the Challenge to Judge Noori, 31 August 1990, *reprinted in* 24 Iran–USCTR 314, 324 (1990).

226 See eg Caron, Caplan and Pellonpää (n 61) 219 ('we view this decision primarily as reflecting the low expectations of impartiality that came to be placed on the Iranian-appointed arbitrators'); Baker and Davis (n 62) 56 ('the rule the claimant sought . . . would simply not have been practical. Nearly all the Iranian arbitrators once were employees of the Iranian government, which is the direct or indirect respondent in nearly every case').

to increase the award against Iran if the Iran-appointed arbitrator continued to dispute the result. The appointing authority found that it was 'not competent to assess the correctness of the arbitrators' judgment whether evidence is or is not convincing nor of their decision to accept some evidence as a basis for their award'.[227] As for the alleged threat to change the award, the appointing authority concluded that Art 31 of the Rules, preserving the confidentiality of tribunal deliberations, precluded a challenge based on such allegations.[228]

16.138 A subsequent challenge by the United States against another arbitrator, Judge Broms, was based precisely on allegations that he disclosed confidential deliberations in his concurring and dissenting opinion in a case. The appointing authority criticized the arbitrator's conduct as violating the Rules but did not find that the particular indiscretions sustained doubts as to Judge Broms' impartiality.[229]

16.139 The question has arisen whether the standard of 'justifiable doubts' should be applied more robustly at an early stage of proceedings (when upholding a challenge would cause less disruption in the case) and, conversely, should be applied more cautiously at a late stage of an arbitration (to avoid the lost time and expense of repeating a proceeding except in egregious cases). It has been held that neither approach would be defensible and that neither is consistent with Art 10(1)'s uniform standard.[230]

16.140 *(1.1.5) The significance of failures to disclose* Two challenges—one brought by the United States and one by Iran—have asserted *inter alia* that the arbitrator failed to disclose circumstances whose disclosure was required by Art 9.[231] Neither challenge resulted in a ruling on the question whether a failure to disclose can itself sustain a challenge, and commentators have expressed divergent views on the question.[232]

16.141 **(1.2) The restriction of parties' ability to challenge arbitrators they appoint** Article 10(2) states that a party can challenge an arbitrator it has appointed but only based on circumstances of which the party becomes aware after making the appointment. The drafters included this provision in recognition that 'circumstances unknown at the time of nomination may emerge thereafter revealing that the arbitrator had a bias against the party nominating him, or in favour of the other party'.[233]

---

[227] Decision of the Appointing Authority on the Second Challenge by Iran of Judge Briner, *reprinted in* 21 Iran–USCTR 384, 388 (1989).

[228] *ibid* at 387.

[229] Decision on Judge Broms Challenge (n 214) 4.

[230] See Caron, Caplan and Pellonpää (n 61) 224–5.

[231] See Reply Memorandum of Iran regarding the Challenge of Judge Briner in Case no 55, 28 November 1988, *reprinted in* 20 Iran–USCTR 260, 282–5 (1988-III); Claimant's Challenge to Assadollah Noori, 20 February 1990, *reprinted in* 24 Iran–USCTR 309, 311 (1990-I).

[232] *Compare* Caron, Caplan and Pellonpää (n 61) 226 ('in our view, a failure to disclose may give rise to justifiable doubts but does not, *per se*, establish such justifiable doubts') and van Hof (n 55) 65 and n 124 (citing Rule 4.1 of the International Bar Association's Rules of Ethics for International Arbitrators (1987) ('Failure to make such disclosure creates an appearance of bias, and may of itself be a ground for disqualification')) *with* Baker and Davis (n 62) 50 ('it must be concluded that a breach of Art 9 is not by itself grounds for disqualification').

[233] *Summary of 8th Session Discussion* (n 55) para 67.

(2) Contemplated revisions

The Working Group does not intend to recommend any substantive revisions in Art 10.[234] 16.142

Article 11

1 A party who intends to challenge an arbitrator shall send notice of his challenge within fifteen days after the appointment of the challenged arbitrator has been notified to the challenging party or within fifteen days after the circumstances mentioned in articles 9 and 10 became known to that party.

2 The challenge shall be notified to the other party, to the arbitrator who is challenged and to the other members of the arbitral tribunal. The notification shall be in writing and shall state the reasons for the challenge.

3 When an arbitrator has been challenged by one party, the other party may agree to the challenge. The arbitrator may also, after the challenge, withdraw from his office. In neither case does this imply acceptance of the validity of the grounds for the challenge. In both cases the procedure provided in article 6 or 7 shall be used in full for the appointment of the substitute arbitrator, even if during the process of appointing the challenged arbitrator a party had failed to exercise his right to appoint or to participate in the appointment.

(1) Commentary on current text

Art 11 specifies (i) the process for initiating a challenge; (ii) the procedure by which the challenge can be resolved without a ruling by the appointing authority; and (iii) how, if the challenge is so resolved, a replacement arbitrator will be selected. 16.143

(1.1) Initiating a challenge

(1.1.1) The 15-day time limit Art 11(1) imposes a strict time limit on a party's initiation of a challenge, which must be brought within 15 days of either an arbitrator's appointment or the date when the circumstances giving rise to justifiable doubts as to an arbitrator's impartiality or independence 'became known to that party'. As has been noted, Art 10(2) prohibits a party that appoints an arbitrator from challenging him or her based on facts the party knew prior to the appointment. Other parties may challenge based on such previously known facts, but they must wait until the appointment occurs, since Art 11(1) only provides for challenges to 'an arbitrator', which (as the text of Art 9 makes clear) is distinct from a 'prospective arbitrator'. 16.144

As was noted in discussing Art 9, the 15-day limit is intended to force challenges to be made at the earliest possible stage, to avoid the greater disruption to the proceedings caused by challenges brought in the midst of an arbitration and to prevent a party from strategically deploying a challenge only when it faces an arbitral result it does not like.[235] The drafters were agreed that 'a waiver will take place automatically when no challenge is made within the applicable . . . period'.[236] 16.145

[234] See *Report of WGII on the work of its 49th session* (15–19 September 2008) para 81, UN Doc A/CN.9/665, recording the adoption of draft Art 10 set forth in UN Doc A/CN.9/WG.II/WP.151, para 24.

[235] See paragraph 16.119, *supra*.

[236] *Commentary on Revised draft Rules* (n 90) 170 (referring to a 30-day period in the then-current draft, which was later revised to a 15-day limit).

16.146 It can be difficult for an appointing authority to determine when certain circumstances 'became known to' a party, particularly if information concerning those circumstances has been in the public domain for some time. This difficulty has led to disputes whether either party bears a burden of proof on this issue. For example, Iran's first challenge to Robert Briner at the Iran-US Claims Tribunal was based on Judge Briner's prior relationship with the Swiss subsidiary of Morgan Stanley, a company that provided expert testimony in Case no 55; the relationship was evidently ascertainable from public records long before the challenge was brought.[237] As a result, the claimant in the case argued that Iran 'has the burden of proof in establishing . . . that it learned of the circumstances that gave rise to the challenge no more than 15 days before acting on that information.'[238] Iran rejected the argument, noting that Art 11(1) 'says nothing about having to fulfill any burden of proof' and that, since the claimant was asserting that the challenge was time-barred, it bore the evidentiary burden since 'the burden of proof . . . lies on him who affirms a fact'.[239] However, Iran also emphasized that it had 'voluntarily agreed to produce evidence to show that it has observed the 15-day time limit . . . because it happened to have ample, readily available proof to establish that fact', which included 'a number of facsimile transmission and letters received in pursuit of the knowledge finally obtained about Mr. Briner's connection with Morgan Stanley'.[240] Judge Briner resigned from Case 55 before the appointing authority could rule on this question.

16.147 Some commentators have suggested that, although Art 11(1) is indeed silent about any burden of proof as to the timeliness of a challenge, an analogy may be drawn to Art 24(1), which provides that 'each party shall have the burden of proving the facts relied on to support his claim or defence'. These commentators believe it may thus be 'appropriate that the party bringing a challenge should be required . . . to make some showing that its awareness of the circumstances . . . arose within the 15-day limit', particularly 'when the facts are wholly within the possession of one party and inaccessible to the other party'.[241]

16.148 At the Iran-US Claims tribunal, the appointing authorities have tended strictly to enforce the 15-day limit. For example, in the second challenge to Judge Briner, the appointing authority found that most bases for Iran's challenge were known to it once its agent received the English version of the award in Case no 39, more than 15 days before the challenge was initiated. Although English and Persian are both official languages of the Tribunal and its practice is thus to issue a Persian translation following the issuance of an award in English, the appointing authority found 'there is no doubt that the Agent of the Islamic Republic has a thorough command of English' and therefore Iran could be assumed to know the

---

[237] See Baker and Davis (n 62) 62.

[238] Memorandum of Amoco Iran Oil regarding the Challenge of Judge Briner in Case no 55 by Iran, 2 November 1988, *reprinted in* 20 Iran–USCTR 233, 234 (1988).

[239] Reply Memorandum of Iran regarding the Challenge of Judge Briner in Case no 55, 28 November 1988, *reprinted in* 20 Iran–USCTR 260, 319 and 266 (1988).

[240] *ibid,* 271. Iran also presented 'a sworn Affidavit by Iran's foreign lawyers preparing the pleadings in . . . Case no 55 . . . that they had not ever heard a single mention of the possible connection between Mr. Briner and Morgan Stanley . . . .' *ibid,* 272.

[241] Caron, Caplan and Pellonpää (n 61) 244 (internal quotes and citation omitted); see also Baker and Davis (n 62) 62.

award's contents 'on the day following the day when the document was received'.[242] Noting the 'modern means of communication—such as telephone, telegraph, telex and telefax', the appointing authority also rejected Iran's argument that its agent could only confer with government officials about a challenge once the award had been transmitted by the government's weekly mail pouch from The Hague to Tehran.[243] A much more recent challenge, filed by the US against all three Iranian arbitrators after one of those arbitrators admitted that he and his colleagues were paying a portion of their salary to Iran, was rejected as time-barred by the appointing authority, based primarily on a third person's handwritten notes of an administrative meeting held in 1984 and attended by the agent for the US. According to those notes, an Iranian arbitrator had stated at that meeting that Iranian arbitrators returned part of their salaries to Iran.[244]

The question has also arisen whether a tribunal or appointing authority can extend or waive the 15-day limit if the circumstances are believed to warrant this. In one instance when the government of Iran made such a request, the President of the Iran-US Claims Tribunal refused on the ground that there was 'no room for extension'.[245] Although Art 15 generally authorizes the tribunal to 'conduct the arbitration in such manner as it considers appropriate', this authority is made 'subject to these Rules', which arguably precludes tribunals from altering deadlines established in those Rules. Nor does any provision in Arts 11 or 12 purport to authorize an appointing authority to extend the time limit for challenges—a deadline that, as already noted, the Rules' drafters regarded as 'automatically' effecting a waiver for parties that do not timely file a challenge. On the other hand, a party that files its challenge within the deadline need not file all of its supporting evidence at that time but may supplement its challenge with further material.[246] **16.149**

(1.1.2) The notification of challenge Article 11(2) requires that the notice of challenge be in writing, that it 'state the reasons for the challenge', and that it be sent to 'the other party', the challenged arbitrator, and 'the other members of the arbitral tribunal'.[247] The drafters' primary intent in specifying the form and content of a notice of challenge was to facilitate the other party's or the challenged arbitrator's response to the challenge, as envisioned under Art 11(3).[248] The appointing authority affirmed this purpose when he reviewed Iran's attempt to 'disqualify' Judge Mangård.[249] The appointing authority found that Iran's **16.150**

---

[242] Decision of the Appointing Authority on the Second Challenge by Iran of Judge Briner, 19 September 1989, *reprinted in* 21 Iran–USCTR 384, 392 (1989-I).

[243] *ibid.*

[244] Decision of the Appointing Authority of the Iran-US Claims Tribunal on the United States' Challenge to the Iranian Arbitrators, 19 April 2006 referred to in and attached to *Mealey's Int'l Arb Rep*, vol 21, issue 7 (July 2006) 14.

[245] Baker and Davis (n 62) 63 (quoting a letter of President Böckstiegel to the Government of Iran's Agent at the Tribunal, Mohammed Eshragh, filed 12 July 1985).

[246] See eg Letter of the Appointing Authority C M J A Moons to the Agent of the Government of Iran, 21 September 1988, *reprinted in* 20 Iran–USCTR 187 (1988-III) (rejecting contention by Judge Briner that Iran had to file with its challenge all evidence on which it relied). See also Caron, Caplan and Pellonpää (n 61) 249–50.

[247] Notwithstanding this last requirement, according to Professor Sanders Art 11 is intended to permit a challenge to the first arbitrator of a three-member tribunal as soon as he or she is appointed. Sanders (n 28) 189.

[248] *Commentary on Revised draft Rules* (n 90) 170 (commentary on draft Art 10(2)).

[249] Decision of the Appointing Authority C M J A Moons on the Objections of Iran to Judge Mangård, 5 March 1982, *reprinted in* 1 Iran–USCTR 509, 518 (1981–82).

submissions did not meet the requirements for a challenge, since they contained neither 'a sufficiently clear description of the circumstances giving rise to the accusation levelled against Mr. Mangård of a "lack of neutrality" nor any indication of the dates on which the actual event on which the disqualification is based took place'.[250]

16.151 (1.2) **Resolving a challenge without recourse to the appointing authority** Article 11(3) provides that a party's challenge of an arbitrator can be resolved in two ways that forestall recourse to the appointing authority: either the other party may agree to the challenge or the challenged arbitrator may withdraw 'from his office'. According to Professor Sanders, at least as at the time when the Rules were drafted, 'in most cases' challenges were resolved by one of these methods.[251] The Rules encourage such resolution by expressly stipulating that neither a party's agreement to a challenge nor an arbitrator's decision to withdraw implies acceptance of the basis for the challenge. If the non-challenging party agrees to the challenge, then the challenged arbitrator will be replaced whether or not he or she agrees to withdraw.

16.152 (1.3) **Replacement of arbitrator removed pursuant to Article 11(3)** Article 11(3) provides that a challenged arbitrator who is either removed by party agreement or agrees to withdraw will be replaced according to the procedure that was specified (under Arts 6 or 7) for initially selecting that particular arbitrator. The text makes clear that this procedure will apply even if, at the time of the original arbitrator's selection, the procedure was not followed. For example, if a sole arbitrator was chosen by an appointing authority because the parties failed to agree on a candidate within the 30 days that Art 6(2) provides, Art 11(3) gives the parties another opportunity to agree upon the replacement arbitrator. Only if they fail to agree within 30 days will the selection again be made by an appointing authority.

16.153 The incorporation by reference of Arts 6 and 7 into Art 11 may result in the parties having to struggle once again with some of the ambiguities in those earlier Articles' wording. For example, in the scenario mentioned in the preceding paragraph, if a sole arbitrator chosen by an appointing authority requires replacement pursuant to Art 11(3) and if the parties are unable to agree on a new sole arbitrator, they would face an anomaly already mentioned in the discussion of Art 6: the appointing authority that appointed the first sole arbitrator would in most instances still be available to act again but, if that appointing authority had been designated by the Secretary-General of the PCA, the literal wording of Art 6(2) would seem to require designation of a second appointing authority because the existing one was not 'agreed upon by the parties'. As discussed previously, this result is likely unintended.[252]

(2) Contemplated revisions

16.154 The Working Group intends to make three changes in Art 11 that implement its general goals of (i) adapting the Rules to the possibility of multi-party arbitration; (ii) relaxing the Rules' various requirements of written form to accommodate electronic communication; and (iii) reorganizing the provisions governing replacement of arbitrators. The Working

---

250 *ibid.*
251 Sanders (n 28) 189.
252 See discussion at para 16.85, *supra.*

Group will also (iv) seek to insert a new paragraph in Art 15, permitting modification of all time limits under the Rules, which could affect the regime governing challenges.

(2.1) Rewording Article 11 to acknowledge multi-party arbitration The Working Group has agreed to recommend that Art 11(2) be reworded to require that notice of a challenge be sent to 'all other parties,' rather than to 'the other party'. It similarly seeks modification of Art 11(3) so that it would require that 'all other parties' (rather than 'the other party') agree on the removal of a challenged arbitrator.[253] **16.155**

(2.2) Modifying Article 11 to accept electronic communication The Working Group will also recommend deletion of Art 11(2)'s requirement that a notice of challenge 'be in writing'. This change conforms to the Working Group's general intention to modify Art 2, clarifying that 'any notice' under the Rules may be delivered 'by any means that provides a record of its transmission' to a party's (or to its representative's) 'designated address'.[254] **16.156**

(2.3) Consolidating provisions governing replacement of arbitrators The Working Group intends to recommend the insertion in Art 13 of a clause establishing the following general rule: that whenever it is necessary to replace an arbitrator during a proceeding, the replacement will be selected according to the procedure set forth in Arts 6 to 9 that applied to the selection of the arbitrator being replaced, even if during the actual appointment of that arbitrator 'a party had failed to exercise its right to appoint or to participate in the appointment'.[255] This revision will result in either the deletion of the last sentence in current Art 11(3) or the modification of that sentence, so that it simply refers to the new provision in Art 13. The Working Group is considering whether this general procedure for replacement of arbitrators should be subject to a discretionary exception, as further described in the discussion of contemplated revisions in Art 13.[256] **16.157**

(2.4) Expanding or abridging deadlines The Working Group intends to recommend a new para 2 in Art 15, authorizing arbitral tribunals to 'extend or abridge . . . any period of time prescribed under the Rules,' after first giving the parties an opportunity to express their views'.[257] The impetus for this change is unrelated to the procedure for handling challenges; rather, the Working Group's focus has been on time periods stipulated in the Rules whose adjustment might be 'necessary for a fair and efficient process of resolving the parties' dispute'.[258] Nevertheless, given the proposed wording quoted above, the revision of **16.158**

---

[253] See *Report of WGII on the work of its 49th session* (15–19 September 2008) paras 84, 88, UN Doc A/CN.9/665, recording the adoption with changes of the version of Arts 11(2) and 11(3) set forth in *Note by the Secretariat*, UN Doc A/CN.9/WG.II/WP.151 para 25.

[254] *ibid*, para 29, adopting with changes the revision of Art 2 set forth in UN Doc A/CN.9/WG.II/WP.151 paras 6–7.

[255] *Report of WGII on the work of its 49th session* para 103 (15–19 September 2008), UN Doc A/CN.9/665, recording the adoption of the revised version of Art 13(1) set forth in UN Doc A/CN.9/WG.II/WP.151 para 30.

[256] *ibid*, paras 104–17, UN Doc A/CN.9/665. See discussion in para 16.184, *infra*.

[257] *ibid*, paras 120–5, reflecting the Working Group's adoption with modifications of a new para provisionally denominated 1 bis to Art 15 as set forth in UN Doc A/CN.9/WG.II/WP.151 para 35.

[258] *Report of WGII on the work of its 45th session* (11–15 September 2006) para 41, UN Doc A/CN.9/614.

Art 15 would seem also to authorize tribunals to extend the 15-day deadline for initiating a challenge, although the Working Group has not thus far mentioned this.

Article 12

1. **If the other party does not agree to the challenge and the challenged arbitrator does not withdraw, the decision on the challenge will be made:**
   (*a*) **When the initial appointment was made by an appointing authority, by that authority;**
   (*b*) **When the initial appointment was not made by an appointing authority, but an appointing authority has been previously designated, by that authority;**
   (*c*) **In all other cases, by the appointing authority to be designated in accordance with the procedure for designating an appointing authority as provided for in article 6.**
2. **If the appointing authority sustains the challenge, a substitute arbitrator shall be appointed or chosen pursuant to the procedure applicable to the appointment or choice of an arbitrator as provided in articles 6 to 9 except that, when this procedure would call for the designation of an appointing authority, the appointment of the arbitrator shall be made by the appointing authority which decided on the challenge.**

(1) Commentary on current text

16.159 Article 12 both (i) establishes the rule that an appointing authority resolves a challenge if the challenged arbitrator has not withdrawn or is not removed by party agreement, pursuant to Art 11; and (ii) clarifies how a replacement arbitrator will be selected if the appointing authority sustains the challenge.

16.160 **(1.1) Having the challenge resolved by an appointing authority** Article 12(1) sets forth the principle that, if a challenge does not result (pursuant to Art 11(3)) in withdrawal by the arbitrator or removal of the arbitrator by party agreement, it will be resolved by decision of the appointing authority. As Professor Sanders described this Article, it 'regulates the procedure that must be followed when the normal consequences of a challenge do not materialize'.[259] Although the appointing authority may itself have chosen the arbitrator that is under challenge, the Rules' drafters concluded that such an authority could still be relied upon to provide a neutral evaluation of the challenge.[260]

16.161 Article 12(1) distinguishes three different methods of identifying the appointing authority that will resolve the challenge. The Article is silent on how or when the challenge will be placed before the appointing authority, but implicitly it is the challenging party that would do so. Unless an appointing authority was called upon to act at a prior stage of the arbitration and remains available or the parties have already agreed upon such an authority, then the appointing authority that will resolve the challenge must be chosen 'in accordance with the procedure for designating an appointing authority as provided for in article 6'. This raises the question whether the parties are to follow that Article's complete procedure, beginning with the 30-day period in which the parties discuss and seek to agree upon an appointing authority pursuant to Art 6(1), or whether the parties are to begin immediately with the procedure in Art 6(2), which provides for 'designat[ion]' of an appointing authority

[259] Sanders (n 28) 190.
[260] *Commentary on Revised draft Rules* (n 90) 171 (commentary on draft Art 11(1)(a)).

by the PCA Secretary-General, at a party's request. The answer appears to be that a party can proceed immediately to request designation.

In the case in which Iran sought to 'disqualify' Judge Mangård from further service on the Iran-US Claims Tribunal, once the tribunal determined this to be equivalent to a 'challenge', the PCA Secretary-General responded to a party request for designation of an appointing authority. Thereafter, Iran objected to the appointing authority's jurisdiction on the ground that the Secretary-General could not designate such an authority 'until the Parties have been unable to reach agreement on the designation by them in mutual consultation of an appointing authority.'[261] The appointing authority rejected that contention, finding that Art 12's reference to Art 6 was 'intended to make it possible . . . to decide on the challenge as quickly and as simply as possible' and therefore that the Secretary-General had properly responded to the party request for designation.[262] 16.162

(1.2) Selecting a replacement arbitrator If the appointing authority sustains the challenge pursuant to Art 12(1), then a new arbitrator must replace the challenged one. Article 12(2) essentially follows Art 11(3) in again providing that the replacement arbitrator will be chosen according to the applicable procedure that is set out in Arts 6 through 9 of the Rules. Article 12(2) differs from Art 11(3) in clarifying that, if an appointing authority is ultimately needed under that applicable procedure for selecting the replacement arbitrator, the appointing authority that has decided the challenge should fill that further role. 16.163

(2) Contemplated revisions

The Working Group intends to recommend (i) a conforming change to adapt Art 12 to the possibility of multi-party arbitration; (ii) the addition of a time limit in Art 12(1) to ensure prompt resolution of challenges; and (iii) the deletion of Art 12(2) because of the addition of similar language in Art 13 that will cover replacements pursuant to Art 12, as well. 16.164

(2.1) Adapting Article 12 to provide for multi-party arbitration The Working Group will recommend that Art 12(1) be reworded to refer to the possible failure of 'any party' to agree to removal of a challenged arbitrator. This would reflect the intended change in Art 11, whereby 'all other parties' (rather than 'the other party') must agree to the removal of a challenged arbitrator. The Working Group also decided that the word 'and' should be changed to 'or,' immediately before the phrase 'the challenged arbitrator does not withdraw', to clarify that, if the parties agree to remove a challenged arbitrator, removal will occur whether or not the arbitrator agrees.[263] 16.165

(2.2) Imposing a time limit on resolution of challenges It was pointed out to the UNCITRAL Secretariat, in a report prepared in advance of the current Rules revision project, that Art 12 contained no time limit within which a party that had initiated a challenge was required to seek a decision on the challenge by an appointing authority. As the 16.166

[261] Decision of the Appointing Authority on Iran's Objection to Judge Mangård, 5 March 1982, *reprinted in* 1 Iran–USCTR 509, 513 (1981–82) (paraphrasing Iran's objection).

[262] *ibid.* See also para 16.84, *supra.*

[263] See *Report of WGII on the work of its 49th session* (15–19 September 2008) paras 93–8, UN Doc A/CN.9/665, recording the adoption with modification of revised Art 12(1) as set forth in *Note by the Secretariat*, UN Doc A/CN.9/WG.II/WP.151 para 28.

authors of that initial report stated, the absence of a time limit 'has on occasion led to delay and, worse, uncertainty on the part of the tribunal, which may feel hesitant to proceed, in the shadow of a possible or likely challenge'.[264] The Working Group agreed that imposition of a time limit was advisable,[265] and subsequently agreed to recommend specific language that requires a party that has initiated a challenge to bring it before an appointing authority that has previously been 'appointed or designated' within 30 days of the date of the notice of challenge. If no such appointing authority has been designated or appointed, the party is to seek a decision within 15 days from the appointment or designation of an appointing authority.[266]

16.167 **(2.3) Consolidating provisions relating to replacement of arbitrators** The Working Group intends to recommend the insertion in Art 13 of a clause establishing the general rule that, whenever it is necessary to replace an arbitrator during a proceeding, the replacement will be selected according to the procedure set forth in Arts 6 through 9 that applied to the selection of the arbitrator being replaced.[267] This revision will result in the modification of Art 12(2), which would simply refer to Art 13's new clause. The Working Group is considering whether this general procedure for replacement of arbitrators should be subject to a discretionary exception, as further described in the discussion of contemplated revisions in Art 13.[268]

REPLACEMENT OF AN ARBITRATOR

Article 13

1 **In the event of the death or resignation of an arbitrator during the course of the arbitral proceedings, a substitute arbitrator shall be appointed or chosen pursuant to the procedure provided for in articles 6 to 9 that was applicable to the appointment or choice of the arbitrator being replaced.**

2 **In the event that an arbitrator fails to act or in the event of the *de jure* or *de facto* impossibility of his performing his functions, the procedure in respect of the challenge and replacement of an arbitrator as provided in the preceding articles shall apply.**

(1) Commentary on current text

16.168 Article 13 explains the method of replacing an arbitrator in four further circumstances in which a substitute arbitrator must be chosen: where (i) the arbitrator resigns or dies; or (ii) the arbitrator fails to act or is placed in a situation in which it is impossible for him or her to perform the arbitrator's functions.

16.169 **(1.1) Death or resignation of an arbitrator** Article 13(1) establishes the rule that, when an arbitrator dies or resigns during an arbitration, he or she will be replaced according to the procedure set forth in Arts 6 to 9 that 'was applicable to the appointment or choice of

264 Paulsson and Petrochilos (n 39) 56.

265 *Report of WGII on the work of its 45th session* (11–15 September 2006) para 66, UN Doc A/CN.9/614.

266 See *Report of WGII on the work of its 49th session* (15–19 September 2008) paras 93–8, UN Doc A/CN.9/665, recording the adoption with modification of revised Art 12(1) as set forth in UN Doc A/CN.9/WG.II/WP.151 para 28.

267 *ibid,* para 103, UN Doc A/CN.9/665, recording the adoption of the revised version of Art 13(1) set forth in UN Doc A/CN.9/WG.II/WP.151 para 30.

268 *ibid,* paras 104–17, UN Doc A/CN.9/665. See discussion in para 16.184, *infra.*

the arbitrator being replaced'. Although this paragraph does not include the additional phrase contained in Art 11(3) (clarifying that the originally applicable selection procedure applies even if, when the first arbitrator was chosen, 'a party had failed to exercise his right to appoint or to participate in the appointment'), the intended meanings of Arts 11(3) and 13(1) appear to be the same.[269]

A question that can arise is how the parties or the tribunal might respond if an arbitrator is believed to have resigned for illegitimate reasons. Article 13(1) is silent on this point, and Professor Sanders' commentary on this Article offered this explanation: 16.170

> The Rules do not give any indication as to the circumstances in which a resignation may be justified, and, indeed, they could hardly be expected to do so. Once the arbitrator has agreed to function he should fulfill his task. Exceptionally there may be good reasons for not continuing, such as a heart attack. If not, an arbitrator who resigns may possibly be sued for damages (costs) consequent upon his resignation.[270]

The Iran-US Claims Tribunal has confronted a significant number of resignations, both those that were unexplained and potentially disruptive, and those that were foreseeable in a tribunal that has now been in existence for more than 25 years.[271] The Tribunal has adopted certain policies and supplemental provisions under Art 13, aimed at curtailing the disruptive effect of resignations, including requirements that arbitrators submit their resignation for acceptance to the Tribunal, that the Tribunal not accept the resignation until a replacement has been appointed or designated, and that resignations only take effect with respect to cases as to which no merits hearing has yet been held.[272] 16.171

However, the efficacy of these measures has depended to some extent on the willingness of the arbitrators (and the government parties) to adhere to them. More importantly, such innovations are not really feasible outside the specialized context of a tribunal that has an ongoing docket and express authority to modify the Rules.[273] In the case of the more typical arbitral tribunal, created to resolve a single set of claims under an arbitration agreement that specifies application of the Rules, it is doubtful such restrictions can be imposed upon the timing and effective date of a resignation.[274] Indeed, as was recognized during the drafting of the Rules, 'even if the reasons for resigning were unsatisfactory, it would be difficult to oblige an arbitrator to fulfill his functions, since the arbitration rules constituted nothing more than a private agreement between two parties'.[275] 16.172

---

[269] See eg van Hof (n 55) 93 (noting that, following the resignation of Judge Riphagen from the Iran-U.S. Claims Tribunal, who had been appointed by an appointing authority, his successor Judge Briner was appointed by agreement of the two governments).

[270] Sanders (n 28) 190.

[271] See eg Caron, Caplan and Pellonpää (n 61) 281–3; Baker and Davis (n 62) 67–70; van Hof (n 55) 92–4.

[272] *ibid.*

[273] Pursuant to The Claims Settlement Declaration, the Iran-US Claims Tribunal has authority to modify the UNCITRAL Rules as they apply to the Tribunal's 'conduct [of] its business'. See Claims Settlement Declaration Art III.2, *reprinted in* Aldrich (n 29) 547.

[274] cf Baker and Davis (n 62) 68–9 (urging that other arbitrators using the Rules should find the Tribunal's practices on resignation 'persuasive').

[275] UNCITRAL Committee of the Whole II, *Summary Record of 5th Meeting* (14 April 1976) para 32, UN Doc A/CN.9/IX/C.2/SR.5.

(1.2) Failure to act or impossibility of performing the arbitrator's functions

16.173 *(1.2.1) Possible basis for removal of arbitrator* An initial draft of Art 13(2) referred not only to failure to act but also to 'incapacity' as the bases for removing the arbitrator. It was understood by the drafters that these factors were distinct from the grounds in Art 13(1) since, unlike death and resignation, they 'covered reasons which, in objective terms, would be more difficult to establish'.[276] Several delegates expressed concern that 'incapacity' was ambiguous or would lead to varying interpretations under different legal systems.[277] This prompted a call for a more objective term to encompass both legal and physical inability to act,[278] which resulted in the present phrasing: '*de jure* or *de facto* impossibility of performing his functions'.

16.174 Thus, Article 13(2) provides that if an arbitrator fails to act or if such action has become legally or practically impossible, the procedure under the Rules for challenging and replacing an arbitrator shall apply. In effect, this means that when a party believes that an arbitrator is failing to act or is unable to fulfill arbitral functions, it is up to that party to set in motion the challenge procedure, so that either the other party can agree, the challenged arbitrator can withdraw, or an appointing authority can decide whether the allegations of failure to act or impossibility of performance are true.

16.175 In a challenge procedure initiated by Iran under Art 13(2) against Judge Arangio-Ruiz at the Iran-US Claims Tribunal, Iran alleged that this presiding arbitrator had spent so little time in The Hague and had worked so little on the backlogged docket that he was 'failing to act' within the meaning of Art 13(2) and should be replaced. The appointing authority held that 'the phrase "fails to act" also covers the situation in which an arbitrator, though not completely inactive, consciously neglects his arbitral duties in such a way that his overall conduct falls clearly below the standard of what may be reasonably expected from an arbitrator'.[279] However, the appointing authority disagreed that the level of Judge Arangio-Ruiz's activity at the Tribunal fell below this standard.

16.176 The United States has alleged that the behaviour of several arbitrators at the Iran-US Claims Tribunal so seriously breached the Rules or so deviated from the norm of judicial conduct that it had become practically impossible for the arbitrators to fulfill their functions within the meaning of the second standard for removal under Art 13(2). The allegation was first lodged against the two Iranian arbitrators who physically assaulted Judge Mangård, but a ruling under 13(2) was avoided in that case by Iran's agreement to replace the arbitrators.[280] Similar allegations against Judges Broms and Oloumi, based on their alleged disclosure of confidential deliberations, were rejected on the merits.[281] As the appointing authority

---

[276] *ibid*, para 41.

[277] *ibid*, paras 37–43.

[278] *ibid*, para 44.

[279] Decision of the Appointing Authority on the Challenge by Iran to Judge Arangio-Ruiz, 24 September 1991, *reprinted in* 27 Iran–USCTR 328, 332 (1991-II).

[280] See Caron, Caplan and Pellonpää (n 61) 188.

[281] Decision on Judge Broms Challenge (n 214); Decision of the Appointing Authority of the Iran-US Claims Tribunal, Sir Robert Jennings, on the Challenge of Judge Hamid Reza Oloumi Yazdi ('Decision on Judge Oloumi Challenge') 2 April 2008; *cited in Mealey's Int'l Arb Rep*, vol 23, issue 4 (April 2008) 7.

noted in considering whether Judge Broms' breach of Art 31 necessarily demonstrated his partiality toward Iran, 'a judge may be strictly and correctly impartial and independent though massively indiscreet and forgetful of the rules'.[282]

(1.2.2) Truncated tribunals A question that has arisen several times in proceedings under the UNCITRAL Rules is how to respond to an arbitrator who ceases to take part in a case, typically during the final deliberations stage and in circumstances that indicate a deliberate or coerced withholding of participation. The most notorious example is recounted in the interim and final awards in *Himpurna California Energy Ltd (Bermuda) v Republic of Indonesia,*[283] where the arbitrator appointed by Indonesia appeared to be prevented by agents of the Indonesian government from attending a witness hearing scheduled in The Hague. After being involuntarily boarded onto a return flight to Jakarta, the arbitrator 'declined' to participate in the remainder of the case. **16.177**

The tribunal in *Himpurna* concluded that it should render a final award notwithstanding the lack of participation by its third member. It thus confronted the question whether it was precluded from proceeding as a so-called 'truncated tribunal' by Art 13(2), because that clause provides a different remedy for an arbitrator who fails or is unable to act, namely, the removal of the arbitrator by means of the challenge procedure and the subsequent replacement of him.[284] The two remaining arbitrators in *Himpurna* cited with approval the conclusion on this point by certain members of the Iran-US Claims Tribunal that Art 13(2) 'is not the exclusive procedure for dealing with the failure of an arbitrator to act' and therefore 'cannot be invoked to disrupt the orderly process of the Tribunal or to obstruct its function'.[285] **16.178**

The *Himpurna* tribunal also relied upon Judge Stephen Schwebel's comprehensive survey of the history of truncated tribunals, extending back well over a century, which concluded that 'withdrawal of an arbitrator from an international arbitral tribunal which is not authorized or approved by the tribunal is wrong under customary international law' and that, 'while the precedents are not uniform, and the commentators are divided, the weight of the international authority . . . clearly favours the authority of an international tribunal from which an arbitrator has withdrawn to proceed and to render a valid award'.[286] Finally, the tribunal noted that, according to a leading practitioner, other Articles of the UNCITRAL Rules supported the possibility of a truncated tribunal: **16.179**

> A key provision of the Rules gives the arbitral tribunal the power to 'conduct the arbitration in such manner as it considers appropriate' (Art. 15(1)). The Rules further provide that decisions and awards can be made by two arbitrators (Art. 31(1)) and can be signed by two arbitrators (Art. 31(4)). Further interpretation of the Rules has led to the conclusion that

---

[282] Decision on Judge Broms Challenge (n 214) 7.

[283] (2000) XXV *Ybk Comm Arb* 11.

[284] No party in *Himpurna* had sought removal pursuant to Art 13(2); the claimant urged the tribunal to render an award as a truncated tribunal, while the respondent argued that the remaining two arbitrators should resign or the entire arbitration should be suspended pending resolution of related court actions in Indonesia. *ibid*, 192.

[285] *ibid*, 197 (quoting *Uiterwyk Corp et al v Islamic Republic of Iran et al* (Award no. 375-381-1, 6 July 1988) (Supplemental Opinion of Judges Böckstiegel and Holtzmann) *reprinted in* 19 Iran–USCTR 107, 170–1).

[286] *ibid*, 194 (quoting Schwebel, S., *International Arbitration: Three Salient Problems* (Cambridge, 1987) 296.

the requirement of the Rules that the Arbitral Tribunal must treat the parties 'with equality' (Art. 15(1)) does not appear to prevent the arbitral tribunal from proceeding without the participation of a party-appointed arbitrator because the Rules clearly establish that that arbitrator must be independent of the parties (Arts. 9 and 10).[287]

16.180 By no means would every instance in which an arbitrator fails to participate in proceedings justify the extraordinary step of acting as a truncated tribunal. As commentators have cautioned, the precipitating circumstances should be not merely a failure to act, which could unfairly be engineered by the joint efforts of the remaining two arbitrators,[288] but rather a 'refusal to act'[289] or, as formulated more broadly by the *Himpurna* tribunal, circumstances in which '*without valid excuse*, one of [a tribunal's] members fails to act, withdraws or . . . even purports to resign'.[290]

16.181 At the Iran-US Claims Tribunal, each chamber has completed work on particular cases as a truncated tribunal when an arbitrator's temporary withdrawal or purported resignation threatened, and was perhaps timed, to frustrate ongoing work.[291] In the first such instance, after a retiring presiding arbitrator had notified his co-arbitrators that he intended the chamber should work through his last month of service to complete work on several awards, the Iranian arbitrator announced that he was taking vacation for that month. When the remaining two arbitrators proceeded to deliberate upon and sign a number of awards, the absent arbitrator protested that he should, instead, have been subject to a challenge procedure pursuant to Art 13(2).[292] As has been subsequently noted with respect to the awards by truncated chambers at the Iran-US Claims Tribunal, 'Iran challenged the resultant awards, sometimes in Dutch courts, but the latter challenges were discontinued, the awards have been treated by the Tribunal as valid, and they have been paid'.[293]

16.182 The Iran-US Tribunal has generally only resorted to truncated tribunals when such absences occurred at the deliberations stage or, later, when an award was ready to be signed. By contrast, '[g]enerally, hearings have been postponed when 'truncation' was the only option for the Tribunal or one of its Chambers'.[294] This is consistent with both Art 14 of the Rules, providing for possible repetition of a hearing upon replacement of an arbitrator, and the

---

287 *ibid*, 196–7 (quoting Szasz, I., 'Arbitration Rules and Practices of Institutions,' in van den Berg (ed), *ICCA Congress series no 5* (1990) 256).

288 See Veeder, V., 'The Natural Limits to the Truncated Tribunal: The German Case of the Soviet Eggs and the Dutch Abduction of the Indonesian Arbitrator,' in *Law of International Business and Dispute Settlement in the 21st Century (Liber Amicorum Karl-Heinz Böckstiegel)* (C Heymanns Verlag, Cologne, 2001) 795, 797–801 (describing arbitration between German and Soviet Union parties in the *Chlebprodukt* case, in which the Soviet chairman contrived—by scheduling on short notice hearing dates that conflicted with the German arbitrator's prior commitments—to ensure the latter's failure to attend, followed by replacement).

289 *ibid*, 801 ('Although perhaps the line is difficult to draw in legal theory, there is an important practical difference between an arbitrator's refusal to act and a mere failure to act'); see also van Hof (n 55) 96.

290 (2000) XXV *Ybk Comm Arb* 11, 193 (emphasis added).

291 See Caron, Caplan and Pellonpää (n 61) 293–7; van Hof (n 55) 95–7.

292 Statement of Judge Shafeiei concerning his failure to sign Cases 83, 188, 220 and 449, *reprinted in* 3 Iran–USCTR 125–6 (1983-II).

293 Schwebel, S., 'The Validity of an Arbitral Award Rendered by a Truncated Tribunal' (1994 Goff Lecture), 6/no 2 *ICC ICArb Bull* 19, 20–1 (1995).

294 Caron, Caplan and Pellonpää (n 61) 296.

Tribunal's adoption of supplemental Rule 13(5), requiring that an arbitrator whose resignation is accepted by the Tribunal shall, 'after the effective date of . . . resignation . . . continue to serve as a member of the Tribunal with respect to all cases in which he had participated in a hearing on the merits'.[295]

(2) Contemplated revisions

The Working Group intends to revise Art 13 by (i) modifying its first paragraph so that it becomes a general clause regarding replacement of an arbitrator that consolidates provisions currently also found on this subject in Art 11(3) and 12(2); and (ii) adding language in a second paragraph that would expressly authorize a tribunal to operate on a 'truncated' basis in limited circumstances. The Group also intends (iii) to move the provision set forth in the current 13(2) concerning the failure of an arbitrator to act or the impossibility of his doing so to Art 12. **16.183**

(2.1) Consolidating provisions governing replacement of arbitrators The Working Group intends to recommend revision of Art 13(1) so that it establishes a general rule that whenever it is necessary to replace an arbitrator during a proceeding, the replacement will be selected according to the procedure set forth in Art 6 through 9 that applied to the selection of the arbitrator being replaced, even if during the actual appointment of that arbitrator 'a party had failed to exercise its right to appoint or to participate in the appointment'.[296] The Working Group is considering whether this general replacement procedure should contain a discretionary exception, permitting an appointing authority itself to choose the replacement arbitrator if, after hearing from all parties and arbitrators, it finds this is appropriate because, for example, an arbitrator resigned in bad faith with the collusion of the party that appointed him.[297] **16.184**

(2.2) Express authorization of truncated tribunals The Working Group is considering combining the discretionary exception referred to in the preceding sentence with a further permission to the appointing authority to authorize a tribunal from which an arbitrator absents himself without valid reasons 'at a late stage of proceedings' to proceed on a truncated basis. The Group is still considering the best wording to describe the 'improper conduct' that would justify exercise of such exceptional authority.[298] **16.185**

(2.3) Relocation of authority to replace arbitrators who fail to act or are unable to act The Working Group has provisionally decided that the basic content of the present Art 13(2) should be transferred to the current Art 12, '[f]or the sake of consistency in the structure of articles 12 and 13 of the Rules'.[299] Thus, all grounds for removing an arbitrator pursuant to the challenge procedure would be grouped together. **16.186**

---

[295] van Hof (n 55) 90.

[296] *Report of WGII on the work of its 49th session* (15–19 September 2008) para 103, UN Doc A/CN.9/665, recording the adoption of the revised version of Art 13(1) set forth in *Note by the Secretariat*, UN Doc A/CN.9/WG.II/WP.151 para 30.

[297] *ibid*, paras 104–17, UN Doc A/CN.9/665.

[298] *ibid*, paras 111–17, UN Doc A/CN.9/665.

[299] *Report of WGII on the work of its 49th session* (15–19 September 2008) para 108, UN Doc A/CN.9/665.

REPETITION OF HEARINGS IN THE EVENT OF THE REPLACEMENT OF AN ARBITRATOR

Article 14

If under articles 11 to 13 the sole or presiding arbitrator is replaced, any hearings held previously shall be repeated; if any other arbitrator is replaced, such prior hearings may be repeated at the discretion of the arbitral tribunal.

(1) Commentary on current text

16.187 Article 14 establishes a basic rule that any hearing held prior to the replacement of a sole or presiding arbitrator will be repeated and, in the case of replacement of any other arbitrator, may be repeated at the discretion of the tribunal.

16.188 The drafters' decision to distinguish between the replacement of sole and presiding arbitrators, on the one hand, and of arbitrators appointed by (or on behalf of) parties, on the other, was justified tersely on the basis of 'the special role that is played in arbitral proceedings' by the former types of arbitrators.[300] The distinction appears to have resulted from a compromise between those delegates, identified as particularly those from the common law background, who placed greater reliance on oral hearings and those who worried about the risk of needless cost and delay if hearings were required to be repeated in all instances.[301]

16.189 The Iran-US Claims Tribunal modified this Article to leave any decision to repeat hearings to the discretion of the Tribunal. As a practical matter, few hearings have been repeated at that Tribunal.[302] It has been noted that Art 14's use of the word 'repeated' serves to prevent a party from using such a hearing to introduce new evidence.[303]

(2) Contemplated revisions

16.190 The Working Group intends to recommend that Art 14 be revised to state, as the default rule, that 'the proceedings shall resume at the stage where the arbitrator who was replaced ceased to perform his or her functions' and to leave any decision whether to repeat a hearing to the tribunal's discretion.[304] The Group's decision follows the lead of the Swiss Rules, which have modified UNCITRAL Art 14 in the same way[305] in order to reflect what was regarded as contemporary practice.[306]

---

[300] *Commentary on Revised draft Rules* (n 90) 171 (commentary on draft Art 12(3)).

[301] UNCITRAL Committee of the Whole II, *Summary Record of 5th Meeting* (14 April 1976) paras 47–56, UN Doc A/CN.9/9/C.2/SR.5.

[302] Baker and Davis (n 62) 71; van Hof (n 55) 99; Caron, Caplan and Pellonpää (n 61) 325–6.

[303] *ibid.*

[304] *Report of WGII on the work of its 49th session* (15–19 September 2008) para 118, UN Doc A/CN.9/665, recording the adoption of the draft of revised Art 14 set forth in UN Doc A/CN.9/WG.II/WP.151, para 33.

[305] *Report of WGII on the work of its 45th session* (11–15 September 2006) para 75, UN Doc A/CN.9/614.

[306] Frey, H., 'Consequences of the Replacement of an Arbitrator,' in Zuberbühler, Müller and Habegger (eds) (n 64) 138 ('[Swiss] Article 14 reflects what has become common practice in international arbitration (Derains/Schwartz, 192). Additional cost and delay associated with repeating procedural steps are probably the main reasons underlying such practice.').

Section III. Arbitral proceedings

GENERAL PROVISIONS

Article 15

1. **Subject to these Rules, the arbitral tribunal may conduct the arbitration in such manner as it considers appropriate, provided that the parties are treated with equality and that at any stage of the proceedings each party is given a full opportunity of presenting his case.**
2. **If either party so requests at any stage of the proceedings, the arbitral tribunal shall hold hearings for the presentation of evidence by witnesses, including expert witnesses, or for oral argument. In the absence of such a request, the arbitral tribunal shall decide whether to hold such hearings or whether the proceedings shall be conducted on the basis of documents and other materials.**
3. **All documents or information supplied to the arbitral tribunal by one party shall at the same time be communicated by that party to the other party.**

(1) Commentary on current text

Article 15 contains a fundamental principle that is essential to the administration of arbitrations under the Rules, conferring authority upon the tribunal (i) to conduct the proceedings as it sees fit, subject to (ii) three principal restraints: (a) the requirements of other provisions in the Rules; (b) the obligation to treat the parties equally and to give them a full opportunity to present their case; and (c) the duty to schedule a hearing, upon request. In addition, Art 15 provides (iii) that each party, when it furnishes any 'documents or information' to the tribunal, must provide these at the same time to the opposing party. **16.191**

(1.1) The principle of flexible authority in conducting arbitrations During the drafting of the Rules, Art 15(1)'s text was described as recognizing the 'two . . . hallmarks of arbitration', namely, 'flexibility during the proceedings and reliance on the expertise of the arbitrators'.[307] Article 15(1) gives the arbitrators both the power to deal with issues or circumstances not addressed elsewhere in the Rules as well as principles to follow in doing so.[308] A good illustration of Art 15(1)'s utility is furnished by certain arbitral decisions that have invoked this provision to resolve third parties' requests to participate as *amici curiae*, a subject that is nowhere adumbrated in the Rules. **16.192**

In *Methanex Corp v United States of America*, an arbitration brought under the Rules pursuant to ch 11 of the North American Free Trade Agreement ('the NAFTA'), a Canadian manufacturer challenged an order by the governor of California banning, on environmental grounds, the use of a fuel-additive in gasoline sold in California. Several environmental organizations sought access to the parties' pleadings in the case as well as the right to attend any hearings and to make written and oral submissions on matters allegedly within the public interest. The tribunal noted that 'there is nothing in either the UNCITRAL Arbitration Rules or Chapter 11, Section B [of the NAFTA], that either expressly confers **16.193**

[307] *Commentary on Revised draft Rules* (n 90) 172 (commentary on draft Art 14(1)).

[308] The invocation of Art 15(1) in various proceedings at the Iran-US Claims Tribunal is summarized in van Hof (n 55) 103–5.

upon the Tribunal the power to accept *amicus* submissions or expressly provides that the Tribunal shall have no such power,' and it thus concluded that 'the Petitioners' requests must be considered against Art 15(1)'.[309]

16.194 The *Methanex* tribunal found that 'the power under Art 15(1) must be confined to procedural matters', so that it did not authorize the tribunal, for example, to add parties to the dispute, but the arbitrators concluded that receiving written submissions from third persons would neither give *amici* the status of parties nor alter the rights of the original parties.[310] Although the claimant opposed the interventions because responding to *amici* submissions would be burdensome, the tribunal noted that any burden would 'be shared by both Disputing Parties'[311] and could be limited by the tribunal's intention to bar *amici* from submitting additional factual evidence. Finally, since it appeared to have the power to accept written *amicus* briefs,[312] the tribunal considered whether it should exercise its discretion to do so and concluded that it was 'minded to receive such submissions' but deferred a final decision until the case had further developed.[313]

16.195 The Iran-US Tribunal has invoked its flexible authority under Art 15(1) to manage much more quotidian matters than the proposed participation of *amici curiae*. These have included whether to allow one party to submit an unauthorized filing without permitting a reply[314] or whether to accept pleadings filed after a final submission deadline established by the Tribunal.[315] Other tribunals operating under the Rules have invoked Art 15(1) in deciding to apply the International Bar Association's Rules on the Taking of Evidence in International Commercial Arbitration.[316]

(1.2) Article 15's restraints upon the tribunal's flexible authority

16.196 *(1.2.1) Other Articles of the Rules* Article 15(1)'s grant of authority to 'conduct the proceedings in such manner as [the tribunal] considers appropriate' is, of course, expressly made 'subject to these Rules'. This appears to mean (for example) that, in managing the

309 Decision of the Tribunal on Petitions from Third Persons to Intervene as 'Amici Curiae,' 12, 15 January 2001, available at <http://naftaclaims.com/Disputes/USA/Methanex/MethanexDecisionReAuthorityAmicus.pdf>

310 *ibid*, 14.

311 *ibid*, 17.

312 The tribunal held that it could not grant the petitioners access to oral hearings, whose privacy was preserved by Art 25.4 unless waived by both parties, and it declined to resolve to what extent that Article also required the parties' pleadings to be kept confidential since the parties had already agreed to a consent order specifying which materials from the arbitration would be made public. *ibid*, 19–21.

313 *ibid*, 23. Ultimately, the parties reached agreement on the scope of *amicus* participation, following a general statement concerning third party participation in NAFTA proceedings by the Free-Trade Commission of the three NAFTA governments. See Disputing Parties' Agreement on *Amicus* Participation, 31 October 2003, available at <http://naftaclaims.com/Disputes/USA/Methanex/MethanexAgreementReScope.pdf>. See also *United Parcel Service v Canada*, Decision of the Tribunal on Petitions for Intervention and Participation as *Amici Curiae*, 17 October 2001, available at <http://www.international.gc.ca/trade-agreements-accords-commerciaux/assets/pdfs/IntVent_oct.pdf>.

314 See eg *Foremost Tehran Inc v Iran* (Order of 15 September 1983), *reprinted in* 3 Iran–USCTR 361, 362 (1983-II).

315 See eg *Harris Int'l Telecommunications Inc v Islamic Republic of Iran et al* (Partial Award), paras 60–75, *reprinted in* 17 Iran–USCTR 31, 45–6 (1987-IV).

316 See eg *CME Czech Republic BV v The Czech Republic* (Final Award, 14 March 2003) (*Ad Hoc* UNCITRAL Proceeding) para 43, available at <http://ita.law.uvic.ca/documents/CME-2003-Final_001.pdf>.

proceedings, the tribunal cannot alter the time limits embedded in the Rules, unless the parties agree to such modification. It has also been noted that, as Art 1(2) confirms, the Rules themselves are subordinate to mandatory provisions of applicable law.[317]

(1.2.2) Equal treatment and the full opportunity to present one's case The principle of equal treatment has been repeatedly considered by the Iran-US Claims Tribunal in deciding whether to accept late or additional pleadings. The Tribunal has identified a range of factors that inform the ultimate decision as to what constitutes equal treatment in such circumstances, including whether there has been 'equal opportunity to make written submissions and to respond to each other's submissions', the 'possible prejudice to either party' of a late submission, which in turn can hinge on 'the character and contents of late-filed documents'.[318] In that regard, 'filings containing facts and evidence are the most likely to cause prejudice', while true 'rebuttal evidence' will be more acceptable than 'largely new material'.[319] **16.197**

Notwithstanding the guarantee of a 'full opportunity of presenting' a case, the Tribunal has not doubted its power to enforce deadlines for submissions, pointing both to Art 22 (tribunal 'to fix the period of time for communicating such statements') and to Art 28(3) (tribunal may make award without considering unexcused late-filed evidence).[320] However, the arbitrators must ensure that the opportunity to submit evidence, prior to such deadline, is a 'full' one. In one case in which a Tribunal chamber discouraged the claimant from submitting voluminous invoices but then denied recovery on the ground that the independent audit of invoices was insufficient evidence,[321] a federal court in New York subsequently refused Iran's request for enforcement of the award against that claimant, finding that the claimant had been 'unable to present its case' within the meaning of Art V(1)(b) of the New York Convention.[322] **16.198**

(1.2.3) The opportunity for a hearing Article 15(2) is worded very broadly, suggesting that a tribunal may be required to hold a hearing 'at any stage' for presentation even of 'oral argument' on any subject. In practice, at least at the Iran-US Claims Tribunal, this provision has been interpreted as having certain implied limitations. The Tribunal has held that a request for a hearing may be denied if it is not made at 'an appropriate time'—for example, if it is made long after the arbitrators have established a deadline for such a request.[323] The Tribunal has also taken the view that, if the subject of a proposed hearing is a 'procedural matter', a hearing may not be called for,[324] although it adopted an interpretive Note to **16.199**

---

[317] See Caron, Caplan and Pellonpää (n 61) 30–2.

[318] *Harris Int'l Telecommunications Inc v Islamic Republic of Iran et al* (Partial Award 2 November 1987), paras 60–2 (citing numerous Tribunal precedents), *reprinted in* 17 Iran–USCTR 31, 46–7 (1987-IV).

[319] *ibid*, paras 63–4 (citing numerous Tribunal precedents).

[320] *ibid*, paras 58–60.

[321] *Avco Corp v Iran Aircraft Industries,* Award 377-261-3 (18 July 1988), *reprinted in* 19 Iran–USCTR 200, 214 (1988-II).

[322] *Iran Aircraft Industries et al v Avco Corp*, 980 F 2d 141 (2d Cir 1992).

[323] See *Dadras Int'l et al v Islamic Republic of Iran et al* (Award no 567-213/215-3, 7 November 1995), *reprinted in* 31 Iran–USCTR 127, 143 (1995) (citing previous cases).

[324] See eg *Component Builders Incet al v Islamic Republic of Iran,* Case no 395 (Order of Chamber Three, 19 February 1985).

support this reading of Art 15(2).[325] It may be difficult for other tribunals (which lack the Iran-US Claims Tribunal's special authority, under the Algiers Accords, to revise the Rules) to implement such a distinction between procedural and substantive hearings. A tribunal will be aware that, if a court were later to find that 'the arbitral procedure was not in accordance with the agreement of the parties', this may be a ground for non-enforcement of an award under Art V(1)(d) of the New York Convention.

16.200 (1.3) **Parties' sharing of filings and pleadings** Article 15(3) requires that, whenever a party supplies 'documents or information' to the tribunal, it shall communicate the same to 'the other party'. This is included in Art 15 because the drafters regarded the provision as reflecting the general principle of equal treatment of the parties.[326]

(2) Contemplated revisions

16.201 The Working Group intends to recommend that Art 15 be modified (i) to clarify the timing of the parties' right to present their case; (ii) to encourage the tribunal to seek efficiency along with fairness; (iii) to allow the tribunal to modify periods of time set in the rules or by the parties themselves; (iv) to qualify the parties' right to insist upon a hearing; (v) to qualify the obligation to give all information simultaneously to the tribunal and other parties; and (vi) to address the possibility of joining third persons to an arbitration.

16.202 (2.1) **Each party's 'opportunity to present its case'** In Art 15(1), the Working Group seeks to modify the current language so that the party is only assured of 'an opportunity' (rather than 'a full opportunity') to present its case at 'an appropriate stage of the proceedings'.[327] The delegates have noted that this modification would largely follow Art 18 of the UNCITRAL Model Law and believe this revision would both 'avoid a situation where a party would insist on submission at an inappropriate stage of the arbitration' and minimize disputes over whether an opportunity had been a 'full' one.[328]

16.203 (2.2) **Efficiency in proceedings** The Working Group recommends adding a final sentence to Art 15(1) to the effect that a tribunal, 'in exercising its discretion, shall conduct the proceedings so as to avoid unnecessary delay and expense and to provide a fair and efficient process for resolving the parties' dispute'.[329] While such hortatory language might have little concrete effect, it was suggested that this could 'be useful to provide leverage for arbitrators both vis-à-vis the other arbitrators and the parties' in moving things along.[330]

[325] See van Hof (n 55) 101 (reproducing the Iran-US Claims Tribunal's 'Notes' to Art 15, including Note 2, authorizing determinations as to 'procedural matters' without a hearing).

[326] See *Preliminary Draft Rules* (n 18) (commentary on draft Art 13(4)) *reprinted in* (1975) VI *UNCITRAL Ybk* at 173.

[327] *Report of WGII on the work of its 49th session* (15–19 September 2008) para 119, UN Doc A/CN.9/665, recording the Group's adoption of revised draft of Art 15(1) as set forth in *Note by the Secretariat,* UN Doc A/CN.9/WG.II/WP.151 para 34.

[328] *Report of WGII on the work of its 45th session* (11–15 September 2006) para 77, UN Doc A/CN.9/614.

[329] *Report of WGII on the work of its 49th session* (15–19 September 2008) para 119, UN Doc A/CN.9/665, recording the Group's adoption of revised draft of Art 15(1) as set forth in *Note by the Secretariat,* UN Doc A/CN.9/WG.II/WP.151 para 34.

[330] UNCITRAL, *Note by Secretariat* (6 December 2006), para 3, UN Doc A/CN.9/WG.II/WP.145/Add.1.

(2.3) Tribunal authority to modify time limits The Working Group seeks to add a new paragraph to Art 15 authorizing the tribunal, after giving all parties an opportunity to express their views, to shorten or extend time limits established in the Rules or set by the parties themselves.[331] The drafters' twin concerns are that (i) because the tribunal's general authority in Art 15(1) to conduct proceedings is 'subject to the Rules,' this may be construed as precluding adjustment of deadlines set in the Rules; and (ii) that a tribunal, after hearing from the parties, should be able to modify, for example, 'an agreement that the arbitration should be completed within a certain period of time'.[332] **16.204**

(2.4) Qualifying parties' right to request a hearing For the same reason that prompted the Working Group to urge a similar modification of Art 15(1), the Working Group seeks to revise Art 15(2) so that a party is only assured of a hearing if it requests one 'at an appropriate stage' rather than 'at any stage'.[333] **16.205**

(2.5) Simultaneous communication of information to other parties The Working Group is considering modifying the requirement that a party must give any information it submits to the tribunal *simultaneously* to the other parties. The modification would seek specifically to accommodate (i) the circumstance of certain institutions administering arbitrations that require parties initially to communicate copies of tribunal submissions to the institution itself, which distributes these to the other parties; and (ii) the possibility in limited circumstances for a party to request a preliminary order on an *ex parte* basis when it is believed that simultaneous disclosure of the request to the opposing party would permit that party to frustrate the order before the tribunal can grant it.[334] The subject of preliminary orders is further discussed in the context of Art 26. **16.206**

(2.6) Joinder The Working Group considered but did not endorse a proposed new clause, modeled on Art 22.1(h) of the LCIA Rules, permitting joinder of a third party that is not a signatory to the arbitration agreement, provided that the third party and at least one of the original parties to the arbitration consent to the joinder. Many in the Working Group expressed concern that this deviated from 'the fundamental principle of consent of parties in arbitration',[335] and the proposal lost further support when it was learned that such joinder had only been sought under the LCIA provision ten times in ten years, usually unsuccessfully.[336] The Working Group instead intends to recommend a more modest **16.207**

[331] *Report of WGII on the work of its 49th session* (15–19 September 2008) paras 120–5, UN Doc A/CN.9/665, recording the Group's adoption, with modification, of revised draft of Art 15(1)bis as set forth in *Note by the Secretariat*, UN Doc A/CN.9/WG.II/WP.151 para 34.

[332] *Report of WGII on the work of its 46th session* (5–9 February 2007) paras 135–6, UN Doc A/CN.9/619.

[333] *Report of WGII on the work of its 49th session* (15–19 September 2008) para 126, UN Doc A/CN.9/665, recording the Group's adoption of revised draft of Art 15(2) as set forth in *Note by the Secretariat*, UN Doc A/CN.9/WG.II/WP.151 para 34.

[334] *ibid*, para 127, UN Doc A/CN.9/619, recording the Group's request that the Secretariat draft language to implement this modification and referring only to the concern about preliminary orders.

[335] *Report of WGII on the work of its 46th session* (5–9 February 2007) paras 122, 126, UN Doc A/CN.9/619.

[336] UNCITRAL, *Note by the Secretariat* (6 August 2008) para 37, UN Doc A/CN.9/WG.II/WP.151. The Working Group also rejected a proposed addition to Art 15 facilitating consolidation of cases between the same parties. It was believed this posed too many difficulties, particularly in *ad hoc* arbitrations and in cases

provision permitting joinder of third persons who are already signatories to the arbitration agreement that underlies the existing arbitration. The Working Group is considering a proposal that such joinder should be subject to the tribunal's review of possible prejudice to any party, rather than simply requiring the consent of the party to be joined.[337]

PLACE OF ARBITRATION

Article 16

1 **Unless the parties have agreed upon the place where the arbitration is to be held, such place shall be determined by the arbitral tribunal, having regard to the circumstances of the arbitration.**

2 **The arbitral tribunal may determine the locale of the arbitration within the country agreed upon by the parties. It may hear witnesses and hold meetings for consultation among its members at any place it deems appropriate, having regard to the circumstances of the arbitration.**

3 **The arbitral tribunal may meet at any place it deems appropriate for the inspection of goods, other property or documents. The parties shall be given sufficient notice to enable them to be present at such inspection.**

4 **The award shall be made at the place of arbitration.**

(1) Commentary on current text

16.208 Article 16 accomplishes three purposes: it (i) authorizes the tribunal to determine the place of arbitration if the parties have not done so (including a locale within a country that the parties have specified); (ii) permits the tribunal to hold hearings, meet for deliberations, or conduct inspections at any place it deems appropriate; and (iii) provides that the award 'shall be made at the place of arbitration'.

16.209 **(1.1) Determining the place of arbitration** Whether determined by the parties or by the tribunal, the choice of the place of arbitration will carry significance for the conduct of the arbitration. Although the parties may sometimes provide otherwise, the law of the place of the arbitration will usually constitute the *lex arbitri*, and may thus affect, *inter alia*, the procedure in the arbitration, the arbitrability of the dispute, and the validity of the arbitration agreement.[338]

16.210 The tribunal's authority to determine the place of arbitration when the parties have not done so is subject to the limitation that the arbitrator(s) must have 'regard to the circumstances of the arbitration'. While this language may serve a negative function in discouraging arbitrators from choosing a place having no connection with the needs of the arbitration merely for its attractiveness, it also affirmatively suggests that there are several aspects of an arbitration's 'circumstances' that should be considered in selecting the place of arbitration.

where the arbitration clauses underlying the two arbitral proceedings differed. See *Report of WGII on the work of its 46th session* (5–9 February 2007) para 119, UN Doc A/CN.9/619.

[337] *Report of WGII on the work of its 49th session* (15–19 September 2008) para 134, UN Doc A/CN.9/665, recording the Working Group's request that the Secretariat prepare new language implementing the proposal.

[338] Redfern, A., Hunter, M., Blackaby, N. and Partasides, C., *Law and Practice of International Commercial Arbitration* (4th edn, Sweet and Maxwell, 2004) paras 2–14 to 2–18; Gaillard, E. and Savage, J. (eds), *Fouchard Gaillard Goldman on International Commercial Arbitration* (Kluwer, Deventer,1999) paras 1 178–92.

Many of these factors were identified in the *Notes on Organizing Arbitral Proceedings*, adopted by UNCITRAL in 1996 as non-binding guidance for arbitrators.

According to the *Notes*, a tribunal determining the place of arbitration should take into account (i) the suitability of the arbitral procedure law in that place; (ii) the existence of any treaty on enforcement of awards between the state of that place and any state where an award might have to be enforced; (iii) convenience to the parties and arbitrators, including travel distance; (iv) availability and cost of support services at the place; and (v) location of subject matter of the dispute or of evidence related to it.[339] **16.211**

These factors have been relied upon by a number of tribunals operating under the UNCITRAL Rules in proceedings brought under ch 11 of the NAFTA.[340] In addition, the consideration of 'neutrality' of the place of arbitration has been cited as a consideration; as one tribunal noted, although this factor 'is not referred to in the UNCITRAL Notes [it] constitutes one of the key features of international arbitration'.[341] **16.212**

In the opinion of Professor Sanders, 'the decision of the arbitral tribunal on the place of arbitration is a majority decision', meaning that 'such a decision is not . . . a decision on a 'question of procedure', and thus Art 31, para 2 [permitting the presiding arbitrator to decide such questions on his own, subject to the tribunal's revision] does not . . . apply'.[342] **16.213**

As is reflected in the Model Arbitration Clause appended to Art 1 of the Rules (which invites parties to consider adding to their arbitration agreement a designation of 'town *or* country' as their place of arbitration), an arbitral tribunal may have to choose what Art 16(2) refers to as the 'locale' of the arbitration within a country that the parties have already named as the place. **16.214**

(1.2) Meeting or deliberating elsewhere than at the place of arbitration Article 16(2) authorizes the tribunal to 'hear witnesses' or to meet for its own deliberations 'at any place it deems appropriate', but once again having 'regard to the circumstances of the arbitration'. Given this wording, it may be wondered whether a hearing without witnesses, ie solely for purposes of oral argument (which parties have a right to request under Art 15(2)), may have to be held at the place of arbitration. Although Art 16(2) does not expressly provide for a hearing without witnesses to be held other than in the place of arbitration, it is doubtful that the drafters consciously excluded it. Rather, it appears that the drafters simply assumed that the convenience of witnesses would be the primary factor prompting a different hearing location.[343] Article 16(3) accommodates another factor that was similarly believed sometimes to require meetings away from the place of arbitration: the need **16.215**

---

[339] UNCITRAL, *Notes on Organizing Arbitral Proceedings* para 22 (1996).

[340] See eg *Canfor Corp v United States of America*, Decision on the Place of Arbitration, Filing of a Statement of Defence and Bifurcation of Proceedings (23 January 2004) 3, para. 13, available at <http://www.naftaclaims.com> (hereafter, *Canfor Corp*). See also Caron, Caplan and Pellonpää (n 61) 98–114 (excerpting several relevant decisions from NAFTA tribunals).

[341] *Canfor Corp* (n 340) at para 16.

[342] Sanders (n 28) 193.

[343] See *Commentary on Revised draft Rules* (n 90) 172 (commentary on draft Art 15(2) and (3)).

to 'inspec[t] goods, other property or documents'. Article 16(3) assures the parties of advance notice of such inspections, so that they may join the tribunal.

16.216 (1.3) **Making the award at the place of arbitration** Article 16(4)'s declaration that 'the award shall be made at the place of arbitration' carries substantial implications for enforcement of any award. First, an award can only be set aside under the law of the place of arbitration, and the grounds for such setting aside vary among jurisdictions. Similarly, the enforcement of an award within the country of the place where the award was made (including the grounds for possible non-enforcement) will normally be regulated by the law of that country, and such law can also vary among jurisdictions although it has been considerably harmonized over the years.

16.217 Secondly, for purposes of enforcing the award in any country other than the country of the place of arbitration, the place at which the arbitral award was 'made' plays a significant role in application of the The New York Convention. Enforcement of an award may be refused under Art V of that Convention because, *inter alia*, (i) the arbitration agreement 'is not valid under the law to which the parties have subjected it, or failing any indication thereon, under the law of the country where the award was made'; (ii) 'the composition of the arbitral authority or the arbitral procedure was not in accordance with the agreement of the parties or, failing such agreement, was not in accordance with the law of the country where the arbitration took place'; or (iii) 'the award . . . has been set aside or suspended by a competent authority of the country in which, or under the law of which, that award was made'.[344] The place where an award will be 'made' pursuant to Art 16(4) of the Rules can be equated with the 'country' or 'place' identified in each of the phrases in Art V of the New York Convention that are quoted in the preceding sentence.

16.218 A further possible consequence of where the award is 'made' arises from the operation of one of the permitted reservations to the New York Convention. Pursuant to Art I(3) of the Convention, a state may limit its adherence to the treaty on the basis of reciprocity, so that it agrees to enforce foreign arbitral awards 'made only in the territory of another Contracting State'. Roughly half of the more than 140 signatory states have adopted this reservation.[345] Thus, in the unlikely circumstance that the place of arbitration is within a state that has not ratified the New York Convention, the enforcement of any resulting award pursuant to that Convention may be substantially curtailed.

16.219 The question arises whether Art 16(4)'s reference to the award's being 'made' at the place of arbitration requires the arbitrators to be present in the place of arbitration when they sign the award. Article 16(4) does not expressly address this, and the *travaux préparatoires* are ambiguous: different delegates indicated contrary views on the matter.[346] However, decisive weight should perhaps be given to the comment near the end of the debate by Professor

344 New York Convention, Art V(1)(a), (d) and (e), respectively.

345 A current list of the ratifying States and the reservations they have adopted can be found on the UNCITRAL website at: <http://www.uncitral.org/uncitral/en/uncitral_texts/arbitration/NYConvention_status.html>.

346 UNCITRAL Committee of the Whole II, *Summary Record of the 6th Meeting* (15 April 1976) paras 70–89 (compare eg the remarks of the United Kingdom's delegate and Mexico's delegate), UN Doc A/CN.9/9/C.2/SR.6.

Sanders, who as Special Consultant to the UNCITRAL Secretariat played a particular role in framing the Rules. Professor Sanders' firm view was that 'the fact that an award stated that it had been made at a particular place did not mean that it had actually been signed there'.[347]

(2) Contemplated revisions

The Working Group intends to recommend (i) consolidation and streamlining of the provisions authorizing meetings elsewhere than at the place of arbitration; and (ii) revision of Art 16(4) (which will be merged with Art 16(1)) to clarify that an award need not be drafted or signed at the place where it is 'made'. The Working Group also (iii) has considered whether to clarify the meaning of the term 'place' of arbitration by using an alternative word, such as 'seat'. **16.220**

(2.1) Meetings other than at the place of arbitration In lieu of the current, somewhat limiting language in Arts 16(2) and 16(3) as to the location of hearings or inspections, the Working Group seeks to insert a more general sentence in a revised Art 16(2), giving the tribunal broad authority to 'meet at any location it considers appropriate for hearings or meetings', unless 'otherwise agreed by the parties'. Thus, the tribunal's express power would no longer be limited to relocating witness hearings nor would it be required to have 'regard to the circumstances of the arbitration'. The new language will be complemented by a general sentence allowing the tribunal to meet at any location for deliberations.[348] In using the word 'location' to identify alternative meeting sites, the Working Group hopes to reduce confusion by reserving the word 'place' to designate only where the arbitration is legally seated.[349] **16.221**

(2.2) Where the award is 'made' The Working Group will recommend revising the text of Art 16(4) to state that 'the award shall be deemed to be made at the place of arbitration'.[350] This revision follows the language used in Art 31 of the UNCITRAL Model Law and is intended 'to avoid the risk that an award might be declared invalid if it was signed in a place other than the seat of arbitration'.[351] **16.222**

(2.3) 'Place' of arbitration The Working Group twice debated replacing the phrase 'place of arbitration' with some term that might better indicate its significance, such as the arbitration's 'legal seat' or even 'juridical seat'.[352] Although it was said that parties often failed to appreciate the legal implications of the 'place' of arbitration and that other arbitration rules use some variant of the term 'seat', the Working Group concluded that **16.223**

---

347 *ibid*, para 86.

348 *Report of WGII on the work of its 49th session* (15–19 September 2008) paras 137–9, UN Doc A/CN.9/665, recording the Working Group's modified adoption of the revised draft of Art 16(2) as set forth in *Note by the Secretariat*, UN Doc A/CN.9/WG.II/WP.151 para 38.

349 UNCITRAL, *Note by the Secretariat* (6 August 2008) para 38, UN Doc A/CN.9/WG.II/WP.151.

350 *Report of WGII on the work of its 49th session* (15–19 September 2008) para 136, UN Doc A/CN.9/665, recording the Working Group's adoption with modifications of the revised draft of Art 16(1) as set forth in *Note by the Secretariat*, UN Doc A/CN.9/WG.II/WP.151 para 38.

351 *Report of WGII on the work of its 45th session* (11–15 September 2006) para 90, UN Doc A/CN.9/614.

352 See *ibid*, paras 87–9, UN Doc A/CN.9/614; *Report of WGII on the work of its 46th session* (5–9 February 2007) paras 139–41, UN Doc A/CN.9/619.

many contracts and contract drafters now rely upon the Rules' use of 'place', which is consistent with usage in the Model Law. However, as noted two paragraphs above, the Working Group seeks to reduce confusion by deleting the Rules' use of the word 'place' to refer as well to the location of meetings or hearings not held at the 'place of arbitration.'[353]

LANGUAGE

Article 17

1 **Subject to an agreement by the parties, the arbitral tribunal shall, promptly after its appointment, determine the language or languages to be used in the proceedings. This determination shall apply to the statement of claim, the statement of defence, and any further written statements and, if oral hearings take place, to the language or languages to be used in such hearings.**

2 **The arbitral tribunal may order that any documents annexed to the statement of claim or statement of defence, and any supplementary documents or exhibits submitted in the course of the proceedings, delivered in their original language, shall be accompanied by a translation into the language or languages agreed upon by the parties or determined by the arbitral tribunal.**

(1) Commentary on current text

16.224 Article 17 accomplishes two objectives: it (i) authorizes the tribunal to determine the language(s) to be used in the arbitration if the parties have not done so; and (ii) designates those submissions that must be made in such language(s) and those that 'may' be ordered to be translated.

16.225 **(1.1) Determining the language of the proceedings** If the parties have not already agreed upon the language(s) to be used in the proceedings, the tribunal is to make the determination 'promptly after its appointment', since parties making submissions (and the tribunal's own orders) will have to conform to the choice of language(s). Commentators agree with Professor Sanders that the tribunal's choice of language involves a 'procedural question' that, pursuant to Art 31(2), can be resolved by the presiding arbitrator (subject to tribunal revision) if there is no majority.[354]

16.226 As the experience of the Iran-US Claims Tribunal demonstrates, a decision that more than one language will be used 'prove[s] to be very expensive and the cause of repeated extension requests'.[355] Moreover, translation can 'substantially reduce[e] the parties' ability to make changes toward the end of the drafting process',[356] and simultaneous interpretation of hearings can complicate and prolong them. Nevertheless, there are some circumstances in which the use of two languages is unavoidable, particularly where there is no agreed common language or where one party's language, though spoken and understood by both parties, cannot be chosen without exacerbating political or cultural tensions in the dispute.

353 *Report of WGII on the work of its 46th session* (5–9 February 2007) paras 139–41, UN Doc A/CN.9/619.

354 Sanders (n 28) 193; Caron, Caplan and Pellonpää (n 61) 363.

355 Baker and Davis (n 62) 81.

356 *ibid.*

The drafters considered inserting in this Article a default rule favouring a choice of the language used for the parties' contract or in their correspondence. However, given complicating factors in particular cases such as the linguistic abilities of the arbitrators, it was decided that no 'rigid rule' would be workable in all cases.[357] Nevertheless, the factors just identified would normally influence a tribunal's determination.[358] **16.227**

(1.2) Translations of submissions Whereas Art 16(1) mandates that certain documents be submitted and that certain proceedings be conducted in the language of the arbitration, Art 16(2) makes the translation of other documents or exhibits from their original language discretionary, stating that the tribunal 'may order' it. Article 16(2)'s reference to documents in their 'original language' signals that this provision's likely purpose is to avoid a blanket requirement that documents originally used by the parties without the need of translation must be translated for the arbitral proceeding. The Iran-US Claims Tribunal implemented a similar distinction in its Guidelines for the Translation of Documentary Evidence, which allowed submission without translation, 'in the first instance', of draft contracts, technical reports, brochures, invoices, accounting statements, shipping documents and blueprints or diagrams (among other documents), provided these 'were not required to be translated at the time [they] came into existence'.[359] **16.228**

A tribunal that chooses a language that is not the native language of one of the parties or that chooses two languages for the proceedings may confront a number of difficult questions concerning the consequences of submissions made without proper translation.[360] The Iran-US Claims Tribunal has often given additional time for a party to supply missing translations or to rectify deficient ones, although it has been willing to render its decision without the translations if they were not filed within the extended deadline,[361] or if it believed no extension should be granted in exceptional circumstances.[362] It has also extended the response deadlines for the party that failed to receive documents in its native language.[363] And, where the Rules oblige a party to file a document by a certain deadline to avail itself of a particular right, the Tribunal has been willing to toll the deadline if the party filed the document in only one of the arbitral languages, pending receipt in a reasonable time of the translated copy.[364] **16.229**

---

357 *Summary of 8th Session Discussion* (n 55) paras 111–12, *reprinted in* (1975) VI *UNCITRAL Ybk* 24, 36.

358 See Caron, Caplan and Pellonpää (n 61) 355.

359 See eg *Fluor Corp et al v Islamic Republic of Iran*, Case no 810 (Order by Chamber One, 16 February 1987), Case no 810; see also Caron, Caplan and Pellonpää (n 61) 361–2, 366-71 (describing application of the Guidelines by the Iran-US Claims Tribunal).

360 Caron, Caplan and Pellonpää (n 61) 356–71 (describing and citing the Iran-US Claims Tribunal jurisprudence on such questions); van Hof (n 55) 115–16 (same).

361 See eg *Juliette Allen v Islamic Republic of Iran*, Award no 541-930-3 (11 December 1992), *reprinted in* 28 Iran–USCTR 382, 384 (1992).

362 See eg *Computer Science Corp v Islamic Republic of Iran*, Award no 221-65-1 (16 April 1986), *reprinted in* 10 Iran–USCTR 269, 272 (1986-I).

363 See eg *Development and Resources Corp v Islamic Republic of Iran*, Case no 60 (Chamber Three Order of 31 January 1985); *The United States of America on behalf of Thomas A. Todd v Islamic Republic of Iran*, Case no 10856 (Chamber One Order of 8 January 1986).

364 *Hood Corp v Islamic Republic of Iran*, Decision no DEC 34-100-3 (1 March 1985) 1–2, *reprinted in* 8 Iran–USCTR 53, 54 (1985-I).

(2) Contemplated revisions

16.230 The Working Group does not intend to make any changes in Art 17. Although the Working Group does seek to delete, in the Model Arbitration Clause appended to Art 1, the suggestion that 'language(s)' might be chosen for the proceeding (see discussion above under Art 1), the Working Group decided not to delete the plural form from Art 17, recognizing that there may be some cases where the tribunal will need to have this option.[365]

STATEMENT OF CLAIM

Article 18

1. **Unless the statement of claim was contained in the notice of arbitration, within a period of time to be determined by the arbitral tribunal, the claimant shall communicate his statement of claim in writing to the respondent and to each of the arbitrators. A copy of the contract and of the arbitration agreement if not contained in the contract, shall be annexed thereto.**
2. **The statement of claim shall include the following particulars:**
   (*a*) **The names and addresses of the parties;**
   (*b*) **A statement of the facts supporting the claim;**
   (*c*) **The points at issue;**
   (*d*) **The relief or remedy sought.**

The claimant may annex to his statement of claim all documents he deems relevant or may add a reference to the documents or other evidence he will submit.

(1) Commentary on current text

16.231 The text of Art 18 has two elements: (i) providing that the Claimant must submit a statement of claim within a certain period; and (ii) establishing both mandatory and optional contents for this statement.

16.232 **(1.1) When the statement of claim shall be filed** Pursuant to Art 3, the Claimant may include its statement of claim in its notice of arbitration. However, if it does not do so it must submit a statement of claim within the time 'determined by the tribunal'. Although it was originally suggested that allowing the notice and statement of claim to be combined 'constituted a bridge between the civil law and common law systems',[366] parties today are more likely to decide whether to combine the two submissions based on strategic considerations in the case. As an UNCITRAL delegate noted during Art 3's formulation, 'it would be pointless to draft a long statement of claim when the possibility of reaching a settlement still existed'.[367] If the claimant defers filing a statement of claim until the tribunal is constituted, the time given by the tribunal to file the statement, pursuant to Art 23, 'should not exceed forty-five days', although the tribunal may extend this period if it is justified.

---

[365] *Report of WGII on the work of its 49th session* (15–19 September 2008) paras 140–1, UN Doc A/CN.9/665.

[366] UNCITRAL Committee of the Whole II, *Summary Record of 2nd Meeting* (15 April 1976) para 36 (remarks of US delegate on draft Art 4), UN Doc A/CN.9/9/C.2/SR.2.

[367] UNCITRAL, *Summary Record of 162nd Meeting* (9 April 1975)128 (remarks of Polish delegate on draft Art 3), UN Doc A/CN.9/SR.162.

(1.2) Contents of the Statement of Claim Article 18(1)'s requirement that the statement be accompanied by 'a copy of the contract and of the arbitration agreement if not contained in the contract' reflects the drafters' assumption (already encountered in Arts 1 and 3) that the Rules would generally be used in disputes over commercial contracts. As for the further contents mandated in Art 18(2), the parties' names and addresses will already have been included in the notice of arbitration pursuant to Art 3(3), while the requirement that 'the points at issue' be stated has been said to result from a drafting oversight and may be difficult to fulfill at an early stage of proceedings.[368] This leaves the statement of 'facts supporting the claim' and of 'the relief or remedy sought' as the primary elements that Art 18(2) requires in the statement of claim. **16.233**

In confronting objections that particular submissions do not meet these requirements, tribunals have held that Art 18's provisions are flexible but cannot be disregarded. Thus, on the one hand, at least three judges of the Iran-US Claims Tribunal suggested a 'two-page business letter' sufficed as a statement of claim if it encompassed the required elements.[369] On the other hand, two tribunals sitting pursuant to ch 11 of the NAFTA have said that a statement of claim 'must be specific enough to put the respondent on notice so that it can reply adequately in its statement of defence' and that, 'as a matter of procedural fairness, [the respondent] is entitled to know precisely the case advanced against it'.[370] If a statement of claim is objected to as insufficiently specific after the respondent has managed to file its statement of defence, the complaint will be less credible and will likely be rejected.[371] In most instances, tribunals have given the claimant an opportunity to correct a deficient statement of claim,[372] but a failure to use that opportunity may result in dismissal on the merits.[373] **16.234**

Finally, Art 18(2) provides that the claimant 'may annex' to the statement of claim documents it considers relevant or 'may add a reference' to documents or evidence 'he will submit'. This flexibility responds to a concern that the claimant should not have to select its evidence before the disputed issues have been joined in the statement of defence.[374] **16.235**

---

368 Baker and Davis (n 62) 85 (suggesting that the drafters meant to delete this provision).

369 *In re Raymond International (UK) Ltd* (Decision no 18-Ref21-FT, 8 December 1982, Dissenting Opinion of Judge Holtzmann, joined by Judges Aldrich and Mosk) *reprinted in* 1 Iran–USCTR 394, 396.

370 *Methanex Corp v United States of America* (Partial Award on Jurisdiction, 7 August 2002) 78, available at <http://www.kluwerarbitration.com/arbitration/DocumentFrameSet.aspx?ipn=80373>, and *United Parcel Service of America Inc v Government of Canada* (Award on Jurisdiction, 22 November 2002) 39, available at <http://www.international.gc.ca/trade-agreements-accords-commerciaux/assets/pdfs/Jurisdiction%20Award.22Nov02.pdf>.

371 See eg, *Motorola Inc v Iran National Airlines Corp et al* (Award no 373-481-3 para 16, 28 June 1988) para 16 (finding Statement of Claim 'not completely' and yet 'sufficiently clear'), *reprinted in* 19 Iran–USCTR 73, 76–7.

372 See eg *Jonathan Ainsworth v Islamic Republic of Iran* (Order of 7 November 1983), *reprinted in* 4 Iran–USCTR 26, 27 (1983-III).

373 See eg *Cyrus Petroleum Ltd v Islamic Republic of Iran* (Award no 230-624-1, 2 May 1986), *reprinted in* 11 Iran–USCTR 70, 71 (1986-II).

374 UNCITRAL Committee of the Whole II, *Summary Record of the 7th Meeting* (19 April 1976) paras 13–15 (remarks of United Kingdom and Mexico delegates on draft Art 17(2)), UN Doc A/CN.9/9/C.2/SR.7.

Nonetheless, the Iran-US Claims Tribunal revised its rules to state that 'it is advisable' that claimants annex 'such documents as will serve clearly to establish the basis of the claim'.[375]

(2) Contemplated revisions

16.236 The Working Group intends to recommend (i) revisions in Art 18 to conform to certain changes it has made elsewhere in the Rules; and (ii) the addition of a requirement that the statement of claim address the legal basis of the claims.

16.237 (2.1) **Conforming changes** Consistent with its general aim of deleting language suggesting that the Rules only apply to contractual disputes (see eg discussion of revisions under Arts 1 and 3), the Working Group recommends amending Art 18 so that a copy of 'the contract' need only be submitted with the statement when this is relevant. Similarly, conforming to changes proposed in the notice of arbitration (see Art 3), the Working Group believes the statement of claim should contain 'contact details' rather than merely 'addresses' for the parties. The Working Group also seeks to add language to the effect that the statement of claim 'should, as far as possible', be accompanied by documents on which the claimant relies.[376] This more forceful language is partly justified by the Working Group's decision to require a response to the notice of arbitration,[377] so that the claimant will be aware of the defence before it has to submit supporting documents with its statement of claim. Finally, the Working Group would amend Art 18 to provide that the claimant can only elect to treat its notice of arbitration as also containing its statement of claim after the respondent has filed its response and may only do so if the notice satisfies Art 18's requirements.[378]

16.238 (2.2) **Legal basis of claims** The Working Group intends to include a fifth sub-para in Art 18(2), requiring that the statement of claim also include the 'legal grounds' supporting the claim.[379] Both this revision and the proposed new language encouraging the annexing of supporting evidence were recommended by the report that the UNCITRAL Secretariat commissioned in advance of the Rules revision project, which suggested that each modification could accelerate presentation of the case.[380]

STATEMENT OF DEFENCE

Article 19

1 **Within a period of time to be determined by the arbitral tribunal, the respondent shall communicate his statement of defence in writing to the claimant and to each of the arbitrators.**

2 **The statement of defence shall reply to the particulars (*b*), (*c*) and (*d*) of the statement of claim (article 18, para. 2). The respondent may annex to his statement the documents on**

---

375 van Hof (n 55) 119; see also Caron, Caplan and Pellonpää (n 61) 395.

376 *Report of WGII on the work of its 46th session* (5–9 February 2007) paras 152–4, UN Doc A/CN.9/619; *Report of WGII on the work of its 50th session* (9–13 February 2009) para 24, UN Doc A/CN.9/669.

377 See discussion of contemplated revisions to Art 3.

378 *Report of WGII on the work of its 49th session* (15–19 September 2008) para 36, UN Doc A/CN.9/665; *Report of WGII on the work of its 50th session* (9–13 February 2009) paras 19–22, UN Doc A/CN.9/669.

379 *Report of WGII on the work of its 46th session* (5–9 February 2007) paras 147–54, UN Doc A/CN.9/619; Note by the Secretariat, *Settlement of commercial disputes: Revision of the UNCITRAL Arbitration Rules* (6 August 2008) para 1, UN Doc A/CN.9/WG.II/WP/151/Add.1 (setting forth text previously approved by Working Group).

380 Paulsson and Petrochilos (n 39) 90.

which he relies for his defence or may add a reference to the documents or other evidence he will submit.

3 **In his statement of defence, or at a later stage in the arbitral proceedings if the arbitral tribunal decides that the delay was justified under the circumstances, the respondent may make a counter-claim arising out of the same contract or rely on a claim arising out of the same contract for the purpose of a set-off.**

4 **The provisions of article 18, paragraph 2, shall apply to a counter-claim and a claim relied on for the purpose of a set-off.**

(1) Commentary on current text

Article 19 accomplishes three purposes: it (i) requires the respondent to file a statement of defence and stipulates how the time for filing should be determined; (ii) establishes the mandatory and optional contents of the statement; and (iii) permits respondents, in their statement of defence (and, if justified, even thereafter), to raise a counterclaim or set-off arising from the same contract on which the claimant has based its claim. **16.239**

(1.1) **Requiring a statement of defence** The respondent must file a statement of defence, and the period within which it must do so will be determined by the tribunal. That decision will be subject once again to the presumptive limit of 45 days that, as set forth in Art 23, can be extended. **16.240**

(1.2) **Contents of the statement of defence** The structure of the statement of defence mirrors that of the statement of claim outlined under Art 18, encompassing a 'reply' to the claimant's statements as to the facts, the points in issue, and request for relief or remedy. A 'global denial of all claims is insufficient to meet . . . the requirements of Article 19'.[381] The respondent, like the claimant, 'may annex' documents on which its statement relies or may simply refer to evidence it intends to submit later. **16.241**

Pursuant to Art 21(3), the statement of defence is also the respondent's last opportunity to raise 'a plea that the arbitral tribunal does not have jurisdiction'. In certain cases, a respondent has successfully argued that it should submit only its jurisdictional objection when its statement of defence becomes due, to avoid possibly wasted effort.[382] The tribunal's power to bifurcate proceedings even before the statement of defence is submitted may be derived from the combined provisions of Art 15 (tribunal's general authority to conduct proceedings as it deems appropriate); Art 21(3) (authorizing the raising of jurisdictional defences before the statement of defence), Art 23 (authorizing extensions of the presumptive 45-day deadline for filing statements of defence); and Art 21(4) (encouraging tribunals to rule on a jurisdictional objection as 'a preliminary question'). **16.242**

---

[381] *Rockwell Int'l Systems Inc v Islamic Republic of Iran* (Award no 438-430-1, 5 September 1989) para 142, *reprinted in* 23 Iran–USCTR 150, 188 (1989-III).

[382] See *United Parcel Service of America Inc v Government of Canada* (Decision of NAFTA Chapter 11 Tribunal on the Filing of Statement of Defence, 17 October 2001) para 20, available at <http://www.international.gc.ca/trade-agreements-accords-commerciaux/assets/pdfs/SD_oct.pdf>; *Canfor Corp v United States of America* (Decision of NAFTA Chapter 11 Tribunal on the Place of Arbitration, Filing of a Statement of Defence and Bifurcation of the Proceedings, 23 January 2004) para 47, available at <http://www.state.gov/documents/organization/28637.pdf> .

16.243 (1.3) **Counterclaims and claims of set-off** The statement of defence should also include any counterclaim or claim of set-off that the respondent wishes to make and that arises 'out of the same contract'. A counterclaim or set-off may not be filed against a person or entity that is not already a party to the proceeding.[383]

16.244 In principle, counterclaims and claims of set-off are distinct. For example, unlike a counterclaim, a claim of set-off is often based on a debt owed in a different transaction. However, several commentators have doubted whether such differences survive under Art 19(3) of the Rules, which requires that any counterclaim *or* set-off 'aris[e] out of the same contract' on which the main claim is based.[384] Indeed, the Iran-US Claims Tribunal has held that, 'as far as its jurisdiction is concerned claims for set-off are generally governed by the same standards as counterclaims'.[385] In a subsequent dissent criticizing the Tribunal's general approach to set-off, Judge Khalilian complained that the majority failed to preserve the distinction between a counterclaim, which 'must be related to [the original claim]', and a set-off, which 'indicates the existence of a debt which in itself . . . sets off and extinguishes all or part of the claimant's claims'.[386] However, as certain commentators have noted, the objection might more properly be directed at the Rules than at the Tribunal's application of them.[387]

16.245 The practical impact of Art 19(3)'s limitation on set-off is illustrated in numerous decisions by the Iran-US Claims Tribunal dismissing claims by Iran for unpaid taxes or social insurance contributions against corporations that presented claims based on business they had done with the Government of Iran. The Tribunal held that such tax claims arose from statutory law, rather than from 'the same contract', unless the contract provided for deduction of taxes from payments due.[388]

16.246 Article 19(3) permits a respondent to raise a counterclaim or claim of set-off even after it has filed its statement of defence, if the tribunal decides that 'the delay was justified'. The Iran-US Claims Tribunal usually based such decisions on whether a valid excuse for the delay had been given and the extent to which the delay prejudiced the claimant or efficient

---

383 See *Itel Int'l Corp v Social Security Organization of Iran et al* (Award no 479-476-2, para 6, 23 May 1990), *reprinted in* 24 Iran–USCTR 272, 275 (1990-I).

384 Baker and Davis (n 62) 89; Caron, Caplan and Pellonpää (n 61) 413.

385 *Computer Science Corp v Islamic Republic of Iran* (Award no 221-65-1, 16 April 1986), *reprinted in* 10 Iran–USCTR 269, 309 (1986-I).

386 *First National Bank of Boston v Islamic Republic of Iran* (Decision no DEC 83-202-2, 19 September 1988) (Separate Opinion of Seyed Khalilian, 23 September 1988), *reprinted in* 19 Iran–USCTR 310, 312 (1938-II). Judge Khalilian cited, among other authorities, the definition of 'set-off' in *Black's Law Dictionary*: 'remedy employed by the defendant to reduce plaintiff's demand by an opposite one arising from transaction extrinsic to plaintiff's cause of action.' *ibid* 311; see also van Hof (n 55) 133–4.

387 Caron, Caplan and Pellonpää (n 61) 413 n 61.

388 See eg *Houston Contracting Co v National Iranian Oil Co* (Award no 378-173-3, 22 July 1988), *reprinted in* 20 Iran–USCTR 3, 36–8 (1988-II) (citing numerous prior decisions to the same effect). The Tribunal rejected such tax claims even though, pursuant to its revision of Art 19(3), it applied the jurisdictional test of the Claims Settlement Declaration ('counterclaim which arises out of the same contract, transaction or occurrence that constitutes the subject matter of [the] claim'), which is obviously broader than the test under Art 19(3) of the Rules. See Art II(1), Claims Settlement Declaration, *reprinted in* Baker and Davis (n 62) 281.

completion of the proceedings.[389] Article 19(4) requires that, in presenting its counterclaim or claim for set-off, the respondent must fulfil the requirements of Art 18(2) regarding a statement of claim.

Article 19 does not mention an opportunity to file a statement of defence in response to a counterclaim, but the drafters apparently believed the claimant's right to make such a submission was assured by Art 15's requirement of equal treatment of the parties.[390] **16.247**

(2) Contemplated revisions

The Working Group will recommend three changes in Art 19 conforming to revisions sought elsewhere in the Rules. The Working Group intends to clarify that the respondent 'should, as far as possible', annex the evidence on which it relies to its statement of claim.[391] This is consistent with a similar change in Art 18. Secondly, in view of the proposed requirement of a response to the notice of arbitration,[392] the Working Group seeks new language in Art 19(1) (cf similar language to be added in Art 18), allowing a respondent to decide (once it has seen the statement of claim) that its response also constitutes its statement of defence.[393] Finally, the Working Group has considered how best to revise the requirement in Art 19(3) that counter-claims or claims of set-off must arise 'from the same contract' as the claim so as to avoid implying that the Rules apply only to contractual disputes.[394] Such a revision would be especially relevant to investor-State arbitrations under bilateral investment treaties (BITs),[395] in which there is often no contractual relationship between the investor and the State. The present text may serve to exclude the arbitrators' jurisdiction over counterclaims in such cases.[396] The Working Group considered several alternative formulations for defining the permissible range of counterclaims and claims of set-off (including a very broad proposal to allow set-off based on claims not even covered by the same arbitration agreement[397]) but concluded that all such alternatives ran the risk of **16.248**

389 See eg *Harris Int'l Telecommunications Inc v Islamic Republic of Iran* (Award no 323-409-1, 2 November 1987), *reprinted in* 17 Iran–USCTR 31, 61 (1987-IV) (no explanation provided); *American Bell Int'l Inc v Islamic Republic of Iran* (Award no 255-48-3, 19 September 1986), *reprinted in* 12 Iran–USCTR 170, 225 (1980-III) (no prejudice to claimant).

390 UNCITRAL Committee of the Whole II, *Summary Report of the 8th Session* (16 April 1976) paras 57–8, UN Doc A/CN.9/9/C.2/SR.8 (remarks of French, USSR and Austrian delegates opposing draft language providing for replies to counterclaims).

391 *Report of WGII on the work of its 50th session* (9–13 February 2009) para 26, UN Doc A/CN.9/669 (approving, as modified, the draft text of revised Art 19(2) set forth in *Note by the Secretariat*, UN Doc A/CN.9/WG.II/WP/151/Add.1 para 2).

392 See discussion of proposed revisions in Art 3, *supra*.

393 *Report of WGII on the work of its 50th session* (9–13 February 2009) para 25, UN Doc A/CN.9/669 (approving, as modified, the draft text of revised Art 19(1) set forth in *Note by the Secretariat*, UN Doc A/CN.9/WG.II/WP/151/Add.1 para 2).

394 *Report of WGII on the work of its 46th session* (5–9 February 2007) paras 156-60, UN Doc A/CN.9/619.

395 *ibid*, para 158.

396 See *Saluka Investments BV v Czech Republic* (Decision on Tribunal's Jurisdiction over The Czech Republic's Counterclaims, 7 May 2004) para 26 (assessing claimant's argument that, in arbitration brought pursuant to Netherlands-Czech BIT, the 'UNCITRAL Rules did not allow counterclaims . . . , since Art 19.3 only allowed counterclaims arising out of the same legal instrument containing the reference to arbitration', ie the BIT), available at <http://ita.law.uvic.ca/documents/Saluka-DecisiononJurisdiction-counterclaim.pdf>.

397 See Note by the Secretariat, *Proposal by the Government of Switzerland* (9 September 2008), UN Doc A/CN.9/WG.II/WP.152.

unduly interfering with procedural domestic law and of being subject to variable interpretations under different legal systems.[398] The Working Group thus determined that Art 19(3) should be revised to permit the respondent to 'make a counterclaim or rely on a claim for the purpose of a set-off provided that the tribunal has jurisdiction over it'.[399]

AMENDMENTS TO THE CLAIM OR DEFENCE

Article 20

During the course of the arbitral proceedings either party may amend or supplement his claim or defence unless the arbitral tribunal considers it inappropriate to allow such amendment having regard to the delay in making it or prejudice to the other party or any other circumstances. However, a claim may not be amended in such a manner that the amended claim falls outside the scope of the arbitration clause or separate arbitration agreement.

(1) Commentary on current text

16.249 Article 20 of the Rules (i) sets forth the parties' general right to amend their claims or defences (provided these remain within the scope of the arbitration agreement), but (ii) subjects this right to the tribunal's authority to reject a particular amendment on grounds of unexcused delay or prejudice to the parties or proceedings.

16.250 (1.1) **The general right to amend claims or defences** The phrasing of Art 20's first sentence signals a presumption in favour of allowing amendments, and this interpretation has been confirmed by relevant tribunals. The Iran-US Claims Tribunal has held that Art 20 'affords wide latitude to a party who seeks to amend a claim',[400] while a NAFTA ch 11 tribunal has stated that, although 'the tribunal may exercise control over amendments, its leave need not be sought in the first instance'.[401] As another *ad hoc* tribunal has warned, the alternative would be an 'unduly static or formalistic rule that would require parties to recommence proceedings every time the adversarial evolution of argument and evidence suggests the need for a different legal articulation of claims'.[402]

16.251 (1.2) **Tribunal's acceptance of amendments** As for the admissibility of particular amendments under Art 20's criteria, the Iran-US Claims Tribunal has generally found no undue delay or prejudice when a party seeks at a reasonable stage to amend the amount[403] or interest rate claimed[404] or to add a new legal theory for recovery if the factual predicate(s)

[398] *Report of WGII on the work of its 50th session* (9–13 February 2009) paras 27–31, UN Doc A/CN.9/669.

[399] *ibid*, paras 31–2.

[400] *Int'l School Services Inc v Islamic Republic of Iran* (Award no ITL 57-123-1, 30 January 1986), *reprinted in* 10 Iran–USCTR 6, 12 (1986-I).

[401] *United Parcel Service of America Inc v Government of Canada* (Award on Jurisdiction, 22 November 2002) para 131, available at <http://www.international.gc.ca/trade-agreements-accords-commerciaux/assets/pdfs/Jurisdiction%20Award.22Nov02.pdf>.

[402] *Himpurna California Energy Ltd v PT. (Persero) Perusahaan Listruik Negara* (Final Award, 4 May 1999) para 58, *reprinted in* (2000) XXV *Ybk Comm Arb* 13, 29.

[403] See eg *Fereydoon Ghaffari (a claim less than US $250,000 presented by the United States of America) v Islamic Republic of Iran* (Order by Chamber Two in Case no 10792, 15 September 1987), *reprinted in* 18 Iran–USCTR 64, 65 (1988-I).

[404] See eg *Cal-Maine Food Inc v Islamic Republic of Iran* (Award no 133-340-3, 11 June 1984), *reprinted in* 6 Iran–USCTR 52, 62–3 (1984-II).

were already pleaded[405] or if the other party has ample time to respond. Usually, the Tribunal has canvassed the views of any affected party before judging the degree of possible prejudice.[406] By contrast, adding a new respondent well after the statement of claim had been filed has been deemed prejudicial,[407] as was addition of a new legal claim based on facts not pleaded before.[408]

(2) Contemplated revisions

The Working Group recommends minor revisions in Art 20 to make clear that amendments may be made to counterclaims, as well as to claims or defences, and to require the tribunal to consider the prejudice to 'all other parties', not just 'the other party'.[409] In addition, in keeping with the new language proposed for Art 19 that would permit any counterclaim or claim of set-off over which the tribunal has jurisdiction, the last sentence of Art 20 would be revised to prohibit only amendments to claims or defences that lie beyond 'the competence of the tribunal' rather than falling 'outside the scope of the arbitration clause'.[410] **16.252**

PLEAS AS TO THE JURISDICTION OF THE ARBITRAL TRIBUNAL

Article 21

1 **The arbitral tribunal shall have the power to rule on objections that it has no jurisdiction, including any objections with respect to the existence or validity of the arbitration clause or of the separate arbitration agreement.**

2 **The arbitral tribunal shall have the power to determine the existence or the validity of the contract of which an arbitration clause forms a part. For the purposes of article 21, an arbitration clause which forms part of a contract and which provides for arbitration under these Rules shall be treated as an agreement independent of the other terms of the contract. A decision by the arbitral tribunal that the contract is null and void shall not entail *ipso jure* the invalidity of the arbitration clause.**

3 **A plea that the arbitral tribunal does not have jurisdiction shall be raised not later than in the statement of defence or, with respect to a counter-claim, in the reply to the counterclaim.**

4 **In general, the arbitral tribunal should rule on a plea concerning its jurisdiction as a preliminary question. However, the arbitral tribunal may proceed with the arbitration and rule on such a plea in their final award.**

---

[405] See eg *Sedco Inc v National Iranian Oil Co et al* (Award no ITL 55-129-3, 28 October 1985, *reprinted in* 9 Iran–USCTR 248, 265–6 (1985-II).

[406] Caron, Caplan and Pellonpää (n 61) 471, 474.

[407] *Bank Markazi Iran v Bank of Boston International, New York*, Case no 733 (Order of Chamber Two, 8 December 1983); cf *Fedders Corp v Loristan Refrigeration Industries* (Decision no DEC 51-250-3, 28 October 1986), *reprinted in* 13 Iran–USCTR 97, 98 (1986-IV) (upholding addition of new respondent that was deemed a 'clarification' of the statement of claim, not an amendment of the claim).

[408] See eg *Arthur Young and Co v Islamic Republic of Iran* (Award no 338-484-1, 1 December 1987), *reprinted in* 17 Iran–USCTR 245, 253–54 (1987-IV). Any amendment that raises the prospect of claimant's filing a new claim faces an additional hurdle at the Iran-US Claims Tribunal that does not arise in other UNCITRAL proceedings, namely the jurisdictional filing deadline imposed by the Claims Settlement Declaration. See eg *Westinghouse Electric Corp v Islamic Republic of Iran* (Award no 579-389-2, para 44, 20 March 1997), *reprinted in* 33 Iran–USCTR 60, 75-6 (1997).

[409] *Report of WGII on the work of its 50th session* (9–13 February 2009) paras 34-5, UN Doc A/CN.9/669 (approving, as modified, the draft text of revised Art 20 set forth in *Note by the Secretariat*, UN Doc A/CN.9/WG.II/WP/151/Add.1 para 4).

[410] *ibid.*

(1) Commentary on current text

16.253 Article 21 affirms two crucial principles: that (i) the tribunal has jurisdiction to determine its jurisdiction and that (ii) in doing so, it shall treat an arbitration agreement as separable from any contract that contains it. Article 21 also regulates objections to jurisdiction: (iii) a party must raise an objection no later than in the statement of defence or the reply to a counterclaim; and (iv) the tribunal should usually resolve such objections as preliminary questions but may defer doing so until the final award.

16.254 (1.1) **Tribunal's authority to resolve jurisdiction** Article 21(1) confirms the well established principle in international arbitration that an arbitral tribunal has jurisdiction to rule upon its own jurisdiction, often referred to as the doctrine of '*competence-competence*'. This has been characterized as 'a legal fiction' that 'evolved to avoid th[e] drawbacks' that would result if a respondent could frustrate any properly agreed arbitration clause by insisting first on a court ruling as to the arbitrators' jurisdiction.[411] The drafters debated whether to add language to this Article making clear that, notwithstanding the arbitral authority just described, the relevant national law (as applied by courts[412]) would ultimately control the question of the arbitrators' jurisdiction. This debate did not alter Art 21 but led instead to insertion of the general provision in Art 1 confirming that the Rules as a whole are subject to mandatory provisions of applicable law.[413] Thus, as Professor Sanders notes in his *Commentary* regarding Art 21, 'notwithstanding the impression this provision might give, the final word on the competence of arbitrators still remains with the [c]ourt'.[414]

16.255 (1.2) **Separability of the arbitration clause** Article 21(2) reaffirms another basic principle of international arbitration, the doctrine of 'separability'. The doctrine holds that a tribunal's finding that the parties' contract is void or invalid does not, in and of itself, entail a holding that an arbitration clause contained in that contract is also invalid. The underlying theory, as expressed during the drafting, is that parties who insert an arbitration clause in a contract actually intend to submit to arbitration all 'disputes arising from or relating to the contractual *relationship*'.[415] This presumption is also reflected in the wording of the Model Arbitration Clause attached to Art 1, which includes among the issues that the parties agree to submit to arbitration any dispute relating to the 'breach, termination *or invalidity*' (emphasis added) of the contract. It has been noted that a further consequence of the separability doctrine is to render a tribunal's finding as to the invalidity of a contract largely beyond the review of courts, since such a finding is no longer bound up with a determination as to the tribunal's competence.[416]

---

411 Lew, J., Mistelis, L. and Kröll, S., *Comparative International Commercial Arbitration* 333 (Kluwer, The Hague, 2003).

412 UNCITRAL, *Summary Record of 165th Session* (11 April 1975) 17–9 (Remarks of the Chairman, the Brazilian delegate and of Professor Sanders), UN Doc A/CN.9/SR.165; see also Caron, Caplan and Pellonpää (n 61) 445; van Hof (n 55) 142–3.

413 UNCITRAL Committee of the Whole II, *Summary Record of the 8th Meeting* (16 April 1976) paras 13–20, UN Doc A/CN.9/9/C.2/SR.8; *Report of Committee of the Whole II* (n 55) 67, para 12.

414 Sanders (n 28) 197.

415 *Commentary on Revised draft Rules* (n 90) 174 (emphasis added) (commentary on draft Art 19(2)).

416 Caron, Caplan and Pellonpää (n 61) 447.

(1.3) Timing of objections to jurisdiction Article 21(3) requires that any objection to jurisdiction 'shall be raised *not later than* the statement of defense or . . . in the reply to the counter-claim' (emphasis added), implying that no objection may be raised thereafter. In practice, however, there are three narrow exceptions. As first drafted, Art 21(3) contained an exception for cases where 'delay in raising a plea of incompetence is justified'.[417] Ultimately, that caveat was dropped, but only because Art 20 already gave parties an opportunity to amend their defence and, more generally, arbitrators have authority to conduct the proceedings as they deem appropriate.[418] Secondly, a jurisdictional objection that cannot be waived under applicable law may be raised after the deadline.[419] Finally, the deadline for parties' objections does not prevent a tribunal from subsequently raising jurisdictional concerns *sua sponte*.[420] **16.256**

(1.4) Jurisdiction as a preliminary issue According to Art 21(4), a jurisdictional objection should 'in general' be resolved by the tribunal 'as a preliminary question', reflecting many drafters' belief that such a practice avoids unnecessary expense.[421] However, as some delegates noted, a separate resolution of jurisdiction may not be the most efficient approach if jurisdiction is ultimately upheld.[422] **16.257**

As certain commentators have noted, after initially favouring preliminary resolution of jurisdictional disputes, the Iran-US Tribunal shifted its practice as it found that the separate briefing, hearing, and deliberation of a challenge to jurisdiction, followed by the writing of an award dismissing the challenge, only prolonged proceedings and expanded their costs.[423] A tribunal may also decide to defer resolving jurisdiction if 'part of the [respondent's] jurisdictional challenge depends critically on issues which are intimately linked to the factual merits of [the claimant's] case'.[424] In addition, based on the Iran-US Tribunal's nearly **16.258**

[417] *Preliminary draft Rules* (n 18) (draft Art 18(2), *reprinted in* (1975) VI *UNCITRAL Ybk* 163, 174. One example given of a justifiable delay was a jurisdictional objection arising from new facts, see *Commentary on Revised draft Rules* (n 90) 174 (commentary on draft Art 19(3)).

[418] *Report of the Committee of the Whole II* (n 55) 74 (discussing revision of draft Art 19(3)). The reliance on the arbitrators' flexibility in conducting proceedings may be misplaced since the authority under Art 15(1) is expressly made 'subject to these Rules', including the seemingly mandatory rule of Art 21(3).

[419] See Baker and Davis (n 62) 105–6. But see *CME Czech Republic BV v Czech Republic* (Partial Award of 13 September 2001; *ad hoc* UNCITRAL proceeding) para 380 ('The majority of the Tribunal is of the opinion that, disregarding possible Czech national law requirements, the clear provision of the UNCITRAL Rules must supersede national law, if deviating. According to the UNCITRAL Rules, a defence of jurisdiction is deemed to be waived, if not raised in time.'), available at <http://ita.law.uvic.ca/documents/CME-2001PartialAward.pdf>.

[420] *Burton Marks et al v Islamic Republic of Iran* (Award no ITL 53-458-3, 26 June 1985), *reprinted in* 8 Iran–USCTR 290, 296–7 (1985-I) (dismissing the claims on grounds first raised by the tribunal after respondent raised no jurisdictional objection in its statement of defence).

[421] See eg UNCITRAL Committee of the Whole II, *Summary Record of 8th Meeting* (16 April 1976) paras 32, 40, A.CN.9/9/C.2/SR.8 (remarks of Nigerian delegate and of observer from the International Council for Commercial Arbitration).

[422] *id* (see, especially, remarks by the Chairman of the Committee and by the Mexican delegate).

[423] Baker and Davis (n 62) 107; van Hof (n 55) 151.

[424] *Methanex v United States of America* (Partial Award on Jurisdiction, 7 August 2002; NAFTA Chapter 11 proceeding) para 167, available at <http://ita.law.uvic.ca/documents/Methanex-1stPartial.pdf>. See also *Glamis Gold v United States* (Procedural Order no 2, 31 May 2005; NAFTA Chapter 11 proceedings) para 12(c) (tribunal 'may decline to [bifurcate jurisdictional issues] when doing so is unlikely to bring about increased efficiency'), available at <http://ita.law.uvic.ca/documents/16Order2_000.pdf>.

uniform practice of not resolving separately any jurisdictional objections relating to counterclaims, Judge Brower believes that Art 21(4) is 'intended to address only main claims'.[425]

(2) Contemplated revisions

16.259 The Working Group will recommend that Art 21 be essentially replaced by most of the text of Art 16 of the UNCITRAL Model Law on International Commercial Arbitration ('the Model Law'), which provides more comprehensive treatment of the same subjects. Thus, the revised Art 21 would contain three paragraphs dealing with (i) the principles of *competence-competence* and separability; (ii) regulation of the parties' right to raise jurisdictional objections; and (iii) the tribunal's prerogative of resolving jurisdiction as a preliminary question.

16.260 (2.1) ***Competence-Competence* and *separability*** The Working Group intends to replace Arts 21(1) and 21(2) with the text of Art 16(1) of the Model Law.[426] The Working Group felt that the Model Law language clarified the tribunal's power to raise jurisdictional concerns *sua sponte* in those unusual circumstances where the parties themselves do not do so.[427]

16.261 (2.2) **Regulating the parties' objections to jurisdiction** The Working Group recommends that the current text of Art 21(3) be replaced essentially by the text of Model Law Art 16(2),[428] which adds three points that are substantively related to the existing requirement that parties raise jurisdictional objections no later than the statement of defence or reply to counterclaim. The Working Group believes it is useful also to clarify, as Model Law Art 16(2) does, that (i) a party's participation in appointment of the tribunal does not waive jurisdictional objections; (ii) a plea that an arbitral tribunal is exceeding the scope of its authority must be raised 'as soon as' the action threatening that result occurs; and (iii) a party may raise a belated jurisdictional objection if the tribunal finds 'the delay justified'. As has been noted, the last addition was proposed for inclusion in the 1976 Rules but ultimately deleted.

16.262 (2.3) **Bifurcating jurisdictional issues** The Working Group seeks to replace the current text of Art 21(4) with two provisions contained in Model Law Art 16(3), the first of which would still permit, but would no longer encourage, the resolution of jurisdiction as a preliminary question. The second provision would confirm an arbitral tribunal's power to

[425] *Islamic Republic of Iran v United States of America*, Case no B-1 (Order of 27 November 2001) (dissenting opinion of Judge Brower), *reprinted in* 36 Iran–USCTR 286, 290 n 14 (2000–2002).

[426] *Report of WGII on the work of its 50th session* (9–13 February 2009) paras 36–44, UN Doc A/CN.9/669, adopting with only two minor edits, the phrasing of draft Art 21(1) as set forth in *Note by the Secretariat*, UN Doc A/CN.9/WG.II/WP.151/Add.1 para 5.

[427] *Report of WGII on the work of its 45th session* (11–15 September 2006) para 97, UN Doc A/CN.9/614.

[428] *Report of WGII on the work of its 46th session* (5–9 February 2007) para 163, UN Doc A/CN.9/619, adopting the draft Art 21(2) as set forth in *Note by the Secretariat*, UN Doc A/CN.9/WG.II/WP.145/Add.1 para 19; see also *Report of WGII on the work of its 50th session* (9–13 February 2009) para 45, UN Doc A/CN.9/669 (confirming earlier decision).

proceed with the case notwithstanding a 'pending challenge to its jurisdiction before a court'.[429]

FURTHER WRITTEN STATEMENTS

Article 22

The arbitral tribunal shall decide which further written statements, in addition to the statement of claim and the statement of defence, shall be required from the parties or may be presented by them and shall fix the periods of time for communicating such statements.

(1) Commentary on current text

Article 22 directs the tribunal to decide whether to have further written submissions, including by fixing any filing dates. In general, international commercial arbitrations will require such further pleadings, and the number and sequencing is left to the discretion of the arbitrator(s). **16.263**

It has been suggested that the principle of equal treatment may require sequential filings, to give each party an equal opportunity of responding to the other.[430] On the other hand, at the Iran-US Claims Tribunal, final submissions were often ordered to be simultaneous, which may be a method of addressing the conflict between common and civil law traditions as to which of the parties—claimant or respondent—should have the last word.[431] Although Art 22 is framed as permitting further written submissions, it has often been invoked by the Iran-US Claims Tribunal in support of its negative power to reject unauthorized or untimely submissions.[432] **16.264**

(2) Contemplated revisions

The Working Group does not intend to recommend modifications in Art 22.[433] **16.265**

PERIODS OF TIME

Article 23

The periods of time fixed by the arbitral tribunal for the communication of written statements (including the statement of claim and statement of defence) should not exceed forty-five days. However, the arbitral tribunal may extend the time limits if it concludes that an extension is justified.

(1) Commentary on current text

Article 23 establishes a presumption that the time given for filing submissions referred to in Arts 18, 19 and 22 should not exceed 45 days. However, the provision also gives the tribunal authority to extend that limit when it deems this 'justified'. During the drafting of this provision it was noted that firm deadlines were important to efficient proceedings but **16.266**

---

429 *Report of WGII on the work of its 50th session* (9–13 February 2009) para 46, UN Doc A/CN.9/669, adopting the draft of revised Art 21(3) as set forth in UN Doc A/CN.9/WG.II/WP.151/Add.1 para 5.

430 van Hof (n 55) 155; Caron, Caplan and Pellonpää (n 61) 502.

431 van Hof (n 55) 153.

432 Baker and Davis (n 62) 96–7; see eg *Vivian Mai Tavakoli et al v Islamic Republic of Iran* (Award no 580-832-3, 23 April 1997) para 9 (citing numerous precedents to demonstrate that the Tribunal 'has in general taken a restrictive approach to the exercise of its discretion' to accept unauthorized late submissions pursuant to Art 22), *reprinted in* 33 Iran–USCTR 206, 211 (1997).

433 *Report of WGII on the work of its 50th session* (9–13 February 2009) para 47, UN Doc A/CN.9/669.

that the 45-day period was intended only 'as a general guideline' since 'it has been found that rigid time periods cannot be imposed [by rule] in domestic commercial arbitrations and of course this holds true even more for international commercial arbitrations'.[434]

16.267 Article 23 does not say what consequence may follow from the failure to meet any final deadline established. (Article 28 does address the impact on the proceedings of a failure to submit a statement of claim or of defence.) The Iran-US Claims Tribunal, which often confronted the problem of late-filed documents or excessive requests for extensions,[435] adopted various responses depending upon such factors as whether there was a legitimate explanation for delay, the nature of the material submitted, and the overall impact on the other party or parties or the proceedings. The responses ranged from outright rejection of the tardy document[436] to allowing a further extension for a document's submission while adjusting subsequent deadlines to mitigate prejudice to the other party,[437] to denying the extension and proceeding to tribunal deliberations but permitting submission of the document during that time, for whatever notice the tribunal could take of it.[438]

(2) Contemplated revisions

16.268 The Working Group has not recommended any revisions to Art 23.[439]

EVIDENCE AND HEARINGS (ARTICLES 24 AND 25)

Article 24

1 **Each party shall have the burden of proving the facts relied on to support his claim or defence.**

2 **The arbitral tribunal may, if it considers it appropriate, require a party to deliver to the tribunal and to the other party, within such a period of time as the arbitral tribunal shall decide, a summary of the documents and other evidence which that party intends to present in support of the facts in issue set out in his statement of claim or statement of defence.**

3 **At any time during the arbitral proceedings the arbitral tribunal may require the parties to produce documents, exhibits or other evidence within such a period of time as the tribunal shall determine.**

(1) Commentary on current text

16.269 Article 24 contains three rules regarding the presentation of evidence during an arbitration: (i) each party bears the burden of proving facts on which it relies to support its claim or defence; (ii) the tribunal may order a party to produce a summary of 'documents and other evidence' it will adduce to support facts set forth in its statement of claim or of defence; and (iii) the tribunal may order a party to 'produce documents, exhibits or other evidence'.

---

434 *Commentary on Revised draft Rules* (n 90) 175 (commentary on draft Art 21).

435 See Caron, Caplan and Pellonpää (n 61) 520–2; Baker and Davis (n 62) 99–100.

436 See eg *Bendix Corp v Islamic Republic of Iran et al,* Case no 208 (Order by Chamber Two, 28 September 1987).

437 See eg *United States of America on behalf and for the benefit of Thomas A Todd v Islamic Republic of Iran,* Case no 10856 (Order of Chamber One, 8 January 1986).

438 See eg *Hoffman Export Corporation v Ministry of National Defence of Iran,* Case no 50 (Order of Chamber Two, 8 December 1983).

439 *Report of WGII on the work of its 50th session* (9–13 February 2009) para 48, UN Doc A/CN.9/669.

(1.1) Burden of proving facts relied upon Professor Sanders has described Art 24(1) as setting forth a 'generally accepted principle' concerning burden of proof, and one may therefore wonder about the need to have included it. Indeed, this provision was added late in the drafting, with no explanation in the *travaux préparatoires*.[440] However, as certain commentators have noted, 'the expectations of parties from different legal systems are never so likely to conflict as with questions of evidence',[441] and this may be sufficient reason for expressly restating a 'generally accepted principle'. Even such a straightforward rule can give rise to disagreement in practice as to whether a given fact is raised by the defence or must be disproved as an element of the claim.[442] Moreover, the obligation to prove facts on which a claim or defence relies does not preclude doing so indirectly, such as by drawing inferences from evidence of other, related facts.[443] **16.270**

Indeed, Art 24(1) is silent on the question of the standard of proof, which, in the practice of the Iran-US Claims Tribunal, 'varies according to the circumstances'.[444] In particular, as another commentator has noted, 'the use of presumptions mitigates and partially shifts the burden'.[445] For example, the Tribunal established a presumption that a corporate claimant could demonstrate its US nationality (a jurisdictional requirement) if it introduced certain evidence concerning the percentage of foreign addresses and the maximum percentage shareholdings among its shareholders.[446] This presumption was subject to rebuttal by the respondent, making it in effect one instance of the Tribunal's willingness on selected issues to shift the burden to the respondent to disprove a fact after the claimant has made a *prima facie* showing that the fact is true. Sometimes, as in the case of a corporation's nationality, the Tribunal resorted to this presumption so as not to 'impose excessive burdens on the Parties and the Tribunal'.[447] In other instances, this approach was adopted because of the 'difficulty which the applicant may have in trying to obtain corroborative evidence'.[448] **16.271**

(1.2) Providing summaries of anticipated evidence Article 24(2) authorizes tribunals to order submission of a summary of evidence a party 'intends to present in support of the facts in issue set out in his state of claim or . . . of defense'. This may again seem superfluous, given the tribunal's general authority under Art 15 to conduct the proceedings in the **16.272**

---

[440] See *Commentary on Revised draft Rules* (n 90) 75 (commenting on a proposed draft Art 21(1)).

[441] Caron, Caplan and Pellonpää (n 61) 565.

[442] See eg *Ultrasystems Inc v Islamic Republic of Iran* (Dissent by Judge Mosk to Award no 89-84-3, 7 December 1983) (objecting that the respondent bore the burden of showing that the claimant's checks had been paid, as this was an affirmative defence and that the majority of the tribunal had erred in requiring the claimant to demonstrate non-payment), *reprinted in* 4 Iran–USCTR 80 (1983-III).

[443] See eg *PEPSICO v Islamic Republic of Iran* (Dissenting opinion of Judge Ameli in Award no 260-18-1, 13 October 1986) (criticizing the majority's willingness to assume that goods shipped by the claimant arrived in Iran 30 days later since the claimant had the burden of proving when the 180-day period for payment following receipt began), *reprinted in* 13 Iran–USCTR 3, 54 (1986-VI).

[444] Caron, Caplan and Pellonpää (n 61) 570; see, generally, *id* 570–2.

[445] van Hof (n 55) 162.

[446] See eg *Flexi-Van Leasing Inc v Islamic Republic of Iran* (Order of Chamber One, 15 December 1982), *reprinted in* 1 Iran–USCTR 455, 457-8 (1981-82); see also Caron, Caplan and Pellonpää (n 61) 571; Baker and Davis (n 62) 110.

[447] *Flexi-Van Leasing Inc v Islamic Republic of Iran* (Order of Chamber One, 15 December 1982), *reprinted in* 1 Iran–USCTR 455, 457 (1981-82).

[448] Caron, Caplan and Pellonpää (n 61) 570.

'manner . . . it considers appropriate' and under Art 22 to 'decide which further written statements . . . shall be required from the parties'. However, it was stated during the drafting that this provision was needed 'in order to prevent surprise at hearings'.[449] Thus, the key words in Art 24(2) are 'evidence which that party *intends to present*'. The provision was evidently not understood as providing for summaries of evidence that had been submitted with the statement of claim or defence, although of course that kind of summary could be ordered.

16.273 (1.3) **Tribunal orders for the production of evidence** The tribunal may order a party to produce evidence that is sought by another party or that the tribunal seeks *sua sponte*. According to certain commentators, Art 24(3)'s reference to 'other evidence' includes evidence from witnesses,[450] such as by affidavit,[451] although orders for production of an affidavit would appear to be rare. The scope of Art 24(3) has been understood to authorize not broad 'discovery' of large categories of documents but rather production orders for specific evidence. Generally, the Iran-US Claims Tribunal has also required a requesting party to describe its own effort to obtain the evidence before granting an order directing production.[452] Although some of the Article's drafters suggested this provision could be deleted because this authority was implicit in the power to control proceedings under Art 15, the counter-argument was successfully raised that, 'since the Rules were intended to be applied by arbitrators of different nationalities and backgrounds throughout the world, the parties might wish to have a prior indication of the powers of the arbitrator'.[453]

16.274 One issue that Art 24(3) does not address is how or whether an order to produce evidence may be enforced if a party fails to carry it out. Assuming a local court has the power (and is willing) to enforce such an order, the question remains whether a party or the tribunal may seek such court assistance. The parties' general authorization under Art 26(3) to seek court-ordered interim measures would seem to extend to measures enforcing tribunal orders to produce evidence. Similarly, a tribunal's general authority under Art 15(1) to conduct an arbitration 'in such manner as it considers appropriate' would appear to encompass the power to seek court enforcement of the tribunal's own orders.[454] It has been noted[455] that the UNCITRAL Model Law, which contains provisions comparable to Art 26(3)[456] and Art 15(1)[457] of the Rules, has a separate provision authorizing the tribunal or a party (with the tribunal's 'approval') to request a court's 'assistance in taking evidence'.[458] However, 'the intent of the Working Group [that drafted this Model Law provision was] that the Article . . . establishes a right to [court] assistance to an arbitration'.[459] Thus, it was the

449 *Commentary on Revised draft Rules* (n 90) 75 (commentary on proposed draft of new Art 21(2)).
450 Sanders (n 28) 202.
451 Caron, Caplan and Pellonpää (n 61) 575.
452 Caron, Caplan and Pellonpää (n 61) 577.
453 UNCITRAL Committee of the Whole II, *Summary Record of the 8th Meeting* (16 April 1976) para 76 (comments of the US delegate), UN Doc A/CN.9/9/C.2/SR.8.
454 Caron, Caplan and Pellonpää (n 61) 579.
455 *id.*
456 See Art 9 of the Model Law on International Commercial Arbitration (2006).
457 See Art 19(2) of the Model Law on International Commercial Arbitration (2006).
458 Art 27 of the Model Law on International Commercial Arbitration (2006).
459 Holtzmann, H. and Neuhaus, J., *A Guide to the UNCITRAL Model Law on International Commercial Arbitration: Legislative History and Commentary* 737 (Kluwer, Deventer, 1989).

power of the courts to grant assistance, not of the tribunal or the parties to seek assistance, that the Model Law drafters seemingly felt the need to establish. Quite apart from any court enforcement of an order to produce evidence, it has been held that the tribunal may draw an adverse inference from non-compliance with its order, concluding that material evidence that, without valid explanation, a party fails to produce is likely adverse to the party's position.[460]

(2) Contemplated revisions

The Working Group intends (i) to recommend the deletion of Art 24(2); and (ii) to recommend relocating the substance of Art 25(5) and (6) to Art 24. The heading above Art 24 would be shortened to 'Evidence,' which would no longer extend as well to Art 25. **16.275**

(2.1) Deletion of Article 24(2) The Working Group favours deletion of Art 24(2) on the ground that it is 'rarely, if at all, used in practice' and that its deletion would not 'diminis[h] the discretion of the arbitral tribunal' to request a summary of evidence pursuant to its general authority under Art 15(1).[461] Retention of the provision is deemed to send the wrong signal to parties 'about the optimal form in which evidence was expected to be submitted',[462] particularly in light of the changes that the Working Group recommends in Arts 18 and 19 to encourage full submission of documentary evidence as exhibits to the statements of claim and of defence. **16.276**

(2.2) Relocation of provisions in Article 25 to Article 24 The Working Group recommends inserting, as a new text of Art 24(2), a modified version of the current text of Art 25(5), stating that 'unless otherwise directed by the arbitral tribunal, statements by witnesses and experts may be presented in writing and signed by them'.[463] Article 24 provides a more appropriate context for this provision since it deals with documentary evidence typically submitted before a hearing, whereas Art 25 deals with evidence presented at 'an oral hearing'. **16.277**

For similar reasons, the Working Group favours relocating the current text of Art 25(6) as a new Art 24(4), since this provision deals with the tribunal's treatment of all evidence—both documentary and oral—and therefore does not relate exclusively to the context of an oral hearing that is the focus of Art 25.[464] **16.278**

Article 25

1 **In the event of an oral hearing, the arbitral tribunal shall give the parties adequate advance notice of the date, time and place thereof.**

2 **If witnesses are to be heard, at least fifteen days before the hearing each party shall communicate to the arbitral tribunal and to the other party the names and addresses of the witnesses**

---

[460] See eg *INA Corp v Islamic Republic of Iran* (Award no 184-161-1, 12 August 1985) (drawing such an inference from the respondent's failure to provide copies of alleged special accounting rules and techniques on which audit report relied), *reprinted in* 8 Iran–USCTR 373, 382 (1985-I).

[461] *Report of WGII on the work of its 47th session* (10–14 September 2007) paras 22, 25, UN Doc A/CN.9/641.

[462] *ibid*, para 22.

[463] *Report of WGII on the work of its 50th session* (9–13 February 2009) paras 69–72, UN Doc A/CN.9/669.

[464] *ibid*, paras 69–75.

he intends to present, the subject upon and the languages in which such witnesses will give their testimony.

3 The arbitral tribunal shall make arrangements for the translation of oral statements made at a hearing and for a record of the hearing if either is deemed necessary by the tribunal under the circumstances of the case, or if the parties have agreed thereto and have communicated such agreement to the tribunal at least fifteen days before the hearing.

4 Hearings shall be held in *camera* unless the parties agree otherwise. The arbitral tribunal may require the retirement of any witness or witnesses during the testimony of other witnesses. The arbitral tribunal is free to determine the manner in which witnesses are examined.

5 Evidence of witnesses may also be presented in the form of written statements signed by them.

6 The arbitral tribunal shall determine the admissibility, relevance, materiality and weight of the evidence offered.

(1) Commentary on current text

16.279 Article 25 contains six paragraphs but broadly deals with two subjects. The first three paragraphs (i) provide for the planning of hearings. Thus, the tribunal must give advance notice of any hearing and must arrange for simultaneous interpretation of oral hearing statements and for the making of a record of the proceedings, when it deems these actions necessary (or, in the case of the making of a record, when the parties jointly so request). For their part, the parties must give advance notice concerning the witnesses they will present. The Article's last three paragraphs (ii) provide guidance on the conduct of the hearing and the receipt of evidence.

16.280 **(1.1) Advance planning for hearings** The Rules do not require that an arbitration include a hearing, unless one of the parties requests it or the tribunal decides there should be one.[465] But, if a hearing is to be held, Art 25(1) requires that the tribunal give the parties 'adequate advance notice' of its date, time and place,[466] and Art 25(2) requires the parties to inform each other and the tribunal at least 15 days beforehand of the identity of any witnesses they will present, the language in which the witness(es) will testify, and the scope of their testimony. The notice as to witnesses was justified, during the drafting, as ensuring that the other party can 'prepare his response to that evidence'.[467] On that basis, the Iran-US Claims Tribunal has sometimes been strict in disallowing testimony from a witness noticed after the deadline (which the Tribunal has increased to 30 days).[468] However, the Tribunal does not apply this rule to what it calls 'rebuttal witnesses' (not a term used in the Rules) or to 'party representatives'.[469]

16.281 This last point raises the tricky question of 'Who is a witness' under Art 25. Some civil law systems, including Iran's, adopt the view that a party or its representative (such as its officer) cannot be a witness because he or she has an interest in the case's outcome. The practice of

[465] See Art 15(2) of the Rules.

[466] The tribunal's options if a notified party fails to attend are addressed in Art 28(2).

[467] *Report of Committee of the Whole II* (n 55) para 123 (discussion of draft Art 22(2)).

[468] See eg *Harris Int'l Telecommunications Inc v Islamic Republic of Iran* (Award no 323-409-1, 2 November 1987) paras 102–7, *reprinted in* 17 Iran–USCTR 31, 62–3 (1987-IV).

[469] *ibid.*

the Iran-US Claims Tribunal takes this position into account by allowing such persons to present 'information' but not to 'testify' as 'witnesses'.[470]

In drafting Art 25(3), delegates ultimately deleted the word 'verbatim', which had appeared before the words 'record of the hearing,' giving more flexibility as to the type of record that the tribunal may arrange in each case.[471] Article 25(3) does not specify what result obtains if only one party seeks a transcript. The Iran-US Claims Tribunal adopted a practice of allowing any party to make a transcript if a copy were given to the Tribunal.[472] **16.282**

(1.2) Conduct of the hearing and receipt of evidence Article 25(4)'s requirement that hearings be held *in camera* (absent contrary agreement by the parties) aims to protect the hearing's privacy[473] but not necessarily the proceedings' confidentiality.[474] Thus, it will at least preclude the tribunal from allowing third parties who seek to act as *amici curiae* from attending a hearing, unless the parties so agree.[475] The further provision in Art 25(4) authorizing exclusion of a witness during other witnesses' testimony again raises the question of 'Who is a witness?'. The Iran-US Claims Tribunal generally allowed parties and party representatives who provided oral 'information' at the hearing to remain in attendance during others' testimony, even as it excluded those who were believed to be serving as proper 'witnesses'.[476] **16.283**

Article 25(4) also allows the tribunal to 'determine the manner in which witnesses are examined', including whether to permit cross-examination. It was noted during the drafting of this clause that, 'where one or both parties are unacquainted with this technique the arbitrators may find it inappropriate to permit'.[477] On the other hand, the concern was also expressed that some jurisdictions might refuse enforcement of an award if a party's right to cross-examine were denied.[478] Such competing considerations reinforce the general point that, pursuant to Art 15(1), a tribunal must conduct hearings in such a way as both to preserve equal treatment of the parties and to afford each party a 'full opportunity of presenting its case'. Finally, the authority to control 'the manner' of examination extends to the type of oath or affirmation that the tribunal may ask witnesses to make, subject to any mandatory provisions in this regard of the applicable law.[479] **16.284**

---

470 See Caron, Caplan and Pellonpää (n 61) 612–13; see also *W Jack Buckamier v Islamic Republic of Iran* (Award no 528-941-3, 6 March 1992) (noting that 'the Tribunal cannot, in the field of evidence, . . . make the domestic rules or judicial practices of one party prevail over the rules and practices of the other, insofar as such rules or practices do not coincide with those generally accepted by international Tribunals'), *reprinted in* 28 Iran–USCTR 53, 74–6 (1992).

471 *Report of Committee of the Whole II* (n 55) para 125 (discussion of draft Art 22(3)).

472 Baker and Davis (n 62) 122.

473 *Preliminary draft Rules* (n 18) (commentary on draft Art 21(4)), *reprinted in* (1975) VI *UNCITRAL Ybk* 163, 174.

474 See eg *Methanex Corp v United States of America*, paras 41–6 (Decision on Petitions from Third Persons to Intervene as '*Amici Curiae*,' NAFTA ch 11 Proceeding, 15 January 2001), available at <http://ita.law.uvic.ca/documents/Methanex-AmiciCuriae.pdf>.

475 *ibid.*

476 Caron, Caplan and Pellonpää (n 61) 617.

477 *Commentary on Revised draft Rules* (n 90) 176 (commentary on draft Art 22(4)).

478 UNCITRAL, *Summary Record of the 166th Meeting* 184 (remarks of the Egyptian delegate, speculating as to the policy of the English courts), UN Doc A/CN.9/SR.166.

479 Caron, Caplan and Pellonpää (n 61) 617–18.

16.285 Article 25(5) authorizes witnesses to provide their evidence by way of signed written statements. The inclusion of this provision in the Rules resulted from the discussion of the preliminary draft Rules in early 1975 at the Congress of the International Council for Commercial Arbitration, where participants urged that written witness statements 'under some circumstances . . . could save considerable time and expense' although it was recognized that such submissions would be 'subject to a possible ruling by the arbitrators . . . request[ing] oral testimony by the person who made the statement'.[480] It has also been noted that reliance on written testimony may, in some legal systems, be contrary to law.[481]

16.286 Notwithstanding that Art 25 generally deals with hearings, Art 25(6)'s broad grant of discretion to the tribunal in evaluating evidence applies to every stage of proceedings. The clause seeks to give the tribunal freedom to disregard local rules of evidence as the particular circumstances warrant, and this was confirmed by a second sentence contained in an early draft, stating that, 'conformity to legal rules of evidence shall not be necessary'.[482] Several delegates felt this might encourage disregard of even mandatory provisions of applicable law, and so this second sentence was deleted.[483] But the text that remains was still characterized as conferring 'complete discretion to decide on the weight [the arbitrators] would give to the evidence offered, in addition to the discretion they had to determine the admissibility, relevance and materiality'.[484] The Iran-US Claims Tribunal has indeed disregarded evidentiary rules of both parties' legal systems, admitting (for example) hearsay evidence as well as the equivalent of testimony from parties,[485] while still upholding other rules, such as the exclusion of evidence of settlement offers.[486]

(2) Contemplated revisions

16.287 Consistent with the revised heading for Art 24 ('Evidence'), the Working Group believes Art 25 should be given the title 'Hearings' and should be revised to give clearer guidance on the organization of hearings.[487] The Working Group recommends five revisions in Art 25, namely (i) to add a new paragraph (denominated '1bis') affirming the tribunal's authority to determine how witnesses *and* experts are heard *and* examined and also clarifying who may be a witness; (ii) to delete Art 25(2) and (3); (iii) to clarify in Art 25(4) that party witnesses should generally not be asked to retire from a hearing; (iv) to revise Art 25(5) to authorize the receipt of oral testimony by means that do not require a witness's physical presence at the hearing; and (v) to relocate Art 25(6) to Art 24(4). The last revision has already been discussed in the context of revisions to Art 24 and requires no further comment.

---

480 *Preliminary draft Rules (Addendum)* (n 20) paras 4, 17–18 (proposal to add a reference in Art 21 to witness statements), *reprinted in* (1975) VI *UNCITRAL Ybk* 184.

481 Caron, Caplan and Pellonpää (n 61) 620 and fn 76.

482 *Preliminary draft Rules* (n 18) (text of draft Art 21(5)), *reprinted in* (1975) VI *UNCITRAL Ybk* 176.

483 UNCITRAL, *Summary Record of 166th Meeting* (11 April 1975) 184-85, UN Doc A/CN.9/SR.166.

484 *Report of Committee of the Whole II* (n 55) 75 (commentary on draft Art 22(6)); see also Sanders (n 28) 202.

485 See summary of cases in Caron, Caplan and Pellonpää (n 61) 621-3, 637-45; Baker and Davis (n 62) 114–15.

486 *ibid*, 115.

487 *Report of WGII on the work of its 50th session* (9–13 February 2009) paras 70–1, UN Doc A/CN.9/669.

(2.1) The Manner of hearing witnesses By inserting a new paragraph '1bis' confirming the tribunal's authority to set the conditions under which 'witnesses and party appointed experts may be heard' as well as the manner in which they may be examined, the Working Group seeks to cover issues beyond the current scope of the last sentence in the current text of Art 25(4), which is essentially merged into this new paragraph.[488] Equally important, the new para 1bis would add a clause stating that any persons 'admitted to testify . . . on any issue of fact or expertise shall be treated as a witness under these Rules'.[489] Recognizing that some legal systems preclude parties (or persons tied to parties, such as officers or employees) from being witnesses, the Working Group favours 'an international standard to overcome these national differences'.[490] After noting that a similar provision is contained in the IBA Rules on the Taking of Evidence in International Commercial Arbitration as well as in other arbitration rules, the Working Group approved the addition of this clause.[491] 16.288

(2.2) Deletion of Article 25(2) and (3) After considering a revision to the wording of Art 25(2) that would have placed responsibility for identifying witnesses in advance of a hearing with the tribunal (after consulting the parties), rather than with the parties, the Working Group ultimately decided to delete Art 25(2) entirely on the ground that the tribunal's obligation to give parties advance notice of the hearing under Art 25(1) would logically include 'the identification of persons who were to be examined at the hearing'.[492] The Working Group also concluded that Art 25(3)'s provision for record transcripts and 'translation of oral testimony' was 'too detailed to be included in modern arbitration rules' and therefore agreed to its deletion apparently believing that arrangements for such services will normally be made without explicit direction from the Rules.[493] 16.289

(2.3) Limiting the authority to require party representatives to retire from a hearing Consistent with the practice developed at the Iran-US Claims Tribunal, the Working Group intends to clarify, in Art 25(4), that party witnesses 'should not generally be requested to retire during testimony of other witnesses',[494] since this could 'affect a party's ability to present its case'.[495] 16.290

(2.4) Hearing a witness by remote means The Working Group has expressed concern that Art 25(5)'s reference to written testimony, coupled with Art 25(4)'s requirement of *in camera* hearings, might be misinterpreted as precluding testimony by videoconferencing. 16.291

---

488 *ibid* at paras 57, 70 and 76-9; see also UN Doc A/CN.9/WG.II/WP.151/Add.1 para 11.

489 *Report of WGII on the work of its 50th session* (9–13 February 2009) paras 70, 77–9, UN Doc A/CN.9/669.

490 *Report of WGII on the work of its 47th session* (10–14 September 2007) para 30, UN Doc A/CN.9/641.

491 *Report of WGII on the work of its 50th session* (9–13 February 2009) paras 58–60, 70, and 77–9, UN Doc A/CN.9/669.

492 *ibid*, paras 70, 80.

493 *ibid*, para 81.

494 *ibid*, para 83.

495 *Report of WGII on the work of its 47th session* (10–14 September 2007) para 41, UN Doc A/CN.9/641.

Therefore, it intends to add a phrase to Art 25(5) expressly permitting oral testimony by means of such a remote electronic link.[496]

INTERIM MEASURES OF PROTECTION

Article 26

1 **At the request of either party, the arbitral tribunal may take any interim measures it deems necessary in respect of the subject-matter of the dispute, including measures for the conservation of the goods forming the subject-matter in dispute, such as ordering their deposit with a third person or the sale of perishable goods.**

2 **Such interim measures may be established in the form of an interim award. The arbitral tribunal shall be entitled to require security for the costs of such measures.**

3 **A request for interim measures addressed by any party to a judicial authority shall not be deemed incompatible with the agreement to arbitrate, or as a waiver of that agreement.**

(1) Commentary on current text

16.292 Article 26 encompasses three very general provisions concerning interim measures, which (i) authorize tribunals to issue such measures; (ii) clarify such measures' possible form and the tribunal's right to require security for their costs; and (iii) confirm that parties may also seek interim measures from courts.

16.293 **(1.1) The Tribunal's authority to issue interim measures** Article 26(1) grants the tribunal broad authority to issue interim measures (except in those (now) rare circumstances where the applicable law restricts such power to courts). Although this clause gives only two examples of such measures (the 'conservation of goods' or 'sale of perishable goods'), the list is framed as being purely illustrative. Thus, the Rules' only substantive constraints on a tribunal's power to grant an interim measure are that a party must have requested the measure and that the arbitrator(s) must deem the measure 'necessary in respect of the subject matter of the dispute'. Although a variety of interim measures have been granted pursuant to that standard,[497] it has sometimes been questioned whether certain types of relief, such as orders to post security or even an injunction against parallel court proceedings, exhibit the requisite link to 'the subject matter of the dispute'.

16.294 Aside from the two requirements just noted, Art 26(1) gives no guidance as to when an interim measure is appropriate. The Iran-US Claims Tribunal has, in practice, identified three further conditions that should be met.[498] First, since interim measures are often

[496] *ibid*, paras 43–4; see also *Report of WGII on the work of its 50th Session* (9–13 February 2009) para 84, UN Doc A/CN.9/669.

[497] See generally Caron, Caplan and Pellonpää (n 61) 539–40, 546–60; van Hof (n 55) 178-89; Baker and Davis (n 62) 134–8. Most interim measures granted by the Iran-US Claims Tribunal relate to conservation or custody of goods or involve a stay of parallel court proceedings. However, Art 26 is broad enough to permit orders on quite different subjects. See eg *Sergei Paushok et al v Government of Mongolia* 16 (Order on Interim Measures, 2 September 2008, *Ad Hoc* UNCITRAL Rules Arbitration pursuant to Russian Federation-Mongolia BIT) (*inter alia*, suspending payments by the claimants' company to the respondent of taxes due under the respondent's windfall profits tax law), available at <http://ita.law.uvic.ca/documents/Paushok-Interim.pdf>.

[498] See generally Caron, D., 'Interim Measures of Protection: Theory and Practice in Light of the Iran-United States Claims Tribunal' 46 *Zeitschrift für ausländisches öffentliches Recht und Völkerrecht* 465 (1986) (detailed examination, in English, of the Iran-US Tribunal's early practice in this area).

sought before jurisdiction over the case has been resolved, the Tribunal requires at least a *prima facie* showing that it has jurisdiction over the underlying claims before granting an interim measure.[499] Second, the Tribunal has held (perhaps as an elaboration of what constitutes a 'necessary' measure) that the requesting party must show a 'threat of grave or irreparable damage'[500] if the measure is not granted. The Tribunal has given somewhat varying views on what constitutes irreparable damage, but it appears that this is mainly but not invariably confined to damage that cannot be compensated by a monetary award.[501] Something less than an absolute position is supported by Art 26(1)'s own reference to a measure ordering the 'sale of perishable goods', which shows, as one commentator has noted, that 'monetary relief does not preclude interim measures'.[502]

Finally, the Tribunal has stated that an interim measure should not overlap with relief sought in the claim on the merits or should not be of such a nature that, if granted, it would preclude certain decisions on the merits.[503] Thus, for example, a claimant's request for an interim payment for storing the respondent's goods was denied because such costs were also sought in the underlying claim.[504] The Iran-US Claims Tribunal has not imposed other conditions for granting interim measures that domestic courts often require, such as a showing of urgency or likely success on the underlying merits. However, a recent *ad hoc* tribunal operating under the UNCITRAL Rules has done so.[505] **16.295**

Notwithstanding the broad authority conferred in Art 26(1), the Iran-US Claims Tribunal has often relied instead (or in addition) upon its 'inherent power' to issue interim measures deemed 'necessary to conserve the respective rights of the Parties and to ensure that this Tribunal's jurisdiction and authority are made fully effective'.[506] Certain commentators believe this reliance on 'inherent power' reflects the fact that 'the scope of Art 26 remains unclear'.[507] Indeed, arbitrators' only guidance comes from Art 26(1)'s narrow examples of interim measures combined with its terse reference to any measure deemed 'necessary'. **16.296**

---

[499] See eg *Bendone-Derossi Int'l v Islamic Republic of Iran* (Award no ITM 40-375-1, 7 June 1984) (finding, under test previously applied by the International Court of Justice, that there was not *prima facie* jurisdiction, although this was 'without prejudice to the final determination of the jurisdictional issue'), *reprinted in* 6 Iran–USCTR 130, 131-2 (1984-II).

[500] *Atlantic Richfield Co v Islamic Republic of Iran* (Award no ITM 50-396-1, 8 May 1985), *reprinted in* 8 Iran–USCTR 179, 181–2 (1985-I).

[501] Compare *Behring Int'l Inc v Islamic Republic of Iran* (Award no ITM/ITL 52-382-3, 21 June 1985) ('the concept of irreparable prejudice in international law arguably is broader than the Anglo-American law concept of irreparable injury' since it 'does not necessarily . . . require' that the injury 'is not remediable by an award of damages'), *reprinted in* 8 Iran–USCTR 238, 276 n 50 (1985), with *Islamic Republic of Iran v United States of America* (Decision no DEC 85-B1-FT, 18 May 1989) ('injury that can be made whole by monetary relief does not constitute irreparable harm'), *reprinted in* 22 Iran–USCTR 105, 109 (1989-II).

[502] See van Hof (n 55) 190.

[503] See eg *United Technologies Int'l, Inc v Islamic Republic of Iran* (Decision no DEC 53-114-3, 10 December 1986), *reprinted in* 13 Iran–USCTR 254, 259 (1986-IV).

[504] *ibid*, paras 24–5.

[505] See eg *Sergei Paushok et al v Government of Mongolia* paras 45–85 (Order on Interim Measures, 2 September 2008, *ad hoc* Proceeding pursuant to Russian Federation-Mongolia BIT), available at <http://ita.law.uvic.ca/documents/Paushok-Interim.pdf>.

[506] *E-Systems Inc v Islamic Republic of Iran et al* (Award no ITM 13-388-FT, 4 February 1983), *reprinted in* 2 Iran–USCTR 51, 57 (1983-I).

[507] Baker and Davis (n 62) 133.

The Tribunal first relied on its 'inherent power' in an interim award directing a respondent to stay parallel court proceedings it had initiated in Iran,[508] but the Tribunal has continued to invoke this justification (even after two of its members pointed out the sufficiency of Art 26[509]) not only in cases involving stays of court proceedings[510] but even when addressing the protection of goods.[511]

16.297 (1.2) **The Form of interim measures and security for their costs** Article 26(2)'s provision permitting interim measures to be issued as interim awards was evidently intended 'to facilitate the enforcement of interim measures'.[512] If the expectation was that measures issued as interim awards would be subject to the enforcement regime for 'awards' under the New York Convention, that expectation has not been met. As the UNCITRAL Secretariat has since acknowledged, '[t]he prevailing view, confirmed . . . by case law in some States, appears to be that the [New York] Convention does not apply to interim awards'.[513] This is one reason why UNCITRAL has recently added a statutory regime for court enforcement of tribunals' interim measures to its Model Law on International Commercial Arbitration.[514] Moreover, framing interim measures as awards is an awkward practice, at best, since interim measures are by their nature provisional and subject to revision,[515] whereas awards, pursuant to Art 32(2), are 'final and binding on the parties'.[516]

16.298 Although the Iran-US Tribunal has issued some interim measures as interim awards, the more common approach of tribunals operating under the Rules is to issue them as orders. Moreover, in circumstances in which the Iran-US Tribunal felt it had to act to avert harm quickly—and, thus, before it could hear from both parties—it adopted the practice of provisionally ordering the party against which an interim measure was sought to maintain the status quo pending the Tribunal's final decision on the interim measure.[517] By thus acting before it heard from one of the parties, the Tribunal essentially adopted a provisional

---

[508] *E-Systems Inc v Islamic Republic of Iran, et al* (Award no ITM 13-388-FT, 4 February 1983), *reprinted in* 2 Iran–USCTR 51, 57 (1983-I).

[509] *ibid* 60–1 (concurring opinion of Judges Holtzmann and Mosk). Judge Holtzmann, having been a delegate to UNCITRAL during the drafting of the Rules, stated that the 'Rules do not restrict the subject-matters appropriate for the granting of interim measures' and that Art 26 is 'appropriate to protect the jurisdiction of the Tribunal'.

[510] Baker and Davis (n 62) 137 n 619 (cases cited therein).

[511] *Behring Int'l v Islamic Republic of Iran* (Award no ITM/ITL 52-382-3, 21 June 1985) (invoking both Art 26 and 'inherent power' in ordering measures to conserve certain goods), *reprinted in* 8 Iran–USCTR 238, 275 (1985-I).

[512] *Commentary on Revised draft Rules* (n 90) 176 (commentary on draft Art 23(2)).

[513] UNCITRAL, *Note by the Secretariat* (6 April 1999) para 121, UN Doc A/CN.9/460, *reprinted in* (1999) XXX *UNCITRAL Ybk* 395, 410.

[514] Arts 17H and 17I of the UNCITRAL Model Law on International Commercial Arbitration (2006).

[515] See eg Art 17D of the UNCITRAL Model Law on International Commercial Arbitration (2006) ('the arbitral tribunal may modify, suspend or terminate an interim measure . . . it has granted').

[516] See *Chas T Main Int'l Inc v Ministry of Energy of the Islamic Republic of Iran et al*, Case no 120 (Order of Chamber Two, 23 November 1983) (rejecting request for modification of an interim award that appointed two experts, on the ground that an award may only be 'interpreted' or 'corrected' following its issuance, pursuant to Arts 35 and 36), *reprinted in* 4 Iran–USCTR 60 (1983-III).

[517] See *Shipside Packing Co Inc v Islamic Republic of Iran* (Award no ITM 27-11875-1, 6 September 1983) (ordering claimant to defer any action on its threat, made during settlement negotiations, to sell disputed goods), *reprinted in* 3 Iran–USCTR 331 (1983-II); *Component Builders Inc et al v Islamic Republic of Iran et al*, Case no 395 (Order by Chamber Three, 10 January 1985) (ordering respondent to seek stay of proceedings

measure on an *ex parte* basis. Judge Brower, concurring in one such order, explained that such a 'temporary restraint' was sometimes necessary for an international tribunal 'to preserve its ability to act effectively on a request for interim measures'.[518]

With respect to the second sentence in Art 26(2), authorizing tribunals to require posting of security 'for the costs of [interim] measures', the drafters may surprisingly have had in mind only 'the costs of arbitration,' ie the costs of having arbitrators and counsel deal with the motion.[519] However, the provision is now understood to authorize something more in keeping with court practice, ie, that the party seeking an interim measure may be ordered to post an amount to compensate the other party for complying with the measure, particularly in case the tribunal later determines that it should not have granted the measure.[520] **16.299**

(1.3) Court-ordered interim measures Article 26(3) confirms that a party may at any time seek interim measures relating to arbitrable disputes from a national court without waiving its right to enforce its arbitration agreement. A party may need to seek an interim measure from a court when, for example, the tribunal is not yet constituted or when the measure (such as an attachment) is of a coercive nature and would affect third parties that lie beyond the tribunal's jurisdiction. **16.300**

(2) Contemplated revisions

The Working Group intends to expand Art 26 substantially, by including most of the elaborated regime for tribunals' issuance of interim measures[521] that has recently been added to the UNCITRAL Model Law on International Commercial Arbitration.[522] An analysis of this lengthy new set of provisions, which reflect the Working Group's efforts to revise the Model Law over a period of more than four years, lies beyond the scope of this commentary.[523] Rather, the discussion below can only (i) summarize the new provisions' essential objectives. That summary is supplemented with descriptions of the five modifications that the Working Group intends to make when importing the Model Law's interim measures regime into Art 26 of the Rules: (ii) removing language that appears to encourage issuance of interim measures as interim awards; (iii) specifying that the identified categories of interim measures are illustrative, not exhaustive; (iv) clarifying the meaning of one of those categories; (v) adding only a general reference to the possible authority (outside of the Rules) **16.301**

---

in Tehran court in which claimant had been summoned to appear only a few days hence), *reprinted in* 8 Iran–USCTR 3 (1985-I).

518 *ibid*, 7 (concurring opinion of Judge Brower, citing such actions by the International Court of Justice).

519 See eg *Commentary on Revised draft Rules* (n 90) 176 (commentary on draft Art 23(2)).

520 Caron, Caplan and Pellonpää (n 61) 543; Baker and Davis (n 62) 143.

521 *Report of WGII on the work of its 47th session* (10–14 September 2007) para 51, UN Doc A/CN.9/641 (recording the Working Group's provisional view that the draft of revised Art 26 set forth in *Note by the Secretariat*, UN Doc A/CN.9/WG.II/WP.145/Add.1 para 25 should be adopted); see also *Report of WGII on the work of its 50th session* (9–13 February 2009) paras 85–119, UN Doc A/CN.9/669 (confirming that initial view with a few editorial revisions).

522 See Arts 17, 17A—17G of the UNCITRAL Model Law on International Commercial Arbitration (2006).

523 The purpose and objective of that revision may be traced in the Reports of the relevant Working Group sessions. The revision of Art 17 of the Model Law (interim measures) was discussed at the 36th, 37th, 38th, 39th, 40th, 41st, 42nd, 43rd, and 44th sessions of Working Group II, and the Reports for these sessions are available at <http://www.uncitral.org/uncitral/en/commission/working_groups/2Arbitration.html>.

for issuing *ex parte* preliminary orders in cases of particular need; and (vi) possibly revising the clause that imposes liability on a party that obtains an interim measure for costs that the measure imposes on the other party if the measure 'should not have been granted'.

16.302 (2.1) **Basic elements of the new provisions** The Model Law's expanded regime governing tribunals' issuance of interim measures contains three main elements. First, the new provisions identify the range of interim measures that a tribunal may grant according to broad functional categories, rather than narrow examples. Thus, the tribunal may issue measures directing a party to (i) maintain or restore the status quo pending determination of the dispute; (ii) take action that would prevent, or refrain from taking action that is likely to cause, current or imminent harm—or prejudice to the arbitral process itself; (iii) provide a means of preserving assets out of which a subsequent award may be satisfied; or (iv) preserve evidence that may be relevant and material to the resolution of the dispute.[524] By identifying these broad categories, the Working Group seeks to eliminate the kind of doubt concerning tribunals' authority in this area that is reflected in the Iran-US Claims Tribunal's frequent reliance on 'inherent power'.

16.303 Secondly, the new regime lists three conditions that the tribunal must establish before granting most interim measures. Before issuing any interim measure (except for the preservation of evidence), the tribunal must find that (i) harm not adequately reparable by an award of damages is likely to result if the requested measure is not ordered; (ii) such harm substantially outweighs the harm likely to result to the party against whom the measure is directed if the measure is granted; and (iii) there is a reasonable possibility that the requesting party will succeed on the merits of the claim.[525] This new text also expressly states that the tribunal's finding on likelihood of success does not bind the tribunal in any future determination.

16.304 Finally, the expanded regime governing interim measures contains a series of ancillary provisions for carrying out this authority. These stipulate that an interim measure may always be modified, suspended or terminated; that the tribunal may require the posting of security 'in connection with the measure'; that a party may be required promptly to disclose any change in the circumstances on which the measure was based; and, that a party shall be liable for other parties' costs and damages if the tribunal ultimately determines it should not have granted the measure.[526]

16.305 Broadly speaking, the Working Group added these provisions to the Model Law for three principal reasons: the growing importance of interim measures in arbitration, the fact that arbitrators are often in doubt as to the extent of their powers in this field, and the belief that court enforcement of interim measures (the subject of a separate but related new section of the Model Law)[527] would be more successful if courts were given a clear picture of tribunals' authority in this area.[528] Although the Working Group expressed some concern about

---

[524] Art 17(2) of the UNCITRAL Model Law on International Commercial Arbitration (2006).
[525] Art 17A(1), *ibid.*
[526] Arts 17D, 17E, 17F and 17G, *ibid.*
[527] See Arts 17H and 17I, *ibid.*
[528] See legislative history for Model Law revisions, cited in n 523.

incorporating such a lengthy set of provisions also into the Rules, on balance it considered that 'the details in Art 26 did not serve only an educational purpose, but were intended to provide necessary guidance and legal certainty to the arbitrator and the parties' which was 'particularly important in respect of many legal systems, which were unfamiliar with the use of interim measures in the context of international arbitration'.[529]

(2.2) The form of interim measures The Working Group intends to depart from the language of revised Model Law Art 17 by deleting a phrase from its second paragraph, stating that an interim measure may be 'in the form of an award or in another form', which parallels the existing phrase in Art 26(2) of the Rules, stating that an interim award 'may be established in the form of an interim award'. The Working Group believes such language is no longer useful, given the new regime in the Model Law for court enforcement of interim measures regardless of their form and given that the issuance of interim measures as awards may pose problems in cases where tribunals subsequently wish to revise them.[530] **16.306**

(2.3) Illustrative rather than exhaustive categories of permissible measures In Art 17 of the revised Model Law, the list of the four functional categories of interim measures that tribunals may issue is exhaustive—the tribunal is only authorized to issue measures within those descriptions. In revising Art 26 of the Rules, however, the Working Group considered that some allowance should be made for 'the possibility of other types of interim measures not identified in the list'.[531] Therefore, Art 26(2) of the Rules will provide[532] that interim measures 'include, without limitation' the four categories of measures described above[533] and set forth in Art 17(2) of the Model Law. **16.307**

(2.4) Clarifying a category of interim measures The second type of possible interim measures described in Art 17(2)(b) of the Model Law is an order directing a party to 'take action that would prevent, or refrain from taking action that is likely to cause, current or imminent harm or prejudice to the arbitral process itself'. On reflection, the Working Group concluded that this wording might leave the scope of the category unclear, since it could be read as encompassing only measures forestalling 'harm or prejudice to the arbitral process' rather than (as was intended) encompassing measures that forestall *either* 'current or imminent harm' *or* 'prejudice to the arbitral process'. Accordingly, the Working Group will insert a '(i)' and '(ii)' before the two objectives of the interim measure in the phrase just quoted.[534] **16.308**

(2.5) *Ex parte* preliminary orders The Working Group has been divided over whether the provisions in the new Art 17B and 17C of the Model Law governing the use of preliminary orders should be incorporated into Art 26 of the Rules.[535] Given that there was **16.309**

---

[529] *Report of WGII on the work of its 50th session* (9–13 February 2009) para 88, UN Doc A/CN.9/669.

[530] *Report of WGII on the work of its 47th session* (10–14 September 2007) para 51, UN Doc A/CN.9/641; *Report of WGII on the work of its 50th session* (9–13 February 2009) para 94, UN Doc A/CN.9/669, adopting the draft of revised Art 26(2) set forth in UN Doc A/CN.9/WG.II/WP.151/Add.1 para 14.

[531] *Report of WGII on the work of its 50th session* (9–13 February 2009) para 92, UN Doc A/CN.9/669.

[532] *ibid* at para 94.

[533] See para 16.302, *supra.*

[534] *Report of WGII on the work of its 50th session* (9–13 February 2009) para 95, UN Doc A/CN.9/669.

[535] See eg *ibid* at paras 100–12.

opposition to including any reference to preliminary orders in the Rules, the Working Group has adopted a neutral approach intended to clarify that the Rules do not alter the extent to which any particular tribunal might otherwise be authorized to issue or prevented from issuing preliminary orders. Thus, the proposed text of new Art 26(5) reads:[536]

> Nothing in these Rules shall have the effect of creating a right, or of limiting any right which may exist outside these Rules, of a party to apply to the arbitral tribunal for, and any power of the arbitral tribunal to issue, in either case without prior notice to a party, a preliminary order that the party not frustrate the purpose of a requested interim measure.

16.310 (2.6) **Liability for damages caused by interim measure that 'should not have been granted'** Article 17G of the revised Model Law provides that the party requesting an interim measure shall be liable for the costs and damages caused by the measure 'to any party if the arbitral tribunal later determines that, in the circumstances, the measure . . . should not have been granted'. In considering whether this language should be imported into Art 26(9) of the Rules, the Working Group considered an alternative proposal that would have left this determination to the applicable law.[537] This discussion persuaded the Group that it would be useful to know how different national laws deal with liability for interim measures before determining what provision should be inserted in the Rules, which will operate within various national legal frameworks. Accordingly, the Working Group has deferred decision on Art 26(9) pending further information to be prepared by the UNCITRAL Secretariat on this issue.[538]

EXPERTS

Article 27

1 **The arbitral tribunal may appoint one or more experts to report to it, in writing, on specific issues to be determined by the tribunal. A copy of the expert's terms of reference, established by the arbitral tribunal, shall be communicated to the parties.**

2 **The parties shall give the expert any relevant information or produce for his inspection any relevant documents or goods that he may require of them. Any dispute between a party and such expert as to the relevance of the required information or production shall be referred to the arbitral tribunal for decision.**

3 **Upon receipt of the expert's report, the arbitral tribunal shall communicate a copy of the report to the parties who shall be given the opportunity to express, in writing, their opinion on the report. A party shall be entitled to examine any document on which the expert has relied in his report.**

4 **At the request of either party the expert, after delivery of the report, may be heard at a hearing where the parties shall have the opportunity to be present and to interrogate the expert. At this hearing either party may present expert witnesses in order to testify on the points at issue. The provisions of article 25 shall be applicable to such proceedings.**

---

536 *ibid* at para 112.

537 See Note by the Secretariat, *Proposal by the Government of Switzerland*, (9 September 2008) UN Doc A/CN.9/WG.II/WP.152.

538 *Report of WGII on the work of its 50th Session* (9–13 February 2009) para 117–18, UN Doc A/CN.9/669.

(1) Commentary on current text

Article 27 regulates certain aspects of a tribunal's appointment of experts, including by providing for experts' access to information from the parties and for the parties' examination of, or comment on such reports (and the documents on which they rely). Article 27 provides no guidance as to when tribunals should appoint their own experts and how they should choose them. It has been found desirable for a tribunal to receive input from the parties on both points (as well as on the formulation of terms of reference for any tribunal expert), which may avoid parties subsequently choosing competing, party-appointed experts.[539] On the other hand, the Iran-US Claims Tribunal found that its own appointment of experts often greatly expanded the cost and length of proceedings and, over time, the Tribunal came to rely more on party-appointed experts to resolve complex issues.[540] **16.311**

The tribunal's authority, under Art 27(2) to resolve an expert's disputed requests for information appears to include a right to resolve, as well, any dispute about the expert's duty to consider, eg late-proffered evidence from the parties.[541] Similarly, the tribunal has authority to interpret the terms of reference to determine whether the expert has strayed beyond them.[542] The tribunal may not delegate its own adjudicatory responsibility, and thus the report of its expert cannot bind the tribunal.[543] **16.312**

Article 27(4) contains the only clear reference in the Rules to party-appointed experts, possibly creating the misimpression that their role is limited to rebutting tribunal-appointed experts. To the contrary, as is implicit in a party's right under Art 15(2) to request a hearing, *inter alia*, for 'the presentation of evidence by witnesses, including expert witnesses', the parties may appoint experts whose presentation will be governed by Art 25. The Rules' failure to make this clear appears to have resulted from a drafting oversight.[544] **16.313**

(2) Contemplated revisions

The Working Group intends to change the title of Art 27 so that it expressly refers to tribunal-appointed experts. It also seeks to make conforming changes in the text of Art 27 to make clear that an expert may be of either gender.[545] **16.314**

DEFAULT

Article 28

1 **If, within the period of time fixed by the arbitral tribunal, the claimant has failed to communicate his claim without showing sufficient cause for such failure, the arbitral tribunal shall issue an order for the termination of the arbitral proceedings. If, within the period of time fixed by the arbitral tribunal, the respondent has failed to communicate his statement**

539 Caron, Caplan and Pellonpää (n 61) 668–71.

540 Baker and Davis (n 62) 128.

541 *Starrett Housing Corp et al v Islamic Republic of Iran et al* (Award no 314-24-1, 14 August 1987), *reprinted in* 16 Iran–USCTR 112, 119 (1987-III).

542 *Richard D. Harza v Islamic Republic of Iran* (Award no 232-97-2, 2 May 1986), *reprinted in* 11 Iran–USCTR 76, 124–5 (1986-II).

543 Caron, Caplan and Pellonpää (n 61) 670, 674.

544 van Hof (n 55) 193; Baker and Davis (n 62) 129 (both treatises noting that clarifying language approved by the Committee of the Whole II somehow failed to be included in Art 27(1)).

545 *Report of WGII on the work of its 47th session* (10–14 September 2007) para 61, UN Doc A/CN.9/641.

of defence without showing sufficient cause for such failure, the arbitral tribunal shall order that the proceedings continue.

2 **If one of the parties, duly notified under these Rules, fails to appear at a hearing, without showing sufficient cause for such failure, the arbitral tribunal may proceed with the arbitration.**

3 **If one of the parties, duly invited to produce documentary evidence, fails to do so within the established period of time, without showing sufficient cause for such failure, the arbitral tribunal may make the award on the evidence before it.**

(1) Commentary on current text

16.315 Article 28 addresses the consequences of three kinds of non-participation by a party: (i) failure to submit its initial statement (of claim or of defence); (ii) failure to appear at a hearing; and (iii) failure to produce requested documentary evidence. Although this Article is captioned 'Default', it does not provide for any default judgment. Rather, unless the case is terminated under Art 28(1), the tribunal must still decide the dispute based on the evidence before it, bearing in mind Art 24(1)'s requirement that each party has the burden of proving the facts on which its claim or defence relies. Moreover, Art 28's sanction for each failure is (except in case of failure to file a statement of claim) limited to the phase of proceedings in which the failure occurs. Thus, if a party (for example) fails without cause to appear at a hearing, Art 27(2) does not permit the tribunal to presume a more general default by excluding that party from subsequent proceedings, such as the filing of post-hearing briefs. Such exclusion would jeopardize enforceability of a final award, since one ground for non-enforcement under Art V(1)(b) of the New York Convention is that a party was 'unable to present his case'.[546]

16.316 **(1.1) Failure to submit a statement of claim or of defence** Although Art 28(1) provides that the tribunal 'shall' terminate the arbitral proceedings upon a claimant's failure to file its statement of claim and 'shall' order the proceedings to continue if the respondent fails to submit its statement of defence, both actions are subject to two conditions that essentially render termination or continuation discretionary. First, the rule refers to a failure to submit the statement 'within the time fixed by the tribunal', and the tribunal may always extend a deadline originally given, as the Iran-US Claims Tribunal has, in fact, done.[547] Second, the delinquent party may 'sho[w] sufficient cause for such failure', in which case a further extension is again likely.

16.317 **(1.2) Failure to attend a hearing** A tribunal's authority under Art 28(2) to proceed with a hearing notwithstanding the non-appearance of a party is also subject to two conditions, one of which is again that the party has failed to 'sho[w] sufficient cause for the failure'. The second condition is that the non-appearing party was properly notified. The Iran-US Claims Tribunal has proceeded with hearings in the absence of any (or any sufficient) explanation for non-appearance at the hearing.[548]

---

[546] See Caron, Caplan and Pellonpää (n 61) 715.

[547] See eg *Amoco Int'l Finance Corp v National Iranian Oil Co* (Case no 56, Order of Chamber 3, 22 February 1984), 1-2, excerpted in Caron, Caplan and Pellonpää (n 61) 723 (giving a final extension for filing a Statement of Defence after 'numerous extensions').

[548] See eg *George J Meyer Manufacturing Division of Figgie Int'l Inc v Zamzam Bottling Co*, Case no 299 (Order of Chamber One, 22 March 1984), *reprinted in part in* Caron, Caplan and Pellonpää (n 61) 724–5.

(1.3) Failure to submit requested documents Article 28(3) allows a tribunal to render an award without waiting further for evidence that a party has failed to produce within the time limit given, subject once again to a party's ability to 'sho[w] sufficient cause'. It has been held that 'this rule equally applies' to allow the tribunal to proceed with an award without considering 'additional, unauthorized material' that a party belatedly offers.[549] The *Himpurna* tribunal[550] considered the meaning of 'sufficient cause' at some length when the respondent failed to submit evidence after an Indonesian court enjoined further submissions in the arbitration. Holding that 'alleged impediments [under Art 28(3)] do not excuse a non-performing party unless they are *insurmountable, irresistible,* and *external* to the will of the defendant',[551] the tribunal concluded that the respondent had not carried its burden of proving the impediment had these characteristics, particularly since the third party that obtained the court injunction was within the control of the arbitral respondent.[552] **16.318**

(2) Contemplated revisions

The Working Group intends to revise each sentence in Art 28(1). The Group is considering modifying the first sentence to permit a tribunal, even when no statement of claim has been filed, to proceed for certain purposes, such as to resolve a counterclaim or to dismiss the claims with prejudice if, eg, the filing of the claims appears abusive.[553] The Group recommends modifying the second sentence of Art 28(1) to authorize a tribunal also to proceed with the arbitration when the respondent fails to file its response to the notice of arbitration (a submission to be newly required under an article to be inserted after Art 3) or when a claimant fails to file a statement of defence to a counterclaim.[554] The Tribunal also intends to add a phrase making clear that failure to file a response or statement of defence is not 'in itself . . . an admission' of allegations in the claim or counterclaim.[555] This language is already contained in the corresponding provision (Art 25) of the Model Law on International Commercial Arbitration. **16.319**

CLOSURE OF HEARINGS

Article 29

1 **The arbitral tribunal may inquire of the parties if they have any further proof to offer or witnesses to be heard or submissions to make and, if there are none, it may declare the hearings closed.**

2 **The arbitral tribunal may, if it considers it necessary owing to exceptional circumstances, decide, on its own motion or upon application of a party, to reopen the hearings at any time before the award is made.**

---

549 *Vera-Jo Miller Aryeh v Islamic Republic of Iran* (Award no 581-842/843/844-1, 22 May 1997), *reprinted in* 33 Iran–USCTR 272, 287 (1997).

550 *Himpurna Calif Energy Ltd (Bermuda) v Republic of Indonesia* (Interim Award, 26 September 1999, *ad hoc* proceeding under the UNCITRAL Rules), *reprinted in* (2000) XXV *Ybk Comm Arb* 109, 166–7.

551 *ibid*, para 108 (emphasis in original).

552 *ibid*, paras 109–48.

553 *Report of WGII on the work of its 51st session* (14–18 September 2009) paras 22–26, UN Doc A/CN.9/684.

554 *Report of WGII on the work of its 47th session* (10–14 September 2007) para 62, UN Doc A/CN.9/641.

555 *ibid*, para 63.

(1) Commentary on current text

16.320 Article 29(1) identifies a mechanism that a tribunal may, but is not required to, use in bringing hearings to a close: having parties confirm that they have nothing more to submit. During the drafting of this provision, delegates noted the provision's advantage (a party's clear statement that it had nothing further to submit might forestall a later challenge to enforcement under Art V(1)(b) of the New York Convention (a party was 'unable to present his case')) but also cautioned that the provision should not be permitted to 'encourage one of the parties to resort to delaying tactics'.[556] Article 29(2) provides that the tribunal may reopen hearings, prior to the final award, 'owing to exceptional circumstances.'

16.321 There is a link between Art 29(2) and Art 15(2), the provision that assures each party the right to request a hearing 'at any time'. As the Iran-U.S. Claims Tribunal held in responding to a request for a second or reopened hearing, 'Article 15, paragraph 2 is primarily applicable to the situation where there has not yet been a hearing and one of the parties requests one'. By contrast, 'where a Hearing has already been held, the reasonableness of the request and the appropriateness of the timing become even more important because the disruption of the arbitral process is that much greater and because the parties have already had an extensive opportunity to present their cases'.[557] In practice, the Tribunal has rarely granted a motion to reopen hearings.[558]

(2) Contemplated revisions

16.322 The Working Group does not intend to recommend any changes in Art 29.

WAIVER OF RULES

Article 30

A party who knows that any provision of, or requirement under, these Rules has not been complied with and yet proceeds with the arbitration without promptly stating his objection to such non-compliance, shall be deemed to have waived his right to object.

(1) Commentary on current text

16.323 Article 30 requires a party that knows a provision of the Rules is being violated to object to the violation promptly or be deemed to have waived the objection.[559] The party must have actual knowledge of the non-observance—the drafters debated whether to deem the objection waived if a party 'should have known' of a derogation from the Rules, but decided against it.[560] The provision's purpose is not only to dissuade parties from sitting on their

[556] UNCITRAL Committee of the Whole II, *Summary Record of the 16th Meeting* (26 April 1976) paras 81, 84, UN Doc A/CN.9/9/C.2/SR.16 (remarks, respectively, of the United States delegate and of Professor Sanders, special consultant to the Secretariat).

[557] *Dadras Int'l v Islamic Republic of Iran* (Award no 567-213/215-3, 7 November 1995) paras 56, 57 (reaffirming that exceptional circumstances warranted reopening a hearing), *reprinted in* 31 Iran–USCTR 127, 143 (1995).

[558] See eg *General Petrochemicals Corp v Islamic Republic of Iran* (Award no 522-828-1, 21 October 1991) (rejecting request for 'rehearing' pursuant to Art 29(2) on grounds, *inter alia*, that claimant made no showing that its belatedly submitted documents were not available to it at earlier stage), *reprinted in* 27 Iran–USCTR 196 (1991-II); see also Caron, Caplan and Pellonpää (n 61) 652.

[559] See eg *Frederica Lincoln Riahi v Islamic Republic of Iran* (Decision no DEC 133-485-1, 17 November 2004) 20–1 (rejecting request to reconsider award because alleged procedural irregularities during arbitration were waived pursuant to Art 30), *reprinted in Mealey's Int'l Arb Rep*, vol 19, issue 12, section C (2004).

[560] *Report of the Committee of the Whole II* (n 55) paras 143–7.

rights and to ensure orderly proceedings but also to recognize that parties may have agreed, pursuant to Art 1(1), on a modification of the Rules in respect of the provision that is not being complied with. A prompt objection to derogation from the Rules clarifies that the objecting party believes it has not so agreed.

(2) Contemplated revisions

The Working Group has taken note that it can be difficult for a non-objecting party to prove that a party that tardily objects to non-compliance with the Rules had prior *actual* knowledge of this non-compliance. To address that difficulty while still avoiding reliance on a 'should have known' standard, the Working Group favours redrafting Art 30 to place the burden of proof on the objecting party to show, eg, that it did not previously know of the non-compliance or that its failure previously to object was excusable in the circumstances.[561] **16.324**

Section IV. The award

DECISIONS

Article 31

1 When there are three arbitrators, any award or other decision of the arbitral tribunal shall be made by a majority of the arbitrators.

2 In the case of questions of procedure, when there is no majority or when the arbitral tribunal so authorizes, the presiding arbitrator may decide on his own, subject to revision, if any, by the arbitral tribunal.

(1) Commentary on current text

Article 31(1) establishes (i) a basic rule of decision-making within three-member tribunals, requiring that any award or decision be made by a majority, but also sets forth (ii) an exception for 'questions of procedure', which can be decided by the presiding arbitrator alone, if the tribunal has delegated such decisions to him or her or if no majority can be formed on a procedural matter. The presiding arbitrator's decision can be overridden by the tribunal. **16.325**

(1.1) General rule requiring majority decisions The drafters recognized that a rule of majority decision for awards or other substantive matters would not avoid all deadlocks but resisted giving the presiding arbitrator a deciding vote. In some delegates' minds, doing so would risk the possibility of extreme awards;[562] it was also noted that the ICC Rules provision allowing the presiding arbitrator a deciding vote had been used once.[563] As Professor Sanders observes, Art 31(1) instead requires arbitrators 'to continue their deliberations until a majority, and probably a compromise solution has been reached'.[564] **16.326**

[561] *Report of WGII on the work of its 51st session* (14–18 September 2009) paras 44–51, UN Doc A/CN.9/684.

[562] UNCITRAL Committee of the Whole II, *Summary Record of the 10th Meeting* (19 April 1976) paras 79–80 (remarks of the United States and Australian delegates), UN Doc A/CN.9/9/C.2/SR.10; see also UNCITRAL Committee of the Whole II, *Summary Record of the 11th Meeting* (19 April 1976) paras 2-20 (discussion following statement of Professor Sanders strongly favouring the majority requirement), UN Doc A/CN.9/9/C.2/SR.11.

[563] *ibid*, para 3 (remarks of Professor Sanders, special consultant to the Secretariat).

[564] Sanders (n 28) 207.

16.327 The Iran-US Claims Tribunal has issued several awards in which one arbitrator disagreed with the reasoning, or some conclusions, or the form, or scope, or amount of the award but nonetheless joined in it to ensure that an award was issued. As Judge Holtzmann explained when concurring 'in order to form a majority for the key finding' as to liability, '[i]n view of the many errors in the Interlocutory Award, it would be easier to dissent from it than to concur in it'. He regarded concurrence as the only alternative to 'accepting the prospect of infinite delay in progress toward final decision of this case'.[565] The fact that forming a majority may require difficult deliberations has been said to underscore the need for preserving their confidentiality.[566] Although the Rules are silent as to the confidentiality of tribunal deliberations, it has been asserted by a tribunal operating under the Rules that the 'secrecy of deliberations . . . [is] a fundamental element of the arbitral process'.[567] To reinforce that point, the Iran-US Claims Tribunal adopted a Note to Art 31 expressly providing for both the privacy and confidentiality of tribunal deliberations.[568]

16.328 (1.2) **The exception for 'questions of procedure'** The presiding arbitrator in a three-member tribunal may decide 'questions of procedure' if he or she is given this authority by the tribunal or if a majority cannot be formed. During the drafting, it was stated that having a chairman resolve procedural matters 'would be quicker and more efficient, and would probably be just as fair to the parties'.[569] The Rules do not say what distinguishes 'questions of procedure'. As was noted in the commentary on Arts 16 (place of arbitration) and 17 (language of arbitration), a determination under the former Article is not deemed a procedural matter while a determination under the latter is, since the seat of arbitration likely determines the law governing the proceeding. This has led some commentators to conclude that 'defining "questions of procedure" . . . should involve consideration of whether the decision could have a measurable impact on the rights of one or both of the parties, which could result in unfair advantage or prejudice'.[570]

(2) Contemplated revisions

16.329 The Working Group considered whether the presiding arbitrator should be authorized to decide all matters alone (including awards) when a majority otherwise cannot be formed.

---

[565] *Starrett Housing Corp et al v Islamic Republic of Iran et al* (Interlocutory Award no ITL 32-24-1, 19 December 1983) (Concurring Opinion of Howard M. Holtzmann), *reprinted in* 4 Iran–USCTR 122, 159 (1983-III); see also *Ultrasystems Inc v Islamic Republic of Iran* (Award no 89-84-3, 7 December 1983) (Dissenting Opinion of Judge Richard M. Mosk) (objecting that the presiding arbitrator had segmented the case to achieve different majorities on its different elements and warning that this practice, 'if misused, conflicts with the spirit, if not the letter, of the rule requiring an award to be made by a majority'), *reprinted in* 4 Iran–USCTR 77, 82 (1983-III).

[566] *Raygo Wagner Equipment Co v Star Line Iran Co* (Award no 20-17-3, 15 December 1982) (Concurring Opinion of Richard M. Mosk) (criticizing Judge Sani's separate statement on his refusal to sign the award because it allegedly disclosed deliberations and noting that 'confidentiality is particularly essential in arbitration proceedings such as these', where deliberations were needed to reach a majority), *reprinted in* 1 Iran–USCTR 411, 424 (1981–2).

[567] *Himpurna California Energy Ltd (Bermuda) v Republic of Indonesia* (Interim Award of *ad hoc* proceeding, 26 September 1999), *reprinted in* (2000) XXV *Ybk Comm Arb* 109, 152.

[568] van Hof (n 55) 211 (setting forth text of Note 2 to Art 31).

[569] UNCITRAL Committee of the Whole II, *Summary Record of the 6th Meeting* (15 April 1976) para 97 (remarks of observer from the International Council for Commercial Arbitration), UN Doc A/CN.9/9/C.2/SR.6.

[570] Caron, Caplan and Pellonpää (n 61) 760–1.

Adoption of such a provision was one of the 'main lines of revision' recommended by the report commissioned by the UNCITRAL Secretariat, prior to the revision project.[571] The report noted that this change would rarely be used but would encourage arbitrators to be more reasonable and would provide a solution to rare cases where no majority could be formed without one arbitrator's compromising on a matter of principle.[572] In response, it was argued in the Working Group, *inter alia*, that awards issued by two arbitrators are more acceptable to parties and particularly valued by states in investment arbitration. The assumption that presiding arbitrators are always more reasonable than party-appointed arbitrators was also questioned, and the concern was expressed that allowing presiding arbitrators to resolve cases by themselves is open to abuse.[573] The Working Group ultimately decided not to revise Art 31(1) except for changing 'when there are three arbitrators' to 'more than one arbitrator' to accommodate the possibility of tribunals of irregular number.[574]

FORM AND EFFECT OF THE AWARD

Article 32

1 **In addition to making a final award, the arbitral tribunal shall be entitled to make interim, interlocutory, or partial awards.**
2 **The award shall be made in writing and shall be final and binding on the parties. The parties undertake to carry out the award without delay.**
3 **The arbitral tribunal shall state the reasons upon which the award is based, unless the parties have agreed that no reasons are to be given.**
4 **An award shall be signed by the arbitrators and it shall contain the date on which and the place where the award was made. Where there are three arbitrators and one of them fails to sign, the award shall state the reason for the absence of the signature.**
5 **The award may be made public only with the consent of both parties.**
6 **Copies of the award signed by the arbitrators shall be communicated to the parties by the arbitral tribunal.**
7 **If the arbitration law of the country where the award is made requires that the award be filed or registered by the arbitral tribunal, the tribunal shall comply with this requirement within the period of time required by law.**

(1) Commentary on current text

Article 32 provides (i) that awards may resolve less than the entire dispute and may be denominated accordingly, (ii) that awards of all types shall be 'final and binding upon the parties' and that the parties undertake to carry out such awards promptly, and (iii) that awards shall satisfy several formal requirements, such as being in writing and signed by the arbitrators. **16.330**

(1.1) Types of awards Article 32(1) identifies three types of award other than a 'final award' that a tribunal may render, namely 'interim', 'interlocutory', and 'partial' awards. **16.331**

[571] Paulsson and Petrochilos (n 39) 9.

[572] *ibid*, 9, 125–8.

[573] *Report of WGII on the work of its 47th session* (10–14 September 2007) paras 70, 72, UN Doc A/CN.9/641.

[574] *Report of WGII on the work of its 51st session* (14–18 September 2009) paras 52–61, UN Doc A/CN.9/684.

Although an early draft of this Article referred only to 'the award', it was suggested that the Article refer expressly to 'interim, interlocutory or partial awards' because 'such a definition might also facilitate enforcement of awards since there would be certainty as to what decisions of arbitrators could be classed as "awards"'.[575] Thus, delegates seemed to intend that even interim awards should benefit from enforcement under Arts III, IV and V of the New York Convention. However, as has been noted in the commentary to Art 26, that expectation has not been realized. The UNCITRAL Secretariat has itself concluded that, '[t]he prevailing view, confirmed . . . by case law in some States, appears to be that the [New York] Convention does not apply to interim awards'.[576]

16.332 During the drafting, 'interim, interlocutory or partial awards' were distinguished from 'final, definitive awards'.[577] Some commentators believe that, in practice, these different forms of interim awards have been given distinct uses[578] while others note that even the Iran-US Claims Tribunal 'did not consistently distinguish among partial, interim and interlocutory awards.'[579] It is clear, however, that in listing the different types of awards, the drafters intended to enhance arbitrators' flexibility to make 'any kind of award they deem appropriate'[580] rather than to limit their application.

16.333 (1.2) **'Final and binding on the parties'** During the drafting of Art 32(2), the words 'final and' were added to 'binding,' but no reason for the insertion was recorded.[581] While one delegate later suggested that 'final' meant beyond judicial review, another delegate noted that a party may always object to enforcement of an award, apparently referring to the grounds for non-enforcement in Art V of the New York Convention.[582] Professor Sanders expresses a similar view of 'final and binding,' noting that the phrase 'does not prevent the parties applying to the Court, under the law applicable to the arbitration, for setting aside the award'.[583] Thus, Art 32(2) signifies that the parties are generally obliged to carry out an award promptly, that an award is not subject to any appeal, but that the parties have not waived their right to object if a basic aspect of arbitral procedure has been disregarded or the arbitration agreement is invalid, such as would justify an award's non-enforcement under the New York Convention or being set aside under the law of the seat of arbitration.

16.334 Quite apart from Art 32(2)'s impact upon the parties, there is a separate question as to this provision's effect on the arbitrators: does the fact that awards are 'final and binding upon the parties' prevent a tribunal that has issued a final award from ever revising it? A tribunal

[575] *Summary of 8th Session Discussion* (n 55) 41 (discussion of draft Art 26(5)).

[576] UNCITRAL, *Note by the Secretariat* (6 April 1999) para 121, UN Doc A/CN.9/460, *reprinted in* (1999) XXX *UNCITRAL Ybk* 395, 410.

[577] *Preliminary draft Rules* (n 18) 177–8 (commentary on draft Art 26).

[578] Caron, Caplan and Pellonpää (n 61) 793 (asserting that the Iran-US Claims Tribunal 'came to develop a practice as to when each appellation was to be used').

[579] Baker and Davis (n 62) 165.

[580] Sanders (n 28) 209.

[581] UNCITRAL Committee of the Whole II, *Summary Record of 10th Meeting* (19 April 1976) para 77, UN Doc A/CN.9/9/C.2/SR.10.

[582] UNCITRAL Committee of the Whole II, *Summary Record of 17th Meeting* (22 April 1976) paras 12, 17 (remarks of Belgian and French delegates, respectively), UN Doc A/CN.9/9/C.2/SR.17.

[583] Sanders (n 28) 208.

may, of course, 'interpret' or 'correct' an award within the limits imposed by Arts 35 and 36, respectively, but can a tribunal go further and actually revise a final award in extreme circumstances, such as upon a showing that the award was obtained by false evidence? Perhaps the strongest declaration in favour of such an authority comes from the *ad hoc* tribunal in *Antoine Biloune et al v Ghana Investments Centre et al*, which declared that 'a court or Tribunal, including this international arbitral Tribunal, has an inherent power to take cognizance of credible evidence, timely placed before it, that its previous determinations were the product of false testimony, forged documents, or other egregious "fraud on the Tribunal"'.[584] However, that tribunal found 'no such evidence has been adduced' in the case before it and thus did not have to modify its earlier award. The Iran-US Claims Tribunal addressed similar questions and came to essentially the same conclusion, though expressed more tentatively. As certain commentators have noted, '[t]he Tribunal seemed to endorse the existence of inherent authority to reopen, but never faced a fact situation sufficiently severe to warrant exercising it'.[585] Thus, '[t]he Tribunal . . . steadfastly defended the finality of awards issued under Art 32(2)'.[586]

A related but somewhat different issue is whether Art 32(2) prevents a tribunal that has not yet issued its final award from revisiting issues decided in an earlier partial award. A threshold question is whether Art 32(2) even ascribes finality to anything other then a final award. The Article states only that 'the award' is final without saying whether this applies not only to a final award but to the other types of awards mentioned in Art 32(1). Neither the wording of Art 32(1) nor the drafting history gives any reason to believe that partial, interlocutory and interim awards were to be distinguished from final awards as somehow not final and not binding. Indeed, at least with respect to partial and interlocutory awards, the Iran-US Claims Tribunal 'has consistently ruled that such awards were final and could not be reopened.'[587] Nonetheless, even if the Rules are correctly read as decreeing all (or nearly all) partial and interim awards to be 'final,' it may not follow automatically that such awards can never 'be reopened' by a tribunal that still has jurisdiction in the case and that may have special reasons for reconsidering its initial findings. **16.335**

[584] Award on Damages and Costs, *ad hoc* UNCITRAL tribunal, 30 June 1990, *reprinted in* XIX *Ybk Comm Arb* 11, 22–3 (1994).

[585] Caron, Caplan and Pellonpää (n 61) 917. *see also* Baker and Davis (n 62) 199 *et seq.*

[586] Caron, Caplan and Pellonpää (n 61) 917.

[587] *id* (n 61) 799. With respect to interim awards that embody interim measures, these commentators suggest that such awards are less 'final' since they may at least be superseded by subsequent interim awards for provisional relief. Indeed, Art 17D, UNCITRAL Model Law on International Commercial Arbitration (2006) expressly provides that a tribunal may 'modify, suspend or terminate' an interim measure, which includes those issued as interim awards. However, the fact that a provisional measure issued as an interim award may be modified or terminated does not necessarily conflict with its being 'final', at least in the sense that, like other awards, it is susceptible to being enforced. See *id*, Arts 17H and 17I; see especially *id* 17H(2) (party obtaining enforcement of interim measure must 'promptly inform the court of any termination, suspension or modification of that interim measure'). See also Born, G., *International Commercial Arbitration* 2023 (3rd edn Wolters Kluwer, The Netherlands, 2009) (noting that 'Provisional measures are "final" in the sense that they dispose of a request for relief pending the conclusion of the arbitration' and that it is no impediment to their enforcement that courts may need to 'readjust their enforcement measures, if an arbitral tribunal altered the provisional relief it ordered').

16.336 Even though it is often said that a tribunal is *functus officio* with respect to any issue that it has resolved on the merits by partial award, nevertheless—in a few cases—tribunals have held that they may revisit such issues when, for example, they believe a change in circumstances or in the factual record renders the initial award untenable. For example, the tribunal in an ICC arbitration decided in its final award (i) that its partial award ordering the respondent to purchase the claimant's share of their joint venture was (to this extent) 'non-final' and could be reconsidered, (ii) that this aspect of the partial award had now become moot as a result of the joint venture's bankruptcy, and thus (iii) that the formerly specified procedure for pricing the buyout would not be implemented. The claimant sued to set aside the final award on the ground, *inter alia*, that the tribunal's reconsideration of the buyout remedy contravened 'applicable arbitration procedure' because the tribunal had been *functus officio* on that remedy once the partial award was issued and that the partial award was *res judicata*. The Quebec court rejected the contention that the arbitral procedure had been violated, apparently relying on expert evidence that the ICC Rules gave the tribunal broad procedural discretion in resolving the case.[588] In sum, although there is scant jurisprudence on the question whether an interim or partial award's 'final' status absolutely precludes a tribunal from revisiting matters resolved in such awards, a blanket conclusion that tribunals lack all such power would be doubtful.

16.337 (1.3) **Formal requirements for awards** Articles 32(2) through 32(7) impose a wide range of formal requirements for an award, including that it shall be in writing, shall state reasons for the result (unless the parties agree otherwise), shall identify the date when and the place where the award is made, shall be signed by all arbitrators (and, if one of a three-member tribunal fails to do so, shall explain why), shall only be publicized if both parties agree, shall be sent to the parties, and shall be filed and registered by the tribunal if the law of the place of arbitration so requires. The application or significance of most of these requirements is relatively straightforward, but a few merit further comment.

16.338 The Rules' silence on the question of including dissents in awards must be read as permissive. The original draft of Art 32(3) prohibited addition of dissenting opinions to awards,[589] but this was deleted,[590] *inter alia*, because it might provoke dissenting arbitrators to refuse

[588] See *Holding Tusculum BV v Louis Dreyfus SAS* (Case no 500-05-017680-966, Decision of the Superior Court of Quebec, Montreal District, 8 December 2008) 54-57 (arbitration governed by the 1988 ICC Rules, Art 24(1) of which declared that 'the arbitral award shall be final'), available at <http://francais.mcgill.ca/files/arbitration/TusculumDreyfus2.pdf>. See also *Employers' Surplus Lines Insurance Co v Global Reinsurance Corp—US Branch,* no 07 Civ 2521(HB), 2008 WL 337317, at *7, (SDNY 6 February 2008) (upholding sole arbitrator's revision of his partial award on liability in his final award concerning damages and noting that, 'the materials on damages submitted by [the claimant] . . . led the Arbitrator to find that determining [the respondent's] damages . . . as instructed by the Partial Final Award was impossible,' which, 'in turn, caused the Arbitrator to realize that his second liability finding was based on an incorrect interpretation of the [insurance] Certificate'). cf *Chas T Main Int'l, Inc v Ministry of Energy of the Islamic Republic of Iran et al,* Case no 120 (Order of Chamber Two, 23 November 1983) (rejecting request for modification of an interim award on the ground that an award may only be 'interpreted' or 'corrected' following its issuance, pursuant to Arts 35 and 36), *reprinted in* 4 Iran–USCTR 60 (1983-III).

[589] *Preliminary draft Rules* (n 18) 177 (draft of Art 26(3)).

[590] UNCITRAL, *Summary Record of 166th Meeting* (11 April 1975) 189, UN Doc A/CN.9/SR.166.

to sign the award to express their dissent.[591] It was noted that the phrase 'shall be signed by the arbitrators' includes dissenting arbitrators, who should sign 'more or less as a notary'[592] and because they are obliged to ensure the award's enforceability in countries requiring signatures of all arbitrators.[593] By contrast, Art 32(4) provides that, where an arbitrator fails to sign an award '*the award* shall state the reason for the absence of the signature' (emphasis added), implying that the explanation shall be included by the signing arbitrators, rather than being appended by the non-signing arbitrator—a point made in certain cases by judges at the Iran-US Claims Tribunal.[594]

Article 32(4)'s further requirement that the award state 'the place where the award was made' must be read in conjunction with Art 16(4). As discussed in the commentary to that Article, regardless of where the arbitrators sign the award, the place where the award 'was made' is the 'place' of the arbitration as designated by the parties or, in default of their designation, by the tribunal, and this designation has important consequences for the enforcement of the award. **16.339**

(2) Contemplated revisions

The Working Group intends to recommend replacing the reference to the different types of awards in Art 32(1) with a basic statement that a tribunal 'may make separate awards on different issues at different times', believing that the current list of different types of awards 'created confusion'.[595] At the end of Art 32(2), the Working Group favours adding language, similar to that contained in the ICC and LCIA Rules,[596] to the effect that parties adopting the Rules thereby waive any appeal, review or recourse to any court with respect to an award. The language would make clear that the waiver does not extend to actions for setting aside an award, and the Working Group agreed that the waiver also would not include grounds for resisting enforcement of an award, eg under Art V of the New York Convention.[597] Finally the Working Group favours modifying Art 32(5) so that a party may make an award public without consent to the extent required by a legal duty or to pursue a legal right (such as enforcement of the award) and the Group also proposes deleting Art 32(7) regarding local registration of an award, on the ground that it was unnecessary to restate in a rule a requirement of (some) national laws.[598] **16.340**

591 *id*, 188 (remarks of the Polish delegate).

592 *id*, (remarks of the Chairman).

593 UNCITRAL Committee of the Whole II, *Summary Record of the 11th Meeting* (19 April 1976) para 27 (remarks of Austrian delegate), UN Doc A/CN.9/9/C.2/SR.11.

594 See eg *Raygo Wagner Equipment Co v Star Line Iran Co* (Award no 20-17-3, 15 December 1982) ('Judge Mosk's Comments on Judge Sani's Reasons for Not Signing Award No. 20-17-3'), *reprinted in* 1 Iran–USCTR 411, 424–8 (1981–2); see also Sanders (n 28) 207.

595 *Report of WGII on the work of its 51st session* (14–18 September 2009) paras 63–6, UN Doc A/CN.9/684; *Report of WGII on the work of its 47th session* (10–14 September 2007) paras 79–80, UN Doc A/CN.9/641. Of related interest is the Working Group's intention, discussed in the commentary on contemplated revisions to Art 26, to delete the language in Art 26(2) providing that interim measures can be established as interim awards.

596 See Art 28(6) ICC Rules (1998) and Art 26(9) LCIA Rules (1998).

597 *Report of WGII on the work of its 51st session* (14–18 September 2009) paras 71–86, UN Doc A/CN.9/684.

598 *Report of WGII on the work of its 47th session* (10–14 September 2007) paras 95–9, 105, UN Doc A/CN.9/641.

APPLICABLE LAW, AMIABLE COMPOSITEUR

Article 33

1 **The arbitral tribunal shall apply the law designated by the parties as applicable to the substance of the dispute. Failing such designation by the parties, the arbitral tribunal shall apply the law determined by the conflict of laws rules which it considers applicable.**

2 **The arbitral tribunal shall decide as *amiable compositeur* or *ex aequo et bono* only if the parties have expressly authorized the arbitral tribunal to do so and if the law applicable to the arbitral procedure permits such arbitration.**

3 **In all cases, the arbitral tribunal shall decide in accordance with the terms of the contract and shall take into account the usages of the trade applicable to the transaction.**

(1) Commentary on current text

16.341 Article 33 addresses two issues: it (i) establishes the method for determining the law governing the merits of the dispute as well as specifying other legal norms to be applied; and (ii) prevents the tribunal from acting *ex aequo et bono* unless expressly authorized by the parties and permitted by applicable law to do so.

16.342 (1.1) **Determining the applicable law** Article 33 applies the principle of party autonomy to determination of the substantive law for resolving the dispute,[599] requiring a tribunal to apply any governing law the parties have designated. While it has been suggested that a tribunal might refuse to apply the parties' choice of law if it risked conflicting with (or was chosen to evade) public policy requirements of the law most closely connected with the disputed matter[600] or if the law of the place of arbitration precludes applying a wholly unrelated legal regime,[601] few if any tribunals appear to have so refused.[602] Indeed, there is generally less arbitral jurisprudence regarding Art 33 than other provisions of the Rules since the Iran-US Tribunal adopted a quite different provision, based on those two governments' agreement in the Claims Settlement Declaration that the tribunal could apply 'such . . . principles of commercial and international law as the arbitral tribunal determines to be applicable'.[603]

16.343 The UNCITRAL drafters evidently understood the parties' designation of a national law to mean (unless otherwise stated) the substantive law of that jurisdiction, ie excluding conflict of law rules.[604] This point is made expressly in Art 28(1) of the UNCITRAL Model Law on International Commercial Arbitration but is only implicit in the Rules.

16.344 Can the parties choose as the governing 'law' something other than a national law, such as the *lex mercatoria* or UNIDROIT legal principles? While the text of Art 33(1) leaves room for much disagreement, an inference might be drawn from the parties' authority under Art 33(2) to require resolution of the dispute *ex aequo et bono* (which derogates to a much greater extent from resolution of the case according to law) that the parties may also submit

599 *Commentary on Revised draft Rules* (n 90) 178 (commentary on draft Art 28(1)).

600 Caron, Caplan and Pellonpää (n 61) 124 (and authorities cited therein).

601 This concern was raised during the drafting of the 1976 Rules, *Commentary on Revised draft Rules* (n 90) 178 (commentary on draft Art 28(1)).

602 Caron, Caplan and Pellonpää (n 61) 125 (and authorities cited therein).

603 van Hof (n 55) 226–8.

604 See *Report of Committee of the Whole II* (n 55) para 172 (discussing draft Art 28(1)).

their disagreement to transnational legal principles, assuming the law of the arbitral seat and of any jurisdiction of likely enforcement of the award does not forbid this.[605]

If the parties have not chosen an applicable law, Art 33(1) requires that the tribunal first determine which system of conflict of laws should apply to this question and then choose the substantive law indicated by those conflicts rules. This suggests that the tribunal should follow the so-called *voie indirecte* although, given that the text of Art 33(1) allows the tribunal to choose the conflicts rules 'it considers applicable' (rather than requiring the tribunal to adopt, for example, the conflicts rules of the place of arbitration), the tribunal has some latitude in its method of proceeding. **16.345**

In addition to applying the substantive law chosen either by the parties or pursuant to the appropriate conflicts rules, the tribunal must (under Art 33(3)) resolve the dispute 'in accordance with the terms of the contract'. This is required 'in all cases', including cases in which the tribunal is authorized to decide *ex aequo et bono*. By contrast, the tribunal need only 'take into account' applicable 'usages of the trade'. This reflects a conscious decision by the drafters as to the hierarchy of legal norms to be applied: trade usages should not prevail over applicable law.[606] **16.346**

(1.2) The power to act *ex aequo et bono* or as *amiable compositeur* Pursuant to Art 33(2), a tribunal's authority to act *ex aequo et bono* depends not only on the parties' express agreement to confer such authority but also on whether the tribunal is permitted to act in this way by 'the law applicable to the arbitral procedure', which is normally the law of the place of arbitration. According to recent commentators, 'no *ex aequo et bono* or *amiable compositeur* award rendered under the UNCITRAL Rules is known'.[607] **16.347**

(2) Contemplated revisions

The Working Group intends to recommend two changes in Art 33(1). Firstly, it will seek to clarify in the first sentence that parties may choose to apply 'rules of law' rather than only a 'law' to govern their dispute, which would allow the choice of such transnational legal rules as the UNIDROIT Principles.[608] The Working Group opposes a similar revision that would allow the tribunal to apply 'rules of law' where the parties have not chosen a governing law, believing that such derogation from national law should be left to the parties. This follows the approach already adopted in Art 28 of the UNCITRAL Model Law on International Commercial Arbitration.[609] Secondly, the Working Group intends to abandon the requirement in the second sentence of Art 33(1) that a tribunal choose the governing law according to the *voie indirecte*, ie by first determining which system of conflict of laws applies. Rather, the Working Group is inclined to insert new language allowing the **16.348**

---

[605] Caron, Caplan and Pellonpää (n 61) 127–8 (noting that 'there is no straightforward answer to this question').

[606] See Baker and Davis (n 62) 176–7.

[607] Caron, Caplan and Pellonpää (n 61) 135 n 64.

[608] *Report of WGII on the work of its 47th session* (10–14 September 2007) para 106, UN Doc A/CN.9/641 (recording approval of alternative wording in the revised Art 33(1) as set forth in *Note by the Secretariat*, UN Doc A/CN.9/WG.II/WP.145/Add.1 para 37).

[609] *ibid*, para 109; *Report of WGII on the work of its 51st session* (14–18 September 2009) para 91, UN Doc A/CN.9/684.

tribunal directly to choose the applicable law it deems appropriate when the parties have not done so.[610] Finally, in Art 33(3), the Working Group would add the words 'if any' after the word 'contract' to conform to amendments in Arts 1 and 3 and elsewhere expanding the Rules' application to non-contractual disputes.[611]

SETTLEMENT OR OTHER GROUNDS FOR TERMINATION

Article 34

1 **If, before the award is made, the parties agree on a settlement of the dispute, the arbitral tribunal shall either issue an order for the termination of the arbitral proceedings or, if requested by both parties and accepted by the tribunal, record the settlement in the form of an arbitral award on agreed terms. The arbitral tribunal is not obliged to give reasons for such an award.**

2 **If, before the award is made, the continuation of the arbitral proceedings becomes unnecessary or impossible for any reason not mentioned in paragraph 1, the arbitral tribunal shall inform the parties of its intention to issue an order for the termination of the proceedings. The arbitral tribunal shall have the power to issue such an order unless a party raises justifiable grounds for objection.**

3 **Copies of the order for termination of the arbitral proceedings or of the arbitral award on agreed terms, signed by the arbitrators, shall be communicated by the arbitral tribunal to the parties. Where an arbitral award on agreed terms is made, the provisions of article 32, paragraphs 2 and 4 to 7, shall apply.**

(1) Commentary on current text

16.349 Article 34 specifies the actions that a tribunal may take when it appears that an arbitration should be terminated before an award on the merits has been issued. The rule addresses (i) circumstances in which the parties have settled their dispute; and (ii) circumstances in which arbitral proceedings should be terminated for some other reason.

16.350 **(1.1) Settlement of disputes** Article 34(1) provides that, when the parties settle their dispute before an award is made, if the parties so request, the tribunal *may* record the terms of the settlement in an award on agreed terms. The drafters understood that an award on agreed terms, by incorporating the terms of the settlement, would enjoy the same benefits of enforceability under, eg the New York Convention as an award on the merits.[612] Pursuant to Art 34(3), all of the provisions governing the making of or the attributes of an award on the merits that are set forth in Art 32 (except for the requirement in Art 32(3) that reasons for the award be stated) also apply to awards on agreed terms.

16.351 Article 34(1) is silent as to how a tribunal should decide whether to issue an award on agreed terms, but the drafters evidently expected the tribunal's discretion to be narrow, since they appeared to discuss only two grounds for refusing a request: 'the settlement

[610] *ibid*, paras 93–6 (discussing alternative wordings proposed in *Note by the Secretariat*, A/CN.9/WG.II/WP.151/Add.1 para 30).

[611] *Report of WGII on the work of its 51st session* (14–18 September 2009) paras 98–100, UN Doc A/CN.9/684.

[612] See *Report of the Committee of the Whole II* (n 55) 179 (referring to draft Art 29). This point is made expressly in Art 30(2) of the UNCITRAL Model Law on International Commercial Arbitration; see also Sanders (n 28) 211; van den Berg, A., *The New York Arbitration Convention of 1958: Towards a Uniform Judicial Interpretation* (Kluwer, Deventer, 1981) 49–50.

agreed on by the parties might be unlawful or contrary to public policy'.[613] At the Iran-US Claims Tribunal, it was argued that the arbitrators should also decline to issue an award if the dispute or its settlement fell outside their jurisdiction or if the settlement was not a reasonable resolution of the matter. In response, the full Tribunal stated generally that 'the power to refuse to record a settlement cannot be exercised in an arbitrary manner,' but it agreed that it should 'make such examination concerning its jurisdiction as it deems necessary'. On the other hand, it declined 'to review the reasonableness of the settlement in the place of the arbitrating parties'.[614] The latter decision was consistent both with the principle of party autonomy in arbitration and with Art 34(1)'s statement that the 'tribunal is not obliged to give reasons' for an award on agreed terms.

If a tribunal rejects a request to issue an award on agreed terms or if the parties reach a settlement but do not seek such an award, then the tribunal must issue an order terminating the arbitration. Parties might decide they do not require an award on agreed terms if, for example, their settlement can be fully implemented before it is notified to the tribunal. **16.352**

(1.2) **Termination for other reasons** Article 34(2) requires the tribunal also to order termination of arbitral proceedings when their continuation 'becomes unnecessary or impossible for any reason' other than settlement, 'unless a party raises justifiable grounds for objection'. Arbitral proceedings can become 'unnecessary or impossible', *inter alia*, because the claimant withdraws its claim,[615] the claimant fails to pursue its case,[616] or the claim is resolved in another forum. Before ordering termination, the tribunal must ask the parties whether they object. The text of Art 34(2) gives no guidance as to what constitute the 'justifiable grounds for objection' that—if raised—preclude termination. One such ground could be that the defendant has raised counterclaims that fall within the tribunal's jurisdiction and remain to be adjudicated. **16.353**

Can a party condition its non-objection to termination upon the tribunal's award of arbitration costs against the claimant seeking to withdraw its claim(s)? The Iran-US Claims Tribunal has implicitly rejected the proposition that the failure to award costs to the party not seeking termination could be a 'justifiable ground for objection'. For example, in *Seaboard Flour Corp v Islamic Republic of Iran*,[617] the respondent stated that it agreed with the claimant's request for termination 'provided that damages for costs and counsel fees be included in the award'. The tribunal ordered termination of the proceedings but also stipulated that '[e]ach Party shall bear its costs of arbitration'. This result seems consistent with Art 40, which ultimately leaves the apportionment of costs to the tribunal's discretion. Art 40(3) expressly requires that a tribunal fix the costs of arbitration even when issuing an order for termination of proceedings (or, for that matter, in issuing an award on agreed **16.354**

[613] *Summary of 8th Session Discussion* (n 55) para 194; see also *Preliminary draft Rules* (n 18), *reprinted in* (1975) VI *UNCITRAL Ybk* at 179 (both documents referring to draft Art 28).

[614] *Iran v United States* (Decision no DEC 8-A1-FT, 14 May 1982), *reprinted in* 1 Iran–USCTR 144, 152-3 (1981–2).

[615] See eg *Reliance Group Inc v National Iranian Oil Co* (Award no 15-90-2, 8 December 1982), *reprinted in* 1 Iran–USCTR 384, 385 (1981–2).

[616] See *eg Isaac Poura v Islamic Republic of Iran,* Case no 323 (Chamber One, Order of 3 March 1993).

[617] Case no 318 (Chamber Three, Order of 9 April 1985).

terms) but does not otherwise indicate any special rule on apportionment of costs. According to the drafting history of a predecessor clause, it was 'expected that, in the absence of special circumstances, the arbitrators will divide the costs of arbitration equally between the parties'[618] in cases resulting in an award on agreed terms or an order of termination.

(2) Contemplated revisions

16.355 The Working Group has not endorsed revisions in Art 34(1), other than a small wording change (substituting 'the parties' for 'both parties'), to conform to the Group's decision that the Rules should expressly refer to multi-party arbitrations. The Working Group is considering whether to modify Art 32(2)'s direction that tribunals 'terminate' certain proceedings for the same reasons that it is considering giving tribunals more flexible authority under Art 28(1).[619] Finally, the Working Group favours deleting cross-references in Art 34(3) to Art 32(6) and (7) since the former provision is duplicative and the latter provision is slated to be removed from Art 32.

INTERPRETATION OF THE AWARD

Article 35

1 **Within thirty days after the receipt of the award, either party, with notice to the other party, may request that the arbitral tribunal give an interpretation of the award.**

2 **The interpretation shall be given in writing within forty-five days after the receipt of the request. The interpretation shall form part of the award and the provisions of article 32, paragraphs 2 to 7, shall apply.**

(1) Commentary on current text

16.356 Article 35 authorizes parties to seek and tribunals to furnish an 'interpretation' of a previously issued award and imposes time limits on both of these actions.

16.357 Once a party timely requests an 'interpretation,' Art 35 provides that the 'interpretation shall be given', implying that the tribunal is obliged to carry out any such request. However, as the Article's wording suggests and as tribunals have held, arbitrators need not supplement their award if what is requested is denominated an interpretation but is in reality something else.[620] As the Iran-US Claims Tribunal explained in one case, 'the legislative history of Art 35, paragraph 1 of the UNCITRAL Arbitration Rules . . . indicates that the term "interpretation of the award" was intended to mean "clarification of the award". Thus, [the article] was intended to apply only where an award contains language that is ambiguous'.[621] On that principle, arbitrators have held that Art 35 does not require interpretation

---

[618] *Commentary on Revised draft Rules* (n 90) 180 (commentary on draft Art 29(2)).

[619] *Report of WGII on the work of its 51st session* (14–18 September 2009) paras 101–3, UN Doc A/CN.9/684; see also discussion in para 16.319, *supra.*

[620] See eg *Pepsico Int'l Corp v Islamic Republic of Iran,* Decision no DEC 55-18-1 (19 December 1986) (tribunal declined to issue requested interpretation because, 'while the Respondents' submission reargues certain aspects of the Case and disagrees with various conclusions of the Tribunal, it fails to point to any element of the Award that is ambiguous'), *reprinted in* 13 Iran–USCTR 328, 329–30 (1986-II).

[621] *Paul Donin de Rosiere et al v Islamic Republic of Iran,* Decision no DEC 57-498-1 (10 February 1987), *reprinted in* 14 Iran–USCTR 100, 101–2 (1987-I).

of an award if the award's original wording is already clear.[622] Similarly, a party's request to order the opposing party to comply with an award has been found not to be a request for interpretation.[623]

Article 35 evidently responds to the drafters' concern that parties' 'obligations and rights' under an award might be unclear, particularly if the award is written in a language that is 'not . . . the mother tongue of all of the arbitrators'.[624] In practice, however, according to one commentator's review of cases at the Iran-US Claims Tribunal, 'requesting parties usually are not in search of an interpretation of an award as much as they are attempting to obtain review on the merits by the Tribunal'.[625] However, other commentators have noted that the Iran-US Claims Tribunal generally 'addressed commercial relations that had been broken abruptly . . . [and] thus set forth few if any continuing obligations of the sort that require clarification for future action', which is where 'Article 35 is most likely to be valuable'.[626] **16.358**

The drafters of Art 35 sought to reconcile the authority to interpret prior awards with the principle that awards are final (see Art 32(2)) and enforceable (see eg the New York Convention) by providing in Art 35(2) that any interpretation issued by a tribunal 'shall form part of the award and the provisions of Art 32, paragraphs 2 to 7 shall apply' to the interpretation. As a result, any enforcement of the original award should also extend to any interpretation of that award. As Professor Sanders has noted, a further consequence of requiring interpretations to satisfy Art 32(2) to (7) is that any interpretation issued by a three-member tribunal must be rendered by a majority.[627] **16.359**

Even though Art 35 extends the competence of the arbitrators past the time when the final award was issued (so that any ambiguity in the award may be redressed),[628] such a power need not conflict with the requirement of finality. This was confirmed by the *ad hoc* tribunal in *Wintershall AG v The Government of Qatar,* which rejected the respondent's argument that local law precluded interpretation of a previously issued award. The tribunal held that 'Article 1059 of the Netherlands Arbitration Act 1986[,] providing for the *res judicata* effect of a partial final award[,] in no sense deprives the parties of the ability to agree to an interpretation of a partial award under Article 35'.[629] **16.360**

---

[622] See eg *Norman Gabay v Islamic Republic of Iran*, Decision no DEC 99-771-2 (24 September 1991), *reprinted in* 27 Iran–USCTR 194, 195 (1991-II) ('The Tribunal cannot identify any ambiguous language in the Award, and the Claimant has pointed to none').

[623] *Islamic Republic of Iran v United States of America*, Case no A/27 (Full Tribunal, Order of 5 August 1998).

[624] UNCITRAL, *Summary Record of the 167th Meeting* (14 April 1975) 205–6, UN Doc A/CN.9/SR.167 (remarks of the Mexican and Hungarian delegates, respectively).

[625] van Hof (n 55) 284. See eg *Eastman Kodak v Government of Iran*, Decision no DEC 102-227-3 (30 December 1991) ('While the Respondent refers to 'the need for interpretation of the Final Award,' it also argues that the Tribunal's findings in the Partial Award and the record of the Case warrant a conclusion different from that reached by the Tribunal in the Final Award'), *reprinted in* 27 Iran–USCTR 269, 270 (1991-II).

[626] Baker and Davis (n 62) 194.

[627] Sanders (n 28) 212 (citing Art 31 of the Rules).

[628] *Commentary on Revised draft Rules* (n 90) 180 (referring to draft Art 30(2)).

[629] *Wintershall AG v The Government of Qatar*, Final Award (*ad hoc* tribunal, 31 May 1988), *reprinted in* 28 ILM 833, 835 (1989).

(2) Contemplated revisions

16.361 The Working Group does not envision any changes in Art 35, other than small wording changes (eg substituting 'other parties' for 'other party'), to conform to the Group's decision that the Rules should expressly permit multi-party arbitrations. The cross-reference to Art 32(7) will also be deleted since that paragraph of Art 32 is itself slated to be removed.[630]

CORRECTION OF THE AWARD

Article 36

1 **Within thirty days after the receipt of the award, either party, with notice to the other party, may request the arbitral tribunal to correct in the award any errors in computation, any clerical or typographical errors, or any errors of similar nature. The arbitral tribunal may within thirty days after the communication of the award make such corrections on its own initiative.**

2 **Such corrections shall be in writing, and the provisions of article 32, paragraphs 2 to 7, shall apply.**

(1) Commentary on current text

16.362 Much as Art 35 authorizes a tribunal to render an 'interpretation' of an award previously issued, Art 36 ensures that a tribunal also retains competence to rectify any unintended errors.

16.363 In contrast to Art 35's regime for interpretations, Art 36 allows arbitrators to make corrections not only when a party so requests but also *sua sponte*, within 30 days following issuance of the award. The description of the types of mistakes that arbitrators are empowered, *post hoc*, to correct is fairly precise: 'errors in computation, any clerical or typographical errors, or errors of a similar nature'. Parties often seek 'corrections' that lie beyond this narrow category of errors,[631] but tribunals have generally refused to make such 'corrections'. For example, in *Petrolane Inc et al v. Government of the Islamic Republic of Iran et al*,[632] the government of Iran requested that a citation in the award be 'corrected'. What the arbitrators had cited was an award in another case that the parties in the other case had subsequently agreed (as part of a settlement) to treat as null and void, and thus Iran sought a 'correction' of what it suggested was akin to a 'clerical error'. The *Petrolane* arbitrators declined the request, seemingly on the ground that they had intentionally cited the award, which did exist, and thus that there was no 'error' that could be corrected.[633] On the other hand, several tribunals have made corrections of the sort that do fall squarely within

---

[630] *Report of WGII on the work of its 51st session* (14–18 September 2009) paras 104–5, UN Doc A/CN.9/684.

[631] See eg *Endo Laboratories Inc v Islamic Republic of Iran et al*, Decision no DEC 74-366-3 (25 February 1988) (the respondents' requests for correction included, *inter alia*, 'a) a request for the Tribunal to correct its alleged failure to take into account in the Respondents' favor gratis samples amounting to 10% of the ordered amount; b) a request for the Tribunal to correct its finding in paragraph 57(b) for which, according to the Respondent, no evidentiary basis exists . . .'), *reprinted in* 18 Iran–USCTR 113, 114 (1988-II).

[632] Decision no DEC 101-131-2 (25 November 1991), *reprinted in* 27 Iran–USCTR 264, 264 (1991-II).

[633] See also eg *Ford Aerospace & Communications Corp v Iran*, Decision no DEC 59-93-1 (22 April 1987) (declining to correct alleged mischaracterization of respondent's statement) *reprinted in* 14 Iran–USCTR 255, 256 (1987-I); see generally Baker and Davis (n 62) 196.

Art 36's ambit, such as for typographical errors, incorrect dates, accidental exclusion of amounts from calculations, inconsistent references to fixed sums etc.[634]

(2) Contemplated revisions

The Working Group intends to revise the relevant phrase in Art 36(1) to read 'or any errors **16.364**
or omissions of a similar nature'. The intent of this change is to 'cover situations such as [an] arbitrator omitting to sign the award or to state the date or place of the award'.[635] The Working Group also expects to make small wording modifications (substituting, in the first sentence, 'any party' for 'either party' and 'parties' for 'party'), so that the Rules expressly accommodate multi-party arbitrations. In Art 36(2), the Working Group favours adding language to impose a time limit for the issuance of a correction and to require that any correction form part of the award, to be consistent with the approach taken in Arts 35 (Interpretation of the Award) and 37 (Additional Awards).[636] Finally, the cross-reference to Art 32(7) will be deleted since that paragraph of Art 32 is itself slated to be removed.

ADDITIONAL AWARD

Article 37

1 **Within thirty days after the receipt of the award, either party, with notice to the other party, may request the arbitral tribunal to make an additional award as to claims presented in the arbitral proceedings but omitted from the award.**

2 **If the arbitral tribunal considers the request for an additional award to be justified and considers that the omission can be rectified without any further hearings or evidence, it shall complete its award within sixty days after the receipt of the request.**

3 **When an additional award is made, the provisions of article 32, paragraphs 2 to 7, shall apply.**

(1) Commentary on current text

Like Arts 35 and 36, Art 37 ensures that the tribunal retains jurisdiction for a fixed time **16.365**
after it issues an award to remedy a possible defect, in this case an unintentional failure to resolve a claim that was previously presented to the arbitrators. The remedy Art 37 authorizes is for the tribunal to 'make an additional award' addressing the omitted claim.

A tribunal must satisfy itself that five conditions are met in order to issue an additional **16.366**
award. First, a party must have requested the further award within 30 days after receiving the allegedly deficient award. Secondly, the claim that the additional award would address must have been 'presented in the arbitral proceedings'. This prevents parties from abusing the procedure by tardily raising new claims, and indeed the Iran-US Claims Tribunal has taken a fairly strict view as to whether a claim allegedly 'omitted' from an award had been properly 'presented'. For example, in *International Schools Services Inc v Iran,* the tribunal concluded that a claim had only been mentioned in a rejoinder brief (in which no new

[634] See cases noted, eg in Caron, Caplan and Pellonpää (n 61) 898–900; Baker and Davis (n 62) 195.

[635] *Report of WGII on the work of its 47th session* (10–14 September 2007) para 116, UN Doc A/CN.9/641, adopting draft revision of Art 36 set forth in UN Doc A/CN.9/WG.II/WP.145/Add.1 para 41.

[636] *Report of WGII on the work of its 51st session* (14–18 September 2009) paras 106–12, UN Doc A/CN.9/684.

issues were to be raised) and thus was not properly 'presented'.[637] Third, the claim must have been 'omitted' from the award that has been issued. The Iran-US Claims Tribunal has not hesitated to point out that claims allegedly 'omitted' were in fact disposed of in the award, even if sometimes obliquely.[638]

16.367 The fourth condition is that the tribunal must find the request for an additional award is 'justified'. The Secretariat's commentary on this provision during the drafting described it as giving arbitrators 'full discretion . . . to decide whether or not to make such an additional award'.[639] Indeed, as one delegate noted, even if an award omits a claim previously presented, the tribunal may be able to explain the omission, in which case 'there was no point in pressing the arbitrators to rectify an omission'.[640] In effect, then, Art 37 only covers unintended omissions, as has been confirmed by certain rulings of the Iran-US Claims Tribunal. For example, in *Avco Corp v Iran,* the respondent sought an additional award on the disposition of certain goods but the tribunal noted that its award expressly directed the parties to seek to negotiate a resolution of this issue and thus the award, in the arbitrators' view, had not 'omitted' the claim.[641]

16.368 Finally, any additional award must be rendered 'without any hearings or evidence'. The inclusion of this condition provoked disagreement among the drafters: some objected that a prior failure to elicit evidence might well reflect 'the arbitrators' performance and omissions', while others responded that, to avoid abuse, additional awards should be limited to claims for which 'all the elements necessary for an award had been submitted',[642] and the latter view prevailed. Ten years later, however, this restriction on additional awards was omitted from the corresponding provision (Art 33(3)) of the UNCITRAL Model Law on International Commercial Arbitration.

(2) Contemplated revisions

16.369 Although the Working Group has not yet adopted final language for this Article, it has provisionally decided to recommend deletion of the clause in Art 37(2) permitting an additional award only if it can be rendered without a further hearing or receipt of further evidence.[643] The Working Group may also add language in Art 37(2) permitting the

---

[637] Decision no DEC 61-123-1 (28 April 1987), *reprinted in* 14 Iran–USCTR 279, 281 (1987-I). See also *Lockheed Corp v Iran* Decision no DEC 84-829-2 (19 September 1988) (reference to other party's duty to return goods did not constitute a claim for delivery of goods), *reprinted in* 19 Iran–USCTR 317, 318 (1988-II).

[638] See eg *Exxon Research and Engineering Co v Islamic Republic of Iran,* Decision no DEC 63-155-3 (29 July 1987) (claim for an award of legal fees was not 'omitted' since the tribunal's award directed each party to bear its own costs), *reprinted in* 16 Iran–USCTR 110, 111 (1987-III).

[639] *Commentary on Revised draft Rules* (n 90) 181 (referring to draft Art 32(2)).

[640] UNCITRAL, *Summary Report of 167th Meeting* (14 April 1975) 208, UN Doc A/CN.9/SR.167 (remarks of Greek delegate).

[641] Decision and Correction to Partial Award 377-261-3 (30 December 1988) para 7, *reprinted in* 19 Iran–USCTR 253, 255–6 (1988-II).

[642] UNCITRAL Committee of the Whole II, *Summary Record of 12th Meeting* (20 April 1976) paras 21-2 (remarks of Soviet Union delegate and of Professor Sanders, respectively), UN Doc A/CN.9/9/C.2/SR.12.

[643] See *Report of WGII on the work of its 47th session* (10–14 September 2007), paras 117-21, UN Doc A/CN.9/641; see also *Note by the Secretariat, Settlement of Commercial Disputes: Revision of the UNCITRAL Arbitration Rules*(6 August 2008) para 36, UN Doc A/CN.9/WG.II/WP.151/Add.1.

tribunal to extend the 60-day deadline for issuing an additional award 'if necessary'.[644] In addition, the Working Group is considering whether to respond to the problem that could arise if a tribunal issues a termination order when there remain issues before it (eg a counter claim) that should be resolved. Article 37's authorization of an '*additional* award' may not redress that situation, and the Working Group thus may recommend either modifying Art 37 to allow requests for 'an award' after termination or modifying Art 34(2) to provide that termination orders may be treated as awards for the purposes of Art 37.[645] Finally, the cross-reference to Art 32(7) will be deleted since that paragraph of Art 32 is itself slated to be removed.

COSTS (Articles 38 to 40)

Article 38

The arbitral tribunal shall fix the costs of arbitration in its award. The term 'costs' includes only:

(*a*) The fees of the arbitral tribunal to be stated separately as to each arbitrator and to be fixed by the tribunal itself in accordance with article 39;

(*d*) The travel and other expenses incurred by the arbitrators;

(*c*) The costs of expert advice and of other assistance required by the arbitral tribunal;

(*d*) The travel and other expenses of witnesses to the extent such expenses are approved by the arbitral tribunal;

(*e*) The costs for legal representation and assistance of the successful party if such costs were claimed during the arbitral proceedings, and only to the extent that the arbitral tribunal determines that the amount of such costs is reasonable;

(*f*) Any fees and expenses of the appointing authority as well as the expenses of the Secretary-General of the Permanent Court of Arbitration at The Hague.

(1) Commentary on current text

Article 38 sets forth an exclusive list of items that make up the 'costs' of arbitration, which arbitrators must fix in any award.[646] Only these costs will be payable by one or more parties (or apportioned between or among the parties) pursuant to Art 40, depending upon the tribunal's allocation of them. **16.370**

Article 38's descriptions of the elements that constitute 'costs' are straightforward and have occasioned little attention in arbitral decisions. Sub-paragraph (a)'s requirement that fees be stated separately for each arbitrator is evidently intended as a further check (complementing the provisions of Art 39, discussed *infra*) against arbitrators' seeking to disguise the extent of their remuneration by aggregating these amounts with other costs.[647] By implication, and as the drafting history confirms, 'all other costs of arbitration may be combined into one figure.'[648] **16.371**

644 *ibid.*

645 *Report of WGII on the work of its 51st session* (14–18 September 2009) paras 113–16, UN Doc A/CN.9/684.

646 As previously noted, tribunals are also required, under Art 40(3), to fix costs when issuing either an award on agreed terms or an order to terminate proceedings prior to issuance of a final award.

647 See Baker and Davis (n 62) 209 (noting that Art 38(a) 'permit[s] easier scrutiny by the parties' of fees).

648 *Commentary on Revised draft Rules* (n 90) 181 (referring to draft Art 33).

16.372 Expenses relating to witnesses are covered by sub-para (d) and must, uniquely, be 'approved by the tribunal', a phrase that was 'added in order to avoid abuse of the right to call witnesses'.[649] Although some drafters feared parties might call too many witnesses,[650] a majority felt that witnesses could be crucial in presenting a case and therefore that their costs should be payable.[651]

16.373 The drafters debated whether 'costs' should include the successful party's legal fees, which was linked to consideration of the provision allocating costs of the arbitration. It was noted that, in many countries, each party bore its own legal expense.[652] On the other hand, a majority of drafters evidently felt that requiring the prevailing party always to bear such costs could be unfair.[653] The wording adopted in (e) (limiting the inclusion of the successful party's legal fees to those that are 'claimed during the arbitral proceedings'[654] and that the tribunal deems 'reasonable') along with the discretionary rule for apportioning legal costs (which became Art 40(2)) were said to create the most 'flexible' approach[655] and, taken together, left the arbitrators 'free to apportion between the parties . . . the legal expenses of the successful party'.[656] Professor Sanders suggests, however, that the discretion not to award the legal fees of the successful party was intended to be exercised in simple cases where legal assistance 'may be regarded as unnecessary'.[657]

16.374 In *Sylvania Technical Systems Inc v Iran*, the tribunal considered the meaning of 'reasonable' fees in Art 38(e), finding that reasonableness should be determined, *inter alia*, in light of the relative complexity of the case and of the fact that 'in commercial cases in the United States the practice is that each party generally bears the costs of its legal counsel'.[658] It is unclear whether the latter factor was invoked simply because the prevailing party in the case was American, but Judge Holtzmann expressly objected that 'the practices as to legal fees in courts in the United States are not relevant to the determination of reasonable costs under the Tribunal Rules'.[659]

---

[649] UNCITRAL Committee of the Whole II, *Summary Record of the 12th Meeting* (20 April 1976) para 72 (remarks of Professor Sanders, special consultant to the UNCITRAL Secretariat), UN Doc A/CN.9/9/C.2/SR.12.

[650] *ibid.* paras 63, 69 and 71 (remarks of the Austrian, French and Philippines delegates) .

[651] *ibid*, paras 67–8, 70, and 75–6 (remarks of United Kingdom, United States, Indian, Hungarian and Mexican delegates, among others).

[652] UNCITRAL Committee of the Whole II, *Summary Record of 13th Meeting* (20 April 1976) paras 1–5, 8 (remarks of United States and Philippines delegates regarding draft Art 33), UN Doc A/CN.9/9/C.2/SR.13.

[653] *ibid*, paras 10, 17 (remarks of the French and Mexican delegates among others regarding draft Art 33).

[654] A tribunal can deny any award of legal costs, pursuant to Art 40(2), if the prevailing party fails to request them; see eg *Futura Trading Inc v Khuzestan Water and Power Authority*, Award no 187-325-3 (19 August 1985), *reprinted in* 9 Iran–USCTR 46, 59-60 (1985-III).

[655] UNCITRAL Committee of the Whole II, *Summary Record of 13th Meeting* (20 April 1976) paras 6, 18 (remarks of French and Soviet Union delegates, respectively, regarding draft Art 33), UN Doc A/CN.9/9/C.2/SR.13.

[656] *Report of the Committee of the Whole II* (n 55) para 218 (referring to draft Art 33).

[657] Sanders (n 28) 216; see also *Sylvania Technical Systems Inc v Iran,* Award no 180-64-1 (27 June 1985), *reprinted in* 8 Iran–USCTR 298, 332 (1985-I) (separate opinion of Judge Holtzmann).

[658] Award no 180-64-1 (27 June 1985), *reprinted in* 8 Iran–USCTR 298, 324 (1985-I).

[659] *ibid*, fn 16. Although the *Sylvania* decision remains 'the leading case expressing the Tribunal's philosophy on awards of costs', Baker and Davis (n 62) 210, its persuasive authority is limited by the Tribunal's exceptional inconsistency on this issue. As the *Sylvania* tribunal itself described the record as of 1985, 'Chamber Two [of the Iran-US Claims Tribunal] has never awarded any costs, Chamber One has awarded relatively

All costs listed in Art 38 are described in the introductory phrase as 'costs of arbitration', but the descriptions of witness costs and legal costs in Art 38(d) and (e) do not expressly limit these costs to ones incurred before the tribunal. Thus, parties may be able to seek recovery under Art 38(d) and (e) of witness and legal costs incurred in related court proceedings. While the Iran-US Claims Tribunal has rejected requests for the costs of actually presenting claims to courts,[660] the result might be different, for example, with respect to 'costs made in obtaining court-ordered provisional measures'.[661] **16.375**

(2) Contemplated revisions

The Working Group intends to recommend that the word 'reasonable' be added as the second word in each of sub-paras (b), (c) and (d), just as it already modifies the costs that may be fixed under Art 38(e).[662] In sub-para (e), the Working Group favours deletion of the word 'legal', since 'representation and assistance' of a party can be provided by non-lawyers, and it has also decided that the words 'successful party' should be replaced by the word 'parties' on the ground that Art 38 'did not deal with the question of the criteria for apportionment of costs, which was dealt with under article 40'.[663] Finally, the Working Group is considering whether Art 38 should be revised to clarify that a tribunal may fix costs of arbitration in more than one award.[664] **16.376**

Article 39

1 **The fees of the arbitral tribunal shall be reasonable in amount, taking into account the amount in dispute, the complexity of the subject-matter, the time spent by the arbitrators and any other relevant circumstances of the case.**

2 **If an appointing authority has been agreed upon by the parties or designated by the Secretary-General of the Permanent Court of Arbitration at The Hague, and if that authority has issued a schedule of fees for arbitrators in international cases which it administers, the arbitral tribunal in fixing its fees shall take that schedule of fees into account to the extent that it considers appropriate in the circumstances of the case.**

3 **If such appointing authority has not issued a schedule of fees for arbitrators in international cases, any party may at any time request the appointing authority to furnish a statement setting forth the basis for establishing fees which is customarily followed in international cases in which the authority appoints arbitrators. If the appointing authority consents to provide such a statement, the arbitral tribunal in fixing its fees shall take such information into account to the extent that it considers appropriate in the circumstances of the case.**

4 **In cases referred to in paragraphs 2 and 3, when a party so requests and the appointing authority consents to perform the function, the arbitral tribunal shall fix its fees only after**

small amounts of costs in only a few cases, and Chamber Three has in general awarded costs to the successful party in an amount well below the one claimed'. Award no 180-64-1, *reprinted in* 8 Iran–USCTR at 324. Seven years later, two commentators agreed that 'Tribunal practice in awarding fees remained inconsistent'. Baker and Davis (n 62) 213.

[660] See eg *Sylvania Technical Systems Inc v Iran* (n 658); see also van Hof (n 55) 295–6 (referring also to other similar Tribunal holdings).

[661] van Hof (n 55) at 296.

[662] *Report of WGII on the work of its 48th session* (4–8 February 2008) para 18, UN Doc A/CN.9/646.

[663] *ibid*, para 19.

[664] *Report of WGII on the work of its 51st session* (14–18 September 2009) para 120, UN Doc A/CN.9/684.

consultation with the appointing authority which may make any comment it deems appropriate to the arbitral tribunal concerning the fees.

(1) Commentary on current text

16.377 Article 39 seeks to guide arbitrators in fixing their fees in two ways: by (i) setting forth general standards that the fees must meet; and (ii) providing that arbitrators must consider fee schedules or fee-calculation methods provided by any appointing authority that has been designated in the case.

16.378 (1.1) **General standards for fees** Article 39(1) establishes the basic standard of reasonableness that arbitrators' fees must meet but then defines this standard in a way that preserves the arbitrators' ultimate discretion, since what is 'reasonable' is to be determined not only by the size of the case, its complexity, and the time required for its adjudication, but also by 'any other relevant circumstance of the case'. What may be 'relevant' is for the arbitrators to decide. Cases from the Iran-US Claims Tribunal offer no guidance on this standard, since all payments to the arbitrators serving on that Tribunal were made by the two governments, pursuant to the Claims Settlement Declaration.[665] In other arbitrations, fee amounts or calculation methods may simply be decreed by the tribunal or agreed with the parties.[666]

16.379 (1.2) **Guidance from appointing authorities** The drafters of the Rules recognized the risk of abuse in certain cases if arbitrators were given complete discretion to fix their own fees,[667] and the delegates debated how best to address the problem. Several drafters favoured inserting a fee schedule into the Rules,[668] but this was ultimately abandoned as impractical for a number of reasons[669] and, instead, the focus shifted to the role that an appointing authority might play in guiding the arbitrators' decisions concerning fees.[670] Article 39 provides for two types of guidance. First, Art 39(2) and (3) provide that, if an appointing authority has been agreed or designated in a case and if that authority either has issued a fee schedule for international arbitrations or has not issued such a schedule but, upon a party's request, is willing to state the basis for setting fees 'customarily followed in international cases' in which it appoints arbitrators, then the tribunal must take either the schedule or the fee basis into account when fixing its own fees, 'to the extent that it considers appropriate

[665] See Art VI(3) of the Claims Settlement Declaration (n 29).

[666] See eg Caron, Caplan and Pellonpää (n 61) 935-41 and cases cited therein.

[667] See eg *Summary of 8th Session Discussion* (n 55) para 214 (noting that, to the extent the draft of what was then Art 31 'empowered the arbitrators themselves to fix their fees, the view was expressed that there should be some limitation on this power').

[668] *ibid;* see also *Report of the Committee of the Whole II* (n 55) paras 206–7 (referring to draft Art 33 and noting that such a schedule 'would prevent the possibility that some arbitrators would charge unreasonably high fees for their services').

[669] The perceived difficulties included the fact that any schedule would have to accommodate conditions in a wide range of legal markets, given the anticipated global application of the Rules, in which case there would need to be broad fee ranges, yet there might be no administering institution to select an appropriate amount within a range for any particular case. See *Note by the Secretariat, Draft UNCITRAL Arbitration Rules: Schedule of Fees of Arbitrators,* UN Doc A/CN.9/114 (1976), *reprinted in* (1976) VII *UNCITRAL Ybk* 190, 191; see generally Caron, Caplan and Pellonpää (n 61) 942–3.

[670] *id,* 943; see also eg UNCITRAL, *Summary Record of 168th Meeting* (14 April 1975) 209 (remarks of United States delegate).

in the circumstances of the case'. Like the standard for 'reasonable' fees in sub-para (1), this precatory language effectively leaves the final determination of fees to the arbitrators' discretion.

Secondly, Art 39(4) provides that in any case where the appointing authority has furnished either a fee schedule or a fee-setting basis to the tribunal, if a party so requests and the appointing authority agrees to serve this further role, the tribunal must consult the appointing authority about the fee amounts it intends to fix and give the appointing authority an opportunity to comment. Since this provision does not require that the tribunal follow the appointing authority's comments, the tribunal again retains full discretion to fix its fees, although obviously it is hoped the tribunal will heed such advice. **16.380**

(2) Contemplated revisions

While final new wording for Art 39 has not yet been adopted, the Working Group intends essentially to preserve sub-paras (1) and (2) but to recommend substantial revisions to (3) and (4), in order to 'provide for a general supervisory power of the appointing authority, or failing its appointment, the [Permanent Court of Arbitration], over the methodology and final computation of fees'.[671] The regime favoured by the Working Group would assign final control over fees (in cases where there was any objection by a party) to the appointing authority or, if there is none, to the Secretary-General of the PCA, which has agreed to perform this role.[672] **16.381**

Reforming the mechanism for setting arbitrators' fees was one of the 'main lines of revision' in the Rules recommended in the report commissioned by UNCITRAL's Secretariat when the Working Group began its current revision project.[673] That report noted that 'there have been disturbing instances of 'negotiations' regarding fees between arbitrators and parties, especially where one party finds it tactically appealing to accept anything the arbitrators say'.[674] This view was echoed in the Working Group, although delegates felt—as did the authors of the report—that instances of abuse were the exception rather than the rule.[675] **16.382**

The proposed revised text of Art 39(3) and (4) that the Secretariat has prepared to reflect the Working Group's deliberations to date (and which awaits the Group's further consideration) would create the following new regime for establishing fees. First, a tribunal would be obliged to inform the parties how it proposes to determine its members fees 'promptly after its constitution', and then, when it subsequently fixes its fees pursuant to Art 38, it **16.383**

[671] See *Report of WGII on the work of its 48th session* (4–8 February 2008) para 26, UN Doc A/CN.9/646; see also *ibid*, paras 20–1.

[672] *ibid*; see also *Note by the Secretariat, Settlement of Commercial Disputes: Revision of the UNCITRAL Arbitration Rules* (6 December 2006) para 45 ('the Permanent Court of Arbitration in the Hague has been approached on that matter and agreed to be involved to a greater extent in practical issues relating to the fixing of the fees'), UN Doc A/CN.9/WG.II/WP.145/Add.1. See *Report of WGII on the work of its 51st session* (14–18 September 2009) paras 122–6, UN Doc A/CN.9/684.

[673] Paulsson and Petrochilos (n 39) 10.

[674] *ibid.*

[675] *Report of WGII on the work of its 48th session* (4–8 February 2008) para 20 ('It was observed that Art 39 had been the source of difficulties in practice when exaggerated fees were charged by arbitral tribunals, leaving parties without practical solutions other than perhaps resorting to State court.').

would be required to state how it had done so.[676] Secondly, if any party contests either the intended approach to fee determination the tribunal announces or the calculation of final fees, the party may refer the matter either to the appointing authority or (in the absence of such authority) to the Secretary-General of the PCA 'for final determination in accordance with the criteria in paragraph (1)'.[677] Any revision, under this procedure, of the final calculation of fees for the tribunal 'shall be deemed to be part of the award'.[678] The Working Group has identified several open questions about the operation of such a new regime that it must still address.[679]

Article 40

1 **Except as provided in paragraph 2, the costs of arbitration shall in principle be borne by the unsuccessful party. However, the arbitral tribunal may apportion each of such costs between the parties if it determines that apportionment is reasonable, taking into account the circumstances of the case.**

2 **With respect to the costs of legal representation and assistance referred to in article 38, paragraph *(e)*, the arbitral tribunal, taking into account the circumstances of the case, shall be free to determine which party shall bear such costs or may apportion such costs between the parties if it determines that apportionment is reasonable.**

3 **When the arbitral tribunal issues an order for the termination of the arbitral proceedings or makes an award on agreed terms, it shall fix the costs of arbitration referred to in article 38 and article 39, paragraph 1, in the text of that order or award.**

4 **No additional fees may be charged by an arbitral tribunal for interpretation or correction or completion of its award under articles 35 to 37.**

(1) Commentary on current text

16.384 Article 40 accomplishes three objectives: it (i) provides guidance for the tribunal's allocation of costs among the parties; (ii) requires a tribunal to fix costs even when it issues an award on agreed terms or an order to terminate proceedings; and (iii) precludes the tribunal from charging any fees for work done in issuing an interpretation or correction of a previous award or in rendering an additional award, pursuant to Arts 35, 36 and 37, respectively. The second of these objectives has already been discussed in the context of Art 34[680] and is not examined further here.

16.385 (1.1) **Allocation of costs** Article 40(1) establishes the rule that, 'in principle', the losing party is to bear the costs of arbitration as defined in Arts 38 and 39—except for legal costs (as defined in Art 38(e)), which are treated separately under Art 40(2). However, the 'principle' of the losing party's bearing the arbitration costs is considerably modified by the second sentence of Art 40(1), providing that the arbitral tribunal may nonetheless

[676] See *Note by the Secretariat, Settlement of Commercial Disputes: Revision of the UNCITRAL Arbitration Rules* (6 August 2008) para 38 and preceding text, UN Doc A/CN.9/WG.II/WP.151/Add.1; *Report of WGII on the work of its 51st session* (14–18 September 2009) paras 123–6, UN Doc A/CN.9/684.

[677] *Note by the Secretariat* (n 676) para 39 and preceding referenced text.

[678] *ibid.*

[679] *Report of WG II on the work of its 51st session* (14–18 September 2009) paras 123–6, UN Doc A/CN.9/684.

[680] See para 16.354, *supra.*

apportion the costs between the parties if this seems 'reasonable, taking into account the circumstances of the case'.

Under Art 40(2), which covers the allocation only of legal costs and which omits the **16.386** general principle that the losing party pays, the tribunal has essentially the same power to apportion costs 'if it determines that apportionment is reasonable', once again 'taking into account the circumstances of the case'. As has already been discussed in the context of Art 38, the primary reason for the distinct rule on the allocation of legal costs was the drafters' awareness that in many legal systems each party traditionally bears its own costs.[681]

Certain commentators have noted that, '[i]n reality, both approaches [ie under Art 40(1) **16.387** and (2)] afford the arbitral tribunal wide discretion to apportion and award the costs of arbitration in almost any manner it chooses.'[682] The same commentators have further noted that, '[b]ecause the . . . standards are so flexible, no clear and consistent practice regarding the awarding of costs under the Rules has emerged'.[683]

Commentators have noted that tribunals operating under the UNCITRAL Rules have **16.388** tended toward 'consideration of three principal factors in interpreting the phrase [circumstances of the case]'.[684] First among these factors, which can inform a tribunal's apportionment not only of arbitration costs under Art 40(1) but also of legal costs, pursuant to Art 40(2), is the extent to which one party succeeded in the arbitration.[685] Success may be demonstrated by resisting claims, as well as prevailing on them.[686] A second 'circumstance' that tribunals have taken into account is the conduct of a party that unreasonably increases the costs of arbitration.[687] Finally, tribunals resist allocating costs in favour of one party

[681] See eg *Summary of 8th Session Discussion* (n 55) para 218.

[682] Caron, Caplan and Pellonpää (n 61) 948.

[683] *id,* 949; see also van Hof (n 55) 302.

[684] Caron, Caplan and Pellonpää (n 61) 951.

[685] See eg *S.D. Myers v Government of Canada,* Final Award Concerning the Apportionment of Costs Between the Parties, (NAFTA Chapter 11 Tribunal, 30 December 2002) para 19 ('The Majority considers that neither party has achieved absolute 'success' in the sense used in Art 40.1 of the UNCITRAL Rules, and that there must be some apportionment as mandated by that Rule'), available at <http://www.international.gc.ca/trade-agreements-accords-commerciaux/assets/pdfs/MyersFinalAward-Final-30-12-02.pdf>; *Pope and Talbot Inc v Government of Canada,* Award on Costs, (NAFTA Chapter 11 Tribunal, 26 November 2002) para 17 ('Taking an overall view of the case, the Tribunal concludes that the success of each party was mixed. In the circumstances the Tribunal has determined that each party should bear its own legal costs under Art 38(d) and (e)'), available at <http://www.international.gc.ca/trade-agreements-accords-commerciaux/assets/pdfs/CostsAward26Nov02.pdf>.

[686] See eg *Electronic Systems Int'l v Ministry of Defense of the Islamic Republic of Iran, et al,* Award no 430-814-1 (28 July 1989) para 63 ('Claimant has successfully discharged the burden of proving only approximately one eighteenth of its total Claim, and in view of the costs incurred by the Respondent in defending itself, the Tribunal considers that the Respondent should be granted US $5,000 as costs of arbitration'), *reprinted in* 22 Iran–USCTR 339, 355 (1989-II).

[687] See eg *Ultrasystems Inc v Islamic Republic of Iran,* Award no 27-84-3 (4 March 1983) ('the Tribunal takes into account the fact that extra costs were incurred by the Claimant through Isiran failure to provide information as to its status until a late stage of the proceedings'), *reprinted in* 2 Iran–USCTR 100, 113 (1983-I); *Near East Technological Services USA Inc v Islamic Republic of Iran Air Force,* Award no 406-845-1 (15 December 1988) para 22, (finding relevant to apportionment the fact that 'Respondent's task of preparing pleadings and evidence was made more difficult by the lack of coherence in the Claimant's written presentation of its

when both parties are state governments, considering that normally each such party should bear its own costs.[688] Variations on these considerations appear in a significant number of decisions under the UNCITRAL Rules.[689]

16.389 (1.2) **No fees for interpretations, corrections or additional awards** Article 40(4) bars a tribunal from charging any fees to the parties for the tribunal's work in issuing an interpretation, a correction or an additional award, pursuant to Arts 35, 36 and 37. The drafters adopted this provision in the belief that a tribunal would only take these further actions because its original award either was vague, contained an error or omitted to cover a presented claim, in which case the arbitrators were responsible and did not warrant further remuneration.[690]

(2) Contemplated revisions

16.390 The Working Group has decided upon one revision in Art 40 and is contemplating another. First, the Group will recommend eliminating the separate rule for apportioning legal costs by deleting Art 40(2) (and the cross-reference to it in Art 40(1)), so that the same standard will apply to the allocation or apportionment of all arbitration costs.[691] Secondly, the Working Group is considering whether Art 40(4) should be deleted or modified, to permit arbitrators to collect fees or at least their costs for some or all of their work in responding to requests for an interpretation, correction or additional award.

16.391 The debate on this second issue has been sharply divided. On the one hand, it is noted that the arbitrators must deal with many unmerited requests for interpretations, corrections or additional awards, which can be time-consuming. Some delegates also doubt whether the tribunal is necessarily at fault if a further ruling is needed and, at least in the case of additional awards, the work required to draft them would have to be done to complete the resolution of the case in any event. On the other hand, it is said that a rule precluding fees for such work establishes an incentive for writing clear and complete awards in the first instance and encourages brevity in any additional award that may be needed.[692] The Working Group has yet to resolve any final revision in Art 40(4).[693]

---

case'), *reprinted in* 21 Iran–USCTR 13, 19 (1989-I); *Dadras Int'l et al v Islamic Republic of Iran et al* (Award no 567-213/215-3, 7 November 1995) paras 280–1 (noting the many prior cases in which, '[i]n determining the appropriate amount of costs to award, the Tribunal has . . . taken into account a party's conduct during the arbitral proceedings', and, in the case before it, referring to the fact that Respondents 'have caused considerable disruption of the arbitral process . . . pursuing their unfounded allegations of forgery and belatedly proffering the unconvincing testimony of Mr. Golzar'), *reprinted in* 31 Iran–USCTR 127, 205 (1995).

688 See eg *Ministry of National Defense v United States, Cases B59/B69* (Award no 247-B59/B69-1, 14 August 1986), *reprinted in* 12 Iran–USCTR 33, 36 (1986-III).

689 See generally Caron, Caplan and Pellonpää (n 61) 956–81 (cases cited therein).

690 *Report of the Committee of the Whole II* (n 55) paras 192, 195, 202.

691 *Report of WGII on the work of its 48th session* (4–8 February 2008) para 28, UN Doc A/CN.9/646; see also *Note by the Secretariat, Settlement of Commercial Disputes: Revision of the UNCITRAL Arbitration Rules* (6 August 2008) para 40, UN Doc A/CN.9/WG.II/WP.151/Add.1.

692 See *Report of WGII on the work of its 48th session* (4–8 February 2008) paras 31–6. UN Doc A/CN.9/646.

693 See *Note by the Secretariat, Settlement of Commercial Disputes: Revision of the UNCITRAL Arbitration Rules* (6 August 2008) para 41, UN Doc A/CN.9/WG.II/WP.151/Add.1.

DEPOSIT OF COSTS

Article 41

1 **The arbitral tribunal, on its establishment, may request each party to deposit an equal amount as an advance for the costs referred to in article 38, paragraphs (*a*), (*b*) and (*c*).**

2 **During the course of the arbitral proceedings the arbitral tribunal may request supplementary deposits from the parties.**

3 **If an appointing authority has been agreed upon by the parties or designated by the Secretary-General of the Permanent Court of Arbitration at The Hague, and when a party so requests and the appointing authority consents to perform the function, the arbitral tribunal shall fix the amounts of any deposits or supplementary deposits only after consultation with the appointing authority which may make any comments to the arbitral tribunal which it deems appropriate concerning the amount of such deposits and supplementary deposits.**

4 **If the required deposits are not paid in full within thirty days after the receipt of the request, the arbitral tribunal shall so inform the parties in order that one or another of them may make the required payment. If such payment is not made, the arbitral tribunal may order the suspension or termination of the arbitral proceedings.**

5 **After the award has been made, the arbitral tribunal shall render an accounting to the parties of the deposits received and return any unexpended balance to the parties.**

(1) Commentary on current text

Article 41 addresses four issues relating to advance funding of certain costs of arbitration: (i) it establishes tribunals' authority to request deposits to cover its own future costs; (ii) it requires a tribunal in some circumstances to consult an appointing authority before fixing the amounts of such deposits; (iii) it allows the tribunal to suspend and ultimately terminate proceedings if requested deposits are not made; and (iv) it obligates the tribunal to render a final accounting of funds deposited by the parties. The last duty is self-explanatory and requires no further comment. **16.392**

(1.1) **Requiring advance deposits** A tribunal is authorized to request advance deposits, in equal amounts from the parties, but only to cover its own costs and those of any experts it may retain, as identified in Art 38(a), (b) and (c). The tribunal may do this when it is first constituted and, also, during the proceedings. Nothing is said concerning deposits for the costs of an appointing authority or administering institution, but the drafters believed that at least the former could separately condition its willingness to serve on its receipt of advance payment.[694] **16.393**

(1.2) **Consultation with appointing authority** Just as the drafters sought, under Art 39, to rely on the appointing authority to curb possible overreaching by tribunals setting fees, so they similarly strove in Art 41 to forestall excessive requests for deposits. Pursuant to Art 41(3), if an appointing authority has been agreed or designated, and if a party so requests and the authority agrees to serve in this role, the tribunal is required to consult the appointing authority and give it an opportunity to comment on any amount of deposit to be requested. **16.394**

694 *Report of the Committee of the Whole II* (n 55) paras 225–6.

16.395 (1.3) **Non-payment of deposits** Article 41(4) provides for two responses if a party does not make a deposit within 30 days of a request to do so. First, the tribunal must notify parties of the non-payment, so that another party may supply the missing deposit, recognizing that the party who has already paid may have an interest in seeing the arbitration proceed to its conclusion. If no party pays the missing deposit, then the tribunal may suspend or terminate the arbitration.

(2) Contemplated revisions

16.396 The Working Group does not recommend any revision in Art 41 except for an insignificant wording change in the first sentence (substituting 'the parties' for 'each party').[695]

(1) Additional proposed provisions

16.397 (1.1) **Additional Article on liability of arbitrators** The Working Group has provisionally decided to add an Article to the Rules that would seek to shield arbitrators from liability for their official actions, although the wording and scope of such a clause has yet to be determined.[696] The Group favours such an addition, *inter alia,* in view of the facts that parties dissatisfied with an award sometimes respond by suing the responsible arbitrators and that arbitrators do not enjoy the kind of immunity afforded judicial officials nor do they have ready access to the kind of liability insurance available to some professionals through professional associations.[697] The Working Group has considered how best to express the level of protection to be provided, so as not to exonerate deliberate wrongdoing while avoiding reliance on particular legal concepts (such as negligence or gross negligence) that are not common to, or uniformly understood among, all legal systems. It has been suggested that perhaps arbitrators should simply be exempted from liability 'to the fullest extent possible under any applicable law.'[698] The Working Group is also debating whether such immunity should be extended to the designating or appointing authority, as well as to experts.

16.398 (1.2) **Additional Article establishing gap-filling principle** The Working Group has considered the advisability of including in a final new provision a general principle to guide tribunals in filling gaps in the Rules, along the following lines: 'Questions concerning matters governed by these Rules which are not expressly settled in them are to be settled in conformity with the general principles on which these Rules are based.'[699] The Working Group has so far been substantially divided over the advisability of adding such a provision, with some delegates worried that this could lead to complex disputes over what general principles might underlie the Rules and believing that, in any event, Art 15 already provides general guidance in conducting the proceedings, including on issues not expressly addressed elsewhere in the Rules.[700] Given the absence of consensus, no decision has been

[695] *Report of WGII on the work of its 48th session* (4–8 February 2008) para 37, UN Doc A/CN.9/646.

[696] *ibid*, paras 38–45, UN Doc A/CN.9/646.

[697] *ibid*, at para 40.

[698] *ibid*, at para 44.

[699] See *Note by the Secretariat, Settlement of commercial disputes: Revision of the UNCITRAL Arbitration Rules* (6 December 2006) para 48, UN Doc A/CN,9/WG.II/WP.145/Add.1.

[700] *Report ofWGII on the work of its 48th session* (4–8 February 2008) paras 50-3, UN Doc A/CN.9/646.

made whether to add such a provision, but the Working Group has reserved the possibility that it may revisit the issue at a later point in its revision work.[701]

III. Bibliography

Aldrich, G., *The Jurisprudence of the Iran-United States Claims Tribunal* (Clarendon Press, Oxford, 1996).

Baker, S. and Davis, M., *The UNCITRAL Arbitration Rules in Practice: The Experience of the Iran-United States Claims Tribunal* (Kluwer, Deventer, 1992).

van den Berg, A., *The New York Arbitration Convention of 1958: Towards a Uniform Judicial Interpretation* (Kluwer, Deventer, 1981).

Besson, S., 'Introduction' in T. Zuberbühler, C. Müller and P. Habegger (eds).

Böckstiegel, K.-H., 'The Relevance of National Arbitration Law for Arbitrations under the UNCITRAL Rules' (1984) 1(3) *J Int'l Arb.*

Böckstiegel, K.-H., 'Applying the UNCITRAL Rules: The Experience of the Iran-United States Claims Tribunal' (1986) 4 *International Tax and Business Lawyer* 266.

Born, G., *International Commercial Arbitration* (3rd edn, Wolters Kluwer, The Netherlands, 2009).

Brower, C., and Brueschke, J., *The Iran-United States Claims Tribunal* (Brill, The Hague, 1998).

Brower, C., 'The Anatomy of Fact-Finding Before International Tribunals: An Analysis and a Proposal Concerning the Evaluation of Evidence' in R. Lillich (ed), *Fact-Finding Before International Tribunals* (Transnational Publishers, Ardsley NY, 1992) 147.

Brower, C., 'The Iran-United States Claims Tribunal,' (1990-V) 224 *Recueil des Cours* 123.

Bühler, M., 'Appointment of Arbitrators in Bi-Party or Multi-Party Proceedings,' in Zuberbühler, Müller and Habegger (eds).

Caron, D., Caplan, L. and Pellonpää, M., *The UNCITRAL Arbitration Rules: A Commentary* (OUP, Oxford, 2006).

Caron, D., '*Interim Measures of Protection: Theory and Practice in Light of the Iran-United States Claims Tribunal*' 46 *Zeitschrift für ausländisches öffentliches Recht und Völkerrecht* 465 (1986).

Caron, D. and Crook, J. (eds), *The Iran-U.S. Claims Tribunal and the Process of International Claims Resolution* (Transnational Publishers, Ardsley NY, 2000).

Derains, Y. and Schwartz, E.A., *Guide to the New ICC Rules of Arbitration* (2nd edn, Kluwer, Deventer, 2005).

Frey, H., 'Commentary on Article 14 of the Swiss Rules' in Zuberbühler, Müller and Habegger (eds).

Gaillard, E. and Savage, J. (eds), *Fouchard Gaillard Goldman on International Commercial Arbitration* (Kluwer, Deventer, 1999).

van Hof, J., *Commentary on the UNCITRAL Arbitration Rules: The Application by the Iran-U.S. Claims Tribunal* (Kluwer, Deventer, 1991).

Holtzmann, H. and Neuhaus, J., *A Guide to the UNCITRAL Model Law on International Commercial Arbitration: Legislative History and Commentary* (Kluwer, Deventer, 1989).

Holtzmann, H., 'Drafting the Tribunal Rules,' in D. Caron and J. Crook (eds).

Holtzmann, H., 'Some Lessons of the Iran-United States Claims Tribunal,' in J. Moss (ed), *Private Investors Abroad—Problems and Solutions in International Business* 16–1 (Matthew Bender, New York, 1988).

Holtzmann, H., 'Fact-Finding by the Iran-United States Claims Tribunal' in R. Lillich (ed), *Fact-Finding By International Tribunals* 101 (Transnational Publishers, Ardsley NY, 1992).

ICC Arb Bull vol 19/no 1 (2008).

[701] *ibid.*

Iran-United States Claims Tribunal Reports (Grotius Publications, Cambridge, 1981).
Lew, J., Mistelis, L. and Kröll, S., *Comparative International Commercial Arbitration* (Kluwer, The Hague, 2003).
Paulsson, J. and Petrochilos, G., *Revision of the UNCITRAL Arbitration Rules* (2006).
Redfern, A. , Hunter, M., Blackaby, N. and Partasides, C., *Law and Practice of International Commercial Arbitration* (4th edn, Sweet and Maxwell, 2004).
Rubino-Sammartano, M., *International Arbitration Law and Practice* (Kluwer, Deventer, 2001).
Sanders, P., 'Commentary on UNCITRAL Arbitration Rules' (1977) II *Ybk Commercial Arb* 172.
Sanders, P., 'Has the Moment Come to Revise the Arbitration Rules of UNCITRAL?' 20 *Arb Int'l* 243 (no 3, 2004).
Sanders, P., 'Procedures and Practices under the UNCITRAL Rules,' (1979) 27 *Am J Comp Law* 453.
Sanders, P., *The Work of UNCITRAL on Arbitration and Conciliation* (2nd edn, Kluwer, 2004).
Selby, J., 'Fact-Finding Before the Iran-United States Claims Tribunal: The View from the Trenches' in R. Lillich (ed), *Fact-Finding Before International Tribunals* 135 (Transnational Publishers, Ardsley NY, 1992).
Selby, J. and Stewart, D., 'Practical Aspects of Arbitrating Claims Before the Iran-United States Claims Tribunal' (1984) 18 *Int'l Lawyer* 211.
Schwebel, S., *International Arbitration: Three Salient Problems* (Cambridge, 1987).
Schwebel, S., 'The Validity of an Arbitral Award Rendered by a Truncated Tribunal' (1994 Goff Lecture), 6/no 2 *ICC Int'l Court of Arb Bull* 19, 20–1 (1995).
Strohbach, H., '*General Introduction*' (1976) I *Ybk Commercial Arb* 4–17.
Szasz, I., '*Arbitration Rules and Practices of Institutions*,' in A. van den Berg (ed), ICCA Congress series no 5 (1990).
United Nations Commission on International Trade Law: Yearbook, Volumes from 1975–1977 and 1999.
United Nations Commission on Trade and Development, '*Investor-State Disputes Arising From Investment Treaties: A Review*' (United Nations, New York, 2005).
Veeder, V., 'The Natural Limits to the Truncated Tribunal: The German Case of the Soviet Eggs and the Dutch Abduction of the Indonesian Arbitrator' in *Law of International Business and Dispute Settlement in the 21st Century* (Liber Amicorum Karl-Heinz Böckstiegel) (C Heymanns Verlag, Cologne, 2001).
Zuberbühler, T., Müller, C. and Habegger, P. (eds), *Swiss Rules of International Arbitration: Commentary* (Kluwer/Schulthess, Zurich, 2005).

17

ICDR INTERNATIONAL ARBITRATION RULES

Martin F. Gusy, James M. Hosking and Franz T. Schwarz

I. Introduction

A. The American Arbitration Association (AAA) and its International Centre for Dispute Resolution (ICDR)

For more than 80 years, the American Arbitration Association (AAA) has provided individuals and businesses with services related to arbitration and other forms of dispute resolution. The International Centre for Dispute Resolution (ICDR) is the AAA's international arm.[1] **17.01**

This chapter primarily addresses the ICDR International Arbitration Rules (ICDR Rules). However, the AAA's and ICDR's work extends beyond administering arbitrations conducted pursuant to those Rules. The institutions also play an important role in various initiatives to promote the use of arbitration, to encourage the enactment of modern arbitration legislation, to develop procedures for the conduct of arbitral proceedings and implement educational programmes for users and neutrals to gain a greater understanding of arbitration practice.[2] **17.02**

(1) The American Arbitration Association (AAA)

The AAA was founded as a not-for-profit public service organization in 1926 and is the result of a merger of three pioneering arbitration groups active in the New York of the early 1920s. **17.03**

---

[1] This chapter has benefited from comments and suggestions made by management at the ICDR. The authors wish to express their gratitude. Statistics and information on the ICDR's standard administrative practices stated in this chapter, unless indicated otherwise, are drawn from various AAA and ICDR public communications, material available on the AAA/ICDR website (<http://www.adr.org>) and/or discussions with ICDR senior management.

[2] See generally <http://www.adr.org/about>.

17.04 Inspired by Julian Cohen's treatise, *Commercial Arbitration and the Law*, the New York Chamber of Commerce and the New York State Bar Association co-sponsored arbitration legislation resulting in the state of New York's enactment of a first modern arbitration statute in 1920. The New York arbitration statute in turn inspired the formation of the Arbitration Society of America in 1922, instrumental in effecting the passage of the 1925 Federal Arbitration Act, the Arbitration Foundation, formed in 1924, and the Arbitration Conference, formed in 1925. The AAA is the result of a merger of these three groups in 1926.

17.05 The AAA administers cases for individuals and organizations that wish to resolve conflicts out of court. The AAA's administrative services include assisting in the appointment of mediators and arbitrators, setting hearings, and providing users with information on dispute resolution options, including settlement through mediation. Ultimately, the AAA aims to move cases through arbitration or mediation in a fair and impartial manner from filing until completion.

17.06 Additional AAA services include the design and development of alternative dispute resolution systems for corporations, unions, government agencies, law firms, and the courts. The AAA also provides election services as well as education, training, and publications for those seeking a broader or deeper understanding of alternative dispute resolution.

17.07 Headquartered in New York, the AAA maintains four Case Management Centers[3] and 23 regional offices in the US.

(2) The International Centre for Dispute Resolution (ICDR)

17.08 For its international services, the AAA established the ICDR in 1996. The ICDR is the AAA's international arm and maintains specialized administrative facilities in New York, where a staff of multilingual attorneys supervises the administration of international cases. In May 2001, the ICDR opened a European office in Dublin, Ireland to serve the growing number of users in Europe, the Middle East and Africa. ICDR case administration capabilities will soon be added in the ICDR's Dublin office. In February 2006, the ICDR opened an office in Mexico City through a joint venture with the Mediation and Arbitration Commission of the Mexico City National Chamber of Commerce (CANACO). In October 2007, the ICDR also opened an office in Singapore through a joint venture with the Singapore International Arbitration Centre (SIAC). In December 2008, the AAA signed an understanding with Bahrain's Ministry of Justice and Islamic Affairs to establish the Bahrain Chamber of Dispute Resolution (BCDR/AAA). The BCDR/AAA will administer domestic arbitrations under a set of rules that has yet to be developed. In addition, an ICDR office will be established in Bahrain to administer international cases under the ICDR Rules.

17.09 The ICDR provides impartial administrative services with respect to international disputes, including arbitration and mediation. The ICDR does not decide any cases. For each case, a new arbitral tribunal is constituted to discharge its mandate of issuing a final and

[3] The Case Management Centers are located in Fresno, California; Dallas, Texas; Atlanta, Georgia; and East Providence, Rhode Island.

binding decision on the parties' dispute and/or a mediator is appointed to try to facilitate a resolution.

The ICDR maintains a world-wide panel of nearly 600 arbitrators and mediators. The ICDR has access to hearing facilities and other services beyond its immediate network through 64 cooperative agreements with arbitral institutions in 45 countries. **17.10**

For arbitrations in the international context, the ICDR is empowered to apply any one of several sets of rules and procedures. First and foremost are the ICDR Rules, which are part of the ICDR's International Dispute Resolution Procedures.[4] The International Dispute Resolution Procedures are available in English, Spanish, French, Portuguese and Chinese, whereas the English language version is the official text for questions of interpretation. **17.11**

Other sets of rules administered by the ICDR include the AAA's Commercial Arbitration Rules, Construction Industry Arbitration Rules and Employment Rules, the ICDR Supplementary Procedures for Internet Corporation for Assigned Names and Numbers (ICANN) Independent Review Process and the ICDR Protocol for Manufacturer/Supplier Disputes. **17.12**

The ICDR also administers *ad hoc* arbitrations pursuant to the Commercial Arbitration and Mediation Center for the Americas Rules (CAMCA) or the Inter-American Commercial Arbitration Commission Rules (IACAC). For *ad hoc* arbitrations under the UNCITRAL Arbitration Rules, the ICDR applies its Procedures for Cases under the UNCITRAL Rules. **17.13**

Since 2003, the ICDR also administers international class action arbitrations in accordance with the Supplementary Rules for Class Arbitrations. On 8 October 2003, in response to the ruling of the US Supreme Court in *Green Tree Financial Corp v Bazzle*,[5] the AAA issued its Supplementary Rules for Class Arbitrations to govern proceedings brought as class arbitrations. In *Bazzle*, the Supreme Court held that, where an arbitration agreement was silent regarding the availability of class-wide relief, an arbitrator, and not a court, must decide whether class relief is permitted. Accordingly, the ICDR administers demands for international class arbitrations pursuant to its Supplementary Rules for Class Arbitrations if the underlying agreement specifies that disputes arising out of the parties' agreement shall be resolved by arbitration in accordance with any of the AAA's rules, the agreement is silent with respect to class claims, consolidation or joinder of claims and the case is international. Demands for class arbitration will not be administered where the underlying agreement prohibits class claims, consolidation or joinder, unless a court orders the parties to the underlying dispute to submit any aspect of their dispute involving such issues to an arbitrator or to the ICDR. **17.14**

B. Statistics on ICDR Arbitration

The AAA maintains the world's largest caseload of any arbitration institution. On average, the AAA provides dispute resolution services in more than 150,000 cases annually: 230,000 **17.15**

[4] Available at <http://www.adr.org/sp.asp?id=33994>; for a full list of the AAA's sets of rules applicable in international cases see <http://www.adr.org/sp.asp?id=28819>.

[5] *Green Tree Financial Corp v Bazzle*, 539 US 444 (2003).

cases in 2002, 173,000 in 2003, 159,000 in 2004, 142,000 in 2005, 137,000 in 2006, nearly 128,000 cases in 2007, and more than 138,000 cases in 2008, including arbitrations (of any sort), mediations, and other alternative dispute resolution processes.

17.16 Internationally, the ICDR recorded an increase in its caseload from 194 international cases in 1996 to 510 in 2000.[6] The ICDR reported an average of more than 600 administered cases annually since 2001, involving total claims and counterclaims in excess of US$35 billion and parties and arbitrators from about 75 nations. The average administration time per case has been approximately 12 months from the commencement of the case through to the submission of the final award.

17.17 In 2001, the ICDR administered 649 cases, involving more than US$10 billion in claims and counterclaims, almost half of which involved claims of more than US$1 million or undisclosed amounts; 672 cases in 2002 involving US$3.4 billion in claims and counterclaims, involving parties from more than 70 countries; 614 cases in 2003 involving arbitrators and parties from 69 nations and 646 cases with parties and arbitrators involved from 72 countries in 2004. In 2005, 580 cases were filed involving $3.25 billion and parties from 79 countries; in 2006, 586 cases involving $6.2 billion and parties from 76 countries; in 2007, 622 cases, involving $4.7 billion and parties from 65 countries and in 2008, 703 cases involving $4.0 billion and 75 countries.

C. Revisions of the ICDR Rules and current status

17.18 The AAA's first set of rules drafted for international cases was the 1986 Supplement for International Commercial Arbitration to the AAA Commercial Arbitration Rules (Commercial Rules).[7] It took until 1991 for the introduction of the first set of rules entitled 'International Arbitration Rules'.

17.19 The 1991 AAA International Arbitration Rules were modelled on the UNCITRAL Arbitration Rules of 1976 (UNCITRAL Rules). A first revision took place in 1993. A subsequent revision was carried out in 1996/1997 and today's ICDR Rules are substantially based on this version.

(1) The 1996/1997 revision

17.20 In 1996, with the introduction of the ICDR, the AAA substantially restructured the manner in which it administers international arbitrations. William K. Slate II, President and CEO of the AAA, appointed a task force to revise the 1993 International Arbitration Rules under the guidance of the late AAA General Counsel, Michael F. Hoellering.[8]

---

[6] See AAA Press Release, 'American Arbitration Association announces International Centre for Dispute Resolution in Dublin', 25 April 2001.

[7] The AAA Commercial Arbitration Rules and Mediation Procedures (including Supplemental Procedures for Large, Complex Commercial Disputes) are commonly used for the AAA's administration of US domestic commercial cases. Cases involving claims exceeding US$500,000 are subject to the Supplemental Procedures for Large, Complex Commercial Disputes, included with the Commercial Arbitration Rules.

[8] Task force members were David W. Rivkin (chair), Charles A. Beach, James H. Carter, Dana H. Freyer, Robert Layton and John M. Townsend. The task force considered other commercial arbitration rules including the WIPO Rules and those of the Commercial Arbitration and Mediation Center for the Americas, and conducted discussions with Robert B. von Mehren and Howard H. Holtzmann, chairs of the AAA

The 1996 revised ICDR Rules continued to reflect the model of the UNCITRAL Rules but contained some important innovations that led to an increase in use of the ICDR Rules. As a jurisdictional matter, before the revision, the 1993 International Arbitration Rules stated that they would apply only where the parties agreed to apply them, while the Commercial Rules provided that they would apply either when specifically chosen or when the parties have provided generally for arbitration by the AAA. After the 1996/1997 revision, the ICDR Rules apply, if the arbitration is international and also if the parties have chosen the ICDR or AAA without designating particular rules. As a result of the revision, the ICDR is charged with the exclusive administration of all of the AAA's international arbitrations. The revised ICDR Rules became effective on 1 April 1997. **17.21**

(2) *Introduction of the International Dispute Resolution Procedures in 2003*

On 1 July 2003, the ICDR released the International Dispute Resolution Procedures, combining in one publication the ICDR Rules with the ICDR's International Mediation Rules.[9] The introduction of the International Dispute Resolution Procedures underlines the ICDR's promotion of dispute resolution through settlement and provides a set of rules for the administrator to encourage disputing parties facing an arbitration to try mediation, both at the commencement of the case and closer to the hearing. Parties often respond favourably to inquiries by the ICDR regarding their interest in mediation. In about 8–10 per cent of all arbitrations administered by the ICDR, parties settle through mediation. The three points in time most likely to facilitate settlement are after the administrative conference, at the end of document disclosure and at the preliminary hearing. Historically, about 85 per cent of domestic and international commercial cases submitted to mediation settle.[10] **17.22**

In an effort to further the study of international arbitration, the ICDR also amended Art 27 to add para 8, which, unless the parties agree to override it, allows publication of ICDR awards that have been edited to conceal the names of the parties and other identifying details or that have been made publicly available in the course of enforcement proceedings or otherwise. **17.23**

(3) *Emergency relief*

On 1 May 2006, the ICDR amended the ICDR Rules to include procedures for emergency relief prior to the formation of the arbitral tribunal.[11] The resulting new Art 37 is based on the AAA's Optional Rules of Emergency Measures of Protection, which had been in existence since 1999. While the Optional Rules of Emergency Measures of Protection could always be expressly adopted in writing by the parties, Art 37 makes pre-tribunal emergency **17.24**

Arbitration Law Committee and International Arbitration Committee, respectively. The draft revised rules were sent to more than 100 experts in the field and responses were received from about 25%. See American Arbitration Association Task Force on the International Rules, 'Commentary on the Proposed Revisions to the International Arbitration Rules of the American Arbitration Association' (1996/1997) 2(1) *ADR Currents*.

[9] The International Mediation Rules provide for means of initiating and terminating mediation, a method for appointment of the mediator, the authority of the mediator and extend confidentiality to the process.

[10] Appel, M., 'Taking Your Case to the International Centre for Dispute Resolution', ICDR paper.

[11] See Sheppard, B., Jr. and Townsend, J., 'Holding the Fort Until the Arbitrators Are Appointed: The New ICDR International Emergency Rule' (2006) 61(2) *Disp Res J* 58.

relief automatically available to all parties to ICDR arbitration agreements entered into on or after 1 May 2006.[12]

(4) ICDR Guidelines for Arbitrators Concerning Exchanges of Information

17.25 All international cases initiated and administered by the ICDR after 31 May 2008 are governed by the ICDR Guidelines for Arbitrators Concerning Exchanges of Information.[13] The Guidelines require parties to exchange in advance of the hearing all documents upon which they intend to rely. Parties may request the arbitral tribunal to order other parties to produce documents in the party's possession, not otherwise available to the party seeking the documents, which are reasonably believed to exist and to be relevant and material to the outcome of the case. Such document production requests need to contain a description of specific documents or classes of documents, along with an explanation of their relevance and materiality to the outcome of the case.

17.26 While stating that 'depositions, interrogatories, and requests to admit, as developed in American court procedures, are generally not appropriate procedures for obtaining information in international arbitration', the Guidelines also limit electronic discovery. Requests for documents maintained in electronic form should be narrowly focused and structured to make searching for them as economical as possible. A requesting party may be required by the arbitral tribunal to justify the time and expense that its request may involve and the arbitral tribunal may condition the granting of a request on the payment of part or all of the costs by the party seeking the information. Finally, the Guidelines specify that where the parties come from jurisdictions in which different privilege rules apply, to the extent possible, the arbitral tribunal should apply the same rule to both sides, giving preference to the rule providing the highest level of protection.

II. Commentary on the ICDR International Arbitration Rules

Article 1

1. **Where parties have agreed in writing to arbitrate disputes under these International Arbitration Rules or have provided for arbitration of an international dispute by the International Centre for Dispute Resolution or the American Arbitration Association without designating particular rules, the arbitration shall take place in accordance with these rules, as in effect at the date of commencement of the arbitration, subject to whatever modifications the parties may adopt in writing.**
2. **These rules govern the arbitration, except that, where any such rule is in conflict with any provision of the law applicable to the arbitration from which the parties cannot derogate, that provision shall prevail.**

[12] As of 1 May 2009, Art 37 has been applied successfully in seven cases. The average emergency relief procedure completion time is three weeks.

[13] Co-chaired by James H. Carter and John Beechey, a 24-member task force of arbitrators, counsel and business people started developing the Guidelines in July 2007. Task force members included Mark Baker, David Haigh, Gabrielle Kaufmann Kohler, Carolyn Lamm, Carole Malinvaud, David Rivkin, Paul Friedland, Claus von Wobeser, Professor William Park, Sally Harpole as well as representatives of John Deer, Daimler-Benz and Hanes. See Gusy, M. and Illmer, M., 'The ICDR Guidelines for Arbitrators Concerning Exchanges of Information—A German/American Introduction in Light of International Practice' (2008) 6 *Int'l Arb L Rev* 195.

3. These rules specify the duties and responsibilities of the administrator, the International Centre for Dispute Resolution, a division of the American Arbitration Association. The administrator may provide services through its Centre, located in New York, or through the facilities of arbitral institutions with which it has agreements of cooperation.

(1) Introduction

Article 1 prescribes the ICDR Rules' scope of application, declares their subordinance to mandatory laws and provides for the ICDR to be the exclusive administrator of all international arbitrations under the auspices of the AAA. **17.27**

(2) 'Where parties have agreed in writing to arbitrate disputes' (Article 1(1))

The cornerstone of the arbitral process is the parties' agreement to arbitrate a dispute in writing. This principle is incorporated in the ICDR Rules at their very start. Article II of the New York Convention on the Recognition and Enforcement of Foreign Arbitral Awards of 1958 (New York Convention) and Art 7(2) and (3) of the UNCITRAL Model Law on International Commercial Arbitration (UNCITRAL Model Law)[14] contain the same form requirement. **17.28**

As a principle matter, without an agreement in writing to arbitrate a dispute, there is no ICDR arbitration. The ICDR's International Mediation Rules allow parties to request the ICDR to invite another party to participate in mediation by voluntary submission, in which case the ICDR will attempt to obtain a submission to mediation from the other side. However, for purposes of starting arbitration under the ICDR Rules, the parties are required to 'have agreed'. Such agreement to arbitrate may be made by means of both parties' completion and filing of the ICDR's Submission to Dispute Resolution Form[15] or the parties' agreement otherwise on or before the claimant's filing of the Notice of Arbitration. **17.29**

The ICDR Rules themselves do not contain any definition of what constitutes an agreement 'in writing'. Whether an arbitration agreement is in writing will depend on the applicable national or international laws. Guidance is given by the 2006 addition of Art7(3) to the UNCITRAL Model Law, which is testament to a change to a more liberal approach in international arbitration practice. Under the revised UNCITRAL Model Law, parties are allowed to agree upon arbitration orally, by conduct, or by other means as long as they record it thereafter in any form in order to satisfy the writing requirement. **17.30**

(3) Institutional arbitration (Article 1(1))

Provided the writing requirement has been fulfilled, arbitration under the ICDR Rules is available in two content-based alternatives: (i) either with an agreement to arbitrate 'under these International Arbitration Rules'; or (ii) if the parties have provided 'for arbitration of **17.31**

---

[14] UNCITRAL Model Law on International Commercial Arbitration 1985, as amended 2006 (United Nations documents A/40/17, annex I and A/61/17, annex I) (As adopted by the United Nations Commission on International Trade Law on 21 June 1985, and as amended by the United Nations Commission on International Trade Law on 7 July 2006).

[15] Available at <http://www.adr.org/si.asp?id=3812>. The ICDR offers the opportunity for parties to take part in telephone conferences prior to the submission of a dispute to the ICDR. As a result of such calls, parties may choose to complete and file the Submission to Dispute Resolution form and thereby initiate the appropriate dispute resolution procedure.

an international dispute by the International Centre for Dispute Resolution or the American Arbitration Association without designating particular rules'.

17.32 In either scenario, the parties agreed to institutional as opposed to *ad hoc* arbitration.[16] More concretely, the parties agreed to an arbitration conducted under the auspices of the AAA's international division, the ICDR, in accordance with these ICDR Rules.

17.33 In practice, arbitration clauses often contain non-existing institution names or are otherwise pathological. If confronted with such clauses, the ICDR may solicit party clarification and ask the parties to complete and file its Submission to Dispute Resolution form prior to the initiation of its case administration procedures.

17.34 In addition, when presented with applications to enforce arbitration agreements by means of motions to compel arbitration under s 2 of the Federal Arbitration Act or similar procedures under US state laws, US federal and state courts often order parties to bring their arbitration to the AAA or ICDR even though the parties' agreement did not provide for institutional arbitration.[17]

(4) '[U]nder these International Arbitration Rules' (Article 1(1))

17.35 The first scenario in which the ICDR will have jurisdiction requires the parties to have mentioned either the 'AAA International Arbitration Rules' or the 'ICDR International Arbitration Rules' in their agreement to arbitrate. Alternatively, the parties may cite the International Arbitration Rules as the 'ICDR Arbitration Rules'.

17.36 Arbitration clauses often seen in practice provide for the AAA or the ICDR to act as the appointing authority for the appointment of one or more arbitrators in accordance with its International Arbitration Rules. In such a case, the ICDR will act as an appointing authority only, unless the parties agree separately and in writing that the ICDR should also act as the case administrator.

(5) '[O]r have provided for arbitration of an international dispute by the International Centre for Dispute Resolution or the American Arbitration Association without designating particular rules' (Article 1(1))

17.37 The second scenario in which the ICDR will obtain jurisdiction was introduced in the 1996/1997 amendments, and essentially provides that the ICDR Rules will apply if the arbitration is international and if the parties chose to have their arbitration administered by the ICDR or the AAA without designating particular rules.

17.38 The key issue is what constitutes an international dispute under Art 1(1) of the ICDR Rules. Provided there is no ambiguity as to the parties' choice of institutional arbitration and there is (little or) no ambiguity that the parties chose the AAA or the ICDR to administer

[16] See Hoellering, M., 'The Institution's Role in Managing the Arbitration Process' (1994) *Am Rev Int'l Arb* 121; see also Aksen, G., 'Ad Hoc Versus Institutional Arbitration' (1991) *ICC Ct Bull* 8.

[17] See eg Supreme Court of the State of New York County of New York, Case no 107131/06, Order dated 23 June 2006 ('The parties may bring their arbitration before the American Arbitration Association in New York City' although the parties' agreement provided 'Any dispute arising . . . will be arbitrated under the laws of the State of New York' only).

the case, the ICDR will act as the case administrator in all cases it deems international in accordance with these ICDR Rules.

(5.1) **'International dispute'** What the ICDR deems as 'international' has its roots in Art 1 of the UNCITRAL Model Law.[18] When starting to administer a case, the ICDR commonly sends a notice to the parties stating: 'There are two main criteria which may be used either alone or in conjunction, in defining the term international. The first requires analysing the nationality or residence of the parties and the second focuses on the nature of the dispute. This may also include the case of a corporation that is incorporated in the United States but is a subsidiary of a foreign corporation.' **17.39**

An international dispute does not necessarily have to be detached from all national legal systems. Although the New York Convention indirectly recognizes the concept of a 'non-national' award, the idea of an arbitration detached from national legal systems will remain of limited relevance so long as the ultimate remedy (enforcement of the arbitral award) is controlled by national courts. **17.40**

By confining its application to 'foreign' or 'non-domestic' awards, the New York Convention made no attempt to provide a direct definition of international arbitration. In addition, it is impossible to determine whether an arbitration is 'international' solely on the basis of its legal regime. An arbitration's legal regime is often the consequence of the fact that the arbitration is international. Substantive rules found in national laws, in international conventions and in non-national sources such as arbitration rules and arbitral awards, concern all the various aspects of arbitration: the arbitration agreement, the arbitral procedure and the merits of the dispute. **17.41**

However, rather than solely relying on criteria subject to party influence, account can also be taken of more objective factors of 'internationality'. For the ICDR Rules to apply, it is necessary and sufficient for the dispute to be genuinely or intrinsically international. **17.42**

One definition of international arbitration is offered by French law. Article 1492 of the New Code of Civil Procedure provides that '[a]n arbitration is international when it involves the interests of international trade'. This economic view of internationality places emphasis on the disputed relationship rather than on the means of resolving it. **17.43**

The attachment to 'international trade' is incorporated in the 1961 European Convention expressly concerned with international commercial arbitration. The Convention applies to arbitration agreements and resulting arbitral proceedings and awards (Art I(1)(b)), entered into 'for the purpose of settling disputes arising from international trade between physical or legal persons having . . . their habitual place of residence or their seat in different Contracting States (Art I(1)(a))'. **17.44**

[18] See AAA Press Release 'ICDR Opens Office in Mexico City - International Division of AAA Reaches Cooperative Agreement with CANACO', 16 February 2006: 'Both institutions will promote the services of CANACO for all domestic cases in Mexico and the ICDR's services for all international cases. When the party agreement allows, any case that only includes parties from Mexico will be administered by CANACO; in turn, when party agreement allows, international cases will be administered by ICDR. Both institutions have agreed to apply Article 1 of the United Nations Commission on International Trade Law (UNCITRAL) Arbitration Model Law as the definition of an international case.'

17.45 As international trade is not defined, it must be considered to include all exchanges of services or assets, whether in the form of debt or equity, involving the economies of at least two countries.[19]

17.46 Even disputes between parties resident of the same country could be genuinely or intrinsically international. This will be the case of a dispute between two companies from the same jurisdiction relating to a contract performed abroad, such as an international freight contract, or a subcontract for a foreign construction project.

17.47 Other circumstances guaranteeing that the dispute is genuinely or intrinsically international include the series of alternative criteria contained in Art1(3) of the UNCITRAL Model Law. In its revised version as amended in 2006, the UNCITRAL Model Law provides:

> An arbitration is international if:
> (a) the parties to an arbitration agreement have, at the time of the conclusion of that agreement, their places of business in different States; or
> (b) one of the following places is situated outside the State in which the parties have their places of business:
> (i) the place of arbitration if determined in, or pursuant to, the arbitration agreement;
> (ii) any place where a substantial part of the obligations of the commercial relationship is to be performed or the place with which the subject-matter of the dispute is most closely connected; or
> (c) the parties have expressly agreed that the subject matter of the arbitration agreement relates to more than one country.

17.48 The vast majority of situations commonly regarded as international will meet these criteria. The UNCITRAL Model Law broadens the notion of 'internationality' to 'cases where the place of arbitration, the place of contract performance, or the place of the subject-matter of the dispute is situated outside the State where the parties have their place of business, or cases where the parties have expressly agreed that the subject-matter of the arbitration agreement relates to more than one country'. Article 1 thus recognizes the freedom of the parties to submit a dispute to the legal regime established pursuant to the UNCITRAL Model Law.[20]

17.49 Thus, the expansive definition of what constitutes an 'international' dispute for purposes of the UNCITRAL Model Law provides a broad mandate for the AAA/ICDR to determine that a particular dispute should be administered by the ICDR. Also, the parties can agree that a dispute is international in nature and thus the ICDR is bound to accept this stipulation.

---

[19] See Gaillard, E. and Savage, J. (eds), *Fouchard Gaillard Goldman on International Commercial Arbitration* (Kluwer Law International, The Hague, 1999) s 102.

[20] Explanatory Note by the UNCITRAL secretariat on the 1985 Model Law on International Commercial Arbitration as amended in 2006, at para 11. This note was prepared by the secretariat of the United Nations Commission on International Trade Law (UNCITRAL) for informational purposes only; it is not an official commentary on the Model Law. A commentary prepared by the Secretariat on an early draft of the Model Law appears in document A/CN.9/264 (reproduced in UNCITRAL Yearbook, vol XVI — 1985, United Nations publication, Sales no E.87.V.4).

(5.2) **Change of residence while case is pending** Not only pre-dispute stipulations will make a case international, a change of residence after the dispute has commenced can lead to the same result. Where a party changes residence after the initiation of an arbitration, this may prompt a change in the applicable set of rules including the application of the ICDR Rules *ex post facto*. **17.50**

In this scenario, the ICDR may send a notice of change in administrator to the parties, which in turn can be understood as a change of the applicable rules upon which the case is being administered. This is best illustrated by the *Malecki v Long* case.[21] **17.51**

In the *Malecki* case, pursuant to a contract entered into with the Longs, the Maleckis had filed a request for arbitration against the Longs with the AAA in Philadelphia under its then existing Commercial Rules. Shortly after the constitution of the tri-partite panel, the Maleckis informed the AAA that their counsel had been dismissed and that they had moved to France, requesting all future communications to be sent to their new address in France. Inviting the parties' comments, the ICDR in New York, rather than the AAA in Philadelphia, informed the parties it had taken note of the changes and that the arbitration would thereafter be administered by the ICDR in accordance with the International Rules. The ICDR invoked the definition of 'international arbitration' in Art 1(3) of the UNCITRAL Model Law. No party commented. Subsequently, the arbitrator appointed by the Maleckis resigned and an award was rendered by the remaining two arbitrators.[22] While the Paris Court of Appeal refused to recognize the award in the end based on the arbitrator's behavior, it found that the Maleckis were barred from relying on the Commercial Rules because they had 'carefully refrained from enquiring' as to the meaning and consequences of the change in administrator and could not therefore allege before the Paris Court of Appeal that they did not understand the implications of that change.[23] **17.52**

(6) '[S]ubject to whatever modifications the parties may adopt in writing' (Article 1(1))

Party control is a guiding principle of international arbitration. The ICDR Rules incorporate this principle by offering that the parties' adoption of the ICDR Rules is 'subject to whatever modifications the parties may adopt in writing.' This is in contrast to the ICC, which does not allow the parties to derogate from certain core procedural characteristics of ICC arbitration, eg, entry into the Terms of Reference (ICC Rules, Art 18) and that the award be subject to the scrutiny of the ICC Court of Arbitration (ICC Rules, Art 27). **17.53**

---

[21] See Bensaude, D., 'Malecki v Long: Truncated Tribunals and Waivers of Dutco Rights' (2006) 23 *J Int'l Arb* 81.

[22] See ICDR Rules, Arts 10 and 11 on truncated tribunals (discussed at ss 17.153 *et seq infra*).

[23] See Bensaude, D., 'Malecki v Long: Truncated Tribunals and Waivers of Dutco Rights' (2006) 23 *J Int'l Arb* 81, criticizing the decision on the basis that the place of arbitration was not in an UNCITRAL Model Law jurisdiction, that no provision in the UNCITRAL Model Law provides that a change of residence of a party in the course of an arbitration procedure entails a change of status in an ongoing arbitration, and international arbitrations with parties residing in, or moving to, different countries may be administered under the AAA Commercial Rules (Art 16 of the Commercial Rules provides: 'Where the parties are nationals or residents of different countries, the AAA, at the request of any party or on its own initiative, may appoint as a neutral arbitrator, a national of a country other than that of the parties. The request must be made prior to the time set for the appointment of the arbitrator as agreed by the parties or set by these rules.').

(7) 'These rules govern the arbitration' (Article 1(2))

17.54 Article 1(2) establishes that 'these rules govern the arbitration'. Similar language can be found in Art 1(2) of the UNCITRAL Rules ('These Rules shall govern the arbitration'). Unlike Art 15(1) of the ICC Rules, the ICDR Rules do not make reference to being bound by 'rules of procedure of a national law'.

(8) 'Law applicable to the arbitration from which the parties cannot derogate' (Article 1(2))

17.55 While Art 28 recognizes the parties' freedom to choose the applicable national substantive law or rules of law, the parties' freedom to agree on the applicable law to the merits is not without limits. Article 1(2) recognizes that the ICDR Rules and the parties' power to choose their own applicable law may be overridden by any applicable mandatory laws. This is consistent with international arbitration practice as evidenced for example in the New York Convention.

17.56 An often-cited decision in the context of mandatory laws applicable in international arbitration is the *Mitsubishi v Soler Chrysler* case decided by the US Supreme Court in 1985.[24] In *Mitsubishi* the Supreme Court acknowledged the important interest of both the public and the litigants in the proper application of US antitrust laws, stating that the arbitral tribunal 'should be bound to decide that dispute in accordance with the national law giving rise to the claim'. But the Court also stressed that the courts 'will have the opportunity at the award enforcement stage to insure that the legitimate interest in the enforcement of the antitrust laws has been addressed'. In a case in which the anti-competitive effects occurred in the US, at the enforcement stage, US courts could thus exercise *a posteriori* control over the arbitrator's application of US antitrust laws and overwrite the parties' choice of Swiss law in the underlying agreement.

17.57 Parties cannot deviate from the effects of the laws of their place of incorporation or legal residence (in the case of a company) or their nationality (in the case of a physical person) with respect to their capacity to enter into an arbitration agreement (New York Convention, Art V(1)(a)). In the absence of party agreement upon the law applicable to the arbitration agreement, the law of the country where the award is made will govern the validity of the arbitration agreement and become a mandatory law. In the absence of a clear definition of what constitutes a 'law applicable to the arbitration from which the parties cannot derogate', it might even be argued that the legal norms of the likely place of enforcement should be observed.

(9) Duties and responsibilities of the administrator and other parties involved (Article 1(3))

17.58 Article 1(3) is unambiguous in that the ICDR is the administrator of all international cases. Its administration mission is 'premised on its ability to move the matter forward, facilitate communications, ensure that qualified arbitrators and mediators are appointed, control costs, understand cultural sensitivities, resolve procedural impasses and properly interpret and apply its International Arbitration and Mediation Rules'.[25]

---

[24] *Mitsubishi Motors Corp v Soler Chrysler-Plymouth Inc* 473 US 614 (1985), YCA XI (1986) 555 *et seq* (also ruling in favour of the extension of arbitrability to antitrust claims).

[25] See Introduction to International Dispute Resolution Procedures; see also Slate, W. II, 'Paying Attention to "Culture" in International Commercial Arbitration' (2004) 59 *Disp Res J* 96.

Central to the ICDR's case management system is the assignment of the case to a case manager. The ICDR also assigns a supervisor to each case. The primary point of contact for the parties is the case manager. The case manager remains involved throughout the proceeding. The case manager coordinates the logistics of the arbitration, conducts the administrative conference call, and serves as a link between the parties and the tribunal in issues such as the arbitrator selection, challenges and compensation, as well as the delivery of the final award to the parties. **17.59**

Under the ICDR's case management system, case management is organized into three specialized teams—the European/African Desk, the Americas Desk, and the Middle East/Asian Desk. A supervisor oversees each team and is responsible for quality control. **17.60**

(9.1) Emergency relief The parties' first contact with the ICDR's case manager may be for the appointment of an emergency arbitrator to handle requests for interim arbitral relief prior to the formation of the arbitral tribunal. The ICDR can appoint an emergency arbitrator within one business day after receipt of the Notice of Arbitration (Art 37).[26] **17.61**

(9.2) Administrative conference In the absence of requests for emergency relief, the ICDR's standard administrative procedure requires that an administrative conference be conducted in all international cases within 10 business days after the Notice of Arbitration has been submitted; international logistics permitting, it may be conducted as soon as 48 hours after the submission thereof. **17.62**

The administrative conference is organizational—as opposed to judicial—in nature and must not be confused with the possible hearing(s) between the arbitrators and the parties. Except for extensions of time under Art 3(4) and decisions on the challenge of an arbitrator (Art 9), the arbitral tribunal is the ultimate decision maker on all legal issues throughout the arbitration. The rules do not require the parties to file their jurisdictional objections within the administrative conference. Jurisdictional objections need to be filed no later than the filing of the Statement of Defense and only further participation in the arbitration without raising jurisdictional objections in the responsive statement may constitute waiver of the right to register such objections at a later date (Art 15(3)). **17.63**

The administrative conference, usually conducted by telephone, affords the parties an opportunity to take control of the management of the case and reach agreements on administrative issues. Administrative issues that may lend themselves to early discussion include: the means of communication between the ICDR and the parties; scheduling issues; establishing the approximate length of the proceeding; handling of time extension requests; the need for interim measures; and the parties' preferences regarding the number of arbitrators, their qualifications, compensation and method of appointment. Depending on the complexity of the case and familiarity of both sides with the factual and legal issues, the administrative conference may also permit an opportunity to arrive at stipulations of uncontested **17.64**

[26] See ss 17.286 *et seq infra*.

facts, identify potential witnesses,[27] provide for advance exchange of information and consider the possibility of utilizing a documents-only process.[28]

17.65 At the administrative conference, the ICDR is also likely to invite the parties to consider mediation for the first time. The ICDR may encourage the parties to reconsider mediation closer to the hearing date.

17.66 **(9.3) *Ex parte* communication and arbitrator selection, disclosure and challenge procedure** The next milestone involving the case administrator may be the arbitrator selection, disclosure and challenge procedure.

17.67 The selection of the arbitrator is rightly regarded as one of the most important decisions in an international arbitration. For this reason, pre-appointment interviewing of a party's prospective arbitrator has become increasingly common in many jurisdictions. Under the ICDR Rules, as with most other institutions, the parties and their counsel are prohibited from engaging in any *ex parte* communications with the arbitrator(s) except to advise the arbitrator candidate of the general nature of the controversy and the anticipated proceedings and to discuss the candidate's qualifications, availability or independence.[29]

17.68 Once appointed, the arbitrator determines whether a limited direct exchange of communications between the parties, the ICDR, and him- or herself is acceptable. Otherwise, all correspondence should be submitted to the case manager for transmittal to the arbitrator, copying in the other parties (Art 12). Beyond the Checklist for Conflicts and the arbitrator ranking list (if applicable), only financial documents such as invoices are permitted *ex parte* communications between the parties and the ICDR.

17.69 The ICDR Rules provide the parties with an opportunity to agree upon the member(s) of the arbitral panel within 45 days from the commencement of the case (Art 6). The ICDR Rules do not require any of the arbitrators to be of a different nationality than the parties.[30]

17.70 Should party agreement prove impossible, in the absence of party agreement on another method of appointment, the ICDR's default administrative practice is to use the list

---

[27] The standard ICDR administrative procedure asks each party to disclose the witnesses it expects to present on its Checklist for Conflicts, which is customarily attached to the ICDR's letter acknowledging receipt of the Notice of Arbitration. This list is confidential, should only be sent to the case manager and helps the case manager to select arbitrators free from conflicts. Having said this, not all cases may be at a stage where witnesses can be readily identified.

[28] Although subject to interpretation, Art 20(1) does not explicitly require that there be an oral hearing on the merits.

[29] See AAA/ABA Code of Ethics for Arbitrators in Commercial Disputes (2004), Canon III para B(1): 'When the appointment of a prospective arbitrator is being considered, the prospective arbitrator: (a) may ask about the identities of the parties, and the general nature of the case; and (b) may respond to inquiries from a party or its counsel designed to determine his or her suitability and availability for the appointment. In any such dialogue, the prospective arbitrator may receive information from the party or its counsel disclosing the general nature of the dispute but should not permit them to discuss the merits of the case.'; see also IBA Rules of Ethics for International Arbitrators (1986) and the UK Chartered Institute of Arbitrators' Practice Direction: The Interviewing of Prospective Arbitrators (2007) (suggesting a tape recording or arbitrator's file note to be made available to the other party and the administering institution as early as possible).

[30] See ICC Rules, Art 9(5) and LCIA Rules, Art 6.

method for the appointment of the sole and presiding arbitrator as well as the party-appointed arbitrators. Under the ICDR list method, the ICDR proposes a list of 10 names for a sole arbitrator and 15 names for a tri-partite panel, all of which are drawn from the ICDR's international roster. On a confidential basis, the parties are invited to submit their ranking of the arbitrators included on the list. Although the ICDR invites the parties to make only a limited number of pre-emptory strikes, there is no limit which could conceivably result in the parties striking the entire list. In that event, and if both sides agree, a second list can be provided. Unless the parties strike the entire list, the parties are asked to list the acceptable arbitrators in the order of their preference. The ICDR will appoint the arbitrator with the closest common preference. If the parties do not ultimately arrive at an agreement on the arbitrators from the list(s) within 45 days, the ICDR will make the appointment.

(9.4) **Preliminary hearing, evidence and party submissions** While involved throughout the proceedings, the administrator's duties and responsibilities are reduced to the logistical facilitation of the arbitral process after the arbitrators have been designated. Once constituted, the arbitral tribunal takes control and routinely holds a preliminary hearing to facilitate the organization and management of the arbitral proceedings. Topics discussed may include: jurisdictional issues, the place and/or locale of the arbitration, the law governing the proceedings, the language of the proceedings, claims, damages, defences, the necessity for pre-hearing information exchange and the scope, method and timing of such exchange, the method and timing for the submission of legal argument, documentary and physical evidence, the necessity for and scheduling of hearings, witness testimony and site visits, the scope, form, and timing of pre-hearing submissions, the need for interim relief and security for costs, the form of the award and opportunities for mediation and settlement. **17.71**

While there are few limits to the parties' agreement and the arbitrators' discretion afforded by Art 16, in all but the simplest cases, a common practice in international commercial arbitrations today includes the exchange of one or two rounds of legal briefs in addition to the already filed Statements of Claim and Defense, to be followed by the exchange of documents each party intends to rely upon and the other side requests as well as fact and expert witness evidence in writing. Witnesses commonly provide a written statement of their testimony in lieu of a direct examination at the hearing. The tribunal may only rely upon the statement if the party offering the testimony makes the witness available for cross-examination. Thereafter, another exchange of legal briefs in preparation of the hearing may be conducted before the hearing on the merits takes place. At the hearing, parties are commonly afforded an opportunity to present their opening arguments. Party submissions may also include closing arguments or post-hearing submissions, or both. **17.72**

(9.5) **Award** The ICDR case administration is concluded with the delivery of the arbitral award to the parties and the payment of the arbitral tribunal. The arbitral award is authored by the arbitral tribunal alone. Although more limited in scope than the review conducted by the ICC Court of Arbitration (ICC Court) as provided for in Art 27 of the ICC Rules, the ICDR does review the tribunal's award for clerical, typographical or computation errors **17.73** and ensures that the awards address all claims presented in the arbitration.[31] Thereafter, the ICDR delivers the award to the parties.

Article 2: Commencing the Arbitration—Notice of Arbitration and Statement of Claim

1. **The party initiating arbitration ('claimant') shall give written notice of arbitration to the administrator and at the same time to the party against whom a claim is being made ('respondent').**
2. **Arbitral proceedings shall be deemed to commence on the date on which the administrator receives the notice of arbitration.**
3. **The notice of arbitration shall contain a statement of claim including the following:**
   - **(a) a demand that the dispute be referred to arbitration;**
   - **(b) the names, addresses and telephone numbers of the parties;**
   - **(c) a reference to the arbitration clause or agreement that is invoked;**
   - **(d) a reference to any contract out of or in relation to which the dispute arises;**
   - **(e) a description of the claim and an indication of the facts supporting it;**
   - **(f) the relief or remedy sought and the amount claimed; and**
   - **(g) may include proposals as to the means of designating and the number of arbitrators, the place of arbitration and the language(s) of the arbitration.**
4. **Upon receipt of the notice of arbitration, the administrator shall communicate with all parties with respect to the arbitration and shall acknowledge the commencement of the arbitration.**

(1) Introduction

17.74 Like the 'Request for Arbitration' under ICC Rules, Art 4 and LCIA Rules, Art 1, Art 2 of the ICDR Rules establishes the requirements for the document by which a case is initiated. Based on UNCITRAL Rules, Art 3 and 18, it is also called the 'Notice of Arbitration'.

(2) Commencement of a case upon the administrator's receipt of the Notice of Arbitration (Article 2(1) and (2))

17.75 ICDR arbitration is commenced by filing a Notice of Arbitration, which contains within it a Statement of Claim.[32]

17.76 Article 2(1) requires the party initiating arbitration to serve the Notice of Arbitration upon the opposing party/parties at the same time as it is served upon the ICDR administrator. The party initiating the arbitration is defined as the 'claimant', the party/parties against whom a claim is being made as the 'respondent(s)'. Despite the wording of Art 2(1) using the word 'party' in singular, the ICDR Rules are commonly used in multi-party arbitrations.[33]

---

[31] See Art 30(1) (permitting the parties to seek correction for 'any clerical, typographical or computation errors or make an additional award as to claims presented but omitted from the award'.) See s 17.261 *infra*.

[32] The ICDR website contains a form Notice of Arbitration that may be used when preparing the Notice of Arbitration, available at <http://www.adr.org/si.asp?id=3849>.

[33] In the Introduction to the International Dispute Resolution Procedures it is stated that '[w]henever a singular term is used in the rules, such as "party," "claimant" or "arbitrator," that term shall include the plural if there is more than one such entity'.

Corresponding with the provision in ICC Rules, Art 4(2) and LCIA Rules, Art 1.2, arbitration proceedings under the ICDR Rules are deemed to commence on the date on which the administrator receives the Notice of Arbitration (Art 2(2)).[34] Receipt of the Notice of Arbitration will be confirmed by the ICDR. This is particularly important where the claimant is experiencing difficulties in effectuating service of the Notice of Arbitration on the proper respondent. It is also important where commencement of the arbitration is being relied upon to toll any relevant statute of limitations or contractual limitation period. **17.77**

Notices may be served by airmail, air courier, fax, telex, telegram, or other written forms of electronic communication addressed to the party or its representative at its last known address or by personal service, unless otherwise agreed by the parties or ordered by the tribunal (Art 18(1)). **17.78**

Despite the unconditional presumption in Art 2(2) that the arbitration 'shall be deemed to commence on the date on which the administrator receives the Notice of Arbitration', it is the claimant that bears the ultimate responsibility for effecting proper service. Further, in the unsatisfactory scenario of a non-delivery of the Notice of Arbitration, it is left to the claimant to proceed with the arbitration while assuming the risk of non-enforcement.[35] **17.79**

Beyond the tolling of the statute of limitations, the commencement date is critical, inasmuch as it establishes the date from which deadlines flow for the filing of a responsive pleading (Arts 3(1) and 3(2)), for responding to a claimant's proposal for such matters as the appointment of arbitrators and the method of their selection (Art 6(3)), and the venue and language of the arbitration (Art 3(3)). The commencement date will also be used to calculate any refund of the initial filing fee. **17.80**

(3) Contents of the Notice of Arbitration—Statement of Claim (Article 2(3))

(3.1) Demand that the dispute be referred to arbitration (Article 2(3)(a)) An arbitration is started by the party requesting the dispute to be submitted to arbitration, as opposed to other forms of dispute resolution, including mediation. The party initiating arbitration must unequivocally announce its election that the dispute be referred to arbitration. A mere request for a dispute to be decided or resolved will not suffice to initiate arbitration under the ICDR Rules. **17.81**

(3.2) Names, addresses and telephone numbers of the parties (Article 2(3)(b)) Article 2(3)(b) requires a proper identification of the party (or parties) against whom the claimant(s) wish(es) to proceed. For natural persons, it is essential for identification purposes to state both the first name(s) and last name as well as the postal address of the party's/parties' residence. Where known, it is also recommendable to include some distinguishing information such as the date of birth. In the case of legal persons, in addition to the name and resident office, the legal nature of that party should not be omitted. If available, a commercial register excerpt or a certificate of good standing might be added. **17.82**

---

[34] cf UNCITRAL Rules, Art 3(2), which provides for the arbitral proceedings to commence on the date on which the Notice of Arbitration is received by the respondent.

[35] See ICDR Rules, Art 23 (discussing default proceedings), ss 17.226 *et seq infra*.

17.83 (3.3) **Reference to 'the arbitration clause or agreement that is invoked', 'any contract out of or in relation to which the dispute arises', and 'a description of the claim and an indication of the facts supporting it' (Article 2(3)(c), (d) and (e))** The Statement of Claim shall contain 'a description of the claim and an indication of the facts supporting it'. As the Statement of Claim represents the first opportunity to advocate the claimant's case and to educate the arbitrators about it, the art of persuasion knows no boundaries in this mission.[36] In the absence of strict pleading requirements, the ICDR Rules encourage presentation of a claim in a narrative style. Although Art 2(3)(c) and (d) require a 'reference' to the arbitration clause or agreement and the contract out of or in relation to which the dispute arises, attaching these documents as complete copies has become common practice and explaining them may further the claimant's cause.

17.84 While the ICDR Rules require only an 'indication' of the supporting facts, a claimant may even at this early stage produce any document it wishes to rely on in support of its claims with the Notice of Arbitration. Of course, a well thought-out plan for winning a case cannot be conceived without understanding the facts and the applicable law from the beginning, but the Notice of Arbitration is only the starting point for articulating a theory of the case. Inherent in the facts are the equities of the case—the human sense of fairness or unfairness when examining the parties' acts or omissions, the wrongs that were committed by one party against another and the injury that was suffered by one or more parties as a result. However, under the ICDR Rules, the Notice of Arbitration does not yet have to contain a full presentation of all legal and factual elements as well as the evidence in support of the facts stated. Notwithstanding the tribunal's powers under Art 16(3) to 'direct the parties to focus their presentations on issues the decision of which could dispose of all or part of the case', the ICDR Rules do not provide for pre-trial motions for the dismissal of a case for a failure to state a case in the Statement of Case, such as a Motion to Dismiss under r 56 of the Federal Rules of Civil Procedure in the US federal legal system.

17.85 A well pled Notice of Arbitration and Statement of Claim may deal with a description of the contractual/legal situation underlying the dispute and provide a historical account of the events leading up to the dispute. It may also deal with the anticipated opposition arguments while not losing focus on the claimant's own arguments.

17.86 (3.4) **Relief or remedy sought, amount claimed and relevance for administrative fees (Article 2(3)(f))** Beyond the relief or remedy sought (payment of money, specific performance, permanent injunction, declaratory judgment), Art 2(3)(f) requires the claimant to state the amount claimed. The amount stated by the claimant will be used primarily by the administrator to determine the initial filing fee, payable in full when the Notice of Arbitration is filed. The fees payable by the claimant are based on the amount of the claim and are subject to increase if the amount of a claim is modified after the initial filing date. Fees are also subject to decrease if the amount of a claim is modified before the first hearing.

17.87 It may be extremely difficult and costly to go through the exercise of quantification of the amount claimed. Claimants sometimes request a bifurcation of the proceedings for the

[36] See generally Bishop, R.D., *The Art of Advocacy in International Arbitration* (Juris Publishing, Huntington, 2004) 445.

arbitral tribunal to rule upon liability in principle before turning to quantification. In such cases, as well as other cases where the amount claimed is unknown, parties are requested to state a range of claims or be subject to the highest possible filing fee, currently $65,000. The ICDR administrative practice therefore discourages a claimant from asserting overblown estimates of recoverable damages.

If no monetary award is claimed, the ICDR will apply pre-set fees for non-monetary claims. Irrespective of the amount claimed, the minimum fees for any case having three or more arbitrators are $2,750 for the filing fee, plus a $1,250 case service fee. Parties on cases held in abeyance for one year by agreement, will be assessed an annual abeyance fee of $300. If a party refuses to pay the assessed fee, the other party or parties may pay the entire fee on behalf of all parties and claim the portion advanced for the other party/parties in the final award. Otherwise the matter will be closed. **17.88**

The ICDR administrative filing fees are apportioned, a feature that may prove useful in mere collection cases. While the Initial Filing Fee is due upon the filing of the Notice of Arbitration, the subsequent Case Service Fee becomes due and payable if the matter proceeds to a first hearing. The administrative conference is not deemed a hearing for these purposes. In addition, arbitrator compensation is not part of the administrative fee. The ICDR's administrative fees are set out in a table in the end of the International Dispute Resolution Procedures. It is restated here below: **17.89**

Amount of Claim	Initial Filing Fee	Case Service Fee
Above $0 to $10,000	$750	$200
Above $10,000 to $75,000	$950	$300
Above $75,000 to $150,000	$1,800	$750
Above $150,000 to $300,000	$2,750	$1,250
Above $300,000 to $500,000	$4,250	$1,750
Above $500,000 to $1,000,000	$6,000	$2,500
Above $1,000,000 to $5,000,000	$8,000	$3,250
Above $5,000,000 to $10,000,000	$10,000	$4,000
Above $10,000,000	Base fee of $12,500 plus .01% of the amount of claim above $10 million.	$6,000
Non-monetary Claims	$3,250 Filing fees capped at $65,000	$1,250

The ICDR also offers a refund schedule on filing fees. For cases with claims up to $75,000, a minimum filing fee of $300 will not be refunded. For all other cases, a minimum fee of $500 will not be refunded. Subject to the minimum fee requirements, refunds will be calculated as follows: **17.90**

- 100 per cent of the filing fee, above the minimum fee, will be refunded if the case is settled or withdrawn within five calendar days of filing;
- 50 per cent of the filing fee will be refunded if the case is settled or withdrawn between six and 30 calendar days of filing;
- 25 per cent of the filing fee will be refunded if the case is settled or withdrawn between 31 and 60 calendar days of filing.

17.91 No refund will be made once an arbitrator has been appointed (this includes one arbitrator on a three-arbitrator panel).

17.92 (3.5) **'[P]roposals as to the means of designating and the number of arbitrators, the place of arbitration and the language(s) of the arbitration' (Article 2(3)(g))** Unlike the other items listed in Art 2(3), the Notice of Arbitration may—but does not have to—include proposals as to the means of designating and the number of arbitrators, the place of arbitration and the language(s) of the arbitration. In well drafted arbitration clauses, these items will have been included and the parties will have agreed upon them in writing already. If not already agreed upon in writing, the claimant may set out its preferences on all of these items in the hope that the respondent accepts one or another of the suggestions.

17.93 Even in cases where the parties have already agreed upon these items in the arbitration agreement, the circumstances of the case may merit an attempt to change the agreements reached in light of possibly different economic interests and factual scenarios at the time the dispute arose as compared to when the business relationship was initiated. Either the Notice of Arbitration or correspondence between the parties prior thereto may be the appropriate instrument to do so.

17.94 Any proposed qualification the arbitrator(s) should have, such as the nationality, residence, profession, legal training, language proficiencies or any other qualification, will aid the administrator in the appointment should the administrator be called upon to do so in accordance with Art 6. The ICDR Rules do not require the party initiating arbitration to nominate its arbitrator with the Notice of Arbitration already. The ICDR Rules do not contain any requirement either that the claimant has to nominate its arbitrator before the respondent. Article 6 allows the parties to designate the arbitrator(s) within 45 days after the commencement of the case.

17.95 One issue when drafting the Notice of Arbitration can be in what language it should be done. Article 14 stipulates that the language shall be that of the documents containing the arbitration agreement. However, the stipulation is subject to the power of the tribunal to determine otherwise based upon the contentions of the parties and the circumstances of the arbitration.

(4) Administrator's acknowledgement of commencement and initial communication (Article 2(4))

17.96 Upon receipt of the Notice of Arbitration, the administrator acknowledges the commencement of the arbitration and starts communicating with all parties with respect to the arbitration. It is the ICDR standard administrative practice to notify the parties of their responsible case manager and supervisor. The first communication by the ICDR also notifies the parties of the time of the administrative conference.

17.97 As early as within the commencement letter, the ICDR distributes its Checklist for Conflicts and encloses an Arbitration Information Sheet, providing basic information about the ICDR arbitration process and sets forth initial dates for the case management. The administrator also invites the respondent to file its written Statement of Defense and any counterclaim in accordance with Art 3.

As part of the ICDR's administrative service, the ICDR maintains a AAA WebFile for each case. With the initial communication to the parties, the ICDR invites the parties to take advantage of the AAA's WebFile. It allows the parties to perform a variety of case-related activities online. These include the filing of additional claims, the completion of the Checklist for Conflicts form, to view invoices and submit payments, share and manage documents, strike and rank the lists of neutrals and to review the case status and hearing dates and times. Cases filed in hard copy format are posted electronically and can then be viewed and managed online as well. **17.98**

Article 3. Statement of Defense and Counterclaim

1. **Within 30 days after the commencement of the arbitration, a respondent shall submit a written statement of defense, responding to the issues raised in the notice of arbitration, to the claimant and any other parties, and to the administrator.**
2. **At the time a respondent submits its statement of defense, a respondent may make counterclaims or assert setoffs as to any claim covered by the agreement to arbitrate, as to which the claimant shall within 30 days submit a written statement of defense to the respondent and any other parties and to the administrator.**
3. **A respondent shall respond to the administrator, the claimant and other parties within 30 days after the commencement of the arbitration as to any proposals the claimant may have made as to the number of arbitrators, the place of the arbitration or the language(s) of the arbitration, except to the extent that the parties have previously agreed as to these matters.**
4. **The arbitral tribunal, or the administrator if the arbitral tribunal has not yet been formed, may extend any of the time limits established in this article if it considers such an extension justified.**

(1) Introduction

Article 3 is the mirror image of Art 2, but focused on the respondent's duties. While Art 2 deals with the Notice of Arbitration and the Statement of Claim, Art 3 deals with the defence thereto. Similar rules can be found in ICC Rules, Art 5, LCIA Rules, Art 2, and UNCITRAL Rules, Art 19. **17.99**

(2) Contents of the Statement of Defense and joinder of third parties (Article 3(1))

The respondent is required to submit a written Statement of Defense responding to the Notice of Arbitration within 30 days after the arbitration has been commenced. The respondent may also reply to any proposals made by the claimant as to the number of arbitrators, the place of the arbitration, or the language of the arbitration. The ICDR Rules do not require the respondent to deviate from previously reached agreements with the claimant. **17.100**

Additionally, the respondent may make counterclaims or assert set-offs at the time it submits the Statement of Defense. The claimant, in turn, has 30 days to file a Statement of Defense to a counterclaim. Such Statement of Defense to the counterclaim will be governed by this Art 3 *mutatis mutandis*. **17.101**

Challenges to the tribunal's jurisdiction must be made at the time of the Statement of Defense or will be considered waived (Art 15). **17.102**

17.103 The respondent is not required to provide a full defence, but may do so if it so wishes. In practice, as a responsive pleading, the contents of the Statement of Defense will depend on the facts and arguments presented by the claimant in the Notice of Arbitration. The respondent is required to 'respond to the issues raised in the notice of arbitration' and must submit its statement to the claimant and any other parties as well as the administrator. In the vast majority of cases, the respondent will request that the claims be dismissed, and that the claimant be ordered to bear the costs of arbitration, including the respondent's legal costs.

17.104 Under Art 3(1), the respondent can submit a written Statement of Defense to any other parties. The ICDR Rules thus provide for the possibility of a joinder of third parties. Since the respondent is required to submit its statement to the claimant, the administrator and 'any other parties', the administrator exercises no scrutiny whether such joinder is admissible. The jurisdictional challenges attached to multi-party arbitrations are for the arbitral tribunal to decide.[37]

(3) Counterclaims (Article 3(2))

17.105 The respondent may have a counterclaim against the claimant. Rather than pursuing such claims as separate counterclaims, the respondent may declare such counterclaim as a set-off against the relief sought. In such a case, to the extent the counterclaim is introduced as a set-off only, the counterclaim is not regarded as an independent claim so that the amount of set-off will not be taken into account when the ICDR fixes the administrative fees. In case the counterclaim exceeds the claim, the ICDR's fee assessment will thus be based on the amount exceeding the claim only if the counterclaim amount equalling the claim was presented as a set-off.

(4) The claimant's answer to counterclaims (Article 3(3))

17.106 If the Statement of Defense or any third party's statement contains a counterclaim, the claimant needs to submit its answer to the respondent, any third party and the administrator within 30 days. Should the claimant challenge the arbitral tribunal's jurisdiction to hear the counterclaim, Art 15(3) requires it to raise such objection within this answer statement.

(5) 30-day time limits and extensions (Article 3(4))

17.107 Whereas the claimant is afforded with virtually unlimited amount of time within which to prepare its Notice of Arbitration, the respondent is required to answer within 30 days of the receipt of the Notice. This might lead to injustice. The respondent may be caught by surprise and may even be unaware that the claimant considered that a dispute had arisen and be submitted to arbitration. Further, it might take a considerable amount of time within the respondent organization to reach the necessary level of decision maker and select outside counsel. In addition, various levels of unfamiliarity may be encountered starting from international commercial arbitration as such, through the language of the arbitration, and

[37] See Hosking, J., 'Non-Signatories and International Arbitration in the United States: The Quest for Consent' (2004) 20(3) *Arb Int'l* 289.

ranging up to the unfamiliarity with the underlying subject matter and/or banal logistical problems such as the unknown location of the relevant files.

In comparison to the claimant's unlimited amount of time to prepare its Notice of Arbitration, it may constitute a denial of equal treatment if the respondent were forced to comply with the 30-day time limit for the preparation of its Statement of Defense in all cases. Article 3(4) addresses this issue and grants the administrator—or the arbitral tribunal if already constituted—the authority to extend any of these time periods. Article 3(4) does not require the administrator to invite the other side's comments and Art 3(4) does not specify how long an extension may be granted by the administrator. In practice, the administrator often grants a first extension of time of seven days without inviting the other side's comments and solicits such input for any additional time requests. **17.108**

Article 4. Amendments to Claims

During the arbitral proceedings, any party may amend or supplement its claim, counterclaim or defense, unless the tribunal considers it inappropriate to allow such amendment or supplement because of the party's delay in making it, prejudice to the other parties or any other circumstances. A party may not amend or supplement a claim or counterclaim if the amendment or supplement would fall outside the scope of the agreement to arbitrate.

(1) Introduction

Within the scope of the arbitration agreement, ie the boundaries of an arbitral tribunal's jurisdiction, Art 4 establishes the principle that amendments and supplements to claims, counterclaims or defences are admissible at any time during the proceedings, so long as the arbitral tribunal considers it appropriate. Article 4 is based on UNCITRAL Rules, Art 20. In contrast, the comparable provision in the ICC Rules, Art 19, addresses new claims and counterclaims after the Terms of Reference have been signed only. Before allowing a party to amend any 'claim, counterclaim, defence and reply' LCIA Rules, Art 22.1(a) even requires the tribunal to give the parties a 'reasonable opportunity to state their views'. No such requirement can be found in the ICDR Rules. **17.109**

(2) Amendment and supplement of claims, counterclaims or defences (Article 4)

Whether amendments and supplements may be considered appropriate or inappropriate depends on the individual circumstances of the case and the arbitral tribunal's exercise of its discretion vested by Art 16(1). Article 16(1) requires the arbitral tribunal to treat the parties with equality and that each party has the right to be heard and is given a fair opportunity to present its case. In discharging their mandate, arbitral tribunals carefully structure procedural directions and it is not for the parties to treat an arbitral tribunal's carefully structured procedural direction with an unwelcome disregard on its own motion. **17.110**

Article 4 is open-ended and applies to both amendments and supplements of claims, counterclaims or defences. Although it spells out the party's delay in making amendments or supplements and the prejudice to the other parties as grounds to consider when ruling whether the amendments or supplements are timely, Art 4 allows for any other circumstances to be considered as well. **17.111**

The initial pleadings and the claims, counterclaims and defences presented therein serve a critical purpose as a basis for all other steps in the proceedings, including the structuring of **17.112** the introduction and adducing of witness and expert evidence and document production requests. In light of the standards of Art 16, the threshold for the admission of an entirely new theory, whether factually or legally, ie an amendment of the claims, counterclaims and defences, at a late stage of the proceedings must be higher than for a mere supplementation of an already presented, yet not fully pled, claim, counterclaim or defence.

(3) Impact on fees (Article 4)

17.113 If admitted by the arbitral tribunal, the administrative fee may be subject to increase if the amount of a claim (or counterclaim) is modified after the initial filing date. Fees are also subject to decrease if the amount of a claim or counterclaim is modified before the first hearing. The ICDR's assessment of fees is based on the parties' presentation of claims after having consulted with the tribunal.

The Tribunal

Article 5: Number of Arbitrators

If the parties have not agreed on the number of arbitrators, one arbitrator shall be appointed unless the administrator determines in its discretion that three arbitrators are appropriate because of the large size, complexity or other circumstances of the case.

(1) Party autonomy and its limits

17.114 As with most other aspects of international arbitration, the appointment of arbitrators is in large part governed by the principle of party autonomy, granting the parties significant freedom to agree amongst them the number of arbitrators to decide their dispute, and the mechanism for appointing them. This principle is fully recognized in the ICDR Rules.

17.115 Parties typically agree on the number of the arbitrators in the arbitration agreement. It is an expression of party autonomy, however, that the parties can reach such an agreement even later, after the arbitration has commenced, for as long as no tribunal has been constituted.

17.116 The parties' agreement on the number of arbitrators is binding like any other contractual commitment. Therefore, a party can in principle not deviate from an earlier agreement, unless it contests the validity or conclusion of the arbitration agreement that contains the agreement on the number of arbitrators. In such a case, it may be arguable that the agreement on the number of arbitrators was never validly concluded.

(2) Default of sole arbitrator

17.117 If there is no consent of the parties on the number of the arbitrators, institutional rules typically provide for a default solution. Some institutions provide that, absent agreement on the number of arbitrators by the parties, the dispute will be decided by three arbitrators.[38] The ICDR Rules provide for one arbitrator as default.[39] The major perceived advantage of appointing a sole arbitrator is the limitation this places on the costs of the arbitration (with a sole arbitrator incurring by definition only about a third of the expense incurred by

[38] UNCITRAL Rules, Art 5; ICSID Convention, Art 37(2)(b).

[39] Other rules also provide for one arbitrator as a rule, but leave it to the institution to appoint three arbitrators where the circumstances so require. See eg LCIA Rules, Art 5(4); ICC Rules, Art 8(2); SCC Arbitration Rules, Art 12.

a three-member tribunal). It is argued that a sole arbitrator may also be able to resolve the dispute with greater speed, without the need to coordinate the busy schedules of three members on the panel.[40] It also removes the risk of a party-appointed arbitrator employing delaying tactics and of the likelihood of an award that is a compromise between the interests of both parties.[41]

Despite this, there is a strong preference in modern arbitration for a three-member tribunal, certainly in bigger and more complex cases. Specifically, it is argued that such a choice facilitates a higher degree of quality in the award, in particular where the case concerns different legal areas and the arbitrators, owing to their possibly different areas of experience and expertise, are able to complement each other in the decision-making process. With three arbitrators deliberating, and discussing each other's approaches,[42] a three-member tribunal is vested with a powerful dynamic of internal quality control.[43] These deliberations can reduce the risk of misunderstandings, facilitate the use of more sophisticated expertise, and, as is generally the case with diverse panels, take account of the different national and legal backgrounds of the parties which in turn may make the award of the tribunal more acceptable to the parties.[44] As Art 5 recognizes, these quality considerations offset some disadvantages associated with three-member tribunals, in particular the risk of higher costs and the potential for delay.[45] **17.118**

Article 6: Appointment of Arbitrators

1. **The parties may mutually agree upon any procedure for appointing arbitrators and shall inform the administrator as to such procedure.**
2. **The parties may mutually designate arbitrators, with or without the assistance of the administrator. When such designations are made, the parties shall notify the administrator so that notice of the appointment can be communicated to the arbitrators, together with a copy of these Rules.**
3. **If within 45 days after the commencement of the arbitration, all of the parties have not mutually agreed on a procedure for appointing the arbitrator(s) or have not mutually agreed on the designation of the arbitrator(s), the administrator shall, at the written request of any party, appoint the arbitrator(s) and designate the presiding arbitrator. If all of the parties have mutually agreed upon a procedure for appointing the arbitrator(s), but all appointments have not been made within the time limits provided in that procedure, the**

[40] Schwarz, F.T. and Konrad, C.W., *The Vienna Rules, A Commentary on International Arbitration in Austria* (Kluwer Law International, The Hague, 2009) s 14-004.

[41] See Derains, Y. and Schwartz, E.A., *A Guide to the ICC Rules of Arbitration* (2nd edn, Kluwer Law International, The Hague, 2005) 147; Lew, J., Mistelis, L. and Kröll, S., *Comparative International Commercial Arbitration* (Kluwer Law International, The Hague, 2003) paras 10-11 *et seq*; Craig, W.L., Park, W.W. and Paulsson, J., *International Chamber of Commerce Arbitration* (3rd edn, Oceana Publications, New York, 2000) 190.

[42] See Craig *et al* (n 41) 191.

[43] Lachmann, J.P., *Handbuch für die Schiedsgerichtspraxis*, (3rd edn, Verlag Dr Otto Schmidt, Cologne, 2008) 208; there is a preference visible in common law countries to choose a sole arbitrator, whereas, in civil law countries, preference is for an arbitral tribunal. See Lew *et al* (n 41) para 10-10, commenting that a three-member tribunal also allows the appointment of arbitrators with particular scientific or technical knowledge when required, s 10-18.

[44] See Craig *et al* (n 41) 191; Lew *et al* (n 41) para 10-18.

[45] Lew *et al* (n 41) s 10-19.

administrator shall, at the written request of any party, perform all functions provided for in that procedure that remain to be performed.

4. **In making such appointments, the administrator, after inviting consultation with the parties, shall endeavour to select suitable arbitrators. At the request of any party or on its own initiative, the administrator may appoint nationals of a country other than that of any of the parties.**
5. **Unless the parties have agreed otherwise no later than 45 days after the commencement of the arbitration, if the notice of arbitration names two or more claimants or two or more respondents, the administrator shall appoint all the arbitrators.**

(1) Party autonomy and the constitution of the tribunal

17.119 The principle of party autonomy is, under ICDR Rules as elsewhere, not limited to the parties' choice of the number of arbitrators, but extends (within the confines of the mandatory law at the seat of the arbitration)[46] to the procedure pursuant to which the tribunal is constituted. Thus, the ICDR Rules leave it to the parties to agree whether, in the case of a three-arbitrator panel, each party designates a co-arbitrator, who in turn designate a chairman; or whether the chairman is designated directly by the parties, or else directly by the arbitral institution; or indeed any other process. Different procedures are also conceivable for the appointment of a sole arbitrator. The parties' agreement will also typically (and indeed should) contain time limits for the various steps in that procedure.

17.120 The parties' agreement on the procedure for the tribunal's constitution is often contained in the arbitration agreement. If not contained therein, Art 6(3) affords the parties an additional 45 days from the commencement to agree on an appropriate procedure.

17.121 Where the parties are in agreement on the procedure of constitution, or indeed able to designate the arbitrators, the role of the ICDR is naturally limited. Article 6(1) merely requires the parties to inform the administrator of any agreement that the parties have reached, and of any designation of arbitrators by the parties that arises from such a procedure. In that case, per Art 6(2), the administrator will notify the arbitrators so designated of their appointment, and provide them with a copy of the ICDR Rules. The wording of Art 6(2) could be read to suggest that a designated arbitrator's first contact with the case is through the administrator. However, neither Art 6(3) nor, more importantly, Art 7(2) prevents a party from approaching a prospective arbitrator to check his or her availability and the existence of conflicts, without of course discussing the substance of the case.

17.122 While the parties are in principle free to agree on the procedure for the appointment of the arbitrators, the arbitration law at the seat of the arbitration may impose some limits. For example, within the scope of the European Convention on Human Rights (ECHR), some countries require that every party agreement on the constitution of the tribunal (including an agreement on the number of arbitrators) needs to ensure a fair and balanced trial within the meaning of Art 6 ECHR. As discussed below, these issues play an important role in multi-party arbitration.

(2) Default procedure and institutional arbitrator appointments under the ICDR Rules

17.123 Article 6(3) is triggered if the parties have not agreed on a procedure for constituting the tribunal, in the arbitration agreement or otherwise within 45 days from the commencement

[46] See ICDR Rules, Art 1(2) (discussed at ss 17.54 *et seq supra*).

of the arbitration. The ICDR Rules provide for the simple solution of the ICDR appointing all arbitrators (ie the sole arbitrator or, where agreement on a panel exists or a panel is deemed appropriate by the ICDR pursuant to Art 5, all members of the tribunal).

The administrator's appointment is made only upon a party's request in writing and includes the designation of the presiding arbitrator. **17.124**

The administrator will also become active if the parties have agreed on a procedure, but fail to designate the arbitrators as required and within the agreed timeframe. In that case, the administrator will follow the agreed procedure, and simply 'perform all functions provided for in that procedure that remain to be performed'. If for example, the parties have agreed that each side shall designate an arbitrator within 30 days and the two co-arbitrators then designate a presiding arbitrator, but only the claimant proceeds to make a designation, the administrator will appoint both the arbitrator for the respondent and the presiding arbitrator: both appointments 'remain to be performed' within the meaning of Art 6(3). **17.125**

In making an institutional appointment, Art 6(4) requires the administrator to designate a 'suitable' candidate. This term is not specified, nor could it be; it is designed to confer significant discretion on the administrator and the freedom to take into account the circumstances of the case. For the chairman or sole arbitrator appointment an increased level of arbitral experience may be required. Knowledge of the substantive law and the subject matter of the dispute will also be taken into account. **17.126**

The administrator may take into account the nationality of the parties but is not required to do so even when so requested by a party. In practice, the nationality may play a prominent role during the appointment of the presiding arbitrator: there is a perception of additional neutrality if the presiding arbitrator is from a different country than the parties and otherwise removed from any national links to the dispute. **17.127**

Although not provided for in the ICDR Rules, the ICDR's default administrative practice is to use the list method for the appointment of arbitrators.[47] Parties are well advised to discuss specific qualifications and requirements for the prospective arbitrators as early as during the administrative conference call.[48] **17.128**

(3) Constituting the tribunal in multi-party arbitrations

One of the fundamental principles of commercial arbitration is the parties' equal treatment.[49] The increasingly common phenomenon of multi-party arbitrations—and in particular the appointment of an arbitrator where multiple parties on one side fail to agree on a joint nomination—raise significant concerns in this regard.[50] If there are, for example, three respondents who may even have divergent interests, why should they be forced to jointly nominate an arbitrator, and what are the consequences if they do not?[51] **17.129**

---

47 See the description of the list method at s 17.70.

48 See ss 17.62–65.

49 Born, G.B., *International Commercial Arbitration Commentary and Materials* (3rd edn, Kluwer Law International, The Hague, 2009) ch 14.

50 Schwarz and Konrad (n 40) s 15-032.

51 Schwarz and Konrad (n 40) ss 15-033 *et seq.*

17.130 The issue is illustrated by the famous case of *Siemens AG/BKMI Industrienanlagen GmbH v Dutco Construction Company* decided by the French *Cour de Cassation* in 1992.[52] In this case, the court was asked to consider the issue of equal treatment of the parties with regard to the constitution of an arbitral tribunal. The French *Cour de Cassation* found that the constitution of the tribunal had been unfair to the respondents because it afforded *Dutco* (who was able to appoint an arbitrator) a better position to influence the final outcome of the arbitration than the respondents (who could not agree on an arbitrator and therefore lost their right of appointment to the institution). The court set aside the award reasoning that 'the principle of the equality of the parties in the appointment of arbitrators is a matter of public policy (*ordre public*) [and] can be waived only after a dispute has arisen'.[53]

17.131 Although the *Dutco* decision has met with considerable scepticism in other jurisdictions,[54] all major arbitral institutions have subsequently amended their rules to ensure equality. Of course, as indicated by the word, equal treatment does not necessarily have to mean identical treatment. But absent indications of bad faith in connection with the non-appointing multi-party side or other circumstances justifying non-identical treatment, such as equality of interest amongst one multi-party side,[55] the institutional appointment of only one side's arbitrator while upholding the other side's appointment would seemingly violate the principle of equality and give one 'side' more influence on the composition of the tribunal than the other.[56] ICDR Rules Art 6(4) leaves it to the parties to agree on a particular procedure within 45 days from the commencement of the arbitration, failing which the administrator will appoint all the arbitrators, both for the claimant and the respondent side. This is now the predominant approach in arbitration:[57] the institution proceeds to appoint an arbitrator for the respondents *and* the claimants (even where the claimants have made a joint nomination), or indeed proceed to immediately appoint all three arbitrators. That way, both sides are treated equally, because both sides are faced with an institutional appointment,[58] in what is a prompt and unequivocal solution that uniformly applies to all cases.[59] Of course, this solution imposes most directly on the claimants who were able to make a joint appointment, but who lose that right if the respondents cannot make a joint appointment as well. Although some have raised concerns that this solution is unfair because by

[52] See Cour de Cassation, 1re Ch Civ, 7 January 1992, *Siemens AG/BKMI Industrienanlagen GmbH v Dutco Construction Company* (1993) XVII YB Comm Arb, 140-2.

[53] *ibid.*

[54] See *Karaha Bodas Company LLC v Perusahaan Minyak Pertambanga Dan Gas Bumi Negara,* (2003) 21(3) ASA Bull, 667–84 (High Court of the Hong Kong Special Administrative Region)); see also BGer, 4 August 2006, BGE 4P.105/2006, (2007) 25(1) ASA Bull, 105–22; see Lew *et al* (n 41) para 16–27.

[55] Weber, D., 'Wider den Verlust des Bestellungsrechts bei Nichteinigung der Mehrparteiengegenseite auf einen Schiedsrichter' in *Grenzüberschreitungen—Beiträge zum Internationalen Verfahrensrecht und zur Schiedsgerichtsbarkeit, Festschrift für Peter Schlosser zum 70 Geburtstag* (Mohr Siebeck, Tübingen, 2005) 1063.

[56] Lew *et al* (n 41) s 16-12.

[57] The other model, which is less favoured today, takes the more traditional approach of leaving the claimants' joint appointment in place, and making an institutional appointment only on behalf of the respondents. See eg VIAC Rules, Art 15.

[58] Schwarz and Konrad (n 40) s 15-043 with further references.

[59] Berger, K.-P., 'Schiedsrichterbestellung in Mehrparteienschiedsverfahren' [1993] *Recht der Internationalen Wirtschaft* 702.

deliberately not agreeing on an arbitrator, the respondents could effectively cancel the appointment of the claimants' arbitrator,[60] a similar standard has also been adopted by the ICC, LCIA, CEPANI, SIAC; and exists in modified form in the DIS and WIPO Rules.[61]

Article 7: Impartiality and Independence of Arbitrators

1. **Arbitrators acting under these Rules shall be impartial and independent. Prior to accepting appointment, a prospective arbitrator shall disclose to the administrator any circumstance likely to give rise to justifiable doubts as to the arbitrator's impartiality or independence. If, at any stage during the arbitration, new circumstances arise that may give rise to such doubts, an arbitrator shall promptly disclose such circumstances to the parties and to the administrator. Upon receipt of such information from an arbitrator or a party, the administrator shall communicate it to the other parties and to the tribunal.**
2. **No party or anyone acting on its behalf shall have any *ex parte* communication relating to the case with any arbitrator, or with any candidate for appointment as party-appointed arbitrator except to advise the candidate of the general nature of the controversy and of the anticipated proceedings and to discuss the candidate's qualifications, availability or independence in relation to the parties, or to discuss the suitability of candidates for selection as a third arbitrator where the parties or party designated arbitrators are to participate in that selection. No party or anyone acting on its behalf shall have any *ex parte* communication relating to the case with any candidate for presiding arbitrator.**

(1) Impartiality and independence

It is an important principle of due process that arbitrators, like any judicial decision maker, must carry out their functions impartially and independently from the parties.[62] Unlike in state courts, parties have the right to select arbitrators of their choosing. Respecting this right, and ensuring a non-partisan decision-making process at the same time has been called the 'crux of arbitration'.[63] **17.132**

All major institutional arbitration rules impose some standard of neutrality on the arbitrator, but there is no unified terminology. Arbitrators acting under ICC Rules must be, and remain throughout the case, 'independent of the parties involved in the arbitration';[64] arbitrators acting under LCIA Rules 'shall be and remain at all times impartial and independent of the parties; and none shall act in the arbitration as advocates for any party',[65] and arbitrators acting under UNCITRAL Rules may simply be challenged for lack of 'impartiality and independence'.[66] Article 7 simply requires that '[a]rbitrators acting under these Rules shall be impartial and independent'. Yet none of these rules provide a definition as to what 'impartiality' or 'independence' means; these terms were developed, and continue to evolve, in academic writing and national precedent. Indeed, national law remains highly **17.133**

[60] Schwarz and Konrad (n 40) s 15-043 with further references.

[61] Under the DIS Rules, Art 13, if multiple respondents fail to jointly appoint an arbitrator, the institution will set aside the claimant's appointment and nominate two arbitrators; but the institution will not appoint the presiding arbitrator.

[62] See eg Art 6 ECHR which requires a hearing by 'an independent and impartial tribunal'.

[63] Matscher, F., 'Schiedsgerichsbarkeit und EMRK' in W.J. Haberscheid and K. Schwab (eds), *Festschrift für Heinrich Nagel zum 75. Geburtstag* (Aschendorff, Münster, 1987) 236.

[64] ICC Rules, Art 7(1).

[65] LCIA Rules, Art 5(2).

[66] UNCITRAL Rules, Art 10.

relevant for these issues: although the arbitral institution (including the ICDR under Arts 7 and 8) will decide a challenge, that decision is usually subject to review by the courts at the seat of the arbitration, either immediately or in the context of a setting-aside proceeding.

17.134 In international doctrine, impartiality is described as the arbitrator's ability to assume a state of mind[67] in which the arbitrator does not adopt a position favourable to either of the parties until the case has been heard and argued in full.[68] Independence, by contrast,[69] is often understood as a more objective factor that refers to the relationship between the arbitrator and the parties. An arbitrator is independent if he or she lacks a close, substantial and recent relationship, whether personal, social, or financial, with either one of the parties that is 'likely to give rise to a personal interest in the result of the arbitration'.[70] At a minimum, arbitrators are prohibited from having any direct relationship with the parties that would give rise to a financial, business or professional interest by the arbitrator.[71] Obviously, a close private relationship to one of the parties may also affect the arbitrator's freedom of judgment.[72]

(2) Disclosure

17.135 Article 7(1) not only requires arbitrators to '*be*' impartial and independent; it also requires them to 'disclose . . . any circumstance *likely to give rise to justifiable doubts as to the arbitrator's impartiality or independence*'. The duty of prompt disclosure exists not only at the time of appointment, but continues to apply 'at any stage during the arbitration'.

17.136 The duty to disclose is a necessary corollary of the duty to be impartial and independent; one cannot exist without the other.[73] Disclosure enables the institution and the parties to make an informed decision if the appointment, or the challenge, of an arbitrator is appropriate under the circumstances. Any prospective arbitrator is therefore required carefully to examine his or her relationship to the parties and the circumstances of the case to ensure that there are no conflicts that would prevent his accepting the appointment.[74] However, the arbitrator cannot be the ultimate judge as to whether his or her service is appropriate

[67] Aksen, G., 'The Tribunal's Appointment' in L.W. Newman and R.D. Hill (eds), *The Leading Arbitrators' Guide to International Arbitration* (Juris Publishing, Huntington, 2004) 32.

[68] Bishop, R.D. and Reed, L., 'Practical Guidelines for Interviewing, Selecting and Challenging Party-Appointed Arbitrators in International Commercial Arbitration' (1998) 14(4) *Arb Int'l* 395, 396.

[69] The term 'neutral' or 'non-neutral' arbitrator is also commonly used in domestic US arbitration. Under that concept, a party-appointed arbitrator may be non-neutral, and, as such, predisposed towards a party. At least conceptually, the idea of a non-neutral arbitrator is difficult to understand, or endorse, from a European perspective. Indeed, the ABA/AAA Code of Ethics for Arbitrators has abandoned the previously applicable principle that party-nominated arbitrators are non-neutral in favour of an assumption of neutrality; thus, parties have to expressly agree to non-neutral arbitrators.

[70] Smith, M.L., 'Impartiality of the Party-Appointed Arbitrator' (1990) 6(4) *Arb Int'l* 320, 323.

[71] Born, G.B., *International Arbitration and Forum Selection Agreements: Drafting and Enforcing* (2nd edn, Kluwer Law International, The Hague, 2006) 72.

[72] Derains and Schwartz (n 41) 127. In this regard, it is irrelevant if the arbitrator is biased against or in favour of either party.

[73] In Switzerland, the Swiss *Bundesgericht* has found that the duty to disclose is an implied contractual duty of the arbitrator. See De Witt Wijnen, O.L.O., Voser, N. and Rao, N., 'Background Information on the IBA Guidelines on Conflict of Interest' (2004) 5 *Bus L Int'l*, n 13.

[74] Alvarez, G.A., 'The Challenge of Arbitrators' (1990) 6(3) *Arb Int'l* 203, 217.

under the circumstances—thus, disclosure affords the parties and the administering institution the opportunity to assess the arbitrator's impartiality and independence.

The standard of disclosure is hotly debated in international arbitration. Most rules and laws advocate a subjective standard that requires arbitrators to disclose those circumstances that give rise to doubts from the parties' perspective. General Standard 3(a) of the IBA Conflict Guidelines, for example, requires the disclosure of facts 'that may, in the eyes of the parties, give rise to doubts as to the arbitrator's impartiality or independence'. **17.137**

Although Art 7(1) does not contain such an express reference to a subjective perspective of the parties, on balance, it is more appropriate to apply a subjective standard to disclosure under the ICDR Rules as well. As a matter of principle, if there is an objective appearance of bias, the arbitrator should simply not serve. If one were to require disclosure under the same criteria that apply to disqualification, however, *every* disclosure by an arbitrator would necessarily lead to disqualification.[75] The arbitral process benefits from disclosures even where the disclosed fact should not and does not lead to disqualification;[76] this facilitates the policy aim of encouraging disclosures in case of doubt[77] and at all stages of the arbitration.[78] **17.138**

Article 7 requires arbitrators to 'be' impartial and independent, and it requires disclosure of circumstances 'likely to give rise to justifiable doubts'. If the arbitrator 'is' not impartial and independent, he or she must not accept the appointment; in addition, if the arbitrator thinks that a certain fact is 'likely to give rise to justifiable doubts', he or she must disclose it. These duties are directly addressed to the arbitrator. **17.139**

Similarly, an arbitrator will be removed under Art 8 'whenever circumstances exist that give rise to justifiable doubts as to the arbitrator's impartiality or independence'. There is a difference between the successful challenge ('circumstances exist that *give* rise to justifiable doubts') and the wider standard for disclosure ('circumstances exist that are *likely to give* rise to justifiable doubts'). The determination of whether certain facts are *likely* to give rise to doubts is broader and more subjective than the assessment as to whether certain facts *actually* give rise to justifiable (ie reasonable) doubts. A prospective arbitrator willing to accept the appointment[79] should therefore disclose all circumstances that 'are likely to' (rather than only those that *actually will*) justify doubts as to the arbitrator's impartiality. The arbitrator will also be required to make all reasonable enquiries as to whether circumstances for **17.140**

---

[75] For a detailed discussion, see Schwarz and Konrad (n 40) para 7-143 *et seq*.

[76] See IBA Conflict Guidelines, General Standard 3(a) which clarifies: 'If facts or circumstances exist that may, in the eyes of the parties, give rise to doubts as to the arbitrator's impartiality or independence, the arbitrator shall disclose such facts or circumstances to the parties, the arbitration institution or other appointing authority (if any, and if so required by the applicable institutional rules) and to the co-arbitrators, if any, prior to accepting his or her appointment or, if thereafter, as soon as he or she learns about them.'

[77] IBA Conflict Guidelines, General Standard 3(c) provides: 'Any doubt as to whether an arbitrator should disclose certain facts or circumstances should be resolved in favour of disclosure.'

[78] IBA Conflict Guidelines, General Standard 3(d) provides: 'When considering whether or not facts or circumstances exist that should be disclosed, the arbitrator shall not take into account whether the arbitration proceeding is at the beginning or at a later stage.'

[79] The arbitrator obviously can decline the appointment without giving any reasons, and thus, without disclosing potentially disqualifying circumstances. Schwarz and Konrad (n 40) s 7-147 (for further references).

disclosure exist.[80] Again, the national law at the seat of the arbitration may also impact on the specific disclosure requirements imposed on arbitrators.

17.141 Under Art 7, the arbitrator will make the disclosure first only to the administrator, who then forwards this information to the parties and, where applicable, to the other arbitrators. This enables the parties to consider the information and decide whether to challenge the arbitrator pursuant to Art 8.

17.142 In implementing these standards, the ICDR requires each arbitrator to complete and file a detailed Notice of Appointment before the arbitrator is confirmed in office. This Notice requires extensive disclosures, prefaced by the statement that

> [i]t is most important that the parties have complete confidence in the arbitrator's impartiality. Therefore, please disclose any past or present relationship with the parties, their counsel, or potential witnesses, direct or indirect, whether financial, professional, social or of any other kind. This is a continuing obligation throughout your service on the case and should any additional direct or indirect contact arise during the course of the arbitration or if there is any change at any time in the biographical information that you have provided to the ICDR/AAA, it must also be disclosed. Any doubts should be resolved in favour of disclosure. If you are aware of direct or indirect contact with such individuals, please describe it below. Failure to make timely disclosures may forfeit your ability to collect compensation. The ICDR will call the disclosure to the attention of the parties.

17.143 On that basis, the Notice sets forth an extensive list of questions. Each arbitrator is specifically asked to confirm whether s/he or his/her law firm presently represents any person in a proceeding involving any party to the arbitration; has represented any person against any party to the arbitration; has had 'any professional or social relationship with counsel for any party in this proceeding or the firms for which they work'; has had 'any professional or social relationship' with any parties or witnesses identified to date in this proceeding or the entities for which they work; has had any 'professional or social relationship of which you are aware with any relative of any of the parties to this proceeding, or any relative of counsel to this proceeding, or any of the witnesses identified to date in the proceeding'; whether s/he or any member of his/her family, or any close social or business associate ever served as an arbitrator in a proceeding in which any of the identified witnesses or named individual parties gave testimony; whether s/he 'or any member of his (her) family, or any close social or business associate has been involved in the last five years in a dispute involving the subject matter contained in the case, which you are assigned'; or whether s/he has 'ever served as an expert witness or consultant to any party, attorney, witness or other arbitrator identified in this case'. The Disclosure Guidelines that are appended to the Notice emphasize that the prospective arbitrator 'must disclose any relationships . . . with any party, attorney, witness or other arbitrator in this case—which includes relationships with their families and household members; current employers, partners, and professional and/or business associates'.

---

[80] See eg IBA Conflict Guidelines, General Standard 7(c) ('An arbitrator is under a duty to make reasonable enquiries to investigate any potential conflict of interest, as well as any facts or circumstances that may cause his or her impartiality or independence to be questioned. Failure to disclose a potential conflict is not excused by lack of knowledge if the arbitrator makes no reasonable attempt to investigate.').

Further, the Notice of Appointment enquires whether any of the party representatives, law firms or parties have appeared before the prospective arbitrator in past arbitration cases; whether the prospective arbitrator is a member of any organization relevant to the arbitration; whether the prospective arbitrator has ever sued or been sued by either party or its representative; whether the prospective arbitrator, or his (her) spouse, own stock in any of the companies involved in the arbitration. If there is more than one arbitrator appointed to the case, the Notice also requires disclosure of whether the prospective arbitrator has had any professional or social relationships with any of the other arbitrators. In an attached 'Arbitrator's Oath', the prospective arbitrator then discloses any relevant circumstances and otherwise attests that he has performed a 'thorough review' of these issues. **17.144**

(3) Ex parte *communications*

It is well accepted in international arbitration that there should principally be no *ex parte* communication between an arbitrator and one party:[81] what cannot be done in the open, before the eyes of all parties, should not be done at all. The only generally accepted exception regards contacts of a party with a prospective arbitrator to assess his or her qualifications and availability, and to discuss the appointment of the presiding arbitrator.[82] A discussion of the merits of the case with one party alone is not permitted.[83] If a party approaches an arbitrator in any fashion during the arbitration, the arbitrator is well advised to immediately communicate that approach to the other arbitrators and the other parties, in order to avoid any appearance of inappropriate conduct on his or her part. **17.145**

These considerations are expressly codified in Art 7(2). Under that provision, *ex parte* communications relating to the case are prohibited with any arbitrator, and expressly with 'any candidate for appointment as party-appointed arbitrator'. It is only permitted to advise a prospective arbitrator 'of the general nature of the controversy and of the anticipated proceedings' and to ascertain whether the prospective arbitrator meets any specific requirements or qualifications and is otherwise able and willing to accept the appointment. As regards the presiding arbitrator, if such a procedure has been agreed, parties are allowed to discuss with 'their' co-arbitrators suitable candidates for that position. However, Art 7(2) is very clear in prohibiting *any ex parte* contact between a party and a candidate for presiding arbitrator. **17.146**

Challenge of Arbitrators

Article 8.

1. **A party may challenge any arbitrator whenever circumstances exist that give rise to justifiable doubts as to the arbitrator's impartiality or independence. A party wishing to challenge an arbitrator shall send notice of the challenge to the administrator within 15 days after being notified of the appointment of the arbitrator or within 15 days after the circumstances giving rise to the challenge become known to that party.**
2. **The challenge shall state in writing the reasons for the challenge.**

---

[81] See IBA Rules of Ethics for International Arbitrators, item 5.3.

[82] See IBA Code of Ethics, see *also* s 17.66 *supra.*

[83] Lachmann (n 43) 218.

3. Upon receipt of such a challenge, the administrator shall notify the other parties of the challenge. When an arbitrator has been challenged by one party, the other party or parties may agree to the acceptance of the challenge and, if there is agreement, the arbitrator shall withdraw. The challenged arbitrator may also withdraw from office in the absence of such agreement. In neither case does withdrawal imply acceptance of the validity of the grounds for the challenge.

Article 9

If the other party or parties do not agree to the challenge or the challenged arbitrator does not withdraw, the administrator in its sole discretion shall make the decision on the challenge.

(1) The Challenge of an arbitrator

17.147 As discussed, Art 7 requires that '[a]rbitrators acting under these Rules shall be impartial and independent'. Article 8 provides that an arbitrator may be challenged 'whenever circumstances exist that give rise to justifiable doubts as to the arbitrator's impartiality or independence'. As also discussed, this standard is different from the standard of disclosure: an arbitrator will be removed under Art 8 if circumstances *exist* that *give* rise to justifiable doubts as to the arbitrator's impartiality or independence, whereas he or she must disclose all circumstances that are *likely to give* rise to justifiable doubts.

(2) Procedure

17.148 In order to minimize the disruption of a challenge to ongoing proceedings and to prevent parties from obstructive tactics, the parties must file a challenge no later than 15 days after having been notified by the ICDR of the appointment or after having learned of the disqualifying circumstance. A party is deemed to have waived its right to a challenge under Art 8 if it waits longer than 15 days to bring its challenge, and such a belated challenge will not be accepted by the administrator. While the position under the ICDR Rules (as under other institutional rules) is clear in this regard, national law at the seat of the arbitration may provide that certain conflicts cannot validly be waived and can therefore be advanced even if the 15-day period has expired.

17.149 A challenge must be filed with the administrator and must contain reasons. Parties would be well advised to provide detailed reasons to make their challenge persuasive, and to refrain from challenges that are unlikely to succeed.

17.150 Article 8 provides that once a challenge is received, the other party is notified. In practice, a challenge is provided to all parties and all arbitrators, including the challenged arbitrator, and all parties are afforded an opportunity to comment. While processed by the ICDR case manager, the challenge is decided by an ICDR officer of at least supervisory status.

17.151 Where a challenge is brought and the parties agree on the arbitrator's withdrawal, the arbitrator must withdraw. Article 8 also gives the challenged arbitrator the opportunity to withdraw voluntarily before the administrator proceeds to decide on the challenge. If disqualifying circumstances exist, the arbitrator is obliged to withdraw. But even where no objective reasons for disqualification exist, a challenged arbitrator may consider that his or her withdrawal in fact benefits the process, the dynamics on the tribunal, or the acceptance of a final award. To protect an arbitrator in such circumstances, Art 8 expressly provides that the voluntary withdrawal (or the withdrawal on the back of the parties' agreement) does not 'imply acceptance of the validity of the grounds for the challenge'. On the other hand, where no reasons for disqualification exist, an arbitrator may well be under the duty to continue his or her service as an arbitrator and to discharge his or her judicial function to the parties, maintaining the appointing party's right to have an arbitrator of its choosing hear the case, and avoiding the delay and disruption (in particular at advanced stages of the proceedings) that are associated with having to appoint a replacement. Since Art 10 requires the administrator to appoint a substitute arbitrator where 'the administrator determines that there are sufficient reasons to accept the resignation of an arbitrator', an arbitrator in principle has to remain in office in cases where no 'sufficient reason' for a resignation exist.

If the parties do not remove the arbitrator, or if the arbitrator does not withdraw voluntarily, the administrator 'in its sole discretion' may decide the challenge according to the standard of impartiality and independence discussed above. If the challenge is rejected, the arbitration will proceed. Of course, this does not preclude the possibility of subsequent challenges in national courts based upon lack of independence and impartiality. If the challenge is granted, the arbitrator will be replaced pursuant to Art 10. **17.152**

Replacement of an Arbitrator

Article 10

If an arbitrator withdraws after a challenge, or the administrator sustains the challenge, or the administrator determines that there are sufficient reasons to accept the resignation of an arbitrator, or an arbitrator dies, a substitute arbitrator shall be appointed pursuant to the provisions of Article 6, unless the parties otherwise agree.

Article 11

1. **If an arbitrator on a three-person tribunal fails to participate in the arbitration for reasons other than those identified in Article 10, the two other arbitrators shall have the power in their sole discretion to continue the arbitration and to make any decision, ruling or award, notwithstanding the failure of the third arbitrator to participate. In determining whether to continue the arbitration or to render any decision, ruling or award without the participation of an arbitrator, the two other arbitrators shall take into account the stage of the arbitration, the reason, if any, expressed by the third arbitrator for such non-participation and such other matters as they consider appropriate in the circumstances of the case. In the event that the two other arbitrators determine not to continue the arbitration without the participation of the third arbitrator, the administrator on proof satisfactory to it shall declare the office vacant, and a substitute arbitrator shall be appointed pursuant to the provisions of Article 6, unless the parties otherwise agree.**
2. **If a substitute arbitrator is appointed under either Article 10 or Article 11, the tribunal shall determine at its sole discretion whether all or part of any prior hearings shall be repeated.**

(1) The replacement of an arbitrator

An arbitrator may for any number of reasons be unable to serve from the beginning of the arbitration through to its final conclusion. Article 10 addresses the replacement of an arbitrator. It bears emphasis that the application of Art 10 is limited to certain, specified circumstances: (i) an arbitrator's voluntary withdrawal after a challenge pursuant to Art 8(3); (ii) an arbitrator's removal after a successful challenge under Art 9; (iii) an arbitrator's **17.153** resignation where this is accepted as justified by the administrator; and (iv) the arbitrator's death.

17.154 Only these—but no other—grounds trigger the application of Art 10, resulting in the appointment of a substitute arbitrator following the appointment procedure of Art 6 (unless the parties agree otherwise). Thus, the substitute arbitrator is in principle appointed according to the same procedure that governed the appointment of the arbitrator who is being replaced. However, the parties can agree otherwise and provide, for example, that the substitute arbitrator is appointed directly by the administrator.[84] If an arbitrator is unwilling or unable to participate in the arbitration for other reasons, the tribunal is deemed 'truncated' and Art 11 applies.

17.155 The grounds for replacement under Art 10 are self-explanatory; but the voluntary resignation of an arbitrator, as a particular feature of the ICDR Rules, deserves special mention. Under Art 8, an arbitrator is entitled to resign if he or she is challenged. However, Art 10 makes clear that the freedom to resign is conditional. In particular at advanced stages of the proceedings, in principle, arbitrators are under an obligation to discharge their judicial function to the parties, and to avoid the disruption associated with having to appoint a replacement. Article 10 therefore effectively limits an arbitrator's right to resign to cases where justifiable grounds exist. It is thus for the administrator to determine whether the resignation should be accepted. This mechanism is designed to deter obstructive arbitrators from forcing the process into the delay caused by seeking a replacement. Thus, where the resignation of an arbitrator is deemed unjustified by the administrator, no substitute arbitrator will be appointed. Rather, the rules for truncated tribunals pursuant to Art 11 will apply.

(2) The authority of a truncated tribunal to render an award

17.156 As discussed, only where an arbitrator on a three-member tribunal is removed or withdraws from office on the grounds specified in Art 10 will a substitute arbitrator be appointed. In all other cases, the two remaining arbitrators are entitled to proceed under Art 11 in what is sometimes referred to as a 'truncated' tribunal. This provision therefore ensures that the arbitration proceeds even if an arbitrator, without proper justification, fails to participate; it saves the parties the delay of a replacement process and the potentially even greater delay of having to repeat part of the proceedings under Art 11(2).[85]

17.157 Article 11 therefore entitles the two remaining arbitrators to proceed with the arbitration and to 'make any decision, ruling or award' without the third arbitrator. The two remaining arbitrators enjoy significant discretion in determining whether they want to stay the arbitration or whether they want to proceed with the case to an award. However, Art 11 specifically requires the truncated tribunal to take into account whether the arbitration has proceeded to an advanced stage—the further advanced the arbitration is, the more delay

[84] Note, for example, the different approach adopted by Art 12 of the ICC Rules, which vest the ICC Court with the power to override the originally-agreed appointment procedure and make a direct appointment if the Court deems this appropriate in the circumstances of the case.

[85] Other rules do not confer such powers on a truncated tribunal, but always provide for the replacement of the defaulting arbitrator. See eg LCIA Rules, Art 11.

without good justification may be perceived as being disruptive and as frustrating the efficient and expedient conduct of the proceedings. The arbitrators are also asked to consider the justification offered by the defaulting arbitrator who fails to participate.

When exercising their discretion and considering the circumstances of the case, the remaining arbitrators can, if they consider it appropriate, insist that they will not continue without their colleague. In that case, the administrator must ('shall') appoint a replacement arbitrator pursuant to Art 6 (unless the parties agree otherwise). However, the administrator must do so only upon receiving 'proof satisfactory to it'—suggesting that the last word in the matter is for the administrator, not for the truncated tribunal. In practice, the administrator always follows the directions of the remaining arbitrators if it is evident that the third arbitrator will no longer participate in the arbitration. **17.158**

(3) Repeating previous proceedings

Article 11(2) allows the newly constituted tribunal to consider and decide if, and if so to what extent, prior hearings should be repeated. The newly constituted tribunal can repeat prior hearings, including witness examinations and oral argument. This authority is at the sole discretion of the newly-constituted tribunal which is likely to consider, but is under no obligation to solicit, the views of the parties. **17.159**

The primary purpose of this provision is to enable the new arbitrator to have an opportunity to address and personally consider prior witness testimony and cross-examination, as opposed to simply consulting hearing transcripts and prior submissions. However, the newly-constituted tribunal may also consider the reason for the removal of the previous arbitrator. Where an arbitrator has been removed for lack of impartiality or independence, or some other misconduct, this may have tainted the previously conducted proceedings and justify their repetition. Thus, the newly-constituted tribunal will need to balance the additional time and cost incurred through repeating hearings against the tribunal's duty to respect each party's right to be heard by an impartial, independent and fully functioning tribunal and to ensure, insofar as possible, that any award it delivers is enforceable at law. **17.160**

As a textual matter, Art 11(2) enables the newly-constituted tribunal to repeat the 'prior hearings'. It does not include the broader application of some other institutional rules which authorize the newly-constituted tribunal to revisit prior 'proceedings'.[86] Open to interpretation, Art 11(2) allows the newly-constituted tribunal to reconsider and repeat all procedural acts and if and to what extent prior decisions or awards can be revisited.[87] This may depend on the effects associated with the award or decision under the applicable *lex arbitri*, although Art 11(2) could also be interpreted as a contractually agreed exception to any principle of *res judicata*.[88] **17.161**

---

[86] ICC Rules, Art 12(4) (stating that the newly constituted tribunal shall 'determine if and to what extent prior proceedings shall be repeated'); VIAC Rules, Art 18.2.

[87] Art 11(2) is based on Art 14 of the UNCITRAL Rules providing that if the sole or presiding arbitrator is replaced, any prior hearings must be repeated, but if a party-appointed arbitrator is replaced 'such prior hearings may be repeated at the discretion of the arbitral tribunal'.

[88] See *ICC Case no 6476*, (1997) 8(1) ICC Ct Bull 59.

Article 12: Representation

Any party may be represented in the arbitration. The names, addresses and telephone numbers of representatives shall be communicated in writing to the other parties and to the administrator. Once the tribunal has been established, the parties or their representatives may communicate in writing directly with the tribunal.

17.162 Although some jurisdictions have traditionally placed restrictions on who can appear on behalf of the parties in an arbitration proceeding conducted on its territory,[89] there is a clear trend in international arbitration towards allowing the parties freely to choose their legal representation as they deem appropriate, whether that be a local lawyer or foreign counsel, or someone not qualified as a lawyer at all.[90] Although national law at the seat of the arbitration may still have an impact on this issue, all major arbitration institutions allow lawyers and non-lawyers alike to represent parties in an arbitration, irrespective of their nationality or connection to a local bar.[91]

17.163 Article 12 does not provide express guidance as to who may or may not represent a party in arbitration. It does provide, however, that each party has the right to representation, and given the liberal approach underlying modern doctrine and the ICDR Rules, this provision should be interpreted to provide each party the freedom to select a representative of its choosing, whether that is a lawyer or a non-lawyer.

17.164 If a party chooses to be represented in the arbitration, it is as a matter of course required to notify the other parties and the administrator and communicate the contact details of its representative. Once those details are communicated, service on the address of the representative is valid service on the party.[92] Article 12 also clarifies that, once the tribunal is duly constituted, the parties' representatives can communicate directly with the tribunal, rather than routing communication through the administrator. In practice, parties will copy the administrator in all correspondence.

Article 13: Place of Arbitration

1. **If the parties disagree as to the place of arbitration, the administrator may initially determine the place of arbitration, subject to the power of the tribunal to determine finally the place of arbitration within 60 days after its constitution. All such determinations shall be made having regard for the contentions of the parties and the circumstances of the arbitration.**
2. **The tribunal may hold conferences or hear witnesses or inspect property or documents at any place it deems appropriate. The parties shall be given sufficient written notice to enable them to be present at any such proceedings.**

---

[89] Born (n 49) 514.

[90] Polkinghorne, M., 'More Changes in Singapore: Appearance Rights of Foreign Counsel' (2005) 22(1) *J Int'l Arb* 75; Polkinghorne, M. and Fitzgerald, D., 'Arbitration in Southeast Asia: Hong Kong, Singapore and Thailand Compared' (2001) 18(1) *J Int'l Arb* 101.

[91] Lew *et al* (n 41) para 21-73 (citing in France see Cour de Cassation, 1re Ch Civ, 19 June 1979, *SARL Primor v Société d'Exploitation Industrielle de Bétaigne* [1979] *Rev arb* 487*;* see also Rivkin, D.W., 'Restriction on Foreign Counsel in International Arbitrations' (1991) XVI *YB Comm Arb* 402. The survey identified Singapore, Turkey, Japan, Portugal and Yugoslavia as arbitration venues which did not allow for foreign legal counsels in the early 1990s. In almost all these countries the practice or law has changed.

[92] See ICDR Rules, Art 18 (discussed at ss 17.203 *et seq infra*).

(1) Importance of the place (or 'seat') of the arbitration

Parties typically agree on the 'place', 'seat' or '*situs*' of the arbitration in the arbitration agreement. This is advisable because the seat of the arbitration is not a matter of mere convenience, in terms of climate, cuisine or culture. Rather, it is one of the most important determinants of the arbitral process. Specifically, while Art 1(2) establishes that '[t]hese rules govern the arbitration', the law of the place or seat of the arbitration may provide the law applicable to the arbitration agreement and determine its validity; it may, by virtue of its mandatory procedural provisions, define the parameters of due process; it may stipulate the rights and duties of the arbitrators and the parties, including standards of impartiality and independence; it may provide for, or limit, the intervention of local courts in the arbitral process; and it may also, through its conflicts of law rules, certain mandatory provisions or its *ordre public*, influence the substantive determination of the parties' dispute. Indeed, the place of arbitration provides the law and forum for applications to set aside the award; and it plays an important role in enforcement proceedings under Art V(1)(a), (d) and (e) of the New York Convention.[93] For all these reasons, parties are well-advised to consider carefully, and then agree on, a legal seat for their arbitration. Article 13 fully respects the parties' autonomy to reach agreement on this important point. **17.165**

(2) Substitute determination of the place of arbitration

Each arbitration needs a legal seat, a place where it is hosted, with all the consequences described above. Where the parties have failed to agree on a seat, the administrator will, at the preliminary call with the parties, proceed to determine the place of the arbitration on the parties' behalf. In doing so, the administrator has to take into account 'the parties' contentions' and 'the circumstances of the arbitration'. Typically, the administrator will strive to determine a place that is perceived neutral from both parties' perspective, and detached from any links to the case. **17.166**

The administrator's determination is binding on the parties, but not on the arbitrators. Rather, the arbitrators can determine a different place within 60 days from the tribunal's constitution. This recognizes that even after such a short period of time, the arbitrators may be better placed to appreciate the circumstances of the case and determine the legal seat of the arbitration accordingly, again taking into account 'the parties' contentions' and 'the circumstances of the arbitration'. Thus, the administrator's preliminary determination of the place of arbitration is designed merely to prevent that the arbitration is without legal seat at any material point in time. The last word in the matter is reserved for the tribunal. **17.167**

(3) Location of hearings and procedural acts

The legal seat of the arbitration does not necessarily coincide with the physical location of where the proceedings are, entirely or in part, actually conducted.[94] In that sense, the seat **17.168**

[93] Redfern, A., Hunter, M., Blackaby, N. and Partasides, C., *Law and Practice of International Commercial Arbitration* (4th edn, Sweet & Maxwell, London, 2004) s 2-11 ('The vital role of the arbitral *situs* in the viability of international arbitration derives in large measure from the enforcement scheme of the New York Arbitration Convention.') See also Park, W.W., 'Judicial Controls in the Arbitral Process' (1989) 5(3) *Arb Int'l* 230, 255.

[94] Schwarz and Konrad (n 40) ss 2-010 *et seq.*

of the arbitration is a legal fiction that attaches the consequences discussed under para 17.165, *supra*, but that can be detached from the place where the arbitration is actually conducted.[95]

17.169 Article 13(2) fully recognizes this well established principle and permits individual procedural acts to be conducted in places other than the seat of arbitration. It specifically allows the tribunal to hold conferences, hear witnesses or inspect property or documents at any place that it deems appropriate. 'Holding conferences' is a deliberately broad term that effectively authorizes the tribunal to conduct a significant range of procedural acts at a different location. Unlike other rules, the ICDR Rules do not require the tribunal first to consult the parties before ordering a hearing or other procedural act at a different location. Rather, the ICDR Rules are concerned with due process and therefore require the tribunal to give sufficient notice in advance of such a hearing, in order to 'enable them to be present at any such proceedings'. The combined effect of Arts 13 and 20 is obvious: they require sufficient advance notice for any hearing.

Article 14: Language

If the parties have not agreed otherwise, the language(s) of the arbitration shall be that of the documents containing the arbitration agreement, subject to the power of the tribunal to determine otherwise based upon the contentions of the parties and the circumstances of the arbitration. The tribunal may order that any documents delivered in another language shall be accompanied by a translation into the language(s) of the arbitration.

17.170 Article 14 recognizes as binding the parties' agreement, in the arbitration clause or otherwise, on a particular language in which the arbitration shall be conducted. However, where the parties have not specified the language of the arbitration, Art 14 provides that the language of the 'documents' (typically, the underlying commercial contracts) that contain the arbitration agreement is in principle determinative of the language of the proceedings.

17.171 This is different from most other major arbitral institution's rules which leave it to the arbitrators' discretion, absent agreement by the parties, to determine the language of the arbitration, perhaps by taking into account the language of the parties' commercial contract. The solution adopted by Art 14 of providing a default language has the advantage that the language of the arbitration can be easily ascertained by the parties even before the arbitral tribunal is constituted. As a matter of practice, this is also commercially sensible. By choosing a particular language for the main contract, the parties have already indicated that they are comfortable to conduct business with each other in that language.

17.172 Article 14 also recognizes that, in the circumstances of a particular case, another language may be more appropriate, and affords the arbitrators the discretion to determine a different language in such cases. Arbitrators will typically take into account the parties' nationality, the language of their previous correspondence, the language (if known) of likely witnesses and documentary evidence (as well as attendant costs of translation) and all other considerations bearing on the fairness and efficacy of the proceedings. The arbitrators' discretion is limited only by considerations of due process, as the determination of the applicable

[95] It is therefore better to speak of the 'seat' of the arbitration, rather than the 'place' of the arbitration.

language should not impede a party's right to be heard, including by imposing prohibitive costs on a party. All of this must be assessed on a case-by-case basis.

Article 14 also permits the arbitrators to determine the '*languages*' of the arbitration, recognizing that it may be appropriate in some cases to conduct the arbitration in more than one language. It is not uncommon, for example, to require the parties to make submissions in one language (eg English) but to allow them to produce documents or witness statements in other languages without having to provide a translation. **17.173**

Under Art 14, the tribunal may determine a different language 'based upon the contentions of the parties'. This seems to suggest that the parties should be heard on the matter before the arbitrators reach a decision. Any directions on the language of the arbitration will typically be in the form of a procedural order, and should be given at the outset of the proceedings in order to permit the parties to prepare their case accordingly. **17.174**

Article 15: Pleas as to jurisdiction

1. **The tribunal shall have the power to rule on its own jurisdiction, including any objections with respect to the existence, scope or validity of the arbitration agreement.**
2. **The tribunal shall have the power to determine the existence or validity of a contract of which an arbitration clause forms a part. Such an arbitration clause shall be treated as an agreement independent of the other terms of the contract. A decision by the tribunal that the contract is null and void shall not for that reason alone render invalid the arbitration clause.**
3. **A party must object to the jurisdiction of the tribunal or to the arbitrability of a claim or counterclaim no later than the filing of the statement of defense, as provided in Article 3, to the claim or counterclaim that gives rise to the objection. The tribunal may rule on such objections as a preliminary matter or as part of the final award.**

(1) Kompetenz-Kompetenz

The arbitrators' authority to decide disputes regarding their own jurisdiction, including disputes over the existence, validity, legality and scope of the parties' arbitration agreement, is usually referred to as the arbitrator's *Kompetenz-Kompetenz* (or *competence-competence*). This principle is widely acknowledged,[96] and it is central to the arbitral process. **17.175**

Conceptually, any decision by the tribunal that no valid arbitration agreement exists would include at the same time a corollary finding that the tribunal lacked jurisdiction in the first place, precisely because the arbitration agreement—the basis for the tribunal's jurisdiction—was found not to exist. The doctrine of *competence-competence* overcomes the conceptual problems arising out of any decision by the arbitrator on his or her own jurisdiction.[97] **17.176**

---

[96] LCIA Rules, Art 23; UNCITRAL Rules, Art 21; Swiss Rules, Art 21. Note an interesting approach under s 23 Czech Court of Arbitration Rules, where '[t]he board of the Arbitration Court shall have the power to decide on issues of jurisdiction. To this end, the arbitrators, if already appointed or, otherwise, the Secretary, shall present the records of the case to the Board with a short report in each case, whenever a decision on the jurisdiction of the Arbitration Court is to be taken in view of an objection to the jurisdiction taken by a party or in view of an objection to the jurisdiction taken by a party or in view of the doubts of the Secretary or the arbitrators, or their opinion that the Arbitration Court lacks the necessary jurisdiction'.

[97] Lew *et al* (n 41) s 14-13.

It allows arbitrators to decide on all jurisdictional issues, and thus seeks to avoid the argument that jurisdictional objections have to be litigated in state courts.

17.177 Commentators note that the modern notion of *competence-competence* subjects the power of the tribunal to rule on its own jurisdiction to later court review.[98] If one adopts this approach, it would be more appropriate to replace the term of *competence-competence* by 'preliminary competence' of the arbitral tribunal to rule on its own jurisdiction.[99]

17.178 Article 15(1) expressly confirms the tribunal's power to rule on its own jurisdiction. By reference, it forms part of the parties' arbitration agreement. However, national arbitration law at the seat of the arbitration may restrict the power nonetheless, or, in most modern jurisdictions, subject the tribunal's decision to the subsequent review of the state courts.

(2) Separability

17.179 Article 15(2) recognizes specifically that 'an arbitration clause shall be treated as an agreement independent of the other terms of the contract. A decision by the tribunal that the contract is null and void shall not for that reason alone render invalid the arbitration clause'. As such, Art 15(2) is an express codification of the 'doctrine of separability' which refers to the principle that an arbitration agreement is at the outset treated as separate from the underlying contract in which it is contained, or to which it refers.

17.180 Treating the arbitration agreement as an agreement separate from the underlying contract has significant consequences. It recognizes that different substantive legal rules may be applicable to the arbitration agreement as opposed to the underlying contract. It also accepts the possibility that the arbitration agreement is valid, although the parties' underlying contract is invalid, void or illegal.

17.181 In international doctrine, the principle of separability is widely acknowledged. Article 16(1) of the UNCITRAL Model Law provides that 'an arbitration clause which forms part of the contract shall be treated as an agreement independent of the other terms of the contract', and both Art II and Art V(1)(a) of the New York Convention treat arbitration agreements as distinct agreements that, at least implicitly, exist separately from the parties' underlying contracts.[100] Article V(3) of the European Convention authorizes arbitrators to examine the 'existence or the validity of the arbitration agreement *or* of the contract of which the agreement forms part', and Art VI(2) of the European Convention provides for specific choice-of-law rules for arbitration agreements.

[98] Born (n 49) 6. See also Schwab, K.H. and Walter, G. (eds), *Schiedsgerichtsbarkeit* (7th edn, C.H. Beck, Munich, 2005) ch 6, ss 9 *et seq.*

[99] Recently confirmed by the German *Bundesgerichtshof,* 13 January 2005, III ZR 265/03, (2005) *Neue Juristische Wochenschrift* 1125 ('the parties will no longer be authorized to exclude the competence of the German courts' and that 'the arbitrator's decision on his competence is always provisional'). See Berger, K.P., 'The New German Arbitration Law in International Perspective' (2000) 26 *Forum Int'l* 1, 9; Böckstiegel, K.-H., 'An Introduction to the New German Arbitration Act Based on the UNCITRAL Model Law' (1998) 14(1) *Arb Int'l* 19, 25. See also Kröll, S., 'Recourse Against Negative Decisions on Jurisdiction' (2004) 20(1) *Arb Int'l* 55; Lachmann, J.P., *Handbuch für die Schiedsgerichtspraxis* (3rd edn, Verlag Dr Otto Schmidt, Cologne, 2008) 187 *et seq.*

[100] Born (n 49) ch 3.

Properly analysed, the separability issue is a conceptual instrument to examine the parties' consent to arbitrate where (or rather, *even* where) the validity of their main contractual relationship is in doubt. In other words, assuming that the main contract between the parties is invalid, or void, would the parties prefer to have the dispute about this issue be decided in arbitration, or before state courts? In international commerce, it is justified to assume that parties would have intended to resolve all of their disputes through arbitration, rather then submitting certain disputes, such as disputes about the validity of the main contract, to the state courts. Thus, commercial parties should be presumed to intend that an arbitration agreement remains valid and binding even though the underlying contract is claimed (or subsequently found) to be invalid, void, illegal, or that it has been terminated.[101] By contrast, denying the presumption of separability would invite obstructive parties to avoid arbitration simply by declaring that the main contract, which contains the arbitration clause, is void. The risk to then have to litigate the validity of the underlying contract not in arbitration, but in a potentially inhospitable state court forum, with attendant risks of delay and partisan decisions, is unwieldy in the context of international trade. Article 15(2) confirms and reinforces that assumption by making it an express part, by reference, of the parties' arbitration agreement. **17.182**

At the same time, it is inaccurate to describe the arbitration clause as entirely 'autonomous' or 'independent' from the parties' underlying contract. The separability doctrine, and Art 15(2), have their natural limits. The parties' lack of consent to enter into an agreement can extend to the arbitration clause contained therein. In these cases, the separability doctrine cannot cure the lack of consent of the parties.[102] The separability doctrine can therefore not provide any basis for the arbitrators' jurisdiction where the main contract is non-existent for lack of consent.[103] **17.183**

[101] See UK Department of Trade and Industry Consultation Document on Proposed Clauses and Schedules for an Arbitration Bill, reprinted in (1994) 10(2) *Arb Int'l* 189, 227 ('Whatever degree of legal fiction underlying the doctrine, it is not generally considered possible for international arbitration to operate effectively in jurisdictions where the doctrine is precluded (. . .) [I]nternational consensus on autonomy has now grown very broad.'). See also Mayer, P., 'The Limits of Severability of the Arbitration Clause' (1999) 9 ICCA Congress Series (Paris) 260, 262. Similarly, a choice-of-law clause is not affected by the cancellation of an invalid agreement because one of its purposes is to specify which law, court or arbitrator should apply in deciding whether the contract is null and void. In the same way, an arbitration clause must be complied with if it reflects the parties' intent to have an arbitrator decide whether the agreement is valid, or null and void.')

[102] In the words of *Mayer*, '[t]he scenario in which an arbitration clause most clearly would not be severed, and hence would be invalid, is where the assent of one of the Parties is lacking. If the person to whom the offer is made does not accept it, then no contract has been formed, and the arbitration clause contained in the offer has not been agreed to any more than any of the other clauses, for there was no specific mutual agreement with respect to that clause' Mayer, P. (*ibid*) 260, 263. 264; Schlosser, P., 'Der Grad der Unabhängigkeit einer Schiedsvereinbarung vom Hauptvertrag' in R. Briner *et al* (eds), *Law of International Business and Dispute Settlement in the 21st Century in Liber Amicorum K.-H. Böckstiegel* (Carl Heymanns Verlag, Cologne, 2001) 704, 706.

[103] Sanders, P., 'L'autonomie de la clause compromissoire' in *Hommage à Frédéric Eisemann, Une initiative de la Chambre de Commerce Internationale, Liber Amicorum* (Paris, ICC, 1978) 31, 33; Jolidon, P., *Commentaire au Concordat Suisse sur l'Arbitrage* (Stämpfli Verlag, Bern, 1984) 139; Schlosser, P., *Das Recht der internationalen privaten Schiedsgerichtsbarkeit* (2nd edn, Mohr Siebeck, Tübingen, 1989) s 393.

(3) Timely objection

17.184 No party can be forced into arbitration without its consent. At the same time, jurisdictional objections are also raised to delay and obstruct the enforcement of the claimant's rights. In any case, it is vital to ascertain the arbitrators' jurisdiction as early as possible, and to prevent dilatory tactics by the parties. In line with all major rules and modern arbitration laws, Art 15(3) therefore provides that a party must object to the jurisdiction of the tribunal (or to the arbitrability of a claim) with its statement of defence under Art 3. Failing such a timely objection, subject to applicable arbitration law, the jurisdictional objection is deemed as having been waived.

17.185 The tribunal may make a decision as 'a preliminary matter or as part of the final award'. Often, it is preferable for reasons of legal certainty and efficiency to address jurisdictional objections at the outset of the arbitration. In some cases, however, the issue of jurisdiction is closely intertwined with the merits of the case; for such cases, the tribunal retains the discretion to address the issue of jurisdiction together with its final determination of the merits.

Article 16: Conduct of the Arbitration

1. **Subject to these Rules, the tribunal may conduct the arbitration in whatever manner it considers appropriate, provided that the parties are treated with equality and that each party has the right to be heard and is given a fair opportunity to present its case.**
2. **The tribunal, exercising its discretion, shall conduct the proceedings with a view to expediting the resolution of the dispute. It may conduct a preparatory conference with the parties for the purpose of organizing, scheduling and agreeing to procedures to expedite the subsequent proceedings.**
3. **The tribunal may in its discretion direct the order of proof, bifurcate proceedings, exclude cumulative or irrelevant testimony or other evidence and direct the parties to focus their presentations on issues the decision of which could dispose of all or part of the case.**
4. **Documents or information supplied to the tribunal by one party shall at the same time be communicated by that party to the other party or parties.**

(1) The tribunal's discretion

17.186 Under Art 16(1), the arbitrators enjoy free discretion to conduct the arbitration as they deem appropriate. However, there are several limitations to that discretion. First, as Art 16(1) expressly provides, the arbitrators' discretion is 'subject to these Rules'. Hence, the arbitrators can only exercise their procedural discretion within the framework of the ICDR Rules.

17.187 Second, the arbitrators' discretion is also limited by the applicable mandatory law at the seat of the arbitration.[104] Third, although Art 16 does not expressly address this issue, the arbitrators' discretion is typically thought to be limited, at least in most respects by the parties' agreement.[105] For example, the European Convention provides in Art IV(1)(b)(iii)

[104] Schwarz and Konrad (n 40) s 20-099; see also ICDR Rules, Art 1(2) (discussed at ss 17.54 *et seq supra*).

[105] The 1923 Geneva Protocol required in its Art 2 that 'the arbitral procedure, including the constitution of the arbitral tribunal, shall be governed by the will of the parties and by the law of the country in whose

that parties shall be free 'to lay down the procedure to be followed by the arbitrators',[106] and Art V(1)(d) of the New York Convention permits a state to refuse the recognition or enforcement of an award on the basis that 'the arbitral procedure was not in accordance with the agreement of the parties'.[107] This view also does most justice to the consensual nature of arbitration, which unlike any state court procedure, cannot be imposed on one of the parties. Indeed, parties choose arbitration specifically because they enjoy the freedom to agree upon a procedure that is flexible and efficient and customized to fit their individual case,[108] and that avoids the formalities of state court litigation.[109] Thus, the parties' express agreement on procedural issues can only be disregarded if it were to force the arbitrators to violate applicable law or fundamental principles of due process.

(2) Due process

The notion of due process and fair trial is an accepted and fundamental feature acknowledged in all major jurisdictions and international instruments.[110] The equal and fair treatment of the parties,[111] as recognized in Art 16(1) is an important part of due process, together with the right to be heard, which means that each party must receive a fair opportunity to present its case.[112] Together, these essential values have been said to represent 'foundation pillars of any judicial procedure'.[113] In most countries, a violation of these principles may lead to the setting aside of the award. **17.188**

Equal treatment, however, must not be understood formalistically. Equality, as a function of procedural fairness, cannot be reduced to a mathematical formula, does not necessarily mean identical treatment and is informed by the circumstances of the case. Equally, the right to be heard is not unlimited.[114] It bears emphasis that the parties must only be afforded **17.189**

---

territory the arbitration takes place'. As discussed above, this provision was understood as requiring compliance with the procedural law of the arbitral seat.

[106] European Convention, Art IV(1)(b)(iii). As discussed below, Art IV(4)(d) also provides that, where the parties have not agreed upon the arbitral procedure, the arbitral tribunal shall determine the arbitral rules. Like Art V(1)(d) of the New York Convention, Art IX(1)(d) of the European Convention provides for the non-recognition of arbitral awards if the procedure followed by the tribunal departed from that agreed by the parties. See Hascher, D.T., 'European Convention on International Arbitration (1961)' (1995) XX *YB Comm Arb* 1,006, 1,017 *et seq*; Gaillard and Savage (n 19) ss 759, 1,184; Bouchez, L.J., 'The Prospects for International Arbitration: Disputes Between States and Private Enterprises' (1991) 8(1) *J Int'l Arb* 81, 96.

[107] New York Convention, Art V(1)(d).

[108] Crawford, J., 'Advocacy Before the International Court of Justice and Other International Tribunals in State-to-State Cases' in R.D. Bishop (ed), *The Art of Advocacy in International Arbitration* (Juris Publishing, Huntington, 2004) 11 *et seq* (describing historic use of 'combination of full written and oral phases').

[109] Petrochilos, G., *Procedural Law in International Arbitration* (OUP, Oxford, 2004) 84; R Pietrowski, 'Evidence in International Arbitration' (2006) 22(3) *Arb Int'l* 373, 374.

[110] For an overview of the issue, see Schwarz, F.T. and Ortner, H., 'Procedural Ordre Public and the Internationalization of Public Policy in Arbitration' in C. Klausegger *et al* (eds), *Austrian Arbitration Yearbook 2008* (Manz, Vienna, 2008).

[111] Lew *et al* (n 41)) s 25-36.

[112] Berger, K.P., *International Economic Arbitration* (Kluwer Law International, Boston, 1993) 663; Lew *et al* (n 41) s 25-36 ('minimum standards').

[113] Reiner, A., 'Schiedsverfahren und rechtliches Gehör' [2003] *Zeitschrift für Europarecht, Internationales Privatrecht und Rechtsvergleichung* 52 *et seq.*

[114] Paulsson, J., 'The Timely Arbitrator: Reflections on the Böckstiegel Method' in R. Briner *et al* (eds), *Law of International Business and Dispute Settlement in the 21st Century, Liber Amicorum K.-H. Böckstiegel* (Carl Heymanns Verlag, Cologne, 2001) 608.

a 'fair' opportunity; the arbitrators are not required to wait until a party actually avails itself of the right to be heard. Thus, a party who simply disregards the opportunities given to it by the tribunal to present its case, can later not complain that its right to be heard has been violated.[115] Similarly, a party is entitled to a fair opportunity to present its case, but is not entitled to an endless procession of written submissions or oral argument. For this reason, the tribunal is entitled to limit the parties' written submissions, and the offering of evidence, to what is appropriate, as long as the parties are put on advance notice of any cut-off date or comparable mechanism.

(3) Duty of expedition

17.190 Article 16(2) serves as a reminder to the arbitrator to conduct the arbitration expeditiously. Of course, speed must not be confused with haste; and each party must be given a fair opportunity to present its case.

17.191 As an encouragement for expeditious and proper organization, Art 16(2) also suggests that a preparatory conference may be held to discuss the precise conduct of the arbitration. Indeed, the arbitral process is more flexible than highly-regulated proceedings before state courts, but by the same token requires a higher degree of organization from the parties and the arbitrators. This is usually done through a preliminary (or 'preparatory' or 'case management') hearing.

17.192 Skilled arbitrators will use the preparatory conference to establish the ground rules that govern the proceeding at the very outset of the arbitration. If properly done, the preliminary hearing will ensure that both parties know how and when exactly they are expected to present their case—which is particularly important when the parties come from different legal traditions with different expectations. Most arbitrators therefore insist on such an early meeting to discuss the organization of the proceedings,[116] in person, or remotely (over the telephone, or through videolink), often following the UNCITRAL Notes.[117] In the practice of the ICDR, arbitrators are provided a Preliminary Hearing and Scheduling Order which invites discussion with the parties of essential elements of the case, such as deadlines for any amendments to the claims or counterclaims; a stipulation of uncontested facts by a certain date; an early notification of witnesses which a party intends to proffer; the exchange of information and documentary evidence by a certain date; and the date of the hearing.[118]

(4) Evidence

17.193 Article 16(3) reinforces the arbitrators' broad discretion in establishing the facts and taking evidence as they deem appropriate. By way of example, but in no way limiting the general

---

115 Schwarz and Konrad (n 40) s 20-076.

116 Redfern *et al* (n 93) ss 6-27 *et seq* (discussion of preliminary meetings and their role and importance). See also Report of the Secretary-General on the Revised Draft Set of Arbitration Rules, UNCITRAL, 9th Session, Add 1 (Commentary), UN Doc A/CN.9/112/Add 1 (1975), (1976) VII UNCITRAL YB 166, 175 (Art 25(3) of the UNCITRAL Rules 'deals with certain preparatory measures for hearings that the arbitrators must take in order to ensure that the hearings run smoothly').

117 See also as for international instruments, the '1996 UNCITRAL Notes on Organizing Arbitral Proceedings' ('UNCITRAL Notes').

118 See s 17.71 *supra*.

discretion conferred on the arbitrators by virtue of Art 16(1), this provision addresses the tribunal's authority with respect to several important elements of the arbitral procedure.

First, the tribunal may in its discretion direct the order of proof. Thus, the tribunal is entitled, on its own accord and without application from the parties, to request the parties to offer certain evidence that the tribunal considers relevant for the case. Included in that authority is of course the power to order such production of documents by way of disclosure as the tribunal deems appropriate, either upon a party's request or its own volition.[119] **17.194**

Second, the tribunal may bifurcate proceedings, where it deems that segmenting the arbitration into different phases would make the proceedings more expeditious. For example, proceedings can often be bifurcated into a jurisdictional phase and a phase on the merits; or in a phase on liability and a phase on quantum. In addition, the tribunal may direct the parties to 'focus their presentations on issues the decision of which could dispose of all or part of the case'. Similar to the rationale underlying the bifurcation of the proceedings, it may not make sense to hear the entire case if the claim stands or falls on jurisdiction, time bar, or other dispositive preliminary issues that can be heard separately without wasting the resources associated with hearing the entire case. **17.195**

Finally, the tribunal can also 'exclude cumulative or irrelevant testimony or other evidence'. As Art 16(3) confirms, emphasizing once more the arbitrators' duty to conduct the arbitration expeditiously, a party is not entitled, in the guise of its right to be heard, to make factual assertions or produce evidence that is irrelevant or immaterial to the dispute at bar.[120] Thus, the right to be heard is not violated if the arbitrators, either *ex officio* or upon the request of a party, exclude or dismiss factual allegations or evidence that fail to make a material contribution to the resolution of the case. **17.196**

Again, these powers are listed in Art 16(3) only by way of example. Beyond those powers, the tribunal enjoys broad discretion under Art 16(1) to conduct the proceedings as appropriate in the individual circumstances of the case.[121] **17.197**

Article 17: Further Written Statements

1. **The tribunal may decide whether the parties shall present any written statements in addition to statements of claims and counterclaims and statements of defense, and it shall fix the periods of time for submitting any such statements.**
2. **The periods of time fixed by the tribunal for the communication of such written statements should not exceed 45 days. However, the tribunal may extend such time limits if it considers such an extension justified.**

---

[119] See also ICDR Rules, Art 19 (for a discussion of the ICDR Guidelines for Arbitrators Concerning Exchanges of Information) (discussed at ss 17.208 *et seq infra*).

[120] See also Art 9(2) of the IBA Rules ('The Arbitral Tribunal shall, *at the request of a Party or on its own motion*, exclude from evidence or production any document, statement, oral testimony or inspection for any of the following reasons: (a) lack of sufficient relevance or materiality . . .') (emphasis added).

[121] In one of the reported ICDR awards, ICDR 4-2004, the tribunal admitted the witness statements of witnesses even though those witnesses did not appear at the hearing. However, the tribunal afforded those written statements decreased probative value because neither the tribunal nor the other side had the opportunity to examine the witnesses orally.

(1) Additional written statements

17.198 There is a clear trend in current arbitration practice to focus heavily on written materials, in order to avoid the costs and inefficiencies of having to bring the parties, witnesses, experts, and their lawyers, often all from different countries, together for a lengthy meeting in person. Written submissions are therefore of central importance in international arbitration.[122]

17.199 Article 17 assumes that normally, the parties will only file a statement of claims and counterclaims and a statement of defence. The tribunal has to approve the filing of additional submissions, re-emphasizing the rationale of Art 16(2) to ensure streamlined proceedings.

17.200 In practice, in particular in larger cases, the parties will normally file further written submissions with the tribunal.[123] This can be efficient as well if these submissions properly prepare the case to the fullest extent, and thus reduce the need for, and ultimately the length of, any oral hearing. Such written submissions will typically contain a detailed description of the factual allegations and will elaborate in detail on the applicable substantive law.

17.201 Sometimes, written briefs are not submitted consecutively, but simultaneously by both parties. This is often done to expedite the arbitration, but exchanging the parties' written briefs on the same day means that neither party can properly respond to the other side's case.[124] Sequential pre-hearing written filings are almost invariably preferable, with the claimant making the first submission.[125] Instead of, or in addition to, oral closing arguments, written submissions are often also submitted after the hearing (so-called 'post-hearing briefs'). These present the parties with the opportunity to summarize their case and apply the facts, as established in their view by the evidence taken throughout the arbitration and specifically at the oral hearing, to the law.[126]

---

[122] Caron, D., Caplan, L. and Pellonpää, M., *The UNCITRAL Arbitration Rules: A Commentary* (OUP, Oxford, 2006) 392 ('In an overwhelming majority of cases, the arbitral procedure begins with an exchange of written submissions. Written pleadings are often given primary emphasis throughout the proceedings, with a short oral hearing or no hearing at all.'); Crawford, J., 'Advocacy Before the International Court of Justice and Other International Tribunals in State-to-State Cases' in R.D. Bishop (ed), *The Art of Advocacy in International Arbitration*, (Juris Publishing, Huntington, 2004) 11, 28.

[123] See the Report of the Secretary-General on the Revised Draft Set of Arbitration Rules, UNCITRAL, 9th Session, Add 1 (Commentary), UN Doc A/CN.9/112/Add. 1 (1975), (1976) VII UNCITRAL YB 166, 173 (1976) (under Article 19(2), the respondent's defence is 'without prejudice to his right to present additional or substitute documents at a later stage in the arbitral proceeding'); Caron *et al* (n 122) 498 ('In most international arbitrations, further written submissions are likely to be useful, unless the case is disposed of on jurisdictional or other preliminary grounds. Provision should therefore usually be made for a second round of written pleadings, consisting of a reply (replique) by the claimant to the Statement of Defense (and any counterclaim) and a rejoinder (duplique) to this by the respondent.'); Wilberforce, W., 'Written Briefs and Oral Advocacy' (1989) 5(4) *Arb Int'l* 348.

[124] Mani, V., *International Adjudication: Procedural Aspects* (Martinus Nijhoff Publishers, The Hague, 1980) 107 (stating that 'where the plaintiff-defendant relationship is discernible simultaneous presentation is illogical in that it requires the defendant to produce a complete defence without knowing fully in advance of the arguments of the claimant').

[125] In some arbitrations, a mixed approach is adopted. Even where pre-hearing memorials are submitted in an alternating order by the claimant and the respondent, respectively, post-hearing briefs will be submitted by both parties on the same day.

[126] In large arbitrations, the arbitrators increasingly require parties to file very comprehensive post-hearing briefs, which then become the central point of reference (containing all facts, evidentiary conclusions, and legal arguments) for the arbitrators' deliberations.

(2) Time limits

Article 17(2) provides for a time limit of 45 days for additional written submissions. Again, those default time limits are ambitious and designed to expedite the proceedings. In many cases, they may be fully appropriate. However, in large arbitrations, written submissions can require several months to prepare, will be hundreds of pages long (not including exhibits, which will entail thousands of additional pages or more) and will be very comprehensive, detailed documents. The tribunal has the discretion, in such cases or if otherwise appropriate, to provide for a more extended timetable. **17.202**

Article 18: Notices

1. **Unless otherwise agreed by the parties or ordered by the tribunal, all notices, statements and written communications may be served on a party by air mail, air courier, facsimile transmission, telex, telegram or other written forms of electronic communication addressed to the party or its representative at its last known address or by personal service.**
2. **For the purpose of calculating a period of time under these Rules, such period shall begin to run on the day following the day when a notice, statement or written communication is received. If the last day of such period is an official holiday at the place received, the period is extended until the first business day which follows. Official holidays occurring during the running of the period of time are included in calculating the period.**

(1) Method of communication

Article 18 allows for a wide range of methods to communicate written submissions and correspondence to the other side. It is preferable to use a method that provides a record of transmission, in order to avoid disputes about whether the submission was properly sent, either at all or in time. Tribunals will therefore often order specific methods of delivery in their first procedural order. **17.203**

Communications can be validly served both on the party or on the party representative, if such a representative has been communicated pursuant to Art 12. Often, tribunals will order at the outset that communications are only served on the parties' legal representatives. In any case, service must be effected either 'at [the] last known address' (protecting the parties from sudden undisclosed changes of address) or 'by personal service' (requiring hand delivery and thus minimizing any likely dispute about whether and when it is received). **17.204**

(2) Calculating time periods

Time periods start to run on the day after a submission is received. If the last day of a period falls on a holiday—importantly, at the place where the submission is received—the period is extended to the next business day. **17.205**

Article 19: Evidence

1. **Each party shall have the burden of proving the facts relied on to support its claim or defense.**
2. **The tribunal may order a party to deliver to the tribunal and to the other parties a summary of the documents and other evidence which that party intends to present in support of its claim, counterclaim or defense.**
3. **At any time during the proceedings, the tribunal may order parties to produce other documents, exhibits or other evidence it deems necessary or appropriate.**

(1) Burden of proof

17.206 Article 19(1) requires each party to carry the burden of proving the facts on which it relies in support of its claim or defence. As a procedural rule, this provision is incorporated by reference into the parties' arbitration agreement. However, the burden of proof is not a purely procedural issue under some laws. Indeed, the substantive law in many civil law jurisdictions contains specific and sometimes elaborate rules about the burden of proof, and how the burden of proof is reversed as a result of substantive law considerations. The relationship between Art 19 and such substantive rules is open to interpretation.

(2) Exchange of information and document production

17.207 As discussed in the context of Art 16, the tribunal may in its discretion direct the order of proof.[127] Article 19 reinforces in express terms that the tribunal is entitled to request the parties to offer specific evidence and to order the production of documents by way of disclosure. The tribunal is entitled to order the production of evidence either upon a party's request or of its own volition where deemed appropriate in the circumstances of the case. The tribunal will in all instances be guided by the relevance of the evidence for the issues in dispute.

17.208 In that regard, the ICDR has recently introduced Guidelines for Arbitrators Concerning Exchanges of Information,[128] aimed at ensuring that document production processes adopted in arbitration do not detract from the arbitrator's duty to ensure that arbitration remains 'a simpler, less expensive, and more expeditious process' than litigation in state courts. Whilst recognizing that each party must have a fair opportunity to present its case, the Guidelines therefore direct the tribunal to 'manage the exchange of information among the parties in advance of the hearing with a view to maintaining efficiency and economy'.[129] Under the Guidelines, each party is required to produce prior to the hearing all documents on which it intends to rely. The tribunal is authorized to order the production of documents in the possession[130] of the other party if these documents are described with specificity and shown to be relevant and material to the outcome of the case.

17.209 On the somewhat controversial subject[131] of the production of 'electronic documents',[132] the Guidelines do not treat such documents any differently,[133] and apply the same concept

---

[127] See ss 17.186 *et seq supra*.

[128] The ICDR Guidelines state that '[u]nless the parties agree otherwise in writing, these guidelines will become effective in all international cases administered by the ICDR commenced after May 31, 2008, and may be adopted at the discretion of the tribunal in pending cases'. See generally Beechey, J., 'The ICDR Guidelines for Information Exchanges in International Arbitration: An Important Addition to the Arbitral Toolkit' (2008) *Disp Res J* 84.

[129] ICDR Guidelines, at 1.a.

[130] This seems to be a narrower standard than the possession, custody and control of Art 3.3 of the IBA Rules on the Taking of Evidence in International Commercial Arbitration. See Gusy and Illmer (n 13).

[131] See Howell, J., 'Electronic Disclosure in International Arbitration', (Juris Publishing, Huntington, 2008); Shore, L., 'Three Evidentiary Problems in International Arbitration' [2004] *SchiedsVZ* 76.

[132] Some authors stress that the reference to electronic 'documents' limits the tribunal's authority to order the production of other electronic data, such as metadata or recovered deleted data. See Gusy and Illmer (n 13) 200. In practice, the Guidelines should not be read to impose an inflexible standard, referring generally to the exchange of information. A party may therefore be able to request the production of electronic data more generally if it can identify that data with specificity; show that its production would be relevant and material to the outcome of the case; and show that the production is justifiable in light of the overarching goals of expediency and cost efficiency.

[133] Electronic documents can be produced in paper form, or in any other form that allows for the most convenient and cost-effective production in the circumstances.

of specificity, relevance and materiality. The Guidelines merely state in addition that 'requests for documents in electronic form should be narrowly focused and structured to make searching for them as economical as possible'.[134] The Guidelines avoid terminology such as 'disclosure' or 'discovery' and instead emphasize that US civil litigation procedures are in principle not appropriate for obtaining information in international arbitration.[135]

The Guidelines also recognize that defences of confidentiality and privilege may be raised against a request for document production. Recognizing the reality in international arbitration that parties and their counsel may be subject to different ethical or professional rules with respect to the documents concerned, the Guidelines direct the Tribunal 'to the extent possible [to] apply the same rule to both sides, giving preference to the rule that provides the highest level of protection'.[136] This approach of a 'most favourable regime' appears quite sensible in international cases involving different legal traditions. **17.210**

Article 20: Hearings

1. **The tribunal shall give the parties at least 30 days advance notice of the date, time and place of the initial oral hearing. The tribunal shall give reasonable notice of subsequent hearings.**
2. **At least 15 days before the hearings, each party shall give the tribunal and the other parties the names and addresses of any witnesses it intends to present, the subject of their testimony and the languages in which such witnesses will give their testimony.**
3. **At the request of the tribunal or pursuant to mutual agreement of the parties, the administrator shall make arrangements for the interpretation of oral testimony or for a record of the hearing.**
4. **Hearings are private unless the parties agree otherwise or the law provides to the contrary. The tribunal may require any witness or witnesses to retire during the testimony of other witnesses. The tribunal may determine the manner in which witnesses are examined.**
5. **Evidence of witnesses may also be presented in the form of written statements signed by them.**
6. **The tribunal shall determine the admissibility, relevance, materiality and weight of the evidence offered by any party. The tribunal shall take into account applicable principles of legal privilege, such as those involving the confidentiality of communications between a lawyer and client.**

(1) Introduction

Article 20 sets out basic procedural rules for the arbitral hearing, including general logistics, notice requirements, witness procedure and grants the tribunal a broad discretion on evidentiary issues. The scope of the article matches that of Art 25 of the UNCITRAL Rules. By comparison, ICC Rules, Art 21 is less detailed and not nearly as prescriptive. No specific deadlines or logistics are laid out and the tribunal is given a general power to be in 'full charge of the hearings.' Similarly, LCIA Rules, Art 19 grants the tribunal a general power of 'fullest authority' to address logistics. **17.211**

134 ICDR Guidelines, at 4.
135 *ibid* at Introduction and at 6.b.
136 *ibid* at 4.

(2) Logistics for hearing (Article 20(1) and (2))

17.212 Paragraphs (1) and (2) of Art 20 provide minimum notice periods for advising of the time and place of the initial oral hearing and of the identity and scope of witness testimony. Beyond these minimum notice rules, the tribunal is given a broad discretion to determine the rules to be applied to a hearing. Consistent with international arbitration practice, the tribunal may well decide to adopt or be guided by internationally accepted rules such as the IBA Rules on the Taking of Evidence in International Commercial Arbitration[137] or the UNCITRAL Notes on Organizing Arbitral Proceedings.[138]

17.213 The general reference in Art 20(1) to giving notice of an 'initial oral hearing', does not explicitly require that there be an oral hearing on the merits or give the parties the power to insist on such a hearing.[139] Article 20(2) of the ICC Rules, in contrast, provides that the tribunal 'shall hear the parties together in person if any of them so requests'.[140] In any event, international commercial arbitration practice suggests that it is typical in most cases for at least some form of hearing to be held.[141]

(3) Witness testimony (Article 20(3)–(5))

17.214 Article 20(3) anticipates that oral evidence in a language other than that of the arbitration shall be interpreted if necessary and, further, that a transcript may be made available of the hearing in its entirety. The provision assigns these duties to the ICDR case administrator, although by agreement the tribunal or the parties may take on these logistical duties. Article 20(4) makes clear that, unless otherwise agreed by the parties or provided by law, the hearing is to be 'private,' ie with access restricted to only those authorized by the tribunal. This is not to be confused with the Art 34 provision relating to confidentiality.[142] Article 20(4) also grants the tribunal a broad discretion to determine the manner in which witnesses are to be examined and explicitly permits ordering that witnesses be excluded from the hearing room pending their testimony. Consistent with common practice, Art 20(5) provides that signed statements by the witnesses may serve as a substitute for live testimony.

(4) Evidence and privilege issues (Article 20(6))

17.215 Last, Art 20(6) empowers the tribunal to rule on evidentiary questions. Uniquely, it also explicitly mandates that the tribunal is to take into account applicable principles of legal privilege when making such determinations.[143] The explicit reference to privilege issues mirrors that found in other rules associated with the AAA.[144] In addition, unless otherwise

---

[137] IBA Rules on the Taking of Evidence in International Commercial Arbitration, International Bar Association (adopted 1 June 1999).

[138] UNCITRAL Notes on Organizing Arbitral Proceedings (finalized 14 June 1996).

[139] See also ICDR Rules, Art 16(1) (each party has the right to be heard and to be given a fair opportunity to present its case).

[140] See also the similar provision in LCIA Rules, Art 19.1.

[141] See Redfern *et al* (n 93) s 6-104 (2004).

[142] See ICDR Rules, Art 34 (discussed at ss 17.278 *et seq infra*).

[143] See generally Sheppard, A. and von Schlabrendorff, F., 'Legal Privilege and Confidentiality in Arbitration,' in M. Koehnen, M. Russenberger and E. Cowling, *Privilege and Confidentiality: An International Handbook* (International Bar Association, London, 2006) 377.

[144] See eg Commercial Arbitration Rules, Art 31(c).

agreed, the ICDR Guidelines for Arbitrators Concerning Exchanges of Information apply to all arbitrations since 31 May 2008. Guideline 7 provides that:

> The tribunal should respect applicable rules of privilege or professional ethics and other legal impediments. When the parties, their counsel or their documents would be subject under applicable law to different rules, the tribunal should to the extent possible apply the same rules to both sides, giving preference to the rule that provides the highest level of protection.

The default rule of providing, to the extent possible, equal treatment to both parties and a preference for the highest level of protection, is consistent with the international practice recommended by leading arbitrators.[145] **17.216**

Article 21: Interim Measures of Protection

1. **At the request of any party, the tribunal may take whatever interim measures it deems necessary, including injunctive relief and measures for the protection or conservation of property.**
2. **Such interim measures may take the form of an interim award, and the tribunal may require security for the costs of such measures.**
3. **A request for interim measures addressed by a party to a judicial authority shall not be deemed incompatible with the agreement to arbitrate or a waiver of the right to arbitrate.**
4. **The tribunal may in its discretion apportion costs associated with applications for interim relief in any interim award or in the final award.**

(1) Introduction

Article 21 empowers the tribunal to order whatever interim measures 'it deems necessary', including but not limited to injunctive relief and measures necessary for the protection of property. The measures may, for example, be intended to preserve evidence for use in the case, prevent property from being interfered with or, more generally, to preserve the status quo pending determination of the dispute.[146] The Article is generally similar to its equivalent provisions in Arts 23, 25 and 26 of the ICC, LCIA and UNCITRAL Rules, respectively, each of which grants fairly broad powers to the tribunal to make interim measures of protection. **17.217**

(2) Broad discretion vested in tribunal (Article 21(1))

The model for Art 21 is Art 26 of the UNCITRAL Rules. However, Art 26 contains some potential limitations on the tribunal's powers, most importantly in that the interim measures must apply to the 'subject matter of the dispute'.[147] To overcome this, Art 21(1) of the ICDR Rules was amended with effect from September 2000 to encompass a broader formulation. Thus, commentators suggest, for example, that the amended Art 21(1) **17.218**

[145] See, eg de Boisséson, M., 'Evidentiary Privileges in International Arbitration,' in J. van den Berg (ed), *International Arbitration 2006: Back to Basics? (ICCA International Arbitration Congress)* (2007) 705.

[146] See, eg *Nordell Int'l Resources Ltd v Triton Indonesia Inc*, Civ no 92-55058, 1993 WL 280169 (9th Cir. 1993) (citing r 34 of the AAA Commercial Rules, permitting 'such orders as may be necessary to safeguard the property which is the subject matter of the arbitration without prejudice to the rights of the parties or to the final determination of the dispute', as empowering the tribunal to make an interim order requiring the parties to continue to perform the agreement pending conclusion of the arbitration).

[147] See Caron *et al* (n 122) 534-9 (discussing UNCITRAL Rules, Art 26.1).

empowers the tribunal to order security for costs.[148] Article 21(1) still retains the requirement that any such interim measures be 'necessary' rather than merely 'appropriate', as provided in the equivalent article of the ICC Rules.[149]

(3) Interim measures may be in form of interim award (Article 21(2))

17.219 Article 21(2) indicates that the measures may be in the form of an interim award so as to encourage enforcement in those jurisdictions in which a mere 'order' may not be enforceable under the New York Convention or local law.[150] The tribunal may also order security for costs related to the measures.

(4) Interim measures may be requested from court and costs (Article 21(3) and (4))

17.220 The ability for parties to request interim measures from competent courts without waiving their rights to arbitrate is also enshrined in the UNCITRAL Model Law[151] and in the arbitration laws of many jurisdictions.[152] As this is a fairly recent development in some jurisdictions,[153] Art 21 may be important evidence to convince a court that interim relief from courts is not inconsistent with the parties' arbitration agreement.[154] Article 37(8) contains the analogue provision in case of requests for emergency relief.

Article 22: Experts

1. **The tribunal may appoint one or more independent experts to report to it, in writing, on specific issues designated by the tribunal and communicated to the parties.**
2. **The parties shall provide such an expert with any relevant information or produce for inspection any relevant documents or goods that the expert may require. Any dispute between a party and the expert as to the relevance of the requested information or goods shall be referred to the tribunal for decision.**
3. **Upon receipt of an expert's report, the tribunal shall send a copy of the report to all parties and shall give the parties an opportunity to express, in writing, their opinion on the report. A party may examine any document on which the expert has relied in such a report.**

[148] See Rubins, R., 'In God We Trust, All Others Pay Cash: Security for Costs in International Commercial Arbitration' (2000) 11 *Am Rev Int'l Arb* 307, 347–8.

[149] See ICC Rules, Art 23(1).

[150] See, eg Widman, S.M., 'When it's Over Before it's Completed: The Finality of Interim Awards' (2006) vol 24 *Alternatives to the High Cost of Litigation* 97. See also *Sperry Int'l Trade Inc v Government of Israel*, 689 F2d 301, 306 (2d Cir 1982) (enforcing an interim award issued under the pre-amendment ICDR International Rules and providing that disputed monies be paid into an escrow fund pending an award on the merits).

[151] See UNCITRAL Model Law, Art 9.

[152] See generally, the arbitration laws of Australia, Bahrain, Belarus, Bermuda, Bulgaria, Canada, Chile, Cyprus, Egypt, France, Greece, Guatemala, Hungary, India, Iran, Ireland, Japan, Kenya, Lithuania, Macau, Madagascar, Malta, Mexico, New Zealand, Nigeria, Oman, Peru, Russian Federation, Scotland, Singapore, Sri Lanka, Tunisia, Ukraine and Zimbabwe.

[153] See eg in New York, Civil Practice Law and Rules, s 7502(c) (a 2005 amendment to the rules of civil procedure authorizing New York state courts to grant provisional remedies in aid of arbitration).

[154] See *Puerto Rico Hospital Supply Inc v Boston Scientific Corp* Civ 05-1523, 2005 WL 1431822 *3 (D. Puerto Rico, 17 June 2005) (referring to ICC Rules, Art 23 as evidence that the court had jurisdiction over a request for a preliminary injunction to preserve the status quo). However, even where resort to court is not 'incompatible' with the arbitration agreement a court may decline to give relief and refer the matter to the arbitrators. See eg *DHL Information Services (Americas) Inc v Infinite Software Corp* 502 F Supp 2d 1082 (DC Cal 2007) (referring to similar language in AAA Commercial Arbitration Rules, r 34(c) as permitting the court to order interim relief but holding that it would be inappropriate to do other than refer the matter to the tribunal).

4. **At the request of any party, the tribunal shall give the parties an opportunity to question the expert at a hearing. At this hearing, parties may present expert witnesses to testify on the points at issue.**

(1) Introduction

Article 22 addresses tribunal-appointed, as opposed to party-appointed, experts. It is closely modelled on the equivalent provision in the UNCITRAL Rules[155] and is broadly similar to the analogous articles of the ICC and LCIA Rules.[156] While it provides the framework for empowering the tribunal to appoint such experts and some basic rules, it leaves to the tribunal's discretion other practical issues, such as the method of selecting the expert, arrangements for payment of the expert's fees and expenses[157] and negotiation of the expert's terms of engagement.[158] **17.221**

(2) Tribunal may appoint independent experts (Article 22(1))

Article 22(1) grants the tribunal a broad power, either on application or *sua sponte*, to appoint one or more experts that are independent of the parties. Unlike in the ICC Rules, there is no obligation to consult the parties concerning the appointment, although this would clearly be prudent. The provision also vests in the tribunal the exclusive power to designate the issues on which the expert will opine. The issues must, however, be communicated to the parties (by way of a terms of reference or otherwise). The expert report must be delivered in writing.[159] **17.222**

(3) Procedure upon appointment by tribunal of an expert (Article 22(2)–(4))

Article 22(2) states that the parties must provide the expert with any relevant information, documents or goods the expert may require. The tribunal is to decide any dispute regarding the relevance of such material. **17.223**

In accordance with the duties of equality and opportunity to present one's case enshrined in Art 16, Art 22(3) provides that the expert report is to be shared with all parties and the parties are to have an opportunity to express 'in writing' their opinions on the report. This is most likely to be done by way of party-appointed expert witnesses. Article 22(3) also states that a party may 'examine any document on which the expert has relied in such a report.' The tribunal may need to make specific orders regarding confidentiality of information exchanged as part of this process. **17.224**

Article 22(4) provides that, if requested, any party shall have an opportunity to question the expert at a hearing and, in so doing, parties may present their own expert witnesses to testify 'on the points at issue'. In practice, the tribunal may also adopt any of the forms of 'witness caucusing' or 'witness conferencing', in which tribunal-appointed and/or party-appointed experts confer to seek to narrow the issues in dispute.[160] **17.225**

155 See UNCITRAL Rules, Art 27.
156 See ICC Rules, Art 20 and LCIA Rules, Art 21.
157 See LCIA Rules, Art 24 with respect to payment of fees.
158 See UNCITRAL Rules, Art 27 with respect to terms of engagement.
159 cf LCIA Rules, Art 21.2, permitting the expert to deliver an oral report.
160 See eg Peter, W., 'Witness "Conferencing"' (2002) 18(1) *Arb Int'l* 47.

Article 23: Default

1. **If a party fails to file a statement of defense within the time established by the tribunal without showing sufficient cause for such failure, as determined by the tribunal, the tribunal may proceed with the arbitration.**
2. **If a party, duly notified under these Rules, fails to appear at a hearing without showing sufficient cause for such failure, as determined by the tribunal, the tribunal may proceed with the arbitration.**
3. **If a party, duly invited to produce evidence or take any other steps in the proceedings, fails to do so within the time established by the tribunal without showing sufficient cause for such failure, as determined by the tribunal, the tribunal may make the award on the evidence before it.**

(1) Introduction

17.226 Article 23 addresses the situation in which one party to a proceeding 'defaults', whether by failing to file a timely Statement of Defense, appear at a hearing, produce evidence or otherwise failing to take a step ordered by the tribunal. Unsurprisingly, such a default occurs only where the errant party has been duly notified of the steps required[161] and where it fails to show 'sufficient cause' to excuse its failure.

(2) Tribunal may proceed where party defaults (Article 23(1)-(3))

17.227 In keeping with international arbitration practice, Art 23 provides that where a party fails to file a Statement of Defense or appear at a hearing, the tribunal 'may proceed with the arbitration'. In other words, while the tribunal retains a broad discretion, the preference is to proceed with the arbitration rather than issue any sort of 'default judgment' as might be the case in court in some jurisdictions.[162] Were the position otherwise, it might be inconsistent with the arbitrators' Art 16(1) duty to ensure that the parties are treated with equality, that each party has the right to be heard and is given a fair opportunity to present its case.[163]

17.228 Article 23(3) provides that where the default is a failure to 'produce evidence or take any other steps in the proceedings' within the time established, the tribunal 'may make the award on the evidence before it.' Again, the purpose of the provision is to ensure that the arbitration is not stymied by a party's lack of cooperation. The tribunal maintains a broad discretion as to how to deal with such a failure. One option may be to sanction the offending party by drawing adverse inferences against it with respect to the evidence not provided.[164]

---

[161] See ICDR Rules, Art 18 (regarding 'Notices') (discussed at ss 17.203 *et seq supra*).

[162] See Caron *et al* (n 122) (discussing analogous UNCITRAL Rules, Art 28). With respect to the analogous default provision in the AAA Commercial Arbitration Rules, see *Choice Hotels Int'l Inc v SM Property Management, LLC*, 519 F3d 200 (4th Cir 2008) (upholding vacatur of a default arbitral award on the basis that the contract's notice provision had not been fulfilled); cf *Gingiss Int'l Inc v Bormet*, 58 F3d 328 (7th Cir 1995) (upholding a default award where the challenging party had been duly notified in accordance with AAA Commercial Arbitration Rules requirements).

[163] Gaillard and Savage (n 19) s 1,363 ('There is no obligation on the arbitrators to simply accept the arguments of the party which is present or represented, nor indeed to increase the burden of proof on that party so as to compensate for the other's failure to participate, provided the other party has been properly invited to attend.').

[164] See generally Sharpe, J.K., 'Drawing Adverse Inferences from the Non-Production of Evidence' (2006) 22(4) *Arb Int'l* 549–71.

For enforcement purposes, and subject to any relevant laws in the enforcing jurisdiction, an award made following default proceedings is to be treated no differently from one made following proceedings in which all parties fully participated.[165] 17.229

Article 24: Closure of Hearing

1. **After asking the parties if they have any further testimony or evidentiary submissions and upon receiving negative replies or if satisfied that the record is complete, the tribunal may declare the hearings closed.**
2. **The tribunal in its discretion, on its own motion or upon application of a party, may reopen the hearings at any time before the award is made.**

(1) Introduction

This provision grants the tribunal broad powers to conclude the hearings and the discretion, before an award is made, to reopen a hearing. 17.230

(2) Tribunal may declare hearings closed (Article 24(1))

The purpose of Art 24(1) is to provide a mechanism for closing the hearing stage of the arbitration but, consistent with international practice, does not preclude filing further written submissions. In appropriate cases, and with the tribunal's consent, further evidence might even be tendered. The provision closely follows UNCITRAL Rules, Art 29(1). Closure of the hearings may serve to preclude any frivolous additional requests for additional hearings. No analogous provision exists to that in the ICC Rules, which, upon closure of the hearing, obligates the tribunal to advise the ICC Secretariat of an approximate date by which the award will be rendered.[166] 17.231

(3) Tribunal may reopen hearings (Article 24(2))

Article 24(2) gives the tribunal the discretion, of its own motion or upon application of one of the parties, to reopen the hearings at any time before the award is made. Unlike Art 29(2) of the UNCITRAL Rules, reopening is not available only where there are 'exceptional circumstances'.[167] While likely only to be rarely applied, reopening may be appropriate where to do so is necessitated by the Art 16(1) obligation to ensure that each party is given a fair opportunity to present its case. 17.232

Article 25: Waiver of Rules

A party who knows that any provision of the Rules or requirement under the Rules has not been complied with, but proceeds with the arbitration without promptly stating an objection in writing thereto, shall be deemed to have waived the right to object.

(1) Waiver of right to object to non-compliance

This provision seeks to avoid the potential problems that could arise if the parties, of their own volition or by order of the tribunal, deviate from the procedures established in the 17.233

165 Gaillard and Savage (n 19) s 1,363 (with reference to CA, Paris, 24 March 1995, *Bin Saud Bin Abdel Aziz v Crédit Industriel et Commercial de Paris*, 1996 *Rev arb* 259).

166 See ICC Rules, Art 22(2).

167 See Caron *et al* (n 122) 652 (noting that exceptional circumstances might include (i) in the course of deliberations the arbitrators realize that a particular point of law or fact has been insufficiently developed; or (ii) new material evidence has been discovered that requires clarification through an additional hearing).

Rules. Article 25 is almost identical to UNCITRAL Rules, Art 30, except that the former requires a waiver to be 'in writing'.

17.234 By comparison, ICC Rules, Art 33 explicitly extends to other instances of waiver, including failure to comply with directions given by the tribunal or requirements under the arbitration agreement. LCIA Rules, Art 32 also refers to non-compliance with any provision of the arbitration agreement.

17.235 Under the ICDR Rules, a party shall be deemed to have waived any objection to non-compliance with the Rules where it has knowledge of the deviation but proceeds nonetheless with the arbitration and, further, fails to raise promptly a written objection to the procedural non-compliance. The onus is therefore on a party to object to any such conduct without delay. As a practical matter, the tribunal's willingness to find there has been a waiver may diminish depending on the seriousness of the non-compliance and the nature of the procedural right at issue.[168]

Article 26: Awards, Decisions and Rulings

1. **When there is more than one arbitrator, any award, decision or ruling of the arbitral tribunal shall be made by a majority of the arbitrators. If any arbitrator fails to sign the award, it shall be accompanied by a statement of the reason for the absence of such signature.**
2. **When the parties or the tribunal so authorize, the presiding arbitrator may make decisions or rulings on questions of procedure, subject to revision by the tribunal.**

(1) Awards, decisions and rulings may be made by majority

17.236 Article 26(1) establishes that in any arbitration other than with a sole arbitrator,[169] 'any award, decision or ruling' shall be made by a majority of the tribunal. There is no requirement that the majority includes the chairperson and nor is the chairperson specifically empowered to make a decision alone if no majority can be achieved.[170]

17.237 Where an arbitrator refuses to sign an award—ie, where the arbitrator dissents—the award must contain a statement of the reasons for his or her refusal to sign. This is consistent with the Art 27(2) obligation on the arbitrators to state the reasons upon which the award is based.

17.238 Article 26(2) provides that upon agreement of the parties or the tribunal, the presiding arbitrator may make procedural decisions subject to revision by the tribunal. Similar to UNCITRAL Rules, Art 31(2), this rule is intended to expedite proceedings by consolidating power in the chairperson to decide merely procedural issues. Thus, procedural conferences

---

[168] See Caron *et al* (n 122) 741.

[169] See ICDR Rules, Art 5 regarding the number of arbitrators (discussed at ss 17.114 *et seq supra*).

[170] cf ICC Rules, Art25(1) (requiring that 'if there be no majority, the Award shall be made by the chairman of the Arbitral Tribunal alone'.) See also LCIA Rules, Art 26 and WIPO Rules, Art 61 (also adopting the so-called 'presiding arbitrator' approach). Art 31 of the UNCITRAL Rules, like the ICDR Rules, requires a 'majority'. However, there is increasing support for amending Art 31 to adopt some form of the 'presiding arbitrator' solution. See *Report of The Working Group on Arbitration and Conciliation*, UN Doc A/CN.9/641 (25 September 2007) 14-16 (noting also that 'the majority rule was not obsolete and that, in a recent review of the International Arbitration Rules of the American Arbitration Association. . ., a proposal to modify the majority requirement had been rejected').

need not necessarily involve the entire tribunal. It is open to debate what constitutes 'questions of procedure'. With respect to the analogous UNCITRAL Rules, Art 31(2), a leading commentator says that the test 'as a practical matter should involve consideration of whether the decision could have a measurable impact on the rights of one or both of the parties . . . [a]n identifiable significant impact should give an arbitral tribunal pause to treat a decision as purely procedural'.[171]

Article 27: Form and Effect of the Award

1. **Awards shall be made in writing, promptly by the tribunal, and shall be final and binding on the parties. The parties undertake to carry out any such award without delay.**
2. **The tribunal shall state the reasons upon which the award is based, unless the parties have agreed that no reasons need be given.**
3. **The award shall contain the date and the place where the award was made, which shall be the place designated pursuant to Article 13.**
4. **An award may be made public only with the consent of all parties or as required by law.**
5. **Copies of the award shall be communicated to the parties by the administrator.**
6. **If the arbitration law of the country where the award is made requires the award to be filed or registered, the tribunal shall comply with such requirement.**
7. **In addition to making a final award, the tribunal may make interim, interlocutory or partial orders and awards.**
8. **Unless otherwise agreed by the parties, the administrator may publish or otherwise make publicly available selected awards, decisions and rulings that have been edited to conceal the names of the parties and other identifying details or that have been made publicly available in the course of enforcement or otherwise.**

(1) Introduction

Modelled on UNCITRAL Rules, Art 32, Art 27 of the ICDR Rules prescribes the basic requirements of the form for, and the effect of, any ICDR arbitral award. The article does not provide a comprehensive list of requirements for a valid award. Rather, it prescribes certain general minimum standards, while also giving some deference to the potential application of the parties' agreement and the specific demands of the law at the place of arbitration or where enforcement is sought. **17.239**

(2) Award is final and binding (Article 27(1))

Article 27(1) requires that the award be 'in writing', following international arbitration practice and the requirements of many jurisdictions interpreting Arts III and IV of the New York Convention.[172] **17.240**

A 'final and binding' award corresponds with the established arbitral practice that such an award is conclusive of the issues determined, may not be appealed or challenged (except on whatever grounds may be provided for in the relevant jurisdiction) and creates obligations on the parties that are potentially enforceable as a matter of law. This may also be seen as the source of a duty on the tribunal to do all it can to ensure that the award is valid and **17.241**

[171] See Caron *et al* (n 122) 760–1.
[172] See eg Gaillard and Savage (n 19) s 1,389.

enforceable.[173] In addition to being 'final and binding' the parties also undertake to 'carry out any such award without delay'. Depending on the relevant applicable law, this obligation might also constitute a waiver of the parties' rights to challenge the award or a waiver of sovereign immunity from enforcement.[174] However, the language of Art 27(1) is not on its face as explicit as that of other analogous rules in this respect.[175]

17.242 Article 27(1) differs from the UNCITRAL Rules in requiring the arbitrators to render their award 'promptly' while leaving the establishment of the time limit for making the award to the discretion of the arbitrators and the institution.[176] This is a less specific requirement than the time limit provided in the ICC Rules (although such time limit is frequently extended).[177] Some jurisdictions may, of course, also have arbitration laws that require an award to be rendered within a certain time period or provide judicial recourse in the event that an arbitrator fails to render an award within a reasonable time.[178]

(3) Award must be reasoned (Article 27(2))

17.243 Article 27(2) requires the tribunal to 'state the reasons upon which the award is based' unless the parties have agreed otherwise. The language is almost identical to UNCITRAL Rules, Art 32(3).[179] This provision represents an important departure from the AAA Commercial Rules in that it recognizes the international practice of expecting a 'reasoned' award.[180] US domestic arbitral practice has, at least historically, been less consistent in expecting that an award will be reasoned.[181]

(4) Award must state date and place made (Article 27(3))

17.244 Article 27(3) requires that the award state the date on which, and place where, the award was made. Unlike other institutional rules, there is no specific requirement that the award

---

[173] See eg discussion of analogous Art 32(2) of the UNCITRAL Rules in Caron *et al* (n 122) 803. See also ICC Rules, Art 35.

[174] See eg *Creighton v Qatar*, Cour de Cassation, Appeal no A98019.068 (hearing on 6 July 2000), reproduced in English in (2000) 15 (10) *Mealey's Int'l Arb Rep* A1 (holding that a state waives its immunity from enforcement when agreeing to carry out the award without delay, and that the arbitration award was 'enforceable' as stated in Art 24 of the (then in force) ICC Rules of Arbitration under the heading 'Finality and enforceability of award').

[175] cf LCIA Rules, Art 26.9 ('All awards shall be final and binding on the parties. By agreeing to arbitration under these Rules, the parties undertake to carry out any award immediately and without any delay . . . and the parties also waive irrevocably their right to any form of appeal, review or recourse to any state court or other judicial authority, insofar as such waiver may be validly made.'). See also ICC Rules, Art 28(6) ('By submitting the dispute to arbitration under these Rules, the parties undertake to carry out any Award without delay and shall be deemed to have waived their right to any form of recourse insofar as such waiver can validly be made').

[176] See Introduction at ss 17 *et seq supra* on average duration of ICDR arbitrations.

[177] See ICC Rules, Art 24(1); Craig *et al* (n 41) 143.

[178] See Gaillard and Savage (n 19) s 1,384.

[179] See also LCIA Rules, Art 26.1. cf ICC Rules, Art 25(2) (requiring that the award state the reasons upon which it is based, which seems a logical necessity in order to pass the scrutiny of the ICC Court).

[180] See AAA Commercial Arbitration Rules, Art 42(b) ('The arbitrator need not render a reasoned award unless the parties request such an award in writing prior to appointment of the arbitrator or unless the arbitrator determines that a reasoned award is appropriate').

[181] See Smit, H., 'International and Domestic Arbitration Procedure: The Need for a Rule Providing a Limited Opportunity for Arbitral Reconsideration of Reasoned Awards' (2004) 15 *Am Rev Int'l Arb* 9, 16. See also *Gerstle v Merry X & Co*, Cour de Cassation, 22 November 1966 (confirming that an AAA arbitral panel's failure to provide a reasoned award was not *per se* contrary to French international public policy).

be signed by the arbitrators. Nevertheless, a signed award is clearly the accepted international arbitration practice and may be required for the award to be recognized in certain jurisdictions. The omission might be intended to side-step the difficulties that can arise where an arbitrator refuses to sign an award.[182] It may also be intended to overcome an argument that the award must be signed at the place of arbitration.[183] Article 27(3) specifically states that the place where the award is made shall be the place designated pursuant to Art 13, ie the seat of the arbitration, although this might have been made clearer by stating that the place where the award is made shall be *deemed* to be the seat.[184] Article 27(5) requires that copies of the award shall be communicated to the parties by the ICDR (rather than the tribunal). Unlike with some other institutions, release of the award to the parties is not dependent on all arbitration costs first having been paid.[185] Receipt of the award triggers the 30-day period for seeking an interpretation, correction or additional award pursuant to Art 30. The date of the award or the date of receipt of the award may also trigger certain deadlines for setting aside or enforcement as provided for in the applicable local laws.[186]

(5) Award is confidential but redacted award may be published (Article 27(4))

Article 27(4) confirms, but provides common limitations on, the presumption that an award shall remain confidential, ie awards may be made public with the consent of all parties or as required by law. This provision addresses only the confidentiality of the award and not other aspects of confidentiality of the proceeding.[187] The inclusion of the 'as required by law' caveat, envisages situations in which a party may need to make an award public, for example, in the course of collateral litigation (eg setting-aside or enforcement proceedings) or due to disclosure obligations incumbent on publicly-traded companies. **17.245**

On a related issue, Art 27(8) provides that the ICDR may 'publish or otherwise make publicly available selected awards, decisions and rulings that have been edited to conceal the names of the parties and other identifying details'. This power exists unless the parties otherwise agree to it.[188] This default rule mirrors ICC Rules, Art 28(2). As with many other institutions, the AAA/ICDR has commenced a project to publish selected awards and decisions in order to assist all users of AAA/ICDR arbitration to understand the various sets of rules and arbitral practice under such rules.[189] Such published awards are available on the Westlaw database. **17.246**

182 See discussion of Art 32(4) of the UNCITRAL Rules in Caron *et al* (n 122) 804–11.

183 See *Hiscox v Outhwaite* [1991] 3 All ER 641 (holding that, despite the seat being London, an award signed by the chairperson of the tribunal in Paris would be considered French).

184 See ICC Rules, Art 25(3).

185 Comment made by ICDR senior management.

186 See eg *Oberwager v McKechnie Ltd* Civ No 06-2685, 2007 US.Dist LEXIS 90869 at *16-*24 (ED Penn, 10 December 2007) (reviewing ICDR Rules, Art 27 in deciding that the three-month statute of limitations under the FAA for filing a challenge to an award ran from the date of the 'Final Award' as opposed to the arbitrator's subsequent decision under ICDR Rules, Art 30 denying a request for interpretation).

187 See Art 34 regarding confidentiality. That provision also places a duty on the 'members of the tribunal and the administrator [to] keep confidential all matters relating to the arbitration or the award'. See also ICDR Rules, Art 20(4) (regarding privacy of hearings) (discussed at ss 17.211 *et seq supra*).

188 To opt out of this requires agreement of the parties. See eg ICSID Arbitration Rules, Art 48(4).

189 See ss 17.23 *et seq supra*.

(6) Award may be registered (Article 27(6))

17.247 If the arbitration law of the seat so requires, Art 27(6) mirrors UNCITRAL Rules, Art 32(7) in requiring the tribunal to file or register the award. This duty arguably is already encompassed within the tribunal's implicit duty to ensure that the award is final and binding for purposes of Art 27(1). While increasingly uncommon, some jurisdictions require that the award be deposited with, typically, a court in order to be recognized as a binding award.[190]

(7) Tribunal may make interim awards (Article 27(7))

17.248 Article 27(7) empowers the tribunal to make not only a 'final award' but also any 'interim, interlocutory or partial orders and awards'. Notably, the rule includes 'orders' and not just 'awards'.[191] There is no agreement on the exact distinctions between these potentially different types of awards and orders. Even in debating the UNCITRAL Rules, the terms were used interchangeably in Committee discussions and 'the flexible nomenclature envisioned by the drafters was meant to promote efficiency, effectiveness and expediency in the tribunal's decision-making process by avoiding overly technical and unnecessarily time-consuming disputes about the appellation of a particular decision'.[192] Whether an interim, partial or interlocutory award is treated any differently than a final award is a matter likely to be determined by the law of the enforcing court.[193]

Article 28: Applicable Laws and Remedies

1. **The tribunal shall apply the substantive law(s) or rules of law designated by the parties as applicable to the dispute. Failing such a designation by the parties, the tribunal shall apply such law(s) or rules of law as it determines to be appropriate.**
2. **In arbitrations involving the application of contracts, the tribunal shall decide in accordance with the terms of the contract and shall take into account usages of the trade applicable to the contract.**
3. **The tribunal shall not decide as *amiable compositeur* or *ex aequo et bono* unless the parties have expressly authorized it to do so.**
4. **A monetary award shall be in the currency or currencies of the contract unless the tribunal considers another currency more appropriate, and the tribunal may award such pre-award and post-award interest, simple or compound, as it considers appropriate, taking into consideration the contract and applicable law.**
5. **Unless the parties agree otherwise, the parties expressly waive and forego any right to punitive, exemplary or similar damages unless a statute requires that compensatory damages be**

[190] See eg discussion in Lew, J. and Mistelis, L., *Arbitration Insights: Twenty Years of the Annual Lecture of the School of International Arbitration* (Kluwer Law International, The Hague, 2006) 19:103–9.

[191] cf UNCITRAL Rules, Art 32(1). Of course, for reasons of enforcement or otherwise, arbitrators may prefer to issue an 'award' rather than an 'order'. See ICDR Rules, Art 21(2), (discussed at ss 17.219 *et seq supra*).

[192] See Caron *et al* (n 122) 792–3.

[193] See eg Yu, C.H., 'Final, Interim, Interlocutory or Partial Award: Misnomers Apt to Mislead' (2001) 13 *Singapore Academy of L J* 467 (discussing *Tang Boon Jek Jeffrey v Tan Poh Leng Stanley* [2001] 3 SLR 237). See also *Metallgesellschaft AG v M/V Capitan Constante*, 790 F2d 280 (2d Cir 1986) (holding that an award that finally and definitively disposes of a separate independent claim may be confirmed although it does not dispose of all the claims that were submitted to arbitration); *Sperry Int'l Trade Inc v Israel*, 532 F Supp 901, 909–10 (D.C.N.Y. 1982) (interpreting the AAA Commercial Rules).

increased in a specified manner. This provision shall not apply to any award of arbitration costs to a party to compensate for dilatory or bad faith conduct in the arbitration.

(1) Introduction

This provision addresses the issue of laws applicable to the arbitration and certain matters relating to remedies available to the tribunal. Its touchstone is 'party autonomy', ie respecting the choice of the parties as expressed in the parties' agreement or before the tribunal. Nevertheless, the parties' freedom may be affected by the laws of the place of arbitration or of enforcement. In addition, Art 1(2) provides that any applicable mandatory law takes precedence over the powers recognized in Art 28. **17.249**

(2) Parties' choice of law to be given effect (Article 28(1))

Article 28(1) provides that the substantive laws or rules of law designated by the parties shall apply to the dispute. Only absent such a designation (or where there is an applicable mandatory rule of law) should the tribunal apply the law(s) 'it determines to be appropriate'. The language is a combination of UNCITRAL Rules, Art 33(1) and ICC Rules, Art 17(1).[194] As with the ICC Rules, the ICDR Rules do not specify what criteria the tribunal should apply to decide what law is 'appropriate' should it be required to make a determination. UNCITRAL Rules, Art 33(1) specifically refers to applying a conflict of laws analysis.[195] Consistent with international arbitration practice, the ICDR Rules appear to permit the arbitrators to make a 'direct' choice of law if they so desire.[196] **17.250**

(3) Tribunal to apply contract terms and usages of the trade (Article 28(2))

Article 28(2) makes clear that the terms of the contract are to take precedence in any contract dispute. The language is the same as that of UNCITRAL Rules, Art 33(3), although expressly limited only to contract disputes. ICC Rules, Art 17(2) contains the more ambiguous directive to 'take account' of the contract.[197] In addition, the tribunal 'shall take into account usages of the trade applicable to the contract'. This formulation suggests that in applying the law, trade usages are of secondary relevance to contract terms. **17.251**

(4) Tribunal may act as an amiable compositeur *Article 28(3)*

Article 28(3) permits the tribunal to decide the dispute as an *amiable compositeur or ex aequo et bono* but only if the parties have 'expressly authorized it to do so'. This reaffirms the primacy of the assumption that the tribunal will apply a substantive law or rules of law unless the parties have expressly—in their arbitration agreement, their submission to arbitration or before the tribunal—permitted a departure to consider notions of fairness and equity. Article 28(3) has omitted the explicit requirement found in UNCITRAL Rules, **17.252**

---

194 ICDR Rules, Art 28(1) differs from UNCITRAL Rules, Art 33(1) by referring not only to 'substantive law(s)' but also 'rules of law', the latter presumably being broader. For this reason, 'rules of law' was adopted in the amendments made in the 1998 ICC Rules. See Craig *et al* (n 41) 111. While in most cases the parties will choose a single national law as the law governing the merits, this need not be the case and 'rules of law' may encompass, for example, *lex mercatoria*, the UNIDROIT Principles of International Commercial Contracts or other sets of rules.

195 See also UNCITRAL Model Law, Art 28(2).

196 See Craig *et al* (n 41) 112.

197 Such ambiguity fuelled suspicion and was apparently the driver behind adopting the stricter language in UNCITRAL Rules, Art 33(3). See Caron *et al* (n 122) 137, n 75.

Art 33(2) that the 'law applicable to the arbitral procedure' must permit such a departure. However, this issue would be relevant regardless of any specific mention in the Rules.[198]

(5) Currency, interest, punitive damages (Article 28(4) and (5))

17.253 Paragraphs (4) and (5) of Art 28 address remedies. Any monetary award will be in the same currency as the contract at issue unless the tribunal considers another currency 'more appropriate'. The tribunal is free to award 'such pre-award and post-award interest, simple or compound, as it considers appropriate, taking into consideration the contract and applicable law'. In other words, the tribunal is given a very broad discretion. LCIA Rules, Art 26.6 is similarly broad, even making clear that the tribunal is not bound by the legal rate of interest that would be imposed by any state court.

17.254 Article 28(5) seeks to avoid a potential, although in practice rare, problem: the possibility of punitive damages being awarded and the fact that such an award may be unenforceable as contrary to public policy in some jurisdictions. The Rules provide that the parties 'expressly waive and forego the right to punitive, exemplary or similar damages unless a statute requires that compensatory damages be increased in a specified manner'. While not unique only to the US, such damages are commonly perceived as a characteristic of US litigation and thus this provision might serve to distance the ICDR Rules from their association with the AAA.[199] Notably, the rule carves out from the prohibition statutory directions to award increased compensatory damages, eg treble damages proscribed by statute.[200] Article 28(5) also makes explicit that the tribunal retains the discretion to award costs as a consequence of dilatory or bad faith conduct.[201]

Article 29: Settlement or Other Reasons for Termination

1. **If the parties settle the dispute before an award is made, the tribunal shall terminate the arbitration and, if requested by all parties, may record the settlement in the form of an award on agreed terms. The tribunal is not obliged to give reasons for such an award.**
2. **If the continuation of the proceedings becomes unnecessary or impossible for any other reason, the tribunal shall inform the parties of its intention to terminate the proceedings. The tribunal shall thereafter issue an order terminating the arbitration, unless a party raises justifiable grounds for objection.**

(1) Introduction

17.255 Similar to UNCITRAL Rules, Art 34 this provision details two instances in which the arbitration may be terminated other than by provision of a final award.

---

198 See ICDR Rules, Art 1(2), (discussed at ss 17.54 *et seq supra*).

199 See Gotanda, J.Y., 'Charting Developments Concerning Punitive Damages: Is the Tide Changing?' [2007] 45 *Columbia J Transnational L* 507; Gotanda, J.Y., 'Awarding Punitive Damages in International Commercial Arbitrations in the Wake of *Mastrobuono v Shearson Lehman Hutton, Inc.*' [1997] 38 *Harvard Int'l LJ* 59.

200 See eg *Investment Partners LP v Glamour Shots Licensing Inc*, 298 F3d 314, 318 (5th Cir 2002) (upholding enforcement of an award where antitrust treble damages were awarded as these were not inconsistent with a contractual prohibition on 'punitive damages').

201 See generally Gotanda, J.Y., 'Awarding Costs and Attorneys' Fees in International Commercial Arbitrations' [1999] 21 *Michigan J Int'l L* 1, 42. See also *Polin v Kellwood Co* 103 F Supp 2d 238, 264–7 (SDNY 2000) (upholding the tribunal's power to award sanctions against counsel in an arbitration governed by the AAA Employment Arbitration Rules).

(2) Termination upon settlement (Article 29(1))

Article 29(1) provides that the tribunal *shall* terminate the arbitration if the parties settle the dispute before an award is made. If the parties so request, the tribunal *may* record the settlement in the form of an award on agreed terms. The advantage of the latter is that, in most jurisdictions, such a consent award is enforceable as an arbitration award.[202] Further, it may give the tribunal an opportunity to review and offer suggestions on the terms of the settlement. Article 29(1) clarifies that the tribunal need not give reasons for such an award. Otherwise, the consent award should be subject to the same requirements of form and have the same effect as any other award under the Rules. ICC Rules, Art 26 and LCIA Rules, Art 26.8 make similar provisions for consent awards. 17.256

(3) Termination where continuation unnecessary or impossible (Article 29(2))

Article 29(2) addresses the situation where the continuation of the arbitration becomes 'unnecessary or impossible for any other reason'. Such reasons might include where the claimant fails to prosecute its case, where the costs of the arbitration are not being paid or where the subject matter of the arbitration becomes moot. In that case, the tribunal must first inform the parties of its intention to terminate the proceeding. Unless a party raises 'justifiable grounds for objection' the tribunal may thereafter issue an order terminating the arbitration.[203] Neither the ICC nor the LCIA Rules have a similarly explicit rule, except in relation to failure to pay the advance on costs or resignation of an arbitrator. 17.257

Article 30: Interpretation or Correction of the Award

1. **Within 30 days after the receipt of an award, any party, with notice to the other parties, may request the tribunal to interpret the award or correct any clerical, typographical or computation errors or make an additional award as to claims presented but omitted from the award.**
2. **If the tribunal considers such a request justified, after considering the contentions of the parties, it shall comply with such a request within 30 days after the request.**

(1) Introduction

As with the other major institutions, the ICDR Rules provide a limited opportunity for interpretation or correction of an award and for an additional award to be made on claims presented but not included within the award. The article provides a strict deadline for any such application and for the tribunal's response. 17.258

(2) Tribunal may interpret, correct or make additional award (Article 30(1))

Article 30 condenses into one article the powers to interpret, correct and make an additional award laid out in Arts 35, 36 and 37, respectively, of the UNCITRAL Rules. Any such application must be made within 30 days of receipt of the award. 17.259

(2.1) **Interpretation of the award** As to what constitutes 'interpretation', commentators on analogous rules have stated that the interpretation process does not permit reargument of a conclusion nor may new arguments or evidence be raised but, rather, it may provide 17.260

[202] See eg UNCITRAL Model Law, Art 30(2) ('The award on agreed terms has the status of any other award on the merits').

[203] The ICDR Rules do not give any guidance on what might constitute 'justifiable grounds'. But see the discussion of UNCITRAL Rules, Art 34(2) in Caron *et al* (n 122) 864–6.

'clarification of the award by resolving any ambiguity and vagueness in its terms'.[204] The LCIA Rules do not permit such interpretation at all.

17.261 (2.2) **Correction of the award** The power to 'correct any clerical, typographical or computation errors' is modelled on the language in the ICC, LCIA and UNCITRAL Rules. However it does not contain the more open-ended language permitting correction of 'any errors of a similar nature'. Interestingly, unlike the other rules, Art 30 also does not grant the tribunal any discretion to make a correction of its own initiative,[205] although one might argue that the tribunal has inherent powers to reconsider its award, especially for the limited purpose of making a correction.[206]

17.262 (2.3) **Making an additional award** The power to make an additional award addressing claims or counterclaims presented in the proceeding but omitted from the award is found in UNCITRAL Rules, Art 37 and LCIA Rules, Art 27.3 but not in the ICC Rules. The UNCITRAL Rules specifically provide that to grant such a request the tribunal must consider the request not only 'justified' but also that the 'omission can be rectified without any further hearings or evidence'.[207] The ICDR Rules do not contain any such specific directive. However, in light of the short timeframe, such a limitation might be implied.

(3) Effect of interpreting, correcting or making additional award (Article 30(2))

17.263 Article 30(2) sets the very ambitious timetable that the tribunal is to comply with such a request 'within 30 days after the request'. In contrast, UNCITRAL Rules, Art 35 provides a deadline of 45 days after receipt of a request for interpretation and 60 days in the case of a request for an additional award. Article 29(2) of the ICC Rules anticipates giving the non-moving party a 'short' time to respond ('normally not exceeding 30 days') and provides that the draft decision must be submitted to the ICC Court not later than 30 days following expiration of the time limit for comments from the other party or within such other period as the ICC Court may decide.[208]

17.264 Notably, Art 30 does not explicitly state that any interpretation or correction is to form part of the award.[209] Noting this, a US court has held that a request for interpretation or correction did not toll the statutory time periods within which a party must challenge the award.[210]

---

[204] See commentary on UNCITRAL Rules, Art 35 in Caron *et al* (n 122) 881–2.

[205] cf UNCITRAL Rules, Art 35(2); ICC Rules, Art 29(1); LCIA Rules, Art 27.2.

[206] See di Ció, C.M., 'Dealing with Mistakes Contained in Arbitral Awards' [2001] 12 *Am Rev Int'l Arb* 121; but see *Danella Construction Corp v MCI Telecoms Corp*, Civ No A91-1053, 1992 WL 82316 (ED Pa 14 Apr 1992); *revs'd Danella Construction Corp v MCI Telecoms Corp*, 993 F2d 876 (3d Cir 1993) (Table).

[207] UNCITRAL Rules, Art 37(2).

[208] See also LCIA Rules, Art 27.1 (providing for the tribunal's decision within 30 days of receipt of the request).

[209] cf UNCITRAL Rules, Arts 35 and 37; LCIA Rules, Arts 27.1 and 27.3 and ICC Rules, Art 29(3).

[210] See *Oberwager v McKechnie Ltd*, Civ No 06-2685, 2007 US Dist LEXIS 90869 at *16-*24 (ED Pa, 10 December 2007) (finding a decision denying a request under Art 30 not to be part of the final award and thus the party's challenge to the award was untimely).

Unlike the UNCITRAL Rules, the ICDR Rules do not specify that the arbitrators may not charge fees for work undertaken on such a request for interpretation, correction or for an additional award.[211] 17.265

Article 31: Costs

The tribunal shall fix the costs of arbitration in its award. The tribunal may apportion such costs among the parties if it determines that such apportionment is reasonable, taking into account the circumstances of the case.

Such costs may include:

(a) **the fees and expenses of the arbitrators;**

(b) **the costs of assistance required by the tribunal, including its experts;**

(c) **the fees and expenses of the administrator;**

(d) **the reasonable costs for legal representation of a successful party; and**

(e) **any such costs incurred in connection with an application for interim or emergency relief pursuant to Article 21.**

(1) Introduction

This provision makes clear that it is the tribunal's duty to fix the costs of the arbitration, grants it a broad discretion to apportion such costs and enumerates what items the costs award may include. Of course, the parties' agreement, the legal culture of the parties and any relevant applicable law may also impact on the tribunal's costs decision. 17.266

(2) Tribunal may apportion costs as it determines is reasonable

(2.1) Taking into account the circumstances of the case Article 31 empowers the tribunal to apportion costs among the parties if it determines that such apportionment is reasonable. This broad and unfettered discretion is not coupled with any explicit expectation that the unsuccessful party shall bear the costs of the arbitration.[212] The reference to 'taking into account the circumstances of the case', which also appears in UNCITRAL Rules, Art 40 has been interpreted to refer to the relative success or failure of each of the parties, the conduct of the parties during the arbitration and the nature of the parties (eg whether an individual, corporation or sovereign entity). 17.267

(2.2) Costs listed are not exclusive As to what constitutes 'costs', the list of items is stated not to be conclusive.[213] Unsurprisingly, it includes the fees and expenses of the arbitrators (which will have been determined in accordance with Art 32), the costs of assistance required by the tribunal (eg tribunal-appointed experts) and the ICDR administrative fees (determined according to the schedule to the Rules). The costs may also include 'the reasonable costs for legal representation of a successful party'. On its face, therefore, only a successful party may seek an award of its legal costs from the losing party but such costs 17.268

[211] cf UNCITRAL Rules, Art 40(4).

[212] cf *ibid*, Art 40 (providing that, except for legal fees, there is a presumption that the unsuccessful party shall bear the costs subject to a general right to allocate).

[213] cf *ibid*, Art 38 ('[t]he term "costs" includes only. . .').

must be 'reasonable'. Unlike in the UNCITRAL Rules, a claim for legal costs need not have been made 'during the arbitral proceedings', although it usually will have been.[214] Another interesting distinction is that Art 31 refers only to the costs for 'legal representation' and not 'legal representation and assistance' as is found in Art 38(e) of the UNCITRAL Rules. Arguably, therefore, Art 31 may not extend to recovery of other third party costs incurred in the course of the arbitration such as party-appointed expert witness fees. The list of costs refers to costs 'incurred in connection with any application for interim or emergency relief pursuant to Article 21'. Since Art 21(3) expressly mentions applications for interim relief to judicial authorities, this language needs to be read as to encompass not only costs associated with seeking interim relief from the tribunal but also any such application to the courts.[215]

17.269 (2.3) **Logistics for claiming costs** Article 31 does not address any of the practical logistics of how a party proves its claim for costs, whether costs should be part of the final award or made in a supplemental award and how to handle disbursement of any amounts paid on deposit.[216] These matters are left to the arbitral tribunal.

Article 32: Compensation of Arbitrators

Arbitrators shall be compensated based upon their amount of service, taking into account their stated rate of compensation and the size and complexity of the case. The administrator shall arrange an appropriate daily or hourly rate, based on such considerations, with the parties and with each of the arbitrators as soon as practicable after the commencement of the arbitration. If the parties fail to agree on the terms of compensation, the administrator shall establish an appropriate rate and communicate it in writing to the parties.

(1) Introduction

17.270 Article 32 represents a different approach than that adopted, for example, in the ICC Rules, in which the costs of arbitration are determined by the ICC Court based on a scale established by reference to the amount in dispute. The LCIA Rules also provide a fixed range of fees, although the tribunal retains discretion to fix its own fees based on various factors and subject to review by the LCIA Court.[217]

(2) Arbitrators' fees to be determined on a case-by-case basis

17.271 In language similar to that of UNCITRAL Rules, Art 39(1), Art 32 lists various factors that should be taken into account in determining an arbitrator's compensation. It makes clear that it is the job of the ICDR administrator to arrange an appropriate rate in consultation with the parties and all arbitrators. In the absence of agreement, the administrator can impose an applicable rate. Rates are normally on a per hour basis and are disclosed to the parties at the time of appointment of the tribunal. The ICDR requires that all other terms

[214] UNCITRAL Rules, Art 38(e).

[215] See also ICDR Rules, Art 37(9) (costs associated with an application for emergency relief are to be initially apportioned by the emergency arbitrator or special master but are subject to final determination by the tribunal).

[216] See generally Gaillard and Savage (n 19) ss 1,253 *et seq*; Gotanda, J.Y., 'Awarding Costs and Attorneys' Fees in International Commercial Arbitrations' [1999] 21 *Michigan J Int'l L* 1, 42.

[217] See LCIA Rules, Art 28 and Schedule of Arbitration Fees and Costs, section 4.

related to arbitrator compensation, such as a cancellation fee, are also disclosed at this point. The ICDR encourages arbitrator compensation to be equal among the different tribunal members, although it may be that the chairperson is entitled to a higher fee than the co-arbitrators.[218]

The arbitrators render invoices for compensation to the ICDR and the case administrator is responsible for collecting funds from the parties and ensuring that sufficient funds are available to meet invoices on an ongoing basis. The ICDR also performs a role in monitoring the reasonableness of the invoices submitted for compensation, as well as ensuring that an arbitrator provides adequate explanation for particular tasks performed. If a party questions an arbitrator's fee, the ICDR will undertake a confidential review and may request further information of the arbitrator. If requested, an arbitrator's invoice may be provided to the parties. **17.272**

Article 33: Deposit of Costs

1. **When a party files claims, the administrator may request the filing party to deposit appropriate amounts as an advance for the costs referred to in Article 31, paragraphs (a), (b) and (c).**
2. **During the course of the arbitral proceedings, the tribunal may request supplementary deposits from the parties.**
3. **If the deposits requested are not paid in full within 30 days after the receipt of the request, the administrator shall so inform the parties, in order that one or the other of them may make the required payment. If such payments are not made, the tribunal may order the suspension or termination of the proceedings.**
4. **After the award has been made, the administrator shall render an accounting to the parties of the deposits received and return any unexpended balance to the parties.**

(1) Introduction

Article 33 sets out the basic rules for when deposits are to be paid as an advance on the costs of the arbitration, consequences for non-payment and the administrator's duty to account to the parties for how the deposits have been used. Article 33 is very similar to UNCITRAL Rules, Art 41. It differs from rules such as the ICC Rules in which the advance on costs is calculated pursuant to a schedule of costs and an associated formula. **17.273**

(2) Advance on costs may be ordered (Article 33(1) and (2))

Article 33(1) makes clear that the advance on costs is to be calculated based on the fees and expenses of the arbitrators, the costs of assistance required by the tribunal and the fees and expenses of the administrator. Unlike with some other institutions, the ICDR does not apply a specific formula to calculate the advance on costs. Instead, the administrator, in close consultation with the tribunal, makes regular ongoing assessments of what the actual anticipated costs of arbitration will be. **17.274**

As a practical matter, the administrator will require an up-front payment at the outset of the arbitration. This is typically calculated on the basis of requiring sufficient funds to cover eight hours of preparation time per arbitrator in advance of the procedural hearing.[219] **17.275**

[218] See generally Gaillard and Savage (n 19) ss 1,158 *et seq.*
[219] Comment made by ICDR senior management.

However, thereafter, the supplemental payments demanded are based on the anticipated likely actual costs of the arbitration.

(3) Consequences of failure to pay advance on costs and accounting of costs (Article 33(3) and (4))

17.276 Consistent with international arbitration practice, if a party fails to make its payment, the administrator must inform the other party or parties and invite one or another of them to make the payment in order for the arbitration to proceed. If the payment is not made, the tribunal is empowered to suspend or terminate the proceedings.

17.277 After the award has been made, the administrator must provide an accounting of the deposits received and return any unexpended funds in amounts proportional to the parties' relative contributions. This duty to provide an accounting also applies where the arbitration is terminated for any other reason prior to an award being rendered.

Article 34: Confidentiality

Confidential information disclosed during the proceedings by the parties or by witnesses shall not be divulged by an arbitrator or by the administrator. Except as provided in Article 27, unless otherwise agreed by the parties, or required by applicable law, the members of the tribunal and the administrator shall keep confidential all matters relating to the arbitration or the award.

(1) Introduction

17.278 This provision is one of the distinguishing features of the ICDR Rules, providing a duty of confidentiality on the arbitrators and the administrator that is not found in either the UNCITRAL or ICC Rules. LCIA Rules, Art 30 imposes a general duty of confidentiality on the parties.

(2) Tribunal and administrator bound by duty of confidentiality

17.279 The Art 34 duty of confidentiality extends to confidential information disclosed during the proceedings by the parties or witnesses. Further, except as provided for in Art 27 (Form and Effect of the Award) or as agreed by the parties, the arbitrators and the administrator shall 'keep confidential all matters relating to the arbitration or the award'. This presumably extends to the hearing, the deliberations and the actual content of the award. LCIA Rules, Art 30.2 specifically affirms that the tribunal's deliberations are confidential, except to the extent that an arbitrator's refusal to participate needs to be disclosed.

17.280 Of course, the practical import of Art 34 will also be affected by the law applicable at the seat of arbitration and potentially elsewhere (eg the place of incorporation of any corporate party).[220]

Article 35: Exclusion of Liability

The members of the tribunal and the administrator shall not be liable to any party for any act or omission in connection with any arbitration conducted under these Rules, except that they may be liable for the consequences of conscious and deliberate wrongdoing.

---

220 See also, Greengrass, L.S., 'Do Arbitrators Have the Power to Impose Confidentiality?' [2004] 11(1) *Arias-US Q* 23.

(1) Introduction

Article 35 absolves the tribunal and administrator of any liability in connection with the arbitration except for consequences of intentional wrongdoing. **17.281**

(2) Arbitrators and administrator enjoy broad exclusion of liability

As a rule, Art 35 is intended to bind parties who select ICDR arbitration as a matter of contract. However, many national arbitration laws have specific provisions relating to liability for arbitrators and administrators that may impact on this. The arbitrators and parties may also enter into specific contractual arrangements to the extent permitted by the applicable law.[221] **17.282**

ICC Rules, Art 34 provides an absolute exclusion of liability for an enumerated list of individuals in connection with the arbitration, without an exclusion for deliberate wrongdoing.[222] LCIA Rules, Art 31 is on similar terms to the ICDR Rules. However, it also provides that the parties undertake not to seek to make any arbitrator or administrator a witness in any legal or other proceedings arising out of the subject arbitration. While not explicitly stated in the ICDR Rules, the AAA has previously taken the position that arbitrators should not be subjected to giving evidence of any sort in post-award litigation.[223] **17.283**

Article 36: Interpretation of Rules

The tribunal shall interpret and apply these Rules insofar as they relate to its powers and duties. The administrator shall interpret and apply all other Rules.

(1) Interpretation falls to arbitrators and administrator

Article 36 provides a division of responsibilities such that the tribunal is charged with interpreting and applying the ICDR Rules to the extent that they impact on the tribunal's powers and duties in a particular case. Otherwise, it falls to the administrator to address such issues. **17.284**

The ICDR Rules do not contain a catch-all 'General Rule' of the sort found in ICC Rules, Art 35 and LCIA Rules, Art 32, in which the tribunal and the institution are directed that in all matters not expressly provided for in the rules, they are to act in the 'spirit of these Rules' and to make every effort to ensure that the resulting award is enforceable. Nevertheless, the ICDR considers that even though not explicitly stated in the ICDR Rules, such principles are intrinsic to the Rules as a whole.[224] **17.285**

---

221 See *Pacific Insurers Employment Co v Moglia*, 365 BR 863 (ND Ill 2007) (holding that arbitrators acting pursuant to the AAA Commercial Arbitration Rules had the authority to require the parties to sign a 'hold harmless' agreement by which the parties undertook not to assert any claims against the arbitrators).

222 See Craig *et al* (n 41) 181 (noting that the ICC rejected a proposal to exclude deliberate wrongdoing); see also Gaillard and Savage (n 19) ss 1,142 *et seq*.

223 See *Gearhardt v Cadillac Plastics Group Inc* 140 F.R.D. 349 (SD Ohio 1992) (refusing to permit an arbitrator to be deposed concerning his preparation of the award and any medical or mental condition that may have affected his conduct in the arbitration, where the defendant was challenging the award on the basis that the arbitrator may have been suffering from senile dementia or some other form of neurological disorder) (the court also relied on an *amicus curiae* brief from the AAA advising that the request was 'unprecedented in the AAA's 65-year history of administering arbitration proceedings' *ibid* 351).

224 Comment made by ICDR senior management.

Article 37: Emergency Measures of Protection

1. Unless the parties agree otherwise, the provisions of this Article 37 shall apply to arbitrations conducted under arbitration clauses or agreements entered on or after May 1, 2006.
2. A party in need of emergency relief prior to the constitution of the tribunal shall notify the administrator and all other parties in writing of the nature of the relief sought and the reasons why such relief is required on an emergency basis. The application shall also set forth the reasons why the party is entitled to such relief. Such notice may be given by e-mail, facsimile transmission or other reliable means, but must include a statement certifying that all other parties have been notified or an explanation of the steps taken in good faith to notify other parties.
3. Within one business day of receipt of notice as provided in paragraph 2, the administrator shall appoint a single emergency arbitrator from a special panel of emergency arbitrators designated to rule on emergency applications. Prior to accepting appointment, a prospective emergency arbitrator shall disclose to the administrator any circumstance likely to give rise to justifiable doubts to the arbitrator's impartiality or independence. Any challenge to the appointment of the emergency arbitrator must be made within one business day of the communication by the administrator to the parties of the appointment of the emergency arbitrator and the circumstances disclosed.
4. The emergency arbitrator shall as soon as possible, but in any event within two business days of appointment, establish a schedule for consideration of the application for emergency relief. Such schedule shall provide a reasonable opportunity to all parties to be heard, but may provide for proceedings by telephone conference or on written submissions as alternatives to a formal hearing. The emergency arbitrator shall have the authority vested in the tribunal under Article 15, including the authority to rule on her/his own jurisdiction, and shall resolve any disputes over the applicability of this Article 37.
5. The emergency arbitrator shall have the power to order or award any interim or conservancy measure the emergency arbitrator deems necessary, including injunctive relief and measures for the protection or conservation of property. Any such measure may take the form of an interim award or of an order. The emergency arbitrator shall give reasons in either case. The emergency arbitrator may modify or vacate the interim award or order for good cause shown.
6. The emergency arbitrator shall have no further power to act after the tribunal is constituted. Once the tribunal has been constituted, the tribunal may reconsider, modify or vacate the interim award or order of emergency relief issued by the emergency arbitrator. The emergency arbitrator may not serve as a member of the tribunal unless the parties agree otherwise.
7. Any interim award or order of emergency relief may be conditioned on provision by the party seeking such relief of appropriate security.
8. A request for interim measures addressed by a party to a judicial authority shall not be deemed incompatible with this Article 37 or with the agreement to arbitrate or a waiver of the right to arbitrate. If the administrator is directed by a judicial authority to nominate a special master to consider and report on an application for emergency relief, the administrator shall proceed as in Paragraph 2 of this article and the references to the emergency arbitrator shall be read to mean the special master, except that the special master shall issue a report rather than an interim award.
9. The costs associated with applications for emergency relief shall initially be apportioned by the emergency arbitrator or special master, subject to the power of the tribunal to determine finally the apportionment of such costs.

(1) Introduction

This new provision was introduced in 2006[225] to provide a unique resource for parties requiring emergency relief prior to constitution of the tribunal. Article 37 details a number of procedural steps a party must take to secure expedited emergency relief, the powers of the emergency arbitrator and the effect of any interim awards and other orders of emergency relief that may be provided. **17.286**

The ICDR's approach to this topic is unique. The ICC offers the ability to have a dispute submitted to a pre-arbitral referee for, amongst other things, emergency orders. However, the ICC Rules for a Pre-Arbitral Referee Procedure must be explicitly agreed upon by the parties. The LCIA permits a party to apply for expedited formation of a tribunal and then relies on the tribunal's powers to make interim awards.[226] The UNCITRAL Rules do not contain an analogous provision. **17.287**

Importantly, note that these emergency measures of protections exist separately from Art 21, empowering a tribunal to make interim measures of protection. Further, and significantly, a party may still choose to go to a court of competent jurisdiction to obtain emergency relief such as a preliminary injunction, temporary restraining order or order to preserve evidence. The utility of Art 37 lies in situations in which a party fears that the appropriate courts will not grant interim relief. **17.288**

As of 1 May 2009, the Art 37 procedures have been formally invoked and emergency awards or orders made on six occasions. It took on average three weeks between filing of the application and issue of the orders. Anecdotal evidence suggests that the threat of these procedures being invoked may also have influenced parties' behaviour such that formal recourse to Art 37 became unnecessary.[227] However, given that Art 37 is relatively new and there is very little publicly available information concerning the details of those cases in which it has been invoked, it is difficult to comment on the specifics of the emergency relief regime. **17.289**

(2) Article 37 applies unless agreed otherwise (Article 37(1))

The Art 37 regime applies to all arbitrations conducted pursuant to agreements entered into on or after 1 May 2006. Unlike the ICC's pre-arbitral provision, Art 37 applies automatically without having to opt into it. **17.290**

(3) Procedure for seeking emergency relief (Article 37(2)-(4))

(3.1) Party makes application Article 37(2) provides that the party seeking emergency relief shall notify the administrator and all other parties in writing of the nature of the relief sought and the reasons why such relief is required on an emergency basis. The notice must include a statement 'certifying that all other parties have been notified or an explanation of **17.291**

225 See s 17.24 *supra.*

226 LCIA Rules, Art 9.

227 Comments made by ICDR senior management.

the steps taken in good faith to notify other parties'. On its face, therefore, there is no provision for making such an application on an *ex parte* basis.

17.292 (3.2) **Administrator to appoint a single emergency arbitrator** Article 37(3) provides that the 'emergency arbitrator' shall be appointed within one business day of the AAA/ICDR's receipt of the notice requesting emergency relief. This extraordinarily fast timetable is made possible by the formation of a standing panel of emergency arbitrators. By referring to the decision maker as an 'arbitrator', it suggests that the emergency relief procedure, the appointment of the emergency arbitrator and the ultimate orders and awards are all to be treated as being part of an arbitration and therefore subject to the applicable local arbitration laws and international arbitration treaties. This is not the same in the ICC's 'referee' procedure, in which at least some courts have held that the referee is not an arbitrator.[228]

17.293 Prior to accepting appointment, it is incumbent on the emergency arbitrator to disclose to the administrator any circumstance likely to give rise to justifiable doubts as to that individual's impartiality or independence. This mirrors the standard of arbitrator impartiality required by Art 7. Any challenge to the emergency arbitrator must be made within one business day of the administrator's communication of the appointment and of the circumstances disclosed.

17.294 (3.3) **Emergency arbitrator to give parties an opportunity to be heard** As soon as possible, but in any event within two business days of appointment, the emergency arbitrator must establish a schedule for considering the merits of the emergency relief application. Article 37(4) specifically states that the emergency arbitrator is to 'provide a reasonable opportunity to all parties to be heard' but a formal hearing may not be necessary as a telephonic conference or written submissions may suffice.

(4) Scope of emergency arbitrator's powers (Article 37(4) and (5))

17.295 Article 37(4) makes clear that the emergency arbitrator has the powers provided under Art 15, including being entitled to rule on his or her own jurisdiction and the applicability of Art 37.[229]

17.296 Article 37(5) grants the emergency arbitrator broad powers to order 'any interim or conservancy measure . . . deem[ed] necessary, including injunctive relief and measures for the protection or conservation of property'. This may be by way of an interim award or an order. The interim award or order must be reasoned. Again, the language evidences a clear intention that such interim awards or orders are to be treated as the product of an arbitration and, as such, should be enforceable where this is permitted under applicable local and international laws relating to international arbitration.

17.297 Article 37(5) also provides that the emergency arbitrator may modify or vacate the interim award or order for good cause shown. This is a pragmatic necessity given that, as with

---

[228] See Kantor, M., 'Arbitration Rules Update: Expedited Emergency Relief Under the AAA/ICDR, ICC and LCIA Rules' [2006] 21 *Mealey's Int'l Arb Rep* 25, 30.

[229] See ICDR Rules, Art 15 (discussed at ss 17.175 *et seq supra*).

applications for emergency relief in court, the decision maker is having to respond very quickly to a potentially uncertain factual and legal scenario.

(5) Tribunal may reconsider once constituted (Article 37(6))

The emergency arbitrator becomes *functus officio* once the tribunal in the merits proceeding is constituted. The emergency arbitrator may not serve as a member of the tribunal unless otherwise agreed by the parties. Once in place, the tribunal may reconsider, modify or vacate the interim award or order. Again, this acknowledges that with a full tribunal in place and an opportunity for more comprehensive analysis, it may be decided that the initial interim award or order is no longer appropriate. **17.298**

(6) Party may seek judicial emergency relief (Article 37(8))

Article 37(8) makes explicit that a party is still free to go to the appropriate courts to seek emergency relief in aid of the arbitration. Doing so is not to be considered a waiver of the right to arbitrate. This mirrors Art 21(3) in which it is confirmed that a request for judicial interim measures is not incompatible with the arbitration agreement. **17.299**

(7) Costs and security for costs (Article 37(7) and (9))

Article 37(7) permits the emergency arbitrator to condition any emergency award or order on the applicant's provision of 'appropriate security'. **17.300**

Article 37(9) states that the emergency arbitrator is to make a decision on the extent to which the costs of dealing with the application are to be apportioned between the parties. This therefore falls in the first instance to the emergency arbitrator's discretion but is subject to the tribunal's ultimate power to make a final determination on apportionment of costs. **17.301**

III. Appendix

A. Contact details for the ICDR

International Case Management Centre

International Centre for Dispute Resolution
Thomas M. Ventrone, Esq.
Vice President
1633 Broadway, 10th Floor
New York, New York 10019
Telephone: +1 212 484 4181
Fax: +1 212 246 7274
Email: VentroneT@adr.org

Europe, Middle East, Africa

International Centre for Dispute Resolution
Mark Appel
Senior Vice President
14 Merrion Square

Dublin 2, Ireland
Telephone: +353 1 676 1500
Fax: +353 1 676 1501
Email: AppelM@adr.org

Asia

International Centre for Dispute Resolution - Singapore
Michael Lee
Director
Maxwell Chambers, ICDR-Singapore
32, Maxwell Road
Singapore 069115
Singapore
Telephone: +65 6334 1277
Fax: +65 6334 2942
Email: LeeM@adr.org

Central and South America

International Centre for Dispute Resolution
Luis Martinez
Vice President
1633 Broadway, 10th Floor
New York, New York 10019
Telephone: +1 212 716 5833
Fax: +1 212 716 5904
Email: MartinezL@adr.org

Mexico and Canada

International Centre for Dispute Resolution
Steve Andersen
Vice President
1108 E. South Union Avenue
Midvale, UT 84047
Telephone: +1 801 569 4618
Fax: +1 801 984 8170
Email: AndersenS@adr.org

B. Model arbitration clauses and other patterns provided by the ICDR

Parties might wish to submit their dispute to an international mediation prior to arbitration. International mediation is administered by the ICDR in accordance with its International Mediation Rules. There is no additional administrative fee where parties to a pending arbitration attempt to mediate their dispute under the ICDR's auspices.

If the parties want to adopt mediation as a part of their contractual dispute settlement procedure, they can insert the following mediation clause into their contract in conjunction with a standard arbitration provision:

> If a dispute arises out of or relates to this contract, or the breach thereof, and if the dispute cannot be settled through negotiation, the parties agree first to try in good faith to settle the dispute by mediation in accordance with the International Mediation Rules of the International Centre for Dispute Resolution before resorting to arbitration, litigation or some other dispute resolution procedure.

If the parties want to use a mediator to resolve an existing dispute, they can enter into the following submission:

> The parties hereby submit the following dispute to mediation administered by the International Centre for Dispute Resolution in accordance with its International Mediation Rules. (The clause may also provide for the qualifications of the mediator(s), method of payment, locale of meetings and any other item of concern to the parties.)

Parties can arbitrate future disputes by inserting either of the following clauses into their contracts:

> Any controversy or claim arising out of or relating to this contract, or the breach thereof, shall be determined by arbitration administered by the International Centre for Dispute Resolution in accordance with its International Arbitration Rules.

or

> Any controversy or claim arising out of or relating to this contract, or the breach thereof, shall be determined by arbitration administered by the American Arbitration Association in accordance with its International Arbitration Rules.
>
> The parties may wish to consider adding:
>
> (a) The number of arbitrators shall be (one or three);
>
> (b) The place of arbitration shall be (city and/or country); or
>
> (c) The language(s) of the arbitration shall be ______________.

C. Bibliography

Aksen, G., 'Ad Hoc Versus Institutional Arbitration' (1991) *ICC Ct Bull* 8.

Aksen, G., 'The Tribunal's Appointment' in L.W. Newman and R.D. Hill (eds), *The Leading Arbitrators' Guide to International Arbitration* (Juris Publishing, Huntington, 2004).

Alvarez, G.A., 'The Challenge of Arbitrators' (1990) 6(3) *Arb Int'l* 203, 217.

American Arbitration Association Press Release, 'American Arbitration Association announces International Centre for Dispute Resolution in Dublin' (25 April 2001).

American Arbitration Association Press Release 'ICDR Opens Office in Mexico City - International Division of AAA Reaches Cooperative Agreement with CANACO' (16 February 2006).

American Arbitration Association Task Force on the International Rules, 'Commentary on the Proposed Revisions to the International Arbitration Rules of the American Arbitration Association' (1996/1997) 2(1) *ADR Currents*.

Beechey, J., 'The ICDR Guidelines for Information Exchanges in International Arbitration: An Important Addition to the Arbitral Toolkit' (2008) *Disp Res J* 84.

Bensaude, D., '*Malecki v Long*: Truncated Tribunals and Waivers of *Dutco* Rights' (2006) 23 *J Int'l Arb* 81.
Berger, K.-P., *International Economic Arbitration* (Kluwer Law International, Boston, 1993).
Berger, K.-P., 'The New German Arbitration Law in International Perspective' (2000) 26 *Forum Int'l* 1, 9.
Berger, K.-P., 'Schiedsrichterbestellung in Mehrparteienschiedsverfahren' [1993] *Recht der Internationalen Wirtschaft* 702.
Bishop, R.D., *The Art of Advocacy in International Arbitration* (Juris Publishing, Huntington, 2004).
Bishop, R.D. and Reed, L., 'Practical Guidelines for Interviewing, Selecting and Challenging Party-Appointed Arbitrators in International Commercial Arbitration' (1998) 14(4) *Arb Int'l* 395, 396.
Böckstiegel, K.-H., 'An Introduction to the New German Arbitration Act Based on the UNCITRAL Model Law' (1998) 14(1) *Arb Int'l* 19, 25.
Born, G.B., *International Arbitration and Forum Selection Agreements: Drafting and Enforcing* (2nd edn, Kluwer Law International, The Hague, 2006).
Born, G.B., *International Commercial Arbitration—Commentary and Materials* (2nd/3rd edn, Kluwer Law International, The Hague, 2001/2009).
Bouchez, L.J., 'The Prospects for International Arbitration: Disputes Between States and Private Enterprises' (1991) 8(1) *J Int'l Arb* 81, 96.
Caron, D., Caplan, L. and Pellonpää, M., *The UNCITRAL Arbitration Rules: A Commentary* (OUP, Oxford, 2006).
Craig, W.L., Park, W.W. and Paulsson, J., *International Chamber of Commerce Arbitration* (3rd edn, Oceana Publications, New York, 2000).
Crawford, J., 'Advocacy Before the International Court of Justice and Other International Tribunals in State-to-State Cases' in R.D. Bishop (ed.), *The Art of Advocacy in International Arbitration* (Juris Publishing, Huntington, 2004).
De Boisséson, M, 'Evidentiary Privileges in International Arbitration,' in J. van den Berg (ed), *International Arbitration 2006: Back to Basics?* (ICCA International Arbitration Congress, 2007) 705.
Derains, Y. and Schwartz, E.A., *A Guide to the ICC Rules of Arbitration* (2nd edn, Kluwer Law International, The Hague, 2005).
De Witt Wijnen, O. L.O., Voser, N. and Rao, N., 'Background Information on the IBA Guidelines on Conflict of Interest' (2004) 5 *Bus L Int'l*.
DI Ció, C.M., 'Dealing with Mistakes Contained in Arbitral Awards' [2001] 12 *Am Rev Int'l Arb* 121.
Document A/CN.9/264 (reproduced in UNCITRAL Yearbook, vol XVI—1985, United Nations publication, Sales no E.87.V.4).
Explanatory Note by the UNCITRAL Secretariat on the 1985 Model Law on International Commercial Arbitration as amended in 2006.
Gaillard, E. and Savage, J. (eds), *Fouchard Gaillard Goldman on International Commercial Arbitration* (Kluwer Law International, The Hague, 1999).
Gotanda, J.Y., 'Awarding Costs and Attorneys' Fees in International Commercial Arbitrations' [1999] 21 *Michigan J Int'l L* 1.
Gotanda, J.Y., 'Awarding Punitive Damages in International Commercial Arbitrations in the Wake of *Mastrobuono v Shearson Lehman Hutton, Inc.*' [1997] 38 *Harvard Int'l L J* 59.
Gotanda, J.Y., 'Charting Developments Concerning Punitive Damages: Is the Tide Changing?' [2007] 45 *Columbia J Transnational L* 507.
Greengrass, L.S., 'Do Arbitrators Have the Power to Impose Confidentiality?' [2004] 11(1) *Arias-US Q* 23.

Gusy, M. and Illmer, M., 'The ICDR Guidelines for Arbitrators Concerning Exchanges of Information—A German/American Introduction in Light of International Practice' (2008) 6 *Int'l ALR* 195.

Hascher, D.T., 'European Convention on International Arbitration (1961)' (1995) XX *Ybk Comm Arb* 1006.

Hoellering, M., 'The Institution's Role in Managing the Arbitration Process' (1994) *Am Rev of Int'l Arb* 121.

Hosking, J., 'Non-Signatories and International Arbitration in the United States: The Quest for Consent' (2004) 20(3) *Arb Int'l* 289.

Howell, J., 'Electronic Disclosure in International Arbitration', (Juris Publishing, Huntington, 2008).

Jolidon, P., *Commentaire au Concordat Suisse sur l'Arbitrage* (Stämpfli Verlag, Bern, 1984).

Kantor, M., 'Arbitration Rules Update: Expedited Emergency Relief Under the AAA/ICDR, ICC and LCIA Rules' [2006] 21 *Mealey's Int'l Arb Rep* 25.

Kröll, S., 'Recourse Against Negative Decisions on Jurisdiction' (2004) 20(1) *Arb Int'l* 55.

Lachmann, J.P., *Handbuch für die Schiedsgerichtspraxis* (3rd edn, Verlag Dr. Otto Schmidt, Cologne, 2008).

Lew, J. and Mistelis, L., *Arbitration Insights: Twenty Years of the Annual Lecture of the School of International Arbitration* (Kluwer Law International, The Hague, 2006).

Lew, J., Mistelis, L. and Kröll, S., *Comparative International Commercial Arbitration* (Kluwer Law International, The Hague, 2003).

Mani, V., *International Adjudication: Procedural Aspects* (Martinus Nijhoff Publishers, The Hague, 1980).

Matscher, F., 'Schiedsgerichsbarkeit und EMRK' in W.J. Haberscheid and K. Schwab (eds), *Festschrift für Heinrich Nagel zum 75. Geburtstag* (Aschendorff, Münster, 1987) 236.

Mayer, P., 'Les limites de la séparabilité de la clause compromissoire' [1997] *Rev arb* 359, 362.

Park, W.W., 'Judicial Controls in the Arbitral Process' (1989) 5(3) *Arb Int'l* 230.

Paulsson, J., 'The Timely Arbitrator: Reflections on the Böckstiegel Method' in R. Briner *et al* (eds), *Law of International Business and Dispute Settlement in the 21st Century, Liber Amicorum for Karl-Heinz Böckstiegel* (Carl Heymanns Verlag, Cologne, 2001).

Peter, W., 'Witness "Conferencing"' (2002) 18(1) *Arb Int'l* 47.

Petrochilos, G., *Procedural Law in International Arbitration* (OUP, Oxford, 2004).

Pietrowski, R., 'Evidence in International Arbitration' (2006) 22(3) *Arb Int'l* 373.

Polkinghorne, M. and Fitzgerald, D., 'Arbitration in Southeast Asia: Hong Kong, Singapore and Thailand Compared' (2001) 18(1) *J Int'l Arb* 101.

Polkinghorne, M., 'More Changes in Singapore: Appearance Rights of Foreign Counsel' (2005) 22(1) *J Int'l Arb* 75.

Redfern, A., Hunter, M., Blackaby, N. and Partasides, C., *Law and Practice of International Commercial Arbitration* (4th edn, Sweet & Maxwell, London, 2004).

Reiner, A., 'Schiedsverfahren und rechtliches Gehör' [2003] *Zeitschrift für Europarecht, Internationales Privatrecht und Rechtsvergleichung* 52 *et seq*.

Report of the Secretary-General on the Revised Draft Set of Arbitration Rules, UNCITRAL, 9th Session, Add 1 (Commentary), UN Doc A/CN.9/112/Add 1 (1975), (1976) VII UNCITRAL YB 166.

Report of The Working Group on Arbitration and Conciliation, UN Doc A/CN.9/641 (25 September 2007).

Rivkin, D.W., 'Restriction on Foreign Counsel in International Arbitrations' (1991) XVI *YB Comm Arb* 402.

Rubins, N., 'In God We Trust, All Others Pay Cash: Security for Costs in International Commercial Arbitration' (2000) 11 *Am Rev Int'l Arb* 307.

Sanders, P., 'L'autonomie de la clause compromissoire' in *Hommage à Frédéric Eisemann, Une initiative de la Chambre de Commerce Internationale, Liber Amicorum* (ICC, Paris, 1978).

Schlosser, P., *Das Recht der internationalen privaten Schiedsgerichtsbarkeit* (2nd edn, Mohr Siebeck, Tübingen, 1989).

Schlosser, P., 'Der Grad der Unabhängigkeit einer Schiedsvereinbarung vom Hauptvertrag' *in* R. Briner *et al* (eds), *Law of International Business and Dispute Settlement in the 21st Century in Liber Amicorum Karl-Heinz Böckstiegel* (Carl Heymanns Verlag, Cologne, 2001).

Schwab, K.H. and Walter, G. (eds), *Schiedsgerichtsbarkeit* (7th edn, C.H. Beck, Munich, 2005).

Schwarz, F.T. and Konrad, C.W., *The Vienna Rules, A Commentary on International Arbitration in Austria* (Kluwer Law International, The Hague, 2009).

Schwarz, F.T. and Ortner, H., 'Procedural Ordre Public and the Internationalization of Public Policy in Arbitration' in C. Klausegger and others (eds), *Austrian Arbitration Yearbook 2008* (Manz, Vienna, 2008).

Sheppard Jr., B. and Townsend, J, 'Holding the Fort Until the Arbitrators Are Appointed: The New ICDR International Emergency Rule' (2006) 61(2) *Disp Res J* 58.

Sheppard, A. and von Schlabrendorff, F., 'Legal Privilege and Confidentiality in Arbitration' in M. Koehnen, M. Russenberger and E. Cowling, *Privilege and Confidentiality: An International Handbook* (International Bar Association, London, 2006).

Shore, L., 'Three Evidentiary Problems in International Arbitration' [2004] *Zeitschrift für SchiedsVZ* 76.

Slate II, W., 'Paying Attention to "Culture" in International Commercial Arbitration' (2004) 59 *Disp Res J* 96.

Smit, H., 'International and Domestic Arbitration Procedure: The Need for a Rule Providing a Limited Opportunity for Arbitral Reconsideration of Reasoned Awards' (2004) 15 *Am Rev Int'l Arb* 9.

Smith, M.L., 'Impartiality of the Party-Appointed Arbitrator' (1990) 6(4) *Arb Int'l* 320, 323.

UK Department of Trade and Industry Consultation Document on Proposed Clauses and Schedules for an Arbitration Bill, reprinted in (1994) 10(2) *Arb Int'l* 189.

UNCITRAL Model Law on International Commercial Arbitration 1985, as amended 2006 (United Nations Docs A/40/17, annex I and A/61/17, annex I).

UNCITRAL Notes on Organizing Arbitral Proceedings (finalized June 14, 1996).

UNCITRAL Yearbook, vol XVI—1985, United Nations publication, Sales no E.87.V.4.

Weber, D., 'Wider den Verlust des Bestellungsrechts bei Nichteinigung der Mehrparteiengegenseite auf einen Schiedsrichter', in *Grenzüberschreitungen—Beiträge zum Internationalen Verfahrensrecht und zur Schiedsgerichtsbarkeit, Festschrift für Peter Schlosser zum 70. Geburtstag, 1063* (Mohr Siebeck, Tübingen, 2005).

Widman, S.M., 'When it's Over Before it's Completed: The Finality of Interim Awards' (2006) 24 *Alternatives to the High Cost of Litigation* 97.

Wilberforce, W., 'Written Briefs and Oral Advocacy' (1989) 5(4) *Arb Int'l* 348.

Yu, C.H., 'Final, Interim, Interlocutory or Partial Award: Misnomers Apt to Mislead' (2001) 13 *Singapore Academy L J* 467.

18

LCIA RULES

Julian D.M. Lew, Loukas A. Mistelis and Josephine C.P. Davies

I. Introduction

A. The LCIA and its Organization

(1) Introduction

18.01 The LCIA is an autonomous, independent and dedicated arbitration institution based in London providing services to the international business community. The LCIA administers arbitrations in accordance with its own rules (the Rules). It also administers *ad hoc* arbitrations under UNCITRAL Arbitration Rules (the UNCITRAL Rules). In addition, it offers the administration of mediation and other forms of ADR[1] and will act as a 'fund-holder'.[2] The LCIA is a not-for-profit organization and is not a branch of the London Chamber of Commerce and Industry.[3]

18.02 The headquarters of the LCIA are in London but there is no requirement that the juridical seat of arbitration be London. Although the Rules do provide for London as the default seat,[4] this is a pragmatic choice reflecting London's role as a centre of international arbitration,[5] as well as the LCIA's enduring connection with the city. Equally, LCIA arbitration does not necessarily entail London-based or English arbitrators, English procedural law, or the control of the English High Court.[6]

---

[1] See para18.21.

[2] See para 18.19.

[3] See n 25.

[4] Art 16, 18.214 ff.

[5] See School of International Arbitration/PricewaterhouseCoopers (2006) *International arbitration: Corporate Attitudes and Practices' survey:* participants rank London number one choice for international arbitration; and Mistelis, L., 'International Arbitration: Corporate Attitudes and Practices' (2004) 15 *Am Rev Int'l Arb* 525, at 564–7.

[6] Delvolvé, J.L., 'Le centenaire de la LCIA' (1993) *Rev arb* 599 [Delvolvé, LCIA] but see reference to '*our own*' LCIA: Goode, R., 'The Adaptation of English Law to International Commercial Arbitration' (1992) 8 *Arb Int'l 11*.

18.03 The present structure of the LCIA was established in the mid 1980s. It consists of three parts: the Company, the Court and the Secretariat. The Court and the Secretariat are the bodies with which users will have most contact.[7]

18.04 In addition, the LCIA is involved in two overseas projects. Since 2008 it has a joint venture with the Dubai International Financial Centre (DIFC) to establish DIFC-LCIA Arbitration and Mediation Centre which operates on rules similar to those of the LCIA. In 2009, a subsidiary LCIA company was established in India to provide those in India and throughout Asia ready accessibility to LCIA services.

(1) The Company

18.05 The first pillar of the LCIA is the corporate body, a private company limited by guarantee (the Company). Its board of directors (the Board) plays no active role in the administration of dispute resolution but is principally concerned with the operation of the LCIA's business and company law matters. Most members of the Board are prominent London-based arbitration practitioners.

18.06 The LCIA Director General is Chief Executive Officer of the Company. He is also a member of the Court and is thus the primary contact between it and the Board.

(2) The Court

18.07 The LCIA Court is the second pillar of the institution. It is governed by the LCIA constitution (the Constitution).[8] In performing its functions, the Court, its officers and members must act independently of the Board.[9]

18.08 The Court performs institutional functions, including as appointing authority in arbitrations administered by the LCIA.[10] It is the final authority for the application of the Rules, keeps the Rules under review and makes recommendations to the Board if new rules are desirable.[11]

18.09 The Court has up to 35 members, including seven Vice Presidents. All are appointed for a five-year term by the Board on the recommendation of the Court and are not generally eligible for reappointment for a consecutive term. The President is appointed for a term of up to three years and is eligible for reappointment.[12]

18.10 The international membership of the Court is ensured by the LCIA Constitution, which provides that no more than six members may be of UK nationality[13] and that due regard

---

[7] For comment on the constitution see: Winstanley, A., 'The LCIA—history, constitution and rules' in A. Berkeley and J. Mimms (eds), *International Commercial Arbitration: Practical Perspectives* (Centre of Construction Law & Management, 2001), 22–6.

[8] The Constitution of the LCIA Arbitration Court, most recently amended in 2000, is available on the LCIA website.

[9] Art D(3), Constitution.

[10] Arts D(1)(a) and D(1)(b), Constitution.

[11] Arts D(1)(c) and D(1)(d), Constitution. For implementation of this, see Winstanley, A., 'The New Rules of the London Court of International Arbitration' (1997) 8 *Am Rev Int'l Arb* 59 [Winstanley, The New Rules].

[12] Arts A and B, Constitution.

[13] Art A(1), Constitution.

must be given to a balance of nationalities among the Vice-Presidents.[14] In early 2009, the President was French, only one Vice President and three of the 25 other members were UK nationals.

The non-administrative functions of the Court are performed by the President, a Vice-President, or by divisions of three members, appointed by the President and chaired by the President or a Vice-President. Administrative functions of the Court are performed by the Registrar (or Deputy Registrar).[15] Thus challenges to arbitrators under Art 10 of the Rules are almost invariably considered by a three-member division while the receipt of Art 1 Requests is handled by the Registrar. **18.11**

(3) The Secretariat and the Registrar

The third pillar of the institution is the Secretariat, which oversees the administration of all disputes referred to the LCIA for arbitration. The actual extent of administration conducted by the Secretariat varies according to the requirements of the tribunal, parties and the nature of the case. **18.12**

The Secretariat is headed by the Registrar (typically a qualified lawyer). The Registrar provides the link between the Secretariat and the Court as well as assisting the Director General with the running of the LCIA. **18.13**

The Registrar has a minimal formal role but, informally, is of great importance for the main LCIA business of case administration. The Registrar is, for example, the point of contact for the parties' representatives if they consider there is a problem with a party nominated arbitrator or the conduct of the arbitration. The Court is supplied with summaries prepared by the Registrar on each pending arbitration (typically about 350 such cases at any time). **18.14**

The LCIA's stated intention is to provide the tribunal and the parties with the administrative support that they require, particularly with regard to case management, and communications and to the parties. **18.15**

The LCIA considers that a secretary to the Tribunal may be of real assistance and save costs although their role should not extend to administrative functions properly carried out by the Secretariat. If a secretary is considered desirable, the LCIA will propose appropriate terms. **18.16**

(4) Users' Councils

The LCIA offers membership of six regionally[16] organized Users' Councils. These organize events additional to those organized by the LCIA centrally. The Users' Councils have no formal control over the LCIA although their feedback is noted by the Board and Court with a view to ensuring the LCIA's international perspective. **18.17**

[14] Art B(1)(b), Constitution.
[15] Art D(2) and G, Constitution. These functions are articulated in Art 3, Rules, see para 18.69 ff.
[16] ie African, Asia-Pacific, Arab, European, Latin-American and Caribbean, and North American.

(5) Charges for arbitration

18.18 The fees of the LCIA and its tribunals are not based on the sum in issue. Instead, the LCIA charges a registration fee[17] payable when the Request for Arbitration[18] is filed. Thereafter, fees are based on the time expended by both the LCIA and its arbitrators. Current fees and charges are set out in a Schedule to the Rules (the Schedule of Costs). The Court determines the costs of each arbitration. Any dispute regarding administrative charges or fees and expenses of the tribunal is decided by the Court (usually as a division).

18.19 Similarly, the LCIA charges for fund-holding services according to the time expended. As at March 2009, the charges were in line with the lower administrative rate for secretariat personnel.[19]

(6) Comparison with the ICC

18.20 The LCIA is less 'institutionalized' and interventionist than the ICC.[20] The most notable differences are its fee structure (the ICC operates an *ad valorem* fee structure for administrative charges and arbitrators' fees) and the level of institutional engagement in the arbitral process (for example, the LCIA neither requires terms of reference[21] nor has a designated counsel team per arbitration case nor scrutinizes awards). The LCIA should not be thought of as competing with the ICC but rather as providing 'an alternative to the ICC system of arbitration'.[22]

(7) Mediation

18.21 The LCIA mediation procedure is available whether parties have only a general mediation obligation, have chosen to mediate, or have chosen the LCIA procedure in advance. The costs of mediation are time based.[23]

B. History of the LCIA and the Rules

18.22 While the institution was created in 1892, the modern existence of the LCIA began in 1975 when the Institute of Arbitrators (now the Chartered Institute of Arbitrators) joined the London Chamber of Commerce and the City Corporation in administering the London Court.[24] In 1981 the institution's name was changed to the London Court of

---

17 £1,500 in March 2009.

18 Art 1.

19 £100 per hour in March 2009, see Schedule of Costs.

20 Poudret , J.F. and Besson, S., *Comparative Law of International Arbitration* (2nd edn, 2007) [Poudret and Besson], s 103. For comment on the less than full institutional nature of the LCIA see Veeder, V.V., 'London Court of International Arbitration, The New 1998 LCIA Rules' (1998) 23 *YCA* 366 [Veeder, 1998 Rules].

21 Although it is not uncommon for a tribunal to hold a preliminary conference to agree on procedure: Rivkin, D., '1997: A Year of Rule Changes' *Int'l Arb L Rev* 1998 1(2) 92 [Rivkin].

22 Tackaberry, J. and Marriott, A.. *Bernstein's Handbook of Arbitration and Dispute Resolution Practice* (4th edn, 2003) [Bernstein's Handbook], s 9-023. For a comparison of the rules see, eg: Craig, W.L., 'The LCIA and ICC Rules: the 1998 revisions compared' in A. Berkeley and J. Mimms (eds), *International Commercial Arbitration: Practical Perspectives* (Centre of Construction Law & Management, 2001), 79.

23 See LCIA Mediation Rules Art 8.

24 A summary of the LCIA's history from its creation in 1892 is provided on its website and in Winstanley, A., 'The LCIA—history, constitution and rules' in A. Berkeley and J. Mimms (eds), *International Commercial Arbitration: Practical Perspectives* (Centre of Construction Law & Management, 2001), 21–2.

International Arbitration to reflect the predominance of international work.[25] At the same time, new rules (the 1981 Rules)[26] were adopted prompted by the English Arbitration Act 1979 and changes in English attitudes to international arbitration.[27] The basic concept behind the new rules was to 'maximise the powers and the jurisdiction of the arbitral tribunal, and to minimize formalities and other restrictions'.[28] This remains the cornerstone of the Rules.

The 1981 Rules consisted of fourteen Articles and a four-paragraph schedule. In 1985, they were revised and expanded to twenty more detailed Articles (the 1985 Rules).[29] The 1985 Rules took into account of the *travaux préparatoires* and the draft of the UNCITRAL Model Law on International Commercial Arbitration (the Model Law). Among other things, the 1985 Rules provided powers for arbitrators and the Court to deal with dilatory conduct by the parties and reflected the right of parties to waive their right of recourse to national courts. **18.23**

The 1985 Rules were replaced by the 1998 Rules, the current version of the LCIA Rules (the Rules) consisting of 32 Articles. The revisions, mainly of a minor nature and adding detail, were prompted by the English Arbitration Act 1996 (the 1996 Act) and by developments in international practice.[30] A further revision of the Rules is anticipated in the foreseeable future. **18.24**

Despite the LCIA's nineteenth century origins in the common law, it is not a common law institution.[31] It is not a 'chasse gardée' of Queen's counsels and the Rules do not presume typically common law procedures such as cross-examination 'ou bizarreries de même sorte inaccessibles au commun des mortels'.[32] **18.25**

C. Statistics on LCIA Arbitrations

In 2008, the LCIA registered some 221[33] new arbitrations. This was the highest annual number of arbitrations up from 137 in 2007.[34] Apparently, 106 new cases had been registered by late April 2009. **18.26**

[25] Where an arbitration agreement refers to the London Court of Arbitration, the LCIA will accept jurisdiction. Special provision is also made where an agreement names the London Chamber of Commerce (and Industry) (LCCI). Although the LCIA is neither part of nor connected to the LCCI, LCCI bye-law 6.01 provides that disputes referred to it are deemed to be references to the LCIA.

[26] Published in Sanders, P. (ed), *YCA vol VII* (1982) 223.

[27] Hunter, J.M. and Paulsson, J., 'Rules of the London Court of International Arbitration A Commentary on the 1985 Rules of the London Court of International Arbitration' in P. Sanders (ed), *YCA vol X* (1985) 167 [Hunter and Paulsson, 1985 Rules].

[28] *ibid.*

[29] Published in Sanders, P. (ed), *YCA vol X* (1985) 157.

[30] Veeder, 1998 Rules, 366. A further aim was to preserve and enhance 'arbitration's edge over litigation in terms of cost and time efficiency' Winstanley, The New Rules, 59.

[31] See the response to a reported criticism from a Swiss participant that civilian lawyers might be disadvantaged: Thompson, D., 'Annual Conference: Chartered Institute of Arbitrators' (1985) 2 *J Int'l Arb* 116.

[32] Delvolvé, LCIA, 600.

[33] 4(1) *Global Arb Rev* (2009) 10, 16, 17, 22 (recording LCIA number up to November 2009. Additional information is also provided in the Director General's annual report).

[34] 4(1) *Global Arb Rev (2009)* 17.

18.27 Since the LCIA fee structure is not based on the value of the claim, about a third of cases are not quantified on referral; many of these are said to be worth in excess of US$10 million. In both 2007 and 2006, around 8 per cent of referrals were for claims between US$10 and 20 million; a similar proportion were for claims over US$20 million. Around 20 per cent were worth between US$1 and 5 million and another 20 per cent were worth less than one million.

18.28 The users of the LCIA are from a diverse range of jurisdictions. In 2007 the largest groups were 16 per cent from the UK and 10 per cent from the USA. A significant number of other jurisdictions are represented including India, Latin America, Switzerland, Russia, and Middle Eastern, and African countries.

18.29 Of the 88 tribunals appointed in 2007, 50 per cent were sole arbitrators. Just over half of those appointed were party nominees. The majority of arbitrators were English but a wide range of nationalities were represented.

II. Commentary on the LCIA Rules

A. Overview and structure of the Rules

18.30 The Rules provide a framework for the procedural stages of the arbitration from initial request to final award. Notwithstanding this, party autonomy regarding the conduct of the arbitration is enshrined in Art 14.1[35] and is fundamental to LCIA arbitrations. The position is summed up thus: 'In many ways, the LCIA occupies an historical position halfway between full institutional arbitration and *ad hoc* forms of arbitration; its two most distinctive features [Article 14.1, party autonomy, and Article 5, the Court's power to appoint arbitrators,] straddle this division.'[36]

18.31 Mandatory supervision is limited to ensuring that the LCIA and the tribunal are in funds to pay the fees and expenses of the arbitrators and the LCIA. The Secretariat, however, can provide a more 'hands on' case management if desired.

18.32 The Rules provide useful guidance to parties and arbitrators,[37] and are sufficiently detailed to be used as the necessary planning instrument, with the need for little or no addition.[38] Nevertheless, they are frequently silent on matters of detail, such as the test to be applied by the tribunal in deciding whether to grant interim relief.[39]

18.33 The Rules and answers to frequently asked questions (FAQ) can be obtained from the LCIA.

---

35 See para 18.171 ff.

36 Veeder, 1998 Rules, 366

37 Redfern, A. and Hunter, M., *Law and Practice of International Commercial Arbitration* (4th edn, 2004) [Redfern and Hunter], s 1-117. Given that the LCIA publishes no decisions (save for those on challenges to arbitrators, see 18.140 ff) which could offer any other guidance to the parties, this guidance in the Rules is clearly necessary and has been expanded with each subsequent revision.

38 Kerr, M., 'London Court of International Arbitration' in *ICCA Congress Series no 7* (1996) 213.

39 See para 18.309 ff.

B. Commentary on the individual LCIA Rules

Article 1 The Request for Arbitration

1.1 Any party wishing to commence an arbitration under these Rules ('the Claimant') shall send to the Registrar of the LCIA Court ('the Registrar') a written request for arbitration ('the Request'), containing or accompanied by:

(a) the names, addresses, telephone, facsimile, telex and email numbers (if known) of the parties to the arbitration and of their legal representatives;

(b) a copy of the written arbitration clause or separate written arbitration agreement invoked by the Claimant ('the Arbitration Agreement'), together with a copy of the contractual documentation in which the arbitration clause is contained or in respect of which the arbitration arises;

(c) a brief statement describing the nature and circumstances of the dispute, and specifying the claims advanced by the Claimant against another party to the arbitration ('the Respondent');

(d) a statement of any matters (such as the seat or language(s) of the arbitration, or the number of arbitrators, or their qualifications or identities) on which the parties have already agreed in writing for the arbitration or in respect of which the Claimant wishes to make a proposal;

(e) if the Arbitration Agreement calls for party nomination of arbitrators, the name, address, telephone, facsimile, telex and email numbers (if known) of the Claimant's nominee;

(f) the fee prescribed in the Schedule of Costs (without which the Request shall be treated as not having been received by the Registrar and the arbitration as not having been commenced);

(g) confirmation to the Registrar that copies of the Request (including all accompanying documents) have been or are being served simultaneously on all other parties to the arbitration by one or more means of service to be identified in such confirmation.

1.2 The date of receipt by the Registrar of the Request shall be treated as the date on which the arbitration has commenced for all purposes. The Request (including all accompanying documents) should be submitted to the Registrar in two copies where a sole arbitrator should be appointed, or, if the parties have agreed or the Claimant considers that three arbitrators should be appointed, in four copies.

(1) Generally

Article 1 sets out the procedure for the initiation of proceedings. By requiring a written agreement to be submitted, it also arguably restricts the scope of the LCIA's jurisdiction.[40] **18.34**

(2) The Request

There is no prescribed form for the Request; all that is required is that it contains the information set out in the lettered sub-paras although the fee due under Art 1.1(f) can be sent direct to the LCIA's bank account. Requests may be a lengthy and fully particularized statement of case or a short statement of the claim and relief sought. **18.35**

40 Samuel, A., 'Jurisdiction, interim relief and awards under the LCIA Rules' in A. Berkeley and J. Mimms (eds), *International Commercial Arbitration: Practical Perspectives* (Centre of Construction Law & Management, 2001), 35 [Samuel].

18.36 One reason a Claimant may chose to make a fuller Request is that, unless otherwise agreed or determined by the tribunal, the Claimant has only 30 days from the appointment of the tribunal to file its Statement of Case.[41]

18.37 The information required is to enable the Respondent and the LCIA to understand the nature of the claim and ensure communication between the parties. The information required is largely self-explanatory.[42] The only possible difficulty is the parenthetic 'if known' in the requirement that the contact information of the parties and any Claimant-nominated arbitrator be provided.[43] As it is quite conceivable that the Claimant will not know several of the items listed (not just the electronic contact details), the words 'if known' must be read as qualifying every piece of information required in Arts 1.1(a) and (e). Thus, the Claimant must provide as much information as is available.

18.38 Article 1.1(c), requiring a brief statement describing the nature and circumstances of the disputes and specifying the claims, is an essential part of due process and is also useful for the selection of appropriate arbitrators.

18.39 Article 1.1(d) is the opportunity for the Claimant to make proposals about the conduct of the arbitration proceedings. This may include indicating the means by which the Claimant would like to present evidence;[44] doing so at this stage may save costs.

18.40 No provision is made in the LCIA rules for the consequence of making a Request which does not contain the required information, save that Art 1.1(f) provides that, if the fee payable under it is not received, the 'Request shall be treated as not having been received by the Registrar and the arbitration as not having been commenced'.[45]

18.41 Failures to comply with the sub-paras to Art 1.1, other than non-payment of the fee will not, therefore, necessarily result in the Request being treated as if it had not been received. The LCIA Court is expressly given discretion to proceed with the formation of the Arbitral Tribunal notwithstanding that the Request is incomplete.[46] While this is perfectly defensible where the failure is minor, there is clearly a point where the Claimant's failure is such that the document submitted cannot properly be treated as a Request.[47] It is suggested that a failure to set out or attach the Arbitration Agreement (Art 1.1(b)), or to set out the nature of the dispute and the claim being made (Art 1(1)(c)), or to confirm that the Request had been served on the other parties (Art 1(1)(g)), would be failures sufficient to prevent the Request being effective.

---

41 Art 15.2.

42 Especially as Art 1 is more detailed than its predecessors under the 1981 and 1985 rules.

43 Arts 1.1(a) and (e).

44 Lörcher, G., 'Improving procedures of Oral and Written Witness Testimony' in *ICCA Congress Series no 7* (1996) 145.

45 Despite this, on occasions (and provided the Respondent is prepared to participate) the arbitration will proceed.

46 Art 5.4.

47 The Rules expressly contemplate that there are circumstances in which the progress of the arbitration will be delayed as the Court seeks documents adjudged to be missing from the Request. Art 9.3 providing that the Court may curtail a time limit in relation to documents adjudged to be missing from the Request.

18.42 Failures, which are sufficiently minor to allow a strictly non-compliant document to be treated as a Request are most likely to occur in relation to Art 1.1(d). For example, the Claimant omits to state matters on which the parties have agreed, such as the language of the arbitration. In such a case, there is unlikely to be any real prejudice to the other parties who will have the opportunity to address the matter in their Response under Art 2.1. In such circumstances, it is probable that the Request will be treated as such.

18.43 If the Claimant fails to nominate an arbitrator where the Arbitration Agreement calls for this (Art 1.1(d)), the Request will almost certainly be treated as effective and, under Arts 7.2 and 5.4, the LCIA Court is empowered to nominate an arbitrator.

18.44 In completing the Request, a prudent Claimant will explain the reasons for the omission of any detail required by Art 1.1.

(3) Service of the Request

18.45 The Request must be in writing and the Claimant should deliver it to the Registrar[48] and to the Respondent. The requirements of Art 4 should be followed.

18.46 Under Art 1.1(g), the Request must be served on the other parties to the arbitration either at the same time as or prior to the time when it is served on the Registrar. In contrast with the default position under the English 1996 Act, and reflecting the importance of consensual arbitration, the arbitration cannot be deemed to be commenced, even if the LCIA is the appointing body, until service has been effected on the Respondent.[49]

18.47 Where service can be effected electronically, there is unlikely to be any difficulty with simultaneous service. Where, however, electronic means are unavailable for service on the other parties, the Claimant will risk being put in a position of alerting the other parties to the intended arbitration proceedings before the date on which the arbitration is formally commenced under Art 1.2.

18.48 If this occurs, the Claimant is exposed to the risk that the Respondent may start substantive or injunctive court proceedings in another jurisdiction before the LCIA arbitration is commenced. Equally, the Respondent might commence arbitration in another forum. Insofar as arbitration or court proceedings are commenced outside the countries to which the Brussels Regulation[50] is applicable, providing the English High Court's jurisdiction can be established, it will be open to the Claimant to apply for an anti-suit or anti-arbitration injunction in support of the arbitration from the English High Court.[51] Such injunctive

---

[48] The Registrar is discussed in the context of Art 3, see 18.70 ff.

[49] s 14(5) of the 1996 Act provides that, if the parties have not agreed when arbitration proceedings are to be regarded as commenced, 'Where the arbitrator or arbitrators are to be appointed by a person other than a party to the proceedings, arbitral proceedings are commenced in respect of a matter when one party gives notice in writing to that person requesting him to make the appointment in respect of that matter'.

[50] European Council Regulation 44/2001/EC on International Jurisdiction and Recognition and Enforcement of Judgments in Civil and Commercial Matters [2001] OJ L012/1.

[51] See eg the discussion in Merkin, R.M., *Arbitration Law* (3rd edn, Informa, 2004) [Merkin, Arbitration Law], ch 8. Also *Shashou & Ors v Sharma,* [2009] EWHC 957 (Comm), (8 May 2009).

relief cannot be obtained, however, if another European Union Court has jurisdiction under the Brussels Regulation.[52]

18.49 In practice, the best course for a Claimant who cannot serve the other parties by electronic means, is to serve the Registrar electronically as soon as it receives confirmation of delivery to the Respondent by hand.

(4) Commencement

18.50 Once the Registrar receives a valid Request, Art 1.2 provides that the arbitration will be treated as commenced 'for all purposes'. This is wide enough to encompass commencement for the purposes of national law rules on limitation of actions. So, for example, under English law, Art 1.2 is an agreement as to commencement under s 14(1), 1996 Act.

18.51 There is no provision in any part of the Rules that service can only be made on a business day or within office hours. Provided, therefore, that the fee had already been received by the LCIA it would be possible to commence an arbitration on a non-business day in London. It is not uncommon for the LCIA to receive funds before the written Request.

18.52 Article 1.2 also requires the Claimant to supply copies of the Request for the tribunal to be appointed. Where there is no agreement for a three-member tribunal, the rebuttable presumption is for a sole arbitrator to be appointed.[53] Clearly, if the Claimant desires a three-member tribunal and there is no prior agreement, it should propose this and supply four copies of the Request.

18.53 If there is a dispute between the parties as to the appropriate number of arbitrators,[54] one party may provide a single copy of its initial document (the Request or Response) while the other provides three copies. If the Court decides there should be three arbitrators, the relevant party will be asked to supply additional copies of the relevant document.

(5) Status of the claim set out

18.54 The requirement for the Claimant to outline its case in the Request, and provision for the Response, has led some practitioners to refer to the LCIA system as one of 'double pleading'. This need not be so. Although the Request may stand as the Claimant's Statement of Case,[55] all that is required for the reference is to provide sufficient detail to specify all the matters in dispute as the Reference.

18.55 Together with any Response, the Request determines the tribunal's jurisdiction. The Rules provide for amendment, but not addition, of claims.[56] In order to avoid later difficulty, it is recommended that the Request contain some general wording to cover all matters in dispute to which the arbitration agreement applies in addition to the specific matters

52 See *Ras Riunione Adriatica di Sicurta SpA v West Tankers Inc (The Front Comor)* Case C-185/07, decided on 10 February 2009, (a reference from [2007] UKHL 4; [2007] 1 All ER (Comm) 794; [2007] 1 Lloyd's Rep 391); and, more generally, Briggs, A. and Rees, P., *Civil Jurisdiction and Judgments* (4th edn, Informa Professional, 2005); and Raphael, T., *The Anti-Suit Injunction* (OUP, 2008).

53 Art 5.4.

54 A matter likely to be raised in the Response under Art 2.

55 See the option under Art 15.3 that the Request may stand as a Statement of Case.

56 Art 22.1(a).

set out.[57] In practice, if matters which appear to be outside the scope of the Request are introduced at the formal pleading stage, the parties are usually able to agree to refer those additional matters to theTribunal already appointed.

Article 2 The Response

2.1 Within 30 days of service of the Request on the Respondent, (or such lesser period fixed by the LCIA Court), the Respondent shall send to the Registrar a written response to the Request ('the Response'), containing or accompanied by:

(a) confirmation or denial of all or part of the claims advanced by the Claimant in the Request;

(b) a brief statement describing the nature and circumstances of any counterclaims advanced by the Respondent against the Claimant;

(c) comment in response to any statements contained in the Request, as called for under Article 1.1(d), on matters relating to the conduct of the arbitration;

(d) if the Arbitration Agreement calls for party nomination of arbitrators, the name, address, telephone, facsimile, telex and email numbers (if known) of the Respondent's nominee; and

(e) confirmation to the Registrar that copies of the Response (including all accompanying documents) have been or are being served simultaneously on all other parties to the arbitration by one or more means of service to be identified in such confirmation.

2.2 The Response (including all accompanying documents) should be submitted to the Registrar in two copies, or if the parties have agreed or the Respondent considers that three arbitrators should be appointed, in four copies.

2.3 Failure to send a Response shall not preclude the Respondent from denying any claim or from advancing a counterclaim in the arbitration. However, if the Arbitration Agreement calls for party nomination of arbitrators, failure to send a Response or to nominate an arbitrator within time or at all shall constitute an irrevocable waiver of that party's opportunity to nominate an arbitrator.

(1) Generally

Article 2 sets out the procedure for the Respondent to respond to the Request. The Respondent has an opportunity, rather than an obligation, to comment on and perhaps to narrow the issues, and to make any counterclaim. **18.56**

(2) Contents and service of the Response

The Respondent is required to respond to the Request within 30 days of service on it of the Request[58] but is not obliged to do so. The 30-day period may be abridged by the Court;[59] however, the Court has no power to extend the period for a Response to be filed.[60] **18.57**

The requirements of Art 2.1 are broadly equivalent to those set out in Art 1.1 save that the Respondent is not required to give contact details or to provide a copy of the written **18.58**

[57] Sutton, D.S.J., Gill, J. and Gearing, M., *Russell on Arbitration* (23rd edn, Sweet & Maxwell, 2007) [Russell on Arbitration], s 5-026.

[58] Also Arts 4 and 1.1(g).

[59] Art 9.

[60] The power of the LCIA Court to abridge time is dealt with in Art 9. No express reference is made to any power to extend time.

agreement said to contain the arbitration clause. The first difference could put the Claimant at some procedural disadvantage if it can be served by email and fax while the Respondent cannot. This is resolved by Art 4.5 which allows the tribunal to direct the means of communication. As to the second difference, unless the Respondent purports to rely on a different Arbitration Agreement, there is no need for an equivalent to Art 1.1(b).

18.59 Any counterclaim which the Respondent may have should be advanced at this stage. A failure to do so will not, however, prevent the Respondent from advancing the claim at a later stage.[61]

18.60 Other points to note are that, under Art 2.1(a), the Respondent can only confirm or deny the statements made in the Claimant's claims. This is directed to indicating what issues are actually in dispute. The Respondent is also given the opportunity to comment on the Request as it considers relevant (Art 2(1)(c)).

18.61 Article 2.2 mirrors Art 1.2.[62]

(3) Failure to file a Response

18.62 The Response is not a mandatory submission. Article 2.3 ensures that the Respondent will not be precluded from denying any matter or advancing a counterclaim in the arbitration if no Response is sent.[63] On the other hand, if the arbitration agreement calls for party nomination of arbitrators, a failure to do so is an irrevocable waiver of the Respondent's right in that respect.

18.63 The two limbs of Art 2.3 are designed to ensure the effectiveness of the arbitration procedure. The first ensures that the Respondent has the opportunity to make its case and thus prevents the award being challenged for failure to comply with requirements of natural justice, particularly the principle of *audi alteram partem*.[64] The second prevents a recalcitrant Respondent stalling the arbitration proceedings.[65]

18.64 The Rules[66] contemplate a failure to 'send a Response or to nominate an arbitrator'. It is suggested that 'or' is disjunctive so a Respondent might fail to file a Response but might nevertheless validly nominate an arbitrator. This is an entirely sensible reading and allows an agreement for party-nominated arbitrators to be effective if at all possible.

18.65 The time provision for nomination is, 'within time or at all' (Art 2.3). This phrase appears to qualify both the sending of a Response and the nomination of an arbitrator and, unless this has been varied by the arbitration agreement, the Respondent should regard itself as having 30 days to nominate an arbitrator. Nevertheless, if a Respondent's nomination is

---

61 See para 18.62 ff.

62 See para 18.50 ff.

63 The provision for a Response was introduced as Art 2, 1985 Rules.

64 Default in arbitration after having been duly notified has invariably been held not to bar enforcement of a Convention award: Butchers, J. and Kimbrough, P., 'The Arbitral Tribunal's Role in Default Proceedings' (2006) 22 *Arb Int'l* 233.

65 See Arts 5.2 and 5.3.

66 Art 2.3.

made after this time but before the Court has actually appointed an arbitrator,[67] the Respondent's nomination will probably, but not certainly,[68] be treated as effective. Since the Court will appoint the Arbitral Tribunal 'as soon as practicable' after the Response is received by the Registrar (or the time for it to be served has expired) the window for this nomination may be very narrow. This balances the object of avoiding unnecessary delay[69] with that of carrying out the parties' chosen arbitration method.

Not infrequently, a Respondent may consider it to be a tactical advantage not to file a Response. A commonly perceived advantage (which may relate to separate but connected proceedings) is that the Respondent can avoid stating any position on the claims advanced by the Claimant until the Claimant's case has been set out in a more detailed form. **18.66**

As the Respondent may nevertheless nominate an arbitrator (if the Arbitration Agreement calls for this), the Respondent will only forgo the opportunity to comment on the conduct of the arbitration by filing no Response. Equally a Respondent might file an incomplete Response dealing with only procedural matters. **18.67**

(4) Partial statement

If the Respondent does submit a Response setting out its answer to the claim advanced in the Request, its right to advance further claims in the arbitration may be subject to dispute. Commonly, the Response is little more than a blanket denial with (to avoid dispute) a reservation of the Respondent's right to put its case following receipt of the Claimant's Statement of Case. As for the Request, general wording should be included to cover all outstanding matters as well as such a reservation of rights.[70] **18.68**

Article 3 The LCIA Court and Registrar

3.1 The functions of the LCIA Court under these Rules shall be performed in its name by the President or a Vice President of the LCIA Court or by a division of three or five members of the LCIA Court appointed by the President or a Vice President of the LCIA Court, as determined by the President.

3.2 The functions of the Registrar under these Rules shall be performed by the registrar or any deputy Registrar of the LCIA Court under the supervision of the LCIA Court.

3.3 All communications from any party or arbitrator to the LCIA Court shall be addressed to the Registrar.

(1) Generally

Article 3 sets out the delegation of authority provisions within the Court. **18.69**

(2) The Court and Registrar

Reflecting the administrative role of the Secretariat, Art 3.3 requires all communications to the Court be addressed to the Registrar. The communication may be by any methods specified in Art 4.1. Once the arbitration is underway communication is normally directly **18.70**

67 Under Art 5.4.
68 See Art 7.2.
69 See Art 14.1.
70 See too para 18.55.

with the tribunal. The Registrar is normally informed of the progress of the arbitration, such as the submissions filed.

Article 4 Notices and Periods of Time

4.1 Any notice or other communication that may be or is required to be given by a party under these Rules shall be in writing and shall be delivered by registered postal or courier service or transmitted by facsimile, telex, email or any other means of telecommunication that provide a record of its transmission.

4.2 A party's last-known residence or place of business during the arbitration shall be a valid address for the purpose of any notice or other communication in the absence of any notification of a change to such address by that party to the other parties, the Arbitral Tribunal and the Registrar.

4.3 For the purpose of determining the date of commencement of a time limit, a notice or other communication shall be treated as having been received on the day it is delivered or, in the case of telecommunications, transmitted in accordance with Articles 4.1 and 4.2.

4.4 For the purpose of determining compliance with a time limit, a notice or other communication shall be treated as having been sent, made or transmitted if it is dispatched in accordance with Articles 4.1 and 4.2 prior to or on the date of the expiration of the time limit.

4.5 Not withstanding the above, any notice or communication by one party may be addressed to another party in the manner agreed in writing between them or, failing such agreement, according to the practice followed in the course of their previous dealings or in whatever manner ordered by the Arbitral Tribunal.

4.6 For the purpose of calculating a period of time under these Rules, such period shall begin to run on the day following the day when a notice or other communication is received. If the last day of such period is an official holiday or a non-business day at the residence or place of business of the addressee, the period is extended until the first business day which follows. Official holidays or non-business days occurring during the running of the period of time are included in calculating that period.

4.7 The Arbitral Tribunal may at any time extend (even where the period of time has expired) or abridge any period of time prescribed under these Rules or under the Arbitration Agreement for the conduct of the arbitration, including any notice or communication to be served by one party on any other party.

(1) General

18.71 Article 4 is designed to 'avoid sterile arguments over the precise date, time and method of service of documents'.[71] It states where and how communications are to be made but maintains the parties' right to agree, and the tribunal's power to order, otherwise. It also states how time periods are to be calculated. In this respect, the parties may vary only some aspects. The tribunal is given absolute discretion to extend or abridge time.

(2) Means of communication

18.72 Under Art 4.1, notices and communication must be in writing delivered by registered post or courier service, or increasingly popularly, by various electronic means. Article 4.1 allows for the advancement of technology by stating that any other means of telecommunication providing a record of transmission may be used.

[71] Winstanley, The New Rules, 60.

The use of electronic communications may cause difficulty if a document is sent in a form that cannot be read by the recipient. If this were to occur the tribunal would almost certainly exercise its discretion under Art 4.7 to extend time to run from the date of readable delivery so as to avoid prejudice to the receiving party. **18.73**

Where physical delivery is effected, a courier service will invariably provide a record of both sending and delivery. The situation is less clear in relation to 'registered post' since each national postal service has its own definition of the phrase. In the context of Art 4.1, however, it can only reasonably mean a postal service under which the mail is tracked, and the sending and delivery are both recorded. **18.74**

The requirements of Art 4.1 are not unusual. Nevertheless, Art 4.5 offers three further possibilities: agreement in writing to another method; a method used in previous dealings; or a method ordered by the tribunal. **18.75**

The commencement of time under Arts 4.3 and 4.6 is triggered by delivery but compliance with a time limit under Arts 4.4 and 4.6 is triggered by sending. Accordingly, parties would be well advised to ensure that any method they choose, including one used in previous dealings, provides a record of the time of both sending and delivery. It would be unwise to rely on an unrecorded oral communication because of the inevitable difficulties of proving its content and existence. **18.76**

(3) Address for communication

The place at which communications and notices are to be sent to each party is specified by Art 4.2. In addition, by implication, Art 4.5 allows other addresses to be used. **18.77**

Article 4.2 is largely self-explanatory, providing that the party's 'last-known' residence or place of business shall be a valid address for the purpose of notice or communication during the arbitration unless notification is given of that change. So, unless and until it has been indicated or agreed otherwise, communications must be to the other party at one of these addresses and not to its legal representative. **18.78**

The Claimant will have set out both its address and, if it can, the addresses of the other parties in the Request.[72] Article 4.2 does not state that these will automatically be treated as the valid address for communication.[73] Accordingly, it appears that parties could communicate via any address that falls within the description of a 'last-known residence or place of business'. In practice, the addresses stated in the Request will often be coincident with this. **18.79**

There are no formal requirements regarding notification of any change of address. Under English law, the question will simply be whether the information was communicated.[74] Ideally, any change should be notified by an appropriate means to all concerned stating the old and new addresses. Nevertheless, a letter on paper headed with a different address is arguably sufficient to effect notification. Such an action might result from a failure to **18.80**

72 Art 1.1(a).

73 Unlike Art 4.4 of the 1985 Rules.

74 See *Mannai v Eagle Star* and *ICC v West Bromwich BS* [1998] 1 WLR 898.

appreciate the need for clarity but it might be used by an unscrupulous Respondent to create delay. In the event of any doubt as to the correct address, the receiving party and the tribunal should request that the other party clarifies its address for communications. Such correspondence should naturally be addressed to both the old and new addresses.

18.81 Finally, the effect of Art 4.5 is that the parties can use another address provided that they have agreed in writing; or this is the address which has been used in the course of previous dealings; or this is ordered by the tribunal. An obvious example is where communication is always made through brokers or agents.

(4) Time

18.82 Articles 4.3, 4.4 and 4.6 set out the rules dealing with time limits.

18.83 A period of time under the rules starts on the day following the day when the notice or communication is received.[75] The notice or communication is treated as having been received on the day it is delivered or, in the case of telecommunications,[76] transmitted provided it is sent in accordance with Arts 4.1 and 4.2. If some other method is used pursuant to Art 4.5, then the notice or communication will be treated as received as agreed, or as customary, or as ordered by the tribunal. If there is no relevant agreement, custom or order, then time will begin under Art 4.6 when the notice or communication is actually received.

18.84 Where compliance with a time limit is concerned, dispatch of the message, rather than its delivery or receipt, is relevant under Art 4.4. The latest time for compliance with a time limit is for the communication to be sent on the last day of the period. If the communication is sent other than in accordance with Arts 4.1 and 4.2, then pursuant to Art 4.5 'unless otherwise agreed, ordered or customary' the actual time of sending will be required to determine whether there has been compliance with the time limit.

18.85 The Rules take account of business days only to a limited extent, that is, in relation to the expiration of periods for compliance. Under Art 4.6, if the last day of a period of time under the rules is an official holiday or a non-business day at the residence or place of business of the addressee who is the party obliged to respond or take a step, the period is extended until the first business day at that place. Generally, though, where official holidays or non-business days occur during the running of the period of time, these are included in calculating that period.

18.86 In contrast with this, neither Art 4.3 nor 4.6 makes reference to the effect of delivery outside office hours or on a non-business day for the purpose of commencement of a time limit. In the overall context of Art 4.6, it is probably strictly correct to treat delivery, even outside office hours or on a holiday, as adequate to start time running on the next day. Tribunals often obviate any problem by specifying the time by which communication must be sent or a hard copy of a submission delivered.

[75] Art 4.6.

[76] ie facsimile, telex, email or other means of telecommunication which records its transmission: Art 4.1.

Finally, it is to be noted that Art 4 does not specify whether the time and date of delivery to be considered is local time. As it is communication to the party who must respond which matters, it is suggested that local time is relevant. Again, tribunals may obviate this problem by stating whether the time for communication by reference to, for example, UTC. **18.87**

(5) Discretion to extend and abridge time

Under Art 4.7, the tribunal has a discretion to extend time under the Rules or the Arbitration Agreement, even where the prescribed periods have expired. No test to be applied by the tribunal in the exercise of this discretion is stated. **18.88**

It is suggested that the tribunal should exercise the discretion consistent with the obligations contained in Art 14. It must therefore ensure the fair, efficient and expeditious conduct of the arbitration, in particular, balancing the need for each party to have an opportunity of putting its case and dealing with that of its opponent with the need to avoid unnecessary delay or expense. The party's explanation for the need for extra time will be crucial (in particular, whether the failure to comply was deliberate and whether this was caused by the party or its representative). The tribunal would also be justified in considering whether the party requiring extra time has previously failed to comply with other time limits and directions, the effect which the delay will have on all parties and whether some form of interim relief is appropriate. **18.89**

In practice, other than in exceptional cases, or to maintain a long-fixed hearing date, it is rare for an extension of time not to be granted. **18.90**

Equally, the tribunal may abridge time where the circumstances of the case require it. This discretion is most likely to be used in the context of the exceptional urgency (where there is need for interim relief or a contract where time of performance affects many parties in a large project) and complements the Court's power to abridge time for the tribunal's formation.[77] Again, the tribunal should exercise the discretion consistent with the Art 14 obligations. **18.91**

Article 5 Formation of the Arbitral Tribunal

5.1 The expression 'the Arbitral Tribunal' in these Rules includes a sole arbitrator or all the arbitrators where more than one. All references to an arbitrator shall include the masculine and feminine. (References to the President, Vice President and members of the LCIA Court, the Registrar or deputy Registrar, expert, witness, party and legal representative shall be similarly understood).

5.2 All arbitrators conducting an arbitration under these Rules shall be and remain at all times impartial and independent of the parties; and none shall act in the arbitration as advocates for any party. No arbitrator, whether before or after appointment, shall advise any party on the merits or outcome of the dispute.

5.3 Before appointment by the LCIA Court, each arbitrator shall furnish to the Registrar a written sum of his past and present professional positions; he shall agree in writing upon fee rates conforming to the Schedule of Costs; and he shall sign a declaration to the effect that there are no circumstances known to him likely to give rise to any justified doubts as to his impartiality or independence, other than any circumstances disclosed by him in

[77] Art 9.

the declaration. Each arbitrator shall thereby also assume a continuing duty forthwith to disclose any such circumstances to the LCIA Court, to any other members of the Arbitral Tribunal and to all the parties if such circumstances should arise after the date of such declaration and before the arbitration is concluded.

5.4 **The LCIA Court shall appoint the Arbitral Tribunal as soon as practicable after receipt by the Registrar of the Response or after the expiry of 30 days following service of the Request upon the Respondent if no Response is received by the Registrar (or such lesser period fixed by the LCIA Court). The LCIA Court may proceed with the formation of the Arbitral Tribunal notwithstanding that the Request is incomplete or the Response is missing, late or incomplete. A sole arbitrator shall be appointed unless the parties have agreed in writing otherwise, or unless the LCIA Court determines that in view of all the circumstances of the case a three-member tribunal is appropriate.**

5.5 **The LCIA Court alone is empowered to appoint arbitrators. The LCIA Court will appoint arbitrators with due regard for any particular method or criteria of selection agreed in writing by the parties. In selecting arbitrators consideration will be given to the nature of the transaction, the nature and circumstances of the dispute, the nationality, location and languages of the parties and (if more than two) the number of parties.**

5.6 **In the case of a three-member Arbitral Tribunal, the chairman (who will not be a party-nominated arbitrator) shall be appointed by the LCIA Court.**

(1) General

18.92 Article 5 is a key provision of the Rules, defining the Court's role in controlling the tribunal's appointment.

(2) Appointment

18.93 The appointment of the tribunal is by the Court[78] even where the parties have agreed to nominate arbitrators. The Court will, however, invariably appoint the party nominees subject to their compliance with the requirements of Art 5.3.[79]

18.94 Under Art 5.4 the Court may proceed with an appointment even where the Request (Art 1) is incomplete or the Response (Art 2) is missing, late or incomplete. The LCIA may thus ensure the effective progress of the arbitration.

18.95 Article 5.6 provides that the chairman[80] of a three-member tribunal shall be appointed by the LCIA Court although if the parties have agreed that the chairman is to be nominated by the two other arbitrators, the Court will have due regard to this mechanism and will usually appoint the arbitrators' nominee.[81]

18.96 The LCIA states that, where it is responsible, it seeks to constitute the tribunal within ten working days of the Response.[82] In some cases of urgency three-member tribunals have been appointed within just a few days. The Rules provide no time limit within which the

---

[78] Arts 5.4 and 5.5. Under the Constitution, the power of appointment vests in the President or a Vice President. On the advantages of institutional appointment see eg Russell on Arbitration, s 4-06.

[79] Arts 5.5 and 7.1.

[80] The chairman may be given power to make procedural rulings alone (Art 14.3 and 18.183 ff) and decisions where there is no majority (Art 26.3 and 18.322 ff).

[81] See n 79.

[82] FAQ Q29.

arbitrators must accept appointment; however, the institutional nature of the LCIA enables it to ensure a swift response from arbitrators.[83]

(3) Impartial and independent

Article 5.2 sets out the standard of behaviour for any arbitrator appointed under the Rules. Crucially, the arbitrator must, as is generally required in international arbitration, be 'at all times impartial and independent of the parties'. In addition, express prohibitions are placed on acting as an advocate for any party and advising any party on the merits or outcome of the dispute. **18.97**

Impartiality and independence are essential as a failure by the tribunal to act judicially may lead to enforcement of an award being refused. Breach of the duty is the dominant basis upon which challenges are made under Art 10 and the requirements of these duties are discussed in that context.[84] Party nomination of an arbitrator is not inconsistent with these obligations. **18.98**

Article 5.2 is reinforced by Art 5.3 which requires each potential appointee to provide the LCIA with a resumé and sign a declaration disclosing any circumstances likely to give rise to any 'justified doubts' as to his impartiality or independence. The obligation to disclose such circumstances was introduced by the 1998 Rules and is inspired by the UNCITRAL Rules.[85] The arbitrator is then under a continuing duty to disclose to the Court, the other members of the tribunal, and the parties, any circumstances arising after the declaration has been made but prior to conclusion of the arbitration which could lead to such doubts. **18.99**

(4) Criteria

Where the parties have specified selection criteria or method for the arbitrators, the Court will give them due regard.[86] This reflects the obligations in the Model Law, Art 11(5), and gives best effect to the parties' intentions and legitimate expectations. The Court will not depart from the parties' criteria without good reason. **18.100**

Article 5.5 sets out the factors which will be considered by the Court in addition to any selection method or criteria specified by the parties. Most are matters of common sense; for example, the languages and locations of the parties are relevant to the question of costs consequent on interpretation and travel. **18.101**

It is generally desirable that the arbitrator has at least a working knowledge of the language of the arbitration[87] to avoid incurring costs consequent on translation both due to the **18.102**

83 Okekeifere, A.I., 'The Parties' Rights Against a Dilatory or Unskilled Arbitrator' (1998) 15 *J Int'l Arb* 129, 131.

84 See 18.143 ff. Challenges may be a delaying tactic during proceedings or made to prevent enforcement after the award has been issued either in the courts of the seat or by resisting recognition and enforcement under, in particular, the New York Convention: Redfern and Hunter, s 4-31.

85 Hunter and Paulsson, 1985 Rules; Art 3.1 merely obliged the arbitrator to decline appointment if there were circumstances likely to give rise to any justified doubts about his impartiality or independence rather than to disclose the circumstances.

86 Art 5.5.

87 Although, unless there is express agreement as to the language of the arbitration, the language may not be determined until after the tribunal has been appointed (Art 17.3).

direct cost and due to the inevitable lengthening of proceedings. Where appropriate, the Court will appoint bilingual arbitrators. Similarly, the IBA Rules of Ethics for International Arbitrators (IBA Rules of Ethics) require a prospective arbitrator to be satisfied that he has an adequate knowledge of the language of the arbitration.

18.103 Where the substance of the dispute is governed by, for example, English law, the Court may be inclined to appoint an English arbitrator.[88] Nevertheless, the Court has determined that a non-English arbitrator was qualified to sit as a sole arbitrator in proceedings arising out of an English insurance contract governed by English law since, *inter alia*, it would run contrary to the practice of international arbitration to have only English arbitrators decide on matters of English law.[89] The arbitrator need not be legally qualified although it is usual that a sole arbitrator, or the chairman, will be in order to meet the expectation that he should be capable of dealing with issues of both substantive and procedural law with ease.[90]

18.104 The LCIA has a database of about 800 arbitrators from whom it will usually make appointments but arbitrators who are not on this database will also be appointed by the Court if appropriate. All members of the Court are eligible for appointment as arbitrators[91] but the President is only eligible if the parties agree to nominate him as the sole arbitrator or chairman and the Vice-Presidents are only eligible if nominated by one or more parties. If the President or a Vice-President is nominated, he will take no further part in the functions of the Court in relation to the arbitration.

(5) One arbitrator or three

18.105 The Rules provide only for a tribunal of one or three.[92] Under Art 5.4, absent a written agreement by the parties for three arbitrators, a sole arbitrator will usually be appointed although the Court may appoint a three-member tribunal if the circumstances require. This presumption in favour of a sole arbitrator[93] is in contrast to the position under Art 10(2) of the Model Law but matches the presumption formalized in English law.[94] While this presumption has been described as 'outmoded'[95] there remain advantages including saving of costs and expedition in fixing hearings. It can be a convenient solution in a multi-party arbitration.[96]

---

[88] In 2007 LCIA appointed 105 UK arbitrators and 57 arbitrators of other nationalities: 4(1) *Global Arb Rev* 22 (2009).

[89] Unsuccessful challenge to an arbitrator (Decision 17, 14 August 2003), see Nicholas, G. and Partasides, C., 'LCIA Court Decisions on Challenges to Arbitrators: A Proposal to Publish' (2007) 23 *Arb Int'l* 1 [Nicholas and Partasides] at 39–40.

[90] See: Redfern and Hunter, s 4-43, s 4-44; and Miles, W., 'Practical Issues for Appointment of Arbitrators' (2003) 20 *J Int'l Arb* 219.

[91] Constitution, Art F(2).

[92] Art 2(2), 1981 Rules, contemplated a situation where the total number of arbitrators was related to the number of parties. (Arguably so did Arts 3.1 and 16.3, 1985 Rules.) Clearly this could rapidly become very costly which is perhaps the explanation for the provision having been dropped although it might play a useful role in multi-party arbitrations (Art 8).

[93] This is articulated by the LCIA in its FAQ Q27. See Delvolvé, LCIA, in which he describes the imperialism of the English position favouring a sole arbitrator.

[94] s 15(3), 1996 Act.

[95] Merkin, Arbitration Law and Merkin, R.M. and Flannery, L., *Arbitration Act 1996* (4th edn, 2008) [Merkin, Arbitration Act] 53.

[96] Factors noted by the Departmental Advisory Committee on Arbitration Law in its *Report on the Arbitration Bill* published in 1996 prior to the enactment of the 1996 Act (DAC Report), s 79, published in, *inter alia*, app 8, Merkin, Arbitration Act. Also see Poudret and Besson, s 242.

Where the sums at stake are large or the legal issues relatively complex, the Court is likely to appoint a panel of three arbitrators.[97] This would be particularly appropriate where the nature of the legal issues makes it desirable for one of the arbitrators to be qualified in the applicable law but it is not possible to find an individual who is so qualified and of a different nationality to one of the parties.[98] **18.106**

(6) Fees

In line with the informal practice before 1998, Art 5.3 requires the arbitrator to agree, in writing and prior to appointment, a fee rate conforming to the Schedule of Costs. **18.107**

Where, as in LCIA arbitrations, arbitrator's fees are on a per hour basis, it has been asserted that some arbitrators have 'fallen into the temptation of dragging proceedings a day, a week, a month or more . . . longer than it ought to have taken, just so as to earn more money from the longer period'.[99] The LCIA maintains that in arbitrations which it administers, this is not a risk since both the Court and the Secretariat 'carefully monitor the charges levied by all arbitrators'.[100] Further, the LCIA is known to have asked arbitrators to reduce or adjust their fee in cases where the amount of dispute is not very high. **18.108**

Article 6 Nationality of Arbitrators

6.1 Where the parties are of different nationalities, a sole arbitrator or chairman of the Arbitral Tribunal shall not have the same nationality as any party unless the parties who are not of the same nationality as the proposed appointee all agree in writing otherwise.

6.2 The nationality of parties shall be understood to include that of controlling shareholders or interests.

6.3 For the purpose of this Article, a person who is a citizen of two or more states shall be treated as a national of each state; and citizens of the European Union shall be treated as nationals of its different Member States and shall not be treated as having the same nationality.

(1) Generally

Article 6 is designed to prevent the appearance of bias. **18.109**

(2) Nationality of arbitrators

In principle, if an arbitrator is independent and impartial as required by Art 5.2, there is no reason why an arbitrator of the same nationality as one of the parties should not be appointed. Indeed, the Model Law states that 'No person shall be precluded by reason of his nationality from acting as an arbitrator, unless otherwise agreed by the parties'.[101] Article 6 nevertheless reflects the suggestion in Art 11(5) of the Model Law, that the appointing authority should take into account 'the advisability of appointing an arbitrator of a nationality other than those of the parties'. **18.110**

---

97 See FAQ Q27.
98 See Art 6 regarding nationality.
99 Okekeifere, A.I., 'The Parties' Rights Against a Dilatory or Unskilled Arbitrator' (1998) 15 *J Int'l Arb* 129, 133.
100 FAQ Q22.
101 Art 11(1), UNCITRAL Model Law.

18.111 The enquiry by the Court into the nationality of a potential arbitrator should be 'substantive and not merely formal' as there may be circumstances where a personal connection to a country is so strong that an arbitrator's technical nationality will not ensure apparent neutrality.[102] This issue arose in a challenge in an arbitration between a Kuwaiti party and a non-Arabic party. The latter challenged the arbitrator on the basis of his alleged cultural affiliation (derived from study rather than nationality) to Arab culture. The challenge was unsuccessful. The Court found that there was not a 'scintilla of evidence' that the arbitrator might be biased as alleged.[103] The risk that factors making an arbitrator particularly well qualified to consider a dispute may give rise to apparent bias is not uncommon in international arbitrations but rarely leads to a justified complaint.

18.112 Where arbitrators are party nominees, it is usual that each party will select an arbitrator who it believes to have some inclination or predisposition to favour its case commonly consequent on a shared cultural background and probably nationality. Provided the arbitrator does not breach his obligations of independence and impartiality this is acceptable.[104] It then, however, becomes particularly important to avoid the appearance of bias in the tribunal's chairman; this is facilitated by Art 6.

18.113 An arbitrator will not be disqualified merely because he is of the same nationality as one of the party's counsel but not the party.[105]

18.114 Theoretically, under Art 6.1, if the Court appointed a tribunal of three, it could appoint two arbitrators of the same nationality as one party provided the chairman was of a different nationality. In practice, it is unlikely that the Court would do so as this is contrary to the spirit of Art 6.1.

18.115 The provisions of Art 6.2 mean that the LCIA will need to know the nationality of the controlling shareholder or interest. The Court will request that the parties provide information about their nationalities and will also perform independent checks insofar as it is able to do so. Equally, the LCIA expects arbitrators to check for possible nationality conflicts insofar as they can.

18.116 The word nationality, rather than citizenship, is used in Art 6.1 and in the Model Law.[106] The Working Group on the Model Law concluded that the word citizenship need not be included in the Article, but that the term 'nationality' should be given a wide interpretation so as to embrace citizenship where such a term was used in a legal system.[107] In consequence,

[102] Statement by the Court in the context of an unsuccessful challenge to an arbitrator (Decision 5, 30 September 1998) on the basis that an arbitrator was a *de facto* British National, see Nicholas and Partasides, 29–30.

[103] Unsuccessful challenge to an arbitrator (Decision 9, 22 November 2001), see Nicholas and Partasides, 35.

[104] Bishop, D. and Reed, L., 'Practical Guidelines for Interviewing, Selecting and Challenging Party-Appointed Arbitrators in International Commercial Arbitration' (1998) 14 *Arb Int'l* 395 [Bishop and Reed].

[105] Unsuccessful challenge to an arbitrator (Decision 6, 10 November 1999), see Nicholas and Partasides, 30.

[106] Art 11.

[107] Report of the Working Group on the work of its seventh session, 6 March 1984, UN-Doc A/CN.9/246 (<http://www.uncitral.org/uncitral/en/commission/sessions/17th.html>), s 31.

Art 6.3 provides that citizenship of the European Union is not to be regarded as nationality for the purposes of the Art 6.1 prohibition.

Article 7 Party and Other Nominations

7.1 If the parties have agreed that any arbitrator is to be appointed by one or more of them or by any third person, that agreement shall be treated as an agreement to nominate an arbitrator for all purposes. Such nominee may only be appointed by the LCIA Court as arbitrator subject to his prior compliance with Article 5.3. The LCIA Court may refuse to appoint any such nominee if it determines that he is not suitable or independent or impartial.

7.2 Where the parties have howsoever agreed that the Respondent or any third person is to nominate an arbitrator and such nomination is not made within time or at all, the LCIA Court may appoint an arbitrator notwithstanding the absence of the nomination and without regard to any late nomination. Likewise, if the Request for Arbitration does not contain a nomination by the Claimant where the parties have howsoever agreed that the Claimant or a third person is to nominate an arbitrator, the LCIA Court may appoint an arbitrator notwithstanding the absence of the nomination and without regard to any late nomination.

(1) Generally

Article 7 makes provision for party-nominated arbitrators while retaining the overall authority of the Court as the appointing authority. **18.117**

(2) Party nomination

Party appointment of arbitrators has been described as a defining aspect of the arbitral system and a powerful instrument when used wisely by a party.[108] Such appointments better reflect the autonomy of the parties as enunciated in the Model Law (Art 11(2)).[109] Accordingly, although only the Court can appoint an arbitrator for the purposes of an LCIA arbitration,[110] under Art 7.1, the parties are free to agree that the arbitrators will be nominated by the parties or a third person. The Court will almost invariably appoint the parties' nominees subject to safeguards in relation to suitability and to prevent the abuse of the nomination procedure by a party reluctant to participate in the arbitration. **18.118**

The Court has a veto on any nominee it considers to be unsuitable for any reason including lack of independence or impartiality.[111] This provision, and that of Art 7.2, was introduced in the 1985 revision of the LCIA Rules.[112] **18.119**

The retention of this power by the Court and the checks imposed by Arts 5.2 and 5.3 mean that 'it serves nothing for a party to nominate an arbitrator who is partial or otherwise unsuitable'.[113] In practice, informal contact between the Registrar and the parties will enable unsuitable nominees to be substituted. In 1998, at the time the current rules were published, no party nomination had ever formally been rejected by the Court on this ground alone.[114] **18.120**

---

108 Bishop and Reed, 395.

109 eg Akseli, O., 'Appointment of Arbitrators as Specified in the Agreement to Arbitrate' (2003) 20 *J Int'l Arb* 247.

110 Art 5.5.

111 Reiterated in Arts 5.5 and 11.1.

112 Arts 3.3 and 3.4, 1985 Rules.

113 Veeder, 1998 Rules.

114 *ibid.*

18.121 If a party is required to nominate an arbitrator but does not know whom to nominate, it may make no nomination and rely on the default provisions of Art 7.2. Alternatively, if both parties agree, the LCIA will provide the parties with a list of suitable arbitrators drawn from its database. A similar facility is available where the parties have provided for agreement of a sole arbitrator. This facility is most likely to be used where the arbitration is under the UNCITRAL Rules which require it.[115]

(3) Failure of appointment method

18.122 Article 7.2 is permissive rather than mandatory. Under it the Court may, but not shall, appoint an arbitrator or arbitrators where the party required to make the nomination under the Arbitration Agreement has failed to do so 'within time or at all'. It is clear from the final words of each sentence ('without regard to any late nomination') that where a late nomination is received, the Court may nonetheless give effect to that nomination. In practice, it will do so if reasonable.[116]

18.123 In circumstances where the Claimant has made its nomination in time but the Respondent has not, and assuming that the nominee is suitable, that arbitrator will be appointed and the Court will appoint an arbitrator in lieu of the Respondent's nomination. This power prevents the Respondent from delaying the arbitration.[117]

18.124 Although the Respondent might claim this is unfair (ie because the Claimant but not Respondent has its chosen arbitrator), because the Respondent has been given due opportunity to make an appointment, it is unlikely that any challenge on this basis would succeed. It is certainly a fairer procedure than allowing the arbitration to proceed in front of a sole arbitrator appointed by one party although even this has been considered not to render an award unenforceable under Art V(2) of the New York Convention.[118]

Article 8 Three or More Parties

8.1 Where the Arbitration Agreement entitles each party howsoever to nominate an arbitrator, the parties to the dispute number more than two and such parties have not all agreed in writing that the disputant parties represent two separate sides for the formation of the Arbitral Tribunal as Claimant and Respondent respectively, the LCIA Court shall appoint the Arbitral Tribunal without regard to any party's nomination.

8.2 In such circumstances, the Arbitration Agreement shall be treated for all purposes as a written agreement by the parties for the appointment of the Arbitral Tribunal by the LCIA Court.

(1) Generally

18.125 Article 8 is designed to deal with multi-party arbitrations and to reconcile the conflict between the presumption that the tribunal will consist of one or three members and the situation where there are more than two parties to an arbitration agreement or to the dispute.

---

115 UNCITRAL Rules, Art 6.3.

116 See commentary to Art 2.3, 18.62 ff.

117 See comments in Hunter and Paulsson, 1985 Rules, 169.

118 See *Shipowner (Netherlands) v Cattle and Meat Dealer (Germany)*, Germany, Bundesgerichtshof (Federal Supreme Court), 1 February 2001, *XXIX YB Comm Arb* 700.

(2) Multi-party arbitrations

Article 8 applies where there are several parties to one contract.[119] It was introduced in response to the *Dutco* case[120] in which the French Cour de Cassation set aside an ICC award which had allowed the claimant to appoint its own arbitrator but required the two respondents to nominate an arbitrator jointly. The French court considered that the failure to allow each respondent to appoint its own arbitrator was a violation of the principle of equal treatment of the parties.[121] 18.126

Under Art 8.1, if the parties cannot agree (in writing) that they effectively represent only two separate sides, the Court must appoint all the members of the tribunal without regard to any party's nomination. Strictly, therefore, the Court could appoint a party nominee if that individual was deemed suitable. In practice, it is unlikely that the Court would do so, not least, because of the risk of a challenge to that arbitrator for lack of independence. While there is no reason why such a challenge should succeed (if Art 5.3 is satisfied), a challenge will, nevertheless, cause delay and it is desirable to avoid it. In certain circumstances, however, there may be only one candidate with suitable experience and expertise. 18.127

Article 8.2 states that the Arbitration Agreement shall be treated as an agreement for the Court to appoint the tribunal. It is designed to prevent enforcement of the award being challenged under Art V(1)(d) of the New York Convention by the losing party arguing that the tribunal has been established *for* rather than *by* the parties. Article 8.2 thus bolsters the argument in response that 'by adopting the institutional rules they had agreed, *inter alia*, to this particular provision'.[122] 18.128

Article 8 has been described as a 'sensible solution'[123] and, from the point of view of time and cost efficiency, this is likely to be correct particularly if a single arbitrator is used as a solution.[124] A system where the LCIA were simply to appoint arbitrators in addition to party nominees would be undesirable, not only because of the costs, but because of the risk 18.129

---

[119] Where there are separate contracts between pairs of parties, consideration may be given to joinder under Art 22.

[120] *Siemens AG and BKMI Industrienlagen GmbH v Dutco Construction Co* Cass Civ 1re, 7 January 1992; (1992) 119 *Journal du Droit International* 707, 2nd document; (1992) *Revue de l'Arbitrage* 470, (comment by Bellet at 473-82), reported in English at [1994] *ADRLJ* 36. See *inter alia* discussion in Lew, J.D.M., Mistelis, L.A. and Kröll, S., *Comparative International Commercial Arbitration* (Kluwer Law International, 2003) (Lew, Mistelis, Kröll), s 16-16; Poudret and Besson, s 242. See too: Greenblatt, J.L. and Griffin, P., 'Towards the Harmonization of International Arbitration Rules: Comparative Analysis of the Rules of the ICC, AAA, LCIA and CIET' (2001) 17 *Arb Int'l* 101 and Akseli, O., 'Appointment of Arbitrators as Specified in the Agreement to Arbitrate' (2003) 20 *J Int'l Arb* 247.

[121] The result might have differed in another jurisdiction; in *Arab Republic of Egypt v Westland Helicopters Ltd* (Cour de justice, Geneva, 26 November 1982, affirmed by Tribunal Federal Suisse, 16 May 1983) the Swiss court upheld the ICC's appointment of a single arbitrator for multiple respondents.

[122] Redfern and Hunter, s 3-76. Also Poudret and Besson, s 242 stating that the solution has been widely accepted.

[123] Redfern and Hunter, s 3-75.

[124] Also see comments in DAC Report s 79. It is to be noted that the LCIA did not revert to the provision of Art 2(2), 1981 Rules, under which that each party was to nominate its arbitrator and the Court would then appoint each of the nominees together with Court-selected arbitrators to ensure that the total number of arbitrators was uneven and that the chairman was an LCIA appointee.

of a perceived imbalance in the tribunal, for example, where more parties might be characterized as Respondents than Claimants.

18.130 Nevertheless, if parties to a multi-party arbitration agreement were to determine that each should have his own arbitrator, and were to make a sufficiently clear provision to this effect, it is presumed that the Court would be prepared to make the necessary appointments in the interests of upholding party autonomy.

Article 9 Expedited Formation

9.1 In exceptional urgency, on or after the commencement of the arbitration, any party may apply to the LCIA Court for the expedited formation of the Arbitral Tribunal, including the appointment of any replacement arbitrator under Articles 10 and 11 of these Rules.

9.2 Such an application shall be made in writing to the LCIA Court, copied to all other parties to the arbitration; and it shall set out the specific grounds for exceptional urgency in the formation of the Arbitral Tribunal.

9.3 The LCIA Court may, in its complete discretion, abridge or curtail any time limit under these Rules for the formation of the Arbitral Tribunal, including service of the Response and of any matters or documents adjudged to be missing from the Request. The LCIA Court shall not be entitled to abridge or curtail any other time limit.

(1) Generally

18.131 Article 9 is an important aspect of the Rules. Most other international arbitration rules have no equivalent. The principal object of Art 9 is to enable parties to obtain urgent relief where they have elected for their dispute to be determined by arbitration.

(2) Exercise of discretion

18.132 The provision for the expedited formation of the tribunal by the current version of the Rules allows a tribunal to be formed, in a case of exceptional urgency, in a matter of hours or days. By 1998, the power had already been used to form a tribunal.[125]

18.133 The application for expedition may be made by the Claimant in its Request for arbitration or thereafter. The application must, under Art 9.2, be made in writing, copied to all other parties, and set out the specific grounds for exceptional urgency.

18.134 Exceptional urgency is not defined. In practice, the power is most commonly used where the Claimant seeks urgent interim relief under Art 25[126] (the primary purpose for which Art 9 was introduced).[127]

18.135 Once the Request is made, the Court may, under Art 9.3, abridge or curtail any time limit in relation to the formation of the tribunal. Although the service of a Response is not a prerequisite, the Respondent will always be given an opportunity to reply to the

---

[125] Veeder, 1998 Rules, 368.

[126] FAQ Q30. A recent case where expedition was sought so that judgment could be obtained before insolvency proceedings against the Respondent had been completed was not regarded as meeting the Art 9 criteria.

[127] The 1932 version of the LCIA's rules had contained a special procedure whereby such rulings could be made before the formation of the Tribunal by an 'Urgency Committee'. The proposal to re-introduce such a committee or power for the Court was rejected, not least because of the attendant risks of the non-enforceability of such rulings (Veeder, 1998 Rules, 368 and Rivkin, 92).

Claimant's application. This is because *ex parte* applications run contrary to the consensual basis of international arbitration and would, in any event, undermine one party's confidence in the tribunal. Similarly to the position in relation to a Response under the normal timetable, if the Respondent fails to respond, the Court may proceed with the expedited appointment in any event.[128]

The Rules do not set out the test to be applied by the LCIA Court in deciding whether to exercise its jurisdiction under Art 9. It appears, however, that the Court must be satisfied that grounds for exceptional urgency have, prima facie, been established by the applicant.[129] If such grounds are made out, the tribunal may be appointed in as little as five days from the date of the application.[130] **18.136**

The existence of this power has led courts, for example in the USA, to refuse to exercise their discretion to grant relief.[131] Similarly, an English court would expect the parties to take steps to arrange for expedition under Art 9 if at all possible.[132] **18.137**

(3) No other discretion to abridge time

The Court is not entitled to abridge or curtail any other time limit. Once the tribunal has been formed, issues of procedure and timetable are within its exclusive remit.[133] **18.138**

Article 10 Revocation of Arbitrator's Appointment

10.1 If either (a) any arbitrator gives written notice of his desire to resign as arbitrator to the LCIA Court, to be copied to the parties and the other arbitrators (if any) or (b) any arbitrator dies, falls seriously ill, refuses, or becomes unable or unfit to act, either upon challenge by a party or at the request of the remaining arbitrators, the LCIA Court may revoke that arbitrator's appointment and appoint another arbitrator. The LCIA Court shall decide upon the amount of fees and expenses to be paid for the former arbitrator's services (if any) as it may consider appropriate in all the circumstances.

10.2 If any arbitrator acts in deliberate violation of the Arbitration Agreement (including these Rules) or does not act fairly and impartially as between the parties or does not conduct or participate in the arbitration proceedings with reasonable diligence, avoiding unnecessary

[128] FAQ Q30.

[129] See the comments of Winstanley, A., 'UNCITRAL heralds the age of ex parte measures' (March 2005) LCIA website.

[130] *ibid.*

[131] A full discussion of the issue of Court and tribunal authority in relation to interim measures is found in Donovan, D.F., 'The Allocation of Authority Between Courts and Arbitral Tribunals to Order Interim Measures A Survey of Jurisdictions, the Work of UNCITRAL and a Model Proposal' in *ICCA Congress Series no 12* (2005) 203. In *Al Nawasi Trading Co v BP Amoco Corp* 191 FRD 57 (SDNY 2000), a district court in the Southern District of New York denied a plaintiff's motion for expedited discovery stating:

> [I]t is one thing to apply to a court to preserve the status quo until a duly constituted arbitrator can act; but it is quite another thing to consciously avoid taking steps that would give the arbitrator the ability to act, and, instead to apply to another court for relief . . . Given the modern preference for international arbitration, such bootstraps are no longer fashionable.

[132] The English High Court has made it clear that, where the Court's power to make an interim order in a case of urgency under s 44, 1996 Act is exercised, the Court's order should require the claimant to undertake to have a tribunal formed as soon as possible so as to give effect to the parties' chosen dispute mechanism: *Econet Wireless Ltd v Vee Networks Ltd* [2006] EWHC 1568 (Comm); [2006] 2 Lloyd's Rep 428. See, in particular, paras 13 and 14.

[133] Under Art 4.7.

delay or expense, that arbitrator may be considered unfit in the opinion of the LCIA Court.

10.3 An arbitrator may also be challenged by any party if circumstances exist that give rise to justifiable doubts as to his impartiality or independence. A party may challenge an arbitrator it has nominated, or in whose appointment it has participated, only for reasons of which it becomes aware after the appointment has been made.

10.4 A party who intends to challenge an arbitrator shall, within 15 days of the formation of the Arbitral Tribunal or (if later) after becoming aware of any circumstances referred to in Article 10.1, 10.2 or 10.3, send a written statement of the reasons for its challenge to the LCIA Court, the Arbitral Tribunal and all other parties. Unless the challenged arbitrator withdraws or all other parties agree to the challenge within 15 days of receipt of the written statement, the LCIA Court shall decide on the challenge.

(1) Importance of the right and the LCIA's decisions

18.139 The right to challenge arbitrators is most important and arises from the right to a fair hearing imported by the tribunal's quasi-judicial function and the due process requirement inherent to the process.[134] Regrettably, challenges are sometimes used for tactical reasons, particularly to induce delay or intimidate an arbitrator.[135]

18.140 By contrast with other arbitration institutions, and although there is no obligation on the Court to give reasons,[136] the Court communicates the reasons for its decisions to the parties. Moreover, the LCIA has decided to publish decisions on challenges.[137] Eventually, abstracts of all such decisions will be published. As the LCIA does not publish (even redacted) awards, the significance of the decision to publish cannot be understated.[138] The fact that the majority of challenges have been unsuccessful probably indicates that the Rules are successful in ensuring the proper behaviour of arbitrators and encouraging parties to behave reasonably in the nomination of arbitrators.[139]

(2) Resignation

18.141 Article 10.1 is self-explanatory. The Court's power to revoke the appointment of an arbitrator who resigns, dies, falls seriously ill, or refuses, or becomes unable or unfit to act is expressed in permissive rather than mandatory terms. This leaves open the possibility that, for example, if a resignation is retracted before his appointment is revoked, the Court could leave that arbitrator in office.[140]

---

[134] eg European Convention on Human Rights, Art 6.

[135] Lew, Mistelis, Kröll, s 13-7.

[136] Art 29.1.

[137] See Nicholas and Partasides, which sets out a survey of the score of decisions rendered by the Court between September 1995 and October 2005.

[138] See n 137.

[139] Hunter and Paulsson, 1985 Rules,169. The publication of the Court's decisions on challenges may even promote the 'acceptable deontology of international arbitration' (*ibid*).

[140] A course taken by the ICC in *Ivan Milutinovic v Deutsche Babcock AG*, ICC Case no 5017, Partial Award of 8 November 1987, discussed in Schwebel, S.M., 'The Validity of an Arbitral Award Rendered by a Truncated Tribunal' (1995) 6 *ICC ICArb Bull* 22. The award was then rendered without the participation of the arbitrator who had attempted to resign. The award was quashed by the Swiss Courts. Equally, in *ATC-CFCO (Congo) v COMILOG (Gabon)*, XXIVa YBCA 281 (1999), Int'l Arb L Rev N-47 (1999) with note by Schwartz, the Cour d'Appel in Paris set aside an award in which one arbitrator had failed to participate on

If an arbitrator resigns, he will give notice of his resignation to the Court, the parties, and other arbitrators. If one of the situations set out in Art 10.1(b) occurs, a request for removal may be made by any remaining arbitrator, or a challenge may be made by a party. These provisions are necessary for practical reasons. For example, a partisan arbitrator might otherwise rely on a claim of ill health in order to delay or otherwise undermine the proceedings.[141] Provisions for the conduct of proceedings if one arbitrator refuses to participate is also made by Art 12. **18.142**

(3) Challenge and unfitness

Under Art 10.3[142] parties may challenge an arbitrator on the grounds that 'circumstances exist that give rise to justifiable doubts as to his impartiality or independence'. This reflects Art 12(2) of the Model Law[143] but does not go as far as the Model Law which also allows a challenge if the arbitrator does not possess qualifications agreed by the parties. This difference arises because, appointment is by the Court, which must do no more than have 'due regard' for criteria imposed by the parties.[144] **18.143**

The concepts of impartiality and independence are not defined in the Rules and there is ongoing debate as to the meaning and extent of the concepts.[145] Some guidance may be found in the Codes of Ethics and academic writings,[146] and, eventually, from the published decisions of the LCIA Court. For the purposes of bringing a challenge under the Rules, the finer points of the distinction should be immaterial since either partiality or a lack of independence is sufficient basis for a challenge. **18.144**

Equally, the phrase 'justifiable doubts' is not defined. It is suggested that the test to be applied is whether the doubts are justifiable on an objective basis; that is: 'Are they reasonable doubts as tested by the standard of a fair minded, rational, objective observer?'[147] It is apparent that in some decisions the Court has applied a similar test, 'would a fair-minded and informed observer have concluded that there was an appearance of bias and that there was a real possibility that the arbitrator was in fact biased'.[148] The first limb of this test does mean, however, that an arbitrator can be entrapped into an appearance of bias **18.145**

the grounds that the tribunal which rendered the award was irregularly constituted. The LCIA Rules make specific provision for an award to be given in similar circumstances are contained in Arts 12 and 26.2.

141 Lew, Mistelis, Kröll, s 13-4.

142 The precursor to this provision was introduced in the 1985 Rules following criticism of the 1981 Rules for omitting such a procedure: Hunter and Paulsson, 1985 Rules, 169.

143 But not the English 1996 Act which calls only for impartiality.

144 Art 5.5.

145 See eg Lew, Mistelis, Kröll, ch 11.

146 AAA *Code of Ethics for Arbitrators in Commercial Disputes* (1977); IBA, *Guidelines on Conflicts of Interest in International Arbitration* (2004). Also Redfern and Hunter, s 4-54 to s 4-57; Poudret and Besson, s 416, s 417; Lew, Mistelis, Kröll, s 13-9 ff; Bernstein's Handbook, s 9-107 ff; Bishop and Reed, 398; Eastwood, G., 'A Real Danger of Confusion? The English Law Relating to Bias in Arbitrators' (2001) 17 *Arb Int'l* 287; Donahey, M.S., 'The Independence and Neutrality of Arbitrators' (1992) 9 *J Int'l Arb* 31.

147 Discussed in Lew, Mistelis, Kröll, s 13-14 and enunciated by the Secretary-General of the Permanent Court of Arbitration in an arbitration under the UNCITRAL Rules, Challenge decision of 11 January 1995, XXII *YBCA* 227 (1997).

148 Decision 18, 21 October 2005 Nicholas and Partasides, 36–8.

and then challenged. The risk that an unbiased arbitrator might thus be disqualified was one the Court has been prepared to run.

18.146 The 'real danger of bias' test used in some English court decisions[149] should not be applied. The intervention of a national legal system should be subject to a higher threshold than LCIA Court review because of the requirement to respect party autonomy and choice of arbitration to resolve their disputes.[150] The same is true of other, similar, national tests.

18.147 Article 10.2 also provides that the Court may consider the arbitrator to be unfit for a range of other reasons (deliberate violation of the Arbitration Agreement, including the Rules, failure to conduct or participate in the arbitration proceedings with reasonable diligence, failure to avoid unnecessary delay or expense). These provisions are largely self-explanatory.[151]

18.148 Article 10.2 itself does not refer to challenges by the parties but it is clear from the reference in Art 10.4 to a challenge on the basis of any circumstance referred to in Art 10.1, 10.2, and 10.3 that this is possible. The same is true of Art 10.1. The right to challenge for breach of the Rules is particularly useful to the parties who may ensure that proceedings accord with their expectations. A challenge might, for example, be made to an arbitrator who delays excessively after the written stage of proceedings has been completed.

18.149 Although each decision of the Court following an Art 10 challenge has different facts, common points can be identified and reported decisions should be considered not least because costs may be awarded against a party bringing an unsuccessful challenge. Points to be noted include:

- (i) a challenge for lack of independence where an arbitrator and barrister were members of the same chambers was rejected, but where an arbitrator is connected to a party by reason of his membership (or prior membership) of a law firm, the Court has on occasion been prepared to uphold a challenge or not appoint that arbitrator;[152]
- (ii) where the arbitration clause provided that the arbitrator should not be based in England, the fact that he was a door tenant of a London barristers' chambers and merely visited from time to time did not disqualify him from appointment;[153]
- (iii) a number of unsuccessful challenges have been made on the basis of nationality;[154]
- (iv) challenges for bias are frequently based on the imposition of a timetable or scheduling of hearings in a manner said to be unfair to one party.[155] In principle, this is a reasonable

149 Stated in the 1979 Act, now replaced by the 1996 Act.

150 In any event, the requirements of English administrative law have undoubtedly coloured the attitude of English judges. Such considerations should have no place in international arbitration.

151 The provision is similar to that under the 1985 Rules save that these referred to 'manifest' rather than 'deliberate' violation of the Rules. The substitution plainly reflects the likelihood that a deliberate breach is likely to be covert.

152 See decisions 2, 1, 6A and 15. Parties should note, however, that following the late disclosure that counsel from the same London chambers as the arbitrator had been appointed led to a decision that the barrister concerned should not participate in the hearing: *Hrvatska Elektroprivreda dd v Republic of Slovenia* (ICSID Case no ARB/05/24 published on the ICSID website: <http://icsid.worldbank.org>).

153 Decision 19, Nicholas and Partasides, 31.

154 See commentary to Art 6.

155 Decisions 7, 8, 13, 14, 16, Nicholas and Partasides, 33–4.

basis of challenge but the evidential burden of proving that the tribunal's conduct gave rise to justifiable doubts as to an arbitrator's impartiality, independence or fairness is difficult to discharge;

(v) where a sole arbitrator met with one party in circumstances where the other had been told that the hearing in London had been cancelled and had not, therefore, travelled to London and so could not attend, the Court concluded that the arbitrator had failed to give adequate notice of the hearing and was in breach of Art 19.2. But for special circumstances and the absence of funds from the Claimant, it appears that the Court would have replaced the arbitrator;[156]

(vi) a failure to consult with co-arbitrators when required to do may lead to a successful challenge;[157] and

(vii) where, prior to the issuance of the final award, an arbitrator disclosed a draft copy to counsel for the Claimant, the Court removed the arbitrator.[158] *Ex parte* communication of any sort is almost always inappropriate and private meetings have been held to be unacceptable.[159]

(4) Limits on the right

There are two limits on the right to challenge. The first is set out in Art 10.3. A party may only challenge an arbitrator it has nominated, or in whose appointment it has participated (presumably by a list or other joint selection process), for reasons of which it becomes aware after the appointment has been made. This provision is effectively identical to that of Art 12(2) of the Model Law. **18.150**

The second limit on the right to challenge is temporal and imposed by Art 10.4. A party must challenge within 15 days of the formation of the tribunal or, if it becomes aware of the basis for challenge at a later stage, within 15 days of that awareness. **18.151**

(5) Procedure for challenge

The only formal requirement for the challenge is that it be made in writing and sent to the Court, the tribunal (including, of course, the arbitrator being challenged) and all other parties. The Court will decide on the challenge if either the challenged arbitrator does not withdraw or all the other parties do not agree to the challenge within 15 days of its receipt. Where the date of receipt of the written statement varies between recipients, for example, because it is sent by post or courier,[160] it is suggested that the Court should not decide the challenge until the latest recipient has had 15 days to respond. **18.152**

Neither the challenged arbitrator, nor other arbitrators, nor parties need file any response to the challenge but any response filed will be considered by the Court. **18.153**

The Court will almost invariably consider the challenge as a three-member division chaired by the President or a Vice-President and generally including at least one member of the **18.154**

156 Decision 10, *ibid*, 39.
157 Decision 12, *ibid*, 35.
158 Decision 11, *ibid*, 37.
159 Decision 18 and Decision 10, *ibid*, 37 and 29.
160 See commentary to Art 4.

Court with previous experience of a challenge. The division will also take account of the geographic and cultural characteristics of the parties involved in the arbitration.[161]

18.155 The decision of the Court can be rendered rapidly. For example, in 2005, a sole arbitrator was appointed on 20 October and challenged by the Respondent by letter dated 24 October. The Claimant filed a response on 26 October and stated the need for urgency; on 27 October the arbitrator commented on the challenge. On 28 October the reasoned decision of the Court was communicated to the parties.[162]

18.156 The costs of a challenge will usually be left to the final award. In a small number of Court decisions, however, a direction is made that the administrative costs of an unsuccessful application shall be borne by the applicant.[163]

18.157 Where information that would support a challenge is discovered shortly before a final award is given, there is a risk that the challenge may not be possible before the arbitrator becomes *functus officio*. In these circumstances, the appropriate course is to challenge the award and seek its annulment.[164] Almost conversely, a challenge to an arbitrator may be a *de facto* challenge to an interim award.[165]

Article 11 Nomination and Replacement of Arbitrators

11.1 In the event that the LCIA Court determines that any nominee is not suitable or independent or impartial or if an appointed arbitrator is to be replaced for any reason, the LCIA Court shall have a complete discretion to decide whether or not to follow the original nominating process.

11.2 If the LCIA Court should so decide, any opportunity given to a party to make a re-nomination shall be waived if not exercised within 15 days (or such lesser time as the LCIA Court may fix), after which the LCIA Court shall appoint the replacement arbitrator.

(1) Generally

18.158 Article 11 complements the Court's powers to appoint and to revoke an arbitrator's appointment.

(2) Original nominating process

18.159 Where an arbitrator has to be replaced, the Court has complete discretion to not follow the original nominating process although it will generally try to give effect to the parties' chosen method in accordance with Art 11.2. This is consistent with the provision of Art 5.5 which does no more than oblige the Court to have 'due regard' to the parties' selection criteria or method.[166]

18.160 The power under Art 11.1 is also consistent with the Rules' purpose in preventing undue delay.[167] The Court may, for example, consider that the original nominating method is unduly time-consuming or will inevitably lead to the appointment of an arbitrator who is

---

161 Nicholas and Partasides, 5.
162 *ibid*, 7–8.
163 *ibid*, 40.
164 See Lew, Mistelis, Kröll, s 13-36 ff.
165 See Decision 4 discussed at para 18.332.
166 See para 18.100 ff.
167 See Hunter and Paulsson, 1985 Rules 169.

unsuitable, possibly because one party has no intention of nominating a suitable arbitrator. In such circumstances, it would be wholly legitimate for the Court not to follow the original nominating process.

(3) Limited opportunity to renominate

Other than in exceptional circumstances considered above, the parties will be given the opportunity to make a re-nomination. Article 11.2 provides that where such opportunity is given, if it is not exercised within 15 days (or a lesser stated period) the party's right is waived. After this, the Court 'shall' appoint the replacement arbitrator. The wording is mandatory indicating that the Court may not appoint the party nominee if the nomination is received after the 15-day (or shorter) period. This protects the other party to the arbitration from prejudice caused by delay. **18.161**

It is to be noted that the default period of 15 days is shorter than the equivalent period under the 1985 Rules (30 days). A shorter period obviously promotes efficiency and is realistic where electronic communication is readily available. **18.162**

Article 12 Majority Power to Continue Proceedings

12.1 If any arbitrator on a three-member Arbitral Tribunal refuses or persistently fails to participate in its deliberations, the two other arbitrators shall have the power, upon their written notice of such refusal or failure to the LCIA Court, the parties and the third arbitrator, to continue the arbitration (including the making of any decision, ruling or award), notwithstanding the absence of the third arbitrator.

12.2 In determining whether to continue the arbitration, the two other arbitrators shall take into account the stage of the arbitration, any explanation made by the third arbitrator for his non-participation and such other matters as they consider appropriate in the circumstances of the case. The reasons for such determination shall be stated in any award, order or other decision made by the two arbitrators without the participation of the third arbitrator.

12.3 In the event that the two other arbitrators determine at any time not to continue the arbitration without the participation of the third arbitrator missing from their deliberations, the two arbitrators shall notify in writing the parties and the LCIA Court of such determination; and in that event, the two arbitrators or any party may refer the matter to the LCIA Court for the revocation of that third arbitrator's appointment and his replacement under Article 10.

(1) Generally

Article 12 provides for a truncated tribunal. Such provisions are controversial but essential for the conduct of international commercial arbitration.[168] **18.163**

(2) The power of a truncated tribunal to continue proceedings

Article 12.1 makes it clear that a truncated tribunal may give a valid award. This is effectively an agreement between the parties which should prevent any effective challenge to the award's validity if made by a truncated tribunal.[169] **18.164**

---

168 Veeder, V.V., 'The Lena Goldfields arbitration: the historical roots of three ideas' (1998) 47 *ICLQ* 747, at 773.

169 See Schwebel, S.M., 'The Authority of a Truncated Tribunal' in *ICCA Congress Series no 9* (1999) 314 at 316. Also discussion of truncated tribunals in Lew, Mistelis, Kröll, s 13-67 to s 13.82.

18.165 There is some ambiguity as to the stage at which Art 12.1 can be used. On the one hand, Arts 12.1 and 12.3 refer to a refusal to participate in deliberations and arguably implicitly limit the article's application to after the close of the hearings.[170] On the other hand, Art 12.2 refers to 'the stage of the arbitration' and also to the making of an order or other decision as well as an award. Theoretically, the power under Art 12.1 is probably available at any time. Procedural impropriety will be prevented by the obligation to give notice to the Court.

18.166 The obligation on the remaining arbitrators to give written notice to the Court, the parties, and the third arbitrator under Art 12.1, and to set out the reasons for their determination under Art 12.2, is designed to protect both the parties and the arbitrators. A third arbitrator who has a good reason for non-participation, and feels that this has been misunderstood by the remaining arbitrators, may respond to the written notification. The remaining arbitrators would be obliged to consider this fairly in compliance with the overriding duty under Art 14.

18.167 The power to proceed as a truncated tribunal should not be confused with the chairman's power under Art 14 to make procedural rulings alone.

(3) A determination not to continue

18.168 In general, a tribunal of three is preferable and exercise of the power under Art 12.3 to refer the matter to the Court for the revocation of the third arbitrator's appointment and his replacement will be the best course provided proceedings are not significantly advanced before the non-cooperation becomes apparent. The power to proceed as a truncated tribunal is most likely to be used close to the end of proceedings where the additional cost and delay of appointing another arbitrator outweighs the benefit. It may also be used where it is necessary to proceed swiftly, perhaps to grant an interim remedy. In any case, the obligation to give written notice means that the parties can make their views known on the course adopted and these will be considered by the tribunal.

Article 13 Communications between Parties and the Arbitral Tribunal

13.1 Until the Arbitral Tribunal is formed, all communications between parties and arbitrators shall be made through the Registrar.

13.2 Thereafter, unless and until the Arbitral Tribunal directs that communications shall take place directly between the Arbitral Tribunal and the parties (with simultaneous copies to the Registrar), all written communications between the parties and the Arbitral Tribunal shall continue to be made through the Registrar.

13.3 Where the Registrar sends any written communication to one party on behalf of the Arbitral Tribunal, he shall send a copy to each of the other parties. Where any party sends to the Registrar any communication (including Written Statements and Documents under Article 15), it shall include a copy for each arbitrator; and it shall also send copies direct to all other parties and confirm to the Registrar in writing that it has done or is doing so.

(1) Generally

18.169 Article 13 is broadly self-explanatory and reflects flexibility in the extent of involvement of the Court and Secretariat.

[170] Rivkin, 93.

(2) Copies of documents

Parties should pay particular attention to the provisions of Art 13.3 requiring them to send copies of all communications to the Registrar to all other parties. This applies even where the tribunal has directed under Art 13.2 that direct communications may be made between it and the parties. **18.170**

Article 14 Conduct of the Proceedings

14.1 The parties may agree on the conduct of their arbitral proceedings and they are encouraged to do so, consistent with the Arbitral Tribunal's general duties at all times:

(a) to act fairly and impartially as between all parties, giving each a reasonable opportunity of putting its case and dealing with that of its opponent; and

(b) to adopt procedures suitable to the circumstances of the arbitration, avoiding unnecessary delay or expense, so as to provide a fair and efficient means for the final resolution of the parties' dispute.

Such agreements shall be made by the parties in writing or recorded in writing by the Arbitral Tribunal at the request of and with the authority of the parties.

14.2 Unless otherwise agreed by the parties under Article 14.1, the Arbitral Tribunal shall have the widest discretion to discharge its duties allowed under such law(s) or rules of law as the Arbitral Tribunal may determine to be applicable; and at all times the parties shall do everything necessary for the fair, efficient and expeditious conduct of the arbitration.

14.3 In the case of a three-member Arbitral Tribunal the chairman may, with the prior consent of the other two arbitrators, make procedural rulings alone.

(1) Generally

Article 14 records a key element or the 'Magna Carta' of LCIA arbitration.[171] This recognizes party autonomy regarding proceedings as 'the guiding principle in determining the procedure to be followed in an international commercial arbitration'.[172] Although it is mentioned specifically only in the context of Art 20.4, Art 14 must form the background for any tribunal decision (procedural or substantive). **18.171**

(2) The tribunal's duties

Article 14.1 adopts the wording of s 33(1), 1996 Act, in setting out the duties of the tribunal in conducting the arbitral proceedings and is consistent with the basic considerations of international public policy.[173] **18.172**

Both (a) and (b) are concerned with ensuring that the tribunal fulfils its task of doing full justice to the parties.[174] Limb (a) sets out the requirements of natural justice. It is crucial to enforcement under the New York Convention and because of the tribunal's quasi-judicial function. **18.173**

In relation to limb (b), it has been pointed out that it is by no means obvious why the tribunal should be concerned with unnecessary delay or expense since this affects both **18.174**

---

171 Veeder, 1998 Rules 367.

172 Redfern and Hunter, s 6-03.

173 Veeder, 1998 Rules, 366. The rules are mandatory if the seat of arbitration is England and Wales and Veeder states expressly that the introduction of these provisions was the result of this.

174 See DAC Report s 150.

parties equally.[175] An answer is that the provision allows the tribunal to protect a weaker party from being bullied by another and reduces the scope for challenge to the validity of the award.

18.175 Further, limb (b) and Art 14.2 support the tribunal's ultimate discretion in procedural matters provided it complies with Art 14.1.[176]

18.176 The duties are based on, but not identical to, the Model Law Art 18; in particular, 'reasonable opportunity' replaces 'full opportunity'. In the equivalent provision of the 1996 Act, this change was to remove any argument that a party might take as long as it wanted.[177] There is a very close resemblance to s 33 of the 1996 Act.

(3) The party autonomy

18.177 Article 14.1 enshrines the principle of party autonomy subject to the limit that the parties cannot agree to dispense with the duty on arbitrators; for example, parties could not, therefore, agree that the arbitrators can act unfairly.[178] The importance of party autonomy in international arbitration means that the parties are expressly 'encouraged' to agree the conduct of proceedings.

18.178 An agreement about the conduct of proceedings must be recorded in writing and, it is clear from the provision for this to be recorded by the tribunal, that the agreement may be reached at any time and can involve the tribunal.

18.179 If the tribunal considers that a party agreement is inconsistent with its duties, it should refuse to carry out the proceedings as agreed. In appropriate circumstances, the tribunal would be justified in resigning if the parties were to refuse to adopt a procedure complying with Art 14.[179] In evaluating whether the parties' agreement is appropriate in view of the tribunal's duties, the tribunal may be assisted by being able to identify the parties' reasons for the agreement.[180]

18.180 If the tribunal does refuse to conduct the proceedings on the basis of the parties' agreement, it is open to them to complain to the LCIA Court that the arbitrators were not acting in accordance with the Rules.[181]

(4) Tribunal's discretion

18.181 Article 14.2 puts beyond doubt the tribunal's discretion over procedural matters. In the absence of agreement between the parties, and subject to the Rules, the tribunal's discretion is limited only by any rules of law which the tribunal determines applicable. Typically these will be any mandatory requirements imposed by national legislation of the seat of the arbitration. They will not, however, be the general procedural law of the seat since the very point is for the tribunal to decide the specific procedure appropriate for the case.

---

175 Pryles, M., 'Limits to Party Autonomy in Arbitral Procedure' (2007) 24 *J Int'l Arb* 327.
176 See DAC Report s 153.
177 See *ibid*, s 165.
178 See *ibid*, s 155.
179 Similarly under s 33, 1996 Act, see Merkin, Arbitration Act, 86.
180 Pryles, M., 'Limits to Party Autonomy in Arbitral Procedure' (2007) 24 *J Int'l Arb* 327, 336 ff.
181 See Pryles, M., 'Limits to Party Autonomy in Arbitral Procedure' (2007) 24 *J Int'l Arb* 327.

Article 14.2 also imposes a duty on the parties to assist in the fair, efficient and expeditious conduct of the arbitration. This adopts, almost verbatim, the provision of s 40(1) of the 1996 Act but does not provide an equivalent to s 40(2) which sets out examples of what is required from the parties.[182] Section 40 of the 1996 Act is mandatorily applicable, albeit to be construed as extending only to those matters which the tribunal is entitled to decide in the absence of contrary agreement.[183] It is suggested that even where s 40 is not mandatory, the matters listed in s 40(2) should be treated as included within Art 14.2. **18.182**

(5) Procedural rulings

Article 14.3 allows the chairman to make procedural rulings without consulting the other members provided that their prior consent for this is obtained. **18.183**

The power is intended to operate without the parties' consent unless they have specifically agreed otherwise. This is practical because, notwithstanding the heated arguments that procedural matters regularly generate, a particular procedural ruling can be said to have determined the outcome of a case. A possible example of a procedural ruling which might generate a challenge is the fixing of a hearing at a time as it was impossible for a particular witness to attend and give oral evidence. **18.184**

It is notable that the prior consent of the other arbitrators does not have to be recorded in writing under Art 14.3. Nevertheless, it would be prudent to obtain a written confirmation. **18.185**

This rule cannot apply in circumstances where the chairman is unavailable. Given the likelihood that the two arbitrators who are not the chairman will be party appointees, it would be inappropriate for one of those individuals alone to rule on procedural matters. **18.186**

Article 15 Submission of Written Statements and Documents

15.1 Unless the parties have agreed otherwise under Article 14.1 or the Arbitral Tribunal should determine differently, the written stage of the proceedings shall be as set out below.

15.2 Within 30 days of receipt of written notification from the Registrar of the formation of the Arbitral Tribunal, the Claimant shall send to the Registrar a Statement of Case setting out in sufficient detail the facts and any contentions of law on which it relies, together with the relief claimed against all other parties, save and insofar as such matters have not been set out in its Request.

15.3 Within 30 days of receipt of the Statement of Case or written notice from the Claimant that it elects to treat the Request as its Statement of Case, the Respondent shall send to the Registrar a Statement of Defence setting out in sufficient detail which of the facts and contentions of law in the Statement of Case or Request (as the case may be) it admits or denies, on what grounds and on what other facts and contentions of law it relies. Any counterclaims shall be submitted with the Statement of Defence in the same manner as claims are to be set out in the Statement of Case.

---

[182] That is, the obligation to do all things necessary includes '(a) complying without delay with any determination of the tribunal as to procedural or evidential matters, or with any orders or directions of the tribunal, and (b) where appropriate, taking without delay any necessary steps to obtain a decision of the court on a preliminary question of jurisdiction or law'.

[183] Merkin, Arbitration Act, 98.

15.4 Within 30 days of receipt of the Statement of Defence, the Claimant shall send to the Registrar a Statement of Reply which, where there are any counterclaims, shall include a Defence to Counterclaim in the same manner as a defence is to be set out in the Statement of Defence.

15.5 If the Statement of Reply contains a Defence to Counterclaim, within 30 days of its receipt the Respondent shall send to the Registrar a Statement of Reply to Counterclaim.

15.6 All Statements referred to in this Article shall be accompanied by copies (or, if they are especially voluminous, lists) of all essential documents on which the party concerned relies and which have not previously been submitted by any party, and (where appropriate) by any relevant samples and exhibits.

15.7 As soon as practicable following receipt of the Statements specified in this Article, the Arbitral Tribunal shall proceed in such manner as has been agreed in writing by the parties or pursuant to its authority under these Rules.

15.8 If the Respondent fails to submit a Statement of Defence or the Claimant a Statement of Defence to Counterclaim, or if at any point any party fails to avail itself of the opportunity to present its case in the manner determined by Article 15.2 to 15.6 or directed by the Arbitral Tribunal, the Arbitral Tribunal may nevertheless proceed with the arbitration and make an award.

(1) Generally

18.187 Article 15 sets out a default procedure for written statements and documents.[184] This gives the LCIA Rules a degree of predictability.[185] After the written stage, the parties and the tribunal have no choice but to decide the further conduct of the arbitration.

18.188 The first procedural issue in every international arbitration is how claims, defences, testamentary and documentary evidence, technical expert reports, legal arguments and supporting legal authorities are brought to the tribunal for its consideration. At the outset this always justifies some thought by both the parties and the tribunal, especially where parties are from different legal and cultural backgrounds.

18.189 Lawyers' views are frequently based on the court practice of the national jurisdiction with which they have most familiarity but blindly to mimic court practice reduces the value of the parties' choice of the autonomy of international arbitration.

18.190 The procedure for written statements and documents should not be considered in isolation from the procedure that will be adopted at the hearing. It is suggested that written submissions be detailed at the outset and supported wherever possible by the evidence on which the parties rely. At the hearing, written documents should be limited to short focused documents, identifying the specific evidence which supports the principal points which the party must prove or disprove to succeed in the arbitration and obtain the relief it has requested. If such procedure is to be adopted, however, the tribunal should suggest it to the parties before any written submissions are produced as it may influence the way in which the statements of case are formulated.

---

[184] In contrast to the ICC Rules Art 20.

[185] See Hunter and Paulsson, 1985 Rules, 170.

In international arbitration, it is now the norm to adopt two rounds of exchange of submissions, (a four-stage exchange of statements) rather than the LCIA default position of a three-stage process. Although this may not be appropriate in all circumstances, if it is adopted, it has the advantage of providing the parties with a full opportunity to indicate where a matter is not contested, thereby saving time and costs. **18.191**

(2) Particular instances in which the default procedure will not be suitable

There are two specific instances where the default procedure set out in Art 15 will not be suitable: 'fast-track' and multi-party arbitrations. **18.192**

The Rules do not contain a separate provision for fast-track procedures.[186] Such procedures are often desirable where the sum in dispute does not merit the costs of a lengthy arbitration or where the dispute is discrete, such as in relation to price and quality determination. If the parties cooperate, a case can be fully argued, the evidence collated and presented, and an award rendered within just a few months. **18.193**

Setting a timetable for the arbitration to be conducted is the most obvious measure to ensure a fast-track procedure but other matters can assist in the swift resolution of a dispute. Consideration should be given to limiting statements of case to exclude statements of reply to statements of defence.[187] It may be appropriate to require that all witness statements and documentary evidence be filed with the statements of case. Requests for document production may be limited or excluded. If the parties require that an oral hearing takes place,[188] there is considerable scope for time to be saved by limiting or excluding witness testimony.[189] In all of these areas, care must be taken that the just disposal of the dispute is not compromised.[190] **18.194**

Where there are more than two parties to the arbitration, the appropriate procedure depends heavily on the nature of the dispute. Even where two parties' interests are broadly aligned, it is possible that the production of simultaneous claim or defence documents will not be suitable. Equally, although rarely, it may be that on some issues two or more of the parties have an identical interest and can make joint submissions. It may also be that one party's liability is wholly dependent on that of another (most frequently in subcontracting situations) and, where both are party to the proceedings, there will probably be little point in the first party providing a statement of defence until the second (usually subcontracting party) has done so. **18.195**

(3) The default procedure

Article 15 sets out a default timetable for the written stage of proceedings. This three-stage pleading process is analogous to that provided for in English court procedures although the time limits, consistently 30 days, are different. **18.196**

186 Party autonomy makes this unnecessary. Compulsory fast-track procedures can be specified in the Arbitration Agreement and the LCIA can propose suitable wording, FAQ, Q21.

187 This limitation is imposed by eg the London Maritime Arbitrators Association (LMAA) in its Fast and Low Cost Arbitration Procedure.

188 It may be dispensed with under Art 19.1.

189 Also Art 20.5.

190 Schwartz, E.A., 'Reconciling Speed with Justice in International Arbitration' in B.G. Davis (ed), *Improving International Arbitration* (International Chamber of Commerce, 1998) 44.

18.197 A four-stage procedure is now commonly adopted.[191] Although the 30-day time limit was adopted to 'give further impetus to the drive for greater speed and efficiency',[192] the time limits often change as 30 days is often insufficient time to review documents, and to prepare submissions and witness statements. The problem is exacerbated where parties are in different time zones and speak different languages.

(4) Form and content of written statements

18.198 The style and content of the Statements of Case is a matter for the parties. They could agree (although rarely do so) that the written documents are to be brief, in the style of an English court pleading, going no further than bare essentials.

18.199 Any agreement by the parties must accommodate the key requirements enunciated in Arts 15.2 and 15.3. The Claimant need not repeat matters already set out in its Request and may simply adopt that document as its Statement of Case. The Statements of Case, Defence and Counterclaim should set out 'in sufficient detail' the facts and law on which each party relies and the relief claimed against all other parties. There are no express requirements for the Reply but plainly any further facts and law relied upon should, likewise, be set out in sufficient detail so that the claims are clear, can be understood and responded to by the other party, and determined by the tribunal.

28.200 The level of detail required will vary. With regard to the facts, if the matter is to proceed to an oral hearing, sufficient facts must still be set out to enable the tribunal to understand what each party says has happened. With regard to the law, the parties should bear in mind the constitution and qualifications of the tribunal as well as the experience of the other parties and their representatives. Where the tribunal is qualified in another law, it is appropriate to set out the law relied upon in a neutral manner and identify the weight which is given to any authority cited.

(5) Documents

18.201 Article 15.6 requires each Statement to be accompanied by copies of the 'essential' documents on which each party relies which have not already been submitted. Arguably this means the parties must produce all those documents upon which they rely to prove their case.[193] The effect of this is to assist the other party in understanding the case it has to answer and to reduce the scope for document disclosure. Nevertheless, submission of further documents is allowed for by the Rules (Arts 20, 21 and 22.1).

18.202 The requirement is modified in the case of particularly voluminous documents which may be listed or, if appropriate, a sample may be provided. For example where a dispute relates to a series of transactions with materially identical paperwork, it would be appropriate to list all documents but provide only one set of documentation with the Statement and, possibly, a schedule identifying any differences. This is an area for pragmatic agreement between the parties or where necessary order by the tribunal.

---

191 See para 18.191.

192 Winstanley, The New Rules, 60.

193 Pietrowski, R., 'Evidence in International Arbitration' (2006) 22 *Arb Int'l* 373 [Pietrowski], at 391.

Where documents are not in the language of the arbitration, the tribunal the Court may require their translation (see Art 17.4). In any case, it is in each party's interest to provide an appropriate translation of any document on which it relies. 18.203

(6) Duty to proceed

Article 15.7 provides that the tribunal must proceed as agreed by the parties or pursuant to its authority under the Rules. This reflects the aim that the dispute be resolved swiftly and fairly. This express provision also facilitates a challenge to a dilatory tribunal under Art 10.2. For both reasons, where the parties agree a different procedure to that set out in Art 15, they should consider including a similar statement. 18.204

(7) Power to proceed

Article 15.8 aims to prevent the proceedings being frustrated by the non-participation of one party, usually the Respondent. Although Art 15.8 is part of the article dealing with the written procedure and the exchange of documents, it is sufficiently wide to cover any non-participation by either party. In particular, since an oral hearing and procedural matters other than those covered in Art 15 will have to be the subject of a tribunal order, these fall within the wording 'or directed by the Arbitral Tribunal'. 18.205

The tribunal has a discretion, not an obligation, to continue the proceedings. If it does so continue, it is crucial that the defaulting party continues to be given notice of the steps and given every opportunity to be heard. Provided each party has been given the opportunity to present its case at each stage (including a hearing), its failure to do so will not prevent a valid award being made or allow enforcement to be resisted. 18.206

Failure by the Claimant to submit a Statement of Claim is not expressly covered, presumably because this is relatively unlikely and, in any event, its claim should have been set out in its Request. There is no provision in the Rules for the claim to be dismissed if the Claimant files no Statement of Case[194] although national legislation, for example the 1996 Act,[195] may confer such power on the arbitrators. 18.207

Without a power to dismiss the claim, the tribunal has three options. The first is to do nothing. This is unlikely to be attractive to the Respondent who will face the possibility that proceedings could be brought against it at any time. The second option is to order that if the Claimant does not serve a Statement of Claim within a set period the Request will be treated as the Statement of Claim. This is most likely to be appropriate if the Request is relatively detailed. The third option is for the tribunal to order the Claimant to serve a Statement of Claim or a statement that its Request is to be treated as its Statement of Claim by a certain time. Under the latter options, the Claimant has been given the opportunity to 18.208

194 In contrast, the Model Law provides by Art 25(a) that, if, without sufficient cause, the claimant fails to communicate his Statement of Claim, the tribunal shall terminate the proceedings.

195 s 41(3), 1996 Act. The detailed operation of this provision is not considered here but it is worth mentioning that inordinate delay by the Claimant in pursuing the claim is a matter of years, not months, and it is rarely appropriate for an award to be made within the limitation period applicable to the claim: see Harris, B., Planterose, R. and Trecks, J. (eds), *The Arbitration Act 1996* (4th edn, Blackwell Science, 2007) and Merkin, Arbitration Law, s 16.22 ff.

present its case. The tribunal may then proceed with the arbitration and accept the Respondent's submissions and evidence without unfairness.

18.209 A failure to participate by the Respondent is more likely but a Statement of Defence which is merely served late will almost invariably be accepted by the tribunal in order to avoid allegations of injustice.[196]

18.210 The tribunal must proceed to a hearing and make an award since its task is to *determine* not 'rubber stamp' claims presented to it.[197] In line with Art 25(b) of the Model Law, there is no provision for the tribunal to treat the Respondent's failure as an admission of the Claimant's claims and, under Art 26.1, the award must be reasoned.

(8) Conduct of an arbitration under Article 15.8

18.211 Where the arbitration proceedings continue in default of one party, it is often considered appropriate for the tribunal to, at the very least, ask witnesses to confirm their evidence on the record, and ask questions to assure themselves that the witnesses' evidence is accurate. The tribunal will invariably ask the party present to make a full presentation of its legal case and question those legal principles so far as is possible. It is not, however, necessary for a tribunal to make the case for a defaulting party, or undertake its own research to challenge law or fact.

18.212 For the purposes of due process, it is invariably good practice either to have a full recorded transcript of the meeting, or at least for minutes to be taken at the end of that meeting, and to send this to the defaulting party.

Article 16 Seat of Arbitration and Place of Hearings

16.1 The parties may agree in writing the seat (or legal place) of their arbitration. Failing such a choice, the seat of arbitration shall be London, unless and until the LCIA Court determines in view of all the circumstances, and after having given the parties an opportunity to make written comment, that another seat is more appropriate.

16.2 The Arbitral Tribunal may hold hearings, meetings and deliberations at any convenient geographical place in its discretion; and if elsewhere than the seat of the arbitration, the arbitration shall be treated as an arbitration conducted at the seat of the arbitration and any award as an award made at the seat of the arbitration for all purposes.

16.3 The law applicable to the arbitration (if any) shall be the arbitration law of the seat of arbitration, unless and to the extent that the parties have expressly agreed in writing on the application of another arbitration law and such agreement is not prohibited by the law of the arbitral seat.

(1) Generally

18.213 The seat of an arbitration is important. It determines the law that regulates the arbitration over the agreement of the parties, and the tribunal's authority; it provides the supporting court system for proceedings and in which an award can be challenged, and it is important for the purposes of enforcement under the New York Convention. Article 16 expresses the parties' right to choose the seat and applicable law (or possibly delocalization)

---

[196] eg Lew, Mistelis, Kröll, s 21-78 n 101.

[197] Redfern and Hunter, s 8-46. See generally on issues of default, Lew, Mistelis, Kröll, s 21-75ff.

of the arbitration. As these are essentially preliminary matters, the Court will deal with them at the stage of the Request and Response.

(2) Default provision

The parties may choose any place as the seat of the arbitration. LCIA-administered arbitrations have had their seats in places as diverse as Mumbai, Sri Lanka, Berlin and Japan.[198] Nevertheless, London is the most popular choice.[199] The LCIA will comment on the advisability of venues from its experience in the administration of arbitration in non-London venues.[200] **18.214**

In making London the agreed seat of the arbitration where there has been no party agreement or Court determination to the contrary, Art 16.1 provides, as the LCIA puts it, a safety net. The requirement for an express choice to defeat the presumption has been described as commendable.[201] London is the obvious default choice not just because of the LCIA's physical link with the city and parties' frequent presumption that LCIA arbitration will have its seat in London[202] but also because the Rules were drafted with the English 1996 Act in mind. **18.215**

(3) Juridical concept

The seat of arbitration is a legal concept; hearings may be held in any location. Article 16.2 puts this beyond doubt. There is no obligation on the tribunal to consult the parties on the location of hearings but, given the consensual foundation of international arbitration, it would be wrong for a tribunal not to do so. **18.216**

Occasionally an arbitration agreement will be worded so as to imply a choice of physical location of hearings as well as of juridical seat, for example, referring to the venue of the arbitration.[203] It is at least arguable that such a choice ousts the right of the tribunal to hold hearings at some other place. In such circumstances, if hearings are held other than in the named location, one party may challenge the award on the basis that the procedure did not conform to the parties' agreement.[204] These difficulties are avoided if the tribunal obtains the parties' agreement to the location of hearings. **18.217**

(4) Applicable law

Article 16.3 specifies 'the law applicable to the arbitration'. This wording might be clearer since different aspects of proceedings may have different applicable laws. The most **18.218**

198 Paulsson, J., 'Arbitration-Friendliness: Promises of Principle and Realities of Practice' (2007) 23 *Arb Int'l* 477. Greig, R.T., 'International Commercial Arbitration in Japan: A User's Report' (1989) 6 *J Int'l Arb* 21. And see 2008 data in 4(1) *GAR*, 22.

199 J. Paulsson (n 198).

200 Bernstein's Handbook, s 9-062.

201 Petrochilos, G., *Procedural Law in International Arbitration* (2004) s 5.44.

202 On its introduction (Art 7, 1985 Rules) it was said that London 'appears best to conform to the parties' expectation when they refer to LCIA arbitration without specifying that they desire a seat or arbitration other than London.' (Hunter and Paulsson, 1985 Rules, 168).

203 See Mistelis, L., 'International Arbitration: Corporate Attitudes and Practices' (2004) 15 *Am Rev Int'l Arb* 525, at 564 ff.

204 See Redfern and Hunter, s 2-18. Conversely, and surprisingly, in *Braes of Doune Wind Farm (Scotland) Ltd v Alfred McAlpine Business Services Ltd* [2008] 1 Lloyd's Rep 608, it was held that the 'seat' denoted the physical location for proceedings, not the juridical seat.

significant possibilities are: the law applicable to the substance of the dispute; the law governing the procedure of the arbitration (or 'curial' law);[205] the law of the agreement to arbitrate (which covers substantive issues in relation to the arbitration agreement such as validity and interpretation of the agreement);[206] and the law governing the reference to arbitration although, in practice, this is almost always identical to the law of the agreement to arbitrate.[207]

18.219 Considered in context, Art 16.3 must provide for the curial law rather than that of the merits or arbitral procedure as these are to be determined by the tribunal under Arts 22.3 and 14.2, respectively.[208] This does not inevitably mean that the same law is applicable to both the arbitration agreement and the procedure of an arbitration, although at least in England, it is rare for the law of the separable arbitration agreement to be different from the law of the seat.[209]

18.220 In respect of procedural law, certainly as a matter of English law, the curial law will be that of the seat, at least as far as its mandatory provisions are concerned.[210] Article 16.3 puts the position beyond doubt. Although it has been suggested that no-one in their right mind would do so,[211] the parties might choose a law applicable to the arbitration which did not coincide with the law of the seat. This would certainly pose some difficulty at least under the 1996 Act since most of the court's powers are only available if the seat of the arbitration is in England and Wales or Northern Ireland.[212] In some jurisdictions, it is not possible to exclude all provisions of national legislation where that jurisdiction is the seat so a choice of a different applicable law would not be wholly effective. England provides one example where parties may exclude only some provisions of national law.[213]

Article 17 Language of Arbitration

17.1 The initial language of the arbitration shall be the language of the Arbitration Agreement, unless the parties have agreed in writing otherwise and providing always that a non-participating or defaulting party shall have no cause for complaint if communications to and from the Registrar and the arbitration proceedings are conducted in English.

17.2 In the event that the Arbitration Agreement is written in more than one language, the LCIA Court may, unless the Arbitration Agreement provides that the arbitration proceedings

205 Often also referred to as the *lex arbitri*. See Mistelis, L., 'Reality rest: current state of affairs in theory and practice relating to lex arbitri' (2006) 17 *Am Rev Int'l Arb* 155.

206 See *Heavy Industries Ltd v Oil and Natural Gas Commission* [1994] 1 Lloyd's Rep 45, 57 and other cases cited in Russell on Arbitration, s 2-097. Also the extensive discussion of the significance of the applicable law in Merkin, Arbitration Law, s 7.5 ff.

207 See Lew, Mistelis, Kröll, chs 17-18, Merkin, Arbitration Law, s 7.60 and Russell on Arbitration, s 2-088.

208 Also Petrochilos (n 201) s 5.43.

209 *C v D* [2007] EWCA Civ 1282; [2008] 1 Lloyd's Rep 239. This was not essential to the decision reached, however, the court gave the matter more than passing consideration (ss 21 to 29).

210 Russell on Arbitration, s 2-101.

211 Samuel, 39.

212 s 2(1) 1996 Act. The exercise of powers under s 2(3) and 2(4) is discretionary see eg *Viking Insurance Co v Rossdale and Ors* [2002] 1 Lloyd's Rep 219 relating to s 44 of the 1996 Act.

213 s 4(2) and 4(3) and Sch 1,1996 Act and see the discussion in *Union of India v McDonnell Douglas Corp* [1993] 2 Lloyd's Rep 48, 51. The selection of any rules by the parties, including the LCIA Rules, or the IBA Rules on the Taking of Evidence in International Commercial Arbitration are subject to the mandatory provisions of the 1996 Act.

shall be conducted in more than one language, decide which of those languages shall be the initial language of the arbitration.

17.3 Upon the formation of the Arbitral Tribunal and unless the parties have agreed upon the language or languages of the arbitration, the Arbitration Tribunal shall decide upon the language(s) of the arbitration, after giving the parties an opportunity to make written comment and taking into account the initial language of the arbitration and any other matter it may consider appropriate in all the circumstances of the case.

17.4 If any document is expressed in a language other than the language(s) of the arbitration and no translation of such document is submitted by the party relying upon the document, the Arbitral Tribunal or (if the Arbitral Tribunal has not been formed) the LCIA Court may order that party to submit a translation in a form to be determined by the Arbitral Tribunal or the LCIA Court, as the case may be.

(1) Generally

Article 17 is a largely self-explanatory and practical provision. **18.221**

(2) Language of the arbitration agreement

Where the parties have not expressly[214] chosen the language of the arbitration, Arts 17.1 and 17.2 provide a workable solution for communications until the tribunal has been constituted. **18.222**

It is not unreasonable to presume that both parties to the arbitration agreement will be conversant with the language of that agreement and so will suffer no prejudice where the initial proceedings are conducted in that language. This may not be true, however, where the agreement is in two languages, each only understood properly by one party. A choice by the Court of a single language might disadvantage one party. In this situation, the Court will seek the parties' views. Equally, if it is a matter of concern to either party, the appropriate language for the arbitration can be raised in the Request and the Response. The party requesting arbitration should do so in the language in which it is most comfortable. **18.223**

In fact, almost all LCIA arbitrations are in English; at the start of 2009, only four LCIA cases were in a language other than English and all of these are bilingual with English. **18.224**

The final default provision is for communications to be in English if only between the Registrar and the non-defaulting party. Implicitly, this is regardless of the language of the agreement. This is primarily for the convenience of the LCIA staff and will not be imposed on the participating party. **18.225**

(3) Tribunal determination of the language of arbitration

Article 17.3 is a change from the earlier rules[215] and provides greater party control of proceedings as it had been found that the language of the contract was frequently neither the most logical nor practical choice for the conduct of proceedings.[216] **18.226**

---

214 The language of the arbitration agreement and associated documents is sometimes argued to be an implied choice (See Lew, Mistelis, Kröll, s 21-60).

215 Under the previous versions of the Rules, the language of the arbitration was fixed for the whole arbitration, possibly reflecting the prevalence of English in commercial agreements see: Fouchard, P., Galliard, E. and Goldman, B., *International Commercial Arbitration 1999* (Kluwer Law International,1999) [Fouchard, Galliard, Goldman] s 1244 and citing Lazareff, S., 'The Language of Institutional Arbitration' (1997) 8 *ICC ICArb Bull* 18.

216 Winstanley, The New Rules, 61.

18.227 The appropriate language is the one that best assists in the just resolution of the arbitration without unnecessary delay or expense.[217] One obvious factor to be taken into account is the extent of translation required as this lengthens proceedings and affects costs considerably. In addition, care should be taken to consider potential prejudice resulting from the extensive translation of oral evidence particularly where the evidence of only one party's witnesses will have to be translated.

18.228 The languages of the arbitrators are similarly important and there is a slight tension between determination of the language after the tribunal has been appointed and the duties of linguistic competence suggested by the IBA Rules of Ethics.[218]

18.229 Further, care may be needed to avoid the suggestion of any ground for bias where one party and the tribunal, or part of it, share a language but the other party does not.

18.230 Arbitrations in multiple languages simultaneously are possible but are very costly and special factors would be required to justify this.[219]

(4) Translation

18.231 Article 17.4 gives the tribunal or the Court power to require documents to be translated in a suitable form (not necessarily certified) but there is no obligation to translate all documents.

18.232 Where parties include voluminous exhibits, tribunals may be prepared to accept documents in the original language, accompanied by 'free translations' of extracts on which the party relies. Only where the accuracy of a translation is disputed need a tribunal order a certified translation. Although not specified in Art 17, it is implicit that written submissions should be in the language of the arbitration unless the contrary is agreed.

Article 18 Party Representation

18.1 Any party may be represented by legal practitioners or any other representatives.

18.2 At any time the Arbitral Tribunal may require from any party proof of authority granted to its representative(s) in such form as the Arbitral Tribunal may determine.

(1) Generally

18.233 Article 18.1 allows the parties greater flexibility as to representation than they would have before most national courts[220] and certain other arbitration systems that preclude the participation of lawyers.[221] Accordingly, a party representative may be qualified in any, or none, of the laws applicable to the arbitration.

18.234 A party may be formally represented at every stage of the arbitration. There is no limit as to the occasions on which the representatives may act and no requirement that the same representative is used throughout the proceedings. A party might, for example, choose to have

217 In accordance with the duties of the tribunal, Art 14.1.
218 See para 18.102.
219 Fouchard, Galliard, Goldman, s 1244.
220 See Bernstein's Handbook, s 2-025 ff for comments on this distinction.
221 This is particularly common in trade association arbitrations.

different issues presented by different representatives, the most obvious example being a separation between technical and legal issues.

The background of the parties' representatives has a significant impact on the conduct of proceedings. The classic example is the emphasis placed on testing witness evidence by cross–examination in the common law tradition. Other common differences affect the length and content of written submissions, and the presence, presentation and examination of witnesses and experts at the hearing. **18.235**

We consider that there is no bar to a party appearing on his own behalf. It is generally unfortunate, however, for a party to do so as it heightens the risk of unequal representation. Where parties are unequally represented, the tribunal must take particular care to ensure that justice is done between the parties while remaining, and appearing to remain, independent and impartial. Under the Rules, at least a partial solution to this may be for the tribunal to exercise the powers provided by Arts 19.3 and 22.1(c). **18.236**

Article 18 provides choice but does not allow a party to insist that a particular individual be his representative. In rare circumstances, the tribunal's powers under Art 14 to manage the arbitration to ensure the fair, efficient and expeditious conduct of the arbitration means that the tribunal may order that a particular representative may not be used. The two circumstances in which this is most likely to occur are: (i) where a reluctant party nominates an unavailable representative to delay the arbitral process;[222] and (ii) where a party nominates a representative whose presence may justify a challenge to one of the arbitrators.[223] **18.237**

There is no requirement that the parties give notice of their intention to be represented at any hearing.[224] It is nonetheless desirable that the parties do give appropriate notice and the tribunal may require them to do so. Not only does an indication of how each party's case is to be presented assist in the efficient conduct of proceedings but there is a possibility that a particular representative could actually, or apparently, render the tribunal partial. Accordingly, it is good practice for the names of representatives to be disclosed once they have been chosen to allow time for any dispute to be resolved.[225] Similarly, the identity of experts who will be assisting the party in the arbitration should be disclosed at an early stage in the proceedings. **18.238**

Article 18.2 requires no elaboration. In practice, it is not unusual for tribunals to require representatives to provide a power of attorney. **18.239**

Article 19 Hearings

19.1 Any party which expresses a desire to that effect has the right to be heard orally before the Arbitral Tribunal on the merits of the dispute, unless the parties have agreed in writing on documents-only arbitration.

19.2 The Arbitral Tribunal shall fix the date, time and physical place of any meetings and hearings in the arbitration, and shall give the parties reasonable notice thereof.

222 In the context of the equivalent provisions of s 36, 1996 Act, see DAC Report, s 184.
223 See *Hrvetska v Slovenia*, note 152.
224 There was such a provision in Art 7(3), 1981 Rules.
225 See n 223.

19.3 The Arbitral Tribunal may in advance of any hearing submit to the parties a list of questions which it wishes them to answer with special attention.

19.4 All meetings and hearings shall be in private unless the parties agree otherwise in writing or the Arbitral Tribunal directs otherwise.

19.5 The Arbitral Tribunal shall have the fullest authority to establish time limits for meetings and hearings, or for any parts thereof.

(1) Right to an oral hearing

18.240 Article 19.1 reflects the LCIA's view that the right to an oral hearing is fundamental, even if the tribunal considers it unnecessary.[226]

18.241 An oral hearing is generally desirable to resolve conflicting factual evidence, particularly witness evidence,[227] and to give the parties the chance to develop their arguments in response to questions from the tribunal. Nevertheless, documents-only arbitrations can be effective and are certainly more economic. In such circumstances, the tribunal may submit written questions to the parties after the first submissions are received. It is often appropriate in any case for some issues, typically quantum, to be dealt with without any oral hearing.

(2) Date, time and physical place of meetings

18.242 Article 19.2 gives the tribunal apparently unfettered discretion in relation to logistics of meetings or oral hearings but we consider that account should be taken of the parties' views.[228] That said, under English law at least, if the tribunal disregards the parties' agreement on the location of hearings, this will only found a successful challenge[229] if it has caused serious injustice, not simply inconvenience.[230]

18.243 The place of the hearing need not be the seat of the arbitration; that the legal seat remains the same is emphasized by the words 'physical place' in Art 19.2.[231] Different stages of the hearing may be held in different locations. Particularly common are situations where witnesses or experts cannot or will not travel to the seat of arbitration, or where there is a need for a visit to the site of the project or dispute.

(3) Questions from the tribunal

18.244 The power to put questions enables the tribunal to take on a more inquisitorial role.[232] The practice will depend on the legal culture and dynamics of the tribunal and parties' counsel. It can be of particular assistance where, for example, written submissions do not address the same issues in a comparable format (commonly a result of different national practice and sophistication of the representatives). Nevertheless, care must be taken that the questions are neither leading nor suggest that the tribunal has already decided any issue.

---

226 Hunter and Paulsson, 1985 Rules, 170. The right was first made express in the 1985 Rules, Art 10.

227 Pietrowski, 394–5.

228 Not least as part of the Art 14 obligations.

229 Under s 68, 1996 Act.

230 *Tongyuan (USA) International Trading Group v Uni-Clan Ltd*, 19 January 2001, QBD Commercial Court, Moore-Bick J.

231 See also Art 16.

232 See Redfern and Hunter, s 6-113.

The tribunal will often ask for an agreed list of issues, probably some weeks after the close of the written process, to which the tribunal may add its questions. Both lists of issues and questions can assist in the expeditious and fair conduct of proceedings. **18.245**

(4) Private hearings

The presumption set out in Art 19.4 reflects the general position that arbitrations are private[233] and complements the confidentiality obligations in Art 30. The provision allowing the parties to agree that the hearing will not be private is, however, unremarkable. **18.246**

The unusual feature of Art 19.4 is that it allows the tribunal to direct that hearings are not to be held in private without the agreement of the parties. This is a notable point of distinction from the UNCITRAL Rules[234] that provide that the only exception to an *in camera* hearing is where the parties agree otherwise. Given that the privacy of the hearing is generally regarded as axiomatic of international arbitration and as one of its major advantages,[235] it is difficult to imagine a situation in which a tribunal would allow non-parties or their representatives to be present if one party objected. Under English law, it is doubtful whether such an order would be upheld by the courts.[236] **18.247**

(5) Time limits

Article 19.5 gives the tribunal the final say over time limits. It does not assume equality of time for the parties; this is often neither practical nor appropriate. Naturally, this power may only be exercised insofar as it is consistent with the overriding obligations on the tribunal under Art 14 and will not derogate from the implicit requirement that account should be taken of the parties' views. **18.248**

Article 20 Witnesses

20.1 Before any hearing, the Arbitral Tribunal may require any party to give notice of the identity of each witness that party wishes to call (including rebuttal witnesses), as well as the subject matter of that witness's testimony, its content and its relevance to the issues in the arbitration.

20.2 The Arbitral Tribunal may also determine the time, manner and form in which such materials should be exchanged between the parties and presented to the Arbitral Tribunal; and it has a discretion to allow, refuse, or limit the appearance of witnesses (whether witness of fact or expert witness).

20.3 Subject to any order otherwise by the Arbitral Tribunal, the testimony of a witness may be presented by a party in written form, either as a signed statement or as a sworn affidavit.

20.4 Subject to Article 14.1 and 14.2, any party may request that a witness, on whose testimony another party seeks to rely, should attend for oral questioning at a hearing before the Arbitral Tribunal. If the Arbitral Tribunal orders that other party to produce the witness and the witness fails to attend the oral hearing without good cause, the Arbitral Tribunal

233 Under English law, see *'The Eastern Saga'* [1984] 2 Lloyd's Rep 373; *Ali Shipping v Shipyard Trogir* [1998] 1 Lloyd's Rep 643; *Emmott v Michael Wilson & Partners Ltd* [2008] EWCA Civ 184, [2008] 1 Lloyd's Rep 616.

234 Art 25.4.

235 eg Redfern and Hunter, s 1-56.

236 Under previous English legislation, a successful challenge was made to the arbitrator's order of concurrent hearings without the consent of the parties as this was contrary to the concept of private arbitration agreed by the parties: *'The Eastern Saga'* [1984] 2 Lloyd's Rep 373.

may place such weight on the written testimony (or exclude the same altogether) as it considers appropriate in the circumstances of the case.

20.5 Any witness who gives oral evidence at a hearing before the Arbitral Tribunal may be questioned by each of the parties under the control of the Arbitral Tribunal. The Arbitral Tribunal may put questions at any stage of his evidence.

20.6 Subject to the mandatory provisions of any applicable law, it shall not be improper for any party or its legal representatives to interview any witness or potential witness for the purpose of presenting his testimony in written form or producing him as an oral witness.

20.7 Any individual intending to testify to the Arbitral Tribunal on any issue of fact or expertise shall be treated as a witness under these Rules notwithstanding that the individual is a party to the arbitration or was or is an officer, employee or shareholder of any party.

(1) Advance notice in relation to witnesses and their evidence

18.249 Articles 20.1 and 20.2 together assist the tribunal and parties in adhering to Art 14. The tribunal can only effectively control the evidence under Art 20.2 if it has notice in advance of that testimony's general nature. Arrangements for the presentation of witnesses should generally be set out in the tribunal's procedural directions.

18.250 Under Art 20.1, the tribunal may order summaries of witness testimonies be exchanged; alternatively, it might rely on the sequential or simultaneous exchange of witness statements. Sworn statements or affidavits are not necessary unless specifically required by the tribunal.[237] Notably, the power under Art 20.1 to require that parties state the relevance of the witness evidence to the issues goes beyond the comparable IBA provisions.[238]

18.251 A two- or multi-stage notification process may, as is increasingly common, be adopted to allow the parties to rely on further witnesses in response (or rebuttal) to new issues or material raised although, by contrast with the IBA Rules on Evidence,[239] the Rules make no specific provision for this.

18.252 It is plain from Art 20.2 that Art 20 covers both factual and expert witnesses.[240]

(2) Written testimony

18.253 Article 20.3 makes it clear that written testimony is acceptable but not mandatory. Written testimony is common but it is not unheard of for proceedings to be conducted relying on oral testimony only where witnesses are reluctant to commit themselves in writing for fear that the documents might become available in unrelated and disadvantageous circumstances.[241] A mix of written and wholly oral primary evidence without a good justification is generally undesirable.[242]

---

237 Provided for by Art 20.3.

238 Art 4(1), IBA Rules on the Taking of Evidence in International Commercial Arbitration, 1 June 1999.

239 Art 4(6).

240 On expert witness see Art 5, IBA Rules on Evidence, and the Chartered Institute of Arbitrators' *Protocol for the Use of Party Appointed Expert Witnesses in International Arbitration* which applies developments in common law litigation to the arbitration framework. See also for comment: Jones, D., 'Party Appointed Expert Witnesses in International Arbitration: A Protocol at Last' (2008) 24 *Arb Int'l* 137.

241 See 'Act III: Advocacy with Witness Testimony' (2005) 21 *Arb Int'l* 589.

242 For a discussion of the merits of written witness testimony see Tallerico, T.J. and Behrendt, J.A., 'The Use of Bifurcation and Direct Testimony Witness Statements in International Commercial Arbitration Proceedings' (2003) 20 *J Int'l Arb* 295. For a civilian lawyer's approach to witness evidence see Oetiker, 253.

There are no requirements as to the written form save that it is signed. The document is testimony, so should include an affirmation of its truth.[243] **18.254**

(3) Appearance of witnesses

Any party may request that its witnesses appear although this is subject to the tribunal's power under Art 20.2 to refuse or limit the appearance of witnesses. That power must be exercised in accordance with Art 14 although it is unlikely that an award will be set aside solely on the basis of a refusal to hear oral testimony.[244] **18.255**

The tribunal's discretion under Art 20.2 is limited where it has appointed an expert under Art 21. In those circumstances, the tribunal may not refuse to allow the parties to call expert witnesses although it may limit that evidence.[245] **18.256**

The Rules contain no presumption that a witness who has given written testimony will appear.[246] Accordingly, Art 20.4 allows each party to require the other's witness to attend for questioning. Notably, and perphaps in recognition of the scope for dispute in this context, Art 20.4 is the only part of the Rules expressly made subject to Arts 14.1 and 14.2. **18.257**

If a witness has been ordered to attend but fails to do so without good cause, the tribunal is empowered by Art 20.4 to reduce the weight given to that testimony. It arguably follows that, unless such an order has been made, the tribunal may not accord less weight to the evidence of a witness who gives no oral testimony. This favours savings in cost since parties will not feel compelled to produce all their witnesses to avoid the weight of evidence being reduced. **18.258**

The tribunal has no express power to require a witness to attend. The ends of justice *inter partes* are unlikely to be damaged; a party who wishes to criticize the reliability of a witness' evidence may request that the witness attend. This reflects the adversarial, not inquisitorial, nature of the proceedings. **18.259**

Oral hearings usually focus on witness evidence. Many, particularly from the civil law tradition, consider that this does no more than put some flesh around the good skeleton of fact provided by the contemporaneous documents.[247] Parties from Asian countries are often suspicious, regarding oral testimony as unreliable and simply an opportunity to inject more advocacy into proceedings.[248] Even where parties have a common law background, practicalities dictate that time limits are almost invariably imposed. **18.260**

---

[243] Parties may refer to the guidance in Art 4(5), IBA Rules on Evidence.

[244] Lew, Mistelis, Kröll, s 22-62. As a matter of English law, the 'right to be heard' does not mean that arbitrators are required to accede to every request for a hearing or submission of evidence (Merkin, Arbitration Law, s 15.24 ff and see Jermini, C., 'Note—Tribunal federal, Ire Cour civile, 7 January 2004 (4P.196/2003)' (2004) 22 *ASA Bull* 605 for a helpful summary of the Swiss courts' approach to the 'right to be heard').

[245] See Hunter and Paulsson, 1985 Rules, §170-1 on the equivalent provisions (Arts 11 and 10) of the 1985 Rules.

[246] Contrast with Art 4(7) of the IBA Rules on Evidence.

[247] Comments made by Pierre A. Karrer in a paper 'Civil Law and Common Law How far apt are we still in international commercial arbitration?' delivered to an invited audience on 17 January 2008.

[248] View expressed by Michael Moser at the 15th Annual International Commercial Arbitration Workshop: Arbitral Advocacy, in: 'Act III: Advocacy with Witness Testimony' (2005) 21 *Arb Int'l* 588.

18.261 Article 20.5 provides that all parties and the tribunal may put questions to a witness who attends to give oral evidence. In each case, the tribunal should develop a procedure for questioning which is appropriate to the specific circumstances.

(4) Witness preparation

18.262 Article 20.6 states that, subject to national law (and, implicitly, applicable professional codes), there is no bar to a party's legal representatives or the party speaking to a witness before he gives his evidence.[249] This includes preparation of witnesses in advance of the hearing. Although it is not clear in Art 20.6, as non-legal representatives are permitted,[250] we consider that such a representative would enjoy a similar right.

(5) A party may be a witness

18.263 Article 20.7 provides that any person may be a witness whether or not he is, or is employed by, a party.[251]

(6) Witness conferencing

18.264 There is nothing in the Rules[252] which expressly allows or prevents witness conferencing or, as it is sometimes known, confrontation.[253] If the tribunal considers it to be appropriate,[254] usually in the context of expert witnesses, it may be ordered and should be expressly provided for by the tribunal's procedural order.

Article 21 Experts to the Arbitral Tribunal

21.1 Unless otherwise agreed by the parties in writing, the Arbitral Tribunal:

(a) may appoint one or more experts to report to the Arbitral Tribunal on specific issues, who shall be and remain impartial and independent of the parties throughout the arbitration proceedings; and

(b) may require a party to give any such expert any relevant information or to provide access to any relevant documents, goods, samples, property or site for inspection by the expert.

21.2 Unless otherwise agreed by the parties in writing, if a party so requests or if the Arbitral Tribunal considers it necessary, the expert shall, after delivery of his written or oral report to the Arbitral Tribunal and the parties, participate in one or more hearings at which the parties shall have the opportunity to question the expert on his report and to present expert witnesses in order to testify on the points at issue.

21.3 The fees and expenses of any expert appointed by the Arbitral Tribunal under this Article shall be paid out of the deposits payable by the parties under Article 24 and shall form part of the costs of the arbitration.

---

249 An attractive outline suggestion for witness preparation is found in Roney, D.P., 'Effective Witness Preparation for International Commercial Arbitration: A practical Guide for Counsel' (2003) 20 *J Int'l Arb* 429.

250 Art 18.

251 It mirrors Art 4(2) of the IBA Rules on Evidence. The provision is present because in some jurisdictions (eg Switzerland: Oetiker, 253) a witness can otherwise only be a person who is independent of the parties.

252 Compare the IBA Rules on evidence which provide for this at Art 5(3).

253 Although it might be argued that this falls within the wide discretion in Art 22.1(f) albeit that it is worded to suggest application to documents rather than witnesses.

254 At least some consider that this technique can 'get the most useful (and truthful) testimony from witnesses' Rees, P.J., 'The Conduct of International Arbitration in England: the Challenge Has Still to be Met' (2007) 23 *Arb Int'l* 505, at 510. Also Peter, W., 'Witness "Conferencing"' (2002) 18 *Arb Int'l* 47.

(1) Effect of the provision

Articles 21.1 and 21.2 are based on Art 26 of the Model Law but Art 21.1(a) has been expanded to make clear that the expert must remain independent. The IBA Rules on Evidence with similar motive require a tribunal-appointed expert to submit a statement of this prior to appointment.[255] **18.265**

The rule is a compromise between civil and common law systems. In the former, experts to the court are common, in the latter they are usually party appointees.[256] The power under Arts 21.1 and 21.2 may be excluded by agreement at any stage of the proceedings. **18.266**

Articles 21.1 and 21.2 are largely self-explanatory. It is to be noted that Art 21.2 effectively provides the parties with an absolute right to present their own expert to testify if the tribunal appoints an expert. This limits the tribunal's power under Art 20.2 such that the expert may not be excluded. **18.267**

(2) Costs

Article 21.3 was introduced in the current version of the Rules. Under it, parties will ultimately bear the costs of the tribunal expert. The tribunal should only appoint an expert when it considers it genuinely necessary to do so but parties concerned about this can and should agree to exclude or limit the right of appointment under Arts 21.1 or 21.2. Under the Rules, it is not possible to exclude the obligation to pay the costs if either of Arts 21.1 or 21.2 applies.[257] **18.268**

Article 22 Additional Powers of the Arbitral Tribunal

22.1 Unless the parties at any time agree otherwise in writing, the Arbitral Tribunal shall have the power, on the application of any party or of its own motion, but in either case only after giving the parties a reasonable opportunity to state their views:

(a) to allow any party, upon such terms (as to costs and otherwise) as it shall determine, to amend any claim, counterclaim, defence and reply;

(b) to extend or abbreviate any time limit provided by the Arbitration Agreement or these Rules for the conduct of the arbitration or by the Arbitral Tribunal's own orders;

(c) to conduct such enquiries as may appear to the Arbitral Tribunal to be necessary or expedient, including whether and to what extent the Arbitral Tribunal should itself take the initiative in identifying the issues and ascertaining the relevant facts and the law(s) or rules of law applicable to the arbitration, the merits of the parties' dispute and the Arbitration Agreement;

(d) to order any party to make any property, site or thing under its control and relating to the subject matter of the arbitration available for inspection by the Arbitral Tribunal, any other party, its expert or any expert to the Arbitral Tribunal;

(e) to order any party to produce to the Arbitral Tribunal, and to the other parties for inspection, and to supply copies of, any documents or classes of documents in their possession, custody or power which the Arbitral Tribunal determines to be relevant;

---

[255] Art 6(2) thereof.

[256] Commission Report, UN-Doc A/40/17, s 219. The inclusion of the provision in the 1985 LCIA Rules has been said to be 'another concession to the internationalisation of the rules', Delvolvé, LCIA 606.

[257] This mirrors the mandatory nature of s 37(2), 1996 Act, intended to avoid the risk of the tribunal being unable to recover the costs and the expert possibly going unpaid; see DAC Report, s 188.

(f) to decide whether or not to apply any strict rules of evidence (or any other rules) as to the admissibility, relevance or weight of any material tendered by a party on any matter of fact or expert opinion; and to determine the time, manner and form in which such material should be exchanged between the parties and presented to the Arbitral Tribunal;

(g) to order the correction of any contract between the parties or the Arbitration Agreement, but only to the extent required to rectify any mistake which the Arbitral Tribunal determines to be common to the parties and then only if and to the extent to which the law(s) or rules of law applicable to the contract or Arbitration Agreement permit such correction; and

(h) to allow, only upon the application of a party, one or more third persons to be joined in the arbitration as a party provided any such third person and the applicant party have consented thereto in writing, and thereafter to make a single final award, or separate awards, in respect of all parties so implicated in the arbitration;

22.2 By agreeing to arbitration under these Rules, the parties shall be treated as having agreed not to apply to any state court or other judicial authority for any order available from the Arbitral Tribunal under Article 22.1, except with the agreement in writing of all parties.

22.3 The Arbitral Tribunal shall decide the parties' dispute in accordance with the law(s) or rules of law chosen by the parties as applicable to the merits of their dispute. If and to the extent that the Arbitral Tribunal determines that the parties have made no such choice, the Arbitral Tribunal shall apply the law(s) or rules of law which it considers appropriate.

22.4 The Arbitral Tribunal shall only apply to the merits of the dispute principles deriving from *ex aequo et bono, amiable composition* or 'honourable engagement' where the parties have so agreed expressly in writing.

(1) General

18.269 Article 22 aims to give the tribunal powers to control and conduct the proceedings effectively. The heading ('additional powers') is not entirely appropriate because some matters covered by Art 22 are inherent to Art 14.2. Article 22 is not exclusive in its effect so far as the conduct of proceedings is concerned. Nevertheless, it functions to provide default powers that might not otherwise be available under the default provisions of national arbitration legislation.[258]

18.270 Without written agreement by the parties, the decision to exercise the powers under Art 22.1 lies with the tribunal subject to a duty to give the parties a reasonable opportunity to state their views.

(2) Amendments

18.271 The need to use the power under Art 22.1(a) will depend on the conduct of the written stage of proceedings.[259] The tribunal may well be cautious in using the power to avoid challenge for illegitimately broadening its jurisdiction.[260] The power to impose terms may discourage parties from unnecessary changes to their written statements.[261]

[258] eg 1996 Act, s 34(3), provides a narrower default jurisdiction than Art 22.1(b).
[259] Art 15.
[260] Samuel, 47.
[261] See para 18.35 ff and para 18.68 regarding the contents of the Request and Response.

(3) Time limits

The discretion to abbreviate or extend time limits under Art 22.1(b) is confined to the conduct of the arbitration. On the other hand, the tribunal cannot affect time limits imposed by national law, for example, laying down limitation periods. **18.272**

(4) Power to conduct enquiries

More than Arts 19.3 and 20.5, Art 22.1(c) allows the tribunal to act inquisitorially in the civilian tradition.[262] The non-exhaustive list of functions covered was introduced in 1998[263] and should allay concern that arbitrators from a non-inquisitorial background might apply the power inappropriately.[264] **18.273**

In practice, a hybrid approach is often most effective[265] and can assist in cases where there is inequality of representation.[266] **18.274**

(5) Inspection of documents and property

Articles 22.1(d) and 22.1(e) deal with document production or disclosure. This is additional to any documents that have been disclosed with written statements.[267] Although there is no automatic right to inspect documents or property, the powers are potentially very wide; the only express limit is relevance.[268] **18.275**

The discretion must be exercised with Art 14 firmly in mind. In practice, the tribunal should also bear in mind its right to rule on admissibility, relevance or weight of material tendered (Art 22.1(f)). **18.276**

In contrast with the IBA Rules on Evidence,[269] the Rules do not state that the tribunal may draw an adverse inference from a failure, without good reason, to produce a document when ordered to do so. It is suggested that the tribunal may nevertheless do so under the discretion conferred by Art 22.1(f) although, to avoid any difficulty, it should advert to the possibility when ordering production (thereby allowing the parties an opportunity to address the issue).[270] **18.277**

(6) Rules of evidence

Article 22.1(f) gives the tribunal discretion over the rules of evidence, if any, to be applied. The form of Art 22.1(f) was probably inspired by s 34(f) of the 1996 Act. The notable difference between the provisions is the time at which the discretion is to be exercised. **18.278**

---

[262] The differences are described in Borris, C., 'Common law and civil law: fundamental differences and their impact on arbitration' (1995) 4 *Arb Disp Res L J* 92.

[263] Compare Art 13.1(f), 1985 Rules.

[264] A similar power is s 34(2)(g), 1996 Act; during the consultation process, 'some anxiety was expressed . . . that arbitrators are unused to such powers and might, albeit in good faith, abuse them' DAC Report, s 171.

[265] See Lew, Mistelis, Kröll, s 21-34 and s 21-35.

[266] See para 18.236 and also Merkin, Arbitration Law, s 14.26.

[267] Art 15. See especially para 18.201.

[268] For a comment on differing national attitudes towards document production: Park, W.W., 'Arbitration's Discontents: Of Elephants and Pornography' (2001) 17 *Arb Int'l* 265.

[269] Arts 9(4) and 9(5), IBA Rules on Evidence.

[270] For the view that the tribunal will and should be reluctant to draw a negative inference unless convinced that the party which has failed to produce the evidence in question is in fact able to do so see: Pietrowski 383-4. For a helpful discussion of the basis and criteria for inferences, see Sharpe, J.K., 'Drawing Adverse Inferences from the Non-production of Evidence' (2006) 22 *Arb Int'l* 549.

The 1996 Act considers it before the tender of documents while the Rules envisage documents having been tendered, reflecting that, historically, international tribunals have had little patience with wrangles over admissibility.[271] It is probably correct that the Rules have 'disposed of the legal concept of admissibility'.[272]

18.279 As with the other powers in Art 22.1, the tribunal must consult the parties as well as meeting the Art 14 requirements, particularly allowing each party a reasonable opportunity of putting its case. In relation to this obligation, admitting but then disregarding evidence is materially distinct from not admitting it.[273]

18.280 The parties may agree on criteria for admissibility possibly by reference to a national law or the IBA Rules on Evidence[274] or by the creation of a bespoke list of categories.

18.281 Notwithstanding the potential breadth of the Rules for the production of documents, tribunals and parties should check that the power is not curtailed by national law, in particular in relation to public interest immunity[275] and so called privileged communications with lawyers.[276]

18.282 The last part of Art 22.1(f) gives the tribunal discretion over the manner of exchange and presentation of evidence. Notably, it allows tribunals to take advantage of modern technology by ordering electronic disclosure.[277]

(7) Rectification of contracts. Other remedies available to the tribunal?

18.283 Article 22.1(g), allowing rectification or correction of a contract, is the only[278] part of the Rules expressly dealing with remedies although Art 26.6 plainly contemplates that the award may be of money and, to the extent that the award is a written and reasoned document,[279] it may also be effective as declaratory relief.[280]

18.284 Arguably the powers of an arbitration tribunal are wider than those of national courts and tribunals may not be confined to remedies known in domestic law. Nevertheless, the lack

---

[271] Pietrowski, 378. Thus, the general approach is for tribunals to read whatever is put forward and then assess the weight to be given to it see: Lew, Mistelis, Kröll, s 22-44; Hunter, J.M., 'The Procedural Power of Arbitrators Under the English 1996 Act' (1997) *13 Arb Int'l* 352 and Sandifer, D.V., *Evidence Before International Tribunals* (1975) 203.

[272] Saleh, S.A., 'Reflections on Admissibility of Evidence: Interrelation between Domestic Law and International Arbitration' (1999) 15 *Arb Int'l* 141, at 152, commenting on Arts 11.2 and 14.3, 1985 Rules.

[273] See presentation to the *Ius and Lex Foundation*, Warsaw, 14 June 2007 by Alexis Mourre, published on the LCIA website. For a comment on the equivalent provision of 1996 Act, see Merkin, Arbitration Law, 88.

[274] See, in particular, Arts 9(2) and 9(3). Rees, P.J., 'The Conduct of International Arbitration in England: the Challenge Has Still to be Met' (2007) 23 *Arb Int'l* 505, at 510, suggests that these rules will 'cut down on wasteful disclosure'.

[275] For the English law position see Hollander, C., *Documentary Evidence* (9th edn, 2003) ch 18.

[276] On the issue of privilege, see eg: Pietrowski, 404-6 and Berger, K.P., 'Evidentiary Privileges: Best Practice Standards and Arbitral Discretion' (2006) 22 *Arb Int'l* 501.

[277] On this, see Smith, R.H. and Robinson, T.B.E., 'Disclosure in International Arbitration' (2008) 24 *Arb Int'l* 105.

[278] It has even been suggested that it be removed: Samuel, 42–3.

[279] Art 26.1.

[280] Similarly Art 23.1 contemplates that the tribunal may effectively grant declaratory relief by finding the agreement containing the arbitration clause to be non-existent, invalid or ineffective.

of detail may make the effect of national law uncertain. Under English law, for example, the extent of displacement of the default provisions of the 1996 Act is not entirely clear.[281]

(8) Joinder of a third party

Article 22.1(h) is intended to provide a partial solution to the problem of connected arbitrations. It allows arbitrators to permit willing non-signatories to the arbitration agreement to be joined provided that one arbitrating party has agreed in writing. The utility of the provision depends on whether governing national legislation allows for joinder, concurrent hearings or consolidation of proceedings. **18.285**

In principle, under Art 22.1(h) the tribunal can override the wishes of a party which disagrees. In reality, tribunals will be reluctant to do so. So far as we are aware, the power has not been exercised to date. When the power was introduced, it was suggested that joinder against the wishes of one party would be limited to cases in which there was no *bona fide* motive for resisting joinder in a case whose ultimate resolution obviously implicates a third party (such as a guarantor) who is willing to join in the arbitration.[282] While this has attractions, the obvious procedural and enforcement difficulties remain regardless of the third party's character. **18.286**

Once a third party is joined, the tribunal may make a single or separate final awards. As ever, the parties should be given a reasonable opportunity to state their views. **18.287**

(9) Agreement not to apply to the courts

Article 22.2 preserves the primacy of the tribunal as the arbiter of the parties' disputes. Where the tribunal has power to act, no application may be made to the courts or judicial authorities without the parties' written agreement.[283] This reduces the scope for a recalcitrant party to obstruct proceedings.[284] **18.288**

(10) Law applicable to the merits

Article 22.3 provides that the tribunal shall determine the dispute under the law or rules of law chosen by the parties or, if no choice has been made, under the law or rules of law it considers most appropriate. It is undoubtedly open to the parties to make submissions on the issue (including at Request and Response stage). **18.289**

Much ink has been spilled addressing the question of what is meant by the merits of a dispute and the law or rules of law that the arbitrator is to apply.[285] The position under the **18.290**

281 We consider that the difficulty is confined to s 48(5), 1996 Act. Art 22.1(g) may only displace s 48(5)(c) which makes specific reference to rectification; a detailed discussion of the issue is outside the scope of this chapter.

282 YCA 1985. Also Salans, C.F., 'The 1985 Rules of the London Court of International Arbitration' (1986) 2 *Arb Int'l* 40, at 40, 43; and Delvolvé, J.L., 'L'arbitrage et les tiers: III—Le droit de l'arbitrage' (1988) *Rev arb* 501. Also Platte, M., 'When should an Arbitrator Join Cases?' (2002) 18 *Arb Int'l* 67 and Diamond, A., QC, 'Procedure and hearings' in A. Berkeley and J. Mimms (eds), *International Commercial Arbitration: Practical Perspectives* (Centre of Construction Law & Management, 2001), 52–5.

283 Many of the powers that would otherwise be available under s 44, 1996 Act are thereby excluded.

284 See Hunter and Paulsson, 1985 Rules.

285 eg Lew, J.D.M., *Applicable Law in International Commercial Arbitration* (1978); Naón, H.G., 'Choice-of-Law Problems in International Commercial Arbitration' (2001) 289 *Collected Courses, Hague Academy of Int'l L* 9; Heiskanen, V., 'Dealing with Pandora: the Concept of "Merits" in International Commercial

Rules is tolerably clear: Art 14.2 provides a general discretion in relation to the applicable law (albeit focused on procedural aspects) while Art 22.3 relates to substantive argument.

18.291 Ultimately, all questions of applicable law save for those which will be mandatorily applicable by virtue of the seat of the arbitration are for the tribunal to determine. The tribunal may even have to decide whether and what conflict of laws rules to apply[286] to determine whether a particular aspect of a claim is within the scope of the parties' agreement as to the law applicable to the merits of their case.[287]

18.292 Article 22.4 requires an express written agreement if the dispute is to be resolved applying principles from '*ex aequo et bono*', '*amiable composition*' or '*honourable engagement*'.[288] It follows that whatever law the tribunal decides to apply under Art 22.3, it should be a so-called strict rule of law. In the context of Art 22.3 we consider this is wide enough to encompass non-national laws, for example, religious laws, transnational rules of law, or *lex mercatoria*.[289]

18.293 In deciding the merits of the dispute the tribunal will also look closely at the terms of the contract between the parties and related trade usages or customary law.

Article 23 Jurisdiction of the Arbitral Tribunal

23.1 The Arbitral Tribunal shall have the power to rule on its own jurisdiction, including any objection to the initial or continuing existence, validity or effectiveness of the Arbitration Agreement. For that purpose, an arbitration clause which forms or was intended to form part of another agreement shall be treated as an arbitration agreement independent of that other agreement. A decision by the Arbitral Tribunal that such other agreement is non-existent, invalid or ineffective shall not entail *ipso jure* the non-existence, invalidity or ineffectiveness of the arbitration clause.

23.2 A plea by a Respondent that the Arbitral Tribunal does not have jurisdiction shall be treated as having been irrevocably waived unless it is raised not later than the Statement of Defence; and a like plea by a Respondent to Counterclaim shall be similarly treated unless it is raised no later than the Statement of Defence to Counterclaim. A plea that the Arbitral Tribunal is exceeding the scope of its authority shall be raised promptly after the Arbitral Tribunal has indicated its intention to decide on the matter alleged by any party

Arbitration' (2006) 22 *Arb Int'l* 597; Mayer, P., 'Reflections on the International Arbitrator's Duty to Apply the Law' (2001) 17 *Arb Int'l* 235; Kaufmann-Kohler, G., 'The Arbitrator and the Law: Does he/she know it? Apply it? How? And a few more questions' (2005) 21 *Arb Int'l* 631.

[286] Usually those of the seat although they need not be: Russell on Arbitration, s 2-092. The 1996 Act, s 46(3) does not fetter the tribunal's choice of conflict rules.

[287] eg the contract provides that it is subject to New York law, it is broken and one party claims damages for loss of profits. New York law sets out the standard of proof required in relation to such damages. Whether this provision of New York law is to be applied will depend on whether the tribunal characterizes the provision as applicable to the merits of the dispute or as a procedural rule, in which case, the tribunal may apply some law other than that of New York to the standard of proof. Whether the provision for the standard of proof is a procedural or merits (or substantive) issue may depend on what, if any, national conflict of laws rules are applied. See Lew, Mistelis, Kröll, chs 17 and 18.

[288] Art 22.4 has no equivalent in the 1985 Rules and was apparently introduced in response to the widening of the 1996 Act to allow the tribunal to decide the dispute in accordance with 'such other considerations' (s 46(1)(b): see Merkin, Arbitration Act, 117).

[289] See *DST v Rakoil* [1987] 3 WLR 1023, CA in which ICC arbitrators' finding of 'internationally accepted principles of law governing contractual relations' as the proper law applicable was upheld by the English courts.

to be beyond the scope of its authority, failing which such plea shall also be treated as having been waived irrevocably. In any case, the Arbitral Tribunal may nevertheless admit an untimely plea if it considers the delay justified in the particular circumstances.

23.3 The Arbitral Tribunal may determine the plea to its jurisdiction or authority in an award as to jurisdiction or later in an award on the merits, as it considers appropriate in the circumstances.

23.4 By agreeing to arbitration under these Rules, the parties shall be treated as having agreed not to apply to any state court or other judicial authority for any relief regarding the Arbitral Tribunal's jurisdiction or authority, except with the agreement in writing of all parties to the arbitration or the prior authorisation of the Arbitral Tribunal or following the latter's award ruling on the objection to its jurisdiction or authority.

(1) Generally

Articles 23.1 and 23.2 are heavily influenced by the Model Law and spell out the near-universally accepted rules of *competence-competence* and separability. **18.294**

(2) Complaints by the parties

Articles 23.2, 23.3 and 23.4 resemble the Model Law, Art 16, and the 1996 Act, s 31. Also to be noted is that the complaint is to the tribunal and not the LCIA.[290] **18.295**

Article 23.2 provides the regime for parties to complain to the tribunal regarding jurisdiction and scope of authority during the proceedings. **18.296**

Where a party wishes to challenge the tribunal's jurisdiction, it must do so no later than when it submits its Statement of Defence under Art 15.3 or, implicitly, the equivalent time under an agreed procedure. The cut-off must be after the tribunal has been appointed or effect cannot be given to the principle of *competence-competence.* **18.297**

Since an LCIA arbitration under the Rules involves a Response, Art 23.1 makes it clear that the Respondent may file a Response and nominate an arbitrator without indicating an intention to challenge the tribunal's jurisdiction, without waiving the right to challenge. Nonetheless, if the Respondent is considering challenging jurisdiction, it would be wise to state that the Response (or nomination) is without prejudice to its right to later challenge the jurisdiction of the tribunal (or validity of proceedings). **18.298**

The equivalent provision for the Claimant allows the Claimant to challenge the scope of the arbitration clause.[291] **18.299**

The second basis for a complaint is that the tribunal is extending the scope of its authority. This may include procedural acts that are not authorized[292] and may also arise where one party seeks to amend its case to include matters that were outside the scope of the original appointment or the arbitration agreement. Such complaint may be made at any time during the arbitration but must be made promptly. Promptly is not defined; its meaning will **18.300**

---

290 Samuel, 40.

291 In England this will be difficult following *Fiona Trust v Privalov* [2007] UKHL 40, where the House of Lords held that arbitration agreements were to be construed as covering a very wide range of disputes in line with their commercial purpose.

292 eg in England, tribunals cannot grant freezing injunctions: *Kastner v Jason* [2004] 2 Lloyd's Rep 233.

depend on the circumstances including the possible prejudice to the other party who may have taken (or not taken) steps and incurred costs relying on the challenged ruling.

18.301 Fairness is ensured by the final sentence of Art 23.2, which allows the tribunal to admit an untimely plea. The circumstances in which this could be invoked will be rare; any such plea would need to include a real and compelling justification why it was not raised at an earlier stage.

18.302 Under Art 23.3, the tribunal may leave its decision on jurisdiction until it makes its final award.[293] If it does not, the ruling on jurisdiction will take effect as an award pursuant to the tribunal's power under Art 26.7. The course chosen will depend on factors such as whether the question of jurisdiction can properly be separated from the issues on the merits, the likely time to complete an award on the merits and the likely delay which would result from a separate ruling on jurisdiction.[294]

(3) Competence-competence

18.303 Article 23.4 ensures *competence-competence* by prohibiting appeal to the courts or judicial authorities before the tribunal has ruled on its own jurisdiction without the written agreement of all parties to the arbitration or the prior authorization of the tribunal. As part of the Rules, it is a contractual obligation that should be recognized even if proceedings are instituted in a jurisdiction (irrespective of whether it is or not the seat of arbitration) that formally does not recognize the principle.

Article 24 Deposits

24.1 The LCIA Court may direct the parties, in such proportions as it thinks appropriate, to make one or several interim or final payments on account of the costs of the arbitration. Such deposits shall be made to and held by the LCIA and from time to time may be released by the LCIA Court to the arbitrator(s), any expert appointed by the Arbitral Tribunal and the LCIA itself as the arbitration progresses.

24.2 The Arbitral Tribunal shall not proceed with the arbitration without ascertaining at all times from the Registrar or any deputy Registrar that the LCIA is in requisite funds.

24.3 In the event that a party fails or refuses to provide any deposit as directed by the LCIA Court, the LCIA Court may direct the other party or parties to effect a substitute payment to allow the arbitration to proceed (subject to any award on costs). In such circumstances, the party paying the substitute payment shall be entitled to recover that amount as a debt immediately due from the defaulting party.

24.4 Failure by a claimant or counterclaiming party to provide promptly and in full the required deposit may be treated by the LCIA Court and the Arbitral Tribunal as a withdrawal of the claim or counterclaim respectively.

(1) Generally

18.304 Article 24 reflects the institutional nature of the LCIA. Details of the LCIA costs are scheduled to the Rules. Sums deposited are applied to pay the arbitrators and any expert to the tribunal,[295] as well as the LCIA's administrative costs. The LCIA credits interest on sums deposited to the parties.[296]

[293] Such a course is often viewed as undesirable: Samuel 41–2.
[294] Which, as an award may be subject to challenge in the relevant national court, eg, under s 67, 1996 Act.
[295] Art 21.
[296] Art 28.1.

The sanctions for non-payment are that: under Art 24.2, the arbitration is not allowed to proceed; and, under Art 24.4, if the payment is not provided promptly by the Claimant or Counterclaimant, that claim or counterclaim will be treated as withdrawn. Non-payment by a Respondent does not have the same effect; the LCIA Court will usually order the Claimant to pay the deposit due from the Respondent under Art 24.3. 18.305

Despite the statement in Art 24.2 that the tribunal shall not continue with the arbitration if the LCIA does not have adequate funds in hand, this is not always practical. For example, after a tribunal is established it may correspond with the parties, and even commence with the procedural aspects of the arbitration while the LCIA is still waiting for the initial deposits to be received. Equally, a tribunal will rarely cease work and not complete an award while the LCIA is seeking additional funds from the parties. 18.306

Ultimately, notwithstanding the debt created under Art 24.3, if the Respondent is without funds, the Claimant may end up out of pocket because their liability to the LCIA is joint and several.[297] 18.307

Article 25 Interim and Conservatory Measures

25.1 The Arbitral Tribunal shall have the power, unless otherwise agreed by the parties in writing, on the application of any party:

(a) to order any respondent party to a claim or counterclaim to provide security for all or part of the amount in dispute, by way of deposit or bank guarantee or in any other manner and upon such terms as the Arbitral Tribunal considers appropriate. Such terms may include the provision by the claiming or counterclaiming party of a cross-indemnity, itself secured in such manner as the Arbitral Tribunal considers appropriate, for any costs or losses incurred by such respondent in providing security. The amount of any costs and losses payable under such cross-indemnity may be determined by the Arbitral Tribunal in one or more awards;

(b) to order the preservation, storage, sale or other disposal of any property or thing under the control of any party and relating to the subject matter of the arbitration; and

(c) to order on a provisional basis, subject to final determination in an award, any relief which the Arbitral Tribunal would have power to grant in an award, including a provisional order for the payment of money or the disposition of property as between any parties.

25.2 The Arbitral Tribunal shall have the power, upon the application of a party, to order any claiming or counterclaiming party to provide security for the legal or other costs of any other party by way of deposit or bank guarantee or in any other manner and upon such terms as the Arbitral Tribunal considers appropriate. Such terms may include the provision by that other party of a cross-indemnity, itself secured in such manner as the Arbitral Tribunal considers appropriate, for any costs and losses incurred by such claimant or counterclaimant in providing security. The amount of any costs and losses payable under such cross-indemnity may be determined by the Arbitral Tribunal in one or more awards. In the event that a claiming or counterclaiming party does not comply with any order to provide security, the Arbitral Tribunal may stay that party's claims or counterclaims or dismiss them in an award.

25.3 The power of the Arbitral Tribunal under Article 25.1 shall not prejudice howsoever any party's right to apply to any state court or other judicial authority for interim or conservatory

[297] Para 9, Schedule of Costs.

measures before the formation of the Arbitral Tribunal and, in exceptional cases, thereafter. Any application and any order for such measures after the formation of the Arbitral Tribunal shall be promptly communicated by the applicant to the Arbitral Tribunal and all other parties. However, by agreeing to arbitration under these Rules, the parties shall be taken to have agreed not to apply to any state court or other judicial authority for any order for security for its legal or other costs available from the Arbitral Tribunal under Article 25.2.

(1) Generally

18.308 The purpose of this provision is to give tribunals the power to order interim and conservatory measures and to obtain the parties' commitment of the tribunal, not the national court, as the principle source of such relief. Such measures enhance the effectiveness of international arbitration and, increasingly, national law systems allow such measures.[298]

(2) Test to be applied

18.309 The test to be applied by the tribunal in making orders under Art 25 is not stated.[299] The power must be exercised in accordance with Art 14 but it is suggested that a more precise test is required to enable the tribunal to achieve these aims. It will naturally be appropriate for the tribunal to invite submissions on the test and state in reasons for the order made and the test actually applied.

18.310 The unstated purpose of each part of Art 25 should influence the test to be applied. It is suggested that the primary motivation of Art 25.1(a) and 25.2 is to ensure the effectiveness of the arbitral process and to discourage the maintenance of unmeritorious defences or claims. The motivation of Art 25.1(b) and (c) probably differs and is primarily to maintain the status quo during arbitral proceedings.

18.311 While it is desirable for the tribunal to have power to make orders to ensure the effectiveness of the arbitral process and to maintain the status quo insofar as is possible,[300] in doing so, the tribunal must be careful not to pre-judge the merits. Should the tribunal do so the final award may be challenged on the basis that the tribunal was not impartial; a carefully reasoned award (and order) should reduce this risk.[301]

18.312 In some, although not many, circumstances interim orders can be made without some assessment of the merits. In practice a test involving the merits has to be adopted as a decision on interim relief cannot be taken in a vacuum.

---

[298] For a more detailed review of the use of such measures, see eg: Lew, Mistelis, Kröll, ch 23, Fouchard, Galliard, Goldman, ch III; Poudret and Besson, ch 6 pt 6.3; Redfern and Hunter, ch 7 pt 3.

[299] By contrast with the UNCITRAL Model Law. Art 17 provides power to grant interim measures while Art 17A sets out a two limb test requiring the tribunal to (i) weigh the likely harm to the parties; and (ii) decide whether there is a reasonable possibility that the requesting party will succeed on the merits.

[300] Mourre (see n 273) gives the example of an order not to call on a bank guarantee. See commentary on Art 22; the relevant *lex arbitri* and any terms agreed by the parties will determine whether the tribunal has this power in any event.

[301] eg the *Norsk Hydro* decision of the French *Cour de Cassation* on 6 November 1998. In one recent case under the LCIA rules, one of the issues was whether the parties' agreement meant that there was an entitlement to withhold payment for goods where there was a dispute about compliance with the contract or whether the party with the goods was obliged to pay and then seek to recover damages. An interim application was made for payment under Art 25.1(c). A challenge to one of the tribunal members who had expressed himself to be in favour of making the order was made but did not succeed.

18.313 It is suggested that the following tests (based on Art 14 and the Model Law) might be applied, modified according to the circumstances of each case and any relevant provisions of national law. The party seeking the interim measure should satisfy the tribunal that:

(i) the measure sought is necessary to ensure a fair and efficient resolution of the dispute avoiding unnecessary delay or expense;
(ii) the measure sought will ensure that each party has a reasonable opportunity to put its case and deal with that of its opponent;
(iii) harm which cannot adequately be compensated by an award of damages is likely to result if the measure is not ordered and that such harm substantially outweighs the harm likely to result to the party against whom the measure is sought;
(iv) on the statements of case and essential documents before the tribunal, there is a reasonable possibility that the party seeking the order will succeed on the merits; and
(v) that the order will not amount to a pre-judgment of the case on the merits.

18.314 Any order made should go no further than is absolutely necessary to achieve the aims of Art 14. Thus under Art 25.1(a), a bank guarantee is usually more appropriate than a deposit, and a cross-indemnity could be considered. Under Art 25.2, the interests of fairness mean that a cross-indemnity should generally be required.[302]

(3) Orders not awards: enforcement and sanctions for non-compliance

18.315 Art 25.1 contains no sanction for a failure to obey the tribunal's order. By contrast, and in parallel with the LCIA Court's power in relation to the payment of deposits,[303] a failure to obey an order made under Art 25.2 entitles the tribunal to stay the party's claims or counterclaims or dismiss them in an award (the former is more common). A parallel distinction is made by Art 25.3 which provides that an application to the court is possible in relation to matters under Art 25.1 but not in relation to Art 25.2.

18.316 The distinction is justifiable as the Claimant has control over whether it brings a claim. This is fully in accordance with the general acceptance of the jurisdiction of the tribunal to determine disputes between the parties and the obligation under the arbitration agreement to recognize and respect the tribunal's award. Failing to do so is arguably a breach of both the arbitration agreement and the agreement to accept and adhere to the provisions of the Rules.

18.317 An order under Art 25.1 is not necessarily an award and so is perhaps neither enforceable under the New York Convention,[304] nor subject to the formalities of an award.[305] Whether it can be enforced, given that the tribunal has no sanctions, will depend on the law governing

[302] See Reid, G., 'Security for costs in international arbitrations—forget it?' 152 *NLJ* 1426 27 September 2002 for a short discussion of factors relevant to an order for security for costs and Gu, W., 'Security for Costs in International Commercial Arbitration' (2005) 22 *J Int'l* Arb 167 for a longer discussion.

[303] Art 24.2.

[304] See Poudret and Besson, s 639 ff for an overview of the debate as to enforceability of interim awards or orders.

[305] Art 26; and two important cases stating that a procedural order may be treated as an award if it is meant to function as an award: *Publicis v True North Communications* (US), 206 F 3d 725, XXV YBCA 1152 (2000) (7th Cir, 14 March 2000) [relating to an LCIA Arbitration]; *and Brasoil and GMRA,* (France*),* XXIVa YBCA 296 (1999).

the arbitration, thus choice of seat is of particular significance. In England, the 1996 Act gives the tribunal an excludable power to make an order including a sanction for non-compliance.[306] Under s 42, 1996 Act, the court has power to order compliance with such an order. In other countries, the existence of an interim relief order or order for conservatory measures whilst not enforceable *per se* may be given effect by an order of the court issued in support of the decision of the tribunal.

(4) Applications to the court

18.318 As noted above, some national arbitration laws[307] allow for applications to the court to enforce tribunal orders. These applications are not intended to be covered by the Art 25.3 provision allowing applications to any state court for interim or conservatory measures before the formation of the tribunal and in exceptional cases thereafter.

18.319 The application of Art 25.3 is clear prior to the tribunal's formation; after this, the right is limited to exceptional cases.[308] These plainly exclude any case where an application could reasonably be made to the tribunal under Art 25. Equally, they exclude any case covered by Art 22.1's specific exclusion of application to the courts. Exceptional cases may be where there is genuine urgency or a justifiable need for an *ex parte*[309] application to be made. The paradigm case is an application for a freezing injunction where both urgency and secrecy are required; moreover, under English law at least, the general view is that the tribunal has no power to make such an order absent an express agreement.[310] Where there is no urgency or need for an *ex parte* application, if a tribunal considers that it has no power to act, then the appropriate step will be for the applicant to seek the tribunal's consent for an application to the court.[311]

(5) Ex parte interim relief?

18.320 Article 25 makes no provision for *ex parte* applications and, as Art 13 requires communications to be copied to all parties, there is no scope for such applications. Although some[312] have suggested that the tribunal might legitimately consider that there is no unfairness in hearing an *ex parte* application, the prevailing view in the arbitral community that such applications are to be avoided is to be preferred and this accords with the right under Art 14 of each party to meet the case against it.[313] In any event, it is difficult to see how the grant of an *ex parte* order would be of any practical use to a party given the limits on

[306] On this power, see Merkin, Arbitration Act, 101.

[307] eg Hong Kong and Switzerland.

[308] On the difficulties of this: Samuel, 44.

[309] See para 18.320.

[310] For a brief outline in relation to the Rules: Styles, *Ex parte applications for interim and conservatory measures* published on the LCIA website.

[311] s 44 of the 1996 Act sets out the English court's powers exercisable in support of arbitral proceedings. Some are clearly excluded by Arts 22.1 and 22.2.

[312] Styles (n 310).

[313] van Houtte, H., 'Ten Reasons Against a Proposal for Ex Parte Interim Measures of Protection in Arbitration' (2004) 20 *Arb Int'l* 85; Mourre (n 273). Also *inter alia* Redfern and Hunter, s 7-17; Lew, Mistelis, Kröll, s 23-72.

enforcement of orders.[314] It is, however, noteworthy that Art 17 of the Model Law, adopted in 2006, allows for short-term *ex parte* preliminary orders.

Article 26 The Award

26.1 The Arbitral Tribunal shall make its award in writing and, unless all parties agree in writing otherwise, shall state the reasons upon which its award is based. The award shall also state the date when the award is made and the seat of the arbitration; and it shall be signed by the Arbitral Tribunal or those of its members assenting to it.

26.2 If any arbitrator fails to comply with the mandatory provisions of any applicable law relating to the making of the award, having been given a reasonable opportunity to do so, the remaining arbitrators may proceed in his absence and state in their award the circumstances of the other arbitrator's failure to participate in the making of the award.

26.3 Where there are three arbitrators and the Arbitral Tribunal fails to agree on any issue, the arbitrators shall decide that issue by a majority. Failing a majority decision on any issue, the chairman of the Arbitral Tribunal shall decide that issue.

26.4 If any arbitrator refuses or fails to sign the award, the signatures of the majority or (failing a majority) of the chairman shall be sufficient, provided that the reason for the omitted signature is stated in the award by the majority or chairman.

26.5 The sole arbitrator or chairman shall be responsible for delivering the award to the LCIA Court, which shall transmit certified copies to the parties provided that the costs of arbitration have been paid to the LCIA in accordance with Article 28.

26.6 An award may be expressed in any currency. The Arbitral Tribunal may order that simple or compound interest shall be paid by any party on any sum awarded at such rates as the Arbitral Tribunal determines to be appropriate, without being bound by legal rates of interest imposed by any state court, in respect of any period which the Arbitral Tribunal determines to be appropriate ending not later than the date upon which the award is complied with.

26.7 The Arbitral Tribunal may make separate awards on different issues at different times. Such awards shall have the same status and effect as any other award made by the Arbitral Tribunal.

26.8 In the event of a settlement of the parties' dispute, the Arbitral Tribunal may render an award recording the settlement if the parties so request in writing (a 'Consent Award'), provided always that such award contains an express statement that it is an award made by the parties' consent. A Consent Award need not contain reasons. If the parties do not require a consent award, then on written confirmation by the parties to the LCIA Court that a settlement has been reached, the Arbitral Tribunal shall be discharged and the arbitration proceedings concluded, subject to payment by the parties of any outstanding costs of the arbitration under Article 28.

26.9 All awards shall be final and binding on the parties. By agreeing to arbitration under these Rules, the parties undertake to carry out any award immediately and without any delay (subject only to Article 27); and the parties also waive irrevocably their right to any form of appeal, review or recourse to any state court or other judicial authority, insofar as such waiver may be validly made.

(1) Generally

Article 26.1 sets down the basic requirement for a written and, unless the parties agree otherwise in writing, reasoned award. The tribunal may make separate awards on different **18.321**

314 See para 18.315.

issues at different times all of which have the same status and effect (Art 16.7). Examples of separate awards include partial final awards on jurisdiction,[315] applicable law, time bar, and damages or other relief. Such awards may focus or limit the scope of the subsequent stage of the arbitration (for example, applicable law), or may provide the parties with a platform from which they may resolve the dispute between themselves (for example, liability).

(2) Majority award

18.322 The Rules allow majority decisions where a three-member tribunal is unable to agree (Art 26.3) or where one arbitrator fails to comply with the mandatory provisions of any applicable law relating to the making of the award (Art 26.2).[316] The rules also provide for the chairman to make a decision if there is no majority decision (Art 26.3).

18.323 Only tribunal members making the award sign it. If the award is not signed by all members of the tribunal, an explanation for this must to be provided in the award (Arts 26.2 and 26.4). This has to be dealt with carefully so as not to prejudice the internal discussions between arbitrators or undermine the award.

18.324 The Rules neither provide for nor preclude the expression of a dissenting opinion. This is recognized as a practice widely adopted in international arbitration.[317]

(3) The LCIA Court

18.325 The LCIA Court is, under Art 26.5, responsible for transmitting the award to the parties. It will not do so if the costs of the arbitration have not been paid. This may have implications for the parties' right to take any action against the award.[318]

18.326 The Court does not scrutinize or review awards although, at the tribunal's request, the Secretariat will review the award for typographical and similar errors.[319] Where the costs of the arbitration are stated,[320] however, these are provided by the LCIA.

(4) Currency of the award and interest

18.327 Article 26.6 gives the tribunal discretion regarding the currency of the award and the rate of interest applied. This is to discourage a paying party from delaying the proceedings to retain what might be cheap money particularly if the award may be in a weak currency.[321] The Rules are the only major institutional rules that permit an award to be expressed in any currency.[322]

18.328 Interest continues to run to the date on which payment is made.

---

[315] Art 23.

[316] For criticism of Art 26.2 see Samuel, 45.

[317] n 7 in Redfern, A., 'Dissenting Opinions in International Commercial Arbitration: The Good, the Bad and the Ugly' (2004) 20 *Arb Int'l* 223.

[318] See para 18.339.

[319] Also para 18.332.

[320] Art 28.

[321] Hunter and Paulsson, 1985 Rules.

[322] Similarly, see s 48(4), 1996 Act and Merkin, Arbitration Act, 121.

(5) Remedies other than the payment of money

The Rules do not list the remedies available.[323] It follows from Art 26.6 that money awards are possible and from Art 22.1(g) that in limited circumstances rectification may be ordered. Further, declaratory relief is effectively within the scope of a written award. Other powers are those set out by the default regime of any applicable national law. **18.329**

(6) Settlement

If a settlement is reached, Art 26.8 allows the arbitration procedure to be ended either by way of a Consent Award or by the discharge of proceedings. The Consent Award need not contain reasons and thus preserves the privilege of the settlement negotiations. Although there is no express discretion the tribunal would almost certainly be entitled to refuse a request for a Consent Award if it considered the settlement agreement a sham, illegal, or drafted to perpetrate a fraud.[324] **18.330**

(7) Finality

Article 26.9 is intended to ensure finality and is self-explanatory. It will only ensure finality to the extent permitted by the applicable national law; in England, for example, parties retain a limited right of recourse to the courts.[325] **18.331**

On several occasions, challenges to arbitrators brought under Art 10 were effectively challenges to an interim award. In decision 7 (22 June 2001), the arbitrator held, in an interim award, that his jurisdiction was limited. In rejecting allegations that the Respondent had been denied a fair hearing because of this, the division reviewed the arbitrator's decision on his jurisdiction. The division not only held that the procedure was fair but expressed its view that the arbitrator was correct. By contrast, in decision 4 (22 July 1998), a challenge based on criticism of the content of the arbitrator's third interim award, the division held that the LCIA Court had no jurisdiction to remove the arbitrator on these grounds and stated the orthodox position that it is not the function of the LCIA Court to look critically at the content of an award.[326] **18.332**

Article 27 Correction of Awards and Additional Awards

27.1 Within 30 days of receipt of any award, or such lesser period as may be agreed in writing by the parties, a party may by written notice to the Registrar (copied to all other parties) request the Arbitral Tribunal to correct in the award any errors in computation, clerical or typographical errors or any errors of a similar nature. If the Arbitral Tribunal considers the request to be justified, it shall make the corrections within 30 days of receipt of the request. Any correction shall take the form of separate memorandum dated and signed by the Arbitral Tribunal or (if three arbitrators) those of its members assenting to it; and such memorandum shall become part of the award for all purposes.

27.2 The Arbitral Tribunal may likewise correct any error of the nature described in Article 27.1 on its own initiative within 30 days of the date of the award, to the same effect.

[323] See paras 18.283 and 18.284.

[324] Tweeddale, A. and Tweeddale, K., *Arbitration of commercial disputes: international and English law practice* (OUP, 2005) s 10.41.

[325] Challenge on jurisdiction and for serious irregularity: ss 68 and 69, 1996 Act.

[326] Described in Nicholas and Partasides.

27.3 Within 30 days of receipt of the final award, a party may by written notice to the Registrar (copied to all other parties), request the Arbitral Tribunal to make an additional award as to claims or counterclaims presented in the arbitration but not determined in any award. If the Arbitral Tribunal considers the request to be justified, it shall make the additional award within 60 days of receipt of the request. The provisions of Article 26 shall apply to any additional award.

(1) Scope

18.333 Article 27 is based on Art 33 of the Model Law but includes no provision for the tribunal to provide interpretations of its award. The difference is deliberate to reduce the risk of delay of enforcement.[327]

(2) Corrections and additional award

18.334 Articles 27.1, 27.2 and 27.3 are to ensure that the award is accurate and covers all that the parties wanted to be addressed. Without such a provision, after rendering the award the tribunal would usually be considered *functus officio* and any correction would require its cumbersome, and possibly costly, reconstitution.

18.335 The time limits to request a correction run from the time the final award is received by the parties not the date of the award or of its despatch.

18.336 In making any additional award, the tribunal will consider whether the issue was properly before it and, if so, whether it is in fact adequately addressed in the award. Care must be taken that the provision of Art 27.3 is not abused to allow disguised requests for clarification, reconsideration, variation, or narrowing of the award. Arguably this power resolves the possible lacuna identified where a properly typed sentence deals with an issue but in an ambiguous fashion.[328]

18.337 Consequent on Art 26.7, any additional award has a separate status to the award from which it was derived and the provisions of Arts 26 and 27 apply to it.

Article 28 Arbitration and Legal Costs

28.1 The costs of the arbitration (other than the legal or other costs incurred by the parties themselves) shall be determined by the LCIA Court in accordance with the Schedule of Costs. The parties shall be jointly and severally liable to the Arbitral Tribunal and the LCIA for such arbitration costs.

28.2 The Arbitral Tribunal shall specify in the award the total amount of the costs of the arbitration as determined by the LCIA Court. Unless the parties agree otherwise in writing, the Arbitral Tribunal shall determine the proportions in which the parties shall bear all or part of such arbitration costs. If the Arbitral Tribunal has determined that all or any part of the arbitration costs shall be borne by a party other than a party which has already paid them to the LCIA, the latter party shall have the right to recover the appropriate amount from the former party.

28.3 The Arbitral Tribunal shall also have the power to order in its award that all or part of the legal or other costs incurred by a party be paid by another party, unless the parties agree

[327] The power was excluded from the Art 17, 1985 Rules: Hunter and Paulsson, 1985 Rules.

[328] Raised in Knutson, R., 'The Interpretation of Arbitral Awards—When is a Final Award not Final?' (1994) 11 *J Int'l Arb* 104.

otherwise in writing. The Arbitral Tribunal shall determine and fix the amount of each item comprising such costs on such reasonable basis as it thinks fit.

28.4 Unless the parties otherwise agree in writing, the Arbitral Tribunal shall make its orders on both arbitration and legal costs on the general principle that costs should reflect the parties' relative success and failure in the award or arbitration, except where it appears to the Arbitral Tribunal that in the particular circumstances this general approach is inappropriate. Any order for costs shall be made with reasons in the award containing such order.

28.5 If the arbitration is abandoned, suspended or concluded, by agreement or otherwise, before the final award is made, the parties shall remain jointly and severally liable to pay to the LCIA and the Arbitral Tribunal the costs of the arbitration as determined by the LCIA Court in accordance with the Schedule of Costs. In the event that such arbitration costs are less than the deposits made by the parties, there shall be a refund by the LCIA in such proportion as the parties may agree in writing, or failing such agreement, in the same proportions as the deposits were made by the parties to the LCIA.

(1) LCIA costs

Under Art 28.1, the LCIA will apply the Schedule of Costs to determine the total costs. The Schedule of Costs was, when introduced, a novelty.[329] It allows the parties to estimate the likely costs of an arbitration. **18.338**

Under Art 28.2, total costs are specified in the award (together with any division deemed appropriate by the tribunal). The LCIA will check that it has sufficient funds in hand before releasing the award.[330] If it does not, it will request that the parties provide further deposits. If one party does not pay its share, the LCIA may ask the other party to pay that sum.[331] If an award is issued by the tribunal but not released by the LCIA, under many laws, time for challenge and for enforcement of the award will have commenced running.[332] **18.339**

Article 28.5 provides for costs in the event of settlement. The parties are not freed from their obligation to pay the LCIA for the fees and expenses that have accrued; any settlement should make allowance for this. The LCIA will refund any sums overpaid (with interest). **18.340**

(2) Apportionment of costs

Under Art 28.2, the tribunal may order one party to pay any proportion of the LCIA Court costs and, under Art 28.3, may make a similar order in respect of the costs incurred by one party (other than those due to the LCIA and covered by Arts 28.1 and 28.2) to be paid by another party. **18.341**

If the tribunal is to determine the amount of each item under Art 28.3, it will usually require a written schedule of costs. This will frequently be requested after the filing of the post-hearing brief (or when no further steps in the arbitration are required) because once the tribunal has issued its award it is *functus officio* and has no further powers (save the limited provisions of Art 27). In some cases it may be appropriate for the tribunal to make its final award subject only to costs which will then be argued subsequently. **18.342**

329 Lebedev, S.N., 'The LCIA Rules for International Commercial Arbitration' (1992) 8 *Arb Int'l* 325.

330 Art 26.5.

331 See para 18.307.

332 eg under English Law, s 70(3), 1996 Act, requires that, generally, an appeal to be brought within 28 days of the date the award is signed.

18.343 The usual apportionment of costs is to reflect success but in any case the tribunal must give its reasons for the apportionment of costs (Art 28.4).

18.344 In determining costs, tribunals generally take a broad brush approach considering the degrees of success of the parties, the behaviour of the parties at various stages of the arbitration, the reasonableness of the fees incurred which may be viewed in light of the fees of the other party, and overall considerations of fairness. This also allows consideration of the fact that lawyers from different jurisdictions have different charge rates and methods for calculating fees.[333]

Article 29 Decisions by the LCIA Court

29.1 The decisions of the LCIA Court with respect to all matters relating to the arbitration shall be conclusive and binding upon the parties and the Arbitral Tribunal. Such decisions are to be treated as administrative in nature and the LCIA Court shall not be required to give any reasons.

29.2 To the extent permitted by the law of the seat of the arbitration, the parties shall be taken to have waived any right of appeal or review in respect of any such decisions of the LCIA Court to any state court or other judicial authority. If such appeals or review remain possible due to mandatory provisions of any applicable law, the LCIA Court shall, subject to the provisions of that applicable law, decide whether the arbitral proceedings are to continue, notwithstanding an appeal or review.

18.345 The effect of Art 29 is to prevent any challenge to a decision by the LCIA Court unless national law provides for a non-excludable right of review or appeal.

Article 30 Confidentiality

30.1 Unless the parties expressly agree in writing to the contrary, the parties undertake as a general principle to keep confidential all awards in their arbitration, together with all materials in the proceedings created for the purpose of the arbitration and all other documents produced by another party in the proceedings not otherwise in the public domain - save and to the extent that disclosure may be required of a party by legal duty, to protect or pursue a legal right or to enforce or challenge an award in bona fide legal proceedings before a state court or other judicial authority.

30.2 The deliberations of the Arbitral Tribunal are likewise confidential to its members, save and to the extent that disclosure of an arbitrator's refusal to participate in the arbitration is required of the other members of the Arbitral Tribunal under Articles 10, 12 and 26.

30.3 The LCIA Court does not publish any award or any part of an award without the prior written consent of all parties and the Arbitral Tribunal.

18.346 Article 30 records the general principle that arbitration is confidential and seeks to extend it positively to the parties by their acceptance of the Rules.

18.347 This Article aims to provide a thorough code for confidentiality so that there should be no need for parties to make express provision for confidentiality in their arbitration clause. However, it is not clear exactly what aspects of the arbitration remain confidential and how this duty can be enforced. For example, the existence of the arbitration is difficult to keep

[333] An examination of costs which might take place in eg the English court before a 'costs judge' is generally both inappropriate and outside the competence of international arbitral tribunals.

secret, if one party wishes to publish it, without some court order. The same is true, albeit to a lesser extent, of the substantive arguments in the case.

Article 30(1) does, however, make it clear that documents prepared for the purposes of the arbitration (for example, submissions, witness statements, and documents produced) are confidential, as is the ultimate award (subject of course to the procedures to challenge or enforce the award). Where there are specific concerns, for example, in relation to 'information' rather than documents, these issues are best regulated by the parties seeking an order for the tribunal specific to the particular issue in that arbitration. **18.348**

The deliberations and discussions of the arbitrators, including memoranda exchanged and drafts of the award prepared and circulated between the arbitrators are also confidential. **18.349**

Although the LCIA's refusal to publish awards has precluded scholarly assessment of LCIA practice, the provision for confidentiality has been said to be valued by LCIA users almost as much as a neutral forum.[334] **18.350**

The only express exception to the provision for confidentiality is where disclosure may be required in relation to other legal proceedings (Art 30.1). The scope of this 'requirement' varies between jurisdictions and the controversy arising from such decisions is outside the scope of this chapter.[335] The Rules go as far as is possible to protect confidentiality; however, the effectiveness of any remedy before a national court for breach of the provision is subject to national law and is questionable once the tribunal becomes *functus officio*.[336] **18.351**

Article 31 Exclusion of Liability

31.1 None of the LCIA, the LCIA Court (including its President, Vice Presidents and individual members), the Registrar, any deputy Registrar, any arbitrator and any expert to the Arbitral Tribunal shall be liable to any party howsoever for any act or omission in connection with any arbitration conducted by reference to these Rules, save where the act or omission is shown by that party to constitute conscious and deliberate wrongdoing committed by the body or person alleged to be liable to that party.

31.2 After the award has been made and the possibilities of correction and additional awards referred to in Article 27 have lapsed or been exhausted, neither the LCIA, the LCIA Court (including its President, Vice Presidents and individual members), the Registrar, any deputy Registrar, any arbitrator or expert to the Arbitral Tribunal shall be under any legal obligation to make any statement to any person about any matter concerning the arbitration, *nor shall* any party seek to make any of these persons a witness in any legal or other proceedings arising out of the arbitration.

(1) Exclusion of liability

Article 31.1 seeks to exclude liability for any officer or employee of the LCIA, or any arbitrator acting under the Rules, for anything to do with the arbitration. The only exception is an act or omission that was a 'conscious and deliberate wrongdoing' on the part of the individual or entity. This records the traditional view of English law relating to immunity **18.352**

[334] Veeder, 1998 Rules, 369. Although it has been argued that the presumption be reversed: Samuel, 47.
[335] See further Mistelis, L., 'Confidentiality and Third Party Participation in Investment Arbitration' (2005) 21 *Arb Int'l* 205.
[336] Veeder, 1998 Rules, 369.

of arbitrators subject to errors that are deliberate. Article 31.1 makes it clear that the burden of proving that the wrongdoing was conscious and deliberate is on the party making the allegation.

18.353 In practice, it is likely that this burden will be discharged only in exceptional circumstances.

(2) Cessation of duties

18.354 Article 31.2 relieves the LCIA in all its aspects, the tribunal, and any expert to the tribunal from any legal obligation to make any statement regarding the arbitration. Not only does this support the provisions of Art 30 regarding confidentiality but it also makes a challenge under Art 31.1 even less likely to succeed.

Article 32 General Rules

32.1 A party who knows that any provision of the Arbitration Agreement (including these Rules) has not been complied with and yet proceeds with the arbitration without promptly stating its objection to such non-compliance, shall be treated as having irrevocably waived its right to object.

32.2 In all matters not expressly provided for in these Rules, the LCIA Court, the Arbitral Tribunal and the parties shall act in the spirit of these Rules and shall make every reasonable effort to ensure that an award is legally enforceable.

(1) Waiver of right to object

18.355 Article 32.1 is designed to ensure certainty and enforceability. Thus, a party aware of any non-compliance will have waived its right to object unless it gives prompt notice of this. Presumably notice should be to the other party together with the tribunal, or Registrar as appropriate. The meaning of 'promptly' depends on the circumstances of the case and how long the knowledge in question has been with, or could have been with, the party complaining of non-compliance. There is no exception to this requirement.

(2) Efforts to ensure that an award is legally enforceable

18.356 Article 32.2 allows the Court, the tribunal and the parties to take any necessary or reasonable steps to ensure enforceability and prevents a recalcitrant party from resisting such a step on the grounds that it is outside the LCIA Court's or tribunal's authority. The steps taken may include actions to ensure that procedural or administrative requirements under national laws have been observed, for example, the award being signed at the seat of the arbitration.

18.357 Doubts have been expressed[337] as to the power of the Court to ensure that the award is legally enforceable given that it does not review the award.[338] This is to overlook the very important power of the Court to remove an arbitrator who fails to fulfil his duties.[339]

[337] On the equivalent provisions of the 1985 Rules: Salans, C.F., 'The 1985 Rules of the London Court of International Arbitration' (1986) 2 *Arb Int'l* 40.

[338] Art 26.5 but also para 18.332.

[339] Art 10.

III. Appendix

A. Contact details

LCIA
70 Fleet Street
London
EC4Y 1EU
United Kingdom
Telephone: 00 44 (0) 20 7936 7007
Fax: 00 44 (0) 20 7936 7008
Email
General: lcia@lcia.org
Casework: casework@lcia.org
Accounts: accounts@lcia.org
Website: <http://www.lcia.org>

B. Model arbitration clauses and other patterns

The LCIA publishes a number of model clauses to cover the various services which it offers. It also states that the Secretariat will be pleased to discuss any modifications to these standard clauses; for example, to provide for party nomination or arbitrators, expedited procedures or a small claims provision. The sample clauses are separated into those relating to future disputes and those relating to existing disputes. Clauses relating to the former are set out below. In the case of future disputes or expert determination, adjudication and other forms of ADR, the LCIA Secretariat will supply suitable wordings on request.

Future disputes

For contracting parties who wish to have future disputes referred to arbitration and/or mediation under the auspices of the LCIA, the following clauses are recommended. Words/blanks in square brackets should be deleted/completed as appropriate.

Arbitration only

> Any dispute arising out of or in connection with this contract, including any question regarding its existence, validity or termination, shall be referred to and finally resolved by arbitration under the Rules of the LCIA, which Rules are deemed to be incorporated by reference into this clause.
>
> The number of arbitrators shall be [one/three].
>
> The seat, or legal place, of arbitration shall be [City and/or Country].
>
> The language to be used in the arbitration shall be [ ].
>
> The governing law of the contract shall be the substantive law of [ ].

Mediation only

> In the event of a dispute arising out of or relating to this contract, including any question regarding its existence, validity or termination, the parties shall seek settlement of that dispute by mediation in accordance with the LCIA Mediation Procedure, which Procedure is deemed to be incorporated by reference into this clause.

Mediation and arbitration

In the event of a dispute arising out of or relating to this contract, including any question regarding its existence, validity or termination, the parties shall first seek settlement of that dispute by mediation in accordance with the LCIA Mediation Procedure, which Procedure is deemed to be incorporated by reference into this clause.

If the dispute is not settled by mediation within [ ] days of the commencement of the mediation, or such further period as the parties shall agree in writing, the dispute shall be referred to and finally resolved by arbitration under the LCIA Rules, which Rules are deemed to be incorporated by reference into this clause.

The language to be used in the mediation and in the arbitration shall be [ ].

The governing law of the contract shall be the substantive law of [ ].

In any arbitration commenced pursuant to this clause,

(i) the number of arbitrators shall be [one/three]; and

(ii) the seat, or legal place, of arbitration shall be [City and/or Country].

Arbitration under the UNCITRAL Rules

Any dispute arising out of or in connection with this contract, including any question regarding its existence, validity or termination, shall be referred to and finally resolved by arbitration under the UNCITRAL Arbitration Rules, which Rules are deemed to be incorporated by reference into this clause.

Any arbitration commenced pursuant to this clause shall be administered by the LCIA.

The appointing authority shall be the LCIA.

The LCIA schedule of fees and costs shall apply.

The number of arbitrators shall be [one/three].

The seat, or legal place of arbitration shall be [City and/or Country].

The language to be used in the arbitral proceedings shall be [ ].

The governing law of the contract shall be the substantive law of [ ].

C. Bibliography

'Act III: Advocacy with Witness Testimony' (2005) 21 *Arb Int'l* 583.

Akseli, O., 'Appointment of Arbitrators as Specified in the Agreement to Arbitrate' (2003) 20 *J Int'l Arb* 247.

Berger, K.P., 'Evidentiary Privileges: Best Practice Standards and Arbitral Discretion' (2006) 22 *Arb Int'l* 501.

Bishop, D. and Reed, L. 'Practical Guidelines for Interviewing, Selecting and Challenging Party-Appointed Arbitrators in International Commercial Arbitration' (1998) 14 *Arb Int'l* 395 [Bishop and Reed].

Borris, C., 'Common law and civil law: fundamental differences and their impact on arbitration' (1995) 4 *Arb Disp Res L J* 92.

Briggs, A. and Rees, P., *Civil Jurisdiction and Judgments* (4th edn, Informa Professional, 2005).

Butchers, J. and Kimbrough, P., 'The Arbitral Tribunal's Role in Default Proceedings' (2006) 22 *Arb Int'l* 233.

Craig, W.L., 'The LCIA and ICC Rules: the 1998 revisions compared' in A. Berkeley, A. and J. Mimms (eds), *International Commercial Arbitration: Practical Perspectives* (Centre of Construction Law & Management, 2001), 79.

Delvolvé, J.L., 'L'arbitrage et les tiers: III—Le droit de l'arbitrage' (1988) *Rev arb* 501.

—— 'Le centenaire de la LCIA' (1993) *Rev arb* 599 [Delvolvé, LCIA].

Diamond, A. QC, 'Procedure and hearings' in A. Berkeley and J. Mimms (eds), *International Commercial Arbitration: Practical Perspectives* (Centre of Construction Law & Management, 2001) 49.

Donahey, M.S., 'The Independence and Neutrality of Arbitrators' (1992) 9 *J Int'l Arb* 31.

Donovan, D.F., 'The Allocation of Authority Between Courts and Arbitral Tribunals to Order Interim Measures A Survey of Jurisdictions, the Work of UNCITRAL and a Model Proposal' in *ICCA Congress Series no 12* (Kluwer, 2005) 203.

Eastwood, G., 'A Real Danger of Confusion? The English Law Relating to Bias in Arbitrators' (2001) 17 *Arb Int'l* 287.

Fouchard, P., Galliard, E., Goldman, B., *International Commercial Arbitration 1999* (Kluwer Law International, 1999) [Fouchard, Galliard, Goldman].

Goode, R., 'The Adaptation of English Law to International Commercial Arbitration' (1992) 8 *Arb Int'l* 11.

Greenblatt, J.L. and Griffin, P. 'Towards the Harmonization of International Arbitration Rules: Comparative Analysis of the Rules of the ICC, AAA, LCIA and CIET' (2001) 17 *Arb Int'l* 101.

Greig, R.T., 'International Commercial Arbitration in Japan: A User's Report' (1989) 6 *J Int'l Arb* 21.

Gu, W., 'Security for Costs in International Commercial Arbitration' (2005) 22 *J Int'l Arb* 167.

Harris, B., Planterose, R. and Trecks, R. (eds), *The Arbitration Act 1996* (4th edn, Blackwell Science, 2007).

Heiskanen, V., 'Dealing with Pandora: the Concept of 'Merits' in International Commercial Arbitration' (2006) 22 *Arb Int'l* 597.

Hollander, C., *Documentary Evidence* (9th edn, Sweet & Maxwell, 2003).

Hunter, J. M., 'The Procedural Power of Arbitrators Under the English 1996 Act' (1997) 13 *Arb Int'l* 345.

Hunter, J.M. and Paulsson, J., 'Rules of the London Court of International Arbitration A Commentary on the 1985 Rules of the London Court of International Arbitration' in P. Sanders (ed), *YCA Vol X* (Kluwer Law International, 1985) 167 [Hunter and Paulsson, 1985 Rules].

Jermini, C., 'Note—Tribunal federal, Ire Cour civile, 7 janvier 2004 (4P.196/2003)' (2004) 22 *ASA Bull* 605.

Jones, D., 'Party Appointed Expert Witnesses in International Arbitration: A Protocol at Last' (2008) 24 *Arb Int'l* 137.

Kaufmann-Kohler, G., 'The Arbitrator and the Law: Does he/she know it? Apply it? How? And a few more questions' (2005) 21 *Arb Int'l* 631.

Kerr, M., 'London Court of International Arbitration' in *ICCA Congress Series no 7* (Kluwer, 1996) 213.

Knutson, R., 'The Interpretation of Arbitral Awards—When is a Final Award not Final?' (1994) 11 *J Int'l Arb* 99.

Landau, T., 'Composition and Establishment of the Tribunal' (1998) 9 *Am Rev Int'l Arb* 45.

Lazareff, S., 'The Language of Institutional Arbitration' (1997) 8 *ICC ICArb Bull* 18.

Lebedev, S.N., 'The LCIA Rules for International Commercial Arbitration' (1992) 8 *Arb Int'l* 321.

Lew, J.D.M., Mistelis, L.A., and Kröll, S., *Comparative International Commercial Arbitration* (Kluwer Law International, 2003) [Lew, Mistelis, Kröll].

Lew, J.D.M., *Applicable Law in International Commercial Arbitration* (Oceana, 1978).

Lörcher, G., 'Improving procedures of Oral and Written Witness Testimony' in *ICCA Congress Series no 7* (Kluwer, 1996) 145.

Mayer, P., 'Reflections on the International Arbitrator's Duty to Apply the Law' (2001) 17 *Arb Int'l* 235.

Merkin, R.M., *Arbitration Law* (3rd edn, Informa Business Publishing, 2004) [Merkin, Arbitration Law].

Merkin, R.M. and Flannery, L., *Arbitration Act 1996* (4th edn, Informa Law, 2008) [Merkin, Arbitration Act].

Miles, W., 'Practical Issues for Appointment of Arbitrators' (2003) 20 *J Int'l Arb* 219.

Mistelis, L., 'International Arbitration: Corporate Attitudes and Practices' (2004)15 *Am Rev Int'l Arb* 525;

—— 'Reality rest: current state of affairs in theory and practice relating to lex arbitri' (2006) 17 *Am Rev Int'l Arb* 155;

—— 'Confidentiality and Third Party Participation in Investment Arbitration' (2005) 21 *Arb Int'l* 205.

Naón, H.G., 'Choice-of-Law Problems in International Commercial Arbitration' (2001) 289 *Collected Courses, Hague Academy of Int'l L* 9.

Nicholas, G. and Partasides, C., 'LCIA Court Decisions on Challenges to Arbitrators: A Proposal to Publish' (2007) 23 *Arb Int'l 1* [Nicholas and Partasides].

Oetiker, C., 'Witnesses before the International Arbitral Tribunal' (2007) 25 *ASA Bull* 253 [Oetiker].

Okekeifere, A. I., 'The Parties' Rights Against a Dilatory or Unskilled Arbitrator' (1998) 15 *J Int'l Arb* 129.

Park, W.W., 'Arbitration's Discontents: Of Elephants and Pornography' (2001) 17 *Arb Int'l* 263.

Paulsson, J., 'Arbitration-Friendliness: Promises of Principle and Realities of Practice' (2007) 23 *Arb Int'l* 477.

Peter, W., 'Witness "Conferencing"' (2002) 18 *Arb Int'l* 47.

Petrochilos, G., *Procedural Law in International Arbitration* (OUP, 2004).

Pietrowski, R., 'Evidence in International Arbitration' (2006) 22 *Arb Int'l* 373 [Pietrowski].

Platte, M., 'When should an Arbitrator Join Cases?' (2002) 18 *Arb Int'l* 67.

Poudret, J.F. and Besson, S., *Comparative Law of International Arbitration* (2nd edn, Sweet & Maxwell, 2007) [Poudret and Besson].

Pryles, M., 'Limits to Party Autonomy in Arbitral Procedure' (2007) 24 *J Int'l Arb* 327.

Raphael, T., *The Anti-Suit Injunction* (OUP, 2008).

Redfern, A., 'Dissenting Opinions in International Commercial Arbitration: The Good, the Bad and the Ugly' (2004) 20 *Arb Int'l* 223.

Redfern, A. and Hunter, M., *Law and Practice of International Commercial Arbitration* (4th edn, Sweet & Maxwell, 2004) [Redfern and Hunter].

Reid, G., 'Security for costs in international arbitrations—forget it?' 152 *NLJ* 1426 27 September 2002.

Rees, P.J., 'The Conduct of International Arbitration in England: the Challenge Has Still to be Met' (2007) 23 *Arb Int'l* 505.

Rivkin, D., '1997: A Year of Rule Changes' *Int'l Arb L Rev* 1998 1(2) 91 [Rivkin].

Roney, D.P., 'Effective Witness Preparation for International Commercial Arbitration: A practical Guide for Counsel' (2003) 20 *J Int'l Arb* 429.

Salans, C.F., 'The 1985 Rules of the London Court of International Arbitration' (1986) 2 *Arb Int'l* 40.

Saleh, S.A., 'Reflections on Admissibility of Evidence: Interrelation between Domestic Law and International Arbitration' (1999) 15 *Arb Int'l* 141.

Samuel, A., 'Jurisdiction, interim relief and awards under the LCIA Rules' in A. Berkeley and J. Mimms (eds), *International Commercial Arbitration: Practical Perspectives* (Centre of Construction Law & Management, 2001), 35 [Samuel].

Sanders, P. (ed), *YCA Vol VII* (Kluwer Law International, 1982) 223.

—— *YCA vol X* (Kluwer Law International, 1985) 157.

Sandifer, D.V., *Evidence Before International Tribunals* (University Press of Virginia, 1975).

School of International Arbitration / Price Waterhouse Coopers (2008) *International arbitration: Corporate Attitudes and Practices Survey.*

Schwartz, E.A., 'Reconciling Speed with Justice in International Arbitration' in B.G. Davis (ed), *Improving International Arbitration* (International Chamber of Commerce, 1998).

Schwebel, S.M., 'The Authority of a Truncated Tribunal' in *ICCA Congress Series no 9* (Kluwer, 1999) 314;

—— 'The Validity of an Arbitral Award Rendered by a Truncated Tribunal' (1995) 6 *ICC ICArb Bull* 22.

Sharpe, J.K., 'Drawing Adverse Inferences from the Non-production of Evidence' (2006) 22 *Arb Int'l* 549.

Smith, R.H. and Robinson, T.B.E., 'Disclosure in International Arbitration' (2008) 24 *Arb Int'l* 105.

Sutton, D.S.J., Gill, J. and Gearing, M., *Russell on Arbitration* (23rd edn, Sweet & Maxwell, 2007) [Russell on Arbitration].

Tackaberry, J. and Marriott, A., *Bernstein's Handbook of Arbitration and Dispute Resolution Practice* (4th edn, Sweet & Maxwell, 2003) [Bernstein's Handbook].

Tallerico, T.J. and Behrendt, J.A., 'The Use of Bifurcation and Direct Testimony witness Statements in International Commercial Arbitration Proceedings' (2003) 20 *J Int'l Arb* 295.

Thompson, D., 'Annual Conference: Chartered Institute of Arbitrators' (1985) 2 *J Int'l Arb* 116.

Turner, P. and Mohtashami, R., *A Guide to the LCIA Arbitration Rules* (OUP, 2009).

Tweeddale, A. and Tweeddale, K., *Arbitration of commercial disputes: international and English law practice* (OUP, 2005).

van Houtte, H., 'Ten Reasons Against a Proposal for Ex Parte Interim Measures of Protection in Arbitration' (2004) 20 *Arb Int'l* 85.

Veeder, V.V., 'London Court of International Arbitration, The New 1998 LCIA Rules' (1998) 23 *YCA* 366 [Veeder, 1998 Rules].

—— 'The Lena Goldfields arbitration: the historical roots of three ideas' (1998) 47 *ICLQ* 747.

Winstanley, A., 'UNCITRAL heralds the age of ex parte measures' (March 2005) LCIA website.

—— 'The LCIA—history, constitution and rules' in A. Berkeley and J. Mimms (eds), *International Commercial Arbitration: Practical Perspectives* (Centre of Construction Law & Management, 2001), 21;

—— 'The New Rules of the London Court of International Arbitration' (1997) 8 *Am Rev Int Arb* 59 [Winstanley, The New Rules].

Yesilirmak, A., *Provisional Measures in International Commercial Arbitration* (Kluwer Law International, 2005).

Seventh session of the Working Group on International Contract Practices, Report of the Working Group on the work of its seventh session, 6 March 1984, UN-Doc A/CN.9/246 (<http://www.uncitral.org/uncitral/en/commission/sessions/17th.html>).

LCIA website Frequently Asked Questions [FAQ].

Global Arb Rev, 2009:4(1).

LCIA *News* 2008:13(1) Kluwer Law International.

—— 2007:12(1) Kluwer Law International.

—— 2006:11(1) Kluwer Law International.

INDEX